THE ENCYCLOPEDIA OF AMERICAN RELIGIONS

SECOND EDITION

THE
ENCYCLOPEDIA
OF AMERICAN
RELIGIONS

SECOND EDITION

J. Gordon Melton

Gale Research Company • Book Tower • Detroit, Michigan 48226

J. Gordon Melton

Charity Anne Dorgan, *Contributing Associate Editor*

Aided by:

Iris Cloyd, Valerie J. Webster, Carol A. Schwartz, Danita L. Wimbush, Jelena Obradovic Kronick,
Robert Thomas Wilson, Emily B. Tennyson, Denise Michlewicz Broderick, Margaret A. Chamberlain,
Colleen M. Crane, Kathleen Droste, Nancy H. Evans, Michael L. LaBlanc, Polly A. Vedder,
Sheila Fitzgerald, Heidi Ellerman, Anne Sharp, and Debra M. Kirby

Dennis LaBeau, *Editorial Data Systems Director*
Donald G. Dillaman, *System Design and Development*
Mary Beth Trimper, *External Production Supervisor*
Dorothy Kalleberg, *Senior External Production Associate*
Arthur Chartow, *Art Director*
Laura Bryant, *Internal Production Supervisor*
Louise Gagné, *Internal Production Associate*
Sandy Rock, *Senior Internal Production Assistant*
Lisa Woods, *Internal Production Assistant*

Frederick G. Ruffner, *Publisher*
Dedria Bryfonski, *Editorial Director*
Ellen T. Crowley, *Associate Editorial Director*
John Schmittroth, Jr., *Director, Directories Division*
Robert J. Elster, *Managing Editor, Directories Division*

Contents

Part 2 - Directory Listings

Indexes

Preface to the Second Edition

The first edition of *Encyclopedia of American Religions,* published in 1979, provided the first comprehensive study of religious and spiritual groups in the United States since the 1936 edition of Census of Religious Bodies. This second edition, reflecting the proliferation and variation of contemporary American religions, expands and updates that coverage, providing current and detailed information on approximately 1,350 groups, ranging from Adventists to Zen Buddhists. In addition to the increased coverage, the second edition introduces several new features to facilitate use of the *Encyclopedia.* These include a new arrangement of historical essays and descriptive directory listings, new entry format, improved typography, and an increase in the amount of information and detail in each directory entry. The second edition also contains six new comprehensive indexes, allowing users of the *Encyclopedia* to access information in a variety of ways.

New Features in This Edition

The second edition of *Encyclopedia of American Religions* contains several new features, including the following:

1) New Arrangement. Information in the *Encyclopedia* is now divided into two parts, in contrast to the single body of text presented in the first edition. The first part contains essays describing the historical development of the major religious families and traditions in the United States. The second part of the *Encyclopedia* comprises directory sections that correspond to the essay chapters in the first part, and they provide names, addresses, contacts, descriptions, and other information about the individual churches, religious bodies, and spiritual groups that constitute each major religious family. In the first edition, this descriptive information— without directory details—was interspersed throughout the essays. The new arrangement separates and highlights these two distinct types of information to make it easier for users seeking only one of the two types. (Of course, the parallel arrangement of chapters in the two parts also allows quick access to those needing both kinds of information.)

2) Convenient One-Volume Format. The second edition has been computer composed, allowing more information to be printed on each page. This, as well as the introduction of a larger page size, permits the expanded second edition to appear in one volume, rather than the two-volume format of the first edition, despite a considerable increase in the amount of information provided.

3) Improved Typography. Computerized photocomposition is now used to produce *Encyclopedia of American Religions.* Computerization permits organization names and subheadings appearing in the directory section and chapter subheadings in the essay section to be rendered in boldface type for easier identification, among other improvements in typography.

4) New Entry Format. As in the supplement to the first edition, the *Encyclopedia*'s directory listings feature a new entry format designed to highlight important items of information within the text. Separate headings are provided for membership data, periodicals published by the group, and other details. In addition, each directory entry is preceded by a sequential entry number that is used in all indexes to refer to the entry.

5) Indexes. Six separate indexes augment and replace the general indexes that appeared at the end of each volume of the first edition. These include the Religious Organization and Institution Index; Publications Index; Geographic Index; Personal Name Index; Educational Institution Index; and Subject Index. These indexes cite items in both the essay section and the directory section, and they are fully described below.

Compilation Methods

Information contained within the entries has been obtained from questionnaire responses from the religious groups and, in some cases, by follow-up telephone conversations. Published sources have also been consulted for additional background information.

Contents and Arrangement

The second edition of *Encyclopedia of American Religions* consists of two parts, the first containing essays providing general historical information, the second containing current directory listings.

The general historical essays are organized into 22 chapters, each covering the development of one of the major religious families and traditions found in the United States. A select list of bibliographic source materials appears at the end of each chapter. These source lists replace the cumbersome footnote sections that appeared in the first edition and are representative of the comprehensive files on each group maintained at the Institute for the Study of American Religion.

The directory listings are also organized into 22 sections. The sections correspond to the essay chapters in the first part of the *Encyclopedia,* and they contain current directory and descriptive information about the individual churches, religious bodies, and spiritual groups that constitute each major religious family. They also contain information on churches for which no current address could be obtained and defunct churches. Typical directory entries contain the following details:

> *Sequential Entry Number* (used in indexes to refer to an entry)
>
> *Religious Organization Name* (including address)
>
> *Description of Organization's Beliefs, History, and Organization*
>
> *Membership* (detailed statistics as reported by the group)
>
> *Educational Facilities* (lists post-secondary educational institutions sponsored and/or supported by the group)
>
> *Publications* (periodicals, newsletters, or other publications issued by the group)
>
> *Remarks* (includes additional information not applicable to the basic headings listed above)
>
> *Sources* (lists selected source materials used to develop the entry as well as sources for further readings)

New Indexes

In the first edition of the *Encyclopedia,* separately alphabetized general indexes appeared at the end of each volume. For the second edition, these indexes have been expanded and replaced by the six new indexes described below. Because of the difference in format between the essay section and the directory section, citations in the indexes refer to both *page numbers* (for items in the essay section) and *entry numbers* (for items in the directory section).

RELIGIOUS ORGANIZATION AND INSTITUTION INDEX. An alphabetical listing of religious groups and other organizations mentioned in both the essay section and the directory section.

EDUCATIONAL INSTITUTION INDEX. An alphabetical listing of post-secondary educational institutions sponsored and/or supported by religious organizations described in the second edition.

PERSONAL NAME INDEX. An alphabetical listing of persons mentioned in the essay section and the directory section.

PUBLICATIONS INDEX. An alphabetical list of periodicals, newsletters, and other publications regularly issued by the religious groups outlined in the directory section. (This index does not cover source materials listed at the end of each essay chapter nor publications listed under the heading Sources within each directory entry.)

GEOGRAPHIC INDEX. Arranges religious organizations listed in the directory section alphabetically by state and then by city. Index entries include organization name and address.

SUBJECT INDEX. Provides access to the material in the essay section and the directory section through a selected list of subject terms.

Supplement Will Add to Coverage

An inter-edition supplement will be published covering newly identified and newly formed religious groups in the United States. The supplement will also supply updated information on groups described in the second edition.

Institute for the Study of American Religion

The Institute for the Study of American Religion, now located in Santa Barbara, California, was founded in 1969 for the purpose of researching and dissemanating information about the numerous religious groups in the United States. The second edition of the *Encyclopedia* has been compiled in part from the Institute's collection of more than 25,000 volumes and their thousands of files covering individual religious groups.

Users with particular questions about a religious group, with suggested changes in the *Encyclopedia,* or information about any group not listed are invited to write to the Institute in care of its director:

> Dr. J. Gordon Melton
> Institute for the Study of American Religion
> Box 90709
> Santa Barbara, CA 93190-0709

Selections from the Introduction
to the First Edition

The Encyclopedia of American Religions explores the broad sweep of American religions and describes over 1,200 [now 1,347] churches. Some churches in the *Encyclopedia,* such as certain Hindu and Jewish bodies, follow a tradition several thousand years old. Others were born yesterday, like Garner Ted Armstrong's Church of God International, formed in the summer of 1978. With few exceptions, if a church existed in the United States in 1976 [now 1986], it is discussed in the *Encyclopedia.*

In my sixteen-year study of American religion I discovered three kinds of religious institutions: primary religious bodies (i.e., churches), secondary organizations which serve the primary bodies, and tertiary organizations which strive to change the primary bodies. The *Encyclopedia* treats only the primary religious bodies, but it does refer to the two other kinds of institutions, so some comment on all three types is necessary here.

In defining primary religious bodies (a church, denomination, sect, or cult), I established certain criteria. First, a church seeks the chief religious loyalty of its members. Second, it meets requirements of size. If it is organized into congregations, it has at least two congregations, or it has one congregation of more than 2,000 members who make a measurable impact on the country through the mass media. If a church is not organized into congregations, it meets the size requirement when its members come from more than one state and from beyond a single metropolitan area. The third criterion concerns faith: a primary religious body tends to promote its particular views. For instance, it may encourage belief or disbelief in the Trinity. Or it may try to discourage the wearing of neckties; some holiness churches consider wearing neckties ostentatious.

I waived the size requirement for primary religious bodies whose beliefs are at odds with those of more people in our culture. For example, some Satanic groups are discussed in the *Encyclopedia* although they do not have enough members to meet my size criterion for primary religious bodies. The vast majority of churches in the *Encyclopedia* do, however, meet my three criteria.

Most primary religious bodies share other traits. Their leaders "marry and bury," as the saying goes. The churches usually hope to expand: they plan to make converts and form additional congregations. Finally, a number of primary religious bodies, though under-represented in America, have large foreign branches.

Much of the money and time given to religious enterprises in the United States is channeled, not into the primary religious bodies, but into secondary and tertiary religious institutions. Secondary religious organizations, service agencies, perform tasks for one or more primary body. The tasks include missionary work, the education of seminarians, the publication of church materials, the sale of religious articles, and care for orphans and the aged.

Tertiary organizations try to change a number of primary religious bodies by promoting one special issue. For example, ecumenical organizations seek the unity of churches. However, few churches supporting the ecumenical organizations have specific plans to merge with other churches; so ecumenists try to change the attitudes of the churches. Among the country's ecumenical groups are several which draw members from various religious families (e.g., the National Council of Churches and the National Association of Evangelicals) and many more whose members are limited to one family (e.g., the Christian Holiness Association, the Pentecostal Fellowship of North America, the World Baptist Alliance, the International New Thought Alliance, the American Council of Witches, the Midwest Pagan Council, and the Buddhist Council of Hawaii).

Tertiary organizations have been formed to promote peace (the Fellowship of Reconciliation), a belief in creation instead of evolution (the Bible Science Association, Inc.), the psychic (the Spiritual Frontiers

Fellowship), spiritual healing (the International Order of St. Luke, the Physician), Pentecostalism (the Full Gospel Businessmen's Fellowship, International), and Sabbatarianism (the Bible Sabbath Association).

Because the country is virtually flooded with secondary and tertiary organizations the primary religious bodies form only a small percentage of American religious institutions. It is to the primary bodies, though, that the secondary and tertiary organizations look for members and support.

In describing America's 1,200 [1,347] primary religious bodies, I am departing from the church-sect-cult categories of Ernst Troeltsch. He pioneered in describing various Christian bodies, not in doctrinal, but in social terms, treating churches as far more than defenders of certain beliefs. In the latter part of his work, *The Social Teachings of the Christian Churches* (New York: Macmillan, 1931), Troeltsch examined the Christian churches of post-Reformation Europe. He discovered three types of groups: the dominant state churches, the sect groups (schismatic groups that broke away from the state churches), and the mystical groups (the latter came to be called cults). Unfortunately, American sociologists applied Troeltsch's categories to American religions. With time, the popular media attached pejorative connotations to the words "sect" and "cult," connotations Troeltsch never intended. To understand Troeltsch properly, one must remember that he described only Christian religions. Furthermore, he studied countries with Christian state churches, to which all citizens were expected to belong. The United States has no state church and has far more non-Christian churches than Europe had before 1800, the terminal point of Troeltsch's study.

American religions do not yield to so simplistic a set of categories as the church-sect-cult triad. Instead of using those three classifications, I examined religions family by family, and have found seventeen distinct families. This approach, I hope, does justice to the amazing variety within the American religious experience. Ten of the seventeen religious families in the United States basically follow Christian beliefs and practices; seven do not.

Within the seventeen families of American religions, the member bodies of each family share a common heritage, thought world (theology in its broadest sense), and lifestyle. These three features define each individual religious body and illuminate its relationship to other churches in the family.

It has become fashionable to use other characteristics in classifying religious bodies, characteristics such as ethnicity, class, racial composition, type of leadership (priest? guru? pastor?), and the degree of acceptance of or hostility to the world. While these characteristics provide useful information, they are entirely inadequate in explaining the formation, development, relationships, and continuing life of the broad spectrum of America's religious bodies. Elements of ethnicity are, for example, most helpful in identifying sub-groups within the older European church traditions brought to America in the eighteenth and nineteenth centuries. Lutheran, Reformed, and Pietist churches split along ethnic lines, each sub-group using its own language. But as language barriers disappeared, the ethnic orientation of the churches diminished. Thus Swedish Baptists in America are more likely to develop joint programs, to merge, or to share missionary concerns with German or English or even black Baptists than with Swedish Lutherans or Swedish Pentecostals. The strength of family relationships overrides ethnic considerations.

In order to understand any family or its members, it is necessary to understand the family's heritage, thought world, and lifestyle. In many families, one of the three features—heritage, thought world, and lifestyle—is dominant. For the Lutheran family and those churches within the liturgical family, heritage is the feature setting them apart from other churches. Lifestyle is the key feature for four families in particular: the Communal, Holiness, Pentecostal, and Psychic families. Group ownership of property and certain self-imposed disciplines put communes into a class of their own. A day-to-day striving for perfect love dominates holiness preaching and teaching, with worldly activities prohibited. Pentecostals seek certain gifts of the Spirit, such as speaking in tongues, prophesying, and healing, so Pentecostals have a distinctive lifestyle in both their worship and their daily lives. Finally, the psychics are set apart from other religious groups because of their interest in extrasensory perception, psychokinesis, and communication with spirits through seances and visions

If heritage and lifestyles distinguish certain families so does the thought world for other families. For fundamentalists and for the Protestant churches, especially those which follow John Calvin's Reformed theology, the features distinguishing them from each other is their thought world. They hold divergent views on these topics in particular: sacrament, ecclesiology, the sovereignty of God, perfection, and the nature of the end time. But even where there is agreement, sharing a thought world does not necessarily mean holding identical views. Rather, it means sharing some beliefs which set the context for constant debate over specifics. Adventists, for example, expect Christ to return soon, but violently argue among themselves about the nature of his return, the possibility of pinpointing the date of his return, and the significance of certain world events as signs of his return.

Of particular interest to me are the families of "hidden religions" outside the country's religious mainstream. The spiritualists who hold seances are within the hidden families; so are the Buddhists, the Sufis, and the witches in their covens. Such groups are invisible to many Americans, but often they have large national followings. Several congregations that belong to these sizable but hidden families meet within a few blocks of my home in Evanston, Illinois. But had I not searched hard for these congregations, I would never have found them.

Many years of searching went into my study of America's religions. I might be better qualified to study the country's religions if I were detective instead of a Methodist minister. I examined endless printed material and interviewed countless church founders and leaders—all with the aim of understanding the heritage, lifestyle, and thought world of the religions. To say the least, the task had its challenges. Some churches exaggerate or deny aspects of their lifestyle or history. Many Pentecostals say their church was founded at Pentecost, in 33 A.D., and hide their recent origins. Other churches try to gloss over the career their founder led before establishing their church. Among such founders, David Berg (of the Children of God), L. Ron Hubbard (of the Church of Scientology), A. A. Allen (of the Miracle Revival Fellowship), and Sun Myung Moon (of the Unification Church), have followed or still follow vocations quite different from that of a spiritual leader. For example, Hubbard was an undercover agent for the Los Angeles Police Department, a fiction writer, and an explorer before founding his church.

Some religious bodies function as such but deny their religious nature. One such is the World Plan Executive Council, popularly called Transcendental Meditation. Other dislike denominational labels and refuse to list themselves in a phone book or give brochures to nonmembers. The Cooneyites, also called the Two-by-Two's, have developed the shunning of publicity into a fine art.

But the most difficult churches to study are those of the American Indian. Authors who treat Indian religions as one religion adulterate history. Each tribe has its own beliefs and practices, often dramatically different from those of nearby tribes. A thorough examination of all Indian faiths is needed—a mammoth task. Because researchers have scarcely begun it, and because I myself am not familiar with Indian religions, I am unable to include them in this work. Similarly, I lack material on the beliefs and religious practices of the American gypsies, and cannot describe them here.

To paint a picture of America's religious bodies in 1978 is not to describe them as they will be in 1988. Families dwindle and expand. The major church in a family (one that claims more than half the family's members) may divide in half in a decade, torn by schism. Smaller churches in a family may consolidate—e.g., through merging all-black and all-white churches. Lutherans, once divided according to European ethnic origins and language, have consolidated in this century and then redivided over doctrinal issues. The Eastern religious bodies in this country—originally composed of Hindu and Buddhist immigrants—have attracted young American devotees, thereby blending the West with the East. Despite changes within families, however, the identity of the families remains the same. An intense conservatism governs religious bodies; they would rather lose dissident members than change. Further, churches rarely jump from one family to another. Theological and organizational patterns tend to perpetuate themselves. True, institutions adjust to the changing society, but only begrudgingly. The division of religions into families (denominationalism) is fundamental to religious life in the United States. We do not live in a post-denominational age. The ideals of ecumenism have swept through American Christianity, firing imaginations, creating cooperation structures, and breaking down walls of intolerance and hostility between religions. But if ecumenism has illustrated anything, it has been this: the religious family is strong. It will endure.

J. Gordon Melton

Part One
Essays

Chapter One

THE WESTERN LITURGICAL FAMILY

Directory listings for the groups belonging to the Western Liturgical
Family may be found in the section beginning on page 171.

A strong liturgical life is the distinguishing feature of the oldest Christian churches that have continued to our day. These churches have other distinguishing characteristics, true—creeds, orders, sacraments, language, and culture. Liturgy, however, is the place where these other characteristics find their expression. So it seems appropriate to group these churches together as the liturgical family.

In this family are the many church bodies of four major traditions: the Eastern Orthodox tradition, the non-Chalcedonian Orthodox tradition, the Western Roman tradition, and the Anglican tradition.

Most of the liturgical churches celebrate seven sacraments: baptism, the eucharist, holy orders, unction, marriage, confirmation, and penance. Few topics exist among Christians on which there is such a variety of thinking as on the sacraments. Some non-liturgical groups, such as the Methodists, celebrate only two sacraments—baptism and holy communion—while other non-liturgical groups, such as the Baptists, have no sacraments. Some churches consider baptism and holy communion not sacraments but ordinances, and add a third ordinance, footwashing. A fully developed sacramental system, however, characterizes the members of the liturgical family.

Other characteristics of the liturgical churches are allegiance to creeds and belief in Apostolic succession. Each creed, a statement of doctrines, originated in the early centuries of the church or is a variation on an early creed. Each church professes that it inherits an unbroken line of authority from the Apostles who founded the church at Pentecost.

Speaking of this unbroken line, Bishop Sion Manoogian says of the Armenian Church, "The Armenian Church was founded by two of the Apostles of Our Lord, St. Thaddeus and St. Bartholomew, in the first century. This is the reason for its sometimes being called the Armenian Apostolic Church" (Sion Manoogian, *The Armenian Church* [n.p., n.d.], 15). Dean Timothy Andrews says of the Greek Orthodox Church, "It is the church founded by Christ, received its mission on Pentecost, propagated throughout the world by the Holy Apostles" (Timothy Andrews, *What Is the Orthodox Church?* [pamphlet, 1964], 7). The Church of the East traces its conversion, establishment, and Apostolic

succession to the seventy disciples (Luke 10:1) and the twelve Apostles, but more particularly to Mar Shimun Koopa (St. Simon Peter), Mar Tooma (St. Thomas), Mar Addai (St. Thaddeus), Mar Mari (St. Mari, one of the seventy disciples), and Mar Bar Thulmay (St. Bartholomew). The Roman Catholic Church traces its origins to St. Peter, the first bishop of Rome.

People hold conflicting views concerning the relationship of the four traditions of the liturgical family to the Apostles and to the first century church. Most agree, however, that the peculiar traits of the traditions evolved as Christianity spread to various cultures and as church councils formulated doctrines. The Conciliar Era, a time of debate and discussion, lasted from 325 A.D. to 787 A.D. Seven councils were held during that time.

The First Ecumenical Council was called in 325 A.D. at Nicea, near Constantinople. Its focus was the teaching of Arius about the nature of Christ. Arius said the Son is not of the same substance as the Father but was created as an agent for creating the world. The Council condemned Arius and declared his teaching heretical. This action caused an immediate defection in the church in Egypt. In various places Arian Christians remained in some force for a number of years, especially during a continuing Arian controversy in the fourth century. The barbarians who sacked Rome in 401 A.D. were Arians, and since the sixth century a beautiful Arian baptistry has stood near the Orthodox one in Ravenna, Italy.

The Second Council met at Constantinople in 381 A.D. and continued the development of the doctrine of the Trinity. It said the Father, Son, and Holy Spirit are coeternal and consubstantial.

The Third Council met at Ephesus in 431 A.D. This Council met to discuss the opinions of Nestorius, who had been made patriarch of Constantinople in 428 A.D. Nestorius believed that Christ was not the Son of God, but that God was living in Christ. The two natures, said Nestorius, were separable. The debate centered upon the use of the phrase "Theotokos" ("Mother of God"). The Nestorians rejected the term, saying that Mary bore Christ, not God. The Council ruled against Nestorius and deposed him as patriarch. A Nestorian

Council was organized a few days later and deposed its opposition. Although Nestorius was imprisoned and eventually banished to Egypt, his followers formed a strong church in Syria and Persia. Later missionary activity pushed the Nestorian church into India and China. It is represented today by the Church of the East, part of the non-Chalcedonian Orthodox tradition.

The Fourth Council met at Chalcedon in 451 A.D. It drafted what came to be known as the Chalcedonian Creed:

"Therefore, following the holy Fathers we all with one accord teach men to acknowledge one and the same Son, our Lord Jesus Christ, at once complete in Godhead and complete in manhood, truly God and truly man, consisting also of a reasonable soul and body; of one substance with the Father as regards his Godhead, and at the same time of one substance with us as regards his manhood; like us in all respects, apart from sin; as regards his Godhead, begotten of the Father before the ages, but yet as regards his manhood begotten, for us men and for our salvation, of Mary the Virgin, the God-bearer; one and the same Christ, Son, Lord, Only-begotten, recognized IN TWO NATURES, WITHOUT CONFUSION, WITHOUT CHANGE, WITHOUT DIVISION, WITHOUT SEPARATION; the distinction of natures being in no way annulled by the union, but rather the characteristics of each nature being preserved and coming together to form one person and subsistence, not as parted or separated into two persons, but one and the same Son and Only-begotten God the Word, Lord Jesus Christ; even as the prophets from earliest times spoke of him, and our Lord Jesus Christ himself taught us, and the creed of the Fathers has handed down to us."

This creed is considered the "orthodox" solution to the Christological problems of the early church by the Roman Catholic, Greek Orthodox, and most Protestant churches. However, some Eastern and Egyptian Christians rejected the creed's emphasis on the two natures of Christ. The non-Chalcedonian Orthodox tradition is one of the four main traditions of the liturgical family. Many non-Chalcedonians were called Monophysites because they felt the human and divine in Christ constituted only one nature. Today the Armenian Church and the Coptic Church represent part of the non-Chalcedonian Orthodox tradition.

The first four councils—at Nicea, Constantinople, Ephesus, and Chalcedon—served to isolate the non-Chalcedonian Orthodox tradition from the Eastern Orthodox and Western Roman traditions. The Eastern Orthodox tradition developed centers of authority in Antioch, Alexandria, and Constantinople. The Western branch's center of authority was in Rome. This East-West division was more a cultural than a doctrinal separation. The churches allowed culture and politics to lead them toward an eventual break. When the official division came in 1054 with mutual excommunications, the churches were declaring to the world what had already been a reality for some time. This explanation is not to say that there are no important differences of doctrine, rites, or ecclesiastical practices between the two churches, or to deny that these differences have grown stronger since 1054. It is merely to show how even these pale into insignificance when set against the glaring differences caused by rival cultures, conflicting empires, and eight hundred years of lack of meaningful communication.

Of the three oldest traditions of the liturgical family—the Eastern Orthodox tradition, the non-Chalcedonian Orthodox tradition, and the Western Roman tradition—only the third failed to remain fairly stable down through the nineteenth century. In the first tradition, the Eastern Orthodox Church split jurisdictions along national and cultural lines. It was able to preserve unity by granting local autonomy to the various national groups. In the non-Chalcedonian Orthodox tradition, the Coptic Church and the Armenian Church fell under the rule of rising Islam after the sixth century. The force of an over-powering enemy served to keep them both small and united. In the Western Roman tradition, however, the Roman Catholic Church attempted an imperial stance, trying to provide a religious blanket to cover all of Western culture. Consequently, it was to suffer when secular power deserted it. Not only did the various Protestant and post-Protestant groups break off from it, but the fourth major liturgical tradition emerged from it: the Anglican.

The church in England had been at odds with the see of Rome as early as Thomas à Becket, the twelfth-century Archbishop of Canterbury. In the sixteenth century, the marriage problem of Henry VIII caused the break with Rome. With few immediate changes in the church beyond confiscation of church property by Henry, the Church of England had to wait for the Protestantizing of Edward and the mediating of Elizabeth for a genuinely new orientation. The development and spread of the Elizabethan prayerbook alone is reason to look upon the Anglicans as a separate liturgical tradition.

THE ANGLICAN TRADITION. The Church of England, also called the Anglican Church, developed in the sixteenth century when King Henry VIII came into conflict with papal authority. Henry had no doctrinal problems with Rome. In fact, because of his early theological writing, he had been given the title "defender of the faith" by the pope. But two issues led to his break with Rome: his desire for a male heir and his financial needs. Rome granted him an annulment for one marriage, but would not later grant him a divorce for another marriage. So he determined to separate the English church from papal jurisdiction. Besides, he knew the wealthy monasteries would be a good source of revenue for running his kingdom and waging war. This made the break from Rome doubly beneficial to him. The Church of England kept its already existing structure, with bishops, clergy, church buildings, and congregations continuing under the archbishop of Canterbury instead of under the pope. The church was still Roman in doctrine, liturgy, and organization.

Not until Edward VII, Elizabeth I, and Oliver Cromwell was the present character of the Anglican Church molded. The pendulum of the church swung from Protestant under Edward to Catholic under Mary, called Bloody Mary for the persecutions accompanying the enforced return to Catholicism. Elizabeth took the throne aware that both Edward and Mary had found strong support for their choice of religions. So Elizabeth adopted a *via media* (middle way), blending both Roman and Protestant elements. During her reign the Thirty-nine Articles of Religion were promulgated, with some articles condemning Roman beliefs and practices, some articles preserving Roman elements. Purgatory, indulgences, venerating saints' relics, and celebrating the liturgy in any tongue other than the vernacular were among the Roman elements condemned. However, Elizabeth retained the traditional episcopal structure even though it had been under attack during her time and Edward's, and even though many English Puritans objected to ordained priests.

The Book of Common Prayer has gone through several editions. The edition published during Elizabeth's reign is crucial: it makes concrete the distinctive character of Anglicanism that has continued to this day. That edition includes the Thirty-nine Articles of Religion, creeds, church calendar, and liturgical services. Material on the sacraments in that edition is intentionally vague, to allow various interpretations of the eucharist. Anglicans recognize only two sacraments—baptism and the Lord's supper. Anglican doctrine on the church shifted from the Roman emphasis on the bishop to the Calvinist emphasis on the congregation. *The Book of Common Prayer* says the church exists where the Word of God is preached, the sacraments are duly administered, and the faithful are gathered.

A certain Anglophilia aligns the church with British tradition. When Rome commissioned St. Augustine to be a missionary in England in 597 A.D., he found Christians already in England, so many Anglicans insist their church was not formed by Rome and that the Anglican Church in England predates the arrival of the Roman Catholic Church in England. Anglicanism is thus a tradition separated from Roman Catholicism by its liturgical differences, its condemnation of some Roman beliefs and practices, and its alignment with British tradition. With the expansion of England in the seventeenth century, the Anglican tradition spread throughout the world.

The Anglican Family has been represented in the United States until recent decades primarily by the Protestant Episcopal Church, a few congregations of the ethnic Philippine Independent Church, and the Reformed Episcopal Church. However, beginning with the Anglican Orthodox Church formed in 1964, protest of the liberal trends within the Protestant Episcopal Church has produced a number of conservative Anglican splinters. Some of these new Anglican groups were able to obtain orders from valid Episcopal and Independent Philippine bishops, while others have had to turn to Old Catholic sources. The New Anglicans have been in a state of constant flux with schisms and mergers regularly religning the parishes currently found across the United States.

THE OLD CATHOLIC MOVEMENT. The Western Roman liturgical tradition suffered other divisions beside that of the Anglicans. The most conspicuous of which developed during the seventeenth century in Port Royal, France, when Jansenists—members of a mystical movement that carried on the work of Dutch theologian Cornelius Jansen (1585–1638)—conflicted with the Jesuits, priests of a religious order obedient to the pope. Jansenists believed that the will is not free and that redemption is limited only to a part of

mankind. Thus Jansenists were condemned by the pope and opposed by the Jesuits. The Jesuits accused the Jansenists of being Protestants, hence heretics; the Jansenists accused the Jesuits of despotism and laxity in doctrine and discipline. In alliance with the French monarchy, the Jesuits began a persecution that eventually broke the power of the Jansenists, many of whom fled to Holland in the territory of the see of Utrecht.

As the Jansenists moved into Holland from Port Royal, Utrecht's newly consecrated bishop, Peter Codde, entered into relations with them. When the pope demanded that Codde subscribe to the condemnation of the Jansenists, he refused and was accused of Jansenism. Rival parties developed—one behind Codde and another behind Theodore de Cock. De Cock, for various reasons, was banished from Holland by the government. Codde was deposed by the pope and ceased exercising his functions.

Without episcopal functionaries, the see soon began to wither, as no ordinations or confirmations could occur. This problem was somewhat alleviated by the unexpected stop over in Amsterdam of Dominique Marie Varlet, newly consecrated bishop of Babylon, on his way to Persia in 1719. In Amsterdam, he confirmed more than six hundred children, the first confirmed in seventeen years. For this act he was suspended from office. He returned to Europe and settled in Amsterdam. In 1724 Varlet consented to consecrate a new archbishop of Utrecht, Cornelius van Steenoven. When van Steenoven died shortly thereafter, Varlet consecrated Cornelius Wuytiers. Several other consecrations for neighboring dioceses such as Haarlem and Deventer followed, insuring that the apostolic succession would not be lost. For approximately 150 years the Church of Utrecht, commonly called the Old Catholic Church, continued with only episcopal supervision as the dividing line between it and Rome.

Though the Old Catholic Movement traces its history back to the see of Utrecht in Holland in 1702, it dates officially from the 1870's and the reaction to the declaration of papal infallability at the First Vatican Council. In 1870 the First Vatican Council declared the pope infallibile when speaking on matters of faith and morals, prompting large numbers of Roman Catholics to leave their church and seek communion with the Church of Utrecht. Even before the Council, opposition in anticipation of the declaration arose, particularly in Germany. In 1871 in Munich a congress of opponents, led by Von Schulte, a professor of canon law, was held. Three hundred delegates, including representatives from the Churches of Utrecht and England, came. These representatives organized the Old Catholic Church along national lines. In 1873 Joseph Hubert Reinkens, a professor of church history at Breslau, was elected bishop and was consecrated by the bishop of the church at Deventer. A Constitution was adopted in 1874 which recognized national autonomy and established an international Synod of Bishops. The archbishop of Utrecht now presides over the episcopal conference.

The Old Catholic Church retained most of the doctrines of Rome but rejected ecclesiastical unity under the pope. In 1874 the Old Catholic Church dropped the compulsory fasting and auricular confession of the Roman Catholic Church, and feast days were reduced. By 1880 vernacular mass began to replace the Latin. The seven sacraments were continued, but baptism and the eucharist were elevated to prime importance. The Roman Catholic Church has recognized the validity of Old Catholic (Utrecht) orders though the exercise of the episcopal powers are illegal.

Because the Church of England (the Anglican Church) was so similar to the Old Catholic Church on the Continent, no attempt was made to introduce the later church into England. However, during the nineteenth century there arose men who wished to function as bishops outside of either the Roman or Anglican communions. In some cases these were former priests in older communions. Some were representatives of ethnic communities expressing nationalistic enthusiasms. The Old Catholic movement developed an anti-authoritarian character. Most of its bishops have been self-appointed and have small followings. They have pressed for recognition of orders while keeping independence of jurisdiction. As an attempt at legitimization, they have sought recognition or reconsecration by bishops of the Eastern Orthodox Church (often after rebuff by the archbishop of Utrecht, the head of the Old Catholic Church). What began as a specific protest against the pope's authority turned into a drive by independent bishops to set up schismatic dioceses.

With the growth of independent dioceses and recognition by various Eastern and Western churches, the variation in ritual and doctrine has increased tremendously.

As the Old Catholic movement developed in America, a chaotic episcopal scene emerged. Many bishops claim dioceses which exist only on paper and ordinations by bishops whose existence cannot be verified. A few churches seem to be oriented to serve the homosexual community. A few have been confidence schemes.

In the United States, most of the Old Catholic Churches derive their orders through two lines of succession, that of Joseph Rene Vilatte or Arnold Harris Mathew. A third faction traces its lineage to miscellaneous Eastern and Western orders through Hugh George de Willmott Newman. Neither Vilatte's nor Mathew's churches remained in communion with the European Old Catholic churches, which in 1932 entered into full communion with the Church of England and by 1936 with most of the churches of the Anglican communion.

Arnold Harris Mathew. Arnold Harris Mathew (1852-1919) began his professional career as a Roman Catholic priest. After serving several parishes, he became a Unitarian. He flirted with the Church of England for a while, changed his name, and married. Eventually he made peace with Rome and settled down as a layman and author. He penned a number of items, including collaboration in editing the third edition of H. C. Lea's *History of Sacerdotal Celibacy in the Christian Church* early in this century. In September 1907 he began corresponding with Bishop Eduard Herzog, an Old Catholic bishop in Switzerland. In these letters, and later ones to Bishop J. J. Van Theil of Haarlem, he suggested the formation of an Old Catholic Church in England.

Mathew had in the years previous to his correspondence become associated with a group of disgruntled ex-Catholics, led by Father Richard O'Halloran. Under O'Halloran's guidance, Mathew was elected bishop of the Old Catholics in England. The problem was to get valid orders. The church at Utrecht, the central see of the Old Catholic Church, was very hesitant, but finally on April 22, 1908, Mathew was consecrated in Utrecht by the Archbishop under protest from the Anglicans.

Mathew returned to England to find that O'Halloran had lied to him and there was no following waiting for Mathew to become their bishop. Mathew immediately wrote the archbishop of Utrecht informing him of the deceit and offering to resign. When his resignation was refused, Mathew accepted his circumstances as a mission. The Rev. W. Noel Lambert turned over his chapel to become St. Willibrord's Procathedral and Mathew's headquarters.

In 1910 Mathew secretly consecrated two ex-Roman Catholic priests as bishops without informing Utrecht and without the assistance of other validly consecrated bishops. Mathew declared his independence from Utrecht and succeeded in building a small church. He died in lonely poverty, but before his death, Mathew set the stage for Old Catholicism in America.

Among Bishop Mathew's significant consecrations were those of Prince de Landas Berghes et de Rache, Duc de St. Winock, who established Mathew's succession in the U.S., and Frederick Samuel Willoughby, who founded the Liberal Catholic Church. Mathew's consecrations also included that of John Kowalski of the Polish Mariavite Church.

The Duc de Landas Berghes was an Austrian nobleman consecrated by Bishop Arnold Harris Mathew of the Old Catholic Church on June 28, 1913, probably with the idea of setting up an independent church in Austria. De Landas Berghes was prevented from returning to Austria from England because of World War I, however, and fled to the U.S. to escape arrest as an enemy-alien. During his short career, before his submission to Rome in 1919, he consecrated as bishops Fathers W.H. Francis Brothers and Henry Carfora, the direct sources of most Old Catholic bodies in America to date because of the many men that they consecrated as bishops.

Joseph Rene Vilatte. The man who first brought the Old Catholic Church to America was Joseph Rene Vilatte. French-born, Vilatte appeared in Wisconsin in the 1880's preaching Old Roman Catholic doctrines among French and Belgian immigrants. He had had a checkered religious education under an ex-Roman Catholic priest, Father Charles Chiniquy, and had come to believe both Roman Catholic and Protestant positions invalid. After marked success in Wisconsin, Vilatte went to Berne and obtained ordination from Bishop Herzog, but a protest from the Anglicans prevented his obtaining consecration from Utrecht, the central see of the Old Catholic Church. He finally, after a long search, obtained consecration as archbishop of the archdiocese of America on May 29, 1892, from Archbishop Alvarez of Ceylon, who had received his orders from the Syro-Jacobite Church of Malabar.

Vilatte briefly returned to Roman Catholicism in 1899–1900, but soon became frustrated, resumed his independent work and for the next twenty years operated as an archbishop for the American Catholic Church. Given his Roman background and his Orthodox orders, it is not surprising that both Old Catholic and independent Eastern Orthodox jurisdictions sprang from his activity. Also, the Syro-Jacobite Church of Malabar refused to recognize the various consecrations he performed, even for leaders in his own church, and he was further removed from the mainstream of American church life. Finally, in 1925, he again returned to the Roman Catholic Church, and renouncing his separatist and independent course of action, died in the arms of *Mater Ecclesia*. His own American Catholic Church, after the death of Archbishop Frederick Lloyd, Vilatte's successor, was taken over by bishops with Theosophical leanings and moved totally into the Liberal Catholic Church community.

Hugh de Willmott Newman. Among the most colorful bishops in the independent Catholic community, Hugh de Willmott Newman (1905-) can be credited with introducing an increasingly common practice among the autonomous bishops, that of seeking numerous re-consecrations in order to legitimize an otherwise miniscule ecclesiastical jurisdiction by having its bishop embody a wide variety of lines of apostolic succession, both East and West. Such jurisdictions would symbolize the ecumenical church.

Newman was originally consecrated in 1944 by Dr. William Bernard Crow, whose orders derived from Luis Mariano Soares (Mar Basilius) of the small Syro-Chaldean Church in India, Ceylon, Socotra, and Messina. However, within the next decade Newman received no less than nine additional consecrations, usually in ceremonies in which he in turn reconsecrated the other bishop (thus passing along the apostolic lineages he had already received). Of the several consecrations swapped by Newman, that with W. D. de Ortega Maxey of the Apostolic Episcopal Church was most important for the American scene, as Maxey not only established an American branch of Newman's Catholicate of the West, but became the prime source for American bishops to receive Newman's lineages.

Episcopally led churches have traditionally based their legitimacy on their ability to trace their line of succession from the original twelve Apostles. That is, for a bishop to be validly consecrated, and thus able to validly ordain priest, that bishop must himself be consecrated by a validly consecrated bishop. Thus the story of the independent Old Catholic jurisdictions in America is the story of the search for legitimacy through ever more valid consecrations. It has become common for independent bishops to receive multiple consecrations, especially after changing allegiance to a different jurisdiction.

The importing of Eastern orders for a Western church, and the intermingling of Eastern and Western lineages in bishops such as Newman, also initiated a complex mixing of liturgies. The independent jurisdictions have felt free to adopt, irregardless of the practices of the body from which they received their apostolic succession, any number of liturgies— Roman, Anglican, Eastern, or even Theosophical, while some have written their own. Since many of the American

jurisdictions are quite small, with an unpaid clergy and congregationally owned property, one of the few real decisions which the bishop can make regards the liturgies which the congregations may use.

Adopting the practice introduced by Mathew of having an unpaid clergy, the Old Catholic (and independent Orthodox) church has splintered into over a hundred jurisdictions. Priests and bishops, since they have no financial tie to any given jurisdiction, can leave at will, and frequently do. The constant flux within the jurisdictions has made the problem of straightening out the line of succession extremely complex; however, the work begun in this area by H. R. T. Brandweth, Peter Anson, and Arthur C. Piepkorn has been expanded in recent years by Karl Pruter, Bertil Persson, and Alan Bain (without whose assistance this chapter could not have been completed).

Since the Roman Catholic Church's Second Vatican Council and the adoption of the new liturgy for the mass, a new set of independent Catholic jurisdictions have appeared which have an allegiance to the Latin liturgy and several practices largely abandoned in the post-Vatican Church. Some of these traditionalist jurisdictions have sought and received Old Catholic orders for their episcopal leadership, while others (such as the followers of Swiss Archbishop Lefebvre) have waited for some kind of recognition from Rome. Their future will be determined by such future acceptance of their continuance of pre-Vatican II practices or the denial thereof by Papal authority. Several of these traditionalist groups seem unlikely to ever receive any Papal approbation as they have become structured around one or more mediumistic individuals who claim to be in regular contact with and receiving frequent messages from the Virgin Mary.

Each of the four major liturgical traditions was brought to the United States by immigration of its Old World disciples, with the exception of the Old Catholics. The traditions came as structures to preserve the Old World customs and cultures in the secular environment of the United States. Churches were founded wherever a significant group of immigrants or their descendants resided. These churches remained under the supervision of ancient sees and kept much closer contact with the sees than with neighboring American churches. There was little attempt to evangelize beyond the boundaries of the immigrants' particular ethnic groups. Schism would wait until the twentieth century for most groups, when Americanization and the desire for native American bishops would become major issues.

SOURCES—WESTERN LITURGICAL FAMILY

THE WESTERN LITURGICAL TRADITION

Alan, Kurt. *A History of Christianity*. Philadelphia: Fortress Press, 1985. 474 pp.

Frankforter, A. Daniel. *A History of the Christian Movement*. Chicago: Nelson-Hall, 1978. 317 pp.

Johnson, Paul. *A History of Christianity*. London: Weidenfeld and Nicolson, 1976. 556 pp.

Mirgeler, Albert. *Mutations of Western Christianity*. New York: Herder and Herder, 1965. 158 pp.

Sheldon, Henry C. *Sacerdotalism in the Nineteenth Century*. New York: Abingdon, 1909. 461 pp.

Thompson, Baird. *Liturgies of the Western Church*. Cleveland: The World Publishing Company, 1962.

Algermissen, Konrad. *Christian Denominations*. St. Louis: B. Herder Book Co., 1946.

ROMAN CATHOLICISM

Bokenkotter, Thomas. *A Concise History of the Catholic Church*. Garden City, NY: Doubleday, 1977. 431 pp.

Brantl, George, ed. *Catholicism*. New York: Washington Square Press, 1962. 277 pp.

Foy, Felician A. *Catholic Almanac*. Huntington, IN: Our Sunday Visitor, issued annually.

————. *A Concise Guide to the Catholic Church*. Huntington, IN: Our Sunday Visitor, 1984. 158 pp.

Frederic, Catherine. *The Handbook of Catholic Practices*. New York: Hawthorn Books, 1964. 320 pp.

McKenzie, John L. *The Roman Catholic Church*. New York: Holt, Rinehart and Winston, 1969. 288 pp.

THE ROMAN CATHOLIC CHURCH IN AMERICA

Catholicism in America. New York: Harcourt, Brace and Company, 1954. 242 pp.

Ellis, John Tracy. *American Catholicism*. Garden City, NY: Doubleday, 1965. 196 pp.

————. *Documents of American Catholic History*. 2 Vols. Chicago: Henry Regnery Company, 1967.

Hennesey, James. *American Catholics*. Oxford: Oxford University Press, 1981. 397 pp.

Kelly, George A. *The Battle for the American Church*. Garden City, NY: Doubleday, 1979. 513 pp.

Maynard, Theodore. *The Story of American Catholicism*. Garden City, NY: Doubleday, 1960.

ROMAN CATHOLIC THOUGHT

Abell, Aaron I. *American Catholic Thought on Social Questions*. Indianapolis: Bobbs-Merrill, 1968. 571 pp.

Abbott, Water, ed. *The Documents of Vatican II*. New York: Guild Press, 1966. 793 pp.

Burghardt, Walter J., and William F. Lynch. *The Idea of Catholicism*. New York: Meridian Books, 1960. 479 pp.

Berkouwer, G. C. *Recent Developments in Roman Catholic Thought*. Grand Rapids, MI: Wm. B. Eerdmans Publishing Company, 1958. 81 pp.

Bokenkotter, Thomas. *Essential Catholicism*. Garden City, NY: Doubleday, 1985. 437 pp.

A Catholic Catechism. New York: Herder and Herder, 1958. 448 pp.

Fremantle, Anne. *The Papal Encyclicals*. New York: New American Library, 1956. 317 pp.

O'Brien, John A. *Understanding the Catholic Faith*. Notre Dame, IN: Ave Maria Press, 1955. 281 pp.

Trese, Leo J. *The Creed—Summary of the Faith*. Notre Dame, IN: Fides Publishers, 1963. 155 pp.

ROMAN CATHOLIC LITURGY

Lefebvre, Gaspar. *The Spirit of Worship*. New York: Hawthorn Books, 1959. 127 pp.

Segundo, Juan Luis. *The Sacraments Today*. New York: Maryknoll, 1974. 154 pp.

The Treasures of the Mass. Clyde, MO: Benedictine Convent of Perpetual Adoration, 1957. 128 pp.

ROMAN CATHOLIC POLITY

McKnight, John P. *The Papacy*. London: McGraw-Hill Publishing Company, 1953. 400 pp.

Scharp, Heinrich. *How the Catholic Church Is Governed*. New York: Paulist Press, 1960. 128 pp.

Tillard, J. M. R. *The Bishop of Rome*. Wilmington, DE: Michael Glazier, 1983. 242 pp.

EASTERN RITE ROMAN CATHOLICISM

Attwater, Donald. *The Christian Churches of the East*. Milwaukee: Bruce Publishing Company, 1961. 232 pp.

————. *Eastern Catholic Worship*. New York: Devin-Adair Company, 1945. 224 pp.

Liesel, N. *The Eastern Catholic Liturgies*. Westminster, MD: Newman Press, 1960. 168 pp.

ANTI-CATHOLICISM

Billington, Ray Allen. *The Protestant Crusade*. New York: Macmillan, 1938. 514 pp.

Chiniquy, Charles. *Fifty Years in the Church of Rome*. Grand Rapids, MI: Baker Book House, 1960. 597 pp.

de la Bedoyere, Michael. *Objections to Roman Catholicism*. Philadelphia: J. B. Lippencott Company, 1965. 185 pp.

McLoughlin, Emmett. *Famous Ex-Priests*. New York: Lyle Stuart, 1968. 224 pp.

OLD CATHOLICISM

Anson, Peter F. *Bishops at Large*. London: Faber and Faber, 1964. 593 pp.

Bain, Alan. *"Bishops Irregular."* Bristol, Eng.: The Author, 1985. 256 pp.

Brandreth, H. R. T. *Episcopi Vagantes and the Anglican Church*. London: S.P.C.K., 1961. 140 pp.

Conger, Yves. *Challenge to the Church*. Huntington, IN: Our Sunday Visitor. 1976. 96 pp.

Davies, Michael. *Pope Paul's New Mass*. Dickinson, TX: Angelus Press, 1980. 673 pp.

Groman, E. Owen, and Jonathan E. Trela. *Three Studies in Old Catholicism*. Scranton, PA: Savonarola Theological Seminary Alumni Association, 1978. 37 pp.

Huelin, Gordon, ed. *Old Catholics and Anglicans, 1931-1981*. Oxford: Oxford University Press, 1983. 177 pp.

Moss, C. B. *The Old Catholic Movement*. Eureka Springs, AK: Episcopal Book Club, 1977. 368 pp.

Piepkorn, Arthur Carl. *Profiles in Belief*. Vol. I. New York: Harper & Row, 1977. pp. 29-56, 73-80.

Pruter, Karl, ed. *A Directory of Autocephalous Anglican, Catholic and Orthodox Bishops*. Highlandsville, MO: St. Willibrord Press, 1985.

Pruter, Karl, and J. Gordon Melton. *The Old Catholic Sourcebook*. New York: Garland, 1983. 254 pp.

CHURCH OF ENGLAND AND THE WORLDWIDE ANGLICAN COMMUNION

Dart, J. L. C. *The Old Religion*. London: S.P.C.K., 1956. 210 pp.

Flindall, R. P., ed. *The Church of England, 1815-1948*. London: S.P.C.K., 1972. 497 pp.

Hardy, E. R., Jr., ed. *Orthodox Statements on Anglican Orders.* New York: Morehouse-Gorham Co., 1946. 72 pp.

Neill, Stephen. *Anglicanism.* London: A. R. Mowbrays, 1977. 421 pp.

Wand, J. W. C. *What the Church of England Stands For.* London: A. R. Mowbray, 1951. 131 pp.

EPISCOPALIANISM IN AMERICA

DeMille, George E. *The Episcopal Church Since 1900.* New York: Morehouse-Gorham Company, 1955. 223 pp.

Herklots, H. G. G. *The Church of England and the American Episcopal Church.* London: A. R. Mowbray & Co., 1966. 183 pp.

Manross, William W. *A History of the American Episcopal Church.* New York: Morehouse-Gorham Co., 1950. 415 pp.

Woolverton, John Frederick. *Colonial Anglicanism in North America.* Detroit: Wayne State University Press, 1984. 331 pp.

THE NEW ANGLICANS

Dibbert, Roderic B. *The Roots of Traditional Anglicanism.* Akron, OH: DeKoven Foundation of Ohio, 1984.

A Directory of Churches of the Continuing Anglican Tradition. Eureka Springs, AK: Fellowship of Concerned Churchmen, 1983-84.

Joseph, Murray, *"Priests Forever."* Valley Forge, PA: The Brotherhood of the Servants of the Lord, 1975. 16 pp.

Opening Addresses of the Church Congress at St. Louis, Missouri, 14-16 September 1977. Amherst, VA: Fellowship of Concerned Churchmen, 1977.

A Retired Priest. *The Broken Body.* N.p.: The Author, 1980. 38 pp.

Chapter Two

THE EASTERN LITURGICAL FAMILY

Directory listings for the groups belonging to the Eastern Liturgical Family
may be found in the section beginning on page 207.

THE EASTERN ORTHODOX TRADITION. The Eastern Church and the Western Roman Church coexisted as two branches of the same church for centuries. However, cultural differences, politics, and doctrinal disagreements finally led to official division and mutual excommunication in 1054. The Eastern Church dominated the eastern Mediterranean basin, spreading through Greece, Egypt, Asia Minor, the Arab countries, and the Slavic nations. In the early Middle Ages, this dominance was weakened by the loss of the "heretical" churches (the non-Chalcedonian Orthodox churches) and then by the Moslem conquests.

In each area, the Eastern Church developed an episcopal structure of national autonomous sees. Certain sees were more prominent and have been designated patriarchates. They include Alexandria, Antioch, Jerusalem, and Constantinople. In more recent years, patriarchates have been designated in Bulgaria, Serbia (Yugoslavia), Russia, and Romania. Autocephalous churches, headed by a bishop but without a patriarchate, exist in the Ukraine, Cypress, Albania, Greece, Poland, and Georgia (U.S.S.R.). Autonomous churches, headed by a bishop, self-governing on internal matters, but dependent on a patriarchate for the appointment of its primate (head bishop) and relations with other churches, exist in Finland, Estonia, Czechoslovakia, Latvia, Lithuania, and Mt. Sinai.

The patriarchs are represented by the "ecumenical" patriarch of Constantinople, though his position of primacy is one of honor, not power. All of the patriarchs are of equal authority and none has the right to interfere with the work in another's territory. They are, however, "in communion" with each other and in the United States the bishops of the churches who directly relate to the ecumenical patriarch work together as the Standing Conference of Canonical Orthodox Bishops in the Americas. Most Orthodox Christians in America are members of these churches.

To most Americans, familiar with only the Roman and Anglican traditions, the Eastern Orthodox tradition presents several distinctive features. The celibate priesthood of the Roman Catholic Church is not demanded. In the East priests marry (though they must do so before ordination). Monks do not. Bishops are drawn from the ranks of the monks. Priests who are not monks are not eligible for the episcopacy. The Eastern Church does not recognize the authority of the bishop of Rome over the various patriarchs of the Eastern Church. The Eastern Churches recognize only the seven ecumenical councils held between 325 A.D. and 787 A.D. because no further councils occurred at which the bishops of Rome and the Eastern patriarchs worked together.

The Eastern Church rejects the *filioque* doctrine of the Roman Catholic Church. *Filioque* is the Latin word for "and the Son," added to the creed to assert that the Holy Spirit proceeds from the Father and the Son. Some theologians of the Eastern Church insisted the Holy Spirit proceeds from the Father through the Son. The Eastern Church rejected the *filioque* doctrine partly because John 15:26 makes no mention of the Son and instead speaks of "the Spirit of truth who proceeds from the Father."

The Greek *Liturgy of St. Chrysostom* is used throughout the Eastern Church. The various national bodies have translated it into their native tongues, and in America English is being increasingly used.

Those areas where Orthodoxy exists only as a small minority religion and geographically removed from the ancient centers are designated Orthodoxy in Diaspora. The largest diaspora community is the three million-plus Orthodox Christians in the United States.

Orthodoxy entered the United States in the eighteenth century following the discovery of Alaska by Russians in 1741. In 1743 an Aleutian by the name of Andreu Islands was baptized. The Russian Orthodox Church was firmly established in 1794 when seven monks came to Paul's Harbor and consecrated the first church. By 1841 a seminary was in operation in the Aleutian Islands. The first diocese, created after Alaska was purchased, was moved to San Francisco in 1872.

Spotty immigration of Orthodox Christians occurred throughout the nineteenth century, but only in the last decades did it become significant. Heavy immigration between 1880 and 1920 was caused by the unrest following the Russian and Turkish expansion and by World War I.

Greek immigration in the second decade of the twentieth century doubled the American-Greek community.

Immigration was largely to Eastern and Midwestern urban centers, and most Orthodox churches are still to be found there. Immigrants developed the various non-English-language "ghettos" held together by periodicals, ethnic fraternities, and the churches. Intermarriage of local families further united the small communities.

Americanization has become the major issue in the various Orthodox communities. The abandonment of Old World languages plus marriage with outsiders, democratic tendencies, and the pressure of a non-Orthodox environment have all brought change and in some cases schism within the Orthodox churches.

The structure of American Orthodoxy was dramatically changed in 1970 with the creation of the Orthodox Church in America by the merger of several of the Russian churches. Russian Orthodoxy, by reason of its early arrival date, has always had a primacy in America. Many of the currently existing independent Orthodox bodies were formed under its care. In recent years the growth of the Greek Orthodox Church in America led to challenges to Russian primacy, challenges based on the claims of the ecumenical patriarch in Istanbul as the first among equals in world Orthodoxy. The argument was somewhat academic since each American church was directly related to a different overseas see. The Orthodox Church in America, unattached to a foreign see, was authorized by Patriarch Alexis in Moscow, whose right to grant such status has been questioned by the Greek Orthodox.

The new body, the Orthodox Church in America, aims at uniting Orthodox of all ethnic groups into a single American Orthodox body. This is the natural result of a growing demand for American autonomy. Archbishop Phillip of the Antiochean Church has been among the new church's most vocal advocates. The new body is the only Orthodox church which has all of the structures necessary to continue without outside help. These structures include seminaries, monasteries, and charitable institutions.

THE EMERGENCE OF INDEPENDENT ORTHODOXY IN THE TWENTIETH CENTURY.

During the nineteenth century, Orthodox believers from many of the European national churches migrated to America. A few, such as the Greeks, remained autonomous and eventually formed their own ethnic church. Others, such as the Syrians, began as an ethnic group under the care of the Russian Church, which, because of its being the first Orthodox church to establish work, had a special hegemony within the United States. Once in the United States with its multi-ethnic atmosphere and geographically removed from its homeland, the Orthodox church became subject to a variety of forces which has split its community into a number of ecclesiastical factions. The first major splinter began as a movement to unite American Orthodoxy.

Aftimios Ofiesh (1890-1971) came to America in 1905 to work among Syrians, then a part of the Russian Orthodox Church. In 1917 he was consecrated bishop for the Syrian work, succeeding Bishop Raphael Hawaweeny. On February 2, 1927, the Russian bishops gave him duty of caring for the American-born orthodox, especially the English-speaking parishes, not otherwise being given proper care. By their action they created a new jurisdiction, the American Orthodox Church, as an autonomous body with filial relationship to the Russian Church.

The project met immediate opposition. The non-Russian bishops were not supportive of a united American Orthodoxy as proposed and the Ecumenical Patriarch, the nominal head of all Orthodox churches, denounced the project as schismatic. The Greeks were angered by Ofiesh's publication of a magazine, *Orthodox Catholic Reporter*. Especially offended were the Episcopalians who considered themselves the American form of Orthodoxy and who were providing the Russians with large amounts of financial support. They applied pressure on Metropolitan Platon to abandon Ofiesh. Even though abandoned by the Russians, Ofiesh continued in his project and, beginning with Emmanuel Ato-Hotab (1927) and Sophonius Bashira (1928), he consecrated four bishops to head his independent work.

The problem with Ofiesh was not the only trouble to disturb the Russian Church during the 1920's. As a result of the Russian Revolution and the coming to power of an antireligious regime, the close allegiance of the Church to the Russian government was called into question, especially after the imprisonment of the Patriarch of Moscow in 1922. Soviet supporters within the Russian Church in 1924 organized a sobor (convention) of what came to be called the Living Church faction. They voiced support of the Soviet government and elected the only American at the Sobor, John Kedrowsky, Bishop of America. He came to America and with his sons, Nicholas (later his successor as Bishop of America) and John, through court action took control of St. Nicholas Cathedral in New York City. However, he was rejected by a Synod of the American Russian Church in 1924 which declared its autonomy in administrative matters from the Church in Russia.

While the Russians were splintering into several factions, the Greeks, never under Russian control, were having their own problems. In 1908, the Greek parishes in America were transferred from the direct authority of the Ecumenical Patriarch to the Holy Synod of the Church in Greece. That arrangement did not provide the necessary leadership for the burgeoning American church, so in 1918, the Ecumenical Patriarch began the process of establishing the American church as an archdiocese, finally accomplished in 1922. However, that arrangement also did not resolve the leadership question, and in 1930 the Ecumenical Patriarch reasserted his hegemony in America by appointing a representative to come to the United States and take over leadership of the Archdiocese.

Meanwhile, as organizational trouble plagued the church, it was further divided by internal problems in Greece. A faction of the American membership opposed the transfer of the allegiance of the American church from the Church in Greece to the Ecumenical Patriarch. In the 1930's they removed themselves from the Archdiocese and sought consecration of a new bishop by the Church in Greece. Thus in 1934, Christopher Contogeorge, with the blessing of the

Church in Greece, was consecrated Archbishop of Philadelphia by Albanian Bishop Fan Noli, assisted by Bishop Sophonius Bashira. Archbishop Christopher was the consecrator of Bishop John Kedrowsky's successor, Nicholas Kedrowsky.

By the mid-1930's Bishops Sophonius, Nicholas (Kedrowsky), Christopher, and Fan Noli constituted a group of independent Orthodox bishops both organizationally and emotionally separated from the larger body of Orthodox bishops and faithful. These four participated in a number of consecrations of new bishops, both in their several jurisdictions and in other independent Orthodox churches. From their lineage come Bishops Joseph Klimovicz, Walter Propheta, and Peter Zurawetzky, who in turn consecrated most of the men who head the presently existing independent Orthodox churches.

There is one strain of independent Orthodoxy which has a history independent of the bishops discussed above, those which derive from Archbishop Joseph Rene Vilatte of the American Catholic Church (discussed in the previous chapter as one of the founders of Old Catholicism in America). Vilatte's episcopal orders came from a small Orthodox body in India and during the later years of his life he consecrated individuals who adopted an Orthodox stance, most notably George A. McGuire, founder of the African Orthodox Church. Also, at least one person from the Vilatte lineage participated in the consecration of Walter Propheta.

Finally, it should be noted that just as both Orthodox and Catholic jurisdictions derived from the work of Vilatte, so too have they both derived from the independent Orthodox bishops. Most notably, Christ Catholic Church derived as an Old Catholic body from under the previous jurisdiction of Peter Zurawetzky.

THE NON-CHALCEDONIAN ORTHODOX CHURCHES. Separating during the years of the great Ecumenical Councils, the Christian churches of Egypt, Armenia, and the Middle East, for a variety of reasons, refused to ratify one or more of the creeds, primarily the Chalcedonian Creed of 451 A.D., which most of the Eastern Orthodox world accepted as a standard of orthodox Christian faith. Both the Roman Catholic Church and the Eastern Orthodox Churches have branded these churches as heretical in faith, though the Armenian Church has vigorously protested such labeling as a misunderstanding of its position both theologically and relationally to the Council of Chalcedon.

The Nestorians. The monk Nestorius, who became patriarch of Constantinople in 428 A.D., believed that Christ was not the Son of God, but that God was living in Christ. The two natures of Christ—divine and human—were separable, said Nestorius. Further, he said Mary bore the human Christ, not God. Thus she was not "Theotokos," the God-bearer. And it was not God who suffered and died. Nestorius preached his doctrines throughout the Eastern Church. In 431 A.D., the Third Council of the early church met at Ephesus to treat the teachings of Nestorius. The Council ruled that Mary was "Theotokos," and that the human and divine natures are inseparably bound together in the one person of Christ. The

Council condemned Nestorius, declared his teachings heretical, and deposed him as patriarch of Constantinople. These actions began a four-year battle of ecclesiastical and imperial politics. The result was Nestorius' banishment and the burning of his books.

The Nestorians continued to spread Nestorius' beliefs. They conducted missionary work in Persia, India, and China, and won followers in Arabia and Egypt. Under the Mohammedans they were essentially free from persecution until the modern era. They survive to this day as the Church of the East. Their largest losses have been to proselytizing efforts by Roman Catholics, Jacobites (to whom they lost much of the church in India), and more recently Protestants.

The Church of the East belongs to the non-Chalcedonian Orthodox tradition in the sense that it opposes the statement of the Council at Chalcedon, 451 A.D., that Christ was "begotten . . . of Mary the Virgin, the God bearer."

When the Nestorians were rediscovered in the 1830's by Protestant missionaries, their preservation of an old Aramaic dialect also became news. They have since made this dialect the language of their Scripture translation. The seven sacraments they observe are baptism, ordination, the holy eucharist, anointing, remission of sins, holy leaven, and the sign of the cross. The holy leaven refers to the belief that a portion of the bread used at the Last Supper was brought to the East by the Apostle Thaddens and every eucharist in the Church of the East is made from bread continuous with that meal. The sign of the cross is considered a sacrament and a very specific formula is prescribed for its rubric.

As with all of the Eastern churches, relation with a particular Apostle is assumed. The Church of the East claims a special relationship with the Apostle Thaddeus, who visited the kingdom of Oshroene soon after Pentecost, and with Mari (one of the seventy disciples). Supposedly, there was correspondence between Abgar, the ruler of Oshroene, and Christ, in which the former invited Jesus to settle at Edessa, the capital city.

The liturgy of the Church of the East is that of the "Holy Apostles Addai and Mari" (Saints Thaddeus and Mari), who brought it from Jerusalem. The leadership of the church is found in the patriarchate, which has since 1350 been hereditary in the family of Mar Shimun. Since the patriarch is celibate, the office passes from uncle to nephew. Under the patriarch are the metropolitans and bishops. The priests are allowed to marry at any time, even after their ordination.

The Monophysites. The Monophysite Churches, like the Eastern Orthodox and Roman Catholic, emphasize liturgy in their church life; they believe strongly in an Apostolic succession; and they derive their doctrinal position from the ancient creeds. Their distinctiveness comes from the content of their creed, which differs more from both Constantinople and Rome than the latter two differ from each other. The Monophysite Churches are united on doctrine, but have lines of succession and liturgy with a national flavor.

The distinct Monophysite doctrines derive from the fifth century discussions on the nature of Christ. It was the Monophysite position that Christ was one person of one (mono) nature (physis), the divine nature absorbing the human nature. In the context of the debate, Monophysitism was opposed to Nestorianism, which said that Christ had two natures but that they were separable.

Monophysitism was condemned by the Fourth Council of the early church, held at Chalcedon in 451 A.D. The Council formulated what came to be called the Chalcedonian Creed, which says Christ is "of one substance with the Father as regards his Godhead, and at the same time of one substance with us as regards his manhood." Rejecting this creed, most of the Armenian, northern Egyptian, and Syrian churches broke away from the main body of the Christian church. In general, the Monophysite churches accept only the first three councils of the early Christian church (those at Nicea, Constantinople, and Ephesus) as valid and binding.

Theologians continue to debate Monophysite Christology. Some writers contend that the Monophysite churches are Eutychean; i.e., that they follow the teaching of Archimandrite Eutyches, a monk of Constantinople, who asserted the unity of nature in Christ in such a way that the human nature was completely fused and absorbed in the divine. Others, however, assert that the Monophysite churches (at least some of them) are not Eutychean, but Orthodox with a very "undeveloped terminology." The Armenian, Syrian, and Coptic Churches represent the Monophysite tradition, but they deny the label "Monophysite" and deny that they teach any submergence of Christ's human nature.

The Armenian Churches. According to tradition Christianity was brought to Armenia by Thaddeus and Bartholomew, two of the original twelve apostles. By 260 A.D., a bishopric had been established in Armenia and was referred to Eusebius's *Ecclesiastical History*. In 301 A.D. Tiridates II, the King of Armenia, became the first Christian monarch. St. Gregory the illuminator, who converted Tiridates, worked with the King's blessing to organize the Armenian Church. Through the church a written language was developed and a literate Armenian culture emerged. As is common with Monophysite churches, the Armenian Church accepted only the first three ecumenical councils (those at Nicea, Constantinople, and Ephesus), and uses the Nicene Creed. Members of the Armenian Church did not attend the Council of Chalcedon in 451 A.D. and rejected its decisions.

Ecclesiastical authority in the Armenian Church was invested in the catholikos who originally resided at Vagharshabat in central Armenia. There, close to the palace, Gregory built Etchmiadzin, the great Cathedral. Because of changing political fortunes, the catholikos was frequently forced to move, first to Dovin (484), then among other places to Argina (944), Tauplour (1054), Domnplov (1065), and finally to Sis, in the Kingdom of Lesser Armenia or Cilicia (1293). In 1441 an assembly was held at Etchmiadzin and a catholikos was installed. The catholikos at Sis at that time took the title catholikos of Cilicia. Both sees—Etchmiadzin and Cilicia—have functioned until the present.

There are several minor peculiarities in the Armenian Church's sacraments, distinguishing it from other churches in the liturgical family. Holy communion is customarily celebrated only on Sunday and on special occasions and cannot be celebrated twice in the same day. Pure wine (without water) and unleavened bread are used and the laity receive the eucharist by intincture. The eucharist is served to infants immediately after baptism by touching the lips with the elements.

Armenians in America. During the last 1500 years Armenia has suffered foreign domination and persecution by Moslems and Russians. The most terrible of these persecutions were the ones begun by the Turks in 1890 and carried on intermittently for the next thirty years. The effect was practically to destroy and scatter the Armenian nation. The arrival of Armenians in America really dates from the immigration begun as a result of the massacres. The anti-religious persecution by the Russians after World War I followed the Turkish onslaughts.

Armenians in America began to form churches in the early twentieth century. The first was organized in 1891 in Worcester, Massachusetts. After 1921 American Armenians began to divide politically into two factions. One group remained intense nationalists, loyal to an independent Armenia and its symbols. The other group, often described as Pro-Soviet, accommodated themselves to and then supported the inevitable Russian dominance of Armenia. The political division was deeply felt throughout the entire American Armenian community, including the church.

Though practically autonomous, the Armenian Church in America recognized the authority of the catholikos of Etchmiadzin. Archbishop Levon Tourian was designated by the see of Etchmiadzin as the supreme prelate of the Armenian Apostolic Church in America. Shortly after his arrival he managed to offend both political parties in contradictory statements concerning the nationalist flag. The continued polarization of the two factions led in 1933 to a split in the church itself.

The split occurred during the annual meeting of the National Church Council. Pro-Soviet lay delegates began to hold rump sessions and from their meeting a second church was, in effect, begun. While there was little doubt of the legal continuance through the Church Council, Archbishop Tourian recognized the Pro-Soviet group and declared some of the nationalist priests "unfrocked." A few months later Bishop Tourian was assassinated during High Mass in New York City. So deep was the split in the Armenian community that as one writer observed, "Armenians have come to hate one another with a passion that has exceeded at times even a hatred for the Turks" (Sarkis Atamian, *The Armenian Community* [New York: Philosophical Library, 1955], 358).

The Syrian Churches. Antioch, an ancient city of Syria, is the place where the followers of Jesus were first called Christians (Acts 11:26). In the early centuries Antioch was the center of a large Christian movement rent by the Monophysite controversy concerning whether Christ had two natures, human and divine, or one (mono) nature (physis). Jacob Baradeus, a resident of Antioch though Bishop of Edessa, was both a favorite of Empress Theodora and a fervent Monophysite. After his consecration in 542 A.D., he toured all of the area from Turkey to Egypt organizing churches. Those churches under his authority were to take his name in later years.

The evangelical zeal of the Jacobites was hindered and much of their gains destroyed in the conquests of Islam. In 1665 the Jacobites gained strength in India and Ceylon when the Nestorian Malabar Christians came under the Antiochean patriarch. This action more than doubled the size of the church and today makes up more than sixty percent of its worldwide membership of 100,000.

The Jacobites have several distinctive practices. Baptism is by triune infusion (pouring). Auricular confession to the priest is not used. During the eucharist the priest waves his hand over the elements to symbolize the operation of the Holy Spirit. The action is also used in ordination ceremonies.

The Coptic Churches of Egypt and Ethiopia. At one time the Church in Egypt, the Coptic Church, was among the largest in Christendom. But in 451 A.D., Dioscurus, the patriarch of Alexandria, was deposed by the Council of Chalcedon, the fourth of the general councils in the early centuries of Christianity. There began an era of persecution of the Copts, first by their fellow Christians and then after 640 A.D. by the Arab conquerors. Beginning with heavy taxes, the persecutions became bloody toward the end of the first millennium A.D. By the end of the Middle Ages, the Coptic Church had shrunk from 6 million to 15,000 members. Growth since that time has been slow, but religious toleration in the nineteenth century helped, and by the middle of the twentieth cetntury, there were 3 to 5 million members.

The Coptic Church developed its own traditions. Its members are proud of Egypt as the childhood home of Jesus and the location of the ministry of St. Mark, who traditionally is credited with Egypt's initial evangelization. Several liturgies are used, but the most popular is the Liturgy of St. Basil, written by St. Basil the Great (b. 330 A.D.). There is particular veneration of the Virgin, and there are thirty-two feasts in her honor during the ecclesiastical year. In 1971 she is said to have appeared over the Coptic Cathedral in Cairo.

The head of the Coptic Church is the patriarch of Alexandria with his see at Cairo. In 1971 this office was assumed by Pope Shenouda III. On May 6, 1973, Pope Shenouda greeted Pope Paul VI with a kiss of peace on a visit to St. Peter's Basilica in Rome.

Ethiopia accepted Christianity in the fourth century and the first bishop, Frumentius, was consecrated by Athanasius, who was the patriarch of Alexandria. The Ethiopian Church came under the jurisdiction of the Coptic Church in Egypt and followed its theological lead. Isolated by its mountains, Ethiopia withstood the advances of Islam but was cut off from the rest of Christendom. It reached its heights of glory in the thirteenth century under King Lalibela, who gave his name to a city of churches, ten of which were hewn from solid rock. Modern history for this church began when Catholic missionaries sought to bring the Abyssinians under the Roman pontiff. They almost succeeded in the seventeenth century when for a few years Roman Catholicism was accepted by the ruler.

The Ethiopian Church differs from the Coptic Church in that it has absorbed strong Jewish traits. It accepts the Apocrypha as scripture, venerates the Sabbath along with Sunday, recognizes Old Testament figures as saints, and observes many Old Testament regulations on food and purification.

SOURCES—EASTERN ORTHODOX FAMILY

EASTERN ORTHODOXY

Adeney, Walter F. *The Greek and Eastern Churches*. New York: Charles Scribner's Sons, 1908. 634 pp.

Attwater, Donald. *The Dissident Eastern Churches*. Milwaukee: The Bruce Publishing Company, 1937. 349 pp.

Benz, Ernst. *The Eastern Orthodox Church*. Garden City, NY: Doubleday, 1963. 230 pp.

Bulgakov, Sergius. *The Orthodox Church*. London: Centenary Press, 1935. 224 pp.

Lau, Emhardt Burgess. *The Eastern Church in the Western World*. Milwaukee: Morehead Publishing Co., 1928. 149 pp.

Handbook of American Orthodoxy. Cincinnati: Forward Movement Publications, 1972. 191 pp.

Kuzmission, Joe. *Eastern Orthodox World Directory*. Boston: Braden Press, 1968. 305 pp.

Le Guillou, M. J. *The Spirit of Eastern Orthodoxy*. Glen Rock, NJ: Paulist Press, 1964. 121 pp.

Orthodoxy, A Faith and Order Dialogue. Geneva: World Council of Churches, 1960. 80 pp.

Parishes and Clergy of the Orthodox, and Other Eastern Churches in North and South America. New York: Joint Commission on Cooperation with the Eastern and Old Catholic Churches of the General Convention of the Protestant Episcopal Church, 1964-65. 187 pp. Rev. ed., 1967-68. 184 pp. Rev. ed., 1970-71. 208 pp.

Schmemann, Alexander. *The Historic Road of Eastern Orthodoxy*. New York: Holt, Rinehart and Winston, 1963. 343 pp.

Zernov, Nicolas. *The Church of Eastern Christians*. London: Society for Promoting Christian Knowledge, 1942. 114 pp.

ORTHODOX LITURGY

Dalmais, Irenee-Henri. *Eastern Liturgies*. New York: Hawthorn Books, 1960. 144 pp.

The Orthodox Liturgy. London: Society for Promoting Christian Knowledge, 1964. 110 pp.

Sokolof, D., comp. *A Manual of the Orthodox Church's Divine Service*. Jordanville, NY: Holy Trinity Russian Orthodox Monastery, 1968. 166 pp.

ORTHODOX THEOLOGY

Allen, Joseph J. *Orthodox Synthesis*. Crestwood, NY: St. Vladimir's Seminary Press, 1981. 231 pp.

Lossky, Vladimir. *The Mystical Theology of the Eastern Church*. London: James Clarke & Co., 1957. 252 pp.

Maloney, George A. *A History of Orthodox Theology Since 1453*. Belmont, MA: Nordland Publishing Company, 1976. 388 pp.

Platon, Metropolitan. *The Orthodox Doctrine of the Apostolic Eastern Church*. London, 1857. Reprint. New York: AMS Press, 1969. 239 pp.

INDEPENDENT ORTHODOXY

Anson, Peter F. *Bishops at Large*. London: Faber and Faber, 1964. 593 pp.

Bain, Alan. *"Bishops Irregular."* Bristol, England: The Author, 1985. 256 pp.

Brandreth, H. R. T. *Episcopi Vagantes and the Anglican Church*. London: S.P.C.K., 1961. 140 pp.

Morris, John W. "The Episcopate of Aftimios Ofeish." *The Word* Part One: 25,2 (February 1981) 5-9; Part Two: 25, 3 (March 1981) 5-9.

Pruter, Karl, and J. Gordon Melton. *The Old Catholic Sourcebook*. New York: Garland Publishing, Inc., 1983. 254 pp.

Tillett, Gregory. *Joseph Rene Vilatte: A Bibliography*. Sydney, Australia: The Vilatte Guild, 1980. 23 pp.

NON-CHALCEDONEAN ORTHODOXY

Butler, Alfred J. *The Ancient Coptic Churches of Egypt*. 2 Vols. Oxford: Claredon Press, 1884.

Elmhardt, William Chauncey, and George M. Lamsa. *The Oldest Christian People*. New York: AMS Press, 1970. 141 pp.

Fortescue, Adrian. *The Lesser Eastern Churches*. London: Catholic Truth Society, 1913. 468 pp.

Issac, Ephraim. *The Ethiopian Church*. Boston: Henry N. Sawyer Company, 1968. 59 pp.

McCullough, W. Stewart. *A Short History of Syriac Christianity to the Rise of Islam*. Chico, CA: Scholars Press, 1982. 197 pp.

Meinardus, Otto, F. A. *Christian Egypt Faith and Life*. Cairo: The American University in Cairo Press, 1970. 513 pp.

Ramban, Kadavil Paul. *The Orthodox Syrian Church, Its Religion and Philosophy*. Puthencruz, Syria: K. V. Pathrose, 1973. 167 pp.

St. Mark and the Coptic Church. Cairo: Coptic Orthodox Patriarchate, 1968. 164 pp.

Sarkissian, Karekin. *The Council of Chalcedon and the Armenian Church*. New York: The Armenian Church Prelacy, 1965. 264 pp.

————. *The Witness of the Oriental Orthodox Churches*. Artelias, Lebanon: The Author, 1970. 91 pp.

Chapter Three

THE LUTHERAN FAMILY

Directory listings for the groups belonging to the Lutheran Family may be found in the section beginning on page 237.

Lutheranism represents the first widely successful western breach of the authority of the Roman Catholic Church. The teachings of Martin Luther, coupled with the power of the German princes who supported him, precipitated a dramatic break with Roman Catholicism throughout Europe in the early sixteenth century. Lutheranism embraces the two basic precepts of Luther's writings: first, that salvation is by grace through faith alone; and second, that the Bible is the sole rule of faith and the sole authority for doctrine. Lutheranism is distinct from other Reformation churches because of its continued emphasis on a sacramental liturgy and because of Luther's understanding of the eucharist.

LUTHERAN DOCTRINE. Word and sacrament are the keystones of Lutheran church life. "Word" refers to the appeal to the Bible instead of to both the Bible and tradition. "Sacrament" refers to the high regard Lutherans have for the two sacraments they observe—baptism and the eucharist—and Luther's theology of the eucharist. Luther's belief that salvation is by grace through faith alone finds expression in Lutherans' interpretation of the Bible and reliance on it, and in their celebration of the sacraments.

A discussion of the importance of the Word to Lutherans must start with Luther's background. He was a Bible scholar and a professor at the University of Wittenburg in what has become East Germany. He translated the Bible into German and based his theology on the Bible. Before he broke with the Roman Catholic Church, he was an Augustinian monk who strove to merit salvation through ascetic practices. In studying the Bible, however, he found that salvation does not come by man's action but only by God's free gift. Thus comes the emphasis on man's sinfulness in Lutheranism: a person who breaks one law is as guilty as a person whose whole life is the breaking of laws. Luther saw that the whole point of Christ's coming was to bring salvation; human beings could not earn it by themselves.

It remains for each person to welcome grace by faith in Christ. This emphasis contrasts with the traditional Roman Catholic emphasis on both faith and good works. Further, this emphasis contradicts a practice popular in Luther's time—the selling of indulgences (by which people paid to cancel the punishment they would receive in purgatory for

their sins). Proceeds from the sale of many indulgences in Germany were being used to finance the building of St. Peter's Basilica in Rome.

Luther's discovery that the righteousness (goodness) of God is man's only reason for hope came during the winter of 1513-14, in what is called his "tower experience," so named because it occurred while he was in the monastery tower. Among Biblical passages supporting his doctrines are these two: "For in it (the gospel of Jesus) the righteousness of God is revealed through faith, for faith. He who through faith is righteous shall live," from Romans 1:17, and "For by grace you have been saved through faith. This is not your own doing, but the gift of God, not because of works, lest anyone should boast," from Ephesians 2:8.

Because of Gutenberg's invention of the printing press in the fifteenth century, Luther's translation of the Bible could be made widely available. His translation of the New Testament was published in 1522, and the Old Testament in 1534, and they quickly became best-sellers in Germany. Lutherans then and now have used the Bible as their only standard for faith and doctrine. Further, Luther used it to counter a range of traditional Catholic elements. First, Luther said only two sacraments, baptism and the eucharist, have a Biblical basis. So Lutherans do not consider the following to be sacraments: penance, confession, holy orders, unction, and marriage. Second, Luther argued against a number of practices that Roman Catholics consider sanctioned by tradition if not by the Bible. Luther used the Bible to denounce doctrines and practices he said were sanctioned only by tradition. For example, he said the celibate priesthood has no Biblical basis. He later left the Augustinian priesthood and married a former nun. Among pious practices Lutherans abandoned were monastic life, the veneration of relics, radical fasting, pilgrimages, hair-shirts, scourges, and the rosary. Lutheran piety instead developed around hearing the Word in the liturgy, receiving the eucharist, and reading the Bible. Third, Luther used the Bible to counteract the authority of the pope, and said the Bible was the source of his own authority to reform the church.

To discuss the importance of "sacrament" for Lutherans involves treating both Luther's understanding of the eucharist, and other elements discussed in the next section that make Lutheran liturgy distinctive.

Luther's doctrine of the eucharist is called consubstantiation, a departure from the Roman Catholic doctrine called transubstantiation. Consubstantiation means Christ is present everywhere, but his presence is especially focused in the eucharist. The bread and wine still exist, but under the guise of bread and wine is Christ, who is received by the believer physically. This reception occurs, said Luther, because of Christ's promise at the Last Supper that it would occur. Transubstantiation, on the other hand, means that the essence of bread and wine are replaced by the essence of Christ, who becomes present physically.

The doctrine of consubstantiation allowed Lutherans to preserve their liturgical worship instead of denying the sacraments altogether. So Lutheran liturgy is distinct from that of the Anabaptists, who do not have any sacraments, although they do observe a memorial meal. The consubstantiation doctrine also kept Lutherans from following the Reformed tradition, which replaces belief in Christ's physical presence in the eucharist with belief only in his spiritual presence in the eucharist.

LUTHERAN LITURGY. Lutheranism vies with the historic Catholic and Orthodox traditions for its emphasis on liturgy. In the early 1520's Luther began revising the Sunday service and found himself in conflict with those reformers, such as Andreas von Carlstadt, who looked for radical changes in the worship. Luther developed a form of worship in Wittenburg which followed the form of the Roman liturgy but which emphasized the vernacular in preaching, in the liturgy, and in hymns. Vestments, candles, and pictures became optional. The church calendar remained in use.

Luther did change the format of the service by bringing the sermon into the worship, and on days when the eucharist was not served, a sermon substituted for it. Gregorian music was continued but gradually was replaced. The medieval outline that was standard for each liturgical service continued and remains basic in Lutheran liturgy. This outline is reflected in the *Agenda*, forms of worship adopted by the Lutheran churches in the United States in 1958.

No discussion of Lutheran liturgy would be complete without mention of Lutheran hymnology. All Protestants are familiar with Luther's "A Mighty Fortress Is Our God," which became the battle hymn of the Reformation. In 1524 Luther published his first hymn book and a second was published before the year was out. The popular hymns not only spread Luther's ideas on man's sinfulness and God's righteousness, but became integral to the worship and distinguish Lutheran liturgy from most other liturgical services.

POLITY. Polity is largely a low-priority subject among Lutherans. Bishops, though rare, have not been entirely unknown. The tendency generally, however, is for churches to operate somewhere between a congregational polity and a form of presbyterianism in which power is vested in the synod or body of ministers.

Luther advocated cooperation between church and state. He said a Christian ruler, acting in a Christian manner, should govern the secular sphere, and the church should govern the religious sphere. Thus the Christian ruler and the church, each in their respective spheres, would oversee the activities of all the people in the state.

THE "CONFESSING" CHURCH. Luther's doctrinal insights and his criticisms of Roman Catholicism were first publicly presented in the Ninety-five Theses he nailed to the church door in Wittenburg in 1517, and then in the three treatises of 1521. His position did not find confessional status until 1530, with the Augsburg Confession. Princes who were following Luther and breaking the unity of the Roman Catholic Church had to account for that to the Holy Roman Emperor. So they presented the Augsburg Confession to him to explain their position. As written by Melanchthon, a professor of Greek and a New Testament scholar at Wittenburg, it has remained the central statement of Lutheran essentials. It includes traditional Christian beliefs such as belief in the Trinity and the resurrection of the body. But it goes further to elaborate on statements concerning humanity, specifically, on man's sinfulness, forgiveness of sin, and justification by grace through faith alone. Lutherans rallied around the Augsburg Confession, and Roman Catholics united against it. It became the standard under which Lutherans later entered the Thirty Years' War.

The Augsburg Confession began the practice of the "confessing" church. Typically, when pressed by a contemporary situation, Lutherans (and Reformed) Churches will summarize a stance in the form of a "confession of faith" which says to the world, "Here we stand; we can do no other." In the twentieth century such statements were issued to counter Nazism.

To the Augsburg Confession were added other confessions and documents which further clarified a Lutheran position as opposed to other religions. These documents include the Larger and Small Catechism (1529), written by Luther, the Smalcald Articles (1537), and the Formula of Concord (1577). These, along with the three ecumenical creeds (the Apostles' Creed, the Nicene Creed, and the Chalcedonian Creed), were collected in 1580 into the *Book of Concord*. This is the basic collection of Lutheran doctrinal writings, a clear statement of the truths Lutherans feel are taught in Scripture and the starting point for other theological endeavors.

ORIGINS. At least three dates vie with each other for the beginning of Lutheranism. The most widely accepted date is October 31, 1517, the day Luther nailed his Ninety-five Theses for debate to the Castle Church in Wittenburg. Outside the scholarly circles of Lutheran seminaries, this date goes virtually unrivaled as the beginning date not only of Lutheranism but also of the entire Reformation. Lutheran scholars have pointed out, however, that other dates are worthy of consideration. Some cite Luther's discovery of the meaning of the righteousness of God during the winter of 1513-14. This was the so-called "tower experience," which supplied the theological insights inherent in the Ninety-five Theses.

The third and most valid year for the origin of Lutheranism is 1530. The years 1514 and 1517 cannot really qualify as dates of origin because no Lutheran Church existed then.

The year 1530 brought the publishing of the Augsburg Confession. What had been an almost chaotic movement had a document around which to rally. The congregations which wished to identify with Luther could be said to have become a public entity. So 1530 was the first year of the Lutheran Church.

LUTHERANS IN AMERICA. After 1530, Lutheranism spread in Germany, Sweden, Denmark, Finland, and Norway. An independent church was established in each country. But when the Lutherans came to the U.S., they entered a vast country compared to the smaller European states. So Lutherans from any one European country were scattered in America, seeking good farm land especially in the Midwest and along the Southern seaboard. Everywhere they spread, each linguistic group established a synod, an autonomous Lutheran church. Each group was independent of the churches of other linguistic groups, and typically was independent of the churches in other American states. The rapid immigration in the nineteenth century led to the creation by 1850 of more than 150 Lutheran church bodies. The history of American Lutheranism is thus the history of the merger of these 150 synods into twenty-one Lutheran churches today.

For no other family of American religions does national origin make such a difference. For example, the Roman Catholics, who came to the U.S. from all over Europe, remained one ecclesiastical entity when they arrived here. Roman Catholic immigrants from various national and linguistic groups did not create diverse denominational bodies. To give another example, most Methodists came to the U.S. from the British Isles and thus did not create churches divergent from the European Methodist churches (with two minor exceptions). For neither Catholics nor Methodists did national origin matter as much as for Lutherans.

Lutheranism was first brought to America by Swedes who established a colony, Fort Christina, on the Delaware River in 1638. Rev. Reorus Torkillus, the first Lutheran pastor in the New World, accompanied them. The Swedes were bolstered by the arrival of German Lutherans who began to settle in Pennsylvania in the last half of the century. By the middle of the eighteenth century, they were firmly entrenched in Pennsylvania and the surrounding territory. In March 1834, the Salzburgers created a third Lutheran center in Georgia.

In 1742 Henry Melchior Muhlenberg came to the colonies, and from his work and ministry, organized Lutheranism in the U.S. is dated. Installed as pastor of three congregations in Pennsylvania, he began to reach out to other parishes and to write Germany for continued help. In 1748 he led in the organization of the Ministerium of Pennsylvania, the first Lutheran synod in the colonies. He also opened his home to ministerial candidates. In 1792 a new constitution was adopted. Lay persons were first allowed to come to meetings of ministers in 1796, and the organizational tie to Germany was effected in that year.

The decades following the war were ones of expansion and the addition of new synods—New York (1786), North Carolina (1803), Ohio (1818), Maryland (1820), and Tennessee (1820). The General Synod (1820) was a cooperating body for the various state synods. Accompanying the growth was the emergence of tension over the issue of Americanization. Theologian Samuel S. Schmucker became a leading "liberal" who advocated the use of English in worship and a strong "pietistic" emphasis (a stress on piety and religious experience instead of on rigid doctrinal conformity). Schmucker was opposed by the newly arriving immigrants, who came in great numbers in the second quarter of the century. They were orthodox and conservative.

Emerging as the leader of the "conservatives" was C.F.W. Walther, who had migrated from Saxony in 1839. He began to publish *Der Lutheraner* to argue for his position and was influential in setting the form of Lutheranism for such synods as Missouri (1846), Buffalo (1845), and Iowa (1854).

During the middle of the century, the Scandinavian Lutherans began to arrive in great numbers and to form their own synods. The first Norwegian Synod was formed in 1846. The Swedes in the General Synod joined with recent immigrants to form the Augustana Synod in 1860. Lars Paul Esbjorn led the Swedish schism. Other synods were formed by the Finns (1890), Danes (1872), Slovaks (1902), and Icelanders (1885).

The great strength of Lutheranism shifted away from the East Coast in the nineteenth century and became dominant in the states north and west of Chicago. Centers were established along the Mississippi River at St. Louis, Rock Island, and Minneapolis.

The large influx of immigrants who took control away from the older, liberal eastern leaders like Schmucker delayed but could not avoid the problems created by Americanization. The use of English and adaptation to "American" mores increasingly plagued the church and reached its culmination during World War I. There is little doubt that English-speaking churches were able to fan the flames of prohibition by attacking their German brethren who supported the German brewers (Schlitz, Anheuser-Busch).

From the last quarter of the nineteenth century until the present time, the major thrust in the Lutheran family has been intrafamily ecumenism. Although Lutherans have entered ecumenical discussions with those of other faiths, these discussions have never reached the stage of definite plans for a merger. Within Lutheranism, however, there has been a century of merger by the multitude of independent synodical bodies established in the nineteenth century. Merger was usually preceded by the formation of cooperative councils. The more conservative Lutheran churches formed the Lutheran Synodical Conference in 1872. The conference included such synods as the Missouri Synod, the Synod of Evangelical Lutheran Churches, the Evangelical Lutheran Synod, and, until 1892, the three synods of Wisconsin, Michigan, and Minnesota. Only the Missouri Synod and the Synod of Evangelical Lutheran Churches remain in the Lutheran Synodical Conference. For all practical purposes, the conference has fallen apart, due to the Missouri Synod's negotiations with more liberal Lutheran bodies. The National Lutheran Council (1918-66) and the American Lutheran

Conference became the arena for the largest number of mergers by various linguistic traditions as they became Americanized. Major mergers in the 1960's made these obsolete and they were replaced by the Lutheran Council in the U.S.A., in which the three larger churches participated: the Lutheran Church in America, the American Lutheran Church, and the Missouri Synod. In 1977, after many years of debate, the Missouri Synod withdrew from the council.

The amalgamation of Lutherans has not been without its reactions, and the decades following World War II have been ones that have seen a number of new Lutheran churches form and others threaten to form. Most of these new churches represent the conservative wing.

THE APOSTOLIC LUTHERANS. One group, the Finnish Apostolic Lutherans, have developed outside of the main thrust of Lutheran history in America. The product of an intense pietistic movement originating in a geographically isolated part of northern Scandinavia, and centered in a relatively isolated part of the United States, the Apostolics have moved along a distinct pathway, though still very Lutheran in faith and life. Their small numbers have, due to their splintering, accounted for a relatively large number of Lutheran church bodies.

In the 1840's, in northern Sweden in the area generally called Lapland, a young pastor, Lars Levi Laestadius, led a revival in the state church, the Swedish Lutheran Church. The movement was based on Laestadius' powerful preaching of repentance. The revival spread from Kaaresuvanto to all of northern Scandinavia. Characteristic of the revival were deep sorrow for sin, public confession of sin before the whole congregation, and the experience of deliverance. Among the leaders of the emerging revival was Juhani Raattamaa, a lay preacher. Raattamaa discovered the Power of the Keys or the practice of absolution by which a representative of the church laid hands on the penitent and pronounced forgiveness. The penitent was to believe these words as if Christ had pronounced them. The Laestadians believed that God sent times of visitation on all peoples and that there were Christians in all churches, but they laid emphasis on the need to follow the Bible to attain salvation.

Finns (Laplanders) and other Scandinavians from near the Arctic area began to migrate to America in the 1860's due to economic problems in Scandinavia. They settled in Minnesota and the Upper Peninsula of Michigan. Antti Vitikka began to preach among the Finns and in 1870 gathered a Laestadian group at Calumet, Michigan. The congregation called Solomon Korteniemi as their pastor and in 1872–73 organized the Solomon Korteniemi Lutheran Society. Korteniemi proved a poor leader and was succeeded by John Takkinen, sent from Sweden. Under his leadership in 1879 the name "Apostolic" Lutheran was chosen.

The Apostolic Lutherans grew and prospered in their American home but quickly became rent with controversy, which splintered them into five separate churches. Each faction goes under the name of Apostolic Lutheran and is distinguished by its nickname and its doctrine and practice. Only one group has organized formally as a church body.

The first schism in the Apostolic Lutheran movement occurred in the Calumet congregation in 1888. Members opposed to the "harsh rule" of Takkinen elected John Roanpaa and seized the church property. In 1890 Arthur Leopold Heideman arrived from Lapland to serve this new congregation.

In Europe in 1897, the Laestadians split into the Church of the First Born and the Old Laestadians. In America, the Takkinen congregation aligned with the Church of the First Born and the followers of Arthur Heideman aligned with the Old Laestadians.

Another schism occurred in Europe when a Pietist party, called the New Awakening, left its Pietist church in Finland. In 1910 the New Awakening sent Mikko Saarenpaa and Juho Pyorre to America.

These three prime groups, the Old Laestadians, the Church of the First Born, and the New Awakening, share the common Laestadian Lutheran doctrinal heritage as transmitted through Raattamaa. Raattamaa had taught that justification and conversion came by hearing the Gospel preached by the church of Christ. The New Awakening, however, believed that conversion could occur without hearing the Word. The New Awakening accused the Laestadians of moral laxity and emphasized a strict moral life. The New Awakening also departed from the other Laestadians on their belief in the "third use of the law," i.e., that the Ten Commandments were in force for Christians. For the Old Laestadians the only law was the law of Christ, the commandments of love. The Old Laestadians tended to believe that the church must be outwardly one. Hence they tended to be ultra-exclusivist.

A fourth schism occurred among the Old Laestadians when an emphasis on evangelism—redemption, forgiveness, and the righteousness of Christ—was opposed to an emphasis on Christian life and conduct and the repentance from sin. The evangelicals were inspired by the fervent preaching of Heideman and felt that the preaching of free grace would produce good fruit of itself.

The Apostolic Lutherans have always had a congregational government, in part a reaction to Scandinavian Lutheran episcopacy. Like other extreme congregationalists, they have resisted organization but can be distinguished by doctrinal position, periodicals, and foreign alignments.

SOURCES—THE LUTHERAN FAMILY

MARTIN LUTHER

Bainton, Roland. *Here I Stand.* New York: Abingdon Cokesbury, 1950.

Booth, Edwin. *Martin Luther, Oak of Saxony.* Nashville: Abingdon Press, 1966.

Luther, Martin. *Three Treatises.* Philadelphia: Fortress Press, 1960.
———. *Works.* Edited by Jaroslav Pelikan and Helmut T. Lehman. 55 Vols. St. Louis: Concordia Publishing House and Philadelphia: Fortress Press, 1958-67.

Ritter, Gerhard. *Luther, His Life and Works.* New York: Harper & Row, 1963.

What Luther Says, An Anthology. St. Louis: Concordia Publishing House, 1959.

THE LUTHERAN CHURCH WORLDWIDE

Bergendoff, Conrad. *The Church of the Lutheran Reformation*. St. Louis: Concordia Publishing House, 1967. 339 pp.

Bodensieck, Julius, ed. *The Encyclopedia of the Lutheran Church*. 3 Vols. Minneapolis: Augsburg Publishing House, 1965.

Lucker, Edwin L., ed. *Lutheran Cyclopedia*. St. Louis: Concordia Publishing House, 1975. 845 pp.

Lutheran Churches of the World. Minneapolis: Augsburg Publishing House, 1972. 333 pp.

Nelson, E. Clifford. *The Rise of World Lutheranism*. Philadelphia: Fortress Press, 1982. 421 pp.

Vajta, Vilmos, ed. *The Lutheran Church, Past and Present*. Minneapolis: Augsburg Publishing House, 1977. 392 pp.

LUTHERANS IN AMERICA: HISTORICAL

Nelson, E. Clifford, ed. *The Lutherans in North America*. Philadelphia: Fortress Press, 1980. 564 pp.

Thorkelson, Wilmar. *Lutherans in the U.S.A.* Minneapolis: Augsburg Publishing House, 1969.

Weideraenders, Robert C., and Walter G. Tillmanns. *The Synods of American Lutheranism*. N.p.: Lutheran Historical Conference, 1968. 209 pp.

Wallace, Paul A. W. *The Muhlenbergs of Pennsylvania*. Philadelphia: University of Pennsylvania, 1950. 358 pp.

Wentz, Abdel Ross. *A Basic History of Lutheranism in America*. Philadelphia: Muhlenburg Press, 1964. 439 pp.

Wolf, R. C. *Documents of Lutheran Unity in America*. Philadelphia: Fortress Press, 1966. 672 pp.

DOCTRINAL

Allbeck, Willard Dow. *Studies in the Lutheran Confessions*. Philadelphia: Fortress Press, 1968. 306 pp.

Gritsch, Eric W., and Robert W. Jenson. *Lutheranism*. Philadelphia: Fortress Press, 1976. 214 pp.

Hamsher, Paul O. *This I Believe, My Lutheran Handbook*. Lima, OH: The C.S.S. Publishing Co., n.d. 86 pp.

Schink, Edmund. *Theology of Lutheran Confessions*. Philadelphia: Muhlenberg Press, 1961.

Schramm, W. E. *What Lutherans Believe*. Columbus, OH: Wartburg Press, 1946. 156 pp.

LITURGY

Reed, Luther D. *The Lutheran Liturgy*. Philadelphia: Muhlenberg Press, 1947. 824 pp.

Stauffer, S. Anita, Gilbert A. Doan, and Michael B. Aune. *Lutherans at Worship*. Minneapolis: Augsburg Publishing House, 1978. 96 pp.

POLITY

Asheim, Ivar, and Victor R. Gold, eds. *Episcopacy in the Lutheran Church*. Philadelphia: Fortress Press, 1970. 261 pp.

Chapter Four

THE REFORMED-PRESBYTERIAN FAMILY

Directory listings for the groups belonging to the Reformed-Presbyterian
Family may be found in the section beginning on page 247.

The Reformed-Presbyterian tradition is based on the work of John Calvin, who established the Reformed Church in Geneva, Switzerland, in the 1540's. The various churches that trace their origins to Calvin are set apart from other Christian churches by their theology ("Reformed") and church government ("Presbyterian").

Calvin's theological system was shaped by his awareness of God's sovereignty in creation and salvation. The other major theological tenets of Calvinism—predestination and limited atonement—are built on the belief in God's sovereignty. Strictly interpreted, predestination means that the number and identity of "the elect" (those who are saved) were ordained by the sovereign God before the beginning of the world. Christ's atonement for sin was thus limited to the elect; salvation is not possible for all humanity, but only for those predestined to be saved. The issue of a strict or lenient interpretation of predestination has divided both European and American Calvinists.

Churches in the Reformed-Presbyterian tradition have a presbyterial form of church government. The presbytery is a legislative and/or judicial body composed of clergy and laity in equal numbers from the churches of a given region. The laity are elected by the members of the church. The word "presbytery" is also sometimes used to refer to the ruling body of the local church, but the name "Presbyterian" derives from the regional governing body.

Thus the name of this tradition is "Reformed" for Calvin's theology (an attempt to reform the Roman Catholic Church) and "Presbyterian" for the form of church government based on the presbytery. The name for this tradition also reflects history. On the continent, Calvinists established Reformed churches. In the British Isles, predominantly in Scotland, Calvinists established Presbyterian churches. In America, the Reformed churches and the Presbyterian churches all belong to the Reformed-Presbyterian tradition, along with the Congregational churches. In this chapter, the word "Reformed" applies to Calvinist theology, worship, and churches using Calvinist theology. The word "Reformed" is not used to refer to the whole Reformation, a movement much broader than Calvinism, although Calvin played a major role in that movement.

Reformed theology involves many beliefs in addition to the distinguishing tenets mentioned above—beliefs in God's sovereignty, in predestination, and in limited atonement. Reformed theology affirms the commitments associated with the creeds of the early centuries of Christianity: beliefs in God, Christ, the Holy Spirit, and the Trinity.

Beyond these beliefs come those shared by Reformed theology with other Protestant theologies: the belief in salvation by grace through faith, and the reliance on the Bible as the sole authority for faith and doctrine. With the followers of Martin Luther and Ulrich Zwingli, Calvinists were Protestants in that they protested various doctrines and practices of the Roman Catholic Church during the sixteenth-century movement called the Reformation. The Protestant emphasis on salvation by grace through faith stands opposed to the Roman Catholic understanding of salvation through faith and good works. Further, when Protestants claim the Bible as their sole authority for faith and doctrine, they negate the Roman Catholic reliance on both the Bible and tradition. Reformed churchmen were generally hostile toward practices sanctioned by tradition unless the practices could be substantiated by Scripture.

Within Reformed theology, the definition of the church makes no reference to bishops or apostolic succession (the line of succession by ordination from the Apostles to modern times), two elements that are crucial to churches in the liturgical tradition. Instead, Reformed theology defines the church as the place where the "pure doctrine of the gospel is preached" and the "pure administration of the sacraments" is maintained. By the "pure doctrine of the gospel" is meant the gospel preached by ordained ministers according to Calvinist emphases (e.g., predestination). By the "pure administration of the sacraments" is meant the administration only of baptism and the Lord's Supper as sacraments. This practice contrasts with Roman Catholicism's celebration of seven sacraments and some churches' rejection of all sacraments. (The Zwinglians and the Anabaptists serve as two examples of those rejecting all the sacraments. Zwinglians considered the eucharist a memorial meal, not a sacrament. The Anabaptists had no sacraments but did have ordinances, including footwashing and adult baptism.)

21

Though not without some differences, Lutherans and Roman Catholics accepted the doctrine of the real physical presence of Christ in the sacraments. The followers of Calvin supplanted this idea with the belief in the spiritual presence apprehended by faith. The effect is to change the sacrament as a special focus of Christ's presence in the world and to move away from the sacramental world of the liturgical churches. The Reformed world is a secular world. God is present and can be apprehended by faith in all activities.

Worship in a Reformed church is centered on the preaching of the sermon, which ideally combines the exposition of Scripture with the ordered presentation of a great truth of the faith. While having been influenced by the emotive appeal of the Methodists in modern times, the Reformed sermon still serves primarily a teaching function. Prayers and hymns rehearse the basic tenets of the Reformed faith—confession, forgiveness, and the acknowledgement of the sovereignty of God. Hymns for many years were limited to the Psalms set to music, and the church produced many editions of Psalters. Most now use hymn books, though the Psalms remain important.

As spelled out in the Second Helvetic Confession (1566), the characteristics of Reformed worship are the Word of God properly preached to the people, decent meeting spaces purged of anything offensive to the church, and services conducted in order, modesty, discipline, and in the language of the people. Gone are the aesthetic/theological/sacramental appeals of worship. Gone are "offensive" elements such as statues, vestments, saints' festivals, indulgences, pilgrimages, and relics. Reformed worship is directed on a cognitive level—preaching, worship understandable to the layman, logical thoughts and ordered behavior, and a disciplined atmosphere.

The Reformed theological position was codified in confessions in the sixteenth and seventeenth centuries. The main Reformed confessions are the First Helvetic Confession (1536), the Belgic Confession (1561), the Second Helvetic Confession (1566), the Canons of the Synod of Dort (1619), and the Westminster Confession of Faith (1647). Also necessary to understanding the Reformed faith is the Heidelberg Catechism (1693). The above description of Reformed theology aligns with these confessions, which all make the same basic doctrinal statements and in addition address whatever current crisis and/or local debate prompted the confessions. Along with other documents written by the Westminster Assembly of Divines in the 1640's, the Westminster Confession is the confession that has had the greatest impact on U.S. churches in the Reformed-Presbyterian tradition. Baptist documents are also derived from the Westminster documents.

Calvin developed the doctrine of two spheres of action, the secular and religious. Although his Reformed Church in Geneva was a state church, he ended any interference of the state in church affairs such as the celebration of church festivals or the appointment of church officials. Calvin set up a theocracy, a form of government designed to have God as its head. The church defined the magistrates' authority as coming from God and the church had power over the magistrates in that magistrates were church members. Thus religion had considerable power over all social activities; Calvin was the most powerful man in Geneva. The theocracy was patterned on Calvin's *Institutes of the Christian Religion*.

The presbyterial system is a state church system and was designed for intimate communion with the secular authority. It was based on a parish system in which the country would be divided into geographic areas with one church to a parish. All people who had been baptized would be members. The church and state together, each in its proper area, would keep order. The most notable example of the interworking of church and state in Geneva concerned a heretic, Servetus. Among other objections to orthodox Christian doctrines, Servetus called the Trinity a three-headed hound of hell. Calvin condemned Servetus as a heretic, but the secular authorities in Geneva tried and executed him.

Within the presbyterial system of the Reformed-Presbyterian tradition, clergy and lay people together rule the church. The preaching orders (ministers) are the pastors and teachers. The ruling elders, lay people, are to assist the teaching elders in discipline and in the governance of the church. Deacons collect the offering and see to its distribution. In the local congregation, the ministers and elders together make up the consistory or session, occasionally called the presbytery. In some cases the deacons also belong to the consistory. All ministers and elders are called and elected by the other elders.

The ministers and elders from a series of judicial and legislative bodies. The local consistories or sessions are grouped into a presbytery or classis or coetus. From this body of all the ministers in a given region, plus an equal number of elected elders, comes the name for the presbyterial form of government. The presbyters, those in the presbytery, have the power within the church. Several presbyters (usually a minimum of three) may come together to form a synod (or classis) and synods may form an even larger body such as the General Assembly of the United Presbyterian Church. Each body has specific functions and usually a protest of a decision at one level can be appealed to a higher level. (In actual practice among some Presbyterian churches, a congregational form of government prevails and the presbytery functions as an advisory forum and facilitates cooperative endeavor.)

Both Luther and Calvin established state churches, as did Ulrich Zwingli. Zwingli died in 1531; his church in Zurich, Switzerland, was soon absorbed into Calvinism. The Anabaptists (discussed in Chapter Eight) opposed all state churches, whether Lutheran, Calvinist, or Roman Catholic, and they were persecuted by the state churches. The Reformation brought its share of bloodshed.

Calvin's doctrine, more than the doctrine of any other religion, moved with the rising mercantile society and justified secular activity in the world. By contrast, Anabaptism was a world-denying view that sheltered the elect against a hostile, sinful secular society. The Anabaptist tradition continues in the Mennonites, the Amish, the Quakers, and the Church of the Brethren. Lutheranism retained a more sacred character than Calvinism; Lutheranism spread by refurbishing Catholic forms.

Calvinism, however, rose on the emerging middle class of Western Europe.

Calvin, who lived from 1509 to 1564, wrote the most influential book ever written in Protestant theology, *Institutes of the Christian Religion*, and was the first Protestant systematic theologian. He gained a reputation for intellectual brilliance while a student in Paris. After a 1533 sermon in which he pleaded for the reform of the Roman Catholic Church, he was forced to leave Paris. In Geneva, he introduced reforms, but in 1538 he was forced to leave Geneva because of the severity of the reforms. (Later his church would be characterized by stern morality, austerity, and insistence on attending church.) A noted preacher, Calvin went to Strassburg for several years and from there he maintained communication with those in Geneva. In 1541 the people of Geneva recalled him. From then on Geneva was the headquarters for Calvin and the Reformed Church.

There the future leaders of Calvin's reform found a haven from non-Calvinist magistrates of other areas. William Tyndale, Miles Cloverdale, and John Knox exported Calvin's ideas from Geneva to the British Isles. By 1600 representatives of the Reformed faith were making themselves heard throughout all of Central Europe.

THE SPREAD OF CALVINISM. As early as 1555 a Protestant congregation was organized in France by a disciple of Calvin. (Followers of Luther, Zwingli, and Calvin were all Protestants, protesting elements of Roman Catholicism.) In 1559 the first synod of the French Reformed Church met. The next centuries for the French Reformed Church, or the Huguenots as they were popularly called, were years of persecution. In 1598, Henry IV issued the Edict of Nantes and began a brief period of toleration. But Louis XIV revoked the edict in 1685, and periods of persecution followed until the Constitution of 1795 granted religious freedom.

Reformed Church advocates entered the Netherlands very soon after Calvin's reign in Geneva began. The religious wars which followed led to revolution by the Protestants and the formation of two countries, predominantly Reformed Holland and predominantly Catholic Belgium. This separation was completed in 1579 under the Protestant leader, William of Orange. It was in the Dutch Church that Jacob Arminius emerged as a leader with a liberal interpretation of predestinarianism and was refuted by the 1618 Synod of Dort. Although a predestinarian, Arminius later became a hero of the anti-predestinarians.

No other centers of Reformed faith on the continent grew as did Switzerland, France, and Holland. However, the faith did seep into the surrounding countries, and synods were formed in Czechoslovakia and Hungary. Also in Italy the Reformed faith began to dominate the Waldensians. Because of its affinity with Lutheranism, the Reformed church moved north into Germany and, while never challenging Lutherans for control, became a large minority religion. It is from this body that the 1693 Heidelberg Catechism emerged; its teaching was to have a profound influence on the interpretation of Calvin in Reformed history.

The leading center of Reformed faith in the British Isles is Scotland. A devout follower of Calvin, John Knox returned to Scotland in 1559 after a year and a half on a French galley and twelve years' exile in Europe. He found the country ripe for Protestantism. He quickly became the leader of the cause which in another year saw the Scottish parliament abolish Catholicism and begin to set up Presbyterianism, the name given the Reformed Church in Scotland. Despite recurrent battles with then Episcopal England, Presbyterianism was firmly settled in Scotland and became the seedbed from which the Reformed movement could spread to Ireland and England.

In 1603 James I of England invited the Scots to settle the rebels' land in Ulster (Northern Ireland) which had been forfeited to the crown. So many came to Ireland that soon Ulster was dominantly Protestant and in spite of James' Catholic preferences, he reasoned that Presbyterians were better than people with no religion at all. Irish Catholics were not so quick to give in to the Protestant intruders and religious wars ensued. By 1642 things had quieted to a point that the first presbytery in Ireland could be formed, but a stable accord has never been reached between Irish Catholics and Presbyterians.

In England Reformed-Presbyterian thinking was labeled Puritanism. This name came as a result of the different Reformed thinkers' uniting around the issue of "further purifying the church," as the latter stages of the Reformation brought Elizabeth to the throne in 1558 with her *via media* solution to religious strife. (For a discussion of Elizabeth's blending of both Roman Catholic and Protestant elements, see the section in Chapter One on the Anglican tradition.) The two major groups within Puritanism were the Independents and the Presbyterians. Most Puritans were Reformed in their thinking, but beyond that they varied from those who merely wished to simplify church vestments and worship to the Independents who wished to set up a congregationally organized church, one in which the highest authority lay within the local church instead of in a regional or national governing body. The years 1558 to 1649 were years of struggle, persecutions, war, and on-again, off-again toleration among proponents of the various churches in England. In 1649, Puritan Oliver Cromwell succeeded in his revolt against the monarchy and established the Puritan Commonwealth. Although Cromwell was an Independent, the Presbyterians were dominant in Parliament, so when Cromwell's reign began, Presbyterianism became the dominant church in England. Up to that time the Presbyterians and Independents had sustained a united front against the Episcopalian state church of the monarchy. However, once Puritanism gained the position of state church, the factions within Puritanism—Presbyterians and Independents—no longer needed to be united against Episcopalianism and their differences with each other intensified. The Congregationalists, a group within the Independents, began to press for a state church based on a congregational system instead of on a presbyterial system. The Congregationalists wanted to remain attached to the Church of England in the sense that the Congregationalists would preach the doctrines of the Church of England but they would choose their own ministers, own their property themselves, and would not come under the authority of the bishops of the Church of England. The Congregationalists were opposed by another party within the Independents, the Separatists. This latter party wished to become separate from any episcopal entanglements.

In 1660 Presbyterianism lost its state church position because the monarchy was restored to power and the Anglican Church returned as the state church. Presbyterians became another small English sect among other sects. The Restoration therefore meant the end of Presbyterian power, but Reformed theology remained dominant in England's Protestant circles, including Presbyterians, Congregationalists, and Separatists.

Years before Cromwell came to power, Parliament paved the way for the establishment of Presbyterianism by abolishing the system of bishops in 1642-43. Parliament also convoked the Westminster Assembly of Divines to reorder the Church of England. This assembly, meeting for a number of years, produced the three most important works in Reformed history (apart from Calvin's *Institutes* from which they derived): The Larger and Shorter Catechisms, the Westminster Confession of Faith, and the Directory of Public Worship. Even though only four Scots were in the Westminster Assembly, the Church of Scotland quickly adopted the Westminster documents. These documents remain to this day the basic works in doctrine and standards for most Presbyterian Churches around the world.

With time, the Separatists, a group within the Independents, divided into Brownists and Baptists. Robert Browne was among the first to move toward the idea of a "sect" church of pure Christians as opposed to a universal or state church of all baptized citizens. The Baptists were even more radical than the Brownists. The Baptists were anti-liturgical, not having any sacraments. For them baptism is an ordinance and is reserved for adults instead of being available also to children.

The various groups mentioned above existed as parties within the Puritan movement in England from the late 1500's until the 1689 Act of Toleration, which allowed them freedom to develop fully as distinct sects. The Brownists, however, did not exist for long.

IN AMERICA. The story of the Reformed-Presbyterian tradition in colonial America is the story of the establishment of American branches of the various European Reformed churches. As early as 1611 the Rev. Alexander Whittaker arrived in Virginia with his Presbyterian views. The Pilgrims and Puritans arrived in the 1620's to establish American Congregationalism. Dutch Calvinists were in New York as early as 1623. French Huguenots settled along the coast of the colonies. Quickly Americanized, they joined the Presbyterian Church. The backbone of American Presbyterianism was the vast migration of the Scottish-Irish Ulsterites. Between 1705 and 1775 more than 500,000 Ulsterites reached America and settled in its middle section, particularly the Carolinas. Germans began to arrive in the late 1600's and settled in Pennsylvania. The Calvinists among them organized the Reformed Church.

Francis Makemie, recognized as the father of American Presbyterianism, landed in the colonies in 1683 to begin organizing the scattered Presbyterians. About 1705, the date is not clear, he organized the first presbytery (of Philadelphia). Makemie died in 1708 as the great Scottish-Irish immigration was beginning. In 1717 the Synod of Philadelphia was organized with nineteen ministers, forty churches, and 3,000 members.

The Reformed traditions have displayed several interesting patterns of growth in America. The churches of the Reformed tradition (with the possible exception of Presbyterianism) are regional churches. Largely continental in their background, they are concentrated in those areas in the Northeast and Midwest where large-scale German migration occurred. The Congregationalists were located largely in the Northeast but gained strength in the Midwest through the mergers of 1931 and 1958.

Significant in the spread of the Reformed churches were the anti-evangelical, anti-revivalistic policies of church leaders in the eighteenth and nineteenth centuries. The Reformed churches gained new members largely through groups of laymen who migrated West, formed congregations, and called a pastor.

Education has been a major contribution of the Reformed tradition to Protestantism. The churches always insisted on a college-trained clergy, and they created numerous colleges for that purpose. They have based their program on a theologically sound teaching ministry. A large number of the outstanding theologians in American history were out of this tradition—Cotton Mather, Jonathan Edwards, John Williamson Nevin, Horace Bushnell, Benjamin Warfield, and Reinhold and H. Richard Niebuhr.

The Plan of Union of 1801 was an agreement between Presbyterians and Congregationalists concerning their frontier congregations. The Plan of Union provided that where there were small groups of Presbyterians and Congregationalists, the groups would unite and be served by a minister from either church. Because more Presbyterian ministers went to the frontier than Congregationalist ministers, most of those united churches became Presbyterian. The "frontier" of the early 1800's was the area west of the Allegheny Mountains.

Splintered into a number of separate denominational bodies in the nineteenth century, Presbyterians made significant strides in bringing members together in one organization during the twentieth century. The most important step in the merging process was accomplished in 1983 when the two largest Presbyterian bodies, split since before the Civil War merged to form the Presbyterian Church (U.S.A.). The story of this church and its antecedents constitutes the majority of Presbyterian history in the United States.

CONGREGATIONALISM—A VARIATION OF THE REFORMED TRADITION. The form of Congregationalism that came to America in the early 1600's with the Pilgrims and Puritans can be traced to one group of Puritans in seventeenth-century England. This group stood between the Presbyterians and the Separatists. The Presbyterians looked for the development of a state church, one modeled on the theocracy Calvin established in Geneva. The Separatists looked for a congregationally organized church divorced from state control and intervention. The Congregationalists, taking a middle position, wanted a state church but one congregationally oriented. All three groups were Reformed in their theology and acknowledged the Westminister documents. They differed in their methods of opposition to the episcopal establishment.

Congregational organization had four distinctive features. First, the church was built on the covenant of people together. A church was not formed until the people constituted it. Second, the church was tied to a place. It was the covenanted people in a specific location. Ideally, the whole countryside would be divided into parishes, geographic areas each with one congregation. The importance of place is reflected in the fact that the Mayflower Compact (a civil version of the church covenant) was not drawn up until the Pilgrims reached the New World. Third, the church was to be an established church. In New England it had intimate ties with the government, and ministers drew their salaries from the civil authority. Finally, the church was to be the sacred institute for the society. The clergy spoke directly to issues of public morals, expected to be consulted on matters of importance to public life, and often represented the colony as political figures.

The early Congregationalists have often been confused with those Independents who desired a church totally cut off from state affiliation, control, and finance. While it is true that Congregationalism later became independent of state authority, it is well to keep in mind the movement's original aim to be a state church.

Meeting at Cambridge, Massachusetts, in 1648, representatives of the four Puritan colonies issued what came to be called *The Cambridge Platform*. It became the basic document of Congregational policy in New England. As stated in the Platform, "The Government of the Church is a mixed Government . . . in respect of Christ the Head and King of the Church, and the sovereign power residing in Him, it is a Monarchy; in respect of the Body of Brotherhood of the Church, and Power from Christ granted unto them, it resembles a Democracy; in respect of the Presbytery, and Power committed unto them, it is an Aristocracy." The basic unit was the visible congregation united into one body by a covenant. The care of the church was left to elders (pastors, teachers, and ruling elders) and deacons, all elected by the congregation.

Churches, though equal, were to maintain communion with one another by means of synods. Synods, though not of the essence of the church, were deemed necessary to the times, to establish truth and peace. Composed of elders and other messengers, synods were to "debate and determine controversies of Faith and Cases of Conscience; to clear from the Word holy directions for the Holy Worship of God, and good Government of the Church; to hear witness against maladministration and corruption of manners in any particular church; and to give Directions for the Reformation thereof." Churches were enjoined not to remove themselves from the communion of the other churches. In its developed form, Congregationalism was very close to Presbyterianism

rather than to the independent congregational policy which later became typical of the Baptists. Developed Congregationalism was also far removed from the free church structure of the Plymouth Brethren.

A key element in Congregationalism was the power granted by the church to the secular magistrate. The magistry was encouraged to restrain and punish idolatry, blasphemy, heresy, schism, and like actions. When the power of the magistry was removed from Congregationalism by the American Revolution, the churches adopted an independent congregationalism, but always with a tendency to presbyterial forms.

It has often been asserted that Congregationalism was a non-creedal church. But the same body that drew up the Cambridge Platform when asked to prepare a creed, adopted the Westminster Confession of Faith, which placed Congregationalism doctrinally within British Calvinism (Puritanism).

The first branch of the Reformed tradition in America was Congregationalism, the church of the Pilgrims and Puritans. They landed in 1620 and 1630 respectively and established their theocracy. Their church operated as a state church until disestablished after the American Revolution. It adopted the Westminster Confession shortly after promulgation by the English divines. It was the church of the New England Patriots, Harvard and Yale Universities, and of famous ministers, Jonathan Edwards, Timothy Dwight, Cotton Mather, Thomas Hooker, and Charles Chauncy. It also became the seedbed upon which Unitarianism, Universalism, and Christian Science were to grow. Only in the twentieth century, as it became a major force in Reformed family ecumenism did it produce schismatic churches.

SOURCES—REFORMED-PRESBYTERIAN FAMILY

HISTORY, EUROPEAN

Grimm, Harold J. *The Reformation Era*. New York: Macmillan, 1954. 675 pp.

Leith, John H. *An Introduction to the Reformed Tradition*. Atlanta: John Knox Press, 1977. 253 pp.

McNeill, John T. *The History and Character of Calvinism*. New York: Oxford University Press, 1954. 466 pp.

Reaman, G. Elmore. *The Trail of the Huguenots*. London: Frederick Muller, 1964. 318 pp.

Reed, R. C. *History of the Presbyterian Churches of the World*. Philadelphia: Westminister Press, 1912. 408 pp.

Thompson, Ernest Trice, and Elton M. Eenigenburg. *Through the Ages*. Richmond, VA: The CLC Press, 1965. 480 pp.

HISTORY, AMERICAN

Armstrong, Maurice, Lefferts A. Loetscher, and Charles A. Anderson. *The Presbyterian Enterprise*. Philadelphia: The Westminster Press, 1956. 336 pp.

Bratt, James D. *Dutch Calvinism in Modern America*. Grand Rapids, MI. William B. Eerdmans Publishing Company, 1984. 329 pp.

Jamison, Wallace N. *The United Presbyterian Story*. Pittsburgh: The Geneva Press, 1958. 253 pp.

Slosser, Gaius Jackson, ed. *They Seek a Country*. New York: Macmillan, 1955. 330 pp.

Trinterud, Leonard J. *The Forming of an American Tradition.* Philadelphia: Westminister Press, 1949. 352 pp.

Watts, George B. *The Waldenses in the New World.* Durham, NC: Duke University Press, 1941. 309 pp.

Lingle, Walter L. *Presbyterians, Their History and Beliefs.* Richmond, VA: John Knox Press, 1944. 127 pp.

THEOLOGY

Beardslee, John W., III, ed. *Reformed Dogmatics.* New York: Oxford University Press, 1965. 471 pp.

Bratt, John H., ed. *The Heritage of John Calvin.* Grand Rapids, MI: William B. Eerdmans Publishing Company, 1973. 222 pp.

Calvin, John. *The Institutes of the Christian Religion.* 2 Vols. Philadelphia: Westminister Press, 1960.

Cochrane, Arthur C., ed. *The Reformed Confessions of the Sixteenth Century.* Philadelphia: Westminister Press, 1966.

Geer, Felix B. *Basic Beliefs of the Reformed Faith.* Richmond, VA: John Knox Press, 1960. 80 pp.

Gettys, Joseph M. *What Presbyterians Believe.* Clinton, SC: The Author, 1953. 128 pp.

Osterhaven, M. Eugene. *The Spirit of the Reformed Tradition.* Grand Rapids, MI: William B. Eerdmans Publishing Company, 1971. 190 pp.

Schaff, Philip. *Creed Revision in the Presbyterian Churches.* New York: Charles Scribner's Sons, 1890. 67 pp.

LIFE AND WORSHIP

Mackay, John A. *The Presbyterian Way of Life.* Englewood Cliffs, NJ: Prentice-Hall, 1960. 238 pp.

Melton, Julius. *Presbyterian Worship in America.* Richmond, VA: John Knox Press, 1967. 173 pp.

Nichols, James Hastings. *Corporate Worship in the Reformed Tradition.* Philadelphia: Westminister Press, 1968.

CONGREGATIONALISM

Hiemert, Alan, and Andrew Delbanco, eds. *The Puritans in America.* Cambridge: Harvard University Press, 1985. 438 pp.

Jenkins, Daniel. *Congregationalism: A Restatement.* London: Faber and Faber, 1954. 152 pp.

Starkey, Marion L. *The Congregational Way.* Garden City, NY: Doubleday, 1966. 342 pp.

Walker, Williston. *The Creed and Platforms of Congregationalism.* Philadelphia: Pilgrim Press, 1960. 604 pp.

Chapter Five

THE PIETIST-METHODIST FAMILY

Directory listings for the groups belonging to the Pietist-Methodist Family
may be found in the section beginning on page 265.

The movement called Pietism gave rise to three groups of churches—the Moravian churches, the Swedish Evangelical churches, and the Methodist (Wesleyan) churches—all of which will be treated in this chapter. First, however, Pietism itself must be considered.

Pietism was an evangelical reaction to trends within Protestantism in the late seventeenth century. The regular church life of the Protestant churches, mainly the Lutheran and Calvinist churches, had taken on a certain rigidity, and their creeds reflected the systematic theology of the second generation Lutheran and Calvinist scholastics. Pietism countered both the rigidity and the sectarian scholasticism. Without abandoning doctrine, Pietism sought to change the emphasis of those churches from divisive formulations to spiritual experience. The dominant characteristics of the movement were (1) a Bible-centered faith, (2) the experienced Christian life (guilt, forgiveness, conversion, holiness, and love within community), and (3) free expression of faith in hymns, testimony and evangelical zeal. The earliest representatives of the movement include Philipp Jacob Spener (1635-1705) and August Hermann Francke (1663-1727).

Spener is credited with originating a basic form taken by Pietists—the *collegia pietatis* (association of piety). In despair over the impossibility of reforming Lutheranism, he began to organize small groups which met in homes for Bible study, prayer, and discussions leading to a deeper spiritual life. These groups spread throughout Europe and were known in England as religious societies.

Francke was Spener's most famous disciple. Forced out of the University of Leipzig, and later dismissed from the University of Erfurt, he became a teacher at the newly formed University of Halle and turned it into a Pietist center. (Leipzig, Erfurt, and Halle are in East Germany.) During the three decades Francke taught there, Halle graduated more than two hundred ministers a year. Besides the deeply experienced faith taught at Halle, Francke encouraged missionary endeavors. He began an orphan house in 1698. Knowledge of his work brought financial help and allowed the work to include a pauper school, a Bible institute, a Latin school, and other facilities to aid destitute children. Most early missionaries came from among Halle's graduates.

From Halle, Pietism spread throughout the world. Correspondence between Francke and Cotton Mather led to the establishment of religious societies in the Boston churches, and Pietistic literature lay directly behind the American revival movement of the 1730's and 1740's called the Great Awakening. In Germany Pietism renewed the Moravian Church, which then began to spread its own version of Pietism. The Moravian Church carried the Pietist faith to England where Pietism became a strong influence on John Wesley, the founder of the Methodist movement. Moravians working in Sweden helped establish the Swedish Evangelical Church. Thus three groups of churches emerged from the Pietist movement: the Moravian churches, the Swedish Evangelical churches, and the Methodist churches.

However, most of Pietism's influence was absorbed by the Lutheran Church and the Calvinist groups (the Reformed Church, the Presbyterian Church, and the Congregational Church). Although Pietism did lead to schism in the American churches, most of the schismatic churches reunited with their parent bodies.

A note of contrast: the Pietist churches are very different from the European free churches. The Latter, discussed in Chapter Eight, include the Mennonites, the Amish, the Quakers, and the Brethren. The Pietists were distinct from the European free churches because the Pietists were open to traditional Christian practices and beliefs, and lacked hostility to their parent bodies. Instead of rejecting the forms of the past, as the European free churches did, the Pietists worked with the forms of the past and sought the life of the spirit within them. In general, the free churches of the past and the present have opposed infant baptism, opposed traditional ideas of church and sacrament, and opposed many liturgical practices. In contrast, Pietists have accepted Reformation ideas of church and sacrament, have baptized infants, and have used simplified versions of liturgical forms. Whereas the European free churches sprang up as a protest to state churches (whether those were Roman Catholic, Anglican, Lutheran, or Calvinist), Pietist groups began as societies within Protestant state churches and only later removed themselves from their parent churches and became independent entities.

THE MORAVIANS. The Moravian churches of today exist only because the Pietist movement gave life to an almost extinguished Moravian church. Thus the Moravians are distinct among Pietists: the Moravians represent not so much a new church created by Pietism as a renewed church recreated by Pietism. That re-creation occurred in 1727. The story of the Moravian churches, however, starts in the ninth century with the founding of the early Moravian church.

Cyril and Methodius, missionaries of the Greek Orthodox Church, arrived in the ninth century in Moravia, an area in what is now called Czechoslovakia. There they established a Greek-based Slavic church. At first the Moravians were encouraged by the Roman Catholic Church, but later Rome forced a Latin rite upon them. The Moravians considered this a repressive move. They became discontented with being Catholic, and their discontent was heightened by a young priest named John Hus (1369-1415). From his pulpit in Prague, he began to throw challenges in the face of the Roman Catholic Church. He questioned the practice of selling indulgences, which were promises of the remission of punishment due for sins. Hus also questioned the denial of the cup to the laity in holy communion, and the moral corruption of the papacy. Hus's career coincided with the time when three men were claiming to be the pope, each having a segment of Europe behind him. In 1414 at the Council of Constance, called to determine the one true pope, Hus was invited (with a safe conduct promise) to state his case. He was arrested and burned at the stake. The Hussite Wars followed and eventually Hus's followers, concluding that Hus's ideas would never positively effect the Roman Church, formed their own church—the Unitas Fratrum or "Unity of the Brethren." The church existed for its early years as a Reformed Roman Church, turning to Bishop Stephen of the Waldensian Church for apostolic ordination. It published the Bible in the Czech vernacular—the Kralitz Bible, which affected Czechoslovakia as strongly as Luther's Bible affected Germany.

The religious was of the late sixteenth and early seventeenth centuries all but destroyed the once prosperous Unitas Fratrum. On June 21, 1621, fifteen Brethren leaders were beheaded in Prague. The persecutions brought an end to all visible manifestation of the Unitas Fratrum.

In 1722 a few families from the former Unitas Fratrum fled from Moravia to Saxony, a region in East Germany. Soon more than three hundred exiles had settled in Saxony on Count Zinzendorf's estate, called Herrnhut. The exiles held conferences and drew up a "Brotherly Agreement." Their bickering, though, led Zinzendorf to invite as many as would come to a communion service at his manor church on August 13, 1727. This date is considered to be the birth of the Renewed Unitas Fratrum (or Moravian Church) as there occurred an amazing "outpouring of the power of God," which Moravians compared to Pentecost. The wranglings and strife were over. Zinzendorf received a copy of the "Discipline" of the old Unitas Fratrum and began to set the church in order. Ordination in the apostolic succession was secured from Daniel Ernest Jablonsky. Jablonsky, a court preacher in Berlin, was one of the ordained bishops in the line of the old Unitas Fratrum. Jablonsky ordained David Nitschman as the first bishop of the Restored Church.

The arrival of the Moravians on the estate of Zinzendorf largely determined the Moravian future. Zinzendorf was a Pietist and he led the Moravians into placing great stress upon religious experience and the relation of the individual with God. Numerous forms were developed to foster this deep faith. Among them was the love feast, an informal service centering on holy communion but also including a light meal, singing, and a talk by the officiating minister. The Litany, a lengthy prayer form for corporate and private devotions, was added to the Herrnhut services in 1731. Its present form is a modified Lutheran litany. The idea of small groups of dedicated Christians meeting together regularly for worship and exhortation and service was taken from the German Pietists and used extensively, especially in the mission field. Moravian meetings were the model of early Methodist societies developed by John Wesley.

The *Daily Texts* was a book which grew from a need of the early Herrnhut settlers, the need for a "watchword" from the Scripture for daily use. They at first copied Scriptural passages by hand on bits of paper to be drawn from a container each day. This practice evolved into an annual volume of texts. For each day there was a text from both the Old and New Testaments and a hymn stanza to amplify the text. This book, printed annually, has had an influence far beyond the membership of the church, as it circulates widely to nonmembers.

The most characteristic aspect of Moravian piety was its mission program. Zinzendorf, early in his life, became convinced that he was destined to do something about the neglected peoples of the world. In 1731 he traveled to Copenhagen, where he met Anthony Ulrich, a black man and slave from the Danish West Indies. Ulrich told Zinzendorf of his people's plight. Back at Herrnhut, Zinzendorf told Anthony Ulrich's story, preparing the way for the slave to arrive and tell it himself. The response was immediate, and David Nitschmann and Leonhard Dober were chosen as the first missionaries to the oldest Moravian mission—St. Thomas. The Moravians then proceeded to establish missions all over Europe. Zinzendorf, a Lutheran himself, gave strict orders for the Moravians not to encroach upon state church prerogatives. They became merely preachers of the Word and were welcomed in many Protestant lands. In England they moved into an established church structure and set up "religious societies" for Bile study and prayer, never encouraging anyone to leave his state church. John Wesley was a member of one of these societies for a while.

In 1872 re-entrance into Czechoslovakia was permitted with the Edict of Toleration, and the first congregation in Bohemia was established in 1872. Other mission work included British Guiana, Surinam, Southern Africa, Java, Nicaragua, Jordan, Alaska, and Labrador, all established before 1900. In 1735 the Moravians came to the American colonies.

Moravians in America. The settling of Moravians in America in 1735 had a two-fold purpose: the securing of a settlement in the New World in case Germany again became intolerant, and a mission to the Indians. The first group of settlers in the New World was led by Bishop August Gottlieb Spangenberg. He traveled to Georgia on the same ship that brought John Wesley, the founder of Methodism, to the colony of George Oglethorpe in Georgia. Wesley was impressed with Spangenberg and the Moravians and records a number of conversations with Spangenberg. Soon after settling in Savannah, the Moravians opened an Indian school. The Moravians were, however, caught in the war between the British (Georgia) and the Spanish (Florida). Their refusal to bear arms led to their being looked down upon. By 1740 the Moravians left Georgia for Pennsylvania. They established the town of Nazareth and the following year Bishop David Nitschmann arrived and began to settle Bethlehem. In December of 1741, Zinzendorf arrived, and on Christmas day he organized the Moravian Congregation in Bethlehem, the first in America.

Under Spangenberg's leadership a semi-communal arrangement was worked out in Bethlehem which soon made it a self-sufficient settlement, able to bear its own mission program to the Indians. Churches were soon organized at Nazareth and Lilitz in Pennsylvania, and Hope, New Jersey.

In 1749 the British Parliament acknowledged the Moravian Church as "an Ancient Protestant Episcopal Church," thus in effect giving an invitation to settle in other British Colonies. The Moravians took advantage of Parliament's recognition of their church and settled in North Carolina on property owned by Lord Granville. Rising persecution in Germany encouraged the Moravians to come to America.

Spangenberg and five others went to North Carolina in 1752 and had surveyors lay out what is now Forsyth County. The first settlers, fifteen in all, arrived in 1753 and settled in Bethabara. In 1766 the permanent settlement of Salem was laid out. From this beginning other churches and settlements developed.

METHODISM. Among Methodist historians there is a wide disagreement about when Methodism began; however, organizational continuity in the Wesleyan movement dates to late 1739 when the first society was formed by John Wesley and eighteen other persons "desiring to flee from the wrath to come . . . and be saved from their sins." The number of societies grew and in 1744 the first Methodist Conference was held as Wesley called his lay ministers together to confer with him. Wesley made all the decisions and assigned the preachers to their tasks.

Methodism's founder, John Wesley (1703-91), the son of an Anglican clergyman, attended Oxford to study for the ministry. While at Oxford he formed a religious society called the Holy Club by other students. To this group was first applied the derisive title "Methodists" party because of their strict daily schedules.

Wesley left Oxford and became a missionary to the Indians in Georgia. This adventure ended in failure. However, while on the voyage to America he encountered the Moravians and was very impressed with their simple piety and their leader Bishop August Gottlieb Spangenberg. In Georgia, he also encountered the writings of Scottish Pietist Thomas Halyburton, whose personal religious experience closely paralleled his own. Arriving back in London, Wesley affiliated with the Moravians and in particular with Peter Bohler, who would soon be on his way to America as a missionary to the slaves. Activity with Bohler led Wesley to his own crisis experience which occurred at the religious society at Aldersgate on May 24, 1738. Wesley described what happened in his *Journal*:

"In the evening, I went very unwillingly to a Society in Aldersgate Street, where one was reading Luther's Preface to the Epistle to the Romans. About a quarter before nine, while he was describing the change which God works in the heart through faith in Christ, I felt my heart strangely warm. I felt I did trust in Christ; Christ alone, for salvation; and an assurance was given me, that he had taken away my sins, even mine, and saved me from the law of sin and death."

This experience became the turning point in Wesley's life. During the next year he visited Germany (seeing the Moravians), broke with the Moravians over several points of practice, and began the United Societies. Innovations for Wesley included field preaching, the use of lay preachers (Mr. Wesley's assistants), and the discipline of the societies.

The United Societies were a group of dedicated Christians within the state church, Anglicanism. As with continental Pietism, doctrine was not at issue as much as the application of doctrine to life. Some doctrinal innovations did occur concerning the Christian life—Wesley's emphasis on the witness of the Spirit and Christian perfection. These doctrines often led to excesses and accusations of "enthusiasm," the eighteenth century euphemism for "fanaticism."

Those who experienced this Evangelical Awakening were organized into societies, the basic document of which was the General Rules. Those in the society were expected to evidence their desire for salvation:

First: by doing no harm, avoiding evil of every kind, especially that which is most generally practiced.

Second: by doing good of every possible sort, and as far as possible to all men.

Third: by attending upon the ordinances of God.

Wesley wrote that following the third rule involved the public worship of God, the ministry of the Word (either read or expounded), the Supper of the Lord, family and private prayer, searching the Scriptures, and fasting and abstinence.

The society was to be thought of as a gathering of people, not as a place. Wherever the society met was where it held its regular worship services and most importantly the quarterly meeting. Once each quarter Wesley visited each society. He inquired into the lives of the members relative to the General Rules and issued quarterly tickets. The tickets admitted members to the society for the next three months. Wesley served communion and usually a love feast was held, an informal service centering on holy communion but also including a light meal, singing, and a talk.

Wesley lived almost the entire century and the issue of doctrinal standards for Methodism came to the fore late in his life. Early doctrinal concerns had been set in the *Minutes of the Conference* but additional doctrinal questions were raised in 1777 by the predestinarian Calvinists and in the 1780's by the establishment of the Methodist Episcopal Church in America. The Calvinist controversy set Methodism firmly against predestinarian doctrines. Wesley opposed the Calvinist idea of irresistible grace: if grace comes, you cannot refuse it; if it does not come, you cannot obtain it. Wesley said grace is freely given to each person and each person can freely respond to the gospel. The formation of American Methodism caused Wesley to set doctrinal standards in his letter to the preachers in America: "Let all of you be determined to abide by the Methodist doctrine and discipline published in the four volumes of *Sermons* and the *Notes on the New Testament*, together with the *Large Minutes of the Conference.*"

These three documents joined the Articles of Religion which Wesley abridged from the Thirty-nine Articles of the Anglican Church. Wesley excluded Articles on hell, creeds, predestination, bishops, excommunication, and the authority of the church. The Articles of Religion printed here are from Wesley's text in *The Sunday Service of the Methodists*, published in 1784.

Articles of Religion

i. Of Faith in the Holy Trinity

There is but one living and true God, everlasting, without body or parts, of infinite power, wisdom, and goodness; the maker and preserver of all things, both visible and invisible. And in unity of this Godhead there are three persons, of one substance, power, and eternity—the Father, the Son, and the Holy Ghost.

ii. Of the Word, or Son of God, Who Was Made Very Man

The Son, who is the Word of the Father, the very and eternal God, of one substance with the Father, took man's nature in the womb of the blessed Virgin; so that two whole and perfect natures, that is to say, the Godhead and Manhood, were joined together in one person, never to be divided; whereof is one Christ, very God and very Man, who truly suffered, was crucified, dead, and buried, to reconcile his Father to us, and to be a sacrifice, not only for original guilt, but also for the actual sins of men.

iii. Of the Resurrection of Christ

Christ did truly rise again from the dead, and took again his body, with all things appertaining to the perfection of man's nature, wherewith he ascended into heaven, and there sitteth until he return to judge all men at the last day.

iv. Of the Holy Ghost

The Holy Ghost, proceeding from the Father and the Son, is of one substance, majesty, and glory with the Father and the Son, very and eternal God.

v. Of the Sufficiency of the Holy Scriptures for Salvation

The Holy Scripture containeth all things necessary to salvation; so that whatsoever is not read therein, nor may be proved thereby, is not to be require of any man that it should be believed as an article of faith, or be thought requisite or necessary to salvation. In the name of the Holy Scripture we do understand those canonical books of the Old and New Testament of whose authority was never any doubt in the Church. The names of the canonical books are:

Genesis, Exodus, Leviticus, Numbers, Deuteronomy, Joshua, Judges, Ruth, The First Book of Samuel, The Second Book of Samuel, The First Book of Kings, The Second Book of Kings, The First Book of Chronicles, The Second Book of Chronicles, The Book of Ezra, The Book of Nehemiah, The Book of Esther, The Book of Job, The Psalms, The Proverbs, Ecclesiastes or the Preacher, Cantica or Songs of Solomon, Four Prophets the Greater, Twelve Prophets the Less.

All the books of the New Testament, as they are commonly received, we do receive and account canonical.

vi. Of the Old Testament

The Old Testament is not contrary to the New; for both in the Old and New Testament everlasting life is offered to mankind by Christ, who is the only Mediator between God and man, being both God and Man. Wherefore they are not to be heard who feign that the old fathers did look only for transitory promises. Although the law given from God by Moses as touching ceremonies and rites doth not bind Christians, nor ought the civil precepts thereof of necessity be received in any commonwealth; yet notwithstanding, no Christian whatsoever is free from the obedience of the commandments which are called moral.

vii. Of Original or Birth Sin

Original sin standeth not in the following of Adam (as the Pelagians do vainly talk), but it is the corruption of the nature of every man, that naturally is engendered of the offspring of Adam, whereby man is very far gone from original righteousness, and of his own nature inclined to evil, and that continually.

viii. Of Free Will

The condition of man after the fall of Adam is such that he cannot turn and prepare himself, by his own natural strength and works, to faith, and calling upon God; wherefore we have no power to do good work, pleasant and acceptable to God, without the grace of God by Christ preventing us, that we may have a good will, and working with us, when we have that good will.

ix. Of the Justification of Man

We are accounted righteous before God only for the merit of our Lord and Saviour Jesus Christ, by faith, and not for our own works or deservings. Wherefore, that we are justified by faith, only, is a most wholesome doctrine, and very full of comfort.

x. Of Good Works

Although good works, which are the fruits of faith, and follow after justification, cannot put away our sins, and endure the severity of God's judgement; yet are they pleasing and acceptable to God in Christ, and spring out of a true and lively faith, insomuch that by them a lively faith may be as evidently known as a tree is discerned by its fruit.

xi. Of Works of Supererogation

Voluntary works—besides, over and above God's commandments—which they call works of supererogation, cannot be taught without arrogancy and impiety. For by them men do declare that they do not only render unto God as much as they are bound to do, but that they do more for his sake than the bounden duty is required; whereas Christ saith plainly: When you have done all that is commanded you, say, We are unprofitable servants.

xii. Of Sin After Justification

Not every sin willingly committed after justification is the sin against the Holy Ghost, and unpardonable. Wherefore, the grant of repentance is not to be denied to such as fall into sin after justification. After we have received the Holy Ghost, we may depart from grace given, and fall into sin, and, by the grace of God, rise again and amend our lives. And therefore they are to be condemned who say they can no more sin as long as they live here; or deny the place of forgiveness to such as truly repent.

xiii. Of the Church

The visible Church of Christ is a congregation of faithful men in which the pure Word of God is preached, and the Sacraments duly administered according to Christ's ordinance, in all those things that of necessity are requisite to the same.

xiv. Of Purgatory

The Romish doctrine concerning purgatory, pardon, worshiping, and adoration, as well of images as of relics, and also invocation of saints, is a fond thing, vainly invented, and grounded upon no warrant of Scripture, but repugnant to the Word of God.

xv. Of Speaking in the Congregation in Such a Tongue as the People Understand

It is a thing plainly repugnant to the Word of God, and the custom of the primitive Church, to have public prayer in the church, or to minister the Sacraments, in a tongue not understood by the people.

xvi. Of the Sacraments

Sacraments ordained of Christ are not only badges or tokens of Christian men's profession, but rather they are certain signs of grace, and God's good will toward us, by which he doth work invisibly in us, and doth not only quicken, but also strengthen and confirm, our faith in him.

There are two Sacraments ordained of Christ our Lord in the Gospel; that is to say, Baptism and the Supper of the Lord.

Those five commonly called sacraments, that is to say, confirmation, penance, orders, matrimony, and extreme unction, are not to be counted for Sacraments of the Gospel; being such as have partly grown out of the *corrupt* following of the apostles, and partly are states of life allowed in the Scriptures, but yet have not the like nature of Baptism and the Lord's Supper, because they have not any visible sign or ceremony ordained of God.

The Sacraments were not ordained of Christ to be gazed upon, or to be carried about; but that we should duly use them. And in such only as worthily receive the same, they have a wholesome effect or operation; but they that receive them unworthily, purchase to themselves condemnation, as St. Paul saith.

xvii. Of Baptism

Baptism is not only a sign of profession and mark of difference whereby Christians are distinguished from others that are not baptized; but it is also a sign of regeneration or the new birth. The baptism of young children is to be retained in the church.

xviii. Of the Lord's Supper

The Supper of the Lord is not only a sign of the love that Christians ought to have among themselves one to another, but rather is a sacrament of our redemption by Christ's death; insomuch that, to such as rightly, worthily, and with faith receive the same, the bread which we break is a partaking of the body of Christ; and likewise the cup of blessing is a partaking of the blood of Christ.

Transubstantiation, or the change of the substance of bread and wine in the Supper of our Lord, cannot be proved by Holy Writ, but is repugnant to the plain words of Scripture, overthroweth the nature of a sacrament, and hath given occasion to many superstitions.

The body of Christ is given, taken, and eaten in the Supper, only after a heavenly and spiritual manner. And the mean whereby the body of Christ is received and eaten in the Supper is faith.

The Sacrament of the Lord's Supper was not by Christ's ordinance reserved, carried about, lifted up, or worshiped.

xix. Of Both Kinds

The cup of the Lord is not to be denied to the lay people; for both the parts of the Lord's Supper, by Christ's ordinance and commandment, ought to be administered to all Christians alike.

xx. Of the One Oblation of Christ, Finished upon the Cross

The offering of Christ, once made, is that perfect redemption, propitiation, and satisfaction for all the sins of the whole world, both original and actual; and there is none other satisfaction for sin but that alone. Wherefore the sacrifice of masses, in the which it is commonly said that the priest doth offer Christ for the quick and the dead, to have remission of pain or guilt, is a blasphemous fable and dangerous deceit.

xxi. Of the Marriage of Ministers

The ministers of Christ are not commanded by God's law either to vow the estate of single life, or to abstain from marriage; therefore it is lawful for them, as for all other Christians, to marry at their own discretion, as they shall judge the same to serve best to godliness.

xxii. Of the Rites and Ceremonies of Churches

It is not necessary that rites and ceremonies should in all places be the same, or exactly alike; for they have been always different, and may be changed according to the diversity of countries, times, and men's manners, so that nothing be ordained against God's Word. Whosoever, through his private judgment, willingly and purposely doth openly break the rites and ceremonies of the church to which he belongs, which are not repugnant to the Word of God, and are ordained and approved by common authority, ought to be rebuked openly, that others may fear to do the like, as one that offendeth against the common order of the church, and woundeth the consciences of weak brethren.

Every particular church may ordain, change, or abolish rites and ceremonies, so that all things may be done to edification.

xxiii. Of the Rulers of the United States of America

The President, the Congress, the general assemblies, the governors, and the councils of state, *as the delegates of the people*, are the rulers of the United States of America, according to the division of power made to them by the Constitution of the United States and by the constitutions of their respective states. And the said states are a sovereign and independent nation, and ought not to be subject to any foreign jurisdiction.

xxiv. Of Christian Men's Goods

The riches and goods of Christians are not common as touching the right, title, and possession of the same, as some do falsely boast. Notwithstanding, every man ought, of such things as he possesseth, liberally to give alms to the poor, according to his ability.

xxv. Of a Christian Man's Oath

As we confess that vain and rash swearing is forbidden Christian men by our Lord Jesus Christ and James his apostle, so we judge that the Christian religion doth not prohibit, but that a man may swear when the magistrate requireth, in a cause of faith and charity, so it be done according to the prophet's teaching, in justice, judgment, and truth.

The Articles of Religion grounded Methodism in traditional Christian doctrines and the *Sermons, Notes*, and *Minutes* stated Methodist opinion on current issues. The Articles are themselves derivative of continental Reformed confessions and, with the exception of predestination, place Methodism in a Reformed theological tradition. The Reformed tradition, based on the work of John Calvin, shows up most clearly in Articles v, ix, xii, xiii, xvi, and of course in the anti-Roman Catholic Articles x, xi, xiv, xv, xix, xx, and xxii. Methodists have always identified with Reformed theologian Jacob Arminius, whom they interpreted as rejecting the Calvinist emphasis on predestination. Wesley named the first Methodist periodical *The Arminian Magazine*. The twenty-five Articles of Religion are a common core of doctrinal agreement for all Methodists and are included in doctrinal statements by almost all Methodist bodies.

In England, Methodism remained as a Society within the Anglican Church and as such, was spread throughout the British Commonwealth by the missionary vision and activity of Rev. Thomas Coke. The British Wesleyans became independent of the Anglican Church in 1795.

Wesleyanism in America. Methodist history in the colonies begins in the 1760's with the migration of Methodist laymen and preachers. The first society on record was in Leesburg, Virginia, in 1766, and the second in New York City. Methodism spread in the middle colonies and developed early centers in Baltimore, Philadelphia, and Wilmington.

The first crisis for American Methodists was the Revolutionary War. Because of their attachment to the Church of England and Wesley's antirevolutionary traits, their loyalty was suspect. After the war, because of the independence of the colonies from England, Wesley decided to allow the American Methodists to set up an independent church. In September 1784, he ordained Thomas Coke as a superintendent and sent him to America with instructions to set up the church and to ordain Francis Asbury. This organization was accomplished at the Christmas Conference held at Lovely Lane Chapel in Baltimore.

Francis Asbury (1745-1816) was second only to Wesley in molding American Methodism. He came to America in 1771 and during his first thirteen years of service emerged as the unquestioned leader of the American bretheren. He was ordained bishop in December 1784 (the American preachers preferred the term bishop to superintendent) and formed the Methodist Episcopal Church. His appointments of ministers to their congregations covered the United States, Nova Scotia, and Antigua.

As the Methodists grew in number, their organization became more sophisticated, but several features important for understanding Methodists and their schisms have remained constant. These features are the conference and itinerary. The basic structure of Methodism is the conference, a name derived from Wesley's practice of having regular meetings with his preachers to confer with them before deciding on issues. The local church charge conference, district conference, annual conference, and general conference form a hierarchy of authority. The local church charge conference is the annual business meeting of the local congregation. There the congregation elects officers and sets the budget. The district conference is primarily a funnel; it lets local congregations know the messages of bishops and annual conferences. The annual conference is a regional conference chaired by the bishop, whose duty it is to assign ministers to their churches (charges) each year, and to publish those assignments at the annual conference. The general conference is made up of representatives of all the annual conferences in the country. The general conference meets quadrennially, is the church's highest legislative body, and writes the Discipline, the book of church order.

The phrase "annual conference" has a meaning in addition to that described above. For a minister to belong to an annual conference means that he or she has contractual relationships with the church in that area. The minister agrees to be available for assignment, and the church guarantees that he or she will receive an appointment to a congregation and also receive a salary. The phrase "annual conference" thus connotes an association of ministers, a fellowship, a sense of belonging.

Itineracy is the second important structural feature of Methodism. Ministers itinerate; that is, they travel to various congregations within their own region (usually part of a state) as they are assigned by the bishop of that region. The assignments were traditionally for one year, but the length of the minister's stay is expanding. In addition to itinerant ministers, Methodists have both ordained and unordained local preachers who do not travel but belong to only one congregation. They are licensed by the church and they preach, assist the minister, and occasionally act as interim pastors.

During the nineteenth century the itinerant, the circuit rider of folklore, would often be assigned to a charge with twenty or thirty preaching points on it. The circuit rider would travel his circuit every two, three, or four weeks. The effect of this type of organization was to cover the land, but it also put the ministers in many places on weekdays—not on Sundays. This became an issue in the nineteenth century as Methodism grew and stable congregations emerged which wanted to meet on Sundays instead of on weekdays.

Attempts of merger between the English-speaking and German-speaking Methodist and Pietist groups in the early 1800's failed. A major factor in the failure was Asbury's belief that there should be no perpetuation of German work since English would quickly be the only language in America. Of course, Asbury was essentially correct, but he failed to foresee the large German migrations of the 1800's. Eventually the Methodist Episcopal Church had to organize its own German-speaking mission to cope with the demand for ministry.

GERMAN METHODISTS. Two Wesleyan churches developed among America's German-speaking population: the United Brethren in Christ, and the Evangelical Association. These two churches merged with each other and then with the United Methodist Church. Prior to these mergers, various schismatic churches formed from the two German-speaking churches.

One of the most interesting schismatic churches is now defunct: the Republican United Brethren Church. It was formed by members of the White River Conference of the United Brethren in Christ during the Mexican War. The church's origin can be traced to an informal meeting of ministers and members of the White River Conference at Dowell Meeting House, Franklin Circuit, Indiana, on March 12, 1848. At the meeting, a resolution was passed protesting conference action concerning Rev. P. C. Parker. (Rev. Parker had been expelled from the ministry for "immorality" because of his participation in the war.) This resolution was refused publication; therefore, an appeal was made to the General Conference. The 1853 General Conference, however, sustained Parker's expulsion and passed a strong anti-war resolution. The convention also acted in support of a belief in "the doctrine of the natural, hereditary, and total depravity of man." That doctrine refers to the sinfulness of man after the fall, by which sinfulness the will is in bondage and is unable to turn to God. The protest of the three actions of the General Conference became the formal basis for withdrawal. At a meeting at Union Chapel, Decatur County, Indiana, on September 8-12, 1853, the new church was organized. The church was small (the first conference listed only two charges) and existed for only a short time. In the 1860's, the church became part of the Christian Union.

BLACK METHODISM. Of the religiously affiliated black people in America, the second largest number belong to Methodist churches. (The largest number belong to Baptist churches.) Blacks were a part of Methodism almost from the beginning; first mentioned by John Wesley, the founder of Methodism, in his *Journal* were servants of Nathaniel Gilbert, the pioneer of Methodism in the West Indies. In America they were members of the earliest societies, a few being named in the records. At least two, Richard Allen and Harry Hoosier, were present at the Christmas Conference in Baltimore in 1784, when the American Methodist church was established as a separate church from English Methodism. Harry Hoosier traveled often with Bishop Francis Asbury, the first Methodist bishop, and Richard Allen emerged as the leader of the Philadelphia black Methodist group. By 1800 a large free black constituency was present in Baltimore, New York, Wilmington, North Carolina, and Philadelphia, quite apart from the large membership among the slaves.

Forms in keeping with the master-slave relationship were adopted as more and more blacks became church members. These included segregated services, church galleries, and later separate congregations. Dislike of practices derogatory of black people became apparent first among the free black members in the Northern urban centers. Only after the Civil War was significant dissent vocalized.

NON-EPISCOPAL METHODISM. No concern—except for the race issue—has led to the number of schisms within Methodism as has the protest against the episcopal polity of the Methodist Episcopal Church. The first group to depart over polity questions and to subsequently form a nonepiscopal church was the Republican Methodists led by James O'Kelley. His small church eventually became a part of the Christian Church (a constituent part of the present-day United Church of Christ). More significant, however, was the Methodist Protestant schism in the 1920's. This created the first major alternative to the Methodist Episcopal Church and finally merged with the two large episcopal branches in 1939. The merger of the Methodist Protestant Church left many of its pastors and members dissatisfied and led to no less than six schisms. Members refused to move from the relatively small denomination into the ten-million-member Methodist Church (1939-1968), now the United Methodist Church. They also rejected the episcopal system and, in the South, feared the possibility of racial integration, which, of course, occurred in the 1960's. Such churches as the Methodist Protestant Church (1939-), headquartered in Mississippi, and the Bible Protestant Church, centered in New Jersey, originated from the merger of the Methodist Protestant Church in 1939.

Besides the schisms growing out of the Methodist Protestant Church, there have been other protests that included rejection of episcopal authority and led to the formation of new church bodies. Most notable was the Congregational Methodist movement in Georgia in the 1880's. More recently the Southern Methodists and the Evangelical Methodists have followed that pattern. One could also see the Holiness Movement (generally regarded as the only doctrinal schism in Methodism) as a polity schism caused by the inability of the bishops and district superintendents to control the numerous holiness associations that had emerged to focus holiness doctrinal concerns. In fact, most holiness churches adopted a nonepiscopal form of government.

SOURCES—PIETIST METHODIST FAMILY

PIETISM

Gerdes, Egon W. "Pietism Classical and Modern." *Concordia Theological Journal*, April 1968, pp. 257-68.

Stoeffler, E. Ernest. *German Pietism During the Eighteenth Century*. Leiden: E. J. Brill, 1973.

SCANDINAVIAN PIETISTS

Covenant Memories, 1885-1935. Chicago: Covenant Book Concern, 1935. 495 pp.

Norton, H. Wilbert, et al. *The Diamond Jubilee Story of the Evangelical Free Church of America*. Minneapolis: Free Church Publications, 1959. 335 pp.

Olsson, Karl A. *By One Spirit*. Chicago: Covenant Press, 1962.

————. *A Family of Faith*. Chicago: Covenant Press, 1975. 157 pp.

MORAVIANS

Schattschneider, Allen W. *Through Five Hundred Years*. Bethlehem, PA: Comenius Press, 1956. 148 pp.

Weinlick. *Count Zinzendorf*. New York: Abingdon Press, 1956. 240 pp.

THE WESLEYAN TRADITION

Bishop, John. *Methodist Worship*. London: Epworth Press, 1950. 165 pp.

Bucke, Emory Stevens, ed. *The History of American Methodism*. 3 vols. New York: Abingdon, 1965.

Davies, Rupert, and Gordon Rupp, eds. *A History of the Methodist Church in Great Britain*. 3 vols. London: Epworth Press, 196—.

Green, Vivian H. H. *John Wesley*. London: Nelson, 1964.

Nagler, Arthur Wilford. *Pietism and Methodist*. Nashville: Publishing House of the M. E. Church, South, 1918. 200 pp.

Schmidt, Martin. *John Wesley, A Theological Biography*. 2 vols. New York: Abingdon, 1963-73.

UNITED METHODISM

Albright, Raymond W. *A History of the Evangelical Church*. Harrisburg, PA: The Evangelical Press, 1956.

Andersen, Arlow W. *The Salt of the Earth*. Nashville; Norwegian-Danish Methodist Historical Society, 1962. 338 pp.

Davis, Lyman E. *Democratic Methodism in America*. New York: Fleming H. Revell, 1921.

Douglas, Paul F. *The Story of German Methodism*. New York: The Methodist Book Concern, 1939. 361 pp.

Eller, Paul Himmel. *These Evangelical United Brethren*. Dayton, OH: The Otterbein Press, 1950. 128 pp.

Godbold, Albea, ed. *Forever Beginning, 1766-1966*. Lake Junaluska, NC: Association of Methodist Historical Societies, 1967. 254 pp.

Graham, J. H. *Black United Methodists*. New York: Vantage Press, 1979. 162 pp.

Harmon, Nolan B. *Encyclopedia of World Methodism*.

————. *Understanding the United Methodist Church*. Nashville: Abingdon, 1977. 176 pp.

Norwood, Frederick A. *Sourcebook of American Methodism*. Nashville: Abingdon, 1982. 683 pp.

————. *The Story of American Methodism*. Nashville: Abingdon, 1974.

Stokes, Mack B. *Major United Methodist Beliefs*. Nashville: Abingdon, 1971. 128 pp.

Tuell, Jack M. *The Organization of the United Methodist Church*. Nashville: Abingdon, 1977. 174 pp.

Wallenius, C. G., and E. D. Olson. *A Short Story of the Swedish Methodism in America*. Chicago, 1931. 55 pp.

Wunderlich, Friedrich. *Methodist Linking Two Continents*. Nashville: The Methodist Publishing House, 1960. 143 pp.

OTHER METHODISTS

Richardson, Harry V. *Dark Salvation*. Garden City, NY: Doubleday, 1976. 324 pp.

Chapter Six

THE HOLINESS FAMILY

Directory listings for the groups belonging to the Holiness Family may be
found in the section beginning on page 283.

The desire to follow Christ's call, "Be ye perfect as my father in heaven is perfect" (Matt. 5:48), has resulted in "holiness churches." These churches take the drive for perfection or holiness as their primary focus. The corollary to this drive has been separation from Christians who did not reach high enough toward the goal of perfection. Thus holiness churches are distinct from other churches because of the primary focus on perfection and because of separatist practices.

John Wesley, the founder of Methodism, gave impetus to the formation of holiness churches. Though the Wesleyan movement of the eighteenth century was only in part a perfectionist movement, Wesley did encourage the ethical life and perfection, and numerous churches now strive for what they call Wesleyan holiness.

Wesley's understanding of perfection developed through two phases: first, an emphasis on sinlessness, and second, on love. While at Oxford as a college student, Wesley formed the "holy club," a group of students in search of the holy life. In his early sermon, "Christian Perfection," Wesley defined perfection as holiness, saying Christians are perfect in that they are free from outward sin. Wesley felt mature Christians are free from evil tempers and thoughts, and such perfection is possible in this life.

Wesley was immediately challenged for his doctrine of perfection. In answers to his accusors he had to emphasize that perfection did not apply to mistakes, infirmity, knowledge or freedom from temptation. Also, he said there was no perfection that did not admit of further progress. Wesley himself began to see the harmful consequences of defining perfection as "absence of sin," and he redefined perfectionism in terms of "love." His ideas on perfection are gathered together in his *Plain Account of Christian Perfection.* The line between the Pietist-Methodist family and the holiness family is difficult to draw. There have always been individual Methodists who stressed holiness and sanctification. Further, many holiness churches are schismatic bodies that broke away from various Methodist churches, and some holiness churches use the word "Methodist" in their titles. However, the holiness churches place greater stress than Methodist churches on the second blessing and on a lifestyle reflecting sanctification.

HOLINESS CREDO. The credo or distinctive hallmark of the holiness churches involves two elements: doctrine and lifestyle.

The doctrine of the holiness churches focuses on the sanctification experience, after which the recipient remains holy. This experience is called the second blessing or the second work of God in the life of man or the second work of grace. It is the culmination of a process of becoming holy, a process that begins with the first work of God in the life of man: justification. That first experience is the "born again" experience in which the recipient discovers Jesus as a personal savior. Various churches call the first experience by different names: the "born again" experience, the new birth, justification, salvation, regeneration, and the first experience of grace.

After a person is justified and discovers Jesus, the person proceeds to grow in grace. Finally, his or her perfection is ratified in the second blessing. Thus the holiness churches contain members who are still yearning for the second blessing and members who have received the second blessing. An opinion with which most holiness churches would have little disagreement is this statement about sanctification adopted by the Wesleyan Church:

"Inward sanctification begins the moment one is justified. From that moment until a believer is entirely sanctified, he grows daily in grace and gradually dies to sin. Entire sanctification is effected by the baptism of the Holy Spirit, which cleanses the heart of the child of God from all inbred sin through faith in Jesus Christ. It is subsequent to regeneration and is wrought instantaneously when the believer presents himself a living sacrifice, holy and acceptable to God, and is thus enabled through His grace to love God with all the heart and to walk in all His holy commandments blameless. The crisis of cleansing is preceded and followed by growth in grace and the knowledge of our Lord and Savior, Jesus Christ. When man is fully cleansed from all sin, he is endued with the power of the Holy Spirit for the accomplishment of all to which he is called. The ensuing life of holiness is maintained by a continuing faith in the sanctifying blood of Christ, and is evidenced by an obedient life."

While the holiness family can be distinguished from most of the Christian world by the emphasis on sanctification, they are particularly distinguished from their closest neighbors by their lifestyle.

In the last half of the nineteenth century personal holiness, symbolized by a rigid code of behavior, became the distinguishing theme in the holiness lifestyle. John Wesley, who wrote the *General Rules* for the Methodists, is the source of this trend. He disapproved of flashy clothes, costly apparel, and expensive jewelry, and in the early nineteenth-century holiness schisms from Methodism, a consistent voice was one deploring the departure of the Methodists from the *General Rules*. The strictest personal codes came in the late nineteenth century. They were in part a reaction to the "social gospel" emphasis in the larger denominations. There is also strong evidence that such codes were and are tied to the frustrations of people left behind by urbanization, mechanization, and population growth. Without status in mass society, people reject it and find virtue in the necessity of their condition. Holiness was and is to be found in asceticism and rejection of worldliness.

The "rejection of worldliness" theme has led to typical "holiness" intrafamily polemics over exactly what constitutes worldliness. Churches have split over the acceptance of television or the style of clothing, such as neckties. Other issues include the attitude toward divorced people, cosmetics, swimming with the opposite sex, dress in high school gym classes, and the cutting of females' hair (I Cor. 11: 1-16).

At one time the holiness movement concentrated much of its attention on social issues and public morality. The Wesleyan and Free Methodists both were abolitionist-oriented and at different times the holiness movement was tied to the great crusades for temperance and women's rights. Beginning with the co-mingling of Wesleyan and Quaker ideas during the era of John Gurney, pacifism has had a strong hold on the holiness movement and is the major remnant of the social imperative. Many Pentecostal churches have inherited this emphasis.

Among the holiness groups, sacraments have not been an important part of church life. Some churches have two sacraments—baptism and the Lord's Supper as the Wesleyan Church does. Some consider baptism and the Lord's Supper to be ordinances, not sacraments. Churches such as the General Eldership of the Churches of God add footwashing as a third ordinance. Finally, other churches, most notably the Salvation Army, have neither ordinances nor sacraments.

HOLINESS MOVEMENT IN AMERICA. The strain of perfectionism in Wesleyan teaching was not the most emphasized doctrine in early nineteenth-century Methodism. On the heels of the great American revival of 1837-38, however, centers of interest in the Wesleyan doctrine of perfection or holiness, as it was termed, emerged. One phase of this interest came in 1839 with the sanctification of Charles G. Finney. Sanctification, in this context, means holiness; it means becoming perfect in love. Finney, a Congregationalist and the most famous evangelist of his day, had learned of sanctification from the Methodists and from reading Wesley's *Plain Account of Christian Perfection*. At the same time, Finney became involved in a search for social holiness, which means making society perfect in love, with justice being the social form of love. Finney defended women's rights, participated in the antislavery crusade, and as a pacifist protested the Mexican War, which started in 1846. After experiencing sanctification in 1839, Finney began to write on it and preach it. In 1844 his colleague at Oberlin, Asa Mahan, published his book, *Scripture Doctrine of Christian Perfection*, which became the major statement of the Oberlin position. Because of his non-Methodist background, Finney had a great effect on other soon-to-be holiness greats—T.C. Upham, William Boardman, and A.B. Earle. Thus, the first wave of holiness in the United States began outside of Methodism, by Methodized Presbyterians, Baptists, and Congregationalists. Prior to 1855 only one Methodist gained any reputation for perfectionist thinking, Timothy Merritt, editor of the *Guide to Christian Perfection* (later called the *Guide to Holiness*), but Finney had raised an issue for the whole Methodist church, and Methodists could no longer ignore their heritage.

Without any weakening or demise of the Oberlin holiness crusade, the holiness movement began a new phase after the revival of 1857–58. The new center of interest was the "Tuesday Meeting for the Promotion of Holiness" led by Mrs. Phoebe Palmer, a member of Allen Street Methodist Church in New York City. Mrs. Palmer's efforts were aided by the publication of two books, *Christian Purity* by Randolph S. Foster and *The Central Idea of Christianity* by Jesse T. Peck. Both men were soon to be bishops. The revival which was spreading from Allen Street to the whole of Methodism was interrupted by the Civil War, but picked up momentum as soon as the hostilities ceased. During the war, the Palmers, Phoebe and her husband, Walter, bought Merritt's *Guide to Holiness* and in 1866 they toured the country, establishing centers of the sanctified wherever they preached.

It was not long until ministers rallied to the cause. The camp meeting proved to be the prime structure to carry on the work and in 1867 William Osborn of the South New Jersey Conference of Methodists and John S. Inskip of New York set up a national camp meeting at Vineland, New Jersey. During this camp meeting the "National Camp Meeting Association for the Promotion of Holiness" was formed, and Inskip became its first president. Bishop Simpson personally aided the work which prospered under episcopal approval.

The holiness movement grew tremendously among Methodists in the first decade after the Civil War. In 1872 Jesse T. Peck, Randolph S. Foster, Stephen Merrill, and Gilbert Haven, all promoters of the holiness revival, were elected Methodist bishops; and, with their encouragement, the movement was given vocal support through the church press. In 1870 a second national press organ was begun by William McDonald of the New England Conference. *The Advocate of Holiness* became the organ of the Camp Meeting Association. The revival reached some of the most influential members of the church: Daniel Steele, first president of Syracuse University and then professor of systematic theology at Boston University; William Nast, father of German Methodism; Bishop William Taylor; wealthy layman,

Washington C. DePauw; and women's rights leader, Frances Willard. A new generation of preachers came along ready to make their mark as ministers of the holiness gospel: Beverly Carradine, J. A. Wood, Alfred Cookman, John L. Brasher, and Milton L. Haney. The movement grew and developed; and, like the Finney revival, there was little or no fear of schism.

While this new work spread quickly among the Methodists, that begun by Finney did not die but continued to bear fruit. While the Oberlin position never really caught on with non-Methodists, leaders from the Quakers, Presbyterians, and Baptists preached the second blessing. William Boardman carried the message to England where, in conjunction with R. Pearsall Smith, a Presbyterian, he began the "Oxford Union Meeting for the Promotion of Scriptural Holiness." The Oxford meetings then formed the base for the Keswick Movement, which became the main carrier of the holiness movement in the Church of England. Smith's wife, Hannah, wrote one of the great classics of the Keswick era, *The Christian's Secret of a Happy Life*. The Keswick brand of holiness, which emphasized the giving of power instead of the cleansing from sin, gained its adherents in the United States: Dwight L. Moody, R.A. Torrey, A.J. Gordon, A.B. Simpson, and evangelist Wilbur Chapman.

At the height of this wave of success something went wrong; schisms began to dominate the movement, and a third phase began: the establishment of independent holiness churches. The voice for schism began to be heard in the 1880's, became dominant in the 1890's, and by 1910 had almost totally removed the holiness movement from the main denominations into independent holiness churches. The movement out of Methodism was a response to at least three forces antagonistic to the holiness movement. First, a theological critique began to be heard. Men such as J.M. Boland, author of *The Problem of Methodism*, attacked the second blessing doctrine and maintained that sanctification was accomplished at the moment of conversion. James Mudge in his *Growth in Holiness Toward Perfection or Progressive Sanctification* argued for progressive rather than instantaneous sanctification. Borden Parker Bowne, representing a growing army of German-trained theologians, simply dismissed the whole issue of sanctification as irrelevant.

The second force of growing concern to Methodist leaders was the mass of uncontrollable literature and organizations which the holiness movement was producing. By 1890 the number of books, tracts, pamphlets, and periodicals coming off the press to serve the holiness movement was enormous. Independent camp meeting associations covered the country and in many places competed with local churches for the allegiance of members. Since camp meetings were independent, bishops and district superintendents had only the power of moral suasion to control what happened at the meetings or what was read throughout the movement. For some, this state of affairs was felt as a direct threat to their power. Others were genuinely concerned with excesses, fanaticism, and heterodox teaching. In either case, the loss of control led to an anti-holiness polemic.

The third cause for the holiness schism is found in the genuine shift of power which occurred between 1870 and 1890 in the Methodist Church and the holiness movement itself. By 1890 the bishops who promoted the holiness movement and gave it official sanction had been replaced largely by others who were cool to the holiness heat. Within the holiness movement itself were regional and national leaders who were unhappy under the yoke of an unsympathetic hierarchy which was moving further away from their position each day. Not wishing to be confined in their ministry, they bolted the church. Among the first to leave were Daniel S. Warner, who founded the Church of God at Anderson, Indiana, and John P. Brooks. Brooks, a leader in the Western Holiness Association, in 1887 published *The Divine Church*, which called for all true holiness Christians "to come-out" of Methodism's church of mammon. *The Divine Church* became the theological guide to lead the way to the formation of independent churches.

The "come-out" movement created pressure on those who chose to stay in to justify their position. Thus, the 1890's saw loyalists publishing books against "come-outism," and calling for strengthening of the camp meetings. Beverly Carradine called for remaining in the church, but favored the establishment of independent holiness colleges. Asbury College, Wilmore, Kentucky, and Taylor University, Indiana, represent the partial success of Carradine's view. These efforts by the loyalists were significantly unsuccessful, however, and by 1910 only minor pockets of holiness teaching (such as the Brasher Campgrounds in Alabama) remained in the larger Methodist churches.

CONTEMPORARY DEVELOPMENTS. Possibly because of the intense controversy during the formative years of the older holiness churches, there is a strong sense of identity with the holiness family among the various members. This image is focused not only in the doctrinal unity and similarity of lifestyle, but in the several ecumenical structures. These structures are home to a wide range of groups, from those who still keep ties with the United Methodist Church (Wesleyans, Free Methodists), all the way over to groups like the Church of God of the Mountain Assembly, which has Baptist origins.

The oldest ecumenical structure is the Christian Holiness Association. This body, which includes most of the larger holiness churches in its membership, is a continuation of the National Holiness Camp Meeting Association, which guided the movement from the 1870's. After the establishment of the various denominational structures it remained as a meeting ground for these new organizations and those who remained in their original churches, primarily Methodists. Increasingly, it served the denominational bodies and in 1970 assumed its present name to recognize that fact.

One longstanding, if minor, theme in the holiness movement was that perpetuated by the Keswick Conventions. Growing up primarily among the holiness supporters of the Church of England, it supported the idea of "suppression" of the evil tendencies in man, as opposed to the "eradication" taught by the Wesleyans. Keswick ideas did not produce many new groups but did find a home among one large body, the Christian Missionary Alliance.

THE GLENN GRIFFITH MOVEMENT. As the holiness movement has grown since World War II, and has become more accommodating to the world, some of its members have begun to protest this accommodation. They say they wish to preserve the "old-fashioned Scriptural holiness" in which they were raised. The leader of this movement is the Rev. Glenn Griffith, a former minister from the Church of the Nazarene. The revival services he held in 1955 between Nampa and Caldwell, Idaho, attracted many people to him. His movement spread, finding advocates in all of the larger holiness churches. Members left those churches to follow Griffith; this splintering from the holiness churches is still continuing.

Even before Griffith gave focus to the protest movement, the Rev. H.E. Schmul facilitated fellowship among conservative holiness churches and ministers. The structure used by Schmul to promote this fellowship was the Interdenominational Holiness Convention. It was begun by Schmul, a Wesleyan Methodist minister, in 1947. Its magazine, *Convention Herald*, served as a placement service for evangelists seeking appointments for revival meetings. Leaders of the various splinter movements within holiness churches had participated in the Interdenominational Holiness Convention. After the new churches were formed, these leaders moved into key positions in the Convention. On the editorial board of the *Convention Herald* are H. Robb French and Glenn Griffith.

The Interdenominational Holiness Convention continues to operate informally with membership open to individuals, congregations, and churches.

SOURCES—HOLINESS FAMILY

GENERAL SOURCES ON SANCTIFICATION AND HOLINESS

Fenelon, Francois de Salignac de La Mothe. *Christian Perfection.* New York: Harper & Row, 1947. 208 pp.

Finney, Charles G. *An Autobiography.* Westwood, NJ: Fleming H. Revell, 1876. 477 pp.

———. *Sanctification.* Fort Washington, PA: Christian Literture Crusade, n.d. 105 pp.

Law, William. *A Serious Call to a Devout and Holy Life.* New York: E. P. Dutton, 1906. 355 pp.

Lindstrom, Harold. *Wesley and Sanctification.* New York: Abingdon, 1946. 228 pp.

THE HOLINESS MOVEMENT IN AMERICA

Bundy, David D. *Keswick: A Bibliographical Introduction to the Higher Life Movements.* Wilmore, KY: B. L. Fisher Library, Asbury Theological Seminary, 1975. 89 pp.

Dayton, Donald W. *The American Holiness Movement, A Bibliographic Introduction.* Wilmore, KY: B. L. Fisher Library, Asbury Theological Seminary, 1971.

Dieter, Melvin Easterday. *The Holiness Revival of the Nineteenth Century.* Metuchen, NJ: Scarecrow Press, 1980. 356 pp.

Jones, Charles Edwin. *A Guide to the Study of the Holiness Movement.* Metuchen, NJ: Scarecrow Press, 1974.

Lambert, D. W. *Heralds of Holiness.* Stoke-on-Trent: M.O.V.E. Press, 1975. 80 pp.

Nazarene Theological Seminary. *Master Bibliography of Holiness Works.* Kansas City, MO: Beacon Hill Press, 1965.

Peters, John Leland. *Christian Perfectionism and American Methodism.* New York: Abingdon, 1956.

Pollock, J. C. *The Keswick Story.* London: Hodder & Stoughton, 1964. 190 pp.

Smith, Timothy L. "The Holiness Crusade." In vol. II of *The History of American Methodism.* Ed. Emory Stevens Buck. Nashville: Abingdon, 1965, pp. 608-59.

———. *Revivalism and Social Reform.* Nashville: Abingdon, 1957. 253 pp.

HOLINESS THOUGHT

Arthur, William. *The Tongue of Fire.* Winona Lake, IN: Light and Life Press, n.d. 253 pp.

Boyd, Myron F., and Merne A. Harris, comps. *Projecting Our Heritage.* Kansas City: Beacon Hill Press of Kansas City, 1969. 157 pp.

Carradine, Beverly. *The Sanctified Life.* Cincinnati: The Revivalkist, 1897.

Foster, Randolph S. *Christian Purity.* New York: Nelson & Phillips, 1869. 364 pp.

Kuhn, Harold B., ed. *The Doctrinal Distinctives of Asbury Theological Seminary.* Wilmore, KY: Asbury Theological Seminary, n.d. 100 pp.

Palmer, Phoebe. *Faith and Its Effects.* New York: Walter C. Palmer, 1854.

Rose, Delbert E. *A Theology of Christian Experience.* Minneapolis: Bethany Fellowship, 1965.

CRITICAL APPRAISALS

Boland, J. M. *The Problem of Methodism.* Nashville: The Author, 1889.

Ironside, Harold A. *Holiness, the False and the True.* New York: Loizeaux Brothers, 1947. 142 pp.

Mudge, James B. *Growth in Holiness Toward Perfection, or Progressive Sanctification.* New York: Hunt and Eaton, 1895.

Nevins, John W. *The Anxious Bench.* Chambersburg, PA: German Ref. Church, 1844. 149 pp.

Warfield, Benjamin B. *Perfectionism.* Philadelphia: The Presbyterian and Reformed Publishing Company, 1958. 464 pp.

Chapter Seven

THE PENTECOSTAL FAMILY

Directory listings for the groups belonging to the Pentecostal Family may
be found in the section beginning on page 309.

The Pentecostal movement claims several million Americans and millions more overseas. In South America, the movement boasts the two largest local congregations in the world: one in Santiago, Chile, with 45,000 members, and another in Sao Paulo, Brazil, with 43,000.

As Pentecostals have taken their place in the world Christian community, they have emphasized their orthodoxy. They have had few doctrinal disagreements with the various churches from which they grew. In fact, the confessions of faith of the Pentecostal churches reflect their heritage, be that heritage Methodist or Baptist or holiness (rooted in the holiness movement and churches, discussed in the preceding chapter). The dividing line between Pentecostal churches and the mainline Protestant churches has been clear, though, from the beginning of modern Pentecostalism in 1901. What makes Pentecostals distinct?—their new form of religious experience highlighted by speaking in tongues.

The Pentecostal experience may be defined as seeking and receiving the gift of speaking in tongues as a sign of the baptism of the Holy Spirit. In turn, that baptism may be defined as the dwelling of the Holy Spirit in the individual believer. From the initial idea and experience of the baptism of the Holy Spirit and speaking in tongues, flows the belief in other gifts of the Holy Spirit manifested in the New Testament church (I Cor. 12:4-11). Those gifts include healing, prophecy, wisdom (knowledge unattainable by natural means), and discernment of spirits (seeing nonphysical beings such as angels and demons).

SPEAKING IN TONGUES. Glossolalia, speaking in tongues, was a part of the experience of Jesus' disciples at Pentecost (Acts 2) and reappeared at several important points in the growing church. In Paul's *Epistle to the Corinthians*, "tongues" are mentioned as one gift or "charisma" among others such as healing, working miracles, and prophecy. "Tongues" usually appear in connection with other "gifts of the Spirit" although, historically, the other gifts have often appeared without the accompanying verbal gift. The experience of "tongues," if not common, was well known in the ancient world. The phenomenon is manifest today in a number of tribal religions, as well as among Pentecostals.

What are "tongues"? To the outsider, hearing "tongues" is like hearing so much gibberish. To the Pentecostal, it is speaking under the control of the Holy Spirit. Pentecostal lore is full of tales of people who have been able to speak in a foreign language at a moment of crisis, although they did not know the language. Believers regard such instances as supernatural occurrences.

Social scientists generally look to a different explanation. Linguist William Samarin would separate glossolalia from zenoglossia. Glossolalia, says Samarin, is not truly a language. It is a verbalized religious experience. Only a few vowels and consonants are used, not enough to make a language as we know it. Glossolalia is the common prayer speech heard at Pentecostal churches. Zenoglossia is the utterance of an existent foreign language by one who has no knowledge of it. A rare occurence, it nevertheless has been noted and recorded in the literature of psychical research. Both telepathy and spirit contact have been hypothesized.

LIFESTYLE AND WORSHIP. Along with the new form of religious experience centered upon speaking in tongues comes the second distinguishing mark of the Pentecostal: a lifestyle reordered around that religious experience. The Pentecostal convert lets his or her religious experience dominate daily life. The Pentecostal encourages others to have the baptism of the Holy Spirit; Pentecostals talk about that experience often; when they pray, they pray in tongues; they see healings as signs of God's immediate presence; they pay attention to other gifts of the Holy Spirit; and finally they tend to look down on those who do not speak in tongues.

Pentecostals are pejoratively called "holy rollers" for their free, loud, participatory style of worship and their constant attention to the gifts of the Spirit, especially tongues. In contrast to the more orderly services in the Methodist and Baptist churches, Pentecostals seem to have a very free, spontaneous service which includes hymns that emphasize rhythm, extemporaneous prayers, and frequent interruption of the service with "Amen's" and "tongues." Those who visit Pentecostal services for the first time are startled by the seeming lack of order. The freedom and spontaneity are limited, however. Even the most free congregation falls into a narrow pattern, repeated week after week with little variation.

It is the worship and the lifestyle keyed to religious experience—the constant search for the experience and the endless talk about it—that really separate Pentecostalism from the more established denominations. Such distinctions are more felt than rationalized and are rarely articulated.

When conservative Christians such as Baptists and the Reformed talk about the doctrinal differences between themselves and the Pentecostal movement, they discuss disagreements about the baptism of the Holy Spirit and the gifts of the Spirit. They say the gifts of the Spirit were given to the early church and disappeared after the Apostles died. Some charge the Pentecostals with demon possession. By contrast, the Pentecostals insist the end of time is near, and the words of the prophet Joel (Joel 3:1) are being fulfilled:

"It shall come to pass in the last days, says God, that I will pour out my Spirit on all mankind: Your sons and daughters shall prophesy, your young men shall see visions and your old men shall dream dreams."

According to Acts 2:17, Peter referred to this passage on Pentecost.

HEALING. If speaking in tongues makes Pentecostals controversial, so does healing. Objections to healing center not as much on the reality of healing as on the form that healing ministers have assumed. Mainline Christians are offended by the seeming overfamiliarity with God assumed in praying for God to heal, as well as the loud, demanding style of many evangelists. The critics also object to the emotional, crowd-psychology-oriented healing services which seem to manipulate those in attendance. The recent controversy centered on the child-evangelist, Marjoe Gortner, is typical of the polemics. Gortner conducted healing services as a child, but came to the decision that what he was doing was not valid. So he invited filmmakers to follow him in a year's work of Pentecostal healing, filming what he did. The resultant movie and book were exposés of Pentecostal healing.

However, the Pentecostals have raised an important issue for contemporary Christians: the question of healing as a sign of God's work among his people. Pentecostals join both Christian Scientists, who refrain from using medicine and doctors, and Episcopalians in raising this issue. An Episcopalian minister, Charles Cullis, held healing services at the turn of this century in his summer camp at Old Orchard, Maine. Many of the spiritual healing ministries in this country can be traced to an additional Episcopalian source: the Order of St. Luke, a spiritual healing group. Thus Pentecostals are not alone in their interest in healing as a gift of the Spirit.

"TONGUES" IN HISTORY. The first manifestation of "tongues" in the modern era occurred in the late seventeenth century in France. The times were a blend of persecution and miraculous events. After the revocation of the Edict of Nantes, state suppression of Protestants began in southern France, among other places. In the mountainous region of Languedoc in the 1680's more than 10,000 people were victims of the stake, galley, and wheel. Partially in reaction to this persecution, strange psychic phenomena began to occur. At Vivaris, in southern France, a man had a vision and heard a voice say, "Go and console my people." At Berne, people saw apparitions and heard voices. There arose prophets who were viewed as miraculous because, although young and untutored, they spoke fluently and with wisdom.

Among the French mountain villages was a poor unlettered girl, Isabella Vincent. The daughter of a weaver, Isabella left home after her father accepted a bribe to become a Catholic and after she witnessed a massacre of Huguenots (French Calvinists). She was a Huguenot, and she fled to her Huguenot godfather. On February 12, 1688, she had her first ecstatic experience. She entered a trance in which she spoke in tongues and prophesied. She called for repentance, especially from those who had forsaken their faith for gold. Her fame spread. People marveled at her perfect Parisian French and her ability to quote the mass *verbatim* and refute it. She was finally arrested, but others rose to take her place. In 1700, a movement began among the youth, and children as young as three entered ecstatic states and prophesied. Continued persecution was followed by war and eventual migration to other parts of Europe, where these people became known as the French Prophets.

There are few manifestations of "tongues" in the eighteenth century among the Quakers in England and the Methodists in America. In the 1830's, two groups emerged who spoke in tongues: in England, the Catholic Apostolic Church, and in America, the Church of Jesus Christ of Latter-Day Saints. Both accepted the experience as part of a gifted, charismatic church life. It was, however, after the Civil War that "tongues" began to manifest themselves within the holiness churches and thus came into historical continuity with the present-day Pentecostal movement. In 1875, the Rev. R.B. Swan, a holiness minister, was one of five people in Providence, Rhode Island, who spoke in tongues. This group grew and soon became known as the "Gift People." Jethro Walthall reported speaking in tongues as early as 1879. This evangelist from Arkansas at first accepted tongues as part of a total experience of "being carried outside of himself," but later identified it with Pentecost and became a superintendent of the Assemblies of God, discussed in this chapter. In 1890, Daniel Awrey, an evangelist from Ohio, experienced "tongues." In the 1890's, members attending the meetings of R.G. Spurling in Tennessee and North Carolina, and W.F. Bryant of Camp Creek, North Carolina, spoke in tongues. The experience was later identified with Pentecost and these two men became leaders in the Church of God (Cleveland, Tennessee), discussed in this chapter. Besides these and other isolated incidents of "tongues," in the 1890's, there appeared a new movement in the holiness church which was to be a direct precursor of Pentecostalism as it exists today—the fire baptism.

As a movement, fire baptism was an "experience" preached by some holiness ministers looking for something more than their "holiness experience" had given them. The first such minister was Reverend B.H. Irwin who had derived the experience from the writings of John Fletcher, an early Methodist. Fletcher, in his works, had spoken of a "baptism of burning love," but it is doubtful if he was implying any of what Irwin was seeking. Fire baptism, a personal religious experience of being filled with and empowered by the Holy Spirit, took its name from the Holy Spirit's descent upon the Apostles in the form of tongues of flame—the first Pentecost. In 1895, the first fire-baptized congregation (the first church to seek and receive fire baptism) was organized at Olmitz, Iowa. From there fire baptism was spread by itinerant evangelists. Holiness leaders labeled this new experience, which they termed "The Fire," heresy and fanaticism. Opposition did not keep the teaching from spreading and, within three years, there were nine state associations organized and six more waiting to form, including two in Canada. Formal organization of the Fire-Baptized Holiness Association took place in 1898 at Anderson, South Carolina, and a periodical, *Live Coals of Fire*, was started in 1899. Later, the Fire-Baptized Holiness Association was to accept as a body the Pentecostal emphasis on speaking in tongues as a sure sign of the Spirit's presence within the believer. The early experience of tongues and the development of the Fire-Baptized Holiness Association set the nineteenth-century stage for the twentieth-century Pentecostal movement. Three years would be significant in its development—1901, 1906, and 1914.

1901—Topeka, Kansas.
The beginnings of the modern Pentecostal movement centered on the Rev. Charles Parnham. After leaving the Methodist Episcopal Church, Parnham opened the Bethel Healing Home in 1898 in Topeka. He had been inspired by the healing ministry of J.A. Dowie of Zion, Illinois. In 1900, he began an extended tour of holiness and healing ministries from Chicago to New York to Georgia. Returning to Topeka, Parnham found his work undermined and usurped. Undaunted, he purchased a building just outside of town and began the Bethel Bible College in the fall of 1900. Over the Christmas holidays, before leaving to speak in Kansas City, he assigned his students the task of investigating the "baptism of the Spirit," sometimes called the Pentecostal blessing. Upon returning, Parnham got a report: "To my astonishment, they all had the same story, that while different things occurred when the Pentecostal blessing fell, the indisputable proof on each occasion was that they spoke with other tongues" (Sarah E. Parnham, *The Life of Charles F. Parnham* [Joplin, MO: Press of the Hunter Printing Co., 1969], 52).

Immediately they turned to seek a baptism with an indication given by utterance in "tongues." On January 1, 1901, the Spirit fell, first on Agnes Oznam, and a few days later on many others, and then on Parnham himself.

Thus Agnes Oznam became the first person in modern times to seek and receive the experience of speaking in tongues (glossolalia) as a sign of being "baptized with the Holy Spirit." At that moment was inaugurated the Pentecostal Movement.

This small beginning, of fewer than forty people, did not portend the growth that was to come. Parnham closed the school and with his students set out to spread the message of the new Pentecost. He traveled and preached through Missouri and Kansas, and climaxed his tour with a revival in Galena, Kansas, which lasted for four months in the winter

of 1903-04. In 1905, he began work in Texas for the first time. He made Houston his headquarters and in December 1905 opened a bible school. Parnham at this point let the mantle of leadership pass to W.J. Seymour, who studied under Parnham in Houston.

1906—Azusa Street, Los Angeles, California.
The Pentecostal scene shifts to the West, to California, where in 1906 W.J. Seymour, a black holiness minister, arrived to preach at a small Baptist church. The church refused to hear him after his first sermon, but he was invited to preach at a member's home on Bonnie Brae Street. After three days of his preaching, the Spirit fell and "tongues" were heard on the West Coast. The meeting quickly outgrew the small home and a former Methodist Church building was rented on Azusa Street. From here was to develop the revival which was to send the Pentecostal experience around the world.

The Pentecostal outpouring in Los Angeles did not occur in a vacuum, but was the culmination of earlier events. From the spring of 1905, Frank Bartlemen and Joseph Smale had been giving wide publicity to the 1904 Wales revival under Evans Roberts. From Armenia, a number of Pentecostals who spoke in tongues had arrived to begin a new life in America. All quickly lent support to the Bonnie Brae phenomena.

After the initial speaking in tongues on April 9, the meeting grew and spread. Significant in this growth was the occurrence on April 18, just nine days after the initial experience, of the great San Francisco earthquake. More than 125,000 tracts relating the earthquake to the Azusa Street happenings and the "endtime" were promptly distributed. News of the revival was also widely circulated in holiness and other religious periodicals. Attracted by the excitement, people came to Los Angeles from across the country. As they received the baptism, they went home to spread the word. Pentecostal centers appeared in Illinois, New York, North Carolina, and as far away as Sweden, England, India, and Chile.

1914—Hot Springs, Arkansas.
From 1901 until 1914, the Pentecostals existed primarily within the holiness movement. The holiness movement was oriented toward an experience that ratified the believer's sanctity, the experience of the "second blessing," after which the believer would be holy forever. As the Pentecostal movement spread, many holiness churches accepted speaking in tongues as a final guarantee of holiness, a more sure sign than the "second blessing," and they called the Pentecostal "baptism of the Holy Spirit" the third experience. (The first, preceding the second blessing, was justification—the discovery of Christ as the personal savior.)

The holiness movement thus had supplied the basic problem (sanctification, life in the Spirit) which had caused concern for the "baptism of the Holy Spirit." The early Pentecostal leaders and members came from holiness churches, and holiness periodicals spread the word of the revival. Most important, the holiness churches, like the synagogues for Paul, became the first centers for Pentecostal evangelism. However, growth of the movement caused many holiness churches to express disapproval of it. Resistance varied from the mild policy of the Christian and Missionary Alliance to radical rejection by the Pentecostal Nazarene Church, which dropped the word "Pentecostal" from its title to manifest its opposition.

Growing hostility, factionalism within the movement, and the need for coordination of activities led in December 1913 to a call for a 1914 meeting of all who desired fuller cooperation at the Grand Opera House, Hot Springs, Arkansas. Out of this meeting grew the Assemblies of God. More important, from this organization came the impetus for the eventual organization of additional independent Churches. Pentecostal denominationalism had begun.

With time, three Pentecostal churches took a special place in the American Pentecostal movement: the Assemblies of God, the Church of God (Cleveland, Tennessee), and the Church of Our Lord Jesus Christ of the Apostolic Faith. Many other Pentecostal churches are offshoots of these three or are modeled on one of these three and deviate from that church on only a few points.

For practical purposes, a parenthetical subtitle is given to some churches in this encyclopedia. Thus the Church of God (Cleveland, Tennessee) calls itself simply the Church of God, but its headquarters are in Cleveland, Tennessee, so that is added to its title to distinguish it from the many other churches also called the Church of God.

As various Pentecostal churches came into existence, they adopted different forms of church government. Some are congregational, some connectional. The congregational churches share four characteristics: the local churches operate autonomously; they choose their own ministers; they own their property themselves; and they allow their regional and national church bodies to have only advisory authority over the local churches. In connectional churches, the regional and national church bodies have varying levels of power to legislate on doctrinal and organizational matters. Some pentecostal churches with a connectional polity are close to a presbyterial system; some are close to an episcopal system with bishops.

CONTEMPORARY DEVELOPMENTS. Among the second and third generation Pentecostal denominations, a marked tendency to lessen the overtly emotional, loud and spontaneous lifestyle is quite noticeable, particularly in urban centers. Symbolic is the regular use of printed weekly church bulletins that contain an order of worship for the Sunday morning service.

Also characteristic of modern Pentecostal bodies is the development of ecumenical structures and the development of neo-Pentecostalism as a movement within mainline Christian churches.

Ecumenical efforts within Pentecostalism began with the World Conference of Pentecostals held at Zurich, Switzerland in May 1947. This conference served as inspiration for the formation of the Pentecostal Fellowship of North America, constituted at Des Moines, Iowa, October 26-28, 1948. This body has among its members all the larger trinitarian Pentecostal denominations (seventeen Canadian and United States bodies representing more than one million members in 1970).

Meetings of Pentecostals around the world have continued (Paris, 1949; London, 1952; Stockholm, 1955; Toronto, 1958; Jerusalem, 1961; Helsinki, 1964; Rio de Janeiro, 1967; Dallas, 1970 and 1974). Along with these conferences have been attempts, increasingly successful, to engage the older ecumenical bodies in dialogue. Emerging as the central figure in the effort has been David J. DuPlessis, a South African Assemblies of God minister currently residing in the United States. DuPlessis was a key organizer of the early world Pentecostal conferences, worked on the staff of the Second Assembly of the World Council of Churches in Evanston, Illinois, in 1954, and has generally served as Pentecostalism's roving ambassador to non-Pentecostal Christians.

SUBFAMILIES. Doctrinal differences and racial discrimination led Pentecostals to divide into six subfamilies. Additional small groups may be discerned, such as the snake handlers, but the far-reaching divisions have resulted in only six subfamilies. In general, Pentecostals fall into three doctrinal groups, all of which split along racial lines with blacks forming large denominations, thus creating a total of six groups.

The earliest doctrinal disagreement occurred between those Pentecostals who came out of the holiness movement, primarily former Methodists, and those who came directly into the Pentecostal experience, primarily former Baptists. The holiness people saw the Pentecostal experience (receiving the baptism of the Holy Spirit and speaking in tongues) as a third experience following justification and sanctification. The Baptists insisted that any believer was capable of receiving the Pentecostal experience, without the intermediate "second blessing" assuring sanctification, the key experience of the holiness movement. Many Pentecostals split over the issue of two experiences (justification and the baptism of the Holy Spirit) or three experiences (justification, sanctification, and the baptism of the Holy Spirit).

No sooner had these two positions become evident than another serious theological issue arose. A group of ministers began to preach a "Jesus only" doctrine which amounted to a monotheism of the second person of the Trinity. This denial of the Trinity by what are generally termed "Apostolic" Pentecostals has been the most serious family split, and the "Jesus only" people generally do not participate in the family ecumenical structures. Blacks have formed especially large denominations of the "Jesus only" type.

This discussion of Pentecostal subfamilies would be incomplete without a mention of neo-Pentecostalism. That is the movement of the 1960's and 1970's to form Pentecostal fellowships within the mainline Christian denominations. Neo-Pentecostalism also goes by the name of charismatic renewal. Its leaders were never a part of the older Pentecostal bodies, and have formed charismatic fellowships within the Roman Catholic, Lutheran, United Methodist, Presbyterian, and Episcopal Churches.

In the 1970's these fellowships have served two functions. First, they have kept Pentecostals within their mainline Christian churches, making unnecessary their move to the older Pentecostal churches. Second, the fellowships have been places where new denominations, separate from the mainline Christian churches, could form. Thus the same fellowships have served two disparate functions, although they were established as organizations for Pentecostals *within* the mainline denominations.

THE APOSTOLIC, ONENESS, OR "JESUS ONLY" MOVEMENT. In 1913 at the Los Angeles Pentecostal camp meeting, the fledgling Pentecostal movement, barely beginning its second decade of existence, came face to face with a new issue. R.E. McAlister, a popular preacher, speaking before a baptismal service, shared his thoughts that, in the apostolic church, baptism was not done with a Trinitarian formula but in the name of Jesus Christ. While raising much opposition, McAlister's message found favor with Frank J. Ewart and John C. Scheppe. Scheppe's emotional acceptance of the "new" idea had a powerful impact on the camp. Ewart afterwards joined McAlister in a revival meeting in Los Angeles and began to note results whenever he called upon the name of Jesus.

The movement spread under the leadership of Ewart and evangelist Glenn A. Cook. They were able to bring in such key leaders as G.T. Haywood of Indianapolis, E.N. Bell, and H.A. Goss, all prominent leaders in the Assemblies of God. Ewart became editor of *Meat in Due Season*, the first oneness periodical.

The vocalization of oneness ideas, mostly by members of the Assemblies of God, came to a head in 1916 at the Assemblies of God General Council meeting in St. Louis. A strong Trinitarian stance was adopted within the Statement of Beliefs. One hundred and fixty-six ministers were expelled by that act and many Assemblies were lost; the era of formation of "oneness" churches began.

The oneness Pentecostals deny the Trinity and uphold the oneness of God. Jesus is identified with God the Father (Isaiah 9:6, John 10:30), God the creator (John 1:1), the bodily presence of God. The Holy Spirit is not considered a third person within the Trinity but the spirit and power of God and Christ. Salvation is by repentance, and water baptism is considered an essential part of salvation. Baptism is by immersion in the name of Jesus only (Acts 2:38).

Apart from the Trinitarian and baptismal questions, oneness people are typical Pentecostals. The oneness message has had particular appeal among black people, and the largest bodies are primarily black in membership. Of the several Apostolic Churches, the United Pentecostal Church is the largest white church.

BLACK PENTECOSTAL CHURCHES. There has been much discussion in both popular and scholarly literature of the tie-in between black religion and Pentecostalism. Much of this discussion has been plainly derogatory and borders on racism. Pentecostalism, distinguished by its emotionalism and escapism, was seen as an example of primitive religious forms. Fortunately, the growth of neo-Pentecostalism has led to a complete re-evaluation of the authenticity of the Pentecostal forms. With the new appreciation comes the opportunity to see, with new perspective, the key role which black people played in the early development of Pentecostalism, and more important, the manner in which they have taken the form far beyond its development by their white brothers and sisters.

Modern Pentecostalism began in the short-lived integrated Topeka Bible School founded by Charles Parnham. Among those students who received the Baptism of the Holy Spirit was a black woman, Sister Lucy Farrow. It was Sister Farrow who took Pentecostalism to Houston and opened the door for Parnham to begin his Bible school there. Among his pupils was one W.J. Seymour, a black minister with the Church of God (Anderson, Indiana).

After Seymour received Parnham's message, he traveled to Los Angeles where in 1906 he gathered a group of black believers into meetings that were eventually held at the Azusa Street Mission. As the gifts of the Spirit became manifest, whites began to attend the meetings and receive baptism from the blacks who led the services.

Racism was overcome for only a short time; almost immediately white leaders began to develop their own movements. Although most Pentecostal churches remained integrated for one or two decades, eventually almost all of the groups split along racial lines. There is little doubt that the early splintering among Pentecostals throughout the country was because the black leadership at Azusa was unacceptable to whites.

The preaching of "Jesus only" by G.T. Haywood, a black minister in Indianapolis, forced the Assemblies of God to deal with the "oneness" doctrine that denied the Trinity. Haywood's congregation became the nucleus of the first "oneness" denomination, the Pentecostal Assemblies of the World. Other black "oneness" groups are among the largest Pentecostal bodies in the world.

Pentecostalism swept the black community and created some large, if hidden, denominations. They compiled impressive figures for foreign mission work in Africa and the West Indies, where Pentecostalism has become the major faith in places. The Church of God in Christ now claims upwards of three million members worldwide.

DELIVERANCE (HEALING) MOVEMENT. Almost from the beginning, healing has been a major emphasis of the Pentecostal movement. It represents the culmination of a healing movement begun in evangelical churches by Charles Cullis, an Episcopal minister in Boston who held healing services at the turn of this century at his summer camp at Old Orchard, Maine. Albert Benjamin Simpson was healed at this camp and later made healing part of his four-fold gospel that presented Christ as savior, sanctifier, healer and coming king. In the early years of this century F.F. Bosworth, Paul Rader, John D. Lake, and Smith Wigglesworth were popular healing evangelists and, of course, Aimee Semple McPherson was the most popular of all. The years between the wars saw the emergence of numerous independent healing evangelists, popular targets of exposé writers.

After the Second World War a group consciousness developed among some of the Pentecostal evangelists. In 1946 Rev. William Branham, then a Baptist minister, claimed a visit by an angel and was told to begin a healing ministry.

That visit was the beginning of a remarkable "supernatural" ministry of healings, prophecies, and other paranormal phenomena. Branham began to tour the country in revival meetings. In 1947, Gordon Lindsey began *The Voice of Healing Magazine.* Gradually, without giving up their independence, other evangelists became associated with Branham and began to be heard through the pages of *The Voice of Healing.* Branham died in 1965. In the years since his passing, deliverance ministers have emerged as a significant force within Pentecostalism.

In many cases, the deliverance evangelists have remained independent and travel at the request of churches or groups such as the Full Gospel Businessman's Fellowship. Others are leaders of large evangelistic missionary organizations. Evelyn Wyatt, T.L. Osborn, and Morris Cerullo head such organizations. Others have become heads of church-forming bodies (both in the United States and abroad) which constitute new primary religious groups. These include Leroy Jenkins, W.V. Grant, Neal Frisby, and the late William Branham, Gordon Lindsey, Kathryn Kuhlman, and A.A. Allen. For most of the above, evangelistic endeavors among members of Pentecostal and mainline Christian churches is still the primary activity, with their deliverance churches forming relatively small bases of operation.

SNAKE HANDLING. One group of Pentecostals are sharply distinguished from the rest by their peculiar practice of "preaching the signs." In the Gospel of Mark 16: 17-18, Jesus promised his followers that certain signs would follow them: speaking in tongues, the ability to heal the sick, and the casting out of demons. Most Pentecostals accept these three. Those who "preach the signs," however, go beyond these to accept Jesus's promise that they may take up venomous serpents and drink poisons without experiencing any harm. This promise has led to the practice popularly called snake handling. The original group that practiced the signs, that is, that handled snakes and drank poison (usually strychnine) in worship services, arose very soon after the Pentecostal movement spread to the Appalachian Mountain region.

In 1909 George Went Hensley, a preacher with the Church of God (Cleveland, Tennessee) in rural Grasshopper Valley, became convinced that the references in Mark 16: 17-19 to taking up poisonous snakes and drinking poison were, in fact, commands. He captured a rattlesnake and brought it to an open air revival meeting for participants to handle as a test of their faith. In 1914 A. J. Tomlinson, head of the Church of God, asked Hensley to demonstrate snake handling to the church's annual assembly, so, with his tacit approval, the practice spread throughout the mountainous and rural South.

Those who engage in snake handling are Pentecostals who accept the basic theology by which people seek and receive the bapitism of the Holy Spirit, evidenced by speaking in tongues. Snake handlers also accept the rigid ethical code of most holiness and Pentecostal bodies: Dress is plain; the Bible is consulted on all questions in an attempt to discern wordly behavoir; the kiss of peace is prominent. The snake handlers, however, go beyond the Pentecostals in their belief that holding venomous reptiles and drinking poison are signs of an individual's faith and possession of the Holy Spirit. The handling of snakes and drinking of poison are done while in an ecstatic state, referred to by members as "being in the Spirit."

The first and crucial test of the practice of snake handling was the near-fatal bite received by Garland Defries, which led to much unfavorable publicity and caused many snake handlers, who thought themselves immune to bites, to reevaluate the practice. Snake handling came under considerable attack within the Church of God, whose leaders denounced it as fanaticism. In 1928 the church formally forbade its continuation, thus forcing the snake handlers into separate congregations and small churches, primarily in rural areas.

A second test of snake handling came in 1945 when Lewis Ford, a member of the Dolly Pond Church of God with Signs Following (Dolly Pond, Tennessee), was fatally bitten. His death brought the first widespread public attention to snake handling and led to Tennessee legislation against it. Despite this legislation the practice continues in clandestine meetings in Tennessee and throughout the South.

SOURCES—PENTECOSTAL FAMILY

GENERAL SOURCES

Hunter, Harold D. *Spirit Baptism, A Pentecostal Alternative.* Washington, DC: University Press of America, 1983. 310 pp.

Kelsey, Morton T. *Tongue Speaking.* Garden City, NY: Doubleday, 1968. 252 pp.

Kydd, Ronald A. N. *Charismatic Gifts in the Early Church.* Peabody, MA: Hendrickson Publishers, 1984. 100 pp.

Roebling, Karl. *Pentecostals Around the World.* Hicksville, NY: Exposition Press, 1978. 120 pp.

Sherrill, John L. *They Speak with Other Tongues.* Westwood, NJ: Fleming H. Revell Company, 1965. 143 pp.

Synan, Vinson, ed. *Aspects of Pentecostal-Charismatic Origins.* Plainfield, NJ: Logos International, 1975. 252 pp.

————. *The Holiness-Pentecostal Movement in the United States.* Grand Rapids: William B. Eerdmans Publishing Company, 1971. 248 pp.

BIBLIOGRAPHICAL SOURCES

Faupel, David W. *The American Pentecostal Movement, A Bibliographical Essay.* Wilmore, KY: B. L. Fisher Library, Asbury Theological Seminary, 1972. 56 pp.

Jones, Charles Edwin. *A Guide to the Study of the Pentecostal Movement.* 2 vols. Metuchen, NJ: Scarecrow Press, 1983.

Martin, Ira J. *Glossolalia, The Gift of Tongues, A Bibliography.* Cleveland, TN: Pathway Press, 1970. 72 pp.

HISTORICAL

Bartleman, Frank. *How Pentecost Came to Los Angeles.* Los Angeles: Privately Printed, 1928.

Davis, George T. B. *When the Fire Fell.* Philadelphia: The Million Testaments Campaign, 1945. 104 pp.

Dayton, Donald. *"From Christian Perfection to the Baptism of the Holy Ghost": A Study in the Origin of Pentecostalism.* Chicago: The Author, 1973. 16 pp.

Ewart, Frank J. *The Phenomenon of Pentecost.* Hazelwood, MO: World Aflame Press, 1975. 207 pp.

Frodsham, Stanley H. *With Signs Following*. Springfield, MO: Gospel Publishing House, 1946. 279 pp.

Gaver, Jessyca Russel. *Pentecostalism*. New York: Award Books, 1971. 286 pp.

Hollenweger, Walter J. *The Pentecostals: The Charismatic Movement in the Church*. Minneapolis: Augsburg, 1972. 522 pp.

Kendrick, Klaude. *The Promise Fulfilled*. Springfield, MO: Gospel Publishing House, 1961. 237 pp.

Nichols, Thomas R. *Azusa Street Outpouring*. Hanford, CT: Great Commission International, 1979. 35 pp.

Riss, Richard Michael. *The Latter Rain Movement of 1948 and the Mid-twentieth Century Evangelical Awakening*. Vancouver, BC: Regent College, 1979. 261 pp.

Strachey, Ray. *Group Movements of the Past*. London: Faber & Faber Ltd., 1934.

Valdez, A. C., and James F. Scheer. *Fire on Azusa Street*. Costa Mesa, CA: Gift Publications, 1980. 139 pp.

Wallace, Mary H. *Profiles of Pentecostal Preachers*. Hazelwood, MO: World Aflame Press, 1983. 281 pp.

Wagner, Wayne, ed. *Touched by the Fire*. Plainfield, NJ: Logos International, 1978. 163 pp.

GLOSSOLALIA AND THE SPIRITUAL GIFTS

Goodman, Felicitas D. *Speaking in Tongues, A Cross-Cultural Study of Glossolalia*. Chicago: University of Chicago Press, 1972. 175 pp.

Kildahl, John P. *The Psychology of Speaking in Tongues*. New York: Harper & Row, 1972. 110 pp.

Samarin, William. *Tongues of Men and Angels*. New York: Macmillan Company, 1972. 277 pp.

Sneck, William Joseph. *Charismatic Spiritual Gifts*. Washington, DC: University Press of America, 1981. 298 pp.

APOSTOLIC OR ONENESS PENTECOSTALS

Clanton, Arthur J. *United We Stand*. Hazelwood, MO: The Pentecostal Publishing House, 1970. 207 pp.

Foster, Fred J. *Their Story: Twentieth Century Pentecostals*. Hazelwood, NJ: World Aflame Press, 1981. 193 pp.

Richardson, James C., Jr. *With Water and Spirit*. Martinsville, VA: The Author, n.d. 151 pp.

BLACK PENTECOSTALS

Nelson, Douglas J. *For Such a Time as This, The Story of Bishop William J. Seymour and the Azusa Street Revival*. Birmingham, England: University of Birmingham, Ph.D. Dissertation, 1981. 346 pp.

Hollenweger, Walter J. *Black Pentecostal Concept*. Special issue of *Concept 30* (1970).

Tinney, James S. "William J. Seymour: Father of Modern Day Pentecostalism." In *Black Apostles*. Ed. Randall K. Burkett and Richard Newman. Boston: 1978. pp. 213-25.

DELIVERANCE MOVEMENT

Harrell, David Edwin, Jr. *All Things Are Possible*. Bloomington: Indiana University Press, 1975. 304 pp.

Melton, J. Gordon. *A Reader's Guide to the Church's Ministry of Healing*. Independence, MO: The Academy of Religion and Psychical Research, 1977. 102 pp.

SIGNS MOVEMENT

Carden, Karen W., and Robert W. Pelton. *The Persecuted Prophets*. New York: A. S. Barns & Co., 1976. 188 pp.

Holliday, Robert K. *Tests of Faith*. Oak Hill, WV: The Fayette Tribune, 1968. 120 pp.

La Barre, Weston. *They Shall Take Up Serpents*. New York: Schocken, 1969. 208 pp.

NEOCHARISMATIC MOVEMENT

Bradfield, Cecil David. *Neo-Pentecostalism, A Sociological Assessment*. Washington, DC: University Press of America, 1979. 75 pp.

A Charismatic Reader. New York: Evangelical Book Club, 1974.

Culpepper, Robert H. *Evaluating the Charismatic Movement*. Valley Forge, PA: Judson Press, 1977. 192 pp.

O'Connor, Edward D. *The Pentecostal Movement in the Catholic Church*. Notre Dame, IN: Ave Maria Press, 1971. 301 pp.

Quebedeaux, Richard. *The New Charismatics*. Garden City, NY: Doubleday, 1976. 252 pp.

Shakarian, Demos. *The Happiest People in the World*. Old Tappen, NJ: Chosen Books, 1975. 187 pp.

NON-PENTECOSTAL EVALUATIONS OF PENTECOSTALISM

Bauman, Louis S. *The Tongues Movement*. Winona Lake, IN: Brethren Missionary Herald Co., 1963. 47 pp.

Charismatic Countdown. Washington, DC: Review and Herald Publishing Association, 1974. 80 pp.

Dollar, George W. *The New Testament and New Pentecostalsim*. Minneapolis: Central Baptist Theological Seminary, 1978. 141 pp.

Gustafson, Robert R. *Authors of Confusion*. Tampa, FL: Grace Publishing Company, 1971. 105 pp.

Kinghorn, Kenneth Cain. *Gifts of the Spirit*. Nashville, Abingdon, 1976. 126 pp.

Noorbergen, Rene. *Charisma of the Spirit*. Mountian View, CA: Pacific Press Publishing Association, 1973. 191 pp.

Robinson, Wayne A. *I Once Spoke in Tongues*. Old Tappen, NJ: Spire Books, 1975. 128 pp.

Stolee, H. J. *Pentecostalism*. Minneapolis: Augsburg Publishing House, 1936. 142 pp.

Chapter Eight

THE EUROPEAN FREE-CHURCH FAMILY

Directory listings for the groups belonging to the European Free-Church
Family may be found in the section beginning on page 363.

Until recently, histories of the Reformation have treated Luther and Calvin as superstars and have described the radical reformers as threats to the Reformation. The radicals, who protested any church tie to the state, have been considered by such historians to be utopian dreamers, revolutionaries, mystics, anarchists, and heretics. According to past historians, the radicals were rightfully the object of scorn for Catholic, Lutheran, and Calvinist alike.

Modern scholarship, however, has rediscovered the radicals, and history is being rewritten to give them their rightful place as makers of the Reformation. (The Reformation occurred in sixteenth-century Europe. It was the movement of protest and reform that began in the Roman Catholic Church and eventually was carried on largely outside of that church.)

One scholar goes so far as to say of the modern publication of radical Reformation documents, "They have the same significance for the interpretation of the whole of modern church history as the discoveries in the Dead Sea caves and in upper Egypt are having for New Testament studies and early church history" (George H. Williams, *The Radical Reformation* [Philadelphia: The Westminster Press, 1962], xix).

Who were the radical reformers? They were men who, like Luther and Calvin, were interested in the reform of the church but who, because of a variety of backgrounds and outlooks and theologies, placed their emphases on much different points as the crux of needed reform. For most, faith, sacrament, and liturgy were not as significant as the doctrine of the church in its relation to the state. The radicals frowned upon involvement in secular activity, and were typically persecuted by the state. Most radicals came from the lower class, so they built upon the traditional adversary relationship between the lower class and the ruling class. The radicals took the ideas of the Reformation (ideas such as the priesthood of believers and the freedom of the Christian man) to such an extreme that Luther and Calvin were horrified.

Most of the radicals came to a bloody end in war or persecution, and many saw their movements entirely destroyed. Because of this destruction, men such as Thomas Müntzer, Hans Denck, and Michael Sattler did not leave a surviving remnant to carry on their work. Others, such as Caspar Schwenckfeld, Jacob Hutter, and Melchior Hofmann, were able to leave movements which survived and exist today. Among the churches that trace their roots to the radical reformers are the Mennonites, the Amish, the Brethren, the Quakers, and the Free Church Brethren. All of these churches belong to the free church family, meaning that they are not state churches but free associations of adult believers. The free churches emphasize free will, contrasting sharply with strict Calvinists who believe in predestination—that the number and identity of the elect was ordained before the beginning of the world.

The radical Reformation can be dated from Christmas Day 1521, more than four years after Luther's Ninety-five Theses were nailed to the church door in Wittenburg. On this day, Andreas Bodenstein of Carlstadt—a man called simply Carlstadt by historians—celebrated the first "Protestant" communion. (Protestant services today follow the trend set by that service.) He preached and without vestments read the "Mass," but omitted all references to sacrifice, did not elevate the host, and gave both bread and wine. Each act was a significant repudiation of the beliefs or practices of the Roman Catholic Church. Behind this communion service was the strong contention of the supremacy of spirit over letter, the supremacy of grace over works, and the common priesthood of all believers. From these events were to flow others initiated by men who were already thinking as Carlstadt.

The career of Thomas Müntzer (1490?-1525) was one of the results of the activity of Carlstadt. In 1520, Müntzer appeared at Zwickau, a town in Saxony, where, as minister to one of the churches, his radicalism began to emerge. He urged people to respond spontaneously and immediately to the leadings of the Holy Spirit. He defined the church as the Spirit-filled saints gathered together in a community. His definition avoided any mention of bishops or sacraments and thus was at odds with a traditional understanding of the church. He aroused the laity in support of him against his more conservative colleagues. After being removed from his pastorate, Müntzer spent several years as a wandering preacher, becoming more and more radical and embittered. In a famous sermon in 1524 before the German princes, he

47

called upon them to take up the sword to defeat the forces of anti-Christ (the pope) and bring in the kingdom.

A number of events, including an astrological conjunction, converged in 1524 and occasioned an uprising of the peasants of Germany. Not the least of these events was the preaching of Müntzer and his radical colleagues. As the Peasants' War began, Müntzer, having given up on the immovable princes, joined the peasants' forces at Mühlhausen. He was ready to wield his sword for the kingdom. He saw the Peasants' War as his instrument. When the revolt was put down, Müntzer was captured. His career ended on the executioner's block and his flock was scattered.

At the time of Müntzer's short career in the north, other radical reformists appeared in southern Germany and Austria. Their first spokesman was Hans Denck. While at Nuremberg as rector of a parish school, Denck had come under the influence of Carlstadt and Müntzer. Denck was expelled from Nuremberg by Lutherans who feared him as a competitor. In the fall of 1525, Denck became the spiritual leader of a group at Augsburg. In the spring of 1526 (under the influence of Swiss refugee Balthasar Hubmaier), he led in the reconstitution of his group as a truly reformed church by the adoption of the apostolic practice of believer's baptism. By that practice only adult believers in Christ were baptized, the procedure believed to have been used by the Apostles. Thus anabaptism, or rebaptism of those who were baptized as infants, emerged as a central factor in the radical reformation. Denck saw the church as an adult, self-disciplined fellowship. His criteria for understanding the church naturally excluded infants, thus *antipedobaptism* (literally against the baptism of infants) became a central teaching of the movement. From this belief and this practice was to come the fully developed Anabaptist understanding of the church as an association of adults (not children) acting freely.

Denck was forced out of several cities as his reputation caught up with him. In 1527, he arrived in Augsburg to participate in a synod of Anabaptist leaders. After the meeting, many were arrested and died martyrs' deaths, so the meeting is called the Martyrs' Synod.

The main item of concern for the synod was the eschatalogical program of John Hut, an Austrian Anabaptist leader who had been rebaptized by Denck. Hut repudiated the peasants for taking up arms and interpreted current events as symbols of the nearness of the end time. God would do his work. The saints, while suffering at present, would live to see the new kingdom appear. Hut proceeded to build an underground movement throughout Bavaria and Austria.

When the synod met, three issues concerning the coming kingdom were under discussion: the manner and time of its approach, the role of Anabaptists to prepare for it, and the role of the magistry in the present time. No clear-cut decisions were reached on these points. After the synod, Hut was arrested and died in a fire in his cell. The inability of the synod to bring the radicals into one mind, the attacks of the Lutherans on some radical excesses in doctrine, and

disillusionment with his role in God's reformation led Denck to recant. He died of the plague a few years later.

Contemporaneous with the rise of South German and Austrian Anabaptists was the rise of Swiss Anabaptists, popularly known as the Swiss Brethren, under the leadership of Michael Sattler. Within the Swiss Brethren a mature, articulate Anabaptist stance would be formed, and from them would come the most important statement of the Anabaptist position.

Swiss Anabaptism arose in the 1520's to protest a state church. The church in question was that of Ulrich Zwingli (1484-1530), the leader of the Reformation in Switzerland. Zwingli took religious control of the canton of Zurich, with the power structures of Zurich establishing the Zwinglian Church for all in the area. The Swiss Brethren insisted that only the righteous should belong to the church, and not all members of any given area. After the vote to establish the Zwinglian Church, the Swiss Brethren withdrew from Zurich.

They determined to continue their efforts to restore the true Church. Two leaders of the Swiss Anabaptists, Conrad Grebel and George Blaurock, became the center of controversy. On January 21, 1525, layman Grebel rebaptized Blaurock, a priest, and that action led to months of disputation. The Brethren grew, even though they were persecuted. Doctrinally, they had a double problem. First, they had to counter Zwingli's ideas, which were very popular. Second, they had to clarify for people their differences with Müntzer and Hut. Müntzer and Hut had poor reputations, and people mistakenly associated the Swiss Brethren with them. It was in the attempt to refute Müntzer and Hut that Michael Sattler came forward as a leader of refugees in Strassburg. Upon his return to Switzerland, Sattler found himself leader of the Schleitheim Synod. There the mature Anabaptist position was hammered out in a document originally called "The Brotherly Union of a Number of Children of God Concerning Seven Articles," now called the Schleitheim Confession. Because of its importance in setting the issues for the whole Anabaptist community, the key sections are quoted below:

Schleitheim Confession

Dear brethren and sisters, we who have been assembled in the Lord at Schleitheim on the Border, make known in points and articles to all who love God that as concerns us we are of one mind to abide in the Lord as God's obedient children, (His) sons and daughters, we who have been and shall be separated from the world in everything, (and) completely at peace.

The articles which we discussed and on which we were of one mind are these 1. Baptism; 2. The Ban (excommunication); 3. Breaking of Bread; 4. Separation from the Abomination; 5. Pastors in the Church; 6. The Sword; and 7. The Oath.

First. Observe concerning baptism: Baptism will be given to all those who have learned repentance and amendment of life, and who believe truly that their sins are taken away by Christ, and to all those who walk in the resurrection of Jesus Christ, and wish to be buried with Him in death, so that they may be resurrected with him, and to all those who with this significance request it (baptism) of us and demand it for themselves. This excludes all infant baptism, the highest and chief abominations of the pope. In this you have the foundation and testimony of the apostles. Mt. 28, Mk. 16, Acts 2, 8, 16, 19. This we wish to hold simply, yet firmly and with assurance.

Second. We agree as follows on the ban: The ban shall be employed with all those who have given themselves to the Lord, to walk in His commandments, and with all those who have been baptized into the one body of Christ and who are called brethren and sisters, and yet who slip sometimes and fall into error and sin, being inadvertently overtaken. The same shall be admonished twice in secret and the third time openly disciplined or banned according to the command of Christ. (Mt. 18.) But this shall be done according to the regulation of the Spirit (Mt. 5) before the breaking of bread, so that we may break and eat one bread, with one mind and in one love, and may drink of one cup.

Third. In the breaking of bread we are of one mind and are agreed (as follows): All those who wish to break one bread in remembrance of the broken body of Christ, and all who wish to drink of one drink as a remembrance of the shed blood of Christ, shall be united beforehand by baptism in one body of Christ which is the church of God and whose Head is Christ. For as Paul points out we cannot at the same time be partakers of the Lord's table and the table of devils; we cannot at the same time drink the cup of the Lord and the cup of the devil. That is, all those who have fellowship with the dead works of darkness have no part in the light. Therefore all who follow the devil and the world have no part with those who are called unto God out of the world. All who lie in the evil have no part in the good.

Fourth. We are agreed (as follows) on separation: A separation shall be made from the evil and from the wickedness which the devil planted in the world; in this manner, simply that we shall not have fellowship with them (the wicked) and not run with them in the multitude of their abominations. This is the way it is: Since all who do not walk in the obedience of faith, and have not united themselves with God so that they wish to do His will, are a great abomination before God, it is not possible for anything to grow or issue from them except abominable things. For truly all creatures are in but two classes, good and bad, believing and unbelieving, darkness and light, the world and those who (have come) out of the world, God's temple and idols, Christ and Belial; and none can have part with the other.

Fifth. We are agreed as follows on pastors in the church of God: The pastor in the church of God shall, as Paul has prescribed, be one who out-and-out has a good report of those who are outside the faith. This office shall be to read, to admonish and teach, to warn, to discipline, to ban in the church, to lead out in prayer for the advancement of all the brethren and sisters, to lift up the bread when it is to be broken, and in all things to see to the care of the body of Christ, in order that it may be built up and developed, and the mouth of the slanderer be stopped.

This one moreover shall be supported of the church which has chosen him, wherein he may be in need, so that he who serves the Gospel may live of the Gospel as the Lord has ordained.

Sixth. We are agreed as follows concerning the sword: The sword is ordained of God outside the perfection of Christ. It punishes and puts to death the wicked, and guards and protects the good. In the Law the sword was ordained for the punishment of the wicked and for their death, and the same (sword) is (now) ordained to be used by the worldly magistrates.

In the perfection of Christ, however, only the ban is used for a warning and for the excommunication of the one who has sinned, without putting the flesh to death,—simply the warning and the command to sin no more.

Now it will be asked by many who do not recognize (this as) the will of Christ for us, whether a Christian may or should employ the sword against the wicked for the defense and protection of the good, or for the sake of love.

Our reply is unanimously as follows: Christ teaches and commands us to learn of Him, for He is meek and lowly in heart and so shall we find rest to our souls.

Secondly, it will be asked concerning the sword, whether a Christian shall pass sentence in worldly dispute and strife such as unbelievers have with one another. This our united answer: Christ did not wish to decide or pass judgment between brother and brother in the case of the inheritance, but refused to do so. Therefore we should do likewise.

Thirdly, it will be asked concerning the sword: Shall one be a magistrate if one should be chosen as such? The answer is as follows: They wished to make Christ king, but He fled and did not view it as the arrangement of His Father. Thus shall we do as He did and follow Him, ... He Himself forbids (the employment of) the force of the sword saying, The worldly princes lord it over them, etc., but not so shall it be with you.

Finally, it will be observed that it is not appropriate for a Christian to serve as a magistrate because of these points: The government magistracy is according to the flesh, but the Christians' is according to the Spirit; their houses and dwelling remain in this world, but the Christians' citizenship is in heaven; the weapons of their conflict and war are carnal and against the flesh only, but the Christians' weapons are spiritual, against the fornication of the devil. The worldlings are armed with steel and iron, but the Christians are armed with the armor of God, with truth, righteousness, peace, faith, salvation and the Word of God.

Seventh. We are agreed as follows concerning the oath: The oath is a confirmation among those who are quarreling or making promises. In the Law it is commanded to be performed in God's Name, but only in truth, not falsely. Christ, who teaches the perfection of the Law, prohibits all swearing to His (followers), whether true or false,—neither by heaven, nor by the earth, nor by Jerusalem, nor by our head,—and that for the reason which He shortly thereafter gives, For you are not able to make one hair white or black. So you see it is for this reason that all swearing is forbidden:

We cannot fulfill that which we promise when we swear, for we cannot change (even) the very least thing on us (W. L. Lumpkin, *Baptist Confessions of Faith* [Chicago: Judson Press, 1959] 22-31).

From the Schleitheim Confession emerges the distinctive doctrinal and ethical position of the Anabaptist churches. This stance would be accepted, with minor modifications, by the various bodies which survived the era of persecution. The church is composed of those united to Christ by believer's baptism and who have separated themselves from the evil world. The church is a minority group, pilgrims in a hostile world trying to isolate themselves from its influence and forces. Specifically, certain items—war, the use of violent force against one's neighbor, civic affairs, courts, oaths, worldly amusements and serving as a magistrate—are to be studiously avoided as things of the world.

Pacifism, in particular, has arisen as the essential point in the avoidance ethic and these churches have been characterized as the historical peace churches. Christians obey the laws of the land, as is possible for pacifists (and any attempting to live withdrawn), but their essential authority is to be found in the church.

The church is the disciplined fellowship. It appoints its own leadership and accepts its authority as the leadership administers it. Its prime force is the ban, a practice based on Matthew 18:15-17, which is similar to excommunication. Menno Simons is credited with emphasizing a modified form of banning termed shunning, in which the church stops all dealing with an erring brother, including eating with him, with the intent of winning him back to the straight and narrow. This practice is based on I Corinthians 5:11.

The church was opposed to both popish and anti-popish works and church services. From this position comes a lay-oriented, non-liturgical, non-creedal, Bible-oriented church. Their opposition to the state church, a position that was articulated as well as manifested by their very existence, led to the appellation, "free church." Non-liturgical worship in its extreme form can be seen in the classic Quaker service.

The Bible is the prime document from which the Anabaptists derive their belief and practice. Their method of Biblical interpretation, which will not utilize tradition and philosophy, becomes literalistic. Sacraments become ordinances, symbolic acts: baptism is an initiatory ceremony and the Lord's Supper a memorial act. Footwashing, for which there is a more unequivocal command than either baptism or the Lord's Supper, is also practiced, especially in those churches of Swiss origin.

Though all the European free churches believe in adult baptism, they have a wide variety of modes. The Mennonites pour water on the person being baptized, while the Church of the Brethren has triune immersion, the practice of entering the water once for each person of the Trinity.

After the Schleitheim Confession, three events were to remold the Anabaptists—the fall of the town of Münster; the death of the martyrs; and the rise of Menno Simons.

The Radical Reformation had continually been punctuated by apocalyptic thinking, including a few instances of militancy.

These tendencies came to a climax in the town of Münster. Radicalization there began with the pastor, Bernard Rothmann. His popular sermons led to the Protestantization of the community in 1531. Rothmann's Lutheran views became more and more radical, and he began to defend believer's baptism. Other Anabaptists heard of Rothmann and began to flock to Münster as the new Jerusalem. Among the immigrants were Jan Mathijs and his major supporter, Jan of Leiden. The immigrants adopted the apocalyptic theory that the end of time was imminent and would be caused by God's direct intervention in human affairs.

By the beginning of 1534, the radicalization of the city was complete and Mathijs was quickly rising to power. All Catholics and Lutherans were expelled, and the city armed itself for the siege that would follow that expulsion. Mathijs imposed his religious beliefs. The town adopted a communist lifestyle while it made military preparations for the siege. In the midst of these reforms Mathijs was killed. Jan of Leiden took over and began to set up a theocracy with himself as God's vicar. The strict discipline worked effectively during the siege. After a particularly heavy battle, Jan introduced polygamy.

The beleaguered city finally was betrayed and captured. Jan had imposed ruthless authority on the people. After his capture, he was tortured to death. With only a few minor exceptions, the Münster episode ended any apocalypticism in the Anabaptism movement.

That episode, however, did not bring to a close the killings of Anabaptists. *The Martyrs Mirror*, a book which functions for Anabaptists much as John Foxe's *Book of Martyrs* functions for English Protestants, records the trail of blood of Anabaptists killed for their faith. The book was first published in 1554. Persecution left a stamp upon the members of the free churches, who came to see themselves literally as wandering pilgrims in a hostile world.

Anabaptists flocked to Menno Simons in the Netherlands. Emerging in 1537 as a leader, Menno began a series of books which set down a moderate free church position and rallied the disintegrating Anabaptist forces. It is to Menno's credit that the forces were held together and survived until 1577 when toleration was granted in Holland. The followers of Menno became, with few exceptions, the surviving Anabaptist community.

In additon to the apocalyptic Anabaptism of Münster and the moderate Anabaptism of the Swiss Brethren was a third form of Anabaptism. It turned inward in what has been termed a spiritualist or mystical movement. Among the first to espouse the spiritualist perspective was Hans Denck. An early leader in the Anabaptist movement, Denck recanted in his despair at its divisions and began to turn inward. He had long been a student of the mystic John Tauler, and to Tauler he turned. He began to preach of the God who meets us as a Light, a Word, and a Presence. He was followed by others such as Sebastian Franck, Johann Bünderlin, and Christian Entfelder.

As a whole, the spiritual Anabaptists collected no following and left no following. One exception was Caspar Schwenckfeld, a Silesian courtier turned prophet. In successive steps, he became a disciple of Luther, a critic of the Reformation as outward and shallow, an Anabaptist theologian with some peculiar views on the sacraments and Christ, and a mystic leader with a large following that still exists. But Schwenckfeld was the exception.

What the spiritual reformers did primarily was to create a literature with Anabaptist devotional and mystic leanings that became (1) the basis of a mystical movement within the free churches much like the one in medieval Catholicism and (2) the inspiration for later mystical, devotional movements, primarily Quakerism and to a certain extent Pietism. Each of these strains was to find a home in colonial Pennsylvania.

SWISS AND DUTCH MENNONITES. The central surviving Anabaptist tradition owes its name to one of its major leaders, Menno Simons (1496?-1561). Simons, a Dutchman, was born in Witmarsum in the Netherlands. While a Roman Catholic priest, Simons was led to believe that the bread and wine were *not* the real body and blood of Christ. A 1531 execution of an Anabaptist led him to investigate infant baptism. An investigation of Anabaptist views convinced him they were right. Finally, in 1536, a year after his own brother's death as an Anabaptist, Menno Simons left his Catholic heritage. Because of his abilities, he immediately became a leader in the Anabaptist community. His main tasks became keeping the community protected from authorities and free from militarism (which had led Anabaptists to take complete control of Münster and wage a long battle to defend it) and from heresies such as apocalyptic beliefs that the world would soon end through God's direct intervention. Some of Menno's followers found toleration in East Friesland in the Netherlands, under the Countess Anne. It was she, in recognizing the peaceful followers of Menno in contradistinction to the militarists and apocalyptics, who first dubbed them "Menists." The main part of Simon's active life was spent writing in defense of his new-found faith and hiding from the authorities, who had put a price on his head.

Menno's views were similar to those outlined by the Swiss Brethren at Schleitheim. It can be argued, and has been, that the Mennonites are the legitimate inheritors of the Swiss-German Anabaptist tradition, as most of the other Anabaptists have disappeared from the contemporary world. In essentials, the Mennonites certainly share the Swiss and German Anabaptists' views on rebaptism, pacifism, religious toleration, separation of church and state, opposition to capital punishment, opposition to holding office, and opposition to taking oaths. On two points only did Menno Simons differ—his use of the ban and his doctrine of incarnation.

Menno joined in the argument with the Brethren on the strict versus the liberal use of the ban. Menno advocated the strict use as the only means to keep the church free of corrupt sects. He also advocated "avoidance" or shunning all who were banned. Shunning was centered upon the idea of not eating with the person under the ban; this practice created a significant ingroup problem when one member of a family was under the ban. The practice of avoidance was liberalized over the years by the main body of Mennonites, but it was their distinguishing feature.

Menno has also been accused of compromising the humanity of Christ by minimizing the human properties said to have been received from Mary. This slight difference in Christology, which led many to accuse him of antitrinitarianism, has not been a major factor in recent Mennonite history.

The Mennonite movement spread slowly, and the late 1500's were a period in which many names were added to the roll of martyrs. The movement spread into Germany and Switzerland, building on small groups of Anabaptists already there. Mennonites settled and migrated as rulers first allowed toleration and then rescinded the privilege. In 1763, Catherine the Great of Russia offered religious toleration to German settlers who would populate the southern Steppes. Moravians, Mennonites, and Hutterites flocked to Russia; the Mennonites, mostly Prussians, settled in Crimea and Taurie. The Mennonites developed in southern Russia a unique history because of the special status granted them by the Russian government. A self-governing Mennonite community arose, the government approaching that of a theocracy. The end of Russian paradise came in the 1870's when the Czar introduced universal military service as a policy among the German colonists. This policy was part of a general Russification program in face of the growing military power of Prussia. The Mennonites, pacifists, did not want to join the military. So in 1874, a six-year mass immigration to the United States and Canada began. Those that remained in Russia prospered until 1917 when they became victims of the Bolsheviks. They still survive, however, in small scattered communities.

Reference to Mennonites in America occurs as early as 1643 in the records of New Netherlands. In 1633, a communal experiment led by Cornelius Pieter Plockhoy appeared on Delaware Bay, then a part of New Netherlands. The first permanent Mennonite colony was established in 1683 at Germantown, Pennsylvania; this date is usually accepted by Mennonites as their date of origin in America. Several factors encouraged Mennonites to come to the U.S. First, religious persecution in Europe caused many to immigrate. Second, William Penn and George Fox were seeking German converts, and appealed to members of Mennonite communities to come to America. Finally, the German Quakers (former Anabaptists) already in America wrote their friends and relatives asking them to move to Pennsylvania.

This growing Mennonite element is credited with American history's first public protest against slavery and was very influential in the later Quaker antislavery position. The Mennonites were an agricultural people and began to spread north and west of Germantown. The group's size was bolstered by immigration from the Palatine in the early eighteenth century.

The Revolutionary War became the first major crisis in the American Mennonite community, leading to their first schism. The issue was support of the Continental Congress. The majority argued that they could not support the Congress because such support would involve them in the war.

One leader, Christian Funk, argued in favor of support, including the special war tax, drawing support from Jesus' words on taxation (Matt. 22:21). Funk was excommunicated and with his followers formed the Mennonite Church (Funkite), which existed until the mid-nineteenth century. It died as all the participants in the original dispute died.

Continued immigration and the natural expansion of the Mennonites, who are prone to have large families, forced them west looking for new land. The early nineteenth century found Mennonites making settlements in Ontario and the Old Northwest Territory, and after the Civil War, the prairie states. This growing migration and wide separation geographically set the stage for formation of schismatic churches that would reach major proportions in the 1880's.

While no distinct and sharp lines can be drawn, there are rough ethnological distinctions within the Mennonite community. Some of the American splintering of churches can be traced to the Swiss, Dutch, or German background of the colonies. The largest distinction among the Mennonites as a whole is between the Western European and Russian settlers. Most of the Western European Mennonites came in the initial wave of settlers into Pennsylvania in the eighteenth century and pushed west into Canada and Indiana. The Russian immigrants are those Mennonites who migrated in the nineteenth century and settled in the western United States, primarily Kansas, and Canada.

Mennonites have been proud of a heritage of Biblical theology and avoidance of hairsplitting, unproductive attempts at philosophical sophistries. Nevertheless, they have a definite theological heritage in Swiss and Dutch Anabaptist ideas. Except for the distinctive themes illustrated in the Schleitheim Confession, Mennonites would have little problem with the major affirmations of mainline Christian churches. These have never been a point of conflict.

Crucial for Mennonites are ecclesiology and separation from the world. Mennonites share a doctrine of the church based on the concept of ecclesia, the called-out fellowship of believers in mission. The tendency is to emphasize the local congregation and to build wider fellowships based on a commonality of belief. Ministers (bishops) arise out of the fellowship as do deacons; the exact methods for choosing them varies. Casting lots was a favorite method.

The most popular Confession of Faith for Mennonites is the Dordrecht Confession of 1632. It was adopted by the American church and is still a standard for most Mennonites. According to the Dordrecht Confession, the Bible is the source of belief, and emphasis is placed upon the believer's direct encounter with the living Christ and the work of the Spirit within. The pietism, emphasis on the practical life in the Spirit, is worked out in the mutual, shared existence of the church. The church is the basic society for the true Christian.

Because of the lack of agricultural employment, youth are required to seek work in the non-Amish community. Such jobs provide an open door to outside influence and operate to destroy the close-knit Mennonite culture, family, and faith.

THE AMISH. Among the more liberal Swiss Mennonites of the late seventeenth century, there arose a party led by one Jacob Amman, a minister in the Emmenthal congregation. Because his family records have not been found, little can be said of him except for the practices he promoted among both the Swiss Mennonites and the Swiss Brethren. Amman insisted upon a strict interpretation of discipline. For his practices he appealed to Menno Simons' writings and to the Dordrecht Confession of Faith of 1632, which, as for the Mennonites, has become the recognized statement of doctrine for both Amish and Old Mennonites in America. The Dordrecht Confession says the Bible is the source of belief, and places prime importance upon the believer's direct encounter with the living Christ and the work of the Spirit within. The Dordrecht Confession insists that the church is the basic society for the true Christian.

In his preaching, Amman stressed the practice of avoidance. A member whose spouse was under the ban was neither to eat nor sleep with him or her until the ban was lifted. Amman also reintroduced footwashing. Non-religious customs of the period—hooks and eyes instead of buttons, shoestrings instead of buttons, bonnets and aprons, broad brimmed hats, and beards and long hair—became identifying characteristics of the church and were seen in terms of religious conformity.

All of the Mennonites during Amman's time were in a loose federation and strove to remain of one mind. Amman's strict interpretation of the "avoidance" clause in the ban led to a division among the Mennonites, with some following Amman and separating themselves from the others. Amman placed under the ban all who disagreed with him. After a few years of separation, Amman and his associates tried to reconcile with the other Mennonites, but the reconciliation efforts failed. Since then, the Amish have been independent of the Mennonites.

In the early 1700's, the Amish began to appear in America, the earliest congregation on record being the one along North Kill Creek in Berks County, Pennsylvania. Colonies were later planted in eastern Pennsylvania, Ohio, Indiana, Illinois, and Iowa. Until recently, their strength had been in Lancaster County, Pennsylvania.

The Amish represent a reactionary faction in the Mennonite movement. They have gone far beyond a practice common to Western Christianity of seeking to actualize an apostolic church. The Amish have attempted to freeze a culture, that of the late seventeenth century. As time has passed and the surrounding culture has discarded more and more elements of Jacob Amman's culture, greater and greater pressure has been placed on the Amish to conform with the modern world. Each generation has brought new issues to Amish leaders. Decisions must constantly be made on accommodating to the prevailing culture on different points. Public school laws, consolidated farming (and the shortage of available farm lands), automobile-oriented road systems, and tourists are just a few of the issues that have joined perennial Amish problems such as in-breeding. A lack of consensus on these issues has produced the several schisms they have experienced.

In order to deal with the various "liberal" trends and local schisms, a general conference was held in Wayne County, Ohio, in 1862, followed by others annually for several years. The conferences only accentuated the various trends. Before the conferences were discontinued, the more conservative "Old Order" Amish withdrew and organized separately. Others formed more liberal bodies which have moved toward the Mennonites in practice.

THE RUSSIAN MENNONITES. Some Anabaptist brethren, instead of coming to America, chose instead to go to Russia at the invitation of Catherine the Great in the 1760's. Catherine wanted colonists to develop newly acquired territory and promised religious freedom and local autonomy. Colonies were settled mainly in southern Russia and the Crimean area. Yet there arose in Russia a "pharaoh who knew not Joseph," Czar Alexander II.

In 1870, a program of Russification was begun by the Czar. Its thrust was directed at German colonists, including the Mennonites, whose presence seemed threatening to the rising Russian military power. Local autonomy was ended, the Russian language was to replace German, schools were to come under Russian tutelage, and exemption from universal military service was dropped. Immigration seemed the only recourse for the Mennonites. Among those who came to America, many belonged to the Mennonite Church, the first church described in this chapter. Other Russian immigrants belonged to churches which, in Russia, had broken off from the Mennonite Church there. The settlers brought these previously formed schismatic churches to America: the Evangelical Mennonite Church (Kleine Gemeinde), the Evangelical Mennonite Brethren Conference, the Mennonite Brethren Church, and the Crimean Brethren, whose members in this country joined the Mennonite Brethren Church in 1960. These churches are described below, as is the General Conference Mennonite Church, which was formed in this country instead of in Russia.

The first immigrants to North America included Bernard Warkentin, Cornelius Jansen, and David Goerz, who were prominent in the resettlement program. New communities were established in open lands from Oklahoma to Manitoba, with the largest settlements in Kansas.

THE BRETHREN. Among those awakened by the Pietist movement of the late seventeenth century, a movement that stressed personal piety over rigid doctrinal conformity, was a group of citizens of the Palatinate, an area now in West Germany. Influenced by the Mennonites in the vicinity, they decided to separate themselves from the state church. Their leader, Alexander Mack, recorded the event:

"In the year 1708 eight persons agreed to establish a covenant of a good conscience with God, to accept all ordinances of Jesus Christ as an easy yoke, and thus to follow after their Lord Jesus—their good and loyal shepherd—as true sheep in joy or sorrow until the blessed end . . . . These eight persons united with one another as brethren and sisters in the covenant of the cross of Jesus Christ as a church of Christian believers" (Donald F. Durnbaugh, *European Origins of the Brethren* [Elgin, IL: The Bretheren Press, 1958], 121).

As a part of the act of forming the new church, they rebaptized themselves, thus placing themselves in the Anabaptist tradition, a tradition reinforced by their German language upon their arrival in America.

While the Palatinate had changed state churches after the religious wars, neither Catholics, Lutherans, nor Reformed were happy with separatists, those who wanted to separate from the state church (whether that church was Catholic, Lutheran, or Reformed). People like the Brethren were subject to persecution and rather than give up their faith, the Brethren migrated, first to Wittgenstein and then the Netherlands. Toleration diminished as they began to receive members from the state church.

During this time, the Brethren became influenced by Gottfried Arnold, the historian. Arnold had written several books on the early life of the church which he believed normative for all Christians. He introduced through his writings the idea of triune immersion as the proper mode of baptism. The believer, on his knees in the water, is immersed three times in the name of the Father, Son, and Holy Spirit. The Brethren also continued a close contact with the Mennonites.

By 1719, little over a decade after their formation, the Brethren began to think about the New World as a home. Having become familiar with William Penn's experiment in Pennsylvania from his continental visits and those of his Quaker followers, they began to migrate to Germantown. The migration was completed by 1735 and the few remaining Brethren in Europe became Mennonites.

The first Brethren Church in America was established in 1723 after the Brethren had corresponded with their European counterparts. They chose Peter Becker (1687-1758) as their pastor. He proceeded to baptize the first American converts and preside over the first love feast, a service which included footwashing, a group meal, and the eucharist. This church is the mother congregation of the present-day Church of the Brethren.

THE FRIENDS (QUAKERS). The middle 1600's in England was a time in which the early stages of the Reformation were beginning to be felt in a practical way. Dissidents whose perspective reflected the religious ferment of the continent began to appear. One of the men whose perspective was in line with that of the continental radical reformers was George Fox—mystic, psychic, social activist, and founder of the Quakers.

Fox (1624-1691) had begun to preach in 1647 after experiencing an inner illumination and hearing a voice which said, "There is One, even Christ Jesus, that can speak to thy condition." The experiences of the inner light came as a psychic-spiritual awakening and Fox developed a reputation as "a young man with a diserning spirit." Fox was a powerful preacher and a charismatic personality. A wide variety of the gifts of the Spirit (I Cor. 12:4-11) appeared regularly throughout his ministry.

Fox was an intense activist on the social scene. He was an early prohibitionist and a preacher against holidays, entertainments, and sports, saying that such activities directed man's thoughts to vanity and looseness. During the wars waged when Oliver Cromwell ruled England, Fox emerged as a peace advocate, a position held by many radical reformers. Thrown into prison for his activities, he converted the jailer and became a pioneer prison reformer.

A group of followers soon gathered around Fox and, in 1667, they were organized into a system of monthly, quarterly, and yearly meetings. Their one doctrinal peculiarity was their belief in the inner light. The Quakers believed that God's revelation was not limited to the Bible but continued in a living daily contact between the believer and the divine Spirit. The light would lead to the road to perfection. Fox's followers, always on the edge of mere subjectivism, escaped it by constantly testing their light by the teachings and example of Jesus.

The Bible is the source book of the Quaker faith and from it Fox drew many ideas which became part of the peculiar ethos of Quaker life and an offense to non-Quakers. For example, Fox believed that much of the activity of the world was vanity. He exhorted Quakers to lead simple lives which were not wasted in frivolity. Dress was to be simple. No wigs were to be worn, nor were gold or vain decorations on clothing. A Quaker costume developed from these injunctions. The Biblical use of the familiar tense (thy and thou) became standard for Quakers, although most have now deserted this practice.

The Quaker organization was built around "meetings" for friends in a certain area. These meetings—monthly, quarterly, and yearly—handled business on an increasingly geographical basis. For many years, the monthly and quarterly meetings handled organization and discipline. They developed as needs manifested themselves. As early as 1668, a "General Meeting of Ministers" was held. This meeting, repeated in 1672, evolved into the yearly meeting as a general organizational body. Thus the word "meeting" can mean "church."

Quaker worship also took on a particular form, in negative reaction to Anglican formality and liturgy and in positive reaction to the inner light doctrine. Without clergy, the Quakers would sit in silence and wait for the Spirit to move. Often, no word would be spoken, but as Francis Howgill noted:

"The Lord of heaven and earth we found to be near at hand, and we waited on him in pure silence, our minds out of all things, His heavenly presence appeared in our assemblies, when there was no language, tongue or speech from any creature."

Through the years under the influence of other Protestants, particularly the holiness churches that take John Wesley as their founder, free church worship patterns began to replace the Quaker meeting. For example, the Quakers adopted such practices of the holiness churches as a more programmed worship service, with a minister who would preach. Contemporary Quakers can be divided into the unprogrammed, who follow the old Quaker meeting format, and the programmed, who have an ordered worship which includes hymns, vocal prayer, Bible reading, and a sermon.

Quakers in the United States. Quakers found their way to America within a decade of the beginning of George Fox's public ministry in England; individuals arrived as early as 1655. They found at first no more favorable home in the colonies than they had left in England. However, soon Rhode Island became their sanctuary and the first meeting was established there in 1661. George Fox's visit in 1671-73 spurred the growth of the infant group.

In the 1660's, the man destined to become the most important figure in the early life of the Quakers in the colonies—William Penn (1644-1718)—joined the British Friends. Penn was the son of a British admiral, and becoming a Quaker after meeting George Fox, he became deeply impressed by the problem of persecution which they faced. Heir to a small fortune from the king, Penn accepted a tract of land (the state of Pennsylvania) instead of the money. Here he established a Quaker colony and began the great experiment of trying to mold a colony on a Biblical model. To the everlasting credit of Penn, religious freedom was the order of the day, even for Jews and Turks.

In the next century, American Quakers would begin to make social history. Believing as they did in social justice, especially as it expressed itself in the equality of man, Quakers would begin a campaign against slavery. One of their number, John Woolman, would be a widely traveled leader in early Christian anti-slavery efforts. A mission was begun among the Indians, in line with the same belief in the equality of man. Friends controlled the Pennsylvania government until 1756, when they gave up their seats rather than vote for war measures during the French and Indian War.

The first General Meeting of Friends was held in 1681 at Burlington, New Jersey, and for several years one was held each year at both Burlington and Philadelphia. In 1685, these two meetings assumed the name "The General Yearly Meeting for Friends of Pennsylvania, East Jersey, and of the Adjacent Provinces." This became the Philadelphia Yearly Meeting, the oldest Quaker group still in existence in the United States.

Quakers, induced by the promise of freedom of conscience, migrated into tracts of land in the southern United States and established large settlements. Slavery soon became an issue and in the decades before and after 1800, most Quakers left the South as a protest and moved to Indiana and Ohio. To this day, Quaker strength lies across the Midwest and is virtually non-existent south of the Ohio River.

As Quakerism expanded westward, regionally based yearly meetings were formed as autonomous units but in harmony with eastern counterparts. As time passed and issues came and went, these yearly meetings became the bases for denominational units and late nineteenth century ecumenical endeavors.

The general unity of American Friends remained until the 1820's, when schism began to rend the Friends and produced the various denominational bodies which exist today. Philadelphia remains as a home of broadly based, if more conservative, Quakerism.

Quakers, while fitting clearly within the free church tradition and following the European spiritual Anabaptist faith, deviate from other groups at several points. The baptism issue, a matter of intense Anabaptist interest, was solved by dropping water baptism entirely. As a natural outgrowth of Schwenckfelder belief in the primacy of the spiritual, Quakers hold that the one baptism of Ephesians 4:4-5 is the inward baptism of the Holy Spirit. (See the article on the Schwenckfelder Church in America, the last church described before the Quakers.) Women also have had an unusual status, their right to full participation having been accepted at an early date. They were accepted into the ministry earlier than in most other churches.

Doctrinally, Quakers have followed a Protestant lead and profess a belief in the fatherhood of God, Jesus Christ as Lord and savior, the Holy Spirit, salvation by faith, and the priesthood of believers. Quakers do, however, take a free church anti-creedal stance, and while most Quaker bodies have a statement of belief, they usually preface it with a disclaimer against a static orthodoxy, and a wide range of beliefs are present. Evangelical practices became a dominant element in the nineteenth century and, as the century closed, Wesleyan holiness became a force. In the early twentieth century, a liberal-conservative split began to emerge, leading to several schisms. The conservative elements tended to identify with holiness ideals and withdrew from the larger Friends' Meetings to form most of the smaller bodies. The Evangelical Friends Alliance formed in 1847 serves as an ecumenical body for the conservatives.

While divided into several denominations, Quakers have been able to keep an intense social activism witness in some intra-family structures. The American Friends Service Committee founded during World War I emerged as an expression of national loyalty seeking to serve in war-alternative activities. It has gained wide respect for its refugee work. The Friends Committee for National Legislation is a non-partisan lobby group.

SOURCES—EUROPEAN FREE CHURCH

GENERAL SOURCES

Durnbaugh, Donald F. *The Believer's Church*. New York: The Macmillan Company, 1968. 315 pp.

Grimm, Harold J. *The Reformation Era*. New York: Macmillan Company, 1954.

Jones, Rufus M. *Spiritual Reformers of the Sixteenth and Seventeenth Centuries*. Boston: Beacon Press, 1914. 362 pp.

Littell, Franklin H. *The Anabaptist View of the Church*. New York: The Macmillan Company, 1952. 231 pp.

Spotts, Charles D. *Denominations Originating in Lancaster County, Pennsylvania*. Lancaster, PA: Franklin and Marshall College Library, 1963.

Williams, George H. *The Radical Reformation*. Philadelphia: The Westminster Press, 1962. 924 pp.

THE MENNONITES

Bender, Harold S. *Two Centuries of American Mennonite Literature, 1727-1928*. Goshen, IN: The Mennonite Historical Society, 1929.

The Complete Writings of Menno Simons, 1491-1561. Scottsdale, PA: Herald Press, 1956.

Hostetler, John A. *Mennonite Life*. Scottsdale, PA: Herald Press, 1959.

The Mennonite Encyclopedia. 4 vols. Scottsdale, PA: Mennonite Publishing House, 1955-59.

Smith, C. Henry. *The Mennonites*. Berne, IN: Mennonite Books concern, 1920. 340 pp.

Smith, Elmer L. *Meet the Mennonites*. Witmer, PA: Allied Arts, 1961.

Springer, Nelson P., and A. J. Klassen. *Mennonite Bibliography, 1631-1961*. 2 vols. Scottsdale, PA: Herald Press, 1977.

Waltner, James H. *This We Believe*. Newton, KS: Faith and Life Press, 1968. 230 pp.

Wenger, John Christian. *The Doctrines of the Mennonites*. Scottsdale, PA: Mennonite Publishing House, 1950.

THE AMISH

Hostetler, John A. *Amish Life*. Scottsdale, PA: Herald Press, 1959.

———. *Amish Society*. Baltimore: The Johns Hopkins Press, 1963. Rev. ed. 1968. 369 pp.

———. *An Annotated Bibliography on the Amish*. Scottsdale, PA: Mennonite House, 1951.

Rice, Charles S., and Rollin C. Stinmetz. *The Amish Year*. New Brunswick, NJ: Rutgers University Press, 1956. 224 pp.

Schreiber, William. *Our Amish Neighbors*. Chicago: University of Chicago Press, 1962. 227 pp.

Smith, Elmer Lewis. *The Amish*. Witmer, PA: Applied Arts, 1966.

———. *The Amish People*. New York: Exposition Press, 1958. 258 pp.

THE RUSSIAN MENNONITES

Smith, C. Henry. *The Coming of the Russian Mennonites*. Berne, IN: Mennonite Book Concern, 1927.

Stucky, Harley J. *A Century of Russian Mennonite History in America*. North Newton, KS: Mennonite Press, Inc., 1974.

THE BRETHREN

The Brethren Encyclopedia. 2 Vols. Philadelphia, PA: The Brethren Encyclopedia, Inc., 1983.

Durnbaugh, Donald F. "A Brethren Bibliography, 1713-1963." *Brethren Life and Thought* 9, 1-2 (Winter and Summer, 1964): 3-177.

———. *The Brethren in Colonial America*. Elgin, IL: The Brethren Press, 1967. 659 pp.

———. *The European Origins of the Brethren*. Elgin, IL: Brethren Press, 1958. 463 pp.

———. "Guide to Research in Brethren History." Elgin, IL: Church of the Brethren General Board, 1977. 16 pp.

Holsinger, H. R. *History of the Tunkers and the Brethren Church*. Lathrop, CA: The Author, 1901.

Mallot, Floyde E. *Studies in Brethren History*. Elgin, IL: Brethren Publishing House, 1954. 382 pp.

Sappington, Roger E. *The Brethren in the New Nation*. Elgin, IL: Brethren Press, 1976. 496 pp.

Willoughby, William G. *Counting the Cost*. Elgin, IL: Brethren Press, 1979. 176 pp.

THE FRIENDS (QUAKERS)

Baltzell, E. Digby. *Puritan Boston and Quaker Philadelphia*. Boston: Beacon Press, 1979. 585 pp.

Barbour, Hugh, and Arthur O. Roberts. *Early Quaker Writings, 1650-1700*. Grand Rapids, MI: William B. Eerdmans Publishing Company, 1973. 622 pp.

Benjamin, Philip S. *The Philadelphia Quakers in the Industrial Age*. Philadelphia: Temple University Press, 1976. 301 pp.

Brinton, Howard H. *Children of Light*. New York: Macmillan Company, 1938. 416 pp.

Comfort, William Wistar. *The Quaker Way of Life*. Philadelphia: The Blakiston Company, 1945. 178 pp.

Elliott, Errol T. *Quakers on the American Frontier*. Richmond, IN: Friends United Press, 1969. 434 pp.

Evans, Thomas. *A Concise Account of the Religious Society of Friends*. Philadelphia: Friends Books Store, n.d.

Finding Friends around the World. London: Friends World Committee for Consultation, 1982. 128 pp.

Holder, Charles Frederick. *The Quakers in Great Britain and America*. Los Angeles: Neuner Company, 1913. 669 pp.

Jones, Rufus. *The Quakers in the American Colonies*. New York: W. W. Norton & Company, 1966. 606 pp.

Kenworthy, Leonard S. *Quakerism*. Durbin, IN: Prinit Press, 1981. 215 pp.

Van Etten, Henry. *George Fox and the Quakers*. New York: Harper, 1959. 191 pp.

Chapter Nine

THE BAPTIST FAMILY

Directory listings for the groups belonging to the Baptist Family may be
found in the section beginning on page 385.

The Baptist churches are free churches, called "free" to show that they are free associations of adult believers. Other free-churches include those in the European free-church family, discussed in the previous chapter, and those in the independent fundamentalist family, discussed in the next chapter. A cursory examination might suggest that the Baptists are a subgroup of the European free-church family, which includes the Mennonites, the Amish, the Brethren, and the Quakers. The Baptists, like that family, are anti-authoritarian, lay-oriented, non-liturgical, non-creedal; they oppose state churches, and they baptize adult believers, not infants.

But the size of the Baptist churches and their continued growth suggest significant differences between the Baptists and the European free-church family. The Baptists make up the second largest family on the American religious scene, second only to Roman Catholics. One difference between the Baptists and the smaller European free churches is historical. The Baptists are related to British Puritanism, whereas the European free churches are related to the continental radical reformers. A second difference is the Baptists' freedom from some hindrances to growth that characterize the European free churches. These hindrances include pacifism, the ban (a form of excommunication), and prohibitions against voting, holding public office, and serving in the armed forces. The Baptists are free of such provisions that tend to limit membership. Finally, the Baptists' evangelistic revivalistic lifestyle has attracted many followers. All of these factors help explain why great numbers of people find the Baptist churches appealing.

HISTORY. History is a problem for the Baptists. When and where did the Baptists originate? Baptist scholars give widely divergent answers to that question.

One school, the earliest to appear in Baptist circles, holds to what one scholar calls the "Jerusalem-Jordan-John theory." These scholars believe that the Baptists can be dated to John the Baptist and his baptism of Jesus in the Jordan River. David Benedict, writing in the second decade of the nineteenth century, expresses this view:

"All sects trace their origin to the Apostles, or at least to the early ages of Christianity. But men, and especially the

powerful ones, have laboured hard to cut off the Baptists from this common retreat. They have often asserted and taken much pains to prove that the people now called Baptists originated with the mad men of Münster, about 1522. We have only to say to this statement, that it is not true. And not withstanding all that has been said to the contrary, we still date the origin of our sentiments, and the beginning of our denomination, about the year of our Lord twenty-nine or thirty; for at that period John the Baptist began to immerse professed believers in Jordan and Enon, and to prepare the way for the coming of the Lord's Annointed, and for the setting up of his kingdom" (David Benedict, *A General History of the Baptist Denomination in America and Other Parts of the World* [Boston: Lincoln and Edmunds, 1813], 1:92).

Followers of this school generally deny that the term Protestant has any reference to them because, they say, they predate Luther. They are also concerned with an "apostolic succession" of Baptist congregations and take great pains to define and locate it.

A second group of scholars criticized the first group for seeking a continuity of organization and called upon them to seek rather a continuity of doctrine. The second group tended to locate Baptist organizational origins in the Anabaptist wing of the Reformation. (Anabaptists called for an adult believer's baptism, which necessitated the rebaptism of those baptized as infants.) This second view was theologically, if not historically, attractive for a church that sought to recreate the first-century church. As Thomas Armitage put it:

"If it can be shown that their churches are the most like the Apostolic that now exist, and that the elements which make them so have passed successfully through the long struggle, succession from the times of their blessed Lord gives them the noblest history that any people can crave. To procure a servile imitation of merely primitive things has never been the mission of Baptists. Their work has been to promote the living reproduction of New Testament Christians, and so to make the Christlike old, the ever delightfully new. Their perpetually fresh appeal to the Scriptures as the only warrant for their existence at all must not be cut off, in a foolish attempt to turn the weapons of the hierarchy against itself. The sword of the Spirit must still be their only arm of service, offensive and defensive. An appeal to false credentials now would only cut them off from the use of all that now remains undiscovered and unapplied in the word of God. The distinctive attribute in the Kingdom of Christ is life; not an historic life, but a life supernatural, flowing eternally from Christ alone by his living truth" (Thomas Armitage, *A History of the Baptists* [New York: Bryan, Taylor and Co., 1887], 11-12).

The final school of thought on Baptist origins, which gained ascendency in the twentieth century, looks to seventeenth-century England for the beginnings of the Baptist movement. Robert Torbet, the contemporary exponent of this view points out in relation to the first school:

"To say, however, that any single one of these early segments of the Christian church may be identified definitively with the communion we now know as Baptists is to make an assertion which lacks convincing historical support. That there are similarities of teaching between each of these groups and the Baptists is not to be denied. Yet, although it is not possible to trace a clear lineage of Baptists as an historical entity back to the early church, Baptist history may certainly be traced from the stirring days of the Protestant Reformation" (Robert G. Torbet, *A History of Baptists* [Chicago: The Judson Press, 1950], 15).

Torbet also refutes the Anabaptist theory by holding up the difference between Baptist and Anabaptist theology:

"Baptists have not shared with Anabaptists the latter's aversion to oath-taking and holding public office. Neither have they adopted the Anabaptists' doctrine of pacifism, or their theological views concerning the incarnation, soul sleeping, and the necessity of observing an apostolic succession in the administration of baptism." (Torbet, 62).

One could also note the lack of vital intercourse and familial attachment between the contemporary Baptist churches and the contemporary Anabaptist churches (i.e., the Mennonites, Hutterites, and Amish) and the lack of Anabaptists in Baptist ecumenical bodies.

Henry C. Vedder is cited by Torbet as an able exponent of the third school. Vedder believed that "after 1610 we have an unbroken succession of Baptist Churches" (Torbet, 201). Further support for this third school is found in the theology of the early Baptists: they continued to operate out of their basic Calvinist theology, deviating at two points—the sacraments and the church—rather than adopt a Mennonite theology which was adjusted for their use. While they differ with their Presbyterian and Congregationalist forefathers on two issues, they disagree with the Anabaptists on a number of issues.

English Baptists can trace their history to Holland where Separatists had located after the execution of some of their leaders in 1593. John Smyth's congregation and another led by John Robinson arrived in Holland in the first decade of the seventeenth century. In a short time Smyth issued a tract, *The Differences of the Churches of the Separation* (1608), in which he explained why the two congregations could not

fellowship. Baptism was not an issue; extemporaneous preaching was. Smyth's congregation became heavily influenced by the Dutch Mennonites and in the winter of 1608-09, Smyth and about forty people were rebaptized. Continued Anabaptist influence led to schism, however, and Smyth, whose congregation was absorbed by the Mennonites, returned to England. The schism resulted from the collision of the Calvinists' belief in predestination and the Mennonites' belief in free will. Thomas Helwys, the leader of the schismatic group, tried to reject both by adopting an Arminian theology. He also rejected any attempt at tracing the Apostolic succession of the true church.

John Smyth founded the first Baptist church on English soil in 1611. In England and later in America, the first Baptists were Arminian in their theology instead of Calvinist. That means the first Baptists believed in a "general" atonement—salvation is possible for all—not in the "particular" atonement or limited atonement—predestination—of the Calvinist Baptists. Thus the first Baptists were called General Baptists; the Calvinist Baptists were called Particular Baptists. The growth of Smyth's church and local squabbles among Baptists led to the founding of five more churches in England by 1630 and forty-one more by 1644.

The founding of the second main grouping of Baptists, the Particular Baptists, came about through the Puritans' move toward a Baptist position in the 1630's. In 1638, a group in the church at Southwark pastored by Henry Jacob rejected Congregational Church baptism because it was of the Church of England. Anabaptism began to emerge; dismissals led to the formation of a Calvinistic Baptist Church pastored by John Spilsbury.

Among these Calvinistic Baptists, called Particular Baptists, the issue of immersion as the correct mode of baptism was raised. In 1644, they promulgated the London Confession of Faith, which provided for immersion and incorporated Calvinist theology with a call for religious freedom. This confession outlined the major issues which were to separate Baptists from other Christian bodies. Baptists would be congregationally governed but completely separated from the state. While being orthodox Christians, they would hold to adult baptism by immersion as the Apostolic, hence correct, mode of baptism. They would divide among themselves on Calvinist and Arminian lines.

A third Baptist group believed that Saturday was the true Sabbath. This belief arose as early as 1617. Seventh-day Baptists have never made up a large percentage of Baptists, overall, but have persisted as one of the oldest continually existing Baptist bodies, and have been the source of almost all Sabbatarian teaching in the United States.

In rejecting affiliation with the state and asserting the sovereignty of the local congregation, Baptists took the major step toward their typical form of congregational government. The next step came in the 1600's when various issues led local congregations to associate together in order to present a united front on an issue. As early as 1624, General Baptists issued a common document against the Mennonites. In 1644, Particular Baptists issued the London Confession. These united-front gatherings eventuated into associations—regular structures for affiliation of congregations. As a rule, General Baptists began to move toward strong associations with more centralized authority, while Particular Baptists tended toward a very loose organization.

BELIEFS. Baptists have generally been among those churches which professed a non-creedal theology. Actually, several "Confessions of Faith" have been significant in forming Baptist theology, not the least of which was the Westminster Confession, which set the issues for English Puritanism. The Baptists produced their own version of this confession in 1677. In addition, the Baptists wrote the London Confessions of 1644 and 1689, and most important for Baptists in the United States, the New Hampshire Confession of Faith in 1833. This confession was produced in the midst of the various controversies of the early 1800's, and became a working document for a majority of Baptists in later decades. Amended versions were adopted as official statements by several associations and by the Southern Baptist Convention (1925). The following is the New Hampshire Confession of Faith with its 1853 additions.

Declaration of Faith

i. Of the Scriptures

We believe [that] the Holy Bible was written by men divinely inspired and is a perfect treasure of heavenly instruction; that it has God for its author, salvation for its end, and truth, without any mixture of error, for its matter; that it reveals the principles by which God will judge us; and therefore is, and shall remain to the end of the world, the true centre of Christian union, and the supreme standard by which all human conduct, creeds, and opinions should be tried.

ii. Of the True God

[We believe] that there is one, and only one, living and true God, [an infinite, intelligent Spirit,] whose name is JEHOVAH, the Maker and Supreme Ruler of heaven and earth; inexpressibly glorious in holiness; [and] worthy of all possible honor, confidence, and love; revealed under the personal and relative distinctions of the Father, the Son, and the Holy Spirit; equal in every divine perfection, and executing distinct but harmonious offices in the great work of redemption.

iii. Of the Fall of Man

[We believe] that man was created in a state of holiness, under the law of his Maker; but by voluntary transgression fell from that holy and happy state; in consequence of which all mankind are now sinners, not by constraint but choice, being by nature utterly void of that holiness required by the law of God, wholly given to the gratification of the world, of Satan, and of their own sinful passions, therefore under just condemnation to eternal ruin, without defense or excuse.

iv. Of the Way of Salvation

[We believe] that the salvation of sinners is wholly of grace; through the Mediatorial Offices of the Son of God, who [by the appointment of the Father, freely] took upon him our nature, yet without sin; honored the [divine] law by his personal obedience, and made atonement for our sins by his death; being risen from the dead he is now enthroned in heaven; and united in his wonderful person the tenderest sympathies with divine perfections, [he] is every way qualified to be a suitable, a compassionate, and an all-sufficient Savior.

v. Of Justification

[We believe] that the great Gospel blessing which Christ of his fulness bestows on such as believe in Him, is Justification; that Justification consists in the pardon of sin and the promise of eternal life, on principles of righteousness; that it is bestowed not in consideration of any works of righteousness which we have done, but solely through His own redemption and righteousness, [by virtue of which faith his perfect righteousness is freely imputed to us of God;] that it brings us into a state of most blessed peace and favor with God, and secures every other blessing needful for time and eternity.

vi. Of the Freeness of Salvation

[We believe] that the blessings of salvation are made free to all by the Gospel; that it is the immediate duty of all to accept them by a cordial, [penitent,] and obedient faith; and that nothing prevents the salvation of the greatest sinner on earth except his own [inherent depravity and] voluntary refusal to submit to the Lord Jesus Christ, which refusal will subject him to an aggravated condemnation.

vii. Of Grace in Regeneration

[We believe] that in order to be saved, we must be regenerated or born again; that regeneration consists in giving a holy disposition to the mind; and is effected in a manner above our comprehension or calculation, by the power of the Holy Spirit, [in connection with divine truth,] so as to secure our voluntary obedience to the Gospel; and that its proper evidence is found in the holy fruit which we bring forth to the glory of God.

viii. Of Repentance and Faith [This article added in 1853]

[We believe] that Repentance and Faith are sacred duties, and also inseparable graces, wrought in our souls by the regenerating Spirit of God; whereby being deeply convinced of our guilt, danger, and helplessness, and of the way of salvation by Christ, we turn to God with unfeigned contrition, confession, and supplication for mercy; at the same time heartily receiving the Lord Jesus Christ as our Prophet, Priest, and King, and relying on him alone as the only and all-sufficient Savior.

ix. Of God's Purpose of Grace

[We believe] that Election is the gracious purpose of God, according to which he [graciously] regenerates, sanctifies, and saves sinners; that being perfectly consistent with the free agency of man, it comprehends all the means in connection with the end; that it is a most glorious display of God's sovereign goodness, being infinitely [free,] wise, holy, and unchangeable; that it utterly excludes boasting, and promotes humility, [love,] prayer, praise, trust in God, and active imitation of his free mercy; that it encourages the use of means in the highest degree; that it is ascertained by its effects in all who [truly] believe the gospel; [that it] is the foundation of Christian assurance; and that to ascertain it with regard to ourselves, demands and deserves our utmost diligence.

x. Of Sanctification [Added in 1853]

We believe that Sanctification is the process by which, according to the will of God, we are made partakers of his holiness; that it is a progressive work, that is begun in regeneration, and that it is carried on in the hearts of believers by the presence and power of the Holy Spirit, the Sealer and Comforter, in the continual use of the appointed means—especially the Word of God, self-examination, self-denial, watchfulness and prayer.

xi. Of the Perseverance of Saints

[We believe] that such only are real believers as endure unto the end; that their persevering attachment to Christ is the grand mark which distinguishes them from mere professors; that a special Providence watches over their welfare; and [that] they are kept by the power of God through faith unto salvation.

xii. [Of the] Harmony of the Law and the Gospel

[We believe] that the Law of God is the eternal and unchangeable rule of his moral government; that it is holy, just, and good; and that the inability which the Scriptures ascribe to fallen men to fulfill its precepts, arises entirely from their love of sin; to deliver them from which, and to restore them through a Mediator to unfeigned obedience to the holy law, is one great end of the Gospel, and of the means of grace connected with the establishment of the visible Church.

xiii. Of a Gospel Church

[We believe] that a visible Church of Christ is a congregation of baptized believers, associated by covenant in the faith and fellowship of the Gospel; observing the ordinances of Christ; governed by his laws; and exercising the gifts, rights, and privileges invested in them by his word; that its only proper officers are Bishops or Pastors, and Deacons, whose qualifications, claims, and duties are defined in the Epistles to Timothy and Titus.

xiv. Of Baptism and the Lord's Supper

[We believe] that Christian Baptism is the immersion of a believer in water, in the name of the Father [and] Son, and Spirit, to show forth in a solemn and beautiful emblem, our faith in a crucified, buried, and risen Savior, with its purifying power; that it is a prerequisite to the privileges of a church relation; and to the Lord's Supper, in which the members of the church, by the [sacred] use of bread and wine, are to commemorate together the dying love of Christ; preceded always by solemn self—examination.

xv. Of the Christian Sabbath

[We believe] that the first day of the week is the Lord's-Day, or Christian Sabbath; and is to be kept sacred to religious purposes, by abstaining from all secular labor and [sinful] recreations; by the devout observance of all the means of grace, both private and public; and by preparation for that rest which remaineth for the people of God.

xvi. Of Civil Government

[We believe] that civil government is of divine appointment, for the interests and good order of human society; and that magistrates are to be prayed for, conscientiously honored, and obeyed, except [only] in things opposed to the will of our Lord Jesus Christ, who is the only Lord of the conscience, and the Prince of the kings of the earth.

xvii. Of the Righteous and the Wicked

[We believe] that there is a radical and essential difference between the righteous and the wicked; that such only as through faith are justified in the name of the Lord Jesus, and sanctified by the Spirit of our God, are truly righteous in his esteem; while all such as continue in impenitence and unbelief are in his sight wicked, and under the curse; and this distinction holds among men both in and after death.

xviii. Of the World to Come

[We believe] that the end of this world is approaching; that at the last day, Christ will descend from heaven, and raise the dead from the grave to final retribution; that a solemn separation will then take place; that the wicked will be adjudged to endless punishment, and the righteous to endless joy; and that this judgment will fix forever the final state of men in heaven or hell, on principles of righteousness (W. L. Lumpkin, *Baptist Confessions of Faith* [Chicago: The Judson Press, 1959], 360-367).

The New Hampshire Confession has been characterized as an attempt "to restate Calvinism in very moderate terms." Such moderation is exemplified by the article on the "Freeness of Salvation." The statement is also representative of typical Baptist positions which distinguish them from their close doctrinal neighbors.

The basically Calvinist stance of the confession is indicative of Baptist ties to the Reformed tradition (through British Presbyterianism and Congregationalism) as opposed to the Anabaptist tradition. As early as 1644, the London Confession rejected Mennonite views against taking oaths, holding government offices, and doing military service.

The points at issue between the Baptists and other English Separatists were believers' baptism and the nature of the church in relation to ecclesiastical authority and to the state. The Baptists rejected the almost universal practice of the Western church in baptizing infants. They first proposed "believers' baptism" as the alternative, feeling that only those who first repent and profess belief could be baptized. This idea led John Smyth in 1609 to baptize himself by pouring. He was serving an English congregation in exile in Amsterdam at the time and had come into contact with the Waterlander Mennonites who influenced him at this point. It was not until 1640 that the idea of immersion as the true mode of baptism emerged. However, after it did, it became inseparable from the idea of believers' baptism. As a matter of fact, it has been the major issue separating Baptists from other family groups.

The sacraments as a whole became a corollary issue between Baptists and the classical Reformation churches. Baptists rejected the concept of sacrament in favor of ordinance. They emphasized the memorial and command-filling aspect of baptism and the Lord's Supper at the expense of a belief in God's presence in the sacramental elements or act.

The second point at issue between the Baptists and their forebears was the doctrine of the church. The Congregationalists, from whom the Baptists had directly emerged, had dissented from both episcopal and presbyterian forms of church government but still saw themselves as an established church with all the rights and privileges. Their ideal was realized in its most nearly perfect form in the New England theocracy that the Puritans established. They retained infant baptism and tried to retain a favorable standing with the state. The Baptists rejected Congregational ecclesiology and opted for an extreme free church ideal. They rejected any connection with the state and any belief in the possibility of a Christian state. Christians would freely associate themselves with Christ's church and live as pilgrims in a hostile world. They would not deny the legitimacy of the worldly structures, but would see them as a part of God's creative, not salvic, action.

For other Baptists, the New Hampshire Confession would become a document to modify, refute, or use as a standard of allegiance.

IN AMERICA. Some Baptists came to America from England; some emerged from the established British churches in the colonies. The earliest Baptist churches were founded by Roger Williams and John Clarke in Rhode Island. First Church in Providence, founded by Williams, dates to 1639, and Clarke's Newport Congregation to 1648. Apart from the Rhode Island churches, the early Baptists were persecuted for not allowing their infants to be baptized. This persecution was all but ended in 1691 with the Americanization of the 1689 Act of Toleration.

In the 1680's, Baptists began to enter the middle colonies. A short-lived congregation was founded in 1684, and, in 1688, the Pennepack Church in Philadelphia was founded. Because of the lack of established churches in the middle colonies, the Baptists were to thrive here in a way not possible in the Northeast or South until after the Revolutionary War.

In 1707, the first Baptist association in the colonies was formed. The Philadelphia Association was patterned on an English model. It was a very loose association acting only as an advisory body. To it was left the task of disciplining the ministers and of acting as a council of ordination. In 1742, the association adopted the London Confession of Particular Baptists of 1689, thus identifying American Baptists with Calvinist doctrine. Benjamin Griffith and Jenkin Jones added a statement on the relation of churches and the association "based on theological agreement."

In the South, Baptists arrived in the late 1600's and formed the first Baptist church in 1714. The earliest Baptists were Arminians, which means they opposed strict Calvinist views on predestination and instead believed people were given free will so they could choose whether or not to follow the gospel. From the Arminian Baptists would come the Free-Will Baptist associations.

In the early 1700's the Great Awakening began to affect the Baptists. Their number increased tremendously, but they also found themselves involved in new controversy. Among the Particular Baptists arose the Separatist Baptists, whose membership requirement was the personal experience of regeneration (in modern terms, the "born again" experience, involving an awareness of Jesus as personal savior). The Separatist Baptists separated themselves from those who practiced anything less. Among both the particularists (now called Regulars) and the Separatists, divisions arose on the emotional appeal of revivalism. The New Lights were for it and the Old Lights against it. A final union of the various Particular groups was effected in 1801. The 1700's also saw the rise of Particular Baptists to predominance over the General Baptists in most areas.

The 1800's were a time of significant growth for Baptists, who were beginning to structure themselves and develop the adjuncts of a succesful church—a publishing concern, a missionary arm, and institutions of higher education. In 1824, the Triennial Convention was formed. This meeting was, at its inception, a convention of associations called together for missionary concerns. "The General Missionary Convention of the Baptist Denomination in America" was the official designation, but the meeting every three years was popularly called the Triennial Convention. While missionary in its base, it became the forum in which many issues would be argued and out of which most schisms would come. Most Calvinistic Baptists, in the beginning, related themselves to the Convention.

THE GROWTH OF THE LARGER BAPTIST BODIES. The founding of the Triennial Convention was a signal for other cooperative efforts to form. The American Baptist Publication Society began in 1824, the American Baptist Home Mission Society in 1832, and the American Foreign Bible Society in 1837. A number of state societies and conventions were also formed. These were the building blocks out of which a national group consciousness could grow and from which a national convention or the equivalent of a national denomination eventually could emerge. It is difficult to say just when that national consciousness emerged, but it was certainly before 1907, when the American Baptist Convention was formed. That convention represents a gradual move toward centralization.

Proceedings in the Triennial Convention moved in the 1830's from missions to educational leadership and publications. In the 1840's, however, a new issue emerged—slavery. In April 1840, an "American Baptist Anti-Slavery Convention" was orgainzed to press the issue which had been resisted as a topic for consideration.

At the 1841 Triennial Convention, the Southerners, led by Richard Fuller, protested the abolitionist agitation and argued that, while slavery was a calamity and a great evil, it was not a sin according to the Bible. The Savannah River Association threatened to withdraw cooperation unless the abolitionists were dismissed from the Board of Managers. The debate began a controversy that would result in the gradual withdrawal of the Southern Baptists from participation in convention activities and from support of the *Missionary Magazine* and missions.

The 1844 session proved decisive; the Southern delegates showed up in force with several test cases. The Alabama Convention sent a query to the Board of Foreign Missions asking "whether or not slaveholders are eligible and entitled equally with non-slaveholders to all the privileges and immunities of the several Unions." The Georgia Baptists chose a slave-owner as a missionary and forwarded his appointment to the Home Missions Society as a test case. The convention dodged the issues by referring them to the respective subsidiary boards.

Because the issue of slavery was raised in the nomination from Georgia, the board ruled that it was not at liberty to consider it. The Alabama query was answered in the negative. Appointment of a slaveholder would make the Northern brethren responsible for an institution they could not conscientiously sanction. The situation of the mission board was further complicated by the formation of a Free Mission Society, which refused "tainted" Southern money. In the face of these two issues, the Southern brethren decided to withdraw, and in 1845, they formed the Southern Baptist Convention.

The split brought to the forefront a second issue between Southern and Northern Baptists, organizational centralization. The Southern Baptist Convention became a single organization overseeing all the activities which were separated in the Northern boards and conventions. Some three hundred churches entered the new church convention, which met every two years.

The Northern and Southern churches are similar in church government, both being congregationally oriented, and in doctrine, both accepting the New Hampshire Confession of Faith. The Southern church, in fact, is more centralized in its aggressive mission activity, and has expanded northward in the twentieth century. The Northern church has been much more open to modern theological trends, the ecumenical movement, and social activism, and it tends to be more "liberal" in its outlook.

As a rule, ecumenical participation by Baptists has been hindered by both the extreme congregational polity and the demand for doctrinal unity with those with whom they fellowship. There is, however, a Baptist World Alliance, with which many Baptists associate.

Predestination, missions, race, and restoration theology became the issues around which subfamilies developed. The old controversy between Particular and General Baptists, between those who believed and those who did not believe in predestination, continued in America, although the predestinarians triumphed in the nineteenth century.

The mission society controversy led to a major schism in the early nineteenth century. Those who broke with the Triennial Convention became known as the Primitive Baptists.

CONSERVATIVE BAPTIST MOVEMENT. In the early decades of the twentieth century, the Northern Baptist Convention, like other large Christian bodies, was rent asunder by the fundamentalist-modernist controversy. Among the Baptists, the fundamentalist movement focused on the issues of social action and the deviation from doctrine by missionaries. The fundamentalists opposed the post-World War I policies which seemed to involve unsuitable social activism, and they opposed the sending of missionaires who did not hold a strong conservative Baptist position. When the Convention turned away from their demands, the members of the Fundamentalist Fellowship organized, in 1920, the Consevative Baptist Fellowship (CBF) to continue their understanding of the gospel.

For many years, the CBF continued within the Northern Baptist Convention, but during World War II, plans for separation were pursued. Over the years, at least five churches have resulted from splintering associated with the CBF.

The Conservative Baptist Movement must also be seen as a reaction to the centralization signaled by the formation of the Northern Baptist Convention, itself, in 1907. An extreme congregational polity exists in churches belonging to the Conservative Baptist Fellowship. Congregations associate freely. Mission work is carried on by separate but approved mission agencies; schools tend to operate similarly.

PRIMITIVE BAPTISTS. In the years following the American Revolution, a great wave of enthusiasm for missions swept across the American church. Among the Baptists, this enthusiasm was occasioned by the acceptance of the Baptist view on immersion by two Congregationalist missionaries on their voyage to the mission field in India. Having lost the support of the American Board of Commissions for Foreign Missions, Adoniram Judson and Luther Rice turned to the Baptists to support their work.

In response to Rice's appeal, a new structure, "the General Missionary Convention of the Baptist Denomination in the United States for Foreign Missions," was created in 1814. In 1815, Elder Martin Ross presented to the Kehukee Association meeting at Fishing Creek, North Carolina, a report on the new mission board. Elder Ross had already built up a reputation for missionary zeal. In 1803, he had placed his concern before the Association in the form of a query:

"Is not the Kehukee Association, with her numerous and respectable friends, called on in Providence, in some way, to step forward in support of that missionary spirit which the great God is so wonderfully reviving amongst the different denominations of good men in various parts of the world?" (Cushing Biggs Hassell and Sylvester Hassell, *History of the Church of God from Creation to A.D. 1885, Including Especially the History of the Kehukee Primitive Baptist Association* [Atlanta, GA: Turner Lassetter, 1962; reprint of original edition, Middletown, NY: Gilbert Beebe's Sons, 1886], 721).

In both 1803 and 1815, Ross met with a favorable response. Similar actions were occurring across the country.

Nevertheless, there remained a minority who viewed the missionary movement as an innovation and who, a decade later, were able to unite in opposition to a number of "new" causes. An eloquent voice arose in the Kehukee to confront the eloquent Martin Ross. Joshua Lawrence, of no formal education but great native ability, authored a "Declaration of

Principles" for the churches of the Kehukee Association. At the 1827 association meeting, a lengthy debate on the declaration was followed by a resolution to "discard all Missionary Societies, Bible Societies and Theological Seminaries, and the practices heretofore resorted to for their support, in begging money from the public." The Kehukee Association further resolved:

"If any persons should be among us, as agents of any of said societies, we hereafter discountenance them in those practices; and if under a character of a minister of the gospel, we will not invite them into our pulpits; believing these societies and institutions to be the inventions of men, and not warranted from the Word of God."

Masonary was one of the issues combined with opposition to the new missionary groups, and the Kehukee reacted against members who joined the lodge. We "declare non-fellowship with them and such practices altogether" (Hassell and Hassell, 736-37). The lengthy action was finally adopted in complete consensus. There were no dissenting votes.

This action did not go unopposed by those who had for years supported the missionary cause, both within and outside of the Kehukee Association. Within the Association, churches began to withdraw and to continue their support of mission societies. Other associations withdrew their letter of correspondence (doctrinal and ethical similarity) with Kehukee. One of these, the Neuse Association (North Carolina), split in 1830-31, and the Contentea Association was formed around the Kehukee position against missionary groups. The Little River and the Nauhunty Associations adopted the Kehukee position at the same time.

In August 1832, the County Line Association came out in opposition to missionary societies. The following month a similar action was taken at an "unofficial" meeting of some churches of the Baltimore Association who gathered at the Black Rock church in Baltimore County in Maryland. The action at Black Rock was significant, as it was bringing the issue close to Philadelphia, home of the Mission Board. In the North, those opposed to mission societies were called "Blackrockers."

No segment of the Baptist Church, particularly in the South, was unaffected by the debates, and, as associations were divided, a unitive consciousness of being the "true," "primitive," or "old school" Baptist church developed among those who refused to support what they termed "innovations." A national body of like-minded believers who registered their consciousness of one another through "letters of correspondence" began to emerge. By 1840, Primitive Baptist associations covered what was then the United States, reaching north into Pennsylvania and west to Missouri and Texas.

Primitive Baptist beliefs were hammered out in debates with the growing Missionary Baptist movement on the one hand and the Arminianism of the United and the Free Will Baptists on the other hand. (Arminians believe salvation is possible for all through free will, a belief opposed to the predestination believed in by the strict Calvinists.) The heritage of the Primitive Baptists was the New Hampshire Confession and British Puritan Calvinism. Primitive Baptists'

response was to affirm their traditional Calvinism and independency. Primitive Baptists are not, as a whole, theologically trained, and their differences have arisen over acceptance or rejection of traditional statements.

The Statement of Faith is included in most copies of annual association minutes. Typically, the statement will include articles on the Trinity, the Scriptures as the only rule of faith and practice, original sin, human depravity, election, perseverance of the saints, baptism by immersion, closed communion, the resurrection, and ordination. Differences among Primitive Baptists will be manifest primarily on the doctrine of election and/or predestination. All hold to a belief in election, that God elected the saved before the foundation of the world. Some go beyond, and hold that God predestined everything that comes to pass. Upon that doctrine, associations have split. Footwashing is practiced by most Primitive Baptists, but very few make it a test for fellowship. Some consider it an ordinance. The King James Version of the Bible is preferred. Secret societies are frowned upon.

Primitive Baptists have an extreme congregational form of government, and many assert in their articles of faith that an association has no right to assume any authority over local churches. For the overwhelming number of Primitive Baptists, there is no organization above the loose associations which typically cover several counties. Associations consist of representative member churches and can sit in advisory capacities only.

Except for the few Primitive Baptist groups which have organized more formally, there are no headquarters, institutions, or official publications. As with the Plymouth Brethren, periodicals become a major means of communication and are identified with various divisions. Generally speaking, each periodical will serve a specific geographic area for a particular doctrinally definable group.

The local church consists of members, deacons, and elders. Members must be adult baptized believers. Deacons oversee the temporal affairs. Ministers have little or no theological training and, typically, no salary. They are expected to study the Scriptures. No musical instruments are used in worship. Sermons are delivered extemporaneously, in a distinctive sing-song voice. Also associated with the Primitives is Sacred Harp singing, a cappella singing in four-part harmony which sounds like eighteenth-century folk music.

While not organized in an hierarchical fashion, there is a definite organizational structure to the Primitive Baptist movement which can be defined by doctrine and by letters of correspondence. Each association has a sister association to which it sends annual letters of greeting. Such letters are recognition of being in communion and professing similar doctrines. Doctrinal differences among associations in correspondence manifest the generally low level of doctrinal freedom allowed. With rare exceptions, associations in correspondence will not overlap geographically. Several groups have taken steps to organize more formally and to form supra-associational structures. Finally, race has also become a means of distinguishing a set of corresponding associations.

If one defines a primary religious body among the Primitive Baptists as an association and those associations with which it is in correspondence and has doctrinal unity, no fewer than 13 distinct Primitive Baptist groups emerge. Each one of these bodies meets the criteria of a primary religious group as outlined in the introduction. Each asks for the primary allegiance of its members, has two or more centers of operation, and has at least one item of doctrine or organizational principle that will be distinctive from its closest neighbor.

BLACK BAPTISTS. Baptist missions among the slaves date to the beg of Baptist history and the efforts made among the black members of Roger Williams' Providence Church. But in the 1700's as Baptists moved into the South, slaves grew to be a large percentage of the membership. The first black Baptist church was formed at Silver Bluff, South Carolina, between 1773 and 1775, and was made up of residents of the plantation of John Galphin. Leadership was provided by a Brother Palmer, the church's founder, the Rev. David George, and the Rev. George Lisle. The late date of this formation is symbolic more of the hesitancy of slave owners to allow separate churches (which could become independent centers for subversive activities) than of any lack of success preaching the gospel among the slaves. Within a few years, a second church was formed at Williamsburg, Virginia, at the initiation of the white Baptists. A third church was formed in Savannah in 1779. From these three, others sprang up across the South.

Northern blacks established Baptist churches after the turn of the century. The Jay Street Church of Boston was founded in 1804, with New York (1808) and Philadelphia (1809) following in quick succession. The Boston and New York churches were formed by the Rev. Thomas Paul. The Abyssinian Baptist Church in New York would later be pastored by Congressman Adam Clayton Powell.

Like their white brethren, the blacks were active in foreign mission work, sending a missionary to Haiti in 1824. In 1821, the Revs. Lott Carey and Collins Teague were sent by the Triennial Convention to work in Liberia. They traveled to their new home with a group of blacks sponsored by the African Colonization Society.

As the reaction of slave owners to slave revolts cut into the freedom of slaves to spread their religion, and as many slaves fled north and west, Baptist churches spread in the Midwest. In 1836, the Providence Baptist Association in Ohio became the first Black Baptist Association in the country. Two years later in Illinois, the Wood River Association was formed. In 1840, the American Baptist Missionary Convention was formed by blacks in the Northeast and mid-Atlantic states. It was active in Freedman's aid as the Civil War drew to a close.

After the Civil War, several organizational attempts met with varying success until, in 1879, the Rev. W.W. Colley returned from Africa with a vision of the role of black Baptist churches. At a meeting in Montgomery, Alabama, in 1880, the Foreign Mission Baptist Convention of the U.S.A. was formed. This Convention became the rallying point of black Baptists, and its organization is usually accepted as the founding date of the National Baptist Convention. Within the Foreign Mission Baptist Convention, machinery was provided for the calling of a meeting at which the American National Baptist Convention was formed in 1886. In 1893, a third body, the Baptist National Educational Convention, was formed. Other regional bodies joined in these national efforts, and the stage was set for the formation of the first national black denomination in 1895.

GENERAL BAPTISTS. The first Baptists in both England and America were Arminian in their theology. This means they held that salvation is possible for all. They believed in a "general" atonement (thus the name "General Baptists") in opposition to the "particular" atonement or strict predestination of the Calvinist Baptists, who said the number and identity of the elect were predetermined before the world began. John Smyth founded the first Baptist church in England in 1611; many General Baptists in America trace their seventeenth-century roots to Smyth. The English Baptists faced persecution, but were able to set up a central organization, "the General Assembly," in the 1660's. By 1699, this assembly included some ten local associations.

In America, the General Baptist history begins in 1639 with Roger Williams' Church at Providence, Rhode Island. Other churches spread in the East over the next century. In the first decade of the eighteenth century, General Baptist centers were established in the South. A group settled in Virginia and, in 1709, applied to England for a minister. The minister died soon after his arrival, and the church moved to North Carolina under the leadership of William Sojourner. In the same year, Paul Palmer baptized nine persons and formed the Chestnut Ridge Church in Maryland. He, too, moved to North Carolina. Through his labors, William Parker was converted; under Palmer, Parker, and Sojourner, a thriving General Baptist movement was organized.

Much of the General Baptist work was lost to the militant Calvinists in the late 1700's. The Philadelphia Association absorbed the Northern Baptists and their missionaries, and organized the Kehukee Association from members in North Carolina. Those not absorbed by the Kehukee became known as "Free-Willers," a name that stuck.

SEVENTH-DAY BAPTISTS. Seventh-Day or Saturday worship has been a recurring issue raised by serious students of the Bible. For the Baptists who were in search of ways to recover the primitive church, it was an early theme. Modern Sabbatarians find it practiced throughout Christian history, but its modern history begins in the 1550's with scattered reports of Sabbatarians among the British reformers. As early as 1595, a book was published on the question by Nicholas Bownd.

The first congregation of Seventh-Day Baptists seems to have arisen in 1617 under the leadership of John Trask in London. The church met at Millyard. and it had a checkered existence as a result of continued persecution. A second congregation was added in 1640 at Nutton, Gloucestershire. The congregation included both Sunday and Saturday worship at first, but by the end of the century, the Sabbatarians were in control. In all, some 15 congregations seem to have existed by 1700.

In 1664, a member of the Bell Lane Seventh-Day Baptist Church of London, the Rev. Stephen Mumford, came to America and affiliated with the Newport, Rhode Island, Baptists. He began to raise the Sabbath issue, encountering both support and opposition, the latter from the church elders. On December 23, 1671, he formed the Newport congregation, the first Seventh-Day Baptist Church in America.

Other individuals migrated to America from various Sabbatarian Baptist churches in England. In most cases, they existed as Baptists until driven out as heretics. Churches were formed at Philadelphia (1680's) and Piscutaway, New Jersey (1705). Over the century, growth was slow but steady. The Sabbatarians spread throughout the colonies, south to Georgia.

Among the pietists of Germany, a second strain of Sabbatarianism developed in the wake of the Bible study promoted by Francke and Spener. Among these Sabbatarians was the famous Woman in the Wilderness Commune that settled on Wissahickon Creek near Germantown, Pennsylvania, in 1694. They were among a number of German dissenters who settled in Pennsylvania at the invitation of William Penn. They were early in communication with both Abel Noble, founder of the Philadelphia Church, and the Newport Brethren. The community dissolved in the early 1700's.

In 1720, Conrad Beissel arrived in Philadelphia ready to join the Wissahickon brethren. Only then did he learn of the community's demise, but he was able to meet with a few of its former members. The following year Beissel went west to Lancaster County and founded a settlement. In 1724, he made a tour of the coastal settlements, visiting the Labadist Community at Bohemia Manor and the Rhode Island Sabbatarian Baptists. Shortly after that visit, he became a Sabbatarian himself. Through the influence of the German Baptist Brethren, he became a Baptist in 1725 and became the leader of the newly organized Conestoga Church near his home. Under Beissel and a Brother Lamech, who kept the diary of the congregation, the Sabbatarian issue was raised to prominence.

In 1728, the split in the congregation became effective, and Beissel formed an independent Sabbatarian church. Beissel immediately published an apology, *Mystyrion Anomias,* on the seventh-day Sabbath. Further activities led to the formation in 1732 of the famous Ephrata Cloister, a communal Seventh-Day Baptist group. From it, others would grow.

CHRISTIAN CHURCH (DISCIPLES OF CHRIST) AND RELATED CHURCHES. Many members of the Christian Church (Disciples of Christ) and its sister bodies would be offended by being thought of as "Baptists," but they would also, upon reflection, find many reasons for being considered in a chapter with the Baptist family. The Christian Church began with three ex-Presbyterian ministers in the early 1800's, two of whom belonged to a Baptist association from 1813 to 1830. The Christian Church holds some beliefs and practices in common with Baptists; for example, believers' baptism by immersion, the celebration of the Lord's Supper

as a memorial meal, and the effort to restore New Testament Christianity.

The Christian Church had its origin in the work of three ex-Presbyterian ministers—Thomas and Alexander Campbell and Barton Stone. The Campbells were Scotch-educated Irishmen who had, during their years of training, become heavily influenced by some Presbyterian leaders who had adopted a free-church position. (Free churches oppose state churches and are anti-authoritarian, lay-oriented, non-liturgical, and non-creedal. They practice adult baptism, not infant baptism.) Presbyterian leaders John Glas, Robert Sandeman, and the Haldane brothers had left their respective churches to establish independent congregations. In America, other anti-authoritarian movements were begun by Methodist James O'Kelly and Baptists Abner Jones and Elias Smith.

Thomas Campbell came to America in 1807 and joined the Philadelphia Synod of the Presbyterian Church, but his name was removed from the rolls in May 1807 under charges of heresy. Thomas founded the Christian Association of Washington (Pennsylvania) to give form to the anti-authoritarian protest. At about the same time, Alexander Campbell broke with the Scotch Presbyters and sailed for America.

The Campbells, repulsed by the Presbyterians, began to form congregations, the first of which was the Brush Run Church. In 1813, the Campbells and their followers united with the Red Stone Baptist Association, a union which lasted until 1830. During those seventeen years, the central ideas of the Campbells crystallized. Some of those ideas were in direct conflict with Baptist precepts, a development which led to the dissolution of fellowship in 1830.

The ideas which eventually caused the schism were clustered around the notion of "Restoration"—the striving to restore New Testament Christianity. While restoration, in itself, would not be objectionable to Bible-oriented Christians, the implementation of restoration with specific programs and notions was not so acceptable. For example, in direct contradiction to Baptist teaching, Alexander Campbell began to teach a distinction between grace and law, and the New Testament versus the Old Testament. He wanted to establish the New. Organizationally, the Campbells were also becoming involved in the same struggle that produced the Primitive Baptist Church in the East and South—the rejection of associations and other supracongregational structures with power to legislate for the member churches. Associations, said the Campbells, were for fellowship and edification only. Alexander Campbell, in the pages of the *Christian Baptist,* which he published, also began to speak against the mission boards.

A major thrust of Campbellite thinking was concerned with the unity of the church, a common problem in early nineteenth-century Protestantism. The Campbellites felt that a restoration of the New Testament would include a union of all Christians as an essential aspect of the primitive order. Of course, other church bodies did not agree on what constituted primitive Christianity. Churches with strong supracongregational structures gave many reasons for their system as opposed to a congregational system. The restoration movement became known for its defense of the congregational system.

While he was among the Baptists, the sacraments or ordinances became a major issue for Alexander Campbell, and believers' baptism by immersion replaced the presbyterial form. The Lord's Supper was viewed as a memorial meal; although as it came to be practiced, it has been a point of distinction between the Christian Church and other churches. The Lord's Supper was commemorated each Sunday and was open to all Christians, even those who had not been immersed.

Barton Stone was the third person chiefly credited for the formation of the Christian Church. In the early 1800's, he began to have doubts about both the doctrine and polity of his Presbyterian church. After his ministering at the camp meeting at Cane Ridge, he and four other ministers were censured by the Synod of Kentucky. They withdrew and formed the Springfield Presbytery. The Presbytery was dissolved on June 28, 1809, and in a celebrated document— "The Last Will and Testament of the Springfield Presbytery"—founders set out their protest of Presbyterian polity. Emphasis was on the independence of the local church, the Scriptures as the only authority, and conferences of churches for fellowship and edification only. The group took the name "Christian Church."

In 1830, the Campbells finally departed from the Baptists, and correspondence with Barton Stone, already initiated, was continued. The two groups following the Campbells and Stone consummated a merger in 1832. No sectarian designation was wanted, so several "non-sectarian" names began to be used—Christian Church and Disciples of Christ being the most common.

At the heart of the Disciples' organization was a protest of certain structures which they saw present in Christendom. They protested the division of Christianity, which they called a result of sectarian ideas (as expressed in creeds) and church polity not based on the Bible. They took the "Bible only" as their uniting creed and an ultracongregational polity as the New Testament form. They did not like any structures which either usurped the duties of the local church (as mission societies did) or which exerted power over the church, as some Baptist associations, presbyteries, or bishops did. They at first saw themselves as independent societies functioning as a leaven for the lump of sectarian Christianity.

Between 1830 and 1849, the Disciples experienced rapid growth. Fellowship was expressed in quarterly and annual meetings of regional gatherings. Independent colleges and publishing interests were founded and continued. Then in 1849, the first general convention was held. Its purpose was to further the work of the societies and to represent them. The convention adopted the name "American Christian Missionary Society," and its task centered on church extension, foreign missions, and evangelism. Over the next sixty years, other agencies were formed to handle specific tasks. They reported to the annual convention.

By the turn of the century, the creation of a number of boards and agencies led to a demand for centralization and coordination. A debate was precipitated when the 1910 Convention adopted a resolution to form one general convention of the Disciples, which would unify all organizations, coordinate the collection of money, and make more efficient the administration. Finally in 1917, the International Convention was organized.

Since 1849, there have been several schisms within the restoration movement. These groups retain a large doctrinal consensus and vary only on a few points at issue in their founding and on polity.

CHRISTADELPHIANS. The Christadelphians date to 1844 when Dr. John Thomas, a physician in Richmond, Virginia, began a monthly magazine, *The Herald of the Future Age*. Dr. Thomas, who had immigrated from England in 1832, became associated with Alexander Campbell and the Christian Church, which Campbell and his brother helped form. Over the years, however, Thomas found himself in disagreement on a number of points of doctrine. He came to feel that knowledge and belief of the gospel must precede baptism, and he was rebaptized. A polemic began which led to a complete break in 1844. Groups began to form and each was given the name *ecclesia* (the Greek word for church).

The Christadelphians hold views similar to those of the Campbells, but are non-Trinitarians and resemble the early Unitarians in Christology. The Holy Spirit is God's power which executes his will. Thomas also denied man's natural immortality and believed that man was unconscious from death to the resurrection. At the end time, Christ will appear visibly; all will be resurrected and judged, and the kingdom will be established. The kingdom will be the kingdom of Israel restored in the Holy Land. The wicked will be annihilated. Most important, Thomas taught that baptism by immersion after receiving knowledge of the gospel was essential for salvation. Closed communion is practiced. The Christadelphians do not participate in politics, voting, war; nor do they hold civil office.

The organization of the ecclesias is congregational. Each ecclesia elects local officers, serving brethren. The serving brethren include managing brethren and presiding brethren. The former conduct the temporal affairs and the latter the speaking, teaching, and pastoral work. Groups of ecclesias meet in fraternal gatherings which have no legislative powers.

In the 1890's, a controversy which developed between Robert Roberts and J.J. Andrew, two leading brothers in England, spread among the Christadelphians. The controversy involved the issue of "resurrectional responsibility" and split the Christadelphians into two factions generally termed the Amended and Unamended.

SOURCES—THE BAPTIST FAMILY

BAPTIST ORIGINS AND HISTORY

Armitage, Thomas. *A History of the Baptists*. New York: Bryan Taylor & Co., 1887.

Baptist Advance. Forest Park, IL: Roger Williams Press, 1964.

Benedict, David E. *A General History of the Baptist Denomination in America and Other Parts of the World*. Boston: Lincoln & Edmunds, 1819.

Collinsworth, J. R. *The Pseudo Church Doctrines of Anti-Pedo-Baptists Defined and Refuted.* Kansas City, MO: Hudson-Kimberly Publishing Company, 1892. 496 pp.

The Encyclopedia of Southern Baptists. 3 vols. Nashville: Broadman Press, 1958.

Newman, Albert Henry. *A History of Anti-Pedobaptism.* Philadelphia: American Baptist Publication Society, 1897. 414 pp.

Torbet, Robert G. *A History of the Baptists.* Philadelphia: Judson Press, 1950. 540 pp.

THE BAPTISTS IN AMERICA

Armstrong, O. K., and Marjorie Moore Armstrong. *The Indomitable Baptists.* Garden City, NY: Doubleday, 1967. 392 pp.

Baker, Robert A. *A Baptist Source Book.* Nashville: Broadman Press, 1966. 216 pp.

Boney, William Jerry, and Glenn A. Iglehart. *Baptists & Ecumenism.* Valley Forge, PA: Judson Press, 1980. 177 pp.

Boyd, Jesse L. *A History of Baptists in America 1845.* New York: The American Press, 1957.

Brackney, William H., ed. *Baptist Life and Thought: 1600-1980, A Source Book.* Valley Forge, PA: Judson Press, 1983. 448 pp.

Gaver, Jessyca Russell. *"You Shall Know the Truth."* New York: Lancer Books, 1973. 368 pp.

Stiansen, P. *History of the Norwegian Baptists in America.* Chicago: The Norwegian Baptist Conference of America and the American Baptist Publication Society, 1939. 344 pp.

BAPTIST THOUGHT

Bush, L. Russ, and Tom J. Nettles. *Baptists and the Bible.* Chicago: Moody Press, 1980. 456 pp.

Carson, Alexander. *Baptism, Its Mode and Its Subjects.* Evansville, IN: The Sovreign Grace Book Club, n.d. 237 pp.

Lumpkin, W. L. *Baptist Confessions of Faith.* Chicago: Judson Press, 1959.

Robinson, H. Wheeler. *Baptist Principles.* London: The Carey Kingsgate Press, 1925.

Wallace, O. C. S. *What Baptists Believe.* Nashville: Broadman Press, 1934.

PRIMITIVE BAPTISTS

Hassell, Sylvester. *History of the Church of God.* Middletown, NY: Gilbert Beebe's Sons, 1886. 1008 pp.

Piepkorn, Arthur Carl. "The Primitive Baptists of North America." *Baptist History and Heritage,* 7, No. 1 (January 1972), pp. 33-51.

Rushton, William. *A Defence of Particular Redemption.* Elon College, NC: W. J. Berry, 1971. 48 pp.

BLACK BAPTISTS

Brawley, Edward M., ed. *The Black Baptist Pulpit.* Freeport, NY: Books for Libraries Press, 1971. 300 pp.

GENERAL BAPTISTS

Latch, Ollie. *General Baptists in Church History.* Poplar Bluff, MO: General Baptist Press, 1968. 130 pp.

SEVENTH-DAY BAPTISTS

Seventh Day Baptists in Europe and America. 2 vols. Plainfield, NJ: American Sabbath Tract Society for the Seventh Day Baptist General Conference, 1910.

THE RESTORATION MOVEMENT

Dowling, Enos E. *The Restoration Movement.* Cincinnati Standard Publishing, 1964. 128 pp.

Ford, Harold W. *A History of the Restoration Plea.* Oklahoma City, OK: Semco Color Press, 1952. 217 pp.

Gates, Errett. *The Early Relation and Separation of the Baptists and Disciples.* Chicago: The Christian Century Company, 1904. 124 pp.

Harrell, David Edwin. *The Social Sources of Division in the Disciples of Christ.* Athens, GA: Publishing Systems, Inc., 1973. 458 pp.

Humbert, Royal. *Compend of Alexander Campbell's Theology.* St. Louis: Bethany Press, 1961. 295 pp.

Murch, James DeForest. *Christians Only.* Cincinnati Standard Publishing, 1962. 392 pp.

CHRISTADELPHIANS

A Declaration of the Truth Revealed in the Bible. London: "The Dawn" Book Supply, 1970. 30 pp.

Roberts, Robert. *Christendom Astray.* London: "The Dawn" Book Supply, n.d. 462 pp.

Thomas, John. *A Brief Exposition of the Prophecy of Daniel.* Birmingham, England: "The Christadelphian," 1947. 122 pp.

————. *The Last Days of Judah's Commonwealth and Its Latter Day Restoration.* West Beach Post Office, South Australia: Logos Publications, 1969. 99 pp.

Chapter Ten

THE INDEPENDENT FUNDAMENTALIST FAMILY

Directory listings for the groups belonging to the Independent
Fundamentalist Family may be found in the section beginning on page 411.

The thought world and lifestyle of the churches in the independent fundamentalist family derive from the work of John Nelson Darby. The movement he began in England in the 1820's attempted a more thoroughgoing revival of primitive Christianity than either the Puritan or Wesleyan movements, which had come earlier. Unlike its Puritan and Wesleyan predecessors, the new movement was not content merely to purify or revive the existing church, but sought to recreate the Apostolic church. The prime methods used to recover Apostolic life were intense concentration on the Bible and the adoption of a Biblical lifestyle, theology, and ecclesiology. The key man in the development of this new approach to the Christian life was John Nelson Darby, and the key idea was dispensationalism.

JOHN NELSON DARBY. Probably no Christian thinker in the last two hundred years has so affected the way in which English-speaking Christians view the faith, and yet has received so little recognition of his contribution, as John Nelson Darby. Why this anonymity? One can only guess. It might be that the theological movement that he began was so ahistorical that it was programmed to forget its roots, its originator. It might be that its disestablishment orientation worked for a breakdown of communication that left the second generation without a knowledge of its heritage. In any case, the thinking of a large number of Chrisitans finds its source in the unique Biblical theology that Darby evolved in the nineteenth century. From his ideas have sprung modern-day fundamentalism, the later work of Dwight L. Moody and the Moody Bible Institute in Chicago, the *Scofield Reference Bible,* the *Companion Bible,* and a number of churches that bear names such as Bible Church, Bereans, Grace Gospel, Brethren, Independent Fundamentalist, and Gospel Assembly. Moreover, as a result of Darby's work, a number of Christians in the larger denominations would one day read with relish the works of such men as I.M. Haldeman, William Graham Scroggie, Clarence Larkin, G. Campbell Morgan, James H. Brooks, and William E. Blackstone, to name a few.

Who was Darby? John Nelson Darby was an Angelican priest ordained in 1826, who, through the study of the Scripture, came to reject the idea of a state church. Darby's dissent led him to withdraw from the Anglican Church in 1827 and begin the pursuit of a non-denominational approach to church life, establishing fellowship groups of Christians who had also come out of the existing denominational structure. It was Darby's view that the true church is a temporary structure, set up by God between the cross and the second coming, and composed of a number of individual believers. This concept dominates Darby's thinking.

In 1827, the Albury Conferences on prophetic studies—conferences held at Albury Park, an estate near London—caused Darby to think about eschatology. The term "eschatology" refers to the end time and includes consideration of death, heaven and hell, judgment, the second coming of Christ, and the millennium (Christ's reign on earth for a thousand years). Darby created a new system of thought called dispensationalism. Dispensationalism is a view of the Bible as a history of God's dealing with man in terms of various periods (dispensations) of history. The church had often seen history, on a theological or numerological basis, as divided into three or seven periods. But it was Darby who began a division of the Biblical story based on God's method of dealing with his people. Darby's system had seven basic dispensations; one period, Israel's, was divided into three subperiods. The system was roughly as follows:

1. (Paradisaical state) to the flood
2. Noah—government
3. Abraham—calling and election
4. Israel
   a. Under the law—Moses
   b. Under the priesthood
   c. Under the kings—Saul
5. Gentiles (begins with Nebuchadnezzar)
6. The Spirit (the present?)
7. The fullness of time

While Darby was fairly clear about the early dispensations, his discussion of the present and future is vague and at times seemingly contradictory. To ease the confusion, Darby's theological successors (particularly C. I. Scofield and H. A. Ironside) refined his system into what has become the basis for most modern discussion of dispensational schemes. Scofield's seven dispensations are:

1. Innocence—from creation to the fall of Adam
2. Conscience—from the fall to the flood
3. Government—from Noah to Abraham
4. Promise—from Abraham to Moses
5. Law—from Moses to Jesus
6. Grace—from the cross to the second coming
7. Personal reign of Christ—from the second coming to and includung eternity

Dispensational schemes solve several basic Biblical problems. They clear up some of the baffling Biblical contradictions by shifting contradictory passages to different dispensations. For example, when one reads all of the passages concerning the end of time and the events surrounding the second coming of Christ, one is left confused as to what will happen. Passages in Thessalonians, the Book of Revelation, and Matthew offer seemingly contradictory pictures of the future which the dispensationalists were able to reconcile by their rather complex outline of future events. The dispensationalists were also able to reconcile the obvious difference between the small New Testament church and the large ecclesiastical organizations by which they were surrounded. The true church (i.e., the church of the dispensationalists) was ever the small body of the faithful called out from Babylon (i.e., large religious organizations). Finally, the dispensationalists offered a rationale for change. Each dispensation was initiated by a renewed action of God toward his people, by which God tries to reach his chosen ones. The failure of each successive action leads inevitably to the cross, said the dispensationalists. And the failure of the New Testament church to realize the promises given to it must lead inevitably to a final dispensation in which Christ is acknowledged as the universal ruler.

Second only to dispensationalism as a key idea of Darby is his ecclesiology. Darby had early come to reject "denominated," primarily state-church, Christianity, and he tackled the problem of the "Nature and Unity of the Church of Christ" in his first pamphlet in 1828. He attacked as the enemy of the work of the Holy Spirit any "who seeks the interests of any particular denomination." No formal union of outward-professing bodies is desirable. Unity is to be found in "the Unity of the Spirit and can only be in the things of the Spirit, and therefore can only be perfected in spiritual persons ... Believers know that all who are born of the Spirit have substantial unity of mind, so as to know each other, and love each other as brethren." Churches influenced by Darby's ecclesiology generally have a statement of belief in the spiritual unity of believers in Jesus Christ.

Darby established assemblies of like-minded believers tied together by their consensus and their fellowship. They accepted no authority except the "charismatic" leadership of Darby and other talented teachers who soon arose in their midst. There were no bishops or overseers.

The gospel assembly became the central building block among Darby's followers and imitators. The assembly was a local gathering of like-minded Christians. Each person was both layman and minister, and each assembly was independent and tied to the other assemblies only by the bonds of doctrinal consensus and fellowship.

No name for the group was accepted, although Biblical designations such as Church of God and, most popularly, "Brethren," were often used. The lack of designation has been a characteristic that has persisted and has often made the Brethren an "invisible" part of the on-going religious life of any community in which they reside. Few groups of Brethren publish their membership statistics.

While they had no formal ministry, the Brethren did display an intense evangelical zeal and began to develop structures that could be used without infringing on the autonomy of the assembly. First, there emerged in the assemblies gifted teachers and evangelists who, by the consent of the assembly, taught the Bible and preached the gospel. The majority of the assembly, of course, had responsibilities in reaching the lost with the gospel. The more talented of the teachers and evangelists began to travel and speak at neighboring assemblies, and, by such informal means, a "professional" ministry developed.

A major new form that evolved as an expression of the Biblical priority in the life of the Brethren was the Bible reading. This sermon-like presentation usually involved the tracing of a key word or idea, such as "creation" or "church," through a series of otherwise disconnected passages, with the speaker commenting on each passage briefly. The Bible reading evolved out of the Reading Meeting of the British Brethren, where students would gather in a home and together search the Scripture.

A very active publishing ministry initiated with the voluminous writings of Darby. Pamphlets and tracts were soon joined by books and periodicals. Last to arise were Brethren-owned printing and publishing houses. These latter were owned by some prominent Brethren who published as a service to the brotherhood, but, in matters of business, functioned as entrepreneurs. As the movement grew and schisms developed, the publishers became the spokesmen for different factions that could be distinguished, primarily, by the literature they accepted as "orthodox." Publishers, in the absence of ministerial associations and national conventions, have become the major molders of opinion in the otherwise informally organized assemblies.

The assemblies, as a rule, reject any doctrinal formulation or creed, though Darby emphasized that unity of mind was an essential feature of the Church of God. There was, and is, informally, however, a very rigid orthodoxy and doctrinal stand, particularly about the nature of the church. Almost all of the schisms within the Darbyite movement were articulated as doctrinal disputes and appeared as a breakdown of doctrinal consensus. Of course, a major disagreement concerns the amount of latitude in belief that is possible without destroying the unity of mind.

Darby accepted the orthodox Protestantism of the Reformation on the central issues of belief in God, the Trinity, the divinity of Christ, the person and work of the Holy Spirit, the Bible as the Word of God, and the necessity of man's repentance, forgiveness, and salvation. Where Darby differed from the Protestants of the Reformation was in the issues of ecclesiology and eschatology.

While never developing an expectancy of Christ's imminent return to the degree that the Adventists did, the Brethren were in the forefront of nineteenth-century emphasis on the approaching end of the age, and they promoted speculative interpretation of Scriptural statements on the nature and order of eschatological events. Their speculations took the form of prophecy. Prominent in the dispensational scheme is a particular form of eschatology, usually termed premillennialism.

It was Darby's belief that people could be divided, for eschatological purposes, into three groups—the Jews, the Church of God (Christians), and the Gentiles (all non-Christians who were not Jews). The first event in the eschatological framework is the invisible coming of Christ to gather his saints, both living and dead, and take them away as described in Paul's First Epistle to the Thessalonians (4:13-18). This event is called the "secret rapture" of the saints. The rapture is the signal of God's rejection of the Gentiles, particularly nominal Christians; but after the rapture, his work is begun among the Jews, who convert and become preachers of Christianity to the lost world for seven years during which Satan is unleashing his most terrible woes. This seven-year period is called the tribulation (Rev. 7:14). At the end of the tribulation period, Christ and his army will come to do battle with Satan and his allies. After Christ's victory, a thousand years (the millennium) of peace will ensue. The remnant who come to Christ during the tribulation shall live on earth while the raptured saints reign with God in heavenly glory.

At the end of the millennium occurs the judgment of the Great White Throne. Satan, bound for the millennium, is loosed for a last bit of activity before his destruction. Finally, the wicked dead (non-Christians) are resurrected and judged, and the saints are given their eternal reward. This was a relatively new eschatological schema, but as it grew in popularity along with the corollary dispensational view of history, it set the issues of debate for other Bible students and conservative Christians. The rapture itself was the main point of attack by Darby's opponents. It involved an "invisible return," or secret rapture, by Christ seven years before the visible second coming.

THE DEVELOPING MOVEMENT. Darby's theology began to influence a large number of Bible students. First, such men as Charles H. Mackintosh (usually designated as C.H.M.), William Trotter, and William Kelly joined Darby's movement, and began to write and expound Darby's system. As early as 1859, Darby visited Canada, with other visits in 1864 and 1866. In 1870, 1872-73, and 1874, he visited most of the major United States cities. In 1872, Moody discovered the Brethren, who spent several days introducing Moody to dispensational thought. As Darby and his associates toured America, such leading clergy as A.J. Gordon and J.H. Brooks opened both their minds and their pulpits to the new truth. As a result of the massive body of literature this movement created, along with its non-denominational character and association with Moody, a large segment of conservative Christianity accepted it. In the 1880's and 1890's, the thought became institutionalized in many Bible colleges, the most famous of which was Moody Bible Institute in Chicago. It should be noted that while Darby's theology became popular, many people who accepted it never accepted the ecclesiology nor became Brethren, a fact that often gave Darby and his followers moments of consternation.

Two books appeared which greatly increased the popularity of Darbyism. The first was *Jesus Is Coming* by William E. Blackstone. This eschatologically oriented book appeared in 1878 and was an immediate success. Though its topic was the second coming, its treatment was thoroughly dispensational. The book after a century is still in print. The second book was the *Scofield Reference Bible*. C.I. Scofield was a St. Louis lawyer converted under Moody's preaching. Later, he moved to Dallas and became a Congregational minister. His first dispensational work appeared in 1888, *Rightly Dividing the Word of Truth*, which is also still in print. In the 1890's Scofield set up a Bible study course used at many of the Bible colleges, including Moody. In 1902, he commenced work on the reference Bible which appeared in 1909. It immediately became the cardinal work in the movement and has become the standard by which to judge the dispensational movement. In 1967, a new *Scofield Reference Bible*, edited by a committee of prominent dispensationalists and with minor additions to Scofield's notes in the light of later research, appeared.

Widespread use of the *Scofield Reference Bible* has led to growth in orthodox dispensationalism, and the book has become the source from which leaders in the movement have deviated to launch new teaching. For instance, Moody Biblical Institute graduate J.C. O'Hair developed the Grace Gospel movement, which rejects water baptism.

Following Scofield's pattern have been a large number of conservative ministers, both denominational and independent. For many years, I.M. Haldeman, pastor of the First Baptist Church of New York City, wrote on dispensationalism. His most significant book in this vein is *A Dispensational Key to the Holy Scriptures*, which was published in 1915. Manifesting the way dispensational teaching readily adapts itself to pictorial presentations, two authors have had great success specializing in publishing diagramic texts of dispensationalism. Clarence Larkin's *Dispensational Truth* and Ray O. Brown's *Truth on Canvas* have become very popular.

In England, two scholars contemporaneous with Scofield produced a major deviation in the Darbyite manner of thinking. They were Ethelbert W. Bullinger and Charles Welch. What Scofield called the dispensation of grace begins with the cross, the resurrection, and Pentecost, and goes to the second coming of Christ. Bullinger divided this period into two dispensations, so that one dispensation covers the era of the Apostolic church. This added dispensation begins with Pentecost and closes with the end of the ministry of the apostles and Paul. In the Bible, this era traces the church from Acts 2 to Acts 28:25-28, and was to be considered separate from the body of Christ mentioned in Colossians and Ephesians. Also, Bullinger identified the bride of Christ in Revelation as being entirely a Jewish remnant church to be built at the end, and not at all the body of Christ. Bullinger, through his popular writings, and Welch, in his continuance of Bullinger's thought, have occasioned discussion and some acceptance of their teachings. A major debate among dispensationalists, producing the Grace Gospel movement discussed below, concerns one's views toward Bullinger's thought. In America, Bullinger's teachings have taken hold and produced several groups. A spin-off of Bullingerism is the work of A.E. Knoch, discussed below.

During the twentieth century, followers of Darby's teaching in the Scofield vein remained a conservative wing in the major churches. However, during the 1920's, as a result of the heated fundamentalist-modernist controversy, groups which were dispensational in their stance began to form. This new emergence of dispensational-thinking, independent bodies, along with the continued splintering of the older bodies, has left no fewer than thirty-nine groups growing out of Darby's teaching.

PLYMOUTH BRETHREN. The Plymouth Brethren is the group originally founded by John Nelson Darby and his associates. The meeting at Plymouth, England, became the most prominent assembly in the movement and, as the group refused to be denominated, it became known as the Brethren from Plymouth. Within the growing movement, a separation began to appear in the 1840's. Benjamin W. Newton and Darby began to differ on eschatology and ecclesiology. Newton denied Darby's idea of the saints' rapture, and emphasized the autonomy of the local assembly as opposed to the unity of the whole movement. Darby's attack on Newton was characterized as violent and vindictive. Division at Plymouth was followed by accusations against Newton for holding a heretical Christology. The assembly at Bethesda, formerly a Baptist congregation, had been received into the Brethren as a group. In 1848, the Bethesda congregation received some of the Newton people at the Lord's Supper. The ensuing controversy led to the permanent division of the movement into the "Open" Brethren and the "Exclusive" Brethren.

The basic division concerns the doctrine of separation. The Exclusive Brethren believe in receiving no one at the Lord's table who is not a true Christian in the fullest sense, including being a member of a fully separated assembly (an assembly of Brethren who associate only with Brethren and not with persons from other churches). The Open Brethren, on the other hand, receive all believed to be true Christians (Brethren), even if other members of their church might hold allegedly false doctrine. The Exclusive Brethren have established several "circles of fellowship", that is, groups of mutually approved assemblies in which the decision of one assembly is binding on all.

Because the Brethren refuse to accept denominational labels, the United States Bureau of the Census chose to designate them with Roman numerals. This mode of reference was followed by Elmer T. Clark in *The Small Sects in America* and by Frank S. Mead in *The Handbook of Denominations in the United States.* (This numerical system of reference is noted for the entries in the directory section of this encyclopedia.)

FUNDAMENTALISM. The arrival of fundamentalism as a movement within American Christianity is usually dated from 1910 and the publication of a series of booklets entitled *The Fundamentals: A Testimony of Truth.* The booklets, printed by two wealthy Presbyterians, Los Angeles oilmen Lyman and Milton Stewart, were distributed freely and were the textbooks for what in the 1920's became the fundamentalist-modernist controversy. Fundamentalism so defined is usually viewed as a reaction to modernism, asserting traditional standards against the new theology and its search for scientific compatibility. While there is much truth in that definition, it is limited. It misses the essentially affirmative nature of fundamentalism and the century-old movement, of which early twentieth-century fundamentalism is but one passing phase.

Fundamentalism was, at its best, an affirmative assertion of certain ideas concerning Bible truth. At its beginning, it was a discovery by clergy and laymen of American Protestant churches of the dispensational theology of John Nelson Darby, discussed early in this chapter. Conservative and evangelical, fundamentalism became a rallying point for church leaders and, during the late nineteenth century, was one of the major thrusts of Christianity in America. Fundamentalism was no more reactionary than neo-orthodoxy or other movements centered upon what are seen to be traditional Christian affirmations.

In the mid-nineteenth century, the ideas of William Miller were prominent, in the form of a public consciousness of the doctrine of the second coming of Christ and the dispensational theology of Darby, with its emphasis upon the premillennial literal return of Jesus. In America, Darby found that people accepted his ideas without leaving their own church to join the Brethren. Outstanding Christian leaders became vocal exponents of dispensational theology. Possibly none was as effective as effective as evangelist Dwight L. Moody, who had been deeply affected by Brethren evangelist Harry Moorhouse. Leading ministers—Adoniram J. Gordon, Arthur T. Pierson, William G. Moorehead, and James H. Brooks—were all changed by Brethren thinking.

THE INDEPENDENT FUNDAMENTALIST FAMILY. In 1869, a group of ministers associated with a millennial periodical, *Waymarks in the Wilderness,* held the first of what became the Believers Meeting for Bible Study. The ministers met to promote belief in the "doctrine of the verbal inspiration of the Bible, the personality of the Holy Spirit, the atonement of (Christ's) sacrifice, the priesthood of Christ, the two natures in the believer, and the personal imminent return of our Lord from heaven." In 1883, the annual meetings were moved to Niagara-on-the-Lake, Ontario, and thus became known as the "Niagara Conference on Prophecy."

Part of the aim of the Niagara Conference was to manifest the primitive idea of the ecclesia, the church. Thus the conference was the ministers' means of forming what Darby called the church, a gathering of believers free of denominational systems. However, the ministers did not leave their mainline denominations. They gathered for the informal closeness and doctrinal purity that Darby said should characterize the church. They used the "Bible reading" as developed by the Brethren, and they accepted Darby's ideas on dispensationalism and his eschatology.

In 1890, a definitive step for the whole course of fundamentalism occurred. The Niagara Conference adopted a credal statement. The fourteen-point statement was highly determinative of the movement's future course and set its priorities. The premillennial return of Christ is asserted as the answer to the impossibility of converting the world in this dispensation. The conference accepted the premillennialist's idea that the world is becoming less Christian, with evolution not bringing real human progress, thus necessitating Christ's direct intervention before the millennium. The conference asserted traditional beliefs that the Bible (in its original text) is inerrant, the Scriptures are Christ-centered, and all of the books of the Bible are equally inspired. Most important, a Calvinist theological emphasis on human depravity and salvation by the blood of Christ was forcefully detailed in six articles. As the movement to support the credal statement developed, it drew the majority of its strength from churches of the Reformed heritage (Baptist, Presbyterian, Reformed, and Congregational). In the 1920's, fundamentalism had its major battle ground in the Baptist and Presbyterian churches. Fundamentalists denied the second blessing (a major idea of the holiness movement—the second blessing is a personal religious experience after which the believer is holy for life), and two ideas of the Adventists—soul-sleep and annihilationism. Soul-sleep is the idea that the soul exists in an unconscious state from death to the resurrection of the body. Annihilationism means the belief that the wicked are destroyed instead of existing in eternal torment. While some Methodists and some Adventists would, in the 1920's, agree on the "five fundamentals," the Methodists and Adventists were not prominent in the fundamentalist movement.

The "five fundamentals" are the beliefs in the inspiration of the Bible, the depravity of man, redemption through Christ's blood, the true church as a body composed of all believers, and the coming of Jesus to establish his reign. These five beliefs are derived from but not inclusive of the fourteen points of the credal statement adopted by the Niagara Conference.

The group consciousness of the leaders of the Niagara Conference was solidified in the several Bible institutes which were founded in the late nineteenth century. The most influential of these was the Moody Bible Institute in Chicago, but others, including the Bible Institute of Los Angeles (BIOLA), Philadelphia Bible Institute, the Toronto Bible Training School, and the Northwestern Bible Training School in Minneapolis, contributed to the cause. These schools institutionalized fundamentalism and, more important, helped train its future leaders.

In the early years of the twentieth century, the most prominent of the fundamentalist leaders was Arno E. Gaebelein, a former Methodist who left the church after accepting the dispensational theology. He began a magazine, *Our Hope*, in 1899. He helped finance the work on the *Scofield Reference Bible*, the single most influential source of Darby's theology in the modern era.

New life flowed into the movement with the publication of *The Fundamentals* in 1910, and Darbyite fundamentalism came into direct conflict with emerging liberalism in the decade before World War I. *The Fundamentals* followed the lead of the Niagara Creed in asserting the verbal inerrancy of Scripture, the Calvinist doctrine of human depravity, and the imminent second coming. As modernist thinking grew, polemic led to polarization within American Protestantism, and polarization was followed by the formation of new denominations. The modernist thinking was highlighted by a theology that accepted the theory of evolution and by higher Biblical criticism, the study of the Bible in the light of the findings of secular historians and archeologists.

The new denominations occasioned by the fundamentalist controversy were of two kinds. First, from the several large Protestant bodies arose "fundamentalist" churches which differed only from their parent bodies by acceptance of a fundamentalist mindset with which to interpret the parent bodies' own doctrinal statements. Second, there emerged new religious bodies that encompassed the total fundamentalist thrust and were the truly American form of the Plymouth Brethren tradition discussed earlier in this chapter. These have been referred to as the "undenominated" churches, since they were organized in loose fellowships. They had a dispensational theology with the Reformed emphasis of Niagara, and became the ecclesiastical products of the Bible Institutes.

Fundamentalism of both kinds has become split into essentially two parties. One group emphasizes separation from all apostasy and from particular forms of evil such as communism, the National Council of Churches, and organizations which compromise the faith. A second group, a later development, is more positive and emphasizes its conservative theology. Neo-evangelicalism is the name generally associated with this new movement, which has tried to be honest with natural science, conversant on philosophy and theology, and socially concerned.

The separatists have been associated with the American Council of Christian Churches (ACCC) and the ministry of Dr. Carl McIntire, whose organ of expression has been the *Christian Beacon*. McIntire is the head of the Bible Presbyterian Church. Membership in the ACCC is made up largely of small separatist bodies. The more inclusive approach is advocated by the National Association of Evangelicals (NAE). It includes a wide range of bodies which accept its minimal statement of faith. The NAE accepts not only church bodies, but also conferences and local churches, or groups not otherwise affiliated. The independent magazine, *Christianity Today*, is the most important periodical of neo-evangelicalism, though the NAE has its own organ, *United Evangelical Action*.

THE GRACE GOSPEL MOVEMENT. As John Nelson Darby's dispensational theology gained acceptance in evangelical circles, it was inevitable that variations would arise. One such variation is attributed to Anglican Ethelbert William Bullinger, who published a new outline of dispensational history in his book *How to Enjoy the Bible*. His seven dispensations are outlined in a symmetrical manner:

A. The Edenic State (Innocence)
  B. Mankind as a whole (Patriarchial)
    C. Israel (under Law)
      D. The Church of God. The Secret.
        The Dispensation of Grace
    C. Israel (Judicial)
  B. Mankind as a whole (Millennial)
A. The Eternal State (Glory)

Evident in much of Bullinger's writings is a desire for symmetry and mathematical order, which influenced greatly his interpretation of the Scriptures. For Bullinger, the Edenic State went from creation to the fall; the patriarchal dispensation went from the fall to Moses; the dispensation of Israel under the law went from Moses through Pentecost to the beginning of Paul's ministry and therefore included the Apostolic church. The fourth dispensation is the present. It is the time of the church of God, the Christian church as influenced by the ministry of Paul and therefore directed not to the Jews but to the Gentiles. Bullinger called this period "the secret" because to Paul was revealed the secret hidden from the ages, the secret of God's grace replacing the law and reaching beyond the Jews to the Gentiles (Ephesians 3:1-6). For Bullinger, the next dispensation is a judgment period for the Jews in which the Jews will be judged according to their own law, not according to the grace of Christianity. The judgment period occurs before the tribulation and is based on Jeremiah 30. The sixth dispensation includes the tribulation and millennium, as discussed early in this chapter with the material on John Nelson Darby, who originated dispensationalism. Bullinger's seventh dispensation is eternity.

The crucial item in Bullinger's work had to do with his interpretation of the transition from the third to the fourth dispensation. Bullinger sees in the Gospels, Acts, and New Testament Epistles a development. The Gospels belong to the third dispensation and have one baptism, John's water baptism. In Acts and the early Pauline epistles, there are two baptisms—John's and the baptism of the Spirit. In the later Pauline epistles, representing the start of the fourth dispensation, there is only one—Spirit baptism (Ephesians 4:5—"There is one Lord, one faith, one baptism"). The significance of so dividing Scripture is to say that, in the church age, water baptism has no place.

Strongly influenced by Bullinger was Charles H. Welch, who, in 1929, began *The Berean Expositor* in London and authored several books. As "Ultradispensationalism" developed, a strict differentiation was made between the church of Acts and the body of Christ which had its beginning with Paul's pronouncements in Acts 28:25-28, telling the church to direct its efforts to the Gentiles instead of to the Jews. The Gospels are purely Israelitish. With Pentecost, the church was unaugurated; its distinctives were the sign-gifts (miracles), water baptism, and the Lord's Supper. However, these ceased with the beginning of the body of Christ with its one baptism. Bullinger and Welch also taught that the body of Christ was distinct from the bride of Christ, which was identified with a remnant of Israel. The Churches of Asia in Revelation 2:3 are seen as future Jewish churches that will become Christian.

Among the beliefs of Bullinger and Welch, for which they were most criticized by fundamentalists, were *annihilationism*, or the belief that the wicked are destroyed instead of existing in eternal torment; *soul-sleep*, or the idea that the soul exists in an unconscious state from death to the resurrection of the body; and the belief that the Lord's Supper is not to be observed in the post-Acts church. There is some dispute concerning whether or not Bullinger actually taught annihilation for the wicked, but Welch certainly did.

In the 1920's, the views of Bullinger began to spread in America. The first advocates were Pastor J. C. O'Hair, a graduate of Moody Bible Institute in Chicago and minister of the North Shore Church in Chicago, and Dr. Harry Bultema of the Berean Church in Muskegon, Michigan. O'Hair, a member of the Independent Fundamental Churches of America and a prolific writer on dispensationalism, published many pamphlets and Bible studies and was active in conferences and a radio ministry. He frequently wrote and spoke of the "blunder of the church," by which he meant the confusion of the hope, calling, and program of Israel with the hope, calling, and program of the church. O'Hair's discussion of Israel includes the early Apostolic church, which existed within the Jewish community. O'Hair did not want Christians to confuse that church with the church as influenced by Paul's later epistles and therefore directed to the Gentiles in a much broader program than the Apostolic church which was directed to Jews. The church influenced by Paul's later epistles is the church of the present, the church existing in the dispensation of grace. Thus O'Hair's teaching came to be called the Grace Gospel position.

During the 1930's there was an increase in the number of ministers and Bible churches which held the Grace Gospel position. Early centers developed in Milwaukee, Paterson (New Jersey), St. Louis, Grand Rapids, Holland (Michigan), Indianapolis, and Evansville (Indiana).

Welch made his first visit to Canada in 1927 and, in 1955, made a trip both to Canada and the United States. After World War II, a following which accepted annihilationism and did not practice the Lord's Supper (as did O'Hair) developed around Welch.

SOURCES—THE INDEPENDENT FUNDAMENTALIST FAMILY

Dispensationalism

Bass, Clarence B. *Backgrounds to Dispensationalism*. Grand Rapids, MI: Baker Book House, 1960. 184 pp.

Bowman, John Wick. "Dispensationalism." *Interpretation*, 10, No. 2 (April 1956), pp. 170-87.

Brown, Roy L. *Truth on Canvas*. Waterloo, IA: The Cedar Book Fund, 1939. 240 pp.

Ehlert, Arnold D., comp. *A Bibliographic History of Dispensationalism*. Grand Rapids, MI: Baker Book House, 1965. 110 pp.

Huebner, R. A. *The Truth of the Pre-Tribulation Rapture Recovered*. Morganville, NJ: Present Truth Publishers, 1973. 81 pp.

Humberd, R. I. *The Dispensations*. Flora, IN: Christian Book Depot, n.d. 116 pp.

Kraus, C. Norman. *Dispensationalism in America: Its Rise and Development*. Richmond: John Knox Press, 1958.

Larkin, Clarence. *Dispensational Truth.* Philadelphia: Rev. Clarence Larkin Est., 1920. 176 pp.

MacPherson, Dave. *The Unbelievable Pre-Trib Origin.* Kansas City, MO: Heart of America Bible Society, 1973. 123 pp.

Scofield, C. I. *Rightly Dividing the Word of Truth.* Westwood, NJ: Fleming H. Revell, 1896.

————. *Scofield Bible Correspondence Course.* 4 vols. Chicago: Moody Bible Institute, 1960.

Sisco, Paul E. *Scofield or the Scriptures.* Alden, NY: The Author, n.d. 65 pp.

Zens, Jon. *Dispensationalism: A Reformed Inquiry into Its Leading Figures and Features.* Phillipsburg, NJ: Presbyterian and Reformed Publishing Co., 1980. 57 pp.

THE PLYMOUTH BRETHREN AND JOHN NELSON DARBY

Coad, Roy. *A History of the Brethren Movement.* Exeter: The Paternoster Press, 1968. 336 pp.

Darby, John Nelson. *The Collected Writings.* 35 vols. Oak Park, IL: Bible Truth Publishers, 1971.

Ehlert, Arnold D. *Brethren Writers.* Grand Rapids, MI: Baker Book House, 1965.

Miller, Andrew. *"The Brethren" (Commonly So-called).* Kowloon, Hong Kong: Christian Book Room, n.d. 213 pp.

Neatby, William Blair. *A History of the Plymouth Brethren.* London: Hodder and Stoughton, 1901.

Noel, Napoleon. *The History of the Brethren.* 2 vols. Denver: W. F. Knapp, 1934.

Pickering, Hy. *Chief Men Among the Brethren.* London: Pickering & Inglis, 1918. 223 pp.

Turner, W. G. *John Nelson Darby.* London: C. A. Hammond, 1944. 88 pp.

FUNDAMENTALISM

Barr, James. *Fundamentalism.* Philadelphia: Westminster Press, 1978. 379 pp.

Blackstone, William E. *Jesus Is Coming.* New York: Fleming H. Revell, 1908. 252 pp.

Cole, Stewart G. *The History of Fundamentalism.* New York: Richard R. Smith, 1931. 360 pp.

Cook, David C. *Memoirs.* Elgin, IL: David C. Cook Publishing Company, 1929. 188 pp.

Curtis, Richard C. *They Called Him Mister Moody.* Garden City, NY: Doubleday, 1962. 378 pp.

Deremer, Bernard. *Moody Biblical Institute, A Pictorial History.* Chicago: Moody Press, 1960. 128 pp.

Dollar, George W. *A History of Fundamentalism in America.* Greenville, SC: Bob Jones University Press, 1973. 411 pp.

English, E. Schuyler. *H. A. Ironside, Ordained of the Lord.* Oakland, CA: Western Book and Tract Company, 1946. 276 pp.

Falwell, Jerry. *The Fundamentalist Phenomenon.* Garden City, NY: Doubleday, 1981. 269 pp.

Furniss, Norman F. *The Fundamentalist Controversy, 1918-1931.* New Haven: Yale University Press, 1954.

Gaebelein, Arno Clemens. *The Conflict of the Ages.* New York: Publication Office "Our Hope," 1933. 171 pp.

Haldeman, I. M. *The Coming of Christ Both Pre-millennial and Imminent.* New York: Charles C. Cook, 1906. 325 pp.

Russell, C. Allyn. *Voices of American Fundamentalism.* Philadelphia: Westminster Press, 1976. 304 pp.

Sandeen, Ernest R. *The Roots of Fundamentalism.* Chicago: University of Chicago Press, 1970.

Two Christian Laymen. *The Fundamentals.* 8 vols. Chicago: Testimony Publishing Co., n.d.

Weber, Timothy P. *Living in the Shadow of the Second Coming.* New York: Oxford University Press, 1979. 232 pp.

GRACE GOSPEL MOVEMENT

Bullinger, E. W. *The Foundations of Dispensational Truth.* London: Lamp Press, 1959. 287 pp.

————. *Selected Writings.* London: Lamp Press, 1960. 296 pp.

Hoste, William. *Bullingerism or Ultra-Dispensationalism Exposed.* Fort Dodge, IA: n.d. 32 pp.

Ironside, Harold A. *Wrongly Dividing the Word of Truth.* Neptune, NJ: Loizeaux Brothers, n.d. 66 pp.

O'Hair, J.C. *Bible Messages of Grace and Glory.* Chicago: The Author, n.d. 17 pp.

————. *The Great Blunder of the Church.* Chicago: The Author, n.d. 70 pp.

Stewart, Alex. H. *Bullingerism Exposed.* New York: Loizeaux Brothers, n.d. 15 pp.

Chapter Eleven

THE ADVENTIST FAMILY

Directory listings for the groups belonging to the Adventist Family may be
found in the section beginning on page 431.

Since the beginning of Christianity, various groups have arisen sporadically to preach a type of faith that has been called apocalyptic, chiliastic, or millennial. The movements have been characterized by the expectation of the immediate return of Christ to bring a final end to "this evil order" and replace it with a new world of supreme happiness and goodness. At every turning point in the history of Christianity, people supporting such movements appeared, sometimes within the mainstream of church activities as disturbers of accepted patterns of life, and sometimes at the outer edge of church activities as critics and reformers. Always their presence is felt because they promote an idea which orthodox Christians have said to be part of the faith.

APOCALYPTICISM IN HISTORY. Christianity inherited its bent toward apocalypticism from its Jewish forefathers. Both the book of Daniel in the Old Testament and the apocryphal works of Jewish apocalypticism, such as the Assumption of Moses and the Books of Enoch, were part of the thought-world in which early Christians lived. For later generations, however, the book of Daniel was to be the important text. Penned in the second century B.C., Daniel purports to be a product of the sixth century B.C. The first half of the book tells the story of Daniel and some friends of his who were faithful to God while living under foreign political control. The last half details some visions of future history, stretching from sixth century Babylon to the reign of Antiochus Epiphanes in the second century. These visions, in and of themselves apocalyptic, provided the material from which future apocalyptics would draw.

Apocalypticism was part of the lifestyle of the early church. Many expected the imminent return of Jesus to finish what was begun on Calvary. The signposts of this belief are found in such Biblical passages as Mark 13, Matthew 24, I Thessalonians 4:13-18, and, preeminently, in the vision of John the Revelator. Just as Daniel emerged as the central piece of Jewish apocalypticism, so Revelation soon pushed aside other Christian apocalypses and became the one book of the vast literature to be canonized (included in the Bible).

Revelation purports to be the ecstatic vision of "John," an official in the Church of Asia Minor (now Turkey). His vision has a special message for each of seven churches, and contains a lengthy scenario of the future course of history, which centers on the church. The vision culminates with a picture of the end of time and the establishment of the kingdom of God in its totality.

A vast amount of work has been done by scholars describing the nature of apocalyptic literature, with a surprising amount of unanimity in their understanding. The apocalyptist has a particular view of time and history, evil, God's relation to the world, the groups of which he is a part, and the worth of man's activity in the world.

The apocalyptist sees history and time as quite lineal. History, begun at some point in the distant past, has continued on a more or less steady course to the present. The present is just short of the climax of the whole scheme of time. The climax will be a great supernatural happening which will destroy the present system and replace it with a new and better divine system.

The cosmic struggle of good and evil, of God and the devil, determines the course of history, and good is losing. The believer feels this loss on a quite personal level as persecution, deprivation, or moral indignation. But while evil seems to be progressing to an ultimate victory, it will be stopped short by the intervention of God, who will completely eliminate its power in the world.

God has a very close and personal relationship to the world. He began the course of history and has never ceased to intervene at various points. He caused the formation of a "remnant" of his people to witness to him. And he will step in to crush the evil forces before they completely conquer the good.

The course of history is personalized and internalized by the apocalyptist. He sees history as made for and centering upon himself and his ingroup. His group has been chosen; although they are on the bottom of the social ladder now, they will be on top as soon as God acts. This reversal of position will take place in the very near future.

The nearness of the end of this age puts a new perspective on man's activity in the world. As the date for the end closes in upon man, the value of "normal" activity decreases. Attention might be given to such Biblical admonitions as,

"For the future, men who have wives should live as though they had none, and those that mourn as though they did not, and those who are glad as though they were not glad, and those who buy as though they did not own a thing, ... For the outward order of things is passing away." (I Cor. 7:29-31). Normal activity is now replaced with a stepped-up campaign to spread the message of the coming cataclysm, for "the gospel must first be published among all nations." Not always, but quite often, an intense moral imperative is associated with the end-time. This phenomenon is seen as apocalyptists combine with the reformers who look to moral and social reform as a means to hold back an impending doom.

This type of moral apocalypticism is seen most pointedly in men such as Jeremiah, Thomas Müntzer, and George Storrs.

The Apostle Paul, himself, had to deal with Christians who fell away from the apocalyptic stance of the early church. In his letter to the Thessalonians he had to answer those who were questioning why so many had died before Christ returned. But as the church grew, what for Paul was a minor incident became for the church a major problem leading it to redefine its faith. As the distance between the believers and Calvary grew, the sensibleness of an apocalyptic lifestyle diminished. So during the second, third, and fourth centuries, a battle raged—a theological battle, but much more, a battle over the whole approach and stance of the church toward the world.

Symbolic of this fight is the issue of the canonization of the book of Revelation. During the second century, this visionary masterpiece circulated from Asia Minor to Antioch and Rome. It found its earliest exponent in Justin Martyr, and about the year 200, the Muratonian Canon lists Revelation as Scripture. Irenaeus in Gaul and Tertullian in North Africa accepted and used Revelation in their writings.

One of the first millennial sects, the Montanists, picked up the apocalyptic stance and made it a central part of its message. Montanus tried to gather in his movement some of the spiritual, prophetic, and visionary attributes of the early church, in what was considered by many an heretical stance. The movement spread from Phrygia and eventually claimed Tertullian as an adherent in North Africa.

The first works rejecting Revelation as Scriptural and of Apostolic authorship were produced by authors who were anti-Montanists. So effective were these writings that, about 215 A.D., Hippolytus wrote a carefully worded defense of the controversial book. Then in the middle of the third century, the great scholar Origen put the Alexandrians behind the canonicity. Origen's allegorizing and spiritualizing of the text gave the church a means of accepting the work while strongly rejecting its literal millennialism (belief that Christ would reign on earth with his saints for one thousand years). Even though the place of Revelation was somewhat open until the fifth century, Origen's acceptance of it, followed a century later by that of Athanasius, assured Revelation a place in the Bible.

By the early fifth century, with few exceptions, the canon was set. There needed only to be stated an authoritative position that the church would accept which would reconcile its four hundred years of waiting for Christ to return, the existence of Revelation in the canon, and the refutation of millennialism. Such a position was stated by Augustine in his magnum opus, *The City of God*. He pointed out that some had misunderstood John's Revelation and had construed it so as to produce "ridiculous fancies." Augustine reworked the literal eschatology of John in such a way that the church, while still remaining in God's history, did not live in the imminent expectation of the climax of history. God still operates in history with his chosen ones, and he is holding back evil even now. In effect, Augustine was saying that John was not painting a picture so much of the end of time as the manner in which the church progresses as it moves through both time and space. Thus, Augustine was able to keep the hope of Christ's coming to the faithful, but was able to push it effectively into the distant future. That Augustine's view could become acceptable to the church as a whole reflects not only Augustine's scholarship but also the change of position the church had undergone from a persecuted sect to the state religion of the Roman Empire. In any case, from Augustine's time to the present, any group which projected an immediate second coming was to find itself on the fringe of the church and, while the church was closely tied to the state, a persecuted minority.

But millennialists continued to arise, and while their leaders were usually of the educated, hence upper classes, the members were usually of the disinherited classes who combined their millennialism with a social protest movement. For example, in seventh-century Syria, the early Christian form of the *Sibylline Oracles* appeared to bring consolation to Syrian Christians living under Moslem oppression. According to these oracles, an emperor, Methodius, is to arise and begin the final battle with the Anti-Christ. This battle results in an Anti-Christ victory, but the victory is short-lived because of the return of Christ for the final judgment. In the Middle Ages, millennial movements arose and then disappeared on numerous occasions, reflecting the high degree of social turmoil which was to result in the social revolutions of the sixteenth century. The eleventh century saw several mass millennial movements, particularly the first crusade in 1095. Led by popular leaders such as Peter the Hermit, large armies were formed to Christianize Jerusalem. One army stopped in the Rhine Valley and performed the first massacre of European Jews. The movement, itself, died, partly in exhaustion after a few miles of travel, partly on the battle fields near Constantinople.

In the twelfth century, a Cistercian monk, Joachim of Flore, produced, between 1190 and 1195, an eschatological scheme which was to be the most influential apocalyptic understanding for the Middle Ages. He identified his new vision of history as the everlasting gospel which according to Revelation was to be preached in the last days. Joachim's scheme pictured history as an ascent in three stages, the Father's law, Christ's gospel, and the Spirit's culmination of history. Taking Matthew 1 as his starting point, Joachim counted forty-two generations from Abraham to Christ and saw this as a "type" of the gospel age. Assuming a generation is thirty years, Joachim reasoned that the movement from the gospel to the Spirit age must take place between 1200 and 1260. A new order of monks must arise to preach this message and thus prepare the way. Twelve patriarchs would arise to convert the Jews. Anti-Christ would reign for three and one-half years, after which he would be overthrown, and the age of the Spirit would begin.

Popular leaders grasped Joachim's ideas and tied them to the popular fallen hero, Frederick I, who was killed on the third crusade in 1190. A new Frederick was to arise, and he was seen as the "emperor of the last days." This movement grew when Frederick I's grandson became Frederick II. This brilliant figure did much to foster the growing messianism about himself. In 1229, he went on a crusade and crowned himself king of Jerusalem, which he had temporarily recaptured. When Pope Innocent IV put Frederick and Germany under the interdict, Frederick retorted by expanding his role to include chastisement of the church. Because Innocent was so immoral himself, his interdict had no effect. In 1240, the writings of Joachim's disciples inflamed the masses, which were heading for a major break with papal power in Europe. The movement was ended suddenly by Frederick's death in 1250. The ideas that started with Joachim were reinterpreted, and for several hundred years the dream of a resurrected Frederick was the vision that supported protest in central Europe.

One of the more famous of the chiliastic sects were the Taborites, the radical wing of the Hussite movement in fifteenth-century Czechoslovakia. These followers of the martyred John Hus united a political and economic revolt with their millennial aspirations soon after Hus's death in 1514. They went beyond Hus in their adherence to literal Biblical authority. The bitter struggle for control of Czechoslovakia helped precipitate doomsday worries. In 1519, a group of ex-Catholic priests began to preach openly the coming of the last days and the destruction in February 1520 of every town by fire (like Sodom). Everyone was called upon to flee to five towns, Taborite strongholds, destined to be saved. When the destruction did not occur, the Taborite leaders called upon their followers to take up the sword in a holy war. It was not until 1534 that the Taborites were finally defeated and, with them, their millennial hopes.

It seems more than coincidence that in Frederick's Germany the Reformation was to occur, and that out of the social upheaval caused by the Reformation, the next great movement of popular millennialism was to arise. Its leader was Thomas Müntzer. He was only one of many who saw the social and religious turmoil of the Reformation era as the sign of the end of an age, but he was the most famous. Others holding up the vision of the millennium were John Hut, Melchior Hofmann, and Augustine Bader.

Müntzer came by his view in study with Nicholas Storch, a weaver in Zwickau, and a former resident of the old Taborite lands. Müntzer believed that the Turks (Anti-Christ) would soon rule the world, but that the elect would then rise up and annihilate all the godless, and the millennium would begin. In his famous 1524 sermon, he called upon the princes of Germany to join him in this righteous war. Rejected by the princes, he turned to the poor. His league of the Elect became a power base from which was built a proletarian army at Mühlhausen and Frankenhausen. In two battles, the princes defeated Müntzer's army, and captured and executed Müntzer, thus ending another phase of millennialism.

England had its share in millennial hopes. Anti-Cromwellian forces found an ally in the Fifth Monarchy Men, a movement that crystallized in the 1650's. This group looked to Jesus to establish a fifth world monarchy. The previous four, following the image in Daniel 2, were Assyria, Persia, Greece, and Rome (which still existed as the Roman Catholic Church). After spending time in evangelical work, the Monarchy Men concluded it was time for them to take up the sword of the Lord. In 1657 and 1661, they attempted two uprisings, both unsuccessful. Their military defeats eventually wiped them off the map.

Various millennial, chiliastic, messianic movements continued to arise, and date-setting for Christ's second coming continued to be a popular activity. With the arrival of religious pluralism, toleration, and freedom, few bloodbaths followed in the wake of the earlier executions and battles. The early nineteenth century saw a renewal of the imminent expectation of the second coming of Jesus. Edward Irving, founder of the Catholic Apostolic Church in the 1830's, proclaimed the second coming in England, setting the date as 1864. Dr. Joseph Wolff, a converted Jew, toured England and the U.S. lecturing on the second coming. Both men had been spurred into action by the French Revolution and Napoleon. Until his martyrdom, Joseph Smith, founder of the Mormons, established locale after locale as the headquarters of the kingdom of God. It was, however, a poor farmer in upper New York State who founded the movement which still exists as American Adventism, and thereby originated the American brand of the millennial hope.

MILLENNIALISM IN AMERICA. The American millennial movement which today is known as Adventism had its beginnings in New York, started there by William Miller, a Baptist layman. Miller had settled in New York after the War of 1812. For awhile Miller was a Deist, denying that God interferes with the laws of the universe, and stressing morality and reason rather than religious belief. Then Miller began to study the Bible. This study, which lasted about two years, seemed to satisfy his major doubts, but also convinced him that he was living near the end of his age. Further study over several more years convinced him not only that the end was near, but also that he had to go and tell the world about it. His first labors were at Dresden, New York, where a revival followed his speaking in 1831.

He continued to speak in the area as pulpits opened to him. Within a year, he was able to accept no more than half of his speaking invitations. In 1832, the *Vermont Telegraph* published a series of sixteen articles written by Miller, the first of many works Miller was to write. The next year, a sixty-four-page pamphlet was widely circulated.

In September 1833, Miller was given a license to preach by the Baptists. For the next ten years, Miller lived the life of an itinerant evangelist, preaching and teaching his message of the imminent return of Jesus. The Methodists, Baptists, and Congregationalists were eager to hear Miller's words. In 1836, Miller published his lecture in his first book, *Evidences from Scripture and History of the Second Coming of Christ about the Year 1843: Exhibited in a Course of Lectures*. This book, plus a new edition of the earlier pamphlet, gave great impetus to the movement. Others began to join Miller and preach his doctrine. Most notably, in 1839, Joshua Himes invited Miller to preach in his Boston church. Himes was the man with promotional and organizational talent to lift the movement out of local interest into national prominence. In March of 1840, Himes began publication of the movement's first periodical, *Signs of the Times*. By autumn, the movement had grown to the point where a decision was made to hold a conference on the second coming of the Lord Jesus Christ. This conference opened October 13, 1840, at Chardon Street Church in Boston. Early leaders were among those in attendance—Josiah Litch, Joseph Bates, and Henry Dana Ward. The conference spent its time discussing the views which Miller had expounded in his pamphlets and book.

Miller believed that "God has set bounds, determined times, and revealed unto his prophets the events long before they were accomplished." These times were revealed by both plain declaration and by figurative language. From his study of Daniel and Revelation, Miller believed that he had deciphered the chronology concerning the end of the age. He began with the principle that a prophetic day is equal to a year (see Ezekiel 4:6). The key passages were Daniel 8:14, "unto 2,300 days, then shall the sanctuary be cleansed, or justified," and Daniel 9:24, "Seventy weeks are determined upon thy people . . . to make an end of sins." Miller saw the end of the seventy weeks (490 days or 490 years) as A.D. 33, at the cross of Jesus. From this date, he pushed backward to 457 B.C. ("the going forth of the commandment to Ezra to restore the law and the people of Jerusalem") as the beginning. Since, as Miller argued, the seventy weeks were part of the 2,300 days, the 2,300 days could be seen to begin also in 457 B.C. Thus, the cleansing of the sanctuary would be in 1843. Though Miller bolstered this chronology with several other figures which also ended in 1843, this set of figures was the basic one.

From these figures, Miller and his associates could build a history based on the events described in Revelation and Daniel, and this chronology of prophetic history worked out mathematically. Miller published such a work covering the Old Testament period and showing that 1843 was the end of the sixth millennium since creation. In his books, he also pointed the way for his followers to fill in the history from A.D. 33 to the present.

The Boston conference was so successful that in ensuing weeks other conferences in other cities were held to explain and discuss Miller's message, which Himes had now renamed "the midnight cry." As the movement grew, opposition increased, and the established denominations began to take action to counteract Miller's influence. Formerly cooperative churches closed their doors to Miller and his associates. Numerous accounts appeared of ministers and laymen being expelled from their churches. In one famous case, L.S. Stockman was tried for heresy before his presiding elders in the Maine Conference of the Methodist Episcopal Church and was later expelled. The *New York Christian Advocate* of 1843 carried a series of articles against Millerism, which vied for space with anti-Romanism (articles against the Roman Catholic Church).

Miller's movement was taking on a more definite shape in this period. Before the end in 1843, the first camp meeting was held at East Kingston, New Hampshire. In November, the second periodical, *The Midnight Cry*, was begun. Miller was also sharpening his views. Until 1843, Miller had been vague about the second coming as being "about the year 1843." But on January 1st, he committed himself to a more definite stance: "I am fully convinced that somewhere between March 21st, 1843 and March 21st, 1844, according to the Jewish mode of computation of time, Christ will come."

With tension running high as March approached, there appeared in the late February sky a large comet. Its appearance was a complete surprise, without a warning from the astronomers. And this was just one of a number of spectacular events of the night sky which found their way into print. March 14, 1843, came and went. Now, new issues began to emerge. The increased opposition of the churches made meeting houses hard to secure. Also, large numbers of Adventists had no prior religious connection from which they could gain nourishment. These two factors, plus the growing size of the movement, led Charles Fitch to start the inevitable "come out" movement, urging those who believed in Christ's imminent return to come out of their denominational churches and form their own churches. Fitch was opposed by Miller, but the pressure to "come out" only increased.

In 1844, as the March 14th deadline passed without the second coming, Miller had approximately 50,000 followers across the East and Midwest. Miller had earlier written of his views, "If this chronology is not correct, I shall despair of ever getting from the Bible and history a true account of the age of the world." In May 1844, Miller wrote to his followers, "I confess my error and acknowledge my disappointment."

But 50,000 enthusiastic followers could not just be turned away. While a few dropped out, most would not. In a short time, adjustments in Miller's chronology were made. In August, Samuel S. Snow put forth the "seventh month" scheme which looked to October 22, 1844, as the real date of return. Tension reached a new high. On October 22, the Adventists gathered to await the Lord. However, as one author put it, "But the day came. And Christ did not."

The Great Disappointment, as the Adventists have termed the reaction to the non-happening of October 22, 1844, left the movement in chaos. Miller again acknowledged the error but remained confident in the imminent return of Jesus. Other leaders also found themselves in the same boat. Miller refuted any further attempts to set dates and gradually retired from active leadership in the movement. But forces already in operation were now prepared to weld these organized believers into a number of denominational bodies. These are treated below.

Adventist theology at any time is usually built upon and accepts the theological perspectives of its parent bodies, making the necessary apocalyptic adjustments. Since almost all American Adventist bodies can be traced directly to Miller, the Baptist lay preacher, it is not surprising to find that popular Baptist theology has had a great influence on Adventism. There is general agreement on the doctrines concerning the Bible, God, Christ, and the sacraments. The idea of ordinances (instead of sacraments), baptism by immersion, and the practice of footwashing, particularly, further manifest Baptist origins. Sabbatarianism was, of course, transmitted directly by the Seventh-Day Baptists.

Eschatology took up two articles in the Baptists' 1833 New Hampshire Confession of Faith and provided a base from which Miller could speculate that "the end of this world is approaching." The Adventists, of course, went far beyond the Baptists in speculations. The Adventists also raised the issue of man's innate immortality by denying it and have, in the twentieth century, been in the forefront of groups proposing a view that has been accepted by many Biblical scholars.

Ethical positions among Adventists have shown two seemingly divergent trends. An emphasis on the Old Testament and on the law as mandatory for Christians has developed out of the acceptance of the Sabbath. Some groups have gone so far as to celebrate Jewish holidays and dietary laws. The celebration of the Sabbath has been promoted by the ecumenical Bible Sabbath Association, which was formed as a counterpart of the Lord's Day Alliance of the United States. Formed in 1945, the Bible Sabbath Association promotes the observance of the Sabbath and publishes a directory of Sabbath-keeping organizations. A second ethical trend emerged as the Adventists became involved in the great social crusades of the two decades preceding the Civil War. Many Adventists were vocal abolitionists and ardent supporters of the peace movements. Pacifism remains a common Adventist position; the well-publicized refusal of the Jehovah's Witnesses to be drafted is derived from their Millerite heritage.

THE SACRED NAME MOVEMENT. No one knows exactly who first raised the issue of God's name as being an important doctrinal consideration. Certainly, in the 1920's the International Bible Students on their way to becoming the Jehovah's Witnesses raised the issue forcefully. Twentieth-century scholarship had, however, begun to emphasize belief that "Yahweh" was the correct pronunciation of the "YHWH," the spelling of God's name in Hebrew. There were slight variations in spelling and pronunciation, as will be noted. By the mid-1930's there were members and ministers, primarily of the Church of God (Seventh-Day), who were beginning to use the "Sacred Name" and to promote the cause actively. One person associated with these efforts was Elder J.D. Bagwell of Warrior, Alabama. By the end of 1938, the Faith Bible and Tract Society had been organized. In July 1939, the Assembly of YHWH was chartered in the state of Michigan. About the same time, the Assembly of Yahweh Beth Israel was also formed.

No single force in spreading the Sacred Name movement was as important as *The Faith* magazine. This magazine was formed to support the Old Testament festivals as being contemporarily valid. Gradually the editor, Elder C.O. Dodd, began to use "Jehovah," then "Jahoveh," "Yahovah,"

"Yahavah," and "Yahweh." Dodd edited *The Faith* from its founding in 1937 until his death in 1955.

During the 1940's, several assemblies were formed and new periodicals begun. Some of these became substantial movements and continue today as primary religious bodies. Having come primarily out of the Church of God (Seventh-Day), the assemblies follow the Adventist and Old Testament emphases, including the observance of the Jewish festivals. The main divergence is over the Name issue and exactly what spelling and pronunciation the Name has. The common designation for local gatherings is "assembly," a literal translation of the Greek "ecclesia."

The Sacred Name movement is often thought of as the "Elijah Message," a reference to Elijah's words in I Kings 18:36 which extol Yahweh as the Elohim of Israel. Many of the churches in the movement do not report exact membership statistics.

CHARLES TAZE RUSSELL'S BIBLE STUDENTS. Following any apocalyptic failure, such as the Millerite disappointment of 1844, there are several options open to the followers. The disbanding of the group and a return to pre-excitement existence is a minority option. Spiritualization—the process of claiming that the prophecy was in error to the extent of its being seen as a visible historical event, and the attempt to reinterpret it as a cosmic, inner, invisible, or heavenly event—is most popular. A final trend for disappointed apocalyptics is to return to the source of revelation (the Bible, psychic-prophet, or analysis of contemporary events) and seek a new date. (An obvious, less committed form is to set a vague date, usually verbalized as "the near future.")

After the 1844 disappointment, leaders and periodicals rose and fell as they projected new dates and had to live with their failures. Few spawned groups that lasted beyond the projected dates. Speculations on the winter of 1853-54 lay behind the formation of the Advent Christian Church. A small group led by Jonas Wendell projected an 1874 date. Disappointed followers spiritualized the 1874 date and projected a new date, 1914. In 1876, Charles Taze Russell came across an issue of *The Herald of the Morning*, Nelson H. Barbour's magazine, which extolled the views of Jonas Wendell, and a whole new era in Adventist thought began.

Russell (1852-1916) was born in Pittsburgh, Pennsylvania, of Scotch-Irish Presbyterians, and was reared in his father's clothing store chain. Shaken by "infidel claims," he began a religious quest that led, in 1870, to Jonas Wendell. He joined Wendell's group, but soon disagreed on the manner of Christ's return. Then, in 1876, he met Barbour and united with him in beginning anew the suspended *Herald of the Morning* and co-authoring *Three Worlds or Plan of Redemption*.

By the time of his association with Barbour, Russell had come to accept three ideas which are thoroughly ingrained in the movement he began and characteristic of it. First, he rejected a belief in hell as a place of eternal torment. Secondly, he left the Wendell Adventists because he had discovered the true meaning of *parousia* (the Greek word usually translated "return"). Russell believed that it meant *presence* and he arrived at the conclusion that, in 1874, the Lord's presence had begun. Finally, Russell began to arrive at a new doctrine of the atonement, or ransom. Adam, he believed, received death as a just sentence, but his offspring received death by inheritance. Jesus' act of sacrifice counteracted the death penalty. Because of Adam, all were born without the right to live. Because of Jesus, all had inherited sin cancelled. Thus, all people were guaranteed a second chance, a trial in which enlightenment and experience would be followed by a choice either to belong to God or be a rebel deserving of death. This "second chance" would be offered during the millennium, Christ's reign on earth with his saints for one thousand years.

Russell's doctrine of the ransom also included a role for the church as an atoning force. Derived in part from Paul's Epistle to the Colossians 1:24 and from an allegorical interpretation of the Hebrew sacrifice of the bull (i.e., Christ) and the goat (i.e., the church) on the day of atonement described in Leviticus 16, Russell taught that the church as the body of Christ is by its present suffering offering a spiritual sacrifice to God.

Inherent in Russell's beliefs was a denial of certain "orthodox" ideas such as the Trinity. He accepted a history that extended to Arius (fourth century A.D.) whose atonement idea was close to Russell's and to that of the ecclesiastical rebels—Luther, Peter Waldo, and John Wycliff.

After meeting Barbour, Russell drew support from other Adventists such as J.H. Paton, A.P. Adams, and A.D. Jones. This coalition lasted until 1878, when Barbour, who had set April as the month when the church would go to heaven, suffered a loss of support by the disconfirmation of his prophecy. (He further deviated with some speculations on the atonement.) Russell, Paton, and Jones withdrew their support of Barbour, and Russell began, with their assistance, *Zion's Watch Tower and Herald of Christ's Presence*, which was sent free to all of Barbour's subscribers. Paton soon was to join the ranks of dissenters, and he left Russell to expound his own speculations in his periodical, *Zion's Day Star*.

The first issue of *Watch Tower* in 1879 is a convenient date to begin the history of Russell's movement. To the *Watch Tower* was soon added abundant literature to help a growing number of Bible students who were popularly called "Millennial Dawn Bible Students." They came together to study the Scriptures with the help of Russell's writings. Russell began to publish tracts, a number of which were combined into *Food for Thinking Christians*. He also called for a thousand preachers to spread the gospel by distributing the *Watch Tower* and his tracts.

In 1881, Zion's Watch Tower Tract Society was set up. In 1886, the first of six volumes of *Studies in the Scripture* appeared. The publishing of Volume I, *The Plan of the Ages*, marked an upward turning point in the development of the movement, as it gave the substantial "theological" base to *Watch Tower* readers. By 1889, more than 100,000 copies of *The Plan of the Ages* were in print.

The pattern of the Bible Student movement's growth was typical of the growth of a number of loosely affiliated religious groups. Local congregations were formed by people

impressed by Russell's views and writings. They were related directly to Russell primarily through the *Watch Tower*. The work was spread mostly by volunteers. Gradually, there arose "colporteurs," who spent from half to all of their time in the work and who earned their living by selling Russell's books (with a 64% discount).

In 1894, "pilgrims" were added to the structure as traveling preachers and teachers to local congregations. Pilgrims were paid by the central office. A plan for local elders or leaders to sell their ideas to new areas was begun in 1911.

Extension of the work also occurred through a number of events that generated a great deal of publicity. In particular, Russell enjoyed debates, at which he was a master. His 1903 debate with E.L. Eaton, a Methodist minister, and with Elder L.S. White of the Disciples of Christ did much to spread the movement.

As the movement emerged, certain ideas came to the fore; none was so prominent as chronology and the 1914 date. *The Plan of the Ages* was God's calendar for dealing with men. Reminiscent of John Nelson Darby's followers was Russell's division of history into a number of eras. According to Russell's chart in *The Plan of the Ages*, the first dispensation from Adam to the flood demonstrated the inability of angels to improve the world. The patriarchal age (from the flood to Jacob's death) was followed by the Jewish age, which lasted until Christ's death. The gospel age of 1845 years ended in 1874. That year marked the dawning of the millennial age, which would begin with a "harvest period" or millennial dawn period of forty years.

The millennial dawn period (1874-1914) would be marked by a return of the Jews to Palestine and the gradual overthrow of the Gentile nations. All would be climaxed in 1914 with the glorification of the saints, the establishment of God's direct rule on earth, and the restoration of man to perfection on earth. The coincidence of the apocalyptic date with World War I was viewed by Russell's followers as a cause for great hope, sharply contrasting the disappointments that had followed other predictions. The war was interpreted as God's direct intervention in the affairs of humanity, and a signal of the beginning of the world's end. (Russell revised the date to 1918 later and, of course, died in 1916, before the second disconfirmation.)

A final significant idea was the doctrine of the future church. Russell believed from his reading of Revelation 7:4-9 that the church consisted of 144,000 saints from the time of Christ to 1914, who would receive the ultimate reward of becoming "priests and kings in heaven." Others would make up a class of heavenly servants termed "the great company." The idea of two classes of believers was illustrated by numerous Biblical characters (most notably Elijah, taken to heaven, and Elisha, his servant), who were seen as types of the classes.

Russell and his ideas would become the subject of much controversy after his death. Some leaders would ascribe to him a cosmic role and identify him with the good and faithful servant of Matthew 25:21. Others would argue over the significance of the harvest, which supposedly ended in 1914. Some would feel that the harvest closed in 1914 and that the 144,000 were all chosen by then. Others would consider the harvest open and continue to gather the 144,000. Similar to the differences on the harvest would be differences on the identification of the Elijah and Elisha classes.

When Russell died, he left behind him a charismatically run organization in the hands of a board of directors and editorial committee. The next decade was marked by controversy, schism, the rise to power of Judge J.R. Rutherford, and the emergence of Jehovah's Witnesses.

THE SOUTHCOTTITES. Before William Miller created an Adventist movement in the United States in the 1830's and 1840's, an Adventist movement flowered in England. The focus of the English movement was Joanna Southcott (1750-1814). In the 1790's, she began to profess visions, to write them down in both prose and verse, and to gather a following. She was convinced that she was a prophetess. Several predictions, including France's conquest of Italy under the unknown general Bonaparte, created some attention.

The thrust of her message was placed within an orthodox Christian framework and centered upon the imminent return of Christ. What made the prophecy distinctive was the peculiar "doctrine of the bride." A feminist, Joanna began to speculate on the crucial role of women in the Bible and the role of the "woman clothed with the sun" (Rev. 12:1), who would bring forth the male child who would rule the nations with a rod of iron. She identified the woman with the bride of the Lamb (Rev. 19:7), and then identified both of them with herself.

She began a movement to mobilize England. Joanna's real impact dates from 1801, when she first published her prophecies abroad in several booklets. These booklets brought her first disciples, among whom she began a practice of sealing. Accepting the apocalyptic vision of a world delivered into the hands of Satan, she believed that the key to the devil's overthrow was to have a sufficient number of people renounce him and be sealed as of the Lord. She distributed the seals to all who would sign up for them. They were written on square sheets of paper upon which a circle was drawn. Inside the circle Joanna wrote "The sealed of the Lord, the Elect and Precious, Man's Redemption to Inherit the Tree of Life, to be made Heirs of God and Joint Heirs with Jesus Christ." The paper would be folded and sealed with wax and with the monogram I. C. and two stars. Critics accused Joanna of selling the seals, but she denied it.

In 1814, at 64 years of age, she had a climactic revelation. Having identified herself with the woman in Revelation 12, she was always concerned with the child the woman was to bear. Joanna's voice told her to prepare for the birth of a son. This child was identified in Joanna's thinking with Shiloh (Genesis 49:10). She began to show signs of pregnancy and was declared pregnant by several doctors. The followers prepared for a new virgin birth. As the time of the delivery approached, she took an earthly husband. When the baby failed to arrive and the symptoms of the hysteric pregnancy left, Joanna's strength ebbed and she died in December of 1814.

Followers and leaders alike were thrown into chaos. Among those who did not leave, there were attempts to regroup the forces, and a number of separate churches resulted. Most were confined to England, but a few found their way to America.

BRITISH ISRAELISM. Growing up largely with Adventist circles, and picking ideas from them at random—nontrinitarian theology, Sabbatarianism, sacred name emphases, and dispensationalism—the British Israelite bible students emerged as a separate distinct group in American religion during the decade after World War I. They experienced a steady growth into the forties but seemed to wane in the 1950's and 1960's. During the 1970's, however, the movement experienced a new wave of revival in its most militant wing, popularly called the "Identity Movement."

Though only visible in the United States since World War I, British Israelism, the Identity Movement, traces its history to ancient Israel. In actual fact, its history begins in the late eighteenth century in England, where one of the more popular avocations of bible students was the attempt to discover the present-day identity of the so-called ten lost tribes of Israel—the ten tribes carried away into captivity by Shalmaneser, the king of Assyria in 721 B.C. (II Kings 17). Since 1800, numerous speculations have appeared, but only two opinions, apart from the generally accepted one that the tribes were assimilated into the peoples of the Middle East, ever gained a wide following. The first of these speculations identified the American Indians as the tribes. That speculation was promulgated by Joseph Smith, the founder of the Church of Jesus Christ of Latter-Day Saints. The second speculation was the identification of the tribes with Anglo-Saxon peoples by the British Israelites.

Scotsman John Wilson, who in 1840 published his theories in *Our Israelitish Origins*, is generally looked upon as the founder of the British Israelites. His appearance of scholarship and his oratorical abilities were enough to sell his notion to the public.

Wilson was by no means the first to make the British-Israelite identification. As early as 1649, John Sadler (b. 1615) speculated on the idea in his *Rights to the Kingdom* and seemed to have advised Oliver Cromwell on readmitting the Jews to England. In the eighteenth century, Dr. Abade of Amsterdam, a Protestant theologian, is reported to have said: "Unless the ten tribes have flown into the air, or have been plunged into the center of the earth, they must be sought for in the north and west, and in the British Isles" (Anton Darms, *The Delusion of British Israel* [New York: Loizeaux Brothers, Bible Truth Depot, n.d.], 15).

The real originator of the idea, however, was Canadian Richard Brothers (b. 1757), a psychic visionary who settled in London in the 1780's. He began to publish the content of revelations that identified Brothers as a descendant of King David and demanded the crown of England. He was found guilty of treason, but insane, and sent to an asylum. Brothers' ideas caught on with some influential men such as Orientalist Nathaniel Brassey Halhed, Quaker psychic William Bryan, and Scottish lawyer John Finleyson. The defeat of Napoleon was the marked confirmation of their ideas.

The basics of British Israelite theology are quite simple, although a working knowledge of the Old Testament is required to trace the intricacies of the logic. The basic premise is that Israel and Judah were two entities, the former comprising the northern ten tribes, and the latter the two southern ones after 922 B.C. Members of the northern kingdom, after being freed from captivity, wandered into Europe and settled in northwest Europe, Scandinavia, and the British Isles. Jeremiah, the prophet, is believed to have transported Tea-Tephi, the daughter of King Zedekiah, to Ireland to marry Prince Herremon, thus continuing Israel's royal lineage. James I was the first descendant of this union to reign in London.

Different countries of Europe are to be identified with the different tribes; Britain and the United States are descendants of Joseph's two sons Ephraim and Manasseh, and, as such, are particularly blessed (Genesis 48). The tribe of Dan has, in fulfillment of prophecy (Genesis 49:17), left numerous signposts of its tribal meanderings—Dan River, Denmark, Danube River, etc.

From this basic theology, other observations are made in correlating Biblical quotes with isolated facts of archaeology, legendary materials, history, and philology. Wilson was the first to note the correlation between the Hebrew word for covenant, "brith," and "Britain." The Stone of Scone is believed to have been from the throne in Jerusalem, brought to Ireland by Jeremiah. (Actually, it was quarried in Scotland.)

British Israelism has attracted much attention because of its racist tendencies, especially in the United States. Implicit in the theory is the superiority of the Anglo-Saxon, which is seen as a "religious" superiority, much as with any "chosen people" doctrine. The Jews were seen as "kin" to the Anglo-Saxons. In a famous quote, J. H. Allen said:

"Understand us: we do not say that the Jews are not Israelites; they belong to the posterity of Jacob, who was called Israel; hence they are all Israelites. But the great bulk of Israelites are not the Jews, just as the great bulk of Americans are not Californians, and yet all Californians are Americans; also, as in writing the history of America we must of necessity write the history of California, because California is a part of America; but we could write a history of California without writing a history of America" (J. H. Allen, *Judah's Sceptre and Joseph's Birthright* [Boston: A. A. Beauchamp, 1930], 71).

However, in twentieth-century America, racial, not religious, superiority has been asserted, and the movement has been anti-Jewish and, by its most successful exponent, anti-black. That exponent is Herbert Armstrong of the Worldwide Church of God, an Adventist Church.

Numerous refutations of British Israelism have been written from a perspective of orthodox history and theology. These have, in spite of their often vitriolic nature, conclusively refuted the bulk of British Israelite speculations. They, however, have missed the point: whatever success British Israelism has had has been as a religious and emotional expression of British imperialism and American manifest destiny. There is a definite correlation between the rise and fall of those ideas and the popularity of British Israelism. The

dismantling of the British Empire has had a devastating effect upon the movement.

John Wilson's book was published in America in 1850 and found isolated disciples, but no real following until after World War I. In 1886, M. M. Eshelman was introduced to British Israelism by an eighty-year-old immigrant to Illinois, William Montgomery. In the pages of *The Gospel Messenger*, published at Mt. Morris, Illinois, Eshelman began to write of his ideas, and in 1887, he published a book, *Two Sticks*. Then in 1902, the Rev. J. H. Allen published his *Judah's Sceptre and Joseph's Birthright*. These two books became the major items selling British Israelism to an American audience.

The British Israel movement was at its height in the 1930's and 1940's. It never reached the development or popularity in America that it had in England, but in the late 1940's, it could boast a national audience among both congregational members and radio respondents. Two seminaries were functioning in 1950. The British Israel hypothesis—that Anglo-Saxons are descendants of the ten lost tribes of Israel—was finding support among people who would by no means identify themselves with the movement itself. What remain today are the remnants of that once healthy national movement.

One of the most important structures created by the movement was Dayton Theological Seminary, which functioned from 1947 into the early 1950's. It was founded by Millard J. Flenner, an ex-Congregational minister and pastor of the Church of the Covenants in Dayton. Among the teachers was Conrad Gaard, who was pastor for many years of the Christian Chapel Church in Tacoma. As head of the Destiny of America Foundation, he was a significant writer and radio minister until his death in 1969. Gaard helped Dayton graduates keep in touch through his travels and tours.

SOURCES—THE ADVENTIST FAMILY

ADVENTISM, MILLENNIALISM, AND APOCALYTICISM

Case, Shirley Jackson. *The Millennial Hope*. Chicago: University of Chicago Press, 1918. 253 pp.

Chamberlin, E. R. *Antichrist and the Millennium*. New York: E. P. Dutton, 1975. 244 pp.

Froom, Edwin Leroy. *The Conditionalist Faith of Our Fathers*. 2 vols. Washington, DC: Review and Herald Publishing Association, 1966.

———. *The Prophetic Faith of Our Fathers*. 4 vols. Washington, DC: Review and Herald Publishing Association, 1950-54.

Harrison, J. F. C. *The Second Coming, Popular Millenarianism, 1780-1850*. London: Routledge & Kegan Paul, 1979. 277 pp.

Hunter, Anthony. *The Last Days*. London: Anthony Blond, 1958. 232 pp.

Rist, Martin. "Introduction to the Revelation of St. John the Divine." In *The Interpreters Bible*. Vol. XII. New York: Abingdon, 1974, pp. 617-27.

Schmithals, Walter. *The Apocalyptic Movement*. Nashville: Abingdon, 1975. 255 pp.

ADVENTISM IN AMERICA

Directory of Sabbath-Observing Groups. Fairview, OK: The Bible Sabbath Association, 1980. 147 pp.

Gaustad, Edwin Scott. *The Rise of Adventism*. New York: Harper & Row, 1974.

Nichol, Francis D. *The Midnight Cry*. Washington, DC: Review and Herald Publishing Association, 1944. 576 pp.

Sears, Clara Endicott. *Days of Delusion*. Boston: Houghton Mifflin Company, 1924. 264 pp.

Seventh-Day Adventist Encyclopedia. Washington, DC: Review and Herald Publishing Association, 1966. 1454 pp.

WILLIAM MILLER

Bliss, Sylvester. *Memoirs of William Miller*. Boston: Joshua V. Himes, 1853. 426 pp.

A Brief History of William Miller, the Great Pioneer in Adventist Faith. Washington, DC: Review and Herald Publishing Association, 1915.

Gale, Robert. *The Urgent Call*. Washington, DC: Review and Herald Publishing Association, 1975. 158 pp.

White, James. *Sketches of the Christian Life and Public Labors of William Miller*. Battle Creek, MI: Steam Press, 1875. 413 pp.

ELLEN G. WHITE AND THE SEVENTH-DAY ADVENTISTS

A Critique of Prophetess of Health. Washington, DC: The Ellen G. White Estate, General Conference of S.D.A., 1976. 127 pp.

Damsteegt, P. Gerard. *Foundation of the Seventh-Day Adventist Message and Mission*. Grand Rapids, MI: William B. Eerdmans Publishing Company, 1977. 348 pp.

Delafield, D. A. *Ellen G. White and the Seventh-Day Adventist Church*. Mountain View, CA: Pacific Press Publishing Association, 1963. 90 pp.

Noobergen, Rene. *Ellen G. White, Prophet of Destiny*. New Canaan, CT: Keats Publishing, 1972. 241 pp.

Numbers, Ronald L. *Prophetess of Health, A Study of Ellen G. White*. New York: Harper & Row, 1976. 271 pp.

CHURCHES OF GOD (SEVENTH DAY)

Hopkins, Joseph. *The Armstrong Empire*. Grand Rapids: William B. Eerdmans Publishing Company, 1974. 304 pp.

Nickels, Richard C. *A History of the Seventh Day Church of God*. Vol. I. Sheridan, WY: The Author, 1977. 397 pp.

———. *Six Papers on the History of the Church of God*. Sheridan, WY: Giving & Sharing, 1977.

SABBATARIANISM

Armstrong, Herbert W. *The Resurrection Was Not on Sunday*. Pasadena, CA: Ambassador College, 1972. 14 pp.

———. *Which Day Is the Sabbath of the New Testament?* Pasadena, CA: Worldwide Church of God, 1971. 23 pp.

Dellinger, George. *A History of the Sabbath Resurrection Doctrine*. Westfield, IN: Sabbath Research Center, 1982. 33 pp.

Haynes, Carlyle B. *From Sabbath to Sunday*. Washington, DC: Review and Herald Publishing Association, 1928. 128 pp.

Love, William Deloss. *Sabbath and Sunday*. Chicago: Fleming H. Revell, 1896. 325 pp.

SACRED NAME MOVEMENT

Dugger, A. N., and C.O. Dodd. *A History of the True Church*. Jerusalem: n.p., 1968. 318 pp.

"Let Your Name Be Sanctified." Brooklyn: Watchtower Bible and Tract Society of New York, 1961. 382 pp.

Meyer, Jacob O. *The Memorial Name—Yahweh*. Bethel, PA: The Assemblies of Yahweh, 1978. 76 pp.

Snow, L. D. "A Brief History of the Name Movement in America." *The Eliyah Messenger and Field Reporter*, May 1966, pp. 1, 4, 7, 12.

Traina, A. B. *The Holy Name Bible*. Brandywine, MD: Scripture Research Association, 1980. 346 pp.

Rutherford, J. F. *Vindication*. Vol. I. Brooklyn: Watchtower Bible and Tract Association, 1931. 346 pp.

CHARLES TAZE RUSSELL AND THE BIBLE STUDENTS

Beckford, James A. *The Trumpet of Prophecy*. Oxford: Basil Blackwell, 1975. 244 pp.

Cole, Marley. *Triumphant Kingdom*. New York: Criterion Books, 1957. 256 pp.

Gruss, Edmond Charles. *Apostles of Denial*. N.p.: Presbyterian and Reformed Publishing Co., 1970. 324 pp.

Rogerson, Alan. *Millions Now Living Will Never Die*. London: Constable, 1969. 216 pp.

White, Timothy. *A People for His Name*. New York: Vantage Press, 1967. 418 pp.

JOANNA SOUTHCOTT

Balleiene, G. R. *Past Finding Out*. New York: Macmillan Company, 1956. 151 pp.

The Life and Journal of John Wroe. Ashton-under-Lyne: Trustees of the Society of Christian Israelites, 1900. 639 pp.

Matthews, Ronald. *English Messiahs*. London: Methuen & Co., 1936. 230 pp.

ANGLO-ISRAELISM

Allen, J. H. *Judah's Sceptre and Joseph's Birthright*. Boston: A. A. Beauchamp, 1930. 377 pp.

Armstrong, Herbert W. *The United States and Britain in Prophecy*. Pasadena, CA: Worldwide Church of God, 1980. 163 pp.

Darms, Anton. *The Delusion of British-Israel*. New York: Loizeaux Brothers, Bible Truth Depot, n.d. 224 pp.

Haberman, Frederick. *The Climax of the Ages Is Near*. St. Petersburg, FL: The Kingdom Press, 1940. 94 pp.

Hate Groups in America. New York: Anti-Defamation League of B'nai B'rith, 1982. 107 pp.

Mackendrick, W. G. "The Roadbuilder." *The Destiny of the British Empire and the U.S.A.* London: Covenant Publishing Co., 1931. 213 pp.

Roy, Ralph Lord. *Apostles of Discord*. Boston: Beacon Press, 1953. 437 pp.

Schwartz, Alan M., et al. "The 'Identity Churches': A Theology of Hate." *ADL Facts* 28, No. 1 (Spring 1983), p. 116.

Swift, Wesley A. *Testimony of Tradition and the Origin of Races*. Hollywood, CA: New Christian Crusade Church, n.d. 34 pp.

Wilson, J. *Our Israelitish Origins*. Philadelphia: Daniels & Smith, 1850. 237 pp.

Chapter Twelve

THE LIBERAL FAMILY

Directory listings for the groups belonging to the Liberal Family may be
found in the section beginning on page 467.

The liberal family of churches has become identified with three key ideas: unitarianism, universalism, and infidelism. Unitarianism means the return to the idea of a unitary God instead of a trinitarian God, and involves the denial of the divinity of Jesus. Universalism affirms that all will be saved, and denies the Christian belief in hell. Infidelism is the movement toward a human-centered philosophy and away from a God-centered philosophy. Liberals fit on a continuum between unitarians and the more radical "infidels." The three ideas of unitarianism, universalism, and infidelism constitute the major tendencies in the liberal tradition; people typically adopt one of the three stances, and not all three.

The origin and much of the continuing life of liberalism lie in its attack upon the dictates of Christian orthodoxy. (Orthodoxy may be described as the mainline Christian religions that follow the Scriptures and the three creeds—the Nicene, Chalcedonian, and Apostles' Creeds.) Thus the liberal tradition has a secondary nature, protesting existent churches. The differences within the tradition can be gauged by how far various liberal groups deviate from orthodox beliefs.

Most liberals defend people's right to believe as they wish, and not to believe at all if reason leads them to disbelief. Liberals therefore have been in the forefront of fights for religious freedom, and dominated such debates on religious freedom as those of the late eighteenth century in France and the United States.

In America, beginning in the eighteenth century, liberals dissented from the established orthodoxy primarily of New England Calvinism and to a lesser extent Protestantism. Before the Civil War, American liberals were judged by themselves and others only in relation to the creed from which they deviated. Therefore they were called, by themselves and others, by such negative names as anti-trinitarian and infidel. After the Civil War, though, liberals began to see themselves in a new light and describe themselves in such positive terms as secularists, humanists, and liberals.

As an intellectual movement, liberalism stresses the power of man's reason to perfect the world. This emphasis on reason is coupled with a high regard for the worth of each human being. Liberals hold the self-image of being on the progressive cutting-edge of human history, striving for the freedom of the individual. Although never very numerous, liberals have had tremendous influence on society as the public accepted their ideals. The Bill of Rights, for example, stands as a landmark of the liberal tradition.

What is liberal for one generation may become conservative for another generation. For example, in the 1920's, to be a liberal meant to be in the labor movement. Today, though, to be a liberal often means to be against the labor movement because labor is seen as part of the "establishment." Thus liberalism takes on new meanings with time. Also, at any given moment in history, liberals are more united by their opposition to orthodoxy than by any positive idea they promote. They have lacked the positive thrust that builds such movements as Methodism or Calvinism. Their common history of protesting orthodoxy, however, does tie them together, so both unitarians and atheists (infidels) belong to the liberal tradition, although both might be unhappy at being classed together.

The Enlightenment of the eighteenth century led liberals to their high regard for reason. As religion shifted away from God and supernaturalism, only two bases for religion were left: man's feelings and man's mind. An arational mysticism became the hallmark of the liberals who chose feelings as the base for their religion. The transcendentalists followed the arational path, developing an idealistic movement that emphasized the union of the individual with the spiritual reality underlying all life. Most liberals, however, opted for the rational. They said man was the product of a law-abiding nature and reasonable thinking could reveal the universal laws which permeated everything.

Science was the product of rationalism. Science discovered the tangible world of indestructible particles. What was real was what could be seen, felt, and, most important, measured. The law-abiding world could be observed and documented. From observation came knowledge, and, by extension, the liberals concluded the only knowledge worth having was that produced by scientific observation. Scientific method, said the liberals, could be applied to the study of religion and from it a scientific religion, acceptable to all, could emerge. Beneath the diversity of ideas and practices could be found the great religious values, some reasoned. Others reasoned that if those values were not found, religion could be destroyed altogether.

The scientist's emphasis on the visible world gave way to secularism as a worldview. The search for values in this world and this life became part of the lifestyle of the liberal tradition.

As comparative religion became a major study, its findings became a major factor in the development of liberalism. As solid information on the major faiths filtered out of the scholarly enclaves, a search for a "universal religion" began. Liberals hoped such a religion, built upon "essentials" or "common" factors or the "natural" religious particles, could command the respect of all. Such books as *The World's Sixteen Crucified Saviors* provided ample material to attack Christianity's distinctiveness.

In the nineteenth century, many liberals adopted the four-fold creed of evolution, reason, science, and materialism. From Darwin and Herbert Spencer, liberals learned to think in terms of progress. Not only nature, but also human culture was progressing. For liberalism, the great stumbling block to progress was ignorance, and the great tool to aid progress was education. The alliance of liberalism and the university was a natural one.

ETHICS. The anti-mystical intellectualism within the main body of the liberal tradition led to a dominance of ethical concerns. Liberals followed their triumphs in the Bill of Rights with active involvement in the great crusades of the pre-Civil War era. Always the liberals could be found standing with those issues that aimed at great freedom for the individual. They swelled the ranks of the abolition, peace, prison reform, and women's rights movements. In the liberal religion camp were Julia Ward Howe, Lucy Stone, Robert Dale Owen, and Lucretia Mott. In the twentieth century, liberals were prominent in the labor, sexual freedom, and civil rights movements.

THE FORMS OF FAITH. The active revolt against specific religious forms, which eventuated in the atheists' attack upon religion itself, does not lead to worship, piety, and prayer. These occur only on the extreme right wing of the liberal movement. The dominant form of liberalism was the communication of information at first in the sermon and as time passed more frequently in the lecture. Great emphasis has been placed upon the education of members and the public, particularly their sensitization on moral issues.

The efforts at education and sensitization have been carried on by the liberal press. Liberal periodicals, most of which were independently published, have been the backbone of the movement from the early nineteenth century. The liberals' oldest periodical still in existence is *The Truth Seeker*, founded in 1873. Books attacking orthodoxy and religion are subsidized and circulated. Some have become popular items.

HISTORICAL DEVELOPMENT. The liberals look to an amazing number of radicals in Christian history as precursors of their movements. Various liberals claim as precursors such figures as Origen, Pelagius, and Leonardo da Vinci. The real beginning of a line of descent, however, is generally conceded

to be Michael Servetus, who published *On the Errors of the Trinity* in 1532. Servetus, martyred by John Calvin, has become a symbol of free religion fighting orthodox intolerance. Other reformers of similar opinions led parts of Europe into a unitarian perspective. Socinius converted Poland, and Francis David a large segment of Transylvania. In 1568 the only Unitarian king in history, John Sigismund, issued the Western world's first edict of religious toleration.

In seventeenth-century Europe, the Enlightenment offered "liberal" alternatives to traditional Christian beliefs. In particular the deists of England preached a religion stripped of orthodox accretions. The deists said the creator does not interfere with the laws of the universe. To the deists, God was like a watchmaker who makes a watch, winds it up, and leaves it to run on its own. God, they said, leaves the world to follow its own course. The deists advocated a natural religion based on human reason and morality rather than revelation. Deism found a ready audience among the educated and upper classes of both England and America. Most of the leaders of the American Revolution identified themselves with the deist "idea world," particularly Washington, Jefferson, and Madison. By the time of the American Revolution the three key ideas of the liberals—unitarianism, universalism, and infidelism—had matured and had come to dominate the liberals' dissenting orientation. With each of these three ideas was carried a fight for religious freedom and a battle against the abuses of clericalism.

Universalism had been preached in America as early as the 1740's by Dr. George de Bonneville in Pennsylvania. In 1770, major impetus was given to the movement by the arrival of John Murray from England. Murray had been raised a Methodist and had become a class leader. Impressed with George Whitefield, he left Methodism and associated himself with Whitefield's independent London tabernacle. While in London he became a universalist and was expelled from the tabernacle membership when he refused to "confine his sentiments to his own bosom." After his arrival in the new world, Murray itinerated and preached his universalism, which had by 1775 created such an impact that pamphlets were written against him. About this time universalist congregations began to appear. Murray's followers in Gloucester, Massachusetts, who had belonged to the Congregational Church, had their membership suspended. So, in 1779, they formed the Independent Church of Gloucester. The movement to form churches grew, and in 1786 the Articles of Association for Universalist Churches were promulgated, although the association itself was short-lived. In the 1790's Hosea Ballou appeared on the scene to continue the leadership of the aging John Murray. His newspaper, the *Winchester Profession*, became the standard for universalist views. In 1790, at a convention in Philadelphia, Articles of Faith and a Plan of Government were adopted. Thus, universalism became the first of the liberal views to solidify into an organizational structure.

In the eighteenth century unitarianism was preached in England and America. Theophilus Lindsey founded the British unitarian movement in 1774 after his resignation from the Anglican priesthood. In New England, unitarianism originated in the Congregational Church, but it was not until 1794, when Joseph Priestley migrated to America, that churches were founded that took the name unitarian.

During the pre-Civil War nineteenth century, three men—William Ellery Channing, Ralph Waldo Emerson, and Theodore Parker—in succession dominated unitarian thought. The liberal debate in America centered around them.

William Ellery Channing, a Congregational minister, in the second decade of the nineteenth century was the leading intellectual among unitarians, a liberal wing in the Congregational Church. His 1819 sermon at the funeral of Jered Sparks became the unitarians' manifesto. Then in 1825 Channing led in founding the American Unitarian Association, a missionary group. Most members of Unitarian churches date their beginnings from one of these two events. Channing is credited with emphasizing ethics instead of theology, an emphasis that has become a hallmark of Unitarian churches.

In the 1830's Ralph Waldo Emerson and the transcendentalists were at their intellectual apex. Emerson's efforts to sell his monist position, most notably through his famous speech to Harvard Divinity School in 1838, were rebuffed for the time. But Emerson, his colleagues at Brook Farm (an experimental, communitarian venture of the transcendentalists), and the raft of romantic literature flooding America from England could not long be denied.

Theodore Parker stands as the symbol of the union of unitarian thinking with transcendentalism. While unitarianism could not contain Emerson, it was forced to accept Parker. He combined three elements: the philosophical, which appealed to unitarians because of their emphasis on the mind; the mystical, which appealed to the transcendentalists; and the practical, which appealed to the liberals because of their desire to improve society. Parker, applying transcendental ideals in concrete situations, was an abolitionist and a spokesman against the fugitive slave law. His sermon at the ordination of Charles Shackford in 1841, entitled "The Transient and Permanent in Christianity," set the tone for liberal Christianity for his generation and served further to drive a wedge between the orthodox and liberal Congregationalists which was to result in the break between them after the Civil War.

For the origins of what in the nineteenth century was called infidelity (the complete rejection of theism, the church, and piety), one immediately turns to France and the works of Voltaire and his contemporaries. These works reached their culmination in the radically anti-clerical, anti-religious aspect of the French Revolution. In its early days in America, the adjective "French" was often used to modify "infidelity." The first exponent on the American scene was Ethan Allen, the revolutionary war hero, who published his *Reason the Only Oracle of Man* in 1784. This publication was essentially a restatement of deism, emphasizing man and his reason. For various reasons the work made little impact. But in 1794 Thomas Paine published his *Age of Reason*, which was an immediate success. The *Age of Reason* became the Bible of the free thought movement and Paine became the symbol of evil infidelity to the orthodox.

The free thought tradition replaced the deist tradition of the eighteenth century. The transition can be marked in the 1790's by the leadership of Elihu Palmer and the beginnings of local free thought societies. The free thought movement stressed the importance of the inquiring mind, scientific methodology, and philosophical thinking. The movement opposed orthodoxy in religion, orthodoxy being the mainline Christian tradition based on Scripture and the creeds. Palmer, from 1791 until his death in 1806, was instrumental in the founding and leadership of at least three different radical societies, the most important being the "Deistical Society" of New York City. This society published the *Temple of Reason*, one of the first periodicals in America supporting an "infidel" tradition. After Palmer's death in 1806, there were about twenty years of silence from the free thought camp. Then in the 1820's Robert Owen founded his New Harmony experiment in Indiana which gave the U.S. many of its firsts in education and community service.

In 1827 the free thought voice was heard again with the establishment of the Free Press Association in New York City. Before the end of the decade, societies were founded in Philadelphia; Woodstock, Vermont; Paterson, New Jersey; Schuylkill, Pennsylvania; Wilmington, Delaware; and St. Louis. In the 1830's and 1840's societies were also founded in a number of other northern and Midwestern communities. Many adopted the name of "Free Inquirers." "Moral Philanthropists" and "Rationalists" were also popular names. Attempts at national organization in 1828 and 1835 failed. A short-lived attempt to form "The Infidel Society for the Promotion of Mental Liberty" began in 1845 but died in 1848.

Other attempts waited until after the Civil War. Meanwhile, the liberals, both Christian and free thought, found themselves caught in circumstances which worked against organization. First, due to the Congregational Church's polity of local independency and the local nature of the "infidel" societies, leaders had no one but their local constituency to please. National organization tended to work against the very freedom which was so highly prized. Secondly, the decades before the Civil War were a period of intense social change; and involvement in anti-slavery, women's rights, and other social causes took much of the energy that could have gone into organizational building. The close of the war ended the era of social activism and two generations of existence had caused a shift of emphasis in liberal thought. It began to turn from its primary emphasis on a critique of its religious origins toward the development of a positive position, setting the stage for the solidification of the liberal forces.

The last four decades of the nineteenth century were a time of organization of liberal churchmen. On April 7, 1865, just five days before the surrender of Lee at Appomattox, a National Convention of Unitarian Churches met in New York City to organize a National Conference of Unitarian Churches. Transcendentalists, not happy with the overly orthodox position of the National Conference, organized in 1867 the Free Religious Association (FRA). Among the leaders of the FRA were John Weiss, Samuel Johnson, Octavius Brooks Frothingham, Thomas Wentworth Higginson, and David Wasson. The radicals who formed the FRA in turn found themselves divided between the mystical transcendentalists and the scientifically oriented members. The latter organized in 1875 as the National Liberal League. The issue around which they organized was a movement in the 1860's by evangelicals for a constitutional amendment which would wed church and state. Specifically, the amendment would tie the Protestant churches closely to national political institutions, from the President and Congress on down. The Liberal League countered with a program to achieve complete separation of church and state. The Liberal League itself divided over support of obscenity laws, and the group favoring a complete lifting of censorship formed the National Liberal League of America.

The thrust of most of these organizations lasted only one generation. As the issues which gave them birth died, they passed from the scene and were often absorbed by more stable bodies such as the Unitarian churches. This absorption liberalized the stable groups. Replacing the organizations that died were new associations that gathered to respond to new issues. One such association was the Union of Liberal Clergymen, formed following the Parliament of Religions in 1893. The Union of Liberal Clergymen promoted progress, reverence for law, science, an openness to new revealments, and said the church should be a school of the humanities.

ATHEISM. Increasingly, since the Renaissance, people have denied the very existence of a God. Generally, these men were intellectuals—scholars and university professors—giants in their own particular disciplines. Included are such figures as Thomas Hariot, Christopher Marlowe, and Pierre Bayle. It was not, however, until the nineteenth century that atheism became a force with significant support.

Many deists walked a tightrope between belief in a God who did not act upon his world and outright denial of his existence. In the nineteenth century the university provided a haven for those who wished to declare themselves as atheists. Like its deistic predecessor, atheism was built upon an attack of the Christian churches in the nineteenth century. Primarily, however, it was an intellectual movement which launched an attack on theology and natural religion. The movement's perspective was that of scientific materialism, the theory that the basic reality of the universe is material and is therefore observable and scientifically measurable.

Among the major atheists in the nineteenth century are Karl Marx, Ludwig Feuerbach, Auguste Comte, and Charles Bradlaugh. Often forgotten, but important in any history of atheism is poet Percy Bysshe Shelley. Shelley was expelled from Oxford in 1811 for writing *The Necessity of Atheism*. His lengthy *Queen Mab* became a poetic reinforcement to his earlier essay. Reflecting on the death of an atheist, he cries:

There is no God!
Nature confirms the faith this death-groan sealed:
Let heaven and earth, let man's revolving race,
His ceaseless generations tell the tale.

The Spirit of Nature was posed as an alternative to God. In the twentieth century Bertrand Russell, A. J. Ayer, and Julian Huxley were among the outspoken atheists. As a whole, however, the atheists mentioned above were isolated individuals who served as background for the organized movements which began to emerge in the years after the Civil War. *The Truth Seeker*, a liberal periodical, while not atheist oriented to begin with, allowed atheist notices to be printed and served as a means of communication. Only after World War I were efforts to affiliate atheist bodies in larger organizations successful. People within the liberal tradition fall roughly into three groups, ranging from conservative to radical. The first group believes in God; the unitarians and universalists belong to this set of liberals. The second group is a humanist, ethical group with a vigorous, positive moral philosophy. The third group is atheistic and proposes a variety of worldviews exclusive of any deity. Atheists insist that first and foremost they are people with a positive approach to life that finds no need to assert the existence of a deity. Their popular designation as people who deny the existence of God is an image created by their necessary attempts to explain their position in the face of a more dominant theistic population.

SOURCES—THE LIBERAL FAMILY

GENERAL SOURCES

Baumer, Franklin L. *Religion and the Rise of Skepticism*. New York: Harcourt Brace and World, 1960. 308 pp.

Bratton, Fred Gladstone. *The Legacy of the Liberal Spirit*. Boston: Beacon Press, 1943. 319 pp.

Brown, Marshall G., and Gordon Stein. *Freethought in the United States, A Descriptive Bibliography*. Westport, CT: Greenwood Press, 1978. 146 pp.

Sheldon, Henry C. *Unbelief in the Nineteenth Century*. New York: Eaton & Mains, 1907. 399 pp.

Stein, Gordon. *Robert G. Ingersoll, A Checklist*. Kent, OH: Kent State University Press, 1969. 128 pp.

UNITARIANISM AND UNIVERSALISM

Albee, Ernest. *A History of English Unitarianism*. New York: Collier Books, 1962. 383 pp.

Parke, David B. *The Epic of Unitarianism*. Boston: Beacon Press, 1957. 164 pp.

Scott, Clinton Lee. *The Universalist Church of America, A Short History*. Boston: Universalist Historical Society, 1957. 124 pp.

Three Prophets of Religious Liberalism: Channing, Emerson, Parker. Boston: Beacon Press, 1961. 152 pp.

Wilbur, Earl Morse. *A History of Unitarianism*. Cambridge, MA: Harvard University Press, 1946. 617 pp.

Williams, George Huntston. *American Universalism*. Boston: Beacon Press, 1971. 94 pp.

DEISM AND FREETHOUGHT

Darrow, Clarence, and Wallace Rice. *Infidels and Heretics*. Boston: Stratford Company, 1929. 293 pp.

Hawke, David Freeman. *Paine*. New York: Harper & Row. 1974. 500 pp.

Ingersoll, Robert G. *Ingersoll's Greatest Lectures*. New York: The Freethought Press Association, 1944. 419 pp.

Koch, G. Adolf. *Republican Religion*. New York: Henry Holt and Company, 1933. 334 pp.

May, Henry F. *The Enlightenment in America*. New York: Oxford University Press, 1976. 419 pp.

Morais, Herbert M. *Deism in Eighteenth Century America*. New York: Russell & Russell, 1960. 203 pp.

Persons, Stow. *Free Religion*. Boston: Beacon Press, 1947. 162 pp.

Tribe, David. *100 Years of Freethought*. London: Elek, 1967. 259 pp.

HUMANISM

Hawton, Hector. *The Humanist Revolution*. London: Barrie and Rockliff, 1963. 247 pp.

Walker, Joseph. *Humanism as a Way of Life*. New York: Macmillan, 1932. 83 pp.

ATHEISM

Brooks, David M. *The Necessity of Atheism*. New York: The Freethought Press Association, 1933. 322 pp.

Stein, Gordon, ed. *An Anthology of Atheism and Rationalism*. Buffalo, NY: Prometheus Books, 1980. 354 pp.

CHRISTIAN ATHEIST CONTROVERSY

Blackie, John Stuart. *The Natural History of Atheism*. New York: Scribner, Armstrong & Company, 1878. 253 pp.

Graham, Lloyd M. *Deceptions and Myths of the Bible*. New York: Bell, 1979. 484 pp.

Lewis, Joseph. *The Bible Unmasked*. New York: The Freethought Press Association, 1926. 236 pp.

McCabe, Joseph. *The Sources of the Morality of the Gospels*. London: Watts, 1914. 315 pp.

Marty, Martin E. *The Infidel: Freethought and American Religion*. Cleveland: World Publishing Co., 1961.

Micelli, Vincent P. *The Gods of Atheism*. New Rochelle, NY: Arlington House, 1973. 490 pp.

Wheless, Joseph. *Forgery in Christianity*. Moscow, ID: Psychiana, 1930. 428 pp.

Chapter Thirteen

THE LATTER-DAY SAINTS FAMILY

Directory listings for the groups belonging to the Latter-Day Saints Family
may be found in the section beginning on page 481.

"After I had retired to the place where I had previously designed to go, having looked around me, and finding myself alone, I kneeled down and began to offer up the desires of my heart to God. I had scarcely done so, when immediately I was seized upon by some power which entirely overcame me, and had such an astonishing influence over me as to bind my tongue so that I could not speak. Thick darkness gathered around me, and it seemed to me for a time as if I were doomed to sudden destruction. But, exerting all of my powers to call upon God to deliver me out of the power of this enemy which had seized upon me, and at the very moment when I was ready to sink into despair and abandon myself to destruction—not to an imaginary ruin, but to the power of some actual being from the unseen world, who had such marvelous power as I had never before felt in any being—just at this moment of great alarm, I saw a pillar of light exactly over my head, above the brightness of the sun, which descended gradually until it fell upon me.

It no sooner appeared than I found myself delivered from the enemy which held me bound. When the light rested upon me I saw two personages, whose brightness and glory defy all description, standing above me in the air. One of them spake unto me, calling me by name, and said, pointing to the other—

'THIS IS MY BELOVED SON, HEAR HIM!'

My object in going to inquire of the Lord was to know which of all the sects was right, that I might know which to join. No sooner, therefore, did I get possession of myself, so as to be able to speak, than I asked the personages who stood above me in the light, which of all the sects was right—and which I should join. I was answered that I must join none of them, for they were all wrong, and the personage who addressed me said that all their creeds were an abomination in His sight: that those professors were all corrupt; that 'they draw near to me with their lips, but their hearts are far from me; they teach for doctrines the commandments of men: having a form of godliness, but they deny the power thereof.' He again forbade me to join with any of them: and many other things did he say unto me, which I cannot write at this time. When I came to myself again, I found myself lying on my back, looking up into heaven. When the light had departed, I had no strength; but soon recovering in some degree, I went home" (Joseph Smith, *History of the Church* [Salt Lake City: Deseret Book Company, 1902-1912], 1:5-6).

Thus is described by the man to whom it occurred the first event that led to the founding in 1830 of the Church of Jesus Christ of Latter-Day Saints; the man—Joseph Smith.

Vermont-born Joseph Smith had moved to western New York in 1815 at the age of ten, along with many others who flooded the area following the War of 1812. With the immigrants came the revival oriented church to stoke the fires of their emotions and burn the Word of God into their pioneer hearts. So successful had the evangelists been that observers would look upon western New York and label it "the burned-over district," the product of wave after wave of evangelical fervor and spiritual fire. It was in this same area that Charles Finney, discussed in the chapter on the holiness movement, made his triumphant tours of the late 1820's and early 1830's.

In this context Joseph Smith began to be moved by religious concerns and, like so many before him, to be confused by the plethora of churches, each claiming to speak God's truth. And in this context Joseph Smith began to see the visions (including the one related above) that resulted in his founding a new church to be the embodiment of God's true revelation. The two personages in the first vision (later identified as Jesus and God the Father) were followed by John the Baptist and various angelic beings in other visions. One of the angels gave to Joseph in 1827 the plates of gold upon which was engraved what is now known as the *Book of Mormon*. The engraving was in what Joseph called a reformed Egyptian language. Also given were two divining stones, the "Urim and Thummim" (Exodus 28:30), used to translate the tablets of reformed Egyptian text. The stones could be compared to crystal balls.

The story related in the *Book of Mormon* purported to be the history of two groups of people: the Jeredites, who came to America directly after the attempt to build the Tower of Babel, and the Israelites, who came following the destruction of Jerusalem in the sixth century B.C. The former group had been destroyed shortly before the arrival of the second group. The second group was essentially destroyed in the fourth century A.D., and the Indians remained as its only remnant. The last of the prophets among the second group was commanded to write a history which was buried in New York.

In 1830, the *Book of Mormon* was published and the church organized. Both events had an immediate impact on the religious community and began a debate that has grown in intensity to this very day. The *Book of Mormon* was attacked and the Mormons became outcasts.

But the *Book of Mormon* was not the only new revelation of Joseph Smith. His other major works were the *Book of Moses*, the *Book of Abraham*, and an inspired translation of the Bible. At regular intervals new revelations were given for specific purposes. These were gathered in a collection in 1833 as the *Book of Commandments*, now called the *Doctrine and Covenants* (D.C.). Also, there were fragmentary works and mention of other major works which were never undertaken because of Smith's untimely death. References to the *Doctrine and Covenants* throughout this chapter will be given with the initials D.C. and the number of the section under consideration. The *Book of Mormon* contains books within it, as does the Bible. References to the *Book of Mormon* will look like Biblical references (e.g., II Nephi 2:46-47).

Smith's many revelations created a number of problems for Mormon theology. They also built into the system a ready-made impetus to schism. It did not take long for others to get the idea, "If Joseph Smith can, then I can also." So that, quite apart from the issue of the truth or falsity of the *Book of Mormon* or other writings produced by Joseph Smith, his example continually excited would-be prophets to action. Common to almost every Mormon group is one or more leaders who receive revelations. These leaders originated as disturbers of the peace in each new church center as the Saints migrated from Kirkland, Ohio, to Independence, Missouri, to Nauvoo, Illinois, and finally, after Joseph Smith's murder, to Salt Lake City, Utah.

The church was hardly organized before Brother Hiram Page began to obtain revelations concerning the church through "a certain stone." Smith soon learned that his confidant, Oliver Crowley, and David Whitmer had been taken in by Page, but Smith was able to handle this situation in a church conference. Page recanted, and he and Crowley were sent on a mission to preach to the Indians.

After the movement of Smith's followers to Kirkland, Ohio, genuine schism began to occur. Wycam Clark led a group of former Saints who established the short-lived Pure Church of Christ. A Mr. Hawley walked barefoot six hundred miles from New York to tell Joseph that he was no longer the prophet. In 1831, Joseph was able to reconcile a group called "the family" to full status in the church. This communal group had joined the Mormons as a body and had to be persuaded to follow "the more perfect law." In 1832, a Mr. Hoton and a Mr. Montague organized a body of which the former was president and the latter bishop. The group fell apart when the bishop accused the president of visiting the "pork barrel" (stored supplies), and the president accused the bishop of visiting his wife.

The years 1837-38 were difficult for Joseph, as two major movements took sheep from his flock. Warren Parrish, treasurer of the Kirkland Safety Society, became disillusioned with Joseph's prophetic ability and withdrew. He and a number of prominent Latter-Day Saints who joined him founded the Church of Christ. Also, there appeared in Kirkland an unnamed woman called the Kirkland seeress. She had a black stone and she prophesied that either David Whitmer or Martin Harris would succeed Joseph, who had fallen into transgression. The movement in support of the anti-Josephite revelations was strong enough to spread to Missouri. No record of the eventual fate of the girl is known. *The History of the Church* by Smith has only a proclamation issued in the fall of 1837 expressing hope for the reclamation of David Whitmer and others. In 1838 the Saints moved to Missouri to a town called Far West. In 1839 they were forced to leave Far West, so they settled in Nauvoo, Illinois, and stayed there until Joseph Smith's death in 1844. In 1840 George M. Hinkle, a colonel in the militia which defended the Mormons at Far West, Missouri, founded the Church of Jesus Christ, the Bride the Lamb's Wife, at Moscow, Iowa. Hinkle, a trusted confidant of Smith, had had a significant role in turning Joseph, his brother, Hiram, and others over to General Lucas of the Missouri militia. "Hinkle" has since been synonymous in Mormon circles with traitor. In 1845 Hinkle's church merged with Sidney Rigdon's Church of Christ.

In the 1840's during the Nauvoo era, Joseph reached the height of his power. Nauvoo, in Hancock County, became the largest city in Illinois and, because of the evenly divided makeup of Illinois politics, it held the balance of power between Democrats and Republicans. Because Joseph kept switching sides, the Mormons became a hated people. Added to the political situation was the jealousy of the people of Hancock County at the success of the whole Nauvoo enterprise. During the entire stay of the Mormons at Nauvoo, tensions were on the rise and schism could always find its support among gentile haters of the Saints.

At least three major schisms occurred here, each contributing to the downfall of the Mormon establishment. In 1842, the High Council excommunicated Oliver Olney, would-be prophet, who moved to nearby Squaw Grove, Illinois, to establish headquarters and to publish his anti-Smith literature. He was still publishing as late as 1845 but his full history is not known. Also in 1842, Gladden Bishop was for a second time excommunicated, this time for "having received, written and published or taught certain revelations not consistent with the Doctrine and Covenants of the Church." Bishop began setting up splinter churches and then rejoining the Saints. He is known to have had followings at various times at Little Sioux, Iowa; in California, Wisconsin, Ohio, and Salt Lake City. After being in and out of the church several times, he was excommunicated permanently.

The major trouble for Joseph Smith at Nauvoo was a schism caused by William Law and his associates—Wilson Law, Robert and Charles Foster, and C.L. Higbee. They and a large following left the church and set up a rival organization in Nauvoo with William Law at the head of it. This schism meant more than just the loss of some members. In May

1844, Law announced a newspaper to support his views. He then got an indictment against Smith for adultery and polygamy. Robert Foster got an indictment against Smith for false swearing. Francis Higbee sued for slander, demanding $5,000. On June 7, 1844, the first and only issue of the *Nauvoo Expositer* appeared. The Nauvoo Legion, after Smith declared the paper a public nuisance, destroyed it. This proved to be a political blunder and as news spread across the state, public pressure mounted against the Saints and Joseph Smith. He was forced to flee from Nauvoo to Iowa. He soon returned to Illinois.

The Law affair was significant in the series of episodes that led in 1844 to the arrest of Joseph, his brother, Hiram, John Taylor, and Willard Richards. On June 27, 1844, a mob broke into the jail at Carthage, Illinois, and killed Joseph and Hiram and wounded Taylor. The sudden and violent death of its leader left the church he founded in chaos. Joseph had left no undeniable successor, only a martyr's image and a history of prophecy. The Saints were essentially united, but there began a power struggle that split the movement into at least four groups that, over the years, spawned more than fifty additional bodies.

The key idea in Joseph's theology was restorationism, the restoring of the Apostolic church which had been lost. Restorationism had been a major concept of the Disciples of Christ (Campbellite) from which Smith's early confidant, Sidney Rigdon, came. Smith believed that the true church died with the first generation of apostles and was restored only with his ordination. The ordination at the hands of John the Baptist occurred on May 15, 1829, when Joseph Smith and Oliver Cowdery were given the Priesthood of Aaron. Subsequently, the Priesthood of Melchizedek was conferred and the church was formally established (April 6, 1830). Along with this restoration of the Apostolic church came a set of doctrines and a church order.

The Articles of Faith, written shortly before Joseph Smith's death and still used by the Church of Jesus Christ of Latter-Day Saints, contain thirteen points of doctrine:

1. We Believe in God, the Eternal Father, and in His Son, Jesus Christ, and in the Holy Ghost.

2. We believe that men will be punished for their own sins, and not for Adam's transgression.

3. We believe that through the Atonement of Christ, all mankind may be saved, by obedience to the laws and ordinances of the Gospel.

4. We believe that the first principles and ordinances of the Gospel are: first, Faith in the Lord Jesus Christ; second, Repentance; third, Baptism by immersion for the remission of sin; fourth, Laying on of hands for the gift of the Holy Ghost.

5. We believe that a man must be called of God, by prophecy, and by the laying on of hands, by those who are in authority to preach the Gospel and administer the ordinances thereof.

6. We believe in the same organization that existed in the Primitive Church, viz., apostles, prophets, pastors, teachers, evangelists, etc.

7. We believe in the gift of tongues, prophecy, revelation, visions, healing, interpretation of tongues, etc.

8. We believe the Bible to be the word of God as far as it has been translated correctly; we also believe the Book of Mormon to be the word of God.

9. We believe all that God has revealed, all that He does now reveal, and we believe that He will yet reveal many great and important things pertaining to the Kingdom of God.

10. We believe in the literal gathering of Israel and in the restoration of the Ten Tribes; that Zion will be built on this (the American) Continent; that Christ will reign personally upon the earth; and that the earth will be renewed and receive its paradisaical glory.

11. We claim the privilege of worshipping Almighty God according to the dictates of our own conscience, and allow all men the same privilege; let them worship how, where or what they may.

12. We believe in being subject to kings, presidents, rulers and magistrates, in obeying, honoring, and sustaining the law.

13. We believe in being honest, true, chaste, benevolent, virtuous, and in doing good to all men, indeed, we may say that we follow the admonition of Paul. We believe all things, we hope all things, we have endured many things, and hope to be able to endure all things. If there is anything virtuous, lovely or of good report or praiseworthy, we seek after these things.

The average non-Mormon needs some interpretation of these statements inasmuch as they were worded to present Mormon doctrine in a form acceptable to mainline Christian denominations. For example, it may seem that the first article professes a belief in the Trinity, but in actuality a tritheism is being affirmed.

The doctrines concerning God and man which relate to the first four articles, some attributed to Joseph and some to those who came later, especially Brigham Young, are complicated, to say the least.

The restoration determined the nature of the church, which was to be organized after a revealed pattern. Two orders of priesthood were set up. The Aaronic Priesthood is the lesser order; all adult males are members, and from it are drawn deacons, teachers, and priests. The Melchizedek Priesthood is the higher order, and from it come the church's leadership—elders, seventies, high priests, and the presidency.

Organizationally, the church is ruled by a series of councils. Leading the church is the first presidency, composed of three people—the president and two other high priests elected by the twelve apostles. When the office of the first presidency is filled, the council of twelve apostles officiates under its direction as a traveling presiding council. Unanimous decisions by the council of twelve have authority equal to the decisions of the first presidency. Thus the first presidency and council of the twelve function very much as the pope and college of cardinals in the Roman Catholic Church.

The presiding quorum of seventy and the presiding bishopric comprise the other two ruling councils. The presiding bishopric holds jurisdiction over the duties of other bishops in the church and over the organization of the Aaronic Priesthood.

Most Mormons may be divided into Utah Mormons and Missouri Mormons, names that refer to their history more than to their current headquarters. The churches discussed under the heading of Utah Mormons either have their headquarters in Salt Lake City, Utah, or were established by a former member of the Church of Jesus Christ of Latter-Day Saints. The churches discussed under the heading of Missouri Mormons rejected the direction of Brigham Young, who led the Saints to Salt Lake City. The Missouri Mormons instead place a strong emphasis on the prophecy (D.C. 51) that the temple was to be built in Independence, Missouri.

POLYGAMY. No turmoil has so affected the Church of Jesus Christ of Latter-Day Saints as the controversy over its practice of polygamy in the post-Civil War era. Twenty years of practice had made polygamy an essential part of the Mormon social system and theology, and it was only after a lengthy battle against overwhelming odds that the church capitulated. This capitulation was in the form of a Manifesto in 1890 by President Wilford Woodruff abolishing the practice of plural marriage. The Manifesto was unanimously adopted by the vote of the Latter-Day Saints Church conference.

It soon became obvious that, at all levels of the church, resistance to the Manifesto was growing. Several polygamy-practicing groups formed but were broken up during World War I. After the war new groups were formed.

Most of the groups of polygamy-practicing Mormons accept a common history which dates to 1886, four years prior to the Manifesto. On September 26, 1886, at a meeting of church leaders to consider a document prepared by George Q. Cannon, the first counselor, on the polygamy question, President John Taylor is supposed to have spent a night in conversation with Joseph Smith and the Lord. The next morning President Taylor denounced the document and asked each to pledge himself to the principle of plural marriage. After the meeting, supposedly, five copies were made of the revelation of the Lord on plural marriage; and five men—Samuel Bateman, Charles H. Wilkins, George Q. Cannon, John W. Woolley, and Lorin Woolley—were given authority to administer the covenant (i.e., plural marriage) and to see that no year passed without some children being born in the covenant. Taylor also prophesied that during the time of the seventh president (Heber J. Grant), the church was to go into spiritual and temporal bondage, and one strong and mighty would appear (D.C. 85). The Latter-Day Saints Church claims this meeting never occurred and was a later fiction of Lorin Woolley.

Among the polygamists are Mormons called fundamentalists. They are distinguished from other polygamy-practicing groups in that they claim only to possess the presidency of the high priesthood, while other groups claim it as well as the presidency of the church.

In 1929 Joseph White Musser, the leader and most prolific writer among the fundamentalists, claimed he had received authority from Taylor's five disciples. He claimed further that after the Manifesto was issued, the office of the president of the church and the president of the high priesthood were separated and the latter given to the fundamentalists. Hence the priesthood has authority apart from the church leadership. Musser felt that the movement away from polygamy was but one of several changes and departures from the faith made by the church. The fundamentalists believe in the Adam-God theory, (taught by Brigham Young) that "Adam is Our Father and Our God and is the literal Father of Jesus." Almost all fundamentalists claim authority through Musser.

The polygamists are living outside the laws of both the Latter-Day Saints Church and the United States, and most have retreated into the desert and mountainous regions to escape legal and social pressure. They are an embarrassment to the Latter-Day Saints Church, which wishes to ignore them.

SOURCES—LATTER-DAY SAINTS FAMILY

GENERAL SOURCES

Arbaugh, George Bartholomew. *Revelation in Mormonism*. Chicago: University of Chicago Press, 1932. 252 pp.

Carter, Kate B. *Denominations That Base Their Beliefs on the Teachings of Joseph Smith*. Salt Lake City: Daughters of the Utah Pioneers. 1969. 68 pp.

Cory, Delbert J. *A Comparison Study of the Basic Thought of the Major "Latter Day Saint" Groups*. Oberlin, OH: The Author, 1963. 42 pp.

Goodliffe, Wilford Leroy. *America Frontier Religion: Mormons and Their Dissenters, 1830-1900*. University of Idaho, Ph.D. Dissertation, 1976. 287 pp.

Rich, Russell B. *Little Known Schisms of the Restoration*. Provo, UT: Brigham Young University, 1967. 76 pp.

———. *Those Who Would Be Leaders*. Provo, UT: Brigham Young University, 1967. 89 pp.

Shields, Steven L. *Divergent Paths of the Restoration*. Bountiful, UT: Restoration Research, 1975. 282 pp.

Tullis, F. LaMond, ed. *Mormonism, A Faith for All Cultures*. Provo, UT: Brigham Young University Press, 1978. 365 pp.

Van Nest, Albert J. *A Directory of the "Restored Gospel" Churches*. Evanston, IL: Institute for the Study of American Religion, 1984. 32 pp.

JOSEPH SMITH, JR.

Anderson, Richard Lloyd. *Joseph Smith's New England Heritage*. Salt Lake City: Deseret Book Company, 1971. 230 pp.

———. "The Reliability of the Early History of Lucy and Joseph Smith." *Dialogue*, 4, No. 2 (Summer 1969), pp. 12-28.

Brodie, Fawn M. *No Man Knows My History*. New York: Alfred A. Knopf, 1945. 495 pp.

Huntress, Keith. *Murder of an American Prophet*. San Francisco: Chandler Publishing Company, 1960. 232 pp.

Nibley, Hugh. *No Ma'am That's Not History*. Salt Lake City: Bookcraft, 1946. 62 pp.

Smith, Lucy Mack. *Joseph Smith and His Progenitors*. Lamoni, IA: Reorganized Church of Jesus Christ of Latter Day Saints, 1912. 371 pp.

Taves, Ernest H. *Trouble Enough, Joseph Smith and the Book of Mormon*. Buffalo, NY: Prometheus Books, 1984. 280 pp.

MORMON HISTORY

Arrington, Leonard J. *Brigham Young: American Moses*. New York: 1985.

————. *Great Basin Kingdom*. Lincoln: University of Nebraska Press, 1966. 538 pp.

————, and Davis Bitton. *The Mormon Experience*. New York: Alfred A. Knopf, 1979. 404 pp.

Backman, Milton V., Jr. *Eyewitness Accounts of the Restoration*. Orem, Ut: Grandin Book Company, 1983. 239 pp.

Mullen, Robert. *The Latter-Day Saints: The Mormons of Yesterday and Today*. Garden City, NY: Doubleday, 1966. 316 pp.

O'Dea, Thomas F. *The Mormons*. Chicago: University of Chicago Press, 1957. 289 pp.

Rich, Russell R. *Ensign to the Nations*. Provo, UT: Brigham Young University Publications, 1972. 663 pp.

Shipps, Jan. *Mormonism, the Story of a New Religious Tradition*. Urnana: University of Illinois Press, 1985. 211 pp.

Stegner, Wallace. *The Gathering of Zion*. New York: McGraw-Hill, 1971. 331 pp.

LATTER-DAY SAINTS BELIEFS

McConkey, Bruce R. *Mormon Doctrine*. Salt Lake City: Bookcraft, 1966. 856 pp.

Living Truths from the Book of Mormon. Salt Lake City: The Sunday School of the Church of Jesus Christ of Latter-Day Saints, 1972. 330 pp.

Richards, LeGrand. *A Marvelous Work and a Wonder*. Salt Lake City: Deseret Book Company, 1968. 452 pp.

Smith, Joseph F. *Gospel Doctrine*. Salt Lake City, Deseret Book Company, 1969. 553 pp.

CHRISTIAN REFUTATIONS OF THE LATTER-DAY SAINTS

Ahmanson, John. *Secret History*. Chicago: Moody Press, 1984. 179 pp.

Anderson, Einar. *Inside Story of Mormonism*. Grand Rapids: Kregal Publications, 1973. 162 pp.

Fraser, Gordon H. *Is Mormonism Christian?* Chicago: Moody Press, 1977. 192 pp.

McElveen, Floyd. *Will the "Saints" Go Marching In?* Glendale, CA: G/L Publications, 1977. 175 pp.

Ropp, Harry L. *The Mormon Papers*. Downers Grove, IL: InterVarsity Press, 1977. 118 pp.

Sackett, Chuck. *What's Going On There?* Thousand Oaks, CA: Ex-Mormons for Jesus, 1982. 64 pp.

Smith, John L. *I Visited the Temple*. Clearfield, UT: The Utah Evangel Press, 1966. 104 pp.

Tanner, Jerald, and Sandra Tanner. *Mormonism—Shadow or Reality?* Salt Lake City: Modern Microfilm Company, 1972. 587 pp.

MORMON SCRIPTURES

Campbell, Alexander. *An Analysis of the Book of Mormon*. Boston: Benjamin H. Greene, 1832. 16 pp.

Kirkham, Francis W. *A New Witness for Christ in America*. Independence, MO: Press of Zion's Printing and Publishing Company, 1951. 429 pp.

Nelson, Dee Jay. *Joseph Smith's "Eye of Ra."* Salt Lake City: Modern Microfilm Company, 1968. 32 pp.

————. *A Translation of Facsimile No. 3 in the Book of Abraham*. Salt Lake City: Modern Microfilm, 1989. 32 pp.

Nibley, Hugh. *Abraham in Egypt*. Salt Lake City: Deseret Book Company, 1981. 288 pp.

Prince, Walter Franklin. "Psychological Tests for the Authorship of the Book of Mormon." *American Journal of Psychology*, 28, No. 3 (July 1917), pp. 373-89.

Tanner, Jerald, and Sandra Tanner. *Did Spalding Write the Book of Mormon?* Salt Lake City: Modern Microfilm Company, 1977. 105 pp.

POLYGAMY

Anderson, J. Max. *The Polygamy Story: Fiction and Fact*. Salt Lake City: Publishers Press, 1979. 166 pp.

Bailey, Paul. *Grandpa Was a Polygamist*. Los Angeles: Western Lore Press, 1960. 181 pp.

————. *Polygamy Was Better Than Monotony*. New York: Ballantine Books, 1972. 180 pp.

Ballard, Melvin J., et al. *Marriage*. Salt Lake City: Truth Publishing Company, n.d. 107 pp.

Beadle, J. H. *Polygamy*. The Author, 1904. 604 pp.

Collier, Fred C. "Re-Examining the Lorin Woolley Story." *Doctrine of the Priesthood*, 1, No. 2 (February 1981), pp. 1-17.

Foster, Lawrence. *Religion and Sexuality*. Urbana: University of Illinois Press, 1984. 363 pp.

The Most Holy Principle. 4 vols. Murray, UT: Gems Publishing Company, 1970-75.

Merrill, Melissa. *Polygamist's Wife*. New York: Paperback Books, 1977. 176 pp.

Musser, Joseph White. *Celestial or Plural Marriage*. Salt Lake City: Truth Publishing Company, 1970. 154 pp.

Openshaw, Robert R. *The Notes*. Pinesdale, MT: Bitterroot Publishing Company, 1980. 616 pp.

Shook, Charles A. *The True Origins of Mormon Polygamy*. Cincinnati: Standard Publishing Company, 1914. 213 pp.

Taylor, Samuel Woollwy. *Family Kingdom*. New York: New American Library, 1951. 254 pp.

Tullidge, Edward W. *The Women of Mormondom*. New York: The Author, 1877. 552 pp.

Wallace, Irving. *The Twenty-seventh Wife*. New York: New American Library, 1962. 400 pp.

Whitney, Helen Mar. *Plural Marriage as Taught by the Prophet Joseph*. Salt Lake City: Juvenile Instructor Office, 1882. 52 pp.

Young, Kimball. *Isn't One Wife Enough*. New York: Henry Holt and Company, 1954. 476 pp.

Chapter Fourteen

THE COMMUNAL FAMILY

Directory listings for the groups belonging to the Communal Family may
be found in the section beginning on page 497.

"The group of believers was one in mind and heart. No one said that any of his belongings were his own, but they all shared with one another everything they had." These verses from Acts 4:32 (along with Acts 2) have inspired countless generations of Christians to forsake society and attempt to find a new style of living in communalism and commonality. Sources in pre-Christian society may have influenced early Christian practice. The ancient Cretes and Greeks adopted certain aspects of the communalist life style. The Essene community at Qumran represents an attempt in the Jewish community at a communal alternative.

It is not until the fourth century, however, that communalism becomes a real force in Western society, and interestingly enough, its form is the same as in the East—monasticism. Like the Christians, Buddhists, particularly in China, developed monastic communities as an attempt at authentic religious living in the face of a culture that was only nominally religious. For Western Christianity, the monastic ideal was a reaction to the establishment of Christianity as the state church, with mass conversions and baptisms which the monks said brought everybody into the church instead of making the church an assembly of true believers. Unlike the early church, which merely pooled its resources, monasticism presented a thorough-going communalism.

Inherent in the monk's life was the acceptance of an equality of life with the other brothers in the community. *Poverty* and the renunciation of the world were the prime means to this end. In the *chastity* rule an alternative to family life, a main distraction to community allegiance, was offered. In *obedience* to the abbot and in acceptance of the rules came the strong social system to replace the one ingrained from youth, as well as a discipline to enforce the new order.

The result was, of course, the success of the movement to which the church responded by the acceptance of some monastic goals for its clergy, principally chastity. However, the very success of the movement had consequences which threatened the existence of the monastic communities. They became wealthy and their wealth became a part of the problem of the Middle Ages as *they became an adjunct to the power structures instead of an alternative.*

Francis of Assisi was the one who raised the issue of poverty in monastic circles. Sophistry had undermined the poverty ideal, thought Francis. While individually giving up all property, collectively the monasteries were rich and the monks (without owning) could *use* all the wealth nevertheless. Francis advocated a poverty of *use*, and this real poverty ideal raised an issue that threatened the medieval church. In the face of this threat, the church hierarchy rejected Francis, burned his books, and rewrote his rules for the order. After Francis, various attempts were made to reform the monasteries, but few, if any, understood the heart of the issue. The inability to reform was a factor in the plundering of monasteries during the Reformation.

In the pre-Reformation and Reformation eras, various communal experiments were tried, mostly as part of the radically militant wing of reformist movements. Typical were the Taborites and Munsterites. The Taborites arose after the execution in 1415 of John Hus, the Czech reformer. In the conflict between papal supporters and Hussites, the Taborites emerged. Communities developed on Bohemian hillsides and a conscious imitation of early Christian communalism was practiced. The most important of these communities, on a hill near Bechyne Castle, was named Mount Tabor. Tabor was to be the site of the second coming of Christ (Mark 14), and the group derived its own name from the new Mount Tabor. Anti-German, intensely nationalistic, anti-Roman Catholic, and Biblicist, the Taborites were attempting a new social order outside that of Bohemia or even Western Europe. For this reason, they were themselves subject to persecution by both Roman Catholics and Hussites. In 1420, Martinek Hauska appeared, preaching the end-time and calling for all to flee to the mountaintops for safety. The mountaintops to which he referred were, of course, the five Taborite communities. The success led to a call for a holy war to exterminate sin and sinners and thus purify the land and bring in the millennium.

The millennium was to be characterized as an anarcho-communism. There would be no authority figures, taxes, rents, or private property. Since it was a classless society, it would begin by a massacre of the rich. Communal coffers were established. When these ran low, the Taborites "took from the enemies of God what God has given for his children" (i.e., they stole what they needed from any nearby non-Taborite). The Taborites, well supplied militarily, continued to exist for a generation, but were broken and splintered by war, messianic figures claiming to be Christ, doctrinal divergences and, primarily, an inability to produce the goods needed to survive. They eventually died out as a social experiment.

During the Reformation, communalism emerged among the radical reformers. In 1534, the New Jerusalem was established at Munster by Bernard Rothmann, Jan of Leiden and Jan Mathijs. The leaders imposed communalism on an essentially reluctant community. They began by collecting all the financial resources into the community treasure, effecting the change by making the surrender of money the test of true Christianity. Demands on food and shelter followed as the ideal became a disappearance of the distinction between thine and mine. Mathijs emerged as the ruling authority, but was killed in a scouting raid against the Catholic forces now besieging the city. Jan of Leiden took over and began the imposition of an exacting moral code. Artisans were commandeered and made community employees. The sexual mores were changed. Jan took advantage of the three-to-one ratio of women to men and declared polygamy the order of the day. Jan, himself, took fifteen wives, and the polygamy soon disintegrated into promiscuity.

After an early victory over the Catholic forces, Jan of Leiden proclaimed himself king of the world and instituted a wave of terror against community dissidents. The early victory of the reformers only led to greater efforts by the Catholic forces, who laid an even stronger siege to Munster. Eventually, they starved the community to death, and Jan of Leiden was executed.

The experiences at Munster and Tabor were typical in many ways of medieval communal groups. Though Munster was an extreme case, communalists associated with the Reformation tended to be militant in their approach to authority structures other than their own. Possibly related to their militancy was their own experience of having been persecuted, and a resulting short life-span. When they gained power, they became the persecutor. The Taborite practice of the appropriation of property of non-communalists was also widespread. The sexual reforms, mostly advocating community of women or polygamy, were common. With such models, it is no wonder that communalism did not experience another revival for several centuries. A few isolated attempts appeared, but only in the early 1800's did a new wave of communalism arise.

THE NINETEENTH-CENTURY COMMUNAL SURGE.
The nineteenth century burst of communalism grew out of the Enlightenment of the eighteenth century and the rise of intellectual concern with social order. The followers of Claude Henri Saint-Simon are usually accredited with the beginning of egalitarian reformist ideas, but roots to Saint-Simon's thought are deep in the trends of eighteenth century philosophy. In the 1820's, followers of Saint-Simon began a community, which after Saint-Simon's death, was moved to Menilmontant by its leader, Enfantin. In 1832, Enfantin was condemned for teaching free love, and communalism suffered a setback from which it never recovered in France.

Among the French socialist writers was Etienne Cabet, who put his communalist ideals in an 1840 book, *Voyage en Icarie*. In 1848, he and some followers settled in Fanin County, Texas, but health problems forced them to Illinois, where they settled at Nauvoo, which had recently been abandoned by the Mormons. Branch colonies were established in Iowa and Missouri, but Cabet's death in 1856 was a nearly fatal blow. One colony in Iowa did survive until the end of the century.

More important for the eventual rise of communal groups were the ideas of Charles Fourier (1772-1837). Fourier saw the world organized in phalanxes (his name for a single community) in which communism would be practiced in both labor and production. A strong order would exist for discipline, and loyalty to the phalanx (a central idea) would replace national and family ties. Marriage would be regulated on a polyandric system, with women having many husbands. The vision of Fourier gripped the imagination of the Western world.

One of the people who adopted Fourier's vision was George Ripley. His concerns were laid down in a lengthy letter to Ralph Emerson on November 9, 1840. Ripley looked for a place where a natural union between intellectual pursuits and labor could be achieved by combining the two. He proposed to do this on a tract of land which would be a farm, garden, and college, all in one. This adventure, thought Ripley, would yield industry without drudgery and equality without vulgarity. It would do away with the evils of capitalism and competition. Each family would retain some private property, thus allowing individuality to continue. About ten to twelve families would start the experiment, which would grow slowly. The adults would be paid interest on their investment and wages for their labor. There would be no great wealth but a comfortable living.

Government would be by consensus expressed in open meetings. On September 29, 1841, the Articles of Association for Brook Farm were drawn up after the members spent a summer near West Roxbury, Massachusetts. The Articles called for full support of children to age ten and their education until age twenty. The youth would work for half wages and, at twenty, would decide to stay as a full member or leave without obligation to the community. Income would come to the community through a boarding school and a farm. Later, printing and manufacturing would be added.

Problems arose in the community. An internal critique identified several sources of the friction. There was a lack of well planned operating procedures. The only real community experience was eating together; there should be more sharing on other levels. No common religious life existed. No confrontation with the basic problem of divided love had been made.

After making this critique, the members revived their interest in Fourier's ideas. Albert Brisbane, an ardent disciple of Fourier, joined Brook Farm, and it was on its way to becoming a successful phalange. Population increased and a house (phalanstery) was begun. But before it could become self-sufficient, a smallpox epidemic took a heavy toll of its members, some of whom died, and some of whom fled. A fire destroyed the phalanstery. In November 1846, Brook Farm was declared a failure and the project ended.

More successful was the phalanx at Hopedale, Massachusetts. Begun in 1841, it prospered for eleven years under the able guidance of Adin Ballou, a Unitarian and Spiritualist. Altogether, one hundred and seventy-five people lived at Hopedale. Its success was built upon Ballou's strong leadership and a strict moral and behavioral code. Religious freedom was allowed. The project failed after Ballou withdrew as leader.

Communities drawing on the enthusiasm of the French philosophers, but based more directly on religious, mainly New Testament, ideals also flourished in the nineteenth century. Significant for their success were the Rappites, German separatists who migrated to Pennsylvania in the early 1800's. In 1803-04, they settled in Butler County, Pennsylvania, and in 1805, promulgated their Articles of Agreement. They were German pietists and millennialists. They were led by George Rapp, who was given almost complete control over the community. Regulation of sexual life began in 1807 when the community became celibate. Equality was a high ideal and a uniform dress was adopted. A community graveyard without markers was also used. In 1814, the group migrated en masse up the Wabash River from Evansville to New Harmony, Indiana.

Here they established one of the most successful communities in American history. In 1818, the final break with the past was made when all property records, hence all claims by individuals on the community's property, were destroyed by vote of the community. The Rappites became known for their innovations. They were the first to develop prefabricated houses, many of which still stand. They diversified their economy and became in a short time entirely self-sufficient. They made wagons, distilled whiskey, cultivated silk, and had an early printing center for the Wabash Valley. Success threatened their faith, so in 1824, they sold the property and returned to Pennsylvania. They built a new town, Economy, near Pittsburgh.

The beginning of the end came in the late 1820's when Father Rapp, without consulting the community, published a second set of Articles of Agreement. While these articles merely said in writing what was happening in practice, discontent at Rapp's impertinence arose. To counter the dissatisfaction, Rapp began to emphasize the nearness of the second coming of Christ in his sermons and to propose a group journey to meet him in the Holy Land. The apocalypticism was rewarded in 1832 by the appearance in Economy of "Count Leon," a professed returned Christ and the anointed of God. He took approximately 250 of the Rappites with him when he left. The "Count Leon" incident was followed by disagreement on celibacy and Rapp's paternal control. Rapp was forced to modify his articles.

In 1834, Father Rapp's adopted son, who had been the financial genius of the community, died. With his passing much of the community's financial success passed also. In 1847, Father Rapp died, and without his unitive personality, the community disintegrated. Both New Harmony and Economy are only tourist spots today.

THE TWENTIETH CENTURY. The first half of the twentieth century saw few communal experiments. The Protestant monasticism of Taizé in France and the Sisters of Mary of Darmstadt in Germany are among the few. Both were begun in the aftermath of World War II and remain successful communities. The Society of Brothers and Koinonia Farm are other exceptions. It was not, however, until the 1960's that a new communal ideal emerged. Beginning in the summer of 1967, a number of young adults flocked to Haight-Ashbury in San Francisco in search of a cultural alternative to the middle-class life in which they had been raised. Labelled flower children because of their habit of giving flowers to people, they soon became distinguished by their use of psychedelic drugs. Both in San Francisco and along Sunset Strip near Los Angeles, they adopted communalism as a way to survive economically in the ghetto they were creating. As communalism grew, the rediscovery of a new quality of living was made. After time and the media destroyed the flower children, the communal quality of living remained as a residue. Since that time, hundreds of communes have been founded. Some have survived the initial birth pangs to become stable, self-supporting communes; most died in the birth agony.

THE MARKS OF A SUCCESSFUL COMMUNITY. Of the many communities begun in America since 1800, only a few have survived any length of time. That is, only a few have survived long enough for a child born in the commune to become an adult member. From those that have survived and from a study of demise of those that failed, some characteristics of successful and unsuccessful communities emerge. As a beginning, it might be noted that sex and close interpersonal relations are rarely the cause of a community's failure. These two items often bring discontent and a change of membership, but in only the rarest of cases do they lead to a total break-up of the community. Even Plato, in the *Republic*, recognized the necessity of a strong order in sexual relations. He proposed a community of wives. It is characteristic of communities either at the beginning or very soon thereafter (sex is a question that does not wait long to be asked), that personal relationships must be put in a social pattern. The human organism has proved adaptable to a seemingly infinite variety of patterns, from monogamy, to polygamy and polyandry, to free love of both traditional and Oneida varieties, to group marriage (which might include homosexual attachments), and to chastity, the most popular regulation. The particular form is not important; that sex be regulated is important.

Among the most influential of the patterns of sexual conduct in American religious groups is the (complex marriage) system developed by the Oneida community. The group was formed in Putney, Vermont, in the early 1840's, and moved to Oneida, New York, in the mid-1840's. The community endured for a generation, dissolving in 1880. The group produced silverware; the Oneida Corporation continues as a business venture. The Oneida community's sexual mores were established by John Humphrey Noyes, the founder of the community. Early in his career Noyes began to preach against monogamy as an exclusive attachment that limited love. As a first step in developing his new system. Noyes discovered what he called male continence, the practice of intercourse without the male reaching climax. (This practice was widespread among Tibetan Buddhists, and was called karezza.) By using this technique, numerous pregnancies could be avoided. Thus men of the Oneida community could cohabit with a number of women without giving the community the burden of many new members. As finally worked out, cohabitation within the Oneida community was regulated by a system of "ascending fellowship." In this system, those seen as more perfect (the older members) tended to have sexual encounters with the younger members. All encounters were arranged by a third party, and records were kept to prevent any exclusive relationships from developing.

A study of the history of many communes that have died out indicates five main reasons for their failure. First, communities *founded for shallow reasons* (i.e., by persons wanting to escape their homes) do not survive. *Poor planning* by those inexperienced in meeting the total needs of people is a prime cause of failure, particularly now, when so many communalists were raised in the city in complete ignorance of rural life. Anarchy, *a lack of order*, is another cause. Production of items (food, money, shelter, restrooms, etc.) necessary to survival becomes everyone's job but no one's responsibility. A common time for communes to dissolve is immediately following the first snow. *Hostility from the surrounding community* has been a prime force in disrupting communal existence. This hostility comes as a reaction to the different styles of life and the often deviant (from the local surrounding community) moral standards of communalists. Refusal to allow Oneida's sexual mores to prevail was a significant factor in its eventual demise. Hostility in New Mexico has all but destroyed many communes there. The final factor in communal disruption is *success*. Communes, if successful in reaching their original goals, financial or otherwise, will pose new goals often drawn from the surrounding world. Thus, keeping the communal ideal before the group is a continuing function. Communities in Zion, Illinois, Amana, Iowa, and New Harmony, Indiana, all suffered from success.

The successful commune (i.e., one that survives) will have several of the following characteristics, no one of which is sufficient in itself. *A strong leader* is present in many surviving communes. He supplies the unity and authority, and functions somewhat as a patriarchal father. His power may be drawn from his psychic, oratorical, or intellectual abilities, or just from his personality. Such present-day communes as the Ananda Cooperative Community of Kriyananda, the One World Family of Allen Noonan, and the Farm of Stephen are good examples. In the absence of a strong leader, *a strong system of social control and behavior* can function in his stead. This system, which may be formal or informal, must regulate enough of the life of the community for the necessities of life to be provided and a quality of life sustained. Many communes survive the death of their leaders by adopting such a system based on his teachings. *Economic self-sufficiency* is vital to a community's existence. Parasites can exist only for a couple of years. *Removal* from the outside world, in its most effective form geographically, is an early necessity. The establishment of a commune means changing habits and mores ingrained since childhood. It is best accomplished in a period of isolation, without old distractions. It can be done by a careful regulation of the possessions and material resources used by the community. After establishment, a careful check on new ideas must be made, and those destructive to the community's life countered.

The basic problem for communal groups is always, then, living as a subculture in a dominant culture which is often hostile and which always aims at assimilation and uniformity. Just as eternal vigilance is the price of freedom, eternal confrontation is the price of continued communal life.

SOURCES—THE COMMUNAL FAMILY

GENERAL SOURCES

Fogarty, Robert S. *American Utopianism*. Itaska, IL: F. E. Peacock Publishers, 1972. 175 pp.

Kanter, Rosebeth Moss. *Commitment and Community*. Cambridge: Harvard University Press, 1972. 303 pp.

Melton, J. Gordon, and Robin Martin. *A Bibliography of American Communalism*. Evanston, IL: Institute for the Study of American Religion, n.d. 23 pp.

Mercer, John. *Communes*. Dorchester, Dorset: Prism Press, 1984. 152 pp.

Muncy, Raymond Lee. *Sex and Marriage in Utopian Communities*. Bloomington: Indiana University Press, 1973. 275 pp.

Rexroth, Kenneth. *Communalism: From Its Origins to the Twentieth Century*. New York: Seabury Press, 1974. 316 pp.

Richter, Peyton E. *Utopias, Social Ideals and Communal Experiments*. Boston: Holbrook Press, 1971. 321 pp.

COMMUNES IN AMERICA PRIOR TO 1860

Bester, Arthur. *Backwoods Utopias*. Philadelphia: University of Pennsylvania Press, 1970. 330 pp.

Lockwood, George B. *The Harmony Movement*. New York: Dover Publications, 1971. 404 pp.

Mandelker, Ira L. *Religion, Society and Utopia in Nineteenth-Century America*. Amherst, MA: University of Massachusetts Press, 1984. 181 pp.

Sashse, Julius F. *The German Pietists of Provincial Pennsylvania*. Philadelphia: The Author, 1895.

Wisby, Herbert A., Jr. *Pioneer Prophetess*. Ithaca, NY: Cornell University, 1964. 232 pp.

COMMUNES IN AMERICA 1860-1960

Hine, Robert. *California's Utopian Communities*. New Haven: Yale University Press, 1966. 209 pp.

Kagan, Paul. *New World Utopias*. New York: Penguin Books, 1975. 191 pp.

Veysey, Laurence. *The Communal Experience*. Chicago: University of Chicago Press, 1978. 495 pp.

COMMUNES IN AMERICA AFTER 1960

Fitzgerald, George R. *Communes, Their Goals, Hopes, Problems*. New York: Paulist Press, 1971. 214 pp.

Fracchia, Charles A. *Living Together Alone*. San Francisco: Harper & Row, 1979. 186 pp.

Gardner, Hugh. *The Children of Prosperity*. New York: St. Martin's Press, 1978. 281 pp.

Hedgepath, William, and Dennis Stock. *The Alternative Life in New America*. New York: Collier-Macmillan, 1970. 191 pp.

Houriet, Robert. *Getting Back Together*. New York: Avon, 1971. 408 pp.

Chapter Fifteen

THE CHRISTIAN SCIENCE-METAPHYSICAL FAMILY

Directory listings for the groups belonging to the Christian Science-Metaphysical Family may be found in the section beginning on page 513.

During the last half of the nineteenth century, two movements, distinct yet distinctly related, emerged in the United States. They shared historical roots in both the Transcendental idealism of New England and the early nineteenth century magnetic healing movement. They also found agreement in the emphasis upon health and the healing of the body and the role of "Mind" in accomplishing such healing. The first to appear, Christian Science, and the Church of Christ, Scientist, in which it became institutionalized, was to a large extent the parent body of the other, a diverse and splintered movement generally called "New Thought."

THE FORERUNNERS—QUIMBY AND EVANS. During the 1920's the magnetic healing ideas of Austrian physician Franz Anton Mesmer were introduced to the United States. Mesmer had postulated the existence of a magnetic cosmic fluid, a subtle substance which could under the proper condition become focused in one person and transferred to another. In the transference, two prominent phenomena occurred, a somnambulistic sleep, known today as a hypnotic trance, and the healing of the physical body.

Once advocated by magnetist Charles Poyen, whose 1837 book, *Progress of Animal Magnetism in New England*, became a best seller, a magnetist movement swept America. It was common for lecturers to travel the land giving demonstrations. The Spiritualist movement came, in part, from people affected by the phenomena produced in magnetist sessions. Among the people whose lives were changed by magnetism was Phineas Parkhurst Quimby (1802-66).

A clockmaker residing in Belfast, Maine, Quimby had developed an early dislike for doctors. During the 1830's while under a physician's treatment for tuberculosis, he had become steadily weaker and almost died. Dismissing the physician, he cured himself. His own experience led him into a singular fascination with mesmerism following the visit of a Dr. Collyer to Belfast in 1838. He began to read and practice mesmerism, and to look for a suitable subject, whom he quickly found in Lucius Burkmer, a person who could easily slip into a deep hypnotic trance. In trance, Burkmer could diagnose and prescribe for illnesses of individuals brought before him. During the next few years Quimby experimented and observed. He saw people healed by taking medicines prescribed by Burkmer, medicines which had no medicinal value. Gradually, he decided that the real agent in illness was the mind of the individual.

Gradually Quimby abandoned much of the magnetist perspective and practice, particularly hypnotism, though he never completely separated himself from mesmerism. He continued to make magnetic passes over his patients, and his mature ideals still reflected the strong influence of magnetist thought.

For Quimby, mind was substance, spiritual matter, a substance produced by the continual agitation and motion of the body. Mind can in turn act upon the body and the state of the body is reflected in the state of the mind. Like seeds planted in the ground, ideas could be planted in the mind. False ideas could grow and mature and then manifest as disease. Quimby observed this process both in himself and his patients. He concluded that illness resulted from the mind's being controlled by false opinions. (In his basic definition of mind, Quimby identifies the magnetic fluid, popularly called "animal magnetism" by his contemporaries, with that element of the individual commonly believed to hold and manipulate ideas, the mind.)

Opposed to the changing ideas and opinions which fill the mind is Wisdom. Wisdom, in contrast to the mind's opinions, never changes. It is God, and creation, the perfect expression of Wisdom, is good. Evil enters the world as a result of human distortion through false belief. Disease is an effect of mind, not a cause. Wisdom is to be found within as Spirit, Principle, and Truth. To drop opinion and adopt Wisdom is to find happiness and health.

Wisdom is also scientific. It can be demonstrated. Science is the Wisdom, God, put into practice. It proves Wisdom and destroys ignorance. Once established, the Science of Truth will bring life and happiness. A central target of Science is manmade religion, including Christianity, which has thoroughly distorted the teaching of Jesus. Jesus taught the Christ, the unseen Principle, God within each person, and demonstrated the Science of the Christ.

In 1859 Quimby moved to Portland, Maine, established an office for healing and for teaching those who came to him for treatment. Quimby exercised a peculiar role as a healer. He claimed through clairvoyance the ability to sense his patient's disease apart from any outward diagnosis of the body. The Wisdom or Truth to which he was attuned destroys the disease. This destruction of error was accomplished, in Quimby's opinion, partly mentally and partly by talking to the patient.

While in Portland, Quimby welcomed as patients and pupils several who were to have the leading role in the development of metaphysical religion: Warren Felt Evans, Julius and Annetta Dresser, and Mary Patterson, later known to the world as Mary Baker Eddy. He treated their illnesses and taught them his ideas, which he circulated as a series of handwritten essays. When he died in 1866, Warren Felt Evans became the first to continue Quimby's healing work.

Evans, about whose early life little is known, was for many years a Methodist minister. Impressed by his reading of Emanuel Swedenborg, he joined the Swedenborgian Church of the New Jerusalem in the 1860's. His becoming a Swedenborgian coincided with an illness for which he placed himself under the care of Quimby. Not only was he healed, but he discovered that he had healing abilities similar to Quimby's. Quimby encouraged him to establish a practice in Claremont, New Hampshire, but following Quimby's death, Evans moved to Salisbury, Massachusetts (a Boston suburb) and continued his healing practice out of his home for the next two decades.

Besides his healing practice, Evans wrote several popular books on mental healing. Since Quimby had never published, his ideas had circulated by word of mouth alone. Evans' first book, *The Mental Cure* (1869), was followed by *Mental Medicine* (1872), in which he acknowledged Quimby as the source for the ideas he was advocating. These were followed by *Soul and Body* (1875); *The Divine Law of Cure* (1881); *Primitive Mind Cure* (1885); and *Esoteric Christianity and Mental Therapeutics* (1886). In his books Evans developed Quimby's ideas in the context of a sophisticated cosmology derived from Swedenborg and the German idealistic philosophers. He also continued some of Quimby's mesmeric practices. However, his writings continuously emphasize the major theme that disease is basically an expression of wrong belief. If the belief can be changed, the patient can be healed.

Evans spent his life in private practice and in writing. He never tried to gather a following; however, his popular books first introduced the general public to mental healing and directly influenced many of the early leaders of what would become the New Thought movement.

MARY BAKER EDDY AND CHRISTIAN SCIENCE. At the commencement of the study of Metaphysical science, we must acquaint ourselves with its Principle whereby to gain the demonstration of this Principle in healing the sick. For the sake of brevity, these first lessons are arranged in questions and answers.

"Question—What is God?

Answer—Jehovah is not a person. God is Principle.

Question—What is Principle?

Answer—Principle is Life, Truth and Love, Substance and Intelligence.

Question—Is there more than one Principle?

Answer—There is not. The varied manifestations of science have but one Principle, for there is but one God. All science expresses God, and is governed by Principle" (Mary Baker Eddy, *The Science of Man by Which the Sick Are Healed* [Lynn, MA: Luther C. Parker, 1879]).

Mary Baker Eddy (1821-1910), the founder of Christian Science, had grown up in a devout New England Congregationalist home. Her early formal education had been limited by her poor health, but she recovered enough in her teen years to attend Holmes Academy and then in 1843 to marry. Her husband died just months before their child was born, an event that signaled another period of poor health for the still youthful Mary.

She married again in 1953. Her husband, George Patterson, joined the Union Army during the Civil War, during which he was captured. Meanwhile, Mary had heard of Phineas P. Quimby and in 1862 she traveled to Portland, Maine to receive treatment. Within a month she was seemingly cured, and wrote in praise of Quimby to the newspaper in Portland. Her first stay in Portland, which lasted for three months, began the most crucial and controversial period of her career. It is evident that Quimby had opened up a new direction for her and that she initially gave him enthusiastic credit for an improvement of health. In later years, she would be accused by early leaders of the New Thought movement of doing little more than taking Quimby's material, recasting it (and on occasion misunderstanding it), and presenting it to the world as her own. Such does not appear to be the case.

Close examination of this period indicates that her health, after an initial marked improvement, continued to fluctuate. Also, while obviously engaged in the study of Quimby's ideas, and actually using his methods on others, she was not an uncritical student. She had trouble accepting the concept of mind as spiritual matter and of reconciling Quimby's thought with the Christian faith in which she had been raised. However, she associated with Quimby until his death in 1865.

The years as a student of Quimby were followed by the series of events that led to the discovery of Christian Science. On February 1, 1866, while visiting in Lynn, Massachusetts, she fell on the ice. She was found the next day to be suffering severe internal spasms. Taken back to her home in Swampscott, she was confined to her bed. Projections varied on the length of her recovery, some even doubting its possibility. However, on Sunday, February 4, given a Bible to read and left to meditate alone, she was overwhelmed with the conviction that her life was in God and that God was the only Life, the sole reality of existence. In that discovery came her healing. She got out of bed, dressed, and walked into the next room to the astonishment of all present.

The next months and years would be ones of personal turmoil, punctuated by her divorcing her husband for desertion, and her growing comprehension of the implication of the insight received at the time of her healing. During the next decade she would engage in intensive Bible study, struggling to understand the implications of God as healer versus Quimby's notion of mind as healer. In 1870 she formed a partnership with Richard Kennedy as a practitioner and teacher, and in August held her first class. She also began the writing that would eventually become *Science and Health with Key to the Scripture*, the first edition of which was published in 1875 (as simply *Science and Health* with the imprint of the Christian Scientist Publishing Company).

The following year the Christian Scientists Association was formed as a fellowship of her students, among whom was Asa Gilbert Eddy, whom she married in 1877. This led in 1879 to the formation of the Church of Christ, Scientist. In 1881 she formed the Massachusetts Metaphysical College, and a few months later was ordained by her students as pastor of the Church. In 1883 she began editing and publishing the *Journal of Christian Science*. In the midst of the organizational development, she found herself the leader of a growing movement, as her students had begun to scatter to cities across the United States. In 1884 she traveled to Chicago to teach a three week class. Two years later she went to New York to form the National Christian Scientists Association.

During the 1880's, teachings and teachers at variance with those of Eddy appeared. These in turn led to internal conflict and schism. Partially in response to the diffusion of these differing ideas, and partially in doubt of the desirability of any organization to carry on her work, in May 1889 Eddy began a process of dismantling the organizational structure she had created. She resigned as pastor of the church. In June she turned the *Journal* over to the National Christian Scientists Association. In September she dissolved the Christian Scientist Association (the Boston student's group) and finally in December the church dissolved. The only stricture to remain, the national student group, adjourned from its meeting in May 1890 not to meet again until 1892.

During this period Eddy turned her attention to a major revision of *Science and Health*, which appeared in 1891, and the following year reorganized the First Church of Christ, Scientist. She also resumed control of the *Christian Science Journal* and the National Christian Scientists Association disbanded. The events of 1892 placed the movement founded by Eddy on a stable organizational course. During the thirteen years since the founding of the original church in 1879, however, former associates and students had begun to form a rival movement which not only drew upon her teachings but continued and revived those of her former teacher P. P. Quimby.

THE NEW THOUGHT MOVEMENT. While Mary Baker Eddy was organizing Christian Science, the writings of Warren Felt Evans were attracting people to a metaphysical healing more closely connected to Quimby's ideals. To Evans' efforts were added those of Julius and Annetta Dresser who moved to Boston and in 1883 began teaching classes using their notes from Quimby. Among their early pupils were former associates of Eddy. The Dressers began to denounce Eddy, charging that she both denied her debt to Quimby and had changed his teachings. She responded by noting the

distinctiveness of her own perspective which she had developed (or discovered) quite apart from Quimby, and by becoming more vocal in her denying specific teachings of Quimby. The controversy thus launched continued at a heated pace well into the twentieth century, and remnants can still be found in the recent scholarly works of Charles Braden, Robert Peel, and Stephen Gottschalk.

The Dressers' efforts were given a significant boost by the defection of two of Christian Science's outstanding leaders, Emma Curtis Hopkins and Ursula Gestefeld. Hopkins, who took Eddy's class in 1883, quickly moved into a position of importance close to her teacher as the assistant editor of the new *Journal of Christian Science*. In August 1884 she became the editor. For reasons never fully clarified, in October 1885, Hopkins was dismissed from her post. She moved to Chicago and became an independent teacher. Within a year she had taught more than six hundred students and had established an Emma C. Hopkins Association. In 1887 she founded the Christian Science Theological Seminary, which became the school for the training of the next generation of future New Thought leaders. It included among its pupils Annie Rix Militz, Harriet Rix, Malinda Cramer, Mrs. Frank Bingham, Charles and Myrtle Fillmore, H. Emile Cady, and Ernest Holmes. Hopkins' continued influence on the movement was assured by the establishment of a teaching center to hold classes based upon her material (Joy Farm) and a publishing concern to keep her books and pamphlets in print (Ministry of the High Watch).

Ursula Gestefeld had attended the first Chicago class taught by Eddy in 1884. She became a popular teacher and in the developing movement in Chicago. Then she began to publish books independently of the Church and, from Eddy's perspective, deviating from her teachings. Gestefeld's 1888 volume, *Ursula Gestefeld's Statement of Christian Science*, was denounced in the *Christian Science Journal*. Gestefeld left Eddy's organization and bitterly attacked it in her pamphlet *Jesuitism in Christian Science*. She went on to become a prominent writer and teacher for New Thought.

Following Hopkins' and Gestefeld's breaks with Christian Science, other leaders, some influenced by them, emerged to provide leadership in the spreading movement. Charles M. Barrows, M. J. Barnett, Horatio Dresser (Julius' and Annetta's son), William J. Colville, Prentice Mulford, Ralph Waldo Trine, and Henry Wood produced an increasing number of books communicating versions of Quimby's and Eddy's ideas to the public. They were joined, especially after the turn of the century by a host of magazines which further popularized the movement. Centers and associations (the initial form of New Thought denominations) appeared in widely scattered locations from Boston to Los Angeles.

Both independent centers and the beginnings of what were to become large denominations met in 1899 in the first "New Thought Convention." The name "New Thought" had become popular in the 1890's and had been widely accepted within the movement, though some preferred such names as Divine Science, Mental Science, Christian Science, or Practical Metaphysics for their own variations on New Thought principles. Some objected to using "New Thought" because they wished to stress the eternal nature of truth and that they had merely rediscovered Jesus' teaching. These objections did not prevail, however. The New Thought Convention developed into the loosely organized "International New Thought Alliance" in 1914.

Individualism has been a keynote of New Thought, and in the twentieth century a number of writers and leaders arose who refused to connect themselves with anything beyond the local independent groups to whom they spoke regularly. The most influential of these leaders was Emmet Fox, long-time pastor of the Church of the Healing Christ in New York City. Born in Ireland and reared a Roman Catholic, Fox was drawn to New Thought and became one of its great propagandists. In his many books and pamphlets, Fox was able, as few have been, to demonstrate the metaphysical meaning in orthodox Christian terminology. He could use phrases like "God, the Father" and interpret them metaphysically—for example, saying the fatherhood of God refers to a feeling of security in the universe. Along the same lines, Job is seen to represent people's development from formal righteousness to inner change of heart. Fox's books sell as well today as when they were first published.

Second only to Fox in influence was Thomas Troward, the British New Thought philosopher. Troward spent all his active life in India and Pakistan, returning to England to retire. He joined a New Thought group and was soon asked to lecture. It was to be the first of many lectures he would give in the remaining years of his life. His *Edinburgh Lectures on Mental Science, Doré Lectures on Mental Science* and *Bible Mystery and Meaning* have been widely used as textbooks by New Thought leaders. His main idea that "the supreme principle of life must also be the ultimate principle of intelligence" fits into Quimby's ideas about mind and God.

The number of independent New Thought centers has grown since World War II. These centers are important sources of new denominational structures. A split in the Religious Science movement has spawned many of these. Typical is the Science of Mind Church, directed by popular author Frederick Bailes. It meets in the large Fox-Wilshire Theatre in Los Angeles, where it carries on an independent work not unlike that of other Religious Science churches. The All Faiths Church/Science of Mind in El Monte, California, is headed by the Rev. David Thompson, who has chosen to emphasize the universal religious aspect of Ernest Holmes' teaching, as well as to publish his own materials. Others can be found listed in the directory of the International New Thought Alliance in each issue of the *Quarterly*.

Also significant in the spreading of New Thought has been the propagation of its ideas and perspectives by ministers in mainline churches. These ministers would be headed by Norman Vincent Peale, whose *Power of Positive Thinking* is a New Thought classic. Others would include Bishop Fulton J. Sheen, Rabbi Joshua Liebman and Methodist Lewis Dunnington. Possibly Glenn Clark made New Thought more popular than all of the above. He founded Camp Farthest Out, an interdenominational group centered upon healing, prayer, and the spiritual life. Even after Clark's death, Camp Farthest Out continues as a strong body, headquartered in St. Paul, Minnesota.

METAPHYSICAL RELIGIOUS THOUGHT AND PRACTICE. During the 1880's a spectrum of ideas developed between those who strictly adhered to the teachings of Mary Baker Eddy and her major book, *Science and Health with Key to the Scriptures*, and those who tried to perpetuate the teachings of P. P. Quimby. Eddy and the members of her Church have attempted, and rightfully so, to separate themselves from what they view as the chaos of opinion that characterizes the metaphysical movement as a whole. However, that has not prevented the movement of ideas from Christian Science into the New Thought movement and the development of a certain commonality of beliefs (such as the emphasis upon the impersonal attributes of God over the personal). Within the larger metaphysical movement, the teachings of the Church of Christ, Scientist, form one major source. Several groups led by former Christian Science practitioners most closely adhere to those teachings. The New Thought movement, on the other hand, has no single teacher or source, but has borrowed widely from Quimby, Eddy, and others, and individual teachers and groups will emphasize different themes. The closest the movement comes to a consensus can be found in the Declaration of Principles adopted by the International New Thought Alliance.

Declaration of Principles

We affirm the inseparable oneness of God and man, the realization of which comes through spiritual intuition, the implications of which are that man can reproduce the Divine perfection in his body, emotions, and in all his external affairs.

We affirm the freedom of each person in matters of belief.

We affirm the Good to be supreme, universal, and eternal.

We affirm that the Kingdom of Heaven is within us, that we are one with the Father, that we should love one another, and return good for evil.

We affirm that we should heal the sick through prayer, and that we should endeavor to manifest perfection "even as our Father in Heaven is perfect."

We affirm our belief in God as the Universal Wisdom, Love, Life, Truth, Power, Peace, Beauty, and Joy, "in whom we live, move, and have our being."

We affirm that man's mental states are carried forward into manifestation and become his experience through the Creative Law of Cause and Effect.

We affirm that the Divine Nature expressing Itself through man manifests Itself as health, supply, wisdom, love, life, truth, power, peace, beauty, and joy.

We affirm that man is an invisible spiritual dweller within a human body, continuing and unfolding as a spiritual being beyond the change called physical death.

We affirm that the universe is the body of God, spiritual in essence, governed by God through laws which are spiritual in reality even when material in appearance.

New Thought is in its essence a religious philosophy, based upon the ideas of Phineas P. Quimby. The basic concept is mind. Mind is the underlying ordering principle in the universe. God is mind, man is mind. Mind is orderly and expresses itself as law. Law is usually man's first contact with the principles and orderliness of God. The universe is abstract, impersonal, giving to all alike. God is unchangeable. Man is created in his image and likeness. Man is the expression or manifestation of God's law being executed in a particular instance. God is a Trinity of mind, idea, and expression—three yet one.

God is being, the *I Am* of the Old Testament. Mind is what is metaphysically real. It is, it exists. But it is dynamic, it is Spirit. It not only orders, it propels. It is conscious. It knows itself. It is the sustaining power in the universe. In creating and sustaining, it is all pervasive, immanent in all that exists. It is the source of all. Charles Fillmore wrote of mind:

"The foundation of our religion is Spirit, and there must be a science of Truth. The science of Truth is God thinking out creation. God is the original Mind in which all real ideas exist. The one original Mind creates by thought" (Charles Fillmore, *Christian Healing* [Kansas City, MO: Unity School of Christianity, 1938], 17).

To mind as source and sustainer, man is to look for all his needs. God is the nexus of all the positive values—goodness, truth, beauty, and love. Mind particularly carries truth as an attribute. Truth is that which is.

Evil is privative. It is the denial of truth, the opposite of Spirit, that which lacks metaphysical reality. Hence, evil is error. The basic error is the belief that evil is real. Ascribing reality to the unreal by giving it time and attention is man's basic problem. It is the reason for sickness, poverty, and unhappiness. According to New Thought proponents, we think poverty and we become poor. We think sick and are ill. We turn from God and are unhappy.

From an understanding of the basic metaphysics, one can gain some understanding of the dynamics of New Thought in showing people how to move from illness, poverty, and unhappiness to health, wealth, and happiness. For each, the process is a variation on the other. Man must turn his attention to God, or attune his mind to Mind and Truth, and the Source of the Universe is open to him. Instead of focusing thought on a bad family relationship which brings on asthma, turn to God and allow the lungs to function normally according to God's laws. Instead of bemoaning one's lack of money, turn to the Creator and become attracted to his abundance. Instead of being unhappy, think on God.

There are a number of techniques to implement the movement-to-God attunement. The Sunday worship is an aid to focus on God. The structure is derived from New England Congregationalism and Unitarianism, and retains the Calvinist emphasis on decency and order. Worship is filled with content (prayers, hymns, meditations, sermon), which tells the worshiper that he is the child of God ready to receive all.

Two forms which are priority items for any New Thought believer are meditations and affirmations. Meditations are short statements which direct one's attention to the positive. For example,

Today I would cleave to that which is good. I would be "kindly affectioned one to another with brotherly love." I would let God love my brother through me. I am humble before the majesty and power of my God.

The affirmation is a type of meditation in which one affirms of the self what is believed to be true on a metaphysical level and which one is seeking to manifest on a visible way. For example, "I am the ever-renewing, ever-unfolding expression of the Christ within."

Finally, the ministry of the New Thought group is oriented to facilitating the manifestation, or in common parlance, the "demonstration," of truth in the believer. The key person in this ministry is the practitioner. The practitioner is one who knows the truth, can demonstrate it, and can be a catalyst for the healing of patients who come for help. The practitioner knows within himself the truth about the patient, and that self-knowing rises into the consciousness of the patient. The practitioner forms within his mind the change to be effected. He then communicates this change to Spirit and to the patient's spirit. This communication may be verbal, but is more centrally a purely mental process. Once the patient's mind is healed, the body adjusts.

The final structure central to New Thought is the class. Ever since Quimby gathered his students and taught the first classes, they have been the major means of conveying the truths of the faith. In Christian Science, the class has become the central means of rising to a leadership position in the church. In New Thought, the class varies in significance.

SOURCES—CHRISTIAN SCIENCE-METAPHYSICAL FAMILY

GENERAL SOURCES

Fuller, Robert C. *Mesmerism and the American Cure of Souls.* Philadelphia: University of Pennsylvania Press, 1982. 227 pp.

Judah, J. Stillson. *The History and Philosophy of the Metaphysical Movements in America.* Philadelphia: Westminster Press, 1967.

Melton, J. Gordon. *A Reader's Guide to the Church's Ministry of Healing.* Independence, MO: The Academy of Religion and Psychical Research, 1977. 102 pp.

Meyer, Donald. *The Positive Thinkers.* New York: Pantheon Books, 1980. 396 pp.

Parker, Gail Thain. *Mind Cure in New England.* Hanover, NH: University Press of New England, 1973. 197 pp.

Podmore, Frank. *Mesmerism and Christian Science.* London: Methuen, 1909. 299 pp.

Zweig, Stefan. *Mental Healers.* New York: Frederick Ungar Publishing Co., 1962. 363 pp.

THE FORERUNNERS-QUIMBY AND EVANS

Clark, Mason Alonzo, ed. *The Healing Wisdom of Dr. P. P. Quimby.* Los Altos, CA: Frontal Lobe, 1982. 127 pp.

Dresser, Anetta Gertrude. *The Philosophy of P. P. Quimby.* Boston: George H. Ellis, 1895.

Dresser, H. W. *The Quimby Manuscripts.* New York: Thomas Y. Crowell, 1921. 474 pp.

Evans, Warren Felt. *The Divine Law of Cure*. Boston: H. H. Carter & Co., 1884. 302 pp.

———. *Esoteric Christianity and Mental Therapeutics*. Boston: H. H. Carter & Karrick, 1886. 174 pp.

———. *The Mental Cure*. Boston: Colby & Rich, 1869.

———. *Mental Medicine*. Boston: 1873. 15th ed.: Boston: H. H. Carter & Co., 1885.

———. *The Primitive Mind Cure*. Boston: H. H. Carter & Karrick, 1885. 215 pp.

———. *Soul and Body*. Boston: H. H. Carter & Co., 1876. 147 pp.

Hawkins, Ann Ballew. *Phineas Parkhurst Quimby*. Los Angeles: DeVorss & Co., 1951. 56 pp.

Quimby, Phineas Parkhurst. *Immanuel*. Mokelumne Hill, CA: Health Research, 1960. 109 pp.

MARY BAKER EDDY AND CHRISTIAN SCIENCE

Beasley, Norman. *The Continuing Spirit*. New York: Duell, Sloan and Pearce, 1956. 403 pp.

———. *The Cross and the Crown*. New York: Duell, Sloan and Pearce, 1952. 664 pp.

Braden, Charles S. *Christian Science Today*. London: George Allen & Unwin, 1959. 432 pp.

Eddy, Mary Baker. *Science and Health*. Boston: Christian Scientist Publishing Company, 1875. 456 pp. Authorized edition: *Science and Health with Key to the Scripture*. Boston: Trustees Under the Will of Mary Baker G. Eddy, 1906. 700 pp.

———. *The Science of Man by Which the Sick Are Healed*. Lynn, MA: Luther C. Parker, 1879. 22 pp.

Gottschalk, Stephen. *The Emergence of Christian Science in American Religious Life*. Berkeley: University of California Press, 1973. 305 pp.

Leishman, Thomas Linton. *Why I Am a Christian Scientist*. Boston: Beacon Press, 1966. 245 pp.

Peel, Robert. *Christian Science, Its Encounter with American Culture*. Garden City, NY: Doubleday, 1965. 224 pp.

———. *Mary Baker Eddy*. 2 vols. New York: Holt, Rinehart and Winston, 1966, 1971.

Studdert-Kennedy, Hugh A. *Christian Science and Organized Religion*. Los Gatos, CA: The Farallon Foundation, 1961. 170 pp.

Swihart, Altman K. *Since Mrs. Eddy*. New York: Henry Holt and Company, 1931. 402 pp.

What Makes Christian Science Christian. Boston: The Christian Science Publishing Society, 1982. 30 pp.

NEW THOUGHT

Anderson, Alan. *Horatio W. Dresser and the Philosophy of New Thought*. Boston: Boston University, Ph.D. dissertation, 1963.

Beebe, Tom. *Who's Who in New Thought*. Lakemont, GA: CSA Press, 1977. 318 pp.

Braden, Charles S. *Spirits in Rebellion*. Dallas: Southern Methodist University Press, 1963. 571 pp.

Dresser, Horatio. *A History of the New Thought Movement*. London: George G. Harrap & Co., n.d. 352 pp.

———. *Spiritual Health and Healing*. New York: Thomas Y. Crowell, 1922. 314 pp.

Larson, Martin A. *New Thought: A Modern Religious Approach*. New York: Philosophical Library, 1939.

Chapter Sixteen

THE SPIRITUALIST, PSYCHIC, AND NEW AGE FAMILY

Directory listings for the groups belonging to the Spiritualist, Psychic, and
New Age Family may be found in the section beginning on page 531.

From the beginning of recorded history, men have claimed powers of mind and spirit far surpassing those commonly recognized by twentieth-century science. Men have claimed knowledge from beyond the capabilities of the five senses: the power to move objects by thought, the ability to talk to beings whose permanent home is not our world. In ancient Greece, the temple at Delphi was a center of this psychic world. There lived the Pythia, a psychic who prophesied for visiting dignitaries. Given in hexametric verse, these prophecies were often of a cryptic nature. Possibly the most famous story of Delphi comes from Herodotus. Croesus, king of Lydia in the time of Cyrus of Persia, was feeling the pressure of Cyrus and decided to do battle with him. Beforehand, he consulted the oracle of Delphi, who told him, "Croesus, having crossed the Halys (River), will destroy a great empire." Confident of victory, Croesus crossed the river and was thoroughly defeated. Croesus demanded an explanation. The Oracle replied bluntly that a great empire, Lydia, had fallen as predicted.

Socrates is often cited in ancient literature as a psychic of note. While a child, he became aware of a voice which spoke to him. The voice never commanded particular acts, but forbade wrong action.

In our own day, parapsychologists, scientists who investigate the psychic, have given the world a vocabulary by which the psychic can better be understood. Dr. J. B. Rhine of Duke University has spearheaded this effort. Extrasensory perception (ESP) is the term Rhine coined to describe man's ability to perceive information and encounter a world beyond the commonly recognized senses. ESP is of several kinds. Telepathy is mind-to-mind (subconscious-to-subconscious) communication. Clairvoyance is perception of the world beyond the senses without any other mind's help. Psychokinesis (PK) is mind over matter; Rhine would include spiritual healing in this category. Precognition is seeing into the future. In years of exacting experiments, Rhine demonstrated the existence of these four phenomena. But beyond these four, psychics describe many other experiences which psychical research is only beginning to explore. Some are plainly categories under these four inclusive terms, as, for example, spiritual healing. Others are not so clearly of these four. Astral travel is the experience of

the conscious self as being outside the body. Mediumship is clairvoyance and/or telepathic communication with beings not of this world.

In the 1960's, investigation of the healing power so long claimed by psychics and some churchmen was begun in earnest. Such people as Bernard Grad of McGill University in Montreal and Justa Smith of Rosary College in Buffalo, New York, have begun to demonstrate the reality of the power in healing mice, in stimulating the growth and yield of plants, and in changing the growth rate of enzymes. From such work as this, a new science, paraphysics, is evolving.

Beyond the realm of the purely psychical is the realm of the *occult*. "Occult" is a word that originally meant "hidden," the opposite of "apocalypse." In contemporary science, however, it has come to be applied generally to practices which were once part of the "hidden wisdom." These practices include various arts of divination—astrology, numerology, tarot cards, palmistry, and tea leaves, to mention a few.

THE BIBLICAL PSYCHIC TRADITION TO 1800. Although aware of the ancient world in general, contemporary psychics are most aware of one aspect of the ancient world—the Biblical tradition. They hold that, from cover to cover, the Bible is a psychic book, replete with incidents which would today be called psychic. These include incidents of spirit communication (Matthew 17:1-9, I Samuel 28), clairvoyance (John 4:16-29), healing (I Kings 5:1-27, Acts 3:3-11), prophecy (Acts 11:28; 21:1-13), and divination (Matthew 2:1-2, Acts 1:15-26).

In the Old Testament, Samuel is the paradigm of the psychic. As a young child, he was taken to Eli, Israel's corrupt psychic, to be dedicated to God. Shortly afterwards, he had his psychic awakening in the famous incident when a voice called out his name (I Samuel 3). Typical of Samuel's career, as he rose to be Israel's psychic, was the time he met Saul (I Samuel 9). Saul, the son of Kish, woke one morning to find his father's donkeys gone. He looked in vain for the lost herd. His servant suggested that Samuel, the prophet, might be able to help, for as the writer of I Samuel noted:

"Before time in Israel when a man went to inquire of God, thus he said, "Come let us go to the seer; for he that is now called a Prophet was before time called a Seer" (v. 9).

Samuel received a clairvoyant vision of Saul long before Saul's arrival and went out to meet him. Instead of speaking to Saul of donkeys, Samuel began to give Saul a precognitive vision of his future as king of Israel. He then anointed him. Only after the anointing did Samuel talk of the lost donkeys, revealing that they had returned home. When Saul became king, Samuel became his chief psychic advisor, a popular office in the ancient world. After Samuel's death, Saul went to a medium, a woman at Endor, to try to contact Samuel's spirit (I Samuel 28).

Psychics studying the New Testament look to Jesus as the paradigm of a psychic, one upon whom they can model their own lives. Jesus' miracles are interpreted in psychic categories. The transfiguration, in which Jesus talks to the visible spirits of several long-dead personages, Moses and Elijah, is seen as a materialization. There are also incidents of psychic healing (Mark 7:31-37, Matthew 20:29-34), PK (Mark 11:12-14, 20-21, Acts 13:6), clairvoyance (Matthew 2:13, Acts 10:1-33), and precognition (Mark 10:32-34, Acts 27:9-44). Psychic talents are given the name "gifts of the Spirit" by Paul (I Corinthians 12:4-11).

Irenaeus noted the continuation of these gifts in the second-century church. Other writers noted the appearance of psychic events century after century until modern times.

The modern psychic community really dates from the new psychical research which began to appear in the late seventeenth century. In the face of Deism, which denied the possibility of miracles or communication with spirits, researchers began to publish accounts of supernatural incidents that "proved" the existence of the invisible world. These included incidents of simple clairvoyance and precognition (often in dreams), astral travel, witchcraft and possession, ghosts, and spirit communication. Among the many writers who contributed to this research are Joseph Glanvill, Cotton Mather, Increase Mather, Richard Baxter, and John Wesley (founder of Methodism).

A contemporary of Wesley, Emanuel Swedenborg, became the first psychic-medium of import in modern times. In the late 1700's, he published many books which he claimed to be accounts of his contacts and visits to another world—the astral world of spirits. A later contemporary of Wesley and Swedenborg was Franz Anton Mesmer, who developed magnetic (or psychic) healing, giving it a scientific frame of reference.

THE PSYCHIC IN AMERICA. The psychic history of America is as old as the settlement by whites. From the beginning, witchcraft and occultism reared their heads in New England in patterns not unlike those of their English homeland. Among the first occultists was Tituba, the slave of the Rev. Samuel Parris of Salem, who taught the Parris children occult practices brought from her West Indian homeland. Voodoo dolls were found in the house of Goodwife Glover during the witchcraft trials of 1692, an indication that occult arts were more widespread than many thought.

Healing, psychic readings, and even black magic were rife among the Pennsylvania Dutch, whose Powwow men were both feared and venerated.

In the 1830's and 1840's, a number of healers, hypnotists, and phrenologists toured America, writing and lecturing. The disciples of Mesmer, most notably Charles Poyen, created a movement of magnetists before the Civil War. They defined animal magnetism as the energy flowing from healer to patient during psychic healing and from hypnotist to client in hypnotism. Their ranks included radical Methodist preacher LeRoy Sunderland. They were followed by the spiritualists, who gave us the first American psychic tradition. Their goal was proof of survival (the person's survival beyond bodily death) through evidence of spirit contact (contact with the dead).

The growth of Spiritualism, coupled with flamboyant press coverage and charges of fraud, caused many scientists and intellectuals to become interested in psychic phenomena. This interest led in 1882 to the formation of the Society of Psychical Research in England and, in 1884, to the establishment of the American Society of Psychical Research (ASPR). Among the leading members of the ASPR were William James and Josiah Royce. The early years of the ASPR were dedicated to research on mediumistic phenomena. In this endeavor, William James believed he had found sufficient proof of survival beyond death.

A new day in psychical research arrived when Dr. J. B. Rhine began his work at Duke University in the 1930's. Rhine completely revamped psychical research, giving it a new name, parapsychology, and a new method. Rhine took the psychic event into the laboratory, demonstrating it in repeatable experiments. In 1968, the Sputnik of the psychic community appeared in a book by two young reporters, Sheila Ostrander and Lynn Schroeder. Their *Psychic Discoveries Behind the Iron Curtain*, which gave the majority of Americans their first look at Russian research in the psychic, has done more to spur research than anything since Rhine's first book.

After the Civil War, psychic alternatives to spiritualism began to appear. Former Spiritualist Helena Petrovna Blavatsky started the Theosophical Society. Rosicrucians appeared. After the turn of the century, non-spiritualist psychic groups appeared. Some of these were oriented to Eastern philosophy; others, to parapsychology. The last to arrive in any number were the revived occultists.

A NOTE ON LIFESTYLE. The contemporary psychic community is oriented to experience: religious experience and much the same experience that Pentecostals seek when they pray for the baptism of the Holy Spirit as signified by speaking in tongues. The experience is itself important. In this respect, psychics differ slightly from New Thought metaphysicians, who are oriented more to results and meaning. In being oriented to religious experience, psychics share a lifestyle with mystics and pietists of all ages.

Psychics have leaned toward scientific demonstration of the truth of their faith. Psychics see their beliefs proved in the everyday repetition of verifiable psychic events. Spiritualists believe that the truth of survival comes in data received through mediums. For some, the truth is in the deep philosophy which comes through an otherwise shallow person who operates as a channel. For others, the truth is found in the very existence of an invisible world of psychic perception, continually demonstrated by clairvoyance.

This *desire for scientific verification* gives the psychic community a peculiar relation to scientists, to whom they are continually looking for verification. To date, there has been a high degree of correlation, and the growth of data from parapsychology has had a profound effect on the religious psychic community. Such data provide content for continual discussion and make the psychic community almost impervious to religious traditions which lack contemporary verification.

SWEDENBORG AND THE NEW JERUSALEM. The life and experience of Emanuel Swedenborg, the son of a Swedish Lutheran bishop, were to make him one of the great religious lights of the eighteenth century. That he is not as well remembered as some of his contemporaries, such as John Wesley and Jonathan Edwards, does not so much belie his significance as illustrate the psychic movement's tendency to belittle history.

Swedenborg, born in 1688, was reared a pious Lutheran. As a young man, he took up the study of science; mathematics and astronomy were his favorite subjects. After a period abroad gaining an education, he settled in Sweden to begin a scientific career and was, in 1724, appointed to a position on the Board of Mines. His publication of several volumes a decade later led to his recognition by the scientific community and an invitation to become a corresponding member of the Royal Academy of Sciences in St. Petersburg, Russia.

His work with the Bureau of Mines led him to concentrate his scientific study in the field of geology. His practical suggestions spurred the improvement of mining procedures throughout Sweden and actually laid the foundation for a science of geology in that country. He published one of the first exhaustive works on metallurgy, and his efforts led to the founding of the science of crystallography. His published works might seem overly philosophical by contemporary standards, but they indicate an ecumenicity of mind, not any lack of scientific acumen.

As early as 1736, however, a different side of Swedenborg began to emerge. He started to take account of unusual dreams and bodily states which he did not fully understand. The crisis in his thinking came in 1744, when he began to realize that intellectual pursuits were ultimately unsatisfying and that he must submit his life to divine guidance. Three years later, he made public his changed perspective, resigned his position with the Bureau of Mines, and devoted the remainder of his life to developing his ideas and publishing them abroad.

At this point, Swedenborg became what today would be called a medium, one who has contact with disincarnate spirit entities. He claimed that, in his visions, he traveled to spirit realms and from spirit entities gained revelatory knowledge of the nature of life, life after death and God. The crux of his philosophy is set forth in five long treatises and a commentary on the Bible.

The central theme in Swedenborg's system is the "law of correspondences." He believed that there were two realms of created existence, the physical (phenomenal) and the spiritual (real). Between the two, there is everywhere an exact correspondence. As a seer/visionary, Swedenborg was able to discern these correspondences. He turned especially to the Scripture; his commentaries were aimed at elucidating the spiritual meaning of the scripture.

The revelatory data upon which Swedenborg spent so much of his time concerned the nature of life after death. He claimed to have gained this knowledge by traveling (astral travel) to the spirit world. From these experiences, he came to believe that man and woman were immortal. He denied the resurrection of the body, and believed that man's soul immediately passes to conscious spirit existence. Souls find themselves moving toward the prime of adult life; that is, the souls of people who died as children will progress to maturity and the souls of those who died in old age will return to the vigor they had in younger adulthood.

As one dies, the soul goes to an intermediate spirit abode between heaven and hell, where preparation for the final state is made. Periodic visits of the soul after reaching heaven or hell are made to this intermediate state, so that appreciation or understanding of the final abode can be heightened by contrast.

Swedenborg deviated from orthodox Lutheranism on several other points. For example, he denied the orthodox doctrine of the Trinity (one God in three persons), avowing instead that God is one in three principles, each of which is manifest in Jesus Christ. Swedenborg believed the Father is the principle of love, "ineffable and exhaustless"; the Son is the principle of divine wisdom; the Holy Spirit is the energy of divinity which operates in humans to inspire, console, and sanctify them.

Between 1749 and 1756, the multi-volume commentary on Genesis and Exodus, *Arcana Coelestia*, was published. Other works followed. The books had little response in Sweden, and Swedenborg did little to proselytize, aside from making his ideas available. A few persons were impressed with his clairvoyance, demonstrated in his famous vision of the Stockholm Fire of 1759 at a time when he was three hundred miles away from that city.

It was in England that his teachings found greatest acceptance. Several men—the Rev. John Clowles, the Rev. Thomas Hartley, and Thomas Cookworthy—began to translate the material into English in the mid-1770's, shortly after Swedenborg's death in 1774. In 1783, Robert Hindmarsh began to search for other interested parties. As a result of his efforts, a weekly meeting, originally called the "Theosophical Society," was established in London. This body was constituted the New Jerusalem Church in 1787. It is often called the New Church.

The publication and spreading abroad of Swedenborg's religious writings was a major thrust of New Church activity from the outset. Under Cowles' leadership, a "Society for

Printing and Publishing the Writing of Emmanuel Swedenborg" was established in 1810.

Members of the New Church migrated to the colonies and formed a society in Baltimore in 1792. Other societies were soon formed along the coast as far south as Charleston, South Carolina, and as far west as Madison Town, Indiana.

SPIRITUALISM. In the First Book of Samuel, Chapter 28, according to Spiritualists, there occurs one of the most famous single incidents of mediumship in the history of the West. As the story goes, Saul, King of Israel, was to face the Philistines and became afraid of their might. After consulting his dreams, his royal psychics, and the Urim and Thummim (an ancient divination device), he visited a medium at Endor, asking that she call up Samuel, Saul's departed psychic counselor. To everyone's surprise, Samuel appeared and condemned Saul.

In Matthew 17, the other famous mediumistic event, popularly known as the transfiguration, is recorded. Jesus and three Apostles were present when two long-dead figures, Moses and Elijah, appeared and conversed with Jesus. In modern Spiritualist terminology, this event would be called a materialization, by which a spirit or something immaterial takes visible form.

Mediumistic phenomena are as old as mankind. Archeological, anthropological, and historical literature is full of references to professed intercourse with the spirit world. In the so-called primitive culture, the shaman was a combination of medium, psychic, and magician, as were psychics operating under various guises in the ancient Mediterranean world. However, in spite of the ancient phenomena and practices to which Spiritualism is an heir, Spiritualism is itself a relatively new phenomenon, related to the peculiar thrust of Western religion since the late 1600's. The true ancestors of Spiritualism are not the ancient mediums, but the Puritan and Wesleyan conservatives who used psychic phenomena to prove the existence of the unseen world. In the late 1600's, as the polemic against witchcraft grew and Deism, which denied the validity of any intercourse with spirit entities, emerged, the Puritan theologians began to issue numerous accounts of the spirit world.

"Spiritualism is the Science, Philosophy and Religion of a continuous life, based upon the demonstrable fact of communication by means of mediumship, with those who live in the Spirit World" (*Constitution and Bylaws* [Washington, DC: National Spiritualist Association, 1930], 7). So the National Spiritualist Association of Churches defines Spiritualism. The demonstration of survival was not a necessity, nor even a major theme of psychic-medium phenomena, until the modern age began to doubt survival. In this respect, Spiritualism is the direct inheritor of Puritan Wesleyan concerns.

In 1681, Joseph Glanvill published his *Saducismus Triumphatus*, which was followed by like books written by Increase Mather, Richard Baxter and Cotton Mather. John Wesley, the founder of Methodism, states the issue of the British evangelicals succinctly in an introduction to his lengthy discussion of the mediumship of Elizabeth Hobson:

"I take knowledge these are at the bottom of the outcry which has been raised, and with such insolence spread through the nation, in direct opposition not only to the Bible, but the suffrage of the wisest and best of men in all ages and nations. They well know (whether Christians know it or not), that the giving up witchcraft is, in effect, giving up the Bible; and they know, on the other hand, that if but one account of the intercourse of men with separate spirits be admitted, their whole castle in the air (Deism, Atheism, Materialism) falls to the ground. I know no reason, therefore, why we should suffer even this weapon to be wrested out of our hands. Indeed there are numerous arguments besides, which abundantly confute their vain imaginations. But we need not be hooted out of one; neither reason nor religion require this" (John Wesley, *The Journal* [London: The Epworth Press, 1914], V:265).

That these men, not the many psychics of every age, are the immediate ancestors of the Spiritualists is amply documented in the literature of Spiritualism as well as in the creedal statements, where continual reference is made to the central emphasis of Spiritualism—*the belief in personal survival of death, which can be demonstrated by mediumship*. This belief and emphasis on survival and mediumship distinguishes Spiritualism from other psychic groups.

Spiritualism is secondarily the child of the psychic activity of the eighteenth century. This activity was centered in the work of two men—Swedenborg (discussed in an earlier section of this chapter) and Franz Anton Mesmer. Mesmer had, in the 1770's and 1780's, discovered and articulated a form of psychic healing that included both magnetic healing and hypnotism. Denounced by the French Academy in 1784, Mesmer died in disgrace, but many of his students took his magnetic philosophy and hypnotism to England and the United States. As the result of the publication of the *Progress of Animal Magnetism in New England* by Charles Poyen in 1837 and wide-spread lecturing by him and other magnetic students, the issue of man's psychic nature was raised across the country in the early 1840's. In 1843, one of these roving Mesmerists spurred interest in a young shoemaker-apprentice, Andrew Jackson Davis. With this encounter, modern Spiritualism can be said to have begun.

Davis was born in Blooming Grove, New York, in 1826. After hearing the lectures on Mesmerism, Davis sought out a local hypnotist, William Levington, and was placed in a trance. He immediately showed clairvoyance; claims were made that he could duplicate the practices of the magnetists. The following year he had a vision of Galen, the famous Greek physician, and soon after, of Emanuel Swedenborg. These visions changed his life, and he began a career as healer and seer. He claimed abilities to diagnose and heal, converse with spirits, and channel knowledge from the omnipotent mind. Davis published a number of books over the next thirty years. Although not widely read today, these books were most influential in the formative years of Spiritualism.

Davis, like Swedenborg, pictured six spheres of existence in the afterlife. At death, man gravitates to that sphere most akin to his state of being at death. From this sphere, he continues to progress toward God through the higher spheres or "summerland." Thus mankind is in a state of continual progression upward. The progression scheme was common in early Spiritualism.

The event to which most American Spiritualists look more than to Davis as the birth of their faith occurred on March 31, 1848. Then Kate Fox, a young woman, began to get a rational response from some mysterious rapping noises in her home in Hydesville, New York. Kate and her two sisters discovered that the rapping sounds would respond to their hand clapping. With a little practice, they were able to work out a code by which they were able to communicate with Mr. Splitfoot, as they called him, supposedly a disincarnate entity. Mr. Splitfoot rapped out his name as Charles B. Roena, and told them he had been murdered in that house some years previously. Neighbors came to witness the rapping. No less famous a person than Horace Greeley supported the veracity of the Fox sisters against charges of fraud. News of the Fox sisters' mediumship spread, and soon other psychics who could communicate began to appear. Some were slate mediums: the spirits wrote their messages with chalk on slates. Other mediums tipped tables. Still others went into trances and allowed spirits to use their voice boxes. Physical mediums, who could produce materialized images of the spirits, appeared. Within a decade of the Civil War, what was to become a spiritualist movement was developing.

The years between 1880 and 1920 were the era of the great mediums. During this time, numerous books purporting to be revelations from the spirit world were produced. These provided alternate material to both Swedenborg and Davis. They included *Oahspe* by John B. Newbrough and the *Aquarian Gospel of Jesus Christ* by Levi H. Dowling. Both are still in print and are heavily read in the spiritualist movement. Among the mediums to be tested with outstanding results in this era were Gladys Osborne Leonard, Alta Piper, and Mrs. Coombe-Tennant.

THE ORGANIZATION. Spiritualism has developed several forms which carry its teachings. These include the camp, the church, the seance, and the development class.

The camp developed in the Chautauqua era and was modeled on that famous camp, which was located in New York and began operating in the mid-nineteenth century. Scattered around the country, the various Spiritualist camps provide a leisurely setting for lectures, mediumistic readings, and general propaganda efforts. These assume major effort in the summer for both churched and unchurched mediums who experience a summer slack.

The local Spiritualist groups are organized into churches, modeled on Protestant churches. The head medium is usually listed as pastor; other mediums are listed as assistants. The Sunday morning service is similar in form to average Protestant church service except (1) the content will be Spiritualist in orientation, (2) at times, the pastor may go into a trance for the sermon, and (3) members of the congregation may receive psychic readings (usually called spirit greetings).

The real heart of Spiritualism is the seance. This meeting is conducted by a medium for as many as fifty people. It is usually in the dark, and the people are seated in a circle. From an entranced state, the medium channels spirit phenomena of a wide variety, including the levitation of objects and materialization. Usually a spirit control speaks through the medium—the spirit control is the person from the spirit realm who regularly speaks through the medium and is thought of as the medium's constant companion. The word "control" is used because the medium's vocal chords are said to be controlled by the person from the spirit realms while the medium is in a trance. The spirit control often gives those at the seance information about their loved ones who have died.

The development class is the final major form of Spiritualism. As the name implies, the class is for the development and training of psychic abilities, especially mediumistic ones. Meditation is basic to development, but other techniques and practices vary, depending on the medium.

Mediums themselves are largely supported by individual readings (the conveying of greetings from the spirit world) for church members. Building on the experiences of contact with the departed, the Sunday worship services take second place to actual experiences of phenomena. Events in which readings occur are always the best attended.

The Spiritualist camp remains a vital force within the movement. A mixture of leisure, lectures, and a number of mediums attract believers during the summer (or local tourist season) and are a vital source of revenue for many mediums serving small churches. Some camps serve as schools for mediums-in-training, providing exposure and a working-learning situation.

The great problem which has hampered the development of Spiritualism is fraud. As soon as Spiritualism emerged, fraudulent practices by various mediums were uncovered; Henry Slade, a famous slate medium, was continually exposed. The most famous case was in 1888, when Margaretta and Kate Fox confessed and then demonstrated how they had made the original rappings. Margaretta retracted her confession the next year and was accepted back into the ranks of Spiritualism, but the confessions still are not forgotten.

In the early years of this century, Harry Houdini, the famous magician, turned his attention to mediums, becoming one of the most famous exposers of fraud in the history of American Spiritualism. A master magician himself, Houdini knew all the devices used to fool the naive sitter at the seance.

Many people assumed that fraudulent mediumship had been driven out of Spiritualism by the likes of Houdini, but in 1960, a major exposé of fraudulent mediums was reported, complete with pictures, in the *Psychic Observer*. Dr. Andrija Puharich and Thomas O'Neill, the editor, discovered Mabel Riffle, one of the most famous mediums in the country and the secretary of Camp Chesterfield, fraudulently giving materialization seances. Besides the removal of some of the mediums from the camp (at least one was still there in 1972), the main result of the exposé was the complete loss of financial support for the *Psychic Observer*, forcing O'Neill to sell out.

Those within the psychic community note that, overall, fraud is little practiced and is, in the main, confined to a few independent mediums and several of the Spiritualist camps. The major practice is the attempt by mediums and psychics to pad a little psychic ability with many bland generalities. Apologists insist that the constant demand for psychic readings is responsible. The mediums have to perform on demand, but the nature of psychic power is such that it does not always function on demand. Still, there is no doubt that fraud has been the one single force keeping Spiritualism from becoming the powerful element in the religious community here that it is in Brazil and Great Britain.

Psychic groups are characterized by their independence and lack of cooperative activity. However, some of the independent Spiritualist churches formed an ecumenical Federation of Spiritual Churches and Associations in 1947. Its purpose is to bring unity to the Spiritualist movement, but the group has so far failed to attract the larger bodies in the United States.

TEACHING SPIRITUALISM. Almost from the beggining there was the impulse within Spiritualism not only to prove the existence of life after death, but also to get into contact with "knowledgeable" spirit entities who could supply detailed information about the nature of spirit existence and the structure of the universe. In other words, there was the desire to understand the Spiritualist metaphysical system derived from spirit communication. Although the primary emphasis in Spiritualism has been to prove "survival," the continuance of life after bodily death, the secondary emphasis to understand the spirit world and the real nature of life on earth has been a determining force in the history of spiritualist groups. Some schisms in early Spiritualism grew out of this secondary emphasis.

The influence of theosophy is marked in the growth of this metaphysical Spiritualism. In general, Teaching Spiritualists disparage overemphasis on communication with departed loved ones and friends, seeing it as unproductive. While they retain the centrality of mediumship, the medium, usually termed a "channel," is in contact with evolved spirit entities, spirits that were once human and now in the spirit world have evolved to higher levels of wisdom and knowledge. These entities are viewed as wise and spiritual masters, who function very much as the bodhisattva in Buddhism who returns from his elevated state to teach mankind.

Common to all the Spiritualist philosophies are evolution and reincarnation. Man is a fallen spirit-being, evolving through many lifetimes to pure spirituality. Karma, interpreted by Spiritualists as "the Spiritual law of cause and effect," is operative. Man must overcome his bad karma, the consequences of his bad actions, usually those of an earlier incarnation. Man must try to add to his good karma, and evolve to a higher spiritual existence through good deeds. Beyond the basic Spiritualist hypothesis, the Teaching Spiritualist groups are highly eclectic. The channel's source (control) is the authority for the group. Actual teachings will make reference to all the major world religions, and much will be drawn from Hinduism via theosophy. Hindu elements in Teaching Spiritualism include beliefs in reincarnation, the view of all existence as a mystic whole, and the

communication with spiritual masters who are similar to the bodhisattva.

In general structure, the teaching mediums have one center, consisting of a small group to aid in the production and transcription of communications, which are sent out across the city, state, and nation. For some, the one center may include a "church" at which regular worship services are held. Most meetings are midweek and in the evening. Some groups would not think of themselves as a new religious group even though they function as primary religious bodies, as described in the Introduction. Such groups as the University of Life Church and the Agasha Temple of Wisdom, which include a traditional Spiritualist church program and publish a set of materials from one or more spirit controls, form a transition to Teaching Spiritualism.

DRUG-ORIENTED GROUPS. Since ancient times religious bodies have made use of various substances which altered consciousness and aided in the production of ecstatic states. According to some scholars, the Hindu god of sacrifice and the rituals associated with him are tied to the *Amanita muscaria*, a mushroom widely used because of its hallucinogenic powers. Most famous of the ancient drug-oriented bodies was the Dionysian religion, based on Dionysius, the god of the vine. Other Greek-based religions became famous for their use of alcohol. In pre-Colombian America, the Aztecs, Huichol, and various Mexican Indians ate peyote and related plants ceremonially.

Throughout Western history, various persons have discovered drugs with differing consciousness-altering properties and have then incorporated these into religious practices. At the turn of the twentieth century, William James mentioned the use of nitrous oxide to stimulate the mystical consciousness. Most famous of the early twentieth-century drug users was Aleister Crowley, who used hashish and opium in his magical work for many years.

A new era in consciousness-expansion by the use of drugs began in 1938 when Dr. Albert Hofmann, a Swiss biochemist, synthesized d-lysergic acid diethylamide (LSD) tartate from the rye fungus called ergot. In 1943, he accidentally absorbed some of the new drug, thus discovering its unusual properties. It caused a distortion of space and time, and produced hallucinations. It also produced a state of consciousness in which the objective world took on a new meaning. The effects have been termed "psychedelic." In the wake of Dr. Hofmann's discovery, other psychedelic drugs were catalogued and became known in medical and academic circles. They began to be used in hospitals for the treatment of neuroses and psychoses.

In the 1950's, widespread experiments with LSD began to occur, and Aldous Huxley wrote a popular account of his use of mescaline, another psychedelic drug, comparing his experiences with those described in the *Tibetan Book of the Dead*. In the early 1960's, reports began to appear of the experiences of those who took LSD. Many reported mystic and religious awakenings. The experiments eventuated in the watershed event of the era, the 1963 firing at Harvard of Professors Timothy Leary and Richard Alpert for involving students in "reckless experiments" with LSD.

Timothy Leary had been introduced in 1960 to tioanactyle, the psychedelic mushroom, by a Mexican anthropologist. His first "trip" was life-shaking and described as the "deepest religious experience" of his life. He proceeded to begin experiments with psychedelic drugs at Harvard. He introduced them to his colleague, Richard Alpert. After their firing, Timothy Leary became the psychological center of a drug-oriented generation, while Alpert traveled to India and emerged as a guru in his own right (Baba Ram Dass). The story of the religious drug movement from this point becomes one of legal battles to establish open practice of psychedelic groups under the Constitution. In 1966, the use of LSD, except for very limited research purposes, was declared illegal. Several of these cases will be discussed below under individual groups. The loss of some of these cases has decimated the ranks of the once-powerful movement.

An early confrontation of the drug groups and the law came in Dutchess County, New York, where Leary and his group (which he founded in 1966 as the League for Spiritual Discovery) along with Art Kleps' Neo-American Church and the non-drug-using Sri Rama Ashrama had taken refuge on the estate of William Mellon Hitchcock, in Millbrook. In December 1966, the Dutchess County police raided Millbrook and arrested Leary, Kleps, Hitchcock, and others. As a result of the raid and the publicity and pressure, Hitchcock evicted the psychedelic groups. Leary's career since then has been one of fleeing the law, jail sentences, and even a jail break in 1970 from the Orange County (California) jail.

While at Millbrook, Leary began to publish the first of the several books he has since written. *Psychedelic Prayers After the Tao Te Ching* became the handbook of the League. Leary describes the psychedelic experience as being on three levels—neural, cellular, and molecular. In the first level, one tunes into patterns of neurological signals which are usually censored from mental life. The cellular consciousness transcends the symbolic game and the sensory apparatus, and people experience raw sensory bombardment and cellular hallucination. The molecular consciousness transcends even further and contacts elemental energies that crackle and vibrate within the cellular structure. The content of molecular consciousness is what, in mystic terminology, is called the "white light," "the ovid," or "the inner light."

Continued legal pressures and unanimous court decisions against psychedelic use have largely driven supporters from the ranks or into an underground existence. If the League for Spiritual Discovery still exists, it does so only as an informal circle of Leary sympathizers. The drug-oriented churches have remained, however, living in hope of a court-reversal or a change in the laws governing the use of psychedelic drugs.

A major result of the drug culture has been to spur work in parapsychology (the study of ESP, psychokinesis, etc.), particularly in the area of altered states of consciousness. The particular experiences of psychedelically induced states also resemble many visionary, mystical, and psychic experiences. Drug users have found more openness to their concerns in areas of the psychic community than in any other religious family.

FLYING SAUCER GROUPS. On June 24, 1947, history was made in the skies of the state of Washington near Mount Rainier when Kenneth Arnold saw a series of nine bright disks flying across the heavens in front of his plane. He described the objects as "saucers," and, when the media repeated his quote, flying saucers became a new reality with which Americans had to contend. Arnold's sighting was followed by others. In July, a picture of a flying saucer, or UFO (unidentified flying object), was given wide coverage in the press before it proved to be a weather balloon. Toward the end of July, the Maury Island (Washington) sighting was followed by the death of two investigators from the Air Force. Only later was the hoax element of the Maury Island incident revealed.

Time and *Life* devoted space to the saucers. The next major incident in the history of UFO's was the death of Captain Thomas Mantell on January 7, 1948. Mantell died in a plane crash as he was chasing a UFO over Louisville, Kentucky. Other major sightings were by two Eastern Airlines pilots, Clarence S. Chiles and John B. Whitted, and by Lt. George F. Gorman of the North Dakota National Guard.

Already, in 1947, Project Sign had been established by the newly created United States Air Force to investigate reports of UFO's. In July 1949, a Project Sign report concluded that UFO's really were "interplanetary vehicles." The investigations were upgraded in 1949, and were called Project Grudge. Investigation proceeded normally until 1952, in spite of charges of coverup made by UFO buffs such as Major Donald Keyhoe. In 1952, however, there were major sightings for several evenings over Washington, D.C. That same year APRO (Aerial Phenomena Research Organization) was founded in Tucson, Arizona, as the first national UFO study organization. The founding of APRO marked the beginning of a movement that was to grow by huge proportions in the next fifteen years.

A major segment of the UFO movement consisted of the growing number of people who claimed to have met and talked with occupants of the UFO's. Emanuel Swedenborg claimed to have conversed with beings of the solar system in the eighteenth century. During the nineteenth and early twentieth centuries, a number of people, mostly psychics, claimed to have had visits with inhabitants of other planets, and wrote about these visits and circulated their writings within the psychic community. These instances of claimed contact with extra-terrestrial beings form a background for modern claims of contact as much as do the UFO phenomena.

After the UFO sightings drew national attention, the first to say he met and talked with UFO occupants was George Adamski. In his first book he detailed 1952 contact with the space brothers, and displayed pictures of their craft. Later books actually included silhouette pictures of Venusians. Adamski's books used many quotes from Theosophic literature, including quotations from the *Book of Dazan*, written by Madame Helena Petrovna Blavatsky, founder of Theosophy, and containing her comments on Venusians. Adamski was quickly followed by others, such as George Williamson, Truman Bethurum, Cedric Allingham, Orfeo M. Angelucci, Carl Anderson, and Buck Nelson. These later contacts varied greatly in their accounts; each contacted visitors from different planets and lived in different parts of the United States. For some, the objects were, plainly, advanced space craft. For others like Angelucci, they were objects from another dimension. In psychic lingo, they were creatures of a high vibratory rate who lowered their vibration in order to contact earth. Bethurum and Anderson were among those who claimed to have ridden in the spaceships.

The emergence of those who said they had contacted the UFO occupants in the early 1950's led to a split among those concerned with the strange objects in the sky. One group, the investigators of unidentified flying objects, continued to seek answers about their nature. The second group, having made contact with what it claimed to be extra-terrestrial entities, knew what the "UFO's" were, and were now engaged in telling others the message of the space brothers. The term "flying saucer" has come to refer to extra-terrestrial craft.

Through these early contacts, the space brothers began to articulate a message. While it varied at many specific points, its central ideas were common. The space brothers were more highly evolved (either culturally or psychically) beings who were coming to aid their younger brothers. They brought a message of concern about the course of man, whose materialistic nature (or some other evil) is leading him to destruction. Through the mediation of the beautiful space people, however, this destruction can be averted by following the message of love they bring. The space brothers are said to be constantly around, in a guiding paternity.

The continued appearance of UFO's and, especially, the messages of contactees (those contacted by UFO occupants), led many to begin a search for UFO's in history. Newly discovered accounts became a standard part of UFO literature. The Fortean Society aided in the explication of these. These followers of Charles Fort had been collecting UFO data for many years. Other students turned to the Bible to find accounts of UFO's there.

Certain events were quickly seen as cryptic accounts of UFO visitors from the skies. The most quoted account is of Ezekiel and the wheels in the air. More sophisticated study pointed to possible UFO involvement in the movement of the Israelites out of Egypt, as described in the Biblical book of Exodus. One author, Presbyterian minister Barry H. Downing, has postulated that the word "cloud" was a code word for Biblical UFO's and "angels" a word for extraterrestial visitors. He cited several incidents where UFO action occurred. These are found in Genesis 32:24-25, Exodus 14:19-20, Exodus 40:33-38, Joshua 10:12-14, II Kings 2:1, Matthew 17:1-8, Luke 2, and Acts 1. Of interest is his understanding of Miriam's leprosy as skin irritation from a UFO contact.

Several later visionary experiences have also come to be seen as UFO landings. For example, Jacques Vallee noted that the last visit of the Virgin at Fatima was accompanied by a bright sun-like object dancing in the sky and the dropping of angel hair, a fluffy substance often associated with UFO's. More recent writers, such as Erich von Däniken, have even speculated that the human race is descended from space beings, not from lower mammalian forms.

Early Contactee Groups. Besides the rather personal effort being made by individuals to spread the space brother gospel through speaking and writing, several people who were in telepathic contact with UFO's began to gather a group around them, channel regular messages, daily or weekly, and publish these messages abroad. These groups were modeled upon the Theosophic/I AM groups, and many of the hierarchiacal orders of Theosophy began to appear as space brothers. The Heralds of the New Age began in the 1950's to send out messages from the saucer world. Even though located in New Zealand, it was the single most influential group. It formed a network, through the mails, of others interested in UFO material. In the United States, a young psychic, Gloria Lee, joined in these efforts. The Cosmon Research Foundation, in the late 1950's rallied to her support. Gloria Lee's guide was an entity from Jupiter, identified only as J.W. Besides the regular mailings from the Foundation, J.W. wrote two books through Gloria Lee entitled, *Why We Are Here* and *The Changing Condition of Your World*. Highly Theosophical in nature, they include much material reminiscent of both Madame Blavatsky and Alice Bailey.

In 1962, the thirty-seven-year-old Gloria went to Washington with the model and plans of a space ship, given her by J.W. Following his instructions, Miss Lee secured herself in a hotel room to await word from government officials on her model. Once in her room, she began a Gandhi-like fast. On November 28, 1962, she lapsed into a coma, ending her sixty-six-day fast in death on December 2. The Cosmon Research Foundation soon died with the loss of its leader, but Gloria Lee became a martyr figure for the cause. Within two months, the Heralds of the New Age began to channel messages from her and soon produced a book, *The Going and the Glory*, purporting to be from her. Other groups followed suit, and, in the wake of Gloria's death, a number of other space brothers began to emerge from oblivion.

Another early UFO group was Christ Brotherhood, Inc., founded in 1956 by Wallace C. Halsey, a World War II veteran and engineer-turned-minister. Both psychic and engineering interests led Halsey to the study of UFO's. In 1962, the space brothers instructed Tarna, his wife, to set up a tape recorder near his bed and to put the microphone on his chest. While asleep in bed, Halsey began audibly to channel the message of coming destruction and the gathering of a remnant who would be saved.

In 1963, on a flight from Utah to Nevada in a light plane, Halsey disappeared. No trace of either him or the plane had been found. However, within a short time, Michael X. Barton, a metaphysical lecturer and writer in Los Angeles who had known Halsey, began to receive messages from him. The messages detailed the location of the missing plane. Though the plane was not found, several UFO's were sighted during the course of the search, and through messages Dr. Halsey described his departure in a UFO to Boston. The story of Barton's search was published, and Halsey joined the list of martyrs. Only in 1977 was Halsey's plane finally located.

THE NEW AGE MOVEMENT. Many psychic/occult bodies in the United States do not readily fit among either the Spiritualists or the Ancient Wisdom (discussed in the following chapter) occult groups. Given the constant ferment of the occult community, new impulses are constantly arising. In the 1970's, however, a new generation of psychic/occult/ spiritual seekers arose, who on the one hand rejected the Spiritualist emphasis upon spirits and mediums and refused the more negative designation "occult," while on the other hand identified strongly with the new wave of Eastern teachers that became visible in the late 1960's. In the fervor of their discovery of the psychic/spiritual dimensions of life, they began to see themselves as the harbingers of a new age for humanity. By the mid-1970's a loosely organized New Age Movement could be clearly discerned.

The New Age Movement originated in 1971-72, the period of the appearance of the first popular book representative of the movement (*Be Here Now* by Baba Ram Dass, 1971), the first national periodical (*East-West Journal*, 1971) and the first national network directories (*Year One Catalog* by Ira Friedlander and the *Spiritual Community Guide*, 1972).

As it emerged, the movement is very loosely organized, though it includes within it some highly structured and even authoritarian groups. The movement is centered upon a vision of radical transformation of society and the individual, though the means for accomplishing that transformation vary widely from group to group and individual to individual. On the individual level the transformation is very personal and mystical. The accomplished personal transformation provides the model for eventual social transformation. New Age theorist Marilyn Ferguson described it as an open conspiracy by transformed people to complete a process of transformation in their neighbor and in society as a whole.

In the New Age, a new universal religion, based not upon creeds and the division of social groups into denominations and religions, but one having as its goal the development of a mystical consciousness or awareness, will arise. God will be seen as the unifying principle that binds nature and humanity together in a whole. Loyalty to humanity as a whole will transcend personal loyalties to more limited social groups, such as nations and clans.

New Agers basically differ among themselves in their opinions on the exact path that will provide the surest way into the New Age, in part related to their alignment with a particular religious tradition. A wide variety of occult-spiritual techniques have been proposed, taught, and adopted by various segments of the movement. These techniques vary from vegetarianism and communalism to different forms of meditation, yoga, and magic.

Included in the directory section of this encyclopedia are some groups within the New Age Movement which have also adopted a complete religious worldview and lifestyle. Such groups will provide the basis for a full religious life for those associated with them, including regular worship, religious literature, learning experiences, and a program oriented around a spiritual practice and/or discipline. It must be noted that many groups from a theosophical tradition, and from the more mystical segment of the Middle Eastern and Eastern traditions also identify with the New Age movement, and their inclusion greatly boosts its size and significance.

SOURCES—THE SPIRITUALIST, PSYCHIC, NEW AGE FAMILY

GENERAL SOURCES

Judah, J. Stillson. *The History and Philosophy of the Metaphysical Movements in America*. Philadelphia: Westminster Press, 1967. 317 pp.

Kerr, Howard, and Charles L. Crow, eds. *The Occult in America*. Urbana: University of Illinois Press, 1983. 246 pp.

Shepard, Leslie. *Encyclopedia of Occultism and Parapsychology*. 3 vols. Detroit: Gale Research Company, 1984-85.

SWEDENBORG AND THE NEW JERUSALEM

Block, Marguerite Beck. *The New Church in the New World*. New York: Henry Holt and Company, 1932.

Pendleton, William Frederic. *Topics from the Writings*. Bryn Athyn, PA: The Academy Book Room, 1928. 249 pp.

Sigstedt, Cyriel Odhner. *The Swedenborg Epic*. New York: Bookman Associates, 1952. 517 pp.

Silver, Ednah C. *Sketches of the New Church in America*. Boston: Massachusetts New Church Union, 1920. 314 pp.

Spalding, Joh Howard. *Introduction to Swedenborg's Religious Thought*. New York: Swedenborg Publishing Association, 1977. 235 pp.

Toksvig, Signe. *Emanuel Swedenborg, Scientist and Mystic*. New Haven: Yale University Press, 1948. 389 pp.

Trobridge, George. *Swedenborg, Life and Teachings*. New York: Swedenborg Foundation, 1907.

SPIRITUALISM—GENERAL SOURCES

Barbanell, Maurice. *This Is Spiritualism*. London: Herbert Jenkins, 1959. 223 pp.

Carter, Huntley, ed. *Spiritualism, Its Present-Day Meaning*. Philadelphia: J. B. Lippincott, 1920. 287 pp.

Davis, Andrew Jackson. *The Harmonial Philosophy*. Chicago: Advanced Thought Publishing Co., n.d. 428 pp.

Keene, M. Lamar. *The Psychic Mafia*. New York: St. Martin's Press, 1976. 177 pp.

Lawton, George. *The Drama of Life After Death*. London: Constable & Company, 1933. 668 pp.

Nelson, Geoffrey K. *Spiritualism and Society*. New York: Shocken Books, 1969.

Pearsall, Ronald. *The Table-Rappers*. New York: St. Martin's Press, 1972. 258 pp.

Skultans, Vieda. *Intimacy and Ritual*. London: Routledge & Kegan Paul, 1974. 106 pp.

PSYCHICAL RESEARCH AND SPIRITUALISM

Ashby, Robert T. *A Guide Book for the Study of Psychical Research*. New York: Samuel Weiser, 1972.

Douglas, Alfred. *Extra-Sensory Powers*. Woodstock, NY: Overbrook Press, 1977. 392 pp.

Gauld, Alan. *The Founders of Psychical Research*. New York: Schocken Books, 1968. 389 pp.

Moore, R. Laurence. *In Search of White Crows*. New York: Oxford University Press, 1977. 310 pp.

SPIRITUALISM—HISTORY

Baer, Hans A. *The Black Spiritual Movement: A Religious Response to Racism*. Knoxville: University of Tennessee Press, 1984. 221 pp.

Brown, Slater. *The Heyday of Spiritualism*. New York: Hawthorne Books, 1970.

Brandon, Ruth. *The Spiritualists*. New York: Alfred A. Knopf, 1983. 315 pp.

Centennial Book of Modern Spiritualism in America. Chicago: The National Spiritualist Association of United States of America, 1948. 253 pp.

Grand Souvenir Book. World Centennial Celebration of Modern Spiritualism. San Antonio: Federation of Spiritual Churches and Associations, 1948. 200 pp.

Pond, Mariam Buckner. *Time Is Kind*. New York: Centennial Press, 1947. 334 pp.

Todorovich, Thomas E., ed. *The Centennial Memorial of Modern Spiritualism Records, 1848-1948*. St. Louis: National Spiritualist Association of U.S.A., 1948. 157 pp.

FLYING SAUCERS AND UFOS

Flamonde, Paris. *The Age of Flying Saucers*. New York: Hawthorn Books, 1971. 288 pp.

Fuller, Curtis G., ed. *Proceedings of the First International UFO Congress*. New York: Warner Books, 1980. 440 pp.

Jacobs, David Michael. *The UFO Controversy*. Bloomington: Indiana University Press, 1975. 362 pp.

Steiger, Brad. *The Aquarian Revelations*. New York: Dell, 1971. 158 pp.

Zinsstag, Lou, and Timothy Good. *George Adamski, the Untold Story*. Kent, England: Ceti Publications, 1983. 208 pp.

PSYCHEDELICS

Castenada, Carlos. *The Teachings of Don Juan*. New York: Ballantine Books, 1969. 276 pp.

DeMille, Richard. *Castaneda's Journey: The Power and the Allegory*. Santa Barbara, CA: Capra Press, 1976. 205 pp.

Kleps, Art. *Millbrook*. Oakland, CA: Bench Press, 1977. 354 pp.

La Barre, Weston. *The Peyote Cult*. New York: Schocken Books, 1969. 260 pp.

Leary, Timothy. *Flashbacks*. Los Angeles: J. B. Tarcher, 1983. 397 pp.

Masters, R. E. L., and Jean Houston. *The Varieties of Psychedelic Experience*. New York: Delta, 1967. 326 pp.

Weil, Gunther M., Ralph Metzner, and Timothy Leary, eds. *The Psychedelic Reader*. New York: Citadel Press, 1971. 260 pp.

THE NEW AGE MOVEMENT

Allen, Mark. *Chrysalis*. Berkeley, CA: Pan Publishing, 1978. 179 pp.

Ferguson, Marilyn. *The Aquarian Conspiracy*. Los Angeles, CA: J. B. Tarcher, 1980. 448 pp.

Joshua. *Journeys of an Aquarian Age Networker*. Palo Alto, CA: New Life Printing Co., 1982. 333 pp.

Raschke, Carl A. *The Interruption of Eternity*. Chicago: Nelson—Hall, 1980. 271 pp.

Satin, Mark. *New Age Politics*. New York: Delta, 1979. 349 pp.

Wilber, Ken. *The Spectrum of Consciousness*. Wheaton, IL: Theosophical Publishing House, 1977. 374 pp.

Chapter Seventeen

ANCIENT WISDOM FAMILY

Directory listings for the groups belonging to the Ancient Wisdom Family
may be found in the section beginning on page 593.

By the end of the nineteenth century, a distinct group of occultists who had separated themselves from Spiritualism could be found in both the United States and England. Rather than contact with spirits of the deceased and a desire to demonstrate the their proof of life after death, these occultists claimed to be the bearers of a hidden (i.e., occult) wisdom which had been passed to them from contemporary representatives of a lineage of teachers whose beginning was in the remote past. Now available for the first time in centuries, it could be given to those individuals prepared to receive it. The idea of an ancient hidden wisdom had a long history in the West, having been perpetuated through Freemasonry and Rosicrucianism. However, it experienced a a revival in the nineteenth century with the formation of two new Rosicrucian bodies, the Theosophical Society, and several occult orders.

The accounts of the emergence of an "ancient wisdom" follow three basic formats. First, a person claims to have made direct contact with the present bearers of the lineage usually in some remote corner of the earth (for example, Tibet, Egypt, Arabia). From the teachers of the lineage that person returns to civilization to disclose its essential truths. Second, the wisdom may be revived through the rediscovery of texts, long hidden away, which contain its teachings. Most frequently, however, rediscovery of the ancient wisdom comes through a special person who is able to enter into the occult realms, not accessible to ordinary persons, and be taught the secret wisdom directly by various occult masters. The Great White Brotherhood is a common designation for those who have kept the ancient wisdom through the centuries. The term may be applied to a groups of noncoporeal beings (some of who may occasionally take a human body) or to a group entirely or partially composed of individuals currently living on earth.

Two main ancient wisdom schools have appeared in the English-speaking West, the Rosicrucians and the Theosophists. The former obtained the ancient wisdom from Christian Rosencreutz who discovered it during travels in the Near East. Madame Blavatsky, the first Theosophist to discourse with the masters extensively, claimed to have recovered an ancient document of which no copies had survived in the mundane world, the *Stanzas of Dyzan*, which summarized occult truth.

Besides the Theosophists and Rosicrucians, and those groups which have derived from them (Arcane School of Alice Bailey and the I AM Religious Activity of Guy and Edna Ballard) are a few which have found an alternative source for acquiring the ancient wisdom. Also, several groups, drawing upon the theosophical model have developed variations on it within other religious traditions. Thus Paul Twitchell, founder of ECKANKAR, while drawing his teaching primarily from the Sant Mat Sikh tradition, claims to have traveled to what he termed "soul realms" to translate and bring humanity various ancient documents. Similarly, flying saucer contactees, most of whom came out of a spiritualist tradition, saw the extraterrestial entities with whom they claimed contact to be, in fact, the Great White Brotherhood.

Typically, ancient wisdom groups are modeled upon the ancient gnostic schools rather than contemporary churches. They offer instruction in occult truth through classes and correspondence courses. Upon manifesting their accomplishment of a body of teachings and mastery of certain occult techniques, the student is awarded a degree and admited to instruction in the next level. Groups vary in the number of levels of work offered, the nature of the oversight given to students, and the strictness in applying any standards by which they judge the completion of a degree by a student. Thus one group may have ten degrees, limit contact with students to correspondence, and be very lax in advancing the student through the degrees. Another group may have only four degrees, do all their work in small groups, and advance students only after the student demonstrates the proper competence level in both occult theory and practice (clairvoyance, psychokinesis).

The Rosicrucians, growing out of a story published in the seventeenth century in Germany, is the oldest of the several ancient wisdom groups with any following in the United States.

ROSICRUCIANS. "The Rosicrucian Order had its traditional conception and birth in Egypt in the activities of the Great White Lodge" (H. Spencer Lewis, *Rosicrucian Questions and Answers*, 9th edition [San Jose, CA: Supreme

Grand Lodge of AMORC, 1969], 33). So begins one account of the history of the Rosicrucians. Actually, if there were historical continuity between any Egyptian secret occult order (or any other ancient group) and modern Rosicrucians, documents attesting to this connection have never been made public. In their actuality in the mid-twentieth century, American Rosicrucian groups appear to be highly eclectic bodies drawing on the Western magical tradition, Theosophy, Freemasonry, and modern parapsychology in varying degrees. The interaction with Theosophy has been extensive and there are many likenesses. But, while Theosophy was founded in 1875, the Rosicrucians attempt to document their organizational continuity with the mystery-schools of the ancient Mediterranean Basin.

The first actual mention of a possible Rosicrucian group was the appearance in the second decade of the seventeenth century of a pamphlet, the *Fama Fraternitatis*, in Germany, written by someone under the pseudonym of Christian Rosencreutz (C.R.). The *Fama Fraternitatis*, translated, is the *Discovery of the Most Laudable Order of the Rosy Cross*. The book detailed the travels of C.R. to the Mediterranean Basin in the early 1400's, where he acquired all wisdom about the microcosm and macrocosm, attunement with the All, the nature of health and disease, and other occult wisdom.

Returning to Germany, C.R. saw the world was not ready for him, so he lived quietly, affiliating with three followers and then four more. These eight were the original Rosicrucians in Germany. They agreed on the following points:

They would not profess anything but curing the sick without reward,

They would wear no special habit,

They would meet every year in the House *Sancti Spiritus*,

The brothers would choose their successors,

The letters "R.C." would be their only seal and character, and

The fraternity would remain secret for one hundred years.

C.R. died in 1484, at age 106. The rediscovering of his secret tomb by a Brother created a great stir. The inscription said that after 120 years he would return. The meaning was that the Rosicrucian Order would surface again in 1604 and take all initiates who were worthy.

There was great response to the pamphlet *Fama Fraternitatis* from doctors, the altruistic, and those who just wanted to live 106 years. In 1615, a second pamphlet, promised by the first, was issued. It attacked the present worldly situation and boasted of the wisdom of C.R. (i.e., the magical world) and the importance of the secrecy of the order.

Many commentators have suggested that a Lutheran pastor, Valentin Andreae (1586-1654), was the author of the pamphlet, since he was admitted author of the 1616 novel, *The Hermetic Romance or the Chemical Wedding; written in High Dutch by Christian Rosencreutz*. From this time forward, sporadic works claiming to be products of a secret fraternity of Rosicrucians appeared. Evidences of other secret fraternities of an occult nature also are in the record. Such a one is the Illuminati, founded in 1676 by Adam Weishaupt. It was feared and finally suppressed because of its murders. In 1670, the Abbé de Villars published *The Count of Gabalis or Extravagant Mysteries of the Cabalists and Rosicrucians*. It was outwardly an attack on the Rosicrucians (thus good evidence of their existence), but many have seen it as an attempt to spread occultism by making public its ideas. De Villars was murdered a few years later, by the Rosicrucians, it was rumored.

English Rosicrucianism was given its direction by Robert Fludd, alchemist and author of the *Apologia Compendiaria Fraternitatem de Rosea Cruce* in 1616. He is the probable source of the rumor that Francis Bacon was a Rosicrucian. Among the founders of the English Rosicrucians was William Lilly, the famous astrologer. British Rosicrucians were pro-alchemy, as opposed to those on the continent at that time.

Rosicrucian lodges proliferated in the eighteenth century. Many were fraudulent, but many were legitimate attempts at forming societies attuned to Rosicrucian ideals. It was also at this time that the free intercourse between the Rosicrucians and Freemasons occurred. The Freemasons added a Rosicrucian degree to their initiations, and the Rosicrucians were greatly influenced by the Freemasons. The Freemasons originated as guilds of bricklayers and stone artisans in the Middle Ages. Each guild had its own professional secrets; these gradually became occult secrets, and the guilds became occult orders.

In 1865, a Masonic-based Rosicrucian body was founded in London by Robert Wentworth Little. The Societas Rosicruciana in Anglia was modeled on the German "Fratres of the Golden and Rosy Cross" of the previous century, and membership was confined to master masons. This group became the breeding ground of the Hermetic Order of the Golden Dawn.

Modern Rosicrucian teachings are like those of Theosophy and Freemasonry, and can be seen as a form of Christian gnosticism and mysticism. Transmutation, psychic development, and meditative/yogic disciplines are stressed. Teachings are differentiated into outer or public teachings (which include most of the philosophic material) and inner, for-member-only, teachings (which include most of the instruction on ritual and development exercises). It is difficult for non-members to obtain the secret materials, especially from the smaller bodies.

As in Masonic rituals, a system of initiation through a number of degrees is used, each initiation admitting members into deeper and more secret knowledge. Most Rosicrucian groups have published books covering their general orientation, which they sell to the general public and place in libraries. Some of these have become widely used, quite apart from any involvement in the group that published it.

The history of Rosicrucians in the United States dates to 1694 with the arrival of the Chapter of Perfection in Germantown, Pennsylvania. The Chapter, composed of Rosicrucians who derived their teachings from mystic Jacob Boehme, the Kabbalah, and several German psychic visionaries, built an observatory and Temple and thrived for a generation, but slowly died away after the death of its leader, Kelpius. The Chapter left no group to carry on its work, but the first powwow magicians once belonged to the Chapter of Perfection. No further reference to Rosicrucians in America occurs until the nineteenth century, when the first founders of the present Rosicrucian bodies appeared.

THEOSOPHY. Helena Petrovna Blavatsky (HPB) has survived the scandal that surrounded her for the last twenty-five years of her life to become one of the most influential writers in the whole psychic/occult world. Through her two major books, *Isis Unveiled* (1877) and *The Secret Doctrine* (1888), she has taught several generations about occult lore, and the Theosophical Society she founded has become a major force in the occult community.

HPB was born in Russia in 1831 of an aristocratic family. She became an early student of the occult and showed mediumistic tendencies. In 1851, she began a life of wandering that took her to India. She claimed contact with the mahatmas, persons who had evolved to a point from which they have become conscious co-workers with the divine plan of the ages and are thus beings of great authority, attainment, and responsibility. Their wisdom guides all movements for growth, particularly the Theosophical Society. During her life, Madame Blavatsky claimed constant contact with them.

HPB went to England and the United States and became deeply involved in Spiritualism (she was later to become a major antagonist). In 1873, she met Henry Steele Olcott, and together they founded the Theosophical Society in New York in 1875. *Isis Unveiled* became the society's central document. As the first president, Olcott became the chief administrator in the movement and HPB's right arm.

The objectives of the Theosophical Society were three:

1. To form a nucleus of the Universal Brotherhood of Humanity without distinction of race, creed, sex, caste, or color.

2. To encourage the study of Comparative Religion, Philosophy, and Science.

3. To investigate the unexplained laws of nature and the powers latent in man. (Alvin Boyd Kuhn, Theosophy/A Modern Revival of Ancient Wisdom [(New York: Henry Holt and Company, 1930], 112-113).

The original society was an outgrowth of Spiritualism, and, in her early writings, HPB still rejects reincarnation. She claimed that Spiritualist phenomena were genuine but were the work of lower astral entities rather than disincarnates.

In 1879, Olcott and HPB sailed for India and established permanent headquarters in Adyar. HPB discovered Hinduism and Buddhism and became fascinated with them as continuations of the ancient wisdom of Egypt and the Mediterranean. Also, at this time, the concept of the mahatmas or masters came to the fore. From a special altar in her home at Adyar and a few other places, letters from the masters in the spirit world began to arrive, and Madame claimed to be in constant contact with them.

Madame Blavatsky's cosmology is the basis of theosophical thought. To the novice, the cosmology is a highly complicated Pleroma of Gods and lesser entitities, organized in a divine hierachy and controlling the overall evolution of the earth. Aiding the hierarchy are the mahatmas or masters, men who have evolved to an almost semi-divine status and who directly represent the hierarchy to the human race. The masters are the key to the theosophical system. As in most Gnostic systems, numerical symmetry is a feature; the numbers three, seven, and ten continually arise.

At the top of the occult hierarchy is God, usually referred to as the Cosmic Logos. He expresses himself as a Trinity, usually thought of in Hindu categories as Creator, Preserver, and Destroyer. (Brahma, Vishnu, and Shiva are the Hindu deities.) There are also seven Planetary Logoi; every star in the universe is assigned to one of these logoi. Our sun and solar system are assigned to the Solar Logos, the Lord of this system and God for mankind. The Solar Logos emanates a Trinity (Father, Son, and Holy Ghost) and seven logoi. Along with these logoi, there are a number of lesser angelic entities called Devas.

Mankind is the product of a lengthy evolutionary process. The earth (and universe) is in the midst of seven-stage cycle. The first three stages are steps toward materialization; the fourth is crystallization, and the last three are spiritualization and return to spirit. We live in the fourth stage now. Mankind appeared at the beginning of the fourth round and has furthered his physical evolvement from lower life forms through the merger of his spirit with the body, welded together with the mind. Thus, physical evolvement of more complicated material animal forms met Spirit being thrust into matter, and, because spirit and matter could not be joined in themselves, Mind became the intermediate principle.

Man's evolvement takes him through seven root races, each of which has seven subraces. The first three root races perfect the union of matter and spirit; the fourth expresses the union; the last three represent the struggle of the spirit to be free of matter. We now live in the Fifth Root Race. The third race was the Lemurian, so named for a mythical submerged continent in the Pacific Ocean, and the fourth was the Atlantean, so named for Atlantis, the paradisaical origin of man. The Fifth Root Race, the Aryan, finds its culmination in the Anglo-Saxon subrace. From this point, mankind will evolve into spiritual adepts.

Man, himself, is a complicated being composed of seven bodies ranking from his pure spirit true self to the gross material body. These planes of existence are outlined thus:

1. Divine — Adi
2. Monadic — Anupadaka
3. Spiritual — Nirvanic
4. Intuitional — Buddhic
5. Mental — Mental
6. Astral — Astral
7. Physical — Physical

In this list, the terms on the right are the proper terms, several of them being the Eastern words for the planes of existence. The terms on the left are explanatory of the proper terms. Level six, the astral, is a low-grade immaterial plane that is not very highly regarded; it is occupied by such lesser figures as ghosts. Level two, the monadic, is the level of union with all that exists.

Man is a spark of divinity which manifests itself as a trinity of spirit, intuition, and mentality. Man assumes a body appropriate to each level of functioning. As he moves downward, each body he assumes is composed of denser substance. The astral and the physical are the densest, and these are discarded at death. It is the Theosophist belief that most Spiritualist phenomena are centered on contact with the astral plane and "discarded astral shells"; Theosophists often complain that Spiritualists are engaged in lower psychism.

In the present evolutionary struggle to become free from matter, man is hindered because his consciousness is stuck in the gutter of the physical plane. The goal of this life is to raise the consciousness to higher levels. Man is hindered in this goal by each body's inability to apprehend the higher vibration rate of the less dense substance above it, but man is helped by various occult practices, reincarnation, and the masters from the spirit world.

Theosophy offers a number of occult practices, such as meditation and yoga, as techniques to help the self to reach life on higher planes. These techniques, common to most religious traditions, overcome the tendency to place attention purely on the physical plane.

Reincarnation is the educative process by which the self is given repeated opportunities to rediscover its true life. Man takes on successive bodies until he overcomes his attachment to the lower planes. Each life is a representation of the state of evolvement of the soul in previous lives.

By far the greatest help to evolvement are the masters. These are spiritual giants, men who have progressed far beyond the human race, who no longer need to incarnate, but who do so in order to aid the struggling race. They form an intermediate hierarchy between man and the Solar rulers. The hierarchy of masters is given a name by position. Each position is currently filled by entities who were once incarnated on this physical plane and who are known, in many cases, as great spiritual giants. The masters are organized in a complicated system, much as the Solar Hierarchy is organized.

At the top is the Lord of the World, the agent of the Solar Logos. Under him is the Trinity of Buddhas. These four are often referred to as Sanat Kumara and the Three Kumaras. The three department heads in the hierarchy are Will, Love Wisdom, and Intelligence. Each of these has a representative: Manu Vaivasvata, Bodhisattva Maitreya, and the Maha Chohan. The hierarchical assistants, who manifest Will, Love Wisdom, and Intelligence to humans, are the Seven Rays. The first three of these Rays (Master Morya, Master Koot Hoomi, and the Venetian Master) are called the Three Aspects or Major Rays. The other four are called the Four Attributes or Minor Rays (Master Serapis, Master Hilarion, Master Jesus, and Master Prince Rakoczi). Morya manifests Will to humans; Koot Hoomi manifests Love Wisdom, and the other five masters manifest Intelligence. (Various Theosophical groups spell Koot Hoomi's name differently—

sometimes Kuthumi, sometimes Kut Hoomi, etc.) Master Jupiter is an assistant to Morya with a special relationship to India. Master Djual Khool is an assistant to Koot Hoomi with a special relationship to the Theosophical Society. The following chart shows the hierarchical arrangement. Those numbered are the Seven Rays.

Sanat Kumara

Three Buddhas

Will	Love Wisdom	Intelligence
Manu Vaivasvata	Bodhisattva Maitreya	The Maha Chohan
1 Master Morya	2 Master Koot Hoomi	3 Venetian Master
Master Jupiter	Master Djual Khool	4 Master Serapis
		5 Master Hilarion
		6 Master Jesus
		7 Master Prince Rakoczi

These masters are very confusing at first until one realizes that they represent positions, not people. The entities who presently hold those positions have reappeared in physical form throughout history, but not always as the individual one might expect from a casual perusal of the chart. For example, the position in the hierarchy called Master Jesus is now filled by the person who was known on earth as the Greek figure, Apollonius. The masters, their characteristics and their most famous incarnations are charted below:

1. Morya	Power and Strength	A Tibetan
2. Koot Hoomi	Wisdom	Pythagoras
3. The Venetian	Adaptability	Plotinus
4. Serapis	Harmony and Beauty	
5. Hilarion	Science	Iambichus
6. Jesus	Purity and Devotion	Apollonius
7. Prince Rakoczi	Ordered Service (Ceremonial Magic)	Rosencreutz and Roger Bacon

The one known on earth as Jesus was a reincarnation of Shri Krishna and is now filling the position of Bodhisattva Maitreya. Master Jupiter is the special guardian of India, and Djual Khool is especially attached to the leaders of the Theosophical Society. The masters work through the leadership of the Theosophical Society and thus become the teachers of the human race. They possess the wisdom which mankind needs to escape the repetition of incarnations and rise to the spiritual home. The Seven Rays use the seven colors of the rainbow in aiding people.

While the masters speak in cognitive language, the wisdom of which they speak is occult (hidden) and, in the long run, available only by the apprehension of the higher self. Like the knowledge that comes in loving another, it cannot be reduced to statements or adequately conveyed by words.

Theosophy, as a movement, developed centers of work in the United States, England, and India, but the major issues were being decided in India. In Adyar, Madame Blavatsky had set up headquarters. From there, her continued contact with the masters grew at an increasing rate. Quite apart from the Theosophical system, the question of the existence of the masters became the issue for the last years of Blavatsky's leadership.

In 1884, while both Olcott and Blavatsky were in England, Mrs. Emma Coulomb and her husband, who were in charge in Madame Blavatsky's home, passed some materials to Christian missionaries, who published them and attacked what they considered fraud in the production of the messages from the masters. The messages, which appeared in the specially designed cabinet with secret openings to Madame Blavatsky's bedroom and to another room in her house, were credited to Madame Blavatsky herself.

The newly founded Society of Psychical Research (SPR), sent Richard Hodson, a young British scholar, to investigate the whole matter. He quickly found the opening from Blavatsky's bedroom into the place where the master's letters were delivered. He reported that Blavatsky's phenomena were fraudulent. The SPR report was a major blow and signaled a period of eclipse for the Theosophical Society.

A problem which beset Blavatsky throughout her life came from the development of the Esoteric Section (ES), formally constituted in 1888. The ES became an inner group of trusted students who practiced what they had been taught. It also, in effect, became an elite controlling group and a source of contention for many years.

Madame Blavatsky settled in London in 1887, where she was visited by Annie Besant, a young radical activist and orator who had made quite a name for herself as a colleague of atheist Charles Bradlaugh. Mrs. Besant was ready to leave her liberal background and become a theosophist. Madame Blavatsky recognized her talent and encouraged her. As a result of their effort during the last five years of Blavatsky's life, the Society recovered and expanded in Europe. Some outstanding workers, such as G.R.S. Mead and Mabel Collins, were attracted to the Society. Colonel Olcott continued to offer his administrative ability.

Upon Madame Blavatsky's death in 1891, Annie Besant's star began to rise. She succeeded Blavatsky as head of the Esoteric Section. During the next decade, with Olcott's help, the Society became a world-wide organization. Shortly before his death in 1907, Olcott received a message from the masters "appointing" Mrs. Besant the new president. With her strong leadership, a new era began, and the Society started a process of slow and steady growth which has resulted in its spread to all parts of the globe. Its literature now is distributed to the entire occult/psychic community. Only three things marred Besant's career—the Leadbeater affair, the Krishnamurti affair, and the loss of strong leaders in America and Germany who disagreed with her on points of administration and doctrine.

Charles W. Leadbeater, a priest in the Church of England, joined the Theosophical Society in 1883. Soon afterward, he went to India, at the insistence of Master K, to aid in its defense. A talented occultist, he became a popular lecturer and writer. In 1895, he became assistant secretary of the European Section and a close friend of Mrs. Besant, with whom he co-authored several books. The primary content of these books was the clairvoyant exploration of the cosmology of Madame Blavatsky. Gradually, these books became the dominant literature of the movement.

The crisis with Leadbeater came in 1906. Charges were preferred against Leadbeater for giving immoral sexual advice to some youths who had been left in his charge. He had taught the boys the practice of masturbation as a means of dealing with their own physical problems. Annie tried to defend her friend, who was being attacked from all quarters. The scandal was eventually overcome, and Leadbeater remained active in the Theosophical Society, but the blot on Annie continued to be used by her adversaries.

During the early years of the century, Mrs. Besant began to talk of the coming to visibility again of an Avatar, a world teacher, in the flesh, to lead the world into a new stage of evolution. In a series of lectures in 1909 on "The Changing World," she declared that a new race was coming and a new Christ was to appear. Then in the winter of 1908–09, a Theosophical Society member in Adyar named Narayaniah asked the Society to care for his motherless boys, among them, Jeddu Krishnamurti.

Leadbeater, now living in Adyar, immediately became attached to Krishnamurti, whom he called Alcyone, meaning the calmer of storms. Convinced that Krishnamurti was destined to be a great spiritual leader, Leadbeater became his teacher. During the next two years, Leadbeater worked with him psychically, and the product was a now-famous little book, *At the Feet of the Master*. Annie Besant soon became convinced that Krishnamurti was the body to be used by the Bodhisattva (Avatar) for his new appearance. In January 1912, a new periodical, *Herald of the Star*, was begun, to announce his appearance. Already formed as a preparatory organization was the Order of the Star of the East. The propaganda material began to roll off the Adyar presses.

But obstacles asserted themselves before the new Christ could begin his mission. Krishnamurti's father began to demand the return of his son; the sexual charges against Leadbeater were revived, and a series of court cases were begun. The cases were finally won by the Theosophical Society. The Order of the Star of the East progressed until Krishnamurti, himself, began to reject the role. The Order of the Star of the East then died for lack of a messiah.

Over the period of the various scandals from the 1880's until the 1930's, schisms were rending the Theosophical Society. As groups jocked for power, particularly with Annie Besant, they became disgusted with Leadbeater and disputed Besant's new ideas. Alternate messages from the masters began to appear, to challenging Besant's authority. The story of these schisms is the story of the development of the Theosophical subfamily of religious groups.

Theosophy in America. The Theosophical Society had been founded in New York City in 1875, at which time William Q. Judge became the group's counsel. The American organization fell into inactivity after Olcott and Madame Blavatsky went to India, but Judge gradually revived it, and it was reconstituted in 1886. Judge also became head of the American Esoteric Section (ES). He wrote a number of books, including the classic *Ocean of Theosophy*, and was editor of *The Path* and *The Theosophical Forum*.

From the first there had been resentment at the control of American Theosophy from India. Judge also hoped to become the international president of the Theosophical Society and hence did not favor the rise of Annie Besant. Her triumphant tour, which included speaking to overflow crowds at the World Parliament of Religions in Chicago, did not help the situation.

Annie did, however, work out a temporary arrangement to share power in the ES—Judge in America, Besant in Europe and India. This arrangement came about partly as a result of Judge's proposal of the plan and the subsequent appearance of a message from Master Morya with the words, "Judge's plan is right." As other messages appeared, rumors that they were emanating from Judge became formal charges. Unfortunately, there was no mechanism for handling such charges, so the supposedly bogus messages were given to the newspapers, which attacked Judge viciously. Judge retorted by declaring that Annie Besant was no longer head of the Theosophical Society and was under the control of dark forces.

In 1895, at the American Theosophists' Convention in Boston, the Americans declared themselves independent of the British headquarters and formed the Theosophical Society in America. Seventy-five American branches went with Judge. Fourteen remained loyal to Adyar and were rechartered as the American Theosophical Society (now called the Theosophical Society of America), with Alexander Fullerton as President. The death of Judge in 1896 set the stage for the formation of new Theosophical groups.

THE ALICE BAILEY MOVEMENT. Alice La Trobe Bateman (1880-1949), a teenage church-school teacher in the Church of England, was stunned one Sunday morning to see the door to her home open and a tall stranger with a turban walk in and speak to her. He told her of important work already mapped out for her future. This event was but one of a number of psychical/mystical happenings that, coupled with world travel for the Young Men's Christian Association (YMCA) and an unsuccessful marriage, brought her to the Theosophical Society in Pacific Groves, California.

Theosophical teachings of a divine plan for humanity, a hierarchy of masters, and reincarnation and karma appealed to her. Also, it was at the Theosophical Society that she saw a picture of the man in the turban, who was identified as the Master Koot Hoomi. He figures in the cosmology of the Theosophical Society, discussed in the preceding section of this chapter. She became active in the Society and there met Foster Bailey, whom she married. He became national secretary of the Society, and Alice, editor of the *Messenger*, the sectional magazine.

In 1919, Alice was approached by a Master Djwhal Khul (D.K.), who requested that he become her control in the transmission by clairvoyant telepathy of a series of books. After first objecting, Alice began to receive *Initiation, Human and Solar*, her first book. Nineteen books in all were dictated between 1919 and 1960; still other books were written by Alice and/or Foster.

At first, the chapters of *Initiation, Human and Solar* were received with some enthusiasm and were serialized in *The Theosophist*, but then publication abruptly stopped. Concurrently, trouble developed within the Esoteric Section of the Theosophical Society over the dictations. Alice complained that Annie Besant, the head of the Society, acted autocratically, demanded that members cut outside ties and swear loyalty to her, and allowed contact with the masters from the spirit world only with her consent. The trouble came to a head at the 1920 convention, when Mrs. Besant's supporters were placed in all the key offices, and both Foster and Alice were dismissed from their positions. They thus became free to pursue their own work of transmitting the material from D.K. (Theosophists spell his name Djual Khool.)

Alice Bailey's teachings resemble Theosophy closely, with the description of the divine hierarchy, the seven rays, and the evolution of man to higher levels. Man had evolved by 1920 to the point where one could look toward the new age when groups of mankind could form advanced training schools to prepare for the real esoteric schools. In the 1930's, this observation took on an eschatological emphasis when it was revealed that, because of the spiritual yearnings of mankind, the new age was coming closer. According to the followers of Alice Bailey, this reappearance of the Christ is being accomplished by the power of the divine hierarchy being brought into this world and by service based on the love of humanity. A two-pronged program is being implemented to carry through the double emphasis.

To encourage the advent of the Christ, meditation groups are set up to help channel the energy from the hierarchy. Each group or person is seen as a "point of light" radiating the power of the world. A particularly effective way of channeling is the use of the Great Invocation. It is repeated slowly and with solemnity while one visualizes the funneling down of power from the hierarchy. Various Bailey groups reprint and distribute this prayer, and it is often used by people with no idea of its origin:

"From the point of Light within the Mind of God/Let light stream forth into the minds of men./Let Light descend on Earth./From the Point of Love within the Heart of God/Let love stream forth into the hearts of men./May Christ return to Earth./From the centre where the Will of God is known/ Let purpose guide the little wills of men—/The purpose which the Masters know and serve./From the centre which we call the race of men/Let the Plan of Love and Light work out./And may it seal the door where evil dwells./Let Light and Love and Power restore the Plan on Earth.

Particular times of the month and year are periods when special spiritual energies are available from the hierarchy. The period of the full moon is such a time, meditation groups always gather on the evening of the full moon to celebrate and meditate. On three of these full moon dates occur the great spiritual festivals. Eventually, all men will celebrate these three festivals as focal points of the hierarchical year. The festival of Easter occurs with the full moon in April and is the time of active forces of restoration of the Christ. The festival of Wesak occurs in May and is the time of Buddha's forces of enlightenment. The festival of Goodwill is in June and the forces of reconstruction are active. The festivals also illustrate Alice Bailey's belief in the synthesis of East and West into a new unity of mankind.

The program of service has found expression in the New Group of World Servers. Within this nebulous body are those who, desiring to be disciples of the masters from the spirit world, work as intermediaries between the hierarchy and the mass of humanity. The second group is composed of people of goodwill who, knowing nothing of the hierarchy, nevertheless strive for goodwill under the guidance of the masters' disciples. From this ideal of service have come a number of practical programs in education and political realignment.

In 1923, the Baileys founded the Arcane School. After Alice's death in 1949, the movement splintered, and a number of full-moon meditation groups emerged. All of the Alice Bailey groups agree on the content of teachings, though few can master the voluminous writings. All gather for the full moon and celebrate the festivals. In southern California, most of the groups cooperate in publicizing and holding the celebrations. The main differences among the groups concern non-acceptance of the Bailey family leadership and local autonomy in spreading the teaching. Among members of the psychic community, the Bailey disciples have the reputation for evangelical fervor and proselyting activity. This proselyting zeal is often based on the Theosophical notion of the astral versus the higher spiritual planes. Non-believers are often seen as enmeshed in lower psychism.

THE I AM RELIGIOUS MOVEMENT. Among the most colorful of the several divergences within the larger Theosophical Movement is the I AM Religious Movement founded by Guy W. Ballard (1878-1939) and his wife, Edna W. Ballard (1886-1971). Guy Ballard, a mining engineer during his early life, had decided, in 1929 upon completion of a job in the West, to visit Mt. Shasta, California. As early as the 1880's, the mountain had been seen as the home of a lost race of mystic adepts from Atlantis who lived inside the massive volcanic structure. Throughout the next half-century, the occult legends had grown, and Ballard, a student of occult metaphysics, was intrigued.

One day during his visit while hiking up the side of the mountain, Ballard knelt to dip water from a mountain stream. A young man appeared and offered him "a much more refreshing drink than spring water." The cup was filled with a vivifying white liquid which the stranger identified as Omnipotent Life itself. The young man continued to talk of abundant supply, reincarnation, and the laws of cause and effect. As he did, he changed into the mystical figure of Saint Germain, the seventeenth-century occultist, now an Ascended Master.

Saint Germain described his task as that of initiating the Seventh Golden Age, the permanent "I AM" Age of Eternal Perfection on Earth. During the previous six centuries he had searched Europe for someone in human embodiment strong enough and pure enough that the Instruction of the Great Law of Life could be released through them. Having failed to find such a person, he turned to America and eventually located Ballard. He designated Ballard, his wife Edna, and son Donald, the only Accredited Messengers of the Ascended Masters.

During the ensuing months, Ballard had numerous experiences with Saint Germain and other Ascended Masters about which he regularly informed his wife through a series of letters. Upon his return to Chicago, where the family dwelt, Edna's position as a Messenger was confirmed and she began regular contact. Using the pen name Godfre Ray King, Guy Ballard recorded his initial experiences with Saint Germain, which were published as two volumes in 1934, *Unveiled Mysteries* and *The Magic Presence*. These were followed by additional volumes, including *The I Am Discourses* (1936), a series of lectures by Saint Germain which summarize the basic teachings; *"I AM" Adorations and Affirmations* (1935), which give the text for the decrees (the peculiar I AM form of prayer); and a hymn book, *"I AM" Songs* (1938). A periodical, *The Voice of the I AM*, appeared in the spring 1936.

In 1932 the Ballards began to release the message of the Ascended Masters to the public. They formed the Saint Germain Foundation to administer the work and the Saint Germain Press to publish their materials. In 1934 they held the first public ten-day class in Chicago at the Civic Opera House. During the next few years similar classes were held from New York, Philadelphia, and Boston, to Miami and Los Angeles. More than seven thousand attended the Los Angeles classes. By the time of Guy Ballard's death in 1939, the movement claimed over one million students.

According to the I Am teaching, in 1929 the Ascended Masters instituted a new thrust of activity. There had, of course, been previous thrusts, such as that initiated through Madame Blavatsky and the Theosophical Society. This new thrust was begun by Saint Germain, the Lord of the Seventh Ray, who in previous incarnations claimed to be the Old Testament prophet Samuel, Saint Alban, and Sir Francis Bacon. As Bacon, he claimed to have authored the Shakespearean plays. In 1684 he "illumined and raised His body" and spent a period of time in the Himalayas only to return to Europe at the time of the French Revolution. During the past centuries, he has worked in America, the seat of the new civilization which is to be the permanent condition on the planet in the future.

Saint Germain taught the nature and importance of the "I AM Presence," the Mighty Presence of Light, God in Action. The I AM Presence emanates from the Mighty Creative Fire, the Great Central Sun, the impersonal Source of reality in our world. Out of its abundance, the Great Central Sun pours forth the Primal Light. That primal light is the basis for all manifested form, both the visible and invisible world. Through the individualization of the light, everything comes into existence.

The term, "I AM," refers to that Primal Light, the Opulence and Energy of God. Individualized, it is the essence of each person. It is to be constantly invoked and activated. The individual's "I AM Presence" is the real point of contact with divine reality, and hence properly referred to as the Presence of God within each person. It is visualized in a chart used by "I AM" students which shows an individual surrounded in a column of purple flame. Above him, connected by a shaft of white light is the "I AM Presence," pictured as a person clothed in golden light surrounded by a circular rainbow of light, a color radiance indicative of the accumulated good of previous lives.

The "I AM Presence" is invoked by the use of decrees, affirmative commands for the "I AM Presence" to initiate action. In calling upon the "I AM Presence," the violet flame pictured around each person is activated as a purifying fire to burn undesirable personal conditions away. A wide variety of decrees for handling both personal and social situations are used by I AM students. Most controversial are the several negative decrees which target specific conditions for annihilation, to be blasted from existence. These come, it should be noted, with instructions that such decrees can be used only for the dissipation of discord and imperfection. They can have no effect upon that which is good, and are not to be directed against any individual, though they may be directed to a negative condition surrounding a person.

Assisting and guiding humanity, both individuals in their personal conditions as well as the human race in it process of evolving, are the Ascended Masters. A Master is an individual who has passed through several human incarnations but, by his own effort, has generated the conditions necessary to rise above human limitations (ascend) and escape the necessity of continued re-embodiment. Such Ascended Masters radiate love and power which can be called upon to correct the various destructive currents which retard humanity. Each master, a visible tangible Being, has a particular quality or talent which is invoked for particular situations.

The steady progress of the "I AM" movement was interrupted by a series of events which began shortly after the sudden death of Guy Ballard in 1939. Several former students became vocal critics of the Activity. One, Gerald B. Bryan, wrote a series of books against the Foundation. Finally in 1941, Edna and Donald Ballard and several members of the staff of the Foundation were indicted for mail fraud, in their the promotion of the "I AM" movement through the mails. In a trial, which began in December 1941, the Ballards were charged with making a variety of fraudulent misrepresentations and false promises to ex-members who testified that the Ballards were not only advocating a false religion but that they knew to be false. They were convicted. Subsequently, the postal department denied both the Foundation and the Press their privilege to use the mail.

The conviction was appealed, and in 1944 a landmark decision in religious liberty was granted in the Supreme Court's ruling which reversed the judgment. Justice Douglas, in stating the opinion of the Court, asserted, "Men may believe what they cannot prove. They may not be put to the proof of their religious doctrines or beliefs." The case, sent down for review was finally dismissed in 1946.

During the period of the initial trial and the subsequent appeals, the "I AM" Religious Activity became the victim of a hostile press, and many students left the movement. The ending of criminal litigation set the stage for the rebuilding of the movement, even though additional legal action over the next decade was required to handle the problems created by the original conviction. For example, eight years of further action were needed to reverse the effects of 1943 decision of the Post Office Department and return full use of the mail system. (During the intervening years, the Foundation and Press had distributed materials through American Express.) The period of rebuilding also set the stage for the formation of new organizations by individuals who agreed with the essentials of the Ascended Masters' teachings, but who also claimed subsequent direct contact with additional teachings.

SOURCES—THE ANCIENT WISDOM FAMILY

GENERAL SOURCES

Braden, Charles S. *These Also Believe*. New York: Macmillan, 1949. 491 pp.

Ellwood, Robert S., Jr. *Religious and Spiritual Groups in Modern America*. Englewood Cliffs, NJ: Prentice-Hall, 1973. 334 pp.

Hall, Manly Palmer. *Great Books on Religion and Eastern Philosophy*. Los Angeles: Philosophycal Research Society, 1966. 85 pp.

Judah, J. Stillson. *The History and Philosophy of the Metaphysical Movements in America*. Philadelphia: Westminster Press, 1967. 317 pp.

ROSICRUCIANISM

Allen, Paul M., ed. *A Christian Rosenkreutz Anthology*. Blauvelt, NY: Rudolph Steiner Publications, 1968. 702 pp.

Clymer, R. Swinburne. *The Rosicrucian Fraternity in America*. 2 vols. Quakertown, PA: Rosicrucian Foundation, 1935.

McIntosh, Christopher. *The Rosy Cross Unveiled*. Wellingborough: Aquarian Press, 1980.

Voorhis, Harold V. B. *Masonic Rosicrucian Societies*. New York: Press of Henry Emmerson, 1958. 146 pp.

Waite, Arthur Edward. *The Brotherhood of the Rosy Cross*. London: Rider, 1924.

————. *The Real History of the Rosicrucians*. London: n.p., 1887

Yates, Frances A. *The Rosicrucian Enlightenment*. London: Routledge & Kegan Paul, 1972.

THEOSOPHY

Campbell, Bruce F. *A History of the Theosophical Movement*. Berkeley: University of California Press, 1980. 249 pp.

Meade, Marion. *Madame Blavatsky*. New York: G. P. Putnam's Sons, 1980. 528 pp.

Murphet, Howard. *Hammer on the Mountain*. Wheaton, IL: Theosophical Publishing House, 1972. 339 pp.

Nethercot, Arthur H. *The First Five Lives of Annie Besant*. Chicago: University of Chicago Press, 1960. 419 pp.

————. *The Last Four Lives of Annie Besant*. Chicago: University of Chicago Press, 1963. 483 pp.

Rogers, L. W. *Elementary Theosophy*. Wheaton, IL: Theosophical Press, 1956. 269 pp.

Ryan, Charles J. *H. P. Blavatsky and the Theosophical Movement*. Pasadena, CA: Theosophical University Press, 1975. 358 pp.

Winner, Anna Kennedy. *The Basic Ideas of Occult Wisdom*. Wheaton, IL: Theosophical Publishing House, 1970. 113 pp.

ALICE BAILEY

Bailey, Alice A. *The Unfinished Autobiography*. New York: Lucis Publishing Company, 1951. 305 pp.

Sapat, Peter. *The Return of the Christ and Prophecy*. Philadelphia: Dorrance & Company, 1978. 293 pp.

Thirty Years Work. New York: Lucis Publishing Company, n.d. 32 pp.

LIBERAL CATHOLIC CHURCH

Cooper, Irving S. *Ceremonies of the Liberal Catholic Rite*. Ojai, CA: St. Alban Press, 1964. 380 pp.

Hodson, Geoffrey. *The Inner Side of Church Worship*. Wheaton, IL: Theosophical Press, 1948. 82 pp.

———. *The Priestly Ideal*. London: St. Alban Press, 1971. 76 pp.

Leadbeater, Charles Webster. *The Hidden Side of Christian Festivals*. Los Angeles: St. Alban Press, 1920. 508 pp.

———. *The Science of the Sacraments*. Los Angeles: St. Alban Press, 1920. 560 pp.

The Liturgy According to the Use of the Liberal Catholic Church. London: St. Alban Press, 1967.

Tillett, Gregory. *The Elder Brother*. London: Routledge & Kegan Paul, 1982. 337 pp.

"I AM" RELIGIOUS ACTIVITY

King, Godfre Ray (pen name of Guy W. Ballard). *The Magic Presence*. Chicago: Saint Germain Press, 1935. 393 pp.

———. *The Unveiled Mysteries*. Chicago: Saint Germain Press, 1935. 260 pp.

Prophet, Elizabeth Clare. *The Great White Brotherhood*. Malibu, CA: Summit University Press, 1983. 356 pp.

OTHER OCCULT ORDERS

Hall, Manly Palmer. *Man, The Grand Symbol of the Mysteries*. Los Angeles: Philosophical Research Society, 1947. 420 pp.

———. *Self-Unfoldment by Disciplines of Realization*. Los Angeles: Philosophical Research Society, 1946. 221 pp.

———. *What the Ancient Wisdom Expects of Its Disciples*. Los Angeles: Philosophical Research Society, 1945. 79 pp.

Jones, Marc Edmund. *Occult Philosophy*. Stanwood, WA: Sabian Publishing Society, 1971. 436 pp.

Perkins, Lynn F. *The Masters as New Age Mentors*. Lakemont, GA: CSA Press, 1976. 228 pp.

Schure, Edouard. *From Sphinx to Christ*. San Francisco: Harper & Row, 1970. 284 pp.

Shepherd, A. P. *A Scientist of the Invisible*. New York: British Book Centre, 1959. 222 pp.

William, Sir. *The Occults in Council or the Great Learning*. Denver: The Smith-Brooks Printing Co., 1901. 408 pp.

Chapter Eighteen

THE MAGICK FAMILY

Directory listings for the groups belonging to the Magick Family may be
found in the section beginning on page 633.

Magick is the life-orientation of a great many persons in contemporary America. Most people, familiar only with stage-show illusions, find it hard to conceive that anyone could live by or even believe in magick—not mere illusion for entertainment, but real magick.

Magick, as one magician defines it, is "the science and art of causing change to occur in conformity to the will" (Aleister Crowley, *Magic Without Tears* [St. Paul, MN: Llewellyn Publications, 1973], 27). Another describes it as "an effect without an observable cause" and owing "nothing to the physical laws of our everyday world" (David Conway, *Magick/An Occult Primer* [New York: E. P. Dutton and Company, Inc., 1972], 19). Neither definition is complete. The latter, for example, could apply as well to PK (psychokinesis), mind over matter. Fr. Richard Woods supplements these definitions by describing magick as the "art of employing the mysterious supernatural forces believed to underpin the universe in order to produce desired effects at will" (Richard Woods, *The Occult Revolution/A Christian Meditation* [New York: Herder and Herder, 1971], 30). Fr. Woods's definition is weakened by its use of the word "supernatural," but does make the point that a particular view of the world is implicit in magick: The world is made up of forces which impinge upon man; the object of magick is to come to terms with the world by coming to terms with these forces.

Inherent in the magical world-view is the notion of control and manipulation: Forces manipulate man, victimizing him until he becomes the controlling agent. One popular witch defines magick as "the art of producing a desired effect or result through the use of various techniques such as incantations and presumably assuring human control of supernatural agencies or the forces of nature" (Sybil Leek, *Diary of a Witch* [Englewood Cliffs, NJ: Prentice-Hall, Inc., 1968], 4). In its demonic aspect such control can lead to the manipulation of people by curses (i.e., black magick), but fortunately, such "black" magick is by no means a major practice among magicians.

Magicians vary widely in their beliefs and are intensely individualistic. Nevertheless, there are a few characteristics (beyond magick) common to the groups herein classified as members of the magick family. These characteristics include ritual, secret ancient wisdom, and a tradition which has its roots in the pre-Christian world.

Ritual, for magicians, is much more than the ordering principle in worship. Ritual is seen as a very useful tool in focusing the power of the individual and in concentrating the thoughts of members of a group on a common object of concern. Beyond these functions, the ritual effects a merging of reality and the mysterious. The climax of the ritual is the evocation or invocation of deity for some specific purpose. Well performed ritual reaches a person on all levels, thus achieving the coordination of outside effects (color, music, meditative practices, chants and words) with inner dimensions of the self. The ritual brings about a change in the state of consciousness. To help produce this state, some groups even use various psychedelic drugs.

Those groups for which ritual is the apex of magical activity wear ritual garb and use elaborate facilities. Such facilities may be anything from the temple of a magical lodge to the circle of a witches' coven (a coven is a small group of witches). Garb ranges from full-length robes to nudity (Gardnerian witches). Implements of worship include various kinds of sacred objects: the athame (ritual knife) of the witch, the rod of hazelwood, the sword, the incense burner. These objects are for ritual use only and are carefully protected from profane eyes. Most magicians also take a ritual name, to be used with other initiated brethren. This name may be that of a great magician of the past, like John Dee, or it may even be a motto. (William Butler Yeats's name was "Daemon est Deus Inversus," which in translation means "the Devil is the reverse side of God.")

Secrecy is a vital part of the magician's life style. Secrecy can be protection from, on the one hand, a hostile world that does not understand magick and, on the other hand, thrill seekers who are attracted to magick for shallow reasons, such as the chance to participate in an orgy. For most, however, secrecy is an element of the faith, which they believe is for the few. (The masses, being neither prepared nor intelligent enough, would misuse, degrade and be unable to understand the teachings. Such vulgarization of the faith would destroy the power of the ritual.)

Secrecy is bolstered by a system of initiations and degrees. New members, after a probationary period, are given a basic initiation. Some groups have only one initiation, others may have three, ten, twenty-three, or even more. Initiation to each higher degree gives one access to a greater amount of secret material and presupposes an added proficiency in the magical arts.

The material which is kept secret is the magical knowledge of the group. This knowledge may consist of rituals, various incantations, metaphysical teachings, and the more powerful magical formulas. There are also the particular group's secrets, such as the magical names of members.

Most magical world-views include a belief in reincarnation, alchemy, the Atlantis myth, and astrology and the other divining arts. Many groups would argue that their tenets constitute not a religion but a philosophy with possible religious overtones. Most groups adopt a new calendar and practice their ceremonies according to an astrological or Egyptian year. Some have begun to articulate their practices in Jungian archetypical terms.

Possibly as important as any characteristic which the magical groups share is their common history. The works of the ancient mystery schools, the Gnostics, and more recently, Francis Barrett, Eliphas Levi, Louis Claude de Saint-Martin, MacGregor Mathers and Aleister Crowley appear in the histories of all the various magical subdivisions. This common history manifests not only a common effort, but also a consensus as to which issues are important enough to generate polemics, a consensus which is most important to the creation of a family group.

The differences between magical groups reflect those issues around which debate centers. Groups vary in particulars of ritual, in organization, in attitudes toward drugs and in the specific calendar used. The major groups vary on the particular aspect of ancient wisdom with which they identify. Related to the particular ancient wisdom (Egyptian, Druidic, Hebrew, etc.) are varying ideas about deity. Some groups are close to Unitarian Christianity; others are unashamedly polytheistic. All shades of belief in between those two are also held by magical groups.

A SHORT HISTORY OF MAGICK. That magick was a common practice of the ancient and even pre-historic world is a truism today. The magical world of the shaman, the alchemist, the magi, the voodoo cult and the medieval witchcraft trials have been given ample treatment in historical, archaeological, anthropological and psychological literature. Most modern magical groups take much inspiration from two magical groups which developed in the Middle Ages—the Knights Templar and the Kabbalists.

The Knights Templar was formed in 1118 by Hugh de Payens and Geoffrey de Saint-Omer. The group was sanctioned in its primal mission to protect Jerusalem for Christian pilgrims by the king of Jerusalem and by the pope. The order developed into a monastic and then a magical group, and much Gnostic-like theology was taught by Hugh and his followers. The group learned the "mysteries of true Christianity" from the Johannites, a magical sect operating in Jerusalem in the twelfth century. Caught in a power play

with the king of France two hundred years after its founding, the wealthy and powerful organization was destroyed almost overnight, and Jacques de Molay, the leader, was burned at the stake. The charges of black magick leveled against them were never really proved, but that they were a magical fraternity is little doubted.

Development of the Kabbalah from older Hebrew sources had begun in Babylon in the early Middle Ages. The most important book, the Book of Zolar, was a thirteenth-century product of Moses de Leon (1250-1305). Kabbalists believe the world can be grasped through numbers and letters, and that their job is to discover the meaning hidden in the numbers and letters through traditional methods. The number "ten" is the basic organizing principle of the universe. Through the ten numbers (sephirot), the basic working principles of life are organized and are pictured in the Sephirotic tree (fig. 1). The Sephirot are emanations of God, who is at the top of the tree. Man climbs the tree, through magick, to the divine.

Each Sephirot represents an aspect of life as well as a realm of attainment for the Kabbalistic student. Above the first Sephirot is the Ein Soph, the ineffable ground of all being, i.e., God. The Ein Soph emanates the ten Sephirot. (The Ein Soph is not pictured in the diagram.) Each Sephirot has a name and quality ascribed to it. They are as follows:

1. Kether—being or existence;
2. Chochmah—wisdom;
3. Binah—intelligence or understanding;
4. Chesed—mercy or love;
5. Geburah—strength and/or severity;
6. Tiphareth—beauty;
7. Netzach—firmness;
8. Hod—glory;
9. Yesod—foundation;
10. Malkuth—kingdom.

An eleventh Sephirot, not pictured, lies concealed behind and between Chochmah and Binah. It is Daath—knowledge (of the sexual kind, as spoken of in the opening chapters of Genesis). Daath often takes prominence in the systems of Kabbalistic groups which practice sex magick.

Also developed in the Middle Ages (the fourteenth century) was the Tarot, though its present form is a nineteenth-century refinement of the work of such men as Eliphas Levi, Aleister Crowley, and A. E. Waite. Each of the seventy-eight cards carries a complicated picture full of occult symbolism, much of it Kabbalistic. Today the Tarot is one of the most popular forms of divination.

The modern history of magick begins in the late eighteenth century when magical groups, no longer fearful of persecution, began to emerge into the public eye concurrently with the rise of a dilettante interest in occultism in Western Europe. In 1784, Ebenezer Sibley published his *Celestial Sciences*, which contained a lengthy section on magick and necromancy. That same year, Count de Gebelin published a book which connected the Tarot with the Egyptian Book of Thoth. At the turn of the century, Francis Barrett gathered a magical group around him, and in 1801 he published *The Magus*, which became that group's textbook on magic and alchemy.

The real impetus to the spread of magick came in the early 1800's when an ex-Catholic seminarian, Alphonse-Louis Constant, rediscovered the Kabbalah, the Tarot and the whole magical tradition. He became familiar with Barrett's work and joined a group called the Saviours of Louis XVII. The leader of this group, a man named Ganneau, believed that he was the reincarnation of Louis XVII and preached a form of revolutionary royalism. Toward the mid-century, Constant left the sect and in the 1850's published his *Dogma and Ritual of High Magic* followed by the *History of Magic* and *Key of the Great Mysteries*. In his writings, he claimed for magick both antiquity and potency and said it was the only universally valid religion. Constant, in publishing these books, took the Kabbalistic pen name Eliphas Levi. Levi was to become over the next decades the teacher of the many magical traditions that began to flourish. Rosicrucians, ritual magicians and witches all would look to Levi for direction, even as they formed highly differentiated groups.

RITUAL MAGICK. The rise of ritual magick is understandable only in light of the blending of several traditions which emerged forcefully in mid-nineteenth century England. On the one hand, Spiritualism and what was to become Theosophy were having a major cultural impact. (Spiritualists and Theosophists said they received messages from the world of the spirits. By 1855, the *Yorkshire Spiritual Telegraph*, England's first Spiritualist newspaper, was functioning.) This helped to stir popular interest in things supernatural. On the other hand, the magical writings of Levi, the existence of the Societas Rosicruciana in Anglia (SRIA) and the continuing impact of speculative Freemasonry provided fertile soil in which new magical orders could grow. In the 1850's and 1860's, a group using Barrett's *Magus* gathered around the psychic, Fred Hockley, trying to make use of magick formulas. In 1888, the two traditions merged to produce the Isis-Urania Temple of the Golden Dawn.

The founders of the Temple and the Hermetic Order of the Golden Dawn (OGD) which it represented included the Rev. A. F. A. Woodford, Kenneth R. H. Mackenzie, Dr. Wynn Westcott and S. L. MacGregor Mathers. All except Woodford had been members of the SRIA, but Woodford had been the one to inherit, in 1885, the magical manuscripts owned by Fred Hockley, upon which the ritual of OGD would be built. Westcott decoded the manuscripts, and Mathers systematized them into a useful form. The material also contained the Nuremberg address of Anna Sprengel, a Rosicrucian of high degree. Mathers corresponded with her, receiving voluminous materials and the charter for the Isis-Urania Temple. Other temples were soon founded in Edinburgh, Weston-super-Mare, Bradford and Paris.

In 1897, Westcott left the Order of the Golden Dawn, and Mathers took complete control. Mathers had already gained a wide reputation for his occult scholarship. He had reworked Barrett's texts and produced a grimore, or magical text, of superior quality. He also published a book on the Kabbalah. By 1892, he had moved to Paris. From there, he conducted the OGD.

Under Mathers' leadership the order developed a ritual and world-view from which other groups would create variations.

This system was called Western magick. The basic idea was the Hermetic principle of the correspondence of the microcosm (the human being) and the macrocosm (the whole, the universe). Any principle that exists in the universe also exists in man. The trained occultist can become attuned to these cosmic forces. In the process, invocation and evocation become standard practices. *Invocation* is the "calling down" into the self of a cosmic force, with a purely psychological result. *Evocation* is the "calling up" of that same force from the depths of the self, and it may result in objective physical phenomena. The correspondences also include relationships between colors, shapes, Kabbalah, etc., and the universe. A second belief is in the will's power. The trained will can do anything. Central to magick is the will, its training and activity.

The ritual magician also looks to other planes of existence, usually referred to as astral planes. These planes are inhabited by entities other than human beings, to which names such as "secret chiefs," "Oliponthic forces" and "gods" are given. Much magical work is in the astral. Finally, most ritual magicians have adopted a Kabbalistic initiation system wherein each grade is given a numerical symbol related to the Tree of Life. The numerical symbol uses two numbers, the number on the right being identical to the number of the Sephirot, and the number on the left being the "opposite" of that Sephirotic number. The names Zelator Adeptus Minor and Theoricus Adeptus Minor are simply two names for the same grade. The chart of the grades and their numerical symbols comes from *Ritual Magic in England* by Francis King.

FIRST ORDER

Grade	Numerical Symbol
Neophyte	0° = 0°
Zelator	1° = 10°
Theoricus	2° = 9°
Practicus	3° = 8°
Philosophus	4° = 7°

(The Link-Lord of the Paths of the Portal in the Vault of the Adepti.)

SECOND ORDER

Grade	Numerical Symbol
Zelator Adeptus Minor	5° = 6°
Theoricus Adeptus Minor	
Adeptus Major	6° = 5°
Adeptus Exemptus	7° = 4°

THIRD ORDER
(The Secret Chiefs)

Grade	Numerical Symbol
Magister Templi	8° = 3°
Magus	9° = 2°
Ipsissimus	10° = 1°

All the founders of the OGD began as 7 degrees = 4 degrees, a degree conferred by Fraulein Sprengel. (Mathers himself claimed to have contacted the secret chiefs in 1892.)

The most famous member of the OGD was Aleister Crowley. Reared in an Exclusive Plymouth Brethren home, Crowley had been introduced to magick in a book by A. E. Waite. His Kabbalistic studies led him in 1898 to the OGD. Crowley rose quickly in the order, but was refused initiation to Adeptus Minor because of his moral turpitude (in this case homosexuality). Crowley gained a reputation through the next two decades for breaking every moral law on the books, from fornication to murder. Crowley went to Paris and was initiated (5° = 6°) by Mathers, which led to a split in the order in London.

In 1904, Crowley received a communication from the astral with instruction for the establishment of a new order, which he set up in 1907. It was called the Astrum Argentinum (silver star). In 1909, he began publishing the *Equinox* to spread his ideas.

Crucial to understanding Crowley and his followers is Crowley's revelation in 1904 in Cairo. At this time an entity called Aiwass communicated a prose poem entitled *Liber al Vel Legis*, i.e., *The Book of Law*. The Egyptian magick favored by Crowley is manifested in this cryptic work, which divides history into the aeon of Isis (or matriarchy) until 500 B.C., the aeon of Osiris (or patriarchy) until 1904, and the aeon of Horus (beginning in 1904). The aeon of Horus, the son, is one of the dominance of Thelema or Will. From the book came Crowley's themes: "'Do what thou wilt' shall be the whole of the Law;" "Every man and every woman is a star," and "Love is the Law, Love under Will." These three phrases constantly reappear in Crowley's writing. By them, Crowley meant that each person is to move in his true orbit as marked out by the nature of his position, the law of his growth and the impulse of his past. One's duty is to be determined to experience the suitable event at each moment. Love is an art of uniting with a part of Nuit, the total possibilities of every kind. Each act must be willed so as to fulfill, not thwart, one's true nature.

Around the turn of the century, Karl Keller, a German, founded the Ordo Templi Orientis (OTO), a ritual magick group which taught sex magick. Crowley joined the OTO and was made the head of its British affiliate. To the heterosexual ninth degree he added a homosexual eleventh degree. OTO sexual magick seems to have been derived from Oriental sources as well as from P. B. Randolph of the American-based Fraternitas Rosae Crucis. It was perfected by Crowley during three years (1920-23) at the Abbey of Thelema in Sicily. Crowley also succeeded Theodor Reuss in 1922 as outer head of the OTO.

Upon Crowley's death in 1947, Karl Johannes Germer succeeded to the outer headship of the order. Germer had been with Crowley in England, but returned to his native Germany in the 1930's. He was arrested in Hitler's purges of occult groups and spent some time in a concentration camp. He was ultimately deported in 1941 and came to the United States. He died in 1962 and was succeeded by Karl Metzger, a Swiss disciple.

RITUAL MAGICK IN AMERICA. Ritual magick was brought to America from Britain by Americans who had joined the OGD. However, the real beginning was Crowley's several visits in 1905 and 1915. Shortly before World War I, C. S. Jones (Frater Achad) opened OTO branches in Vancouver, Los Angeles and (possibly) Washington, D.C. C. S. Jones was Crowley's magical child, but the two soon split. Crowley visited the Vancouver lodge in 1915. He met Winifred T. Smith (Frater 132) while there and gave him permission to open an OTO lodge, which he did. Smith moved to Pasadena, California, and, upon Achad's fall from favor with Crowley, became head of the American OTO. Smith's move to Pasadena begins one of the most bizarre episodes in American religious history.

Once in Pasadena, Smith seduced Helen Parsons, the wife of Frater 210, known in public life as John W. (Jack) Parsons, an explosives expert and key man at California Institute of Technology, who had joined Smith's OTO lodge in Pasadena. After Helen had a child by Smith, Parsons took Betty, Helen's younger sister, as his mistress and magical partner. At this point, probably in 1945, a new Frater in the person of L. Ron Hubbard appeared on the scene, and two distinct accounts exist as to what happened between Parsons and his new "assistant."

According to recent accounts published by OTO, Parsons developed an immediate liking for Hubbard and took him into the OTO work, though Hubbard never formally became a member, nor was he properly initiated. The two worked together on several magical operations, including an attempt to produce a moonchild. In this process, while Parsons engaged in ritual intercourse, Hubbard acted as a seer to describe the concurrent events on the astral plane. The act was supposed to induce a spirit into the child produced by the intercourse.

Early in 1946, Parsons and Hubbard had a parting of the ways. Parsons claimed that Hubbard had persuaded him to sell the property of the Agape Lodge, after which Hubbard, along with Parsons' sister-in-law Betty, absconded with the money. Hubbard's wife filed for divorce. He reappeared on a newly purchased yacht off the Florida coast. Parsons pursued him, and on July 5, 1946, a confrontation occurred. Hubbard had sailed at 5 p.m. At 8 p.m., Parsons performed a full invocation to "Bartzabel." At that same moment a squall struck the yacht and ripped the sails, thus forcing Hubbard to port. Parsons was able to recover only a small percentage of the money, however. The confrontation in Miami did not end the relationship. The latter part of 1946 finds Hubbard "forgiven" and doing work with Parsons again.

Hubbard's account (and that of the present day Church of Scientology that he founded), denies any attachment of Hubbard to the OTO. Rather, Hubbard claims that he was sent to investigate Parsons because the Pasadena headquarters of the Lodge also housed a number of nuclear physicists who lived there while working at Cal Tech. These physicists were among sixty-four later dismissed from government service as insecure. Hubbard asserts that due to his efforts the headquarters were torn down, a girl rescued from the group, and the group ultimately destroyed.

Both stories stand and in fact may be genuine perceptions of the events since Hubbard obviously did not make his "investigative" function known until some years later. Hubbard's story is consistent with the observation that the present Church of Scientology shows no direct OTO influence.

Though weakened by Hubbard's actions, the Agape Lodge was not destroyed by him. Parsons did that himself. In 1949 he took the oath of AntiChrist and adopted the magical name "Belarion Armiluss Al Dajjal AntiChrist." Then in 1952, in a still unexplained occurrence, he was killed when his home laboratory exploded. According to the late Louis Culling, Parsons had been making bootleg nitroglycerine to sell to get money to keep the work going after the loss of the Lodge's treasury.

Besides the Agape Lodge, several other lodges were formed in the years after World War I. One of these was the Choronzon Club, or Great Brotherhood of God (GBG), formed in Chicago in 1931. The head of the GBG was C. F. Russell, who had been with Crowley at Thelema. Russell, an American, split with Crowley. Among the Choronzon Club's members was Louis T. Culling, who in 1969 published its ritual as the *Complete Magical Curriculum of the GBG*. Its three degrees were preceded by some basic occult training. The sexual magick began with Alphaism, a discipline of complete chastity in thought, word and deed; moved to Dianism, or Karezza, prolonged sexual relations without orgasm, and finished with Quodosch, similar to the completed heterosexual activity of the OTO ninth degree. Culling, head of the San Diego Lodge of the Great Brotherhood of God, left in 1938 to join the OTO.

Another derivative of the Order of the Golden Dawn was the Order of the Portal, a lodge headquartered in Boston in the late 1920's and early 1930's. It was headed by Aleta Baker and was the most overtly Christian of the various OGD offshoots. Of central importance was the belief in the bisexuality of God and the equality of woman.

Little information is available on the present practices of ritual magick groups. They are secret material, given in written form to only a few leaders and carefully guarded by the members. However, rituals used by a number of defunct lodges have become available. The publication of the OGD rituals resulted in the dissolution of two groups that were using them. The published rituals show a remarkable similarity; present rituals are most certainly derivatives of these, with changes suitable to particular needs and uses. Francis King has published a number of the sexual rituals used by Crowley.

WITCHCRAFT. The current growth of witchcraft (the craft of the *wicca* or wise ones) can be dated to 1951, when the last of the British witchcraft laws was repealed, and to the subsequent publication in 1954 of *Witchcraft Today* by Gerald Gardner, a self-proclaimed witch from the Isle of Man in Britain. Gardner's book signaled to the world that witches still existed. His work was based upon the thesis of Margaret Murray that witchcraft had existed since pre-Christian times in small, scattered, occult groups practicing the old pagan religion and hidden in fear of persecution.

Most contemporary witches have accepted Murray's historical thesis, but the legitimacy of her conclusions is now a matter of intense debate in the occult community.

There can be little doubt that various, mostly agricultural religions existed in Europe at the time that the Christian Church was in the process of becoming the dominant religious form of Europe. There is also little doubt that in the 1400's, the church turned its inquisitional powers on something called witchcraft. What was described as witchcraft was a mixture of the local religions, a number of things the church wished to suppress, and some things wholly in the imaginations of the early inquisitors. It was during this era that various new images of witchcraft, particularly the one connecting it with Satan worship, were published.

Many men, women, and even children died in the witch scare that gripped Europe in the sixteenth and seventeenth centuries. In the face of the myth of satanic witchcraft, some genuine Satanists and even genuine witches arose. The most famous incident was the Black Mass scandal which rocked the court of Louis XIV and led to the arrest of more than three hundred persons. In the 1670's, Madame LaVoisin, one of Louis XIV's mistresses, suspected she was losing Louis' affection and hired a priest to say Black Masses, hoping thereby to win back the king. Some of the masses included the killing of babies; some of the masses were offered on Madame LaVoisin's nude body. Louis imprisoned or banished the participants in the heinous affairs.

Contemporary witchcraft bears little resemblance to the witchcraft described in the literature of the witchcraft trials. Going beyond the medieval image, modern witches try to separate themselves from any connection with Satanism. Rather than reacting to Christianity (i.e., being anti-Christians), they see themselves as an alternative faith (like Buddhism or Islam). As magicians, they have selected the old faiths of Europe with which to identify.

Just what are the elements of wicaan faith? This question is not an easy one to answer, there being a wide variety of definitions in the literature. First, witchcraft is a religion. There is much more to the adherents' faith than just magick. Witchcraft offers a world-view, a relationship to deity and an ethical code. Of course, magick and psychic development are a part of the religion; much of the ritual and energy of witches is spent in their practice. "Witchcraft is the raising and manipulation of psychic power," says one witch.

Wicca is polytheist, finding its pantheon in various European pre-Christian nature religions. The prime deities are the Goddess and God, usually represented as the Triple Goddess and Horned God. The triple aspects of the Goddess are maiden, mother, and crone. There are different explanations of the origin of these gods, although most agree that the Goddess is ascendent in modern cultic expressions. Psychic development, besides being training for magick, is also for communion with the deity. (The Horned God was connected with Satan by medieval witch-hunters, and Satan has been pictured since with a goatee and cloven hoofs.)

The two essential books of the witch are the grimoire and the book of shadows. The grimoire is the book of spells and magical procedures. The best known grimoires are medieval: the *Greater Key of Solomon the King* and *The Book of the Sacred Magic of Abra-Melin the Mage*. The book of shadows is the traditional book of rituals. According to custom, it is copied by hand by each individual witch, and thus no two copies are alike.

The basic organization of witches is the coven, though there is also an associational tie between covens of like belief and practice, especially where one coven has broken off from another and owes its initiation to the other. Such a relationship exists in the Gardnerian covens. The coven consists of thirteen people (an optimum number which may vary from four to twenty) who meet regularly to practice witchcraft. The regular meeting of the coven is called an esbat; but eight times a year there are seasonal festivals, sabbats. The most famous festival is October 31, Halloween. Others include Candlemas or Oimelc (February 2), May Eve or Beltane (April 30), August Eve or Lammas (August 1), and the lesser sabbats—the two solstices (June 22 and December 22) and the equinoxes (March 21 and September 21). The eight festivals are reflected in the common practice of publishing witch-oriented periodicals eight times a year.

Most covens have both a basic initiation and higher initiations which are reserved for potential and actual priests and priestesses, who are the coven leaders. There are usually three degrees which require a year and a day between each initiation. Work within the coven is done with the magick circle, a circle nine feet in diameter, drawn on the floor or ground. Magick is done within the circle, which functions both for protection and concentration. Within the circle are placed the various magical items. They include the *athame*, a ritual knife; the *pentacle*, a disc-shaped talisman; a chalice; and a sword. These items vary from coven to coven. The *athame* is most ubiquitous. Many covens worship in the nude (i.e., skyclad); but in most, street clothes or ritual robes are worn. When the robe is worn it is bound with a cord, the color of which designates the degree of initiation. The work of the coven covers all religious practices (psychic healing and problem-solving playing a big part) and includes hand fasting (marriage).

Witches share with all magicians a belief in reincarnation and the manipulative world-view. They also place belief in the power of spells. They cast spells for the healing of themselves and others, for their own betterment (financially, sexually) and, on rare occasions, against someone else. For most witches, the magical world-view is tempered by a poetic-mystical appreciation of nature. In their writings are numerous references to ecology, being natural and, in a few cases, vegetarianism. For most, acceptance of the gods is a poetic expression of attunement with the forces of life.

African Witchcraft. Voodoo, the major folk religion of Haiti, is an African form of magick and witchcraft mixed with New World elements, complete with the ruling mother goddess, a pantheon of lesser deities (correlated to specific human needs), a psychic ritual and a manipulative world-view. Voodoo has a significant history in the eighteenth and nineteenth centuries, particularly in the Creole country. In the nineteenth century, Dr. John and, later, Marie Laveau, the voodoo queen of New Orleans, openly flaunted their magical powers in public. They were followed by Dr. Alexander and Lou Johnson.

For a number of reasons, modern witchcraft practice has had little input from voodooism, apart from the romantic aura of the word. This lack of intercourse can be traced to a number of elements, the same that have prevented many books on voodoo from appearing. Voodoo is not a literary religion; this source material must be gathered directly from practitioners. Practitioners are few in number and hard to find. They are mostly members of the black community or recent immigrants from the Caribbean. The latter often have a language problem.

As the term "voodoo" is found in popular American usage, it refers to at least four distinct phenomena. The first, *voodoo* proper, is the magical religion brought from Haiti in the late 1700's. It is a mixture of French Catholicism and the religion of the Ibos, Magos and Dahomeans. Its leading god is Damballah, the serpent. The second, *Santeria*, is a mixture of Iberian Catholicism and Yoruba religion. Its main god is Chango, god of fire and stone. It is found throughout most of Latin America, and in Brazil is called Macumba. The third, the *Conjure Man* or *Root Doctor* in the Southern United States, is an adoption by blacks of European magick but is associated with voodoo because of the mystique of New Orleans. This phenomenon does not seem to produce groups, as such. The fourth, the *Bruja* or Latin American witch, is often placed under the voodoo label, but is more closely related to the folk witchcraft traditions. Besides the widespread practice of voodoo and Santeria, as evidenced by the numerous botanicas (stores which sell magical ingredients) in most urban centers, there are at least three public voodoo-like groups.

Voodoo and its relatives exist in America today; its outward manifestations can be found in the black, Puerto Rican, and Cuban communities of major cities of the United States and in the occult supply shops which sell magical items. Such items include yerbabuena and perejil, herbs which, when used properly, are assumed to have powers to keep away evil. Other items, such as bat's blood and graveyard dust, are also available.

Witchcraft in America. The history of witchcraft in America begins with the first settlers. As early as 1636, New England colonists felt a need to pass a law against witchcraft. In 1648, the first execution under this law occurred. (There is little similarity between witches as defined by seventeenth-century Puritans and contemporary practitioners of the craft.) New England persecution of witches reached a climax at Salem in 1692. Spurred by confessions of occult practices by a Jamaican servant and the finding of voodoo dolls at the home of Goodwife Nurse, the community launched a massive witch-hunt which led to the death of a number of persons. In the wake of the killings, realization by the community of what it had done led to reaction against any belief whatsoever in the existence of witches. The history of American witchcraft then switches to Pennsylvania.

Among the Pennsylvania Dutch there is the survival of what seems to be a genuine "witchcraft-like" practice, locally termed powwowing. One must call it witchcraft-like because, while it involves magick and the psychic, it is theologically a Christian derivative with Kabbalistic elements. The practitioners are Bible believers, who feel themselves to be supernaturally endowed with their powers. The most obvious manifestations of the powwow power are the many colorful hex signs on the farmhouses in Eastern Pennsylvania. Each sign is a circle; within the circle are birds, hexagonal stars, etc.

Powwowers are, in essence, Christianized witches working in the agricultural society of the Pennsylvania Dutch. They have a grimoire (a book of spells and magical procedures), *The Long Lost Friend*, by John Hohman and they are as feared for their ability to hex as they are liked and sought after for their ability to heal. *The Long Lost Friend*, first published in 1819, is an eclectic compilation from the Kabbalah, Albertus Magus (a magician), German folklore, folk medicine, etc.

No group of what could be called a powwow cult exists, but the power of powwow belief is amply demonstrated by the sporadic trials of people for murder and various lesser offenses because of "victims' " beliefs that they were hexed.

The magical folklore which produced the powwow practices can be traced to medieval Germany and seems to have been brought to America by immigrants in the seventeenth and eighteenth centuries. The lore included a belief in astrology, amulets and charms, herbal medicine and the psychic powers of gifted people.

Prior to the 1960's, there were only a few manifestations of witchcraft in America apart from the powwow men. There were isolated areas that had the equivalent of the powwower, but not in such strength or prominence. Such an area was the Shenandoah Valley in Virginia and Pennsylvania, where practitioners had a German heritage. Occasionally there was a witchcraft trial such as the one which occurred in Omaha, Nebraska, in 1939. A woman accused a local "witch" of casting spells against her. The "witch" was found guilty and expelled from the community.

THE GARDNERIAN REVIVAL. Many contemporary witches claim associations with witches, covens, and/or a faith which they can trace backward for many generations. However, little evidence to substantiate those claims has been brought forward and several have proved to be without any basis in fact. Most witches are converts who have come into the movement since 1960. While a few can trace their ancestry to individuals accused of witchcraft in the sixteenth and seventeenth centuries, there is no evidence of any survival of the practice within the families during the intervening centuries.

During the 1970's, a very few active covens with a history pre-dating 1960 were located, but overwhelmingly, modern witchcraft can be traced to the work of Gerald Gardner (1884-1964), a retired British civil servant. A sickly child, Gardner had only a minimal amount of education and in his teen years moved to Ceylon (now Sri Lanka) where he worked on a plantation. During the next thirty-nine years he worked at various government and private jobs throughout India and Southeast Asia. He became an accomplished amateur anthropologist and authored the standard work on the *kris*, the Indonesian ceremonial weapon. In Palestine, he participated in the excavation of a site centered upon the worship of the goddess Astaroth.

Upon his return to England just before World War II, Gardner associated himself with the Corona Fellowship of Rosicrucians, founded by Mabel Besant-Scott, daughter of theosophist Annie Besant. Through the group, he met some witches who introduced him to one Dorothy Clutterbuck. According to Gardner, "Old Dorothy," as she was affectionately known, initiated him into witchcraft. After the death of the priestess of the coven to which he belonged, he was allowed to describe some of the life of the group in a novel, *High Magic's Aid* (1949), published under his magical name, "Scire." Then in 1954, following the repeal of the Witchcraft Laws in England in 1951, he published *Witchcraft Today*, which gave a more detailed picture of what Gardner described as a dying religion. The book, however, initiated a revival of interest, and led to a new generation of witches who turned to Gardner for initiation.

Recent research has done much to discredit Gardner's account of the rise of modern witchcraft. Examination of his papers sold to "Ripley's Believe It or Not" by his daughter and the publication of several sets of rituals which he and his associates gave to various initiates, have disclosed a radically different account of the origin of Gardnerian witchcraft. Rather than being initiated into a pre-existing Wiccan religion, it appears that Gardner created the new religion out of numerous pieces of Eastern religious and Western occult and magical material.

Basic rituals were adapted from ritual magic texts such as the *Greater Key of Solomon* and the writings of Aleister Crowley and upon Freemasonry (into which Gardner had been initiated in Ceylon). Beginning with the eight ancient Pagan agricultural festivals (called "sabbats") as major holy days, he added regular biweekly gatherings at the full and new moon (esbats). From the Malayan *kris*, he developed the *athame*, the witch's ritual knife. Having become a practitioner of nudism as a result of sunbaths taken while recovering from a illness, he ordained that rituals were to be done in the nude, or *skyclad* (a term used to describe the nude sadhus of India). He also incorporated several Eastern religious practices (ritual scourging) and beliefs (karma and reincarnation).

By 1954 Gardner and the small group he had gathered around him had created Wicca (or Wica), a religion more accommodating to a popular audience than ritual magic could ever be. During the late 1950's and early 1960's, Wiccan initiates took Gardner's rituals and formed separate covens, and slowly the movement began to spread. One initiate, Alexander Sanders, revised the rituals and began a new "Alexanderian" lineage of witchcraft. Though beginning entirely from Gardnerian rituals, Sanders created a fictionalized story of his having begun his career in witchcraft after being initiated as a child by his grandmother. Sybil Leek, another witch who began her practice with Gardnerian rituals, came to America in the late 1960's. Before becoming famous as a professional occultist, she formed several covens in different locations around the United States.

The Gardnerian origin of contemprary covens is often obscured by the adoption of designations such as "traditional" and "hereditary" to indicate their allegiance to a "nonGardnerian" form of witchcraft. However, while covens will deviate at particular points, they tend to perpetuate Gardner's original belief system and overall set of practices. In particular, numerous variations of his original rituals have been developed and not a few entirely new sets of rituals composed. Such rituals, however, almost always retain the patterns he established in the 1950's.

Witches may practice alone, as solitaries, but most are organized into covens, small groups which meet biweekly at the new and full moon and eight times a year for the major holidays. Most covens have abandoned nudity and do their rituals in robes, though strict Gardnerians and Alexanderians retain the practice.

Gardnerian Wicca in the United States. Gardnerian Wicca or Witchcraft was brought to the United States in the mid-1960's by Raymond and Rosemary Buckland. Longtime students of the occult, they heard of Gardner and traveled to the Isle of Man, where he operated a witchcraft and magic museum. While there they went through a intensive program in Gardner's witchcraft and were initiated into both the first and second degrees (which is contrary to standard practice that requires a year and a day between initiations). Upon their return, they formed a coven on Long Island and became the center of a burgeoning movement. Much of the spread of the movement was due to the Bucklands' availability to the media whose interest was sparked both by the witchcraft museum they owned and their willingness to be interviewed and photographed as witches.

Soon after Witchcraft spread across America, other people attracted to the Goddess faith began to create variations on it. One set of variations became known as "Neo-Paganism." Donna Cole, a Chicago witch who had received her initiation in England in the late 1960's, composed a set of rituals, similar to Gardner's, but much more worshipful and celebrative and less focused upon magic. These rituals circulated through the witchcraft community in the United States and became the basis of a set of "Pagan Way" temples, several of which served as outer courts for the more secret and exclusive witchcraft groups. The term "Neo-Paganism" was actually coined by Tim Zell (now known as Otter G'Zell) who also composed a set of alternative rituals and founded a new group, the Church of All Worlds.

Neo-Pagan groups differ primarily from witchcraft groups by their rejection of the designation "witch." They will also occasionally vary by their use of a term other than coven to designate groups (nest, grove, etc.) or by their adoption of a particular pre-Christian tradition (Druidic, Norse, Egyptian) from which to draw the inspiration and symbology of their ritual life. For purposes of this encyclopedia, however, all witchcraft and Neo-Pagan groups will be treated as products of the Gardnerian revival, from which they are believed to have originated.

SATANISM. Often confused with witchcraft is the worship of Satan; witches, however, are quick to protest such identification and to assert the strong distinction between the two. The basic distinction is the relation to Christianity. Witchcraft logically (if not chronologically) "pre-dates" Christianity. That is, it exists in its own right, much as other non-Christian religions. (There is some doubt that any religion can grow up in Western culture without direct reaction to Christianity, but the witches are certainly articulating the possibility.) Witchcraft exists as an alternative to the Christian faith, much as do Buddhism and Hinduism.

Satanism, on the other hand, is logically subsequent to Christianity and draws on it in representing an overthrow of the Christian deity in favor of his adversary. It stands in polemical relation to Christianity and, in both belief and ritual, uses Christian elements, which are changed and given new meaning. The most famous element used by Satanists is the Black Mass, an obvious corruption of Christian liturgies.

Apart from their allegiance to Satan and resultant dislike for the Christian church, Satanists do share in common the magical world-view of witches. Many Satanists openly claim witchcraft as their own. Their most vocal exponent, Anton LaVey, has entitled one of his books, *The Compleat Witch.* Satanists have as an unwitting ally the conservative Christian press, which would like to brand witches as Satanists (and lump all psychics in with them). They are also aided by a tradition stemming from the era of the great witch trials, when witchcraft was defined as the worship of Satan. One could easily make the case that contemporary Satanism is a produce of Christian polemics. Paranoid perceptions of "the enemy" have led to irrational accusations concerning beliefs, obscenities, profanities, rituals and behavior patterns. These accusations merely gave people new ideas; the anti-witch books became the textbooks for Satanic practices.

Contemporary Satanism seems to have little connection organizationally with earlier Satanism. Books on black magick, Satanism, and the psychic in general seem to provide the source, and the contemporary psychic scene, the setting, from which Satanic practices could emerge. The magical writings of Aleister Crowley have been influential in many areas.

Satanists do share a number of symbols (and ritual practices) with all magical religions, but several are unique and distinctive. The inverted pentagram, the five-pointed star with the single point down, is the most frequently used. The Horned God in the form of the goat of Mendes is common. The pentagram is often mixed with the goat, stamped upon the goat's forehead. Not seen as often as some might think is the black inverted cross. With the decline in power of the Roman Catholic Church (since the days of the Holy Roman Empire), from which most Satanists come, the Black Mass is not practiced much.

As one studies the contemporary Satanist scene, two distinct realities emerge. On the one hand are what are frequently termed the "sickies." These are disconnected groups of occultists who employ Satan worship to cover a variety of sexual, sado-masochistic, clandestine, psychopathic and illegal activities. From these groups come grave-robberies, sexual assaults and blood letting (both animal and human). These groups are characterized by lack of theology, disconnectedness and short life, and informality of meetings.

Usually they are discovered only in the incident that destroys them.

On the other hand are the public groups which take Satanism as a religion seriously and have developed articulate theologies which do not resemble in many ways what one might expect. Their systems closely resemble liberal Christian theologies with the addition of a powerful cultural symbol (Satan), radically redefined. There is a wide gulf between the second type of Satanist and his "sick" cousin. While, theologically, the Christian might find both reprehensible, their behavior is drastically different and the groups should not be confused.

In the mid-1970's, Satanism as a whole waned in strength in the U. S., though several new Satanic groups appeared. These include the Temple of Set, headquartered in San Francisco and the Fraternity of the Goat, headquartered in Wheaton, Illinois.

SOURCES—THE MAGICK FAMILY

GENERAL SOURCES

Bonewits, P. E. I. *Real Magic.* Berkeley, CA: Creative Arts Book Company, 1979. 282 pp.

Green, Marian. *Magic for the Aquarian Age.* Wellingborough: Aquarian Press, 1983. 144 pp.

Mauss, Marcel. *A General Theory of Magic.* New York: W. W. Norton & Company, 1972. 148 pp.

Melton, J. Gordon. *Magic, Witchcraft and Paganism in America, A Bibliography.* New York: Garland Publishing, 1982. 231 pp.

HISTORY OF MAGIC

Cavendish, Richard. *A History of Magic.* New York: Taplinger Publishing Company, 1977. 180 pp.

Gilbert, R. A. *The Golden Dawn, Twilight of the Magicians.* Wellingborough: Aquarian Press, 1983. 144 pp.

Howe, Ellic. *The Alchemist of the Golden Dawn.* Wellingborough: Aquarian Press, 1985. 112 pp.

————. *The Magicians of the Golden Dawn.* London: Routledge and Kegan Paul, 1972. 306 pp.

King, Francis. *Ritual Magic in England.* London: Neville Spearman, 1970. 224 pp.

McIntosh, Christopher. *Eliphas Levi and the French Occult Revival.* New York: Samuel Weiser, 1974. 238 pp.

Thomas, Keith. *Religion and the Decline of Magic.* New York: Charles Scribner's Sons, 1971. 716 pp.

Webb, James. *The Occult Establishment.* LaSalle, IL: Open Court Publishing Company, 1976. 535 pp.

————. *The Occult Underground.* LaSalle, IL: Open Court Publishing Company, 1974. 387 pp.

RITUAL MAGICK

Ashcroft-Nowicki, Dolores. *First Steps in Ritual.* Wellingborough: Aquarian Press, 1982. 96 pp.

Conway, David. *Magic, An Occult Primer.* New York: E. P. Dutton, 1972. 286 pp.

Crowley, Aleister. *Magick in Theory and Practice.* New York: Castle Books, n.d. 436 pp.

King, Francis. *Techniques of High Magic.* New York: Warner Destiny Books, 1976. 254 pp.

Levi, Eliphas. *The History of Magic.* London: W. Rider & Sons, 1913. 535 pp.

————. *Transcendental Magic.* London: G. Redway, 1896. 406 pp.

Regardie, Israel. *Ceremonial Magic,* Wellingborough: Aquarian Press, 1980. 127 pp.

WITCHCRAFT

Baroja, Julio Caro. *The World of the Witches.* Chicago: University of Chicago Press, 1965. 313 pp.

Boyer, Paul, and Stephen Nissenbaum. *Salem Possessed.* Cambridge: Harvard University Press, 1974. 231 pp.

Hansen, Chadwick. *Witchcraft at Salem.* New York: New American Library, 1969. 318 pp.

Kieckhefer, Richard. *European Witch Trials.* Berkeley: University of California Press, 1976. 181 pp.

Monter, E. William. *European Witchcraft.* New York: John Wiley & Sons, 1969, 177 pp.

Russell, Jeffery Burton. *A History of Witchcraft.* London: Thames and Hudson, 1980. 192 pp.

AFRO-CARIBBEAN RELIGION

Gonzalez-Wippler, Migene. *Santeria.* New York: Julian Press, 1973. 181 pp.

Haskins, James. *Witchcraft, Mysticism and Magic in the Black World.* Garden City, NY; Doubleday, 1974. 156 pp.

Langguth, A. J. *Macumba.* New York: Harper & Row, 1975. 273 pp.

Pelton, Robert W. *The Complete Book of Voodoo.* New York: G. P. Putnam's Sons, 1972. 254 pp.

MODERN WITCHCRAFT AND PAGANISM

Adler, Margot. *Drawing Down the Moon.* New York: Viking Press, 1979. 455 pp.

A Book of Pagan Rituals. New York: Samuel Weiser, 1978. 142 pp.

Bracelin, J. L. *Gerald Gardner: Witch.* London: Octagon Press, 1960. 224 pp.

Farrar, Janet, and Stewart Farrar. *Eight Sabbats for Witches.* London: Robert Hale, 1081. 192 pp.

————. *The Witches' Way.* London: Robert Hale, 1984. 349 pp.

Farrar, Stewart. *What Witches Do.* New York: Coward, McCann & Geohegan, 1971. 211 pp.

Gardner, Gerald. *Witchcraft Today.* London: Jarrolds, 1968. 192 pp.

Miller, David L. *The New Polytheism.* New York: Harper & Row, 1974. 86 pp.

Starhawk. *Dreaming in the Dark.* Boston: Beacon Press, 1982. 242 pp.

————. *The Spiral Dance.* San Francisco: Harper & Row, 1979. 218 pp.

Valiente, Doreen. *An ABC of Witchcraft.* New York: St. Martin's Press, 1973. 416 pp.

SATANISM

Ashton, John. *The Devil in Britian and America.* Ann Arbor, MI: Gryphon Books, 1971. 363 pp.

Laver, James. *The First Decadent.* New York: Citadel Press, 1955. 278 pp.

Lyons, Arthur. *Satan Wants You.* London: Rupert Hart-Davis, 1970. 211 pp.

Wolfe, Burton H. *The Devil's Avenger.* New York: Pyramid Books, 1974. 222 pp.

Chapter Nineteen

THE MIDDLE EASTERN FAMILY

Part I—JUDAISM

Directory listings for the groups belonging to the Middle Eastern Family
(Judaism) may be found in the section beginning on page 667.

"O give thanks to the Lord of lords,
for his steadfast love endures forever;
to him who alone does great wonders,
to him who by understanding made the heavens,
for his steadfast love endures forever;
to him who spread out the earth upon the waters,
to him who made the great lights,
the sun to rule over the day,
the moon and stars to rule over the night,
to him who smote the first-born of Egypt,
and brought Israel out from among them,
with a strong hand and an outstretched arm,
to him who divided the Red Sea in sunder,
and made Israel pass through the midst of it,
but overthrew Pharaoh and his host in the Red Sea,
to him who led his people through the wilderness,
to him who smote great kings,
and slew famous kings,
Sihon, king of the Amorites,
and Og, king of Bashan,
and gave their land as a heritage,
a heritage to Israel his servant,
for his steadfast love endures forever."
(Psalm 136)

In this song to the steadfast love of Yahweh written in a later era, the story of the origin of the Jewish community is told. Recounted are the events during the life of Moses, a Hebrew and the adopted son of Pharaoh of Egypt. Reared a prince, Moses forsook his palace to lead his enslaved people out of Egypt, into the wilderness and to the very edge of their new home in Canaan, where he mediated to them the Covenant Law (Torah). These events and the subsequent movement into Canaan welded the nomadic tribes into a nation and made Moses the founder of one of the world's great faiths. While there is a history before Moses, it was the Exodus-Sinai event that made the people. The history of the Jewish people is found in the *Torah, Prophets*, and *Writings*, which together comprise what Christians call the "Old Testament." A second great body of writings, the *Talmud*, begun as an exegetical commentary on scripture, and including other religious wisdom, was written over the period of a millennium following the time of exile.

The next major event which changed the course of Israel's history was the Diaspora, the scattering of the Jews beyond Jerusalem. Never a happy people under outside rulers or occupation armies, the Jews had continuously made trouble for Rome. In A.D. 70, in an attempt to solve the problem, a Roman army destroyed Jerusalem and the Temple. With the destruction of the Temple, Jewish worship and religious life was changed. It now centered upon the synagogue (congregation), and the Jews were scattered abroad as never before. There had, of course, been Jewish communities throughout the Mediterranean basin before this time, but now the center of Jewish life shifted to these dispersed communities.

During the Middle Ages, Jews established communities throughout Europe. Times of tolerant acceptance were interspersed with persecution, attempts at forced conversion, and the emergence of a few Jews as prominent money lenders. Lending money for profit, an almost necessary practice in modern states, was denied Christians at this time.

Throughout modern history, Jews have settled in Europe, looking for a home in the midst of exile. They rose to positions of power. Always committed to education, they produced many of the molders of Western culture—Sigmund Freud, Karl Marx, Martin Buber, Samuel Weiss, Ludwig Wittenstein. Nonetheless, they periodically suffered intense persecution.

One cannot understand contemporary American Jews without grasping their reaction to the most brutal episode of the Diaspora: the Holocaust. In Germany during World War II the Nazis exterminated more than six million Jews—men, women, and children—in an almost successful attempt to eliminate them from the continent.

As a result of the Holocaust, an independent Jewish state was finally established in Palestine. The establishment of Israel was both the aftermath of the Holocaust and the culmination of a Zionist movement which had begun in the late nineteenth century. Among the Jews, the overwhelming majority is now at least nominally Zionist; there is only one small anti—Zionist organization in the United States.

141

Jewish beliefs begin and end in the Exodus. It was this event which called the community together and it is from this event that the community draws its life. Beliefs and morals, ritual and custom, all are derived from the covenant made at Sinai. Central to these beliefs is the Shema, which is repeated in the morning and evening synagogue service: "Hear O Israel, the Lord Our God is One Lord" (Deut. 6:4).

Also basic are the beginning sentences in the Covenant document of Sinai, popularly known as the Ten Commandments (Exodus 20:1-7):

"And God spoke all these words, saying,

'I am the Lord your God, who brought you out of the land of Egypt, out of the house of bondage.

'You shall have no other gods before me.

'You shall not make yourself a graven image, or any likeness of anything that is in heaven above, or that is in the earth beneath, or that is in the water under the earth; you shall not bow down to them or serve them, for I the Lord your God am a jealous God, visiting the iniquity of the fathers upon the children to the third and the fourth generation of those who hate me, but showing steadfast love to thousands of those who love me and keep my commandments.

'You shall not take the name of the Lord your God in vain, for the Lord will not hold him guiltless who takes his name in vain.

'Remember the sabbath day, to keep it holy. Six days you shall labor, and do all your work, but the seventh day is a sabbath to the Lord your God, in it you shall not do any work, you, or your son, or your daughter, your manservant, or the sojourner who is within your gates; for in six days the Lord made heaven and earth, the sea, and all that is in them and rested the seventh day; therefore, the Lord blessed the sabbath day and hallowed it.

'Honor your father and your mother, that your days may be long in the land which the Lord your God gives you.

'You shall not kill.

'You shall not commit adultery.

'You shall not steal.

'You shall not bear false witness against your neighbor.

'You shall not covet your neighbor's house; you shall not covet your neighbor's wife, or his manservant, or his maidservant, or his ox, or his ass, or anything that is your neighbor's.' "

While making creeds has never been a Jewish preoccupation, and Jews recognize no doctrinal statement as normative, the statement of Rabbi Moses Maimonides of the twelfth century A.D. is a handy synopsis of Jewish belief:

"I believe with perfect faith that God is; that he is one with a unique unity; that he is the incorporeal; that he is eternal; that to him alone prayer is to be made; that all the words of the Prophets are true; that Moses is the chief of the Prophets; that the law given to Moses has been transmitted without alteration; that this law will never be changed or superseded; that God knows all the deeds and thoughts of men; that he rewards the obedient and punishes transgressors; that the Messiah will come; that there will be a resurrection of the dead" (Charles S. Braden, *The World's Religions*, rev. ed. [Nashville: Abingdon Press, 1954], 177–178).

Basic to Judaism is the concept of "Torah." Narrowly, Torah is the Book of Moses, the five Old Testament books—Genesis, Exodus, Leviticus, Numbers, and Deuteronomy. It is the story of God's calling a nation. More broadly, however, Torah is a teaching, a way of life based on the dictates of Israel's God given in the written Torah. Most broadly, however, Torah is the covenant of Israel by which Yahweh became their God and Israel became Yahweh's people.

No description of Jewish life would be complete without mention of the notion of the "chosen people." Always undergirding Jewish actions has been the belief, more or less articulated, that Yahweh had chosen the Jews for a special role. This choosing occurred at the time of Abraham and was reaffirmed at the Exodus—Sinai event and, while the exact significance of this new status has been widely debated, it remains a controlling concept. The effect on Jewish life of this idea has been tremendous, both in keeping the Jews from too ready an assimilation in their many surrounding cultures and in making them easy targets for persecution.

Also important to Judaism are the five great feasts. Passover, in early spring, is a commemoration of the Exodus—Sinai event with specific reference to the Lord's passing over Jewish homes when he slew the first—born in each household in Egypt (Exodus 12). Pentecost, in late May or early June, commemorates the giving of the Ten Commandments to Moses. The Feast of Tabernacles marks the Jewish wanderings in the desert (Exodus 23:14, 34:23). The Feast of Lights of Hanukkah celebrates the purification of the Temple in 164 B.C. by the Maccabees after its defilement by Antiochus Epiphanes, a Syrian ruler. Purim honors the rescue of the Jewish people by Mordecai and the heroine, Esther.

The important days in the Jewish calendar begin with Rosh Hashana, New Year's Day, which is followed by ten days of penitance. This period culminates in the single most important day of the Jewish year, Yom Kippur, the Day of Atonement.

The basic organization of Judaism is the congregation or synagogue, which may be constituted wherever there are ten males. This is the basic governing body in Judaism, which is congregationally structured. The synagogue has as its pastor a rabbi (teacher). The congregation usually sponsors a school for its children. The school may be conducted only one day a week for several hours to give minimum preparation for Bar Mitzvah, the coming of age ceremony for Jewish youth, but ideally, the synagogue would have a total educational system to meet both secular and religious needs.

JEWS IN AMERICA. The story of Jews in America began in the fifteenth century with the arrival of Columbus. Several of the members of the crew were converted Jews, victims of the Spanish persecution. There are even some who have attempted to make a case that Columbus was a Jew, though the evidence is far from convincing at present. The Spanish and Portuguese Jews helped finance Columbus' voyages, and many early Jews in America were Marranos, secret Jews who had accepted Christian baptism but still practiced their Jewish faith in the privacy of their homes, a practice kept alive in the face of the Inquisition in Spain. Others were refugees, Jews who were exiled for not converting to Christianity.

Many refugees fled to Holland, became prosperous and produced many great scholars and thinkers, such as Baruch Spinoza. When the Dutch made war in Brazil and South America in the early 1600's, many Marranos there sided with them as a fifth column. The first openly Jewish community in America—Kahal Kodesh, the Holy Congregation—was founded in Recife, Brazil, in the 1630's. Recife fell to the Portuguese in 1654 and the Jews had to immigrate. Many returned to Holland; others moved to new Dutch settlements in America. Curacao, a Dutch island off Venezuela, became the location of a congregation in 1656, the oldest still in existence in the New World.

Some of the fleeing Jews came to New York City, then New Amsterdam, where they joined the few Jews who had migrated directly from Holland to continue their trading. Peter Stuyvesant, the governor, was not happy to have Jewish refugees; it was only over a period of time that a cemetery, a congregation, and a synagogue were allowed. A corner of the old cemetery can still be visited in Manhattan.

In 1682, after New York had become English property, toleration was granted and a building was rented for use as a synagogue. In 1728, the group organized as Congregation Shearith Israel, the Remnant of Israel, and built the first synagogue. The second settlement of Jews in an area now part of the United States, often claiming precedence over the New York settlement, was in Newport, Rhode Island. Religious toleration and the opportunity to trade were the two attractions for Jewish settlers. The cemetery, founded in 1677, is older than New York's. The synagogue, built in 1763, still stands, but the congregation was dispersed during the Revolution when the British captured Newport. The Jews were rebels and only a few returned after the war. At present, the old synagogue is being used by a new group of Eastern European immigrants who are completely unrelated to the original settlers.

Other Jewish communities in the United States began to appear after the Revolution, composed of immigrants and the few Jews scattered throughout the colonies. Evidence of Jews in New England before 1780 is sparse, though one Judah Morris got his M.A. at Harvard in 1820. In 1822, he became a Christian and taught Hebrew at the Cambridge School. Other early centers of Judaism were Philadelphia and Lancaster, Pennsylvania; Richmond, Virginia; Charleston, South Carolina, and Savannah, Georgia. The Jews thus were here at the founding of the nation and the group has grown with the nation as an integral part of its history. In this respect, the Jews differ radically from other non—Christian bodies, which were post—Civil War arrivals.

All the early Jews in America were Sephardim; that is, they came from Spain and Portugal or were descendants of Jews from these countries. All six pre—nineteenth century congregations (New York, Newport, Philadelphia, Savannah, Charleston and Richmond) were Sephardic in ritual. The Sephardim were soon joined by Ashkenazim, Jews from Germany and central Europe, mostly Poland. There were differences of rite between the two, and there was also a feeling among the Sephardim that they were the elite of the Jewish community. In 1802 in Philadelphia and in 1825 in New York City, the Ashkenazim withdrew to form their own organization.

Before 1836, immigration of Jews had been an individual matter. After 1836, immigrations of entire groups of Jews from single locations in Europe, primarily Germany or German-speaking areas in Central Europe, began. These poor immigrants, mostly retail merchants, were the source of most Jewish communities in inland American cities.

Eastern European Jews had arrived in small numbers in the eighteenth century and, in 1848, the first European synagogue was formed in Buffalo, New York. Mass immigrations began in 1881, motivated by pogroms and Russia's anti-Jewish decrees. To the 250,000 Jews in the United States in 1880 were added almost two million from Eastern Europe. In 1880, there were 270 synagogues; in 1916 before World War I halted the immigration, there were 1,902.

With the arrival of the Eastern European Jews, a new issue arose within the American Jewish community-Zionism. In contradistinction to German Jews who saw Judaism as primarily a religion, Russian Jews saw it as a religious culture and nationality. Following the lead in 1896 of Viennese journalist Theodor Herzl, they began to clamor for a Jewish homeland. The first American Zionist Congress was held in 1897. The Central Conference of American Rabbis reacted by unanimously condemning Zionism. The climax to the growth of Zionism was the 1917 Balfour Declaration, which committed England to the Zionist cause. The United States endorsed the declaration in 1922 in its acceptance of the British protectorate of Palestine. These actions, and the to the cause by outstanding Jewish leaders such as Louis D. Brandeis, finally swung the support of American Jews behind Zionism. By 1945, eighty percent swung the support of American Jews behind Zionism. By 1945, eighty percent of American Jews favored a Jewish commonwealth in Palestine. The founding of Israel has turned Zionism mainly into a program of support for Israel, a program of fund-raising and political lobbying.

During the twentieth century, the Jewish community became a settled and stable feature of American life and began to build synagogues and schools in urban centers throughout the land. Various national fellowships of rabbis and congregations formed as divisions on ritual law and the nature of Judaism developed. The main organizations were formed around the well-known distinctions of Orthodox, Conservative, Reform and, more recently, Reconstructionist Judaism. Less well known was the development of the Hasidic community in Brooklyn after World War I. This community was small until 1946, when large migrations of survivors of the Holocaust began. The Hasidim, at one time nearly half of European Jewry, now appear to be remaking the Jewish community as it grows, through both evangelistic efforts and a high birth rate.

HASIDISM. The phenomenon of the mystic, reacting to formal religion by seeking a closer direct experience of the divine, is common in religious history. Judaism has had its share of mysticism. In the late Middle Ages, the Messianic claimant, Shabbetai Zevi (b. 1676), offered such a direction. In the following century, a more stable form would appear in Hasidism, a Kabbalistic Judaism attributable to the efforts of Israel Baal Shem Tov (1700-1760), a rabbi in the Ukraine.

Hasidic teachings are plainly Orthodox but also mystical. Baal Shem Tov taught that all men were equal before God and that piety, devotion and purity, prayer and the Torah were more important than study, learning or ascetic practices. The Kabbalah provided a framework for mystic integration of the Bible. The Kabbalah is discussed as a Jewish magical system in the preceding chapter. The virtues of *Shiflut* (humility), *Simcha* (joy), and *Hillahavut* (enthusiasm) were emphasized. The movement spread rapidly and, at its height, attracted about half the Jews in Europe, particularly those in Poland and the Slavic countries.

Organizationally, the movement began to focus on local charismatic leaders called "zaddikim," or "righteous ones." Unlike the rabbi, or teacher, known for his scholarship and wisdom, the zaddik, who might also be a rabbi, was honored for his mystic powers—miracle working, shamanism and personal magnetism. Organizationally, zaddikim came to lead segments of the movement and created dynasties by passing on the charisma to sons or followers. Thus schools or sub-sects, as in Sufism, were formed.

The Hasidic movement aroused the indignation of non-Hasidic Jews, and a lengthy, bitter era of polemic followed. Eventually, Hasidism was forced to retreat. The twentieth century brought new problems as pogroms began in Russia. Many Hasidim migrated. The Holocaust, of course, all but wiped out European Hasidism. Fortunately, many of the "rebbes," a common title for the zaddikim, escaped and sought to make new homes for their followers in Israel and America.

The first Hasidim in America were members of the first major wave of Eastern European immigrants to America beginning in the 1880's. For lack of an Hasidic synagogue or zaddik (all of whom were still in Europe), they often became indistinguishable from other Orthodox Jews. Separated from their zaddik, they became discouraged in the attempt to perpetuate Hasidism. After World War I, several zaddikim came to the United States, including the Ukrainian Twersky Zaddik. They gathered followers, but did not begin to reach outward to seek new believers. The real era of Hasidic growth in the United States began after World War II. Led by the Lubavicher Rebbe, Hasidic zaddikim, especially from Poland and Hungary, came to the United States after escaping from Hitler.

The Hasidim, as a whole, settled in Brooklyn in that section designated as Williamsburg. Here they have created a unique social structure—an isolated urban religious culture.

Williamsburg is a haven of "true" Judaism. They have been able not only to survive but even prosper, in spite of an economic system which seeks to assimilate them. The vitality of Hasidism is shown in the emergence of new Hasidic groups among younger Jews. A strong emphasis on tradition, social service, celebration, communal life and experiment with radical ideas is characteristic of their lifestyle. Though largely ignored by most writers on American Judaism, the Hasidim are currently the fastest growing segment of American Judaism. This growth comes from both proselytization within the wider Jewish community and a high birth rate.

BLACK JEWS. Among the black population of the early nineteenth century were some individuals who became legends as regular worshipers at the local synagogues. Possibly the most famous was "Old Billy," who in the first half of the nineteenth century was a "faithful attendant" at the Charleston, South Carolina, synagogue. He described himself as a Rachabite (Jeremiah 35:2ff) and, accordingly, abstained from all wines and liquor. Other black members have been noted by various authors. To this day, and in growing numbers, there are black members of white Jewish congregations.

A real spur to blacks to elect Judaism as an alternative to Christianity was the discovery in the late nineteenth century of the Falashas, Black Jews of Ethiopia, by Joseph Halevy, a Frency explorer. There had long been a legend that Black Jews, descendants of the Queen of Sheba, had existed but had long ago disappeared. Knowledge of their present existence became more widely spread in the 1920's, when Jacques Faitlovitch of the University of Geneva followed up earlier pro-Falasha committee activities with a passionate revival of efforts to aid them. While American black Jews like to identify with them, the Falashas have no direct connection with Judaism in the Afro-American community. As a matter of fact, most recent scholarship has concluded that the Falashas are not Negroid. In addition to the Falashas, isolated pockets of African Black Jews, products of interracial marriages, have been discovered.

While the African Jews supplied much inspiration for the American Black Jewish movement, the Biblical faith of rural America supplied the content. Black people, Bible students, were quick to identify with the Ethiopians and, in their search for identity and status in the white culture, began to see a special place for themselves as Jews. Proponents cite all the references to the Ethiopians (such as I Kings 10, Isaiah 18:1-2, Amos 9:7 and Acts 8:26-40); attempts are also made to prove that the true Jews were black. Psalm 119:83 in which the author (David?) see himself as becoming like a bottle (King James Version) in the smoke, is a passage popularly quoted as proof of black Jews in Biblical times.

The Christian Biblical origin of the movement is made by the early leaders who articulated its postulates. Warren Roberson, an early prophet of Black Jewishness, spoke of himself as a second Jesus Christ. Another called his group the Church of God and Saints of Christ. It would be hard to find a more "Christian" designation.

The origin of the Black Jewish movement dates to three men who appeared in Northern urban black centers at the turn of the century. Two of these, F.S. Cherry and William S. Crowdy, founded movements which still exist and are discussed below. The third, the first of several New York City-based leaders, was Elder Warren Roberson. Roberson was a notorious charismatic leader who alternated between being Messianic and being a sex cult priest. He spent several terms in jail, which only added to his aura as a persecuted black savior.

Roberson's group and its several spin-offs, such as Rabbi Ishi Kaufman's Gospel of the Kingdom Temple, were swept up into the Garveyite movement. Coming from the West Indies, Marcus Garvey instilled within his followers and admirers a dream of a black nation where black men would rule. Since white Christianity had enslaved and tamed black people, an alternative had to be found. Judaism provided one such alternative. With the encouragement of Arnold Josiah Ford, Garvey's choirmaster and self-proclaimed Ethiopian Jew, a new phase of history began.

Ford tried to get Garvey to accept Judaism, but he refused, whereupon Ford organized the Moorish Zionist Church, in which he taught that all Africans were Hebrews. He followed Garvey's nationalistic program. He united his efforts with another self-professed Jew, Mordecai Herman, but they soon parted ways. Ford then organized, in 1924, the Beth B'nai Abraham congregation (BBA). Both groups obtained funds from white Jews during the remainder of the decade. Elements of Islamic lore (possibly also from the Garvey movement) crept into Ford's theology.

The BBA came to an abrupt end in 1931 when Ford decided to sail for Europe. He gave his blessing to a new leader, Wentworth Arthur Matthew, whose career initiated the present phase of Black Judaism. Ford disappeared to Africa, but had laid the groundwork for a widespread Black Judaism. Today, a number of independent synagogues are located in black urban areas around the country.

SOURCES—THE MIDDLE EASTERN FAMILY, PART I

GENERAL SOURCES

Bamberger, Bernard J. *The Story of Judaism*. New York: Schocken Books, 1964. 484 pp.

Rosenthal, Gilbert S. *The Many Faces of Judaism*. New York: Behrman House, 1978. 159 pp.

Seldin, Ruth. *Image of the Jews, Teachers' Guide to Jews and Their Religion*. New York: KTAV Publishing House, 1970. 151 pp.

Werblowsky, R. J. Zwi, and Geoffrey Wigoder. *The Encyclopedia of the Jewish Religion*. New York: Holt, Rinehart and Winston, 1965. 415 pp.

JUDAISM IN AMERICA

Feldstein, Stanley. *The Land That I Show You*. Garden City, NY: Doubleday, 1979. 606 pp.

Glazer, Nathan. *American Judaism*. Chicago: University of Chicago Press, 1957. 176 pp.

Hardon, John A. *American Judaism*. Chicago: Loyola University Press, 1971. 372 pp.

Learsi, Rufus. *The Jew in America: A History*. Cleveland: World Publishing Company, 1954. 382 pp.

Lebeson, Anita Libman. *Pilgrim People*. New York: Minerva Press, 1975. 651 pp.

Neusner, Jacob. *Understanding American Judaism*. 2 vols. New York: KTAV Publishing House, 1975.

Ruderman, Jerome. *Jews in American History, A Teacher's Guide*. New York: KTAV Publishing House, 1974. 224 pp.

JEWISH THOUGHT

Barish, Louis, and Rebecca Barish. *Basic Jewish Beliefs*. New York: Jonathan David, 1961. 222 pp.

Eisenstein, Ira. *Varieties of Jewish Belief*. New York: Reconstructionist Press, 1966. 270 pp.

Fackenheim, Emil L. *God's Presence in History*. New York: Harper & Row, 1970. 104 pp.

Gordis, Robert. *Judaism for the Modern Age*. New York: Farrar, Straus and Cudahy, 1955. 368 pp.

Heschel, Abraham Joshua. *God in Search of Man*. New York: Meridian Books, 1959. 437 pp.

Neuser, Jacob. *Understanding Jewish Theology*. KTAV Publishing House, 1973. 280 pp.

JEWISH LIFE AND CUSTOMS

Maslin, Simeon J., ed. *Gates of Mitzvah*. New York: Central Conference of American Rabbis, 1979. 165 pp.

Posner, Raphael, Uri Kaploun, and Shalom Cohon, eds. *Jewish Liturgy*. New York: Leon Ameil Publisher, 1975. 278 pp.

Trepp, Leo. *The Complete Book of Jewish Observance*. New York: Behrman House, 1980. 370 pp.

HASSIDISM

Abelson, J. *Jewish Mysticism*. New York: Hermon Press, 1969. 182 pp.

Aron, Milton. *Ideas and Ideals of the Hassidim*. New York: Citadel Press, 1969. 350 pp.

Bokser, Ben Zion. *The Jewish Mystical Tradition*. New York: Pilgrim Press, 1981. 277 pp.

Buber, Martin. *The Origin and Meaning of Hassidism*. New York: Horizon Press, 1960. 254 pp.

Dresner, Samuel H. *The Zaddik*. New York: Schocken Books, 1974. 312 pp.

Rabinowitz, H. *A Guide to Hassidism*. New York: Thomas Yoseloff, 1960. 163 pp.

Rubenstein, Aryeh. *Hassidism*. Jerusalem: Ketter Books, 1975. 120 pp.

ANTI-SEMITISM AND THE HOLOCAUST

Cohn, Norman. *Warrant for Genocide*. Baltimore: Penguin Books, 1970. 336 pp.

Levin, Nora. *The Holocaust*. New York: Schocken Books, 1973. 768 pp.

Littell, Franklin H. *The Crucifixion of the Jews*. New York: Harper & Row, 1975. 153 pp.

Poliakov, Leon. *The History of Anti-Semitism*. New York: Schocken Books, 1974. 340 pp.

Singerman, Robert. *Antisemitic Propaganda*. New York: Garland Publishing, 1982. 448 pp.

Tumin, Melvin M. *An Inventory and Appraisal of Research on American Anti-Semitism*. New York: Freedom Books, 1961. 185 pp.

Black Judaism

ben-Jochanman, Josef. *We: The Black Jews*. New York: Alkebu-lan Books and Educational Materials Associates, 1983. 408 pp.

Goitein, S. D. *From the Land of Sheba*. New York: Schocken Books, 1973. 142 pp.

Rapoport, Louis. *The Lost Jews*. New York: Stein and Day, 1980. 252 pp.

Winsor, Rudolph R. *From Babylon to Timbuktu*. New York: Exposition Press, 1969. 151 pp.

Chapter Twenty

THE MIDDLE EASTERN FAMILY

PART II—ISLAM, ZOROASTRIANISM, AND BAHA'I

Directory listings for the groups belonging to the Middle Eastern Family
(Isalm, Zoroastrianism, and Baha'i) may be found in the section beginning
on page 683.

With less than a million adherents in 1965, when the emigration barriers were liberalized, Islam has growth to be the second largest religious tradition in America, eclipsing Judaism by the end of the 1970's. In like measure, it has moved from the faith of a few ethnic enclaves to a powerful presence in every segment of urban society, due in no small measure to its association with oil and the turmoil of the Middle East. While not yet as well organized as the Jewish community, it has gained ground quickly.

ORIGINS. "There is but one God and Muhammed is His Apostle" is the great standard under which Islam has become the religion of one-seventh of the world's population. Islam means submission, in this case submission to Allah, the creator-ruler God of Muslim faith. Islam can be said to date from 622, the year of Muhammed's removal from Mecca to Medina in Saudi Arabia. The Hegira marked the change in Muhammed from the role of itinerant preacher to head of a definite community of faith.

Belief in Allah, the supreme God, is the essential component of Islamic faith. He is seen as the transcendent Being, creator and sustainer of the universe. He is the law-giver, the arbiter of good and evil, and the judge at the end-time. Existing with God are his angelic messengers. Chief among these is Gabriel, who communicated the *Koran* to Muhammed. (Opposing the angels are the *satans* or devils.) The *Koran* is the written revelation of God, accepted as transcribed by Muhammed. It is to be distinguished from Muhammed's teachings, which are based on the *Koran* and are the prime tool for understanding it. The *Koran*, a book of some 300 pages, is divided into 114 suras or chapters, which are arranged (with the exception of Sura I) in order of length, the longest first. These suras were given at various periods throughout Muhammed's life.

Muhammed himself is seen as the last of a series of apostles who have preached the unity of God and warned of the end-time judgment. The twenty-eight earlier prophets include Adam, Noah, Moses, John the Baptist and Jesus. The judgment they described is a cataclysmic event when the trumpet will sound for men to stand and be called to account. Paradise and hell wait to receive the just and the damned.

The law of Allah is a central concept of the faith, and the *Koran* and writings about Muhammed have yielded to codification. The law has become a basic unifying force in the Muslim world. Outward manifestation of the law is most readily seen in the five central observances of Muslim life: 1) the observance of ritual prayer five times daily; 2) the giving of alms to the poor; 3) fasting during the month of Ramadan; 4) a pilgrimage to Mecca, holy city of the Muslims, at least once in each lifetime and 5) striving in the way of God. Beyond these, are a number of ritual and legal requirements, such as refraining from eating pork and from usury.

From Medina, Islam spread steadily in what today are Saudi Arabia, Syria, Iraq, Jordan and Egypt. The rise of the new faith released a tremendous amount of cultural and intellectual energy which produced a new Arab religious culture. The spread of Islam in the Middle Ages carried it west across North Africa into Spain, north into Turkey, south along the African coast, and east into Persia. Further expansion carried the faith into what are today the southern provinces of the USSR. The movement into Europe was turned back at Vienna in the sixteenth century.

Within orthodox Islam, numerous schools of thought have developed, but in the seventh century, a major schism developed among the followers of Ali, the fourth caliph of Islam and son-in-law of Muhammed. Ali assumed the role of caliph, the spiritual and temporal ruler of Islam, in 656 A.D. He moved his capital to Kufa in present-day Iraq. Upon his death in 661, the political power shifted back to Syria, a move disliked by the Iraqi Arabs. Their political goals found religious expression in a new doctrine—the exclusive right of the house of Ali to the caliphate. In forming this doctrine, the House of Ali had to repudiate the first three caliphs: Abu Bakr, Omar and Othman, three reverend companions of Muhammed. The Arabs who held this doctrine are called Shi'a and are distinguished from the main body of orthodox or Sunni Muslims.

MUSLIMS IN AMERICA. There is probably no group whose presence in American history has been as well hidden as that of the Muslims. Like many minority groups, the Muslims appeared in the New World in the days of the

Colonies. "Istfan the Arab" was a guide to Franciscan explorer Marcos de Niya in Arizona in 1539. Nosereddine, an Egyptian, settled in the Catskills of New York in the 1500's and was burned at the stake for murdering an Indian princess. One Arab has even become a folk hero: Haj Ali, in 1840 a camel driver for U.S. Army experiments with breeding camels in the Arizona desert. He is remembered under his corrupted name, Hi Jolly:

"Hi Jolly was a camel driver, long time ago.
  He followed Mr. Blaine a way out West.
He didn't mind the burning sand,
  In that God forsaken land,
But he didn't mind the pretty girls the best.

Hi Jolly! Hey Jolly!
  Twenty miles today, by golly.
Twenty more before the morning light.
  Hi Jolly, Hey, I
Gotta be on my way
  I told my gal I'd be home Sunday night."

As early as the 1860's, Syrians and Lebanese, fleeing the invading Turks, came to the United States. But the first serious attempt to establish Islam in America followed the conversion of Muhammed Alexander Russell Webb in 1888. Webb was the American Consul in Manila at the time of his conversion, but returned to New York in 1892. The following year, he opened the Oriental Publishing Company and began a periodical, *The Moslem World*, of which he was editor. He also wrote a number of booklets. In the same year, he was the only defender of Islamic faith presented at the Parliament of Religions at Chicago. He died in 1916.

Contemporaneous to Muhammed Alexander Russell Webb's activities was the beginning of large scale immigration from the Eastern Mediterranean—Syria, Lebanon, Iran, India, Turkey and other predominantly Muslim countries. Three thousand Polish Muslims and a small community of Circassian (Russian) Muslims also settled in New York. The American Muslim community was distinguished by two characteristics: it was heavily male in population and extremely clannish. National and sub-national communities formed in Northern urban centers, particularly Detroit. Little effort to keep records or to reach out toward non-Muslim neighbors was made.

Early organization attempts were made wherever large Muslim population centers developed. After Detroit and New York City came Pittsburgh, Cleveland, Worcester, Boston, and Providence. Detroit work was begun in 1912, and there are now four societies in the Detroit-Windsor area. By 1920, centers were operating in Michigan City, Indiana; Chicago; Toledo; Cedar Rapids; Milwaukee; Akron; Philadelphia, and Baltimore. Within communities, divisions developed along national lines.

A major event in the American Muslim community was the completion in 1956 of the Islamic Center in Washington, D.C. Built in part with money from fifteen sponsoring countries with the idea of serving the diplomatic community, its potential as a major focus for missionary endeavor and education is being explored by American followers.

Shi'a Muslims emerged in the 1970's as Iraqi immigrants arrived in large numbers in the U.S. They are served by the Shi'a Association of North America, which publishes the *Islamic Review*; the Midwest Association of Shi'a Organized Muslims, which publishes the *Masom Newsletter*; and the Islamic Seminary in New York City. Centers are located in Atlanta; Allentown, Pennsylvania; Lanham, Maryland; Chicago; Houston; and California (where three centers are located). The Shi'a Muslims distribute a large number of pamphlets supportive of Islam in general and the Shi'a position in particular.

BLACK MUSLIMS. No one knows when the first Black Muslim came to America, but it is well known that Africans south of the Sahara had developed Islamic centers prior to the time of the slave trade, and that among the slaves in the United States were Muslims. Morroe Berger notes that such slaves tended to be viewed as superior by both themselves and other slaves; they were often educated, and they resisted acculturation and assimilation, thus retaining their faith longer.

Timothy Dwight, while in New York, recorded a visit with a slave from the South who told him stories of other Muslims. William B. Hodgson, an ethnologist, mentions five Muslim slaves in a 1852 work. One, Bul-Ali, was a slave-driver on a Sapelo Island, Georgia, plantation. C. C. Jones, a missionary who authored *The Religious Instruction of the Negroes in the United States*, noted that Muslim slaves, under pressure from Christianizing forces, would try accommodations to the new faith by equating God with Allah and Jesus with Muhammed. Berger concludes that, while no definite connection can be made between twentieth century Black Muslims and those who might have survived the slave era, nevertheless, "It is quite possible that some of the various American Muslim groups of the past half century or so had their roots in these vestiges, that the tradition was handed down in a weak chain from generation to generation" (Morroe Berger, "The Black Muslims," *Horizon* 6 [January 1964]: 49-64).

One non-Muslim movement generally conceded to underlie present Black Muslim organizations is the Universal Negro Improvement Association of Marcus Garvey. Among Garvey's confidants was a half-black Egyptian, Duse Mohammed Ali, and in his newspaper, *Negro World*, Garvey paid homage to the blacks of ancient Egypt and the medieval Moorish empires.

Between the wars, contact between blacks in America and the Near East increased. Blacks migrated in the 1930's to Turkey and Egypt. One arrived in 1932 in Cairo, announcing his allegiance to Islam and his intention to go to Mecca.

Black Muslims are to be partly understood in terms of black nationalism, the perspective from which most studies have originated. The concomitance of these two movements cannot be denied. The Muslim faith became an avenue by which blacks expressed a rebellious feeling against the white majority religion.

SUFISM. The word "Sufism" is used to describe a wide variety of mystical and more-or-less disciplined orders found throughout the Islamic world. No one knows the origin of the term, and several explanations vie for acceptance. Some relate the term to *suf*, or wool, denotative of the wool garments worn by some Sufis. Others see a connection to the Hebrew *en sof*, the name for the infinite Divine in Jewish mysticism. While still others derive it from *safa*, the Arabic word for purity, or from *sophia*, the Greek word for wisdom. These several explanations do not exhaust the options.

Whatever the origin of their name, the Sufis appear to have developed from the ascetic pietism evident from the very first generation of the followers of Muhammed. From these early ascetics arose the *gussas* or storytellers, popular preachers of the Koran, and from the storytellers came the idea of the Madhi, the divinely guided one who will help bring the ultimate victory of Islam by means of a cosmic event. In the eighth century, the ascetic movement began to take on a mystical aspect, and true Sufism emerged.

Once launched, Sufism became a popular religious movement which developed its own forms and peculiarities. The *dhikr* and *sama*, the recitation of and meditation upon the Koran by the congregations, began to rival the Mosque. The ecstatic experience offered the immediate knowledge of God, as compared to the second-hand knowledge of the theologians, who were replaced by the Sufi leaders, the *shaikhs*. These official teachers gained their position through charismatic authority. Outstanding shaikhs became founders of new schools of Sufism and were often regarded as saints after they died. Also, in contradistinction to the Koran, which is against the unmarried state, many Sufi leaders practiced celibacy.

Sufism was an eclectic movement drawing on Christian and Gnostic elements. A pantheistic theology began to emerge, a possibility in any mystical system. More popular was a non-theological approach which accepted orthodoxy, but practiced mysticism on the side. One major innovation was the development of a gnostic-like spiritual hierarchy, populated with the saints, and headed by the *Qutb*, the Pole of the World. The Qutb, who superintends the world through his hosts, resembles closely the Platonic "demiurge," a subordinate deity who is the creator of the material world.

Love and fear vie in Sufi mysticism as the motivating force. Fear was the early focus of Sufi pietism, and the horror of hell was held up to men. Later, love assumed a dominant position. Rabi'a al-Adawiya (b. 801), a woman saint and mystic, summed up the emphasis in a poem:

"I love Thee with two loves, love of my happiness,
And perfect love, to love Thee as is Thy due.
My selfish love is that I do naught
But think on Thee, excluding all beside,
But that purest love, which is Thy due,
Is that the veils which hide Thee fall, and I gaze on Thee.
No praise to me either this or that,
Nay, Thine the praise for both that love and this."

Sufism was in a constant battle for existence with the ruling, orthodox, religious leaders until the twelfth century. The change from persecution to acceptance is possibly attributable to the career of al-Ghazali (b. 1111), a man of marked intellectual acumen and religious insight. Beginning with a search for ultimate reality, he pursued a course through theology and philosophy and ended with the personal experience of God and Sufi mysticism. Al-Ghazali's great contribution seems to have been the creation of a religious synthesis, through which Sufism could be accepted in an orthodox system and orthodoxy could become an acceptable framework for the Sufis.

The changes that came with al-Ghazali allowed the development of the Sufi schools. He promoted the idea that disciples should move in close association to their shaikh, who then began to assume a status like that of a Hindu guru. Brotherhoods built around a shaikh grew, and initiation ceremonies were adopted. Initiates would often leave to found affiliated groups. A popular school thus could spread (and on occasion did) throughout the Islamic world. When the leader died, an initiate would inherit the former leader's role and prayer rug.

According to Sufi tradition, twelve orders were founded prior to the establishment of the Ottoman Empire. The first was the Uwaisi, founded by Uwais following a vision of the Angel Gabriel in 659 C.E., less than forty years after the Hegira. Uwais pulled all of his teeth out in memory of Muhammed, who lost two teeth in a battle. His imposition of that same sacrifice for members insured that the Uwaisi remained small in size. The remaining eleven schools or orders, most of whom have taken the name of their founder are: Illwani, Adhani, Sustami, Saqati, Qadiri, Rifai, Nurbakhshi, Suharwardi, Qubrawi, Shazili, Mavlana, and Badawi. (Spelling of the names of the various Sufi orders varies from author to author as each tries to render the sound of the name into English. No standard spelling has yet been developed.)

Since the establishment of the Ottoman Empire and the subsequent spread of Islam from Indonesia to Albania, the number of orders has grown immensely and no catalog exists (though detailed lists for some countries do exist). The main orders in India at present are the Chishti, the Qadiri, the Suharwardi, and the Naqshbandi, two of which are of later origin. Other orders are prominent in other countries. Orders also have split into suborders. For example, both the Nizami and Sabiri suborders of the Chishti Order have a following in the United States in the Chishti Order in America and the Sufi Order (headed by Pir Vilayat Khan) respectively.

In their homeland, members of orders can frequently be distinguished by the peculiar clothes they wear. Apparel will vary in color and style, especially the head gear. Several of the orders have become famous for their peculiar ritual formats which include the whirling dances of the Jerrahi and the howling of the Rifai.

The first Sufi group to become visible in America was the Sufi Order founded in the early twentieth century by Hazrat Khan. He was followed by George Gurdjieff, the spiritual teacher so influenced by Sufism, who created a unique modern variation on the Sufi orders. During the 1970's representatives of many Sufi groups migrated to the United States and organized in the United States. Also, since the end of World War II, the Middle East, like India, has become the site for pilgrimages by spiritual seekers looking for mystic teachers. Several who found their gurus in a Sufi shaikh returned to the United States to be found American branches of their shaikh's orders.

ZOROASTRIANISM AND THE MAZDAZNAN MOVEMENT.

Zoroaster (or Zarathustra) was a Persian prophet and religious teacher of the seventh century B. C. who worked a monotheistic revolution in his native land. According to tradition, Zoroaster, when he was about thirty years of age, was admitted into the presence of Anuru Mazda, the supreme being, and was personally instructed in the doctrines of the new faith. Over the next few years, he received visions of the six archangels, the chief attendants and agents of Mazda. After eleven years of frustrating work, he was able to convert Vishtapa (Hystaspes), one of the rulers of Iran, who aided Zoroaster in spreading the new faith with two holy wars.

Zoroaster's faith was monotheistic. Mazda is the all-wise creator and absolute sovereign. Mazda demands righteousness and promises help to men who follow truthfulness, and justice, and foster agriculture. The righteous will attain heaven. In the oldest Zoroastrian texts, Angra Mainyu appears as an evil spirit, but only in later years was he to arise as the evil counterpart of Mazda and to make Zoroastrianism a thorough-going dualism. The main representatives of this dualistic Zoroastrianism are the Parsees.

BAHA'I WORLD FAITH.

Among the newest of the several religious traditions to grow beyond the country of its founding into an international movement, the Baha'i World Faith originated in Persia (now Iran) in the mid-nineteenth century. Baha'is generally date their founding to the work of Siyyad Ali Muhammad of Shiraz (1819-1850), a prophet who declared himself the Bab, i.e., the Gate, through whom people would know about the advent of another messenger of God. His proclamations were done within a context of Islamic expectation of the Madhi, the successor of the previous Messenger, Muhammed, the founder of Islam. The Bab began his prophetic work in 1844, but, after gaining a large following, encountered the opposition of the country's Muslim leaders. He was eventually imprisoned by the Shah and in 1850 executed.

Among the Bab's followers was Mirza Husayn-Ali (1817-92). During the time of the Bab's imprisonment, at a conference of his followers, he assumed the title "Baha," and emerged as one of the principle spokespersons of the Babi community. In 1852, Jinab-i-Baha, as he was then called, was imprisoned in another wave of anti-Babi persecution. While languishing in a Tehran jail, he received the first intimations that he was, in fact, the one of whom the Bab spoke, "Him Whom God shall make manifest." Soon released from prison, he gradually assumed the prime leadership role among the Babis. Finally, in 1863, to a small group of family and friends, he announced his conviction that he was the Promised One foretold by the Bab.

Jinab-i-Baha's initial proclamation came just as a large segment of the Babi community were beginning an exile first in Constantinople and then in Adrianople (now Edirne, Turkey). In Adrianople, he openly proclaimed his new role and new name, Baha'u'llah, "the Glory of God," through a series of letters, called "tablets," sent to many world rulers and political leaders.

In 1868, Baha'u'llah and his family were further banished to Akka (now Acre) in Palestine, where he lived the remainder of his life, first at the penal colony and from 1879 in a residence in the city. During this period he authored his most important book, the *Kitab-i-Agdas* (the Most Holy Book), the book of laws for Baha'is, as well as numerous other shorter works, all now considered to have the authority of scripture.

Baha'u'llah was succeeded by his son, Abbas Effendi (1844-1921), who took the name, Abdu'l-Baha, "the Slave of Baha." A devoted follower of his father even before the initial proclamation of his role in 1866, he followed Baha'u'llah into exile, and authored the first history of the movement in 1886. He assumed control of the movement under the authority of his father's will.

As the Center of the Covenant, Abdu'l-Baha directed the international spread of the movement. Following his confinement from 1901 to 1908, and the discontinuance of travel restrictions in 1911, he made the first of several foreign tours. A world tour the following year brought him to the United States, where he dedicated the grounds for the Baha'i temple in Wilmette, Illinois. Returning to Palestine just before World War I, he settled in Haifa, where Turkish authorities again confined him, until the British took control.

As the Interpreter of Baha'u'llah, Abdu'l-Baha summarized the major themes of the new Faith revealed by his father. He emphasized its universal character: that all religions were essentially one and that all the prophets of God, the Great Manifestations, taught the same religion. He expounded the eleven principles of the Baha'i Faith: (1) the independent investigation of truth; (2) the oneness of the human race; (3) religion should be the cause of love and affection (not hate); (4) the conformity of religion to science and reason; (5) the abolition of religious, racial, political, and patriotic prejudice; (6) the equal opportunity to the means of existence; (7) the equality of persons before the law; (8) universal peace; (9) the noninterference of religion in politics; (10) the equality of the sexes; and (11) the power of the Holy Spirit as the means of spiritual development. He also advocated a universal language and universal compulsory education.

Abdu'l-Baha was succeeded by his nephew Shoghi Effendi, who did much to develop the international organization and administration of the Faith. Under Shoghi Effendi, the Baha'is established a following on every continent. Since his death, a more collective form of leadership has emerged.

BAHA'IS IN AMERICA.

The Baha'i Faith was brought to America in 1892 by a Lebanese convert, Ibrahim Kheiralla. A former businessman, Kheiralla proved to be an energetic teacher and soon gathered groups of eager students. The first Baha'i groups were formed in Chicago, New York, Boston, and Kenosha, Wisconsin.

During the 1890's, there was almost no copies of English translations of the writings of Baha'ullah in print. In the absence of published volumes, Kheiralla taught a full course on the Baha'i faith, but presented it within the context of his own occult speculations. Eventually Kheiralla published his peculiar teachings in several books. Kheiralla's deviations from Baha'i teachings reached a crisis during a pilgrimage by American Baha'is to meet Abdu'l-Baha during the winter of 1898-99. Kheiralla argued with Andu'l-Baha who rejected his speculative presentation of the faith. Kheiralla in turn rejected Abdu'l-Baha and, continuing in his own presentation of the faith, took his supporters from the Chicago and Kenosha groups and formed a rival organization. The Behaists, as Kheiralla termed his followers, existed for several decades, but then disbanded. Kheiralla is now remembered as a "covenant breaker," a term applied to individuals who attempt to establish rival Baha'i organizations, and American Baha'is generally remember their history as beginning with Thornton Chase, the first American convert.

SOURCES—MIDDLE EASTERN FAMILY, PART II

ISLAM—GENERAL SOURCES

Abdalati, Hummudah. *Islam in Focus*. N.p.: The Author, n.d. 211 pp.

Ede, David. *Guide to Islam*. Boston: G. K. Hall & Co., 1983. 261 pp.

Farah, Ceasar E. *Islam*. Woodbury, NY: Barron's Educational Series, 1968. 306 pp.

Galwash, Ahmad A. *The Religion of Islam*. 2 vols. Doha, Qatar: Educational and Cultural Ministry, 1973.

Geddes, C. L. *An Analytical Guide to the Bibliographies on Islam, Muhammad, and the Our'an*. Denver: American Institute of Islamic Studies, 1973. 102 pp.

———. *Books in English on Islam, Muhammad, and the Our'an: A Selected and Annotated Bibliography*. Denver: American Institute of Islamic Studies, 1976. 68 pp.

Haneef, Suzanne. *What Everyone Should Know About Islam and Muslims*. Chicago: Kazi Brothers, 1979. 202 pp.

Hussain, Asaf. *Islamic Movements in Egypt, Pakistan and Iran*. London: Mansell Publishing, 1983. 168 pp.

Islam in Paperback. Denver: American Institute of Islamic Studies. 1969. 70 pp.

Maududi, Sayyid Abul Ala. *Towards Understanding Islam*. Lahore, Pakistan: Idara Tarjuman-Ul-Quran, 1974. 179 pp.

Nomani, M. Manzoor. *Islamic Faith and Practice*. Lucknow, India: Academy of Islamic Research and Publications, 1973. 168 pp.

Rahman, Fazlur. *Islam*. Garden City, NY: Doubleday, 1968. 331 pp.

MUSLIMS IN AMERICA

Elkholy, Abdo A. *The Arab Moslems in the United States*. New Haven, CT: College and University Press, 1966. 176 pp.

Richardson, E. Allen. *Islamic Cultures in North America*. New York: Pilgrim Press, 1981. 64 pp.

SHI'ITE MUSLIMS

Khomeini, Ruhollah. *Islamic Government*. New York: Manor Books, 1979. 154 pp.

Tabatabai, Allamah Sayyid Muhammad Husayn. *Shi'ite Islam*. Houston, TX: Free Islamic Literature, 1979. 253 pp.

ul-Amine, Hasan. *Shorter Islamic Shi'ite Encyclopedia*. Beirut: n.p., 1969. 355 pp.

SUFISM

Arberry, A. J. *Sufism*. New York: Harper & Row, 1950. 141 pp.

Grisell, Ronald. *Sufism*. Berkeley, CA: Rose Books, 1983. 112 pp.

Nicholson, Reynold A. *The Mystics of Islam*. New York: Schocken Books, 1975. 178 pp.

Rastogi, T. C. *Islamic Mysticism Sufism*. London: East-West Publications, 1982. 126 pp.

Shah, Indries. *The Diffusion of Sufi Ideas in the West*. Boulder, CO: Keysign Press, 1972. 212 pp.

———. *The Sufis*. Garden City, NY: Doubleday, 1971. 451 pp.

Shah, Sirdar Ikbal Ali. *Islamic Sufism*. New York: Samuel Weiser, 1971. 299 pp.

Subhan, John A. *Sufism, Its Saints and Shrines*. New York: Samuel Weiser, 1970. 412 pp.

Trimingham, J. Spencer. *The Sufi Orders of Islam*. London: Oxford University Press, 1971. 333 pp.

Williams, L. F. Rushbrook. *Sufi Studies: East and West*. New York: E. P. Dutton, 1974. 260 pp.

BLACK MUSLIMS

Austin, Allan D. *African Muslims in Antebellum America, A Sourcebook*. New York: Garland Publishers, 1984. 759 pp.

Craig, H. A. L. *Bilal*. London: Quartet Books, 1977. 158 pp.

Essien-Udom, E. U. *Black Nationalism*. New York: Dell, 1962. 448 pp.

Lincoln, C. Eric. *The Black Muslims in America*. Boston: Beacon Press, 1961. 276 pp.

Mansour, Khalid Abdullah Taria Al, and Faissal Fahd Al Talal. *The Challenges of Spreading Islam in America*. San Francisco: The Authors, 1980. 213 pp.

AHMADIYYA

Ahmad, Mirza Bashiruddin Mahmud. *Ahmadiyyat or True Islam*. Washington, DC: The American Fazl Mosque, 1951. 246 pp.

Dard, A. R. *Life of Ahmad*. Lahore: Tabshir Publication, 1948. 629 pp.

Khan, Muhammad Zafrulla. *Ahmadiyyat, The Renaissance of Islam*. Lahore: Tabshir Publications, 1978. 360 pp.

Nafwi, S. Abul Hasan Ali. *Oadianism, A Critical Study*. Lucknow, India: Academy of Islamic Research and Publications, 1974. 167 pp.

ZOROASTERIANISM

Bode, Dastur Framroze Ardeshir, and Piloo Nanavutty. *Songs of Zarathushtra*. London: George Allen & Unwin, 1952.

Dawson, Miles Menander. *The Ethical Religion of Zoroaster*. New York: AMS Press, 1969. 271 pp.

Masani, Rustom P. *The Religion of the Good Life, Zoroasterianism*. London: George Allen & Unwin, 1938. 189 pp.

Modi, Jivanji J. *The Religious Ceremonies and Customs of the Parsees*. New York: Garland Publishing, 1979. 536 pp.

BAHA'I FAITH

Balyuzi, H. M. *'Abdu'l-Baha*. London: George Ronald, 1971. 560 pp.

———. *Baha'u'llah, The King of Glory*. London: George Ronald, 1980. 539 pp.

———. *Edward Granville Browne and the Baha'i Faith*. London: George Ronald, 1970. 142 pp.

Gayer, Jessyca Russell. *Baha'i Faith*. New York: Award Books, 1967. 222 pp.

Miller, William McElwee. *The Baha'i Faith: Its History and Teachings*. South Pasadena, CA: William Carey Press, 1974.

Perkins, Mary, and Philip Hainsworth. *The Baha'i Faith*. London: Ward Lock Educational, 1980. 96 pp.

Sears, William. *The Prisoner of Kings*. Toronto: General Publishing Company, 1971. 240 pp.

——. *Release the Sun*. Wilmette, IL: Baha'i Publishing Trust, 1971. 250 pp.

Chapter Twenty-one

THE EASTERN FAMILY

PART 1, HINDUISM, JAINISM, SIKHISM

Directory listings for the groups belonging to the Eastern Family
(Hinduism, Sikhism, and Jainism) may be found in the section beginning
on page 705.

HINDUISM. What is Hinduism? Of no major religious community is this question more difficult to answer. It is without an individual founder, has only a vaguely defined relation to an authoritative scripture, and has no single set of issues around which it can orient itself. Some writers, in the face of this frustration, have tried to turn these problems into a positive polemic for Hinduism by seeing its "systematic anarchy" as a sign of Hinduism's universal character. "Hinduism is absolutely indefinite . . . It rejects nothing. It is all-comprehensive, all-absorbing, all-complacent," says one Hindu writer.

Yet on a second look, Hinduism is not so vague as might first appear. While there is a great diversity of opinion among Hindus, it is no greater than among Christians. While Hinduism has no founders, it does have some mythological figures to which it relates. Despite a variety of ideas and emphases, Hindus do possess certain ideas in common, such as a belief in reincarnation and karma, and they do practice certain disciplines, the most common of which is yoga. Hindus also relate to a common history, that of India. Certain writings have a great value for them although the *Vedas* and *Upanishads* have only rarely functioned as the *Bible* or *Koran* has. Hinduism might thus be defined as a set of religions that positively relate to several mythological figures (Krishna, Rama), some metaphysical ideas and practices (reincarnation, karma, yoga), two writings (the *Vedas* and *Upanishads*), and a people's history. That definition seems to describe justly the Hindus while distinguishing them from other religious groupings, particularly the Jains and Sikhs.

Indian and Hindu history can be divided roughly into four periods. The first is defined as pre-Vedic. Prior to the invasion of India by the Aryans, or Indo-Europeans, a culture on a par with that of the ancient Mediterranean basin existed, the artifacts of which have only recently and partially been uncovered. While religious articles have been found, no picture of this people's religious faith has emerged.

The second or Vedic period begins with the invasion of India by the Indo-Europeans. The waves of Aryan migration have been variously dated from 5000 B.C. to 1500 B.C. The primary document of this period is the *Rig Veda*, the oldest

of India's existing sacred books. The *Rig Veda* is actually ten books of hymns and prayers to the gods, collected probably about 1000 B.C. The *Vedas* present a very vigorous, worldly religion oriented to nature and a pastoral, agricultural life. These people of the Vedic period had a positive view of the world and saw their survival of death as a continuation of the good life. Along with the various gods, particular attention was paid to Soma, the deified intoxicant of the soma plant.

The third period of India's history begins in the several centuries following 1000 B.C. and represents a significant shift in religious outlook, which the Aryan invasion must have brought to the previous Indian culture. The change in outlook is from a positive view of life to a pessimistic world-fleeing one. The two ideas which symbolized this change are transmigration or reincarnation and karma. Transmigration is the idea that a person may go through a succession of earthly lives, in some of which he may be an animal (and in more extreme forms of Hinduism, a plant). All of life is on the wheel of rebirth, and the goal of life is to escape physical rebirth by reaching spiritual perfection. Part of the rationale for the rebirth theory is karma. Karma is the principle of retribution, an inexorable law of justice which brings upon the individual the consequences of his actions—whether the actions were performed in his current life or in an earlier life. The goal in life is to escape karma, good or bad.

Escape from karma is by absorption in the world-soul, Brahman. How can absorption be accomplished? The most common answer given is yoga, a discipline designed to lead man to self-integration and then to integration with Brahman. The best known of the several forms of yoga in the West is hatha yoga, which includes such bodily postures as the lotus position. Hatha yoga is a discipline used in the East for body integration and control, and as a preliminary to the four higher forms of yoga. In the West, hatha yoga has been put to all kinds of uses in physical culture quite apart from Hindu notions.

The four paths to God by yoga are bhakti yoga (to God through love), jnana yoga (to God through knowledge), karma yoga (to God through work) and raja (royal) yoga (to God through meditative exercises). These four, more advanced, yogas are designed for the various types of people, according to Hindu analysis. Some people, being basically reflective, find the ideas and the philosophical, logical demonstrations of jnana yoga suited to their innate patterns. By taking thought, the jnana yoga student can come to a realization that many levels of self are finite, and the student can discern his eternal self beyond the finite qualities of size, shape, emotions, etc. For the basically emotional person, bhakti yoga gives direction to man's most powerful emotion, love. Man tends to become like that which he loves; thus, bhakti yoga directs man's amazing potentials of love toward God. A major feature of bhakti yoga is japa, the practice of repeating the name of God. (A Christian form of this practice is the Jesus prayer in classical Russian Orthodoxy.) The active person can be guided on a path to God through work. The smallest activity of life can be done wisely as a Godward practice—karma yoga. The highest path to God is through raja yoga, the royal road to reintegration. By meditation, the self penetrates the layers of man until it reaches the beyond that is within. While bhakti yoga is most popular in India, raja is most popular in the United States.

Associated with the *Upanishads* were several subsidiary developments. The most important was the rise of the Brahmins, the priestly class, as the highest level of the caste system in India. The rule of the Brahmins would dominate Indian life and lead to reactions by later movements. The idea of *maya* or illusion developed at this period. Common to most Hinduism is the belief that outward life and suffering are mere illusion and that realization of this fact will lead to release from suffering. *Ahimsa* is the highest of ethical precepts for Hinduism (it is also popular in several other religions) and is the vow of non-injury to life, non-killing. Ahimsa is the foundation of vegetarianism.

Later Developments. The collecting of the *Upanishads* became a watershed in Hindu history as it completed the writings to which Hindus would give a more or less universal authority. From these writings the various schools of interpretation would arise, and to these writings later movements would react. Development proceeded at a normal pace until the early 1800's when a disjunctive event, the invasion and conquest of India by England, changed the whole course of Indian history. The coming of the British marked the arrival of an alien culture and an alien religion, backed by political power. In the face of the development of a vigorous Christian mission, an initial defensive reaction was followed by a creative Hindu Renaissance, which produced a number of outstanding leaders (such as Ram Mohan Roy and Sri Ramakrishna) and movements. These movements, in many cases, were important in the nationalist drives of the twentieth century and in Hinduism's movement into the U.S.

Within Hindu circles, four figures are particularly important—*guru, swami, avatar,* and *chela*. A guru is a religious teacher who teaches basically out of the knowledge he has received by becoming an accomplished yoga practitioner. The ideal of the guru is to become a satguru or perfect master. The knowledge to be imparted by the guru to the chela (pupil) is both technique and the mystic reality (Brahman) which is the goal of yogic life. The swami is a Hindu monk who also functions as teacher and religious leader. The avatar is an incarnation of God and thus properly an object of veneration and worship.

Increasingly, since the British made Christianity a force in India, the guru and swami have taken on a new function. In pre-Christian India, there was little or no congregational worship apart from the large seasonal festivals. The guru arose as a leader of an isolated ashram (retreat center) inhabited by only a few close disciples. Increasingly, the guru has become a resident of a population center and the leader of mass movements. Influenced by Christian worship, the urban ashram with regular gatherings of the guru's followers is becoming a dominant mode of religious expression.

THE HINDU SAMPRADAYAS. Like American Christianity, Indian Hinduism is divided into a number of denominational-like groups, *sampradayas*. The prime three, roughly analogous to the Christian divisions of Catholic, Protestant, and Orthodox, are the Vaishnava, Shaiva, and Shakta. The Vaishnavas worship Vishnu as the primary deity in the Hindu pantheon and emerged as a recognizable group around the fifth century B.C.E. In India, the majority of temples seen throughout the countryside are Vaishnava centers, and Vaishnava holymen, both monks and individual renounciates, can be seen in their typical white robes and vertical markings (*tilaks*) on their forehead. Over the centuries Vaishnavas have focused their attention upon a variety of Vishnu's incarnations; however, that of Krishna has been the most popular. The merger of Vishnu, the hero of the Hindu classic the *Mahabharata*, Vasudeva-Krishna occurred over the period of the writing of the *Mahabharata* and becomes complete in the *Bhagavad Gita*, a late insertion into the text.

The *Gita* also introduces a prime emphasis of Vaishnava Hinduism, bhakti yoga or devotional service. The volume, a dialogue between the god Krishna and his human devotee Arjuna, discusses the more traditional approach to the deity through gifts, sacrifices, and austerities (i.e., jnana and raja yoga), and then points the reader to the truer path of devoted service as the means to really approach Vishnu-Krishna.

Over the centuries, four main Vaishnava sampradayas (denominations) have arisen. The Sri Vaishnavas, traditionally considered the oldest of the four, is said to have started with Vishnu and his wife ShriLakshmi (hence the popular name of the group), but emerged as a distinct path under Ramanuja in the early twelfth century. Ramanuja most clearly established both the position of theistic worship as opposed to the allegiance to an impersonal divine reality of the Saivites and the legitimacy of devotional service as the way of salvation.

The Nimbarki (or Namawat) Sampradaya was founded by Nimbarkiacharya who taught a theology which might be termed dualistic monism. Human souls (and the world in general) are seen as both different from God, being endowed with their own qualities and limitations, but at the same time not different since God is omnipresent and souls depend upon Him.

The Madhwaguariya Sampradaya was founded by the famous Bengali fifteenth-century saint Chaitanya Mahaprabhu. Centering his activity upon the Gita and the *Srimad*

Bhagavatam, a voluminous devotional work on Krishna, Chaitanya taught the practice *sankirtan*, the multiple recitation of the God's name, as the most acceptable form of devotional activity in the present age. His perspective became well known in the America in the 1970's through the high visibility of the Hare Krishna Movement, one of several representatives of the Madhwaguariya in the West.

The Brahma Sampradaya, generally traced to Madhwacharya in the thirteenth century, centers its worship on Vayu, the Air god. According to Madhwacharya, regarded as an incarnation of Vayu, Vishnu communicated his truths to Brahma who in turn spread them to humanity through the aid of Vayu. Present day salvation comes by worship of Vayu.

Competing with the Vaishnavas for the loyalties of Hindus are the Shaivas, those who worship Shiva (or Siva) as the one great God. Shiva appears very early in the *Vedas* and *Upanishads* as a principle deity, but the *Mahabharata* contains a full description of the popular Shiva. He is seen as both the great yogi who practices jnana and raja yoga in his mountain home and the creative deity symbolized by his lingam (phallus), a symbol centrally located in many Shaiva temples and worn (as is the yoni of his wife) by many devotees.

Two figures stand out in Shaiva history, Patanjali and Shankaracharya. Patanjali, about whom almost nothing is known (including the century in which he lived), brought together the scattered teachings on yoga and organized them into a system of practice, the following of which constituted the major method by which an individual could become united or yoked to God. Within the Shaiva community, yoga is given varying degrees of emphasis from those who practice it as the major avenue of spiritual enlightenment, to those who integrate it into a larger salvic scheme, to those who discount its significance. The practice of hatha yoga (asanas) is much more prominent in the American Hindu community than in India.

The goal of Patanjali's system was *samadhi*, a state of cosmic awareness reached through the control of body and mind. Practice begins with the negative discipline of *yama* (abstention from violence, falsehood, theft, incontinence, and acquisitiveness) and the positive observance of *niyama* (purity, contentment, austerities, study, and dedicated activity). Accompanying these overall disciplines was the practice of *asanas* (postures) of hatha yoga, *pranayama* (disciplined breathing), and *pratyahara* (detachment of the mind from senses by which it is connected to the outside world). Once the mind and body are suppressed, the yogi can progress to the ultimate three stages, *dharana* (contemplation), *dhayna* (meditation), and *samadhi*.

A major reorganization of Shaiva thought and worship occurred in the eighth century under Shankaracharya (788-820 B.C.E.). Shankaracharya became the major exponent of *advaita* (nondualistic or monistic) philosophy centered upon the sole reality of the impersonal Brahman. Brahman, the really real, is devoid of qualities. The phenomenal world with its qualities, designations, and forms is *maya*, illusion, believed to be real because of *avidya* (ignorance). If the world

is illusion, so are most religious practices and beliefs, such as that in a personal god. The avenue beyond ignorance is jnana (knowledge) resulting from withdrawal from maya and contemplation on Brahman.

Shankaracharya's perspective led in two directions. First and foremost, he had little concern for lay Hindus and believed that jnana could only true be practiced by one living a renounced life. He thus gave a great impetus to the orders of renounciates, the sanyasis. On a practical level, he reorganized the sanyasin around four monastic centers (one in each part of India) and ten orders, two or three of which were attached to each math (or monastery). The leaders of the four Sankara maths are among the most respected leaders in all of Hinduism, though their ultimate power is more informal that organizational. The four centers and the orders attached to each are as follows:

Jyotir Math (North)	Giri
	Parwat
	Sagar
Shringeri (South)	Saraswati
	Bharati
	Puri
Govardhan (East)	Arayna
	Van
Sharda (West)	Tirtha
	Ashram

A sanyasi renounces any connection with the world, including his family and any means of worldly occupation and support, and dons a orange (ochre) robe. He may lead a nomadic life for part of all of his life. He may also engage in religious teachings, and many of the twentieth century Hindu sampradayas have been formed by a sanyasi (or his Vaishnava counterpart) gathering of a personal following.

While Sankaracharya discounted most religious practice, he did recognize its possible value as a preparation for jnana and the renounced life. Thus Sankara's philosophy mixed with the popular temple worship of Shiva and the associated deities in what is termed the Smarta tradition. Smartas, followers of the sutras or aphorisms of the Smriti, or "memorized tradition." These detail the practices of accompanying proper worship of the Vedic deities and the Smartas emphasize the *dharmma* (duties) of *puja* (worship).

Typical of Smarta ritual is the "*puja of the five shrines*" centered upon the worship of five deities: Shiva; Vishnu; Genesh (Genesa), the elephant-headed god who removes obstacles; Surya, the sun-god; and Durga, the consort of Shiva. The Smarta tradition has been brought to the United States by Hindu immigrants since 1965.

The third major group of Hindus, present in the United States in much greater proportion than in India, the Shaktas worship Shakti, one name of the female consort of Shiva. The practices of the Shaktas dramatize within the human the reunion of the passive Shiva with the dynamic Shakti thus bringing enlightenment. This tradition emerged out of the Shaiva tradition around the fifth century B.C.E. with the production of a new set of ritual books called Agamas or Tantras.

The Shaktas or Tantrics, as they are popularly called, emphasize the presence of the Shakti or female power within the human body. Commonly referred to as kundalini, a coil of power resting in potential at the base of the spine, it can be activated by specific practices and ritual procedures. Like a snake, kundalini awakens and springs upward.

Tantrics have also developed a unique view of the human body as possessing, in addition to the physical body, a subtle anatomy consisting of seven *chakras* (cosmic energy centers) located along the spine from its lower tip to the crown of the head, tied together by *nadas* (energy pathways). The practice of kundalini yoga releases the Shakti to rise through the *chakras* to the crown *chakra*. By thus bringing the dynamic Shakti back into union with the more passive Shiva, enlightenment is produced.

The Shaktas are also to be distinguished from the Shaivas by their acceptance of the world. Enlightenment is to be received by using the world, not by denying it. The most controversial practice of the Shaktas has been the ritual use of the very items Shaivas avoid as most harmful to the person seeking spiritual progression since they excite the outward senses. The so-called *pancamakara* (five m's) ritual involves the partaking of wine, meat, fish, grain (considered an aphrodisiac), and sexual intercourse (in Sanskrit each word begins with "m"). In the West, the word "tantra" has become (though quite incorrectly) synonymous with any form of sexual magic.

HINDUISM IN AMERICA. The history of Hinduism in America begins long before any guru came to the United States to expound his tenets. During the seventeenth century, colonists and missionaries began an active relationship with India that led to the translation into English of many of the Hindu sacred writings. Some of these, particularly the *Bhagavad Gita*, had a direct and powerful influence upon New Englanders, particularly Ralph Waldo Emerson and the other leaders of the Transcendentalist Movement.

As the Transcendentalists absorbed the insights of Hindu literature, Hindus were responding to the impact of Christianity. Among the reformist movements was one led by Ram Mohan Roy which developed the Brahmo Samaj, a movement based upon the monotheism of the *Upanishads* and the abandonment of all image worship. Roy's first book, *The Precepts of Jesus* (1820), reprinted in America in 1825, aroused a great deal of controversy and acceptance among early Unitarians. In the 1850's, Unitarian Charles Dall and Keschub Chunder Sen, a leader of the Brahmo Samaj, developed a friendship that led to a relationship between the two organizations that is still active.

The first Hindu guru to come to America was a representative of the Brahmo Samaj. Protap Chunder Mozoomdar delivered his first American address on September 2, 1883, in the parlor of the widow of Ralph Waldo Emerson in Concord, Massachusetts. His brief tour was the only appearance by a Hindu teacher until the monumental events of 1893.

In 1893, Mozoomdar was one of several Hindus who came to America for the World Parliament of Religions. His appearance at this first international conclave between representatives of the major Eastern and Western faiths was eclipsed, however, by that of Swami Vivekananda, the young flamboyant disciple of the late Swami Ramakrishna. His impact was so great that he left the Parliament to tour the country for two years and eventually founded the first Hindu movement in America, the Vedanta Society. Returning to India in 1895, he organized the scattered disciples of Ramakrishna and found two, Swamis Abhedananda and Turiyananda, to head the Vedanta groups already formed in New York and San Francisco respectively.

A small wave of immigration from India beginning in the 1890's brought other teachers. Swami Rama Tirtha, a young sanyasi arrived in 1902 and lectured throughout America for the next two years. That same year Baba Premanand Bharati, a Bengali disciple of Sri Chaitanya, began a five year stay during which time he organized the Krishna Samaj. He left behind disciples who carry his memory into the 1980's.

These early teachers from India were joined by Westerners who adopted Hindu teachings and expounded them through writings and the formation of groups. No writer surpassed the popularity of William Walker Atkinson who in 1903 began to write books on Hindu teachings under the pseudonym of Swami Ramacharacka. His thirteen books have remained in print since their initial appearance. Pierre Bernard, known by his followers by his religious name, Oom the Omnipotent, founded possibly the first Tantric organization, the Tantrick Order of America. In spite of the several scandals he had to survive, Bernard's group lasted for several decades, and his nephew Theos wrote several classical texts in yoga.

The growth of Hinduism was stymied in the decades during and after World War I. A growing anti-Asian sentiment, primarily directed against Chinese and Japanese, included the Indians in its attack that led to the passing of the Asian Exclusion Act of 1917. This action effectively cut off Asian immigration for several generations and stymied what would have become, in all likelihood, the steady growth of Hinduism in the United States. Several years later, as the result of a lawsuit brought by Bhagat Singh Thind, an Indian Sikh, the Supreme Court ruled Indians ineligible for citizenship and denied citizenship to some who had already received it. Then, in 1927, Hinduism was viciously attacked in a best-selling volume, *Mother India,* by Katherine Mayo, a book credited with affecting Indian-American relations for a generation.

The Hindu community grew very slowly in the half century after the passing of the Asian Exclusion Act, but it did grow. A number of teachers were able to emigrate and several founded movements. For example, Besudeb Bhattacharya, a young playwright, came to New York, where he assumed the religious name Pundit Acharya and founded the Temple of Yoga, the Yoga Research Institute, and Prana Press. The most successful of the several gurus was Paramahansa Yoganananda who arrived in 1924 to attend an interfaith conference, but stayed to found the Yogada-Satsang, known today as the Self-Realization Fellowship. His *Autobiography of a Yogi* (1946) was immensely popular and assisted the spread of Hinduism far beyond the Fellowship.

Besides those mentioned above, other teachers who founded movements upon which modern American Hinduism is built were A. K. Mozumdar (Messianic World Message); Swami Omkar (Shanti Ashrama); Sri Deva Ram Sukul (Dharma Mandal); Rishi Krishnanada (Para-Vidya Center; Sant Ram Mandal [Universal Brotherhood Temple and School of Eastern Philosophy]); and Swami A. P. Mukerji (Transcendent Science Society). Joining them were a number of teachers who did not found their own groups but wrote a number of books which enjoyed a circulation among those interested in Eastern and esoteric philosophies, such as Bhagwan Singh Gyanee and Rishi Singh Grewal. Theosophy also contributed greatly to the growth of Hinduism through its continued dissemination of Indian books through the American occult community and its promotion of Jeddu Krishnamurti and the coming world savior.

Krishnamurti, a young Indian boy, had been picked out in the early twentieth century to be the cosmic figure predicted in Theosophical literature. He lectured in the early 1920's on behalf of the Theosophical cause, while for health reasons he settled in Ojai, California. Then in 1927 he renounced his messianic role and began a career as an independent teacher. Beginning with the remnants of his Theosophical following, his gradually attracted both an international audience and a following among academics. He became a forceful element in the build up of interest in Hinduism noticeable after World War II, whose most visible component was, a far cry from Krishnamurti's emphases, the spread of hatha yoga.

Just as 1893 and 1917 had become years of dramatic junctures in the history of American Hinduism, so was 1965. In the fall of that year, the Asian Exclusion Act was repealed and the immigration quotas from Asia were placed on a par with those of Europe. The number of Indian immigrants jumped dramatically. Also during the years that the Exclusion Act was in force, Indian teachers who were not opposed to teaching Hinduism to Westerners emerged in significant numbers. As quotas allowed, they came to America and began to build movements primarily among young adults. Though Shaiva yoga teachers and Shakta tantric teachers were most successful, Vaishnavas were also represented.

The greatest number of Indian immigrants have not been teachers motivated by goals of building an American following; they have been Hindu lay people faced with the task of reestablishing traditional and familiar temple structures in the West. As their numbers have increased, they have banded together to erect both Shaiva and Vaishnava temples and have brought priests from India to lead the ritual activities. The emergence of these traditional temples has completed the spectrum of Indian religion in North America. At present, the only significant element of Indian religious practice not evident in the larger Western Hindu community are the bands of holy men which roam the Indian countryside, many without clothes, living off of the alms of the working people.

Also serving the Indian-American community is the Vishwa Hindu Parishad, an ecumenical group which has provided contact for Hindus across the boundaries created both by sectarian differences and the several Indian languages.

SIKHISM. The early sixteenth century was a time of bitter conflict in North India. A series of invasions which culminated in 1526 established Muslim supremacy. The Punjab area was one of the most hotly contested regions and it was here that Nanak (1469-1539), the founder of Sikhism, was born. One day while bathing in a river, he had a vision of God's presence in which he was told to go into the world and teach the repetition of the name of God, the practice of charity, meditation and worship, and the keeping of ritual purity through absolution.

According to tradition, after a full day of silence, he uttered the pronouncement, "There is no Hindu (follower of the native faith of India) and no Musselman (Muslim)." He adopted a unique garb which combined both Hindu and Muslim features, and developed an eclectic faith which took elements from many religions, mainly from Hindus and Muslims. From Islam he taught of One Creator God, called the True Name to avoid such designations as Allah or Vishnu. From Hinduism he taught the ideas of karma, reincarnation, and the ultimate unreality of the world. Nanak also emphasized the unique role of the guru (teacher) as necessary to lead people to God. After Nanak's death, nine gurus followed him in succession.

The fourth guru, Ram Dass, began the Golden Temple of Amritsar, the present headquarters of the world Sikh community. The fifth guru, Arjan, completed the temple and installed the SIRI GURU GRANTH SAHIB, or ADI GRANTH, the collected writings of Nanak, within it.

The tenth guru, Gobind Singh (1666-1708), had the second most significant role in molding the Sikh community—second only to Nanak. Gobind Singh completed the ADI GRANTH and militarized the Sikhs by forming the Khalsa, the Community of the Pure. Members were initiated by baptism in which they drank and were sprinkled with sweetened water stirred with a sword. They changed their name to Singh (Lion) and adopted the five K's: (1) Kesh, or long hair, a sign of saintliness; (2) Kangh, a comb for keeping the hair neat; (3) Kach, short pants for quick movement in battle; (4) Kara, a steel bracelet signifying sternness and restraint; (5) Kirpan, a sword of defense.

After Gobind Singh's death, the ADI GRANTH became the guru and no further human guru's were allowed. The military emphasis continued, however, and Sikhs served with distinction in British army units.

Sikhism in America. The first East Indians to come to the United States were some unnamed visitors to Salem, Massachusetts, in 1790. No significant migration occurred until the first decade of the twentieth century. Canadian railroads recruited large numbers of Punjabi Sikhs to work in the West. Within a short time, however, many drifted south into Washington, Oregon, and California. Over the next 20 years, immigration was sporadic and the East Indians, easily spotted because of their turbans, were the object of severe discrimination. In 1917, legal immigration was curtailed and few people from the Punjab area of India arrived until the 1946 and 1964 laws, which lifted migration bans. Immigration then increased dramatically.

Early history of the East Indians, almost all Sikhs from the Punjab, is spotted by such events as the 1907 riots in Seattle, Bellingham, and Everett, Washington, and the 1923 case of Bhagat Singh Thind, in which East Indians were declared ineligible for United States citizenship because they were not "free white persons."

JAINISM. Jainism developed in the sixth century B.C. out of the teachings of Vardhamana Mahavira (599-527 B.C.) who, like his contemporary, Buddha, was born of a wealthy family which he rejected to become an ascetic. After some twenty years of meditation and mortification, he discovered enlightenment and became a *jina*, a "conqueror," from which the name of the community he founded took its name. By the time of Mahavira's death, his followers numbered about ten thousand.

Jain theology is atheistic. It poses the existence of two realities—*jivas*, eternal souls, and *ajivas*, eternal, non-living, material elements. Humans are forced into cycles of reincarnation because their jiva has attached itself to ajiva. Attachment is by *karma*, the energy of the soul. Liberation is by directing one's life to reducing karma. Among the practices which aid liberation are: *Ahimsa*, the non-hurting of life; *preservation*, proper control over the mind, speech, and body; *carefulness*, proper care in walking, speaking, eating, lifting, and lying; ascetic *observances; meditation*; and *right conduct*.

The austere practices required of Jains have led to some extremes. For example, the Digambara Jains reject the ownership of all property, including clothes, and encourage the practice of going naked. One recent visitor to the United States, Muni Sushil Kumarji, a Jain monk, made news because of the mask he wore (to prevent inhaling flies) and the brush he used (to gently sweep insects from his path so he would not step on them).

In 1893, Virchand A. Gandhi traveled to Chicago to address the World Parliament of Religions, a most impressive task. Like Jains to follow, Gandhi was opposed by many co-religionists who felt that any travel, other than by foot, was morally wrong. From that time to 1972, only a few Jains, such as Champat Rai Jain, who ventured to England in the 1930's, found their way to the West. By 1975, a community of some 200 was reported in Chicago, with others scattered in various urban centers.

SOURCES—THE EASTERN FAMILY, PART I

GENERAL SOURCES

Dasgupta, Shashibhusan. *Obscure Religious Cults*. Calcutta: Firma K. L. Mukhopadhyay, 1969. 436 pp.

Farquhar, J. N. *An Outline of the Religious Literature of India*. Dehli: Mitilal Banarsidass, 1967. 451 pp.

Ghurye, G. S. *Indian Sadhus*. Bombay: Popular Prakashan, 1964. 260 pp.

Griswold, Henry DeWitt. *Insights into Modern Hinduism*. New York: Henry Holt and Company, 1934. 288 pp.

Hopkins, Thomas J. *The Hindu Religious Tradition*. North Scituate, MA: Duxbury Press, 1971. 156 pp.

Pararignanar, Saiva Ilakkia. *The Development of Saiviam in South India*. Dharmapuram Adhinam, 1964. 359 pp.

Pereira, Jose. *Hindu Theology*. Garden City, NY: Doubleday, 1976. 558 pp.

Renou, Louis. *The Nature of Hinduism*. New York: Walker and Company, 1962. 155 pp.

Santucci, James A. *An Outline of Vedic Literature*. Missoula, MT: Scholars Press, 1976. 69 pp.

Tripathi, B. D. *Sadhus of India*. Bombay: Popular Prakashan, 1978. 258 pp.

Uban, Sujan Singh. *The Gurus of India*. London: Fine Books, 1977. 175 pp.

Wilson, H. H. *Religious Sects of the Hindus*. Calcutta: Susil Gupta, 1958. 1958. 221 pp.

HINDUISM IN AMERICA

Fisher, Maxine P. *The Indians of New York*. Columbia, MO: South Asia Books, 1980. 165 pp.

Jackson, Carl T. *The Oriental Religions and American Thought*. Westport, CT: Greenwood Press, 1981. 302 pp.

Kamath, M. V. *The United States and India, 1776-1976*. Washington, DC: The Embassy of India, 1976. 222 pp.

Riepe, Dale. *The Philosophy of India and Its Impact on American Thought*. Springfield, IL: Charles C. Thomas Publisher, 1970. 339 pp.

Thomas, Wendell. *Hinduism Invades America*. Boston: Beacon Press, 1930. 300 pp.

SIKHISM

Cole, W. Owen, and Piara Singh Sambhi. *The Sikhs*. London: Routledge & Kegan Paul, 1978. 210 pp.

Juergensmeyer, Mark, and N. Gerald Barrier, eds. *Sikh Studies*. Berkeley, CA: Graduate Theological Union, 1979. 230 pp.

Kaur, Sardarni Premka. *Guru for the Aquarian Age*. Albuquerque, NM: Brotherhood of Life Books, 1972. 131 pp.

Macauliffe, Max Arthur. *The Sikh Religion*. 6 vols. New Delhi: S. Chand & Company, 1978.

Singh, Gopal. *The Religion of the Sikhs*. Bombay: Asia Publishing House, 1971. 191 pp.

SANT MAT

Fripp, Peter. *The Mystic Philosophy of Sant Mat*. London: Neville Spearman, 1964. 174 pp.

Johnson, Julian. *The Path of the Masters*. Punjab, India: Radha Soami Satsang Beas, 1972. 572 pp.

————. *With a Great Master in India*. Beas, India: Radha Swami Sat Sang, 1953. 200 pp.

Lane, David Christopher. *Radhasoami Parampara in Definition and Classification*. Berkeley: M.A. thesis, Graduate Theological Union, 1981. 132 pp.

JAINISM

Gopalan, Subramania. *Outlines of Jainism*. New York: Halsted Press, 1973. 205 pp.

Jain, Muni Uttam Kamal. *Jaina Sects and Schools*. Delhi: Concept Publishing Company, 1975. 162 pp.

Stevenson, Mrs. Sinclair (Margaret). *The Heart of Jainism*. New Dehli: Munshiram Manoharlal, 1970. 336 pp.

Chapter Twenty-two

THE EASTERN FAMILY

PART 2, BUDDHISM, SHINTOISM, JAPANESE NEW RELIGIONS

Directory listings for the groups belonging to the Eastern Family (Buddhism, Shintoism, and Japanese New Religions) may be found in the section beginning on page 745.

BUDDHISM. Buddhism arose as a reformist movement in Brahmanistic India. Siddhartha Gautama, Buddhism's founder, was born a prince of the realm about 560 B.C. at Lumbini near the capital of the Kingdom of Shakya. Thus Gautama is often called Shakyamuni or Sakyamuni. According to early accounts of his life, Gautama led a typical princely life, protected from contact with the real world. He was married at seventeen and fathered a child. His life changed in 529 B.C. when he departed from the palace, abandoned his worldly existence, and began a career as a wandering seeker for the meaning of life. Gautama spent the next six years visiting various Indian religious groups, sitting with several teachers of renown, and experimenting with many religious practices, such as asceticism and meditation. His search ended in 523 B.C., while he was in meditation and contemplation at the foot of the "Bodhi tree," the location of which is still a famous Buddhist shrine. As this period of meditation began, Gautama is said to have made the following vow:

"Let my body be dried up on this seat,
Let my skin and bones and flesh be destroyed
So long as Bodhi is not attained . . .
My body and thought will not be removed from
  this seat."

The Bodhi, or enlightenment, was attained in 523 B.C., and Gautama became the Buddha or enlightened one. After this enlightenment, Buddha began to preach and teach, and a group of disciples gathered around him. A movement began to grow, particularly in northwest India. Buddha died of dysentery about 480 B.C.

Much of the essence of Buddhism is found in the teachings of the Buddha, which outline the Dharma, the true way of life. The Dharma is remarkably simple, for all its profundity, and lends itself easily to a brief summary. All Buddhists share a belief in the Buddha's Dharma which centers upon the four basic truths and the "noble eightfold path." The four basic truths are: 1) all existence entails suffering; 2) the cause of suffering is desire, i.e., the thirst for pleasure, prosperity, and continued life (it is this thirst for continued life that begets rebirth); 3) the way to escape suffering, existence, and rebirth is to rid one's self of desire; and 4) to be emancipated from desire, one must follow the eightfold path.

The noble eightfold path is pictured in the eight-spoked wheel, a symbol second only to the seated Buddha as a sign of Buddhist faith. The path consists of: 1) right understanding, 2) right resolve, 3) right speech, 4) right conduct, 5) right livelihood, 6) right effort, 7) right attention, and 8) right concentration. Various Buddhist groups would accept the eightfold path but disagree on their interpretation of it and the emphasis on, and priority of, certain aspects of it. This difference will often be manifest in the words that English Buddhist groups use to translate the language of the eightfold path in their literature.

For example, some groups, leaning toward a more intellectualized Buddhism, will translate the first step of the path as right belief or knowledge. Zen Buddhists, pointing to the mystic and indescribable nature of Buddhist experience, will often translate it as right vision. Interpretations of right concentration, or the goal of nirvana, range from the present-mindedness of mystic Buddhism, which finds nirvana in the mystical experience, to the other-worldliness of various groups of Buddhists. Some of the variations will become evident below.

The basic scriptures of Buddhism, the *Tripitaka* or *Three Baskets*, are divided into the Vinaya, the Sutras, and the Abhidhamma. The Vinaya consists basically of rules for the monks and information on Buddha's life. The Sutras are a collection of material attributed to the Buddha and his close disciples. How much is actually Buddha's words is a matter of debate. The Abhidhamma is composed of discourses of Gautama. Other scriptures have been added to the *Tripitaka* by various national Buddhist bodies, and each particular group has its own interpretive material.

SPREAD OF BUDDHISM. Buddhism, as noted above, arose as a sect of Hinduism and included many elements of Hindu thought within it, although it modified greatly certain ideas, such as the transmigration of the soul. After the crisis of Buddha's death, a council, which has become known in Buddhist history as the First Council, was held under the leadership of Kashyapa, a disciple of Buddha. Some basic decisions about doctrine and discipline were made; it was these actions which enabled the Buddhist movement to be organized and to spread. The Second Council was held in 377 B.C. after a group of monks revolted against the strict rules of the order and decided to "reinterpret" them. The Vaishali Council decided in favor of the strict interpretation and the lax monks seceded from the order. They represent the first major schismatic school.

The next significant date in Buddhist history is 270 B.C. This year saw the emergence of the "Indian Empire" with its ruler Asoka, the man who did more for the spread of Buddhism than anyone since its founder. In remorse and regret produced by his wars of conquest, Asoka was led to become a Buddhist monk (while still the emperor). Until Asoka, Buddhism was a local Indian sect, but with Asoka's help it was spread throughout his kingdom, to all of India and into Ceylon, Nepal, and central Asia. Asoka had inherited an intensely missionary understanding of his faith from Buddhist scripture and implanted it within the movement. This missionary zeal has distinguished Buddhism from almost all other indigenous faiths of Southern Asia.

By the time of Asoka, Buddhism had begun to develop an extensive literature. First steps toward the development of a canon were probably made during Asoka's time at the so-called Third Council. This council was called to deal with the problems created by the large increase in nominal members, a result of the extensive growth following Asoka's missionary endeavors.

After Asoka's death the center of Buddhism shifted to the Northwest (Kashmir, Kabul, Bactria, etc.), where a Greek friendly to Buddhism had established himself in power. The role of the Greek king, Menander, was doubly important. He provided a haven for Buddhists from Asoka's successors who were less than devoted admirers of the growing faith. He also provided the influence that led to Buddhist art, particularly statues of Gautama. No representations of the Buddha survive prior to this period.

In the centuries before and after Asoka the two main schools of Buddhism began to take a more pronounced form. The first of the schools to emerge was called Hinayana or the Lesser Vehicle. Hinayana looks to the writings of Sariputra, an early disciple of Buddha whose method of interpreting Buddha's teachings was very conservative and emphasized the role of the monk and the monastic life as the way to nirvana. In reaction to the monk-oriented faith of Hinayana there arose Mahayana Buddhism, the Greater Vehicle, which dates itself to Ananda and other early disciples of Buddha who did not accept the interpretations of Sariputra. Mahayana was much more open to the role of non-monks in the faith and held as a goal the ultimate salvation of all living beings. This universalist tendency made it a more efficient vehicle in which to carry the faith across Southeast Asia to Japan. As Buddhism spread, it not only took upon itself the national characteristics of each country but also generally related itself to one of the two major schools.

A term often used interchangeably with Hinayana is "Theravada." The term applies to the *Tripitaka* or *Pali Canon* of Buddha's writing. The *Tripitaka* was finally put into writing during the first century B.C. The Hinayanists accepted it but the Mahayanists accepted only part of it and developed their own canon, which included various sutras that have become the basis of the various Mahayana groups. Included would be such writings as the Lotus Sutra (used by Nichiren), the Diamond Sutra (used by some Zen groups) and the Sukhavati-Vyuha (used by the Pure Land groups).

South-East Asian (Theravoda) Buddhism. Asoka's son, Prince Mahinda, took Buddhism to Ceylon. Although the exact details of the conversion process are buried in legendary material, there is no doubt that Mahinda's activity established Buddhism in Anuradhapura, the capital, and among the royal family. Asoka sent to the new converts a scion of the sacred Bohdi tree, which is still preserved and venerated. The monastery established by Mahinda became a center from which the stricter Hinayana could be spread.

Burma, like Ceylon, probably first heard of Buddhism as a result of Asoka's missionaries. A small Buddhist community was established by Mahayanists. Hinayana became firmly established as the dominant faith, however, in the sixth century A.D. after a Hinayanist revival in Madras.

Thailand, formerly Siam, represents the other main center of the Hinayanist school. The origin of Buddhism in Thailand has been lost, but early in the Christian era it was co-existing with Brahmanism (Hinduism). Mahayana could possibly have entered from Cambodia in the era that the Cambodians ruled most of Indo-China. (The Cambodians had received Buddhism from Indian merchants and settlers just as they had received Brahmanism.) The Siamese began their rise to power in the eleventh century A.D. and controlled the country by the end of the thirteenth century. In the complexity of war and its resulting chaos, Hinayana entered the country and in a short time had supplanted both Mahayana and Brahmanism. As Hinayana grew in Thailand, it spread also to Cambodia. Hinduism was already yielding to Mahayana there, and both then gave way to Hinayana.

By the modern era, Hinayana Buddhism had a firm control from Ceylon along the southern coast of Asia to Indo-China. This growth, while impressive, was eclipsed by that accomplished by Mahayana with its more universal appeal. Several cases have been noted in which Hinayana came into a country only after Mahayana had been present for some time.

Chinese Buddhism. China received Buddhist missionaries possibly as early as 200 B.C. and quickly became the great center of Mahayana Buddhism. The importance of China was heightened as Hinduism reasserted itself in India in the face of a growing Buddhism and all but drove Buddhism from its Indian homeland. As Buddhism interacted with the religions of China, numerous variations of it (including what was to become Zen) sprang up. But over the centuries, the various Buddhist groups have evolved into what is usually the eclectic mixture of Buddhism, Confucianism, and Taoism which had been popularized throughout mainland China. The faith is a form of Buddhism centered on bodhisattvas who function somewhat like saints in Roman Catholicism. Religious structures, temples, are dedicated to a particular bodhisattva; Kwan Yin, the goddess of mercy, is a popular one. Other bodhisattvas have lesser positions, and a temple thus gives the appearance of having a pantheon represented in the statuary. The popular most form of Buddhism in China (as in Japan) centers on Amida Buddha with his promise of a Pure Land, or the Lotus Heaven, to which men are brought by faith in the Buddha. In China, Amida is known as Omito Fu.

Confucius, the Latinized name given Master K'ung, born in China in 551 B.C., was the great teacher of morals, practical religion, and philosophy. During his early twenties, he entered a time of seclusion to mourn his mother's death and found it a time of deep thought. By the age of thirty he was a teacher and later became chief judge of his own district of Lu. After a life of success and failures, he died in 479 B.C. His teachings—emphasizing family (including ancestor worship), morality, and respect for authority—became part of the Chinese way of life.

Lao-Tzu, the reputed founder of Taoism, was an early contemporary of Confucius. His name, which means "little old child," derives from a legend that he was born an old man. We know little about him beyond his retirement from public life and his composition of the *Tao Te Ching*, the chief religious book of the Taoists. A disciple, Chuang-tse, wrote a commentary on his master's work, which is also a part of the sacred writing. The teachings center on the nature of the Tao or Way. The Way is mystical, natural, and highly ethical but vague and open to wide interpretation. The influence of Taoism has largely survived through the sacred writings, which are widely read, and a folk religion which merged the mystical faith of Taoism with the ancient polytheistic, magical religion of pre-Taoist China.

The common form of presenting Chinese religion as a separate topic in itself is legitimate. Yet, in its American manifestations, Chinese religion should be considered within a Buddhist context. John F. Mulholland in his survey, *Hawaii's Religions*, reflects upon the Buddhist affiliation of many members of America's Oriental community:

"When the Chinese immigrants prospered, the children went to private schools. If the school was Catholic or Episcopal and required or expected all students to be baptized, the children were baptized. The second and third generations found that in Hawaii they were expected to have a religion, and since the lack of religious designation in China was confusing, many Chinese simply said they were Buddhist. There were no organized Buddhist groups and no membership requirements as Christian churches had. The temples were privately owned or existed in connection with Chinese societies. As the Japanese Buddhists built temples which related them to Japan, so the Chinese began to emphasize the Buddhist part of their multiple religion" (John F. Mulholland, 292).

Korean Buddhism. From China, Buddhism spread to Korea. Buddhism in Korea differs markedly from Buddhism in other Oriental societies in that, during the modern era, the various schools of Buddhist thought began to emphasize their commonality over their differences. As a result, the several organizations were able not only to reverse the process of splintering but finally, in 1935, to unite into a single organization, the Chogye sect, from which most contemporary groups derive.

Buddhism entered what is today called Korea in 372 C.E., when it was brought from China to the Kingdom of Koguryo, a state covering the northern portion of the peninsula. From there it spread southward to the kingdoms of Paekche and Silla. It flourished in the united kingdom created by Silla in 668 C.E. during which time Zen was introduced along with the original Mahayana (called "Chiao" in Korea) forms. Nine schools of Zen developed around nine outstanding masters and six schools of Chioe emerged.

Through the next centuries, Buddhism waxed and waned, always remaining in competition with Confucius's thought and popular folk religion. Zen experienced a revival in the twelfth century when Master Pojo (1158-1210) advocated a union of thought which found favor with the varying Zen schools. A century and a half later, in 1356, under Master T'aego (1301-1382), a merger of all the Zen schools into the Chogyejong was accomplished. Master T'aego was one of several priests who had risen to prominence in the land and had been given the title "national teacher" by the king.

The Yi Dynasty (1392-1910) became a time of great suffering for Korean Buddhism, as the ruling powers generally assumed a hostile posture toward it. Buddhism was suppressed and Zen almost died out, though in the face of opposition Buddhism became more united. In 1424 two of the Chiao sects united with the Chogyejong to form the Sonjong while the remaining Chiao sects united into the Kyojong. Only in the late eighteenth century did government policies toward Buddhism relax. King Chongyo began to lift negative government regulations and in the nineteenth century Buddhism began a revival, further spurred in the 1890's by the arrival of many Japanese Buddhist priests. In 1904, for the first time, the government ended its control of Buddhist temples. The revival of Buddhism, the cooperation with the Japanese priests, and the new freedom, however, came to an abrupt halt in the second decade of the twentieth century after Japan occupied Korea in 1910. The occupation government reclaimed control of the temples. Nationalistic feelings led to a new sense of unity by Korean Buddhists over against the Japanese. The growth of those sentiments led in 1935 to the merger of the Sonjong and Kyojong into the single Chogye sect which dominates Korean Buddhism to this day.

Japanese Buddhism. From China, Buddhism spread to Korea and then to Japan. Japanese Buddhism is very important to American Buddhists because the overwhelming majority of American Buddhists are Japanese in their orientation. Buddhism at first was not strong enough to win many converts from Shinto, the national religion of Japan, but Buddhism did receive toleration from the emperor. The building of the new capital at Nara in 710 A.D. marked the turning point in Japanese Buddhist history. During the Nara period, the emperor became Buddhist and made Buddhism the state religion. A number of the Chinese Buddhist sects, including Jojitsu, Sanron, Hosso, Kusha, Ritsu, and Kegon, were introduced. Only a few of these are represented in the United States. In 807, the Tendai sect was brought to Japan. It was more open to the laity than the Nara sects, which tended to be rather exclusive. Esoteric (tantric) Buddhism was introduced in the following century.

In the twelfth century, Honen and his disciple Shinran brought the Pure Land Sect from China to Japan. Long before Honen (1133-1212) organized the Jodo or Pure Land Sect, there had been a belief in the Amitabha (Amida), a benevolent deity who dwells in a Western paradise to which men may gain access by calling upon his name. But it was Honen who gave the idea an independent form, thereby establishing a new school of thought. Various groups whose beliefs derive from Honen are called Shin groups.

Honen's basic disagreement with most Buddhists of his day was over whether one gained salvation by jiriki, one's own strength, or by tariki, another's strength. He believed firmly in the strength of tariki, in this case by calling upon the bodhisattva Amida. The practice of calling upon Amida is named "nembutsu." Those calling upon Amida would be reborn into the Western paradise. In the Pure Land, all enjoy powers and bliss. It is a step toward nirvana. The nembutsu, according to Honen, should be repeated often and with sincerity, deep belief, and longing.

The most important of Honen's students was Shinran (1173-1262), a monk and friend of Honen. The innovative Shinran abolished monasticism, permitted priests to marry and promoted the worship of Amida and, to a lesser extent, Shakya (Shakyamuni—Gautama Buddha). Only the relics and images of Amida are allowed. Salvation is attained through faith alone, as a gift of Amida. Honen believed that man is saved by faith, but that ritual and working for others help.

The central act of all Shin groups is the repetition of the nembutsu. "Namu Amida Butsu" (to bow or submit to the one who is enlightened) is repeated often and is said before the statue of Amida Buddha. To repeat the nembutsu is to be one with Amida.

The Shin group gradually split after Shinran's death into the Jodo (or Jodo-shu) and Shinshu groups. The Jodo look to Honen and the Shinshu to Shinran. The Shinshu grew slowly and in the medieval period fell victim to the various political upheavals and wars. Shinran's daughter supervised construction of the Hongwanji or Temple of the Original View in Kyoto, which became the headquarters of the True Pure Land Sect. In 1496, a temple, which became the new Shinshu center, was founded at Yamashina. Yamashina was destroyed in 1532 and the headquarters were moved to Ishiyama. In 1570, Oda Nobunaga, a feudal lord who was spreading Christianity to counteract Buddhism's power, attacked Ishiyama and eventually (after ten years) destroyed Ishiyama. Oda Nobunaga (1532-1582) "defended" Christianity in conjunction with the missionary work of Francis Xavier, but Nobunaga's aim was less to spread Christianity than to destroy Buddhism. He considered the Buddhists a threat to his power. As a result of the evacuation by the chief abbot from Ishiyama, a disagreement arose among his sons as to how long the Shinshu should have fought Nobunaga, and a split developed. Ieyasu, the shogun of Japan, fearing the growth of the Shinshu among the people, took advantage of the split to divide the group. He sided with the elder son and gave him a tract of land upon which to build an Hongwanji. The supporters of the younger son are now known as the Honpa Hongwanji and the

supporters of the elder as the Higashi Hongwanji. Their differences were largely administrative, but, as time has passed, the Honpa groups have been the more progressive and adaptive to change.

The thirteenth century saw the appearance of Nichiren, another outstanding Buddhist teacher who began as a reformer and Buddhist ecumenist but became the founder of the Nichiren-shu. ("Shu" means "religion.") Nichiren believed that in the teachings known as the Lotus Sutra he had found the primitive, true Buddhism that could unite the many sects. He attacked the other sects' beliefs and won many followers as he traveled around Japan.

One of the central ideas in Japanese Buddhism, usually associated with Nichiren, is mappo, or end of the law. Nichiren divided history into three millennia, the first of which began with Buddha's death. The last phase or mappo began in 1050 A.D. In this last period, salvation is to be obtained through belief in the Lotus Sutra. Nichiren's ideas are discussed at greater length later in this chapter.

Zen Buddhism. Zen was also introduced into Japan about this time. Zen is the mystical school of Buddhism. It stands in relation to Buddhism much as Sufism does to Islam and contemplative Catholicism does to Christianity. It arose in the interaction of Buddhist philosophy with Taoist meditative techniques. The actual founder was Tao-sheng (360-434), who added to Buddhist meditative techniques the doctrine of instantaneous enlightenment—the attainment in one single act of illumination of the goal of mystical truth in both its objective and subjective aspects.

Recognized by many Zen students as the founder of Zen is Bodhidharma (d. 534), who came from his native India to teach Zen in China during most of his mature life. He is termed the first patriarch and is credited with the addition of "wall-contemplation" to Zen practice. He was followed by five other patriarchs—Hui-k'o, Seng-ts'an, Tao-hsin, Hung-jen, and Hui-neng. Hui-neng is ranked next to Bodhidharma as the second (and actual) founder of Zen.

As Zen continued to develop in China, it went through the familiar process of schism and adoption of new ideas and practices. Among the new practices develoed was the koan. The koan is an anecdotal event or utterance of the masters given to disciples as problems. It is used as a means to enlightenment. The koan led to the development of the two major schools of Zen which still exist. One school, Lin-chi, accepted the koan and used it extensively. In reaction, a second school, Ts'ao-tung, emerged and was characterized by its doctrine of silent illumination. Ts'ao-tung saw the koan as "gazing on the word." Transported to Japan, the Lin-chi sect became Rinzai Zen, and Ts'ao-tung became Soto Zen. These two schools were both transferred to the United States. In pure Rinzai Zen, people use the koan; in pure Soto Zen, people do not. Most groups are neither pure Rinzai or Soto, but lie between those two extremes.

One popular koan often used as the first exercise for Rinzai students is the "mu" koan. Mu, meaning "no" or "nothing" in Sino-Japanese, is understood as the nothing that contains everything. Mu is to be experienced, not intellectualized.

Dogen (1200-1253), the founder of Japanese Soto, is the originator of the typical Zen method of meditation, zazen. As described by Dogan, zazen proceeds thus:

"If you wish to attain enlightenment, begin at once to practice *zazen*. For this meditation a quiet chamber is necessary, while food and drink must be taken in moderation. Free yourself from all attachments, and bring to rest the ten thousand things. Think of neither good nor evil and judge not right or wrong. Maintain the flow of mind, of will, and of consciousness; bring to an end all desires, all concepts and judgements. Do not think about how to become a Buddha.

"In terms of procedure, first put down a thick pillow and on top of this a second (round) one. One may chose either a full or half cross-legged position. In the full position one places the right foot on the left thigh and the left foot is placed on the right thigh. In the half position only the left foot is placed upon the right thigh. Robe and belt should be worn loosely, but in order. The right hand rests on the left foot, while the back of the left hand rests in the palm of the right. The two thumbs are placed in juxtaposition.

"The body must be maintained upright, without inclining to the to the left or to the right, forward or backward. Ears and shoulders, nose and navel must be kept in alignment respectively. The tongue is to be kept against the palate, lips and teeth are kept firmly closed, while the eyes are to be kept always open.

"Now that the bodily position is in order, regulate your breathing. If a wish arises, take note of it and then dismiss it. In practicing thus persistently you will forget all attachments and concentration will come of itself. That is the art of *zazen*. *Zazen* is the Dharma gate of great rest and joy." (Heinrich Dumoulin, *A History of Zen Buddhism* [Boston: Beacon Press, 1969], 161).

The essence of zazen is to achieve the full and perfect equilibrium of the organism.

Next to Dogen, Hakuin (1685-1768) was the greatest Zen master and was the one who revived Rinzai Zen in Japan. Hakuin described the tension of the disciple when confronted with the koan. This tension is the "great doubt." Hakuin also described satori, the great enlightenment, which is a central concern of Zen. In the various reports of satori, one again finds the range of reflections on mystical experience, this time described in Buddhist categories.

The roshi is the prime official in Zen. The roshi is the master, the one who has attained the goals of Zen meditation and has the knowledge and maturity to aid others in attaining them. There is a tendency toward a Buddhist version of apostolic succession in Zen, the roshis tending to see themselves in a lineage of Zen masters and to be in a school formed by a succession of patriarchs. In America, most Zen is derived from Jito Gasan, a Japanese Zen master and head of Engaku Temple. He passed on the Rinzai tradition to Imakita Kosen (1816-1892), a Japanese master whose students included Soyen Shaku.

Tibetan Buddhism. The last place that Buddhism invaded as a conquering missionary faith was Tibet. The date traditionally given is 747 A.D., when Padmasambhava brought tantric Buddhism to Tibet. In the mountainous terrain, Buddhism mixed with Bon, the native religion, the aim of which was the magical control of evil spirits and the use of cosmic powers. Tibetan Buddhism thus emerged as a magical faith, distinct from either Chinese or Indian Buddhism.

The older sects still emphasize the magic tantra and make wide use of the mantra and the mandala. The mantra is a phonetic form (the most popular being "om" and "om mani padme hum"—meaning the jewel in the heart of the lotus, the center of truth). The very sound of the mantra has a psychological effect and is aimed at producing deep mystical experience. A mandala is a circular drawing representative of the universe, a cosmogram whose center is thought to be the metaphysical center of the universe. It is used as an aid in worship.

Tantric Buddhism is based on the belief that everything is permeated by a single power (Shakti) emanating from God. This force manifests itself in three ways: positive masculine, negative feminine, and most important, the union of the two. What is true on a cosmic level is considered true on a human, individual level. The union of opposites, a major goal in tantric practice, is accomplished by the disciplines of yoga, the most controversial aspect of which includes ritual sexual intercourse.

Tantric sexual ritual involves the male practitioner's partaking of the 5 M's (True Things)—madya (wine), mamsha (meat), matsya (fish), mudra (parched grain), and maithuna (coitus). Tantric rituals can be practiced in three modes. The Sattvio Sadhana or symbolic school has spiritualized tantra. The Rajasic Sadhana uses material substitutes for the 5 M's. The Kaula Sadhana practices a literal partaking of the 5 M's. The symbolic and substitutionary partaking of the 5 M's are usually termed "right-hand" tantra. Such practice is typical of the Japanese Shingon sect. The literal school, which performs ritual sexual intercourse, is generally said to practice "left-hand" tantra. The object of tantra is twofold: the union of the individual with the divine, and the gaining of magical power which can be used to do miraculous works.

A reform, led by Tsong-kha-pa at the turn of the fifteenth century, created a second major Buddhist school in Tibet. It attempted to tighten the monastic discipline, insisted on celibacy, reduced the emphasis on magic, and effected strong organization. The latter was accomplished at the time when the reformists were teaching that the heads of the chief monasteries were bodhisattvas. When a lama, or monastery ruler, died, a search was made for a new incarnation of him born at the time of his death. The chief lama in Tibet was the Dalai Lama. The Dalai Lama sect was thoroughly disrupted by the Chinese invasion of Tibet in 1959. Various reforms have led to the founding of two other major sects, and numerous schisms have resulted in the formation of many smaller groups.

BUDDHISM IN AMERICA. Buddhism in America is difficult to understand apart from the international spread of Buddhism since most Buddhist bodies in the United States represent transplanted forms of the many varied schools of thought and practice. New bodies formed as a result of schism by American Buddhists are present but in the minority.

Southeastern Asian (Theravada) Buddhism in America. Prior to 1965, the story of Buddhism in America was largely the story of the emigration of Japanese Buddhists to Hawaii and the West coast and the spread of Japanese forms of Buddhism in the Caucasian population. The presence of Theravada Buddhism was limited to a few intellectuals and the diplomatic mission personnel from the several Southeast Asian countries in New York City and Washington, D.C. The situation changed dramatically after the beginning and the spread of the Vietnam War to surrounding countries and the rescission of the Asian Exclusion Act. During the 1970's, a great wave of immigrants from Vietnam (increased by special legislation passed after the withdrawal of United States forces from the country), Cambodia, Laos, and Thailand moved to the West Coast and the northern American urban centers. Slowly, they have organized congregations, established temples, and developed national associations. The Theravada centers consist almost entirely of first generation, non-English-speaking, Asian-Americans. As of the 1980's, language remains a barrier to the spread of Theravada Buddhism to the Caucasian population, though initial signs of its spreading have begun to emerge around the followers of the few English-speaking Theravada teachers.

Chinese Buddhism in America. The Chinese came to the United States before the Japanese, their major immigration occurring between 1854 and 1883, when a law regulating Chinese migration was passed. By 1880, more than 100,000 Chinese had settled in America, primarily on the West Coast.

The 1850's saw the arrival of the first large groups of "coolies" to labor in the United States. Family altars and shrines were set up immediately. They were the source of complaints about "heathen Mongolians" and led to reinforced Christian missions. As early as 1878, a Chinese monk brought a Kwan Yin statue and a Kwan Tai statue to Honolulu and built a temple or joss house to Kwan Yin. (Kwan Tai was a military hero of the third century B.C. who was later canonized.) In 1887, three joss houses were reported. During World War II, one observer reported seven temples on Oahu and another on Kauai. Chinese joss houses appeared on the West Coast before 1900. Much of the Chinese faith is centered on these joss houses, particularly the small family shrines still to be found in California and Hawaii.

A modern revival of Buddhism in a Chinese mode has resulted in the establishment of a number of centers across the country, many of which have been formed by expatriates from the Maoist revolution. Some of these serve Chinese-Americans; others were formed by American converts or by Americans who found themselves in China as missionaries or soldiers and were converted abroad. Independent Chinese Buddhist associations have formed to serve each of these groups.

Most Chinese Buddhist centers are located in Honolulu, San Francisco, and New York City. The existence of these centers, often only blocks apart but administratively independent, manifest the variety within Chinese Buddhism, as well as the distinctions formed by migration at different times and from different sections of China.

Korean Buddhism in America. Korean migration since 1965 has been proportional to that of other Asian countries, but most of the new Korean-Americans are Christians. However, a few Korean Buddhist priests have come to the United States and at least one Zen priest, Master Seung Sahn Sunim, has been able to create a national organization within a few short years.

Japanese Buddhism in America. Japanese immigration began with the arrival of large numbers of laborers in Hawaii on June 19, 1868. Further immigration was encouraged until 1907, when Japanese immigration was limited. At present, approximately one-third of the Hawaiian population is Japanese. Because the early Japanese came there as plantation laborers, the work of establishing Buddhism began in the country-side, usually on a plantation, and then moved to Honolulu as plantation life soured for the Japanese. Buddhist settlement in California came only a short time after that in Hawaii, as Japanese immigrants also settled on the West Coast. In many cases, the Buddhist missionary from Japan would stop in Hawaii on his way to California. The growth of the community, however, was stymied by the 1907 law.

The name of the first Buddhist in America is lost to history, but in 1889 Soryu Kagahi of the Honpa Hongwanji arrived in Honolulu to minister to Buddhists on the plantations. Under his leadership a temple, the first in America, was built in April 1889, in Hilo, where he had found many former Buddhists ready to reactivate their faith. In the fall, he returned to Japan and soon disappeared from history. The following ten years, things did not go well for Hawaiian Buddhists. Particularly, they were continually visited by renegade Buddhist priests who took their hard-earned wages and then skipped town. Such practices left the Japanese open to the very active Christian mission.

Pleas for help were finally heard by the Buddhists in Japan, who sent their official representatives. To Hawaii came Jotei Matsuo, a Jodo-shu priest (1894), and Ejun Miyamoto of the Honpa Hongwanji (1897). Within a decade, four more of the Buddhist sects—the Higashi Hongwanji, the Shingon, the Nichiren, and the Soto Zen—arrived. In 1899, Yemyo Imamura, the bishop who was to dominate Buddhism in Hawaii until his death in 1932, took up residence in Honolulu.

As early as 1898, the Honpa Hongwanji sent two priests to survey possibilities for an American mission. A mission in San Francisco was established after the arrival of the Reverends Shuyei Sonoda and Kakuryo Nishijimi in September, 1899. These two men organized the Young Men's Buddhist Association and, by 1905, had consecrated a church, which became the mainland headquarters of the Jodo Shin Buddhists.

Zen Buddhism in America. Zen came to America in 1893 when a Renzai monk, Soyen Shaku, addressed the World Parliament of Religions in Chicago. A graduate of the Western-oriented Keio University, he, despite strong opposition, traveled to the land of the "barbarians" to speak on "The Law of Cause and Effect, as Taught by the Buddha." After his brief visit, during which he did not make the impact of a Vivekananda or Annie Besant, he returned to Kamakura. In 1905 he returned to the United States as the guest of the Alexander Russells in San Francisco. After a year of hospitality, he ended his stay with a national and then a world tour. The remainder of his life was spent as a leader in Japanese Zen.

Soyen (1859-1919) had been a student of Imakita Kosen, renowned in nineteenth-century Buddhism as one who took Western thought and culture seriously. After Kosen's death, his students came to the West and became the real founders of American Zen. One of these students was Daisetz Teitaro Suzuki, a lay scholar, who, through his books, has done more to enlighten American audiences about Zen than any other single person. Another of Kosen's students, Sokatsu Shaku (1869-1954), became a teacher in Tokyo. In 1906, he came to America with six disciples. The group settled in Berkeley but soon moved to a farm in Hayward, California. After discovering their inability to farm profitably, they moved to San Francisco. Gradually, each returned to Japan, leaving no visible organization behind. The last of the group to return was Shigetsu Sasaki, who completed his Zen training in Japan and came again to the United States as a roshi with the new name of Sokei-an. His settlement in New York in 1928 marked the beginning of a continuous Rinzai history in America.

Soto Zen came to the United States in 1903. It began in Hawaii when the Reverend Senyei Kawahara came to Honolulu and erected a temple on the West Loch side of Pearl Harbor. Within a few years Ryuki Hirai, another Soto priest, joined him and built a temple at Waialua to the north of Oahu. Other temples were added on Maui and Kauai as later priests arrived. Then, in 1913, Bishop Hosen Isobe was sent to Honolulu, where a temple was built under his direction the following year. The mission spread to Kona on the Big Island, Hawaii, in 1916. (Soto Buddhists look upon the arrival of Bishop Isobe as the real beginning of Soto Zen in America.)

After beginning the work in Hawaii, Bishop Isobe brought Soto to California. He organized Zenshuji Mission (now called the Soto Mission) in the home of Toyokichi Nagasaki in Los Angeles in 1922. The history of Soto Zen in America is continuous from that time.

The history of Zen in America, like the history of Buddhism, would be incomplete without mention of those non-Oriental Americans who played a significant role in its spread and influence. Notable is Ruth Fuller Everett Sasaki, possibly the first American student of Zen in Japan. She came to New York in 1938 after work in a Japanese monastery and became a prime supporter of the First Zen Institute and editor of *Cat's Yawn*, its first magazine. In 1944 after four years of widowhood, she married Sokei-an Sasaki Roshi, a move which stabilized the Institute during the final year of the war. Widowed a second time, she moved to Japan where she became the first non-Oriental priest and abbess of a temple, the Ryosen-an, and spent her life translating her late husband's work.

Chester F. Carlson, who discovered the process of xerography, was typical of several wealthy benefactors of Zen Buddhism. He was the first founder of the Zen Mountain Center of Tassajara Springs, California, but kept his support of Buddhist causes quiet during his lifetime.

Tibetan Buddhism in America. Since the Chinese occupation of Tibet in 1959, each of the four major Tibetan Buddhist sects has arrived in the United States and their several representatives have established a number of separate organizations. Unlike Southeast Asian Buddhism, language has not been as significant a factor in slowing the spread of Tibetan Buddhism in the Caucasian population, and by the mid-1980's, Caucasian disciples far outnumbered Tibetan-American Buddhists.

Much support for Tibetan Buddhism was generated by American sympathy for their plight in the face of the Chinese. Groups such as the Tibetan Friendship Group, headquartered in Ojai, California, have combined efforts with the Dalai Lama's Office of Tibet in New York City to focus attention upon the political and humanitarian side of the Tibetans' situation.

Western Buddhists. The growth of Buddhism in America as a result of Japanese emigration coupled with the increase of world religious studies in American universities set the stage for a number of Americans to become Buddhists. They were largely attracted by Buddhist philosophy and ethics, but followed their studies with full identification with the faith. Often gaining their understanding from books, instead of Buddhist religious teachers, they found like-minded believers and formed Buddhist study societies. Typical of the Western–led Buddhist societies, such as the English language groups founded by Ernest Hunt after World War I in Hawaii, has been a desire to transcend the sectarian rivalries within Buddhism.

Among the first Westerners attracted to Buddhism, though never a professing Buddhist, was Paul Carus of the Open Court Publishing Company in LaSalle, Illinois. Attracted to Zen Master Soyen Shaku at the World Parliament of Religions in 1893, he saw Buddhism as a worthy non-theistic alternative to the Christianity he had already rejected. In 1894 he published his compilation of Buddhist texts, *The Gospel of the Buddha*. He sent it to Soyen Shaku in Japan, who gave it to Daisetz Teitaro Suzuki to translate into Japanese. Carus later brought Suzuki to Illinois and from their collaboration came one of the first major thrusts of American Buddhist history.

Central to the rise of Buddhism in America has been the work of a number of non-Orientals who were attracted to the philosophy of Buddhism and became articulate spokesmen to an audience never reached by the Oriental priests. Such a person was Dwight Goddard, who formed the Fellowship Following Buddha, which operated out of his home in Thetford, Vermont. Ernest Hunt (1876-1967), who became a Buddhist on the eve of taking his orders as an Anglican priest, settled in Hawaii in 1915 and became head of the English Department of the Honpa Hongwanji in 1927. He was the main interpreter to the English-speaking Hawaiians for the next forty years. Mrs. Thomas Foster, a wealthy Honolulu heiress, was typical of several wealthy converted Buddhists who contributed financially to its promulgation. The Fosters had become interested in Buddhism through Dr. Wilhelm Hillebrand of Germany, and they became heavy investors in the Banaras excavations in India at the place where Buddha was enlightened. (The Soto Temple in Honolulu is built on an Indian model.) The botanical gardens in Honolulu are named for Mrs. Foster.

Like many non-Christian religions, Buddhism profited greatly from participation in the 1893 Parliament of Religions in connection with the Columbian Exposition in Chicago, Illinois. In all, seven papers were given, two by Mr. A. Dharmapala of India. They covered the basics of Buddha's life, Hinayana (of Siam), Mahayana (of Japan), and Buddha's teaching. Dharmapala particularly tried to show Buddhism's superiority, and the several Japanese speakers tried to counter what they believed to have been unjust criticism of Buddhism by non-Japanese. "There are very few countries in the world so misunderstood as Japan," began Kinza Riuge Hirai ("What Buddhism Teaches of Man's Relation to God, and Its Influence on Those Who Have Received It," in *The World's Congress of Religions*, ed. J.W. Hanson [Chicago: The Monarch Book Company, 1894], 395). The special program on Buddhism to the whole congress on the evening of September 26 featured addresses by Soyen Shaku, Jitsuzen Ashitzu, K. R. Hirai, and Swami Vivekananda, a Hindu who offered his own appreciation of Buddha. Of significance was the absence of any representative of Buddhism from China.

Buddhist groups in America are of three kinds. Most are transplanted Chinese, Japanese, and other Oriental sects which keep more or less close contact with a parent body. This contact may be formal and organizational, or may be merely by the continuation of a teaching. The second kind are the schismatic groups of the first kind. Schisms have occurred over differences of practice and emphasis, beliefs, and race. A common pattern in Buddhist groups is for a basically Oriental body to grow by additions of Caucasians, only to find itself splintering along racial lines as soon as the Caucasian members are a large enough group. The third type of body is the philosophical Buddhist center formed usually around one or more leaders who have settled in the United States after study in Japan.

SHINTOISM. Shinto, the state religion of Japan, emerged from native folk religions. The "Way of the Gods," Shinto was originally a nature-worship faith, which added a pantheon over the years by a process of deifying heroes. Festivals were centered on seasons and the agricultural cycles. Highly synthetical, Shinto has absorbed elements from other religions and has changed with time. The introduction of Buddhism into Japan in the sixth century seems to have been the major force which led Shinto to become an organized religion.

The central diety is *Kami*, the Japanese name for the life force. The Land of the Rising Sun is Kami's land. Kami's main attribute is the inspiration of awe and wonder; hence, any high object (i.e., Mt. Fuji) can be worshipped as an embodiment of Kami. Two books, *Kojiki* and *Nihongi*, provide the basic texts necessary to understand Kami.

Two major concerns around which ritual expressions are focused are fertility and purity. A nature religion tends to revolve around agricultural seasons; Shinto is no exception. Festivals of planting and harvesting predominate, and one can often see at Shinto shrines offerings of rice, fruit; and other foods on and around the altar. These are a thank offering and/or attempts at sympathetic magic, in which the offering is analogous to the favor requested of the god.

The basic creation myth in Shinto is sexual in that it involves the production of the gods by Izanagi, the primal male, and Izanami, the primal female. Japan, itself, and the line of the imperial family were also their product and, as such, are due reverence.

Worship in Shinto is individual; there is no congregational worship. The entrance to the sacred place, the place of Kami, is through the *torii*, the gate. Cloth strips are tied to trees to scare away evil spirits and offerings are made to court the favor of the good ones. The worshipper washes upon entering, claps his (or her) hands, says the prayer, and departs.

The magic elements in Shinto come to the fore in the attempts of the believers to purify themselves by ceremonial ablutions. There are a number of purifying rituals, one of which is to take a piece of paper, rub it over the body, and send it out to sea with one's impurities.

The history of Shinto is the story of its rise and fall in the eyes of the emperor at various periods. Shinto was weakest in the twelfth century when Honen was spreading the Amida cult and Buddhism was enjoying the favor of the emperor. The height of Shinto power came prior to World War II. In the early nineteenth century, a passionate nationalism, which centered on a "Pure Shinto," *Fakko*, arose in Japan. *Kojiki* and *Nihongi* were restored as sacred texts. A revolution in 1867-68 set Shinto up as a national religion and brought about the persecution of Buddhists. The nationalism eventually led Japan into World War II. Since 1945, religious freedom has reigned in Japan, and Shinto has suffered in defeat along with the emperor.

Early in the twentieth century, the Japanese government recognized thirteen Shinto sects and all Shintoists had to be of these, but this rule ended in 1945. The thirteen sects can be divided into several groups, such as the mountain sects, which recognize the high places as the abodes of deity, or the purification sects and healing sects.

Shinto came to America with the Japanese immigrants. A Shinto shrine was constructed in Hilo, Hawaii, in 1898. In 1906, a temple was opened in Honolulu. Shintoism prospered until the 1930's, when growing concern over Japanese imperialism led to criticism of the Shinto priests as agents of a foreign power. After Pearl Harbor, the shrines were confiscated and the priests arrested. One temple, to avoid confiscation, donated its building to the city of Honolulu and was able to recover it in court in 1961. Other groups had to rebuild.

JAPANESE NEW RELIGIONS. Recently there has been a significant amount of literature devoted to studying what have come to be called the Japanese "new religions." These are religions which have been founded since 1800, but which have made their impact in the twentieth century, particularly since religious freedom was declared after World War II. These religions do share a number of characteristics, the most important being their inroads into the membership of the older Buddhist and Shinto faiths.

However, the new religions do not share a common heritage, thought-world, or lifestyle. Groups such as Nichiren Shoshu and Rissho Kosei Kai are clearly variations on a theme by Buddha. A second set of groups, such as Tenrikyo and Konko Kyo, is clearly Shinto in basic faith. Seicho-No-Ie is an example of a third grouping, which are psychic and metaphysical (New Thought). This third group has shown in America a movement toward psychic and New Thought advocates. Therefore Seicho-No-Ie is discussed in the chapter on New Thought. A fourth grouping is made up of the few miscellaneous bodies, of which only one, Perfect Liberty Kyodan, has found its way to America.

Characteristic of many of the new groups is the influence of Christianity, though different groups have picked up different elements. "Church," the idea of group worship, has been picked up by many Buddhists. As in India, with the ashram, "church" has been a powerful concept. The Konko Kyo seems to have been influenced by the Roman Catholic confession in its toritsugi, a form of group confession and meditation. In no case, at least in those which have come to America, has Christianity become the dominant element.

SOURCES—THE EASTERN FAMILY, PART II

GENERAL SOURCES

Ch'en, Kenneth K. S. *Buddhism*. Woodbury, NY: Barron's Educational Series, 1968. 297 pp.

Conze, Edward. *Buddhism: Its Essence and Development*. New York: Harper & Row, 1959. 223 pp.

————, trans. *Buddhist Scriptures*. Baltimore: Penguin Books, 1959. 250 pp.

Dutt, Nalinaksha. *Buddhist Sects in India*. Delhi: Motilal Banarsidass, 1978. 297 pp.

Jayatilleke, K. N. *The Message of the Buddha*. New York: The Free Press, 1974. 262 pp.

Kalupahana, David J. *Buddhist Philosophy*. Honolulu: University Press of Hawaii, 1976. 189 pp.

March, Arthur C. *A Buddhist Bibliography*. London: The Buddhist Lodge, 1935. 257 pp.

Robinson, Richard H. *The Buddhist Religion*. Belmont, CA: Dickenson Publishing Company, 1970. 136 pp.

Saunders, E. Dale. *Buddhism in Japan*. Philadelphia: University of Pennsylvania Press, 1964. 328 pp.

Schuman, Hans Wolfgang. *Buddhism*. Wheaton, IL: Theosophical Publishing House, 1973. 200 pp.

Shojun, Bando, et al., eds. *A Bibliography of Japanese Buddhism*. Tokyo: CIIB Press, 1958. 180 pp.

The Teaching of Buddha. Tokyo: Bukkyo Dendo Kyokai, 1966. 300 pp.

Yoo, Yushin. *Books on Buddhism*. Metuchen, NJ: Scarecrow Press, 1976. 251 pp.

BUDDHISM IN AMERICA

Fields, Rick. *How the Swans Came to the Lake*. Boulder, CO: Shambhala, 1981. 433 pp.

Hunter, Louise H. *Buddhism in Hawaii*. Honolulu: University of Hawaii Press, 1971. 266 pp.

Kalbacker, Catherine Elmes. *Zen in America*. Lansing: Ph.D. dissertation, University of Michigan, 1972. 213 pp.

Keshima, Tetsuden. *Buddhism in America*. Westport, CT: Greenwood Press, 1977. 272 pp.

Layman, Emma McCoy. *Buddhism in America*. Chicago: Nelson-Hall, 1976. 342 pp.

Melton, J. Gordon. *A Bibliography of Buddhism in America, 1880-1940*. Santa Barbara, CA: Institute for the Study of American Religion, 1985. 13 pp.

Peiris, William. *The Western Contribution to Buddhism*. Delhi: Motilal Bonarsidass, 1973. 287 pp.

Prebish, Charles S. *American Buddhism*. North Scituate, MA: Duxbury Press, 1979. 220 pp.

THERAVADA BUDDHISM

Dhiravamsa, V. R. *The Way of Non-Attachment*. New York: Schocken Books, 1975. 160 pp.

Dutt, Sukumar. *Buddhism in East Asia*. New Delhi: Indian Council for Cultural Relations, 1966. 225 pp.

Hamilton-Merritt, Jane. *A Meditator's Diary*. New York: Harper & Row, 1976. 155 pp.

Jumsai, M. L. Manich. *Understanding Thai Buddhism*. Bangkok: Chalermnit Press, 1973. 124 pp.

JAPANESE MAYAHANA BUDDHISM

Anesaki, Masaharu. *Nichiren, The Buddhist Prophet*. Cambridge: Harvard University Press, 1949. 160 pp.

Nakai, Gendo. *Shinran and His Religion of Pure Faith*. Kyoto: Shinshu Research Institute, 1937. 260 pp.

Suzuki, Beatrice Lane. *Mahayana Buddhism*. New York: Macmillan, 1969. 158 pp.

ZEN BUDDHISM

Becker, Ernest. *Zen: A Rational Critique*. New York: W.W. Norton, 1961. 192 pp.

Dumoulin, Heinrich. *A History of Zen Buddhism*. Boston: Beacon Press, 1963. 335 pp.

Humphreys, Christmas. *A Western Approach to Zen*. Wheaton, IL: Theosophical Publishing House, 1972. 212 pp.

Suzuki, D. T. *Zen Buddhism*. Garden City, NY: Doubleday, 1956. 294 pp.

Watts, Alan. *The Way of Zen*. New York: Pantheon Books, 1968. 236 pp.

CHINESE BUDDHISM

Pachow, W. *Chinese Buddhism*. Washington, DC: University Press of America, 1980. 260 pp.

Thompson, Laurence G. *Chinese Religion: An Introduction*. Belmont, CA: Dickenson Publishing Company, 1969. 119 pp.

Yu, Lu K'uan (Charles Luk). *Practical Buddhism*. Wheaton, IL: Theosophical Publishing House, 1973. 167 pp.

KOREAN BUDDHISM

Seo, Kyung-Bo. *A Study of Korean Buddhism Approached through the Chidangjip*. Walnut Creek, CA: Walnut Creek Zendo, 1960(?).

TIBETAN BUDDHISM

Anderson, Walt. *Open Secrets*. New York: Viking Press, 1979. 230 pp.

Bloefeld, John. *The Tantric Mysticism of Tibet*. New York: Causeway Books, 1974. 257 pp.

Dasgupta, Shashi Bhushan. *An Introduction to Tantric Buddhism*. Boulder, CO: Shambhala, 1974. 211 pp.

Hoffman, Helmut. *The Religions of Tibet*. New York: Macmillan, 1961. 199 pp.

Sopa, Lhundup, and Jeffery Hopkins. *Practice and Theory of Tibetan Buddhism*. New York: Grove Press, 1976. 164 pp.

SHINTO

Aston, W. G. *Shinto, The Way of the Gods*. London: Longmans Green & Co., 1905. 390 pp.

Ballou, Robert O. *Shinto, The Unconquered Enemy*. New York: Viking Press, 1945. 239 pp.

Ross, Floyd Hiatt. *Shinto, The Way of the Gods*. Boston: Beacon Press, 1965. 187 pp.

Sectarian Shinto (The Way of the Gods). Tokyo: The Japan Times & Mail, 1939. 62 pp.

TAOISM

Blofeld, John. *Taoism, The Road to Immortality*. Boulder: Shambhala, 1978. 195 pp.

Legge, James, trans. *I Ching Book of Changes*. New Hyde Park, NY: University Books, 1964. 448 pp.

Waley, Arthur. *The Way and Its Power*. New York: Grove Press, 1968. 262 pp.

Welch, Holmes. *Taoism, The Parting of the Way*. Boston: Beacon Press, 1965. 194 pp.

CONFUCIANISM

Chai, Ch'u, and Winberg Chai. *Confucianism*. Woodbury, NY: Barron's Educational Series, 1973. 202 pp.

The Wisdom of Confucius. New York: Books, Inc., 1960. 236 pp.

NEW RELIGIONS OF JAPAN

Ellwood, Robert S., Jr. *The Eagle and the Rising Sun*. Philadelphia: Westminster Press, 1974. 224 pp.

McFarland, H. Neill. *The Rush Hour of the Gods*. New York: Macmillan, 1967. 267 pp.

Offner, Clark B. *Modern Japanese Religions*. New York: Twayne Publishers, 1963. 296 pp.

Thomsen, Harry. *The New Religions of Japan*. Rutland, VT: Charles E. Tuttle Company, 1963. 268 pp.

Part Two
Descriptive Directory Listings

Western Liturgical Family

An historical essay on this family is provided beginning on page 1.

The Roman Catholic Church

★1★

ROMAN CATHOLIC CHURCH
National Conference of Catholic Bishops
1312 Massachusetts Ave., N.W.
Washington, DC 20005

[Introductory note: The Roman Catholic Church is by far the largest ecclesiastical community in the United States, more than three times as large as the Southern Baptist Convention, its closest rival. That fact, coupled with its position as the largest Christian body in the world and as such the bearer of much of the Christian tradition, gives it a special position in any survey of religious bodies. Overwhelmingly Western Christian churches can trace their origins to dissent from Roman Catholicism, on one or more points. Even within a predominantly Protestant country such as the United States, the Roman Catholic Church provides a measuring rod by which other Christian groups (approximately two-thirds of those treated in this *Encyclopedia*) can locate themselves. Understanding the lives of these groups presupposes some knowledge of their variation from Catholicism. The Roman Catholic Church was also one of the first churches to come to America, bringing with it the long history of Western Christianity. The matter of the origin of the Roman tradition and of the emergence of the See of Rome as the dominant body in the West is a matter of intense debate among ancient-church historians. Most agree, however, that by the fifth century Rome was the ecclesiastical power in the West, and Rome's bishop was the leading episcopal authority. Further, for the next millennium, the story of Christianity in the West is largely the story of Rome. The detailing of this story and the elaboration of this developing tradition is far beyond the scope of this volume. Interested readers are referred to the volumes cited at the end of this entry for a sample of the volumes that treat those topics. This volume will merely provide a summary of basic material about the Church and its historical development in the West, the emergence of religious orders, its history in the United States, its

basic beliefs and practices, and its organization. The long history of the Church and some of its sanctioned but less than universal practices (Eastern rite liturgies, localized forms of piety, etc.) will be treated primarily as background for understanding those groups that have dissented with the Church.]

The Roman Catholic Church is that Christian religious community whose members are "baptized and incorporated in Christ, profess the same faith, partake of the same sacraments and are in communion with and under the government of the successor of St. Peter, the pope, and the bishops in union with him." (quoted from *A Concise Guide to the Catholic Church* by Felician A. Foy). The rise of the Roman Catholic Church to a position of dominance within the Christian community can be traced through a series of steps beginning with the geographical spread of the Church throughout the Roman Empire and beyond and the emergence of an authority structure built around bishops (mentioned in the New Testament, but hardly the figures of authority as exist today). Then the conversion of the Emperor Constantine pulled the Church out of its role as just another religion competing in the Roman forum.

In 303 A.D. Diocletian initiated a plan designed to stabilize the vast empire he ruled. He divided it into Eastern and Western sections. Over each section he placed a senior emperor assisted by a junior emperor with the right of succession. Diocletian then voluntarily resigned and the four appointees took his place: the senior emperor Constantius Chlorus and his junior partner, Severus in the West, and Galerius and his junior partner, Maximinus, in the East. However, upon the death of the emperor in the West, his son Constantine usurped the power and Severus, the rightful successor, was killed.

In the midst of his rise to power Constantine identified himself with (only much later was he baptized) what was at the time a very small Christian community. According to Christian historian Eusebius, he saw avision over the Milvian bridge where he was to meet his rival. The vision was of a cross in the sky with words around it saying, "In this sign you will conquer." Constantine ordered this sign painted on the shields of his soldiers; defeated his rival, and emerged as sole ruling power in the West. One of his first acts was to give Christianity freedom by granting it an equal legal status with paganism. In the East, Galerius followed Constantine's lead. Under Constantine, the idea that Christianity best flourished under the protection of the empire began its ascendancy along with its corollary that the empire and the emperor were not only capable but were in fact divinely appointed to rule and to render that protection. Both the centuries of intimate union between the "Christian" state and the Christian Church and the church-state theory based upon that union were initiated at this time, even before the Church became the dominant religious power in the empire.

Then in 330 C. E., Constantine transferred his capital from Rome to Byzantium (now Istanbul) in the East. He renamed it Consantinople and over the next decades initiated a whole new thrust in culture. But in so doing, he abandoned Rome and created a severe power vacuum throughout the West. The Church and the bishop of Rome, the Pope, emerged as the organization with both the will and the ability to accomodate to the new situation. Christian bishops took up temporal authority and, given the emperors' acceptance of their role, became an elite ruling class. The bishops in the more important towns of the empire came to be known as archbishops and those in the major cities, such as Antioch, Alexandria, Constantinople, Rome, were known as patriarchs. the Roman patriarch assumed some preeminence both as successor to Peter, who died in Rome, and patriarch of the significant urban center in the West.

But while the bishop of Rome claimed a primacy of honor and privilege, the Eastern patriarchs, claimed a similiar prestige as well. The emperor resided in the East. The ecumenical councils were held there. Most Christians lived there, where Christinity had begun and had its longest history. However, the Western Church had an opportunity for growth and development that it would not miss.

Pope Gregory the Great, elected in 590, in a very real sense the founder of the modern papal structure, began the process of centralizing the entire Western Church, then loosely organized into a set of dioceses, upon Rome. He brought to the office a vision, discipline, missionary instinct, and sense of order and rule to the church. If the pope's power of jurisdiction and supremacy had been ill defined previously, it was Gregory who sharpened the definition. A high civil official before becoming a monk, he used his organizational ability to reorganize church finances, thus making it financially independent. He consolidated and expanded the Church's power. He exercised hegemony for the Church throughout the West and sent forth missionaries (usually monks) to claim lands for the faith. He took major steps to convert the Germanic tribes, end Arianism in Spain, and gain the loyalty of the Irish church. Gregory sent Augustine to England where he converted the king and established the

see at Cantebury. The papacy emerged as the international center of the Western Church in power as well as prestige. The church that emerged under Gregory's successors looked to Rome, not to the Emperor in Constantinople nor his representative at Revenna.

Two centuries after Gregory, the emperor Charlemagne (742- 814) consolidated secular political rule in almost all of Europe and reestablished an empire to match the spiritual realm delineated by the Church. A bond was forged, and the marriage between the Western Church and the Western empire took place. The Eastern emperor became a mere figurehead to the West.

The dissipation of Charlemagne's empire into the hands of numerous local monarchs set the stage for Pope Gregory VII, elected in 1073, the founder of the papal monarchy. By Gregory's time, Western Christendom had grown "larger" than the territory of any empire. Gregory, monarch of his own country, but more importantly, the representative of a religion that transcended the boundaries of both his country and the empire as it then existed, began to assume more universal powers, full political and spiritual supremacy. He encouraged remote territories such as Spain, Denmark, and Hungary to accept the protection of the Holy See, implying that he, the pope, was the real universal center of things rather than any emperor. He insisted that the pope could be judged by none; that the pope alone could depose, move and/or restore bishops. He took authority to depose rulers or to absolve subjects from their allegiance to their rulers. Under Gregory and his successor, the Papacy exercised its greatest temporal authority in the West. The extensive corruption of that power, felt throughout the church at every level, created the need for reform and set the stage for Martin Luther, John Calvin, and the Protestant and Radical Reformers.

The Reformation can best be seen as the convergence of numerous factors upon Northern and Western Europe in the sixteenth century. The Church was beset with numerous internal problems. The Church was also filled with numerous voices calling for its reform and a new emphasis upon spirituality in place of its preoccupation with political involvement. Several centuries of reform efforts had also coincided with the rise of strong national states which further stripped the Holy Roman Emperor of real power to hold structures together in the West. Once Luther's cause gained support, other independent reform efforts proceeded, ranging from those of Calvin in Switzerland and Henry VIII in England to the more radical Swiss Brethren (Mennonites) and Unitarians. Once the political power supporting the Roman Catholic Church was broken, the establishment of numerous independently controlled bodies of Christianity became possible.

The Reformation divided the West among five Christian traditions (Roman, Lutheran, Reformed, Anglican, and Free Church) and fostered the further division of the non-

Roman traditions into the many individual organizations with linguistic, political, nationalistic, and doctrinal divergences, leading, of course, to the numerous churches seen in this century (and described in various sections of the *Encyclopedia*). While Rome remained in control of the largest block of territory, it had to devise new ways of relating to religiously divided societies, especially in those countries which had both a Roman Catholic presence and a hostile Protestant ruler.

The Reformation also occurred at the same time as the discovery, exploration, and settlement of the Americas. Roman Catholicism settled in most of South and Central America and became the dominant religious force. In North America, with the early settlers, the Church found a much different situation, i.e., a predominantly Protestant society moving quickly toward a religious freedom and pluralism not hinted at since the days of the Roman Empire.

A note about religious orders: the forces of reform that disrupted the Church in the sixteenth century were not new to Western Christianity. Reform had been expressed and acted upon by numerous movements throughout its history. Some of these reformers became rival movements, largely remembered today as the great heretical movements (Gnosticism, Montanism, etc.) When the Church gained access to political power, it turned upon those movements and left a record of persecution that came back to haunt it in later centuries. However, with reformist, mystical, and enthusiastic movements not defined as heretical (but nevertheless potentially schismatic) the Church had a more creative solution in the formation of ordered religious communities. The tendencies of, for example Protestantism and the Free Church families, constantly lead to the formation of new sects. In Roman Catholicism, however (and to a lesser extent in Eastern Orthodoxy), these tendencies resulted in the various orders of monks, nuns, and lay brothers and sisters. Many such orders show all of the characteristics of sectarian bodies, including liturgical and theological peculiarities, distinctive dress, special missional emphases. The only difference is that theses groups remain in allegiance to the bishop of Rome. Many orders operate effectively outside of local diocesan control and report directly to the orders' officials, who in turn report directly to the Pope or curia. Of course, by accepting new religious movements as ordered communities, the Church is able both to nurture geniune religious enthusiasms and control their excesses.

From the fifth to the twelfth centuries, there was practically only one religious order in the church: the Benedictines. Then, in the twelfth century, a variety of new types of religious communities appeared on the scene with many derivative branches. Not only was the Benedictine Order no longer held to be the only safe road to heaven but, by the twelfth century, a noticeable decline had set in. Some monasteries had become socially exclusive and had become fossilized into great symbols of stability from which no innovations could be expected.

New orders were needed. First, there were the Augustinians (Luther's order), an informal group compared to the structured Benedictines, dedicated to practical service to others (in contrast to self perfection of the former monks) and to survival in a world of change. The Cistercians, on the other hand, wanted to flee change, flux, and the world and return to pristine Benedictine rigor and purity. They moved into the some of the uninhabited lands of Europe, first growing rapidly, then like the Benedictines before them, succumbing to success.

The new town culture of the late Middle Ages brought into existence the two most influential orders of the time, the Franciscans and Dominicans. Founded by middle class men (Francis of Assisi was the son of a merchant) as an order of brothers (fratello in Italian) or friars, they were not, as older orders, to withdraw from the world but to penetrate it. They gave to the age the common spectacle of the traveling friar and itinerant preacher.

The Roman Catholic Church came to America with the early Spanish and French explorers. Priests accompanied Hernando de Soto and Francisco Coronado, and some, like Jacques Marquette and Junipero Serra, became explorers in their own right. The first missions were begun in Florida after the founding of St. Augustine in 1565. Spanish priests and (after 1573) Franciscans developed the missions. The settlement of large segments of America by European Catholic countries largely determined the earliest religious development of America. Florida, the Gulf Coast of present-day Alabama and Mississippi, California, and the Southwest were Spanish territory. The French settled Louisiana and the Mississippi Valley. The early Catholic hegemony is reflected in the many towns named for the saints they revered.

Under the leadership of an English Catholic convert, George Calvert (who became the first Baron of Baltimore) a small band of British Catholics settled on the East Coast and, in 1634, founded the colony of Maryland. In stark contrast to their neighbors in Pennsylvania, many of whom had come to America fleeing Roman Catholic persecution, these Catholics had come fleeing Protestant attacks. In 1649 Calvert issued the famous Act of Toleration offering the "free exercise" of religion to residents. Unfortunately, Catholic control of the colony was soon lost, and in 1654 the Act was repealed and Catholicism prohibited. Four Catholics were executed and the Jesuits driven out. Not until 1781 were Catholics allowed to participate in public life.

Catholicism existed in America for over two centuries without a bishop. There had been no confirmations and all clergy were ordained abroad. Since 1757, the colonies had been nominally under the bishop in London, but after the American Revolution a resident bishop was needed. The person chosen for the task was John Carroll, a member of the most prominent Catholic family in the colonies and a cousin to Charles Carroll, one of the signers of the Declaration of Independence. By the end of the century Carroll would have approximately 50,000 Catholics under his care.

During the nineteenth century, several factors shaped the life of the Church. First, the dominance of people of British and German ancestry, both with a strong anti-Catholic bias from the days of the Reformation, meant that Catholics would frequently have to exist in a hostile environnment. (This reached its height in the mid-nineteenth century during the so-called Know Nothing era.) Secondly, the Church grew massively as literally millions of immigrants from predominantly Roman Catholic countries poured into the United States. At the same time, the Church became divided internally into many ethnic groupings, as Catholics from different countries and speaking different languages settled into homogeneous communities. They tended to locate in pockets in the cities and recreated (as much as possible) life in the old country. To this day many of the nation's leading cities retain a large Catholic element and many neighborhoods retain remants of these immigrant communities. The many ethnic groups also contrasted strongly with the predominantly Irish clergy and hierarchy. Attempts to play down ethnicity and "Americanize" parishes (in part by assigning priests from outside the predominant ethnic group in a parish) caused considerable friction. It was also the cause of the only major schism from within the Church in the United States, the Polish National Catholic Church. The parochial school system, mandated in 1884, was originally established to assist Catholic immigrants as they adjusted to life in non-Catholic America.

Growth of the Church during the nineteenth century (which lasted until immigration from mostly Catholic countries was curtailed in 1921) was spectacular. By 1822 Baltimore had been designated an archepiscopal see and bishops resided in Boston; New York; Philadelphia; Norfolk, Virginia; New Orleans; and Bardstown, Kentucky. By 1900 there were over 12,000,000 Catholics in the United States (eclipsing by far the largest Protestant church), and by 1930 there were over 20,000,000. During the next half-century, Church membership would more than double in size

The Roman Catholic Church bases its beliefs on the revelation of God as given through the Bible, and on tradition handed down from the Apostles through the Church. The essential beliefs have come to be summarized in several creedal statements, especially those developed by the early ecumenical councils: the Apostles Creed, Nicene Creed, and Athanasian Creed. Until recently, new converts to the Church were asked to sign a "Profession of Faith," which included a rejection of a number of false doctrines, a promise of obedience to the Church, and a statement of belief. Though no longer required, the statement of belief, printed below, remains an authoritative guide to the Church's essential belief:

"One only God, in three divine Persons, distinct from and equal to each other, that is to say, the Father, the Son, and the Holy Ghost; the Catholic doctrine of the Incarnation, Passion, Death, and Resurrection of our Lord Jesus Christ; the personal union of the two natures, the divine and the human; the divine maternity of the most holy Mary, together with her spotless virginity; the true real and substantial presence of the Body and Blood, together with the Soul in the Eucharist; the seven Sacraments instituted by Jesus Christ for the salvation of mankind, that is to say, Baptism, Confirmation, Eucharist, Penance, Extreme Unction, Orders, and Matrimony; Purgatory, the Resurrection of the Dead, Everlasting Life; the primacy, not only of honor, but also of jurisdiction, of the Roman Pontiff, successor of St. Peter, prince of the apostles, Vicar of Jesus Christ, the veneration of the saints and their images; the authority of the Apostolic and Ecclesiastical traditions, and of the Holy Scriptures, which we must interpret and understand, only in the sense which our holy mother, the Catholic Church, has held, and does hold; and everything else that has been defined, and declared by the Sacred Canons, and by the General Councils, and particularly by the holy Council of Trent and delivered, defined and declared by the General Council of the Vatican, especially concerning the primacy of the Roman Pontiff and his infallible teaching authority.

Defined by the first Vatican Council, the doctrine of papal infallibility remains the most controversial of Roman Catholic beliefs. It grows out of and is an expression of the Church's long held belief in its being kept from error by the power of the Holy Spirit. The Pope's words are considered infallible only when speaking *ex cathedra*, i.e., in his office as pastor and doctor of all Christians, and when defining doctrine on matters of faith or morals to be held by all Christians. More often than not, Papal statements do not fall into this category. However, Catholics are enjoined to give heed to Papal messages as part of their obedience to the Church's teaching authority.

Two relatively recent papal statements in which the Pope has been deemed to have spoken *ex cathedra* concerned what is possibly the second most controversial area of Roman Catholic doctrine (at least to most Protestant Christians), the understanding of the Virgin Mary. During the nineteenth century the veneration of the Virgin Mary took on a new importance within Roman Catholicism, and it found expression in numerous new pietistic forms and practices, many built around the several apparitions, such as those at Lourdes (France) and Fatima (Portugal). In the last century the doctrine of the Immaculate Conception (the sinless birth of Mary) was declared. In 1950 her bodily assumption into heaven was defined.

Supplementing the beliefs of the Church are the moral precepts which are considered binding upon each Church member. They are required to do the following: 1) participate in Mass on Sundays and specified holy days and to abstain from work and business concerns that impede worship; 2) fast and abstain on appointed days (primarily during the Lenten season); 3) confess their sins at least annually; 4) receive the Eucharist during the Easter season (for American Catholics between the first Sunday of Lent and Trinity Sunday); 5) contribute to the support of the Church; and 6) observe the laws of the Church concerning marriage.

Worship in the Catholic Church is centered upon the liturgy, the major components being the following: the Eucharist (the Mass) and the other six sacraments; sacramentals (sacramental-like signs such as holy water, rosaries, holy medals, etc.); sacred art; sacred music; the prayer cycle of the Liturgy of the Hours (the Divine Office); and the designation of the liturgical year and calendar.

Individuals are brought into the Church through baptism, through which original sin is washed away. The Mass, instituted by Christ at the Last Supper, is a real sacrifice of Christ using the elements of bread and wine. During the liturgy of the Mass, the Church teaches that the bread and wine change (the change is termed "transubstantiation") into the body and blood of Christ. The Eucharist is the major sacramental expression encountered by Church members on a regular basis. Confirmation, usually given to youth or adult converts immediately after finishing a period of instruction in the faith, is generally conferred by the bishop, and it empowers individuals with the force of the Holy Spirit. Penance is the means by which the faithful confess and receive forgiveness for present sin. Holy Orders sets aside Catholic males (unmarried and celibate) for specified priestly functions. The annointing of the sick (unction) is performed when the individual is in danger of death, in hope of an improvement in the state of health, as well as for forgiveness of sins at the time of death. Finally, matrimony binds two people together in God's eyes.

Over the years, supplementing the sacramental life, the Church has broadly defined the life and structure of faith through the liturgical calendar. The calendar focuses attention on the essentials of the faith and commemorates the life of the Virgin Mary and the saints. The liturgical year begins with Advent and includes as its high points Christmas, Lent, Easter, and Pentecost. Worship is further enhanced by the promotion of a variety of devotional practices, inluding prayers said using the rosary, novenas, and meditation on the stations of the cross (picturing Christ's passion and death).

The Roman Catholic Church derives its authority as the Church founded by Christ through the Apostles. The signs of Christ's Church are its oneness in doctrine, worship, and practice; its holiness by the indwelling of the Holy Spirit; its apostolic nature; and its catholicity or universal aspect. The Apostolic authority has been passed, generation by generation, through the bishops of the Church, especially the Pope, the successor to Peter, the first bishop of Rome. The Pope resides in Vatican City, a small sovereign state outside of Rome, Italy. The curia is located there, where the college of cardinals meets.

The Pope, the Supreme Pastor of Christians, is elected by the College of Cardinals. The College, which evolved out of the synod of the clergy of the diocese of Rome, includes the principal advisors and assistants to the Pope, who help administer the affairs of the Church. It was officially constituted in 1150, and twenty-nine years later the selection of its members was left to the reigning Pope. Members of the College are of three types: cardinal bishops, the bishops of dioceses geographically neighboring the diocese of Rome; cardinal priests, bishops of dioceses away from Rome who have been assigned to a church in Rome; and cardinal deacons, bishops assigned to administrative of fices in the Roman curia. Generally, the archbishops of the most important sees in the United States are appointed cardinal priests.

The offices of the Roman Catholic Church that administer its affairs worldwide are called the curia. It includes the Secretariat of State, the Council for the Public Affairs of the Church, and numerous other departments, congregations, tribunals, and secretariats. Worldwide, the Church is divided into a number of dioceses. The largest and most important are designated archdioceses, with an archbishop who generally has some supervisory rights over the neighboring dioceses. Dioceses are grouped into provinces, provinces into regions, and regions into conferences. In 1966, bishops in the United States were formed into the National Catholic Conference in the United States. The Church as a whole is governed according to canon law, the rules of the Church. A revised edition of that law, written during the Second Vatican Council, was issued in 1981. The 1,752 canons cover all aspects of Church life, from the nature and structure of the Church to the rights and obligations of the faithful.

In the years after the split between the Roman Catholic Church and the Eastern Orthodox Churches in the eleventh century, communities that had a history as Eastern Orthodox were converted to Catholicism, and they came under the jurisdiction of the Pope. In many cases these churches were allowed to keep their Eastern liturgical life. There are six patriarchs who preside over nongeographical dioceses of all of the faithful of their respective rite, wherever in the world they might be found. These churches retain a married priesthood. Eastern rite Catholics began to emigrate to the United States in the late 1700s, and parishes were founded in the nineteenth century. The presence of Eastern Catholic and Eastern Orthodox parishes so close together in the relatively free environment of the United States facilitated the movement of members (and sometimes even whole parishes) from one church to another.

Membership: In 1982 the Church reported 52,088,774 members, 24,071 parishes, and 57,870 priests.

Educational facilities: For a complete list of institutions of higher learning supported by the Roman Catholic Church see the latest edition of either *The Official Roman*

Catholic Directory (New York: P. J. Kenedy & Sons) or *Catholic Almanac* (Huntington, IN: Our Sunday Visitor). Each is regularly revised and updated.

Periodicals: There are over 500 Church-related newspapers and 300 magazines published in the United States. For a complete list see the latest edition of either the *Catholic Almanac* or *The Official Roman Catholic Directory.*

Sources: Felician A. Foy, *A Concise Guide to the Catholic Church.* Huntington, IN: Our Sunday Visitor, 1984; Aloysius J. Burggraff, *Handbook for New Catholics.* Glen Rock, NJ: Paulist Press, 1960; Daughters of St. Paul, *Basic Catechism with Scripture Quotations.* Boston: St. Paul Editions, 1984; Sister M. Catherine Frederic, *The Handbook of Catholic Practices.* New York: Hawthorn Publishers, 1964; Matthew F. Kohmescher, *Catholicism Today.* New York: Paulist Press, 1980. John Tracy Ellis, *American Catholicism.* Garden City, NY: Doubleday, 1965; John Tracy Ellis, ed., *Documents of American Catholic History.* Chicago: Henry Regnery, 1967. 2 Vols.; James Hennesey, *American Catholics.* Oxford: Oxford University Press, 1981; Theodore Maynard, *The Story of American Catholicism.* Garden City, NY : Doubleday, 1960. Walter J. Burghardt and William F. Lynch, *The Idea of Catholicism.* New York: Meridian, 1960; John L. McKenzie, *The Roman Catholic Church.* New York: Holt, Rinehart and Winston, 1969; J. M. R. Tillard, *The Bishop of Rome.* Willmington, DE: Michael Glazier, 1983; Heinrich Scharp, *How the Catholic Church is Governed.* New York: Paulist Press, 1960.

Old Catholicism

★2★

AMERICAN ORTHODOX CATHOLIC CHURCH - WESTERN RITE MISSION, DIOCESE OF NEW YORK

% Most Rev. Joseph J. Raffaele
318 Expressway Dr., S.
Medford, NY 11763

Joseph J. Raffaele, a Roman Catholic layperson, founded St. Gregory's Church, an independent traditionalist Latin-rite parish, in Sayville, New York, on August 28, 1973. Three months later, he was ordained by Bishop Robert R. Zaborowski of the Archdiocese of the American Orthodox Catholic Church in the U.S. and Canada (now called the Mariavite Old Catholic Church). Raffaele developed a congregation among traditionalists who felt spiritually alienated from the post-Vatican II Roman Catholic Church. The parish grew slowly, and Raffaele and his assistants continued to work in secular jobs (the standard Old Catholic pattern), devoting evenings and weekends to the church. The parish moved from Sayville to Shirley to Ronkonkoma, New York. During the mid-1970s Bishop Zaborowski insisted upon the acceptance of Mariavite (i.e. Polish) liturgical patterns by the congregations under his

jurisdiction. Both St. Gregory's and Fr. Raffaele left the Mariavite Old Catholic Church. Shortly after, Archbishop Zaborowski issued an excommunication decree.

Raffaele joined the Mount Athos Synod under Bishop Charles C. McCarthy (a bishop in the American Orthodox Catholic Church under Archbishop Patrick J. Healy). On July 18, 1976, McCarthy consecrated Raffaele and raised his associate priest, Gerard J. Kessler, to the rank of monsignor. Six months later, in December 1976, St. Gregory's and Raffaele, due to some personal disagreements with McCarthy, left the Mt. Athos Synod and became an independent jurisdiction, the American Orthodox Catholic Church-Western Rite Mission, Diocese of New York.

The new jurisdiction continues as a traditionalist Latin Rite Catholic Church, though Eastern Rite usage is allowed. The jurisdiction accepts the Baltimore Catechism (minus the papal references) as a doctrinal authority and uses the 1917 Code of Canon Law (again minus the papal references). Clerical celibacy is not demanded, but female priesthood is rejected. No collection is taken on Sunday at worship services. Communion is open to all.

In 1978 St. Matthias Church, in Yonkers, New York, was begun as the first mission parish. In 1979 St. Gregory's moved into a newly purchased building in Medford, New York. That same year, Raffaele consecrated Elrick Gonyo as an independent Uniate bishop in Stuyvesant, New York. In 1979, Raffaele and Gonyo consecrated Kessler as the auxiliary bishop for the jurisdiction.

The Congregation of the Religious of the Society of St. Gregory the Great provides a structure for priests, brothers, and nuns who wish to live an ordered life. There is also a third order, a lay fraternal organization for women (deaconesses).

Membership: In 1985 the American Orthodox Catholic Church-Western Rite Mission reported one congregation in New York with statewide outreach, serving approximately 200 members and a Spanish-speaking parish in Miami, Florida. It had two active bishop-priests and five priests.

Periodicals: *Glad Tidings*, 318 Expressway Drive South, Medford, Long Island, New York 11763.

Sources: *"Milestones,"* *American Orthodox Catholic Church.* Medford, N.Y.: St. Gregory's Church, 1983.

★3★
ARCHDIOCESE OF THE OLD CATHOLIC CHURCH OF AMERICA
% Most Rev. Walter X. Brown
2450 N. 50th St.
Milwaukee, WI 53210

The Archdiocese of the Old Catholic Church of America began in 1941 when Francis Xavier Resch, who had been consecrated by Archbishop Carmel Henry Carfora of the North American Old Roman Catholic Church (Rogers), broke with that jurisdiction and began the independent Diocese of Kankakee centered upon his parish in Kankakee, Illinois. In a short time the new Church had parishes in Illinois, Indiana, Michigan, and Wisconsin. However, these parishes, consisting of first generation Eastern European immigrants, were lost as the second generation became Americanized. In 1963 Bishop Resch consecrated the Rev. Walter X. Brown, who ultimately succeeded Resch as archbishop. In 1970 Brown moved the Church's headquarters to Milwaukee where it maintains a seminary and several charitable institutions.

The Archdiocese accepts the Western Roman tradition of the seven ecumenical councils and the church Fathers. The seven sacraments are practiced, and their "Statement of Faith of the Old Catholic Church of America" follows the outline of the Nicene Creed. In a Statement of Principles, the Church takes a stand on nuclear disarmament, stating that "a Christian must be committed to unilateral nuclear disarmament." It opposes abortion and euthanasia but "does not believe civil laws are as efficacious in these regards as they may seem to appear." The Archdiocese supports three monastic enterprises, a Franciscan Friary in Chicago, and two monastic communities (one Eastern and one Western) in Milwaukee.

Membership: In 1984, the Archdiocese reported 2,300 members, 14 congregations, and 26 clergy. Churches of the Archdiocese are located in Dallas and Brownsville, Texas; Erie, Pennsylvania; Chicago; Racine, Madison, and Milwaukee, Wisconsin; Brooklyn, New York; and Ottawa, Ontario, Canada. Affiliated branches are found in Germany, Belgium, and England.

Educational facilities: Holy Cross Theological Seminary, Milwaukee, Wisconsin.

Periodicals: *The Messenger*, 2450 North 50th Street, Milwaukee, WI 53210.

Sources: John Cyprian Holman, *The Old Catholic Church of America*. Milwaukee, WI: Port Royal Press, 1977; Francis X. Resch, *Compendium Philosophiae Universae*. Lake Village, IN: The Author, 1950.

★4★
CANONICAL OLD ROMAN CATHOLIC CHURCH
% Most Rev. John J. Humphreys
5501 62nd Ave.
Pinellas Park, FL 33565

The Canonical Old Roman Catholic Church began as a reaction to changes not enacted by the Roman Catholic Church at the Second Vatican Council in the 1960s. Fr. Anthony Girandola, a Roman Catholic priest, announced in 1966 that he was married, had been for some time, and intended to remain married and continue to function as a Roman Catholic priest. Since no Roman Catholic bishop would accept him as a married priest he began, independently, to organize a parish in St. Petersburg, Florida.

Girandola became something of a celebrity for his stance and was much in demand as a speaker and as a guest on radio and television talk shows. He later wrote a famous book, *The Most Defiant Priest*. In order to meet the demands the media was making on his time, he arranged for one of his followers, John J. Humphreys, to be ordained a priest. Shortly thereafter Humphreys separated from Fr. Girandola. He formed Our Lady of Good Hope Old Roman Catholic Church and went under the jurisdiction of Archbishop Richard A. Marchenna of the Old Roman Catholic Church, and for several years he served as the jurisdiction's Vicar General. He served under Marchenna's jurisdiction until 1974 when Marchenna consecrated Robert Clement as bishop of the Eucharistic Catholic Church, an openly homosexual church.

Marchenna's action in consecrating Clement resulted in his excommunication by Archbishop Gerard George Shelley, who regarded himself as Marchenna's superior as Primate of the Old Roman Catholic Church in England and America. Fr. Humphreys then accepted consecration by Archbishop Shelley and organized the Historical and Canonical Old Roman Catholic Church as Shelley's jurisdiction for America. One of Bishop Humphreys' priests, Fr. Michael Farrell of San Jose, California was selected to succeed Shelley, who died in 1980. Humphreys consecrated Farrell on June 13, 1981, but a short time later Farrell resigned. Emile Rodriguez y Fairfield, pastor of a small church in East Los Angeles, with orders from the Mexican National Catholic Church emerged as the senior bishop. However, in 1983, when he became the single surviving bishop with the lineage of the Mexican Church, Rodriguez y Fairfield left the jurisdiction to re-assert his position in that body. In 1984 Humphreys was elected primate.

Membership: This small jurisdiction has one parish in Florida and one in Massachusetts, headed by Bishop John J. Greed.

Sources: John J. Humphreys, ed., *Questions We Are Asked*. Chicago: Old Roman Catholic Information Center, 1972.

★5★

CATHOLIC CHRISTIAN CHURCH
% Most Rev. Alan S. Stanford
316 California Ave., Suite 713
Reno, NV 89509

W. D. de Ortega Maxey began his episcopal career on January 2, 1927, when he was consecrated by William Montgomery Brown, a bishop in the Old Catholic Church in America, at that time headed by Archbishop W. H. Francis Brothers. Maxey functioned in various capacities during the next two decades, including a period as general secretary of the Temple of the People, an international theosophical body headquartered in Halcyon, California. During the 1940s he became associated with the Apostolic Episcopal Church founded by Arthur Wolfort Brooks. He traveled to England at the close of World War II and was consecrated again by Hugh George de Willmott Newman and named Supreme Hierarch of the Catholicate of the Americas. Upon Maxey's return to New York, Brooks, who had previously accepted the title of Hierarch of the Catholicate of the United States, reconsecrated Maxey and placed him in charge of the Apostolic Episcopal Church on the West Coast. Maxey served the two intertwined bodies and, for a period following Brooks death in 1948, he headed them. However, in 1951, he resigned his episcopal positions and joined the Universalist Church.

In 1977 Archbishop Maxey again assumed authority as an archbishop and founded the Christian Catholic Church. With the assistance of Archbishop Joachim of the Western Orthodox Church in America, he consecrated Alan S. Stanford as his co-adjutor. Stanford now heads ministries in San Francisco through the Church's chapel, the Holy Order of the Society of St. Jude Thaddeus, and the National Catholic Street Ministry Project. In addition to the work in San Francisco, the Church reports three mission stations. There are two bishops and three priests.

Membership: Not reported.

★6★

CATHOLIC LIFE CHURCH
% Most Rev. A. L. Mark Harding
1955 Arapahoe St., Suite 1603
Denver, CO 80202

The Catholic Life Church was founded in 1971 by the Rev. A. L. Mark Harding and the Rev. Peter A. Tonella, a former Roman Catholic priest who had married in the 1950s. Tonella first joined the Protestant Episcopal Church but soon left it to become bishop of St. Petersburg, Florida, under Bishop Peter A. Zurawetzky of the Christ Orthodox Catholic Patriarchate. The Church grew quickly, ministering to Latinos in Denver where the Church had gathered several congregations. Mark

Harding, who was consecrated bishop by Tonella and Walter X. Brown of the Archdiocese of the Old Catholic Church, supported the small denomination with funds he earned as the owner and operator of four pornographic bookstores in Denver. The Church virtually disappeared when Harding, who had become its patriarch, was arrested and sentenced to prison. After his confinement ended in the fall of 1981, Harding resumed his ministry as Patriarch and Presiding Bishop.

Membership: Not reported.

★7★

CHRIST CATHOLIC CHURCH (PRUTER)
% Most Rev. Karl Pruter
Box 98
Highlandville, MO 65669

Christ Catholic Church was founded by the Rev. Karl Pruter, a Congregationalist minister deeply involved in the liturgically-oriented Free Catholic Movement, a fellowship among ministers and lay people of the Congregational and Christian Churches in the 1940s. The movement did not fair well after the merger of the Congregational-Christian Churches with the Evangelical and Reformed Church to form the United Church of Christ. The subsequent splintering found leaders of the Movement in different denominations. Despairing of the situation, in 1965, the Rev. Pruter, made a pilgrimage to Europe, where he met with many Old Catholic leaders. He returned to the United States, settled in Boston and searched for a free Catholic Church and/or bishop. Finding neither, he turned to independent Orthodox Archbishop Peter A. Zurawetzky and under his authority began a church in Boston's Back Bay area. He emphasized the contemplative life, mysticism, and an experiential faith. The growing congregation soon opened a mission in Deering, New Hampshire.

In 1967 Archbishop Peter, assisted by Archbishop Uladyslav Ryzy-Ryski of the American World Patriarchs, consecrated Fr. Pruter to the episcopacy as Bishop of the Diocese of Boston. The next year, he designated the Diocese as an independent communion. The two jurisdictions met in Synod, and accepted the Constitution and Canons given to the new body by Archbishop Peter.

Bishop Pruter has been a most aggressive publisher and distributor of literature for the several interests which have dominated his life. St. Willibrord's Press, founded by Bishop Pruter, has become the major publisher of Old Catholic literature, and Pruter has become a major author, having written many tracts and pamphlets as well as more substantive books such as *The Teachings of the Great Mystics* and *A History of the Old Catholic Church*. He also operates Tsali Bookstore which specializes in American Indian literature and Cathedral Books which specializes in peace material.

Christ Catholic Church is Old Catholic in faith. It adheres to the Holy Scriptures, the ecumenical creeds, the seven ecumenical councils, and the Confession of Utrecht. Both lay and clergy retain the right of private judgment on matters of doctrine, but a clergyman found to be heterodox by the Presiding Bishop may be deprived of clerical faculties. The Church uses a venacular liturgy, "The Christ Catholic Mass," which follows the Old Catholic pattern. Bishop Pruter has been an energetic advocate for peace, while equally opposed to abortion.

Headquarters of the Church have moved from Boston to New Hampshire to Scottsdale, Arizona to Chicago to its present location in Highlandsville, Missouri, where Bishop Pruter serves as pastor for the Cathedral Church of the Prince of Peace, a small chapel described as the smallest catherdal in the world.

Membership: In 1984 Christ Catholic Church reported 165 members in six parishes, one each in Biddleford, Maine; Kingston, Rhode Island; Chicago; Aurora, Illinois; Phoenix and Scottsdale, Arizona.

Periodicals: *The Cathedral Voice*, Box 98, Highlandsville, MO 65669.

Sources: Karl Pruter and J. Gordon Melton, *The Old Catholic Sourcebook*. New York: Garland, 1983; Karl Pruter, *The Story of Christ Catholic Church*. Chicago: St. Willibrord's Press, 1981; Karl Pruter, *The Teachings of the Great Mystics*. Goffstown, NH: St. Willibrord's Press, 1969; Karl Pruter, *A History of the Old Catholic Church*. Scottsdale, AZ: St. Willibrord's Press, 1973.

★8★
COMMUNITY OF CATHOLIC CHURCHES
Most Rev. Thomas Sargent
3 Columbia St.
Hartford, CT 06106

The Community of Catholic Churches is a small jurisdiction formed in 1971 as a result of a group of Old Catholic priests and bishops deciding to abandon the traditional Catholic hierarchical structure. They removed the purely administrative functions from their ecclesiastical offices and formed a fellowship of clergy and parishes. Priests kept their sacradotal functions and provided priestly leadership for the parishes, most of which are house churches. The groups is led by Senior Bishop Thomas Sargent and Convenor, the Most Rev. Lorraine Morgenson.

The Community generally follows Catholic doctrine and practice, but sets no particular doctrinal standard for members. It also allows the option of dual membership in other churches. It differs from other Old Catholic groups in that it had been willing to ordain both females and homosexuals to the priesthood.

Membership: In 1984 the Community of Catholic Churches claimed 5 churches, 9 clergy and 60 confirmed members.

★9★
ECUMENICAL ORTHODOX CATHOLIC CHURCH-AUTOCEPHALOUS
% Most Rev. Francis J. Ryan, Primate-Apostolos
   Western Rite
Box 637, Grand Central Station
New York, NY 10017

The Ecumenical Orthodox Catholic Church-Autocephalous was formed in the 1970s by its Archbishop Francis J. Ryan. Ryan had been consecrated by Archbishop Uladyslav Ryzy-Ryski of the American World Patriarchs in 1965. It is a small jurisdiction. During the 1970s, the Secular Brothers of the Poor, currently an independent Old Catholic apostolate in Paterson, New Jersey, was an integral part of the church.

Membership: Not reported.

★10★
EVANGELICAL CATHOLIC COMMUNION
% Most Rev. Marlin Paul Bausum Ballard
8648 Oakleigh Rd.
Baltimore, MD 21234

The Evangelical Catholic Communion was formed in 1960 by Michael A. Itkin and other members of the Eucharistic Catholic Church. The new organization took its name from the group formed by Ulric Vernon Herford in England in 1902 following his consecration by Mar Basilius of the Syro-Chaldean Church in India, Ceylon, Socotra, and Messina, a small Orthodox Church headquartered in southern India. Itkin's second consecration by Christopher Maria Stanley carried the apostolic lineage from Herford through British Archbishop Hugh George de Willmott Newman. In 1968 the Itkin-led group split. Itkin founded the Community of the Love of Christ, while the remaining members reorganized under Marlin P. B. Ballard.

The Communion describes itself as an independent body of believers, catholic in faith, standing for social justice, peace and goodwill among men. It emphasizes the love of God and neighbor; the communion of man with man; the living of a sacramental life; and the uniting of humanity into one sacramental faith. It is governed by a Holy Synod.

Membership: Not reported. As a policy, the Communion does not give out statistics of membership.

★11★
EVANGELICAL ORTHODOX (CATHOLIC) CHURCH IN AMERICA (NON-PAPAL CATHOLIC)

% Most Rev. Perry R. Sills
3110 W. Voltaire Ave.
Phoenix, AZ 85029

The Evangelical Orthodox (Catholic) Church in America (Non-Papal Catholic) was originally founded as the Protestant Orthodox Western Church in 1938 by Bishop Wilhelm Waterstraat in Santa Monica. When he retired in 1940 he chose as his successor Father Frederick Littler Pyman. In 1943 Pyman was consecrated Bishop by Archbishop Carmel Henry Carfora, of the North American Old Roman Catholic Church (Rogers). Under Bishop Pyman the Protestant Orthodox Western Church remained an integral part of Archbishop Carfora's jurisdiction until 1948, when Pyman withdrew and changed the name of the Church to The Evangelical Orthodox (Catholic) Church in America (Non-Papal Catholic).

Bishop Pyman had hoped to create a "bridge church," and he led his small denomination in adopting the Leipsic Interim of 1548, a document drawn up as part of a sixteenth-century process to create reconciliation of Protestant and Catholic differences. But the twentieth century promulgation under Bishop Wilhelm Waterstraat and Bishop Pyman drew no reaction from either Protestants or Catholics.

In most respects the Church adheres closely to the Old Catholic position. The Church recognizes the office and authority of the Supreme Pontiff, but only Christ is considered infallible. Clerical celibacy is optional. Oral confession is not required. Both the Latin and vernacular mass is said.

Upon Bishop Pyman's retirement in the 1970s, the leadership of the Church passed to Archbishop Perry R. Sills, who had been enthroned as Bishop Pyman's successor and Second Regionary Bishop on June 30, 1974. On the previous day he had been consecrated by Archbishop Pyman, and Bishops Larry L. Shaver, William E. Littlewood and Basil. In 1984 Sills affiliated with the Patriarchial Synod of the Orthodox Catholic Church of America, an association of independent bishops.

Membership: In the early 1980s the Church reported six parishes and ten clergy, but gave no membership figures.

Sources: *The Evangelical Orthodox (Catholic) Church.* Santa Monica, CA: Committee on Education, Regionary Diocese of the West, 1949.

★12★
GOD'S BENEVOLENCE ORTHODOX CATHOLIC CHURCH

% Rt. Rev. Patrick K. McReynolds
801 Levering Ave., #3
Los Angeles, CA 90024

God's Benevolence Orthodox Catholic Church was formed by Patrick K. McReynolds, a bishop with the Independent Catholic Church (now the Independent Old Roman Catholic Hungarian Orthodox Church of America, headed by Archbishop Edward Paine. Patrick Keven McReynolds received his MA in theology from Fordham in 1978. His ministerial career began, however, even prior to his finishing his education, as he was originally ordained by Bishop Michael A. Itkin in 1974. The next year he joined Archbishop Payne in the Independent Catholic Church and was reordained. A year later he was consecrated by Payne, assisted by Uladyslav Ryzy-Ryski of the American World Patriarchs and six others.

McReynold's early religious training included comparative religion and studies in the occult, yoga, and mysticism. While remaining in the Catholic tradition he attempts to take and use elements from his study of other religious traditions and to balance freedom and tradition, tolerance and orthodoxy. He believes that many Eastern and occult practices are central to the Christian mystical tradition, though called there by different names.

McReynolds believes that women should be involved in ministry but not assume the role of men, i.e., the priesthood. He advocates the revival of the ancient order of the deaconess. He believes that using stereotypes such as homosexuality as an exclusive label for people is both psychologically and socially disastrous. Hence people should not be lumped into categories such as "straight" and "gay."

Membership: This jurisdiction has one congregation, which is located in Los Angeles, California.

Educational facilities: God's Benevolence Institute, Los Angeles.

Periodicals: *Mater Benevola*, 801 Levering Avenue, #3, Los Angeles, CA 90024.

★13★
INDEPENDENT ECUMENICAL CATHOLIC CHURCH (SHOTTS)
(Defunct)

The Independent Ecumenical Catholic Church was formed in 1976 by Rev. John Michael Becket, a former Universalist minister, and Bishop David E. Shotts. Fr. Becket was placed in charge of Saint Jude Abbey and the Brothers of the Sacred Rosary, however, the year after its founding, Fr. Becket left the Church and placed himself under the Ecumenical Catholic Communion headed by M. P. B. Ballard.

The Church followed the Tridentine Roman Catholic liturgy, but used the English translation of 1951. Its doctrine was Catholic, all Seven Sacraments were served. No excommunication was recognized. Flowing from its commitment to ecumenicity, members of a variety of Christian groups, including some Protestant churches, were allowed to take communion.

Membership: In 1977 the Church reported 4 churches, 200 members and 8 ordained clergy. However, in 1979 Shotts, who had been charged in a child molestation case, also abandoned the Church and placed himself under Archbishop Edward Stelik of the North American Old Catholic Church, Ultrajectine Tradition, headquartered in Necedah, Wisconsin. The Independent Ecumenical Catholic Church is presumed to have dissolved.

★14★
INDEPENDENT OLD ROMAN CATHOLIC HUNGARIAN ORTHODOX CHURCH OF AMERICA
% Most Rev. Archbishop Edward C. Payne,
Catholicos-Metropolitan
Box 261
Weatherfield, CT 06109

The Independent Old Roman Catholic Hungarian Orthodox Church of America was founded in 1970 as the Independent Catholic Church by Edward C. Payne. Payne was consecrated in 1969 by Archbishop Hubert A. Rogers of the North American Old Roman Catholic Church (Rogers). Originally, he rejected the liturgy used by the N.A.O.R.C.C. and decreed that the Anglican Rite be used by his congregations as it most nearly corresponded to the Scriptural norm of St. Paul's First Letter to the Corinthians.

Soon after the establishment of the Independent Catholic Church, Payne was attracted to Eastern Orthodoxy. He associated himself with Archbishop Uladyslau Ryzy-Ryski and the American World Patriarchs and in 1972 the Archbishop elevated Payne as the archbishop of an affiliated "Archdiocese of New England." Ryzy-Ryski was at that time beginning a process of establishing an international association of ethnic Orthodox jurisdictions and appointing Archbishops over each national group. Thus in 1975 he appointed Payne Metropolitan of Urgo-Finnic Peoples and Patriarch of the Hungarian Autocephalous Catholic Church in Exile.

Payne was part Hungarian by birth and had about twenty Hungarian families in his Connecticut congregation at that time. During the intervening years, Payne has asserted the Hungarian roots of the Church, both through the orders that can be traced through the N.A.O.R.C.C. to the Austro-Hungarian Duc and Bishop Landas Berghes and the role assigned by Archbishop Ryzy-Ryski. That

heritage led to the adoption of the jurisdiction's present name in 1984.

The Church is Old Catholic in doctrine and practice and accepts the Declaration of Utrecht. It rejects papal infallibility as well as the universal pastorship of the Pope. It also rejects the recent doctrinal statements on the Immaculate Conception and Bodily Assumption of the Virgin Mary. Open communion is practiced. No ordination of homosexuals is allowed.

Membership: In 1984 the Church reported 9 congregations, 11 clergy and 400 members.

Educational facilities: Independent Catholic Seminarium, Hartford, Connecticut.

Periodicals: *The Independent Catholic*, 171 Colby, Hartford, CT 06106.

★15★
MARIAVITE OLD CATHOLIC CHURCH, PROVINCE OF NORTH AMERICA
% His Eminence, Most Rev. Robert R. J. M. Zaborowski
2803 Tenth St.
Wyandotte, MI 48192

The Mariavite Old Catholic Church was incorporated in 1972 as the American Orthodox Catholic Church (changed in 1973 to the Archdiocese of the Old Catholic Church in America and Canada). It assumed its present name in 1974. The founder of the Church is the Robert R. J. M. Zaborowski who claims apostolic lineage from the Mariavite Old Catholic Church headquartered at Plock, Poland. The Mariavite Movement can be traced to the mid-nineteenth century in Poland and the founding of a variety of new monastic communities within the Roman Catholic Church which stressed the inner life and spirituality. Among these was a sister house opened in 1883 at Plock, by Feliksa Magdalena Kozlowska (1862-1921), known more popularly by her religious name, Mother Maria Francis. The new community followed the second rule of the Franciscians (originally written for the Sisters of St. Clare) to which was added a particular devotion to the Most Blessed Sacrament exposed to view in the monstrance, a form of devotion attributed to the Virgin Mary during her life at Nazareth. The name Mariavite derives from the Latin words meaning "Mary's life."

Mother Maria Francis was also a visionary, and her visions received a considerable amount of publicity. As a result the community at Plock grew into a movement throughout Poland which included both men and women and attracted a number of priests. It's spread also attracted the attention of Church authorities who began to attack both the visions of Mother Maria Francis and the appropriateness of such a movement being led by a female. The appointment of Fr. John Michael Kowalski to the position of Minister General of the Congregation of Mariavite Priests in 1903 did little to ease the tension. In 1904 the Church demanded the disbanding of the Order which was followed in 1906 by the excommunication of Kowalski and Mother Maria Francis. While most of their former following disavowed their relationship with them, the pair decided to continue their movement. They formed the independent Mariavite Catholic Church. Kowalski traveled to Holland and in 1909 was consecrated to the episcopate by Archbishop Gerard Gul of the Old Catholic Church. The Church was renamed the Mariavite Old Catholic Church. Following the death of Mother Maria Francis, Bishop Kowalski assumed full leadership of the Church. During his reign a number of controversial practices were introduced including a married priesthood and the ordination of females to the priesthood. Also the Latin mass was rendered into Polish. The new practices were largely opposed by both the Church's membership and leadership, and several schisms occurred. In 1923 one group led by four priests left the church and founded the Old Catholic Church in Poland. A few years later a second group founded the Old Catholic Church of Poland. Finally, in 1935, the several bishops under Kowalski separated themselves and took control of the Mariavite Old Catholic Church. (Kowalski then moved with his following to the town of Felicianow and reorganized as the Mariavite Catholic Church.)

As a former Roman Catholic who had affiliated with the Old Catholic movement, Zaborowski became acquainted with the Old Catholic Church of Poland and was ordained by one one of its episcopal leaders, Archbishop Joseph Anthony Mazur. At the time of his ordination he also became acquainted with Archbishop Francis Ignatius Boryszewski of the Polish Catholic Church, an independent jurisdiction headquartered in Jersey City, New Jersey. In 1972, assisted by some French bishops with Mariavite orders, Boryszewski (who also possessed Mariavite orders) consecrated Zaborowski. Upon the death of Archbishop Mazur later that year, Zaborowski succeeded to the role of archbishop and the following year changed the name of the jurisdiction to reflect its Mariavite heritage.

The Mariavite Old Catholic Church follows the orthodox theological heritage of the Mariavite Old Catholic Church of Plock. It accepts the early creeds of the undivided Catholic Church, but considers the statement of papal infallibility erroneous and the recent pronouncement of the dogmas of the Immaculate Conception and the Assumption of the Virgin Mary as invalid. It recognizes the seven sacraments. Auricular confession is optional. Special devotion is paid to the the Lord Jesus Christ as present in the Blessed Sacrament and members are obliged to render such devotion a minimum of one hour per week plus a hour per month in a congregational gathering. Special devotion to Mary as Our Lady of Perpetual Help is also practiced. The Church is headed by its Prime Bishop (Archbishop Zaborowski) and the Council. The Council is selected by the General Chapter of the Church (composed of all bishops and clergy). All clergy belong to

the Religious Order of St. Francis of Assisi. However, they do no live together in a monastery. Rather they serve as parish priests and missionaries. Clergy, who follow the first and third Rule of St. Francis, are assisted by lay brothers who adhere to only the third Rule and sisters who follow the Rule of St. Clare.

Membership: The Mariavite Old Catholic Church has reported a spectacular rate of growth. From its modest beginnings (it reported only 487 members, in 8 centers and 32 clergy in 1972), it claimed, by 1980, to have 301,009 members in 117 churches served by 25 clergy in the United States. An additional 48,990 members were claimed for the 58 churches in Canada and several hundred members were claimed for churches in France and West Germany. By 1984, the Church claimed 358,503 members, 48 clergy, and 157 parishes in the United States as well as an additional 29,350 members in two congregations in Paris, France and West Germany.

Educational facilities: The Mariavite Academy of Theological Studies, 2803 Tenth Street, Wyandotte, MI 48192-4994.

Periodicals: *The Mariavita Monthly,* 2803 Tenth Street, Wyandotte, Michigan 48192-4994.

Remarks: A number of factors have raised doubt about the accuracy of the facts and figures reported by the Mariavite Old Catholic Church. In spite of its reported growth from 1972 to 1975, observers have been unable to locate any of the congregations affiliated with the Church except the small chapel in Archbishop Zaborowski's residence in Wyandotte, Michigan. Zaborowski has consistently refused to share with inquirers the names and address of any of the claimed parishes or their priests. Doubts have also been raised about Archbishop Zaborowski's ordination and consecration. During the early 1970s he circulated copies of his ordination (1968) and consecration (1972) certificates. They bore the names of Bishop Francis Mazur and Ambrose as prime officiants, and they were on forms bearing the title "Antiqua Ecclesia Romanae Catholicae" (i.e. "Old Roman Catholic Church"). It was supposed by observers (and claimed by Zaborowski) that he had been ordained by the same Bishop Francis Mazur who had been consecrated by Archbishop Carmel Henry Carfora of the North American Old Roman Catholic Church. More recently, Zaborowski has circulated a different set of certificates bearing the title of the Mariavite Old Catholic Church, Province of North America (a name not used until two years after his consecration) and bearing signatures of Archbishop (not bishop) Francis A. Mazur and Archbishop Francis Ignatius Boryszewski as prime officiants. The signatures on the two ordination certificates do not resemble each other in the least. (Archbishop Zaborowski had claimed that he himself had confused the Bishop Mazur consecrated by Carfora and Archbishop Mazur of the Old Catholic Church of Poland.) The earlier ordination certificate also carries no signatures of any other bishops who might have assisted in the ordination. In like measure, Zaborowski claims that Archbishop Boryszewski wished his role in the consecration service suppressed until his death, and hence it was not revealed until 1975. However, the signatures of those bishops whose names appear on both consecration certificates vary in great detail. It should also be noted that even a third ordination certificate exists which claims that Zaborowski was ordained in 1965 by a Roman Catholic bishop, Most Rev. G. Krajenski (living in exile) and signed by Most Rev. Cardinal Wojtyla, Ordinary of the Diocese of Kracow. Neither exist on any registry of Roman Catholic bishops.

Sources: Jerzy Peterkiewicz, *The Third Adam*. London: Oxford University Press, 1975; Robert R. R. Zaborowski, *What Is Mariavitism?* Wyandotte, MI: Ostensoria Publications, 1977; Robert R. Zaborowski, *Catechism.* Wyandotte, MI: Ostensia Publications, 1975; Robert R. Zaborowski, *The Sacred Liturgy.* Wyandotte, MI: Ostensoria Publications, 1975.

★16★
MEXICAN NATIONAL CATHOLIC CHURCH
% Rt. Rev. Emile F. Rodriguez-Fairfield
4011 E. Brooklyn Ave.
East Los Angeles, CA 90022

During the presidency of General Plutarco E. Callas (1924-28), Mexico put into effect provisions of the 1917 Constitution aimed at curbing the political power of the Roman Catholic Church. With Callas' tacit consent, a rival Mexican-controlled Catholic body free from any connection to foreign interests was formed. The leaders turned to Archbishop Carmel Henry Carfora of the North American Old Roman Catholic Church (Rogers) for episcopal orders. On October 17, 1926 Carfora consecrated successively Jose Joaquin Perez y Budar, Antonio Benicio Lopez Sierra, and Macario Lopez y Valdez. Perez y Budar became Primate and Patriarch.

Before returning to Mexico, Bishop Lopez y Valdez visited his family in Los Angeles and contacted a Bishop Roberto T. Gonzalez, pastor of El Hogar de la Verdad, an independent spiritualist church operating within the Mexican community in East Los Angeles. Lopez developed a friendly relationship with Gonzalez. Gonzalez died in 1928, and two years later, Lopez consecrated Gonzalez's successor, Alberto Luis Rodriguez Y Durand. By this act the Mexican National Catholic church was able to extend its territory into Southern California. El Hogar de la Verdad gradually became known as the Old Catholic Orthodox Church of St. Augustine of the Mystical Body of Christ.

Over the next decades, as church-state relations improved in Mexico, the National Church, which by 1928 had claimed 120 priests and parishes in fourteen Mexican states, began to dissolve. The largest remnant united with the Orthodox Church in America and became its Mexican

Exarchate in 1972. Its bishop, Jose Cortes y Olmas was named Exarch. The Los Angeles parish survived as the single American outpost of the Church. In 1955, Bishop Rodriguez, being in poor health, consecrated Emelio Federico Rodriguez y Fairfield as his successor.

In 1962, Fairfield decided to affiliate with the Canonical Old Roman Catholic Church, the American branch of the Old Roman Catholic Church headed by British Archbiship Gerard George Shelley. Following Shelley's death, Fairfield joined Bishop John J. Humphreys in consecrating a new archbishop in 1982. When Shelley's successor, Michael Farrell, resigned a month after his consecration, Fairfield emerged as the senior bishop of the Church. Then in 1983, with the dea th of Jose Cortes y Olmas, Fairfield became the sole possessor of episcopal orders from the Mexican National Catholic Church. On September 13, 1983, he was installed as Archbishop-Primate of the Iglesia Ortodoxa Catolica Apostolica Mexicana.

Membership: Only one parish, in East Los Angeles, California, of the Mexican National Catholic Church remains. It has less than 100 members.

Sources: Paul Schultz, *A History of the Apostolic Succession of Archbishop Emile F. Rodriguez-Fairfield from the Mexican National Catholic Church, Iglesia Ortodoxa Catolica Apostolica Mexicana.* Glendale, CA: The Author, 1983.

★17★
NORTH AMERICAN OLD CATHOLIC CHURCH, ULTRAJECTINE TRADITION
% For My God and My Country
Necedah, WI 54646

The North American Old Catholic Church, Ultrajectine Tradition was formed in the late 1970s by a group of former members of the Roman Catholic Church associated with the Queen of the Holy Rosary Mediatrix of Peace Shrine, an independent shrine at Necedah, Wisconsin, created as a result of the visions of the Virgin Mary seen by Mary Ann Van Hoof. Van Hoof had her first apparition of the Virgin on November 12, 1949, one year after a reported apparition in Lipa City, Philippines. Then on April 7, 1950 (Good Friday), a series of apparitions were announced by the Virgin and as promised occurred on May 28 (Pentecost), May 29, May 30, June 4 (Trinity Sunday), June 16 (Feast of the Sacred Heart), and August 15 (Feast of the Assumption). As word of the apparitions spread, crowds gathered. Over 100,000 people attended the events of August 15, 1950.

On June 24, 1950, the chancery office of the Diocese of LaCrosse (Wisconsin) released information that a study of the apparitions had been initiated. In August, Bishop John Treacy announced that preliminary reports had questioned the validity of the apparitions, and he placed a temporary ban on special religious services at Necedah. He lifted the ban for the announced event on August 15. In spite of the ban, an estimated 30,000 people attended a final apparition on October 7, at which it was claimed that the sun whirled in the sky just as at the more famous site of Marian apparitions at Fatima, Portugal in 1917. On October 18, the group that had grown around Van Hoof published an account of the visions and announced that a shrine was to be built and completed by May 28, 1951, the anniversary of the first public apparition.

In spite of the negative appraisal by Bishop Treacy and an editorial in the Vatican's newspaper in 1951 condemning the visions, the activity at Necedah continued, and people attended the public events at which Van Hoof claimed to be conversing with the Virgin Mary. Finally, in June, 1955, Treacy issued a public statement declaring the revelations at Necedah false and prohibiting all public and private worship at the shrine. Approximately 650 pilgrims attended the August 15, 1955 (Feast of the Assumption), apparition in defiance of Treacy's ban. In September, details of the exhaustive study of the shrine (by then operating under the corporate name For My God and My Country, Inc.) were released. The report attacked Van Hoof as a former spiritualist who had never been a practicing Roman Catholic. While the report of the diocese lessened support, worship at the shrine continued, and efforts were made to have a second study conducted. Finally, in 1969, Bishop F. W. Freking, Treacy's successor as bishop of LaCrosse, agreed to reexamine the case. For a time during the study, the shrine was closed to visitors. In 1970 the commission again produced a negative report, and in June, 1972, Freking warned the corporation officers to cease activities or face church sanctions. Such sanctions were invoked in May, 1975, when seven people were put under an interdict.

The break with the Roman Catholic Church was formally acknowledged in May, 1979, with the presentation to the shrine's supporters of Old Catholic Bishop Edward Michael Stehlik as archbishop and metropolitan of the North American Old Catholic Church, Ultrajectine Tradition. On May 28, 1979, Stehlik dedicated the shrine, twenty-nine years after the first public apparition. The church is at one in doctrine with the Roman Catholic Church, except in its rejection of the authority of the papal office. Stehlik had been consecrated by Bishop Julius Massey of Plainfield, Illinois, pastor of an independent Episcopal Church. Massey had been consecrated by Denver Scott Swain of the American Episcopal Church (now the United Episcopal Church of America).

The North American Old Catholic Church, Ultrajectine Tradition faced one crisis after another. During 1980 Stehlik and the priests he brought around him came under heavy attack in the press for falsifying their credentials. Stehlik's assistant, Bishop David E. Shotts, formerly of the Independent Ecumenical Catholic Church, was arrested for violation of parole from an earlier conviction for child molestation. Then in January, 1981, Stehlik quit the church, denounced the apparitions as a hoax, and

returned to the Roman Catholic Church. He was succeeded by Francis diBenedetto, whom he had consecrated. However, on May 29, 1983, diBenedetto, in the midst of a service at the shrine, announced his resignation, further labeled the shrine a hoax, and returned to the Roman Catholic Church. In the wake of diBenedetto's leaving, a large number of the adherents also quit and returned to communion with the Roman Catholic Church.

On May 18, 1894, Mary Ann Van Hoof died. Without her leadership, the future of the shrine is in doubt, as is the future of the North American Old Catholic Church. Over the years the shrine itself has developed into a complex of structures. In line with a strong anti-abortion polemic, the Seven Sorrows of Our Sorrowful Mother Infant's Home was created to assist unwed mothers and unwanted children. The construction on the St. Francis of Assisi Home for Unfortunate Men continued through 1984.

Membership: Not reported. As of 1984 over 300 members of the Church resided in the Necedah area with several thousand suporters (none organized into parishes) scattered around the United States and Canada.

Periodicals: *Shrine Newsletter,* For My God and My Country, Necedah, WI 54646.

Sources: Swan, Henry H., *My Work at Necedah.* 4 Vols. Necedah, WI: For My God and My Country, 1959; Mary Ann Van Hoof, *The Passion and Death of Our Lord Jesus Christ.* Necedah, WI: For My God and My Country, 1975; Mary Ann Van Hoof, *Revelations and Messages.* 2 Vols. Necedah, WI: For My God and My Country, 1971, 1978.

★18★

NORTH AMERICAN OLD ROMAN CATHOLIC CHURCH (ROGERS)

% Most Rev. Archbishop James H. Rogers
118-09 Farmer Blvd.
St. Albans, NY 11412

The North American Old Roman Catholic Church (Rogers) dates to October 4, 1916, when the Duc de Landas Berghes, in the United States to escape confinement in England during World War I, consecrated the Rev. Carmel Henry Carfora at Waukegan, Illinois. The Italian-born Carfora had come to the United States to do Roman Catholic mission work among the immigrants in West Virginia, but by 1911 had broken with Rome. In 1912 he sought consecration from Bishop Paulo Miragalia Gulotti, who had been consecrated by Archbishop Joseph Rene Vilatte, and proceeded to form several independent Old Catholic parishes. After his second consecration, he broke with Bishop W. H. Francis Brothers, also consecrated by Landes Berghes, settled in Chicago and began to organize his own jurisdiction, which he named the North American Old Roman Catholic Church. (Brothers organized the Old Catholic Church in America.)

During his lengthy life, Carfora was able to build a substantial church which may have had as many as 50,000 members. He absorbed numerous independent parishes, many of an ethnic nature. He also consecrated numerous bishops (at least thirty) most of whom left him to found their own jurisdictions, both in the United States and in foreign lands. In the mid 1920s a shortlived union with the American Catholic Church was attempted under the name The Holy Catholic Church in America.

Even before Carfora's death in 1958 the North American Old Roman Catholic Church began to collapse, and remnants of what was once a growing ecclesiastical unit now exist as several small jurisdictions. Most have simply disappeared. Splintering began with Samuel Durlin Benedict, who left Carfora a few years after his 1921 consecration to found the Evangelical Catholic Church of New York, a small group that did not survive his death in 1945. In 1924 Carfora consecrated Edwin Wallace Hunter, who in 1929 assumed the title of archbishop of the Holy Catholic Church of the Apostles in the Diocese of Louisiana. This church also died with its founder in 1942. In 1931 Carfora consecrated James Christian Crummey, who, with Carfora's blessing, founded the Universal Episcopal Communion, an ecumenical organization that attempted to unite various Christian bodies (with little success). Crummey broke relations in 1944 and died five years later. The Communion did not continue into the 1950s. This pattern continued throughout Carfora's lifetime. Over twenty jurisdictions trace their lineage to Carfora.

The pattern of Carfora's consecrating priests beyond any ecclesiastical substance to support them, followed by their leaving and taking their meager diocese to create an independent jurisdiction, continued throughout Carfora's life. The major loss of strength by Carfora's N.A.O.R.C.C., however, came in 1952 when thirty parishes under Bishop Michael Donahue, moved, with Carfora's blessing, into the Ukrainian Orthodox Church. Donohue was received as a mitered archpriest.

Carfora was succeeded as head of the North American Old Roman Catholic Church by Cyrus A. Starkey, his Coadjutor, but before the year was out, the synod met and set aside Starkey's succession. It elected Hubert A. Rogers (1887-1976) who had served for five years as Coadjutor but had been deposed by Carfora just a few months before his death. Rogers, while proving a most capable leader, was a West Indian. Most of the nonblack priests and members refused to accept his position and withdrew. This final splintering of the Church left it predominantly black in membership, which it remains. H. A. Rogers was succeeded by his son James Hubert Rogers, the present Archbishop.

The N. A. O. R. C. C. advocates a faith in complete agreement with pre-Vatican I Roman Catholicism: "The Old Roman Catholic Church has always used the same ritual and liturgy as the early Church practiced, abiding by the same doctrines and dogmas; following the exact teaching given by the Apostles of Christ, and continuing through valid historical succession down to the present time." In one point it follows Old Catholic rather than Roman Catholic practice: Carfora married, and a married priesthood is allowed at all levels in the N.A.O.R.C.C. The practice has been passed on to those churches that derived from it.

Membership: In 1965 the Church reported 30 parishes, 18,500 members, and 112 clergy. However, by 1982 it could report only 4 parishes, 750 members, and 15 clergy.

Periodicals: *The Augustinian*, Box 1647, G.P.O., Brooklyn, NY 11202.

Sources: Jonathan Trela, *A History of the North American Old Roman Catholic Church*. Scranton, PA: The Author, 1979.

★19★
NORTH AMERICAN OLD ROMAN CATHOLIC CHURCH (SCHWEIKERT)

% Most Rev. John E. Schweikert
4200 N. Kedvale
Chicago, IL 60641

The North American Old Roman Catholic Church (Schweikert) is one of several Old Catholic jurisdictions which claims to the legitimate successor to the North American Old Roman Catholic Church formed by Archbishop Carmel Henry Carfora. Archbishop John E. Schweikert bases his claim upon his consecration by Bishop Sigismund Vipartes a Lithuanian bishop who had served in Westville, Illinois, under Bishop Carfora beginning in 1944.

Archbishop Carfora died in 1958 and was succeeded by Cyrus A. Starkey, his coadjutor. However, the synod of the N.A.O.R.C.C. put aside his succession in favor of Hubert A. Rogers, who had been Coadjutor until a few months before Carfora passed away. Starkey left the N.A.O.R.C.C. in 1960, and Richard A. Marchenna, claimed that Starkey named him as his successor (see Old Roman Catholic Church (Marchenna)). According to the records of the N.A.O.R.C.C., Schweikert was consecrated by Marchenna on June 8, 1958.

Following Starkey's death in 1965, Schweikert asserted a claim to be his successor against that of Marchenna. He also claimed that Vipartes, not Marchenna, consecrated him in 1958. Through Vipartes (consecrated by Carfora in 1944) and Starkey, Schweikert claims to be Carfora's legitimate successor.

Headquarters for the church are in Chicago in a building complex that also houses a sisterhood of nuns: the Order of Our Most Blessed Lady, Queen of Peace. The sisters operate a school for retarded children. Belief and practice follow that of the North American Old Roman Catholic

Church, though Bishop Schweikert is discontinuing the practice of an unpaid clergy and is promoting a more democratic church structure. In 1962 Schweikert consecrated Robert Ritchie as bishop of the Old Catholic Church of Canada, founded in 1948 by the Rt. Rev. George Davis. The two jurisdictions remain in communion.

Membership: In 1982 the North American Old Roman Catholic Church (Schweikert) reported 130 parishes and missions, 62,383 members, and 150 clergy, figures that reflect the continuing increase in numbers reported during the last decade.

Remarks: It must be noted that during the past decade researchers have been unable to locate any parishes under Archbishop Schweikert's jurisdiction other than the single parish and affiliated mission, both in the Chicago area, over which he serves as pastor. Archbishop Schweikert has consistently refused to reveal the names of any priests or the addresses of any parishes under his jurisdiction.

★20★

NORTH AMERICAN OLD ROMAN CATHOLIC CHURCH-UTRECHT SUCCESSION
% Rt. Rev. E. R. Verostek
3519 Roosevelt Ave.
Richmond, CA 94805

The North American Old Roman Catholic Church-Utrecht succession dates to 1936 when Bishop A. D. Bell, who had been consecrated in 1935 by Archbishop W. H. Francis Brothers of the Old Catholic Church in America, accepted reconsecration from Archbishop Carmel Henry Carfora of the North American Old Roman Catholic Church. In 1938 Bell consecrated E. R. Verostek who succeeded Bell. Then in 1943 Carfora commissioned Elsie Armstrong Smith (d. 1983) as Abbess of a new order, the Missionary Sister of St. Francis. As an independent order the sisters have conducted a ministry of visiting the sick, offering intercessory prayers and service to the Church--making vestments and publishing pamphlets and prayerbooks. Over the years the congregations under their leadership separated from the main body of the North American Old Roman Catholic Church, though it continues to follow its lead in theology and practice. The Missionary Sisters are headquartered in Mira Loma, California where they maintain a chapel.

Membership: In the early 1980s, the Church reported 6 parishes with less than 200 members.

★21★

OLD CATHOLIC CHURCH IN AMERICA (BROTHERS)
% Metropolitan Hilarion
1905 S. Third St.
Austin, TX 78704

The Old Catholic Church in America is one of the oldest independent Catholic bodies in the United States having been founded in 1917 by W. H. Francis Brothers (1887-1979). Brothers, prior of a small abbey under the patronage of the Protestant Episcopal Church, began to move under the umbrella of several independent Catholic bishops. He was ordained in 1910 by Archbishop Joseph Rene Vilatte and the next year took the abbey into the Polish Old Catholic Church headed by Bishop J. F. Tichy. Tichy resigned due to ill health, and in 1914 Brothers became bishop-elect of the now miniscule body which had lost most of its members to the Polish National Catholic Church. Then Brothers met the Duc de Landas Berghes, the Austrian Old Catholic bishop, spending the war years in the United States. He consecrated Brothers and then Carmel Henry Carfora (later to found the North American Old Roman Catholic Church) on two successive days in October 1916.

Brothers broke with both Landas Berghes and Carfora, renamed the Polish Old Catholic Church and assumed the titles of Archbishop and Metropolitan. He began to build his jurisdiction by appointing bishops to work within ethnic communities. He consecrated Antonio Rodriguez (Portuguese) and attracted Bishops Stanislaus Mickiewicz (Lithuanian) and Joseph Zielonka (Polish) into the Church. Most importantly, former Episcopal Bishop William Montgomery Brown joined his college of bishops. The church grew and prospered, and in 1927 the Episcopal Synod of the Polish Mariavite Church gave Brothers oversight of the Mariavites in the United States. In 1936, the Church reported 24 parishes and 5,470 members.

By the 1950s, the once prosperous Church began to suffer from the Americanization of its ethnic parishes and the defection of his bishops. In 1962 Brothers took the remnant of his jurisdiction in to the Russian Orthodox Church and accepted the title of mitred archpriest. However, five years later he withdrew from the Russian Church, and reconstituted the Old Catholic Church in America. He consecrated Joseph MacCormick and his successor. Brothers retired in 1977, and MacCormack organized the Synod which now administers the affairs of the Church. He also began the slow process of rebuilding the jurisdiction. An important step was the acceptance of the Old Catholic Church of Texas, Inc., an independent jurisdiction formerly associated with the Liberal Catholic Church International, and its leader Robert L. Williams, Metropolitan Hilarion, into the church in 1975. The Old Catholic Church in America follows the beliefs of the Roman Catholic Church, prior to Vatican II, with the exception of a belief in papal infallibility. Both Western and Eastern rites are allowed.

Membership: In 1984 the Church claimed 4 congregations, 500 members and 12 clergy. Affiliated congregations in Yugoslavia have approximately 2,000 members.

Sources: William H. F. Brothers, *Concerning the Old Catholic Church in America.* 1925; William H. F. Brothers, *The Old Catholic Church in America and Anglican Orders.* 1925; John LoBue, "An Appreciation, Archbishop William Henry Francis Brothers, 1887-1979." *The Good Shepherd.* 1980.

★22★

OLD CATHOLIC CHURCH IN NORTH AMERICA (CATHOLICATE OF THE WEST)
% Rev. Dr. Charles V. Hearn
2210 Wilshire Blvd., Suite 582
Santa Monica, CA 90403

The Old Catholic Church in North America was established in 1950 by Grant Timothy Billet and several Old Catholic bishops. Billet had been consecrated by Earl Anglin James of Archbishop Carmel Henry Carfora's North American Old Roman Catholic Church. Billet established headquarters in York, Pennsylvania, and organized the interdenominational American Ministerial Association which attracted a wide variety of clergy under its umbrella. During the 1970s, he reported a membership of the Church at approximately 6,000, a highly inflated figure. Billet died in 1981. He was succeeded by the present Archbishop and Patriarch, Charles V. Hearn, a psychotherapist and noted counselor on alcoholism. He reorganized the Church and reincorporated both it and the American Ministerial Association in California. The church generally follows Roman Catholic doctrine and practice. However, celibacy is not a requirement for the priesthood.

Membership: In 1984 the Church reported 26 churches in the United States with affiliated work in seven countries. There were 43 clergy and 188 members.

Educational facilities: Trinity Hall College & Seminary, Louisville, Kentucky and Denver, Colorado.

★23★

OLD CATHOLIC CHURCH-UTRECHT SUCCESSION
% Most Rev. Roy G. Bauer
Box 1981
Boston, MA 02105

Bishop Roy G. Bauer was consecrated in 1976 by Bishop Armand C. Whitehead of the United Old Catholic Church and Bishop Thomas Sargent of the Community of Catholic Churches, but served as a bishop under Archbishop Richard A. Marchenna of the Old Roman Catholic Church. In 1977, he, along with Bishops John Dominic Fesi, of the Traditional Roman Catholic Church in the Americas, and Andrew Lawrence Vanore, accused

Marchenna of usurping authority, and resigned their positions in the church. Bauer together with Vanore went on to found the Old Roman Catholic Church-Utrecht Succession, following the faith and practice of the parent body. They were later joined by Bishop LeBlanc of Holy Annunciation Monastery. Bauer was elected Presiding Archbishop in 1979.

The Church accepts the Baltimore Catechism and, in general, pre-Vatican II Roman Catholic theology with the exception of the dogmas of papal infallibility, the Immaculate Conception, and the Bodily Assumption of the Virgin Mary. The doctrines on the Virgin Mary are acceptable as pious belief. The Church is headquartered in Boston, and parishes are located in Denver, Colorado;Washington, D.C.; Orlando, Florida; and several locations in Massachusetts. There is one mission in Japan. In 1984 Bishop Bauer affiliated with the Patriarchial Synod of the Orthodox Catholic Church America, an association of independent Orthodox and Catholic bishops.

Membership: In 1984, the Church reported 12 congregations and approximately 1,000 members. The Archbishop is assisted by 2 bishops and 16 priests.

★24★

OLD ROMAN CATHOLIC CHURCH IN NORTH AMERICA
% Most Rev. Francis P. Facione
3827 Old Creek Rd.
Troy, MI 48084

The Old Roman Catholic Church in North America was formed in 1963 as the Old Roman Catholic Church (English Rite) by Bishop Robert Alfred Burns. Burns was ordained in 1948 by Archbishop Carmel Henry Carfora of the North American Old Roman Catholic Church. He left the N.A.O.R.C.C. and joined the Old Roman Catholic Church. On April 14, 1961 he was appointed Metropolitan Vicar General by the Church's Presiding Archbishop Richard A. Marchenna. A month later he was elected bishop-auxillary and consecrated on October 9, 1961. He left Marchenna's jurisdiction in 1963 and aligned himself with British Bishop W. A. Barrington-Evans, Primate of the Old Roman Catholic Church (English Rite), a small British jurisdiction. Burns was appointed Archbishop of Chicago. In 1973, the year before his death, Burns reported to the *Yearbook of American Churches* that there were 186 churches, 65,128 members and 201 clergy in his jurisdiction. In fact, he had only a few clergy, most of whom were bishops, and only one or two parishes.

After Archbishop Burns' death in 1974, a Synod elected Bishop Andrew Johnston-Cantrell, whom Burns had consecrated in 1973, to succeed him. That same synod elected Dr. Francis C. Facione, a professor at Wayne State University, as Suffragan Bishop. Bishop Facione was consecrated several weeks later on St. Andrew's Day. Early in 1975, Johnston-Cantrell resigned, due to health reasons, and Bishop Facione was elected by the Synod to a ten-year term as Presiding Bishop. He was also appointed ordinary of the newly created Diocese of Michigan and the Central States.

The tranquility of the Old Roman Catholic Church (English Rite) was disturbed in 1978 by publicity surrounding the activities of Chicago Bishop Richard A. Bernowski. Bernowski, who had been accorded canonical recognition for an independent ministry in 1977, was accused of a variety of immoral and illegal actions in the Chicago press. The council of bishops attempted a formal ecclesiastical inquiry into the allegations but were refused any cooperation by Bernowski. The council of bishops, accordingly, withdrew their recognition of him. Then in October 1978, Bernowski was shot to death in front of his home. As the investigation into his death proceeded, Bernowski was revealed to be the manager of a bar in suburban Chicago, head of a male prostitution ring, and the "front" for a crime syndicate. Operator of a state-funded program for youth, Bernowski had originally come under investigation because of a beating that had taken place at St. Martin's Center on Chicago's southside.

Membership: Not reported.

★25★

OLD ROMAN CATHOLIC CHURCH (HAMEL)
% H. H. Claudius I
Box 2608, Station D
Ottawa, ON, Canada K1P 5W7

The Old Roman Catholic Church (Hamel) was founded by Earl Anglin James who had been consecrated as Bishop of Toronto by Archbishop Carmel Henry Carfora of the North American Old Roman Catholic Church in 1945. The following year, however, he associated himself with Hugh George de Willmott Newman (Mar Georgius) of the Catholicate of the West. During the summer of 1946, Mar Georgius had extended the territory of the Catholicate to the United States through W. D. de Ortega Maxey. In November, by proxy, he enthroned James as Exarch of the Catholicate of the West in Canada. James was given the title Mar Laurentius and became Archbishop and Metropolitan of Acadia.

Mar Laurentius led a colorful career as an archbishop. He claimed a vast following, at times in the millions. He collected degrees, titles and awards, and as freely gave them out to those associated with him. He became affiliated with a wide variety of international associations. In 1965, he consecrated Guy F. Hamel and named him his coadjutor with right of succession. After James' retirement in 1966, Hamel was enthroned as the Universal Patriarch and assumed the title of H. H. Claudius I.

Guy F. Claude Hamel became one of the most controversial figures in Old Catholic circles. He was ordained in 1964 by Bishop William Pavlik of the Ontario Old Roman Catholic Church. However, before the year

was over, Pavlik excommunicated him. Hamel then spent a short period under Michael Collin, a French prelate who had assumed the title of Pope Clement XV. He then went under Mar Laurentius.

After becoming head of the Old Roman Catholic Church, Hamel began to appoint an international hierarchy, a list of which was published in the April 1968 issue of *C. P. S. News*, the Church's periodical. The list included not only most of the Old Catholic bishops in the United States and Canada (many of whom have taken pains to denounce Hamel) but also many people who were never associated with him--the Rev. Arthur C. Piepkorn (Lutheran theologian), Archbishop Irene (Orthodox Church in America), and Bishop Arthur Litchtenberger (Protestant Episcopal Church). The publication of this list, which enraged many whose names were listed and amused others who recognized the names of many long-dead prelates, was followed in 1970 by a conviction for fraud in an Ontario court. In the years since the conviction, Hamel has continued to lead the Old Roman Catholic Church, but lost most of the genuine support he had gained prior to 1970.

The Old Roman Catholic Church follows the creeds of the early Christian Church and the Pre-Vatican II rituals. All seven sacraments are administered, and devotion to the Virgin Mary, as well as the veneration of images and relics of the saints is espoused.

Membership: Not reported.

Periodicals: *C. S. P. World News*, Box 2608, Station D, Ottawa, Ontario, Canada K1P 5W7.

Sources: *Disciplinary Canons and Constitutions of the Old Roman Catholic Church (Orthodox Orders.* Havelock, Ont.: C.S.P.News, 1967; Guy F. Claude Hamel, *Broken Wings.* Cornwall, Ont.: Vesta Publications, 1980 Guy F. Claude Hamel, *The Lord Jesus and the True Mystic.* Toronto: Congregation of St. Paul, (1968).

★26★

OLD ROMAN CATHOLIC CHURCH (MARCHENNA)
% Most Rev. Derek Lang
2103 S. Portland St.
Los Angeles, CA 90007

The Old Roman Catholic Church was founded by Richard A. Marchenna who had been consecrated by Archbishop Carmel Henry Carfora in 1941. Marchenna's consecration began a stormy relationship to the North American Old Roman Catholic Church and its first Archbishop. In 1948 Carfora deposed him, but he was reinstated two years later. Then in 1952 he was once more deposed and excommunicated. This time he left and took several of the clergy and four parishes. He entered into communion with Gerard George Shelley. Marchenna had consecrated Shelley in 1950, after which Shelley returned to England where he succeeded B. M. Williams, who as Archbishop of Caer-Glow, claimed to be the direct British successor to Archbishop Arnold Harris Mathew. He called his group the Old Roman Catholic Church in England. Marchenna stayed in communion with Shelley until 1974.

Marchenna also claims that Cyrus A. Starkey, the former Coadjutor to Carfora, who had left the North American Old Roman Catholic Church) after Carfora's death, asked Marchenna to assume the duties as Supreme Primate of the "Old Roman Catholic Church." Thus through Starkey, Marchenna asserted a claim to Carfora's ecclesiastical succession.

Marchenna had slowly put together one of the larger Old Catholic jurisdictions. Then in 1974, he consecrated a homosexual priest, Fr. Robert Clement, head of the Eucharistic Catholic Church. That action angered many of his bishops and priests and led to considerable splintering of the Old Roman Catholic Church.

The Old Roman Catholic Church follows the belief and practice of the North American Old Roman Catholic Church (Rogers), differing from it only in matters of administration. Bishop Marchenna often used Old Roman Catholic Church, Ultrajectine, as the title of his church. "Ultrajectine" refers to the anti-ultra montane (anti-papal) position of the Old Catholic Church of Utrecht. The essentials of the tradition are as follows: 1) conscience (not authority) is the final arbiter of moral and ethical questions and 2) unity with the Apostolic See in Rome in what is de fide (matters of faith) as well as fidelity to the Roman pontiff as the center of Christian unity with no acknowledgement of the Pope's infallibility. Marchenna died in 1984 and was succeeded by Derek Lang, who he had consecrated and named Coadjutor.

Membership: The group is estimated to have approximately a half-dozen parishes, double that number of clergy, and as many as several hundred members.

★27★

OLD ROMAN CATHOLIC CHURCH, ARCHDIOCESE OF CHICAGO (FRIS)
Current address not obtained for this edition.

In 1970 Archbishop Robert A. Burns, of the Old Roman Catholic Church (English Rite), now the Old Roman Catholic Church in North America, consecrated Howard Fris, giving him the right to succession. However, three years later he removed Fris and replaced him with Andrew Johnston-Cantrell. Fris proceeded to found his own Church and took some of Burns' small following with him. After Burns' death, the corporation of the Old Roman Catholic Church (English Rite) lapsed, as no one filed the annual reports during the bickering and in-fighting of that period. Fris revived the corporation and had it assigned to himself.

It is unknown if Burns knew of Fris' personal problems at the time of the consecration in 1970, but there is no doubt that they led to his deposition. They did not stop his continuing to function as the leader of his small flock. Though an alcoholic himself, in the late 1970s Fris opened St. Teresa's Manor, described as a home for alcoholics and wayward men. Because of Fris' ecclesiastical connections, social service agencies in the city began to refer men to the Manor. Then in 1979 Fris was arrested for contributing to the sexual delinquency of a child and the theft of credit cards. In the publicity accompanying his arrest and conviction, it was discovered that both of the priests working with him at the manor also had long records of arrest and conviction for felonies. Fris died in 1981, reportedly of cirrhosis of the liver.

Fris' conviction and the public scandal accompanying it did not destroy his jurisdiction, and he continued to lead his diocese. He performed at least one consecration, and after his death, his coadjutor John Kenelly, succeeded him. St. Teresa's Manor was closed, but Bishop Kenelly heads the Missionaries of St. Jude who minister to the residents of a private hotel for the mentally disturbed, alcoholics, and elderly, located on the north side of Chicago.

Membership: In 1979 the Archdiocese claimed 13 clergy and 2 parishes. It considers the residents of the hotel as lay members.

Sources: *Old Catholic Church (Utrecht Succession)*. Chicago, Old Catholic Press of Chicago, (1980).

★28★

OLD ROMAN CATHOLIC CHURCH (ENGLISH RITE) AND THE ROMAN CATHOLIC CHURCH OF THE ULTRAJECTINE TRADITION
% Most Rev. Robert Lane
4416 N. Malden
Chicago, IL 60640

A single church body with two corporate names, the Old Roman Catholic Church (English Rite) and the Roman Catholic Church of the Ultrajectine Tradition is headed by Bishop Robert W. Lane. Lane, a priest in the Old Roman Catholic Church (English Rite) headed by Archbishop Robert A. Burns, was consecrated by Howard Fris on September 15, 1974. Both Burns and Lane perceived that Fris had failed to follow the correct form for the ceremony, and later that same day, Burns reconsecrated Lane.

Burns died two months later. Lane left Fris's jurisdiction and placed himself under Archbishop Richard A. Marchenna of the Old Roman Catholic Church. Meanwhile, during the last year of his life, Burns had allowed the corporation papers of his jurisdiction to lapse. Lane learned of the situation and assumed control of the corporate title. He was at this time serving as pastor of St. Mary Magdelen Old Catholic Church in Chicago.

According to Lane, in 1978 Marchenna offered him the position of co-adjutor with right to succession. He had, however, developed some disagreements with Marchenna and both refused the position and left the Old Roman Catholic Church. He had previously incorporated his work for Marchenna in Chicago as the Roman Catholic Church of the Ultrajectine Tradition. Upon leaving the Old Roman Catholic Church, Lane formed an independent jurisdiction which continues both former corporations.

The Old Roman Catholic Church (English Rite) and the Roman Catholic Church of the Ultrajectine Tradition are thus two corporations designating one community of faith maintaining a Catholic way of life. It is like the Roman Catholic Church in most of its belief and practice. It retains the seven sacraments and describes itself as "One, Holy, Catholic, Apostolic, and Universal." It differs in that it uses both the Tridentine Latin mass (in both Latin and English translation) and the Ordo Novo. It has also dropped many of the regulations which govern Roman Catholic clergy, most prominently the provision prohibiting the marriage of clergy.

Membership: In 1984 Bishop Lane reported four congregations in the United States, including one each in Chicago; New York City; Nashville, Tennessee; and Anchorage, Alaska. In addition, a congregation in Hamburg, Germany and a mission in Poland were reported.

Educational facilities: Seminary of St. Francis of Assisi, Chicago, Illinois (currently inactive).

★29★
OLD ROMAN CATHOLIC CHURCH IN THE U. S. (HOUGH)
(Defunct)

Joseph Damien Hough, while under the jurisdiction of Bishop Richard A. Marchenna of the Old Roman Catholic Church, formed a congregation of Oblates of St. Martin of Tours and was designated bishop-elect in 1964. However, following a dispute with Marchenna in 1966, Hough obtained Marchenna's permission to withdraw, and founded the Old Roman Catholic Church in the U.S. In early 1969 Hough was consecrated by Bishop Robert Raleigh of the American Catholic Church (Malabar Succession) with right of succession. Following Raleigh's death, Hough, being the only ultrajectine bishop in California, gathered the faithful into his reorganized church, which combines both Marchenna's and Raleigh's traditions. The ultrajectine element predominates, and worship and belief follow the ultrajectine tradition. Headquarters were established in Venice, California, and all members of the church resided in the state. Both Roman and ultrajectine Catholics were admitted to the services and holy communion. Bishop Hough was in communion with the Old Catholic Church in England, then under Bishop Gerard George Shelley. Hough retired

in the early 1980s, and the jurisdiction he headed dissolved.

★30★
ONTARIO OLD ROMAN CATHOLIC CHURCH
% Most Rev. Nelson D. Hillyer
5 Manor Rd., W. Suite 5
Toronto, ON, Canada M5P 1E6

The Onatario Old Roman Catholic Church was founded in 1962 following the consecration of William Pavlik (d. 1965) by Archbishop Richard A. Marchenna of the Old Roman Catholic Church. For a brief period Pavlik was in communion with Bishop Robert A. Burns of the Old Roman Catholic Church (English Rite), but eventually became autonomous. The faith and practice of the Old Roman Catholic Church are continued. The ceremonies are like those of the Roman Catholic Church before the Second Vatican Council. The present head of the Church, Archbishop Nelson D. Hillyer, was consecrated by Pavlik in 1964 and served as coadjutor until Pavlik's death.

Membership: In 1970 the Church reported 3 parishes, one each in Toronto, Erie, Pennsylvania and Niagara, New York. At that time, there was one bishop, three priests and three candidates for holy orders.

★31★
OUR LADY OF THE ROSES, MARY HELP OF MOTHERS SHRINE
Box 52
Bayside, NY 11361

Our Lady of the Roses, Mary Help of Mothers Shrine emerged from the visionary experiences of Veronica Lueken (b. July 12, 1923), a New York housewife, which began in 1968. Initial visitations from St. Therese of Lisieux (1873-1897) were followed on April 7, 1970, by a visit from the Blessed Virgin Mary. The Virgin announced that beginning April 7, 1970, nine years to the day after the initial apparitions of the Virgin to some children at Garabandal, Spain, she would begin regular visits to Lueken. As announced, she appeared to Lueken outside St. Robert Bellarmine Catholic Church in Bayside, Queens, New York. At the first apparition, the Virgin announced she would return on the eve of the major feast days of the church, especially those dedicated to her. She requested that a shrine and basilica be erected on the grounds occupied by St. Robert's. She revealed herself as "Our Lady of the Roses, Mary Help of Mothers," and designated Lueken as her voicebox to disseminate the future messages.

The messages have focused upon the denouement of many modern trends, especially changes within the Roman Catholic Church. Prediction of an imminent chastisement of the world on the level of the destruction of Sodom and Gomorrah or the flood in Noah's time have added an urgency to the warnings against doctrinal and moral disintegration. Admonitions have been given against abortion, the occult, immodest dress, and freemasonry. Within the church, the messages have denounced the taking of communion in the hand instead of the mouth, the Catholic Pentecostal Movement, the use of recent Bible translations (which replaced the Douay-Rheims version), and religious textbooks which omit vital teachings of the Church.

As the apparitions continued, Lueken's following grew. The Roman Catholic Diocese of Brooklyn instituted an investigation and, in an official statement, the chancery office denied any miraculous or sacred qualities to the apparitions and messages. However, the crowds attending the frequent vigils grew beyond the lawn of St. Robert's and into neighboring yards. In April 1975 a restraining order against any outside vigils was obtained, and during the following month St. Robert's refused the use of the building for vigils. This crisis forced the moving of the site away from the location of the mandated shrine. Since that time, gatherings have been held at Flushing Meadows Park in Queens.

The break with the Roman Catholic Church was followed by continued polemics. The messages have become increasingly critical of the church. In the fall of 1975, the messages endorsed the idea, popular among some traditionalist Catholics, that an imposter had been substituted for Pope Paul VI. Periodic denounciations of the apparitions came from various Catholic bishops, especially those whose members continued to frequent the shrine. Renewed attempts to vindicate the miraculous nature of the apparitions have centered upon successful prophecies of events, such as the New York blackout and the death of Pope John Paul I and a set of unusual photographs which show what many people believe to be supernatural lights and manifestations. The Bayside apparitions have been widely publicized, and accounts of the events and reprints of the messages have appeared in numerous independent Marian publications. Support for the apparitions has come from the Center of Our Lady of the Smile in Lewiston, Maine; the Apostles of Our Lady in Lansing, Michigan; Faithful and True, a publishing center in Amherst, Massachusetts; and *Santa Maria*, an independent periodical published in Ottawa, Canada. For several years (1973-77), the Order of Saint Michael, a Catholic lay group in Quebec, Canada, supported Lueken in its quarterly publication *Michael*, but the group broke with her after a disagreement.

Lueken withdrew from her followers and the public during the mid-1970s. She speaks to no one except her closest followers, though she regularly appears at the site of the apparitions. At such times she is surrounded by a cadre of male followers distinguished by their white berets. Women followers wear blue berets.

Membership: Not reported. Depending upon the weather, as many as several thousand people attend the vigils in Bayside. Schedules are publicized around the United States and Canada. Literature is mailed to many thousands across North America, though the majority remain otherwise members of the Roman Catholic Church.

Sources: de Paul, Vincent, *The Abominations of Desolations: AntiChrist Is Here Now*. St. Louis, MO: The Author, 1975; Grant, Robert, "War of the Roses" in *Rolling Stones*, no. 113 (February 21, 1980), pp. 42-46; *Our Lady of the Roses, Mary Help of Mothers*. Lansing, MI: Apostles of Our Lady, 1980.

★32★
POLISH CATHOLIC CHURCH
(Defunct)

The Polish Catholic Church existed throughout most of the twentieth century as one remnant of the organization begun by independent Polish Bishop Stephen Kaminski which did not join with the Polish National Catholic Church. Kaminiski died without designating a successor or consecrating a bishop for his jurisdiction. Several of his priests, however, continued to serve their parishes awaiting a new opportunity to reestablish Kaminski's diocese. One such priest was Francis Ignatius Boryszewski. During the 1920s, Boryszewski worked under Archbishop Carmel Henry Carfora of the North American Old Roman Catholic Church (Rogers) but in 1927 affiliated with the American Catholic Church, headed by Archbishop Frederick E. J. Lloyd. Like Kaminski, Lloyd had been consecrated by Archbishop Joseph Rene Vilatte. In 1928 Boryszewski began a new parish in New York City, St. Peter and St. Paul Polish Catholic Church. The following year Bishop Lloyd, assisted by Bishops Gregory Lines and Daniel Hinton, consecrated Boryszewski to head an independent Polish Catholic Church in communion with the American Catholic Church. (It appears that Polish Mariavite Bishop J. M. P. Prochniewski consecrated Boryszewski a second time in a separate ceremony in 1930.)

The Polish Catholic Church followed Roman faith and practice but rejected the authority of the Roman Catholic Church. The small jurisdiction never grew very large, but Bishop Boryszewski continued to pastor the church in New York City until his death in the 1970s.

Sources: *Fifth Year Book*. New York: St. Peter and St. Paul Polish Catholic Church, 1933; *Church Directory and Year Book*. New York: St. Peter and St. Paul Polish Catholic Church, 1933.

★33★
POLISH OLD CATHOLIC CHURCH IN AMERICA
(Defunct)

The Polish Old Catholic Church in America derived from the Polish Mariavite Church. The Mariavite movement dates from 1893 when Sister Felicia (Maria Franciska Kozlowska), a member of the Third Order of St. Francis, a Roman Catholic order, claimed to have had a vision of the Blessed Virgin. In the vision she was told to establish a mixed order of men and women dedicated to the Blessed Virgin. Thus Sister Felicia founded the Mariavites and the order spread, carried by its strong mystical element. Polish Roman Catholic bishops denounced the vision and labeled it hallucinatory. They ordered the disbanding of the Mariavites, but the members refused to obey. They were excommunicated in 1906. They found support from the Russian Church and were eventually able to obtain priestly orders from the Old Catholic Church at Utrecht. Denied a place in the Roman Catholic Church, the order transformed into a large denomination. Freed from Roman authority, they made several innovations on traditional Roman Catholic practices. They ordained females to the priesthood and episcopacy. They placed a great emphasis upon the veneration of the Virgin. It is estimated that over a half million Mariavites can be found in Poland.

During the first decades of the twentieth century, Mariavites began to migrate to the United States. Many joined the Polish Old Catholic Church of America, founded in 1913 by Joseph Zielonka, a former priest of the Polish National Catholic Church. Zielonka sought consecration from Paolo Miragalia Gulotti, an independent Italian bishop. In 1925 Zielonka brought his jurisdiction into the Old Catholic Church in America, headed by Archbishop W. H. Francis Brothers. After fifteen years with Brothers, Zielonka left the Old Catholic Church in America and established the Old Catholic Archdiocese for the Americas and Europe. In 1960 the church had 22 parishes and 7,200 members.

In 1961 Zielonka died and was succeeded by his suffragan Peter A. Zurawetzky, a Ukrainian by birth. His leadership was immediately questioned by Fr. Felix Starazewski, pastor of the parish in South River, New Jersey, who claimed to be Zielonka's true successor. Many of the Polish parishes, opposed to Zurawetzky's attempt to make the Church more inclusive followed Starazewski in founding the Polish Old Catholic Church in America.

In the decades since its founding, the church, consisting originally of a few parishes in the northeast (primarily New Jersey and Massachusetts), found it was unable to overcome the forces of Americanization and a mobile society, and the parishes declined in strength. No evidence of the Polish Old Catholic Church in America had been found during the 1980s, and it is presumed to have ceased to exist.

★34★
POLISH NATIONAL CATHOLIC CHURCH
% Most Rev. Francis C. Rowinski
529 E. Locust St.
Scranton
Scranton, PA 18505

In the last decades of the nineteenth century, nationalistic enthusiasms engulfed the Polish communities in the U.S.

Tension developed from the assignment of non-Polish priests to predominantly Polish parishes. Efforts directed toward autonomy developed in Chicago, Buffalo, and Scranton. In Chicago an independent Polish parish, All Saints Catholic Church, whose formation had been encouraged by Old Catholic Bishop Joseph Rene Vilatte, had developed under Father Anthony Kozlowski. In Buffalo an independent congregation was formed and called Father Stephen Kaminski as its priest. Other independent parishes developed in Cleveland and Detroit.

All of these churches were placed under Vilatte. Kaminski was elected bishop and sought consecration from Vilatte. Kozlowski challenged Kaminski's claims and went to Europe where he sought consecration from Bishop Herzog of the Old Catholic Church. Vilatte consecrated Kaminski in 1898 and two factions, often bitter rivals, developed.

A third group of Polish nationals emerged in Scranton, Pennsylvania, where the issue was local control of church property. In consultation with Father Francis Hodur, their former priest, the Poles constructed an independent church and in 1897 Hodur accepted the pastorate. After unsuccessful attempts to remain within the Roman Catholic Church, the Poles organized a second church in nearby Dickson City.

Other independent congregations followed, and in 1904 a synod met in Scranton. At that time the Polish National Catholic Church of America was organized and Hodur was elected bishop. In 1907 he received orders from Utrecht, the central see of the Old Catholic Church. That same year Kozlowski died, and most of his followers were received into Hodur's diocese.

The Polish National Catholic Church of America differs little from the Roman Catholic Church as it was before the changes brought about by the Second Vatican Council of the 1960s. It has added some feast days of a nationalistic flavor and elevated the preaching of the gospel to the status of a sacrament. Bishop Hodur became known for his rejection of a doctrine of eternal hell. There is local control of property and the congregation does have a say in naming their priest. The liturgy, which for many years was said in Polish, has been translated into English and is being used in a higher percentage of the masses year by year.

In 1914 Hodur helped to start a Lithuanian National Catholic Church and in 1924 he consecrated Father John Britenas as its bishop. The body became independent but was eventually reabsorbed. The Polish National Catholic Church of America grew steadily through the first half of the twentieth century. It became the only substantial American Old Catholic jurisdiction and the only one in communion with the Old Catholic See of Utrecht. For many years it was in communion with the Protestant Episcopal Church but broke fellowship after the later decided to accept female priests. During the last two decades it has suffered greatly from Americanization, especially the abandonment of the Polish language by younger members, and the mobility of its members, many of whom have moved into areas not served by a PNCC parish. From a peak of 162 churches in 1960, the church has experienced a loss of almost one-third of its parishes.

The PNCC is organized into four American dioceses: Central (headquartered in Scranton); Eastern (headquartered in Manchester, New Hampshire); Western (headquartered in Chicago); and Buffalo-Pittsburgh (headquartered in Buffalo, New York). There is also a Canadian diocese headquartered in Toronto. A very active mission, begun after World War I, produced a growing National Church in Poland. A bishop was appointed in 1924. Cooperation has also been initiated between the Polish National Catholic Church of America and the Puerto Rican National Church. The PNCC is a member of both the World Council of Churches and National Council of Churches.

Membership: In 1980 the PNCC reported 110 churches and approximately 280,000 members.

Educational facilities: Savonrola Theological Seminary, Scranton, PA.

Periodicals: *Rola Boza* (God's Field), 529 E. Locust St., Scranton, PA 18505.

Sources: *A Catechism of the Polish National Catholic Church.* [Scranton, PA]: Mission Fund Polish National Catholic Church, 1962; Paul Fox, *The Polish National Catholic Church.* Scranton, PA: School of Christian Living, [1955]; Laurence Orzell, *Rome and the Validity of Orders in the Polish National Catholic Church.* Scranton, PA: Savonarola Theological Seminary Alumni Association, 1977; Stephen Wlodarski, *The Origin and Growth of the Polish National Catholic Church.* Scranton, PA: Polish National Catholic Church, 1974; Robert William Janowski, *The Growth of a Church, A Historical Documentary.* Scranton, PA: The Author, 1965.

★35★

SERVANT CATHOLIC CHURCH

% Most Rev. Robert E. Burns
50 Coventry Lane
Central Islip, NY 11722

The Servant Catholic Church first convened on the Feast of All Saints in 1978 and finalized its formation and polity in January 1980. Its bishop-primate, Robert E. Burns, SSD, (not to be confused with Robert A. Burns of the Old Roman Catholic Church (English Rite)) was consecrated on July 13, 1980, by Archbishop Herman Adrian Spruit of the Church of Antioch. On November 2, 1980, Patricia deMont Ford was consecrated. She and Ivan MacKillop-Fritts, OCC, abbot-general of the church-sponsored religious order, the Order of the Celtic Cross, constitute the present college of bishops.

The core theology of the Servant Catholic Church is rooted in the perception that the essence of the Christian kerygma lies in the proclamation of Christian freedom. Thi s belief is technically termed "eleutheric theology." This theology is impressed upon the church's liturgy as contained in *The Sacramentary and Daily Office.* The church recognizes the sacraments of initiation (baptism), reconciliation (penance), restoration (for healing and wholeness), and the Eucharist. Confirmation and marriage are designed as sacramental rites. Though receiving their orders from Liberal Catholic sources, the Servant Catholic Church has rejected theosophy as "a heresy and cancer within the church" and adopted a more orthodox theological perspective. It reaches out ecumenically to other orthodox sacramental bodies who share its commitment to justice, effective pastoral ministry, and the admission of women to all priestly orders.

Membership: In 1984 the church reported three congregations, five priests, and seventy-eight members.

Educational facilities: The Whithorn Institute, Ronkonkoma, New York.

Periodicals: *The Fourth Branch*, 50 Coventry Lane, Central Islip, New York 11722.

Sources: *The Sacramentary and Daily Office of the Servant Catholic Church.* Central Islip, NY: Theotokos Press, 1981.

★36★

THEE ORTHODOX OLD ROMAN CATHOLIC CHURCH (BROWN)

% Rt. Rev. Peter Charles Brown
Box 49314
Chicago, IL 60649

The Orthodox Catholic Old Roman Church was founded in the mid-1970s by Peter Charles Caine Brown (a.k.a. William C. Brown), more popularly known by his ecclesiastical title, Archbishop Simon Peter. The Archbishop claims to have been consecrated on June 1, 1973 by Bishops Robert A. Burns, James Lashley, G. D. M. Vorhis and Leo Christopher Skelton. He had previously been ordained to the priesthood by Archbishop Herman Keck of the Calvary Grace Christian Church of Fort Lauderdale, Florida. The group operates a senior citizen center on Chicago's southside.

Membership: In 1983 the Church claimed a membership of 2,369 in 19 congregations served by 36 clergy.

Remarks: Certificates concerning Archbishop Simon Peter indicate that he was consecrated on August 12, 1973 by Leo Christopher Skelton, known currently by his ecclesiastical title, Markus I, leader of the Byzantine Catholic Church. Skelton was assisted by Bishops William Nesslerode and Nicholaus Gularte. Unique to Catholic procedure, the certificates also indicate that on the next day, August 13, 1973, Brown was ordained to the priesthood by Skelton.

TRADITIONAL CHRISTIAN CATHOLIC CHURCH
Current address not obtained for this edition.

The Traditional Christian Catholic Church was founded by Archbishop Thomas Fehervary and is built around a group of immigrants from Austro-Hungarian stock who came to Quebec in 1965 following the failure of the Hungarian revolt. Fehervary had been consecrated in 1945 by Archbishop James R. Prochniewski of the Polish Mariavite Church, and he had served an independent Hungarian church since 1939. The faith and practice accord with that of the Roman Catholic Church before the Second Vatican Council of the 1960s, and the church opposes the innovations of that Council. Priests are unsalaried, but (unusual among Old Catholics) they are university-trained.

Membership: In 1972 the Church reported one parish in Canada, three missions in the United States, three missions in Western Europe, two missions in Eastern Europe and one mission in Hong Kong. One mission in New York City became independent in 1976 as the Tridentine Catholic Church currently headed by Archbishop Leonard J. Curreri. No current statistics have been reported.

TRADITIONAL ROMAN CATHOLIC CHURCH IN THE AMERICAS
% Most Rev. John D. Fesi
Friary Press
Box 470
Chicago, IL 60690

The Traditional Roman Catholic Church in the Americas was formed in 1977 by John Dominic Fesi, a bishop in the Old Roman Catholic Church headed by Archbishop Richard A. Marchenna. During his brief membership in the Old Roman Catholic Church, Fesi had risen to the post of chancellor. In 1976 he voiced his disapproval of Marchenna's leadership of the church by resigning his post as chancellor and calling a council meeting to reform the church. Two other bishops, Andrew Lawrence Vanore and Roy G. Bauer, attended the meeting and joined Fesi in issuing a declaration of independence from Marchenna. The document accused Marchenna of "unlawful actions" and the "personal usurpation and misuse of authority and jurisdiction." After issuing the declaration, the three bishops each adopted alternative paths. Fesi formed the Traditional Roman Catholic Church in the Americas.

Fesi had begun his ecclesiastical career as a Franciscan friar in the Archdiocese of the Old Catholic Church in America headed by Archbishop Walter X. Brown. In 1973 Brown created the Vicariate of Illinois and consecrated Msgr. Earl P. Gasquoine as its bishop.

Gasquoine appointed Fesi vicar general with the title of reverend monsignor. Fesi, as part of his work, ran Friary Press which printed a quarterly periodical, *The Franciscan*, and pamphlets for the archdiocese.

In 1974 Fesi left Brown's jurisdiction and sought consecration from Damian Hough, head of the Old Roman Catholic Church in the U. S.. Assisted by Bishops Roman W. Skikiewicz and Joseph G. Sokolowski, Hough consecrated Fesi on June 30, 1974. Fesi took his friars into the Old Roman Catholic Church headed by Marchenna. Though *The Franciscan* was discontinued, Friary Press became the church's major publishing arm.

During his years with Brown and Marchenna, Fesi and the Franciscans assisted at the Church of St. Mary Mystical Rose, an independent Old Catholic parish in Chicago. Bishop Skikiewicz pastored the congregation which had been founded in 1937 in response to a vision of Maria Kroll, a young Polish immigrant. The church was in effect an independent Old Catholic jurisdiction. Eventually, Fesi was appointed associate pastor. Marchenna appointed Fesi head of the Vicariate of Illinois and eventually the Church of St. Mary Mystical Rose became part of the vicariate. Though a strong congregation, after Skikiewicz's death the support dwindled and the building was sold.

The Traditional Roman Catholic Church in the Americas follows the Old Catholic tradition. It keeps the seven sacraments and teaches that baptism is essential for salvation. Veneration of images and pictures of the saints (who are present in a mystical manner in their image) and especially the Blessed Virgin Mary (whose intercession is essential to salvation) is promoted. Abortion is condemned. The church is organized hierarchically. Under the bishop is an ecclesiastical structure which includes priests, deacons, subdeacons, acolytes, exorcists, lectors, and doorkeepers. Priest are allowed to marry. A synod meets annually.

Membership: In 1984, the church reported eleven parishes, twenty-three priests and 780 members.

Educational facilities: Our Lady of Victory Seminary, Chicago, Illinois.

Periodicals: *The Larks of Umbria*, Friary Press, Box 470, Chicago, Illinois 60690.

Sources: John Dominic Fesi, *Apostolic Succession of the Old Catholic Church*. Chicago: Friary Press, [1975?]; John Dominic Fesi, *Canonical Standing of Religious in Regards to the Sacred Ministry*. Chicago: Friary Press, 1975; John Dominic Fesi, *Reasons for Divorce and Annulment in Church Law*. Chicago: Friary Press, 1975.

★39★

TRIDENTINE CATHOLIC CHURCH

% Archbishop Leonard J. Curreri, Primate
Sacred Heart of Jesus Chapel
1740 W. Seventh St.
Brooklyn, NY 11223

The Tridentine Catholic Church was formed in 1976 by Fr. Leonard J. Curreri, formerly a priest in the Traditional Christian Catholic Church headed by Archbishop Thomas Fehervary. In 1974 Fehervary moved to extend his Canadian-based jurisdiction to the United States by ordaining and commissioning Curreri and two other priests. However, the following year, on April 13, 1977, Curreri was consecrated a bishop by Francis J. Ryan of the Ecumenical Catholic Church of Christ. (He was subsequently reconsecrated subconditionally in December, 1976, by Archbishop Andre Barbeau of the Catholic Charismatic Church of Canada.) Then in 1976 Curreri called a synod at which the Tridentine Catholic Church was organized as a separate jurisdiction.

The Tridentine Catholic Church follows the doctrines and practices of the pre-Vatican II Roman Catholic Church. It rejects the Novus Ordo. It also rejects the doctine of papal infallibility, the ordination of women to the priesthood, and abortion under any circumstances. It leaves the matter of birth control to individual consciences.

Membership: In 1984 the church reported twelve congregations and/or missions, ten clergy, and 165 members, all in the United States.

Sources: Leonard J. Curreri, *De Sacramentis.* Brooklyn, NY: n.d.; Leonard J. Curreri, *More Questions and Answers on the Tridentine Catholic Church.* Brooklyn, NY: n.d.; Leonard J. Curreri, *Questions and Answers on the Tridentine Catholic Church.* Brooklyn, NY: n.d.; Leonard J. Curreri, *Seccessio Apostolica.* Brooklyn, NY: 1984.

★40★

TRIDENTINE OLD ROMAN COMMUNITY CATHOLIC CHURCH (JONES)

% Most Rev. Jacques A. Jones
10446 Highdale St.
Bellflower, CA 90706

The Tridentine Old Roman Community Catholic Church was organized in 1976 by Fr. Jacques A. Jones. Jones was consecrated in 1980 by Bishops Lawrence E. Carter, of the North American Old Roman Catholic Church-Utrecht Succession, headed by E. R. Verostek, and Thomas Sargent, of the Community of Catholic Churches. The Church adheres to the Roman Catholic Catechism of Trent and use a variety of liturgies, primarily an orthodox amended Tridentine liturgy said in both Latin-English and Spanish. The Church is in communion with the Old Calendar Greek Orthodox Church (headquartered on Mt. Athos) and the North American Old Roman Catholic Church-Utrecht Succession.

Membership: In 1984 the Church reported one parish, St. John the Apostle Catholic Church, in Bellflower, California, but it was establishing a second, St. Francis of Assisi Cathoic Church in Chula Vista, California. Bishop Jones was assisted by 3 priests and claimed approximately 25 members.

★41★

UNITED HISPANIC OLD CATHOLIC EPISCOPATE IN THE AMERICAS

% Most Rev. Hector Roa y Gonzalez
10 Stagg St.
Brooklyn, NY 11206

The United Hispanic Old Catholic Episcopate in the Americas can be traced to December 8, 1958, when Fr. Hector Roa y Gonzalez formed the Puerto Rican National Catholic Church as a Spanish-speaking Old Catholic body for the Commonwealth. The original intentions and hope were to affiliate with the Polish National Catholic Church, and the new church adhered strictly to the Declaration of Utrecht of September 24, 1889, one of the definitive documents of Old Catholicism. Roa opened negotiations with the primate of the Polish National Catholic Church in 1959.

The PNCC withdrew from the negotiations in 1960, in part due to the presence of the Protestant Episcopal Church (with whom, at that time, it was in full communion) on the island. Roa then turned to Eastern Orthodoxy, and in 1961 was received into the Patriarchial Exarchate of the Russian Orthodox Church in the Americas. The next year his church was registered as La Santa Iglesia Catolica Apostolica Orthodoxa de Puerto Rico, Inc., i.e.. The Holy Catholic Apostolic Church of Puerto Rico. The church for a time kept its revised tridentine ritual, with a few necessary Orthodox alterations. However, within a short time, the Orthodox liturgy was translated into Spanish and introduced into the Puerto Rican parishes. Gradually, other changes were introduced, and some members began to feel that the church had lost its identity and was being totally absorbed into Russian Orthodoxy, as its Spanish Western Rite Vicariate.

Roa led the fight against the Russification of the vicariate, but after the replacement of Archbishop John Wendland as head of the Exarchate, he found that he had lost his major support within the jurisdiction. In 1968, with his followers, Roa withdrew and reestablished the Puerto Rican National Catholic Church. Roa then turned to the Catholic Apostolic Church in Brazil, founded by Dom Carlos Duarte Costa, to receive episcopal orders. He was consecrated by Bishop Luis Silva y Viera in 1977. In 1979, in recognition of the geographical spread of the church, its name changed to the United Hispanic Old Catholic Episcopate in the Americas.

The United Hispanic Old Catholic Episcopate in the Americas continues to use the revised tridentine liturgy and accepts the seven traditional sacraments. Following the eastern practice, clergy are allowed to mary prior to ordination, but bishops are chosen from among the unmarried clergy. Clerical celibacy is encouraged.

Membership: In 1982 the episcopate claimed 21,000 members scattered throughout the Western Hemisphere.

★42★
UNITED OLD ROMAN CATHOLIC CHURCH (WHITEHEAD)

% Most Rev. Armand C. Whitehead
527 82nd St.
Brooklyn, NY 11209

The United Old Catholic Church resulted from the 1963 merger of three independent jurisdictions, the Catholic Episcopal Church and two other churches. The archbishop and head of the new merged body was Armand C. Whitehead, consecrated in 1960 by Michael A. Itkin, soon left Itkin's jurisdiction to found the Catholic Episcopal Church. Whitehead was consecrated a second time by James Edward Burns in 1970.

In general, doctrine and practice conform to the seven ecumenical councils held between 325 A.D. and 787 A.D., and the canons of the Roman Catholic Church prior to 1880. Distinctive features of the church include a vernacular liturgy, non-obligatory use of the sacrament of penance, and recognition of the primacy (though not the supremacy or infallibility) of the Pope. None of the newer doctrines of the Virgin Mary are accepted, such as her bodily assumption into heaven. Also, "individual bodily parts of our Blessed Lord" such as the "Sacred Heart" are not held in special veneration.

Membership: In 1967, the United Catholic Church reported 3 parishes and approximately 100 members. As of 1984, Archbishop Whitehead was living in semi-retirement and recent information on activities of the church have not been reported.

Anglicanism

★43★
AMERICAN EPISCOPAL CHURCH

% The Most Rev. Anthony F. M. Clavier
Box 373
Deerfield Beach, FL 33441

The American Episcopal Church was formed in Alabama in 1968 by a group of former clergy and members of the Protestant Episcopal Church and the Anglican Orthodox Church. They sought a more loosely organized structure than that offered by the Anglican Orthodox Church and organized the new jurisdiction with a congregational polity. The Church turned to James Charles Ryan, better known by his Indian name, K. C. Pillai, for episcopal orders.

An Indian nationalist and convert to Christianity, Pillai sought an alternative to the Anglican Church in India which in the 1940s still resisted placing Indians in episcopal positions. Pillai journeyed to England and received episcopal orders from the Evangelical Church of England (an offshoot of the Reformed Episcopal Church) and then met Hugh George de Willmott Newman. In 1945 he was consecrated *sub conditione* by Newman, who commissioned him to head an Indian Orthodox Church under Newman's leadership. In 1948, the year India became independent, Pillai came to the United States where he eventually settled.

The congregations that made up the infant American Episcopal Church turned to Pillai, and he responded by becoming their first primate. The Indian Orthodox and the American Episcopal Church merged. In December 1968 Pillai consecrated James H. George as "Bishop of Birmingham." Bishop George succeeded Pillai as Primate when he died in 1970.

On February 11, 1970, George consecrated Anthony F. M. Clavier as suffragan bishop. Having found the very loose structure of the church unworkable, the pair spearheaded a reorganization plan which led to the adoption of a more centrally organized polity. To accomplish the reorganization, it proved necessary for all of the clergy to resign from the church and to reconstitute it anew. Then the new American Episcopal Church, meeting in a General Convention in April 1970, ratified a constitution and Canon more in keeping with Anglican tradition. After the reorganization, Bishop George resigned as Primate and Clavier succeeded him. The following year, George resigned from the church altogether and joined in the formation of the Anglican Church in America now a part of the Anglican Episcopal Church. Clavier served as Primus until 1976 when Harold L. Trott succeeded him. In 1981, Trott resigned both as Primus and as a member of the church, and Clavier once again resumed duties as Primus.

While following traditional Episcopal practice and using the Book of Common Prayer, the American Episcopal Church has adopted a conservative theological stance and has written a new doctrinal statement which replaces the traditional 39 Articles. They do not admit women to the priesthood and do not involve themselves in political affairs.

In December 1983, the Diocese of the Southwest, which had withdrawn from the Anglican Catholic Church, united with the American Episcopal Church. Bishop Robert C. Harvey, former head of the Diocese, retired and H. Edward Caudill was installed as the new bishop. The Diocese of the Southwest joins the other three dioceses in the Church, the Diocese of the South, the

Diocese of the Eastern States, and the Diocese of the West.

Membership: In 1983 the American Episcopal Church reported 36 congregations and the Diocese of the Southwest 26. There are an estimated 5,000 to 7,000 members.

Periodicals: *Ecclesia*, 3153 Cheryl Drive, Hendersonville, NC 28739.

Sources: Anthony F. M. Clavier, *The American Episcopal Church*. Valley Forge, PA: Brotherhood of the Servants of the Lord, 1975. (Revised ed.: Greenville, SC: American Episcopal Church, 1976); Anthony F. M. Clavier, *The Principles of Reformed Catholicism*. Cincinati: Diocese of the Eastern States, American Episcopal Church, 1976.

★44★
ANGLICAN CATHOLIC CHURCH
% The Most Rev. Louis W. Falk
4807 Aspen Dr.
West Des Moines, IA 50265

While dissent over what many felt was theological and moral drift in the Protestant Episcopal Church led to the formation of several small protesting bodies, large-scale dissent occurred only after a series of events beginning in 1974 gave substantive focus to the conservative protest. In 1974 four Episcopal bishops (in defiance of their colleagues and the church) ordained eleven women to the priesthood. The following year, the Anglican Church of Canada approved a provision for the ordination of women. Then in 1976, with only a token censure of the bishops, the Protestant Episcopal Church regularized the ordinations of the eleven women. It also approved the revised *Book Of Common Prayer* which replaced the 1928 edition most Episcopalians had used for half a century.

The events of the mid 1970s led to the calling of a Congress of Episcopalians to consider alternatives to the Protestant Episcopal Church and to find a way to continue a traditional Anglican Church. In the months leading up to the congress, several congregations and priests withdrew from the Episcopal Church and formed the provisional Diocese of the Holy Trinity. They designated James O. Mote as their bishop elect. Eighteen hundred persons gathered in St. Louis in September 1977 and adopted a lengthy statement, the "Affirmation of St. Louis," which called for allegiance to the Anglican tradition of belief (as contained in the Thirty-nine Articles of Religion) and practice (as exemplified in the 1928 edition of the Book of Common Prayer). It specifically denounced the admission of women to the priesthood, the liberal attitudes to alternative sexual patterns (especially homosexuality), and both the World Council of Churches and the National Council of Churches. It affirmed the rights of congregations to manage their own financial affairs and expressed a desire to remain in communion with the See of Canterbury.

Throughout 1977 more congregations left the Protestant Episcopal Church, and others were formed by groups of people who had left as individual members. Following the September congress, three more provisional dioceses were established, and bishops elected. The Diocese of Christ the King elected Robert S. Morse; the Diocese of the Southwest elected Peter F. Watterson; and the Diocese of the Midwest elected C. Dale D. Doren. Bishops were sought who would consent to consecrate the new bishops-elect, and four finally agreed. Of the four Paul Boynton, retired suffragan of New York, was the first to withdraw from the consecration service, due to illness. Then Mark Pae of the Anglican Church of Korea, a close personal friend of Dale Doren, withdrew under pressure from his fellow bishops. But he did send a letter of consent to the consecration. On January 28, 1978, with Pae's letter to confirm the action, Albert Chambers, former bishop of Springfield, Illinois and Francisco Pagtakhan, of the Philippine Independent Church, consecrated Doren. Doren in turn joined Chambers and Pagtakhan in consecrating Morse, Watterson, and Mote.

Having established itself with proper episcopal leadership, the new church, unofficially called the Anglican Church of North America, turned its attention to the task of ordering its life. A national synod meeting was held in Dallas in 1978. Those present adopted a name, the Anglican Catholic Church, and approved a constitution which was sent to the several dioceses (by then seven in number) for ratification. In May 1979, the bishops announced that five of the seven dioceses had ratified the actions of the Dallas synod; thus, the Anglican Catholic Church had been officially constituted.

The early 1980s was a period of flux for the Anglican Catholic Church. It emerged as the single largest body of the St. Louis meeting, claiming more than half of the congregations and members. But along the way, it lost two of its original dioceses and three of its original bishops. The dioceses of Christ the King and the Southeast and their bishops (Morse and Watterson) refused to ratify the constitution. They instead continued under the name "Anglican Church of North America." The Diocese of the Southeast soon broke with the Diocese of Christ the King and became an independent jurisdiction. Then, in 1984, Watterson resigned as bishop and joined the Roman Catholic Church. His action effectively killed the diocese, and member churches were absorbed by the other Anglican bodies, primarily the Anglican Catholic Church.

While dealing with the loss of the dioceses of Christ the King and the Southeast, the church continued to grow as new and independent congregations joined; additions more than made up for losses. Bishop Doren resigned in 1980, but only two congregations followed him. In 1981 several priests and parishes left to form the Holy Catholic Church, Anglican Rite Jurisdiction of the Americas. The largest schism occurred in 1983 when the Diocese of the Southwest under Bishop Robert C. Harvey withdrew and took twenty-one congregations in Arkansas, Texas,

Oklahoma, New Mexico, and Arizona. Later that year they joined the American Episcopal Church.

The Anglican Catholic Church describes itself as the continuation of the traditional Anglicanism as expressed in the Nicene and Apostles' Creeds, and it holds to the liturgy of the Book of Common Prayer, 1928 edition. It rejects women in the priesthood and holds to traditional standards of moral conduct, condemning specifically "easy" divorce and remarriage, abortion on demand, and homosexual activity.

At its national convention in 1983, Louis W. Falk, bishop of the Diocese of the Missouri Valley, was elected as the ACC's first archbishop. While serving as archbishop he continues as pastor of St. Aldan's parish in Des Moines, Iowa.

Membership: In 1983 the Anglican Catholic Church had 135 congregations and an estimated 3,000 to 5,000 members.

Educational facilities: Holyrood Seminary, Liberty, New York.

Periodicals: *The Trinitarian*, 3141 South Josephine, Denver, CO 80210.

Sources: *A Directory of Churches of the Continuing Anglican Tradition.* Eureka Springs, AK: Fellowship of Concerned Churchmen, 1983-4; Perry Laukhuff, *The Anglican Catholic Church.* Eureka Springs, AK: Fellowship of Concerned Churchmen, 1977; *Opening Addresses of the Church Congress at St. Louis, Missouri, 14-16 September 1977.* Amherst, VA: Fellowship of Concerned Churchmen, 1977.

★45★
ANGLICAN CHURCH OF NORTH AMERICA
% Rt. Rev. Robert T. Shepherd
Chapel of St. Augustine of Canterbury
1906 Forest Green Dr., N.E.
Atlanta, GA 30329

The Anglican Church of North America traces its origin to the Independent Anglican Church founded in Canada in the 1930s by William H. Daw. Later he led his jurisdiction into the Liberal Catholic Church headed by Bishop E. M. Matthews and in 1955 was consecrated by Matthews. In 1964 Daw and Bishop James Pickford Roberts left Matthews to found the Liberal Catholic Church International. Daw assumed the role of primate, but withdrew in 1974 in favor of Joseph Edward Neth. He resumed the primacy in 1979, when Neth was forced to resign after consecrating a priest of another jurisdiction without church approval.

In 1981 Daw participated in the formation of the Independent Catholic Church International, which brought together a number of independent Old Catholic, Anglican, and Liberal Catholic jurisdictions in both North America and Europe. Meanwhile, the Liberal Catholic Church International and Daw reasserted its Anglican roots in the wake of the formation of the Anglican Catholic Church in Canada and the consecration and untimely death of its first bishop, Carmino M. de Catanzaro. The Liberal Catholic Church International repudiated Theosophy and changed its name to the North American Episcopal Church. In 1983 P. W. Goodrich, primate of the ecumenical Independent Catholic Church International, resigned to become primate of the North American Episcopal Church. Goodrich had originally been consecrated by Daw as bishop for the small Independent Catholic Church of Canada.

Goodrich's leadership of the North American Episcopal Church was shortlived, however, and within a year he was forced out and Archbishop Daw again resumed the primacy. Two bishops, Rt. Rev Robert T. Shepherd and Rt. Rev. M. B. D. Crawford, have been consecrated to administer the work of the church in America and Canada respectively. The first American parish was established in Atlanta, Georgia, in 1983. In June 1984, the church's name was changed to Anglican Church of North America.

The Anglican Church of North America, as other continuing Anglican Bodies, accepts the 1977 affirmation of St. Louis and follows the practices of the Protestant Episcopal Church and the Anglican Church of Canada prior to the changes of the 1970s. It differs from other continuing Anglican bodies in that it believes that a single jurisdiction should be established for all of North America rather than several jurisdictions divided along national and regional lines. It also stresses the collegiality of all levels of the clergy and the laity.

Membership: In 1984 the Church reported 10 congregations, 8 priests and 250 members in the United States and Canada.

Educational facilities: St. Matthias' Cathedral Seminary, Hamilton, Ontario, a correspondance school.

Periodicals: *Our Anglican Heritage.* 43 Medina Sq. East, Keswick, Ontario, Canada L4P 1E1.

★46★
ANGLICAN EPISCOPAL CHURCH OF NORTH AMERICA
% Most Rev. Walter Hollis Adams
789 Allen Ct.
Palo Alto, CA 94303

The Anglican Episcopal Church of North America was founded in 1972 by Most Rev. Walter Hollis Adams. That same year on two successive days, Adams had been consecrated, first by William Elliot Littlewood of the Free Protestant Episcopal Church and then by Herman Adrian

Spruit of the Church of Antioch. In 1975 Adams spearheaded the organization of the Anglican Episcopal Church but they considered themselves as Anglican in worship and belief -- The Anglican Church of America, the Episcopal Church (Evangelical) and the Protestant Episcopal Church. As a step toward eventual union, in 1977 the bishops of these churches reconsecrated each other thus mingling their several lines of apostolic succession. By the end of 1980, all of the member churches had merged into the Anglican Episcopal Church and the Council became dormant.

The Anglican Church of America had been founded in 1971 by Bishop James H. George, after his withdrawal from the American Episcopal Church. George remained head of the Church until his death in a car accident in 1977. He was succeeded by John A. Perry-Hooker who had headed the Province of New England. Perry-Hooker had formed the Evangelical Catholic Communion in 1965 in association with Archbishop Julian E. Erni, and in communion with the order of the same name founded in 1902 in England by Ulric Vernon Herford. After Bishop George founded the Anglican Church of America, Perry-Hooker brought his work under George's jurisdiction. A psychiatrist as well as bishop, Perry-Hooker has been active in counseling and a rehabilitation program sponsored by the Church.

The Episcopal Church (Evangelical) was formed in 1977 by Rt. Rev. M. Dean Stephens and former members of the Protestant Episcopal Church who wished to continue to "teach the faith of Our Father as given to the Church in England and subsequently to the Episcopal Church in America" but which had been abandoned by the Protestant Episcopal Church. Stephens, formerly associated with the American Episcopal Church, had edited their periodical *Ecclesia*. In 1982, Stephens left the Anglican Episcopal Church and was reconsecrated in the Holy Catholic Church, Anglican Rite Jurisdiction of the Americas.

The United Episcopal Church was founded in 1973 by former members of the Anglican Orthodox Church under the leadership of bishops Troy A. Kaichen, Thomas J. Kleppinger, and Russell G. Fry. Under Kleppinger's leadership the church joined the Anglican Episcopal Council and subsequently merged with the Anglican Episcopal Church. Kleppinger served as suffragan to Bishop Adams and continued to edit the periodical *Episcopal Tidings*, which he had begun several years before. (Most recently, Kleppinger has transferred to the Anglican Catholic Church.)

The Anglican Episcopal Church describes itself as traditional. It uses the King James Version of the Bible and the Book of Common Prayer, 1928 edition, and it holds to the Apostles' and Nicene Creeds and the articles of Religion. The Church is Evangelical and can be said to have its roots in the low church party of the Protestant Episcopal Church. As can be seen in its history, it has aggressively reached out of various splinter groups that came out of the Episcopal Church during the 1970s.

During the 1980s, the Anglican Episcopal Church continued its efforts at bringing together the fragments of traditional Anglicanism. In 1981 intercommunion was established with both the American Episcopal Church and the Holy Catholic Church, Anglican Rite Jurisdiction of the Americas. In May 1982, the American Episcopal Church and the Anglical Episcopal Church met in a joint synod. A disagreement developed among the leaders of the Anglican Episcopal Church, two bishops of which wanted immediate union with the American Episcipal Church. The disagreement led to the withdrawal of Bishops John M. Hamers and Frank H. Benning who led their diocese into the American Episcopal Church. Then in 1983 the Anglican Episcopal Church signed documents of intercommunion with the Anglican Catholic Church. In discussions which project merger of the Anglican Episcopal Church into the ACC, agreement was reached to allow the Anglican Episcopal Church to come into the ACC as an nongeographical diocese, the Diocese of St. Paul, with Adams as bishop.

Membership: In 1982 the Anglican Episcopal Church reported 25 congregations, but it lost approximately 15 congregations to the American Episcopal Church. It has an estimated 1,000 members.

Periodicals: *Episcopal Tidings*, Box 11521, Alexandria, VA 22312.

★47★
ANGLICAN ORTHODOX CHURCH
% Most Rev. James Parker Dees
323 E. Walnut St.
Box 128
Statesville, NC 28677

Rev. James Parker Dees, a priest in the Protestant Episcopal Church, was the first of the modern spokespersons to call the members of that Church who opposed the changes in liturgy and program to come out and separate themselves from apostasy. A low church Episcopalian, he had trouble with both liberalism which he felt denied Biblical authority, and sacerdotalism among high church members. He therefore left the Episcopal Church and in 1963 formed the Anglican Orthodox Church. The following year he received episcopal orders from autocephalous Ukrainian Bishop Wasyl Sawyna and Old Catholic Bishop Orlando J. Woodward (who later joined the United Episcopal Church of America). Formed in the southern United States in the early 1960s, the North Carolina-based group found its greatest response in the South among Episcopalians who rejected the Church's involvement in social and political issues, particularly the racial turmoil of the mid-60s.

The Anglican Orthodox Church follows the low church in a very conservative manner. It adheres to the Thirty-nine articles and uses the 1928 edition of the Book of Common Prayer. The polity is episcopal, but local congregations are autonomous and own their own property. Much power has been placed in the hands of the presiding bishop, so much that other Episcopalians desiring to leave the Protestant Episcopal Church refused to join the Anglican Orthodox Church which they termed "dictatorial."

The Anglican Orthodox Church was able to bring together many pockets of dissent, however, and has created a strong Church. By 1972 it had 37 congregations, though some were lost to other Anglican splinters as the decade progressed. Dees established Cranmer Seminary, which in 1977 had four full-time students. He also has brought the Church into communion with like-minded churches in Pakistan, South India, Nigeria, the Fiji Islands, Rhodesia (Zimbabwe), Madagascar, and Colombia.

As other Anglican groups have formed, Dees was pressed to draw sharp lines of distinction. He has argued against the doctrinal "looseness" and high church tendencies in other groups of Anglicans. He has continued his campaign against the growing "apostasy" he sees within the Protestant Episcopal Church, and has concentrated his attention upon building the Anglican Orthodox Church as a viable and continuing denomination.

Membership: In 1983 the Church reported 7 congregations and 1,325 members.

Educational facilities: Cramner Seminary, Statesville, North Carolina.

Periodicals: *The News*, Box 128, Statesville, NC 28677.

Sources: James P. Dees, *Reformation Anglicanism.* Statesville, NC: Anglican Orthodox Church, 1971.

★48★
APOSTOLIC EPISCOPAL CHURCH
℅ Dr. Bertil Persson
St. Ephrem's Institute
Box 7048
Solna,

The Apostolic Episcopal Church was formed in 1932 in New York City by Arthur Wolfort Brooks. Brooks, a Protestant Episcopal Church clergyman, was originally consecrated in 1925 by Mar Antoine Lefberne who had received orders from the Chaldean Church. He resigned from the Episcopal Church in 1926, and that same year, at the First Annual Convocation of the Anglican Universal Church, later the Holy Orthodox Church in America, he was elected bishop of Sardis. In 1927 he became pastor of the Christ's Church-by-the-Sea, a parish on Long Island. Then in 1930 he left the Anglican Universal Church and formed his own jurisdiction, the Apostolic Episcopal Church. In 1932 Mar Georgius (George Winslow Plummer), head of the Anglican

Universal Church, issued a statement repudiating Brooks' claims of Chaldean orders. Brooks, meanwhile, had been reconsecrated by William Montgomery Brown of the Old Catholic Church in America and assumed the religious name of Mar John Emmanuel.

The church began to spread through consecrations of a number of people, among them Harold F. Jarvis in 1934 and Hermann F. Abbinga in 1946. In 1936 it reported 12 churches and 6,389 members. After his consecration, Abbinga moved to Europe and began to establish the church there, and gradually the center of the church began to shift away from the United States. Three dioceses were eventually established for England, Sweden and the rest of Europe (headquartered in Norway). The American body, following Brooks' death in 1948, was active for several years in New York, Hawaii, and Los Angeles. Archbishop W. D. de Ortega Maxey (Mar David I), patriarch of Malaga, succeeded Brooks as presiding bishop. He resigned three years later and was succeeded by Bishop Jarvis. Over the next two decades, the American branch dwindled to but a single parish, the continuation of the one originally headed by Brooks. During the early 1980s this parish was headed by Fr. Francis C. Spataro, but upon his resignation from the church, all American work has for the moment ceased to exist.

Present leader of the Church is Bishop Bertil Persson, well known as a scholar of and among the various independent catholic, anglican and orthodox jurisdictions. Persson succeeded Perry N. Cedarholm who in turn had succeeded Abbinga.

Membership: Not reported.

Sources: Beril Persson, *A Collection of Documentation on the Apostolic Succession of Joseph Rene Vilatte with Brief Annotations.* Solna, Sweden: The Author, 1974; Bertil Persson and Shmouel Warda, *Armaic Idioms of Eshoo (Jesus) Explained.* Solna, Sweden: St. Ephrem's Institute, 1978.

★49★
CELTIC EVANGELICAL CHURCH
℅ Rt. Rev. Wayne W. Gau
1666 St. Louis Dr.
Honolulu, HI 96816

The Celtic Evangelical Church is a small Anglican body formed by its bishop-abbot, Wayne W. Gau. It is evangelical in its theological approach.

Membership: In 1984 the Church had one congregation in Hawaii.

Periodicals: *The Celtic Evangelist*, 1666 St. Louis Drive, Honolulu, HI 96816

★50★
DIOCESE OF CHRIST THE KING
℅ Rt. Rev. Robert S. Morse
St. Peter's Pro-Cathedral
6013 Lawton
Oakland, CA 94618

The Diocese of Christ the King shares the history of that larger conservative movement which participated in the 1977 congress at St. Louis and approved the "Affirmation" adopted by the delegates. The diocese was one of the four original provisional dioceses that were formed. Its bishop-elect, Robert S. Morse, was consecrated along with the other new Anglican bishops in Denver, Colorado on January 28, 1978, by Bishops Albert Chambers, Francisco Pagtakhan, and C. Dale D. Doren. However, Bishop Morse and other members of his diocese were among those most opposed to the new constitution adopted by the synod at Dallas in 1978 by the group which took the name Anglican Catholic Church. Neither the Diocese of Christ the King nor the Diocese of the Southeast ratified the constitution, preferring instead to work without such a document. They called a synod meeting for Hot Springs, Arkansas, on October 16-18, 1978, two days immediately prior to the opening of the Anglican Catholic Church synod at Indianapolis, Indiana. Those gathered at Hot Springs decided to continue informally to use the name "Anglican of North America." They adopted canons (church laws) but no constitution.

The new jurisdiction immediately faced intense administrative pressures. In response to the "Anglican Church of North America" claiming many congregations in California and the South, the Anglican Catholic Church established a new structure, the patrimony, to facilitate the movement of existing congregations into the church and to assist the formation of new congregations in areas not covered by existing diocesan structures. Both Bishop Morse and Bishop Watterson viewed the patrimony as an attempt to steal the congregations under their jurisdiction.

The pressure from the Anglican Catholic Church did not keep the two dioceses in the "Anglican Church of North America" from facing crucial internal issues. Bishop Watterson argued for a strict division of the Anglican Church of North America into geographical dioceses with the understanding that neither bishop would attempt to establish congregations or missions in the other's diocese. The diocese of Christ the King rejected Watterson's suggestions, and the Diocese of the Southeast became a separate jurisdiction. The Diocese of Christ the King proceeded to initiate work in the South.

Once separated, the Diocese of the Southeast experienced continued internal problems. In 1980 nine congregations withdrew with the blessing of Bishop Francisco Pagtakhan (who was becoming increasingly dissatisfied with the Anglican Catholic Church) and formed the Associated Parishes, Traditional Anglo-Catholic. Pagtakhan named Fr. J. Bruce Medaris as archdeacon. This new jurisdiction dissolved very quickly and merged back into Anglican Catholic Church. Finally, in 1984, Bishop Watterson resigned his office and joined the Roman Catholic Church. His jurisdiction dissolved and the remaining congregations realigned themselves with the other Anglican bodies. The dissolution of the Diocese of the Southeast left the Diocese of Christ the King the only diocese in the "Anglican Church of North America."

The Diocese of Christ the King is at one in faith and practice with the other Anglican bodies, holding to the faith of the undivided primitive church to which Episcopalians have always belonged, as spelled out in the affirmation of St. Louis. It rejects both the National Council of Churches and the World Council of Churches. It differs from the Anglican Catholic Church only in matters of administration.

Membership: In 1983 the Diocese of Christ the King had thirty-five parishes with an estimated 3,000 to 5,000 members.

Educational facilities: Saint Joseph of Arimathea Anglican Theological College, Berkeley, California.

Sources: *A Directory of Churches in the Continuing Anglican Tradition 1983-84.* Eureka Springs, AK: Fellowship of Concerned Churchmen, 1983-84.

★51★
DIOCESE OF THE SOUTHWEST
(Defunct)

The shortlived Diocese of the Southwest was originally formed in 1978 as a constituent part of the Anglican Catholic Church. In 1982 it left the ACC and for several months existed as an independent jurisdiction. In December 1983 it merged into the American Episcopal Church. It no longer exists as a separate body.

★52★
FREE PROTESTANT EPISCOPAL CHURCH
Current address not obtained for this edition.

The Free Protestant Episcopal Church was established in 1897 by the union of three small British episcopates: the Ancient British Church (founded 1876/77); Nazarene Episcopal Ecclesia (founded in 1873); and Free Protestant Church of England (founded in 1889). Leon Checkemian, an Armenian, the first primate of the new church, was supposedly consecrated by Bishop A. S. Richardson of the Reformed Episcopal Church in 1890, though present claims indicate that he was consecrated in 1878 by an Archbishop Chorchorunian. In either case, no papers have been produced, and the validity of the consecration is questioned by many. In 1952, Charles D. Boltwood became the fifth person to hold the post of primate.

The faith of the Free Protestant Episcopal Church is the same as the Protestant Episcopal Church. The Thirty-nine Articles are accepted. There are, however, seven doctrines condemned as contrary to God's word: 1) that the church exists in only one order or form of polity; 2) that ministers are "priests" in any other sense than that in which all believers are a "royal priesthood;" 3) that the Lord's table is an altar on which the oblation of the body and blood of Christ is offered anew to the Father; 4) that Christ is present in the elements of bread and wine in the Lord's Supper; 5) that regeneration and baptism are inseparably connected; 6) that the law should punish Christians with death; and 7) that Christians may wear weapons and serve in war except in aiding the wounded or assisting in civil defense. In these seven objections, the sacramentalism of Anglo- Catholicism is explicitly denied and conscientious objection to carrying arms in war is elevated to dogma.

The Free Protestant Episcopal Church came to America in 1958 when Boltwood, on a trip to Los Angeles, consecrated Emmet Neil Enochs as archbishop of California and primate of the United States. On the same trip, John M. Stanley was consecrated bishop of Washington; subsequently four additional bishops were consecrated for the United States. The primate was directly responsible to the bishop primus in London. In 1967 the Free Protestant Episcopal Church reported 23 congregations plus a number of affiliated missions, and there were an estimated 2,000 members in the United States and Canada.

The Free Protestant Episcopal Church dissipated as various bishops passed orders to men who established other jurisdictions. These included such groups as the Autocephalous Syro-Chaldean Church of North America, which received orders from Bishop Stanley; the Anglican Episcopal Church, whose founder was consecrated by a Free PEC bishop, W. E. Littlewood; and the Apostolic Catholic Church of the Americas, formed by former Free Protestant Episcopal Bishop Gordon I. DaCosta. The last United States Primate Albert J. Fuge, retired without naming a successor.

★53★

HOLY CATHOLIC CHURCH, ANGLICAN RITE JURISDICTION OF THE AMERICAS

℅ Most. Rev. G. Wayne Craig, Archbishop
2535 Sunbury Dr.
Columbus, OH 43219

In the several years following the 1977 St. Louis congress, the Anglican Movement grew to encompass over 200 congregations. However, as it grew, it splintered into several factions due to administrative disagreements as well as the issued of the domination of the Anglican Catholic Church by the Anglo-Catholic (high-church) perspective. Some congregations remained outside of the various diocesan structures altogether. Bishop Francisco Pagtakhan of the Philippine Independent Church, who had participated in the original consecrations of the four Anglican bishops in 1978, became increasingly disturbed at the splintering and lack of unity in the Anglican Movement. In 1980, asserting his role as the ecumenical and missionary officer for the Philippine Independent Church, Pagtakhan decided to create an "umbrella" for those in the Anglican Movement who were searching for a home where they could "belong to a genuinely canonical part of the One, Holy, Catholic and Apostolic Church." Thus in March, 1980, in Texas, he initiated the incorporation of the Holy Catholic Church, Anglican Rite Jurisdiction of the Americas.

On September 26, 1981 (with the permission of the Supreme Bishop of the Philippine Independent Church, Most Rev. Macario V. Ga) Bishop Pagtakhan, assisted by retired bishops Sergio Mondala and Lupe Rosete, consecrated Robert Q. Kennaugh, G. Ogden Miller, and C. Wayne Craig, all former priests in the Anglican Catholic Church. Kennaugh became head of the Diocese of St. Luke, centered in Corsicana, Texas, and archbishop for the jurisdiction . Miller was named bishop of the Diocese of St. Matthew with headquarters in California. Craig became bishop of the Diocese of St. Mark with headquarters in Columbus, Ohio. In 1982 Herman F. Nelson was consecrated as bishop for the Diocese of St. John the Evangelist with headquarters in Venice, Florida. Shortly thereafter, Kennaugh retired as archbishop, and Craig was named to that post. In 1985 the Anglican Rite Jurisdiction received Bishop Harold L. Trott into the Church as the Bishop of the Missionary Diocese of Reconciliation. Trott had left the American Episcopal Church in 1979 and had formed the Pro-Diocese of Reconciliation (consisting of several congregations in California and New Mexico) while waiting for a larger body with which to affiliate.

The Anglican Rite Jurisdiction of the Americas has no differences in doctrine and practice with the larger Anglican Movement and emphasizes its thorough commitment to "the unity of genuine continuing Anglicanism." The jurisdiction has moved to establish intercommunion with other Anglican bodies and to accept otherwise independent congregations under its umbrella.

Membership: In 1985 the jurisdiction reported eighteen congregations and more than 1,500 members.

Periodicals: *The Evangelist*, The Dekoven Foundation of Ohio, 82 Frederick Avenue, Akron, Oh 44310.

Sources: Roderic B. Dibbert, *The Roots of Traditional Anglicanism*. Akron, Oh: Dekoven Foundation, 1984; *The Prologue*. Akron, OH: DeKoven Foundation, 1984; *Official Directory of Bishops, Clergy, Parishes*. Akron, OH: Holy Catholic Church, Anglican Rite Jurisdiction of the America, Office of the Secretary of the ARJA Synod, 1985.

★54★
OLD EPISCOPAL CHURCH
% Rt. Rev. Jack C. Adam
Box 2424
Mesa, AZ 85204

The Old Episcopal Church is a small diocese in the Southwest headed by Rt. Rev. Jack C. Adam, Bishop of Arizona. A former Protestant Episcopal Church priest, he left the Episcopal Church and was consecrated by Archbishop Walter Propheta of the America Orthodox Catholic Church in 1972.

Membership: Not reported. There are several parishes in Arizona and New Mexico.

★55★
PROTESTANT EPISCOPAL CHURCH IN THE U.S.A.
815 Second Ave.
New York, NY 10017

The Church of England came into the American colonies with the first British settlers. The first church was established at Jamestown in 1607, and in 1619 an act of the Virginia legislature formally declared Virginians to be members of the Church of England. By the time of the American Revolution, more than 400 Anglican parishes were spread along the coast from Georgia to New Hampshire.

The American Revolution created a crisis for the church in the new nation because, in spite of the large number of parishes, the church in the colonies had no bishop. War with England meant England would not be sending a bishop to America, so there was no way to ordain new priests or consecrate future bishops. Further, many priests (already in short supply) sided with England in the Revolution and returned to England. Thus the war left Anglican congregations highly disorganized. In 1783 the Connecticut churches sent Samuel Seabury to England to be consecrated. But, because he would not swear allegiance to the British Crown, he could not be consecrated. He was finally consecrated by the Non-juring Church of Scotland in 1784. Upon Seabury's return in 1785, the Connecticut priests held a convocation to organize their parishes.

Meanwhile, a second movement to reorganize the American parishes was undertaken in the Middle Colonies (mainly in Pennsylvania and Virginia) under the leadership of William White. A series of meetings over the next several years resulted in the adoption of the "Ecclesiastical Constitution of the Protestant Episcopal Church in the United States." William White and Samuel Provoost were chosen as bishops. They sailed for England and were consecrated by the archbishop of Canterbury in 1787, after Parliament had rescinded the requirement of an oath of loyalty to the Crown for any consecrated bishop from "foreign parts." In 1789 the new constitution was adopted by all the American churches (including Bishop Seabury's diocese). The Protestant Episcopal Church was born, the church that represents the Anglican tradition in the U.S.

The Protestant Episcopal Church, popularly called the Episcopal Church, grew and became a national body during the nineteenth century. Within its membership three informally organized but recognizable groups developed: the high church of the Anglo-Catholic group; the low church evangelicals; and the broad church party (the group between the high church and low church groups). The differences between these groups was largely based upon their approach to liturgy and the Eucharist. Episcopalians have followed the liturgy of the Prayer Book which is built upon a belief in the Real Presence of Christ in the Eucharist. The Church of England passed to American Episcopalians a repudiation of the particular explanation of that doctrine of the Real Presence called "transubstantiation." High Church Episcopalians have tended to emphasize the forms and ceremonies associated with the Roman tradition and have tended toward a Roman explanation of the Real Presence. In contrast, Low Church Episcopalians have emphasized the "Puritan" element introduced into the Anglican Church after the Reformation. They have opposed the emphasis on outward ceremony, centering their attention upon the reading and preaching of the Word.

During the 1840s the American Church began to receive the influence of the Oxford Movement, a high church revival in the Church of England. Among the personages identified with the movement was John Henry Newman, who later joined the Roman Catholic Church. In the wake of the revival, church architecture and sanctuary furnishings began to change. The Gothic church became common. The common arrangement of furniture in the sanctuary centered upon a table, and the pulpit was replaced with a center altar, the common arrangement today.

The broad church party, which reached into both high-church and low-church camps was identified mostly by its liberalism in matters of discipline, doctrine, and Biblical interpretation. Broad churchmen generally avoided too much emphasis upon ceremony and found their identification in their enclusive spirit. They were open to a variety of creedal interpretations and would often open their pulpit and altar to non-Episcopalians.

During the mid-twentieth century new issues began to become prominent in the church, and these led to new lines of division that cut across the older groupings. Dissent within the church appeared around the issues of laxity in church moral standards (especially an acceptance of sexual immorality), the ordination of women priests, the reported use of funds contributed to the National Council of Churches and World Council of Churches for "far-left" political causes, and the church's involvement in various social crusades (from civil rights and women's liberation to gay liberation). In addition, disagreements evolved over the introduction of extensive revisions of the 1928 edition of the *Book of Common Prayer*, made available in a revised prayer book. These issues came to a head in 1976 when the General Convention of the church approved the ordination of women and the revised *Book of Common Prayer*. Several thousand who disapproved of the changes left the church in the late 1970s. (Following the movement out of the Episcopal Church, the Anglicans, as the conservatives called themselves, tended to split along the older party lines).

Membership: In 1982 the Protestant Episcopal Church reported 2,794,139 members in 7,095 congregations served by 12,974 priests.

Educational facilities: Seminaries: Berkeley Divinity School at Yale, New Haven Connecticut; Church Divinity School of the Pacific, Berkeley, California; General Theological Seminary, New York City, New York; George Mercer Jr., Memorial School of Theology, Garden City New York; Nashotah House, Nashotah, Wisconsin; Protestant Episcopal Theological Seminary in Virginia, Alexandria, Virginia; Seabury-Western Theological Seminary, Evanston, Illinois; University of the South, School of Theology, Sewanee, Tennessee. Colleges and universities: Bard College, Annandale-on-the- Hudson, New York; Hobart and William Smith College, Geneva, New York; Kenyon College, Gambier, Ohio; St. Augustine's College, Raleigh, North Carolina; St. Paul's College, Lawrenceville, Virginia; Trinity College, Hartford, Connecticut; University of the South, Sewanee, Tennessee; Voorhees College, Denmark, South Carolina.

Periodicals: *The Episcopalian*, 1930 Chestnut Street, Philadelphia, PA 19103; *The Living Church*, 407 E. Michigan Street, Milwaukee, WI 53202; *Historical Magazine*, Box 2247, Austin, TX 78705.

Remarks: In 1967 the General Convention adopted the designation "Episcopal Church" as an official alternative name.

Sources: William & Betty Gray, *The Episcopal Church Welcomes You*. New York: Seabury Press, 1974; William W. Manross, *A History of the American Episcopal Church*. New York: Morehouse-Gorham, 1950; Edward Lambe Parsons and Bayare Hale Jones, *The American Prayer Book*. New York: Charles Scribner's Sons, 1946; W. Norman Pittenger, *The Episcopalian Way of Life*. Englewood Cliffs, NJ: Prentice-Hall, 1957: Massey H. Shepherd, Jr., *The Worship of the Church*. Greenwich, CT; Seabury Press, 1954; William Synder, Looking at the Episcopal Church. Wilton, CT: Morehouse-Barlow, 1980.

★56★
PROVISIONAL DIOCESE OF ST. AUGUSTINE OF CANTERBURY
(Defunct)

The Provisional Diocese of St. Augustine of Canterbury was formed in 1978 by Canon Albert J. duBois (1906-1980), former head of the American Church Union, and five former parishes of the Diocese of the Holy Trinity (of what is now the Anglican Catholic Church). It was the desire of the parishes to unite with The Roman Catholic Church, though they wished to retain their own liturgy, forms of piety, and their traditional lay involvement in the life of the Church. The group was led by its "senior priest," Canon duBois; the Rev. John Barker, head of the "Clericus," a priests' conference; and Dr. Theodore L. McEvoy, head of its "Laymen's League."

In 1980 Archbishop John R. Quinn, Roman Catholic Archbishop of San Francisco, announced a plan by which Anglicans could come into the Roman Catholic Church and keep their own priests, an approved Anglican liturgy, and a common identity. In 1981, James Parker became the first priest to move from the Protestant Episcopal Church to the Roman jurisdiction. By 1985, twenty-three married priests had been re-ordained as Roman priests. Five parishes had been received by the Vatican.

★57★
REFORMED EPISCOPAL CHURCH
% Board of National Church Extension
4225 Chestnut St.
Philadelphia, PA 19140

The Reformed Episcopal Church was formed in 1873 in New York City by Bishop George David Cummins, the assistant bishop of Kentucky for the Protestant Episcopal Church. The immediate cause of its formation was to protest the growing sacramentalism of the high church group. Sacramentalists emphasized the importance of the real presence of Christ in communion, and it said priests were necessary for the celebration of the eucharist. This priestly exclusivity was criticized.

An ecumenical communion service in 1873 also led to the formation of the Reformed Episcopal Church. At a conference of the Evangelical Alliance of the World, both Cummins and the Dean of Canterbury, Dr. Payne Smith, participated in a Union Communion service at the Fifth Avenue Presbyterian church in New York City. For this act they were severely criticized. Cummins felt this criticism deeply, and he announced his intention of transfering his work outside the Protestant Episcopal Church. He was finally deposed from his office and ministry.

Prior to Cummins' being deposed, however, the Reformed Episcopal Church was organized, and the Rev. Charles Edward Cheney was elected and consecrated bishop. This act ensured the continuance of the line of validly consecrated bishops. The doctrine, polity, and practices of the Protestant Episcopal Church (the parent body) are continued, with a few exceptions. The Reformed Episcopal Church values the episcopacy, but it does not consider other churches' lack of apostolic succession a bar to fellowship. The church is thoroughly reformed in its approach to the sacraments and does not have a priesthood. Confirmation is maintained. The Reformed Episcopalians revised the liturgy of the Protestant Episcopal Church to remove any Romanizing elements in the liturgy (a revision contrary to the influential nineteenth century Oxford Movement of high church Episcopalians).

The Church is governed by a triennial general council, but most authority lies at the synodical and parish levels. The theological seminary of the Reformed Episcopal Church is located in Philadelphia, Pennsylvania. Mission work is maintained in India, Zaire, Uganda, Zimbabwe, and Germany.

Membership: In 1980 the Church reported 6,200 members in 70 congregations with 101 clergy.

Educational facilities: Reformed Episcopal Church Theological Seminary, Philadelphia, Pennsylvania.

Periodicals: *Episcopal Recorder*, 4225 Chestnut Street, Philadelphia, PA 19140; *The Reformed Episcopalian*, 4225 Chestnut Street, Philadelphia, PA 19140.

Sources: *The Book of Common Prayer*. Philadelphia: The Reformed Episcopal Publication Society, 1932; Charles Edward Cheney, *What Reformed Episcopalians Believe*. N.p. (Philadelphia?): Christian Education Committee, Reformed Episcopal Church, 1961; Charles Edward Cheney, *A Neglected Power and Other Sermons*. New York: Revell 1916; Robert L. Peck, "A Brief Study of the Reformed Episcopal Church." *American Church Quarterly* vol. 3, no.4 (1963) pp. 153-62; Paul A. Carter, "The Reformed Episcopal Schism of 1873: An Ecumenical Perspective." *Historical Magazine of the Protestant Episcopal Church* vol. 33, no.3 (September, 1964) pp.225-38.

★58★
SOUTHERN EPISCOPAL CHURCH
℅ Most Rev. B. H. Webster
2315 Valley Brook Rd.
Nashville, TN 37215

The Southern Episcopal Church was formed in 1953 by ten families of All Saints Episcopal Church in Nashville, Tennessee. Its constitution was ratified in 1965. The presiding bishop is the Rt. Rev. B. H. Webster. He is assisted by fellow bishops William Green, Jr., Webster B. Hoyle, and Huron C. Manning, Jr.. The church is governed by the National Convention composed of all bishops (House of Bishops) and the lay and clerical delegates. The 1928 *Book of Common Prayer* is standard

for worship. The church sponsors an American Indian mission as well as foreign work in four countries. American parishes can be found in Tennessee, Alabama, Georgia, the Carolinas, Florida, Ohio, Indiana, Oklahoma, and New York.

Membership: In 1984 the Church reported 72,000 members in 14 congregations with 17 priests.

Educational facilities: Holy Trinity College, Nashville, Tennessee.

Periodicals: *The Southern Episcopalians*, 2315 Valley Brook Road, Nashville, TN 37215.

★59★
UNITED EPISCOPAL CHURCH OF AMERICA
℅ Rt. Rev. Richard C. Acker
6317 N. Trenholm Rd.
Columbia, SC 29206

The United Episcopal Church of America can be traced to the American Episcopal Church founded in the early 1940s by Denver Scott Swain (not to be confused with the current American Episcopal Church formed by K. C. Pillai in 1968). Swain had been ordained to the priesthood in 1942 by Archbishop Carmel Henry Carfora of the North American Old Roman Catholic Church, but he was soon suspended from the priesthood for going beyond Carfora's jurisdiction while seeking someone to consecrate him. Eventually (around 1943) Francis V. Kanski of the American Catholic Church raised Swain to the episcopacy. During the 1940s, the American Episcopal Church applied for membership. Upon investigation, it was discovered that Swain had misrepresented the nature and strength of the church.

It was widely reported that the American Episcopal Church had dissolved in the 1950s. However, in 1945 Swain consecrated William H. Schneider, who in turn consecrated James Edward Burns in 1948. Eventually Burns became primate and the name of the church was changed to the United Episcopal Church. Burns established the Church's headquarters at All Saints Church in East Hanover, New Jersey. He was subsequently consecrated by Hubert A. Rogers (who succeeded Carfora as head of the North American Old Roman Catholic Church) in 1967 and by Walter Propheta of the American Orthodox Catholic Church in 1968.

In 1976 Burns, assisted by Bishop Edward G. Marshall and Archbishop John W. Treleaven (of the Apostolic Catholic Church of North America), consecrated Richard C. Acker to the episcopacy. Several months later Acker succeeded Burns as archbishop in charge of the United Episcopal Church of America. Acker's parish, St. James Church, (located in Hopkins, South Carolina) became the new national cathedral of the jurisdiction. In 1984, Acker, assisted by Bishops Marshall and Orlando Woodward, consecrated Charles Edward Morley of Pensacola, Florida.

The United Episcopal Church of America describes itself as a conservative independent church which uses the King James Bible, the 1928 edition of the *Book of Common Prayer*, and the 1940 Hymnal of the Protestant Episcopal Church. The church combines traditional liturgical form with the widest possible measure of intellectual freedom.

Membership: Not reported. The church has several congregations and an estimated membership of several hundred.

Remarks: As this publication goes to press, the editor has received word that Bishop Acker died on October 29, 1985. It is assumed that Bishop Morley has succeeded him.

★60★
UNITED EPISCOPAL CHURCH OF NORTH AMERICA
% Most Rev. C. Dale D. Doren
2293 Country Club Dr.
Upper St. Clair, PA 15241

In 1980 C. Dale David Doren, senior bishop of the Anglican Catholic Church and head of its mid-Atlantic diocese, resigned. He contended that the Anglican Catholic Church was becoming exclusively "high-church" or "Anglo-Catholic" in its stance. With only two congregations, he formed the United Episcopal Church of the U.S.A. (known since 1985 as the United Episcopal) and the United Episcopal Church of North America. It adheres to the traditional beliefs and practices of the Protestant Episcopal Church as exemplified in the 1928 *Book of Common Prayer* and the Thirty-nine Articles of Religion.

The UEC tends to the "low-church" end of the Anglican spectrum. Each parish is independent and holds title to properties and control over temporal affairs. The jurisdiction adopted the 1958 Protestant Episcopal Church Constitution and Canons (with specific changes in relation to church properties) as its own. The presiding bishop was given the title of archbishop, but the church invested little power in the office. In 1984 Archbishop Dorn consecrated Albion W. Knight as a missionary bishop to assist him in leadership of the jurisdiction's affairs.

Membership: Not reported. Parishes of the church are found in Pennsylvannia, Ohio, New York, Maryland, New Hampshire, and Florida. In 1984, membership was estimated to be less than 1,000.

Periodicals: *Glad Tidings*, Box 4538, Pensacola, Florida 32507.

Eastern Liturgical Family

An historical essay on this family is provided beginning on page 9.

Orthodoxy

★61★
AFRICAN ORTHODOX CHURCH
℅ Most Rev. Stafford J. Sweeting
15801 N.W. 38th Place
Opa-Locka, FL 33054

The Protestant Episcopal Church, like all American denominations with both episcopal leadership and a significant black membership, faced the problems and pressures related to electing and elevating their first black member to the bishopric. Within the Episcopal Church the cries for a bishop drawn from among black members grew even louder after the Civil War. They were refused, the leadership arguing that, since the church did not recognize racial distinctions, it could not elevate a man to the bishopric just because he was black. A step toward the solution came in 1910 with the creation of black "suffragan" bishops, bishops without right to succession and without vote in the house of bishops.

Among those who complained that suffragans were not enough was Dr. George A. McGuire (1866-1934), an Episcopal priest who had emigrated from the West Indies. In 1921 he left the Protestant Episcopal Church and founded the Independent Episcopal Church. McGuire had had a distinguished career in the Episcopal Church, serving parishes in both the United States and Antigua, and he had been considered for the post of Suffragan Bishop of Arkansas. He declined in order to study medicine at Jefferson Medical College, where he graduated as a Doctor of Medicine in 1910. Upon graduation, he served at St. Bartholomew's Episcopal Church in Cambridge, Massachusetts. He was then called to be the Secretary of the Commission for Work among the Colored People under the Church's Board of Missions.

After several years as Secretary, he moved back to Antigua, where he remained for six years building the church where he was baptized, St. Paul's in Sweets. When fellow West Indian Marcus Garvey formed the United Negro Improvement Association, McGuire returned to the United States to support him. Working with Garvey only strengthened his dissatisfaction in serving a church where black people were systematically denied positions of leadership, and he became determined to pursue an independent course.

On September 2, 1921, in the Church of the Good Shepherd in New York City, a meeting of independent black clergy resolved itself into the first Synod of the African Orthodox Church, and designated McGuire as its bishop elect. The Synod then entered into negotiations with the Russian Orthodox Church in America in their search for their episcopal orders for their newly elected bishop. The Russians indicated a willingness to consecrate McGuire, but only if they controlled the newly created jurisdiction. The idea of non-Black control had no appeal to either McGuire or his followers. They then turned to the American Catholic Church, headed by Archbishop Joseph Rene Vilatte. Vilatte was willing to confer orders and ask little or nothing in the way of control. On September 29, 1921, Bishop Vilatte, assisted by Carl A. Nybladh, consecrated Dr. McGuire in the Church of Our Lady of Good Death in Chicago.

The Church experienced slow but steady growth, although most of the individual congregations were small. The priests were seldom full-time clergy, although every church was encouraged to contribute something to their support. McGuire emphasized education and led in the organization of a seminary for the training of clergy. The first class numbered fourteen men. The school provided professional training for its students, while accommodating to the generally lower educational level of its applicants. It has not tried to become an accredited degree-granting institution.

Archbishop McGuire led the Church until his death in 1923, and it enjoyed peace and stability. After his death the leadership of the church fell into the hands of Archbishop W. E. J. Robertson. Shortly after his elevation to the archbishopric, dissatisfaction arose among the group of clergy, and a schism, the Holy African Church was created. The dissidents were led by Bishop R. G. Barrow, who had been McGuire's closest associate. In time, Barrow was succeeded by Bishop F. A. Toote and then Bishop Gladstone St. Claire Nurse. Bishop Nurse led the efforts to reunite the two factions. On February 22, 1964, the two bodies joined together under Robertson, who adopted the Patriarchal name of Peter IV. Just prior to the merger he consecrated several bishops, an obvious effort to insure his continued control of the Church. Nurse did not protest Robertson's action, and upon the death of the Patriarch was elected by the bishops to be the new primate of the Church. He quickly brought all the elements of the Church together and upon his death, leadership passed very easily to Archbishop William R. Miller, who served as the Church's Primate from 1976 until August of 1981. At the Annual Synod of the Church, he resigned and was succeeded by Archbishop Stafford J. Sweeting.

The denomination remains small in the United States, but it has affiliated parishes in the West Indies and Africa (Nigeria, Ghana, and Uganda). Recently, the Church lost one of its strongest parishes when Bishop G. Duncan Hinkson of Chicago left to found the African Orthodox Church of the West.

Membership: In 1983 the Church reported 17 parishes and 5,100 members in the United States.

Educational facilities: Endich Theological Seminary, New York, New York.

Periodicals: *The Trumpet*, Rev. Fr. Harold Furblur, Box 1925, Boston, MA 02105.

Sources: Arthur C. Terry-Thompson, *History of the African Orthodox Church*. New York: The Author, 1956; *The Divine liturgy and Other Rites and Ceremonies of the Church*. Chicago: African Orthodox church, 1945; Randall K. Burkett, *Garveyism as a Religious Movement*. Metuchen, NJ: Scarecrow Press, 1978; Richard Newman, "The Origins of the African Orthodox Church" in *The Negro Churchman*. Millwood, NY: Kraus Publishing Co., 1977.

★62★
AFRICAN ORTHODOX CHURCH OF THE WEST
% Most Rev. G. Duncan Hinkson
St. Augustine's African Orthodox Church
5831 S. Indiana St.
Chicago, IL 60637

In 1984 Bishop G. Duncan Hinkson, a physician and pastor of St. Augustine's African Orthodox Church, on the southside of Chicago, left the African Orthodox Church and formed a new jurisdiction. While following the teachings and ritual of its parent body, it is administratively independent. Bishop Hinkson consecrated Bishop Franzo King to lead work in San Francisco.

Membership: In 1985, the Church had two parishes, one in Chicago and one in California with several hundred members.

★63★
ALBANIAN ORTHODOX ARCHDIOCESE IN AMERICA
% Metropolitan Theodosius
529 E. Broadway
Boston, MA 02127

The Albanian Orthodox Archdiocese in America can be traced to 1908, when the first Albanian parish in the U.S. was established in Boston. In the same year, an Albanian-American immigrant, Fan S. Noli, was ordained to the priesthood by Metropolitan Platon of the Russian Orthodox Church. Father Noli returned to Albania in 1920 where he had a prominent political career, eventually becoming prime minister. He became a bishop in 1923, but in 1930 (due to Turkish domination of Albania), he returned to the United States and organized the American parishes into the Albanian Orthodox Archdiocese in America. The Archdiocese remained in communion with the Church in Albania until after World War II when a Communist government hostile to the Church took control of the country, and, inthe eyes of the Archdiocese, subverted the leadership of the Church. While retaining orthodox belief and practice, the Archdiocese became independent. Noli was succeeded by Metropolitan Theodosius.

Membership: In 1978 the Archdiocese reported 16 parishes, 40,000 members and 25 priests.

Periodicals: *The Vineyard (Vreshta)*, 529 E. Broadway, Boston, MA 02127.

★64★
ALBANIAN ORTHODOX DIOCESE OF AMERICA
% The Rev. Ik. Ilia Katra, Vicar General
54 Burroughs St.
Jamaica Plain, MA 02130

In 1949 His Grace Mark I. Lipa came to the United States with authority from the Ecumenical Patriarch in Constantinople to organize the Albanian faithful (which had become independent under Fan Noli of the Albanian Orthodox Archdiocese in America). The following year he formed the Albanian Orthodox Church in America, now known as the Albanian Orthodox Diocese of America. It is a member of the Standing Conference of Canonical Orthodox Bishops in America.

Membership: In 1982 the Diocese reported 10 parishes, 5,250 members and 3 clergy.

Periodicals: *The True Light*, 54 Burroughs Street, Jamaica Plain, MA 02130.

★65★
AMERICAN CARPATHO-RUSSIAN ORTHODOX GREEK CATHOLIC CHURCH
℅ Most Rev. John R. Martin
312 Garfield St.
Johnstown, PA 15906

The American Carpatho-Russian Orthodox Greek Catholic Church was founded in the 1930s by a group of former members of the Roman Catholic Church who had migrated to the United States from Carpatho-Russia. Carpatho-Russia had been forcefully converted from Eastern Orthodoxy to the Roman Catholic Ruthenian Rite by a series of rulers who basically followed the Latin Rite. Once in the United States, a process of further Latinizing Ruthenian Rite parishes began. Among other issues, attempts were made to curtail the assignment of married priests to American parishes.

As early as 1891, a Carpatho-Russian Catholic parish sought to return to Eastern Orthodoxy. It was soon joined by others. Then in 1936, approximately forty parishes which had left Roman jurisdiction organized and selected Orestes P. Chernock as their leader. The next year they designated him their bishop-elect and turned to the ecumenical patriarch in Constantinople for recognition. In 1938 the patriarch consecrated Chernock and authorized the American Carpatho-Russian Orthodox Diocese as an independent body. In 1966 the patriarch elevated Chernock to the dignity of a metropolitan and consecrated John R. Martin, formerly the chancellor of the Roman Catholic Byzantine Diocese of Pittsburgh, as his assistant bishop.

The American Carpatho-Russian Orthodox Greek Catholic Church is an independent autonomous body directly under the authority of the ecumenical patriarch. It has a working relationship with the Greek Orthodox Archdiocese of North and South America, whose archbishop is the exarch of the patriarch. The archbishop intercedes when the appointment of a new bishop is requested by the church and has the task of consecrating him. The Church is at one with Eastern Orthodox faith and practice, though its liturgy still retains a few minor peculiarities reflective of its Roman Catholic history. The Church is a member of the Standing Conference of Canonical Orthodox Bishops in the Americas.

Membership: In 1976 the Church reported 70 parishes, 100,000 members and 68 priests.

Periodicals: *Cerkovny Visnik--Church Messenger*, 127 Chandler Avenue, Johnstown, PA 19506.

★66★
AMERICAN CATHOLIC CHURCH, ARCHDIOCESE OF NEW YORK
℅ Most Rev. Michael Edward Verra
238 Mott St.
New York, NY 10012

The American Catholic Church, Archdiocese of New York was formed in 1927 by James F. A. Lashley. In 1932, Bishop William F. Tyarcks (having been recently deposed from the African Orthodox Church by Archbishop George A. McGuire), consecrated Lashley. Lashley, a black man, built a substantive independent jurisdiction which in the mid-1960s reported 20 churches under its leadership. These included nine in the United States and 11 in the West Indies. Bishop Verra succeeded to leadership upon the death of Archbishop Lashley.

The Church takes as its standards of faith the Holy Bible, the first Seven Ecumenical Councils, the Synod of Jerusalem of 1692, and the accumulated teachings of the Church Fathers. An Eastern liturgy is used. Icons are allowed for veneration and clergy can marry.

Membership: In 1984 the Archdiocese reported five parishes, 400 members, and eight priests. There is affiliated work conducted in Trinidad.

★67★
AMERICAN EASTERN ORTHODOX CHURCH
Current address not obtained for this edition.

Since the second century, India has had Eastern Orthodox churches that call themselves Mar Thomas churches. They claim that St. Thomas the Apostle founded them. In the 1930s the Church of England was India's state church. When the Christian Missionary Society of the Church of England attempted to convert members of the Mar Thomas churches, a controversy arose. One of its results was that Bishop Anthony Devan left India and came to the U.S. to locate members of the Mar Thomas churches residing there. He succeeded in locating a few families, and he ordained four priests, thus establishing the American Eastern Orthodox Church. It continues the tradition of the Mar Thomas Christians. It is one in faith and practice with the Orthodox churches. St. Thomas is honored on the Sunday after the Resurrection (Easter), July 19 (his birthday), and October 19 (anniversary of his martyrdom). The Liturgy of St. Basil is used.

Membership: In 1973 there were 5 parishes, 5 mission stations and 1,240 members.

Sources: *Following Christ in the American Eastern Orthodox Church*. Las Vegas, NV: St. George Monastery, 1967.

★68★
AMERICAN HOLY ORTHODOX CATHOLIC EASTERN CHURCH
(Defunct)

The American Holy Orthodox Catholic Eastern Church was incorporated in 1933 under the leadership of Cyril John Clement Sherwood, popularly known by his ecclesiastical name, Clement I. His Holiness Clement I had previously belonged to the Benedictine community founded by Archbishop W. H. Francis Brothers of the Old Catholic Church in America. In 1927, however, he received priestly orders from Archbishop Frederick E. J. Lloyd of the American Catholic Church and three years later was consecrated by Bishop William F. Tyarks of the African Orthodox Church. He was then reconsecrated in 1932 by Bishop George A. McGuire of the African Orthodox Church, and throughout the rest of his life he considered this latter consecration as his true one. The American Holy Orthodox Catholic Eastern Church followed Eastern Orthodox faith and practice, but it was established as a completely autocephalous jurisdiction, autonomous of all foreign bishops and church bodies. Headquarters of the church were established in Sts. Peter and Paul Church in New York City. For a while Clement issued a periodical, *The Voice of the Community*. Clement founded a coalition of various independent orthodox and catholic bishops, the Orthodox Catholic Patriarchate of America. Clement died in 1969. Following his death, leadership of the Patriarchate passed to Archbishop George A. Hyde of the Orthodox Catholic Church of America. In succeeding years, the already weakened organization ceased to exist though it has recently been re-established by Archbishop Alfred Lankenau who succeeded Hyde as head of the Orthodox Church in America. At the same time, the American Holy Orthodox Catholic Apostolic Eastern Church was received into the Orthodox Catholic Church in America as its Eastern Rite Diocese, and it ceased to exist as a separate body.

★69★
AMERICAN INDEPENDENT ORTHODOX CHURCH (BRIDGES)
2301 Stanford Ave.
Los Angeles, CA 90011

The American Independent Orthodox Church was founded in 1976 by Richard W. Bridges, whose episcopal orders were conferred in 1980 by Bishops Gregory Voris, C. Engel, and Hans B. Kroneberg. It adheres to the faith of the Seven Ecumenical Councils and the Three Ecumenical Creeds, and it is designed to use both Eastern and Western rites. While not open to ordaining females to the priesthood, it is open to receiving homosexuals into Holy Orders.

Membership: In the early 1980s, the Church claimed 2 parishes, 3 priests and 75 members.

★70★
AMERICAN ORTHODOX CATHOLIC CHURCH (PROPHETA)
% Archbishop John A. Christian
675 E. 183rd St.
New York, NY 10458

The American Orthodox Catholic Church was incorporated in 1965 by its newly consecrated bishop, Walter A. Propheta (1912-1972). Propheta had been a Ukrainian Orthodox priest since 1938, but left the Ukrainian Church and in 1964 was consecrated bishop by Archbishop Theodotus (DeWitow) of the Holy Orthodox Church in America and Archbishop Joachim Souris, an independent Greek bishop. The following year he was elevated to Archbishop and began the task of building an independent and indigenous American Orthodoxy.

He considered as essential the doctrinal decrees of the Seven Ecumenical Councils, but left to each bishop the choice of ritual, language, calendar, vestments and other details the churches under their jurisdiction would use. His only requirement was that th e liturgy be an expression of common faith and the commonly-accepted seven sacraments.

Within the loose structure, lacking any real central authority, and given the eagerness of Propheta to build the jurisdiction by consecrating new bishops, many men accepted episcopal orders only to leave within a few years to found their own jurisdictions. Severe splintering of the jurisdiction began even before Propheta's death. At a Synod in November 1972, those remaining elected John A. Christian to succeed Propheta. As of 1985, Archbishop Christian has retired without naming a successor.

In 1982 Archbishop Christian consecrated Harold Donovan, who took the name Archbishop Aftimios, and in January 1983, in cooperation with the Orthodox Church in the Philippines, established an exarchate now known as the American Orthodox Church. The new church body operates independently of Archbishop Christian, though a friendly relationship is maintained.

Membership: In 1985, no active parishes were reported within the Church. The jurisdiction, having lost most of its bishops to other independent bodies, has almost ceased to exist.

Sources: *American Orthodox Catholic Church, Ecclesiatical History*. Los Angeles: Archdiocese of So. California and the Western Province, 1974; Walter M. Propheta, *Divine Liturgy for 20th Century Christians*. New York: American Orthodox Church, 1966.

★71★
AMERICAN ORTHODOX CATHOLIC CHURCH (HEALY)
(Defunct)

One of the several jurisdictions formed by clergy who were with Archbishop Walter M. Propheta's American Orthodox Catholic Church, this jurisdiction of the same name was formed by Bishop Lawrence Pierre, formerly the Auxiliary Bishop for New York and the Eastern States. It continued the beliefs and practices as well as the name of Propheta's Church, being bi-ritualistic (i.e, it allowed both Eastern and Western liturgies be used in its parishs' worship services). Archbishop Pierre was succeeded by Archbishop Patrick J. Healy as primate. Upon the death of Healy in 1984, the jurisdiction disolved.

★72★
AMERICAN ORTHODOX CATHOLIC CHURCH (IRENE)
% Most Rev. Milton A. Pritts
851 Leyden St.
Denver, CO 80220

The American Orthodox Catholic Church (Irene) was founded in 1962 and incorporated three years later. Its presiding head is a female-bishop known only as Archbishop Irene, consecrators unknown. Spokesperson of the Church is Bishop Emeritus Milton A. Pritts, who had been consecrated by Archbishop Walter Propheta of the American Orthodox Catholic Church.

The Church is orthodox in faith and practice, accepting the forms presented in the *Service Book* edited by Isabel Florence Hapgood, and the principles enuciated in such standard orthodox volumes as Fr. John Meyendorff's *The Orthodox Church*. The Revised Standard Version of the Bible is used. It differs in the following: 1) it would consider otherwise qualified women and homosexuals for the priesthood and 2) it believes that apostolic succession is not necessary to the establishment of a valid church or ministry. A resolution passed by the Grant Synod of the Church, January 6, 1979 stated, "We now hold with the Churches of England, Sweden, Congregational, Presbyterian, Lutheran, Methodist, Christian Scientists and others who are determined to revive lay selection and authority of the congregation to avoid the further creation of hierarchies."

Although renouncing the necessity of apostolic succession and the idea of building further hierarchies, the church has claimed to have a ministry with valid apostolic episcopal orders and claims to have built an elaborate hierarchy. The jurisdiction, divided into 53 dioceses, is spread over all of North America. Apart from Bishop Pritts, the names of Church officers and bishops and the addresses of their diocesan headquarters have not been available for publication.

Membership: Not reported. There is some doubt as to the size of this Church in light of the unverifiable nature of its claims and the inability to locate any parishes associated with Bishop Pritts or Archbishop Irene.

★73★
AMERICAN ORTHODOX CHURCH
% Archbishop Aftimios Harold J. Donovan, Exarch
3332 S. Kings Ave.
Springfield, MO 65807

The American Orthodox Church was established in 1981 by Harold Donovan as the Orthodox American Catholic Church, Diocese of the Ozarks under a charter from the Orthodox Church of the Philippines. Donovan was originally consecrated by Bishops Howard Fris and John Kenelly of the Old Roman Catholic Church, Archdiocese of Chicago. However, in 1982, Donovan was reconsecrated by Archbishop John A. Christian of the American Orthodox Catholic Church (Propheta) in order to establish formal continuity with the original American Orthodox Church established by Archbishop Aftimios Ofiesh in the 1920s. Donovan took the religious name of the late archbishop and is currently known as Archbishop Aftimios Donovan. On January 1983, Archbishop Christian, in cooperation with the Orthodox Church in the Philippines, established an exarchate known as the North American Synod of the Holy Eastern Orthodox Catholic and Apostolic Church (shortened to its present name the following year).

The Church follows Eastern Orthodox belief and practice. The liturgy of St. Germain is used and sacraments are administered according to the American Rite of St. Germain, an abbreviated and modified formula based upon the Byzantine Rite.

The exarchate retains formal ties to both the Orthodox Church in the Philippines and the American Orthodox Catholic Church headed by Archbishop Christian. Its parish work includes two missions in Los Angeles, one to Oriental-Americans and one to Hispanic-Americans.

Membership: In 1984 the Church reported 3 parishes, 3 clergy, and less than 150 members.

Educational facilities: Seminary of the Orthodox Catholic Church in the Philippines, Manila, Philippines.

Periodicals: *The Orthodox Catholic*, Box 389, Ozark, MO 65721.

Sources: *The Liturgy*. Springfield, MO; American Orthodox Church, 1983.

★74★

ANTIOCHIAN ORTHODOX CHRISTIAN ARCHDIOCESE OF NORTH AMERICA
℅ Metropolitan Philip, Primate
358 Mountain Rd.
Englewood, NJ 07631

In 1892 the Russian Orthodox Church began a Syrian Mission in the United States to provide spiritual guidance for Orthodox Christians from the Eastern Mediterranean basin. In 1904 the first Orthodox bishop ever consecrated in America, Archimandrite Bishop Raphael Hawaweeny, became the leader of the Syrian Mission of the Russian Orthodox Church. Then in 1914 Metropolitan Germanos came to the United States and began organizing Syrian churches. These two efforts paralleled each other until 1925 when an independent church was created. In 1936, Archimandrite Anthony Bashir was elected and consecrated bishop by the American Syrian churches. He became Metropolitan of New York and All America in 1940 and provided leadership for almost thirty years.

In the 1936 election in which Anthony Bashir was elected to the bishopric, Archimandrite Samuel David of Toledo, Ohio, polled the second highest number of votes. On the same day that Archbishop Anthony Bashir was consecrated in New York, Russian bishops consecrated Samuel David as archbishop of Toledo. Archbishop Samuel David was condemned and excommunicated by Archbishop Anthony Bashir in 1938 but then recognized the following year. The Antiochean Orthodox Archdiocese of Toledo, Ohio, and Dependencies which he led existed as a separate body until 1975.

In 1966 Most Reverend Philip Saliba succeeded Bashir and became primate of the Antiochean Orthodox Christian Archdiocese of New York and all North America. Archbishop Philip has been a leader in promoting the use of English in the liturgy. He has given priority to missions and has extended his work to Australia and the South Seas.

In 1958, Archbishop David died, and hope for reunion of the two Antiochean Churches emerged. Archbishop Michael Shaheen succeeded Archbishop David and conducted talks toward union which was finally consummated in 1975. The new Antiochean Orthodox Christian Archdiocese of North America selected Archbishop Philip as head of the church with the title of metropolitan.

Membership: In 1977 the Archdiocese reported 110 parishes, 152,000 members and 132 priests.

Periodicals: *The Word*, 54 Howitt Road, Boston, MA 02132.

Sources: John vonHolzhausen, *The Complete Toledo Primer*. Toledo, OH: Theophany Orthodox Publications, 1964.

★75★

AMERICAN WORLD PATRIARCHS
℅ Most Rev. Emigidius J. Ryzy
19 Aqueduct St.
Ossining, NY 10562

Uladyslau Ryzy-Ryski, a Byelorussian priest, was consecrated in 1965 by Archbishop Walter A. Propheta of the American Orthodox Catholic Church as the Bishop of Laconia, New Hampshire and the New England States. During this period he also met Archbishop Peter A. Zurawetzky of the Old Orthodox Catholic Patriarchate of America, who on November 4, 1967, in the presence of a congregation of four, elevated him to the status of Archbishop. Without leaving Propheta's jurisdiction, Ryzy-Ryski began to create archbishops-patriarchs for each national/ethnic group and, quite apart from any laity demanding leadership, to build a hierarchy which he envisioned as international in scope. The World Patriarchate was very loosely structured, and established in large part by the elevation to patriarchial status of other independent bishops not otherwise required to recognize Ryzy-Ryski's authority or come under his jurisdiction. In 1972, as one of the last acts before his death, Propheta excommunicated Ryzy-Ryski from the American Orthodox Catholic Church, an action which merely spurred the growth of the American World Patriarchs, who established patriarchs for Puerto Rico, Colombia, Haiti, Santo Domingo, Brazil, Peru, Argentina, El Salvador, Nigeria, the West Indies, Norway, Sweden, Formosa, and the Ukraine. Only rarely were new congregations established as a result of a patriarch being named. Occasionally, the new patriarch could claim a small following.

In connection with the American World Patriarchates, the Ryzy-Ryski organized a Cathedral of Learning, an educational center designed to meet the needs of various ethnic and immigrant groups in the Bronx, New York. A well-educated man, with a good academic background, he led a faculty which offered a wide variety of courses in the humanities, and especially in English as a second language. The school also provided the World Patriarchates with a seminary.

Since the death of Patriarch Uladyslau Ryzy-Ryski in 1980, the work has continued under his brother, Archbishop Emigidius J. Ryzy, who holds the title of Apostolic Administrator of All American World Patriarchates. He is assisted by Archbishop Adam Bilecky, Patriarch II of the American World Patriarchate.

Membership: In 1984 the American World Patriarchs reported 22 parishes, 254 members and 52 priests/bishops.

★76★

APOSTOLIC CATHOLIC CHURCH OF THE AMERICAS

% Most Rev. Gordon I. DaCosta
408 S. 10th St.
Gas City, IN 46933

The Apostolic Catholic Church of the Americas dates to a 1976 merger of two jurisdictions headed by Bishops Robert S. Zeiger and Gordon I. DaCosta. Zeiger had been consecrated in 1961 by Archbishop Peter A. Zurawetzky of the Old Orthodox Catholic Patriarchate of America as an Orthodox bishop for Westerners. However, in 1962 Zieger left Zurawetzky's jurisdiction and formed the American Orthodox Catholic Church headquartered in Denver, Colorado. The church was conceived as American in its autonomy, Orthodox in its faith and practice, and Catholic in its universality.

Gordon I. DaCosta was a priest and bishop of the Free Protestant Episcopal Church. He left that jurisdiction in 1971 and formed the Anglican Church of the Americas, in Indiana. The Anglican Church of the Americas was designed to continue the work of, and update the structure of, the Free Protestant Episcopal Church (then in the process of losing any American presence) and to avoid any conflict over the similarity of name with the Protestant Episcopal Church. Over the first few years of its existence, the Anglican Church moved toward Orthodoxy in both faith and liturgy and in 1976 merged into the American Orthodox Catholic Chruch headed by Bishop Zeiger. At the time of the merger, the American Orthodox Catholic Church took on a second name, the Apostolic Catholic Church of the Americas. This second name became its most frequently used designation, though both names are officially correct.

Soon after the merger, Zieger resigned both his office and membership in the church and joined the Roman Catholic Church as a layman in a Uniate Ruthenian congregation. DaCosta was elected as his successor. (As of 1984 Zeiger remains connected to the church as its registered agent. The church is registered in Colorado while DaCosts resides in Indiana.)

The Apostolic Catholic Church of the Americas describes itself as Western Orthodox. It is Orthodox in that it accepts as authority the Sacred Scriptures, the Apostolic Tradition, the doctrinal decrees of the Seven Ecumenical Councils, and the writings of the church fathers. It follows Eastern practice in making clerical celibacy optional. It rejects females as candidates for the priesthood. The Church is Catholic, but not Roman; Evangelical but not Protestant; and Orthodox, but not Eastern.

As of 1985, the church is headed by two bishops: Gordon I. DaCosta and Herbert Robinson of Bellingham, Washington. A third bishop, C. F. Quinn, who headed a large congregation in Dallas, Texas, recently died. Church property is owned locally by the boards of individual congregations. Thus, church government is a complex mixture of episcopal and congregational polity.

Membership: In 1984 the church reported nine parishes, missions, and chaplaincies and had an estimated membership of less than 500.

Periodicals: *The Door*, 4201 Fairmount Street, Dallas, Texas 75219.

Sources: *The Order of Daily Prayer*. Dallas: Diocese of Texas, Apostolic Catholic Church, n.d.

★77★

ASSOCIATION OF OCCIDENTAL ORTHODOX PARISHES

Father Stephen Empson
57 Saint Marks Place
New York, NY 10003

The use of the Western Rite in Orthodox Churches has experienced a revival during the twentieth century as Eastern Orthodoxy has flourished in the West. It has a long history, though little noticed due to the predominance of the Roman Rite. It was the opinion of some, verified by such examples as the Western Rite Vicariate within the Antiocean Orthodox Church, that Western Rite parishes do not remain Western within a predominantly Eastern Rite church body. The Orthodox Church of France is a totally Western Rite diocese founded in 1953 by Fr. Evgraph Kovalevsky and several other priests who withdrew from the Russian Orthodox Church. As priests in Lithuania they had followed a Western Rite and Fr. Kovalevsky had pastored a Western Rite parish opened in 1944 in Paris. That parish became the source of several others.

After leaving the Russian Orthodox Church, the priests and their parishes affiliated with the Russian Orthodox Church Outside of Russia. Bishop John Maximovitch ordained several new Western Rite priests and saw to the publication of the liturgy, the old Gallican Rite according to Saint Germain, Bishop of Paris (555-576), not to be confused with the eighteenth-century occultist of the same name. The death of Bishop John led to a break with the Russian Church, and, as relations worsened, Kovalevsky, who had been consecrated in 1964, led his followers in forming an autonomous diocese. But he died in 1970 without having a successor consecrated. Finally, in 1972, the Patriarch of Romania agreed to consecrate Pere Gilles Hardy as the new bishop of the Orthodox Catholic Church of France. He is known as Bishop Germain. The Western Rite was reintroduced to America by Father Stephen Empson who founded a parish in New York City. In 1981 he organized the Association of Occidental Orthodox Parishes to further promote Western Rite Orthodoxy.

Membership: In 1984 the Association had five parishes (New York City; Brooklyn, NY; Chicago; Dorchester, MA; and Fullerton, CA) and a monastery in Jacksonville, Florida. Internationally, the Western Orthodox Church had 60 parishes, most in France, but including two each in Switzerland and Spain and one each in Germany, Belgium, and Argentina.

Periodicals: *Axios*, 800 S. Euclid St., Fullerton, CA 92632 (unofficial publication).

★78★

AUTOCEPHALOUS SLAVONIC ORTHODOX CATHOLIC CHURCH (IN EXILE)
2237 Hunter Ave.
New York, NY 10475

The Autocephalous Slavonic Orthodox Catholic Church (In Exile) dates its existence to the coming of Saint Cyril and Saint Methodius to Moravia in the ninth century and to Saint Gyle's coming to Hungary in the tenth century. A Greek Orthodox church was established and in 1620 a jurisdiction of the Podcarpathian Church was established which existed until World War II and has since gone underground. It was granted autocephalic status in 1951.

In 1968, fearing for their church, Primate Philotej and his auxiliaries, Bishop Ianofan and Bishop Vladimir, came to the United States and established the Slavic Church in Exile by consecrating Archimandrite Andrew Prazsky and making him bishop-heir to the title of the Church. Archbishop Andrew was enthroned in 1969 as metropolitan-archbishop in Canada by His Eminence Spyridon of the Autocephalous Greek Orthodox Church of America. Archbishop Andrew took up residence in the Bronx, from where he, with the assistance of two auxiliary bishops, presided over the Metropolitan Synod. He established a monastery on Long Island and a priory in Connecticut.

Membership: In 1970 the Church reported 30 parishes, including one on the Island of Atka in the Aleutians.

★79★

AUTOCEPHALOUS SYRO-CHALDEAN CHURCH OF NORTH AMERICA
% Most Rev. Bertram S. Schlossberg (Mar Uzziah)
9 Ellington Ave.
Rockville, CT 06066

The Autocephalous Syro-Chaldean Church of North America traces its origins to Hugh George de Willmott Newman, popularly known by his ecclesiastical name Mar Georgius. Mar Georgius was the first of the independent bishops to have himself consecrated numerous times in order to embody the several episcopal lineages both East and West, which he in turn passed on to the many individuals he consecrated. Among the people to whom he passed these various lines of apostolic succession was Charles D. Boltwood, a bishop in the British-based Free

Protestant Episcopal Church. In 1959, three years after his reconsecration by Newman, Boltwood became primate of the church. Among his first actions, Boltwood consecrated John M. Stanley (May 3, 1959) as bishop of the state of Washington.

During the 1960s, Stanley withdrew from the Free Protestant Episcopal Church and formed the Syro-Chaldean Archdiocese of North America. In so doing he claimed the lineage of the Church of the East received by Newman from W. S. M. Knight who had received the lineage from Ulric Vernon Herford (Mar Jacobus). Stanley, as archbishop of the new jurisdiction, took the ecclesiastical name Mar Yokhannan.

The series of events which led to the formation of the Autocephalous Syro-Chaldean Church of North America began at the meeting of the Holy Synod of Syro-Chaldean Archdiocese, December 13-14, 1974. The synod designated Archpriest Bertram S. Schlossberg as bishop-elect with the task of organizing a Diocese of New York. By that action Schlossberg came under the direct authority of Archbishop James A. Gaines who had authority from the archdiocese for the eastern half of the United States. Together, on April 16, 1976, they incorporated their new work as the Autocephalous Syro-Chaldean Archdiocese of the Eastern United States of America. On October 31, 1976, Gaines consecrated Schlossberg as bishop of the Northeast and in December erected the Diocese of the Northeast, over which Schlossberg was assigned.

The actions of Gaines and Schlossberg were followed by a split with Mar Yokhannan, who attempted to dissolve both the Autocephalous Eastern Archdiocese and the Diocese of the Northeast. Eventually, on April 2, 1977, Mar Yokhannan released Schlossberg and Gaines from "all canonical obedience" and then withdrew from the Syro-Chaldean Archdiocese and joined the Church of the East. Gaines (Mar Jacobus) and Schlossberg (Mar Uzziah) then reorganized all of the work formerly under Mar Yokhannan and in October 1977 incorporated the Autocephalous Syro-Chaldean Church of North America, with Mar Jacobus as metropolitan and Mar Uzziah as bishop of the Northeastern Diocese.

The Syro-Chaldean Church follows the Orthodox theology of the Church of the East. It affirms the Bible as the Word of God and both the Apostles' and Nicene Creeds. It keeps seven sacraments: baptism, confirmation, holy communion, reconciliation, annointing for healing, holy matrimony, and holy orders. It uses the Liturgy of Mar Addai and Mar Mari as its official liturgy, but allows parishes great freedom in choosing other forms of worship.

Membership: In 1984 the church reported 400 members and 18 clergy in four parish churches and two missions. It sponsors one missionary in Papua, New Guinea.

Educational facilities: Christ the King Seminary and School of Discipleship, Rockville, Connecticut.

★80★

BULGARIAN EASTERN ORTHODOX CHURCH (DIOCESE OF NORTH AND SOUTH AMERICA AND AUSTRALIA)

Metropolitan Joseph
550 A, W. 50th St.
New York, NY 10019

Bulgarians arrived in the United States throughout the nineteenth century and by 1907 were numerous enough to begin establishing congregations independently of the Russian Orthodox Church parishes in which they had mainly worshipped. The first parish was formed in Madison, Illinois. Soon, the Holy Synod in Sophia established a mission to oversee their American members. Finally, in 1938, a diocese was created and Bishop Andrey Velichky came from Bulgaria as its head. Bishop Andrey returned to Bulgaria during World War II and worked on various projects among which was the handling of negotiations between the ecumenical patriarch in Istanbul and the Bulgarian patriarch which led to the healing of a seventy year-old broken relationship. During this period, the ecumenical patriarch elevated the diocese in America to a metropolia and gave it jurisdiction for Bulgarians in North and South America and Australia.

Soon after the war ended, Archbishop Andrey returned to America. In 1947 he incorporated the Bulgarian Eastern Orthodox Diocese of America, Canada and Australia. The constitutional assembly meeting in March of that year realigned its relationship to the Church in Bulgaria by declaring that while it saw itself as part of the whole of Bulgarian Orthodoxy, it could not accept orders from the church leaders in Sophia as long as a Communist regime ruled their homeland. They then proceeded to formally elect Andrey as their leader. The Holy Synod reacted by declaring the election null and void. The American diocese ignored the Synod and for the next fifteen years the diocese operated independently of the church leaders in Sophia. In 1962 the Church in Bulgaria recognized the Metropolia and reestablished a working relationship. In 1972 the Church was divided into two dioceses, and Bishop Joseph Znepolski succeeded Archbishop Andrey as Metropolitan. The Bulgarian Eastern Orthodox Church follows standard Orthodox faith and practice. It is a member of the Standing Conference of Canonical Orthodox Bishops in the Americas.

Membership: In the mid-1970s (latest report available) the Church had 18 parishes and an estimated membership of 105,000.

★81★

BULGARIAN EASTERN ORTHODOX CHURCH, DIOCESE OF NORTH AND SOUTH AMERICA

519 Brynhaven Dr.
Oregon, OH

The reestablishment of relations between the Orthodox Church in Bulgaria and the Bulgarian Eastern Orthodox Church (Diocese of North and South America and Australia) and the resultant manifestation of that accord in the joint visitation of North American parishes in 1963 by Bishop Andrey (Velichky), metropolitan of the American church and Bishop Preiman, metropolitan of Nevrokop, Bulgaria, led to major protests throughout the Church. Bishop Andrey was accused of violating the declaration made in 1947 that the Bulgarian Church in America would not accept any orders from the Church in Bulgaria. In March 1963, protesting leaders representing eighteen churches and missions met in Detroit, Michigan and reconstituted themselves as the Bulgarian Eastern Orthodox Church (Diocese of the United States of America and Canada) and elected Archimandrite Kyrill Yonchev as their bishop.

They turned to the Russian Orthodox Church Outside of Russia for support. The Russians, also cut off from their homeland by a hostile regime, gave the new Bulgarian jurisdiction their canonical protection and their bishops consecrated bishop-elect Yonchev in 1964 at their monastery in Jordanville, New York.

The Bulgarian Eastern Orthodox Church differs from its parent body only in matters of administration. It lays claim to all properties belonging to the undivided Church in America though it has not been able to take control of them. It is staunchly anti-Communist.

Membership: In the mid-1970s, the Church reported 21 parishes and missions.

★82★

BYELORUSSIAN AUTOCEPHALIC ORTHODOX CHURCH IN THE U.S.A.

% Archbishop Mikalay, Primate
Church of St. Cyril of Turau
524 St. Clarens Ave.
Toronto, ON, Canada

Byelorussia is that section of the U.S.S.R. directly north of the Ukraine and East of Poland. A national church had been organized there in 1291 under Greek jurisdiction. With time, it came under the control of the patriarch in Moscow, the head of the Russian Orthodox Church. In 1922 a split developed in the Byelorussian church when the Minsk Council of clergy and laity, under the leadership of Metropolitan Melchizedek, attempted to organize an autonomous Byelorussian church free of Moscow. Such action met the disapproval of both the government and the patriarch of the Russian Church. Within a short period of time, all the Byelorussian leaders had been arrested and sent to Siberia, and the church reverted to its dependent status. During the Nazi occupation of Byelorussia, the church attempted again to organize independently, but their efforts ended with the defeat of the German occupation forces.

The Byelorussian Autocephalic Orthodox Church in the U.S.A. is one of two Orthodox groups among Byelorussian immigrants. It emerged among refugee Byelorussians in Germany after the War. Their own bishops having returned to the Russian Church, clergy and laity turned to the Ukrainian Church. Metropolitan Polikarp not only blessed the reorganization of an autonomous church among the Byelorussians, but in 1948 granted permission for one of his bishops, Bishop Siarhej, to leave his jurisdiction and join the new church. In 1949, accompanied by his former Ukrainian colleagues, Sierhej consecrated a second bishop for the church, Bishop Vasil. As the church spread among immigrants around the world, two more bishops were consecrated in 1968.

Present Primate of the Church is Archbishop Mikalay, elected in 1984 at a convention at the church in Highland Park, New Jersey. He resides in Toronto, Canada. In the United States, parishes are located in Cleveland, Ohio; Detroit, Michigan; and Dorothy, New Jersey. The Church also oversees parishes in England (3), Belgium, and Australia.

★83★
BYELORUSSIAN ORTHODOX CHURCH
190 Turnpike Rd.
South River, NJ 08882

When refugees and immigrants from Byelorussia came to the West after World War II, some organized as the Byelorussian Autonomous Orthodox Church and elected their own bishops. Others formed independent congregations and sought the canonical blessings of other Orthodox bishops. The Byelorussian Orthodox Church consists of three congregations who placed themselves under the jurisdiction of Archbishop Iakovos, head of the Greek Orthodox Archdiocese of North and South America, in his role as Exarch in America for the ecumenical patriarch. Besides the congregation in South River, New Jersey, parishes are found in Chicago and Toronto.

Membership: Not reported.

★84★
BYZANTINE CATHOLIC CHURCH
℅ Most Rev. Mark I. Miller
Box 3642
Los Angeles, CA 90078

The Byzantine Catholic Church was formed in 1984 by a merger of the Byzantine Old Catholic Church and the Holy Orthodox Catholic Church, Eastern and Apostolic, a small jurisdiction headed by Bishop Richard B. Morrill.

The Byzantine Old Catholic Church was a jurisdiction from out of the Old Catholic tradition whose history is intimately tied to the career of its leader, Bishop Mark I. Miller.

As a child, Miller was adopted and, taking the name of his new parents, was raised as Oliver W. Skelton. He joined the American Orthodox Catholic Church. Upon ordination as a priest, he assumed the religious name Leo Christopher (Skelton), as he became known throughout the Old Catholic movement after his consecration as a bishop by Christopher J. Stanley in 1965. In 1966 Skelton left Stanley and the American Orthodox Catholic Church, of which he was then a part, and became a cardinal in the Orthodox Old Catholic Church headed by Claude Hamel. Headquartered in Enid, Oklahoma, Skelton functioned under the name, Old Roman Catholic Church (Orthodox Orders), a corporation he had formed in 1964. Upon leaving Hamel, whom he accused of exercising capricious and authoritarian leadership, Skelton changed the name of his organization to the Orthodox Old Roman Catholic Church II and assumed the ecclesiastical name Mark I. He established headquarters in Hollywood, California.

In the mid-1970s, Skelton reorganized the Orthodox Old Roman Catholic Church II and changed its name to the North American Orthodox Catholic Church. During this period he was moving, both theologically and liturgically, away from Old Catholicism and toward Eastern Orthodoxy. In April 1975 he had his secular name changed legally to that of his natural parents and became Mark I. Miller.

Two further reorganizations of his jurisdiction in 1981 and 1983 transformed the North American Orthodox Catholic Church into the Byzantine Old Catholic Church. The major reorganization in 1981 resulted from clergy engaged in what were termed "unOrthodox actions." Miller promulgated a number of additions to the Disciplinary Canons, most notably new regulations prohibiting the ordination of females and the assumption of the bishopric by married clergy. The name was changed to the World Independent Orthodox Catholic Church (and Her Dependencies). Finally in 1983 the World Independent Orthodox Catholic Church assumed the name which it took into the 1984 merger, the Byzantine Old Catholic Church.

After the new church was formed, His Beatitude Metropolitan Richard (B. Morrill) became the president of the Sacred Synod of Bishops and administrator of the church. His Beatitude Mark (I. Miller) became vice-president of the Sacred Synod of Bishops and ecclesiastical administrator and chief justice of the Spiritual Court of Bishops. The Byzantine Catholic Church is Orthodox in faith and practice. It uses the several Eastern liturgies (most prominently St. John Chrysostom's, St. Basil's).

Membership: In 1984 the Byzantine Catholic Church reported 1,600 members in ten congregations served by twenty priests. Affiliated parishes are also found in England, France, Italy, Nigeria, Brazil, and Chile.

Educational facilities: The International Theological Seminary, Van Nuys, California.

Periodicals: *Maranatha! The Lord Cometh.* 14617 Victory Blvd., Van Nuys, CA 91411.

★85★
CATHOLIC APOSTOLIC CHURCH IN AMERICA
% Most Rev. Jerome Joachim
540 Jones St., Suite 504
San Francisco, CA 94102

Though officially reconstituted in 1983, the Catholic Apostolic Church in America continues an unbroken existence from 1950 when Stephen Meyer Corradi-Scarella established an American outpost of the Catholic Apostolic Church in Brazil. The Catholic Apostolic Church in Brazil was formed in 1946 by Dom Carlos Duarte Costa, a former bishop of the Roman Catholic church who had been excommunicated by Pope Pius XII because of his criticism of the church during World War II. Corradi-Scarella was consecrated by Costa in 1951 and established the church as an exarchate with headquarters in New Mexico. During the 1960s, following the death of Costa, Corradi-Scarella lost touch with the Brazilian group and began to associate with the various Old Catholics in the United States. By 1970 he called his jurisdiction the Diocese of the Old Catholic Church in America.

The church grew slowly until the 1970s. In 1973 Corradi-Scarella was joined by Francis Jerome Joachim, a priest ordained by Archbishop Bartholomew Cunningham of the Holy Orthodox Church, Diocese of New Mexico. Joachim brought an Eastern Orthodox perspective with him, in contrast to Corradi-Scarella's Catholic tradition, but soon became his chief associate. Corradi-Scarella arranged for Joachim's consecration by Archbishop David M. Johnson of the American Orthodox Church, Diocese of California, on September 28, 1974. Two months later, on December 1, 1974, Corradi-Scarella, then almost seventy years old, resigned in favor of Joachim.

Under Joachim the small jurisdiction grew, at one point having almost 100 clergy, but lost significant strength due to the defections of many to other independent jurisdictions. In 1980 Joachim renamed his jurisdiction the Western Orthodox Church in America (formerly the National Catholic Apostolic Church in America).

Membership: In 1984 the Church reported approximately 15 parishes and six missions served by 32 clergy. Bishops are located in Savannah, Georgia; New York City; Ft. Lauderdale, Florida; and San Francisco. Bishop Forest E. Barber is ordinary for the Dominican Republic.

Educational facilities: Chrysostom University, St. Louis, Missouri; St. John Chrysostom Theological Seminary, San Francisco, California.

Periodicals: *Chrysostomos*, 808 Post Street, Suite 1021, San Francisco, CA 94109; *Western Orthodox Voice*, 808 Post Street, Suite 1021, San Francisco, CA 94109.

★86★
EASTERN ORTHODOX CATHOLIC CHURCH IN AMERICA
% Most Rev. Dismas Markle
321 S. Magnolia Ave.
Sanford, FL 32771

Among the several bodies claiming to carry on the mission of Archbishop Aftimios Ofiesh, the Eastern Orthodox Catholic Church in America can make one of the strongest cases for being the real antecedent body of Aftimios' independent jurisdiction. The first bishop consecrated by Aftimios was Bishop Sophonius Bashira in 1931. Aftimios' retirement and Bishop Joseph Zuk's unexpected death just months after his consecration by Ofiesh, left Sophronius in charge. He turned to Metropolitan Benjamin Fedchenkov of the Moscow Exarch (now the Patriarchal Parishes of the Russian Orthodox Church in the United States and Canada), one of several warring Russian Orthodox factions, and with his blessing, consecrated John Chrysostom More-Moreno in 1933. Sophronius soon left the United States and More-Moreno took up the task of creating an American Orthodox church, in 1951, by forming the Eastern Orthodox Catholic Church in America.

The church follows the practice of Orthodoxy in both liturgy and theology. For many years it published the influential monthly periodical, the *American Review of Eastern Orthodoxy* (suspended in 1980).

Membership: In 1974 the Church reported 4 churches, 13 clergy and 315 members.

★87★
ESTONIAN ORTHODOX CHURCH IN EXILE
% Rev. Sergius Samon
5332 Fountain Ave.
Los Angeles, CA 90029

In 1944 the Union of Soviet Socialist Republics gained political hegemony over Estonia. Primate of the Estonian Orthodox Church Archbishop Alexander fled to Sweden where he organized The Estonian Orthodox Church in Exile. The church is under the Greek Orthodox Church's ecumenical patriach in Constantinople and at one in faith and worship with the Greek Orthodox Church.

In 1949 the Very Reverend Sergius Samon established the first congregation of the Estonian Church in North America at Los Angeles. Large numbers of Estonians had come to the United States and Canada following World

War II. Congregations were subsequently established in San Francisco, Chicago, and New York City. Canadian parishes were established in Vancouver, Toronto, and Montreal.

Membership: In the mid-1970s, the Church reported 1,700 members in North America.

★88★

EVANGELICAL ORTHODOX CHURCH
% Rt. Rev. Peter Gillquist, Presiding Bishop
Box 17074
Seattle, WA 98107

The Evangelical Orthodox Church, founded in February of 1979, began with Campus Crusade for Christ, a conservative evangelical ministry among the nation's college students. In common with most evangelical groups, they laid stress on being born again, on the bible as the sole source of religious truth, and they pursued a strong evangelistic program. They sought also to bring any converts into membership in a conservative evangelical church where they would receive the proper care and nurture. The church was viewed as important only because it helped people in their service to Christ. The Catholic and Orthodox view that a relationship with Christ is impossible apart from the Church was quite foreign to their thinking.

The leaders of the movement tended to be scholarly people and in the 1970s they began to ask some questions among themselves, via correspondence and through various publications. One popular view of history held by many Protestants disturbed many of them. Many evangelical groups lay claim to adhering to the first century Christian Church. According to this view Christ did establish a Church, but shortly after his death it began to become corrupted by false doctrine and worldliness. Then for centuries, except for an occasional, so-called heretical sect, the true faith disappeared. It was not to appear again until the Reformation, when it reappeared and, again, the light slowly began to flicker out. It remained for the modern Evangelical Revival to once gain restore the gospel to a few churches and denominations. Thus evangelical Christians could separate themselves from the predominantly Catholic phase of the Church's 2,000 year history.

To many of the leaders in the movement this appeared as a mistake, and they met in Chicago in February of 1979 to call evangelicals back to their historic roots. They felt evangelicals were denying too much of their history and they were led to the observation that much they had accepted as evangelicals about the church's history had been inaccurate. Prominent among their discoveries was the antiquity of Christian liturgy. So, in addition to restoring some lost history the group came to believe that it must also restore discarded liturgy.

In their review of Church history, they studied historical theology, covering questions rarely treated in conservative evangelical theological inquiries such as the "filioque" controversy. In reviewing this particular controversy, which split the Eastern and Western Church in the eleventh century, they gradually accepted the Eastern view, in part because it agreed with their view of Scriptures and the nature of the Godhead, and in part because of a bias against Roman Catholicism. They found it convenient to stand with Eastern Orthodoxy in a common rejection of the Roman Catholic Church's claim of Papal supremacy.

During the late 1970s, the Church began seeking Eastern Orthodox orders, and in 1979 at Santa Barbara, California, representatives met initially with Bishop Dmitri of the Orthodox Church in America. Discussion focused upon several issues which have been perennial problems for Protestants. The representatives of the Evangelical Orthodox Church, taking a great leap toward Orthodoxy, confessed their belief in the Blessed Virgin Mary as *theotokos*, the Mother of God, and were quite open on the issue of her ever-virginity, which they had found to have been a confession of the Church from the beginning. They also found that they had no trouble with the Orthodox position on the communion of saints. Finally, the Church fully accepted the idea of apostolic succession, stood ready to receive it from Orthodox Church in America, and OCA, and was willing to come under that Church's jurisdiction. They already used the Liturgy of St. John Chrysostom. The initial talks with the Orthodox Church in America eventually deadlocked over the question of the Evangelical Orthodox Church's bishops. The Orthodox Church in America was unwilling to compromise on the acceptance of married bishops. This issue has left the Church further exploring an acceptable alternative within Orthodoxy.

Membership: In 1984 the Church reported 53 parishes and several thousand members.

Periodicals: *Again*, Conciliar Press, Box 106, Mt. Hermon, CA 95041.

Sources: *The Divine Liturgy of Saint John Chrysostom.* Santa Barbara, CA: Evangelical Orthodox Church, Santa Barbara Diocese, n.d.; Jon E. Braun, *It Ain't Gonna Reign No More.* Nashville: Thomas Nelson, 1978; Jack Sparks, *The Mind Benders.* Nashville: Thomas Nelson, 1977.

★89★

FINNISH ORTHODOX CHURCH
% Fr. Denis Ericson
Box 174
Lansing, MI 48901

The first Orthodox missionaries reached Finland in the tenth century and founded Valamo Monastery. While the church has remained small, it has persisted. Finland gained independence from Russia in 1919 and a wave of nationalism swept the church. In 1923 the church was given autonomy under the Greek Orthodox Church's ecumenical patriarch in Constantinople. The following year a non-Russian bishop was named primate. The church is Orthodox in faith and practice and uses the Finnish and Russian languages. The selection of archbishops must be submitted to Constantinople for approval.

In 1955 the first attempts to call together Orthodox Finns residing in the United States found most already attached to Russian congregations, but a small mission chapel was established in the Upper Peninsula of Michigan. It was not able to minister to the 1,300 Orthodox Finns and ceased to exist in 1958. A new plan was implemented in 1962 by Father Denis Ericson of Lansing, Michigan. Using Lansing as a base, he travels to four worship stations. Services are in English, but Finnish hymns and customs are preserved.

Membership: Not reported.

★90★
GREEK ORTHODOX ARCHDIOCESE OF NORTH AND SOUTH AMERICA
% His Eminence Archbishop Iakovos
8-10 E. 79th St.
New York, NY 10021

As early as 1767 Greek Orthodox Christians settled in New Smyrna, Florida. Greek merchants in New Orleans established Holy Trinity, the first Greek Orthodox Church in America, in 1864. Other parishes sprang up across the country. No attempt was made to organize the parishes until 1918 when the Greek Orthodox Archdiocese of North and South America was organized. Archbishop Alexandros headed the archdiocese from 1922. He began the extensive work of bringing the many Greek parishes under his jurisdiction. The greatest progress in this direction was made by his successor, Metropolitan Athenagoras Spiru, who became the ecumenical patriarch in 1948.

The Greek Orthodox Archdiocese has over the years become the largest in the United States. It has seven districts, each headed by a bishop, and Archbishop Iakovos, as chairman of the Standing Conference of Canonical Orthodox Bishops and Exarch for the ecumenical patriarch, has been a recognized spokesman of the Greek Orthodox community to the outside world.

Currents of change which have flowed through the Orthodox world have made Archbishop Iakovos a subject of intense controversy. As criticism has been directed against the growing openness of Patriarch Athenagoras toward Rome and the World Council of Churches, Archbishop Iakovos has been criticized for approving this openness and initiating contact on his own in the United States with various Protestant and Catholic bodies. Ultra-traditionalists see such ecumenical activity as

compromising Orthodox faith. Mt. Athos, the most famous Orthodox monastery, has become a center of traditionalism and has produced spokesmen critical of Archbishop Iakovos and of changes in the contemporary church.

Liturgy being the most important aspect of Orthodox church life, changes affecting liturgy are met with extreme resistance. The Greek Archdiocese follows the Eastern Rite and the Liturgy of St. John Chrysostom. However, traditionally the Orthodox liturgy has followed the Julian calendar, which twentieth century liturgists have largely replaced with the Gregorian. Many of those who have left the Greek Archdiocese reject his use of the Gregorian calendar.

Membership: In 1977 the Archdiocese reported 1,950,000 members, 535 churches and 655 priests.

Educational facilities: Holy Cross School of Theology, Brookline, Massachusetts; Hellenic College, Brookline, Massachusetts.

Periodicals: *Orthodox Observer*, 8-10 E. 79th Street, New York, NY 10021.

Sources: *The Divine Liturgy of St. John Chrysostom.* Brookline,MA: The Greek Orthodox Theological Institute Press, 1950; Demetrios J. Constantelos, *An Old Faith for Modern Man.* New York: Greek Orthodox Archdiocese, 1964; Demetrios J. Constantelos, *The Greek Orthodox Church.* New York: Seabury Press, 1967; George Poulos, *A Breath of God.* Brookline, MA: Holy Cross Orthodox Press, 1984.

★91★
GREEK ORTHODOX ARCHDIOCESE OF VASILOUPOLIS
Current address not obtained for this edition.

The Greek Orthodox Archdiocese of Vasiloupolis is a small jurisdiction headed by His Eminence Metropolitan Pangraties Vrienis. His headquarters are in Woodside, New York. During Holy Week in 1972 he ordained Father Jose G. Oncins Hevia, an executive in a Spanish airlines, as priest for a Missionary Orthodox Church in Spain.

Membership: Not reported.

★92★
GREEK ORTHODOX CHURCH OF AMERICA
Current address not obtained for this edition.

The Greek Orthodox Church of America was formed on December 1, 1971, at a meeting held in Miami, Florida, for the purpose of forming a federation of independent Greek Orthodox Churches. Many of these churches had grown out of local schisms and were headed by priests who had left the jurisdiction of Archbishop Iakovos. Members object to what they see as a movement "to Catholicize and Protestantize the church." They hope to preserve Greek faith, language, and traditions. They believe in local control of property, not archdiocesan ownership. As of 1974 the church was without episcopal supervision but was seeking it from various sources.

A moving force in the Greek Orthodox Church of America is Father Theodore Kyritsis. He was defrocked by Archbishop Iakovos and went under the jurisdiction of Bishop Petros of the Hellenic Orthodox Church in America. Bishop Photios of the Greek Orthodox Diocese of New York was installed as archbishop in Memphis in St. George's Greek Orthodox Church which Kyritsis pastored, and has since then been a vocal opponent of Archbishop Iakovos.

Membership: In the mid-1970s the Church had 10 parishes scattered around the United States from Miami to Rhode Island, Pennsylvania, Michigan, and Tennessee.

★93★
GREEK ORTHODOX DIOCESE OF NEW YORK
Current address not obtained for this edition.

The Greek Orthodox Diocese of New York was formed in 1964 at Philadelphia, Pennsylvania, by priests and laity formerly under the jurisdiction of Archbishop Iakovos of the Greek Orthodox Archdiocese pf North and South America. They objected to the administration of Archbishop Iakovos and are the only Orthodox body in the West which allows the laity the sole right to elect the bishops and to keep the monies of church under the control of the members. Oxford-educated Bishop Photios was elected archbishop, and Theocletos of Salimis, auxiliary bishop. The installation of the archbishop took place in St. George's Greek Orthodox Church in Memphis, where Archbishop Photios resided for several years.

Archbishop Photios has gathered the largest group of Greek Orthodox followers not under Archbishop Iakovos. In 1965 jurisdiction was extended to Australia. Archbishop Photios was in communion with the late Bishop Dionisije of the Serbian Orthodox Free Diocese of the United States and Canada and Bishop Alexis of Adelaide, Australia, of the Byelorussian Autocephalic Church.

Membership: Not reported.

★94★
HELLENIC ORTHODOX CHURCH IN AMERICA
Current address not obtained for this edition.

In 1952 Archimandrite Petros, a monk from Mt. Athos, arrived in the United States and began to gather scattered groups of independent communities which follow the Julian calendar. In 1962 he was consecrated Bishop of

Astoria (Long Island, New York) by two Russian bishops who use the Julian calendar, Archbishop Leontios of Chile and Bishop Serapim of Venezuela, and the Hellenic Orthodox Church came into existence. It is at one with Orthodoxy except on the calendar issue.

Bishop Petros began a monthly periodical, *The Voice of Orthodoxy*. By 1967 he directed five churches and missions and 9,000 members. In each parish he established a parochial school to teach the Orthodox faith and the Greek language. The New York headquarters produced a radio show which carries the same name as the periodical.

Membership: Not reported.

★95★
HOLY APOSTOLIC ORTHODOX CATHOLIC CHURCH
(Defunct)

The Holy Apostolic Orthodox Catholic Church was founded in the mid-1960s with headquarters in Fort Lauderdale, Florida. During the 1970s it claimed to have a seminary and an elaborate hierarchy, including two archbishops and one bishop in the United States, and additional archbishops in West Germany, the Canal Zone, Hong Kong, and Switzerland. During the 1980s, no manifestation of the church or its founder Archbishop Mark Cardinal Evans has been seen. The Church professed the Orthodox faith as based in the Nicene Creed without the filoque clause and used the Liturgy of St. John Chrysostom without alteration.

Sources: *Ecclesiatical Proclamation, Divine Liturgy*. N.p.: Home Missions Department of the Holy Apostolic Orthodox Catholic Church, 1965.

★96★
HOLY EASTERN ORTHODOX CHURCH, ITALIO-BYZANTINE
Current address not obtained for this edition.

Orthodoxy established itself in southern Italy and Sicily in the Greek communities which had established themselves in ancient times. Most of these Greek churches came under the authority of the Roman Catholic Church after the Synod at Bari in 1097 A.D. Only two bishops refused to submit and they led their Orthodox followers into what became an increasingly underground church. The church survived in spite of severe measures to convert its members to Catholicism. Cut-off from mainline Orthodoxy, however, it developed several peculiarities, including a married bishopric. It also has a mobile episcopacy, in part due to the persecution it felt, and began to designate their bishops as being "in" a See location rather than "of" a See City. Thus, their present Primate is Bishop Umile Natalino, Bishop in Venetio. The Church became fullhy autonomous in 1428.

The first Italian Orthodox priests came to America in 1904 and established parishes in Brooklyn, Newark and Philadelphia. Progress was slow until 1979 when two men, Emilio Rinauldi and Luciano Gaudio, were elected Bishop in Newark (NJ) and Las Vegas (NM) respectively. They were consecrated by a deputation of bishops from Italy headed by the late Primate Constantino, Bishop in Catania.

The Church is Orthodox in theology. The two bishops have administrative responsibility for that section of the United States in which they reside. Bishop Gaudio announced plans to build a monastic complex New Mexico. The Church was affiliated with the Holy Orthodox Church, American Jurisdiction headed by Bishop James Francis Miller which merged into the Orthodox Catholic Church of America.

Membership: Not reported.

★97★

HOLY EASTERN ORTHODOX CHURCH OF THE UNITED STATES
% Most Rev. Trevor W. Moore
1611 Wallace St.
Philadelphia, PA 19130

The Holy Eastern Orthodox Church of the United States was founded in 1970 by Trevor Wyatt Moore, who had been ordained by Old Catholic Bishop Christopher Jones. On July 11, 1971, he was consecrated by Archbishop Ulanyslau Ryzy-Ryski and Bishop Y. K. Kuang. In August 1971 Ryzi-Ryski, in his plan to establish a hierarchy of patriarchs representing the various ethnic groups, elevated Moore to be an archbishop with jurisdiction for the English-speaking world. Though an archbishop in the American World Patriarchs, Moore's jurisdiction remained autonomous. in the years since his elevation, Archbishop Trevor has become one of the few of the independent bishops to gain some recognition in the larger Christian community, through his authorship of several books and service as an editor-at-large for the *Christian Century* magazine.

The Church is strictly Eastern Orthodox in faith and practice, and it adheres to the Byzantine rite. It is organized into the Archepiscopal See of Philadelphia, the Diocese of Providence (Rhode Island), and the Missionary Eparchy of New Jersey. Parishes are centered in Pennsylvania, New Jersey, and Rhode Island but are also located in Massachusetts, Illinois, California, and Puerto Rico.

The Church has been most atuned to the issues that have dominated the established churches, particularly the many social concerns. It has spoken out forcefully of peace and nonviolence. It operates a social service center in Spring Garden, an Hispanic area of Philadelphia, and a parish within Leesburg Prison in New Jersey. It has been active in civil rights and interracial and intercultural efforts, particularly in Spanish-speaking communities.

Membership: In 1983 the Archdiocese reported 10 parishes, 15 priests and 1,500 members.

★98★

HOLY ORTHODOX CATHOLIC CHURCH
% Most Rev. Paul G. Russell
5831 Tremont
Dallas, TX 75214

This body began in 1965 as the American Orthodox Church but changed its name in 1972 to the Holy Orthodox Catholic Church. It is headed by Bishop Paul G. Russell, who was consecrated on August 22, 1976 by Bishops David Baxter and William Henry. The group accepts the idea of female priests and would ordain a homosexual to Holy Orders, but in all other respects the Church holds to the Orthodox-Catholic faith. It is headquartered in Dallas, and claims six priests and three parishes. Membership is unknown.

Membership: In 1983 the Church reported 3 parishes and 6 priests.

★99★

HOLY ORTHODOX CHURCH, AMERICAN JURISDICTION
% Most Rev. W. Francis Forbes
Box 400
Antioch, TN 37013

The Holy Orthodox Church, American Jurisdiction, was formed in 1974 by Bishop William Francis Forbes, who had been consecrated by Archbishop Colin James Guthrie of the American Orthodox Catholic Church and John Mary Kendra. Though formed in the mid-1970s, it lays claim to continue the lifework of Bishop Aftimios Ofiesh, and dates its lineage to the work begun by Ofiesh in the 1920s. The Church is Orthodox theology and uses both the Eastern and Western liturgy in its parishes.

The Church is led by a synod of bishops. The Synod is viewed as a free association of independent archbishops, and thus a cooperative structure more than a formal jurisdictional entity. Each bishop has jurisdictional authority for the entire United States and may establish parishes and missions anywhere, except in the see city of another bishop, without their permission. The tranquility of the Church was disturbed in 1981 when a group of bishops and priests attempted a reorganization of the church which included the abolishment of the office of Primate. The disruption occasioned a splintering with several bishops, including James Francis Miller, Bishop of Louisville (Kentucky) leaving and establishing a separate jurisdiction with the same name. That jurisdiction has recently merged into the Orthodox Catholic Church of America.

Membership: Not reported.

Periodicals: *The Communicator*, Box 400, Antioch, TN 37013.

★100★
HOLY ORTHODOX CHURCH, DIOCESE OF NEW MEXICO (CUNNINGHAM)

Current address not obtained for this edition.

The Holy Orthodox Church, Diocese of New Mexico was formed by Archbishop Bartholomew Cunningham a former priest of the Roman Catholic Church and seminary professor. Cunningham was consecrated by Bishops Colin James Guthrie and Robert S. Zeiger of the American Orthodox Catholic Church on June 23, 1968 and served under Guthrie until the present Holy Orthodox Church, Diocese of New Mexico, was established in 1970. The church is Orthodox in faith and practice. It is open to the ordination into the priesthood of otherwise qualified homosexuals but rejects females for holy orders.

Archbishop Batholemew died in 1984 and the future status of the Diocese is in question.

Membership: In the early 1980s, the Church reported 15 parishes and a few hundred members, primarily in New Mexico and Illinois.

★101★
HOLY ORTHODOX CHURCH IN AMERICA

% Most Rev. Mother Serena
321 W. 101st St.
New York, NY 10025

The Orthodox Church in America grew out of the early interest in Christian Mysticism of Rosicrucian George Winslow Plummer. Plummer had been one of the founders of the Societas Rosicruciana in America, covered in a separate item in this Encyclopedia, in 1907 and became its leader when Sylvester Gould died two years later. In the 1920s Plummer's particular interest in mysticism led him to found the Seminary of Biblical Research through which he issued lessons on Christian mysticism. About this same time he founded the Anglican Universal Church and sought consecration from a Puerto Rican bishop, Manual Ferrando.

In 1934 Plummer was reconsecrated by Bishop William Albert Nichols of the American Orthodox Church originally founded by Lebanese Orthodox bishop, Aftimios Ofiesh and took the religious name, Mar Georgius. Following his consecration, he reconsecrated three of his bishops of the Anglican Universal Church and incorporated as the Holy Orthodox Church in America. The Holy Orthodox Church in America (Eastern Catholic and Apostolic) accepted through Nichols the mandate of Bishop Ofiesh to develop an American Eastern Orthodoxy.

The Holy Orthodox Church, while endorsing the canons of the Seven Ecumenical Councils, has remained intimately connected to the Rosicrucian organization which Plummer headed. The original episcopal leadership was drawn from the S.R.I.A. and the original parishes were all located in cities with an S.R.I.A. group. The liturgy of the church is that of St. John Chrysostom, however, a special emphasis is placed upon spiritual healing and special services for that purpose are held weekly.

Plummer died in 1944 and was succeeded by Archbishop Theodotus Stanislaus DeWitow (formerly Witowski). From his death in 1973 to 1981 the church was without a bishop. The work was carried on by three deaconesses, two of whom, Mrs. G. E. S. DeWitow (a.k.a. Mother Serena), widow of the last archbishop, and Lucia Grosch were consecrated in 1981 by Archbishop Adrian H. Spruit of the Church of Antioch. Mother Serena is the current presiding bishop.

Membership: In 1983 the Church reported that it had one church, and one chapel, and a membership of less that 100.

★102★
HOLY UKRAINIAN AUTOCEPHALIC ORTHODOX CHURCH IN EXILE

103 Evergreen St.
West Babylon, NY 11714

The Holy Ukrainian Autocephalic Orthodox Church in Exile was organized in New York City in 1951 among immigrants who had left the Ukraine, primarily that part formerly controlled by Poland, as a result of the disruptions of World War II. A diocese was formed under the guidance of Archbishop Palladij Rudenko, former Bishop of Krakiv, Lviv and Lemkenland, and Archbishop Ihor Huba. former Bishop of Poltava and Kremenchuk, both refugees then living in the United States. The church was incorporated in 1960. Following the death of Archbishop Ihor, Archbishop Iakovos of the Greek Orthodox Archdiocese of North and South America consecrated a new bishop for the Church, Rt. Rev. Andrew Kusch, in 1967. It is a member of the Standing Conference of Canonical Orthodox Bishops.

Membership: In 1972 the Church had only two parishes, one in West Babylon and one in Syracuse, New York.

★103★
MACEDONIAN ORTHODOX CHURCH

% Rev. Spiro Tanaskaki
51st & Virginia Sts.
Gary, IN 46409

Another schism in the Serbian Church occurred in 1947 when under pressure of the government a new church was created to serve the geographic area of Macedonia, now existing in Yugoslavia, Greece, and Bulgaria, though its strength was in South Serbia. In 1959 the patriarchate was "forced" to recognize it as autonomous but under the Belgrade patriarch, and Bishop Dositej was placed at its head. In 1967 Dositej proclaimed separation and independence, an act not recognized by the patriarch (or anyone but Marshall Tito) and thus became schismatic.

The Macedonian Church was begun in Gary, Indiana, in 1961 during a visit of Rev. Spiridon Tanaskovski. Other parishes were established in Syracuse, New York, and Columbus, Ohio. They are under the jurisdiction of Bishop Kiril who resides in Skoplje, Yugoslavia. In 1972 a schism developed in the Sts. Peter and Paul Macedonian Orthodox Church in Gary, Indiana. As a result of disputes, Rev. Tanaskovski left and founded a new church, St. Clement Ohridski, which he claims is loyal to the American flag and not to Tito.

Membership: Not reported.

★104★

OLD ORTHODOX CATHOLIC PATRIARCHATE OF AMERICA

% Most Rev. Peter A. Zurawetzky
5520 W. Dakin St.
Chicago, IL 60641

Not all of the independent Polish Catholic Churches founded in the late-nineteenth and early-twentieth century joined with the Polish National Catholic Church. Some of these parishes had associated with independent Old Catholic bodies which had grown out of the work of Archbishop Joseph Rene Vilatte and his American Catholic Church, especially the Old Catholic Church in America headed by Archbishop W. H. Francis Brothers and the Polish Catholic Church of Bishop Stephen Kaminski. In 1937 some of these churches joined with several parishes of Slavic (Lithuanian) background and came together to form the Polish Old Catholic Church. They incorporated in New Jersey and elected Bishop Joseph Zielonka as their leader. Zielonka had been consecrated some years previously by Paolo Miraglia-Gulotti and had served as a bishop under Brothers.

Under Zielonka's capable leadership the church grew and by the time of his death in 1961 consisted of 22 parishes. Most were located in New Jersey with others in Pennsylvania and Massachusetts. The growth phase under Zielonka, however, was completely reversed under his successor, Peter A. Zurawetzky. Zurawetzky, Zielonka's suffragan, had been consecrated in Springfield, Massachusetts, in 1950. Patriarch Joseph Klimowicz of the Orthodox Catholic Patriarchate of America, Archbishop Konstatin Jaroshevich (a Byelorussian prelate who had been consecrated by Archbishop Fan Stylin Noli of the Albanian Orthodox Church), Archbishop Zielonka, Metropolitan Nicholas Bohatyretz of the Ukrainian Orthodox Church, and Old Catholic Bishop Peter M. Williamowicz participated in the consecration service.

Among his first acts, Zurawetzky changed the name of the Church to Christ Catholic Church of the Americas and Europe, an expression of a desire to move beyond ethnic and language barriers in his jurisdiction so that all nationalities might feel welcome. The future looked promising, but problems began to plague the newly named Church almost immediately. First some churches and clergy did not accept Archbishop Peter's leadership. They also did not like the name change. Second, Fr. Felix Starazewski asserted a claim to be the legitimate successor of the late Bishop Zielonka, and he and his church in South River, New Jersey, refused to honor the jurisdiction of Archbishop Peter. His defection led the way and other congregations departed for either the Polish National Catholic Church or one of the other independent Catholic or Orthodox bodies.

Third, and most importantly, Zurawetzky shifted his attention away from building his jurisdiction from expanding parishes and membership to growth by uniting with other independent Old Catholic and Eastern Orthodox bodies. He thus brought into his jurisdiction the divisiveness which had led to the splintering of these independent groups in the first place, and exacerbated the situation by assuming the title of Patriarch in America. Gradually all of his time and energy were poured into the actualization of a dominating vision, an American Patriarchate. At the same time his churches, consisting largely of Eastern European ethnic parishes, were being further reduced by the inevitable processes of Americanization.

By 1965, the Church having been reduced to a handful of communicants and clergy, a new possibility emerged. Rev. Karl Pruter, who had come from the Free Catholic Movement in the Congregational Church, was ordained by Archbishop Peter, and organized a nonethnic congregation in Boston, out of which a second congregation emerged. The Church of St. Paul was organized in Hobbs, New Mexico, by Fr. Daniel Smith. Then Zurawetzky moved to enlarge the Patriarchate. Assisted by Archbishop Uladyslau Ryzy-Ryski, he consecrated Pruter who consented to the consecration only on the condition that they be set aside as an independent jurisdiction to be called, Christ Catholic Church, Diocese of Boston, now known simply as Christ Catholic Church. Then, Smith was consecrated, but after a short while in Hobbs, he moved to Denver and withdrew from Archbishop Peter's jurisdiction altogether. Another briefly successful venture was the establishment of the Monastery of Our Lady of Reconciliation at Glorieta, New Mexico, in 1969. Fr. Christopher William Jones was a successful author and minister to many of the disenchanted youth of the late 60s and early 70s. However, shortly after Archbishop Peter consecrated him, he too left to form an independent, self-governing jurisdiction.

As of the mid-1980s, Archbishop Peter has no congregations in his jurisdiction, but maintains a chapel at Vineland, New Jersey, and a home in Chicago. He continues his efforts to build the Patriarchate.

Membership: As of 1985 there are no parishes in the Patriarchate, though several clergy remain affiliated.

Periodicals: *Our Missionary*, 5520 West Dakin, Chicago, IL 60641.

★105★
ORTHODOX CATHOLIC CHURCH OF AMERICA
% Most Rev. Alfred Lankenau
Box 1222
Indianapolis, IN 45206

Several jurisdictions derive their orders from Archbishop Joseph Rene Vilatte, founder of the American Catholic Church through the orders given to the African Orthodox Church. In 1926 William F. Tyarks, a priest in the American Catholic Church who had been ordained by Vilatte's successor, Archbishop Frederick E. J. Lloyd in 1916, left Lloyd's jurisdiction and with other priests and members formed the American Catholic Orthodox Church. The group applied to the African Orthodox Church for orders and Archbishop George A. McGuire consecrated Tyarks in 1928.

In 1930 Tyarks consecrated one of the priests who had come from the American Catholic Church with him, Cyril John Clement Sherwood (1895-1969). Sherwood soon left Tyarks and was reconsecrated by McGuire in 1932. The next year he formed the American Holy Orthodox Catholic Apostolic Eastern Church. Sherwood's career overlapped that of Archbishop Aftimios Ofiesh's greatest activity, and Sherwood became acquainted with his vision of a united American Orthodoxy. He incorporated it in an ecumenical organization, the Orthodox Catholic Patriarchate of America.

Among Sherwood's bishops was George A. Hyde, whom the Patriarch consecrated in May 1957. Hyde had formed the Eucharistic Catholic Church in Atlanta, Georgia in 1946. This first exclusively gay ministry in America continued until 1959 when Hyde moved to Washington, D.C. and formed the Society of Domestic Missionaries of St. Basil the Great, an order of priests. The following year he left Sherwood and formed the Orthodox Catholic Church of America. He believed that Sherwood was too narrowly Eastern in his approach to liturgy and theology and wanted to restructure the church making it open to Western rite orthodox practice. In spite of leaving Sherwood's jurisdiction, Hyde continued to participate in the ecumenical Orthodox Catholic Patriarchate of America.

In 1969 Sherwood died. At a meeting of the Synod the next year, Hyde was elected to succeed him as head of the Patriarchate, and the Holy Orthodox Catholic and Apostolic Eastern Church voted to become the Eastern Rite Diocese of the Orthodox Catholic Church of America. Thus Archbishop Hyde took control of all the work begun by Sherwood.

Doctrinally, the Orthodox Catholic Church of America follows the teachings of the Seven Ecumenical Councils and rejects the doctrinal innovations such as purgatory, Papal infallibility, the immaculate conception, communion in one kind only, and an unmarried clergy. The Church uses both the Eastern and Western rites in its liturgy. Under Hyde's administration, the Church was active in promoting a ministry to homosexuals and is the ultimate source of the presently-existing Eucharistic Catholic Church.

In 1983 Hyde retired and Alfred Louis Lankenau, bishop of the Diocese of Indianapolis and Chicago, was elected to succeed him. Under the new Archbishop, the Orthodox Catholic Patriarchate of America, which had ceased to function during the 1970s, has been revived and several Catholic and Orthodox jurisdictions have affiliated. In 1983, the Holy Orthodox Church, American Jurisdiction headed by Archbishop James Francis Miller, which had broken from the church of the same name headed by Archbishop William Francis Forbes, merged into the Church.

Membership: In 1984 the Church reported parishes located in Maine, New York, Rhode Island, Indiana, Illinois, Georgia, South Carolina, Florida, New Mexico, and the District of Columbia with mission parishes in Pennsylvania, Ohio and California.

Periodicals: *U. S. Orthodox Life*, Box 1273, Anderson, SC 29622.

Sources: George Augustine Hyde, ed., *The Genesis of the Orthodox Catholic Church of America*. Indianapolis: Orthodox Catholic Church of America, 1981; George Augustine Hyde, ed., *The Courage to Be Ourselves*. Anderson, SC, Ortho-Press, 1972; R. J. Bernard, *A Faith for Americans*. Anderson, SC: Ortho, 1974; *The Divine Liturgy*. Elberton, GA; Orthodox Catholic Church of America, 1966.

★106★
ORTHODOX CHURCH IN AMERICA
% Most Blessed Theodosius, Archbishop of
    Washington, Metropolitan of All America and
    Canada
Very Rev. Daniel Hubiak, Chancellor
Box 675
Syosset, NY 11791

The Orthodox Church in America is the oldest continuously existing Eastern Orthodox body in North America in general and the United States in particular. As the first Orthodox church to arrive, it assumed a hegemony over what became in the nineteenth century a multi-ethnic Orthodox community, and many of the presently existing independent Orthodox churches in America began as parishes and/or a diocese within what is today known as the Orthodox Church in America.

The OCA began in Alaska with the arrival of missionaries of the Russian Orthodox Church. In 1794 eight monks and two novices arrived on Kodiak Island to follow up on the work of converting the Native Americans already begun by a generation of Russian lay people in the Aleutians. Among these ten was Father Herman, later canonized by the Church. In 1824 John Veniaminov, a married priest, was sent to the Aleutians. After the death of his wife, he was consecrated the first bishop of a missionary diocese. Bishop Innocent had an outstanding career in Alaska, building the first cathedral at Sitka, among other accomplishments. He was called in 1868 to be the Metropolitan of Moscow, the highest office in the Church and finally in 1977 canonized.

The sale of Alaska to the United States left the Missionary Diocese on its own. It moved its headquarters to San Francisco in 1872 and changed its name to the Russian Orthodox Church, Diocese of the Aleutian Islands and North America. The period during the episcopacy of Bishop Nicolas beginning in 1891 was a time of noted growth. The Alaskan Mission was expanded, and the work in Canada and the Eastern United States began.

In 1905 the diocese moved its headquarters from San Francisco to New York City. Its growth was recognized by its elevation to the rank of archdiocese. Under the archbishop was a bishop for Alaska and an Arabic-speaking bishop, Bishop Raphael Hawaweeny, who as Bishop of Brooklyn had oversight of Orthodox from the Middle East. Two additional bishops in Cleveland and Pittsburgh were soon added. The church progressed steadily until disrupted by events in Russia during World War I.

The Russian Revolution proved a disaster for the American Russian church. Russian Orthodox Christians ahd always carried a special loyalty for the royal family which had been executed by the new government in Moscow. Also, money from Russia which had always assisted in the support of the archdiocese was abruptly curtailed, to be almost immediately followed by a wave of immigration by refugees looking to the Church for spiritual guidance and support. The patriarch of Moscow was arrested and the American church split over loyalty to him versus acceptance of the new govenment. Representative of what was termed the "Living Church," those supportive of the Communist regime arrived in the United States in 1923. At a synod of the Russian Church in 1924 in Detroit the credentials of the Living Church were rejected and the Church asserted its administrative, judicial and legislative independence from Russia. It assumed a new name, the Russian Orthodox Greek Catholic Church of America and declared the imprisoned Archbishop Platon, "Metropolitan of All America and Canada," an action which led then to be popularly called the "Metropolia." Their major loss came in court. Before they were able to legally validate their separation from Moscow, the Living Church representatives were able to win the transfer of the title of St. Nicolas Cathedral in New York City into their hands.

In 1925 Archbishop Platon died. He was succeeded by Archbishop Sergius who in 1927 issued a Declaration calling for loyalty and cooperation with the new Russian government. Prior to this Declaration, the bishops of the Russian Orthodox Greek Catholic Church of America had cooperated with other Russian bishops around the world caught outside of Russia and also cut off by the Revolution. Following the Declaration, Metropolitan Platon declared his loyalty to Sergius but specifically denied him any power to make administrative decisions concerning the American church. In spite of the challenges of the several competing branches of Russian Orthodoxy, one stanchly opposed to any cooperation with the Church under Communist domination (Russian Orthodox Church Outside of Russia), and the other administratively tied to the Patriarch of Moscow (the American Exarchate of the Russian Orthodox Catholic Church), the Russian Orthodox Greek Catholic Church in America retained the support of most American believers.

During the years following the turmoil of the Russian Revolution, the Metropolia assumed the position that it would give recognition to the spiritual authority of the patriarch in Moscow, if he would recognize its administrative autonomy. However, the Church in Russia continued its support of those parishes in the Exarchate who recognized his complete authority. Finally, in 1970, the separation of the Metropolia from the Church in Russia was ended when the patriarch of Moscow, His Holiness Alexis, granted autonomous status to the Russian Orthodox Greek Catholic Church of America, renamed the Orthodox Church in America. The Exarchate was disolved and most of its parishes moved into the OCA.

For quite different reasons, the creation of the Orthodox Church in America created a controversy within the larger American Orthodox community. For many years there had been various attempts to move away from the ethnic divisions within American Orthodoxy. In creating the Orthodox Church in America, rica, the Russian community asserted its status as the oldest Orthodox church in North America and as such the most fitting focus of Orthodox unity. Other Orthodox groups, particularly the Greek Archdiocese, saw the emergence of the OCA as a unilateral effort not deserving of recognition.

The OCA is headed by its archbishop, Metropolitan Theodosius, whose jurisdiction extends throughout the western hemisphere. There are nine dioceses in the United States, one in Canada and an exarchate in Mexico. Also under its canonical jurisdiction are the autonomous Albanian Orthodox Archdiocese and the Romanian Orthodox Episcopate of America. The latter places the OCA in a peculiar position, having a relationship with the Romanian Episcopate while holding membership in the Standing Conference of Canonical Orthodox Bishops which includes the rival Romanian Orthodox Church of America.

Membership: In 1978 the Church reported 440 parishes, 1,000,000 members and 531 priests.

Educational facilities: St. Tikhon's Orthodox Theological Seminary, South Canaan, Pennslyvania; St. Vladimir's Orthodox Theological Seminary, Tuckahoe, New York.

Periodicals: *The Russian Orthodox Messenger*, 59 East 2nd Street, New York, NY 10003; *The Orthodox Church*, Box 39, Pottstown, PA 19464.

Sources: Sophie Koulomzin, *The Orthodox Christian Church through the Ages*. New York: Russian Orthodox Greek Catholic Church of America, 1956; *The Orthodox Liturgy...according to the Use of the Church of Russia*. London: Society for Promoting Christian Knowledge, 1964; Constance Tarasar, Orthodox America, 1794-1976: Development of the Orthodox Church in America. Syosset, NY: Orthodox Church in America, 1975.

★107★
ORTHODOX CHURCH OF AMERICA
% Most Rev. David Baxter
502 East Childress
Morrilton, AR 72110

The Orthodox Church of America was formed on June 29, 1970 by Bishop David M. Baxter. Bishop Baxter had been consecrated the previous year by Archbishop Walter M. Propheta of the American Orthodox Catholic Church, assisted by bishops John A. Christian, and Foster Gilead. The church uses the Western Rite, but places emphasis upon its Eastern orders and Eastern spirituality. Its basis of faith is the Nicene Creed, the Seven Sacraments and the necessity of Orders in the Apostolic Succession.

Membership: In 1983 the Church reported 5 parishes, 14 priests, and 214 members.

Educational facilities: St. Herman Seminary, Morrilton, Arkansas, a correspondance school.

★108★
ROMANIAN ORTHODOX CHURCH IN AMERICA
% His Eminence The Most Rev. Archbishop Victorin
  (Ursache)
19959 Riopelle
Detroit, MI 48203

The first Romanian Orthodox parish in North America was formed in Regina, Saskatchewan in 1902. It was followed two years later by a parish in Cleveland, Ohio, the first in the United States. These parishes and others to follow functioned under the hegemony of the Russian Orthodox Church. A diocese was created in 1929 and a bishop assigned in 1935. Bishop Policarp Morusca

returned to Romania at the beginning of World War II and after the war was detained and finally in 1948 involuntarily retired by the new Romanian government. In 1950 a new bishop, consecrated and sent by the Church in Romania arrived. The appearance of Bishop Andrei Moldavan divided the American church which had a by-law providing for the consecration of a bishop only after the election by a diocesan congress.

The majority of the American Romanian Orthodox reject Moldovan. The Romanian Orthodox Church of America began with the twelve parishes that accepted him. They organized as the Canonical Missionary Episcopate in the United States, Canada, and South America. The Church is fully Orthodox in faith and practice, a member of the Standing Conference of Canonical Orthodox Bishops in the United States, and differs from the larger Romanian Orthodox Episcopate of America in administration.

Membership: In 1980 the Church had 13 parishes and 12,835 members in the United States, with 19 additional parishes in Canada and one in Venezuela.

Periodicals: *Credinta--The Faith*, 19959 Riopelle, Detroit, MI 48203.

★109★
**ROMANIAN ORTHODOX EPISCOPATE OF
  AMERICA**
% His Eminence Archbishop Valerian (D, Trifa)
2522 Frey Tower Rd.
Jackson, MI 49201

The first Romanian Christians came to America at the end of the nineteenth century. A parish of the Romanian Orthodox Church was organized in Regina, Saskatchewan, in 1902, and two years later St. Mary's Church was founded in Cleveland. Individual congregations cooperated with Russian bishops and were related directly to the hierarchy in Romania. After a quarter of a century, a church congress was held in Detroit and in 1929 the Romanian Orthodox Episcopate (diocese) of America was organized. In 1935 the first bishop, His Grace Policarp Morusca, came to the United States and settled in Grass Lake, Michigan.

In 1939 Bishop Policarp went to Romania but due to political events could not return. After World War II he was detained by the Romanian government and in 1948 placed in retirement. The Romanian patriarchate, without the knowledge or consent of the American diocese, consecrated a new bishop, the Reverend Andrei Moldovan. His arrival in the U.S. created a major crisis. The statutes and bylaws of the diocese provided for ordination of bishops only after election by the diocesan congress. The majority of the congregations rejected Moldovan and a split occurred. The majority party (48 parishes) declared themselves in full separation from the Romanian patriarchates and elected Valerian D. Trifa as their bishop. Trifa had, like Moldovan, just arrived in the

United States. Through a fraternal tie, Trifa was able to bring the Episcopate under the canonical protection of the Russian Orthodox Greek Catholic Church of America (now the Orthodox Church in America, which recognized Trifa's church as a self-governing body.

Membership: In 1982 the Episcopate reported 34 parishes, 40,000 members and 69 priests.

Periodicals: *SOLIA, Roumanian News,* 11341 Woodward Avenue, Detroit, MI 48202.

Remarks: In the mid-1970s the Episcopate underwent a period of disturbance when Bishop Trifa was charged with concealing his role in Nazi atrocities in Romania. In 1980 Trifa was stripped of his United States citizenship, and in 1984 he was deported to Portugal.

Sources: *Holy Liturgy for Orthodox Christians.* Jackson, MI: Roumanian Orthodox Episcopate, n.d.; Valerian D. Trifa, *Holy Sacraments for Orthodox Christians.* Jackson, MI: Roumanian Orthodox Episcopate, n.d.; Beliefs of Orthodox Christians. Jackson, MI: Roumanian Orthodox Episcopate, n.d.

★110★
RUSSIAN ORTHODOX CHURCH IN THE U.S.A., PATRIARCHIAL PARISHES OF THE

St. Nicholas Patriarchal Cathedral
15 E. 97th St.
New York, NY 10029

Following the Russian Revolution, the members of the Russian Orthodox Church in both Russia and the United States were split over rejecting or acknowledging the new government which had risen to power. Within the United States, especially after the arrest of the Patriarch of Moscow, the sentiment was largely against any accommodation and the American archdiocese declared itself administratively autonomous of the homeland. Meanwhile, within the Soviet Union, a reorganization of the church by leaders of the so-called "Living Church," those who supported accommodation to the Communist government occurred. With government backing, they assumed control of the Church and elected John Kedrowsky as the new bishop for the West. Kedrovsky arrived in America in 1923 prepared to take up his leadership role. However, at the same synod meeting in 1924 at which the Church declared its autonomy, Kedrovsky's credentials were rejected. As the official representative of the Church in Russia, however, he did find some support, and in 1926 won possession of the headquarters cathedral in New York City.

Kedrovsky's situation was further complicated in 1933 by the arrival of Metropolitan Benjamin Fedchenkov. In the year that Bishop John had lived in the United States, the Church in Russia had regained some stability and the Living Church faction had died away. Metropolitan Benjamin represented a more acceptable accommodationist position and he gained some support. He established the American Exarchate of the Russian Orthodox Catholic Church. However, for another decade Bishop John, succeeded by his son Nicolas Kedrovsky, whom he had consecrated, kept possession of St. Nicholas Cathedral. Finally in 1945, after the death of both Bishop John and Nicolas, the Kedrovsky faction was left without either support of the Church in Russia or an episcopal leader. Rev. John Kedrovsky, Bishop John's other son signed the cathedral over to the Exarchate.

Negotiations continued sporadically in an attempt to work out differences between the church authorities and the larger autonomous Russian Orthodox Greek Catholic Church of America. These reached fruition in 1970. The Russian Orthodox Greek Catholic Church of America became the Orthodox Church in America and recognized the Patriarch of Moscow as its spiritual authority. The Patriarch, in turn, recognized its autonomous status. As part of the agreement, the Exarchate was disolved. At the time of the disolution of the Exarchate, it was agreed that any parishes which wished to remain under the direct administrative authority of the Moscow patriarchy could remain outside of the Orthodox Church in America. These several parishes reformed as the Patriarchal Parishes of the Russian Orthodox Church in the United States and Canada. A vicar bishop was placed in charge of the approximately 40 parishes. St. Nicholas remained with the Patriarchal Parishes and served as its headquarters. Over the years parishes have been allowed to transfer to the OCA.

Membership: In 1975 the Patriarchal Parishes reported 51,500 members in 41 parishes headed by 60 priests.

Periodicals: *One Church,* 727 Miller Avenue, Youngstown, OH 44502.

Sources: M. Pokrovshy, *St. Nicholas Cathedral of New York, History and Legend.* New York: St. Nicholas Cathedral Study Group, 1968.

★111★
RUSSIAN ORTHODOX CHURCH OUTSIDE OF RUSSIA

% His Eminence Philaret, Metropolitan
75 E. 93rd St.
New York, NY 10028

Following the Russian Revolution and the cutting of lines of authority and communication between the Patriarch of Moscow and bishops serving Russian Orthodox communities outside of Soviet control, attempts were made to reorganize the church. In 1921 a conference of Russian Orthodox bishops in exile met at Sremski Karlovtsy, Yogoslavia. Among the participants was Metropolitan Platon, leader of the American archdiocese. Metropolitan Platon continued to work with the Council of Bishops Abroad until 1926 when he ran into conflict over the movement toward autocephalous status of the

American church. Metropolitan Platon declared the Council of Bishops an uncanonical organization. The Council dismissed Platon and assigned Bishop Apollinary in his place.

Bishop Apollinary was elevated to archbishop in 1929 and, after a short period of leadership, he died in 1933. He was succeeded by Bishop Vitaly. Efforts to heal the schism between the Church Abroad and the autonomous Russian Orthodox Greek Catholic Church of America (popularly called the Metropolia) led to a temporary reproachment in 1935 which continued through the period of World War II. In the mid-1940s, however, it became evident that the larger body wished some realignment with the Patriarch of Moscow and, in 1946, it broke completely with the Church Abroad. The American followers of the Church Abroad asserted their continuity with Russian Orthodoxy in America and declared the Metropolia schismatic. Since that time the Russian Orthodox Church Outside of Russia has been the major voice of the anti-Soviet faction of Russian Orthodoxy, and it has tried to continue the practices of the Church (including the veneration of the Russian royal family) as they were prior to the Revolution.

Membership: In 1972 the Church reported 95 parishes in the United States, 29 parishes in Canada, and 37 parishes in South America. There were over 50,000 members in the United States.

Educational facilities: Holy Trinity Orthodox Seminary, Jordanville, New York.

Periodicals: *Orthodox Life*, Holy Trinity Monastery, Jordanville, NY 13361; *The Orthodox Word*, St. Herman of Alaska Brotherhood, Platina, CA 96076.

Sources: M. Rodzianko, *The Truth About the Russian Church Abroad*. N.p.: 1975; *A Cry of Despair from Moscow Churchmen*. New York: Russian Orthodox Church Outside of Russia, 1966; *Fiftieth Anniversary of the Russian Orthodox Church Outside of Russia*. Montreal: Monastery Press in Canada, 1971.

★112★
SACRED HEART CATHOLIC CHURCH (ARRENDALE)
1475 Walton Ave.
New York, NY 10452

The Sacred Heart Catholic Church was founded in 1980 by Archbishop James Augustine Arrendale and other former members of Archbishop James Lashley's American Catholic Church, Archdiocese of New York. Arrendale was consecrated on August 10, 1981 by Bishop Pinachio, who was assisted by Bishops Donald Anthony and William Wren. The group adheres to the teachings of the Seven Ecumenical Councils and the three Ecumenical Creeds. Archbishop Arrendale died in 1985 and the future course of the Archdiocese is in doubt.

Membership: In 1983 the Church reported three parishes, two priests, and 50 members.

★113★
SERBIAN EASTERN ORTHODOX CHURCH FOR THE U.S.A. AND CANADA
% Rt. Rev. Bishop Firmilian
St. Sava Monastery
Box 519
Libertyville, IL 60048

Few churches have been so affected by the changes in modern Europe as the Serbian Church. Present maps (if they show it at all) reveal Serbia as a part of Yugoslavia, a country welded together out of a number of pre-World War II, pre-Tito states. An independent Serbian Orthodox Church had been established in 1219 under Archbishop St. Sava. A patriarchate was established in the fourteenth century. From 1389 to 1815 Serbia was under Turkish rule and the church suffered severe persecution, but a nineteenth century revival followed independence from Moslem control.

In 1765 Serbian autonomy was ended and the church returned to the jurisdiction of the ecumenical patriarch in Constantinople, who began a Hellenization program. In 1832 the archbishop of Belgrade was given the title metropolitan and in 1879, as a result of the Congress of Berlin, the Serbian Church regained autonomy. In 1920 it joined with the independent Serbian churches in Montenegro, Bosnia, Herzegovina, Dalmatia, and Croatia to form the Serbian patriarchate. The seat was established in Belgrade and its independence recognized by the ecumenical patriarch in 1922.

Immigrants from Serbia began to arrive in the U.S. in significant numbers in the 1890s. In 1892 Archimandrite Firmilian arrived and began to organize parishes. The first was in Jackson, California, but others soon followed in Chicago; Douglas, Alaska; and McKeesport, Steelton, and Pittsburgh, Pennsylvania. All of these early parishes were placed under the jurisdiction of the Russian Orthodox Church in America. The Serbian Church began to seek autonomous status as early as 1913. With Russian encouragement, Serbian Father Mardary was sent to the United States to organize an independent diocese in 1917. In 1919 the Russians elevated him to archimandrite. In 1921 the Serbs separated from the Russian Orthodox Church and Mardary became the administrator. In 1926 he was consecrated bishop for the American diocese. The Serbian Church grew slowly in this country until World War II, when a flood of refugees came into the United States. St. Sava Monastery at Libertyville, Illinois, was built soon after Bishop Mardary's consecration and the church headquarters are currently established there. On November 14, 1970, King Peter, deposed monarch of Yugoslavia, died; he was buried in the Monastery.

The changes in political structure in Yugoslavia after World War II drastically altered the American diocese. In

1940 Bishop Dionisije Milivojevitch was sent to the United States to assume authority for the church. Because Dionisije was a vocal anti-Tito spokesman and defender of the Serbian monarchy, Marshall Tito, the new ruler of Yugoslavia, encouraged the Belgrade patriarch to release Dionisije. At the same time, Tito moved against the church by confiscating all church property, thus placing the church under his financial control. The American Archdiocese was divided into three dioceses. Dionisije was left in charge of the Midwest. He rejected the actions of the patriarch in Belgrade, which he interpreted as coming from an atheist government bent on absolute control of the church. He was suspended from office and the following year excommunicated. He appealed the actions of the Belgrade patriarch to the clergy and laity of the American church and individual congregations, and priests began to take sides. Each side filed suit against the other, and two churches have evolved: the Serbian Orthodox Church in the United States and the Serbian Orthodox Church in Diaspora.

The Serbian Orthodox Church in the United States of America and Canada is the canonical body loyal to the Mother Church with its Patriarchal See in Belgrade, Yugoslavia. In 1963 it was reorganized into three dioceses. Leading the church is Bishop Firmilian of the Midwestern American Diocese headquartered at Libertyville, Illinois. During the period of the 1960s and 1970s when the headquarters property of the church at St. Sava Monastery was being contested in the court and under the control of Bishop Dionisiji, the Midwestern Diocese erected a large church building in Chicago which served (until 1980) as its temporary headquarters. The Western American Diocese is headquartered in Alhambra, California and the Eastern American Diocese in Edgeworth, Pennsylvania. In 1983 the Canadian parishes were separated from the Eastern Diocese and organized into a new Canadian Diocese. The Serbian Orthodox Church in the United States of America and Canada is a member of the Standing Conference of Canonical Orthodox Bishops.

Membership: In 1984 the Church reported 97,123 members, 78 parishes and missions and 73 priests.

Periodicals: *The Path of Orthodoxy,* Box 36, Leesdale, PA 15056.

Sources: Djoko Slijepchevich, *The Transgressions of Bishop Dionisije.* Chicago: The Author, 1963; Nicholai D. Velimirovich, *The Life of St. Sava.* Libertyville, IL: Serbian Eastern Orthodox Diocese, 1951; Nicholai D. Velimorovich, *The Faith of the Saints, Catechism of the Eastern Orthodox Church.* (Libertyville, IL): The Serbian Eastern Orthodox Diocese for the United States of America and Canada, 1961.

★114★
SERBIAN ORTHODOX CHURCH IN DIASPORA
% Metropolitan Iriney Kovachevic
Box 371
Grayslake, IL 60030

The Serbian Orthodox Church in Diaspora, formerly the Serbian Orthodox Free Diocese of the United States and Canada, like the Serbian Orthodox Church in the United States and Canada, claims the history of Serbian Orthodoxy in America since the 1890s. It remains, however, as that branch which remained loyal to Bishop Dionisiji Milivojevitch after he was excommunicated and defrocked by the Belgrade Patriarch. That action began a lengthy series of court battles between Bishop Dionisiji's followers and the appointed representatives of the Belgrade church authorities. In 1978 the courts finally awarded the property at Libertyville, Illinois to the Belgrade representatives. Bishop Dionisiji died in 1979, a few months before his followers abandoned the property.

The Free Serbian Church, as it was popularly called, purchased property at nearby Grayslake, Illinois and began to build a new headquarters complex. The massive Gracanica Monastery was dedicated in 1984. Dionisiji was succeeded by Bishop Iriney. Under his leadership the stanch anti-Communist and anti-Tito stance adopted by his predecessor has continued. The Church is in communion with the Orthodox Church of Greece under the jurisdiction of Metropolitan Auxentios of Athens.

Membership: In 1984 the Church reported 48 parishes, 30,000 members and 45 priests.

Educational facilities: St. Sava Seminary, Lake Villa, Illinois.

Periodicals: *Diocesean Observer,* Box 371, Grayslake, IL 60030; *Orthodox Missionary,* Box 404, Chilliwack, British Columbia, Canada.

Sources: *A Time to Choose.* Third Lake, IL: Monastery of the Most Holy Mother of God, 1981; *Gracanica.* Grayslake, IL: Serbian Orthodox Free Diocese of the United States and Canada, 1984; Jovan Todorovich, *Serbian Patran Saint, Krsna Slava.* Merrilville, IN: The Author, 1978; Bishop Dionisije, *Patriarch Gherman's Violations of the Holy Canons, Rules and Regulations of the Serbian Orthodox Church in Tito's Yugoslavia.* Libertyville, IL: The Serbian Orthodox Diocese in the U.S.A. and Canada (Free Serbian Orthodox Church in Free World, 1965.

★115★
TURKISH ORTHODOX CHURCH
Current address not obtained for this edition.

The Turkish Orthodox Church was established in 1926 when excommunicated priest Paul Eftymios Karahissaridis claimed to have had his sentence of excommunication lifted by two members of the Holy Synod of the Greek Orthodox Church and that Bishops Cyril of Erdek and Agathangelos of Prinkipo consecrated him. Karahissaridis became popularly known as Papa Eftim. The new church grew out of a controversy begun by Papa Eftim's demanding a Turkish Church independent of the Greek Orthodox ecumenical patriarch in Constantinople. In 1933 Papa Eftin introduced a Turkish language version of the Divine Liturgy and ordained his son Socrates Ermis Karahissaridis and nephew Nicholas Doren to the priesthood. (Ermis became Eftim II.) The relations of the Turkish movemei t and the ecumenical patriarch have remained shaky and very much tied to Turkish-Greek relations. In 1962 Eftim II succeeded his ailing father as head of the church. Papa Eftim died in 1968.

On December 6, 1966, the Turkish Orthodox Church came to the United States with the appointnment of the Most Rev. Civet Kristof (a.k.a. Christopher M. Cragg) as metropolitan archbishop of New York and patriarchal exarch and primate of the Turkish Orthodox Church in America. Cragg, a well-educated black American of Ethiopian ancestry, had been consecrated by Archbishop Christopher Maria Stanley in 1965 and named Auxiliary Bishop of New York for the American Orthodox Catholic Church headed by Archbishop Walter M. Propheta. He edited the jurisdiction's periodical, the *Orthodox Catholic Herald*, which became the first periodical for the Turkish Orthodox Church. Kristof issued the first copies of *Orthodoks Mustakil*, the new periodical for the Turkish Orthodox Church, in 1969.

Membership: In 1969 the church reported 14 churches and 6 mission parishes.

Remarks: The Turkish Church continued to exist throughout the 1970s but during the early 1980s, Archbishop Cragg moved to Chicago and opened a health clinic. His stationary carried the title, American Orthodox Church, Diocese of Chicago and North America.

Sources: Most Reverend Metropolitan Kristof, *A Brief History of the Turkish Orthodox Church in America (Patriarchal Exarchate)*. New York: Turkish Orthodx Church in America, Exarchal Office, (1967?).

★116★

UKRAINIAN ORTHODOX CHURCH IN THE U.S.A.

% Most Rev. Mstyslav Skrynpyk
Box 495
South Bound Brook, NJ 08880

Ukrainian Christians, primarily Roman Catholic followers of the Uniate Eastern Rite, arrived in the United States and organized parishes in the nineteenth century. However, they soon encountered efforts of the Church in America to further Latinize the Uniate parishes. Some left and joined the Russian Orthodox Church, in spite of what many felt were imperial designs against Ukrainians. In 1915 an independent Ukrainian National Church was founded. It placed itself under independent Catholic bishop Carmel Henry Carfora, head of the National Catholic Diocese in North America and later primate of the North American Old Roman Catholic Church, with the understanding that it would affiliate with the Ukrainian Orthodox Church when and if it was allowed to exist in the Ukraine. In 1917, as the Russian Revolution progressed, the Ukrainian National Republic came into existence and, in 1919, it proclaimed the Ukrainian Autocephalous Orthodox Church the official church of the land. The Ukrainian-Americans immediately began to establish an independent church. An initial All-Ukrainian Orthodox Church Council of the American Ukrainian Orthodox Church met in 1922. It petitioned for a bishop and two years later John Theodorovich arrived to head the new church.

As Theodorovich was organizing the new diocese, a second split in the ranks of the Roman Catholic Church's Ukrainian-American members occurred, after the Western Ukraine was given to Poland in the 1920s. This intensified the issue of Latinization and clerical celibacy. By the end of the decade, American dissenters had organized the Independent Greek-Catholic Church. They renamed the Ukrainian Orthodox Church in America. The new Church was taken under the care and protection of independent Lebanese bishop Aftimios Ofiesh of the American Orthodox Church, who consecrated their first bishop, Joseph Zuk, who unfortunately died in 1934. He was succeeded by Bohdan T. Shpilka.

The two dioceses led by Theodorovich and Shpilka existed side-by-side for several decades until a church council elected Mystyslaw Skrypnyk as the new archbishop of the Ukrainian Orthodox Church of America. Shpilka became his auxiliary bishop. Shrypnyk opened negotiations with Theodorovich, and they resulted in the union of the churches in 1950 as the Ukrainian Orthodox Church in the U.S.A. Theodorovich submitted to reconsecration and was named the new church's first metropolitan. The church also declared its freedom from dependence upon the ecumenical patriarch.

Membership: In 1966 the Church reported 107 parishes, 87,745 members, and 131 priests.

Periodicals: *Ukrainian Orthodox Word*, Box 495, South Bound Brook, NJ 08880.

Sources: Peter Bilon, *Ukrainians and Their Church*. Johnstown, PA: Western Pa. Regional Branch of the U.O.L., 1953.

★117★

UKRAINIAN ORTHODOX CHURCH IN AMERICA (ECUMENICAL PATRIARCHATE)

St. Andrew's Ukrainian Orthodox Diocese
% Most Rev. Metropolitan Andrei Kuschak
90-34 139th St.
Jamaica, NY 11435

In 1950 the two branches of the Ukrainian Orthodox Church in America united. The initial attempts toward union had followed the replacement of Bishop Bohdan T. Shpilka as ruling bishop of one branch of the church by Mystyslaw Skrypnyk. At the time of the union, Bishop Bohdan declined to participate in the new church and withdrew with his following and reorganized as the Ukrainian Orthodox Church in America. Bishop Bohdan had led the Ukrainian Orthodox Church from 1934 to 1950 and had been consecrated in 1937 on orders of the ecumenical patriarchate. He retained that relationship after he broke with Bishop Skrypnyk.

Bohdan died in 1965. He was succeeded by Andrei Kuschak, but not before a document in which Bohdan aledgedly passed his succession to Demetius Sawka was declared invalid. The Church is identical in faith and practice to the Ukrainian Orthodox Church in the U.S.A.

Membership: In 1977 the Church reported 28 parishes, 25,000 members and 35 priests. A 1980 survey indicated 23 parishes 3,465 confirmed members and an additional 2,000 adherents.

Periodicals: *Ukrainian Orthodox Herald*, 90-34 139th Street, Jamaica, NY 11435.

★118★

UNIVERSAL SHRINE OF DIVINE GUIDANCE

% Most Rev. Mark A. G. Karras
30 Malta St.
Brooklyn, NY 11207

Father Mark Karras, the son of a Greek priest, was consecrated by Archbishops Peter A. Zurawetzky of the Old Catholic Patriarchate of America, assisted by independent Greek bishop, Joachim Souris, Archbishop of Byzantium, on July 18, 1955, and the following month founded the Universal Shrine of Divine Guidance. He was assisted in this enterprise by Veronica Perweiler, whom he consecrated as "abbess" the following year. The teachings of the Universal Shrine are based upon the idea that humanity has entered a third and final state of spiritual and moral evolution. Thus, the Universal Shrine is a continuation, with significantly new emphases, of the Pentecostal Church, and the Apostolic episcopacy. The first stage was the regulatory period of Judaism and the second the instructional stage of Christianity. In the third stage, a period of fulfillment through enlightenment and grace will ensue. Bishop Mark promulgates a pure philosophy of faith in God and spiritual values, a universal faith emphasizing moral achievement and merit.

At the heart of the doctrine is the Christian teaching of love.

Membership: Not reported.

Sources: Mark Karras, *Christ Unto Byzantium*. Miami, FL: Apostolic Universal Center, 1968.

★119★

WESTERN ORTHODOX CHURCH IN AMERICA

% Most Rev. C. David Luther
1529 Pleasant Valley Blvd.
Altoona, PA 16602

The Western Orthodox Church grew out of the Catholic Apostolic Church of Brazil founded by former Roman Catholic Church bishop, Carlos Duarte Costa, which had been brought to the United States by Bishop Stephen Meyer Corradi-Scarella, an independent bishop in New Mexico. In 1973 Corradi-Scarella gave Fr. Charles David Luther, a priest he had ordained, directions to found the Community of the Good Shepherd as a fellowship of priests and priest in training. In 1977 the name was changed to Servants of the Good Shepherd. The Community accepts qualified men into the priesthood, trains them and assists them in starting mission churches, usually as worker-priests.

In 1977 Luther was consecrated by Bishop Charles R. McCarthy assisted by Jerome Joachim and W. D. de Ortega Maxey. In 1974 Joachim had succeeded Corradi-Scarella as head of the National Catholic Apostolic Church in America. In 1980 he renamed his jurisdiction the Western Orthodox Church in America. After his consecration Luther brought the Servants of the Good Shepherd into Joachim's jurisdiction. He became bishop of the Diocese of Altonna and was later (l981) made archbishop. In 1983, however, Joachim and Luther decided to become independent of each other. Joachim and his following became the Catholic Apostolic Church in America, while Luther retained the name, Western Orthodox Church in America.

The Western Orthodox church in America, while possessing Catholic orders, is Orthodox while following a Western Rite. In 1984, Luther consecrated Richard James Ingram as Bishop of Hobart (Indiana) and James Franklyn Mondok as Bishop of Euclid (Ohio). The Church is affiliated with the Ecumenical Church Fedration, a fellowship of independent bishops and other Christian leaders organized by Bishop Alan Bain, Archbishop for the British Isles of the Apostolic Episcopal Church.

Membership: In 1981 there were 25 priests and over 100 seminarians studying for the priesthood affiliated with the Servants of the Good Shepherd.

Educational facilities: Duarte Costa University, Altoona, Pennsylvania; Duarte Costa School of Religion, Altoona, Pennsylvania.

Sources: *A Brief Description of the Servants of the Good Shepherd.* Altoona, PA: n.p., (1980?).

Non-Chalcedonian Orthodoxy

★120★
ARMENIAN APOSTOLIC CHURCH OF AMERICA
℅ Archbishop Mesrob Ashjian
138 E. 39th St.
New York, NY 10016

In 1933, the Armenian Church in America split along political lines as a result of the Soviet dominance of Armenia. The Armenian Apostolic Church of America continues that Church which began to form in the 1890s among Armenian-Americans and whose members were most commited to a free and independent Armenia. This Church existed without official sanction until 1957 when Zareh I, the newly elected Catholicos of the See of Cilicia, took it under his jurisdiction. Located in Sis, the capital of Lesser Armenia, since the fifteent century, the See of Cilicia moved to Lebanon in the twentieth century.

In 1972, the Prelacy of the Armenian Apostolic Church of America was divided into the Eastern States and Canada, and the Western States. His Grace, Bishop Yeprem Tabakian is Prelate of the Western Prelacy and His Eminence, Archbishop Mesrob Ashjian of the Eastern. Archbishop Ashjian succeeded Archbishop Karekin Sarkissian in 1977.

Membership: In 1984, the Church reported 300,000 members in 33 churches with 37 priests.

Periodicals: *The Outreach*, 138 E. 39th St., New York, NY 10016.

Sources: Karekin Sarkissian, *The Council of Chalcedon and the Armenian Church.* New York: Armenian Church Prelacy, 1965; Karekin Sarkissian, "Armenian Church in Contemporary Times" in A. J. Arberry, ed., *The Church in the Middle East.* Cambridge: Cambridge University Press, 1969; Karekin Sarkissian, *The Witness of the Oriental Orthodox Churches.* Antelias, Lebanon: The Author, 1970.

★121★
ARMENIAN CHURCH OF AMERICA
℅ His Eminence Torkom Manoogian, Primate
630 Second Ave.
New York, NY 10016

The Armenian Church of America is the continuing faction of the Armenian Church, which since 1933 has attempted to accomodate to the merger of Armenia into the Union of Soviet Socialist Republics. It is under the jurisdiction of the See of Etchmiadzin in Soviet Armenia. It is headed by Archbishop Torkom Manoogian, with a western diocese under the leadership of Bishop Elisha Simonian.

Membership: In 1979, the Church reported 66 churches, 61 clergy, and 4500,000 members.

Periodicals: *Bema*, 630 Second Ave., New York, NY 10016; *The Mother Church*, 1201 N. Vine St., Hollywood, CA 90038.

Sources: *The Handbook on the Divine Liturgy of the Armenian Apostilic Holy Church.* Boston: Baikar, 1931; Sion Manoogian, *The Armenian Church and Her Teachings.* N.p.: The Author, n.d.; Papken Gulesserian, *The Armenian Church.* New York: Diocese of the Armenian Church in America, 1966; Hogop Gurlekian, *Christ's Religion in Every Branch of Life and the Armenians Really Alive.* Chicago: The Author, 1974.

★122★
APOSTOLIC CATHOLIC ASSYRIAN CHURCH OF THE EAST, NORTH AMERICAN DIOCESE
℅ His Grace, Mar Aprim Khamis, Bishop of the
     North American Diocese
744 N. Kildare
Skokie, IL 60076

Alternate address: His Holiness Mar Dinkha IV, Catholicos Patriarch, Box 3257, Sadoun, Baghdad, Iraq.

Victims of Turkish expansion, the Church of the East was dispursed in the late nineteenth century and its headquarters in northern Kurdistan was abandoned. Scattered members of the church began to arrive in America in the 1890s, but for many years were without organization. Early in this century, there were several visitations by the bishops. They found a flock served by an insufficient number of priests and deacons meeting whenever space was available. All of this changed in 1940 when Mar Eshai Shimun XXIII, the 119th patriarch of the church, moved his headquarters to Chicago. A church-reorganization program was initiated. Priests and deacons were ordained; churches were purchased and built; administration was put in efficient order; and a publishing program, including a new periodical, was begun. The progress of the Church has continued under the present patriarch, who has reestablished the international headquarters in Iraq.

Membership: In 1983, the Diocese reported 13 churches, 35,000 members, and 65 clergy.

Periodicals: *Voice from the East*, Box 25264, Chicago, IL 60626.

Sources: *The Liturgy of the Holy Apostles Adai and Mari.* London: Society for Promoting Christian Knowledge, 1893. Mar O'Dishoo, *The Book of Marganita (The Pearl) on the Truth of Christianity.* Kerala, India: Mar Themotheus Memorial Printing & Publishing House Ltd., 1965; Yulpana M'Shikhay D'eta Qaddishta Washlikhayta O'Qathuliqi D'Mathnkha, *Messianic Teachings.* Kerala, India: Mar Themotheus Memorial Printing & Publishing House Ltd., 1962; *Rules Collected from the Sunhados of the Church of the East & Patriarchial Decrees.* San Francisco: Holy Apostolic and Catholic Church of the East, 1960.

★123★

COPTIC ORTHODOX CHURCH
℅ Archpriest Fr. Gabriel Abdelsayed
427 West Side Ave.
Jersey City, NJ 07304

Since World War II, an increasing number of Copts have left Eqypt because of Moslem discrimination. Many of these have come to the United States. In 1962, the Coptic Association of America was formed to serve the Coptic Eqyptians in New York City and vicinity and to work for the establishment of regular pastoral care. The following year Bishop Samuel, bishop of public, ecumenical, and social services, was delegated to come to the United States by Pope Kyrillos VI to meet with the Coptic Association and implement pastoral care. In 1965 Father Marcos Abdel-Messiah was ordained in Cairo and sent as a priest to Toronto to establish the Diocese of North America. In 1967 Father Dr. Rafael Younan arrived in Montreal. By 1974 there were nine priests serving four churches in New York, plus other churches in Los Angeles, Houston, Detroit, Jersey City, St. Paul, Indianapolis, Milwaukee, Chicago, and several smaller centers. There are fewer than 2,000 adult Copts in North America. An English translation of *The Coptic Orthodox Mass and the Liturgy of St. Basil* has been produced and educational literature has been initiated by Father Marcus Beshai of Chicago.

Membership: In 1983, the Church reported 9 churches, 2,332 members, and 17 priests.

Sources: Fayek M. Ishak, *A Complete Translation of the Coptic Orthodox Mass and Liturgy of St. Basil.* Toronto: Coptic Orthodox Church, Diocese of North America, 1973; *St. Mark and the Coptic Church.* Cairo: Coptic Orhtodox Partriarchate, 1968; *The Agprya.* Brooklyn, Abdelsayed, "The Coptic-American: A Current African Cultural Contribution in the United States of America." *Migration Today* 19 (1975) 17-19.

★124★

ETHIOPIAN ORTHODOX CHURCH IN THE UNITED STATES OF AMERICA
℅ His Eminence Abuna Yeshaq, Archbishop
Holy Trinity Ethiopian Orthodox Church
140-142 W. 176th St.
Bronx, NY 10453

Alternate address: His Holiness Abuna Tekle Haimanot, Box 1283, Addis Ababa, Ethiopia.

The beginning of the twentieth century saw a developing nationalism within the Ethiopian Church, at that time still under the Patriarch of Alexandria. Due in part to the diplomacy of Emperor Haile Selassie, in 1929 , five native bishops were consecrated, though they were without dioceses and could not perform other consecrations. In 1944, the Emperor established the Theological College in Addis Ababa. Immediately after World War II, the Emperor negotiated an agreement with the Egyptians that led, in 1948, to the promulgation of the Statue of Independence of the Ethiopian Orthodox Church, thus freeing it from Alexandria and the Coptic Orthodox Church in Eqypt. That same year, it joined the World Council of Churches. Finally, in 1959 the bishop of Addis Ababa was raised to the rank of patriarch and chosen from among the Coptic monks. This action gave the church its actual autonomy.

Following the overthrow of Haile Selassie in 1974 and the establishment of a Marxist government in Addis Ababa, the Church came under severe attack. In 1976, His Holiness Abuna Theopolis, the Patriarch was removed from office, arrested, and has not been seen since. Whether he is still alive is unknown. Several other high ranking church leaders were exiled or remain under detention. In 1978, Archbishop Abba Matthias, head of the Ethiopian monastery in Jerusalem, defected to the United States and began a compaing to alert the Western world to the religious persecution in Ethiopia.

In 1959, the same year the Ethiopian Church attained full independence, Laike Mandefro, was one of several Ethiopian priests who came to the United States to study. Originally associated with Abuna Gabre Kristos Mikeal of the Ethiopian Coptic Orthodox Church of North and South America, who sponsored their entrance into the United States, they soon broke relations with him and under the authority of His Grace Archbishop Theopolis, began to gather Ethiopian-Americans into a congregation in Brooklyn, later relocated to the Bronx. As his work grew, he was raised to the rank of Archimadrite and placed in charge of the Ethiopian Church in the West. He moved t Jamaica in 1970, where by 1977, there were congregations in Kingston, Montego Bay, Ocho Rios, Linsted, and St. Ann, with missions throughout the Carribean. In 1974, the American branch became an "affiliated communion" with the National Council of Churches. The Jamaican branch is a full member of both the Jamaica Council of Churches and the Caribbean

Conference of Churches. More recently Archimadrite Mandefro was consecrated a bishop and made Archbishop of the Western Hemisphere Diocese.

Membership: In 1984, the Church reported 34 parishes and missions, 5,000 members, and 15 clergy. There are approximately 10,000 members in 7 parishes and 3 missions in Jamaica.

Periodicals: *The Structure of the Church*, 140-142 West 176th St., Bronx, NY 10453.

Sources: Enrico S. Molnar, *The Ethiopian Orthodox Church*. Pasadena, CA: Bloy House Theological School, 1969; K. M. Simon, *The Ethiopian Orthodox Church*. Addis Ababa: n.p., (195-?); Lisa Bessil-Watson, comp., *Handbook of Churches in the Caribbean*. Bridgetown, Barbados: Cedar Press, 1982.

★125★

ETHIOPIAN ORTHODOX COPTIC CHURCH, DIOCESE OF NORTH AND SOUTH AMERICA
1255 Bedford Ave.
Brooklyn, NY 11216

The Ethiopian Orthodox Coptic Church, Diocese of North and South America, was formed by Most Rev. Abuna Gabre Kristos Mikael, an Ethiopian-American who established his jurisdiction under the authority of the Archbishop Walter M. Propheta of the American Orthodox Catholic Church. In 1959, he traveled to Ethiopia, was ordained, and then elevated to the rank of Chorepistopas by Abuna Basilios. late patriarch of Ethiopia. He then served as sponsor for a group of three priests and five deacons sent by Abuna Basilios to the United States for advanced study and to develop an American branch of the Ethiopian Orthodox Church. However, the priests, led by Fr. Laike Mandefro, broke relations with Mikael and centered their efforts on a parish in Brooklyn, New York, later relocated to the Bronx, which was directly under the authority of the Patriarch in Addis Ababa. The Ethiopian Orthodox Coptic Church remains in communion with the American Orthodox Catholic Church, from which some of the clergy were drawn.

In the few years of its existence it has established churches in Trinidad, Mexico, and Pennsylvania; in Brooklyn there are two churches, one with a Latin and one with a Coptic Ethiopian rite, the rite commonly followed by the church. The worship is in English. The priests are both celibate and married and all bishops are celibate, the common Eastern church practice. Most of the members and clergy are black, but the church made news in 1972 by elevating a white man to the episcopate as bishop of Brooklyn.

Friction has developed between the two "Ethiopian" churches, each questioning the legitimacy of the other.

Membership: Not reported. It is estimated that several hundred members can be found in the three parishes in New York and Pennsylvania.

★126★

HOLY APOSTOLIC-CATHOLIC CHURCH OF THE EAST (CHALDEAN-SYRIAN)
℅ Metropolitam Mar Mikhael
190 Palisades Dr.
Daly City, CA 94015

The Holy Apostolic-Catholic Church of the East (Chaldean-Syrian) is one of several bodies to grow out of the work of Mar Jacobus (Ulric Vernon Herford). Herford was consecrated by Mar Basilius Soares, Metropolitan of the Syro-Chaldean Church in India, Ceylon, Socotra, and Messina, in 1902. Though raised a Unitarian, Herford was led to Mar Basilius by a desire to find a meeting point for Eastern and Western Christianity. Several years before Herford's death in 1938, Mar David (not to be confused with Mar David I, W. D. de Ortega Maxey), brought the jurisdiction to the United States and established it in Florida. The present metropolitan is the fourth in direct linage.

The belief and practice of the Church is Orthodox. It holds to the doctrines of the first two Ecumenical Councils and affirms the virgin birth of Jesus, His incarnation and sacrificial atonement, and the Holy Trinity. The Bible, consisting of the Old and New Testaments, is the authority for the Church which uses the Peshitta, the Bible translated directly from the ancient Aramaic texts. This jurisdiction differs from some Eastern bodies in that it entered into the Charismatic Renewal in 1947 and continues to believe and teach that the Gifts of the Holy Spirit (I Corinthians 12) are meant for today.

Membership: In 1983, the Church reported 15 parishes and 3,500 members in the United States.

Remarks: This author's volume, *The Old Catholic Sourcebook* (Garland, 1983), co-authored with Karl Pruter, incorrectly identified Mar Mikhael with Michael A. Itkin, a bishop whose church also derives from the Syro-Chaldean lineage of Mar Jacobus. Itkin's Church, however, is oriented to ministry within the homosexual community and accepts homosexuals into the priesthood. In this respect it is to be distinguished from the Holy Apostolic-Catholic Church of the East.

★127★

ORTHODOX CATHOLIC SYNOD OF THE SYRO-CHALDEAN RITE
℅ Most Rev. Bashir Ahmed
100 Los Banos Ave.
Daly City, CA 94014

The Orthodox Catholic Synod of the Syro-Chaldean Rite was formed in 1970 by Bishop Bashif Ahmed and is one of several bodies to continue the tradition of Mar Jacobus

(Ulric Vernon Herford), who brought the Syro-Caldean Church to the West in 1902. Raised a Unitarian, Herford journeyed to the Orient on a quest to find a means of uniting East and West. In 1902 he was consecrated by Mar Basilius Soares, Bishop of Trichur, and head of a small body of Indian Christians called the Mellusians. Mar Basilius had been ordained to the priesthood by Julius Alvarez (who had consecrated Joseph Rene Vilatte) and consecrated to the episcopacy by Mar Antonius Abd-Ishu of the Nestorian linage. Upon his return to England, Herford founded the Evangelical Catholic Communion.

The Orthodox Catholic Synod of the Syro-Chaldean Rite derives from a schism of the Evangelical Catholic Communion, an American church founded by Michael A. Itkin. Itkin had led his orgainzation to take a positive activist stance in support of homosexuals. Rejecting Itkin's leadership, Ahmed founded an independent jurisdiction within the same tradition.

Membership: Not reported.

★128★
SYRIAN ORTHODOX CHURCH OF ANTIOCH (ARCHDIOCESES OF THE UNITED STATES AND CANADA) (JACOBITE)
% Archbishop MarAthanasius Y. Samuel, Primate
49 Kipp Ave.
Lodi, NJ 07644

The Syrian Orthodox Church of Antioch (Archdiocese of the United States and Canada) dates from the migration of Syrian Christians to the United States in the late 1800s, principally after the Turkish persecutions began in 1893. The demand for worship services led the American community to send Deacon Hanna Koorie to Jerusalem. He was ordained to the priesthood and later consecrated a bishop. He returned home on September 28, and began to call together the dispersed flock for a first worship service at St. Luke's Episcopal Church, Paterson, New Jersey.

The Archdiocese was established in 1924 with Koorie as the archbishop. He was succeeded on his death by Mar Athanasius Y. Samuel, the present archbishop.

Membership: In 1982, the Archdiocese reported 15 parishes in the United States and 4 in Canada, 30,000 members, and 18 clergy.

Periodicals: *Beth Nahrin (Mesopotamia)*, 49 Kipp Ave., Lodi, NJ 07644.

Sources: Mar Ignatius Ephrem I, *The Syrian Church of Antioch, Its Name and History.* Hackensack, NJ: The Archdiocese of the Syrian Church of Antioch in the United States and Canada, n.d.; Mar Severius Ephrem Barsoun, *The Golden Key to Divine Worship.* West New York, NJ: 1951; Anaphora. Hackensack, NJ: Metropolitan Mar Athanasius Yeshue Samuel, 1967.

★129★
SYRIAN ORTHODOX CHURCH OF MALABAR
% Dr. K. M. Simon
Union Theological Seminary
Broadway and 120th St.
New York, NY 10027

From the time of the ancient church, there has existed on the southwest Malabar coast of India a people who by legend were first evangelized by the Apostle Thomas. Relations with the Roman See were established in the Middle Ages. In the fifteenth century when the Protugeuse began to colonize the Malabar coast, they attempted to Latinize the church, and after a period of tension most of the church withdrew from papal jurisdiction in 1653. In 1665 the Syrian Jacobites sent their representative to the Malabar coast and eventually many of the Malaber Christians were brought under the Syrian patriarch of Antioch. A Malabar bishop was consecrated in 1772 and there are approximately 1,500,000 Christians in his jurisdiction today.

The Syrian Orthodox Church of Malabar has established a mission in New York directly under the patriarch of Antioch. There is only one congergation (as of 1967) which meets at Union Theological Seminary every Sunday and on holidays. Its approximate 150 members are drawn from students, diplomatic personnel, and permanent residents. Periodic services are also held in Philadelphia, Washington, DC. and Chicago. Dr. K. M. Simon is the vicar-in-charge.

Membership: Not reported.

Sources: *An English Translation of the Order of the Holy Ourbana of the Mar Thoma Syrian Church of Malabar.* Madras, Diocesan Press, 1947; Kadavil Paul Ramban, *The Orthodox Syrian Church, Its Religion and Philosophy.* Vadayampady, Puthencrez: K. V. Pathrose, 1973.

Lutheran Family

An historical essay on this family is provided beginning on page 15.

Lutheranism

★130★
AMERICAN LUTHERAN CHURCH
422 S. 5th St.
Minneapolis, MN 55415

The American Lutheran Church was formed in 1960 by the merger of three Lutheran bodies: the United Evangelical Lutheran Church, the Evangelical Lutheran Church, and the American Lutheran Church (1930-1960). The merged church retains the name of the group formed in 1930 by the merger of the Ohio (1818), Buffalo (1845), Texas (1851), and Iowa (1854) Synods. All were of German background. The United Evangelical Lutheran Church was founded in 1896 by the union of two separate synods of Danish background. The Danish Evangelical Lutheran Association had been formed in 1884 by pastors seceding from the Norwegian-Danish Conference of 1870. The Danish Evangelical Lutheran Church in North America had been created in 1894 by a group which withdrew from the DanishEvangelical Lutheran Church of America (now in the Lutheran Church in America). The Evangelical Lutheran Church was the result of a merger in 1917 of the different Norwegian churches brought to America in the nineteenth century: the United Norwegian Church, the Norwegian Synod, and the Hague Synod. The American Lutheran Church (of 1960) was the first Lutheran body to merge across ethnic lines.

The official doctrinal position is that held in common by all Lutheran bodies. It has been considered however, to hold a slightly more conservative interpretation of the basic Lutheran documents, from the Lutheran Church in America, considered to be the most liberal of Lutheran Churches. The American Lutheran Church has remained aloof from many non-Lutheran bodies, and has stayed outside of the National Council of Churches. Though, it did join the World Council of Churches.

The highest authority in the American Luthern Church is the biennial general convention made up equally of lay and clerical delegates. It elects a president (presiding-bishop), vice-president, and secretary. There is also a church council comprising general officers of the church and a layperson and a clergy member from each district. Advisory members include the district presidents, youth delegates, and representatives from the Board of Trustees. There are five divisions, four administrative offices, and three boards which implement the program of the church.

The American Luthern Church has four seminaries, ten colleges, and two universities. Missions are operated in 18 countries. There are homes for children and the aged across the country. Augsburg Publishing House is a major book concern.

Membership: In 1984, the American Lutheran Church reported 2,343,411 members in 4,906 congregations being served by 7,314 mimisters.

Educational facilities: Augustana College, Sious Falls, South Dakota; California Lutheran College, Columbus, Ohio; Concordia College, Moorhead, Minnesota; Dana College, Blair, Nebraska; Luther College, Decorah, Iowa; Pacific Lutheran University, Tacoma, Washington; St. Olaf College, Northfield, Minnesota; Texas Lutheran College, Seguin, Texas; Waldorf College, Forest City, Iowa; Wartburg College, Waverly, Iowa. Seminaries: Trinity Lutheran Seminary, Columbus, Ohio; Wartburg Theological Seminary, Dubuque, Iowa; Pacific Lutheran Theological Seminary, Berkeley, California.

Periodicals: *Lutheran Standard*, 426 S. 5th St., Minneapolis, MN 55415.

Remarks: The American Lutheran Church recently voted to join the Lutheran Church in America and the Association of Evangelical Lutheran Churches in a three-way merger, effective January 1, 1988.

Sources: Fred W. Meuser, *The Formation of the American Lutheran Church*. Columbus, OH: The Wartburg Press, 1958; G. Everett Arden, *Augustana Heritage* Rock Island,

IL: Augustana Press, 1963; E. Clifford Nelson, *The Lutheran Church Among the Norwegian-Americans* Minneapolis: Augsburg Publishing House, 1960; *Yearbook of the American Lutheran Church* Minneapolis: Augsburg Publishing House (issued annually).

★131★
APOSTOLIC LUTHERAN CHURCH (OLD LAESTADIANS)

% Rev. George Wilson, President
New York Mills, MN 56567

The Apostolic Lutheran Church is the only branch of the Laestadian (Finnish Apostolic Lutheran) movement to organize formally. Since 1908 the Old Laestadians had held an annual "Big Meeting." It was primarily a time for theological discussions and for affirming consensus. In 1928 the Old Laestadians announced the intention of establishing a national church. In 1929 the constitution and by-laws were adopted, asserting the authroity of the Bible and the Book of Concord. A congregational government and a mission program were established. The church body ordains ministers, establishes institutions, and helps found new congregations. The Old Laestadians practice the laying-on-of hands for absolution after the confession of felt sin to a confessor. They also believe in the three baptisms: of water (establishing the covenant between God and his children), of the Holy Spirit (the bond of love), and of blood (godly sorrow).

The Apostolic Lutheran Church is headed by a president and a central board. There are two districts. Congregations are located in Michigan, Minnesota, the Dakotas, Massachusetts, Washington, Oregon, and California.

Membership: In 1982 the Apostolic Lutheran Church reported 6,500 members in 52 congregations and 38 ministers.

Educational facilities: Apostolic Lutheran Seminary, Hancock, Michigan.

Periodicals: *Christian Monthly*, Apostolic Book Concern, Rte. 1, Box 150, New York Mills, Minnesota 56567.

Sources: Uuras Saanivaara, *The History of the Laestadian of Apostolic-Lutheran Movement in America* Ironwood, MI: National Publishing Company, 1947; *Constitution and By-Laws*. n.p.: Finnish Apostolic Lutheran Church of America, 1929.

★132★
APOSTOLIC LUTHERANS (CHURCH OF THE FIRST BORN)

Current address not obtained for this edition.

The branch of the Apostolic Lutherans, generally called the First Borns, are a continuation of the congregation headed by John Takkinen. They are aligned with the followers of Juhani Raattamaa headquarted at Gellivaara, Finland. They differ from the Old Laestadians (i.e., the Apostolic Lutheran Church) by their emphasis on the simplicity of the Christian life. They turn to the elders of Gellivaara for particular decisions on moral questions. They forbid neckties, pictures on walls, taking photographs, hats on women, Christmas trees, life insurance, and flowers at funerals.

The First Borns were among the first to introduce English in worship and to publish English books. They hold Big Meetings every summer. They print their church news in Valvoju, an unofficial publication circulated among Apostolic Lutherans. By latest count (made in the 1940's) there were approximately 2,000 members. Churches are located in Michigan; Wilmington, North Carolina; Wilmington, Deleware; Brush Prairie, Washington; and Gackle, North Dakota. There are approximately twenty-five congregations.

Membership: Not reported.

Sources: Uuras Saanivaara, *The History of the Laestadian or Apostolic-Lutheran Movement in America*. Ironwood, MI: National Publishing Company, 1947.

★133★
APOSTOLIC LUTHERANS (NEW AWAKENING)

Current address not obtained for this edition.

Possibly the smallest branch of the Laestadians or Apostolic Lutheran Movement is the New Awakening group. They teach the "third use of the law," i.e., that Christians must abide by the Ten Commandments in addition to Christ's two laws of love of God and love of neighbor. They also teach a second experience following conversion. The second experience is the "circumcision of the heart," in which one's heart is deeply broken but then experiences a fuller knowledge of Christ's redemptive work and of sanctification.

Membership: Not reported.

Sources: Uuras Saanivaara, *The History of the Laestadian or Apostolic-Lutheran Movement in America*. Ironwood, MI: National Publishing Company, 1947.

★134★
APOSTOLIC LUTHERANS (EVANGELICALS NO. 1)

Current address not obtained for this edition.

That branch of the Apostolic Lutheran Movement generally referred to as the Evangelicals No. 1 began under the inspiration and preaching of Arthur Leopold Heideman who emphasized positive evangelism. Among the Apostolic Lutherans, they lay the least emphasis on confession and sanctification. They use, but do not consider important, public confession. The Evangelicals No. 1 have experienced two splits. In 1921-22 a group led by Paul A. Heideman returned to the beliefs of the Old Laestadians. In 1940 a split occurred over the place of the commands and counsels of Christ and the Apostles and the use of confession. The Evangelicals No. 1 represent those who hold that the commands of Christ are necessary as a norm for Christian living. They believe themselves to be the one church of true believers.

Membership: Not reported.

Sources: Uuras Saavinaara, *The History of the Laestadian or Apostolic-Lutheran Movement in America.* Ironwood, MI: National Publishing Company, 1947.

★135★
APOSTOLIC LUTHERANS (EVANGELICALS NO. 2)
Current address not obtained for this edition.

Formed in 1940 and having broken from the Apostolic Lutherans (Evangelicals No. 1), that branch of the Apostolic Lutheran Movement generally called the Evangelicals No. 2 rejects the need of the commands and counsels of Christ because, they say, the grace of God works in believers to bring about a denial of unrighteousness and worldly lusts, and it works to instill godly and righteous behavior. They reject the confession of sins as a Roman Catholic institution, and they do not emphasize absolution. The law, they believe, should be preached to unbelievers, but only the gospel of free grace, to believers.

Like the Evangelicals No. 1, this group believes itself to be the one true church of Christ. Founders of the group include John Koskela, Victor Maki, John Taivalmaa, and Andrew Leskinen.

Membership: Not reported.

★136★
APOSTOLIC LUTHERANS (THE HEIDMANS)
Current address not obtained for this edition.

The Heidemans are the second largest group of Apostolic Lutherans. The group was formed in 1921-22 by members of the Apostolic Lutherans (Evangelicals No. 1) who separated and returned to the Old Laestadian position. Thus they resemble the Old Laestadians group, but they remain outside of its organization. The leader of the group was Paul A. Heideman, son of A.L. Heideman, who was for many years the only ordained minister in the group. He was assisted by a number of preachers.

Membership: Not reported.

Periodicals: *Rauhan Tervehdys*; *Greetings of Peace*.

★137★
ASSOCIATION OF EVANGELICAL LUTHERAN CHURCHES
St. Louis, MO 63131

The withdrawal of the Federation for Authentic Lutheranism only slightly lessened the tensions of doctrinal controversy within the Lutheran Church-Missouri Synod. Conservatives leveled several complaints against Missouri Synod policy. They sought withdrawal by the Missouri Synod of its pulpit and altar fellowship from the liberal American Lutheran Church. (Pulpit fellowship refers to the practice of exchanging ministers, and altar fellowship means members of the churches sharing fellowship can receive communion in each other's churches.) Further, the conservatives asked for an end to cooperation with the American Lutheran Church, the Lutheran Church in America, and the Lutheran Council in the U.S.A.. Finally, they demanded an investigation of Concordia Theological Seminary, whose faculty, they alleged, was teaching doctrine contrary to official Lutheran doctrine.

The question of the Missouri Synod's ability to control the teaching at the seminary came to a head in 1972. J.A.O. Preus, president of the Missouri Synod, issued a report accusing some teachers at the seminary of teaching false doctrines. Seminary president John Tietjen was singled out for particular criticism. This action increased the polarization of two parties in the Missouri Synod. A conservative group became increasingly vocal in demanding that the Missouri Synod enforce doctrinal standards, particularly a literal Bible interpretation. A liberal wing, centered on the faculty at Concordia, insisted on greater freedom in both Bible interpretation and theology . Following defeat at the 1973 convention of the Synod, the more liberal group organized what came to be known as Evangelical Lutherans in Missouri (ELIM). Early in 1974, Tietjen was suspended as president of Concordia. In reaction, 43 of 48 professors went on strike, and three-fourths of the student body voted to boycott classes. Forced to leave Concordia, the faculty and students set up Concordia Seminary in Exile (popularly called Seminex). ELIM supported the exiled students and faculty, and prepared itself to remain as an organized dissenting group within the Missouri Synod. The next two years saw an even greater polarization as conservatives now in control of the Missouri Synod pressed for total conformity with traditional doctrinal standards and threatened removal of voices of dissent. The liberals fought a defensive action until early in 1976 to form the Association of Evangelical Lutheran Churches. The new association is one in doctrine with its parent body, the Missouri Synod, but emphasizes ecumenism and diversity. Rejecting its parent body as "separatist," the association has moved into dialogue with other Christian groups, has opened pulpit and altar fellowships with the two larger Lutheran churches (the Lutheran Church in America and the American Lutheran Church), and has vocalized hopes that it might merge with these two churches. Within the limits of fidelity to the Lutheran doctrinal consensus, the association encourages a diversity of perspectives as a sign of health in the church.

The association of Evangelical Lutheran Churches supports Partners in Mission, a foreign missionary agency originally formed by ELIM.

Membership: In 1984 AELC reported 550 ministers, 110,000 members, and 275 congregations.

Educational facilities: Christ Seminary-Seminex, Chicago, Illinois.

Periodicals: *Foreword*, 12015 Manchester Road, Ste. 80LL, St. Louis, Missouri 63131.

Remarks: Recently, the Association of Evangelical Lutheran Churches has voted to join with the American Lutheran Church and the Lutheran Church in America in a three-way merger, effective January 1, 1988.

Sources: Kurt E. Marquart, *Anatomy of an Explosion*. Fort Wayne, IN: Concordia Theological Seminary Press; Paul G. Bretscher, *After the Purifying*. River Forest, IL: Lutheran Educational Association, 1975; Frederick W. Danker, *No Room in the Brotherhood*. St. Louis: Clayton Publishing House, 1977.

★138★
ASSOCIATION OF FREE LUTHERAN CONGREGATIONS
3170 E. Medicine Lake Blvd.
Minneapolis, MN 55427

The Association of Free Lutheran Congregations was formed in 1962 by congregations that refused to enter the merger of the Lutheran Free Church with the American Lutheran Church. Among the organizers was the Rev. John P. Strand who became president at its founding. The dissenting congregations (about 40 in number) met at Thief River Falls, Minnesota, for the organization. They opposed the American Lutheran Church's membership in the World Council of Churches; the liberal theology reflected in new attitudes toward the Bible and the Roman Catholic Church; compromises of congregational polity; high-churchism; and the lack of emphasis on personal Christianity (including the condoning of social dancing and social drinking).

Doctrinally the Association is one with the rest of Lutheranism because it accepts the Book of Concord, the doctrinal standard for all Lutherans. But the association will not affiliate with any churches or people who do not agree with its very conservative interpretation of the Book of Concord.

Mission work is maintained in Brazil.

Membership: In 1974, the Association reported 125 congregations.

Educational facilities: Free Lutheran Bible School, Minneapolis, Minnesota.

Periodicals: *The Lutheran Ambassador.*

★139★
CHURCH OF THE LUTHERAN BRETHREN OF AMERICA
1007 Westside Dr.
Box 655
Fergus Falls, MN 56537

The Church of the Lutheran Brethren of America resulted from a revival in the 1890s among the Lutherans of the Midwest. Many people began to question certain practices in their parishes concerning church order. Most of their questions dealt with the "unconverted," those who had not had a personal conversion experience that infused them with an awareness of Christ as their savior. Some people, such as K.O. Lundelberg, said practices like the following had no basis in Scripture: the acceptance of the "unconverted" into church membership, requiring the oath in confirmation from "unconverted" youth, elaborate ritual worship, and admitting the "unconverted" to communion. Some independent congregations were begun and Rev. Lundelberg began to publish a Norwegian-language newspaper. *Broderbaandet.* In 1900, at a convention in Milwaukee, Wisconsin, the Church of the Lutheran Brethren was organized.

The Brethren differ from other Lutherans in that they accept only those who profess a personal experience of salvation. Confirmation has been discontinued; rather, children are instructed and wait until they have individual conversions before becoming members. Worship is simple and non-liturgical with free prayer and testimonies, and with lay participation. Communion elements are distributed by the elders to communicants in their pews. Otherwise, the church accepts basic Lutheran doctrine.

The policy is congregational. Together the congregations form the synod with a president and other officers. A board of foreign missions oversees work in Japan, Africa, and Formosa. The Lutheran Bible Schools begun in 1903 moved to Fergus Falls in 1935. In 1948, the name was changed to Lutheran Brethren Schools, which includes Hillcrest Lutheran Academy and the Lutheran Bible School and Seminary. Two homes for the aged, Sarepta Home and Broen Memorial Home, are supported by the church.

Membership: In 1983, The Lutheran Brethren reported 10,580 members in 106 congregations and a total of 136 ministers.

Educational facilities: Lutheran Bible School and Seminary, Fergus Falls, Minnesota.

Periodicals: *Faith and Fellowship*, 704 Vernon Avenue, W., Fergus Falls, Minnesota 56537.

Sources: A.A. Petersen, *Questions and Answers about the Church of the Lutheran Brethren of America*. Fergus Falls, MN: Lutheran Brethren Publishing Company, 1962.

★140★
CHURCH OF THE LUTHERAN CONFESSION
460 75th Ave.
Minneapolis, MN 55432

The Church of the Lutheran comfession began in 1957 when over thirty pastors and congregations of the Wisconsin Evangelical Lutheran Synod withdrew to form the Interim Conference. In 1960 they were joined by two pastors and congregations of the Evangelical Lutheran Synod to form the Church of the Lutheran Confession.

Membership: In 1983, The Church of the Lutheran Confession reported 8,986 members in 67 churches with 74 ministers.

Educational facilities: Immanuel Lutheran College, Eau Clair, Wisconsin.

Periodicals: *The Lutheran Spokesman*, 2015 N. Hastins Way, Eau Clair, WI 54701; *Journal of Theology*, Immanuel Lutheran College, Eau Claire, WI 54701.

★141★
CONCORDIA LUTHERAN CONFERENCE
Central Ave. at 171st Place
Tingley Park, IL 60477

The Concordia Lutheran Conference was formed in 1956 by former members of the Lutheran Church-Missouri Synod who wished to "continue in the former doctrinal position of the Missouri Synod" in the face of what they saw as a deviation. They particularly emphasize the Bible as the inerrant word of God and as the only source and norm of Christian doctrine and life. Like their parent body, they accept the Book of Concord as the proper exposition of the Word of God. The church is nonseparatist in orientation and seeks unity with all other Lutherans and Christians on a basis of unity of faith.

Membership: In 1984, the Concordia Lutheran Conference reported a membership of seven congregations, 350 members, and eight ministers.

Educational facilities: Concordia Theological Seminary, Tingley Park, Illinois.

Periodicals: *The Concordia Lutheran*, Central Ave. at 171st St., Tingley Park, IL 60477.

Sources: H. David Mensing, *A Popular History of the Concordia Lutheran Conference*. n.p.: 1981.

★142★
EVANGELICAL LUTHERAN CHURCH IN AMERICA
% Truman Larson
Rte. 1
Jackson, MN 56143

Elling Eielsen was a young Norwegian immigrant who was ordained in America. He led the formation of the Evangelical Lutheran Church in America, the first Norwegian Lutheran synod in the New World, in 1846. Growth of the synod was slow partly due to the demand for proof of conversion prior to admission to membership. Controversy arose as some clergy demanded the admission of all who accepted the Christian faith and led a moral life. In 1876 a constitution revised along these lines was accepted and the name changed to Hauge's Norwegian Evangelical Lutheran Synod (which became part of the American Lutheran Church). At this time Eielsen and his supporters withdrew and formed the Evangelical Lutheran Church in America according to the Old Constitution. Eielsen himself died in 1883 but the Synod has continued as a small body.

Doctrine is at one with other Lutheran bodies. Liturgy is simple. (Eielsen had also protested domination by university-trained clergy, clerical garb, and a too formal liturgy.)

Membership: In 1985, the Church reported on two congregations with a total membership of 50. There are no ordained ministers.

★143★
EVANGELICAL LUTHERAN SYNOD
% Rev. George Orvick, President
2670 Milwaukee St.
Madison, WI 53704

The Evangelical Lutheran Synod was formed at Lake Mills, Iowa, in 1918 by a group of 40 pastors and laymen (the conservative wing of Norwegian Lutherans) who declined to enter the merger of other Norwegian Lutherans deciding instead to establish an independent synod. The name Norwegian Synod of the American Evangelical Lutheran Church was adopted. The present name was assumed in 1957. In 1920 it was received into the conservative-oriented Lutheran Synodical Conference but withdrew along with the Wisconsin Evangelical Lutheran Synod in 1963. It rejects fraternizing with all who deny the essence of Lutheran belief.

Doctrine is the same as the Lutheran consensus with a conservative interpretation (similar to the Wisconsin Synod) and the Evangelical Lutheran Synod has in the past used the Wisconsin and Missouri Synods' seminaries for training its ministers. It is congregational in polity. Resolutions passed by the synod are not binding until sent to the congregations for acceptance. The officers of the synod direct the work of common interest. Home missions are conducted in nine states, and the Kasota Valley Home (for the aged) is located at Kasota, Minnesota. Foreign mission work is conducted in Lima, Peru.

Membership: In 1983, the Synod reported 20,025 members in 110 congregations being served by 97 ministers.

Educational facilities: Bethany Lutheran College, Mankato, Minnesota; Bethany Lutheran Theological Seminary, Mankato, Minnesota.

Periodicals: *Lutheran Sentinel*, Bethany Lutheran College, 734 Marsh St., Mankato, MN 56001.

★144★
FEDERATION FOR AUTHENTIC LUTHERANISM
Current address not obtained for this edition.

The Federation for Authentic Lutheranism was formed in 1971 by members of the Lutheran Church-Missouri Synod. They had signaled their intention to withdraw prior to the 1971 meeting of the Missouri Synod if it did not stop fellowship relations with the liberal American Lutheran Church, withdraw from the Lutheran Council in the U.S.A., (which included both the Lutheran Church in America and the American Lutheran Church), and discipline "errorists" in the synod. (An attempt at the latter action has resulted in the recent controversy in the Missouri Synod.) Seven congregations formed the original federation. Eleven more joined within two years.

Theology is exteremely conservative and pulpit fellowship was immediately declared with the Wisconsin Evangelical Lutheran Synod and the Evangelical Lutheran Synod. Positions have been taken against women's suffrage, the ordination of women, the Boy Scouts, and military chaplaincies. The federation is congregational in polity and run by a board of directors (half lay and half clerical) elected by the entire federation.

Membership: Not reported.

Periodicals: *Sola Scriptura,*

★145★
LATVIAN EVANGELICAL LUTHERAN CHURCH
IN AMERICA
% Rev. Arturs Voitkus, President
3438 Rosedale Ave.
Montreal, PQ, Canada H4B 2G6

The takeover of several European countries by Marxist-Communist governments after World War II placed minority Lutheran Churches in a precarious position. Nationals who had fled Communist rule, and refugees who had left during the war and felt unable to return, established a church-in-exile with headquarters in Germany. Latvian Lutherans in the United States organized in 1957 as the Federation of Latvian

Evangelical Lutheran Churches in America. The churches reorganized in 1976 to become the Latvian Evangelical Lutheran Church in America. It is the North American affiliate of the Lutheran Church of Latvia in Exile.

The Latvian Lutheran Church follows Lutheran doctrine and affirms the three ancient creeds (Apostles, Nicean, and Athanasian) as well as the unaltered Augsburg Confession, Luther's Small and Large Catechisms, and the other parts of the Book of Concord.

The synod, presided over by the church's president, meets every three years.

Membership: In 1983 the church reported 60 congregations served by 52 clergy and 12,526 members in America with an additional 12 congregations, 10 clergy, and 2,600 members in Canada.

Periodicals: *Cela Biedrs*, 425 Elm St., Glenview, IL 60025.

Sources: *Lutheran Churches of the World*. Minneapolis: Augsburg Publishing House, 1957.

★146★
LUTHERAN CHURCH IN AMERICA
231 Madison Ave.
New York, NY 10016

The Lutheran Church in America, the largest of several Lutheran churches in the United States, was formed in 1962 by the merger of four Lutheran bodies: the United Lutheran Church, the Finnish Evangelical Lutheran Church (Soumi Synod), the American Evangelical Lutheran Church, and the Augustana Evangelical Lutheran Church. The merger was the culmination of no fewer than eight previous mergers. The United Lutheran Church in America had been formed in 1918 by the merger of the General Synod, the General Council, and the General Synod of the South (created by the merger of some Southern synods) and was for the next 40 years the largest Lutheran body in America. The General Sy nod had been created in 1820 by the merger of the Pennsylvania Ministerium, the North Carolina Synod, and part of the New York Ministerium. The General council had been formed in 1867 by the merger of the New York Ministerium and the Augustana Synod. The Augustana Synod became independent again in 1918.

The American Evangelical Lutheran Church dated to 1872 when Danish Lutherans founded the Kirklig Missions Forening. The Finnish Evangelical Lutheran Church was formed in 1890 at Calumet, Michigan. It used the liturgy of the Church of Finland. The Augustana Evangelical Lutheran Church originated in 1851 when the Synod of Illinois was established by Swedish and other immigrants. Some Swedish and Norwegian elements pulled out nine years later to form the Scandinavian Augustana Synod. The word "Scandinavian" was dropped in 1894. (Thus the Lutheran Church in America represents the most complete amalgamation of Lutherans across ethnic boundaries and signals their completed Americanization, a process through which all immigrant religious bodies eventually pass.)

In working out the merger of 1962, an affirmation of the traditional Lutheran doctrinal stance was made in a new Confession of Faith. the ancient creeds and the Book of concord were accepted as "valid interpretations of the confession of the church." The Gospel (the good news of Jesus Christ that comes to humanity through the Scriptures) is the heart of the confession.

The Lutheran Church in America is loosely organized into 33 synods in the United States and Canada. There is a biennial convention which elects a president as the chief administrative officer. The president presides over the executive council which supervises the work of the church. There are eight boards and agencies and seven commissions. Fortress Press is a major publishing concern. There are nine seminaries, 16 colleges, and three universities. The church oversees more than 200 social service agencies. Mission work is carried on in 20 countries.

Membership: In 1983, the Lutheran Church in America reported 2,925,655 members in 5,815 congregations being served by 8,216 ministers.

Periodicals: *The Lutheran*, 2900 Queen Lane, Philadelphia, PA 19129.

Sources: Johannes Knudsen, *The Formation of the Lutheran Church in America*. Philadelphia: Fortress Press, 1978; Albert P. Stauderman, *Our New Church* (Philadelphia: Lutheran Church Press, 1962; Amos John Traver, *A Lutheran Handbook*. Philadelphia: Fortress Press, 1964; *Faith of Our Fathers*. Mankato, MN: Lutheran Synod Book Company, 1953.

★147★
LUTHERAN CHURCH-MISSOURI SYNOD
International Center
1333 S. Kirkwood Rd.
St. Louis, MO 63122

Of the largest Lutheran bodies, the Lutheran Church-Missouri Synod, often called simply the Missouri Synod, is by far the most conservative. In 1839 a group of Saxon Lutherans who were fleeing the rationalism which had captured the Lutheran Church in Germany arrived in New Orleans, Louisiana. They eventually settled south of St. Louis, Missouri on a large tract of land in Perry County. They were led by the Rev. Martin Stephan who had been elected bishop. Also among the group was Carl Ferdinand Wilhelm Walther, a young Lutheran minister. Soon after settling in Perry County, Stephan was banished when the colonists discovered he had misappropriated funds to support his opulent lifestyle.

After Stephan's banishment, Walther became the acknowledged leader. He fought what he felt were the theological errors of Stephan's preaching. Cheif among these were the beliefs that Lutheran Church was the church, without which there was no salvation; that the ministry was a mediatorship between God and man, hence, ministers we re entitled to obedience in all things not contrary to the Word of God; and that questions of doctrine were to be decided by the clergy alone. Walther helped found the small school in Altenburg, Missouri, which eventually became Concordia Seminary in St. Louis. In 1841 he went to St. Louis as pastor and in 1844 began to publish the *Lutheraner*, which issue after issue, championed orthodox Lutheranism as opposed to rationalism (a reliance on reason instead of faith). The *Lutheraner* fought for the rights and responsibility of the congregation in the church. In 1847 the Missouri Synod was founded on the principle of the autonomy of the congregation. There were 14 congregations and 22 ministers.

The Synod had been joined by some Franconians in Michigan and Hanoverians in Indiana. Over the years they were joined by other small synods, including the Illinois Synod (1880) and the English Synod of Missouri (1911). In 1963 the National Evangelical Lutheran Church merged into the Missouri Synod. In 1971 the Synod of Evangelical Lutheran Churches joined the Missouri Synod as one of its districts.

Doctrinally, the Missouri Synod is one with the other large Lutheran bodies but generally is considered more conservative. Polity is congregational. The General Convention meets biennially. There are 39 districts represented. The convention elects a president and oversees the vast institutional and missional program. There are four seminaries (including Concordia in St. Louis) and 13 colleges. A number of hospitals and homes dot the nation. Mission work is engaged in with missionaries and partner churches in Australia, Belgium, Botswana, Brazil, Chile, Denmark, France, Germany, Ghana, Great Britian, Hong Kong, India, Japan, Korea, Lebanon, Liberia, the Middle East, Mexico, New Guinea, New Zealand, Nigeria, Paraguay, Philippines, Sierra Leone, Sri Lanka, Taiwan, Thailand, Togo, Uruguay, and Venezuela.

Membership: In 1984 the Missouri Synod reported 2,660,000 members in 5,800 congregations. There were 8,000 ministers.

Educational facilities: Christ College, Irvine, California; Concordia College (with campuses at Ann Arbor, Michigan; Austin, Texas; Bronxville, New York; Mequon, Wisconsin; Portland, Oregon; River Forest, Illinois; St. Paul, Minnesota; Selma, Alabama; Seward, Nebraska; and Edmonton, Alberta, Canada); St. John's College, Winfield, Kansas; and St. Paul's College, Concordia, Missouri. Seminaries: Concordia Theological Seminary (with campuses at St. Louis, Missouri; Ft. Wayne, Indiana; St.

Catherines, Ontario, Canada; and Saskatoon, Saskatchewan, Canada).

Periodicals: *The Lutheran Standard*, 1333 S. Kirkwood Rd., St. Louis, MO 63122; *Witness*, 1333 S. Kirkwood Rd., St. Louis, MO 63122.

Remarks: During the 1960's, the Missouri Synod was racked with doctrinal controversy which found its focus in differing views on just how the Bible can be considered the Word of God. The conservatives believe the Bible to be the inerrant Work of God and interpret quite literally. The more liberal members considered the Bible to bear the Word of God, i.e., Jesus Christ, to the church, and, as such, to be properly the object of historical and textual criticism.

This debate led to several schisms. Impatient with the slowness with which the Synod resolved the debate, several small groups of conservatives left and formed their own synods. In the end (and for the first time in the twentieth century) the conservative viewpoint prevailed, but only after a decade of discussion. As a result, 200 of the 6,100 congregations, representative of the liberal faction, left the Synod to form the Association of Evangelical Lutheran Churches.

Sources: Carl S. Meyer, *A Brief Historical Sketch of the Lutheran Church-Missouri Synod*. St. Louis: Concordia Publishing House, 1938; A. Grabner, *Half a Century of True Lutheranism*. Chattanooga, TN: J. A. Fredrich, n.d.; W. Arndt, *Fundamental Christian Beliefs*. St. Louis: Concordia Publishing House, 1938; *The Lutheran Annual 1984*. St. Louis: Concordia Publishing Company (issued annually); *Handbook*. St. Louis: Lutheran Church-Missouri Synod (issued biennially); Kurt E. Marquart, *Anatomy of an Explosion*. Fort Wayne, IN: Concordia Theological Seminary Press, 1977.

★148★
LUTHERAN CHURCHES OF THE REFORMATION
Current address not obtained for this edition.

In 1964, several congregations in the Midwest (formerly a part of the Lutheran Church-Missouri Synod) joined to form the Lutheran Churches of the Reformation. These congregations had protested what they considered the growing theological liberalism of the Missouri Synod. They follow the doctrine and life of their parent body but take a conservative position on doctrinal questions.

Membership: Not reported.

★149★
THE PROTESTANT CONFERENCE
728 N. 9th St.
Manitowoc, WI 54220

In the 1920's a controversy developed in the Wisconsin Evangelical Lutheran Synod that led a number of pastors and members to accuse the synod of a departure from the faith. In 1926 Pastor W. F. Beitz set the issues clearly in "God's Message to Us in Galatians," a paper read to the Wisconsin River Chippewa Valley Conference. He accused the Synod of legalism, a departure from the life of faith as spelled out in Galatians and evidenced by the Synod's over-emphasis on formalism, institutionalism, and membership-building. He called for repentance and a life lived by faith. The controversy resulted in the formation of the Protestant Conference in 1928.

Its doctrine is like the Wisconsin Synod's, but there is a strong emphasis on dependence on God, forgiveness of sin, and life lived by faith. The General conference meets semiannually.

Membership: In 1984, the Conference reported 960 members in six congregations and one mission being served by 10 ministers.

Periodicals: *Faith-Life*, Box 2141, LaCross, WI 54644.

Sources: *The Wauwatosa Gospel: Which Is It?* Marshfield, WI: The Protestant Conference Press, 1928.

★150★
SYNOD OF EVANGELICAL LUTHERAN CHURCHES
(Defunct)

Lutherans from Czechoslovakia began to migrate to the United States in the 1870s and early congregations were formed at Streator, Illinois; Freeland, Pennsylvania; and Minneapolis, Minnesota. Attempts to organize began in the 1890s, and the Slovak Evangelical Lutheran Synod was finally established at Connellsville, Pennsylvania, in 1902. Theologically, it declared itself at one with the Lutheran Synodical Conference. The move into the Synodical conference proveed the first step toward full merger with the Missouri Synod, which was accomplished in 1971. Thus the Synod of Evangelical Lutheran Church ceased to exist as a separate denomination and became a district within the Missouri Synod.

★151★
WISCONSIN EVANGELICAL LUTHERAN SYNOD
2929 N. Mayfair Rd.
Milwaukee, WI 53222

The Wisconsin Evangelical Lutheran Synod (popularly called the Wisconsin Synod) was established as a result of calls for pastoral service form German immigrants to

Wisconsin in the 1840s. Ministers answered the call, and in May, 1950 the First German Evangelical Lutheran Synod of Wisconsin was organized under the direction of President John Muelhaeuser at Salem Evangelical Lutheran Church, Milwaukee (Granville), Wisconsin.

In the 1840s, a Michigan Synod had also been organized among the Wuerttembergers by Stephan Koehler and Christoph Eberhardt. A Minnesota Synod was organized by "Father" J. C. F. Heyer and others in 1860. The Wisconsin, Michigan, and Minnesota Synods became conservative theologically and staunch defenders of Lutheran doctrine against the "compromises" of the larger bodies. In 1892, after all three had withdrawn from the Lutheran Synodical Conference, they federated to form the Joint Evangelical Lutheran Synod of Wisconsin, Minnesota, and Michigan. A merger in 1917 led to the formation of the Evangelical Lutheran Joint Synod of Wisconsin and Other States. The present name was adopted in 1959.

Doctrinally, the Wisconsin Synod is like the rest of Lutheranism but takes a stance slightly more conservative than the Lutheran Church-Missouri Synod. It is especially opposed to merger without doctrinal unity on all points. It had been active in the Synodical Conference for almost a century but withdrew in 1963. In 1962 it absorbed the Orthodox Lutheran Church, a 1951 Missouri Synod splinter.

The Synod meets biennially. It is divided into 12 districts spread across the nation, though membership is concentrated in Wisconsin and the Midwest. There is a network of parochial schools, three synodical preparatory high schools, 19 area high schools, and three colleges. The Northwestern Publishing House in Milwaukee publishes books, Sunday school literature, and religious materials. A vigorous mission program is supported both at home and abroad. Missions are supported in Arizona among both the Apaches and the Latin Americans. Latin Americans missions are also conducted in Mexico, Columbia, Puerto Rico, and in stateside cities. Foreign work is carried on in Nigeria, Malawi, Zambia, Japan, Hong Kong, Taiwan, India, and Indonesia.

Membership: In 1984 the Wisconsin Synod reported 415,000 members in the United States (with an additional 20,000 outside America), in 1,172 congregations served 1,044 ministers.

Educational facilities: Northwestern College, Watertown, Wisconsin; Dr. Martin Luther College, New Ulm, Minnesota. Seminaries: Wisconsin Lutheran Seminary, Mequon, Wisconsin.

Periodicals: *The Northwestern Lutheran*, 2929 N. Mayfair Rd., Wauwatosa, WI 53222; *Wisconsin Lutheran Quarterly*, 11831 N. Seminary Dr., 65 W., Mequon, WI 53092.

Sources: *Continuing in the Word*. Milwaukee, WI: Northwestern Publishing House, 1951); *This We Believe*. (24 page pamphlet) 1967.

Reformed–Presbyterian Family

An historical essay on this family is provided beginning on page 21.

Reformed

★152★
**CHRISTIAN REFORMED CHURCH IN NORTH
    AMERICA**
2850 Kalamazoo Ave.,S.E.
Grand Rapids, MI 49560

The Christian Reformed Church began in the Netherlands in the 1830's. At that time, some members of the Reformed Church of the Netherlands rejected an attempt to bring the church under the control of the Dutch monarchy. Despite the objections of these churchmen, the church was brought under state control. This led in 1834 to the Succession (the formation of a church independent from the monarchy). Succession leaders were Hendrik DeCock, Henrik Scholte, and Albertus C. van Raalte. They saw themselves as defenders of the historical faith that was being lost because of the indifference of the main body of the Reformed Church of the Netherlands. Following persecution and the failure of the potato crop in 1846, the dissidents supporting the Succession made plans to immigrate.

In 1847 the settlers arrived in western Michigan and by 1848 had formed the Classis Holland. Having been aided by members of the Reformed Church in America with whom they shared the same faith, they affiliated with them in 1850, becoming a classis within the Reformed Church in America. Members of the Classis Holland had the understanding that they could leave the Reformed Church in America if the ecclesiastical connection should prove a threat to their interests. For most it never did. However, one church that belonged to the Classis Holland did leave the classis and the Reformed Church in America in 1857, and others followed, eventually forming the Christian Reformed Church. The background of the schism starts with Gysbert Haan. Within a few years of the 1850 affiiation, Haan began to suggest that the Reformed Church in America was not sound. In 1857 four documents of Succession were received by the classis, urging the classis to leave the Reformed Church in America. The documents charged the Reformed Church in America with open communion, the use of a large collection of hymns, and the neglect of catechism preaching. Further, the documents asserted that the Reformed Church in America believed the Succession in the Netherlands had been unjustified. The classis received but did not approve these documents. One church left the classis in January 1857 and was soon joined by others. In 1859 these congregations became known as the Dutch Reformed Church. Growth was slow at first, and came primarily from additional immigration from the Netherlands. Immigration and growth were particularly heavy in the closing decades of the nineteenth century. Through a series of name changes the church became the Christian Reformed Church in 1904 and has retained that name.

The doctrine is strict and based on the Belgic Confession, the Heidelberg Catechism and the Canons of the Synod of Dort. In 1906 the Conclusions of Utrecht were adopted which recognized that some questions were open for disagreement. Only the children of confessing members are baptized. The church is staunchly anti-lodge and is a major supporter of the National Christian Association. Worship is ordered and derived from the practice of the church in the Netherlands. The early hymnology was largely confined to the Psalms but an expanded hymnology has developed in the twentieth century. Catechistic instruction is stressed. Polity is presbyterial. The general synod is the highest body and is composed of two ministers and two members of each of the 30 classes. There is no intermediate or particular synod between the classis and general synod. Classes meet biannually or quarterly.

There is an active mission program. Home missions include an active Jewish evangelism program, the Reformed Bible Institute, the Back to God Hour, and American Indian Missions. Foreign work is active in Nigeria, Japan, Taiwan, Sri Lanka (Ceylon), Argentina, Brazil, Australia, the Philippines, Mexico, Korea, Indonesia, and Guam. There are also a number of hospitals and homes.

Membership: In 1982 the Church reported 223,976 members, 648 congregations and 1,014 clergy.

Educational facilities: Calvin College, Grand Rapids, MI; Calvin Theological Seminary, Grand Rapids, MI.

Periodicals: *The Banner*, 2850 Kalamazoo Avenue, S.E., Grand Rapids, MI 49560; *De Wachter*, 4850 Kalamazoo Avenue, S.E., Grand Rapids, MI 49560.

Sources: *One Hundred Years in the New World*. Grand Rapids: Centennial Committee of the Christian Reformed Church, 1957.

★153★
CHURCH OF THE GOLDEN RULE
Current address not obtained for this edition.

The Church of the Golden Rule continues the French Huguenot tradition of the Alsacian Protestants who look to Martin Bucer and the city of Strassburg as the source of their faith. A congregation of Alsacian immigrants was formed in 1939 at Hempstead, Long Island, New York, under Pastor Alfred E. Huss. He was authorized by Pastor Boegner of the Alsacian Churches. When Huss died, the congregation relocated in California. In 1971 there were four congregations with about 600 families, all in California, under the leadership of Dr. Pierre Duval. The Church of the Golden Rule is under the Unite Huguenotte Francaise.

Membership: Not Reported.

★154★
CHURCHES OF GOD, GENERAL CONFERENCE
700 E. Melrose Ave.
Box 926
Findlay, OH 45839

The Churches of God, General Conference was formed by John Winebrenner (1797-1860), a German Reformed pastor of four churches in and around Harrisburg, Pennsylvania. Winebrenner, though a reformer in many areas, never intended to form a new denomination. However, in attempting to reform what he perceived as the spiritual apathy in the Reformed Church, he and other Reformed pastors adopted some of the "new measures" which had become popular during the Second Great Awakening. They began to preach the importance of personal acceptance of Jesus Christ as savior; they introduced prayer meetings in the homes of those concerned about their salvation; they prayed for people by name in their services; they initiated altar calls.

The vestry of the Harrisburg congregation served by Winebrenner took exception to these new devices. Their concern was heightened by their pastor accepting invitations to preach in the local Methodist church and by his refusal to baptize the children of unbelieving parents.

He was locked out of the church building in 1823, though he continued to serve other Reformed congregations and remained a member of the synod for several years.

In 1825 a Harrisburg congregation of persons loyal to Winebrenner and others attracted by his preaching was formed. The General Conference dates its beginning from this event. The name Church of God was adopted after a search of the scripture showed it to be the New Testament name of the church. The name was considered to be inclusive of all true believers. (Winebrenner was one of several early nineteenth-century movements which attempted to return to the New Testament model of the church. It was the first of many to follow which adopted the name "Church of God" as an element in their self-reformation.)

The essential teachings of the New Testament Church were taken to be redemption and regeneration through belief in Jesus Christ, justification by faith and the free moral agency. Three "ordinances" instituted by Jesus were followed: believer's baptism by immersion, the observation of the Lord's Supper, and footwashing. A presbyterial polity was followed, with preachers ordained as "teaching elders," assisted by "ruling elders" and deacons in the local congregation. The first organization of a group of churches into an eldership was accomplished in 1830. For many years the group was known as the Churches of God in North America, General Eldership.

While pastors and elders still participate with each other in the sixteen regional annual business meetings, most are now called "conferences" rather than "elderships." The triennial meeting of ministerial, lay and youth delegates from local conferences and elderships is called the General Conference.

An administrative council functions between the triennial meetings of the general conference. There are seven commissions which implement programs. The Commission on Church Vocations relates to the conference's educational facilities. The Commission on World Mission oversees work abroad. The Commission on Education oversees Christian education, leadership development and youth and children's ministries. A Commission on Church Development and a Commission on Evangelism direct and promote outreach and church growth ministries. The Commission on national Ministries oversees cross-cultural ministries, ministries to the aging and family life, and coordinates ministries of national lay organizations of the church. The Commission on Stewardship directs stewardship education.

Membership: In 1985 the conference reported 35,000 members, 353 congregations and 390 ministers. There are an additional 4,000 members in missions in Haiti, India and Bangledesh.

Educational facilities: Findlay College, Findlay, Ohio; Winebrunner Theological Seminary, Findlay, Ohio.

Periodicals: *The Church Advocate*, 700 East Melrose Avenue, Findlay, OH 45839; *The Missionary Signal*, 700 East Melrose Avenue, Findlay, OH 45839.

★155★
FREE AND OLD CHRISTIAN REFORMED CHURCH OF CANADA AND AMERICA
% Jacob Tamminga
950 Ball Ave., N.E.
Grand Rapids, MI 49503

The Free and Old Christian Reformed Church of Canada and America was formed in 1926 as the Free Reformed Church. In 1947 the church members developed corresponding relations with the Christian Reformed Church in the Netherlands (Christelijke Gereformeerde Herken in Nederland) and in 1949 adopted their present name. A synod of Canadian churches was organized in 1950. A synod for the congregations in Canada and the U.S. met for the first time in 1961. Their doctrine and organization (adjusted to size) are similar to the parent body, the Christian Reformed Church. A *Psalter* contains the creeds, forms of worship and hymns.

Membership: In 1966 the church had 3 congregations in the United States (one each in Michigan, New Jersey and California) and eight congregations in Canada.

★156★
HUNGARIAN REFORMED CHURCH IN AMERICA
% Rt. Rev. Dezso Abraham
18700 Midway Ave.
Allen Park, MI 48101

Hungarian Reformed congregations were established in the United States in the late nineteenth century and in 1904 the Hungarian Reformed Church in America was formed under the care of the Reformed Church in Hungary. Following World War I, however, there was a series of negotiations with the Reformed Church in the United States which resulted in the 1924 Tiffin Agreement. This agreement, made at Tiffin, Ohio, joined the Hungarian Reformed Church in America to the Reformed Church in the United States. The merged body is now a part of the United Church of Christ. Three congregations of the Hungarian Reformed Church did not wish to accept the Tiffin Agreement. These congregations and four new ones united to form the Free Magyar Reformed Church in America, which in 1958 adopted the name, Hungarian Reformed Church in America.

Doctrinally the church follows the Second Helvetic Confession and the Heidelberg Catechism. The constitution includes elements of both the presbyterian and episcopal systems. There is a diocese headed by a bishop and a lay curator. The New York, Eastern, and Western Classes are headed by a deacon and lay curator. The diocese meets annually, with a constitutional meeting every three years.

Membership: In 1982 the Church reported 11,000 members, 31 congregations, and 43 ministers.

Periodicals: *Magyar Egyhaz* (Magyar Church).

★157★
NETHERLANDS REFORMED CONGREGATIONS
% Rev. A.M. Doer
Main St., Box 42
Norwich, ON, Canada N0J 1P0

The Netherlands Reformed Congregations date from 1907 when their founders seceded from the state church in Holland, the Reformed Church of the Netherlands. The purpose of forming the new church was to emphasize the soveriegn grace of God and predestination and to combat teachings on free will. In that same year the Netherlands Reformed Congregations were brought to the United States and an American synod was organized. Doctrinal standards of the church are the Belgic Confession, the Heidelberg Catechism, and the Canons of the Synod of Dort. Though small, the church has been active in publishing. The Macedonia Mission Society publishes a series of pamphlets of sermons by the various pastors.

Membership: In 1975 the Church reported 13 congregations, 4,878 members, and four ministers. Most of the congregations were located in the northeastern United States.

★158★
ORTHODOX CHRISTIAN REFORMED CHURCHES
3268 S. Chestnut
Grandville, MI 49418

In the late 1960's within the Protestant Reformed Churches, charges of sin against some members of the First Protestant Reformed Church of Grand Rapids resulted in the excommunication of some of its members. Feeling the excommunication to be unjust and to be a denial of their rights, members of the First Protestant Reformed Church of Grand Rapids organized the Orthodox Reformed Church (unaffiliated) in the fall of 1970. As other congregations became affiliated, the present name was adopted. In doctrine and polity the church is like its parent body though it does not "subscribe to the church political policies of the Protestant Reformed Churches after the year 1965." Worship is simple and expresses a love of decency and order.

The leader of the Church until his death in 1984, the Rev. Gerald Vanden Berg, had previously been the stated clerk of the Protestant Reformed Church. He had been active in forming the Fellowship of Reformed Churches, an ecumenical group of independent reformed congregations.

Periodicals: *The Reformed Scope*, 3268 S. Chestnut, Grandville, MI 49418.

Sources: Gerald VandenBerg, *Why Orthodox Reformed?* Grandville,MI: The Orthodox Reformed Publishing Society, n.d.

★159★

PROTESTANT REFORMED CHURCHES OF AMERICA
15615 S. Park Ave.
South Holland, IL 60473

In 1924 there arose in the Christian Reformed Church what has come to be known as the Common Grace controversy. Mr. J. Vander Mey, a member of Eastern Avenue Christian Reformed Church of Grand Rapids, Michigan, filed a protest against his pastor and objected to five views the pastor had been preaching. According to Mr. Vander Mey, Rev. Herman Hoeskema 1) believed that the grace of God was at all times particular and that he is gracious to the elect only; 2) placed excessive emphasis on the doctrine of election; 3) denied the good in the natural man (science and social reform); 4) failed to sound the earnest invitation to salvation in his preaching; and 5) stated that we must hate those that hate God, hence there is no fellowship with the world in the battle for truth. The articles represent a significant disagreement within Calvinist theology.

Soon after Mr. Vander Mey's protest the Rev. J. K. Van Baalen filed a similar protest against Hoeksema and the Rev. H. Danhof. All of the protests were referred to the Classis Grand Rapids East and Classis Grand Rapids West. In the course of the discussion the question of the consistory's rights versus the classes' rights was also raised. The Classis Grand Rapids West referred the matter to the Synod. The Synod adopted "The Three Points" which put it on record in favor of a view that God did show his grace to all men apart from the grace to the elect and that an unregenerate man was capable of civic good. Danhof and Hoeksema were seen as holding views contrary to "The Three Points" and the Utrecht Conclusions, and they were admonished to conform their doctrine to the Synod's position.

Tension contined and in 1925 four consistories-- Coopersville, Eastern Avenue, Hope, and Kalamazoo-- were deposed. In 1926 the deposed consistories formed the Protestant Reformed Church. For doctrinal standards, the church uses the same documents as the Christian Reformed Church uses, but the particular grace interpretion is accepted. Government is presbyterian, but with greater emphasis on the autonomy of the local congregation. The general synod meets annually.

A theological seminary is located at Grand Rapids, Michigan.

Membership: In 1980 the Church reported 4,544 members, 21 churches, and 31 ministers.

Periodicals: *The Standard Bearer*, Grand Rapids MI; *The Reformed Messenger*, 15615 South Park Avenue, South Holland, IL.

Sources: Herman Hoeksema, *The Protestant Reformed Churches In America*. Grand Rapids, MI: The Author, 1947; Herman Hoeksema, *Why Protestant Reformed?* Grand Rapids, MI: the Sunday School of the First Protestant Reformed Church, 1949.

★160★

REFORMED CHURCH IN AMERICA
475 Riverside Dr.
New York, NY 10115

The first Dutch settlers in America, members of the Reformed Church in the Netherlands, brought that church to this country. A minister, the Rev. Jonas Michaelius, arrived here in 1628 and organized the first congregation, now known as the Collegiate Church of the City of New York. Because of a shortage of ministers, some people began to advocate ministerial training in the colonies. Queens College (now Rutgers University) was founded and a theological seminary established there. The independence of the American church was achieved in 1770 when John Henry Livingston returned from his theological work at Utrecht with a plan of union. In 1792 a constitution was adopted, and in 1819 the church was incorporated as the Reformed Protestant Dutch Church. It took its present name, the Reformed Church in America, in 1867.

The church spread through New York and New Jersey during the colonial era. In the middle of the nineteenth century a new wave of Dutch immigrants arrived. They settled primarily in Michigan and Iowa and from there moved to other states, particularly South Dakota.

Doctrinally the church remained very conservative and accepted as its standard doctrine the Belgic Confession, the Heidelberg Catechism, and the Canons of the Synod of Dort. Worship is outlined in the *Liturgy* and is supplemented by the church's hymnal, *Rejoice in the Lord*. The liturgies of the Lord's Supper, baptism, and ordination are obligatory; those for the Sunday service and marriage are not.

The polity is presbyterial. The highest authority is the General Synod which meets annually in June. A 24-member executive committee functions between sessions. The General Synod is divided into 45 classes. These classes are distributed in six particular synods made up of lay and clerical members of each classis. The voting members of the classis are all the ministers and an elder from each church in the classis. The ruling body at the congregational level is the consistory, composed of the ministers and elected elders and deacons.

Education has always been given high priority by the Reformed Church, and a Board of Theological Education keeps oversight of its seminaries. The General Program Council oversees work among American Indians; social services; Southern Normal High School in Brewton, Alabama; and foreign work in Mexico, several African countries, Japan, Arabia, Kuwait, Oman, Taiwan, Hong Kong and the Philippines. The church is a member of the National Council of Churches and the World Council of Churches.

Membership: In 1984 the Church reported 351,356 members, 947 churches, and 1,618 ministers.

Educational facilities: Colleges: Hope College, Holland, Michigan; Northwestern College, Orange City, Iowa; Central College, Pella, Iowa.

Periodicals: *The Church Herald*, 1324 Lake Dr., S.E., Grand Rapids, MI 49506.

★161★
REFORMED CHURCH IN THE UNITED STATES
% Rev. Vernon Polleme, President
3930 Masin Dr.
Lincoln, NE 68521

In 1934 the Reformed Church in the United States merged with the Evangelical Synod. (In 1961 that merged body joined the United Church of Christ.) One classis of the Reformed Church in the United States, the Eureka Classis in South Dakota, decided not to enter the 1934 merger. So the Eureka Classis adopted the name of its parent body, the Reformed Church in the United States, and stayed separate from all the other classes that joined the 1934 merger. The present Reformed Church in the United States continues the polity and doctrines (adherence to the Heidelberg Confession) of the former Reformed Church in the United States. The classis meets annually.

Membership: In 1982 the Church reported 3,710 members, 30 congregations and 32 ministers.

Periodicals: *The Reformed Herald*, Box 276, Eureka, SD 57437.

Presbyterian

★162★
ASSOCIATE REFORMED PRESBYTERIAN
CHURCH (GENERAL SYNOD)
Associate Reformed Presbyterian Center
One Cleveland St.
Greenville, SC 29601

The Associate Reformed Presbyterian Church (General Synod) stems from the Associate Reformed Presbyterian Church. In 1822, the Synod of the Carolinas broke with the Associate Reformed Presbyterian Church. It eventually became part of the United Presbyterian Church of North America and then the Presbyterian Church (U.S.A.).

The story of the Synod of the Carolinas starts with the Seceder Church formed in Scotland in 1743 as a dissenting body from the established Church of Scotland. Seceders, in America called Associate Presbyterians, settled in South Carolina following the Revolutionary War. They were joined by a few Covenanter congregations, which along with the Seceders had protested Scotland's established church. The Covenanters took their name from the Solemn League and Covenant of 1643, the guiding document of Scotch Presbyterians. In 1790 some Seceders and Covenanters formed the Presbytery of the Carolinas and Georgia at Long Cane, South Carolina. Rev. Thomas Clark and John Boyse led in the formation of this presbytery, a unit within the Associate Reformed Presbyterian Church. The presbytery represented the southern segment of that church in the late eighteenth century.

In 1822 the southern branch became independent of the Associate Reformed Prebyterian Church in the northern states and formed the Associate Reformed Presbyterian Church of the South. "Of the South" was dropped in 1858 when the northern group joined the United Presbyterian Church. The General Synod of the church, its highest governing body, was created in 1935. That is when the church added the words "General Synod" to its title. The General Synod is the denomination's highest court; it is composed of all the teaching elders and one ruling elder from each congregation.

Doctrinally, the church holds to the Westminster Confession of Faith. In 1959 the presbyteries approved some 15 changes in the confessions, including the addition of new chapters on the Holy Spirit and the gospel. Liturgically, the synod has been distinguished by its use of only Psalms as hymns. In 1946 this practice became optional and a new hymn book was approved. Worship is based on the Westminster Directory of Worship. The church is organized on a presbyterial system. Recently the trend has been toward greater congregational autonomy. Foreign mission work is carried on in Mexico and Pakistan.

Membership: In 1980 the Church reported 31,518 members in 156 congregations served by 171 clergy.

Educational facilities: Erskine College and Theological Seminary, Due West, South Carolina.

Periodicals: *The Associate Reformed Presbyterian*, One Cleveland St., Greenville, SC 29601.

★163★
BIBLE PRESBYTERIAN CHURCH
756 Haddon Ave.
Collingswood, NJ 12771

The Rev. Dr. Carl McIntire had been a student at Princeton Theological Seminary when J. Gresham Machen left to found the independent Westminster Theological Seminary. McIntire graduated from Westminster in 1931 and became pastor of the Presbyterian congregation in Collingswood, New Jersey. He was suspended from the Presbyterian Church in the United States along with Machen and left with him to establish what became the Orthodox Presbyterian Church. In 1937, however, McIntire found himself in disagreement with Machen on three points. The Orthodox Presbyterian Church refused to take a stand against intoxicating beverages, refused to become distinctly premillennial in eschatology, and refused to continue to support the Independent Board for Presbyterian Foreign Missions. (A premillennial eschatology refers to the belief that before the millennium--Christ's reign on earth with his saints for 1,000 years--Christ will come to earth to fight the Battle of Armageddon and bind Satan.) In 1937 McIntire and his supporters formed the Bible Presbyterian Church.

The personality of McIntire seemed to have been a more significant factor in the formation of the Bible Presbyterian Church than did his three objections to the Orthodox Presbyterian Church. He has manifested a zealous crusade against modernism, communism, and pacifism, and has led what he termed the "Twentieth Century Reformation" to root out apostasy and build true churches. Prime targets have been the National Council of Churches and its sister organization, the World Council of Churches. McIntire called all true Christians to separate themselves from the apostasy of the members of those councils.

McIntire provided followers with a variety of alternative organizations to support. In 1937 he founded Faith Theological Seminary. Four years later he organized the American Council of Christian Churches (ACCC) to bring together "Separatist" churches from across the country. "Separatist" churches refuse to deal with liberal churches or with conservative churches that cooperated with liberal churches in any way. After the Amsterdam meeting of the World Council of Churches in 1948, McIntire organized the International Council of Christian Churches (ICCC). Because of criticism by some outstanding conservative Presbyterian leaders, the ACCC and the ICCC lost much support, and in 1956 were repudiated by some leaders who had been close followers of McIntire. In that same year, the synod of the Bible Presbyterian Church terminated its support of Faith Theological Seminary, the Independent Board for Presbyterian Foreign Missions, the ACCC, and the ICCC. The seminary and board, though largely supported by the Bible Presbyterians, were both independent interdenominational corporations. The ICCC and the ACCC were both interdenominational and had been criticized for some of their activities in the early

1950s such as the "Bible Balloon" project to send religious literature behind the Iron Curtain by balloon. In repudiating these organizations, the church repudiated McIntire, who had founded the organizations as well as the church. The Bible Presbyterian Church then split into two factions. The larger group, those objecting to McIntire and the organizations, soon changed its name from Bible Presbyterian Church to Evangelical Presbyterian Church. It is now a constituent part of the Presbyterian Church in America.

The smaller group, the supporters of McIntire, included the presbyteries of New Jersey (of which McIntire was moderator), California, and Kentucky-Tennessee. They declared themselves independent and free of the 1956 synod. At a meeting in Collingswood, New Jersey, they created the new synod of the Bible Presbyterian Church. They returned support to the ACCC, the ICCC, Faith Theological Seminary, and the Independent Board for Presbyterian Foreign Missions. However, in 1969, McIntire was removed from the executive committee of the ACCC and he then founded the American Christian Action Council (ACAC) with his few remaining followers.

Doctrinally, the Bible Presbyterians accept the Westminster Confession of Faith and the Larger and Smaller Catechisms. They are premillennial, which means they believe Christ will come before the millennium, that period of 1,000 years when he will reign on earth with his saints. Premillennialists look for Christ to come unexpectedly in the near future to fight the Battle of Armageddon (cf. Revelation) and bind Satan, thus ushering in the millennium. The Bible Presbyterians have taken stands against intoxicating beverages, the new evangelism, the Revised Standard Version of the Bible, evolution, civil disobedience, and the United Nations. The polity is presbyterial but there is a strong assertion of congregational autonomy. The general synod meets annually. The church supports the Friends of Israel Testimony to Christ, the Navaho Bible School and Mission; Reformation Gospel Publications; "The Twentieth Century Reformation Hour," a radio program; and the Christian Admiral Bible Conference and Freedom Center, all independent corporations. Many of these agencies were founded by and are headed by McIntire. The church also supports the Bible Presbyterian Home and the Bible Presbyterian Guest Home.

Membership: Not reported.

Educational facilities: Independent schools supported by the Bible Presbyterian Church are Shelton College, Cape May, New Jersey; Highland College, Pasadena, California; and the Reformation Bible Institute.

Periodicals: *The Christian Beacon* (unofficial publication).

Sources: Margaret G. Harden, *Brief History of the Bible Presbyterian Church and Its Agencies.* N.p.:(1965). *The*

Constitution of the Bible Presbyterian Church Collinswood, NJ: Independent Board of Presbyterian Missions, 1959.

★164★
CUMBERLAND PRESBYTERIAN CHURCH
Cumberland Presbyterian Center
1978 Union Ave.
Memphis, TN 38104

Before the American Revolution, most of the colonies had state churches, some Congregational, many Episocpal (Anglican). All the colonists supposedly belonged to the state church established by their colony. Immediately after the American Revolution, when state churches no longer existed in America, only fifteen per cent of the new nation chose to belong to a church. The remaining eighty-five percent had no religious affiliation. Around the turn of the nineteenth century, this situation ushered in a great drive to "save the nation," a wave of revivalism usually called the Second Great Awakening. One revivalist was the Rev. James McGready, who worked in Kentucky. While preparing to be a Presbyterian minister, he had a mystical conversion experience and became a strong evangelist. He was licensed by the Redstone Presbytery of the Presbyterian Church and moved to Logan County, Kentucky, where he began to preach regeneration, faith, and repentance. Through his work, revivals flourished and by 1800 spread beyond McGready's congregations. The Great Awakening in Kentucky became ecumenical, including Presbyterians, Methodists, and Baptists. Among the new practices that developed were the group meeting and the anxious seat or mourner's bench. Those in attendance at the revivals exhibited signs of emotional excess, loud, spontaneous behavior, and what today would be called altered states of consciousness (such as trances).

The issue of using unordained, uneducated men to fill leadership posts in the growing church had risen. Some of these men were ordained by the Cumberland Presbytery, which had been formed in 1802 from the Transylvania Presbytery of the Presbyterian Church. Critics of the Great Awakening protested the ordination of uneducated ministers and also complained that ministers did not believe in the Westminister Confession. In 1805 the Kentucky Synod judged against the ordinations of the Cumberland Presbytery and decided to examine those irregularly licensed and ordained and to judge their fitness. The Cumberland Presbytery, however, refused to submit to the Kentucky Synod's judgment. In 1806 the Synod dissolved the Cumberland Presbytery, but McGready and the ministers continued to function while appeal was made to the General Assembly of the Presbyterian Church. The efforts for appeal went unresolved and finally in 1810 three ministers- Finis Ewing, Samuel King, and Samuel McAdow- constituted a new presbytery, again called the Cumberland Presbytery. In 1813, those still unable to find reconciliation with the Kentucky Synod formed two more presbyteries, Elk and Logan, and created the Cumberland Synod.

Growth was quick and the Cumberland Synod spread in every direction from its Kentucky base. By 1829, when the General Assembly of the Cumberland Presbyterian Church was organized, the church had reached into eight states.

Post-Civil War efforts at reunion came to fruition in 1906 when the main body of the Cumberland Presbyterian Church reunited with the Presbyterian Church in the United States of America, now an integral part of the Presbyterian Church (U.S.A.). From the Cumberland point of view, though, the union was not altogether a happy one. The union carried by only a slight majority of 60 presbyteries to 51, and a large segment of the church refused to go into the united church. They reorganized themselves as the continuing Cumberland Presbyterian Church, and took that name.

The theology of Cumberland Presbyterianism is derived from the Westminster Confession and is described as the middle ground between Calvinism and Arminianism, a theology which defends free will and opposes the belief in strict predestination. The Cumberland Presbyterians deny the five points of Calvinism with the exception of the perseverance of the saints. (The other four points of Calvinism, which this church rejects, are the utter depravity of man, total predestination, limited atonement, and irresistible grace.) The Cumberland Presbyterians have a presbyterian polity. Their General Assembly meets annually.

After 1906 the women took complete control of Cumberland Presbyterian missions. Foreign work is supported in Columbia, Hong Kong and Japan. Domestic work is centered on a Chinese (American) Cumberland Presbyterian Church in California, and a Choctaw Indian mission in Oklahoma. The church participated in the development of the Covenant Life Curriculum for church schools. Frontier Press issues books and religious literature for its Board of Publication and Education.

Membership: In 1982 the Church reported 97,813 members, 856 congregations and 739 clergy.

Educational facilities: Bethel College, McKenzie, Tennessee; Memphis Theological Seminary, Memphis, Tennessee.

Periodicals: *The Cumberland Presbyterian*, 1978 Union Avenue, Memphis, Tennessee 38104.

Sources: Thomas J. Campbell, *Good News on the Frontier* Memphis: Frontier Press, 1965; E. K. Reagin, *We Believe So We Speak*. Memphis: Department of Publication, Cumberland Presbyterian Church, 1960; Confession of Faith and Government of the Cumberland Presbyterian Church. *Memphis: Frontier Press, 1963; John H. Hughey,* Lights and Shadows of the C. P. Church. *Decatur, IL: The Author, 1906.*

★165★
ORTHODOX PRESBYTERIAN CHURCH
7401 Old York Rd.
Philadelphia, PA 19126

In the early years of the twentieth century the Presbyterian Church in the United States of America became a major focus of the the fundamentalist-modernist controversy. Conservatives felt that liberals were leading the church into compromise with the world and away from the witness to the gospel. Conservatives traced liberalism to the Plan of Union of 1801 between Presbyterians and Congregationalists. The Conservatives said that plan aligned Presbyterians with Congregationalists infected with the "New School theology" of Samuel Hopkins. Late in the nineteenth century the issues of compromise with the world and lack of witness to the gospel were raised anew by the heresy trials of Professors Charles A. Briggs and Henry Preserved Smith. In 1903 doctrinal standards were revised to facilitate the merger with the Cumberland Presbyterian Church.

In reaction against liberal Baptist Harry Emerson Fosdick's preaching in First Presbyterian Church in New York City, a group of conservatives drew up a document presented to and passed by the 1923 General Assembly calling for the ministry to uphold the essentials of the faith, namely the five fundamentals-the infallibility of the Scriptures, the virgin birth of Christ, the substitutionary atonement, Christ's bodily resurrection, and Christ's miracles. Although the assembly passed the conservative document, many of the church leaders were liberals and held key positions on the boards and agencies of the church. In protest of the assembly's vote, they joined with the 1,300 ministers who signed the Auburn Affirmation. This signpost of liberal faith created a storm of controversy, and the two sides were locked in battle.

The publication of *Re-Thinking Missions* by W.E. Hocking in 1932 began the final stage of the church's liberal-conservative battle. Hocking asserted, among other controversial opinions, that missionaries should not take conversions as their only goal, but should provide social services and do medical missionary work in addition to preaching the gospel. J. Gresham Machen, a theology professor at Princeton Theological Seminary, opposed Hocking's suggestion. With other conservative Presbyterians, in 1932 Machen charged the Board of Foreign Missions with no longer preaching that Christ is the exclusive, unique way of salvation. In 1933 Machen and others formed an independent agency that would send out only conservative missionaries; this agency was called the Independent Board for Presbyterian Foreign Missions. The church countered with a mandate comparing non-support of the church boards with refusal to take communion. The fundamentalists replied with charges against other boards, and they condemned participation in the Federal Council of Churches. Machen was tried and convicted of disturbing the peace of the church. Machen and his supporters then left the Presbyterian Church in the United States and formed the Orthodox Presbyterian Church.

Doctrine of the new church is the Westminster Confession of Faith and the Westminster Larger and Shorter Catechisms which are accepted literally and in light of the five fundamentals. Organization is like the United Presbyterian Church. A general assembly meets annually. Over the years support for the Independent Board for Presbyterian Foreign Missions was dropped and a denominational board created. Great Commissions Publications produces a complete line of church school materials. The church participates in the Reformed Ecumenical Synod and the North American Presbyterian and Reformed Council.

Membership: In 1981 the Church reported 17,108 members, 157 congregations and 288 clergy.

Educational facilities: Westminster Theological Seminary, Philadelphia, Pennsylvania.

Sources: John P. Galbraith, *Why the Orthodox Presbyterian Church?* Philadelphia, PA: Committee on Christian Education, The Orthodox Presbyterian Church, 1965; *The Standards of Government, Discipline and Worship of the Orthodox Presbyterian Church.* Philadelphia: Committee on Christian Education, the Orthodox Presbyterian Church, 1965; Gary G. Cohen, *Biblical Separation Defended.* Nutley, NJ: Presbyterian and Reformed Publishing Co., 1977.

★166★
PRESBYTERIAN CHURCH IN AMERICA
℅ Stated Clerk
Box 1428
Decatur, GA 30031

During the 1960s tensions began to rise between liberals and conservatives within the Presbyterian Church in the United States. Among expressions of this rift was the conservatives' protest of denominational support of the National Council of Churches and involvement in social issues, possible union with the United Presbyterian Church in the U.S.A. (which would put the conservatives in an even smaller minority position and which eventually occurred in 1983), liberal theology in *The Layman's Bible* published by the church, the ordination of women, and liberal churchmen in positions of authority in the denomination.

In 1972/73 several presbyteries were formed by congregations that left the denomination (the Vanguard Presbytery in Virginia and Warrior Presbytery in Alabama). In December 1973 delegates gathered in Birmingham, Alabama, and organized the National Presbyterian Church. Rev. Frank Barker, pastor of Briarwood Presbyterian Church in Birmingham, had a powerful voice in the formation of the new body and hosted the conference. In 1976, the church adopted its present name, the Presbyterian Church in America.

In 1982 the Reformed Presbyterian Church, Evangelical Synod merged into the Presbyterian Church in America. The Reformed Presbyterian Church, Evangelical Synod, had been formed in 1965 by a merger of the Evangelical Presbyterian Church and the Reformed Presbyterian Church in North America, General Synod.

Evangelical Presbyterian Church was the name taken by the larger segment of the Bible Presbyterian Church following the split in that church in 1956. (See the discussion of the split in the entry on the Bible Presbyterian Church.) The name for the larger group had been adopted in 1961 to avoid confusion with Dr. Carl McIntire's smaller group. At the time of the split, the synod, controlled by the larger group, had voted to establish an official periodical, the *Evangelical Presbyterian Reporter*; a synod-controlled college and seminary, Covenant College and Covenant Seminary in St. Louis; and its own mission board, World Presbyterian Missions. Immediate efforts were directed toward healing the rift with the Orthodox Presbyterian Church and opening correspondence with the Reformed Presbyterian Church in North America. In 1960 the constitution was amended to allow any view of eschatology, not just premillennialism.

The Reformed Presbyterian Church in North America, General Synod, was of the Covenanter tradition-the church which adhered to the Solemn League and Covenant of 1643 which spelled out the doctrine and practices of Scotch Presbyterians. The General Synod (as the church was often called) dated to 1833 when the Reformed Presbyterian Church split over the issue of participation in civic affairs. One group within the church took the name Reformed Presbyterian Church in North America, General Synod, and allowed its members to vote and hold office. The General Synod also adopted the practice of allowing hymns as well as psalms to be sung at services and allowed instrumental music to be used in worship. Those who did not allow members to vote or hold office, and opposed hymns and instrumental music, are known today as the Reformed Presbyterian Church of North America. In 1965 the Reformed Presbyterian Church in North America, General Synod, merged with the Evangelical Presbyterian Church. The merged body became known as the Reformed Presbyterian Church, Evangelical Synod.

The theology of the Presbyterian Church of America adheres closely to Westminster documents. Organization of the church is presbyterial. The General Assembly meets annually. Originally the Presbyterian Church of America adopted *The Presbyterian Journal*, long-time unofficial independent voice in the Presbyterian Church in the U.S.A., as the official organ of the new body, but it was more recently superseded by a denominational periodical.

Membership: In 1982 the Church reported 149,548 members, 797 congregations and 1,415 clergy.

Educational facilities: Covenant College, St. Louis, Missouri; Covenant Theological Seminary, St. Louis, Missouri.

Periodicals: *The PCA Messenger*, Box 39, Decatur, GA 30031.

Sources: *The Book on Church Order of the National Presbyterian Church.* Montgomery, AL: Committee for Christian Education and Publications, 1973; Donald J. MacNair, *Hallmarks of the Reformed Presbyterian Church, Evangelical Synod.* St. Louis: National Presbyterian Missions, n.d.

★167★
PRESBYTERIAN CHURCH (U.S.A.)
475 Riverside Dr.
New York, NY 10115

The Presbyterian Church (U.S.A.) was formed in 1983 by the union of the United Presbyterian Church in the United States of America and the Presbyterian Church in the United States, the two largest Presbyterian bodies in the United States. It continues the beliefs and practices of the two churches, which originally had split over the same issues that divided the United States at the time of the Civil War.

The United Presbyterian Church in the United States of America was formed in 1958 by a merger of the Presbyterian Church in the United States of America and the United Presbyterian Church of North America. The Presbyterian Church in the United States of America inherited the tradition of early Presbyterianism in the colonies and is in direct continuity with the first synod organized in 1706. In the 1700s the Presbyterians were split between the revivalism of the Methodist, George Whitefield, who had influenced William Tennent and his brother, Gilbert Tennent, and the more traditional, creedal Calvinism with its ordered worship. The Tennents were the founders of a seminary which later became Princeton University. A split developed in the church in 1741 which lasted until 1758.

The church supported the Revolution and afterward reorganized for western expansion. On the heels of the cooperative Plan of Union of 1801 with the Congregationalists and the Second Great Awakening, the Presbyterians moved West and in the forty years after the Revolution grew more than tenfold. The nineteenth century, an era of expansion westward, saw the development of an impressive educational system and large-scale schism over revivalism and slavery. Other schisms would grow out of the fundamentalist debates in the early twentieth century.

The United Presbyterian Church of North America was formed in 1858 by a merger of the Associate Presbyterian Church and the Associate Reformed Presbyterian Church. These two churches continued the Scottish Covenanter and secession movements. The Covenanters were Scottish Presbyterians who seceded from the Church of Scotland, which was Reformed in theology but episcopal in government. The Covenanters formed their independent secession into a church in 1733. The Covenant to which the new church adhered was the Solemn League and Covenant ratified in 1643; it spelled out the doctrine and practices of Scottish Presbyterians.

People who followed the Covenant of 1643 found their way to the American colonies during the seventeenth century. These early Covenanters formed "societies" for worship because they had no minister. The first pastor was the Rev. Alexander Craighead, a Presbyterian attracted to the Covenanters because of their passion for freedom. In 1751, John Cuthbertson landed and began long years of work on a large circuit of Covenanters. He was joined in 1773 by Matthew Linn and Alexander Dobbin and the three constituted the Reformed Presbyterian Church.

The Covenanters represented one branch of the Scottish secession movement; the Seceders represented another. The Seceders developed from the revival movements of the 1700s in Scotland which attacked the patronage system of the established church and its lack of spiritual awareness. The Seceder Church was not formed in Scotland until 1743, although Seceders began to arrive in the colonies in the 1730s. In 1742 a plea for a minister was issued by a congregation in Londonderry, Pennsylvania. The problem of providing leadership was compounded by the Scottish split into Burgher and anti-Burgher factions. The two parties resulted from the requirement of an oath to hold public office in Scotland. The anti-Burghers felt the oath legitimized episcopacy and they therefore objected to it; the Burghers saw nothing wrong with taking the oath. Most of the Americans were anti-Burghers. Two anti-Burgher ministers, Alexander Gellatly and Andrew Arnot, arrived and in 1753 organized the Associate Presbyterian Church.

In 1782 the Associate Presbyterian Church and the Reformed Presbyterian Church merged to form the Associate Reformed Presbyterian Church. A few members of both merging churches declined to enter the merger and continued to exist under the names of their respective churches before 1782. Then in 1822 the Associate Reformed Presbyterian Church split into northern and southern branches. The southern branch continues today as the Associate Reformed Presbyterian Church (General Synod). The northern branch continued to be called the Associate Reformed Presbyterian Church. In 1858 this northern branch merged with the majority of the continuing Seceders, called the Associate Presbyterian Church. The new church formed in 1858 took the name the United Presbyterian Church of North America. In 1958, the United Presbyterian Church of North America

united with the Presbyterian Church in the United States of America to form the United Presbyterian Church in the United States of America.

The Presbyterian Church in the United States arose out of the same controversies which had split the Methodists and Baptists in the years prior to the Civil War. Presbyterians were able, as a whole, to remain in the same ecclesiastical body until War actually broke. The General Assembly of the Presbyterian Church in the United States of America, meeting in Philadelphia only days after the firing on Fort Sumter and devoid of most southern delegates, declared its loyalty to the United States. Presbyterians in the South claimed the Assembly had no such right to make such a political statement. One by one the Southern presbyteries withdrew, and in December 1861 they organized the Presbyterian Church in the Confederate States (later changed to the Presbyterian Church in the United States).

The war divided the north from the south and feeling created by the conflict did much to keep the churches apart. The two churches had little disagreement on either doctrine or church polity. The southern church tended to be more conservative in its doctrinal stance and adopted a more loosely organized structure. It had replaced the church boards created by the Presbyterian Church in the United States of America with executive committees, unincorporated and devoid of permanent funds.

The merger of 1983 left many of the important questions of merging geographically overlapping synods and presbyteries and national offices, boards and agencies to be resolved in the future meetings of the annual General Assembly. For the moment, both national offices and much of the individual programs have been retained in the united church. The structure will remain in flux for several years into the future.

In 1967 the United Presbyterian Church adopted a new confession of faith. The Confession was a very present-minded document though it begins with a statement of continuity with the Reformed Confessional tradition. It is focused on the reconciling work of Christ through the grace of God. A significant section deals with the mission of the church, particularly in society, and has a vague eschatology. The Confession was published along with the Apostles' and Nicene Creeds, five Reformed Confessions, and the Shorter Catechism in a *Book of Confessions. The Book of Common Worship* contains the liturgical resources.

Membership: In 1983 the Church reported 3,131,228 members, 18,969 ministers, and 11,662 congregations. Partnership efforts in Christian mission exists with churches in sixty-three nations.

Educational facilities: Theological seminaries; Austin Presbyterian Theological Seminary, Austin, Texas; Columbia Theological Seminary, Decatur, Georgia; University of Dubuque Theological Seminary, Dubuque,

Iowa; Johnson C. Smith Theological Seminary, Atlanta, Georgia; Louisville Presbyterian Theological Seminary, Louisville, Kentucky; McCormick Theological Seminary, Chicago, Illinois; Pittsburgh Theological Seminary, Pittsburgh, Pennsylvania; Presbyterian School of Christian Education, Richmond, Virginia; Princeton Theological Seminary, Princeton, New Jersey; San Francisco Theological Seminary, San Anselmo, California; Union Theological Seminary in Virginia, Richmond, Virginia.

Educational Institutions: Agnes Scott College, Decatur, Georgia; Alma College, Alma Michigan; Arkansas College, Batesville, Arkansas; Austin College, Sherman, Texas; Barber-Scotia College, Concord, North Carolina; Beaver College, Glenside, Pennsylvania; Belhaven College, Jacskon, Mississippi; Blackburn College, Carlinville, Illinois; Bloomfield College, Bloomfield, New Jersey; Buena Vista College, Storm Lake, Iowa; Carroll College, Waukesha, Wisconsin; Centre College of Kentucky, Danville, Kentucky; Coe College, Cedar Rapids, Iowa; Davidson College, Davidson, North Carolina; Davis & Elkins College, Elkins, West Virginia; University of Dubuque, Dubuque, Iowa; Eckerd College, St. Petersburg, Florida; College of Ganado, Ganado, Arizona; Grove City College, Grove City, Pennsylvania; Hampden-Sydney College, Hampden Sydney, Virginia; Hanover College, Hanover, Indiana; Hastings College, Hastings, Nebraska; Hawaii Loa College, Kaneohe, Oahu, Hawaii; Huron College, Huron, South Dakota; College of Idaho, Caldwell, Idaho; Illinois College, Jacksonville, Illinois; Jamestown College, Jamestown, North Dakota; Johnson C. Smith University, Charlotte, North Carolina; King College, Bristol, Tennessee; Knoxville College, Knoxville, Tennessee; Lafayette College, Easton, Pennsylvania; Lake Forest College, Lake Forest, Illinois; Lee Junior College, Jackson, Kentucky; Lees-McCrae College, Banner Elk, North Carolina; Lewis & Clark College, Portland, Oregon; Lindenwood College, St. Charles, Missouri; Macalester College, St. Paul, Minnesota; Mary Baldwin College, Staunton, Virginia; Mary Holmes College, West Point, Mississippi; Maryville College, Maryville, Tennessee; Missouri Valley College, Marshall, Missouri; Monmouth College, Monmouth, Illinois; Montreat-Anderson College, Montreat, North Carolina; Muskingum College, New Concord, Ohio; Occidental College, Los Angeles, California; College of the Ozarks, Clarksville, Arkansas; Peace College, Raleigh, North Carolina; Pikeville College, Pikeville, Kentucky; Presbyterian College, Clinton, South Carolina; Queens College, Charlotte, North Carolina; Rocky Mountain College, Billings, Montana; St. Andrew's Presbyterian College, Laurinburg, North Carolina; School of the Ozarks, Pt. Lookout, Missouri; Schreiner College, Kerrville, Texas; Sheldon Jackson College, Sitka, Alaska; Southwestern at Memphis, Memphis, Tennessee; Sterling College, Sterling, Kansas; Stillman College, Tuscaloosa, Alabama; Tarkio College, Tarkio, Missouri; Trinity University, San Antonio, Texas; Tusculum College, Greeneville, Tennessee; University of Tulsa, Tulsa, Oklahoma; Warren Wilson College, Swannanoa, North Carolina; Waynesburg, College, Waynesburg, Pennsylvania; Westminster College, Fulton, Missouri;

Westminster College, New Wilmington, Pennsylvania; Westminster College, Salt Lake City, Utah; Whitworth College, Spokane, Washington; Wilson College, Chambersburg, Pennsylvania; College of Wooster, Wooster, Ohio.

Periodicals: *Presbyterian Survey*, 341 Ponce de Leon Avenue, N.E., Atlanta, Georgia.

Sources: *Minutes* of the 195th General Assembly, United Presbyterian Church in the United States of America, 123rd General Assembly, Presbyterian Church in the United States, 195th General Assembly, Presbyterian Church (U.S.A.). Atlanta: Office of the General Assembly, Presbyterian Church (U.S.A.), 1983; *Study Draft, A Plan for Union of the Presbyterian Church in the United States and the United Presbyterian Church in the United States of America*. New York: Stated Clerk of the Presbyterian Church in the United States, 1974; Wallace N. Jamison, *The United Presbyterian Story*. Pittsburgh: The Geneva Press, 1958; Park Hays Miller, *Why I Am A Presbyterian*. New York: Thomas Nelson & Sons, 1956.

★168★
REFORMED PRESBYTERIAN CHURCH OF NORTH AMERICA
% Louis D. Hutmire, Stated Clerk
7418 Penn Ave.
Pittsburgh, PA 15208

The eighteenth-century Reformed Presbyterian Church was the embodiment of the Covenanter tradition in North America, those adhering to the Scotch Presbyterians' Solemn League and Covenant of 1643. In 1782 the majority of the Covenanter tradition merged with the Seceder Church, originally formed in Scotland in 1743 as a group seceding from the established Church of Scotland. The 1782 merger of Covenanters and Seceders resulted in the Associate Reformed Presbyterian Church, which is now a constituent part of the Presbyterian Church (U.S.A.).

However, some Reformed Presbyterians (Covenanters) did not join the 1782 merger. They remained Reformed Presbyterians and in 1833 they split over the issue of participation in government, specifically, over whether members would vote and hold office. The New Lights, those who allowed such participation, formed the Reformed Presbyterian Church, General Synod, which merged with the Evangelical Presbyterian Church in 1965. The merged church, the Reformed Presbyterian Church, Evangelical Synod recently merged into the Presbyterian Church in America, discussed above. The Reformed Presbyterian Church of North America is the continuing old school body, the group opposed to the New Lights in the 1833 split. The church is working for a constitutional amendment which recognizes Christ as king of men and nations. Until such reform is accomplished, members refuse to vote or hold office.

The Westminster Confession of Faith is the standard of doctrine. Worship is centered on the reading and exposition of the Bible. Hymns are limited to Psalms and there is no instrumental accompaniment. Organization is presbyterian. The synod meets annually. Foreign missions are conducted in Syria, Cyprus, China, Japan, Australia, and Ethiopia.

Membership: In 1981 the Church reported 16,000 members in 50 churches being served by 23 clergy.

Educational facilities: Geneva College, Beaver Falls, Pennsylvania; Reformed Presbyterian Theological Seminary, Pittsburgh, Pennsylvania.

Periodicals: *The Covenanter Witness*, 800 Wood Street, Pittsburgh, PA 15221.

Sources: *Adventures in Psalm Singing*. Pittsburgh: Christian Education Office, 1970.

★169★

SECOND CUMBERLAND PRESBYTERIAN CHURCH IN U. S.
226 Church St.
Huntsville, AL 35801

In the early years of the Cumberland Presbyterian Church, following a pattern of the Methodist Episcopal Church, South, ministers of the Presbyterian Church established a slave mission throughout the South. White ministers served segregated black congregations as well as segregated white congregations. By 1860 some 20,000 black members were on the church rolls. Among these was Edmond Weir, who was sent as a missionary to Liberia. After the Civil War, attempts were accelerated to train black ministers, thus providing blacks with an adequate ministry. Separate regional synods were established for black members. Between 1871 and 1874, synods in such states as Tennessee, Kentucky, and Texas organized. By 1874, following again a pattern set by the Methodists, these regional synods established their broader governing unit, the general assembly, and the Colored Cumberland Presbyterian Church became a church separate from the Cumberland Presbyterian Church. The parent church, though, continued moderate financial and educational support of the new church, which is now called the Second Cumberland Presbyterian Church in the U. S.

The church is similar to its parent body in doctrine and organization. The General Assembly meets regularly. There are 19 presbyteries and four synods.

Membership: Recent statistics have not been reported. In 1959 the Church reported 221 church, 30,000 members and 125 ministers. There was an affiliated Presbytery in Liberia.

Educational facilities: Educational opportunities and ministerial training are pursued through the schools of the Cumberland Presbyterian Church.

Periodicals: *The Cumberland Flag*, 226 Church Street, Huntsville, AL 35801.

Sources: Thomas H. Campbell, *Good News on the Frontier*. Memphis, TN: Frontier Press, 1965.

★170★

UKRAINIAN EVANGELICAL ALLIANCE OF NORTH AMERICA
% Rev. Wladimir Borosky
690 Berkeley Ave.
Elmhurst, IL 60126

The Ukrainian Evangelical Alliance of North America was formed in the United States in 1922 by Ukrainian Protestants of several denominations. The purpose of the Alliance was to spread the gospel among Ukrainians in both North America and the Ukraine. The Alliance was thus a missionary organization, and was not meant to be a separate denomination. However, over time the Alliance established mission congregations and in that sense has become a separate denomination. The member congregations typically retain their Ukrainian culture and language and are located in large cities. Most of the Ukrainian Reformed congregations in North America have become members of the larger Presbyterian bodies but two congregations of post-war immigrants, one in Detroit and one in Toronto, carry on the independent tradition and are under the direct guidance of the Ukrainian Evangelical Alliance of North America.

In 1925, the Ukrainian Evangelical Alliance of North America, with the aid of Several Reformed and Presbyterian churches, organized a Ukrainian Reformed Church in what was at that time Polish territory in the Western Ukraine. This church was virtually destroyed by the Communist take-over in World War II.

The Alliance is interdenominational in scope and has passed a resolution declaring denominational missions obsolete and unrealistic in their approach to Ukrainian-Russian relations, especially in their neglect of the native language. The Alliance wishes to be invited to cooperate in all missionary efforts. It has as a major part of its mission, the publication of Ukrainian literature which it distributes in both North America and the Ukraine.

Membership: At last report there were only two congregations solely attached to the Alliance, though congregations consisting of Ukrainian-Russian immigrants of the Reformed faith can be found in several of the larger Presbyterian bodies.

Periodicals: *News Bulletin*.

★171★
UPPER CUMBERLAND PRESBYTERIAN CHURCH
% Roaring River Upper Cumberland Presbyterian
  Church
Gainesboro, TN 38562

The Upper Cumberland Presbyterian Church was formed in 1955 by Rev. H. C. Wakefield, Rev. W. M. Dycus, Lum Oliver, and laymen from Sanderson's, Russell Hill, Pleasant Grove and Poston's Cumberland Presbyterian Churches, all of the Cooksville Presbytery in Tennessee. At the 1950 General Assembly of the Cumberland Presbyterian Church, the Board of Missions and Evangelism reported its application for membership in the Home Missions Council of the National Council of Churches. This application raised the issue of support of the "liberal" social activist theology imposed by the National Council of Churches, and strong opposition to the application developed within the church. In 1952 a Fellowship of Conservative Presbyterians was formed which included Rev. Wakefield and Rev. Dycus. In assembly in the following year, the Fellowship elected a moderator and a stated clerk, urged organization on a presbyterial level, and objected to the Revised Standard Version of the Bible newly issued by the National Council of Churches. Rev. Dycus and Rev. Wakefield were deposed from the ministry of the Cumberland Presbyterian Church. IN 1955 they formed the Carthage Presbytery of the Upper Cumberland Presbyterian Church at a session with the Russell Hill Congregation in Macon County, Tennessee. Thus the Upper Cumberland Presbyterians came into existence. At the first session Lum Oliver was ordained.

The Upper Cumberland Presbyterians adopted the Confession of Faith of the Cumberland Presbyterian Church, with the addition of questions on the virgin birth of Christ and his visible return to the church covenant. Ministers must use the King James Bible.

Membership: In 1970 there were 9 churches and 300 members in the Upper Cumberland Presbyterian Church.

★172★
WESTMINSTER BIBLICAL FELLOWSHIP
% Rev. Earl Pinckney
Bristol, TN 37620

Following the 1969 meeting in which Dr. Carl McIntire was removed from his responsibilities with the American Council of Christian Churches (ACCC), several former leaders of the McIntire-led Bible Presbyterian Church also withdrew support from him. These included J. Phillip Clark, former General Secretary of the Independent Board for Presbyterian Foreign Missions and pastor of Calvary Bible Presbyterian Church in Glendale, California. After the 1969 ACCC meeting, Clark announced the formation of the Westminster Biblical Felllowship in order to provide a vehicle for Bible Presbyterians to remain with the ACCC. Other Bible Presbyterian leaders-Richard E.

Smitley, Jack Murray and Arthur Steele-joined Clark. The Westminster Biblical Fellowship continues the faith of the Bible Presbyterian Church in general, but it objects to the strong crusading stance of Carl McIntire.

Membership: Not reported.

Sources: Carl McIntire, *A Letter to Bible Presbyterians*. Collinwood, NJ: Bible Presbyterian Church, 1969.

Congregationalism

★173★
**CONSERVATIVE CONGREGATIONAL CHRISTIAN
  CONFERENCE**
7582 Currell Blvd., Suite 108
St. Paul, MN 55125

The Conservative Congregational Christian Conference can be dated to 1935 when Rev. Hilmer B. Sandine, then pastor of First Congregational Church of Hancock, Minnesota, began the publication of the *Congregational Beacon*. Beginning as a monthly parish publication, the *Beacon* became the organ for communication among theologically conservative Congregationalists. Emphasis was placed on Biblical evangelism and evangelical Christianity. Growing concern about liberal theology and social activism within the Congregational and Christian Churches led in 1945 to the formation of the Conservative Congregational Christian Fellowship at Minneapolis. During the previous year a plan of union with the Evangelical and Reformed Church had been published. In 1948, during the lengthy process of the formation of the United Church of Christ, the Conservative Congregational Christian Fellowship became the Conference, a separate body from the Congregational and Christian Churches.

Among Congregationalists, the Conference represents the most theologically conservative group. The Conference is committed to the five fundamentals: the infallibility of the Scriptures, the virgin birth of Christ, the substitutionary atonement, Christ's bodily resurrection, and Christ's miracles. The Conference also emphasizes the historical Puritan beliefs in the sovereignty of God, the sinfulness of man, redemption through Christ, the indwelling Holy Spirit, the sacraments, the life of love and service, and the future life. They restricted membership to those who profess regeneration. The Conservative Congregational Christian Conference is a member of the National Association of Evangelicals.

In polity the Conservative Congregational Christian Conference accepts the interpretation that true congregationalism is to be identified with the independent or separated Puritan tradition. The local church is the seat of power. It joins in fellowship with other churches for cooperative endeavors. Ecclesiastical bodies or officers have no right to interfere in local church affairs. There is an annual meeting of the Conference.

Membership: In 1983 The Conference reported 26,968 in 152 affiliated member congregations with 532 ministers and Christian workers, which includes congregations in Canada.

Periodicals: *Foresee*, 7582 Currell Blvd., St. Paul, MN 55125.

★174★
INTERNATIONAL COUNCIL OF COMMUNITY CHURCHES
% Rev. J. Ralph Shotwell, Executive Director
900 Ridge Rd., Suite LL 1
Homewood, IL 60430

The International Council of Community Churches was formally organized in 1946, but possesses a history which begins in the early nineteenth century when nonsectarian community churches began to appear as an alternative to the formation of separate denominationally-affiliated congregations. Such community churches were especially welcomed in communities too small to support more than one viable congregation. Over the years, such congregations have frequently retained a fiercely independent stance. To their number were added other independent congregations which had separated from denominational structures and adopted a nonsectarian stance.

In the wake of the ecumenical movement in the early twentieth century, the most visible symbol being the Federal Council of Churches of Christ formed in 1908, many congregations merged across denominational lines, some forming independent federated or union churches, dropping all denominational affiliation. During this period, some community churches began to see, in light of their years of existence apart from denominational boundaries, that they had a particular role vis-a-vis Christian unity.

A first attempt to build a network of community churches was known as the Community Church Workers of the United States. At a national conference of individuals serving community churches in Chicago in 1923, a committee formed to hold a second conference and outline plans for a national association. Organization occurred the next year and Rev. Orvis F. Jordan of the Park Ridge (Ill.) Community Church was named as secretary. He later became the first president of the group. The organization continued for over a decade, but died in the 1930s due to lack of support.

A second organization of community churches was also begun in 1923 among predominantly black congregations. Representatives of five congregations gathered in Chicago in the fall of 1923 to form the National Council of the Peoples Community Churches (incorporated in 1933 as the Biennial Council of the People's Church of Christ and Community Centers of the United States and Elsewhere). Rev. William D. Cook, pastor of Metropolitan Community Church in Chicago, served as the first president.

Unable to gain recognition from the Federal Council of Churches, the independent community churches began a second attempt at organization in the last days of World War II. Rev. Roy A. Burkhart, pastor of First Community Church of Columbus, Ohio, led in the formation of the Ohio Association for Community Churches in 1945. The next year representatives from nineteen states and Canada met and formed the National Council of Community Churches.

Almost immediately, the black and white groups began to work toward a merger. The merger, accomplished in 1950, created the International Council of Community Churches with a charter membership of 160 churches. By 1957 the several foreign congregations had ceased their affiliation with the council and the word "International" was dropped. In 1969 the name was changed to National Council of Community Churches. In 1983, however, foreign congregations in Canada and Nigeria affiliated and in 1984 the original name was again assumed.

There is no doctrinal statement shared by the council or its member churches, though most churches share a liberal ecumenical-minded protestant perspective. The council describes it self as committed to Christian unity and working "toward a fellowship as comprehensive as the spirit and teachings of Christ and as inclusive as the love of God."

The council is a loosely organized fellowship of free and autonomous congregations. The national and regional officers facilitate communication between congregations and serve member congregations in various functions, such as representing them at the Consultation on Church Union and coordinating the securing of chaplains in the armed services.

Membership: In 1984 the council reported 250 member congregations with 175,000 members and 350 ministers. In addition the council serves more than 1,000 other congregations (membership unknown). The council allows dual membership, and approximately five percent of the congregations have a denominational affiliation.

Educational facilities: As a matter of policy the council has no educational institutions or mission projects of its own. It endorses and encourages member churches to support individual schools and missions that meet a council standard of being "postdenominational" and of promoting Christian unity while meeting human need.

Periodicals: *The Christian Community*, 900 Ridge Road, Suite LL1, Homewood, IL 60430; *The Pastor's Journal*, 900 Ridge Road, Suite LL1, Homewood, Il 60430.

Sources: *National Council of Community Churches, Directory.* Homewood, IL: National Council of

Community Churches, 1982; J. Ralph Shotwell, *Unity without Uniformity*. Homewood, IL: Community Church Press, 1984.

★175★
MIDWEST CONGREGATIONAL CHRISTIAN CHURCH

℅ Rev. Robert Schmitz
Rte. 1, Box 68
Union City, IN 47390

The Midwest Congregational Christian Fellowship was formed in 1958 by former members of the Congregational and Christian Churches. During the years of negotiating the forming of the United Church of Christ, one center of dissatisfaction was in the Eastern Indiana Association. Theologically conservative members of the association were opposed to the church's theologically liberal leadership. They felt there was too much emphasis on social action. The first meetings were held in 1957 in which attempts were made to withdraw the entire Association. Having failed, laymen devised a plan by which individual congregations could withdraw. Thirty churches, primarily small rural congregations removed themselves from the rolls in 1958. These quickly organized as the Midwest Congregational Christian Fellowship (now Church).

The doctrinal statement of the church reflects the Puritan heritage, the Christian non-creedal bias, and the evangelical perspective of the members. The statement affirms belief in the Trinity, salvation, the ministry of the Holy Spirit, the resurrection, and the unity of believers. The polity is a loose congregationalism with emphasis on local ownership of property. The church meets quarterly, with one meeting designated the annual meeting. There is an eight-man committee which includes the moderator and officers who oversee the work of the church.

Membership: In 1970 the Church reported 33 churches, 23 ordained ministers and 26 licensed ministers. Only three churches had a membership exceeding 100.

★176★
NATIONAL ASSOCIATION OF CONGREGATIONAL CHRISTIAN CHURCHES

8473 S. Howell Ave.
Box 1620
Oak Creek, WI 53154

Almost as soon as the merger of the Congregational and Christian Churches and the Evangelical and Reformed Church was proposed, opposition arose among Congregationalists in the Midwest. (The merger occurred in 1948, and the new church took the name, the United Church of Christ.) Opposition came, primarily from members who felt that the proposed merger would replace congregational government with a presbyterial form. One of the first protest meetings was held in 1947 at First Congregational Church, Evanston, Illinois. Several

committees began to publish anti-merger materials, including the Committee for the Continuation of Congregational Christian Churches headed by Malcom K. Burton. The National Association of Congregational Christian Churches was formed in 1955. Among the prominent leaders of the new organization was Harry Butman.

There is little theological difference between members of the United Church of Christ and those of the National Association. Association spokespersons have described the United Church of Christ as a means for expressing and perpetuating Neo-Orthodoxy, a theological perspective originating with German theologian Karl Barth, and lacking the evangelical theological goals of other groups that did not join the united church. However, the Association leaders also saw the United Church of Christ as basically presbyterial, not congregational in government. In contrast, the polity of the National Association emphasizes local autonomy and the fellowship of the local churches. The National Association meets annually. It is seen as purely a spiritual fellowship. While it does not make pronouncements for the member churches, it does undertake a mutually cooperative program. The missionary society oversees work in 14 countries including Bolivia, England, West Germany, Italy, Greece, Hong Kong, India, Taiwan, and the Philippines.

Membership: In 1984 The Association reported 106,000 members in 463 congregations being served by 812 clergy.

Educational facilities: Olivet College, Olivet, Michigan; Piedmont College, Georgia.

Periodicals: *The Congregationalist*, 8473 So. Howell Avenue, Box 1620, Oak Creek, WI 53154.

Sources: Manfred Waldemar Kohl, *Congregationalism in America*. Oak Creek WI; The Congregational Press, 1977; Harry R. Butman, *The Lord's Free People*. Wauwatosa, WI; Swannet Press, 1968; Malcolm K. Burton, *Destiny for Congregationalism*. Oklahoma City: Modern Publishers, 1953.

★177★
UNITED CHURCH OF CHRIST

105 Madison Ave.
New York, NY 10016

The United Church of Christ was formed in 1961, at the end of twenty years of negotiating its formation. It inherits the legacies of four major nineteenth-century church bodies: the Congregational Church, the Christian Church, the Reformed Church in the United States, and the Evangelical Synod of North America.

The Congregational Church had continued the tradition of the Puritan fathers. It was this church which entered the Plan of Union with the Presbyterian Church in 1801. The practical effect of the plan was to leave most of the West to the Presbyterians and spur the development of a foreign missionary zeal in Congregationalism. The American Board of Commissioners for Foreign Missions was founded in 1810 and took the church around the world. The Plan of Union was abandoned in 1852, under the complaint that some Congregationalists were becoming Presbyterians.

Until the early nineteenth century the state associations were the largest unit of government in Congregationalism. But the spread of the church led to the call for a national organization. In 1852 a national council met, marking the first time since 1648 that representatives of all of the churches gathered together. They began the process which led in 1861 to the first of what became triennial national councils. In 1913 at the council in Kansas City, a Congregational platform was adopted which included a preamble, a statement of faith, a form of polity, and a stand on wider fellowships.

Various statements of doctrine drawn by Congregational bodies (1648, 1708, 1865, and 1880) affirmed a Reformed theological base. The Confession of 1913 declared the "steadfast allegiance of the churches composing this council to the faith which our fathers confessed." Polity had by this time become an independent congregationalism. The statement, as a whole, reflects nineteenth century theological trends and openness to modernism, and reflects the American cultural ethos of individualism and progress. The new theological trends include an immanental theology (an emphasis on God's presence in the world instead of on his transcendance), a stress on Christ's humanity instead of on his divinity, and social activism. In 1931 the Congregational Church united with the Christian Church.

The Christian Church was the product of the revivals of the post-Revolutionary War period and of t he democratic thinking of that era. In 1792 James O'Kelly withdrew from the Methodist Episcipal Church and formed the Republican Methodists as a protest to the authoritarian power given Bishop Francis Asbury. Asbury was America's first Methodist bishop, and as bishop had the power to appoint ministers to their congregations. O'Kelly objected to the appointments he received from Asbury, labeled Asbury a "pope," and set up an anti-episcopal church. In 1794 O'Kelly and his followers resolved to be known as "Christians" only. A similar movement arose among the Baptists of New England, where Abner Jones decided that sectarian names and human creeds should be abandoned and that true piety alone should be the test of Christian fellowship. He organized a "Christian" fellowship in 1800 and was soon joined by others.

In 1818 beginning steps toward union among various churches calling themselves "Christian" led to the decision to hold a general conference. It met in Portsmouth, New Hampshire, in 1819 at the call of Frederick Plummer and Edward B. Rollings. In 1833 a General Convention was organized; it formed the Christian Church. The following year the church established a Christian Book Association. From 1854 to 1890, the Southern branch of the Christian Church was separate from the rest of the church. The split was occasioned by an anti-slavery resolution adopted by the General Convention.

The General Convention adopted no doctrinal statement, although the central perspective of Protestantism was assumed as the correct interpretation of Scripture. That perspective stresses salvation by grace through faith and accepts the Bible as the sole authority for faith and doctrine. Reformed theology predominated in the church, but wide variation was allowed even in the matter of the sacraments. The Christian Church united with the Congregational Church in 1931 and the new body was named the Congregational and Christian Churches.

In the united church a purely congregational polity was adopted in which the associations and conferences (extra-congregational organizations) were for fellowship, admonition, and cooperation only. The associations' only power was the withdrawal of fellowship. The ruling eldership and diaconate were merged into the diaconate. The united Congregational and Christian Churches entered the United Church of Christ in 1961.

The second church that formed the United Church of Christ in 1961 was also a merged church, representing the union of the Reformed Church in the United States with the Evangelical Synod of North America.

The Reformed Church in the United States began in 1725 when it was established by German immigrants scattered along the East Coast. In 1748 Michael Schlatter organized the coetus in Philadelphia under the synod of the Reformed Church in Holland. In 1793, however, this group reorganized as the Synod of the German Reformed Church. In 1819, because of growth, the U.S. Synod divided into eight classes and began its development into a large denominational body, the Reformed Church in the United States. Polity was presbyterial. Doctrine was according to the Heidelberg Catechism.

The Evangelical Synod of North America dates to the attempt in 1817 of King Frederick Wilhelm III of Prussia to unite the rival Lutheran and Reformed churches and by decree bring them together in a common form of worship. The new church became known as the Evangelical Union of Prussia. Within a few years Evangelical churches were founded in the Western United States, the first by a German minister, Herman Garlichs. In 1840 a meeting of Evangelical Ministers (and a German Reformed missionary, Karl Daubert) led to the founding of Der Kirchenverein des Westens (The German Evangelical Church Society of the West) with Daubert as president. Early assistance was rendered by the Congregational Home Missionary Society which negotiated with the Basel Missionary Society for support of the American work. Ker Kirchenverein began as a ministerial association; gradually a church developed from it.

Doctrinal standards for the new church included the Heidelberg Catechism, the Augsburg Confession of Faith (in the revised form subscribed to by John Calvin) and Luther's Catechism; where these documents disagreed, there would be liberty of conscience for members to decide what doctrine to adopt. The first congregation moved under the ministerial association in 1849. Other like associations and independent churches also joined the original body which in 1872 became the Evangelical Synod of North America. In 1934 the Evangelical Synod united with the Reformed Church in the United States to become the Evangelical and Reformed Church. A presbyterial form of government was adopted. The units were the general synod, synods, and consistories. In 1961 the Evangelical and Reformed Church united with the Congregational and Christian Churches to become the United Church of Christ. This new church represents one if not the major accomplishment of that part of the ecumenical movement which has as its goal the organic union of Christian churches. The United Church of Christ has within its background the widest range of Protestant traditions of any church currently in existence in this country. But even within the United Church of Christ, the four merging churches had a similar theological base (mild Calvinism) and a loose organizational structure. So the differences among the four merging churches were not as great as they might superficially seem.

The United Church of Christ adopted its constitution in 1961. The constitution provides for a general synod as the representative body of the United Church of Christ, the general synod is thus the symbol of the member churches' unity. It is composed of delegates (ministerial and lay) who administer the national program. The delegates elect an executive council which acts for the synod between meetings and establishes specific program agencies such as the Board for Homeland Ministries and the Council of Christian Social Action. Below the synod are conferences (usually state-wide) and associations. These may adopt any form of government they choose, and at least one, the Southern Convention (Conference), operates on a presbyterial system. It owns the property of the member churches. The local church may organize as the members wish but usually the local church has a ruling council composed of the pastor, the deacons, and the heads of standing committees.

Though envisioned as an ecumenical Protestant church, the Reformed theological image still remains dominant in the United Church of Christ. The creed is open to a variety of interpretations but the Reformed theological background of most of its ministerial leadership is still evident. Only with the second generation of leadership will the over-all direction of the United Church of Christ become evident.

The vision of a united Protestant (or even Christian Church) which came to the fore in the creating of the United Church of Christ and which has made it a unique body in American religion has not been without its problems. Frequently, the membership has voiced disapproval of the synod's work and liberal positions on certain issues, especially those related to social action. One result was the vote in the early 1970s to disband the Council on Social Action. Also the *United Church Herald* steadily lost subscribers to the point that it was forced to merge with the *Presbyterian Life* into a new denominational periodical *A.D,* since discontinued altogether.

In spite of these problems, the church continues a vigorous ministry. The Board of Foreign Ministers oversees work in 27 countries.

Membership: In 1982 the Church reported 1,716,723 members, 6,461 churches and 10,029 clergy.

Educational facilities: Colleges and Universities: Beloit College, Beloit, Wisconsin; Carleton College, Northfield, Minnesota; Cataba College, Salisbury, North Carolina; Cedar Crest College, Allentown, Pennsylvania; Defiance College, Defiance, Ohio; Dillard College, New Orleans, Louisiana; Doane College, Crete, Nebraska; Drury College, Springfield, Missouri; Elmhurst College, Elmhurst, Illinois; Elon College, Elon College, North Carolina; Fisk University, Nashville, Tennessee; Franklin and Marshall College, Lancaster, Pennsylvania; Grinnell College, Grinnell, Iowa; Heidelberg College, Tiffin, Ohio; Hood College, Frederick, Maryland; Illinois College, Jacksonville, Illinois; Huston-Tillotson, Austin, Texas; Lakeland College, Sheboygan, Wisconsin; LeMoyne College, Memphis, Tennessee; Maunaolu College, Paia, Maui, Hawaii; New College, Sarasota, Florida; Northland College, Ashland, Wisconsin; Olivet College, Olivet, Michigan; Pacific University, Forest Grove, Oregon; Prescott College, Prescott, Arizona; Ripon College, Ripon, Wisconsin; Rocky Mountain College, Billings, Montana; Talladega College, Talladega, Alabama; Tougaloo College, Tougaloo, Mississippi; Ursinus College Collegeville, Pennsylvania; Westminster College, Salt Lake City, Utah; Yankton College, Yankton, South Dakota. Seminaries: Andover Newton Theological Seminary, Newton Center, Massachusetts; Bangor Theological Seminary, Bangor, Maine; Chicago Theological Seminary, Chicago, Illinois; Eden Theological Seminary; St. Louis, Missouri; Hartford Theological Seminary, Hartford, Connecticut; United Theological Seminary of the Twin Cities, Twin Cities, Minnesota.

Sources: David Dunn et al., *A History of the Evangelical and Reformed Church.* Philadelphia: Christian Education Press, 1961; Louis E. Gunnemann, *The Shaping of the United Church of Christ.* New York: United Church Press, 1977; Douglas Horton, *The United Church of Christ.* New York: Thomas Nelson, 1962; Marion L. Starkey, *The Congregational Way.* Garden City, NY:

Doubleday, 1966; Hanns Peter Keiling, comp., *The Formation of the United Church of Christ (U.S.A.): A*

Bibliography. Pittsburgh: Clifford E. Barbour Library, Pittsburgh Theological Seminary, 1970.

Pietist-Methodist Family

An historical essay on this family is provided beginning on page 27.

Scandinavian Pietism

★178★
EVANGELICAL COVENANT CHURCH OF AMERICA
5101 N. Francisco Ave.
Chicago, IL 60625

The Pietist movement in Sweden was opposed almost from the beginning by the Lutheran state church as being offensive to order and breeding ground for heresy. The movement had been constantly suppressed but periodically re-emerged. In the early nineteenth century a new revival was started by several non-Swedish agents. One of these, George Scott from England, was brought to Sweden to minister to English industrial workers in Stockholm and influenced Carl Olof Rosenius, a layman, Andrew Wilberg, a Lutheran priest, and Oscar Ahnfelt, a musician. Rosenius became editor of *Pietisten*, Scott's periodical. Rosenius also began to hold conventicles, meetings similar to the English religious societies of the early eighteenth century, and aided the development of a revived hymnody. Under Rosenius' leadership a national revival swept Sweden.

Members of the revival movement migrated to America in the mid-nineteenth century. The Swedes attempted to stay within the Augustana Synod of Lutherans in the Midwest and within other synods. After these attempts failed, the Swedes began to organize their own churches. Two synods were formed, the Swedish Lutheran Mission Synod in 1873 and the Swedish Lutheran Ansgarius Synod in 1884. In 1885 the two synods merged to form the Swedish Evangelical Mission Covenant Church of America. In 1937 the word "Swedish" was dropped; in 1957 the word "Mission" was dropped.

Doctrinally the church is essentially Lutheran, but no statement of faith has been officially adopted. A report on "Biblical Authority and Christian Freedom" presented in 1963 to the annual meeting of the church emphasized the double theme of the Bible as the Word of God and the only perfect rule for faith and practice, and of freedom within that authority. They accept as biblical truth the life and significance of Christ and a relationship with him by faith. They believe in the dedicated life and the unity of all Christians.

The church is organized on a congregational polity, which means that local churches operate autonomously and that congregations call their own ministers. The Covenant holds an annual meeting, and a Covenant Ministerium oversees ordination. There are 11 regional conferences. An Executive Committee of twenty members oversees activities during the year. A Council of Admnistrators includes the heads of the several boards. The Board of Benevolence oversees eight hospitals and homes. Foreign missions are conducted in Alaska, Zaire, Taiwan, Japan, Hong Kong, Indonesia, and Korea. Covenant Press is the publishing arm.

Membership: In 1982 the Church reported 550 congregations, 81,324 members and 847 ministers.

Educational facilities: North Park Theological Seminary, Chicago, Illinois; North Park College, Chicago, Illinois.

Periodicals: *Covenant Companion*, Chicago, IL; *Covenant Home Altar*, Chicago, IL *Covenant Quarterly*, Chicago, IL.

Sources: Karl A. Olsson, *A Family of Faith*. Chicago: Covenant Press, 1975; *Covenant Memories*. Chicago: Covenant Book Concern, 1935; C. V. Bowman, *The Mission Covenant of America*. Chicago: The Covenant Book Concern, 1925; P. Matson, E. B. Larsson, and W. D. Thornbloom, eds., *Covenant Frontiers*. Chicago: Board of Mission, Evangelical Mission Covenant Church of America, 1941.

★179★
EVANGELICAL FREE CHURCH OF AMERICA
1551 E. 66th St.
Minneapolis, MN 55423

The Evangelical Free Church of America was formed in 1950 by the merger of two Scandinavian independent Pietistic churches which had grown out of nineteenth-century revivals: the Swedish Evangelical Free Church and the Norwegian-Danish Evangelical Free Church Association. The Swedish Evangelical Free Church came into existence in 1884. It was composed of congregations that did not want to enter the merger of Swedish synods that took place the following year, the merger forming the Swedish Evangelical Mission Covenant Church of America. These congregations had strong feelings about maintaining their own autonomy, and at the same time desired to sponsor missionary ministry overseas through an association of churches rather than the typical synodical structure. This association was established at a meeting in Boone, Iowa in 1884. An independent religious periodical, *Chicago-Bladet*, established by John Martenson, was a catalyst that brought together the 27 representatives at Boone.

The Norwegian-Danish Evangelical Free Church Association was formed by immigrants from Denmark and Norway who had been influenced by the pietistic revivals in their homeland. The ministry of Rev. Fredrick Franson of Bethlehem Church in Oslo led to the formation of the Mission Covenant Church of Norway, to which some of the immigrants had belonged. In 1889 a periodical *Evangelisten*, was launched in Chicago; and in 1891 the Western Evangelical Free Church Association was organized. Later that same year an Eastern Association of Churches was formed. A merger of the Eastern and Western groups was made in 1909, with the church taking the name of the Norwegian-Danish Evangelical Free Church Association.

The church formed in 1950, the Evangelical Free Church of America, adopted a Confession of Faith which stresses the essentials of the Reformation tradition, though the definite influence of evangelicalism is evident. The Bible is declared to be "the inspired Word of God, without error in the original writings." The second coming is seen as personal (meaning Jesus will come in person), premillennial (he will come before the millennium to bind Satan, and he will reign for a thousand years with his saints on earth), and imminent. Polity is congregational. There is an annual conference to oversee the cooperative endeavors of the church, including the credentialing ministers and a ministerial fellowship.

Mission work is carried on in Japan, Singapore, the Philippines, Malaysia, Zaire, Hong Kong, Peru, Venezuela, Belgium, Austria, and Germany. The church has two children's homes in the United States, and six nursing home facilities. Overseas there are two hospitals, a children's home, a seminary, a Bible institute, and other related institutions.

Membership: In 1984 the Church reported 900 churches with a membership of 106,000 (constituency 146,000).

Educational facilities: Trinity Evangelical Divinity School, Deerfield, Illinois; Trinity College, Deerfield, Illinois; Trinity Western College, Langley, British Columbia, Canada.

Periodicals: *The Evangelical Beacon*, 1515 E. 66th Street, Minneapolis, MN 55423.

Sources: Arnold Theodore Olson, *Believers Only*. Minneapolis: Free Church Publications, 1964; W. Wilbert Norton, et al, *The Diamond Jubilee Story*. Minneapolis: Free Church Publications, 1959; Arnold Theodore Olson, *This We Believe*. Minneapolis: Free Church Press, 1961.

★180★
MORAVIAN CHURCH IN AMERICA
Northern Province
69 W. Church St.
Box 1245
Bethlehem, PA 18018

The Moravian Church in America dates to the arrival of Bishop August Gottlieb Spangenberg in Georgia. After the Georgia work was established, he traveled to Pennsylvania and began work there, setting the stage for the arrival of Bishop David Nitschamann and the settlements of Nazareth, Bethlehem, and Lilitz. From these three centers a concentrated effort was made to bring into the Moravian Church the many groups which William Penn had brought to Pennsylvania: Quakers, Mennonites, and Brethren. The church spread as other Moravian settlements were established.

In 1752 Spangenberg began work in North Carolina, in a town first called Bethania, later called Salem, now called Winston-Salem. The town is in what is now Forsyth County. Salem became the headquarters for the Southern Province. In the 1850s work was begun in Wisconsin among the German and Scandinavian immigrants, and just before the turn of the century in California.

No discussion of the Moravians would be complete without mentioning their missionary zeal. They were among the first of the modern churches to realize that the world would remain essentially un-Christian and that Christians would therefore always have to be missionaries. Before the Moravians, Christians believed Christianity eventually would become the dominant religion of the whole world. The Moravians saw that belief as unrealistic and, recognizing Christians as a minority, saw the implications for ministering to the non-Christians. They began work in the West Indies in 1732 and a main motive in coming to America was to preach to the Indians. The Moravians began the first missions to the slaves and stand behind the whole nineteenth-century Christian mission enterprise.

In order to make American Moravians self-supporting, a plan by Spangenberg called the "Economy" was established. It amounted to a communal system with Bishop Spangenberg and a Board of Directors as supervisors. All the church members placed their time, talents, and labor at the church's disposal. In return they were assured of a home, food, and clothing, as well as the fellowship of the church. By this means affluent agricultural and industrial centers were established, missionaries supported, and books printed and circulated. The missionaries itinerated throughout the colonies and abroad. The "Economy" was used for a century but was abandoned in the mid-nineteenth century.

Presently the church is organized into two provinces, northern and southern. Each province is headed by a bishop and provincial Synod consisting of all active ministers and congregational representatives. Each local church has a council council of elders (who handle the spiritual) and trustees (who handle the temporal). Ministers are placed through the provincial governing board. Each decade there is a meeting of the Unity, that is, the representatives of all the provinces world-wide.

Doctrinally the Moravians follow the motto: "In essentials unity; in non-essentials liberty; in all things charity." The Moravian Church holds to the essentials of Protestant doctrine, which they see to include the Bible as the source of Christian doctrine; the depravity of human nature; the love of God for man; the Trinity, and the divinity and humanity of Christ; reconcilation and justification; the work of the Holy Spirit; good works as the fruit of the Holy Spirit; the fellowship of believers; and the second coming of Jesus.

The Moravians are distinguished by certain practices developed to reflect Pietist concerns. The love feast, a simple meal shared before communion, became an expression of communal oneness. They use the church year and have developed a simplified liturgy and litany. Infant baptism and holy communion (on certain designated feast days) are practiced. While most clerical vestments were abandoned, the surplice is still worn by ministers. The Holy Week service, culminating in the Easter Sunrise Service, is the height of the Christian year. Christmas is celebrated in all Moravian churches with a decorative, many-pointed star and the Christmas putz, a decoration which pictures the Christmas story. Music, which was an important part or the Pietist renewal, was furthered among the Moravians by Zinzendorf and James Montgomery, both prolific hymn writers.

Congregations of the Moravian Church continue to be concentrated in Pennsylvania and North Carolina, though some are scattered around the country. An active mission program continues in many countries around the world, especially in the western hemisphere. Both provinces have an active church history and archive program, one of the best among American church bodies.

The Moravian Church is a member of both the National Council of Churches and the World Council of Churches. Affiliated provinces in the Caribbean are affiliated with the Caribbean Conference of Churches.

Membership: In 1984, the Northern Province reported a membership of 34,791 and the Southern Province reported 21,726 for a total membership of 56,517. There were 178 a ctive ministers in 160 churches. Worldwide membership was 445,659.

Educational facilities: Moravian College and Theological Seminary, Bethlehem, Pennsylvania; Salem Academy and College, Winston-Salem, North Carolina; Linden Hall School for Girls, Lititz, Pennsylvania; Moravian Academy, Bethlehem, Pennsylvania.

Periodicals: *The North American Moravian*, 5 W. Market Street, Bethlehem, PA 18018.

Sources: J. Taylor Hamilton and Kenneth G. Hamilton, *A History of the Moravian Church--The Unitas Fratrum, 1722-1957*. Bethlehem, PA: Interprovincial Board of Christian Education/Moravian Church in America, 1957; George Neisser, *A History of the Beginnings of Moravian Work in America*, translated by William N. Schwarze and Samuel H. Gapp. Bethlehem, PA: The Archives of the Moravian Church, 1955; Allen W. Schattschneider, *Through Five Hundred Years*. Bethlehem, PA: Comenius Press, 1974; John S. Groenfeldt, *Becoming a Member of the Moravian Church*. Winston-Salem, NC: Comenius Press, 1954; Walser H. Allen, *Who Are the Moravians*. Bethlehem, PA: The Author, 1966.

★181★
UNITY OF THE BRETHREN
% Rev. John Baletka, President
3829 Sandstone
San Angelo, TX 76904

While many of the Moravians fled to Saxony, following the persecutions in the eighteenth century, some remained behind in Moravia and Bohemia. In the mid-nineteenth century, some of these Brethren migrated to Texas. There, under the leadership of the Rev. A. Chumsky and H. Juren, they organized the Evangelical Union of Bohemian and Moravian Brethren in North America. A Mutual Aid Society was organized in 1905 and the Hus Memorial School, to train church school teachers, in 1914. In 1924 the Hus Memorial Home was founded in Temple, Texas. An independent group, organized by A. Motycha joined the Evangelical Union 1919, and the name Evangelical Unity of Bohemian and Moravian Brethren in North America (later shortened to Unity of the Brethren) was adopted.

Doctrinally, the Unity uses the 1608 Moravian Catechism and the Confessions of the Luthern and Reformed Churches. It emphasizes the Protestant consensus of theological belief. It practices infant baptism and open communion with all Christians; it's ministers are seminary trained. Government is presbyterian, with power invested in a biennial synod of ministers and church delegates. The synod meets in July on the anniversary of Hus's death. Ministers are called by the congregations.

Membership: At last report in 1971, the Brethren had 27 churches and 3,249 members, a significant decrease from 1964 (32 churches and 6,142 members).

Periodicals: *Brethren Journal*, 5905 Carleen Drive, Austin, TX 78731.

United Methodism

★182★
UNITED METHODIST CHURCH
% Council on Ministries
601 W. Riverside Ave.
Dayton, OH 45406

In 1968 with the formation of the United Methodist Church, for the first time in over a century a majority of those Americans in John Wesley's lineage found themselves in one organization. The United Methodist Church is the successor to five of the larger formerly existing bodies in the Wesleyan tradition, namely, the Methodist Episcopal Church, Methodist Episcopal Church, South, United Brethren in Christ, Evangelical Association, and Methodist Protestant Church. (Three of these churches merged in 1939; the other two formed one church in 1946; then those new churches formed the United Methodist Church in 1968.)

Apart from the Methodist Episcopal Church, those formed earliest were the church of the United Brethren in Christ and the Evangelical Association. The United Brethren in Christ formed as a result of the work of Philip Otterbein, a German Pietist, with the help of Martin Boehm. Otterbein and Boehm began evangelistic work among the German immigrants in Pennsylvania. The growth of the work led in 1789 to a first meeting of preachers connected with the work. In 1800 these meetings became an annual affair and the ministers agreed that Otterbein and Boehm should superintend the work. They began to use the name United Brethren in Christ. Otterbein had been associated with Francis Asbury and the Methodists: he took part in the ordination of Asbury, the first bishop of the Methodist Episcopal Church.

A second German-speaking group developed through the work of Jacob Albright in Pennsylvania. A movement gathered around his preaching and in 1803 a conference of those acknowledging Albright as leader was held. This meeting was the beginning of what became the Evangelical Association.

The Evangelical Association suffered a schism in 1894 when the United Evangelical Church was formed. This schism was largely overcome by the 1922 merger that produced the Evangelical Church. In the 1930s, the United Brethren in Christ entered into merger negotiations with the Evangelical Church, and in 1946 a merger was effected which resulted in the formation of the Evangelical United Brethren.

Within the Methodist Episcopal Church agitation on lay rights and the appointment system (by which a bishop assigns a minister to his church) led to widespread protest, particularly in New England and the Western states. Several dissident periodicals were begun and leaders such as Asa Shinn, Dennis Dorsey, and Nicholas Snethen pressed for reform along more democratic lines. Following the 1828 General Conference, when it became obvious that the church was not going to move in the direction of reform, schism occurred.

Congregations using the name Associated Methodist Churches were formed. These in turn formed the Methodist Protestant Church two years later. A non-episcopal form of government termed "connectionalism" was worked out. Lay representation at conference (the legislative body) was given. The annual conference assumed the duty of stationing the ministers, a duty formerly left to the bishop.

A second schism of the Methodist Episcopal Church occurred in 1844, when the General Conference voted to divide itself and form two General Conferences of one church. This split, one of the most unusual in church history, was prompted by heated debates about slavery and the power of bishops. The result was two churches, the Methodist Episcopal Church (North) and the Methodist Episcopal Church, South, and a tremendous amount of animosity in those areas where both had congregations. A major issue, long blocking reunion, was the denial by many northern Methodists of the legitimacy of the General Conference action and the right of the Methodist Episcopal Church, South to share the tradition. (In general, until 1939 the Methodist Episcopal Church (North) continued to call itself the Methodist Episcopal Church, and that is how it will be referred to throughout this work.)

Continual attempts at reunion of the Methodist Protestant Church and the Methodist Episcopal Churches, North and South, were frustrated until the 1930s. Finally in 1939 a reunion did occur and The Methodist Church (1939-1968) was organized. It was this body that merged with the Evangelical United Brethren in 1968 to form the United Methodist Church.

Since the middle of the nineteenth century, Methodist women have served their congregations as unordained evangelists. When the Methodist Church was established in 1939, it was decided that women could be trained for the ministry and ordained, but that they could not become "members of conference," that is, ministers guaranteed an appointment to a congregation and thereby guaranteed a salary. In 1956 women were given full ministerial status. Ordained women thereafter could be "members of conference" and received annual appointments to churches.

Schism in Methodism has centered around two issues: centralized government and race. The protest of episcopal and clerical authority was the first issue to disturb the harmony of the Methodists. The first protest centered on the Rev. James O'Kelly, a prominent minister, who refused to accept Asbury's appointments. O'Kelly broke away in 1792 and formed the Republican Methodist Church, which eventually became part of the Christian Church. Other schisms, now defunct, based on protest of the centralized authority of the Methodist Episcopal Church, occurred in 1792 in Charleston, South Carolina, where William Hammett led a group in forming the Primitive Methodist Church, not to be confused with the presently existing church of the same name); in 1814 with the Reformed Methodist Church led by Pliny Brett of Vermont; and in 1820 in New York City where Samuel Stillwell and his nephew William Stillwell formed the Methodist Society.

During the twentieth century, Methodists became affiliated with the ecumenical movement. This movement, in tune with the reunionist tendencies of Methodism otherwise, became the occasion of schisms, protesting the growth of a "super" church or the loss of Methodist distinctives. In 1939 when the non-episcopal Methodist Protestant Church moved into the Methodist Episcopal Church, a number of congregations remained out of the reunion and formed new denominations.

Race has been the second point at issue among American Methodists. The first blacks joined the Methodist Episcopal Church during Wesley's lifetime; Methodism moved freely among blacks in the 1700s and early 1800s. In the decades prior to the Civil War, the church established a slave mission which brought many thousands of black people into the church. The Methodist Episcopal Church became the major tool for the education of blacks and the development of their organizational skills. The church's very success in evangelizing both slaves and free black people prior to the Civil War made it a victim of the same social upheavals which split the nation at various times. It should be noted that racial schisms have affected American religion whenever a large proportion of non-Caucasians have become part of a family group. Methodists join Baptists, Holiness churches, Pentecostals, and Buddhists in racial separations. Some Methodist churches are segregated; some are integrated. The United Methodist Church is integrated.

During the period 1880-1914, Methodism was rent by a number of schisms related to the Holiness Movement, a revivalistic movement centered on Wesley's doctrine of perfection. According to that doctrine, after a person is saved, he or she should go on to be perfected in love and receive the "second blessing," an experience certifying holiness. The growth of the holiness movement and of its child, the Pentecostal movement, resulted in two new family groups: the holiness churches, discussed in chapter seven, and the Pentecostal churches, discussed in chapter eight.

While affirming the central theological propositions of Western Christianity, Methodists have generally placed greater emphasis upon piety and religious experience than doctrine. While accepting the faith as defined in the Twenty-five Articles of Religion sent by John Wesley to the American church, it has done so in a spirit of freedom, accepting no statement of doctrine as final or free from error. Generally, Methodists accept four landmark documents as definitive of the Wesleyan tradition: the Twenty-five Articles, the early minutes of the British Wesleyan Conference, John Wesley's Sermons (in which he outlined his basic doctrinal stance), and Wesley's *Explanatory Notes on the New Testament*. There are two sacraments, baptism (form optional but usually by sprinkling) and holy communion. Communion is open to all Christians, and congregations vary widely on the number of communion services held (some quarterly, some monthly and a few weekly). To these are added the General Rules of the Methodist Church, an early definition of Methodist practice. During the twentieth century, the Social Creed, first adopted by the Methodist Episcopal Church and quadrennially revised, has become the major statement of Methodist policy in the political, economic and social arenas.

The United Methodist Church is governed by the General Conference, a representative body of an equal number of lay and clerical members, which meets quadrennially. This body legislates for the entire church and its decisions are printed in *The Discipline*, the church's rulebook. It assigns tasks to the various boards and agencies and sets policy within which every organization within the church operates. Between meetings, the Council on Ministries guides and coordinates the church nationally and internationally. The United Methodist Publishing House is a major publisher of religious literature through Abingdon Press.

Geographically, the church is divided into a number of annual conferences, to whom is assigned the tasks of implementing the church's program in a particular area through the numerous congregations. The annual conference has the responsibility, through the bishop and the district superintendents, of appointing all ministers to pastor churches or to various special tasks. Ministers join one annual conference and assume a covenant of reciprocal accountability. The annual conferences have broad freedom for developing their own program within the guideline of *The Discipline*. Annual conferences are organized locally along the same pattern of boards and agencies as established by the General Conference.

Within the United States, conferences are divided into five geographical jurisdictions. A jurisdictional conference meets quadrennially following General Conference. It is assigned the major task of electing new bishops for the jurisdiction. (Conferences outside the United States are organized into seven central conferences which meet for the election of bishops.) Following the jurisdictional conference, the bishops collectively assign each to a particular episcopal area, consisting of one or two annual conferences in the jurisdiction.

The work of the United Methodist Churchworldwide is delegated to the Board of Global Ministries. Missionary work is carried on in most countries of the world, though there has been an increasing tendency to grant foreign conferences (of which there were 31 as of 1983) an autocephalous status. In those areas, the Board of Global Ministries works cooperatively under the guidance of local leadership in establishing and staffing any work. Also under the Board of Global Ministries is the United Methodist Committee on Relief (UMCOR) which has gained international acclaim for its ability to respond to emergencies and natural disasters with relief assistance.

The United Methodist Church has been a leader in the ecumenical movement. It is a member of both the National Council of Churches and the World Council of Churches. It has signed a corcordat with the Methodist Church in the Caribbean and the Americas (directly represented in the United States by the United Wesleyan Methodist Church of America, a member of the Caribbean Conference of Churches.

Membership: In 1983 the Church reported 9,405,164 members, 38,181 churches, and 36,676 ministers.

Educational facilities: Theological seminaries: Boston School of Theology, Boston, Massachusetts; Candler School of Theology, Atlanta, Georgia; Drew University, the Theological School, Madison, New Jersey; Duke University, the Divinity School, Durham, North Carolina; Gammon Theological Seminary, Atlanta, Georgia; Garrett Evangelical Theological Seminary, Evanston, Illinois; Iliff School of Theology, Denver, Colorado; The Methodist Theological School of Ohio, Delaware, Ohio; Perkins School of Theology, Dallas, Texas; Saint Paul School of Theology, Kansas City, Missouri; School of Theology at Claremont, Claremont, California; United Theological Seminary, Dayton, Ohio; Wesley Theological Seminary, Washington, D.C. (Gammon Theological Seminary participates with three other schools in the Interdenominational Theological Center, the largest facility for training black ministers in the United States.) Predominantly black colleges: Bennett College, Greensboro, North Carolina; Bethune-Cookman College, Daytona Beach, Florida; Claflin College, Orangeburg, South Carolina; Clark College, Atlanta, Georgia; Dillard

University, New Orleans, Louisiana; Huston-Tillotson College, Austin, Texas; Meharry Medical College, Austin, Texas; Morristown College, Morristown, Tennessee; Paine College, Augusta, Georgia; Philander Smith College, Little Rock, Arkansas; Rust College, Holly Springs, Mississippi; Wiley College, Marshall, Texas.

Periodicals: *The Circuit Rider*, United Methodist Publishing House, Box 801, Nashville, TN 37202.

Sources: Jack M. Tuell, *The Organization of the United Methodist Church*. Nashville: Abingdon, 1977; Nolan B. Harmon, *Understanding the United Methodist Church*. Nashville: Abingdon, 1977; Roy I Sano, *From Every Nation without Number*. Nashville: Abingdon, 1982; *The Structure of the United Methodist Church*. Evanston, IL: United Methodist Communications, 1983.

Non-Episcopal Methodism

★183★
APOSTOLIC METHODIST CHURCH
Current address not obtained for this edition.

The Apostolic Methodist Church was organized in 1932 in Loughman, Florida, by E. H. Crowson and a few others. In 1931, Rev. Crowson, an elder in the Florida Conference of the Methodist Episcopal Church, South, had been located (deposed from the itinerant ministry) for "unacceptability." The new group published a *Discipline* in which they complained about episcopal authority and the departure of the Methodist Episcopal Church, South, from its standards of belief and holiness. The Apostolic Methodists believe in the premillennial return of Jesus, his return to earth to bind Satan before his one-thousand-year reign on earth with his saints. The church emphasizes holiness of a "second blessing" type: after being justified or saved, a person can proceed to be perfected in love and have that ratified by a personal religious experience called the "second blessing." In 1933 F. L. Crowson, the father of E. H. Crowson, was tried by the Florida Conference and suspended. He withdrew and joined his son's new group.

The Church operates the Gospel Tract Club at Zephyr Hills, Florida.

Membership: At its peak in the 1960s, the Church had only a few congregations and less than 100 members.

★184★
ASBURY BIBLE CHURCHES
% Rev. Jack Tondee
Box 1021
Dublin, GA 31021

The Asbury Bible Church parallels the John Wesley Fellowship in most ways, but is organizationally separate. Like the John Wesley Fellowship, the Asbury Bible

Churches were organized in 1971 by former members of the Southern Methodist Church who withdrew when that church dropped its membership in the American Council of Christian Churches. They follow the same conservative interpretation of Wesleyan doctrine and loose congregational polity and draw on the Francis Asbury Society of Ministers for their pastors. The Churches are also members of the American Council of Christian Churches.

Membership: Not reported.

★185★
ASSOCIATION OF INDEPENDENT METHODISTS
Box 4274
Jackson, MS 39216

The Association of Independent Methodists (AIM) was organized in 1965 in Jackson, Mississippi, by former members of Methodist Church (1939-1968) which in 1968 merged into the United Methodist Church. The organization rejected the Methodist Church's episcopal polity, the doctrinal liberalism felt to exist in the ecumenical movement, and the social activism as represented in the church's support of the civil rights movement. Two churches, both in Mississippi, participated in the founding of the association.

Doctrinally, the association accepts the Articles of Religion common to all Methodists. However, the statment on sanctification was deleted and new articles on the separation of church and state and the separation of the races were added. This latter article affirms "racial pride" as "a rational, normal, positive principle, as essentially constructive and moral." The association has only white members.

The association has experienced steady growth through its first decade. At the first annual meeting of the association, the original congregations had grown to five churches and 582 members. By 1974 they reported twenty-five churches, more than 2,000 members, and twelve ministers. The association endorses the World Gospel Mission of Marion, Indiana, as the recommended mission agency for the association. The association supports one AIM family at a mission station in Honduras.

Membership: In 1984 the association reported 3,000 members in 27 congregations being served by 26 ministers.

Educational facilities: Wesley Biblical Seminary, Jackson, Mississippi.

Periodicals: *The Independent Methodist Bulletin*, Box 4274, Jackson, Mississippi 39216.

Sources: Ivan C. Howard, *What Independent Methodists Believe.* Jackson, MS: Association of Independent Methodists, n.d.; *Constitution of Churches Organized as*

Independent Methodists Churches by the Association of Independent Methodists. (Jackson, MS): Association of Independent Methodists, (1967).

★186★
BIBLE PROTESTANT CHURCH
Rte. 1, Box 12
Port Jarvis, PA 12771

The Bible Protestant Church is the continuing Eastern Conference of the Methodist Protestant Church which, as a body, refused to join that church's merger with the Methodist Episcopal Church and Methodist Episcopal Church, South to form the Methodist Church (1939-1968) in 1939. They withdrew and organized at Scullville, New Jersey, and in 1940 adopted their present name.

The church is conservative in its interpretation of the Wesleyan tradition. Its members believe in the verbal inspiration of the Bible, i.e., the inspiration of each word, and they also await the premillennial return of Jesus, i.e., his return to earth to bind Satan before his millennial (thousand year) reign on earth with his saints. Bible Protestants think Satan exists as a person, and they ascribe to the bodily resurrection of the dead and the eternal conscious punishment of the wicked. They separate themselves from people who do not share their same understanding of orthodox Christianity.

The polity is similar to that of the former Methodist Protestant Church with the exception that the general conference is no longer in existence. There is one annual conference in which authority is vested. Local congregations are autonomous but freely accept the Bible Protestant standards.

Conference grounds have been located at Port Jervis, New York. Bible Protestant Mission, Inc., has work in Japan, the Philippine Islands, Mexico, and at Seabrook Farm, Bridgeton, New Jersey. The church is a member of the American Council of Christian Churches and the International Council of Christian Churches.

Membership: Not reported. In 1968 the Church had 42 congregations, 2,254 members and 59 ministers.

Periodicals: *Bible Protestant Messenger*, Rd 1, Box 12, Port Jarvis, NY 12771

★187★
CHURCH OF DANIEL'S BAND
% Rev. Duane Koontz, President
5950 Dale Rd.
Beaverton, MI 48612

The Church of Daniel's Band was formed in 1893 at Marine City, Michigan, as an effort to revive primitive Methodism and continue the class meeting, the regular meeting of small classes for discussion, exhortation, Bible study, prayer, confession, and forgiveness. The doctrine and polity are Methodist with a strong emphasis on evangelism, perfectionism, Christian fellowship, religious liberty, and abstinence from worldly excess. Several articles of faith have been added to the standard twenty-five emphasizing belief in the resurrection and judgment of the dead, divine healing, and the laying on of hands for the gift of the Holy Spirit.

Membership: Not reported. In 1951 there were 4 churches, 200 members and 10 ministers.

Sources: *The Doctrine and Discipline of the Church of Daniel's Band.* N.p.: 1964.

★188★
CONGREGATIONAL METHODIST CHURCH
Box 155
Florence, MS 39073

The Congregational Methodist Church was formed by a group of laymen led by local preachers who withdrew from the Georgia Conference of the Methodist Episcopal Church, South. The group met in the home of Mickleberry Merritt on May 8, 1852, and organized. William Fambough was elected chairman. Rev. Hiram Phinazee was appointed to draw up a *Discipline*, which was approved and published soon afterward. Three main issues seemed to disturb those who withdrew: the itinerant system, as then practiced, which was plagued with large circuits and weekday preaching to empty pews; the Church's neglect of the local preachers who did most of the work with the congregations and received no credit; and the government of the Methodist Episcopal Church, South, which deprived laymen of a voice in church business.

On August 12, 1852, a conference was convened. Except for local church conferences, this was the first Methodist conference composed of more laymen than ministers and the first body of Methodists whose total representation was by election of the local congregations. By 1880, the church expanded to include conferences in six states and work in several surrounding ones, with a total membership of approximately 6,000.

The Congregational Methodist Church is conservative in its theology. Its members are premillennialists (they believe Christ will come to earth to bind Satan before the millennium, his reign for one thousand years with his saints on earth). They believe in a literal "heaven" and "hell" and use only the King James Version of the Bible. The addition of Articles of Religion on regeneration and on sanctification in 1941 became the occasion for a dissenting group to leave and form the First Congregational Methodist Church of the United States of America. In 1957, these two articles plus ones on tithing, eternal retribution, and the resurrection of the dead, were formally adopted by the Congregational Methodist Church.

The publishing board of the church oversees Messenger Press, which publishes the church's periodical and the church school literature. In 1953, Westminster College and Bible Institute at Tehuacana, Texas, was established; it later moved to Florence, Mississippi. A mission program in cooperation with World Gospel Mission has missionaries in Africa and South America and among American Indians. Though not a member, the Church cooperates with the Christian Holiness Association.

Membership: Not reported. In 1961 the Church had 14,879 members and 242 congregations organized in 10 conferences.

Educational facilities: Westminster College and Bible Institute, Florence, MS 39073.

Periodicals: *Congregational Methodist Messenger*, Box 555, Florence, MS 39073.

Sources: *Minutes of the General Conference of the Congregational Methodist Church, 1869-1945.* Tehuacana, TX: Westminister College Print Shop, 1960; S.C. McDaniel, *The Origin and Early History of the Congregational Methodist Church.* Atlanta: Jas. P. Harrison, 1881.

★189★
CUMBERLAND METHODIST CHURCH
(Defunct)

The Cumberland Methodist Chruch withdrew from the Congregational Methodist Church in 1950 because of a disagreement on both polity and doctrine. It was organized at Laager, Grundy County, Tennessee, in the mountainous country near Chattanooga. Membership never reached beyond the several counties in southeastern Tennessee. Since its founder's death, no trace of the existence of the Cumberland Methodist Church has been found.

★190★
EVANGELICAL METHODIST CHURCH
3000 W. Kellogg Dr.
Wichita, KS 67213

The Evangelical Methodist Church was founded by former members of the Methodist Church led by Dr. J. H. Hamblen of Abilene, Texas. In 1945, Dr. Hamblen began serving an independent congregation in Abilene. Calls from other congregations led to the founding of the Evangelical Methodist Church at a Memphis, Tennessee, conference on May 8, 1946. The main cause of dissatisfaction was the "modernism" that had infiltrated the parent body.

At the first Annual Conference at Kansas City, Missouri, in 1946, Dr. Hamblen was elected the first general superintendent. E. B. Vargas brought the Mexican

Evangelical Mission into the new church as the first mision district. In subsequent sessions Lucien Smith and Ralph Vanderwood were elected to the office of general superintendent.

The church holds a conservative theological perspective and believes very strongly the Articles of Religion of the former Methodist Episcopal Church, South, to which it has added an article on "perfect love." In describing themselves, members say, "The Church is fundamental in belief, premillennial regarding the second coming, missionary in outlook, evangelistic in endeavor, cooperative in spirit, and Wesleyan in doctrine."

Organizationally the Church is congregational yet connectional. It is congregational in that each congregation owns its own property and calls its own pastor. It is connectional in that all member churches agree to abide by the *Discipline* of the Evangelical Methodist Church. The denomination, as a whole, is governed by the conference system. The General Conference, presided over by the General Superintendents, is the highest legislative body in the church. It meets every four years and oversees the two annual conferences, the several district conferences, and the local churches.

In cooperation with the World Gospel Mission and the Oriental Mission Society, the church has sent more than fifty missionaries. Home mission work is being conducted in Simmesport, Louisiana. The church is also affiliated with both the National Association of Evangelicals and the Christian Holiness Association.

Membership: Not reported. In 1974 the Church had 10,502 members, 139 churches and 218 ministers.

Periodicals: *The Voice of Evangelical Methodism*, 3000 W. Kellogg Dr., Wichita, KS 67213.

★191★
EVANGELICAL METHODIST CHURCH OF AMERICA
Box 751
Kingsport, TN 37662

Largest of several fellowships of independent fundamentalist Methodist churches, the Evangelical Methodist Church of America was established in 1952 by dissenting members of the Evangelical Methodist Church. The issues that led to withdrawal centered around a longstanding doctrinal and organizational disagreement between Dr. J. H. Hamblen and Rev. W. W. Beckbill (d.1974). Rev. Beckbill and his followers did not accept the doctrine of holiness proposed by Dr. Hamblen. There was also conflict over membership in the National Association of Evangelicals.

The withdrawing body, led by Beckbill, established an organization similar to that of the parent body. Membership was established in the fundamentalist American Council of Christian Churches and International Council of Christian Churches, and close working relations were set up with the Southern Methodist Church, the Fundamental Methodist Church, and the Methodist Protestant Church which jointly sponsored Bible Methodist Missions and the International Fellowship of Bible Methodists. Following the withdrawal of the Southern Methodist Church from the American Council of Christian Churches, the Evangelical Methodist Church aligned itself with the Asbury Bible Churches and the Fellowship of Independent Methodists.

Missions are conducted in Jamaica, Argentina, Chile, and Paraguay.

Membership: Not reported.

Educational facilities: Maranath School of Theology, Hollidaysburg, Pennsylvania.

Periodicals: *The Evangelical Methodist.*

Sources: *Discipline.* Altoona, PA: Evangelical Methodist Church, 1962.

★192★
FILIPINO COMMUNITY CHURCHES
838 Kanoa St.
Honolulu, HI 96827

The Filipino Community Churches of Hawaii began when the Rev. N. C. Dizon, a Methodist minister, went to Hawaii after World War I to establish a mission. In 1927 he withdrew from the Methodist church and formed the First Filipino Community Church at Honolulu. In 1957 a congregation was added at Wahiawa, and a congregation in Hilo is informally associated. Joseph H. Dizon became pastor of the headquarters church in Honolulu. Its membership consists almost entirely of Filipino-Americans.

Membership: Not reported.

★193★
FIRST CONGREGATIONAL METHODIST CHURCH OF THE U.S.A.
Decatur, MS 39327

The First Congregational Methodist Church of the U.S.A. was formed by members of the Congregational Methodist Church who withdrew from that body in 1941. Disagreement had arisen about the addition in 1933 of Articles of Religion on regeneration and sanctification and paragraphs on the duty of pastors' collecting superannuate funds (for retired ministers), ladies' work, youth work, trials of ministers charged with misconduct, and the prohibition of special sessions of the general conference called to reverse action of a regular session. Following eight years of conflict, Rev. J. A. Cook, then president of the General Conference, led a segment of the church to withdraw immediately after the 1941 General Conference, at which a two-thirds majority approved adding the articles and paragraphs in dispute.

The new body adopted the pre-1933 *Discipline* and followed essentially the polity and doctrine of the parent body.

Membership: Not reported. In 1954 the Church had 7,500 members in 100 congregations, all in the South.

★194★
FUNDAMENTAL METHODIST CHURCH
1034 N. Broadway
Springfield, MO 65802

The Fundamental Methodist Church was formed by former members of the Methodist Protestant Church who withdrew from the Methodist Church (1939-1968) following the union in 1939. The schism began with John's Chapel Church in Missouri on August 27, 1942, under the leadership of Rev. Roy Keith. Two years later, after having been joined by other congregations, they established an organization.

The church is both congregational and connectional in polity. It is congregational in that the local congregations associate with each other as free and autonomous bodies, and retain the power to hold property and call (appoint) pastors. They are connectional in that their General Conference is the highest legislative body in the church. It is composed of one lay delegate and one minister from each church.

The Fundamental Methodists are fundamentalists theologically. They are members of the American Council of Christian Churches, Bible Methodist Missions, and the International Fellowship of Bible Methodists. They cooperate with other independent fundamentalist Methodist groups in a variety of activities. They are also one of the few Methodist groups to retain the class meeting structure devised by John Wesley, the founder of Methodism. He divided the early societies (congregations) into classes of about twelve members and a class leader. The classes met weekly for mutual discussion, exhortation, prayer, confession and forgiveness, Bible study, and growing in grace. Each person tried to bring to the class a penny a week to help the poor. It is said that some early class leaders supplied the penny for the class member who could not afford to make the contribution.

Membership: Not reported. In 1975 there were 15 churches, 19 ministers, and 745 members. The church supports a mission in Matamoros, Mexico.

Periodicals: *The Evangelical Methodist*, Street, MD 21154 (with the Evangelical Methodist Church of America).

Sources: Roy Keith and Carol Willoughby, eds., *History and Discipline of the Faith and Practice*. Springfield, MO; The Fundamental Methodist Church, 1964.

★195★
JOHN WESLEY FELLOWSHIP AND THE
FRANCIS ASBURY SOCIETY OF MINISTERS
Current address not obtained for this edition.

The John Wesley Fellowship and the Francis Asbury Society of Ministers are two structures formed by former ministers and members of the Southern Methodist Church in 1971 following the Southern Methodist Church's withdrawal from the ultra-fundamentalist American Council of Christian Churches. The John Wesley Fellowship is a loose fellowship of independent congregations, and the Francis Asbury Society of Ministers is an association of pastors. While officially two separate organizations, ministers of the Society serve churches of the Fellowship.

The Society has added to the twenty-five Articles of Religion (printed earlier in this chapter) statements on the Bible as the Word of God (an affirmation not specifically made in the original article on the sufficiency of Scripture), separation from apostasy, and the premillennial return of Jesus. *The Guidelines for Independent Methodist Churches*, published by Rev. Thomas L. Baird, serves unoffically as a discipline for the congregations. Beyond the Articles of Religion are seventeen statements which make a significant departure from Wesleyan emphases. The statement on the church defines the invisible church as all who are known of Christ, "Whether they have joined the visible church or not." The premillennial return of Christ, segregation of the races, and the impossibility of back sliders to be reclaimed (based on Hebrew 6:4-6) are all affirmed. The church has only white members.

The Francis Asbury Society began publication of the *Francis Asbury Society Evangel* in 1971. Both the Society and Fellowship cooperate with Bible Methodist Missions organized by the Evangelical Methodist Church of America. Maranath School of Theology, also sponsored by the Evangelical Methodist Church of America, and Bob Jones University are recommended schools. The Society and Fellowship belong to the American Council of Christian Churches.

Membership: Not reported.

Periodicals: *Francis Asbury Society Bulletin.*

Sources: Thomas L. Baird, ed., *Guidelines for Independent Methodist Churches*. Colonial Heights, VA: The Author, 1971.

★196★
METHODIST PROTESTANT CHURCH
% Rev. F. E. Sellers
Monticello, MS 55362

The continuing Methodist Protestant Church was formed by ministers and members of the Mississippi Conference of the former Methodist Protestant Church who did not wish to join in the 1939 Methodist merger because of the liberalism of the newly formed church, The Methodist Church (1939-1968). They emphasize theBible as the literal word of God, the indwelling of the Holy Spirit subsequent to regeneration (subsequent to being "born again"), and the premillennial return of Jesus Christ. All members of the church are white and believe that racial segregation best serves the interest of both blacks and whites. The church's motto is, "Earnestly contend for the faith which was once delivered to the saints."

The church has congregations in Mississippi, Alabama, Missouri, Louisiana, and Ohio, in three conferences. Mission work has been established in Korea and in two locations in British Honduras. A church camp is located at Collins, Mississippi. The Church is a member of the American Council of Christian Churches and the International Council of Christian Churches. It is not a member but cooperates with the Christian Holiness Association.

The government is a representative democracy modeled on the United States government. Equal representation is given laymen in all functions of the church. There are no bishops.

Membership: Not reported.

Educational facilities: Whitworth College, Brookhaven, MS.

★197★
NEW CONGREGATIONAL METHODIST CHURCH
% Bishop Joe E. Kelley
354 E. 9th St.
Jacksonville, FL 32206

Not a direct schism but related to the Congregational Methodist Church is the New Congregational Methodist Church. It was formed in 1881 by members of the Waresboro Mission and others involved in a rural church consolidation enforced by the Board of Domestic Missions of the Georgia Conference of the Methodist Episcopal Church, South. In protest of the consolidation, the group withdrew and formed the new body at Waycross, Georgia, using the constitution of the Congregational Methodist Church as a model. They adopted a loosely connectional system, rejecting particularly the system of annual conference assessments. They also baptized by immersion and allowed foot washing at communion.

An early period of growth was stopped by the death of several leaders and the withdrawal of a number of congregations who joined the Congregational Methodist Church. They have no connections with any ecumenical bodies.

Membership: Not reported. In 1967 there were 13 congregations (7 in Georgia and 6 in Florida).

★198★
PEOPLE'S METHODIST CHURCH
Current address not obtained for this edition.

The People's Methodist Church was formed in North Carolina by members of the Methodist Episcopal Church, South, who did not wish to join the Methodist merger of 1939. (That merger united the Methodist Episcopal Church, South, with the Methodist Episcopal Church and the Protestant Methodist Church.) The People's Methodist Church is conservative and stresses "the second blessing," an experience ratifying one's perfection in holiness.

Membership: Not reported.

Educational facilities: John Wesley Bible School, Greensboro, NC.

★199★
REFORMED NEW CONGREGATIONAL CHURCH
(Defunct)

The Reformed New Congregational Methodist Church was organized in 1916 by the Rev. J. A. Sander and the Rev. Earl Wilcoxen, a minister in the Congregational Methodist Church. A large following was built in southern Illinois and Indiana; however, no data has been located since 1936 when there were eight churches.

★200★
SOUTHERN METHODIST CHURCH
% Rev. W. Lynn Corbett
Box 132
Orangeburg, SC 29116-0132

The Southern Methodist Church was formed in 1934 by members of several congregations of the Methodist Episcopal Church, South, who did not wish to participate in the 1939 merger with the Methodist Episcopal Church. They felt that the Methodist Episcopal Church was apostate and full of heresy and infidelity and also that merger, forming The Methodist Church (1939-1968), would event uate in the racial integration of the annual conferences and churches. (That integration did occur.)

The withdrawing members, meeting in convocation at Columbia, South Carolina, set up plans to perpetuate what they considered to be the Methodist Episcopal Church, South. In attempting to retain local church property and the name "Methodist Episcopal Church,

South," the group became the center of a series of landmark court decisions culminating in the mandate of Judge George Bell Timmerman on March 12, 1945. The group lost its case to the merged church, The Methodist Church. The bishops of The Methodist Church were legally established as representatives of the membership of the former Methodist Episcopal Church, South with control over property; and the name "Methodist Episcopal Church, South," was the property of its legal successor, The Methodist Church (now the United Methodist Church). The name Southern Methodist Church was then adopted by the withdrawing group.

The church adopted the Methodist Episcopal Articles of Religion printed earlier in this chapter. The church added statements of belief on prevenient grace (grace is shed abroad in the hearts of all), the witness of the Spirit, Christian perfection, and the evangelization of the world. It has also added statements on the creation account of Genesis, premillennialism, Satan and a lengthy statement on the continued segregation of the races. The church has only white members.

Departing from its episcopal heritage, the new body is congregational in polity. It has four annual conferences and a general conference, but it has dropped the office of district superintendent and replaced the bishop with a quadrennially elected president.

The Southern Methodist Church was a member of both the American Council of Christian Churches and International Council of Christian Churches but withdrew in 1971. Missions are supported in Cyprus, Italy, Mexico, Sri Lanka, Venezuela, and Zimbabwe.

Membership: Not reported.

Educational facilities: Southern Methodist College, Orangeburg, SC.

Periodicals: *The Southern Methodist*, Foundry Press, Orangeburg, SC 29115.

Sources: *The Doctrines and Discipline of the Southern Methodist Church*. Orangeburg, SC: Foundry Press, 1970; Jerry Ballard, *To the Regions Beyond*. Orangeburg, SC: Board of Foreign Missions, the Southern Methodist Church, 1970.

Black Methodism

★201★
AFRICAN METHODIST EPISCOPAL CHURCH
500 8th Ave., S.
Nashville, TN 37203

A short time after the founding of the Methodist Episcopal Church in 1784, friction developed between the blacks and the whites of St. George's Church in Philadelphia. The situation was intensified by the erection of a gallery to which the blacks were relegated. The long-standing grievances came to a head on a Sunday morning in November 1787, when whites tried to pull several blacks from their knees at the altar rail. Richard Allen led the group of blacks out of the church, and they formed a church of their own.

Allen was a former slave whose master had been converted by Freeborn Garrettson (a Methodist preacher). His master allowed Allen to buy his freedom. As a freeman he became a prosperous businessman and a licensed Methodist preacher. After leaving St. George's, Allen purchased an abandoned blacksmith shop, and in 1744 Methodist Bishop Francis Asbury dedicated it as Bethel Church. In 1799 Allen was ordained a deacon, the first black so honored.

Differences continued between the leaders of Allen's Bethel Church and St. George's. The former wished to be independent but with a nominal relation to the Methodists. Finally, in 1816, the issues were settled in a court suit when Bethel was granted full independence.

In Baltimore, blacks at the two white churches formed an independent Colored Methodist Society after they had been put in galleries and not allowed to take communion until after the whites. In 1801 Daniel Coke arrived in Baltimore and took over the leadership of the Society. Through his work an independent Methodist Church, also named Bethel, was formed. A call was issued in 1816 for a national meeting of black Methodists for the purpose of forming an African Methodist Episcopal (AME) Church. The *Discipline*, Articles of Religion, and General Rules of the Methodist Episcopal Church were adopted, and Richard Allen was elected bishop. The AME Church remains close in doctrine, practice and polity to the United Methodist Church, the successor to the Methodist Episcopal Church, with whom it has engaged in some serious merger conversations.

Growth in the church throughout the North and Midwest was steady through 1865. After the Civil War a rapid expansion throughout the South occurred, and conferences were established across the territory of the former confederacy.

A missionary imperative was an e arly part of African Methodist concern, and in 1827 Scipio Bean was ordained as an elder and sent to Haiti. From that small beginning (and slow growth due to lack of funds), a twentieth-century mission program has emerged with stations in Africa, South America, and the West Indies. The primary work is with other people of African descent.

Publishing was seen as an integral part of the evangelistic, missionary and cultural life of the church from the beginning, and the items published by this church have had a major impact on the black community. The AME

Book Concern was the first publishing house owned and operated by black people in America. *The Christian Recorder*, a newspaper begun as *The Christian Herald*, published continuously since 1841, is the oldest black periodical in the world; *The AME Review*, started in 1883, is the oldest magazine published by black people in the world. Education joined publishing as an early concern, and the first AME affiliated college, Wilberforce University, was established in 1856. Educational concerns have been carried to the mission field as well, and the church has established a number of schools from the primary grades through college for its African membership. West Africa Seminary was founded in Sierre Leone

The Church is a member of both the National Council of Churches and the World Council of Churches. Affiliated congregations in Barbados and the Caribbean are members of the Caribbean Conference of Churches.

Membership: In 1981 the Church reported 2,210,000 members, 6,200 churches, and 6,550 ministers.

Educational facilities: Payne Theological Seminary, Wilberforce, Ohio; Wilberforce University, Wilberforce, Ohio; Allen University, Columbia, South Carolina; Paul Quinn College, Waco, Texas; Edward Waters College, Jacksonville, Florida; Morris Brown College, Atlanta Georgia; Kittrell College, Kittrell, North Carolina; Shorter College, Little Rock, Arkansas; Campbell College, Jackson Mississippi; Payne University, Birmingham, Alabama; Western University, Quindaro, Kansas. In 1958 Turner Theological Seminary in Atlanta, Georgia joined three other schools to form the Interdenominational Theological Seminary, the largest complex for the education of black Christian ministers in the nation.

Periodicals: *A.M.E. Christian Recorder*, 500 8th Avenue South, Nashville, Tennessee 37203; *A.M.E. Review*, 468 Lincoln Drive, N.W., Atlanta, Georgia 30318; *The Voice of Missions*.

Sources: Andrew White, *Know Your Church Manual*. Nashville, TN: Division of Christian Education, African Methodist Episcopal Church, 1965; George A. Singleton, *The Romance of African Methodism*. New York: Exposition Press, 1952; Carol V. R. George, *Segregated Sabbaths*. New York: Oxford University Press, 1973; Richard Allen, *The Life Experience and Gospel Labors of the Rt. Rev. Richard Allen*. Nashville: Abindon Press, 1960; Joseph Gomez, *Polity of the African Methodist Episcopal Church*. Nashville: Division of Christian Education, African Methodist Episcopal Church, 1971; R. R. Wright, Jr., comp., *Encyclopedia of African Methodism*. Philadelphia, PA: The Book Concern of the AME Church, 1947.

★202★
AFRICAN METHODIST EPISCOPAL ZION CHURCH
Box 23843
Charlotte, NC 28232

In the late 1790s a movement for independence among New York blacks was begun when a group petitioned Bishop Francis Asbury, the first bishop of the Methodist Episcopal Church, to let them hold separate meetings. They complained of not being allowed to preach or join the conference and itinerate. Asbury granted the request, and meetings were held immediately. In 1801 a charter was drawn up for the "African Methodist Episcopal Church (called Zion Church) of the City of New York." It was to be supplied with a minister from the white John's Street Church. Zion Church was thus assured of regular preaching and the sacraments.

In 1813 Zion Church split and Asbury Church was formed as a second black Methodist congregation. Both churches were being served by William Stillwell of John's Street Church in 1820, when Stillwell left the Methodist Episcopal Church with about 300 white members. Blacks, afraid of losing their property to the Methodist Episcopal Church, separated themselves from John's Street Church. They also voted not to join the African Methodist Episcopal Church. Several independent black churches in New Haven and Philadelphia petitioned them for ministers. A *Discipline*, based upon the one of the Methodist Episcopal Church, was drawn up.

Several attempts at reconciliation were made, the most important being a petition to establish the several black congregations as an annual conference within the Methodist Episcopal Church. This request was refused, and the African Methodist Episcopal Zion (AMEZ) Church emerged. Ordination was accepted from William Stillwell, and in 1822 James Varick was elected the first superintendent.

Doctrinally, the AMEZ Church accepts the twenty-five Articles of Religion common to Methodists and has an episcopal polity similar to the Methodist Episcopal Church. Church boards implement programs of the quadrennial General Conference. The Publishing House and Book Concern are located in the headquarters complex in Charlotte, North Carolina, and publish a complete line of church school material. The Church is a member of both the National Council of Churches and the World Council of Churches.

Membership: In 1982, the Church reported 1,134,179 members in 6,023 churches served by 6,269 ministers.

Educational facilities: Hood Theological Seminary, Salisbury, North Carolina; Livingston College, Salisbury, North Carolina; Clinton Junior College, Rock Hill, South Carolina; Lomax-Hannon Junior College, Greenville, Alabama.

Periodicals: *Star of Zion*, Box 31005, Charlotte, NC 28231; *Quarterly Review*, 1814 Tamarack St., N.W., Washington, DC 20012.

Sources: William J. Walls, *The African Methodist Episcopal Zion Church*. Charlotte, NC: The A.M.E. Zion Publishing House, 1974; David C. Bradley, *A History of the A.M.E. Zion Church*. Nashville: Parthenon Press, I, 1956. II, 1970.

★203★

AFRICAN UNION FIRST COLORED METHODIST PROTESTANT CHURCH
515 Jefferson, Plymouth Township
Morristown, PA 19401

The African Union First Colored Methodist Protestant Church of America or Elsewhere was formed by the merger of the African Union Church and the First Colored Methodist Protestant Church. The African Union Church grew out of a lawsuit between Ezion Church, a predominantly black congregation in the Methodist Protestant Church, and Asbury Church, the parent and a predominantly white congregation, in Wilmington, Delaware. The suit emerged because the members of Ezion Church did not wish to accept a white minister sent to them to preach. Peter Spencer and his followers left Ezion and started the Union Church of Africans. In 1850, shortly after the death of Peter Spencer, a schism occurred when a minority faction left to form a church with an episcopal polity. This later body became the Union American Methodist Episcopal Church. The Union Church of Africans emerged from this struggle as the African Union Church.

The First Colored Methodist Protestant Church has an obscure origin but probably originated from a schism in the African Methodist Episcopal Church. On November 25, 1865, representatives met with representatives of the African Union Church and hammered out the merger that formed the African Union First Colored Methodist Protestant Church.

The doctrine is Wesleyan, and the polity of the church is similar to that of the Methodist Protestant Church before 1939. There is no foreign mission program, and home missions are cared for by the women.

Membership: As of 1957 the Church reported 5,000 members in 33 churches.

Sources: Daniel James Russell, *History of the African Union Methodist Protestant Church*. Philadelphia: Union Star Book and Job Printing and Publishing House, 1920.

★204★

CHRISTIAN METHODIST EPISCOPAL CHURCH
564 Frank Ave.
Memphis, TN 38101

From 1844 until the end of the Civil War, slaves formed a large percentage of the membership of the Methodist Episcopal Church. In South Carolina they were in the majority. The proselytizing activity of both the African Methodist Episcopal Church and the African Methodist Episcopal Zion Church claimed many of these former slaves as soon as they were free; others remained with the Methodist Episcopal Church, South (MEC,S), the southern branch of the Methodist Episcopal Church which had split in 1844. Many white Methodists felt that given the blacks' new freedom, a new relationshp must follow. In 1870, following the wishes of their black members, the Methodist Episcopal Church, South helped them form a separate church named the Colored Methodist Episcopal Church (CME). In 1954 the church changed its name to the Christian Methodist Episcopal Church.

At the first General Conference nine annual conferences were designated, the *Discipline* of the MEC,S adopted with necessary changes, a publishing house established, and a periodical, *The Christian Index*, begun. Two MEC,S bishops ordained two colored Methodist Episcopal bishops. Throughout its history the Colored Methodist Episcopal Church has been aided financially in its program by the MEC,S and its successor bodies. Today, the Church is very similiar to the United Methodist Church in belief and practice.

One of the keys to Colored Methodist Episcopal success was the forty-one year episcopate of Isaac Lane. Besides traveling widely and bolstering the poverty-ridden church, he initiated the educational program by founding the CME High School, now (Lane College) in 1882. Education of former slaves and their children, a major enterprise of all Methodists, has been carried through the CME Church in the establishment of a number of schools across the South. Paine College, established MEC,S has been a traditional focus of CME and MEC,S. Growth and expansion beyond the 200,000 initial members was slowed by lack of funds. Movement northward followed the major migration of blacks into northern urban centers in the early twentieth century.

The CME Church is a member of both the National Council of Churches and the World Council of Churches.

Membership: In 1981 the Church reported 786,707 members, 2,883 churches and 2,877 ministers.

Educational facilities: Lane College, Jackson Tennessee; Paine College, Augusta, Georgia; Miles College, Birmingham, Alabama; Mississippi Industrial College, Holly Springs, Mississippi; Texas College, Tyler, Texas. In 1959 Phillips School of Theology moved from Jackson,

Tennessee to Atlanta Georgia to become part of the Interdenominational Theological Center, a complex of four theological schools, the largest educational facility in the nation for the training of black Christian ministers.

Periodicals: *Christian Index*, Box 665, Memphis, TN 38101.

Sources: Othal Hawthorne Lakey, *The Rise of Colored Methodism*. Dallas, TX: Crescendo Book Publications, 1972; Joseph A. Johnson, Jr., *Basic Christian Methodist Beliefs*. Shreveport, LA: Fourth Episcopal District Press, 1978; Horace C. Savage, *Life and Times of Bishop Isaac Lane*. Nashville, TN: National Publication Company, 1958; Eula Wallace Harris and Naomi Ruth Patterson, *Christian Methodist Episcopal Church Through the Years*. Jackson, TN: Christian Methodist Episcopal Church Publishing House, 1965.

★205★

FREE CHRISTIAN ZION CHURCH OF CHRIST
1315 Hutchingson
Nashville, AR 71852

The Free Christian Zion Church of Christ was formed on July 10, 1905, at Redemption, Arkansas, by Rev. E. D. Brown, a conference missionary of the African Methodist Episcopal Zion Church. He and ministers from other Methodist churches objected to what they considered a taxing of the churches for support of an ecclesiastical system and believed that the primary concern of the church should be the care of the poor and needy.

The doctrine is Wesleyan and the polity Methodist with several minor alterations. The bishop, who is called the chief pastor, presides over the work and appoints the ministers and church officers. Pastors and deacons are the local church officers. There are district evangelists to care for the unevangelized communities.

Membership: In 1965 there were 16,000 members in 60 churches.

Periodicals: *Zion Trumphet*.

★206★

REFORMED METHODIST UNION EPISCOPAL CHURCH
% Rt. Rev. Leroy Gethers
1136 Brody Ave.
Charleston, SC 20407

The Reformed Methodist Union Episcopal Church was formed in 1885 by members of the African Methodist Episcopal Church who withdrew after a dispute concerning the election of ministerial delegates to the Annual Conference. Rev. William E. Johnson was elected the first president. A strong sentiment approving of the non-episcopal nature of the new church was expressed.

However, in 1896, steps were taken to alter the polity, and in 1919 after the death of Rev. Johnson, E. Russell Middleton was elected bishop. He was consecrated by Rt. Rev. Peter F. Stevens of the Reformed Episcopal Church. Following Middleton's death, a second bishop was elected and consecrated by the laying on of hands of seven elders of the church.

Doctrine was taken from the Methodist Episcopal Church. The polity has moved in the episcopal direction and was fully adopted in 1916. Class meetings and love feasts are also retained. Class meetings are regular gatherings of small groups for exhortation, discussion, confession and forgiveness, Bible study, and prayer. Love feasts are informal services centering on holy communion but also including a light meal, singing, and a talk by the officiating minister.

Membership: In 1976 the Church reported 3,800 members, 17 churches and 26 ministers.

Sources: *The Doctrines and Discipline*. Charleston, SC: Reformed Methodist Union Episcopal Church, 1972.

★207★

REFORMED ZION UNION APOSTOLIC CHURCH
% Deacon James C. Feggins
416 South Hill Ave.
South Hill, VA 23970

The Reformed Zion Union Apostolic Church was founded by a group from the African Methodist Episcopal Church interested in setting up a religious organization "to aid in bringing about Christian Union, whose fruit will be Holiness unto the Lord." Led by Rev. James Howell, the group met at Boydton, Virginia, in April of 1869 and organized the Zion Union Apostolic Church with Rev. Howell as the president. Harmony and growth prevailed until 1874, when changes in polity led to the election of Rev. Howell as bishop with life tenure. Dissatisfaction with this action nearly destroyed the organization, even though Bishop Howell resigned. In 1882 a re-organization was effected, the four-year presidential structure reinstituted, and the present name adopted.

The representative conference structure is maintained with the law-making power invested in the quadrennial General Conference. Over the years the four-year presidency has again been dropped in favor of life-tenure bishops. A Board of Publication has control over church literature and prints the church school material and the *Union Searchlight*, a periodical.

Membership: Not reported. In 1965 the Church reported 1,832 members and 27 churches.

Periodicals: *Union Searchlight*.

Sources: *General Rules and Discipline of the Reformed Zion Union Apostolic Church.* Norfolk, VA: Creecy's Good-Will Printery, 1966.

German Methodism

★208★
CHURCH OF THE UNITED BRETHREN IN CHRIST
% Bishop C. Ray Miller
302 Lake St.
Huntington, IN 46750

The United Brethren in Christ grew out of the German pietism and revivalism of such preachers as Philip Otterbein (of the German Reformed Church) and Martin Boehm (of the Mennonite Church), both of whom had been affected by Methodism and eighteenth-century Evangelicalism and who became the first bishops of the United Brethren. Their evangelistic efforts led to the formation of a church in 1800. Its earliest concentration of membership was in Maryland, Virginia, and eastern Pennsylvania.

In 1841 the United Brethren adopted its first constitution. During the next four decades the church was disrupted by the debate over the issues of freemasonry and membership in secret societies and pro rata representation and lay representation at General Conference. The crisis came to a head when the General Conference of 1889 was asked to ratify a new constitution which liberalized the rule against belonging to a secret society, allowed for pro rata and lay representation at General Conference and altered the Church's Confession of Faith.

The majority ratified the new constitution. They continued to exist as the United Brethren in Christ until 1946 when they merged with the Evangelical Church to form the Evangelical United Brethren which in turn merged in 1968 with The Methodist Church (1939-1968) to form the United Methodist Church. The minority objected both to the changes and the method of ratification which they felt were illegal. Bishop Milton L. Wright (father of the Wright brothers) led the minority in conserving the original United Brethren in Christ along the lines of an allegiance to the original constitution. The minority group tried to claim property, but was unsuccessful. They opened a new publishing house which moved to Huntington, Indiana in 1897. *The Christian Conservator*, a paper which had supported their cause since its founding in 1885, was adopted as the official newspaper of the church. (In 1954 *The Christian Conservator* was combined with several other periodicals to become the present periodical, *The United Brethren.*

The continuing minority adhered to the original constitution. They believe in the Trinity and the deity, humanity and atonement of Christ. Observance of strict scriptural living is required of all members, who are fobidden the use of alcoholic beverages, membership in secret societies, and participation in aggressive nondefensive war. Baptism and the Lord's supper are observed as ordinances of the church.

Local, annual and general conferences are held; the general conference meets quadrennially and is composed of ministers, district superintendents (presiding elders), general church officials, bishops, and lay delegates. Both men and women are eligible for the ministry and are ordained only once as elders. Missionary societies administer work in evangelism and church aid in the United States and on foreign fields in Sierra Leone, Jamaica, Honduras, Nicaraugua, and Hong Kong. Elementary and secondary schools have been opened in Honduras and Sierra Leone. A Bible Institute is operated by the Church in Honduras and a bible college, affiliated jointly with the Missionary Church, Wesleyan Church, and European Baptist Church, is supported in Sierre Leone.

Since 1974, the United Brethren have developed a close relationship with the Primitive Methodist Church and the Evangelical Congregational Church, and they work together with them in a federation arrangement. They share support of missionaries, publish church school literature, and hold seminars and consultations. The church is a member of the National Association of Evangelicals. The Sandusky Conference of the United Brethren is a member of the Christian Holiness Association.

Membership: In 1984 the Church reported 28,035 members in 281 churches.

Educational facilities: Huntington College Graduate School of Christian Ministries, Huntington, IN; Huntington College, Huntington, IN.

Periodicals: *The United Brethren*, 302 Lake St., Huntington, IN 46750.

★209★
EVANGELICAL CONGREGATIONAL CHURCH
100 W. Park Ave.
Box 186
Myerstown, PA 17067

The history of this church goes back to the 1894 schism in the Evangelical Association, now a constituent part of the United Methodist Church. The schismatic church took the name of the United Evangelical Church, and reunited with the parent body in 1922, when the two formed the Evangelical Church. The many deep scars created by the 1894 schism, however, were not all healed before the 1922 reunion. Therefore, as efforts toward the 1922 reunion progressed, voices of dissent were raised in the United Evangelical Church, opposing merger. Some United Evangelical Church members were still bitter over the loss of their church buildings to the Evangelical Association in court battles. By the 1920s, congregations of the United Evangelical Church had built new churches, which they did not want to share with or give to those who had taken their buildings in the court cases. After merger was voted, a special session of the East Pennsylvania Conference was called and a motion to refrain from merger passed, and the Evangelical Congregational Church formed. an independent anti-merger periodical, *The United Evangelical*, was taken over as a church organ. Former Bishop W. F. Heil was elected bishop and editor of the church paper.

Doctrinally the Evangelical Congregational Church is Arminian-Wesleyan, against the theory of p redestination and for the theory of free will, the belief that grace is available to all and all can exercise free will to accept grace. The church upholds the twenty-five Articles of Religion adopted in 1894 by the United Evangelical Church. The polity is episcopal, but the churches are autonomous and the bishops' powers are strictly limited. There are two Annual Conferences divided into districts. Bishops and district superintendents are elected quadrennially. Ministers are appointed to their charges. Boards and Divisions implement the program of the General Conference.

Missions are located in Colombia, Surinam, Spain, Kenya, Japan, India, Zaire, France, Indonesia, New Guinea, Turkey, Philippines, Mexico, Austria, Malaysia, Germany, Australia, and Liberia. In the United States there are missions to the Jews, Latin Americans, and the mountain people in Kentucky. A retirement village is located near the headquarters complex at Myerstown.

In 1974 the Evangelical Congregational Church entered a federation agreement with the Primitive Methodist Church and the Church of the United Brethren in Christ which led to joint support of missionaries, shared production of church school literature and mutually supported conferences and seminars. The church is a member of the National Association of Evangelicals.

Membership: In 1984 the Church reported 755 churches and 276 ministers. There were 26,769 members in the United States and 92,029 members worldwide.

Educational facilities: Evangelical School of Theology, Myerstown, PA.

Periodicals: *The United Evangelical*, Church Center Press, 100 W. Park Avenue, Myerstown, PA 17067.

★210★
UNITED CHRISTIAN CHURCH
% Elder Henry C. Heagy, Moderator
Lebanon R.D. 4
Lebanon County, PA 17042

The United Christian Church was the second schism of the United Brethren in Christ. Formed also during a war,

this time the Civil War, some members felt that the voluntary bearing of firearms was wrong. They had interpreted certain resolutions of the East Pennsylvania Conference as justifying military service. The withdrawing group, led by George W. Hoffman, also opposed infant baptism, secret societies, and human slavery. The withdrawing group also dissented from the position of the United Brethren on the issue of human depravity. A long debate, lasting several years in the Church of the United Brethren, was highlighted by that church's decision to support the doctrine of total depravity in 1853 and to reaffirm its support of the doctrine in 1857. In 1857 reaffirmation became additional cause for the withdrawal of the people who formed the United Christian Church. (The 1857 reaffirmation statement had been adopted by the United Brethren by only one vote.)

Organization of the United Christian Church was informal for more than a decade; then in January 1877, at a meeting in Campbelltown, Pennsylvania, a Confession of Faith was adopted. The name was chosen the following year and a Constitution and Discipline in 1894. The *Discipline* of the 1841 United Brethren in Christ was accepted; the last revision was in 1947. Footwashing is one of the ordinances recognized.

Activities of the church include an annual camp meeting, mission support (through the Church of the United Brethren in Christ) in Africa, Japan, Austria, Jamaica and India, and services at prisons and homes for the elderly. An annual conference has the power to legislate for this small church body. The Church is a member of the National Association of Evangelicals.

Membership: In 1984 the Church reported 11 churches, 11 ministers, and approximately 430 members.

Sources: *Origin, Doctrine, Constitution and Discipline of the United Christian Church*. Myerstown, PA: Church Center Press, 1950.

British Methodism

★211★
PRIMITIVE METHODIST CHURCH
40 E. Northampton St.
Wilkes-Barre, PA 18702

The Primitive Methodist Church is one of the two Methodist bodies in the United States which does not trace its history to the Methodist Episcopal Church, an American church, but to the British Wesleyan Methodist tradition. The Primitive Methodist Church grew from the work of two English ministers, Revs. Hugh Bourne and William Clowes. They had been influenced by a somewhat eccentric American Methodist minister, Lorenzo Dow, who had gone to England and taken the idea and practice of camp meetings with him. Out of their evangelistic efforts and new church itself developed in England.

Connecticut-born Dow became a successful preacher among various British schismatic groups: independent Protestants and schismatic Methodists. Dow's desire to promote American frontier camp meetings in England caused many to condemn him, but others accepted him warmly, particularly Broune and Cowles. At their request he held a camp meeting at Harriseahead, a gathering place for English Methodists of the Wesleyan Methodist Connection, Broune and Cowles were expelled from the Wesleyan Methodist Connection, and their expulsion led to the formation of the Primitive Methodist Church in 1811. The church accepted the polity of the Wesleyan Methodists and did not create bishops as did its American counterpart, but it did allow women into the ministry, an action unheard of in its day. By 1829, the call for ministers by Primitive Methodists who had migrated to the United States was heard. Four missionaries were sent-- William Summersides, Thomas Morris, Ruth Witkins, and William Knowles. Growth was slow and confined to New York, New Jersey, Pennsylvania, and Connecticut. In 1840 the American group separated itself from its British parent but kept fraternal relations. Growth increased, particularly in the Pennsylvania coal fields. In 1842 a Primitive Methodist Church was founded in Galena, Illinois, and became the base for a second conference in the Midwest. The two conferences existed in close relation but operated autonomously until 1889 when the General Conference was organized. The Primitive Methodist Conference meets annually and is both the administrative and legislative body for the church. It has direct oversight of all the boards and committees. As of 1984, there were six districts: Eastern, Wyoming, Schuylkill, Pittsburgh, Western, and Florida. They provide administrative guidance along with the district and local church quarterly conference. The Conference is presided over by the president, who is elected to a four-year term. There is equal representation of clergy and laity at all levels of administration. There is one fulltime officer--the Executive Director, who is in charge of promotion of the denomination. Mission work is carried on in Spain and Guatemala. The Church is a member of the National Association of Evangelicals and though not a member cooperates with the Christian Holiness Association. In 1974 it entered into a federation agreement with the Evangelical Congregational Church and the Church of the United Brethren in Christ which had led to the mutual support of church conferences and seminars and missionary activities and the production of church school material.

Membership: In 1984 there were 85 churches, 9,617 members, and 109 ministers.

Periodicals: *The Primitive Methodist Journal*, 4 Longmeadow Drive, R.D. 2, Straatsburg, NY 12580.

Sources: Julia Stewart Werner, *The Primitive Connection.* Madison: University of Wisconsin Press, 1984; *Primary Helps and Biblical Instruction for Primitive Methodists.* N.p.: (1958); Paul R. Wert, J. Allan Ranck, and William C. F. Hayes, *The Christian Way.* Dayton: The Otterbein Press, 1950.

★212★
UNITED WESLEYAN METHODIST CHURCH OF AMERICA

% Rev. David S. Bruno
270 W. 126th St.
New York, NY 10027

The United Wesleyan Methodist Church of America was formed in 1905 by Methodists who immigrated to the United States from the West Indies and wished to carry on the tradition of the Methodist Church in the Caribbean and the Americas, a Wesleyan church with historical ties to British Methodists. Their doctrine is Wesleyan, and their polity is like its West Indian counterpart (nonepiscopal). A general conference meets biennially. In 1976 the Methodist Church in the Caribbean and the Americas entered into a concordant with the United Methodist Church which aligned their work and led to a number of jointly sponsored projects in the Islands. The church is a member of both the World Council of Churches and the Caribbean Conference of Churches.

Membership: In 1978 there were 4 congregations, all in New York City. In 1982, the church in the West Indies reported 68,898 members.

Sources: Lisa Bessil-Watson, comp., *Handbook of the Churches in the Caribbean.* Bridgetown, Barbados: The Cedar Press, 1982.

Holiness Family

An historical essay on this family is provided beginning on page 35.

Nineteenth Century Holiness

★213★
AMERICAN RESCUE WORKERS
% General Paul E. Martin, Commander-In-Chief
2827 Frankford Ave.
Philadelphia, PA 19134

The American Rescue Workers was formed in 1882 following a controversy between William Booth, founder of the Salvation Army, and Thomas E. Moore, who had been given the charter as head of the American branch of the Army. Moore felt that money raised in America should stay here and not be sent to England as Booth demanded. Booth disagreed, arguing that the work of the Army was worldwide, and no Salvationist should call any country his own. Moore and a number of the American officers withdrew from Booth and incorporated independently as the Salvation Army in America. In 1889 Moore left the American Salvation Army to become a Baptist minister and was succeeded by Col Richard Holz who almost immediately opened negotiations with Ballington Booth, William Booth's son who had been appointed head of those Salvationists in America still loyal to Booth. Before the year was over, an agreement was reached, and most of the officers returned to the parent organization. About 25 posts remained independent of the Booth organization and reorganized under Major Gratton. In 1896 they reincorporated as the American Salvation Army. Headquarters were established first in Mohawk and then in Saratoga Springs, New York. (It is of interest to note that in 1896, Ballington Booth left the Salvation Army to found the Volunteers of America.)

Gratton was succeeded as Commander-In-Chief by Staff Captain William Duffin, who remained in that post until 1948 and his death at the age of 86. During this period, the organization assumed its present name (1913) and later moved its headquarters to Philadelphia.

The American Rescue Workers are headed by their General and Commander-in-Chief. He is elected for a five-year term by the Grand Field Council. The Council also elects a Board of Managers who administer the ongoing affairs of the Workers. All properties are in the name of the national organization. Doctrinally, the American Rescue Workers are the same as the Salvation Army with the exception of practicing the sacraments of baptism and the Lord's Supper. They believe in equal rights for women, and in the organization's constitution the term "man" is understood to include women.

Membership: In 1984 the Workers reported 4,000 members in 45 centers, served by 200 ministers.

Periodicals: *The Rescue Herald*, 2827 Frankford Ave., Philadelphia, PA 19134.

Sources: *Ritual and Manual.* The American Rescue Workers, n.d.

★214★
**ASSOCIATION OF FUNDAMENTAL MINISTERS
    AND CHURCHES**
Springfield, MO

The Association of Fundamental Ministers and Churches, Inc. was formed in 1931 by Reverend Fred Bruffett, Hallie Bruffett (his wife), Reverend Paul Bennett, Reverend George Fisher, and six other former ministers of the Church of God (Anderson, Indiana). Bennett had been disfellowshipped because of his fellowshipping with other churches. The Association believes that the new birth is the only necessity for fellowship.

Doctrine is like that of the Church of God (Anderson, Indiana). Healing is stressed and the ordinances are not emphasized. The Association meets annually and elects four officers to handle business affairs. There are 25 state conventions. Missions are conducted in Guatemala, Hong Kong, and Alaska.

Membership: Not reported.

Periodicals: *The Fundamental News.*

★215★
BIBLE FELLOWSHIP CHURCH
℅ Pastor W. B. Hottel
404 W. Main St.
Terre Hill, PA 17581

The Bible Fellowship Church was formed in 1947 by churches withdrawing from the Mennonite Brethren in Christ when the Brethren changed their name to the United Missionary Church and dropped all Mennonite connections. Members of the Bible Fellowship Church see themselves as continuing the tradition of the Mennonite Brethren in Christ and date their origin to 1883. Their doctrine follows that of the parent body. They abide by the Dort Confession of Faith (common to most Mennonites), but add statements on sanctification as a second work of grace received instantaneously (the uniquely "holiness" doctrine), divine healing, and the millennium. Baptism is by immersion.

All the churches of the Bible Fellowship Church are in Pennsylvania and are organized into two districts, each headed by a superintendent. There is an annual conference of the entire church. Polity is congregational. Mission work is supported in Colombia, Venezuela, Kenya, and Sweden. Recent statistics are not available.

Membership: Not reported. In 1966 there were 37 churches and 48 ministers.

★216★
BIBLE HOLINESS MOVEMENT
Box 223
Postal Station A
Vancouver, BC, Canada V6C 2M3

The Bible Holiness Movement, originally called the Bible Holiness Mission, was formed as a church in 1949. It grew out of the earlier work of William J. Wakefield. He and his wife had been Salvation Army officers. Upon their retirement as active officers, due to health, the Wakefields took charge of a city mission (an urban center for transients) in Vancouver, British Columbia. William Wakefield developed several doctrinal emphases distinct from those of the Salvation Army. For example, he believed the sacraments were real means of grace, not just symbolic ordinances. The Army does not practice the sacraments at all. The Wakefields directed the mission until Wakefield's death in 1947.

Wesley H. Wakefield succeeded his father, William, and formed the Bible HolinessMission in 1949. The name changed to the Bible Holiness Movement in 1971. Wesley H. Wakefield continues to direct the church as its international leader.

The church recognizes the possibility of instantaneous divine healing, and while it does not emphasize the charismatic gifts of the spirit, it does recognize their validity and does not prohibit them. (Thus, speaking in tongues is not prohibited).

The Bible Holiness Movement combats poverty, racial injustice, and the infringement of human rights. Its members actively assist in programs of drug rehabilitation, alcohol counseling, and aiding runaway youths. The members are noncombatants. The church (headquartered in Vancouver, British Columbia, Canada) is interracial and has a large non-white membership. The church belongs to the Christian Holiness Association, the Evangelical Fellowship of Canada, and the National Black Evangelical Association. Membership in secret societies such as the John Birch Society and labor unions requiring secret oaths is forbidden.

Mission work began as a result of the circulation of Movement material around the world. In some incidents, people were converted as a result of reading Movement literature, and in other places, leaders of independent holiness churches overseas contacted the Movement for affiliation. Currently, the church conducts overseas work in Liberia, Ghana, Kenya, Egypt, the Philippines, and India. The two congregations in the United States are found in Phoenix, Arizona, and Kent, Washington.

Membership: In 1984 the Movement reported 538 members in 36 congregations served by 17 ministers in the United States and Canada. Worldwide there are 12,961 members.

Periodicals: *Truth on Fire*, Box 223, Postal Stn. A, Vancouver, BC, Canada V6C 2M3; *On the March*, Box 223, Postal Stn. A, Vancouver, BC, Canada V6C 2M3.

Sources: *Triumph with Christ.* Vancouver: The Bible Holiness Movement, 1984; Wesley H. Wakefield, *Bible Doctrine.*

★217★
CHRISTIAN AND MISSIONARY ALLIANCE
350 N. Highland Ave.
Nyack, NY 10960

The Christian and Missionary Alliance grew out of the work of the Reverend Albert Benjamin Simpson, a Presbyterian minister who was healed under the ministry of Episcopal minister Charles Cullis, who ran a summer campground at Old Orchard, Maine. Simpson left the Presbyterian Church and began an independent ministry that was both evangelistic and missionary in character. In 1887 two societies--the Christian Alliance for home work and the International Missionary Alliance for foreign missions--were begun by Simpson. In 1897 these two societies were united as the Christian and Missionary Alliance, the present name.

The Alliance tried to remain a mission agency and not become another denomination. However, congregations were established and institutions created, and the denominational character of the group was slowly accepted. Cooperation with other Christian bodies continues to be a major goal, however.

The organization is centered on the annual council which enacts all legislation. The council, composed of delegates of the society's members, elects the board of managers and regulates the Alliance's affairs. As a polity there are no high-paid executives or officials. The use of un-Scriptural or undignified methods of money raising is avoided.

Simpson preached a simple doctrine, usually referred to as the four-fold gospel--Christ as savior, sanctifier, healer and coming Lord. The Christian and Missionary Alliance was among the first of the holiness churches to emphasize the role of spiritual healing in the Christian life. The mission thrust of the Christian and Missionary Alliance has carried its representatives all over the world, and current work is sustained in almost every area of the world and includes a variety of home missions.

Membership: In 1982 the Alliance reported 204,713 members, 1,485 churches and 1,819 ministers.

Educational facilities: Missionary Training Institute, NY; St. Paul Bible Institute, St. Paul, MN; Simpson Bible Institute, Seattle, WA.

Periodicals: *Alliance Witness*, 350 N. Highland Ave., Nyack, NY 10960.

Sources: Albert B. Simpson, *The Four-fold Gospel*. Harrisburg, PA: Christian Publications, n.d.; Albert B. Simpson, *A Larger Christian Life*; Harrisburg, PA: Christian Publications, n.d.; *Manual*. New York: Christian and Missionary Alliance, 1965.

★218★

CHRISTIAN NATION CHURCH, U.S.A.
% Rev. Harvey Monjar, General Overseer
Box 142
South Lebanon, OH 45065

In 1892 eight young evangelists who called themselves "equality Evangelists" began to work in central Ohio. Their efforts met with success, and in 1895 the Christian Nation Church was incorporated at Marion, Ohio. Doctrinally, the group is related to the Christian and Missionary Alliance, and preaches the four-fold gospel of its founder Albert Benjamin Simpson. It is very strict in forbidding worldly amusements, fashionable attire, Sabbath desecration, and divorce. Marriage with non-members is discouraged. Large families are encouraged as being divinely sanctioned.

The polity of the Christian Nation is congregational with district and annual conferences. The pastors' licenses are

renewed annually. Camp meetings are an active part of the program.

Membership: In 1982 the Church reported 226 members, 5 churches and 18 ministers.

★219★

CHRIST'S SANCTIFIED HOLY CHURCH (LOUISIANA)
S. Cutting Ave. at E. Spencer St.
Jennings, LA 70546

In 1903 members of Christ's Sanctified Holy Church (South Carolina) came to West Lake, Louisiana, and proselytized a group of black people, who in 1904 organized the Colored Church South. Among the leaders were Dempsey Perkins, A. C. Mitchell, James Briller, Sr., and Leggie Pleasant. The church soon changed its name to Christ's Sanctified Holy Church Colored. Over the years the church members dropped the word "Colored" from their title and returned to using the same name as their parent body, Christ's Sanctified Holy Church. The parent body is white and has headquarters in South Carolina, whereas the church under discussion here is headquartered in Louisiana. Organization and doctrine are as in the parent body, except that the ministers in Christ's Sanctified Holy Church (Louisiana) are salaried.

Membership: Not reported. At last report (1957) there were 600 members in 30 churches.

★220★

CHRIST'S SANCTIFIED HOLY CHURCH (SOUTH CAROLINA)
CSHC Campground
Perry, GA 31068

Two bodies use the name Christ's Sanctified Holy Church. The earlier of the two, described in this paragraph, was founded in 1887 when Joseph B. Lynch, a Methodist class leader, became convinced he could not be saved without holiness, even though he was living in a justified state. With this conviction he sought and obtained the experience of entire sanctification, and, having found it, he began to preach it. The resistance of the Methodist Church leadership to the holiness movement led to a schism, and the new church was organized on February 14, 1892. There are two stages to membership. Those who are justified and seeking sanctification may be accepted on probation. Only sanctified persons may be received into full membership. The church is governed by Board 1, which has the powers of ordination, decides disputed cases in the local congregations, and examines deacons and deaconesses. A conference of the whole church elects Board 1. Each local congregation has a board of managers with nine to nineteen members who operate by consensus. Each local church's board is numbered according to when it came into existence.

The doctrine of Christ's Sanctified Holy Church is Trinitarian and centered on the experience of sanctification. The members differ from most holiness churches in not using the ordinances of baptism and the Lord's Supper, a practice the church shares with the Salvation Army. They believe that the one baptism of Ephesians 4:5 is baptism of the Holy Spirit (sanctification) and that no act of ritual is necessary to establish a relationship between God and man. Clothing is regulated; jewelry and items made from gold are forbidden. The church is pacifist and believes no members should take part in war. Women are given equal rights in all church matters. A campground near Perry, Georgia, is the scene of annual camp meetings in August. At the grounds is a Home for the Aged.

Membership: Not reported. In 1970 there were approximately 21 churches.

★221★
CHURCH OF GOD (ANDERSON, INDIANA)
Box 2420
Anderson, IN 46018

Daniel Warner, a minister of the General Eldership of the Churches of God in North America, now called the Church of God, General Council, was affected by the holiness movement. He became an ardent advocate of sanctification as a second work of grace. For that belief he was tried and expelled from the church. Warner argued that sanctification led to an identification of the invisible church with the visible church, the concrete embodiment of the spiritual body of Christ.

The new Church of God was organized in 1880 by Warner. Like its parent body, the Church of God has no creed, but it follows the holiness theological consensus. It believes in the inspiration of Scripture, the Trinity, the divinity of Jesus, the indwelling of the Holy Spirit, sin, repentance, and atonement in Christ. There is a distinctive eschatology. While the members look for the second coming of Christ, they hold that it has no connection with a millennial reign. The kingdom of God is here and now. There will be a judgment day with reward for the righteous and punishment for the wicked.

Three ordinances, symbolic of acts of obedience and experience with Christ, are commonly practiced: baptism, the Lord's Supper, and footwashing. Baptism is by immersion. Footwashing is usually practiced on Maunday Thursday by separate groups of men and women. These symbolic acts are but highlights of a Christian life of stewardship and high moral and ethical conduct. Spiritual healing is practiced, as is tithing.

Warner's distinctive doctrine of the church led to a rejection of the presbyterial system. The church uses a congregational form of government as the form that allows only the authority of God to operate. No membership is held in a formal way: there is no formal

initiation rite for members, and membership lists are not made. Beyond the local church there are state and regional associations, and each year a General Assembly is held in connection with the International Convention. Anderson, Indiana, is home to the church. Located there are its headquarters, college, theological school, and Warner Auditorium (site of the International Convention). There is an active outreach program conducted by the general church. The Christian Brotherhood Hour is heard over three hundred stations, including some Spanish-speaking stations. Missions are conducted in Kenya, Egypt, Lebanon, Greece, Switzerland, West Germany, Denmark, England and Ireland, India, Korea, Japan, and throughout Central and South America. Warner Press publishes many books, pamphlets and tracts, and most of the educational material used by the church. The church is a member of the National Association of Evangelicals, and many of its congregations are associated with the Christian Holiness Association.

Membership: No formal membership figures are kept, but an informal count is made periodically. In 1984 the church reported 182,190 members, 2,286 congregations and 3,840 ordained ministers. There are an additional 183,989 members worldwide.

Educational facilities: Anderson College, Anderson, IN; Warner Pacific College, Portland, OR; Gulf-Coast Bible College, Houston, TX.

Periodicals: *Vital Christianity*, Warner Press, Box 2420, Anderson, IN 46018; *Leadership*, Warner Press, Box 2420, Anderson, IN 46018; *Missions*, Warner Press, Box 2420, Anderson, IN 46018.

Sources: Barry L. Callen, ed., *The First Century*. Anderson, IN: Warner Press, 1979. 2 vols.; Milburn H. Miller, *"Unto the Church of God"*.Anderson, IN: Warner Press, 1968; R. Eugene Sterner, *We Reach Our Hands in Fellowship*. Anderson, IN: Warner Press, 1960.

★222★
CHURCH OF GOD (GUTHRIE, OKLAHOMA)
% Faith Publishing House
7415 W. Monsur Ave.
Guthrie, OK 73044

The Church of God (Guthrie, Oklahoma) was formed by some ministers and laymen of the Church of God (Anderson, Indiana) who separated in 1910-/11 over what they felt had been compromises and changes in doctrine and practice, and drifting into worldliness. Among the new practices coming into the Church of God (Anderson, Indiana) were the segregation of the races and the wearing of neckties. In 1910 C. E. Orr began publishing *The Herald of Truth* in California, advocating the original position of Daniel S. Warner, founder of the Church of God (Anderson, Indiana). A movement supporting schism developed around Orr.

In doctrine and practice the Church of God (Guthrie, Oklahoma) is almost identical with the Church of God (Anderson, Indiana), but it is stricter in its practice of holiness and refusal to compromise with the world. Like the members of the parent body, the members of the Church of God (Guthrie, Oklahoma) believe in healing and reject the idea of a literal millennium.

In 1923 Fred Pruitt moved from New Mexico to Guthrie and began to print *Faith and Victory* which continues as the organ of the movement. Today from the Faith Publishing House, Lawrence D. Pruitt continues his father's work and also publishes many tracts and *The Beautiful Way*, a children's quarterly. A vigorous mission program i s supported in the Philippines, Nigeria, Mexico, and India. A national camp meeting has been held each July since 1938. Lesser camp meetings are held across the United States and in Mexico and Canada.

Membership: Not reported.

Periodicals: *Faith and Victory*, Faith Publishing House, 920 W. Monsur Avenue, Guthrie, OK 73044; *The Beautiful Way*, Faith Publishing House, 920 W. Monsur Avenue, Guthrie, OK 73044.

Sources: Fred Pruitt, *Past, Present and Future of the Church*. Guthrie, OK: Faith Publishing House, n.d.; Daniel S. Warner, *The Church of God*. Guthrie, OK: Faith Publishing House, n.d.; S. O. Susag, *Personal Experiences*. Guthrie, OK: Faith Publishing House, 1976.

★223★
CHURCH OF GOD (HOLINESS)
7415 Metcalf
Overland Park, KS 66204

The origin of the Church of God (Holiness) dates to the very beginning of the "come-out" crisis of the early 1880s, a movement whose leaders advocated coming out of the mainline Protestant churches in order to establish independent holiness congregations. The ideal of the one New Testament church, a divine institution headed by Christ, was opposed in their thinking to what they saw as denominational, man-made organizations. Thus local congregations organized in conformity to the New Testament ideal became the movement's immediate goal. The first independent congregations which were established served primarily those holiness people with no previous church (denominational) affiliation, but eventually included people leaving the older churches.

During the decades when holiness advocates had been welcome in the mainline denominations, holiness associations had formed. These were not churches, but simply groups loosely affiliated with the non-holiness churches. As the come-out movement intensified, these associations fell into disfavor among many holiness proponents. Among those most strongly affected by come-outism were members of the Southwestern Holiness

Association covering the states of Kansas, Missouri and Iowa. By 1882 six ministers, leaders of the Association, had decided to withdraw from their parent denominational bodies as soon as it was convenient. A minister in the Methodist Episcopal Church, South, A. M. Kiergan, emerged as their leader and spearheaded the drive toward independent holiness congregations. The dominance of the come-outers in the Southwestern Holiness Association caused its dissolution in 1887 and the formation of a new church, the Independent Holiness People, the following year. In 1895 the name was changed to Church of God (known as Independent Holiness People). *The Good Way*, formerly serving the Southwestern Holiness Association, became the church newspaper.

Almost as soon as the church formed, two factions arose. One wanted complete local congregational sovereignty. The other said the elders should interpret doctrine and be spiritual rulers for the church, and should in turn be subject to a presbytery of elders. Kiergan and John P. Brooks, an early leader of the come-outers in Illinois, led the sovereignty faction. The crux of the issue was representation in the annual convention. In 1897 a "Declaration of Principles" was published by the sovereignty faction. The local sovereignty supporters wanted representation of the congregations at the annual meeting, and the others wanted the elders represented. Following the publication of the Declaration, the church split into the Independent Holiness People (sovereignty faction) and Unity Holiness People (elder faction). A reunion of the two factions was accomplished in 1922. The name of the reunited church is Church of God (Holiness). The new church merged with the Missionary Bands of the World, now a constituent part of the Wesleyan Church, but the merger fell through in 1938.

Four doctrines are central in the Church of God (Holiness)--the New Birth, Entire Sanctification, the one New Testament church, and the second coming followed by a literal millennium. The first two doctrines are common to all holiness churches. The last two doctrines are not held by many holiness churches. The one New Testament church idea is a distinctive feature of the Church of God (Holiness). The doctrinal statement in the reunited church reads:

The New Testament Scriptures teach that there is one true Church, which is composed only of those who have savingly believed in the Lord Jesus Christ, and who willingly submit themselves to His divine order concerning the ministries of the Church through the instrumentalities of God--chosen elders and deacons, ordained in the Chruch by laying on of the hands of the presbytery. The attributes of the Church are unity, spirituality, visibility, and catholicity. (Matt. 16:18; Eph 4:4;Col. 1:18; I Tim. 3: 1-7; Titus 1:5).

The government of the Church of God (Holiness) is congregational, but a delegated annual convention has charge of church-wide ministries. The Board of Publication oversees Herald and Banner Press, the Church's publishing arm. A Home and Foreign Mission Board oversees missions in Jamaica, the Cayman Islands, the Virgin Islands, and Bolivia. There are also missionary efforts along the Mexican border and among West Indian immigrants in England.

Membership: Not reported. The church is estimated to have approximately 3,000 members in approximately 100 congregations.

Educational facilities: Kansas City College and Bible School, Overland Park, Kansas: Cedaredge Bible School, Cedaredge, Colorado; Fort Scott Christian Heights, Fort Scott, Kansas; Holiness Bible School, Beulah, Oklahoma; Kirksville Bible School, Kirksville, Missouri; Mount Zion Bible School, Ava, Missouri; Mountain State Christian School, Culloden, West Virginia; Rocky Mountain Christian School, Littleton, Colorado.

Periodicals: *The Church Herald and Holiness Banner*, 7415 Metcalf, Overland Park, KS 66204.

Sources: Clarence Eugene Cowen, *A History of the Church of God (Holiness)*. The Author, 1948; John P. Brooks, *The Divine Church*. El Dorado Springs, MO: Witt Printing Company, 1960.

★224★
CHURCH OF THE NAZARENE
6401 The Paseo
Kansas City, MO 64131

When the hostility of leaders in both the Methodist Episcopal Church and the Methodist Episcopal Church, South, the two denominations in which most holiness advocates were originally members, made the holiness people feel that a new church was their only option, small schisms began to occur. Independent congregations and holiness associations came into existence. By the turn of the century these smaller groups began to seek wider fellowship by way of mergers. The Church of the Nazarene is the product of a set of such mergers.

Phineas Bresee is looked upon as the founding father of the Church of the Nazarene. In 1895 Bresee, a former Methodist pastor, organized the First Church of the Nazarene, which superceded the Peniel Mission in Los Angeles, California, where he had been preaching for a year. Coincident with Bresee's efforts, the Association of Pentecostal Churches was formed in New York. In 1896 this group united with the Central Evangelical Association with member congregations primarily located in New England. In October, 1907, the Association of Pentecostal Churches and the First Church of the Nazarene merged to form the Pentecostal Church of the Nazarene. On October 13, 1908, the Holiness Church of Christ united with the Pentecostal Church of the Nazarene in their joint meeting at Pilot Point, Texas; they retained the name of

the latter group. This date is accepted as the official beginning of the Church of the Nazarene. In 1915 the Pentecostal Church of Scotland united with the Pentecostal Church of the Nazarene.

In 1919 the word "Pentecostal" was dropped to avoid confusion with the "tongues" sects. Over the years other groups have united with the Church of the Nazarene, including the Laymen's Holiness Association (1922); the International Holiness Mission, an English group (1952); the Calvary Holiness Church, also English (1955); and the Gospel Workers Church of Canada (1958).

The Church of the Nazarene looks upon itself as firmly Wesleyan in doctrine and practice and keeps in essence the Articles of Religion and General Rules as sent to America by Methodist founder, John Wesley. The church has, however, added statements on the plenary inspiration of Scripture, regeneration, entire sanctification, divine healing, and eschatology and has changed completely Wesley's article on the church. The major emphasis is upon the "second blessing" of entire sanctification and the personal holiness of the believer.

Government in the groups which formed the Church of the Nazarene was of all types: congregational, representative, and episcopal. The final outcome was a representative government. The highest law-making body is the general assembly, composed equally of ministerial and lay delegates elected by the district assemblies. A general board, elected by the general assembly, has oversight of specialized general assembly concerns: evangelism, missions, publication, education, and ministerial benevolences. The general assembly, presided over by the general superintendents who are elected every four years, has final authority in all matters except changes in the constitution. Such changes must be voted upon by the district assemblies, as well as the general assembly. The district assembly orders the work of the district, having direct supervision over the local churches and ministers. The local church calls its pastor and conducts its own affairs in accordance with general asembly guidelines.

Missions began in what was to become the Church of the Nazarene as far back as 1897 when Mr. and Mrs. M. D. Wood, Miss Carrie Taylor, Miss Lillian Sprague, and Mr. F. P. Wiley sailed for India. The work has grown until, at present (1983), there are more than 70 countries with work under the direction of the Department of World Missions of the General Board.

Publishing began in the Church of the Nazarene in 1896 with the monthly *Nazarene Messenger*. Early in 1900, the Nazarene Publishing Company was founded to carry on the work of the growing denomination. After the 1908 mergers, plans were made to establish a centrally located Nazarene publishing house, which was done in 1911. The new publishing house--Beacon Hill Press in Kansas City, Missouri--is now the largest publisher of holiness literature in the world. The Church of the Nazarene is a member of the Christian Holiness Association.

Membership: In 1984 the Church reported 507,574 members, 4,931 congregations and 10,775 ministers. There were 729,989 members worldwide.

Educational facilities: Nazarene Theological Seminary, Kansas City, Missouri; Bethany Nazarene College, Bethany, Oklahoma; Eastern Nazarene College, Quincy, Massachusetts;Mid-America Nazarene College, Olathe, Kansas; Mount Vernon Nazarene College, Mt. Vernon, Ohio; Nazarene Bible College, Colorado Springs, Colorado; Northwest Nazarene College, Nampa, Idaho; Olivet Nazarene College, Kankakee, Illinois; Point Loma Nazarene College, San Diego, California; Trevecca Nazarene College, Nashville, Tennessee; Nazarene Indian Bible College, Albuquerque, New Mexico; Canadian Nazarene College, Winnipeg, Manitoba, Canada; British Isles Nazarene College, Manchester, England; Korea Nazarene Theological Seminary, Chonan City, Korea.

Periodicals: *Herald of Holiness*, 6401 The Paseo, Kansas City, MO 64131; *World Mission*, 6401 The Paseo, Kansas City, MO 64131.

Sources: M. E. Redford, *The Rise of the Church of the Nazarene*. Kansas City, MO: Beacon Hill Press, 1948; Ross E, Price, *Nazarene Manifesto*. Kansas City, MO: Beacon Hill Press, 1968; E. A. Girvin, *Phineas F. Bresee: A Prince in Israel*. Kansas City, MO: Pentecostal Nazarene Publishing House, 1916.

★225★
CHURCHES OF GOD, GENERAL CONFERENCE
700 E. Melrose Ave.
Box 926
Findlay, OH 45839

The Churches of God in North America (General Eldership) was founded by John Winebrunner, a pastor of four German Reformed Church parisheses in and around Harrisburg, Pennsylvania. Shortly after his pastorate began, a revival started and opposition to its "disorder" arose. In 1825 Winebrunner, who supported the revival, was forced to give up his pastorate, but the revival continued. As a result of the revival, independent congregations began to form and in 1830 the Church of God was organized. The new body had several distinctions from its Reformed parent. First, in reaction to the growing sectarian spirit, it desired to be non-sectarian and to profess no name or creed that could distinguish it from other churches. Winebrunner became the first to popularize the idea of using the Churcb of God as the only Biblical name. There was only one church established by Christ; the members of the Church of God proposed to be that one church.

Winebrunner saw the Church of God in three ways. It was first a congregation, second a community of saints, and third the sum total of believers everywhere. By congregtion, Winebrunner meant the Church of God was one group gathered at one place, with the group including believers and sinners. By community of saints, Winebrunner meant the Church of God was smaller than a congregtion and was composed of the believers who lead holy lives. As a community, the Church of God needs a government, bishops (elders) and deacons, the former to teach and rule, the latter to assist in temporal matters. The presbyterial form is proper. The church is also visible, unified, sanctified, universal, and perpetual.

The Churches of God take the Bible as their only standard. The churches insist that the Bible teaches that man is depraved (unable to turn to God through intellect and will because of Adam's sin). Further, the Bible teaches redemption in Jesus Christ; the gift of the Holy Spirit; the free agency of man, as opposed to unconditional election; justification by faith; three ordinances--baptism, the Lord's Supper and footwashing; sanctity of the Sabbath; the various means of effectively proclaiming the gospel, including missionary societies, Sunday schools, and the religious press; the holy life; and the second coming.

The Churches of God have sown certain ideas as almost no other body. Numerous schismatic churches have adopted the name "Church of God" as the only true name of the true church. They were a major popularizer of the practice of footwashing. They are a major source of ecumenicity because they were formed to be nonsectarian churches where all Christians could fellowship. This ecumenical thrust, though, instead of promoting the unity of churches, has given rise to a new sect. Winebrunner meant to develop a nonsectarian church, but he created a separate sect by insisting that members foolow his teachings.

While continuing to seek the goals outlined by Winebrunner, the contemporary Churches of God have been drawn into the holiness family at several points. The Churches of God have been a source for much holiness doctrine and practice; primarily through the holiness schism led by Daniel Warner. In 1941 the Churches of god began to cooperate with the Church of God (Anderson, Indiana) on mutually prepared church school materials. Formal conversations looking toward merger began in 1959 and have continued since at more serious levels.

The national organization of the Churches of God, called the General Eldership, meets every three years. On the regional level elderships function like presbyteries, regional legislative bodies. An Administrative Council functions between the triennial meetings of the General Eldership. There are seven commissions which implement programs. The Commission on Education oversees Findley College and Winebrunner Theologıcal Seminary at Findley, Ohio. The Commission on World Mission oversees work in India, Pakistan, and Haiti. The Commission on

Publications controls Central Publishing House and Book Store and publishes the Christ Advocate and a complete line of church school materials. In 1975 they reported 347 churches, 3336,016 members, and 383 ministers.

Membership: In 1984 the General Conference reported 35,000 members, 352 congregations, and 390 ministers. There were 39,000 members worldwide.

Educational facilities: Winebrunner Theological Seminary, Findlay, Ohio; Findlay College, Findlay, Ohio.

Periodicals: *The Church Advocate*, 700 E. Melrose Ave., Findlay, OH 45839; *T he Missionary Signal*, 700 E. Melrose Ave., Findlay, OH 45839.

★226★
CHURCHES OF GOD (INDEPENDENT HOLINESS PEOPLE)
1225 E. First St.
Fort Scott, KS 66701

In 1922 the Church of God (Independent Holiness People) and the Church of God (Unity Holiness People) united to become the Church of God (Holiness). However, some members of the Church of God (Independent Holiness People), those often referred to as the sovreignty faction and most committed to the strong sovreignty of the local congregation, did not join the merger. They reorganized and established headquarters at Ft. Scott, Kansas. The continuing church has no doctrinal differences with the Church of God (Holiness), only distinctive by its firm allegiance to a congregational government. The church has stanchly advocated a pacifist position and has annually at its conventions passed resolutions against Christian participation in war. Membership is concentrated in the Southwest. Missionary work is conducted in Japan and Mexico and among American Indians in South Dakota and Wyoming.

Membership: Not reported. In 1972, 15 churches were represented at the annual convention.

Periodicals: *The Church Advocate and Good Way*, 1225 E. First St., Fort Scott, KS 66701.

★227★
EMMANUEL ASSOCIATION
West Cucharas at 27th St.
Colorado Springs, CO 80904

The Emmanuel Association was formed in 1937 by Ralph G. Finch, a former general superintendent of Foreign Missions of the Pilgrim Holiness Church, now a constituent part of the Wesleyan Church. The Emmanuel Association was run by Finch until his death in 1949. Now, the Association is run by the general conference made up of all ordained and licensed ministers. It establishes all rules and elects the officers. Local churches

function under the general conference. There is also a provision for affiliated membership for both ministers and congregations.

Doctrine is like that of the Pilgrim Holiness Church, but with a very rigid behavior code, the "Principles of Holy Living." Members are conscientious objectors, believing that war is murder. Foreign missionary work is carried on in Guatemala.

Membership: Not reported. In the 1970 there were 17 churches in the United States and Canada and an estimated membership of 400.

Educational facilities: People's Bible College, Colorado Springs, CO.

Periodicals: *Emmanuel Herald*, W. Cucharas at 27th, Colorado Springs, CO 80904.

Sources: *The Guidebook of the Emmanuel Association.* Colorado Springs, CO: Emmanuel Association, 1966; *Ralph Goodrich French, the Man and His Mission.* Colorado Springs, CO: Emmanuel Press, 1967.

★228★
FAITH MISSION CHURCH
% Rev. Ray Snow
1318 26th St.
Bedford, IN 47421

In 1958, when the main body of the Missionary Bands of the World (a small holiness church formed in 1885) merged into the Wesleyan Methodist Church, now a constituent part of the Wesleyan Church, some members of the Bands elected to continue as an independent body. In 1963 they took their present name. All the congregations are in Ohio and Indiana.

Membership: Not reported. There are approximately 100 members.

★229★
FIRE-BAPTIZED HOLINESS CHURCH (WESLEYAN)
600 College Ave.
Independence, KS 67301

The Fire Baptized Holiness Church (Wesleyan) was established in 1890 by holiness people in the Methodist Episcopal Church of southeastern Kansas. The original name, the Southeast Kansas Fire Baptized Holiness Association, was changed in 1945. The church is organized in an episcopal mode taken from the Methodist Episcopal Church. A general assembly meets annually. The Wesleyan holiness doctrine is emphasized, and strong prohibitions exist against alcohol, tobacco, drugs, secret societies, television, immodest clothing, jewelry, and frivolous ammusements. Members regularly tithe. The church is opposed to war and members are conscientious objectors. The church is aggressively evangelistic. Missions are supported on Grenada, Windward Islands.

Membership: Not reported. In the 1970s there were 50 congregations and approximately 1,200 members.

Periodicals: *The Flaming Sword*, 10th & Country Club Road, Independence, KS 67301; *John Three Sixteen*, 10th Street & Country Club Road, Independence KS 67301.

★230★
FREE METHODIST CHURCH OF NORTH AMERICA
901 College Ave.
Winona Lake, IN 46590

The Free Methodist Church dates from a holiness protest in the Genesee Conference (in western New York) of the Methodist Episcopal Church. The Reverend Benjamin Titus Roberts was the leader of the protesting Nazarites, as they were called. In 1856 they began a new periodical, *The Northern Independent*, and in it Roberts published his famous article, "New School Methodism." He accused the ruling structure of the Genesee Conference of departing from Old School Methodism by adoping "modern" theology, showing distrust of deep Christian experience, building Gothic churches, selling pews, and patronizing the world. Roberts was sent to a small rural church at Pekin. He was expelled in 1858, but continued to travel through the Genesse Conference.

Criticisms similar to those of Roberts came from John Wesley Redfield in northern Illinois. In July 1860 those who supported Redfield met at St. Charles, Illinois, to organize as Free Methodist Churches. In August, Roberts and his followers formalized their separation from the Methodist Episcopal Church and chose the name Free Methodist Chur ch. The groups led by Roberts and Redfield organized a national Free Methodist Church, now called the Free Methodist Church of North America. The groups chose to be called Free Methodists to signify freedom from secret societies, slavery, rented pews, flashy clothes and jewelry.

Doctrinally, the Free Methodist Church of North America follows the Wesleyan heritage of the Methodist Episcopal Church, from which it derives its Articles of Religion. The Free Methodists adopted an Article of Religion on entire sanctification which accepted the "instantaneous" interpretation of Wesleyan sanctification. This statement on sanctification has been a position characteristic of the holiness movement in general.

The Free Methodists have adopted a modified episcopacy. Bishops are elected every five years. A general conference has legislative powers. The Commission on Missions has responsibility for missions in 21 countries (1984). The Commission on Christian Education oversees work in higher education. Life and Light Press is a major publisher of holiness literature, including a full-line of Sunday school material.

Membership: In 1983 the church reported 72,920 members in the United States (189,681 worldwide), 997 congregations and 1,733 ministers.

Educational facilities: Central College, McPherson, Kansas; Greenville College, Greenville, Illinois; Roberts Wesleyan College, Rochester, New York; Seattle Pacific University, Seattle, Washington; Spring Arbor College, Spring Arbor, Michigan; Azusa Pacific University, Azusa, California; Aldersgate College, Moose Jaw, Saskatchewan, Canada. The Church also financially supports two independent holiness schools: Asbury Theological Seminary, Wilmore, Kentucky; and Western Theological Seminary, Portland, Oregon.

Periodicals: *Light and Life*, 901 College Avenue, Winona Lake, IN 46590; *The Missionary Tidings*, 901 College Avenue, Winona Lake, IN 46590.

Sources: Leslie R. Marston, *From Age to Age a Living Witness*. Winona Lake, IN: Life and Light Press, 1960; Wilson T. Hogue, *History of the Free Methodist Church*. Chicago: Free Methodist Publishing House, 1918. 2 Vols.; J. Paul Taylor, *Holiness, the Finished Foundation*. Winona Lake, IN: Life and Light Press, 1963; B. T. Roberts, *Holiness Teachings*. Salem, OH: H. E. Schmul, 1964.

★231★
HOLINESS CHRISTIAN CHURCH OF THE UNITED STATES OF AMERICA
Gibraltar, PA 19524

The Holiness Christian Church of the United States of America was formed as an evangelistic endeavor by three men and two women known as the Heavenly Recruits, who were doing street preaching and conducting tent revivals and camp meetings in the Philadelphia area. The need for pastoral care for the many converts became pressing. In 1889 resolutions were passed calling for a presiding elder. Several crises led to the call for a centralized polity, and in 1894 C. W. Ruth was elected president. The name was changed in 1889 from the Heavenly Recruit Association to the Holiness Christian Association and finally to Holiness Christian Church in 1897. Work in Indiana as a separate conference and home missions in the West were begun as a prelude to moving the headquarters to Indiana. As the church spread, Ruth encountered the groups then merging into the Pentecostal Church of the Nazarene (later called the Church of the Nazarene) and in 1908 took most of the Holiness Christian Church into the Pentecostal Church of the Nazarene. Then in 1919 the Holiness Christian Church voted to merge with the International Apostolic Holiness Church, now a constituent part of the Wesleyan Church. Only a remnant of the original Heavenly Recruits Association in eastern Pennsylvania remained out of the merger, but it slowly began to rebuild and is today the

Holiness Christian Church of the United States of America. A periodical was begun in 1937, and mission work in Jamaica was initiated in 1945.

The church is headed by a general superintendent. The conference of churches meets annually.

Membership: Not reported. In the 1970s there were approximately 30 congregations and 1,000 members.

Periodicals: *Holiness Christian Messenger*, Gibraltar, PA 19524.

★232★
METROPOLITAN CHURCH ASSOCIATION
323 Broad St.
Lake Geneva, WI 53147

The Metropolitan Church Association was formed in 1894. It grew out of a holiness revival at the Metropolitan Methodist Episcopal Church in Chicago. It was first known as the Metropolitan Holiness Church and adopted its present name in 1899. Members had a reputation for emotional displays at worship and ascetic behavior patterns. Early in its life, it adopted a communal form of organization, a factor which slowed its growth in the long run.

Besides its early emphasis upon inner city missions, foreign missions were begun around the globe. The one in India has been most productive, and a school and hospital are supported there. Other missions are supported in Mexico and in Cape Town and Swaziland (South Africa). There is an annual camp meeting for revival and fellowship, held since 1971 at the Salvation Army's Camp Wonderland at Camp Lake, Wisconsin. Business is conducted by an annual general assembly.

Membership: Not reported. In the 1970s there were 15 churches and approximately 400 members.

Periodicals: *The Burning Bush*, 323 Broad St., Lake Geneva, WI 53147.

Sources: G. W. Henry, *Shouting: Geniune and Spurious.* Chicago: Metropolitan Church Association, 1903.

★233★
MISSIONARY CHRISTIAN AND SOUL WINNING FELLOWSHIP
350 E. Market St.
Long Beach, CA 90805

The Missionary Christian and Soul Winning Fellowship was formed in 1957 by Reverend Lee Shelley, a minister of the Christian and Missionary Alliance. It continues the evangelistic and missionary interests of the Christian and Missionary Alliance, but its doctrinal statement has deleted any reference to healing, a particular interest of CMA founder, A. B. Simpson.

A missionary program has work in nineteen countries. In the United States there is a single congregation (Christian in Action Chapel) at Long Beach, California. A school provides vocational training for Christian workers. Within the United States a Jewish ministry in Los Angeles led by Abe Schneider is supported, as is an Apache Indian Mission.

Membership: There is a single congregation in California.

★234★
MISSIONARY CHURCH
3901 S. Wayne Ave.
Fort Wayne, IN 46807

The Missionary Church was formed in 1969 by the merger of the United Missionary Church and the Missionary Church Association. The Missionary Church Association was formed in 1898 at Berne, Indiana, by a group headed by J. E. Ramseyer. It was similar to the Christian and Missionary Alliance in both faith and practice. The United Missionary Church dates to an evangelistic effort in Lehigh County, Pennsylvania, among the Mennonites. In 1858 a conference formed using the name Evangelical Mennonites. In 1869 a Canadian Mennonite minister professed conversion after some years in the ministry and instituted protracted meetings in his effort to spread the new experience of grace. He was censured, but his movement spread and in 1874 took the name Reformed Mennonites. The next year they were joined by a small body called the New Mennonites and took the name United Mennonites. The United Mennonites and the Evangelical Mennonites merged in 1879 to form the United Evangelical Mennonites. This body merged with a small splinter of the River Brethren called the Brethren in Christ in 1883 to become the Mennonite Brethren in Christ. The change of name in 1947 to United Missionary Church was a recognition of its having moved away from its Mennonite background. In 1969 it merged with the Missionary Church Association to form the Missionary Church.

The Missionary Church Association generally followed the four-fold gospel emphasis presenting Christ as savior, sanctifier, healer, and coming king. This presentation of the gospel derived from the teachings of Albert Benjamin Simpson, founder of the Christian and Missionary Alliance. Without moving from the truths so held, the Missionary Church has adopted a more comprehensive presentation of its evangelical, conservative and holiness faith. Government is congregational. A general conference meets every two years to elect a president and other officers. The Board of Overseas Missions has work in Brazil, the Dominican Republic, Ecuador, France, Haiti, India, Jamaica, Mexico, Nigeria, and Sierre Leone.

Membership: In 1984 the Church reported 25,371 members, 294 churches, and 482 ministers in the United States and 5,872 members, 131 churches, and 84 ministers in Canada. There were 24,098 baptized members and 18,038 adherents overseas.

Educational facilities: Bethel College, Mishawaka, Indiana; Fort Wayne Bible College, Fort Wayne, Indiana; Emmanuel Bible College, Kitchner, Ontario; Mountain View Bible College, Didsbury, Alberta.

Periodicals: *Emphasis*, 3901 South Wayne Street, Fort Wayne, IN 46807; *Catalyst*, 3901 South Wayne Street, Fort Wayne, IN 46807.

Sources: Eileen Lageer, *Merging Streams*. Elkhart, IN: Bethel Publishing Company, 1979.

★235★
MISSIONARY METHODIST CHURCH OF AMERICA
Rte. 7
Morganton, NC 28655

The Missionary Methodist Church was formed in 1913 in Forest City, North Carolina, by Reverend H. C. Sisk and four other former members of the Wesleyan Methodist Church. (The Wesleyan Methodist Church subsequently merged with the Pilgrim Holiness Church to form the Wesleyan Church.) The Missionary Methodist Church was originally called the Holiness Methodist Church, but the name was changed upon learning of another group with the same name. The original disagreement that led to the founding of the church was over the number of rules and regulations of the Wesleyan Methodist Church. A two-paragraph Creed includes belief in sanctification, which burns out all inbred sin; living every day above sin; keeping the self unspotted from the world; a personal devil; a literal, burning hell; and the premillennial return of Christ. "There are," states the Creed, "no hard man-made rules to bind one down, you can have freedom in the Missionary Methodist Church...." In 1939 the Oriental Missionary Society was adopted as the missionary agency of the church.

Membership: In 1984 the Church reported 1,708 members, 12 congregations, and 32 ministers.

Sources: *Doctrine, Creed and Rules for the Government of the Missionary Methodist Church of America.* (Morganville, NC): 1969.

★236★
NEW TESTAMENT CHURCH OF GOD
% Rev. G. W. Pendleton
307 Cockrell Hill Rd.
Dallas, TX 75211

The New Testament Church of God, Inc. was founded in 1942 by G. W. Pendleton and Martha Pendleton, his wife, both former members of the Church of God (Anderson, Indiana). They opposed the Church of God's cooperation and financial support of the National Council of Churches, but kept the doctrines of the parent body. The members hold camp meetings and state and regional conventions, publish gospel literature, and have regular radio broadcasts.

Membership: Not reported. Congregations are found across the United States, but no membership count has been made.

Periodicals: *Seventh Trumpet*, 307 Cockrell Hill Road, Dallas, TX 75211.

★237★
PENIEL MISSIONS
606 E. 6th St.
Los Angeles, CA 90021

The first Peniel Mission was founded by T. P. Ferguson and his wife Manie Ferguson in Los Angeles in 1886. Ferguson had been influenced by the preaching of Charles G. Finney, an early nineteenth century holiness theologian and evangelist. In 1880 he experienced sanctification under some holiness evangelists. Given the success of the Los Angeles work, he established rescue missions in the urban areas of the West Coast in attempts to win the urban masses to Christ. The missions have been marked by intense evangelistic endeavor, spiritual guidance, and stress on sanctification and sinlessness. For a short time, Phineas Bresee, founder of the Church of the Nazarene, worked at the Los Angeles center. By 1900 work had spread north along the West Coast and in Alaska, Hawaii, and Egypt. In 1949 responsibility for the Egyptian mission was assumed by the National Holiness Missionary Society, currently known as the World Gospel Mission, located in Winona Lake, Indiana.

Membership: Not reported.

Periodicals: *Peniel Herald*, 606 E. 6th Street, Los Angeles, CA 90021.

★238★
SALVATION ARMY
799 Bloomfield Ave.
Verona, NJ 07044

William Booth, a British Methodist minister-evangelist, inspired with a vision of service in the slums of London, left his church in 1865. He organized a Christian Mission, which in spite of success did not find acceptance in the free churches of Britain. To meet the war-on-poverty needs of his community of service, Booth modeled his mission on a "military" organization. In 1878 it became became the Salvation Army. The Army soon added a program of social service which has made it famous and respected even by many who do not know or think of it as a conservative holiness church body. Within two years it spread through the British Isles. In the United States, the Salvation Army was begun in 1880 by Commissioner Scott Railton and seven women officers, known as the "Seven Hallelujah Lassies."

The Army is organized on a military model. Each recruit becomes a cadet and after indoctrination begins to rise in rank. A national commander has charge of a number of divisions which are in turn broken into corps. There are four divisions in the United States. The Salvation Army has broad-reaching social programs, including emergency aid, thrift shops, alcohol rehabilitation, and half-way houses.

Booth believed that the ultimate goal of the Army was the salvation of the world. The social program was based on the belief that basic human needs must be met before man can begin to express a need for God. The doctrine of the Salvation Army is a Wesleyan evangelical holiness system very similar to that of the Wesleyan Church. Distinctive to Salvationists is their opinion on the sacraments. They believe the sacraments are neither essential to spiritual progress nor necessary to salvation, and hence do not observe them; for them Christianity is a spiritual religion, not a ceremonial one (John 4:24).

Membership: In 1982 the Army reported 419,475 members, 1,060 churches and 5,119 ministers.

Periodicals: *War Cry*, 799 Bloomfield Ave., Verona, NJ 07044.

Sources: Edward H. McKinley, *Marching to Glory*. New York: Harper & Row, 1980; Sallie Chesham, *Born to Battle*. Chicago: Rand McNally & Company, 1965; Robert Sandall, *The History of the Salvation Army*. London: Thomas Nelson, 1947; Milton S. Agnew, *Manual of Salvationism*. New York: The Salvation Army, 1968; Bernard Watson, *A Hundred Years' War*. London: Hodder and Stoughton, 1964; Cyril Barnes, *God's Army*. Elgin, IL: David C. Cook, 1968; *The Sacraments, the Salvationist's Viewpoint*. London: Salvationist Publishing and Supplies, 1960; Samuel Logan Brengle, *The Way of Holiness*. London: Salvationist Publishing and Supplies, 1960.

★239★
STANDARD CHURCH OF AMERICA
Brockville, ON, Canada

Ralph G. Horner had been an evangelist in both the Methodist Church in Canada and the Wesleyan Methodist Church, now a constituent part of the Wesleyan Church, in the late nineteenth century, but left them to found his own organization, the Holiness Movement Church, in 1895. As its bishop, he ruled with all the authority of both a bishop and charismatic personality, and within five years there were 118 places of worship. Churches were planted across Canada, into New York, with foreign work in Ireland, Egypt, and China. Then in 1918 the aging bishop was asked to retire. Not satisfied with the request of the church, he, with his supporters, left and founded the Standard Church of America, incorporated at Watertown, New York, in 1919. (The Holiness Movement Church eventually merged with the Free Methodist Church, which accounts for that church's large membership in Egypt.)

Like the Holiness Movement Church, the Standard Church of America is Methodist in doctrine with a strong emphasis on holiness and evangelism. Polity is episcopal. Pastors are stationed by the annual conferences for four-year terms. There are four conferences: Western, Kingston, New York, and Egyptian. A Bible School and printing establishment are maintained adjacent to the headquarters. There is missionary work in China and Egypt.

Membership: Not reported.

Educational facilities: Brockville Bible College, Brockville, Ontario, Canada.

Periodicals: *Christian Standard*, Brockville, Ontario, Canada.

★240★
UNDENOMINATIONAL CHURCH OF THE LORD
% Pastor Robert Wallace
Box 291
Placentia, CA 92677

The Undenominational Church of the Lord was founded at Placentia, California in 1918 by Pastor Jesse N. Blakeley, a holiness minister. Previously, he had helped form the Pentecost Pilgrim Church at Pasadena (which merged into what became the Pilgrim Holiness Church, now a constituent part of the Wesleyan Church). Blakeley became pastor of the Independent Holiness Mission in Placentia following a revival in Santa Ana. He felt the Holy Spirit leading him south and discovered the pastorless congregation in Placentia praying for the Lord to send them the right person. The Independent Holiness Mission became the Undenominational Church of the Lord.

A second branch of the church was founded in 1920 in Anaheim and became the headquarters. In 1922 the Placentia church was consolidated with the Anaheim church. In 1930 Blakeley was succeeded by Elsie Heughan, and in 1941 the headquarters returned to Placentia.

Doctrine of the Undenominational Church of the Lord is holiness. Evangelism, especially by the printed word, is emphasized. Mission churches have been established in Nigeria, India, and Korea, all of which are not autonomous. Though there are fewer than 100 members in the United States, there are many thousands in the foreign fields.

Membership: At last report (1970s) there were 3 congregations: Placentia, California; Chillicothe, Ohio; and Sheridan, Oregon. There were less than 100 members.

Periodicals: *The Second Comforter*, Box 291, Placentia, CA 92677.

★241★
VOLUNTEERS OF AMERICA
3813 N. Causeway Blvd.
Metairie, LA 70002

The Volunteers of America was formed in 1896 by Ballington Booth and Maud Booth, the son and daughter-in-law of William Booth. While very much like the Salvation Army from which it sprang, it differs in several ways; it is more democratic, though keeping the quasi-military organization; it practices both baptism and the Lord's Supper; the early emphasis on sanctification and holiness has lessened in favor of a more general evangelical faith.

Membership: In 1984 the Volunteers reported 70 centers served by 290 ministers.

Periodicals: *The Gazette*, 3813 N. Causeway Blvd., Metairie, LA 70002.

★242★
WESLEYAN CHURCH
Box 2000
Marion, IN 46952

The Wesleyan Church was formed in 1968 by the merger of the Wesleyan Methodist Church and Pilgrim Holiness Church. In the merger two diverse streams of holiness tradition (one pre-Civil War and the other from the late nineteenth century) were brought together.

The Wesleyan Methodist church had been formed in 1843 by ministers and laymen who withdrew from the Methodist Church during the height of the slavery controversy. Reverends Orange Scott, LeRoy Sunderland (later to join the Unitarian Association), and L. C. Matlock were all abolitionists who continually fought the compromise on the slavery issue made by the Methodist Episcopal Church in the early nineteenth century. (A note on that compromise: the eighteenth-century Methodist Episcopal Church did not allow any of its members to have slaves. Over the years, the church reneged on that strong anti-slavery position and allowed slaveholders to membership in the church.) Along with slavery, the reformers also began to attack the abuses of the episcopacy and the failure to teach and practice various forms of piety. By 1843 tension had reached such a level that, feeling no redress of grievances was possible, the reformers withdrew and took twenty-two ministers and 6,000 members and formed the Wesleyan Methodist Church in America. In the first *Discipline*, their book of church order, statements were made against slavery, against the use of alcohol and tobacco, against secret societies, and for modesty in dress. The new structure provided for annual conferences with lay delegates and an elected president (instead of a bishop). There was also a General Conference.

The Pilgrim Holiness Church grew out of the holiness movement of the late nineteenth century. Martin Wells Knapp, a former minister in the Methodist Episcopal Church, and Rev. Seth Cook Rees organized the International Holiness Union and Prayer League in 1897 in Cincinnati, Ohio. The Union was to be a fellowship, not a church. It was established as a completely Wesleyan movement with emphases on holiness, healing the sick, the premillennial coming of Christ, and evangelization. From a small beginning, rapid growth ensued, augmented by mergers with several other holiness bodies. In 1900 foreign missionary work was begun. The growth of the Union led to a change of character, and the fellowship became a church. It underwent several name changes, and 1922 finally took the name of the Pilgrim Holiness Church. The other holiness groups that merged with the Union (later called the Pilgrim Holiness Church) were the following (with merger dates): Indiana Conference of the Holiness Christian Church (1919); Pilgrim Church of California (1922); Pentecostal Rescue Mission (1922); Pentecostal Brethren in Christ (1924); People's Mission Church (1925); and Holiness Church of California (1946).

The Wesleyan church has a modified episcopal government headed by the general superintendent. The general conference is the supreme governing body and elects the general superintendent to four-year term(s). A General Board of Administration operates between general conference sessions. The church is divided into districts. Headquarters of the Wesleyan Church are in Marion, Indiana. The Wesleyan Publishing House located there is responsible for a wide range of books, religious literature, and church school material. The Commission on World Mission oversees a vast foreign mission program, including the work of the Africa Evangelistic Mission, an independent work in South Africa which was received into the Pilgrim Holiness Church in 1962.

Membership: In 1984 the Church reported 113,054 members, 1,821 churches, and 3,086 ministers in the United States. Worldwide there were 2,733 churches and 172,188 members.

Educational facilities: Bartlesville Wesleyan College, Bartlesville, Oklahoma; Central Wesleyan College, Central, South Carolina; Houghton College, Houghton, New York; Marion College, Marion, Indiana; United Wesleyan College, Allentown, Pennsylvania; Wesleyan Seminary Foundation (affiliated with Asbury Theological Seminary), Wilmore, Kentucky.

Periodicals: *The Wesleyan Advocate*, Box 2000, Marion, IN 46592; *Wesleyan World*, Box 2000, Marion, IN 46592.

Sources: Ira Ford McLeister and Roy S. Nicholson, *History of the Wesleyan Methodist Church*. Marion, IN: Wesley Press, 1959; Paul Westphal Thomas and Paul William Thomas, *The Days of Our Pilgrimage*. Marion, IN: , 1976; Martin Wells Knapp, *Holiness Triumphant or Pearls from Patmos*. Cincinnati: God's Bible School Book Room, n.d.

Twentieth Century Holiness

★243★
CALVARY HOLINESS CHURCH
3415-19 N. Second St.
Philadelphia, PA 19140

The Calvary Holiness Church is a small church formed in 1934 by four ministers of the British-based International Holiness Mission. These four men--Maynard James, Jack Ford, Clifford Filer, and most known in America, Leonard Ravenhill--had been engaged in itinerant evangelism, and congregations formed among their converts. Trouble developed because of the refusal of the International Holiness Mission to allow any speaking in tongues, those converted by the four ministering withdrew from the International Holiness Mission to form their own church.

Over the next twenty years, an aggressive program saw other congregations established, a periodical (*The Flame*) begun, a missionary program initiated in Columbia, South America, and a school opened at Uppermill England. However, financial problems after World War II led to merger talks, and in 1955 the Calvary Holiness Church merged with the Church of the Nazarene. Speaking in tongues, frowned upon by the Nazarenes, became an issue again, and a half dozen ministers refusing to join the union, continued the Calvary Holiness Church.

Membership: Not reported.

Sources: Jack Ford, *In the Steps of John Wesley; the Church of the Nazarene in Great Britian*. Kansas City, MO: Nazarene Publishing House, 1968.

★244★
CHRISTIAN PILGRIM CHURCH
Coldwater, MI 49036

The Christian Pilgrim Church was formed in 1937 by a group of holiness people, including Reverends Fannie Alldaffer, C. W. Cripps, and Tracy Alldaffer. They gathered at Coldwater, Michigan, to build a holiness church that could function without "so much law and order or machinery in the church." Officers were elected for life or as long as they remained in agreement with the Bible and the church.

The doctrine is Trinitarian and holiness (i.e., in essential agreement with the other churches discussed in this chapter). Healing is stressed but speaking in tongues is considered contrary to the Word of God; Baptism by any mode is desired; tithing is insisted upon; secret societies are condemned; Christ's imminent premillennial second coming is expected.

There is a General Assembly which meets annually. The church is divided into districts. A general superintendent has general oversight of the work and is aided by two assistants. Congregations are found in the South and Midwest.

Membership: Not reported. In the mid-1970s, the Church had 15 congregations and approximately 250 members.

Periodicals: *The Christian Voice*, Coldwater, MI 49036.

★245★
CHURCH OF THE GOSPEL
% Marion Green
20 1/2 Walnut St.
Hudson Falls, NY 12839

The Church of the Gospel was formed in 1911 in Pittsfield, Massachusetts, by the Reverend and Mrs. C. T. Pike and members of the Advent Christian Church. In 1912 the group incorporated as the Church of God but adopted its present name in 1930 to avoid confusion with other groups. Basic doctrinal perspective is drawn from the Wesleyan holiness tradition. The members practice baptism by immersion and believe in the imminent second coming. The church has distributed "Narrow Way" tracts by the thousands across the country.

Membership: Not reported. Never a large body, in the 1940s there were only four or five churches. In 1971 there was only a single congregation in Virginia and scattered remnants in New England.

★246★

CHURCHES OF CHRIST IN CHRISTIAN UNION
1427 Lancaster Pike
Circleville, OH 43113

As a result of a holiness dispute within the Christian Union (described elsewhere in this volume), those who held the holiness doctrine withdrew and in 1909 organized the Churches of Christ in Christian Union of Ohio at Washington Court House, Ohio. In 1952 the Reformed Methodist Church, an 1814 splinter from the Methodist Episcopal Church over episcopal polity, joined the Churches of Christ in Christian Union as the Northeastern District.

The Reformed Methodist Church was formed in 1814 in Readsborough, Vermont, by a group of Methodists led by Pliny Brett, a local preacher. At their first conference, February 4, 1814, they adopted the Methodist "Articles of Religion" and some democratic rules for church government. The government was essentially congregational with no sharp distinctions being made between ministers and laymen. While the Methodist system of representative conferences was kept, ministers were delegates only if elected, not ex-officio. The local church was the focus of power, having the right to ordain elders, select its own ministers, and do whatever else was necessary to carry on its work. Ministers, likewise, could pick their field of service.

Doctrine of the Churches of Christ in Christian Union is holiness in emphasis (i.e., similar to the other churches discussed in this chapter). It stresses healing and the second coming of Jesus. Polity is congregational. Spiritual officers are the pastor and the elders, and business affairs are conducted by a board of trustees. An annual general council is held. There is an active world-wide mission program.

Membership: In 1980 the Churches reported 11,943 members, 261 congregations, and 482 ministers.

Educational facilities: Mount of Praise Bible School, Circleville, OH.

Periodicals: *Advocate*, 1426 Lancaster Pike, Circleville, OH 43113; *Missionary Tidings*, 1426 Lancaster Pike, Circleville, OH 43113.

★247★

EVANGELICAL CHURCH OF NORTH AMERICA
7525 S.E. Lake Rd., Suite 7
Milwaukie, OR 97222

The Evangelical Church of North America was formed in 1968 by members of the Evangelical United Brethren who did not wish to follow the Brethren into the merger with the The Methodist Church (1939-1968) the created the United Methodist Church, described in the preceding chapter. The schism in the Evangelical United Brethren involved 50 congregations in the church's Northwest Conference and 23 churches from the Montana Conference. For several decades the Northwest Conference had been a center of holiness theology with many of the pastors being trained in the Seattle-Pacific College (of the Free Methodist Church) and the Western Evangelical Seminary (established in 1945 and firmly holiness in its doctrine and emphases).

Almost as soon as the Evangelical Church of North America was formed, the Holiness Methodist Church, with headquarters in Minneapolis, voted to join the new church, and in 1969 it became the North Central Conference of the new church. The Holiness Methodist Church was a result of the "holiness" revival movement that swept the United States in general and Methodism in particular during the late 1800s. The Northwestern Holiness Association was formed at Grand Forks, North Dakota, on March 24, 1909, as a fellowship of those following the holiness way. This informal association changed its name to the Holiness Methodist Church in 1920, recognizing that the association had become a denomination. In 1977 the small Wesleyan Covenant Church, with congregations in Detroit and in Brownsville, Texas, but an extensive Mexican Mission, merged into the Evangelical Church.

The doctrine of the Evangelical Church of North America follows the tradition of Methodism as developed within the Evangelcial United Brethren. It includes a special emphasis on entire sanctification.

The Evangelical Church of North America has seven annual conferences--the Pacific, the Eastern, the Western, the East Central, the North Central, and Canada. A council of superintendents consisting of the superintendents of the various conferences coordinates programs. The highest executive office, that of general superintendent, was created in 1976. Missions are primarily conducted through independent holiness mission agencies, but support is given to the Bolivian Mission of the former Holiness Methodist Church and the Mexican Mission of the former Wesleyan Covenant Church. The Church is a member of the National Holiness Association.

Membership: In 1984 the Church reported 16,000 members, 183 churches, and 235 ministers.

Educational facilities: Wesley Biblical Seminary, Jackson, Mississippi; Western Evangelical Seminary, Portland, Oregon; Hillcrest Christian College, Medicine Hat, Alberta, Canada.

Periodicals: *The Evangelical Excerpts*, 7525 S.E. Lake Rd., Suite 7, Milwaukie, OR 97222.

Sources: John M. Pike, *Preachers of Salvation.*

★248★

GOSPEL MISSION CORPS
Box 175
Hightstown, MD 08520

The Gospel Mission Corps was founded by Robert S. Tarton II, a graduate of the Pillar of Fire Bible Seminary of Zarephath, New Jersey. He began a mission at Hightstown, Maryland, which grew into the Gospel Mission Corps in 1962. Its doctrine is like that of the Pillar of Fire, and the ministers are nonsalaried.

Membership: Not reported. In 1972 there were seven churches, 175 members, and seven ministers.

Periodicals: *Gospel Missionary*, Box 175, Hightstown, MD 08520.

★249★

GRACE AND HOPE MISSION
45 Guy St.
Baltimore, MD 21202

The Grace and Hope Mission was founded in 1914 by Miss Marnie E. Caske and Miss Jennie E. Goranflo , who opened a gospel mission in Baltimore. The work grew so that by the late 1960s there were 14 centers, mostly in large cities. The doctrine is Wesleyan-Protestant with an emphasis on evangelism, holiness, and the hope of the second coming. The officers, all single females, wear a black uniform with red trimming and the Mission's emblem. There is an annual conference at which the assignments of officers for the coming year are made.

Membership: Not reported. In the early 1970s there were 14 centers, all in the northeast and approximately 800 members.

★250★

HOLINESS CHURCH OF GOD, INC.
% Bishop B. McKinney
602 Elm St.
Graham, NC 27253

The Holiness Church of God, Inc., is a small body established in 1920 at Madison, North Carolina, and incorporated eight years later at Winston-Salem. It holds an annual general assembly. There is a president, bishop, vice bishop and general secretary. Overseers are appointed for five areas in the South and East.

Membership: Not reported. At last report (1968) the Church had 28 churches, 36 ministers, and 927 members.

★251★

HOLINESS GOSPEL CHURCH
Rte. 2, Box 13
Etters, PA 17319

The Holiness Gospel Church was founded in 1945 by former members of the Evangelical United Brethren and the Church in God. Its theology is Wesleyan holiness. The church sponsors camp meetings and conducts a radio ministry.

Membership: Not reported. In the 1970s there were 3 congregations and 180 members.

★252★

KENTUCKY MOUNTAIN HOLINESS ASSOCIATION
Star Rte. 1, Box 350
Jackson, KY 41339

The Kentucky Mountain Holiness Association was begun in 1925 by Lela G. McConnell, a deaconness in the Methodist Episcopal Church. Following her ordination in 1924 she began a vigorous ministry in the mountains of eastern Kentucky. She preached a Wesleyan-Protestant doctrine with a strong emphasis on sanctification. The Association maintains a high school and a three-year college level Bible Institute, a radio station, and a camp ground.

Membership: In 1984 the Association reported 17 churches served by 24 ministers, evangelists, and teachers. No count on membership is made.

Educational facilities: Kentucky Mountain Bible Institute, Jackson, KY.

Sources: Lela G. McConnell, *The Pauline Ministry in the Kentucky Mountains*. Jackson, KY: The Author, 1942.

★253★

LUMBER RIVER ANNUAL CONFERENCE OF THE HOLINESS METHODIST CHURCH
% Bishop C. N. Lowry
Rowland, NC 28383

The Lumber River Annual Conference of the Holiness Methodist Church was organized in 1900 by members of the Methodist Episcopal Church, South, at Union Chapel Church, Robeson County, North Carolina. The members of the Lumber River Annual Conference had an intense interest in the holiness movement with its stress on the second blessing, a religious experience certifying holiness. At the time, the holiness movement was criticized by many Methodists, so the holiness advocates among the Conference decided to form a new church. In addition to their interest in the holiness movement was their concern for home missions.

The Church follows Wesleyan-Protestant doctrine and has adopted an episcopal polity. Some features of nineteenth-century Methodism--attendance at class meetings (regular gatherings of small classes for mutual discussion, Bible study, confession and forgiveness, and prayer) and six months' probationary membership--are retained. The itinerant ministry has been dropped.

Membership: Not reported. In the early 1970s there were 7 churches and slightly over 500 members.

★254★
MEGIDDO MISSION
478 Thurston Rd.
Rochester, NY 14619

L. T. Nichols was an independent Bible student who became a minister, believing he had discovered truths long obscured by orthodox ministers. The key truth was the responsibility of every man for his sins and the fact that "No man could be saved apart from knowing and keeping the Commandments of God." First in Oregon in 1880 and then in Minnesota in 1883, Nichols proclaimed this truth and gathered followers. He was spurred in his work by a belief, based on Bible chronology, that the end time was near. In the 1890s he conceived the idea of building a mission boat which would bring the followers together in a common home. This boat, the "Megiddo," a Mississippi River steamer, was launched in 1901 and gave the movement its name.

The boat traveled the Mississippi and Ohio Rivers and their tributaries. It was sold in 1903 and the group moved to new mission fields. In 1903 a community was established in Rochester, New York. Nichols died in 1912. He was succeeded by Maud Hembree, a former nun in the Roman Catholic Church. She developed an active mission program with several boats on the Great Lakes and began its periodical, *Megiddo Messenger*, in 1914.

The community in Rochester currently worships in a building on the church's estate and carries on an active program. From their facilities a large literature ministry is carried on throughout the whole country. Through advertisements in periodicals, a set of eleven booklets on their teachings have become a major item in their evangelistic efforts.

The crusade of the Megiddo Mission is based upon the members' belief in the imminence of the second calling. Its imminence is heralded, they say, by contemporary signs and political corruption, the craze for pleasure, universal fear, the armaments race, and the peace movement. Elijah the prophet will return to signal Christ's return as king. The judgment will lead to a revolt by all who will not acknowledge him. This revolt is the great Battle of Armageddon mentioned in the Bible. The millennium will follow the battle.

Members of the Megiddo Mission deny the Trinity. Jesus is considered God's son and the Holy Spirit is seen as a force, not a person. Man is mortal; immortality comes after a life of righteous living. There is no eternal hell, only death for the wicked. Distinctive is their belief that man did not fall in Adam, but each person is responsible only for himself. If a person follows Christ's example, he will be saved.

Membership: In 1984 two ministers served the approximate 300 members in its single congregation in Rochester. There were approximately 1000 members worldwide. More than 3,000 receive the *Megiddo Messenger*.

Periodicals: *Megiddo Messenger*, 478 Thurston Road, Rochester, NY 14619.

Sources: *History of the Megiddo Mission*. Rochester, NY: Megiddo Mission Church, 1979; *Millennium Superword*. Rochester, NY: Megiddo Mission Church, 1980; Maud Hembree, *The Known Bible and Its Defense*. Rochester, NY: The Author, 1933, 2 vols.

★255★
ORIENTAL MISSIONARY SOCIETY HOLINESS
CONFERENCE
3660 South Gramercy Place
Los Angeles, CA 90018

The Oriental Missionary Society was founded in 1901 by the Reverend Charles E. Cowman (1868-1924) and his wife, Nettie Cowman (d. 1960). Raised a Methodist, Charles E. Cowman was sanctified and was inspired to be a missionary. He felt, however, that he must go out unheralded and alone without a mission board backing his effort. In 1900 he accepted a call from God to Japan. The work in Japan was holiness based and aimed at building an indigenous church. In 1925 a mission in China was established, and then missions were established in India, Colombia, Greece, Brazil, Taiwan, Ecuador, Hong Kong, Haiti, and Indonesia.

Included in the concern of the Oriental Missionary Society were the Japanese immigrants in California. In 1920 six seminarians-- Henry T. Sakuma, George Yahiro, Paul Okamoto, Aya Okuda, Toshio Hirano, Hatsu Yano and Hanako Yoneyama--formed a prayer fellowship whose goal became the evangelization of Japanese-Americans. In 1921 they formed the Los Angeles Holiness Church. The work spread to Japanese communities throughout California, neighboring states, and Hawaii in 1932. Two years later the Oriental Missionary Society Holiness Conference of North America was formed to oversee the work of the several congregations. Though completely disrupted by the internment of Japanese during World War II, the Conference reconstituted itself at the end of the war.

Members of both the Conference and Society follow the Wesleyan- Protestant doctrine with special emphasis on holiness and entire sanctification. They believe the Holy Spirit is the witness to salvation and imparts inner assurance to the child of God. The fullness of the Spirit is the work of grace by which the believer is cleansed from sin and empowered for holy life and service. The experience is instantaneous but is followed by a process of growth in Christian maturity, Christliness, and practical Godliness. Society and Conference members believe in asking God for healing but do not believe it is always God's will to heal (Gal. 6:11, II Cor. 12: 7-9). They say the church is the body of Christ, composed of all true believers. It is built by Christ. The fractures into denominations do not split it, and union does not necessariy make it one.

The Conference is directed by an annual general conference. A nine-person executive committee implements the decisions of the annual conference.

Membership: Not reported. In the 1970s there were seven congregations in California and one in Hawaii and approximately 1,500 members.

Sources: B. H. Pearson, *The Vision Lives*. Grand Rapids, MI: Zondervan Publishing House, 1961; Lettie B. Cowman, *Charles E. Cowman, Missionary, Warrior*. Los Angeles, CA: The Oriental Missionary Society, 1939.

★256★
PILLAR OF FIRE
1302 Sherman St.
Denver, CO 80203

The existence of the Pillar of Fire is due in part to the reluctance of the Methodist Episcopal Church to allow female ministers in its churches in the late nineteenth century. Alma White, a Methodist minister's wife, began to preach both in revivals and in her husband's pulpit. Her success led to notoriety and then opposition from Methodist officials, so she began to organize her converts into independent missions modeled on the early Methodist societies within the Church of England. After initially cooperating with the Metropolitan Church Association, she incorporated the missions in 1902 as the Pentecostal Union, which gradually emerged as a body separate from the Metropolitan Church Association. The name Pillar of Fire was adopted in 1917.

The doctrine of the church is typically Wesleyan holiness. Healing is stressed, as is the immortality of the soul and premillennialism. In organization the church is episcopal, and Alma White was its first bishop. Women can occupy all ministerial roles.

During the revival of the Knights of the Ku Klux Klan in the 1920s, Mrs. White became a writer-polemicist for the Klan and even declared the Klan to be God's agent in maintaining social and racial distinctions.

Headquarters are in Zarephath, New Jersey, but Denver, Colorado (the original headquarters) functions as a second center of activity. At both locations there is a college, Bible seminary, prep school, radio station (KPOF in Denver and WAWZ in Zarephath), and a branch of Pillar of Fire Press. Other schools are located in Cincinnati, Ohio; Jacksonville , Florida; Los Angeles, California; and London, England. Mission work is conducted in Liberia. There is one congregation in England.

Upon Mrs. White's death, her two sons inherited the leadership of the Pillar of Fire. Arthur K. White became the new bishop of the Church and continues to direct its activities.

Membership: In 1980 there were 21 congregations, down from 61 in 1949.

Educational facilities: Bellview College, Westminister, Colorado; Zarephath Bible Seminary, Zarephath, New Jersey.

Periodicals: *Pillar of Fire*, Zarephath, NJ 08890; *Women's Chains*, Denver, CO; *Dry Legion*, Denver, CO.

Sources: Alma White, *The Story of My Life*. Zarephath, NJ: Pillar of Fire, 1919-34. 6 vols.; Alma White, *Guardians of Liberty*. Zarephath, NJ: Pillar of Fire, 1943. 3 vols.; Alma White, *The New Testament Church*. Zarephath, NJ: Pillar of Fire, 1929.

★257★
SANCTIFIED CHURCH OF CHRIST
2715 18th Ave.
Columbus, GA 31901

The Sanctified Church of Christ was formed in 1937 at Columbus, Georgia, by a group of former members of the Methodist Episcopal Church. The group was led by Brother E. K. Leary and Sister Jemima Bishop, and their purpose was to preserve the rich heritage of true scriptural holiness. Their doctrine was Wesleyan-Protestant with a distinct emphasis upon entire sanctification. Particular rules were made against secret oathbound societies, immodest dress such as shorts, jewelry, make-up, public and mixed bathing, women cutting their hair, television, and divorce. Members are conscientious objectors.

There is an annual conference that elects the general superintendent, secretary, treasurer, and the council of twelve members, which is the chief legislative body of the church. The council approves all candidates for the ministry.

Membership: Not reported. In the early 1970s there were 7 congregations spread across the deep south. There were approximately 1,000 members.

★258★
WESLEYAN TABERNACLE ASSOCIATION
626 Elliott Ave.
Cincinnati, OH 45215

The Wesleyan Tabernacle Association is a small holiness church. It was formed in 1936 for the purpose of promoting Christian love and fellowship among godly leaders of various undenominational bodies and to open a greater field of service for holiness evangelistic preachers and singers. The Association asserts belief in the Trinity, salvation and sanctification by God's free grace, divine healing, baptism and the Lord's Supper as ordinances, and the premillennial return of Christ. Polity is congregational. There is an annual Association Convention which elects officers to oversee publications, missions, and cooperative endeavors with like-minded groups. Women are freely admitted to the ministry. The Association supports a children's home and an extensive mission in Haiti.

Membership: Not reported. In the 1970s the Association had 26 congregations in the United States. It supports 173 ordained ministers, 53 licensed ministers, 10 song evangelists and 19 commissioned Christian workers, some of whom are under the direction of independent holiness mission agencies.

Periodicals: *The Evangel.*

Sources: *Yearbook.* N.p.: Wesleyan Tabernacle Association, 1965.

Black Holiness

★259★
ASSOCIATED CHURCHES OF CHRIST (HOLINESS)
1302 E. Adams Blvd.
Los Angeles, CA 90011

On the West Coast the Church of Christ (Holiness) U.S.A. was formed in 1915 by Bishop William Washington and work was carried on independently of the work in the east and south by the church's founder, C. P. Jones. A few years later, Jones went to Los Angeles and held a revival meeting. At that time the two men worked out an agreement for cooperative endeavor. The agreement was in effect until 1946-47. Because of what the manual of the Associated Churches of Christ (Holiness) calls the "manipulating of some administrative problems in the upper circles of the Church," the West Coast churches withdrew from the Church of Christ (Holiness) U.S.A. They now continue under the original incorporation of Bishop Washington. Doctrine and polity are identical with the Church of Christ (Holiness) U.S.A.

Membership: Not reported. In the early 1970s there were 6 churches and 1 mission in the Associated Churches.

★260★
CHURCH OF CHRIST (HOLINESS) U.S.A.
329 E. Monument St.
Jackson, MS 39202

In 1894 C. P. Jones and C. H. Mason formed the Church of God in Christ as a holiness body, following their exclusion from fellowship with black Baptists in Arkansas. Mason took most of the body into pentecostalism in 1907. Those who remained were reorganized by Jones as the Church of Christ (Holiness) U.S.A. Jones himself, residing in Jackson, Mississippi, became well known as a composer and publisher of holiness gospel songs. Doctrinally, the Church of Christ (Holiness) U.S.A. is very close to the Church of the Nazarene, with which it almost merged. It follows the Methodist Articles of Religion printed elsewhere in this volume, and stresses the second blessing of the Holy Spirit which imparts sanctification to the believer. Race issues prevented close relations between the Church of Christ (Holiness) U.S.A. and predominantly white holiness churches.

The church is episcopal in structure with a senior bishop as the highest official. There are seven dioceses. A convention held every two years is the highest legislative authority. Missionary work is sponsored in Mexico. There is a publishing house in Los Angeles. Present leader of the church is Bishop M. R. Conic.

Membership: In 1984 the Church had over 10,000 members and 170 congregations.

Educational facilities: Christ Missionary and Industrial College, Jackson, MS; Boydton Institute, Boydton, VA.

Sources: Otho B. Cobbins, *History of the Church of Christ (Holiness) U.S.A., 1895-1965.* New York: 1966; C. P. Jones, *His Fulness.* Jackson, MS: 1901; C. P. Jones, *The Story of My Songs.* Los Angeles: n.d.

★261★
CHURCH OF GOD (SANCTIFIED CHURCH)
1037 Jefferson St.
Nashville, TN 37208

In the early years of the Church of Christ (Holiness) U.S.A., discussed elsewhere in this chapter, the church existed as an unincorporated entity called the "Church of God" or the "Holiness Church." It was only after the schism over Pentecostalism in 1907 that the church was incorporated and its present name was adopted. Before the incorporation, one of the ministers, Elder Charles W. Gray, established the church in Nashville, Tennessee, and the surrounding areas. When the Church of Christ (Holiness/ U.S.A. incorporated, Gray continued his work independently as the Church of God (Sanctified Church). The doctrine was the same as that of the Church of Christ (Holiness) U.S.A., but the polity was congregational with local churches operating autonomously and appointing their own ministers. The associated churches remained unincorporated. In 1927 there arose a move within the Church of God (Sanctified Church) to incorporate and to consolidate the work under a board of elders. Among those who constituted the newly incorporated church were Elders J. L. Rucker, R. A. Manter, R. L. Martin, M. S. Sowell, B. Smith, and G. A. Whitley. The move to incorporate led to further controversy and a schism. However, under the incorporation, the elders retained the rights to direct the church, and it continues as the Church of God (Sanctified Church). Elder Gray, founder of the church, withdrew to found the Original Church of God (or Sanctified Church).

The Church of God (Sanctified Church) is headed by a general overseer. The first was Elder Rucker. He has been suceeded by Elder Theopolis Dickerson McGhee (d.1965) and Elder Jesse E. Evans. Mission work is conducted in Jamaica.

Membership: Not reported.In the early 1970s the Church reported 60 congregations, approximately 5,000 members.

★262★
**CHURCH OF UNIVERSAL TRIUMPH/THE
   DOMINION OF GOD**
% Rev. James Shaffer
8317 LaSalle Blvd.
Detroit, MI 48206

Rivaling Daddy Grace and Father Divine as charismatic leaders in the black community was the Rev. James Francis Marion Jones, better known as Prophet Jones (1908-1971). Born in Birmingham, Alabama, the son of a railroad brakeman and a school teacher, he was raised in Triumph the Church and Kingdom of God in Christ. Even as a child, he preached (he did so regularly after his eleventh birthday). In 1938 he was sent to Detroit as a missionary and became successful quickly. Tension with headquarters arose before the year was out, however, when members began to shower Jones with expensive gifts. The headquarters claimed them. Rather than surrender his new affluence, Jones left the church and founded the Church of Universal Triumph/the Dominion of God.

The new church, modeled on the parent body, was built upon Jones' charisma. During the 1940s and 1950s he became known for his wealth. He possessions included a white mink coat, a 54-room French chateau which had been built in 1917 by a General Motors executive, five Cadillacs each with its own chauffeur, jewelry, perfumes, and wardrobe of almost 500 ensembles. Jones claimed to be in direct contact with god, who instructed him in the form of a breeze fanning his ear. Among his practices was dispensing solutions to personal problems after inviting individuals to mount his dais and whisper their problems in his ear. Most of Prophet Jones' wealth came from people grateful for Jones' healing ability. Followers were to be found in all the large northern cities. Jones was titled, "His Holiness the Rev. Dr. James F. Jones, D.D.,

Universal Dominion Ruler, Internationally known as Prophet Jones."

The Church, like the parent body, is very strict. Members are not allowed to smoke, drink, play games of any kind, use coffee or tea, fraternize with non-Dominionitetry, attend another church, or marry without the consent of the ruler of the church. Women must wear girdles and men health belts. The major theological tenet concerns the beginning of the millennium in 2,000 A.D. All alive at that time will become immortal and live in the heaven on earth.

The upward path of Prophet Jones came to an abrupt end in 1956 when a vice raid on his home led to his arrest and trial for gross indecency. He was acquited, but the damage had been done and his following declined from that time. During the year prior to his death in 1971, he commuted between Detroit and Chicago. Following his death, his assistant, the Rev. Lord James Schaffer became the Dominion Ruler. He was named by the Dominion Council and Board of Trustees. Some 20 ministers and 5,000 members attended the funeral of Prophet Jones in 1971.

Membership: Not reported.

★263★
CHURCHES OF GOD, HOLINESS
170 Ashby St., N.W.
Atlanta, GA 30314

The Churches of God, Holiness, were formed by Bishop King Hezekiah Burruss (d.1963), formerly of the Church of Christ (Holiness) U.S.A. Burruss began a church in Atlanta in 1914 that belonged to that organization, and by 1920, the Atlanta congregation was large enough that it hosted the national convention of the Church of Christ (Holiness) U.S.A. Shortly after that Atlanta meeting, however, Burruss formed his own church. Doctrine is like the doctrine of the parent body.

The highest authority is the national convention. There are also annual state conventions. Practically speaking the government developed during the period of strong leadership exercised the founding bishop. The bishop appoints the state overseers who assign all pastors. The present bishop is Titus Paul Burruss.

Membership: Not reported. In 1967 there were 42 churches, 16 ministers abd 25,600 members, mostly along the East Coast.

Periodicals: *The Bethlehem Star.*

★264★

GOSPEL SPREADING CHURCH
2030 Georgia Ave., N.W.
Washington, DC 20003

The Gospel Spreading Church, sometimes called Elder Michaux Church of God or the Radio Church of God, was founded by Lightfoot Solomon Michaux (1885-1968), a minister in the Church of God (Holiness). At one point he served as the church's secretary-treasurer. However, he came into conflict with C. P. Jones, founder of the Church of God (Holiness) and left to found an independent church in Hampton, Virginia in 1922, retaining the name he had previously used, the Gospel Spreading Tabernacle Association. In 1928 he moved to Washington, D. C. and established the Church of God and Gospel Spreading Association.

His early success continued in the nation's capital, and he had discovered the potential of radio while in Virginia. In 1929 he began broadcasting on WJSV. Shortly thereafter CBS bought the station and his show expanded through the system. By 1934 he was on over 50 stations nationwide, with an estimated audience of 25,000,000. His show was also carried internationally by shortwave. He was the first black person to receive such exposure. He mixed holiness themes with positive thinking. His magazine was entitled *Happy News*.

From his radio audience, congregations began to form in black communities, primarily in the East. However, by the beginning of World War II his radio ministry had declined and he was heard only a few stations, in those cities where congregations had formed. In 1964 he reorganized his followers as the Gospel Spreading Church, but most of the congregations continued to call themselves the Church of God.

Membership: Not reported.

Sources: Lilian Ashcraft Webb, *About My Father's Business.* Westport, CT: Greenwood Press, 1981; Pauline Lark, ed. *Sparks from the Anvil of Elder Micheaux.* Washington, DC: Happy News Publishing Company, 1950.

★265★

KODESH CHURCH OF EMMANUEL
% Rev. Fred Almond
5104 Haverford Ave.
Philadelphia, PA 19131

The Kodesh Church of Emmanuel is a black holiness sect that was formed by Reverend Frank Russell Killingsworth when he withdrew from the African Methodist Episcopal Church in 1929 along with 120 followers. In common with other holiness churches, this church emphasizes entire sanctification as a second definite work of grace conditioned upon a life of absolute consecration. The church forbids use of alcohol, tobacco and prideful dress;

membership in secret societies; and profaning the Sabbath. In 1934, a merger was effected with the Christian Tabernacle Union of Pittsburgh.

The church is governed by a quadrennial general assembly. Regional assembly assemblies annually. There is mission work in Liberia.

Membership: Not reported. There are less than a dozen congregations found in and around Washington, D.C., Philadelphia and Pittsburgh.

★266★

**MOUNT CALVARY HOLY CHURCH OF
   AMERICA**
% Bishop Harold Williams
1214 Chowan St.
Durham, NC 27713

The Mt. Calvary Holy Church is a small black holiness church headquartered in Boston, Massachusetts, founded by Bishop Brumfield Johnson. Its doctrine is similar to that of the United Holy Church of America. Churches are located in North Carolina; Baltimore, Maryland; New York; Boston; and other cities on the east coast.

Membership: Not reported.

★267★

**TRIUMPH THE CHURCH AND KINGDOM OF
   GOD IN CHRIST**
Box 77056
Birmingham, AL 35228

Triumph the Church and Kingdom of God in Christ was founded by Elder E.D. Smith in 1902. The founding followed by five years a divine revelation given to Smith. According to the literature of the church, the 1902 organization of the church marked the time when the revelation was "speeded to earth." Finally, in 1904, the content of the revelation was announced. Headquarters for the church were established in Baton Rouge, Louisiana, then were moved to Birmingham, Alabama, and later to Atlanta, Georgia. The founder was in charge of the church until 1920, when he moved to Addis Ababa, Ethiopia.

The church follows the holiness beliefs common to holiness churches, but also believes in fire baptism, a spiritual experience of empowerment by the Holy Spirit. Fire baptism was first received by the Apostles in the upper room on Pentecost, when tongues of fire appeared above their heads (Acts 2). As practiced by the several nineteenth and twentieth century "fire- baptized" churches, fire baptism is similar to the pentecostal experience of the baptism of the Holy Spirit, except it is typically not accompanied by speaking in tongues. (See separate entry on the Fire-Baptized Holiness Church, Wesleyan.)

Triumph the Church and Kingdom of God in Christ holds a unique view of itself as a church in relation to Christendom, traditionally called the church militant. This view is reflected in the following passage from the church's catechism: *Question* Was their another Church in the earth before Triumph? *answer*. Yes. Church Militant; *Question* Is there any difference between the Triumph Church and Church Militant? *answer* Yes. Church Militant is a Church of warfare, and Triumph is a Church of Peace; *Question* What happened to Church Militant when Triumph was revealed? *answer* God turned it upside down and emptied His Spirit into Triumph; *Question* Is Triumph just a Church only? *answer* No. It has a Kingdom with it.

Polity is episcopal with bishops elected for life. Under the bishops is a hierarchy of state and local workers. Every four years the church holds an International Religious Congress.

Membership: Not reported. At last report (1972) there were 475 churches, 53,307 members, and 1,375 ministers.

The Glenn Griffith Movement

★268★
ALLEGHENY WESLEYAN METHODIST
   CONNECTION
2161 Woodsdale Rd.
Salem, OH 44460

The Allegheny Wesleyan Methodist Connection (originally the Allegheny Conference) was formed in 1966 by the members of the Allegheny Conference of the Wesleyan Methodist Church in eastern Ohio and western Pennsylvania. Prominent among the leaders of the new Conference was Rev. H. E. Schmul, editor of the *Convention Herald*, the periodical of the Interdenominational Holiness Convention, a conservative holiness ecumenical group wich had provided lines of communication among holiness leaders since its founding in 1947. Schmul and others were opposed to the merger of the Wesleyan Methodist Church with the Pilgrim Holiness Church to form the Wesleyan Church. As with the other conservative holiness churches, there is a strong commitment to strict standards of behavior and congregational government. The connection serves as an agency for cooperative endeavor. A missionary program is carried out among American Indians in Montana and South Dakota and in Haiti.

Membership: Not reported. In 1971 there were 98 church and 2,908 members.

Educational facilities: Northwest Indian Bible School, Alberton, Montana.

Periodicals: *Convention Herald*, Salem, OH 44460 (unofficial publication).

Sources: *Discipline of the Allegheny Wesleyan Methodist Connection.* Titusville, PA: 1970; H. C. Morrison, *Baptism with the Holy Ghost.* Salem, OH: The Alleghany Wesleyan Methodist Connection, 1978.

★269★
BIBLE HOLINESS CHURCH
Current address not obtained for this edition.

The Bible Holiness Church is a small group which separated from the Bible Methodist Connection of Tennessee. The members include a statement on healing among their beliefs, which otherwise are staunchly conservative and holiness in content.

Membership: Not reported. In 1968 there were 9 congregations and approximately 200 members in Tennessee and Virginia.

★270★
BIBLE METHODIST CONNECTION OF
   CHURCHES
Rev. George Vernon
Box 187
Brent, AL 35304

Bible Methodists in Alabama and southwestern Ohio organized in 1966 as the Bible Methodist Church and the Wesleyan Connection of Churches, respectively. In 1970 these two bodies merged to form the Bible Methodist Connection of Churches. The doctrine is conservative and holiness.

Membership: Not reported. In 1970 there were 27 churches in Alabama, 17 in Ohio, 794 members, 21 conference preachers and 48 elders.

Periodicals: *Bible Methodist*, Brent, AL.

★271★
BIBLE METHODIST CONNECTION OF
   TENNESSEE
Box 10408
Knoxville, TN 37919

Protesting both the centralization of authority and the lack of holiness for years in the Wesleyan Methodist Church was D. P. Denton, editor of the *Evangelist of Truth*, an independent monthly out of Knoxvillle, Tennessee. On October 17, 1966, Denton led a meeting in Knoxville with represenatatives of the various factions opposed to the merger of the Wesleyan Methodist Church and the Pilgrim Holiness Church into the Wesleyan Church, a merger finally effected in 1967. At the Knoxville meeting, representatives opposed to merger decided to organize a new "connection," a new association of churches. The new group would continue the use of Wesleyan Methodist *Discipline* (a book of church order), with the exception that each church would be completely autonomous. The new connection would be formed as the merger was consummated. After the negotiations were completed and those who stayed out of the merger settled on the price of buying their property from the new Wesleyan Church, three new bodies emerged: the Bible Methodist Connection of Tennessee, the Bible Holiness Church, and the Bible Methodist Connection of Churches.

From the former Wesleyan Methodist Church, the members of the Tennessee Conference led by Denton became the Bible Methodist Connection of Tennessee. Denton was elected president. The former Conference paper, *Tennessee Tidings*, became the new church's organ. A campground outside of Knoxville serves the church. The *Evangelist of Truth* continues as an independent monthly.

Membership: Not reported. In 1970 there were 19 churches, 136 members, and 28 ministers.

Periodicals: *Tennessee Tidings*.

★272★
BIBLE MISSIONARY CHURCH
822 S. Simms
Denver, CO 80211

Following the successful revival led by Church of the Nazarene minister, Rev. Glenn Griffith near Nampa, Idaho, the group of conservative holiness people attracted to Griffith's message were organized into the Bible Missionary Union. Word of the action spread quickly and within ten months congregations of like minded people had been established in twenty states. Joining Griffith were J. E. Cook, Spencer Johnson, and H. B. Huffman. The first general conference of the church was held in Denver in 1956, at which the present name was selected. Membership in the church has been augmented by the failure in 1956 of conservatives to have the Nazarene Council Assembly condemn television.

Like its parent, the Church of the Nazarene, doctrine is Wesleyan with an emphasi s on holiness. Entire sanctification, as freedom from original sin and a state of entire devotion to God, is stressed. The future life, heaven and hell, and the premillennial return of Jesus are also central beliefs. The church is understood as "composed of all spiritually regenerated persons whose names are written in heaven." The general rules have also been expanded with the addition of much detail on points of behavior. The difference between the Bible Missionary Church and the parent body, the Church of the Nazarene, is primarily on strictness of personal holiness regulations. The Church has endorsed the King James Version of the Bible for use in its churches and has gone on record against modern versions of the Bible, especially the Revised Standard Version, the Living Bible, the New English Translation, the Readers' Digest Condensed Version, and the New International Version.

The Church is headed by two general moderators who preside over the general conference, the highest law making body for the church. Foreign mission work is supported in Guyana, Venezuela, St. Vincent (West Indies), Canada, Nigeria, Honduras, Japan, the Philippines, Papua New Guinea, Barbados, and Mexico; a home mission project is on the Navaho Reservation at Farmington, New Mexico. A children's home is operated in Beulah Heights, Kentucky.

Membership: Not reported. There are 14 district conferences overseeing churches across the United States.

Educational facilities: Bible Missionary Institute, Rock Island, IL.

Periodicals: *The Missionary Revivalist*, 822 S. Simms, Denver, CO 80211

Sources: *Manual*. Rock Island, IL: Bible Missionary Church, periodically revised; Mrs. Roy Keene, *"Love-Threads Reaching"*. (Rock Island, IL): Bible Missionary Church, 1979; J. E. Cook, *W. M. Tidwell (A Life that Counted)*. Ann Arbor, MI: Mallory Lithographing, Inc., n.d.

★273★
CHURCH OF THE BIBLE COVENANT
Rte. 8, Box 214
450 N. Fortville Pike
Greenfield, IN 46140

In 1966 four Indiana-based ministers of the Church of the Nazarene (Marvin Powers, Amos Hann, Donald Hicks, and Granville Rogers) formed a steering committee that led to the establishment of the Church of the Bible Covenant the following year at the John T. Hatfield Campground near Cleveland, Indiana. The four invited their former district superintendent, Remiss Rehfeldt, to join them. On August 10, 1967, the new church elected Rehfeldt and Powers as general presiding officers. Those who gathered for that meeting then spread across the country under the leadership of twelve regional presiding officers to develop local congregations.

The Church's doctrine follows essentially that of the Wesleyan-Protestant tradition, with a strong emphasis on holiness and a high code of ethical standards. A general convention meets quadrennially, during which time elections are held and legislation considered. In 1982 Rehfeldt retired and was granted emeritus status. Donald Hicks was elected as new general presiding officer.

Membership: In 1984 the church reported 90 churches in the United States and 75 churches and preaching points overseas. Total membership was 2,000 but approximately 4,000 attended church school each Sunday.

Educational facilities: Covenant Foundation College, Greenfield, Indiana. The church maintains three Bible-training institutions overseas.

Periodicals: *The Covenanter*, New Castle, Indiana 47352.

Sources: *Articles*. Knightsville, IN: Church of the Bible Covenant, 1970.

★274★
EVANGELICAL WESLEYAN CHURCH
Grand Island, NE 68801

The Evangelical Wesleyan Church was formed in 1963 by the merger of the Evangelical Wesleyan Church of North America and the Midwest Holiness Association, both churches composed of members who had left the Free Methodist Church. The Evangelical Wesleyan Church of North America was organized at a convention held near Centerville, Crawford County, Pennsylvania, with a dedication to restore old-time Free Methodism. (The members sought a stricter interpretatin of personal moral codes; e.g., they were concerned about women's hair styles, makeup, and the length of dresses.) The Midwest Holiness Association was formed in 1962 as a protest against worldliness and apostasy in the Free Methodist Church. The organizing convention of the Midwest Holiness Association was held in Ansley, Nebraska. The Evangelical Wesleyan Church is set against the compromise of old doctrines and standards of Free Methodism and follows its patterns.

Membership: Not reported. Membership is concentrated in Nebraska, Pennsylvania, and New York.

Educational facilities: Adirondack Bible College, Northville, New York; John Fletcher Bible College, Kearney, Nebraska.

Periodicals: *The Ernest Christian*, Grand Island, NE 68801.

★275★
GOD'S MISSIONARY CHURCH
% Rev. Paul Miller
Swengal, PA 17880

God's Missionary Church is one of the older conservative holiness bodies. It was formed in 1935 as a result of a dispute in the Pennsylvania and New Jersey District of the Pilgrim Holiness Church.

It has become a conservative body, very strict in discipline. It is also opposed to participation in war, somewhat reflective of the Quaker influence in the founding of the Pilgrim Holiness Church. The church is congregational, but headed by a general superintendent. There is missionary work in Haiti and among Cuban refugees in

Florida. It cooperates with the Interdenominational Holiness Convention.

Membership: Not reported. In 1971 there were 595 members, 532 of which resided in Pennsylvania.

Educational facilities: Penn View Bible Institute, Penns Creek, PA.

Periodicals: *God's Missionary Standard*.

Sources: *Official Handbook and Discipline*. Watsontown, PA: God's Missionary Church, 1971.

★276★
LOWER LIGHTS CHURCH
Ann Arbor, MI

The Lower Lights Church was formed in 1940 as a single congregation (the Lower Light Mission) in Ann Arbor, Michigan. It subsequently branched out to neighboring communities and now cooperates with the Interdenominational Holiness Convention.

Membership: Not reported. There are several congregations in Michigan and Ohio with several hundred members.

★277★
NATIONAL ASSOCIATION OF HOLINESS
   CHURCHES
% Rev. Dale L. Hallaway, General Secretary
60 Averyville Rd.
Lake Placid, NY 12946

The National Association of Holiness Churches was formed in the 1970s. H. Robb French (1891-1985), a former pastor in the Wesleyan Methodist Church and one of the founders of the Interdenominational Holiness Convention, was the chief moving force in its founding and early development. He was the first general chairman, a post held until his retirement in 1973. The Association exists as a loose confederation of independent ministers and churches formed for purposes of promoting holiness and providing fellowship. An annual camp meeting and association general conference is held in July. Missionary work is supported in Mexico. The bible college supports work in the Bahamas, Haiti, Taiwan, and the Turks and Caicos Islands.

Membership: Not reported. Many of the ministers and churches affiliated with the Association are also affiliated with other conservative holiness church bodies.

Educational facilities: Hobe Sound Bible College, Hobe Sound, Florida; Aldersgate School of Religion, Hobe Sound, Florida.

Periodicals: *The NAHC Bulletin*, Box 1065, Hobe Sound, FL 33455.

★278★
PILGRIM HOLINESS CHURCH OF NEW YORK
32 Cadillac Ave.
Albany, NY 12205

The Pilgrim Holiness Church of New York traces its history to the Pentecostal Rescue Mission organized in 1897 in Binghamton, New York. In 1922 that Mission affiliated as an autonomous district with the International Holiness Church which the following year took the name Pilgrim Holiness Church. During the 1960s the Pilgrim Holiness Church began a process of centralizing authority in the national headquarters and preparing for merger with the Wesleyan Methodist Church (a merger which was completed in 1968 with the creation of the Wesleyan Church). In 1963, asserting its autonomous status, the New York Conference left the Pilgrim Holiness Church and has continued as an independent organization.

The Church is very conservative in doctrine and strict in practice, as are those churches which are affiliated with the Interdenominational Holiness Convention. Missions are directly supported in Brazil, Haiti, and Winnepeg, Manitoba, Canada and other locations through various missionary agencies. Churches are located in New York, New Jersey, Ohio, Pennsylvania, and Massachusetts.

Membership: In 1984 the Church reported 1,100 members, 56 churches, and 101 ministers.

Educational facilities: The Church has no school of its own, but financially supports and recommends God's Bible School, Cincinnati, Ohio; Hobe Sound Bible School, Hobe Sound, Florida (sponsored by the National Association of Holiness Churches); and Penn View Bible Institute, Penns Creek, Pennsylvania (sponsored by God's Missionary Church).

Periodicals: *Pilgrim News*, 32 Cadillac Ave., Albany, NY 12205.

★279★
PILGRIM HOLINESS CHURCH OF THE MIDWEST
Current address not obtained for this edition.

The Pilgrim Holiness Church of the Midwest was formed in 1970. Three years earlier ten congregations affiliated with the Pilgrim Holiness Church had withdrawn to become the Midwest Conference of the Pilgrim Holiness Church of New York. But the ten congregations eventually decided to remain independent, though they have stayed friendly with the New York group. They adopted their own *Discipline* (a book of church order). Mission work is through the Evangelical Faith Missions and Evangelical Bible Missions.

Membership: Not reported. In 1969 there were 13 churches and 246 members.

★280★
UNITED HOLINESS CHURCH OF NORTH AMERICA
Cedar Springs, MI 49319

The United Holiness Church of North America was formed in 1955 by conservatives within the Free Methodist Church at a camp meeting at Carson City, Michigan. Headquarters are at the Bible College at Cedar. It resembles its parent body, but is more strict in its standards of holiness. The Church cooperates with the Interdenominational Holiness Convention.

Membership: Not reported.

Educational facilities: Jordan College, Cedar Springs, MI.

Periodicals: *United Holiness Sentinel*, Cedar Springs, MI 49319.

★281★
VOICE OF THE NAZARENE ASSOCIATION OF CHURCHES
Box 1
Finleyville, PA 15332

One focus within the Church of the Nazarene of the post-World II conservative holiness movement was a magazine, *The Voice of the Nazarene*, published at Finleyville, Pennsylvania by W. L. King. Following the 1956 decision in the Church of the Nazarene in favor of television, some groups in the East against watching television associated with King. They formed the Voice of the Nazarene Association of Churches. It is a loosely congregational organization. The literature from the Finleyville headquarters has been characterized by its extreme conservatism, politically as well as religiously. It is strongly opposed to Communism, the National Council of Churches, and the Roman Catholic Church.

Membership: Not reported. In 1967 there were 8 members congregations (plus 18 cooperating congregations) and 31 Association evangelists.

Periodicals: *Universal Challenger*, Finleyville, PA 15322; *Voice of the Nazarene*, Finleyville, PA 15322.

★282★
WESLEYAN HOLINESS ASSOCIATION OF CHURCHES
108 Carter
Dayton, OH 45405

After only four years with the Bible Missionary Church, Rev. Glenn Griffith left it in protest of its alleged compromise of receiving divorced persons as members and/or ministers. Then, at Muncie, Indiana, he and his followers organized the Wesleyan Holiness Association of Churches. At the first general conference at Colorado Springs, Glenn Griffith was elected general moderator (now general superintendent). Polity is congregational. Small in size, the Association is affiliated with the Interdenominational Holiness Convention.

Membership: Not reported.

Educational facilities: Wesleyan Holiness College, Phoenix, AZ.

Sources: *Declaration of Principles*. Phoenix, AZ: Wesleyan Holiness Association of Churches, 1969; Glenn Griffith, *I Sought a Man*. Phoenix, AZ: The Author, n.d.

Pentecostal Family

An historical essay on this family is provided beginning on page 39.

White Trinitarian Holiness Pentecostal

★283★
THE APOSTOLIC FAITH
6615 S.E. 52nd Ave.
Portland, OR 97206

Among those receiving the baptism of the Holy Spirit during the early Pentecostal revival meetings at the Pacific Apostolic Faith Movement's mission on Azusa Street in Los Angeles was Florence L. Crawford, a Methodist laywoman. At her baptism in the Spirit, she related that God "permitted me to speak in the Chinese tongue which was understood by a Christian Chinese who was present." She also experienced a healing of her eyes, which had been damaged by spinal meningitis. Crawford became an active worker, assisting Mission leader W. J. Seymour. Her first ministries were along the West Coast where she worked as an itinerant home missionary. In Portland, Oregon, the people were so taken with her ministry that the pastor of a little independent church turned the pulpit over to her permanently. She immediately discontinued taking offerings at meetings and began to rely solely on tithes and free-will gifts. She also broke with Seymour, but continued to use the name Apostolic Faith, claiming as her heritage the work begun by Rev. Charles Parham and Seymour. She began to travel under her own sponsorship throughout the West and into the Midwest and Canada. In 1908, having brought the mailing list of the Mission with her, she distributed the first issue of a new periodical, *The Apostolic Faith*. Portland was established as headquarters of the growing movement. In 1922, the large headquarters building, a landmark in downtown Portland, was erected and a large neon sign saying "Jesus the Light of the World," first erected in 1917, was transferred to the new structure.

Following Seymour's teachings, Crawford preached a holiness doctrine like that of the Church of God (Cleveland, Tennessee). Her followers practice a very strict moral code, keeping from worldliness and refraining from being "unequally yoked" in marriage with unbelievers. Footwashing as a third ordinance joins baptism and the Lord's Supper.

The church is governed by a board of five trustees headed by a general overseer. There is also a board of twenty-four elders. The polity is presbyterian and each local congregation is under the leadership and direction of the Portland headquarters. Both home and foreign missions have emerged on a large scale, with work in 21 countries in Africa, Asia, and Europe. Camp meetings remain a central feature of the program, and there are denominational campgrounds in Portland, Oregon; Murfrysboro, Illinois; and Century, Florida.

Membership: In 1984 the Church reported 4,100 members in 45 congregations and 75 ministers. The overseas membership greatly exceeds that in the United States.

Periodicals: *The Light of Hope*, 6615 S.E. 52nd Avenue, Portland, OR 97206.

Sources: *A Historical Account of the Apostolic Faith.* Portland, OR: Apostolic Faith Publishing House, 1965; *The Light of Life Brought Triumph.* Portland, OR: Apostolic Faith Publishing House, 1955; *Saved to Serve.* Portland, OR: Apostolic Faith Publishing House, 1967.

★284★
CAROLINA EVANGELISTIC ASSOCIATION
200 Tuckaseegee Rd.
Charlotte, NC 28208

Dr. A. G. Garr was the first foreign missionary of the Church of God (Cleveland, Tennessee). He left the church in 1906, immediately after receiving the baptism of the Holy Spirit. He continued to do foreign missionary work until 1912, when he returned to the United States and began to operate as an evangelist in the days when Pentecostals were still a small, scattered group. He was particularly active in the early years of the Angelus Temple, the Los Angeles center for the International Church of the Foursquare Gospel headed by Aimee

Semple McPherson. In 1930, he went to Charlotte, North Carolina, to conduct a tent revival. After three months, those who had been saved, healed, and helped asked him to remain. Fifty-six years old then, he remained and built a tabernacle. An abandoned city auditorium was bought, remodeled, and named Garr Auditorium; it remains as the headquarters of the association. Dr. Garr died in 1944 and was succeeded by his wife and son as pastors.

The Carolina Evangelistic Association carries on an active program through Garr Auditorium and Faith Chapel, both in Charlotte. There are missionaries supported by the Association in numerous countries. A regular program of services is conducted in the county jail and the county home. The "Morning Thought for the Day Magazine" radio show is their radio ministry. Camp Lurecrest for youth is located at Lake Lure, North Carolina. The church is a member of the Pentecostal Fellowship of North America.

Membership: Not reported. Approximately 1,000 people regularly attend worship at Garr Auditorium.

★285★
CHURCH OF GOD (CLEVELAND, TENNESSEE)
Keith St. at 25th St., N.W.
Cleveland, TN 37311

Most of the Pentecostal churches which bear the name "Church of God" can be traced to a holiness revival in the mountains of northwest Georgia and eastern Tennessee. In 1884, R. G. Spurling, a Baptist minister in Monroe County, Tennessee, began to search the Scriptures for answers to the problems of modernism, formality, and spiritual dryness. An initial meeting of concerned people was held on August 19, 1886, at the Barney Creek Meeting House to organize a new movement that would preach primitive church holiness and provide for reform and revival of the churches. Christian Union was the name accepted by the first eight members enrolled that day. Spurling died within a few months and was succeeded in leadership by his son, R. G. Spurling, Jr.

After ten years of little growth, three laymen influenced by the Spurlings' work claimed a deep religious experience similar to that written about by John Wesley, the founder of Methodism, and as a result began to preach sanctification. (Wesley attended a service at Aldersgate Street in London in 1738 where he "felt his heart strangely warmed." He and his followers interpreted this as a work of God which again sanctified the person who had already experienced a justifying faith in Christ). The three laymen began to hold services at Camp Creek, in Cherokee County, North Carolina, among a group of unaffiliated Baptists. Spurling and the Christian Union moved their services to Camp Creek and united with the group in North Carolina. During the revival that followed this merger, spontaneous speaking in tongues occurred. After searching the Scriptures, the group recognized the

phenomena as a Biblical occurrence and as a new outpouring of the Holy Spirit.

The Christian Union, as it grew, suffered from both persecution and fanaticism: as its unrestrained members spoke in tongues and held noisy services, various members of the local community complained. Some leaders of the Christian Union, responding to the criticism, decided to make the services more orderly. They devised a simple plan of government at a meeting in the home of W. F. Bryant. The group's name was changed to the Holiness Church. In 1896, during the revival, Ambrose J. Tomlinson, an Indiana Quaker and agent of the American Bible Society, came to the hill country to sell Bibles and religious literature. In 1903, he cast his lot with the group and became pastor of the Camp Creek Church. This event can be viewed as the real beginning of the Church of God movement. Having been influenced by the Church of God (Anderson, Indiana), Tomlinson persuaded the Holiness Church to accept the Biblical name the Church of God. He is also the probable source for the pacifist emphasis which permeates many Pentecostal churches. Tomlinson began a publishing enterprise and printed for distribution the doctrines of the new church. Headquarters were soon established in his home at Culbertson, Tennessee, and he emerged as the dominant leader. Tomlinson later settled in Cleveland, Tennessee, and eventually led a congregation there to unite with the Holiness Church. The church's period of expansion had begun.

With the establishment of further congregations, the members saw the necessity of an assembly for dealing with questions of mutual concern. The first assembly convened in 1906 at Camp Creek and decisions were made about footwashing--it was to be observed at least annually. Mid-week family services were to be encouraged. At the 1907 assembly, the name was officially changed to the Church of God.

The 1908 assembly was attended by G. B. Cashwell, who was to introduce many holiness people to the baptism of the Holy Spirit and the experience of speaking in tongues which had occurred at the mission of the Pacific Apostolic Faith Movement on Azusa Street in Los Angeles. After the assembly, he preached a revival. Tomlinson received the baptism and spoke in tongues. The following year, in a gesture symbolic of the church's acceptance of the new truth preached by Cashwell and experienced by Tomlinson, he was selected general moderator of the young church, a position he held until 1922. In 1914, he was elected general overseer for life. Accelerated growth, with the exception of losses of schismatic bodies, has continued unabated.

Doctrinally, the Church of God believes in the baptism of the Holy Spirit as an experience subsequent to sanctification. Practices include baptism by immersion, the Lord's Supper, and footwashing. Members believe in holiness-of-life, which excludes the use of cosmetics, costly apparel, and shorts or slacks on women. They accept a premillennial second coming (the coming of Christ to bind Satan before Christ's thousand-year reign on earth with his saints).

Government of the Church of God is centralized. Authority is vested in the general assembly, which meets every two years and is chaired by the general overseer. A supreme council operates between general assemblies, and a general executive committee oversees the boards and agencies. State overseers have charge over the churches in their areas and appoint the pastors. Tithing is a central feature in finances. The height of centralization came in 1914 when the annual elections of the general overseer were discontinued and Tomlinson became overseer for life.

Tomlinson's authority was attacked in the 1920s. In 1922, a committee ordered to investigate the church's finances (which Tomlinson completely controlled) reported unfavorably, and Tomlinson was impeached and removed from office. The overseer's authority had been reduced earlier by the addition of two new offices to control functions previously controlled by Tomlinson (publishing and education). These were supplemented in 1922 by the new constitution, adopted despite Tomlinson's opposition.

The Church of God Publishing House produces a large selection of books, pamphlets and tracts, and a full line of church school material. Missions, both foreign and domestic, are widespread (in seventy-two countries) and supported by the tithe of members. The Church is a member of the National Association of Evangelicals.

Membership: In 1982 the Church reported 463,992 members, 5,284 churches, and 10,985 ministers.

Educational facilities: Lee College, Cleveland, Tennessee; Northwest Bible and Music Academy, Minot, North Dakota; West Coast Bible School, Pasadena, California.

Periodicals: *Church of God Evangel*, Church of God Publishing House, 1080 Montgomery Avenue, Cleveland, TN 37311; *Lighted Pathway*, Church of God Publishing House, 1080 Montgomery Avenue, Cleveland, TN 37311.

Sources: Charles W. Conn, *Like a Mighty Army*. Cleveland, TN: Church of God Publishing House, 1955; Charles W. Conn, *Pillars of Pentecost*. Cleveland, TN: Pathway Press, 1956; James L. Slay, *This We Believe*. Cleveland, TN: Pathway Press, 1963; Ray H. Hughes, *Church of God Distinctives*. Cleveland, TN: Pathway Press, 1968; June Glover Marshall, *A Biographical Sketch of Richard G. Spurling, Jr.* Cleveland, TN: Pathway Press, 1974.

★286★
CHURCH OF GOD (JERUSALEM ACRES)
% John A. Looper, Chief Bishop
Box 1207
1826 Dalton Pike (Jerusalem Acres)
Cleveland, TN 37311

The Church of God (Jerusalem Acres) began in 1957 when Grady R. Kent initiated a "reformation" of the Church of God of Prophecy aimed at a reestablishment of its "biblical order." Kent had been a pastor in the Church since 1933. In 1943 he was placed in charge of the Church of God of Prophecy Marker Association begun by A. J. Tomlinson, the church's founder, as an auxiliary to locate, mark, beautify, and maintain prominent places in the world connected with the Church of God of Prophecy. One place of particular interest was the Fields of the Wood-a mountainside Bible monument, based on Psalms 132:6 and Habakkuk 2:2-3, located on Berger Mountain in western North Carolina. The monument includes a replica of the Ten Commandments in seven foot-tall letters and an altar on the top of the mountain. The altar marks the spot where A. J. Tomlinson prayed, received the gift of tongues, and declared the Church of God to be in existence. Kent also supervised the White Angel Fleet, pilots and airplanes used for public demonstrations of public ministry at airports throughout the United States. Between 1948 and 1957, Kent objected to the Church of God of Prophecy replacing the general overseer with the general assembly as the highest authority in the church (which in effect, repeated the history of the Church that led to the formation of the Church of God of Prophecy in the early 1920s). Faced with having to recant his objection to the actions of the general assembly, as well as other controversial ideas he had developed, Kent resigned in 1957. With 300 supporters, many from South Carolina, Kent established a new Church of God, with himself as general overseer.

The doctrine of the Church of God of Prophecy is followed to a large extent. The church leads members into an experiential understanding of justification by faith, sanctification as a second work of grace, and the baptism of the Holy Spirit evidenced by speaking in tongues. It also believes in the restoration of both ministerial (Ephesians 4:11) and spiritual (I Corinthians 12) gifts to the Church.

In areas of worship and service, the church has developed a comprehensive program termed "New Testament Judaism," a term coined by Kent in 1962 on a visit to Israel. The Church observes the Biblical (Old Testament) calendar that includes the sabbath as a day of worship , Passover as a time for celebrating the communion, Pentecost as a festival for spiritual renewal and dedication to the work of the church, and Tabernacles (observed on December 25) as a remembrance of the time of Christ's birth and a foreshadowing of His return. Various symbols generally associated with Judaism are used alongside of the cross. The church also rejects the "pagan" holidays of Easter, Halloween, and Christmas. The Lord's Supper is practiced thrice annually, at Passover and two other times. Missing three straight celebrations of the Lord's Supper is grounds for disfellowshipping. Wine is used in the communion.

The polity is theocratic, government by God through an annointed leader. There is a chief bishop who sits as the final authority (as contrasted to the total authority) in matters of both judicial and executive government. The church has no legislative body, but has a Council of Apostles and Elders, the purpose of which is judicial--that is, to interpret the laws of God in the Bible, both Old and New Testaments, as they relate to the church. The primary officers in the Council are the chief bishop, the twelve apostles, the seven men of wisdom, and the seventy elders.

Membership: In 1984 the church reported 23 churches, 3 missions and 92 ministers. Membership was unknown.

Periodicals: *The Vision Speaks*, Jerusalem Acres, Cleveland, TN 37311.

Sources: John D. Garr, *The Lost Legacy.----. Manual of Apostles Doctrine and Business Procedure, The Church of God.* Cleveland, TN; The Church Publishing Company and Press, n.d.; Grady R. Kent, *Treatise on the 1957 Reformation Stand.* Cleveland, TN: Church Publishing Company, The Church of God, n.d.

**★287★
CHURCH OF GOD OF PROPHECY**
Bible Place
Cleveland, TN 37311

The problems which led to the withdrawal from the Church of God (Cleveland, Tennessee) of A. J. Tomlinson in 1922 are described quite differently by the two sides. According to A. J.'s son, Homer Tomlinson, the occasion for the schism was the desire of some church leaders to organize a "Golden Rule Supply Company" to operate as a co-op for church members, and to use the profits to support the missions. Reportedly, the Rev. Joe S. Lewellyn and others interested in the project were beginning a campaign against Tomlinson which undermined his support and confidence in his leadership. In any case, A. J. Tomlinson strongly objected to the reorganization of the Church of God in 1921 which stripped him of some of his previous powers as general overseer. Following the vote of the general assembly to remove him from office, Tomlinson began again and started the Church of God anew, following the church order adopted in 1914, with himself as general overseer. There were no doctrinal changes. Tomlinson established a new tabernacle in Cleveland, Tennessee, and continued to work with his followers. After a court fight, the name Tomlinson Church of God was adopted. That name was changed to Church of God of Prophecy in 1952.

After A. J. Tomlinson's death and an internal controversy over succession, Milton A. Tomlinson became general overseer. Under his leadership the Church has been rebuilt into a substantial national organization. Missions are supported in over 40 countries on every continent and include many European countries. White Wing Publishing House publishes numerous books and a variety of Christian literature (in several languages), including a full line of church school materials.

Membership: In 1983 the Church reported 74,385 members, 4,567 churches, and 7,495 ministers. Membership worldwide was 214,966.

Educational facilities: Tomlinson College, Cleveland, Tennessee.

Periodicals: *White Wing Messenger*, Bible Place, Cleveland, TN 37311; *Happy Harvester*, Bible Place, Cleveland, TN 37311.

Sources: Harry Lee Moore, ed. *Memoirs of Our Ministry.* Cleveland, TN: The White Wing Publishing House and Press, 1975; James Stone, *The Church of God of Prophecy, History and Polity.* Cleveland, TN: White Wing Publishing House and Press, 1977; Raymond M. Pruitt, *Fundamentals of the Faith.* Cleveland, TN: White Wing Publishing House and Press, 1981; M. A. Tomlinson, *Basic Bible Beliefs.* Cleveland, TN: White Wine Publishing House and Press, 1961; Lillie Dugger, *A. J. Tomlinson.* Cleveland, TN: White Wing Publishing House, 1964.

**★288★
CHURCH OF GOD OF THE APOSTOLIC FAITH**
2530 W. Cameron
Tulsa, OK 74127

The Church of God of the Apostolic Faith was organized in 1914 by four independent Pentecostal ministers who saw the need for some organization and church government. Not wishing to follow the plan of government adopted by the Assemblies of God, which had been formed that year in nearby Hot Springs, Arkansas, the Reverends James O. McKenzie, Edwin A. Buckles, Oscar H. Myers, and Joseph P. Rhoades held a meeting which led to the creation of the Church of God of the Apostolic Faith at Cross Roads Mission near Ozark, Arkansas. They adopted a presbyterial form of government based on Acts 15. The Church also had a doctrinal difference with the Assemblies of God, believing as did the Church of God (Cleveland, Tennessee) that one must seek sanctification before having the baptism of the Holy Spirit. Like the Church of God, healing, tithing, and nonparticipation in war are emphasized.

The general conference of the Church meets annually. It elects the general presbytery of seven ministers, including the general overseer and two assistants. The conference owns all the property and the presbytery controls the ministry. The church is currently divided into five districts. There is a mission in Mexico.

Membership: Not reported. In the mid-1970s there were approximately 1,400 members in 27 congregations.

Periodicals: *Church of God Herald*, 2530 West Cameron, Tulsa, OK 74124; *Christian Youth*, 2530 West Cameron, Tulsa, OK 74124.

★289★
CHURCH OF GOD OF THE MOUNTAIN
  ASSEMBLY
Jellico, TN 37762

The Church of God of the Mountain Assembly grew out of a holiness revival in 1895 in the South Union Association of the United Baptist Church. From 1895 until 1903, members and ministers who adopted the holiness belief in a second work of grace which imparts sanctification by the power of the Holy Spirit, remained within the United Baptist Church. However, in 1903, the Baptists decided to revoke the licenses of all ministers who were preaching sanctification according to the holiness movement. In 1906, these holiness ministers-- Reverends J. H. Parks, Steve Bryant, Tom Moses, and William O. Douglas--met at Jellico, Tennessee, with members of their several churches and organized the Church of God. The words "Mountain Assembly" were added in 1911 after the group heard of other Church of God groups. In 1906-07, the group learned of the baptism of the Holy Spirit as evidenced by speaking in tongues and accepted it as a fuller expression of their ideas. At the second assembly in 1907, S. N. Bryant was elected moderator, a post he held until 1938, except for two years.

The doctrine of the Church of God of the Mountain Assembly is similar to that of the Church of God (Cleveland, Tennessee). The Church is very conservative in its faith, and only the King James Version of the Bible is used. Present polity was adopted in 1914. The offices of general overseer, assistant overseer, and state overseer were established and filled. The overseers operate in a basically congregational system. The assembly meets annually. From its headquarters in Jellico, Tennessee the Church of God of the Mountain Assembly has spread throughout the South and into the Midwest as far as Ohio, Michigan, and Wisconsin.

Membership: Not reported.

Periodicals: *Gospel Herald*, Jellico, TN.

Sources: Luther Gibson, *History of the Church of God Mountain Assembly*. The Author, 1954.

★290★
CHURCH OF GOD OF THE ORIGINAL
  MOUNTAIN ASSEMBLY
Williamsburg, KY 40769

In 1939 Steve N. Bryant, longtime leader of the Church of God of the Mountain Assembly died. He was succeeded by A. J. Long, who led the Church in a reorganization in 1944. However, in 1946, Long was not reelected as moderator. That same year, with his supporters, he left and founded the Church of God of the Original Mountain Assembly. Approximately one fourth of the membership (fifteen ministers, eight deacons, and approximately 300 people) established the new church on the original structure of the parent body. The church is headed by a general overseer and a council of twelve. The first meeting of the Church of God of the Original Mountain Assembly was held at Williamsburg, Kentucky. The doctrine of the parent body was adopted, from the covenant originally made when it was incorporated in 1917, but articles were added on the need for harmony between pastors and deacons (lay leaders), the subordinate role of women and opposition to snake handling.

Membership: Not reported. In 1967 there were 11 churches and 17 ministers.

★291★
CHURCH OF GOD OF THE UNION ASSEMBLY
Box 1323
Dalton, GA 30720

The Church of God of the Union Assembly is a small schism formed in 1920 from the Church of God of the Mountain Assembly. It began when the congregation in Center, Jackson County, Georgia withdrew. The immediate occasion for the split was the issue of tithing. The Union Assembly rejects the tithing system established in 1919 by the Mountain Assembly, believing it to be an Old Testament practice not taught by Jesus or his apostles. The group also believes the kingdom of God is a spiritual kingdom; that David's throne is established in heaven, not on earth; and that Christ's coming will be followed by the end of time, not the millennium (Christ's reign on earth for 1,000 years with his saints). The Union Assembly's present leader is Jesse Pratt, who has written a number of pamphlets disseminated through the church. Congregations have spread to seventeen states.

Membership: Not reported.

Periodicals: *Quarterly News*, Box 1323, Dalton, GA 30720.

★292★
CHURCH OF GOD, THE HOUSE OF PRAYER
% Rev. Charles Mackenin
Markleysburg, PA 15459

Harrison W. Poteat joined the Church of God (Cleveland, Tennessee) in its early years and was an overseer in the Northeast for more than twenty years. In 1933, he established churches on Prince Edward Island. In 1939, he broke with the Cleveland headquarters and founded the Church of God, the House of Prayer. Many of the churches which Poteat had established went with him. A suit was brought by the parent body, which was able to recover occupancy in many of the church properties, and the loss of the property cut deeply into Poteat's support. Some congregations withdrew from the Church of God, the House of Prayer, and became independent. Doctrine follows that of the parent body.

Membership: Not reported. In 1967 the church reported 24 churches in the northeast and 2 in Canada, with a total membership of 1,200.

★293★
CHURCH OF GOD (WORLD HEADQUARTERS)
% Voy M. Bullen, General Overseer
2504 Arrowwood Dr., S.E.
Huntsville, AL 35803

A. J. Tomlinson, founder of the Church of God (Cleveland, Tennessee) and the Church of God of Prophecy died in 1943. His eldest son, Homer Tomlinson claimed that his father had appointed him his successor. However, the General Assembly set aside that appointment and selected the younger son, Milton A. Tomlinson as the new general overseer. Homer Tomlinson rejected their action, called his followers to a meeting in New York and reorganized the Church of God, generally distinguished from other similarly-named groups by the additional phrase, "World Headquarters." A struggle in court over control of the Church resulted in Milton and his followers being recognized as the legal successors. They were awarded all properties and trademarks. Homer continued as head of the group of loyal followers and rebuilt the Church which he led until his death in 1968. He was succeeded by Voy M. Bullen.

The doctrine, which follows closely that of the other Church of God bodies, is contained in the *Book of Doctrines/1903-1970*. The only doctrinal divergence in the entire Church of God movement occurs in the Church of God (World Headquarters). Its members replace the premillennialism of the other branches with a belief that the Church of God has the keys to bring the kingdom of God on earth, and that the kingdom will come by the setting up of the saints of God in the governments of the nations of the world now, here upon earth. Saints are encouraged to become responsible rulers and to preach the gospel of the kingdom. This doctrine was based upon the Bible as interpreted by A. J. Tomlinson, who gave Homer

a commission to plant the church flag in every nation of the earth. Given that commission, Homer established the "World Headquarters" of the Church of God in Jerusalem, as Israel is to be the center of the re-established kingdom of God.

After Bishop Homer's death in 1968, the American headquarters was moved from Queens, New York, to Huntsville, Alabama, a location more central to the congregations. The church's administrative offices are there. An annual assembly is held at Cape Girardeau, Missouri. A vigorous mission program, attributed in part to Homer's tireless traveling, has seen affiliated Churches of God established in England, Scotland, Panama, Nigeria, Barbados, Canada, Egypt, Haiti, Greece, and Ghana. The Theocratic Party, associated with the Church, runs candidates for both state and national offices in the United States.

Membership: Not reported. In 1973, there were 2,035 churches, 75,890 members and 2,737 ministers, worldwide.

Periodicals: *The Church of God*, 2504 Arrowwood Drive, S.E., Huntsville, AL 35803.

Sources: *Book of Doctrines, 1903-1970.* Huntsville, AL: Church of God Publishing House, 1970; Homer A. Tomlinson, *The Shout of a King*. Queens Village, NY: The Church of God, 1968.

★294★
CONGREGATIONAL HOLINESS CHURCH
3888 Fayetteville Hwy.
Griffin, GA 30223

In 1920 a controversy over divine healing arose in the Georgia Conference of the Pentecostal Holiness Church, now known as the International Pentecostal Holiness Church. One faction contended that the healing provisions in the atonement were sufficient, and that human aids (doctors) were unnecessary. While this faction admitted the therapeutic value of effective remedies, such remedies were not considered necessary for God to heal. The other faction, led by Rev. Watson Sorrow, insisted that God had placed medicine on earth for man's use. The group against doctors relied on the Biblical phrase about Christ's passion, "By his stripes you are healed."

The names of the Rev. Watson Sorrow and Hugh Bowling were dropped from the ministerial roll of the Pentecostal Holiness Church without their first being tried by the board of the Georgia annual conference of which they were members. A number of ministers withdrew with them, and together they organized the Congregational Holiness Church. They expressed differences with their parent body on the concentration of power in a few hands, so they attempted to democratize the church government. Consequently their polity is not episcopal, like that of the Pentecostal Holiness Church. Their polity is a moderate connectional system: local churches are grouped in associations which elect delegates to a general association with legislative powers. Pastors are called by vote of the congregation. Only men may be ordained. Mission work is going forth in Nigeria and Cuba.

Membership: In 1981 the Church reported 8,347 members, 174 churches, and 488 ministers.

Periodicals: *Gospel Messenger*, 3888 Fayetteville Hwy., Griffin, GA 30223.

Sources: B. L. Cox, *History and Doctrine of the Congregational Holiness Church*. Gainesville, GA: The Author, 1959; B. L. Cox, *My Life Story*. Greenwood, SC: C. H. Publishing House, n.d.

★295★
DOOR OF FAITH CHURCHES OF HAWAII
Current address not obtained for this edition.

In the 1930s, Rev. Mildred Johnson Brostek, formerly a minister with the Pentecostal Holiness Church, now known as the International Pentecostal Holiness Church in the South, came to Hawaii and, in 1937, began to hold evangelistic services on Molokai in the home of a native Hawaiian. The services prospered and, in 1940, the Door of Faith Churches of Hawaii was chartered and work expanded to other islands. Over the decades, the only major setback in the church's growth was the tragic murder of Reverend Elizabeth Trager, who conducted a store-front mission in Wahiawa. Foreign work is supported in Okinawa, the Philippines and Indonesia.

Membership: In 1979 the church reported 40 churches and 3,000 members in Hawaii.

Educational facilities: Door of Faith Bible School, Honolulu, HI.

★296★
EMMANUEL HOLINESS CHURCH
Box 818
Bladenboro, NC 28320

In 1953, controversy over standards of dress among the members of the Pentecostal Fire-Baptized Holiness Church led to a vote to divide the church. One issue which occasioned the split was the use of neckties, which the Pentecostal Fire-Baptized Holiness Church explicity forbids. Those who voted for the split elected Rev. L. O. Sellers chairman and formed the Emmanuel Holiness Church. It differs from its parent body only on minor points of dress, a more congregational form of government, and tithing which is required of members. A general assembly of all ministers and one delegate from each church has limited legislative powers.

Membership: Not reported. In 1967 there were 72 congregations and 118 ministers.

Periodicals: *Emmanuel Holiness Messenger*.

★297★
EVANGELISTIC CHURCH OF GOD
Current address not obtained for this edition.

The Evangelistic Church of God was incorporated at Denver, Colorado in 1949. It grew out of the work of Norman L. Chase, former minister of the Church of God (Cleveland, Tennessee) and of the (Original) Church of God. By 1955 the group claimed 774 members in twelve churches. The general assembly meets annually.

Membership: Not reported.

Periodicals: *The Church of God Final Warning*, Soddy, TN.

★298★
FIRST INTERDENOMINATIONAL CHRISTIAN
  ASSOCIATION
Calvary Temple Holiness Church
1061 Memorial Dr., S.E.
Atlanta, GA 30315

In 1946, the Rev. Watson Sorrow, who had been one of the founders of the Congregational Holiness Church, formed the First Interdenominational Christian Association, centered upon his own congregation, Calvary Temple in Atlanta. The Association is like the Congregational Holiness Church but less definite in doctrine. The parent body's statements on war, eschatology, and the forbidding of varying doctrinal beliefs among ministers were dropped. Retained were statements on healing, footwashing, and Pentecostalism. Several churches have joined Sorrow by adopting the congregational polity and policies of Calvary Temple.

Membership: Not reported. In the late 1960s, Calvary Temple had about 100 members.

★299★
FREE WILL BAPTIST CHURCH OF THE
  PENTECOSTAL FAITH
Box 278
Elgin, SC 29045

The Free Will Baptist Church of the Pentecostal Faith was formed in the 1950s when some members of the South Carolina Pentecostal Free Will Baptist Church Conference decided not to participate in the reorganization that led to the formation of the Pentecostal Free Will Baptist Church. Those who abstained adopted a constitution and chose a new name. They are at one doctrinally with the other Pentecostal Free Will Baptists.

The polity is congregational. The annual conference is to approve teachings, methods and conduct, and to encourage fellowship and evangelism. A general board headed by the conference superintendent functions between conference meetings. The Foreign Missions Department oversees work in Costa Rica. Camp meetings are periodically sponsored.

Membership: Not reported. In 1967 there were 33 congregations and 39 ministers.

Sources: *Faith and Government of the Free Will Baptist Church of the Pentecostal Faith.* 1961.

★300★
FULL GOSPEL CHURCH ASSOCIATION
Box 265
Amarillo, TX 79105

The Full Gospel Church Association, Incorporated, was organized by the Rev. Dennis W. Thorn at Amarillo, Texas, in 1952 for the purpose of bringing together a number of small, independent Pentecostal churches and missions, most of them with fewer than 100 members in the South and Southwest.

Doctrinally, the Full Gospel Church is similar to the Church of God (Cleveland, Tennessee). It emphasizes healing, tithing, and a literal heaven and hell, and uses only the King James Version of the Bible. It practices footwashing. Bearing arms is a matter of individual judgment. It does forbid disloyalty, insubordination, and criticism of the Association by its individual members. One unique element is the requirement that each church have an "Altar of God" in its building as a condition of its recognition by the Association.

The Association is congregational in polity. A general convention meets regularly. The general board of directors meets quarterly; its executive directors are the supreme council of the Association. Mission workers were active in Mexico, the Philippines, and Africa.

Membership: Not reported. In 1967 there were 67 churches with a total combined membership of 2,010.

★301★
GENERAL CONFERENCE OF THE EVANGELICAL
  BAPTIST CHURCH
Kavetter Bldg.
3400 E. Ash St.
Goldsboro, NC 27530

The General Conference of the Evangelical Baptist Church was organized in 1935 as the Church of the Full Gospel, Inc. It is Pentecostal and holiness in emphasis, following a theology close to that of the Pentecostal Free Will Baptist Church. It stresses spiritual gifts, healing, and the pretribulation, premillennial return of Christ. Four ordinances are recognized--baptism by immersion, communion, the dedication of children, and tithing. The

dedication of children is a form of christening that is distinct from baptism.

The polity is congregational. There is an annual conference which elects officers. In the local church, the pastor is the chief officer. He is elected by the congregation and has the power to appoint or nominate all church officers.

Membership: Not reported. In 1952 there were 31 churches, 2,200 members and 37 ministers.

Educational facilities: Evangelical Theological Seminary, Goldsboro, North Carolina; William Carter College, Goldsboro, North Carolina.

Periodicals: *Evangelical Baptist*, 2400 E. Ash Street, Goldsboro, NC 27530.

Sources: *Discipline of the General Conference of the Evangelical Baptist Church.*

★302★
HOLINESS BAPTIST ASSOCIATION
Douglas, GA 31533

The Holiness Baptist Association can be traced to 1893 when, because of their teaching on "sinless perfection," two congregations and several ministers were expelled from the Little River Baptist Association. The next year, together with two additional newly-organized churches, representatives met at the Pine City Church in Wilcox County, Georgia and formed the Association. The Association mixes the Wesleyan understanding of sanctification with traditional Missionary Baptist standards of faith and decorum. Tongues-speech, while permitted by the group, is not regarded as evidence of the baptism of the Holy Spirit. The Association operates a campground on the Alma Highway seven miles east of Douglas, Georgia. Association business is transacted there annually during camp meeting.

Membership: Not reported. In the mid-1970s there were 46 congregations (all in Georgia and Florida) and approximately 2,000 members.

★303★
HOLINESS CHURCH OF GOD
% Bishop B. McKinney
602 E. Elm St.
Graham, NC 27253

The Holiness Church of God was formed in 1920 by members from several holiness churches which had received the baptism of the Holy Spirit. Three years before, a revival, called the Big May Meeting, led by Elder James A. Foust had occurred in Madison, North Carolina. The entire membership of several congregations became Pentecostals, including the Kimberly Park

Holiness Church in Winston-Salem. The church incorporated in 1928. Churches are found in New York, Virginia and West Virginia.

Membership: Not reported. In 1968 there were 28 congregations and 927 members.

★304★
INTERNATIONAL PENTECOSTAL CHURCH OF CHRIST
Box 439
2245 U.S. 42, S.W.
London, OH 43140

The International Pentecostal Church of Christ was formed in 1976 by a merger of the International Pentecostal Assemblies and the Pentecostal Church of Christ. The International Pentecostal Assemblies was formed in 1936 by the merger of the Association of Pentecostal Assemblies and the National and International Pentecostal Missionary Union. The former body was an outgrowth of a periodical, *The Bridegroom's Messenger*, which had been founded in 1907. The Association of Pentecostal Assemblies was founded in 1921 in Atlanta by Elizabeth A. Sexton, Hattie M. Barth, and Paul T. Barth. The National and International Pentecostal Missionary Union was founded in 1914 by Dr. Philip Wittich.

In 1908, evangelist, John Stroup of South Solon, Ohio, received the baptism of the Holy Spirit, signified by his speaking in tongues. In 1913, he began to travel through southeastern Ohio and the adjacent territory in Kentucky and West Virginia, organizing churches in that area. In 1917 at Advance (Flatwoods), Kentucky, a group of ministers met, organized the Pentecostal Church of Christ, and appointed Stroup bishop. In 1927, the Pentecostal Church of Christ was incorporated.

The doctrine of the merged church follows closely that of the Church of God (Cleveland, Tennessee). Members believe in healing, the premillennial return of Christ, a personal devil, Sunday as the Lord's rest day, and two ordinances--baptism and the Lord's Supper. Footwashing is optional for local assemblies and believers. War is denounced as incompatible with the gospel.

Organization of the small church is congregational with a bishop or general overseer elected every two years. A female ministry (prophetess) is recognized, but women cannot administer the ordinances. *The Bridegroom's Messenger* continues as the official periodical and is now the oldest continuously published Pentecostal publication. Missions are supported in Hong Kong, Japan, India, Uganda, South Africa, Nigeria, Puerto Rico, Mexico and Brazil.

Membership: In 1984 the Church reported 4,000 members, 81 churches and 210 ministers.

Educational facilities: Beulah Heights Bible College, Atlanta, GA 30316.

Periodicals: *The Bridegroom's Messenger*. Box 308, Hartford, MI 49057; *The Pentecostal Leader*, Box 439, London, OH 43140.

★305★
INTERNATIONAL PENTECOSTAL HOLINESS CHURCH
7300 N.W. 39th Expressway
Bethany, OK 73008

In addition to those Pentecostal churches which derive from Rev. Charles Parham and the Apostolic Church and the Topeka Bible School, which he founded, there is a Pentecostal group which begins with Benjamin Hardin Irwin. He was a Baptist who had received the experience of sanctification under the influence of the Iowa Holiness Association, a group made up mostly of Methodists. As a holiness minister, he began to delve into Methodist writings, in particular those of John Fletcher, the eighteenth-century Wesleyan divine. In Fletcher he found what he felt to be an experience for sanctified believers, described as a "baptism of burning love." Eventually Irwin claimed to have received this "baptism of fire" and he began to teach and preach about it. Also called "fire baptism," the experience was related to the Apostles' reception of the Holy Spirit in the form of tongues of fire on Pentecost, as recorded in the Acts of the Apostles. Irwin's preaching of a third experience beyond justification and sanctification (called the "second blessing" in the holiness churches) led to controversy. He and his followers were the objects of intense criticism.

The "third blessing" spread across the Midwest and South. In 1885, the Fire-Baptized Holiness Association was organized in Iowa. Other state and local organizations followed. Irwin exercised authority over each and appointed the presidents. From July 28 to August 8, 1898, a First General Convention was held at Anderson, South Carolina, and formal organization of the Fire-Baptized Holiness Association occurred. Among those in attendance was one black man, W. E. Fuller, who later founded the Fire-Baptized Holiness Church of God of the Americas. The 1898 convention adopted a *Discipline*, which provided for life tenure for the general overseer who was given wide-ranging authority and control over the work. The Association soon took the name of the Fire-Baptized Holiness Church. Within two years, involved in a personal scandal, Irwin left the church and turned it over to J. H. King, a former Methodist minister who had been assisting him in running the church.

Contemporaneous with the ministry of Irwin was that of A. B. Crumpler. Crumpler, a Methodist minister in North Carolina, had received the second-blessing sanctification experience (the "second blessing" was the basic distinguishing mark of the holiness movement). Crumpler received his sanctification experience through the ministry of the Rev. Beverly Carradine, a famous Southern Methodist holiness preacher. He became the leading exponent of the "second blessing" in North Carolina, and in 1896, a great holiness movement began there. In 1899, Crumpler was tried for "immorality," withdrew from the Methodist Church, and the following year formed the Pentecostal Holiness Church at Fayetteville, North Carolina.

In 1906, the Reverend G. B. Cashwell, a Pentecostal Holiness minister, attended the Pentecostal revival services which were occurring on Azusa Street in Los Angeles, and received the baptism of the Holy Spirit evidenced by his speaking in tongues. Cashwell headed eastward to introduce the experience to his brothers and sisters. On New Years's Eve, 1906, he began a revival at Dunn, North Carolina, and introduced the experience to the Pentecostal Holiness Church. He also led J. H. King into the experience. Not without controversy, both the Pentecostal Holiness Church and the Fire-Baptized Holiness Church accepted the new experience in 1908. A merger under the name of the former occurred in 1911. It became the International Pentecostal Holiness Church in 1975.

The Pentecostal Holiness Church insists that the Pentecostal experience of the baptism of the Holy Spirit, signified by speaking in tongues, is valid only as a "third blessing." In other words, the Pentecostal experience can come only to those who have already been justified (accepted Jesus as their personal savior) and sanctified (received the "second blessing" which was the key experience of the holiness movement). By contrast, most Pentecostals believe the baptism of the Holy Spirit is available to any believer at any time, and brings with it power for a holy life. Most Pentecostals seek only "two experiences," while the Pentecostal Holiness Church seeks three.

The Pentecostal Holiness Church is a direct outgrowth of the holiness movement: that explains why it retains the "second blessing." The church also has a Methodist heritage, so it derives its doctrinal statement from the Methodist Articles of Religion (printed in the introductory section on the Pietist-Methodist Family). In line with its Methodist roots, the church is among the few Pentecostal bodies to allow baptism by methods other than immersion. Footwashing is optional.

The polity of the Pentecostal Holiness Church is episcopal. One bishop elected by the general conference and other officers form a general board of administration to administer the affairs of the denomination. Under the administrative board are various other boards and agencies. Property is owned by the general church. Among the boards are those on education, missions, and publication. The Board of Education oversees the work at the three colleges. The Foreign Mission Board, created in 1904, oversees missions in 32 countries. A vigorous publishing program is pursued by the Advocate Press.

Membership: In 1984 the Church reported 108,229 members, 1,443 congregations, and 3,000 ministers.

Educational facilities: Emmanuel College, Franklin Springs, Georgia; Southwestern College of Christian Ministries, Oklahoma City, Oklahoma; Holmes College of the Bible, Greenville, South Carolina.

Periodicals: *The Advocate*, 7300 N. W. 39th Expressway, Bethany, OK 73008; *The Helping Hand*, 7300 N. W. 39th Expressway, Bethany, OK 73008.

Sources: A. D. Beacham, Jr., *A Brief History of the Pentecostal Church of God*. Franklin Springs, GA: Advocate Press, 1983; Joseph E. Campbell, *The Pentecostal Holiness Church, 1898-1948*. Franklin Springs, GA: Publishing House of the Pentecostal Holiness Church, 1951; Joseph H. King, *Yet Speaketh*. Franklin Springs, GA: Publishing House of the Pentecostal Holiness Church, 1949.

★306★
(ORIGINAL) CHURCH OF GOD
Box 3086
Chattanooga, TN 37404

The first schism in the Church of God (Cleveland, Tennessee) occurred in 1917, and was led by the Rev. Joseph L. Scott, a pastor in Chattanooga. Among the issues involved were local autonomy, the tithe (obligatory versus voluntary), and the reception of divorced persons into the church. After the schism a less centralized government was established in the newly formed church. Each congregation is autonomous and takes the name of its location; for example, "The Church of God at Chattanooga." Above the local church is a general office which serves as headquarters and publishing house, which publishes Sunday school literature and the church's two periodicals. A presbytery has oversight of the ministry. The official name of the church includes the word "Original" in parentheses.

There are five ordinances in the (Original) Church of God, Inc.- baptism by immersion, Biblical church government, footwashing, the Lord's Supper, and tithing. Previously divorced persons can be accepted by pastors as church members.

Membership: Not reported. In 1971 there were 70 churches (including one in Trinidad), 20,000 members and 124 ministers.

Periodicals: *The Messenger*, Box 3086, Chattanooga, TN 37404; *The Youth Messenger*, Box 3086, Chattanooga, TN 37404.

Sources: *Manual or Discipline of the (Original) Church of God*. Chattanooga, TN: General Office & Publishing House, 1966.

★307★
PENTECOSTAL FIRE-BAPTIZED HOLINESS CHURCH
Taccoa, GA 30577

The enforcement of discipline in the Pentecostal Holiness Church, now the International Pentecostal Holiness Church, led in 1918 to a schism by those who wanted stricter standards concerning dress, amusements, tobacco, and association between the sexes. In the Pentecostal Fire-Baptized Holiness Church, the schismatic church, women's dresses are to be at least mid-calf in length; women are not to bob or wave their hair, or wear jewelry, gold, or costly apparel. Men are not to wear neckties. Attending fairs, swimming pools, and theaters is forbidden. The strict group was joined by a few who never approved the 1911 merger of the Pentecostal Holiness Church and the Fire-Baptized Holiness Church. The pre-1911 name was adopted and the word "Pentecostal" added. The group also was joined in 1921 by the North Carolina Conference of the Pentecostal Free Will Baptist Church.

The church had 1,929 members in 85 churches in 1952. However, the next year more than half the members left to form the Emmanuel Holiness Church. That schism began a period of unabated decline.

The polity is connectional. A general convention meets biennially, with power to legislate. A seven-member board of missions, elected at the general convention, oversees work in Haiti and Mexico. A campgrounds and printing establishment are owned at Toccoa Falls, Georgia, where the church headquarters are located.

Membership: By 1981 the church had decreased to 298 members.

Periodicals: *Faith and Truth*, Nicholson, GA.

★308★
PENTECOSTAL FREE WILL BAPTIST CHURCH
Box 1081
Dunn, NC 28334

The Pentecostal Free Will Baptist Church was formed in a merger and reorganization of several Free Will Baptist Associations, mainly in North Carolina. Pentecostalism had entered the Free Will Baptist Church through the efforts of the ubiquitous G. B. Cashwell. In 1907 he conducted a revival in Dunn, North Carolina, and persuaded many members of the Cape Fear Conference of the Free Will Baptist Church of the truth of his position. The Conference accepted a Pentecostal doctrine, but remained within the national Free Will Baptist Association. In 1907, the Cape Fear Conference split into two geographic associations; the second body became the Wilmington Conference, and the first retained the original name. In 1911, a third association was formed in southeastern North Carolina as the New River Conference. The following year, the Cape Fear Conference split over the Pentecostal issue. Finally, in 1912 a South Carolina Conference was organized.

In 1943, a group of ministers and laymen of the four Pentecostal conferences: Cape Fear, Wilmington, New River, and South Carolina Conferences, met. They formed a general conference but the organization proved unsatisfactory. In 1959, it was decided to dissolve all the conference structures and organize under one charter and one name. Thus, in 1959, the Pentecostal Free Will Baptist Church was formed.

The doctrine is almost identical to that of the Church of God (Cleveland, Tennessee), and includes belief in three experiences of grace: baptism by immersion, footwashing, and premillennialism. It is this group's position that Benjamin Randall, the founder of the Free Will Baptist Church, taught sanctification as an instantaneous act of God, and that the idea of sanctification as a growing process commencing at birth and lasting throughout life (as became popular in the nineteenth century) is a departure from Randall's teaching.

The church is congregational in structure with an annual conference. The general superintendent heads an executive board for implementing the program. There are six districts; the World Missions Board oversees missions in Hawaii, India, Mexico, Venezuela, Nicaragua, the Philippines and a radio ministry in North Carolina. Churches are primarily in North Carolina, with congregations in Virginia, Georgia, and Florida.

Membership: Not reported. In 1978 there were 128 churches and 12,272 members.

Educational facilities: Heritage Bible College, Dunn, North Carolina.

Periodicals: *The Pentecostal Free-Will Baptist Messenger*, Box 1081, Dunn, NC 28334.

Sources: *Discipline of the Pentecostal Free Will Baptist Church.* 1962; Dan Sauls, *The Ministerial Handbook of the Pentecostal Free Will Baptist Church.* N. P.: 1971; Herbert Carter, *The Spectacular Gifts, Prophecy, Tongues, Interpretations.* Dunn, NC: The Author, 1971; *Faith and Practices of the Pentecostal Free Will Baptist Church, Inc..* Franklin Springs, GA: Advocate Press, 1971.

White Trinitarian Pentecostal

★309★
AMERICAN INDIAN EVANGELICAL CHURCH
1823 Emerson Ave., N.
Minneapolis, MN 55411

During the early twentieth century, conditions forced many American Indians into the cities. By 1945, 8,000 had settled in the Minneapolis/St. Paul metropolitan area. In that year a group of Indians organized the American Indian Mission. In 1956, the Mission became the American Indian Evangelical Church, and Iver C. Grover (a Chippewa) was elected president. He was joined by seven others. In 1959, a committee on ordination was appointed to facilitate the development of an Indian ordained ministry, and four men were ordained.

Doctrine is in line with fundamental evangelicalism. The doctrinal statement of the church begins with the Apostles' Creed and moves on to affirm the Trinity, the divinity of Jesus, and the conscious suffering of the wicked. Baptism by immersion and the Lord's Supper are practiced. The polity is congregational, but the pastor is viewed as the spiritual overseer of the congregation.

Membership: Not reported.

★310★
ANCHOR BAY EVANGELISTIC ASSOCIATION
Box 188
New Baltimore, MI 48047

Roy John Turner and his wife Blanche A. Turner became Pentecostals in 1916. Dr. Turner was a medical doctor and his wife a nurse, and they continued to function as medical professionals while leading prayer meetings. Following a revival campaign in 1918 by evangelist, Mrs. M. B. Woodworth-Etter, a church was formed in New Baltimore. In 1923, Dr. Turner was ordained and became pastor of the congregation. The old opera house in New Baltimore, Michigan, was purchased and remodeled as Bethel Temple. From 1938 to 1940, Turner served as an executive with the International Church of the Foursquare Gospel, the congregation in New Baltimore remained independent. Finally, in 1940, the Turners left the Foursquare Gospel and the Anchor Bay Evangelistic Association was formed and incorporated. After the Turners' deaths, they were succeeded by their daughter, Lucy Evelyn Turner.

The doctrine of the Anchor Bay Evangelistic Association is like that of the International Church of the Foursquare Gospel. Mission work is conducted in Belize, Turkey, the Philippines, South India, West Africa, Indonesia, and Mexico. The church is a member of the Pentecostal Fellowship of North America.

Membership: In the late 1960s there were 320 ministers and 115 churches worldwide.

Educational facilities: Anchor Bay Institute, New Baltimore, Michigan.

★311★
APOSTOLIC CHURCH
142 N. 17th St.
Philadelphia, PA 19103

The Apostolic Church was formed by members, mostly in Wales, who had left the Apostolic Faith Church which had been formed in Great Britain in 1908 by W. O. Hutchinson. In 1916 the Rev. Daniel Powell Williams and others deno4

Sources: *Manual or Discipline of the (Original) Church of God*. Chattanooga, TN: General Office & Publishing House, 1966.

★312★
APOSTOLIC FAITH (KANSAS)
1009 Lincoln Ave.
Baxter Springs, KS 66713

In 1898, Rev. Charles Parham left the Methodist Episcopal Church and established a home for divine healing in Topeka, Kansas. That same year he began to publish a periodical, *Apostolic Faith*, and two years later opened Bethel Bible College. It was at Bethel that Agnes Oznam had the initial experience of speaking in tongues, an event from which the modern Penetecostal movement is dated. After Mrs. Oznam's experience and its acceptance by others, Parham began to spread the word of modern Pentecostalism in Kansas, Oklahoma, Missouri, and Texas. In 1905, he established a Bible school in Houston. Among those who attended was W. J. Seymour, a black holiness preacher affiliated with the Church of God (Anderson, Indiana), who related the experience at Azusa Street, Los Angeles, California.

Parham is hardly mentioned in Pentecostal history after 1906 (when accusation of scandalous behavior ruined his reputation in large segments of the movement), but he continued to work and to consolidate his remaining support into a loose fellowship in the south-central United States. The result was the Apostolic Faith, currently headquartered in Baxter Springs, Kansas. The body keeps no membership rolls and has never incorporated.

Beliefs of the Apostolic Faith are similar to those of the Assemblies of God, and include a strong emphasis on spiritual healing. Footwashing, baptism, and the Lord's Supper are observed as ordinances. No collections are taken, the ministry being supported by tithes. Organization is informal and congregational. There is a three-person board trustees which oversees the Bible college.

Membership: Not reported. In 1974 there were 100 churches and 118 ministers.

Periodicals: *Apostolic Faith Report*, Box 653, Baxter Springs, KS 66713.

Sources: Sarah E. Parham, *The Life of Charles F. Parham*. Joplin, MO: Hunter Printing Company, 1930; Charles F. Parham, *A Voice of One Crying in the Wilderness*. Baxter Springs, KS: Apostolic Faith Bible College, 1910; W. F. Carothers, *The Baptism with the Holy Ghost*. Zion City, IL: The Author, 1907.

★313★
GENERAL COUNCIL OF THE ASSEMBLIES OF GOD
1445 Boonville Ave.
Springfield, MO 65802

The December 20, 1913, issue of *Word and Witness*, an independent Pentecostal periodical published by editor E. N. Bell, issued a call for "A General Convention of Pentecostal Saints and Churches of God in Christ," to be held in Hot Springs, Arkansas, from April 2 to 12, 1914. The purpose was to decide upon some doctrinal standards; a policy of cooperation; missionary, ministerial, educational, and publishing interests; and government religious requirements for business. Bell and J. Roswell Flower, editor of the *Christian Evangel*, quickly emerged as dominant figures in the meeting attended by more than 300 delegates from twenty states and several foreign countries. A loose organization was effected and the new church took the name of the Assemblies of God. The General Council, representative of Pentecostal assemblies and churches, was formed. *The Word and Witness* was accepted as the official periodical and the *Christian Evangel* was combined with it.

During the next two years, the doctrinal position of the Assemblies of God was hammered out in heated debate on the "Jesus only" or "oneness" issue. Oneness Pentecostals believed that Jesus was "Jehovah rediscovered" and demanded re-baptism in Jesus' name, thus opposing baptism in the name of the Trinity. The assemblies adopted a strong statement on the Trinity as integral to the church's belief. The statement, finally adopted in 1916, also reflected the absence of "Holiness theology of the Holy Spirit," and recognized that the baptism of the Holy Spirit is by no means limited to the sanctified, nor is santification viewed as a distinct work of grace. The church's statement of fundamental truths includes belief in the Bible as the Word of God, the fall of man, salvation in Christ, baptism by immersion, divine healing, and the resurrection.

The organization of the Assemblies of God is congregational, but the General Council has centralized control over missionary, educational, ministerial, and publishing concerns. One of the first acts of the Hot Springs meeting was the appointment of a twelve-person presbytery to oversee mission work. The Division of Foreign Missions was created in 1919, and the missionary effort has seen the spread of the Assemblies to 113 countries of the world. The Division of Home Missions oversees work among American Indians, Jews, the deaf, the blind, and in various ethnic groups. It also supervises military and institutional chaplains. The first publishing efforts of the Assemblies of God have grown into the Gospel Publishing House, one of the major publishers of Christian literature in the United States. There is also a vast Sunday School Department and a Radio Department which produces the popular "Revival Time" broadcast on radio.

Membership: In 1984 the Assemblies reported 1,879,182 members (i.e. individuals of all ages who identified with an Assemblies church), 10,386 congregations, and 28,878 ministers.

Educational facilities: American Indian Bible College, Phoenix, Arizona; Assemblies of God Graduate School, Springfield, Missouri; Bethany Bible College, Santa Cruz, California; Central Bible College, Springfield, Missouri; Evangel College, Springfield, Missouri; Latin America Bible College of California, La Puente, California; North Central Bible College, Minneapolis, Minnesota; Northwest College of the Assemblies of God, Kirkland, Washington; Southeastern College of the Assemblies of God, Lakeland, Florida; Southern Arizona Bible College, Hereford, Arizona; Southern California College, Costa Mesa, California; Southwestern Assemblies of God College, Waxahachie, Texas; Trinity Bible Institute, Ellendale, North Dakota.

Periodicals: *Pentecostal Evangel*, Gospel Publishing House, 1445 Boonville Avenue, Springfield, MO 65802; *Assemblies of God Heritage*, Assemblies of God Archives, 1445 Boonville Avenue, Springfield, MO 65802.

Sources: William W. Menzies, *Anointed to Serve*. Springfield, MO: Gospel Publishing House, 1971; Carl Brumback, *Suddenly from Heaven*. Springfield, MO: Gospel Publishing House, 1961; Mario G. Hoover, *Origin and Structural Development of the Assemblies of God*. Southwest Missouri State College, M.A. Thesis, 1968; Noel Perkin and John Garlock, *Our World Witness*. Springfield, MO: Gospel Publishing House, 1963; Ralph W. Harris, *Our Faith and Fellowship*. Springfield, MO: Gospel Publishing House, 1963.

★314★
BETHEL TEMPLE
2033 Second Ave.
Seattle, WA 98121

The Bethel Temple was formed in 1914 as the first Pentecostal congregation in the state of Washington. Its doctrine is like that of the Assemblies of God, and it holds to a premillennial eschatology. Loosely affiliated with the Temple are some 14 congregations--eleven in the state of Washington, two in Minnesota, and one in Wisconsin. Missions are conducted in Japan and Indonesia. A Bible school founded in 1952 offers a two-year course of study.

Membership: Not reported. In the mid-1970s there were 14 congregations.

Educational facilities: Bethel Temple Bible School, Seattle, Washington.

Periodicals: *Pentecostal Power*, 2033 Second Avenue, Seattle, WA 98121.

★315★
BIBLE CHURCH OF CHRIST
New York, NY

The Bible Church of Christ is a small Pentecostal body founded March 1, 1961, by Bishop Roy Bryant. The several congregations support mission work in Africa. Doctrine is like that of the Assemblies of God.

Membership: Not reported. In 1978 it reported 5 churches, 19 ministers and approximately 1,800 members.

Periodicals: *Voice*, New York, NY.

★316★
B'NAI SHALOM
Gospel of Peace Camp Ground
5607 S. 7th St.
Phoenix, AZ 85040

During the 1950s, Elder Reynolds Edward Dawkin, an elder in the Gospel Assemblies (Sowder), had several visions, among them one in which he was instructed to begin work in Palestine, looking toward the restoration of Israel and the end of the Gentile age which began in 1959. Following the death of William Sowder, founder of the Gospel Assemblies, the movement reorganized with a presbyterial form of government. Dawkins rejected that polity in favor of an apostolic order of the five-gifted ministry of Romans 13, the church led by pastor, teacher, evangelist, and prophets, and (over all) the apostle. Dawkins was accepted by his followers as an apostle and his revelations are highly revered.

Dawkins died in 1965 and was succeeded by Elder Richard Tate. He leads a core membership called "overcomers," members who have given three years in living wholly for the body of Christ or who give at least fifty-one percent of their time, money and life for the body. Membership has spread to Jamaica, the Netherlands, Hong Kong, India, Nigeria and Israel. The Peace Publishers and Company serves as the body's financial and publishing structure.

Membership: Not reported. In the early 1970s, there were 8 congregations in the United States and 11 outside, with a total membership of approximately 1,000.

Periodicals: *B'nai Shalom*, 6401 Eighth Place, Phoenix, AZ.

★317★
CALIFORNIA EVANGELISTIC ASSOCIATION
1800 E. Anaheim Rd.
Long Beach, CA 90815

The California Evangelistic Association began in 1933 (incorporated, 1934) as the Colonial Tabernacle of Long Beach California. The tabernacle had been established by Oscar C. Harms, a former pastor in the Advent Christian Church. Additional assemblies became associated with it, and in 1939, it assumed its present name. It is in essential doctrinal agreement with the Assemblies of God, except that it is amillennial. Polity of the Association is congregational, with affiliated congregations remaining autonomous. Churches are found along the West Coast. The California Evangelistic Association supports missionaries in Italy, Zambia, Brazil, Colombia, and Mexico.

Membership: Not reported. In the 1970s there were 62 associated congregations and approximately 4,700 members.

Sources: *Constitution and By-Laws*. Long Beach, CA: California Evangelistic Association, 1939.

★318★
CALVARY PENTECOSTAL CHURCH
% Rev. Leroy Holman
1775 Yew, N.E.
Olympia, WA 98506

The Calvary Pentecostal Church was formed in 1931 by a group of Pentecostal ministers in the northwestern United States who were dissatisfied by what they regarded as "a sad departure from the entire dependence on the power of God that had brought the Pentecostal revival." They formed a ministerial fellowship in Olympia, Washington, which was the following year named the Calvery Pentecostal Church. What was originally intended as an interdenominational fellowship became a denomination as churches began to affiliate.

The doctrine is like that of the Assemblies of God. Healing is emphasized. Adult baptism by immersion is practiced, but when parents request it, infants are dedicated to God (not baptized). The literal second coming is awaited. The church is governed in a loose presbyterial system headed by a presbyterial board and the general superintendent. A general meeting of all ministers and local church delegates is held annually. The local church is governed by the minister, elders, and deacons.

The church supports a home for the aged in Seattle. Foreign work is done in Brazil and India.

Membership: Not reported. In the early 1970s there were 22 churches and approximately 8,000 members.

★319★
CHRISTIAN CHURCH OF NORTH AMERICA, GENERAL COUNCIL
Rte. 18 & Rutledge Rd.
Box 141-A, R.D. 1
Transfer, PA 16154

The Christian Church of North America was formed by the merger of two former Italian-American Pentecostal denominations, both developed from work begun in 1907: the Italian Pentecostal Assemblies of God and the Unorganized Italian Christian Churches of North America.

Pastor William H. Durham of the North American Mission in Chicago was among the first to receive the baptism of the Holy Spirit at the original Pentecostal revival on Azusa Street in Los Angeles. In 1907 Durham began to share his experience with the Italians who attended his mission and encouraged them to start an autonomous work. Among those who received the baptism of the Holy Spirit were John Santamaria and his son, Rocco Santamaria, who had in 1904 begun work among Italians. The Santamarias organized the Italian Pentecostal Assemblies of God. In 1932, a general council was started to unite the approximately 200 independent Pentecostal missions across the country.

In 1907, Louis Francescon began to work in Chicago and became another major force in spreading Pentecostalism among the Italian-Americans. In 1927, he pulled together his followers to form the Unorganized Italian Christian Churches of North America and adopted a confession of faith. The church was incorporated in 1948. With the later merger of the two Italian bodies, the consolidation of Italian Pentecostals outside of the larger English-speaking bodies was completed. The name of the merged church is the Christian Church of North America.

The doctrine is like that of the Assemblies of God. The church believes in abstaining from things offered to idols, from consuming blood, from consuming things strangled, and from fornication (Acts 15:28, 29; 16:4, 21, 25). The code of ethics is based on refraining from all appearance of evil and on the passage, "whatsoever you do, do all to the glory of God." Dress is modest. Women are expected to cover their heads at worship. Intermarriage with non-Christians is forbidden.

Polity is congregational. Congregations are organized into five districts. An annual general convention and an executive board of twelve members are both headed by the general overseer. The general overseer and four assistants are ministers for the five districts. Seven presbyters, who complete the executive board, oversee the seven departments. The Institution Department oversees the denominational rest home in Florida. There is currently foreign work in the Dominican Republic, Barbados, Argentina, Uruguay, Venezuela, Ghana, Ivory Coast, India, Australia, the Philippines, Italy and North Europe.

Membership: In 1982 the Church reported 12,500 members, 101 congregations and 156 ministers.

Periodicals: *Il Faro*, Box 66, Herkimer, NY 13350; *Vista*, R. D. #4, West Middlesex, PA 16159.

Sources: Louis De Caro, *Our Heritage*. Sharon, PA: General Council, Christian Church of North America, 1977; Steven Galvan, ed., *Fiftieth Anniversary, Christian Church of North America*. Sharon, PA: General Council, Christian Church of North America, 1977.

★320★
ELIM FELLOWSHIP
Lima, NY 14485

In 1924, the Rev. and Mrs. Ivan Q. Spencer opened a Bible school in Endicott, New York, to train Pentecostal ministers. Graduates formed the Elim Ministerial Fellowship in 1932 and the Elim Missionary Assemblies in 1947. In 1951, the school was moved to Lima, New York, where it occupies the campus of the old Genesee Wesleyan College, founded in the nineteenth century by the Methodist Episcopal Church.

Doctrine is like that of the Assemblies of God, with a strong emphasis on divine healing and the sanctified life. Ivan Spencer was among those individuals strongly affected by the Latter Rain revival which began in Canada in 1948. He brought the revival to the school, publicized it through the Assemblies periodical and took a leadership role in spreading the renewed emphasis upon the gifts of the Spirit being poured out on God's people in the last days. The premillennial return of Christ is expected. Government is congregational. There is an annual meeting held each summer at Lima. Institute-trained missionaries are currently at work around the world under the auspices of the World Missionary Assistance Plan, Elim's missionary arm. The founder was succeeded by his son, Carlton Spencer. Membership is held in both the Pentecostal Fellowship of North America and the National Association of Evangelicals.

Membership: In 1983 the Fellowship reported 35 congregations and 185 ministers.

Educational facilities: Elim Bible Institute, Lima, New York.

Periodicals: *Elim Herald*, Lima, NY 14485.

Sources: Marion Meloon, *Ivan Spencer, Willow in the Wind*. Plainfield, NJ: Logos International, 1974.

★321★
FELLOWSHIP OF CHRISTIAN ASSEMBLIES
% Fellowship Press
657 W. 18th St.
Los Angeles, CA 90015

Formed in 1922 as the Independent Assemblies of God, the Fellowship of Christian Assemblies adopted its present name in 1973. The Assemblies was disrupted in 1948 by the adherence of many members and pastors to the Latter Rain movement, a revival movement which had begun in Canada and had placed a new emphasis upon the manifestation of the gifts of the Spirit, particularly prophecy and healing. Those opposed to the revival viewed it as possessed of fanatical elements. The group which eventually became the Fellowship of Christian Assemblies is that element of the Independent Assemblies that did not follow the Latter Rain.

Organization of the Fellowship is congregational and its basic principle is fellowship among autonomous churches. The pattern in mission work has also been to establish autonomous churches. National gatherings for counsel and fellowship are held and are planned by a committee working with the local churches. A secretary compiles and publishes a directory. Some of the churches have become members of the Fellowship Press Publishing Corporation; its main function is to publish the monthly periodical, *Conviction*. Mission work is supported in Africa, South America, Japan, and India.

Membership: Not reported. There are an estimated 10,000 members in the churches affiliated with the Fellowship.

Periodicals: *Conviction*, Fellowship Press, Seattle, WA.

★322★
FILIPINO ASSEMBLIES OF THE FIRST BORN
1229 Glenwood
Delano, CA 93215

The Filipino Assemblies of the First Born was founded at Stockton, California, by the Rev. Julian Barnabe, an immigrant to the United States. The organization took place at a convention which met June 26 to July 4, 1933. Headquarters were established in Fresno and moved to San Francisco in 1942 and to Delano, California, in 1943. Doctrine and practice are like those of the Assemblies of God; the group is primarily an ethnic church with preaching often done in the Filipino language.

Membership: Not reported. In 1969 there were 15 churches in California and 17 in Hawaii.

★323★
FREE GOSPEL CHURCH, INC.
% Rev. Chester H. Heath
Box 477
Export, PA 15632

The Free Gospel Church was founded in 1916 as the United Free Gospel and Missionary Society by two brothers, the Reverends Frank Casley and William Casley. It adopted its present name in 1958. An early emphasis upon missions led to initial efforts in Guatemala, though the work was lost to the Church of God (Cleveland, Tennessee). In doctrine, it is similar to the Assemblies of God. Missions are conducted in Sierra Leone, India, and the Philippines.

Membership: Not reported. In the early 1970s there were approximately 25 churches and 2,000 members.

Educational facilities: Free Gospel Institute, Export, Pennsylvania.

★324★
FULL GOSPEL EVANGELISTIC ASSOCIATION
5828 Chippewa Blvd.
Houston, TX 70086

In the late 1940s a controversy developed in the Apostolic Faith Church over issues of taking offerings in church, visiting churches not in fellowship, foreign mission work, and using doctors. Some who supported these activities formed the Ministerial and Missionary Alliance of the Original Trinity Apostolic Faith, Inc., for which they were disfellowshipped. In 1952, they formed the Full Gospel Evangelistic Association. Except for the points at issue, the doctrine is like that of the Apostolic Faith.

Headquarters, established at Kuty, Texas, were moved to Webb City, Missouri, in 1967. The Association supports missions in Mexico, Peru, Guatemala, and Taiwan. Annual camp meetings are held in Oklahoma and Texas.

Membership: Not reported. In the mid-1970s there were 30 congregations and approximately 4,000 members.

Educational facilities: Midwest Bible Institute, Houston, Texas.

Periodicals: *Full Gospel News*, 5828 Chipawa Blvd., Houston, TX 70086.

★325★
GENERAL ASSEMBLIES AND CHURCH OF THE FIRST BORN
Donald C. Hobbs
1008 Center Cross St.
Edinburgh, IN 46124

The General Assembly and Church of the First Born, formed in 1907, is a small Pentecostal body without church headquarters or paid clergy. It has about 30 congregations across the country. Congregations are concentrated in Oklahoma and California, with individual congregations at Montrose and Pleasant View, Colorado, and Indianapolis, Indiana. Members believe in the Trinity, deny original sin, believing that we will be punished only for our own sin, and assert that man can be saved by obedience to the laws and ordinances of the gospel. There are four ordinances--faith in Jesus Christ, repentence, baptism by immersion, and laying-on-of-hands for the gift of the Holy Spirit. The group makes use of all of the gifts of the Spirit and holds the Lord's Supper in conjunction with footwashing , but does not seek the help of doctors.

Elders oversee the local congregations, which are organized very informally. Some elders are ordained and serve as preachers. No membership rolls are kept. The Indianapolis church has published a hymnal. There is an annual campmeeting in Oklahoma each summer.

Membership: Not reported. In 1976 there were approximately 6,000 members.

Remarks: In 1976 the Church of the First Born was involved in a controversy following the death of a member's child after medical treatment was withheld. A district court in Oklahoma made a second child a ward of the court, ruling that the state had a right to intervene when religious beliefs might lead to harm of a minor.

★326★
GOSPEL ASSEMBLIES (JOLLY)
St. Louis, MO

In 1952, Elder Tom M. Jolly became pastor of the Gospel Assemblies (Sowder) congregation in St. Louis, succeeding Dudley Frazier. In 1965, Jolly led supporters to separate from the older, larger Gospel Assemblies group. Under his leadership there has been a marked tendency to centralized congregations in or near major urban areas, followed by the centralization of funds in preparation for the purchase of land upon which the congregations can settle away from the evil influences of contemporary cities. Twice yearly, members gather for pastoral conferences, fellowship meetings and youth rallies. Doctrine follows that of the parent body. The number of congregations (originally twelve) had more than doubled in the first five years.

Membership: Not reported. In 1970 there were approximately 30 congregations and 4,000 members.

★327★
GOSPEL ASSEMBLIES (SOWDER)
Gospel Assembly Church
7135 Meredith Dr.
Des Moines, IA 50322

The phrase, "Gospel of the Kingdom Churches Movement," refers to several religious bodies which have grown out of the work of Elder William Sowders of Louisville, Kentucky. These eclectic but basically Pentecostal groups have no official name, but local congregations are usually called Gospel Assemblies. Sowders was a nominal Methodist who had a call to preach and founded a church in 1907 in Elbo, Illinois. Five years later, he moved to Evansville, Indiana, and founded a Bible school. Among those who were associated with him in the early years were Robert Shelton, George Aubrey, and Dudley Frazer. In 1914, a church in Louisville, which eventually became the informal headquarters of the movement, was founded. The most ambitious project was Gospel of the Kingdom Campgrounds in Shepherdsville, Kentucky. At its height, the 365 acres served as the summer home of as many as 9,000 church members. A home for the aged was also built.

Doctrinally, the group was very eclectic, borrowing from Pentecostalism, the Plymouth Brethren, and even the Millennial Dawn (now the Jehovah's Witnesses), founded by Charles Taze Russell. The church is non-Trinitarian but has not moved toward the Sabellianism of the "oneness" doctrine, identifying Jesus with the Father. It has moved instead toward the Arian Unitarian views (held by the Millennial Dawn) that Jesus is not god but is the first created work of God. The group believes in God the Father and in Jesus, God's Son, and in the Holy Spirit as the life of the Father and Son. Thus it denies that the Holy Spirit is the third person of the Trinity. The Gospel Assemblies also believe in dividing the history of the world into dispensations, periods of time distinct from each other according to the way God acts toward his people during each dispensation. The Gospel Assemblies follow closely Russell's time scheme for various dispensations, including the importance placed upon 1914 as the beginning of the end time. Therefore, the premillennial second coming is considered imminent. (A full discussion of Russell's time scheme is presented in the introductory section of this *Encyclopedia*). The Gospel Assemblies represent the remnant entrusted with God's word in this generation.

Speaking in tongues as evidence of the baptism of the Holy Spirit is stressed, but is distinguished from the gift of tongues (I. Cor. 12: 4-11) which only a few people have. Healing is also emphasized. The Spirit is seen as an inspiring agent and is an authority in addition to the Bible for faith and doctrine.

Approximating the teachings of the Evangelical Bible Church, the Gospel Assemblies teach that there are three baptisms--one by water, one by the Holy Spirit, and one of persecution by the ungodly world (Mark 10:39). There is no set formula for the baptismal act. The Lord's Supper is not practiced.

As with the Plymouth Brethren, the movement has considered itself undenominated and is organized into independent, unincorporated Gospel Assemblies. Within the Church are the seven pillars supporting the church-God, Christ, apostles, prophets, pastors, evangelists, and teachers. The group sees itself as having "no membership, just fellowship; no book but the Bible, and no creed but Christ." Pastors are trained within the movement in an intern system which includes attendance at pastoral conferences. One distinction of the movement was the School of Prophets, the regular gatherings of the pastors to confer with Sowders on matters of doctrine and other concerns. The school centered upon Sowders' answers to questions but allowed much time for debate and discussion.

There is no central headquarters. The Gospel Assembly Ministers' Fund in Norfolk, Virginia issues a directory of churches and ministers periodically. In recent years, the Gospel Assembly Church in Des Moines, Iowa, pastored by Rev. Lloyd L. Goodwin, has emerged as a leading congregation and site of an annual convention. Its periodical lists other conventions and fellowship meetings around the United States.

Membership: Not reported. In 1970 there were 90 congregations and approximately 10,000 members.

Periodicals: *The Gospel of Peace Newsletter*, Gospel Assembly Church, 7135 Meredith Drive, Des Moines, IA 50322.

Sources: Lloyd L. Goodwin, *Prophecy Concerning the Church*. Des Moines, IA: Gospel Assembly Church, 1977. 2 Vols.; Lloyd L. Goodwin, *Prophecy Concerning the Resurrection*. Des Moines, IA: Gospel Assembly Church, 1976; Lloyd L. Goodwin, *Prophecy Concerning the Second Coming*. Des Moines, IA: Gospel Assembly Church, 1979; *Ministers' Address Directory*. Norfolk, VA: Gospel Assembly Ministers' Fund, 1970.

★328★

INDEPENDENT ASSEMBLIES OF GOD, INTERNATIONAL
3840 5th Ave.
San Diego, CA 92103

Among the many independent Pentecostal churches that did not join the Assemblies of God in 1914, were congregations consisting primarily of Scandinavian immigrants, converts of the Scandinavian Pentecostal movement. Petrus Lewi Johanson of Stockholm and Thomas Ball Barrett of Oslo were the dominant figures in the Scandinavian Pentecostal movement. The Scandinavians were extreme congregationalists and

believed that all discipline, even of ministers, should be vested in the local level.

In the United States, the extreme congregationalism worked for a while, but gradually loose federations began to develop. In 1918, a Scandinavian Assemblies of God in the United States, Canada and Other Lands was formed in the northwestern states. In St. Paul, Minnesota, in 1922, a fellowship of independent churches was formed. A third group, the Scandinavian Independent Assemblies of God, was formed around Pastor B. M. Johnson, who had founded the Lakeview Gospel Church in Chicago in 1911, and A. A. Holmgren, who published the *Scanningens Vittne*, a periodical for Scandinavian Pentecostals. In 1935, the latter group dissolved its corporation, and the three groups united to form the Independent Assemblies of God. They began to Americanize and to move beyond their ethnic exclusiveness.

In 1947-1948, there was a division in the Independent Assemblies of God over participation in the "Latter Rain" Movement, a revival that swept western Canada and which became known for extreme doctrine and practices in some phases. The words "Latter Rain" refer to the end of the world when God will pour out his Spirit upon all people. One group accepted the revival as the present movement of God, as God's deliverance promised in the Bible. This group, under the leadership of A. W. Rasmussen, became the Independent Assemblies of God, International. Missions are supported in seventeen countries around the world.

Membership: Not reported. In the mid-1970s there were approximately 300 congregations affiliated with the Assemblies.

Periodicals: *The Mantle*, 3840 Fifth Avenue, San Diego, CA 92103.

Sources: A. W. Rasmussen, *The Last Chapter*. Monroeville, PA: Whitaker House, 1973.

★329★

INTERNATIONAL CHURCH OF THE FOURSQUARE GOSPEL
% Angelus Temple
1100 Glendale Blvd.
Los Angeles, CA 90026

No discussion of the International Church of the Foursquare Gospel is possible without reference to its flamboyant founding pastor, Aimee Semple McPherson. Aimee's mother, reared a Methodist and for a while a member of the Salvation Army, dedicated Aimee to the ministry. At seventeen, Aimee was converted, baptized with the Holy Spirit, and married to the evangelist, Robert Semple. Semple soon died while serving as a missionary in China, leaving Aimee with a one-month-old child. She returned to the United States and had an unfortunate second marriage to druggist H. S. McPherson which ended in divorce. Then she began an independent, itinerant Pentecostal ministry.

Unsupported and berated by other ministers who did not believe in women's speaking from a pulpit, Aimee won success through her oratorical abilities, charisma, the message of the Foursquare Gospel, and her flair for the spectacular which brought widespread publicity. In her early ministry she spent much time with T. K. Leonard and W. H. Durham, both early Pentecostal leaders.

Doctrinally, the Foursquare Gospel is similar in content to the beliefs of the Assemblies of God, but the formulation of its four points was taken directly from the fourfold gospel of A. B. Simpson, founder of the Christian and Missionary Alliance. Simpson had emphasized Christ as savior, sanctifier, healer, and coming king. Aimee simply changed sanctifier to baptizer with the Holy Spirit.

In 1923, Aimee settled in Los Angeles and dedicated the Angelus Temple. Throughout the remainder of her career, the Angelus Temple was the focus of numerous extravaganzas which brought Sister Aimee, as she was affectionately called, a reputation for outlandish, unconventional, religious performances. In 1926, Aimee disappeared for more than a month and upon her return claimed that she had been kidnapped. Such a controversy developed that there is still doubt about what really happened.

An Evangelistic and Training Institute was created almost simultaneously with the Angelus Temple and began training leaders who in turn created branch churches. The creation of some thirty-two churches in southern California by 1925 spurred steps toward formal organization of the Evangelistic Association, which in 1927 took the name of the International Church of the Foursquare Gospel.

The organization of the church is vested in the president, a position held by Aimee until her death in 1944 and now held by her son, Rolf K. McPherson. A five-man board of directors which includes the president and four appointees is the highest administrative body and controls all the departments. A convention meets annually for legislative matters. Publishing has been a major concern and a periodical, *Bridal Call*, was begun in 1917. The church operates KFSG, the first church-owned radio station in America, which was the third station commissioned in Los Angeles. A missionary program established early in the Church's life now sends missionaries around the world.

Membership: In 1980 the Church had 832 congregations and 160,074 members.

Educational facilities: L.I.F.E. (Lighthouse of International Foursquare Evangelism, Los Angeles, California.

Periodicals: *Foursquare Magazine.*

Sources: Raymond L. Cox, ed., *The Four-Square Gospel*. Los Angeles: Foursquare Publications, 1969; Aimee Semple McPherson, *The Story of My Life*. Waco, TX: Word Books, 1973; Lately Thomas, *The Vanishing Evangelist*. New York: Viking Press, 1959; Nancy Barr Mavity, *Sister Aimee*. Garden City, NY: Doubleday, 1931.

★330★
LAMB OF GOD CHURCH
612 Isenburg St.
Honolulu, HI 96817

The Lamb of God Church was founded in 1942 by Rev. Rose Soares, formerly of the Assemblies of God. It is a small church with its several congregations all located on Oahu, Hawaii. The faith and practice are like those of the Assemblies. The churches primarily serve native Hawaiians.

Membership: Not reported. In the mid-1970s there were 3 congregations and approximately 300 members.

Educational facilities: Lamb of God Bible School, Honolulu, Hawaii.

★331★
OPEN BIBLE STANDARD CHURCHES, INC.
2020 Bell Ave.
Des Moines, IA 50315

The Open Bible Standard Churches, Inc., was founded in 1935 by the merger of two evangelistic movements--the Open Bible Evangelistic Association and Bible Standard, Inc.. The former body had been founded by John R. Richey in Des Moines, Iowa, in 1932 and the latter in Eugene, Oregon, by Fred Hornshuh in 1919. At the time of the merger there were 210 ministers. Doctrine is like that of the Assemblies of God (discussed elsewhere in this volume) with a strong emphasis on healing, a literal heaven and hell, resurrection, tithing, and the belief that every Christian should identify with the visible church of Jesus Christ.

The polity is congregational. Congregations are grouped into districts and regions. A general conference meets annually and includes all ministers and a layman from each church. There are fourteen administrative departments. Missions are conducted in twenty-seven countries around the world. Inspiration Press prints both general religious literature and the Bible Truth Series for the Sunday school.

Membership: In 1984 the Church reported over 40,000 members in 290 congregations, and 856 ministers. There were also 1,000 members in Canada and 26,000 members overseas.

Educational facilities: Open Bible College, Des Moines, Iowa; Eugene Bible College, Eugene, Oregon; Dayton Bible College, Dayton, Ohio.

Periodicals: *Message of the Open Bible*, 2020 Bell Avenue, Des Moines, IA 50315; *The Overcomer*, 2020 Bell Avenue, Des Moines, IA 50315.

Sources: Robert Bryant Mitchell, *Heritage & Horizons.* Des Moines, IA: Open Bible Publishers, 1982; *Policies and Principles.* Des Moines, IA: Open Bible Standard Churches, Inc., 1983.

★332★

PENTECOSTAL CHURCH OF GOD OF AMERICA
Box 850
602 Main St.
Joplin, MO 64802

Not all Pentecostals, even those present at the 1914 Hot Springs, Arkansas, meeting to establish the Assemblies of God, agreed on the basis of union. The Assemblies registered even more dissent when the detailed doctrinal position was spelled out in 1916. Dissenters John C. Sinclair of Chicago and George Brinkman, editor of the *Pentecostal Herald*, called a meeting held in Chicago on December 30, 1919, to organize on a basis of acceptance of the Bible as the all-sufficient rule of faith and practice. At this meeting, a congregationally-organized, loose fellowship, the Pentecostal Assemblies of the U.S.A., was established. This name was changed to the Pentecostal Church of God in 1922. The ending "of America" was added in 1934.

Organizationally, the church has developed slowly and, in the early years, functioned primarily as an office to hold ministerial licenses. At present, it is governed by a general convention that meets every two years. An executive board handles administration between conventions. Congregations retain their autonomy, however, and participation in any program is strictly voluntary. Doctrine is like that of the Assemblies of God, but it was not until the 1940s that a doctrinal statement was adopted. In 1949, the convention authorized a book on the church's beliefs.

The Messenger Publishing House was established in Kansas City shortly after the the headquarters moved there in 1933. At first only the periodical was printed, but a Sunday School curriculum was added in 1938. One high school, one grammar school, and two bible schools (Pentecostal Bible College and Southern Bible College) were eventually established. A vigorous missionary program included thirteen fields in 1950. In 1949, a separate department on American Indian work was established. In 1951, the general offices were moved to their present location.

Membership: In 1984 the Church reported 40,867 (constituency 89,559), 1120 congregations and 2,970 ministers.

Educational facilities: School of Bible Theology, San Jacinto, California; Messenger College, Joplin, Missouri.

Periodicals: *The Pentecostal Messenger*, Box 850, Joplin, MO 64802; *The Helper*, Box 850, Joplin, MO 64802.

Sources: Elmer Louis Moon, *The Pentecostal Church.* New York: Carlton Press, 1966; Howard G. Tadlock, *This We Believe.* Joplin, MO: Messenger Publishing House, 1979; *General Constitution and By-Laws.* Joplin, MO: Pentecostal Church of God, 1984.

★333★

PENTECOSTAL CHURCH OF ZION
% Zion College of Theology
Box 110
French Lick, IN 47432

As a youth in Kentucky, Luther S. Howard was converted by an independent Pentecostal minister and, in 1920, was ordained a minister of the Holy Bible Mission at Louisville. He served as a minister and then vice-president. Upon the death of its founder, Mrs. C. L. Pennington, the Mission was dissolved. Its ministers felt the need to continue their work and, in 1954, formed a new organization, the Pentecostal Church of Zion, Inc. Elder Howard was elected president and, in 1964, bishop. Since most of the work of the Holy Bible Mission was in Indiana, the new organization was headquartered at French Lick, Indiana.

The Pentecostal Church of Zion is like the Assemblies of God in most of its doctrine but differs from it on some points. The group keeps the ten commandments, including the Saturday Sabbath, and the Mosaic law concerning clean and unclean meats. (Cows and sheep are clean and may be eaten; pigs and other animals with cloven hooves may not be eaten because they are considered unclean). Most important, the group does not have a closed creed, but believes that members continue to grow in grace and knowledge. Anyone who feels that he has new light on the Word of God is invited to bring his ideas to the annual convention, where they can be discussed by the executive committee. By such a process, a decision was made in the 1960s to drop the Lord's Supper as an ordinance. The church now believes in the celebration of Passover by daily communion with the Holy Ghost.

Polity is episcopal. There is one bishop with life tenure and an assistant bishop elected for a three-year term. An annual meeting with lay delegates is held at the headquarters.

Membership: Not reported. In 1974 there were 5 congregations in Indiana and 1 in Oregon.

Educational facilities: Zion College of Theology, French Lick, Indiana.

Periodicals: *Zion's Echoes of Truth*, Box 110, French Lick, IN 47432.

★334★

PENTECOSTAL EVANGELICAL CHURCH

% Rev. Ernest Beroth
Box 4218
Spokane, WA 99202

The Pentecostal Evangelical Church was founded in 1936. Its first bishop, G. F. C. Fons, had been the moderator of the Pentecostal Church of God of America in the period directly preceeding the formation of the new body. Its doctrine is similar to that of the Pentecostal Church of God of America, and its polity is a mixture of congregationalism and episcopal forms. Each local church is autonomous. The general conference meets every two years and elects a general bishop (for a four-year term), a vice-president (for two years), and a district superintendent (as an assistant bishop). Missions are supported in the Philippines, Bolivia, India and Guyana.

Membership: Not reported.

Periodicals: *Gospel Tidings*, Box 4218, Spokane, WA 99202.

★335★

PENTECOSTAL EVANGELICAL CHURCH OF GOD, NATIONAL AND INTERNATIONAL

Riddle, OR 97469

The Pentecostal Evangelical Church of God, National and International was founded at Riddle, Oregon in 1960. It holds to beliefs similar to those of the Assemblies of God. It ordains women to the ministry. A General Convocation meets annually.

Membership: Not reported. In 1967 there were 4 congregations and 14 ministers.

Periodicals: *Ingathering*, Riddle, OR ; *Golden Leaves*, Riddle, OR.

★336★

SEVENTH DAY PENTECOSTAL CHURCH OF THE LIVING GOD

1443 S. Euclid
Washington, DC 20009

The Seventh Day Pentecostal Church of the Living God was founded by Bishop Charles Gamble, a Pentecostal who had adopted some of the Old Testament practices including the seventh-day Sabbath. Gamble was a Roman Catholic and Baptist before becoming a Pentecostal. The church follows the Jesus-Only nonTrinitarian theology of the Apostolic churches.

Membership: Not reported. In the early 1970s there were 4 congregations with an estimated membership of less than 1,000.

★337★

UNITED FULL GOSPEL MINISTERS AND CHURCHES

Los Angeles, CA

The United Full Gospel Ministers and Churches was incorporated May 16, 1951. Arthur H. Collins was the first chairman. Within a few years it had grown to include more than fifty clergy and a number of congregations. The church is governed by four executive officers, one of whom faces election at each annual meeting. The group has an affiliate in India--the Open Bible Church of God, founded by Willis M. Clay, who at one time also served as treasurer of the United Full Gospel Ministers and Churches.

Membership: Not reported.

★338★

UNITED FUNDAMENTALIST CHURCH

Current address not obtained for this edition.

The United Fundamentalist Church was organized in 1939 by the Rev. Leroy M. Kopp of Los Angeles. It was at one time a member of the National Association of Evangelicals and accepts the Association's doctrinal position. In addition, it is Pentecostal, and prophecy and healing are emphasized. Members are expected to believe that "The divine healing of the sick is not only to honor the prayer of faith (James 5:14, 15) but is to be a sign to confirm the word as it is preached at home and abroad (Mark 16:15-20)." Signs are given until the end of this age, when they will no longer be needed.

The general officers of the United Fundamentalist Church, together with the territorial supervisors and state district superintendents, constitute a council which settles all doctrinal disputes. Zion Christian Mission is sponsored in Jerusalem. Proselyting other Christian denominations is not practiced. A radio ministry was begun in 1940 by Kopp and still continues. The Rev. E. Paul Kopp has succeeded his father as head of the group.

Membership: Not reported. In 1967 there were approximately 250 ministers and missionaries.

Deliverance Pentecostal

★339★

BRANHAM TABERNACLE AND RELATED ASSEMBLIES
% Spoken Word Publications
Box 888
Jeffersonville, IN 47131

William Marrion Branham (1909-1965) was a Pentecostal healer and prophet who as a child began to hear the voice of one he claimed to be an angel of the Lord. Healed as a young man in a Pentecostal Church, he became a preacher and his success led to the building of a tabernacle in his home town of Jeffersonville, Indiana. Another angelic visitation in 1946 launched his evangelical career as a healer and seer. He began to travel around the country leading revival services. He met Gordon Lindsey, a young Assemblies of God pastor in Oregon, who joined Branham and in 1948 began *The Voice of Healing*, to publicize Branham's work and bring supporters together. As Branham's tours and fame spread nationally and internationally, other ministers with a gift of healing associated themselves with him and *The Voice of Healing*. During the 1950s, Branham led the revival in healing that would project such people as Oral Roberts, Morris Cerullo, and A. A. Allen into the spotlight as leaders of their own organizations.

Around 1960 Branham became separated from the majority of the healing evangelists. He allowed divergent opinions which he had always held but had rarely spoken about to become frequent topics in his sermons. He denounced denominationalism as the mark of the beast of the Book of Revelation. He openly preached the non-Trinitarian views of the Jesus Only Pentecostals. Then in 1963 he declared himself the messenger of the last days, endowed with the spirit if Elijah, as prophesied by Malachi 4 and the Book of Revelation 11:3. That last declaration alienated Branham from the majority of his supporters in mainline Pentecostalism. His attempt at recovering widespread support was stopped by his death in a car accident two years later.

Those who followed Branham's message, who believed him the one with the spirit of Elijah, began immediately to preserve and perpetuate Branham's message. Copies of sermon tapes and transcripts of sermons have been reproduced and are circulated by several ministries, primarily Spoken Word Publications and The Voice of God, both in Jeffersonville, Indiana, which between them house the most complete archive of Branham tapes and written materials. Pastors of independent churches have an informal fellowship which circulates not only Branham's works, but the writings and tapes of others who follow his emphases. Branham's son Billy Paul Branham heads the Rev. William Branham Evangelistic Campaigns centered in Branham Tabernacle in Jeffersonville. Other leaders associated with Branham's ministry include Raymond Jackson of Faith Assembly

Church, Jeffersonville, Indiana; Ed Byshal of Bible Believers Inc. in Blaine, Washington and William N. Podaras of the Tabernacle of God in Gastonia, North Carolina. Besides support from across North America, followers can be found in Australia, New Zealand, and India.

Membership: Not reported. Over 100 pastors and churches regularly receive the materials circulated by Spoken Word Publications.

Periodicals: Unofficial but representative of Branham and his teachings: *The Contender*, Faith Assembly Church, 1715 Potters Lane, Jeffersonville, IN 47130; *Thus Saith the Lord*, Tabernacle of God, Box 956, Gastonia, NC 28052.

Sources: David Edwin Harrell, Jr., *All Things Are Possible*. Bloomington: University of Indiana Press, 1975; Gordon Lindsey, *William Branham, A Man Sent from God*. Jeffersonville, IN: William Branham, 1950; William Branham, *Footprints on the Sands of Time*. Jeffersonville, IN: Spoken Word Publications, n.d.; Terry Sproule, *A Prophet to the Gentiles*. Blaine, WA: Bible Believers, n.d.; William Marrion Branham, *Conduct, Order, Doctrine of the Church*. Jeffersonville, IN: Spoken Word Publications, 1974.

★340★

FIRST DELIVERANCE CHURCH OF ATLANTA
65 Hardwick St., S.E.
Atlanta, GA 30315

The First Deliverance Church was founded in Atlanta in 1956 by the Reverends Lillian G. Fitch and William Fitch, two deliverance evangelists. The church teaches three experiences (justification, sanctification, and baptism of the Holy Spirit), emphasizes healing, and practices tithing. Fasts are an important feature of church life. Occasionally members hold a shut-in fast, when they stay at the church for three days over the weekend. Among distinctive practices is their kneeling in prayer upon entering the church. Congregations headed by licensed ministers are located in Georgia, Florida, Oklahoma, and California.

Membership: Not reported.

★341★

FULL GOSPEL FELLOWSHIP OF CHURCHES AND MINISTERS INTERNATIONAL
1545 W. Mockingbird Ln., Suite 1012
Dallas, TX 75235

Gordon Lindsey was the first editor of *The Voice of Healing*, the early magazine of the deliverance-healing movement which grew around William Marrion Branham. A pastor in the Assemblies of God, he became president of the Voice of Healing Publishing Company which assisted in coordinating and announcing the revival meetings of the evangelists as they traveled the country. In 1949, Lindsey called together the first annual gathering of the healing evangelists associated with Branham and the magazine. That same year he began a missionary thrust, the Native Church Crusade, which was to lead to the formation of congregations and the building of meeting houses around the world. He supplemented that effort with a native evangelist program to train indigenous ministers in those areas where churches were being established. Jews and Arabs in the Middle East have been a particular focus for such efforts. Finally, efforts were made to build evangelistic centers in strategic urban centers in the United States. As many of the evangelists associated with *The Voice of Healing* in the beginning developed their own publishing ministries, they discontinued their support of Lindsey's ministry and of the annual conventions. The last one was held in 1961. The following year the Full Gospel Fellowship of Ministers and Churches was formed and held its first annual convention.

The work begun by Lindsey through *The Voice of Healing* was renamed Christ for the Nations Ministry in 1967. Christ for the Nations provides a central focus for the Full Gospel Fellowship of Churches and Ministers educational and missionary concerns. It operates two schools and oversees missions in numerous countries around the world. Its publishing arm has kept Gordon Lindsey's books in print and has published other authors as well. Upon Lindsey's death in 1973, leadership of Christ for the Nations was assumed by his wife, Freda Lindsey.

The Fellowship meets annually in convention. It is congregational in organization. The Fellowship does not ordain or license ministers, that being a perogative of the local churches, but it does offer recognition of ministerial credentials on the national and international level. The Canadian-based United Pentecostal Faith Church is affiliated with the Full Gospel Fellowship of Churches and Ministers.

Membership: Not reported. In 1967 there were 265 churches, 21,000 members and 1,650 ministers and evangelists, with an additional 300 ministers of nonaffiliated churches.

Educational facilities: Christ for the Nations Institute, Dallas, Texas; CFN Institute for Biblical Studies, Stony Brook, New York.

Periodicals: *Fellowship*, Suite 1012, 1545 W. Mockingbird Lane, Dallas, TX 75235; *Christ for the Nations*, Box 24910, Dallas, TX 75224.

Sources: Gordon Lindsey, *The Gordon Lindsey Story*. Dallas: The Voice of Healing Publishing Company, n.d. (1970?); Gordon Lindsey, *Bible Days Are Here Again*. Shereport, LA: The Author, 1949; Freda (Mrs. Gordon)

Lindsey, *My Diary Secrets*. Dallas: Christ for the Nations, 1976.

★342★
HALL DELIVERANCE FOUNDATION
Box 9910
Phoenix, AZ 85068

The Hall Deliverance Foundation was established in 1956 in San Diego as the focus of the ministry of the Reverend Franklin Hall, an independent Pentecostal minister, who began his ministerial career in 1946 as a Methodist. Hall preaches what he terms "body-felt salvation." It is Hall's belief that salvation is for the body as well as the soul. He based his teachings on the Biblical text, "by his stripes we are healed." When one understands the idea of body-felt salvation, he is clothed anew in the power of Christ which renews the body, protects it from sickness, and gives physical strength.

Those who participate in the body-felt salvation also participate in a miracle ministry which finds its demonstration in a wide variety of healings and deliverance from natural disasters and dangerous situations. Also, the experience of the Holy Spirit when it comes upon the person is felt tangibly as a pleasant warmth to heal the body or to bring healing protection energy. This sensation is related to the fire portion of the Holy Spirit baptism (Acts 2:3), which Jesus urged his disciples to obtain (Acts 1:8). Hall also recommends prayer and fasting. The latter enables one to become a powerful conductor of divine and spiritual forces, according to Hall.

Hall continues to travel the United States from his base in Phoenix. He distributes numerous pieces of literature and has recently begun a television ministry. Affiliated work takes place in Mexico, Canada, the Bahamas, Australia, New Zealand, Great Britain, West Germany, France, Sweden, the Philippines, Nigeria, Ghana, the Ivory Coast Ethiopia, Tanzania, Kenya, Malaya, South Africa, and India.

Membership: In 1984, The Foundation reported 42 associated churches, 30 ministers and 2,800 members across the United States. There are approximately 100,000 members overseas.

Educational facilities: Glory Knowledge Bible School Phoenix, Arizona.

Periodicals: *Miracle Word*, Box 9910, Phoenix, AZ 85068; *The Healing Word News*, Box 9910, Phoenix, AZ 85068.

Sources: Franklin Hall, *The Body-Felt Salvation*. Phoenix: Hall Deliverance Foundation, 1968; Franklin Hall, *Our Divine Healing Obligation*. Phoenix: The Author, 1964.

★343★

INTERNATIONAL CONVENTION OF FAITH CHURCHES AND MINISTERS
4500 S. Garnett
Exchange Tower, Suite 910
Tulsa, OK 74146

The International Convention of Faith Churches and Ministers was founded in 1979 by Dr Doyle Harrison and a number of independent Pentecostal pastors and evangelists, some of whom head their own national and international ministries, and a few of whom had become very well known for their work on Christian television-- Kenneth Hagin, (Tulsa, Oklahoma), Kenneth Copeland (Fort Worth, Texas), Frederick K. C. Price (Los Angeles), Norvel Hayes (Cleveland, Tennessee), Jerry J. Savelle (Fort Worth, Texas) and John H. Osteen (Houston, Texas). Hagin is pastor of RHEMA Bible Church and heads Kenneth Hagin Ministries, Inc.. Copeland, assisted by Gloria Copeland, his wife, heads Kenneth Copeland Ministries and Publications. Price, a black minister, heads Ever Increasing Faith Ministries and pastors Crenshaw Christian Center. Savelle heads Jerry Savelle Ministries and founded the Overcoming Faith Churches of Kenya in Africa. Osteen heads the John Osteen World Satellite Network. Norvel Hayes, a successful businessman, is also an independent healing evangelist. Doyle Harrison pastors Faith Christian Fellowship International Church in Tulsa.

Not only does their work center upon healing, but they subscribe to the "faith confession" doctrine which holds that a child of faith can publically confess or claim something from God and be assured of getting it. The Convention admits both churches and individuals to membership. Many of the students trained at RHEMA Bible Training Center, started in 1974 by Hagin, have created new congregations partially drawing upon listeners of the television programs of the Convention founders. In 1975 Harrison, founded Harrison House, a book concern, which publishes many of the healing evangelists' materials.

Membership: In 1985 the Convention had over 800 ministers and churches on its rolls.

Educational facilities: RHEMA Bible Training Center, Tulsa, Oklahoma; Crenshaw Christian Center School of Ministry, Box 90000, Los Angeles, CA 90009.

Periodicals: *International Faith Report*, 4500 South Garnett, Exchange Tower, Tulsa, OK 74146. Unofficial (periodicals issued by ministries associated with the Convention): *The Word of Faith*, Kenneth Hagin Ministries, Box 50126, Tulsa, OK 74150; *Ever Increasing Faith Messenger*, Crenshaw Christian Center, Box 90000, Los Angeles, CA 90009; *Believers Voice of Victory Magazine*, Kenneth Copeland Ministries, Box 2908, Fort Worth, TX 76113.

Remarks: Some of the leading ministers of the Convention (Hagin, Copeland, Price) are among a group of evangelists-teachers who have been attacked by other Pentecostal leaders for what has been termed "faith formula theology," that is a belief that by publically confessing (claiming) something from God, believers will be given it according to their faith.

Sources: Kenneth E. Hagin, *How You Can Be Led by the Spirit of God*. Tulsa, OK: Kenneth Hagin Ministries, 1978; Gloria Copeland, *God's Will for You*. Fort Worth: Kenneth Copeland Publications, 1972; Frederick K. C. Price, *How to Obtain Strong Faith*. Tulsa, OK: Harrison House, 1980; John H. Osteen, *This Awakening Generation*. Humble, TX: The Author, 1964; Norvel Hayes, *7 Ways Jesus Heals*. Tulsa, OK: Harrison House, 1982.

★344★

INTERNATIONAL DELIVERANCE CHURCHES
Box 353
Dallas, TX 75221

Among the deliverance evangelists associated with William Marrion Branham was W. V. Grant. After several years as an active evangelist, he settled in Dallas because of health problems and became a prolific writer of deliverance literature. He became pastor of the Soul's Harbor Church in Dallas and the leading force in the International Deliverance Churches.

From the Dallas Center, annual conventions have been held each summer since 1962. During this period, classes are held for two weeks, and ministers are ordained. In recent years Grant has been joined by his son, W. V. Grant Jr.

Membership: Not reported.

Periodicals: *Dawn of a New Day*, Box 353, Dallas, TX 75221.

Sources: W. V. Grant, *The Grace of God in My Life*. Dallas: The Author, 1952; W. V. Grant, *Faith Cometh*. Dallas: The Author, n.d.; W. V. Grant, *The Truth About Faith Healers*. Dallas: Faith Clinic, n.d.

★345★

KATHRYN KUHLMAN FOUNDATION
(Defunct)

Kathryn Kuhlman emerged in the 1970s as the most famous and sought-after spiritual healer in the country. Born in Concordia, Missouri, and reared in the Methodist church, she could not preach for the Methodists because she was a woman, so she became a Baptist and was ordained by the Evangelical Church Alliance. While she pastored a church in Franklin, Pennsylvania, spontaneous healings began to occur. These were coincidental with some personal mystical/psychical experiences of Mrs. Kuhlman, experiences that included a trancelike state in which her consciousness left her body. From that time on, spectacular healing activity was characteristic of her services. She was reported to have cured such illnesses as muscular dystrophy, emphysema, terminal cancer, and blindness. In 1947, she moved to Pittsburgh where her work was later institutionalized as the Kathryn Kuhlman Foundation. She died in 1976.

Kuhlman was pastor of a congregation in Pittsburgh and once, a month held Sunday morning services in Los Angeles. She was a popular speaker for the Full Gospel Businessmen's Fellowship International. In 1970, the Foundation was subsidized by approximately 21 churches in countries around the world. The Foundation operated a vigorous radio and television ministry, a food assistance program, and a college scholarship program.

Sources: Allen Spraggett, *Kathryn Kuhlman, The Woman Who Believes in Miracles*. New York: New American Library, 1970; Helen Kooiman Hosier, *Kathryn Kuhlman*. Old Tappan, NJ: Fleming H. Revell, 1971; Kathryn Kuhlman, *Nothing Is Impossible with God*. Englewood Cliffs, NJ: Prentice-Hall, 1974; Kathryn Kuhlman, *God Can Do It Again*. Englewood Cliffs, NJ: Prentice-Hall, 1969; Kathryn Kuhlman, *I Believe in Miracles*. Englewood Cliffs, NJ: Prentice- Hall, 1962.

★346★
LEROY JENKINS EVANGELISTIC ASSOCIATION
Box F
Delaware, OH 43015

Leroy Jenkins is a healer who has become known as "the man with the golden arm" for his healing work. When he was five years old, so the story goes, the Lord spoke to him in an audible voice. Four years later, God spoke to him again and he levitated and floated through the air. In an accident in 1960, his arm was almost cut off. He was healed instantly (after refusing amputation) in a meeting conducted by A. A. Allen in Atlanta. With Allen's encouragement, he began to preach and his evangelistic association was formed in 1960. Originally headquartered in Tampa, Florida, he moved to Delaware, Ohio, where a large tabernacle was build in the 1970s. In 1971, his radio ministry was being heard over 57 stations.

Membership: Not reported. The magazine of the Association is mailed to over 100,000 supporters.

Periodicals: *Revival of America*, Delaware, OH.

Sources: Leroy Jenkins, *How I Met the Master*. Delaware, OH: Leroy Jenkins Evangelistic Association, n.d. (1970?); Leroy Jenkins, *God Gave Me a Miracle Arm*. Delaware, OH: Leroy Jenkins Evangelistic Association, 1963; Leroy Jenkins, *How You Can Receive Your Healing*. Delaware, OH; Leroy Jenkins Evangelistic Association, 1966.

★347★
MIRACLE LIFE REVIVAL, INC.
Box 20707
Phoenix, AZ 85036

Associated with W. V. Grant of the International Deliverance Churches is the evangelist Neal Frisby, who became known in the early 1960s for possessing a gift of prophecy. In 1967, he began regularly to release prophetic scrolls which, by 1974, numbered sixty and were published in book form. In 1972, Capstone Cathedral, a large square church capped with a pyramid, was completed on the outskirts of Phoenix, Arizona. It serves as the publishing center and headquarters. The number of Frisby's followers is not known. Recently, Frisby has become noted for releasing a number of pictures in which strange lights appear on the film. While some of these appear to be light refractions and film defects, many are similar to the psychic photography produced in spiritual circles.

Membership: Not reported.

Sources: Neal Frisby, *The Book of Revelation Scrolls*. Phoenix: The Author, n.d.; W. V. Grant, *Creative Miracles*. Dallas: Faith Clinic, n.d.

★348★
MIRACLE REVIVAL FELLOWSHIP
℅ Don Stewart Evangelistic Association
Phoenix, AZ

Asa Alonzo Allen was born of a poor Arkansas family, saved in a Methodist revival, and later baptized with the Holy Spirit in a Pentecostal meeting. He joined the Assemblies of God and felt called to preach. In the early 1940s, he began to seek a ministry of signs and wonders, particularly healing. He had what amounted to a theological conversion when, during a prayer time, he formulated the thirteen requirements for a powerful ministry. He became convinced that he could do the works of Jesus, and do more than Jesus did; that he could be flawless and perfect (in the Biblical sense), and should believe all the promises. During World War II, his throat became, according to one throat specialist, "permanently ruined," but Allen was healed.

In 1951, he purchased a tent and began the crusade in earnest. Headquarters of A.A. Allen Revivals, Inc., were established in Dallas and *Miracle Magazine* was begun. From that time until his death, Allen was an immensely popular evangelist speaking both to integrated and predominantly black audiences. As early as 1960, he was holding fully integrated meetings in the South. In 1958, he was given 1,250 acres near Tombstone, Arizona, which were named Miracle Valley and which became the international headquarters. Allen died in 1970 and was succeeded by Don Stewart, who chose the new name for the organization: Miracle Revival Fellowship.   Miracle Valley was created as a totally spiritual community. Allen founded a Bible school and publishing house, located adjacent to radio and television studios, the healing pool of Bethesda, and the headquarters. He also operated a telephone Dial-a-Miracle prayer service. The church seats 2,500. As a result of Allen's accomplishments and success, missionary churches were begun and independent ministers have become associated wtih him. Miracle Revival Fellowship, at first a department of A.A. Allen Revivals, was established as a ministerial fellowship and licensing agency. After Allen's death, the Bible college was turned over to the Central Latin American District Council of the Assemblies of God and is now known as Southern Arizona Bible College. A. A. Allen Revivals became the Don Stewart Evangelistic Association.

Membership: Not reported. By 1971 the fellowship of ministers had a reported 8,000 affiliated members.

Periodicals: *Miracle*, Miracle Valley, AZ 85645.

Sources: A. A. Allen, with Walter Wagner, *Born to Lose, Bound to Win*. Garden City, NY: Doubleday, 1970; A. A. Allen, *My Cross*. Miracle Valley, AZ: A. A. Allen Revivals Inc., n.d.; Don Stewart with Walter Wagner, *The Man from Miracle Valley*. Long Beach, CA: The Great Horizons Company, 1971; Don Stewart, *Blessings from the Hand of God*. Miracle Valley, AZ: Don Stewart Evangelistic Association, 1971.

★349★
MITA MOVEMENT
Calle Duarte 235
Hata Rey, PR 60919

The Mita Movement is a Puerto Rican Pentecostal movement imported to the continental United States by the immigration of some of its members. It was founded in 1940 by Mrs. Juanita Garcia Peraga, who saw in her sudden healing after a long illness, a divine revelation and a sign that God had chosen her body to be the dwelling place of the Holy Spirit. The name Mita, which she adopted, was given in the revelation.

The Mita Movement was built upon the personality of Mita, who has been an instrument of physical healings and moral conversions. Her followers see her as a sanctified messenger of God, an equal of the Old Testament prophets. Among other things, she is thought able to affect the weather. Worship services are very spontaneous. The main gathering is on Saturday. Hymns that are used were written either by Mita in an inspired state or by several composers ordained for their work by the church.

At the headquarters in Hato Rey, there is a complex of buildings which includes a home for men, a hospice for women, two restaurants, a supermarket, and some shops. In nearby Arecibo is a home for the aged. The movement was brought to the United States after World War II and currently has churches in New York City; Jersey City,

Passaic, and Paterson, New Jersey; Washington, D.C.; Philadelphia, and Chicago.

Membership: Not reported.

Apostolic Pentecostal

★350★
APOSTOLIC ASSEMBLIES OF CHRIST, INC.
Current address not obtained for this edition.

The Apostolic Assemblies of Christ was formed in 1970 by former members of the Pentecostal Churches of the Apostolic Faith led by Bishop G. N. Boone. During the term of presiding bishop Willie Lee, questions of his administrative abilities arose. In the midst of the controversy, he died. In the organizational disaray the church splintered, and one group formed around Bishop Boone and Virgil Oates, the vice-bishop. The new body is congregational in organization and continues in the doctrine of the parent body, since no doctrinal controversy accompanied the split.

Membership: In 1980 the Assemblies had approximately 3,500 members, 23 churches and 70 ministers.

★351★
APOSTOLIC CHURCH OF CHRIST
2044 Stadium Dr.
Winston-Salem, NC 27107

The Apostolic Church of Christ was founded in 1969 by Bishop Johnnie Draft and Elder Wallace Snow, both ministers in the Church of God (Apostolic). Draft, for many years an overseer in the church and pastor of St. Peter's Church, the denomination's headquarters congregation, expressed no criticism of the Church of God (Apostolic); rather, he stated that the Spirit of the Lord brought him to start his own organization. The church differs from its parent body in its development of a centralized church polity. Authority is vested in the executive board, which owns all the church property. Doctrine follows that of the Church of God (Apostolic).

Membership: In 1980 the Apostolic Church of Christ had 6 churches, 300 members, 15 ministers, and one bishop.

★352★
APOSTOLIC CHURCH OF CHRIST IN GOD
% Bethlehem Apostolic Church
1217 E. 15th St.
Winston-Salem, NC 27105

The Apostolic Church of Christ in God was formed by five elders of the Church of God (Apostolic): J. W. Audrey, J. C. Richardson, Jerome Jenkins, W. R. Bryant, and J. M. Williams. At the time of the split, the Church of God (Apostolic) was formally led by Thomas Cox, but, due to his ill health, Eli N. Neal was acting as presiding bishop. The dissenting elders were concerned with the authoritarian manner in which Neal conducted the affairs of the church as well as with some personal problems that Neal was experiencing. Originally, three churches left with the elders, who established headquarters in Winston-Salem, North Carolina. J. W. Audrey was elected the new presiding bishop.

The new church prospered and in 1952 Elder Richardson was elected as a second bishop. In 1956 Audrey resigned and Richardson became the new presiding bishop. Under his leadershp the Apostolic Church enjoyed its greatest success. He began The *Apostolic Gazette* (later the *Apostolic Journal*) which served the church for many years. He also instituted a program to assist ministers in getting an education. However, his efforts were frustrated by several schisms that cut into the church's growth, most prominently the 1971 schism led by former-bishop Audrey.

The church retained the doctrine and congregational polity of the Church of God (Apostolic).

Membership: In 1980 the church had 2,150 members in 13 congregations being served by five bishops and 25 ministers.

★353★
APOSTOLIC CHURCH OF JESUS
1825 E. River St.
Pueblo, CO 81001

The Apostolic Church of Jesus was founded by Antonio Sanches, who had been converted in an evangelistic meeting led by Mattie Crawford in Pueblo, Colorado in 1923, and his brother George Sanches. The Sanches brothers began to preach to the Spanish-speaking population of the city and in 1927 organized the first congregation of the Apostolic Church of Jesus. In subsequent years, congregations were established throughout the state and elsewhere and can now be found in Denver, Westminister, Fountain, Walsenbury, and Ft. Garland, Colorado; Palo Alto, California; San Luis, Trinidad; and Velarde, New Mexico. The group, presently under the leadership of Raymond P. Virgil, has a weekly radio ministry.

Membership: Not reported.

Periodicals: *Jesus Only News of the Apostolic Faith.*

★354★
APOSTOLIC CHURCH OF JESUS CHRIST
Current address not obtained for this edition.

The Apostolic Church of Jesus Christ is a second body that grew out of the Pentecostal Assemblies of the World after the death of G. T. Haywood, who founded the "oneness" work in Indianapolis, Indiana. The Church believes in the indispensability of baptism for salvation.

Membership: Not reported.

Periodicals: *The Voice of the Wilderness*, Indianapolis, IN.

★355★
APOSTOLIC FAITH (HAWAII)
1043 Middle St.
Honolulu, HI 96819

The Apostolic Faith Church, a local congregation in Honolulu, was founded by the Rev. Charles Lochbaum and his wife, Ada Lochbaum, who came to Honolulu in 1923. They began to hold services emphasizing the baptism of the Holy Spirit and divine healing. A tent was set up, services were held throughout the islands, and a building was erected in 1924. An aggressive evangelism program, which included street preaching and evangelizing the planatations, was begun. The first branch of the Apostolic Faith was set up in Kaimuki.

The Apostolic Faith preaches the kingdom of God message, emphasizing entrance into the kingdom by baptism (immersion) in Jesus' name, healing, and the imminent coming of Jesus. The Apostolic Church is a "Jesus only" group which preaches three experiences-- justification, sanctification, and baptism of the Holy Spirit. Divorce and participation in secret societies are not condoned. Tithing and free will offerings are stressed; unlike many Pentecostal churches, this one sees conscientious objection as disloyalty to the established government.

The Apostolic Faith is run by a five-member board of trustees who succeeded Lochbaum in 1959. Branch churches in Hawaii were established in Kaimuki, Lahainia, Kuhului, Kanunakakai, and Hilo. A radio ministry was begun in 1969.

Membership: Not reported.

Periodicals: *Kingdom of God Crusader*, 1043 Middle Street, Honolulu, HI 96819.

Sources: *Kingdom of God Crusader.* Honolulu: Apostolic Faith Church of Honolulu, 1969.

★356★
APOSTOLIC FAITH MISSION CHURCH OF GOD
Current address not obtained for this edition.

Among the people who visited the early Pentecostal revival which occurred in 1906-08 in Los Angeles was F. W. Williams (d.1932), a black man from the deep south. He received the Baptism of the Holy Spirit under the ministry of William J. Seymour and returned to Mississippi to establish an outpost of the Apostolic Faith

Mission. Not having great success, he moved to Mobile, Alabama, where a revival occurred under his ministry. Among those converted was an entire congregation of the Primitive Baptist Church. The members gave him their building as the first meeting house for the new mission parish. The church was organized on July 10, 1906.

In 1915 Bishop Williams became one of the first to adopt the Oneness or non-Trinitarian theology which had been espoused through Pentecostal circles. He broke with Seymour and renamed his church the Apostolic Faith Mission Church of God. He incorporated the new church on October 9, 1915. The church continues to place a strong emphasis upon divine healing, allows women preachers, and practices footwashing with communion. Baptism is in the name of the "Lord Jesus Christ," and without the use of the name, the baptism is considered void. Intoxicants, especially tobacco, alcohol and drugs are forbidden. Members are admonished to marry only those who have been "saved." The church is headed by the Senior Bishop and a Cabinet of Executive Officers composed of the bishops, overseers and the general secretary.

Membership: In 1982 there were 16 congregations (11 in Alabama, 3 in Florida, and 1 each in Ohio and Massachusetts).

★357★
APOSTOLIC GOSPEL CHURCH OF JESUS CHRIST
Current address not obtained for this edition.

The Apostolic Gospel Church of Jesus Christ was founded in Bell Gardens, California, in 1963 by the Rev. Donald Abernathy. During the next five years, four other congregations, all in the Los Angeles area, were added and a new denomination emerged. In 1968, Abernathy reported a series of visions in which it was revealed to him that the entire West Coast of North America would be destroyed in an earthquake. He reported the vision to the other congregations, and one pastor, the Rev. Robert Theobold, reported a confirming vision. As a result, the five congregations decided to move East. Abernathy took his congregation to Atlanta. The church at Avenal went to Kennett, Missouri; the church at Porterville to Independence, Missouri; the church at Port Hueneme to Murfreesboro, Tennessee; and the Lompoc congregation to Georgia.

The church accepts "oneness" doctrines, identifying Jesus with the Father. It does not approve of the use of medicines, doctors, or hospitals--only divine healing. Footwashing is practiced. Members are pacifists. There is a strict code of dress that prohibits bathing suits, slacks, shorts, tightly fitting or straightcut skirts, dresses with hemlines shorter than halfway between the knee and ankle, jewelry, and short hair for women. Long hair, short sleeves, and tightly fitting pants are prohibited for men.

The church is ruled by bishops (or elders) and deacons, and includes in its structure apostles, prophets, evangelists, pastors, and teachers. The attempt is to build a perfect church to which Christ will return. The perfect church will manifest both the fruits and gifts of the Spirit.

Membership: There are five congregations.

★358★
APOSTOLIC OVERCOMING HOLY CHURCH OF GOD
% Bishop Jasper C. Roby
514 W. 10th Ave., N.
Birmingham, AL 35204

William Thomas Phillips (d. 1974) was a black minister in the Methodist Episcopal Church in Mobile, Alabama, who joined the pentecostal Apostolic Faith Mission but eventually broke with its predominantly white body. In 1919, he founded the Ethiopian Overcoming Holy Church of God. The present name was adopted in 1927 to reflect both the "Jesus Only" theology and the inclusion of non-Ethiopians, i.e., white people, among the membership. A small percentage of the church membership is still white. The Apostolic Overcoming Holy Church is a "oneness" Pentecostal church but follows the Church of God (Cleveland, Tennessee) in believing that sanctification is a necessary experience preceeding the baptism of the Holy Spirit. There is a strong holiness code which forbids among other items, narcotics, all appearances of evil, and slavery. Women are given positions as ordained ministers. Divorce and remarriage is allowed under some conditions. Divine healing is stressed.

Influenced by black Jewish ideas, the church has constructed a history of the Ethiopians from the Bible and has reached the conclusion that Christianity existed in Ethiopia even in the days of Enoch.

Organization is episcopal. There is a presiding bishop, vice bishop and executive board which administer the affairs of the church. There is a national conference which takes place annually. Ministers are supported by tithes, and in turn, tithe to support the bishops. Most bishops also serve large churches and their tithe goes to the poor. Sunday school materials and the church periodical are published monthly by the Phillips Printing Company in Mobile, Alabama. Missions are supported in Haiti, India, Africa and the West Indies. There is a retirement home maintained.

Membership: Not reported. In 1956 the Church reported 300 churches, 75,000 members and 35 ministers.

Periodicals: *The People's Mouthpiece.*

★359★
ASSEMBLIES OF THE LORD JESUS CHRIST, INC.
Current address not obtained for this edition.

The Assemblies of the Lord Jesus Christ was formed in 1952 by the merger of three "Jesus only" groups which had sprung up around the country--the Assemblies of the Church of Jesus Christ, the Jesus Only Apostolic Church of God, and the Church of the Lord Jesus Christ. The Assemblies closely resembles the United Pentecostal Church in doctrine. The group preaches two experiences-- justification and the baptism of the Spirit, emphasizes healing, washes feet, tithes, and forbids participation in secret societies. While holding respect for the civil government, members do not participate in war. Worldly amusements are forbidden, as are school gymnastics and clothes which immodestly expose the body.

The government is congregational in form. There is an annual general conference. A general board oversees the church during the year. The church is divided into state districts which are located in the South, Midwest, and Southwest. The Foreign Mission Committee oversees the mission program in Uruguay and Columbia.

Membership: Not reported. In 1971 there were approximately 350 churches.

Periodicals: *Apostolic Witness*, Memphis, TN.

★360★
ASSOCIATED BROTHERHOOD OF CHRISTIANS
Current address not obtained for this edition.

Described as an "association of churches and ministers working together for the up-building of the Church of the Lord Jesus Christ, and the Spread of the New Testament Gospel," the Associated Brotherhood of Christians is a "oneness" Pentecostal body. It was formed under the leadership of E. E. Partridge and H. A. Riley to facilitate fellowship among all "blood-bought" people, those who believe Christ atoned for sins through the blood he shed in the crucifixion. Formation of the Associated Brotherhood of Christians was necessary because other Pentecostal churches were refusing fellowship to the ministers who eventually formed this church. The other Pentecostal churches objected to the ministers' divergence from the churches' doctrines. The original meetings to consider forming the Associated Brotherhood of Christians were held in 1933, with the incorporation taking place during World War II. (This facilitated exemption from military duties for ministers.)

While attempting to facilitate wider fellowship, the group has a definite doctrinal perspective. The "oneness" Pentecostalism of this church is of the "two-experiences" variety, focusing on justification and the baptism of the Holy Spirit. Baptism in Jesus' name is the only ordinance; the church's statement of beliefs includes a specific article on why foot-washing is not practiced. The group accepts the so-called "Bread of life" message, or what is termed spiritual communion. The emphasis of the message is not on the literal eating of literal elements but on the proper discernment of the body of Christ in the church. The church is pacifist, and conscientious objection is recommended to members.

Polity is congregational. There is an annual conference. The association is headed by an official board of three members: a chairman, vice-chairman, and secretary- treasurer. State presbyters are appointed by the official board. Churches are located across the South and Midwest and along the Pacific Coast.

Membership: Not reported. In the early 1970s there were 40 congregations, approximately 2,000 members and 100 ministers.

Periodicals: *Our Herald*, Wilmington, CA.

★361★
BETHEL MINISTERIAL ASSOCIATION
Box 5353
Evansville, IN 47715

The Bethel Ministerial Association is a small fellowship of ministers and churches formed in 1934 by some Baptist ministers headed by the Rev. A. F. Varnell, pastor of the Bethel Temple in Evansville, Indiana. It has gone through several name changes: Evangelistic Missionary Alliance, Bethel Assembly, Bethel Baptist Assembly, and finally became the Bethel Ministerial Association.

Doctrinally, the Bethel Ministerial Association resembles the "oneness" or "Jesus only" Pentecostals. It denies the Trinity and immerses believers in the name of Jesus. Members also believe in the gifts of the Spirit, especially healing, and in a second experience of grace when the Holy Spirit possesses or fills a person. They speak in tongues, but they differ from other Pentecostals by denying that speaking in tongues is a sign of being filled with the Holy Spirit.

Membership: In 1982 the Association reported 1,500 members, 15 congregations and 81 ministers.

★362★
BIBLE WAY CHURCH OF OUR LORD JESUS CHRIST WORLD WIDE, INC.
1130 New Jersey Ave., N.W.
Washington, DC 20001

The Bible Way Church of Our Lord Jesus Christ World Wide, Inc., was formed in 1957 by former members of some seventy churches of the Church of Our Lord Jesus Christ of the Apostolic Faith. Smallwood E. Williams became the presiding bishop. The purpose of organizing the new body was to effect a less autocratic leadership than in the parent body. (Prior to that time, Bishop R. C. Lawson had refused to consecrate other bishops for his church.) Besides Bishop Williams, John S. Beane, McKinley Williams, Winfield A. Showell, and Joseph Moore were also consecrated as bishops. A bishop of the Pentecostal Assemblies of the World officiated at the consecration service. Doctrine remains the same. A general conference meets annually. Williams has become best known for his work on social conditions within the black community in Washington, DC.

Membership: Not reported. In 1974 the Church had approximately 300 congregations and 250,000 members.

Periodicals: *The Bible Way News Voice*, 1130 New Jersey Avenue, Washington, DC.

Sources: Smallwood Edmond Williams, *This Is My Story*. Washington, DC: Wm. Willoughby Publishers, 1981; Smallwood E. Williams, *Significant Sermons*. Washington, DC: Bible Way Church Press, 1970.

★363★
BIBLE WAY PENTECOSTAL APOSTOLIC CHURCH
Current address not obtained for this edition.

The Bible Way Pentecostal Apostolic Church was founded by Curtis P. Jones. Jones began as a pastor in North Carolina in the Church of God (Apostolic), but left that church to join the Church of Our Lord Jesus Christ of the Apostolic Faith under Robert C. Lawson. He became pastor of the St. Paul Apostolic Church in Henry County, Virginia. Jones left during the internal disruption within Bishop Lawson's church in 1957, but did not join with Smallwood Williams' Bible Way Church of Our Lord Jesus Christ. Rather, in 1960, with two other congregations in Virginia, he founded a new denomination. A fourth church was soon added.

Membership: In 1980 the Church had four congregations, all in Virginia.

★364★
CHURCH OF GOD (APOSTOLIC)
Saint Peter's Church of God (Apostolic)
125 Meadows St.
Beckley, WV 25801

The Church of God (Apostolic) was formed in 1877 by Elder Thomas J. Cox at Danville, Kentucky, as the Christian Faith Band. It was one of a number of independent holiness associations of the late nineteenth century. In 1915, it voted a name change, and in 1919 became the Church of God (Apostolic). In 1943, Cox was succeeded by M. Gravely and Eli N. Neal as co-presiding bishops. Headquarters were moved to Beckley, West Virginia. Two years later Gravely divorced his wife and remarried. He was disfellowshipped from the church. In 1964 Neal was succeeded by Love Odom who died two

years later and was succeeded by David E. Smith. These two bishops did much to put the national church in a firm financial condition. They were suceeded by the present general overseer, Ruben K. Hash.

It is a strict church, opposing worldliness and practicing footwashing with the monthly Lord's Supper. Baptism by immersion is in the name of Jesus. The church is headed by a board of bishops, one of whom is designated the general overseer who serves as the church's executive head. There is a general assembly annually.

Membership: In 1980 the church had 15,000 members, 43 congregations and approximately 75 ministers.

★365★
CHURCH OF OUR LORD JESUS CHRIST OF THE APOSTOLIC FAITH
2081 Seventh Ave.
New York, NY 10027

The Church of Our Lord Jesus Christ of the Apostolic Faith was founded in Columbus, Ohio, in 1919 by Robert Clarence Lawson (d. 1961), who as a pastor in the Pentecostal Assemblies of the World had founded churches in Texas and Missouri. At one point in his early life when he was ill he had been taken to the Apostolic Faith Assembly Church, a leading church of the Pentecostal Assemblies, and its pastor, G. T. Haywood. Healed, Lawson joined the Assemblies, and adopted their non-trinitarian theology. However, in 1913 he left Haywood's jurisdiction and, moving to New York City, founded Refuge Temple, the first congregation in his new independent church. Given Lawson's effective leadership, the organization grew quickly. Other congregations were established and a radio ministry, a periodical, a day nursery, and several businesses were initiated. In 1926 he opened a Bible school to train pastors.

In the 1930s, Lawson began a series of trips to the West Indies which led to congregations being formed in Jamaica, Antigua, the Virgin Islands, and Trinidad. His lengthy tenure as bishop of the Church was a time of steady growth, broken only by two schisms by Sherrod C. Johnson, (Church of the Lord Jesus Christ of the Apostolic Faith, 1930) and Smallwood Williams, (Bible Way Church of Our Lord Jesus Christ, 1957). Lawson was succeeded by Hubert J. Spencer and by the present presiding apostle, William Bonner.

Doctrine is like the older Pentecostal Assemblies of the World. Footwashing is practiced and the baptism of the Holy Spirit is believed to be necessary for salvation. The church is headed by the presiding apostle, who is assisted by four regional apostles. There is an annual convocation held in New York City. Affiliated churches can be found in the West Indies, Africa, England and Germany.

Membership: In 1980 there were approximately 450 churches and 300,000 members.

Educational facilities: Church of Christ Bible Institute, New York, New York.

Periodicals: *The Contender for the Faith*, 2081 Seventh Avenue, New York, NY 10027.

Sources: Arthur M. Anderson, ed., *For the Defense of the Gospel*. New York: Church of Christ Pub. Co., 1972.

★366★
CHURCH OF THE LORD JESUS CHRIST OF THE APOSTOLIC FAITH (PHILADELPHIA)
22nd & Bainbridge Sts.
Philadelphia, PA 19146

The Church of the Lord Jesus Christ of the Apostolic Faith was founded in 1933 by Bishop Sherrod C. Johnson, formerly of the Church of Our Lord Jesus Christ of the Apostolic Faith. Johnson protested what he felt were too liberal regulations espoused by Bishop Robert C. Lawson in regard to the appearance of female members. Lawson allowed the wearing of jewelry and make-up. Johnson insisted upon female members wearing cotton stockings, calf-length dresses, unstraightened hair and head coverings. Johnson also opposed the observance of Lent, Easter and Christmas. Upon Bishop Johnson's death in 1961, he was succeeded by S. McDowell Shelton, the "Bishop, Apostle, and Overseer of the Church." This church has been most aggressive and has approached its parent body in membership.

The doctrine is a typical "oneness" doctrine, though the church is known for its conservatism. It does demand that baptism must be in the name of the "Lord Jesus" or "Jesus Christ," but not just "Jesus." This exacting formula is to distinguish the Lord Jesus from Bar Jesus (Acts 13:6) and Jesus Justas (Col. 4:11), two other Biblical characters. The church members also believe one must be filled with the Holy Ghost in order to have the new birth. The church's conservatism is most manifest in its rigid behavior code. Prohibited are women preachers and teachers, remarriage after divorce, dressing like the world, and wearing costly apparel.

The church is episcopal. There is a national convention annually at the national headquarters in Philadelphia. Lay people have an unusually high participation level in the national church, holding most of the top administrative positions. There is an active radio ministry, "The Whole Truth," carried on 50 stations. Missions are conducted in Liberia, West Africa, England, Honduras, Jamaica, Haiti, Bahamas, Jordan, Portugal, and the Maldives.

Membership: In 1980 there were approximately 100 congregations.

Periodicals: *The Whole Truth*, 22nd and Bainbridge Streets, Philadelphia, PA 19146.

★367★
GLORIOUS CHURCH OF GOD IN CHRIST APOSTOLIC FAITH
Current address not obtained for this edition.

The Glorious Church of God in Christ Apostolic Faith was founded in 1921 by C. H. Stokes, its first presiding bishop. He was succeeded in 1928 by S. C. Bass who was to head the church for over a quarter of a century. However, in 1952, after the death of his first wife, Bass remarried a woman who was a divorcee. It had been taught for many years that marrying a divorced person was wrong. Bass' actions split the fifty-congregation church in half. Those who remained loyal to Bishop Bass retained the name, but the founding charter was retained by the other group, which took the name Original Glorious Church of God in Christ Apostolic Faith.

★368★
GOD'S HOUSE OF PRAYER FOR ALL NATIONS
Current address not obtained for this edition.

God's House of Prayer for All Nations, Inc., was founded in 1964 in Peoria, Illinois, by Bishop Tommie Lawrence, formerly of the Church of God in Christ. The doctrine is "oneness" Pentecostal, identifying Jesus with the Father, and the polity is strongly episcopal. Great stress is placed on healing as one of the signs of the spirit and there is much fellowship with the churches of the Miracle Revival Fellowship founded by the late A. A. Allen.

Membership: Not reported. There are several congregations, all in northern Illinois.

★369★
HIGHWAY CHRISTIAN CHURCH OF CHRIST
436 W St.,N.W.
Washington, DC 20001

The Highway Christian Church of Christ was founded in 1929 by James Thomas Morris, formerly a minister with the Pentecostal Assemblies of the World. Relations between the two groups remained cordial, and in 1941 Bishop[J. M. Turpin of the Assemblies consecrated Morris to the episcopal leadership of the Highway Church. Morris died in 1959 and was succeeded by his nephew, J. V. Lomax, formerly a member of the Church of Our Lord Jesus Christ of the Apostolic Faith.

The Highway Church has a reputation as one of the more conservative Pentecostal church bodies. Members are encouraged to wear only black (suits and skirts) and white (shirts and blouses), and to avoid bright colors as too ostentatious. The church will accept ordained women from other denominations, but will neither ordain females nor allow them to pastor congregations.

Membership: In 1980 there were 13 congregations and about 3,000 members.

★370★
INTERNATIONAL MINISTERIAL ASSOCIATION
4003 Bellaire Blvd.
Houston, TX 77025

The International Ministerial Association, Inc. was formed in 1954 by W. E. Kidson and twenty other pastors formerly with the United Pentecostal Church. It practices baptism by immersion and foot-washing. Tithing is believed to be the financial plan of the church. A strong belief in the Second Coming is taught, and the group believes in a distinct judgment where believers only will be rewarded.

An annual international conference is the place for fellowship of the ministers, who hold credentials through the Association and the members of the autonomous congregations which accept the statement of faith. Herald Publishing House is located in Houston, Texas.

Membership: Not reported. In the early 1970s, there were 440 ministerial members and 117 affiliated congregations.

Periodicals: *The Herald of Truth,* 4003 Bellaire Blvd., Houston, TX.

★371★
MOUNT HEBRON APOSTOLIC TEMPLE OF OUR LORD JESUS OF THE APOSTOLIC FAITH
Mount Hebron Apostolic Temple
27 Vineyard Ave.
Yonkers, NY 10703

The Mount Hebron Apostolic Temple of Our Lord Jesus of the Apostolic Faith was founded in 1963 by George H. Wiley III, pastor of the Yonkers, New York, congregation of the Apostolic Church of Christ in God. As his work progressed, Wiley came to feel that because of his accomplishments for the denomination he should be accorded the office of bishop. He had had particular success in the area of youth work, and his wife, Sister Lucille Wiley, served as president of the Department of Youth Work. However, the board of the Apostolic Church denied his request to become a bishop. He left with his supporters and became bishop of a new Apostolic denomination.

Wiley has placed great emphasis upon youth work and upon radio work, establishing an outreach in New York, one in North Carolina, and another in South Carolina. The temple continues the doctrine and polity of the Apostolic Church of Christ in God and has a cordial relationship with its parent organization.

Membership: In 1980 the temple reported 3,000 members in nine congregations being served by 15 ministers. There are two bishops.

★372★
NEW BETHEL CHURCH OF GOD IN CHRIST (PENTECOSTAL)
Current address not obtained for this edition.

In 1927, the Rev. A.D. Bradley was admonished by the board of bishops of the Church of God in Christ to refrain from preaching the "Jesus only" doctrine. (The Church of God in Christ was the oldest and among the largest of the predominantly-black trinitarian Pentecostal churches.) He refused, and with his wife and Lonnie Bates established the New Bethel Church of God in Christ (Pentecostal). Bradley became the church's presiding bishop. Doctrine is similar to other "Jesus only" groups. The three ordinances of baptism, the Lord's Supper, and foot-washing are observed. The group is pacifist but allows alternative noncombatant positions to be held by law-abiding church members. The group disapproves of secret societies and of school activities which conflict with a student's moral scruples.

The presiding bishop is the executive officer and presides over all meetings of the general body. A board of bishops acts as a judicatory body and a general assembly as the legislative body.

Membership: Not reported.

★373★
ORIGINAL GLORIOUS CHURCH OF GOD IN CHRIST APOSTOLIC FAITH
Current address not obtained for this edition.

The Glorious Church of God was founded in 1921. However, in 1952 its presiding bishop, S. C. Bass married a divorced woman. Approximately half of the fifty-congregation church rejected Bass and reorganized under the leadership of W. O. Howard and took the name Original Glorious Church of God in Christ Apostolic Faith. The term "Original" signified their claim to the history of the church, demonstrated by their retention of the founding charter. Howard was succeeded by Bishop I. W. Hamiter, under whose leadership the church has grown spectacularly and developed a mission program in Haiti, Jamaica and India. Hamiter has also led in the purchase of a convention center for the church's annual meeting in Columbus, Ohio.

Membership: In 1980 the Church had 55 congregations in the United States, 110 congregations overseas, 200 ministers and approximately 25,000 members worldwide.

★374★
PENTECOSTAL ASSEMBLIES OF THE WORLD
% Willard W. Saunders, Presiding Bishop
3040 N. Illinois St.
Indianapolis, IN 46208

Oldest of the Apostolic or "Jesus Only" Pentecostal churches, the Pentecostal Assemblies of the World began as a loosely-organized fellowship of trinitarian pentecostals in Los Angeles in 1906. J. J. Frazee (occasionally incorrectly reported as "Frazier") was elected the first general superintendent. Early membership developed along the West Coast and in the Midwest. From 1913 to 1916, the annual convention was held in Indianapolis, soon to become the center of the organization. Growth in the organization was spurred when it became the first group of pentecostals to accept the "Jesus Only" Apostolic theology, which identified Jesus as the Jehovah of the Old Testament and denied the Trinity. Many ministers from other pentecostal bodies joined the Assemblies when the group within which they held credentials rejected Apostolic teachings. In 1918, the General Assemblies of the Apostolic Assemblies, a recently formed Apostolic body, which included such outstanding early movement leaders as D. C. O. Opperman and H. A. Goss, merged into the PAW.

From its beginning the Pentecostal Assemblies of the World was fully integrated racially, though predominantly white in membership. In 1919, following the influx of so many ministers and members, especially the large newly-merged body, the Pentecostal Assemblies reorganized. Four of its twenty-one field superintendents were black, among whom were Thomas Garfield Haywood, who would later become presiding bishop. In 1924, most of the white members withdrew to form the Pentecostal Ministerial Alliance, now an integral part of the United Pentecostal Church. The remaining members, not totally, but predominantly black, reorganized again, created the office of bishop, and elected Haywood to lead them. He remained presiding bishop until his death in 1931.

Shortly after Haywood's death, the Apostolic Churches of Jesus Christ, a name briefly assumed by the former Pentecostal Ministerial Alliance that was then in a phase of consolidatiing various Apostolic groups into a single organization, invited the Assemblies to consider merger. The merger attempt failed, but the Assemblies again lost individual congregations and members to the Apostolic Churches of Jesus Christ, and a large group who formed a new church, the Pentecostal Assemblies of Jesus Christ, as a prelude to the merger which failed. In the face of the new losses, a third reorganization had to occur in 1932. For several years, the church was led by a small group of bishops, enlarged to seven in 1935. Two years later, Samuel Grimes, a former missionary in Liberia, was elected presiding bishop, a post he retained until his death in 1967. Under his guidance, the Pentecostal Assemblies church experienced its greatest era of expansion. Contrary to most black Pentecostal bishops, Grimes did not also serve a parish, hence he was able to devote himself full-time to his episcopal duties.

Doctrine of the Assemblies is similar to that of the Assemblies of God except that it does not believe in the Trinity. Holiness is stressed and the group believes that for ultimate salvation, it is necessary to have a life wholly sanctified. Wine is used in the Lord's Supper. Healing is stressed and foot-washing practiced. Members are pacifists, though they feel it is a duty to honor rules. There is a strict dress and behavior code. Divorce and remarriage are allowed under certain circumstances.

There is an annual general assembly which elects the bishops and the general secretary. It also designates the presiding bishop, who heads a board of bishops. The church is divided into 30 districts (dioceses) headed by a bishop. The Assemblies are designated joint members of each local board of trustees. A missionary board oversees missions in Nigeria, Jamaica, England, Ghana, and Egypt.

Membership: In 1980 the Assemblies had 450,000 members in 1,000 churches divided into 30 districts, each headed by a bishop.

Educational facilities: Aenon Bible School, Indianapolis, Indiana.

Periodicals: *Pentecostal Outlook*, 3040 N. Illinois Street, Indianapolis, IN 46208.

Sources: Morris E. Golder, *History of the Pentecostal Assemblies of the World*. Indianapolis: The Author, 1973; Paul P. Dugas, comp., *The Life and Writings of Elder G. T. Haywood*. Portland, OR: Apostolic Book Publishers, 1968; Morris E. Golder, *The Life and Works of Bishop Garfield Thomas Haywood*. Indianapolis: the Author, 1977; James L. Tyson, *Before I Sleep*. Indianapolis: Pentecostal Publications, 1976.

★375★
PENTECOSTAL CHURCHES OF APOSTOLIC FAITH
Current address not obtained for this edition.

The Pentecostal Churches of Apostolic Faith was formed in 1957 by former members of the Pentecostal Assemblies of the World under the leadership of Bishop Samuel N. Hancock. Hancock was one of the original men selected as a bishop of the Assemblies following its reorganization in 1925. In 1931 he was one of the leaders in the attempt to unite the Assemblies with the predominantly white Pentecostal Ministerial Alliance, and he helped form the Pentecostal Assemblies of Jesus Christ, a body whose polity was more acceptable to the Alliance. Within a few years, Hancock returned to the Assemblies as an elder and was elected as a bishop for the second time.

However, soon after Hancock's return, it was discovered that he had deviated on traditional Apostolic doctrine in that he taught that Jesus was only the son of God, not that he was God. His position forced the Assemblies to issue a clarifying statement of its position, but Hancock's teachings were tolerated. Hancock also felt that he should have become the presiding bishop. Disappointment at not being elected seems to have fueled the discontent felt throughout the 1950s. Hancock carried two other bishops into the new church formed in 1957, including Willie Lee, pastor of Christ Temple Church, the congregation pastored by Thomas Garfield Haywood, the first presiding bishop of the Assemblies. Lee succeeded Hancock as presiding bishop of the Churches upon the latter's death in 1963. The following year, a major schism occurred when the majority of the Churches rejected the doctrinal position held by Hancock and also taught by Lee. Elzie Young had the charter and claimed the support of the Churches to become the new presiding bishop. The church returned to the traditional Apostolic theology.

The Pentecostal Churches of the Apostolic Faith are congregational in polity, and headed by a presiding bishop (Elzie Young) and a council of bishops. Under Young's leadership, the Churches have grown and stablized their original shaky financial condition. A mission program developed, and the Churches support missionaries in Haiti and Liberia, where they have built a school.

Membership: In 1980 the Churches had approximately 25,000 members, 115 churches and 380 ministers.

★376★
REDEEMED ASSEMBLY OF JESUS CHRIST, APOSTOLIC

% Bishop Douglas Williams
734 1st St., S.W.
Washington, DC 20024

The Redeemed Assembly of Jesus Christ, Apostolic was formed by James Frank Harris and Douglas Williams, two bishops of the Highway Christian Church who rejected the leadership of that church by Bishop J. V. Lomax. They complained of his control, bypassing other bishops and pastors and making decisons in conference with the elders of the congregation he headed in Washington, D.C. The new church is headed by a presiding bishop, assistant presiding bishop, and an executive council consisting of the bishops and all the pastors. There was no doctrinal conflict in the split.

Membership: In 1980 the Church had six congregations, one in Richmond, Virginia, one in New York City, and four in the Washington, D.C. area.

★377★
SHILOH APOSTOLIC TEMPLE

1516 W. Master
Philadelphia, PA 19121

The Shiloh Apostolic Temple was founded in 1953 by Elder Robert O. Doub, Jr., of the Apostolic Church of Christ in God. In 1948 Doub had moved to Philadelphia to organize a new congregation for the Apostolic Church of Christ in God. He not only succeeded in building a stable congregation, Shiloh Apostolic Temple, but assisted other congregations throughout the state to organize. In light of his accomplishments, Doub felt that he should be made a bishop and so petitioned the church. He believed that the state overseer was taking all the credit Doub himself deserved. Doub's petition was denied. He left with

but a single congregation in 1953 and incorporated separately in 1954.

The energetic work that characterized Doub's years in the Apostolic Church of Christ in God led Shiloh Apostolic Temple to outgrow its parent body. Doub began a periodical and purchased a camp, Shiloh Promised Land Camp, in Montrose, Pennsylvania. He also took over foreign work in England and Trinidad. The doctrine, not at issue in the schism, remains that of the parent Church of God (Apostolic) from which the Apostolic Church of Christ in God came.

Membership: In 1980 the church had 4,500 members of which 500 were in the congregation in Philadelphia. The church reported 23 congregations, of which 8 were in England and 2 in Trinidad.

Periodicals: *Shiloh Gospel Wave*, 1516 West Master, Philadelphia, Pennsylvania 19121.

★378★
TRUE VINE PENTECOSTAL CHURCHES OF JESUS

% Dr. Robert L. Hairston
New Bethel Apostolic Church
Martinsville, VA 24112

Dr. Robert L. Hairston had been a pastor in several trinitarian Pentecostal groups and had been a co-founder with Willaim Monroe Johnson of the True Vine Pentecostal Holiness Church. However, in 1961 Hairston accepted the Apostolic "Jesus Only" teachings. He left the church he had founded and formed the True Vine Penetcostal Churches of Jesus. Also causal factors in the formation of the new denomination were differences between Hairston and Johnson over church polity and Hairston's marital situation. Hairston rejected the idea of local congregations being assessed to pay for the annual convocation of the church. Also, he had divorced his first wife and remarried, an action frowned upon in many Pentecostal circles.

The Church follows standard Apostolic teachings. Women are welcome in the ministry. Growth of the group was spurred in 1976 by the addition of several congregations headed by Bishop Thomas C. Williams.

Membership: In 1980 the Church reported 10 churches and missions, two bishops, 14 ministers and approximately 900 members.

★379★
UNITED CHURCH OF JESUS CHRIST (APOSTOLIC)
℅ Monroe E. Saunders, Presiding Bishop
2136 32nd Place, S.E.
Washington, DC 20020

The United Church of Jesus Christ (Apostolic) dates to 1945 when Randolph Carr left the Pentecostal Assemblies of the World to found the Church of God in Christ (Apostolic). During the 1960s, Monroe Saunders, chief assistant to Carr, criticized him for contradicting in action his stated position on divorce and remarriage. Carr asked Saunders to leave the Church, and most of the group followed him. They reorganized as the United Church and elected Saunders the presiding bishop. Doctrine stresses the authority of the Bible and the unity of the Godhead. There are three ordinances, including foot-washing.

The Church is headed by a presiding bishop, a vice-bishop, and three other bishops. As presiding bishop, Saunders, who completed his post-graduate education, has led the church in emphasizing an educated ministry, and with the development of The Center for a More Abundant Life, which provides a variety of social services to people living in Baltimore. Missions are supported in Mexico, Trinidad, Jamaica, and other West Indian Islands.

Membership: In 1985 the Church had 75 congregations, approximately 100,000 members and over 150 ministers in the United States. There were approximatly 50,000 additional members overseas.

Educational facilities: Institute of Biblical Studies, Baltimore, Maryland.

Sources: Monroe R. Saunders, Sr., *The Book of Church Order and Discipline of the United Church of Jesus Christ (Apostolic)*. Washington, DC: 1965.

★380★
UNITED CHURCHES OF JESUS, APOSTOLIC
Current address not obtained for this edition.

The United Churches of Jesus, Apostolic was formed by several bishops of the Apostle Church of Christ in God who rejected the leadership of presiding bishop J. C. Richardson Sr. Richardson had married a divorced woman. The church is headed by a general bishop, J. W. Ardrey (one of the founders of the Apostle Church) and a board of bishops. Doctrine is like the parent body.

Membership: In 1980 the United Churches had 2,000 members, 20 churches, 30 ministers and six bishops.

★381★
UNITED PENTECOSTAL CHURCH
8855 Dunn Rd.
Hazelwood, MO 63042

The United Pentecostal Church was formed in 1945 by the union of the Pentecostal Assemblies of Jesus Christ and the Pentecostal Church, Inc. The Pentecostal Assemblies of Jesus Christ had been formed by some "oneness" Pentecostals who had not joined the Assemblies of God. The Pentecostal Church, Inc. was formed by white members who withdrew from the interracial Pentecostal Assemblies of the World.

The United Pentecostal Church teaches two experiences (justification and the baptism of the Holy Spirit) and practices foot-washing, healing, and conscientious objection. There is a rigid holiness code which includes disapproval of secret societies, mixed bathing, women cutting their hair, worldly amusements, home television sets, and immodest dress, especially at school.

Government is congregational. A general conference meets annually. A general superintendent, two assistants and a secretary/treasurer are members of the general board consisting of superintendents, executive presbyters, and division heads. A foreign missions division oversees missions around the world in 90 countries. World Aflame Press, formerly the Pentecostal Publishing House in Hazelwood, Missouri publishes books, Sunday school material, and a wide variety of religious literature. The church is divided into 47 districts which include churches in every state and all ten Canadian provinces.

Membership: In 1984 the Church reported 400,000 members, 3,289 ministers and 6504 ministers. There were 850,000 members worldwide.

Periodicals: *The Pentecostal Herald*, 8855 Dunn Road, Hazelwood, MO 63042; *The Global Witness*, 8855 Dunn Road, Hazelwood, MO 63042.

Sources: Fred J. Foster, *Their Story: 20th Century Pentecostals*. Hazelwood, MO: World Aflame Press, 1981; Arthur L. Clanton, *United We Stand*. Hazelwood, MO; Pentecostal Publishing House, 1970; Andrew D. Urshan, *My Study of Modern Pentecostals*. Portland, OR: Apostolic Book Publishers, 1981.

★382★
UNITED WAY OF THE CROSS CHURCHES OF CHRIST OF THE APOSTOLIC FAITH
Current address not obtained for this edition.

The United Way of the Cross Churches of Christ of the Apostolic Faith was founded by Bishop Joseph H. Adams of the Way of the Cross Church of Christ and Elder Harrison J. Twyman of the Bible Way Church of Our Lord Jesus Christ World Wide, Inc. The new church was formed when the two founders, both pastors of congregations in North Carolina, discovered that God had given each a similar vision to form a new church. Also, Adams, a bishop in North Carolina for the Way of the Cross Church of Christ, had developed some concerns with the administrative procedures of the church. The church grew, in part, from the addition of pastors and their congregations who had previously left other Apostolic bodies.

Membership: In 1980 the United Way of the Cross Churches had 1,100 members in 14 churches. There were 30 ministers and four bishops.

★383★
WAY OF THE CROSS CHURCH OF CHRIST
332 4th St., N.E.
Washington, DC 20003

The Way of the Cross Church of Christ was founded in 1927 by Henry C. Brooks, an independent black Pentecostal minister. Brooks had founded a small congregation in Washington, D.C. which became part of the Church of Our Lord Jesus Christ of the Apostolic Faith founded by R.C. Lawson. At that time there was another small congregation under Bishop Lawson in Washington headed by Smallwood Williams, and Lawson wanted Brooks' congregation to join Williams'. Brooks rejected the plan, left Lawson's jurisdiction and founded a separate organization. A second congregation in Henderson, North Carolina became the first of several along the East Coast. Brooks pastored the mother church for forty years and built a membership of over 3,000.

The Way of the Cross Church is headed by by a presiding bishop. John L. Brooks, the son of the founder, succeeded to that post. He is assisted by twelve other bishops. Missions are supported in Ghana and Liberia.

Membership: In 1980 the Way of the Cross Church of Christ had 48 affiliated congregations and approximately 50,000 members.

★384★
YAHWEH'S TEMPLE
Box 652
Cleveland, TN 37311

Yahweh's Temple was founded in 1947 as the Church of Jesus and has through the decades of its existence sought the name that best expressed its central doctrinal concern of identifying Jesus with the God of the Old Testament. In 1953 the Church became The Jesus Church, and it adopted its present name in 1981. The Temple is headed by Samuel E. Officer, its bishop and moderator, a former member of the Church of God (Cleveland, Tennessee). The Temple follows the "oneness" doctrine generally, but has several points of difference from other bodies. From the Sacred Name Movement it has accepted the use of the Hebrew transliterations of the names of the Creator. It also keeps the Saturday Sabbath. It derives its name from

a belief that Jesus is the "new and proper name of God, Christ, and the church." Specifically rejected are names such as "Church of God," "Pentecostal," and "Churches of Christ." The organization of the Temple is based upon an idea that all the members have a special place to work in a united body. From Ezekiel 10:10, a model of four wheels within wheels has been constructed. Each wheel consists of a hub of elders, spokes of helpers, a band for service, and the rim of membership. At the center is the international bishop, who exercises episcopal and theocratic authority. There are national and state bishops, and local deacons.

Membership: Not reported. In 1973 there were approximately 10,000 members.

Periodicals: *The Light of the World*, Box 652, Cleveland, TN 37311.

Black Trintarian Pentecostal

★385★
AFRICAN UNIVERSAL CHURCH
% Archbishop Clarence C. Addison
14 Webster Place
East Orange, NJ 07018

The African Universal Church was established in 1927 in Jacksonville, Florida, by Archbishop Clarence C. Addison. The movement which became the African Universal Church was founded in the Gold Coast, West Africa, by a number of tribal chiefs. Among the leaders was Laura Adanka Kauffey, a Christian and daughter-in-law of an African king. Unfortunately, Princess Kauffey was assassinated in 1928 in Miami.

The church is Pentecostal, but believes in four experiences: justification, sanctification, baptism of the Holy Ghost, and baptism with fire. The baptism of the Holy Ghost is for the sanctified. The baptism with fire is seen as a "definite Scriptural experience, obtainable by faith on the part of the Spirit-filled believer." The church also believes in healing and the Second Coming. The church does not baptize with water nor does it use wine in the Lord's Supper.

A subsidiary of the African Universal Church is the Commercial League Corporation formed in 1934. It operates as an insurance company for members and pastors. Its motto, printed on all church literature, is, "You need our protection; we need your cooperation; we protect our members financially as well as spiritually." The League has been an expression of black nationalism, which Addison constantly preached. He opposed both "civil rights" and integration, but believed in a black nation in Africa. His anti-integration position made him a popular speaker for conservative white groups such as the Congress of Christian States of America.

The polity of the church is episcopal. There is a general assembly which meets every four years. The church is divided into state districts headed by overseers. Parish mothers (deaconesses) are organized under a senior mother and district mothers.

Membership: Not reported. In 1970 there were fewer than 100 congregations.

★386★

ALPHA AND OMEGA PENTECOSTAL CHURCH OF GOD OF AMERICA, INC.
3023 Clifton Ave.
Baltimore, MD 21216

The Alpha and Omega Pentecostal Church of God of America, Inc., was formed in 1945 by the Rev. Magdalene Mabe Phillips, who withdrew from the United Holy Church of America and, with others, organized the Alpha and Omega Church of God Tabernacles, soon changed to the present name. Like the Church of God (Cleveland, Tennessee), the church's doctrine reserves the baptism of The Holy Spirit for the sanctified.

Membership: Not reported. In 1970 there were three congregations, six missions, and approximately 400 members, all in Baltimore.

★387★

CHURCH OF GOD IN CHRIST
% Mason Temple
939 Mason St.
Memphis, TN 38103

The Church of God in Christ was established in 1894 in Jackson, Mississippi by Charles H. Mason, at that time an independent Baptist minister who four years previously had been affected by the holiness movement and sanctified. With a colleague, Elder C. P. Jones, he had founded the Church of Christ (Holiness) U.S.A.. He had as a child of twelve been healed suddenly of a sickness that almost killed him. In 1907, two events further changed his life. Elder Jones convinced him that he did not yet have the fullness of the Holy Spirit, for, if he did, he would have the power to heal the sick, cast out devils, and raise the dead. He also heard of the meetings at Azusa Street in Los Angeles, went there, was baptized in the Spirit and spoke in tongues.

In August, 1908, the new doctrine and experience was presented to the representatives of the Church of Christ (Holiness) U.S.A. convention in Jackson. At a meeting of those who accepted Pentecostalism, a General Assembly of the Church of God in Christ was organized. Mason was elected general overseer. (This brief history is at odds with the history presented in the item elsewhere in this *Encyclopedia* on the Church of Christ (Holiness) U.S.A.; the two churches involved tell two different stories.)

The Church of God in Christ was organized in an ascending hierarchy of overseer (pastor), state overseer, and general overseer. There are annual state convocations which decide on disputed matters and assign pastors, and a general convocation for matters of the general church.

Upon the death of Bishop Mason in 1961, a series of reorganizational steps began. Power reverted to the seven bishops who made up the executive commission. This group was extended to twelve in 1962 and O. T. Jones, Jr., was named "senior bishop." An immediate controversy began over the focus of power and a constitutional convention was scheduled. In 1967, a court in Memphis ruled that the powers of the senior bishop and executive board should remain intact until the constitutional convention in 1968. That year reorganization took place and power was invested in a quadrennial general assembly and a general board of twelve with a presiding bishop to conduct administration between meetings of the general assembly.

Doctrine is similar to that of the Pentecostal Holiness Church. The group believes in the Trinity, holiness, healing, and the premillennial return of Christ. Three ordinances are recognized: baptism by immersion, the Lord's Supper, and foot-washing.

Membership: In 1982 the Church reported 3,709,661 members, 9,982 congregations and 10,425 ministers.

Educational facilities: Charles H. Mason Theological Seminary, Atlanta, Georgia; Saints Junior College, Lexington, Mississippi. The theological seminary is now a part of the Interdenominational Theological Center.

Periodicals: *Whole Truth*, 67 Tennyson, Highland Park, MI 48203; *The Voice of Missions*, 1932 Dewey, Evanston, IL 60201.

Sources: J. O. Patterson, German R. Ross, and Julia Mason Atkins, *History and Formative Years of the Church of God in Christ with Excerpts from the Life and Works of Its Founder--Bishop C. H. Mason*. Memphis, TN: Church of God in Christ Publishing House, 1969; W. A. Patterson, *From the Pen of W. A. Patterson*. Memphis, TN: Deakins Typesetting Service, 1970; Lucille J. Cornelius, *The Pioneer History of the Church of God in Christ*. The Author, 1975; Mary Esther Mason, *The History and Life Work of Elder C. H. Mason and His Co-Laborers*. Privately printed, n.d. 93 pp.

★388★
CHURCH OF GOD IN CHRIST, CONGREGATIONAL
1905 Bond Ave.
East St. Louis, IL 62201

The Church of God in Christ, Congregational, was formed in 1932 by Bishop J. Bowe of Hot Springs, Arkansas, who argued that the Church of God in Christ should be congregational, not episcopal, in its polity. Forced to withdraw, Bowe organized the Church of God in Christ, Congregational. In 1934, he was joined by George Slack. Slack had been disfellowshipped from the church because of his disagreement with the teaching that if a saint did not pay tithes, he was not saved. He was convinced that tithing was not a New Testament doctrine. He became the junior bishop under Bowe. In 1945, Bowe was wooed back into the Church of God in Christ, and Slack became senior bishop.

Doctrine is like that of the Church of God in Christ, but with disagreements on matters of polity and tithing. Members are conscientious objectors.

Membership: Not reported. In 1971 there were 33 churches in the United States, 4 in England, and 6 in Mexico.

Sources: George Slack, William Walker, and E. Jones, *Manual.* East St. Louis, IL: Church of God in Christ, Congregational, 1948.

★389★
CHURCH OF GOD IN CHRIST, INTERNATIONAL
% Rt. Rev. Carl E. Williams, Presiding Bishop
170 Adelphi St.
Brooklyn, NY 11025

In 1969, following its constitutional convention and reorganization, a major schism of the Church of God in Christ occurred when a group of fourteen bishops led by Bishop Illie L. Jefferson rejected the polity of the reorganized church, left it and formed the Church of God in Christ, International, at Kansas City. The issue was the centralized authority in the organization of the parent body. The new group quickly set up an entire denominational structure. The doctrine of the parent body remained intact.

Membership: In 1982 the Church reported 200,000 members, 300 congregations and 1,600 ministers.

Periodicals: *Message*, Hartford, CT; *Holiness Code*, Memphis, TN.

★390★
CHURCH OF THE LIVING GOD (CHRISTIAN WORKERS FOR FELLOWSHIP)
% Bishop F. C. Scott
801 N.E. 17th St.
Oklahoma City, OK 73105

The Church of the Living God (Christian Workers for Fellowship) was formed in 1889 by a former slave, the Rev. William Christian (1856-1928) of Wrightsville, Arkansas. Christian was an early associate of Charles H. Mason, also a Baptist minister who left the Baptist Church to form the Church of God in Christ. Christian claimed to have had a revelation that the Baptists were preaching a sectarian doctrine and he left them in order to preach the unadulterated truth. He created the office of "chief." Mrs. Ethel L. Christian succeeded her husband after his death and was, in turn, succeeded by their son, John L. Christian. Mrs. Christian claimed that the original revelation came to both her husband and herself.

The doctrine is trinitarian and somewhat Pentecostal. The group rejects the idea of "tongues" as the initial evidence of the baptism of the Holy Spirit, although "tongues" are allowed. However, "tongues" must be recognizable languages, not "unintelligible utterance." Footwashing is a third ordinance. Salvation is gained by obeying the commandments to hear, understand, believe, repent, confess, be baptized, and participate in the Lord's Supper and in foot-washing.

The Church of the Living God also has a belief that Jesus Christ was of the black race because of the lineage of David and Abraham. David in Psalms 119:83 said he became like a bottle in the smoke (i.e., black). The church members also hold that Job (Job 30:30), Jeremiah (Jer. 8:21), and Moses' wife (Numbers 12:11) were black. These teachings were promulgated at a time when many Baptists were teaching that blacks were not human, but the offspring of a human father and female beast. The Church of the Living God countered with the assertion that the saints of the Bible were black.

The polity is episcopal and the church is modeled along the lines of a fraternal organization. Christian was very impressed with the Masons, and there are reportedly many points of doctrine known only to members of the organization. Tithing is stressed. Churches are called temples.

Membership: Not reported. In 1964 there were 276 churches, 43,320 members and 376 ministers.

Periodicals: *Fellowship Echoes*, St. Louis, MO.

★391★

CHURCH OF THE LIVING GOD, THE PILLAR AND GROUND OF TRUTH (LEWIS DOMINION)
4520 Hydes Ferry Pike
Box 5735
Nashville, TN 37208

The Church of the Living God, the Pillar and Ground of Truth traces its beginning to 1903 when Mary L. Tate (1871-1930), generally referred to as Mother or Saint Mary Magdalena, a black woman, began to preach first at Steel Springs, Tennessee and Paducah, Kentucky and then throughout the South. By 1908, when a number of holiness bands had been formed by people converted under her ministry, she was taken ill. Pronounced beyond cure, she was healed and given the baptism of the Holy Spirit and spoke in tongues. She called an assembly in Greenville, Alabama during which the Church of the Living God was organized. She became the Chief Overseer. The Church quickly spread to the surrounding states of Georgia, Florida, Tennessee and Kentucky and by the end of the next decade had congregations across the eastern half of the United States.

In 1919 the first of two major schisms occurred. Led by the church in Philadelphia, some members left to found the House of God, which Is the Church of the Living God, the Pillar and Ground of Truth. Then in 1931, following Mother Tate's death, the church reorganized, with three persons ordained to fill the office of Chief Overseer. The three chosen were Mother Tate's son F. E. Lewis, M. F. L. Keith (widow of Bishop W. C. Lewis), and B. L. McLeod. These three eventually became leaders of distinct church bodies. Lewis' following is the continuing Church of the Living God, Pillar and Ground of Truth (Lewis Dominion). Keith's group became known as the House of God Which Is the Church of the Living God, Pillar and Ground of Truth without Controversy, (Keith Dominion). Bishop F. E. Lewis headed the church until his death in 1968. He was succeeded by his widow, Bishop Helen M. Lewis. She administers the affairs of the church with the assistance of the Supreme Executive Council consisting of the other bishops and seven elders. There is an annual assembly.

Sources: *The Constitution, Government and General Decree Book*. Chattanooga, TN: The New and Living Way Publishing Co., n.d.; Helen M. Lewis and Meharry H. Lewis, *75th Anniversary Yearbook*. Nashville, TN: Church of the Living God, Pillar and Ground of Truth, 1978.

★392★

FIRE-BAPTIZED HOLINESS CHURCH OF GOD OF THE AMERICAS
556 Houston St.
Atlanta, GA 30312

W. E. Fuller (1875-1958), the only black man in attendance at the 1898 organizing conference of the Fire-Baptized Holiness Church, became the leader of almost a thousand black people over the next decade. Feelings of discrimination led to their withdrawal and they organized the Colored Fire-Baptized Holiness Church at Anderson, South Carolina, on May 1, 1908. The white body gave them their accumulated assets and property at this time. Rev. Fuller was elected overseer and bishop. Doctrine is the same as in the International Pentecostal Holiness Church, the body that absorbed the Fire-Baptized Holiness Church.

Legislative and executive authority are vested in a general council that meets every four years and in the eleven-member executive council (composed of bishops, district elders, and pastors). Mission work is under one of the bishops.

Membership: Not reported. In 1968 the Church reported 53 churches and 9,088 members.

Periodicals: *True Witness*, 556 Houston Street, Atlanta, GA 30312.

Sources: *Discipline*. Atlanta: The Board of Publication of the F. B. H. Church of God of the Americas, 1962.

★393★

FREE CHURCH OF GOD IN CHRIST
Current address not obtained for this edition.

The Free Church of God in Christ dates from 1915 when J. H. Morris, a former pastor in the National Baptist Convention of the U.S.A., Inc., and a group of members of his church experienced the baptism of the Holy Spirit and spoke in tongues. The group, mostly members of Morris' family, founded a Pentecostal group which they called the Church of God in Christ. They chose as their leader the founder's son, E. J. Morris, who believed he was "selected" for the role. In 1921, the group united with the larger body led by Bishop Charles H. Mason, which had the same name. The union lasted for only four years, and Morris' group adopted its present name when it again became independent in 1925. It has the same doctrine and polity as the Mason body. By the late 1940s the church had 20 congregations.

Membership: Not reported.

Remarks: No direct contact has been made with the Church since the 1940s and its present condition is unknown. It may be defunct.

★394★

HOUSE OF GOD WHICH IS THE CHURCH OF THE LIVING GOD, THE PILLAR AND GROUND OF TRUTH
Current address not obtained for this edition.

Not to be confused with the church of the same name which derives from the movement begun by Mary L. Tate known as the Church of the Living God, the Pillar and Ground of Truth, the church presently under discussion derives from the work begun by William Christian. In the early twentieth century, the Church of the Living God (Christian Workers for Fellowship), which Christian founded, was splintered on several occasions. In 1902, a group calling itself the Church of the Living God, Apostolic Church, withdrew and, six years later under the leadership of Rev. C. W. Harris, became the Church of the Living God, General Assembly. It united in 1924 with a second small splinter body. In 1925, a number of churches withdrew from the Church of the Living God (Christian Workers for Fellowship) under the leadership of Rev. E. J. Cain and called themselves the Church of the Living God, the Pillar and Ground of Truth. The Harris group joined the Cain group in 1926 and they later adopted the present name. The Church is one in doctrine with the Church of the Living God (Christian Workers for Fellowship). Polity is episcopal and there is an annual general assembly.

Membership: Not reported.

Remarks: The last independent source on this body is the 1936 *Census of Religious bodies*. Later sources often confuse it with the Philadelphia-based group of the same name. Its present location and strength is unknown.

★395★

HOUSE OF GOD, WHICH IS THE CHURCH OF THE LIVING GOD, THE PILLAR AND GROUND OF TRUTH, INC.
6107 Cobbs Creek Pkwy.
Philadelphia, PA 19143

In 1919 the Church of the Living God, the Pillar and Ground of Truth founded by Mary L. Tate, experienced a schism led by the congregation in Philadelphia. The new group, the House of God, the Church of the Living God, the Pillar and Ground of Truth continues the doctrine and episcopal polity of the parent body, but is administratively separate. The general assembly meets annually.

Membership: Not reported. In the early 1970 the Church reported 103 churches and 25,860 members.

Periodicals: *The Spirit of Truth Magazine*, 3943 Fairmont Street, Philadelphia, PA 19104.

★396★

HOUSE OF GOD WHICH IS THE CHURCH OF THE LIVING GOD, THE PILLAR AND GROUND OF TRUTH WITHOUT CONTROVERSY (KEITH DOMINION)
% Bishop J. W. Jenkins, Chief Overseer
Box 9113
Birmingham, AL 36108

In 1931, following the death of founder Bishop Mary L. Tate, the Church of the Living God, the Pillar and Ground of Truth, appointed three chief overseers. Eventually, each became the head of a distinct segment of the church and then of an independent body called a dominion. One of the three chief overseers was M. F. L. Keith, widow of Bishop Tate's son, W. C. Lewis. Her dominion became known as the House of God Which is the Church of the Living God the Pillar and Ground of Truth Without Controversy (Keith Dominion).

The church is headed by a Chief Overseer (Bishop J. W. Jenkins succeeded Bishop Keith in that post) and a Supreme Executive Council.

Membership: Not reported.

★397★

HOUSE OF THE LORD
Current address not obtained for this edition.

The House of the Lord was founded in 1925 by Bishop W. H. Johnson, who established headquarters in Detroit. The doctrine is Pentecostal but departs on several important points. A person who enters the church is born of water and seeks to be born of God by a process of sanctification. The Holy Ghost may be given and is evidenced by speaking in tongues. But sanctification is evidenced by conformity to a very rigid code which includes refraining from worldly amusements, whiskey, policy rackets (the "numbers game"), becoming bell hops, participating in war, swearing, secret organizations, tithing, and life insurance (except as required by an employer). A believer is not sanctified if he owns houses, lands, or goods. Water is used in the Lord's Supper. Members are not to marry anyone not baptized by the Holy Ghost.

The church is governed by a hierarchy of ministers, state overseers, and chief overseer. There is a common treasury at each local church from which the destitute are helped.

Membership: Not reported.

★398★

LATTER HOUSE OF THE LORD FOR ALL PEOPLE AND THE CHURCH OF THE MOUNTAIN, APOSTOLIC FAITH

Current address not obtained for this edition.

The Latter House of the Lord for All People and the Church of the Mountain, Apostolic Faith, was founded in 1936 by Bishop L. W. Williams, a former black Baptist preacher from Cincinnati. The founding followed an enlightenment experience and spiritual blessing realized in prayer. The doctrine is Calvinistic, but adjusted to accommodate Pentecostal beliefs. The Lord's Supper is observed, with water being used instead of wine. The Church members are conscientious objectors. The chief overseer is appointed for life.

Membership: Not reported. In 1947 there were approximately 4,000 members.

★399★

MOUNT SINAI HOLY CHURCH

% Bishop Mary E. Jackson
1601 Broad St.
Philadelphia, PA 19148

Ida Robinson grew up in Georgia, was converted at age seventeen, and joined the United Holy Church of America. She moved to Philadelphia where she became the pastor of the Mount Olive Holy Church. Following what she believed to be the command of the Holy Spirit to "Come out on Mount Sinai," she founded the Mount Sinai Holy Church in 1924. Women have played a prominent role in its leadership from the beginning.

The doctrine is Pentecostal, with sanctification a prerequisite for the baptism of the Holy Spirit. One must be converted before becoming a member. Bishop Robinson believed that God ordained four types of human beings: the elect or chosen of God, the compelled (those who could not help themselves from being saved), the "who so ever will" who can be saved, and the damned (ordained for hell). Spiritual healing is stressed. Foot-washing is practiced. Behavior, particularly sexual, is rigidly codified and rules are strictly observed. Short dresses, neckties, and worldly amusements are frowned upon.

The Mt. Sinai Holy Church is episcopal in government. Bishop Robinson served as senior bishop and president until her death in 1946. She was succeeded by Bishop Elmira Jeffries, the original vice-president, who was, in turn, succeeded by Bishop Mary Jackson in 1964. Assisting the bishops is a board of presbyteries, composed of the elders of the churches. There are four administrative districts, each headed by a bishop. There is an annual conference of the entire church, and one is held in each district. Foreign missions in Cuba and Guinea are supported.

Membership: Not reported. In 1968 there were 92 churches, and approximately 2,000 members.

★400★

ORIGINAL UNITED HOLY CHURCH INTERNATIONAL

% Bishop H. W. Fields
Box 263
Durham, NC 27702

The Original United Holy Church International grew out of a struggle between two bishops of the United Holy Church of America. The conflict led to Bishop James Alexander Forbes and the Southern District being severed from the organization. Those put out of the church met and organized on June 29, 1977 at a meeting in Raleigh, North Carolina. The new body remains in essential doctrinal agreement and continues the polity of the United Holy Church

The Original United Holy Church is concentrated on the Atlantic coast from South Carolina to Connecticut, with congregations also found in Kentucky, Texas, and California. Bishop Forbes also serves as pastor of the Greater Forbes Temple of Hollis, New York. The church supports missionary work in Liberia. On January 24, 1979, in Wilmington, North Carolina, an agreement of affiliation between the Original United Holy Church and the International Pentecostal Holiness Church was signed, which envisions a close cooperative relationship between the two churches.

Membership: In 1985 the church had approximately 210 congregations and over 15,000 members.

Educational facilities: United Christian College, Goldsboro, North Carolina.

Periodicals: *Voice of the World.*

★401★

SOUGHT OUT CHURCH OF GOD IN CHRIST

Brunswick, GA 31520

The Sought Out Church of God in Christ and Spiritual House of Prayer, Inc., was founded in 1947 by Mother Mozella Cook. Mother Cook was converted in a service led by her physical mother, an ecstatic person who was once hauled into court to be examined for lunacy because of her mystical states. Mother Cook's mother seemed to go into trances and was "absent from this world while she talked with God." Mother Cook moved to Pittsburgh and there became a member of the Church of God in Christ founded by Charles H. Mason, but left it to found her own church, which she formed in Brunswick, Georgia, after feeling a divine call.

Membership: Not reported. In 1949 the Church had four congregations and 60 members.

★402★
TRUE FELLOWSHIP PENTECOSTAL CHURCH OF GOD OF AMERICA
4238 Pimlico Rd.
Baltimore, MD 21215

The True Fellowship Pentecostal Church of God of America was formed in 1964 by the secession of the Rev. Charles E. Waters, Sr., a presiding elder in the Alpha and Omega Pentecostal Church of God of America, Inc.. Doctrine is like the Church of God in Christ, differing only in the acceptance of women into the ministry as pastors and elders. Bishop Waters and his wife operate a mission for those in need in Baltimore.

Membership: Not reported. In 1948 the church reported three congregations and about 120 members, all in Baltimore.

★403★
TRUE GRACE MEMORIAL HOUSE OF PRAYER
205 V St., N.W.
Washington, DC 20001

In 1960 after Bishop Marcelino Manoel de Graca (Sweet Daddy Grace) died, Walter McCoullough was elected bishop of the United House of Prayer for All People, but approximately six months later criticism was directed at him for his disposal of church monies without explanation to the other church leaders. The elders relieved him of his office and a lawsuit ordered a new election, at which time he was re-elected. Complaints continued that he was assuming false doctrines, such as claiming that he and only he was doing God's work or that he had power to save or condemn people. Shortly after the second election, he dismissed a number of the church leaders. Twelve dissenting members, with Thomas O. Johnson (d. 1970) as their pastor, formed the True Grace Memorial House of prayer in Washington, D.C. (Elder Johnson had been dismissed after 23 years of service as a pastor.)

Membership: Not reported. In the 1970s there were eight congregations which could be found in Washington, D.C., Philadelphia, New York City, Baltimore, Savannah, Hollowood, Florida and in North Carolina.

★404★
UNITED HOLY CHURCH OF AMERICA
Box 19846
Philadelphia, PA 19144

The United Holy Church of America was formed as the outgrowth of a holiness revival conducted by the Rev. Isaac Cheshier at Method, North Carolina (near Raleigh), in 1886. In 1900, the group became known as the Holy Church of North Carolina (and as growth dictated, the Holy Church of North Carolina and Virginia). In the early twentieth century, the church became Pentecostal and adopted a theology like the Church of God

(Cleveland, Tennessee). The present name was chosen in 1916.

Membership: Not reported. In 1970 there were approximately 50,000 members in 470 churches and over 400 ministers.

Periodicals: *The Holiness Union*, Box 19846, Philadelphia, PA 19144.

★405★
UNITED HOUSE OF PRAYER FOR ALL PEOPLE
1721 1/2 7th St., N.W.
Washington, DC 20001

Sweet Daddy Grace, as Bishop Marcelino Manoel de Graca (1884-1960) was affectionately known by his followers, was born in 1884 on Brava, Cape Verde Islands, and was a former railroad cook who began preaching in 1925. He founded the United House of Prayer for All People, which in the 1930s and 1940s was one of the most famous religious groups in the black community.

In doctrine, the church resembles the holiness Pentecostal bodies. It teaches the three experiences-conversion, sanctification, and baptism with the Holy Spirit. There is a strict behavior code. What sets the House of Prayer apart is the role that Daddy Grace assumed in the group, i.e., that of a divine being. In an often repeated quote, he was heard to have admonished his worshippers:

Never mind about God. Salvation is by Grace only...Grace has given God a vacation, and since God in on His vacation, don't worry Him...If you sin against God, Grace can save you, but if you sin against Grace, God cannot save you.

Thus, while the House of Prayer derives from and continues to grow in relation to the Pentecostal framework, the framework was significantly changed by Grace's assumption of deific powers. Grace reigned supreme as an autocrat until his death. He appointed the ministers and all church officials. A line of Daddy Grace Products included soap, toothpaste, writing paper, face powder, shoe polish, and cookies. There is an annual convocation.

Grace died in 1960 and, after a period of court fights, Bishop Walter McCoullough was acknowledged as head of the church. He has assumed Grace's powers, if not his divine claims. Under his leadership, the church has assumed more traditional Pentecostal stance. In 1974, it launched a $1.5 million housing project in Washington, D.C.

Membership: Not reported. In 1974 Bishop McCollough claimed 4,000,000 members. There were four congregations in Washington, D.C., and others throughout the nation.

★406★
UNIVERSAL CHRISTIAN SPIRITUAL FAITH AND CHURCHES FOR ALL NATIONS
Los Angeles, CA

The Universal Christian Spiritual Faith and Churches for All Nations was founded in 1952 by the merger of the National David Spiritual Temple of Christ Church Union (Inc.) U.S.A., St. Paul's Spiritual Church Convocation, and King David's Spiritual Temple of Truth Association. National David Spiritual Temple of Christ Church Union (Inc.) U.S.A. had been founded at Kansas City, Missouri, in 1932 by Dr. David William Short, a former Baptist minister. He became convinced that no man had the right or spiritual power "to make laws, rules or doctrines for the real church founded by Jesus Christ" and that the "denominational" churches had been founded in error and in disregard of the apostolic example. Bishop Short claimed that the temple was the true church, and hence dated to the first century.

The merged church differs from many Pentecostal churches in that it denies that only those who have spoken in tongues have received the Spirit. It does insist, however, that a full and complete baptism of the Holy Ghost is always accompanied by both the gift of "tongues" and other powers. The members of the church rely on the Holy Spirit for inspiration and direction. The church is organized according to I Corinthians 12:1-31 and Ephesians 4:11. It includes pastors, archbishops, elders, overseers, divine healers, deacons, and missionaries. Bishop Short is the chief governing officer. In 1952, he became archbishop of the newly merged body. He is assisted by a national executive board which holds an annual assembly.

Membership: Not reported. In the mid-1960s there were reportedly 60 churches and 40,816 members.

Educational facilities: St. David Christian Spiritual Seminary.

Periodicals: *The Christian Spiritual Voice.*

Signs Pentecostal

★407★
CHURCH OF GOD WITH SIGNS FOLLOWING
Current address not obtained for this edition.

The Church of God with Signs Following is a name applied to an informally organized group of Pentecostal churches, ministers and itinerant evangelists popularly known as snake-handlers, who are distinguished by their practice of drinking poison (usually strychnine) and handling poisonous serpents during their worship services.

Among those who handle snakes and drink poison, the actions are called "preaching the signs." The terms "signs" refers to Jesus' remarks in Mark 16: 17-18: "And these signs will accompany those who believe: in my name they will cast out demons; they will speak in new tongues; they will pick up serpents; and if they drink any deadly thing, it will not hurt them; they will lay their hands on the sick, and they will recover." The practice, an object of curiosity scorned and ridiculed by outsiders, is a commonplace to believers.

The practice of snake-handling began with George Went Hensley, a minister with the Church of God (Cleveland, Tennessee) in the very early days of the spread of the Pentecostal message throughout the hills of Tennessee and North Carolina. Converted, Hensley erected a brush arbor at Owl Holler outside of Cleveland and began to preach. One day during a service in which he was preaching on Mark 16, some men turned over a box of rattlesnakes in front of Hensley. According to the story, he reached down, picked up the snakes and continued to preach.

A. J. Tomlinson, then head of the Church of God, having become convinced that his ministry was a further proof of the pouring of power on the Church in the last days, invited Hensley to Cleveland to show church members what was occurring. By 1914 the practice had spread through the Church of God, though practiced by only a small percentage of members. Hensley settled in Grasshopper Valley, near Cleveland, and pastored a small congregation. A number of years later, after a member almost died from a bite, Hensley moved to Pine Mountain, Kentucky

Meanwhile, the Church of God was growing and in the 1920s, after Tomlinson's leaving the Church, the early support for the practice of snake-handling turned to strong opposition. In 1928 the Assembly of the Church of God denounced the practice, and it became the activity of a few independent churches, primarily scattered along the Appalachian Mountains. It was largely forgotten until the 1940s.

During the 1940s new advocates of snake-handling appeared. Raymond Hays and Tom Harden started the Dolly Pond Church of God with Signs Following in Grasshopper Valley not far from where Hensley had worked two decades earlier. Over the years since, that church has been the focus of the most intense controversy concerning the practice and become the most best known congregation of the signs people. In 1945 Lewis Ford died of a bite received at the Dolly Pond Church. His death led to the passing of a law against the practice by the state of Tennessee and the subsequent suppression of the group by authorities. Persecution against and demonstrations for the group led to the arrest of Hensley in Chattanooga (convicted of disturbing the peace in 1948) and the disruption of an interstate convention of believers in Durham, North Carolina in 1947. Following these events the group again withdrew from the public eye, and, except for the death of Hensley, bitten in a service in Florida in 1955, was forgotten for several decades.

Then in 1971 the group again was in the news when Buford Peck, a member of the Holiness Church of God in Jesus' Name, a second snake-handling church located not far from the Dolly Pond Church, was bitten. Though he did not die, he did loose his secular job. Over the next few years three persons in Tennessee and Georgia died, two, including Peck and Jimmie Ray Williams, his pastor, from strychnine poison taken during a service. Subsequent court battles, in part to test the law against the practice, led to a 1975 ban on snake-handling and the drinking of poison in public religious services by the Tennessee Supreme Court. Followers vowed to continue the practice.

Members of the snake-handling churches are Pentecostals who accept the basic theology by which people seek and receive the baptism of the Holy Spiirt, evidenced by speaking in tongues. The snake-handlers, however, go beyond the Pentecostals in their belief that snake-handling and the drinking of poison (and for some, the application of flames to the skin) are a sign of an individual's faith and possession by the Holy Spirit. It should be noted that the handling of snakes and the drinking of poison are done only while the believer is in an ecstatic (trance-like) state, referred to by members as being "in the Spirit." Scholars who have examined the movement have frequently questioned the low frequency of bites, given the number of occasions the snakes are handled and the generally loud atmosphere of the services.

The snake-handlers accept the rigid holiness code of the Pentecostal and holiness churches. Dress is plain. The Bible is consulted on all questions having to do with the nature of "worldly behavior." The kiss of peace is a prominent feature of gatherings. Worship is loud, spontaneous and several hours in length.

Congregations of signs people can be found from central Florida to West Virginia and as far west as Columbus, Ohio. Each church is independent (and a variety of names are used, mostly variations on the Church of God). They are tied together by evangelists who move from one congregation to the next. They produce no literature.

Membership: Observers of the snake handlers estimate between 50 to 100 congregations and as many as several thousand adherents.

Sources: Weston La Barre, *They Shall Take Up Serpents.* New York: Schocken Books, 1969; Robert K. Holliday, *Test of Faith.* Oak Hill, WV: The Fayette Tribune, 1966; Karen W. Carden and Robert W. Pelton, *The Persecuted Prophets.* New York: A. S. Barnes, 1976; J. B. Collins, *Tennessee Snake Handlers.* (Chattanooga): the Author, (1947).

★408★
ORIGINAL PENTECOSTAL CHURCH OF GOD
Current address not obtained for this edition.

Rarely recognized by observers of snake-handling groups, the Original Pentecostal Chruch of God represents a significant departure from the commonly accepted belief and practice of signs people. They do not believe in "tempting God" by bringing snakes into church services. However, should the occasion arise where the handling of a serpent provides a situation for a test and witness to one's faith, it is done. Members recount times in which they have encountered rattlesnakes or copperheads outside the church and have picked them up as they preached to those present.

The Original Church of God emerged from the Free Holiness people, the early Pentecostals, in rural Kentucky during the first decade of the twentieth century. Tom Perry and Tom Austin founded churches in rural Tennessee. Perry carried the Pentecostal message to Alabama and in 1910 converted P. W. Brown, then president of the Jackson County Baptist Association. Brown became the pastor of the Bierne Avenue Baptist Church in Huntsville, Alabama, one of the leading congregations of the Original Pentecostal Church. There is little formal organization nor are there "man-made rules." Congregations are scattered throughout the deep South.

Membership: Not reported.

Spanish-Speaking Pentecostal

★409★
CONCILIO OLAZABAL DE IGLESIAS LATINO AMERICANO
1925 E. First St.
Los Angeles, CA 90033

The revival on Azusa Street in Los Angeles which launched the Pentecostal movement soon spread and attracted some Spanish-speaking Christians. Most were affiliated with the Assemblies of God, formed in 1914. Among the early leaders was the Rev. Francisco Olazabal (1886-1937). Mexican-born Olazabal had became a Methodist minister and worked among the Methodists of southern California. In 1917, however, he received the baptism of the Holy Spirit in a prayer meeting in the home of George Montgomery and his wife Carrie Judd Montgomery. As a minister in the Christian and Missionary Alliance, George Montgomery had had a direct influence on Olazabal's conversion and entry into the ministry. By 1917 the Montgomerys had become Pentecostals. He left the Methodists and became an Assemblies pastor. He experienced great success in establishing new churches and recruiting pastors. Then in 1923 he led a movement out of the Assemblies, which he had come to feel had placed an insensitive Anglo in charge of the Spanish-speaking work. With his supporters he began independent work along the West Coast and the Mexican border. In 1931, he came to New York, after which he made visits to Mexico City and in 1934 to Puerto Rico. In 1936 he organized the Concilio Olazabal de Iglesias Latino Americano. In 1937, Rev. Olazabal died and was succeeded by Reverend Miguel Guillen. The present name was adopted after Olazabal's death as a means to honor his life work.

Rev. Olazabal had close contact with A. J. Tomlinson and his son Homer Tomlinson then with the Church of God of Prophecy, and he noted Olazabal's natural affinity to Church of God doctrine rather than that of the Assemblies of God. Olazabal followed the emphasis upon the three experiences of justification, sanctification and the baptism of the Holy Spirit. The Assemblies position negated the necessity of sanctification prior to the baptism. The Council is also, like the Church of God, pacifist in orientation.

Membership: Not reported. In 1967 there were seven churches with 275 members with an additional four churches in Mexico.

Periodicals: *El Revelator Christiana*, Los Angeles, CA.

Sources: Homer A. Tomlinson, *Miracles of Healing in the Ministry of Rev. Francisco Olazabal.* Queens Village, NY: The Author, 1939; Victor DeLeon, *The Silent Pentecostals.* Taylor, SC: Faith Printing Company, 1979.

★410★
DAMASCUS CHRISTIAN CHURCH
℅ Rev. Enrique Melendez
179 Mt. Eden Parkway
Bronx, NY 10473

The Damascus Christian Church is a small Pentecostal body formed in 1939. It grew out of the work of Francisco Rosado and his wife Leoncai Rosado in New York City. By 1962 it had spread to New Jersey, with foreign affiliated congregations in Cuba and the Virgin Islands. The Church is headed by a bishop who is assisted by a council of officers and a mission committee.

Membership: Not reported. In 1962 the Church had 10 congregations and approximately 1,000 members.

★411★
DEFENDERS OF THE FAITH
928 Linwood Blvd.
Kansas City, MO 64109

The Defenders of the Faith was formed in 1925 by an interdenominational group of pastors and laymen headed by Dr. Gerald B. Winrod, an independent Baptist preacher. Winrod gained a reputation in the 1930s not only for his fundamentalism but also for his support of right-wing political causes. The Defenders of the Faith

became the instrument by which Winrod promoted his ideas, and during his lifetime it was a large organization. After Winrod's death in 1957, the group lost many members. However, in 1963, it began a three-year revival under Dr. G. H. Montgomery, who died suddenly in 1966. Since then, it grew slowly and steadily under Dr. Hunt Armstrong, its new leader.

Its main program consists of publishing a magazine, *The Defender*, and numerous pamphlets and tracts; administering six retirement homes in Kansas, Nebraska, and Arkansas; maintaining a school (opened in 1957) and headquarters in Kansas City and conducting a vigorous mission program.

The Defenders of the Faith was not intended to be a church-forming organization nor to be associated with Pentecostalism. In 1931, however, Gerald Winrod went to Puerto Rico to hold a series of missionary conferences. He met Juan Francisco Rodriguez-Rivera, a minister with the Christian and Missionary Alliance. Winrod decided to begin a missionary program and placed Rodriguez in charge. A center was opened in Arecibo, and *El Defensor Hispano* was begun as a Spanish edition of *The Defender*. Rodriguez's congregation became the first of the new movement. In 1932, Rodriguez accompanied Francisco Olazabal founder of the Concilio Olazabal de Iglesias Latino Americano on an evangelistic tour of Puerto Rico. The Defenders of the Faith received many members as a result of the crusade and emerged as a full-fledged Pentecostal denomination. A theological seminary was opened in 1945 in Rio Piedras. Members of the Defenders of the Faith migrated to New York in the late 1930s. In 1944, the Defenders' first church in New York was begun by J. A. Hernandez. From there the movement spread to other Spanish-speaking communities in the United States.

Doctrinally, the churches are not specifically Pentecostal; e.g., they do not insist that speaking in tongues is the sign of the baptism of the Holy Spirit. They are fundamentalist, believing in the Bible, the Trinity, salvation by faith, and the obligation of the church to preach the gospel, to carry on works of charity, and to operate institutions of mercy. Baptism is by immersion. Beyond the basic core of theological consensus, there is a high degree of freedom. Many congregations have become Pentecostal. Others are similar to Baptist churches. Premillennialism is accepted by most.

A central committee directs the work of the Defenders of the Faith. An annual assembly is held. Ties to the national office in Kansas City, which in 1965 discontinued all specific direction for the Spanish-speaking work, are very weak. It does continue support of missionaries and pastors. American congregations are located primarily in the New York City and Chicago metropolitan areas.

Membership: Not reported. In 1968 there were 14 churches and approximately 2,000 members in the United

States, and 68 churches and 6,000 members in Puerto Rico.

Educational facilities: Defenders Seminary, Kansas City, Missouri.

Periodicals: *The Defender*, 928 Linwood Blvd., Kansas City, MO 64109.

★412★
IGLESIA BANDO EVANGELICO GEDEON/ GILGAL EVANGELISTIC INTERNATIONAL CHURCH
636 N.W. 2nd St.
Miami, FL 33128

The Iglesia Bando Evangelico Gedeon was founded as the Gideon Mission in the early 1920s in Havana, Cuba, by Wisconsin-born Ernest William Sellers, known among his followers as Daddy John. He was assisted by three women-Sister Sarah, Mable G. Ferguson, and Muriel C. Alwood. Successful efforts led to the spread of the mission throughout the country. In 1939, a periodical, *El Mensajero de los Postreros Dias* (Last Day's Messenger), was begun. Until 1947, Daddy John had functioned as the bishop, but in that year at the annual convention, Daddy John was named apostle and a three-man board of bishops selected. In 1950, the church sent its first missionary, Arturo Rangel Sosa, to Panama and Mexico.

In 1953, Daddy John died. He had named as his successor Bishop Angel Maria Hernandez y Esperon. During Hernandez' eight years as apostle, special attention was given to overseas missions, which were started in nine countries, and to missions in the United States.

After the death of Apostle Angel M. Hernandez, Bishop A. R. Sosa became the third apostle. He was in office during the Cuban revolution. The church opposed the spread of communism and was persecuted by the Castro regime. The periodicals were cancelled, and many churches were closed and/or destroyed. Then in 1966, Apostle Sosa and two bishops disappeared and have not been heard of since. The remaining members of the board took control of the church and, in 1969, transferred its headquarters to Miami, Florida.

The Gilgal Church is a Sabbaterian Pentecostal body. Members believe in keeping the Old Testament laws, including the dietary restrictions on unclean food (Gen. 7:2, Lev. 11), so they do not eat pork. They beleive in baptism as the first step to salvation; and washing the feet as a sign of humility. They believe strongly in the gifts of the Spirit, especially prophecy and revelation by means of dreams and visions. Ministers are not to be involved in politics.

After Apostle Sosa disappeared, Bishops Florentino Almeida and Samuel Mendiondo headed the church. They were designated archbishops in 1971. They revived the

Last Day's Messenger. In the United States, because of the similarity of name with the Gideons International, the Gideon Mission uses the word "Gilgal." The church conducts work in seventeen Latin American countries.

Membership: Not reported.

Periodicals: *Last Days Messenger*, 636 NW 2nd Street, Miami, FL 33128.

★413★
LATIN-AMERICAN COUNCIL OF THE PENTECOSTAL CHURCH OF GOD OF NEW YORK
115 E. 125th St.
New York, NY 10035

The Latin-American Council of the Pentecostal Church of God of New York, Inc. (known also as the Concilio Latino-Americano de la Iglesia de Dios Pentecostal de New York, Incorporado) was formed in 1957 as an offshoot of the Latin American Council of the Pentecostal Church of God. (The latter is a Puerto Rican church without congregations in the U.S., and therefore not discussed in this encyclopedia.) Work in New York had begun in 1951 and the New York group became autonomous in 1956, though it remains loosely affiliated with the Puerto Rican parent body.

Doctrinally, it is like the Assemblies of God. Healing, tithing, and a literal heaven and hell are stressed. The matter of participation in war is left to the individual members. Secret societies are forbidden and no political activity is advised beyond voting. An unaccredited three-year school of theology with an average enrollment of 500 trains Christian workers. Mission activity is carried on in Central America and the Netherland Antilles, among other places.

Membership: Not reported. In 1967 there was an estimated 75 churches, most in the New York metropolitan area.

Miscellaneous Pentecostal

★414★
ALPHA AND OMEGA CHRISTIAN CHURCH
96-171 Kamahamaha Hwy.
Pearl City, HI 96782

The Alpha and Omega Christian Church was formed in 1962 by Alezandro B. Faquaragon and other former members of the Pearl City Full Gospel Church. A congregation, primarily of Filipino nationals, was established in Pearl City. Four years later, a few members of the church returned to the Philippines and established a congregation at Dingras, Ilocos Norte. In 1968 a flood struck Pearl City and destroyed the meeting hall of the church. Many of the members withdrew after that event, though the church has survived and been rebuilt. The group is small, restricted to the Hawaiian Islands, and completely independent.

Membership: There are only two congregations, one in Hawaii and one in the Philippines.

Educational facilities: Alpha and Omega Bible School, Pearl City, Hawaii.

★415★
AMERICAN EVANGELISTIC ASSOCIATION
2200 Mt.Royal Terrace
Baltimore, MD 21217

The American Evangelistic Association was founded in 1954 in Baltimore, Maryland, by the Rev. John E. Douglas, its president, and seventeen other independent ministers. Many of these had been affected by the Latter Rain Movement which had begun in Canada in the late 1940s. It licenses independent pastors, mostly Pentecostals, but also some other conservtive evangelical ministers. Government is congregational, with congregations affiliating with the national headquarters. The Association is headed by a five-man executive committee. The Association was formed to promote doctrinal, ethical, and moral standards for independent ministers and churches, many of whom had come out of Pentecostal "denominations."

The American Evangelistic Association is missionary in outlook and oversees more than 1,000 workers outside of the United States, mostly in India, Korea, Hong Kong, and Haiti. Headquarters for the Association are in Baltimore, and for the missionary department, World Missionary Evangelism, in Dallas. Its periodical, *World Evangelism*, primarily an informational and promotional work for its many missions, circulates over a half-million copies The group sponsors the annual Christian Fellowship Convention.

Membership: Not reported. In 1968 there were a reported 2,057 ministers whose congregations had over 100,000 members.

Periodicals: *World Evangelism*, Box 222813, Dallas, TX 75222.

★416★
ASSOCIATION OF SEVENTH-DAY PENTECOSTAL ASSEMBLIES
% Elder Garver C. Gray, Chairman
4700 N.E. 119th St.
Vancouver, WA 98665

The Association of Seventh-Day Pentecostal Assemblies (incorporated in 1967) had existed as an informal fellowship of congregations and ministers since 1931. It is a very loose association headed by a chairman and a co-

ordinating committee. The committee has a responsibility for joint vetures, but has no authority over local church programs or affairs. Doctrinally, the Association has taken a non-sectarian stance, affirming some minimal beliefs commonly held but leaving many questions open. No stance, for example is taken on the Trinity, though most ministers hold an non-Trinitarian position. Baptism is by immersion, but a variety of formulas are spoken. The Association believes in sanctification by the blood, Spirit and the Word, the baptism of the Holy Spirit, the ten commandments (each of equal worth) and the millennium. Missions are supported in Canada, Ghana, and Nigeria.

Membership: Not reported.

Periodicals: *The Hour of Preparation*, 4700 N. E. 119th Street, Vancouver, WA 98665.

★417★
BODY OF CHRIST MOVEMENT
% Foundational Teachings
Box 6598
Silver Spring, MD 20906

Along with the neo-Pentecostal movement of the 1960s, there deveoped what can be termed the Body of Christ movement, focused in the ministry of Charles P. Schmitt and Dorothy E. Schmitt of the Fellowship of Christian Believers in Grand Rapids, Minnesota. The basic idea is that God has moved among his people in each generation and has poured out his Spirit upon them in a vital manner. In the eighteenth century, this outpouring occurred through the Wesleyan revival, and in the early twentieth century, through the Pentecostal revival. In the late 1940s, the "Latter Rain" movement swept Canada. According to Schmitt, the outpouring on the present generation is the most momentous of all because this is the last generation and in it shall be manifest the full intent of God (I Cor. 4:1).

Initiation into the "mysteries" is through the baptism of the Holy Spirit. The central mystery of the church as the Body of Christ is that God is preparing a glorious church for himself. God is pouring out his Spirit in every denomination to bring forth the bride of Jesus Christ in this hour. The church as the Body of Christ is the very fullness of Jesus, who fills everything, everywhere with himself.

Doctrine, beyond the core of Pentecostal and Protestant affirmation, is not emphasized. The true basis of fellowship is in God and Jesus Christ. The Body of Christ Movement is organized on a family model, under the care of the responsible brethren (elders) and the ones possessed of spiritual gifts (I Cor. 12:11- 14.

The Body of Christ Movement originated in Grand Rapids, Minnesota. Fellowship Press was established and it has issued numerous pamphlets on a wide variety of topics. The Schmitts began a tape ministry and a home

Bible study course, "Words of Truth and Life." From Grand Rapids, ministers were sent out to cities across the United States. Centers were rapidly established. In the early 1980s, the Schmitts moved their headquarters to the Washington, D. C. area where a strong following had developed. Among the leaders of the Movement is Larry Tomczak, popular Christian speaker and author, a leader of the Covenant Life Christian Community of Greater Washington, D. C., and editor of *People of Destiny Magazine*. Camp Dominion in rural northern Minnesota is the scene of national gatherings during the summer.

Membership: In 1984 there were several hundred congregations and tens of thousands of people involved in the movement.

Periodicals: *Fellowship Together*, Box 6598, Silver Spring, MD 20906. Unofficial: *People of Destiny Magazine*, People of Destiny International, 3515 Randolph Road, Wheaton, MD 20902.

★418★
CHRIST FAITH MISSION
Los Angeles, CA

Christ Faith Mission continues the work begun in 1908 by Dr. Finis E. Yoakum, a Denver Methodist layman and medical doctor. In Los Angeles in 1895 following a near fatal accident, he was healed in a meeting of the Christian and Missionary Alliance, the holiness church founded by Albert Benjamin Simpson, which had been among the first modern churches to emphasize divine healing. As a result of his healing, he dedicated himself to the work of the Lord and began his efforts among the derelicts, outcasts and street people of the city. In 1908 he opened Old Pisgah Tabernacle in Los Angeles. He began to hold gospel services and to provide meals for the hungry. In 1909, he began to publish the *Pisgah Journal*.

Yoakum had a utopian spirit, and envisioned a series of communities that would embody the life of the early church. He opened Pisgah Home for the city's hungry and homeless; Pisgah Ark in the Arroyo Seco, for delinquent girls; and Pisgah Gardens in the San Fernando Valley for the sick. His most famous experiment was Pisgah Grande, a model Christian commune estalished near Santa Susana, California in 1914. The community attracted people from across the United States, including some who had formerly lived at Zion, Illinois, the community built by John Alexander Dowie, several decades earlier. Piscah Grande, already weakened by charges of financial mismanagement and unsanitary conditions, was thrown into further confusion by Yoakum's death in 1920. They eventually incorporated and took control of the Los Angeles property. They bought property in the San Bernadino Mountains and then moved to Pikesville, Tennessee.

In 1939 James Cheek, formerly the manager of Pisgah Grande, took control of the Pisgah Home property in Los Angeles and founded Christ Faith Mission, continuing the heritage of Yoakum's inner city work. He began a periodical. In 1972, the surving Pisgah group in Tennessee united their work with that of Cheek and merged their periodical into *The Herald of Hope*, which he published.

Under Cheek's leadership, the old Pisgah movement reborn as Christ Faith Mission has become a world-wide full gospel (Pentecostal) ministry. He continued the healing emphasis, and the present-day mission sends out prayer cloths to any sick person who requests them. The Mission operates the Christ Faith Mission Home near Saugus, California, and the Pisgah Home Camp Ground at Pikeville, Tennessee. A radio ministry is heard over stations in Los Angeles and Long Beach, California. Foreign language editions of *The Herald of Hope* are sent to mission stations in Korea, Mexico, India, Indonesia, and Jamaica.

Membership: Not reported. In 1984 several hundred attended the headquarters center in Los Angeles.

Periodicals: *The Herald of Hope*, Los Angeles, CA.

Sources: Paul Kagan, *New World Utopias*. Baltimore: Penguin Books, 1975.

★419★
CHURCH OF GOD BY FAITH
3220 Haines St.
Jacksonville, FL 32206

The Church of God by Faith was organized in 1919 by Elder John Bright and chartered in 1923 at Alachua, Florida. Its doctrine is like that of the Church of God (Cleveland, Tennessee) It believes in one Lord, one faith and one baptism, and in the Word of God as the communion of the body and blood of Christ. Members isolate willful sinners from the church. Polity is episcopal and officers consist of the bishop, general overseer, and executive secretary. A general assembly meets three times a year. Matthews-Scippio Academy (grades 1-12) was opened in 1963 in Ocala, Florida. Churches are located in Florida, Georgia, Alabama, South Carolina, Maryland, New Jersey, and New York.

Membership: Not reported. In 1970 there were 135 churches, 5,000 members and 155 ministers.

Periodicals: *The Spiritual Guide*, 3220 Haines Street, Jacksonville, FL 32206.

★420★
CHURCH OF THE LITTLE CHILDREN
Current address not obtained for this edition.

The Church of the Little Children was formed in 1916 by John Quincy Adams (1890-1951) in Abbott, Texas, following his withdrawal from the Baptist ministry. In

1930, he transferred his headquarters to Gunn, Alberta. After his death, his widow succeeded him, remarried, and returned to the United States (Black Rock, Arkansas).

The church is "oneness" Pentecostal--denying the Trinity and identifying Jesus with the Father--and has picked up elements of doctrine from a number of traditions. The writings of Adams constitute the sole source of doctrinal teachings. The group practices foot-washing. Wine is used in communion. The Trinity, Sunday Sabbath, Christmas, Easter, shaving the male beard, wearing neckties, and using the names of the pagan deities for the days of the week are viewed as vestiges of pagan phallic worship. Conscientious objection is required and no alternative service allowed. Healing is emphasized and modern medicine is rejected. There is a major thrust toward acts of love for little children; members try to prevent any child from suffering want or hunger.

The church is headed by a superintendent. Organization is loose and informal. Congregations are located in Arkansas, Missouri, Nebraska, Montana, Wyoming, and Saskatchewan. Each congregation is quite small and meets in a home. Contact between congregations is by correspondence.

Membership: Not reported. In the early 1970s there were eight congregations and fewer than 100 members.

★421★
COLONIAL VILLAGE PENTECOSTAL CHURCH OF THE NAZARENE
Flint, MI

The Colonial Village Pentecostal Church of the Nazarene grew out of an independent congregation founded in 1968 by Bernard Gill, a former minister in the Church of the Nazarene. There followed an attempt to form the true church composed solely of "wholly sanctified holy people with the gifts of the Spirit operating among them," who then accepted as their goal and mission the reformation of the parent denomination.

Gill had begun to think of himself as "God's Prophet of the Latter Rain," and he received numerous revelations directly from God, as did one of the members, Mescal McIntosh. These were published in a periodical, the *Macedonian Call* in 1974. In the July 3rd issue, a resurrection was predicted. Two weeks later, Gill died. On August 11 a letter to readers of the *Macedonian Call* announced the belief of Gill's faithful followers that the prophecy obviously applied to their pastor, and that they were waiting in faith.

Membership: Not reported. No recent information has been received and the present status of the Church is unknown.

★422★
ENDTIME BODY-CHRISTIAN MINISTRIES, INC.
Miami, FL

The Endtime Body-Christian Ministries Inc. (a.k.a. the Body of Christ Movement and Maranatha Christian Ministries) was founded in the early 1960s by Sam Fife (d. 1979). A former Baptist minister, Fife became a Pentecostal after his involvement in the Latter Rain Movement, a Pentecostal revival movement which began in Canada in the late 1940s. Fife founded his organization in New Orleans, but soon moved to Miami where he had formerly worked as a contractor and singer. Fife's messages emphasized what he believed was the approaching end of the world. One sign of the end was the emergence of visions among Christians. In one vision, he was told that he would father a child who would be a great prophet. The woman designated as the mother was not his wife; however, with the consent of his wife and the church, he lived with her for a year, until he became convinced of the error of the vision.

Fife also called his members to prepare for the second coming of Christ by separating themselves from the world. They are in the process of preparing a perfected bride (i.e., church body) for Christ to find upon his return to earth. To accomplish this task, he organized a series of communal farms in the United States, Canada and Latin America. Many of the church members have sold their possessions and moved into these rural communities. The group also established a set of parochial schools for its children. The process of separation from the world led to the disruption of many families, especially where only one spouse was a strong member of the group. Also, the presence of single young adults in the group, often living at rather primitive (by middle class standards) levels, in the 1970s led to several deprogrammings and the focus of attention on the group by segments of the anti-cult movement.

Membership: Not reported. There were reported to be between 6,000 and 10,000 members at the time of Fife's death. Approximately 25 communal farms had been established.

★423★
EVANGELICAL BIBLE CHURCH
2499 Washington Blvd.
Baltimore, MD 21230

The Evangelical Bible Church was founded by the Rev. Frederick B. Marine in 1947. The doctrine is similar to that of the Assemblies of God discussed earlier in this chapter, but great emphasis is placed on the three baptisms for New Testament believers--the baptism into Christ when a person is "born again," water baptism, and Spirit baptism. The church teaches that any doubtful practice that is not forbidden in the New Testament should be left to individual judgment. There are definite statements on meat, drinks, observing the Sabbath, and dressing for show. The church teaches conscientious objection and is against worldly organizations. A pretribulation, premillennial eschatology is taught.

The polity is congregational and there is an annual convention of both ministers and laity. Officers of the church include the general superintendent, the assistant general superintendent, and the general secretary. There are four orders of ministers-- novice, deacon, evangelist, and ordained elder. Foreign missions are conducted in the Philippines where the Church is known as the Evangelical Church of God.

Membership: Not reported. In 1960 there were four churches (three in Maryland and one in Pennsylvania) and 250 members.

★424★

FULL GOSPEL DEFENDERS CONFERENCE OF AMERICA

% Grover S. Smith
3311 Hartel Ave.
Philadelphia, PA 19152

The Full Gospel Defenders Conference of America is a small Pentecostal body with headquarters in Philadelphia. Its emphasis is on evangelism and Christ's authority as manifested by the miracles and signs.

Membership: Not reported.

★425★

FULL GOSPEL MINISTER ASSOCIATION

East Jordan, MI 49727

The Full Gospel Minister Association is a fellowship of Pentecostal ministers and churches believing in the infallibility of the Bible, the Trinity, the fall of man and his need for redemption in Christ, the necessity of holy living, and heaven and hell. Members are conscientious objectors to war. The group sees ministry as being two-fold: the evangelism of the world and the edifying of the body of Christ and the "confirming of the Word with Signs Following and evidence of the power of God." The Association meets annually and elects officers. It issues credentials for both churches and ministers.

Membership: Not reported.

★426★

GLAD TIDINGS MISSIONARY SOCIETY

3456 Fraser St.
Vancouver, BC, Canada

The Latter Rain Movement, a revival movement within the larger Pentecostal movement, began in 1948 in a bible school in North Battleford, Saskatchewan. Among the first places which leaders of the new movement were invited to speak was the Glad Tiding Temple in Vancouver, British, Columbia, where Reg Layzell pastored. Layzell became an enthusiastic supporter of the revival and the Temple became a major center from which the revival spread around the continent. The Glad Tidings Missionary Society began as an extension of the Glad Tidings Temple of Vancouver, British Columbia. Over the years, other congregations affected by the Latter Rain (in Canada and the state of Washington) became associated witht the Temple through it. It has become a primary religious body itself. Mission work is conducted in Africa, Taiwan, and the Arctic.

Membership: Not reported. In the 1970s there were eight churches, three in Washington and five in Canada.

★427★

GOSPEL HARVESTERS EVANGELISTIC ASSOCIATION (ATLANTA)

1710 De Foor Ave., N.W.
Atlanta, GA 30318

The Gospel Harvesters Evangelistic Association was founded in 1961 in Atlanta, Georgia, by Earl P. Paulk, Jr. and Harry A. Mushegan, both former ministers in the Church of God (Cleveland, Tennessee). Mushegan is a cousin of Demos Shakarian, founder of the Full Gospel Businessmen's Fellowship International, while Paulk's father had been the General Overseer of the Church of God. Each man began a congregation in Atlanta. Gospel Harvester Tabernacle, founded by Paulk, moved to Decatur, an Atlanta suburb, and changed its name to Chapel Hill Harvester Church. The Gospel Harvester Chapel, begun by Mushegan, became Gospel Harvester Church, and in 1984 Gospel Harvester Church World Outreach Center, at the time of its move to suburban Marietta, Georgia. To traditional Pentecostal themes, inherited from the Church of God, the Gospel Harvesters have added an emphasis upon the message of the endtire Kingdom of God. According to Paulk, creation has been aiming at a time when God will raise up a spiritually mature generation who will be led by the Spirit of God speaking through his prophets. Given a clear direction from God, that generation, represented by the members of the Gospel Harvester Church and others of like spirit, will overcome many structures in society opposed to God's will.

Both congregations in the Gospel Harvesters Evangelistic Association have developed a variety of structures to make visible the kingdom. The churches support Alpha, a youth ministry; House of New Life, for unwed mothers (an alternative to abortion); a drug ministry; a ministry to the homosexual community; and the K-Center, a communications center.

The government of the Association is presbyterial, though the two senior pastors-founders have been designated bishops. They are members of the International Communion of Charismatic Churches, formerly the World Communion of Pentecostal Churches, that includes congregations in Brazil, Nigeria, and Jamaica. Bishop John L. Meares, pastor of the Evangel Temple in Washington, D.C. and head of the International Evangelical Church and Missionary Association, is also part of the Communion.

Membership: In 1984 there were two churches in the United States; the church in Marietta had 1,000 members, and the one in Decatur, 6,000.

Periodicals: *The Fire*, Gospel Harvester Church, 1710 DeFoor Avenue, NW, Atlanta, GA 30318; *Harvest Time*, Chapel Hill Harvester Church, 4650 Flat Shoals Road, Decatur, GA 30034

Remarks: In 1985 Bishop Paulk became the object of attack by popular (non-Pentecostal) evangelical writer, Dave Hunt. Hunt labeled Paulk one of a number of "seductive forces within the contemporary church." Paulk was included along with a number of popular pentecostal leaders including Oral Roberts, Kenneth Hagin, Kenneth Copeland and Fred Price. Hunt, one of several who have attacked Paulk's kingdom message, was quickly answered by Pentecostal leaders, who came to Paulk's defense.

Sources: Harry A, Mushegan, *Water Baptism*. Atlanta: Gospel Harvester World Outreach Center, n.d.; Earl Paulk, *Ultimate Kingdom*. Atlanta: K Dimensions Publications, 1984; Earl Paulk, *Satan Unmasked*. Atlanta: K Dimensions Publications, 1984.

★428★
GOSPEL HARVESTERS EVANGELISTIC ASSOCIATION (BUFFALO)
Current address not obtained for this edition.

A second Pentecostal body, identical in name to the church headquartered in Atlanta and completely separate in organization, is the Gospel Harvesters Evangelistic Association in Buffalo, New York, founded in 1962 by Rose Pezzino. No information on doctrine or polity is available. Foreign work has been started in Manila and India.

Membership: Not reported. There are two congregations, one in Buffalo and one in Toronto. There are individual believers in the South. In the mid-1970s, there were an estimated 2,000 adherents.

★429★
GRACE GOSPEL EVANGELISTIC ASSOCIATION INTERNATIONAL INC.
% Rev. John D. Kennington
909 N.E. 30th St.
Portland, OR 97232

The Grace Gospel Evangelistic Association International, Inc. was formed in the mid-1930s by Pentecostals of a Calvinist theological background who rejected the

Arminianism of the main body of Pentecostals. (Members stress predestination instead of free will.) Members describe themselves as Calvinist, congregational, and Pentecostal. Churches are located in Pennsylvania, Oklahoma, and along the West Coast. Foreign congregations are located in Canada, Jamaica, Colombia, Japan, Formosa, and India. *Grace Evangel* is a now-defunct periodical. There are approximately seventy ministers and missionaries.

Membership: Not reported. In the early 1970s there were approximately 70 ministers and missionaries.

★430★
INTERNATIONAL CHRISTIAN CHURCHES
2322-22 Kanealii Ave.
Honolulu, HI 96813

The International Christian Churches, founded in 1943 by Rev. Franco Manuel, is a Pentecostal group formed by former members of the Disciples of Christ Church in Hawaii. Members consider themselves "Disciples by Confession and Pentecostal by Persuasion." They accept the Pentecostal doctrines and place emphasis on the life in the Spirit.

In Honolulu, where there is" a single congregation consisting mainly of Filippino-Americans. There are, however, an additional seven churches in the Philipines. The church functions on the loose congregational polity typical of the Disciples of Christ.

Membership: Not reported. In the 1970s there was one congregation with several hundred members.

★431★
INTERNATIONAL EVANGELICAL CHURCH AND MISSIOANRY ASSOCIATION
Washington, DC

The International Evangelical Church and Missionary Association is a charismatic fellowship of churches centered upon the Evangel Temple in downtown Washington, D.C.. The leader is Bishop John L. Mears, a leading advocate of inner-city ministry among Pentecostals. The Association is part of the International Communion of Charismatic Churches that includes the bishops of the Gospel Harvesters Evangelical Association.

Membership: Not reported. Evangel Temple had approximately 4,000 members in 1985.

★432★
INTERNATIONAL EVANGELISM CRUSADES
7970 Woodman Ave.
Van Nuys, CA 91402

The International Evangelism Crusades was founded in 1959 by Dr. Frank E. Stranges, its president, and Revs.

Natale Stranges, Bernice Stranges, and Warren MacKall. Dr. Stranges has become well-known as president of the National Investigations Committee on Unidentified Flying Objects and for his claims that he has contacted space people. The International Evangelism Crusades was formed as a ministerial fellowship to hold credentials for independent Pentecostal ministers. As a denomination, it is loosely oranized as an association of ministers and congregations and unhampered by a dictating central headquarters.

The doctrine of the organization is similar to the Assemblies of God. A Canon of Ethics is stressed, the breaking of which constitutes grounds for expulsion from the fellowship.

Membership: In 1984 the International Evangelism Crusades reported forty congregations and 125 ministers in the United States and a worldwide membership of 350,000. Associated foreign congregations can be found in 57 countries.

Educational facilities: The International Evangelism Crusades formed the International Theological Seminary, in Van Nuys, California. Three seminaries serve the congregations in Asia: Heavenly People Theological Seminary, Hong Kong; International Christian Seminary of South Korea; and International Theological Seminary of Indonesia.

Periodicals: *IEC Newsletter*, 14617 Victory Boulevard, Suite 4, Van Nuys, California 91411.

Sources: Frank N. Stranges, *Like Father-Like Son*. Palo Alto, CA: International Evangelism Crusades, 1961; Frank E, Stranges, *My Friend from Beyond Earth*. Van Nuys, I. E. C. Inc, 1960; Frank E. Stranges, *The UFO Conspiracy*. Van Nuys, CA: I.E.C. Publishing Co., 1985.

★433★
LIGHTHOUSE GOSPEL FELLOWSHIP
% Lighthouse Gospel Center
636 E. 3rd St.
Tulsa, OK 74120

The Lighthouse Gospel Fellowship is a Pentecostal church founded in 1958 by Drs. H. A. Chaney and Themla Chaney of Tulsa, Oklahoma. There are a set of beliefs held in common by ministers and members. The fellowship is trinitarian. It believes in the virgin birth, the bodily resurrection of Jesus, baptism of the Holy Spirit evidenced by speaking in tongues, the laying on of hands for the confirmation of ministry and imparting of the gifts of the Spirit. However, the group also conceives of itself as nonsectarian and hence home to a variety of views on less essential beliefs.

Membership: Not reported. In the 1970s there were approximately 100 congregations and 1,000 members.

★434★
THE NEVERDIES
Current address not obtained for this edition.

Known locally in the communities of West Virginia as the Church of the Living Gospel or the Church of the Everlasting Gospel, the Neverdies are Pentecostals who believe in immortality not only of the soul but also of the body. The soul, they believe, returns to earth in a series of reincarnations until it succeeds in living a perfect life. At that point, the body can live forever. The origin of the group has been lost, but among the first teachers was Ted Oiler, born in 1906, who in 1973 was still traveling a circuit through the mountains of Virginia and North Carolina. The congregations are rather loosely knit, held together by their acceptance of what is a rather unusual doctrine for the mountain area. Among the leaders is Rev. Henry Holstine of Charleston, West Virginia.

Membership: Not reported.

★435★
ROMANIAN APOSTOLIC PENTECOSTAL CHURCH OF GOD OF NORTH AMERICA
7794 Rosemont
Detroit, MI 48203

The Romanian Apostolic Pentecostal Church of God of North America is a small ethnic fellowship of churches serving Romanian Pentecostals in the United States. There is much concern for work behind the Iron Curtain. The general superintendent is Emmanual A. D. Deligiannis, a professor at California State University.

Membership: Not reported.

★436★
UNITED CHRISTIAN MINISTERIAL ASSOCIATION
Box 754
Cleveland, TN 37311

The United Christian Ministerial Association was formed by the Rev. H. R. Hall as a Pentecostal fellowship of churches and ministers. The Association offers ordination to all charismatics who feel called to a ministry in any one of sixteen categories, including bishops, apostleship, evangelism, pastoring, teaching, missions, and the various gifts of the Spirit. It is the Association's belief that thousands ordained by God have not been recognized by religious groups. The Association hopes to correct that situation.

There are no doctrinal standards in the United Christian Ministerial Association though it is described as charismatic, fundamental, and Pentecostal. Ministers are told, upon applying for a license, that a wide variety of doctrinal differences exists within that framework. The Rev. Hall has published four widely publicized booklets which support the mainline Pentecostal perspective that speaking in tongues is a sign of being baptized with the Spirit.

Membership: Not reported.

Educational facilities: United Christian Bible Institute, Cleveland, Tennessee.

Periodicals: *The Shield of Faith*, Box 754, Cleveland, TN 37311.

★437★
UNITED EVANGELICAL CHURCHES
Box 28
Monrovia, CA 91016

The United Evangelical Church was formed in 1960, one of the first structural responses to the neo-Pentecostal revival. It is made up especially of those ministers and laymen from mainline churches who, since their baptism with the Holy Spirit, have not felt free to remain in their mainline churches. As a fellowship, they hope to avoid some of the evils of institutionalism, namely, the excessive control of man that prevents control by the living Spirit of God. Because of its origin, the church continues to be open to charismatics who choose to remain in their own churches.

The tenets of faith of the United Evangelical Church profess belief in the Bible as the Word of God, the Trinity, the virgin birth and resurrection of Christ, the inability of man to save himself, salvation in Christ, regeneration by the Holy Spirit, the present ministry of the Holy Spirit which empowers Christians and manifests itself in gifts and ministries, and the judgment of Christ.

The church is governed by an executive council and there is a conference of the church every two years. Churches are divided into three regions-Western, Central, and Eastern. Churches (in 1970) were found in twenty-four states. Foreign work was located in India, Korea, Formosa, Hong Kong, Singapore, Japan, Ghana, Kenya, Jamaica, Guatemala, El Salvador, Colombia, Mexico, Costa Rica, Honduras, and Iran.

Membership: Not reported.

★438★
**UNIVERSAL CHURCH, THE MYSTICAL BODY
   OF CHRIST**
Box 874
Saginaw, MI 48605

The Universal Church, the Mystical Body of Christ, is an interracial Pentecostal group which emerged in the 1970s. It is distinguished by its belief that in order to serve God freely, members must come out of a corrupt government, society, and churches of this land, and establish a separate government on another continent where a theocratic

system can be constructed. Only then, can perfection exist in society. Members call upon all Christians to join them. They believe that these are the end-times and that God is calling together his 144,000 mentioned in Revelation.

The church has a strict moral code and disapproves of short dresses for women, long hair for men, and women preachers and elders. Women cover their heads during worship. The group fasts, uses wine and unleavened bread at the Lord's Supper, and believes in baptism for the remission of sins, divine healing, speaking in tongues, and the unity of the church. The Universal Church is headed by Bishop R. O. Frazier. Members do not think of themselves as another denomination, but as the one true body of Christ.

Membership: Not reported.

Periodicals: *The Light of Life Herald*, Box 874, Saginaw, MI 48605.

★439★
UNIVERSAL WORLD CHURCH
123 N. Lake St.
Los Angeles, CA 90026

The Universal World Church was formed in 1952 by former Assemblies of God minister Dr. O. L. Jaggers, its president. It differs from other Pentecostal bodies primarily in organization and its doctrine of the sacrament. Under Jaggers are twenty-four elders who form the governing executive body. Their role is taken from Exodus and from Revelations 4:4, 10; 5:6-8. The elders' custom of wearing robes and golden crowns is based on these texts. There are 144 bishops, one for each state of the United States and the rest for the various countries of the world. Elders and bishops must be graduates of the University of the World Church.

One is received into the church by baptism following repentance and faith in Jesus Christ as personal Lord and savior. The reception is the first process of new birth and new creation. Following the new birth, one may receive the genuine baptism with the Holy Spirit of resurrection power and fire, a baptism called the second process. After the second process, one is allowed to partake of the third, the transubstantiation communion which is offered once every three months. At that time twenty-four elders, by faith in Christ and the power of God, perform the miracle of changing bread and wine into the sacred body and blood of the Lord Jesus Christ. This act is done before the golden altar of the church in Los Angeles.

The World Church has come under considerable attack for its flamboyance, which some feel smacks more of showmanship than religion. In spite of these attacks, however, the church has grown. There were 11,315 members of the mother church in 1969. There were approximately 800 congregations in the United States and around the world. The 3,170 ministers are organized into the World Fellowship of the World Church. The World Church schools operate on the elementary and high school levels, and the university on the college level. All ministers are university graduates.

Membership: Not reported. In 1969, the Church reported 11,315 members in the mother church in Los Angeles. There were 800 congregations in the United States and the world, with 3,170 ministers organized into a World Fellowship of the World Church. These figures have been questioned by many who claim that the movement consists merely of the single congregation in Los Angeles.

Educational facilities: University of the World Church, Los Angeles, California.

European Free-Church Family

An historical essay on this family is provided beginning on page 47.

German Mennonites

★440★
CHURCH OF GOD IN CHRIST, MENNONITE
420 N. Wedel
Moundridge, KS 67107

John Holdeman, a member of the Mennonite Church, had, at the age of 21, an intense religious experience which changed his life. He felt that he had been called to preach and, following his baptism, began a period of serious study of the Bible and of the writings of Menno Simons. As a result of his studies, he came to believe that his church had departed from the true way. Holdeman emerged as a young rebellious prophet and visionary. His self-assertion at such an age (his early 20s) and his visions caused controversy.

He began to hold meetings at his home, and spread his concerns through the writing and publishing of his major books. He felt that the Mennonite Church had grown worldly and departed from the true faith; it did not rigidly screen candidates for baptism to insure that they had been born again; the avoidance of the excommunicated was neglected, and members took part in political elections. He also objected to choosing ministers by lot, especially since he had been called to the ministry through his visions. He also felt it was wrong to receive money on loans. While he found much agreement with his observations, few would join him in reformative action.

Growth of his church was slow until the late 1870s when he encountered the German-speaking immigrants who had just arrived from Russia. In 1878 the first church was built, and the first conversion of many people to his church occured in the Long Tree Community of McPherson County, Kansas. Holdeman became the first minister to successfully introduce revivalism into a Mennonite framework. Revivals accounted for much of the rapid growth of his movement in the late nineteenth century, especially in the immigrant communities in Kansas and Manitoba. A slow and steady growth period followed through the early twentieth century, followed by a rapid expansion in both North America and abroad after World War II. Concentrations of members have recently emerged in Alberta and Mexico.

The Church follows the Anabaptist-Mennonite doctrinal concensus with strong emphasis upon repentance and the new birth, a valid believer's baptism, separation from the world, excommunication of unfaithful members, a humble way of life, nonresistance, plain and modest dress, the wearing of the beard for men and devotional covering for women.

The Church is headed by a delegated General Conference which meets every five years. It is composed of all ministers and deacons (all unsalaried) and lay people. Its decisions are binding on the congregations. It oversees Gospel Publishers, the publishing arm of the church, and three mission boards. There are congregations in 21 states, 5 Canadian provinces, Brazil, Belize, the Dominican Republic, Guatemala, Haiti, India, Mexico, Nigeria, and the Philippines. In keeping with Holdeman's concern for the religious nurture of the young, most North American congregations have an elementary parochial school attached to them. The Church supports one hospital, eight nursing homes, four children's homes, and one outpatient home for American Indians.

Membership: In 1984 the Church reported 8,504 members in the United States and 2,889 in Canada. There are a total of 12,421 members worldwide in 95 congregations and 70 mission stations served by 430 ministers.

Periodicals: *Messenger of Truth*, 420 N. Wedel, Moundridge, KS 67107; *Christian Mission Voice*, 420 N. Wedel, Moundridge, KS 67107.

Sources: Clarence Hiebert, *The Holdeman People*. South Pasadena, CA: William Carey Library, 1973.

★441★

CONGREGATIONAL BIBLE CHURCH
% Congregational Bible Church
Marietta, PA 17547

The Congregational Bible Church was formed in 1951 at Marietta, Pennsylvania, as the Congregational Mennonite Church. The name was changed in 1969. The original members of the churdh were from six congregations of the Mennonite Church. The statement of faith is at one with Mennonite belief, but includes a statement on anointing the sick and emphasizes separation from the world. The group has an aggressive evangelistic ministry. The church is organized with a congregational government as a fellowship of like-minded churches. The bishop or pastor is the chief officer.

Membership: Not reported.

★442★
CONSERVATIVE MENNONITE FELLOWSHIP
(NON-CONFERENCE)
Box 36
Hartville, OH 44632

The Conservative Mennonite Fellowship (nonconference) was the result of a protest movement in the main branches of the Mennonite Church in the mid-1950s. The conservatives were concerned that Mennonites were conforming to the world (e.g., women were neglecting to cover their hair or were letting it fall down to their shoulders instead of being tied into a knot), that Mennonites were not resisting the military (e.g., the young men were joining the Army as noncombatants instead of staying out of the Army), and that Mennonites were becoming involved in civil affairs (e.g., they were voting or holding office or becoming policemen). The conservatives were also concerned about the growing acceptance of neo-orthodox theology in Mennonite circles. The Fellowship was formed in 1956. It added to the prior disciplinary standards (the Apostles' Creed, the Dordrecht Confession and the Schleitheim Confession) the Christian Fundamentals, which emphasize strict discipline and separation from the world. These were adopted at a fellowship meeting in 1964.

Membership: Not reported. In 1967 there were 23 congregations with 980 members and an additional 50 cooperating congregations with 2,400 members.

★443★
MENNONITE CHURCH
528 E. Madison St.
Lombard, IL 60148

The largest of the Mennonite bodies is the Mennonite Church. It is the oldest and was for many years the only Mennonite body. Most other U.S. Mennonite groups derive from it. Organization within the church was slow since each congregation tended to be autonomous. In 1727, a conference of Pennsylvania congregations was called to consider, among other things, an English translation of the Confession of Dordrecht. Other conferences were called in particular regions to deal with controversy. Formal conferences began to emerge in the nineteenth century. At present, a biennial General Assembly meets as an advisory body for the entire church. District conferences counsel and provide resources at a local level.

Developing autonomously, but cooperating with the conferences, have been various service and mission agencies. The Mennonite Board of Missions now supervises a program that includes five hospitals, deaf ministries and media ministries. Twenty-three countries are served by 130 workers and more than 130 voluntary service workers. Herald Press is the publishing arm of the church and operates under the Publication Board. The Board of Education oversees the several colleges and seminaries. Other services are provided by the Board of Congregational Ministries and the Mennonite Mutual Aid Board. A General Board coordinates and oversees the five program boards.

While still holding to Anabaptist separatist practices--pacifism, a disciplined membership, believers' baptism--the church has endeavored to minister to urban society. It carries on a vast mission program with congregations on every continent. In the United States, home mission work is conducted among American Indians, Jews, the Spanish-speaking, Asian refugees and the deaf.

Membership: In 1984 the Church reported 114,149 members, 1,354 churches and 3,414 ministers.

Educational facilities: Goshen Biblical Seminary, Goshen, Indiana; Eastern Mennonite Seminary, Harrisonburg, Virginia; Eastern Mennonite College, Harrisonburg, Virginia; Goshen College, Goshen, Indiana; Rosedale Bible Institute, Irwin, Ohio.

Periodicals: *Gospel Herald*, Scottdale, PA 15683; *Mennonite Historical Bulletin*, Goshen, IN 46526.

Sources: J. C. Wenger, *The Mennonite Church in America*. Scottdale, PA: Herald Press, 1966. *An Invitation to Faith*. Scottdale, PA: Herald Press, 1957; James E. Horsch, ed., *Mennonite Yearbook*. Scottdale, PA: Mennonite Publishing House, issued annually; *Mennonite Church Polity*. Scottdale, PA: Mennonite Publishing House, 1952.

★444★
OLD ORDER (REIDENBACH) MENNONITES
% Henry W. Riehl
Rte. 1
Columbiana, OH 44408

During World War II, the issue of the draft was of great concern to the Old Order Mennonites. There was a consensus that all the draft-age youths should be conscientious objectors. However, among the Old Order (Wenger) Mennonites there developed a group who felt that prison, not alternative service (medical work, etc.) should be the only course in reaction to the draft. This group further insisted that those youths who accepted alternative service should be excommunicated.

This group was not supported by the majority of the Wengerites. Thirty-five members of the group began to build a separate meeting house near Reidenbach's store in Lancaster County (hence the name). They remain the most conservative of the Pennsylvania Mennonites. They still use candles instead of coal oil for lighting. Rubber tires on carriages are prohibited. They are the only Pennsylvania group which currently opposes the use of school buses.

Among the Reidenbach Mennonites there are a number of specific regulations to keep them separate from the world. Farm equipment is restricted; for example, manure spreaders are not allowed. Children go only to the one-room school and not beyond the elementary grades. The group has only one congregation.

Membership: Not reported. There is only one congregation, in Lancaster County, Pennsylvania.

★445★
OLD ORDER (WENGER) MENNONITES
% Henry W. Riehl
Rte. 1
Columbiana, OH 44408

Among the Old Order (Wisler) Mennonites of Southeastern Pennsylvania, several schisms have developed over the continuing issue of accommodation to change. In the 1930s, the use of the automobile on a limited basis was advocated by Bishop Moses Horning. Bishop Joseph Wenger rejected the idea, believing automobiles should not be used for either occupational transportation or coming to worship. Wenger's group became the more conservative wing of the Old Order Mennonites. The group holds no evening services and uses only German in the pulpit. Jail, rather than alternative service, is advocated for boys of draft age.

Membership: Not reported. There are an estimated 1,000 members in southeastern Pennsylvania.

★446★
OLD ORDER (WISLER) MENNONITE CHURCH
% Bishop Henry W. Riehl
Rte. 1
Columbiana, OH 44408

In the 1860s the Yellow Creek congregation of the Mennonite Church, located near Elkhart, Indiana, found itself caught between two vocal leaders. Daniel Brenneman demanded a progressive policy and the

adoption of such innovations as English preaching, Sunday schools, protracted meetings, and four-part singing. He was opposed by Jacob Wisler, who opposed all innovations and deviations. Wisler began to place under the ban anyone deviating from the past. Wisler's arbitrary manner of enforcing his ideas resulted in a church trial and he was removed from his office. He then took his followers and formed a new congregation in 1870.

During the following decades, other churches of like perspective were founded and then these united with Wisler's group. A group in neighboring Medina County, Ohio, was the first. A Canadian group headed by Bishop Abraham Martin from Woolwich Township, Waterloo County, Ontario, who opposed speaking in English, sunday schools, evening meetings, "falling"-top buggies, and other modernisms, formed a separate church and later allied itself with the Wislerites. In 1901 followers of Bishop Jonas Martin and Gabriel D. Heatwole formed a church; that church later joined the Wislerites. Bishop Jonas Martin had been the leader of the Mennonite Church in Lancaster County, Pennsylvania, until controversy arose about installing a new pulpit in the church. Martin opposed the new pulpit because he was against innovations, and with a third of the congregation he left the Mennonite Church. A separate group of Mennonites in Rockingham County, Virginia, led by Gabriel D. Heatwole, joined Martin's group and then this church joined the Wislerites.

As a group, the Old Order Mennonites remain among the most conservative in dress, forms of worship, and social customs. They are very close to the Amish in their thinking, but meet in church buildings instead of homes and do not wear beards.

Membership: Not reported. In 1972 they reported 38 congregations, 8,000 members and 101 ministers.

★447★
REFORMED MENNONITE CHURCH
% J. Henry Fisher
448 N. Prince St.
Millersville, PA 17551

The oldest splinter from the Mennonite Church that still survives dates from 1812. It grew out of a previously existing separatist congregation headed by Francis Herr, who had been expelled from the church for irregularities in a horse trade. After Herr's death, his son John Herr, never a religious man, took up his father's faith, became convicted of sin, was baptized, and soon rose to a position of leadership. He was then chosen bishop. John Herr and his associates immediately began to issue a set of pamphlets charging the Mennonite Church with being worldly and corrupt. They complained of laxity in enforcing discipline and separation from the world. Based on Herr's ideas, the Reformed Mennonite Church was created.

In relation to the Mennonite Church, the Reformed Mennonites emphasize the exclusive claims of their particular faith, practices and community. All who are not Reformed Mennonites are considered to be of the world. The Reformed Mennonites practice the ban and avoidance rigidly. They dress plainly and tend to live in plain surroundings. Membership is located primarily in southeastern Pennsylvania.

Membership: Not reported. In 1970 there were 12 churches, 21 clergy and approximately 500 members in the United States and several hundred in Canada.

Sources: *Christianity Defined.* Lancaster, PA: Reformed Mennonite Church, 1958; John F. Funk, *The Mennonite Church and Her Accusers.* Elkhart, IN: Mennonite Publishing Company, 1878; Robert Bear, *Delivered Unto Satan.* Carlisle, PA: the Author, 1974; Clara Qualls, *Adam and Lizzie, Reformed Mennonites.* Auberry, CA: the Author, 1981.

★448★
STAUFFER MENNONITE CHURCH
% Bishop Jacob S. Stauffer
Rte. 3
Ephrata, PA 17522

Jacob Stauffer, a minister in the Mennonite Church at Groffdale, Pennsylvania, was the leader of a group in a progressive-conservative split. The issue was the ban, which Stauffer and colleague Joseph Wenger of the Old Order (Wenger) Mennonites believed should be applied more strictly. About forty members withdrew from the Mennonite Church, demanding that when the ban was used there should be no communion between the church and the offender.

The Stauffers have continued in their conservative ways. They are part of the horse and buggy culture but, unlike the Amish, are cleanshaven and will ride trains on long trips. They prefer the one-room school and refrain from politics (even voting). Though never large, and hurt by one major schism, the group has grown steadily by maintaining a rather high birth rate.

Membership: Not reported. There are three congregations (Lancaster County, Pennsylvania; Snyder County, Pennsylvania and St. Mary's County, Maryland) and approximately 750 members.

★449★
WEAVER MENNONITES
% Pike Meeting House
New Holland, PA 17557

The one schism affecting the Stauffer Mennonite Church was occasioned by the issue of the strictness of the ban. In 1916, the son of aged Bishop Aaron Sensenig married outside the faith. The girl was received into the Stauffer Mennonite Church but later returned to her earlier

heritage. The church was split over the strictness of the ban to be applied to the girl. The lenient group, led by Sensenig and John A. Weaver, left and began a new congregation and constructed a meeting house near New Holland, Pennsylvania.

Membership: Not reported. There is one congregation of approximately 60 members.

★450★
WEAVERLAND CONFERENCE OLD ORDER (HORNING OR BLACK BUMPER) MENNONITES
% Bishop H. O. Weaver
Weaverland Meeting House
New Holland, PA 17557

Bishop Moses Horning (1870-1955) established a liberal wing of the Old Order (Wisler) Mennonites. His followers use automobiles, but only for necessary purposes. The car must be black and without "frivolous" trim. Most of the members cover the chrome with black paint to avoid further ostentation.

Membership: Not reported. There are five congregations, all located in southeastern Pennsylvania, and approximately 1,700 members.

Russian Mennonites

★451★
EVANGELICAL MENNONITE BRETHREN CONFERENCE
5800 S. 14th St.
Omaha, NE 68107

The Evangelical Mennonite Brethren Conference grew out of a merger in 1889 of two conservative Mennonite groups which had been founded by Elders Isaac Peters and Aaron Wall respectively. Isaac Peters (1826-1911) had migrated from Russian in 1874 and settled in Henderson, Nebraska and joined the Bethesda Mennonite Church. As an elder he began to voice some of the ideas which had previously led to a break with the Brethren in Russia. He was a vigorous proponent of evangelism and all the means to accomplish that task, including lively preaching, indoctrination of the youth, prayer meetings and Bible study. He saw a separated life as a sign of regeneration. He also opposed baptism by immersion and the doctrine of the millennium. With a minority of the Henderson congregation, he withdrew in 1880 and formed the Ebenezer congregation.

Aaron Wall (1834-1905) had migrated from Russia in 1875 and settled near Mountain Lake, Minnesota. After his election as elder in 1876 of the Bergfelder Church, he stressed the need for regeneration and the new life in Christ to an extent that he and his followers felt compelled to leave the Bergfelder Church. In 1889 he founded an independent congregation. In October of that year, he led in the union of the congregation with that led by Peters and the resulting formation of the United Mennonite Brethren of North America. The name was soon changed to Defenseless Mennonite Brethren of Christ in North America. The present name was assumed in 1937.

Born in an evangelical awakening, the Evangelical Mennonite Brethren Confrence gave early emphasis to church schools and world missions. From early congregations in Nebraska, Minnesota and South Dakota, the church spread throughout the Midwest and Canada. Missions are currently supported in Europe, Africa, India, Southeast Asia, Japan, Taiwan, and South America. The Church is a member of the National Association of Evangelicals.

Membership: In 1984 the Brethren reported 14 congregations, 2,023 members and 24 ministers in the United States. Worldwide membership is 4,382. There are 26 congregations in Canada and South America.

Periodicals: *Gospel Tiding*, 5800 S. 14th Street, Omaha, NE 68107.

★452★
**EVANGELICAL MENNONITE CONFERENCE
  (KLEINE GEMEINDE)**
Box 1268
400 Main St.
Steinbach, MB, Canada R0A 2A0

Within the self-governing Russian colonies of the second decade of the nineteenth century, the issues of Mennonites becoming magistrates and the use of force against fellow Mennonites were raised by Klaas Reimer. Reimer preached in favor of a more rigorous, disciplined life in the Russian colonies and was particularly spiteful toward any cooperation with the magistracy. The personality of Reimer, who was described as hypercritical and self-willed, was a significant factor in the schism which occurred over a period of several years. Small groups, following Reimer's ideas, seceded in various settlements, and what was called the "Kleine Gemeinde" (small fellowship) was formed. The Kleine Gemeinde was characterized by strict discipline, simplicity of home life, and more somber social life. The group also laid stress on spontaneity, dreams and visions, and outward display of emotion. The Kleine Gemeinde was brought to America in the 1870s by immigrants who settled primarily on either side of the Canadian border, with most in Canada.

Membership: In 1982 the Church reported 5,247 members, 45 churches, and 112 ministers in North America.

Periodicals: *The Messenger*, Box 1268, Steinbach, Manitoba, Canada R0A 2A0; *Familienfreund*, Box 1268, Steinbach, Manitoba, Canada R0A 2A0.

★453★
GENERAL CONFERENCE MENNONITE CHURCH
722 Main St.
Newton, KS 67114

John H. Oberholtzer was an educated young minister in the Franconia District (located in Pennsylvania) of the Mennonite Church. Oberholtzer being of a progressive nature, encountered trouble soon after entering the ministry by protesting the plain, collarless coat worn by most ministers. He felt that the coat was an arbitrary requirement from outside the Mennonite creed. He next asked for the Conference of the Franconia District to adopt a written constitution so proceedings could be conducted more systematically. The result of Oberholtzer's agitation was a parting of the ways. He withdrew in 1847 from the Franconia District at the same conference which proceeded to expel him. With sixteen ministers and several congregations, he led in the organization of a new conference. A major thrust of Oberholtzer's movement was the union of all Mennonite congregations. New practices were initiated, including a more liberal view of the ban, open communication, intermarriage with persons of other denominations and, within a short time, a salaried clergy. Oberholtzer proved a zealous advocate and founded the first Mennonite paper in America, the *Religioeser Botschafter* (later *Das Christliche Volksblat*). Meanwhile, other liberal leaders were emerging and bringing into existence new churches. Daniel Hoch, a minister to several Mennonite churches in Ontario, had joined hands with an Ohio congregation led by Rev. Ephraim Hunsberger to form, in 1855, the Conference Council of the Mennonite Communities of Canada-West and Ohio. In Lee County, Iowa, two congregations found themselves in isolation, banded together, and called for united efforts in evangelism among members who had settled at some distance from the main body in the East. At a meeting in 1860 in Iowa, representatives of some of the above groups met. Oberholtzer was chosen chairman and the General Conference Mennonite Church was organized. Their vision was the union of all Mennonite congregations in the United States and Canada. Its basis was to be a liberal enforcement of the ban and understanding of heresy. What, in effect, happened was the coming together of a number of liberal elements. The doctrine of the General Conference is in accord with the other Mennonite bodies with two exceptions: John 13:4-15 is not interpreted as a command to institute footwashing as an ordinance, and I Corinthians 11:4-15 is not understood so as to make obligatory the covering of female heads. Polity is congregational. The General Conference meets triennially. A Commission on Education oversees the production of Church school materials and Faith and Life Press and Mennonite Press. The Commission on Home Ministries oversees both Spanish-language ministries and American Indian ministries. The Commission on Overseas Missions sponsors work in Bolivia, Botswana, China, Colombia, France, Germany, Hong Kong, India, Japan, Korea, Lesotho, Mexico, Taiwan, Transkei (South Africa), Upper Volta, and Zaire. Canadian Members have organized as the Conference of Mennonites in Canada. The South American Conference includes chruches in Brazil, Paraguay and Uruguay.

Membership: In 1984 the Church reported 37,000 members, 250 congregations and 225 ministers in the United States. Worldwide membership was set at 65,600.

Educational facilities: Associated Mennonite Biblical Seminaries, Elkhart, Indiana; Bethel College, North Newton, Kansas; Bluffton College, Bluffton, Ohio; Freeman Junior College, Freeman, South Dakota.

Periodicals: *The Mennonite*, 722 Main Street, Newton, KS 67114; *Der Bote*, 722 Main Street, Newton, KS 67114.

Sources: Samuel Floyd Pannabecker, *Open Doors, A History of the General Conference Mennonite Church*. Newton, KS: Faith and Life Press, 1975; Edmund G. Kaufman, *General Conference Mennonite Pioneers*. North Newton, KS: Bethel College, 1973; H. P. Krehbiel, *The History of the General Conference of the Mennonite Church of North America*. Newton, KS: the Author, I, 1889. II, 1938; James H. Waltner, *This We Believe*. Newton, KS: Faith and Life Press, 1968; *Constitution and Charter of the General Conference Mennonite Church*. (Newton, KS): 1984; Burton G. Yost, *Finding Faith and Fellowship*. Newton, KS: Faith and Life Press, 1963.

★454★
MENNONITE BRETHREN CHURCH OF NORTH AMERICA (BRUEDERGEMEINDE)
Hillsboro, KS 67063

In the mid-1800s, Pastor Edward Wuest, a fiery evangelical preacher, toured the German colonies in Russia. His message was the free grace of God and the need for a definite religious experience. His influence led a number of Mennonites to become dissatisfied with the formality of their church meeting. They also felt themselves too pure to participate in the communion with others and demanded a separate sacramental service. When the elders refused their request, they began to hold secret sacramental meetings. When they were discovered, opposition was intense and they withdrew, and on January 6, 1860, wrote a statement of protest. After bitter controversy, the government accepted their separate existence and they took the name Mennoniten Bruedergemeinde (Mennonite Brethren). They were one in doctrine with other Mennonites, but did emphasize religious experience. Among the Russian Mennonites they introduced footwashing (with the Lord's Supper) and baptism by immersion (backwards), the latter a unique practice among Mennonites. The Bruedergemeinde members began to arrive with the first immigrants in America. In 1879, Elder Abraham Schellenberg arrived and began to tour the settlements and organize strong congregations. By 1898, the group was supporting a German Department at McPherson College and in 1908, founded Tabor College in Hillsboro, Kansas. A vigorous

mission program was established. As the Brudergemeinde was developing, Jacob Wiebe, a member of the Kleine Gemeinde, now the Evangelical Mennonite Conference, in the Crimea, organized in 1869 the Crimean Brethren, similar in nature to the Bruedergemeinde. The Crimean Brethren came to America in 1874 and settled in Kansas. They were similar to the Mennonite Brethren but had a few differences. They prohibited excessive worldliness, buying of land, and attendance at public amusements. They took Biblical positions against life insurance, voting, and oaths. Marriage with non-members was forbidden. In 1960, the Mennonite Brethren Church absorbed the Krimmer Mennonite Brethren Church (as the Crimean Brethren became known).

The Church is a member of the National Association of Evangelicals.

Membership: Not reported. In 1975 the Church had 120 churches, 16,155 members, and 131 ministers.

Periodicals: *The Christian Leader*, Hillsboro, KS 60763.

Sources: John H. Lorenz, *The Mennonite Brethren Church*. Hillsboro, KS: Mennonite Brethren Publishing House, 1950; *Fundamentals of Faith*. Hillsboro, KS: Mennonite Brethren Publishing House, 1963.

Amish

★455★
BEACHY AMISH MENNONITE CHURCHES
9675 Iams Rd.
Plain City, OH 43064

A split in the Pennsylvania Amish was occasioned by the refusal of Bishop Moses Beachy to pronounce the ban and avoidance on some former Old Order Amish who left to join a Conservative Mennonite congregation in Maryland. The conservative element withdrew fellowship with the bishop, who then, with his supporters, separated and formed a new association. The Beachy Amish have become more accommodating to modern culture. Churches have been built, and in recent years, the automobile has been allowed, as are tractors and electricity. Missionary-aid work for needy people has become a project in contrast to the strictly separatist Old Order group.

Membership: In 1981 the Beachy Amish reported 5,460 members, 79 congregation and 241 ministers.

Periodicals: *Calvary Messenger*.

★456★
CONFERENCE OF THE EVANGELICAL MENNONITE CHURCH
1420 Kerrway Court
Fort Wayne, IN 46805

In the mid-1860's, Henry Egli (also spelled Henry Egly), an Amish minister in Adams County, Indiana, began to emphasize the necessity for a definite conversion experience for all church members. Because of the inherited nature of the Amish culture and religion, few members could honestly profess such a conversion. Egli also complained of the "too liberal dress" of his brethren. In 1866, Egli and his followers withdrew and formed a new congregation. His movement spread to Illinois and Ohio.

The Defenseless Mennonite Church of North America, as Egli's following was known until 1948, was ultrastrict in dress and rebaptized all who came into the movement who could not confess a true conversion experience. They introduced optional immersion. Their strictness has lessened with the years, as has their distinctiveness.

This small movement is largely confined to Illinois, Indiana and Ohio. The holiness movement, which looked for a sanctification by the Holy Spirit subsequent to the regeneration of the believer, found some support within the Church. Members led by J. A. Ramseyer left in 1898 to found the Missionary Church Association (now part of the Missionary Church). The Conference is a member of the National Association of Evangelicals.

Membership: In 1982 the Church reported 3,832 members, 24 churches, and 58 ministers.

Periodicals: *Build*, 1420 Kerrway Court, Fort Wayne, IN 46805.

Sources: Stan Nussbaum, *A History of the Evangelical Mennonite Church*. The Author, 1980.

★457★
CONSERVATIVE MENNONITE CONFERENCE
% Ivan J. Miller
Grantsville, MD 21536

After the establishment of the Old Order Amish Mennonite Church, more liberal Amish gradually began to separate from the church. Some of these congregations became associated and, in 1910, met at Pigeon, Michigan, for a first general conference. These congregations took the name Conservative Mennonite Conference. They introduced innovations to the Amish community such as the use of meeting houses, Sunday schools, protracted meetings, and English language services. Conservative Mennonites are located primarily in the Midwest, but congregations are located as far away as Florida, Arizona, and Delaware.

Membership: Not reported.

★458★
OLD ORDER AMISH MENNONITE CHURCH
Pathway Publishers
Rte. 4
Aylmer, ON, Canada N5H 2R3

The Old Order Amish are in practice the continuation of the original Amish who settled in America. They are strictly conservative and may be identified by their horse-and-buggy culture. The men must grow beards but moustaches are forbidden. The plain black suit for men and bonnet and apron for women are uniforms. There are no buttons on clothes. Marriage with non-Amish is forbidden.

The Amish society is an agricultural community in which church life and worldly life are not separated. Symbolic of their life are the Amish barn raisings in which the congregation gathers to build a member's barn, usually in a single day. Worship is held in the homes of the members every other Sunday on a rotating basis. During the three-hour service, the congregation is divided according to sex and marital status.

Schooling beyond the "3R's" is frowned upon, and trouble with various state governments has been a major cause of migration (both westward and out of the country). Ministers are chosen by lot from a nominated few. Since this is not a missionary church, new members must come into the community from the children.

Membership: Not reported. In 1976 there were 24,000 members in the United States and 900 in Canada.

Periodicals: *The Dairy*.

Sources: John A. Hoestetler, *Amish Society*. Baltimore: Johns Hopkins University Press, 1968; William I. Schreiber, *Our Amish Neighbors*. Chicago: University of Chicago Press, 1962; Clyde Browning, *Amish in Illinois*. The Author, 1971; Charles S. Rice and Rollin C. Steinmetz, *The Amish Year*. New Brunswick, NJ: Rutgers University Press, 1956; *Amish Life in a Changing World*. York, PA: York Graphic Services Incorporated, 1978.

Brethren

★459★
ASSOCIATION OF FUNDAMENTAL GOSPEL CHURCHES
9189 Grubb Court
Canton, OH 44721

The Association of Fundamental Gospel Churches was formed in 1954 by the coming together of three independent Brethren congregations: Calvary Chapel of

Hartsville, Ohio; Webster Mills Free Brethren Church of McConnellsburg, Pennsylvania; and Little Country Chapel of Myersburg, Maryland. Prime leader in the new association was G. Henry Besse (d.1962), a former member of the Reformed Church who had in 1937 become a minister among the Dunkard Brethren. He withdrew from their fellowship in 1953 complaining about their strictures agains wearing neckties, wristwatches and jewelry and their demands that women always wear the prayer veil or cap. Former members of the Church of the Brethren were also opposed to that Church's participation in the National Council of Churches.

In general, members of the Association follow Brethren doctrine and practice. They reject as unbiblical participation in war, but allow members to accept noncombatant military service. They do not allow the taking of oaths, suing at law (including for reason of divorce), or wearing ornamental adornment. They do not practice the kiss of peace.

The association meets annually to elect officers and conduct business. Ministers are chosen from among the congregation's members. They are not required to have advanced education. G. Henry Besse was succeeded by his two sons, Lynn Besse and Clair Besse, both of whom have pastored Calvary Chapel.

Membership: In 1980 there were an estimated 150 members in three congregations.

★460★
BIBLE BRETHREN
Current address not obtained for this edition.

The Bible Brethren was formed in 1948 by a small group who withdrew from the Lower Cumberland (Cumberland County, Pennsylvania) congregation of the Church of the Brethren. Clair H. Alspaugh (1903-1969), a farmer and painter who had been called to the ministry in the congregation in 1942, led the group that assumed a traditional Brethren posture. Alspaugh protested the Church of the Brethren's association with the Federal Council of Churches (now the National Council of Churches and the failure of the Brethren to endorse doctrinal preaching as inspired by the Holy Spirit.

The original group constructed a church building following simple nineteenth-century Brethren patterns (with a long preachers' desk and straight-back pews) at Carlisle Springs, Pennsylvania. A second congregation was formed at Campbelltown, Pennsylvania. It was strengthened by the addition of a group under Paul Beidler which had withdrawn from the Dunkard Brethren, but was lost when Biedler led the entire congregation away in 1974 to form Christ's Ambassadors. A third congregation of Bible Brethren formed in 1954 at Locust Grove Chapel, near Abbotstown, York County, Pennsylvania.

Membership: In 1979 there were approximately 100 members of the Bible Brethren in two congregations.

Sources: Elmer Q. Gleim, *Change and Challenge: A History of the Church of the Brethren in the Southern District of Pennsylvania.* Harrisburg, PA: Southern District Conference History Committee, 1973.

★461★
BRETHREN CHURCH (ASHLAND, OHIO)
524 College Ave.
Ashland, OH 44805

Agitation among the Brethren began in the late nineteenth century against what some considered outmoded practices. The lack of educational opportunities, an unlearned clergy, and the plain dress were main objections. The crisis came to a head with the expulsion in 1882 of Henry R. Holsinger of Berlin, Pennsylvania. Holsinger had objected to the authority of the annual meeting over the local congregation. Others left with him and formed what was called the Progressive Dunkers (named Dunkers in reference to baptism).

The Progressive Dunkers are like the Church of the Brethren in most respects, with the exceptions of having been the first to move toward an educated and salaried ministry, modern dress, and missions. While generally conservative in theology, and expecting a high degree of doctrinal consensus among its ministers, the Church has refused to adopt a statement of faith (though it does have a doctrinal statement) on the grounds that the New Testament is its creed. During the 1930s, a group supportive of a dispensational fundamentalist doctrinal position left the Church to found the National Fellowship of Brethren Churches, now the Fellowship of Grace Brethren. The Church practices baptism by triune immersion, a communion service usually in the evening which includes footwashing, and the laying on of hands for ordination, confirmation and/or healing. Elders (ordained ministers) lead the church in spiritual affairs. Deacons, who may be or either sex, handle local church affairs.

The church follows a congregational polity and an annual conference conducts common business. Missionary activity is supported in Argentina, Columbia, India, Malaysia and Mexico. The Brethren Publishing Company produces church school materials and other literature. Three retirement homes (Ashland, Ohio; Flora, Indiana; and South Bend, Indiana) are supported. The Church is a member of the National Association of Evangelicals.

Membership: In 1982 the Church reported 14,857 members, 125 churches and 179 ministers.

Educational facilities: Ashland Theological Seminary, Ashland, Ohio; Ashland College, Ashland, Ohio.

Periodicals: *The Brethren Evangelist*, 524 College Avenue, Ashland, OH 44805.

Sources: The Task Force on Brethren History and Doctrine, *The Brethren: Growth in Life and Thought*. Ashland, OH: Board of Christian Education, the Brethren Church, 1975.

★462★
BRETHREN IN CHRIST
% Bishop R. Donald Shafer
Box 245
Upland, CA 91786

The Brethren in Christ derive from the informally organized River Brethren who formed in the intense religious atmosphere of Lancaster County, Pennsylvania, in the 1770s. The Brethren, influenced by the Dunker tradition, accepted triune immersion. The first immersions were by Jacob Engel and Peter Witmer for each other. The original group of fourteen met in the upper room of Engel's home at Lobata, Pennsylvania, and had a love feast. The Anabaptist practice of a beard without moustache was continued.

At a later meeting, organization was effected and Jacob Engel was elected bishop. Triune immersion was a central feature. Doctrine was drawn from the Anabaptist-Brethren consensus, but with a strong emphasis on evangelism. The consensus remained until the mid-nineteenth century when three groups emerged from the original one because of doctrinal and accommodationist differences. The three groups were the Brethren in Christ, the Old Order (or Yorker) River Brethren, and the United Zion Church.

The Brethren in Christ was the last of the three groups to organize, but represented the largest wing of the River Brethren. The name was adopted in 1863 although the church was not incorporated until 1904. The church through its continued evangelistic thrust, has spread across the United States and Canada.

The Brethren in Christ is congregationally organized, but six regional conferences and a General Conference serve to carry out churchwide programs. A Board for World Missions overseas missions in India, Japan, Nicaragua, Zimbabwe, Zambia, Cuba, and Venezuela. Evangel Press, Nappanee, Indiana, is the church's publishing house. Two retirement centers, Messiah Village, in Mechanicsburg, Pennsylvania and Upland Manor, in Upland, California are supported by the Church. The Brethren are members of both the National Association of Evangelicals and the Christian Holiness Association.

Membership: In 1983 the Brethren reported 14,782 members in the United States and 2,594 in Canada, 400 congregations and 435 ministers.

Educational facilities: Messiah College, Grantham, Pennsylvania; Niagara Christian College, Fort Erie, Ontario.

Periodicals: *Evangelical Visitor*, Nappanee, IN 46550.

Sources: Carlton O. Wittlinger, *Quest for Piety and Obedience*. Nappanee, IN: Evangel Press, 1978; *Manual of Doctrine and Government*. Nappanee, IN: Evangel Press, 1968; *Manual for Christian Youth*. Nappanee, IN: Evangel Press, 1959; Paul Hostetler, ed., *Perfect Love and War*. Nappanee, IN: Evangel Press, 1974.

★463★
CHRIST'S AMBASSADORS
Current address not obtained for this edition.

Christ's Ambassadors traces its origin to a dispute in 1968 within the Dunkard Brethren congregation at Lititz, Pennsylvania. Leaders in the congregation protested an unauthorized prayer meeting conducted by some of the members under the leadership of Paul Beidler. Beidler led the members in withdrawing and forming an independent congregation. The small group affiliated with the Bible Brethren congregation at Campbelltown, Pennsylvania, in 1970. However, four years later Beidler led the entire congregation to withdraw from the Bible Brethren and formed Christ's Ambassadors. The group follows traditional Dunkard Brethren practice and beliefs, but places great emphasis upon the freedom of expression in worship.

Membership: In 1980 Christ's Ambassadors had approximately fifty members meeting in two congregations, one at Cocalico and one at Myerstown, Pennsylvania.

★464★
CHRIST'S ASSEMBLY
Current address not obtained for this edition.

Krefeld, Germany, in the lower Rhine Valley, was one place that dissenting Pietists found relative safety and toleration during the eighteenth century, and several groups, including the one which would later become the Church of the Brethren upon its arrival in America, had members among the Krefeld residents. In 1737 two Danes, Soren Bolle and Simon Bolle, visited Krefeld and joined the Brethren. They soon returned to Copenhagen and began to preach and gather a following. While they had been baptized by the Brethren, they had been influenced as well by other Pietist Groups, most notably the Community of True Inspiration (which later migrated to America and formed the colonies at Amana, Iowa). The movement under the Bolles, Christ's Assembly, spread through Sweden, Norway, and Germany.

During the 1950s Johannes Thalitzer, pastor of Christ's Assembly in Copenhagen, learned of the continued existence of the Brethren in America through his encounter with some remnants of the recently disbanded Danish Mission of the Church of the Brethren. He initiated contact with several Brethren Groups, especially the Old German Baptist Brethren, who sponsored a visit by Thalitzer to the United States in 1959. In subsequent visits he became acquainted with all of the larger Brethren factions, but felt each was deficient in belief and/or practice. In 1967 he organized a branch of Christ's Assembly at a love feast with nine Brethren (from several Brethren groups) at Eaton, Ohio.

Christ's Assembly largely follows Brethren practice, but like the Community of True Inspiration places great emphasis upon the revealed guidance of an apostolic leadership. In more recent years it has been further influenced by the Pentecostal (Charismatic) Movement which has swept through most major denominations.

As Christ's Assembly grew it included members from four states and all the major Brethren branches. A second congregation was formed in the 1970s in Berne, Indiana.

Membership: Christ's Assembly has two congregations and an estimated 100 members.

Sources: F. W. Benedict and William F. Rushby, "Christ's Assembly: A Unique Brethren Movement" in *Brethren Life and Thought*, vol.18 (1973), pp. 33-42.

★465★
CHURCH OF THE BRETHREN
Church of the Brethren General Offices
1451 Dundee Ave.
Elgin, IL 60120

The Church of the Brethren, popularly called Dunkers (or Tunkers or Taufers, from the German *tunken*, to dip, referring to baptism), began from the original Germantown, Pennsylvania, congregation organized by Brethren immigrants from Germany. It was formally begun on Christmas Day 1723, when Peter Becker baptized six persons and officiated at a love feast service. Becker was soon joined by Alexander Mack, Sr., Alexander Mack, Jr., and Christopher Sauer II, as leaders of the first generation in America. The Church grew quickly by immigration and evangelization. Within a decade, other congregations were formed within the interior of Pennsylvania. The church shared with the brethren of the earlier-formed Mennonite Church the plain dress and pacifism, and with the Quakers, an abhorrence of slavery. The pacifism caused persecution and imprisonment in both the Revolutionary and Civil Wars. Fleeing from local pressure, many Brethren moved to the remote West.

Although Brethren were much influenced by Anabaptism, their equally important Pietist roots resulted in some distinctions between Anabaptists and the Brethren. The Brethren have not used the ban, and they baptize by immersion. They have been abstainers from alcohol and are more open to urban life and occupations. While they do not take oaths or enter lawsuits, they are not anti-magistry. Central to the worship life of the Brethren is the agape or love feast. It is held in the evening and begins with footwashing. A full meal is followed by unfermented wine and unleavened bread.

Following a Quaker pattern, the Brethren began to meet in an annual meeting, at which time business could be transacted. This meeting always opened on Pentecost. The growth of the church led in the 1840s to the establishment of a delegated annual conference which assumed the authority previously held by the annual meeting that all members could attend. The annual meeting still continues as a meeting for fellowship and worship. The conference, which consists of ministerial and lay delegates from each church, is the final authority in the church. Under the conference is an elected General Board which employs administrative staff in charge of the various areas of service, education, finance, and missions. The Brethren Press, located in the headquarters complex at Elgin, Illinois, annually issues a large number of books. It is one of the oldest religious publishing efforts in the country.

The extensive missionary program begun in the nineteenth century began to change dramatically in 1955 when the Annual Conference approved a policy of creating indigenous, independent self-supporting churches later coupled with the idea of working cooperatively with national Christian groups. In 1965 Brethren churches in Ecuador joined in the formation of the United Evangelical Church of Ecuador. The Indian mission became a constituent part of the Church of North India in 1970. The Nigerian churches became the independent Church of the Brethren in Nigeria. Formerly, missions were supported in Sweden and Denmark. The church is also open to cooperation with other Christian bodies and has joined the National Council of Churches and the World Councils of Churches.

Membership: In 1982 the Church reported 168,844 members, 1,063 churches, and 1,913 ministers.

Educational facilities: Bethany Theological Seminary, Oak Brook, IL.

Periodicals: *Messenger*, Church of the Brethren General Offices, 1451 Dundee Avenue, Elgin, IL 60120.

Sources: Roger E. Sappington, ed., *The Brethren in the New Nation*. Elgin, IL: Brethren Press, 1976; Floyd E. Mallot, *Studies in Brethren History*. Elgin, IL: Brethren Publishing House, 1954; *Manual of Brotherhood Organization and Polity*. Elgin, IL: Church of the Brethren, General Offices, 1965; *Book of Worship, The Church of the Brethren*. Elgin, IL: Brethren Press, 1964.

★466★
CONSERVATIVE GERMAN BAPTIST BRETHREN
Current address not obtained for this edition.

The Conservative German Baptist Brethren is a small Brethren body body which dates to the 1931 withdrawl of a group under the leadership of Clayton F. Weaver and Ervin J. Keeny from the Dunkard Brethren Church in Pennsylvania. In 1946 Loring I. Moss, a prominent exponent of the conservative element of the Brethren Movement and one of the organizers of the Dunkard Brethren Church, withdrew and formed the Primitive Dunkard Brethren. Noting the similar concern to keep stricter Brethren standards, Moss led his new group into the Conservative German Baptist Brethren, though personally, he later withdrew and joined the Old Brethren.

Membership: In 1980 the Conservative German Baptist Brethren had two congregations, one at New Madison, Ohio, with ten members and one at Shrewsbury, Pennsylvania, with twenty-five members.

★467★
DUNKARD BRETHREN CHURCH
% Dale E. Jamison, Chairman
Board of Trustees
Quinter, KS 67752

The Dunkard Brethren Church grew out of a conservative movement within the Church of the Brethren which protested what it saw as a worldly drift and a lowering of standards in the church. The movement formed around *The Bible Monitor*, a periodical begun in 1922 by B. E. Kesler, a minister who had joined the Church of the Brethren in the first decade of the twentieth century. He was one of seven people chosen to write the report on dress standards adopted by the church in 1911. However, in the ensuing decade he saw the dress standards being increasingly ignored. Men began to wear ties and women were adopting fashionable clothes and modern hair styles. Kesler also protested the acceptance of lodge and secret society membership, divorce and remarriage, and a salaried educated ministry (which was pushing aside the traditional lay eldership).

The emergence of the *Bible Monitor* movement led to much tension within the Church of the Brethren. In 1923 Kesler was refused a seat at the annual conference. That same year he met with supporters at Denton, Maryland, to further organize efforts to reform the church. Subsequent meetings were held in different locations over the next few years. However, by 1926 it became evident that the church would not accept the movement's perspective, and at a meeting at Plevna, Indiana, the Dunkard Brethren Church was organized.

The Dunkard Brethren Church follows traditional Brethren beliefs and practices, and until recently has rebaptized members who joined from less stict branches of the church. The Dunkard Brethren adopted and enforces the dress standards accepted by the Church of the Brethren in 1911. Modesty and simplicity (though not uniformity) of dress is required. No gold or other jewelry is worn. Women keep their hair long and simply styled. They generally wear a white cap. Men cut their hair short. Divorce and remarriage are not allowed. Life insurance is discouraged. No musical instruments are used in worship.

The church has three orders of ministry. Elders marry, bury, and administer the ordinances; ministers preach and assist the elders in their sacramental role; deacons attend to temporal matters. All are laymen elected by their local congregations. The standing committee, composed of all the elders of the church, has general oversight of the church. Together with the ministers and elders elected by the local churches as delegates, they form the general conference, the highest legislative body in the church. Its decisions are final on all matters brought before it. The church is organized into four districts which meet annually.

The Dunkard Brethren Church also supports the Torreon Navajo Mission in New Mexico.

Membership: In 1980 the Dunkard Brethren reported 1,035 members in twenty-six congregations.

Periodicals: *The Bible Monitor*, c/o Editor, 1138 E. 12th St., Beaumont, CA 92223.

Sources: *Dunkard Brethren Church Manual.* Dunkard Brethren Church, 1971. Dunkard Brethren Church Polity. *1980;* Minutes of the General Conference of the Dunkard Brethren Church from 1927 to 1975. *Wauseon, OH: Glanz Lithographing Company, 1976.*

★468★
EMMANUEL'S FELLOWSHIP
% Rev. Paul Goodling
Rte. 2
Greencastle, PA 17275

Emmanuel's Fellowship was formed in 1966 by members of the Old Order River Brethren, under the leadership of Paul Goodling of Greencastle, Pennsylvania. Goodling rejected the Brethren's insistence on baptism by immersion and their allowing members to accept social security benefits. The Fellowship baptizes by pouring, as the candidate stands in water. There are very strict dress requirements.

Membership: Not reported. In 1967 there was one congregation of 15 members.

★469★
FELLOWSHIP OF GRACE BRETHREN CHURCHES
Winona Lake, IN 46590

The movement which led to the founding of the Fellowship of Grace Brethren Churches developed within the Brethren Church (Ashland, Ohio) during the 1930s. Conservatives within the Church voiced concern over liberal tendencies within the church and more particularly at the church-supported school, Ashland College. Led by ministers such as Alva J. McClain, the National Ministerial Association drew up and adopted the "Message of the Brethren Ministry," a statement of the Brethren position. The entire church refused to adopt the statement on the grounds that it seemed to be a substitute for their adherence to the New Testament as their only creed.

Conservatives scored a second victory in 1930 when a graduate school of theology opened at Ashland under McClain's leadership. However, in 1937, both McClain, then dean of the school, and Professor Herman A. Hoyt were dismissed. Their supporters organized Grace Theological Seminary as a new institution for ministerial training, which set the stage for a confrontation at the 1939 General Conference of the Church. After the exclusion of some of the new seminary's supporters, all walked out and formed the National Fellowship of Brethren Churches, which in 1976 assumed its present name.

The new church adopted the 1921 "Message of the Brethren Ministry" as its doctrinal position. That document was replaced in 1969 by a revised and expanded "Statement of Faith." The new statement affirms the conservative evangelical theology of the original document but adds a lengthy statement on various eschatological issues such as the premillennial return of Christ, eternal punishment for nonbelievers and a belief in a personal Satan. The church practices baptism by triune immersion and a threefold communion that includes footwashing, a meal, and partaking of the elements of bread and the cup.

The Fellowship adopted a congregational polity. The Conference of the Fellowship meets annually and oversees the several schools and a vigorous mission program. The Foreign Mission Society operates in Argentina, Brazil, Africa, France, Germany, Hawaii, Mexico, and Puerto Rico. The National Council of Churches is staunchly opposed.

Membership: In 1981 the Fellowship reported 42,023 members and 284 congregations.

Educational facilities: Grace Theological Seminary, Winona Lake, Indiana; Grace College, Winina Lake, Indiana.

Periodicals: *[Brethren Missionary] Herald*, Winona Lake, IN 46590.

Sources: Louis S. Baumann, *The Faith*. Winona Lake, IN: Brethren Missionary Helard Co., 1960; Herman A. Hoyt, *Then Would My Servants Fight*. Winona Lake, IN: Brethren Missionary Herald Company, 1956; Alva J. McClain, *Daniel's Prophecy of the Seventy Weeks*. Grand Rapids, Zondervan Publications, n.d.

★470★
FUNDAMENTAL BRETHREN CHURCH
Current address not available for this edition.

The Fundamental Brethren Church was formed in 1962 by former members of four congregations of the Church of the Brethren in Mitchell County, North Carolina, under the leadership of Calvin Barnett. The doctrinally conservative group adopted the "Message of the Brethren Ministry," a statement written by some ministers in the Brethren Church (Ashland, Ohio) in the 1920s as their doctrinal standard. Among the issues involved in their leaving the Church of the Brethren, its participation in the National Council of Churches and use of the Revised Standard Version of the Bible were prominent. The group added to its doctrinal statement that the King James Version of the Bible is authoritative. It also adopted a fundamental premillennial dispensational theological stance. By 1967, there were four congregations with 200 members.

Membership: In the 1970s there were 3 congregations of less than 200 members.

★471★
INDEPENDENT BRETHREN CHURCH
Current address not obtained for this edition.

The Independent Brethren Church was formed in 1972. On February 12 of that year, the Upper Marsh Creek congregation at Gettysburg, Pennsylvania, of the Church of the Brethren withdrew and became an independent body. Later that year, members from the Antietam congregation left and established the independent Blue Rock congregation near Waynesboro, Pennsylvania. These two congregations united as the Independent Brethren Church. They are conservative in their following of Brethren belief and practice. They have kept the plain dress and oppose any affiliation with the National Council of Churches.

Membership: In 1980 the Independent Brethren Church had approximately 85 members in two congregations.

★472★
OLD BRETHREN CHURCH
Current address not obtained for this edition.

The Old Brethren Church, generally termed simply the Old Brethren, is a name taken by two congregations which split from the Old German Baptist Brethren in 1913 (Deer Creek congregation in Carroll County, Indiana) and in 1915 (Salida congregation in Stanislaus County, California). Though widely separated geographically, the two congregations banded together and in 1915 published *The Old Brethren's Reasons*, a twenty-four page pamphlet outlining their position. The Old Brethren dissented from the Old German Baptist Brethren's refusal to make annual meeting decisions uniformly applicable and from their allowing divergences of practice and discipline among the different congregations. Also, the Old Brethren called for greater strictness in plain dress and called for houses and carriages shorn of any frills which would gratify the lust of the eye.

In particular, the Old Brethren denounced the automobile and the telephone. Use of either caused a believer to be hooked into the world and inevitably led to church members being yoked together with unbelievers. In practice, over the years, the Old Brethren have been forced to change and have come to closely resemble the group from which they originally withdrew. Even prior to World War II, they began to make accommodation to the automobile.

Members of the Old Brethren meet annually at Pentecost, but keep legislation to a minimum. They allow the congregations to retain as much authority as possible.

Beginning with two congregations, the Old Brethren Church has experienced growth in spite of a schism in 1930 that led to the formation of the Old Brethren German Baptist Church. A third meeting house was built in the 1970s.

Membership: In 1980 the Old Brethren had approximately 130 members and three congregations (Salida, California; Deer Creek, Indiana; Gettysburg, Ohio). Individual members could be found in Tennessee, Mississippi, and Brazil (where a group of Old German Baptist Brethren had settled in 1969).

Periodicals: *The Pilgrim*, 19201 Cherokee Road, Tuolumne, California 95379.

★473★
OLD BRETHREN GERMAN BAPTIST CHURCH
Current address not obtained for this edition.

The Old Brethren German Baptist Church originated among the most conservative members of the Old Brethren Church and the Old Order German Baptist Brethren Church. Around 1930 members of the Old Brethren Deer Creek congregation near Camden, Indiana, began to fellowship with the Old Order Brethren in the Covington, Ohio, area. However, by 1935 the traditionalist Old Brethren found themselves unable to continue their affiliations with the Ohio Brethren. They continued as an independent congregation until they made contact with a few Old Order Brethren near Bradford, Ohio, who met in the home of Solomon Lavy. In 1939 the two groups merged and adopted the name Old Brethren German Baptist Church. They were joined in 1953 by a group of Old Order Brethren from Arcanum, Ohio.

The Old Brethren is the most conservative of all Brethren groups. They use neither automobiles, tractors, electricity, or telephones. Their only accommodation to modern mechanization is that they do permit occasional use of stationary gasoline engines and will hire nonmembers for specific tasks requiring machinery. Members follow a strict personal code of nonconformity to the world. Homes and buggies are plainly furnished and simply painted. No gold or jewelry is worn. Farmers do not raise or habitually use tobacco. Members do not vote or purchase life insurance.

Membership: Among the smallest of Brethren groups, the Old Brethren, in 1980, reported 45 members in three congregations: Camden and Goshen, Indiana and Arcanum, Ohio.

★474★
OLD GERMAN BAPTIST BRETHREN
% Elder Clement Skiles
Rte. 1, Box 140
Bringhurst, IN 46913

The Old German Baptist Brethren represents the conservative wing in the Brethren movement. This group withdrew in 1881, the year before Henry R. Holsinger, a leader of what became known as the Progressive Brethren (now the Brethren Church (Ashland, Ohio)) was expelled from the Church of the Brethren.] The group was protesting innovative tendencies and was opposed to Sunday schools, missions, higher education, and church societies and auxiliaries. It has lessened its opposition to higher education among members and now sponsors parochial schools. No missions are supported, and children attend the regular services of the church instead of having a church school.

The Old German Baptist Brethren retain plain garb and are committed to non-participation in war, government, secret societies, and worldly amusements. They do not object to participation in government (i.e., voting) by members whose conscience allows it. They remain conservative on oaths, lawsuits, non-salaried ministry, and veiled heads for women at worship.

Membership: In 1982 the Brethren reported 5,254 members in 52 churches served by 236 ministers.

Periodicals: *The Vindicator*, Covington, OH 45318.

Sources: H. M. Fisher, et al., *Doctrinal Treatise*. Covington, OH: The Little Printing Company, 1954.

★475★
OLD ORDER GERMAN BAPTIST CHURCH
Current address not obtained for this edition.

As the Old German Baptist Brethren continued to deal with questions of accommodating to a fast-moving society in the early twentieth century, a group of members withdrew in 1921 because of the departure of the Old German Baptist Brethren from the established order and old paths. The petitioners, as they were informally called, could be found throughout the brethren, but were concentrated in the congregations at Covington and Arcanum, Ohio.

Staunchly set against most modern conveniences, the Old Order German Baptists have over the year been forced to accommodate. Automobiles are forbidden, but tractors are now allowed for farm work. Members do not use electricity or telephones. Increasingly, younger members have been forced to leave the farm and seek employment in nonfarm occupations.

Membership: In 1980 the church had less than 100 members and three congregations, all in Ohio (Gettysburg, Covington, and Arcanum).

★476★
OLD ORDER (OR YORKER) RIVER BRETHREN
% Bishop Daniel M. Sipling
356 E. High St.
Elizabethtown, PA 17022

The Old Order (or Yorker) River Brethren separated in 1843 from their parent church, the River Brethren (now known as the Brethren in Christ), protesting what they saw as laxity in matters of nonconformity to the world and non-resistance to the military. The group was led by Bishop Jacob Strickler, Jr., of York County, Pennsylvania (hence the nickname). It was joined in the 1850s by a Franklin County group headed by Bishop Christian Hoover, who had been expelled for being "too orthodox."

The Old Order River Brethren remain the smallest of the River Brethren groups, having only four congregations, all in southeastern Pennsylvania. Three small independent congregations have split off at various times in disputes over modes of transportation. All worship is conducted in home, not in churches. The Old Order River Brethren are also agriculturists.

Membership: Not reported. In 1963 there were 4 congregations and 340 members.

Sources: Laban T. Brechbill, *Doctrine, Old Order River Brethren*. The Author, 1967.

★477★
UNITED ZION CHURCH
% Bishop Alvin H. Eberly
Rte. 2
Denver, PA 17517

The United Zion's Children originated in 1855 following the expulsion of Bishop Matthias Brinser from the River Brethren (i.e., the Brethren in Christ) for building and holding services in a meetinghouse. Other than the use of church buildings, there were no doctrinal differences. An annual conference is held but the government is congregational. The United Zion's Children was strengthened within a few years by some churches formed by Henry Grumbein and Jacob Pfautz. These groups accepted Brinser because of a revelation, but remain a separate unit within the church. They constitute one of three districts which send representatives to the annual conference. Mission work is supported through the Brethren in Christ. One home for the aged is maintained.

During the twentieth century several attempts have been made to improve the relationship between the United Zion Church and the Brethren in Christ, and even to look toward a future reunion. In 1967 the Brethren in Christ passed a resolution asking for the forgiveness of the United Zion Church for the action of the Church's council in 1855 and the continued lack of humility on their part which has kept the two groups apart. The next year the United Zion Church issued a formal statement offering complete forgiveness. These resolutions became the basis for cooperative action on the mission field and in higher education. A member of United Zion Church currently sits on the board of Brethren in Christ-founded Messiah College.

Membership: In 1983 there were 13 churches, 929 members, and 20 ministers.

Educational facilities: Messiah College, Grantham, PA.

Periodicals: *Zion's Herald*.

Sources: Carlton O. Wittlinger, *Quest for Piety and Obedience*. Nappanee, IN: Evangel Press, 1978.

Quakers (Friends)

★478★
ALASKA YEARLY MEETING
Box 268
Kotzebue, AK 99752

As early as 1897 Quaker missionaries from the California Yearly Meeting, an independent programmed meeting of

Friends, began work among the Eskimo people in Alaska. In 1970 the work had grown to the point that it was organized as a yearly meeting affiliated with the California Meeting, which maintained a Bible Training School. A goal of turning the work of the Meeting entirely over to its Eskimo constituency was completed in 1982 when the last of the missionaries were withdrawn and the Alaska Yearly meeting became fully independent. The California Meeting has joined the Friends United Meeting.

Membership: In 1981 there were 11 congregations and 2,860 members.

Educational facilities: Bible Training School.

★479★
CENTRAL YEARLY MEETING OF FRIENDS
Box 215
Westfield, IN 46074

The Central Yearly Meeting of Friends was formed in 1926 by several meetings in eastern Indiana who were protesting the liberalism of the Five Years Meeting. Doctrinally, the Central Yearly Meeting of Friends is evangelical and very conservative in matters of personal holiness. Worship is programmed. Churches of this small body are found in Indiana, Arkansas and Michigan. Missionary work is sponsored in Bolivia.

Membership: In 1981 the Meeting reported 11 congregations (monthly meetings) organized into 3 quarterly (district) meetings and 446 members.

Educational facilities: Union Bible Seminary, Westfield, IN.

Periodicals: *Friends Evangel*, Box 215, Westfield, IN 46074.

★480★
EVANGELICAL FRIENDS CHURCH, EASTERN DIVISION
1201 30th St., N.W.
Canton, OH 44709

Prior to 1971 known as the Ohio Yearly Meeting of Friends, the Evangelical Friends Church is that branch of the Friends most influenced by the holiness movement (discussed in chapter seven). The Evangelical Friends have a programmed worship service with a minister who preaches. Formed in 1813, the Ohio Yearly Meeting of Friends supported the Gurneyites, followers of Joseph John Gurney, a promoter of beliefs in the final authority of the Bible, atonement, justification, and sanctification. After the Civil War, the Ohio Yearly Meeting became open to the holiness movement through the activities of such workers as David B. Updegraff, Dougan Clark, Walter Malone and Emma Malone. The latter founded the Cleveland Bible Insititute (now the Malone College) in 1892, and it now serves an interdenominational holiness constituency. Worship is programmed.

The Evangelical Friends Church, never a member of the Five Years Meeting, has become a haven of conservative congregations who have withdrawn from the Friends United Meeting in both the United States and Canada. Mission work is sustained in Taiwan and India. The Church participates in the Evangelical Friends Alliance.

Membership: In 1981 there were 8,612 members in 86 churches.

Educational facilities: Malone College, Canton, OH.

Periodicals: *The Facing Bench*, 1201 30th Street N.W., Canton, OH 44709.

Sources: Charles E. DeVol, *Focus on Friends*. Canton, OH: The Missionary Board of the Evangelical Friends Church--Eastern Division, 1982;*Faith and Practice, the Book of Discipline*. Canton, OH: Evangelical Friends Church--Eastern Region, 1981.

★481★
FRIENDS GENERAL CONFERENCE
1520-B Race St.
Philadelphia, PA 19102

In the 1820s, there appeared among the Quakers of New York an eloquent minister, Elias Hicks. As his ideas developed, his emphasis on asceticism, rationalism, and subjectivism irritated many quaker faithfuls. Hicks's followers placed great emphasis on the "light within," to the extent of considering all outward forms useless and even harmful. Worship remains unprepared. Hicks attacked the divinity of Christ and expounded an exemplary theory of Christ's work. He was strong in his condemnation of amusements and any activities for self-gratification.

Controversy over Hicks's unsound views became public in 1823 at the Philadelphia Yearly Meeting, where complaints were lodged by some orthodox members. Four years of polemic ensued in which many non-theological factors (sociological differences, personal feelings, etc.) led to a polarization of the two groups. In 1827, the Hicksite following made what was termed a "quiet retreat" from the controversy. They called a conference and organized a separate yearly meeting. Separations occurred in New York, Ohio, and other yearly meetings across the East and Midwest. Seven yearly meetings were established. In 1868, a Sunday school conference began efforts to coordinate and communicate among the various yearly meetings and, in 1900, the mature General Conference emerged to aid in a social witness. It is purely a fellowship endeavor; the Conference has no legislative power over its member meetings. Members may also hold membership in other Friends associations, and some yearly meetings have a joint membership in the Friends United Meeting.

The program of the General Conference is through seven standing committees. While socially active, the Conference does little in the way of missions as these are traditionally understood. The Religious Education Committee publishes a variety of church school material. The Conference maintains an active but informal relationship to the World Council of Churches. The Philadelphia Yearly Meeting, a constituent part of the Conference, is a member of the National Council of Churches.

Membership: In 1982 the Meeting reported 26,184 members in 233 congregations.

Periodicals: *FQC Quarterly*, 1520-B Race St., Philadelphia, PA 19102; *Friends Journal*, 1501 Cherry St., Philadelphia, PA 19102 (unofficial publication).

Sources: Elsie Boulding, *My Part in the Quaker Adventure*. Philadelphia: Religious Education Committee, Friends General Conference, 1958; Jane P. Rushmore, *Testimonies and Practice of the Society of Friends*. Philadelphia: Friends General Conference, 1945.

★482★
FRIENDS UNITED MEETING
101 Quaker Hill Dr.
Richmond, IN 47374

The largest of all the Quaker bodies, the Five Years Meeting of Friends was formed in 1902 as a loose coordinating agency by twelve yearly meetings. By the addition of programs and agencies, a full denominational structure has developed. There are now fourteen yearly meetings in what became in 1965 the Friends United Meeting.

The Friends United Meeting represents the continuation of the "orthodox" Friends who had survived the Hicksite (Friends General Conference) and Wilburite (Religious Society of Friends (Conservative)) schisms, but who had existed throughout the nineteenth century as independent, geographical yearly meetings. Most worship is programmed. Ecumenical efforts began in the 1880s and a series of conferences every five years led to the formation of the Five Years Meeting.

The statement of faith of the Meeting, based upon the teachings of Jesus as "we understand them," includes beliefs in 1) true religion as a personal encounter with God rather than ritual and ceremony; 2) individual worth before God; 3) worship as an act of seeking; 4) essential Christian vitures of moral purity, integrity, honesty, simplicity, and humility; 5) Christian love and goodness; 6) concern for the suffering and unfortunate; and 7) continuing revelation through the Holy Spirit.

The work of the Meeting is carried out through its General Board and three commissions. The Wider Ministries Commission oversees missions in Mexico, East Africa, Cuba, Jamaica, Jordan, and the United States (Tennessee mountains and American Indians). The General Services Commission oversees Friends United Press and Quaker Hill Bookstore. The Meeting Ministries Commission serves the local congregations. There are 15 annual meetings: Baltimore, California, Indiana, Iowa, Nebraska, New England, New York, North Carolina, Southeastern, Western, Wilmington, Canadian, Cuba, East Africa, and Jamaica. It is a member of both the National Council of Churches and the World Council of Churches.

Membership: In 1981 the Meeting had approximately 57,000 members in the United States and Canada with an additional 40,000 in East Africa and 1,300 in Cuba, Jamaica, Mexico, and Jordan.

Educational facilities: Earlham College, Richmond, IN.

Periodicals: *Quaker Life*, 101 Quaker Hill Dr., Richmond, IN 47374.

Sources: Francis B. Hall, "Friends United Meeting" in Francis B. Hall, ed., *Friends in the Americas*. Philadelphia: Friends World Committee, Section of the Americas, 1976.

★483★
INTERMOUNTAIN YEARLY MEETING
% Sante Fe Friends Meeting
630 Canyon Rd.
Sante Fe, NM 87501

In the early 1970s, the Pacific Yearly Meeting devised a plan to divide its widely scattered membership into more geographically workable units. Members in Arizona and New Mexico joined with otherwise independent friends in Arizona, New Mexico, and Colorado, as well as Colorado Friends who had withdrawn from the Missouri Valley Yearly Meeting, to form the Intermountain Yearly Meeting. The group had its first annual session in 1975. Most congregations are unprogrammed. The Mexico City congregation affiliated with the Pacific Yearly Meeting also participates in the Intermountain fellowship.

Membership: In 1981 the Meeting reported 655 members in 15 monthly meetings and 10 worship groups.

★484★
LAKE ERIE YEARLY MEETING
% Clerk, Samuel B. Pellwitz
572 Briar Cliff Rd.
Pittsburgh, PA 15221

The Lake Erie Yearly Meeting began in 1939 as the Association of Friends Meetings. In 1963 it became a yearly meeting and assumed its present structure in 1969.

Congregations are located in Pennsylvania and Ohio with one in Ann Arbor, Michigan. Most meetings are in urban areas or college towns. Worship is unprogrammed. While independent, it has undertaken ecumenical efforts with a wide variety of Friends' groups. It carries on work in Korea with the Ohio Yearly Meeting of the Conservative Friends.

Membership: In 1981 the Meeting had 1,061 members in 23 congregations and worship groups.

Periodicals: *The Lake Erie Bulletin*, 572 Briar Cliff Rd., Pittsburgh, PA 15221.

★485★
MID-AMERICA YEARLY MEETING
2018 Maple
Wichita, KS 67213

The movement westward brought Friends into the South Central states in the early 1800s. The Kansas Yearly Meeting was formed in 1872 and includes churches in Texas, Oklahoma, Colorado, and Missouri. The doctrine is one with other Friends and a pastoral ministry is supported. Worship is programmed. From 1900 to 1937, the Kansas Meeting was in the Five Years Meeting, but withdrew as conservative evangelical elements became dominant in the Kansas Meeting. In 1934, an African mission in the Congo (now Zaire) was established. Camp Quaker Haven at Arkansas City, Kansas, serves the youth. In 1957, the Kansas Meeting joined the Evangelical Friends Alliance.

Membership: In 1981 the Meeting reported 8,000 members in 75 congregations.

Educational facilities: Friends Bible College and Academy, Haviland, Kansas; Friends University, Wichita, Kansas.

Periodicals: *Scope*, 2018 Maple, Wichita, KS 67213; *Quaker Bonnet*, 2018 Maple, Wichita, KS 67213.

Sources: Ralph E. Choate, *Dust of His Feet*. The Author, 1965; *Discipline*. Kansas Yearly Meeting of Friends, 1966; Paul W. Barnett, *Educating for Peace*. Board of Publications, Kansas Yearly Meeting of Friends, n.d.

★486★
MISSOURI VALLEY FRIENDS CONFERENCE
℅ Corky Stark
719 Brookfield Rd.
Wichita, KS 67206

The Missouri Valley Friends Conference was formed in 1955 as an association of otherwise unprogrammed congregations scattered throughout the middle of the United States. As the association grew, it lost participation due to more localized annual meetings being formed. Congregations in this loosely organized Conference are free to leave for another meeting, while keeping an affiliation to the Conference.

Membership: In 1981 the Conference had approximately 100 members.

★487★
NORTH PACIFIC YEARLY MEETING
℅ University Friends Center
4001 9th Ave., N.E.
Seattle, WA 98105

In the early 1970s the Pacific Yearly Meeting, which had congregations spread over a cumbersome distance, divided into several yearly meeetings. In 1972 members in Oregon and Washington became the North Pacific Yearly Meeting and held the first session in 1973. Since its formation groups have been added in Idaho and Montana. The meeting keeps close ties with the parent body with whom it jointly supports a periodical. It also participates in the Pacific Yearly Meeting's Friend-in-the-Orient Program.

Membership: In 1981 the Meeting reported 425 members in 32 congregations and worship groups.

Periodicals: *Friends Bulletin*.

★488★
NORTHWEST YEARLY MEETING OF FRIENDS CHURCH
Box 190
Newberg, OR 97132

Quaker settlers in the Northwest first gathered together in the fertile Willamette Valley in Oregon and were associated with the Iowa Yearly Meeting. They separated from the Iowa Yearly Meeting and became an independent entity in 1893 but, in 1902, joined the Five Years Meeting, which included many quakers from the East. Conservative Oregon and the liberal East did not mix, however, and in 1936, the Oregon Friends withdrew and formed the Oregon Yearly Meeting (now Northwest). The doctrine of the Oregon Friends is evangelical with a touch of Wesleyan holiness. The emphasis on piety and guidance can be seen in their stance that "beliefs should never be static, as merely articles of faith to be subscribed to, but should be dynamic in the lives of God's people, lived out before the world."

From the headquarters in Newberg, Oregon, an active mission program in the Andes Mountains and among the Klamath Indians of Oregon is carried out. The Church supports Friends View Manor for senior citizens. Barclay Press, located in the headquarters building, prints a variety of books and and other materials including mission material in Spanish and the Indian languages. A pastoral ministry is promoted and supported.

Membership: In 1981 the Meeting reported 8,465 members in 47 congregations and 4 missions.

Educational facilities: George Fox College, Newberg, Oregon.

Periodicals: *Northwest Vision*, Box 190, Newberg, OR 97132; *Keeping Current with Missions*, Box 190, Newberg, OR 97132.

Sources: *This is the Story of the Friends in the Northwest.* Newberg, OR: Barclay Press, n.d.

★489★
PACIFIC YEARLY MEETING OF FRIENDS
% The Clerk
2160 Lake St.
San Francisco, CA 94121

Quakers began to establish congregations on the West Coast in the 1880s. In 1931, with impetus from Howard H. Brinton and Mary Brinton, a meeting was called which led to the formation of the loosely organized Pacific Coast Association of Friends. In 1947, the Pacific Year Meeting was established within the Association. Over the next decade it grew to include forty congregations as far apart as Mexico City, Honolulu and Canada. Is a result, a committee recommended the division of the meeting into three meetings which led to the establishment of the North Pacific Yearly Meeting (1972) and the Intermountian Yearly Meeting (1973). Though each is independent, there are close familial ties and they jointly publish a periodical.

Its worship is unprogrammed. Membership though concentrated in California includes congregations in Mexico City and Honolulu. Interest in Asia led to the establishment of a Friends-in-the-Orient Program which annually sends a several members to different Asian locations for a year. The Committee publishes *Windows: East and West* to keep interested Friends informed of developments along the Pacific rim.

Membership: In 1981 the Meeting reported 1,452 members in 35 congregations.

Periodicals: *Friends Bulletin*.

Sources: *Faith and Practice*. San Francisco: Pacific Yearly Meeting of the Religious Society of Friends, 1973; Howard H. Brinton, *Guide to Quaker Practice*. Wallingford, PA: Pendle Hill Publications, 1955.

★490★
RELIGIOUS SOCIETY OF FRIENDS (CONSERVATIVE)
% Olney Friends School
Barnesville, OH 43713

Conservative Friends grew out of the teaching and ministry of John Wilbur. A Quaker minister in New England, Wilbur had become upset at the departure from traditional Quaker faith by the English Friend Joseph John Gurney. When Gurney, who had absorbed much from the Methodists and the Evangelical Revival, came to America preaching the final authority of the Bible, atonement, justification, and sanctification, Wilbur saw a Gurneyite creed replacing the inner light. Strict discipline was instituted by Wilbur's supporters to keep Gurney out, but Wilbur's activity proved unacceptable to most. Wilbur's followers separated in 1845 and set up independent yearly meetings. They were joined by other minority groups over the succeeding decades, though their overall numbers have decreased.

The Conservative Friends are the most persistent in continuing Quaker practices such as the unprogrammed meeting where all wait in silence for the movement of the Spirit. They are one in doctrine with most Quakers. The responsibility for ministry is shared by all and is unpaid. There is no permanent organization representative of Conservative Friends. Approximately every two years there is a joint meeting of the three conservative yearly meetings (Iowa, North Carolina, and Ohio) and several independent congregations for worship and fellowship. Without any direct missional program, the yearly meetings support the several Quaker service agencies such as the American Friends Service Committee.

Membership: In 1979 the Conservative Friends reported 1,832 members and 27 congregations.

Educational facilities: Olney Friends School, Barnesbille, OH.

Periodicals: *The Iowa Friend*, Box 552, Oskaloosa, IA 52577.

Sources: William B. Taber, Jr., "Conservative Friends" in Francis B. Hall, ed., *Friends in the Americas*. Philadelphia: Friends World Committee, Section of the Americas, 1976.

★491★
ROCKY MOUNTAIN YEARLY MEETING
29 N. Garland
Colorado Springs, CO 80909

The Rocky Mountain Yearly Meeting was established in 1957 by separation from the Nebraska Yearly Meeting and did not continue the latter's affiliation with the Friends United Meeting. Worship is programmed. Mission work is carried on among the Navajos at the Rough Rock

Mission in Chinle, Arizona. A campground is maintained north of Woodland Park, Colorado.

Membership: In 1981 the Meeting reported 1,583 members in 26 congregations.

Periodicals: *Rocky Mountain Friend.*

Sources: *Faith and Practice of the Rocky Mountain Yearly Meeting of Friends Church.* Pueblo, CO: Riverside Printing Co., 1978; 25th Anniversary Committee, *Friends Ministering Together.* Pueblo, CO: Riverside Printing Co., 1982.

★492★
SOUTHEASTERN YEARLY MEETING
SEYM Office
1375 Talbot Ave.
Jacksonville, FL 32205

The Southeastern Yearly Meeting is a small body established in 1962 and is composed mostly of Friends who migrated south to Florida. They support a retreat and study center near Orlando, Florida. In 1967, there were ten congregations, one of which was in Georgia, with a membership of 389. Membership is from various Friends' traditions.

Membership: In 1981 the Meeting reported 445 members and 22 congregations and worship groups.

Periodicals: *SEYM Newsletter,* 1375 Talbot Ave., Jacksonville, FL 32205.

★493★
**SOUTHERN APPALACHIAN YEARLY MEETING
   AND ASSOCIATION**
% Mrs. Ruth O. Szittya
Box 545
Swannanoa, NC 28778

The Southern Appalachian Yearly Meeting and Association of Friends was formed in 1970 at Crossville, Tennessee. It was established by congregations in Alabama, Tennessee, Georgia, Kentucky, West Virginia, South Carolina, and North Carolina, some of which had been associated together as early as 1940 in the South Central Friends Conference (and later in the Southern Appalachian Association of Friends). Congregations are unprogrammed, and there are no paid ministers. Annual meetings, held in May, center on silent worship, a search together on a chosen theme, and social concerns. While existing for some years as an independent Meeting, the Southern Appalachian Association has recently become a constituent part of the Friends General Conference.

Membership: See Friends General Conference (separate entry).

Periodicals: *Southern Applachaian Friend,* Box 1, Micaville, NC 28755.

Miscellaneous European Free

★494★
APOSTOLIC CHRISTIAN CHURCH (NAZAREAN)
Apostolic Christian Church Foundation
Box 151
Tremont, IL 61568

The Apostolic Christian Church (Nazarean) traces its history to the movement begun by Samuel Heinrich Froelich (1803-1857), a Swiss clergyman who led a revival in the late 1820s. In 1830, he was deprived of a pulpit by the Swiss state church for preaching the "Gospel of reconciliation in its original purity." The movement, called "Nazarean" on the Continent, spread throughout Europe and was persecuted. Many immigrants flocked to America and congregations were established: Froehlich himself came in 1850 and began immediately to organize his followers as the Apostolic Christian Churches of America. Around 1906/1907 some members of the Apostolic Churches withdrew over several points of doctrine. They adopted the designation "Nazarean," the popular name by which the group is known on the Continent.

Members of the church believe in Christ, are baptized in the name of the Father, Son and Holy Spirit, and form a covenant with God to live a sanctified life and to seek to become rich in good works. They reject the priesthood, infant baptism and transubstantiation, and refuse to be bound with oaths or to participate in war. The church consists only of baptized believers, but affiliated with it are "Friends of Truth," those being converted. Apart from refusing to bear arms and kill in the country's wars, the church is completely law-abiding.

The church is congregationally governed. Elders serve the local church with powers to baptize, lay on hands, administer the Lord's Supper and conduct worship. The Apostolic Catholic Church Foundation is a service organization. It recently moved from Akron, Ohio to its present location.

Membership: In 1981 the Church reported 2,684 members, 46 congregations, and 153 ministers.

Periodicals: *Newsletter,* Box 151, Tremont, IL 61568.

★495★
**APOSTOLIC CHRISTIAN CHURCHES OF
   AMERICA**
3420 N. Sheridan Rd.
Peoria, IL 61604

The Apostolic Christian Churches of America began in the protest of a new catechism introduced in 1830 by the

Reformed Church in Switzerland. Samuel Heinrich Froelich (1803-1857), a Reformed minister, rejected the new catechism as too rationalistic and in the resulting controversy was dismissed. Rebaptized by Mennonites, he organized the Community of Evangelical Baptists. The nonresistance stance (including the refusal to bear arms) adopted by the Community led to considerable tension with the government and occasioned the migration of many members beginning in the 1840s.

The first congregation in America began among members of the Old Order Amish Mennonites of Lewis County, New York. They requested leadership from Froelich, and he sent an elder, Benedict Weyeneth, t o found a congregation at Croghan. He ordained Joseph Virkler to the ministry and returned to Switzerland. He soon returned to the United States and established a second congregation in Woodford County, Illinois. Froelich visited the churches in 1850. Growth came slowly, primarily from German-speaking immigrants to the Midwest.

Following Froelich, the Church draws upon the Reformation concensus of the Reformed and Mennonite churches. It preaches the salvation of souls, the change of heart through regeneration, a life of godliness guided and directed by the Holy Spirit, and a striving for entire sanctification. Members are non-combatants, but loyal to the laws of the United States. A mission in Japan is supported.

Membership: In 1984 the Churches reported 11,173 members worldwide, 84 congregations, and 273 ministers.

Periodicals: *The Silver Lining*, Graybill, IN.

Sources: *Footsteps to Zion, A History of the Apostolic Christian Church of America*; S. H. Froelich, *The Mystery of Godliness and the Mystery of Ungodliness*. Apostolic Christian Church, n.d.; S. H. Froelich, *Individual Letters and Meditations*. Syracuse, NY: Apostolic Christian Publishing Co., 1926.

★496★

CHRISTIAN APOSTOLIC CHURCH (FOREST, ILLINOIS)
Forrest, IL 61741

The Christian Apostolic Church grew out of unrest within the German Apostolic Christian Church during the 1950s. Elder Peter Schaffer, Sr., one of the founders of the German Apostolic Christian Church, protested the attempts of church leaders in Europe to direct the life of the American congregations. Taking members in Illinois and Oregon, he organized independent congregations at Forest, Illinois and Silverton, Oregon in 1955. Doctrine and practice of the parent body were continued.

Membership: Not reported. There are an estimated several several hundred members and constituency in the two congregations.

★497★

CHRISTIAN APOSTOLIC CHURCH (SABETHA, KANSAS)
Sabetha, KS 66534

The Christian Apostolic Church was founded in the early 1960s when members of the German Apostolic Christian Church in Illinois and Kansas withdrew under the leadership of William Edelman. The members were protesting several points of "interpretation of the statues and customs" of the Church.

Membership: Not reported. There are three congregations.

★498★

GERMAN APOSTOLIC CHRISTIAN CHURCH
Current address not obtained for this edition.

The German Apostolic Christian Church is the result of a schism in the Apostolic Christian Churches of America. During the 1930s the pressure to discard the German language in worship, pressure which had greatly intensified since World War I, led the majority of the church to begin to use English. A group led by Elder Martin Steidinger protested that the loss of German would be accompanied by a loss of piety and lead to the influx of worldliness. With the encouragement of some European church leaders, he led members in the founding of the German Apostolic Christian Churches with initial congregations in Sabetha, Kansas, Silverton and Portland, Oregon and several locations in Illinois. Support came primarily from first generation immigrants. Doctrine and practice are like that of the parent body.

Membership: Not reported. There are an estimated 500 members.

★499★

MOLOKAN SPIRITUAL CHRISTIANS (POSTOJANNYE)
841 Carolina St.
San Francisco, CA 94107

The Postojannye are those Molokan Spiritual Christian who reject the practice of enthusiastic jumping during worship services which characterize their Pryguny Molokans. The split in the Molokan community into the Postojannye (the Steadfast) and the Jumpers occurred in the mid-nineteenth century in Russia. The Postojannye also reject the authority of the charismatic- prophetic leaders who arose at that same time, such as Maksim Gavrilovic Rudometkin. Otherwise the beliefs and practices of the Postojannye and Pryguny are similiar.

The first Postojannye came to the United States in 1905. They tried to work in the sugar field of Hawaii, but in 1906, shortly after the earthquake, moved to San Francisco and settled on Potrero Hill.

Membership: Not reported. There were an estimated 2,000 Postojannye Molokans in the mid 1970s. They live in San Francisco, the greater Bay area and in Woodburn, Oregon.

Sources: Ethel Dunn and Stephen P. Dunn, "Religion and Ethnicity: The Case of the American Molokans" in *Ethnicity* vol.4, no.4, (December 1977) pp. 370-79.

★500★
MOLOKAN SPIRITUAL CHRISTIANS (PRYGUNY)
% Paul I. Samarin
944 Orme St.
Los Angeles, CA 99923

Among numerous free evangelical groups which derived from the Russian Orthodox Church, only a few have come to the United States. Among these few are the Molokans, founded by Simeon Uklein (b.1733). He was a son-in-law of a leader of the Dukhobors, a mystical Russian group which is now found in western Canada. Forsaking mysticism, Uklein returned to the Russian Orthodox Church, and began to preach a Bible-oriented faith. He claimed that the church fathers had diluted the true faith with pagan philosophy. The true church, which existed visibly until their time, disappeared and survived only in scattered and persecuted communities. Uklein taught a form of unitarianism and gnosticism. Both the Son and the Holy Spirit were seen as subordinate to the Father; Christ was clothed in angelic, not human, flesh. Uklein tended to be anti-ritualistic and denied the sacraments and rites. Baptism means hearing the word of God and living accordingly; confession is repentance from sin; and the anointing of the sick is prayer. A ritual was constructed from Scripture and hymns. Molokans drink milk during Lent (from which the name Molokans or Milk Drinkers is derived), a practice forbidden in the Russian Orthodox Church. Uklein also adopted some of the Mosaic dietary law.

In the 1830s a great revival, an outpouring of the Holy Spirit, began in the Molokan community. It led to much enthusiastic religious expression, especially the jumping about of worshippers and the appearance of a number of charismatic prophetic leaders, the most popular one being Maksim Gavrilovic Rudometkin (d.1877). The acceptance of these new emphases which grew out of the revival split the Molokans into the Postoiannye (the Steadfast) who reject the practice of jumping and the teachings of Rudometkin and the Pryguny (jumpers). The urge to migrate to America began among the Molokans after the introduction of universal military service by the Russian government in 1878, but came to a head with their refusal to bear arms during the Russo-Japanese War. Over 2,000 left, primarily between 1904 and 1914 (when Russia stopped legal immigration) and settled in California. After World War I, some 500 more who had originally settled in the Middle East were allowed into the United States.

The Pryguny Molokons, the largest group to migrate to the United States, settled in Los Angeles from which they have moved into surrounding suburbs and communities. Various studies of the community found an estimated 3,500 (1912), 5,000 (late 1920s), and then 15,000 (1970). Churches can be found in Kerman, Porterville, Sheridan, Shafter, Delano, Elmira, and San Marcos, California. There is also a group in Glendale, Arizona and a small group in Baja California.

Membership: Not reported. There are an estimated 15,000 to 20,000 Prygun Molokons as of the mid-1980s.

Sources: Paul I. Samarin, comp., *The Russian Molokan Directory.* Los Angeles: the Author,(issued annually); Willard Burgess Moore,*Molokan Oral Tradition.* Berkeley: University of California Press, 1973; Stephen P. Dunn and Ethel Dunn, *The Molokan Heritage Collection. I, Reprints of Articles and Translations.* Berkeley: Highgate Road Social Science Research Station, 1983.

★501★
SCHWENKFELDER CHURCH IN AMERICA
Pennsburg, PA 18073

A surviving group of the followers of Caspar Schwenkfeld (1489-1561) left Silesia in 1734 because of persecution and came to America. In 1782 they organized the Schwenkfelder Church. The present general conference is a voluntary association of five churches, all in southeastern Pennsylvania. It meets semi-annually.

The Schwenkfelders follow the spiritual-mystical lead of their founder. Schwenkfeld, at one time a wealthy German nobleman, came to believe that all externals, though to be used, are of the perishable material world, and he sought to discover the spiritual imperishable reality behind them. He found them in the inner word, the church of those redeemed and called, the invisible spiritual sacrament, faith, and liberty--all emphasized by contemporary Schwenkfelders. Baptism is for adult believers only, but communion is open to all. No distinctive dress is worn. Both public office and military service is allowed (a practice which separates them from many of the Pennsylvania German groups).

Membership: In 1982 there were 5 churches, 2,700 members and 13 ministers.

Periodicals: *The Schwenkfeldian*, Pennsburg, PA 18073.

Sources: Howard Wiegner Kriebel, *The Schwenkfelders in Pennsylvania.* Lancaster, PA: Pennsylvania-German Society, 1904; Peter C. Erb, *Schwenkfeld in His Reformation Setting.* Valley Forge, PA: Judson Press,

1978; Selina Gerhard Schultz, *A Course of Study in the Life and Teachings of Caspar Schwenkfeld von Ossig (1489-1561) and the History of the Schwenkfelder Religious Movement (1518- 1964)*. Pennsburg, PA: The Board of Publication of the Schwenkfelder Church, 1964.

★502★
SMITH VENNER
Current address not available for this edition.

The Smith Venner, more popularly known as the "friends" of Johann Oscar Smith (b. 1871), is a Norwegian pietist group (The pietist movement emphasizes piety more than doctrine.) The Smith Zenner has spread throughout Europe. It is very loosely organized, but has several thousand adherents in Scandinavia, and as many as 3,500 have gathered at the annual assembly representing 20 countries. It has been introduced into the Pacific Northwest and has a small following centered at Salem, Oregon.

Membership: Not reported.

Periodicals: *Skjulete Skatter.*

Baptist Family

An historical essay on this family is provided beginning on page 57.

Calvinist Missionary Baptist

★503★

AMERICAN BAPTIST ASSOCIATION
4605 N. State Line Ave.
Texarkana, AR 75501

No sooner had the Southern Baptist Convention (SBC) been formed than it became disturbed by the controversy over what came to be called "Old Landmarkism." Dr. James R. Graves, editor of *The Tennessee Baptist*, in an attempt to restore Apostolic purity to the churches, called on them to reject non-Baptists, who could not rightly be considered Christian. This view was shared by Dr. J. M. Pendleton of Bowling Green, Kentucky.

The issues of "Old Landmarkism" centered on alien baptism, pulpit affiliation, closed communion, and missions. Supporters of Landmarkism opposed recognition of any baptism by a non-Baptist, the allowing of non-Baptists to join the Lord's Supper, the exchange of pulpits with non-Baptist ministers, and missions controlled by boards beyond the local church. The Southern Baptist Convention never accepted Landmarkism, but for many years supporters of Landmarkism remained as a dissenting minority within the SBC, strongly affecting its policy toward centralization. The Landmark position involved a theory of "Apostolic succession" of Baptist churches similar to the Jerusalem-Jordan-John theory. The succession begins with the Biblical church and continues through the Montanists, Novatians, Donatists, Paulicians, Waldenses, and Anabaptists.

Until 1899, when the Missionary Baptist Association of Texas was formed, Landmarkism remained unorganized. In 1905, however, churches both inside and outside the SBC formed a Landmark denomination, the General Association, which in 1924 became the American Baptist Association (ABA). It is doctrinally like the SBC, except for the Landmark ideals.

The ABA is congregationally governed. It maintains a publishing concern in Texarkana and a campground at Bogg Springs, Arkansas. There are twelve Bible schools and one seminary (at Texarkana) recognized by the ABA, but all are locally owned and controlled, as are several periodicals, including the *Missionary Baptist Searchlight* published by the Missionary Baptist Seminary.

Membership: In 1982 the association reported 225,000 members and 1,641 churches.

Educational facilities: Missionary Baptist Seminary, Texarkana, TX.

Periodicals: *Missionary Baptist Searchlght*, Box 663, Little Rock, AR 72203.

Sources: William Manlius Nevins, *Alien Baptism and the Baptists*. Ashland, KY: Press of Economy Printers, 1962.

★504★

AMERICAN BAPTIST CHURCHES IN THE U.S.A.
Valley Forge, PA 19481

The organization of Baptists in America proceeded in stages. While churches were organized in the 1600s, they were too few to formally organize above the congregational level. In 1707, however, five churches (three in Philadelphia and two in the countryside) organized the Philadelphia Baptist Association. That association at one point included churches from Connecticut and South Carolina. Then, in 1751, the Charleston (South Carolina) Association was formed. The number of Baptists began to grow significantly after the Revolution. The association became the typical structure by which Baptist congregations affiliated. Tensions emerged among those who saw the association strictly for fellowship and those who saw it as a structure through which the congregations could extend their ministry. Most Baptists have been content to emphasize the autonomy of the local church, while assigning specific tasks such as higher education and foreign missions (not generally possible for a congregation) to the association.

The next major step in Baptist organization was spurred by the New World missionary zeal that emerged in the early nineteenth century. Among the first missionaries sent out by the Congregational Church were Adoniram Judson, his wife Ann Judson, and Luther Rice. Rice returned to America to organize support among the churches. As a result of his efforts, the General Missionary Convention of the Baptist Denomination in the United States for Foreign Missions was organized in 1814. This organization was the first to draw support from Baptists nationally. It met every three years and became popularly known as the Triennial Convention. In 1932 it was joined by the American Baptist Home Mission Society, which directed its activity primarily toward the Western United States. A third major national society, the Woman's American Baptist Home Mission Society was formed in 1877.

Over the next decades Baptists were served by several mission agencies, each of which developed its own program and appealed to individual congregations. The need for coordination and the elimination of duplicated efforts was evident. In 1845 when the congregations in the South organized the Southern Baptist Convention, a cohesive convention structure had finally been formed. In 1907, the Northern Baptist Convention was organized, and the several missionary agencies became cooperating organizations of the convention. While retaining their official autonomy, the mission boards agreed to hold their regular meetings at the same time and place and to accept representatives of the congregations as voting delegates. The convention gave new national coherence to the majority of Baptists. The Northern Baptist Convention became known as the American Baptist Convention in 1950, and it assumed its present name in 1973.

Doctrinally, Baptists grew out of the Puritan-Reformed tradition in England. The reliance upon the Puritans is visible in the early Baptist confessions of faith, the First and Second London Confessions (1677 and 1689), the Philadelphia Confession (1742) and the New Hampshire Confession (1833). The first major break with the Reformed theological heritage came after the Revolution when attempts were made to move away from a strong doctrine of predestination. The theology of Andrew Fuller was among the most prominent statements of Baptists attempting to provide a place for the free response of men and women to the gospel. This changing emphasis was embodied in the New Hampshire Confession. Eventually, however, confessional statements fell into disuse. The need for doctrinal uniformity was no longer emphasized, and a variety of theological opinions appeared.

The lack of theological unity allowed several new perspectives to become prominent among American Baptists. An emphasis upon social reform in the cities merged with the new discipline of sociology to produce the social gospel movement. Baptists such as Walter Rauschenbush became leading exponents. Prominent Baptist scholars were among the first to absorb the new German higher criticism of the Bible. As both movements gained support within the denomination, the reactions of conservatives threatened the very existence of the new Northern Baptist Convention. It became one of the most heated and bitter battlegrounds for what became known as the fundamentalist-modernist controversy in the early twentieth century. The losses of conservatives at the convention meetings and the resultant decrease of influence in the mission societies led to several major schisms and the formation of such bodies as the General Association of Regular Baptist Churches and the Conservative Baptist Association.

The American Baptists Churches in the U.S.A. are organized congregationally. Delegates from the individual churches meet annually. Between conventions, a general council oversees the affairs of the churches. The work of the convention is delegated to the agencies that have charge of foreign missions, home missions, education and publication, and ministerial and missionary benefits. Under each of the agencies are a variety of specialized divisions. Judson Press is the publishing arm of the churches.

Membership: In 1983 the churches reported, 5,773 congregations, 1,591,412 adult members, and 8,411 ministers.

Educational facilities: Seminaries include the following: American Baptist Seminary of the West, Berkeley, California; Andover-Newton Theological Seminary, Newton Centre, Massachusetts; Central Baptist Theological Seminary, Kansas City, Missouri; Eastern Baptist Theological Seminary, Philadelphia, Pennsylvania; and Northern Baptist Theological Seminary, Lombard, Illinois. Colleges and universities include the following: Alderson-Broaddus College, Phillipi, West Virginia; Bates College, Lewiston, Maine; Benedict College, Columbia, South Carolina; Bishop College, Dallas, Texas; Bucknell University, Lewisburg, Pennsylvania; Colby College, Waterville, Maine; Denison University, Granville, Ohio; Eastern College, St. Davids, Pennsylvania; Florida Memorial College, Miami, Florida; Franklin College of Indiana, Franklin, Indiana; Hillsdale College, Hillsdale, Michigan; Judson College, Elgin, Illinois; Kalamazoo College, Kalamazoo, Michigan; Keuka College, Keuka Park, New York; Linfield College, Salisbury, North Carolina; Morehouse College, Atlanta, Georgia; Ottawa University, Ottawa, Kansas; University of Redlands, Redlands, California; Shaw University, Raleigh, North Carolina; Sioux Falls College, Sioux Falls, South Dakota; Stephens College, Columbia, Missouri; Virginia Union University, Richmond, Virginia; William Jewell College, Liberty, Missouri.

Periodicals: *American Baptist*, Box 851, Valley Forge, PA 19482; *The Secret Place*, Box 851, Valley Forge, PA 19482.

Sources: Norman H. Maring, *American Baptists, Whence and Whither*. Valley Forge, PA: Judson Press, 1968; Hillyer H. Straton, *Baptists: Their Message and Mission*. Chicago: Judson Press, 1941; Paul M. Harrison, *Authority and Power in the Free Church Tradition*. Princeton, NJ: Princeton University Press, 1959; Ambrose M. Bailey, *Manual of Instruction for Baptists*. Philadelphia: American Baptist Publication Society, 1951; Norman H. Maring & Winthrop S. Hudson, *A Baptist Manual of Polity and Practice*. Valley Forge, PA: The Judson Press, 1963.

★505★
ASSOCIATION OF EVANGELICALS FOR
    ITALIAN MISSIONS
314 Richfield Rd.
Upper Darby, PA 19082

The Association of Evangelicals for Italian Missions was formed by sixteen Baptist ministers meeting in New York City in 1899 as the Italian Association of America. The new association was the product of mission work among Italian immigrants undertaken by the Northern Baptist Convention, now the American Baptist Churches in the U.S.A., after the Civil War. The association became the Italian Baptist Association of America and recently adopted its present name. The association remains on good terms with its parent body, but carries on a mission to Italian-Americans. *The New Aurora* is published five times yearly. Most churches are in the North and East. There is an annual conference that elects officers.

Membership: Not reported.

Periodicals: *The New Aurora*, 314 Richfield Road, Upper Darby, PA 19082.

★506★
BAPTIST BIBLE FELLOWSHIP
Box 191
Springfield, MO 65801

The Baptist Bible Fellowship was begun in 1951 by former members of the World Baptist Fellowship, including Rev. Beauchamp Vick, who had succeeded J. Frank Norris as pastor of the Temple Baptist Church in Detroit. In 1948 he was made president of the debt-ridden Bible Baptist Seminary. Within two years he was able to wipe out most of the debt. He also discovered that Norris retained and would not surrender to him the ultimate power to run the school. In 1950 Vick was dismissed, and open schism soon occurred as pastors and churches lined up behind either Norris or Vick. Vick led in the founding of a new school, the Baptist Bible College, and a new periodical, the *Baptist Bible Tribune*.

Doctrinally, the Bible Baptists are in the main line of traditionally Baptist beliefs. But, while strongly fundamentalist, they are not separatists. There is a firm statement on the supernatural inspiration and verbal inerrancy of Scripture. Their Calvinism is very mild. The Bible Baptists believe in God's electing grace, but also teach that blessings of salvation are made free to all by the gospel. The main way in which the Bible Baptists differ from some other Baptists is in their ecclesiology. They emphasize the autonomy of the local church combined with the placing of strong authority in the pastor as shepherd of his flock. Any congregation which accepts the doctrinal statement may affiliate with the Fellowship.

Work of the denomination is centered on its college, its periodical, and, primarily, its missions. A part of the doctrinal statement is a belief in the command to give the gospel to the world. Also, scriptural giving is one of the fundamentals of faith. A director of missions and a mission committee oversees responsibility for the mission work of the Fellowship. In 1972, there were 387 missions operating in 41 countries. The Baptist Bible Fellowship has grown tremendously both through its evangelistic activities and by acquisition of independent congregations who choose to join. Among its member churches are some of the largest in the country; their congregations have almost one-fourth of the 100 largest Sunday schools in the country. Congregations are concentrated in the South and Midwest and are divided into nine fellowship districts.

Membership: Not reported. In 1972 there were more than 2,000 churches and 1,000,000 members affiliated with the fellowship.

Educational facilities: Baptist Bible College, Springfield, MO.

Periodicals: *Baptist Bible Tribune*, 2591 W. Beaver, Jacksonville, FL 32205.

Sources: Hollis Cook, *Bible Baptist Doctrines*. Springfield, MO: The Author, [1981]; Noel Smith, *There'll Always Be Moonlight on the Wabash*. Springfield, MO: Baptist Bible Tribune, 1973; Jerry Falwell and Elmer Towns, *Church Aflame*. Nashville, TN: Impact Books, 1971.

★507★
BAPTIST MISSIONARY ASSOCIATION OF
    AMERICA
716 Main St.
Little Rock, AR 72201

In 1949, a protest was lodged within the American Baptist Association (ABA) against the practice of seating some messengers to association meetings who were not members of the churches which elected them. The matter was referred to the churches. In 1950, the issue was ignored. After that session, a call meeting of the "church equality" people was held at the Park Place and Temple Baptist Churches in Little Rock, Arkansas, and the North American Baptist Association was organized. It changed its name in 1969 to the Baptist Missionary Association of America. It varies from the ABA only in designating that the association will recognize three messengers chosen from the membership of its member churches.

Headquarters were established in Little Rock. A publication board oversees the publishing of books, Sunday school material and Spanish literature. A vigorous mission program has 80 workers in the field.

Membership: In 1982 the association reported 226,953 members, 1,386 congregations and 3,500 ministers.

Educational facilities: North American Theological Seminary, Jacksonville, TX.

Periodicals: *The Advancer*, 712 Main St., Little Rock, AR 72201; *Baptist Trumpet*, Box 9502, Little Rock, AR 72209.

Sources: Sherman Harmon, comp., *A Fire Was Kindled*. N.p., n.d.; D. N. Jackson, *Studies in Baptist Doctrines and History*. Little Rock, AK: Baptist Publications Committee, n.d.

★508★
CHRISTIAN UNITY BAPTIST ASSOCIATION
% Elder Thomas T. Reynolds
Thomasville, NC 27360

The Christian Unity Baptist Association dates to 1901, when the Mountain Union Regular Association passed a resolution dropping from membership all churches which practiced open communion. Those who opposed the action walked out and for many years functioned as independent congregations. Over the years, only two ministers, F. L. Sturgill and Eli Graham, and three churches survived. In 1932, these churches organized as the Macedonia Baptist Association. In 1935, they were joined by other churches who had left the Mountain Union Regular Association, and the Christian Unity Baptist Association was organized.

Doctrinally, a mild Calvinism prevails. The article on the security of the believer was amended to read that all who are saved and endure to the end sh all be saved. Footwashing and open communion are practiced. The polarity is congregational and the association acts in an advisory role.

Membership: Not reported. In 1965, there were eleven churches in the association in Virginia, Tennessee, and North Carolina, with 623 members and 17 ministers.

★509★
CONSERVATIVE BAPTIST ASSOCIATION
25W560 Geneva Rd., Box 66
Wheaton, IL 60189

The Fundamentalist Fellowship (Conservative Baptist Fellowship) existed in the Northern Baptist Convention (now the American Baptist Churches in the U.S.A.), disturbed only by the withdrawal of the General Association of Regular Baptist Churches (GARBC) until the 1940s. Then concern for the doctrinal position of the missionaries sent out by the Convention caused some members to ask that none be sent who did not hold to fundamentalist doctrine. When this request was turned down, the Fellowship proceeded to form the Conservative Baptist Foreign Missionary Society (CBFMS) to operate within the Convention. Plans began to be forged for a new association which was formed in 1947: the Conservative Baptist Association (CBA).

The emergence of the CBA meant that the fundamentalist wing of the Northern Baptist Convention had in fact become a new body. It was a loose fellowship of independent churches. A most important principle enunciated by the General Director, Myron Cederholdm, was the lack of organic relationship between the CBA and the organizations which the churches support. Thus, the CBA was a confessing body in communion with certain agencies (such as the CBFMS). Churches could support what they wished, there being no unified budget.

Since the CBA had taken over the functions of the Fundamentalist Fellowship (after 1946, called the Conservative Baptist Fellowship), it was assumed by many that the Fellowship would die. But new life was given tothe CBF by its hiring Chester Tulga as research director, and by the popularity of a series of what were termed "Case" books on several topics of theology and ecclesiology which he authored.

Though racked by controversy in the 1950s which eventually led to the loss of two large segments of the movement, the CBA continued to grow. The major issue to disturb it was the degree of separation from other Christians and Baptists. Because of its rejection of strict separation, it declined merge with the GARBC, which promoted separatism. Separtists within the CBA would soon leave to form their own group. A major event was the acceptance of a doctrinal statement in 1953 called the "Baptist Manifesto."

In 1984 the Conservative Baptist Foreign Missionary Society reported missionaries in twenty-three countries. A Conservative Baptist Home Missionary Society oversees programs in the United States tates which include missions to urban centers, Mormons, and to other countries. The Conservative Baptist Press is the publishing arm.

Membership: In 1984 the association reported 220,000 members and 1,087 churches.

Educational facilities: Denver Conservative Baptist Seminary, Denver, Colorado; Southwestern Baptist Bible College, Phoenix, Arizona; Western Conservative Baptist Seminary, Portland, Oregon; Judson Baptist College, Portland, Oregon; International College, Honolulu, HI 96817.

Periodicals: *Conservative Baptist*, Box 66, Wheaton, IL 60189; *Impact*, Box 5, Wheaton, IL 60189.

Sources: Bruce R. Shelley, *Conservative Baptists*. Denver, CO: Conservative Baptist Theological Seminary, 1962; *Founded on the Word, Focused on the World*. Wheaton, IL: Conservative Baptist Foreign Mission Society, 1978; Walter A. Pegg, *Historic Baptist Distinctives*. Wheaton, IL: Conservative Baptist Foreign Mission Society, 1952; *A Baptist Primer in Church Discipline*. Chicago: Conservative Baptist Fellowship, n.d.; Chester E. Tulga, *The Independence of the Local Church*. Chicago: Conservative Baptist Fellowship, 1951.

★510★
DUCK RIVER (AND KINDRED) ASSOCIATION OF BAPTISTS

Duck River Association
  Elder A. B. Ray, Moderator
500 Regan St.
Tullahoma, TN 37388

The Duck River (and Kindred) Association of Baptists separated from the Elk River Association in 1825. The issue was the atonement, and the "liberals" who believed in a general atonement withdrew from the Elk River Association, which was a member of the Triennial Convention, the initial missionary organization which later evolved into the American Baptist Churches in the U.S.A.. Another issue soon divided churches in the Triennial Convention, the issue of compulsory mission support. In 1843 that issue caused some people to withdraw from churches in the Triennial Convention and from another Duck River Association. With further divisions within churches associated with the Triennial Associations, more Duck River Associations were formed. Now there are four Duck River Associations and three Kindred Associations included in the general association. Most of the churches are in Tennessee. All mission work is local. Doctrine is mildly Calvinistic. Members practice footwashing. Polity is congregational. Letters are a standard means of communication. Ministers are ordained by two or more of their colleagues.

Membership: Not reported. In 1975 there were 85 churches, 8,632 members and 148 ministers.

★511★
FUNDAMENTAL BAPTIST FELLOWSHIP
Current address not obtained for this edition.

The Fundamental Baptist Fellowship was formed as a result of conflict and controversy in the Conservative Baptist Association. At issue was what was termed the "new evangelicalism," a trend in conservative Christian circles toward cooperation and accommodation to certain modern situations, without giving up any essentials of the faith. However, some within the Conservative Baptist Association (CBA) saw the new evangelicalism as a departure from Baptist traditions. The critics also believed in a premillennial eschatology and in separation from those who do not hold to fundamentalist doctrine. The controversy centered on the Denver Conservative Baptist Seminary in Denver, Colorado, founded in 1950 and strongly staffed with exponents of the new evangelicalism.

During the 1950s, controversy centered on attempts to control the seminary by the Separatists. Conservative Baptist churches in Colorado began to take sides. The separatist strength was concentrated in the Conservative Baptist Fellowship (CBF), one of the constituent agencies of the CBA. The CBF was headed by Research Secretary Chester Tulga, who spelled out the separatist position in a number of "Case" booklets which attacked modernist and centralizing trends. The new evangelical position was concentrated in the CBA and the Conservative Baptist Foreign Missionary Society. During the 1950s, the distance between the two sides grew. The Colorado Conservative Baptists withdrew support from the seminary, and individual churches and leaders began to support either the CBA or the CBF.

The split became final in 1961 when the leadaers of the CBF formed the World Conservative Baptist Mission. An aggressive stance toward the CBA was taken, and pre-CBA convention sessions were held to try to woo churches to the CBF position. The name was eventually changed to the Fundamental Baptist Fellowship.

The Fundamental Baptist Fellowship established headquarters in Denver from which it issued the *Information Bulletin*, its periodical. The Baptist Bible College offers a two-year curriculum. Close relations are kept with the Minnesota Baptist Convention as a sister organization.

Membership: Not reported.

Educational facilities: Baptist Bible College, Denver, CO.

★512★
GENERAL ASSOCIATION OF REGULAR BAPTIST CHURCHES
1300 N. Meacham Rd.
Schaumburg, IL 60195

Among the conservative elements in the Northern Baptist Convention (now the American Baptist Churches in the U.S.A.) were a number whose main concern was doctrine. After the failure in 1922 of the convention to adopt the New Hampshire Confession of Faith, T. T. Shields of the Jarvis Street Church in Toronto led in the formation of the Baptist Bible Union, a union of individuals interested in the purging of modern elements in the Convention. In 1932, the Baptist Bible Union gave way to the General Association of Regular Baptist Churches (GARBC), formed in Chicago by delegates from eight states.

The GARBC considers itself an association of sovereign Bible-believing Baptist churches. The New Hampshire Confession of Faith was used as a model for the Articles of Faith, though emphasis is placed on the fundamentalist issues of the Bible and Christology. A single article concerns the "Resurrection, Personal, Visible Premillennial Return of Christ, and related events."

The GARBC is also a vocal exponent of separation. Churches in the fellowship are required to withdraw fellowship from and refuse cooperation with any organization or group which permits modernists in its ranks. Their separatist position was included in the name of the GARBC; the term "Regular" was adopted to oppose the other, "irregular" Baptist churches.

Missions are promoted through six independent mission agencies which hold to the GARBC doctrinal position. They are the Association of Baptists for World Evangelism, Baptist Mid-Missions, Evangelical Baptist Missions, Fellowship of Baptists for Home Missions, Continental and Galilean Baptist Mission and Hiawatha Baptist Missions. Together, in 1983, they supported more than 2,000 missions. There are nine independent college/seminaries which are accredited by the GARBC. Four social agencies, two children's homes, a senior citizen's home, and a residential school for the retardedare also approved.

Membership: In 1983 the association reported 260,000 members, 1,593 congregations and 1,600 ministers.

Educational facilities: Approved educational facilities include the following: Baptist Bible College of Pennsylvania and Baptist School of Theology, Clarks Summit, Pennsylvania; Cedarville College, Cedarville, Ohio; Denver Baptist Bible College, Denver Baptist Theological Seminary, Denver, Colorado; Faith Baptist Bible College, Ankany, Iowa; Grand Rapids Baptist College and Seminary, Grand Rapids, Michigan; Los Angeles Baptist College, Newhall, California; Northwest Baptist Seminary, Tacoma, Washington; Spurgeon Baptist Bible College, Mulberry, Florida; Western Baptist College, Salem, Oregon.

Periodicals: *Baptist Bulletin*, 1300 N. Meacham Rd., Schaumburg, IL 60195.

Sources: Merle R. Hull, *What a Fellowship?* Schaumburg, IL: Regular Baptist Press, 1981; *The Biblical Faith of Baptists*. Des Plaines, IL: Regular Baptist Press, 1966. 3 Vols.; J. Murray Murdoch, *Portrait of Obedience*. Schaumburg, IN: Regular Baptist Press, 1979; W. W. Barndollar, *The Validity of Dispensationalism*. Des Plaines, IL: Regular Baptist Press, 1964; [R. T. Ketcham], *The Answer: What Are Non-Convention Baptists Doing?*. Waterloo, IA: General Association of Regular Baptist Churches, 1943.

★513★
INDEPENDENT BAPTIST CHURCH OF AMERICA
% Elmer Erickson, President
2646 Longfellow
Minneapolis, MN 55407

The Independent Baptist Church of America dates to the 1870s, when Swedish Free Baptists emigrated to the United States and settled in the Midwest. In 1893, an annual conference began to be held under the name Swedish Independent Baptist Church, later changed to Scandinavian Independent Baptist Denomination of America. In 1912, a split occurred when part of the group incorporated. The incorporated group called themselves the Scandinavian Independent Baptist Denomination in the United States of America. The unincorporated group continued as the Scandinavian Free Baptist Society of the United States of America. In 1927, the two groups united at a conference at Garden Valley, Wisconsin, and adopted their present name.

Doctrinally, the churches are pietistic and evangelical. Like the Six-Principle Baptists, they practice the laying-on-of-hands at the time a member is received into the church. Members believe in the authority of and obedience to the civil government in all of its demands, except those contrary to the Word of God, such as participation in war.

Membership: Not reported. In 1965 there were two congregations and 70 members (down from 13 congregations in 1926).

Periodicals: *The Lighthouse*, 2646 Longfellow, Minneapolis, MN 55407.

★514★
KYOVA ASSOCIATION OF REGULAR BAPTISTS
Current address not obtained for this edition.

The Kyova Association of Regular Baptists was formed in 1924 from the New Salem Association of Regular

Baptists. In the 1940s, a controversy arose over whether the United Mine Workers (or any union) was in fact a secret society. As a result of this controversy, the Kyova Association dropped correspondence with the New Salem Association in 1945 and then splintered. Some churches moved into other Regular Baptist Associations. The group uses the King James version of the Bible and forbids members to belong to secret societies.

Membership: Not reported. In 1960 the association had 4 congregations and 140 members.

★515★

MINNESOTA BAPTIST ASSOCIATION
% Rev. Richard L. Paige, Jr., Executive Secretary
5000 Golden Valley Rd.
Minneapolis, MN 55422

As the fundamentalist debate arose anew in the 1940s, Minnesota emerged as one of the few areas where, under the leadership of such men as William Bell Riley (1861-1947), conservatives were in the majority. Controversy developed over support of the mission program of the Northern Baptist Convention (now the American Baptist Churches in the U.S.A., and in 1944 a "special account" was created by the Minnesota Convention to channel funds to the Conservative Baptist Foreign Missionary Society (CBFMS). Other objections to the Northern Baptist Convention's program were focused on ecumenism, youth work, and the distribution of funds in the unified budget. The break came in 1948 when the Minnesota Convention became independent of the Northern Baptist Convention.

After the formation of the Conservative Baptist Association (CBA) in 1947, there was a period of cooperation between it and the Minnesota Convention. Individual churches and leaders (such as Dr. Richard V. Clearwaters) were active in both. The Minnesota Convention continued to function, for the CBA accepted only churches (not conventions) as members.

Cooperation with the CBA continued, but the Conservative Baptists were criticized in 1955 when an article in a Minnesota Convention magazine complained that CBFMS missionaries did not believe in the pretribulation, pre-millennial return of Christ. Later that year, a pretribulation position was adopted by the Minnesota Convention. The Convention began to move in a separatist direction; criticism of the CBA continued. The CBA was accused of interfering with local autonomy in the churches and of allowing inclusivist thinking in the early 1960s. (Inclusivist thinking pertained to association with those in liberal associations.) The break between the Minnesota Convention and the Conservative Baptist Association was completed in 1963. The name was officially changed to the Minnesota Baptist Association in 1974.

The Association publishes a church school curriculum and vacation Bible school material as well as various tracts and booklets through the publication ministry of North Star Baptist Press.

Membership: In 1984 there were 76 churches and approximately 100 ministers.

Educational facilities: Pillsbury Baptist Bible College, Owatonna, MN.

Periodicals: *The North Star Baptist*, 5000 Golden Valley Rd., Minneapolis, MN 55422.

Sources: David Becklund, *A History of the Minnesota Baptist Convention*. Minneapolis: Minnesota Baptist Convention, 1967; Marie Acomb Riley, *The Dynamic of a Dream*. Grand Rapids, MI: William B. Eerdmans Publishing Company, 1938.

★516★

NEW ENGLAND EVANGELICAL BAPTIST
   FELLOWSHIP
% Dr. John Viall
40 Bridge St.
Newton, MA 02158

The New England Evangelical Baptist Fellowship is a small body in the Northeast. It is a conservative body and was formally a member of the National Association of Evangelicals. The president in 1965 was Dr. John S. Viall of Boston.

Membership: Not reported. In 1965 there were 10 churches, 20 pastors and 1,022 members.

★517★

NEW TESTAMENT ASSOCIATION OF
   INDEPENDENT BAPTIST CHURCHES
1079 Westview Dr.
Rochelle, IL 61068

The New Testament Association of Independent Baptist Churches was formed in 1965 at a meeting in Denver. Twenty-seven churches affiliated at the organizational meeting. A previous meeting had been held in 1964 by members of the Conservative Baptist Association who supported a premillennial, pretribulationist, separatist position. Among leaders of the newly formed association was Dr. Richard V. Clearwaters of the Minnesota Baptist Convention (now the Minnesota Baptist Association). The polity is a loose congregationalism. An annual meeting is held in which each pastor and five lay delegates have voting power. They elect a president, other officers, and members of a board of trustees to implement Association programs.

Doctrinally, the Association resembles the Conservative Baptist Association. The New Testament Association has adopted a Confession of Faith based on the New Hampshire Confession, but with emphasis on separation and pre-tribulation eschatology. The group is opposed to speaking in tongues. The schools of the Minnesota Baptist Association are approved for students.

Membership: Not reported.

Periodicals: *New Testament Testimonies*, 1079 Westview Dr., Rochelle, IL 61068.

Sources: Richard V. Clearwaters, *The Ten Commandments*. Minneapolis, MN: Central Seminary Press, 1975; Richard v. Clearwaters, *The Local Church of the New Testament*. Chicago: Conservative Baptist Association of America, 1954; Richard V. Claerwaters, *The Great Conservative Baptist Compromise*. Minneapolis, MN: Central Seminary Press, n.d.

★518★
NORTH AMERICAN BAPTIST CONFERENCE
1 S. 210 Summit Ave.
Oakbrook Terrace, IL 60181

The North American Baptist Conference (formerly the North American Baptist General Conference originated in the early ninetenth century with German-speaking Americans who had been influenced by English-speaking Baptists to work among the growing number of immigrants from the fatherland. While tracing their history to a number of efforts begun independently of each other, the German Baptists look to Konrad Anton Fleischmann as the first of their number. A Bavarian, Fleischmann had been converted in Switzerland and joined a separatist church molded on the English model. On a request from George Mueller of Bristol, England, he traveled to America and became pastor of a German Protestant church at Newark, New Jersey, in the spring of 1839, but was fired for refusing to baptize infants. In October, he baptized three people, his first converts, and sent them to an English Baptist church. He traveled throughout eastern Pennsylvania and New York, where he established groups of believers and preaching stations. In 1843, he drew up a series of "Articles" for use by the church at Philadelphia which he founded. It was Baptist in all points except closed communion.

Other missionaries were also at work in the 1840s. Aided by the American Baptist Home Missionary Society, John Eschmann was working in New York City. Alexander Von Puttkamer was converted by English Baptists at Lawrenceville, New York, and began to organize a German Baptist Church in Buffalo while an agent of the American Tract Society. Churches in the Midwest were begun in the late 1840s.

The first conference of German Baptists met in 1851 representing eight churches and 405 members. With the cooperation of the American Baptist Publication Society, they were able to produce a hymnal and a German

translation of the New Hampshire Confession. A Western Conference was formed in 1859, and a General Conference met in 1865.

Doctrinally, the North American Baptists affirm the standard Baptist faith as embodied in the New Hampshire Confession, though only a brief statement has been adopted. Polity is congregational. There is a general conference every three years, with 21 associations in the United States and Canada. Higher education has been a major concern from the beginning, and as early as 1858, August Rauschenbusch went to the Baptist Seminary at Rochester and became one of the outstanding exponents of the social gospel. Missions are carried on in Cameroon, Nigeria, Japan, and Brazil. Home missions are directed toward American Indians and Spanish-speaking Americans in Colorado and Texas. The long-time German-language periodical, *Der Sendbote*, has been absorbed by the English *Baptist Herald*. The conference is affiliated with the Baptist World Alliance.

Membership: In 1982 the Conference reported 29,638 members, 411 congregations, and 673 ministers.

Educational facilities: North American Baptist Seminary, Sioux Falls, South Dakota; North American Baptist College, Edmonton, Alberta, Canada.

Periodicals: *The Baptist Herald*, 1 S. 210 Summit Ave., Oakbrook Terrace, IL 60181.

Sources: Frank H. Woyke, *Heritage and Ministry of the North American Baptist Conference*. Oakbrook Terrace, IL: North American Baptist Conference, 1979; Reinhold Johannes Kerstan, *Historical Factors in the Formation of the Ethnically Oriented North American Baptist General Conference*. Evanston, IL: Northwestern University, Ph.D. dissertation, 1971; Albert John Ramaker, *The German Baptists in North America*. Cleveland, OH: German Baptist Publication Society, 1924.

★519★
REGULAR BAPTISTS
% Tom Marshall
9023 Contee Rd.
Laurel, MD 20810

In the 1740s during what was called the Great Awakening in the American colonies, the new Baptists were divided into Regular Baptists and Separate Baptists. The Separatists were former Congregationalists who had been affected by the revival and particularly the preaching of George Whitefield. Regular Baptists were members of the Philadelphia Association and adhered to the Philadelphia Convention. The Separate and Regular Baptists spent the second half of the eighteenth century engaging in polemics and attempting union. In 1765, the first Regular Baptist Association was formed by churches in Virginia and given the name Ketocten. The Regular Baptists spread into Kentucky and the surrounding states.

In 1801, the Separate and Regular Baptists were able to overcome their differences and merge. They formed various associations with the terms "united" in the association names. Some second generation members of these associations, however, became dissatisfied with the term "united" and many associations dropped it from their name. Larger Baptist bodies absorbed many of these associations.

Toward the middle of the nineteenth century, a move to reconstitute the Regular Baptists began. In 1854, the New Salem Association of United Baptists changed its name to the New Salem Association of Regular Baptists. In 1870 this association adopted another name, Old Regular Baptists. In 1867 the Burning Springs Association of United Baptists changed the term "united" in its name to "regular." Other associations followed suit. Regular Baptists now live in all sections of the country, with the heaviest concentration of them living in the area from Virginia to Indiana.

The reason for the formation of the Regular Baptists is not clear. By the end of the nineteenth century, though, they clearly represented a rejection of the organizational and methodological innovations of most nineteenth-century Baptists. The group rejects Sunday schools, a trained ministry, secret societies, missionary societies, and organization beyond the associational level.

A doctrinal consensus exists among the Regular Baptists, a body of beliefs very close to the doctrine of the United Baptists. Most statements of the beliefs of Regular Baptists affirm belief in the Trinity, the bible as the written word of God, election, man's depravity, the eternal security of the believer, believers' baptism by immersion (often specified as "back foremost," so water covers the whole person), closed communion, the resurrection, and a properly ordained ministry. Beyond that consensus, there is a wide variety of freedom and belief. The statements on salvation and justification are so worded as to be open to both Calvinistic and Arminian interpretations. (Calvinists say the number and identity of the elect was predetermined before the world began; Arminians say salvation is possible for all who, by free will, choose to follow the gospel.) However, the Regular Baptists have no fellowship with those who reject their statements of beliefs. Government is extreme congregationalism with no central headquarters and no structure beyond the association. Among the periodicals serving the churches are *The Regular Baptist* from Annandale, Virginia, and the *Regular Baptist Messenger* of Whitestown, Indiana.

The Regular Baptists have allowed Arminianism but not hyper-Calvinism, and in the 1890s, they split over absolute predestination. (See separate entry on Regular Baptists-Predestinarian.) The following Regular Baptist associations are in correspondence with each other, display doctrinal similarity, and reject absolute predestination: the New Salem, Union, Indian Bottom, Mud River, Sardis, Friendship, Philadelphia, Thornton Union, and Northern Salem Associations.

Membership: Not reported. In the early 1970s there were an estimated 266 churches and 17,186 members.

Periodicals: *The Regular Baptist*, 9023 Contee Rd., Laurel, MD 20810.

Sources: Rufus Perrigan, *History of Regular Baptists and their Ancestors and Accessors*. Haysi, VA: The Author, 1961; Ron Short, "We Believed in the Family and the Old Regular Baptist Church" in *Southern Exposure*, vol. 4, no.3, (1976) pp. 60-65; John Wallhausser, "I Can Almost See Heaven From Here" in *Katallagete* vol. 8, no. 3, (Spring 1983), pp. 2- 10.

★520★
REGULAR BAPTISTS (PREDESTINARIAN)
Current address not obtained for this edition.

In 1894, the Union Association of Regular Baptists split over the question of predestination. The majority was Calvinist, holding to strict predestination. Both the majority and minority groups continue with the same name, the Union Association of Regular Baptists, and have equal claims on the pre-1984 history.

The Sandlick Association of Regular Baptists was formed in 1876 from the New Salem Association of Regular Baptists. In 1896, it became involved in the Calvinist controversy. The Calvinist majority prevails in the Sandlick Association. The Arminian minority, holding that salvation is possible for all, formed the Indian Bottom Association.

Other associations were also racked with the controversy. In 1893, the Mates Creek Association of Regular Baptists was divided, the Arminian group becoming the Sardis Association. Although called Regular Baptists, the following groups are strongly predestinarian and fit the description of Regular Baptists (Predestinarian): the Union Association, the Sandlick Association, and the Mages Creek Association. Most members of these associations live where the Regular Baptists live, that is, from Virginia to Indiana. The predestinarian associations have grown, though some have possibly been lost to the Primitive Baptists. There are no current statistics; figures quoted (22 associations, 7,000 members) in the *Encyclopedia of Southern Baptists* may refer only to Calvinistic associations.

Membership: Not reported.

★521★
RUSSIAN/UKRAINIAN EVANGELICAL BAPTIST UNION OF THE U.S.A., INC.
Roosevelt Blvd. & 7th St.
Philadelphia, PA 19120

The Russian/Ukrainian Evangelical Baptist Union of the U.S.A., Inc., dates from 1901 when Baptists migrated from Russia to Kiev, North Dakota. During the next twenty years, the Baptists absorbed other evangelical groups, many of which were lost in transition to English-language worship. In 1919, the Union was organized at Philadelphia. Missionary work was begun worldwide among Russian immigrants. A Slavic missionary society supported 21 missionaries in Western Europe, South America, and Australia. An English branch works among English-speaking Slavic people. The Evangelical Baptist Camp Home for the Aged is operated by the Union.

Membership: Not reported. In 1968 there were approximately 40 churches of Russian/Ukrainian-speaking Americans.

Periodicals: *Evangelical Baptist Herald* (in English), Roosevelt Blvd. & Seventh St.t, Philadelphia, PA 19120; *The Sower of Truth* (in Russian), Roosevelt Blvd. & Seventh St., Philadelphia, PA 19120.

★522★
SEPARATE BAPTISTS IN CHRIST
% Rev. Roger Popplewell, Moderator
Rte. 5
Russell Springs, KY 42642

The Separate Baptists emerged in the "First Great Awakening" as a result of the hostility of some Congregationalists to the revivalism that swept New England. These former Congregationalists were rebaptized, including Isaac Backus, who became an outstanding theologian and historian. The Separatist movement spread, but the Separatists were not for a long time accepted by many Baptists, in part because of their acceptance of those baptized but not immersed. In 1801, a union was effected between the Regular and Separate Baptists. Some Separatists did not accept the union, and continued to exist west of the Allegheny Mountains. In 1912, several of these associations came together as the General Association of Separatist Baptists.

The Separatist Baptists are similar to the Regular Baptists. A mild Calvinism is generally held. There is no universally accepted creed. Footwashing is an ordinance. Immersion is the only form of baptism. The government is congregational. Sunday schools and home missionary work are supported on a local level. Education is more highy rated than with the Regular Baptists.

Membership: In 1982 the Separate Baptists reported 8,800 members, 100 congregations, and 160 ministers.

Periodicals: *The Messenger.*

★523★
SOUTH CAROLINA BAPTIST FELLOWSHIP
% Rev. John Waters
Faith Baptist Church
1600 Greenwood Rd.
Laurens, SC 29360

The South Carolina Baptist Fellowship was formed at a meeting in 1954 in Greenville, South Carolina, called by the Rev. John R. Waters and the Rev. Vendyl Jones. It was known as the Carolina Baptist Fellowship until its incorporation in 1965. Eleven independent Baptist pastors were present at the 1954 meeting. Rev. Waters was editor of *The Baptist Bible Trumpet*, and in 1955 at the Fellowship meeting, it was adopted as the official organ. Doctrine is fundamental and premillennial; polity is congregational. Meetings of the Fellowship are held monthly. It is a member of the International Council of Christian Churches and individual congregations are affiliated with the American Council of Christian Churches. Missions are supported through independent fundamentalist faith mission organizations such as Baptist Mid-Missions.

Membership: In 1984 there were over 150 churches with a membership of approximately 25,000 affiliated with the fellowship, though no formal membership list is kept.

Educational facilities: Approved educational facilities: Bob Jones University, Greenville, South Carolina; Tennessee Temple University, Chattanooga, Tennessee.

Periodicals: *The Bible Baptist Trumpet*, 1607 Greenwood Rd., Laurens, SC 29360.

★524★
SOUTHERN BAPTIST CONVENTION
% Executive Committee
460 James Robertson Pkwy.
Nashville, TN 37219

The Southern Baptist Convention was formed in 1845 by the Baptist congregations in the southern United States. Underlying the separation of the southerners were the variety of tensions that would fifteen years later divide the nation and lead to the Civil War. Some of those tensions had become focused in the American Baptist Home Mission Board which many felt had neglected the south and southwest in the appointment of missionaries. The immediate occasion for the separation of the southern Baptists was the refusal in 1844 of the American Baptist Foreign Mission Board to appoint a slaveholder as a missionary and American Baptist Home Mission Board to appoint a slaveholder to a mission in Georgia. These refusals seemed to violate longstanding practice and the agreement of the Triennial Convention (the meeting of the foreign mission board), that cooperation in the foreign mission enterprise would sanction neither slavery nor anti-slavery.

Delegates met in Augusta, Georgia in May 1845 to form the convention which would in turn coordinate and direct the churches as a whole in the propogation of the gospel. A constitution was adopted and both a foreign and domestic mission board established. Thus, from the beginning, the southerners, without infringing upon traditional Baptist emphases upon congregational polity, provided a more unified approach in structuring their denominational work. After several attempts to establish a publishing concern failed, a Sunday school board was created in 1891. It provided a single set of materials for the churches' educational program, a major force in unifying southern Baptist thought.

Significant in the life of the convention was the adoption in 1925 of the Cooperative Program by which all the boards, commissions and programs (with the exception of the Sunday School Board) supported by the church came under a unified budget. The program provided stable financial support for all the church's ministries and eliminated competitive fund-raising among the congregations.

Southern Baptists inherited the Puritan-Reformed theological tradition which had been passed through the Baptist confessions of London (1677 and 1689), Philadelphia (1742) and New Hampshire (1833). The New Hampshire Confession was slightly revised and adopted by the convention as the Baptist Faith and Message in 1925, and it was again slightly revised in 1963. These statements, which place Southern Baptists clearly within the Reformed theological tradition, are balanced on the one hand by the frequently articulated belief in the freedom of the individual to interpret Scripture not bound by any creedal statement, and on the other hand by the dispensational theological perspective of fundamentalism which has the support of many Southern Baptist leaders.

During the twentieth century, the convention has been embroiled in a series of battles between those who have championed a variety of innovative perspectives that the more conservative elements of the convention have seen as deviating from traditional Baptist standards of doctrine. The controversy over evolution which began before the turn of the century sharply divided Baptists during the 1920s but gradually gave way to an accomodation to the several forms of theistic evolution as a means of reconciling science with Genesis. During the early 1960s, conservatives attacked *The Message of Genesis*, a book by Midwestern Baptist Theological Seminary professor Ralph H. Elliott. Elliott advocated a critical view of Genesis which sees it as a compilation of various documents rather than a unitive volume written by Moses. In the resulting controversy, Elliott was forced out of his teaching position.

Crucial to Baptist thought has been the authority of the Bible. The Baptist Faith and Message declares the Bible to be divinely inspired with God as its author. In recent decades that belief as been interpreted by some in terms of Biblical inerrancy. Among conservatives that has led to debates on exactly how inerrancy is to be defined. More moderate and "liberal" positions have rejected errancy as a means of defining Biblical inspiration.

The Southern Baptist Convention has a congregational polity. Congregations are related sucessively to three levels of cooperative affiliation. Associations operate on the county level. State conventions organize churches in one or more states. Nationally, the annual convention is composed of from one to ten messengers from each congregation which cooperates that the work of the convention and contributes to its support. The national convention has direct oversight of the national boards and commissions: the Foreign Mission Board, the Home Mission Board, the Sunday School Board, the Christian Life Commission, the Education Commission, the Historical Commission, the Radio and Television Commission and the Stewardship Commission. It also oversees the several seminaries. Broadman Press, one of America's major publishers of religious literature, is officially the Sunday School Board's publishing arm. The mission program has over 2,000 missionaries in over 50 countries.

The Southern Baptist Convention has not been among the most active church bodies in the twentieth-century ecumenical movement that has drawn so many of the larger denominations into cooperative actions. It has preferred to work cooperatively within the larger Baptist family and has been active in the World Baptist Alliance and has helped fund and staff the Baptist Joint Committee on Public Affairs. It has, however, refrained from participation in such organizations as the World Council of Churches, the National Council of Churches or the National Association of Evangelicals.

Membership: In 1982 the Convention reported 13,991,709 members, 36,246 congregations, and 61,600 ministers.

Educational facilities: Seminaries: Golden Gate Baptist Theological Seminary, Midwestern Baptist Theological Seminary, Kansas City, Missouri; New Orleans Baptist Theological Seminary, New Orleans, Louisiana; Southeastern Baptist Theological Seminary, Wake Forest, North Carolina; Southern Baptist Theological Seminary, Louisville, Kentucky; Southwestern Baptist Theological Seminary, Fort Worth, Texas. Colleges and Universities: Baptist College at Charleston, Charleston, South Carolina; Baylor University, Waco, Texas; Belmont College, Nashville, Tennessee; Blue Mountain College, Blue Mountain, Mississippi; Bluefield College, Bluefield, West Virginia; California Baptist College, Riverside, California; Campbell University, Buies Creek, North Carolina; Campbellsville College, Campbellsville, Kentucky; Carson Newman College, St. Louis, Missouri; Cumberland

College, Williamsburg, Kentucky; Dallas Baptist College, Irving, Texas; East Texas Baptist College, Marshall, Texas; Furman University, Greenville, South Carolina; Gardner-Webb College, Boiling Springs, North Carolina; Grand Canyon College, Phoenix, Arizona; Hannibal-La Grange College, Hannibal, Missouri; Hardin-Simmons University, Abilene, Texas; Houston Baptist University, Houston, Texas; Howard Payne Unoversity, Brownwood, Texas; Judson College, Marion, Alabama; Louisiana College, Pineville, Louisiana; Mars Hill College, Mars Hill, North Carolina; University of Mary Hardin-Baylor, Belton, Texas; Mercer University, Macon, Georgia; Mercer University in Atlanta, Atlanta, Georgia; Meredith College, Raleigh, North Carolina; Mississippi College, Clinton, Mississippi;Missouri Baptist College, St. Louis, Missouri; Mobile College, Mobile, Alabama; Oklahoma Baptist University, Shawnee, Oklahoma; Ouachita Baptist University, Arkadelphia, Arkansas; University of Richmond, Richmond, Virginia; Sanford University, Birmingham, Alabama; Shorter College, Rome, Georgia; Southwest Baptist University, Bolivar, Missouri; Stetson University, De Land, Florida; Tift College, Forsyth, Georgia; Union University, Jackson, Tennesssee; Virginia Intermont College, Bristol, Virginia; Wake Forest University, Winston-Salem, North Carolina; Wayland Baptist College, Plainview, Texas; William Carey College, Hattisburg, Mississippi; William Jewell College, Liberty, Missouri; Wingate College, Wingate, North Carolina.

Periodicals: *The Baptist Program*, 460 James Robertson Pkwy., Nashville, TN 37219; *Home Missions*, 1350 Spring St., Atlanta, GA 30303.

Sources: C. Brownlow Hastings, *Introducing Southern Baptists, Their Faith and their Life*. New York: Paulist Press, 1981; Robert A. Baker, ed., *A Baptist Source Book*. Nashville, TN: Broadman Press, 1966; Albert McClellan, *Meet Southern Baptists*. Nashville, TN: Broadman Press, 1978; Albert W. Wardin, Jr., *Baptist Atlas*. Nashville, TN: Broadman Press, 1980; O. C. S. Wallace, *What Baptists Believe*. Nashville, TN: Sunday School Board of the Southern Baptist Convention, 1934.

★525★
SOUTHWIDE BAPTIST FELLOWSHIP
% Rev. John Waters
Faith Baptist Church
1607 Greenwood Rd.
Laurens, SC 39360

In 1955 at the meeting of the Carolina Baptist Fellowship at Aiken, South Carolina, Dr. Lee Roberson, pastor of the Highland Park Baptist Church of Chattanooga, Tennessee, the main guest speaker, was asked to lead in the formation of a fundamental Baptist church that would draw from the entire South. At a conference the following year at Dr. Roberson's church, and with the support of the South Carolina group, such a fellowship was formed as the Southern Baptist Fellowship. One hundred and forty-seven clergy and laymen registered as charter members. Though heavily supported by the Carolina Fellowship, the Southern Baptist Fellowship became a separate body. Many of the South Carolina churches are members in both bodies. The present name was adopted in 1963.

A statement of f aith continues the Baptist consensus and emphasizes the autonomy of the local church. The group professes belief in premillennialism. It also holds that the Revised Standard Version of the Bible is a "perverted translation." It demands separation from all forms of modernism, especially the National Council of Churches.

The Headquarters of the Southwest Baptist Fellowship is in Laurens, South Carolina. The fellowship cooperates with the Radio Commission of the American Council of Christian Churches and the Commission on Chaplains of the Associated Gospel Churches. Fellowship churches are found in all the Southern states, Wyoming, New Mexico, Iowa, Maine, Oregon, New York, New Jersey, and Wisconsin. Foreign work is being carried out in Ghana, Nigeria, Puerto Rico, Canada, Nassau, Nicaragua, Brazil, Japan, St. Lucia, Cayman Islands, and Spain.

Membership: Not reported.

★526★
SOVEREIGN GRACE BAPTIST CHURCHES
% Rev. E. W. Johnson
Calvary Baptist Church
Pine Bluff, AR

Out of the post-World War II theological liberalism which many saw as having permeated the churches of the Reformed theological tradition (particularly the large Baptist and Presbyterian denominations), there arose a reaction which emphasized Calvinist theological distinctions, particularly the sovereign grace of God. In 1966, Grace Baptist Church in Pine Bluff, Arkansas, invited people known to be sympathetic to what was becoming a growing movement to a conference at Carlisle, Pennsylvania. The conference became the focus around which cooperative action by otherwise independent churches and pastors could begin. Most of those attending had come out of either the Southern Baptist Convention or, to a lesser extent, the Presbyterian churches. A few were from independent evangelical congregations. Approximately 100-250 ministers attended the Pennsylvania Conference. By 1969, the loosely organized movement had grown large enough to initiate regional conferences, and no less than three periodicals emerged.

Doctrinally, Sovereign Grace congregations are Calvinistic, accept the Philadelphia Baptist Confession of Faith of 1772, and use the great works of the Reformed theologians such as Calvin, Edwards, and Charles Hodge. An extreme congregational polity has been accepted. Local churches are headed by pastors (who are seen as teaching elder and ruling elder and lay elders.

Besides the annual conference in Pennsylvania, other conferences have grown up, including ones at Ashland, Kentucky, and Pine Bluff, Arkansas. E.W. Johnson, pastor of Calvary Baptist Church in Pine Bluff, edits *Sovereign Grace Message*. The Trinity Reformed Baptist Church of Allentown, Pennsylvania, publishes *The Sword and Trowel*. Among the most substantive of the Sovereign Grace periodicals is the quarterly *Baptist Reformation Review*, begun by Robert Ward of Nashville, Tennessee. Ward identifies with the Sovereign Grace Movement as a result of his former position within the Primitive Baptist Church. Before 1972, as a Primitive Baptist, he edited *Inquirer*.

Membership: Not reported. Sovereign Grace Churches are located throughout the United States and number in the hundreds.

Educational facilities: Spurgeon Theological Seminary, Memphis, TN.

Periodicals: *Baptist Reformation Review*, Jon Zens,, Box 548, St. Croix Falls, WI 54024; *The Sword and Trowel*; *Sovereign Grace Message*, Grace Baptist Church, Pine Bluff, AR.

Sources: Jay Green, *God's Everlasting Love for His Chosen People*. Marshallton, DE: Sovereign Grace Publishers, n.d.

★527★
UKRAINIAN EVANGELICAL BAPTIST CONVENTION
% Rev. Barbuiziuk
690 Berkeley Ave.
Elmhurst, IL 60126

The Ukrainian Evangelical Baptist convention (UEBC) was formed in 1945 as the Ukrainian Missionary and Bible Society by a group of Ukrainian Baptists meeting at Chester, Pennsylvania. The first official assembly was in 1946; the present name was adopted in 1953. The Rev. Paul Bartkow was the first president, serving in that post for twenty years. The UEBC is the conservative branch of the Ukrainian Baptists and is a member of the separatist American Council of Christian Churches.

In line with the anti-communist stance of the American Council of Christian Churches, the convention has developed a program aimed at Iron Curtain countries. Misssionaries have been sent behind the Iron Curtain, and in 1966, the Ukrainian Voice of the Gospel, a biweekly radio program over Trans World Radio in Monte Carlo, began. A publishing House, Doroha Prawdy (The Way of Truth), established in 1954, is operated in cooperation with the sister organization in Canada. Missionary work is carried on among Ukrainian communities in Argentina, Brazil, Paraguay, Australia, France, and Germany. The UEBC supports the Ukrainian Bible Institute in Argentina.

Membership: Not reported. In 1970 there were more than 20 churches scattered across the United States.

Periodicals: *The Messenger of Truth*, 690 Berkeley Ave., Elmhurst, IL 60126.

★528★
WORLD BAPTIST FELLOWSHIP
3001 W. Division
Arlington, TX 76012

The World Baptist Fellowship emerged around the followers of J. Frank Norris (1877-1952), longtime pastor of First Baptist Church of Fort Worth (1909-1952) and Temple Baptist Church in Detroit (1934-1948). During the 1920s, Norris arose as one of the most charismatic leaders of the fundamentalist movement. Then in 1926, he killed a Fort Worth businessman, the climax to a quarrel he was waging with Roman Catholics in Texas. Though acquitted in court, his name was dropped from the officiary of the Bible Baptist Union. That act, which cut him off from a large segment of the movement, did not stop his active work which only ended with his death in 1952.

The World Baptist Fellowship was organized around an annual meeting held at Norris' Fort Worth Church. In 1939 he began the Bible Baptist Institute which later moved to Arlington, Texas, and became the Bible Baptist Seminary. After Norris' death, the headquarters of the Fellowship moved on campus. In early the 1970s they reported over 550 churches with 800 more supporting the work. The main strength is in Texas and Ohio. Most recently the Seminary has added a liberal arts curriculum and is now known as the Arlington Baptist College.

Doctrine is Baptist, with an extremely conservative-fundamentalist approach assumed. Mission work is carried out through Fellowship Missions. Polity is congregational.

Membership: Not reported. There are approximately 500,000 members.

Educational facilities: Arlington Baptist College, Arlington, TX.

Periodicals: *The Fundamentalist*, 3001 W. Division, Arlington, TX 76012.

Sources: J, Frank Norris, *Practical Lectures on Romans*. Fort Worth, TX: First Baptist Church, n.d.; C. Allyn Russell, *Voices of American Fundamentalism*. Philadelphia: Westminister Press, 1976.

Primitive Baptists

★529★

BLACK PRIMITIVE BAPTISTS
% Primitive Baptist Library
Rte. 2
Elon College, NC 27244

Until the Civil War, blacks were members of the predominantly white Primitive Baptist associations and worshipped in segregated meeting houses. After the Civil War, the blacks were organized into separate congregations, and associations were gradually formed. In North Alabama, the Indian Creek Association was formed as early as 1869. Among the leaders was Elder Jesse Lee. He was ordained after the War, and in 1868, organized the Bethlehem Church in Washington, Virginia. In 1877, he became the moderator of the newly formed Second Ketocton Association.

Doctrine and practice of the Black Primitive Baptists are like those of the Regulars. They have no periodical. *The Primitive Messenger*, partially underwritten by Elder W. J. Berry, editor of *Old Faith Contender*, lasted only four years in the early 1950s.

Membership: Not reported. In the early 1970s there were 43 associations which averaged approximately five churches per association and 20 members per church. There are approximately 3,000 members.

★530★

NATIONAL PRIMITIVE BAPTIST CONVENTION OF THE U.S.A.
Box 2355
Tallahassee, FL 32301

Around the turn of the century, there was a movement among the Black Primitive Baptists to organize a national convention. In 1906, Elders Clarence Francis Sams, George S. Crawford, James H. Carey, and others called on their colleagues to join them in a meeting at Huntsville, Alabama, in 1907. Eighty-eight elders from seven Southern states responded. In organizing the convention, of course, the members departed from a main Primitive Baptist concern-that there should be no organization above the loose associations that typically cover several counties.

Doctrinally, the National Primitive Baptist Convention follows the Regular Primitive Baptists. The Convention's creeds profess belief in the "particular election of a definite number of the human race." Footwashing is practiced. The organization is congregational, and at the local level there are two offices-pastor (elder) and deacon or deaconess (mother). The convention meets annually and sponsors Sunday schools and a publishing board.

Membership: Not reported. In 1975, it claimed 606 churches with 250,000 members and 636 ministers.

Sources: *Discipline of the Primitive Baptist Church.* Tallahassee, FL: National Primitive Baptist Publishing Board, 1966.

★531★

PRIMITIVE BAPTISTS-ABSOLUTE PREDESTINARIANS
% Primitive Baptist Library
Rte. 2
Elon College, NC 27244

The smallest of the three larger groups of Primitive Baptists is composed of those who differ from the Regulars only on the issue of predestination. While all Primitive Baptists believe that god chose the elect before the foundation of the world, the "Absoluters," as they are often called, believe that God decreed in Himself from all eternity all things that will come to pass from the greatest to the smallest event. A lengthy exposition of their belief, including numerous Scriptural references, is found annually in the Upper County Line Association Minutes. Some of the Absolute Predestinarians practice footwashing.

Most Absoluters are to be found in Texas, Alabama, North Carolina, Virginia, and the Northeast. Among the periodicals reflecting the Absolute Predestination position are *Zion's Landmark* issued in Wilson, North Carolina, and *Signs of the Times*, the oldest Primitive Baptist periodical, begun in 1832 and now issued from Danville, Virginia.

Membership: Not reported. Fifty-one associations have been located. There are approximately 10 churches to each association, but the average is only about 17 members per church. Thus, a rough estimate of Absoluters would be approximately 8,500, with several hundred in independent churches.

Periodicals: *Signs of the Times*, Rte. 1, Box 539, Beechwood Lane, Danville, VA 24541; *Zion's Landmark*, 117 N. Goldsboro St., Wilson, NC 24065.

★532★

PRIMITIVE BAPTISTS-PROGRESSIVE
% Banner Bookstore
Box 4
Jessup, GA 31545

The most easily defined group of Primitive Baptists is the Progressive. In doctrine, Progressives are like the Regulars; where they differ is in the emergence of innovative forms of congregational life. Included in the congregational life are youth fellowships and Bible study classes, men's brotherhoods and women's societies, vacation Bible schools and youth camps. The Progressives' periodical has carried ads for books not written by

Primitive Baptists. Beyond the church, the Primitive Baptist Foundation is a non-profit corporation underwriting denominational projects. The Primitive Baptist Builders helps new and struggling churches to build and purchase. In the summer, Bible conferences are held in Georgia and Indiana, and a music workshop is conducted in Georgia. "The Lighthouse" is a television program heard over stations in Savannah and Augusta. Two Bethany Homes--one for men in Millen, Georgia, and one for women in Vidalia, Georgia--serve senior citizens.

Progressive churches are predominantly in Georgia, with a few associations overlapping in Florida, Alabama (1) and Tennessee (1), and one located in Indiana. Scattered congregations are also found in Mississippi, Texas, Louisiana, California, Missouri, Illinois, and South Carolina. A ministerial association functions among the non-associational churches of Florida.

Membership: In 1986 there were 138 churches and 146 ministers.

Periodicals: *The Banner Herald*. Box 155, Culloden, GA 31016.

★533★
PRIMITIVE BAPTISTS-REGULARS
% Primitive Baptist Library
Rte. 2
Elon College, NC 27244

The largest single grouping of Primitive Baptists is composed of the moderate Calvinist Regulars. They are to be found throughout the South and Midwest, and are most heavily concentrated in North Carolina, Michigan, West Virginia, Georgia, Alabama, and Tennessee. They believe in the depravity of man, often stated as the imputation of Adam's sin to his posterity. The chosen are elected before the foundation of the world; are called, regenerated and sanctified, and are kept by the power of God. Good works are the fruits of faith and are evidence of salvation. In general, evangelism is not engaged in, since God will call his elect. Most practice footwashing. They oppose secret orders, missionary socities, Bible Societies, theological seminaries, and related institutions, and will not fellowship with churches which are connected with those organizations.

Among the periodicals serving the Regulars are the *Old Faith Contender*, issued bimonthly from Elon College, North Carolina; *The Christian Pathway*, monthly from Atlanta, Georgia; *Baptist Witness*, from Cincinnati; *The Christian Baptist*, from Atwood, Tennessee; and the *Primitive Baptist*, from Thornton, Arkansas. Elder W. J. Berry, editor of *Old Faith Contender*, also operates the Primitive Baptist Library north of Elon College, North Carolina, and publishes the *Primitive Baptist Library Quarterly*. He has been a major force in Primitive Baptist circles as a publisher of annual associationminutes. Besides

publishing the *Baptist Witness*, Elder Lasserre Bradley, Jr., publishes the *Primitive Baptist Directory*, with more than 1,000 churches listed, and broadcasts the "Baptist Bible Hour" over stations in the South, Midwest, and California. Elder S. T. Tolley is compiling a library at Atwood, Tennessee.

Membership: Not reported. No recent census of Primitive Baptists has been made. In the 1970s, 150 Regular associations were located. They vary in size from two churches to more than 20. The average size is seven. The average church has fewer than 50 members, all baptized. On that basis, there are more than 50,000 members, not including the membership of almost five hundred churches of the Regular position which are not affiliated with any associations. Those churches would add another 25,000.

Periodicals: *Old Faith Contender*, Rte. 2, Elon College, NC 27244; *The Christian Pathway*, Box 601, Paris, AK 72855; *Baptist Witness*, Baptist Bible Hour, Box 17-37, Cincinnati, OH 45217; *The Primitive Baptist*, Cayce Publishing Co., Thornton, AR 71766; *The Christian Baptist*, Box 168, Atwood, TN 38220.

Sources: W. J. Berry, *Tracing the True Worship of God*. Elon College, NC: Primitive Publications, 1971; *Historical Facts on the Origin of "Campbellism"*. Atwood, TN: The Christian Baptist Library, n.d.;Samuel Lee Rives, *Meditations Upon Religious Subjects*. Elon College, Primitive Baptist Publishing House, n.d.; A. D. Wood, *The Book of Acts*. Atwood, TN: Christian Baptist Publishing Concern, n.d.; Lasserre Bradley, Jr., *What Do Primitive Baptists Believe?*. Cincinnati, OH: Baptist Bible Hour, n.d.

Black Baptists

★534★
FUNDAMENTAL BAPTIST FELLOWSHIP ASSOCIATION
Current address not obtained for this edition.

The Fundamental Baptist Fellowship Association was formed in 1962 by black members of the General Association of Regular Baptist Churches (GARBC). The black members came into the GARBC as a result of missionary work but felt that the GARBC would not accept them into the full fellowship. They presently cooperate with the Conservative Baptist Association.

Membership: Not reported. In the early 1970s there were approximately 10 churches.

★535★

**NATIONAL BAPTIST CONVENTION OF
  AMERICA**
% Dr. James C. Sams, President
954 Kings Rd.
Jacksonville, FL 32204

In 1915, an issue arose in the National Baptist Convention
of the U.S.A., Inc. over the ownership of the publishing
house. Early in the Convention's life, the Rev. R. H.
Boyd, a brilliant businessman, was made corresponding
secretary of the publication board. Under his leadership,
the publishing house did over two million dollars in
business in the first decade. As time passed, however,
some members of the Convention realized that the
publishing interest had been built on Boyd's property, and
all the materials had been copyrighted in his name.
Further, no proceeds were being donated to other
Convention activities.

In a showdown, the 1915 Convention moved to correct its
mistake by adopting a new charter which clarified the
subservient position of the boards. Refusing to comply,
Boyd withdrew the publishing house from the Convention
and made it the center of a second National Baptist
Convention, called the National Baptist Convention of
America. Because of its refusal to accept the charter, it is
usually referred to as "unincorporated." Missions are
carried on in Jamaica, Panama, and Africa. Ten colleges
and seminaries are supported.

Membership: Not reported. The latest statistics are from
1956 when there were a reported 2,668,799 members,
11,398 churches, and 28,574 ministers.

Educational facilities: Central Baptist Theological
Seminary, Indianapolis, Indiana; Morehouse School of
Religion, Atlanta, Georgia.

Sources: R. H. Boyd, ed., *The National Baptist Hymn
Book*. Nashville, TN: National Baptist Publishing Board,
1906; R. H. Boyd, *Boyd's National Baptist Pastor's Guide*.
Nashville, TN: National Baptist Publishing Board, 1983;
N. H. Pius, *An Outline of Baptist History*. Nashville, TN:
National Baptist Publishing Board, 1911.

★536★

**NATIONAL BAPTIST CONVENTION OF THE
  U.S.A., INC.**
% Dr. T. G. Jemison, President
915 Spain St.
Baton Rouge, LA 70802

The National Baptist Convention of the U.S.A. came into
existence after the adoption of a resolution before the
Foreign Mission Baptist Convention of the U.S.A. to
merge itself, the American National Baptist Convention,
and the Baptist National Educational Convention. To
these three would be added a publications board for
Sunday school literature. The Convention was formed in

Atlanta, Georgia, in 1895. Elected president and
corresponding secretary of foreign missions were Rev. E.
C. Morris and Lewis G. Jordan, respectively. Both were
able men; the National Baptist Convention's survival,
stability, and success were in no small part due to their
long terms in office.

Doctrine and government were taken over from the white
Baptists. The congregational form of church life allowed a
ready adaptation to the black culture, which used religious
forms as a socially accepted way to express their
frustration and to protest their conditions. The worship
developed a high degree of emotional expression, making
little reference to traditional liturgical forms. (While freed
from the rituals of their white parents in the faith, the
local church developed its own "forms," which seem
spontaneous to the occasional visitor. In fact, the black
Baptists allowed themselves to create a new religious
culture, the pattern of which they follow weekly in their
service.)

Within two years of its founding, the new National
Baptist Convention ran into trouble when Jordan moved
its offices from Richmond to Louisville. The Virginia
Brethren, fearing a loss of power, withdrew support. They
formed the Lott Carey Missionary Convention, which still
exists as an independent missionary society. A more
serious disagreement split the denomination in 1915.

For twenty-nine years (1953-1982) the National Baptists
were led by J. H. Jackson. He was succeeded in 1982 by
T. J. Jamison, the son of the convention's president from
1941-1953, D. V. Jemison. There is mission work in
Africa and the Bahamas. The group operates five colleges,
a theological seminary, and a training school for women
and girls.

Membership: Not reported. In 1984 there were an
estimated 7,000,000 memebrs in over 30,000
congregations.

Educational facilities: Shaw University, Raleigh, North
Carolina; Shaw Divinity School, Raleigh, North Carolina;
National Baptist College, Nashville, Tennessee; Central
Baptist Theological Seminary, Indianapolis, Indiana;
Morehouse School of Religion, Atlanta, Georgia; Selma
University, Selma, Alabama; American Baptist
Theological Seminary, Nashville, Tennessee.

Periodicals: *National Baptist Voice*, 2900 Third Ave.,
Richmond, VA 23222.

Sources: J. H. Jackson, *A Story of Christian Activism*.
Nashville, TN: Townsend Press, 1980; *The National
Baptist Pulpit*. Nashville, TN: Sunday School Publishing
Board, 1981; J. H. Jackson, *Unholy Shadows and
Freedom's Holy Light*. Nashville, TN: Townsend Press,
1967; Owen D. Pelt & Ralph Lee Smith, *The Story of the
National Baptists*. New York: Vantage Press, 1960; A. W.

Pegues, *Our Baptist Ministers and Schools.* Springfield, MA: Willey & Co., 1892.

★537★
NATIONAL BAPTIST EVANGELICAL LIFE AND SOUL SAVING ASSEMBLY OF THE U.S.A.
441-61 Monroe Ave.
Detroit, MI 48226

The National Baptist Evangelical Life and Soul Saving Assembly of the U.S.A. was founded by A. A. Banks in 1920 in Kansas City, Missouri. It was begun as a city mission and evangelical movement within the National Baptist Convention of America, with which it remained affiliated for 15 years. Differences arose in the mid-1930s, and in 1936 at Birmingham, Alabama, the Assembly declared itself independent. Centers were established in cities across the nation.

No official statements regulate the doctrine of the Assembly, but generally the doctrine follows that of the National Baptist Convention of America. Relief work, charitable activity, and evangelizing are the main concerns of the Association. Each member hopes to add one member to the kingdom annually. Correspondence courses have been developed in evangelism, missions, pastoral ministry, and the work of deacons and laymen. Degrees are awarded for these studies.

Membership: Not reported. In 1951 there were 57,674 members, 264 churches and 137 ministers.

★538★
PROGRESSIVE NATIONAL BAPTIST CONVENTION, INC.
39-7 Georgia Ave., N.W.
Washington, DC 20011

The Progressive National Baptist Convention was formed in 1961 following a dispute over the tenure of the presidency at the 1960 meeting of the National Baptist Convention of the U.S.A., Inc. In 1957, Dr. J. H. Jackson, who had been elected president in 1953, declined to step down and ruled the four-year tenure rule out of the Constitution. Prior to the adoption of the rule in 1952, presidents had served for life. At the 1960 Convention session, dissatisfaction came to a head in the attempt to elect Dr. G. C. Taylor as Dr. Jackson's successor. The failure of Dr. Taylor's supporters led in 1961 to the call for a meeting to form a new National Baptist Convention by Dr. L. V. Booth of Zion Baptist Church, Cincinnati, Ohio. He was elected the first president of the new Progressive National Baptist Convention.

Also at issue in the 1961 break was denominational support for the Civil Rights Movement, then gaining momentum in the South. Those who formed the ne convention represented the strongest backers of Martin Luther King, who was among those who left to join the Progressives, who in turn gave King their full support.

The Convention is in agreement on doctrine with its parent body, the disagreements being concerned with organization and social policy. It has organized nationally with two-year terms for all officers, except the executive secretary, who has an eight-year term. The women's auxiliary was formed in 1962 and a Department of Christian Education, Home Mission Board, and Foreign Mission Bureau were soon added.

Membership: Not reported. In 1984 there were over 1,000,000 members.

Educational facilities: Central Baptist Theological Seminary, Indianapolis, Indiana; Morehouse School of Religion, Atlanta, Georgia.

Periodicals: *Baptist Progress*, 712-14 Quincy St., Brooklyn, NY 11221.

Sources: Martin Luther King, Jr., *Strength to Love.* New York: Harper & Row, 1963; Martin Luther King, Jr., *Why We Can't Wait.* New York: Harper & Row, 1964.

General Baptists

★539★
BAPTIST GENERAL CONFERENCE
2002 S. Arlington Heights Rd.
Arlington Heights, IL 60005

Gustaf Palmquist was a Swedish Luthern preacher and teacher who migrated to America in the mid-nineteenth century. In 1852, he baptized three persons and organized a Swedish Baptist church in Rock Island, Illinois. The church grew and spread as the Swedish community grew and spread. Churches were established in Village Creek, Iowa; New Sweden, Maine; New York City, Chicago, Illinois, and throughout Minnesota. There were eleven churches by 1864.

Doctrine is Arminian Baptist. There are two ordinances, baptism and the Lord's Supper. The polity is congregational. There is an annual delegated meeting of the churches. An eighteen-member board of trustees is drawn from representatives of the various church boards and the membership at large. The boards implement the program of the conference. The home missions board oversees work in Alaska, the Virgin Islands, Mexico, and among American Indians. The board of foreign missions was first appointed in 1944. Before that time, mission work had been carried on through various independent agencies and the American Baptist Foreign Mission Society. Since 1944, work has been established in India, Japan, the Philippines, Ethiopia, Brazil, and Argentina.

Membership: In 1982 the conference reported 129,928 members, 721 churches, and 1,145 ministers.

Educational facilities: Bethel College, St. Paul, Minnesota; Bethel Theological Seminary, St. Paul, Minnesota; Vancouver Bible Institute, Vancouver, British Columbia, Canada.

Periodicals: *The Standard*, 2002 S. Arlington Heights Road, Arlington Heights, IL 60005; *Missions in Action*, %Home Mission Board, 2002 S. Arlington Heights Road, Arlington Heights, IL 60005.

Sources: Gordon H. Johnson, *My Church*. Chicago: Harvest Publications, 1963; Adolf Olson, *A Centenary History*. Chicago: Baptist Conference Press, 1952; C. George Ericson, *Harvest on the Prairies*. Chicago: Baptist Conference Press, 1956; David Gustafson and Martin Erikson, *Fifteen Eventful Years*. Chicago: Harvest Publications, 1961

★540★
COLORADO REFORM BAPTIST CHURCH
% Bishop William Conklin
Box 12514
4344 Bryant St.
Denver, CO 80211

The Colorado Reform Baptist Church was formed in 1981 by a small group of Baptist congregations that agreed to share a mutual commitment to a loose and free association in order to further common aims, including cooperation in mission and educational work. The church finds its basis in the Reformist tradition of Roger Williams and Anne Hutchinson. Not to be confused with Reformed theology, the Reformist tradition is Arminian and stresses the mission of Christ to correct and address the social condition of humanity. Tenets of civil rights and religious liberty are strongly affirmed.

The church is Trinitarian in its theology. It departs from many Baptists by its observance of seven ordinances: baptism, the gifts of the Holy Spirit, marriage, repentance, healing, communion (the Lord's Table) and spiritual vocations (ordination). The church has a congregational polity. A conference, representing all the congregations, meets annually. It selects a board of directors and a bishop to lead the church and oversees the boards and agencies. A very active social action ministry to address the problems of racism, sexism, hunger, poverty, political prisoners, and other issues is supported. Ecumenical activities are carried out through the Association of Baptist Fellowships.

Membership: In 1984 the church reported 43 member congregations with 96 ordained ministers. Each of the approximately 2,200 members is considered a lay minister. Missions are currently supported in Costa Rica, Mexico, Colombia, Grand Cayman, and West Germany.

Educational facilities: Colorado Reform Theological Seminary/Reform Baptist Theological Seminary, Denver, Colorado.

Periodicals: *Baptist Voice*; Box 12514, Denver, CO 80211; *Roger Williams Review*, Box 12514, Denver, CO 80211.

★541★
GENERAL ASSOCIATION OF GENERAL BAPTISTS
100 Stinson Dr.
Poplar Bluff, MO 63901

The General Association of General Baptists dates to the work of Benoni Stinson. He was a member of a United Baptist group formed in Kentucky in 1801 by a union of Separate Baptists and Regular Baptists. These United Baptists adopted an article of faith that allowed Arminian preaching, which emphasized free will, not predestination. Stinson was baptized in 1820, joined a United Baptist Church in Wayne County, Kentucky, and was ordained in 1821. He then moved to Indiana. The Wabash Association would not tolerate his Arminian free-will views, so he organized the New Hope Church near Evansville, Indiana. He soon had a thriving congregation. Tension with Indiana's predominantly Calvinistic Baptists led to the founding of other churches with an Arminian bias.

The articles of the second church, Liberty Church, professed faith in the unlimited atonement which must be apprehended through faith and the final perseverance through grace to glory. The church practiced closed communion. In 1824, the churches that followed Stinson's Arminian tenets organized the Liberty Association of General Baptists. The associations's growth was sporadic for a decade but became steady in the 1830s. The movement spread south and west.

Doctrinally, the General Baptists are similar to the Methodists. The general atonement is believed in, and open communion has been accepted. Some churches practice footwashing. The polity is congregational and churches are organized in local and state associations and a general association, organized in 1870. Ordinations are approved by local bodies of ministers and deacons.

The general association is the highest cooperative agency in the church. The association's program is implemented by a general board composed of the officers--moderator, clerk, and executive secretary--plus one member from each denominational board and six at-large members from the denomination. The Christian education and publications board publishes the *General Baptist Messenger*. The foreign mission board conducts work in Guam, Saipan, Jamaica, and the Philippines, and there is a Bible college at Davao City in the Philippine Islands. The association sponsors two nursing homes, one in Campbell, Missouri, and the other in Mt. Carmel, Illinois.

Membership: In 1984 the association reported 75,133 members, 860 congregations, and 1,398 ministers. There were an additional 5,671 members overseas in churches in Jamaica, India, the Philippine Islands, and the Marianas.

Educational facilities: Oakland City College, Oakland City, Indiana; General Baptist Bible College, Davao City, Philippines.

Periodicals: *General Baptist Messenger*, 100 Stinson Drive, Poplar Bluff, MO 63901; *Capsule*; 100 Stinson Drive, Poplar Bluff, MO 63901; *Voice*, 100 Stinson Drive, Poplar Bluff, MO 63901.

Sources: Ollie Latch, *History of the General Baptists*. Poplar Bluff, MO: General Baptist Press, 1954; *Doctrines and Usages of General Baptists and Worker's Handbook*. Poplar Bluff, MO: General Baptist Press, 1970.

★542★
GENERAL CONFERENCE OF THE ORIGINAL FREE WILL BAPTIST CHURCH
Ayden, NC 28513

In 1935, when the Free Will Baptists in the Eastern General Conference merged with the General Association of Free Will Baptists, the National Association of Free Will Baptists was the name they gave their new association. Most churches in North Carolina declined to join the new association. They decided to continue as the General Conference of the Original Free Will Baptist Church. The conference headquarters are at Ayden, North Carolina. The conference maintains a seminary, Eureka College.

Membership: Not reported.

Educational facilities: Eureka College, Ayden, NC.

Periodicals: *The Free Will Baptist*, Free Will Baptist Press Foundation, 811 North Lee St., Adyen, NC 28513.

Sources: J. M. Barfield and Thad Harrison, *History of the Free Baptists of North Carolina*. Ayden, NC: Free Will Baptist Press, [1960]. 2 vols.; Robert E. Picirilli, *History of Free Will Baptist State Associations*. Nashville, TN: Randall House Publications, 1976.

★543★
GENERAL SIX-PRINCIPLE BAPTISTS
Rhode Island Conference
% Edgar S. Kirk, President
38 Church St.
West Warwick, RI 02893

In 1652, the historic Providence Baptist Church, once associated with Roger Williams, split. The occasion was the development within the church of an Arminian majority who held to the six principles of Hebrews 6:1-2: repentance, faith, baptism, the laying-on-of-hands, resurrection of the dead, and a final judgment. Soon other churches were organized, and conferences were formed in Rhode Island, Massachusetts, and Pennsylvania.

The distinctive doctrine of the six principles is the laying-on-of-hands. This act is performed when members are received into the church, as a sign of the reception of the gifts of the Holy Spirit. Polity is congregational, but the conference composed of delegates of the various churches retains specific powers. A council of the ordained ministers appr oves all ordinations. Decisions of the conference on questions submitted to it are final. Never a large denomination, the Six-Principle Baptists had dwindled to three congregations, all in Rhode Island, by 1969. There were 134 members.

Membership: Not reported. In 1970, there were 7 churches, 175 members and 7 ministers.

★544★
NATIONAL ASSOCIATION OF FREE WILL BAPTISTS
Box 1088
Nashville, TN 37202

The National Association of Free Will Baptists dates to 1727 when Paul Palmer organized a church at Perquimans, Chowan County, North Carolina. The church grew and spread. A yearly meeting was formed in 1752 and included 16 churches. A general conference was formed in 1827; a doctrinal statement was issued in 1834. For many years, these churches were in communion with the Free Will Baptists in the North. But most of the northern brethren were abosrbed by the inclusive Northern Baptist Convention, now the American Baptist Churches in the U.S.A..

In 1916, the general conference expanded by the addition of non-aligned churches in Oklahoma, Texas, Missouri, Kansas, and North Carolina, and formed the General Association of Free Will Baptists. Controversy developed between the churches in Tennessee and North Carolina over footwashing as an ordinance, and in 1921 the churches in the South withdrew and formed the Eastern General Conference. Working out a settlement took fourteen years, but in 1935, the National Association of Free Will Baptists was formed.

Missions are conducted in Spain, Panama, Cuba, Brazil, Uruguay, France, the Ivory Coast, India, and Japan. North American missions are located in Canada, Mexico, Alaska, Hawaii, Puerto Rico, and the Virgin Islands.

Membership: In 1984 the association reported 226,422 members, 2,480 churches, and 4,351 ministers.

Educational facilities: Free Will Baptist Bible College and Graduate School, Nashville, Tennessee; Hillsdale Free Will Baptist College, Moore, Oklahoma; California Christian College, Fresno, California.

Periodicals: *Contact*, Box 10088, Nashville, TN 37202; *Heartbeat*, Box 1088, Nashville, TN 73202.

Sources: *A Treatise of the Faith and Practices of the Free Will Baptists.* Nashville, TN: Executive Office of the National Association of Free Will Baptists, 1981; John Buzzell, *The Life of Elder Benjamin Randall.* Hampton, New Brunswick: Atlantic Press, 1970; Violet Cox, *Missions on the Move.* Nashville, TN: Woman's National Auxiliary Convention, [1966]; Robert E. Picirilli, *History of Free Will Baptist Associations.* Nashville, TN: Randall House Publications, 1976.

★545★
PRIMITIVE BAPTIST CONFERENCE OF NEW BRUNSWICK, MAINE AND NOVA SCOTIA
% St. John Valley Bible Camp
Box 355
Harland, NB, Canada

The Free Will Baptist movement developed in the maritime provinces of Canada in the early nineteenth century. In 1832, a number of groups came together to form the Christian Conference Church, which became the Free Christian Baptists in 1847. Among the ministers of the latter half of the century was the capable George W. Orser of Carleton County, New Brunswick. Orser found himself in the middle of controversy as he began to call for an "Apostolic" or "primitive" church order. He opposed salaries and, in large part, education for ministers. In the 1870s, Orser withdrew and formed the Primitive Baptist Conference of New Brunswick, Maine and Nova Scotia.

The beliefs of the church follow Free Will Baptist emphases, but make special note of sanctification and the perseverance of the saints. The conference is evangelical, opposes modernism, and does not participate in any ecumenical body. Headquarters are at the Saint John Vally Bible Camp at Hartland, New Brunswick.

Membership: Not reported. In the late 1960s there were 1,500 members in 50 congregations, only one of which, a congregation in Maine, was in the United States.

Periodicals: *Gospel Standard*, Saint John Valley Bible Camp, Harland, New Brunswick, Canada.

★546★
UNITED BAPTISTS
% Omer E. Baker
8640 Brazil Rd.
Jacksonville, FL 32208

The United Baptists were formed by a union of the Separate Baptists and the Regular Baptists in 1786. The Separate Baptists were former Congregationalists who became Baptists. The Regular Baptists claimed to represent the Baptists before dissension over Calvinist and Arminian beliefs split many Baptist bodies. In 1772, the Kehukee Association of Regular Baptists made the first overtures toward union with the Separate Baptists. Because there was little difference between the groups,

union was consummated in 1786. Most of the United Baptist groups dropped the term "united" after awhile, and they exist within the larger Baptist bodies. But several associations in Kentucky, West Virginia, and Missouri persist.

The churches follow a congregational polity and are organized into eleven associations. They follow the early Baptists in doctrine; they lean toward Arminianism. They practice footwashing. Communion is closed. The Cumberland River Association supports the Eastern Baptist Institute in Somerset, Kentucky.

Membership: Not reported. At last report, there were 63,641 members in 568 churches in 26 associations.

Educational facilities: Eastern Baptist Institute, Somerset, KY.

★547★
UNITED FREE-WILL BAPTIST CHURCH
% Kingston College
Kingston, NC 28501

Racial division did not escape the Free Will Baptists, but did wait until the twentieth century. The predominantly black United Free Will Baptist Church was established in 1901. Like its parent body, it is Arminian in theology and practices footwashing and anointing the sick with oil. The congregational polity was modified within a system of district, quarterly, annual, and general conferences. The local church is autonomous in regard to business, elections, and form of government, but the conferences have the power to decide the questions of doctrine.

Membership: Not reported. In 1952 there were 836 churches and 100,000 members.

Educational facilities: Kingston College, Kingston, NC.

Periodicals: *The Free Will Baptist Advocate*, Kingston, NC 28501.

Seventh-Day Baptists

★548★
SEVENTH-DAY BAPTIST GENERAL CONFERENCE USA AND CANADA LTD.
Seventh Day Baptist Center
3120 Kennedy Rd., P.O. Box 1678
Janesville, WI 53547

The English-speaking Sabbatarian Baptists organized their conference in 1801. Headquartered in Plainfield, New Jersey, the conference is composed of autonomous churches which meet together annually. The conference is divided into eight associations. They differ from other

Baptists only in the keeping of the Sabbath, although they tend to be Arminian instead of Calvinistic.

The Seventh Day Baptists established an headquarters for the first time in the 1920s in the Seventh-Day Baptist Building in Plainfield, New Jersey. In 1982 the headquarters were moved to Janesville, Wisconsin, and the Plainfield property sold. The new center houses the various denominational agencies, including the publishing house. The American Sabbath Tract Society is a major distributor of Sabbath literature in America and the world. There are an active historical society, missionary society, and board of Christian education.

Affiliated Seventh-Day Baptists are also found in 16 countries of Europe, Africa, Asia and Latin America. The General Conference is a member of the Baptist World Alliance, the North American Baptist Fellowship and the Baptist Joint Committee on Public Affairs. It was formerly a member of the World Council of Churches and the National Council of Churches, but has withdrawn.

Membership: In 1985 the Conference reported 5,200 members in 69 churches served by 52 ministers. There are over 50,000 members worldwide.

Educational facilities: Alfred University, Alfred, New York; Milton College, Milton, Wisconsin; Salem College, Salem, West Virginia.

Periodicals: *The Sabbath Recorder*, 3120 Kennedy Road, Box 1678, Janesville, WI 53547.

Sources: Russel J. Thomsen, *Seventh-Day Baptists--Their Legacy to Adventists.* Mountain View, CA: Pacific Press Publishing Assn., 1971; Herbert E. Saunders, *The Sabbath: Symbol of Creation and Re-Creation.* Plainfield, NJ: American Sabbath Tract Society, 1970; *A Manual for Procedures for Seventh Day Baptist Churches.* Plainfield, NJ: Seventh Day Baptists General Conference; Katl G. Stillman, *Seventh Day Baptists in New England, 1671-1971.* Plainfield, NJ: Seventh Day Baptist Historical Society, 1971; *Seventh Day Baptists in Europe and America.* Plainfield, NJ: The Seventh Day Baptist General Conference, 1910. 2 vols.

★549★

SEVENTH-DAY BAPTISTS (GERMAN)
% Crist M. King
238 S. Aiken St.
Pittsburgh, PA 15206

In 1764, as the work of Johann Beissel at the Ephrata colony declined, a group of German Seventh-Day Baptists settled at Snow Hill, Pennsylvania. In 1800, a Society was organized. From here, other congregations were organized (five by 1900). The German Baptists differ from their English counterparts in their practice of triune forward immersion, footwashing at the communion service, the anointing of the sick, the blessing of infants, and induction into the ministry by a personal request for ordination rather than election by the congregation. They are also non-combatants. An annual delegated general conference is held.

Membership: Not reported. During twentieth century, the group has experienced a steady decline, going from five to two churches with presently only about 100 members.

Christian Church

★550★

AMENDED CHRISTADELPHIANS
% Christadelphian Ecclesia
206 Stanley Dr.
Santa Barbara, CA 93105

In 1886, the prominent Birmingham, England ecclesia of the Christadelphians accepted an amended text of the statement of faith which affirmed that some who had not been justified by the blood of Christ would be resurrected for judgment by Christ prior to His establishment of His kingdom. The revised text had been drawn up by Robert Roberts, the editor of *The Christadelphian*, the group's leading periodical. The majority of Christadelphians accepted Roberts' position. It is their belief that those judged to be unworthy to receive immortality and life in the kingdom will be annihilated. *The Christadelphian* remains the prime organ among those who accept the amended statement.

In the United States, the majority also accepted the amendment. During the twentieth century the position was championed for many years by *The Faith*, edited by A. H. Zilmer of Morrilton, Arkansas (until his retirement in the 1960s). More recently the Amended assemblies have been served by the *Christadelphian Tidings of the Kingdom of God*, published by Robert J. Lloyd in Pasadena, California. The Santa Barbara Ecclesia publishes two periodicals *Christadelphian Focus on the News* and *Christadelphian Messenger*. Associated with the San Mateo, California Ecclesia is the Christadelphian Joy Fund which publishes *Christadelphia* (formerly *Christadelphia Newsletter*, and *The Seed*. The Joy Fund was established to bring aid and comfort to needy Christadelphians. Also located at San Mateo is the Christadelphia Retirement Community, Inc., supported by the Am ended ecclesias. Week-long, regional Bible schools are held around the country.

Affiliated amended assemblies in Australia publish materials through the Gospel Publicity League.

Membership: Not reported. There are approximately 90 amended assemblies in the United States.

Periodicals: *Christadelphian Focus on the News*, The Christadelphians, 206 Stanley Dr., Santa Barbara, CA

93105; *Christadelphia*, Christadelphian Joy Fund, Box 1058, San Mateo, CA 94405.

Sources: *A Declaration of the Truth Revealed in the Bible.* Birmingham, England: The Christadelphian, 1967; *Christadelphian Hymn Book.* Birmingham, England: The Christadelphian, 1964; *One Hundred Years of The Christadelphian.* Birmingham, England: The Christadelphian, 1964.

★551★
CHRISTIAN CHURCH (DISCIPLES OF CHRIST)
222 S. Downey Ave.
Box 1986
Indianapolis, IN 46206

Continuing the thrust of the International Convention of Christian Churches (described in the introductory material for this volume) is the Christian Church (Disciples of Christ). At the 1968 annual assembly of the International Assembly, a restructuring of the Convention was accomplished. The Convention was voted out of existence and was replaced with a strong national structure. The Disciples were no longer a loosely formed confederation of individuals and congregations with a delegated general assembly. The change is a recognition by the Disciples that they have become another religious body.

The general assembly meets every two years and is composed of representatives from each congregation and all ministers. It elects the general board of 250 members, which in turn elects an administrative committee to implement programs.

Membership: In 1982 the church reported 1,156,458 members, 4,291 congregations, and 6,608 members.

Educational facilities: Atlantic Christian College, Wilson, North Carolina; Bethany College, Bethany, West Virginia; Brite Divinity School, Forth Worth, Texas; Butler University, Indianapolis, Indiana; Chapman College, Orange, California; Christian Theological Seminary, Indianapolis, Indiana; Columbia College, Columbia, Missiouri; Culver-Stockton College, Canton, Missouri; Drake University, Des Moines, Iowa; Eureka College, Eureka, Illinois; Hiram College, Hiram, Ohio; Jarvis Christian College, Hawkins, Texas; Lynchburg College, Lynchburg, Virginia; Northwest Christian College, Eugene, Oregon; Phillips University, Enid, Oklahoma; Texas Christian University, Fort Worth, texas; Transylvania University, Lexington, Kentucky; William Woods College, Fulton, Missouri.

Periodicals: *The Disciple*, Box 179, St. Louis, MO 63166.

Sources: Lester G. McAllister and William E. Tucker, *Journey in Faith.* St. Louis, MO: Bethany Press, 1975; David Edwin Harrell, Jr., *The Social Sources of Division in the Disciples of Christ, 1865-1900.* Atlanta, GA: Publishing Systems, Inc., 1973; Winfred Garrison,

Heritage and Destiny. St. Louis, MO: Bethany Press, 1961; Willaim L. Sprague and Jane Heaton, eds, *Our Christian Church Heritage: Journeying in Faith.* St. Louis, MO: Christian Board of Publication, [1978]; Howard Elmo Short, *Doctrine and Thought of the Disciples of Christ.* St. Louis: Christian Board of Publication, 1951.

★552★
CHRISTIAN CONGREGATION
℅ Rev. Ora Wilbert Eads, General Supt.
804 W. Hemlock St.
La Follette, TN 37766

Closely associated with the Barton Stone movement is the Christian Congregation formed in 1887 at Kokomo, Indiana, from independent Christian Church (Disciples of Christ). The original members sought a means of union on a noncreedal, nondenominational basis. Beginning with the new commandment of John 13:34-35, they asserted that the church is not founded upon doctrinal agreement, creeds, church claims, names, or rites, but solely upon the individuals's relation with God. The basis of Christian fellowship is love toward one another. The congregation is pacifist. Bible study is encouraged.

The Christian Congregation is organized on a congregational polity, as a "centralized congregational assembly." The Bible Colportage Service distributes the *Christian Indicator*, a quarterly publication series, Bibles and Bible helps, and literature for field workers. Most churches are located in those areas where the Christian Church had its strength--the Carolinas, Virginia, Kentucky, Pennsylvania, Ohio, Indiana, and Texas. Congregations are now found across the country.

Membership: In 1982 the Christian Congregation reported 1,435 churches, 100,694 members and 1,443 ministers

★553★
CHURCHES OF CHRIST (NON-INSTRUMENTAL)
℅ Firm Foundation
Box 610
Austin, TX 78767

Even before the Christian Church (Disciples of Christ) formed the American Christian Missionary Society in 1849, opposition to this innovation developed. Some saw within the movement toward the first central organization an attempt to create a "general church," a new entity apart from the local congregations. These critics condemned the American Christian Missionary Society as a modern expedient with no Biblical basis. Among the leading exponents of the anti-mission faction was Tolbert Fanning of Tennessee. Tied to the anti-mission issue was the controversy over instrumental music. The addition of organs in churches was an issue across Protestantism, but nowhere gained the significance that it did with the Christians. Organs were a sign of affluence coming to Western churches.

Instrumental music was attacked as early as 1851 in the *Millennial Harbinger*. In 1860, a debate between Ben Franklin and L. L. Pinkerton set many of the arguments. The Bible was silent and the Christian Church should be silent. David Lipscomb, editor of the *Gospel Advocate*, became a champion of the anti-instrumental faction. He saw instrumental music as a sign of the fashionable church built on monied societies, eloquent sermons void of the gospel, and fine houses of worship. All were in contrast to the Churches of Christ, said Lipscomb.

The tensions heightened through the 1890s and a separate yearbook of noninstrumental congregations was published in 1906, the date generally accepted for their separation from the Disciples of Christ. Today the Churches of Christ represent a large national movement which finds its focus in a doctrinal/ideological consensus and a consciousness of oneness. Without a national or even regional headquarters, it is served by various independent publishing concerns, colleges and Bible schools and missionary agencies.

Issues which arose as soon as the congregations separated in 1906 began to fragment the congregational fellowship and led to the emergence of at least six discernible divisions. The largest set of congregations of the Churches of Christ belongs to the centrist noninstrumental congregations which are associated with the Firm Foundation Publishing House of Austin, Texas, which publishes the weekly *Firm Foundation* and a yearbook listing Church of Christ congregations.

Centrist congregat ions do not use instrumental music, but do have Sunday schools and use individual communion cups when serving the Lord's Supper. They support a number of colleges and schools, and foreign congregations are found in every continent and in over eighty countries.

Membership: In 1982 the Church of Christ reported 1,605,000 members and 12,750 churches.

Educational facilities: Abilene Christian University, Abilene, Texas; Amber University, Garland, Texas; Columbia Christian College, Portland, Oregon; Dallas Christian College, Dallas, Texas; David Lipscomb College, Nashville, Tennessee; Freed-Hardeman College, Henderson, Texas; Harding Graduate School of Religion, Memphis, Tennessee; Harding University, Searcy, Arkansas; Lubbock Christian College, Lubbock, Texas; Minnesota Bible College, Rochester, Minnesota; Oklahoma Christian College, Oklahoma City, Oklahoma; Pacific Christian College, Fullerton, California; Pepperdine University, Malibu, California.

Periodicals: *Firm Foundation*, Box 610, Austin, TX 78767; *Gospel Advocate*, Box 150, Nashville, TN 37202; *Christian Chronicle*, RR1, Box 141, Oklahoma City, OK 73111.

Sources: Lerow Brownlow, *Why I Am a Member of the Church of Christ*. Fort Worth, TX 76105; A. T. De Groot, *New Possibilities for Disciples and Independents*. St. Louis: Bethany Press, 1963; Forest Reed, *Background of Division, Disciples of Christ and Churches of Christ*. Nashville, TN: Disciples of Christ Historical Society, 1968; Herbert E. Winkler, *Congregational Cooperation of the Churches of Christ*. Nashville, TN: The Author, 1961.

★554★
CHURCHES OF CHRIST (NON-INSTRUMENTAL, LIBERAL)
% Restoration Review
1201 Windsor Dr.
Denton, TX 76201

Serving as a bridge between the Churches of Christ (Non-Instrumental), the Christian Church (Disciples of Christ) and the congregations of the North American Christian Convention is a liberal "faction" of the movement. This faction emerged after World War II around such ministers as Norman L. Parks. The congregations are distinguished by their strong stand on the unity of the entire Restoration Movement and their willingness to be "candid" in describing it. This stand on unity has led them to develop fellowship with the wider Restoration Movement ministers as exemplified in the formation in 1973 of Fellowship, Inc., which has drawn leadership from the three larger branches (the Churches of Christ (Non-Instrumental) and the Disciples of Christ and the congregations of the North American Christian Convention). The willingness to be candid about the Restoration Movement led many liberal ministers to give up the notion that the Churches of Christ were non-denominational. They advocated instead that the Churches of Christ had become another "sect."

The liberals are served by several periodicals, including *Integrity*, edited by Hoy Ledbetter of Grand Blanc, Michigan; *Restoration Review*, edited by Leroy Garrett of Denton, Texas; and *Mission*, edited by Ron Durham of Austin, Texas.

Membership: Not reported.

Periodicals: *Fellowship*, 1699 Court St., Salem, OR 97301; *Integrity*, 8494 Bush Hill Court, Grand Blanc, MI 48439; *Restoration Review*, 1201 Windsor Drive, Denton, TX 76201.

★555★
CHURCHES OF CHRIST (NON-INSTRUMENTAL, ONE CUP)
% Old Paths Advocate
R.R. 1
Lebanon, MO 65536

Following a growing trend in American Protestantism, Church of Christ minister G. C. Brewer, introduced the use of individual cups during communion (instead of one cup for all) into the Churches of Christ in a congregation in Tennessee early in the twentieth century. Over the first three decades, the practice spread and, not without controversy, became dominant, especially among newly forming congregations. In the 1920s those who refused to adopt individual cups began to pull away and tighten lines of fellowship. Dr. G. A. Trott and H. C. Harper were leading spokesmen in the *Apostolic Way*, the early "one cup" periodical (currently being published as the *Old Paths Advocate*). The one cup Churches of Christ remain a small segment, with strength in California and Te xas.

Membership: Not reported.

Periodicals: *Old Paths Advocate*, RR1, Lebanon, MO 65536.

★556★
CHURCHES OF CHRIST (NON-INSTRUMENTAL-PREMILLENNIAL)
Current address not obtained for this edition.

Premillennialism became a major issue in American Protestantism in the late nineteenth century as fundamentalism developed. Premillennialism means Christ will return before the end of the world and the establishment of his thousand year reign. In the first quarter of the twentieth century it invaded the Churches of Christ and a periodical, *Word and Work*, emerged in Louisville, Kentucky, with a premillennialist perspective. A radio show, "Words of Life," begun in the early 1930s, is now heard in many of the eastern United States.

Among premillennialist congregations, several schools and one Christian home are supported. Missionaries are active in Africa, Japan, the Philippines, Hong Kong, and Greece. Approximately 100 congregations support the annual Louisville Christian Fellowship Week every August. Churches are concentrated in Indiana, Kentucky, Louisiana, and Texas.

Membership: Not reported. There is an estimated 12,000 members.

★557★
CHURCHES OF CHRIST (NON-INSTRUMENTAL, NON-SUNDAY SCHOOL)
% Gospel Tidings
500 E. Henry
Hamilton, TX 76531

The issue of Sunday schools has plagued the Churches of Christ during the entire twentieth century. An increasingly smaller group of leaders held that anything practiced by the church without command, example, and/or necessary inference from Scripture was wrong, particularly Sunday schools. In 1936, *Gospel Tidings*, edited by G. B. Shelburne, Jr., was begun in support of the non-Sunday school cause. Jim Bullock has succeeded Shelburne as editor. It has been joined by the *Christian*

Appeal and the *West Coast Evangel.* Churches are concentrated in Texas, Oklahoma, Arkansas, Indiana, California, and Oregon. Missions are supported in Malawi, India, Mexico, and Germany.

Membership: Not reported. There are an estimated 500 to 600 congregations and 25,000 to 30,000 members.

Educational facilities: West Angelo School of Evangelism, San Angelo, Texas.

Periodicals: *Gospel Tidings*, 500 E. Henry, Hamilton, TX 76531.

★558★
CHURCHES OF CHRIST (NON-INSTRUMENTAL, CONSERVATIVE)
% Florida College
119 Glen Arven Ave.
Tampa, FL 33617

With the growth of institutions serving large segments of the Churches of Christ (Non-Instrumental), voices arose protesting church support for institutions and various projects. The dissent became a movement in the 1950s, and became a separate "group" in the 1960s. *The Gospel Guardian* of Lufkin, Texas, remains a major voice of the group, but its initial effort has been joined by a dozen more periodicals. Conservatives vary from total isolation from non-conservatives, to fellowshipping with individual non-conservatives on the basis of attitude.

Missions are supported in numerous areas around the world. Florida College at Temple, Florida, and the associated CEI bookstore serve the Conservatives. The college's annual lectureship serves as a time for many members to gather around conservative issues. They hold strongly to the pattern principle, that is, that the sum total of what God has said about any matter becomes the pattern for it. Patterns are discovered in the Bible by considering direct commands (such as the command to go into the whole world and preach the gospel), approved example (such as monogamy), and necessary inference from Scriptural passages (such as inferring from Scripture that the Trinity exists.)

Membership: Not reported.

Educational facilities: Florida College, Tampa, Florida.

★559★
NATIONAL ASSOCIATION OF FREE, AUTONOMOUS CHRISTIAN CHURCHES
Current address not obtained for this edition.

Among the people who strongly opposed the restructuring of the Christian Church (Disciples of Christ) in the 1960s was Dr. Alvin E. Houser, pastor of a large congregation at Centex, Texas. As the debate on restructuring continued, he formed the National Association of Free Christians. His position was conservative theologically and focused on the radical congregationalism of traditional Christian Church thinking. After restructuring became inevitable, the Association of Free Christians became the National Association of Free, Autonomous Christian Churches, with most of its strength in the Southwest.

★560★

NORTH AMERICAN CHRISTIAN CONVENTION
3533 Epley Rd.
Cincinnati, OH 45239

In 1909, the Christian Publishing House, which along with the Standard Publishing Company had served the Christian Churches, was purchased by the Christian Church (Disciples of Christ). This act left Standard without a sanction it had previously enjoyed and made it fiercely competitive with the rivals. Among causes which the *Christian Standard*, the main periodical of Standard Publishing, began to champion was non-cooperation with non-Disciple Christians, especially with the Federal Council of Churches, and its successor, the National Councils of Churches. It also opposed any trend toward open membership for believers not properly immersed, and called for breaking fellowship with all who practiced it.

Several attempts at organizing the supporters of Standard's concerns were attempted, but the first real success came in 1927 with the meeting of the North American Christian Convention (NACC). This meeting, for fellowship and inspiration, gave impetus to the development of a second set of schools, mission agencies, and benevolent establishments as alternatives to those reporting to the International Conventions of the Disciples. Since 1951, the NACC has met annually.

Other structures arose to serve the independent brethren. The Christian Restoration Association of Cincinnati was formed in 1923 and publishes *Christian Restoration*. There are a number of institutions of higher learning, benevolent institutions, and periodicals. The NACC has become a stable organization with a convention committee, executive committee and convention director, who edits the quarterly *N.A.C.C. Update*.

In 1955, the first of several directories, *A Directory of the Ministry of the Undenominated Fellowship of the Christian Churches and Churches of Christ*, was published. This date is taken by many to have signaled the break between the Disciples of Christ and Christian churches affiliated with the NACC. But in 1968, the Disciples of Christ restructured themselves and more than 2,000 congregations formally requested their names to be taken from the list of congregations affiliated wth the Disciples of Christ. They are the bulk of the independent Christian Churches listed in the directory.

Membership: In 1981 the fellowship of Christian Churches had 1,063,254 members and 5,605 churches served by 8,074 ministers.

Educational facilities: Cincinnati Bible Seminary, Cincinnati, Ohio; Lincoln Christian College and Seminary, Lincoln, Illinois; Manhattan Christian College, Manhattan, Kansas; Midwest Christian College, Oklahoma City, Oklahoma; Milligan College, Milligan College, Tennessee; Ozark Bible College, Joplin, Missouri; Puget Sound College of the Bible, Edmonds, Washington; Roanoke Bible College, Elizabeth City, North Carolina; St. Louis Christian College, Flourissant, Missouri; San Jose Bible College, San Jose, California.

Periodicals: *Christian Standard*, 8121 Hamilton Avenue, Cincinnati, OH 45231; *Restoration Herald*, 5664 Cheviot Road, Cincinnati, OH 45329; *N.A.C.C. Update*, Box 39456, Cincinnati, OH 45239.

Sources: *NACC, History and Purpose*. [Cincinnati, OH]: North American Christian Convention, 1973; Enos E. Dowling, *The Restoration Movement*. Cincinnati, OH: Standard Publishing, 1964; James DeForest Murch, *The Free Church*. Louisville, KY: Restoration Press, 1966; James DeForest Murch, *Christians Only*. Cincinnati, OH: Standard Publishing, 1962

★561★

TIOGA RIVER CHRISTIAN CONFERENCE
% Rev. George Kyrk
Bible School Park, NY 16837

The Tioga River Christian Conference was formed in 1844 at Covington, Tioga County, Pennsylvania. It was for many years a constituent part of the Christian Church. In 1931, however, the Conference rejected the merger of the Christian Church with the Congregational Church. The Conference adopted articles of faith manifesting belief in the trinity, the Bible as the Word of God, sin and salvation, the local church, Satan, resurrection, and eternal life. There is an annual meeting of the conference for fellowship and business. A nine-man mission board oversees missions in Bolivia, Peru, and India. *His Messenger* is a quarterly periodical. There are 13 churches in New York and Pennsylvania. Headquarters are in Binghamton, New York.

Membership: Not reported. There are approximately 13 congregations located in New York and Pennsylvania.

Periodicals: *His Messenger*.

★562★
UNAMENDED CHRISTADELPHIANS
% Lawrence Dodl
5104 Cavedo Lane
Richmond, VA 23231

In 1886 the prominent Birmingham, England Ecclesia of the Christadelphians adopted an amendment drafted by Robert Roberts, longtime editor of *The Christadelphian*, the prominent Christadelphian magazine published in the same city. Roberts taught that at the end of time all the dead will be raised, whether faithful to Christ or unfaithful, and will be judged. Those found unworthy to enter the kingdom will be annihilated. While many if not most Christadelphians accepted that position, some vehemently argued against it, asserting that only those justified by Christ will be raised. Leading the opposition to the amendment was the most prominent American Christadelphian periodical, *The Christadelphian Advocate*. From its focus of the position, some American ecclesias reorganized around allegiance to the "Unamended" position that only those who die in Christ will be raised. One Unamended statement reads, "At the appearing of Christ prior to the establishment of the Kingdom the responsible (faithful and unfaithful) dead and living of both classes will be summoned before the judgment seat ₉to be judged according to their works,' and receive in body according to what they have done, whether it be good or bad." The split in America eventually spread to assemblies in England and around the world. In England, the unamended position is represented by the "Dawn" Book Supply in London and in Canada by the Brethren of Messiah of Acton, Ontario.

Talks looking toward reunion of the Christadelphians were pursued in the early 1970s, and agreement was quickly reached on various points of dispute concerning fellowship, inspiration, baptism, and the nature of man. No agreement on resurrectional responsibility acceptable to both sides was forthcoming, however, and the splintered condition remains.

Membership: Not reported. There are approximately 90 assemblies of unamended ecclesias.

Periodicals: *The Christadelphian Advocate*, The Advocate Committee, Lawrence Dodl, 5104 Cavedo Lane, Richmond, VA 23231.

Sources: *A Declaration of the Truth Revealed in the Bible.* London: Dawn Dawn Book Supply, 1970; Robert Roberts and J. J. Andrew, *Resurrectional Responsibility.* Birmingham, England: The Authors, 1894.

Independent Fundamentalist Family

An historical essay on this family is provided beginning on page 69.

Plymouth Brethren

★563★
CHURCHES OF GOD IN THE BRITISH ISLES
AND OVERSEAS (NEEDED TRUTH)
% Mr. J. Ramage
44 Tweedsmuir Ave.
Dundas, ON, Canada

In the 1870s questions began to arise among the Plymouth Brethren (Open Brethren) as to just how far they should go in their openness. Discussions led to several separations by groups with different solutions. One strict group formed around the periodical *Needed Truth*, which began in 1889. The bulk of separations of *Needed Truth* supporters began in 1892-1893. Early in the present century, the movement spread from England to North America, primarily to Canada. The Needed Truth groups, called Churches of God, are most properly described as open, in that they will fellowship with likeminded believers who are not members of the Churches of God, and constitute a bridge between the Open and the Exclusive Brethren groups.

The distinctive teaching of the Churches of God concerns ecclesiology. This group beleives that the "church which is Christ's body" is composed totally of believers in Christ. The fellowship of the Churches of God in the British Isles and Overseas is composed of those who received the Word and who live in obedience, having been baptized by other disciples (Churches of God elders) and having been "added" by the Lord. "Addition" means that a believer is associated with the churches where the proper authority of Christ is expressed, i.e., with churches in fellowship with the Churches of God. There is a tendency toward exclusivism in that assemblies of the Churches of God feel that all brethren (ultimately, all Christians) ought to be a part of their fellowship. Members live a strict life. Television is frowned upon, though radios are tolerated. Members marry within the group. They are conscientious objectors.

The Churches of God constitute the only group of Brethren who have developed what approaches a presbyterial polity. Elders of the Churches of God have powers similar to those of presbyters in the Presbyterian Church, with the duty of leading the worship services, setting doctrinal standards, ruling on governmental matters, and teaching. Government in the Churches of God is placed in the hands of a united elderhood. Local assemblies function as the constituencies of elders who operate on both the local and regional levels. A premium is placed on consensus of the elders. The elders or overseers form a self-perpetuating body. They appoint deacons, and from the deacons, choose new elders. Regular meetings of the overseers occur.

Membership: Not reported. While the Churches of God became a substantive movement in England, there were in the 1970s only eight churches in North America, all but one in Canada. The single United States congregation was in Trinidad, Colorado. There is some question of its continued existence.

Periodicals: *Needed Truth*, Needed Truth Publishing Office, Assembly Hall, George Lane, Hayes, Bromley, Kent, Great Britain.

Sources: G. Willis and B. R. Wilson, "The Churches of God: Pattern and Practice" in Bryan R. Wilson, ed., *Patterns of Sectarianism*. London: Heinemann, 1967.

★564★
PLYMOUTH BRETHREN (EXCLUSIVE: AMES
BRETHREN)
% Christian Literature, Inc.
Box 23082
Minneapolis, MN 55423

The Ames Brethren originated in 1949, when the Plymouth Brethren (Exclusive: Booth Brethren) experienced a schism by a group supporting a preacher named Ames. Ames distrusted the teachings and practice of the Plymouth Brethren (Exclusive: Glanton Brethren), a British group with whom the Booth Brethren were closely associated.

Membership: Not reported.

Sources: Hamilton Smith, *Perspectives on the True Church*. Minneapolis, MN: Christian Literature, Inc., n.d.

★565★
PLYMOUTH BRETHREN (EXCLUSIVE: BOOTH-CONTINENTAL)
% Grace and Truth, Inc.
210 Oak St., Hillery
Danville, IL 61832

The Booth-Continental Brethren are the result of a merger in the mid-1970s of the Plymouth Brethren (Exclusive: Booth Brethren) and the Plymouth Brethren (Exclusive: Kelly-Continental). These, in turn, are the result of several schisms and prior mergers. In 1928, a major controversy erupted in Philadelphia which divided the Plymouth Brethren (Exclusive: Grant Brethren) (named for Frederick W. Grant) three ways. One reason for the controversy was the alleged heresy of James Boyd, a visiting British preacher who had written a tract denying that Christ had a human spirit. A second controversy developed within the Philadelphia assembly between two people: C. A. Mory and a business partner and member of the assembly. Boyd accused the partner of deceit, fraud, and misuse of funds. The failure of the assembly (and the Grant Brethren) to excommunicate Mr. Mory's partner and reject Boyd's teaching led to schism. Adding fuel to the fires of controversy was the growing tension caused by the movement by some of the Grant Brethren toward the position of the Plymouth Brethren (Open Brethren). This movement constituted the third cause of controversy.

One small group of assemblies (designated "VII" by the 1936 *Religious Census*) withdrew fellowship from Boyd and any who did not agree with their strong stand. One leader was R. J. Little, editor of *Holding Fast and Holding Faith*, who later moved to an Open stand and worked at Moody Bible Institute. This group united with the Kelly-Continental Brethren in 1953.

A larger group of assemblies was led by A. E. Booth, who accepted Boyd's retraction of his "heretical" position but rejected the Open Brethren assemblies among the Grant Brethren. Under his leadership, the Erie Bible Truth Depot of Erie, Pennsylvania, was formed. In 1932, with the assistance of Frank B. Tomlinson, he began *Things Old and New*, a periodical that still serves the Brethren. (The Booth Brethren were numbered "VIII" in the 1936 *Religious Census*).

The Kelly-Continental Brethren are the product of a 1926 merger of the Plymouth Brethren (Exclusive: Kelly Brethren) and the Plymouth Brethren (Exclusive: Continental Brethren). William Kelly (1820-1906), an Irishman, was editor of the *Bible Treasury* for fifty years

and of John Nelson Darby's *Collected Writings*. In the 1870s he became associated with a party that became known as New-Lumpism. The group attacked the worldliness of other Brethren and looked with disfavor on the evangelism that was swelling the ranks with new converts. The group yearned for a pure fellowship and advocated the high church principle, namely, that the assembly has the supreme judicial power and its decisions which are in accord with Scripture must be accepted. This group was limited to England.

The Continental Brethren were so named because of their strength on the Continent. They were the surviving Exclusive Brethren who did not accept either Frederick Grant of the Plymouth Brethren (Open Brethren) or F. E. Raven, founder of the Plymouth Brethren (Exclusive: Raven-Taylor Brethren) (see separate entries). They had also sided with C. Strange and W. J. Lowe in 1909 in the Turnbridge Wells Controversy (see Plymouth Brethren (Exclusive: Turnbridge Wells). The Continental Brethren had churches scattered across the United States, though they have never recovered from the Turnbridge Wells schism. They were called "III" in the 1936 *Religious Census*.

With the merger of the small group in 1953 and of the Booth and Kelly-Continental Brethren in the 1970s, the new body has become, by learned estimate, the largest of the Exclusivist groups. Besides those publications mentioned above, they are served by Grace and Truth, Inc., a tract publisher headquartered in Danville, Illinois, and the Believers Bookshelf of Sunbury, Pennsylvania, both former Continental publishers. They also support a vigorous missionary enterprise.

Membership: Not reported.

Periodicals: *Things Old and New*, Box 85, Erie, PA 16512; *Life and Life*, Box 85, Erie, PA 16512.

Sources: William Kelly, *Lectures on the Church of God*. Oak Park, IL: Bible Truth Publishers, n.d.

★566★
PLYMOUTH BRETHREN (EXCLUSIVE: EX-TAYLOR BRETHREN)
Current address not obtained for this edition.

In 1960, several assemblies left the Plymouth Brethren (Exclusive: Raven-Taylor Brethren) because of the restrictions enunciated by the James Taylor, Jr. faction. This group is small, probably divided among itself, and is in correspondence with some similar assemblies in Britain.

Membership: Not reported.

★567★

PLYMOUTH BRETHREN (EXCLUSIVE: RAVEN-TAYLOR BRETHREN)
% Stow Hill Bible and Tract Depot
5 Fife Rd.
Kingston-on-Thames, England

In 1905, after the death of F. E. Raven, James Talyor, Sr., a New York businessman, assumed leadership of this group. Under Taylor's leadership the group became more and more separatist. The elder Taylor was succeeded by his son, James Taylor, Jr., who demanded a rigorour separation from the world. The Taylor Brethren prefer a secluded existence and refuse to list their centers in the telephone directories. They encourage their members to withdraw from professional associations and to resign offices in business corporations and dispose stock. They refuse to eat with any not in their fellowship. Taylor's critics have claimed he advocates divorce if any member of a household loses religious fervor. They have made him a public figure with their fervent denunciation of him. One British newspaper, reporting his return to the United States from England in 1969, commented, "The harsh tenets of this sect have broken up homes and led to misery and suicide. Now he has gone home, Britain's parting message is good riddance and don't come back.'"

The strength of the Taylor Brethren is in New York and California. Other congregations are located in the Northeast and Midwest, while a very few are located in the South. Stow Hill Bible and Tract Depot has been their publisher in England for many years. This group is "IV" in the 1936 *Religious Census* list.

Membership: Not reported.

Sources: F.E.R. [F.E. Raven], *Readings and Addresses in the United States.* Kingston-on-Thames: Stow Hill Bible and Tract Depot, 1902; James Taylor, *Administration in the Assembly.* London: Stow Hill Bible and Tract Deport, 1937; James Taylor, *Christ's Personal Service for the Saints.* Wellington, NZ: Whitcombe & Tombs Limited, Printers, 1925; A. J. Gardiner, *The Substantiality of Christianity.* Kingston-on-Thames, England: Stow Hill Bible and Tract Depot, 1954; A. J. Gardiner, *The Recovery and Maintenance of the Truth.* Kingston-on-Thames, England: Stow Hill Bible and Tract Depot, n.d.; Bryan Wilson, "A Sect at Law" in *Encounter*, vol. 60, no. 1 (January 1983), pp. 81-87.

★568★

PLYMOUTH BRETHREN (EXCLUSIVE: THE TUNBRIDGE WELLS BRETHREN)
% Bible Truth Publishers
59 Industrial Dr.
Addison, IL 60101

The Tunbridge Wells Brethren date to 1909 when a schism occurred among the Plymouth Brethren (Exclusive: Continental Brethren) over the work of a Mr. C. Strange, an old and respected worker who moved to Tunbridge Wells from London in 1896. A personality dispute developed between Strange and W. M. Sibthorpe, and led in a few years to schism locally. When Sibthorpe's supporters disfellowshipped Strange and in 1909 disfellowshipped all who communed with him, the Continental Brethren sided with Strange and with W. J. Lowe, who supported him. The Tunbridge Wells Brethren continue the group begun by Sibthorpe. An opinion growing out of this schism is that two circles of fellowship may not be reunited but that reunion must be done on an individual basis. Those who withdrew (the Sibthorpe party) formed a new group and the cleavage spread to America. There was no doctrinal dispute involved. In 1940, most of the British group returned to the Continentals and left only the American section and a few Brethren in mission fields.

The Tunbridge Wells Brethren's activity is centered on Bible Truth Publishers of Addison, Illinois. It publishes two periodicals and numerous books and pamphlets. It also distributes many of the nineteenth-century Brethren writings. There are several retail books stores managed by group members and a Canadaian affiliate. The group is "V" in the 1939 *Religious Census* list.

Membership: Membership statistics are not available. In 1984 there were just under 100 assemblies.

Periodicals: *Echoes of Grace*, 59 Industrial Drive, Addison, IL 60101; *Christian Truth for the Household of Faith*, 59 Industrial Drive, Addison, IL 60101.

Sources: G. H. S. Price, *Church History.* Addison, IL: Bible Truth Publishers, 1982; Charles Stanley, *The Church of God.* Oak Park, IL: Bible Truth Publishers, n.d.; H. E. Hayhoe, *Present Truth for Christians.* St. Louis, MO: Bible Truth Publishers, 1950; Paul Wilson, *A Defense of Dispensationalism.* Oak Park, IL: Bible Truth Publishers, n.d.; W. T. P. Wolston, *The Church: What Is It?.* Oak Park, IL: Bible Truth Publishers, 1971.

★569★

PLYMOUTH BRETHREN (OPEN BRETHREN)
% Stewards Foundation
Box 294
Wheaton, IL 60189

The Plymouth Brethren came to the United States in the mid-nineteenth century. They prospered in part because John Nelson Darby's ideas were being accepted by many mainline American Protestants, and dispensational thinking was spreading. The Plymouth Brethren grew by evangelistic efforts, and, in the case of the Open Brethren, by the movement of followers of the Exclusivist groups into their ranks.

While there is no generally accepted statement of faith for the Open Brethren, one statement used in some assemblies affirms the Bible as the inerrant Word of God; the

Trinity; the depravity of man, and the necessity of salvation by grace through faith; the church as composed of all true believers in Jesus Christ; two ordinances, baptism by immersion and the Lord's Supper; the security of the believer (once a person is truly a child of God, that status is secure for all time); and pretribulation premillennialism (that is, Christ will return before the tribulation and before the millennium. For a discussion of various positions on the millennium see the introductory material for this volume.) Circles of fellowship are rejected, and concerted efforts to fellowship with like-minded Christians in such other groups as InterVarsity Fellowship and the Billy Graham crusades have been made. Theological perspectives include the new evangelicalism, as well as separatist fundamentalism. The new evangelicalism is the more open wing of fundamentalism.

Many members of the Open Brethren have come from assemblies that were originally a part of the Plymouth Brethren (Exclusive: Grant Brethren), named after Frederick W. Grant. He was a nineteenth-century leader among the Exclusive Brethren in the northeast. He was a student of the Psalms and believed that he had discovered therein a five-fold internal relationship which, he then perceived, ran through the Bible. Out of his work he produced the Brethren classic, the *Numerical Bible*. Critical to his mature theology, Grant advocated the opinion that God had worked his saving grace with his people in all dispensations. This position found much disfavor in both England and Canada, and in 1885, the Montreal assembly led by Alfred Mace and Lord Adelbert Cecil excommunicated Grant for heresy. After the excommunication, many Exclusive Brethren sided with Grant, and the Grant Brethren emerged as a separate branch of the Exclusive Brethren. They were denoted as "I" by the 1939 *Religious Census*. By 1920 they had absorbed the Plymouth Brethren (Exclusive: Glanton Brethren) ("VI" in the *Census*) who had separated from the Plymouth Brethren (Exclusive: Raven Brethren). By the late 1920s, in the wake of controversy, many Grant assemblies moved toward a more open position and have in succeeding years become an integral part of the Open Brethren. Some of the Grant Brethren remained Exclusive, but have now become part of Exclusive groups and no longer exist as separate entities. The Loizeaux Brothers, Bible Truth Depot, long identified with the Grant Brethren as a publishing house, also identified with the Open Brethren.

There are no central headquarters for the Open Brethren, but several structures have become the focus of the assemblies' cooperative endeavor. *Interest*, a monthly periodical, is the major organ of communication and is published by Letters of Interest Associates of Wheaton, Illionis. Letters of Interest Associates also represents the Open Brethren with the United States Government on such matters as chaplaincy, conscientious objection, and tax exemption. *Interest* carries announcements of meetings for Open Brethren organizations. Finally, Letters of Interest Associates serves as a channel for moneys directed to various evangelists, missionaries, and workers. Closely associated is the Stewards Foundation of Wheaton, Illinois, which lends money for chapel construction, issues bonds, provides annuities for investors, operates hospitals, and is an advisor to several nursing homes.

The extensive foreign missionary work of the Open Brethren is publicized and served by Christian Missions in Many Lands, Inc., which publishes a periodical by the same name from headquarters in Wall, New Jersey. The corporation does not designate missionaries, a function left to local assemblies, but does transmit funds and facilitate relations with foreign governments. Other missionary agencies include Workers Together of Wheaton, Illinois, which publishes a newsletter that bears its name. Literature Crusades operates a Bible and missionary center and sponsors teams of short-term missionaries from its headquarters in Prospect Heights, Illinois.

Walterick Publishers of Kansas City, Kansas, is a main publisher and book distributor for the Open Brethren. Gospel Perpetuating Publishers publishes the main Open Brethren Hymnal, *Hymns of Truth and Praise*. There are a number of small, independent publishers who publish tracts, booklets and an annual directory of assemblies in North America and the Caribbean. Emmaus Bible School, formerly of Oak Park, Illinois, was founded in 1945 and provides a three-year curriculum. There are also several one-year Bible schools. Ministers use some of the conservative theological seminaries such as Dallas Theological Seminary or Trinity Theological Seminary in Deerfield, Illinois, for further training. *The Address Book*, published by Walterick Publishers, lists nineteen homes for the elderly and one children's home. In Great Britain, the Open Brethen are served by the publishing firm of Pickering & Inglis of Glasgow and London. It publishes a directory of assemblies worldwide.

The Open Brethren were designated "II" by the 1936 *Religious Census*.

Membership: Not reported. In 1985 there were approximately 750 assemblies in the United States and 350 in Canada. Additional assemblies listed in the annual address books were located in Antigua, the Bahamas, Barbados, Bermuda, Cuba, Grenada, Jamaica, Mexico, Nevis Island, Puerto Rico, St. Lucia, St. Vincent, Tobago, Trinidad, and the Virgin Islands. Missions are located around the world.

Educational facilities: Emmaus Bible College, Dubuque, Iowa.

Periodicals: *Interest*, Letters of Interest Associates, 218 W. Willow Street, Wheaton, IL 60187; *Christian Missions in Many Lands*, Box 13, Spring Lake, NJ 07762.

Sources: Anton Darms, *The Abundant Gospel*. New York: Loizeaux Brothers, Bible Truth Depot, 1941; William

MacDonald, *What the Bible Teaches*. Oak Park, IL: Emmaus Correspondance School, 1949; John Smart, *Historical Sketch of Assembly Missions*. New York: Christian Missions in Many Lands, 1966; Harold B. Barker, *Why I Abandoned Exclusivism*. Fort Dodge, IA: Walterick Printing Company, n.d.; A Younger Brother [A. Rendle Short], *The Principles of Christians Called "Open Brethren"*. Glasgow, Scotland: Pickering & Inglis, 1913.

Fundamentalist

★570★
AMERICAN EVANGELICAL CHRISTIAN CHURCHES
Waterfront Dr.
Pineland, FL 33945

The American Evangelical Christian Churches was founded in 1944 as an interdoctrinal ecclesiastical body. It has tried to remain open to both Calvinist and Arminian theological trends, with the Calvinists believing in predestination and the Arminians insisting that people can exercise free will and choose to follow the gospel. Each church member must accept the seven articles of faith which are seen as the "essentials." They are the Bible as the written word of God; the virgin birth; the deity of Jesus, the Christ; salvation through the atonement; the guidance of our life through prayer; and the return of the savior. All other points are optional.

The polity is congregational, and the American Evangelical Christian Churches seems to function primarily to offer orthodox evangelical ministers a chance to preach without the "restrictions of man-made doctrines imposed by so many religious bodies today." A retreat center known as Pala Mar is located on an estate at Pineland, Florida. The Bible school specializes in home-study courses. There are five regional offices in the United States and one in Canada. Headquarters were moved from Chicago to Pineland, Florida, in the 1970s.

Membership: In 1984 the church had approximately 500 member pastors of whom half were full-time pastors.

Educational facilities: American Bible College, Pineland, Florida.

★571★
ASSOCIATED GOSPEL CHURCHES
1919 Beach St.
Pittsburgh, PA 15221

The Associated Gospel Churches (AGC) was begun by about 25 congregations of the Methodist Protestant Church which refused to enter the merger in 1939 which led to the formation of the Methodist Church, now the United Methodist Church. The congregations against merger adopted the name American Bible Fellowship.

Their leader was Dr. W. O. H. Garman, a former minister of the United Presbyterian Church and later president of the Independent Fundamental Churches of America. Dr. Garman led the Associated Gospel Churches into the fundamentalist family. He had been president of the American Council of Christian Churches (ACCC), but the AGC is not affiliated at present with the ACCC.

Doctrinally, the AGC accepts the fundamental dispensationalist theology (though there is no article on human depravity) and believes in the maintenance of good works. Baptism is by immersion. Separation from apostasy is adamantly affirmed. Polity is congregational with the central headquarters serving as a service agency for chaplains, missionaries, pastors, and schools. A major function is to represent fundamentalist chaplains in the armed forces. Member churches are located in more than 20 states, and overseas work is supported in Italy, Spain, the Philippines, Sri Lanka, Kenya, Nigeria, South Africa, and South America.

Membership: Not reported.

Periodicals: *The AGC Reporter*, 1919 Beach Street, Pittsburgh, PA 15221.

★572★
BERACHAH CHURCH
5139 W. Alabama
Houston, TX 77056

The Berachah Church began as an independent congregation formed by former members of the Norhill Methodist Episcopal Church, South of Houston. C. Y. Colgan, a layman in the Norhill congregation, disagreed with the modernist tendencies of a new pastor and withdrew to found the Berachah Church, named for a congregation Colgan had attended previously in Philadelphia. Over the next several years, the congregation became associated with Dallas Theological Seminary and turned to it for assistance in locating a new pastor in 1936 when Colgan returned to Philadelphia. J. Ellwood Evans became the first of several pastors to serve the church between 1936 and 1950, at which time Robert B. Thieme (b. April 1, 1918) became pastor.

Robert Thieme had just finished college with a major in Greek literature and entered Dallas Theological Seminary when World War II broke out. He went into the Army Air Force and rose to the rank of lieutenant colonel. After the war he returned to Dallas and graduated from Dallas Theological Seminary summa cum laude in 1949. He entered the doctoral program but never finished. He accepted the call to Berachah Church in May 1950, took charge of the congregation, and immediately reorganized it. On the Sunday of his first worship service, he asked for and received the resignation of the entire board of deacons. Under Thieme's strong leadership Berachah Church has continued to grow as an independent congregation; but also, through its publication and dissemination of Thieme's books and tapes, the church has become the fountainhead of a national movement built around Thieme's teachings.

Thieme, as a graduate of Dallas Theological Seminary, carried the school's fundamental dispensational theology to a congregation which already had accepted that theological perspective. The eighteen article statement of beliefs of the church agrees with the twenty-one articles of the doctrinal statement of the school. However, since 1969 Thieme has become the target of theological controversy due to statements in several of his books and lectures. This controversy has alienated Thieme, the Berachah Church, and Thieme's supporters around the United States from many within the Fundamentalist Movement, some of whom have denounced his teachings as heresy.

The prime point of controversy and disagreement concerns Thieme's position on the nature and effects of Christ's death. Based upon his very sophisticated study of the Greek texts, Thieme argues that Christ's physical death was for himself alone, a result of his bearing our sins on the Cross. His spiritual death, i.e., his separation from God, was substitutionary and hence efficacious for humanity's salvation. This position leads Thieme to further assert that the blood of Christ is to be understood in a symbolic manner and was not literally shed for humanity's salvation.

Besides the main point of theological controversy concerning Christ's death, Thieme's teaching material has become noteworthy for its use of a distinctive jargon not found elsewhere in fundamentalist writings. He has also taken strong positions in favor of a "just" war and the legitimate participation of the Christian in the military. He has denounced anti-Semitism as incompatible with Christian faith. Through his doctrine of "right pastor," he has developed the concept of the role of the pastoral minister. As reflected in the constitution of Berachah Church, Thieme teaches that the leadership of the local congregation is vested in the pastor "whose absolute authority is derived from Scripture (Hebrews 13: 7, 13)."

The Berachah Church has made a concerted effort to publish and distribute Thieme's many books and tracts, as well as tapes of his sermons and lectures. Thieme regularly tours the United States, speaking at Bible conferences sponsored by Berachah Church. As a result of the response to his teachings, congregations and less formal groups of people who accept Thieme's teachings have arisen across the United States. Each congregation is, like Berachah Church, an independent congregation.

Distribution of Thieme's material is carried out by Berachah Tapes and Publications, Houston, Texas, which issues several hundred thousand copies per year. Several tape franchises have been authorized, such as Bible Doctrine Tape Supply in Tucson, Arizona. Foreign distributors can be found in England, Australia, Canada, South Africa, and New Zealand. The church supports

missionaries through Operations Grace World Missions, a subsidiary.

Membership: Not reported. There are an estimated several thousand members of Berachah Church within the greater Houston area and several dozen congregations which have accepted Thieme's basic doctrinal emphases.

Educational facilities: Berachah Church supports the independent Tulsa Seminary of Biblical Languages in Tulsa, Oklahoma.

Sources: George William King, *Robert Bunger Thieme, Jr's Theory and Practice of Preaching*. Urbana, IL: University of Illinois, Ph.D. Thesis, 1974; Joe Layton Wall, *Bob Thieme's Teaching on Christian Living*. Houston, TX: Church Multiplication, Inc., 1978; Robert G. Walker, *The False Teachings of R. B. Thieme, Jr.*. Collinwood, NJ: The Bible for Today, 1972; R. B. Thieme, *Anti-Semitism*. Houston, TX: Berachah Tapes and Publications, 1979; R. B. Thieme, *Blood of Christ*. Houston, TX: Berachah Tapes and Publications, 1979; R. B. Thieme, *Freedom Through Military Victory*. Houston, TX: Berachah Tapes and Publications, 1973; R. B. Thieme, *The Integrity of God*. Houston, TX: Berachah Tapes and Publications, 1979.

★573★
BEREAN FUNDAMENTAL CHURCHES
Box 549
North Platte, NE 69101

The Berean Fundamental Churches were formed in 1936 by Dr. Ivan E. Olsen, a graduate of Denver Bible Institute. Olsen had moved to North Platte, Nebraska, to do independent work following graduation. The Berean Churches are fundamentalist in theology and evangelical in program. They are non-pentecostal. They are governed by a church council composed of each pastor and one lay delegate from each church. Congregations are located in Nebraska, Kansas, Colorado, Wyoming, California, and South Dakota. Due the small size of the fellowship, the churches have not developed their own denominational structures but have developed their program by utilizing the services of various faith missions, fundamentalist-conservative Bible schools, and church school literature.

Membership: In 1981 the churches reported 49 churches, 3,350 members and 53 ministers.

Periodicals: *Berean Digest*, Box 213, Basalt, CO 81621.

★574★

BETHANY BIBLE CHURCH AND RELATED INDEPENDENT BIBLE CHURCHES OF THE (ARIZONA) AREA
6060 N. Seventh Ave.
Phoenix, AZ 85013

The Bethany Bible Church, a single congregation, was begun in the 1950s by members of some Baptist and Presbyterian churches who felt that these churches had deviated from their stated theological stand. Dr. John Mitchell, a graduate of the fundamentalist Dallas Theological Seminary, was called by the members to preach. Since that time, four other graduates from Dallas have found similar churches in the Phoenix area. These churches have formed an informal fellowship based upon a unity of doctrinal position.

The doctrine is dispensational and fundamentalist. The *Scofield Reference Bible* is used as a major reference. Baptism by immersion and the Lord's Supper as a monthly ordinance are practiced. Both individual and corporate Bible study are stressed. A mission program has developed through independent faith missions.

Membership: In 1984, the fellowship built around Bethany Bible Church included six congregations, 30 pastors, and approximately 6,000 lay members.

Periodicals: *Window on Bethany*, 6060 N. Seventh Avenue, Phoenix, AZ 85013.

★575★

CHURCH OF CHRISTIAN LIBERTY
203 E. Camp McDonald Rd.
Prospect Heights, IL 60070

Paul Lindstrom, a graduate of Trinity Seminary in Deerfield, Illinois, founded the Church of Christian Liberty in 1965 with the combined purposes of preaching salvation, contending for the faith, and defending God-given liberties. Since that time, both the pastor and the church have been involved in controversy. Lindstrom identified himself with several right-wing political causes which can be grouped under the heading "anti-communist." He received an award from the Republic of China, and the Anti-Communist League of America gave him a statue of John Birch. He has featured in his pulpit conservative leaders such as Dr. Charles S. Poling, Richard Wurmbrand, and George Bundy.

Pastor Lindstrom's activism in forming the "Remember the Pueblo Committee" brought national headlines. (The Pueblo was an American ship seized by North Korea in January 1968.) Lindstrom formed the committee in the summer of 1968, and by 1971 another committee developed from the Remember the Pueblo Committee. The second committee was the Douglas MacArthur Brigade, formed to seek the release of prisoners of war in Vietnam. In 1972, Lindstrom formed the Christian

Defense League to take up the defense of persecuted Christians behind the Iron Curtain.

Doctrinally, the Church of Christian Liberty is reformed fundamentalist, and it has adopted a seven-article statement of faith, adding the following four articles on "Responsibilities of the United States of America":

"1) We believe that we have been endowed by our Creator 9with certain unalienable Rights, that among these are Life, Liberty, and the Pursuit of Happiness.' 2) We believe in a Constitutional Republic as set up by our founding fathers and the responsibilities inherent in such upon its citizens. 3) We believe that individual responsibility and a free economy is the best way to achieve the highest standard of living among all men. 4) We believe in combating Socialism, godless Communism, and all forms of collectivistic tyranny alien to our way of life.

There were, in 1974, three congregations. The first was formed in Prospect Heights, Illinois, with others added in Milwaukee, Wisconsin, and Rockford, Illinois. Parochial schools (Christian academies) are attached to each church and take children through the eighth grade. The supplementary Basic Education Associates, a home-study course, has also been developed. Half the offerings at the church go to missions, and missionaries are supported in Japan, India, Kenya, Mexico, Surinam, and Arizona (Indians). The Westminster Biblical Missions to Korea is headquartered at the Prospect Heights Church.

Membership: Not reported.

Periodicals: *The Christian Militant*, 203 E. Camp McDonald Road, Prospect Heights, IL 60070; *The Church of Christian Liberty Messenger*, 203 E. Camp McDonald Road, Mt. Prospect, IL 60070.

Sources: Paul Lindstrom, *Armageddon, The Middle East Muddle*. Mt. Prospect, IL: Christian Liberty Forum, 1967.

★576★

EVANGELICAL MINISTERS AND CHURCHES, INTERNATIONAL, INC.
105 Madison
Chicago, IL 60602

The Evangelical Ministers and Churches, International, Inc. was formed in 1950 by a group of independent ministers. They are evangelical and fundamentalist in belief. Government is congregational, but the fellowship is headed by an executive board elected by the national convention. Missions are conducted in South Korea, Portugal, and Spain.

Membership: Not reported. In the 1970s there were approximately 150 affiliated ministers.

Educational facilities: Colorado Bible College and Seminary.

Periodicals: *EMCI Herald*, 106 Madison, Chicago, IL 60602.

★577★
FELLOWSHIP OF INDEPENDENT EVANGELICAL CHURCHES
% Howard Boyll
2311 Anderson St.
Bristol, TN 73620

The Fellowship of Independent Evangelical Churches was formed in 1949 by independent fundamentalist ministers, including Dr. L. P. McClenny of Wheaton College Church in Illinois. The group is fundamentalist and premillennial, and professes a belief in angels and Satan. Members hold to separation from evil in all forms. Government is congregational. There is an annual meeting which elects officers.

Membership: Not reported. In 1970 there were 45 ministers and 10 churches, most in the South or Midwest.

★578★
INDEPENDENT BIBLE CHURCH MOVEMENT
% Church Multiplication, Inc.
Box 79203
Houston, TX 77279

During the early twentieth century as the Fundamentalist-Modernist controversy reached its peak, many independent fundamentalist Bible churches were founded, as congregations withdrew from the older denominational bodies and isolated groups formed new congregations. While many of these congregations affiliated with one of the fundamentalist associations, others have remained independent and have affiliated informally over the years with other congregations, publishing houses, missionary enterprises, and schools as deemed expedient. Among the most popular schools have been the Moody Bible Institute (Chicago, Illinois) and Dallas Theological Seminary (Dallas, Texas).

During the 1970s the number of independent Bible churches increased and leadership from the more prominent fundamentalist colleges and seminaries added impetus to the movement to plant independent fundamentalist congregations throughout the United States. Among those taking the lead in this new impulse, Church Multiplication, Inc., was formed in 1977 by people associated with Dallas Theological Seminary. It grew directly out of the New Church Development Committee of the Spring Branch Community Church in Houston, Texas. Its purpose has been to enchance church growth and assist in the formation of new independent Bible Churches. Operating in the Southwest, it has a primary focus in Texas, Arkansas, Louisiana, Oklahoma and New Mexico.

Independent Bible churches are fundamentalist in theology and believe in the infallibility of the Bible and the deity of Christ (exemplified in his virgin birth, his substitutionary atonement, literal resurrection from the dead, and his premillennial second advent). They basically accept the dispensational approach to Scripture as outlined in the *Scofield Reference Bible*. Most distinctively, such churches are congregationally unaffiliated to any denomination or congregational association.

Membership: Unknown. The directory published by Church Multiplication, Inc., in 1983 lists 248 congregations in the states of Texas, Oklahoma, Arkansas, Louisiana, and New Mexico.

★579★
INDEPENDENT FUNDAMENTAL CHURCHES OF AMERICA
1860 Mannheim Rd.
Westcester, IL 60153

The Independent Fundamental Churches of America is one of the oldest and largest of the fundamental church groups. It dates to 1922 when Dr. R. Lee Kirkland, pastor of Lake Okoboji Community Tabernacle in Arnold's Park, Iowa, organized the American Conference of Undenominated Churches. Kirkland had previously participated in the Conference of Union, Federated, and Community Churches, but he opposed its modernism. In 1930, a number of Congregational Churches joined with the American Conference of Undenominated Churches to form the Independent Fundamental Churches of America (IFCA). At the organizational meeting at the Cicero Bible Church in Cicero, Illinois, O. B. Bottorff was elected president of the IFCA. For a time, the IFCA was a member of the American Council of Christian Churches (ACCC), but he left in 1953 in a dispute over differences in personalities and policies.

Doctrine of the IFCA follows five fundamentals closely: the beliefs in the inspiration of the Bible; the depravity of man;, redemption through Christ's blood; the true church as a body composed of all believers; and the coming of Jesus to establish his reign. The IFCA is dispensationalist, but it rejects the ultra-dispensational views of Ethelbert W. Bullinger regarding the sacraments and soul-sleep, the belief that the soul exists in an unconscious state from death to the resurrection of the body. Whereas Bullinger said the church should not practice water baptism or the Lord's Supper, the IFCA practices both as ordinances. The total depravity of man and the eternal security of the believer (once the believer becomes a child of God, that status is secure forever) are emphasized. The IFCA believes that ecumenism, ecumenical evangelism, neo-orthodoxy, and neo-evangelicalism are contrary to faith. It believes strongly in separatism from religious apostasy. In 1970, an addition to the statement of faith was made affirming the ordinances of baptism and the Lord's Supper, and the theory of dispensationalism as divinely ordered stewardships by which God treats man according to his purpose. Polity is congregational; independent churches organize for fellowship and mutual helpfulness. The IFCA meets in convention annually. Each church can send two or more male delegates. A twelve-man executive committee plus the president are active between annual conventions. The national executive director and the editor of the *Voice* magazine are ex-officio members of the executive committee. Missions are conducted through the 20 missionary agencies approved and affiliated with the IFCA.

Membership: In 1983, the Church reported 692 congregations and 1,378 ministerial members. There were over 120,000 lay members.

Educational facilities: There are seven schools affiliated with the IFCA, including the following: Appalachian Bible College, Bradley, West Virginia; Southeastern Bible College, Birmingham, Alabama; Carver Bible College, Atlanta, Georgia; San Diego Bible College and Seminary, San Diego, California; Sacramento Bible Institute, Sacramento, California; and Grand Rapids School of the Bible and Music, Grand Rapids, Michigan. Other independent colleges of a similar doctrinal position are accepted and used by IFCA members.

Periodicals: *The Voice*, 1860 Mannheim Road, Westcester, IL 60153.

Sources: James O. Henry, *For Such a Time as This*. Westchester, IL: The Independent Fundamental Churches of America, 1983; *This We Believe*. Wheaton, IL: Independent Fundamental Churches of America, 1970; Dorothy Martin, *The Story of Billy McCarrell*. Chicago: Moody Press, 1983.

★580★
INDEPENDENT FUNDAMENTALIST BIBLE CHURCHES
% Dr. M. H. McReynolds, Jr.
205 N. Union Ave.
Los Angeles, CA 90026

The Independent Fundamentalist Bible Churches was formed in 1965 by a group of leaders active in the American Council of Christian Churches (ACCC). Among the founders were Dr. Marion H. Reynolds, the first president, the Rev. W. E. Standridge, the Rev. Henry Campbell, and the Rev. Kenneth L. Barth. Rev. Reynolds, formerly of the Independent Fundamental Churches of America (IFCA), was president of the ACCC, an organization from which the IFCA withdrew. Doctrine in the new church is, as the name implies, fundamentalist and Bible-oriented. It differs from the Independent Fundamental Churches of America only on its stand on the necessity of purity of doctrine in the church and on the separation of the church from all "apostasy and scripturally-forbidden alliances" (cooperation with unbelievers). Government is completely congregational (i.e., churches are independent) and the

Independent Fundamentalist Bible Churches is composed of those congregations which accept its doctrinal statement.

Membership: Not reported. In 1967 there were 11 churches and 1,700 members.

★581★
INTERNATIONAL MINISTERIAL FEDERATION, INC.
723 Clark St.
Fresno, CA 93701

The International Ministerial Federation was founded in 1930 by Dr. J. Kellog and Dr. W. E. Opie as a fellowship of independent ministers. It has as its purpose the giving of "ministerial status and authorization to whoever wants it without affiliating with a specific denomination." There is a strong antidenominational bias. Members must be "Evangelical believers in the basic Christian concepts," but there is no statement of doctrine by which that concept could be made specific. The president of the International Ministerial Federation is Dr. Sidney Cornell of St. Petersburg, Florida, and the executive director is Dr. Opie of Fresno, California.

Membership: Not reported. In 1968 there were over 400 members, all ministers.

★582★
MOODY CHURCH
1630 N. Clark
Chicago, IL 60614

The Moody Church is named for famed evangelist Dwight L. Moody (1837-1899). In 1858 Moody began a Sunday school in an old saloon building, which later moved to Illinois Street. That initial group formally became the Illinois Street Church in 1864, and J. H. Harwood served as the first pastor. The unordained Moody served as deacon. After the Chicago fire, a new tabernacle was built and the church regrouped as the Chicago Avenue Church in 1873-74. The Church assumed its present name in 1901 to honor Moody, who had died in 1899. In the early 1920s, construction was begun on the present church, which was dedicated in 1925. It has been the pulpit for some of the leading fundamentalist voices in the land, including Charles A. Blanchard, R. A. Torrey, A. C. Dixon, Paul Radar, H. A. Ironside, Alan Redpath, George Sweeting (current president of Moody Bible Institute), and Warren Wiersbe. Worship activities continue to center on the Memorial Church.

Doctrinally, the church follows dispensationalism, which Moody learned from the Plymouth Brethren. Members are asked to give their assent to an eight-article doctrinal statement which includes belief in the depravity of man and the eternal security of the believer. The members also accept the responsibility to win others to Christ. Polity is congregational.

The church sponsors the weekly "Songs in the Night" radio show, begun in 1943 and heard over 300 stations in 1984. Present pastor of the church is Dr. Edwin W. Lutzer. Associated with Moody Church, but completely separate in operation, are the Moody Bible Institute in Chicago and the *Moody Monthly*, the prominent fundamentalist periodical.

Membership: In 1984 the church reported 1,269 members and supported a ministerial staff of seven.

Periodicals: *Moody Church News*, 1609 N. La Salle Street, Chicago, IL 60614.

★583★
OHIO BIBLE FELLOWSHIP
% Rev. John Ashbrook
5733 Hopkins Rd.
Mentor, OH 44060

The Ohio Bible Fellowship was formed in 1968 by thirteen former members of the Independent Fundamental Churches of America (IFCA) (see separate entry.) The Ohio Bible Fellowship rejected the IFCA's failure "to see the dangers inherent in mediating positions" and claimed it had "wavered under the pressue of the prevailing cooperative spirit of the age." Doctrinally, there is little difference between the fellowship and the IFCA. The pre-1970 IFCA statement of faith was adopted. To it was added a statement on baptism, professing belief in immersion as the proper mode of baptism, although baptism is not seen as essential for salvation. At least three fellowship conferences are held each year. A campground is being developed near Chesterville, Ohio. The Ohio Bible Mission aids new churches.

Membership: Not reported.

Periodicals: *The Ohio Fellowship Visitor*.

★584★
REX HUMBARD MINISTRY
Akron, OH 44331

Rex Humbard came out of a radio preacher's family. The Humbard family has broadcasted over the Mutual network for more than thirty years. At age 15, Rex became the master of ceremonies. He was ordained by his father. In 1952, the Humbard family stayed for five weeks in Akron, Ohio, and Rex decided to remain there. Having been impressed with the power of television to communicate, he decided to build a congregation, go on television with its services and expand the coverage around the world. With brother-in-law Wayne Jones, he created Calvary Temple and built a stable congregation. Calvary Temple was superceded by the Cathedral of Tomorrow founded in 1958, and Humbard began the erection of the $35 million dollar building. The Cathedral was to be the center of a large complex, which was to include a retirement home, television station, library, and youth park.

The center of the Cathedral's activity became the weekly worship service, which by 1971 was televised over 335 stations. One of the unique practices of the Cathedral was the communion service held periodically and televised. Its uniqueness lay in that a week before the broadcast, the television audience was invited to participate, and participants were given instructions on preparing the elements in their homes. The Cathedral had approximately 2,000 families who worshiped at the Cathedral from the Akron area.

Doctrinally, Humbard is evangelical and conservative, but refuses to be pinned down on a specific creed. He opposed the Cathedral's pushing any "sectarian" ideas. During Humbard's tenure as pastor, the Cathedral was operated by a six-person board of trustees which included Humbard and his wife. Humbard's salary was not paid by the Cathedral, but by a special offering. There were eleven ministers on the staff. As the Humbard ministry grew, the Cathedral issued a monthly magazine, *The Answer*. Humbard kept a busy schedule of traveling, preaching and writing. By the end of the decade, the Cathedral services were broadcast over 650 television stations in North America, 700 radio stations and 62 foreign stations covering every continent. In 1976, a special Christmas program became the first religious program carried worldwide by satellite.

In 1983, Humbard resigned as pastor of the Cathedral of Tomorrow and was succeeded by Wayne Jones. He separated the Rex Humbard Ministry from the church, though a strong filial tie continues. The ministry is now focused in the worldwide evangelistic preaching services, the weekly television programs supported by the Life-Line Partners, and the Humbard Family Seminars, aimed at supporting and rebuilding family life. The Cathedral has developed a broad program of service to the Akron community.

Membership: Not reported.

Periodicals: *Rex Humbard Family Ministry*, %Rex Humbard, Akron, OH 44331.

Sources: A. E. Humbard, *My Life Story*. Akron, OH: Cathedral of Tomorrow, 1945; Rex Humbard, *The Ten Commandments Plus 1*. Akron, OH: Cathedral of Tomorrow, n.d.; Rex Humbard, *Where Are the Dead?*. Akron, OH: Rex Humbard World Outreach Ministry, 1977.

Grace Gospel Movement

★585★
BEREAN BIBLE FELLOWSHIP
52nd & E. Virginia Sts.
Phoenix, AZ 85008

Centered in the Pacific Southwest is the Berean Bible Fellowship. It accepts only two vast dispensations but otherwise is in concert with Charles Welch and Ethelbert W. Bullinger (whose views are discussed in the essay section of this volume). Faith in God in Christ is stressed and is differentiated as faith that receives Christ, faith that motivates the believer to walk in love, faith that constrains believers to set their minds on things above, and faith that is humble-minded when believers have among themselves the mind that was in Christ. The Phoenix center operates the Berean Tape Ministry, which distributes more than 1,000 different tapes by Oscar M. Baker (founder of the Truth for Today Bible Fellowship), Welch, Stuart Allen, Arthur E. Lamboune (the leader of the Fellowship), and others. Associated with the fellowship is Scripture Research, Inc., formerly the Ewalt Memorial Bible School, of Atascadero, California, and the Bible Fellowship Church of South Holland, Illinois.

The use of the word "Berean" by this church and a number of other groups stems from the Bible. The Acts of the Apostles mentions that members of the church at Berea in Greece were students of the Scriptures. Because the Bible is so important in the fundamentalist movement, many fundamentalist groups adopted the name "Berean."

Membership: Not reported.

Periodicals: Unofficial publications include *Scripture Research, Inc.*, Box 518, Atascadero, CA 93423; *The Scripture Research Greek Tutor*, Box 518, Atascadero, CA 93423.

Sources: E. W. Bullinger, *The Book of Job*. Atascadero, CA: Scripture Research, Inc., 1983; Harold P. Morgan, *Christian Values and Principles*. Atascadero, CA: Ewalt Memorial Bible School, n.d., 3 vols.

★586★
BEREAN BIBLE FELLOWSHIP (CHICAGO)
7609 W. Belmont
Chicago, IL 60635

In 1970, the Grace Gospel movement experienced its first major schism when Cornelius Stam, head of the Berean Bible Society headquartered in Chicago, severed his relationship with the Grace Gospel Fellowship, discussed elsewhere in this chapter. Stam had begun to publish the *Berean Searchlight* in 1940. The Berean Bible Society developed as an independent arm of Grace Gospel Fellowship. Stam was a prolific author and headed a radio ministry, Bible conferences and a tape library. When J. C.

O'Hair, one of the early exponents of the Grace Gospel position, died, Stam served the North Shore Church in Chicago (of which O'Hair had been the pastor) for a year and a half.

In the 1960s, Stam began to question "trends toward permissivism and liberalism" at Grace Bible College. Criticism was directed at articles in college periodicals which leaned toward the new evangelicalism, advocated the reading of explicitly sexual novels such as those by D. H. Lawrence, condoned the turning to secular movements in search of truth, and (in an article commenting on Psalms 8:5 which used the Revised Standard Version of the Bible) suggested that man was a little lower than God (thus attacking the doctrine of utter depravity). Grace Gospel Fellowship was criticized for commending J. B. Phillips' popular book, *Your God Is Too Small*. As early as 1966, Stam and his followers attempted to express these concerns and seek repudiation of the articles and actions. When no reconciliation proved possible, Stam and his followers broke relations with the Grace Gospel Fellowship and formed the Berean Bible Fellowship.

Doctrine and polity remain the same, since the issues in the split were not doctrinal. An annual assembly is held each August. Churches of the Fellowship are scattered across the country. In 1985, there were over 110 radio stations in the United States (plus one in Manila, the Philippines) carrying Stam's "Bible Time" broadcast.

Membership: Not reported.

Periodicals: *Berean Searchlight*, 7609 W. Belmont, Chicago, IL 60635.

Sources: Cornelius R. Stam, *Things That Differ*. Chicago: Berean Bible Society, 1951; Cornelius R. Stam, *The Controversy*. Chicago: Berean Bible Society, 1963; Cornelius R. Stam, *Satan in Derision*. Chicago: Berean Bible Society, 1972; Cornelius R. Stam, *True Spirituality*. Chicago: Berean Bible Society, 1959.

★587★
BIBLE CHURCHES (CLASSICS EXPOSITOR)
% Dr. C. E. McLain
1429 N.W. 100th St.
Oklahoma City, OK 73114

In Oklahoma, there are four churches (three in Oklahoma City and one in Moore) which are associated with C. E. McLain, pastor of the Northside Bible Church and editor of *The Classics Expositor*. A radio ministry by the Rev. David Webber was heard over eight stations in the South Central states in 1968. *The Classics Expositor* is republishing some dispensational items formerly out of print.

Membership: Not reported.

Periodicals: *The Classics Expositor*, 1429 N. W. 100th, Oklahoma City, OK 73114.

★588★
CONCORDANT PUBLISHING CONCERN
15570 W. Knochaven Drive
Canyon Country, CA 91351

Adolph Ernst Knoch (1874-1965) was a preacher with the Plymouth Brethren (discussed elsewhere in this volume) who was excommunicated over his deviation on points of Scriptural interpretation. In 1909, the first issue of *Unsearchable Riches* appeared as an instrument of Knoch's ideas. It was printed in Minneapolis by Vladimir M. Gelesnoff, its co-editor, who soon moved to southern California, where permanent headquarters were established. Knoch launched his life-work, which was to be a new translation of the Scripture called the Concordant Version. The first part, Revelation, was published in 1919; other portions followed until 1926, when the entire New Testament was issued. In 1939, a German version was issued. Though he had finished his translation work, Knoch lived to see only two portions of the Hebrew Scriptures published before his death: Genesis in 1957 and Isaiah in 1962.

The thrust of the Concordant Version is: 1) to correct the faults of past translations, particularly the King James, American Revised (1901), and the Revised Standard versions; 2) to fix the meanings of the inspired words of Scriptures; and 3) to produce a literal translation. In the process, a new Concordance, which became the basis of the translation, was produced. The appearance of the Concordant Version created a great deal of controversy in conservative evangelical circles and its use has been limited to those people associated with Knoch through *Unsearchable Riches*.

Knoch's study of the Scripture, bolstered in part by his correspondence with British dispensationalist scholar Ethelbert W. Bullinger, led to a new form of dispensationalism based upon the eons (a transliteration of the Greek word usually translated "ages"). Our knowledge of God begins in his decrees before eonian times. The first eon is from creation to the disruption of Genesis 1:2. The eonian times begin with Adam and continue through five periods: innocence (Adam), conscience (Seth), government (Noah), promise (Abraham), law (Moses). The sixth period, that of Jesus' life, begins the eon of the fullness of times (Gal. 4:4). After Jesus comes the eon of the nations, which includes the periods of Pentecost, transition (with Paul as Priest), and the secret (with Paul the prisoner) or Grace. Currently, we are in the period of the secret. Yet to come is the period of indignation (the tribulation) and the eschatological events of the eon of eons, which includes the binding of Satan, the millennial kingdom, the white throne judgment, the new heavens and earth, and the consummation when God is all in all (I Cor. 15:28).

Knoch's thinking had become centered upon Paul, who, Knoch was convinced, had been commissioned to reveal truths that Jesus was unable to reveal to his disciples. These truths concern the glories of Christ and appear in Paul's prison epistles. From these writings, a "creed" can be constructed. Paul believed in the deity of God (Rom. 11:36), the glories of Christ (Col. 1:25), the believer's share in that glory (Eph. 1:3-5), the justification of all mankind (Rom. 5:18-19), the reconciliation of all (Col. 1:18-20), the abolition of death (I Cor. 15:20-26), and the subjection of all to God (I Cor. 15:27-28), including Satan. Knoch thus departed from most of his former brethren by a belief in universal salvation. He felt that the believer is justified when he believes, and that the unbeliever must wait until the consummation.

Unsearchable Riches found readers who grouped around it as a tool for Bible study, and thus a national following of the eonian interpretation of Scripture developed. A song book, *Scriptural Songs*, was produced for these groups.

Membership: Not reported. In 1980, *Unsearchable Riches* listed 23 groups in the United States, and an additional 33 groups in 15 countries. Over half of the foreign groups were to be found in Canada, Australia and Great Britain.

Periodicals: *Unsearchable Riches*, 15570 W. Knochaven Drive, Canyon Country, CA 91351.

Sources: *Concordant Literal New Testament*. Saugus, CA: Concordant Publishing Concern, 1966; *The Concordant Version in the Critics' Den*. Los Angeles: Concordant Publishing Concern, n.d.; *Scriptural Songs*. Saugus, CA: Concordant Publishing Concern, n.d.; *Adolph Ernst Knoch, 1874-1965*. Saugus, CA: Concordant Publishing Concern, 1965.

★589★
GRACE GOSPEL FELLOWSHIP
1011 Aldon St., S.W.
Grand Rapids, MI 49509

Organization of the independent centers which preach the Grace Gospel message of J. C. O'Hair, an early exponent of the Grace Gospel position in Chicago, proceeded in several stages. First, in 1938, a group of pastors and laymen met to formulate a structure to implement the spread of this message at home and abroad. A doctrinal statement was agreed upon; a constitution was formulated, and, in January 1939, the World Wide Grace Testimony (later Grace Mission and now Grace Ministries, International) came into being. The following year, the Milwaukee Bible Institute was founded by a fundamentalist pastor and was operated as a function of the local congregation. This school developed a full curriculum in the mid-1940s, and in 1968, it moved to Grand Rapids, Michigan, as Grace Bible College.

In 1944, the Grace pastors met in Evansville, Indiana, and formally organized the Grace Gospel Fellowship. J. C.

O'Hair and Harry Bultema continued as prominent leaders. At first a ministers' fellowship, it was later opened to laymen.

The doctrine of the Grace Gospel Fellowship follows fundamental Calvinism with emphasis on the total depravity of man and eternal security (once a person is a child of God, that status is secure). Specific doctrine affirms the temporary nature of both the gifts of the Spirit (I Cor. 12:4-11) and baptism. There is a departure from the beliefs of Ethelbert W. Bullinger and Charles Welch in the acceptance of the Lord's Supper to be "observed" "until He comes," and in the specific denial of annihilationism. Eschatology follows the doctrine of John Nelson Darby, founder of the Plymouth Brethren, concerning the secret-rapture doctrine, discussed elsewhere in this volume.

The Fellowship maintains offices in Grand Rapids. *Truth*, the bimonthly periodical, is edited by Dr. Charles F. Baker, a prominent writer and president emeritus of Grace Bible College. Grace Mission has work in Puerto Rico, Africa, and New Mexico. Grace Gospel churches are located across the nation and usually go under the name "Berean." They are extreme congregationalists, approaching the Plymouth Brethren in polity. An annual assembly is held at the Winona Lake Campgrounds in Indiana.

Two independent Grace Gospel efforts are the Missionary Literature Distributors, Inc. of Godfrey, Illinois, which distributes the books of J. C. O'Hair, and Grace Fellowship in Buffalo, New York, which publishes *The Message* and distributes Grace literature. The Grace Fellowship also offers a Gospel of Grace Bible course on a correspondence basis.

Membership: Not reported.

Educational facilities: Grace Bible College, Grand Rapids, Michigan.

Periodicals: *Truth*, 1011 Aldon Street, S.W., Grand Rapids, MI 49509.

Sources: Charles F. Baker, *Bible Truth*. Grand Rapids, MI: Grace Bible College, Grace Gospel Fellowship, Grace Mission, Inc., 1956; Charles F. Baker, *Dispensational Relations*. Grand Rapids, MI: Grace Line Bible Lessons, n.d.; Charles F. Baker, *God's Clock of the Ages*. Grand Rapids, MI: Grace Line Bible Lessons, 1937; C. V. Egemeier, ed., *Grace Mission Story*. Grand Rapids, MI: Grace Missions, Inc., 1967.

★590★
LAST DAY MESSENGER ASSEMBLIES
Box 17056
Portland, OR 97217

Nels Thompson, born in Denmark, immigrated to the United States in the early 1900s and, in 1912, was converted in a meeting of the Plymouth Brethren (Exclusive: Grant Brethren) under the leadership of Harry A. Ironside, later pastor of Moody Church. Thompson became an evangelist, but a conflict arose with the Brethren over the control of his evangelical activity. He also came to accept the Grace Gospel position and dropped water baptism (as of the Jewish dispensation). He founded an assembly at Oakland, and, soon, others were formed.

The Gospel Tract Distributors was founded as an independent, but associated, publishing concern, and began publishing *Outside the Camp* (now *Last Day Messenger*) as a nondenominational dispensational periodical. Each issue carries a seven-point statement of belief in the verbal inspiration of the Bible, the Trinity and the deity of Christ, total depravity, redemption by grace, the security of the believer, the personality and punishment of Satan, and the pretribulation second coming. The group does not practice baptism and is opposed to celebrating Christmas and Easter. Headquarters for Gospel Tract Distributors are in Portland, Oregon, with affiliated assemblies spread from Phoenix, Arizona, to Saskatchewan, Canada.

Membership: In the mid-1970s, the Assemblies reported approximately 15 congregations associated with the *Last Day Messenger*.

Periodicals: *Last Day Messenger*, Box 17056, Portland, OR 97217.

★591★
TIMELY MESSENGER FELLOWSHIP
% R. B. Shiflet
Box 473
Mineral Wells, TX 76067

The Timely Messenger was begun in 1939 by pastor Ike T. Sidebottom of Fort Worth, Texas, as a periodical expounding the Grace Gospel position in the Southwest. Sidebottom had been a student at Moody Bible Institute in Chicago and served as an associate pastor for J. C. O'Hair, the early Grace Gospel pastor in Chicago. Sidebottom returned to Fort Worth in 1928 with the intention of establishing himself as a radio evangelist. His following in a Bible class, however, grew into a church on College Avenue. Work continued to grow from the pulpit of College Avenue Church (rebuilt in 1950), the periodical, and the radio program. Through College Avenue Church, other men were prepared for the ministry, and independent congregations began to emerge.

Most ministers work full-time at a secular job and serve as pastors on the weekends.

The Timely Messenger Fellowship is an informal, cooperative endeavor. It differs from the Grace Gospel Fellowship, discussed elsewhere in this chapter, in that it neither baptizes nor partakes of the Lord's Supper. Mission work is done through Grace Gospel Missions. The Timely Messenger Fellowship sponsors summer camps and mid-winter conferences for high school and college students.

Membership: Not reported. In 1968 there were seven congregations in the fellowship.

Periodicals: *The Timely Messenger*, Box 473, Mineral Wells, TX 76067.

★592★

TRUTH FOR TODAY BIBLE FELLOWSHIP
2508 N. 400, E.
Lafayette, IN 47905

The beliefs of Ethelbert W. Bullinger and Charles Welch were passed to Stuart Allen, who succeeded Welch as pastor of the Chapel of the Opened Book in London. He edits *The Berean Expositor* and has written a number of books and pamphlets. In the United States, Welch's theological disciples are grouped in local fellowships built around several periodicals. *Truth for Today* was begun in 1948 by Oscar M. Baker of Warsaw, Indiana. Baker had been a student of Dr. S. E. Long, an early follower of Bullinger and an extension teacher at Moody Bible Institute. He began his preaching in an abandoned church in Lulu, Michigan. Baker distributes Bullinger's, Welch's, and Allen's books, and supports a tape ministry located in Richmond, Indiana. A radio ministry is heard over a station in Phoenix, Arizona. The correspondence course is distributed from Fort Wayne, Indiana. Congregations in fellowship with the fellowship are located in Alabama, Tennessee, Illinois, Iowa, Indiana, Wisconsin, Michigan, New York, Oklahoma, California, and Canada. A very active group associated with the Berean Chapel in Mobile publishes *Plainer Words* monthly and has radio ministries in Dallas, Lansing (Illinois), and Mobile. *Truth for Today* is mailed to all fifty states and over 40 foreign countries.

Membership: Not reported. In 1984, *Truth For Today* circulated more than 5,000 copies per issue.

Periodicals: *Truth for Today*, 2508 N. 400 E, Lafayette, In 47905.

★593★

THE WAY INTERNATIONAL
Box 328
New Knoxville, OH 45871

The Way International was founded by Victor Paul Wierwille in 1942 as the Vesper Chimes, a radio ministry over a station in Lima, Ohio. Wierwille was a minister in the Evangelical and Reformed Church (now a constituent part of the United Church of Christ) into which he had been ordained the previous year. The radio ministry became The Chimes Hour and then The Chimes Hour Youth Caravan. During these years Wierwille became an avid student of the Bible. In 1951 he manifested the reception of God's holy spirit which manifested in the gifts of the spirit. All of his study culminated in the first Power of Abundant living class, a series of sessions presenting his basic perspective on biblical truth, in 1953. Two years later his ministry was chartered as The Way, Inc. (changed to The Way International in 1975). In 1957 Wierwille resigned from the Evangelical and Reformed Church to devote himself full-time to his growing work. The family farm outside New Knoxville, Ohio, was donated to the ministry as its headquarters.

The Way, Inc. grew steadily during the 1960s and then experienced a sudden growth in the 1970s as the Jesus People revival spread across the United States. The facilities at New Knoxville were expanded and hosted the first national Rock of Ages Festival, the annual gathering of people associated with the ministry, in 1971. The Way considers itself to be a Biblical research, teaching, and household fellowship ministry. It neither builds nor owns any church buildings but holds its meetings in home fellowships. Often overlooked by those who write about the Way's development is the role that Wierwille's research in Aramaic has played. He was spurred on by his contact with and personal relationship to Dr. George M. Lamsa, translator of the Lamsa Bible. Among the activities of the Way have been the establishment of a large Aramaic facility (completely computerized) and the training of a group of scholars in the Aramaic (Syrian) language.

Like other Grace Gospel churches, The Way teaches a form of dispensationalism, although Wierwille preferred the term administration. According to Wierwille, present believers live under the Church administration that began at Pentecost. Scripture from before Pentecost is not addressed to the Church but is for our learning. Pre-Pentecost scripture includes the Old Testament, the Four Gospels, the epistles of Hebrews and James, and Acts (which serves as a transition volume). The Gospels belong to the previous Christ Administration.

Doctrinally, the Way could be considered both Arian and Pentecostal. It rejects the Trinitarian orthodoxy of most of Western Christianity. It believes in the divinity of Jesus, the divine conception of Jesus by God, and that he is the Son of God but not God the Son. It also believes in receiving the fullness of the Holy Spirit, God's power, which may be evidenced by the nine manifestations of the Spirit: speaking in tongues, interpretation of tongues, prophecy, word of knowledge, word of wisdom, discerning of spirits, faith (believing), miracles, and healing.

The Way International is organized on the model of a tree, from the root (international headquarters) to trunks (national organizations) to limbs (state and province organizations) to branches (organizations in cities and towns) to twigs (small, individual fellowship groups). Individual members are likened to leaves. Administratively, the ministry is directed by a three-member board of trustees. Founding president Wierwille was succeeded by L. Craig Martindale. Donald E. Wierwille, son of the founder, is the vice-president. The board appoints the cabinet which oversees the headquarters complex. Each of the five properties in the United States (New Knoxville, Ohio; Emporia, Kansas; Rome City, Indiana; Tinnie, New Mexico; and Gunnison, Colorado) are the designated root locations.

New members usually come into the Way through taking the basic 12-session course developed by Wierwille, called "Power for Abundant Living"(PFAL), in which the teachings of the Way are presented. Several options are open to graduates of the course. Many continue to attend twig fellowships. Others become more involved by attending the Way College, in Emporia, Kansas; by joining the Way Corps; or by becoming a "Word over the World Ambassador" for one year. Each program is designed to give practical application to the Way's biblical teachings. In 1983 PFAL classes were being conducted in Zaire, Argentina, and Venezuela.

Membership: At the beginning of 1983, the Way reported 2,657 twigs with approximately 30,000 people involved. There were slightly over 2,000 Word Over the World Ambassadors.

Educational facilities: The Way College, Emporia, Kansas; The Way College of Biblical Research, Rome City, Indiana.

Periodicals: *The Way Magazine*, Box 328, New Knoxville, OH 45871.

Remarks: Criticism of the Way has been mounting and intense. Most has focused on the standard anti-cult theme, accusing the Way of brainwashing youthful members and Wierwille of growing rich from the movement. In addition, critics claim that Wierwille has been training the Way members in the use of deadly weapons for possible future violent activity against the group's enemies. This criticism derived from the Way College's cooperation with the State of Kansas program to promote hunting safety, in which all students had the choice (but were not required) to enroll. No evidence of any violent motivations, intent, or actions has been produced to back up this criticism.

In 1985 the U.S. Internal Revenue Service revoked The Way International's tax exempt status. The case is under appeal.

Sources: Victor Paul Wierwille, *Power for Abundant Living.* New Knoxville, OH: American Christian Press, 1971; Victor Paul Wierwille, *Receiving the Holy Spirit Today.* New Knoxville, OH: American Christian Press, 1972; Victor Paul Wierwille, *Jesus Christ Is Not God.* New Knoxville, OH: American Christian Press, 1975; Victor Paul Wierwille, *Jesus Christ, Our Promised Seed.* New Knoxville, OH: American Christian Press, 1982; Elena S. Whiteside, *The Way, Living in Love.* New Knoxville, OH: American Christian Press, 1972. Polemical works: John P. Juedes & Douglas V. Morton, *From "Vesper Chimes" to "The Way International."* Milwaukee, WI: C.A.R.I.S., n.d.; Douglas V. Morton & John P. Juedes, *The Integrity and Accuracy of The Way's Word.* St. Louis, MO: Personal Freedom Outreach, [1980]; J. L. Williams, *Victor Paul Wierwille and The Way International.* Chicago: Moody Press, 1979.

Miscellaneous Bible Students

★594★
THE CHURCH WHICH IS CHRIST'S BODY
Current address not obtained for this edition.

The nondenominational theme which was so pronounced in Plymouth Brethren thinking found an ally in the person of Maurice M. Johnson, a former minister with the Methodist Episcopal Church, South (MECS). Licensed to preach in Texas in 1912, he moved to Los Angeles, California, in 1921 as assistant pastor at Trinity, the congregation of Robert Schuler, the Methodist pastor. In 1925, he withdrew from the MECS, objecting to the Church's church-school literature and its ministerial training course. With seventy-five followers, he established an independent Maranatha Tabernacle, but two years later withdrew from it and from his role as a salaried pastor and "began to preach only as a minister of Jesus Christ in the church which is Christ's Body." As he traveled about preaching, a fellowship of Christians, both members and those called to preach, emerged.

The distinctive feature of this fellowship is its refusal to be known by "any denominational name," even such a nondescript name as the "brethren." The group also refuses to incorporate. Members do not use any titles, such as "Reverend," which would distinguish clergy and laity, though they do recognize divinely given offices of pastor, evangelist, teacher, elder, and deacon. In this age, there are no longer apostles and prophets. Members believe that all people who have been convicted of their sins, have personal faith in Christ, and have been added to his body are fellow-members of the church which is Christ's Body. Members of the fellowship think of themselves as merely "some members of the church which is Christ's Body," outside all man-made organizations.

Whenever two or more Christians gather for fellowship they constitute a Christian assembly, a local manifestation of the church.

The fellowship teaches fundamental Christianity, including belief in the Trinity, the incarnation of Christ and his finished work on the cross, and the Bible as the only guide. Members see the Bible interpreted in terms of God's successive dispensations. We live in the dispensation begun at Pentecost, when believers began to be baptized by the Lord with one Spirit into one body. Ordinances of baptism and the Lord's Supper are not practiced in the present dispensation. Ordination is considered an act of recognition by an assembly that God has called an individual to the office of elder. Members do not object to saluting the flag and do not endorse conscientious objection to military service.

Assemblies are centers of aggressive evangelism. Ministers are supported by the assemblies, but do not receive a regular salary. A vigorous tract and radio ministry has been established. Maurice Johnson received mail in Orangeville, California, though there are no formal headquarters of the autonomous assemblies. Other leaders include Berl Chisum of Los Angeles, James Cox of Charlottesville, Virginia, and Jack Langford of Fort Worth, Texas. There are assemblies in Los Angeles, San Diego, Riverside, San Luis Obispo, Sacramento, and other places in California; Fort Worth, Texas; Tulsa, Oklahoma; and Charlottesville, Virginia. No membership records are kept because identifying church members is considered a prerogative of God, the head of the church.

Membership: No membership records available.

Sources: *A Federal Court Acknowledges Christ's True Church.* Fort Worth, TX: The Manney Company, N.d. [1963].

★595★
THE (LOCAL) CHURCH
% Living Stream Ministry
1853 West Ball Rd.
Anaheim, CA 92804

The (Local) Church movement was founded by Ni Shu-tsu, known today as Watchman Nee (1903-1972), in China in the early 1920s. Watchman Nee was a product of the nineteenth-century missions in China. He attended an Anglican school in Fuchow and was converted under a Methodist evangelist, Miss Dora Yu. She introduced him to an independent missionary, Margaret E. Barber, who introduced him to the writings of John Nelson Darby, one of the founders of the Plymouth Brethren. After his conversion, Nee began to use the name To Shen (Watchman) and in 1922 entered the ministry. For the next five years he served as a member, and then a leader, of an informal band of young Christians. As this movement grew and spread, it became the Local Church. Between 1923 and 1950 (when the Revolution prevented

further spread of Nee's church), more than 200 churches were founded by Nee. He wrote and published a score of books, most on ecclesiology, the Holy Spirit, and the Christian life. He also founded *The Present Testimony*, a periodical.

Nee first heard of the Plymouth Brethren soon after beginning his movement and in the late 1920s came into contact with the Plymouth Brethren (Exclusive: Taylor Brethren). At their request, Nee in 1933 visited England and for a while considered merging his movement into the Brethren. However, after he returned to China, trouble developed. The Brethren rejected Nee's allowing women to speak in meetings, his relaxation of the requirements for baptism, and a variety of Nee's opinions on minor points of eschatology. Most importantly, Nee had "fellowshipped" with Theodore Austin-Sparks, head of the Witness and Testimony Literature Trust and leader of a ministry at a small meeting hall at Honor Oak, outside of London. Nee's refusal to disavow Austin-Sparks became grounds for his disfellowshiping by the Taylor Brethren. After his break with the Brethren, he turned his attention fully to the development of the movement in China. He authored a number of books, among the most important being *The Spiritual Man* and *The Normal Christian Church Life*.

During World War II, Nee took a secular job in order not to become a burden to the church. He returned to full-time ministry work after the war. At that time he donated some industrial properties to the church, a practice which became an example to others. By the time of the Chinese Revolution, the church had become entangled with "capitalism," thus leading to the arrest of Nee and the suppression of the movement on the mainland. Nee died in prison, where he lived the last twenty years of his life.

Even before the war, Nee's movement had spread beyond China. After the war the movement continued to spread to Hong Kong, the Philippines and throughout Chinese communities in Southern Asia. Most importantly, after the war, Nee sent his longtime associate, Witness Lee, to Taiwan to lead the movement there. After the revolution, Taiwan became the center of the movement and Lee its titular head.

The movement was brought to America by Stephen Kuang, who arrived in 1954 and settled in New York. Another of Nee's co-workers, Bakht Singh, leader of some 200 churches in India, toured the United States in 1960, preaching to the then small constituency of the (Local) Church. Then in 1962, Witness Lee moved to Los Angeles and founded the Living Stream Ministry. His role as Nee's successor quickly made him the focus of the church in America, and over the years his work earned him the respect of the church. His writings are given the same authority as those of Nee, whom the majority of the present membership never knew. (In more recent years both Kuang and Singh have separated themselves from Lee and the Local Church.)

Nee and Lee accepted the basic fundamentalist and dispensational doctrinal position which affirms belief in the authority of the Bible, the Trinity, the atonement in Christ, the Virgin Birth and the Second Coming of Christ. From the Brethren, the movement also inherited the basis for what became its unique ecclesiology. There is a strong nondenominational stance and a refusal to cooperate with denominational bodies or even recognize denominational structures. Nee's basic innovative insight, derived from his study of the New Testament, concerned the relative importance of the local church. Nee taught that geography was the only basis upon which separate groups of Christians could organize. There was, he believed, only one church per city, and all Christians were to meet under its aegis. Christians were not to gather around denominational or sectarian differences. Typically, a congregation will be called "the Church in Los Angeles" or "the Church in Chicago." Each local church was autonomous and under the leadership of elders drawn from its membership. Certain members, who felt called, could become co-workers, teachers who developed a ministry that served many congregations. Such ministries were supported directly by those individuals and congregations who benefitted from them, though such ministries have no official role in administering the affairs of the congregations. However, they have assumed the apostolic role of guiding the movement's growth, teaching and establishing standards of belief and conduct, training local leaders, and mediating local disputes. The two most prominent ministries in the United States are the Living Stream Ministry of Anaheim, California, led by Witness Lee and the Northwest Christian Publications, led by William T. Freeman of Seattle, Washington.

Prominent in the churches' understanding of dispensations is the idea of recovery (or restoration). Over the centuries, they believe, biblical faith and practice were lost. A recovery began with Martin Luther and the Reformation and continued through the such movements as the Wesleyan revival and the Brethren. The most recent stage of this recovery is through the Local Churches which are calling the Church universal to unity and which have rediscovered the experience of the enjoyment of life in Christ. The latter is experienced in a veriety of "new" pietistic practices such as "pray-reading." Pray-reading is a devotional practice of praying by using the words of scripture. This practice is followed by individual believers in private prayer as well as well as by the congregations in group prayers. Pray-reading is integrated into the spirited worship of the Local Churches, which, except for the absence of speaking-in-tongues, is reminiscent of Pentecostalism.

Membership: In 1985 the Local Church reported 98 congregations and 10,260 members and an additional 7 congregations and 735 members in Canada. There were 605 congregations and 129,042 members worldwide, with more than half located in Taiwan.

Periodicals: *The Firstfruit*, 3931 West Irving Park Road, Chicago, IL 60618; *The True Report*, Box 13791, Sacramento, CA 95853.

Remarks: As the Local Churches grew in the United States, the movement came under extreme criticism by other evangelical Christians. Several books and pamphlets appeared accusing it and Witness Lee of deviating from standards of orthodoxy, particularly in its use of the concept of "mingling" in describing the relationship of God and humanity in Christ and the Church. Lee and prominent church members protested their innocence. One volume, devoted entirely to Lee and the Local Church, titled *The God-Man* by Neil T. Duddy and the Spiritual Counterfeits Project, went far beyond doctrinal matters suggesting, among other observations, that Lee's teachings had led to great harm of those associated with the church and that Living Stream Ministry had mishandled funds.

The harm done by two of the anti-Local Church writings, *The Mind Benders* by Jack Sparks and *The God-Man*, led to lawsuits by Lee and others accusing the authors of libel. The first suit against *The Mind Benders* led to an out-of-court settlement, the book's withdrawal, and an apology by the publisher. An uncontested hearing against *The God-Man* led to an $11,000,000.00 judgment against its authors and publisher. Subsequently, other publishers of anti-Local Church material announced their withdrawal

Sources: *The Beliefs and Practices of the Local Churches.* Anaheim, CA: Living Stream Ministry, 1978; Watchman Nee, *The Normal Christian Church Life.* Washington, DC: International Students Press, 1969; Angus I. Kinnear, *Against the Tide.* Ft. Washington, PA: Christian Literature Crusade, 1973; Dana Roberts, *Understanding Watchman Nee.* Plainfield, NJ: Haven Books, 1980; Witness Lee, *How to Meet.* Taipei, Taiwan: Gospel Book Room, 1970; Witness Lee, *The Practical Expression of the Church.* Los Angeles: Stream Publishers, 1970; Witness Lee, *Gospel Outlines.* Anaheim, CA: Living Stream Ministry, 1980; Bill Freeman, *The Testimony of Church History Regarding the Mystery of the Mingling of God with Man.* Anaheim, CA: Stream Publishers, 1977; Bill Freeman, *The Testimony of Church History Regarding the Mystery of the Triune God.* Anaheim, CA: Stream Publishers, 1976. Controversial and polemical works include the following: William T. Freeman, *In Defense of Truth.* Seattle, WA: Northwest Christian Publications, 1981; Neil T. Duddy and the Spiritual Counterfeits Project, *The God-Men.* Downers Grove, IL: InterVarsity Press, 1981; J. Gordon Melton, *An Open Letter Concerning the Local Church, Witness Lee and the God-Men Controversy.* Santa Barbara, CA: Institute for the Study of American Religion, 1985; Jack Sparks, *The Mind Benders.* Nashville, TN: Thomas Nelson, 1977; Gene Ford, *Who Is the Real Mindbender?* Anaheim, CA: The Author, 1977.

★596★
THE TWO-BY-TWO'S
Current address not obtained for this edition.

The group of Christians called "Two-by-Twos" in this text are also referred to as Cooneyites, Go Preachers, and Tramp Preachers, but they claim no name but Christian. All of these names have been placed upon this somewhat anonymous group by outsiders. The group itself, though numbering in the tens (some suggest hundreds) of thousands of members in the United States, has remained virtually invisible. Members shun publicity, refuse to acquire church property, and issue no ministerial credentials or doctrinal literature, believing that the Bible (King James Version) is the only textbook and that, to be effective, the communication of spiritual life must take place orally, person-to-person. The only printed documents are hymnals. The distinctive feature of the movement has been sending forth, two by two, unmarried teams of preachers who, "as they go, preach" (Matt. 10:7).

The Two-by-Two's originated with William Irvine (1863-1947), a Scotsman and member of the Faith Mission founded in 1886 by Mr. John George Govan (1861-1927). The mission, which worked in neglected rural communities, spread to Ireland. Irvine was a leader at Menagh in County Tipperary. Taking his direction from a literal reading of the Gospel of Matthew, chapter 10, Irvine began to feel that the Faith Mission's practices related to renouncing the world were not as strict as called for in the scripture. By 1899 he had begun independent work and in 1901 formally severed any connection with the Faith Mission. Among the young preachers who joined him was Edward Cooney, a strong leader and zealous worker, from whom one of the derisive names comes. Cooney and Irvine, unfortunately, had differences, and Cooney withdrew from working with Irvine.

In 1903 Irvine held a convention at which the pattern for the next decades were set. Ministers were to give over their possessions to the work, renouncing their former life. They took vows of poverty, chastity and obedience. Following the meeting, ministers were dispersed to carry the gospel around the world--Australia, New Zealand, South Africa, China, South America and the European mainland. Irvine, George Walker and Irving Weir brought the movement to the United States. They were soon joined by Jack Carroll, his sister Mae Carroll, William Cleland, Tom Clarke, George Beatty, Tom Grooms, John Burns and Alfred Magowan. By the end of the decade the movement had spread across the eastern half of the United States. In the South, black preachers added their efforts. By 1923, the movement reached Hawaii.

During the years just prior to World War II, Irvine began to predict the end of the dispensation of grace in 1914. His prophetic zeal, as well as conflict over his role as a general overseer of the movement, led to schism and the ouster of Irvine from leadership of the movement which has since been led collectively by the overseers in the various fields. Irvine moved to Jerusalem and lived there for the rest of his life, supported by a small number of followers.

The Two-by-Two's originated not as a doctrinal movement, but as a response by young Christians to follow the example and admonitions of Christ in their life. Membership in the group involved the acceptance of a pattern of renunciation of the world rather than allegiance to a creed. Beginning with the evangelical faith common to free church Protestants in England at the turn of the century, the group took the Bible as their only creed and have allowed considerable variation in expression and belief. The most orthodox presentation of their faith appears in their hymnbook. Critics, primarily former members, have published excerpts of sermons of leading preachers which indicate that a unitarian theology which denies the Trinity and emphasizes the role of Jesus and human example is a prominent perspective and that further doctrinal variation from evangelical belief is present. Two ordinances are observed: adult believers baptism by immersion (including rebaptism of those who come from other church bodies) and the Lord's Supper, which is observed weekly. Most emphasis is placed upon a holy life indicated by modes of dress, no jewelry (except wedding rings), and generally, no television. Women wear no makeup and do not cut their hair. Conscientious objection to war is general, but not mandatory.

The fellowship has an "episcopal" polity. The United States and Canada are divided into fields, typically a state or province, each with an overseer (also called "senior servant" or "elder brother"). The overseers acting in fellowship exercise general supervision of the movement as a whole. The members are organized into house churches of from 12 to 20 members presided over by a bishop (or local elder). Members meet on Sunday for the breaking of bread and during the week for Bible study.

The missionary and evangelistic arm of the movement is supplied by the preachers. These unmarried "servants" travel in teams of two as successors of the Apostles (Matt. 10:1-7). They move into a new community, hold evangelistic services and gather a following. Members of the house churches will support any evangelistic services in their area. The preachers do not draw a salary, but are supported by the free-will gifts of the members.

There is an annual group meeting, or convention, of each field. It typically is held on a large farm, with members camping while in attendance. In these meetings, matters of work, doctrine, discipline, and policy are aired, and decisions are made. There are house churches in all 50 states and throughout Canada. George Walker, the last of the original preachers in America, died in 1981.

Reportedly, Edward Cooney, following his break with Irvine, came to the United States and began his own variation on Irvine's movement. Recent reports indicate that a few members survive, some in North America, but that there are no preachers, and that it is a dying group.

Membership: Not reported. In the mid-1980s there were 96 annual conventions held in the United States, with an average attendance of from 500 to 2,000 each. That attendance would indicate between 10,000 and 100,000 members in the United States, and possibly twice that number in other countries.

Remarks: Only in the late 1970s did substantive literature on the Two-by-Two's become available. Since that time, individual researchers have appeared who have gathered the scant literature (such as notices of conventions). To date only one book, by an ex-member and his wife, has appeared (though at least one other major study is projected). In the United States, Threshing Floor Ministries, headed by a former member, is collecting data (which has been reviewed in preparing this item for the *Encyclopedia*).

Critics of the movement have charged that it has concealed its origins, especially hiding its association with Irvine and its recent origin, and that it has presented a false front of evangelical orthodoxy when in fact it is completely heterodox. Because of the difficulty in gaining authoritative material about the group, and the contradictory reports on its normative beliefs, no assessment of the doctrinal issue is possible. There is, however, little doubt of its rejection of its early (and to some extent) unhappy history.

Sources: *Hymns Old and New*. Glasgow, Scotland: R. L. Allan and Son, 1951; Doug Parker and Helen Parker, *The Secret Sect*. Pandle Hill, N.S.W., Aust.: The Authors, 1982; Keith W. Crow, *The Invisible Church*. Eugene, OR: University of Oregon, M.A. Thesis, 1964; William E. Paul, *They Go About "Two by Two."* Denver, CO: Impact Publications, 1977.

★597★
**WITNESS AND TESTIMONY LITERATURE
 TRUST AND RELATED CENTERS**
Testimony Book Ministry
Box 34241, Bethesada Dr.
Washington, DC 20034

Theodore Austin-Sparks was a former member of the Baptist Church who left to found an independent meeting-place in the Honor Oak suburb of London, England, for Christians who wished to fellowship together and receive the benefits of Austin-Sparks' ministry. That ministry was conceived to be apart from and above traditional denominational barriers. The nondenominational approach manifests the influence of the Plymouth Brethren. The group which gathered at the meeting hall became informally known as the Honor Oak Christian Fellowship.

In 1922 Austin-Sparks began the publication of a periodical, *A Witness and A Testimony* and later established the Witness and Testimony Literature Trust. Over the years he wrote a number of books and pamphlets. In 1939-40, he discovered his close agreement with Watchman Nee, Chinese founder of the Local Church Movement. Nee spent eighteen months with Austin-Sparks while the first edition of one of his most important books, *The Normal Christian Church Life*, was translated with the assistance of the Fellowship's members. While Austin-Sparks' ministry was never merged with the Local Church, the groups remained on cordial terms for many years.

Austin-Sparks absorbed many of Nee's emphases such as those on the two-fold expression of the church (universal and local) and the importance of the local assembly, which are reflected in his writings. However, he preferred to see himself as part of an even more loosely-organized movement of God which had many centers of likeminded Christians. Over the years such centers have been tied together filially and distinguished by their circulation of the literature of an informally "approved" set of teachers. When in England, such teachers would speak at the Honor Oak centre, and Autin-Sparks would speak at their centers when traveling around the world, but no direct "responsibility" was shared for the separate ministries. The various ministries would also circulate the literature produced by Austin-Sparks and other associated writers. Some of these teachers, such as Bakht Singh, popular Indian leader, were associated with Watchman Nee but not with Witness Lee, the recognized leader of the largest segment of Nee's Movement.

Austin-Sparks' materials began to reach America soon after the Fellowship was organized, and he made his first visit to the United States in 1925. Among the early centers of his support was the Hepzebah House in New York City and the Almquist Christian Book Nook in Northfield, Minnesota, which distributed Austin-Sparks literature. By the 1960s the trust regularly recommended three American centers which distributed its literature: M.O.R.E. (Mail Ordering Religious Education), the Westmoreland Chapel in Los Angeles and Convocation Literature Sales in Norfolk, Virginia. M.O.R.E. was headed by Dean Baker of Indianapolis. It absorbed the Northfield work as well as a periodical, *The Ultimates*, edited by DeVern Fromke, an early friend and supporter of Austin-Sparks. M.O.R.E. was supported by the Sure Foundation. Westmoreland Chapel was an independent congregation in Los Angeles, pastored for a decade by Mr. Carl B. Harrison, formerly of the Honor Oak Centre.. Convocation Literature Sales was headed by Ernest L. Chase, who also organized the Atlantic States Christian Convocation, held annually since 1966 at Camp Wabanna, Mayo, Maryland. More loosely affiliated was the Rev. John Myers and Voice Christian Publications of Northridge, California. During the 1960s and 1970s Myers edited a quarterly, *Voice in the Wilderness. The Voice* (after 1970, *Recovery*) promoted the views of both Nee and Austin-Sparks, but is not limited to supporting them.

Austin-Sparks was in fellowship with Nee for a while but did not follow Nee's ideas completely on the local church. He broke off relations with Witness Lee's followers in 1958. In recent years Austin-Sparks literature has been reprinted and kept in circulation by Testimony Book Ministry of Washington, D.C. while that of Watchman Nee has been reprinted primarily by Christian Literature Crusade, an international ministry whose American headquarters are in Fort Washington, Pennslyvania. Testimony Book Ministry also distributes the books of Bakht Singh. In England, long-time associate of Austin Sparks, Harry Foster, currently publishes *Toward the Mark*, a periodical originating in Weston-Super-Mare, Avon.

Those congregations and centers most closely associated with Honor Oak and the Witness and Testimony Literature Trust are distinguished from the Local Church founded by Watchman Nee in that the former generally does not accept the writings and teachings of Witness Lee.

Membership: Not reported.

Periodicals: *A Witness and A Testimony*, Witness and Testimony Literature Trust, 39 Honor Oak Road, London, England, S.E.23.

Sources: *"This Ministry,"* Messages Given at Honor Oak, London. London: Witness and Testimony Literature, n.d. 2 vols.; T. Austin-Sparks, *The Recovery of the Lord's Testimony in Fullness*. Washington, DC: Testimony Book Ministry, n.d.; T. Austin-Sparks, *The Work of God at the End Time*. Washington, DC: Testimony Book Ministry, n.d.; T. Austin-Sparks, *The Battle for Life*. Washington, DC: Testimony Book Ministry, n.d.; T. Austin-Sparks, *The Centrality and Supremacy of the Lord Jesus Christ*. Washington, DC: Testimony Book Ministry, n.d. *No Other Foundation*. Indianapolis, IN: Sure Foundation, 1965; John Myers, *Voices from Beyond the Grave*. Old Tappan, NJ: Spire Books, 1971; Frances Roberts, *Dialogues with God*. Northridge, CA: Voice Christian Publications, 1968; Bakht Singh, *David Recovered All*. Bombay: Gospel Literature Service, 1967.

Adventist Family

An historical essay on this family is provided beginning on page 77.

Sunday Adventists

★598★
ADVENT CHRISTIAN CHURCH
Box 23152
Charlotte, NC 28212

Among the earliest attempts to organize the scattered believers in William Miller's message of the second coming of Christ after the Great Disappointment in 1844 were those of John T. Walsh, who began preaching in Wilbraham, Massachusetts, in the late 1840s. Walsh had some distinctive ideas--namely, that the wicked dead would not be resurrected and that the millennium had already occurred. The saints were now in a period of waiting for Christ's return. After the advent, the earth would be renovated and become the home of the righteous.

At about the same time (following the Great Disappointment), a party arose which believed Miller was in error by ten years in his calculations and that Christ would return in 1854. Simultaneously, there arose a third party which did not believe in the immortality of the soul. This latter party held that man had lost his potential immortality after the fall. They believed that the dead were in an unconscious state in the grave--a belief contrary to the notion that the body dies and the immortal soul lives on. The second party was headed by Jonathan Cummings and the third by George Storrs, editor of *The Bible Examiner*. These two forces united in the late 1840s. Following the failure of Christ to return in 1854, an attempt to unite the Adventists who had split off because of the date-setting failed because of the immortality issue. Those who believed in immortality formed the Evangelical Adventist Church.

In 1855, those who believed in conditional immortality formed the Advent Christian Church, headed by Cummings. Cummings, who followed the independent Bible study of Philadelphia businessman Henry Grew, taught that the Christian's hope of immortality was in Christ's atoning death alone and was not inherent in humankind. Furthermore, he believed that immortality was conditional--it would apply only to those who through faith in Christ could qualify for it. Finally, immortality and its subsequent rewards would be withheld until Christ's second coming.

In the late 1850s, George Storrs began to accept and publicize the peculiar ideas of Walsh, particularly the non-resurrection of the wicked. He left the Advent Christian Church and, with Walsh, formed the Life and Advent Union in 1863. For many years, the two groups existed as separate bodies, though the Life and Advent Union remained small and was confined to New England. In 1964, a merger was effected and the Life and Advent Union became part of the parent body.

Doctrinally, the Advent Christian Church continues Miller's views about the imminent coming of Jesus, with the exception of the date-setting aspects. It also accepts his general or freewill Baptist theological perspective (i.e., being against strict predestination ideas, such as God's knowledge before the world began of the number and identity of the elect, and being in favor of free-will ideas that said salvation is meant for all humankind and people can choose to follow the gospel). Members of the Advent Christian Church worship on Sunday. They are hesitant to set new dates, but believe that Christ's return is imminent, a belief based on the fact that "Bible prophecy has indicated the approximate time of Christ's return."

Organizationally, a congregational government prevails. The general conference meets annually and has charge of the mission and education program. Missions are currently under way in Nigeria, Japan, the Phillippines, Malaysia, and India. Two retirement centers--Vernon Advent Christian Home, Vernon, Vermont, and the Advent Christian Village, Dowling Park, Florida--are supported by the denomination.

Membership: In 1984 the Church reported 30,000 members, 356 churches, and 490 ministers.

Educational facilities: Aurora College, Aurora, Illinois; Berkshire Christian College, Lenox, Massachusetts.

Periodicals: *Advent Christian Witness*, Box 23152, Charlotte, NC 28212; *Maranatha Devotions*, Box 23152, Charlotte, NC 28212; *Advent Christian News*, Box 23152, Charlotte, NC 29212.

Sources: Clyde E. Hewitt, *Midnight and Morning*. Charlotte, NC: Venture Books, 1983; Clarence J. Kearney, *The Advent Christian Story*. The Author, 1968; *The Advent Christian Manual*. Charlotte, NC: Venture Books, 1984; Clarence H. Hewitt, *The Conditional Principle in Theology*. Boston: Clyde and Robert Hewitt, 1954.

★599★
**CHURCH OF GOD GENERAL CONFERENCE
(ABRAHAMIC FAITH)**
313 N. Third St.
Box 100
Oregon, IL 61061

After the Great Disappointment in 1844, when Christ failed to return as predicted by William Miller, small groups of Adventists associated and continued to exist apart from the larger bodies. Scattered around the country, they only learned of each other's existence as they began to publish independent periodicals. Attempts at merger began in the late 1800s. One such group which was formed with a degree of unity in the 1800s, though a permanent general conference was not effected until 1921, was the Church of God General Conference headquartered in Oregon, Illinois, also called the Church of God (Abrahamic Faith).

The Church of God differs from other Adventists in its view on Christology and eschatology. As it had become increasingly common among Adventists, the Church of God emphasizes the one God, denying the Trinity, and seeing Jesus as the son of God but not God. The Church of God believes Jesus came into existence by birth of the Virgin Mary. Members believe that when Jesus returns he will set up his reign as king in Jerusalem, and the church will be his joint heir. Israel will be established in Palestine as the head of nations. The Christian, through repentance, faith and baptism for the remission of sins, enters into a covenant with God. A persevering life of usefulness and good works leads to a position of honor in the coming earthly kingdom.

An inability to agree on questions of the rights of congregations versus the national body led to the national body's ceasing to function from 1889-1921. Then a general conference was organized at Waterloo, Iowa. A congregational government is the accepted polity. A general conference meets annually. Missions are operated in Nigeria, Ghana, England, the Philippine Islands, India, and Mexico.

Membership: In 1984 the Church reported 5,781 members, 19 ministers, and 94 congregations.

Educational facilities: Oregon Bible College, Oregon, Illinois.

Periodicals: *The Restitution Herald*, Oregon, IL 61061; *Progress Journal*, Oregon, IL 61061; *Challenge*, Oregon, IL 61061.

Sources: *Historical Waymarks of the Church of God*. Oregon, IL: Church of God General Conference, 1976; James Mattison, *The Abrahamic Covenant and the Davidic Covenant*. Oregon, IL: The Restitution Herald, 1964; Alva C. Huffer, *Systematic Theology*. Oregon, IL: Church of God General Conference, 1961.

★600★
PRIMITIVE ADVENT CHRISTIAN CHURCH
% Eliza Moss, President
Sissonville, WV 25185

The Primitive Advent Christian Church developed out of a controversy centering on the preaching of a Rev. Whitman, a minister of the Advent Christian Church in Charleston, West Virginia. The Rev. Whitman opposed both footwashing and rebaptizing reclaimed backsliders. Proponents of these two practices organized the Primitive Advent Christian Church. On these two points alone do they differ doctrinally from the parent body.

An annual delegated conference meets to carry on the business of the church. It ordains ministers and elects officers. The pastor is the presiding officer in the local church. There are also deacons and elders. The church is small, and all the congregations are in central West Virginia.

Membership: Not reported. In 1966 there were 10 churches and 597 members.

Seventh-Day Adventists

★601★
BRANCH SDA'S
Box 4666
Waco, TX 76705

The Branch SDA's carry on the work begun by Victor T. Houteff, a member of the Seventh-Day Adventist Church in Los Angeles. In 1930, he wrote a book, *The Shepherd's Rod*, from which the group derived its popular name. Houteff considered himself a divinely inspired messenger of God with the task of calling for reformation and the gathering of the 144,000 mentioned in Revelation. In 1935, Houteff and eleven followers moved to the Mount Carmel Center, established near Waco, Texas, as a temporary assembling point of the 144,000. Their goal was

Palestine, where they would establish the Davidic kingdom with a theocratic regime and direct the closing work of the gospel prior to the second coming of Christ.

Though denounced by the Seventh-Day Adventist Church in which many congregations were disfellowshipping adherents to *The Shepherd's Rod*, Houteff and his followers tried to remain within the Seventh-Day Adventist Church until the beginning of World War II. After the attack on Pearl Harbor, members began to be called for conscription, and the Seventh-Day Adventists refused to back up the requests for conscientious objector status or ministerial deferment. In a crisis, Houteff hastily organized, issued membership certificates, and distributed ministerial credentials. A formal theocratic organization was created, with Houteff as its leader, and in 1942 the name of the organization was changed to the Davidian Seventh-Day Adventists Association

At its height, there were 125 members at Mount Carmel. Houteff died in 1955 and was succeeded by his wife. She, inturn, announced that on April 22, 1959, the 1,260 days (Revelation 11) would end and that, on that day, God would intervene in Palestine. He would clear out both Jews and Arabs and set the state for the entrance of the Davidic kingdom. In answer to an official call, the faithful gathered for an assembly during April 16-22, 1959, in readiness to move to Palestine. They never recovered from the disappointment, and splintering occurred. On December 12, 1961, Mrs. Houteff acknowledged her error and the lack of soundness of the group's teachings. In March 1962, she and her associate leaders resigned, declared the Davidic SDA's dissolved, and put the Mount Carmel property up for sale.

The Branch SDA's were one of several splinters which broke with the main body of Davidic SDA's following Houteff's death. They did not accept Mrs. Houteff, opposing her leadership and prophecies. Many of her followers joined them in 1959. At one point, the Branch sent colonizers to Israel, but their attempts were unsuccessful. They continued as a small body with headquarters near Waco. Annual convocations following the Old Testament feast days (Leviticus 23) are held at the center. They also manage an organic gardening and farming experimental station for the production of foods free of pesticides and commercial fertilizer.

Membership: Not reported.

Sources: V. T. Houteff, *The Great Controversy Over "The Shepherds Rod"*. Waco, TX: The Universal Publishing Association, 1954.

★602★
DAVIDIAN SEVENTH-DAY ADVENTISTS ASSOCIATION
Bashan Hill
Exeter, MO 65647

The Davidian Seventh-Day Adventist Association is possibly the largest of the several factions which emerged following the disruption in 1959 of the movement begun in the 1930s by Victor T. Houteff. It views its task as sounding the "eleventh hour" call (Matthew 20: 1-7) and preparing the Laodicean Church of Revelation 3 (i.e., the Seventh-Day Adventist Church) for the final proclamation of the gospel in the world.

The Association is headed by a president, vice-president, secretary, and treasurer who oversee the missional and publishing efforts, much of which is directed toward Seventh-Day Adventists. It publishes several series of booklets explaining its position, a set of church school guides, and several periodicals.

Membership: Not reported.

Educational facilities: The Davidian-Levitical Institute, Exeter, Missouri.

Periodicals: *The Symbolic Code*, Exeter, MO 65647; *The Timely-Truth Educator*, Exeter, MO 65647.

Sources: *The Keys to the Kingdom at the Eleventh Hour*. Exeter, MO: The Universal Publishing Association, n.d.; V. T. Houteff, *The Great Controversy Over "The Shepherds Rod"*. Exeter, MO: The Universal Publishing Association, 1954.

★603★
GENERAL ASSOCIATION OF DAVIDIAN SEVENTH-DAY ADVENTISTS
Rte. 1, Box 174
Salem, SC 29676

The General Association of Davidian Seventh-Day Adventists is one of several groups which emerged when the followers of Victor T. Houteff broke apart in 1959. Houteff had left the Seventh-Day Adventist Church during World War II as an advocate of conscientious objection to war. His followers took the name Davidian SDA's in 1942. He was succeeded by his wife, but the failure of a prophecy in 1959 disrupted the work and led to its splintering.

The Association sees its task as being to preach the message of the third angel of Revelation 18:1 (Houteff) and to seal the 144,000 members of the Seventh-Day Adventist Church and to call out the multitude from the world (Babylon) into God's kingdom.

Membership: Not reported.

★604★

PEOPLE'S CHRISTIAN CHURCH
402 Melrose St.
Schenectady, NY 12306

Elmer E. Franke (1861-1946), a member of the Seventh-Day Adventist Church, rejected the claims of Ellen G. White as a prophetess and, in 1916, left to found the People's Christian Church in New York City. Seven years later, a second congregation was founded in Schenectady, New York, and, the following year, a third congregation was established in New Bedford, Massachusetts. The beliefs are similar to those of the Seventh-Day Adventists. Members believe in God, Jesus as one in nature with the Father, and the Holy Spirit as one with the Father and Son. Baptism by immersion is practiced, and the Lord's Supper is celebrated as an ordinance on the first Sabbath of each month. While accepting the ten commandments, members believe man was released from the Mosaic Ceremonial law.

Each church is autonomous, though the New York congregation is spoken of as the mother church. Ministers, deacons, and elders are ordained. There were four churches in 1968, two in New York and two in Massachusetts, with members in California, Florida, Maryland, and elsewhere. There were approximately 1,000 members, in all, in 1968. Present (1985) leader of the church is A. Warren Burns, pastor of the congregation in Schenectady, who edits the quarterly periodical and speaks for the church's radio show, "A Faith that Lives."

Membership: Not reported. In 1980 there were three congregations: New York City; Schenectady, New York; and Bedford, Massachusetts.

Periodicals: *Light*, 401 Melrose Street, Schenectady, NY 12306.

Sources: E. E. Franke, *Pagan Festivals in Christian Worship*. Schenectady, NY: People's Christian Church, 1963; E. E. Franke, *The "2300 Days" and the Sanctuary*. Schenectady, NY: People's Christian Church, 1964; A. Warren Burns, *Civilization*. Schenectady, NY: Peoples Christian Church, n.d.

★605★

SEVENTH-DAY ADVENTIST CHURCH, REFORM MOVEMENT
American Union
6380 63rd St.
Sacramento, CA 95824

As World War I approached, a controversy arose among members of the Seventh-Day Adventist Church concerning participation as combatants. The controversy became most severe in Germany. After the beginning of the conflict in 1914 and mobilization in Germany, the president of the East German Union Conference informed the German war ministry that Seventh-Day Adventist (SDA) members would serve as combatants even on the Sabbath. One man, however, John Wieck, claimed to have been shown in a vision that the earthly probation for all men would end in the spring of 1915. He was joined by others making a similar date-setting prediction. They also denounced the SDA leadership for refusing to publish their predictions.

The stance of the German SDA leaders was contrary to the official position of the church, which was one of conscientious objection, and their action was never approved by any other church body. The dissenters met in Switzerland in 1919 and, the following year, presented their case before a general conference delegation. The president of the general conference sided with the dissidents, and subsequently the German leaders acknowledged their error and expressed their regret. In 1923, the reorganized European division issued a "Declaration of Principles," declaring agreement with the worldwide SDA stance on noncombatancy.

With the issuance of the declaration the matter should have ended, and for most it was. However, some pushed for a stand which would make conscientious objection a test of fellowship. When this action was refused, they established the Seventh-Day Adventist Reform Movement. Support came primarily from Germans and German people in Russia, Australia, and the United States, The American branch of the movement is very small, having splintered during the 1930s. Currently, in North America, field offices can be found in Vancouver, British Columbia; Hamilton, Ontario; Franklinville, New Jersey; Montebello, California; and Sacramento, California. The Religious Liberty Publishing Association is located in Denver. Worldwide, branches of the movement can be found in Australia, England, Greece, India, Indonesia, the Philippines, South Africa, and Sri Lanka.

Membership: Not reported. In the mid 1970s there were ten congregations and approximately 200 members in the United States.

Periodicals: *The Sabbath Watchman*, Box 20234, Sacramento, CA 95820.

Sources: *The Principles of Faith of the Seventh-day Adventist Church "Reform Movement" and Her Church By-laws*. Mosbach/Baden, West Germany: General Conference, Seventh-day Adventist Church, Reform Movement, n.d.; *Church Manual*. Denver, CO: International Missionary Society, Seventh-day Adventist Reform Movement, General Conference, n.d.; International Missionary Society, *Bible Study Handbook*. Denver: Religious Liberty Publishing Assn., 1974.

★606★
SEVENTH-DAY ADVENTIST CHURCH
6840 Eastern Ave., N.W.
Washington, DC 20012

The Seventh-Day Adventist Church (SDA) is an evangelical sabbatarian church whose teachings have been supplemented by insights drawn from the prophecies and visions of its founder, Ellen G. White. The Church views the ministry and writings of Mrs. White as prophetic gifts of the Holy Spirit. After the Great Disappointment of 1844, when Christ's second coming did not occur as William Miller had predicted, a group including Mrs. White, her husband James White, Hiram Edson, Joseph Bates, Frederick Wheeler, and S. W. Rhodes, began to meet at Washington, New Hampshire. The visionary Mrs. White saw in a trance the Adventists going straight to heaven. She was soon accepted as a prophetess by the disheartened Adventists. About this same time, under the influence of a member of the Seventh-Day Baptist Church, whose opinions were confirmed by their own Bible study, the group accepted the idea of a Saturday Sabbath. Mrs. White confirmed this correctness in a vision she had of Jesus and the tables of stones upon which the ten commandments were written. The fourth one, on keeping the seventh day holy, was surrounded by a light.

Mrs. White also confirmed for the group the interpretation of the 1844 date set by William Miller for the return of Christ, as originally proposed by Hiram Edson. Taking a clue from Hebrews 8:1-2, Edson proposed that Miller was correct in his date, but wrong in the event. Christ came not to cleanse the early sanctuary, i.e., did not come in visible presence to earth, but initiated the cleansing of the heavenly sanctuary discussed in the text. After this heavenly work is completed, in an indeterminable but short time, he would return to earth.

With the exception of their belief in the seventh day and the sanctuary work of Christ, the Seventh-Day Adventists accept a general Protestant faith, which they received from their background as Baptists and Disciples of Christ. A statement of belief includes an acceptance of the Bible as their rule of faith and practice, the Trinity, creation ex nihilo (from nothing), baptism by immersion, and salvation by the atonement of Jesus Christ. They believe that Christ's soon return will be followed by a thousand year period of peace on earth (the millennium). They do not believe in the innate immortality of the soul; they believe that the dead await the resurrection in an unconscious state. Their acceptance of the seventh-day Sabbath has also led to a strong emphasis on the other Old Testament commandments. They abstain from alcohol and tobacco.

By 1855, the Whites established the Review and Herald Publishing Association in Battle Creek, Michigan, and a periodical, *Review and Herald*, was begun advocating sabbatarianism and tieing the loose band of Millerites together. In 1860, as those who accepted both sabbatarianism and Mrs. White's teachings were distinguished from other Adventists, the name Seventh-Day Adventist Church was adopted. The Church, which originally included approximately 3,500 members in 125 congregations, was officially organized in 1863.

The Church is organized as a representative democracy. Authority for administering the church is delegated through a system of conferences from the local churches which form biennial conferences which combine into larger, regional (termed union) conferences which meet every four years. The General Conference, which meets every five years, and the Executive Committee of the General Conference, which continues between Conference sessions, are the highest administrative bodies in the Church. They set policies and run the extensive missionary, educational, benevolence and publishing activities. The Church has work in 185 countries plus home mission activities among a variety of ethnic groups. The Church's educational system includes 12 colleges and universities, 90 secondary schools and 1,201 primary schools. The Church has attained an outstanding reputation for its hospitals (5 in the United States) and work in health-related activities. Four publishing houses-- the Southern Publishing Association (Nashville, Tennessee); Pacific Press Publishing Association (Mountain View, California); Review and Herald Publishing Association (Washington, D.C.); and Christian Record Braille Foundation (Lincoln, Nebraska) publish the church's 67 periodicals (in 14 languages) and numerous books and general church literature. The affiliated Religious Liberty Association has continued the church's concern for church-state issues and publishes a leading periodical in the field, *Liberty*.

Membership: In 1984 the Church reported 631,255 members, 3,914 churches and 3,1010 ministers in the United States. There were 4,261,499 members worldwide.

Educational facilities: Andrews University, Berrien Springs, MI 49104; Atlantic Union College, South Lancaster, Massachusetts; Canadian Union College, College Heights, Alberta; Columbia Union College, Takoma Park, Maryland; Home Study Institute, Takoma Park, Maryland; Kettering College of Medical Arts, Kettering, Ohio; Loma Linda University, Loma Linda, California; Oakwood College, Huntsville, Alabama; Pacific Union College, Angwin, California; Southern Missionary College, Collegedale, Tennesssee; Southwestern Adventist College, Keene, Texas; Union College, Lincoln, Nebraska; Walla Walla College, College Place, Washington.

Periodicals: *The Adventist Review*, 6840 Eastern Avenue, N.W., Washington, DC 20012; *Ministry*, 6840 Eastern Avenue, N.W., Washington, DC 20012; *Signs of the Times*, Pacific Press Publishing Association, Mountian View, CA 94042; *These Times*, 55 W. Oak Ridge Drive, Hagerstown, MD 21740.

Remarks: During the 1970s, the Seventh-Day Adventists experienced a major period of internal turmoil by the dissent of members (including ministers and intellectuals) who questioned the legitimacy of Ellen G. White's revelation and/or argued for the Church moving further toward a more traditional Protestant theological stance, dropping some of the Adventist distinctives. Some of these members left the Church, others were disfellowshipped. The Church has in the meantime reaffirmed its theological stance and faith in White's work.

Sources: C. Mervyn Maxwell, *Tell It to the World.* Mountain View, CA: Pacific Press Publishing Association, 1976; *Seventh-Day Adventist Church Manual.* (Washington, DC): General Conference of Seventh-Day Adventists, 1981 (quadrennially revised); Edwin Leroy Froom, *The Conditionalist Faith of Our Fathers.* Washington, DC: Review and Herald, 1966; Edwin Leroy Froom, *The Prophetic Faith of Our Fathers.* Washington, DC: Review and Herald, 1950-54. Geoffrey J. Paxton, *The Shaking of Adventism.* Wilmington, DE: Zenith Publishers, 1977; Arnold V. Wallenkampf and W. Richard Lesher, eds., *The Sanctuary and the Atonement.* Washington, DC: Review and Herald Publishing Association, 1981; Ronald L. Numbers, *Prophetess of Health.* New York: Harper & Row, 1976; *A Critique of Prophetess of Health.* Washington, DC: The Ellen G. White Estate, General Conference of S.D.A., 1976; Walter T. Rea, The White Lie. *Turlock, CA: M & R Publishers, 1982; John J. Robertson,* The White Truth. *Mountian View, CA: Pacific Press Publishing Association, 1981.*

★607★
SEVENTH-DAY CHRISTIAN CONFERENCE
246 W. 138th St.
New York, NY 10030

The Seventh-Day Christian Conference was founded in 1934 in New York City as an independent Trinitarian sabbath-keeping body. The Bible (Old and New Testament) is its only rule of faith and practice. It observes three ordinances: baptism by immersion, the Lord's supper and fellowship. Members tithe. The Church holds that war is immoral and members are conscientious objectors. Only males may hold positions of leadership-- bishop, pastor or elder.

Membership: In 1979 congregations were located in New York City, Montclair, New Jersey; and St. Louis, Missouri. There are three affiliated congregations in Jamaica.

★608★
UNIFICATION ASSOCIATION OF CHRISTIAN SABBATH KEEPERS
255 W. 131st St.
New York, NY 10027

In the early 1940s in Manhattan a movement was started among black Adventists to unite independent Sabbath-keeping congregations. It was begun by Thomas I.C. Hughes, a former minister in the Seventh-Day Adventist Church and pastor of the Advent Sabbath Church, formed in 1941 in Manhattan. The missionary-minded Hughes conceived the idea of both home and foreign endeavors and began to gather support from his congregation. In 1956, the Unification Association of Christian Sabbath Keepers was formed, bringing together Hughes's parish and the New York United Sabbath Day Advent Church. Others joined, including the Believers in the Commandments of God.

There is a wide range of doctrinal belief in the various churches. Immersion is practiced and the Sabbath kept. A general adventist theology prevails. The polity is congregational. There are annual meetings for fellowship and general conferences every four years for business. At the second general conference, the title "bishop" was created, but there is no episcopal authority accompanying that title. A twenty-three member board of evangelism operates between general conferences.

The Unification Association is very missionary-minded. Missions had been established by its founders even before the Association was formed. Affiliated fellowships can be found in Nigeria, Liberia, Jamaica, Antigua and Trinidad.

Membership: In 1979 there were two congregations, one in New York City and one in Elizabeth, New Jersey, and approximately 350 members plus 500 constituency members.

Periodicals: *Unification Leader*, 255 W. 131 Street, New York, NY 10027.

Church of God Adventists

★609★
A CANDLE
(Defunct)

A Candle was a small sabbatarian body which became known in the 1960s for its wide circulation of a number of one-page tracts, which detailed its theological perspective. A Candle's beliefs were similiar to those of the Worldwide Church of God and advocated the observance of the Old Testament law, the seventh- day Sabbath, and the Hebrew feast days. A Candle opposes evolution, voting, healing by medicine, the Good Friday hoax, Christmas, and Easter. Members believe that hell is the grave, baptism is necessary for salvation, and that parts of the Bible (specifically those books mentioned in the Old Testament, but not preserved) are missing. Headquarters of A Candle were in Lehigh Valley, Pennsylvania.

★610★
ASSOCIATED CHURCHES OF GOD
% Association for Christian Development
The Pine Building
Winslow, WA 98110

As schism developed in 1974 and ministers were either disfellowshipped or quit, a national fellowship of former Worldwide Church of God ministers and laypeople developed. Headquarters were established at Columbia, Maryland. While making note of the accusations against the ministry of Garner Ted Armstrong, son of the founder of the Worldwide Church of God, as part of the reason for their leaving the fellowship, they placed greater emphasis upon doctrinal issues. Among their first actions, they established a committee to review all of the various theological questions under dispute at the time of their leaving. They issued a 24-item doctrinal statement, which continued many Worldwide Church of God emphases, but rejected tithing in favor of financing by freewill offering and offered a congregational church government instead of the theocratic government of the Worldwide Church of God. Questions on other issues were assigned to a Biblical Studies Committee for discussion and review.

Congregations initially made up of former Worldwide Church of God members were established across the United States and a periodical, *Impact*, and a radio ministry were begun. In 1977 an evangelistic-teaching auxiliary organization, the Association for Christian Development (ACD), was formed and much of the work beyond the local congregations shifted to it. Through ACD, the Associated Churches issue a newsletter and numerous booklets, circulate cassette tapes, conduct radio broadcasts, and offer a Bible course (all of which introduce nonmembers to the doctrine of the Associated Churches).

Membership: Not reported.

Periodicals: *Newsletter*, Association for Christian Development, The Pine Building, Winslow, WA 98110.

Sources: *Fundamental Beliefs of the Associated Churches of God.* Columbia, MD: Associated Churches of God, 1974; *Christian Giving or Tithing?.* Columbia, MD: Associated Churches of God, 1974; *What Is Christ's Commission to His Church?.* Columbia, MD: Associated Churches of Christ, 1974.

★611★
CHURCH OF GOD, BODY OF CHRIST
Rte. 1
Mocksville, NC 27028

The Church of God, Body of Christ, is a sabbatarian adventist group, which, unlike many adventist bodies, believes in the Trinity. In common with other Church of God adventists, members do believe in baptism by immersion, keeping the ten commandments, celebrating the Lord's Supper annually on the day corresponding to the fourteenth day of the Hebrew month of Nisan, and in the bodily, personal, and imminent return of Christ, as well as in tithing, gifts of the spirit, divine healing, abstaining from pork, and the holy life. The church, as the Body of Christ, is organized into a general assembly and state assemblies, with a general overseer and state overseers.

Membership: Not reported.

Periodicals: *The True Gospel Advocate*, Route 1, Mocksville, NC 27028.

Sources: *Church of God, Body of Christ Manual.* Mocksville, NC: Church of God, Body of Christ, 1969.

★612★
CHURCH OF GOD (CLEVELAND, OHIO)
% Pastor M. L. Bartholomew
Box 02026
Cleveland, OH 44102

The Church of God (Cleveland, Ohio) was founded in 1972 by a group of sabbatarian Church of God members who hoped to unite the various factions of the Church of God following the principles of the church in the New Testament. They stood opposed to all divisions and sectarianism. They also opposed all forms of control above the local church. Hence, the Church of God follows a loose congregational polity; each church is completely autonomous. There are no denominational officers or general governing board. Christ is seen as the only head, and all who are in Him are considered members. Regular unity conventions are held for fellowship among the members around the United States. The Church in general follows the doctrine of the General Conference of the Church of God, but a great latitude of belief is allowed on all but the most essential doctrines. The Lord's Supper is celebrated annually at Passover.

Membership: Not reported. Members can be found throughout the United States and affiliate congregations in Nigeria, India, Canada, Jamaica, and the Philippines.

Periodicals: *The Voice of Unity*, Box 02026, Cleveland, OH 44102.

★613★
CHURCH OF GOD (O'BEIRN)
Box 81224
Cleveland, OH 44181

The Church of God (Cleveland, Ohio) was founded in 1970 by Carl O'Beirn, a minister in the Worldwide Church of God. O'Beirn had argued that the Church should not only keep the Old Testament sabbath and feast days but the observation of the monthly new moon days. He also argued for a more correct calculation of Abib, the first month of the Old Testament year. His pressing these issues led to his being disfellowshiped from the Church. From the headquarters in Cleveland, O'Beirn keeps in contact with members and a sympathetic constituency around the United States through regular open letters, supplying information on the correct days for celebrating the various feast days.

Membership: Not reported.

Sources: *Abib.* Cleveland, OH: Church of God, 1976; *The Israel Mystery.* Cleveland, OH: Church of God, 1975; *Understanding the Law.* Cleveland, OH: Church of God, 1974.

★614★
CHURCH OF GOD EVANGELISTIC ASSOCIATION
11824 Beaverton
Bridgeton, MO 63044

The Church of God Evangelistic Association is an association of Church of God congregations formed in 1980. Many of the founders were former members of the Worldwide Church of God. Initially four congregations supported the association leadership of David J. Smith, the editor of *Newswatch Magazine.* Smith, later joined by associate editor John W. Trescott, has produced numerous booklets, a Bible correspondence course, and many cassette tapes for distribution. Evangelistic efforts have been assisted by a radio show heard on stations in Arkansas, Missouri, and Tennessee.

The Church of God Evangelistic Association follows the non-Trinitarian beliefs of other adventist Church of God groups. The association teaches that God's church is a spiritual organization and not limited to any one earthly organization. Christian believers should be organized to effectively serve God and carry out their commission of evangelism, baptising those who repent, and of teaching, but such organizations should not impede the individual's spiritual growth or subvert personal conscience. The association is sabbatarian and observes the annual Passover feast as a time to partake of the memorial Lord's Supper.

Membership: Not reported. In 1982 the association listed thirty-three congregations supporting the association, though some of these were also members of other Church of God congregational associations. The periodical circulated 1250 copies.

Periodicals: *Newswatch Magazine,* 11824 Beaverton, Bridgeton, Missouri 63044.

Sources: John W. Trescott, *The Gospel of the Kingdom of God.* St. Ann, MO: Church of God Evangelistic Association, 1983; John W. Trescott,*Was Jesus an Imposter.* St. Ann, MO: Church of God Evangelistic Association, n.d.

★615★
CHURCH OF GOD, INTERNATIONAL
Box 2525
Tyler, TX 75710

In the summer of 1978, following his second suspension from the Worldwide Church of God, Garner Ted Armstrong, son of Herbert W. Armstrong, formed the Church of God, International. From his leadership role in the Worldwide Church of God, particularly his years of speaking on its television program, he carried a large following which he began immdiately to consolidate and organize. He began broadcasting over the radio from San Antonio. Though not yet gaining a membership approaching that of the Worldwide Church, the Church of God, International has grown quickly into a strong organization in the United States and an international body with membership in Jamaica, Europe, Australia, and South Africa. The radio and television ministry has been rebuilt and Garner Ted Armstrong is seen and heard across North America. A vast body of literature, including two periodicals, doctrinal booklets, and Bible study material, is supplemented by a cassette tape ministry.

The Church of God, International follows Worldwide Church of God doctrine closely but dropped much of the hierarchical structure. It denies the ruling apostolic authority of Herbert W. Armstrong. While not discouraging tithing by members, the Church does not require and does not monitor membership giving. The feasts are kept and in 1984 four feast sites in the United States and one in Canada were required for the membership.

Membership: Not reported. Congregations are found across the United States and membership is estimated to be between 7,000 and 10,000.

Periodicals: *Twentieth Century Watch,* Box 2525, Tyler, TX 75710; *The International News,* Box 2525, Tyler, TX 75710.

Sources: Garner Ted Armstrong, *Where Is the True Church.* Tyler, TX: Church of God, International, 1982; Garner Ted Armstrong, *Sunday-- Saturday...Which?.* Tyler TX: Church of God, International, 1982; Garner Ted Armstrong, *Work of the Watchman.* Tyler, TX: Church of God, International, 1879; *Constitution and Bylaws.* Tyler, TX: Church of God, International, 1979.

★616★
CHURCH OF GOD (SABBATARIAN)
Current address not obtained for this edition.

In 1969, there was an unsuccessful attempt to unite the various factions of the Church of God (Seventh-Day), initiated by members of the Denver body led by Elder Roy Marrs of Los Angeles and his uncle, Elder B. F. Marrs of Denver. The issue of local autonomy, denied to the congregations by the General Conference of the Church of God had originally led to schism. In Denver, the group became known as the Remnant Church of God, and in Los Angeles, as the Church of God (Sabbatarian). Missions are supported in India, Nigeria, and the Philippines.

Membership: Not reported. In the mid 1970s there were 7 congregations.

Periodicals: *Facts of the Faith*.

★617★
CHURCH OF GOD (SEVENTH-DAY, SALEM, WEST VIRGINIA)
79 Water St.
Salem, WV 26426

In the twentieth century, several schisms have rent the General Conference of the Church of God. In the early 1930s, a group within the church began to advocate what it considered a more "Apostolic" form of church government. The new form included twelve apostles, a council of seventy, and a board of seven business stewards. In 1933, the Apostolic group formed a new church with headquarters at Salem. A unity meeting of the two churches was held in 1949 at Fairview, Oklahoma, at which a compromise polity was worked out, and the several factions of the Church of God were reunited. An executive council of twelve members and a ministerial council of seventy became part of the church structure. Headquarters were established in Denver.

However, the compromise proved unsatisfactory to members on both sides. Almost immediately, a group began a "Back to Salem" movement and reorganized along the "Apostolic" mode. In 1950, The *Advocate of Truth* was begun as the official church publication. The apostolic council meets biannually.

Membership: Not reported. In 1970 the Church had 7 congregations, 9 ministers, and approximately 2,000 members.

Periodicals: *The Advocate of Truth*, Box 328, Salem, WV 26426

Sources: Richard C. Nickels, *A History of the Seventh Day Church of God*. The Author, 1977.

★618★
CHURCH OF GOD, THE ETERNAL
Box 755
Eugene, OR 97440

Because of the controversies within the Worldwide Church of God in the early 1970s, several doctrinal changes were authorized. Pentecost was changed to Sunday and, under certain circumstances, remarriage was allowed for those who had divorced. Some saw these changes as a sign of a general doctrinal decline. Among those who disagreed with the changes, in favor of the "faith once delivered," was Raymond C. Cole. In 1975 he left the Worldwide Church of God and formed the Church of God, the Eternal, with headquarters in Eugene, Oregon, where Herbert W. Armstrong had founded the original Radio Church of God in 1934. Cole briefly affiliated his work with Garner Ted Armstrong and the Church of God, International, but he soon returned to an independent status.

It is Cole's position that God revealed the truth to Armstrong in the early years of the Radio Church of God and appointed him to a special position to teach that truth. Such truth is unchangeable, and no allegiance is owed to a church organization that departed from truth. From the headquarters in Eugene, the church sends out a monthly newsletter with much content on the feast days, numerous doctrinal papers and tapes to an unspecified number of members across the United States. Foreign offices are located in Vancouver, British Columbia, Canada and Lausanne, Switzerland. The Church sponsors an annual Feast of Tabernacles gathering each fall.

Membership: Not reported.

Periodicals: The church publishes a newsletter. The address is Box 775, Eugene, OR 97440.

★619★
CONGREGATION OF YAH
Box S
Beebe, AR 72012

The Congregation of Yah was founded as the Church of God 7th Era in July, 1973, by Larry Johnson, a former member of the Worldwide Church of God. He had been disfellowshipped in January, 1973, after sending a 160-page manuscript detailing his opinions on the organization of the Church to the Pasadena headquarters. In December, 1973, Johnson left his home in Buffalo, Missouri, and traveled to California to meet Herbert W. Armstrong, the Church's founder and apostle. He hoped to explain that, just as the Worldwide Church of God claimed to be the Church of Philadelphia (spoken of in Revelation 3:7-13) and claimed Herbert W. Armstrong one of the two witnesses of Revelation 11:3, Johnson was the other witness. Rebuffed, he continued for several years to contact Armstrong. As the internal turmoil disturbed the Church, and Garner Ted Armstrong (Herbert Armstrong's son) was disfellowshipped, Johnson began to revise his understanding of the meaning of the Book of Revelation. He concluded that the Worldwide Church of God was not the Philadelphia Church, but the Church of Sardis (Revelation 3:1-6) and that Garner Ted Armstrong, not Herbert Armstrong, was the witness. Over the years he also absorbed some Sacred Name Movement ideas and, in 1978, changed the name of the Church of God 7th Era to the Congregation of Yah. To date, Garner Ted

Armstrong and the Church of God International have made no acknowledgement of Johnson. The Congregation of Yah is built around an inner family of supporters and a far larger group who receive Johnson's mailings. The Feast of Tabernacle is celebrated annually.

Membership: Not reported. In 1978 about 400 people supported the Congregation as coworkers. A smaller number were active supporters. About 7,000 people receive Johnson's material with some regularity.

Periodicals: *Activity Bulletin*, Box S, Beebe, AR 72012.

★620★
FOUNDATION FOR BIBLICAL RESEARCH
Box 499
Pasadena, CA 91102

Among the most popular of the Worldwide Church of God leaders was Dr. Ernest L. Martin, former chairman of the theology department at Ambassador College. With several colleagues and a group of supporters in the Pasadena area, he formed the Foundation for Biblical Research and began to circulate tapes and literature on such topics as tithing, marriage, the Sabbath, and church government. A monthly Foundation Newsletter was established, now called the *Foundation Commentator*, and regular research papers are issued on a wide variety of topics. Bible history, theological topics, and Christian living have been emphasized. The Foundation program encourages small groups of believers to meet in their homes regularly for prayer and study. Dr. Martin and his associates also travel widely, speaking to believers around the country. Exact membership figures have not been reported.

The Foundation has departed from Worldwide Church of God doctrine on several points: they believe in congregational church government and see autocratic forms as being condemned by Christ; doctors are allowed; tithing has been dropped in favor of free-will offerings; baptism is no longer practiced.

In 1985 the Board of the Foundation voted to change the format of publication to reflect a broader set of opinions and publish a much higher percentage of material not authored by Martin. This occasioned a split in the Foundation with Martin leaving to found the Associates of Scriptural Knowledge. The new arrangement represents not so much a change in doctrinal perspective as a new administrative order.

Membership: Not reported. In 1985 there were over 2,000 on the Foundation mailing list receiving its publications.

Periodicals: *The Foundation Commentator*, Box 499, Pasadena, CA 91102.

Sources: *Church Government and Church Organization.* Pasadena, CA: Foundation for Biblical Research, 1974; Ernest L. Martin, *Passover, Lord's Supper, Communion.* Pasadena, CA: Foundation for Biblical Research, 1975; *The Sabbath and the Christian.* Pasadena, CA: Foundation for Biblical Research, 1974; Ernest L. Martin, *The Tithing Fallacy.* Pasadena, CA: Foundation for Biblical Research, 1979.

★621★
FOUNTAIN OF LIFE FELLOWSHIP
Valley Center, KS 67147

The Fountain of Life Fellowship was organized in 1970 by James L. Porter, a former member of the Worldwide Church of God. Five years previously he had published a study of the feast days of the Old Testament and the seventh day sabbath. The study began with a discussion of his discovery of what he felt to be the proper method of entering the Kingdom of God, calling directly upon the name of Jesus in prayer. (This method of prayer had led to his being disfellowshipped from the Worldwide Church of God in 1958.) In 1972 Porter began a study of the doctrine of the baptism of the Holy Spirit which led him to believe in the necessity of Christians' having the baptism of the Holy Spirit with the accompanying sign of speaking in tongues. He places an emphasis upon the centrality of all nine gifts of the Spirit (I Corinthians 12) and the fruits of the Spirit (Galatians 5:22-23).

The fellowship was organized as a fellowship of believers. Initially Porter began a radio program but soon dropped it in favor of printing and circulating a periodical. The fellowship is headed by a board. No membership roll is kept, but supporters gather annually for the Feast of Tabernacles. Believers meet locally in fellowship groups. Teachings follow Church of God emphases. Worship is weekly on the sabbath, and the Old Testament festivals are celebrated annually. Porter travels around the United States to meet with believers.

Membership: Not reported. Several hundred people receive regular mailings from the fellowship.

Sources: James L. Porter, *The Sabbaths of God.* New York: Exposition Press, 1965; James L. Porter, *Knowing the Father through the Spring Feasts.* Valley Center, KS: Fountain of Life, 1985; Virginia Porter, *The Gifts of the Spirit.* Valley Center, KS: Fountain of Life Fellowship, 1984; Virginia Porter, *Man's Substitute Gifts of the Spirit.* Valley Center, KS: Fountain of Life, 1985.

★622★
GENERAL CONFERENCE OF THE CHURCH OF GOD

General Conference Offices
Box 33677
Denver, CO 80233

During the two decades following the Great Disappointment of 1844, the followers of William Miller became grouped into what became the larger Adventist churches. However, numerous Adventists remained independent of the larger churches. Many sabbatarians, in particular, rejected the "visions" of Ellen G. White of the Seventh-Day Adventist Church. Some of these independents associated together in 1863 around a periodical, *The Hope of Israel*, published in Hartford, Michigan. Enos Easton, Samuel Davison, and Gilbert Cranmer were among the leaders. *The Hope of Israel* continued intermittently for several years and, in 1866, was formally established at Marion, Iowa, and under the aegis of the Christian Publishing Association. By this time, the name Church of God was in general use and was eventually adopted as the "denominational" name.

During the nineteenth century, the movement grew around the periodical and the evangelical endeavor of its leaders. In 1889, the headquarters were moved to Stanberry, Missouri. The periodical continues as *The Bible Advocate*. In 1906, the associated congregations registered as the Churches of God (Adventist) Unattached Congregations.

The General Conference of the Church of God, as the church is known today, has emerged with a decidedly Old Testament emphasis. It believes that the Christian, in order to have the benefit of the redemption, must lead a life of obedience to God, which includes the observance of the Ten Commandments, especially the Sabbath, and footwashing and the dietary laws. The use of tobacco, alcohol, and narcotics is forbidden as is worldliness--attendance at movie theaters, pool halls, and dances. Christmas, Easter, Lent, Good Friday, and Sunday are considered pagan holidays. The group believes that tithing is the method of church financing. The church is popularly called the Church of God (Seventh-Day), and will be referred to by that title frequently in this chapter.

Organization is congregational, and a general conference meets every two years. A ministerial council of seventy members oversees ministerial licensing. Bible Advocate Press and the Church of God Publishing House publish numerous booklets, church school materials, and several periodicals.

Membership: In 1979 the Conference reported 126 congregations and 6,800 members in the United States and Canada.

Educational facilities: Summit School of Theology, Bloomfield, Colorado.

Periodicals: *Bible Advocate*, Box 33677, Denver, CO 80233; *Harvest Field Messenger*, Box 33677, Denver, CO 80233.

Sources: Richard Nickels, *A History of the Seventh Day Church of God*. The Author, 1977; *Doctrinal Beliefs of the Church of God (Seventh Day)*. Denver: Bible Advocate Press, 1974; Robert Coulter, *The Story of the Church of God (Seventh Day)*. Denver: Bible Advocate Press, 1983; *Church Manual of Organization and Procedure*. Stanberry, MO: Church of God Publishing House, 1962; *The 2300-Day Prophecy of Daniel Eight*. Stanberry, MO: Bible Advocate Press, 1960.

★623★
GENERAL COUNCIL OF THE CHURCHES OF GOD

1827 W. 3rd St.
Meridian, ID 83642-1653

In summer of 1950, a meeting was called in Meridian, Idaho, for former members of the General Conference of the Church of God who wished to continue the congregational polity followed by the Church in the years before its 1949 merger with the Church of God (headquartered at Salem, West Virginia) and the Church's subsequent adoption of some aspects of the "apostolic" church government of the Salem body. The doctrine remained without change, but a spirit of freedom in the Lord is emphasized. Mission work is supported in Jamaica, St. Vincents (West Indies), the Philippines, and Africa.

Membership: In 1979 there were 25 congregations in the United States, two in Canada, and three in the West Indies.

Educational facilities: Maranatha College, Meridian, Idaho.

Periodicals: *The Fellowship Herald*, Church of God Publishing House, 1827 W. 3rd Street, Meridian, ID 83642-1653; *Acts*, Church of God Publishing House, 1827 W. 3rd Street, Meridian, ID 83642-1653.

Sources: *A Declaration of Things Most Commonly Believed Among Us*. Meridian, ID: Church of God Publishing House, 1963; Richard C. Nickels, *History of the Seventh Day Church of God*. The Author, 1977; Frank M. Walker, *The Beast, His Image, and the Two-Horned Beast*. Meridian, ID: Church of God Publishing House, n.d.

★624★
SEVENTH DAY CHURCH OF GOD

Box 804
Caldwell, ID 83606-0804

The Seventh Day Church of God was formed in 1954 by several ministers of the Church of God (Seventh Day) headquartered in Salem, West Virginia. They rejected that Church's stance on divorce (allowing divorced and remarried ministers and/or spouses to continue to serve as ministers). They also wanted to keep the Old Testament feast days. Otherwise the new church follows the doctrine of the several sabbatarian Church of God groups. The church is headed by a chairman and secretary, apostles, elders, evangelists, and teachers. Mission work is supported in Nigeria, Jamaica, the Philippines, India, St. Lucia, the Dominican Republic.

Membership: In 1979 the Church reported six congregations: Watsonville, California; Wallingford, Connecticut; Caldwell, Idaho; and three congregations in Chicago, Illinois.

Educational facilities: Zion Faith College.

Periodicals: *The Herald of Truth*, Box 804, Caldwell, ID 83606-0804.

Sources: Richard C. Nickels, *A History of the Seventh Day Church of God*. The Author, 1977.

★625★
TWENTIETH CENTURY CHURCH OF GOD
Box 129
Vacaville, CA 95688

Among the church leaders to leave the Worldwide Church of God in 1974 was Al Carrozzo, regional director of the western half of the work in the United States and director of the Counseling and Guidance Office in Pasadena. He accused Garner Ted Armstrong, son of founder-apostle Herbert W. Armstrong, of adultery (citing numerous instances over a period of years) and continued to raise the issue in his monthly *Newsletter*. He also had pushed for a change in the church's demand that people living with a second spouse following a divorce and remarriage leave their spouse because they would be living in adultery.

After leaving the church, Carrozzo formed the Twentieth Century Church of God, began a tape and literature ministry, started a radio show over several stations, and traveled around the country talking to groups who had left the Worldwide Church of God. The monthly newsletter contained two sections. One part discusses continuing concerns within the Worldwide Church of God. The other part centers upon the Twentieth Century Church of God's main emphases-spiritual growth, prayer, Christian living, and preaching the gospel of reconciliation. These emphases emerge within a context of general agreement with Worldwide Church of God doctrine.

Membership: Not reported.

Periodicals: *Newsletter*, Box 129, Vacaville, CA 95688.

Sources: Al Carrozzo, *Who Is Qualified to Be Your Minister?*. Vacaville, CA: Twentieth Century Church of God, n.d.; *Our Christian Responsibilities*. Vacaville, CA: Twentieth Century Church of God, n.d.; Al Carrozzo, *Christmas*. Vacaville, CA: Twentieth Century Church of God, n.d.; Al Carrozzo, *How to Study the Bible*. Vacaville, CA: Twentieth Century Church of God, n.d.

★626★
UNITED SEVENTH-DAY BRETHREN
% Myrtle Ortiz
Box 225
Enid, OK 73701

The United Seventh-Day Brethren was formed in 1947 by two independent congregations and several individuals who banded together for greater effect in the fields of evangelism, publication, Sabbath promotion, and fellowship. Each local church in the fellowship remains autonomous. Views held generally in common include the following: the Bible is the inspired Word of God and the final authority in faith and conduct; there is one God; Jesus is God's son, who was born of a virgin, died, was resurrected, and ascended; man has no hope apart from the blood of Christ; the Sabbath Day remains in effect, as do the Ten Commandments; and the local church is autonomous. Members deny the immortality of the soul. They do not use unclean meats.

For several years, *The Vision* was the official periodical for the group, though it was owned privately. In 1966, it was bought by W. Allen Bond and, soon after, the official relationship was ended. *The Vision* continues to reflect Seventh-Day Brethren ideology, however.

Membership: Not reported. In 1980 there was only one congregation.

★627★
WORLD INSIGHT INTERNATIONAL
Box 35
Pasadena, CA 91102

World Insight International was formed in 1977 by Kenneth Storey, a former minister of the Worldwide Church of God who had been associated with Ernest L. Martin's Foundation for Biblical Research, as a Christian service organization offering insight into the full scope of God's plan for the world. A strong evangelistic program was announced as well as provision for the establishment of local fellowship groups. Underlying World Insight International was the discovery by Storey and his wife of the manifestation of the spiritual gifts discussed in I Corinthians 12. The first mailing from the new organization announced both the beginning of the Latter Reign of the Holy Spirit before the end of time and warned against counterfeits (which he believes are manifest throughout the contemporary Charismatic Movement). While looking for the manifestation of spiritual gifts, Storey rejected the basic Pentecostal idea of the primacy of speaking in tongues.

Over the years, Storey received support from other prominent Worldwide Church of God leaders such as David Orr, who had initiated the work of the Foundation for Biblical Research in England, Brian Knowles, and Richard Plache. Since its founding, a program of biblical research and publication has led World Insight into fellowship with more orthodox Christians and has produced a critique of Worldwide Church of God ideas. There is a strong emphasis upon prophetic themes and the inner life. Norman Grubb of Union Life has joined the list of contributing editors to *World Insight*.

Membership: Not reported. There is a mailing list of several thousand and fellowship groups around the United States.

Periodicals: *World Insight*, Box 35, Pasadena, CA 91102.

Sources: Ken Storey, *Worldwide Church of God in Prophecy*. Pasadena, CA: World Insight International, 1979; Ken Storey, *Love Feasts of the Church*. Pasadena, CA: World Insight International, 1978.

★628★
WORLDWIDE CHURCH OF GOD
300 W. Green St.
Pasadena, CA 91123

One of the more successful of the Adventist bodies is the Worldwide Church of God. It was founded by Herbert W. Armstrong, a former advertising man who, in 1931, was ordained in the Oregon Conference of the Church of God (Seventh-Day), a small splinter from the General Conference of the Church of God which had developed during the Depression of the 1930s. Members of the Oregon Conference did not wish to send their money to General Conference headquarters in Stanberry, Missouri. Shortly after moving to Oregon, in the mid-1920s, Armstrong's wife had become influenced by Ora Runcorn, a member of the General Conference of the Church of God, who taught her the "truth" of Sabbath observation. Guided by his wife's enthusiasm, Armstrong became an avid Bible student and was convinced of the beliefs of the Church of God. Without formally joining the Church of God, Armstrong became active in it in 1927 and preached his first sermon in 1928.

After his ordination, he began to preach actively. Then in 1934, without leaving the Church of God, he founded an independent radio ministry, the Radio Church of God, and began publishing *The Plain Truth* magazine. By this time, Armstrong had absorbed a belief in British-Israelism, the identification of the modern Anglo-Saxon people with the descendants of the ten lost tribes of Israel referred to in the Old Testament. Anglo-Israel ideas had been present among Church of God ministers for several decades ,though never accepted by the Church as a whole.

At the time Armstrong began his radio ministry, he had become involved in the several debates within the Church of God movement over church government and the observation of the Old Testament feast days. On both issues he sided with the minority faction which argued for the observance of the feast days and the abandonment of the democratic process in the governance of the church as a whole. Armstrong participated in the founding of the Church of God (Seventh-Day) headquartered at Salem, West Virginia. He was selected as one of the "seventy" leaders chosen by lot in 1933. However, the Salem faction after following the feast days for a few years, dropped the practice. It also separated itself from British-Israel belief. At this point, around 1937, Armstrong withdrew from any further participation in the Church of God (Seventh-Day). Armstrong's following grew slowly but steadily. Following World War II he moved to Pasadena, California, and in 1947 launched Ambassador College. During the 1960s, growth allowed the expansion of the radio broadcast, "The World Tomorrow," and the addition of a television ministry. The voice of Garner Ted Armstrong, Herbert's son, became familiar to many. The name of the Radio Church of God was changed to the Worldwide Church of God in 1968.

Doctrinally, the Worldwide Church of God represents one extreme in the Church of God movement. From the Church of God it received its name, its doctrine of God, an understanding of ordinances (including footwashing), an emphasis on the Old Testament law, and a feeling that certain holidays (Christmas and Easter) are pagan. From the Church of God it also absorbed its emphasis upon the practice of the Jewish festivals and British-Israelism. The Worldwide Church of God observes all seven Old Testament feasts--Passover and the Days of Unleavened Bread, Pentecost, Trumpets, Atonement, Tabernacles, the Last Great Day, and the First Day of the Sacred Year. Across the United States and in the lands where foreign work has been pursued, camp grounds have been constructed for the large gatherings involved in these celebrations.

Even before he left the Church of God, Armstrong had imbibed deeply of British-Israelism, having encountered it through books and its advocates in the Church of God in those early years of Bible study. The racial implications of the theory have not escaped attention and can be seen in the church's pattern of growth throughout the white world.

While rejecting the democratic government of the General Conference of the Church of God, Armstrong did not fully accept the "biblical" government, with leaders chosen by lots, of the Church of God (Seventh-Day). As his independent ministry grew, he began to see himself as God's chosen apostle-messenger of the last days. He became the absolute authority for the Church and ordained and appointed all of its ministers. Just as he saw himself in a special role in God's endtime plans, so too did the Church he led. Drawing a picture of church history from the Book of Revelation, chapters 2-3, he saw the Worldwide Church of God as God Church of the endtime. As a God's agent its life was molded into preordained cosmic cycles of nineteen years each. The church is seen as the historical reality of the Philadelphian church of the Book of Revelation. This Philadelphian church was to appear just before the final apocalyptic happenings during the last cycles.

God gave the first-century Church just two nineteen-year cycles to carry the gospel to the whole world of its day. Nineteen years after the beginning of Jesus' ministry, God opened a door to the apostle Paul at the beginning of a second nineteen-year cycle by which the gospel went to Europe. Armstrong's own ministry began in 1927, exactly 100 cycles after the beginning of Jesus' ministry. At the beginning of the 1934 ministry God marked off two nineteen-year time-cycles before Christ returns for the restoring of the knowledge of the same Gospel!

In January 1953, at the beginning of the second cycle, expansion of the church to Europe was accomplished. In spite of the fact that no significant cosmic event accompanied the end of the second cycle in 1972, the work continues.

The move to Pasadena was followed by several decades of steady, even spectacular, growth, especially during the 1960s. Circulation of *The Plain Truth* jumped from 500,000 to 2,000,000 between 1964 and 1974. However, the 1970s proved a time of tremendous internal discord, complete reorganization of the the the ministerial staff and major schisms. The trouble began with the disappointment over the nonoccurrence of any event marking the end of the second nineteen-year cycle, i.e., the initiation of God's Kingdom visibly and the beginning of a time of turmoil so great as to cause God's people to flee into hiding. This disappointment was accompanied by intense theological debates over the dating of the feast of Pentecost and over divorce and remarriage among members, as well as a massive scandal surrounding Garner Ted Armstrong. The scandal and his eventual disfellowshipping and became the occasion for a group of ministers and members to leave. Several rival church organizations were established, and one group of ex-members began an anti-Worldwide Church of God periodical, *The Ambassador Report*. It became a focus of continuing discontent surrounding the governance of the Church and the elder Armstrong's marriage to a young divorcee followed several years later by their divorce.

In 1978 several ex-members filed a lawsuit against the Church. Gaining the cooperation of the state's attorney in California, they were able to have the Church placed in receivership pending the trial. The controversy was ended abruptly by the intervention of the state legislature which passed new laws prohibiting such action by the state's attorney. The period of controversy has been followed by a time of recovery in which the Church has resumed a normal life and has recovered most of the losses from the 1970s.

By the beginning of 1985, circulation of *The Plain Truth* had topped 7,500,000 and a second magazine, meant for more serious readers, *The Good News*, circulated 700,000 copies (in five languages). Circulation of *The Plain Truth* has been stimulated by the establishment of numerous stands in public establishments across the United States and some European countries. In 1984, over 300,000 enrolled in the Ambassador College Correspondance Course, teaching basic church doctrine. Offices in over 30 countries on every continent oversaw foreign work.

Educational facilities: Ambassador College, Pasadena California; Ambassador College, Big Sandy, Texas.

Periodicals: *The Plain Truth*, Pasadena, CA 91101-9988; *The Good News of the World Tomorrow*, Pasadena, CA 91123; *Youth*, Box 11, Pasadena, CA 91123; (for members only: *The Worldwide News*, Pasadena, CA 91101.

Remarks: In 1979 there were 60,000 members in over 300 congregations.

Sources: Herbert W. Armstrong, *The United States and British Commonwealth in Prophecy*. Pasadena: Worldwide Church of God, 1980; *This Is the Worldwide Church of God*. Pasadena: Ambassador College Press, 1971; Herbert W. Armstrong, *The Autobiography*. Pasadena: Ambassado College Press, 1967; Herbert W. Armstrong, *Mystery of the Ages*. Pasadena: Worldwide Church of God, 1985; Joseph Hopkins, *The Armstrong Empire*. Grand Rapids: Eerdmans, 1974; David Robinson, *Herbert Armstrong's Tangled Web*. Tulsa, OK: John Hadden Publishers, 1980; John Tuit, *The Truth Shall Make You Free*. Freehold Township, NJ: The Truth Foundation, 1981.

Jehovah's Witness Groups

★629★
BACK TO THE BIBLE WAY
(Defunct)

Long-time pioneer for the International Bible Students Association and the Jehovah's Witnesses, Roy D. Goodrich was excommunicated in 1944. To put his case before the public and to serve as a rallying point for other "free" Bible Students, he began publishing a periodical, *Back to the Bible Way*, in 1952. Goodrich departed from the main body of Bible Students at two points. He denied that Charles Taze Russell, founder of the Bible Student movement, is to be considered the "wise and faithful servant" of Matthew 25: 45-47. He also rejected Russell's thinking relative to the ransom, and to the significance of 1914. Headquarters were established in Fort Lauderdale, Florida, from which a large amount of literature was distributed to a mailing list of as many as 3,000.

Goodrich died in 1977 and the movement centered upon him dissolved.

Periodicals: *Back to the Bible Way* was published in Fort Lauderdale, Florida from 1952 through 1973.

★630★
CHRISTIAN BIBLE STUDENTS ASSOCIATION
(Defunct)

Gradually separating from the Dawn Bible Students Association in the late 1960s was the Christian Bible Students Association headquartered in Warren, Michigan. This group began publication of the periodical *Harvest Message* in 1969 and subsequently published several booklets and tracts. Like the Dawn Bible Students Association and the Pastoral Bible Institute, the group emphasized the writings of Pastor Charles Taze Russell and carried the same statement of beliefs. A radio program, "The Harvest Message Broadcast," was heard in Chicago, Nashville, and Detroit. The group disbanded in 1978, and members were absorbed back into the Dawn and other Bible Student groups.

★631★
CHRISTIAN BELIEVERS CONFERENCE
% Berean Bible Students Church
5930 W. 29th St.
Cicero, IL 60650

Since Charles Taze Russell (whose work led to the founding of the Jehovah's Witnesses), raised the issue of the atonement in a most "unorthodox" way, it was no surprise that dissent from a more "orthodox" perspective would appear. J. H. Paton was the first to break with Russell. Paton promulgated his own speculations in both a book and a magazine. In 1909 a significant challenge to Russell arose from three prominent leaders (pilgrims) within his movement-- H.C. Henninges, M.L. McPhail, and A.E. Williamson. They rejected Russell's teaching on the ransom atonement in that it elevated the church to the place of Christ as the redeemer and mediator for humanity. They said Russell's theology spoke of Christ as only a part of the sin-offering presented to God. They also rejected Russell's identification of himself with "that servant" of Matthew 25:45-47.

In the midst of the controversy, which lasted for some two years, Henninges led many of the Australian brethren out of Russell's Millennial Dawn Bible Students and McPhail and Williamson led out groups in New York and Chicago. In America, the groups took the name of the Christian Believers Conference. Continuing polemics by descendants of Henninges and McPhail have brought into focus the sharp distinction which the Christian Believers draw between themselves and Russell. They reject the idea of the elect being limited to 144,000 as "mere assummption." They insist the Lord did not come in 1914 (or 1925) invisibly; he has always been present (Matthew 18:20).

The Christian Believers Conference is structured very loosely, being held together by its peculiar doctrine. For many years a Publications Committee published *The Kingdom Scribe*, discontinued in 1975. The most active ecclesia as of the 1980s is the Berean Bible Students Church in Cicero, Illinois, which publishes the main periodical serving the group nationally. Since 1910 an annual conference has been held, in most recent years in Grove City, Pennsylvania. The conferees meet for mutual edification and Bible instruction, and they have no legislative authority.

Membership: Not reported. In the early 1970s there were 13 ecclesias scattered across the United States from Massachusetts to Wisconsin and Florida.

Periodicals: *The Berean News*, The Berean Bible Students Church, 5930 West 28th Street, Cicero, IL 60650.

Sources: M. L. McPhail, *The Covenants: Their Mediators and the Sin-Offerings.* Chicago: the Author, 1919; *What Say the Scriptures about the Ransom, Sin Offering, Covenants, Mediator, Scapegoat?.* Melbourne, Austr.:Covenant Publishing Company, 1920.

★632★
CHRISTIAN MILLENNIAL CHURCH
307 White St.
Hartford, CT 06106

Two groups are in agreement theologically but separate administratively. They are the Christian Millennial Church and Western Bible Students. The former began as the Associated Bible Students of L'Aurora Millenniale soon after the break by M. L. McPhail that led to the formation of the Christian Believers Conference. It later became known as the Millennial Bible Students Church and is still popularly designated the New Creation Bible Students. It is centered on a single congregation in Hartford, Connecticut, and the national readership of its monthly magazine, *The New Creation*, begun in 1940 by its editor, Italian-American Gaetano Boccaccio. There are cordial relations between the Christian Believers Conference and the New Creation Bible Students. They announce each other's conferences and exchange speakers, but attempts at merger have failed. During the 1980s, Boccaccio has strongly advocated the unity of all the Bible Student groups.

Italian-American Bible Students in Connecticut and Massachusetts began work in Italy in 1939. A periodical, *L'Aurora Millenniale* was begun in Hartford and mailed to subscribers in the homeland. Growth of the work allowed the periodical to be transferred to Italy for publication in 1962. It is now known as *La Nuova Creazione* and is published by the Mensile della chiesa Cristiana Millenarista.

Membership: Not reported.

Periodicals: *The New Creation*, 307 White St., Hartford, CT 06106; *Newsletter for Christian Millennial Church Members*, 307 White St., Hartford, CT 06106.

Sources: *"We Believe"*. Hartford, CT: Christian Millennial Church, 1980.

★633★
DAWN BIBLE STUDENTS ASSOCIATION
199 Railroad Ave.
East Rutherford, NJ 07073

The Dawn Bible Students Association grew up among younger members of the Brooklyn ecclesia of the Pastoral Bible Institute (PBI) in the late 1920s. Some energetic members led by former radio broadcaster W. N. Woodworth, who had worked with Charles Taze Russell, wished to begin a radio ministry. Without any hostility toward the work, the PBI felt genuinely unable to sponsor it. The group, joined by some recent additions from the Bible Students led by Judge J. F. Rutherford (soon to be renamed the Jehovah's Witnesses), withdrew, formed the Dawn Publishers, and began radio work. The very popular "Frank and Ernest" radio show has become a major outreach effort and has more recently been joined by a television show, "The Bible Answers."

The Dawn carries on the most extensive outreach ministry of any of the Bible Student groups other than the Jehovah's Witnesses. Their monthly periodical, *The Dawn*, was begun in 1932. Over the years, the group has published numerous booklets and pamphlets and a few books. The Association is the most avid reprinter of Russell's works and keeps most of the other Bible Students supplied.

Doctrinally, the Dawn is at one with the PBI, differing only in being more strict concerning doctrinal divergences among its members. The PBI is much more open to fellowship with other Bible Students groups. The Dawn carries in each issue the same statement of beliefs as the PBI's *Herald of Christ's Kingdom*.

From Dawn ecclesias across the country, an extensive outreach program is conducted. *The Dawn* is circulated for only a token subscription cost (or with no price) to readers far beyond the membership, and the radio and television shows cover the nation. A tract and literature ministry is pursued, including Spanish language work in the Southwest and Mexico. Foreign work reaches Great Britain, Australia, France, Greece, Denmark, Germany, Italy, New Zealand, Uruguay, and St. Kitts (West Indies). Australian work is coordinated through the Berean Bible Institute headquartered in Melbourne. The South India Bible Students Committee headquartered in Bangalore has developed a working relationship with the Dawn Bible Students, especially in the production of literature.

Membership: Not reported. The Dawn is the largest of the Bible Student groups with ecclesias across the United States and Canada. Membership is in the thousands.

Periodicals: *The Dawn*, East Rutherford, NJ 07073

Sources: *Our Most Holy Faith*. East Rutherford, NJ: Dawn Bible Students Association, 1948; *The Book of Books*. East Rutherford, NJ: Dawn Bible Students Association, 1962; *The Creator's Grand Design*. East Rutherford, NJ: Dawn Bible Students Association, 1969; *When Pastor Russell Died*. East Rutherford, NJ: Dawn Bible Students Association, 1946.

★634★
EPIPHANY BIBLE STUDENTS ASSOCIATION
Box 97
Mount Dora, FL 32757

After the death of Paul S. L. Johnson in 1950, the Layman's Home Missionary Movement began to experience troubles in its leadership. In the spring of 1955, charges of fraud and dishonesty in business were circulated against John J. Hoefle, a prominent leader who had spoken at Johnson's funeral. Hoefle, in turn, accused the leadership of the Layman's Home Missionary Movement of slander and lying, and, in the ever growing polemics, some doctrinal distinctions between Hoefle and Raymond Jolly, who had succeeded Johnson as head of the organization, began to appear. They disagreed on the nature and validity of John's baptism (Acts 19:1ff), which Hoefle saw as an excuse for Jolly to accuse him of being out of harmony with both Johnson and Charles Taze Russell, founder of the Bible Student Movement. Hoefle was formally disfellowshipped on February 8, 1956.

Hoefle began to publish the correspondence on the controversy and his opinions on the ongoing administration of Jolly. By the end of 1957, these letters had become a regular monthly publication. In 1968, the title Epiphany Bible Students Association began to appear on the masthead. Hoefle continues in the Russell/Johnson theological school with only minor differences with the Laymen's Home Missionary Movement, primarily of an administrative nature and concerning variations on the interpretation of specific texts. For example, Hoefle disagreed with the Layman's Home Missionary Movement on whether people new to the truth can presently attain the "Spirit" plane, as members of the Ancient Worthies class can.

The Epiphany Bible Students Association is organized around individuals who receive the monthly newsletters.

Membership: Not reported

Periodicals: The Association publishes an untitled newsletter. The address is Box 97, Mount Dora, FL 32757.

JEHOVAH'S WITNESSES
25 Columbia Heights
Brooklyn, NY 11201

Following the death of Charles Taze Russell in 1916, J. F. Rutherford was elected to succeed him as president of the Watch Tower Bible and Tract Society, the corporate entity which had guided the developing Bible Student Movement. At the convention of Bible Students connnected with the Society in 1931 at Columbus, Ohio, those gathered passed a resolution declaring that from that time foward they would be known as "Jehovah's Witnesses." This resolution crowned the rise of Judge R. R. Rutherford to a position of absolute authority in the society's affairs. For more than decade, he had, step-by-step, molded the loosely organized Bible Students into a tight hierarchical organization, the "theocratic kingdom" of the witnesses to Jehovah. Along the way he lost most of the former Bible Students to the various groups discussed elsewhere in this chapter. However, in so doing, he created an organization that soon eclipsed them in membership and worldwide appeal.

Rutherford's first struggle was to gain official leadershp of the society, overcoming those who also laid claim to it. His strongest opponent was Paul S. L. Johnson, who was finally defeated in 1918 at the election of the Society's board of directors. Johnson left the society with his following and eventually formed the Layman's Home Missionary Movement. Once in control, Rutherford began to purge the society and its Brooklyn headquarters (popularly known as Bethel) of any who did not support him. Rutherford was hindered for a while because of imprisonment on sedition charges. (The society had come under government scrutiny as the war began because of its pacifist position and anti-government apocalyptic rhetoric.) The imprisonment worked to his good in the long run, giving him a martyr's image.

The steps to power included the initiation of some new publications. In 1918, the "so-called" seventh volume of the *Studies in the Scripture*, Russell's popular teaching series, was released. Bible Students immediately rose to denounce it as a departure from Russell. In 1919, *The Golden Age* was begun as a second periodical, in explicit contradiction, many claimed, to Russell's desires.

Rutherford continued Russell's practice of date-setting-- first 1920, then 1925 and, lastly, 1940. As is true of all Adventists, Rutherford was caught in the bind of having to discern the future by relating contemporary events to Biblical passages of prophecy. The continual disconfirmation required continual adjustment, until adjustments could not work. At that time, a complete overhaul was needed.

A process of replacing Russell's writings with Rutherford's began in 1921 with the publication of Rutherford's *The Harp of God*. Between 1921 and 1941,

Rutherford was to write twenty books and numerous pamphlets, which would slowly revise the doctrine and structure left him by Russell. Among the doctrines abandoned were Russell's beliefs in the gathering of the Jews and the great pyramid prophecies. Rutherford revised Russell's view of Armageddon; it was no longer an anarchistic struggle, but rather a universal war. Most important, Rutherford led the Witnesses into the settled condition of a people in the second generation expecting a third, more likely to live out their lives on earth rather than be alive at the end of the world. Ethics emerged as a concern of importance in addition to eschatology. Since Rutherford's death during World War II, all of his books and writings have been replaced by more recently written volumes. New books and pamphlets authorized by the board of the Watch Tower appear regularly. Most are now collectively written.

The new settled condition of the Witnesses' life was reflected in administrative changes. A hierarchical organization replaced the congregational structure of Russell's days. All members were given the job of selling and distributing Watch Tower literature. Money began to be put into purchasing buildings for meetings, kingdom halls, across the land. Rutherford's legacy was a solid organization ready to survive for many generations.

Theologically, the Witnesses are unitarians. They deny the Trinity and the divinity of Christ. The dialogue with traditional Christianity is a significant part of their lifestyle; while agreeing upon the Bible as a source of theology, they interpret it much differently. They have attacked the theologically orthodox churches as instruments of Satan, and in return they have been answered in a vast body of anti-Witness literature, much just as vitrolic, produced largely by evangelical Christians who denounce the Witnesses as a "cult."

In recent decades, Witnesses have produced a new translation, *The New World Translation of the Holy Scriptures*, as an aid in defending their exegetical and doctrinal position. Among the interesting features of this translation is the rendering of the Greek "statos" as "stake" instead of its traditional rendering as "cross." Christ is pictured as dying on a stake, his hands above his head, not on a cross. Also denied is the traditional doctrine of hell. The wicked are believed to be destroyed, not sent to eternal torment.

Eschatology is continually shifting with the Witnesses as 1914 recedes further into the past. Believing as they do that the 144,000 were sealed in 1914, they face the problem of a dwindling number of people alive from that time. They annually record the ever smaller number receiving the bread and wine at the annual Passover service. (Only the 144,000 can partake.) Their belief led to a major prophetic disaster in the 1970s. It had been taught that at the end of one generation, before all those sealed in 1914 have died (approximately 1975), the end would come in a recognizable way. A great expectation was created as 1975 approached. The disappointment following the disconfirmation of that prediction led to a number of defections, including a number of leaders and at least one board member. [It should be noted that most present-day Witnesses, especially those who have entered the kingdom since 1914, do not think of themselves as destined for heaven as are the 144,000, but are all among the great multitude who will live forever on earth to be ruled by the heavenly sealed (the 144,000)].

Ethics and lifestyle have become predominant aspects of the Witnesses' life. Every free moment is taken up with the kingdom-hall activity. Witnesses spend their time in selling and distributing literature, claiming the lost, or learning how. They lead an increasingly separatist existence; a devout Witness has no fellowship with non-Witnesses beyond showing them the truth. Their separatism has manifested itself in a number of traditional ways, such as pacifism, downgrading public education, and withdrawal from political involvement. It has also produced several beliefs which have drawn public scorn--refusal to use blood transfusions or to salute the flag.

In the several decades following World War II, the Witnesses had a spectacular growth. In the first decade, they went from 142,000 publishers (active members selling literature) to 643,000 and they went to more than 1,000,000 by 1965, under the leadership of Nathan H. Knorr, Rutherford's successor. An education program to train Witnesses has been instituted, and Rutherford's goals have been pursued with great success. In 1970, the Witnesses reported work in 206 lands by 1,483,430 Witnesses in 26,523 congregations. In the U.S. alone, in 1975, there were 560,807 Witnesses in 7,117 congregations. Growth since 1975 in the United States was slowed by the failure of the prophecy.

Membership: The 1982 *Yearbook of Jehovah's Witnesses* reported 588,503 publishers (active members) and 7,590 congregations; 1,463,070 attended the annual Passover memorial services. Worldwide the Witnesses reported 2,361,896 publishers and 43,870 congregations.

Periodicals: *The Watchtower Announcing Jehovah's Kingdom*, 25 Columbia Heights, Brooklyn, NY 11201; *Awake!*, 25 Columbia Heights, Brooklyn, NY 11201.

Sources: *Jehovah's Witnesses in the Divine Purpose.* Brooklyn, NY: Watchtower Bible and Tract Society, 1959; *"Make Sure of All Things".* Brooklyn, NY: Watchtower Bible and Tract Society, 1957; *Organization for Kingdom-Preaching and Disciple Making.* Watchtower Bible and Tract Society, 1972; *The Truth that Leads to Eternal Life.* Brooklyn, NY: Watchtower Bible and Tract Society. Jerry Bergman, *Jehovah's Witnesses and Kindred Groups, A Historical Compendium and Bibliography.* New York: Garland, 1985. Timothy White, *A People for His Name.* New York: Vantage Press, 1967; Alan Thomas Rogerson, *Millions Now Living Shall Never Die.* London: Constable & Co., 1969; Heather Botting and Gary Botting, *The Orwellian World of Jehovah's Witnesses.* Toronto: University of Toronto Press, 1984; Edmond Charl es Gruss, *Apostles of Denial.* Nutley, NJ: Presbyterian and Reformed Publishing Co., 1970.

★636★
LAODICEAN HOME MISSIONARY MOVEMENT
Rte. 38
9021 Temple Rd., W.
Fort Myers, FL 33912

John W. Krewson was a member of the Layman's Home Missionary Movement who withdrew in protest over the leadership of Raymond Jolly, who had succeeded Paul S. L. Johnson. In 1955, within months of Johnson's death, Krewson was disfellowshipped and soon began to publish a periodical, *The Present Truth of the Apocalypsis.* He offered LHMM members an option to John J. Hoefle, who had also been disfellowshipped and had formed the Epiphany Bible Students Association. They began to argue, each casting doubt on the other's right to preach and asserting that the other was not a pilgrim (preacher with proper credentials). As time passed, Jolly, Hoefle and Krewson have continued the intrafamily feud; sometimes Jolly and Krewson agree against Hoefle, and sometimes Hoefle and Jolly agree against Krewson. Krewson and Hoefle disagreed on Johnson's status as the last saint, Hoefle arguing that Charles Taze Russell's appointments of other pilgrims (who were still alive) was ample refutation. Both Hoefle and Jolly joined in refuting Krewson's teaching on the apocalypse.

The Laodicean Home Missionary Movement is loosely structured around Krewson's periodical by individuals and small groups who use it for study and edification.

Membership: Not reported. Readership of the magazine is estimated in the hundreds.

Periodicals: *The Present Truth of the Apocalypsis*, Rte. 38, 9021 Temple Road, W., Fort Myers, FL 33912.

★637★
LAYMAN'S HOME MISSIONARY MOVEMENT
Chester Springs, PA 19425

Shortly before Pastor Charles Taze Russell died in 1916, Paul S. L. Johnson, a Jew who had become first a Lutheran minister and then a Bible Student pilgrim (teacher/preacher), was sent to England to straighten out troubles among the British students. In order to facilitate Johnson's work, Russell gave him "enlarged powers." Johnson, in November, proceeded to England and, under the authority received from Russell, fired two of the managers of the London office. Judge J. F. Rutherford, confirmed as president of the Watch Tower corporation while Johnson was in still in England, saw Johnson as a major threat to his consolidation of leadership control. Johnson believed that the "special authority" given by Russell was still valid.

The issue came to a head at the 1918 board meeting of the Watch Tower Bible and Tract Society, the corporate entity of the Bible Students, at which Rutherford's authority was decisively confirmed. Johnson, Raymond Jolly, and a host of Bible Students withdrew from the Rutherford-led organization and joined in the formation of the Pastoral Bible Institute (PBI). Differences soon arose among the PBI leaders, so Johnson left and formed the Layman's Home Missionary Movement. The major strength was in the Philadelphia ecclesia. Two periodicals, *The Herald of the Epiphany* (for general readership) and the *Present Truth*(an in-group periodical and major polemic organ), were begun.

The Layman's Home Missionary Movement believes Russell was that faithful and wise servant of Matthew 25:45-47 and was labelled by Johnson the "parousia messenger." Johnson viewed himself as Russell's successor. As Russell brought word of the presence, so Johnson, as the "epiphany messenger," brought word of Christ's appearance. Raymond Jolly, Johnson's successor, is the "epiphany scribe." Like Russell, Johnson published voluminously. During Johnson's lifetime, fifteen of the seventeen volumes of the *Epiphany Studies in the Scriptures*, volumes following the format and appearance of Russell's *Studies in the Scriptures*, appeared.

The Layman's Home Missionary Movement remains one of the "orthodox" Bible Student groups which still uses Russell's writings and follows Russell's pattern of finding Biblical types of current events and groups. Other Bible Student groups were typed as divisions of the tribes of Levites (Numbers 3:17-37). PBI students were seen as Shimite Gershonites, revolutionists changing Russell's charter into an ecclesiastical, anti-Christ document. Johnson's main disagreement with the PBI and the Dawn Bible Students Association, which he saw merely as the PBI masked under another name, concerned the harvest. Johnson believed that, in 1916, the door of salvation (Luke 13:24-25) closed as an entrance into consecration and spiritual-begettal for high calling purposes. He also believed that the entrance into suffering with Christ and, therefore, the preaching the harvest message was now due. The door, he believed, is closed for entrance into the kingdom. The PBI believed that the door was still open. In essence, the Layman's Home Missionary Movement closed the inner circle, but allowed new members.

Membership: Not reported. There are conflicting claims on membership, ranging from 10,000 to 50,000. The lower estimate more closely approaches the LHMM's real strength.

Periodicals: *The Bible Standard and Herald of Christ's Kingdom*, Chester Springs, PA 19425; *The Present Truth and Herald of Christ's Epiphany*, Chester Springs, PA 19425.

Sources: Paul S. L. Johnson, *Meratiism*. Chester Springs, PA: Layman's Home Missionary Movement, 1938; Paul S.

L. Johnson, *Gershonism*. Chester Springs, PA: Layman's Home Missionary Movement, 1938; Raymond Jolly, *The Chart of God's Plan*. Chester Springs, PA: Layman's Home Missionary Movement, 1953.

★638★
PASTORAL BIBLE INSTITUTE
Box 15031, Chouteau Station
St. Louis, MO 63110

"Harvest siftings," was a term used by the Bible Students led by Charles Taze Russell to describe a period of controversy which resulted in the loss of doctrinal or organizational dissidents. Such a period followed the death of Russell, whose work with Bible Students eventually led to the formation of the Jehovah's Witnesses. Judge J. F. Rutherford, who succeeded Russell as president of the Watch Tower Bible and Tract Society, the Bible Students' corporate entity, was opposed in his rise to power by a number of board members, including R. H. Hirsh, I. F. Hoskins, A. I. Ritchie, and J. D. Wright. They opposed Rutherford's issuance of Volume VII of the *Studies in the Scripture*, the first six volumes of which had been Russell's central teaching materials. They fought Rutherford's power until the elections at the convention in 1918. After his decisive victory, they withdrew and with some fifty colleagues and supporters set up the Pastoral Bible Institute (PBI). A committee of seven was appointed to supervise the work and R. E. Streeter was made editor of a new periodical, *The Herald of Christ's Kingdom*.

Doctrinally, the PBI and those groups which have come out of it are the most conservative of the Bible Student groups and the most attached to Pastor Russell's works. While PBI, like all groups, produces its own literature, it continues to sell and use Russell's books and to keep his writings in print. Each issue of the *Herald* carries a creed-like statement summarizing the truths which "To us the Scriptures Clearly Teach." These include the following:

"That the church is the 'Temple of the Living God'-peculiarly 'his workmanship'; that its construction has been in progress throughout the Gospel Age--ever since Christ became the world's Redeemer and the chief corner stone of this Temple, through which, when finished, God's blessings shall come to 'all people,' and they find access to him. I Cor. 3:16, 17; Eph. 2:20-22; Gen. 28:14; Gal. 3:29.

"That meantime the chiseling, shaping, and polishing of consecrated believers in Christ's atonement for sin, progresses, and when the last of these 'living stones, elect and precious,' shall have been made ready, the great Master Workman will bring all together in the first resurrection; and the temple shall be filled with his glory, and be the meeting place between God and men throughout the Millennium. I Pet. 2:4-9; Rev. 20:4,6.

"That the basis of hope for the church and world lies in the fact that 'Jesus Christ, by the grace of God tasted death for every man,' 'a ransom for all,' and will be 'the true light which lighteth every man that cometh into the world,' in due time. Heb. 2:9; John 1:9; I Tim. 2:5,6.

"That the hope of the church is that she may be like her Lord, 'see him as he is,' be a 'partaker of the divine nature,' and share his glory as his joint-heir. I John 3:2; John 17:24; Rom. 8:17; II Pet. 1:4.

"That the present mission of the church is the perfecting of the saints for the future work of service to develop in herself every grace, to be God's witnesses to the world; and to prepare to be the kings and priests in the next age. Eph. 4:12; Matt. 24:14; Rev. 1:6, 20:6.

"That the hope for the world lies in the blessings of knowledge and opportunity to be brought to all by Christ's Millennial Kingdom-the restitution of all that was lost in Adam, to all the willing and obedient, at the hands of their Redeemer and his glorified Church-when all the willfully wicked will be destroyed. Acts 3:19-23; Isaiah 35."

The import of the statement for PBI, by which it is distinguished from most other Bible Student groups, comes in its belief that the membership in the church is still open. The harvest is not yet closed, and evangelism, not just the perfecting of those believers left in 1918, is a major thrust. The invitation is to the fullness of the heavenly hope, not just to an earthly paradisiacal state, as with the Jehovah's Witnesses. Because of their evangelistic endeavors, PBI and related groups are the largest of the Bible Student bodies other than the Witnesses.

Organization of the PBI is very loose, with individuals and autonomous local ecclesias affiliated through the *Herald* and an annual membership meeting at which the seven-member board and five-member editorial committee are elected. The *Herald* circulates approximately 10,000 copies per issue. Ecclesias are mostly located in the Northeast and Midwest, with a few in the West. Affiliated ecclesias are found in 30 countries. Active correspondence and interchange with the British Bible Students of the Bible Fellowship Union are promoted.

Membership: Not reported.

Periodicals: *The Herald of Christ's Kingdom*, Box 15031, Chouteau Station, St. Louis, MO 63110.

Sources: R. E. Streeter, *The Revelation of Jesus Christ*. Brooklyn, NY: Pastoral Bible Institute, 1923, 1924, 2 Vols.; R. E. Streeter, *Daniel the Beloved of Jehovah*. Brooklyn, NY: Pastoral Bible Institute, 1928.

★639★
PHILANTHROPIC ASSEMBLY
709 74th St.
North Bergen, NJ 07047

F. L. Alexander Freytag (1870-1947) was in charge of the Swiss Bureau of the International Bible Students Association. Though an able leader, he was never an exponent of founder Charles Taze Russell's theology, and in 1917 he began to criticize Russell's main teaching books, the six-volume *Studies in the Scripture*. Then in 1920 he published the *Message of Laodicea* as an attack on the society, and Judge J. R. Rutherford, who succeeded Russell, took up the debate in *The Harp of God*, his first major book, before the year was out. In 1921, Freytag withdrew and set up the Church of the Kingdom of God, also known as the Philanthropic Assembly of the Friends of Man, taking with him many Swiss, German, and French Bible Students.

Freytag concentrated on the religious problem of death. He believed that he had found the answer in his intimate relationship with the person of Christ. One overcomes death by conforming to the form of Jesus. By eschewing sin and following Jesus, one escapes the wages of sin. Freytag's message of death conquered was set within a framework of Russell's theology. He added an important point: eternal happiness is God's goal for all mankind, without exception. The replacement of death with hell's torment was not good enough for Freytag, who demanded the conquering of death itself. The idea is further supported by allegiance to the Universal Law-"God is love." This characteristic is the supreme fact of creation.

Freytag's movement main strength was in central Europe (Switzerland, Germany, France, Spain, Austria, Belgium and Italy), but it found some adherents among Bible Students in the eastern United States. The American headquarters circulates English-language editions of Freytag's books and two periodicals.

Membership: Not reported. American adherents are estimated to be in the hundreds. Internationally, the *Monitor*, the main periodical, circulates 120,000 copies in several languages.

Periodicals: *The Monitor of the Reign of Justice*, 709 74th St., North Bergen, NJ 07047; *Paper for All*, L'Ange de l'Eternal, Le Chateau, 1236 Cartigny, Switzerland.

Sources: F. L. Alexander Freytag, *The Divine Revelation*. Geneva, Switz.: Disciples of Christ, 1922; F. L. Alexander Freytag, *The New Earth*. Geneva, Switz.: Bible and Tract House, 1922; F. L. Alexander Freytag, *Eternal Life*. Geneva, Switz.: The Messenger of the Lord, 1933.

★640★

WESTERN BIBLE STUDENTS ASSOCIATION
12739 14th St.
Seattle, WA 98125

The Western Bible Students Association centered in Seattle, Washington, is at one in doctrine with the Christian Believers Conference but administratively separate. It holds an annual conference at Mission Springs, Santa Cruz, California.

Membership: Not reported.

Sacred Name Movement

★641★

ASSEMBLIES OF THE CALLED OUT ONES OF YAH
231 Cedar St.
Jackson, TN 38301

The Assemblies of the Called Out Ones of Yah began in 1974 when Sam Surratt, a believer who had previously been convinced that "Yah" was the correct name of the Creator and "Yeshuah" that of His son, the Messiah, felt compelled to create a unity of the truly Called Out Ones of Yah. Surratt felt that the true church would be guided by Yah through Yeshuah and the Holy Spirit, rather than by one leader, and that leaders would be chosen by casting lots. Following a Biblical pattern, the Called Out Ones are led by twelve apostles, the seven, and the seventy. The seven, which constitute the officers for the assemblies, are elected for two-year terms and, together with the seventy (directors at large), comprise the board of directors for the assemblies.

The assemblies follow the main ideas of the Sacred Name Movement and are very clear in their rejection of both the Trinitarian position and the "Oneness" or "Jesus Only" position of some Pentecostals. The assemblies are Pentecostal and teach the importance of the baptism of the Holy Spirit and the reception of the gifts of the Spirit (1 Corinthians 12). Members of the assemblies refrain from military duty but will accept alternative humanitarian government service. Members tithe ten percent of their increase (net income) annually. A second tithe is given at the annual feast days (Deuteronomy 14: 22-26), and every third year there is a poor fund tithe. Baptism is by immersion. Weekly worship is on the Sabbath.

In the early 1970s Surratt began to send literature to Sacred Name and Sabbatarian believers across the United States and into foreign fields. He built a mailing list of many thousands that has produced some new members who have begun local assemblies. Branch chapters were designated wherever two or more of the Called Out Ones gathered.

Membership: Not reported. According to the assemblies, the Called Out Ones of Yah consists of the great multitude (which no one can number) from all nations being called out by Yah from all Babylonish religions to serve with Yeshuah in the coming kingdom. It numbers more than 144,000.

Periodicals: *Called Out Ones Bible Thought Provoker Messenger*, 231 Cedar Street, Jackson, TN 38301.

Sources: Sam Surratt, *"Judge" or "Be Judged," That's the Question*. Jackson, TN: Assemblies of the Called Out Ones of Yah, (1977?); Sam Surratt, *The Point of No Return*. Jackson, TN: Assemblies of the Called Out Ones of Yah, (1977?); Sam Surratt, *Virgin Lamps*. Jackson, TN: Assemblies of the Called Out Ones of Yah, 1977.

★642★

ASSEMBLIES OF YAH
Current address not obtained for this edition.

The Assemblies of Yah was a small group headquartered in Albany, Oregon. Its aims were to present Yah's name to the world; to teach the laws, statutes and judgments of the Most High; and to foster growth of the Assemblies throughout the world. Its present status is unknown. During the 1960s, it published a periodical, *The Word*.

★643★

ASSEMBLY OF YAHVAH (OREGON)
% Elder L. D. Snow
Box 1010
Stilwell, OK 74960

Among the first people to accept the ideas of the Sacred Name movement were Elder L. D. Snow and his wife, members of the Seventh Day Church of God at Fort Smith, Arkansas. He affiliated with the original Assembly of Yahweh led by C. O. Dodd and was licensed by them in the early 1940s. In 1945 he began publishing *The Yahwist Field Reporter*. Four years later he moved to Emory, Texas, where he and other Sacred Name followers attending a camp meeting formed the Assembly of Yahvah, using the spelling of the Creator's name Snow had come to feel was most correct. Elder Snow, who moved to Oregon, served as overseer for seventeen years and was succeeded in 1968 by Elder Wilburn Stricklin of Winfield, Alabama.

The statement of belief includes reference to observance of the law of clean and unclean meats (with pork being unclean), Passover (an annual Lord's Supper), tithing, and modesty in dress. Healing of the sick and prayer are believed in strongly.

Around 1970 the Assembly was disturbed by the influx of Pentecostalism which split the membership. Stricklin and James Pridmore, General Secretary of the Assembly, who had accepted the pentecostal position, took over *The Elijah Messenger* and continued their work under the original name. In 1970 Elder Snow moved from Oregon to Oklahoma and the following year began issuing a new periodical, *The World Today Analyzed*, serving those who did not accept the pentecostal perspective. An annual gathering for the Feast of Tabernacles is held each fall at Pilgrim Acres near Emory, Texas, where the Assembly was first constituted. Foreign members are found in the Philippines, England, India, and Jamaica.

Membership: Not reported. Membership is small and scattered around the United States.

Periodicals: *The World Today Analyzed*, World Today Publishers, Box 1010, Stilwell, OK 74960.

Sources: *The Restoration of Original Sacred Name Bible.* Buena Park, CA: Missionary Dispensary Bible Research, 1973; *The Major Beliefs of the Assembly of Yahvah.* Junction City, OR: The Assembly of Yahvah, 1967.

★644★
ASSEMBLY OF YAHVAH (ALABAMA)
Box 89
Winfield, AL 35594

The Assembly of Yahvah (Alabama) dates to 1945 and the organization of the Assembly of Yahvah by a group of Sacred Name believers gathered at a camp ground near Emory, Texas. Elder L. D. Snow, who had first reached the conclusion that "Yahvah" was the correct spelling of the Creator's name, was chosen as Overseer. Wilburn Stricklin was chosen as Assistant Overseer. Stricklin succeeded Snow in 1968. At about this time the Assembly was split over the acceptance by some members, including Stricklin and James Pridmore, the General Secretary, of pentecostalism, the belief in the Baptism of the Holy Spirit and the resulting sign of speaking in unknown tongues. The majority of the group followed Stricklin and Pridmore. Elder Snow, still editor of the Assembly's periodical, *The Elijah Messenger and Field Reporter*, led those who did not accept the new teaching. The Assembly of Yahvah (Alabama), continues the beliefs and practices of the other Sacred Name bodies. It believes in keeping the Saturday sabbath and in baptism by immersion. Members are admonished to keep a holy life, with particular emphasis upon decent dress and the avoidance of the habitual use of intoxicating substances. An annual camp meeting is held each fall.

Membership: Not reported. In 1985, the assembly had two congregations affiliated with it, one in Winfield and one in Jackson Gap, Alabama. There were less than 200 members. Members of independent assemblies from a number of states participate in the annual camp meeting.

Periodicals: *The Elijah Messenger*, Box 89, Winfield, AL 35594.

Sources: *Directory of Sabbath-Observing Groups.* Fairview, OK: Bible Sabbath Association, 1980.

★645★
ASSEMBLIES OF YAHWEH
Bethel, PA 19507

Jacob O. Meyer, a former member of the Church of the Brethren, left the church of his childhood and began a spiritual pilgrimage that led him to a small independent Sacred Name assembly meeting in Hamburg, Pennsylvania. In 1964 he moved to Idaho to become assistant editor of the *Sacred Name Herald*. He attended his first Feast of Tabernacles meeting, in Nevada, Missouri, in 1965, at which time he was consecrated for the ministry. For a while he was associated with the Assemblies of Yah in Albany, Oregon. Then in 1966, he moved to Baltimore and began his radio ministry, the Sacred Name Broadcast. A magazine, *The Sacred Name Broadcaster*, was begun the following year. In 1969, to facilitate the bringing together of the widely scattered Sacred Name believers, he founded the Assemblies of Yahweh. Ten ministers were ordained. As the membership grew, a second periodical for members only, *The Narrow Way* was added. Under Meyer's leadership the Assemblies has grown into the largest Sacred Name organization in North America.

Doctrinally, the Assemblies of Yahweh have several peculiarities. Members affirm "that in order to interpret correctly the Inspired Scriptures, we must use the Old Testament as a basis of our faith." This hermeneutical position completes the shift begun in the writings of Ellen G. White, founder of the Seventh-Day Adventist Church, toward the dominance of the Old Testament in Biblical interpretation. The Assemblies teach the necessity of believers' affirming the divine names, Yahweh and Yahshua, the marks of the Divine Father which stand in contrast to the mark of the beast (Revelation 13: 16-17). As with most Sacred Name groups, a non-Trinitarian position is maintained. All the Old Testament commandments, including the feast days and excepting only the ritual and annual sacrifice laws, must be kept. Tithing is stressed. Remnants of Meyer's heritage among the German Brethren are reflected in emphases upon women's covering their heads for worship, modest dress, nonviolence, and conscientious objection to war.

The Assemblies is headed by the Directing Elder as the earthly shepherd under the Savior, Yahshua the Messiah. Under his direction are the ordained preaching elders who serve in spiritual matters and the deacons who handle temporal affairs. Under these members (who are always males) are the senior missionaries and missionaries (who may be either male or female). Affiliated assemblies are located in twelve countries around the world. The missionary thrust, both foreign and domestic, is concentrated through the Sacred Name Broadcast, heard over twenty-four stations across the United States (as of 1984) and in fifty-three foreign countries. Listeners may receive a wide variety of literature and enroll in a correspondence course. Foreign offices are maintained in England and the Philippines. Affiliated members are found in twelve countries.

Membership: The Assemblies do not count members but (as of 1984) they estimate the number to be several thousand. There are 30 congregations and 6 elders (ministers).

Periodicals: *The Sacred Name Broadcaster*, Bethel, PA 19507; *The Narrow Way*, Bethel, PA 19507.

Sources: Jacob O. Meyer, *The Memorial Name--Yahweh*. Bethel, PA: Assemblies of Yahweh, 1978; *The Sacred Scriptures, Bethel Edition*. Bethel, PA: Assemblies of Yahweh, 1981; *Psalms, Anthems, Spiritual Songs for the Assemblies of Yahweh*. Bethel, PA: Assemblies of Yahweh, n.d.; *Statement of Doctrine*. Bethel, PA: Assemblies of Yahweh, 1981; Jacob O. Meyer, *Exploding the Inspired Greek New Testament Myth*. Bethel, PA: Assemblies of Yahweh, 1978.

★646★
ASSEMBLIES OF YAHWEH (MICHIGAN)
Box 102
Holt, MI 48842

The Sacred Name movement began among members of the Seventh Day Church of God during the 1930s. Possibly the oldest surviving assembly is the Assembly of Yahweh, of Eaton Rapids, Michigan, originally chartered as the Assembly of Y.H.W.H. in 1939. Among its charter members were Joseph Owsinski, John Bigelow Briggs, Squire LaRue Cessna, Harlan Van Camp, George Reiss, Daniel Morris, William L. Bodine, John M. Cardona, Edmond P. Roche, and Marvin Gay. The original charter allowed some variation in the spelling of the Sacred Name, but Yahweh came to be accepted. It associated with other independent assemblies, in large part through the efforts of C. O. Dodd, an early Sacred Name advocate.

Dodd founded a magazine, *The Faith*, at Salem, West Virginia, in 1937, originally to promote the observance of the Old Testament feasts among the members of the Seventh Day Church of God. In 1938 he organized the Faith Bible and Tract Society. Within a few years Dodd had become convinced of the Sacred Name position and began using it on the pages of *The Faith* but moved to Michigan after associating with the Sacred Name movement. The magazine tied together the growing movement and became a major instrument in its spread. After Dodd's death it was passed to several assemblies until 1969 when the assembly at Eaton Rapids took responsibility for publishing it. The Faith Bible and Tract Society was continued by Dodd's widow.

A lengthy statement of faith asserts the Assemblies' aim to remove the names substituted by man for the true names: Yahweh, Elohim, and Yahshua. The Assemblies uphold the Ten Commandments, including the seventh-day Sabbath, and practice footwashing, baptism by immersion, and the Jewish festivals. The Old Testament food laws are advocated, as are tithing and divine healing.

The church is non-Trinitarian. The group is loosely organized, and congregations are found around the country.

Membership: Not reported.

Periodicals: *The Faith*, Box 102, Holt, MI 48842.

★647★
ASSEMBLY OF YHWHOSANA
% David K. Johnson
50006 Olson Rd.
Boone, CO 81025

The Assembly of YHWHOSANA is a small Sacred Name group in Colorado. It differs from other Sacred Name groups in its designation of YHWH (as opposed to Yah, Yahweh, or Yahvah) as the true revealed name of the Almighty and YHWHOSHUA (YHWH plus HOSHUA) for the name of the Messiah (as opposed to Yahshua or Yahoshua). The Assembly of YHWHOSANA is not affiliated with any other Sacred Name body.

The Assembly is Pentecostal in that it accepts the baptism of the Holy Spirit, evidenced by speaking in new tongues and shown by a marked improvement in life as manifested by the fruits of the Spirit (Galatians 5:22-23). It is also separatist: members refrain from participation in any other religious group since all other religious groups exist in disobedience of the law of YHWH. The Roman Catholic Church is especially criticized as it is identified with the Great Whore (Revelation 17-18). The United States government is identified with the Beast of Revelation 13.

Within the assembly, sex gender roles are sharply defined. Only men may become ministers. Holidays are forbidden, though Passover is celebrated. Natural foods are eaten when possible, and, among other artificial foods, soda pop is expressly forbidden. Members are expected to show their separation by paying no income tax or social security and by not voting, using doctors, or attending Bible Schools. Baptism is by immersion.

Membership: The assembly has two congregations, one in Boone and one in Pueblo, Colorado.

★648★
CHURCH OF GOD (JERUSALEM)
Box 10184
Jerusalem, Israel

Elder A. N. Dugger was one of the leaders of the Church of God (Seventh Day) who advocated a more Biblical form of church government and who helped organize the Church of God with headquarters at Salem, West Virginia, in 1933. For several years he edited that church's periodical, *The Bible Advocate*. In spite of the controversies in which he was involved, the Church of God had, in 1931, sent Dugger to Jerusalem to begin work on moving the world headquarters there when possible. The work was established with the help of Elder Henry Cohen, a Hebrew Christian. At the reorganization meeting at Salem in 1933, a resolution passed to reaffirm movement of the headquarters to Jerusalem, and money was collected for a headquarters building. Then in the late 1930s Dugger became closely identified with C. O. Dodd, editor of the independent magazine *The Faith*, founded to promote the observance of the Old Testament feast days and then the Sacred Name movement. However, unlike Dodd, Dugger did not leave the Church of God. In 1950, following the merger of the Salem organization with the Church of God (Seventh Day), Dugger became a leader of one faction of the "Back to Salem" Movement, a small group which rejected the merger. However, the Seventh Day Church of God, reestablished in Salem, voted to reject the idea of a headquarters in Jerusalem. It was Dugger's goal to implement the original resolution looking toward the establishment of such a world headquarters. Spurred by Israel becoming an independent state, Dugger formed his own group, which goes under various names-- Church of God, Congregation of Elohim, and Family of Elohim. He moved to Jerusalem and, in 1953 began to publish *The Mount Zion Reporter*.

Dugger represented a middle ground between the Church of God (Seventh-Day) and the Sacred Name movement. While accepting basically the same theology as C. O. Dodd, with whom he coauthored an important apology for the Church of God (Seventh-Day), and using the Sacred Names, he did not emphasize the names as do other branches of the movement. He noted his distress at the various names for the mighty Creator and his Son which were being used in the Holy Land. "This is surely not pleasing to them, or to the Holy Angels in their presence...These names are in the Hebrew language."

Dugger's emphasis was much more on eschatology, particularly as it relates to the prophetic significance of reestablished Israel. According to Dugger's interpretation of prophecy, the Abomination of Desolation (Daniel 11:31) occurred in 622, the date of Mohammed's choosing of his disciples and beginning of his flight from Mecca. The exact date is either 622 or 632. Moslem calendars begin at that point, the Hegira. From that time, there would be 1,290 days (or years) until the consummation. In 1912, World War I began in the Balkans. After this began, there could be only one generation (45 years) until the end. Thus, the end is imminent.

In Jerusalem, Dugger began a Hewbrew-Christian ministry and publishing concern which prints books, numerous booklets and tracts, church school material, a correspondence course, and several periodicals. Members are scattered around the world. Following Dugger's death in 1975, the work of the church passed into the hands of his wife, Effie Dugger, his daughter Naomi Dugger Fauth, and his son-in-law, Gordon Fauth. They keep in touch with members and assemblies around the world and in the United States through their regular mailing and voluminous correspondence.

A. N. Dugger'sson Charles Andy Dugger broke with the family and began another group, Workers Together with Elohim.

Membership: Not reported.

Periodicals: *The Mount Zion Reporter*, Box 10184, Jerusalem 91101, Israel.

Sources: A. N. Dugger and C. O. Dodd, *A History of the True Religion*. Jerusalem: Mt. Zion Reporter, 1968; A. N. Dugger, *A Bible Reading for the Home Fireside*. Jerusalem: "Mt. Zion" Press. Rept. Decatur, MI: Johnson Graphics, 1982.

**★649★
HOUSE OF YAHWEH (ABILENE, TEXAS)**
Box 242
Abilene, TX 79604

Among the people with whom Jacob Hawkins, founder of the House of Yahweh (Odessa, Texas), communicated his discovery of the true organization of the Called Out Ones of "Yah" was his brother Bill. Israyl Bill Hawkins joined his brother Jacob in building the sanctuary of the House of Yahweh in Odessa. However, in 1980, Israyl Bill Hawkins began to hold Sabbath services in his mobile home in Abilene, Texas. He had become convinced of the necessity of establishing the House of Yahweh according to Micah 4: 1-2. He taught that the formation of the House of Yahweh in Odessa by his brother was but the initial stirring by Yahweh that led to the establishment of Yahweh's true house, the House of Yahweh in Abilene. Israyl Bill Hawkins asserted that the chartering of his house in Abilene by the state of Texas and its recognition as a church by the Internal Revenue Service fulfilled Micah's prophecy. Through the IRS, the United States, a powerful nation, recognized the House of Yahweh and fulfilled the prophecy that the house would be established on the tops of the mountains (i.e., nations. Micah 4:1-2). Also, the house was established in Abilene, a place of gathering at a point due west of Jerusalem, to prepare the world for the second coming of Yahshua, just as the Biblical Abilene (Luke 3:1) had been the starting point of John the Baptist's preparation of Yahshuah's first coming.

The House of Yahweh in Abilene is organized similarly to the House of Yahweh in Odessa, with which it shares a common set of beliefs.

Membership: Not reported. The bimonthly periodical is mailed to several hundred believers around the United States.

Periodicals: *The Prophetic Word*, Box 2442, Abilene, TX 79604.

Sources: *Yahweh's Passover and Yahshua's Memorial*. Abilene, TX: House of Yahweh, n.d.

★650★
HOUSE OF YAHWEH (ODESSA, TEXAS)
% Jacob Hawkins
Box 4938
Odessa, TX 79760

The House of Yahweh was founded in 1973 in Nazareth, Israel, by Jacob Hawkins, an American who had gone to Israel in 1967 to work on a kibbutz in the Negev. Hawkins learned of the discovery in 1973 of an ancient sanctuary dating to the first century that had "House of Yahweh" engraved over its entrance in Hebrew. In his own study of Scripture, he had determined that the name of the people called out by Yahweh was the "House of Yahweh." Thus he was led to found Yahweh's House anew. He began to correspond with people about his discovery and his subsequent actions. In 1973 he returned to the United States and built a sanctuary of the House of Yahweh in Odessa, Texas.

Members of the House of Yahweh direct their worship to Yahweh the Father, whose title is Elohim, and His son Yahshua, whose title is Messiah. Yahshua's shed blood cleanses believers from sin if they keep the Ten Commandments, Yahweh's law. Members tithe one-tenth of their income to the support of the ministry. They are sabbatarians.

The House of Yahweh observes the Old Testament feast days as mentioned in Leviticus 23. Further, it teaches that all believers must come together for the feasts of Passover, Pentecost, and Tabernacles, and members travel from around the United States and the world for these events. In like measure, holidays such as Christmas, Easter, Halloween, and Sunday as a day of worship are condemned as pagan and un-Biblical. Yahshua was born in the spring (around Passover), not in December.

The House of Yahweh is organized on a Biblical pattern with twelve apostles and seventy elders.

Membership: Not reported. In 1980 the House of Yahweh reported congregations in the United States, Israel, India, South Africa, West Africa, Burma, Australia, and Belgium.

Periodicals: *The Prophetic Watchman*, Jacob Hawkins, Box 4938, Odessa, TX 79760.

Sources: *Directory of Sabbath-Observing Groups.* Fairview, OK: Bible Sabbath Association, 1980.

★651★
MISSIONARY DISPENSARY BIBLE RESEARCH
Box 5296
Buena Park, CA 90622

Associated with the Assembly of Yahvah is the Missionary Dispensary Bible Research, headquartered in Buena Park, California. The group is responsible for the production of *The Restoration of Original Sacred Name Bible* which used Yahvah, Elohim, and Yahshua for the Sacred Names. It is based on Joseph B. Rotherham's translation but uses the King James Version's form of paragraphing. Rotherham was widely employed by the Jehovah's Witnesses and included a paragraph entitled "The Name Suggested" in the introduction to his translation. No reference is made to *The Holy Name Bible* translated by A. B. Traina of the Scripture Research Asociation.

Membership: Not reported. Centers of operation were reported in Ward, Arkansas; Winfield, Alabama; and Winston, Ontario, Canada.

★652★
NEW LIFE FELLOWSHIP
Box 75
Natural Dam, AR 72948

The New Life Fellowship was formed by nine ministers, representing four Sacred Name congregations, who gathered at Van Buren, Arkansas, and drew up the doctrinal statement "A Declaration of Those Things Most Commonly Believed Among Us." This group differs from most other Sacred Name organizations in its adoption of a Pentecostal perspective that places strong emphasis upon the gifts of the Spirit as outlined in Corinthians 1:12 and initially evidenced by speaking in tongues. They also believe in the organization of the church under the five-fold ministry as outlined in Ephesians 4:11: apostles, prophets, evangelists, pastors, and teachers lead the church fellowship as a whole. Locally, elders and deacons lead individual congregations.

At the time of the fellowship's formation, a 260-acre tract of land near Natural Dam, Arkansas, was purchased for the purpose of establishing an intentional community. The New Life Community is attached to the congregation at Van Buren. The New Life Fellowship accepts the Sacred Name emphases and acknowledges Yahweh as the Father Creator and Yahshua as His son and humanity's Savior. Weekly worship is on the seventh-day Sabbath (Saturday), and the Old Testament feasts are kept. The annual feast of tabernacles is a time for members of the fellowship to gather from around the United States. Missionary work is supported in Haiti and in Europe.

Membership: The fellowship began with four congregations in Van Buren, Arkansas; Henryetta, Oklahoma; Murrysville, Pennsylvania; and Jim Falls, Wisconsin. In 1983 a congregation in Eaton Rapids, Michigan was added.

Periodicals: *The Olive Tree*, Box 805, Henryetta, OK 74437.

Sources: *Directory of Sabbath-Keeping Groups.* Fairview, OK: Bible Sabbath Association, 1980.

★653★

SCRIPTURE RESEARCH ASSOCIATION
14410 S. Springfield Rd.
Brandywine, MD 20613

Among the first people to accept the ideas of the Sacred Name movement was A. B. Traina, pastor of the independent sabbatarian Gospel Kingdom Assembly in Irvington, New Jersey. For many years Traina was affiliated with the Assembly of Yahweh at Eaton Rapids, Michigan and frequently wrote for *The Faith*, the magazine begun by C. O. Dodd. One of the early projects of the Assemblies of Yahweh was to be the publication of a translation of the Bible using the Sacred Name, but none was ever forthcoming. Hence, during the 1940s, Traina organized the Scripture Research Association from his New Jersey assembly, and in 1950 issued the *Sacred Name New Testament*. The complete *Holy Name Bible* appeared in 1963.

Traina, the Scripture Research Association and the Gospel Kingdom Assembly, follow the beliefs of the Assemblies of Yahweh (Michigan), who use his translation. It was Traina's opinion that the New Testament was originally written in Hebrew, not Greek, and that only in the fourth century did the Nicolaitanes substitute the names of the Greek deities "Kurios" and "Theos" for the originals. "God" came into the language from German in the seventh century.

Membership: Not reported.

Sources: A. B. Traina, *The Holy Name Bible*. Brandywine, MD: The Scripture Research Association, 1980.

★654★

WORKERS TOGETHER WITH ELOHIM
Box 14411
Jerusalem, Israel

Following the death of A. N. Dugger, his son Charles Andy Dugger was accused of doctrinal deviation as well as adultery and was removed from the board of the Church of God (Jerusalem). With his followers, he quickly established his own organization and began to publish *The Jerusalem Reporter*, similar in appearance and format to *The Mount Zion Reporter* published by his father's church. He called his new group Workers Together with Elohim.

Workers Together with Elohim are thorough-going Sacred Name people and use all of the Hebrew transliterations in referring to the deity. (Elohim is the Hebrew word commonly translated as "God" in most English-language Bibles.) Church members also follow the Old Testament ritual and food laws. In particular, they take quite literally the admonition in Numbers 15:38-40 and add blue fringes to all their garments.

Operating out of Jerusalem, the Workers Together with Elohim continue to operate an organization quite similar to the Church of God (Jerusalem), and they relate to an American constituency. In Jerusalem, they have a strong mission which distributes Bibles in both Hebrew and Russian languages. No membership figures are available.

Membership: Not reported.

Periodicals: *The Truth*, Box 14411, Jerusalem, Israel.

★655★

YAHWEH'S ASSEMBLY IN MESSIAH
Rte. 1, Box 364
Rocheport, MO 65279

Yahweh's Assembly in Messiah was incorporated in 1980 as the Assemblies of Yahweh in Messiah in Kansas, by former elders of the Assemblies of Yahweh, led by Jacob O. Meyer. Following the settlement of a lawsuit for trademark infringement, the Assembly took its present name in 1985. The Assembly follows the doctrine of its parent body. There were only administrative disagreements leading to the formation of the new organization. The Assembly is led by a Board of Directors.

The Assembly initiated a publication program which includes a correspondence course, a number of booklets, and several magazines. Cassettes of Sabbath messages are sent to those not affiliated with a local assembly, and traveling elders meet regularly with scattered members. Affiliated assemblies are found across the United States and Canada, in the Philippines, and in the Virgin Islands.

Membership: Not reported.

Periodicals: *The Master Key*, Box 578, Columbia, MO 65205-0578; *Beginning Anew*, Box 578, Columbia, MO 65205-0578.

Sources: *The Heavenly Father's Great Name*. Columbia, MO: Assemblies of Yahweh in Messiah, n.d.

Southcottites

★656★

CHRISTIAN ISRAELITES
% Mrs. M. Shafer
4592 Shafer Dr.
LaFayette, IN 47905

One of the largest groups of Joanna Southcott's followers came under the leadership of George Turner, who had previously been a disciple of visionary Richard Brothers. Southcott's visions and prophecies center upon a prediction that she would bear a son, Shiloh. After her false pregnancy, when no son was born, her followers awaited an answer to their disappointment. Turner's message to them was simple: "Shiloh lives! When old enough, he will return. Then Armageddon will begin. Get ready to play your part." A voice had told him that Shiloh had been taken to paradise, directly from the womb. He would appear on October 16, 1820, as a boy of six. When he did not appear, a second date, April 10, 1821, was set for his epiphany. In September of that year, Southcott and Turner died from disappointment at Shiloh's nonappearance.

John Wroe was a wool comber converted to Joanna's prophecies after having a vision of her with the child Shiloh. He had gained some recognition by his prophecies, especially several which foretold a death. In 1820, he gained even more recognition when he declared Turner's October 16th date a lie. His final step to leadership of Turner's followers came after he discerned adultery in the leader of a committee charged with examining him. In 1822, he organized those of Joanna's followers who accepted his leadership as the Christian Israelites.

Wroe's teachings were based upon the idea that Shiloh would return, but was awaiting a testing period of his people. The testing involved the observance of the Old Testament laws. All males were circumcised. Only kosher meat was to be eaten. Men and women were to wear distinctive (Quaker-like) dress, and men were forbidden to shave. There was to be total abstinence from spirits and tobacco. Everyone began Hebrew lessons.

Wroe's teachings had their ups and downs. He sent out missionaries to America and Australia, and groups were established throughout the island continent and northeastern United States. A branch in New York City was begun in 1844, and John L. Bishop organized the church a few years later. Wroe himself made four round-the-world tours. He lost most of his British movement to later prophets, but in America and Australia the movement has continued. By 1906, there were were 17 churches and almost 6,000 members, mostly in the Midwest.

Present-day Christian Israelites believe Wroe was a prophet. They are orthodox in their beliefs about God, Christ, and salvation, but differ in their belief about the special role of Israel in the last days. It is their belief that the 144,000 of Revelation 7:4 are a special class of Christians who will constitute physically redeemed Israel. These 144,000 will have redeemed physical bodies of flesh. The Christian Israelites aspire to be one of the 144,000 and, in order to attain that position, must live in harmony with Christ and in obedience to his word (Amos 3:3). This obedience includes observing and fulfilling the Old Testament laws as Jesus did (John 5:46-47). Only the sacrificial laws have been superseded. Members observe the Jewish holidays, but give them Christian meaning. While worshiping on Sunday, they believe that, eventually, Sabbath worship will be established, which they acknowledge with a Friday evening sabbath service. They believe that most Christians will be resurrected with spiritual bodies and will join the great multitide (Rev. 7:9). The unrighteous also will be resurrected, but shall "stand by" for 1,000 years until the second resurrection, at which time, Satan being overthrown, they will repent and be welcomed in the kingdom, though at a lower status than the righteous.

The mission of the Christian Israelite Church is to bring together "Israel" out of the nations and prepare it for the literal second coming. The church has a message for a Christian who wants to go on to perfection. Baptism by immersion for cleansing, after believing, is practiced, but the Lord's Supper is not. There is a naming ceremony for children. Members are conscientious objectors, but do vote. There is no paid clergy, only self-trained leaders. Members support the work by tithing.

Membership: In 1984 there were five congregations in Australia and one in Indianapolis, Indiana.

Periodicals: *Notes from Out Church Organ*, Christian Israelite Church, Goulburn Street, Singleton, N. S. W. 2330, Australia.

Sources: G. R. Balleine, *Past Finding Out*. New York: Macmillan, 1956; *The Life and Journal of John Wroe*. Ashton-Under-Lyne: Society of Christian Israelites, 1900.

★657★
ISRAELITE HOUSE OF DAVID
Box 1967
Benton Harbor, MI 49022

The Israelite House of David was founded in 1903 by Benjamin Purnell, believed by his followers to be the seventh messenger of Revelation 10:7. He is also identified as Shiloh (Revelation 12:5), the child born to Joanna Southcott and immediately taken into heaven for a period. Preceeding Purnell were six other messengers, beginning with Richard Brothers and then Southcott, each of whom sounded their message in order. After Southcott came George Turner, William Shaw, John Wroe and James Jezreel. Members of the Israelite House of David believe that in this present age the work of ingathering is occurring around the message of the seventh messenger.

After the death of John Wroe, founder of the Christian Israelites, other leaders appeared in England to claim his followers. Among these were a Mr. and Mrs. Head, leaders of the New House of Israel. Another leader was James White, known to his followers as James Jershom Jezreel, a name derived from Hosea's son (Hosea 1:4,11). Jezreel was the author of a book, *The Flying Scroll* (Zech. 5:1). In it, he asked of himself if he was Shiloh, the son whom Joanna Southcott had awaited. He answered "No!" Rather, he identified Shiloh with the seventh angel of the Book of Revelation. Jezreel was the sixth angel. A seventh angel (messenger) was yet to come. Jezreel's message prepared the way for Benjamin Purnell.

The Flying Scroll was addressed to the ten lost tribes of Israel. In it, creation was described. When the world was made and Satan rebelled (Isaiah 14:12), some spirits joined him willingly and some joined him through ignorance; others remained loyal to God. All these spirits are on earth today. The first are redeemable; the second can be saved by repentance; the third will be rewarded by redemption of the body. They will escape death and reign with Christ as the 144,000 Israelites during the millennium. Jezreel's followers become known for their long hair, looped in back and tucked under violet caps.

In his ideas about God, Jezreel departed from his orthodox precedessors. He taught that the Great Father-Spirit descended on Christ at baptism and left him on the cross. Jezreel's main emphasis, however, was the Divine Mother. Drawing on a number of Biblical texts (for example Gal. 4:23), he talked of a Great Mother-Spirit who shall help men and women withstand Satan's power.

Among Jezreel's converts was Clarissa Rogers, a fifteen-year-old. In 1878, three years after her conversion, she declared a voice had told her to go to America; thanks to her beauty and zeal, many converts were won. A second trip, this time with Jezreel, was made in 1880. Progress was rapid until Jezreel died in 1885 and splintering began.

In Detroit, Michael Keyfor Mills, a Baptist businessman, was converted. He sold everything, sent his money to England, and began a career selling *The Flying Scroll* door-to-door. In 1891 he had a Spirit baptism experience in which he fell into a trance and, along with other unusual happenings, his beard fell to the floor. He arose from this trance believing it his duty as Michael the Archangel to gather the 144,000 for the battle of Armageddon mentioned in Revelation. His belief was strengthened by the discovery that he possessed the power of healing. He gathered the Jezreelites into a commune, with himself as leader.

Detroit was stirred by his miracles, but even more by his proclamation that as Eve had seduced Adam into sin, he would seduce women into virtue. He was arrested, and when he refused to explain his meaning, was sentenced to four years' imprisonment. After being released, he took what followers were left to England. Though not considered a messenger, Mills introduced Purnell to the movement.

Purnell had been a member of Mills' colony but was expelled after three years. After eight years as an itinerant preacher, he founded a colony of his own, the Israelite House of David, in 1903. He purchased 800 acres at Benton Harbor, Michigan, and wrote a book, *The Star of Bethelem*. He identified himself as the seventh messenger whom Jezreel had said was yet to come. Purnell toured the world and gathered the followers of the previous messenger to God's chosen place in the United States. In 1913, eighty-six of the Christian Israelites from Australia

joined him. An Israelite House of David was also established in Australia.

The colony at Benton Harbor grew and prospered with an economy built on fruit growing and canning. Buildings, including a printing office, were erected. The heyday of the colony was the early 1920s, when there were 900 members. Then in 1922 Purnell was indicted for rape and disappeared. Two members filed suit for return of property and wages for their years of work without pay. The case created a national scandal, in which the court found that Purnell was using the House of David for personal gain and to cover his own vices, and that he had debauched a number of innocent young girls. Purnell surfaced in 1926 and was brought to trial the following year. Both he and his wife Mary were ordered to leave the colony was placed under a receivership. Within a few weeks however, he died of tuberculosis. Members did not believe the accusations brought against him. A more immediate problem, however, faced them. A division arose within the membership between Mary Purnell and Thomas Dewhirst. In 1930 Mary left the colony, taking possession of some former colony buildings across the street and establishing a rival center, now known as the Israelite House of David as Reorganized by Mary Purnell.

The House of David believes itself to be the gathering of the twelve of the Children of Israel who are to be carried over alive into the millennium (Revelation 7 & 14). The message of the seventh messenger is one of redemption of the body without death by following the Law of the Spirit of Life. It requires abstainance from all fleshly lusts. The group is also vegetarian; members do not cut their hair or beard; they are pacifists, and as a group live according to an apostolic order (communally).

Both the Australian and American branches remain. During the 1930s, under Dewhirst's leadership, though never gaining the strength they had during Purnell's lifetime, they had a prosperous period and became known for their several sports teams which toured the nation. An amusement park was a popular attraction for the region. During the succeeding decades, the colony has dwindled steadily. By the 1970s, fewer that 100, mostly elderly, remained.

Membership: In the mid-1980s there were less than 50 members.

Periodicals: *Shiloh's Messenger of Wisdom*, Box 1067, Benton Harbor, MI 49022.

Sources: Robert S. Fogarty, *The Righteous Remnant*. Kent, OH: Kent State University Press, 1981; *The What? Where? When? Why? and How? of the House of David*. Benton Harbor, MI: Israelite House of David, 1931; Francis Thorpe, *House of David Victory and Legal Troubles Reviewed*. Benton Harbor, MI: The Author, n.d.; Benjamin Purnell, *The Book of Dialogues*. Benton Harbor, MI: Israelite House of David, 1912. 3 Vols.; Benjamin

Purnell, *The Book of Wisdom*. Benton Harbor, MI: Israelite House of David. n.d. 7 Vols.

★658★
ISRAELITE HOUSE OF DAVID AS
 REORGANIZED BY MARY PURNELL
Box 187
Benton Harbor, MI 49022

Following the death of Benjamin Purnell, the founder of the Israelite House of David, members were divided in their loyalty between Mary Purnell, Benjamin's widow, and prominent leader Thomas Dewhirst. Following her being locked out of the group's facilities, Mary Purnell filed suit. In 1930 an out-of-court settlement awarded Mary some of the colony's property, across the street from the present Israelite House of David. With her supporters, Mary formed a new orgaization incorporated as the Israelite House of David as Reorganized by Mary Purnell. She has come to be identified by her followers as the woman clothed with the sun and with the moon at her feet, the mother of Shiloh (Benjamin Purnell). Beliefs generally follow those of the Israelite House of David with theexception of the opinions held concerning the role of Mary Purnell. Her books are now distributed, along with those of her husband, by the group. She died in 1953.

Membership: There were less than 50 members in the mid-l980s.

Periodicals: *The New Shiloh Messenger*, Box 187, Benton Harbor, MI 49022.

Sources: Robert S. Fogarty, *The Righteous Remnant*. Kent, OH: Kent State University Press, 1981; Mary Purnell, *The Comforter, The Mother's Book*. Benton Harbor, MI: Israelite House of David, 1926. 4 Vols.; Francis Thorpe, *House of David Victory and Legal Troubles Reviewed*. Benton Harbor, MI: The Author, n.d,; Benjamin Purnell, *Shiloh's Wisdom*. Benton Harbor, MI: Israelite House of David as Reorganized by Mary Purnell, n.d. 4 Vols.

Miscellaneous Adventists

★659★
REMNANT CHURCH
Current address not obtained for this edition.

The Remnant Church originated in the early 1950s in the visions of Mrs. Tracy B. Bizich of Sewickley, Pennsylvania. In 1951, Ellen G. White, founder of the Seventh-Day Adventist Church reportedly appeared and told her that that church had backslidden beyond recovery. She was also told that her spiritual name was "the Bee" and that she would soon be joined by a man whose spiritual name would be "the Fly." Together, they would begin to gather the 144,000 mentioned in Revelation 14:1-3, who would be the only ones to enter the new earth after its destruction, which is imminent.

In 1957, Mrs. Bizich met Elsworth Thomas Kaiser (b. 1901), a railroad worker from Rochester, New York. He, too, had many visionary experiences, which Mrs. Bizich was able to interpret for him. She recognized him as "the Fly" and designated him an elder and the first minister of the Remnant Church. That same year, a congregation was founded in Rochester.

According to the Remnant Church, 1957 marked the beginning of the end of the world. In 1962, the first angel blew his trumpet (Rev. 8:7); 1965 brought a foretaste of the burning up of all the green grass. The Remnant Church is very strict. Members are required to be obedient to superiors, observe the Sabbath, dress modestly, share a community of goods, live in sinless purity, eat without question the food placed before them, clean their quarters, be diligent in study, and wear uniforms (gray for women and tan for males). Members are forbidden to go to physicians (although the use of herbs and leaves is permitted, since these are for the healing of the nations); take others to court except in defense of the Remnant; make distinctions on the basis of race; use drugs, alcohol, or tobacco; or attend other church services. The Lord's Supper is celebrated annually. Baptism is by immersion, and full baptism includes baptism with the Spirit.

The 144,000 will perform active spiritual work in the world until they are all caught up in the Spirit. Some souls have already risen from their graves and have preached in the spirit to friends and relatives.

Membership: Not reported. When last encountered in the mid-1970s, the church had only a few members.

★660★
SHILOH TRUE LIGHT CHURCH OF CHRIST
% Elder James Ronnie Purser
4001 Sheridan Rd.
Charlotte, NC 28205

Shiloh True Light Church of Christ was formed in 1870 by Cunningham Boyle, a Methodist layman. Boyle had been a student of Bible chronology and reported that he had received an understanding of God, through the study of Revelation, that 7,000 years was the full time allotted by God from creaton to judgment. The seven days of creaton (1,000 years each) are symbolic of the period. Members further believe that we are living in the last generation (of 100 years), which began in 1870. In 1970, Jesus Christ was supposed to appear and the millennium begin. The judgment will follow the millennium.

The articles of faith of the church profess belief in God, whose attributes are mercy, justice, truth, omniscience, omnipotence, omnipresence, and immutability; the Bible; Jesus as God's Son; the personal devil; man as body and soul; the one true church of Christ; and the ordinances of baptism and the Lord's Supper. The group also states that all non-material things were not created, and hence cannot be destroyed. Jesus is seen as the offspring of God, existing in the Father as an embryo until the beginning of creation, at which time he was separated and made equal to God by the gift of the divine attributes. Man was separated on the sixth day of creation so that a time of probation could be allowed. Man was created as an angel, but fell by yielding to temptation.

Headquarters of Shiloh True Light Church are in Charlotte, North Carolina. The group accepted the failure of the 1970 prophecy and is continuing in spite of it. The Church is congregationally ruled and meets in annual conferences.

Membership: Not reported. At last report, in the early 1970s, there were approximately 450 members in 4 congregations, all in Union and Mecklenburg Counties, North Carolina.

★661★
SHILOH TRUE LIGHT CHURCH OF CHRIST (BRASWELL)
Monroe, NC 28110

In 1969, a dispute arose within the leadership of Shiloh True Light Church when Elder Herman Flake Braswell and Mr. Clyde M. Huntley claimed to have been elected bishop and elder, respectively, of the church. At a meeting on December 26, 1969, Braswell was elected bishop and appointed Huntley as elder. James Rommie Purser, the church's elder, disputed Braswell's claims. The court ruled in Purser's favor. It declared that Shiloh True Light Church was congregationally ruled and enjoined Braswell from disturbing its life and worship.

The disruption occurred just prior to the date in which a hundred-year old prophecy made by Cunningham Boyle, founder of the Shiloh True Light Church, was to be fulfilled. Jesus was to appear in 1970. The Braswell faction of the church approached the date of Christ's coming in a more radical way that did the main body. Braswell closed his upholstery business; others left their jobs. Huntley committed suicide in May, 1970, apparently because of the failure of the prophecy. After the failure, some left the church, but most tried to reestablish their normal church activities and secular activities. Braswell, at last report, had reopened his business.

Membership: Not reported. There is estimated to be less than 100 members.

★662★
STAR OF TRUTH FOUNDATION
(Defunct)

The Star of Truth was the ministry of Ruth H. Lang and V. Jean Mallatt of Galena, Kansas. It was their belief that the fullness of time had come (Eph. 1:10, Mk. 16:7), and

a new age was upon us. Each new age (or period of administration) is initiated by God's representatives giving birth to the Christ. The previous age was begun by Mary, who conceived and brought forth the Son of the most high God. This Son was not a physical birth, but a spiritual being which she conceived within the consciousness of her own being. As God's representative, Mary was told to go and tell the brethren (Matt. 28:7), and a new pattern was set for the age.

It was the Foundation's belief that This period was the day for a new birthing of the Christ. The representative of God for this new birth would be Ruth Lang. In the passing dispensation, the Comforter was given; in the new age, the Spirit of truth which will abide forever would be given. Paul ran ahead of time and saw this new age. He is thus the establisher of it. At one time, Ruth thought of herself as a reincarnation of Paul. She then came to see him as the resurrected one in Christ, who has come in her to resurrect her also.

The Star of Truth Foundation published *The Sparkler* bimonthly. Ms. Lang also wrote a number of pamphlets. The publications tied together the small band of believers, who were scattered across the United States. As of 1984, the Star of Truth Foundation has been disbanded.

★663★
TRUE CHURCH
Current address not obtained for this edition.

The True Church began in 1930 in the home of Mina Blanc Orth in Seattle, Washington. Ms. Orth, the daughter of Baptist home missionaries in Julian, California, had opened her home to George J. Sherwin (b. 1879) to teach a Bible class. In 1937, she took over leadership of the group, becoming the authoress of a dozen books and pamphlets which contain the basics of the True Church's teaching. Beginning in 1950, she engaged in an extensive radio ministry.

The beliefs of the True Church were based upon an allegorical (spiritual) interpretation of Scripture. The church taught that God's Word is understood in "God's three-way light," the literal light, the historical light, and the symbolic, or spiritual light. Numbers are a focus of the interpretation which holds that the Bible is "formed over a numeric system divisible by seven," the number of perfection. Typical elucidation of texts is seen in the Song of Solomon 6:8, an allegorical description of churchanity: There are sixty queens (Catholicism) and eight concubines (Protestantism) and maidens without number (Modernism). God is Father and Son. The personhood of the Holy Spirit is denied."

There was a strong expectancy of the imminent return of Christ. During the 1940s, a date between 1950 and 1967 seemed a possible time for that return. World War III, the third War of Revelation 11:14, would begin in the near future. Churchanity would be destroyed; only a remnant of Anglo-Saxon nations (Israel) and the Jews in Palestine would survive. Upon Christ's return, he would destroy all systems of men in opposition to him and set up a new government, symbolized by Job's seven new sons (Job 43:13) to rule during the millennium.

Membership: Not reported. The True Church is organized into small groups meeting in homes. There were an estimated 600 such centers in the United States and Canada in 1968. Headquarters were in Seattle.

British Israelism

★664★
ANGLO-SAXON FEDERATION OF AMERICA
Box 177
Merrimac, MA 01860

The longest-lived and largest group of the Anglo-Israel movement is the Anglo-Saxon Federation of America headed by Howard B. Rand, lawyer and Bible student. Rand started a small Anglo-Saxon group in his home in 1928, and as the group grew he began to publish *The Bulletin* as a periodical. He also met W. C. Cameron (editor of Henry Ford's *Dearborn (Michigan) Independent*) who, by 1933, had become president of the newly founded Anglo-Saxon Federation. With Cameron's help, a convention of the Anglo-Israelite groups met in Detroit under Rand's leadership. While unable to unite the groups, Rand was able to launch the Federation.

The position of the Federation is spelled out in *The Pattern of History*, an introductory pamphlet. The Bible is the central document; it is to be understood as the history of Israel, past, present and future, and therefore presents quite literally a pattern of history. The key item in Biblical interpretation is identifying Israel. The history of Israel really begins with God's covenant and promises to Abraham (Genesis 15ff.) and passes on through Isaac, Jacob (who was given the name Israel), and the ten tribes. The covenant was especially focused in Joseph's sons, Ephraim and Manasseh, who were to become the head of all of Israel (Genesis 48). Present-day Israel is found by determining which nation or race fulfills God's promises made in the Old Testament. Israel was to be a powerful nation living northwest of Palestine, a mistress of the earth who holds a great heathen empire in dominion, the chief missionary power of the earth, a nation immune to defeat in war. Part of Israel was to have split off and become a great people in its own right. Such a description can fit only Great Britain and the United States, who split off from her.

In the 1930s and 1940s, groups affiliated with the Federation could be found around the country. From the Destiny Publishers, a large number of books and pamphlets were produced, as were the monthly issues of *Destiny Magazine*. The contents of these materials dealt largely with current events interpreted in terms of the British-Israelite stance. As of the mid-1970s, most of this following had dissolved. Precise statistics are not available. *Destiny Magazine* ceased publication in 1969 and has been replaced with a much more modest newsletter. Books are still published and distributed, and membership is still open in the Federation.

Membership: Not reported.

Periodicals: *Destiny Editorial Letter Service*, Box 177, Merrimac, MA 01860.

Sources: *The Pattern of History*. Merrimac, MA: Destiny Publishers, 1961; *The Covenant People*. Merrimac, MA: Destiny Publishers, 1966; Howard B. Rand, *Digest of Divine Law*. Haverhill, MA: Destiny Publishers, 1943; M. H. Gayer, *The Heritage of the Anglo-Saxon Race*. Haverhill, MA: Destiny Publishers, 1941.

★665★
CALVARY FELLOWSHIPS, INC.
Box 128
Rainer, WA 98576

The Calvary Fellowships, Inc., is a ministry centered upon Woodbrook Chapel pastored by the Reverend Clyde Edminster in Tacoma, Washington. Calvary Fellowships differs from other British-Israel ministries in that it has allowed Pentecostalism to become established in its midst--it seeks the baptism of the Holy Spirit as signified by speaking in tongues. Each summer it sponsors the Western Bible Conference which brings together followers of like-minded churches in the Northwest and British Columbia.

Edminster was one of several graduates of the short-lived Dayton Theological Seminary. Through his periodical, *Christ Is the Answer*, he keeps in touch with other graduates, often leading independent congregations. These graduates include Pastor David Bruggeman of the Church of the Covenants in River Forest, Illinois; Pastor Robert Thornton of Christ's Gospel Fellowship of Spokane and editor of *Trumpet*, a monthly periodical; and Pastor Warren Stewart of Kent, Washington.

Membership: Not reported.

Periodicals: *Christ Is the Answer*, Box 128, Rainer, WA 98576.

★666★
CHRISTIAN RESEARCH, INC.
Current address not obtained for this edition.

Christian Research, Inc., was a British-Israelite congregation based in Minneapolis, Minnesota headed by Gerka Koch and formed "for the purpose of aligning citizens to needed action to preserve our Christian heritage." The major documents circulated and studied by

Christian Research students are the following: 1) *Christian History of the Constitution of the United States of America*, compiled by Verna M. Hall, a massive volume on Christian values behind the Constitution, and 2) *An Open Letter to Ministers Who Believe the Jews are Israel* by Sheldon Emry. The Emry tract takes the position that Judaism is a product of the Babylonian exile and, hence, cannot be pre-exilic Israel. Israel is the Caucasian race.

The ideas of Christian Research were being spread through a group in Minneapolis. inneapolis. They published the bimonthly periodical *Facts for Action*, worked for conservative political candidates, distributed literature around the country, and took part in public programs. Closely associated with Christian Research is the Lord's Covenant Church of Phoenix, Arizona, led by former Christian Research vice-president Sheldon Emry. Emry is a prolific writer, and he speaks weekly over a Phoenix station on the "America's Promise" broadcast.

Membership: Not reported.

Periodicals: *America's Promise Newsletter*, Box 30000, Phoenix, AZ 85046.

Sources: Verna N. Hall, comp., *Christian History of the Constitution*. San Francisco, CA: The American Christian Constitution Press, 1960.

★667★
CHURCH OF ISRAEL
Box 62-83
Schell City, MO 64783

Though born within the context of Mormonism, the Church of Israel has largely dropped the elements of Latter Day Saint belief and moved into an acceptance of the Identity message of British Israelism. The church was formed in 1972 by Daniel Gayman and approximately thirty-five members of a small congregation called the Church of Christ at Halley's Bluff (a.k.a. the Church of Christ at Zion's Retreat), located in rural Vernon County, Missouri (discussed elsewhere in this volume). This Church of Christ was a splinter of the Church of Christ (Temple Lot) which claims to be the original Church of Christ founded by Mormon prophet Joseph Smith, Jr.. During the 1960s, Daniel Gayman, the son of one of the church's founders, became a pastor and was appointed to edit the church's periodical, *Zion's Restorer*. Gayman began almost immediately to come into open conflict with the church leaders because he promoted some extreme racist views on white supremacy. He also used the church's youth camp as a seminary for white supremists and as a training ground in the use of weapons and military defense. Both anti-black and anti-Semitic articles appeared regularly in *Zion's Reporter*.

Tension within the church culminated in 1972 when Gayman called a church meeting in which two bishops were deposed and new officers elected. The name of the church's periodical was changed to *Zion's Watchman* and the priesthood totally dissolved. The bishops dismissed at this meeting, together with their supporters, filed suit. Eventually the court ruled in their favor, and Gayman's faction was forced to return most of the property (all but 20 of the 441 acres) and was denied use of the name "Church of Christ." In 1974 Gayman's group reincorporated as the Church of Our Christian Heritage. It adopted its present name in 1981.

The Church of Israel has almost completely left its Mormon roots and no longer uses the Book of Mormon or other Mormon writings. It does use both the Apocrypha and the Old Testament pseudophygraphal literature, but does not ascribe to the authority of the Bible. The teachings of Joseph Smith have been replaced with the Kingdom Identity Message and its white Anglo-Saxon supremacy perspectives, which identifies Anglo-Saxons as the literal descendents of the Israel of the Old Testament. Gayman also sees the British people as the principle bearers of the first-century Christian Church's apostolic succession which was brought to England by Joseph of Arimathea soon after Jesus's resurrection.

Gayman has also developed a variation of the two-seed-in-the-spirit theory first popularized by Daniel Parker, a nineteenth-century Baptist minister. Basing his interpretation on Genesis 3:15, Parker argued that Abel and Cain represented two seeds carried by the human race, the former of God and Adam, the latter of Satan. Every person was born of the two seeds and was thus predestined from the beginning to be part of God's family or Satan's dominion. Gayman developed Parker's idea along racial lines. He taught that white Anglo-Saxons have descended from Seth (the substitute for the murdered Abel). Blacks and Jews descend from Cain, a product of Satan's impregnating Eve.

Following the court's decision and the resultant loss of land and buildings, Gayman recovered quickly. In 1977-78, a chapel was constructed at Nevada, Missouri, and both Christian Heritage Academy (an elementary school) and a ministerial training school were opened. Gayman actively promoted the church around the country as a popular speaker at Kingdom Identity gatherings. A Home Bible Study Program had enrolled 125 by 1982.

In 1981, at the time the present name was adopted, a total reorganization took place. The church was divided into twelve dioceses, each designated by one of the twelve tribes of Israel. (Note: There is no diocese for Joseph; rather, there are two tribes for Joseph's son, Manasseh and Ephraim. There is also no tribe for Levi. The Levites, seen as scattered throughout the nations, represent a continuing priesthood.) Each diocese is headed by a bishop. Gayman assumed the bishopric over the tribe of Manasseh, i.e. the United States. Ephraim is equated with the British Commonwealth, and the other dioceses represent the various northern and western European nations. Only the diocese of Manasseh has been activated.

Membership: At last report, the Church of Israel has two congregations, one in Schell City , Missouri and one in York, Pennsylvania. The Church has an estimated several hundred members.

Periodicals: *The Watchman*, Box 62-83, Schell City, MO 64783.

Sources: Dan Gayman, *The Holy Bible, the Book of Adam's Race*. Nevada, MO: The Church of Our Christian Heritage, 1978; Dan Gayman, *The Two Seeds of Genesis*. Nevada, MO: The Church of Our Christian Heritage, 1978; Dan Gayman, *White Christian Roots*. Nevada, MO: The Church of Our Christian Heritage, 1978; Alan M. Schwartz et al., "The ‚Identity Churches': A Theology of Hate" in a special issue of *ADL Facts*, vol. 28, no. 1 (Spring 1983).

★668★
COVENANT, THE SWORD AND THE ARM OF THE LORD
Rte. 1, Box 128
Pontiac, MO 65729

The Covenant, the Sword and the Arm of the Lord (C.S.A) was founded in the mid-1970s by James D. Ellison, an Identity minister in San Antonio, Texas. He had had a vision of the coming collapse of the American society and decided to flee the city and establish a survivalist community in the Ozark Mountains. He moved to Elijah, Missouri, and then in 1976 purchased a 224-acre tract of land in Arkansas, adjacent to the Missouri border, near Pontiac, Missouri. The commune, called Zarephath-Horeb, is viewed as a purging place, the name having been adopted after its Biblical counterpart.

The C.S.A. teaches the Kingdom Identity Message; i.e., it identifies the white Anglo-Saxon race as the literal descendents of Ancient Israel and hence the heir to the covenants and promises God made to Israel. The Anglo-Saxons have been called to be the light of the world, and black people were created for perpetual servitude. The C.S.A. also believes the Bible teaches that the two-edged sword of God's Spirit is coming soon in judgment to the earth, and God's Arm will be manifest to administer that judgment. The C.S.A. will be that Arm of God. In preparation for the difficult times ahead, the community is storing food and stockpiling weapons and ammunition.

The C.S.A., in line with Ellison's vision, expects the imminent collapse of America, the sign of judgment, and an ensuing war. In that war (Armageddon) whites will be set against Jews, blacks, homosexuals, witches, Satanists, and foreign enemies. At that point, the settlement in Arkansas will become a Christian haven.

The community is largely self-supporting. A farm produces much of the food. Education and medical services are provided internally, and most families live without electricity or plumbing.

Since its founding, the C.S.A. has been a matter of concern for law-enforcement officials. Following a revelation in 1978, the group began to acquire sophisticated weaponry adequate for modern warfare. In 1981 it opened a survival school and gave training to the public in the use of firearms and survivalism. In 1984 a warrant was issued for Ellison's arrest when he failed to appear before a grand jury investigating the murder of an Arkansas state trooper. A gun found in the possession of the accused was registered to Ellison. In spite of a splintering in the winter of 1981-82 over the continuance of paramilitary training and the leaving of those most in favor, the tension which has grown out of the C.S.A.'s potential for violence remains an unresolved concern.

In April 1985 agents of the F.B.I. surrounded C.S.A. and arrested Ellison and several members on federal racketeering charges.

Membership: Less than 100 people live at the Zarephath-Horeb settlement, but several hundred nonresident supporters can be found across the South and Midwest.

Periodicals: *C. S. A. Journal*, Route 1, Box 128, Pontiac, MO 65729.

Remarks: Recently, four members of C.S.A. were sentenced to prison terms. Ellison received 20 years for racketeering. Others receiving lesser sentences were Kerry Noble, Kent Michael Yates, and William Thomas.

Sources: Alan M. Schwartz et al., "The Identity Churches': A Theology of Hate." in a special issue of *ADL Facts* vol. 28, no. 1 (Spring 1983).

★669★
HOUSE OF PRAYER FOR ALL PEOPLE
Box 837
Denver, CO 80201

The House of Prayer for All People was founded in Denver, Colorado by William Lester Blessing (1900-1984) in 1941. A member of the Church of the United Brethren in Christ, he withdrew in 1927 and became an independent evangelist. He began to use the name House of Prayer for All People as early as 1932. He identified his audience as "Anglo-Saxon, Cymric, and Scandinavian Israelites" with a definite interest in establishing the Kingdom politically and economically on earth. The goal of his work was the restoration of the church (The temple of Yahveh) in the heart of Israel and the earth as his dominion. Great Britain and the United States are the latter-day Israel of Yahveh.

Blessing considered himself, the House of Prayer, and *Showers of Blessing*, the monthly periodical established in 1942, to be together the Voice of the Seventh Angel (VOTSA) of Revelation 10:7 and 11:15. VOTSA will usher in the reestablishment of the Church and the Kingdom of Yahveh. (Early in his work he had been influenced by the Sacred Name movement and decided that Yahveh and Yahshua to be the proper name of the Creator and Messiah respectively (see the discussion of the Sacred Name movement elsewhere in this volume).

According to Blessing's teachings, the First Recovery of Israel took place between the birth of Yahshua (Jesus) and 70 C.E.. After His crucifixion, Christ and 12,000 members from each tribe of Israel were resurrected. They returned in power on Pentecost, and the Apostolic ministry was begun. During this time, all of the New Testament was written under the work of the Holy Spirit, the Mother. The second coming occurred in 70 C.E., at which time the temple in Jerusalem was destroyed, the dead raised, and the saints raptured. The age came to an end. Since that time, there has not been a true church of Christ on earth; the world has existed in the "times of the Gentiles." However, there has been a remnant on earth, through whom Yahveh has spoken. In 1809, the first of the seven angels began to be heard in the person of Alexander Campbell. He was followed by Joseph Smith, Jr., Ellen G. White, Charles Taze Russell, Benjamin Purnell, and A. P. Adams. In 1962 the desolation was ended according to the prophecy of Daniel 12:12, and mankind is now in the wilderness, the time between the end of the present evil world and the coming of the righteous world. In the near future is a One World government--Babylon, the Mother of Harlots. Yahshua, the messiah, is also already here and will before 2000 A.D. reestablish the kingdom, to be administered by the remnant of his people.

The House of Prayer for All People believes that salvation is a contact between Yahwveh and the believer. Baptism is the last step in the plan of salvation. Members practice tithing and the kingdom meal, and worship on Sunday. Blessing had an interest in the Great Pyramid, unidentified flying objects, the hollow earth theory, and the psychical, and wrote on all of these.

From the headquarters in Denver, two periodicals are sent auto to adherents around the United States. Members have established local congregations. The minimum number for each h congregation is seventy adults, but ideally this includes seventy heads of family. Each local congregation is headed by seven servants and two bishops who are ordained by the evangelist (Blessing), the head of the church. Blessing was succeeded by his son, John David Blessing.

Membership: Not reported.

Periodicals: *Showers of Blessing*, Box 837, Denver, CO 80201; *Blessing Letter*, Box 837, Denver, CO 80201.

Sources: William Lester Blessing, *VOTSA*. Denver, CO: House of Prayer for All People, 1965; William Lester Blessing, *The Supreme Architect of the Universe*. Denver, CO: House of Prayer for All People, 1956; William Lester Blessing, *The Trial of Jesus*. Denver, CO: House of Prayer

for All People, 1955; William Lester Blessing, *Hallowed Be Thy Name*. Denver, CO: House of Prayer for All People, 1955; Willaim Lester Blessing, *More About Jesus*. Denver, CO: House of Prayer for All People, 1952.

★670★
NEW CHRISTIAN CRUSADE CHURCH
Box 426
Metairie, LA 70004

The New Christian Crusade Church was formed in 1971 by James K. Warner. In the 1960s Warner had been a member of the American Nazi Party headed by George Lincoln Rockwell. He broke with Rockwell and later associated himself with the National States Rights Party led by J.E. Stoner and with the Knights of the Ku Klux Klan. The New Christian Crusade Church teaches the Kingdom Identity Message, i.e., British Israelism, which identifies the present day Anglo-Saxon people as the literal racial descendents of Ancient Israel. The church believes that the present-day Jews come from the Khazars, a warrior people of Turkish-Mongol origin who inhabited the Volga River valleys near the Black Sea in the tenth century. The church is both anti-Semitic and antiblack.

Associated with the church is the Christian Defense League, an open membership organization founded by Warner for individuals who support the church's racial policies. Warner also established the Sons of Liberty, a publishing and literature-distribution company. The Knights of the Ku Klux Klan use the church's post office box as their mailing address.

Membership: The New Christian Crusade Church consists of a single independent congregation, which serves as the literature and information dissemination center for other independent British-Israel Churches in North America. Through its affiliated Christian Defence League, the church is in direct contact with people who share its beliefs throughout North America.

Periodicals: *The CDL Report*, Box 426, Metairie, LA 70004; *Christian Vanguard*, Box 426, Metairie, LA 70004. *The Crusader*, the periodical of the Knights of the Ku Klux Klan, is also distributed from the Church's headquarters.

★671★
PROPHETIC HERALD MINISTRY
(Defunct)

The Northwest has been a center of British-Israelite activity partly because of a strong concentration of believers in Vancouver, British Columbia, Canada. . Bethel Temple in Spokane, Washington, was one of the most active British-Israel centers serving, as headquarters of the Prophetic Herald Ministry and its leader, Alexander Schiffner. Founded in 1933, the ministry has concentrated on anti-Communism and anti-Roman Catholicism as major themes in its British-Israel message.

Schiffner taught that the United States is "branded as God's servant nation, Israel." Jacob gave his name "Israel" to both Ephraim and Manasseh, making thirteen tribes instead of the original twelve. The number thirteen is prominent in the history and founding of the United States. *The Prophetic Herald* proclaimed the new consummation of history, at which time true Israel and true Judah (Romans 2:28-29) will be restored as the terrestrial kingdom and head of nations over unrepentant Gentiles and heathen nations. The ministry also advocated the celestial restoration of true Israel to be joint heir with Christ. In an emphasis missing in other British-Israel ministries, Schiffner taught that "only those who receive God's Holy Spirit through repentance and faith in the Lord Jesus Christ" can be a part of the "chosen people," and that a consecrated life is essential to celestial glorification.

In 1970 approximately 40 radio stations carried the Prophetic Herald broadcasts from coast to coast. The monthly *Prophetic Herald* is mailed out to subscribers around the nation. Schiffner wrote a variety of pamphlets and booklets. His death ended the ministry, and in 1973 Bethel Temple was sold.

Liberal Family

An historical essay on this family is provided beginning on page 87.

Liberal

★672★
AMERICAN ASSOCIATION FOR THE ADVANCEMENT OF ATHEISM
Box 2832
San Diego, CA 92112

The oldest of the several atheist bodies in the United States is the American Association for the Advancement of Atheism founded by Charles Lee Smith (1887-1964) as an anti-religion/anti-God body. Smith, a lawyer, was converted to atheism from his reading of freethought books. After World War I he began to write for *The Truth Seeker*, an independent freethought journal published in New York City. In 1925, with his friend Freeman Hopwood, he founded the Association. Starting with little support and surrounded by a hostile environment, Smith engaged in a number of controversial activities, beginning with his involvement in the debates over Arkansas's antievolution law in 1928. He debated Christian ministers when the opportunity arose, the most famous being Aimee Semple McPherson, the flamboyant leader of the International Church of the Foursquare Gospel. From the publicity given his various activities, the Association grew. It peaked with approximately 2,000 members, and chapters could be found on some 20 college and university campuses. It sponsored periodic lectures, the Ingersoll Forum (named for Robert G. Ingersoll, the famous nineteenth-century freethinker), in New York City. In 1930 Smith purchased *The Truth Seeker*, which remained independent but closely identified with the Association. Hard hit by the Depression, the Association shrank, and most of his organized activities disappeared, though Smith continued to publish the magazine monthly.

Around 1950 Smith began to let his dislike of Jews and blacks become visible on the pages of *The Truth Seeker*, which began to publish an increasing number of racist and anti-Semitic articles. These led to further loss of support and the isolation of the Association from other atheist organizations. In 1964 Smith sold *The Truth Seeker* to James Hervey Johnson, and he moved it and the Association to San Diego. A few months later, Smith died and Johnson has continued as head of the Association and editor of the magazine.

The association believes religion to be a fraud and God nonexistent. It also teaches that the civilized white race is superior to Jews and blacks and actively distributes such books as *The Biological Jew*, by Eustace Mullins, *The International Jew*, by Henry Ford, *The Protocols of the Learned Elders of Zion*, and *Our Nordic Race*, by R. K. Hoskins. The association also stands for law and order, honest government, real liberty, freedom of the press and of speech, absolute separation of religion and government, and taxation of churches. All members must be atheists, a requirement which distinguishes the AAAA from many freethought organizations.

During the 1970s there were approximately 200 members, but no regular meetings. As with most atheist groups, there are too few members in most cities to support a separate meeting, thus members attend any local freethinkers' gathering available to them. In San Diego, the freethinkers gather on the birthdays of Thomas Paine (January 29) and Robert Ingersoll (August 7).

Membership: Not reported. It is estimated that there are only a few hundred members. In 1968 *The Truth Seeker* had about 1,000 subscribers.

Periodicals: *The Truth Seeker*, Box 2832, San Diego, CA 92112.

Sources: James Hervey Johnson, "Charles Smith: 1887-1964" in *The Truth Seeker* vol. 91, no. 11 (November 1964); Aimee Semple McPherson and Charles Lee Smith, *Debate: There Is a God!* Los Angeles: Foursquare Publications, n.d.; James Hervey Johnson, *Superior Men.* San Diego: The Author, 1949; Ira D. Cardiff, *"If Christ Came to New York."* New York: The American Association for the Advancement of Atheism, n.d. (1932); Kersey Graves, *The World's Sixteen Crucified Saviors.*

New York: The Truth Seeker, 1875; Frank Swancara, *Separation of Religion and Government*. New York: Truth Seeker Company, 1950.

★673★

AMERICAN ATHEISTS, INC.
% Madalyn Murray O'Hair
Box 2117
Austin, TX 78767

Possibly the most famous contemporary atheist in the United States is Madalyn Murray O'Hair (b.1919). She heads American Atheists, Inc., founded in 1969 in Austin Texas. O'Hair became a national figure in 1963 when the Supreme Court upheld her suit, which had been joined with a second like case, and ruled against the recitation of the Lord's Prayer and the Bible in the public schools, often mistakenly reported as outlawing prayer in the public schools. She next instituted a suit aimed at eliminating tax-exempt status for church-owned property. Soon after the second suit was filed, she moved from Baltimore to Honolulu, where she formed the International Free Thought Association of America. She eventually settled in Austin, Texas, where she founded Poor Richard's Universal Life Church, the Society of Separationists, and the Charles E. Stevens American Atheist Library and Archives. The Society of Separationists was superceded by American Atheists, Inc., the headquarters of which moved into the American Atheist Center in Austin, Texas in 1977. During the 1970s, O'Hair emerged as a popular and controversial speaker on atheism, frequently debating ministers in public meetings and on television. She instituted a number of lawsuits built around atheistic concerns, most of which failed. Her activities also led to many false rumors, including one that she had petitioned the U.S. Federal Communications Commission to ban religious broadcasting, the persistency of which forced several formal retractions by the FCC. In the midst of building American Atheists, she discovered members who rejected what they considered her autocratic leadership. She dropped some of these from membership, and they, joined by others who left, formed other atheist groups, the most prominent being the Freedom from Religion Foundation.

The group stands free from theism, which is equated with religion. Religion is viewed as a crutch which healthy people do not need. It is called superstitious and is considered to be supernatural nonsense. O'Hair has become deeply involved in various social causes: civil rights, peace, etc. She is actively anti-Christian and rejects the historicity of Jesus, a life after death, and the authority of the Bible.

The American Atheists' library, founded in 1965 and now housed at the Atheist Center, has more than 10,000 volumes and related material. The American Atheist Radio Series (1968-1973) was being heard on over 20 stations in 12 states at its peak. American Atheists is organized into a number of local chapters. Members in Petersburg, Indiana have opened an atheist museum. The organization promotes an annual national membership meeting.

At the annual convention in 1986, O'Hair resigned as president of American Atheists, but she continues to serve as presiding officer of its board of dirctors.

Membership: Not reported. In 1980 there were 25 chapters of American Atheists, Inc. across the United States. In 1986 the organization claimed 30,000 member families.

Periodicals: *The American Atheist*, Box 2117, Austin, TX 78768.

Remarks: Around 1980, William J. Murray, O'Hair's son and the subject of the lawsuit which first brought O'Hair into the public eye, converted to Christianity and left his mother's organization. He subsequently wrote a book about his life, one of several by former O'Hair associates which accuse her of presenting a distorted picture of some of her activities and the relative success of her organizational efforts.

Sources: Madalyn Murray O'Hair, *Bill Murray, the Bible and the Baltimore Board of Education*. Austin, TX: American Atheist Press, 1970; Madalyn Murray O'Hair, *What on Earth is an Atheist*. Austin, TX: American Atheist Press, 1969; Jane Kathry n Conrad, *Mad Madalyn*. Brighton, OH: The Author, 1983; William J. Murray, *My Life without God*. Nashville, TN: Thomas Nelson, 1982.

★674★

AMERICAN ETHICAL UNION
2 W. 64th St.
New York, NY 10023

Felix Adler (1851-1933), the son of a German-born rabbi in New York City, returned to Germany for his graduate education. During this time he encountered the higher criticism of the Bible and German philosophy, which together forced him to give up supernaturalism, God and religion, though leaving him with a strong sense of moral duty and a zeal to implement his ethical ideals. Upon his return to the United States, Adler joined the Free Religious Association (FRA), which had been formed by a group of radical Unitarians, and eventually became their president. During his time with the FRA, in 1876, Adler moved to New York City where he had found a group ready to put his activist philosophy into practice. He initiated the Ethical Culture Society on May 15, and almost immediately began work on educational projects-- first a kindergarten (at the time a radical educational notion) and then a Workingman's school, a grade school that perpetuated some of Adler's new ideas about educating children.

Adler's activist orientation led to a break with the FRA and in 1882 he resigned his presidency and left the FRA to devote all his full time to the Society. In succeeding years social settlements, legal aid, visiting nurse corps, and child law came under the society's attention.

Within a year of leaving the FRA, Adler saw a second Ethical Culture Society formed in Chicago. Another was formed in Philadelphia in 1885, and the fourth in St. Louis a year later. In 1892 the movement became international with the formation of a London society. These ethical societies, and later ones, banded together as the American Ethical Union.

The ethical societies are built on the belief that a creed or belief concerning God is relatively unimportant and not necessary to a meaningful life. The societies say a common basis for life and faith is the affirmation of the worth of every human being and the search for personal relationships in which that worth will be respected. Religion is seen as a way of life in this world, not an afterlife. Such perspectives have led to liberal social involvement on issues of racism, war and peace, citizenship training, and urbanization.

The societies in the American Ethical Union hold Sunday meetings for adults and children. The adult meeting centers on talks by a society leader on various ethical issues. An annual national assembly of the Ethical Cultural societies is held. Adler brought the American and European societies that had been formed under his guidance together as the International Humanist and Ethical Union in 1896.

Membership: Not reported. In 1972 there were 21 societies and fellowship groups.

Periodicals: *The Ethical Outlook*, 2 W. 64th Street, New York, NY 10023; *Ethical Platform*, 2 W. 64th Street, New York, NY 10023; *AEU Reports*, 2 W. 64th Street, New York, NY 10023.

Sources: Benny Kraut, *From Reform Judaism to Ethical Culture*. Cincinnati: Hebrew Union College Press, 1979; *The Fiftieth Anniversary of the Ethical Movement, 1876-1926*. New York: A. Appleton and Company, 1926; Howard B. Radest, *Toward Common Ground*. New York: Frederick Unger Publishing Co., 1969; David Saville Muzzey, *Ethical Religion*. New York: American Ethical Union, 1943.

★675★
AMERICAN HUMANIST ASSOCIATION
7 Harwood Dr.
Box 146
Amherst, NY 14226-0146

In the early twentieth century an aggressive humanist orientation developed among supporters of the American Unitarian Association, the Free Religious Association, and the American Ethical Union. At the time, members of these groups were still theistic. By the 1920s, however, some unitarians had become anti-theists. Their greatest spokesmen were John H. Dietrich, a Unitarian minister in Minneapolis, and Curtis W. Reese, secretary of the Western Unitarian Conference. Taking a keynote from science and from pragmatic philosophy, the anti-theists saw humanism as the only possible alternative to traditional re ligion. While Dietrich and Reese remained within the Unitarian structure, others of like mind left to found humanistic societies. The first two were founded in 1929, in New York by Charles Francis Potter and in Hollywood by Theodore Curtis Abell.

In 1933 eleven prominent humanist leaders issued "A Humanist Manifesto," the definitive statement of the movement. Among its signers were John Dewey, Harry Elmer Barnes, C. F. Potter and John Herman Randall. The statement called for a radical change in religious perspectives. Religion was seen as a tool for realizing the highest values in life. A religion adequate to the twentieth century regards the universe as self-existing, not cre ated, and regards man as part of nature evolved in its processes. Mind-body dualism, supernaturalism, theism, and even deism are rejected. The goal of life is the complete realization of human personality. Social and mental hygiene are priority items. Social control is a means to the abundant life for all. That statement was updated in 1973 by a "Humanist Manifesto II," which adds an additional emphasis on human responsibility toward humanity as a whole.

To bring some co ordination and fellowship nationally to the various independent humanist efforts, the American Humanist Association was formed in 1941. It accepts the basic perspective of the Humanist Manifesto, especially its call for the use of science for social welfare. Its social program has included a defense of human rights, religious freedoms, and freedom of thought; separation of church and state; planned parenthood; funeral reform; penal reform; conservation; and support of the United Nations.

The American Humanist Association is organized democratically; officers are elected by the general membership. Chapters are located across the country. An annual conference is held at various locations around the country. Over twenty percent of its members are students who are organized into campus chapters of the Humanist Student Union of North America. The church is also a member of the International Humanist and Ethical Union.

Among the most active advocates of humanism is Paul Kurtz, former editor of *The Humanist* and head of Prometheus Books, the major American publisher of humanist and freethought literature in recent decades. During the 1970s he led in the formation of the Committee for the Scientific Investigation of the Paranormal, whose quarterly *Skeptical Inquirer* is a major voice in the debunking of psychic and paranormal phenomena. After leaving *The Humanist* staff, he formed the Council for Democratic and Secular Humanism and began *Free Inquiry*. He also became a leading force in the formation of the Academy of Humanism, an organization to recognize leading humanists and disseminate humanist ideals and beliefs, and the Religion and Biblical Criticism Research Project, to disseminate the results of biblical criticism, especially claims seen by many humanists as unfounded, such as the divine inspiration of the Bible and the historicity of Jesus.

Membership: Not reported.

Periodicals: *The Humanist*, 7 Harwood Drive, Box 146, Amherst, NY 14226-0146.

Sources: Curtis W. Reese, *Humanism*. Chicago: Open Court Publishing Company, 1926; Curtis W. Reese, ed., *Humanist Sermons*. Chicago: Open Court Publishing Company, 1927; Paul Kurtz, ed., *The Humanist Alternative*. Buffalo, NY: Prometheus Books, 1973; Corliss Lamont, *Voice in the Wilderness*. Buffalo: Prometheus Books, 1975; H. J. Blackham, *Modern Humanism*. Yellow Springs, OH: American Humanist Association, 1964; *Humanist Manifestos I and II*. Buffalo, NY: Prometheus Books, 1973

★676★
AMERICAN RATIONALIST FEDERATION
2001 St. Clair Ave.
St. Louis, MO 63144

The American Rationalist Federation, formed in 1955 by a number of rationalist groups (mostly limited to a single urban area) and individuals, continues the organized rationalist movement in America which dates to the middle of the nineteenth century. As early as 1857 (St. Louis), German-America rationalists had begun to organize local societies. (That early St. Louis group may have grown out of an even earlier group called Licht-freunde, formed in 1832.) In 1859 several such societies came together to form the Bund der duetschen Freien Gemeinden von Nordamerika (the Federation of German Free Communities of North America). At the time of the second national convention in 1871, societies could be found in Hoboken, New Jersey; New York City; Milwaukee, Painesville, and Maryville, Wisconsin; Frankfurt, Missouri; and New Ulm, Minnesota. The organization of the German-American rationalists was followed by the Czechs and a number of English-speaking groups such as the Friendship Liberal League. These groups seemed to thrive in the late-nineteenth century, but by the time of the formation of the Federation, had dwindled noticeably, many finding it difficult just to continue to exist.

In 1947 many of the surviving rationalist groups had banded together in the United Secularists of America. However, many members began to protest the secretive financial policies adopted by the Secularists, and in 1955 most of the local societies in the United States withdrew

and reorganized as the American Rationalist Federation. Representatives of twelve societies gathered in Chicago, in the building owned by the Czech Rationalist Federation (and previously used as the address of the United Secularists) for the organizing convention.

Rationalism is defined as the mental attitude which "unreservedly accepts the supremacy of reason and aims at establishing a system of philosophy and ethics verifiable by experience and experiment and independent of all arbitrary assumptions of authority." The Federation believes in the complete separation of church and state; in free public education; and that the improvement of civilization can come only by combating all forms of political, social, religious, and economic tyranny.

At the organizing meeting of the American Rationalist Federation, delegates from Chicago and St. Louis formed the Rationalist Association, Inc., whose main task has been the publication of *The American Rationalist*, a bimonthy periodical and the circulation of rationalist-atheist books and literature. Through the years the magazine, though completely independent, has been closely associated in the public mind with the Federation and is often mistakenly seen as its official organ.

Included within the American Rationalist Federation are several surviving German groups and the Czech Rationalist Federation of America, centered in Chicago where a monthly periodical, *Vekrozumu*, is published. Local organizations of rationalists are also found in San Francisco, Chicago, and Cleveland (Czech).

Membership: Not reported. Their were 11 independent rationalist-freethought organizations and 20 state organization in the Federation in the early 1980s.

Periodicals: *The American Rationalist*, 2001 St. Clair Ave., St. Louis, MO 63144, is an unofficial publication of the rationalist movement.

Sources: Eldon School and Walter Hoops, "Going Back to the Beginning: Twenty-five Years Ago" in *The American Rationalist* vol. 25, no. 1 (May-June 1980), pp. 17-19; Thomas Capek, *The Czechs in America*. Boston: Houghton Mifflin Company, 1920.

★677★
AMERICANS FIRST, INC.
(Defunct)

Kent Meyer was a member of the Society of Separationists, now known as the American Atheists, Inc., but he resigned in 1969 and formed his own organization. The small group operated within the state of Oklahoma as an atheist/freethought organization. Within weeks of the founding of Americans First, Meyer made national headlines for his instigation of a lawsuit to have a fifty-foo t lighted cross removed from the state fairgrounds in Oklahoma City. He charged that the presence of the cross is a violation of the state constitution. No recent information on Americans First has been forthcoming and it has been reported defunct.

★678★
CHRISTIAN UNIVERSALIST CHURCH OF AMERICA
(Defunct)

The Christian Universalist Church of America was founded in 1964 by Universalists with a Christian emphasis. Headquarters of this small organization was in Deerfield Beach, Florida. In 1967 there were reported an estimated 200 churches and missions (some of which were also affiliated with the Unitarian Universalist Association) located in 21 states with more than 15,000 members. The subsequent disappearance of the Church has cast some doubts on the reported figures.

★679★
CHURCH OF ETERNAL LIFE AND LIBERTY
Box 622
Southfield, MI 48037

The Church of Eternal Life and Liberty is a libertarian church founded on June 2, 1974, by Patrick A. Heller, Anna Bowling, and James Hudler. It has no creed but espouses a noncoercive libertarian philosophy. Confirming its strong belief in individual freedom, the church has offered support for tax protesters, draft resistance, and alternative schooling for children in the home. The church also has a strong interest in cryogenics, the practice of freezing the body at death in hopes of its being brought back to life at a future point in time when science has conquered physical death and disease.

The church cooperates with other libertarian churches, particularly the Church of Nature, with whom it holds regular joint meetings. Since the early 1980s, the church has engaged in a constant battle with the U.S. Internal Revenue Service, which has questioned the group's legitimacy as a church body and has moved to deny it tax-exempt status.

Membership: In 1984 the church reported approximately 100 members in three congregations, two in Michigan and one in California.

Periodicals: *Live and Let Live*, Box 622, Southfield, Michigan 48037.

Sources: Patrick A. Heller, *As My Spirit Beckons*. Pontiac, MI: The Church of Eternal Life and Liberty, 1974; Patrick A. Heller, *Because I Am*. Oak Park, MI: The Church of Eternal Life and Liberty, 1981.

★680★
CHURCH OF NATURE
Box 407
Dryden, MI 48428

The Church of Nature was founded in 1979 in Dryden, Michigan, by Rev. Christopher L. Brockman. It is described as a libertarian humanist church which espouses a naturalistic philosophy. The church places a high value upon individual freedom and believes that "living up to one's best nature as a human being is the standard of goodness." Freedom is essential to goodness. The church has established two sacraments: marriage and affirmation. The latter consists of providing a ceremonial context in which an individual (or group of individuals) can offer an affirmative statement of some truth or concern to members of the church.

The church is part of a growing movement within the larger Libertarian Movement to provide a religious context for libertarian thinking, and the Church of Nature cooperates closely with other libertarian churches such as the Church of Eternal Life and Liberty and the United Libertarian Fellowship.

Membership: The Church of Nature reported approximately 100 members in a single congregation in 1984.

Periodicals: *Exegesis*, Box 407, Dryden, Michigan 48428.

★681★
CHURCH OF THE HUMANITARIAN GOD
% Ron Libert
Box 13236
St. Petersburg, FL 33733

The Church of the Humanitarian God was founded in 1969 in St. Petersburg, Florida, as an alternative to yielding to the prevailing military-industrial complex. The church teaches that it is man's purpose in this life to aid his fellow man as best as he can. Such service to others establishes man's status in the life hereafter. Sustaining life is the natural law of God. Therefore, only self-defensive aggression can be participated in by members of the church. Nonviolent change is part of the new direction in which the church wishes to lead people.

The church says introspection is man's means of facing himself and allowing his conscience to guide him. Thus, questions of sex, nudity, divorce, drinking, and smoking are largely left to individuals. Drug use is disapproved. Ministers must be eighteen years old, but there are no other restrictions because of age, sex, or marital status.

Membership: Not reported.

★682★
CONFRATERNITY OF DEISTS, INC.
Box 179
Homosassa Springs, FL 32647

The Confraternity of Deists was begun in 1967 in St. Petersburg by Paul Englert, a former Roman Catholic. Deism is belief in one God, the supreme intelligence, as contrasted with belief in Scripture or atheism. Without God, believes the Deist, man is defenseless against himself. The Creed of Confraternity includes the beliefs that the constructive exercise of human intelligence contributes to the glorification of God; that all man-made Scriptures are mere literary works, without religious, historical or chronological value; that the church of the Deist should constitute the free university, disseminating scientific knowledge and nurturing the arts; and that the social duty of the Deist is to work for the spiritual and temporal elevation of the people.

Membership: Not reported. In 1969 there were 3 centers of the Confraternity, one at the headquarters and two at universities.

★683★
FREEDOM FROM RELIGION FOUNDATION
Box 750
Madison, WI 53701

During the mid-1970s complaints began to arise within the membership of American Atheists, Inc.; members accused its founder, Madalyn Murray O'Hair, of undemocratic management of the organization and overt efforts to stifle dissent. Some members were dropped from the membership, and they were soon joined by others who withdrew in protest. In 1978 a group of former members, under the leadership of Anne Nicol Gaylor, organized the Freedom from Religion Foundation. Gaylor was elected president, and within the year over 200 people had joined.

Like its parent organization, the foundation is atheistic in its belief and practice, but includes in its membership people who hold a broad range of freethought, i.e., nontheistic perspectives--humanism, agnosticism, secularism, and atheism. There is no statement of belief, but members generally assert that there is no evidence for the existence of a deity and attack the credibility of the Bible and the adequacy of its moral teachings. The foundation also takes a strong stance in favor of feminist concerns; Gaylor's daughter is editor of a feminist newspaper, *The Feminist Connection.*

Equally important to its goal of educating the public on matters relating to nontheistic belief, the foundation advocates a rigid separation of church and state. It has sought removal of religious objects from public property and has backed lawsuits in which it saw the state unduly supporting a religion. In 1983 it filed a suit challenging President Ronald Reagan's declaration of that year as "The Year of the Bible."

The foundation is headed by an executive council. Gaylor has remained its president. Membership is open to nontheists, and chapters which meet regularly have been formed around the United States. A national meeting is held annually, usually in the fall.

Membership: In 1984 the foundation reported over 1,800 members throughout the United States and Canada.

Periodicals: *Freethought Today,* Box 750, Madison, Wisconsin 53701; *Newsletter of the New Jersey Chapter,* Box 40, Asbury, New Jersey 08802.

Sources: Annie Laurie Gaylor, *Woe to Women--the Bible Tells Me So.* Madison, WI: Freedom from Religion Foundation, 1981; Ruth Green, *Born Again Skeptic's Guide to the Bible.* Madison, WI: Freedom from Religion Foundation, 1979; Gordon Stein, *An Anthology of Atheism and Rationalism.* New York: Prometheus Books, 1980.

★684★
FREETHINKERS OF AMERICA
(Defunct)

The Freethinkers of America was a small freethought group founded in New York in 1915. Around 1920 Joseph Lewis (1889-1968), destined to become one of the leading exponents and popularizers of atheism in the United States, moved from his home in Alabama to New York. Already an atheist, he joined the group and became its leader. During the next decade he wrote several classic statements of the atheist position, all published by the Freethought Press Association which he had founded: *The Tyranny of God* (1920); *The Bible Unmasked* (1926) and *Atheism and Other Addresses* (1930). During this period he also became interested in the study of sexuality, and in the early 1930s he initiated a second publishing concern, Eugenics Publishing Company, which published low-cost books S on sexology written by specialists.

Lewis's books addressed a host of major atheist concerns. He attacked religion, particularly the Judaism he had forsaken early in life. He denied the necessity of religion as a basis for either the individual moral life or social order. He argued for the separation of church and state. He publicized the life of America's founding fathers as a means of arguing for the patriotic role of freethought.

Lewis continued to write into the 1950s. Possibly his two most important books appeared after World War II, *The Ten Commandments* (1946) and *An Atheist Manifesto* (1954). The Freethinkers of America were headquartered in New York, though Lewis lived in Miami for a brief period (and frequently appeared on local radio programs to speak on atheist themes). In the 1960s there were branches in San Diego and Milwaukee and as many as several thousand members. The size of the group had shrunk significantly after the exclusion of the Communists, rejected because they tended to dominate meetings with their own brand of atheism. The

Freethinkers had close relations with the American Association for the Advancement of Atheism for many years, but differed in that it did not demand members to be atheists. The Freethinkers published a periodical, *Age of Reason*, which ceased publication after Lewis's death in 1968. The organization survived Lewis's death only a few years.

Sources: Arthur H. Howland, *Jeseph Lewis--Enemy of God*. Boston: Stratford, 1932; Joseph Lewis, *An Atheist Manifesto*. New York: Freethought Press Association, 1954; Joseph Lewis, *The Bible Unmasked*. New York: Freethought Press Association, 1926; Joseph Lewis, *The Tyranny of God*. New York: Freethought Press Association, 1921; Joseph Lewis, *The Ten Commandments*. New York: Freethought Press Association, 1926.

★685★
GODDIAN ORGANIZATION
(Defunct)

The Goddian Organization was formed in 1965 by Lawrence A. Whitten of Portland, Maine. It was begun as a back-to-God movement, started because other religious organizations were not doing their work of bringing people back to God. Whitten consolidated all religious belief into one affirmation--God as the creator. He sought the union of all people in one brotherhood of man. That union could be achieved if each person will stop insisting that those who differ from him must believe as he does.

There were no ministers or churches. Whitten attempted to unite all Goddians through the headquarters in Portland around a mutual allegiance to the program of good works. In the monthly periodical, *The Goddian Message*, an attack upon Christianity and the Bible followed traditional free thought ideas. While people from around the country responded to ads about the organization, it never received enough support to make it a viable concern. After a few years, it was discontinued.

★686★
SOCIETY OF EVANGELICAL AGNOSTICS
Box 515
Auberry, CA 93602

The Society of Evangelical Agnostics was founded in 1975 by William Henry Young. Young had called himself an agnostic for several years and had harbored a hope that an agnostic organization would emerge. After developing the idea of the society, he placed ads in a number of liberal, religious journals such as *The Humanist* and mass circulation periodicals such as *Nation* and the *Saturday Review*. He also began to champion the cause of agnosticism, frequently speaking to audiences on the subject and writing letters to periodicals whenever he thought agnosticism had been misrepresented.

The society defines agnosticism by reference to a tradition of outstanding freethinkers who called themselves by that label, most notably Thomas Henry Huxley (who coined the term), Bertrand Russell, and Robert G. Ingersoll. Its principles consist of three statements: One should approach all questions and issues with an open mind; One should avoid advocating conclusions without adequate or satisfactory evidence; One should accept not having final answers as a fundamental reality in one's life. According to Young, agnosticism is to be distinguished quite strongly from atheism. The latter flatly denies the existence of God while the former affirms God is both unknown and an unknowable factor. Atheism, like Christianity, violates the second principle of agnosticism by advocating conclusions without adequate evidence.

The society is headed by a board of directors and its administrator, William Henry Young. Young is also the librarian of the Cedar Springs Library, in Auberry, California, which has developed a special collection of freethought literature. The library is the official archive of the society and distributes numerous inexpensive items related to the society's concerns. The society has reprinted many classic statements of agnosticism as well as original material writtten by its members. Membership is open to all who consider themselves agnostics and who contribute a modest annual membership fee. Members are also encouraged to form chapters and hold meetings in their local neighborhoods.

Membership: In 1984 the society reported 860 members in the United States (plus an additional 20 foreign members) and six chapters.

Periodicals: *SEA Journal*, Box 515, Auberry, California 93602.

Sources: *Huxley on Agnosticism*. Auberry, CA: Cedar Springs Library, n.d.; William Henry Young, "The Agnostic as Prophet" in *Faith and Thought*, vol.1, no.2, (Summer 1983) pp. 27-31; Robert G. Ingersoll, *Ingersoll's Greatest Lectures*. New York: The Freethought Press Association, 1944; Leslie Stephens, *An Agnostic's Apology*. New York: G. P. Putnam's Sons, 1903.

★687★
UNITARIAN UNIVERSALIST ASSOCIATION
25 Beacon St.
Boston, MA 02108

Unitarian Universalist Association was formed in 1961 by the merger of the American Unitarian Association and the Universalist Church in America. The merger represents the coming together of the two oldest and most conservative segments of the liberal tradition. It is the only body that affirms its base within the Judeo-Christian heritage. Many of its ministers can be found in local ministerial associations.

The basis of modern Unitarian belief is the free search for truth. Truth is found in the universal teachings of the great prophets and teachers of all ages and traditions, but summarized in the Western tradit ion as love to God and man. Members believe in the worth of every human and in the democratic method in human relationships. A world community based on brotherhood, justice and peace is the goal of all actions. While varying widely in belief structures, Unitarian Universalists generally believe in God as the source of mind and spirit, Jesus as a great prophet, the Bible as a collection of valuable religious writings, science as a source of knowledge, and prayer as a means to lift the mind beyond the ordinary. There are no sacraments.

Following the pattern of their Congregational parents, the Unitarian Universalists are congregationally governed. A national Association meeting is held annually and each minister and local church is represented. The Unitarian Universalist Service Committee was established in 1940 to aid refugees of Nazi persecution and has continued as a means to embody social concerns. The Beacon Press is a major publisher of religious books. oks.

Membership: In 1982 the Association reported 131,844 members, 935 churches, and 949 ministers

Periodicals: *UU World*, 25 Beacon Street, Boston, MA 02108.

Sources: Earl Morse Wilbur, *Our Unitarian Heritage*. Boston: Beacon Press, 1963; Sydney E. Ahlstrom and Jonathan S. Carey, *An American Reformation*. Middletown, CT: Wesleyan University Press, 1985; Prescott B. Wintersteen, *Christology in American Unitarianism*. Boston: The Unitarian Universalist Christian Fellowship, 1977; George Huntston Williams, *American Universalism*. Boston: Beacon Press, 1976; Henry H. Cheetham, *Unitarianism and Universalism*. Boston: Beacon Press, 1962; Robert B. Tapp. *Religion Among the Unitarian Universalists*. New York: Seminar Press, 1973.

★688★
UNITED LIBERTARIAN FELLOWSHIP
% Will Buckley, President
1220 Larnel Place
Los Altos, CA 94022

The United Libertarian Fellowship was incorporated in 1975 in Los Altos, California, by William C. White, Kathleen J. White, and C. Douglas Hoiles. The fellowship is a religious order which espouses libertarian ideals of individual freedom and responsibility within a religious context, and it offers a broad framework within which libertarians can develop religiously following their own initiative and perspectives.

The fellowship has a simple statement of beliefs. God is acknowledged as the fundamental force in the universe.

Human beings possess the capacity to think and act. That capacity places a duty upon people to search for truth and to act in accord with that truth. Individuals, being capable of influencing their own destiny, must also accept responsibility for their actions and the consequences which flow from them. The guidance of personal conduct begins in refraining from the initiation of the use of force or fraud on another person and the general assumption that others are free and should be allowed that freedom to develop their own religious nature.

The fellowship describes worship as "focusing the mind in search for truth." Five sacraments are observed as outward manifestations and public observances of the sacred realm in human life. Affirmation, parallel to confirmation in other churches, is a declaration of adulthood and acceptance of adult responsibility. Marriage is contracting to share lives. Consecration is the dedication of a person or property to sacred purposes. The final two sacraments attempt to integrate religious ideals into everyday life by infusing otherwise mundane activity with sacred worth. Transformation is the act of changing physical materials into a new form with more utility and/or value than the original materials possessed. Exchange is the voluntary giving and receiving of objects or labor.

The direction of the fellowship is in the hands of a board, officers, and its ministers. A three-person board of elders manages the fellowship. Membership on the board is for life, and individual members retain the right to name a successor. The Board appoints the officers: a president who directs the religious work, a secretary-treasurer who keeps the records, and bishops who manage the temporal affairs. The board also appoints and ordains ministers who have sacramental functions and can, if they choose, establish churches. In keeping with libertarian principles, neither bishops nor ministers are assigned tasks; rather, they are encouraged to work in accordance with libertarian beliefs and spread its fellowship as their individual creativity dictates.

Membership: Not reported. However, in 1982 the church reported that membership had spread throughout the United States and missions had been established in various parts of the world. Membership is estimated to be several hundred.

Sources: *The United Libertarian Fellowship, A Religious Order*. Los Altos, CA: United Libertarian Fellowship, 1982.

★689★
UNITED SECULARISTS OF AMERICA
(Defunct)

The United Secularists of America was formed in 1946 as an anti-God, anti-religion organization by William McCarthy. It is the secularists' belief that religion is a great hoax, and the organization opposed the "dangerous" encroachments of religion in education and other areas of life. Among the group's outstanding members was ex-priest Joseph M. McCabe, one of the major popularizers of atheism in the twentieth century. Prior to his death in 1955, he had written more than 200 books against the church and translated 30 others. Titles include *The Sources of Morality of the Gospel, Crime and Religion*, and *A Rationalist Encyclopedia*.

The United Secularists of America advocated the complete separation of church and state; the right not to believe as part of freedom of religion; the exclusion of all religion from public schools; and the taxation of church property. Opposing all supernaturalism and superstition, the United Secularists of America believed in the free intellectual growth of man and the advancement of society toward a rational civilized existence.

During its first decade, the United Secularists were among the largest of the rationalist/atheist bodies, drawing support from many independent rationalist and secularists societies. In 1947 they had begun a magazine *Progressive World*. However, in the early 1950s, protests against secretive financial policies led most of the groups to withdraw and in 1955 form the American Rationalist Federation. After that year, the United Secularists lacked support to even hold an annual meeting. By 1970 there were only three centers, 1,000 active members, and 1,000 at-large members. Over the decade the United Secularists steadily lost their remaining support. In 1981 they finally disbanded and the magazine ceased publication.

Mail Order Churches

★690★
AMERICAN FELLOWSHIP CHURCH
183 Sargent Court
Monterey, CA 93940

The American Fellowship Church (originally named the Mother Earth Church, was formed in 1975 by T. H. Swenson, as an independent church which believes in individual responsibility for spiritual growth and development. Described as a church without walls whose members are widely scattered, ministers are invited to unite daily in prayer and meditation at 7 a.m.and 7 p.m. (Pacific Standard Time). The International Clergy Association is a division of the church open only to ordained ministers. It publishes a directory of members.

Membership: Not reported.

Periodicals: *Newsletter*, 183 Sargent Court, Monterey, CA 93940.

★691★
BROTHERHOOD OF PEACE AND TRANQUILITY
Current address not obtained for this edition.

The Brotherhood of Peace and Tranquility was a fellowship of semi-autonomous churches which included local autonomous congregations and a "Church of the Brotherhood," a single worldwide congregation of individuals. Individual churches varied widely in belief and practice. The Brotherhood operated the Academy of the Brotherhood, its teaching arm, which offered training to ministers as well as courses for members who wish merely to improve their religious knowledge. Both resident and nonresident instruction was offered, and the curriculum was slanted toward the psychic. Both the academy and the church were headquartered in Costa Mesa, California.

★692★
CALVARY GRACE CHURCHES OF FAITH
Box 333
Rillton, PA 19140

Among the first of the mail-order churches is the Calvary Grace Churches of Faith formed in 1954 (chartered in 1958) by Angelo C. Spern of Irwin, Pennsylvania. It issues ordination certificates on application to "worthy Christians who have accepted (the) Lord Jesus Christ as the Savior." The International Chaplain's Association functions as the churches' missionary arm.

Membership: Not reported. In 1971 there were a reported 70 congregations.

Educational facilities: Calvary Grace Bible Institute, Box 333, Rillton, PA 15678.

★693★
CALVARY GRACE CHRISTIAN CHURCH OF FAITH
% Rev. Herman Keck Jr.
271 N.E. 57th St.
Fort Lauderdale, FL 33308

The Calvary Grace Christian Church of Faith was formed in 1961 by the Rev. Dr. Herman Keck Jr. of Ft. Lauderdale, Florida, who began his ministry as a member of the Calvary Grace Churches of Faith. In 1962, he began calling himself the international superintendent and established Faith Bible College. The Church resembles its parent body.

Membership: Not reported.

Educational facilities: Faith Bible College, 271 N.E. 57th St., Fort Lauderdale, FL 33308; Faith Theological Seminary, 271 N.E. 57th St., Fort Lauderdale, FL 33308.

Sources: Bill Bruns, "Praise the Lord and Pass the Diploma" in *Life* (November 14, 1970), pp. 69-78.

★694★
THE CHURCH OF HOLY LIGHT
Box 4478
Pittsburgh, PA 15205

The Church of Holy Light is a small mail-order church that ordains ministers and charters congregations. The Church asks only that candidates feel called to preach. An initial $50.00 offering is asked of new applicants.

Membership: Not reported.

★695★
CHURCH OF THE HOLY MONARCH
Box 1116
Port Orange, FL 32019

Describing itself as a "church without walls," the Church of the Holy Monarch is headed by Dr. Robert Walker and Archbishop R. M. LeRoux. It was founded in 1976 and ordains ministers and charters churches. Ministers are asked to respond to a nominal accessment to remain active clergy in the church.

Membership: Not reported.

Periodicals: *The Monarch Messenger*, Box 116, Port Orange, FL 32019.

★696★
CHURCH OF UNIVERSAL BROTHERHOOD
6311 Yucca Street
Hollywood, CA 90028

The Church of Universal Brotherhood offers (for $10.00) a kit that includes an ordination certificate, a Doctor of Divinity certificate, and complete instructions on forming a church. The Church was founded by Michael Valentine of Hollywood, California, with the purpose of helping people become aware that they are in charge of their own beliefs. The Church admonishes members to love themselves, love their brothers and sisters as they do themselves, and take control of their lives as they see fit. Their Church believes that all is one. The goals of life are best attained, according to the Church, by getting high and staying there, raising the vibes, cherishing the world, and praising God for his grace.

Freedom is a keynote with the church, which encourages ordinations as a means of releasing power for good. Members of the Church say people are in prison, but they deserve to be free and must get the necessary help. The prime virtue is the constant striving for self-mastery. Three tools available to aid the seeker are mirrors, water beds, and hypnosis.

Membership: Not reported.

★697★
CROWN OF LIFE FELLOWSHIP
Route 2, Box 190
Albany, OR 97321

The Crown of Life Fellowship was formed in 1967 at Pullman, Washington, by the Rev. D. H. Howard. It functioned for several years as a fellowship at the University of Washington and then moved to Spokane, and more recently to Oregon. In 1970, the small Spokane group began to place advertisements offering ordination and, by 1972, had ministers in most of the states and provinces. The Fellowship functions as an association of ministers drawn from a diverse theological spectrum. There are no doctrinal requirements for membership.

The church supplies a short course leading to a Doctor of Divinity degree. Through its periodical, *Crown of Life Fellowship News*, it informs members of their privileges as ordained ministers. Many of the churches function as house churches and study groups.

The Crown of Life Fellowship sees itself as continuing the work of A. K. Mozumdar, who began a teaching ministry in Spokane in 1914. For the next 40 years, from the southern California headquarters of the Messianic World Message, Mozumdar preached a "universal message" of the God within. His teachins represented an attempted synthesis of Hinduism and Christianity. The Fellowship has sponsored the republishing of Mozundar's major work, *The Triumphant Spirit*.

Membership: Not reported.

Periodicals: *The Universal Message*, Rte. 2, Box 190, Albany, OR 97321.

Sources: A. K. Mozumdar, *The Triumphant Spirit*. Marina Del Rey, CA: DeVorss & Co., 1978.

★698★
HILLTOP HOUSE CHURCH
(Defunct)

On November 1, 1971, newspapers across the United States carried pictures of Sadie, a Labrador retriever in Terre Linda, California, who has been ordained a minister in the Hilltop House Church by Archbishop Ben F. Gay, its founder. Gay, former president of Holiday Magic, Inc., a cosmetics firm founded by the late William Penn Patrick, founded the Hilltop House Church in 1970 in San Rafael, California. He had formerly been ordained by the Missionaries of the New Truth, a Chicago-based group. The guiding precepts of the Hilltop House Church were the golden rule and John 8:32, "Ye shall know the truth and the truth shall set you free."

Inherent within the Hilltop House Church was a certain cynicism toward religion as a whole. Ministers were ordained for $15.00 and a registration form. They were then promised promotions for recruiting other ministers (a structure quite similar to Holiday Magic's program). The church's stated goal was to ordain 48 bishops, 24 monsignors, and 12 vicars. Ministers were offered ordination simply because of all the benefits ordination brings.

On January 8, 1973, after a year of protesting tax shelters offered to churches, Gay, in a letter to the U.S. Internal Revenue Service, asked that the tax-exempt status of his church be canceled. This act was a dramatic protest of the large, nonreligious, tax-free holdings of other churches.

★699★
LIFE SCIENCE CHURCH
Current address not obtained for this edition.

Similar to the Universal Life Church is the Life Science Church, formed by Archbishop Gordon L. Cruikshank. He offers to ordain "those gifted people that have been called to the ministry and for various reasons have been denied the right to fulfill their mission because of lack of formal education and/or college or seminary training." Ministers may be ordained by sending in $25.00, an application form, and a short thesis on "what the Ministry means to me and how I can serve." All ministers receive an ordination certificate and a Doctor of Divinity degree from the Life Science College. Churches are chartered for $35.00.Ministers may become bishops by recruiting others for ordination.

According to Cruikshank, the science of life consists of learning to live to the fullest. Freedom is the most important part of life, especially freedom of religion. Although the church is not doctrinally oriented and stresses freedom of belief, each minister makes a "non-denominational affirmation of faith."

Since the 1970s, the Life Science Church has become associated with the Posse Comitatus, a right-wing tax protest group in the Midwest. Ministers have been accused of using the church as a tax-dodge and of involvement in several violent confrontations between members of the Posse and the legal authorities.

Membership: Not reported.

★700★
MISSIONARIES OF THE NEW TRUTH
(Defunct)

The Missionaries of the New Truth was formed in 1969 by Frederich W. Zurndorfer and David A. Muncaster of Chicago. The organization immediately began to advertise, offering respondents ordination and a Doctor of Divinity degree. Advantages offered included the right to ordain others in the church's name, the authority to conduct weddings, tax exemption, cash grants for doing missionary work, draft exemption, and reduced rates for ministers at hotels, theaters, and on public transportation. A statement of belief says man is a seeker of truth. The church urges its ministers and members to seek truth, recognizing that subjective truth will differ from person to person. The higher truth is synonymous with God. By 1971, the Missionaries of the New Truth had ordained 7,000 ministers, signifying the church's success. However, the organization was beset with problems. Following an expose in the *Chicago Tribune*, the Illinois state's attorney general filed suit, charging the group with fraud in soliciting funds to establish schools and churches that never materialized. In addition, Muncaster and several leaders of the church were seized in a drug raid and were accused of running the largest hallucinogenic drug factory in the Midwest. Following their conviction, the church dissolved.

★701★
OMNIUNE CHURCH
309 Breckenridge
Texarkana, TX 75501

The Omniune Church was formed by the Rev. M.S. Medley, former international president of public relations for the Life Science Church. The Omniune Church is based upon the ideal of building a church from the bottom up, democratically. Individual member participation is stressed. Beliefs are drawn from ethical liberalism and include emphasis on freedom of belief. The Omniune Church Creed asserts the following: "Believe what ye will, so long as ye do good to thy fellow man: for verily, he that doeth Godly deeds is a Godly man: and he that hath loving kindness in his heart hath God in his soul." The seven great laws of life further enlarge the Omniune perspective: 1) do unto others what you would have done unto you; 2) give the world love and kindness, for you reap what you sow; 3) believe ve in your own worth and turn from error toward improvement; 4) take nothing which the owner has need of, neither his property nor his life; 5) love and honor God and your fellow man-- harm neither by word or deed; 6) seek wisdom, justice, peace and a better life for all; and 7) live joyfully, simply, naturally, sharing God's bounty, moderate in all but love of God and God's creation.

The church stresses function over form in organization and advises congregations, instead of hiring a paid minister, to divide the minister's duties and appoint unpaid volunteers to fulfill those duties. Any person can then become the speaker, conductor, clerk, organizer, instructor, steward, or counselor. These seven officers are designated elders and any assistants are deacons. Congregations are small and close-knit. They are advised to split rather than become too big. In 1973, there were 17 missionary ministers. There were missions in Los Angeles, Houston, Chicago and Atlanta. There were approximately 500 members. Headquarters are in Breckenridge, Texas.

Membership: Not reported. In 1973 there were approximately 500 members and 17 missionary ministers with missions in Los Angeles, Houston, Chicago, and Atlanta.

★702★
UNITED CHURCH OF THE APOSTLES
Lindenhurst, NY 11757

The United Church of the Apostles is a small mail order church that charters congregations and ordains ministers. The Church believes in freedom of religion. It sees its purpose as seeking to unite people and to open them to the beauty and great handiwork of God in everyday life.

Membership: Not reported.

Periodicals: *Church Newsletter*, Lindenhurst, NY 11757.

★703★
UNIVERSAL FREE LIFE CHURCH
Hollywood, FL

The Universal Free Life Church was formed in 1969 by the Rev. Dr. Arthur H. Fox, assisted by the Rt. Rev. Richard H. Kerekes and the Rev. Diane Fox. There is no doctrine; the Free Life Church recognizes the individual's right to his own beliefs. In 1970, the Church reported 1,100 centers in the United States (912 on college campuses) and 43,000 members. No verification of these claims was ever made, and no centers of the church's activity have been located during the 1980s.

★704★
UNIVERSAL LIFE CHURCH
601 Third St.
Modesto, CA 95351

Kirby J. Hensley (b. 1911) was an illiterate Baptist minister from North Carolina. He educated himself and, in the process, was influenced by his readings in world religion. Over the years, he conceived the idea of a universal church that would bring people of all religions together, rather than separating them. In 1962, he founded the Universal Life Church, having previously opened a "church" in his garage in Modesto, California. Though Hensley had his own ideas about theology, he felt others had a right to their own theories. He began to ordain ministers for no fee, for life, without question. He would present a signed ordination certificate and a one-page information sheet covering the ordination ceremony merely for the asking.

In the late 1960s, Hensley attained the status of a minor folk hero as the media discovered his activity and gave it national news coverage. He would often address large college classes and ordain the audience instantly and en masse. Though ordination was free, a Doctorate of Divinity cost $20.00 and was offered with ten lessons explaining how to set up and operate a church. In the state of California, however, he was enjoined from issuing a degree from an unaccredited institution, so the Church's Department of Education was moved to Phoenix, Arizona.

While the Universal Life Church has no doctrine of its own, Hensley has developed an eclectic theology that includes the following beliefs: people are reincarnated; the soul is the continuing essence of man; God is substance manifest in natural laws; Christ is a man more intelligent than most men; heaven is nothing more or less than the position of having what you want; and hell is when you do not have what you want. He has also developed an elaborate concept of history. According to Hensley, two thousand years before the Biblical flood man began to multiply on the earth, and church and state became separate. Thus began a 6,000-year spiritual dispensation which will end in thirty years of turmoil around 2000 A.D. By that time, the church and state will be reunited under the Universal Life banner. To implement his ideas, Hensley has formed the People's Peace Prosperity Party and has run for both governor of California and president of the United States. Hensley has also initiated several "reforms" by marrying a couple in a trial marriage and marrying two girls at the 1971 Universal Life Church Festival.

The Church is organized very loosely. An annual convention is held. Subsidiary structures include the Universal Life Church Press Association. By 1974, churches belonging to the Universal Life Church were functioning in most states, and ministers were located in every state and many foreign countries. By 1977, the Universal Life Church claimed to have ordained more than six million ministers, some 25,000 of which had reportedly formed congregations that met regularly, usually as small groups in house churches. Among the churches which either originally had or presently have charters from the Universal Life Church are the Temple of Bacchus, Wells, Maine; the Thelemic Temple of the Double Vortex, Ithaca, New York; the Venusian Church, Seattle, Washington; the Church of the Eleventh Commandment, Kansas City, Missouri; the Church of World Peace, Denver, Colorado; and several Witchcraft groups.

Membership: Not reported.

Educational facilities: Universal Life University, Modesto, California.

Periodicals: *Universal Life*, 601 Third St., Modesto, CA 95351.

Remarks: The Universal Life Church has remained a constant source of controversy, having been targeted by the U.S. Internal Revenue Service as a tax-dodge. Congregations that claimed a Universal Life charter and ministers that claimed a Universal Life ordination have been carefully scrutinized, and charges of profit-making businesses and various clandestine organizations operating under the Universal Life Church's protection have been periodically reported. The Church has responded to the IRS and resulting negative image of the Church by filing suits against the IRS, moving to overturn denials of state-tax exemption and seeking recognition of its ministers to perform marriages. While the problems with the Internal Revenue Service have done little to slow the Church nationally, they have led many congregations originally chartered by the Church to seek their own charters.

Sources: Lewis Ashmore, *The Modesto Messiah*. Bakersfield, CA: Universal Press, 1977.

★705★
UNIVERSAL LIFE MISSION CHURCH
610 N. Second St.
Sapulpa, OK 74066

The Universal Life Mission Church, also known as the General Council of the Apostolic Sabbatarian Baptist Churches of America, Inc., was founded by Kenneth Russell Lyons, its bishop. The Church was originally chartered by the Universal Life Church, but in 1977 the Church was independently incorporated. The Church is a sabbatarian group. It believes in the Bible as its only guide, preferring the New International or World Version published by the Jehovah's Witnesses.

Membership: In 1984 there were 4 congregations.

Latter-Day Saints Family

An historical essay on this family is provided beginning on page 93.

Utah Mormons

★706★
AARONIC ORDER
℅ Dr. Robert J. Conrad
Box 7095
Salt Lake City, UT 84107

The Aaronic Order was organized by followers of Dr. Maurice Lerrie Glendenning. While still a young man, Glendenning began to receive messages and insights pertaining to God's work for Israel and for Levi and Aaron. Some of these messages, together with some of his letters and epistles, were later assembled into a book known as the *Levitical Writings*. (This book is also referred to as the *Book of Elias* or the *Record of John*.) The Bible, however, is considered the basic scripture of the Aaronic Order and the final authority in all matters of doctrine and practice. The *Levitical Writings* are seen as consistent with and supportive of the Biblical revelation.

In 1928 he and his family moved to Provo, Utah where he continued to receive revelations from Elias and to share them with interested people, many of whom became convinced of their divine origin. His followers increased over the years, and in 1942 incorporated the Aaronic Order under the laws of the State of Utah.

The Aaronic Order has a Chief High Priest who functions primarily in the spiritual area; a First High Priest who functions primarily in the temporal area; a Second High Priest who is in charge of ordinance and ceremonial work; and a Branch Priest who is appointed over each congregation. The ruling legislative body is the Supreme Council of seventy members. The church organization derives from a chart known as the Aaronic Wheel which was given to Glendenning by revelation.

The Aaronic Order stresses discipleship and consecration which require full members to relinquish title to all goods and property. Any property or goods held by a full member constitutes a stewardship under direction of the Supreme Council of the Aaronic Order. The church also has several communal settlements, known as Levitical communities, which practice the Biblical teachings of "all things common." These practices are in harmony with the ministry of Levi and Aaron in early Israel which required that this tribe could have no ownership or inheritance of the temporal things in Israel. The priesthood and the service at the altar were the heritage of Levi and Aaron for all time.

According to the Order's teachings, the beginning of the Levitical priesthood dates to 1736 B.C.E., when the priesthood was granted to Levi and his descendents forever. The priests were known as Levites, Aaronites, Zadokites and Essenes at various times, and many of them became Christians in the New Testament period. One line of the Aaronic priesthood continued through the Middle Ages by lineage of Robert Bruce, king of Scotland, and through one branch of his family known as Glendowyn, brought to America by the Glendennings (or Glendonwyns) in 1742. This family maintained a constant awareness of their lineage and priesthood heritage and passed this on from father to son by written blessings, some of which are in possession of the Order.

The headquarters and a branch of the Order are located in Murray, Utah (a Salt Lake City suburb). Other branches are located in Springville and Partoun, Utah, and in Cheyenne, Wyoming. One of the most important thrusts of the work, however, is in the Levitical community of Eskdale, Utah, which was established in 1956 in the western desert area near the Utah-Nevada Border. In the 1980s, the Order came into contact with a Sacred Name group, Bet HaShem Midrash, headed by Shmuel ben Menachem of New Haven, Indiana. The Indiana group merged into the Order and brought the issue of the Hebrew names of the deity and of Jesus into the larger community. Members not associated with a branch are located across the United States.

Membership: Not available. There are six centers of activity.

Periodicals: *Aaron's Star*, Bet HaShem Midrash, 14809 Bremer Road, Route 1, New Haven, IN 46774.

Remarks: The Aaronic Order is not affiliated with the Church of Jesus Christ of Latter-Day Saints nor does it consider itself as having been derived from it. It should be noted, however, that Glendenning was a member of the church, and was excommunicated from it because of his revelations. Also, the *Levitical Writings* begin with chapter 137 while the LDS edition of the *Doctrine and Covenants* ends with section 136. The *Levitical Writings* parallel in format the *Doctrines and Covenants*.

Sources: *Levitical Writings*. Eskdale, UT: Aaronic Order, 1978; Ralph D. Erickson, *History and Doctrinal Development of the Order of Aaron*. Provo, UT: Brigham Young University, M. A. Thesis, 1969; Blanche W. Beeston, *Purified as Gold and Silver*. Idaho Falls, ID: The Author, 1966.

★707★
CHURCH OF JESUS CHRIST (BULLA)
% Art Bulla
2928 S. State St.
Salt Lake City, UT 84115

Art Bulla joined the Church of Jesus Christ of Latter-Day Saints around 1970. While a member he had come to believe that he was the "One Mighty and Strong" who was spoken of in Mormon scriptures who was to come and set God's house in order. He organized the Church of Jesus Christ in the early 1980s.

Membership: Not reported.

Sources: Art Bulla, *The Revelations of Jesus Christ*. Salt Lake City, UT: The Author, 1983.

★708★
CHURCH OF JESUS CHRIST OF LATTER-DAY SAINTS
50 E. North Temple
Salt Lake City, UT 84150

The main body which carries the history and theology of the Latter-Day Saints tradition described in the introductory material on this chapter is the Church of Jesus Christ of Latter-Day Saints (LDS), headquartered in Salt Lake City, Utah.

After Joseph Smith's death in 1844, the Saints were forced to evacuate Nauvoo, Illinois, and most of them moved into Iowa. The inevitable power struggle ensued. Brigham Young (1801-1877), who had been president of the Council of Twelve Apostles during Smith's time, was elected president of the Church in 1847. Heber C. Kimball and Willard Richards were elected as the other two high priests in the first presidency. Early in 1847, the majority of the Mormons who had fled Nauvoo followed Brigham Young to the present site of Salt Lake City and settled there. Under Young's leadership the Saints colonized over three hundred settlements in Utah and surrounding states.

During the early years in Utah, polygamy, which had begun as a practice among church leaders in Nauvoo, became openly practiced and advocated. Possibly more than any other issue, polygamy thwarted Young's plans for a western state of Deseret, the original name proposed for Utah, while bringing the power of the federal government down upon the Church. During the 1880's laws were passed against polygamy and eventually forced the church to stop the practice and move against those members who participate in plural marriages.

In 1849 the Saints stepped up their worldwide mission, previously initiated during the period in Nauvoo. They concentrated on Western Europe, primarily England and Scandinavia. The many converts they made constituted the basis for the spectacular spread of the church throughout the world in the twentieth century. While becoming an international religion of some importance, the church spread along the Rockies from Phoenix to Boise, and westward to the Pacific. From their western base, the Saints have gradually spread across the U.S. and currently have stakes in every section of the country.

For many years the church was criticized for its stance on admitting black people to the priesthood, an essential structure in the church. That condition changed in 1978, following a revelation given to President Spencer W. Kimball.

The church is organized along patterns revealed to Joseph Smith, Jr. Leading the church internationally is the First Presidency, comprising three men (the president and two counselors) who are assisted by the Council of Twelve Apostles. Brigham Young succeeded Joseph Smith, Jr., the first president of the Church. Since Young's tenure, the church has been served successively by following: John Taylor (1880-1887); Wilford Woodruff (1889-1898); Lorenzo Snow (1898-1901); Joseph F. Smith (1901-1918); Heber J. Grant (1918-1945); George Albert Smith (1945-1951); David O. McKay (1951-1970); Joseph Fielding Smith (1970-1972); Harold B. Lee (1972-1973); Spencer W. Kimball (1973-1985); and Ezra Taft Benson (1985-present).

The First Presidency and the Twelve regulate the affairs of the church generally. The Patriarch and the First Council of the Seventy (seven men) guide the missionary work of the church and regulate the local centers of the church through the local councils of seventy. The Presiding Bishopric (three men) has charge of the property and buildings owned by the church and heads the Aaronic Priesthood in which most of the young men of the church are ordained. The structure of the international organization is somewhat repeated in structures at the regional (stakes) and local (ward) levels.

Integral to the belief and practice of the church are temples. Such structures are used for special ceremonial work rather than being centers for the weekly gathering of worshippers. The four main services performed in the temple are the baptism for the dead (in which the living are baptized as proxies for those who died in generations past); the temple endowments (leading to ordination to the priesthood); temple marriage; and sealings (which establish family structures in the life beyond earthly existence).

The church has expanded rapidly, especially in the decades since World War II. It now has missions in most countries of the world. Wherever the church is, its ministry is assisted by the Relief Society (the women's auxiliary organization), the Primary Association (a children's organization), the Mutual Improvement Association (for youth) and the Church Welfare Program (to assist church members in need).

Membership: In 1982 the church reported 3,521,000 members and 7,839 congregations worldwide.

Educational facilities: Brigham Young University, Provo, Utah and Laie, Hawaii; Ricks College, Rexburg, Idaho; LDS Business College, Salt Lake City, Utah.

Periodicals: *Deseret News*, Box 1257, Salt Lake City, UT 84110; *The Ensign*, 50 East North Temple Street, Salt Lake City, UT 84150; *New Era*, 50 East North Temple Street, Salt Lake City, UT 84150.

Remarks: Beginning with the polygamy era in the nineteenth century, the church of Jesus Christ of Latter-Day Saints have been the objects of evangelical Christian missionaries. Since the 1960s, efforts to convert Mormons and to denounce the church have increased in proportion to the church's growth. Prominent among the anti-Mormons have been Jerald Tanner and Sandra Tanner, former Mormons who live in Salt Lake City and head Utah Lighthouse Ministry and Walter Martin of Christian Research Institute in San Juan Capistrano, California. The growth of anti-Mormon groups has led to the production of literature defending the Church and attempts to counter evangelical Christian material. Besides that produced by the church specifically for use of its missionaries are the independent efforts of Mormon Miscellaneous which prints a variety of tracts and the substantive polemical texts of Robert L. Brown and Rosemary Brown, which both answer and attack the Tanners and Walter Martin.

Sources: General sources include the following: Leonard J. Arrington and Davis Bitton, *The Mormon Experience*. New York: Alfred A. Knopf, 1979; LeGrand Richards, *A Marvelous Work and a Wonder*. Salt Lake City, UT: Deseret Book Company, 1968; Joseph S. Smith, *Gospel Doctrine*. Salt Lake City, UT: Deseret Book Company, 1969; Robert Gottlieb and Peter Wiley, *America's Saints*. New York: G. P. Putnam's Sons, 1984. Anti-Mormon

literature includes the following: Gordon H. Fraser, *Is Mormonism Christian?* Chicago: Moody Press, 1977; Floyd McElveen, *Will the "Saints" Go Marching In?* Glendale, CA: G/L Regal Books, 1977; Harry L. Ropp, *The Mormon Papers*. Downers Grove, IL: InterVarsity Press, 1977; Jerald Tanner and Sandra Tanner, *Mormonism--Shadow or Reality?* Salt Lake City, UT: Modern Microfilm, 1962. Controversial pro-Mormon literature includes the following: Robert L. Brown and Rosemary Brown, *They Lie In Wait to Deceive*. Mesa, AZ: Brownsworth Publishing Company, 1981. 2 vols.; Dean C. Jesse, *The Writing of Joseph Smith's History*. Sandy, UT: Mormon Miscellaneous, 1984; *A Latter-Day Saint Historian, Jerald and Sandra Tanner's Distorted View of Mormonism: A Response to Mormonism--Shadow or Reality?* Salt Lake City, UT: Privately Printed, 1977; Grant Von Harrison, *Converting with the Book of Mormon*. Provo, UT: Aaron Publishing and Indexing, 1981.

★709★
LDS SCRIPTURE RESEARCHERS
(Defunct)

Also known as the Believe God Society and Doers of the Word, the LDS Scipture Researchers was a small group headed by Sherman Russell Lloyd, a music teacher in Salt Lake City. They believed that the present age is the time for the promised return of Joseph Smith, Jr., in the flesh reincarnated. He was believed to be a member of their group. While accepting the basic Mormon scripture, they also read the writings of Emanuel Swedenborg. The group was organized under the authority of the one spoken of in Third Nephi 20:23, who would come forth with fabulous information. They did not publish a periodical but did publish several pamphlets.

★710★
ZION'S ORDER OF THE SONS OF LEVI
% Douglas Kilgore
Rte. 2
Mansfield, MO 65704

In 1938, Dr. Marl Kilgore felt called by the Lord to work among the older Mormon churches; the Church of Jesus Christ of Latter-Day Saints, the Reorganized Church of Jesus Christ of Latter-Day Saints, and the Church of Jesus Christ (Strangites). He wanted to call them back to the United Order, the communal structure practiced in the early days of the church, which must be lived when Christ returns (D.C.104). He worked with the LDS Church until 1950 when differences with his bishop led him to join the Aaronic Order. He moved to Bicknell, Utah, to aid a Mr. Taylor in his sawmill. Once there, he persuaded Taylor to leave the Aaronic Order and help him form a new church, which they called "Zion's Order of the Sons of Levi." After several moves, they bought a farm near Mansfield, Missouri, in 1953. There are slightly over fifty members governed by a presidency, counselors, a bishop, and a patriarch. They use all the Mormon scripture with the exception of Section 132 of the Doctrine and Covenants. They have adopted a communal lifestyle.

Zion's Order claims more than 650 revelations through Mr. Kilgore since 1951. Most of these have to do with the particularities of the life of the group. They claim the site of their commune as the place referred to by Isaiah (2.2) where the Lord's house should be built. They have tried to have other groups join them in building Zion anew, but these attempts have been unsuccessful to date. However, Kilgore resigned as president in 1969 to do mission work among Indians in the Southwest, which has brought a number of members into the church.

Membership: Not reported. There are approximately 50 residents on the farm in Missouri. There are a reported 11 churches in the Indian Mission.

Polygamy-Practicing

★711★
APOSTOLIC UNITED ORDER
1194 W. 16600, S.
Bluffsdale, UT 84065

The Apostolic United Brethren was formed in 1951 when the majority of the members and leaders of the United Effort Order, the largest of the polygamy-practicing groups, rejected the actions of its president, Joseph White Musser (1872-1954). Musser, who had become a polygamist in the early twentieth century, had been among the original leaders of the group established in 1929 by Lorin C. Woolley. During the several decades of the leadership of the Order by John Barlow, Musser had arisen as the major writer-apologist for polygamy. He ran the Truth Publishing Company in Salt Lake City, from which he published a number of books and a periodical, *The Truth*. In 1951, when Barlow died, Musser became the new president.

Two years prior to Barlow's death, Musser had suffered a stroke that left him partially incapacitated. The initial mistrust of his ability to provide adequate leadership was heightened when he appointed his personal physician, Rulon C. Allred, as his chief assistant. This mistrust became open revolt when he added a Mexican, Margarito Bautista, to a leadership position among the informal ruling elite. Musser met the resistance by dismissing the leadership, appointing a new set made up entirely of his supporters, and naming Allred as his successor. Most of the membership, including the residents at Short Creek, Arizona, where several of the dismissed leaders resided, rejected Musser, but several thousand followed him. He reorganized his followers as the Apostolic United Brethren. He also began a new periodical, *The Star of Truth*, which he edited until his death in 1954.

During the period of Rulon Allred's leadership, the Apostolic United Brethren grew several times over. A respected naturopathic physician in the Salt Lake City suburb of Murray and a polygamist since the 1930s, Allred moved quickly to consolidate the Apostolic United Brethren among polygamists, particularly in Mexico. He led in the establishment of a colony in Pinesdale, Montana, where a large meeting hall was dedicated in 1970. His leadership came to an abrupt end on May 10, 1977, when members of a rival polygamist group, the Church of the Lamb of God, led by Ervil LeBaron, assassinated him. He was succeeded by his brother, Owen Allred.

The Apostolic United Brethren is among the more liberal of the polygamy-practicing groups in that it allows sexual activity apart from any intent to produce children. It has also moved far beyond the polygamy issue in its criticism of the Church of Jesus Christ of Latter-Day Saints. It has condemned the larger Mormon body for its changes in traditional practice and belief, specifically its changing the garment worn during temple services, allowing blacks into the priesthood, and granting leadership concessions to women.

Membership: Not reported. Of approximately 30,000 polygamists, 5,000 to 7,000 are believed to be affiliated with the Apostolic United Brethren.

Sources: Rulon C. Allred, *Treasures of Knowledge*. 2 vols. Hamilton, MT: Bitteroot Publishing Co., 1982; Ben Bradlee, Jr. and Dale Van Atta, *Prophet of Blood*. New York: G. P. Putnam's Sons, 1981.; *The Most Holy Principle*. 4 vols. Murrary, UT: Gems Publishing Co., 1970-75; Joseph W. Musser, *Celestial or Plural Marriage*. Salt Lake City: Truth Publishing Co., 1944; Joseph W. Musser, *Michael Our Father and Our God*. Salt Lake City: Truth Publishing Company, 1963.

★712★
CHURCH OF JESUS CHRIST IN SOLEMN
  ASSEMBLY
% Alexander Joseph, Presiding King
Long Haul, Box 151
Big Water, UT 84741

Alexander Joseph was a member of the Apostolic United Brethren. He withdrew in 1975 and led a group of thirteen families in homesteading a colony in southern Utah. Unsuccessful, he moved to Glen Canyon City, now Big Water, Utah. He was elected mayor of Big Water in 1983. After leaving the Brethren, Joseph founded the Church of Jesus Christ in Solemn Assembly. In 1978 Joseph also founded the Confederate Nations of Israel, conceived of as an operational govenment comprising 144 seats, each to be filled by the current king of the particular nation that owns that seat. The nations are divided into three quorums: judges (24), senate (70), and the Council of Fifty (50). Each king acts as an independent sovereign and acts upon his own patriarchial authority. The quorums are not as yet filled, but among those slated to hold seats are Dennis Short, Gilbert A. Fulton, and Ogden Kraut (independent writers known for their defense of polygamy) and Norman LeBaron and Keith Bateman, formerly with the Church of the First Born of the Fullness of Times.

Joseph has issued a brief statement of belief, "Alexander's Creed," which espouses belief in posterity, reality, freedom, responsibility, justice, grace, and patriarchial government. The Church teaches polygamy, and many members enter celestial marriage contracts, but it is not a requirement for members. The Church does teach that the kingdom of God is fully comprehended in the marriage relationship and cannot be fully comprehended apart from it. Joseph has married over 20 times, and as of 1984 he had eighteen children.

Membership: In 1984 the Confederate Nations reported 250 members and 1 congregation with 70 ministers.

Educational facilities: University of the Great Spirit, Big Water, Utah.

Periodicals: *The Laws That Govern the Confederate Nations of Israel*, Box 151, Big Water, UT 84741.

Sources: Alexander Joseph, *Dry Bones*. Big Water, UT: University of the Great Spirit Press, 1979; Gilbert A. Fulton, Jr., *That Manifesto*. Kearns, UT: Deseret Publishing Co., 1974; Odgen Kraut, *Polygamy in the Bible*. Salt Lake City, UT: Kraut's Pioneer Press, 1983; Dennis R. Short, *For Men Only*. Sandy, UT: The Author, 1977.

★713★
CHURCH OF THE FIRST BORN
(Defunct)

When Joel LeBaron, founder of the Church of the First Born of the Fullness of Times, claimed Patriarchal Priesthood for himself, his brother, Ross Wesley LeBaron, rejected Joel's claim in favor of himself. He thus left his brother's church and formed the Church of the First Born. The statement of beliefs published by Ross Lebaron emphasized belief in Michael, the Eternal Father, and in his Son, Jesus Christ, and in Joseph Smith, the witness and testator. The Church of the First Born was established originally by Adam and restored in Joseph Smith. A belief in One Mighty and Strong to come was firmly held. LeBaron disincorporated the church in the early 1980s.

Sources: Verlan M. LeBaron, *The LeBaron Family*. Lubbock, TX: the Author, 1981; Ross W. LeBaron, *The Redemption of Zion*. Colonia LeBaron: Chih., Mexico: The Church of the First-Born, [1962].

★714★
CHURCH OF THE FIRST BORN OF THE FULLNESS OF TIMES
5854 Mira Serana
El Paso, TX 79912

Church of the First Born of the Fullness of Times dates to the participation among Mormon fundamentalist groups of the LeBaron family--Alma Dayer LeBaron, his sons Floren LeBaron, Benjamin F.LeBaron, Alma LeBaron, Jr., Ross Wesley LeBaron, Ervil LeBaron, Joel LeBaron, Verlan M. LeBaron, and a cousin, Owen LeBaron. Alma Dayer LeBaron who, with his family, was a member of the Church of Jesus Christ of Latter-Day Saints was affiliated with polygamist leader Joseph White Musser as early as 1936. In 1934, Benjamin claimed to be the One Mighty and Strong, the prophetic figure mentioned in the Mormon writings known as the *Doctrines and Covenants 85*, and heconvinced several members of the family to substantiate his claims as a prophet. In 1944 the LeBaron family was excommunicated. From then until 1955, most of the family associated with the "fundamentalist" colony in Mexico, directed by Rulon C. Allred, leader of the Apostolic United Brethren. The LeBaron family members were in the process of setting up a united order (a communal economic style of living) when, in 1955, they decided to leave Allred's Mexican colony.

Joel, Ross Wesley, and Floren worked out the basic order of their own church and incorporated on September 1, 1955, under the name of the Church of the First Born of the Fullness of Times. Joel claimed to have the "Patriarchal Priesthood" and had a revelation directing Allred to become his councilor. Allred rejected the invitation. Both Benjamin and Ross Wesley also rejected his claims.

Joel claimed a line of priesthood succession through his father, Alma, Sr., to Alma's grandfather, Benjamin F. Johnson, who was secretly ordained by Joseph Smith. (Mormon authorities point out that Johnson accepted the Manifesto of 1890 abolishing polygamy.) Joel claimed that the priesthood was superior to the presidency of the church, the apostles, and seventies.

Joel LeBaron led the Church of the First Born of the Fullness of Times until he was murdered in 1972. He was succeeded by his brother Verlan, who was killed in an automobile accident in 1981. The current leader of the Church is Siegfried Widmar. For a number of years the Church published a magazine, *Ensign*, in which most of its doctrinal and polemical works were published.

Educational facilities: The group is small, containing several hundred members at most. Most of the membership is located in Mexico.

Sources: Verlan M.LeBaron, *The LeBaron Story*. Lubbock, TX: the Author, 1981; Verlan M. LeBaron,

Economic Democracy Under Eternal Law. El Paso, TX: Church of the Firstborn of the Fullness of Time, 1963; Henry W. Richards, *A Reply to "The Church of the Firstborn of the Fullness of Times".* Salt Lake City: The Author, 1965; Stephen M. Silver, "Priesthood and Presidency, An Answer to Henry W. Richards" in *Ensign* vol. 2, no. 11 (January 1963) pp. 1-127; Siegfried J. Widmar, *The Political Kingdom of God.* El Paso, TX: The Author, 1975; *Priesthood Expounded.* Mexican Mission of the Church of the Firstborn of the Fullness of Times, 1956.

★715★
CHURCH OF THE LAMB OF GOD
Current address not obtained for this edition.

The Church of the Lamb of God was formed in 1970 by Ervil LeBaron, who had held the second-highest office in the Church of the First Born of the Fullness of Times, founded by his brother, Joel LeBaron. In that year Ervil was dismissed from the Church of the First Born of the Fullness of Times. As the leader of his new church, he claimed full authority over all of the polygamy-practicing groups, and asserted an authority to execute anyone who would refuse to accept him as the representative of God.

Beginning at the time of the establishment of the Church of the Lamb of God, a string of murders and feloneous attacks plagued the polygamy-practicing Mormons. On August 20, 1972, Joel LeBaron was shot to death in Ensenada, Mexico. On June 16, 1975, Dean Vest, an associate of Joel LeBaron, was killed near San Diego. On May 10, 1977, Dr. Rulon C. Allred, leader of the Apostolic United Brethren, a rival polygamy group, was brutally murdered in his chiropractic office in Salt Lake City while attending patients. On May 14, 1977, Merlin Kingston, another polygamy leader, narrowly survived an attempt on his life. At least thirteen other polygamy-practicing Mormons were killed before Ervil was arrested, tried, convicted, and sentenced in 1980 for the death of Allred. He died in prison the following year of natural causes.

Membership: Not reported. Since the death of Ervil LeBaron, there have been conflicting reports of the disbanding of the Church. Its present status is unknown.

Sources: Ervil LeBaron, *Priesthood Expounded.* Buenaventurea, Mex: Mexican Mission of the Church of the Firstborn of the Fullness of Times, 1956; Ervil LeBaron, *An Open Letter to a Former Presiding Bishop.* San Diego: The Author, 1972; Michael Fessier, Jr., "Ervil LeBaron, the Man Who Would Be God" in *New West* (January 1981), pp. 80-84, 112-17.

★716★
MILLENNIAL CHURCH OF JESUS CHRIST
% Leo Peter Evoniuk LeBaron
177 Webster St.
Monterey, CA 93940

Claiming to be the spiritual successor to Ervil Lebaron, founder of the Church of the Lamb of God, Leo P. E. LeBaron organized the Millennial Church of Jesus Christ in the mid-1980s. According to a revelation given him in 1984, Ervil LeBaron was delivered by the Lord God from his enemies and now sits on God's right hand. The keys held by Ervil LeBaron have passed to Leo LeBaron. The revelation asserted the necessity of the restoration of the Melchizedek Priesthood and the Patriarchial Order, or damnation will follow. LeBaron and his associate Grand Patriarchs, Paul L. Gardunio, Bill Rios and Raul Rios, have inherited the sealing keys formerly held by Ervil LeBaron. Their task is to seal the 144,000 Grand Patriarchs of the Twelve Tribes of Israel, whom God had hidden from the world previously. They are the only persons entrusted with that sealing power.

Membership: Not reported.

★717★
PERFECTED CHURCH OF JESUS CHRIST
IMMACULATE LATTER-DAY SAINTS
(Defunct)

Among the most unusual of the polygamy-practicing churches was the Perfected Church of Jesus Christ Immaculate Latter-Day Saints, founded by William C. Conway, D.D., of Redondo Beach, California, who claimed to be "the scribe and goodwill ambassador for 500,000 Indians," members of the Perfected Church. Conway claimed that when the Church of Jesus Christ of Latter-Day Saints rejected the six commandments given to Joseph Smith (concerned with the united order and plural marriage primarily), Jesus Christ walked out of the church to Walker Lake, Nevada. There, in the spring of 1890, directed by visions and dreams, several hundred Indians had assembled. Jesus re-established the kingdom as it was in pre-Edenic days and gave Joseph Smith's authority to one of their members, a young white Indian from Yu-ka-tan, named Eachta Eacha Na. He is identified with the One Mighty and Strong, the prophetic personage mentioned in the Mormon scriptures, the *Doctrines and Covenants 85.* The reincarnated Joseph Smith and Angel Moroni (an angel mentioned in the Book of Mormon) are with the One Mighty and Strong.

In 1930, additional keys of authority were transferred by Lorin Woolley, founder of the United Order Effort, largest of the Mormon fundamentalist groups. Woolley was supposedly one of the five authorized to continue plural marriage by President John Taylor of the LDS Church.

Mr. Conway also claims that Moroni "succeeded in perfecting a plan of instruction that abolished menstruation among the woman folk," and that Jesus had explained the technique of immaculate conception. Babies conceived immaculately stay for twelve months in the womb and are immune to all disease. No count on membership in the United States is available.

Membership: This Church is presumed to be defunct as of 1985.

★718★

SONS AHMAN ISRAEL
Box 186
Washington, UT 84780

Sons Ahman Israel was founded at Saratoga Hot Springs, Utah, at dawn on January 25, 1981, by presiding Patriarch David Israel and four other former members of the Church of Jesus Christ of Latter-Day Saints. The group believes in the continued visitation of and revelation by angels, and David Israel regularly receives such revelations in the form of morning and evening oracles. Besides the Bible and the *Book of Mormon*, a wide variety of materials are accepted as scripture, including ancient apocryphal writings (such as the *Gospel of Thomas*, the *Gospel of Philip*, the *Book of Enoch*, the writings found at Nag Hammadi) and modern Mormon revelations (such as the *Oracles of Mohonri* and *The Order of the Sons of Zadok*). Members believe in a secret oral tradition which passed from Moses to the Essenes, the Gnostics, and eventually to Joseph Smith, Jr. That tradition is preserved in such books as the *Pistis Sophia*, an ancient Gnostic text, and the *Sephir Yetzira*, a prime text from Hassidic Judaism.

A 22-item statement of "S.A.I. Beliefs" affirms belief in a heavenly hierarchy consisting of a Heavenly Father and Mother, their son, Jesus Christ, the Holy Spirit, angels and archangels, and ministers of the flame (just men made perfect). Human beings are the literal offspring of the heavenly Parents and have come into earthly existence to experience the mystery of mortality. Redemption for humans comes only through surrendering their life to Yetshuah the Christ and subsequently developing a relationship to Him in the holy temple ordinances and ritualistic ceremonies. The Sons Ahman Israel also follows the Old Testament feasts and holy days.

The Sons Ahman Israel had absorbed much of its ritual practice from the Christian Kabbalah. A monthly ritual cycle begins with each new moon when baptisms are held. On the second lunar day, charisms (holy annointings) are made and on the third day a eucharistic supper is prepared. The fourth through the fifteenth days are for participation in ceremonial priesthood rituals. The full moon is a time for a monthly feast.

The Sons Ahman Israel is headed by a presiding patriarch and matriarch, under whom function (when the organization is at full strength) a first presidency (of three people), a council of twelve apostles, seven arch seventies, and twelve stake princes. Each stake is headed by twelve high counselmen, a quorum of seventy, and twelve bishops. The church practices polygamy but also believes in the perfect equality of the sexes. Women are accepted into the priesthood on an equal basis with men.

Membership: Not reported. As of 1984 it is estimated to be less than 100.

Educational facilities: School of the Prophets, Mt. Kolob, Utah.

Periodicals: *Stone Magazine*, Box 186, Washington, UT 84780.

Sources: *The Sacred Scrolls of the Sons Ahman Israel.* LaVern, UT: Sons Ahman Israel, n.d.

★719★

UNITED ORDER EFFORT
% Leroy Johnson
Colorado City, AZ 86021

The United Effort Order, the largest of the polygamy-practicing groups among the Mormons, began in 1929 when Lorin C. Woolley organized a council of people dedicated to seeing that no year passed without at least one child being born within a plural marriage. Woolley, who claimed to have been commissioned by Mormon Church President John Taylor in 1886, acted only after all of the others present at that time were dead. Woolley had been actively publishing and spreading the story of the authority he and others had from the late-president of the Church of Jesus Christ of Latter-Day Saints since 1912 but experienced only modest success until 1929, when Joseph White Musser compiled the various accounts of the 1886 revelation and published them. He also joined J. Leslie Broadbent, John Y. Barlow, Charles Zitting, Legrand Woolley, and Louis Kelsh as a member of the council.

Lorin Woolley died in 1934. He was succeeded by Broadbent, who died a few months later, who in turn was succeeded by Barlow, the man most known for his early leadership of the group and of its main colony in rural Arizona, Short Creek (presently known as Colorado City). Short Creek had become a haven for polygamists who had gathered there in the late 1920s to escape the problems created by both law enforcement agents and the increased discipline of the Church of Jesus Christ of Latter-Day Saints. Soon after becoming leader of the group, Barlow contacted some of the more vocal advocates of polygamy at Short Creek and worked out an agreement between them and the council. Eventually he moved to Short Creek with some of his followers, and within a few years the polygamists dominated the settlement. Barlow created the United Trust, incorporated formally in 1942 as the United Effort Plan, but commonly known as the United

Effort Order. Meanwhile, Musser, who remained in Salt Lake City, began publication of *The Truth*, the periodical for the group, and the most influential organ promoting polygamy by any group.

Under Barlow's leadership the colony at Short Creek flourished and the United Effort spread throughout Mormon communities in the West, particularly in Idaho, Montana, and Southern California. Many of the polygamists who had fled to Mexico in previous years also accepted Barlow's authority. Having survived a 1935 raid which attempted to destroy the Short Creek community, the only major trouble for the United Effort came in 1944 when an antipolygamy crusade swept through Salt Lake City. Musser and other leaders were arrested and spent several months in jail while the crusade lasted.

Barlow's death in 1951 led to internal crisis and schism within the United Effort. Musser, the new president of the ruling council, was in poor health, and many people rejected his appointments of his physician, Rulon C. Allred, and a Mexican leader, Margarito Bautista, to fill council vacancies. In response, Musser disbanded the entire council and appointed a new one made up of his supporters. That action split the group, the majority of which supported the leadership at Short Creek. The older members of the council elected a new president, Charles Zitting, while Musser organized his following as the Apostolic United Brethren.

Zitting died within months of his election and was succeeded by Leroy Johnson, a council member added by Barlow. Johnson was almost immediately plunged into a new crisis. On July 26, 1953, the governor of Arizona conducted a massive raid on Short Creek. Most of the men were arrested and the women and children placed in the state's custody. Only after several months, during which time the governor realized the political and financial disaster of his actions, were the colonists allowed to return to their homes where they have lived quietly in recent decades.

The United Effort Order is among the strictest of the several polygamy-practicing groups. It approves of sex only for the intention of producing children and demands abstinence while a female is either pregnant or breast-feeding.

Membership: Not reported. Of the approximately 30,000 polygamists, it is estimated that 7,000 to 10,000 are affiliated with the United Order Effort. Several hundred reside at the colonies at Colorado City, Arizona and nearby Hilldale, Utah.

Sources: Max J. Anderson, *The Polygamy Story: Fiction or Fact*. Salt Lake City: Publishers Press, 1979; Ben Bradlee, Jr. and Dale Van Alta. *Prophet of Blood*. New York: G. P. Putnam's Sons, 1981; Joseph White Musser, *Celestial or Plural Marriage*. Salt Lake City: Truth Publishing Co.,

1944; Kimball Young, *Isn't One Wife Enough*. New York: Henry Holt and Company, 1954.

Missouri Mormons

★720★
CHURCH OF CHRIST (BIBLE AND BOOK OF MORMON TEACHING)
1515 S. Harvard
Independence, MO 64052

The Church of Christ (Bible and Book of Mormon Teaching) represents a movement toward orthodox Christianity by former members of the Temple Lot group discussed above. Pauline Hancock, a former church schoolteacher with the Church of Christ (Temple Lot) and daughter of one of the seventy, began to teach that God the Father, Son, and Holy Ghost were one personage. Her Trinitarianism conflicted with the tritheism of most Mormon groups. She was excommunicated and in 1946 organized her own church, called the Church of Christ.

The disagreement over the doctrine of the Trinity was not the only point of difference between the Church of Christ and other Mormons. The newly-organized Church of Christ accepted only the Book of Mormon as valid and taught that Joseph Smith, Jr., founder of the Mormons, was a man called of God but became a wicked man and taught polygamy. Also, in a more orthodox sense, the Church of Christ believed in the Fall; no baptism for the dead was used and only adults were baptized. Mrs. Hancock felt she was called to preach and cited Joseph Smith's "ordination" of Emma Smith as a precedent. Her authority for organizing the church came in her call and subsequent visions.

The doctrinal transition that was noticeable in the founding of the church made a significant move toward orthodox Christianity in 1973 when, having come to believe that Joseph Smith was a fraud, the Book of Mormon was discarded. The Bible alone was accepted as the group's scripture. The church now sees itself as a non-denominational Bible church. The doctrines of the Trinity, the divinity of Christ and the ultimate destiny for all as either heaven or hell is affirmed.

A congregation exists in Independence, Missouri, with members scattered in Michigan, Wisconsin, and California. The church regularly places ads in the *Independence (MO) Examiner*, advertising its position and inviting its consideration by Mormons.

Membership: Not reported.

Sources: *Correspondence between Israel Smith and Pauline Hancock on Baptism for the Dead*. Independence, MO: Church of Christ, [1955]; Pauline Hancock, *The Godhead, Is There More Than One?* Independence, MO: Church of

Christ, n.d.; Pauline Hancock, *Whence Came the Book of Mormon?* Independence, MO; Church of Christ, [1958]; Samuel Wood, *The Infinite God.* Fresno, CA: The Author, 1934.

★721★
CHURCH OF CHRIST (FETTING/BRONSON)
1138 East Gudgell
Independence, MO 64055

On February 4, 1927, Otto Fetting, one of the twelve apostles of the Church of Christ (Temple Lot), claimed that John the Baptist had appeared to him and told him that it was time to build the temple. Other messages gave instructions concerning the building of the temple.

The twelth message became the matter of lengthy controversy. It said, "Let those who come to the church of Christ be baptized, that they may rid themselves of the traditions and sins of men." The members of the Temple Lot church had great difficulty with this passage. Many had come into the church by transfer from the Reorganized Church of Jesus Christ of Latter-Day Saints, and had not been baptized upon entering the Temple Lot Church. They intepreted the message to call for a rebaptism of the entire church membership. A conference held in October 1929 denounced the idea of rebaptizing the Church. Fetting was not allowed to speak on the baptism question. After the conference he was silenced and told to wait for a referendum vote at the conference the following April. For whatever reason, he did not wait, and after the conference, he, Apostle Walter L. Gates, and Thomas B. Nerren were baptized. Others also received a new baptism and in the fall of 1929, all who had been baptized were disfellowshiped. The Church of Christ (Fetting) was begun by Fetting's followers, approximately 1,400 or about one-third of the Temple Lot Church at the time.

Fetting continued to receive messages until his death in 1933. There were thirty messages in all. Several years after Fetting's death, a member in Colorado, W. A. Draves, began to receive messages. At first these messages were received by the larger body of the Church. However, some members, especially those in Louisiana and Mississippi, rejected Draves almost from the beginning and before the end of the decade reorganized as the Church of Christ (Restored). Eventually, in 1943, the church rejected Graves. After a court suit, which the Draves' supporters lost, they reorganized as the Church of Christ with the Elijah Message.

During years following the departure of Draves' supporters, leaders began to advocate the keeping of the Saturday Sabbath. The issue was debated for many years until 1956 when, the Twelve Apostles having reached an agreement on the issue, adopted sabbatarianism for the entire church. It is organized like the Church of Christ (Temple Lot).

Membership: Not reported.

Periodicals: *The Voice of Warning,* 1138 E. Gudgell, Independence, MO 64055.

Sources: *The Word of the Lord.* Independence, MO: Church of Christ, 1935; Willard J. Smith, *Fetting and His Messenger's Messages.* Port Huron, MI: The Author, [1936]; Otto Fetting, *The Midnight Message.* Independence, MO: Church of Christ (Temple Lot), [1930].

★722★
CHURCH OF CHRIST (RESTORED)
% Mr. Uel Sisk
609 C Lilac Place, John Knox Village
Lee's Summit, MO 64063

During the late 1930s the Church of Christ (Fetting), which had been built according to messages received by Otto Fetting prior to his death in 1933, was split over the messages being received by R. A. Draves. At first the main body of the Fettingite Church accepted the messages as like those of Fetting. One branch of the church centered in Louisiana and Mississippi, however, did not accept them and reorganized as the Church of Christ (Restored) independently of the main body of Fettingites. This small body has continued to the present and claims to be the true Fettingite church. (The larger body eventually rejected Draves; however, it also accepted the Saturday-sabbath which the Church of Christ (Restored) views as further error).

Membership: In 1984 the church reported approximately 300 members in the United States. There were 8 congregations and 16 ministers. There were also approximately 25 foreign members in Wales, Germany, and the Netherlands.

Periodicals: *The Gospel Herald,* Mr. Uel Sisk, 609 C Lilac Place, John Knox Village, Lee's Summit, MO 64063.

★723★
CHURCH OF CHRIST (TEMPLE LOT)
Temple Lot
Independence, MO 65051

In the winter of 1852, a number of LDS members met in the home of Granville Hedrick near Bloomington, Illinois. Word of polygamy in Utah had reached these Saints and they withdrew their fellowship from the Utah brethren. Over the next three year they met sporadically and in 1867 Granville Hedrick was set apart as their presiding elder. The group further declared their belief in the Book of Mormon and the 1835 *Book of Commandments.* They took their stand against "polygamy" and "baptism of the dead" as practiced in Utah, and against the idea of "lineal succession of the presidency," which the Reorganized Church of Jesus Christ of Latter Day Saints (then called the New Organization) advocated. They adopted the name of the Church of Christ.

In 1863, Hedrick was elected president, and shortly thereafter he received a revelation which said that the Saints should be gathered back to Missouri, specifically to Independence, Missouri, which had been declared by Joseph Smith, Jr. to be the headquarters of the New Zion (Doctrine and Covenants 57:3). But the Saints had been driven out to Nauvoo, Illinois in 1838-39. In the winter of 1866-67, the members began to return quietly to Independence, and individually began to buy up the land which had been designated for the building of the temple. On that land, they put up a small structure which now serves as the headquarters. The church grew slowly and steadily and in good relations with the Reorganized Church until the 1890s. At that time, the Reorganized Church took the Church of Christ to court to try and recover the temple lot. To do this, the Reorganized Church produced a false deed which had supposedly been made out to Oliver Cowdery's children. Eventually, the Church of Christ was able to furnish proof that the deeds were false and the children non-existent.

In 1925 the Church of Christ voted to accept the 1833 *Book of Commandments* instead of the 1835 edition used prior to that time. Finding no mention of a first presidency, they abolished that office in favor of the twelve apostles.

The church reached its highest membership of approximately 4,000 about 1930. This followed some dissension in the Reorganized Church. In 1884, the Church of Christ had recognized other churches of the Restoration and declared their baptism valid. Thus, members of the Reorganized Church could easily transfer.

The influx of members was a short-lived boon as the church was immediately thrown into turmoil over the revelations of one of its twelve apostles, Otto Fetting. Fetting had been receiving revelations since 1927. The church had acknowledged the revelation which centered upon instructions to begin building the temple. Excavations were begun on the temple in 1929 and foundation stones were uncovered. In 1930, a revelation was received which was interpreted to mean that all the church members would have to be rebaptized. After this revelation, the church refused to accept Fetting, and in 1930 disfellowshipped him and his followers.

The Church of Christ (Temple Lot) is presided over by twelve apostles, a secretary, a few bishops, seventies, and other officers. In 1864 a periodical, *The Truth Teller*, was begun. Its name was changed to *The Search Light* (1896) and *The Evening and Morning Star* (1900). The present periodical took its name in 1922.

Membership: Not reported. At last report (1972), the Church had 2,400 members, 32 congregations, and 188 ministers.

Periodicals: *Zion's Advocate*, Box 472, Independence, MO 64051.

Sources: B. C. Flint, *An Outline History of the Church of Christ (Temple Lot)*. Independence, MO: Board of Publication, Church of Christ (Temple Lot), 1953; B. C. Flint, *Autobiography*. [Independence, MO]: Privately printed, n.d.; *A Book of Commandments for the Government of the Church of Christ*. Independence, MO: Church of Christ, Temple Lot, 1960; Arthur M. Smith, *Temple Lot Deed*. Independence, MO: Board of Publication, Church of Christ (Temple Lot), 1963; B. C. Flint, *What About Israel?*. Independence, MO: Board of Publication, Church of Christ (Temple Lot), 1967; Clarence L. Wheaton and Angela Wheaton, *The Book of Commandments Controversy Reviewed*. Independence, MO: Church of Christ (Temple Lot), 1950.

★724★
CHURCH OF CHRIST AT HALLEY'S BLUFF
Schell City, MO 64783

The Church of Christ at Halley's Bluff, also known as the Church of Christ at Zion's Retreat, was founded in 1932 by former members of the Church of Christ (Temple Lot) who left in a dispute over the messages of Otto Fetting. A group centered in Denver, Colorado, and led by E. E. Long and Thomas Nerren had accepted Fetting's messages but had remained within the Temple Lot when the majority of his followers had left. The original congregation was located in Denver, Colorado, but by the end of the decade five other congregations had joined the small denomination. Nerren began to receive revelations. In 1941, in response to such a revelation, the church moved its headquarters to Zion's Retreat, a 441-acre tract of land in northeast Vernon County, about seventy miles south of Independence, Missouri, the site of Zion according to Mormon prophet Joseph Smith, Jr.

In 1942 the congregation in Cranston, Rhode Island, moved to Zion's Retreat. They were soon joined by the remaining members in Denver, and the group in Independence came in 1946. The remaining congregation, located in Delevan, Wisconsin, separated from the group in Missouri in 1966 and continues to exist today as an independent congregation.

The peace within the church in Missouri was disturbed in the 1960s after Daniel Gayman, one of its pastors, became editor of the church's periodical. He began to advocate strong racist and antiblack sentiments. Then in 1972 Gayman called a meeting of the church, deposed several bishops, and had himself elected to lead the church. The deposed bishops, General Hall and Duane Gayman, and their supporters filed suit and the court returned the property and the use of the church's several names to them. Meanwhile, the Hall-Gayman group had reincorporated as the Church of Christ at Halley's Bluff.

With the loss of its members in Wisconsin and the defection of Daniel Gayman's supporters, the Church of Christ at Halley's Bluff remains as but a small remnant within the family of Latter Day Saint Churches.

Membership: There are less than 100 members.

★725★
CHURCH OF CHRIST WITH THE ELIJAH MESSAGE (DRAVESITES)
608 Lacy Rd.
Independence, MO 64050

The Fettingite Church discussed above received no revelations from 1933 to 1937. In October of 1937, however, a member, W. A. Draves, in Nucla, Colorado, began to experience visits from John the Baptist. These were at first accepted, at least through message No. 56. One message placed Draves among the twelve apostles. But in 1943 some doubts were raised about Draves. He was accused of fraud (in obtaining information about members to use in his messages) and of living with two wives. A battle over control of the church began at the 1943 assembly and led to a court suit which the supporters of Draves lost. They then reorganized and incorporated as the Church of Christ Established Anew. The present name was adopted in 1965.

The Dravesites are basically like the Temple Lot Church members in belief, accepting Temple Lot history to 1930 and Fettingite history to 1943. They do accept a Saturday Sabbath and have their own edition of the Book of Mormon which they call *The Record of the Nephites*. The church has apostles who reside in various areas. A council of bishops manages the church and the council's secretary is the only full-time employee. The church supports an active mission program and has congregations in India, Uganda, Kenya, Tasmania, Nigeria, France, Germany and Italy.

Membership: In 1984 the church reported 1,200 members, 9 congregation and 20 ministers in the United States. There were 11,200 members worldwide.

Periodicals: *The Voice of Peace*, Box 199, Independence, MO 64051.

Sources: *The Record of the Nephites*. Independence, MO: Board of Publications, Church of Jesus Christ with the Elijah Message, 1970; Daniel MacGregor, *Changing of the Revelations*. Independence, MO: W. A. Draves, n.d.; *Foot-Prints in the Sands of Time*. Nucla, CO: W. A. Draves, 1942; *The Word of the Lord*. Independence, MO: Church of Christ with the Elijah Message, 1971.

★726★
REORGANIZED CHURCH OF JESUS CHRIST OF LATTER-DAY SAINTS
The Auditorium
Box 1059
Independence, MO 64051

Few churches have as complicated an early history as the Reorganized Church of Jesus Christ of Latter-Day Saints. It was formed in 1860 by remnants of the Saints left in the East and Midwest; the prime movers of the new church were Jason Briggs, Zenos Gurley, and William Marks.

Briggs had been an elder in the Church of Jesus Christ of Latter-Day Saints (LDS) at Nauvoo, Illinois, and remained loyal until the trek West. He then joined Jesse Strang in 1848. He soon rejected Strang and joined in William Smith's short-lived church in 1850. In 1851, he left Smith and in November claimed a revelation in which the Lord affirmed that He had not cast off His people and that in due time, from the seed of Joseph would come forth one mighty and strong (II Nephi 2:46-47).

Zenos Gurley was senior president of one of the seventies in Nauvoo. He remained loyal to Brigham Young until a few days before the departure west. He joined Strang and was a bishop, but like Briggs he left Strang in 1852. He claimed a revelation similar to Brigg's concerning Joseph's son.

William Marks was the Nauvoo stake president who was excommunicated when he supported the claims of Sidney Rigdon, who founded the precursor to the Church of Christ (Bickertonite). Marks joined Rigdon, then Strang, then several other Mormon groups.

In 1852 Gurley and Briggs came together to form the New Organization, basically from some of Strang's followers. They decided that Joseph Smith III should lead the new church. The organization was effected in 1853 and Briggs was chosen to preside. Young Joseph refused the presidency at first, but in 1859 accepted it. In 1859, William Marks was admitted to the New Organization, and it was he who ordained Smith president. On April 6, 1860, the New Organization became the Reorganized Church of Jesus Christ of Latter-Day Saints with 300 members.

The Reorganized Church agrees with the Utah Church in a number of important points. Members of the Reorganized Church accept all the scriptures that Joseph Smith wrote and their statement of belief is very close to that of the Utah brethren. In particular, they accept the idea of the restoration of the ministerial, priestly, and prophetic offices in the nineteenth century; the gifts of the Spirit; and salvation by faith, repentance, baptism by immersion, and the laying on of hands.

The Reorganized Church draws sharp distinctions on several points on which it feels the Utah Church has fallen into error. The Reorganized Church rejects polygamy, and all the associated doctrines-sealing of marriages for eternity and marriage by proxy to persons deceased-are rejected most strongly. The doctrine that "As man is now is, God once was; as God now is, so man may become," the Adam-God theory, is felt to conflict plainly with the monotheism of the Bible. The members of the Reorganized Church consider abhorrent the practice of "blood atonement" as enunciated by Brigham Young, by which apostates were killed to save them from damnation. In the Reorganized Church, there are no closed temples nor services from which the public is barred, nor any special temple garments.

The most significant difference in the Reorganized Church is its adoption of a hereditary prophetic office in the descendants of Joseph Smith, Jr. Since 1860, the president-prophets of the church have been successively Joseph Smith III (1860-1914), Frank Madison Smith (1914-1946), Israel Alexander Smith (1946-1958), and W. Wallace Smith (1958-). The president-prophets have, unlike the Utah Church presidents, added periodic revelations which appear as additions to the *Doctrine and Covenants.*

The Reorganized Church is described as a theocratic democracy-a government of God directed divinely under the law of "common consent" of the people. There is a world conference held every two years in the church headquarters auditorium, located across the street from the Church of Christ (Temple Lot) in Independence, Missouri. The church has been the most open of all Mormon bodies to mainline Protestantism and one finds books by outstanding Protestants (of a noncontroversial nature) in the catalogue of the church book service. Herald House serves as both the publishing arm of the church and as a retail book distributor. Foreign work is being conducted in Nigeria, Japan, South Korea, Okinawa, South India, the Philippines, Brazil, Mexico, Haiti, New Zealand, Australia, French Polynesia, England, and Germany.

Membership: In 1982 the church reported 201,480 members, 1,061 congregations, and 16,533 ministers.

Educational facilities: Graceland College, Lamoni, Iowa.

Periodicals: *Saints Herald*, Box 1059, Independence, MO 64051.

Sources: Aleah G. Koury, *The Truth and the Evidence.* Independence, MO: Herald Publishing House, 1965; Alvin Knisley, *Infallible Proofs.* Independence, MO: Herald Publishing House, 1930; Daniel MacGregor, *A Marvelous Work and a Wonder.* N.p.: The Author, 1911; F. Henry Edwards, *Fundamentals, Enduring Convictions of the Restoration.* Independence, MO: Herald Publishing House, n.d.

Miscellaneous Mormons

★727★
CHURCH OF JESUS CHRIST (BICKERTONITE)
Sixth & Lincoln Sts.
Monogahela, PA 15603

Sidney Rigdon had been the First Counselor to Joseph Smith, Jr. during the early years of the church. In spite of his health problems which began with the incident in which he and Smith were tarred and feathered and his falling out with the Church over Smith's proposing plural marriage to his daughter, Rigdon retained his formal position in the church. Based upon his office in the church, after Smith's assassination, he claimed to be his successor. Though rejected by the other church leaders, Rigdon found some followers which he led to Pennsylvania. In 1844 he reorganized the church which had but a short life. In the fall of 1846 disagreements appeared that led to its disintegration.

William Bickerton, who never knew Joseph Smith, had joined Sidney Rigdon's church in 1845. Left without a church by the disintegration of Rigdon's following, he joined the Church of Jesus Christ of Latter-Day Saints congregation at Elizabeth, Pennsylvania, in which he became an elder. Sometime shortly after the public announcement of the doctrine of polygamy, Bickerton denounced Brigham Young and the Utah apostles and left the church. He formally organized a new church in July, 1862, claiming he did so in obedience to a revelation. Bickerton gathered some of Rigdon's followers as his first members.

The small Church of Jesus Christ has had a rather tumultuous history. A branch was established in Kansas in 1875, and Bickerton moved there with the church headquarters. Friction arose between the Pennsylvania and Kansas branches, and Bickerton, accused of adultery, was disfellowshipped from his own church. (He returned in 1902.) William Cadman was elected president. In 1904, the year before Cadman's death, a reorganization took place. In 1907, further friction resulted in half the leaders leaving and forming the short-lived Reorganization Church of Jesus Christ. A second schism occurred in 1914.

The doctrine of the Bickertonite Church follows closely that of the Church of Jesus Christ of Latter-Day Saints prior to Joseph Smith's death. The members are strongly opposed to polygamy. They do practice the Lord's Supper weekly (a reflection of Sidney Rigdon's continued attachment to the ideas of Alexander Campbell), the washing of feet, and the holy kiss. The church is ruled by a president, two councilors, a secretary, financial secretary, and treasurer. There is an annual conference of elders which elects officers.

Membership: In 1981 the church reported 2,654 members, 53 congregations, and 243 ministers.

Periodicals: *Gospel News,* 8423 Boettner Road, Bridgewater, MI 48115.

Sources: W. H. Cadman, *A History of the Church of Jesus Christ.* Monogahela, PA: The Church of Jesus Christ, 1945; F. Mark McKiernan, *The Voice of One Crying in the Wilderness: Sidney Rigdon, Religious Reformer, 1793-1876.* N.p.: Herald House, 1979; Willaim Cadman, *Faith and Doctrines of the Church of Jesus Christ.* Roscoe, PA: Roscoe Ledger Print., 1902.

★728★
CHURCH OF JESUS CHRIST (CUTLERITE)
819 S. Cottage St.
Independence, MO 64050

Alpheus Cutler was an elder in the LDS Church and gained some prominence for his efforts in building the Nauvoo Temple. In 1841, he was by revelation (D.C. 12:132) appointed to the Nauvoo State High Council. After Joseph Smith's death, Cutler began a mission to the Indians. The Church of Jesus Christ of Latter-Day Saints claims that the mission was given by Brigham Young. Cutler claimed later that he was given the call by Joseph Smith, Jr. who had given him sole authority to preach the gospel to the Lamanites, the American Indians. When the group under Young went to Utah, Cutler stayed behind and claimed authority from Smith to carry on as an elder in the church.

As a recent church member wrote: "Joseph Smith had organized a group of men into an order of seven, a kingdom order. Joseph was number one in that order and Alpheus Cutler was number seven, and Joseph ordained all six of those men to hold the keys, powers and authorities which he held. So they each held the kingdom authority. As time went on all of the men in that order of seven except Alpheus Cutler either died or joined some of the factions. Alpheus Cutler was number seven and he waited his turn to work. He had been promised he would be given a sign, a certain sign when it was time for him to begin his work, and when he received that sign he began to prepare for organization."

In 1849, Cutler and some followers established a settlement in Iowa which was named Manti. A formal organization of the Church of Jesus Christ followed in 1853, after a number of Saints from Council Bluffs swelled the growing community. There was constant fluctuation in membership during the remainder of Cutler's lifetime because of periodic arguments with other groups of Mormons operating in the Midwest.

In 1864, following Cutler's death, Chauncey Whiting, Cutler's successor, led a group to Minnesota (according to a revelation which Cutler had received) where the town of Clitherall was established. Here they tried to establish a communal existence (the United Order) but were unsuccessful. In 1910, Isaac Whitney, the new first councilor and president of the high priesthood, called all to return to the United Order, which was accomplished in 1913.

In 1928, a branch of the church was established in Independence, Missouri, the site of Zion (Doctrine and Covenants 57:3). A home and a church building were paid for by the United Order in Clitherall, Minnesota, and about half the group took possession of them. Conflict arose almost immediately. Some members in Missouri wanted to give up the communal life. Emery Fletcher, the church president, returned to Clitherall and convinced the Minnesota group to excommunicate the Missouri group, including Erle Whiting, the first councilor. The excommunication was not recognized by the Missouri group. Then in 1953 Emery Fletcher died. The Minnesota groups elected Clyde Fletcher as the new president. The Missouri group rejected the election and recognized Earl Whiting, who as first councilor had the assumed right of succession to that office. This set of events completed the separation between the two groups.

Whiting served as president until 1958 and was succeeded by Rupert J. Fletcher and Julian Whiting (1975). Clyde Fletcher served the Minnesota group until his death in 1969. During the 1970s the Minnesota congregation dwindled steadily and eventually had no one to perform priesthood functions. In recent years it has been reconciled to the Missouri group. During the years of the separation, the Minnesota group referred to itself as the True Church of Jesus Christ.

The main distinctive mark of the Church of Jesus Christ is a belief in the authority of Alpheus Cutler. Under that authority a priesthood was set up in successive groups of twelve priests, forty-eight in all forming the council. The president or chief councilor and his first and second councilors are the main officers. There have not been enough males to fill the forty-eight council seats. Upon the death of the first councilor, the second succeeds him. Besides believing in the authority of Cutler, the Church of Jesus Christ believes that the Lord rejected all Gentiles who did not accept Joseph Smith's message and therefore there is to be no preaching to them. They also treat all days between Christmas and New Years' Day as Sabbath days and do not work that week. They are the only group besides the LDS Church in Utah to perform temple rites; Cutler had known them from his days at Nauvoo.

Membership: As of the early 1980s, there were two centers of the church. The congregation in Missouri has approximately 30 members. There are only a very few members in Minnesota, and they no longer hold regular services.

Sources: Daisy Whiting Fletcher, *Alpheus Cutler and the Church of Jesus Christ.* Independence, MO: The Author, 1970; Rupert J. Fletcher, *The Way of Deliverance.* Independence, MO: The Author, 1969; Rupert J. Fletcher, *The Scattered Children of Zion.* Independence, MO: The Author, 1959.

★729★
CHURCH OF JESUS CHRIST OF LATTER-DAY SAINTS (STRANGITE)
% Vernon Swift
Box 522
Artesia, NM 88210

James Jesse Strang (1813-1856), a Baptist and a lawyer, first heard of Joseph Smith, founder of the Mormons, in 1843 while living at Voree, Wisconsin. In February, 1844, Strang was baptized by Joseph Smith, Jr. and was ordained elder in the Melchizedek Priesthood. The church asked him to survey the Burlington, Wisconsin, area as a possible new home for the Saints. While Strang was on this mission, Smith was killed (June 27, 1844). On this day, Strang later claimed, an angel of the Lord appeared to him, saluted him and said, "Fear God and be strengthened and obey him for great is the work which he hath required at thy hands." The angel then touched him with oil. On July 9, 1844, Strang claimed that he received a letter (dated June 18, 1844) from Joseph Smith. The letter named Strang as his successor, appointed Aaron Smith as Strang's councilor, and designated Voree as the new gathering place of the Saints. Strang first presented his claims at a meeting held August 5, 1844, at Florence, Michigan. The twelve apostles at Nauvoo, Illinois, after receiving a report, excommunicated Strang.

The organization of the Church of Jesus Christ was effected June 5, 1845, at Voree. A dispute with the supporters of Brigham Young arose when Strang attempted to discourage the Saints from traveling West. After the trek West began, Strang received new members who did not join the march. Dissension developed, however, and Strang decided to take his loyal followers and go to Beaver Island, Michigan. Here he set up a theocracy, with himself at its head. More than 2,000 Saints came to Beaver Island, and Strang emerged as the most politically powerful man in the area. By 1856, the Church of Jesus Christ was the largest of the Mormon groups that did not follow Brigham Young. The church suffered a severe setback in 1856 when Strang was shot and died several weeks later in Voree, where he had been taken by his followers.

Strang's death cost the church most of its members, many of whom joined the Reorganized Church of Jesus Christ of Latter-Day Saints. Further, Strang failed to name a successor. The five apostles carried on without a leader. Finally, L. D. Hickey, the last surviving apostle, began to function as their leader. The small group held together under the successive leadership ordained by Hickey before his death in 1897. Wingfield Watson served from 1897 to 1922 and was succeeded by Samuel H. Martin, Moroni Flanders, Lloyd Flanders, and the present head, Vernon Swift.

The Strangite Church currently works out of two centers-- Artesia, New Mexico, and Voree (Burlington), Wisconsin.

A periodical, *The Gospel Herald*, published at Voree in the 1970s has been discontinued.

Membership: In 1984 the Church reported 200 members in 2 congregations. The were 3 priests.

Remarks: Though not accepted by the church, charges of fraud and/or forgery have been leveled by historians from Dale Morgan to, more recently, Lawrence Foster. They have accused Strang of forging the letter upon which his authority rests.

Sources: William Shepard, Donna Falk and Thelma Lewis, eds., *James J. Strang, Teaching of a Mormon Porphet*. [Burlington, WI]: Church of Jesus Christ of Latter Day Saints (Strangite), 1977; Mark A Strang, ed., *The Diary of James J. Strang*. East Lansing, MI: Michigan State University Press, 1961; James J. Strang, *The Prophetic Controversy*. Lansing, MI: 1969; *The Revelations of James J. Strang*. N.p.: Church of Jesus Christ of Latter Day Saints, 1939; Lawrence Foster, "James J. Strang: The Prophet Who Failed" in *Church History*, vol. 50, no. 2, (June 1981), pp. 182-92.

★730★
PRIMITIVE CHURCH OF JESUS CHRIST (BICKERTONITE)
(Defunct)

In 1914 a schism occurred in the Church of Jesus Christ (Bickertonite). A schismatic group, led by James Caldwell, formed the Primitive Church of Jesus Christ at Washington, Pennsylvania. They were joined shortly by another Bickertonite schism, the Reorganized Church, which had formed in 1907 under the leadership of Elder Allen Wright. Caldwell was succeeded by his nephew, Lawrence Dias. The Primitive Church largely followed the beliefs and practices of the parent body, but held that the institution in 1830 of the office of the first presidency was an introduction of an alien institution. The members opposed polygamy, plurality of gods, and baptism for the dead.

By the 1970s, the church has dwindled to a single congregation in Erie, Pennsylvania. More recently the congregation disbanded; some of the members rejoined the parent group.

★731★
RESTORED CHURCH OF JESUS CHRIST (WALTON)
Box 1651
Independence, MO 64055

The Restored Church of Jesus Christ was founded by Eugene O. Walton following a revelation in 1977. Walton, raised a Baptist, had joined the Reorganized Church of Jesus Christ of Latter-Day Saints, but had increasing problems with what he saw as a growing liberalism and a discarding of essentials of the faith. His opposition to the church's president led to his excommunication. He joined the Church of Jesus Christ (Cutlerite), and was ordained an elder. While with the church, he oversaw the printing of a three volume compendium of writings entitled *The Book of Commandments and Covenants*. It contained the 1835 edition of the Doctrine and Covenants, one of the Mormon scriptures, and some doctrinal materials by Walton.

In 1977 Walton received a revelation that he was the one mighty and strong predicted in the Doctrine and Covenants to come to set the house of God in order. This revelation led to disagreements with the church membership. In 1978 Walton and two other elders left and formed Restorationists United. Following a revelation to Walton at the beginning in 1979, his small band of followers held a general conference at which Walton was named High Priest, Apostle and Prophet. Jack Winegar and James Rouse were named First and Second Counselor respectively. Restorationists United became the Restored Church of Jesus Christ. At a later date the entire church was rebaptized into a New and Everlasting Covenant.

The Church espouses belief in a Godhead of two personages: God the Father and Christ the Son. The Holy Ghost is seen as the life and power of God. Members are called to follow and believe the doctrine of Jesus Christ: faith in God and Christ; repentance, baptism by immersion, laying-on-of-hands for the gift of the Holy Ghost; the resurrection of the dead; and eternal life. The church practices a communal life, a necessary step in the establishment of Zion. Christ will not return until Zion is established. Members look forward to the temple of Zion being built in Independence, Missouri. The Inspired Translation of the Bible (as revised by Joseph Smith, Jr.) is used.

Membership: In 1982 there were approximately 25 members.

Sources: *The Book of the Lord's Commandments.* Independence, MO: Restored Church of Jesus Christ, n.d. 3 Vols.

★732★
TRUE CHURCH OF JESUS CHRIST RESTORED
1533 E. Mechanic
Independence, MO 64050

David L. Roberts was ordained to the priesthood in 1966 in the Church of Christ Established Anew (now called the Church of Christ with the Elijah Message. While visiting the congregation in Wellston, Michigan, in 1967 he had a visitation by the Angel Nephi who told him of a future as a healing evangelist and told him to preach baptism in Jesus' name. Later that year he went to Independence, Missouri for the first time and visited the temple lot, the location where, according to the Mormon scriptures, the temple of Zion is ultimately to be built. In another vist by the angel, he was told to rededicate the temple lot. He returned to his home in Columbus, Ohio. Seven years later, in 1974, he and his wife, Denise Roberts, were visited by the Prophet Elijah, who came to give David Roberts the keys to the salvation of the dead and ordained him to the office of Moses and king over the kingdom of God until Jesus returns to earth. At Elijah's bidding, they began new work in Newark, Ohio, out of which the True Church of God Restored emerged.

Roberts came to feel that his ordination represented a third restoration of the Church of Jesus Christ, the first two having been through Joseph Smith, Jr. and James Jesse Strang. Roberts is the successor to both. The True Church uses the Bible, the Book of Mormon, *The Book of the Lord's Commandments*, *The Book of Abraham*, *The Voree Plates* (translated by Strang), and *The Oracles of God Book* (revelation given through Roberts).

The Church is sabbatarian. Roberts also preaches the baptism of the Holy Ghost and Fire, which brings a new birth to the body. This blessing, also called body-felt salvation, changes the body in such a way as to prevent sickness and tiredness. It is experienced as a general feeling of comfort and completeness and the continuous healing process become established in the body.

Membership: Not reported. There is one congregation in Independence.

Periodicals: *The Voice of Eternal Life*, 1533 East Mechanic, Independence, MO 64050.

Remarks: Robert's concept of body-felt salvation is very close to that of Pentecostal evangelist Franklin Hall, discussed elsewhere in this volume as the founder of the Hall Deliverance Foundation.

Sources: David L. Roberts, *The Angel Nephi Appears to David L. Roberts.* Independence, MO: True Church of Jesus Christ Restored, [1974]; *Articles of Religion.* Independence, MO: True Church of Jesus Christ Restored, n.d.

Communal Family

An historical essay on this family is provided beginning on page 99.

Communal — Before 1960

★733★

AMANA COMMUNITY OF INSPIRATIONISTS
% Charles L. Selzer, President
Homestead, IA 52236

The Amana Community of Inspirationists originated in Germany in the year 1714 among the Pietists who rejected Lutheran state- church polity and ritualism, as well as state laws on military service and oath taking. Their leaders were Eberhard Ludwig Gruber and John Friedrick Rock. These men gathered a following attracted to the notion the divine revelation and prophecy were as operative in their day as in Biblical days. All the sayings of the spiritual leaders were recorded and circulated among the faithful.

The eighteenth and early nineteenth centuries were times of persecution of nonconformists, so in 1842, Christian Metz was placed in charge of a Committee of Four to find a new home in America. An initial tract of land was purchased in New York and Ebenezer Society organized. After twelve years, the Society outgrew its land. In 1855, the move began to Iowa. Amana was first settled. Then five other villages-West Amana, South Amana, High Amana, East Amana, and Middle Amana -were established on a 26,000-acre tract. A new constitution establishing communal ownership of property, similar to the Ebenezer Constitution, was adopted, In 1861, the land of the whole community of Homestead was purchased in order for the Society on the railroad line.

Belief of the Amana Society is contained in the *Twenty-four Rules forming the Basis of the Faith*, a short document channeled through J.A. Gruber. Subsequent revelations, paricularly those of Metz and his later contemporary, Barbara Heinemann, also have been published. Except for the orientation on the "Instruments" of revelation, the Amana Society's beliefs closely resemble those of the German Brethren. The *Twenty-four Rules* deal with the strict observance of the holy life and the community ethic.

In 1932, the Amana Society went through a thorough reorganization which separated the church and the temporal enterprises. Each member of the community was given a share in the business enterprises, a very successful appliance corporation and farming. The community assets were distributed to members of the Society in the form of stock certificates, in proportion to years of service. A community representative system of church government was adopted and power invested in a thirteen-member board of directors elected by the members.

The Amana Society continues as a church consisting of the members who live in the seven Amana communities. Economic communalism has been replaced by a wage system.

Membership: In 1984 the Society reported 1241 members in 2 congregations. There were 15 ministers.

Periodicals: *Amana News Bulletin.*

Sources: Diane L. Barthel, *Amana, From Piest Sect to American Community.* Lincoln: University of Nebraska Press, 1984; Lawrence Rettig, *Amana Today.* South Amana, IA: The Author, 1975; Bertha M. H. Shambaugh, *Amana That Was and Amana That Is.* Iowa City, IA: State Historical Society of Iowa, 1932; Janet W. Zuber, trans., *Barbara Heineman Landmann Biorgaphy/E. L. Gruber's teaching on Divine Inspiration and Other Essays.* Lake Mills, IA: Graphic Publishing Company, 1981; Gottlieb Scheuner, *Inspirations--Historie.* Trans. by Janet W. Zuber. Amana, IA: Amana Church Society, 1976-77. 2 vols.

★734★
CHURCH OF THE BROTHERHOOD
Box 606
Orange City, FL 32763

The Church of the Brotherhood is a Hutterite-like body which no longer professes any formal or ethnic ties with the Hutterite Brethren. The two groups hold in common the fundamental doctrines: adult confession and baptism, reliance on Scripture rather than theology or doctrine, pacifism, and the effort to duplicate the communal Apostolic church. The Church of the Brotherhood differs from the Hutterites in its belief that communities must maintain their apartness while living in the world and transacting business with non-believers, all the while ginig witness to the gospel. Members believe it idolatrous to adopt any practice which makes symbols, not life, the means of giving and maintaining identity. Thus they speak a contemporary language and wear no special clothing. Full members live in complete discipline, and dedicate all work and wealth to the community. Confessional members devote a minimum of a tithe of goods and wealth and a full day of work in service projects.

Ministers work in secular pursuits and are not salaried. No separate worship houses are built. Love feasts, washing of feet, and baptism are ordinances. The group operates four centers for emotionally disturbed children and has created more than fifty centers for slum families and migrants, which operate as autonomous faciletes.

Membership: Not reported. In 1969 there were 200 disciplined members and 30,000 confessional members.

★735★
CHURCH OF THE SAVIOR
2025 Massachusetts Avenue, N.W.
Washington, DC 20036

The Church of the Savior was formed in 1946 in Washington, D.C., by a group of nine, headed by Gordon Cosby, a former Baptist. The vision of the new misistry was one of ecumenicity and evangelism, and total commitment of life and resources to Christ. The new communal existence was seen as representative of new humanity- reconciled and reconciling men. The result has been a community dedicated both to the nurture of the inner spiritual life and to the outward life of service.

The Church has identified four missional thrusts: to Christ's church throughout the world, to the poor and oppressed, to the stranger in our midst, to the building of our common life. To carry out its missions, it has divided itself into seven faith communities and an Ecumenical Service and Council which coordinates and oversees the communities. Located in Washington, D.C. in the same headquarters as the Council is Dunamis Vocations Church and the Seekers Church. Also located in Washington at various locations are the Eighth Day Church, the Jubilee Church, the New Community Church, and the Potter's

House Church. In Maryland is the Dayspring Church. Each of the seven faith communities has several mission groups which involve the members in specific tasks. For example, Dayspring, through its Wellspring mission groups provides programs and a newsletter which attempt to build and nurture church growth among Christians not necessarily affiliated with the Church of the Savior. The Jubilee Church ministers within the Jubilee apartments, a multi-family dwelling established and managed by the Council. Other missional thrusts are concerned with peace, the rights of the elderly, feeding the hungry and education of underprivileged youth.

Each faith community is under the guidance of one or more elders. Members in Washington, D.C. gather for an ecumenical service on Sunday morning, but each community has its own worship services during the week.

Membership: Not reported. The church has grown considerably since 1971 when it reported 80 members and 100 in the preparatory membership process.

Periodicals: *Wellspring*, 11301 Neelsville Church Rd., Germantown, MD 20874.

Sources: Gordon Cosby, *Handbook for Mission Groups*. Washington, DC: The Potter's House, 1973; Elizabeth O'Connor, *Call to Commitment*. New York: Harper & Row, 1963; Elizabeth O'Connor, *Journey Inward, Journey Outward*. New York: Harper & Row, 1968; Elizabeth O'Connor, *The New Community*. New York: Harper & Row, New York: Harper & Row, 1976; Elizabeth O'Connor, *Eighth Day of Creation*. Waco, TX: Word Books, 1971.

★736★
THE COLONY
Burnt Ranch, CA 95527

The Colony was begun August 18, 1940 by its prophet and founder, Brother John Korenchan (1886-1982), and eighteen members who settled on the Trinity River near Hawkins Bar, California. Brother John had his spiritual awakening in 1912, when, after five days of fasting and prayer, he was made to feel as a child without fault or law-breaking against the Creator. He wandered through the Siskiyou and Trinity Counties for years, and spent a few months in jail for his pacifism during World War I. As World War II began, he gathered a group of followers in Seattle. This group was finally led to California. Over the years, the group turned the area into a bountiful farm. Brother John was succeeded by Sister Agnes, the only surviving member of the original group.

There are no rules, not even grace at meals. Moderation, not abstinence, is the goal. Brother John taught that religion is meaningless unless it comes from within and is lived. Emphasis is placed on the guidance of the Power. The Power guided members to the Colony, brings in new members as it will, and discerns who is ready for the Truth, Christ.

Membership: As of 1984, there were 16 members living on the farm or on adjacent property, but others come in regularly from the countryside to participate in group activities.

★737★
ESOTERIC FRATERNITY
Box 37
Applegate, CA 95703

The Esoteric Fratenity was founded in 1887 in Boston, Massachusetts, by Hiram Erastus Butler (d. 1916). Butler, after losing several fingers in a saw-mill accident, became a hermit in a New England forest for fourteen years and , as a hermit, began to receive revelations from God. In the late 1880s, he began to tell these revelations to others, gathering around him a dozen followers, all single men and women. They pooled their resources, moved to Applegate, California, and established a monastic-like community. The basic ideas of the Fraternity was that to believe in God one must live the life of a celibate. When man gives up the sex act, the kingdom of God will be established on earth. This belief has tended to keep the group small. At its height, around the beginning of this century, there were only forty members.

The Esoteric Faternity teaches Esoteric Christianity. Members believe in reincarnation and that the population of the world remains constant, as old souls are constantly reborn. They believe that the Fraternity consists of the chosen ones, the Order of Melchizedek as prophesied in the Book of Revelation. They will grow to be 144,000 in number and then the kingdom of God will begin. They would be rulers of the earth for eternity.

Following Butler's death, Enoch Penn, a prolific writer (as was Butler), succeeded him. Penn was editor of the *Esoteric Christian*, the popular periodical of the fraternity which ceased when Penn died in 1943. The next leaders were Lena Crow (d.1953), William Corecco (d.1972), and Fred Peterson, the current president. Peterson, a former Mormon, had converted to the group in the 1950s. A large business in Butler's and Penn's books continues.

In August 1973, one elderly male member of the fraternity was murdered. His killer has not been apprehended.

Membership: Not reported. In 1981 there were only three members.

Sources: Hiram E. Butler, *The Goal of Life*. Applegate, CA: Esoteric Publishing Company, 1908; Hiram E. Butler, *The Narrow Way of Attainment*. Applegate, CA: Esoteric Publishing Company, 1901; Hiram E. Butler, *The Seven Creative Principles*. Applegate, CA: Esoteric Publishing Company, 1950; Hiram E. Butler, *Special Instructions for Women*. Applegate, CA: Esoteric Fraternity, 1942; Enoch Penn, *The Order of Melchisedek*. Applegate, CA: Esoteric Fraternity, 1961.

★738★
HUTTERIAN BRETHREN-DARIUSLUET
% Rev. Elias Walter
Surprise Creek Colony
Stanford, MT 59479

The second group of Hutterites to settle in the United States purchased a section of land in South Dakota on Silver Lake, north of the original Hutterite colony. (For the early history of the Hutterites, see separate entry on Hutterian Brethren-Schmiedeleut.) Under the leadership of Darius Walter, this second colony and those which sprang from it took his name. While establishing seven colonies in South Dakota, they had also spread to Montana (two colonies) and Manitoba, Canada (one colony) by the beginning of World War I. Abandoning all of their colonies, they moved to new colonies in Alberta, Canada. Not unitil 1935 did they reestablish a colony in the United States, in Montana. Since then they have become the most geographically spread out of the luets, having colonies in Washington and Montana and Alberta, Saskatchewan, and British Columbia in Canada. There is also an affiliated colony in Japan. The Dariusleut affiliated with the Society of Brothers for a short period (1931-1950).

The Dariusleut is the most loosely affiliated leut, as symbolized by the ability of new colonies to be founded without prior consent. Hooks and eyes are required on clothing. The minister is the first to enter the worship service.

Membership: In 1983 there were 133 Dariusleut colonies.

Sources: David Flint, *The Hutterites*. Toronto: Oxford University Press, 1975; Paul S. Gross, *The Hutterite Way*. Saskatoon, SK: Freeman Publishing Company Limited, 1965; William Albert Allard, "The Hutterites, Plain People of the West" in *National Geographic*, vol. 138, no. 1, 9 July 1970 pp. 98-125; Michael Holzach, "The Christian Communists of Canada" in *Geo*. vol. 1, (November 1979), pp. 126-54.

★739★
HUTTERIAN BRETHREN-LEHRELEUT
% Rev. Joseph Kleinsasser
Milford Colony
Wolf Creek, MT 59648

The Lehrerleut dates to 1877, when the third group of Hutterites to migrate to America in the 1870s settled near Parkston, South Dakota. (For information on the early history of the Hutterites, see the item on the Hutterian Brethren-Schmiedeleut.) Upon arrival in the United States, the group decided to live communally under its leader, Jacob Wipf. Wipf was an accomplished teacher (lehrer), and the group derived its name from his ability. Slow to expand, the group had only four colonies at the beginning of World War I. Like the other leuts, however, it abandoned the American colonies and migrated to Alberta. Only after World War II was a new American colony established, in Montana. Present-day colonies are scattered across Alberta, Saskatchewan and Montana.

The Lehrerleut is the most liberal of the Hutterite leuts. From their founder's formal education, members have inherited a preference for high German, in which they are thoroughly schooled. They wear buttons on their clothes. Unlike ministers of other leuts, the Lehrerleut minister is the last to enter worship services.

Membership: In 1983 the Lehrerleut had 82 colonies.

Sources: *The Hutterian Brethren of Montana.* Augusta, MT: Privately Printed, 1965; John Horst, *The Hutterian Brethren, 1528-1931.* Cayley, Alberta: Macmillan Colony, 1977.

★740★
HUTTERIAN BRETHREN-SCHMIEDELEUT
% Rev. David D. Decker
Tachetter Colony
Olivet, SD 57052

The Hutterite Brethren are the only surviving group which adopted communal living in response to an Anabaptist vision of establishing a Christian community in which private property would be abolished. They were founded in 1528 among a group of Anabaptist refugees fleeing to Austerlize. (A word on the Anabaptists: They believed the church was the society of adult believers gathered together freely. They thus opposed infant baptism and protested the state church of any area in which they resided. They were continually persecuted by state churches. Menno Simons, founder of the Mennonite Church, was an Anabaptist. He did not urge a comunal lifestyle, however.) For the early Hutterites, the introduction of "community of goods" was at the time a religiously sanctioned necessity. The first colony or Bruderhof (common household) was founded in Austerlitz in Monrovia. The group is named for Jacob Hutter. Not the founder, he became an early leader and organizer and was martyred at the stake in 1536. The pattern of persecution in Moravia became a common one for several centuries. Hutterites were tolerated, became successful and grew in numbers, were objects of jealousy, and finally were persecuted because of their success and their pacifism. This pattern repeated itself in Slovakia, Wallachia, and the Ukraine.

In the nineteenth century, living in close proximity to the Mennonites in Russia, the Hutterites' ideal was lost for a time, but in the 1850's, a renewal of communal living developed around the person and ministry of Michael Waldner. Waldner was a visionary, noted for his trances and psychic experiences. In a vision, an angel told him to reinstitute the *Gemeinshaft* of the Holy Spirit after the pattern of Jesus and the apostles. The phrase *Gemeinshaft* has no exact English equivalent; loosely translated, it is a brotherhood, a very closely knit group. The renewal took place in Hutterdorf, a Hutterite village in the Crimea. Two communal groups were established, one at each end of the village, and they became the basis of the division of the Hutterites into leuts (people) or colonies. The renewal of communal living among the Hutterites ran up against a renewal of nationalism in Russia. In 1871, universal compulsory military service was introduced and the Hutterites' requests for exemption were ignored. In 1874, migration to the United States and Canada was accomplished.

The Hutterites' beliefs arise from the Anabaptist tradition and in general follow the Schleitheim Confession. Like the Amish, the Hutterite Brethren adopted a plain dress. Some of them use hooks-and-eyes instead of buttons, a tradition symbolizing their rejection of the soldiers, their persecutors, who wore large buttons on military uniforms. The Hutterites use electricity, drive cars, have powered farm equipment and telephones. However, they have no televisions and dancing, smoking, and playing musical instruments are forbidden. They are pacifists and follow the radical Anabaptist theology. While there is as similarity among all Hutterites, the three leuts (discussed below) show marked distinctions in dress and discipline, and they do not intermarry.

Approximately 800 Hutterites migrated to America between 1874 and 1876. Approximately one half of these homesteaded family farms and eventually affiliated with Mennonite churches and ceased to be apart of the Hutterite community. The remainder settled in three colonies in South Dakota. These three colonies gave rise to the three "leuts" (people), each named for its founder. Each leut developed its own pecularities and each serves as an organizing unit for fellowship, discipline and administering the religious life of the colonies. The oldest of the luets is the Schmiedeluet.

The Schmiedeleut dates to the original renewal under Michael Waldner and was named for Waldner, who was called "Schmied- Michel" because he was a blacksmith. Upon arrival in the United States, Waldner's people settled the Bon Homme County in South Dakota in 1874. Waldner's continual visions remained a major motivating force in the communal patterns. By 1918, the Schmiedeleut had founded nine colonies. With the coming of World War I, the Hutterites German background conbined with their pacifism led to heightened tension. One by one they abandoned their colonies and relocated in Manitoba. Only in 1934 did a group settle a new American colony (Rockport, near Alexandria, South Dakota).

Among the Hutterites, the Schmiedeleut is considered the most conservative, though it has dropped the requirement for hooks and eyes as a means of fastening clothes. In its worship, the minister is the first to enter the gathering place. Colonies are tied closely together, and the consent of all is required before a new one can be created.

Membership: In 1983 there were 138 Schmiedeleut colonies.

Sources: Douglas S. Cobb, "The Jamesville Bruderhof: A Hutterian Agricultural Colony" in *Journal of the West*, vol. 9, no. 1, (January 1970), pp. 60-77; Lori Sturdivant, "The People of Jacob Hutter" in *The Minneapolis Tribune* (October 16, 1977; Victor Peters, *All Things Common*. New York: Harper & Row, 1971.

★741★
KORESHAN UNITY
% Claude J. Rahn
2012 28th Avenue
Vero Beach, FL 32960

The Koreshan Unity was formed in 1888 in Chicago by the followers of Cyrus Read Teed (1839-19906), a physician and metaphysician who developed a religious system termed the cellular cosmology. The group was organized as a celibate religious organization. The followers of Koresh (Hebrew for Cyrus) moved into a home and, the next year, began to publish the *Guiding Star*, which after six months became the *Flaming Sword*. In 1894, a colony was established in Estero, Florida, where the climate was mild and communal living was tolerated. In 1903, the entire group arrived from Chicago. At its height the organization had more than 300 residents on 6,000 acres, and more than 4,000 followers throughout the United States. A press was established, and numerous books, pamphlets, and periodicals were produced up until 1949, when the press was destroyed by fire.

The cellular cosmology is based upon the belief that the earth's surface is concave and that man lives on the inside of a sphere, not on a ball in space. The earth is not four and one-half billion years old, but eternal. God is an eternal being dwelling in the central brain cells of aggregate humanity. God is both male and female, in one eternal form. Jesus Christ is God perpetuating himself in an individual person formed by parthenogeneis (virgin birth).

The cellular cosmology contains theories on the macrocosm and the microcosm. The macrocosm is viewed as a cosmic egg, a hollow egg. The inside of the "eggshell" is the surface of the earth; in the hollow center of the egg floats the sun, from which flow light, heat and the influence of gravity. The shell of the earth forms a limitation to the effects of the sun, expressed in the materialization of metallic and mineral substance. In a reciprocal relation, the shell of the physical cosmos gives forth the energies, decomposed from material substance, which by Levic force (the opposite of gravity) move toward the sun. By such reciprocity, eternal perpetuity is ensured.

Mankind is a microcosm of the macrocosm, having as its central sun, God, who has his eternal habitation in the enviromental circumfernce of humanity. From God, flow truth and love, which are reciprocated by worship-the highest and purest moral thoughts.

Membership: By 1940 the Unity had been reduced to 36 members. In 1963, the group deeded its property to the state with the provision that the members could live there for the rest of their lives. By 1967 only Hedwig Michael, the president, and Vesta Newcomb (then 88 years old) remained. They continued to publish *The American Eagle*, a monthly newspaper which retained a subscription of upwards of 1,000. Like the Shakers, the group continues through its few surviving members. But, for all practical purposes, the Unity is defunct as an organization.

Sources: *Koreshanity, the New Age Religion*. Miami, FL: The Koreshan Foundation, 1971; James E. Landing, "Cyrus R. Teed, Koreshanity, and Cellular Cosmology" in *Communal Societies*, vol. 1 (Autumn 1981), pp. 1- 17; Cyrus R. Teed, *The Alchemical Laboratory of the Brain*. Chicago: The Eta Company, n.d.

★742★
PEOPLE OF THE LIVING GOD
Rt. 2 Box 423
McMinnville, TN 37110

The People of the Living God was formed in 1932 by Harry Miller (a former minister in the Assemblies of God) and his father-in-law (a former minister in the Presbyterian Church). They saw their action as rebellion against sectarianism, and they opened a Bible training school in Los Angeles to prepare "non-sectarian" missionaries. During the next eighteen years in Kentucky operating a free school in a bankrupt county and then going into the mountains of Tennessee. The group finally settled in New Orleans, where it remained for many years.

Sectarianism is defined as holding dogmatic opinion. To keep free from it, the group maintains an open pulpit, from which laymen and ministers who wish to contest doctrinal beliefs can speak. Conduct, not opinion, is the rule in matters of fellowship (Acts 15:28-29). The doctrinal consensus of the group is close to the beliefs of the Assemblies of God. Members are Trinitarian Pentecostals and practice two ordinances-baptism by immersion and the Lord's Supper (which is open to all). They believe that speaking in tongues is a sign of receiving the baptism of the Holy Spirit.

The fellowship remains small. Headquarters moved from New Orleans to rural Tennessee in 1985. Members work outside the group, turning their earnings into a common treasury. All buying is done by a purchasing agent. Members receive no personal allowance. They run a communal school which the children attend. The simple life-style allows a large percentage of money to be put into literature and into the support of nonsectarian missionaries overseas. The group publishes a series of booklets, mostly of a controversial nature, which is sent out across the country.

Membership: Not reported.

Periodicals: *The Marturion*, Rte. 2, Box 423, McMinnville, TN 37110.

Sources: Harry R. Miller, *Community, A Way of Life*. New Orleans, LA: People of the Living God, n.d.; Harry R. Miller, *Enchantments*. New Orleans, LA: People of the Living God, n.d.; Harry R. Miller, *A Man of Like Passions*. New Orleans, LA: People of the Living God, n.d.

★743★
SHILOH TRUST
℅ Rev. James Janisch
Sulfur Springs, AR 72763

The Rev. Eugene Crosby Monroe (1880-1961) was a businessman who in 1923 was ordained in the Apostlic Church, a British-based pentecostal body. Monroe served as a pastor of the Apostolic Church in Philadelphia until ill health forced his retirement from both his pastoral duties and his business career, which he had continued. He settled on a farm near Sherman, New York, to which young men and women came to continue under his ministry. Out of this situation evolved Shiloh Trust, a self-supporting Pentecostal commune. A large-scale food business was established, through which baked goods, cheese, and other foods were distriguted to retail outlets.

Monroe died in 1961, by which time Shiloh Trust had grown into a sucessful operation. He was succeeded by his son, who was later killed in a plane crash. James Janisch is the current leader. In 1963, the wholesale distribution of health foods to retail stores began to dominate the group's business interests. In 1968, headquarters were moved to Sulphur Springs, Arkansas. Members of the community gather daily for meetings. Beliefs are like those of the Apostolic Church.

Membership: As of 1984, there were a small group of members in Arkansas and a second group in New York.

★744★
SOCIETY OF BROTHERS
Rifton, NY 12471

The Society of Brothers was formed in post-World War I Germany around the leadership of Eberhard Arnold (1883-1935), who rented Sannerz Farm in 1920. Arnold had a background in the Christian Socialist Movement and the Student Christian Movement. He began to preach

a radical form of Christianity based upon the demands of the Sermon on the Mount. On the farm, work at both publishing and farming was begun and the writings of the Anabaptists and Hutterian Brethren studied. Upon learning of the continued existence of the Hutterites in the United States and Canada, the group instituted a fellowship with the Hutterian Brethren-Dariusleut which led, in 1931, to merger. The merger continued until 1950.

During the nineteen years with the Hutterites, Hutterite communal forms were adopted. In 1935, Arnold died and a collective leadership emerged. His death was followed by moves to England (1937), Paraguay (1940), and the United States (1954). The group's initial move from Germany was forced by the Gestapo, who would not allow the Society to be pacifist. Both the break with the Hutterites and the move to the United States spurred modernization. Hutterite forms (beards, confession of faith, plain dress) were replaced. By 1956, the society had reached its greatest expansion, with 1,171 residents in six communes in the United States, Paraguay, Uraguay, Germany, and England.

The first settlement in the United States was on a hundred-acre site near Rifton, New York, named Woodcrest. The group was joined almost immediately by half of the members of an already existing commune, Macedonia, who brought with them a light industry, community Playthings, which was soon to become the major souce of income for the Society. In 1955, the Forest River, North Dakota, colony of the Hutterian Brethren-Schmiedeleut decided to join the Society. A third colony was begun at Oak Lake near Pittsburgh.

The early 1960's were years of crisis in the Society. Contradictions between Hutterite forms and spontaneity, democratic versus authoritarian decision making, United States versus Paraguayan primacy, and other tensions erupted, and by 1962, the top leaders and half the membership had either been purged or withdrawn. From nine, only four centers (called hofs) remained. Strength of the society was consolidated in America and in one British colony. The crisis was accompanied by the rise of David Arnold, Eberhard's son. Recently, the North Dakota colony was closed and a new colony, Evergreen, established near Norfolk, Connecticut.

The Society of Brothers remains in the anabaptist theological tradition and close to the Hutterites, the Society takes a strong stand on pacifism, community activity and regulation of sexual conduct. The common life, which the society believes is ordained by God and has Him as its center, is emphasized in work, learning, play and worship.

Worship is centered in the Gemeindestunde (a brotherhood gathering, very much like a prayer meeting) held once or twice a week and in the evenings. It includes a talk by a servant of the word, silent prayer writing on the Spirit (resembling a Quaker meeting), and a closing prayer by a servant. The religious experience of the Society is joy, expressed in singing and dancing and the closeness of life together. The society is governed by a chief servant or "Vorsteher," the elders or servants of the Word(usually two at each colony), and the stewards, witness brothers ands house mothers. Great emphasis is place, however, on the consensus of the community in decision making.

The differing work loads that sustain the society are distributed to the different centers. Woodcrest and Farmington are the locations of Community Playthings, which supports the society. Plough Publishing is located at Oak Lake, with the sales department at Woodcrest.

Membership: In 1983 there were approximately 1250 residents of the several hofs.

Sources: Emmy Arnold, *Torches Together*. Rifton, NY: Plough Publishing House, 1971; Benjamin Zablocki, *The Joyful Community*. Baltimore, MD: Penguin books, 1971; Ebehard Arnold and Emmy Arnorl, *Seeking for the Kingdom of God*. Rifton, NY: Plough Publishing House, 1974; Eberhard Arnold, *Foundation and Orders of Sannerz and the Rhoen Bruderhof*. Rifton, NY: Plough Publishing Company, 1976; Hutterian Society of Brothers and John Howard Yoder, eds., *God's Revolution*. New York: Paulist Press, 1984.

★745★

TEMPLE SOCIETY
% Dr. Richard Hoffman
152 Tucker
Bentleigh, Australia A

The Temple Society, also known as the Friends of the Temple, or Jerusalem Friends, was founded by Christopher Hoffmann (1815-1885) in 1853 in Wurttemberg, Germany. Hoffmann had attacked the established church conventicles (meetings) as being unable to heal the spiritual decay in the church. Hoffmann's alternatives were a literal adherence to the Old Testament prophecies and a demand that the Davidic kingdom be reestablished as the only avenue to a moral and spiritual refomation. He believed that Christ would return soon, establish his kingdom at Jerusalem, and destroy the enemies of his church. Hoffmann began to gather the true followers and prepare them to go to the Holy Land, but the political situation made the settlement impossible.

In the town of Kirschenhardthof, a society which became the prototype of the New Jerusalem was organized along theocratic lines. A coworker named Hardegg claimed to possess the gifts of the Spirit and professed to be able to expel demons and to set the time of Christ's coming. In a series of writings, Hoffmann presented a version of Christianity very much viewed from an Old Testament perspective. His main work was *Sendschreiben uber den Temple und die Sakramente, Das Dogma von der Dreieinigkeit und von der Gottheit Christi sowie uber die*

Versohnung der menschen mit Gott. He ridiculed some commonly held Christian views, including belief in the trinity and the deity of Christ and the Holy Spirit. The incarnation is viewed as the expression of God's creative thought in the mind and body of Christ. Through the resurrection, Christ became a "man-made God." Christ showed the possibilities of human nature, changed humanity's attitude toward God, and thus established his kingdom as a better mental and social relationship among people. Sin is a disorder; faith is obedience to Christ and the courage to improve the world despite many obstacles. A socialized theocratic state is the goal. The sacraments are rejected. The true sacrament is manifested when a society decides to dedicate all its resouces (time, talents, and material goods) to spreading Christ's kingdom.

Beginning in 1869, three colonies were planted in Palestine before Hoffmann's death. Amazingly, they have survived the century of turmoil, though their growth has not been helped by the internal dissension since Hoffmann's death. Within the first decade after the 1853 founding of the Temple Society, immigrants brought the Society to America, and formal organization occurred in 1866. By 1890, there were four congregations. This number had dwindled to two by 1916. These two congregations survived into the 1970s, but recent efforts to contact then have not succeeded.

Membership: Not reported.

★746★

UNITED SOCIETY OF BELIEVERS IN CHRIST'S SECOND APPEARING
Sabbathday Lake, ME 04274

Mother Ann Lee (1736-1787) was a psychic-visionary who gathered a group of followers around her while still in her native England. Included in her teaching was a deep sense of the sinfulness of humnanity. After the death of her four children in infancy, she began to manifest her sense of sin by a vocal attack on the indecent act of sexual union. The name given to the group was the United Society of Believers in Christ's Second Appearing; the members are popularly called the Shakers.

In the 1750's Mother Ann Lee became associated with a group of Quakers who had been influenced by the French Prophets, people who prophecied and sometimes had visions. She gradually became their leader. Her leadership led to the group's acceptance of celibacy as a sign of following Christ. In 1774, encouraged by persecution, the group sailed for America. Because of their pacifism, Shakers became the object of scorn during the Revolution.

After the Revolution, they began to prosper, especially under the leadership of Joseph Meacham, who came to power in 1787 following Ann's death. The Shakers established communities across America. At the height of their development around 1830, they had 19 communities stretching from southern Kentucky to Maine, with 6,000 resident members. Books were being published and widely circulated. Products of various community interests further spread their reputation.

Shaker theology centers upon the belief that in the coming of Ann Lee, Christ had appeared. They accepted the common millennialist use of the 2,300-days prophecy (Daniel 8:14). They dated the beginning of this prophecy from 533 B.C. when it was given, and 2,300 years brought them to 1747, when James Wardley and his wife began their work in Manchester. It was out of this independent French Prophet/Quaker Society that Ann Lee rose to prominence. The most famous activity of the Shakers and the one from which they got their nickname was ecstatic dance. This activity was ritualized in to a communal exercise and has often been viewed as sublimation of the prohibited sexual activity.

The United Society has become an important aspect of American history, and one of its abandoned communities at Pleasant Hill, Kentucky, is being reconstructed. A museum exists in the Shaker church at South Union, Kentucky and at Old Chatham, New York. The community at New Lebenon, New York was sold to the Sufi Order headed by Pir Vilayat Khan.

Membership: In 1983, only eight Shakers, all women, remained. The last male member died in 1960. Five reside at Sabbathday Lake, Maine, and three reside at Cantebury, New Hampshire.

Sources: Henri Desroche, *The American Shakers*. Amherst: University of Massachusetts Press, 1971; Edward Deming Andrews, *The Gift to Be Simple*. New York: Dover, 1962; Doris Faber, *The Perfect Life*. New York: Farrar, Straus and Giroux, 1974; R. Mildred Barker, *The Sabbathday Lake Shaker*. Sabbathday Lake, ME: Shaker Press, 1978; R. Mildred Barker, *Poems and Prayers*. Sabbathday Lake, ME: Shaker Press, 1983.

★747★
WFLK FOUNTAIN OF THE WORLD
(Defunct)

Francis H. Pencovic (1911-1958) was born in obscurity, but as Krishna Venta, he died a martyr's death amongst followers who still thought of him as the reincarnated Christ. Pencovic spent part of his early life in Utah, where he both married his second wife, Ruth, and became enamored of Joseph Smith and the *Book of Mormon*. According to belief, as Krishna Venta, he landed in America from the Himalayas in 1932. He had been sent from heaven to work among the Indians one hundred and forty-four years previously. Krishna established his group in Box Canyon in the San Fernando Valley of California, where it gained a reputation for fire-fighting activities. Venta was rumored to have developed an openly promiscuous sexual life, which seems to have been his downfall, for on December 10, 1958, two dissident sexual partners of Venta set off an explosion in the group's administration building, killing themselves, Venta, and seven others.

Members of the Fountain of the World believed that Venta was the latest of a series of "saviors" of mankind who have come from heaven. The first was Adam, then Enoch, Methuselah, Noah, Abraham, Moses, Elijah, Jesus, Constantine, Abraham Lincoln, and Joseph Smith. One by one, each gave up in disgust as the sins of men overcame them both spiritually and physically. Members lived communally, turning over any prior possessions to the group. Thus, they became united with one another spiritually, mentally, and through sharing their belongings. They were called upon to practice the virtues of wisdom, knowledge, faith, and love. The Fountain was headed by Krishna and twelve apostles.

Krishna's death in 1958 was a setback, but it did not destroy the group. Mother Ruth Panovic assumed leadership of the Fountain of the World. The group survived into the early 1980s near Canoga Park, California. There was also second center near Homer, Alaska, set up by Krisha before his death.

Sources: Richard Mathison, *Faiths, Cults and Sects of America*. Indianapolis, IN: Bobbs-Merrill, 1960; Arthur Orrmont, *Love Cults & Faith Healers*. Ballantine Books, 1961.

Communal — After 1960

★748★
AQUARIAN RESEARCH FOUNDATION
5620 Morton St.
Philadelphia, PA 19144

The Aquarian Research Foundation (ARF), an outgrowth of the work and vision of Arthur Rosenblum, combines radical politics, psychical research, occult studies, and communalism. It was Rosenblum's feeling that the United States was heading for a second Civil war, an observation growing out of the counterculture world of the late 1960's. A product of sixteen years of communal living with the Society of Brothers, in 1969 Rosenblum formed the ARF to do research to help the new age which is dawning come so fast that the need for revolt would pass. A central concern is learning how to break down society's resistance to change.

In order to do the new kind of research requiring the total involvement of the researcher, a communal structure was created. It allows members to help one another with the kind of personal problems which make people afraid to do something different. Drugs are prohibted as detracting from the work. Meditation, the use of intuitive methods, and learning to listen to others are basic techniques. The monthly newsletter features stories on various psychic and alternative science breakthroughs, including pyramid power, acupuncture, biofeedback, plant telepathy, and flying saucers. In the early 1970s, the group became involved in a major project in astrological birth control, a technique worked out by Dr. Eugen Jonas of Czechoslovakia.

The ARF is open to new members of all ages and sexes who are willing to prepare themselves through a reading course in psychic research. ARF is financed through its publications lectures and classes.

Membership: Not reported. The ARF has a small number of resident members at its commune in north Philadelphia.

Periodicals: *Aquarian Research Foundation Newsletter*, 5620 Morton, Philadelphia, PA 19144.

Sources: Art Rosenblum, *The Natural Birth Control Book*. Philadelphia, PA: Aquarian Research Foundation, 1976; Arthur Rosenblum, *Unpopular Science*. Philadelphia: Running Press, 1974; Art Rosenblum, *Aquarian Age or Civil War?*. Philadelphia: Aquarian Research Foundation, 1970.

★749★
THE BUILDERS
Box 2278
Salt Lake City, UT 84110

Norman Paulsen was an early student of Paramahansa Yogananda, the founder of the Self-Realization Fellowship, one of the early successful Hindu organizations in the United States. At age 17, Paulsen joined the monastic order of the Self-Realization Fellowship, in which he spent five-years. As a member of the order, he learned the meditation techniques and Hinduism of Yogananda. As a meditator, he had deep meditative experiences in which he attained a state which he termed Christ consciousness. He left the order and, after several years as a brick mason, began to teach meditation in the early 1960s. He worked particularly with people on drugs. A community began to gather around him. From his monastic days, Paulsen had retained a vision of communal living but wanted a community that could include men, women, and children.

The Brotherhood of the Sun was established in 1970 at Sunburst Ranch near Santa Barbara, California. The teachings are derived from Yogananda, but they have a distinctly Christian emphasis. Meditation is a twice daily communal activity. Vegetarianism is practiced, and all drugs, tobacco, and alcohol are forbidden. It is Paulsen's belief that the second coming of Christ began January 1, 1961. The second coming is equated with the Aquarian Age, the translation into which was signaled by the turmoil begun by the drug scene. The second coming is equated with the emergence of the younger generation of the 1960s. Membership in the community is through "receiving meditation and initiation" after three weeks without drugs and a one to three-day fast. The new

member makes a symbolic offering of fruit and flowers at that time.

Having grown to include approximately 300 members, the Brotherhood of the Sun prospered through the 1970s in Santa Barbara, but by the end of the decade began to experience a heightened level of tension with the community. In 1977 several members were kidnapped as part of an attempted deprogramming by anticultists. By the end of the decade there was internal unrest, as somme members wanted the communal structure dissolved. Finally, in 1981 several exmembers filed suit, demanding that the community be dissolved and that they receive a share of the assets. In 1981 it sold its Santa Barbara area holdings, which included three food markets, a general store, and a restaurant, and moved to the Big Springs Ranch, near Wells,Nevada. After the move, the group became known as Sunburst Farms and then assumed its present name. Buildings were purchased in Salt Lake City, Utah, where some members have moved to manage the businesses that support the group.

Membership: Not reported. There are approximately 300 members of the Builders.

Sources: Norman Paulsen, *Sunburst, Return of the Ancients*. Goleta, CA: Sunburst Farms Publishing Farms, 1980. Revised and retitled as *Christ Consciousness*. Salt Lake City, UT: The Builders Publishing Company, 1984; Dusk Weaver and Willow Weaver, *Sunburst, A People, A Path, A Purpose*. San Diego, CA: Avant Books, 1982; Susan Duquette, *Sunburst Farm Family Cookbook*. Santa Barbara, CA: Woodbridge Press Publishing Company, 1978; Jan Hansen-Gates, "Growing Outdoors: The Brotherhood of the Sun" in *Santa Barbara Magazine*, vol. 1, no. 3, (Winter 1975-76), pp. 64-71.

★750★
CHURCH OF ARMAGEDDON
617 W. McGraw St.
Seattle, WA 98119

The Church of Armageddon was founded in Seattle, Washington, in 1969 by Paul Erdmann, known to his followers as Love Israel. It was established to "fulfill the New Testament as revealed to Love Israel in the form of visions, dreams, and revelations received by members of the church. The members of the church have all had heavenly Visions...." The name of the church is based on Revelation 16:16 where Armageddon is mentioned as the gathering place of the end-time. The members of the church think of themselves as the Love Family, drawn together out of the world and recognizable by mutual love of the members. They are the one body, the family of God, which can never dissolve.

New members of the church give all they possess, to be distributed as needed. Each person takes a new name. Since Israel is the name of God's people, Israel is the surname of all members of the church. A "virtue" name is assumed as a first name and former names suppressed. Upon joining, members renounce all "worldly traditions of matrimony." As one body, the church is married to Christ, both collectively and individually, and members are married one to another in Christ. The men, as husbands, have authority over the women, as wives. Love Israel and the leaders have the perogative of permitting couples temporary bonding for the purpose of having children.

The church sees itself as the continuation of Israel (Old Testament) and following the lifestyle and beliefs of Jesus Christ (New Testament). Eating and drinking are sacramental, as whatever is eaten is the body of Christ and whatever is drunk is his blood. Joining the church represents a freeing from the past and the world of sin and death. Baptism by immersion is practiced.

During the 1970s the church enjoyed a steady growth, reaching around 300 members by 1980. It became an official observer (not a member) of the Church Council of Greater Seattle. Around 1978 it acquired a rural farm center near Arlington, Washington. It developed a free restaurant and a guest hostel in Seattle and assisted in the distribution of food surpluses to the needy. It began its own school, staffed by teachers drawn from the group. The Church was also involved in continual controversy. In 1972 two men died from an overdose of toluene, a substance which had occassionally been used in religious services. Among the first individuals kidnapped and deprogrammed (unsuccessfully) was Cathy Crampton, one of the group's school teachers. Her parents had allowed the kidnapping and the deprogramming to be filmed by CBS. Crampton's was but the first of several deprogrammings throughout the decade.

Membership: Not reported. There were approximately 300 members in 1980.

Remarks: Recently, a major split (following several years of internal dispute) was being reported. Some predicted the end of the Church, following intense criticism of Love Israel. It appears that a smaller core of his following is reorganizing and continuing at the group's major compound in Seattle.

Sources: Love Israel, *Love*. Seattle: Church of Armegeddon, 1971; Steve Allen, *Beloved Son*. Indianapolis: Bobbs-Merrill Company, 1982.

★751★
THE FARM
156-C Drakes Lane
Summertown, TN 38483

The Farm grew out of the weekly Monday-evening teaching sessions in the 1960s in San Francisco led by Stephen Gaskin, known simply as Stephen. He soon became a well known spiritual philosopher and published two books, *Monday Night Class* and *Caravan*. Attendance at the Monday night class increased from a handful to more than 1,000. In October, 1970, several hundred of the class joined Stephen in a cross-country tour, dubbed the Caravan. In four months, the Caravan covered the nation, gathering converts as it went. At the close of the tour, more than five hundred decided to join Stephen in a commune near Summertown, Tennessee.

The emphasis of Stephen's teaching was on bringing some order out of the chaos that was the counterculture of the 1960s. "Putting it all together" is a common testimony of residents at the Farm, who have responded to the force of both a common life in an agricultural setting and a mystic religious experience. The religious life of the Farm is based on an eclectic, mystical faith, but draws major elements from Mahayanan Buddhism. Included are beliefs in tantra, karma, bodhisattvas, mandalas, and mantras. Vegetarianism is practiced.

The experience shared by all is being stoned, a term drawn from the drug culture to describe the mystical consciousness produced by psychedelic drugs. Marijuana is an intimate part of the Farm's common life. It is used in meditation. Members are also free to use it individually through the week. The mystical worldview is applied to all aspects of life and includes ahimsa, or respect for all life. In 1974, state narcotics agents raided the farm, confiscated the marijuana, and arrested Stephen and three members. They were convicted and served a year in jail after losing appeals to the Supreme Court based on First Amendment religious freedom provisions.

Though living communally, the farm has attempted to contribute to the solving of world problems. Project Plenty, founded in 1974, aims to provide food self-sufficiency for the world. Model projects were established in the Bronx, New York and Bangladesh, Guatemala, the Caribbean, and Lesotho. The multiplication of food protein by vegetarianism is a basic principle of Plenty's approach. It is recognized as a United Nations nongovernmental agency. An emphasis on natural healing led to participation in the national revival of mid-wifery. Stephen's wife, Ina May Gaskin has become a prominent author and advocate of the practice.

By the mid-1970s the Farm had grown to approximately 1,000 members, peaking at approximately 1,500. Besides the commune in Tennessee, ten other independent communes (including one in Canada) formed around Stephen's teachings. Though administratively autonomous, they considered themselves familially tied to the Farm. The Farm Band was formed and accompanies Stephen on his speaking tours. The Book Publishing Company publishes Stephen's books and writing of other commune members.

In 1982-83, the Farm suffered a reaction to the national recession. As income dropped, approximately half the residents left. Those remaining reorganized the commune as a cooperative. Members are now allowed to own personal property and have checking accounts. A board of elders was elected to manage the group's affairs.

Membership: As of 1983, there were approximately 550 residents at the Farm. Associated communes are found in Nashville, Tennessee; Franklin County, New York; Lanark, Ontario, Canada; and southern France.

Periodicals: *The Practicing Midwife*, 156 Drakes Lane, Summertown, TN 38483; *Plenty News*, 156 Drakes Lane, Summertown, TN 38483.

Sources: Stephen Gaskin, *Monday Night Class*. San Francisco: Book Publishing Company, [1974]; Stephen Gaskin, *The Caravan*. New York: Random House, 1972; Stephen Gaskin, *Volume One*. Summertown, TN: Book Publishing Company, 1975; Stephen Gaskin, *Rendered Infamous*. Summertown, TN: Book Publishing Company, 1981; Ina May Gaskin, *Spiritual Midwifery*. Summertown, TN: Book Publishing Company, 1978; Cris Popenoe and Oliver Popenoe, *Seeds of Tomorrow*. San Francisco: Harper & Row, 1984.

★752★
KATHARSIS
(Defunct)

Kartharis was established in 1971 by a group wishing to establish an alternative community with an emphasis on harmony and spiritual growth. In 1974, the members purchased twenty acres near Nevada City, California, for their community and research center. The goals of Katharsis include the following: 1) spiritual growth and self-realization through the study of yoga and related sciences; 2) the development of a natural lifestyle based on diet; 3) cooperative living; and 4) promotion of the practice of astrology as an aid to a fuller life. The group annually published the "Solar Lunar Calendar" and a line of related astrology products. After several years Katharsis disappeared and no sign of their existence has surfaced for several years. The organization is presumed to be defunct.

★753★
LAMA FOUNDATION
Box 44
San Cristobal, NM 877564

The Lama Foundation, located on a mountain near San Cristobal, New Mexico, serves as a coming-together point for the New Age mystical/psychical/Eastern religious perspectives which spread so widely in the counterculture in the 1960s. The Lama Foundation began when Steve Durkee, his wife, and three children settled on the one-hundred-and-fifteen acre tract in the Sangre de Cristo Mountains in 1967. Eventually, a community of approximately 20 adults and their children gathered at the Foundation. Adherents follow different paths, including yoga, Zen, Sufism, Native American Church, and Christianity. During the summer, the community enlarges to more than 100 people, and a vigorous teaching program is maintained. A wide variety of spiritual teachers spends time at the Lama Foundation.

Identified strongly with the Lama foundation is Baba Ram Dass (formerly known as Richard Alpert). Through the Foundation, he published *Be Here Now*, Lama's first publication venture. Sufism has been a strong influence. Murshid Samuel L. Lewis is buried at Lama. The Foundation also recently published *Towards the One* by Pir Vilayat Khan, head of the Sufi Order.

Activities at the Foundation center on the main Dome, which includes a library, prayer room, and bath house. The residents gather three times daily for meditation prayer sessions. Work is spread among the residents and includes construction and maintenance of the various buildings, the preparation of food, publishing, working for the Bountiful Lord's Delivery Service (a book service) and Flag Mountain (which sells silk-screened Tibetan prayer flags).

Membership: Approximately 25 people live year round at Lama Foundation.

Periodicals: *Lama Views*, Box 240, San Christobal, NM 87564.

Sources: Baba Ram Dass, *Be Here Now*. San Christobal, NM: Lama Foundation, 1971; Hugh Gardner, *The Children of Prosperity*. New York: St. Martin's Press, 1978; Robert Houriet, *Getting Back Together*. New York: Avon, 1972; William Hedgepeth and Dennis Stock, *The Alternative*. New York: Macmillan, 1970.

★754★
MU FARM
Box 143
Yoncalla, OR 97499

Mu Farm is named for the ancient continent of Lemuria or Mu, made famous in theosophical lore. It was begun in 1971 when Fletcher Fist and two other people purchased land near Yoncalla, Oregon. A goat-milk farm was established as an economic base, and other works are developing. The beliefs of Mu Farm are eclectic and derive from the many psychical and mystical teachings that developed in the 1960s. The group lists sources of belief as the Bible, the I Ching, the *Aquarian Gospel of Jesus Christ* by Levi, and the writings of Martin Buber,

Swami Yogananda, Einstein, and others. The golden rule is emphasized as replacing a set of specific rules and regulations.

Membership: Not reported. In 1972 there were 30 resident members.

Periodicals: *Mu Eggs Press*, Box 143, Yoncalla, OR 97499.

★755★
RAINBOW FAMILY OF LIVING LIGHT
Route 1, Box 6
McCall, ID 83638

Growing out of the counterculture movement of the late 1960s and conceptualized in the thinking of the Rev. Barry Adams, also known as Barry Davis, the Rainbow Family of Living Light is a loosely organized network of individuals, informal groups, and communes which share in common an attachment to what is termed New Age consciousness. The Family is truly a rainbow in its eclectic mixture of differing beliefs, concerns, and practices, but united in its vision that humanity is passing into a new age of spiritual consciousness. The Rainbow Family sees itself and is seen as a harbinger of the new age and a major component of the New Age movement which has its exponents in many of America's alternative religions.

The major activity of the Family during the 1970s was the sponsorship of an annual "gathering of the tribes." (New Age people often describe the essence of community as a new tribal consciousness.) These annual meetings began with a small "Vortex" gathering in Oregon around 1970. The first large gathering to attract several hundred attendees (and significant media coverage) was held in 1972 at Strawberry Lake, east of Granby, Colorado. It called together the "tribes" to give honor and respect to anyone or anything that has aided in the positive evolution of humankind and nature upon this, our most beloved and beautiful world.

The belief world of the Rainbow Family centers upon ecology and the psychic/spiritual world much discussed in the 1960s. Basic is a nature-pantheism expressed in the belief, "God is you, God is me, God is the World, God is the Sky, God is the Sun." The ecologiclal emphasis is expressed in a love of nature and of the out-of-doors. Adherents believe that everything in nature was placed there for man's use (not abuse). Marijuana is one of the God-created herbs, and it viewed as having sacramental value. All forms of pollutants are opposed.

The psychic world view is expressed in the incorporation of numerous practices from various bodies. The great invocation (channeled through Alice Bailey) is freely used, as is the distinction between Jesus the man and the mystic Christ consciousness. Followers believe in reincaration but with a distinct, this-worldly interest. Christ consciousness

is a mystic state, but it is signalled by a person's making others happy, doing good, and giving more than is taken.

Love is an important goal. Loving someone is equated with heaven, and hating someone is equated with hell. Sex is considered to be an expression of love. Legal aspects of marriage are no longer considered necessary, for when two people love each other, they are thought to be married. There are no formal acts of worship, and the formality of most religious acts is condemned. A wide mixture of Hindu chants, Christian hymns, and meditative techniques are employed to reach God consciousness.

Membership: No membership roles are kept, but a directory of the family's network is published irregularly. Several thousand people are involved. The family claims as many as 10,000 among those who share its free lifestyle. In 1984, 28,000 attended the Family's summer gathering in Modoc County, California.

Sources: *The Rainbow Nation Cooperative Community Guide.* McCall, ID; The Rainbow Nation, 1972; Phil Garlington, "The Return of the Flower Children" in *California*, vol. 9, no. 10, (October, 1978), pp. 81-83, 137-38.

★756★
REBA PLACE FELLOWSHIP AND ASSOCIATED COMMUNITIES
727 Reba Place
Evanston, IL 60602

The Reba Place Fellowship was formed by a group of Mennonite students at Goshen College, Goshen, Indiana, in the mid-1960s. Beginning in 1966 as an off-campus ministry, the members were reacting against the sterility of the church and were operating out of a vision of the church as a disciplined brotherhood in small communities of spiritual consensus. Among the leaders were John Miller, Don Mast, and Virgil Vogt. In 1967, the move to 727 Reva Place, Evanston, Illinois was made. Growth in the Fellowship has been steady, as like-minded individuals, spurred by the communal thrust of the 1960s, were drawn to Reba Place. Other buildings were purchased and community activity accelerated.

In 1971, the Plow Creek Fellowship was established by three families of the Reba Place Fellowship. They purchased a one-hundred-and-ninety acre farm in Bureau County, Illinois, and by 1974, it had grown into an independent congregation in its own right. The Fellowship of Hope was formed by nine people at the Mennonite Seminary at Elkhart, Indiana. From their struggle to find meaning in their church participation, and partially inspired by the Reba Place model, a communal life emerged. In 1971, three families in Newton, Kansas, joined together to "concentrate resources for the work of peacemaking and care for the families at the same time." In 1974, the communes in Bureau County, Illinois, Elkhart, Indiana, and Newton, Kansas joined with Reba

Place in a mutual covenant of dependency. According to the covenant, the basis for membership is a commitment to Jesus and to his radical teaching. Membership specifically involves renunciation of property; love as an alternative to anger, violence, and war; faithfulness in marriage as the context for sex; a servanthood stance in all human relationships; and a communal organization of personal affairs. Each community is seen as a local church, with all the rights and privileges thereof. Within the circle of communities, encouragement is given to the sharing of spiritual gifts and resources, responding to words of correction, visiting between communities, allowing transfer of members between communities, sharing finances, and scheduling occasional intracommunal gatherings.

Each of the associated communities has grown out of a Mennonite base, though strong emphasis is place on the multi-traditional nature of their present membership. A general Mennonite theological perspective remains, along with concerns for peace and social service. Emphasis is placed on the radical teachings of Jesus in the Sermon on the mount. The impetus to communal forms has also been present in Anabaptism, partially as a means of survival in a hostile world. At Reba Place, it is seen as a positive means to fulfill the teachings of Jesus. The communes differ from their Mennonite neighbors primarily in their spontaneous style of worship, which includes guitars, folk music, and the free expression of emotion. Priority is given to learning to live together in a family-like existence. Basic teachings are found in the *Christian Way*, authored by John Miller, one of the founders.

Members of the fellowships work at jobs within the surrounding community. A group associated with the Plow Creek Fellowship, The Builders, helps finance the group through various kinds of construction work. Income is pooled, and each individual or nuclear family receives an allowance. Social structures supported by the Reba Place Fellowship include a day nursery and a commonwork industry. Support is also given to indiviuals in the community. Reba Place is located in a racially mixed neighborhood, and it includes both black and Puerto Rican Americans in its Fellowship.

Membership: Not reported. In 1973 there were more than 160 members/residents at Reba Place; 45 at Plow Creek; approximately 10 at New Creation in Newton, Kansas; and 30 at Fellowship of Hope at Elkhart, Indiana.

Sources: John W. Miller, *The Christian Way*. Scottdale, PA: Herald Press, 1969; Dave Jackson and Neta Jackson, *Living Together in a World Falling Apart*. Carol Stream, IL: Creation House, 1974.

★757★
RENAISSANCE CHURCH OF BEAUTY
Box 112
Turner's Falls, MA 01376

The Renaissance Church of Beauty and the Renaissance Community was founded in 1969 as the Brotherhood of the Spirit near Leyden, Massachusetts by Michael Metelica. Still in his teens and having just returned from California, he built and moved into a tree-house. Soon he was joined by eight friends. They began to work for farmers for wages of food or goods instead of money. When vandals burned down the tree-house, they moved into a cottage on the land of a farmer for whom they had been working. The Brotherhood was born there.

Metelica, who chose the name Michael Repunzal, by which he is currently known, was greatly influenced by Spiritualist medium Elwood Babbitt, who also introduced him to *The Aquarian Gospel of Jesus the Christ* by Levi Dowling, a major source of group beliefs. Babbitt specializes in psychically providing information about an individual's previous incarnations on earth. The beliefs center upon the seven immutable laws: order within the universe; balance of the mind (positive) and brain (negative); harmony (a direct alignment with all vibration of electrical energy); growth from carnal to celestial; God-perfection; spiritual love; and compassion. From the early days of vegetarianism and abstinence from alcohol, a much less strict diet has been adopted.

During the first years of the 1970s the group expanded rapidly, number 365 by 1973. By 1972, the movement decentralized and moved into new centers near four northwest Masschusetts towns. To provide an economic base, several businesses were created. Though most eventually failed, several have survived: Rockets, which outfits buses for touring musicians, and Renaissance Builders and Renaissance Excavating supply most of the current income. By 1974 two separate organizational structures emerged. The Renaissance Church of Beauty was created so that all residents and nonresidents could participate in the support of the beliefs and practices of the former Brotherhood of the Spirit. The Renaissance Community, consisting of the resident members, was then created for church members who wished to practice the church's beliefs on a full-time basis.

In 1975 a eighty-acre tract at Gill, Massachusetts was purchased. The group began to reassemble there and construct the 2001 Center, conceived in part as a haven against the coming time of troubles predicted by Edgar Cayce as the twentieth century comes to an end. An organic farm has been started on the property.

Membership: In 1983 there were approximately 105 members of the Community.

Periodicals: *The Renaissance Community Newsletter*, 71 Avenue A, Turners Falls, MA 01376.

Sources: Karol Borowski, *Attempting an Alternative Society.* Norwood, PA: Norwood Editions, 1984; Cris Popenoe and Oliver Popenoe, *Seeds of Tomorrow.* San Francisco: Harper & Row, 1984.

★758★

SALEM ACRES
R.R.1, Box 175A
Rock City, IL 61070

Salem Acres is an eclectic commune founded in the late 1960s. It combines elements of Pentcostalism and Sacred Name Adventism. Its founder was Lester B. Anderson, a former Baptist minister. The purpose of creating Salem acres was to provide a place where a group could grow in the Spirit and be free to accept new truth as it came. From the Pentecostals, the group at Salem Acres has accepted an emphasis on the baptism of the Spirit and speaking in tongues, and it has adopted a New Testament church order. The various gifts of the spirit are manifest and these ministries are functioning. Women partake in the minsitry but not over men. Spirited singing, testimonies, and prayer for the sick characterize services. From the Sacred Name movement, the group has derived an emphasis on the Old Testament laws, particularly keeping the Sabbath and diet. Both the Lord's Supper and baptism by immersion are practiced.

Membership: Not reported. There were approximately 50 residents in 1974.

Periodicals: *Yahweh Nissi,* R.R.1, Box 175A, Rock City, IL 61070.

★759★

THE SYNANON CHURCH
46216 Dry Creek Rd.
Box 112
Badger, CA 93603

The Synanon Church began in 1958 as Synanon Foundation, Inc., a therapeutic group for alcoholics and drug addicts. Charles E. Dederich, a former member of Alcoholics Anonymous, began the organization informally in his apartment in Ocean Park, California. As the group grew and began to experience some benefits, it rented a clubhouse and incorporated. The following year it moved to Santa Monica and over the next few years gained a reputation for reeducating drug addicts. From its base in Santa Monica, during the 1960s Synanon communities formed along the West Coast, particularly San Francisco, Marin County, and Oakland, and outposts opened in the East, Midwest, and Puerto Rico. Residents totaled 1,400 by decade's end. In 1968 Dederich moved to Marin County, where within a few years three rural Synanon communities developed near the town of Marshall.

The religious nature of Synanon, coming as it did out of another religious organization, Alcoholics Anonymous, had been tacitly recognized from almost the beginning of its existence. However, Dederich also recognized that many of the people Synanon was attempting to assist had rejected organized religion; therefore, Synanon was not formally called a religion. Those outside Synanon tended to view it as another therapeutic community. As community life developed, the religious nature of Synanon life could not be denied. Discussions of Synanon's role as a religion in the 1960s led to a change of Articles of Incorporation in January, 1975, which designated the Synanon Foundation as the organization through which the Synanon religion and church is manifest. On November 17, 1980, the present name, The Synanon Church, was formally adopted.

Synanon derives its theological perspective from Eastern thought (Buddhism and Taoism) and from those Western mystics who had absorbed a prominent Asian religious component in their teachings, most notably Ralph Waldo Emerson and Aldous Huxley. As a community, Synanon seeks to manifest the basic principles of oneness, and members seek to manifest that integration (or oneness) in themselves and in their relations with each other. The Synanon Game, described as the group's central sacrament, is the principal tool utilized in adherents' search for unity. Similar to encounter groups, the Synanon Game is "played" by a small group of people who meet together as equals in a circle to share in an intense and emotionally expressive context. When successful, the game leads to mutual confession, repentence, and absolution while providing overall pastoral care.

Synanon residents follow the golden rule, and helping others is basic in the practical philosophy that all residents attempt to follow. Residents also believe that the most effective way to redeem humanity from alienation and achieve unity and integration is to form religious communities based upon the beliefs of the Synanon religion and church.

The Synanon Church is organized hierarchically. It is headed by a six-member executive committee of the board of directors. The board is composed of the ministers of the church. The ministers oversee the communities, schools, and offices of the church, besides performing their normal ministerial functions.

Membership: In 1984 The Synanon Church had three communities, two at Badger, California and one in Houston, Texas. Approximately 550 adherents reside in one of the communities. Other nonresident adherents can be found across the United States and in several countries.

Educational facilities: Synanon College, Badger, California; Charles E. Dederich School of Law, Badger, California.

Remarks: Since its earliest days, Synanon has been subject to controversy. In December, 1961, Dederich went to jail, for the first time, on a zoning code violation. Synanon has also been attacked in articles by individuals who disagreed with its practices and techniques. One such attack, considered particularly defamatory, led to a libel suit against the *San Francisco Examiner*. Synanon received not only a large cash settlement but an additional $2,000,000 in damages from the Hearst Corporation, the newspaper's publisher for, among other things, burglarizing the Synanon offices.

Possibly the most controversial event affecting Synanon occured in 1978 when an attorney, representing a person suing The Synanon Church, was bitten by a rattlesnake. In the year following this incident, Dederich, who along with two church members had been charged in the case, suffered three strokes. As the trial date approached, and with Dederich's health failing and unable to pursue the defense of the case, those charged settled the case by pleading no contest.

During the last several years, over forty people associated with The Synanon Church have been indicted on various charges by grand juries. None of these well-publicized indictments went to trial, as charges were dropped in each case for lack of evidence. (It is the position of The Synanon Church that, had Dederich's health permitted a trial, he and the others charged in the rattlesnake incident would also have been found innocent). As of 1984, The Synanon Church continues a process of adjudication of charges leveled by various government agencies, especially the U.S. Internal Revenue Service, which has questioned its tax-exempt status.

Sources: Charles E. Dederich, *The Tao Trip Sermon*. Marshall, CA: The Synanon Publishing House, 1978; Guy Endore, *Synanon*. Garden City, NJ: Doubleday, 1968; Howard M. Garfield, *The Synanon Religion*, Marshall, CA: Synanon Foundation, 1978; David U. Gerstel,*Paradise Incorporated: Synanon*. Novato, CA: Presidio Press, 1982; Dave Mitchell, Cathy Mitchell, and Richard Ofshe, *The Light on Synanon*. New York: Seaview Books, 1980; William Olin, *Escape form Utopia*. Santa Cruz, CA: Unity Press, 1980; Lewis Yblonsky, *The Tunnel Back: Synanon*. New York: Macmillan, 1965.

★760★
UNIVERSAL INDUSTRIAL CHURCH OF THE NEW WORLD COMFORTER (ONE WORLD FAMILY)
Box 3
Stockton, CA 95201

The Universal Industrial Church of the New World Comforter, usually called the One World Family and also known as Messiah's World Crusade, is an urban communal group built around the teachings and person of its leader, Allen Michael Noonan. The commune burst into public light in 1968 when Allen was arrested for posssesssion of marijuana. Allen received his call to be messiah or messenger for this planet in 1947, at which time a psychic revelation told him what was wrong with the planet and how he could make things better. Several unsuccessful attempts at organizing a commune carried Allen to Haight-Ashbury in 1966, when a band of flower children formed the core of the present group. In 1969, the group moved to Larkspur, Marin County, California, and the following year to Berkeley, where it opened an organic vegetarian restaurant, the Mustard Seed, several blocks from the University of California campus. In the late 1970s it moved to Stockton, California.

Allen believes that in 1947 he took an astral trip to another planet, where higher exra-terrestrial beings confronted him with the possibility of being the world's messenger. They keep in contact through automatic writing, which guides the group. The thrust of the group is to raise the self above slavery to matter by heightening the consciousness through service to humanity. Each Sunday morning, the whole group gathers for meditation and, when Allen is present, to receive the guidance from the higher realms. These higher beings offer the guidance are equated with both the angels of the Bible and the inhabitants of flying saucers. Unlike most communes, the Messiah's World Crusade is evangelistic and includes the whole world in its vision of the One World Family. There is a core membership of about twenty and about that many more who are transients. Besides the restaurant, a traveling musical group is a major communal project.

Membership: Not reported.

Sources: Allen Michael, *The Everlasting Gospel, to the Youth of the World*. Berkeley, CA: Universal Industrial Church of the Divine Comforter, 1973; Allen Michael, *UFO-ETI World Master Plan*. n.p.: Starmast Publications, 1977; Allen Michael, *ETI Space Beings Intercept Earthlings*. n. p.: Starmast Publications, 1977; Allen Michael, *The Everlasting Gospel, God, Ulyimated Unlimited Mind Speaks*. Stockton, CA: Starmast Publications, 1982; Kathryn Hannaford, *Cosmic Cookery*. Stockton, CA: Starmast Publications, 1974.

Christian Science-Metaphysical Family

An historical essay on this family is provided beginning on page 105.

Christian Science

★761★
CHURCH OF CHRIST, SCIENTIST
Christian Science Service Center
Boston, MA 02115

The Church of Christ, Scientist, grew out of the experiences, work and writings of Mary Baker Eddy. Following her healing in 1866, which happened concurrently with her discovery of God as the sole reality of life, Eddy began a period of study during which she tested her new discovery against scripture, as well as the earlier teachings on mental healing she had received from Phineas P. Quimby. The result was the development of her mature thought, first expressed in a booklet, *The Science of Man* (1870) and later embodied in her textbook, *Science and Health with Key to the Scriptures* (1875). She began almost immediately to put the principles of Christian Science to the test and to teach them informally to others. Her work led her to seek a letter of dismissal from the Congregational Church in which she was raised, and in 1876 she founded the Christian Science Association, the first organization for her students.

The next sixteen years were ones of the development of a variety of organizational expressions, followed by their abandonment and reorganization. A final reorganization in 1892 and the development of the church's by-laws in the *Church Manual* (1895), resulted in the church as it is known today. These sixteen years were punctuated by the formation of the Church of Christ, Scientist, in 1879, Eddy's ordination in 1881, the dissolution of the church in 1889 and its reorganization in 1892. This reorganization placed the governance of the Christian Science movement in the First Church of Christ, Scientist, of Boston, generally known as the Mother Church. The remainder of Eddy's life was spent in perfecting the textbook of the movement which went through several revisions and in completing by-laws as codified in the *Church Manual*. The texts of these two volumes were frozen following Eddy's death and remain the prime sources of the church's doctrine and polity.

The beliefs of the Church of Christ, Scientist, are summarized in the Tenets printed in both *Science and Health* (p.497) and the *Church Manual* (p.15). The Church defines itself as Christian in essence, a major difference between it and most other "metaphysical" churches with which it is often compared. The Tenets affirm the Church's allegiance to the inspired Word of the Bible as the sufficient guide to Life; one God; God's Son; the Holy Ghost; and man as being in God's likeness and image. Forgiveness for sin comes in spiritual understanding that casts out evil as unreal. Jesus is acknowledged as the Way-shower. His atonement, as the evidence of God's love and salvation, comes through the Truth, Life and Love he demonstrated in his healing activity and by his overcoming sin and death.

Healing activity following the principles laid down in the Bible and in *Science and Health* have been the keynote of the Christian Science movement. Such healing is done by authorized practitioners and is in accord with Eddy's experience of the allness of God. It is distinct from other forms of healing, especially psychic or magnetic healing.

Eddy is held in high regard by Christian Scientists. She is considered to be God's appointed messenger for this age, chosen to discover Christian Science and reveal it to the world. She is represented in the Bible (Revelation 12) as the one who fulfilled prophecy by giving the full and final revelation of truth. The church does, however, carefully distinguish Eddy's status and role as the discoverer of Christian Science from that of Jesus as the Savior of humanity. In like measure, while acknowledging the essential and central role of the Christian Science textbook, it does not understand *Science and Health with Key to the Scriptures* to be a second Scripture or a revelation equal in authority to the Bible. Rather, *Science and Health* is considered a tool for understanding the Bible.

The governance of the Christian Science movement is vested in the Mother Church, whose rules of operation are spelled out in the Church Manual. Administration is placed in a five-member self-perpetuating Board of Directors. The Board charters branch churches, which are run according to their own democratic control (apart from any matters not covered in the *Church Manual*). Worship in all branch churches is conducted by approved readers, each of whom must be a member in good standing of the Mother Church. Services in the branch churches consist solely of readings from scripture and *Science and Health*. The exact passages for each week are delineated in *The Christian Science Quarterly*. Publications of the Church are under the control of the Christian Science Publishing Society and its Board of Directors. Included in its publications are its award-winning newspaper *The Christian Science Monitor*, its prime foreign language periodical *The Herald of Christian Science* (published in 12 languages and braille for the blind), and numerous books and pamphlets. Eddy's writings are controlled and published by the Trustees Under the Will of Mary Baker Eddy. Under the Board of the Mother Church is a Board of Lecturers which approves speakers who travel the world offering free public lectures on Christian Science. The Committee on Publication is charged with correcting false information on the church and injustices done to Christian Scientists.

Headquarters of the Church are in the Christian Science Church Center, a large complex in Boston, Massachusetts, which has become one of the city's most-visited tourist stops. Branch churches are found in over fifty nations of the world (though approximately seventy-five percent of the membership is in North America).

Membership: Not reported. In the early 1980s there were approximately 3,000 Christian Science centers worldwide. In 1972 there were a reported 3,237 branch churches worldwide of which approximately 2,400 were in the United States. Worldwide constituency was 633,000, with 475,000 in the United States.

Educational facilities: Principia College, Elsah, Illinois.

Periodicals: *The Christian Science Monitor*, One Norway Street, Boston, MA 02115; *The Christian Science Journal*, One Norway Street, Boston, MA 02115; *Christian Science Sentinel*, One Norway Street, Boston, MA 01225; *Christian Science Quarterly*, One Norway Street, Boston, MA 02115; *The Herald of Christian Science*, One Norway Street, Boston, MA 02115.

Remarks: Since its founding, the Church of Christ, Scientist, has been the subject of intense controversy. Its healing emphasis brought criticism from a variety of perspectives, both those who shared the emphasis but followed a different set of teachings and practice, and those who disapproved of any form of spiritual healing. The most intense criticism found its way into various legal proceedings and has led to an extensive body of legal opinion defining the rights and limits of Christian Science practice. Courts have defined Christian Science healing as a legally protected activity of the church as a form of worship. Deductions for some Christian Science services are allowed by the U.S. Internal Revenue Service. Various state-level committees on publication have issued handbooks defining the legal rights and obligations of Christian Scientists in some detail.

During the 1880s Eddy was accused of drawing her teachings from Phineas P. Quimby, first by Annetta Dresser and her husband, Julius Dresser who, like Eddy, had been students of Quimby, and later by numerous members of what became known as the New Thought movement. An examination of Eddy's writings and the publications of the Church of Christ, Scientist, reveals an essential difference between Eddy's teachings on healing and those of Quimby and finds the major similarity to be in the area of terminology, particularly their shared preference for the impersonal categories of the Divine (though both retained some place for the personal) and the attempt to struggle with the same questions of religion and health.

The Church of Christ, Scientist has attempted over the years to separate itself from the New Thought movement. It has denounced Quimby's adherence to magnetic healing and the movement's abandonment of Eddy's essential Christian orientation. The Church also disapproves of the emphasis in the movement on prosperity and the openness to various psychic and occult practices most evident in some of the larger New Thought groups. Christian Science retains a focus on healing and has denounced Spiritualism and animal magnetism, the forms of the occult most evident in Eddy's lifetime, from its earliest years. Some obvious differences between New Thought and Christian Science can be seen by comparing the Tenets of the Church with the Declaration of the International New Thought Alliance. At the same time the connection between the two movements is very real, as New Thought was to a great extent build upon Eddy's early students, particularly Emma Curtis Hopkins, and used *Science and Health* as a major sourcebook. Today New Thought groups vary considerably, from those who are close to Eddy's teaching to those who more closely follow Quimby while developing their own form of metaphysical thought.

Finally, over the years the Church has had to face formal and informal challenges to its authority, beginning with the various individuals and groups claiming to have inherited Mary Baker Eddy's authority. These challenges led to the formation of several movements, such as the Christian Science Parent Church, none of which prospered more than a few years. There is, of course, a small but steady stream of practitioners who have left the church and who continue to practice independently. Many have built a successful personal following (possibly the most prominent being Joel S. Goldsmith). Most, however, have been anti-organization and their following has continued only briefly after their retirement and/or death.

Sources: Mary Baker Eddy, *Science and Health with Key to the Scriptures*. Boston: Trustees Under the Will of Mary Baker Eddy, 1906; Mary Baker Eddy, *Church Manual of the First Church of Christ, Scientist, in Boston, Mass.* Boston: Trustees Under the Will of Mary Baker Eddy, 1908; Stephen Gottschalk, *The Emergence of Christian Science in American Religious Life*. Berkeley: University of California Press, 1973; Robert Peel, *Mary Baker Eddy*. New York: Holt, Rinehart and Winston, 1971. 3 vols.; Charles S. Braden, *Christian Science Today*. Dallas: Southern Methodist University Press, 1958; Altman K. Swihart, *Since Mrs. Eddy*. New York: Henry Holt and Company, 1931.

★762★

INFINITE WAY
Box 215
Youngtown, AZ 85363

The Infinite Way is the name given to the teachings of Joel S. Goldsmith (1892-1964). A nonpracticing Jew, Goldsmith encountered Christian Science as a young man. The father of a woman he was dating was a practitioner. When Joel's father was healed by that practitioner in 1915, Joel began seriously to study Christian Science. Later, consulting a practitioner for help with a cold, he found himself cured not only of the cold, but also of smoking and drinking. The experience changed his life. He began to pray for people, and to his amazement, they were healed. He joined the Church of Christ, Scientist, and became a practitioner, a practice he pursued for sixteen years. In the early 1940s, however, he began to feel the pressure of the organization, and in 1946 withdrew from the Church. He began working on the book which became *The Infinite Way*. Reluctantly at first, he accepted invitations to teach and lecture, primarily on the West Coast and in 1950 for the first time in Hawaii.

In 1946, a year after withdrawing from Christian Science, he experienced a mystic "initiation" which lasted over several months and which has been described as lifting him to a new dimension of life, a God-experience. Most of the Infinite Way emphases derive from that incident. The Infinite Way represents a mystical form of Christian Science. Without rejecting healing or prosperity demonstration, Goldsmith centered his teaching on the experience of God. "The Infinite Way is not to give the world a new teaching, but to give the world an experience." It was Goldsmith's belief that the seeker of truth begins with solving problems and overcoming discords. When these endeavors become futile, he can then perceive that one can transcend them. Desiring to improve his human condition, he moves out of the less pain/more pleasure syndrome into spiritual consciousness.

Methodologically, spiritual consciousness is attained by meditation. Contemplative meditation, the primal step, is the holding of spiritual truth in the consciousness. Pure meditation is the state of complete silence within. God is

within. We cannot make it so; we can only come to the realization.

God is the one, hence he is all-presence, all-power and all-wisdom. To establish a relationship with the god within is to be able to tap the ready supply of all that makes life worthwhile. God appears as the many, but appearance must not be confused with reality. Christ is the activity of truth within each individual consciousness. The revelation brought by Jesus is the revelation of the Christ.

Goldsmith rejected the idea of founding another organization, and during his lifetime the "Infinite Way" existed only as an informal circle of his students. However, he did fall into a pattern of offering regular classes which were taped and transcribed (an later became the bases for several books). A weekly (later monthly) newsletter was begun and provided a means to keep the scattered students in regular contact. The first of several Infinite Way study centers appeared in Chicago in 1954. For several years after Goldsmith's death, his wife, Emma Goldsmith, continued to issue the newsletter from Hawaii, with the editorial assistance of Lorraine Sinkler, a longtime student. She has more recently moved to Arizona, and with the assistance of Geri MacDonald, her daughter (by a previous marriage), continues to make available the tapes of his lectures. The majority of Goldsmith's material has been edited by Sinkler and published in book form. Individual students such as Sinkler travel around the United States lecturing to groups of people who follow Goldsmith's teaching and others facilitate gatherings which make Goldsmith's material available to local audiences.

Membership: The Infinite Way is not an organization. Rather, it is a designation given to Goldsmith's teachings and, collectively, to the unnumbered people who have accepted them.

Periodicals: *The Infinite Way Letter*, Box 215, Youngtown, AZ 85363.

Sources: Joel S. Goldsmith, *The Infinite Way*. San Gabriel, CA: Willing Publishing Company, 1961; Joel S. Goldsmith, *The Art of Spiritual Healing*. New York: Harper & Row, 1959; Lorraine Sinkler, *The Spiritual Journey of Joel S. Goldsmith*. New York: Harper & Row, 1973; Lorraine Sinkler, *The Alchemy of Awareness*. New York: Harper & Row, 1977.

★763★

**INTERNATIONAL METAPHYSICAL
   ASSOCIATION**
20 E. 68th St.
New York, NY 10021

Among the various independent Christian Science groups, the International Metaphysical Association (IMA), formed in 1955, is perhaps the largest and most influential. It was formed by a number of ex-members of the Church of

Christ, Scientist, who saw that the often individual, fragmentary and undisciplined study of independent followers of Mary Baker Eddy was inadequate. The Association has as its purposes to bring to public notice Eddy's scientific revelation, and to encourage students of Christian Science to regard the teachings as a science and approach them in an orderly way.

To accomplish these goals, it sponsors television and radio work, lectures and special schools, and publishes a number of pamphlets and books. Closely associated is the independent Rare Book Company, which has reprinted the first three editions of *Science and Health* by Mary Baker Eddy and serves as a clearinghouse and distributor of much Christian Science literature.

The IMA is headed by a seven-member board of trustees which included Ethel Schroeder, a popular speaker and writer. In 1966, it sponsored its first international conference, which featured popular independent Christian Scientists from Europe: Peggy Brook, Max Kappeler and Gordon Brown. A second conference was held in California in 1968. The mailing list of the IMA includes students from around the United States, some of whom are banded into study groups which use IMA material.

Membership: Not reported.

Periodicals: *Independent Christian Science Quarterly*, 20 East 68th Street, New York, NY 10021.

Sources: Ethel Schroeder, *Science of Christianity*. New York: International Metaphysical Association, n.d.; W. Gordon Brown, *Christian Science Nonsectarian*. Haslemere, Surrey, England: Gordon & Estelle Brown, 1966; Max Kappeler, *Animal Magnetism--Unmasked*. London: Foundational Book Company Limited, 1975.

**★764★
MARGARET LAIRD FOUNDATION**
(Defunct)

Margaret Laird was a practitioner at the first Church of Christ, Scientist, in Evanston, Illinois. In the late 1930s, she was accused of erroneous teachings. These charges led to a decade of negotiations between the board of directors of the mother church and herself, ending with the removal of her name from the list of practitioners. In 1957 she resigned from the Mother Church. Mrs. Laird continued to teach and operate as an independent Christian Science practitioner. Then in 1959, she incorporated the Margaret Laird Foundation in California. The stated purposes were research into the science of being and dissemination of the results of such research. A world-wide fellowship with other independent Scientists was established and centers were opened in Liverpool and Bombay. The British group published *The Liverpool Newsletter of the Margaret Laird Foundation* a bimonthly periodical.

Among the former Christian Scientists associated with Laird was Harold Woodhull Lund of Bridgeport, Connecticut. Lund published *The Lund Re-View* beginning in 1963 and authored a number of pamphlets. He maintained a cordial relation with the Margaret Laird Foundation and each distributed the other's writings.

Sources: Margaret Laird, *Christian Science Re-explored*. Los Angeles: The Margaret Laird Foundation, 1971; Margaret Laird, *The Personal Concept*. Los Angeles: The Maragret Laird Foundation, 1969; Harold Woodhull Lund, *Four Steps in the Evolution of Religious Thought*. Bridgeport, CT: The Author, 1964.

**★765★
SEED CENTER**
Box 591
Palo Alto, CA 94302

Among the popular metaphysicians in the United States is William Samuel. Since 1968 Mr. Samuel has been publishing *Notes from Woodsong* (originally *Notes from Lollygog*), which is sent to an unspecified number of students across the United States. In several areas groups have formed to study the letters and/or Mr. Samuel's book, *A Guide to Awareness and Tranquility*. Mr. Samuel professes a profound sense of well-being and a surprising abilily to pass that well-being on to others. He asserts that tranquility is acquired not through step-by-step methods but rather by simplicity and honesty in a childlike approach.

Membership: Not reported.

Periodicals: *Notes from Woodsong*.

Sources: William Samuel, *A Guide to Awareness and Tranquility*. Lakemont, GA: CSA Press, 1967; William Samuel, *2 Plus 2=Reality*. Lakemont, GA: CSA Press, 1963; William Samuel, *The Melody of the Woodcutter and the King*. Palo Alto: Seed Center, 1976.

**★766★
UNITED CHRISTIAN SCIENTISTS**
Box 8048
San Jose, CA 95125

United Christian Scientists was founded in 1977 by David James Nolan, who had the year previously been dropped from membership at the First Church of Christ, Scientist, in Palo Alto, California. Church officials claimed, among other things, that Nolan had adopted the teachings of independent Christian Science teacher, Joel S. Goldsmith, founder of the Infinite Way. The prime issue raised by the United Christian Scientists concerns church polity, and the group has challenged the legitimacy of the church's ruling powers, specifically the powers exesiced by the Board of Directors of the Mother Church over the branch churches. To this end a lawsuit, still pending as this volume goes to press, has been filed claiming a breach of trust in the assumption of powers by the Board following the death of Mary Baker Eddy.

Membership: Not reported.

New Thought

★767★
AMERICAN SCHOOL OF MENTALVIVOLOGY
Cedar Heat of the Ozarks
Thornfield, MO 65762

The American School of Mentalvivology was founded in the 1960s by Dr. Merle E. Parker. It grew out of the Foundation for Divine Meditation founded in 1948 and headquartered in Santa Isabel, California. Mentalvivology is described as a science of mind and a practical application of the law of mind. The goal of mentalvivology is producing whole men and women. The basic course involves teaching the student to produce any sensation at will, the use of mind to effect "faith healing," the use of the inner mind to set goals and accomplish them, and the practical application of mind. Advanced courses deal with mysticism and the ritual magic of the ancient wisdom. These advanced lessons were originally published by the now-defunct Aquarius School of the Masters, also of Santa Isabel, California. All courses are by correspondence.

Membership: Not reported. Students are found around the country.

Sources: Merle E. Parker, *The Mentalvivology Story.* Thornfield, MO: The Author, 1969; Merle E. Parker, *Instant Healing Now!.* Santa Isabel, CA: The Foundation for Divine Meditation, 1955.

★768★
ANTIOCH ASSOCIATION OF METAPHYSICAL SCIENCE
Current address not obtained for this edition.

The Antioch Association of Metaphysical Science is a metaphysical church founded in 1932 by Dr. Lewis Johnson of Detroit, Michigan. It serves a predominantly black membership.

Membership: Not reported. In 1965 there were 6 churches.

★769★
CHRIST TRUTH LEAGUE
2400 Canton Dr.
Fort Worth, TX 76112

H. B. Jeffery was a popular New Thought leader in the 1930s. He authored several books, including *Coordination of Spirit, Soul, and Body* and *The Spirit of Prayer.* In content, his teachings were close to those of pioneer New Thought teacher Emma Curtis Hopkins, and he followed her *High Mysticism* closely in his own *Mystical Teachings.* After his death, Alden Truesdale and his wife, Nell Truesdell, acquired the rights to his books and now carry on his ministry both nationally and locally as the Christ Truth League. The League is a member of the International New Thought Alliance.

Membership: Not reported.

Sources: H. B. Jeffery, *Coordination of Spirit, Soul and Body.* Fort Worth: Christ Truth League, 1948; H. B. Jeffery, *The Spirit of Prayer.* Cambridge, MA: Ruth Laighton, 1938; H. B. Jeffery, *Mystical Teachings.* Forth Worth, TX: Christ Truth League, 1954; H. B. Jeffery, *The Principles of Healing.* Fort Worth, TX: Christ Truth League, 1939.

★770★
CHRISTIAN ASSEMBLY
72 N. 5th St.
San Jose, CA 95112

Among the most specifically Christian of the several New Thought groups is the Christian Assembly. It was founded by William Farwell in 1900 in San Jose, California, as a branch of the Home of Truth, the loose association of centers led by Annie Rix Militz. Around 1920 Farwell's congregation separated from the Home of Truth and took its present name. The Christian Assembly believes Christianity is founded upon the doctrines of Jesus Christ and the Bible, and these are used by the Assembly as a source of teaching. The Bible contains a spiritual sense within its historical/literal sense, and this spiritual meaning can be discerned by the Spirit of truth working upon the understanding.

Unlike many New Thought groups, the Christian Assembly has attempted to produce a summary statement of its beliefs. The fundamental principles of the teaching of the Christ include: God is Spirit, whose nature is love and wisdom; the kingdom of God is within; Jesus is the Christ, the Son of the living God; he is divine and human (a perfect unity) and, as the risen Lord, he abides in his kingdom within; true faith comes from God and makes all things possible; evil has no power from God; love is the fulfillment of the law which is constitutional to man; Christian healing is properly a part of the gospel; the kingdom is known through works of faith and love. The work of the Christin Assembly is centered upon a weekly Sunday morning worship service, prayer groups, and Bible classes and truth lectures through the week. The sacraments have been discontinued so that concentration can be upon inner meaning.

Over the years, branches of the Christian Assembly were established in the San Francisco Bay area. Ministers trained and ordained by the Christian Assembly are pastors of branch churches in Gilroy, Palo Alto, Oakland,

Redwood City, and San Jose (2). Farwell was also a prolific writer, and the Assembly has published much of his material.

Membership: Not reported. In 1971 there were 6 congregations.

Sources: William Farwell, *The Paraclete*. San Jose, CA: Christian Assembly, 1928; William Farwell, *Be Thou a Blessing*. San Jose, CA: First Christian Assembly, 1936.

★771★

CHURCH OF HAKEEM
Current address not obtained for this edition.

The Church of Hakeem was founded by Clifton Jones, better known to his followers as Hakeem Abdul Rasheed, in Oakland, California, in January 1978. Jones, a Detroit-born black man, attended Purdue University as a psychology major. In the mid-1970s he ran a weight-reduction clinic, which was closed in 1976 when the state Board of Medical Quality Assurance reported that he was using "psychology" rather than diet and exercise to treat clients. He was practicing psychology without a license.

Hakeem turned from weight-reduction to religion and assumed his new name. Like his colleague, Rev. Frederick Eikerenkoetter II (Rev. Ike), founder of the United Church and Science of Living Institute, Hakeem built upon New Thought emphases that health, wealth, and happiness came from positive mental attitudes put into positive action. He emphasized positive action as a means to wealth. In contrast to Rev. Ike, however, Hakeem implemented his teachings through a variation of what is known as the Ponsie game, a standard confidence scheme. Members paid into the church with the promise of a 400 percent return within three years. Members would in turn recruit further investors. The early investors receive their promised return. People who joined last receive nothing, not even their original investment. Such schemes are illegal.

In May 1979 Hakeem was indicted and later convicted on six counts of fraud. A group of members signed a class action suit against the church, and the Internal Revenue Service moved against the church for taxes. The cumulative effect of these actions have paralyzed the Church of Hakeem, and its future is doubtful.

Membership: By 1979 congregations of the church had been established in San Diego, Los Angeles, San Francisco, and Sacramento, California. There were an estimated 5,000 to 10,000 members.

★772★
CHURCH OF INNER WISDOM
% Joan Gibson
Box 4765
San Jose, CA 95126

The Church of Inner Wisdom was founded in San Jose, California, in 1968 by a metaphysician, Dr. Joan Gibson. Prior to 1968, she had been a member of the Rosicrucians (Ancient Mystic Order of the Rosy Cross) and had studied with Clark Wilkerson, founder of the Institute of Cosmic Wisdom . The church combines the teachings of New Thought with a major secondary emphasis on the psychic. The teachings are described as "macro-ontology," the study of the nature of a child of God, forgiveness, expansion of awareness, Jesus and the major religious prophets as examples for living, and sharing truth received. The psychic is seen as a tool in expanding awareness and as spiritual. However, without the perspective of metaphysics, it becomes a means of mere ego-gratification. Lessons, which may be taken in classes or by correspondence, are the main means of disseminating the church's teachings. The church is governed by a board of directors, Dr. Gibson being the permanent chairman. An annual business meeting is open only to officers, directors and ministers.

Membership: Not reported. In 1972 ministers of the church were at work in Alameda, Alhambra, Concord, and Burlingame, California; Phoenix, Mesa, and Wickenburg, Arizona; Chicago, Illinois; Erie, Pennsylvania; and Atlanta, Georgia.

Periodicals: *The Voice*, Box 4765, San Jose, CA 95126.

★773★
CHURCH OF THE FULLER CONCEPT
Current address not obtained for this edition.

The Church of the Fuller Concept is a New Thought group headed by Dr. Bernese Williamson, a doctor of metaphysical science. Dr. Williamson teaches that we live in the God dispensation. God is our Father and Mother, our natural parents being God caring for us. God has a body (I Cor. 11:30) and is manifested in body-form on earth. Man's body is the image and likeness of God. In recognizing God's body, man can have the blessing of a healthy, whole body. Members of the church do not carry insurance, because in God, where man lives and moves and has his being (which is the body of God), there can be no illness. Dr. Williamson teaches that every meal is a communion and that what one visualizes as he eats and drinks will materialize.

Headquarters of the church are at the Hisacres New Thought Center in Washington, D.C. Members live by a pledge to remember their spiritual nature. They greet each other with the word, "Peace." They adopt spiritual names, because they want to acquire the nature, characteristics and attributes of God. All students sign a pledge to give honest service to their employer for their pay, not accepting tips or vacation-with-pay, nor using intoxicants on the job. This pledge is given to the employers.

Membership: Not reported.

★774★
CHURCH OF THE SCIENCE OF RELIGION
(Defunct)

The Church of the Science of Religion was founded in 1922 by the Rev. Carolyn Barbour Le Galyon, a former practitioner with the Church of Christ, Scientist, who had been healed of a broken wrist. She became a student of various New Thought leaders--Charles Fillmore, Ernest Holmes, and others. The Church of the Science of Religion teaches an eclectic New Thought perspective drawn from the numerous early metaphysical teachers. Headquarters were in Cleveland, Ohio, at the New Thought Temple of Christ. The Church dissolved following Le Galyon's death in the 1970s.

Sources: Carolyn Barbour Le Galyon, *All Things New.* New York: The Analysts' Publisher, 1963.

★775★
CHURCH OF THE TRINITY (INVISIBLE MINISTRY)
% A. Stuart Otto
Box 37
San Marcos, CA 92069

Friend Stuart (i.e., A. Stuart Otto) was a West Coast publisher who, in 1954, had a religious awakening that started his metaphysical search. Over the next few years, he was able to study with many of the outstanding New Thought leaders. In 1957, a series of additional enlightenment experiences began, culminating in 1963 with an inward ordination in what is called the invisible ministry. Three years later, Stuart began to conduct private metaphysical practice under the name "invisible ministry," and, in 1967, obtained a charter and began issuing *Tidings* as a quarterly bulletin. Work was primarily by mail at a distance, though classes were held at the San Marcos center. In 1972, Church of the Trinity was established as an outgrowth of the healing ministry.

The theology of Church of the Trinity is based upon the work of James Allen, Henry Drummond, Emmet Fox and Friend Stuart. The church is grounded in the faith that the Christian doctrine of the Father, Son and Holy Spirit is the ultimate spiritual truth, and that all things proceed from these three aspects of almighty God. The church calls its theology the science of dominion, the Christ-Jesus way. According thereto, man fulfills his destiny by achieving dominion and glorifies God in so doing. Jesus came to overcome death, and, as we recognize truth, we are freed of disease, disharmony and lack. Those on the way are members of the fifth kingdom. The Church of the Trinity thus is similar to the Unity School of Christianity

in its emphasis on specifically Christian tenets which are allegorized in a New Thought framework. However, the church is strictly trinitarian, an aspect not strongly emphasized by Unity.

The Church of the Trinity is purely spiritual and refrains from involvement in secular matters. It enjoins its members to obey the law and to be good citizens. Healing is the major concern, and the church sees itself as a balancing influence with Christ's church as a whole. Seven sacraments are practiced by members: baptism, confirmation, communion, matrimony, holy orders, cognition of divine life, and expiation. As of 1972, there was only one center of the Church of the Trinity, but others were imminent and a school of theology has been opened.

Membership: Not reported. The church considers all baptized Christians as members. In 1984 there were two ministers and one center with an affiliated work in Nigeria led by lay members. Affiliated individuals and supporters of the ministry, especially those involved in the healing work, can be found across the United States. They stay in contact through the mail.

Educational facilities: Trinity School of Theology, Box 37, San Marcos, CA 92069-0025.

Periodicals: *Tidings*, Box 37, San Marcos, CA 92069-0025; *Theologia 21*, Box 37, San Marcos, CA 92069-0025; *Master Thoughts*, Box 37, San Marcos, CA 92069-0025; *The Theologia 21 Encyclopedia*, Box 37, San Marcos, CA 92069-0025.

★776★
CHURCH OF THE TRUTH
% Dr. John L. Baughman
154 W. 5th St.
New York, NY 10019

The Church of the Truth was formed by Albert C. Grier, a minister in the Universalist Church who was healed of stomach ulcers following the reading of a New Thought book. His preaching of spiritual healing was unacceptable to his church, so he withdrew and founded the Church of the Truth in Spokane, Washington. Other leaders were attracted to him and carried the work to various cities. Edward Mills took it to Portland, Oregon, where the work continues as the University of Metaphysics under Mary Pendergast. Leaving the Spokane Church in the hands of Erma Wells (who later became president of the International New Thought Alliance), Grier moved to Pasadena and founded the church there. Grier's last church was in New York City. Upon his retirement, he left the work with his daughter, who was in turn succeeded by Ervin Seale. After the death of Emmet Fox, Seale moved the church to Carnegie Hall, where Fox's Church of the Healing Christ had met. Seale became known for his work in publishing the writings of Phineas P. Quimby, from whom the New Thought movement stemmed. Seale was succeeded in 1973 by J. L. Baughman.

The Church of the Truth currently exists as a loose fellowship of churches and ministers. The Spokane work was lost after an automobile accident incapacitated Erma Wells. There are now churches in Pasadena and New York City; Calgary, Alberta; Victoria, British Columbia; Alameda, California, and Everett, Washington. The teachings of the church are those of the International New Thought Alliance, of which it is a member. Each leader and congregation expresses belief in the church's teachings through making individual statements.

Membership: Not reported. In the early 1980s, congregations existed in New York City, Pasadena and Alameda, California; Victoria, British Columbia: Calgary, Alberta; and Tacoma, Washington.

Sources: Albert C. Grier, *The Spirit of the Truth*. New York: Theo. Gaus' Sons, 1930; Ervin Seale, *Learn to Live*. Los Angeles: Science of Mind Publications, 1967; Erwin Seale, *This Business of Living*. New York: The Builder Press, n.d.; *Church of Truth, Spokane, Washington, A Short History of Its Time and Work*. Spokane: The Fountian Press, 1938.

★777★

DISCIPLES OF FAITH
Box 50322
Nashville, TN 37205

Similar to the Life-Study Fellowship (see separate entry) is the Disciples of Faith of Nashville, Tennessee. As with Life-Study Fellowship, no mention of the leadership is made in the group's literature. Members are related through the mail and by printed testimonials. United prayer with a world-wide prayer fellowship is stressed. Members are asked to rate themselves according to health, prayer life, use of time, faith and relation to God. Members work on receiving the full abundance of God.

Central to the Disciples of Faith are lessons which train the member to prepare the prayer-time, to understand the power of prayer, and to know the laws of abundant living, faith and spiritual healing. The mystical teachings of Jesus on the necessity of prayer as "holy communion" are stressed. Miracles happen to people after their prayers are offered in Jesus' name.

Membership: Not reported.

★778★

DIVINE SCIENCE FEDERATION INTERNATIONAL
1400 Williams St.
Denver, CO 80218

The Divine Science Federation International was formed in 1889 by the merger of two movements, one headed by Malinda Cramer and the other by Nona L. Brooks and her sister, Fannie James. Malinda Cramer had been an invalid for twenty-five years when, in 1885, she discovered metaphysical truth and went from being an incurable patient to being a teacher of the science of health. In 1888, she chartered the Home College of Divine Science and began to publish *Harmony*, a monthly periodical. Nona Brooks and Fannie James had moved to Pueblo, Colorado. There, their father died, leaving them poverty-stricken. While there, they attended lectures by Mrs. Frank Bingham, a student of Emma Curtis Hopkins, the famous early teacher of New Thought. Nona was cured of a throat condition which was preventing her from eating. The healing came through the realization of the omnipotence of God. Nona began to treat people; Fannie began to teach classes. They moved to Denver; then in 1889, Malinda Cramer made her first visit to Denver. Fannie and Nona discovered that their ideas matched hers. They asked permission to use the "Divine Science" name, and the cooperation which began then has continued.

In 1898 they incorporated as the Divine Science College. Under pressure from followers, Fannie went to San Francisco and was ordained by Malinda Cramer. In 1899 she began to hold Sunday morning service s. The work grew slowly, first in the West and then in the East. It was not until 1957, however, that the Divine Science Federation International was formed, as a union of cooperative Divine Science organizations.

Keynote of Divine Science is the omnipotence of God. God fills all and is infinite Spirit. God is the one and only substance. All Divine Science thinking starts from this reality. The omnipresence, omnipotence and omniscience of God prove the unreality of evil. Evil cannot exist by itself. It only exists as we support its existence by our belief. Creation is God in self-expression. Creation is Spirit. Man is the image and likeness of God, at one with his creator. By realizing the true nature of the self, man realizes eternal life.

The Federation is governed by a House of Delegates composed of representatives of the various churches. Any member can attend meetings of the House of Delegates, but only delegates can vote. A General Council of five members handles federation affairs between meetings. The Federation publishes *Aspire*, descendant of *Daily Studies in Divine Science*, the oldest of the New Thought daily devotional guides, begun in 1915. Also published is a selection of books and religious literature. It is a member of the International New Thought Alliance.

Membership: Not reported. In 1981 there were 30 churches and 53 practitioners listed and 1 church each in England and South Africa.

Periodicals: *Aspire*, 1819 East 14th Avenue, Denver, CO 80218.

Sources: Louise McNamara Brooks, *Early History of Divine Science*. Denver: First Divine Science Church, 1963; Fannie B. James, *Truth and Health*. Denver; The Colorado College of Divine Science, 1922; Irwin Gregg, *The Divine Science Way*. Denver: Divine Science Federation International, 1975; Hazel Deane, *Powerful Is the Light*. Denver: Divine Science Federation International, 1965; Malinda Cramer, *Divine Science and Healing*. San Francisco: The Author, 1905.

★779★
ESP PICTURE PRAYERS
Current address not obtained for this edition.

ESP Picture Prayers is headed by Murcie P. Smith of Gary, Indiana. Like the Life-Study Fellowship (see separate entry) ESP Picture Prayers offers printed prayers based upon the idea of God as a loving father. The ESP Picture Prayers organization offers private ESP readings to members as an added incentive. Included in the prayers are special ones for those in the armed services, a "Blessed Sacred Heart of Jesus Christ Prayer" (with a picture of the Sacred Heart included), and a "Blessed Sacred Eyes of Jesus Christ Prayer" (with a picture of the sacred eyes included).

★780★
FIRST CHURCH OF DIVINE IMMANENCE
2109 Broadway
Apt. 8L/144
New York, NY 10023

The First Church of Divine Immanence was founded in 1952 by Dr. Henry Milton Ellis (d. 1970). Ellis was a journalist who studied at the College of Divine Metaphysics, from which he received a doctorate. He was for a while a Religious Science practitioner. He became aware that no New Thought group was serving the scattered believers not close to urban areas, so he founded the First Church of Divine Immanence as a mail order denomination. Ellis wrote *Bible Science: the Truth and the Way* as a textbook. At its height, before Ellis' death, the church numbered close to 1,000 members, but with a much larger constituency. Ellis sent a newsletter, *From the Pastor's Study*, regularly to the membership.

Teachings of the church, Bible Science, draws heavily upon the works of Ernest Holmes, founder of the Church of Religious Science. God is Spirit, the original life-essence. "Infinite mind" is the animative life principle, and we think, decide and act with this omniscient mind. Man is an expression of God in activity. The law of mind is the power of authority in the natural order of law. Man enters the kingdom of heaven by being "born again," in Greek, metanoia, changing the mind. That change occurs when man realizes his true nature.

Membership: Not reported.

★781★
HOME OF TRUTH
% Rev. Gloria Baltes
1300 Grand St.
Alemeda, CA 94501

Annie Rix Militz (d. 1924) was an early student of pioneer New Thought teacher, Emma Curtis Hopkins. After hearing Hopkins in 1887, Militz quit her schoolteaching job and began to conduct classes at a San Francisco metaphysical bookstore. Outgrowing the store, she founded the Christian Science Home, which became the Home of Truth. The "home" was to communicate the mothering spirit which goes out to all people, teaching them the truth of the Godhead of Man. Militz taught for three years in the Chicago Theological Seminary founded by Emma Curtis Hopkins after she left the Church of Christ, Scientist. Militz left her sister Harriet Rix and Eve Elton in charge of the Home. Upon her return, the San Francisco center was flourishing, so Militz went to Los Angeles to found the second center. While there, she began to publish *Master Mind*, one of the most influential metaphysical magazines in the early twentieth century.

The teaching of Militz is based upon the allness of God and the notion that man, as the idea of God, is exactly what God is: good, perfect, immortal. God is man's health. Man's purpose is to manifest God. Healing is conducted by purely spiritual means through silence, prayer and the word of God spoken in both affirmation and denial.

The organization of the Home of Truth was a very loose fellowship. In keeping with the idea that the church consists of the whole body of divine humanity everywhere, no membership rolls are maintained. People affiliate as they find affinity with the teaching and activity. During the 1930s, Homes could be found along the West Coast and with scattered congregations as far east as Miami and Boston. Many of these became independent congregations, and a few, such as the Christian Assembly of San Jose, California, grew into separate New Thought denominations in their own right.

Membership: As of 1985, there was only one Home of Truth center known. It is located in Alameda, California.

Sources: Annie Rix Militz, *Primary Lessons in Christian Living and Healing*. Los Angeles: Home of Truth Publishing Company, 1904; Annie Rix Militz, *The Renewal of the Body*. Holyoke, MA: Elizabeth Towne Co., 1920; Harriet Hale Rix, *Christian Mind Healing*. Los Angeles: Master Mind Publishing Co., 1918; Annie Rix

Militz, *Spiritual Housekeeping*. New York: The Absolute Press, 1910.

★782★

INNER POWERS SOCIETY
Yucca Valley, CA 92284

The Inner Powers Society was founded by Alfred Pritchard, its president. Metaphysician Pritchard contacts prospective members through advertisements in metaphysical and psychic publications. The Society is organized by members relating to the home office in Yucca Valley, California. It offers courses which Pritchard wrote on a wide variety of New Thought topics. Pritchard teaches that one must become attuned to the "inner environment" of "cycling cosmic forces." As these forces of inner powers flow through mankind, the distortions of past reversals of truth will be eliminated, and a new age of super-intelligence will be established. Man is entering a new age, an occurrence which is repeated every 2,155 years.

Membership: Not reported.

Sources: Alfred W. Pritchard, *Man...God's Helpmate*. Los Angeles: Inner Powers Society, 1958.

★783★

INSTITUTE OF ESOTERIC
TRANSCENDENTALISM
℅ Mr. Robert W. C. Burke
3278 Wilshire Blvd.
Los Angeles, CA 90005

Dr. Robert W. C. Burke is a New Thought teacher in Los Angeles. In 1956, he founded the Robert Burke Foundation and, nine years later, Christology. These were combined in 1969 as the Institute of Esoteric Transcendentalism. There is no formal statement of belief. The right to hold divergent religious tenets is acknowledged.

The basis of the Institute's teachings is Christology, the science of the knowledge of Christ, which rests alone upon the words credited to Jesus. All else in the Bible is considered history and stories for guidance and inspiration. Jesus is described as the man who spoke the illumined Word, Christ, and laid before mankind a foundation for spirituality. Mankind is a creature of divinity and thus "of God." He has within him the divine power that moves the universe, but man misuses the abundant gift of God. Intellectual awareness is the first step in building toward a spiritual consciousness. When spiritual consciousness is put into action, complete self-awareness occurs. Meditation is emphasized as a way to spiritual consciousness.

The program of the Institute is centered upon its headquarters at the William Penn Hotel, Whittier, California, where a full program of lectures, classwork

and individual counseling is offered. The two periodicals, both of which follow a lesson format, are mailed to several states.

Membership: Not reported. The Whitter location is the only center.

Periodicals: *The Christext*, 3278 Wilshire Blvd., Los Angeles, CA 90005; *The Transcendentalist,*3278 Wilshire Blvd., Los Angeles, CA 90005.

★784★

LIFE STUDY FELLOWSHIP FOUNDATION, INC.
Noroton, CT 06820

The Life Study Fellowship Foundation, Inc. was begun in 1939. It differs from other New Thought groups in that its members are related to each other and to the headquarters only through the literature sent out regularly. Recent literature carries no mention of the founders or present leaders, but often quotes from testimonials of members who have been helped. Several of the more substantial early books were written by Herbert R. Moral. Basis of the Fellowship is the "new way of prayer," which, while simple, will open the power of prayer to all.

The new way is based on "Unity Prayer," the thrice daily prayer by all members for others in the Fellowship. The prayer to be used at each period is printed in the bimonthy *Faith* magazine. At 8 a.m., the prayer is for God's guidance, at 12 noon, for prosperity, and at 9 p.m., for healing. A second aspect of the "new way of prayer" is the special printed prayers which are sent to members with problems in particular areas. These prayers articulate needs, requests for blessings, and affirmations. They are to be read daily at a regular prayer-time. The third part of the new way is the special-help department devoted to short-term special problems. Members may write to headquarters for help at any time. Members of the Fellowship are urged to use the prayers as a means for problem-solving and obtaining particular goals. A golden key is distributed for good fortune. Each key has letters which can bring good luck when understood and used.

Membership in the Fellowship is solicited in numerous ads in the printed media. Members fill out a lengthy form. The work is supported by offerings of the members. The Teachings Department has, since the mid-1960s, published a series of books and booklets containing prayers on particular themes of prosperity, healing,and peace of mind.

Membership: Not reported.

Periodicals: *Faith*, Noroton, CT 06820.

Sources: [Herbert R. Moral], *"With God All Things Are Possible."* Noroton, CT: Life Study Fellowship, 1945;

Power for Peace of Mind. Noroton, CT: Life Study Fellowship, n.d.; Herbert R. Moral, *How to Have Better Health through Prayer.* Noroton, CT: Life Study Fellowship, n.d.

★785★

MIRACLE EXPERIENCES, INC.
Box 158
Islip Terrace, NY 11752

The Foundation for Inner Peace was founded in 1976 to publish and distribute *A Course In Miracles,* a three-volume textbook in New Thought metaphysics. The material in the *Course* had been received by Dr. Helen Schucman (d. February 9, 1981), a psychologist at the Neurological Institute of Columbia University in New York City. Born a Jew, Dr. Schucman had become an atheist, but in 1965 began to receive the material for the Course as dictated by an inner voice. The voice claimed to be Jesus Christ. The dictations occurred over a seven-year period.

In 1975 Dr. Schucman met Judith Skutch, a well-known leader in New York City's psychic-metaphysical community and head of the Foundation for Parasensory Information. During the next year Skutch read the material and was so impressed that she established the Foundation for Inner Peace. During that year she also met Saul Steinberg, owner of Coleman Graphics, a printshop on Long Island, who offered to print the book. It was published in 1976 without any mention of Dr. Schucman. Though given little fanfare and informally promoted, largely by word of mouth, it quickly found an audience. By 1977 groups studying *A Course in Miracles* sprang up from New York to California. In addition to Coleman Graphics, Steinberg founded a publishing company, Miracle Life, Inc. (now Miracle Experiences, Inc.), and began a newsletter, *Miracle News,* which promotes the *Course* through conferences and workshops and has fostered the emergence of a network of study groups.

The movement which grew around the *Course* soon attracted leaders from among people already accepting of New Thought metaphysics, including some medical and psychological professionals previously aligned with the human potential movement. Several of these professionals, most notably Dr. Gerald G. Jampolsky, founder of The Center for Attitudinal Healing in Tiburon, California, have become national promoters and spokespersons for the *Course.*

As the movement grew, Saul Steinberg emerged as the national conference coordinator and national group coordinator for the *Course.* Regional coordinators and moderators of study groups guide the movement in local communities. Miracle Experiences, Inc., of which Steinberg is the president, coordinates and promotes the national and regional conferences, publishes a newsletter,

and distributes the growing body of materials which has appeared in response to the *Course.*

The *Course,* summarized in fifty brief statements in the first chapter of the three-volume work, is a complete presentation of New Thought metaphysics using as a basic metaphor the image of a miracle. A miracle is redefined from its common definition of God's particular and extraordinary action above and beyond the laws of nature; it is a correction introduced into false thinking by an individual. Miracles are examples of correct thinking which attune the individual's perceptions to Truth.

Membership: Not reported. By the early 1980s over 200 Miracle Groups were reported in the listing circulated by Miracle Experiences, Inc. Over 100,000 copies of *A Course in Miracles* had been sold.

Periodicals: *Miracle News,* Miracle Experiences Inc., Box 158, Islip Terrace, New York 11752. *Miracles,* San Francisco Miracles Foundation, 1040 Masonic Avenue, Apt. #2, San Francisco, California 94117; *Inner Peace,* %Coleman Publishing, 99 Milbar Blvd., Farmingdale, NY 11735.

Sources: *A Course in Miracles.* New York: Foundation for Inner Peace, 1975. 3 Vols.; Sondra Ray, *Drinking the Divine.* Berkeley, CA: Celestial Arts, 1984; John Koffend, "The Gospel According to Helen" in *Psychology Today,* vol. 14 (September 1980), pp. 74-78; Robert Skutch, "A Course in Miracles, the Untold Story" in *New Realities,* vol. 4, no. 1 (July/August 1984), pp. 17-27 (part 1); vol. 4, no. 2 (September/October 1984), pp. 8-15, 78 (part 2).

★786★

NOOHRA FOUNDATION
% Dr. Rocco Enrico
720 Paularino Ave.
Costa Mesa, CA 92626

The Noohra (Light) Foundation was founded in 1970 by Rocco Enrico, a student of George M. Lamsa, an Assyrian-born Bible scholar and translator. It grew out of and supercedes the Aramaic Bible Society, founded by Lamsa in 1927, and Calvary Missionary Church, a congregation formed by Lamsa in 1947 in San Antonio, Texas. Lamsa had migrated to the United States in 1917. He attended Virginia Theological Seminary (Episcopal) and the University of Pennsylvania and then began his career as a Bible translator. It was Lamsa's claim that Greek was not the original language of Scriptures. He believed that Aramaic was spoken by Jesus and the Apostles, that they wrote in Aramaic and that the Eastern Peshitta Bible was the original version. He feels that only by understanding the Aramaic background could the many idioms of the New Testament be understood. Most important, Lamsa claimed that the language, customs and manners of his home country, Assyria (the Assyrian language is the modern form of Aramaic), have not changed since the time of Jesus and could be studied for direct light on Scripture.

Lamsa's scholarship has been embodied in a series of translations of Biblical literature and commentaries on the New Testament which deal with Aramaic customs. Both the Calvary Missionary Church and the affiliated Aramaic Bible Society were created to teach Lamsa's insights and distribute his writings. In the mid-1950s, Rocco Enrico became the co-pastor of the congregation, and in 197 0 founded the Aramaic Bible Center as an educational arm of the church to further expand the knowledge of Lamsa's work. Two years later Enrico resigned as co-pastor of the church to devote full time to the center, which subsequently separated completely from the church.

During the 1960s and 1970s, Lamsa's work was increasingly identified with metaphysical movements. Lamsa's interpretation of Scripture leaned toward a more universal, monistic world view. In the 1960s, Lamsa became a popular speaker for metaphysical groups, especially the Unity School of Christianity. As Lamsa's health failed during the early 1970s, Enrico increasing became the spokesman for his ideas. In 1977 the Center adopted it present name and the following year moved its operations to California, first to Newport Beach, into facilities provided by the Community Church by the Bay, a New Thought congregation headed by Dr. William Parker, and more recently to its present location. The Foundation's stated purpose is to encourage humanity's potential through the study of the scriptural, spiritual, mystical and practical aspects of Truth, using the Lamsa translation of the Bible. Besides its regular on-going classes at various locations in southern California, Enrico is a popular speaker-teacher and has attracted members to the Foundation from across the nation. The Foundation is a member of the International New Thought Alliance.

Membership: Not reported.

Periodicals: *Noohra-Light*, 720 Paularino Avenue, Suite 210, Costa Mesa, CA 92626.

Sources: Tom Alyea, *The Life of George Lamsa*. Tulsa, OK: Abundant Life Publications, 1961; George M. Lamsa, *My Neighbor Jesus*. Philadelphia: Aramaic Research, 1932; George M. Lamsa, *New Testament Commentary*. Philadelphia: A. J. Holman, 1945; George M.Lamsa, *The Kingdom on Earth*. Lee's Summit, MO: Unity Books, 1966.

★787★

PHOENIX INSTITUTE
976 Chalcedony St.
San Diego, CA 92109

The Phoenix Institute was founded in 1966 in San Diego by metaphysician Kathryn Breese-Whiting, its president. It has three stated purposes: to teach the inner creative action of science, art, and religion; to encourage an

intercultural atmosphere; and to provide a place for those who wish to live a life of dedicated service. It implements these goals through a basic course in mind science and through its affiliated structures, the School of Man, the International Friendship Club and the Church of Man. The Church of Man is the specifically religious aspect of the Institute; its statement of belief forms the basis for the Institute's ideals.

The church believes that there is only one presence, God; that God and man cannot be separated; that man hungers for oneness with the self of his own being; that this "one" acts reciprocally and man is the evidence of this action; that man experiences the finding of himself; that every man is the church; and that the principle "Ye are Gods" is verified by both esoteric and exoteric experience.

Membership: Not reported.

Sources: Kathryn Breese-Whiting, *The Phoenix Rises*. San Diego: Portal Publications, 1971.

★788★

PSYCHOPHYSICS FOUNDATION
(Defunct)

The Psychophysics Foundation was headed by Ingra Raamah and taught the science of abundant living. Psychophysics teachings centered upon the great laws of being which, when known and practiced, lead to healing, success and fulfilled dreams. In the most ancient times, the Golden Age, man lived in direct contact with God and in accord with his laws. Since that time, man's history has been one of losing his interior contact with the Word. Truth has remained alive, however, in every age and was made available through psychophysics. Psychophysics accepted a particular mission, seeing the mid-twentieth century as the time immediately preceeding the return of a second Golden Age, at the very time when humanity seemed to have lost hope of such an event.

Psychophysics was a mixture of metaphysics and concern for bodily health. New students were given exercises and adjustments in diet from the beginning of their affiliation. The basic law of the universe was seen to be love. Headquarters of the Psychophysics Foundation were in Glendora, California.

Sources: Ingra Raamah, *The Science and Fine Art of Creative Living*. Glendora, CA: The Psychophysics Foundation, n.d.; Ingra Raamah, *The Science of Abundant Life*. Glendora, CA: The Psychophysics Foundation, n.d.

★789★

RELIGIOUS SCIENCE INTERNATIONAL
3130 5th Ave.
San Diego, CA 92103

In 1949, the Religious Science movement founded by Ernest Holmes was reorganized. However, many ministers and churches refused to join the new United Church of Religious Science, with which most of the movement affiliated. They continued in the formerly independent fellowship of churches originally called the International Association of Religious Science Churches. There is an annual meeting of the churches which includes the ministers and representatives from the churches. A monthy periodical, *Religious Science International*, has been published by the church since 1972. There are no differences of belief between Religious Science International and the United Church of Religious Science, merely a difference of polity. Affiliated congregations are found in Canada, England, South Africa, Jamaica, and Barbados. The Church is a member of the International New Thought Alliance.

Membership: Not reported. In 1984 there were 76 churches in the United States and 10 in foreign countries. There were over 300 practitioners.

Periodicals: *Creative Thought*, 3130 5th Avenue, San Diego, CA 92103.

Sources: Ernest Holmes, ed., *Mind Remakes Your World*. New York: Dodd, Mead, 1941.

★790★

SCHOOL OF ESOTERIC CHRISTIANITY
(Defunct)

The School of Esoteric Christianity was a coalition of independent Science-of-Mind (Religious Science) churches in the Denver, Colorado, area. The School offered classes for both interested lay students and those seeking licenses as practitioners and ministers at several churches in metropolitan Denver. Among the leading ministers was Dr. Helen V. Walker, pastor of the Esoteric Truth Center in suburban Englewood and publisher of *The Esoterian News*. In the 1970s there were churches in Englewood (1), Pueblo (1), and Denver (3). Though the School is defunct, the participating congregations continue as independent churches.

★791★

SCHOOL OF TRUTH
% Dr. Nicol Campbell
Box 5582
Johannesburg, South Africa

New Thought invaded the Union of South Africa in the 1930s through the influx of literature and the visits of various leaders. One person affected was Dr. Nicol C. Campbell, who, in 1937, founded the School of Practical Christianity in Johannesburg. It later changed its name to School of Truth. By the late 1960s, it had saturated South Africa and moved into Rhodesia. In the early 1960s, a center was opened in Los Angeles.

The teachings of the School of Truth are more heavily drawn from the Bible than are those of many New Thought bodies. The basis is "Seek first the kingdom of God" (Matt. 6:33). The kingdom of God is within. Jesus longed for the manifestations of the kingdom, which in latent form is within every person. Finding the kingdom is a state of awareness, the consciousness of love's omnipresence. As we attune to love, we bring the kingdom into expression on earth. Love is the omnipresent law that rules supreme. Live the law by thinking and feeling good thoughts: love, health, happiness, peace and goodwill to all men, and you will reap their benefits in your own life.

All the literature and meetings of the School of Truth are offered without charge. The two monthly periodicals are sent world-wide without request of subscription. Members of the School of Truth are taught to tithe, and it is from their gifts and tithes that the work is sustained. Affiliated centers and study groups are found in England and several African countries. The School is a member of the International New Thought Alliance.

Membership: Not reported. As of 1985 there were no centers in the United States (the Los Angeles center having closed). Adherents kept in contact through periodicals.

Periodicals: *The Path of Truth*, Box 5582, Johannesburg, ZA 2000; *Young Ideas*, Box 5582, Johannesburg, ZA 2000.

★792★

SEICHO-NO-IE
North American Missionary Headquarters
14527 S. Vermont Ave.
Gardena, CA 90247

New Thought was organized in Japan through the efforts of Dr. Masaharu Taniguchi. Dr. Taniguchi (b. 1893), as a youth, was a student of English literature at Waseda University, where he became a devotee of Omoto, one of the new religions of Japan. He took a job as an editor of Omoto's publications and used his leisure time to continue his education in Western philosophy, spirituality, Buddhism and psychotherapy. In 1921, he left Omoto and, among other things, edited a magazine on psychic phenomena. Then in 1928, he obtained a copy of *The Law of Mind in Action* by Fenwicke Holmes, brother of Ernest Holmes, founder of Religious Science. Putting the principles into practice, he was able to improve his financial situation and heal his daughter. He also had a mystical experience with an influx of a brilliant light.

In 1930, Seicho-No-Ie (the home of infinite life, wisdom and abundance) was begun, and Taniguchi inaugurated a periodical. Material from the magazine was later collected into a book, *Seimei No Jisso (Reality in Life)*, now comprising some forty volumes. In 1931, the Holy Sutra, Nectarean Shower of Holy Doctrine, now recited by all the members, was given to Taniguchi by an angel. Seicho-No-Ie's growth has slowed only during a period after World War II, when Dr. Taniguchi was stopped from teaching because of his expression of extreme Japanese nationalism during the war.

Seicho-No-Ie's teaching is similar to that of Religious Science, but it is unique in its use of Shinsokan, the art of prayerful meditation. Members gathered together or in the privacy of their own homes begin each day by reciting the Holy Sutra. It is described as a means of self-remembering to clear the mind so that the real man can shine forth. Shinsokan begins in a correct posture, sitting with the palms together in prayer, and contemplating reality. A closing prayer ends the sesson. Elements from many sources which Taniguchi has encountered during his studies mold the basic New Thought thrust.

Seicho-No-Ie came to the United States in 1938 when Masaharu Matsuda, Tsuruta Yojan and Mrs. Taneko Shimaza began work among the Japanese Americans on the West Coast. These leaders had been through the 15-day training session, an intensive experience in the divine nature through which all leaders are trained. After the war, a church was opened in Los Angeles, later moved to suburban Gardena which serves as headquarters. Other churches were founded in Seattle, Washington, Honolulu, Hawaii, and San Jose, California. By 1974, approximately 7,000 members and 24 missionaries were under the leadership of Rev. Paul K. Kumoto, appointed by Dr. Taniguchi.

Membership: Not reported. In 1985, there were 13 centers in the United States and 3 in Canada.

Periodicals: *Siecho-No Ie Truth of Life*, 14527 S. Vermont Ave., Gardena, CA 90247.

Sources: Roy Eugene Davis, *Miracle Man of Japan.* Lakemont, GA: CSA Press, 1970; Masaharu Taniguchi, *Seimei No Jisso.* Denver: Smith-Brooks Printing Company, 1945; Masaharu Tanaguchi, *Recovery from All Diseases.* Tokyo: Seicho-No-Ie Foundation, 1963.

★793★
SOCIETY OF PRAGMATIC MYSTICISM
200 W. 58th St.
New York, NY 10019

The Society of Pragmatic Mysticism was formed by Mildred Mann, a metaphysical teacher in New York City. She was the author of several books, lesson pamphlets and tracts. She died in 1971 and was succeeded by a group which is carrying on her work and teaching. The Society

has one meeting center in New York City, where a library, bookstore and offices are located. Teaching work is centered upon the textbook, *How to Find Your Real Self*, and several lesson-series. Members in a corresponding relationship are located around the country.

Metaphysics, the combination of science and religion, is taught by the Society. Metaphysics teaches that man is a child of God, the great mind, and has been given everything he needs for complete self-expression and dominion over his own life. The only issue in life is the self's dealing with its own acceptance and belief. Love and fear are the two emotions from which other issues derive. Our task is to express love and overcome fear. Fear arises from the belief that we will lose. When one changes his belief to love and acts on that belief and self-acceptance, he finds that God is life.

Membership: Not reported.

Periodicals: *S. P. M. Newsletter*, 200 E. 58th Street, New York, NY 10019.

★794★
TODAY CHURCH
Box 832366
Richardson, TX 75083-2366

The Today Church was formed in 1969 as the Academy of Mind Dynamics by Bud Moshier and his wife, Carmen Moshier in Dallas, Texas. Bud Moshier was a former Southern Baptist minister who was influenced by New Thought ideas, particular the secular ideas concerning success motivation. Carmen Moshier was a music teacher in the public school and formerly a minister with the Unity School of Christianity. The present name of the Moshier's church was adopted in 1970.

The theology is like that of the Unity School of Christianity, and much Unity material is used in teaching. The oneness of God and the Christ within are affirmed. Man's problems are considered to be due to his having lost sight of his spiritual origin and of his dominion over thought and feelings. Man manifests oneness in three phases-spirit (Christ mind), soul (awareness) and body (vehicle of expression). Man is responsible for finding the inner awareness of God that leads to prosperity, peace and health.

The Today Church is governed by the members while the program is implemented by the pastors and board of trustees (and a vigorous program of classes and book-publishing has developed. The weekly periodical circulates around the country. A tape library of lessons and lectures has been established, and copies are available on request. The aim of the program is to help people help themselves. The Moshiers have developed a new liturgy and hymnology to express the work of the church. They have authored syllabi for the classes on some of the classic books of the New Thought tradition.

Membership: Not reported.

Periodicals: *The Voyager*, Box 832366, Richardson, TX 75083-2366.

Sources: Bud and Carmen Moshier, *Freeing the Whole Self*. Dallas, TX: The Today Church, 1971; Bud & Carmen Moshier, *A Syllabus for the Study of "Science of Succeeding."* Dallas, TX: Academy of Mind Dynamics; Carmen Moshier, *Success Programming Songs for You!* Dallas, TX: Academy of Mind Dymanics, 1970.

★795★
UNITED CHURCH AND SCIENCE OF LIVING INSTITUTE

% Rev. Frederick Eikerenkotter II
Box 1000
Boston, MA 02103

The United Church and Science of Living Institute was formed in 1966 by the Rev. Frederick Eikerenkoetter II, a former Baptist minister, popularly known as Rev. Ike. The Church has become the major Thrust of New Thought into the Black community. After graduating from the American Bible School in Chicago in 1956, Rev. Ike spent a time in evangelism and faith healing and became influenced by New Thought. "Science of Living" is the term used to describe the teachings of Rev. Ike, which focus upon the prosperity theme in New Thought thinking. He believes the lack of money is the root of all evil.

Rev. Ike emphasizes the use of mind-power. Members are urged to rid the self of attitudes of "pie-in-the-sky," and postponed rewards. Instead, they should begin thinking of God as the real man in the self. Turning one's attention to the self allows God to work. Believing in God's work allows one to see the self as worthy of God's success. Visualization is a popular technique to project desires into the conscious mind as a first step to the abundant life. A prosperity "blessing plan" emphasizes believing, giving, and prospering. Rev. Ike developed an extensive media ministry and is heard over 89 radio and 22 television stations in the Eastern half of the United States and in California and Hawaii.

Membership: Not reported. In 1974 there were two congregations, one in New York (over 5,000 average attendance) and one in Boston. However, Rev. Ike regularly spoke to audiences around the United States.

Periodicals: *Action*, Box 1000, Boston, MA 02103.

★796★
UNITED CHURCH OF RELIGIOUS SCIENCE

3251 W. 6th St.
Box 75127
Los Angeles, CA 90075

Ernest Holmes and his brother, Fenwicke Holmes, were raised in a pious home. Early in their careers, they became influenced by the work of W. W. Atkinson (who frequently wrote as Swami Ramacharaka), Christian D. Larson and Thomas Troward, all early New Thought metaphysicians. In 1917, the brothers founded the Metaphysical Institute in Los Angeles and began a periodical, *Up Lift*. Two years later, both published their first books, *Creative Mind* by Ernest and *The Law of Mind in Action* by Fenwicke. Both works are still in print. Ernest settled in Los Angeles; Fenwicke enjoyed the lecture circuit. In 1927, Ernest, from his then large base, founded the Institute of Religious Science and *Science of Mind Magazine*. Other branches of the Institute were formed, mostly in the West, and began to use the name "Church." The ministers of these churches established an informal association which, in 1949, became the International Association of Religious Science Churches. A working, if informal, arrangement with the Institute, which trained the ministers, was arranged. In 1949, a reorganization was effected by which a new entity, the Church of Religious Science, was created. (The word "United" was added later.) The new church included the Institute, the founder's church (the congregation in Los Angeles where Ernest spoke), and as many of the other churches as would join. Some churches in the International Association refused to join and continued their independent organization, which is now called Religious Science International.

The teachings of the United Church are found essentially in the first four chapters of *Science of Mind*, Ernest Holmes' most important textbook, published in 1938. Freedom, says Ernest Holmes, is the birthright of every man. So why is man bound by poverty, weakness and fear? The answer to man's problem, says Holmes, is love and law. The love and law of God are perfect. Science of Mind is the study of God, the "Thing-in-Itself," the intelligence and power behind creation. To learn of God, his love and law, and to apply what is learned, is the way to freedom. This application is a scientific process, neither supernatural nor mysterious. Spirit is in us, according to Holmes. As we become consciously aware of it, it can pass into expression. Mental treatment is a method used to demonstrate truth. The law embodies our desire; law works for us as we work with it.

Because of Holmes' leadership in the International New Thought Alliance (INTA), there has been a large confluence of its ideas and those of Religious Science. Also, Religious Science leaders have continued to hold prominent positions with the Alliance since Ernest Holmes' death in 1960.

Though Holmes had little formal education as a youth, he emphasized continuing education for the churches leaders. That emphasis continued after his death. In 1972, a School of Ministry was begun as a major step in raising the educational level of the clergy. Previously the Church had founded the Ernest Holmes Research Foundation, now known as the Holmes Center for Research in Holistic Healing. Also, as the Church has expanded, ministers have, independently (though with the support and encouragement of the national church) developed Science of Mind radio and television shows to air on stations across the United States. Affiliated churches can be found in Nigeria, Zimbabwe, South Africa, Australia, Belgium, Brazil, Canada, England, France, Germany, India, Mexico, the Philippines, Sweden, Switzerland, and the Virgin Islands.

Membership: In 1984 there were 295 churches and study groups in the United States and 42 groups in foreign countries.

Educational facilities: Ernest Holmes College, Los Angeles, California.

Periodicals: *Science of Mind*, Box 75127, Los Angeles, CA 90075; *Daily Guide to Richer Living*, Box 75127, Los Angeles, CA 90075.

Sources: Fenwicke L. Holmes, *Ernest Holmes, His Life and Times*. New York: Dodd, Mead, 1970; Reginald C. Armor, *Ernest Holmes, the Man*. Los Angeles: Science of Mind Publications, 1977; Ernest Holmes, *The Science of Mind*. New York: Dodd, Mead and Company, 1944; *Practitioner's Manual*. Los Angeles: United Church of Religious Science, 1967.

★797★
UNITY SCHOOL OF CHRISTIANITY
Unity Village, MO 64065

The only New Thought body that is a national organization with strength in all parts of the country is the Unity School of Christianity, founded in 1889 by Charles Fillmore and his wife Myrtle Fillmore. In 1886, they attended a New Thought lecture given by Dr. E. B. Weeks in Kansas City. The tubercular Myrtle learned that she was a child of God and not an inheritor of sickness. She began to follow the teachings and, within two years, was completely well. Charles, a cripple with tuberculosis of the hip diagnosed as incurable, began to practice New Thought and lived into his eighties.

In 1889, Charles Fillmore quit his work to devote himself to exploring what he had learned. He began a periodical, *Modern Thought* (now *Unity*). In 1890, the Society of Silent Help (now Silent Unity) was formed to offer prayer for those requesting help. The following year, the name Unity was adopted for the work.

While the largest of New Thought bodies, Unity has had only nominal relations with the International New Thought Alliance (INTA). Fillmore felt that too many beliefs were encompassed in the INTA, a number of which he could not support. Unity withdrew from the INTA in 1922, and only a few individual ministers remained involved. Over the years, however, many ministers and their churches have affiliated.

Unity is distinctive within the New Thought movement on two points: an emphasis on Jesus as the Christ and reincarnation. Apart from these two notions, Unity teachings are nearly identical to those of the other New Thought bodies. There is no creed, as such, but the writings of the Fillmores and other Unity leaders are the source for the teachings. Fillmore, while heavily leaning on Hinduism at points, was one of the most Christ-oriented teachers in New Thought. His works are liberally sprinkled with references to the Gospels. He saw Unity as Scientific Christianity. Christ is the Word, perfect as the expression of God. Reincarnation was taught but not emphasized by Fillmore, though it is reported that he believed himself a reincarnation of St. Paul. Since Fillmore's death, reincarnation has become a major teaching. Ernest C. Wilson, a prominent minister, was the author of a popular Unity book, *Have You Lived Other Lives?* The popularity of the Unity work led to demands for more instruction. A Unity correspondence course was begun in 1909. In 1925, "The Unity Annual Conference" was formed to insure that Unity centers taught the Fillmores' ideas. In 1920, Unity Farm was purchased. This land, a few miles southeast of Kansas City, Missouri, at Lee's Summit, became the headquarters of the Unity School in the 1940s. It has grown into one of the largest religious centers in the country specializing in mail order service and summer conferences.

The Unity School has developed its program around several foci. Unity Village in Lee's Summit is home to a major publishing establishment. The three English-language periodicals, *Unity*, *Daily Word*, and *Wee Wisdom* (the oldest continuously published children's magazine in America) have a combined subscription total of over two million. Numerous books appear under theSchools imprint, Unity Books. Silent Unity is a twenty-four hour intercessory-prayer facility which can be contacted for help. Unity Radio broadcasts a short meditation, "The Word," over numerous stations, coast-to-coast.

Unity centers apart from Kansas City grew slowly, but since World War II, Unity churches have grown steadily. The Association of Unity Churches services these congregations and supervises the School of Ministerial and Religious Studies for the training of ministers. Unity literature is printed in 14 languages and has assisted the spread of the movement around the globe.

Membership: Not reported. In the early 1980s there were over 300 Unity centers across the United States.

Educational facilities: Unity School for Religious Studies, Unity Village, Missouri.

Periodicals: *Unity Magazine*, Unity Village, MO 64065; *Daily Word*, Unity Village, MO 64065.

Sources: Marcus Bach, *The Unity Way of Life*. Unity Village, MO: Unity Books, 1972; James Dillet Freeman, *The Story of Unity*. Unity Village, MO: Unity Books, 1978; Hugh D'Andrade, *Charles Fillmore*. New York: Harper & Row, 1974; Thomas E. Witherspoon, *Myrtle Fillmore, Mother of Unity*. Unity Village, MO: Unity Books, 1977.

★798★
UNIVERSAL CHURCH OF SCIENTIFIC TRUTH
1250 Indiana St.
Birmingham, AL 35224

The Universal Church of Scientific Truth is headed by its founder, Dr. Joseph T. Ferguson, and headquartered in Birmingham, Alabama. Ferguson also operates the Institute of Metaphysics, in Birmingham. It offers both resident and correspondence courses on a wide variety of metaphysical topics, including metaphysical healing, philosophy, sacred theology and psycho-vaxeen. Dr. Ferguson is the author of the textbooks from which the material for lessons comes. In 1970, the church had congregations in Birmingham and Harrisburg, Pennsylvania, and Dallas, Fort Worth, Brownsville and Waco, Texas.

Metaphysical healing is the major thrust of the church's program. A basic course explains the laws and principles as well as the disciplines and techniques by which the individual attains the "superconscious mind" wherein all is attained. The church offers a Christ universal healing service which involves the sacrament of Christ healing. In the service, the inner light or divinity is released in the individual.

Membership: Not reported.

Educational facilities: Institute of Metaphysics, Birmingham, Alabama.

Sources: Joseph T. Ferguson, *Manual on Metaphysical Healing*. Birmingham, AL: Institute of Metaphysics, 1959.

★799★
WISDOM INSTITUTE OF SPIRITUAL EDUCATION
1236 S. Marlborough
Dallas, TX 75208

The Wisdom Institute of Siritual Education (WISE) was founded by Frank and Martha Baker in Dallas, Texas. Martha Baker is a prolific writer and poet. Associated with WISE is the Allison Non-profit Press, which publishes the church's materials. From the Dallas headquarters, lessons and books are distributed locally and nationally through correspondence courses and mail order.

WISE teaches the "life message," aimed at perfection of the spirit, mind and body, and offers techniques to accomplish this perfection. Self-knowledge of the power within is stressed. In classes, pupils are taught to control their thoughts and feelings and to locate their inner selves and God.

Sources: Martha Baker, *Sermonettes in Rhyme*. Little Rock, AK: Allison Press, 1960; Martha Baker, *Wake Up the God In You and Live*. Dallas, TX: Allison Press, 1958.

Spiritualist, Psychic, and New Age Family

An historical essay on this family is provided beginning on page 111.

Swedenborgian Groups

★800★
GENERAL CHURCH OF THE NEW JERUSALEM
% Rt. Rev. L. B. King, Executive Bishop
Bryn Athyn, PA 19009

The Rev. Richard De Charms, a pastor in Cincinnati, began in 1836 a magazine, the *Precursor*. In its pages, he began to agitate for what he considered true New Church principles. He protested the adoption of an episcopal form of government. In 1838 the General Convention of the New Jerusalem adopted a rule which required all societies to organize under the same rules of order. This rule led to schism. De Charms, then pastor of the New Church in Philadelphia, pulled his church out of the General Convention and, in 1840, led in the founding of the Central Convention. In part, the cause of the schism was a growing conflict between Boston and Philadelphia. The Boston church had proposed a theory of the General Convention as spiritual mother, to which all owed allegiance. Since New England votes (primarily Bostonian votes) controlled the General Convention, the theory was interpreted as an attempt by the New Englanders to run the church. The Philadelphia Society also was moving toward the view that the works of Swedenborg were the only authority of the new dispensation and contained no contradiction or untruth. This was a view opposed by many General Convention members.

The General Convention reacted to the growth of the Central Convention by loosening its rules. The rules of order were declared merely recommendations; closed communication was rejected; a new system of equitable representation was established; and the assumption of any spiritual authority by the General Convention was renounced. The Central Convention was formally dissolved in 1852, but some of its key ideas led eventually to the foundation of a new group within the General Convention--the Academy Movement.

In 1859, William Benade, a younger contemporary of De Charms, proposed the formation of an Academy as an inner circle of scholars devoted to the study of Swedenborg, the propagation of the belief in divine origins and the training of young men for the priesthood. Most members of the General Convention were opposed to the idea of "priesthood," even though it was contained in Swedenborg's writings. The Academy was begun on an informal basis in 1874. To carry the movement, a periodical, *Words for the New Church*, was begun. A theological school and children's day schools were proposed. The Academy students were pulled together in Philadelphia.

Benade, unlike his elder sponsor, was an advocate of episcopal authority and, in 1882, took advantage of a ruling on associational organization to become bishop of the General Church of Philadelphia, the reorganized Philadelphia Association with its seven societies. Others soon joined. Tension developed between the General Church of Philadelphia and the General Convention with which it associated. Other issues affecting relations were the Academy's liberal views on conjugal love (sex) and its antitemperance stance. In 1890, the General Church of Philadelphia made the final break with the General Convention. The General Church of Philadelphia is now called the General Church of the New Jerusalem, a name often shortened to General Church.

Polity of the General Church is episcopal; only the bishop has the power to ordain. There are three bishops. The Executive Bishop is elected at the general assembly and is assisted by a council of the clergy, and the directors of the corporation (laymen). A director of General Church Religious Lessons oversees production of church school course material on New Church themes. An active book-publishing program is also pursued. Affiliated congregations are found in Canada, England, New Zealand, Australia, Denmark, Sweden, Norway, Holland, South Africa, Brazil, and France.

Membership: In 1983 the Church reported 2,618 members, 31 congregations, and 85 ministers. There were an additional 1,157 members worldwide.

Educational facilities: Academy of the New Church College, Bryn Athyn, Pennsylvania; Academy of the New Church Theological School, Bryn Athyn, Pennsylvania.

Periodicals: *New Church Life*, Bryn Athyn, PA 19009; *New Church Home*, Bryn Athyn, PA 19009.

Sources: *The General Church of the New Jerusalem, A Handbook of General Information.* Bryn Athyn, PA: General Church Publications Committee, 1965; *Liturgy and Hymnal.* Bryn Athyn, PA: General Church of the New Jerusalem, 1966; George de Charms, *The Distinctiveness of the New Church.* Bryn Athyn, PA: Academy Book Room, 1962; George de Charms, *The Holy Supper.* Bryn Athyn, PA: General Church Publication Committee, 1961; *What the Writings Testify Concerning Themselves.* Bryn Athyn, PA: General Church Publication Committee, 1961.

★801★
GENERAL CONVENTION OF THE NEW JERUSALEM IN THE UNITED STATES OF AMERICA
48 Sargent St.
Newton, MA 02158

The oldest of the several Swedenborg churches in America is the General Convention, formed in 1817. A call was issued by the Philadelphia Society to the seventeen societies then in existence. Plans were laid for regulating ordination and missionary work west of the Allegheny Mountains. The Convention (the simplified name of the church) is governed by a modified episcopacy, but local affairs are in the hands of the congregation. The Convention meets annually. Any member may attend and speak, but only ministers and delegates may vote.

The doctrine of the Convention follows Swedenborg's writings on the Bible and Christian doctrine. Convention members believe in a Trinity, not of persons but of principle, and teach that the Bible was dictated by God and inspired as to every word and letter. Most important, the Bible contains a spiritual sense. God came to earth to subject the enemies of the human race. Salvation is open to all who will cooperate with God by faith and obedience. When a man dies, he immediately passes to judgment and to either heaven or hell, depending on the spiritual character acquired on earth. Both baptism and the Lord's Supper are administered. Worship in the New Church is liturgical. (A liturgy was published by the Convention as early as 1822.) Chants are used extensively.

The Convention elects a president and other officers, and oversees a board of missions. Foreign work is supported in Europe, Japan, Guyana, and Canada. In 1966 the Convention joined the National Council of Churches.

Membership: In 1981 the Convention reported 39 congregations, 1,820 members, and 53 ministers.

Educational facilities: Swedenborg School of Religion, Newton, Massachusetts; Urbana College, Urbana, Ohio.

Periodicals: *The Messenger*, Box 2642 Stn. B, Kitchener, Ontario, Canada N2H 6N2; *Studia Swedenborgiana*, 48 Sargent St., Newton, MA 02158; *Our Daily Bread*, Swedenborg Book Center, 2129 Chestnut St., Philadelphia, PA 19103.

Sources: Paul Zacharias, *Insights into the Beyond.* New York: Swedenborg Publishing Association.

★802★
LORD'S NEW CHURCH WHICH IS NOVA HIEROSOLYMA
Rev. Philip Odhner
Box 4
Bryn Athyn, PA 19009

The Lord's New Church Which Is Nova Hierosolyma was formed in 1937 by the Rev. H. D. G. Groeneveld, as a result of further developments in the General Church position on the authority of Swedenborg's writings. In Holland in 1929, articles began to appear in a periodical, *De Hemelsche Leer (The Celestial Doctrine)* taking the position that the writings of Swedenborg were like the Bible in being both authoritative and having an internal sense. A primary task was to come to an understanding of the Swedenborg. Thus viewed, the doctrine of the New Church is seen to be from the Lord, not merely of human production. A corollary to that position is the belief that, as understanding deepens and the church follows the Lord, there can be growth and development of these ideas to eternity. When the General Church rejected Groeneveld's ideas, a split occurred.

Societies of followers of Groeneveld were formed in Holland, Sweden, South Africa, Japan, England and America. In the United States, the Rev. Theodore Pitcairn was the main exponent. His efforts have led to the formation of two congregations in the United States, one at Yonkers, New York, and one at Bryn Athyn, Penn., where the only bishop, Rev. Philip N. Odhner, resides.

Membership: There are only two congregations in the United States with a combined membership of less than 100 members. There are between 500 and 1,000 members worldwide.

Sources: Theodore Pitcairn, *My Lord and My God.* New York: Exposition Press, 1967; Theodore Pitcairn, *The Bible, or Word of God, Uncovered and Explained.* Bryn Athyn, PA: The Lord's New Church, 1964; Theodore Pitcairn, *The Seven Days of Creation.* Bryn Athyn, PA: The Lord's Church Which Is Nova Hierosolyma, 1940;

Theodore Pitcairn, *The Book Sealed with Seven Seals*. Bryn Athyn, PA: Cathedral Book Room, 1927.

Spiritualism

★803★
AGASHA TEMPLE OF WISDOM
460 Western Ave.
Los Angeles, CA 90004

The Agasha Temple of Wisdom in Los Angeles was formed in 1943 by the Rev. Richard Zenor (1911-1978), medium and mouthpiece for a spirit entity called Agasha. Zenor had begun to show psychic ability as a child in Terre Haute, Indiana. He attained some degree of fame from being featured in a 1950 book, *Telephone Between Two Worlds*, by popular writer James Crenshaw. The Temple, located on Western Avenue, was the center from which Zenor travels and spreads the teaching of Agasha. Following Zenor's death, his work has been carried on by Dr. Barry Lane, pastor of the Sanctuary of Revelations in Woodland Hills, California. Lane occasionally speaks at the Los Angeles center and works as a medium for the same spirit teachers who spoke through Zenor; however, he has transferred the thrust of the work to Woodland Hills. Members still gather in Los Angeles to play the many tapes made by Zenor before his death. Beginning in the late 1970s, William Eisen, who had been affiliated with Zenor and the Temple since the 1950s, began writing a series of books based upon the Agasha material. Those books have brought a new national following to the late medium's work.

Activity at the Temple includes communication with the departed, but is primarily directed toward master teachers, advanced individuals who communicate teachings from the other side. From Agasha and other master teachers, a distinct philosophy has been developed. Its keynote is individual responsibility and spiritual democracy within the plan of unchanging laws. The basic law is the law of compensation, "For every action, there is an equal and opposite reaction." Man spends many lifetimes seeking to understand this law, by which his life is governed.

Evolution through self-realization is the process by which man returns to a Garden of Eden-like existence, from which he fell into the material world, the "original sin." According to Zenor, the purpose of life is to discover its purpose.

Membership: Not reported. There are two centers, one in Los Angeles and one in Woodland Hills, California.

Sources: James Crenshaw, *Telephone Between Two Worlds*. Los Angeles: DeVorss & Co., 1950; Richard Zenor, *Margie Answers You*. San Diego, CA: Philip J. Hastings, 1965; William Eisen, *Agasha, Master of Wisdom*. Marina del Rey, CA: 1977; William Eisen, *The English Cabalah*. Marina del Rey, CA: DeVorss & Co., 1980-82. 2 Vols.

★804★
AQUARIAN FELLOWSHIP CHURCH
(Defunct)

The Aquarian Fellowship Church was formed in 1969 by the Rev. Robert A. Ferguson, who was until that time president of the Universal Church of the Master, one of the larger Spiritualist organizations. Ferguson founded the new church as a result of inspiration received through dreams. He also felt a growing concern about the doctrine of reincarnation, which most ministers in the Universal Church of the Master accepted but which he, their leader, denied.

The Aquarian Fellowship Church centered its teachings upon Bible, the writings of Andrew Jackson Davis (the founder of modern spiritualism) and the writings of Ferguson as primary sources of belief. Ferguson has initiated a project of reprinting Davis' works. Like Davis, Ferguson rejected the Christian beliefs in the Trinity and the deity of Christ, but considered Jesus the most perfect of men and a pattern for all to copy. This life is the beginning of a process of continual growth. After death, individuals go to one of seven heavens, to which they gravitate according to their earthly character, and from where they continue to work out their salvation. Communication with those in "summerland" (the afterworld) is emphasized. There are no sacraments, though infant dedication occurs.

The headquarters of the Aquarian Fellowship Church was in San Jose, California, and in 1972, there were three congregations, one each in Los Angeles, San Jose, and Dayton, Ohio. Lessons in Spiritualism were offered on a correspondence basis. Ferguson authored several books on psychic themes. Sometime during the 1980s, the church seems to have dissolved.

Sources: Robert A. Ferguson, *Adventures in Psychic Development*. London: Regency Press, 1972; Robert A. Ferguson, *Universal Mind*. West Nyack, NY: Parker Publishing Company, 1979; Walter F. Ferguson as told to Robert A. Ferguson, *The Celestial Telegraph (A Message from Beyond)*. New York: Carlton Press, 1974.

★805★
CHRISTIAN SPIRIT CENTER
Box 114
Elon College, NC 27244

The Christian Spirit Center is headed by S. J. Haddad, its president, and is centered in Elon College, North Carolina. The Center is primarily devoted to translating messages received by Brazilian mediums from Portuguese into English. It also publishes books and distributes literature on spirit doctrines. Spiritualism came into Brazil through the writings of French medium Allen Karnac.

His particular teachings were distinctive, at the time, by their introduction of reincarnation into Spiritualism.

The main tenets of the Center are the continuity of life after death (first taught and demonstrated by Christ in his own resurrection, and now proven by mediumship), the laws of reincarnation and cause and effect ("karma"), and people's free will and responsibility for their actions.

In accordance with the words of Christ, "Freely ye have received, freely give," and based upon spirit teachings to the same effect, the center advocates mediumship as a free service. The same principle is applied to lectureships and other spiritual work. Active followers of the Spirit doctrine earn their living in secular occupations.

Membership: Not reported.

★806★
CHURCH OF COSMIC SCIENCE
Box 61
Jamul, CA 92035

The Church of Cosmic Science is a small Spiritualist body formed in 1959 at Rialto, California, by the Rev. William Dickensen, Reginald Lawrence, and Mrs. Josephine Dickensen of Jamul, California. For many years, the associated Cosmic Light Press issued the monthly *Cosmic Light*, which was widely circulated among the independent Spiritualist churches. They use it for advertising. The group also circulates *Awareness for Cosmic Truth*, lessons in psychic development. The headquarters in Jamul, California, grant ordinations, healer's certificates, and church charters to otherwise autonomous ministers.

Membership: Not reported. In 1970 there were 500 members and 7 churches.

★807★
CHURCH OF ESSENTIAL SCIENCE
℅ Rev. Brian Seabrook
Box 31022
Phoenix, AZ 85046

The Church of Essential Science was founded in Detroit in 1965 by the Rev. Kingdon L. Brown, a medium, ordained originally by the National Spiritual Aid Association. Brown was an early member and developed in an informal study group with the Detroit-area chapter of the Spiritual Frontiers Fellowship. In January, 1964, he received his first message from the Silent Brotherhood of Ascended Masters. Eventually one of their number, Master Manta Ru, became Brown's guide and teacher. Brown slowly became noted for his mediumistic ability, and followers were drawn to him. They became the original members of the new church.

From Manta Ru were received the basic principles of essential science, the system taught by the church. Essential science is a religion responsive to the new data available to twentieth century man--parapsychology, philosophy, sociology, metaphysics and mysticism. God is seen as the cause that sustains and protects all who seek God. Man comes to know God as the Divine Mind Power as he widens his awareness to include spiritual impressions. Man is body, mind and soul. The soul is man's divine inheritance, a part of divinity. Through the Soul, man aligns himself with the God power, the basic atomic pattern structure of the universe itself, the basic energy of the universe. A significant part of creation is the Silent Brotherhood, the fellowship of all seekers of truth. Some are in the body, some have ascended. The ascended ones become our teachers as we decide to put our spiritual development above all else.

Headquarters of the Church of Essential Science are in Scottsdale, Arizona, where Brown became pastor of the Desert Shadows Church. Other centers are located in Detroit, Michigan; Columbus, New Mexico; Little Rock, Arkansas; Fort Wayne, Indiana; Tijeras, New Mexico; and Palo Alto, California. Foreign centers are in Curacao, Nigeria, and Canada. Members are scattered around the country. Many were drawn to the church by the numerous personal appearance of Brown, who in recent years changed his name to Brian Seabrook.

Membership: Not reported. In 1974 there were 35 ministers associated with the church.

Periodicals: *The New Age Forum*, Box 31022, Phoeniz, AZ 85046.

Sources: Kingdon L. Brown, *The Power of Psychic Awareness*. West Nyack, NY: Parker Publishing Company, 1969; *The Metaphysical Lessons of Saint Timothy's Abbey Church*. Grosse Pointe, MI: St. Timothy's Abbey Church, 1966.

★808★
CHURCH OF THE FOUR LEAF CLOVER
(Defunct)

The Church of the Four Leaf Clover was founded in 1925 by the Rev. M. E. Claas. The four leaf clover is a symbol of humility, its four leaves standing for eternal life, everlasting light, divine love and truthfulness. The church emphasized the fatherhood of God, the brotherhood of man, the Ten Commandments and the Sermon on the Mount. The church was among the early Spiritualist bodies which taught reincarnation and karma. There were, in the 1950s, four churches, all on Long Island. Headquarters were at Jamaica, New York.

★809★

CHURCH OF METAPHYSICAL CHRISTIANITY
2717 Browning St.
Sarasota, FL 33577

The Church of Metaphysical Christianity was founded in 1958 by the Revs. Dorothy Graff Flexer and Russell J. Flexer, two prominent mediums in the Spiritualist Episcopal Church. Dorothy Flexer had led the Spiritualist Episcopal Church in its break with Camp Chesterfield in 1956, which resulted in a number of churches and ministers leaving the church. She also became independent two years later.

Metaphysical Christianity, a combination of religion, philosophy and science, disseminates the spiritual truths as manifested in the life and teachings of the master, Jesus. It seeks to study the laws of nature--mental, physical and spiritual. Obedience to these laws is said to constitute the highest form of worship. The church also teaches and gives evidence of the continuity of life after death, encouraging each member to develop his own gifts of the spirit so that communion between the two worlds will become natural.

The basic spiritual laws are: the law of life, the law of love (the creative force of life), the law of truth or right thinking, the law of compensation, the law of freedom, the law of abundance, and the law of perfection. After death, the spirit continues and has a possibility of communicating with those still on the earth-plane. Healing is emphasized as a spiritual art.

Headquarters of the church are in Sarasota, Florida. A second congregation is located in Bradenton, Florida. In 1973, there were on the rolls some 20 spiritual healers, many of whom kept two residences, one in Florida and one in the Northern United States.

Membership: Not reported. In the 1970s there were two congregations.

Periodicals: *The Metaphysical Messenger*, 2717 Browning St., Sarasota, FL 33577.

Sources: Alda Madison Wade, *At the Shrine of the Master*. Philadelphia: Dorrance & Company, 1953.

★810★

CHURCH OF REVELATION (CALIFORNIA)
517 E. Park Paseo
Las Vegas, NV 89104

The Church of Revelation was formed in 1930 at Long Beach, California by the Rev. Janet Stine Lewis (Wolford) (d. 1957). It is not to be confused with the church of the same name formed in 1974 by Harrison Roy Hasketh in Honolulu. In 1945, the headquarters were moved to Hanford, California. The church teaches the Old Christian Initiate, a set of beliefs which the church calls a world-religion and a non-sectarian philosophy. The Old Christian Initiate, based on scientific truth, shows how to find spirit, understand the natural law and have everlasting life without death. The Old Christian Initiate teaches that people survive death in a conscious state, that they can communicate with mortals through mediumship, that as a man sows on earth he will reap in the life to come, that the future life is constructive, social and progressive, and that peace and brotherhood are to be extolled and war decried. After the Rev. Wolford's death in 1957, she was succeeded by the Rev. Winifred Ruth Mikesell.

Membership: Not reported. There has been no information since a 1966 report which listed congregations in Hanford, Sacramento, Burlingame and Apple Valley, California; Toccoa, Georgia; Phoenix, Arizona; and Toledo, Ohio. There were approximately 500 members and 30 ministers. Recent attempts to locate congregations have been unsuccessful.

★811★

CHURCH OF REVELATION (HAWAII)
21475 Summit Rd.
Los Gatos, CA 95030

The Church of Revelation was founded in Honolulu 1974 by Harrison Roy Hesketh. It is an eccletic mystical Spiritualist group whose teachings center upon the one God, who is all in all as all. Hesketh calls his higher or transcendental consciousness "Tattenaiananda," generally shortened to "Tat," the name by which most of his students refer to him. The centers connected with the church teach a wide variety of psychic development techniques, among the most important being the Rainbow Bridge Meditation, by which the leaders take students over the rainbow bridge (that part of the inner consciousness which connects the conscious self with the spiritual realms) to the White Light of God. Tat is also in contact with the ascended masters, those spiritual beings spoken of by Guy Ballard, founder of the I AM Religious Activity.

The church is headed by a board of directors. Hesketh is the president of the church. In 1983 the headquarters were moved to Los Gatos, California. The educational arm of the church is the Astral Physics School. Affiliated centers and churches are found in Honolulu; Seattle, Washington; Vancouver, British Columbia, Canada; and Pambrook East, Bermuda.

Membership: Not reported. In 1984 there were 5 centers/churches.

Periodicals: *The New Spirit*, 21475 Summit Road, Los Gatos, CA 95030.

★812★
CHURCHES OF SPIRITUAL REVELATION ASSOCIATION
Current address not obtained for this edition.

The Churches of Spiritual Revelation Association was a small fellowship of Spiritualist churches and mediums functioning in the 1970s. Though possessing a loosely organized structure, they had an episcopal polity. Most of the churches were in the Northeast and headquarters were in Reading, Pennsylvania, at the residence of Bishop Edward M. Leighton. No evidence of the continuance of the association in the 1980s had been available.

★813★
CHURCH OF TZADDI
2885 Aurora Ave.
Boulder, CO 80303

Amy Merritt Kees was a semi-invalid cripple, victim of an accident to the spine as a teenager. Shortly after the birth of her first child in 1936, however, she began to experience contacts from the spirit world. In 1958, Amy was healed completely. She dedicated her home as a center for study, meditation and healing and, in 1959, formed a study group, "The Open Door of Love." She also became a student of Unity School of Christianity, the Universal Church of the Master and the Self-Realization Fellowship. The growth of her work, along with the spiritual communications received through her daughter, Dorothe, led in 1962 to the founding of the Church of Tzaddi. (Tzaddi is the 18th letter of the Hebrew alphabet and is identified with the Aquarian Age.)

The purpose of the Church of Tzaddi is "to teach sciences, ancient wisdom, ideals and principles, philosophy, psychology, psychometry, and spiritual truths; to promote the brotherhood of man, the universal law of truth and all educational subjects; to solemnize marriages and officiate at funerals; to perform and administer divine healing, give inspirational counsel and communications and prophesy." An extensive course for the ministry includes material drawn from Unity School of Christianity, the Bible, parapsychology, Hermeticism, and world religion. It may be taken by correspondence. Headquarters of the church recently moved from Orange, California to Colorado. Branches are located around the country, among the most prominent being the church in Phoenix, Arizona. Its pastor, Dr. Frank Alper, is also the founder of the Arizona Metaphysical Society.

Membership: Not reported.

Sources: Frank Alper, *An Evening with Christos.* Phoenix, AZ: Arizona Metaphysical Society, 1979; Ann B. Slate, "Your Daughter Shall Prophecy" in *Fate,* vol. 23, no. 4, (August, 1970), pp. 68-78.

★814★
COSMIC CHURCH OF LIFE AND SPIRITUAL SCIENCE
% Rev. M. Russo
2885 Homestead Rd., Suite 1
Santa Clara, CA 95051

The Cosmic Church of Life and Spiritual Science is a small Spiritualist body headed by a Rev. M. Russo of San Francisco, California. Ordinations and healing certificates are granted.

Membership: Not reported.

★815★
ECLESIA CATOLICA CRISTIANA
Current address not obtained for this edition.

The Eclesia Catolica Cristiana is an eclectic body founded by Delfin Roman Cardona in 1956 as a Spiritualist center. The present name was adopted in 1969. Cardona was born in Puerto Rico and reared as a member of the Roman Catholic Church. As a teenager, he encouraged Spiritualism and developed both psychic healing and clairvoyant abilities. He came to New York in 1953 and, after settling in the Bronx, founded the church with the help of Nicolas Guray.

The Eclesia Catolica Cristiana combines Spiritualist doctrine with Roman Catholic ritual and polity. Both masses and seances are held. A full hierarchy has been developed which, in 1974, included a Catolica Cristiana pontiff, a cardinal, a bishop, two reverends and four subsidiary reverends. Women are allowed to hold all offices, including cardinal, a position now held by the Rev. Mother Olga Roman.

The Spiritualism of Allan Kardec, which includes a belief in reincarnation, is taught. There are also elements of yoga, metaphysics, (New Thought) and theosophy; parapsychology is strongly supported. Stressed is the practice of love, compassion, justice, and humility.

Membership: Not reported. In 1974 there were three churches, one each in the Bronx and Brooklyn, New York and Bridgeport (Connecticut).

★816★
FOUNDATION FOR SCIENCE OF SPIRITUAL LAW
% Rev. Alfred Homer
Tonopah, AZ 85354

The Foundation for Science of Spiritual Law was founded in 1968 at Tonopah, Arizona, by Dr. Alfred Homer and the Rev. Gladys A. Homer. From Tonopah, they tour the country as spiritualist mediums, teaching and speaking to small groups of followers. The winter is spent at Tonopah (the Foundation headquarters are only a short distance from the Sun Spiritualist Camp).

Membership: Not reported.

Periodicals: *Foundation Newsletter*, Tonapah, AZ 85354.

★817★
GENERAL ASSEMBLY OF SPIRITUALISTS
% Rev. Rose Ann Erickson
Ansonia Hotel
2107 Broadway
New York, NY 10023

In 1930, after passing of a statement against reincarnation by the National Spiritualist Association of Churches, the membership in New York withdrew to become the General Assembly of Spiritualists of New York. The New Yorkers accused the National Association of eliminating the rights of state associations. The N.S.A.C. declaration of principles was retained, but the schism occurred before the final statement on prophecy was adopted, thus it is missing from the Assembly's Declaration. The Assembly believes in reincarnation. Churches are located in New York, several surrounding states and Canada.

Membership: Not reported.

Sources: Paul R. Lomaxe, *What Do Spiritualists Believe?*. New York: General Assembly of Spiritualists, 1943; *General Assembly of Spiritualists, State of New York*. New York: Flying Saucer News, n.d.

★818★
HALLOWED GROUNDS FELLOWSHIP OF SPIRITUAL HEALING AND PRAYER
% Rev. George Daisley
629 San Ysidro Rd.
Santa Barbara, CA 93108

The Hallowed Grounds Fellowship of Spiritual Healing and Prayer was established in 1961 by the Rev. George Daisley, an outstanding British medium who settled in Santa Barbara, California. Beginning with a mailing list of 1,500 names accumulated on previous lecture tours, Daisley began to travel around the country and to issue *The Witness*, a small quarterly journal. Using Santa Barbara as a base of operation, Daisley tours the country teaching on Spiritualism. Only one center exists, but adherents and supporters are found across the country. *The Witness* ceased with the December, 1973 issue.

Emphasis of Daisley's teachings is a form of Christian Spiritualism with particular interest in the nature of the next life. The new insights are derived from material received in spirit communication. The Bible is interpreted in Spiritualist terminology. The next life is a discarding of the physical body and a manifesting of its duplicate spiritual body. After death, the soul continues on several planes of existence, each of a higher vibration, hence invisible. Those with a gift of discerning spirits can communicate. Spirit life is much like this life.

Membership: Not reported. There is only one center, located in Santa Barbara, California.

★819★
HOLY GRAIL FOUNDATION
% Rev. Leona Richards
1344 Pacific Ave., Suite 100
Santa Cruz, CA 95060

The Holy Grail Foundation was founded in Fresno, California, in the early 1940s by the Rev. Leona Richards. The Rev. Richards was one of a group of twelve who sat in meditation, seeking guidance. Messages received were recorded, and the Foundation grew out of this shared experience. In the early 1960s, the headquarters were moved to Santa Cruz, California. Messages emphasize man's essential divinity and the awareness of the divine as a part of one's life. Classes, using the messages received from spirits, teach self-development by spiritual enlightenment. The goal is that each member will know the presence of God within, the Holy Grail, and his or her own personal guardian angel.

There are three centers of the Foundation, in Fresno, Santa Cruz, and Portland, Oregon. Heading the Foundation are its officers: President Leona Richards, Vice-president Robert Isaacson, Secretary Gerry Isaacson and Treasurer Ruth Musiel. The foundation is affiliated with the International Spiritualist Alliance, headquartered in Vancouver, British Columbia, Canada.

Membership: Not reported.

★820★
INTERNATIONAL CHURCH OF AGELESS WISDOM
Box 502
Wyalusing, PA 18853

The International Church of Ageless Wisdom was founded by Beth R. Hand (1903-1977), a spiritualist minister, in the 1920s. She was also an early student of Paramahansa Yogananda, the founder of the Self-Realization Fellowship, one of the first Hindu organizations established in America. From Yogananda, who came to the United States in 1924, and other studies. She became convinced of the truth of reincarnation and karma. The Spiritualists requested her resignation, and she was forced to abandon the three churches she had founded in New Jersey. She moved to Philadelphia and opened the first Church of Ageless Wisdom in 1927.

Soon after the formation of the Church of Ageless Wisdom, Hand met the Rev. George Haas, leader of the Universal Spiritual Church, a British Spiritualist body which shared Hand's ideas about reincarnation. She brought her church into commmunion with his. She later sought, but did not receive, a formal charter from that church. Meanwhile, in 1956, Haas was consecrated a bishop by John Beswarick, bishop of the Catholic Apostolic Church (United Orthodox Catholicate), an independent British Orthodox-Catholic body, who had received orders from the famous independent bishop, Hugh George de Willmott Newman. In 1958 he consecrated Hand. In spite of the consecration, the inability to receive a formal charter led Hand to become independent of the Universal Spiritual Church. In 1962 she received a charter from the State of Pennsylvania. Subsequently, she consecrated other bishops of the Church, one of whom, Muriel E. Matalucci, succeeded her as Archbishop Primate in 1977. That same year Archbishop Metalucci changed the name of the organization to its present designation.

The Church's teachings are eclectic, drawing upon Spiritualist, Hindu, Buddhist and ancient occult wisdom teachings, though there is a primary emphasis upon Christianity. It teaches that God is the father of all that exists; that all men are brothers (hence no discrimination is allowed); souls are immortal and there is always the opportunity for reformation; reincarnation and karma; and the planet and humanity can be saved by the power of prayer and love. God is not conceived in anthropomorphic terms. Jesus is considered the Wayshower, who manifested the way for individuals, all of whom are sons of God, to become one with God. Humans evolve by following the Universal laws of the universe. Finally, the church believes in and uses the wide variety of psychic gifts as tools for human progress and service in God's work.

The Church is headed by the Archbishop Primate, assisted by the other archbishop, three bishops, the canons-of-states and the canons-at-large, which together comprise the Holy Synod. There is an annual meeting.

Membership: In 1980 the the church reported 26,000 members in 9 congregations.

Educational facilities: The International Church of Ageless Wisdom Esoteric Seminary, Wyalusing, Pennsylvania.

Periodicals: *Aquarian Lights*, Box 502, Wyalusing, PA 18853.

Remarks: Associated with the International Church of Ageless Wisdom is the Michigan Metaphysical Society, headed by popular Detroit-area psychic teacher, Sol Lewis, who was ordained by Hand. Another famous member of the church is popular occult lecturer Col. Arthur Burks.

Sources: Lawrence R. Barrett, *10 Principles.* Atlanta, GA: The Author, 1982; *Ritual Book.* Wyalusing, PA: The International Church of Ageless Wisdom, 1979.

★821★
INTERNATIONAL GENERAL ASSEMBLY OF SPIRITUALISTS
1809 E. Bayview Blvd.
Norfolk, VA 23503

The International General Assembly of Spiritualists (IGAS) was incorporated in 1936 in Buffalo, New York, by the Rev. Arthur Ford (1897-1971), Fred Constantine and eight other Spiritualist ministers. Arthur Ford was the first president. The Rev. Fred Jordan, a retired Navy commander, was ordained by Ford in 1937 and served as president of the IGAS from 1938 to 1974. Rev. Jerry Higgins was elected to succeed Jordan, but died before assuming the post. The Rev. Fred Jordan Jr., the vice-president, was then elected to succeed his father.

In 1946, the IGAS adopted a "Declaration of Principles" which is word-for-word that of the National Spiritualist Association of Churches. Emphasis is placed on prayer, healing, and spiritual unfoldment and development. Communion is served regularly. There are affiliated congregations in Africa, Korea, and Taiwan.

Membership: In 1984 the church reported 25 congregations, 250 members and 210 ministers.

Periodicals: *The I.G.A.S. Journal*, 1809 East Bayview Blvd., Norfolk, VA 23503.

Sources: Clifford M. Royce, Jr., *To the Spirit...From the Spirit.* (Chicago): The Author, 1975; Allen Spraggett with William V. Rauscher, *Arthur Ford: The Man Who Talked with the Dead.* New York: New American Library,1973; Arthur Ford, *Why We Survive.* Cooksburg, NY: The Gutenberg Press, 1952; Arthur Ford with Margueritte Harmon Bro, *Nothing So Strange.* New York: Harper & Row, 1958.

★822★
INTERNATIONAL SPIRITUALIST ALLIANCE
% Rev. Beatrice G. Bishop
3381 Findlay St.
Vancouver, BC, Canada

The International Spiritualist Alliance is a Canadian-based Spiritualist church headquartered in Vancouver, British Columbia. It was founded to "bring into closer Brotherhood and Unity Spiritualists the world over." Churches are located across Canada and the British Isles and include two churches in California, one in San Bernardino and the Holy Grail Foundation in Santa Cruz. There is an annual convention. The current president is the Rev. Beatrice Gaulton Bishop.

The Alliance has a loose belief-structure, accepting as "Principles of Spiritualism" seven affirmations on the fatherhood of God, the brotherhood of man, the immortality of the soul, communion with the departed, personal responsibility, compensation for good and evil, and eternal progress of the soul. Members are Christian, accepting the belief in God and the creator, who is love, and in Jesus, the Lord who was incarnated for the salvation of men. Jesus became perfected in suffering and thus became both Lord and Christ.

Membership: Not reported.

Periodicals: *International Spiritualist News Review*, 3371 Findlay Street, Vancouver, BC, Canada.

★823★
INDEPENDENT ASSOCIATED SPIRITUALISTS
% Rev. Marion Owens
124 W. 72nd St.
New York, NY 10023

The Independent Associated Spiritualists was incorporated in 1925. It is headquartered in New York City, but has churches across the country. Notable among its members was the late psychic surgeon Tony Agapoa of Bagio City, Philippines.

Membership: Not reported.

Sources: Tom Valentine, *Psychic Surgery*. Chicago: Henry Regnery Company, 1973.

★824★
INDEPENDENT SPIRITUALIST ASSOCIATION
% Rev. Harry M. Hilborn
5130 W. 25th St.
Cicero, IL 60650

The Independent Spiritualist Association was formed in 1924 by Amanda Flowers, who with others withdrew from the National Spiritualist Association of Churches (NSAC) because of her objection to the rule which forbade NSAC mediums to work in non-NSAC churches. She also wanted greater freedom of belief, particularly in the areas of reincarnation and other theosophical emphases. At one time, the Independent Spiritualist Association had more than 700 mediums, healers and missionaries, but it lost a large number in 1941 when John Bunker and Clifford Bias left to form the Spiritualist Episcopal Church.

Membership: Not reported.

★825★
LOTUS ASHRAM
% Rev. Noel Street
Box 39
Fabens, TX 79838

The Lotus Ashram was established in 1971 in Miami, Florida, by Noel and Coleen Street. Noel is a medium originally from New Zealand and ordained by the Universal Church of the Master. Coleen is a yoga teacher.

Noel became a popular figure in the psychic community in the United States through his annual tour and his many books and writings. He specializes in psychic healing, which he learned from the Maori natives of New Zealand, and past-life reading by which he is able to trace an individual's previous incarnations on earth. Coleen's work stresses physical fitness through yoga, vegetarianism and food preparation.

In 1975 a second center for the Ashram was opened in Chillicothe, Ohio and named "Springtime." A chapel, healing sanctuary and bookstore are part of the complex. In 1977 the Ashram headquarters moved to Texas, at a location near the Mexican border. The Ashram is governed by an eight-person board of directors.

Membership: Not reported.

Periodicals: *Lotus Leaves*, Box 39, Fabens, Texas 79838.

Sources: Noel Street, *Reincarnation, One Life-Many Births*. Fabens, TX: Lotus Ashram, 1978; Noel Street, *Karma, Your Whispering Wisdom*. Fabens, TX: Lotus Ashram, 1978; *The Story of the Lotus Ashram*. Miami, FL: Lotus Ashram.

★826★
METROPOLITAN SPIRITUAL CHURCHES OF CHRIST, INC.
4315 S. Wabash
Chicago, IL 60653

The Metropolitan Spiritual Churches of Christ, Inc. was founded in 1925 by Bishop William Frank Taylor and Elder Leviticus Lee Boswell. (The word "Spiritual" often differentiates black "Spiritualist" churches from their white counterparts.) The church is Trinitarian and baptizes "in the name of Jesus and in the name of the Father and the Son." It affirms the Apostles' Creed, but replaces the word "catholic" with "universal." It has also drawn from elements of Christian Science and Pentecostalism. The gospel is described as "four-square"-- preaching, teaching, healing, and prophecy. Reincarnation is taught.

Membership: Not reported. In 1965 there were 125 churches and 10,000 members. More recent observation of the movement (while indicating that the 1965 statistics may no longer be true) do disclose a substantive organization with concentrations of members in the Midwest and the Northeastern sections of the United States.

Sources: Hans A. Baer, *The Black Spiritual Movement: A Religious Response to Racism*. Knoxville: University of Tennessee Press, 1984.

★827★
NATIONAL COLORED SPIRITUALIST ASSOCIATION OF CHURCHES
% Rev. Nellie Mae Taylor
1245 West Watkins Rd.
Phoenix, AZ 85007

Shortly after World War I, the growing black membership in the National Spiritualist Association of Churches separated from the parent body and, in 1922, formed the National Colored Spiritualist Association of Churches. Doctrine and practice follow closely those of the parent body. Churches are located in Detroit, Chicago, Columbus (Ohio), Miami, Charleston (South Carolina), New York City, Phoenix and St. Petersburg.

Membership: Nor reported.

Periodicals: *The Nationalist Spiritualist Reporter*, 1245 West Watkins Road, Phoenix, AZ 85007.

★828★
NATIONAL FEDERATION OF SPIRITUAL SCIENCE CHURCHES
(Defunct)

The National Federation of Spiritual Science Churches was a Spiritualist association founded in 1927 whose member churches were primarily on the West Coast. In the 1930s, a periodical, *Spiritual Science Magazine*, was inaugurated. In the 1940s, churches were to be found in the states of California and Washington. The federation taught a form of Christian Spiritualism and affirmed a belief in God revealed in Nature, the teaching of Jesus the Christ, and the worthiness of the Bible as a source of inspirational truth (to be tested by reason and the Laws of God). Spiritual healing was emphasized as was spirit communication. The small federation granted ordination and church charters and offered study courses to the ministry. The mother church was in Los Angeles; however, no sign of its continuance has been observed in recent years. It is presumed to be defunct.

Sources: *Textbook of Spiritual Science*. Los Angeles: National Federation of Spiritual Science Churches, 1932.

★829★
NATIONAL SPIRITUAL AID ASSOCIATION
5239 40th St., N.
St. Petersburg, FL 33714

The National Spiritual Aid Association, Inc. was formed in 1937 and incorporated at Springfield, Illinois. It functions as a central office to certify and hold certification credentials for otherwise independent Spiritualist ministers. Beliefs are not specified beyond the insistence that Spiritualism is the true religion that God sent Christ on earth to teach. Headquarters are in St. Petersburg, Florida, where its president, Charles E. Lyons, resides.

Membership: Not reported.

★830★
NATIONAL SPIRITUAL ALLIANCE OF THE U.S.A.
RFD 1
Lake Pleasant, MA 01347

The National Spiritual Alliance of the U.S.A. was formed in 1913 by the Rev. G. Tabor Thompson, previously a medium with the National Spiritualist Association of Churches (NSAC), and an advocate of belief in reincarnation, a n opinion at variance with the NSAC. Otherwise, the Alliance is similar to its parent body. Baptism is practiced. An annual convention is held at Lake Pleasant, Massachusetts. Polity is congregational. An official board of directors conducts missionary work.

Membership: Not reported. ,In 1971 there were 34 churches, 3,230 members and 54 ministers.

★831★
NATIONAL SPIRITUALIST ASSOCIATION OF CHURCHES
% Rev. Joseph H. Merrill
13 Cleveland St.
Lily Dale, NY 14652

Oldest and largest of the Spiritualist churches is the National Spiritualist Association of Churches (NSAC) formed in 1893 at Chicago. Among its leaders were Harrison D. Barrett and James M. Peebles, both former Unitarian clergymen, and Cora L. Richmond, an outstanding medium and author. The association was formed both for fellowship and to deal with fraudulent mediumship. The Association is also important for its adoption of a number of statements on Spiritualism which have become a standard to which other Spiritualist bodies more or less adhere.

In 1899, a six-article "Declaration of Principles" was adopted. (Three other articles were added at a later date.) Because of its significance in setting the beliefs of modern Spiritualism, all nine articles are quoted in full below. (The influence of Unitarianism is obvious in the definition of God in article one.)

l) We believe in Infinite Intelligence. 2) We believe that the phenomena of Nature, both physical and spiritual, are the expression of Infinite Intelligence. 3) We affirm that a correct understanding of such expression and living in accordance therewith constitute true religion. 4) We affirm that the existence and personal identity of the individual continue after the change called death. 5) We affirm that communication with the so-called dead is a fact, scientifically proven by the phenomena of Spiritualism. 6) We believe that the highest morality is contained in the Golden Rule: "Whatsoever ye would that others should do unto you, do ye also unto them." 7) We affirm the moral responsibility of the individual, and that he makes his own happiness or unhappiness as he obeys or disobeys Nature's physical and spiritual laws. 8) We affirm that the doorway to reformation is never closed against any human soul here or hereafter. 9) We affirm that the precept of Prophecy contained in the Bible is a divine attribute proven through Mediumship.

Over the years, other statements have been adopted on "What Spiritualism Is and Does" and "Spiritual Healing." A set of "Definitions" has also been approved. The two issues of "reincarnation" and the relation of Spiritualism to Christianity have been the major questions dividing Spiritualists. Differing answers to these two questions have split the NSAC on several occasions, and dissent led independent Spiritualists to form their own organizations instead of joining the NSAC. Reincarnation, gaining popularity through theosophy, began to find favor among some mediums in the early twentieth century, but was specifically condemned by the NSAC in 1930. "Are Spiritualists also Christians?" was debated by the NSAC and generally decided in the negative. While the NSAC has drawn heavily on the Christian faith, from which most members came, it identifies its members as Spiritualists. The specifically "Christian" Spiritualists were found in other bodies such as the Progressive Spiritualist Church.

The polity of the Association is congregational. There are loosely organized state associations and an annual national convention. Among Spiritualists, the Association has the highest standards for ordination. The NSAC is noteworthy as the only Spiritualist body to attempt to develop work among youth. The lyceum was originally promoted and shaped by Andrew Jackson Davis in 1863. Children's materials have been developed and many churches have an active lyceum (Sunday school) program. Such efforts have given the NSAC a stability lacking in most Spiritualist bodies.

Membership: Not reported. There were 140 churches listed in 1984. Four churches affiliated with the National Spiritualist Churches of Canada were also listed.

Educational facilities: Morris Pratt Institute, Milwaukee, Wisconsin.

Periodicals: *The National Spiritualist Summit*, Box 30172, Indianapolis, IN 46230.

Sources: Verna Kathryn Kuhnig, *Spiritualist Lyceum Manual*. Milwaukee: The National Spiritualsit Association of Churches, 1962; A. Campbell Holms, *The Fundamental Facts of Spiritualism*. [Indianapolis, IN]: Stow Memorial Foundation, n.d.; H. D. Barrett, *Life Work of Cora L. V. Richmond*. Chicago: Hack & Anderson, 1895; *One Hundredth Anniversary of Modern American Spiritualism*. Chicago: National Spiritualist Association of Churches, 1948.

★832★
NATIONAL SPIRITUAL SCIENCE CENTER
5605 16th St., N.W.
Washington, DC 20011

The National Spiritual Science Center was founded in 1941 by Alice W. Tindall, a student of Julia Forest who had in 1923 founded the Spiritual Science Mother Church. For many years the center was a part of the Ecclesiastical Council of the Spiritual Science Mother Church. The center was also a charter member and for many years active in the Federation of Spiritual Churches and Associations, an ecumenical organization of Spiritualist groups. It was in 1969, while attending a Federation meeting, that Tindall had an accident that disabled her, and led her to turn the center over to two people she had trained over the 1960s, the Revs. Henry J. Nagorka and Diane S. Nagorka. During the 1970s, the center was reorganized, independent of the Spiritual Science Mother Church, and under the Nagorkas emerged as a prominent national Spiritualist organization.

In 1968, the Rev. Tindall had taken over the editorship of the *Psychic Observer*, a once popular Spiritualist periodical which almost became defunct after its exposure of fake mediumship at Camp Chesterfield, Indiana. Under the Nagorka's guidance, it regained much of its former prominence, and in 1974, merged with *Chimes*, another formerly prominent Spiritualist magazine. The church created ESPress, Inc., which has become a significant Spiritualist publishing concern, and operates the School of Spiritual Science, which offers a four-year course of study leading to a diploma and certification as a minister or missionary.

Beliefs of the center are summarized in a nine-point statementwhich affirms belief in God as the Universal Creative Energy; the dynamic growing nature of the universe; the drive of every entity to unite with God; human immortality; individual free will; the reality of communication with spirit; self-unfoldment as the purpose of life; and God as just, accepting, and impersonal.

Membership: In 1979 the Center in Washington, D.C. had 250 members.

Educational facilities: School of Spiritual Science, Washington, D.C.

Periodicals: *Psychic Observer*, 5606 Sixteenth St., N.W., Washington, DC 20011.

Sources: Diane S. Nagorka, *Spirit as Life Force*. Washington, DC: ESPress, Inc., 1983; Margaret R. Moum, *Guidebook to the Aquarian Gospel of Jesus the Christ*. Washington, DC: ESPress, Inc., 1974.

★833★
PROGRESSIVE SPIRITUAL CHURCH
Current address not obtained for this edition.

The Progressive Spiritual Church was formed in 1907 by the Rev. G. V. Cordingley, who had been one of the organizers of the Illinois State Spiritualist Association of the National Spiritualist Association of Churches (NSAC). The Rev. Cordingley had rejected the NSAC's adoption of a "Declaration of Principles" instead of a "Confession of Faith" based upon the authority of the Bible. An aggressive policy of proselytization brought steady growth during the first decade of the Progressive Spiritual Church.

The doctrine of the church is derived from Christian affirmations as modified by divine revelations received through spirit communication. The Confession of Faith affirms belief in communication with spirits, the resurrection of the soul (but not of the body), God as absolute divine spirit, and angels or departed spirits, who communicate through mediums. Members further hold that Jesus was a medium, that spirits have desires, that the Bible is the inspired word of God, and that heaven and hell are conditions, not locations. Four sacraments are practiced: baptism, marriage, spiritual communion and the funeral.

A mother church was established. Officers--a supreme pastor, a board of trustees, a secretary and a treasurer--are elected by it. Individual congregations elect their own officers, but are subject to the mother church. Churches are located mainly in the Midwest.

Membership: Not reported. Multiple attempts in recent years to contact individuals associated with the church have proved futile. It is not known if the church is still functioning.

Sources: Paul McArthur, *Text Book, Ritual, Valuable Data and Selected Poems.* Progressive Spiritualist Association of Missouri, 1908.

★834★
PYRAMID CHURCH OF TRUTH AND LIGHT
2426 G St.
Sacramento, CA 95816

The Pyramid Church of Truth and Light was formed in 1941 by the Revs. John Kingham and Emma Kingham in Ventura, California. They continued at its head until 1962, when the leadership was passed to Dr. Steele Goodman. During the pre-1962 era, four churches were chartered, but none has survived. The teachings of the church center upon individual unfoldment. The church says the basic principle of the universe is vibration or love, which is manifest in many laws. In 1973, there were two churches, the headquarters church in Sacramento and a second in Phoenix, headed by Isaiah Jenkins, a black

man and popular medium. A third church is projected for Santa Ana.

Membership: Not reported.

★835★
ROOSEVELT SPIRITUAL MEMORIAL BENEVOLENT ASSOCIATION
% Rev. Nellie M. Pickens
Box 68-313
Miami, FL 33138

The Roosevelt Spiritual Memorial Benevolent Association was formed in 1949 by a group of independent Spiritualists. Its main purpose in forming was to provide a home for otherwise independent mediums and churches, which it certifies and charters. Doctrinally it is Spiritualist, believes in communication as taught in the Bible and promotes psychical research. It does provide, for any seeking it, a study course in Spiritualism. President of the Association is the Rev. Nellie M. Pickens.

Membership: Not reported.

★836★
ST. PAUL'S CHURCH OF AQUARIAN SCIENCE
312 S. Texas Blvd.
Weslaco, TX 78596

The Rev. Harold C. Durbin is a Spiritualist medium and was formerly a pastor in the Spiritualist Episcopal Church. In the 1960s, he became independent and founded St. Paul's Church of Aquarian Science in St. Petersburg, Florida. In 1970, his book, *Someone Asked, He Answered*, was published. The name of the church is derived from the zodiacal sign of Aquarius. According to the church, humanity is now moving into the Aquarian Age. The "man with the waterpot," Aquarius, is referred to by Jesus in Mark 14:13-15.

The church teaches that God is Universal Spirit with the attributes of power and intelligence; that God is a trinity of Father (creator), Son (created), and Holy Spirit (the process of creation); that man is a trinity of body, soul or mind, and spirit; that Jesus the master r gave the highest teachings, and we grow as we practice these teachings; that man is divine creation, with all the divine attributes and access to God through Jesus; that all life is eternal and must grow and evolve; that the door of reformation is never closed; and that by developing the divine attributes, attunement of the world of spirit (mediumship) is developed. Reincarnation is accepted.

Besides the original congregation in St. Petersburg, a second congregation was established in Tampa, and, in 1970, a third was projected for Sarasota. However, in the late 1970s, headquarters were moved to Texas.

Membership: Not reported. There were over 800 people affiliated with the several congregations prior to the move to Texas.

Sources: Harold C. Durbin, *Someone Asked, He Answered.* Lakemont, GA: 1970.

★837★
SOCIETY OF CHRIST, INC.
% Bishop Dan Boughan
3061 Harrington St.
Los Angeles, CA 90006

The Society of Christ is a small spiritualist body founded by Bishop Harriette Leifeste and Bishop Dan B. Boughan, the president. Teachings are derived from the Bible and the "wisdom teachings of all the great religions," which are interpreted esoterically. God is seen as infinite intelligence manifested in nature and as love and goodness. Members believe in the moral responsibility and free choice of the individual; that science and religion have proved the continuity of life after death, as demonstrated through mediumship; that the highest morality is the golden rule; that the possibility of reformation is never closed, and that man can unfold and manifest the gifts of the spirit. The church grants ordinations, healing certificates and church charters.

Membership: Not reported. At last report there were 2 congregations and 4 ministers.

★838★
SPIRITUAL PRAYER HOME, INC.
Current address not obtained for this edition.

The Spiritual Prayer Home was incorporated in 1939 in California as a Spiritualist organization. The Home issues ordinations and charters, and offers students training courses. The president during the 1970s was Norman C. Fredriksen and the headquarters were in San Dimas, California. Recent attempts to locate the church have failed.

Membership: Not reported.

★839★
SPIRITUAL SCIENCE MOTHER CHURCH
Carnegie Hall
56th St. & 7th Ave.
New York, NY 10019

Mother Julia O. Forrest, a former Christian Science practitioner, became a Spiritualist and, with Dr. Carl H. Pieres, organized a new body modeled on the Christian Science Mother Church in Boston. The Spiritual Science Mother Church is headquartered in New York City. From its ruling ecclesiastical council, it issues charters and runs the Spiritual Science Institute for training ministers. Forrest was succeeded by Glenn Argoe as president of the council and pastor of the mother church in New York City.

From Christian Science the idea of the mother church is retained, as is the concept of demonstration of spiritual realities in this life. Three principles of demonstration are emphasized: preaching, or the giving out to each one through messages (clairvoyance) what God has for him to do; communications from other realms, and healing through the channelling of healing power. Spiritual Science is specifically Christian in its orientation, holding that Jesus Christ is lord and master and dispenser of the law of love. The Trinity of God the Father and creator, the virgin-born Son and Holy Spirit is affirmed. Man is a free agent on a spiritual path which has included past reincarnations. A major emphasis is on soul-unfoldment. Salvation comes as a cleansing process through intelligent prayer.

Membership: Not reported. In the 1970s there were approximately 40 churches.

Educational facilities: Spiritual Science Institute, New York, NY.

★840★
SPIRITUALIST EPISCOPAL CHURCH
% Rev. Ivy M. Hooper
727 N. Capital Ave.
Lansing, MI 48906

The Spiritualist Episcopal Church was formed in 1941 by the Revs. Clifford Bias, John Bunker and Robert Chaney, all prominent mediums at Camp Chesterfield in Indiana. Bias and Bunker were members of the Independent Spiritualist Association and Chaney was a member of the National Spiritualist Association of Churches (NSAC). The founders expressed dissatisfaction with an overemphasis on phenomena within Spiritualism; they wanted a greater emphasis on philosophy, particularly that channeled from the spirit realm.

The beliefs of the church resemble those of the NSAC. Reincarnation is not accepted. Inspiration is drawn from the world's religions, especially Christianity and Buddhism. For many years, the summer seminary at Camp Chesterfield was conducted by the Spiritualist Episcopal Church, and lessons leading toward ordination were developed. The Rev. Ivy Hooper was prominent in the production of this material, which while basically Spiritualist, incorporates material from the Rosicrucian and theosophical traditions.

Significant in the history of the Spiritualist Episcopal Church was the disruption in 1956. In that year, a morals charge was brought against a prominent medium, a candidate for a church office. Camp Chesterfield, where the church had its headquarters, was split between those supporting and those opposing the medium. After attempting to dissuade the medium from seeking office, the Rev. Dorothy Flexer moved the church headquarters to Lansing, Michigan, hoping to keep the divisiveness at Camp Chesterfield from spreading throughout the church. The break between the camp and the leaders of the Spiritualist Episcopal Church was complete when the church was forbidden to hold classes at the camp's summer seminary, and the church's mediums were forbidden to work there.

Membership: Not reported.

Sources: Robert G, Chaney, *"Hear My Prayer"*. Eaton Rapids, MI: The Library, The Spiritualist Episcopal Church, 1942; *Development of Mediumship*. Dimondale, MI: Spiritual Episcopal Church, n.d. (1965?)

★841★
SUPERET LIGHT CENTER
2512-16 W. Third St.
Los Angeles, CA 90059

The Superet Light Center was founded in Los Angeles in 1925 by Dr. Josephine De Croix Trust, called Mother Trust by her followers. According to Superet Light belief, Mother Trust was a Light Scientist who found Jesus' religion because she had the gift to see the light, vibration and aura of Jesus' words. At the age of four, Mother Trust was able to see auras. Twelve years later, she developed tuberculosis. In a vision, Jesus healed her and gave her the mission of bringing to the world his light teachings. She gained a reputation around New York City as a miracle healer. She also began to study the Bible and discovered that only Jesus' words shone with light.

Soon she began to realize the secret of the Mother God. In a revelation, she was told, "This is the new name, Superet, which is the everlasting Fire in God's sacred purple Heart." She discovered that there are two purple hearts united in one, and that the Holy Ghost is the Mother God. This doctrine was not heretofore revealed, because men looked upon women only as breeders.

The Superet Science is the manifestation of God's light through our light atom aura. All substances that possess magnetism, especially all life, have an aura, an invisible emanation. Mother Trust, as an aura scientist, was able to see both the outer and inner aura (or light of the soul). The light atom aura, capable of receiving God's light, is produced by developing one's inner aura. Through use of the aura light, healing is effected and people are made successful in their daily lives.

The Superet Light Center is headquartered in Los Angeles, but has centers around the country in such locations as New York City, Washington, D.C., Barnardsville, N.C., and overseas in England, Nigeria and Panama. Associated is the Prince of Peace Movement inaugurated by Mother Trust in 1939 in Jerusalem. It has clubs and field workers around the country. A monthly

Newsletter is issued from the Los Angeles Center. Mother Trust has written more than 25 books and pamphlets.

Membership: Not reported.

Sources: *Superet Light Doctrine Ministry*. Los Angeles: Superet Press, 1947; Josephine C. Trust, *Superet Light*. Los Angeles: Superet Light Center, 1953; *Miracle Woman's Secrets*. Los Angeles: Superet Press, 1949; Josephine C. Trust, *Superet Light Doctrine*. Los Angeles: Superet Press, 1949; Josephine C. Trust, *Bible Mystery by Superet Light Science*. Los Angeles: Superet Press, 1950.

★842★
UNITED SPIRITUALIST CHURCH
813 W. 165th Place
Gardena, CA 90247

The United Spiritualist Church was founded in 1967 by the Rev. Floyd Humble, Edwin Potter and Howard Mangan. The Rev. Humble had earlier served several independent Spiritualist Churches. The United Spiritualist Church differs from most Spiritualist churches by its adoption of a centralized form of government. Power is invested in the presidency which includes the president, first advisor-secretary and second advisor-treasurer. Under the presidency is the board of governors. There is also a board of publication, education, and church extension and missions. There is a general conference which elects the board of governors.

The beliefs and practices of the church are out of the consensus of Spiritualism. Members believe in mediumship, both mental and physical, and follow the practices of Jesus in preaching, healing, teaching and prophecy. Man is considered immortal; the unfoldment and development of individuals are means to bring the kingdom of God on earth.

Membership: Not reported.

Sources: Floyd Humble, *Bible Lessons*. Gardena, CA: United Spiritualist Church, 1969.

★843★
T.O.M. RELIGIOUS FOUNDATION
Box 52
Chimayo, NM 87522

The T.O.M. Religious Foundation was founded in the 1960s by the Rev. Ruth Johnson of Velarde, New Mexico. The Rev. Johnson achieved her leadership through knowledge gained from study, experience and previous lives. In 1970, the Foundation was moved to Canon City, Colorado. The Teachings are transmitted primarily through the correspondence studies, "Moon Time Studies in Spiritual Culture." Students receive instructions in dreams and the Bible, ESP and psychic development, and "Atlantis" and "Original Christianity." God is conceived as the divine one, or Whole, or Spirit, who knows, loves and cares for us. He manifests his love through spiritual guidance. Students learn the language of the soul, which supplies lines of communication with the spirit world. Graduates may be ordained as ministers and receive a franchise from the foundation.

Membership: Not reported.

★844★
TEMPLE OF UNIVERSAL LAW
5030 N. Drake
Chicago, IL 60625

The Temple of Universal Law was founded in 1936 by the Rev. Charlotte Bright. The Rev. Bright is a medium under the guidance of Master Nicodemus, the control and directing voice who speaks through the Rev. Bright. In 1965, a temple was erected in Chicago, on the North Side. Teachings were given through the Rev. Bright by the Masters of the Great White Brotherhood.

The Temple believes in God who expresses himself as a Trinity. God the Father is the universal law of life which creates, sustains, and progresses to eternal life. Christ is the perfect demonstration of divine mind. The Holy Spirit is the action of divine mind within. Worship can come in many forms. Truth is found in the Bible and in all spiritual traditions. Man in immortal. The essential duty of man is to look within and begin to awaken the Christ Spirit. Only by learning and understanding universal law can we come into oneness with God. The Lord's Supper is celebrated on the first Sunday in each month.

A complete program of classes, special workshops and lectures, and various services emphasizing communication with spirits supplement the Sunday worship. A library is maintained, and numerous booklets have been published. Branch temples are located in Northbrook, and Round Lake, Illinois, and in Wisconsin near Winter Watch. The Temple is informally connected with Camp Chesterfield in Indiana and uses its speakers and mediums.

Membership: Not reported. In the 1970s there were four associated congregations.

Periodicals: *Temple Messenger*, 5030 N. Drake, Chicago, IL 60625.

★845★
UNIVERSAL CHRIST CHURCH, INC.
1704 W. Venice Blvd.
Los Angeles, CA 90006

The Universal Christ Church was formed in 1970 by the coming together in fellowship of several Spiritualist churches in the Los Angeles area. Doctrine is Spiritualist, and reincarnation is accepted. There is an element of ritualism in the worship; the clergy wear clerical

vestments. The Rev. Anthony Benik is the head of the church.

Membership: Not reported. In 1971 there were 5 churches, all in the Los Angeles area, and one 500-member congregation in Australia.

Periodicals: *U.C.C. Spokesman*, 1704 Venice Blvd., Los Angeles, CA 90006.

★846★
UNIVERSAL CHURCH OF THE MASTER
% Rev. Birdie Peterson
45 N. First St.
Box 6100
San Jose, CA 95113

The Universal Church of the Master (UCM) was formed in 1908 in Los Angeles, California, and was incorporated in 1918. Until recently, it was largely a West Coast association of ministers and churches, but it began to spread across the nation in the 1960's. Among its early leaders was Dr. B. J. Fitzgerald, author of *A New Text of Spiritual Philosophy and Religion*, the basic book of the UCM. In 1930, the headquarters were moved to Oakland and then, in 1966, after Dr. Fitzgerald's transition (death), to San Jose.

The church sees itself as both Christian and Universal in its religious philosophy. While it uses much out of liberal Christianity, it also is eclectic, allowing a wide range of beliefs to exist. Its ten-point statement, drawn from the Text, affirms belief in the fatherhood of God and the brotherhood of man, the laws of nature and living in harmony with them, life after death, commmunication with the unseen world, the golden rule, individual responsibility and the continual possibility of improvement, prophecy, and the eternal progress of the soul. The emphasis on the laws of nature denies any supernaturalism or miraculous nature in the communication phenomena. The church also uses *The Aquarian Gospel of Jesus the Christ* by Levi Dowling as a source for its teachings.

The UCM is headed by a governing board including the president, other officers and trustees. There is an annual membership meeting. An examining committee approves all ordinations and certifications. The board of trustees grants charters. The polity is congregational.

Membership: In 1980 the church reported 300 congregations, 1,300 ministers and 10,000 members.

Periodicals: UCM Magazine, 45 North First Street, San Jose, CA 95113.

Sources: B. J. Fitzgerald, *A New Text of Spiritual Philosophy and Religion*. San Jose, CA: Universal Church of the Master, 1954; Levi Dowling, *The Aquarian Gospel of Jesus the Christ*. Los Angeles: Leo W. Dowling, 1925.

★847★

UNIVERSAL CHURCH OF PSYCHIC SCIENCE
4740 Taconey St.
Philadelphia, PA 19124

The Universal Church of Psychic Science is a small Spiritualist body headquartered in Philadelphia and headed by W. L. Salisbury, its president, and Clarence Smith, its secretary. The group is limited to the states of New Jersey, Maryland and Pennsylvania. The Church issues ordinations and church charters.

Membership: Not reported.

★848★

UNIVERSAL HARMONY FOUNDATION
% Rev. Helene Gerling
5903 Seminole Blvd.
Seminole, FL 33542

The Universal Harmony Foundation grew out of and superceded the Universal Psychic Science Association, founded in 1942 by the Rev. Helene Gerling and her husband, J. Bertram Gerling. Both had been prominent mediums at Lily Dale Spiritualist Camp near Rochester, New York. Headquarters were later moved to St. Petersburg, Florida, where a seminary was opened, offering nine courses leading to ordination as minister, healer, missionary, or teacher. Headquarters are now in Seminole, Florida.

Teachings of the Foundation are eclectic, drawn from the universal revelation and the tested teachings of all the world's prophets. Study is directed toward metaphysics, healing, comparative religion, Bible, yoga and mysticism. The seven affirmation-tenets present a religion premised upon the religious and scientific demonstrations of the talents and powers of the Living Spirit. They affirm the fatherhood of God and brotherhood of man, the eternality of life, the power of prayer, spiritual healing, the reality of the psychic, soul-growth as the purpose of life, and fraternal service as the way of life. The Torch of Truth, the symbol of universal harmony, is lighted at the beginning of all services.

There is a mother church, the first chartered by the foundation, and members are encouraged to join it by participation in an annual free-will offering. Ministers are organized into a ministerial fellowship. They may apply for temple (i.e., congregation) charters. The Rev. Gerling is the author of correspondence lessons, offered through the seminary, and a number of books.

Membership: Not reported.

Educational facilities: Universal Harmony Foundation Seminary, Seminole, Florida.

Periodicals: *The Spiritual Digest*, 5903 Seminole Blvd., Seminole, FL 33452.

Sources: Helene A. Gerling, *Healthy Intuitive Development*. New York: Exposition Press, 1971.

★849★

UNIVERSAL RELIGION OF AMERICA
Merritt Island, FL 32953

The Universal Religion of America was founded in 1958 by the Rev. Marnie Koski, pastor of a church in Kenosha, Wisconsin, and a former minister of the Spiritual Science Mother Church. The body is Spiritualist and Pentecostal, and emphasizes ESP and the spiritual gifts such as speaking in tongues. Koski is also known to her followers as Soraya (meaning a "Solar Ray"), because she has served as a medium for some contemporary messages from Jesus. Leaving the Kenosha congregation to assistants, Koski moved the headquarters to Rockledge, Florida, and then more recently to the Metaphysical Center in Merritt Island.

Membership: Not reported. In 1968 there were 500 members. There are two congregations, one in Wisconsin and one in Florida.

Sources: Marnie Koski, *Person Talks with Jesus*. Washington, DC: ESPress, Inc., 1979.

★850★

UNIVERSAL SPIRITUALIST ASSOCIATION
% Rev Clifford Bias
5836 Pendleton Ave.
Anderson, IN 46011

In 1956, Rev. Dorothy Flexer, in the midst of a dispute with the leader of Camp Chesterfield, the Spiritualist camp near Anderson, Indiana, moved the headquarters of the Spiritualist Episcopal Church to Lansing, Michigan. This move led to a disruption of the Spiritualist Episcopal Church. Those who sided with the Camp against Flexer formed the Universal Spiritualist Association. Leaders in the formation were Robert Chaney, Clifford Bias and Lillian Dee Johnson; there were originally 26 churches, nationwide. Ms. Johnson supplied the lesson material which replaced the Spiritualist Episcopal lessons at the summer seminary (held at the camp). Since no doctrinal disputes were involved, the teachings are similar to those of the parent body. Since the death of Mabel Riffle, who for many years was the secretary and pioneer behind Camp Chesterfield and who ardently opposed teachings on reincarnation and karma, reincarnation has become an open and popular teaching. (Flexer left the Spiritualist Episcopal Church two years later and formed the Church of Metaphysical Christianity.)

The Universal Spiritualist Association is among the few associations still attempting materializations of spirits in seances. In 1960, the *Psychic Observer*, a leading Spiritualist journal, published pictures of fake materializations involving many of the prominent mediums including Mabel Riffle and Universal Spiritualist Penny Umbach. The onus of this expose remains over both church and camp.

The Universal Spiritualist Association is governed by a General Board, composed of the president, vice president, secretary, and three trustees. An annual general conference elects the officers. Churches are autonomous, but chartered by the association. Rev. Bias recently moved from New York City, where he had pastored for many years, to a site near Camp Chesterfield.

Membership: Not reported.

Periodicals: *The Universal Spiritualist*, Box 158, Chesterfield, IN 46017.

Sources: Clifford Bias, *The Way Back*. New York: Samuel Weiser, 1985.

★851★
UNIVERSITY OF LIFE CHURCH
% Rev. Richard Ireland
5600 Sixth St.
Phoenix, AZ 85040

The University of Life Church was formed by renowned psychic Richard Ireland of Phoenix, Arizona. After serving a number of Spiritualist churches in the Midwest and East, he moved to Phoenix in 1955. Ireland gained a reputation during the 1960's as a nightclub entertainer, conducting ESP shows in which he read serial numbers of dollar bills while blindfolded. At the church he is a full trance medium; several guides, a Dr. Ellington and an Indian, speak through him. They answer questions for members and visitors, prophesy future events and give spiritual teaching. Reincarnation is stressed.

The center of the church is the congregation in Phoenix, which has 1,450 members. A healing shrine is being built in South Mountain in Phoenix. Lessons written by Ireland and/or his guides are sent out around the country. Ireland tried unsuccessfully to inherit the estate of James Kidd of Miami, Arizona, who willed his money for research on the existence of the human soul. The money went to the American Society for Psychical Research (ASPR).

Membership: Not reported.

Sources: Richard Ireland, *The Phoenix Oracle*. New York: Tower Books, 1970.

Teaching Spiritualism

★852★
AMERICAN GRAIL FOUNDATION
% Verlag Alexander Bernhardt
Vomperberg, A-6134 Vomp
Tirol, Australia A

The American Grail Foundation is the structure for disseminating the teachings of Oskar Ernest Bernhardt (1875-1941) of Bischofswerda, Germany. In 1924, he moved to Bavaria, where he began to write lectures under the pen-name Abd-ru-shin. In 1928, he settled in Austria, where he wrote *In the Light of Truth*. He continued writing until he was expelled by the Nazis in 1938. Abd-ru-shin's message is termed the Grail Message, a reference to the Holy Grail of Arthurian legend.

According to Abd-ru-shin, God created man equal and set him in search of self-consciousness and maturity. In his search, man was led to the world of gross matter. The physical bodies were fashioned for our true selves to function within while on earth. The purpose of man is to learn to live in harmony with the divine laws that brought forth the creation and now maintain it. Eventually, man will return to the spiritual realm as a mature human spirit, ready to enter life-eternal as a fully seasoned and self-conscious entity capable of helping the creator with further creations.

The Grail Message is contained in the three volumes of *In the Light of Truth* and in the other writings of Abd-ru-shin. They are circulated by the Foundation through its two headquarters formerly located in Mount Morris and Lapeer, Michigan. The Foundation works also in most European countries and in Australia.

Membership: Not reported.

Sources: Abd-ru-shin, *The Light of Truth*. Vomperberg, Tyrol, Austria: The Maria Bernhardt Publishing Co., 1954; Abd-ru-shin, *Awake! Selected Lectures*. Vomperberg, Tyrol, Austria: the Maria Bernhardt Publishing Co., n.d.

★853★
ANTHROPOLOGICAL RESEARCH FOUNDATION
(Defunct)

In 1967 William Ralph Duby, the leader and channel for the Organization of Awareness (see Cosmic Awareness Communications), died. Over the several years following his death, the organization splintered into several groups. The Anthropological Research Foundation was founded in the early 1970s in San Diego by Jack T. Fletcher and Pat Fletcher. Among the members of the group was Danton Spivey, a trance medium who claimed to be a continuing voice for "Cosmic Awareness", the universal mystical voice who spoke through Duby. In 1972, the foundation began to issue a magazine, *Aware*, and announced plans for the organization based upon the messages given through Spivey.

The foundation saw itself as composed of ordinary people who had been exposed to extraordinary information. It viewed its task to expose those forces which divide humans from each other and from the divine, and to discover the new culture which is characterized by wholeness. To this end it proposed projects that looked at ancient cultures, especially those of Atlantis and Lemuria.

There is no indication that the foundation survived more than a few years.

★854★

ASSOCIATION FOR THE UNDERSTANDING OF
   MAN
(Defunct)

The Association for the Understanding of Man (AUM) was formed in 1971 as an organization to focus the psychic accomplishments of Ray Stanford (b. 1938). He is the brother of noted parapsychologist Rex Stanford. Ray Stanford began to manifest psychic abilities in his youth. In 1960, meeting with a meditation group, he slipped into an unconscious trance-like state from which he was able accurately to answer questions by group members. The next year he began giving readings to the general public. Over the years, five types of readings evolved: self-help, question-and-answer, dream-interpretation, group-help and research-reading. The self-help readings include reflections upon past lives; research-readings explore various issues in depth. In 1972, a book containing the research-readings on the Fatima prophecy was published. The book discusses the significance of the appearance and words of Mary, the mother of Christ, at Fatima, Portugal, in 1917.

The "Source" of the Stanford readings is not a disincarnate entity, but is described as the unconscious and superconscious of Stanford, which contacts the object of the reading (the person the reading concerns). Recordings of all the readings have been kept. While no creed or dogma has been established, a consistent world-view has emerged. It includes Hindu concepts. The basic psychic/spiritual nature of man and the universe is accepted. Transcending the earth plane are various spiritual regions, including the lower astral and causal planes and, at the top, the "Abode of the Most High." From the higher planes emanates Aum, the great sound, and the music of the spheres, the audible life stream which underlies and sustains all creation, called by Hindus, "Nam." Among the inhabitants of the high planes are the Great White Brotherhood, beings advanced beyond the need of reincarnation.

Man is a spiritual entity, spirit individualized. Soul is the enduring vehicle of individual form which records all past experiences. Component parts of the self are the seven psychic centers (chakras) which serve as contact points between soul and body. The third-eye center (in the forehead, above the nose) is a point of contact with higher levels of consciousness.

Headquarters of AUM were established in Austin, Texas. Members could be found across the country and were of two kinds: recipient and full-participant members. Both a *Newsletter* and the *Journal of the Association for the Understanding of Man* were published, as were a number of books and booklets. AUM was disbanded in the early 1980s.

Remarks: Stanford also possessed a lifelong interest in UFOs (Unidentified Flying Objects). As teenagers in the 1950s, both he and his brother had professed contact with the space beings. Associated with AUM during its years of existence was Project Starlight International (also established by Ray Stanford), a sophisticated UFO detection system in Austin, Texas. It published the shortlived *Journal of Instrumented UFO Research*.

Sources: *Speak Shining Stranger.* Austin, TX: Association for the Understanding of Man, 1975; Ray Stanford, *The Spirit Unto the Churches.* Austin, TX: Association for the Understanding of Man, 1977; Ray Stanford, *Fatima Prophecy, Days of Darkness, Promise of Light.* Austin, TX: Association for the Understanding of Man, 1974; Ray Stanford, *What Your Aura Tells Me.* Garden City, NY: Doubleday, 1977; John McCoy, Ray Stanford, & Rex Stanford, *Ave Sheoi...From Out of This World.* Corpus Christi, TX: The Authors, 1956.

★855★

CIRCLE OF INNER TRUTH
(Defunct)

Marshall Lever was a Presbyterian seminarian who developed the ability of trance mediumship. As a medium, he began to receive messages from a guide, Chung Fu. Chung Fu is viewed as a spirit last incarnated as a student of Lao Tzu in China. The Circle of Inner Truth was begun in 1970 by Marshall and his wife, Quinta Lever, as an instrument for the expression of Chung Fu's work and teaching. Through counseling in trance, Chung Fu offered help to individuals on personal problems, particularly health, and works with groups to teach spiritual truths. Health readings resembled those given through Edgar Cayce, the founder of the Association of Research and Enlightenment.

Lever taught that man has an immortal spirit within, which has evolved through many life forms and previous incarnations. This spirit is continually reincarnating until it breaks the cycle of reincarnations; man must identify with his spiritual self or God-Force during an earth cycle, after which he is spiritually free, eternal and universal, and will not again incarnate. To aid its members, circles were developed for inner awareness through affirmative meditation, nutrition and health, and direct lessons from Chung Fu.

During the 1970s, the Levers had no home and spent all their time traveling among the several groups of the Inner Circle, which were widely scattered across the United States. One was located in London, England. A monthly, *Our News and Views*, was issued from San Francisco and mailed to approximately 600, of which 400 were in the United States. During the 1980s the Circle has ceased to exist and the Levers have moved into other psychic endeavors.

Sources: Chung Fu, *Evolution of Man*. N.p.: Circle of Inner Truth, 1973.

★856★
COSMERISM
(Defunct)

Cosmerism was the name of a short-lived group which began in September, 1972, when the *Book of Cosmer* was channeled by seven angels, the most important of whom was named "Ashram." Receiving the communications were a couple simply known as Luke and Mark (the latter a female). In accordance with the entities' instructions, an original group of thirteen was collected and each member received a Cosmerite name: Matthias, Matthew, Judas Secarius, Josephus, Ananda, Peter, James the Elder, Thomas, Paul, Thaddeus, John the Beloved, and Luke and Mark. In the summer of 1974, the first circle to begin the formal study of the *Book of Cosmer* was held, and the first issue of *The Moon Monk*, a periodical, was issued.

Cosmerites termed their message "the Way" of Cosmer, the creative force,innate in all things and the source of creation. The power of Cosmer focuses in small groups and goes out with them into the world. The Way is a beginning toward peace, both external and internal. Under the oversight of Cosmer, man is on a path toward final absorption, or the building into oneness of men and angels creative force.

Headquarters of Cosmerites in 1974 were at Winter Park, Florida, and the small group of followers was drawn from eastern Florida and Canada. Plans include the building of Ichikama, a wilderness Ashram (a secluded retreat) of peace and tranquility. These plans were never brought to fruition as a brief time later the group's address became obsolete and the periodical discontinued. No sign of the group has appeared since the mid-1970s, and it is presumed to have disbanded.

★857★
COSMIC AWARENESS COMMUNICATIONS
Box 115
Seattle, WA 98507

In 1962, a voice describing itself as "From Cosmic Awareness" began to speak through the body of ex-army officer, William Ralph Duby. In response to the question, "What is Cosmic Awareness?" the group with Duby was told it was "total mind that is not any one mind, but is from the Universal Mind that does not represent any unity other than that of universality."

As the voice continued to speak, its words of wisdom were collected. In 1963, instructions were received for the formation of an Organization of Awareness as a means of giving to individuals the teaching of the voice. The real organization is said to be composed of 144 entities on that inner plane known as Essence.

Communications from Awareness have covered the whole scope of subjects about which people have questions, but, through it all, a few central ideas have emerged. God is seen not as a personal deity, but as natural cosmic law. The spiritual life is stressed, as is compassion in our dealings with men. Man's purpose is to move toward cosmic awareness.

A summary of the voice's stance is contained in the "Laws and Precepts of Cosmic Awareness," printed below:

The Universal Law is that knowledge, that awareness, that all living things, all life has within it that vitality, that strength to gather into it all things necessary for its growth and its fruition.

The Law of Love is that law which places the welfare and the concern and the feeling for others above self. The Law of Love is that close affinity with all forces that you associate with as good. The Law of Love is that force which denies the existence of evil in the world, that resists not evil.

The Law of Mercy is that law which allows one to forgive all error, to forgive equally those who err against you as you err against them. This is to be merciful. To be merciful is akin to the Law of Love, and if one obeys the Law of Mercy there can be no error in the world.

The Law of Gratitude is that sense of satisfaction where energy which has been given receives a certain reward.

Judge Not. Be Humble. Deny Self. Never Do Anything Contrary to the Law of Love. Resist Not Evil. Do Nothing Which Is Contrary to the Law of Mercy.

Duby died in 1967 and a major splintering occurred in the organization. No fewer than seven bodies were formed, each claiming to be the continuation of the original. Disagreement over the publication of materials which some thought should remain secret was one major issue in the schisms. Largest of the several splinters is Cosmic Awareness Communications, which continues the 1963 organization. About four months after Duby's death, a channel emerged through which Cosmic Awareness continued to speak. In the late 1960s, messages received through this new channel, Paul Shockley, both clarified and altered the older material. The new voice revealed that the Organization of Awareness has helped to accomplish a vast shift of consciousness-- a return to the Godhead, which for thousands of years Essence has willed would eventually occur. The return to the Godhead is equated with the return of Lucifer, the fallen angel of light.

Associated with Cosmic Awareness Communications is USA Communications headed by Fred Anthony Warren of Royal Oak, Michigan.

Membership: Not reported. In the 1970s, Cosmic Awareness Communications claimed 75 centers (including three in Canada) and 144,000 members.

Sources: *Cosmic Awareness Speaks.* Olympia, WA: Servants of Awareness, n.d. Vol. II. Olympia, WA: Cosmic Awareness Communications, 1977.

★858★

DIVINE WORD FOUNDATION
26648 San Felipe Rd.
Warner Springs, CA 92086

The Divine Word Foundation was founded in 1962 by Dr. Hans Nordewin von Koerber (1886-1979), formerly professor of Asiatic studies at the University of Southern California. The purpose of the Foundation is to disseminate the revelation of Jakob Lorber (1800-1864). An Austrian-born musician, Lorber in his fortieth year heard a voice in his heart, "Jakob, get up, take your pencil and write." Obeying, he began to function as the scribe to this Voice, which he believed to be none other than the Lord Jesus Christ. Through Lorber, the Voice dictated twenty-five books and other, shorter works. The revelations did not end with Lorber. In 1870, Gottfried Meyerhofer (1807-1877), a retired Army officer living in Trieste and a student of the Lorber literature, heard the Voice, which began to dictate through him. Since Meyerhofer's death, others have continued in succession: Leopold Engel, Johanne Ladner, Bertha Dudde, Johannes Widmann, Max Seltmann, Johanna Henzsel, George Riehle, Johannes Friede, and others.

The works of Lorber were published primarily by Christoph Friedrich Landbeck of Bietigheim, West Germany, who headed the Neutheosophischer Verlag (after 1907 Neusalems-Verlag or New Jerusalem Publication House). In 1924, the Neusalem Gesellschaft (New Jerusalem Society) was formed. Adolf Hitler suppressed the Lorber work, but it was quickly re-established. The Society became the Lorber Gesellschaft and the publishing arm, the Lorber Verlag. In 1921, the Lorber revelations were discovered by Dr. von Koerber. As he accepted them, he began to translate them into English and introduce them to others.

The new revelation fills 42 volumes of approximately 450 pages each. For Lorber, God is the Infinite Spirit behind the universe. The Holy Spirit is the "external life ether" that permeates the universe. The universe is the expression of God, made up of tiny spiritual primordial sparks created to grow into the divine likeness. It is God's desire to create a society of living love.

The plan of God was thwarted by Lucifer who revolted with the spirits below him and became entrapped in matter: impure spirit condensed. God is using matter as a filtering plant through which the impure spirits can be purified. Earth is the place where the rebellious spirits are being given the chance to return voluntarily to God. God became man in Jesus to accelerate the redemptive process. The cross is a perfect example of love.

A human being is intended to learn, through the imitation of Christ, to love God and his neighbor as himself. He thus achieves rebirth and is allowed to participate in the work of redemption. At death, each soul discards the body and begins life as a spirit. It ascends, beginning from its point of development in the body, ultimately to the New Jerusalem. Christ will return in the near future to recreate the earth and establish the millennium, the first signs of which are worldly conflict and turmoil. The present period will culminate in Lucifer's making his final choice and a war of destruction of the most rebellious ones.

The membership of the Lorber Society is concentrated in German-speaking Europe, but has spread to every free continent. In the United States, individuals around the country study the revelation in the books published by the Divine Word Foundation. Study groups are located in San Diego and Newark, California; Denver, Colorado and Salt Lake City, Utah. Since Dr. von Koerber's death, his widow, Hildegard von Koerber, has continued his translating efforts. There is also a translator residing in Salt Lake City. Dr. Fred S. Bunger, the Foundation's first president, died in 1979 and was succeeded by Earl G. Fox of Melba, Idaho. Bunger co-authored with Dr. von Koerber the Foundation's basic text, *A New Light Shines Out of Darkness.*

The Foundation has a friendly relationship with the Lorber-Verlag in Germany, though organizationally independent. It is also associated with another English-language translator in Great Britain.

Membership: There were in 1984 approximately 200 people studying the Lorber material in several study groups in the United States and another 100 people worldwide.

Sources: Jakob Lorber, *The Three-Days-Scene at the Temple of Jerusalem.* Bietigheim, Wuerttemberg, Germany: Neu-Salems-Society, 1932; Fred S. Bunger & Hans N. Von Koerber, *A New Light Shines Out of the Present Darkness.* Philadelphia: Dorrance Company, 1971.

★859★
FATHER'S HOUSE
(Defunct)

Ralph F. Raymond (d. 1984) was a channel for spirit teachers. In the late 1960s he operated the Universal Link Heart Center in Los Angeles. In 1968, he was sent by the "Master" to England and Scotland to visit all the Universal Link centers and people. The centers in the United States were included in the tour. His findings were published in a booklet, *The Universal Link Concept.* Upon his return to the United States, he established the Father's House. The original seven-person board of trustees included several of the Link personalities.

The Father's House publishes *The Father's House Quarterly* and, through its pages, ties together the several hundred subscribers. A plan was initiated in 1973 to acquire a Center for Healing and Meditation. Brother Francis, as Raymond was commonly known, was joined in this endeavor by Ms. Carole Freeman. These plans had not materialized at the time of Brother Francis' death. Foreign affiliated groups were to be found in New Zealand and England.

The thrust of Brother Francis' thought was to provide guidance and leadership as the earth moves into the Aquarian Age. Though the Father's House was independent of other Link groups, informal contact was frequent. Selections of writings from other Link writers appeared in each issue of the quarterly. For example, Tarna Halsey regularly submitted articles channeled from the space people (beings in outer space). Brother Francis also circulated *The Three Day Scene*, one of the books of Jakob Lorber, whose American followers have founded the Divine Word Foundation. Almost every issue carried material from Illiana of New Age Teachings.

Sources: Brother Francis [Ralph Raymond], *Universal Link Concept.* Los Angeles: Universal Link Heart Center, 1968.

★860★
FELLOWSHIP OF THE INNER LIGHT
Rte. 1, Box 390
New Market, VA 22844

The Fellowship of the Inner Light was formed in Atlanta, Georgia, in October, 1972, by psychic Paul Solomon and his associates. In February, 1972, in a hypnotic trance, Solomon began to speak in a stern voice, a voice later to be labeled "the Source." As the trance sessions continued and Solomon began a vigorously disciplined life, the material which came through the readings began to provide for treatment of disease, prophecies which proved accurate, spiritual philosophy and a complete system for the development of "Inner Light Consciousness." The Fellowship was organized as a structure to further the work of Solomon and to disseminate the Inner Light Consciousness. In 1974, the Fellowship moved to Virginia

Beach, Virginia, the home of Edgar Cayce, to whom Solomon is likened by his followers. Cayce founded the Association of Research and Enlightenment, discussed elsewhere in this volume.

The material in the transcripts of the Solomon readings cover a wide range of topics--Atlantis, diet and health, healing, reincarnation, sex, spiritual development and prophecies. The world-view closely parallels that of the Cayce readings. Man is a son of God trapped in material forms which had their first manifestation on Atlantis. By spiritual growth, the cleansing of the body and evolvement, the trapped soul can come back to be one with God. Also in the material are those who came to aid those who are trapped and who wish to return. Reincarnation allows time for the growth of the soul.

The Source for the information coming through Solomon is the Universal Mind and the Akashic records. All thoughts and actions are said to be recorded on the "universal ethers" of the Akashic records, and psychics "tap into" those records to obtain information. In the Fellowship of the Inner Light, contact with spirits is discouraged. From the readings, a course that places the student on the mystic path to cosmic consciousness has been constructed. The course emphasizes the Light Within (or Holy Spirit). Consciousness of the Light is the key to overcoming the limitations of the material. The methods of the course, including relaxation, meditation, prayer, self-control, occult law and psychic development, lead to mastery of one's psychic nature, to integration of the total person and to spiritual development.

The Fellowship is conceived of as a religious association serving the needs of the New Age community. During the 1970s, the Fellowship was headquartered in Virginia Beach, from where a vigorous local program was offered. Closely affiliated was the Heritage Store and Heritage Publications, which issued the material from the readings, the first volume of which appeared in 1974. Heritage Store began in 1969 to make available the remedies suggested in the Cayce readings to the general public. In 1978, however, a thirteen-acre tract of land near New Market, Virginia, was dedicated as "Carmel-in-the-Valley." Headquarters shifted to the rural site, and ambitious plans for the development of a new age community as the center of the fellowship were announced. Publication offices remained in Virginia Beach. Affiliated fellowships can be found across the United States, and in England, Holland, and several other countries.

Membership: Not reported.

Periodicals: *Reflections on the Inner Light*, 620 14th Street, Virginia Beach, VA 23451.

Sources: *Spiritual Unfoldment and Psychic Development through Inner Light Consciousness.* Atlanta, GA: Fellowship of the Inner Light, n.d.; *A Healing*

Consciousness. Virginia Beach, VA: The Master's Press, 1978.

★861★
FELLOWSHIP OF UNIVERSAL GUIDANCE
1674 Hillhurst Ave.
Los Angeles, CA 90027

The Fellowship of Universal Guidance was founded in 1960 by Dr. Wayne A. Guthrie and Dr. Bella Karish, both of whom serve as channels for the "great sources of light," teachers from the spirit world who guide Fellowship activities. The Fellowship has been associated with the Universal Link on occasion, but the thrust of the Fellowship's concern is the harmonizing of the three levels of consciousness. The Fellowship teaches that there are three separate entities within each person--the high self, the conscious self, and the basic self. The ultimate goal is to bring them into alignment for the eventual good of the karmic pattern by blending them for physical, emotional, mental and spiritual development. The high self is part of the super conscious structure and is located about three inches above the head. The conscious self functions in interpersonal relationships, and the basic self is that part that just evolved from the animal kingdom, according to the Fellowship.

Man reincarnates on earth once but is re-embodied until his goal is reached. The high self chooses where to incarnate. The basic self carries memory, emotions, and the masculine/feminine consciousness. Unfulfilled karma from previous embodiments can cause the basic self to open to negative forces that can cause disease, which can be healed only by discharging the karmic pattern. The Fellowship offers a "Three Selves Evaluation" to aid the individual in growth.

The insights of the Fellowship are given to the world through several series of lessons, beginning with the *Wisdom Workshop Series I.* Students may take these lessons by correspondence, and groups have formed to study the material collectively.

Membership: Not reported. As of 1974, Fellowship chapters were located in San Francisco and San Diego, California. Groups in the process of becoming chapters are functioning in Phoenix, Arizona; Omaha, Nebraska; Mooresville, North Carolina; and Summerville and St. John's Island, South Carolina.

Periodicals: *Uniguidance,* 1674 Hillhurst Avenue, Los Angeles, CA 90027.

Sources: *The Prophetic Word. Revelation Number Two.* Los Angeles: Fellowship of Universal Guidance, [1980?]; *Master Apollonius Speaks.* Los Angeles: Fellowship of Universal Guidance, 1970; *Wisdom Workshop Lessons.* Los Angeles: Fellowship of Universal Guidance, n.d. Series I, 12 Vols.

★862★
FOUNDATION CHURCH OF THE NEW BIRTH
Box 996, Benjamin Franklin Station
Washington, DC 20044

James Edward Padgett (1852-1923), a Methodist Sunday-school teacher, became interested in Spiritualism after the death of his wife in 1914. He was told by a medium to begin practicing automatic writing (writing or typing words dictated by spirits), and he became proficient in a very short time. Within the year, Padgett began to receive messages purporting to be from Jesus, urging him to pray for the Father's love. On October 5, 1914, the Master from the spirit world told Padgett he had been selected to disseminate the Father's truths to mankind. The result was a series of volumes which contained the messages of Jesus and the celestial beings. The sum total of these messages were said to constitute the second coming of Jesus. Padgett continued to receive messages regularly until his death. After his death, the manuscripts were given to Dr. Leslie R. Stone, a close associate. It was not until after World War II that the suggestion of preserving and publishing the material was made by John Paul Gibson, a recent convert.

In 1958, the first edition of what became the *True Gospel Revealed Anew by Jesus* appeared. Its appearance represented the second coming of Jesus on earth. A summary of the material received through Padgett is found in the "Tenets" of the church, given as a direct revelation by Jesus and his apostles and disciples in the celestial heavens. True to the Spiritualist heritage, the first tenet concerns the continuity of the soul after death. The soul enters the spirit world and continues to progress until it reaches paradise. Paradise, the sphere of the celestial heavens, is the goal of purified souls, beyond which no progress occurs. It is open only to those souls who seek the divine love of the heavenly Father. Jesus' mission was to teach that divine love had been made available to all, and that immortality comes in the soul's obtaining his love through prayer to him. The potentiality for reception had been lost in the fall.

In 1982, John Paul Gibson died. He was succeeded as president of the church by Victor Summers. A reorganization of the church occurred and all working in an official capacity of the church were relocated in the Washington, D.C. metropolitan area.

Membership: Not reported. Churches are located across the United States.

Periodicals: *New Birth Christian Newsletter,* Box 996, Benjamin Franklin Station, Washington, DC 20044; *New Age Christian Newsletter,* Box 87051, San Diego, CA 92138.

Sources: James D. Padgett, *True Gospel Revealed Anew by Jesus.* Washington, DC: Foundation Church of the New Birth, 1958-1972. 4 vols.

★863★
INNER CIRCLE KETHRA E'DA FOUNDATION, INC.
Box 11672
Palo Alto, CA 94306

The Inner Circle Kethra E'Da Foundation was established in 1945 by Mark Probert and his wife, Irene Probert of San Diego, California. Mark Probert, an orphan with little formal education, one evening began to speak aloud in his sleep. As described by his wife, he spoke in foreign languages and sang arias from operas. Dr. Meade Layne, founder-director of the Borderland Science Research Society, a large southern California psychic organization, recognized Probert as a trance medium and helped guide his development. Gradually, teachers from the spirit world began to contact Probert. One afternoon, five of his teachers appeared to him and told him that they wished to bring their teaching to the world using him as their channel. Many of the teachings were published in 1954 and 1955 in *Mystic, the Magazine of the Supernatural* and later collected in a book, *The Magic Bag*.

In all, eleven teachers manifested themselves in light bodies (figures similar to shining, brilliant ghosts), and Mark was able to make sketches of them. The three main ones were Professor Alfred Luntz, a Anglican clergyman, Ramon Natall, a contemporary of Galileo, and Yada di Shi'ite, who lived half a million years ago in the ancient civilization of Yu in the Himalayas. Yada has reincarnated many times since then. These teachers are members of an Inner Circle, having been one time in a previous reincarnation, together with Probert, on earth. Reincarnation is at the heart of the teachings of the Inner Circle. The goal of life is to attain one's original state as a divine being. Earth experiences are seen as movement through a series of initiations into higher and greater states of awareness. When one attains a state where there is no break in consciousness, freedom is accomplished and there is no necessity to return to the physical. Work with love and sincerity is the way to awareness. Yoga practices, secret mantras, sitting in meditation and deep concentration are considered futile attempts to hurry progress. The basic entity in the universe is the individual. The plan of the universe lies within the individual, as he solves his own riddle of the universe. God is said to be the impersonal soul with which one becomes aware of the unification.

The foundation has preserved the numerous tapes of Probert's trance-lectures and disseminates them in both cassettes and transcripts. Members gathered on Friday evening for dictation prior to Probert's death in the 1970s, and now gather to listen to tapes and for discussions.

Membership: Not reported.

Sources: Mark Probert, *The Magic Bag*. San Diego: The Inner Circle Kethra E'Da Foundation, 1963.

★864★
INTERNATIONAL ORGANIZATION OF AWARENESS
(Defunct)

In 1967, William Ralph Duby, leader of the Organization of Awareness (see Cosmic Awareness Communications died. Within a short time, the organizations splintered into a number of factions. The International Organization of Awareness was one such, founded in Honolulu by Edward Young. This small body survived into the 1970s.

★865★
LIGHT OF THE UNIVERSE
161 N. Sandusky Rd.
Tiffin, OH 44883

The Light of the Universe group was formed in the early 1960s as a psychic interest group in Tiffin, Ohio. Its investigations included ESP, health foods and UFO's. Gradually, a more formal organization emerged, and a teacher, known publically as Maryona (one who has received teachings of light from a higher source) became the leader. In 1965, Maryona published a book, *The Light of the Universe* I, and in 1966, a quarterly periodical began. In December, 1969, the first branch of the group was formed in Cortland, Ohio. Others have organized since then. Correspondence lessons are mailed to students around the country.

Behind the L.O.T.U. group lie a number of books which impressed both members and teacher. These books include *The Aquarian Gospel* by Levi Dowling, *The Life and Teachings of the Masters of the Far East* by Baird Spalding and *Breathing Your Way to Youth* by Edwin John Dingle (of Mentalphysics). A strong emphasis is placed upon helping those dissatisfied with false and outmoded traditions and upon teachings which include the problems in translating the Bible, information on the hidden years of Jesus, and corrections in Christian teachings, especially some corrections previously asserted in the *Aquarian Gospel*.

Great emphasis is placed on the great cosmic law of reincarnation. The soul progresses through various experiences and lessons. It is Maryona's teachings that a soul never goes backward; progress is ever upward. Each person is a master within himself, possessing unlimited power and potential. The god within is pointed to in the words of the Old Testament, "Ye are Gods." This power within, a shining inner presence, man's true self, the divine soul, rules the universe. As man turns from the mud and filth in which he is mired, he can turn to the light and claim his divine birthright. To accomplish this turning, a series of cleansing exercises and meditation techniques is offered to students.

Membership: Not reported.

Periodicals: *The L.O.T.U.S.*, 161 N. Sandusky, Tiffin, OH 44883.

Sources: Maryona, *The Light of the Universe*. Tiffin, OH: The Light of the Universe, Inc., 1965.

★866★
MARTINUS INSTITUTE OF SPIRITUAL SCIENCE
94-96 Mariendalsvej
Copenhagen, Denmark

Martinus (born 1890) is a Danish author who underwent a profound mystical initiation experience. After that he was able to understand and communicate, by means of colored diagrams and symbols, the spiritual principles and laws of the universe. While claiming no new knowledge beyond that which the sages have always taught and which many people already know, Martinus does claim to have analyzed the structure of the universe in "logical chains of thought accessible to the intelligence." The Martinus Institute was founded in Copenhagen in order to spread his teachings. In 1935, the Kosmos Holiday Centre was founded at Klint, a seaside resort center where summer lectures and courses could be given. In the 1960s, Martinus' work spread to Germany, Holland, England and finally, in 1969, to the United States. At the end of July every year, a week of English-language programming is offered at the Holiday Centre.

It is Martinus' teaching that logical conclusions about metaphysical truth can be drawn from the experience of terrestrial man, despite his trials and tribulations. The spiritual science developed by Martinus gave a picture of the cosmic world-plan. The development of energy in nature is an expression of life--the mental energy which animates nature, the consciousness and vitality of every living creature. Because of its ability to get beyond material science in its conclusions, spiritual science can answer metaphysical questions logically. For example, spiritual science can demonstrate that life is eternal and manifested in alternating physical and spiritual existences (i.e., reincarnation). Belief in immortality gives us a longer view from which to evaluate the justice of life as it is worked out in man's evolving situation. Martinus' teachings are definitively presented in his two main books, *The Book of Life* and *The Eternal World Picture*, as well as a series of booklets and pamphlets.

Membership: Not reported.

Periodicals: During the 1970s a magazine, *Kosmos*, was published in Danish, German, Swedish, and Esperanto. The *News from Martinus Institute* and *Contact* were published in English.

Sources: Martinus, *The Principle of Reincarnation*. Copenhagen: Martinus Institute, 1938; Martinus, *The Immortality of Living Beings*. Copenhagen: Martinus Institute, 1970.

★867★
MORSE FELLOWSHIP
Current address not obtained for this edition.

The Morse Fellowship was founded in 1959 by Louise Morse of Silver Springs, Maryland, and was named for Elwood Morse, her husband, who had died the year before. In 1961, the headquarters were moved to Alamogordo, New Mexico. Mrs. Morse began to travel, teach and publish lessons, mostly of material which had been channeled through her. In 1967, she met and married James Spence and, in 1968, they moved to Richardson, Texas (a suburb of Dallas). Two years prior to the founding of the Fellowship, Mrs. Morse had begun to publish the lessons.

The "Portals of Light" was the name given to the ministry of Mrs. Morse, who was seen as a channel for the Holy Spirit. Her ministry was seen as a fulfillment of Biblical prophecy concerning the last days when the spirit of truth would be poured out on all flesh. The whole range of psychic issues has been dealt with in the lessons given by the celestial teachers. The teachers, who have spoken through Mrs. Morse while she was in trance, were never identified, but were of both sexes.

According to the teachings, man had come forth from the God nature. The disobedience in the Garden of Eden had allowed sin to enter the race, for, through disobedience, the consciousness was lowered. The race entered the kingdom of Satan. In Jesus, man is given the chance to enter God's kingdom through obedience. By consciously identifying with Jesus, man is drawn back into the nature of God. The way back is through love. The reorientation to God's will allows one to become aware of the still, small voice within. As this voice becomes clearer and one follows it, one will be moving closer to God's will.

Mrs. Morse gave weekly trance sessions with a more or less stable group of sitters from the 1950s into the 1970s. The lessons are made available on tape and in printed form. By 1968, approximately 250 persons were receiving the lessons regularly. During the last years of her work, Morse was able to receive messages from the spirit world without going into trance.

Sources: *The Living Water*. Richardson, TX: Morse Fellowship, 1970.

★868★
NEW AGE TEACHINGS
37 Maple St.
Brookfield, MA 01506

New Age Teachings was established in 1967 in Brookfield, Massachusetts by Anita Afton (b. 1922), better known as Illiana, the name she uses as a channel. Illiana is referred to as the "soul which is in this body." In the beginning of her work as a channel, entities from a planet called Jamal spoke through her, but after a few years, as her own consciousness was "Uplifted", the "I AM THAT I AM" was and remains the only voice which speaks through her.

Illiana had become influenced by Eastern philosophy while attending a Unitarian Church. She later joined the Self-Realization Fellowship of Paramahansa Yogananda (discussed in the chapter on Hindus) and went through the entire set of lessons in Kriya Yoga. She learned of her past lives in India and how to meditate. In 1965, while in meditation, she received her first message as a channel. It was a rather mundane message concerning a lecture topic. A second, later message was a complicated code-like message, drawn from several languages. Messages began to be received regularly from then on.

At the request of the cosmic being who issued messages through her, Illiana began to publish regular bulletins. They carry the messages from the cosmic hierarchy, the "I AM THAT I AM," which emphasizes the increasing Light coming into earth as a result of the New Age vibrations being poured forth upon the planet.

From the headquarters in Massachusetts, the bulletin and other publications are mailed to followers across the United States and around the world to every continent. Some members have formed study groups and centers from which the bulletins can be circulated locally. The bulletin is considered a "Universal Organ for World Upliftment though study and spiritual understanding." In 1976, a Spanish edition of the bulletin appeared and segments of the messages are regularly translated into several languages. Headquarters for the Spanish-language work are in Houston, Texas.

Membership: As of 1985, approximately 2,000 people in the United States received *New Age Teachings*. There are 30 study groups who use the material channeled by Illiana. It is mailed to some 3,500 followers in 35 countries around the world.

Periodicals: *New Age Teachings*, 35-37 Maple Street, Brookfield, MA 01506; *Ensenznzas de la Mueva Era*, 35-37 Maple Street, Brrokfield, MA 01506.

★869★
ORGANIZATION OF AWARENESS (CALGARY)
(Defunct)

In 1967 the Organization of Awareness which had formed in the early 1960s splintered when its main leader and spiritual channel, William Ralph Duby, died. Three branches retained the name of the original group, among them a small group in Calgary, Alberta headed by Nick Chwelos. It survived into the 1970s.

★870★
ORGANIZATION OF AWARENESS (FEDERAL WAY)
(Defunct)

The Organization of Awareness (Federal Way) was one of three groups which splintered from the original Organization of Awareness after the death of its leader and spiritual channel, William Ralph Duby, in 1967. This branch was headed by Frances Marcx and headquartered in Federal Way, Washington. It was a small body which survived into the 1970s.

★871★
ORGANIZATION OF AWARENESS (OLYMPIA)
(Defunct)

One of three splinters of the original Organization of Awareness formed in the early 1960s (see Cosmic Awareness Communications which retained the name under which the organization operated until the death of its main spiritual channel, William Ralph Duby. In 1967, this branch was formed and headed by David DeMoulin. It was a small group headquartered in Olympia, Washington. It survived into the 1970s.

★872★
RADIANT SCHOOL OF SEEKERS AND SERVERS
(Defunct)

The Radiant School of Seekers and Servers was founded in 1963 by a small group led by Kenneth Wheeler at Mt. Shasta, California. The mystic mountain had brought them together the previous year and, as a group, they moved to the village at the mountain's base. In the 1890s, an entity, Phylos the Tibetan, began to speak through Frederick Spencer Oliver, his amanuensis. The material by Phylos was collected into a book, *A Dweller on Two Planets*. It described the existence of a mystic brotherhood of survivors of Atlantis, who live inside the mountain. The existence of Phylos was further highlighted in 1940 by the appearance of *An Earth Dweller Returns*, a second book by Phylos. The Radiant School began channeling from Phylos in 1963 and offered to its members the material from Phylos in lesson form.

The material advocated belief in God's divine plan, which is for all and enwrapped in the "folds of every life pattern." Every life pattern is interwoven in a great universal pattern. Each person is expected to unfold his plan in full. There is opportunity to meet all others with whom we have interfered and created karma. Each divine plan includes the rights to health, happiness and prosperity.

Man resides in his physical body as a "Temple" and the Temple is the means of contacting the higher self. The self is overshadowed by angels and is thus never alone. Prayer is the expression of desires. Abundance comes in longing to know the great love of God. To be patient, willing, forgiving and enduring is the key to the soul's progress of perfection.

Headquarters of the Radiant School were in Mt. Shasta, California. The School was run by a six-person board of directors, a president, bishop and assistant bishop. Members received monthly lessons from Phylos. The school disbanded in the early 1980s.

Sources: Phylos the Tibetan [Frederick Spencer Oliver], *A Dweller on Two Planets*. Los Angeles: Borden Publishing Co., 1899.

★873★
ROBIN'S RETURN
Current address not obtained for this edition.

Dorothy and Ray Davis founded Robin's Return from their home in Grand Rapids, Michigan. In the mid-1960s, they began to receive messages from Paramahansa Yogananda (discussed in the chapter on Hindus). At the time, they did not know who Yogananda was. Then, in 1965, Robin, Dorothy Davis' son by a previous marriage, was killed when his bomber was shot down over Vietnam. After his death, both Ray and Dorothy began to receive messages from him, as well as from Yogananda and other masters. They gathered the messages together and began to publish them, first as a booklet entitled *Robin's Return* and then in a newsletter sent to a contact across the United States. During the last six months of 1966, *Chimes*, the Spiritualist magazine, ran a series of articles by the Davises on their experiences. Reader response led to the establishment of a national network of people who receive the Davis material. Though many of the early messages were from Robin, over the years the majority came from master spiritual teachers and a divine Spirit usually referred to as "I AM."

According to the Davises, light and love are the basic reality of the universe. The soul is evolving toward God through a series of incarnations in which the attempt is made to raise the vibrations of the soul. As one moves in the light of God, one is growing spiritually. Death is the gateway to a new sphere of light. Love is a means of raising one's vibrations, thus creating a channel of communication with the masters. The purpose of life is to become a living expression of love. Growth through the light and love are the essence of the great plan of the universe. Although Ray died in 1976, Dorothy continues spreading their beliefs.

The Davises have been close friends of Nellie Cain of the Spiritual Research Society and Illiana of New Age Teachings (discussed elsewhere in this chapter), and have moved freely in the Universal Link circles.

Membership: Several hundred people receive mailings from the Davis home in Grand Rapids, Michigan.

★874★
SCHOOL OF NATURAL SCIENCE
25355 Spanish Ranch Rd.
Los Gatos, CA 95030

The School of Natural Science was established in Stockton, California, in 1883 by John E. Richardson, a practicing attorney. According to Richardson, in the summer of 1883, he was encountered by a stranger at the Grand Central Hotel in Stockton. He had been drawn by a voice telling him, "There is someone at the hotel who wants to see you." The stranger, who identified himself as Hoo-Kna-Ka, told Richardson that he had known him all his life and had come over continents and oceans to see him. He described Richardson's spiritual journey from Baptist to Spiritualist to the decision that both hypnotism and mediumship were the results of the same destructive process. Hoo-Kna-Ka then invited Richardson to become an initiate of the School of the Master, headquartered in India, on the condition that he would begin an education movement of that school in the Western world. He was taught by Hoo-Kna-Ka without pay, and was instructed always to give the teachings as a gift: "By an endless chain of Gifts shall the Great Work be established."

In 1894 Richardson (popularly known as "TK") moved to Chicago and associated himself with Mrs. Florence Huntley. In 1907 he founded the Indo-American Book Company which became the publishing arm of the "Great Work," the name of the movement that spread Hoo-Kna-Ka's teachings. The company issued the Harmonic Series, still the basic teaching materials of the School of Natural Science. In 1916, after what was termed "certain disclosures," (which included charges of financial mismanagement), TK withdrew from the School and the Great Work, and the School moved to California. In California, he reestablished the School and continued to teach and publish his books.

The School of Natural Science teaches that the Universal Intelligence is revealed through his immutable laws, that nature is engaged in the evolvement of individual intelligences, that nature impels individuals to higher levels of consciousness, that the soul is immortal and passes successively into physical and spiritual bodies, that man's free will works within a law of compensation (karma), that willing conformity to the laws of nature leads to self-mastery, poise and happiness, and that by living the laws of nature, people come to know instinctively that spiritual reality exists and that life continues after death. Correspondence courses based upon these teachings are offered to students.

Membership: Not reported. Students are located across the United States.

Periodicals: *Life In Action*, 25355 Spanish Ranch Road, Los Gatos, CA 95030.

Sources: J. E. Richardson, *The Great Work*. Chicago: Indo-American Book Co., 1907; J. E. Richardson, *The Great Message*. N. p.: The Great School of Natural Science, 1950; J. E. Richardson, *Who Answers Prayer?*. N.p.: The Great School of Natural Science, 1954; Sylvester A. West, *TK and the Great Work in America*. Chicago: The Author, 1918; W. Stuart Leech, *The Great Crystal Fraud or the Great P.J.*. Chicago: Occult Publishing Company, 1926.

★875★
SERVANTS OF AWARENESS
(Defunct)

In 1967, following the death of William Ralph Duby, the Servants of Cosmic Awareness (see Cosmic Awareness Communications) split into several groups. The Servants of Awareness was formed by David E. Worcester and was headquartered in Seattle. It continued into the 1970s with several groups around the United States, but has not been heard from in the 1980s. It is presumed defunct.

★876★
SISTERS OF THE AMBER
(Defunct)

As the message of the Universal Link spread in the United States, a number of informal centers developed. Some evolved into independent teaching organizations built around a single teacher-spiritual channel-writer, which published independently, though the teachings remained similar to those of the Universal Link. During the 1970s, the name most connected with the Universal Link operation in North America was Merta Mary Parkinson (d. 1983). Parkinson was, like Liebie Pugh, the British leader of the Link, a journalist and writer and, because of her interest in metaphysics, became an early devotee of the Link.

Parkinson created two more-or-less informal organizations to tie together students. The more general audience received material from the Dena Foundation. Many of the women were brought together as the Sisters of the Amber. Ms. Parkinson became intrigued with amber after a friend asked help in locating some for healing purposes. The Sisters are linked to each other by their dedication to loving service to each other and by the amber each has been given by Ms. Parkinson. She was directed by inner light to begin the work.

★877★
SPIRITUAL RESEARCH SOCIETY
740 Hubbard St., N.E.
Grand Rapids, MI 49505

Edwin Cain, Sr., was the son of a Spiritualist medium. Shortly after their marriage, he and his wife, Nellie Cain recognized some spirit rappings (rhythmic noises made by spirits to communicate messages), which led to a "developing circle" and the emergence of Mr. Cain's mediumship in the early 1940s. Mrs. Cain also began to develop and to contact a group of Masters from the White Brotherhood (spirits who were once human and who, after death, evolved to levels of spiritual excellence and teach humans about spiritual reality). She was accepted by them as a novice and was presented with the robe of the initiate. The Cains founded the Spiritual Research Society, which evolved from the original circle.

The teachings, which came through the Masters, are based upon the evolution and progression of life and of the soul. The universe is organized on an upward spiral from electronic and mineral to vegetable, animal and human, to Christ-Buddhic or divine. The levels are likened to the rising frequency of the musical scale. The soul also evolves to higher levels of consciousness. The universe is organized on seven-fold structures and according to the universal laws of vibration, correspondence, cause and effect, rhythm, polarity and gender.

Following the publication of the first book on the Masters, a copy was sent to Merta Mary Parkinson of the Sisters of the Amber and an American representative of the Universal Link. Parkinson then forwarded a copy to Liebie Pugh, of the Universal Link in England. Subsequent correspondence brought the Cains into close association with Parkinson and Pugh. They were both disappointed by the nonoccurrence of the momentous event predicted for Christmas, 1967. They soon came to view the period since then as a time of great siftings in every area of man's life, a time of renewal and reevaluation and spiritual discoveries. In 1971, they received a message that the Linking had been completed on the outer levels, and the work now is one of radiating light in a collective "Nuclear Evolution" Operation.

Membership: Not reported.

Sources: Nellie B. Cain, *Exploring the Mysteries of Life*. Grand Rapids, MI: Spiritual Research Society, 1972; Nellie B. Cain, *Gems of Truth from the Masters*. Grand Rapids, MI: Spiritual Research Society, 1965.

★878★
UNIVERSAL BROTHERHOOD OF FAITHISTS
℅ Universal Faithists of Kosmon
Box 664
Salt Lake City, UT 84110

John Ballou Newbrough (1828-1891) was a Spiritualist medium. In the year 1882, he received by automatic writing on a typewriter a revelation published under the title *Oahspe*. He rose early each morning for fifty weeks and, as the "lines of light" rested on his hands, he typed for an hour. The first edition of the resultant book was published that same year. In 1883, a convention was held in New York City to work toward founding a communal group to care for orphans and foundlings, as directed in *Oahspe*. A colony was founded in New Mexico, but failed after only a couple of years. Since that time, small bands of followers have kept *Oahspe* in print.

Oahspe is a large volume, written in the style of the King James Version of the Bible. It contains the story of man's creation some 78,000 years ago and the upward struggle of the race. Man originated on Pan, a Pacific continent much like Lemuria, which was the sole victim of the Biblical flood. Religion evolved through eleven prophets, beginning with Zarathustra and continuing through Joohu (Jesus). All religion and effort have been guided by angelic forces toward the Kosmon Era. During this era, which began in the nineteenth century, a new people will emerge, and will transform the world into a place of joy and beauty.

Over the decades, a wide variety of Faithist groups have emerged and disappeared. The movement is sustained through a number of independent groups and periodicals who stay in touch through several informal networks. The *Faithist Journal*, published in Arizona, has provided continuity for America Faithists, though in recent years, no person has arisen of the stature of a Wing Anderson, the leading Faithist spokesperson in the mid-twentieth century. *Search Magazine*, published by the widow of Ray Palmer, a *Oahspe* devotee, carries a regular column through which Faithists may stay in contact. *The Kosmon Church Service Book*, published by the British Faithists, provides guidance for rituals from church services to baptisms and funerals.

Membership: Not available. There are an estimated several thousand Faithists in the United States.

Periodicals: *The Faithist Journal*, 2324 Suffock Avenue, Kingman, AZ 86401.

Sources: *Oahspe*. Los Angeles: Essenes of Kosmon, 1950; Jim Dennon, *Dr. Newbrough and Oahspe*. Kingman, AZ: Faithist Journal, 1975; Jim Dennon, *The Oahspe Story*. Kingman, AZ: Faithist Journal, 1975; K. D. Stowes, *The Land of Shalam, Children's Land*. Evansville, IN: Frank Molinet Print Shop, n.d.

★879★
UNIVERSAL LINK
1, St. Georges Square
St. Annes, Lancashire, England

The Universal Link and the Universal Foundation are two closely related British organizations which trace their history to April 11, 1961, to the visionary experience of Richard Grave of Worthing, England. While working on a newly-rented house, he saw "a bearded Christlike figure" who blocked his path. Pointing to a picture, the figure touched the glass, causing it to explode and pulverize, driving fragments into the picture. The being then disappeared in a blaze of orange light. The picture, a representation of an angel announcing the birth of Jesus, soon gained reknown as the "Weeping Angel of Worthing" as salty drops of moisture formed on its surface.

The being, who called himself "Truth," visited Grave often after that and left him a series of messages. The messages were apocalyptic, concentrating on the imminent second coming of the Christ as mankind seems on the brink of disaster. The message and events were carried in a *Psychic News* article on May 4, 1961. Liebie Pugh, an artist of St. Anne's, England, heard of Grave through the articles. After meeting Pugh, Grave realized the spiritual being that had visited him was the one portrayed in a sculpture by Ms. Pugh which she called simply "Limitless Love."

Ms. Pugh is regarded as the architect of the Universal Link, a linking of a number of individuals and groups to the Highest, who in this period is breaking through in an ever-increasing way. The Link developed as an informal fellowship of like-minded individuals centered upon a number of "channels." These channels were delivering revelations of the cosmic operation ushering in the new age.

The critical period in the revelation was from 1961 to 1967. An early revelation through Grave said the following: "No one can know the day nor the hour of MY COMING, or when the great Universal Revelation will be enacted; however by Christmas morning 1967, I will have revealed myself through the medium of nuclear evolution. This is MY PLAN which is absolute."

During the six years, a major effort was made to spread the message and tie together other channels, primarily through the travel and work of Anthony Brooke. Brooke, a descendant of Sir James Brooke, the first "White Rajah of Sarawak," ruled that land before it became a British colony in 1946. In the mid and late 1960s, Brooke traveled widely, locating and tying together individuals and groups. In England, the Universal Foundation was formed, with Brooke and Monica Parish at its head.

As December, 1967 approached, a great feeling of expectancy pervaded the movement. There was hope for an objective event, a spectacular change-over in universal thinking, which would signal the coming new age. When no event occurred, a spiritualized explanation was sought. For Brooke, attention was focused on the purpose of Liebie Pugh. Liebie had become identified with the entity known as Limitless Love, and, as early as 1964, the hypothesis had been put forth that Limitless Love was Liebie herself in the form of a constellated fragmentation of her own personality. Liebie was, reasoned Brooke, "an extension or a projection--a secondary personality, if you like--of Truth or Limitless Love." In January, 1966, Liebie was given a prophecy of her death in December, 1966. After she died in December, members of the Universal Link groups discovered that "Limitless Love is appearing with ever greater frequency in the actions and to the vision of more and more people."

Thus the work of the Universal Foundation became the linking together of groups and individuals who were working toward the spiritual evolution of mankind around the world. These people form a vanguard who are attuned to the cosmic lights and are awaiting the yet-to-appear day of manifestation which will mark the Christing of the whole earth and the beginning of the Golden Age.

The Universal Link was brought to the United States in the late 1960s, primarily through the visits of Anthony Brooke. Initial centers were formed in Elkins, Pennsylvania; Grand Rapids, Michigan; Kansas City, Missouri; Brookfield, Massachusetts; Denver, Colorado, and Los Angeles, California. During the 1970s several of these centers died out, but others became independent centers in their own right, publishing their own books and newsletters. In effect, their work superceded that of the Foundation for North America, though they remained more or less loosely affiliated with the work in England and acknowledged their debt to it. In Grand Rapids, Nellie Cain and Ed Cain developed the Spiritual Research Society. In Kansas City, Merta Mary Parkinson began to issue material under the name of the Sisters of the Amber and the Dena Foundation. In Brookfield, Illiana (Anita Afton) developed an international network receiving her New Age Teachings. From Los Angeles, Brother Francis (Ralph Raymond) moved the Universal Link Heart Center to Santa Monica, where it was renamed the Father's House and then later in the decade to Santa Clara, California, where it existed for many years. Each of these centers is covered elsewhere in this chapter.

Membership: Not reported. There is no direct affiliate of either the Universal Foundation or Universal Link currently functioning in America.

Sources: Anthony Brooke, *The Universal Link Revelations*. London: Universal Foundation, 1967; Brother Francis [Ralph Raymond], *The Universal Link Concept*. Los Angeles: Universal Link Heart Center, [1967]; Liebe Pugh, *Nothing Else Matters*. St. Anne's-by-the-Sea, Lanc.: The Author, 1964.

Flying Saucers

★880★
GEORGE ADAMSKI FOUNDATION
314 Lado de Loma Dr.
Vista, CA 92083

The first person to become widely known for his claims to having talked to the beings who flew the flying saucers and who taught what was purported to be their wisdom was George Adamski (1891-1965). On November 20, 1952, he claimed to have conversed with a human-like man from Venus, the first of several contacts and subsequently wrote three of the most popular flying saucer books ever penned: *Flying Saucers Have Landed* (co-authored with Desmond Leslie); *Inside the Space Ships*

(reprinted as *Inside the Flying Saucers*); and *Flying Saucers Farewell* (reprinted as *Behind the Flying Saucer Mystery*). The two most important of the several groups which emerged to perpetuate his teachings were the George Adamski Foundation and the UFO Education Center.

Polish-born Adamski first assumed a role as a metaphysical teacher in the 1930s when he issued several publications from the Royal Order of Tibet, an order which he claimed to represent and for whom he lectured. He was also briefly associated with the Order of Loving Service, another metaphysical group centered on Laguna Beach, California. For many years he lived in Southern California and lectured to interested audiences.

Soon after his contact with the space people and his first two books appeared (1953 and 1955), Adamski attained a broad following among people not only interested in his contact stories, but the wisdom which the space brothers had to offer. In 1957 he organized his following into the International Get Acquainted Club. The next year his metaphysical teachings, the cosmic wisdom of the saucer people, began to appear first in a telepathy course and then in its more systematic form in *Cosmic Philosophy* (1961) and the *Science of Life Study Course* (1964).

Adamski, while a popular lecturer, was not organizationlly minded. He turned his early organization over to C. A. Honey, who broke with Adamski shortly before his death. However, in 1965, Alice Wells (d. 1980), Adamski's daughter, and Charlotte Blob, his secretary and editor, both formed organizations to keep his teachings alive. The George Adamski Foundation brought together the largest group of Adamski followers. After Wells' death, Fred Steckling, a longtime associate of Adamski, became head of the Foundation. The UFO Education Center with headquarters in Valley Center, California and Appleton, Wisconsin has a similar program to to the Foundation.

Membership: Not reported.

Remarks: Adamski was plagued throughout his life by charges of fraud. In the 1950s several expose articles claimed that Adamski had faked the photographs he claimed to have taken of the flying saucers. Noting the resemblance of his *Inside the Space Ships* to a science fiction novel he wrote in the 1940s led to further accusations. The most damaging attack upon Adamski's credibility came from his close associate, C. A. Honey. He published material from Adamski's own copy of Royal Order of Tibet materials (edited for reissuance in the *Science of Life Study Course*) as if it originated from the space brothers.

Sources: Lou Zinsstag and Timothy Good, *George Adamski, The Untold Story*. Beckenham, Kent: Ceti Publications, 1983; *George Adamski, Questions and Answers by the Royal Order of Tibet*. Laguna Beach, CA:

Privately Printed, 1936; George Adamski, *Cosmic Philosophy*. Freeman, SD: Pine Hill Press, 1971; Desmond Leslie and George Adamski, *Flying Saucers Have Landed*. London: T. Werner Laurie, 1953; Fred Steckling, *Why Are They Here?* New York: Vantage Press, 1969.

★881★

AETHERIUS SOCIETY
6202 Afton Place
Hollywood, CA 90028

The Aetherius Society was begun in London in 1954 by George King, medium and long-time student of occultism and yoga. He was told to prepare himself to become the voice of the Interplanetary Parliament. In 1955, he was named by Master Aetherius of Venus as the "primary terrestrial mental channel." Since that time, he has regularly channeled messages form Aetherius and the Master Jesus. They and other members of the Great White Brotherhood oversee the activities of the Society. A center was opened in Los Angeles within a year of the first messages. King's teachings are the focus of the Society.

According to the Aetherius Society, earth is engaged in a cosmic warfare focused on the activities of certain "black magicians" seeking to enslave man. The cosmic brotherhood, the space hierarchy, wages war on these magicians. Members of the Society cooperate with the Brotherhood by channeling spiritual energy to particular concerns. Channeling activities are centered on certain periods when a space ship orbits earth and sends out special power. These periods are termed "spiritual pushes," and all members help direct the energy. These pushes are typically given military titles, such as Operation Bluewater, which ended on November 27, 1976. During this operation, the cosmic masters poured vital spiritual power into a psychic center through a spiritual-power radiating instrument at sea.

Still celebrated is Operation Starlight, begun at Holdstone Down in England in 1958 and continued for three years and one month. During this time, King, directed by a vision of the Master Jesus, climbed eighteen designated mountains to charge them with spiritual power, to be used by anyone making a pilgrimage to them. August 23 is the date of the annual convention.

The most important date in the annual calendar is July 8, commemorating the 1964 initiation of earth by a gigantic space ship and the ship's manipulation of cosmic energies. Other days in the annual calendar are King's birthday, the end of Operation Karmalight (a phase of Armageddon) and the Master Jesus' birthday. The push dates are announced annually and are usually for periods of three to four weeks.

As described by King, the Interplanetary Parliament is headquartered on Saturn, the tribunal of the solar system. The agents from Mars and Venus are making a metaphysical survey of earth. The saucers have also saved earth from the damage of terrestrial scientists to earth's ionosphere.

King has accepted consecration as an archbishop through the Independent Liberal Catholic Church headed by Richard Earl Quinn. He has also received a number of titles and awards, most of them conferred by the "cosmic" sources or the Society which he heads. He has been a prolific writer, the author of several books and numerous pamphlets, all published by the Aetherius Society.

Membership: There are two centers of the Society in the United States, one in Hollywood and one in Detroit, Michigan. Several hundred members are involved. The Society has several centers in England.

Periodicals: *Cosmic Voice*. 6202 Afton Place, Hollywood, CA 90028; *Spiritual Healing Bulletin*, 6202 Afton Place, Hollywood, CA 90028.

Sources: *The Story of the Aetherius Society*. Hollywood, CA: The Aetherius Society, n.d.; George King, *The Practices of Aetherius*. Hollywood, CA; Aetherius Society, 1964; George King, *A Book of Sacred Prayers*. Hollywood, CA: Aetherius Society, 1966; George King, *The Twelve Blessings*. London: Aetherius Press, 1958; George King, *The Nine Freedoms*. Los Angeles: Aetherius Society, 1963; George King, *You Are Responsible*. London: Aetherius Press, 1961.

★882★

ASSOCIATION OF SANANDA AND SANAT KUMARA
Box 35
Mount Shasta, CA 96067

The Association of Sananda and Sanat Kumara is headed by Sister Thedra (Dorothy Martin), for many years a channel for the ascended masters. Very early in her career, she became the object of a famous sociological study, *When Prophecy Fails*. She also reports that in 1954 that she was healed and restored to a life of usefulness by Sananda, an ascended master, and she was instructed to go to Peru and Bolivia, where for the next five years she experienced great trials and tribulations. She spent some time at the monastery established by the Brotherhood of the Seven Rays headed by George Hunt Williamson. During this period she lived with the natives, observing and experiencing their hardships, squalor and unbelievable poverty. Through this period of training under the tutelege of the masters, she learned the "true meaning of divine love towards human beings, regardless of their status in life." The ensuing years were interspersed with moments of ecstastic communication with the masters-- Sibors, the Elohim (council of Gods), John the Beloved, the Angel Moroni (mentioned in the *Book of Mormon*), beings from other planets, and, primarily, Sananda, who most people know as the Christ. Thedra was given the prediction of the reincarnation of the Angel Moroni, which occurred in 1965. The child was to begin to manifest his powers in August, 1975.

While still in Peru, Thedra began to send the inspired messages back to interested people in the United States. Through her, Christ continues to reveal and call out to those who wish wholeheartedly to come to Him. These people will be sibored--illumines of the Father. A sibor is a teacher in the higher realms.

Sister Thedra returned to the United States from South America in 1961 and established the association in 1965. The material channeled through her is sent across the United States and to a number of foreign countries to those students who request it. The basic material is contained in three sets of material: "The Sibors Portions," "The Fundamentals," and "The Order of Melchezdek." These are constantly supplemented by ongoing revelation from the masters. In 1985, the association hosted the first annual Gathering of the Children of Light, a convocation of individuals who receive Sister Thedra's material and/or are related to similar groups.

Membership: The association does not keep statistics on the number of students who regularly request material channeled by Sister Thedra. It is estimated to be in the thousands. There is one center in Mt. Shasta.

Educational facilities: University of Melchezedek, Castleton, VA 22716.

Sources: Sananda, as recorded by Sister Thedra, *I, the Lord God Say Unto Them.* Mt. Shasta, CA: Association of Sananda and Sanat Kumara, [1954]; Thedra, *Excerpts of Prophecies from Other Planets Concerning Our Earth.* Mt. Shasta, CA: Association of Sananda and Sanat Kumara, [1956]; Edward L. Watkins, *The Teachings and the Liberation.* Mt. Shasta, CA: Association of Sananda and Sanat Kumara, 1977; Leon Festinger, Henry W. Riecken and Stanley Schachter, *When Prophecy Fails.* New York: Harper & Row, 1956.

★883★
BROTHERHOOD OF THE SEVEN RAYS
(Defunct)

Among the early contactees was George Hunt Williamson (1926-1986), an archeologist and student of Theosophical literature. He and his wife were among those who watched from a distance as George Adamski made his first contact with a Venusian in the California desert on November 12, 1952. Then, in 1953, Williamson published his own story, *The Saucers Speak*, in which he claimed contact with Martians by way of automatic writing (writing what a spirit dictates) as early as August 2, 1952. The messages were, initially, from Kadar Laqu, the head of the Interplanetary Council-Circle. The messages called for cooperation to prevent the death of human civilization. The Telonic Research Center was established by Williamson to study the new science of space-visitation.

All of Williamson's interests were brought together in the Brotherhood of the Seven Rays. Besides contact with the space beings, Williamson had been in touch with the ascended masters, those mysterious beings first described by Guy Ballard, founder of the I AM Religious Activity. As early as 1955, Lake Titicaca had been mentioned as a sanctuary of the Great White Brotherhood, the hierarchy of ascended masters who were once human and who now as spirits teach humans about spiritual realities. In 1956, it was decided that an outer retreat of the sanctuary (as well as the others around the world) would be established by dedicated individuals. The inner sanctuaries for full-fledged members date to the submergence of Lemuria, when the secrets of that advanced civilization were deposited in secluded centers the world over. Araru-Muru, now an ascended master in the spirit world, was in charge of Titicaca. The other retreat, or abbey, was to be located near the inner sanctuary on the Peruvian side of Lake Titicaca, and was to have priories at spots around the world as contact points with the populace.

In December, 1956, Williamson, under his religious name, Brother Philip, and others made a trip to Peru to establish the Abbey of the Seven Rays, Lord Muru's primary outer retreat. The expedition extended through most of 1957. The ruins of the area were viewed as partially the result of contact and cooperation between the Great White Brotherhood and the space masters. The contact has continued, and is focused in the Brotherhood of the Abbey. It was Williamson's belief that "the space confederation has a gigantic base there near the remains of the lost cities," which survived from the time of the original contacts.

The Brotherhood of the Seven Rays, referring to the spectrum of light rays administered by the ascended masters, was established at the time of the destruction of Lemuria between 10,000 and 12,000 B.C., but not until 1956 did it have outward expression in a monastic system in which students could come together. Since each student would be most attuned to one of the seven rays, the grouping of students would bring a harmony of the seven colors symbolic of the spiritual life of the monastery. The monastery was established in the 1960s and continued into the 1970s. Students who came to live at the center in Peru had to accept the cosmic Christ as one who came to earth and who is due to return in the near future. The Essene way of life--meditation, fasting, and contemplation--was followed. The communal meal, or supper, of the Essenes was observed daily. Novices underwent water-baptism by immersion before becoming friars and were anointed with oil before becoming monks. No narcotics or stimulants (including chocolate) were used, and monks were vegetarians. Hair was worn long. Both sexes were welcome to all levels, and marriage was acceptable.

Associated with the Brotherhood were its two orders. The Order of the Red Hand was dedicated to the preservation of the arcane knowledge through the ages, particularly through the Scriptorium at the Monastery in Peru. The

Ancient Amethystine Order was the prime group associated with the Brotherhood and has reference to the vibrations of the seventh ray of violet, into which the earth is moving. Its hoped-for effects were to be the cure of humanity's ills and earth's drunken state. United States headquarters of Williamson's small following was in Corpus Christi, Texas.

Membership: Not reported.

Remarks: It was Williamson's claim that his real name was Michael d'Obrenovic and that he was a descendent of a Yugoslavian royal family. During the last years of his life, Williamson reasserted that claim and, as Michael d'Obrenovic, was consecrated to the episcopacy by an unnamed bishop claiming orders from the Nestorian (Syro-Chaldean) Church. He moved to Santa Barbara, California and established an independent jurisdiction called the Holy Apostolic Catholic Church, Syro-Chaldean Diocese of Santa Barbara and Central California. There was but one small parish which existed for several years in the early 1980s.

Williamson was also profiled in several issues of *Who's Who* in which he claimed degrees from at least three institutions of higher learning which deny ever having issued degrees to him.

Sources: George Hunt Williamson, *The Saucers Speak.* London: Neville Spearman, 1963; George Hunt Williamson, *Secret Places of the Lion.* London: Neville Spearman, 1959; George Hunt Williamson, *Road in the Sky.* London: Neville Spearman, 1959; Brother Philip (George Hunt Williamson), *The Brotherhood of the Seven Rays.* Clarksburg, VA: Saucerian Books, 1961; John McCoy, *They Shall Be Gathered Together.* Corpus Christi, TX: The Author, 1957.

★884★
COSMIC CIRCLE OF FELLOWSHIP
% Edna Valverde
4857 N. Melvina Ave.
Chicago, IL 60630

The Cosmic Circle of Fellowship was formed in 1954 by William Ferguson and a group of followers in Chicago, Illinois. Ferguson, a former mail carrier, was taken in 1938 to the center of all creation, where he was permitted to see Pure Universal Substance, described as a cube containing all forms and colors. Although the experience began with his physical body laying on a studio lounge in his home, upon return to his home his wife and a friend could neither see nor hear him, and his physical body was not on the lounge. He, then, placed himself upon the lounge and remained quiet until his being was transformed back into this three-dimensional dense matter projection.

In 1947, Khauga, the chief uniphysicist of our solar system, took Ferguson on a trip to Mars. Upon his return to earth, members of his family and a friend could neither see nor hear him. In his eagerness to tell his experience, he had not first allowed himself to return to three dimensions. Remembering what was occurring, he went into the next room, lay on a cot, and was transformed into three dimensions. He then went into the next room and told his account.

The matter of the physical body had been raised into a four-dimensional frequency, then he had been teleported to Mars at the speed of consciousness. He returned with a message that the Martians were sending an expedition to earth. Within a few months many UFOs were reported, and several people made personal contacts with their inhabitants.

In 1954 Ferguson was taken aboard a Venusian spacecraft and given a message from the Oligarchs of Venus for the people of earth. They noted that spacecraft normally function in four dimensions (and are hence invisible) but can also function in three dimensions by changing their frequency or their density. When they disappear suddenly, they have merely changed back into the fourth dimension.

In the 1940s, Ferguson began to gather a group primarily related to the cosmic healing techniques and the "clarified water device" taught to Ferguson by Khauga. The latter device, thought to impart healing properties to water, got Ferguson in trouble with the American Medical Association. Eventually, he was convicted of fraud (1947) and served a year in prison. Upon his return from prison, he decided to go public with his story and organized the Cosmic Circle. In 1958, he commenced a journey to found circles in other cities and gained a following in Washington, Philadelphia, New York and San Francisco.

According to Ferguson, at the center of creation are the Father and Mother of creation. A sphere of Pure Intelligent Energy exists inside a cube of Pure Universal Substances. Creation commences as the rays of life of the Father impregnate the substance of the Mother. Khauga is described as the Comforter, the Spirit of Truth, the angel who gave the Book of Revelation to St. John, a perfected being from the Holy Triune. Khauga is the leader in the Universal Brotherhood of the Sons of the Father, members of which are drawn from the various solar systems. They are preparing earth for the next evolutionary step--the second coming of Jesus.

A war of consciousness, symbolized by the war in heaven of Revelation 12, has been created as man makes the next step in evolution. As the New Age comes in, the dragon of materialism and evil will be overthrown. It will be replaced as man is lifted into a fourth-dimensional consciousness. Ferguson had been a long-time teacher of relaxation, and his techniques remain the major way to consciousness expansion.

Ferguson died in 1967. Leadership passed to the Chicago group, which still publishes his booklets. Associated with it is the Cosmic Study Center, headed by Cloe Driscoll of Potomac, Maryland.

Membership: Not reported.

Sources: William Ferguson, *A Message from Outer Space*. Oak Park, IL: Golden Age Press, 1955; Willaim Ferguson, *My Trip to Mars*. Chicago: Cosmic Circle of Fellowship, 1954; William Ferguson, *The New Revelation*. N.p.: The Author, 1959; *The Comforter Speaks*. Potomac, MD: Cosmic Study Center, 1977; William R. Ferguson, *Relax First*. Chicago: Bronson-Canode Printing Co., 1937.

★885★
COSMIC STAR TEMPLE
Current address not obtained for this edition.

The Cosmic Star Temple was founded in 1960 by Violet Gilbert of Santa Barbara, California, who claims that her first contact with the space brothers was in 1937. Prior to that time, she was a student of Theosophy and "I AM" Religious Activity, and is described as having a "rich background of service for the Brotherhood since childhood." As an adult, she was made aware of the space brothers in 1937 and in January, 1939, after an eight-month preparation, she was given a three-and-one-half-week excursion to Venus. This trip was a physical visit. Her initial contact had been arranged by her previous teachers, following a request for healing. She received a complete physical healing. Since her initial visit, she has returned in the astral (not physically, but through her consciousness). She also acquired a control, Dr. Winston of the Ashtar Command. Her first trip to Mars was in 1955. She was not allowed to go public until 1960.

While on Venus, she was given instructions in healing, which forms a major aspect of the Temple's works, and in reading the Akashic records. (The Akashic records are the records of all that has happened, and are inscribed on the "universal ethers.") Mrs. Gilbert reads the Akashic records of individuals, which give information about their previous incarnations. The teachings of the Temple are eclectic and include material from the New Thought metaphysics, Spiritualism and the dominant Theosophy. Color-healing has become a major emphasis.

Mrs. Gilbert teaches that the coming of the space brothers is entirely beneficial. Their overall purpose is to keep us from destroying ourselves and to share their advanced knowledge. Mankind now is in a transition to a new age and is currently experiencing a cleansing in preparation.

Membership: Not reported.

Sources: Violet Gilbert, *My Trip to Venus*. Grants Pass, OR: Cosmic Star Temple, 1968; Violet Gilbert, *"Love Is All."* Grants Pass, OR: Cosmic Star Temple, 1969.

★886★
LAST DAY MESSENGERS
Current address not obtained for this edition.

The Last Day Messengers is a small group centered in Fort Lauderdale, Florida, headed by Dave W. Bent. Bent became interested in psychic phenomena and began to develop his psychic consciousness. During this process, he encountered the material from the Mark-Age Meta Center and other groups in contact with the spiritual hierarchy. He became a channel for the White Brotherhood, and formed the Last Day Messengers. It is his belief that we are in the last days prior to Christ's physically cleansing the earth. Man must cleanse his consciousness before that time. The Messengers point to positive signs of the New Age: technological progress, the youth who are seeking love and simplicity in life, the spread of psychic development and healing, the popularity of reincarnation and the flying saucers.

Membership: Not reported.

★887★
MARK-AGE
Box 290368
Fort Lauderdale, FL 33329

Mark-Age was initiated by spiritual communications received in 1956 by Charles Boyd Gentzel and formally organized in 1960 by Gentzel and Pauline Sharpe to channel the messages of the "Hierarchical Board" (the spiritual government for the solar system) during the last forty years of this century (1960-2000 A.D.). This is the transition coordinating group for the movement from the Piscean Age to the Aquarian. The original leaders of the group included several psychics who channeled the data from the hierarchy. They were Yolanda (Pauline Sharpe), who has channeled most of the messages; Mark (Charles Boyd Gentzel); Astrid (Jeanene Moore); Wains (James Hughes Speed), and Zan-Thu (Holden Lindsey). In 1962, the Mark-Age Meta Center was established in Miami. As early as 1949, the name Mark-Age was revealed. A subsequent revelation in 1955 concurred in its significance.

Mark-Age sees itself as one of numerous focal points of contact with the higher spiritual forces. By automatic writing and telepathic communications, the hierarchy speaks. Messages have come through from Gloria Lee (founder of the Cosmon Research Foundation and early contactee who died during a fast in 1962), famous individuals such as John F. Kennedy, and the Theosophical masters El Morya, Nada, Sananda (Jesus) and Djual Khool. Mark-Age was corresponding with Gloria Lee just prior to her death in 1962. After her death, their communications with her and the publication, *Gloria Lee Lives*, were major steps forward in Mark-Age's growth.

Space-craft are one means of communication between the Hierarchical Board and earth. They are not physical craft, but exist in the etheric realms. Jesus (Sananda) has been in orbit around earth since 1885 in the etheric realms and will take on material form as the planet is cleansed. Through telepathy with the spaceships, contact is made with beings of other planets.

Since 1960, Mark-Age has published a large amount of teaching material, much of which is condensed in the standard introductory book, *Mark-Age Period and Program*. The content of the messages, besides outlining the minimal organization of Mark-Age, has been toward a defining of the roles of the hierarchy (which, apart from the emphasis on flying saucers, is very Theosophical) and raising man's spiritual consciousness as the Aquarian Age dawns. The latter involves a process of meditation and psychic development. Instructions for groups associated with Mark-Age have also been published.

In 1977 a site near Ft. Lauderdale, Florida was purchased as a site for a headquarters complex. That same year an estate in Santa Monica Canyon, near Los Angeles, was opened as a West Coast retreat center.

Membership: Not reported.

Periodicals: *Mark-Age Inform-Nations (MAIN)*, Box 290368, Ft. Lauderdale, FL 33329.

Sources: Nada-Yolanda (Pauline Sharpe), *Mark Age Period and Program*. Miami, FL: Mark-Age, 1970; Nada-Yolanda, *Visitors from Other Planets*. Miami, FL: Mark-Age, 1974; *Group Guidelines for New Age Light Centers*. Miami, FL: Mark-Age MetaCenter, 1971; *1000 Keys to the Truth*. Miami, FL: Mark-Age, 1976; *Plan a Nation*. Miami, FL: Mark-Age, 1975; "History of Mark-Age" in *Mark-Age Inform-Nations*, vol. 22, June-July 1975 (special issue).

★888★
SOLAR LIGHT CENTER
7700 Avenue of the Sun
Central Point, OR 97501

Marianne Francis is the "Telethought Channeler" of the Solar Light Center established in the mid-1960s at Central Point, Oregon. Miss Francis became interested in UFOs in 1947, the first year UFOs were seen in modern times. She moved to the United States in 1954 and settled in Santa Barbara, California, where she became a yoga student. She met Kenneth Keller, and her sensitivity began to develop as they conducted experiments aimed at contacting outer-space intelligence. They became associated with an early space brothers group, the Solar Cross Fellowship, headed by Rudolph H. Pestalozzi, a channel for Baloran, a space brother. The Solar Cross and Solar Light worked together, but the former's work was eventually absorbed by the latter. Miss Francis' main contact in the spirit world is a highly evolved being, Sut-Ko, who first contacted the Solar Cross from his space craft "SY-7."

Beliefs of the Solar Light Center are focused on the spiritual hierarchy. Members believe in the creator or all-knowing one, the cosmic chart, and the Great White Brotherhood. They accept the eternal truths given by the world avatars (Jesus, Buddha, Krishna) and spiritual masters, and the reality of space-beings which are superior to anything on earth and which can be contacted by telepathy. The teaching of the evolved beings includes reincarnation (cause and effect, karma--the notion that the consequences of good or evil actions are seen in one's later incarnations); a freedom of attitude toward the infinite creator, the self and others; the tenet that the present time ime is the end of a 26,000-year cycle, and the assertion that a cleansing is taking place as a result of the light-energies received. The light-charge heralds the second coming of Christ and the beginning of a Golden Age.

Miss Francis serves as the Director of the Solar Light Center/Retreat in Central Point, Oregon. A full program of channeling sessions and symposiums is conducted. *Starcraft*, a quarterly, has been published since 1965. Miss Francis, now known as Aleuti Francesca, is a popular speaker.

Membership: Not reported.

Periodicals: *Starcraft*, 7700 Avenue of the Sun, Central Point, OR 97501.

★889★
STAR LIGHT FELLOWSHIP
Current address not obtained for this edition.

The Star Light Fellowship was founded in 1962 in New York City by Sterling Warren and Mrs. Jackie Altisi as a "continuing Spiritual Education Program, initiated, directed and transmitted by Etheric Master Teachers of this and Other Planets, Galaxies and Realms of the Universe." Mrs. Altisi functions as Jackie White Star and is the main direct-voice channel of messages from the spirit world, but is assisted by Phyllis Veronica. Messages have been received from departed spirits, the ascended-master hierarchy, and the space brothers, including Gloria Lee (discussed elsewhere in this volume). One of the central communications has been from Christopher, aide to the King of the Moon and spokesman for the Luna Moon Government Headquarters of United Cosmic Planets. Ch ristopher described the moon as a "complete authority in itself, but working with an interplanetary confederation."

Within the context of emphasis on communication with the space brothers, the general "ascended master" theology is accepted, and there is much correspondence with the "I AM" ascended master groups (discussed elsewhere in this volume). Ascended masters were once human and now, as spirits, teach humans about spiritual realities. During the 1970s, activities of the Fellowship were centered in New York City, where regular meetings were held and a semi-annual periodical, *The Star Light Messenger*, was published.

Membership: Not reported.

★890★
UNDERSTANDING, INC.
Box 614
Alamagordo, NM 88311

Daniel Fry, an explosives technician and employee of Aerojet General Corporation, became one of the most famous of the flying saucer contactees following his experience on July 4, 1950. Out walking on a hot evening near the Organ Mountains and White Sands Proving Grounds, New Mexico, he saw an "ovate spheroid about thirty feet in diameter." He encountered a space-being, A-Lan, and took a ride in the saucer. The trip to New York and back took less than an hour. The purpose of the visit was to determine the basic adaptability of the earth-race to concepts completely foreign to the customary mode of thinking. Fry was described as open. The entire visit was discussed in a book, *The White Sands Incident*, in 1954. The following year, Understanding, Inc., was founded.

Unde rstanding, Inc. has been one of the most eclectic of UFO groups but has been very much shaped by the teachings of A-Lan through Daniel Fry. Major purchases are the charting of the area of worldwide agreement in "spiritual" science and those tenets accepted as valid by all races and creeds, leading toward a guide for the behavior of man. Hypnotism has been highly recommended when properly used. The group has promoted the UFO cause generally, and Fry is a popular speaker in psychic circles.

During the 1970s headquarters of Understanding, Inc. were moved from Oregon to Tonapah, Arizona, where the Universal Faith and Wisdom Association, founded by the Rev. Enid Smith (and centered upon some saucer-shaped buildings adjacent to Sun Spiritualist Camp) was absorbed into Underst anding, Inc. More recently the headquarters moved to New Mexico. The organization is administered by its officers who are elected in the annual membership meeting.

Membership: Not reported. During the 1970s, there were approximately 60 units worldwide.

Periodicals: *Understanding*, Box 614, Alamagordo, NM 88311.

Sources: Daniel W. Fry, *Atoms Galaxies and Understanding*. El Monte, CA: Understanding Publishing Co., 1960; Daniel W. Fry, *The Curve of Development*. Lakemont, GA: CSA Printers and Publishers, 1965; Daniel W. Fry, *Alan's Message: To Men of Earth*. Los Angeles: New Age Publishing Co., 1954; Daniel W. Fry, *The White Sands Incident*. Los Angeles: New Age Publishing Co., 1954.

★891★
UNARIUS-SCIENCE OF LIFE
143 S. Magnolia
El Cajon, CA 92022

Unarius was founded in 1954 by Ernest L. Norman, a former Spiritualist medium, shortly after his meeting with Ruth Norman, his future wife. Ernest, the Unarian moderator, is described in the Unarius literature as "the greatest intelligence ever to come to earth" and is believed to be a reincarnation of the entity who was also Pharaoh Amenhotep IV and Jesus. Mrs. Norman, in previous lives, had been the pharaoh's mother, the betrothed of Jesus, the woman who found Moses in the bullrushes and the woman who sat for Leonardo da Vinci/ as Mona Lisa. The beginning of Ernest's mission was on ancient Atlantis and Lemuria, to which Ernest came via a space ship. The mission is also seen as the return of Jesus and the renewal of his work, so abruptly cut off 2,000 years ago. During his life, Ernest dictated material which Ruth copied and published.

The teachings of Unarius are encompassed in the many books channeled by Ernest after he met Ruth, the books written through Ruth since Ernest's death and the Unarius lessons which contain teachings not otherwise published. Ernest's mission began when he materialized on earth and was guided by the evolved beings, now residing on other planets. From these teachers, he dictated seven books, which contain information about and teachings from the planets Venus, Mars, Hermes, Eros, Orion and Muse. The techings comprise the true science of life and deal with spiritual development and healing. Healing is accomplished by Ray-Booms, the projected light beams from the great intelligences on the higher worlds. Besides detailed descriptions of the various planets in Ernest's books, Ruth has given a picture of the Intergalactic Confederation. The Confederation consists of planets, advanced beyond earth, with which Ruth has been in touch. As the Confederation was formed, earth was invited to join. The polarization (joining) of earth occurred on September 14, 1973, with Ioshanna (Ruth) as the central contact. Earth is progressing more rapidly since it became part of the Confederation.

From Unarius headquarters, Ruth Norman conducts a healing ministry through the subsidiary Academy of Parapsychology, Healing and Psychic Sciences, which is a prime means of relating to the public. Lessons are sent out from headquarters, as most students are by correspondence. A library of tapes is maintained.

Membership: Not reported.

Sources: The Universal Hierarchy, *A Pictorial Tour of Unarius*. El Cajon, CA: Unarius Educational Foundation, 1982; Ernest L. Norman, *The Elysium*. Pasadena, CA: Unarius, 1956; Ioshanna (Ruth Norman), *A Space Woman Speaks from Outer Space*. El Cajon, CA: Unarius, n.d.; Ernest L. Norman, *The Voice of Venus*. Santa Barbara,

CA: Unarius-Science of Life, 1956; Ruth E. Norman and Vaughn Spaegel, *Who Is the Mona Lisa?* El Cajon, CA: Unarius-Science of Life, 1973.

★892★

UNIVERSARIUN FOUNDATION
4360 North Bear Claw Way
Tucson, AZ 85749

The Universariun Foundation was formed in 1958 and for many years headquartered in Portland, Oregon. Among the small group, Zelrun Karsleigh and his wife, Daisy Karsleigh, then still in her teens, began to receive telepathic material. Meetings were held regularly in their home, and the work grew steadily. For several decades, the Karsleighs remained the primary channels of messages from the spirit world, though eventually others have developed within the group.

Messages have been received from both the ascended masters and the masters from outer space. The principle communicators have been Sri Soudah, Koot Hoomi and Lord Michael. The material follows the perspective of the I AM Religious Activity and is aimed at the illumination and emancipation of earth from its fear, chaos and confusion.

The Universariun Foundation is governed by a board of seven directors elected by the membership at an annual meeting. The board oversees publication of the monthly periodical. A sanctuary for weekly meditation and telepathic channeling and a bookstore are maintained in Tucson. The recommended reading list of books, sold on a mail-order basis, includes a wide variety of metaphysical works.

Membership: Not reported.

Periodicals: *The Voice of Universarius*, 4360 Bear Claw Way, Tucson, AZ 85749.

Sources: Ethera Prins, *Miracle of Love and Life*. Portland, OR: Universariun Foundation, 1974. Djwhal Khul, *The Prophecies of the Tibetan*. Tucson, AZ: Universariun Foundation, 1983; *Universarius as Given in Space Messages of 1960*. Portland, OR: Sadhana-Western Publishers, 1961; *Oh1 Urantia*. Portland, OR: Universariun Foundation, [1967]; *How the Forces of Love Can Overcome the Forces of Hate*. Portland, OR: Universariun Foundation, n.d.

★893★

WHITE STAR
Box 307
Joshua Tree, CA 92252

Located close to Giant Rock in the Yucca Valley of California is White Star, founded by Doris C. LeVesque of Joshua Tree, California. (Giant Rock is the location of the Ministry of Universal Wisdom founded by George Van Tassel, a center discussed elsewhere in this chapter.) LeVesque began to channel messages from unseen entities in the mid-1950s after having read a book on saucers in 1954. In 1957, she began publication of the *White Star Illuminator*. She developed contact with the Ashtar Command, previously contacted by Van Tassel.

Ms. LeVesque teaches that earth is in a transition period created by the atomic age. Cataclysm is to be avoided by moving away from the destruction of nature. Universal laws, especially that of divine love, must be expressed. Love i s the prime motivating force in the universe. The universe is organized on the principles of density and substance. Man evolves by assuming more density which vibrates at high rates. Life on all planets is at differing points of evolvement. A key evolutionary concept is light, which is said to be created by vibration traveling in substance. Evolvement to higher spiritual levels accompanies the presence of more light. Followers are encouraged to meditate and to visualize the coming of the light into various needful situations.

Membership: Not reported. Mailings go out to followers across the United States.

Periodicals: *Times of the Signs*, Box 307, Joshua Tree, CA 92252.

Drug-Related Groups

★894★

CHURCH OF THE AWAKENING
(Defunct)

The Church of the Awakening was formed in 1963 by John W. Aiken and Louisa Aiken, both retired physicians. The Aikens lost their sons in 1951 and 1957, and were led into the realm of the psychic to seek an answer to why their sons were taken from them. They also began to experiment with peyote, using it as early as 1955. The year after the Church of the Awakening was formed, they sold their home and became active in speaking to psychic and psychedelic groups around the country.

The church had no formal statement of doctrine, but six affirmations formed a common core of accepted ideas: the unity of mankind, the reality of man's spiritual nature, the importance of experiencing that reality, the importance of the properly directed psychedelic sacrament as a means of achieving the unitive experience, the practical application of the unitive experience in everyday life, and the extension of the awareness of the reality as a factor in the solution of both personal and world problems. A great deal of control was exercised over the taking of the sacrament. Members were required to make application, after which an experienced monitor was secured, and a proper environment arranged.

The church was a loosely organized fellowship. Ten or more members of the church in a given area could apply for a charter to operate as a branch. Among the outstanding members were Dr. Huston Smith, professor of religion at Massachusetts Institute of Technology, and Dr. Walter Houston Clark, professor emeritus of the psychology of religion at Andover-Newton Theological Seminary. Clark has remained a major advocate of the religious psychedelics.

The Church suffered heavily from the 1966 ruling which made psychedelic drugs illegal. In 1969, looking for a status like that of the Native American Church, the group had a hearing with the Bureau of Narcotics, but received a negative verdict. Further rulings against the church later in the decade proved fatal to it. In 1970, there were 400 members, nationwide.

Sources: Walter Houston Clark, *Chemical Ecstasy: Psychedelic Drugs and Religion.* New York: Sheed & Ward, 1969; Walter Houston Clark, "What Light Do Drugs Throw on the Spiritual and the Transpersonal?"in *The Journal of Religion and Psychical Research*, vol. 4, no. 2, (April, 1981), pp. 131-37.

★895★

CHURCH OF THE TREE OF LIFE
451 Columbus Ave.
San Francisco, CA 94133

Apart from the Native American Church, the only psychedelic church to survive into the 1980s with its legal status intact has been the San Francisco-based Church of the Tree of Life, formed in 1971. It is a non-dogmatic church believing that each person is sovereign of his or her own mind and body and must have the right to do with himself or herself, or with any consenting adults, whatever he or she pleases, as long as those actions do not violate the rights of others. This sovereignty includes the use of psychedelic drugs.

It is the belief of the church that all substances are God's gifts, to be used as one may elect. However, since LSD and marijuana are illegal, they are not "officially" embraced as sacraments, rather a number of alternative legal mind-altering substances are listed as sacraments. They include nutmeg, kava, soma, peyote, ginseng and calamus. The church feels a responsibility to impart information to members and has published *The First Book of Sacraments* as a guide to legal mind-alterants. Ritual is practiced in connection with the individual's taking of psychedelic substances as a means of organizing one's life and thus gaining the most from the experience.

Membership: Not reported. In 1972 the church reported 1,500 members.

Periodicals: *Bark Leaf*, 451 Columbus Avenue, San Francisco, CA 94133.

Sources: John Mann, ed., *The First Book of Sacraments of the Church of the Tree of Life.* San Francisco: Church of the Tree of Life, 1972.

★896★

NATIVE AMERICAN CHURCH
Current address not obtained for this edition.

Long before the white man came to America, psychedelic substances were used by the various American Indian tribes that came into what is now the United States from Mexico. Some time prior to 1870, the use of psychedelic drugs entered the United States by way of the Mescalero Apaches. The practice spread northward to the Kiowa, Comanche and Caddo. Its spread followed the demise of the Ghost Dance, for which it substituted. The prime psychedelic source was peyote, a small, spineless, carrot-shaped cactus which grows wild in the Southwest. The dried peyote button is ingested during the ceremony and produces effects similar to those of LSD.

Legal measures and hostility of both whites and fellow Indians led to the quest for legally guaranteed security of worship. In the second decade of the twentieth century, Jonathan Koshiway, son of an Oto mother and a former missionary for the Church of Jesus Christ of Latter-Day Saints, discovered in peyotism a way of affirming both his Indian heritage and his Christian tendencies. He viewed peyote as one of God's creations, which he pronounced "good," seeing the button and the peyote tea as a reflection of sacramental bread and wine. Under his leadership, the First Born Church of Christ was formed in 1914 with 411 members. This group was later absorbed by the Native American Church.

The Native American Church dates to 1906, when a loose intertribal association of peyote groups in Oklahoma and Nebraska was formed. In 1909, the name "Union Church" was adopted. In 1918, the U.S. Bureau of Indian Affairs began campaign to declare peyote illegal. In reaction to this effort, the Native American Church was incorporated. Present at the formation was Jonathan Koshiway, who attempted to get the group to join the First Born. Koshiway's church was rejected as too Christian; eventually, Koshiway joined the Native Americans.

Although the actual practices of the Native American Church vary widely, there is a considerable core of commonality. The central figure is the shaman, who keeps the peyote buttons and controls their use. As with all mediumistic figures, he is endowed with psychic powers. Peyote ritual begins with the pilgrimage by members of the tribe to collect the buttons, which are returned to the shaman.

The ceremony occurs in the evening in a tepee. The "father peyote" is placed on a crescent-shaped mound. The mound is in the West, with the crescent horns facing East. Before participants eat the peyote, prayer and smoking occur, and singing and drumming follow. The ritual lasts until morning.

Legal battles for peyote began as early as 1899, when Oklahoma outlawed its use. Following the conviction of three Indians in 1907, the law was repealed in 1908. Anti-peyote laws were passed in Colorado, Utah and Nevada in 1917. Similar laws were passed in other Western states. A significant case was that of Mary Attakai, arrested for peyote use in 1960. In his decision, the judge ruled that peyote was non-habit forming and not a narcotic, and found the anti-peyote statute unconstitutional. In 1964, the California Supreme Court ruled that the Native American Church could not be deprived of peyote for religious ceremonies. Finally, when the psychedelic drugs were made illegal by federal law in 1966, peyote and the Native American Church were excluded from the strictures of the law. Since the court rulings of the 1970s, many non-Indians have attempted to affiliate with the church. In reaction, it has tended to exclude non-Indians from its rituals, both to protect its special status and to keep people believed to be merely seeking a drug experience from distorting its rituals.

The church is headed by a national president elected for a two-year term. An annual convention elects officers and is the chur ch's highest legislative body. State and local chapters are autonomous.

Membership: Not reported. In 1977 the church had approximately 225,000 members.

Sources: David F. Aberle, *The Peyote Religion among the Navaho*. New York: Wenner-Glen Foundation for Anthropological Research, 1966; Edward F. Anderson, *Peyote, the Divine Cactus*. Tucson, AZ: University of Arizona Press, 1980; Antonin Artaud, *The Peyote Dance*. New York: Farrar, Straus and Giroux, 1976; Weston La Barre, *The Peyote Cult*. New York: Schocken Books, 1969; Bernard Roseman, *The Peyote Story*. No. Hollywood, CA: Wilshire Book Company, 1963.

★897★
NEO-AMERICAN CHURCH
Current address not obtained for this edition.

The Neo-American Church was formed in 1964 by Arthur Kleps, the son of a Lutheran minister. Kleps can be (and is viewed by his critics as) an irreverent clown, drug addict and con-artist. One of his supporters, Timothy Leary, called him an "authentic American anarchist, nonconformist, itinerant preacher." The target of this diatribe and praise is one who calls himself the Chief Boo Hoo, primate of the East and proponent extraordinary of the sacramental use of psychedelic substances. Kleps was converted to the religious use of psychedelics at Millbrook, New York, at the estate which became an early gathering place for religion-oriented drug users. He incorporated his church in California, but settled in Millbrook until ejected.

Symbol of the Neo-American Church is the smiling three-eyed toad. It is Klep's belief that modern man is too corrupt to be illuminated as were the ancients. He needs LSD. The church believes that the use of psychedelic drugs is a sacramental act.

The Neo-American Church considers itself "to the left" of other psychedelic churches in that it has no set ritual, has no condition for membership other than agreement with its principles, and does not regulate the frequency or intensity of the sacramental experience. Regular services are not held; rather, the focus is upon lodges and retreats where the faithful can go for days or weeks at a time.

In rejection of over-institutionalization, Kleps injected massive doses of "absurdity into the church form." As Chief Boo Hoo he appoints and consecrates state primates, who are in charge of sacks. The primate ordains local Boo Hoos. Members must have cards and ordination certificates signed by the Chief Boo Hoo, and membership is renewable annually. A Boo Hoo heads a lodge at which members can receive the sacrament.

Kleps has authored the *Boo Hoo Bible*, the scripture of the church, and also edited *Divine Toad Sweat*, a periodical. A eucharistic guide details the preparation and use of various psychedelic substances. In the late 1960s, Kleps claimed 6,000 members but this included a highly transient membership. By the end of the 1970s, the courts had spoken definitively against religious exemptions for the use of otherwise illegal psychedelic substances, apart from the use of peyote by the Native American Church. Such rulings brought the viability of organizations like the Neo-American Church into question. During the 1980s, little evidence of the continued existence of the Neo-American Church has appeared and its present status is difficult to access. If it exists, it does so with a very small informal membership.

Membership: Not reported.

Sources: Art Kleps, *The Boo Hoo Bible*. San Christobal, NM: The Author, 1971; Art Kleps, *Millbrook*. Oakland, CA: Bench Press, 1977; Robert E. Brown, et al., eds., *The Psychedelic Guide to Preparation of the Eucharist*. Austin, TX: Linga Shirira Incense Co., 1975; Arthur Kleps, "Synchronicity and the Plot/Plot" in *Psychedelic Review*, vol. 8, (1966), pp. 123-24; Ed Dwyer and Robert Singer, "Interview: Art Kleps, Chief Boo Hoo, Neo American Church" in *High Times*, vol. 8, (March 1976), pp. 21-24.

Miscellaneous Psychic New Age

★898★

AMERICAN UNIVERSALIST TEMPLE OF DIVINE
WISDOM
Rte. 4, Box 301
Escondido, CA 92025

The American Universalist Temple of Divine Wisdom was founded in 1966 by a group of esoteric Christians living in the vicinity of Escondido, California. It is known as a Christ-centered point of light from which the love of God pours forth. It was prophesied by John the Revelator on the Isle of Patmos, who established the Order of the Golden Grail for the preservation of the original, unadulterated Christian doctrine of the inner life. The teachings of the Temple are "clairsentiently" received from ascended beings, and the Temple has instituted courses based upon the divine wisdom as a means of reaching sincere seekers of spiritual truth. The Temple is governed by a board of trustees.

Membership: Not reported. In 1968 there were 2 centers, one in California and one in Chicago.

Periodicals: *Light of the Crystal Ray*, Route 4, Box 301, Escondido, CA 92025.

★899★

ASSOCIATION FOR RESEARCH AND
ENLIGHTENMENT
Box 595
Virginia Beach, VA 23451

Edgar Cayce (1877-1945), one of the great psychics of the twentieth century, was born in 1877 in Hopkinsville, Kentucky. As a young man, he discovered that he could sleep on his books and gain a photographic memory of their content. At the age of twenty-one, he cured himself of a throat condition by taking advice given while in a trance-like state. Cayce soon gained a reputation for what, in the nineteenth century, was called traveling clairvoyance: the ability to "tune in" to another, even at some distance, and diagnose his condition and prescribe for it. A popular form of psychic phenonmenon in the nineteenth century, it was dying in popularity by the twentieth, and Cayce was its last major exponent. (As a result of Cayce's fame, other psychics revived traveling clairvoyance in the 1970s.)

In 1922, during a reading for Arthur Lammers, a Theosophist, astrologer and student of Eastern religions, Cayce began to talk about reincarnation and to describe what he claimed were the past lives on earth of various individuals. The "life readings," as these were called, joined the health readings in his repertoire. Most unusual for psychics in his day, Cayce had all of his readings recorded and transcribed. The Association for Research and Enlightenment (A. R. E.) was founded in 1931 to preserve, research and act upon the readings. When Cayce died, he left records of more than 14,000 readings given to more than 8,000 people.

Since Cayce's death, the A. R. E. has been cross-indexing, publishing and presenting the teachings of the readings. A number of biographies of Cayce, books on various topics in his thought and numerous pamphlets have been produced. Interest shifts between the health readings and the various remedies recommended for different illnesses, and the metaphysical readings which center on reincarnation and a theosophical cosmology.

Under Edgar Cayce's son, Hugh Lynn Cayce (1906-1983), A. R. E. grew to be one of the largest psychic organizations in the United States with study groups in every major city across the country. Most use basic *Search for God* (Volumes I and II) as their texts, supplemented by Cayce's readings, kept on file at the library in Virginia Beach, Virginia. Associated but independent of A. R. E. are the Edgar Cayce Foundation, a private corporation which owns the Cayce papers and much of the property used by A. R. E. in Virginia, and the A. R. E. Clinic in Phoenix, Arizona.

Membership: In 1984 A.R.E. reported 39,500 members in the United States and an additional 2,000 in other countries.

Periodicals: *Venture Inward*, Box 595, Virginia Beach, VA 23451; *Pathways to Health*, The A. R. E. Clinic, 4018 N. 40th Street, Phoenix, CA 85018.

Remarks: The Association for Research and Enlightenment does not consider itself a religion. It is included in this volume, however, because, like other organizations which also do not consider themselves a religion (World Plan Executive Council, Ancient and Mystical Order of the Rosae Crucis), it meets the definition of religion being used by this volume. A. R. E. does present through its publications a distinct spiritual-religious worldview, unique in its derivation from the Cayce readings, and a program of action analogous to the other groups and organizations included throughout this volume. Many of the members of the A. R. E. are also members of other churches and religious groups.

Sources: Thomas Sugue, *The Story of Edgar Cayce*. New York: Dell Publishing Company, 1945; Brett Bolton, ed., *Edgar Cayce Speaks*. New York: Avon, 1969; Hugh Lynn Cayce, ed., *The Edgar Cayce Reader*. New York: Paperback Library, 1969. 2 Vols.; Stern, Jess, *Edgar Cayce, the Sleeping Prophet*. New York: Bantam Books, 1968; Herbert B. Puryear, *The Edgar Cayce Primer*. New York: Bantam Books, 1982.

★900★
ASTROLOGICAL, METAPHYSICAL, OCCULT, REVELATORY, ENLIGHTENMENT CHURCH
Current address not obtained for this edition.

The Astrological, Metaphysical, Occult, Revelatory, Enlightenment Church (AMORE) was formed in 1972 by the Reverend Charles Robert Gordon, formerly a minister of the African Methodist Episcopal Zion Church(AMEZ). His father was Bishop Buford Franklin Gordon of the AMEZ Church. The church is Bible-based and views Jesus as the embodiment of cosmic consciousness. The AMORE Church believes in using the occult arts as a means to enlightenment in the coming Aquarian Age. Headquarters of the AMORE Church were established in Meriden, Connecticut. In recent years the church has moved and no contact has been made. Its present status (1985) is unknown.

Membership: Not reported.

★901★
AUM TEMPLE OF UNIVERSAL TRUTH
(Defunct)

The Aum Temple of Universal Truth was founded by Elizabeth Delvine King (1858-1932) as the Church Truth Universal-Aum in 1925 in Los Angeles. A metaphysician for many years, in 1907, as an answer to prayer, she received "the infilling of the Holy Spirit, which is the New Birth." Three days after her experience, "The Voice of the Infinite" spoke to her, saying, "Child, thy ministry is to be among what is called advanced thinking people." Over the next seven years, she wrote five books, which are the basic texts of the movement. In 1912 she headed a center for Practical Christianity in Manhattan Beach, California and in 1916 moved to Los Angeles and began a ministry of "Primitive Christian Teachings." In 1925, the first Sunday services were held.

Work progressed, and, by 1930, 22 ministers had been ordained. In 1929, the idea of a temple in the LaCrescenta Valley outside Los Angeles led to the beginning of construction. An Ashram was built as an adjunct of the Temple. At the time of Dr. King's death, there were two centers in Los Angeles and one in the Valley. Dr. King was succeeded by Dr. E.W. Miller and he, by Nina Fern Brunier (now Dennison), who has served as the leader beginning in 1940. Under her guidance, the present name of the church was adopted and, in 1956, she relocated the temple in the Mojave Desert where she had found a site for a new sanctuary and retreat complex. In 1964, the move was made to Newberry Springs, California, the La Crescenta Temple having previously been sold. In 1967, a new temple was completed. The center at Newberry Springs served the group through the 1970s, but in the early 1980s, the Temple was disbanded.

The Aum Temple taught Esoteric Christianity as given by the Great White Brotherhood, of which Jesus Christ is the active head. Truth is the light and wisdom divine, given to assist men to the kingdom of God. To enter the kingdom, the self must be cleansed and purified through scientific prayer, renunciation of carnal beliefs and meditation. By cleansing, not bodily death, one escapes the cycle of reincarnation in the dense material world and the law of cause and effect.

Aum is God's own name for himself, is God in unmanifested and manifested form. The repetition of the name of God attunes one to the vibration of the spirit. In speaking the word, one wields the power of the universe. The word is but part of the "Secret Heart Way," the discipline of mind, body, and spirit through which one attains union. It is the path of Bhakti Yoga, first taught in the United States by Baba Premanand Bharati, a Krishna devotee who worked in the United States from 1902 to 1907. Healing is an integral aspect of the work.

The Sanctuary and Retreat in Newberry Springs housed a self-contained community of disciples, who lived their love and devotion and kept an organic garden, bee hives, goats and chickens. Besides the disciples, there were a few members of the Temple who did not reside at Newberry Springs, but supported the work and frequently attended the weekly services on Sunday and Thursday. At various times periodicals, *The Greeting Messenger* and *AUM, The Cosmic Light* were published.

Sources: Elizabeth Delvine King, *The Flashlights of Truth*. Los Angeles: AUM Temple of Universal Truth, 1918; Elizabeth Delvine King, *The Lotus Path*. Los Angeles: J. F. Rowny Press, 1917; *New Age Songs*. Newberry Springs, CA: AUM Temple of Universal Truth, 1972; Nina Brunier, *The Path to Illumination*. Highway Highlands, CA: The Author, 1941; Leh Rheadia Althma, *The Garden of the Soul*. Newberry Springs, CA: AUM Temple of Universal Truth, 1943.

★902★
CHIROTHESIAN CHURCH OF FAITH
1757 N. Normandie
Los Angeles, CA 90027

The Chirothesian Church of Faith was formed in 1917 in Los Angeles by the Reverend D. J. Bussell, its president and senior bishop. Chirothesia is described as a natural religion based on the original form of the law of God. A Chirothesian is one who observes and obeys the law of God. The law of God was laid down in the beginning, has always had its followers and accepts Jesus as a modern messiah presenting the laws of God in a more modern manner and adapting them to a more modern world. The four Gospels and the Books of James and Jude contain the presentation of the law, according to Chirothesians. The account of creation in Genesis illustrates the law of God: "A fully concentrated thought must produce its kind." Man was created according to this law. Man is body (earthly) and soul and spirit (godly). The physical part of man is to be subject to the intellectual part. As an expression of God, "Man becomes what he thinks." The way of the law is the way of harmony and indicates a way back for any who has missed the original plan. Practicing the law allows one to overcome discord, unrighteousness and disease. Healing has been especially emphasized.

The Chirothesian Church does not proselytize, is not evangelistic and does not invite membership. However, the church is open to those who seek membership, and most meetings are open to the public. Closed meetings are business meetings and classes of instruction in which prior sessions are necessary to understand the class subject. Headquarters are in Los Angeles, with branch churches across the United States.

Membership: Not reported. There are several congregations across the United States.

Sources: D. J. Bussell, *Chirothesia.* Los Angeles; Chirothesian Church of Faith, n.d.; E. E. Garlichs, *The Life Beautiful.* Long Beach, CA: Aquarian Church of Chirothesia, [1946].

★903★
CHRIST MINISTRY FOUNDATION
Box 1103
Santa Cruz, CA 95061

The Christ Ministry Foundation was established in 1935 by Eleanore Mary Thedick (1883-1973) of Oakland, California. Ms. Thedick received her initial vision in 1926, when she was told that she would be a channel for a "spiritual broadcasting station." As the plan unfolded, the ministry was seen to illustrate the Christ-Light within. The outer foundation was to have 48 dual sects, each to be named for the Christ-qualities displayed in persons. Over the years, Ms. Thedick wrote several books. In 1970, Ms. Thedick merged her efforts with those of one of her students, Woods Mattingley. Mattingley had been involved in psychic/spiritual work for many years and had founded the Seeker's Quest. As the merger of efforts occurred, the Seeker's Quest Ministry was seen as being in an exoteric role, and the Foundation as being in an esoteric one.

The Christ Ministry Foundation teaches a form of esoteric Christianity. Christ is the great teacher who brought love into the world. The soul is envisioned as growing slowly toward at-one-ment with the Father. This process takes many incarnations, but, as with the prodigal, all will eventually return. During incarnation, we attempt to overcome character weakness, pay karmic debts and bear witness to the Light of God. Healing is a major practice; it is done by channeling the Light of God, often envisioned as the Triune Ray (Father, Son and Holy Spirit). In 1970, Ms. Thedick retired from active work, and the ministry was headed by Mattingley. In 1972, she gave her students, Geneva D. Seivertson and her husband, Wayne Seivertson, charge over the Foundation, and Mattingley's Seeker's Quest Ministry became independent,

though affiliated, in San Jose. He continued to publish his quarterly periodical.

Membership: Not reported.

Periodicals: *The Seeker's Quest Newsletter*, Box 8188, San Jose, CA 95155.

Sources: Eleanor Thedick, *The Christ Highway*. Oakland, CA: Christ Ministry Foundation, n.d.; Eleanor Thedick, *Light on Your Problems*. Oakland, CA: Christ Ministry Foundation, n.d.; Eleanor Thedick, *Jewels of Truth and Rays of Color*. Oakland, CA: Christ Ministry Foundation, n.d.; Genevah D. Seivertson, *The Christ Highway*. Marina del Rey, CA: DeVorss & Company, 1981.

★904★
CHURCH OF BASIC TRUTH
Box 6084
Phoenix, AZ 85005

The Church of Basic Truth was founded in 1961 in Phoenix, Arizona and is headed by Dr. George H. Hepker. It teaches huna (power), the beliefs of the pre-Christian religious leaders of Hawaii, with an emphasis on healing via "Meda-Physical Dynamics." This therapy was developed on the theory that any disorder the mind can allow to develop can be controlled and often cured.

Membership: Not reported. A second center is in Gary, Indiana.

★905★
CHURCH OF EDUCTIVISM
3003 Santa Monica Blvd.
Santa Monica, CA 90404

Jack Horner (b. 1927) worked from 1950 to 1965 with L. Ron Hubbard, founder of the Church of Scientology. A prominent member of the church, he was awarded the first Doctor of Scientology degree. Then in 1965, he left the church over what he considered a authoritarian ethics policy. After a period of non-association with Scientology, he began to develop Dianology, viewed as an improved Scientology drawing from a number of various sources. In 1970, Horner moved to Los Angeles and founded the Personal Spiritual Freedoms Foundation. In 1971 he changed the name Dianology to Eductivism with emphasis placed on "educing" latent potentials and uncovering what is hidden. The Church of Eductivism, formerly the Church of Spiritual Freedoms, is the religious adjunct to the Foundation; both are aspects of the umbrella corporation, the Association of International Dianologists.

Eductivism is an applied philosophy aimed at evoking the individual's infinite spiritual potentials. Individuals (usually referred to as "life sources") are infinitely capable of total creation and total cessation, simultaneously. But individuals do not use that potential. Through classes and exercises, the potentials are released in a meaningful context.

The creed of the church emphasizes the freedoms believed to be implicitly denied in the Church of Scientology--to seek God, however he may be perceived; to create alternatives, to possess opinions, thoughts and sanity; to communicate freely with others, and to join voluntary associations. Like Scientology, the Horner teaches that humans are basically "well disposed" and that "occlusions which mar and blemish the human spirit can be removed by the application of Spiritual technology."

Horner had an immediate response to his efforts, and associated centers have been established and independent clearing consultants trained. Horner is a leader in the California Association of Dianetic Auditors, a fellowship of independent cousultants.

Membership: Not reported.

Sources: Jack Horner, *Dianology*. Westwood Village, CA: The Association of International Dianologists, 1970; Jack Horner, *Eductivism and You*. Westwood, CA: Personal Creative Freedoms Foundation, 1971; Jack Horner, *Clearing*. Santa Monica, CA: Personal Creative Freedoms Foundation, 1982; Jack Horner and J. Rey Geller, *What an Eductee Should Know*. Santa Monica, CA: Personal Creative Freedoms Foundation, 1974.

★906★
CHURCH OF GENERAL PSIONICS
204 N. Catalina
Redondo Beach, CA 90277

The Church of General Psionics was founded by John L. Douglas and Henry D. Frazier. Douglas was an amateur hypnotist and student of the psychic. Over the decade preceding the church's founding in 1968, Douglas had been evolving a pragmatic view of "psi"--the psychic. "Does it work?" became his criterion for things psychic. Then, in a visionary experience in 1968, a new understanding of the nature and purpose of humanity was given and a group was formed by those who were of like mind.

The purpose of Psionics is to help a person develop his own philosophy. Since the path to enlightenment is loaded with obstacles, General Psionics aids the individual by offering training to help him to become aware of his immortality. Man is a soul inhabiting a body, as it has inhabited other bodies previously. The various techniques of becoming aware are termed psionics engineering. New members of the church, before they are introduced to psionic engineering, are asked to agree to the "code of an immortal." The code acknowledges the dignity of all entities, quite apart from the body, and the fight of each entity to self-determination. From the church center in Redondo Beach, California, a program of classes, workshops, and counseling is offered.

Membership: Not reported. There was only a single center in the 1970s.

★907★
CHURCH OF SCIENTOLOGY
Flag Service Org(anization)
Box 23751
Tampa, FL 33630-3751

Few of the new religious bodies of the 1960s have aroused so much controversy as the Church of Scientology, founded in 1952 by L. Ron Hubbard (1911-1986). From its beginning, it has been attacked, questioned and not infrequently defamed. The controversy has in like measure helped mold the church, which has geared itself to defend its rights and to refute all charges and false statements about itself, its teachings or its founder.

L. Ron Hubbard first became a public figure as a science fiction writer and explorer. As early as 1949, however, he established an organization to spread his emerging ideas about the human mental processes, ideas which were published the following year in *Dianetics/the Modern Science of Mental Health*, the basic text of the present church. Hubbard wanted to offer dianetics as a mental health discipline, so in the summer of 1950 he journeyed to Washington, D.C., and made a presentation to a group of psychiatrists and educators. The effect was negative as the American Psychological Association called upon psychologists not to use dianetic therapy. Dianetics also came under attack by the American Medical Association. During this period, considered by Scientologists a time of self-interest-motivated persecution, Hubbard was building the organization by establishing centers in Los Angeles and Wichita, while dealing with several internal disputes. More importantly he continued to expand the more practical and mundane areas of concern covered by dianetics into the more metaphysical speculations which became Scientology. Scientology is the logical extension of dianetics. Just as Scientology was outlined, Hubbard, confronted by attacks on every side, moved to Washington, D.C. and founded the Church of Scientology in 1955. This evolution of the movement had the added effect of creating a new religion.

Dianetics is described as a science leading to the source of all psychosomatic ills and human aberrations. Hubbard postulates the existence of the mind in two aspects. The analytical mind perceives, reasons and remembers. The reactive mind simply records engrams, completely detailed impressions on protoplasm of perceptions present in a past moment of unconsciousness. Engrams can be recorded at any traumatic moment. Significant engrams are lodged by the fetus before birth at moments when the mother is expressing strong emotions. Dianetics was a set of techniques for discovering and getting rid of engrams.

The person who has gotten rid of all his engrams is called a clear. One becomes clear by going through a series of courses leading to self-discovery, and by a process called auditing. Auditing is done with an E-Meter, actually a modified Wheatstone Bridge, which measures resistance to electric currents. The student takes hold of lines connected to the E-Meter, and the instructor, called an auditor, takes him through various drills, all aimed at freeing one from engrams.

After becoming clear, one proceeds to various levels of Scientology. Scientology is concerned with the isolation, description and handling of the human spirit. Hubbard discovered the means of separating the human personality from the body and mind (a process called astral travel by non-Scientologists). He names the "thing" which separated from the body, the theta, after the Greek letter. The theta has the power to create MEST, that is, matter, energy, space and time, or the basic stuff of existence. The thetan who has the power to exteriorize is termed an operating thetan. The thetan reincarnates through a series of lifetimes. The Church's beliefs are uniquely presented in the christening ceremony which is seen as a means to get the theta oriented after its taking over a new body.

Hubbard acknowledged that the founding of the church was to allow Scientology access to areas where only religion can go--prisons, hospitals and institutions. Its leaders are ministers. *Ceremonies of the Founding Church of Scientology* describes basic services, which follow traditional patterns.

General oversight of Scientology is invested in the International Church of Scientology, headquartered in the church complex in Hollywood. The Guardian's Office is the administrative arm of the church. It is assigned a variety of tasks not the least of which is that of ensuring that the teachings and practice of the church follow the strict procedures prescribed in the various books written by Hubbard and/or issued by the Church. The office charters the various churches, missions and other units of the church. In this regard it has organized the church's thrust into social concerns, having fostered structures: Narconon (anti-narcotics), the Citizens Commission on Human Rights, the Committee on Public Health and Safety, American Citizens for Honesty in Government, the Committee for a Safe Environment, and the National Commission on Law Enforcement and Social Justice. Finally, it is in charge of defending the church from attack, which has made it the focus of most of the controversy surrounding the church.

The church is divided regionally, there being two regions (The Church of Scientology--Western United States and the Church of Scientology--Eastern United States) designated in America. Under the regions are the local churches and missions. The Flag Organization (popularly called the Sea Org, from the years it was located on an ocean-going vessel), is an elite fraternity of people who (prior to Hubbard's death) engaged with him in the continuing development of Scientology. tology. The Advanced Organization has oversight of the advanced

levels of Scientology instruction, specifically those leading to clear and the development of the operating thetan.

The goal of Scientology is a clear planet and the elimination of the effects of engrams and the reactive mind. Members believe that dianetics and scientology are the only path for humanity to become totally free.

Membership: In 1985 the church claimed approximately 3,000,000 members worldwide, of whom 1,000,000 were in America. That figure represents a cumulative number of people who have participated in one or more of the church's programs or availed themselves of the church's services over a period of several years. In the United States there are approximately 125 churches and missions.

Periodicals: *Advance*, The Advanced Organization of Los Angeles, 1306 N. Berendo Street, Los Angeles, CA 90027; *The Auditor*, Church of Scientology Western United States, 1413 N. Berendo Street, Los Angeles, CA 90027; *Cause*, American Saint Hill Organization, 1413 N. Berendo Street, Los Angeles, CA: 90027; *Freedom*, Church of Scientology of California, 1306 N. Berendo Street, Los Angeles, CA 90027.

Remarks: The years since the founding of the Church in 1955 have been ones of seemingly unending, intense controversy. Controversy began with ex-members who claimed that the organization had defrauded them of large sums of money (an average student spends a minimum of $2,500 to become a clear). Governments became hostile to Scientology. In 1963, officers of the Food and Drug Administration raided the Washington, D.C. church and seized the E-Meter. Only in 1969 was a decision reached that E-Meters and auditing were valid religiously. In 1968, England placed a restriction on all non-English nationals who were entering the country just to study or practice Scientology. The 1965 ban of Scientology by the Australian government led to a lengthy legal battle resolved in the Church's favor in 1983.

One pattern repeated frequently in the Scientologist controversies has been strong assertions against the Church (or Hubbard), followed by press exposure, lawsuits, and the clear establishment of the falsity of the original assertions. Such assertions filled several early books on Scientology. The Church has also been the frequent victim of raids by government agencies. Partially in response to the build-up of questionable documents on the Church in various government files (the direct cause of some raids), the Church has become one of the most vigorous users of the Freedom of Information Act. The Church has even published a booklet aimed at helping individuals and Church members gain access to files on themselves.

During the 1960s and 1970s, the Church pursued a variety of legal procedures to stop government action (particularly action by the U.S. Internal Revenue Service) against it and to defend itself against the attacks of exmembers and other opponents. Prior to the 1980s, the Church won a majority of such cases. However, during the first half of the 1980s, the Church suffered some major defeats in court. Criminal charges filed against Church leaders following a raid of Church offices in 1977 led eventually to their conviction. Those sentenced for stealing government documents included the church's top official, Guardian Jane Kember and Hubbard's wife, Mary Sue Hubbard. In 1984 the Church's tax-exempt status was taken away in a federal court decision. The trial, which highlighted the financial dealings of the Church, created a significant amount of bad publicity , and led the church to place ads in newspapers asking for informants with information on illegal actions by the Internal Revenue Service.

In the midst of major legal setbacks and a reflection of the public's attitude toward the Church, two juries awarded multimillion dollar judgments against it in the suit brought by ex-member Julie Christofferson, who had been deprogrammed by her parents. Both judgments have been overturned and no decision on the possibility of a third trial of the suit has been announced (as of the end of 1985).

Sources: *What Is Scientology.* Los Angeles: Church of Scientology of California, 1978; L. Ron Hubbard, *Dianetics, The Modern Science of Mental Health.* New York; Hermitage House, 1950; Roy Wallis, *The Road to Total Freedom.* New York: Columbia University Press, 1977; Trevor Meldal-Johnson and Patrick Lusey, *The Truth About Scientology.* New York: Tempo Books, 1980; *Scientology: A World Religion Emerges in the Space Age.* [Los Angeles]: Church of Scientology Information Service, Department of Archives, 1974.

★908★
CHURCH OF THE GENTLE BROTHERS AND SISTERS
Box 346
Bolinas, CA 94924

Frank Douglas was a trance medium in New York City who moved to London to continue his work. While in London in January of 1971, he received messages through other mediums that Mexico was an ideal place to begin a spiritual center and healing group. He arrived at Puerto Angel and there met Martin Myman, who agreed to join forces in forming a center. Healing work commenced, and the center's fame spread throughout both Mexico and California. A community formed around Douglas. Healing was done by a combination of spiritual healing, zonal therapy, counseling, massage and even drugs. After two years, the Mexican government began to suppress the efforts, and the center moved to San Francisco, where it incorporated as the Church of Gentle Brothers and Sisters. Because of legal restrictions, the laying-on-of-hands has been the main method employed in healing since the move. Prior to healing, palm readings are done on patients. The group is Theosophic in outlook and

studies the Alice Bailey books. Emphasis is placed on spiritual unfoldment (religious growth), as opposed to psychic development (through telepathy, clairvoyance, etc.).

★909★
CHURCH OF THE GIFT OF GOD
(Defunct)

The Church of the Gift of God was a nonsectarian group whose prime manifestation occurred through the New England Conservatory of Health headquartered in Magnolia, Massachusetts. There, the Conservatory operated a retreat house that offers a program "dedicated to restoring your natural and spiritual good health." The church was headed by Professor James A. Dooling II, who based it upon the teachings of St. Luke, St. Benedict and St. Dorothy. It was Dooling's belief that good health is within the reach of all who will merely abide by the laws of the creator of nature.

Various healing techniques were offered at the Conservatory. They ranged from the more accepted medical and physical therapy practices to less orthodox approaches such as medical astrology, color therapy and psychic healing. Emphasis is placed on natural diet and exercise, and on human ecology as the correct ordering of the total environment of physical and spiritual man. The Church seems to have dissolved in the early 1980s.

★910★
CHURCH OF THE LORD JESUS CHRIST (ISHI TEMPLE)
(Defunct)

The Church of the Lord Jesus Christ (Ishi Temple) was founded by bishop Robert N. Skillman, known to his followers as the Prophet Saoshyant. The church was described as Christoid, that is, in the image of Christ. It honored the holy name of God, Ishi (Hosea 2:16), meaning "My Husband." It was a church which recognized the necessity of having living prophets to govern it: "Saoshyant" is the name in Avestan (Zoroastrian) literature of the great coming Prophet. The church also taught that miracles were needed to demonstrate the power of God in extraordinary ways and that revelation was needed as a vehicle for bringing greater truth to the world today. Finally, the church taught the truth of the Latter Rain, the movement from the divine light of the Sixth Ray to the Seventh Ray (a reference to theosophic teaching on the light which emanantes from the divine).

Skillman was assisted in the Ishi Temple by Archdeacon Robert S. Kimball. Headquarters were established in Brisbane, California, from where a periodical, *The Christoid Evangel*, was published irregularly. The church offered correspondence lessons in "prosperity" and distributed talismans for a variety of needs. Saoshyant authored several booklets--*The Grand Affirmation, The Healing Affirmation* and *The Sayings*.

★911★
CONGREGATIONAL CHURCH OF PRACTICAL THEOLOGY
Star Route, Box 28
Ponchatoula, LA 70454

The Congregational Church of Practical Theology was formed in 1969 by Dr. E. Arthur Winkler, a former United Church of Christ and United Methodist minister. There are no creeds, though there is a set of beliefs which members and ministers are asked to use as guidelines for individual spiritual search. God is seen as continually revealing himself in the open-minded search for truth. The Bible is a textbook for Truth, but not the final word. Jesus is divine, but each person is also a divine son of God. The theology is practical and seeks to apply religion to all of life. The diginity of all people is affirmed; service to individuals and society is extolled. Ministers are seen as catalysts to the spiritual quest of individuals.

The church was not founded for the purpose of establishing congregations (though it has chartered a number of congregations) but to provide a ministry of guidance for all people who seek its varied forms of ministry as well as to promote the dignity and love of all humankind--people of all colors, races, religions, social backgrounds, and economic levels. Ministers are ordained for the purpose of putting their religion into action in all areas of their life. Ministers, being needed in all professions, are not necessarily pastors of congregations but may be counselors, psychologists, medical doctors, hypnotherapists, lawyers, law officers, or they may follow other careers and earn their living in the occupation of their choice.

Membership: In 1984 the church reported 165 ministers and 21 chartered congregations. Membership figures are not kept. Affiliated members can be found in Canada, Sweden, the West Indies, and Africa.

Educational facilities: St. John's University, Ponchatoula, Louisiana (with branches in St. Louis, Missouri; Florence, Kentucky; St. Petersburg, Florida; and Sweden and Nigeria).

Periodicals: *Attain: Health, Happiness and Success*, Star Route, Box 28, Ponchatoula, LA 90454.

Sources: Arthur Winkler, *Hypnotherapy*. Valley, NB: Eastern Nebraska Christian College, 1972; *The Congregational Church of Practical Theology*. Ponchatoula, LA: The Congregational Church, [1970].

★912★
COPTIC FELLOWSHIP OF AMERICA
1735 Pinnacle, S.W.
Wyoming, MI 48509

The Coptic Fellowship of America was founded in Hollywood, California, in 1927 by Hamid Bey (d. 1976). Bey was born in Egypt and, as a five-year-old child, met a master of the hidden temples of the Christian religion. According to Bey, due to persecution and the destruction of early Christian temples, Christians built seven hidden temples that could not be found. The churches remained as mere outside schools. In the temple, Bey was trained in self-control, in how to subdue the body, concentration, the essentials of personality and clairvoyance. The most important temple is the Head Masters Temple, which is 9,000 years old and hewn out of rock on the Nile. It is headed by the Great Eleven Ring Master. Having finished his temple education, Bey was sent to America to show that Houdini's claim to be able to reproduce any occult phenomenon was false. Though Houdini died soon after Bey's arrival, Bey stayed to tour the country, demonstrating his yogic abilities, particularly the feat of being buried for several days.

The Coptic Fellowship teaches an esoteric Christianity. The universe expresses polarity. Eastern and Western civilizations are manifestations of the polarity. Egypt is of the East. Nature is the handiwork of the creator. Man is the epitome of creation. His purpose is to bring into manifestation his latent potential powers of conscious awareness-cosmic consciousness. Christ was one of the major teachers of the one law, and beheld the law more completely than any other master. In Christ, we see the essentials of the upward path--health of the physical body, work, science and love. It is the belief of the fellowship that truth is eternal and eternally available and that it was passed on to the Coptic Order. All of life, creation, progress and evolution emanate from God's love, the same reality which leads humans and societies to perfection. Individual souls grow through a continous progression (reincarnation and karma), but are often hidden from truth by ignorance and misdirection.

During the 1970s, the fellowship had become aligned to the New Age Movement, and saw its work as a catalyst in the transformation to a new planetary civilization the Spiritual Unity of Nations (SUN). SUN was founded in England by Joseph Bushby with the purpose of uniting spiritual powers to bring about a world spiritual bonding of nations. SUN's American headquarters are located at the fellowship's headquarters.

Bey was suceeded as head of the fellowship by John Davis, formerly its Midwest Director. The fellowship is guided by a four-person board of directors. Work within the fellowship is divided among four orders: the Light Ministry is a body of teachers who publicly disseminate the orders teachings, often through opening centers; the World Service Order conducts seminars on New Age concerns; the Devotional Order is an inner order of people who follow a meditative discipline; and Star Rise, a program for the nurturing of children. Correspondence lessons for new members are offered via mail.

Membership: Not reported.

Sources: Hamid Bey, *My Experiences Preceding 5000 Burials*. Los Angeles: Coptic Fellowship of America, 1951.

★913★
DAWN OF TRUTH
Current address not obtained for this edition.

The Dawn of Truth was the name used by the teaching ministry of Mikkel Dahl, of Windsor, Ontario, described as a nondenominational Christian. Dahl is the author of a number of booklets and lessons, which are published by his organization. Publicity literature describes Dahl as "the 20th Century Revelator," Bible teacher extraordinary, and the preliminary messenger of the New Age. The writings cover a wide range of Biblical, prophetic and current-interest topics. The heart of the Dawn of Truth, however, is in the Tabracana Lessons, which reveal the spiritual laws of successful living. The lessons cover metaphysics, the Great Pyramid, an allegorical interpretation of the Bible and an esoteric Christianity. These lessons are mailed out across the United States and Canada. The present status of the ministry is unknown.

Membership: Not reported.

Sources: Mikkel Dahl, *God's Master Plan of Love for Man*. Windsor, Ont.: Dawn of Truth, 1961; Mikkel Dahl, *The Coming New Society*. Windsor, Ont.: Dawn of Truth, n.d.

★914★
EMBASSY OF THE GHEEZ-AMERICANS
Mt. Helion Sanctuary
Rock Valley Rd., Box 53
Long Eddy, NY 12760

The Embassy of the Gheez-Americans is headed by Empress Mysikiitta Fa Senntao, who runs the Mt. Helion Sanctuary at Long Eddy, New York. She is also titled "The Ambassadress of the Sun God and Resurrector of the Gheez-Nation [Ethiopia]." She is believed to have come from the sun in a space ship, leaving her husband behind and taking over a body upon arrival. Her mission is to redeem her people, who have been lost on earth for thousands of years and during that time have reincarnated in many nationalities.

According to Her Majesty, Satan and his brother, Tao, the god of love, fought for control of earth. After man chose Satan and the tree of good and evil in the garden, Satan took control. The tree of life (wisdom) was hidden

among the few occult. Taoism, the wisdom of eternal life, came to Ethiopia at the beginning of the Age of Taurus. From there, it went to Egypt and survived the flood with Noah. Of Noah's sons, only one, Ham, accepted the ministry of the wisdom, a burden Hamites have had to bear. With Egyptian decline, Abraham and Israel were chosen the custodians of the wisdom. When Moses saw his people, who were worshipping Taurus, not able to keep the law, he gave them a lesser law.

The empress is calling together the ancient Gheez-Nation. Members are united by a common language (Gheez), a history, culture and a cosmic link of God. Her Majesty has bound Satan on the planet Uranus. The chosen people, the Gheez-Nation, will become the leaven in lifting all of humanity. The new nation learns the Gheez language, engages in ecstatic dancing and practices the martial arts of the Priest Kurahti. Most members are black people and number in the hundreds. Her Majesty functions as a psychic and a teacher of occult wisdom.

Membership: Not reported.

★915★
EMISSARIES OF DIVINE LIGHT
5569 N. Country Rd. 29
Loveland, CO 80537

The Emissaries of Divine Light (formerly known as the Ontological Society and the Universal Institute of Applied Ontology) was formed in 1932 in Tennessee by Lloyd Arthur Meeker, its first bishop. Bishop Meeker, who wrote under the pen-name Uranda, established Sunrise Ranch, a community and home base of the Society, in rural Colorado, near Loveland. He was succeeded by Martin Cecil, bishop of the Society. In 1951, a second Ontological community was begun at 100 Mile House, British Columbia. In the 1960s, George Emery, a former Methodist minister who headed his own psychic organization, the Foundation for Spiritual Development, in Tombstone, Arizona, joined the Society as its international field representative.

The basic stance of the Emissaries is spelled out in a pamphlet, "The Divine Design." According to the Society, man was created in the image and likeness of the body of God, i.e., he was created to manifest the divine design. God is the one focus of all being. Distortions appear when the mind allows evil influences (fear, hate, jealousy, anger, resentment, etc.) to gain control. Since man has free will, the mind can select the influences which will be allowed to enter and control his body. The mind can choose to accept divine control.

Collectively, mankind manifests the distortions of evil influences in societal problems. But the return to divine control is the immediate possibility of every individual. The re-emergence of the divine design is called healing. Ontology, defined as the science of true being, is the art of manifesting reality in the world of chaos. That reality

(God) manifests as truth (the design of form) and love (the power of life). Form is constantly in process, a fact which allows for healing.

A goal of members of the Emissaries is to experience reality, to know the identity of one's true being, to know oneness. The experience of oneness is an experience of the image and likeness of God in the present, without reference to past or future. The Emissaries of Divine Light helps its members find atonement with reality. Jesus is seen as a demonstration of ontological truth.

The Emmisaries are centered in the two communities in Colorado and British Columbia. They serve as models for the numerous smaller local centers scattered throughout North America and around the world. The Emmisaries do not proselytize. Members have been active in cooperative activities with other groups of like mind and purpose, especially those who constitute the New Age Movement, in which its members have been very active. One structure for such cooperative endeavor is Emissary Foundation International which supports a variety of programs such as the Association for Responsible Communication, Renaissance Business Associates, Renaissance Educational Associates, and Whole Health Institute.

Periodicals: *Integrity International.* Box 9, 100 Mile House, British Columbia, Canada V0K 2E0.

Sources: Lord Martin Cecil, *Being Where You Are.* New Cannan, CT: Keats Publishing Inc., 1974; Lord Martin Cecil, *On Eagle's Wings.* New York: Two Continents Publishing Group, 1977; Michael Cecil et al, *Spirit of Sunrise.* London: Mitre Press, 1979; Aumra, *As of a Trumpet.* Loveland, CO: Eden Valley Press, 1968.

★916★
ESSENE CENTER
(Defunct)

The Essene Center was founded in 1972 in Hot Springs, Arkansas, by the Reverend Walter Hagen. In 1970 Hagen had a vision of Christ, and the stigmata (marks similar to those in Jesus' hands after the crucifixion) were placed on his hands as a sign of his acceptance of his mission. In other visions, he was given the power to work miracles. Hagen is also a prophet and regularly makes predictions of coming events.

According to Hagen, Jesus was an Essene, and the order of Essenes actually dates to the time of Moses. The House of Prophets on Mt. Carmel was the center of the order. Essenes were characterized by abstinence from slavery, by communal living, disdain for commerce and industry, longevity, belief in reincarnation, healing by God's power, and psychic abilities. As modern-day Essenes, Hagen taught his followers to believe that war is wrong, that waste is a misuse of what God had given, that all religions are acceptable to God, that respect for the rights of all men includes disdain of slavery, and that it is a duty to help other Essenes. He accepted the Dead Sea Scrolls and believed that the coming messiah will arise from among the Essenes.

During the 1970s there was only one Essene group, that one associated with the Center at Hot Springs, but members were located around the country. They were tied together by *The Guide*, a monthly periodical. Hagen's workshops and a variety of services were offered through the Center. No evidence of the continuance of the center into the 1980s has been found.

★917★
ETHERIAN RELIGIOUS SOCIETY OF
**   UNIVERSAL BROTHERHOOD**
Box 446
San Marcos, CA 92069

The Etherian Religious Society of Universal Brotherhood was formed in 1965 in California by its director, the Reverend E. A. Hurtienne, and has its source in the mental visions given Mr. Hurtienne earlier in his life. While no being or form was seen in these visions, there were present waves of love and the awareness of universal consciousness. The purpose of the Society is to minister through love so as to insure dignity, equality and justice for all mankind throughout the universe and help establish the future root races (developmental stages) of mankind upon earth and assure the entrance of earth into the Planetary Federation of Light of our solar system.

The basic philosophy of the Society recognizes a consciousness that is divine and manifested in four principles of omnipresence, omnipotence, omniscience and love. It further holds that all men are brothers throughout the universe; all forms of life on all planes are related; all religions, though under the direction of God, are man-made; love is the unifying force and must become a living reality, for only through it can eternal life by achieved; karma and reincarnation are universal laws, man is divine and is entitled to free throught and action; man is a spiritual being with seven complete bodies, and all life is to be held in reverence. Behavior is to center upon sincerity, tolerance, integrity, kindness and affection.

The Society has among its immediate goals the establishment of primary classes in metaphysics and esoteric studies and the formation of light and meditation groups for healing, unity , and harmony between nature and mankind. Membership is open to all; after a year, members may become a part of the Brotherhood of Light, an inner group with the Society. The group circulates copies of *Man, Know Thy Divinity*, published by the Living Christ Movement of New Zealand. Among future goals are the establishment of a university, a healing center and a religious community of advanced spiritual beings.

Membership: Not reported.

Periodicals: *The Etherian Bulletin*, Box 446, San Marcos, CA 92069.

Sources: *Man, Know Thy Divinity*. Auckland, NZ: Living Christ Movement, n.d.

★918★
FIRST CENTURY CHURCH
(Defunct)

The Reverend David N. Bubar was a Southern Baptist minister and graduate of New Orleans Baptist Theological Seminary. After a seven-year pastorate during which he became more and more aware of his psychic abilities, he resigned his parish and, in 1969, opened the Spiritual Outreach Society (later renamed the First Century Church). During the 1970s he developed a national reputation as a clairvoyant, prophet and psychic counselor, and he kept a heavy schedule of lectures around the country.

In 1975 Bubar was involved in the arson case of the Sponge Rubber Plant in Shelton, Connecticut. Plant owner Chrles Moeller had been a longtime client of Bubar's and Bubar had predicted a plant "disaster" shortly before it was bombed. As of 1977, Bubar was serving a prison term foll owing his conviction as a participant in the arson.

There was only a single congregation of the First Century Church, but it had a significant outreach through its nationally circulated periodical, *Flaming Sword*. Weekly services and classes were held at the church, which survived only a short time after Bubar began his long sentence.

★919★
FOUNDATION FAITH OF GOD
Faith Center
3055 S. Bronco
Las Vegas, NV 89102

The Foundation Faith of God was formed in 1974 when the majority of the leaders of the Process Church of the Final Judgment rejected the direction being taken by Process prophet Robert de Grimston, withdrew their support and reorganized as the Foundation Church of the Millennium. Subsequently it has progressed through several doctrinal positions and internal reorganizations reflected in the change of names, first to the Foundation Faith of the Millennium (1977) and then to its present name (1980).

A dissatisfaction with the growing emphasis on Satan was the immediate problem which led to the ousting of de Grimston and the formation of the Foundation Faith by most of the following of the Process Church. A hierarchical order has been retained. Heading the Faith is a nine-member Council of Luminaries who in turn delegate temporal administration to the Office of the Faithful. Ministers are ranked from luminaries and celebrants (both ordained) to mentors, covenanters and covenantors. Those preparing for the ministry are termed founders. The uniforms, consisting of a blue suit with a white shirt, so evident in the 1970s, have been largely abandoned. Laity is composed of aides and disciples.

The Foundation Faith has moved steadily toward an orthodox Christian belief, expressing belief in the Trinity, the deity of Jesus, salvation from sin, the necessity of the new birth and the second advent. There is a strong emphasis upon the soon second coming of Christ and the establishment of the Kingdom of God.

The Faith has established Foundation centers and missions across the United States. The Faith is also spread through prayer fellowship and outreach ministries. There is a wide and diverse program of social programs, conceived as part of a healing ministry. Spiritual healing has been a consistent part of the Faith's belief and practice, and ministers make themselves available for healing prayer at all Faith centers. Spiritual consultations are also offered for their healing value.

Periodicals: *Newsletter*, 3055 S. Bronco, NV 89102.

Sources: *Hymns and Chants*. N.p.: The Foundation Faith of the Millennium, n.d.; *Hymns and Chants*. N.p.: Foundation Faith of God, 1977.

★920★
FUTURE FOUNDATION
Box 26
Steinauer, NE 68441

The Future Foundation was formed in 1969 in Steinauer, Nebraska, by Gerard W. Gottula and an associated group which had been meeting for several months. The history of the group actually dates to the 1950s and the healing works of Jennings Ruffing, who lived in a small Wyoming town. Ruffing discovered that one of his patients was clairvoyant and, under the direction of Ruffing, could give psychic readings. The eight members of the original foundation group gathered for a reading from Ruffing and his associate, at which time the formation of the Foundation was announced to them.

The first issue of the *Future Foundation*, a newsletter, appeared in 1969. A board of twelve members was formed to govern the work, which would consist of giving health, life, and guidance rea

Membership: Not reported. Members are scattered around the United States. In 1971, the healing center was begun in Hot Springs, South Dakota. Plans were being considered to establish a permanent headquarters in Lush, Wyoming. A fourth center is in North Glenn, Colorado.

Sources: *Prophecies of Cyrus*. Steinauer, NB: Future Foundation, 1970.

★921★
HAIKIM INTERNATIONAL MEDITATION SOCIETY
(Defunct)

The Haikim International Meditation Society is/was a small group headquartered in Houston, Texas, and headed by Mary Beatrice Gunn, its director/counselor. Its world headquarters were in Zurich, Switzerland. No sign of its continuance into the 1980s has been observed.

★922★
HOLY ORDER OF EZEKIEL
(Defunct)

The Holy Order of Ezekiel was founded in 1969 by Dr. Daniel Christopher. Dr. Christopher was a student of Dr. Judith Tyberg, who had been a disciple of Sri Autobindo and later taught at the East-West Cultural Center in San Francisco, California. Christopher graduated from the Center and later studied in Europe at the Prasura Institute and the Guggenheim Academy. The Order, founded upon Christopher's return to the United States, was composed of two parts, the Celestial and Terrestrial Circles. The Celestial Circle, composed of three masters, seven practitioners and other initiates, is the center of guiding light that radiates celestial illumination to every attuned being. The masters are the spiritual gurus of all members. Christopher was the First Master. The Terrestrial Circle consisted of the scribes, secretaries and members and was to be the growing branch of the Order. Members who manifest assimilation of and dedication to the precepts of the Order were welcomed as initiates.

The Order's basic teachings centered upon the knowledge of God's power and the techniques of achieving personal success and fulfillment through that power. The Divine Life Lessons distributed by the Order prepared the seeker to receive the power promised by Christ. These include instruction in meditation, breathing, the use of "Aum" (a mantra), mystical symbolizing, spiritual healing and numerology. There was a strong belief in reincarnation and karma. The masters were seen as helpful in the student's progress. The Order taught that God assumes one-half of the student's burden and the master, one-fourth. The members must generate the initial spark.

In the 1970s, headquarters of the Holy Order were in Glendale, California. From there, the lessons were sent out to students across the country.

★923★
HOLY SPIRIT ASSOCIATION FOR THE UNIFICATION OF WORLD CHRISTIANITY
4 W. 43rd St.
New York, NY 10036

The Holy Spirit Association for the Unification of World Christianity was brought to the United States in 1959 from South Korea. After a period of slow growth, it mushroomed during the early and mid-1970s and became a controversial and significant religious force because of its non-conventional beliefs, accusations of improper recruitment techniques and its attempts to build coalitions of scholars around the church's idealistic programs and ideals. The church first gained national attention as a result of a speaking tour which its founder, the Reverend Sun Myung Moon, made across the country in 1972. The Unification Church, as it is usually called, came to the United States in 1959 in the person of Young Oon Kim, who produced the first English translation of the *Divine Principle*, the basic scripture of the church revealed through Moon. During its early years, it was the subject of one major sociological study, and Mr. Moon was proclaimed a voice for the New Age by Spiritualist medium Arthur Ford.

The Reverend Moon was born in a Presbyterian family in what is now North Korea in 1920. At the age of 16, he had a vision of Jesus in which he was told to carry out Jesus' unfinished task. This vision occurred and was nurtured at a time when Korean Pentecostal Christians were predicting a Korean messiah. In 1944, Moon began to collect a following and, in 1946, founded the Broad Sea Church. He also spent six months at Israel Soodo Won (Israel Monastery), established by Paik Moon Kim, a self-proclaimed messiah, and changed his name from Yong Myung Moon to Sun Myung Moon (meaning shining sun and moon). From 1946 to 1950, Moon was in a prison, in part for his anti-Communist activities, and, in 1950, became a refugee. He settled in Pusan and founded the Unification Church in 1954.

The new church grew slowly. By 1957, a Korean edition of the *Divine Principle* was in print. Missionaries were sent to Japan and had their greatest success. Meanwhile, Moon became the head of several corporations which deal in such varied products as ginseng tea and titanium. In 1972, he moved to the United States. During the early 1970s, as the church began to grow, a variety of buildings were purchased to house its expanding program. Facilities for the Unification Church Seminary were acquired near Barrytown, New York and an estate, used both for training sessions and as a residence for Moon, who had acquired a permanent resident visa, were also purchased near Tarrytown, New York. In Manhattan a headquarters building and mission center (the former New Yorker Hotel) completed its major organizational centers.

Unification Church belief is built around the three principles of Creation, Fall, and Restoration. The

Principle of Creation asserts that God created the world and by that act became known. The world, reflective of God, has two expressions as Sung Sang (inner, invisible, feminine) and Hyung Sang (outer, visible, masculine). God created the world out of his inner nature, his heart, his impulse to love, and to be united in love. The purpose of creation is to experience the joy that comes in loving.

The Principle of the Fall begins with Adam and Eve's lack of realization of God's purpose. They fell away from God because of their adultery (a misuse of love), and their resultant inability to create a perfect family. Their failure placed Satan in control of the world. Since that time God has been trying to restore his primal intention and replace the rule of Satan.

The Principle of Restoration outlines the condition for restoration to occur. God will honor human freedom but must deal honestly with sin. Hence a Messiah is necessary. The Messiah must meet a variety of qualifications. He must be fully human. He must conquer sin and manifest God's masculine nature. He must marry a woman who will manifest God's feminine nature. Jesus accomplished only half of the task since he never married. Jesus accomplished only the spiritual salvation of humankind.

Rev. Moon has come to fill the conditions of the Lord of the Second Advent. In 1960 he married Han Ja Han, and she has had twelve children. Moon offers a complete restoration. Individuals participate in the restoration through their alignment with the Messiah. The alignment begins in a period of sacrificial work and personal celibacy. At the end of that period, church members are matched with a suitable mate and married in a public ceremony conducted by Rev. Moon and his wife. The events surrounding the marriage are the primary rituals in the life of the church. Following their matchings, members participate in a wine ceremony (analogous to Christian communion) and begin a period of engagement. Couples are married in large mass ceremonies, the most recent having been in 1983 (in New York City and Seoul, Korea). After the wedding, couples separate for a period of no less than forty days before the union is consummated. The so-called three-days ritual during which the consummation occurs, ritually dramatizes the restoration.

The Unification Church is headed by Rev. Moon who has complete authority. The church is administered by the Board of Trustees, most of whom reside in America. The board appoints the national president for each country or region. Moishe Durst is the current president of the American church. To carry out the Messiah's program for restoration and bring forth the kingdom of God, the church has created a variety of programs of evangelistic, political, cultural, charitable, and religious programs. The large number of these programs (literally in the hundreds), and their frequently ephemeral nature, have led many to accuse the church of merely establishing a host of "front groups."

Evangelistic programs include the Collegiate Association for the Research of Principles (referring to the church's basic principles), a prime recruiting structure on the nation's campuses. Church centers around the United States reach out through the Home Church program. The church's political program finds expression in an intense anti-Communism. One reason Korea is identified as the land in which the New Lord will appear is that it is on God's front line as well as Satan's front line. The 38th parallel is called the confrontation line between Communism and democracy. The major expression of the anti-Communist program in the 1970s, the Freedom Leadership Foundation, has been replaced largely by CAUSA, which has found great success in Latin America.

The cultural program was reorganized in 1982 under the International Cultural Foundation, the most important aspects being the International Conference on the Unity of the Sciences (the church's single most successful program) which has annually brought scientists together to discuss the convergence of science, morals, and values. Growing out of the Conference has been the Professors World Peace Academy and the Washington Institute for Values in Public Policy. Like the cultural activities, the ecumenical religious programs have been reorganized under the International Religious Foundation. The prime charitable activities, finding their greatest response in the urban minority communities, are Project Volunteer and the National Council for the Church and Social Change.

The church grew very slowly until 1972. By 1976 it had grown from a few hundred to approximately 6,000 members. It also began a worldwide expansion that has seen church centers opened in many countries on every continent. In the United States and western Europe, the church became an object of controversy and public hostility, and suffered much internal tension because of unrealized expectations experienced by many members, especially by many couples following the last mass wedding. Church membership in the United States dropped below 5,000 by the end of the decade and continued to decline. During the early 1980s, centers were established in every state; most, however, remain small.

Membership: In the mid-1980s the church had less than 5,000 members in the United States. Worldwide membership was in the tens of thousands.

Educational facilities: Unification Theological Seminary, Barrytown, New York.

Periodicals: *Today's World*, 481 8th Ave., New York, NY 10001; *Unification News*, 4 W. 43rd St., New York, NY 10036.

Remarks: Alarmed by the growth of the Unification Church in the early 1970s, opponents have organized and carried on a steady program of opposition that has succeeded in making the church an object of continued controversy. By the 1970s the church had become the prime reference for the popular derisive term "cult." Attacks have been launched from a variety of sources. These attacks culminated in the conviction of Moon for tax evasion. For details on other controversies the church has been involved in, please refer to the volumes listed below as well as other titles covering the church and/or contemporary cult controversies.

Sources: *Divine Principle.* New York: Holy Spirit Association for the Unification for World Christianity, 1973; *Outline of the Principle, Level 4.* New York; Holy Spirit Association for the Unification of World Christianity, 1980; Mose Durst, *To Bigotry, No Sanction.* Chicago: Regnery Gateway, 1984; Eileen Barker, *The Making of a Moonie.* Oxford: Basil Blackwell, 1984; David G. Bromley and Anson D. Shupe, Jr., *"Moonies' in America.* Beverly Hills, CA: Sage Publications, 1979.

★924★
HOMEBRINGING MISSION OF JESUS CHRIST
% Charlotte E. Suprenant
Box 13
Pelham, NH 03076

The Homebringing Mission of Jesus Christ emerged from the activity of Gabriele Wittek, a German prophetess, who has since 1975 been the instrument for two spirit entities identified as Jesus Christ and as the Cherub of Divine Wisdom, Brother Emmanuel. Wittek was born in the 1930s near Augsburg, West Germany, and raised a Roman Catholic. After World War II, she married and moved to Wurzburg. By this time she had rejected the religion of her childhood. The first anniversary of her mother's death, November 11, 1970, became a crucial turning point in her life. She saw her mother's spirit and was convinced of life after death. She began to attend meetings with a medium through whom the spirit of Christ spoke. The spirit of Christ told her of a great mission to which she had been called.

During the Christmas holidays of 1974, Wittek was contacted by an inner spiritual teacher, Brother Emmanuel, and in January, 1975, by Jesus Christ. Several months later, for the first time, Christ spoke through her in the presence of a group of people. Wittek soon began to speak before a small group in Nuremberg and before the year was out held the first public gathering. The first Christ-cell, as groups that receive and study the teachings are called, was formed in Munich. During these first months of the mission, a process of growth was established. Advertisements were placed in newspapers and magazines, and literature explaining the mission and containing the messages received through Wittek was circulated free of charge.

The work of the mission is to bring the messages revealed by Jesus Christ and His servants through the prophetess, Wittek, to the world. The connection with God that allows the revelation is the "Inner Word," God's language of light that a few purified souls are able to perceive in their mother tongue. The mission, in publishing the material, provides a course of instruction for all who wish to practice contemplation within their inner self, to the end that they may be brought home by Jesus Christ after the temporal body has passed away.

The mission is founded upon four pillars. First, the revelations through Wittek and others provide, in concentrated form, the deeper spiritual knowledge (largely lost in the West) that has been the sole possession of a few initiated persons. The revelations describe a spiritual path that leads the pilgrim on a path of unfoldment. Second, the mission meetings represent the Inner Spirit-of-Christ Church, not founded upon statutes, dogmas, creeds, rituals, or priests. At these gatherings, all people may be instructed directly by Christ through the Inner Word. Third, the seeker may receive instruction in meditation from the Prayer-Healing-Meditation Center. Fourth, upon completing the courses from the Meditation Center, the student may begin the sevenfold path of soul evolution under the direct guidance of Jesus Christ. The mission's primary goal is to make available once again the completely Christian-mystical path to the Godhead to all who sincerely strive for God.

The Homebringing Mission has been quick to translate the revelations into English, and by the early 1980s advertisements began to appear in American periodicals informing the public of its existence. Most materials are distributed free of charge, though donations are accepted for larger booklets and cassette tapes. The mission has had a significant response and experienced a steady growth.

Membership: By 1984 communities of the Inner Spirit of Christ Church had been formed in New York City; New Haven, Conn.; Boston, Mass.; and Denver, Colorado. An unreported number across North America receive church material.

Sources: *The Divine Mystical Method of Instruction in the Homebringing Mission of Jesus Christ.* Pelham, NH: Homebringing Mission of Jesus Christ, 1980; *A Former Spiritually Unknown Person on the Path to God, the Course of Life of the Prophetess in the Homebringing Mission of Jesus Christ.* Pelham, NH: Homebringing Mission of Jesus Christ, 1980; Gabriele Wittek, *In Harmony with the Absolute Spirit, the Source of All Life.* 1983.

★925★
HUNA RESEARCH ASSOCIATES
126 Camillia Drive
Cape Girardeau, MO 63701

The religion of Hawaii prior to the coming of the white man in great numbers was a magical polytheism. There were four main deities; Kane, the creator; Lono, the fertility god; Ku, the war god; and Kanaloa, the god of the sea and death. They headed a large pantheon, or assembly of gods. *Mana*, power, was the basic idea that tied the religion together. Mana was the object of ritual. It could be stored and used. The mana in certain places was protected by *kapu*, or taboo. Kapu prevents mana from harming anyone.

The main religious functionary of the Hawaiian religion was the priest, called a kahuna. The word "kahuna" also was used to designate the rituals which went with religion. Heavy Kahuna was an ancient ritual which included human sacrifice. It was replaced with light kahuna, simply ritual and chants, after white people came to Hawaii. The centers of the ancient religion were the *heiaus*, open areas in which ritual and sacrifices were practiced.

In 1819, the old religion was overthrown when Queen Keopuolani broke kapu by eating with her son, Kauikeaouli. Liholiho, her son who was king, joined them and in the months that followed put down the defenders of the ancient faith and destroyed many of the heiaus.

In spite of the destruction of the religion, the beliefs, particularly that of mana (power), persisted. Mana was associated with healing, and healing became the main thrust of the surviving huna tradition. In the early 1920s, the only active heiau in the Islands was a healing heiau operated by Sam Lono on the back side of Oahu. For many years, David Bray, Sr. was the main practitioner of huna. His son now carries on the work. At Kapua, Kauai, Margaret Kupihea is a famous kahuna, and in Hawaii, Charlie Kenn is another famous kahuna. In recent years, there has been a growing interest in huna religion on the mainland.

The great student of Hawaiian religion in the twentieth century was Max Freedom Long. Long went to Hawaii in 1917 as a teacher. While there, he became fascinated with the (secret) huna practices which had survived since 1819, when the Hawaiian queen and her family destroyed many traditional religious practices, as discussed in the preceding paragraphs. He probed unsuccessfully until 1931, when he left the Islands. Four years later, he awakened in the middle of the night with the clue that allowed him to discover and probe the world of huna. The secret lay in the double meaning of several Hawaiian words. Subsequently, he published his findings and solicited help. In a letter from William Reginald Steward, he discovered that the Berber tribesmen of North Africa used the same word (with dialect shifts) in the same way, for their magic.

According to Long, huna is magic. It involves the superconscious (*aumakua*), which uses mana (power), which is transmitted through a fine substance called *aka*, "shadowy body stuff." This material was published in detail in *The Secret Science Behind Miracles* in 1948. Response to the second book led directly to the founding of Huna Research, Inc. around 1950. The membership, Huna Research Associates, was scattered across North America, England and Australia. The basic task was to explore the possibility of using huna magic. As Huna Research, Inc. continued, other books were published, covering the practical use of huna magic, exploration of the relation of huna to Christianity, psychical research and hypnotism. It was Long's belief that huna had been worked into the New Testament.

Long died in 1971, and was succeeded by Dr. E. Otha Wingo. The Max Freedom Long Library and Museum has been established in Fort Worth, Texas. Affiliated groups can be found in 20 countries.

Membership: In 1984 Huna Research, Inc. reported 11,000 members in 30 centers with 65 ministers. There were an additional 4,000 members worldwide.

Periodicals: *The Huna Work*, Huna Research, Inc., 126 Camillia Dr., Cape Girardeau, MO 63701.

Sources: Max Freedom Long, *The Secret Science Behind Miracles*. Vista, CA: Huna Research Publications, 1954; Max Freedom Long, *The Secret Science at Work*. Vista, CA: Huna Research Publications, 1953; Max Freedom Long, *Recovering the Ancient Magic*. Cape Girardeau, MO: Huna Press, 1978; Max Freedom Long, *Introduction to Huna*. Sedona, AZ: Esoteric Publications, 1975; E. Otha Wingo, *The Story of the Huna Work*. Cape Girardeau, MO: Huna Research, Inc., 1981; Enid Hoffman, *Huna, A Beginner's Guide*. Rockport, MA: Para Research, 1976.

★926★
INNER LIGHT FOUNDATION
Box 761
Novato, CA 94948

The Inner Light Foundation was founded in the 1960s by psychic Betty Bethards of Novato, California, with the objective of developing in all people a conscious awareness of God through knowledge and use of ESP. It is Ms. Bethards' belief that within each individual are extrasensory faculties, the development of which can lead to the greater brotherhood of man. The Foundation teaches a technique of concentration and meditation called "The Way to Awareness," given to Ms. Bethards by Uvalla, her spirit-guide and a former Peruvian Indian. This process of quieting allows for inner awareness, psychic development and the emergence of channeling abilities.

The Foundation has grown steadily and, by 1972, was holding regular meetings in the San Francisco Bay area at Ignacio, San Francisco and Oakland. Meditation groups are also scattered throughout the area. Ms. Bethards remains a popular lecturer and has written several books presenting the Foundation's teachings.

Membership: Not reported.

Sources: Betty Bethards, *The Sacred Sword*. Novato, CA; The Inner Light Foundation, 1972; Betty Bethards, *There Is No Death*. Novato, CA: Inner Light Foundation, 1975; Betty Bethards, *Sex and Psychic Energy*. Novato, CA: Inner Light Foundation, 1977.

★927★
INNER PEACE MOVEMENT
Box 4897
Washington, DC 20008

Francisco Coll had been a student of the psychic and spiritual. In the early 1960s, he became involved with the ecumenical church-psychic group, Spiritual Frontiers Fellowship, and began to develop his own psychic potentials. In 1964, he established the Inner Peace Movement (IPM) to help people develop their abilities by awakening the potentials of the inner man. IPM was founded in Washington, D.C., but headquarters were established in Osceola, Iowa, a suburb of Des Moines. As the program developed, lectures, workshops, small groups and personal (psychic) counseling became integral to the program.

The basic perspective of IPM is contained in Coll's book, *Discovering Your True Identity*, the text for the IPM orientation course. Individuals are taught to confront their self-images mages and to see their uniqueness. Human beings are seen as essentially spirit-electromagnetic energy, who create by thought or energy. Their basic purpose is self-realization, awareness or growth. The spirit directs the body. The material world, including the body, is present to aid the process of awareness of spiritual growth. The unaware person is separated from his true self. By gaining self-respect, and through the techniques of self-awareness, a oneness of the self is achieved.

In 1972, headquarters of IPM moved to Washington, D.C. IPM is governed by a sixty-seven-person board which meets annually. Coll is the president. Among the several subsidiary organizations are the American Leadership College and the International Brotherhood of Spiritual Movements. The latter orga nization is made up of leaders who head local organizations of IPM groups.

Membership: In 1984 IPM reported 60,000 members in the United States and an additional 20,000 in 21 foreign countries.

Periodicals: *Expression*, Box 4897, Washington, DC 20008.

Sources: Francisco Coll, *Discovering Your True Identity*. Osceola, IA: American Leadership College, 1968; Francisco Coll, *Discovering Your True Identity Leadership Training Manual*. Osceola, IA: American Leadership College, 1972.

★928★
INSTITUTE OF COSMIC WISDOM
3528 Franciscan Lane
Las Vegas, NV 89121

The Institute of Cosmic Wisdom was founded by the Reverend Clark Wilkerson. It combines New Thought metaphysics with the magical religion of the huna. Wilkerson began as a metaphysician, and the main class offered students of Cosmic Wisdom was in "Mental Expansion." Wilkerson's teachings differ from those of most metaphysicians in his emphasis on the use of the mind to gain control of not only the self but others. He also believes that mastery of metaphysics comes in the deep meditative or hypnotic state.

In the early 1950s Wilkerson began to emphasize Hawaiian huna (the ancient magical practices of Hawaii) as an occult science which leads to success and happiness with less effort. The course emphasizes concentration and entering into the meditative silence as well as adjusting the mind to open concepts. Exercises are offered in how to enter the silence and use this ability.

Members of the Institute are drawn primarily through advertisements, mostly in psychic periodicals. Most students begin with correspondence courses in metaphysics or huna. Classes taught by Wilkerson are held periodically. Students who have completed the courses become the core of continuing members. An Inner Circle of ordained ministers constitutes the leadership.

Membership: Not reported.

Sources: Clark Wilkerson, *Hawaiian Magic*. Playa Del Rey, CA: Institute of Cosmic Wisdom, 1968; Clark L. Wilkerson, *Celestial Wisdom*. Gardena, CA: Institute of Cosmic Wisdom, 1965.

★929★
INSTITUTE OF MENTALPHYSICS
59700 - 29 Palms Hwy.
Box 640
Yucca Valley, CA 92284

The Institute of Mentalphysics was founded in 1927 in Los Angeles by Edwin John Dingle (1881-1972). A correspondent and explorer in early life, he seems to have been one of the few American metaphysical teachers actually to have spent time in Tibet. His birth in England coincided with the death of a lama of whom Dingle was said to be the reincarnation. According to Dingle, Tibet existed as the depository of the ancient Aryan wisdom. The Aryans, a white people who lived in Siberia some 60,000 years ago, spread and became the source of Indian, Mediterranean and Anglo-Saxon culture. The Aryans are responsible for the Vedas, a Greek philosophy and modern science. In India, the caste system was instituted to keep them racially pure, but the system failed and the ancient wisdom was taken to Tibet. The Mongolians were to preserve the white man's own wisdom.

Once in Tibet, Dingle described his meeting with a master who helped him recall his memory (i.e., of previous incarnations). He was taught proper breathing and the remaining disciplines, which became the basis of mentalphysics. In 1921, Dingle retired to Oakland, California. In 1927 he gave a series of lectures in New York City. Some who attended asked that he give a class on the wisdom he had learned in the East. That class is viewed as the beginning of the institute and of the new career of Ding Le Mei (Dingle's religious name). The institute was incorporated in 1934.

The teachings of mentalphysics combine New Thought metaphysics, breathing exercises, diet control and exercises, and meditation. New students are introduced to the universal laws of the creator which, if followed, will lead to mastery of oneself and all of life. Proper breathing is a key; it is the means of extracting prana, the energy of life, from the air. A strict vegetarian diet is followed. The healthy body prepares one to have a perfect mind.

Mentalphysics teaches that just as there is prana, life energy, there is a mind-substance, a subtle form of energy. It is universally distributed and is what the soul uses to think with. Using the mind-substance, as activated through breathing, one is able to activate the creative powers within. The student is also instructed in meditation, which leads toward a mystic view of the universe.

Basic mentalphysics is taught in a series of twenty-six lessons available through correspondence--the "Initiate Group Course." Beyond this basic course are a wide range of advanced lessons. Headquarters of the Institute is located at the 25-building complex at Yucca Valley, California. Sunday services are held there at the First Sanctuary of Mystic Christianity. The Institute's Teaching and Spiritual Center is also located there. It is used for the Meditation Center and the Preceptory of Light. Rev. Donald L. Waldrop succeeded Dingle as president and chancellor. The organization is headed by a board of trustees.

Membership: In 1984 the institute reported that it had enrolled over 216,000 members in the United States and had an additional 1,000 members in foreign countries (Iceland, India, Spain, Trinidad, and Equador). There were 25 ministers and 6 centers.

Periodicals: *Light of the Logos*, 59700 - 29 Palms Highway, Box 640, Yucca Valley, CA 92284.

Sources: Edwin J. Dingle, *Borderlands of Eternity*. Los Angeles: Institute of Mentalphysics, 1939; Edwin John Dingle, *The Voice of the Logos*. Los Angeles: Institute of Mentalphysics, 1950; Edwin J. Dingle, *Breathing Your Way to Youth*. Los Angeles: Institute of Mentalphysics, [1931].

★930★
INTERNATIONAL CHURCH OF SPIRITUAL VISION, INC. (WESTERN PRAYER WARRIORS)
Current address not obtained for this edition.

The International Church of Spiritual Vision, Inc., was formed by Dallas Turner who as Nevada Slim became a country-music star in the 1960s. In 1959, he received the Pentecostal "baptism of the Holy Spirit" and spoke in tongues, in an actual foreign language. A long-time student of psychical metaphysics, numerology and hypnotism, Turner has built an eclectic system of belief which combines elements of the psychic, Pentecostalism and Sacred Name Adventism in a blend called Aquarian Metaphysics.

The essence of the church's beliefs are included in the Yahwist Creed: "I believe in Yahweh the Father Almighty, creator of all things. And in Yahoshua--whom the world knows as Jesus Christ--Yahweh's only begotten Son our Savior; who was conceived by the Holy Ghost, born of the blessed virgin, suffered under Pontius Pilate, was crucified, died and was buried. He descended into hell; preached to the spirits in prison. The third day He arose from the physical dead. He ascended into the World of Spirit, sits at the right hand of Yahweh the Father Almighty; from there He shall come to judge the living and the so-called dead. I beleive the original message of our Saviour and Wayshower. I accept the Scriptural and Metaphysical Truths of all religions. I give no place to the devil. I believe that Yahweh is the only power that exists. I believe in the Holy Ghost, the nine gifts of the Spirit, the communion of believers, the resurrection of the spiritual body, and life everlasting. Amen." Members relate to the church through the mail. Turner solicits the prayer concerns from members and sends blessed cloths (Acts 19:12) and includes absent members in metaphysical healing prayers. He also offers lessons in Aquarian Metaphysics.

Membership: Not reported.

★931★
LORIAN ASSOCIATION
Box 147
Middleton, WI 53562

The Lorian is an association of people dedicated to the vision of the New Age, defined as the spirit of wholeness upon the earth. Members have discerned that humanity is striving for a new level of completeness expressed in a new sense of partnership with creation, the emergence of a wholistic spirit within individuals and a new covenant between God and the godliness in each person.

The catalyst for the formation of the Lorian Association was the return of David Spangler (b. 1945) to the United

States in 1973 after three years as the co-director of the Findhorn Community in northern Scotland, a new age community founded by Peter Caddy, his wife, Eileen Caddy and Dorothy McLean. Along with the Universal Link, Findhorn has been one of the most important groups fostering the larger New Age Movement. Spangler led in the founding of the Association soon after his arrival in America. Over the next few years, he authored several books which for many people provided the definitive statements of the New Age vision.

The beliefs of the association are summarized in their fifteen-part "Statement of Interdependence" which commits members to a dedication to sacred, cooperative decision making, the process of growth, one world, harmless interaction with the environment, the building of a planetary village, conservation and wise use of energy, diversity in cultural expressions, an open social order, and the communication with and learning from preaterhuman intelligences who also inhabit earth. Since the 1960s Spangler has been in contact with a spiritual entity named "John," and he views much of his literary production as a synthesis of John's insight and his words.

Headquarters of the association are near Madison, Wisconsin. An active program built around educational events for the public, publication of new age literature, encouragement of music and the arts and networking with people who share one or more common concerns. The Association is made up of a small and dedicated community and encourages the development of likeminded groups over the growth of the association.

Membership: Not reported. There are less than a hundred full members of Lorian, but there are many associate members who support its work and regularly receive its publications.

Periodicals: *Lorian Journal*, Box 147, Middleton, WI 53562.

Sources: David Spangler, ed., *Conversations with John*. Elgin, IL: Lorian Press, 1980; David Spangler, *Festivals in the New Age*. Forres, Moray, Scotland: Findhorn Publications, 1975; David Spangler, *Reflections on the Christ*. Forres, Moray, Scotland: Findhorn Publications, 1977; David Spangler, *Revelation, the Birth of a New Age*. San Francisco: The Rainbow Bridge, 1976; David Spangler, *Towards a Planetary Vision*. Forres, Scotland: Findhorn Foundation, 1977.

★932★
LOVE PROJECT
Box 7601
San Diego, CA 92107

The Love Project, headed by Arleen Lorrance and Diana K. Pike, is an outgrowth of the Foundation of Religious Transition, formed originally in 1969 by Episcopal Bishop James A. Pike and Diane, his wife. The formation of the

Foundation came after Pike's well-publicized problems throughout the 1960s with a traditional statement on Christian doctrine, his trial for heresy, his re-marriage and his involvement in the psychic. Bishop Pike's main doctrinal disagreements with orthodox Christianity centered on the doctrine of the Trinity and the inerrancy of the Bible. In the spring of 1969, the Pikes decided to leave the institutional church and begin a ministry to other "church alumni and those on the ,inside edge' of the church." The Foundation's program was multi-faceted, with major themes in such diverse areas as social activism, parapsychology, clergy-training and the study of Christian origins.

The death of Bishop Pike in September, 1969, less than a year after the formation of the Foundation, necessitated a reorientation. The name was changed to the Bishop Pike Foundation, but during the next two years it became increasingly clear that, without the bishop, the specific missions of the Foundation were not materializing. In 1972, the Foundation was merged into a structure already being formed by Arleen Lorrance, the Love Project. The Love Project grew out of a teacher-student experience of sharing which turned a violence-ridden ghetto into a center of love, concern and positive action after the 1970-71 school year. This experience led to a realization zation of the distinction between inspiring people with a story and facilitating the emergence of love. As the Love Project matured, it was conceived as an active process of creating love.

The Love Project is an alternative to negative, destructive, violent living and a way in which all seekers of such alternatives may link energies in a universal chain of caring--a chain forged with the strength of the uniqueness of each individual. The way of the seeker is to make his very life an alternative, that of being changed rather than seeking to "make it." The Love Project has various structures--workshops, group travel experiences, and training people in love. The very nature of the Love Project keeps seekers on the move, though headquarters are kept in San Diego.

Membership: Not reported.

Periodicals: *The Seeker Newsletter*, Box 7601, San Diego, CA 92007.

Sources: Arleen Lorrance, *The Love Project*. San Diego, CA: LP Publications, 1972; Diane Kennedy Pike, *Cosmic Unfoldment*. San Diego, CA: LP Publications, 1976.

★933★
NEW AGE CHURCH OF TRUTH
Star Route 2
Box CLC
Deming, NM 88030

Gilbert N. Holloway (b.1915) began his career as a lecturer and metaphysical teacher in the 1930s. He became aware, as a result of studies in Rosicrucianism and Theosophy, that he had psychic powers. In the 1960s, he became prominent as a psychic on radio and television, and large audiences flocked to hear his lectures and to obtain readings (the statements he uttered while in a psychic state). In 1967, he received a Pentecostal experience and spoke in tongues. In the mid-1960s Holloway had begun to establish a community and center in Deming, New Mexico. After his conversion, this center became the Christ Light Community.

Since 1967, Holloway and his wife, June Holloway, who specializes in healing work, have continued to travel, lecture and give psychic demonstrations. They have also built the Deming community into a New Age Center. There is a free movement in the programming between Pentecostal and psychic categories. Holloway has written books and booklets and publishes a monthly newsletter for members and friends of the church. He is particularly adept at prophecy; predictions of future events compose much of the content of his publications.

Membership: Not reported.

Periodicals: *Newsletter*, Star Route 2, Box CLC, Deming, NM 80030.

Sources: Gilbert Holloway, *E.S.P. and Your Super-Conscious*. Louisville, KY: Best Books, Inc., 1966; Gilbert N. Holloway, *Seven Prophetic Years*. Deming, NM: New Age Truth Publications, 1969; Gilbert N. Holloway, *New Ways of Unfoldment*. Deming, NM: New Age Truth Publications, n.d.

★934★
NEW AGE SAMARITAN CHURCH
Current address not obtained for this edition.

The New Age Samaritan Church was incorporated in 1961 by the Reverend Ruth McWilliams of Everett, Washington. The doctrine is eclectic, a combination of material from the New Testament, New Thought, metaphysical beliefs, Theosophy, Zen and Spiritualism. The church espouses no system of beliefs, but professes to help its students and members to discover for themselves the spiritual laws. Its goals include helping the poor in body and spirit, relieving the suffering in the world, eliminating prejudice and teaching the interrelation of all creatures. It practices the various psychic arts, including "treasure mapping" as a means to achieving your heart's desire. This involves visualizing what you want and how to get it.

Membership: Not reported. In 1967 there were 4 study groups and students engaged in correspondence across the United States. Attempts at contact have not been successful for several years and the present status of the church is unknown.

★935★
NEW PSYCHIANA
% Psychiana Study Group
4069 Stephens St.
San Diego, CA 92103

The New Psychiana was formed in 1967 by Jack E. Gardner of San Diego, California. Gardner was an early student of Frank B. Robinson, the founder of Psychiana, a popular New Thought group which had its greatest growth in the 1930s and 1940s. Gardner completed both the regular and advanced courses. Gardner has accepted the role of the student who would arise to continue Robinson's work following his death in 1948. In the years since Robinson's death, the whole field of ESP has emerged, and Gardner has added teachings on conscious evolution to Psychiana to bring it up to date.

Conscious evolution is the "divine cybernetics to spiritual growth." It teaches techniques of becoming fully aware of the powerful God-presence within you. By learning to control this power, one can heal bodily and spiritual wounds, bring peace and break free from poverty and defeat.

Membership: Not reported.

★936★
THE ONLY FAIR RELIGION
Current address not obtained for this edition.

The Only Fair Religion was founded by Saint Kenny and a group of his followers. Neither the identity of Saint Kenny, not any of his group, is disclosed in the literature. The group teaches modern reincarnationism. The universe is in constant flux, governed by natural laws. Souls progress through lower life-forms to higher ones. When a being evolves to a point of gaining a sense of awareness, it simultaneously acquires an immortal soul. It then moves through a series of incarnations which are necessary for its development. It eventually evolves to become a planetary ruling spirit. The system is the "Only Fair Religion" because it assures a balance of woe and happiness, explains evil and assures eventual salvation for all.

New groups form for the discussion of issues in light of modern reincarnationism. Members seek to unite in their concept of God and in their concern for justice, and true communion results. Telepathy and psychic phenomena will often occur during this process.

Membership: Not reported. In 1972, the "Only Fair Religion" claimed 10,000 members in Southern California, a figure based on the number of people successfully qualified to be group leaders.

★937★
PEOPLE'S TEMPLE CHRISTIAN (DISCIPLES) CHURCH
(Defunct)

The People's Temple Christian (Disciples) Church was formed in 1955 in Indianapolis by the Rev. Jim Jones. (Though formally a member congregation in the Christian Church (Disciples of Christ), the People's Temple, in the 1970s, developed beliefs and practices that were very much different than those of its parent body.) Jones emerged in the 1960s as a charismatic leader who cared for the poor and the black people of the city and preached a message of equality, brotherhood and socialism.

In 1965, a year after being ordained in the Christian Church (Disciples of Christ) he migrated with his following to Ukiah, California. From there the People's Church became a communal group modeled on the Peace Mission of Father Divine, whom Jones had known and revered. Though white himself, Jones gathered a largely black following who came to view him as a prophet and miracle worker. By 1972 Jones claimed that over forty people had been raised from the dead. Church services featured psychic readings and healings by Jones, spirited singing, testimonies and sermons. A wide range of social services was supported.

By 1972 congregations flourished in San Francisco, Los Angeles, and Indianapolis and followers were to be found in cities around the United States. That same year Jones leased land in Guyana which became a farming community, Jonestown. Jones became a prominent, controversial, but powerful figure in the California religious community, but also became an object of government investigation because of reports of violence directed toward ex-members and abuse of children under his care. Coincidental with the publication of several major media reports on the church and with the filing of several lawsuits, Jones moved with many of his members to Guyana.

By 1977 when Jones moved to Guyana, Jonestown had swelled to a thousand residents. This town was the scene, in 1978, of the murder of Congressman Leo J. Ryan and several of his party, who came to Jonestown to investigate the charges which had been brought against it. Immediately following Ryan's murder was the mass suicide/murder of over 900 of the town's residents, including Jones. In 1978 the church was formally disbanded by the remaining members in California.

In the years since the deaths in Guyana, the People's Temple and its leader have become symbols of the possibilities inherent in religious groups and have frequently been invoked as the end result of cultic practice. As most of the papers assembled for the investigation of Congressman Ryan's death have remained unpublished, the likelihood of substantive future revelations about Jones, the temple, and the deaths in Guyana remains high.

★938★
PROCESS CHURCH OF THE FINAL JUDGMENT
(Defunct)

The Process Church dates to 1963, when a group began to gather around the charismatic Robert de Grimston, then a resident of London. The group was primarily psychologically oriented to begin with, but its search led to a spiritual quest. IN 1966, members spent several months at Xtul, Yucatan, which is viewed as a place of miracles and a shared religious experience. Those who went were welded into a closely-knit group. Over the next seven years, a theology-in-process developed, primarily through the continued revelations of de Grimston. Development was rapid; significant changes could be noted annually and with each issue of the irregularly-issued *Process*.

As the theology appeared in 1973, the central emphasis was a dualism of Christ and Satan overcome by a reconciliation expressed in the formula, "The Unity of Christ and Satan is Good News for You. If that conflict can be resolved, then yours can be too." Behind this theme was a belief in the four deities: Jehovah, Lucifer, Christ and Satan--each representative of a personality-type and a spiritual path. All doctrine was set within the context of a Biblical apocalypticism.

To perpetuate the teaching, a strong hierarchical organization was established. Topping the hierarchy with de Grimston was a twelve-member Council of Masters. Ministers were called messengers. Initiated lay members were disciples, and joined the ranks of the Inside Processeans, as opposed to the Outside Processeans who lived according to process teaching without initiation. Inside Processeans dressed in the black uniform and wore the cross with a snake entwined upon it.

The Process Church was delt a fatal blow in 1974 when the majority of the Council of Masters rejected de Grimston's prophetic leadership (particualrly his emphasis on Satanic themes) and reorganized as the Foundation Church of the Millennium (now the Foundation Faith of God). Most of the members, including de Grimston's wife, aligned themselves with the new church.

The Process Church did not die completely with the schism. de Grimston reorganized the Process in a loose fashion and attempted to gather the remnant of followers into a very loose organization. He sent an open letter to his followers from his new home in New Orleans, encouraging them to form local autonomous groups around his teachings. Chapters formed in Boston and Toronto and smaller groups in Chicago, New Orleans, New York City, San Francisco, and London, England. A periodical, *The Process*, was published from the Boston headquarters. After several years in which it became evident that the organization could not be rebuilt, de Grimston returned to England and obscurity and all sign of the Process disappeared before the end of the decade.

Sources: *Facts and Figures, Some Questions and Answers about the Process Church.* Chicago: The Process Church, 1973; *Assemblies and Hymns.* N.p.: Process Church of the Final Judgment, n.d.; Robert de Grimston, *Exit.* Letchworth, Herts., England: Garden City Press, 1968; Robert de Grimston, *The Gods and Their People.* Chicago: Process Church of the Final Judgment, 1970; William Sims Bainbridge, *Satan's Power.* Berkeley: University of California Press, 1978.

★939★
QUIMBY CENTER
Box 453
Alamogordo, NM 88310

The Quimby Center dates to 1946 when its founder, Dr. Neva Dell Hunter (d. 1978), began working in the field of ESP. Though part of her spiritual work assignment from the beginning, the Center did not materialize until 1966 in Alamogordo, New Mexico. The purpose of the Center, besides being a vehicle of Dr. Hunter's continued work, was fourfold: to promote the fatherhood of God and the brotherhood of man, to promote spiritual understanding among men, to provide education by holding classes and to provide facilities for the general public. Like its namesake, Phineas P. Quimby, the founder of New Thought, the Center teaches that man is a direct expression of God. By applying metaphysical teachings, man can gain self-mastery.

Man lives within a universe governed by spiritual laws. These impersonal cosmic laws hold man responsible for every choice. Through the cycle of reincarnation, man becomes aware of the nature of life, assumes his responsibility and becomes attuned to the oneness of life. He realizes that there is life on other planets. He realizes that the present upheavals are preparation for movement into the Aquarian Age.

The Center programs stress workshops, seminars and lectures. A large library is maintained, and books, records and tapes are available to members on loan. One of the unique practices of the Center is a form of spiritual healing called "aura balancing," in which healers work on the patient's auric emanations. (Auras are waves that bodies project.) A booklet on the work, *The Auric Mirror*, by Ellavivian Power, has been published. Dr. Hunter was a psychic with a wide reputation in the psychic community. She gave karmic live-readings and psychic counseling both at the Center and at her many lectures around the country. When in Alamogordo, she gave weekly channeled classes.

The Center is run by a president-director, a vice-president, treasurer, secretary and nine-member board. Hunter was succeeded as president by Robert D. Waterman. Members are found both in Alamogordo and scattered around the United States in small study groups. Study groups have focused on aura-balancing. An annual Memorial Day picnic is held in Michigan by the Midwestern members.

Membership: Not reported.

Periodicals: *Quimby Center Newsletter*, Box 453, Alamogordo, NM 88310.

★940★
SAVITRIA
2405 Ruscombe
Baltimore, MD 21209

Savitria, formed in 1970 by a group led by artist Robert Hieronimus, is dedicated to sowing the seeds for the Aquarian Age. The spiritual heart of Savitria is a three-and-one-half-acre estate in North Baltimore, Maryland, which houses the core communal group, the Aum Esoteric Study Center and the New Morning School. Hieronimus began with a meditation group at Johns Hopkins University. Savitria was an outgrowth of that group.

It is Savitria's belief that man is a dual being, both mental and immortal. Man's goal is to allow the immortal aspect of being to overshadow the mental. This goal is accomplished through the study of esoteric sciences, which allow man to understand the cosmic process, and meditation, which raises his consciousness without the use of drugs. The high consciousness allows the two aspects of man to work in harmony and will lead to the era of the brotherhood of man and fatherhood of God, the golden age spoken of in all ancient esoteric writings.

Hieronimus had, in the early 1970s, gained a reputation in the psychic community because of his interest in the esoteric history of the United States. He believes that the Masons and Rosicrucians had a large part in the founding of the country. Evidence of their influence is to be be found in the reverse of the Great Seal of the United States (found on the back of the one-dollar bill), which features the eye of God in the great triangle, a Rosicrucian symbol.

The Aum Esoteric Study Center is a state-approved institution and functions as a branch of the World University, founded by Howard John Zitko headquartered in Tucson, Arizona. It was formed as the first step in providing a total alternative education curriculum for all grades through college. At this point, the center has a three-year curriculum, with classes on the mystic arts, occult sciences and religion metaphysics. Certificates are offered in each area. New Morning School was formed in 1971 as a day-care/nursery school for pre-school children. In the mid-1970s, the Savitria community included approximately 15 people, who follow a strict code of conduct which includes meditation before sunrise and abstinence from drugs, extramarital sex, and wearing shoes in the house.

Membership: Not reported.

Sources: Robert Hieronimus, *The Two Great Seals of America*. Baltimore, MD: Savitriaum, 1976; Howard John Zitko, *New Age Tantra Yoga*. Tucson, AZ: World University Press, 1974.

★941★
TEACHING OF THE INNER CHRIST, INC.
% Inner Christ Administrative Center, Inc.
3009 Grape St.
San Diego, CA 92102

The Teaching of the Inner Christ, Inc. (also previously known known as the Brotherhood of Followers of the Present Jesus and the Society for the Teaching of the Inner Christ) was founded in 1965 and incorporated in 1977 as the Inner Christ Administration Center. The founders were the Reverends Ann Meyer Makeever and Peter Victor Meyer. Makeever, who is a "sensitive," claims constant contact with the master teachers, Jesus and Babaji, and with her own I AM Self. The ministers and members accept guidance from these masters and from their own I AM Selves. Counseling, in which the counselor contacts the deeper levels of the patient through the invisible teachers, and a wide range of classes in prayer therapy, inner sensitivity and Western Yoga are offered.

Headquarters of the center are in San Diego. The group supports a World Healing Ministry. There are centers and study groups in San Diego, San Francisco, Long Beach, Escondido Aptos, Berkeley, Los Altos, Orange County, Santa Monica, Saratoga and West Marin County, California; Salt Lake City, Utah; Las Vegas, Nevada; Boise, Idaho; Burlington, Vermont; Merrillville, Indiana; and Victoria, British Columbia.

Membership: In 1984 the center reported 1,200 members in 18 centers. There were 39 ministers.

Educational facilities: West Coast Ministerial Directorate, San Diego, California; Rocky Mountain Ministerial Directorate, Salt Lake City, Utah.

Periodicals: *The Double Heartline*, 3009 Grape Street, San Diego, CA 92102.

Sources: Ann Meyer, *Ann, A Biography*. San Diego, CA: T.I.C. Books, 1982; Ann Meyer and Peter Meyer, *Being a Christ!*. San Diego, CA: Dawning Publications, 1975; *God's Will*. San Diego, CA: The Brotherhood, 1968; *Jesus' Love*. San Diego, CA: The Brotherhood, 1964.

★942★
THEOCENTRIC FOUNDATION
3341 E. Cambridge Ave.
Phoenix, AZ 85008

The Theocentric Foundation was founded in 1959 in Phoenix, Arizona, but is the successor to a series of prior structures dating to the 1920s: The Shangrila Missions of Ojai, California, the Eden Foundation, the Manhattan Philosophical Center and the Theocentric Temple. The basic teachings of the Foundation are Hermetic, based on the writing of Hermes Mercurious Trismegistus. The Bible and other metaphysical books are also used.

The Theocentric Foundation teaches basic truth, the understanding of the divine self. In this understanding, the seventy-three "Gods of the walking dead," such as anger, fear, grief, domination, limitation, prejudice, etc., and the five basic questions (What am I? What is my origin? Why am I here? Where do I go? and What am I doing about it?) can be dealt with. Before man can recognize his divine origin, he must become fully human and possess attributes such as affection, discrimination, enthusiasm, justice, kindness and tenderness. These attributes lead into the attributes of pure awareness, possessed by the self-governing identity. The self-governing identity has conquered the outside forces that would dominate a person and embodies love, certainty, consideration, understanding, empathy and admiration.

The headquarters of the Theocentric Foundation are in Phoenix. It has established branch centers around the country, and classes are offered in Hermetic theology. Degrees are issued after completion of the courses. Inner-order courses of ten degrees are also offered to students.

Membership: Not reported.

Sources: Orpheus, *The Poimandres of Hermes Mercurius Trimegistus*. Phoenix, AZ: The Theocentric Foundation, 1960.

★943★
TRUE CHURCH OF CHRIST, INTERNATIONAL
Box 2, Station G
Buffalo, NY 14213

The True Church of Christ, International, was formed by Christian Weyand of Buffalo, New York. It is described as the "non-profit establishment of religion authorized by ecclesiastical authority of the True Bible Society International" (also headed by Weyand) and "the only existing Christian Church founded upon and teaching the True Complete Christian Bible and the True Complete Teachings and Scriptures of God and Christ." The church has published the True Complete Bible, which contains the Old and New Testaments translated from Aramaic; the True New Testament, containing the secret unwritten teachings of Jesus; the *Lost Books of the Bible* and the

Forgotten Books of Eden, a collection of apocryphal writings, and the *Apocrypha*.

The True Church teaches psychic development and mediumship, and that the reason why no miracles occur in today's churches is because churches limit themselves to the Old and New Testament. The True Church believes Jesus taught hypnosis, miracle power and ESP. Man's soul, his life spirit, is part of God, the great creative intelligence. Psychic powers are natural to the soul and it is through these powers that all miracles are wrought. The church believes also that the water baptism of John has been replaced with spirit baptism.

The True Church advertises widely and offers its members around the country correspondence courses in the True Scriptures, hypnotism and the psychic. The church also has formed the World Roster of Psychic Contact, a prayer group.

Membership: Not reported.

★944★
UNIVERSAL BROTHERHOOD
Box 366, Grand Central Station
New York, NY 10017

The Universal Brotherhood is an occult group headquartered in New York City and headed by the Reverend Ureal Vercilli Charles. The Order is under the guidance of the Great White Brotherhood and offers lessons on the "Seven Immutable Laws of the Universe," man's key to health, success, and happiness. These laws are the laws of gender, cause/effect, rhythm, polarity, vibration, correspondence, and mentalism. Mr. Charles runs the First Church of Spiritual Vision in New York City. Other centers of the Brotherhood are in Jamaica, New York City, and the Bronx. *Lessons from the Great Masters* is a correspondence course taken by students across the United States. The Brotherhood also publishes *Wake Up and Learn!*, a series of pamphlets by Krishnahara, a Master of the Great Lodge who dictates through Elizabeth Dean.

Membership: Not reported.

Periodicals: *The Light Beyond*, Box 366, Grand Central Station, New York, NY 10017.

★945★
URANTIA BROTHERHOOD
533 Diversey Pkwy.
Chicago, IL 60614

The Urantia Foundation was formed in 1950 in Chicago, Illinois, for the dissemination of the principles, teachings and doctrines of *The Urantia Book*, a work of 2,097 pages of material received from numerous celestial beings. The name of the person who received the content of the book has never been revealed. It represents the first major revelation since the coming of Christ. The contents "differ from all previous revelations, for they are not the work of a single-universe personality, but a composite presentation of many beings." *The Urantia Book* was first published in 1955.

The Urantia Book, one of the lengthiest of psychic revelations, is divided into four parts. Part I describes the central and super universe. Our planet, Urantia, is located in super universe Orvonton, whose capital is Uversa. Part I deals also with God as Father, Universal Spirit and Trinity, and with the plethora of spirit entities. Part II deals with our local universe, Nebadon, whose capital is Salvington. Part III is a history of Urantia. Part IV contains a biography of Jesus, including a detailed discussion of the hidden years (from age twelve to the beginning of his public ministry). According to *The Urantia Book*, Jesus was born August 21, 7 B.C., had an excellent education, became a skilled carpenter, began a Mediterranean tour in his twenty-eighth year and began his public ministry in 27 A.D. After more than three years, his ministry ended in the crucifixion and resurrection. Objectives of the Urantia Foundation are to promote the true teachings of Jesus, primarily the appreciation of the fatherhood of God and the brotherhood of Man, and to lead to the increase of the comfort, happiness and well-being of man.

Associated with the Foundation, and growing out of its publication and circulation of *The Urantia Book* is the Urantia Brotherhood, a fellowship of those people who have found truth and meaning in *The Urantia Book* and its teachings. The Brotherhood is composed of numerous local societies. Every three years the societies send delegates to the General Assembly, at which a General Council is elected. Operating under the General Assembly is the Urantia Brotherhood Corporation which handles the fiscal affairs of the Brotherhood. The societies have as their objective the protection and dissemination of the message of *The Urantia Book*. The Brotherhood emphasizes its nonsectarian nature. It holds out the possibility that members of diverse religions may be members of the Brotherhood and receive its revelation as an enrichment rather than a contradiction of their own faith. It is a free religious brotherhood.

Membership: Not reported.

Periodicals: *Urantia Brotherhood Bulletin*, 533 Diversey Pkwy., Chicago, IL 60614 ; *Urantian*, 533 Diversey Pkwy., Chicago, IL 60614.

Sources: *The Urantia Book*. Chicago: Urantia Foundation, 1955; Clyde Bedell, *Concordex of the Urantia Book*. Laguna Hills, CA: The Author, 1980; Martin W. Myers, *Unity, Not Uniformity*. Chicago: Urantia Foundation, 1973; Ruth E. Renn, *Study Aids for Part IV of the Urantia Book, The Life and Teachings of Jesus*. Chicago: Urantia Foundation, 1975.

WORLD CATALYST CHURCH
Current address not obtained for this edition.

The World Catalyst Church seeks to be a catalyst in moving from old ideas to new. The church believes that there is an inner light that is beyond ourselves in wisdom, power and scope. The church's job is to lead men from their present ignorant state to the eternal something within. Man's forward movement can be accomplished through his own efforts. Man is bound, however, by natural law and by his oneness with others. No man will enter eternal perfection until all are able to. Man is a microcosm of the macrocosm. He is reincarnated in any given dimension long enough to learn the necessary lessons. Prayer and meditation are useful tools in learning to live.

The World Catalyst Church has members around the country, drawn from those who have taken the basic correspondence study course , "That Man May Find Himself." The course also is the beginning material for any who wish to become teachers for the church. The church refuses to put money into religious edifices. There is no charity assistance of a material nature. All monies go into communities. The church was formed in 1967 at Butte, Montana by Helen Muschell (author of *Wells of Inner Space*), Margot Jones, Ese Jasper, Ernest Hanson, Ruth Adams, Beata Kamp and Matt Gleason.

Membership: Not reported.

Ancient Wisdom Family

An historical essay on this family is provided beginning on page 121.

Rosicrucianism

★947★
**ANCIENT AND MYSTICAL ORDER OF THE
 ROSAE CRUCIS**
San Jose, CA 95191

The Ancient and Mystical Order of the Rosae Crucis (AMORC) was founded in 1915 by H. Spencer Lewis (1883-1939) in New York City, as an esoteric fraternal order. Lewis was a young occultist who had been associated with the various British occult orders and who met, if briefly, Aleister Crowley. Active attempts to establish the Rosicrucian Order began in 1909. In that year, Lewis states, in Toulouse he met French members of the International Rosicrucian Council. He was initiated, returned to America and began holding meetings. In 1915, the Order was firmly established, and the massive publicity campaign, which has made this branch of the Rosicrucian the most well known to the general public, was begun.

Lewis' early affiliations with various occult groups, especially th e Ordo Templi Orientis (O.T.O), headed by Crowley for many years, is clearly reflected in his frequent inclusions of material from them in the teachings and symbolism of the AMORC. For example, the Rose Cross emblem was taken from the *Equinox* III (Crowley's periodical), and other emblems were borrowed from other issues. (Lewis was not above pure plagiarism; whole chapters of his *Mystic Life of Jesus* were taken from the *Aquarian Gospel of Jesus* by Levi Dowling.) In 1916, after the German O.T.O. split with Crowley over *The Book of the Law* it gave its recognition to the AMORC in a document Lewis proudly displayed (in spite of O.T.O.'s association with the practice of sex magic, which AMORC has never advocated). ated.

Rapid growth led to the conflict with the other Rosicrucian bodies. In 1928, shortly after the move of the AMORC to San Jose, the older Fraternitas Rosae Crucis launched an attack on Lewis, challenging the Order's right to the designation "Rosicrucian." Lewis accused R. Swinburne Clymer, a lifelong advocate of alternative healing practices, of receiving an M.D. from a diploma mill and of fraudulent behavior. An intense polemic, which at times has involved the Rosicrucian Fraternity in Oceanside, California, has continued to the present.

The teachings of the Rosicrucians center on God's purpose for life. Rosicrucians believe God created the universe according to his immutable laws. Man's success is through mastership, the ability to bring into material expression one's mental imaging. The techniques taught to students lead to mastery. For example, students are taught to "image" or imagine such things as health, wealth, and happiness, and thereby draw those things to themselves. Progress in the teaching and knowledge of the accompanying practices comes through a series of correspondence lessons mailed regularly to members. Completion of a set of lessons admits students to a higher degree in the work and makes available the next, more advanced, set of lessons. Members may also attend local centers (designated lodges, chapters or pronaoi, depending upon their strength) for group activities.

The AMORC sees itself as a continuation of the ancient mystery schools of Amenhotep IV and Solomon; listed among famous Rosicrucians are Isaac Newton , Rene Descartes, Benjamin Franklin, and Francis Bacon. The Fraternity works on one-hundred-and-eighty-year cycles, first acting in silence and secrecy and then acting in public. A new public cycle began in 1909. The Grand Lodge has jurisdiction for the Americas, the British Commonwealth, France, Germany, Switzerland, Sweden, and Africa. Head of the Order is the Grand Imperator, a post held by Ralph M. Lewis, Spencer Lewis' son, since 1939.

H. Spencer Lewis was interested in Egypt, and, through the Rosicrucian Egyptian Museum in San Jose, which he founded, made many significant contributions to Egyptology. The museum is located in Rosicrucian Park, a square block in San Jose which houses the other departments of the Order, and which has become a major tourist stop in California.

Membership: Not reported. Membership figures are not published. In 1985 the Order listed 162 chartered lodges, chapters, and pronaoi in the United States, including Puerto Rico. Members were also reported in 85 countries worldwide. More than 6,000,000 pieces of literature are mailed out annually from the San Jose headquarters. The AMORC is by far the largest Rosicrucian organization in the world.

Educational facilities: Rose-Croix University, San Jose, California.

Periodicals: *Rosicrucian Digest*, Rosicrucian Park, San Jose, CA 95191; *Rosicrucian Forum*, Rosicrucian Park, San Jose, CA 95191 (available to members only).

Sources: H. Spencer Lewis, *Rosicrucian Manual*. San Jose, CA: Rosicrucian Press, 1941; H. Spencer Lewis, *Rosicrucian Questions and Answers*. San Jose, CA: Supreme Grand Lodge of AMORC, 1969; H. Spencer Lewis, *The Mystical Life of Jesus*. San Jose, CA: Supreme Grand Lodge of AMORC, 1929.

★948★
AUSAR AUSET SOCIETY
   Oracle of Thoth, Inc.
Box 281
Bronx, NY 10462

The Ausar Auset Society is a Rosicrucian body serving the black community of the United States. It was founded in the mid-1970s by R. A. Straughn, also known by the name Ra Un Nefer Amen, formerly head of the Rosicrucian Anthroposophical League in New York City. He is the author of several occult texts in spiritual science, each offering methods drawn from the Kabbalah and eastern religions to facilitate the orderly transition to the enlightened state.

The Society has directed its program to blacks and *The Oracle of Thoth* regularly features, alongside of its occult articles, items of general interest and concern to black people. The Society advocates the appropriation of the positive accomplishments of African ancestors by the contemporary black community. The Socie ty offers free public classes in a variety of occult topics. Currently such classes are being held in New York City, Brooklyn, Chicago, Philadelphia, New Haven, Washington, DC, and Norfolk, VA.

Membership: Not reported.

Periodicals: *Oracle of Thoth*,   Oracle of Thoth, Inc., Box 281, Bronx, NY 10462.

Sources: R. A. Straughn, *The Realization of Neter Nu*. Brooklyn, NY: Maat Publishing Company, 1975; R. A. Straughn, *Meditation Techniques of the Kabalists, Vedantins and Taoists*. Bronx, NY: Maat Publishing Company, 1976; R. A. Straughn, *Black Woman's, Black Man's Guide to a Spiritual Union*. Bronx, NY: Oracle of Thoth, Inc., 1981.

★949★
FRATERNITAS ROSAE CRUCIS
Beverly Hall
Quakertown, PA 18951

This, the oldest of the several existing Rosicrucian bodies, dates to 1868 when it was founded by P. B. Randolph (1825-1875). The first lodge was established in San Francisco three years later. On three occasions, the grand lodge was closed and reestablished: first in Boston (1871), then in San Francisco (1874), and finally in Philadelphia (1895). Randolph was succeeded by Freeman B. Dowd who in turn was succeeded by Edward H. Brown (1907) and R. Swinburne Clymer (1922). Clymer was recently succeeded by his son, Emerson M. Clymer. Randolph, a physician, had for many years lectured upon issues of sexuality. The inner teachings of the order he established included a system of occult sexuality, which he termed Eulistic, a word derived from the Greek Eleusinian mysteries, which Randolph believed to be mysteries of sex. In 1874 he established a Provisional Grand Lodge of Eulis in Tennessee, but he had to dissolve it because of internal problems among the membership. Translations of Randolph's writings, disseminated through his European followers, became a source for the sex magick system developed by the Ordo Templi Orientis. As presented in the English-speaking world by Aleister Crowley, the O.T.O.'s sex magic stood in contradiction to Randolph's teachings at several points, particularly on the moral level. Randolph had advocated the practice of his teachings only by married couples. Twentieth-century followers of Randolph have denounced the O.T.O. teachings as black magick.

In the Fraternitas Rosae Crucis, the member begins his work and is taught the basic ideas of the "secret schools," which include reincarnation and karma, and the Law of Justice and the non-interference with the rights of others. He begins to learn the process of transmutation (of the base self into the finest gold) and the acquisition of health and strength by casting out thoughts of weakness and age. He is also taught to contact the hierarchies of the heavenly realm. Members believe in the fatherhood of God and the ultimate brotherhood of man. The inner circle of the Fraternity is the Aeth Priesthood, in which is taught "the highest occultism known to man." Associated with the fraternity is the Church of Illumination, an outer court group, which means it interacts with the public and from which a select few may be chosen to join the inner group. The church emphasizes the establishment of the "Manistic" Age, which began in the late nineteenth century and follows the previous Egyptian and Christian ages. Manism is the recognition of the equality of man and woman. It is also the name of the new world leader who teaches the divine law with its five fundamentals: As ye sow so shall ye reap; talents as gift and responsibility; the golden rule; honesty; and the new birth as the awakening of the Christos or divine spark within.

"Many are called but few are chosen" is a watchword with the Fraternitas Rosae Crucis, which does not advertise in the manner associated with the Ancient and Mystical Order of the Rosae Crucis (AMORC). Numerous books by R. Swinburne Clymer, who revived the all but moribund fraternity in the early twentieth century, have attracted members. Authority of the Fraternity rests with the Council of Three. The highest office is held by the Hierarch of Eulis. The Beverly Hall Corporation in Quakertown, Pennsylvania, handles the distribution of literature. Continuing the lifelong health concerns of R. Swinburne Clymer, like Randolph, a physician, are the Humanitarian Society and the Clymer Health Clinic, both located at the fraternity's headquarters complex in Quakertown.

Membership: Not reported.

Sources: R. Swinburne Clymer, *The Rosicrucian Fraternity in America.* Quakertown, PA: Rosicrucian Foundation, 1935. 2 Vols.; R. Swinburne Clymer, *The Rose Cross Order.* Allentown, PA: The Philosophical Publishing Co., 1916; Paschal Beverly Randolph, Eulis, *Affectional Alchemy.* Quakertown, PA: Confederation of Initiates, 1930; R. Swinburne Clymer, *The Rosy Cross, Its Teachings.* Quakertown, PA: Beverly Hall Corporation, 1965; R. Swinburne Clymer, *The Age of Treason.* Quakertown, PA: Humanitarian Society, 1959.

★950★
HOLY ROSICRUCIAN CHURCH
(Defunct)

The Holy Rosicrucian Church was a small shortlived Rosicrucian body known primarily through a single literary remain, a booklet, *Rosikrucianism*, published in 1915. The Church, and its associated orders were founded by a person known only as Sergius Rosenkruz and headquartered in Los Angeles. The Church and Brotherhood taught a method of liberation, the awakening to the knowledge of unity with the One. The Church advocated a series of preparatory methods which included study, twice daily baths, the practice of charitable works, the avoidance of frivolous activities, and the adoption of a variety of occult meditative techniques. The associated Order of the Knights of the Golden Circle which through rites and ceremonies prepared members for either a favorable reincarnation, or safety in the beyond.

Sources: Sergius Rosenkruz, *Rosikrucianism*. Los Angeles: The Author, 1915.

★951★
LECTORIUM ROSICRUCIANUM
Box 9246
Bakersfield, CA 93309

Newest of the Rosicrucian bodies is the Lectorium Rosicrucianum, formed in 1971 by former members of the Rosicrucian Fellowship. International headquarters are in Holland, where the founder, J. Van Rijckenborgh, resides. He is the author of *Dei Gloria Intacta*, a way of initiation for this period of harvest, a self-emancipation path. The teachings are based upon the universal doctrine as taught by Jesus Christ to his intimate disciples. A central concept is transfiguration, ending the ceaseless change of nature and returning to static nature-order. The move of the Lectorium Rosicrucianum is away from occultism and toward a form of Gnosticism, a secret knowledge said to lead to salvation.

The organization spread quickly throughout Europe with particular areas of concentration in France, Sweden, West Germany, Switzerland, and Austria. Moving into the English-speaking countries, a strong following developed in Australia and New Zealand. The American branch of the Lectorium Rosicrucianum was established in Bakersfield, California, by Mae C. Wells, the American representative.

Membership: Not reported.

Sources: *The Way of the Rosycross in Our Times.* Haarlem, Neths.: Rozekruis-Pers, 1978; J. Van Rijckenborgh, *Elementary Philosophy of the Modern Rosycross.* Haarlem, Neths: Rozekruis-Pers, 1961.

★952★
ROSICRUCIAN ANTHROPOSOPHICAL LEAGUE
Current address not obtained for this edition.

Membership: The Rosicrucian Anthroposophical Society was formed in 1932 by Samuel Richard Parchment (b.1881), a former leader in the San Francisco Center of the Rosicrucian Fellowship. Parchment, continuing the astrological emphasis of the Fellowship, wrote a classic textbook, *Astrology, Mundane and Spiritual*, and even before leaving the Fraternity began writing the books which were to guide the League: *The Just Law of Compensation, The Middle Path, the Safest, Ancient Operative Masonry*, and *Steps to Self-Mastery*. Early centers were in California and New York. (In the late 1970s the surviving New York City center broke away to become the Ausar Auset Society.

The principles of the League commit it to an investigation of occult laws, the brotherhood of man, the dissemination of spiritual truth, and the attainment of self-conscious immortality. Recent contact with the League has not been made and its present status is uncertain.

Educational facilities: Not reported.

Sources: S. R. Parchment, *Steps to Self-Mastery.* Oceanside, CA: Fellowship Press, 1927; S. R. Parchment, *Ancient Operative Masonry.* San Francisco: San Francisco Center--Rosicrucian Fellowship, 1930; S. R. Parchment, *The Just Law of Compensation.* San Francisco: San Francisco Center-Rosicrucian Fellowship, 1932; S. R. Parchment, *Astrology, Mundane and Spiritual.* San Francisco: Anthroposophical Rosicrucian League, 1933.

★953★
ROSICRUCIAN FELLOWSHIP
2222 Mission Ave.
Box 713
Oceanside, CA 92054

The most Theosophical of the various Rosicrucian bodies is the Rosicrucian Fellowship founded in 1907 by Carl Louis Van Grasshof, better known under his pen-name, Max Heindel (1865-1919). Born in Germany, Heindel moved to the United States and, in 1903, settled in Los Angeles. He became active in that branch of the Theosophical Society headed by Katherine Tingley. He was president of the local lodge in 1904 and 1905 and a popular lecturer. He also became acquainted with Rudolf Steiner, founder of the Anthroposophical Society just as the Society was beginning to experience the controversy caused by its leader's promotion of Jeddu Krishnamurti as the new World Teacher. Steiner, a leader in the German section of the society, actively opposed the focus upon Krishnamurti.

Traveling to Germany in 1907, Heindel encountered a being, identified as an Elder Brother of the Rosicrucian Order, who appeared in his room and promised to help him. He was led to the Temple of the Rosy Cross near the Germany-Bohemia border, where he was given the material contained in his first book, *The Rosicrucian Cosmo-Conception*, the basic text of the fellowship. Returning to the United States, he opened the first center of what was to become his new order in Columbus, Ohio, in 1908, and before the end of the decade work spread to Seattle, North Yakima (Washington), Portland (Oregon) and Los Angeles.

The teachings of *The Rosicrucian Cosmo-Conception* are heavily theosophic; one finds a discussion of the seven lodges, the evolution of the worlds and races, and the spiritual hierarchy. Heindel's system differs from Theosophy by its greater emphasis on Christianity and Christian symbols (which show the influence of Steiner), and acceptance of a Rosicrucian heritage. Heindel took over the emphasis upon astrology which had been centered in the British theosophical lodges. New rituals for temple service, healing, marriage and burial were written and are published in the *Manual of Forms*.

In 1911, headquarters were established at Mt. Ecclesia near Oceanside, California, where a sanctuary, administrative offices, a women's dormitory, cottages and a vegetarian cafeteria were erected. A correspondence course and numerous books, booklets and tracts pour from the press. The Fellowship became a major force in the spread of astrology in the twentieth century, and many astrologers not connected with the fellowship use the annual *Ephemeris* and the *Table of Houses* published at Oceanside. Excluded from membership in the Fellowship are hypnotists and professional mediums, psychics, and palmists. Those accepted as members must abstain from meat, tobacco and alcohol. Heindel was succeeded in leadership by his wife, Augusta Foss Heindel (d.1938), an accomplished occultist in her own right.

Membership: Not reported.

Periodicals: *Rays from the Rose Cross*, 2222 Mission Avenue, Box 713, Oceanside, CA 92054.

Sources: Max Heindel, *Rosicrucian Cosmo-Conception.* Oceanside, CA: Rosicrucian Fellowship, 1937; Mrs. Max (Augusta Foss) Heindel, *The Birth of the Rosicrucian Fellowship.* Oceanside, CA: The Rosicrucian Fellowship, n.d.; Max Heindel, *Rosicrucian Philosophy in Questions and Answers.* Oceanside, CA: The Rosicrucian Fellowship, 1922; Max Heindel, *Simplified Scientific Astrology.* Oceanside, CA: The Rosicrucian Fellowship, 1928.

★954★
SOCIETAS ROSICRUCIANA IN AMERICA
321 W. 101st St.
New York, NY 10025

Sylvester C. Gould was an early member of the Societas Rosicruciana in Civitatibus Foederatis, the masonic Rosicrucian society. He was admitted into the Boston college in 1885. However, it was his desire to create a Rosicrucian organization that would admit non-Masons. In 1907, with the assistance of George Winslow Plummer (1876-1944) he created the Societas Rosicruciana in America (S.R.I.A.) adapting the masonic materials for general use. He also began *The Rosicrucian Brotherhood*, a periodical. Gould died in 1909. Plummer succeeded to the leadership role, a position he held until his death.

Plummer incorporated the S.R.I.A. in 1912 and four years later founded the Mercury Publishing Company and *Mercury*, a quarterly magazine for the society. During the decade six colleges were chartered in the United States, and one in Sierre Leone. In 1921 two more were added. Plummer authored the lessons and other material distributed by the society. His interests in Christian mysticism and ritual also led him to create a Seminary of Biblical Research (through which he wrote and published a series of lessons on Christian mysticism) and to found two churches: the Anglican Universal Church and the Holy Orthodox Church in America, treated elsewhere in this encyclopedia. These organizations were intimately intertwined with the S.R.I.A. Colleges and church congregations were frequently located in the same cities with the church's members being drawn primarily from society adherents.

The booklet, *Principles and Practices of the Rosicrucians* by Plummer details the affirmations and duties of members. The group affirms the existence of one infinite intelligence, the incarnation of Spirit in matter, the continuousness of all life in evolution, the possibility of the mental attaining knowledge of the spiritual while yet incarnate, and reincarnation. Each student is expected to experiment, and to demonstrate knowledge of concentration, meditation, contemplation, prayer, dietetics, exercise, rest, rituality, sexual faculties, healing, cheerfulness, fasting and individual development; vegetarianism is not demanded, but alcohol is forbidden. New members in the Societas Rosicruciana in America are called postulants. After a year, they become fraters (brothers) or sorores (sisters). Progress is through ten degrees.

Following Plummer's death, the Society and the Holy Orthodox Church in America were headed by Stanislaus Witowski (de Witow), who married Plummer's widow. Glady Plummer. Gladys Plummer de Witow, now known as Mother Serena, became head of the society and the church after her second husband's death.

Membership: Not reported. Only one center of the S.R.I.A. remains, and it is located in New York City.

Periodicals: *Mercury*, 321 W. 101st St., New York, NY 10025.

Sources: George Winslow Plummer, *Principles and Practice for Rosicrucians*. New York: Society of Rosicrucians, Inc., 1947; George Winslow Plummer, *The Art of Rosicrucian Healing*. New York: Society of Rosicrucians, Inc., 1947; Serena, *Lettergrams*. New York: Society of Rosicrucians, Inc., 1976.

★955★

SOCIETAS ROSICRUCIANA IN CIVITATIBUS FOEDERATIS
Current address not obtained for this edition.

The Societas Rosicruciana in Anglia was formed in England in 1865 by Robert Wentworth Little. It seems to have been based on eighteenth-century Rosicrucian texts. Among its members were Kenneth R. H. Mackenzie, Dr. Wynn Westcott and W. R. Woodmen, who were among the founders of the Hermetic Order of the Golden Dawn, the group most credited with initiating the revival of magic in the twentieth century. Members of the Societas were required to be masons prior to beginning their work. During the late nineteenth century, colleges were opened in London (1867), Bristol (1869), Manchester (1871), Cambridge (1876), Sheffield (1877), Middlesex (1877), and Newcastle (1890). In 1873 the East of Scotland College was inagurated in Edinburgh.

News of the formation of the Rosicrucian organization spread through masonry to the American lodges. In 1978 a group led by Charles E. Meyer (1839-1908) of Pennsylvania traveled to England and were initiated at Sheffield. They applied for a charter, but getting no response, turned to Scotland and received a charter from the college in Edinburgh in 1879. A second charter was granted for a college in New York and in 1880 the two colleges formed the Society Rosicruciana Republicae Americae. A Boston and a Baltimore college were chartered later that year. The organization's name was changed to the Societas Rosicruciana in the United States of America, also known as the Societas Rosicruciana in Civitatibus Foederatis. Later charters were granted for Duluth, Minnesota (1911), Texas (1918), New Jersey (1931), North Carolina (1932), Virginia (1933), Illinois (1934), Colorado (1935), Long Island, New York (1935), Nova Scotia, Canada (1936)), and Ontario, Canada (1937). Membership from the 1930s to the 1950s remained steady at between 200 and 300 members. Membership has remained small and, like the British and Scottish counterparts, it is limited to masons. From 1951 to 1973, the society issued a biannual report, *The Rosicrucian Fama*. Recent information on the society has not been available.

Membership: Not reported. In 1973 the society reported 31 members.

Sources: Harold V. B. Voorhis, *Masonic Rosicrucian Societies*. New York: Press of Henry Emmerson, 1958.

Occult Orders

★956★

ASTARA FOUNDATION
800 W. Arrow Hwy.
Box 5003
Upland, CA 91786

The Astara Foundation was formed in 1951 by Robert and Evelyn Chaney, both former Spiritualists. Robert Chaney had been active at Camp Chesterfield and instrumental in the founding of the Spiritualist Episcopal Church. While still a Spiritualist, he became interested in Theosophy and began to profess a belief in reincarnation, which was, in the 1940s, still a minority idea within Spiritualist circles and which met with strong disapproval at the Camp. Evelyn, as a child clairvoyant, had held conversations with a being she called simply "Father." When she asked his name, he replied "Kut-Hu-Mi." When she later discovered Koot Hoomi in Theosophical literature, he revealed that he had chosen her for special hierarchical work--to write the teachings of the ancient wisdom for the new age. After resigning from their church in Eaton Rapids, Michigan, the Chaneys moved to Los Angeles and began their independent endeavor.

Astara is one of the most eclectic of bodies. The eclecticism is both a reflection of the varied strong influences on the Chaneys at points in their lives-- Spiritualism, Theosophy, yoga, Christianity--as well as the expressed desire to allow Astara to be a center of all religions and philosophies. These various tendencies have found unity, however, in the teaching of Hermes Mercurious Trismegistus, the ancient Egyptian magician said to have organized the mystery schools from which all others have derived. Astara conceives of itself as a mystery school in the Hermetic tradition. The name is from the Greek goddess of divine justice, Astraea, and was chosen as a sign of the renewal of the Golden Age.

Hermes taught of God, the cosmos and man, each in relation to the others. God is the only uncreated who emanates his seven attributes and all that is. He also taught seven laws. Basic is the matical law of correspondence, "As above, so below." According to Hermes, our world is a microcosm of the macrocosm, the universe. This law is the basis of alchemy. The law of vibration says everything is in motion. Other laws deal with polarity, cycles, cause and effect, gender and mind.

These laws encompass a number of practices. Lama Yoga is a consciousness expanding method taught originally to Evelyn Chaney by the masters. The chanting of the holy name, "Om," is encompassed under the law of vibration. A natural food diet, preferably vegetarian, is encouraged. The arcane rhythm techniques include numerous yogic practices.

For many years, the center for Astara was a congregation in Los Angeles where regular Sunday services were held. The real heart of Astara, however, has always been the correspondence school. It is Astara's belief that written instructions by a mystery school can function as a guru in teaching the student. Astarians are led through ascending degrees of twenty lessons each. An active healing ministry is conducted by Evelyn Chaney. In 1978 the headquarters were moved from Los Angeles to Upland, California. Astara has become well-known through its large ads in major psychic periodicals such as *Fate Magazine*. The Chaneys are also popular lecturers around the country.

Membership: Not reported.

Periodicals: *Voice of Astara*, 800 W. Arrow Hwy., Box 5003, Upland, CA 91785.

Sources: Robert Galen Chaney, *The Inner Way*. Los Angeles, CA: DeVorss & Co., 1962; Earlyne Chaney, *Remembering*. Los Angeles: Astara's Library of Mystical Classics, 1974; Robert Chaney, *Mysticism, the Journey Within*. Upland, CAL Astra's Library of Mystical Classics, 1979; Earlyne Chaney and William L. Messick, *Kundalini and the Third Eye*. Upland, CA: Astara's Library of Mystical Classics, 1980; Earlyne Chaney, *Shining Moments of a Mystic*. Upland, CA: Astara, Inc., 1976.

★957★
BROTHERHOOD OF THE WHITE TEMPLE
Sedalia, CO 80135

The Brotherhood of the White Temple was formed in Denver in 1930 by Morris Doreal, a long-time student of occultism and a "channel for bringing the ancient wisdom to the Western Student." Doreal claims contact with the Great White Lodge, the Elder Brothers of man (figures similar to the ascended masters, spirits who were once human and now teach humans about spiritual reality). Doreal is the agent for the coming Golden Age in which the brotherhood of man will be established on earth. Integral parts of the Brotherhood of the White Temple are the White Temple Church, which emphasizes the "Original Gnostic Teachings of Jesus," and the Shamballa Ashrama, a tract of 1,560 acres at Sedalia, Colorado, where a community of Brotherhood members is housed and the headquarters are located. From the publishing plant the numerous booklets and lessons written by Doreal are printed and distributed. The booklets cover the whole range of occult topics.

The teachings of the Brotherhood come from the central core of occult teachings, drawing heaviily on kabbalistic images. (The Kabbalah is a Jewish magical system.) God is conceived as the all-pervasive one, and man is a spark of the divine. The soul is incarnate for the purpose of overcoming negation and darkness and changing itself into order and light. The fall of man was caused by his being overwhelmed by inharmony after his creation. The teachings of the White Brotherhood emphasize methods of establishing harmony and cover various topics in the occult tradition (Atlantis, Lemuria, the Masters of Tibet and the Great Pyramid). In keeping with the occult tradition, an allegorical approach to the Bible is offered.

From the headquarters in Sedalia, booklets and lessons are offered by correspondence to members around the country. Lessons are divided into four neophyte grades and twelve temple grades. After completion (approximately four and one-half years), a member is invited into the inner work.

Membership: Not reported. Approximately 50 families live at the Ashrama, and corresponding students are located across the United States.

Periodicals: *Light on the Path*, Sedalia CO 80135.

Sources: M. Doreal, *Personal Experiences amongthe Masters and Great Adepts in Tibet*. Sedalia, CO: Brotherhood of the White Temple, n.d.; M. Doreal, *Man and the Mystic Universe*. Denver: Brotherhod of the White Temple, n.d.; M. Doreal, *Maitreya, Lord of the World*. Sedalia, CO: Brotherhood of the White Temple, n.d.; M. Doreal, *Secret Teachings of the Himalayan Gurus*. Denver: Brotherhood the White Temple, n.d.

★958★
CHURCH OF LIGHT
Church of Light
Los Angeles, CA

The Church of Light was incorporated in 1932 in Los Angeles by Elbert Benjamine (also known by his pen name, C. C. Zain), but actually dates to 1876, when Emma Harding Britten (who the year previously had participated in the founding of the Theosophical Society) published the teachings of the occult Brotherhood of Light in her book, *Art Magic*. The Brotherhood of Light was, according to the Church of Light tradition, formed in 2400 B.C. by a group which separated from the theocracy of Egypt. It has existed since that time as a secret order and is called the source of the science upon which Western civilization rests. Its initiates are said to have included Thales, Pythagoras, and Plato. It has continued to exist on the inner planes as well as the outer. (The outer plane is the one people live on; the inner plane contains ghostly bodies and is visible only to psychics.)

In the nineteenth century, one M. Theon was the head of the Brotherhood of Light in Europe. He was contacted by T. H. Burgoyne (1855-1894), a Scot, who originally contacted the Brotherhood on the inner plane. He came to America in 1880s. Joining him was Captain Norman Astley, a retired British army officer who married Genevieve Stebbins, a member of the Brotherhood in New York. Burgoyne, while living with the Astleys in Carmel, California, wrote an original series of lessons, *Light of Egypt*, Vol. I. With the help of Dr. Henry Wagner and Mrs. Belle M. Wagner, a branch of the Brotherhood, the Hermetic Brotherhood of Luxor was formed. The Hermetic Brotherhood was always governed by a scribe, an astrologer and a seer. Burgoyne was the original scribe. In 1909 when Minnie Higgins, the original astrologer, died, Elbert Benjamine was called to the home of a Mrs. Anderson, the seer, to become the council's astrologer.

The teaching of the Brotherhood was the ancient Religion of the Stars, and Benjamine was appointed to prepare a complete system of occult studies by which men could become conversant with the religion in the coming Aquarian Age. He was guided in this task by members on the inner plane, and wrote the twenty-one series of lessons for the twenty-one areas of occult science. In 1915, he began to hold classes, which were opened to the public in 1918. The lessons were completed in 1934. In 1913, the Hermetic Brotherhood of Luxor was closed and its mission was turned over to Benjamine.

The Church of Light teaches that there are two orders of truth- religion and science-between which there can be no true antagonism. The only book infallible in interpreting the will of deity is the book of nature. There is but one religion, nature's laws. Astrology is stressed as a means of interpreting nature, though all occult arts are recognized. The main program of the church consists of twenty-one courses, the member is given an Hermetic certificate.

Service to others is stressed as a means to evolution from man to angel. The life of service to others is the life of the Spirit. Reincarnation is not a belief of the church.

The Church of Light is headed by a president. Upon Benjamine's death in 1951, he was succeeded by Edward Doane, the present president. There are a vice-president and secretary-treasurer. An annual meeting of the church is held at the headquarters in Los Angeles. Ordained ministers may establish branch churches where interest warrants, and individual members taking correspondence courses are located across the United States.

Membership: Not reported.

Periodicals: *The Church of Light Quarterly*, Box 76762, Los Angeles, CA 90076.

Remarks: According to occult historian A. E. Waite, Thomas Burgoyne is a pseudonym adopted by one Thomas Henry Dalton, a convicted felon (on fraud charges) who actually came to America to escape a scandal concerning the Hermetic Brotherhood. M. Theon, also according to Waite, was a man named Peter Davidson, possibly identical with Norman Astley.

Sources: Thomas H. Burgoyne, *The Light of Egypt*. Albuquerque, NM: Sun Publishing Company, 1980. 2 Vols.; H. O. Wagner, comp., *A Treasure Chest of Wisdom*. Denver, CO: H. O. Wagner, 1967.

★959★
HOLY ORDER OF MANS
20 Steiner St.
San Francisco, CA 94117

The Holy Order of MANS was begun in San Francisco in the early 1960s, having grown out of a revelation received by its founder, Father Paul W. Blighton. It was incorporated in 1968. The word "MANS" is an acronym standing for "Mysterion, Agape, Nous, Sophia," four Greek words meaning mystery, love, mind, and wisdom. The order considers itself Pauline Catholic, in that it takes the Apostle Paul's work as its own and the Master Jesus as the master of the order, and the Nicene Creed is accepted as the full statement of the community's Christian faith. Within the Order, students are provided the atmosphere required for spiritual growth and the ultimate realization of the God SELF leading to the attainment of ultimate freedom from all earthly bondage.

The Holy Order of MANS is an ordered community much like the orders in the Roman Catholic Church but completely independent organizationally. The order is under the guidance of the Esoteric Council (of active priests within the order) and the Director General. Both men and women may participate in the order at all levels. Potential members are accepted into a into a three-month novitiate. Following successful completion of the novitiate, individuals enter the Student Training Program which lasts approximately one year. Also after the novitiate, students take their first vows. After the training period, they must decide whether or not to take second vows of humility, obedience, poverty, purity and service, which are for life. Immediately after second vows, new members spend a year in either the Brown Brothers (males) or Immaculate Sisterhood of Mary (females, the missionary arms of the order. After a year in missionary service, members are eligible for several forms of advanced training. Some, after completion of their schoolwork within the order, are accepted for further training leading to ordination into the priesthood. There is also an Outer Order of Discipleship for those who wish to receive the teachings but cannot enter into the ordered life.

The teachings of the order are summarized in the tenets which teach the Universal Law of Creation in accordance with the teachings of Jesus Christ and the other great avatars. The tenets afirm the existence of both the seen and unseen plane of the life force (derived from the Creator when It created the world and humanity); the continuity and ever-evolving nature of Life; spiritual healing; and the unity of the Great Creator in God, Mind and matter, throughout the solar system. The tenets affirm the equality of men and women, the desirability of confession of sins to a qualified priest, baptism of the Holy Spirit as the lifting of consciousness. The sacrament of the giving of Communion on both the physical and spiritual level is practiced. These tenets are further explained and expanded upon in the books and training programs of the order, which cover the topics common to esoteric groups--the Great White Brotherhood, consciousness and psychic-spiritual develoment. The order has also published its own Kabbalistic interpretation of the Tarot. The Holy Order of MANS is unique among esoteric groups both for its ordered life and its focus upon service to the Creator, through service to humanity in the world. The order maintains community aid stations to provide counselling and direct care for those in need. Administration of the Order is handled by the corporate board which sits at the central headquarters in San Francisco. Spiritual matters are under the guidance of the Esoteric Council. Centers are maintained across the United States and in several foreign countries. Fr. Blighton was followed as Director General by his widow, Ruth Blighton. That post is currently held by Rt. Rev. Andrew Rossi.

Membership: Not reported. In 1977 there were approximately 600 people who had taken lifelong vows in the order, 299 in traning and approximately 1,000 lay adherents. There were more than 60 centers in the United States. Foreign centers were located in Canada, Japan, Germany, France, Holland, England, and Spain.

Periodicals: *onflowers*, Box 308, Cheyenne, WY 82001.

Sources: *Uniting All Faith*. San Francisco: Holy Order of MANS, 1973; *The Golden Force*. San Francisco: Holy Order of MANS, 1967; Paul Blighton, *Memoirs of a*

Mystic. San Francisco: Holy Order of MANS, 1974; *Keystone of Tarot Symbols*. San Francisco: Holy Order of MANS, 1971; *History of the Great White Brotherhood and Its Teachings*. San Francisco: Holy Order of MANS, n.d.; *Book of the Master Jesus*. San Francisco: Holy Order of MANS, 1974. 3 vols.; *Book of Order*. San Francisco: Holy Order of MANS, n.d.

★960★
LEMURIAN FELLOWSHIP
Box 397
Ramona, CA 92065

Lemuria, the Pacific counterpart of the lost continent of Atlantis, forms the homeland of the Lemurian Fellowship. On Lemuria, according to the Fellowship, Christ first enunciated the Lemurian philosophy. He reigned for a thousand years as Melchizedek, the emperor of Atlantis. After the destruction of Atlantis, all that had been taught, both philosophical and scientific, was stored away in the archives of the secret brotherhoods-the Rosicrucians, the Essenes, etc. The oldest of the brotherhoods was the Lemurians. Their duty was to compile the information for the integration of a New Age civilization. The Lemurian Fellowship is considered the mundane channel for releasing the information of the Brotherhood.

The Lemurian Fellowship was formed in 1936 in Chicago. Its public inauguration was on September 16, a date derived from reading the Great Pyramid of Gizah, believed to contain a map of the plan of the ages. Within a few months, the Fellowship moved to Milwaukee and, in 1938, to Chula Vista, California. Then in 1941, the group purchased property near Ramona, California, where it is now located in 260 acres in two tracts of land, eight miles apart.

The Lemurian philosophy was developed in the early publications of the Fellowship--*The Earth Dweller Returns* and *The Sun Rises*. The former book was seen as a sequel to *A Dweller on Two Planets* by Phylos (pseudonym of Frederick William Oliver), one of the first books (1899) to discuss Lemuria. *The Sun Rises*, written by Robert D. Stelle, who founded the Fellowship, describes the founding of the Mukulian civilization on Lemuria. The philosophy is described as a balanced practical philosophy centered on the basic laws. These include: The law of precipitation, by which one brings into his environment whatever is desired; the law of cause and effect; the law of compensation; the law of correspondence, and the law of transmutation. There is a strong belief in reincarnation and karma.

The work of the Lemurian Fellowship is the building of the New Age, the kingdom of God. The key to the new society will be a communalism in which the society prospers through the individual's prosperity and the individual prospers through society's prosperity. Members of the Fellowship are expected to participate in the new economic order and to work gradually toward becoming full participants in the communal structure.

On the land near Ramona are the buildings for the school, administrative faculty, dining room, laundry, workshops, garages and storage. On the larger tract of land, Gateway (the actual headquarters), Gateway Chapel, a library and Lemurian Crafts are located. Lemurian Crafts, founded in 1948, creates jewelry and accessories for the home, both as an expression of Lemurian philosophy and a source of income. The main program of the Fellowship in its correspondence school, by which lessons are mailed to students across the country. Non-resident students can become members of the Lemurian Order.

Leadership of the Fellowship is invested in the Council of Elder Brothers and in the Advanced Ego (Robert D. Stelle). Since Stelle's death in 1952, the administration has been in the hands of the selected board of governors.

Membership: Not reported.

Periodicals: *Lemurian View Point*, Box 397, Ramona, CA 92065.

Sources: Phylos the Tibetan, *An Earth Dweller Returns*. Milwaukee: Lemurian Press, 1940; Robert D. Stelle, *The Sun Rises*. Ramona, CA: Lemurian Fellowship, 1952; The Lemurian Scribe, *Be It Resolved*. Milwaukee: Lemurian Prass, 1940; Teofilo de la Torre, *Psycho-Physical Regeration, Rejuvenation and Longevity*. Milwaukee: Lemurian Press, 1938.

★961★
MAYAN ORDER
Box 2710
San Antonio, TX 78299

The Mayan Order, it is claimed, was founded by people who had rediscovered the teachings of an ancient group of holy men (H'Men) who dominated Mayan culture and to whom the greatness of the civilization was due. These men possessed great knowledge of astrology, the calendar, medicine, mathematics and occult wisdom. Only a few H'Men survived the Spanish conquest, and only three copies of the ancient books have survived. What is known of the ancient wisdom is preserved today by the Mayan Order.

Mayan material is distributed in degree-lessons through correspondence. Early in the work, the student is taught a very simple code; in succeeding lessons, key words are printed in that code. Reincarnation is stressed within a framework of New Thought metaphysics, with the New Thought emphasis on light, mind, and the power of positive thinking. Psychokinesis in practiced by each student. Appropriate rituals are learned at each initiation; content is heavily biblical.

Like Astara, the Mayan Order has become known through its ads in various psychic periodicals. It is under the guidance of Rose Dawn, the registrar and supreme leader.

Membership: Not reported.

Periodicals: *Daily Meditation*, Box 2710, San Antonio, TX 78299.

Sources: Rose Dawn, *The Miracle Power*. San Antonio, TX: The Mayan Press, 1959.

★962★
PHILOSOPHICAL RESEARCH SOCIETY
3910 Los Feliz Blvd.
Los Angeles, CA 90027

The Philosophical Research Society was founded in 1934 by Manly Palmer Hall, the most prolific and widely-read occult writer of the twentieth century. He began as a young occult scholar and lecturer in the 1920s as a leader in the Church of the People in Los Angeles. During these years he began to publish his own books under the imprint of the Hall Publishing Company. The Philosopher Research Society was the culmination of a dream to establish a philosophical/religious institution modeled on the ancient philosopher/religious schools of Pythagoras, Plato, and the Serapeum of Alexander. Its goals include research, application of the occult heritage to modern problems and the dissemination of the ancient wisdom by a variety of means.

Hall's basic position is closely related to an Eastern idealism. Life is eternal, it is an endless unfoldment towards the real. It has its beginnings in the immeasurable past and its ultimates in the immeasurable future. Man's present individual existence is but one episode of innumerable ones. Law brings us into life and is the purpose of living. The seven laws of life are evolution, cause and effect, polarity, reincarnation, harmony and rythym, generation and vibration. Man may come into harmony with these, but they are immutable. All of Hall's lecturing and writing has been an explication of this perspective. He has also published a number of historical studies of occultism and occultists.

The Philosophical Research Society is centered at its headquarters complex in Los Angeles. Included are a research library, bookstore and publishing facilities. Books, booklets and lecture transcripts are distributed across the United States. Correspondence courses are offered in a wide variety of topics. Regular classes and Sunday morning services are offered weekly. Through his publications, Hall continues to make a significant impact on the psychic/occult community.

Membership: Not reported.

Periodicals: *PRS Journal*, 3910 Los Feliz Blvd., Los Angeles, CA 90027; *P.R.S. News*, 3910 Los Feliz Blvd., Los Angeles, CA 90027; *Contributor's Bulletin*, 3910 Los Feliz Blvd., Los Angeles, CA 90027.

Sources: Manly Palmer Hall, *Man, the Grand Symbol of the Mysteries*. Los Angeles: The Philosophical Research Center, 1947; Manley Palmer Hall, *The Mystical Christ*. Los Angeles: The Philosophical Research Society, 1951; Manley Palmer Hall, *Reincarnation, the Cycle of Necessity*. Los Angeles: The Philosophical Research Society, 1946; Manly Palmer Hall, *Questions and Answers*. Los Angeles: The Philosophers Press, 1937.

★963★
SABIAN ASSEMBLY
2324 Norman Rd.
Stanwood, WA 98292

The Sabian Assembly dates to 1922 and a class in astrology led by Marc Edmund Jones in New York City. That class was the culmination of a decade of work which included a "meeting with a master." The following year, a second class was held at Manly Palmer Hall's Church of the People in Los Angeles. On October 17, 1923, a group who had found some direction in the occult truths and who wished to test them in their life created the Sabian Assembly. The astrological emphasis broadened to include the entire area of occultism, and, in 1925, Jones's *Key Truths of Occult Philosophy* appeared. *The Ritual of Living*, the manual of the Assembly was published in 1930. Since then, the Sabian Assembly has continued as a group oriented to the Sabian philosophy as enunciated by Jones. Until after World War II it was a very small group, but within the occult community, it has gradually spread with the increasing popularity of Jones' books and lectures. Jones emerged as, intellectually, one of the strongest occultists in the public eye.

The Sabian Assembly is an openly eclectic body. Jones acknowledged that he had drawn from New Thought, Theosophy, Kabbalism and Spiritualism, as well as from both Eastern and Western theological and philosophical traditions. The occult tradition is seen as a special way of understanding and self- dedication, especially as expressed in astrology, the Kabbalah and Tarot. The Kabbalah, the medieval Jewish mystical-occult teaching, is predominant, and the Sabian project is basically the application of the Kabbalah to all of life. Since the occult is easily warped into a pyramid of illusions, the group-effort allows the student to keep in mind the need for verifiable experience in direct proportion to spiritual realization.

The Sabian Assembly is a solar group whose occult discipline derives its authority from within the self (as opposed to a lunar group which sees authority as represented outwardly by a hierarchical system). The individual Sabian attempts to become a laya center, defined as "the persisting reality of an original potential...the nothing that constitutes the continuum or core genius of every particular something." A laya center is equated with the philosopher's stone, the item alchemists search for so they will be able to turn lead into gold. An "adapt" is a laya center for an entire group. The effort centered in or at a laya center is defined as work in consciousness and includes meditation, concentration and retrospection. Healing occurs in the meditative consciousness.

Rituals were developed at the specific request of the sponsors, who constitute the invisible council of the Assembly. Rituals are provided for all Sabian activities. There are rituals for the dedication of a life (baptism), a departure from this life (funeral), a partnership (marriage, as well as other cooperative endeavors), and projects. The most important rituals occur at the four quarterly meetings (Palm Sunday, July 3rd, October 17th, and December 31), the monthly full-moon meetings, and the healing work.

The Sabian Assembly exists as a loosely organized fellowship of aspirants, each pursuing his own course of study in Jones' material and in psychic/occult development. A prime working-principle of the fellowship is "myob" or "mind your own business." Membership is open to any who wish to participate in the invisible fellowship, the fellowship of the masters in moving toward the goals of the spiritual history of the race. The aspirant becomes a neophyte. After two years, the aspirant may become an acolyte and, after another five years, a legate. Acolytes participate in work in consciousness daily, as well as in specific volunteer work for the Assembly for three years. The acolyte must also attend sixty-three consecutive full-moon meetings. When the legate state is reached, a mystery-name is selected and is used in all nine inner phases of group procedure. Legates are organized in groups of four for work in consciousness.

Jones served as chancellor of the Assembly until his death in the early 1980s. Students receive weekly lessons on a variety of philosophical/occult topics. The lessons are published in *Letter to the Neophytes and Regular Students* and *Fortnightly News Notes*.

Membership: Not reported. There are several hundred regular students of the Assembly.

Periodicals: *The Sabian News Letter*, 1324 Tulane Rd., Wilmington, DE 19803.

Sources: Marc Edmund Jones, *The Ritual of Living*. Los Angeles, CA: J. F. Rowny Press, 1930; Marc Edmund Jones, *The Sabian Manual*. New York: Sabian Publishing Society, 1957; Marc Edmund Jones, *The Sabian Book*. Stanwood, WA: Sabian Publishing Society, 1973.

SOULCRAFT, INC.
Box 192
Noblesville, IN 46060

William Dudley Pelley (1890-1965) made his mark on American history during the 1930s. On January 31, 1933, the day after Hitler took control of Germany, Pelley organized the Christian American Patriots, more popularly known as the Silver Shirts. The body was anti-Jewish and pro-Nazi and, through the Christian Party, proposed the disenfranchisement of the Jews to prevent their holding property and to limit their participation in the professions. In 1942, Pelley's activities were stopped when he was jailed for sedition. He spent the next seven years in federal prison.

Pelley had a second life, as an occultist. In 1929 in the *American Mercury*, he published his oft-reprinted article, "Seven Minutes in Eternity," an account of his astral travel experiences. From these initial experiences, Pelley developed into a channel through which a number of "mentor minds" spoke, and left a legacy of 32 books. These books spell out in great detail an occult system. Earth is supervised by the high mentors. Man evolves by the expansion of consciousness through many lifetimes. Integral to the Soulcraft system were Pelley's racial theories and social goals. The Christian Commonwealth was a new social environment by which the nation would be incorporated and each citizen made a shareholder with a political voice and an economic stake.

Pelley was against Soulcraft's becoming an organization and he let his writings create any structures that might emerge. Since his death, the work of distributing his writings has been carried on by his daughter and son-in-law, Adelaide Pearson and his son-in-law, Melford Pearson, at the Fellowship Press in Noblesville, Indiana. The social philosophy, as it appears in one book, *No More Hunger*, is published by Aquila Press, a separate corporation. The periodicals *Valor* and *Over There* have been discontinued.

Membership: Not reported.

Sources: William Dudley Pelley, *Seven Minutes in Eternity*. Noblesville, IN: Soulcraft Chapels, 1954; *The Golden Scripts*. Noblesville, IN: Soulcraft Chapels, 1951; Willaim Dudley Pelley, *Star Guests*. Noblesville, IN: Soulcraft Press, 1950; Willaim Dudley Pelley, *No More Hunger*. Noblesville, IN: Aquila Press, 1961; Donald S. Strong, *Organized Anti-Semitism in America*. Washington, DC: American Council on Public Affairs, 1941.

★965★
STELLE GROUP
405 Mayfield Ave.
Garland, TX 75041

The Stelle Group, named for Robert D. Stelle, founder of the Lemurian Fellowship, and its sister society, the Adelphi Organization, were founded by Richard Kieninger (b. 1927). As early as 1953, Kieninger had been associated with the Lemurian Fellowship, from whom he received his initial occult training, but in 1963 he broke with it and formed the Stelle Group. The same year the group was formed, *The Ultimate Frontier*, written by Kieninger under a pen-name, Eklal Kueshana, was released. It is an autobiography and discussion of the basic philosophy of the Stelle Group. In 1966, the Lemuria Builders was formed to acquaint the public with the group's philosophy and to recruit new members. Stelle School was opened in 1968. Originally the headquarters of the Group was in Kieninger's home in Chicago, but in 1973, with the official founding of the community of Stelle, Illinois, the offices shifted there.

Essential to an understanding of the Stelle Group is the reported experience of his leader. Kieninger claims his first contact with non-physical beings was on his twelfth birthday. The contact, Dr. White, taught reincarnation, told Kieninger of his past lives, including ones as the Biblical King David and Pharaoh Akhnaton, and began to explain Kieninger's mission to found a new nation. Later that year, he was given a secret name, permanently incised into his skin, and at the same time was taught of the twelve brotherhoods (five greater and seven lesser). In 1945, Dr. White gave him the place of the ideal community--Stelle City. Stelle is a community near Kankakee, Illinois, to which the activity and life of the group gradually shifted over the 1970s. As an intentional community, it is seen as one preparatory model of the new society which will be formed in the next decades. From 1973 to 1982, the focus of the Stelle group was upon the community of Stelle. However, in 1976, Kieninger formed a sister organization to the Stelle Group, the Adelphi Organization. It purchased 78 acres of land 35 miles east of Dallas, Texas upon which a community open only to a dedicated core of disciples of Kieninger's teachings (i.e. members of either the Adelphi Organization or the Stelle Group) is being developed. Residents must have lived in the vicinity of either Stelle or Dallas to attend a weekly orientation for a year prior to their moving into the community. Then in 1982, the headquarters of the Stelle group were moved to suburban Dallas and the community of Stelle was opened to non-members who nevertheless wanted to participate in the experimental community life. The Stelle Community Association was chartered in 1983.

The Stelle Group, itself, functions as an outer expression of the brotherhood. The masters, who have been guiding history, are awaiting the development of the communities of Stelle and Adelphi, at which time they will begin to incarnate as children of the citizens. At the end of the twentieth century, a massive natural catastrophe leading to a rearrangement of the land masses will be triggered by the alignment of the planets in this solar system on May 5, 2000 A.D. It will be preceded by an economic depression which was to begin in 1975 and by the Battle of Armageddon, an atomic war to end in 1999. The people of Stelle and Adelphi will be among the ten per cent of the world's population to survive this catastrophe. After the worst is past, members of the brotherhood will rebuild a new Philadelphia.

The Stelle Group is now seen as a school which offers basic training for citizens of the new community and spiritual initiation. It leads individuals into the Adelphi Organization and the future community of Philadelphia.

The Stelle Group is headed by a board of trustees which is headed by both a president and a chairman, Kieninger holding the latter position. The Adelphi Organization and the Stelle Community Association have separately elected boards. Kieninger is president of th e Adelphi board. Both Stelle and Adelphi operate a school. A radio show "In Pursuit of the Ultimate Frontier" is aired in Dallas. Both the Stelle Group and the Adelphi Organization are orienting their activity upon preparation for the coming troubles due at the end of the century and the development of resources and skills to rebuild the new society.

Membership: Not reported. As of 1981, there were 42 residental housing unites at Stelle City, with slow growth proceeding. There are an estimated several hundred members of the two organizations.

Periodicals: *The Lemuria Builder*, Box 75, Quinlan, TX 75474.

Sources: Eklal Kueshana (pseudonym of Richard Kieninger), *The Ultimate Frontier*. Chicago: The Stelle Group, 1963; Richard Kieninger, *Observations*. The Stelle Group, 1971-79. 4 vols.; Tom Valentine, *The Great Pyramid: Man's Monument to Man*. New York: Pinnacle Books, 1975.

Theosophy

★966★
INTERNATIONAL GROUP OF THEOSOPHISTS
634 S. Gramercy Place, Suite 301
Los Angeles, CA 90005

The International Group of Theosophists is a small group which grew out of the American Theosophical movement in southern California. It was founded in the 1940s by Boris Mihailovich de Zirkoff (1902-1981), the grand-nephew of Helena Petrovna Blavatsky. Its objectives are to uphold and promote the original principles of the modern Theosophical movement and to disseminate the teachings of the esoteric philosophy as set forth by

Blavatsky and her teachers. The group has tried to operate outside of the disagreements of the more established lodges and has cooperated with them in Zirkoff's major life work, the editing and publishing of Blavatsky's collected writings. For over thirty years it published *Theosophia*, a quarterly journal (1944-1981), but issued a final volume in the summer of 1981 as a tribute issue to its founder.

Membership: Not reported.

★967★
TEMPLE OF THE PEOPLE
Box 528-H
Halcyon, CA 93420

The Temple of the People began in Syracuse, New York during the period of disruption of the American branch of the Theosophical Society following the death of founders Helena Petrovna Blavatsky and William Q. Judge. Following Judge in leadership of the American society was Katherine Tingley, who many, including the group in Syracuse, rejected. Under the leadership of Dr. William H. Dower (1866-1937) and Francis A. LaDue (1849-1922), they became independent and formed the Temple of the People in 1898. Within a few years they purchased a tract of land at Halcyon, California (near Pismo Beach) and moved there in 1903. In 1904, Dower opened a sanitorium, which became famous during the generation of its operation for its treatment of alcoholics and drug addicts. In 1905 a portion of the residents organized as a co-operative colony, the Temple Home Association; however, the utopian venture lasted less than a decade. It demise did not stop the growth of the community which during the 1920 numbers around 50.

The Temple began with the contact from the mahatmas or masters through LaDue and Dower, known respectively as "Blue Star" and "Red Star," the designations given them by the masters. They were told to abandon the Tingley-led society, and through their reception and publishing of continuing material from the masters, to carry on the work begun by Madame Blavatsky. Over the years they produced an impressive set of materials, including a large volume, *Theogenesis*, a third volume of Blavatsky's magnus opus, *The Secret Doctrine*, the two previous volumes of which were entitled *Anthropogenesis* and *Cosmogenesis*.

According to the Temple, the spiritual hierarchy is led by Central Spiritual Sun, the Christos, the expression of the Infinite Godhead. Other masters, members of the Great White Brotherhood, embody aspects of the divine light, key members being the masters of the seven rays (of the color spectrum). Integral to the original teachings given to The Temple's founders from the Master Hilarion, Regent of the Red Ray, was a prophecy concerning the soon-to-occur birth of an avatar, an incarnation of the Christos, an event which only happens once every two thousand years. The first generation of the Temple was to a great extent motivated by that expectation and the belief that members were the spearhead of the Messianic Age into which humanity was moving. These emphases, which still undergird the Temple's understanding of its educational mission and work in the world, are summarized in the *Teachings of the Temple* volumes.

During the first generation the life of the community in Halcyon revolved around the sanitorium and the Temple building built 1923-24. Groups which received and studied the material produced through the temple sprang up around the country, and every summer a national convention was held. Dower succeeded LaDue as the guardian-in-chief of the Temple. He was in turn succeeded by Pearl F. Dower and the present leader, Harold Forgostein. The Temple has kept the material originally received by Dower and LaDue in print and their work revolves around it.

The Temple of the People is still focused upon the community at Halcyon, now occupied by 20 to 30 members. Groups, originally termed "squares," are located around the United States, and there is a lively following in both England and Germany. The Temple is led by four officers: the guardian-in-chief (Harold Forgostein), the inner-guard (Eleanor Shumway), the treasurer (Carolyn Forgostein), and the scribe.

Membership: Not reported. Approximately 70 people attended the 1985 convention in Halcyon. An estimated 200 people are actively participating in Temple activities worldwide.

Periodicals: *The Temple Artisan*, Box 528-H, Halcyon, CA 93420.

Sources: *Teachings of the Temple.* Halcyon, CA: Temple of the People, 1947-1985. 3 vols.; *Theogenesis.* Halcyon, CA: Temple of the People, 1981; *From the Mountain Top.* Halcyon, CA: Temple of the People, 1974-1985. 3 vols.; Bob Burns, et al., *The Temple of the People, Halcyon.* California Polytechnic State University, 1972; Paul Kagan, *New World Utopias.* Baltimore: Penguin Books, 1975.

★968★
THEOSOPHICAL SOCIETY (HARTLEY)
Covina, CA

In 1951, following the death of A. L. Conger, the Theosophical Society headquartered in Pasadena, California split. Conger appointed William Hartley to succeed him. The ruling cabinet, however, rejected Hartley in favor of J. A. Long. The Long faction retained control of the Society, and Hartley and his few supporters formed a new society. It is possibly the smallest branch of theosophists. It has had no leader since Hartley's death in 1956, and publishes no materials.

Membership: Not reported.

★969★
THEOSOPHICAL SOCIETY
Post Office Bin C
Pasadena, CA 91109

The Theosophical Society with headquarters at Altadena, California, is the successor to the Theosophical Society of America, headed by William Q. Judge. Upon Judge's death in 1896, E. T. Hargrove was elected president and Katherine Tingley became head of the esoteric work. Mrs. Tingley had met Judge in the early 1890's after a time as a Spiritualist. At the convention that elected Hargrove, she as a medium brought word from the departed leader. She also laid plans for a utopian community built around a school, and formed the International Brotherhood League to emphasize humanitarian concerns. In 1898, the Theosophical Society and the League merged to become the Universal Brotherhood and Theosophical Society, and Tingley was elected leader and official head. The merger stripped Hargrove of power, while giving Tingley her post for life.

Mrs. Tingley moved the headquarters to Point Loma, California, speedily built up the school and community and, in 1919, opened the Theosophical University. The Point Loma experiment drew Theosophists from around the country. They were attracted by Tingley's leadership in both cultural and humanitarian activities.

In the 1920s, however, financial trouble began to plague the work. In 1929, Mrs. Tingley was killed in an auto accident in Europe. She was succeeded by Dr. Gottfried de Purucker, but the situation at Point Loma was past saving. De Purucker was an able leader and scholar. He attempted to revive the lodges which had been abandoned when Tingley called the Theosophists to California. A decade of decline, climaxed by de Purucker's sudden death in 1942, led to a move from Point Loma to Covina, a Los Angeles suburb. In the early 1950s headquarters were moved to Altadena.

Under the leadership of Col. A. L. Conger, who succeeded de Purucker, an even more conservative line was asserted, one holding to the teachings of Helena Petrovna Blavatsky, founder of the Theosophical movement. The problem of lack of formal means to elect a new leader led to a power struggle after Conger's death. Conger appointed William Hartley, but the ruling cabinet rejected him, aligning itself with J. A. Long, instead. A split ensued. The Long faction continues in the Altadena headquarters. The Hartley faction has headquarters at Covina.

The Theosophical Society follows the teachings of Blavatsky but not those of Annie Besant. It has adopted no ritual and has remained free of any association with the Liberal Catholic Church (were de Purucker's works are read and used). There are only a few meetings and members left in the United States, though a weekly lecture program is offered at the library in Altadena.

Internationally, the society is affiliated with Theosophists in Australia, Germany. Great Britain, the Netherlands, Sweden, and South Africa.

Membership: Not reported.

Periodicals: *Sunrise*, Post Office Bin C, Pasadena, CA 91109.

Sources: William Q. Judge, *Echoes of the Orient*. San Diego: Point Loma Publications, 1975; William Q. Judge, *The Ocean of Theosophy*. Point Loma, CA: Aryan Theosophical Press, 1926; Katherine Tingley, *Theosophy: the Path of the Mystic*. Pasadena: Theosophical University Press, 1977; Gottfried de Purucker, *Fountain-Source of Occultism*. Pasadena, CA: Theosophical University Press, 1974; Gottfried de Purucker, *H. P. Blavatsky*. San Diego: Point Loma Publications, 1974; Charles J. Ryan, *H. P. Blavatsky and the Theosophical Movement*. Pasadena, CA: Theosophical University Press, 1974.

★970★

THEOSOPHICAL SOCIETY OF AMERICA
Box 270
Wheaton, IL 60187

After the death of Theosophical founder, Helena Petrovna Blavatsky, the American branch asserted its independence of the British and Indian branch and their new leader, Annie Besant. Only fourteen lodges remained loyal, but with these, President Alexander Fullerton began the process of rebuilding the newly constituted Theosophical Society of America. Annie Besant came to America in 1897 to help the struggling work, and by the end of the year there were 50 lodges. Growth has been steady, and this branch eventually reclaimed its position as the largest of the several theosophical groups functioning in the United States. Many members around the country rejoined this group after rejecting the new leader of the American branch, Katherine Tingley, and her call to concentrate Theosophist activities in Point Loma, California.

Headquarters, originally in California, were moved to Wheaton, Illinois, where a vital program emanates to lodges across the country. An active publishing work is centered on the Theosophical Publishing House. A large selection of the paperback volumes under the imprint "Quest Books" (many reprints of Theosophical classics) has spread the work in recent years. The Krotona School at Ojai, California, and three summer camps are also operated. At the Wheaton headquarters is a large library of both theosophical and world-religions books. Social concerns (family life, animal welfare, peace, social service, Tibetan refugees, and the arts) are focuses in the Theosophical Order of Service, founded in 1908 by Annie Besant. The Tibetan Friendship Group, founded in 1960 by Muriel Lewis is one department of the order.

The Esoteric Section of the Theosophical Society continues and is headquartered at Ojai. To be admitted one must have been a Theosophist for three years and must refrain from tobacco, alcohol, and meat. Members practice a secret meditation method. The original materials of the Esoteric Section have recently been published in the final volume of Madame Blavatsky's *Collected Writings*.

Membership: Not reported. In 1970 there were 5,436 members with concentrations in New York, Illinois, and California.

Periodicals: *The American Theosophist*, Box 270, Wheaton, IL 60187; *For the Love of Life*, Theosophical Order of Service, Star Route, Box 6854, Pahrump, NV 89041.

Sources: Bruce F. Campbell, *Ancient Wisdom Revived*. Berkeley: University of California Press, 1980; Marion Meade, *Madame Blavatsky*. New York: G. P. Putnam's Sons, 1980; Josephine Ransom, *A Short History of the Theosophical Society*. Adyar: The Theosophical Publishing House, 1938; Howard Murphet, *When Daylight Comes*. Wheaton, IL: Theosophical Publishing House, 1975.

★971★

UNITED LODGE OF THEOSOPHISTS
% Theosophy Hall
245 W. 33rd St.
Los Angeles, CA 90007

In 1909, after his rejection by Theosophists at the Point Loma, California, headquarters for insubordination, Robert Crosbie organized the United Lodge of Theosophists and began to gather into autonomous lodges those theosophists dissatisfied with both Katherine Tingley, leader of the continuing American branch of the Theosophical Society, and Annie Besant, international leader of the Theosophical Society, headquartered in Adyar, India. The Lodge was also an attempt to be informal in organization. Crosbie was himself a popular author and wrote several books, including *Friendly Philosopher* and *Answers to Questions on the "Ocean of Theosophy."* The literature of Helena Petrovna Blavatsky, founder of the Theosophist movement, and William Q. Judge, an American co-founder, are the main sources for the United Lodge. The Lodge is against hypnotism and has published a pamphlet labeling it as a modern form of sorcery.

Members of the Lodge are requested to sign a declaration which pledges the Lodge to dissemination of the "Fundamental Principles of the Philosophy of Theosophy." The declaration says the basis of union for Theosophists is a "similarity of aim, purpose and teaching." The Lodge has rejected controversies over leadership and authority, and personal interpretations of the work.

Noteworthy among United Lodge centers is the Santa Barbara, California, lodge, also known as the Universal Theosophical Fellowship. Under the leadership of Raghavan N. Iyer, it has developed a series of interlocking structures. Through Concord Grove Press it is pursuing an aggressive program of publishing materials on theosophy, eastern religion, and classical philosophy. The related Institute of World Culture promotes dialogue on classical traditions, modern science, art, and social structures as they relate to an emerging world culture. Foreign lodges are located in France, England, Australia, Holland, India, Italy, Belgium, and Canada. The Theosophy Company is the United Lodge's publishing concern in Los Angeles.

Membership: Not reported. In 1985 there were 10 lodges in the United States and 12 foreign lodges.

Periodicals: *Theosophy*, 245 W. 33rd Street, Los Angeles, CA 90007; *Hermes*, Universal Theosophy Fellowship, Box 1085, Santa Barbara, CA 92102.

Sources: Emmett A. Greenwalt, *California Utopia: Point Loma: 1897-1942*. San Diego: Point Loma Publications, 1978; Robert Crosbie, *Answers to Questions on the Ocean of Theosophy*. Los Angeles: The Theosophy Company, 1937; *The United Lodge of Theosophists, Its Mission and Its Future*. Los Angeles: The Theosophy Company, n.d.

★972★
WORD FOUNDATION
Box 18235
Dallas, TX 75218

Harold W. Percival (1868-1953) was a psychically attuned person from his early youth. In 1892, he joined the Theosophical Society. Membership in that group served as a springboard for his own development as a philosopher/ metaphysician and mystic. In 1893, he had a mystic experience which he described as being conscious of the presence of consciousness. He was conscious of consciousness as the ultimate and absolute reality and was thereby enabled to know about any subject. Thinking occurs when one selects a subject and holds it in the conscious light. As the light is focused, the subject is known. By this process, Percival began to dictate messages to Benoni B. Gattell. Between 1904 and 1917, Percival published twenty-five volumes of *The Word*. From 1912 to 1932, he dictated the material which became his most famous book, *Thinking and Destiny*. The popularity of the massive volume led to its having been reprinted five times by 1971. The Word Foundation was formed by readers who became disciples of Percival and wished to see his ideas spread abroad.

Thinking and Destiny lays out an impressive metaphysical system and includes reflections upon many topics covered in New Thought metaphysics and the psychic/occult world. Percival taught that the goal of life is to become conscious of consciousness. The triune (or real) self is the indivisible unit of a trinity (a knower, doer and thinker) incarnate within a body. Most often, this self is bound by thoughts initiated in the bodily desires. The underlying law of the universe is the law of thought; that which exists is an exteriorization of thought. By gaining knowledge of the triune self, one becomes no longer dependent on the bodily desires. The knower of the triune self is led to consciousness of consciousness and, hence, to conscious immortality.

Membership: Not reported.

Sources: Harold W. Percival, *Thinking and Destiny*. New York: Word Publishing Company, 1950; Harold W. Percival, *Democracy Is Self-Government*. New York: Word Publishing Company, 1952; Harold W. Percival, *Man and Woman and Child*. New York: Word Publishing Company, 1951; Harold W. Percival, *Masonry and Its Symbols*. New York: Word Publishing Company, 1952.

Alice Bailey

★973★
AQUARIAN EDUCATIONAL GROUP
30188 Mulholland Hwy.
Agoura, CA 91301

The Aquarian Educational Group dates to 1955, when a group began informally to meet in a garage in Van Nuys, California, to study the ancient wisdom, i.e., the occult teachings of such people as Helena Petrovna Blavatsky, founder of the Theosophical Society, Helena Roerich, co-founder with her husband, Nicolas Roerich, of the Agni Yofa Society, and Alice Bailey, founder of the Arcane School. The group grew, taking the name Aquarian Educational Foundation in 1963. Its leader is Haroutiun Saraydarian, more recently known as Torkom Saraydarian, a student of Eastern and occult religion, who settled in the United States in 1959. His early books have become the central texts for the Group.

The nineteen-paragraph creed professes belief in an evolutionary plan of the universe. Man is a spark of the almighty one. This life, the fourth kingdom, is the step to the fifth or superhuman kingdom. From there, man continues through two higher levels of awareness before graduating from the planetary school into the solar one. From the solar school man steps into cosmic evolution. The superhuman kingdom begins as a fountain of love and light and power. Through love and sacrificial service, man can touch the superhuman kingdom and thus purify his heart. From the superhuman kingdom come the immortals who periodically enlighten humanity and restore the law of love.

The symbol of the Group is a five-pointed star inside three concentric circles with an arrow in its midst. Man is a five- pointed star who must reach perfection and must communicate with the three circles-personality, soul and monad (a unifying element). The arrow, made of a tau cross and pyramid, symbolizes the path of sacrificial love and the transfigured life. Once attained, the cross becomes a bridge to Antahkarana, the thread of continuity of consciousness.

After the formal organization of the Group in 1963, work expanded into other communities. Land was purchased in Agoura, California, and a permanent center complex begun. The first building was started in 1972, and work began on a library, Sunday school, college and temple. A full program of classes and channeling from the masters are conducted, and two correspondence courses offered. Both the new moon and full moon are celebrated.

Membership: Not reported.

Periodicals: *Akbar Journal*, 12212 N. 58th Place Scottsdale, AZ 85254 (unofficial publication).

Sources: Haroutiun Saraydarian, *The Science of Meditation*. Reseda, CA: Aquarian Educational Group, 1971; Haroutiun Saraydarian, *The Magnet of Life*. Reseda, CA: Aquarian Educational Group, 1968; Torkom Saraydarian, *The Triangles of Fire*. Aguora, CA: Aquarian Educational Group, 1977.

★974★
ARCANA WORKSHOPS
Box 605
Manhattan Beach, CA 90266

Among the largest of the groups promoting the teachings of Alice Bailey in Southern California groups is the Arcana Workshops. The group has developed a meditation training-program based upon workshops and correspondence courses on a wide variety of topics and publications. Through the workshops, offered in the Los Angeles area, groups of people around Southern California have formed full-moon meditation groups. Through correspondence courses, numerous pamphlets, books and regular mailings, the organization has been able to establish a network around the country. The Arcana Workshops pioneered the intergroup cooperation that led to the annual celebration of the three linked festivals of Wesak, Humanity and Easter among occult groups in southern California every spring.

Sources: *The Full Moon Story*. Beverly Hills, CA: Arcana Workshops, 1974; *For Full Moon Workers*. Beverly Hills, CA: Arcana Workshops, n.d.; *What Is Arcana?* Beverly Hills, CA: Arcana Workshops, n.d.

★975★
ARCANE SCHOOL
866 United Nations Plaza
Suite 566-7
New York, NY 10017

The original group continuing the work and thought of Alice Bailey is the Arcane School, founded by Alice and Foster Bailey. In spite of the many divisions which have occurred among the students, it remains the largest of the full-moon meditation groups. All of the Alice Bailey books are published through its Lucis Publishing Trust, which publishes her books for the entire movement.

Several subsidiary programs were created to implement the program of the hierarchy. Triangles was founded in 1937 to build groups of three people who would unite daily in a mental chain radiating energy into the world. World Goodwill was established in 1932 with the purpose of establishing right human relations in the world. It is an "accredited non-governmental organization" with the United Nations in New York and Geneva.

Groups of the Arcane School are now found in all the major United States urban centers, and the Alice Bailey books have risen in circulation as a result of recent paperback editions. During the later years of her life, Alice, with the help of some leading students, began the preparation of correspondence lessons which are now mailed out around the country. They are based on Alice's books and lead the student through various degrees. Offices are located in the United Nations Plaza adjacent to the U.N. Building. Following Alice's death in 1949, Foster Bailey took charge of the work. Mary Bailey assumed the leadership role after Foster's death in 1977.

Membership: Not reported.

Periodicals: *The Beacon*, Lucis Publishing Company, 866 United Nations Plaza, Suite 566-7, New York, NY 10017; *World Goodwill Newsletter*, World Goodwill, 113 University Place, 11th Floor, New York, NY 10003.

Sources: John R. Sinclair, *The Alice Bailey Inheritance*. Wellingsborough, Northamptonshire: Turnstone Press, 1984; Alice A. Bailey, *The Unfinished Autobiography*. New York:Lucis Publishing Company, 1951; *Thirty Years' Work*. New York: Lucis Publishing Company, n.d.

★976★
MEDITATION GROUPS, INC.
Box 566
Ojai, CA 93023

Of the several groups which have separated from the Arcane School, the original organization established by Alice Bailey to perpetuate the teaching she had received from the Great White Brotherhood, Meditation Groups, Inc. seem to be the largest. It was formed in 1950 by Florence Garrique (1888- 1985) and was headquartered in

Greenwich, Connecticut. With the assistance of Ray Whorf, MGNA began a center on a mountain precipice overlooking the Ojai (California) Valley in 1968. The center has functioned as a site for new-moon and full-moon gatherings since its dedication in 1971.

While following the same teachings as the Arcane Scool and centering its teachings on the books of Alice Bailey, Meditation Groups Inc. has developed its own programs which function as the Meditation Group of the New Age, the Group for Creative Meditation and the Specialized Groups. Meditation Group for the New Age is the instructional arm of Meditation Groups, Inc. It teaches a comprehensive three-year course in meditation which presents its basic principles and introduces the student to the occult perspective of the books Alice Bailey received from the Tibetan, the master from the spiritual hierarchy with whom she had extensive contact. Following completion of the three-year course, the student may elect to continue in an on going advanced meditation course with materials mailed out quarterly. MGNA also sponsors regular symposia in Ojai annually and at various locations on the East and West Coast.

The Group for Creative Meditation encompasses the numerous meditation groups actually working on the program of service to the Christ, humanity and the planet earth by following a cycle of meditation based upon the call of the Tibetan for unanimous and simultaneous meditation. In this endeavor, the group provides a number of materials for conducting new and full moon meditation group sessions and a meditation calendar with full information for necessary adjustments within the various time zones in the United States.

The teachings at MGNA have been heavily influenced by Robert Assagioli, an Italian psychologist whose book, *Psychosynthesis*, and therapy system of the same name, aim at an integration of the personality. His is one of the few contemporary psychological schools of thought which give consideration to man's psychic a nd spiritual nature and needs. The Group for Creative Meditation sponsors an annual transpersonal conference which draws heavily on Assagioli's perspectives.

Conceived as the most subjective of the three activities, the Specialized Groups combine disciplined meditation with a focus upon a particular area of endeavor, one of the ten originally discussed by the Tibetan: telepathic communication, recognition of reality, healing, education, politics, religion, science, psychology, finance, and creativity. Students must have completed the first year of the Meditation Group for the New Age course before they can join a specialized group.

Meditation Groups, Inc. has affiliated members and groups in Canada, Britain, Germany, Belgium, Italy, Holland, and Argentina.

Membership: Not reported.

Sources: Raymond B. Whorf, *The Tibetan's Teaching*. Ojai, CA: Meditation Groups, Inc., n.d.; Frances Adams Moore, *A View from the Mount*. Ojai, CA: The Group for Creative Meditation, 1984.

★977★
SCHOOL OF ESOTERIC STUDIES
40 E. 49th St., Suite 1903
New York, NY 10017

The School for Esoteric Studies was established in 1956 by former staff members of the New York headquarters of the Arcane School. Each had been a close co-worker of Alice Bailey. The school is located in New York City and offers training for discipleship in the New Age. Its course, given via correspondence to students through the world, focuses on study of the ancient wisdom teachings, meditation, and service as a way of life. Discipleship is seen not as devotion towards any individual or group, but as intelligent cooperation with the spiritual hierarchy (i.e. the masters of wisdom, or the Christ and His Disciples) towards the working out of the Plan of Light and Love within humanity.

The teaching staff at the school has written its own lesson material, which is used by students reading the various texts by Alice Bailey. The School is led by its president, Jan van der Linden, and a teaching staff of twenty-two members.

Membership: In 1984 the school reported 227 students of whom 176 were in the United States. It is not organized into local groups.

Sources: Norman Gregor, *Whither Man?*. New York: School for Esoteric Studies, n.d.

★978★
SCHOOL OF LIGHT AND REALIZATION (SOLAR)
Route 1, Box 72
Suttons Bay, MI 49682

The School of Light and Realization (Solar) dates to 1969, when the concept of the school emerged in a conversation between Hamid Bey of the Coptic Fellowship in America and Norman Creamer, the founder of Solar. Following the conversation, Creamer, who had been searching for the right course for his life, and his wife, Katy Creamer, purchased a farm north of Traverse City, Michigan. The vision of Solar emerged largely out of a reading of the works of Alice Bailey and Theosophy. There is strong belief in the imminent reappearance of the Christ and coming of the Aquarian Age. Solar is conceived to be one of the "New Group of World Servers" that will create the new society on the principles of goodwill and basic human character.

Solar's program is centered upon training men and women for life in the new age, and training them to raise the level of consciousness in order to come in touch with the world of ideas and intuition. Solar teaches the growth of the communal ideal; the coming of the one Christ; the removal of limitations and the development of potentials; that there is no original sin, that each individual has his own set of liabilities, assets and responsibilities; that to give the soul its freedom is the goal of human life, that discipline is self-imposed and that Eastern philosophy is useful for Western man.

A school for both children and adults is being established on the farm near Traverse City. The first session of the adult training school was held in the summer of 1972. Centers for the dissemination of Solar concepts are being established across the country; the first is in St. Petersburg, Florida. Solar offers correspondence lessons in its teachings.

Membership: Not reported.

Periodicals: *The Solarian*, Route 1, Box 71, Sutton's Bay, MI 49682.

Sources: Norman Creamer, *The Aquarian Cosmic Vision*. Suttons Bay, MI: School of Light and Realization, n.d.; Norman Creamer, *Song of Solar*. Sutton's Bay, MI: School of Light and Realization, 1972.

★979★
TARA CENTER
Box 6001
North Hollywood, CA 91603

Within the Theosophical tradition, Charles W. Leadbeater and Annie Besant first promoted the expectation of a world savior whose appearance was equated with the Second Advent of Christ and the arrival of Lord Maitreya, the Buddhist bodhisattva who would assist humanity in making its next forward evolutionary step. They identified Jeddu Krishnamurti as that savior and organized the Order of the Star of the East to communicate their hope. In 1948, almost two decades after Krishnamurti had renounced his messianic role, Alice Bailey, founder of the Arcane School, published the *Reappearance of the Christ*, in which she argued that the time was ripe for the appearance of a new world teacher (avatar) who would come as both Son of God and head of the spiritual hierarchy, the group of exalted beings believed by Theosophists to form the cosmic government of the universe. She also suggested that preparatory work for the appearance would begin in 1975.

In 1975 a Scottish-born student of Bailey's teachings began to proclaim the imminent appearance of the Christ. Benjamin Creme first voiced his expectations in London and then traveled throughout Europe and to North America. He claimed to have originally come into contact with the Spiritual Hierarchy in 1959. He later received instructions to begin his mission of publicity announcing Maitreya's appearance in 1975. In 1977 he began receiving

messages from Maitreya which could be relayed to the general public. The substance of the messages was brief: Humanity has arrived at a situation in which it must either change or die. Humans must begin to manifest their divinity in new ways, specifically through the more traditional values of love and justice, but especially in the sharing of the world's resources with the poor and starving.

According to Creme, the anti-Christ has come and gone. The anti-Christ, an energy not a person, the destructive force which destroys the old in preparation for the positive forces of the Christ, wreaked its havoc during the period of 1914-1945 and was fully embodied in Adolf Hitler and his closest associates. With anti-Christ out of the way, Christ/Maitreya is is ready to appear.

During the 1970s, according to Creme, Maitreya materialized a human body into which he incarnated. In 1977 he flew from Karachi to London and took up residence in the Indian-Pakistani community of London, where he began to speak regularly to audiences numbered in the hundreds. On April 24-25, 1982, through advertisements taken out in a number of the world's prominent newspapers, Creme announced that Maitreya's "Day of Declaration" would occur within two months. Followers expected it on or before June 21, 1982. When the Declaration failed to occur and Maitreya failed to appear, Creme blamed the apathy of the media (a sign of general human apathy). He also announced that the Day of Declaration was still imminent though no new specific date was set. In the meantime, the followers were urged to continue their main task of announcing that Christ is in the world and soon to appear.

As people accepted Creme's message, an organization began to emerge, and by 1980 Tara Centers had been established in New York and Hollywood to distribute books and tapes, facilitate Creme's tours and speaking engagements, and develop "transmission groups," small groups of followers who work in meditation to transform the energy emanating from the Spiritual Hierarchy. That transformation makes the energy accessible to the planet to carry on the work of the Christ. Groups now exist across North America and Europe.

Membership: Not reported.

Periodicals: *Share International*, Box 971, North Hollywood, CA 91603.

Sources: Alice Bailey, *The Reappearance of the Christ*. New York: Lucis Publishing Company, 1848; Benjamin Creme, *Messages from Maitreya the Christ*. Los Angeles: Tara Press, 1980; Benjamin Creme, *The Reappearance of the Christ and the Masters of Wisdom*. Los Angeles: Tara Center, 1980; Benjamin Creme, *Transmission, A Meditation for the New Age*. North Hollywood, CA: Tara Center, 1983; *Update on the Reappearance of the Christ*. North Hollywood, CA: Tara Center, 1983.

Liberal Catholic Churches

★980★

AMERICAN CATHOLIC CHURCH
℅ Most Rev. Simon Eugene Talarczyk
430 Park Ave.
Laguna Beach, CA 92651

On December 29, 1915, as one of the first acts after founding his fledgling American Catholic Church, Joseph Rene Vilatte, consecrated Frederick E. J. Lloyd (1859-1933), an Episcopal clergyman whose distinguished career included his election and then rejection of the post of Bishop Coadjutor of Oregon. In 1915, after four years as pastor of Grace Episcopal Church in Oak Park, Illinois, he resigned to go with Vilatte. In 1920 at a Synod of the Church held in Chicago, Vilatte retired and turned the Church over to Lloyd who assumed the titles of Primate, Metropolitan and Archbishop.

Lloyd proved to be an able leader, but, following the pattern of other independent bishops, he attempted to build the American Catholic Church by drawing priestly colleagues around him and consecrating them to the episcopacy. He hoped that bishops would generate a jurisdiction, and appointed them before there were congregations over which they could give oversight. Among the eight bishops he consecrated Gregory Lines (1923), Francis Kanski (1926), Daniel C. Hinton (1927) and Ernest Leopold Peterson (1927). Each of these would at one point leave the American Catholic Church and establish a different jurisdiction.

Lloyd was succeeded in 1932 by Hinton. Hinton in turn consecrated Percy Wise Clarkson the following year. Clarkson opened a very successful church in Laguna Beach, California, but he was a Theosophist and brought a Theosophical theological perspective which came to dominate American Catholic Church life and thought.

Bishop Lines had problems with Hinton. He withdrew from the American Catholic Church in 1927 in reaction to Hinton's consecration as Bishop-Auxiliary to Lloyd, and formed the Apostolic Christian Church. He returned a few years later only to leave again when Hinton became Primate. During his first year separated from the Church, he consecrated Justin A. Boyle (a.k.a. Robert Raleigh). In 1930 Raleigh consecrated a Theosophist, Lowell Paul Wadle. Wadle soon left Raleigh and placed himself under Clarkson who had succeeded Hinton. In 1940 Wadle succeeded Clarkson, and served as Primate of the American Catholic Church for the next twenty-five years. During these years the Theosophical perspective initially brought in by Clarkson became the only perspective in the church and interaction with the Liberal Catholic Church branches has been strong. Wadle participated in a number of Liberal Catholic consecration services. In 1965 Wadle was succeeded by Hanlon Francis Marshall, who served only one year before being replaced by Hugh Michael

Strange. The present Primate is Archbishop Simon E. Talarczyk.

During this same period, the other bishops, now separated from Clarkson and Wadle, initiated their new jurisdictions: The American Catholic Church (Syro-Antiochean) (Peterson); The Church of Antioch (Lines/Raleigh); the Traditional Roman Catholic Church in the Americas (Kanski): and the Apostolic Episcopal Church (Kanski).

The beliefs of the American Catholic Church are very close to that of the Liberal Catholic Church. It views itself as holding to an "orthodox" faith but interpreting it in the light of some basic truths: that our ignorance of God and nature is due to the lack of the spirit and life of God within us; that the way to the divine knowledge is the way of the gospel that leads to a new birth; and that the way of new birth is totally within the will of man to grasp.

Membership: Not reported. There are only one or two churches and several hundred members remaining in the church.

Sources: Lowell Paul Wadle, *In the Kight of the Orient*. Long Beach, CA: the Author, 1951; *The Holy Liturgy*. American Catholic Church, 1955; Odo A. Barry, *Outline History of the American Catholic Church*. Long Beach, CA: American Catholic Church, 1951.

★981★

CHURCH OF ANTIOCH
℅ Most Rev. Herman Adrian Spruit
Box 219
Mountian View, CA 94042

During the 1930s the American Catholic Church on the West Coast became thoroughly infused with Theosophical metaphysics. One instrument for moving the Church in that direction was Justin A. Boyle, more popularly known as Robert Raleigh. Boyle, a Roman Catholic priest, joined the Apostolic Christian Church, a splinter of the American Catholic Church schism formed by Gregory Lines in 1927. Lines consecrated Boyle on April 7, 1928, and appointed him coadjutor with right of succession. Lines returned for a few years to Lloyd's Church, but seceded again upon Lloyd's retirement. After Lines' death Raleigh continued as head of his independent jurisdiction. Over the years he also headed several Christian metaphysical organizations, St. Primordia's Guild and the Mystical Prayer Shrine.

At the time of Bishop Raleigh's retirement in 1965, his coadjutor was Herman Adrian Spruit (b. 1911). Spruit was a former Methodist minister who had developed a broad experience in metaphysical-religious leadership through his affiliation with the Church of Religious Science and the Theosophical Society. In 1955 he began the independent Parish of Saint Michael, The Church

Universal. He first explored the possibility of associating with the Liberal Catholic Church but rejected it for organizational reasons. At this point he became aquainted with independent Liberal Catholic bishop Charles Hampton. Recognizing Spruit's potential, Hampton ordained him to the deaconate (1955) and priesthood (1956) and then consecrated him to the bishopric (1957).

Partially as a result of his contact with Bishop Lowell Paul Wadle, who had joined Hampton in ordaining Spruit, he met Robert Raleigh. And in the Apostolic Christian Church, he found the wider Christian community with which he could relate. He merged his work into Raleigh's jurisdiction and became his coadjutor. In 1965 he succeeded Raleigh. He also changed the name of the jurisdiction to the Church of Antioch Malabar Rite, thus affirming his succession through Frederick E. J. Lloyd and Joseph Rene Vilatte, the first archbishops of the American Catholic Church, to Mar Julius the Metropolitan of Malabar, and the authorization of Vilatte's consecration by Ignatius Peter III of Antioch.

In faith and practice the Church of Antioch emphasizes the Theosophical perspective of the Liberal Catholics. Although it relies on the authority of the Holy Scripture and the Ecumenical Creeds, it is quick to state that it "seeks further light on the mystery and wonder of faith, by searching in the spirit of disciplined scholarship for those aspects of Christian Evidences that preceded and followed the Apostolic Period." The Church has not only ordained women to the priesthood, but Spruit consecrated his first wife, Helene Seymour, as the first woman bishop in modern times. In early 1986, he consecrated his present wife, Mary Spruit, as matriarch of the church, the feminine counterpart of his role as patriarch.

Membership: Not reported. Parishes under the jurisdiction of the Church of Antioch are scattered along the West Coast. A strong parish, the Church of the Divine Presence (pastored by John Joseph Rankin) is located in Houston, Texas. There are an estimated several thousand members.

Educational facilities: Sophia Divinity School, Mountain View, California.

Periodicals: *Prism*, Church of Antioch, Box 1015, Mountain View, CA 94042.

Sources: Edward C. Sullivan, *A Short History of the Church of Antioch and Its Apostolic Succession*. Bellingham, WA: Holy Order of the Rose and Cross, 1981; Herman Adrian Spruit, *Constitution and Statement of Principles*. Mountian View, CA: Church of Antioch Press, 1978; Mary Spruit, ed., *The Chalice of Antioch*. Mountain View, CA: Archbishop Herman Adrian Spruit, 1979.

★982★
ECCLESIA GNOSTICA
% Most Rev. Stephan Hoeller
4516 Hollywood Blvd.
Los Angeles, CA 90028

Stephan A. Hoeller has for many years been a popular writer of occult literature and has written extensively on gnosticism and the wisdom tradition. Very early in his career, he became acquainted with the writings of James Morgan Pryse. Pryse, a leader of the independent Theosophical movement in New York City early in the century, later moved to Los Angeles and became a popular lecturer and writer on the occult and gnosticism. The Gnostica Ecclesia continues, in a religious vein, the gnostic tradition of the Gnostic Society founded by Pryse in 1928. The Society is now a chartered lay organization of the church.

In 1959 Hoeller was appointed to oversee the work of the Brotherhood and Order of the Gnosis and the Pre-Nicene Church as the American representative of Richard, Duc de Palatine. After de Palatine's death, he and many members of the Order left and formed the Ecclesia Gnostica. Hoeller had been consecrated in 1967 by de Palatine, assisted by Bishops John Martyn-Baxter and Gregory F. E. Barber. He was reconsecrated subconditione by Archbishop Herman Adrian Spruit (of the Church of Antioch), assisted by Bishop Barber and Neill P. Jack, Jr., in 1972.

The Ecclesia Gnostica continues the teaching of the Brotherhood and Order of Pleroma, but has a much more open approach. From the headquarters, the Sophia Gnostic Center in Hollywood, California, regular classes and lectures and weekly worship is offered to the public, and a worshipping community has gathered. Following Bishop Spruit's lead, the Church has been in the forefront of welcoming women to the priesthood and has one female bishop.

Membership: In 1984 the church reported approximately 250 affiliated lay people, 10 priests, and three congregations.

Periodicals: *ABRAXAS*, 4516 Hollywood Blvd., Hollywood, CA 90027.

Sources: Stephan A. Hoeller, *The Gnostic Jung*. Wheaton, IL: Theosophical Publishing House, 1982; Stephan A. Hoeller, *The Royal Road*. Wheaton, IL: Theosophical Publishing House, 1975; Stephan A. Hoeller, *The Enchanted Life*. Hollywood, CA: Gnostic Society, n.d.; James M. Pryse, *Spiritual Light*. Los Angeles: The Author, 1940.

★983★

ECCLESIA GNOSTICA MYSTERIUM
% Most Rev. Rosa Miller
3437 Alma, #23
Palo Alto, CA 94306

The Ecclesia Gnostica Mysteriorum is an independent jurisdiction formed originally as the Northern California diocese of the Ecclesia Gnostica led by Stephan A. Hoeller. In 1983, however, the Ecclesia Gnostica Mysteriorum became a separate legal entity, though it remains in a federated relationship with the parent body. Founder of the new jurisdiction is Rosa Miller, who was ordained by Hoeller in 1974 and consecrated to the episcopacy in 1981 by Bishops Hoeller, Forest Barber and Homer Jack.

Bishop Miller claims a primal apostolic succession through the Mary Magdalene lineage. According to her account, Mary Magdalene had received her "hierophantic power" at the time of Christ's last supper. Later she was the first to see the resurrected Christ. Unable to function in the immediate area because of sexist attitudes, she traveled west with Joseph of Arimathea, first ot England and later to the Continent, where she lived out her life. She left behind a secret sisterhood which survived to this day. During the 1960s, Miller made contact with this sisterhood and was consecrated in it. She promised to keep her association confidential until after she had received the more recognized male lineage. She has now, however, ordained the first male priests in the Mary Magdalene order. Teachings of the church are similar to the Ecclesia Gnostica and derive from various gnostic sources. A liturgy was developed that draws freely on George Mead's collection of gnostic texts, *Fragments of a Faith Forgotten*. The church is a member of the Synod of Independent Sacramental Churches.

Membership: In 1984, the church reported three congregations and 17 clergy. Membership is not counted but approximately 600 people are loosely affiliated. There is one foreign parish, in Seville, Spain, with approximately 100 affiliated members.

Periodicals: *The Gnostic.* 3437 Alma, No. 23, Palo Alto, CA 94306.

Sources: Rose Miller, *The Gnostic Holy Eucharist.* Palo Alto, CA: Ecclesia Gnostica Mysteriorum, 1984; *The Gnostic Holy Eucharist.* Palo Alto, CA: Sanctuary of the Holy Shekinah, 1984; George R. S. Mead, *Fragments of a Faith Forgotten.* New Hyde Park, NY: University Books, 1960.

★984★

FEDERATION OF ST. THOMAS CHRISTIAN CHURCHES
% Dr. Joseph L. Vredenburgh
6656 Trigo Road, B
Goleta, CA 93117

The Federation of St. Thomas Christian Churches was formed in 1980 as a loose fellowship of independent non-papal apostolic priests and ministries, some of whom were former members of the Church of Antioch led by Archbishop Herman Adrian Spruit. All of the member churches were gnostic in their belief, mystical in their worship, open to feminine leadership at all levels, and generally agreed on "New Age" philosophical concepts such as reincarnation and karma. Included in the federation by 1938 (among thirty ministries and churches) were the MeBasrim Fellowship, the Ecclesia Gnostica Mysteriorum, and the Order of Antioch.

Disruption of the Fellowship began in 1984. That year Bishop Michael Zaharakis, a leading member of the federation died, and presiding Bishop Joseph L. Vredenbregh, who had moved to Hawaii, and Bishop Lewis P. Keizer of the MeBasrim Fellowship had a disagreement on policy which led to a disintegration of the federation as it was then constituted. Many of the member churches withdrew and formed the Synod of Independent Sacramental Churches. Bishop Vredenbrugh reorganized the federation as a umbrella for the remaining independent ministries. In 1984 the Reformed Catholic Church in America, led by Most Rev. Brian G. Turkington, its founder, merged into the Federation. Turkington was named Archbishop-Metropolitan of the Federation and shares leadership with Vredenburgh. An annual synod convenes on the July 4th weekend.

Membership: Not reported. Membership consists primarily of priests who are chaplains or who conduct other independent noncongregation-oriented ministries.

Educational facilities: College of Seminarians, Goleta, California.

Periodicals: *St. Thomas Journal*, 6656 Trigo Road, B, Goleta, CA 93117.

★985★

GNOSTIC ORTHODOX CHURCH
% Abbot-Bishop George Burke
3500 Coltrane Rd.
Oklahoma City, OK 73121

The pilgrimage of Abbot George Burke and the group of monastics that surround him at the Monastery of the Holy Protection of the Blessed Virgin Mary in suburban Oklahoma City, Oklahoma, is among the most fascinating of all of the independent apostolic churches. Burke was raised a conservative Protestant but among people with a mystic bent who had prophetic powers and practiced spiritual healing. As a young adult he discovered the *Bhagavad Gita*, the ancient Hindu scripture from India, to which he was immediately attracted. He began a study of Eastern religious literature. He finally traveled to India and was initiated into the classical Hindu monastic order of Shankaracharya.

He returned to the United States and resided for three years in a Greek Orthodox monastery where he discovered the convergence of mystical Eastern Christianity with much Hindu spirituality. Upon leaving the Monastery he gathered a small group around him and in 1968 they went to India. They became disciples of Sri Sri Anandamayi (b. 1895), a famous female guru. Upon their return in 1969, they settled in Oklahoma City and created the Sri Ma Anandamayi Monastery. As disciples of Anandamayi they practiced japa (or mantra) yoga, a spiritual discipline which requires the repetition of a mantrum, word(s) of power. The practice leads to the spiritual liberation that all seek.

By 1974 19 disciples had gathered at the monastery and a periodical, *Ananda Jyoti*, was being published. Then in the early 1970s Burke, known then as Swami Nirmalananda Giri became acquainted with Jay Davis Kirby of the Old Catholic Episcopal Church. Under Kirby's guidance, he was led to Old Catholicism. On August 23, 1975 he was consecrated by Kirby and Robert L. Williams of the Liberal Catholic Church International, working with a letter of concurrence from Archbishop E. R. Verostek of the North American Old Roman Catholic Church-Utrecht Succession.

During the mid- and late 1970s Burke and the Monastery functioned under the episcopal authority of Bishop Williams as the American Catholic Church. They created Rexist Press, from which flowed some of the most substantive material produced by Old Catholics in America. Burke's catechetical text, *Faith Speaks*, remains the most complete theological text produced by any American Old Catholic. He also wrote several booklets, reprinted several classical Old Catholic works, produced a series of *Bible Guides*, and in 1976 began *The Old Catholic* (later renamed *The Good Shepherd*) which gave Old Catholicism one of its few high-quality periodicals. During this period Burke's writings were traditional Catholic in its theological perspective and widely read and appreciated by Old Catholics.

More recently, Burke has openly moved toward Liberal Catholicism in belief, while the early attunement to Eastern Orthodoxy has asserted itself in practice. He remains a member of the Shankaracharya Order and has sought an affiliation that will provide an ideological compatibility. The concept of reincarnation and karma are integral to his theology. Finally, in 1984 he founded the Gnostic Orthodox Church. It is in communion with the Liberal Catholic Church, Province of the U.S.A.

Membership: Not reported. Besides the monastery in Oklahoma City, Oklahoma there is a congregation in Dallas, Texas.

Sources: George Burke, *Faith Speaks*. Oklahoma City, OK: Rexist Press, 1975; George Burke, *Magnetic Healing*. Oklahoma City, OK: Saint George Press, 1980; Edward C. Sullivan and Jeffrey A Isbrandtsen, "An Interview with Abbot George Burke" in *AROHN*, vol. 3, no. 3 (1980) pp. 26-29 (part 1); vol. 3, no. 4 (1981) pp. 24-30 (part 2).

★986★
JOHANNINE CATHOLIC CHURCH
Archbishop J. Julian Gillmon
Box 8098
San Diego, CA 92102

The Johannine Catholic Church was organized in 1968 (incorporated in 1971) by J. Julian Gillman and his wife, Rita Anne Gillman, as a ministry to those rejected by or disillusioned with the traditional churches. Initially it was directed to the hippie culture of the late 1960s. Gillman was consecrated "sub-rosa" by a 'renegade' (unnamed) Episcopal bishop, but in 1977 both he and his wife were consecrated by H. Ernest Caswell of the North American Old Roman Catholic Church-Utrecht Succession.

The church is described as new age in orientation, open to clergy of both sexes and making no distinctions due to sexual preferences. The designation Johannine refers to the Gospel of John and its central message of love. Love, not theology, is considered the overriding principle of Christianity.

The church sponsors several religious orders, all open to men and women, both married and single. The Order of Saint John the Evangelist is the order of clergy whose ministry is to the rejected. The Order of Saint John Bernadone is a street ministry to street people. The Paracelsian Order is a new age community seeking to develop an alternative life style. The Community of the Resurrection ministers in the homosexual community. The church is a member of the Synod of Independent Sacramental Churches. Gillman edits *SISCOM*, the journal of the synod. Saint Dionysius' Press is the church's publishing arm.

Membership: Not reported. The church has centers in San Diego, Santa Barbara, Dulzura, and San Francisco, California.

Sources: William Nihle, *A True History of Celtic Britain*. San Diego, CA: Saint Dionysius Press, 1982.

★987★

INTERNATIONAL LIBERAL CATHOLIC CHURCH
% Rt. Rev. Edmund W. Sheehan
480 Fairview Rd.
Ojai, CA 93023

The International Liberal Catholic Church was founded in 1966 by Bishop Edmund Walter Sheehan and others who left the Liberal Catholic Church branch led by Bishop Edward M. Matthews. He had previously served as an auxiliary bishop under Bishop Charles Hampton. His disagreement with Matthews concerned administrative matters.

Sheehan linked the International Liberal Catholic Church to the Brotherhood of the Blessed Sacrament, a Dutch group which had broken with the British headquarters of the Liberal Catholic Church. The Brotherhood had originally sided with Matthews but had broken relations with him in 1962.

The International Liberal Catholic Church follows the Matthews faction in doctrinal and liturgical matters. While reporting 9 bishops, 25 clergy, and 3,000 members in 1969, the International Church dwindled to only a few parishes during the 1970s.

Membership: Not reported.

Sources: *International Liberal Catholic Church, Origins, Principles, Worship, Theology, Sacraments.* Ojai, CA: St. Raphael's Printing Guild, 1968; Edmund Sheehan, *Teaching and Worship of the Liberal Catholic Church.* Los Angeles, CA: St. Alban Press, 1925.

★988★

LIBERAL CATHOLIC CHURCH INTERNATIONAL
% Rt. Rev. Dean Bekken
741 Cerro Gordo Ave.
San Diego, CA 92102

The Liberal Catholic Church (being the American Province of the Liberal Catholic Church International) was constituted in 1983 by the merger of the Liberal Catholic Church and the Liberal Catholic Church International. The Liberal Catholic Church was one of two groups claiming to continue the original Liberal Catholic Church incorporated in 1928. In that church (under the second regionary bishop Charles Hampton) a strong division of opinion developed. Hampton articulated an independent stance regarding the Theosophical Society. As a result, he was deposed in 1944.

Some clergy and congregations supported him, and a schism was created. Then, the Presiding Bishop of the Church, F. W. Pigott (d. 1956), in London appointed John T. Eklund as the new regionary bishop. Eklund in turn consecrated two priests as bishops without obtaining the required approval of the priests and deacons of the Province. This act precipitated a second schism under Bishop Ray Marshall Wardall (d. 1954).

In response to the Eklund consecrations, Wardall consecrated Edward M. Matthews (1898-1985), whom the Eklund faction had deposed from his position as Dean of the Liberal Catholic Cathedral in Los Angeles. Nevertheless Matthews retained possession of the Cathedral. In 1950 Matthews succeeded Wardall as head of those clergy and congregations under his control. At that point the Eklund faction filed suit against the Wardall-Matthews faction asking the court to deny Matthews use of either the name Liberal Catholic Church or the title Regionary Bishop. In 1955 Matthews exercised his powers as head of the jurisdiction by consecrating two priests to the episcopacy, William H. Daw and James Pickford Roberts.

The litigation took over a decade, by which time Pigott, Eklund, Hampton and Wardall had all died. The court ruled in favor of Matthews, who it declared to be the Presiding Bishop of the Liberal Catholic Church. However, during the years of litigation most of the clergy and congregations were now aligned with other jurisdictions. (Also, detached from the organizational strength of the Theosophical Society, the Matthews' faction had lost a major source for new members.) In 1964, shortly after the ruling, Bishops Daw and Roberts left the Mathews' jurisdiction to form the Liberal Catholic Church International.

Matthews eventually sold the Los Angeles Cathedral property and moved his headquarters to Miranda, California, where it remained until 1976, at which time Matthews reported 8 churches, 8 clergy, and 4,000 members. (In fact the church had only two parishes, one in Miranda and one in San Diego, California, and several priests.) The Church splintered and Matthews, along with the congregation in Miranda, returned to the Liberal Catholic, Province of the United States. The San Diego parish under the leadership of then Very Rev. Dean Bekken, Vicar General of the Province, retained the corporate structure, and began to rebuild the Church.

Meanwhile, the International Liberal Catholic Church had picked up strenght internationally. In 1974, Daw, the presiding bishop resigned in favor of Joseph Edward Neth. It also developed a close working relationship to the Old Catholic Episcopal Church headed by Bishop Jay Davis Kirby.

On July 4, 1983, the Liberal Catholic Church merged with the Liberal Catholic Church International and became its American Province. Neth remained as the Presiding Bishop but also became the Provincial Bishop for the United States. Affiliated parishes are reported in England, Canada, Belgium and the Netherlands.

Among the important documents produced by Bishop Matthews, the 1959 Encyclical *"Freedom of Thought"* outlined the distinctives of this branch of Liberal Catholicism. Matthews attempted to move the Church away from Theosophical distinctives by affirming traditional Catholic ones. He specifically attacked the doctrine of reincarnation and noted that Liberal Catholicism does not now nor ever has at any time insisted or prescribed the dogma or teaching of the principle known as reincarnation, "Christian" or otherwise, as a tenet of belief and practices. Reincarnation is often a basic "text" belief in one's acceptance or rejection of Theosophy.

Membership: In 1984 the Church reported 5,000 members in the United States, 10 priests, and five congregations. There were an additional 1,500 members worldwide.

Educational facilities: St. Alban Theological Seminary, San Diego, California.

Sources: *The Holy Eucharist and Other Services.* San Diego, CA: St. Alban Press, 1977; Edward M. Matthews, *The Liberal Catholic Church and Its Place in the World.* Los Angeles: St Alban Book Shop, n.d.; Edward M. Matthews. *"Freedom of Thought," An Encyclical.* Los Angeles: Liberal Catholic Church, 1959; *Statement of Principles.* San Diego, CA: Liberal Catholic Church, 1977.

★989★
LIBERAL CATHOLIC CHURCH, PROVINCE OF THE UNITED STATES
% Rt. Rev. Lawrence J. Smith
9740 S. Avers
Evergreen Park, IL 60642

Bishop James Ingall Wedgwood brought the Liberal Catholic Church to the United States on the round-the-world tour he took his first year as Primate. Crossing the United States and meeting with Theosophists, he ordained as priests Charles Hampton (Los Angeles, August 19, 1917), Dr. Edwin Burt Beckwith (Chicago, September 16, 1917) and Ray M. Wardall (New York City, October 4, 1917). In 1919 Charles W. Leadbeater joined Wedgwood in consecrating Irving Steiger Cooper as the first regionary bishop for the United States. That consecration led to a war of words. Independent American Theosophists, especially those led by Katherine Tingley, used the emergence of the Liberal Catholic Church as an opportunity to denounce the Annie Besant-led Theosophists for selling out to Catholicism.

The Liberal Catholic Church prospered and spread under Cooper, but ran into trouble under its second regionary bishop, Charles Hampton (d. 1958). Hampton questioned the necessity of the close tie of the church to the Theosophical Society and its beliefs. As the controversy continued, Hampton was deposed, and John T. Eklund was appointed to succeed him. Eklund's consecration of Newton A. Dahl and Walter J. Zollinger led to a second schism by priests led by Bishop Wardall, who objected to the legality of the action. Among those opposed to Eklund

was Edward M. Mathews, the priest in charge of the leading congregation of the church in Hollywood, California. Eklund instituted suit against the schismatic group in hopes of denying it use of the Church's name. The suit was lost in a ten- year court battle, but in spite of the loss, most Liberal Catholics adhered. In 1973 it could report 29 congregations, 61 clergy and 2,393 members. The church retained the recognition of the international church headquartered in London, but it was forced to reincorporate in 1968 in Maryland in order to continue the use of its original name in the United States.

This branch of Liberal Catholicism is most closely tied to the Theosophical Society, a point at issue in its deposing Hampton. A house, traditionally the residence of the presiding bishop, is located at Krotona, the Theosophical community at Ojai, California. Nearby is the cathedral church of Our Lady and All Angels. It is aligned with the world headquarters of the Church in England. International leader of the church is Rt. Rev. Sten von Krusenstierna. In 1985, Rt. Rev. Lawrence J. Smith of Chicago became the Regionary Bishop for the Province of the United States, succeeding Rt. Rev. Gerrit Munnik.

Membership: In 1984 there were 77 priests and approximately 2,500 members. The 1985 directory listed 18 churches.

Periodicals: *Ubique,* The Liberal Catholic Church, Box 2546, Eugene, OR 97402; *The Voice of the Synod,* Very Rev. William Holme, Box 7042, Rochester, MN 55903.

Sources: *The Liturgy of the Liberal Catholic Church.* London: St. Alban Press, 1983; Irving S. Cooper, *Ceremonies of the Liberal Catholic Rite.* London: The St. Alban Press, 1964; James Ingall Wedgewood, *The Beginnings of the Liberal Catholic Church.* Lakewood, NJ: Ubique, 1967; William H. Pitkin, *Credo, First Steps in Faith.* Ojai, CA: St. Alban Press, 1977; Charles Webster Leadbeater, *The Science of the Sacraments.* Los Angeles: St. Alban Press, 1920.

★990★
MEBASRIM FELLOWSHIP
% Mar Petros
495 Ellis, #137
San Francisco, CA 94102

MeBasrim Fellowship dates to 1976 when several former priests of the Church of Antioch left. On Thanksgiving Day of that year, one of their number, Michael G. Zaharakis(1946-1984) was consecrated by Lewis P. Keizer to lead the small band. An initial congregation of twenty-two members was formed in Santa Cruz, California. The Fellowship shared the gnostic-mystical doctrine of the Church of Antioch, but had placed their priority on social action and community service. In Portland, Oregon, a ministry to alcoholics began and in Santa Cruz, an outreach to migrants led to the development of a jail ministry. These were but the first of a variety of outreach projects. A 1980 "Day of Solidarity with Jewish Congregations" resulted in the validation of the Santa Cruz chapel.

The Fellowship led in the formation of the ecumenical Federation of St. Thomas Christian Churches in 1980 and Bishop Zaharakis provided much of its leadership. However, in 1984, the federation was disrupted by internal disagreements. MeBasrim Fellowship withdrew and led in the formation of the Synod of Independent Sacramental Churches, which considered itself the continuation of the federation.

Membership: Not reported. There are several congregations along the West Coast and a number of priests in noncongregationally oriented ministries.

Sources: Lewis S. Keizer, *Initiation: Ancient & Modern.* San Francisco: St. Thomas Press, 1981.

★991★
NEW ORDER OF GLASTONBURY
Box 324
Rialto, CA 92376

The New Order of Glastonbury began in 1979 when seven independent Old and Liberal Catholic priests decided to establish an ordered community. The previous year, one of their number, Frank Ellsworth Hughes, had been consecrated by Archbishop Herman A. Spruit of the Church of Antioch. The group incorporated in 1980 and only later decided to add a missionary ministry as a means of serving the lay public. Several of the clergy have established chapels and begun to build a congregation.

The order is very eclectic but generally follows a Liberal Catholic perspective. Their statement of principles espouses a belief in One God, manifest as the Creator; the Cosmic Christ, the Son; and the Holy Spirit, the Comforter. In life and worship, the order combines emphases from Catholic (apostolic succession, seven sacraments); Protestant (freedom of belief and mode of worship); and Metaphysical (the study of comparative religion, occult and psychic reality) traditions. A variety of liturgies are approved from the more orthodox (such as the Tridentine Latin or Byzantine) to the theosophical liturgy of the American Catholic Church written by Lowell Paul Wadle.

The order is governed by a six-member board of directors. Most Rev. Frank Ellsworth Hughes was elected as the first presiding bishop. The order admits both married men and women to all levels of its ministry. Fr. Merle D. Mohring, Sr. served as the first president of the board of directors, while his wife, Most Rev. Martha Theresa (Martha Jo Mohring) served as secretary-treasurer, and more recently she was appointed acting presiding bishop.

Membership: In 1984 the order reported five congregations and 100 members served by 13 priests.

Educational facilities: Seminary of Our Lady, St. Mary of Glastonbury, Rialto, California.

Periodicals: *Gateways*, Box 324, Rialto, California 92376.

Sources: *The New Order of Glastonbury, History and Apostolic Succession.* Rialto, CA: New Order of Glastonbury, [1980?].

★992★
OLD CATHOLIC EPISCOPAL CHURCH
% Most Rev. Jay Davis Kirby
923 1/2 E. Briadway
Glendale, CA 91205

The Old Catholic Episcopal Church was founded in 1951 by Jay Davis Kirby, a chiropracter and a priest with Liberal Catholic and American Catholic backgrounds. He broke with his former Churches, however, as he wished to serve a truly Catholic Church "unadulterated by theosophy, parapsychology, tarot cards, homosexual congregations, women priests and women bishops." In 1970, Kirby was consecrated by Archbishop Herman Adrian Spruit of the Church of Antioch. Kirby also heads the Order of Christus Rex. A Laguna Beach parish is served by Suffragan Bishop John Charles Maier.

Membership: In 1984 there were 3 congregations and 5 priests in the church.

★993★
OLD HOLY CATHOLIC CHURCH, PROVINCE OF NORTH AMERICA
% Most Rev. George Brister
Box 69235
Oklahoma City, OK 73146

The Old Holy Catholic Church, Province of North America was founded in 1979 by Rev. George W. S. Brister. Brister had been ordained to the priesthood by Bishop James A. J. Taylor of the Order of St. Germain, Ecclesia Catholica Liberalis in 1969. He headed the Maranatha Ministry Church and the Order of St. Timothy, Ecclesia Catholica Liberalis, both in Oklahoma City, Oklahoma. By 1975 Maranatha Churches could also be found in Tulsa and Las Vegas. He was consecrated by Bishop Stephan A. Hoeller of the Ecclesia Gnostica in 1980. His Church, as is true of Liberal Catholic congregations, was quite eclectic and combined teaching drawn from Theosophy, Buddhism, New Age metaphysics and Religious Science.

At the time of the founding of the new jurisdiction he announced that he would "preach no doctrine except that which had been given us by Jesus Christ and handed down by the Apostles." This statement represented a movement toward orthodoxy, even though the Church continues to offer members classes in such topics as Kabbalah, Gnosticism, and psychogenics.

The jurisdiction is headquartered in Oklahoma City where Bishop Brister pastors St. Timothy's Church. He also edits the quarterly periodical, *The Lamp*, which recently replaced *Continuum* and *The Old Catholic Newsletter* as the church's official publication.

Membership: In 1984 there were six congregations and approximately 500 members served by 23 priests.

Periodicals: *The Lamp*, Box 60235, Oklahoma City, OK 73146.

★994★
ORDER OF ST. GERMAIN, ECCLESIA CATHOLICA LIBERALIS
(Defunct)

The Order of St. Germain, Ecclesia Catholica Liberalis was founded in 1969 as the Order of St. Germain. Its more recent name was adopted two years later. Its founder was James A. J. Taylor, also known as James Matthews, a former member of the Holy Order of MANS, an esoteric-metaphysical group modeled on the structure of a Roman Catholic religious order. Like traditional orders, the Order of St. Germain had no lay members, but is made up entirely of priests, ministers and "practitioners." Taylor asserted that although he "was consecrated by a Bishop (unnamed) of the Liberal Catholic Church, the Order claims no genetic connection with that Church."

The Order existed to forward the work of the Masters, the Christs, in the world. It was a sacramental church but differed in that it attempted to offer the widest latitude in matters of intellectual liberty and respect for individual conscience. Theologically it was Liberal Catholic in perspective.

The small order was headed by the Archbishop, assisted by other bishops appointed to administer state jurisdictions. A board of directors assisted in administrative matters. The order never grew beyond northern California.

★995★
PARACLETIAN CATHOLIC CHURCH
(Defunct)

The Paracletian Catholic Church was founded in 1982 by Leonard R. Barcynski and Vivian Barcynski, two bishops in the Church of Antioch. The Barcynskis had become well-known during the 1970s for their many books on magick and the occult written under their pseudonyms, Melita Denning and Osborne Phillips. They have been leaders for over a decade in the Aurum Solis, a ritual magick organization which they helped reconstitute in 1971.

In 1978 the Barcynskis moved to the United States and soon after met Archbishop Herman Adrian Spruit, who in June 1982 consecrated them and established a Diocese of St. Paul (Minnesota) which the Barcynskis jointly administered. However, in October of that year, they broke with the Church of Antioch and established an independent jurisdiction. The Church never became firmly established, however, and several years later they abandoned any further effort to establish its parishes.

The articles of association of the Paracletian Catholic Church indicated that the church's main purposes were "to spread the love and knowledge of Christ, to administer the sacraments of the Catholic and Apostolic tradition in their plenitude, and to perform charitable works." The church was an attempt to give expression through the forms of the Catholic liturgical tradition to the teachings of Western Occultism as transmitted through the Aurum Solis. As defined by the Aurum Solis, the purpose of life in this world is to discover one's True Will and to do it. God is envisioned as the Divine Spark within, which motivates people to search out their true Vocation or Will.

★996★
PRE-NICENE CHURCH (DE PALATINE)
% Most Rev. Seiji Yamauchi
8136 Ginzaga Ave.
Los Angeles, CA 90045

The Brotherhood and Order of the Pleroma was founded in 1953 in England by Ronald Powell, better known by the name he adopted, Richard, Duc de Palatine. The year previous to his founding of the Order he had been given the office of archon (ruler) of an Italian-based order, The Ancient Mystical Order of the Fratis Lucis. The Church is a liturgical community open only to members of the Order. It has its apostolic succession from Hugh George de Willmott Newman, who consecrated de Palatine in 1953.

The Order and Church differs from many Liberal Catholic groups by their emphasis upon gnosticism. The Gnostics were second century Christians who rejected the humanity of Jesus. They said he never became human, i.e. fleshly, and only seemed to have a material body. "Gnosis" means "knowledge," and the Gnostics sought salvation through the secret knowledge (occult wisdom) teachings.

The Order and Church emphasize a Western approach to the ancient wisdom, as opposed to Theosophists who draw heavily upon Eastern occultism.. It emphasizes Jesus' role as the bringer of gnosis and de-emphasizes the Oriental yogic disciplines. It is an active system, calling members to strive for enlightenment and push aside any self-abnegation. God is identified with nature and is pictured as fragmented into billions of parts, which are the spiritual selves, sparks of the divine, which man is. This spark is buried in the tomb of flesh. Humanity's task is to realize his God-nature and actualize his divine potentials. Reincarnation is a part of this scheme of actualization.

The method of actualization is the arcane (hidden) discipline, a way known to mystics of all ages. It includes the esoteric sacramental rituals of the Church which are based upon the allegorical interpretation of Holy Scripture.

The Order and Church are headquartered in London. The Sanctuary of the Gnosis is the corporate body created to give legal and civil status to the Order in America. The present President of the Sanctuary is George Ricci. The apostolic succession was passed by Powell to John Martyn-Baxter, who has passed it to the present bishop leaders of the Church.

Membership: Not reported. There are only a few hundred members of the Order in America and no more than 1,000 worldwide.

Sources: Richard, Duc de Palatine, *You and Reincarnation.*Sherman Oaks, CA: Aeon Press, 1976; Richard John Chretien Duc de Palatine, *The Inner Meaning of the Mystery School.* London: Pre-Nicene Publishing House, 1959.

★997★

ST. RAPHAEL'S OLD CATHOLIC CHURCH OF BRITISH COLUMBIA AND SOCIETY
715 E. 51st Ave.
Vancouver, BC, Canada V5X 1E2

St. Raphael's Old Catholic Church separated from the Canadian jurisdiction, the Liberal Catholic Church of Ontario, in an effort to take a more Catholic and Orthodox stance. However, the new jurisdiction moved into communion with the Liberal Catholic Church, Province of the U.S.A. Unlike many of the jurisdictions which share a Liberal Catholic perspective, this jurisdiction is against ordaining females. It also is opposed to admitting homosexuals into the priesthood.

Bishop J. Gerard A. Laplante was consecrated September 30, 1979 by Bishops D. M. Berry and H. V. Russell of the Liberal Catholic Church. He pastors the headquarters church in Vancouver, an attractive, if modest, cathedral.

Membership: In 1984 the church claimed two congregations and 300 members served by four priests.

I AM Groups

★998★

ASCENDED MASTER FELLOWSHIP
Box 603
162 Look-a way
Yarnell, AZ 85362

The Ascended Master Fellowship was founded in 1972 by the Rev. Theodore M. Pierce, a former minister in the Cosmic Church of Life and Spiritual Science. In 1954, he had been called by Ascended Master Saint Germain through a vision in which he was shown the word "Freedom" written across the universe. The basic teachings of the church are found in two volumes written by A.D.K. Luk, *Law of Life*. The volumes are a variation on the original I AM teachings as presented by Guy Ballard, founder of the I AM Religious Activity. Volume II includes a minute description of the spiritual hierarchy and the personages that fill the positions. The Fellowship works especially under Saint Germain, the Chohan of the Aquarian Age, but also is in cooperation with Ascended Masters Jesus and Mother Mary.

The Rev. Pierce has entered the realm of spiritual healing, and practices cosmic surgery through several spirit doctors. According to the Fellowship, in January, 1969, during a healing session, he was taken out of his body and taken back in time so as to be able to release "misqualified energy" (karma) from the individual. Pierce subsequently became a karmic eraser, one who can remove the consequences of evil that was done in former incarnations.

Regular services are held at the headquarters at Yarnell, Arizona. Affiliated groups are found in South Carolina, North Carolina, Phoenix; individual members are found across the United States. The periodical is sent to Canada, New Zealand, and Saudi Arabia.

Membership: Not reported.

Periodicals: *Temple Notes*, Box 603, 162 Look-a-way, Yarnell, AZ 85362.

Sources: A. D. K. Luk, *Law of Life*. Baltimore, MD: The Author, 1959-60. 2 Vols.

★999★

LAW OF LIFE ASCENDED MASTER GROUPS
% A. D. K. Luk
1124 N. Meta Ave.
Oklahoma City, OK 73107

A. D. K. Luk is an independent exponent of the I AM teachings who wrote and published the *Law of Life*, a popular variant treatment of I AM themes. It was also a summary of the information scattered through the discourses given by the masters through Guy Ballard, founder of the I AM Religious Activity. During the 1960s a number of independent groups such as those advocated in the first volume of *Law of Life* formed to study, meditate, and decree. In 1971 Luk issued an instruction manual for group leaders to guide their efforts. Beliefs and practice follow those of the I AM Activity. A. D. K. Publications issues a wide variety of materials for use by related groups. The books by Guy Ballard issued by the I AM Activity are also used, but there is no organizational affiliation.

Membership: Not reported.

Periodicals: *Law of Life Enlightener*, A. D. K. Publications, 1124 N. Meta Avenue, Oklahoma City, OK 73107.

Sources: A. D. K. Luk, *Law of Life*. Oklahoma City, OK: A. D. K. Publications, 1959-60. 2 Vols.; A. D. K. Luk, *Law of life Instruction for Group Directors*. Oklahoma City, OK: A. D. K. Publications, 1983.

★1000★
CITY OF THE SUN FOUNDATION
Box 356
Columbus, NM 88029

The City of the Sun grew out of Christ's Truth Church and School of Wisdom, founded in 1968 by the Rev. Wayne Taylor as a New Age community under guidance and direction of the spiritual hierarchy, particularly Master Hilarion. The City of the Sun, as the growing community is known, is near Columbus, New Mexico, on the Mexican border. A former member of the Bridge to Freedom, Taylor was for two years president of Sologa, Inc., and then helped edit *The Mentor*, published by the Sanctuary of the Master's Presence. During the time he was with Sologa, Inc. his wife, Grace Taylor, functioned as a channel. The move to New Mexico came as a result of messages received through that channeling. Preparation was made in the form of the acquisition of a tract of 159 acres near Columbus.

The basic teachings which led to the foundation are contained in Taylor's book, *Pillars of Light*. In it is told the story of man's fall, which has resulted in his being set back spiritually for missions of years. Taylor explains that through the "Light bearers of all ages the veil of spiritual darkness is being lifted. Man is about to enter the Golden Age, and the City of the Sun is one structure to prepare for transition."

The first official service of the church occurred in 1970 and included messages from Ascended Masters Hilarion, Martin Luther King, Mahatma Gandhi, Bishop James A. Pike, and Pope John XXIII. A periodical, which keeps interested students informed of on-going activity and attempts to coordinate the various independent groups receiving messages from the masters, was begun. The

foundation is one of the most ecumenical of the ascended master groups.

Membership: Not reported.

Periodicals: *The Golden Dawn*, Box 356, Columbus, NM 88029.

Sources: Wayne H. Taylor, *Pillars of Light*. Columbus, NM: The Author, 1965.

★1001★
CHURCH UNIVERSAL AND TRIUMPHANT
Box A
Malibu, CA 90265

Though often confused with the I AM Religious Activity, from which it drew some inspiration, the Church Universal and Triumphant (CUT), was founded by Mark Prophet and his wife, Elizabeth Clare Prophet, neither of who had been affiliated with the I AM Religious Activity or the Saint Germain Foundation. While founded by two individuals, who like Guy Ballard (founder of the I AM Activity), have been designated Messengers of the Ascended Masters, the teachings of the Church are at considerable variance with those held by the Saint Germain Foundation.

CUT had its beginning in 1958 when Mark Prophet was appointed as a Messenger by the Master, El Morya, who wished to initiate a new thrust of ascended master activity. In the early 1960s he was joined by Elizabeth Clare Wulf, who he married, and she was also appointed a Messenger. The Keepers of the Flame Fraternity was formed to provide students with systematic lessons in the teachings of the Masters. The work became known as the Summit Lighthouse, and in 1966 headquarters were moved from Washington, D.C. to Colorado Springs, Colorado. Mark Prophet died in 1973 and Elizabeth assumed full responsibility for the work.

During the 1970s, as the work grew, new departments were created, and in 1975 a reorganization of the entire structure was made. Summit International became the structure under which the various departments were tied together. The Church Universal and Triumphant, incorporated in 1974, had already replaced the Summit Lighthouse as the main structure of the work. Summit Lighthouse became the publishing arm of the organization. Montesorri International provides parochial education for children and youth, primarily of church members. Summit University provides advanced intensive education in a retreat-like atmosphere for members of the Keepers of the Flame Fraternity. In 1976 the headquarters moved to Pasadena, California and two years later to Malibu. Presently, a second headquarters complex is being prepared in Montana.

The Church Universal and Triumphant is a new activity of the Great White Brotherhood, as the ascended masters are often called. According to the masters', in the beginning, light came forth from the Great Central Sun, the metaphysical center of our cosmos, and was individualized as many individual sparks, each a personalized fragment of deity. These sparks are the "I AM Presence," the essence of each person. Each person was created a soul destined to return to its source of life. While on earth, the soul can choose to follow a path of return or to wander aimlessly in the mire of existence. Mediating for the soul seeking to return is the Christ consciousness, the real self of each child of God. (Jesus of Nazareth and other very saintly figures walked on earth in complete atunement with their Christ consciousness.)

To assist chels (students on the path of return), the church teaches a number of helpful disciplines which include the lost arts of healing and the science of the spoken word. The latter includes prayers, affirmations and decrees to invoke light. Eventually, each soul will unite with its Christ consciousness and ascend, though this process may involve a number of earthly incarnations.

The church has inherited a strong sense of patriotism and places emphasis upon America's role as the birth place of modern freedoms in the plans of the masters. Members are also involved in social issues especially as related to abortion, child pornography, nuclear warfare, terrorism, and world communism, all of which the church opposes.

Individuals may relate to the church on three levels. Members of the geneal public may receive church teachings, participate in most of its religious services and conferences, and send their children to the Montesorri school located at the church's headquarters complex. Next, they may join the Keepers of the Flame Fraternity, in which they pledge to nurture the flame of the inner self. As members, they receive regular lessons, may attend special weekly services and become eligible to attend Summit University. Finally, members of the fraternity may also choose to become full communicant members and be formally baptized. Full church members must formally subscribe to the tenets of the church and tithe their income.

In 1975 the Church initiated a number of teaching centers around the United States. Such centers which provide live-in facilities give members, the majority of whom relate to the church through correspondence lessons and by receiving the regular communications from the masters channeled through Elizabeth Clare Prophet in the weekly *Pearls of Wisdom*.

The Church is headed by Elizabeth Clare Prophet, the Messenger of the Masters, who regularly received guidance for the Church from the ascended masters. Administratively the church is headed by a board of trustees who manage its affairs. The Church sponsors three different cable television shows featuring Elizabeth Clare Prophet that are seen on over 100 stations nationwide: "The Coming Revolution in Higher Consciousness," "Everlasting Gospel," and "Summit University Forum."

Membership: Not reported.

Educational facilities: Summit University, Malibu, California.

Periodicals: *Pearls of Wisdom*, Box A, Malibu, CA 90265; *Heart*, Box A, Malibu, CA 90265; *The Coming Revolution*, Box A, Malibu, CA 90265; *Royal Teto n Ranch News*, Corwin Springs, MT.

Sources: Elizabeth Clare Prophet, *The Great White Brotherhood in the History, Culture and Religion of America*. Los Angeles: Summit University Press, 1976; Mark Prophet and Elizabeth Prophet, *Climb the Highest Mountain*. Colorado Springs, CO: Summit Lighthouse, 1972; Mark Prophet and Elizabeth Prophet, *My Soul Doth Magnify the Lord*. Colorado Springs, CO: Summit Lighthouse, 1974; El Morya, as dictated to Elizabeth Clare Prophet, *The Chela and the Path*. Colorado Springs, CO: Summit University Press, 1976; Mark Prophet and Elizabeth Prophet, *The Science of the Spoken Word*. Colorado Springs, CO: Summit Lighthouse, 1974.

★1002★
ESSENE TEACHINGS INC.
% Mary Myers
3427 Denison Place
Charlotte, NC 28215

The Essene Teachings, Inc. began as the Teachings of the Angelic Host within the Kingdom of Heaven, which was formed in 1973 by the merger of two previously existing Ascended Master organizations, the Teachings of the New Age and Christ's Love Retreat. The Teachings of the New Age had emerged in the late 1960s as the instrument of Mary L. Myers, a channel of the masters and former member of the Bridge to Freedom, now known as the New Age Church of Christ. She was the channel of *My Truth*, given as "the Bible of the new age" to open up the passages of "the Holy Bible," and more a more recent sequel, *My Peace*. Also associated is Dr. C. H. Yeang, a Malaysian, who also cooperates with the Ruby Focus of Magnificent Consummation. In 1978 there was an internal reorganization of the group and the present name adopted.

From the hierarchy, Aeolus and Pallas Athena claim the particular attention of the Essenes. Aeolus was considered by the Bridge to Freedom as the Cosmic Holy Spirit ranking above the Maha Chohan. Pallas Athena was of the Cosmic Board. They are the administrators of the Teachings of the Angelic Host and are identified as the Father and Mother god. The goal of the Teachings group is the unity of all the Light (I AM) centers in "the Christ Consciousness of the Father Mother Fire Flame Light." The group believes the angelic host will build an etheric temple over the Retreat Center in Lakemont, Georgia.

The by-laws of the Teachings admonish the members to have no gods but Aeolus. They should look to the Father as creator and the Mother as the supply in the world, and they shall recognize them in all the children of mankind.

Membership: Not reported. In 1978 there were four centers, one each in North Carolina, Florida, California, and Utah.

Sources: Mary L. Myers, *My Truth.* Nuremberg, Germany: W. Tuemmels Buchdruckerei und Verlag GmbH, 1965; Mary Kumara, *The Higher Meaning of the Ten Commandments.* Charlotte, NC: Artistic Letter Shop, n.d.; *The Cosmic Holy Spirit Introduces the Holy Mother Venus and the New Beginning in 1978.* Charlotte, NC: Essene Teachings, Inc., 1978.

★1003★
I AM RELIGIOUS ACTIVITY
Saint Germain Foundation
1120 Stonehedge Dr.
Schaumberg, IL 60194

The "I AM" Religious Activity is the oldest branch of the Ascended Master thrust which was begun by Guy Ballard. It is also the most conservative branch, adhering strictly to the dictates of the masters as brought forth through their only accredited Messengers, Guy W. and Edna W. Ballard. Through them was released a threefold truth not previously disclosed outside of the Masters' secret retreats: the knowledge of the "Mighty I AM Presence," the individualized presence of God; the use of the Violet Consuming Flame of Divine Love; and the use of God's Creative Name, "I AM."

The "I AM" Activity believes that the "I AM Presence" emanated from the heart of the cosmos and as it individualized, creation resulted. The "I AM Presence" is the essence of each individual. However, over the centuries, the misuse of God's energy has led to the present discord and evil present in the world. In spite of that discord and evil, a few individuals have risen above the world's situation and, by completely attuning themselves to their "I AM Presence" ascended into the light. Eventually, each person will follow them. In the meantime these Ascended Masters, also known as the Great White Brotherhood, work to lift humanity out of their present situation.

The central focus of the "I AM" Activity is contact and cooperation with the work of the Ascended Masters. The Messengers left over 3,000 dictations from the Masters which present a total program for both individual and social life. The Saint Germain Foundation and Saint Germain Press work to publish and present this material to the public and its student body.

The primary means of attuning oneself to the "I AM Presence" is quiet contemplation and the repetition of affirmations and decrees. Affirmations are sentences which both affirm the individual's attunement to God usually in relation to a specific aspect of life and recount the blessings due as a result of that attunement. Decrees are fiats spoken from the perspective of the essential self, the "I AM Presence." They call forth the visible manifestation of a divine condition or the dissolution of an evil one. They are always given in the Name of God. Decrees are given daily.

Almost as definitive as decreeing, the patriotism of the "I AM" Activity is noteworthy. Freedom has been a persistent theme throughout the decrees dictated to the Ballards. America is seen as having a special role in the Masters' plans. Reflective of this emphasis are the prominent display of of American flags at I AM centers and the special programs on patriotic holidays.

New students are introduced to the Activity by their reading the first three books of the eleven volume Saint Germain series. The first two volumes, *Unveiled Mysteries* and *The Magic Presence,* tell the story of Guy Ballard's original contacts with the Masters. Volume three, a series of dictations from Ascended Master Saint Germain, outline the basic beliefs of the "I AM" Activity. After reading the books, they may attend an introductory class, held periodically in Chicago.

The Saint Germain Foundation was led by Guy Ballard until his death in 1939. His wife Edna Ballard then led the work until her death in 1971. At that time the board of directors assumed collective leadership of both the Foundation and the Press. That board, orginally five members, was expanded to eighteen in 1982. The board charters the local centers and sanctuaries, which otherwise are independent and autonomous. It also oversees the work of Appointed Messengers (who teach introductory classes), field workers and regional counselors. The Foundation sponsors a variety of national and regional gatherings, several of which are held at the Shasta Springs, the retreat center located at the base of Mt. Shasta in northern California.

Since 1978 headquarters of the Activity have been in a new building complex in Schaumburg, Illinois, a Chicago suburb. The Press, previously located in Santa Fe, New Mexico, moved there in 1982, thus consolidating all the national offices. A radio show begun by Edna Ballard has been continued and is heard on over twenty-five stations. There is an independent "I AM" school in Denver, Colorado.

Membership: Not reported. In 1985 there were over 300 "I AM" sanctuaries and centers, most in the United States.

Periodicals: *The Voice of the "I AM",* 1120 Stonehedge Drive, Schaumburg, IL 60194.

Remarks: Greatly affected by the court cases in the 1940s and the subsequent litigation to recover the Foundation's tax-exempt status and the Press' right to use the mails, the I AM Activity assumed a very low profile. Under Edna Ballard's leadership it cut itself off from the media and refused contact with reporters and/or religious researchers. As a result, all of the material available about the Activity either was written during the period of controversy or is heavily reflective of that period. That material is generally hostile and unreflective of the present status and beliefs of the Activity.

Sources: Godfre Ray King (pen name of Guy W. Ballard), *Unveiled Mysteries*. Chicago: Saint Germain Press, 1934; Godfre Ray King, *The Magic Presence*. Chicago: Saint Germain Press, 1935; Saint Germain (through Guy W. Ballard), *The "I AM" Discourses*. Chicago: Saint Germain Press, 1935; *"I AM" Fundamental Group Outline*. Schaumburg, IL: Saint Germain Press, 1982.

★1004★
NEW AGE CHURCH OF CHRIST
Kings Park, NY 11754

Possibly the first group that closely followed the I AM teachings of Guy Ballard (while organizationally independent of the Saint Germain Foundation and the I AM Religious Activity) was the Bridge to Freedom, formed in 1954 by Thomas Printz. The organization, more recently renamed the New Age Church of Christ, was to "span" the way over which man's consciousness could proceed into the Consciousness of the Great White Brotherhood (the hierarchy of ascended masters, spirits who were exceptional human beings and who now, from the spirit world, tell humans about spiritual reality). Students are urged to put the law of forgiveness into effect to purge the soul of karma, the consequences of evil done in former incarnations. To accomplish this end, students invoke the Divine Presence "I AM" through decrees, rhythmic breathing and monthly Transmission Flame Classes, when the power of a particular ascended master is available.

The Great White Brotherhood is the name given to the spiritual hierarchy headed by Sanat Kumara, Lord Gautama, and Lord Maitreya. The Brotherhood dwells in "Shamballa," a heavenly region said to be physically located in the mountains of Tibet. Its goals are world brotherhood and the elevation of humanity above disease, limitation and imperfection. Under the Brotherhood is the karmic board, which renders justice to all human beings. Semi-annual meetings of this board are held in conjunction with the semi-annual church gatherings in the Grand Tetons in Wyoming. Particular spots on earth, for example the Arizona desert, are considered foci of light from the Brotherhood. In defining the extent of the Brotherhood, the spiritual hierarchy first popularly presented by Helena Petrovna Blavatsky and the Theosophical Society and elaborated upon by Guy Ballard, attention is paid to a variety of spiritual entities including angels, devas, Helios and Vesta (the god and

goddess of the solar system), the seven archangels, the seven Elohim (each drawn from Greek mythology, and Manus (in charge of root races-stages of humanity's development). Since the beginning of the era of freedom on earth in 1954 (the year of the founding of the Bridge to Freedom) activity has been directed toward the transmuting Violet Flame which will change all the negative into love, peace, harmony, and freedom. An order of service centered on candlelighting (a symbol of Light), visualization of the Violet Flame and decrees has been distributed.

Membership: Not reported. Groups are located around the country.

Periodicals: *The Bridge to Freedom*, Kings Park, Long Island, NY 11754; *Hope*, Kings Park, Long Island, NY 11754.

Sources: Thomas Prinz, *The Student's Handbook*. King's Park, NY: Bridge to Freedom, 1972; Ascended Master Kuthumi, *The Wisdom of the Ages*. St. James, NY: The Bridge to Freedom, n.d. 2 Vols.; *The Violet Transmuting Flame*. Kings Park, NY: The Bridge to Freedom, 1968; Thomas Printz, *Memoirs of Beloved Mary, Mother of Jesus*. Philadelphia: Bridge to Freedom, 1955.

★1005★
RUBY FOCUS OF MAGNIFICENT CONSUMMATION
P.O. Drawer 1188
Sedona, AZ 86336

The Ruby Focus of Magnificent Consummation, Inc. was founded in the mid-1960s by Garman Van Polen and Evangeline Van Polen, both former students of the I AM Religious Activity and the Bridge to Freedom, now the New Age Church of Christ. Evangeline eventually became a channel of the ascended masters, and in the late 1950s began to issue discourses under the aegis of the New Age Clinic of Spiritual Therapy in Phoenix, Arizona. Influential in the emergence of the Magnificent Consummation were the writings of Dr. C. H. Yeang. Yeang agreed with the Bridge to Freedom that over the years a number of changes had occurred in the makeup of the spiritual hierarchy. Specifically, he noted that in 1955, Gautama Buddha replaced Sanat Kumara as Lord of this World, that Lord Maitreya, formerly the World Teacher, now held the office of Buddha, and that Jesus and Koot Hoomi, formerly Chohans (ascended masters) of the Sixth and Second Rays, respectively, jointly function as the World Teacher. Yeang also believed that Saint Germain had been elevated and that Godfre-Ray King and Lotus King (i.e., Guy Ballard and Edna W. Ballard) had replaced him as Chohan of the Seventh Ray. St. Germain, in 1965, proclaimed himself as Eolia, now radiating the Golden Liquid Snow of Eolian Consciousness, the Light of the Central Sun. From that position, he will continue to direct the Seventh Ray and its new Chohan.

The Magnificent Consummation is the particular child of the Ruby Light of the Sixth Ray. Sananda and Lady Nada, Chohans of the Sixth Ray, are the directors. (Sananda is so labeled on all the literature.) The special work is to aid the descent of the Ruby Light of freedom, justice, peace, confidence, balance and magnificence into the physical world. Almost all of the literature of the Ruby Focus is on pink paper, usually with red ink.

In the early 1970s, new additions to the hierarchy were recognized in the persons of Ruby and Christos, two additinal Rays of Light. Ruby's color is iridescent ruby and Christos' is iridescent mother of pearl. They represent the negative and positive electric polarities and, together, are said to be the perfect laser beam of light. They will bring in the Magnificent Consummation of all seven colors plus themselves as the Rainbow Ray Consciousness and thus usher in the Aquarian Age.

From its headquarters, the Ruby Focus issues a variety of books and materials, including monthly lessons for its students. An order of service is built around a call upon one of the Seven Rays (plus the Eighth and Ninth Rays daily), songs, a message from one of the masters, and the taking in and radiation of light into the country and the world. Decrees are used extensively.

Membership: Not reported.

Periodicals: *Open Letter.*

Sources: Garman Van Polen & Theresa Martin, *A Treatise on Father-Mother Light as Golden Experiences.* The Author, 1966; Garman Van Polen & Evangeline Van Polen, *Catechism of Light.* Sedona, AZ: Magnificent Consummation, Inc. (1965). 2 Vols.; C. H. Yeang, *Who Am I? I Am That I Am.* Privately Published, (1965).

★1006★
SACRED SOCIETY OF THE ETH, INC.
Box 3
Forks of Salmon, CA 96031

The Sacred Society of the Eth, Inc. is the creation of Walter W. Jecker, known by his celestial name, Jo'el of Arcadia. During the 1960s, he went into the Siskiyou Mountains (a range in California and Oregon) and for seven years compiled volumes of words regarding love, light, and life. The words were published in 1967. He also founded the Society. His particular contact was with Jesus the Christ, known as the Ascended Master Sananda.

According to Jo'el, man is an emanation (sun) of God. While living in a body, man must know that he is the God of his being. Basic to man is Breath. The intelligence, says Jo'el, is in the Breath. Breath is thought and breathing is mind. Through Breath is the constant flow of the water of life. The etheric body is the fallen Breath of life. The Breath is creational. Man's life is determined by the hate or love within his mind.

Membership: Literature is distributed to study groups and individuals around the country.

Sources: Walter W. Jecker, *The Words of Light.* Forks of Salmon, CA: The Sacred Society of the Eth, 1967; Walter W. Jecker, *God Speaks, I Hear His Voice.* Forks of Salmon, CA: Sacred Society of the Eth, 1967; Walter W. Jecker, *God in Man Alive.* Forks of Salmon, CA: Sacred Society of the Eth, 1972.

★1007★
SANCTUARY OF THE MASTER'S PRESENCE
Two Larkin Rd.
Scarsdale, NY 10583

Closely related to other I AM groups is the Sanctuary of the Master's Presence. The Sanctuary was formed in the 1960s, but the public manifestation was not made until 1966 with the appearance of *The Mentor*, a periodical which carried the messages from the ascended masters. The Mentor was one of the entities from the spirit world who spoke through Mary Myneta, the principal percipient and teacher.

According the Mentor, man is evolving to a greater awareness of his creator. The present age is a time of man's becoming aware of a truth and reality not known previously. This step is precipitated by the powerful radiations of spiritual light from ascended masters' spheres of activity. The masters are projecting a golden radiance into earth to stir up our awareness.

Originally, the Sanctuary was headquartered in New York City and its periodical, edited by the Rev. Wayne Taylor, was published from Melbourne, Florida. However, in 1968, both were moved to Scarsdale, New York. From 1965 to 1968 Taylor had been president of Sologa, Inc., for whom his wife Grace Taylor was a channel. However, in 1968 the Taylors moved to Columbus, New Mexico to found Christ's Truth Church and School of Wisdom. Besides the group in Scarsdale, there are a few classes and group meetings, though they are no longer as strong as they were in the 1960s.

Membership: Not reported. The Sanctuary peaked in support in the 1960s, and there remains only a group in Scarsdale and few students around the United States.

Periodicals: *The Mentor*, Two Larkin Rd., Scarsdale, NY 10583.

Sources: *The Order of the Service.* New York: The Sanctuary of the Masters' Presence, [1969].

★1008★
SOLOGA, INC.
Box 759
Melbourne, FL 32901

Sologa, Inc., was established in 1959 by Dr. Ruth Scoles Lennox and included among its members Wayne Taylor, who succeeded to the presidency of the group upon Lennox's death in 1965, and Grace Taylor, his wife, a channel for the masters. In 1968, Taylor left Melbourne and Sologa for New Mexico, where he founded Christ's Truth Church and School of Wisdom and the City of the Sun Foundation.

Membership: Not reported. In 1968 there were two Sologa groups, one in Miami and one in Melbourne, Florida.

Periodicals: *The Solograph*, Box 759, Melbourne, FL 32901.

Miscellaneous Theosophical Groups

★1009★
AGNI YOGA SOCIETY
319 W. 107th St.
New York, NY 10025

The Agni Yoga Society was founded in the mid-1920s, beginning informally as a group of students who gathered to study a book *Leaves of M's Garden*, published in 1924. The Society was founded by Nicolas Roerich (1874-1947) and his wife, Helena Roerich. The Roerichs had left Russia at the time of the Revolution, he being an outstanding artist. They came to the United States in 1920 on the invitation of the Art Institute of Chicago. Very early in their new life in the West, the Roerichs had joined the Theosophical Society, and Helena translated Helena Petrovna Blavatsky's major work, *The Secret Doctrine*, into Russian. She also began to receive regular communications from one of the masters originally contacted by Blavatsky, the Master Morya. Her first book, received from him, was *The Leaves from M's Garden*. It and the subsequent volumes have become the prime teaching material of the Agni Yoga Society. Prior to founding the Society, Nicolas had founded several organizations to embody his ideal of art as a unifying force for humanity, the Master Institute of the United Arts and the Nicolas Roerich Museum.

The Roerich's settled permanently in the Punjab in 1929. Helena produced thirteen volumes of material from the Master Morya. Nicolas also wrote numerous books on his continuing concerns of art, peace, and spirituality. A building purchased to house a collection of his art, the museum, also houses the Agni Yoga Society. Membership in the Society is open after one to three years of study of the books. The esoteric group meets bimonthly, and is not open to the general public. Study groups meet at various locations around the country.

Membership: Not reported.

Sources: Garabed Paelian, *Nicolas Roerich*. Agoura, CA: Aquarian Educational Group, 1974; *Nicolas Roerich*. New York: Nicolas Roerich Museum, 1974; Nicolas Roerich, *Realm of Light*. New York: Roerich Museum Press, 1931; *Letters of Helena Roerich, 1929-1938*. New York: Agni Yoga Society, 1954. 2 Vols.; Guru R. H. H., *Talk Does Not Cook the Rice*. York Beach, ME: Samuel Weiser, 1982.

★1010★
AMICA TEMPLE OF RADIANCE
Box 304
Ojai, CA 93023

The Amica Temple of Radiance dates to the early 1930s and the experience of Ivah Bergh Whitten. As a young child stricken with an incurable disease, Ms. Whitten was cured through "colour awareness" and began to explore and teach on its potentials. The initial course was first published in 1932. Among Ms. Whitten's students were Roland Hunt and Dorothy Bailey, who structured the Amica Temple in Los Angeles in 1959. Roland Hunt, while in England in 1952, had described to him inwardly two strangers with whom he would become associated upon his return to the United States. The two, Paola Hugh and John Hugh, were, with Hunt, taken under the guidance of an elder brother of the inner wisdom schools. They joined in the formation of Amica. In 1971, an affiliate organization, the Fleur de Lys Foundation of East Sound, Washington, was founded. It is seen as a reflection of an inner order of illumined ones who are seeking the victory of man's higher self over his ego.

The Amica Temple is a continuation and expansion of the colour awareness teachings. As man has evolved, he has become aware of the various aspects of God-the Father principle, the Son, the Holy Ghost-and, in this new era, of the Spirit made manifest in seven colours. Each colour, or ray, as taught by the Theosophical Society, rules an aspect of existence and is in turn ruled by a master. By understanding which ray you were born under, you can discover your proper work and place in life. Each ray also has a healing potential. Overriding the seven rays is the white ray, which shines di rectly from the Logos. The Amica Temple continues as a structure to present Hunt's teachings to the world. Lessons are offered in color awareness to students around the country.

Membership: Not reported. Centers are located in California and Washington.

Sources: Ivah Bergh Whitten, *The Initial Course in Colour Awareness*. London: Amica, n.d.; Dorothy A. Bailey, *The Light of Ivah Bergh Whitten*. Southampton: A.M.I.C.A., n.d.; Roland T. Hunt, *The Seven Rays to Colour Healing*. Ashingdon, Essex: C. W. Daniel Company, 1954; Roland T. Hunt, *Man Made Clear for the Nu Clear Age*. Lakemont, GA: CSA Press, 1969; Roland T. Hunt,

Fragrant and Radiant Healing Symphony. Ashingdon, Essex: C. W. Daniel Company, 1949.

★1011★

ANN REE COLTON FOUNDATION OF NISCIENCE
336 W. Colorado
Glendale, CA 91209

The Ann Ree Colton Foundation of Niscience was formed in 1953 by Ann Ree Colton (b. 1898) and Jonathan Murro. Psychic from childhood, Ms. Colton in her twenties began to contact the Theosophical masters. At twenty-four, she began to receive instructions from Master Morya. She learned that she and Murro were mediators to unite men with the great mediator, the Lord Jesus. Along the way, she was given information on her past lives, in which she was among others. Madame Helena Petrovna Blavatsky (the founder of Theosophy) and Joan of Arc. She was taught the occult arts-astrology, healing, prophecy-and relived her initiatory experiences. In 1932, she began her public ministry and became well-known as a prophet. A church was formed in 1936 in Florida, and continued for nine years. In 1945, the church was closed, and Ann Ree entered a transition period. She began to read Blavatsky's books and to accept the record of her previous life. In 1952, she met Jonathan Murro, who came to her for counseling.

According to Ms. Colton, we are moving into the age of science. In this age, the masters will no longer incarnate. Thirty-three cosmic disciples scattered throughout the world mediate the higher worlds. They communicate through thirteen telepathic disciples. (All the disciples are men advanced in their sciences or humanities, but their spiritual work is unknown to their colleagues.) When a cosmic disciple ascends to the spirit world, a telepathic disciple replaces him and an advanced student becomes a telepathic disciple. Beyond the disciples, in the second heaven in the realms of light dwell the masters and the recording angels. In the third heaven dwell the archangels and the archetypes of God, the very blueprints for the creation of the earth. Through the archangels, God controls the universe and initiates the new. The time when men are open to the third heaven of the archangels and the archetypes is a time of receiving the Holy Spirit.

Ms. Colton was permanently united with the Niscience Archetype and was told that the "hum" of his archetype will bring a new spiritual impulse. It will unite men with the Jesus Ethic, thus bringing them closer to the Christ. The revelation of Niscience led directly to the establishment of the Foundation of Niscience and the Church of the Jesus Ethic.

The ministry of the Foundation has found outward e xpression in the formation of chapels to teach Niscience and the Jesus Ethic, the main one being at the Glendale, California, headquarters. ARC Publishing Company has published and distributed Ms. Colton's books and the monthly White Paper sent to all members. Members are organized into Niscience Units. New members receive The Mediator series, a seven-month orientation course. Advanced students can qualify to become lay ministers through the Niscience Guild and the lessons in *The Contributor*; ministry and Bible study using Niscience interpretation are stressed. Teachers offer a wide variety of classes on Niscience topics.

Membership: Not reported.

Sources: Ann Ree Colton, *Men in White Apparel.* Glendale, CA: ARC Publishing Company, 1961; Ann Ree Colton and Jonathan Murro, *Prophet for the Archangels.* Glendale, CA: ARC Publishing Company, 1964; Ann Ree Colton, *The Soul and the Ethic.* Glendale, CA: ARC Publishing Company, 1965; Ann Ree Colton, *The Venerable One.* Glendale, CA: ARC Publishing Company, 1963; Ann Ree Colton, *Vision for the Future.* Glendale, CO: ARC Publishing Company, 1960.

★1012★

ANTHROPOSOPHICAL SOCIETY
Rudolf Steiner Information Center
211 Madison Ave.
New York, NY 10016

Even before the death of Helena Petrovna Blavatsky, the Theosophical Society (which she had founded) had expanded from its strong center in England to other European countries. A branch of the Theosophical Society was established in Germany in the early 1890s and chartered in 1902. The same year of its chartering, the German Theosophical Society elected to its leadership Rudolf Steiner. Forty-one years old at the time, he had already distinguished himself as a scholar, having previously edited an issue of Goethe's scientific writings and having worked on the standard edition of Goethe's works. His writing, editing, and teaching increasingly led him into a mystic philosophy and experience, a decidedly Christian mysticism.

Invited to address an audience of Theosophists in the winter of 1901/02, he lectured on "Christianity as Mystical Fact," in which his thesis was that the ancient mystics had served to prepare the way for Christ on earth and that Christ was the focus of earth's evolution. Theosophists had generally been taught to regard Jesus as just another avatar. In spite of this disagreement, Steiner's intellectual and charismatic leadership was desired by the still small group. Steiner accepted a leadership role, while reserving his independence, because the Theosophists were the only ones with any interest in his work. In the next decade, he began to publish his ideas on the nature of man, the evolution of the earth and initiation. In 1909, he published *Spiritual Hierarchies*, which elucidated his teachings on the centrality of Christ. This work focused his growing dissatisfaction with Annie Besant, the recently elected president of the Theosophical Society.

Steiner's differences with Annie Besant and the Theosophical Society were fundamental. The Society was becoming more and more involved in Eastern mystical occult practices. It practiced a system of withdrawal from the manifest material world and centered on meditative yogic disciplines. It regarded Christ as just another God-embodied teacher and Christianity as just another religion. Steiner approached the spiritual in a world- affirming scientific spirit, based upon his research in medieval forms, particularly those of the West. Eastern religion he saw as a way of the past, replaced by Christianity. For Steiner, Christ summed up the Eastern search and launched the new era of finding the spiritual in the material (science). The disagreements between Steiner and the Society climaxed after Annie Besant announced the return of Christ in Jeddu Krishnamurti. Steiner declared that no one could be a member of the German Theosophical Society and the Order of the Star of the East, an organization formed to prepare for the coming of a new Christ in Krishnamurti, then still a youth. Besant revoked the charter of the German Theosophical Society in 1912. Steiner took fifty- five of the sixty-five lodges and formed the Anthroposophical Society.

Headquarters of Anthroposophy were moved to Dornach near Basel, Switzerland, where a Goetheanum, a huge center designed by Steiner, was built. The world-affirming approach of Steiner led to the development of a number of programs which illustrate Anthroposophy in all of life. The arts are of a particular interest, and Steiner developed Eurythmy, a new form of rhythm movement. Education was a central focus, and the Waldorf schools were begun in 1919 to show how a new education-system, based on Steiner's understanding of human nature, could be applied.

Immediately after World War I, Anthroposophy began to spread on the continent and to England and, by 1925, had been brought to America. It spread initially among German immigrants and was soon to be found in urban centers across the North and Midwest, California and Canada. With the translation and wide circulation of Steiner's books since World War II, for the first time non-German-speaking students came into the movement in significant numbers. The program of the Society is built on lectures, study groups discussing Steiner's writings, and the various education and artistic programs.

As the Anthroposophical Society developed, Christian pastors and theological students began to press Steiner for a liturgical- communal form in which Anthroposophy could find expression. An outline of his feelings on such things as Christianity's ritual, priesthood, organization, social impact and the equality of women was given in some lectures in 1921. The key man in the movement was Dr. Friedrich Rittelmeyer, an outstanding German Lutheran pastor. In the fall of 1922 at a meeting at Dornach, the Christian Community was formed, and Rittelmeyer was ordained by Steiner. Rittelmeyer then ordained the remaining leaders. Steiner gave them a statement of faith and a ritual form, the *Act of Consecration of Man*. The aim of the ritual is to help people turn actively to the spiritual world and to teach that to become human is the true aim of life. A full sacramental system is also offered. The teachings of the community are Anthroposophy, with an emphasis on the mystical and spiritual world and Steiner's understanding of Jesus.

The Christian Community has followed in the footsteps of the Anthroposophical Society, but its growth has not been as spectacular. In 1928, a German priest, Wilhelm Hochweber, visited Chicago and celebrated the *Act of Consecration of Man* for the first time in America. But it was not until 1948 that Verner Hegg and Alfred Heidenreich established the Christian Community permanently in the U.S. The first congregation drew primarily upon refugees who had fled Nazi oppression. Congregations have spread throughout the Eastern cities where Anthroposophical societies are located.

The Christian Community is congregational in structure, but it does have central ruling figures. For example, the Christian Community in each country is headed by a community-priest, and the Oberlenker (entire church) is headed by the Erzoberlenker, whose office is in Stuttgart, Germany. A theological training center is located in Sussex, England. *The Christian Community Journal* is published in England for the English-speaking church; the New York group publishes a newsletter.

The Christian Community is a separate entity, not formally connected with the Anthroposophical Society. There continue strong informal ties, and many people are members of both. In fact, both groups function as a religious body, the Christian Community being the liturgical form. Both deal with Steiner's spiritual/religious philosophy, have social forms and an ethical life, and, as two forms of the same basic body, deserve mention among America's religious bodies.

The Society is headquartered in a center in New York City which also houses a library, a book store and a eurythmy training school. Spring Valley, New York, the second most active center, is the location of a number of affiliated structures, including the following: Anthroposophic Press; several therapuetic structures (Fellowship of Physicians; Anthroposophical Therapy and Hygiene Association; and Weleda, Inc.); the Fellowship Community, a retirement home; Bio-chemical Research Laboratory; and the Pfeiffer Foundation. North American headquarters have also been opened in Toronto, Ontario, Canada and Mexico. There were 15 Waldorf schools in North America.

Membership: Not reported. In the early 1980s, the Society had four branches (Los Angeles, California; Chicago, Illinois; and New York City and Spring Valley, New York) and 29 groups scattered around the country. The Christian Community reported 10 congregations, including two in Canada.

Periodicals: *New York Newsletter,* The Christian Community, 309 West 74th Street, New York, NY 10023; *Journal for Anthroposophy,* 211 Madison Avenue, New York, NY 10016.

Sources: A. P. Shepherd, *A Scientist of the Invisible.* New York: British Book Centre, 1959; Guenther Wachsmuth, *The Life and Work of Rudolf Steiner.* New York: Whittier Books, 1955; *Rudolf Steiner, An Autobiography.* Blauvelt, NY: Rudolf Steiner Publications, 1977; Alfred Heidenreich, *Growing Point.* London: The Christian Community Press, 1965; *The Creed.* London: Christian Community Press, 1962; Evelyn Derry, *Seven Sacraments in the Christian Community.* London: Christian Community Press, 1949; Floyd McKnight, *Rudolf Steiner and Anthroposophy.* New York: Anthroposophical Society in America, 1967.

★1013★
BODHA SOCIETY OF AMERICA
(Defunct)

The Bodha Society of America was incorporated in 1936 by its president, Ms. Violet B. Reed. She described it as a movement fostering spiritual consciousness through self-realization and world service. Spiritual virility can be attained only through a better outlook on life and a deeper realization of the spiritual realm. According to the Society, the Bodha movement was begun in 1907 under the direction of the Sanctuaries of Tibet and Sikkim and assumed "the full responsibility which once rested in the Theosophical Society, this organizatin being no longer patronized by its founders, inspirers and real leaders: the masters." The Bodha Society was seen as the vehicle of the Great Brotherhood, the ascended masters who were once humans and who now as spirits teach people about spiritual realities.

The Society kept the three spiritual festivals associated with Buddhism, particularly Wesak. Associated centers were opened in France and Cuba; world headquarters were claimed to be in Tibet. National headquarters were in Long Beach, California. *Sun Rays,* a periodical was published.

★1014★
CHRISTWARD MINISTRY
Route 5, Box 206
Escondido, CA 92025

The Christward Ministry was founded by Flower A. Newhouse, a long-time teacher in the southern California psychic community. Current headquarters of the ministry are at Christhaven, a retreat center founded in 1940 and located near Escondido, California. Ms. Newhouse has centered her teachings on meditation and angels. Man is considered an embodied soul in a process of development and growth. Meditation helps him establish his spiritual identity in the realm of unceasing reality through conscious memory.

Ms. Newhouse believes in the hierarchy of angels (instead of masters) and describes Christ as the Hierarch of angels and men. The angelic kingdom is above the human as the next step in evolution. Angels are found throughout the world as unseen guides and influences in society and nature. Each person is under watchfulness of an archangel who guides his incarnations. Closest to each is his guardian angel, a spiritual mother who trains him in the spiritual life. The angels have been described minutely in Newhouse's various books.

A program of Sunday worship and retreats is held at Questhaven, including annual retreats for ministers preparing for ordination in the Christward Ministry. "The Quest for Spiritual Awareness" is the title of lessons sent out monthly from Escondido. All the literature is published by Christward Publications.

Membership: Not reported.

Educational facilities: Questhaven Academy, Escondido, California.

Sources: *The Christward Ministry.* Vista, CA: The Christward Ministry, 1947; Flower A. Newhouse, *The Christward Way.* Four vols. (lessons 1-208). Vista, CA: Christward Publications, n.d.; Flower A. Newhouse, *The Meaning and Vaue of the Sacraments.* Escondido, CA: The Christward Ministry, 1971; Stephen Isaac, *The Way of Discipleship to Christ.* Escondido, CA: The Christward Ministry, 1976.

★1015★
CHURCH OF COSMIC ORIGIN AND SCHOOL OF THOUGHT
Box 257
June Lake, CA 93529

The Church of Cosmic Origin was founded in 1963 at Independence, California, by Hope Troxell (b. 1906), who had for thirty years been lecturer on "expanded concepts." In her early life, she received three major healings from the angelic host, and during the 1950s, she received instructions from the masters and published several books of their material. *From Matter to Light* contains messages from several different masters, including Djual Khool, Alcyon, Univera of Jupiter, Melchizedek and Nerfertiti. *The Mohada Teachings from the Galaxies* contains a series of messages from Mohada, a particularly significant master for Ms. Troxell.

The church teaches what is termed "cosmic Christianity." Man is considered an evolving being whose purpose is to become one with Light and escapethe continual reincarnation and involvement in matter. Man originally fell from grace into matter after his creation by the Elohim, the family of God. Jesus came from the Elohim, is now a master and is due to return for judgment and to lift those who have followed the God-Way. In the coming age, America will lead the world in the spiritual plane of God's laws, according to the Church of Cosmic Origin.

The cosmic wisdom given by Jesus and the masters illumines the Bible. The Church of Cosmic Origin also use the writings from Qumran and models itself upon the resident community model of the Essenes. The symbol of the church is the Greek cross in a circle with a rose on it, symbolizing the risen Christ. The masters gave the format for the church services, which is, as in the original Christian church, the circle. The directors of the church are in the center, with members, students and visitors around them. Services include Scripture readings, readings from the masters, and a sermon as received by Ms. Troxell (without a trance-state). There are no ministers.

The church and school are headquartered at June Lake, California. Since the main work is the preparation of teachers, the number of residents at the school is very small. An adult community participates in daily classes for both advanced and beginning studies. Twice a day, prayer circles are held; church services are each Sunday. The bulk of students are those taking correspondence lessons across the United States and in several other English-speaking countries.

Membership: Not reported.

Periodicals: *Cosmic Frontiers.*

Sources: Hope Troxell, *The Mohada Teachings.* Independence, CA: School of Thought, [1963]; Hope Troxell, *From Matter to Light.* June Lake, CA: School of Thought, 1968; Hope Troxell, *Through the Open Key.* El Monte, CA: Understanding Publishing Co., n.d.

★1016★
LIGHTED WAY
Current address not obtained for this edition.

The Lighted Way is described as a "New Age School for Discipleship Training." It was founded in 1966 by Muriel R. Tepper (known as Muriel Isis), under the direction of Master D.K. of the White Brotherhood. It is guided and inspired by the cosmic mother Isis. Muriel is the outer symbol of the mother principle-truth and inspiration. The mother as Isis reveals the cosmic laws and pure truths for the building of the immortal light body and the resurrection of the physical form. These laws include the laws of light radiation, magnetism, cause and effect, polarity and correspondence.

The Lighted Way is the highway back to divinity. To help the members in their return, a variety of services is offered. Light Radiation Circles allow each person a chance to gain direct awareness of the Universal Mind. Individual counseling in Akashic records, in the aura and in personal soul evolvement is offered by Muriel, either in person or by mail on cassette tape. (Akashic records are the recordings on the "universal ethers" of all thoughts

and actions; psychics can "tap into" these records. The auras are psychic emanations from the human body; psychics can see and interpret auras.) Full moon meditations are held monthly. Classes are offered in meditation, Yoga and the lessons of Isis on metaphysical truths. Healing services are held weekly.

Membership: Not reported. In 1973 centers were functioning in Los Angeles, Pacific Palisades, Costa Mesa, and Hollywood, California.

Sources: Muriel R. Tepper, *Mechanisms of the Personality through Personology.* Pacific Palisade, CA: Lighted Way, n.d.; Muriel R. Tepper, *The Lighted Way Road to Freedom.* Los Angeles: Lighted Way Press, n.d.

★1017★
OASIS FELLOWSHIP
Box O
Florence, AZ 85232

The Oasis Fellowship began in the home of George White and his wife, Alice White. While meditating, they began to make contact with several spirit entities named "Elawa," "Malala" and "Yeban," believed to be teachers from a higher plane of evolvement. As messages began to come through, friends of the Whites began to attend the sessions. Healing prayer was a major concern. As time passed, the Whites disposed of their business and went in search of a place for a center to which those dedicated to the program could gravitate. After a year of searching, such a spot was located near Florence, Arizona, and the Oasis Fellowship began.

At Florence, on the seventeen-and-a-half acres, members of the fellowship lead a communal-like existence in separate mobile homes and travel trailers. Many leave during the summer months. Soon after the establishment in Arizona, weekly "Lessons in Living" began to come through the channels. These lessons were taped, transcribed and sent out across the country without any request for money. Study groups have formed at several points across the country and the lessons are mailed to adherents in almost every state and province. Members of the community at Florence gather twice daily for meditation, reading of the lessons and discussion.

Beliefs of the Oasis Fellowship resemble a "Christian Spiritualism." The lessons are often comments by one of the spirit teachers on a Bible passage. A psychic/spiritual interpretation is offered. There is strong emphasis on reincarnation and the spiritual evolvement of the individual. God is viewed both as the creator of life and the presence shining as light within.

Membership: Not reported.

★1018★
OPEN WAY
Box 217
Celina, TN 38551

The Open Way is a New Age group centered in Celina, Tennessee, and headed by Lovie Webb Gasteiner. There is a close affinity with Mary L. Myers of the Essene Teachings Inc. The Open Way teaches that God manifests as Father and Mother and lives in all. God is the source of life, love, peace, strength and abundant life. Man's goal is a return to God in self- realization. The law of life is giving and receiving, and the Open Way teaches exercises on giving and receiving divine energy. The secret is tensing and relaxing the muscles, nerves, and tissues of the body in combination with the human voice, used in speaking, chanting, humming, and singing.

Membership: Not reported.

★1019★

PHILO-POLYTECHNICAL CENTER
(Defunct)

The Philo-Polytechnical Center of Los Angeles had aims similar to those of the Bodha Society of America. It was headed by Ronald Clifton and published *The Bodha Renaissance*.

★1020★

UNIVERSAL GREAT BROTHERHOOD
Administrative Council of the U. S. A.
Box 9154
St. Louis, MO 63117

The Universal Great Brotherhood was formed by Serge Raynaud de la Ferriere (b. 1916), a Frenchman who had been involved in the esoteric from his childhood. As a young man, he traveled to Egypt, where, according to his biography, he was initiated as the "Sublime Crowned Cophto and Great Priest Khediviar." At the age of 22, in London, he received a degree of Doctor of Hermetic Science and the next year, in Amsterdam, Doctor of Universal Science. During World War II he became closely identified with the Theosophical Society in France and joined the Theosophical and Astrological Lodge in London. After the war, his occult work expanded and he became active in a Masonic body.

De la Ferriere's early esoteric work prepared him for an encounter with Master Sun W. K., described as the "Superior Power of Tibet," who gave da la Ferriere his mission to begin the exposition of initiatic principles to the general public. De la Ferriere founded the Universal Great Brotherhood and for the next three years traveled widely, establishing the brotherhood in centers around the world. Very early in his travels, he went to Venezuela where he met Jose Manuel Estrada, who was to become his leading student.

Estrada (b. 1900) had, for nine years, announced the arrival of an avatar (an incarnation of God) and had gathered a group waiting upon the avatar. After their meeting, Estrada accepted de la Ferriere, who spent eighteen months with Estrada and his group, and on March 21, 1948, reopened the Universal Great Brotherhood in a public manner.

In 1950, de la Ferriere turned over the management of the brotherhood to Estrada and retired to a quiet life of esoteric work and writing. Estrada assumed the title of director general. The work grew steadily in Latin America through the 1950s and 1960s. In 1969 Estrada sent Rev. Gagpa Anita Montero Campion to the United States. She settled in St. Louis and began to teach yoga classes. She shared the teachings of the brotherhood with her pupils and in 1970 organized the first brotherhood center. It soon spread to Ann Arbor, Michigan; Chicago; and New York City.

The brotherhood describes itself as an educational organization rather than a religion. It is an initiatic school designed to assist humanity in its transition to a new age, often spoken of as the transition from the Age of Pisces to the Age of Aquarius. The birthplace of this new age is the Americas, hence the reopening of the brotherhood of the West.

The Brotherhood is dedicated to the attainment of peace by raising the consciousness of humanity both individually and collectively. The brotherhood offers a number of services to pre-initiates. It sponsors health care programs with special emphasis on preventive medicine and natural cures. The organization strongly advocates vegetarianism. It also sponsors a variety of classes to promote personal growth, such as hatha yoga, martial arts, astrology, and meditation. In this regard it also promotes the Cosmic Ceremony, a Universal form of worship that allows each person to get in touch with his or her own highest concept of the divine.

Participants in brotherhood public programs, designated followers, may be invited to become initiates. Once initiated they become members of the Esoteric College and receive the title Gegnian, or Little Novice. Afterward they pass upward through several degrees: first degree, Getuls or Novice; second degree, Reverend Gag-pa, or affiliated; third degree, Right Reverend Gelong, or Adept; and the fourth degree, Respectable Guru, or Instructor. Currently held by only the international leaders, still higher degrees are, in principle, open to all. The fifth degree, Honorable Sat Chellah, or Disciple, is held by Domingo Dias Porta; and the sixth degree, Venerable Sat Arhat, or Missionry, is held by Estrada. Only one person can hold the seventh degree as Sat Guru, the Master, presently de la Ferriere. Administratively, the brotherhood is headed by the superior council, which operates under the Sat Guru and makes all the decisions concerning the activities of the brotherhood internationally. Under it are national and regional councils.

Membership: Not reported. The Brotherhood has opened centers in seventeen countries. In the United States, centers can be found in St. Louis, Missouri; Chicago, Illinois; Ann Arbor, Michigan; Brooklyn, New York; Oklahoma City, Oklahoma; Shaker Heights, Ohio; Los Angeles, California; and Jamaica Plains, Massachusetts.

Sources: *Biography, the Sublime Maestra, Sat Guru, Dr. Serge Raymaud de la Ferriere.* St. Louis, MO: Educational Publications of the I. E. S., 1976; Montero-Campion, Anita, *My Guru from South America: Sat Arhat Dr. Jose Manuel Estrada.* St. Louis: The Author, 1976.

★1021★
UNIVERSAL WHITE BROTHERHOOD
Prosveta U. S. A.
Box 49614
Los Angeles, CA 90049

The Universal White Brotherhood, named for the spiritual hierarchy of advanced esoteric adepts, was brought to France in 1937 by Omram Michael Aivanhov (b. 1900), a Bulgarian esoteric teacher. According to Aivanhov, the true brotherhood is a line of masters who periodically appear to give humanity its lofty impulses. In secret for several thousand years, it was reestablished in its outer form in the nineteenth century in Bulgaria through Peter Deunov (d. 1944). As Deunov's student, Aivanhov brought the brotherhood to France and, upon Deunov's death, succeeded him as its master.

The brotherhood is seen not as a new religious sect, but as a new form of the eternal religion of Christ, thus continuing the Church of St. John, the embodiment of the tradition of true Christian spirituality. By the Church of St. John, the brotherhood refers to the small number of spiritual elites, working in secret, alongside of the larger Church of St. Peter, i.e. official and public religion. The meaning of life is to discover the elder brothers (the spiritual elites) of the brotherhood and to participate in their work of helping humanity become one family. The brotherhood exists to give to the perfected beings an opportunity to act through humanity to bring about the Kingdom of God on earth.

The Universal White Brotherhood was brought to America after the appearance of the English translations of Aivanhov's work in the early 1980s. Aivanhov made his first visit to America in 1983.

Membership: In 1983 the Brotherhood had approximately 4,000 members in France, Belgium, and Switzerland; 2,000 in French Canada; and several hundred in the United States.

Sources: Peter Dunoff, *The Great Law.* Sofia (Bulgaria): J. Panayotoff, 1925; Beinsa Douno (Peter Dunoff), *The Great Master.* Los Angeles: Sunrise Press & Books, 1970; Omraam Mikhael Aivanhov, *Complete Works.* Frejus, France: Editions Prosveta, 1978-198?. 24 Vols. (in progress); Agnes Lejbowicz, *Omraam Mikhael Aivanhov, Master of the Great Univeral White Brotherhood.* Frejus, France: Editions Prosveta, 1982; *Who Is the Master Omraam Mikhael Aivanhov.* Frejus, France: Editions Prosveta, 1982; Pierre C. Renard, *The Solar Revolution and the Prophet.* Frejus, France: Editions Prosveta, 1980.

★1022★
WHITE LODGE
(Defunct)

Lady Elizabeth Carey was an agent of the White Eagle Lodge, a British New Age group, who was sent to the United States to open the work. In 1941 while in Los Angeles, she became aware that she was being guided by spirits, and, on Grouse Mountain near Vancouver, a group became aware through her of the imminent return of Christ. In 1943, a tract of land near Del Mar, California, was purchased as a site for a sacred shrine. The guidance was received from the Great White Brotherhood, a group of elder brothers identical to the Buddhist bodhisattvas or the Theosophical ascended masters. These brothers have often incarnated in the past and have existed as a group since the first godman walked the earth. Roselady, as Ms. Carey was known, was in contact with a Great White Brotherhood initiate, Azrael.

Through the shrine at Del Mar called the White Lodge, the message of Azrael began to be published through a monthly periodical, *Angelus.* Growing popularity led to the publication in the 1960s of four *Books of Azrael* containing collections of Azrael's messages. Advertising in such psychically oriented periodicals as *Chimes* made the shrine well known throughout the United States.

The teachings of Azrael are concerned with the work of the White Brotherhood and its role in bringing in the New Age of Aquarius. Azrael is helping to creat a new humanity by raising the consciousness of those who receive the teachings. The content of Azrael's message is summed up in two words, "love" and "light." Love is the cohesive force of the universe, the principle by which God acts, judges and heals. Light is the symbol of man's path back to God. The Brotherhood dwells in the light and teaches the path to illumination through prayer and meditation. Reincarnation and karma were strongly held beliefs, and prayer for healing through the white light was a major practice. Healing prayer was accompanied by a "linking in," during which members scattered across the country joined in prayer at the same hour.

In the late 1960s, tension arose among the supporters of the shrine. On Easter Sunday, 1969, Eloise Mellor, the guardian of the shrine, asserted that she was the channel for Azrael and St. John the Beloved. According to the fourth Book of Azrael, a special work by St. John was directly to precede the coming of Jesus, the world teacher. Eloise also replaced members of the shrine's board of trustees. These changes were made with the claimed blessing of White Eagle, a guide from the spirit world, but without going through Roselady. Almost immediately, two factions arose and, in 1971, open schism appeared.

After Easter of 1969, Joseph E. Hall, deposed vice president of the shrine at Del Mar, California called the White Lodge, continued to receive the communications from Azrael and to circulate them among former supporters of the work. Then, in 1970, Philip Schraub of Corpus Christi, Texas, was confirmed by the aging Roselady as her successor as the channel of Azrael and the one to be used to carry forward the New Age teachings of John the Beloved. In the spring of 1971, public announcement of Philip's role, as well as a denoucement of Eloise, was made by Mr. Hall and nine other leading supporters of the Shrine in the first issue of a new monthly, *The New Angelus for the New Age*. A letter from the White Eagle Lodge denied support of Eloise. Through Philip, the Brotherhood announced its temporary withdrawal from the Shrine and the movement of the work to Corpus Christi.

Efforts began to recover the Shrine, at first through negotiation with Eloise, Mari Mae Napier and her husband, who at that time constituted the Shrine's board. In the midst of these negotiations, Eloise fell ill. Durng her convalescence, she repented of her activity and began to support Philip. She was also deposed as guardian of the Shrine, and five trustees appointed in her place. *Rays of Wisdom* replaced the *Angelus* as the periodical.

Upon her recovery, a court fight was initiated by Eloise to regain her guardianship, but she died in 1974, before the matter could be resolved. Several years later, the trustees turned the work and the property over to Elizabeth Clare Prophet and the Church Universal and Triumphant, into which it was completely absorbed.

Philip Schraub continued to publish *The New Angelus for the New Age* first in Corpus Christi and then in West Sedona, Arizona until 1983, after which the work was discontinued.

Sources: *Book of Azreal*. Santa Barbara, CA: J. F. Rowny Press, 1965-67. 4 Vols.; Eloise [Mellor], *Youth: Open the Door*. Los Angeles: DeVorss & Co., 1969.

Magick Family

An historical essay on this family is provided beginning on page 131.

Ritual Magick

★1023★
AURUM SOLIS
% The Administrator General
Box 43383-OSV
St. Paul, MN 55164

Aurum Solis, the Order of the Sacred Word, was founded in England in 1897 by Charles Kingold and George Stanton as a school of Western Kabbalistic magick. Like the Hermetic Order of the Golden Dawn, the Aurum Solis teaches a system of high magick, i.e., a disciplined approach to self-transformation. Its system, much of which has been published in the five-volume set *The Magical Philosophy* by Melita Denning and Osborne Phillips, centers upon the myth of the sacred king (i.e., the magician), who chooses of his own free will the path of sacrifice but subsequently rises again and passes into the light of attainment.

Melita Denning and Osborne Phillips are the pen names of Vivian Barcynski and Leonard R. Barcynski, who currently serve as grand master and administrator general of the order. Both had encountered the order while living in England and participated in its reconstitution in 1971. They brought the order to America in 1978 when they moved to St. Paul, Minnesota. Under their pen names they have authored numerous books on various occult topics.

Membership in the order is by invitation only, through inquiries are invited. The Barcynskis also headed the Paracletian Catholic Church, a liturgical church in the Liberal Catholic tradition, based upon the Christian expression of Aurum Solis teachings. but disbanded it to concentrate on the order.

Membership: Not reported, but estimated at no more than a few hundred.

Sources: Melita Denning and Osborne Phillips, *The Magical Philosophy*. St. Paul: Llewellyn Publications, 1974-81. 5 Vols.; Melita Denning and Osborne Phillips, *The Magick of Sex*. St. Paul, MN: Llewellyn Publications, 1982; Melita Denning and Osborne Phillips, *The Magick of the Tarot*. St. Paul, MN: Llewellyn Publications, 1983.

★1024★
BAVARIAN ILLUMINATI
(Defunct)

The Bavarian Illuminati was founded in 1776 by the infamous Dr. Adam Weishaupt, a professor of canon law at the University of Ingoldstadt in Germany. The group associated with the Masons and gained a reputation as a secret revolutionary body. The group was present in England as the Hell-Fire Club headed by Sir Francis Dashwood. (This English group is supposedly the source of a flirtation with Masonry by the founding fathers of the United States, who allegedly placed the Illuminati pyramid and the Eye of Horus on the Great Seal of the United States.)

A modern version of the Order of the Illuminati was established during the 1970s with headquarters in San Francisco, California, and Nantes, France. It was one of a variety of half-serious/half-joking organizations created by magician-author Robert Anton Wilson, more recently a resident of Ireland. Wilson has authored a series of books on magick and occult philosophy using the Illuminatus metaphor, but drawing its content from the twentieth century Thelemic magick of Aleister Crowley and modern psychical and consciousness studies. Since Wilson's leaving the United States there are no formal representatives of the modern order, though it could be seen to have continued informally among Wilson's large reading audience. Even in the 1970s, the order existed only as a loose confederation of independent but like-minded magicians. It existed primarily to pursue Thelemic magick, as Wilson thought of Aleister Crowley as the twentieth-century inventor of the Illuminati tradition. Adherents were also devotees of Eris, the goddess of chaos and discord. The Order was a confederation of like-minded magicians who help each other over any times of problems in magical practice.

Sources: Neal Wilgus, *The Illuminoids*. New York: Pocket Books, 1978; Robert Anton Wilson, *Masks of the Illuminati*. New York: Pocket Books, 1981; Robert Anton Wilson, *Cosmic Trigger*. Berkeley, CA: And/Or Press, 1977; Robert Anton Wilson, *The Illuminati Papers*. Berkeley, CA: And/Or Press, 1980; Robert Anton Wilson, *Schroedinger's Cat*. New York: Pocket Books, 1980-81. 3 Vols.

★1025★

BENNU PHOENIX TEMPLE OF THE HERMETIC ORDER OF THE GOLDEN DAWN
(Defunct)

A shortlived attempt to revive the Hermetic Order of the Golden Dawn emerged in the early 1970s, led by John Phillips Palmer. The Bennu Phoenix Temple continued the tradition of the H.O.G.D. prior to the revelations of its secrets by Aleister Crowley. Crowley is viewed as a former member "impervious to discipline...consequently degraded to the Paths of the Portal in the Vault of Adepti and expelled." The group also follows the tradition which rejected S. L. MacGregor Mathers' leadership. He is believed to have fallen to the dark powers of the left-hand path.

The Bennu Phoenix Temple follows the ten rituals of the Order of the Golden Dawn and used forms of the rituals published by Israel Regardie. Sex magick was allowed if practiced within the context of marriage. Sex magick outside of marriage with a homosexual partner or as a mystic masturbation was strictly condemned. Homosexual behavior was regarded as impure. Drugs and animal sacrifice were also forbidden.

Sources: Israel Regardie, *The Golden Dawn*. St. Paul, MN: Llewellyn Publications, 1969.

★1026★

FELLOWSHIP OF MA-ION
(Defunct)

In 1904, Aleister Crowley received *The Book of the Law*, which became the new revelation for Thelemic magicians. The revelation included the prediction of a "child" who would "discover the key of it all." In 1915 Crowley carried out a series of sex magic workings with Jane Foster. Nine months later Charles Stansfeld Jones (d. 1950), known within thelemic circles as Frater Achad, proclaimed his assumption of the magical grade of Master of the Temple. Crowley accepted Achad as a magical child, i.e., a product of his own magical workings. Over the next eighteen months, Achad worked out the kabbalistic formulas which allowed Crowley to interpret some of the obscure passages of *The Book of the Law*.

In spite of Crowley's acceptance of Achad as the child, in 1919 the y broke relations, never to be associated again (though they periodically corresponded.) Achad wrote several books based upon his speculations on the kabbalah (qabala), but his interpretations never gained wide acceptance. Achad moved to London in the late 1920s. He initiated a period of intense self-reflection which issued forth in a new perspective which he termed the "arising of the Silver Star," artistically depicted as a silver pentaegram in a blue circle. In 1932 he composed a set of magical rituals and in the spring opened the Immanual Lodge. The work of the lodge bore magical fruit sixteen years later when Achad proclaimed the arrival of the Aeon of Ma, the manifestation of Truth and Justice. (Maat was the ancient Egyptian goddess of Truth and Justice.) The Aeon of Ma superceded the Aeon of Horus proclaimed by Crowley in 1904. The Aeon was never announced publicly, but communicated to a few magicians in private letters.

According to some sources, a small following who responded to the proclamation of the Aeon of Ma and who followed Achad's unique interpretation of the kabbalah formed an informal Fellowship of Ma-Ion which had members in both England and America. No verification of the existence of this group has been located. In the 1970s, in the wake of the publication of much of Aleister Crowley's materials and material on the Aeon of Ma(at), several groups have arisen which have developed a Maatian perspective, but these have arisen without any connection with or even knowledge of a Fellowship of Ma-Ion. (See separate entry on Ordo Adeptorum Invisiblum.)

Sources: Frater Achad [Charles Stansfeld Jones], *The Anatomy of the Body of God*. New York: Samuel Weiser, 1969; Frater Acad, *The Egyptian Revival*. New York: Samuel Weiser, 1969; Francis King, *Ritual Magic in England*. London: Neville Spearman, 1970.

★1027★

FOUNDATION, AN HERMETIC SOCIETY
Current address not obtained for this edition.

The Foundation was organized in 1971 by W. E. Stone, Jr., for the purpose of establishing a definite procedure for the study of ritual magick. Study was based upon the work of the Hermetic Order of the Golden Dawn, as updated and edited. Insights of such magicians as W. E. Butler, W. G. Gray, Gareth Knight and Israel Regardie were utilized. Membership in the Foundation was not solicited, but the leadership was quite open in sharing its findings with a wider audience through published articles and open lectures. In 1972, there were fewer than 20 members. The organization lasted only a few years.

The Foundation offered students a method of ceremonial magick as a "determined effort to establish a working relationship through himself between his lower and higher selves." The form was modernized in line with what was viewed as the natural evolution of the art. Group work was stressed; several working together increase the power available. Beginning as a neophyte, the student passed through four degrees to the portal series. Along the way, he learned the basics of occultism, meditation, astrology, Tarot, Kabbalah, various forms of divination and psychic development. The portal series was training in pure magick. Headquarters were in Houston, Texas.

★1028★
MONASTERY OF THE SEVEN RAYS
Box 1554
Chicago, IL 60690-1554

The Monastery of the Seven Rays is the organizational umbrella given to the various magical activities focused in the person of Michael Bertiaux, a noted Chicago occultist-magician. Bertiaux is the inheritor of the French Martinist tradition which he received through his magical training in Haiti and by his ordination and consecration as bishop of the Neo-Pythagorean Church.

Louis Claude de Saint-Martin (1743-1803) was a Roman Catholic raised in France. As a soldier, he met Martines de Pasqually, a disciple of Emanuel Swedenborg and Rosicrucianism. De Pasqually founded an occult order, the Order of the Elect Cohens, which Saint-Martin joined in 1768. After de Pasqually's death in 1774, Saint-Martin became the focus of a group of occultists. He began to write books (published posthumously), and a movement, the history of which is still known only in fragments, was born.

By the end of the eighteenth century, a branch of the Martinist Order had been established in Haiti. This group continued to function after Haiti gained its independence. It tended to blend with voodoo. In the 1890s, there was a revival movement in the Martinist Order, emphasizing a purist strain of Gnostic philosophy. In the years between the world wars the Gnostic Church was established in Leogane, Haiti, and was brought to the United States after World War II. In General, the Gnostic philosophy emphasizes a secret knowledge that humans can attain, and denies the divinity of Christ.

The Monastery of the Seven Rays, which became widely known through its advertisments in *Fate Magazine* in the 1970s, is a magical order drawing upon modern thelemic magick (derived from the writings of Aleister Crowley), voodoo, and the nineteenth-century French gnostic-occult tradition. Bertiaux wrote the lessons which teach a basic magical system and lead the student into the higher levels of magical working.

The Neo-Pythagorean Gnostic Church is the ecclesiastical structure which, along with six other fraternal and psychically oriented structures with which it is interlocked, focus the Martinist occult/mystical tradition in North America. The tradition began in France, was brought to Haiti, and from there came to the United

States in the mid-1950s. Bertiaux was consecrated by Bishop Hector Francois Jean-Maine, a Haitian who had received orders from the Spanish Albegensian Church which in turn had orders from the French gnostics. The famous French occultists Joseph-Antoine Boullan (1824-1893) and Pierre Michel Eugene Vintras (1807-1875) are included in the lineage.

The Neo-Pythagorean Gnostic Church is a ritual theurgic body in which the eucharist is the center of initiation. Through it, the invocation of angels and planetary spirits is made, and spirit communication often takes place during the mass. Purity of ritual is emphasized, and no tallow (i.e. nothing that carries the suffering of animals) is used in the candles. All members of the clergy are clairvoyant and often have visions during mass. Also, during worship a mystical language is intuitively (i.e. clairvoyantly) perceived and mystically spoken.

A Gnostic hierarchical system is headed by the Absolute, similar to the Kabbalist Ein Soph. The Absolute emanates a Trinity, which in turn is the source of lucifer and sophia, the basic male/female polarity. Lucifer is the morning star, inferior to Christ but not to be confused with Satan. Sophia is paid homage in the cult of the Virgin, the archetypical divine being. She is often revered as Our Lady of Mt. Carmel. Satanism and black magick are strongly opposed.

The church is subject to a supreme heliophant (in 1984, Dr. Hector Francois Jean Maine, residing in Madrid). The American jurisdiction is under Bishop Pierre-Antoine Saint-Charles of Boston, who has direct authority over all Haitian-American members. Michael Bertiaux in Chicago is over the Caucasian- American members and BishopMarc Lully of Chicago heads overseas development in South America and the West Indies. In 1979 Bertiaux exchanged consecrations with Bishop Forest Gregory Barber of the Catholic Apostolic Church in America.

Associated with the church are the Ancient Order of Oriental Templars, the Arithmosophical Society, Zotheria and the Esoteric Traditions Research Society. The Ancient Order of Oriental Templars is a lodge with credentials derived from the pre-Crowleyite Ordo Templi Orientis in Germany. It teaches a 16-degree system of magick. The Arithmosophical Society concentrates on Saint-Martin's philosophy of numbers. Numbers form a key to Saint-Martin's system of magical correspondences and tie Saint-Martin to Pythagoras. Both Zotheria and the Esoteric Traditions Research Society are outer courts of the various esoteric structures.

Membership: Not reported.

Sources: Docteur Bacalou Baca [Michael Bertiaux], *Lucky Hoodoo*. Chicago: Absolute Science Institute, 1977; Kenneth Grant, *Cults of the Shadow*. New York: Samuel Weiser, 1976; Christopher McIntosh, *Eliphas Levi and the French Occult Revival*. New York: Samuel Weiser,1974.

★1029★
NEW ENGLAND INSTITUTE OF METAPHYSICAL STUDIES
(Defunct)

The New England Institute of Metaphysical Studies was founded in the early 1970s by Ron Parshley and Mark Feldman as a correspondence school dedicated to the pursuit of occult knowledge. It was the Institute's perspective that Aleister Crowley placed magick in a system open to all. Through its own P-F Publications, it published the five-volume *Theorems of Occult Magick* by Feldman and Parshley as a study in Crowley's teachings. It also offered seventeen courses in occultism, divination, witchcraft and magick. A quarterly *Newsletter* was sent to all students. Also associated was *Tamlacht*, published three times a year by Victor Boruta of Linden, New Jersey. Headquarters were in Methuen, Massachusetts.

Sources: Mark Feldman and Ron Parshley, *Theorems of Occult Magick*. Methuen, MA: P-F Publications, 1971. 10 Vols.

★1030★
ORDER OF THE LILY AND THE EAGLE
(Defunct)

The Order of the Lily and the Eagle was the "guardian" of the Eonian tradition cradled in India and Egypt and passed through Orpheus, Pythagoras, Plotinus, Christian Rosencreutz, Paracelsus, Thomas Vaughn and Louis Claude de Saint-Martin (among others). It was founded in 1915 when its two masters--Deon (d. 1924), the prototype of wisdom, and Dea (d. 1918), the prototype of Love-- reestablished the order. Their goal was to work for the liberation of humanity and to announce the coming of the Holy Spirit as promised by our Savior.

The work of the order was to help individuals become initiates. The process begins in purification and continues through a knowledge of self and nature (the mysteries) to mastery of alchemy and theurgy (practical magick) and the initiatic sciences. The initiate struggles against evil, instructs others, and engages in healing of his fellow creatures. He is united with the invisible world and the masters, spirits who were once human and now teach humans about spiritual realities.

The Order of the Lily and the Eagle disseminated the teachings of the founders. They are structured in seven grades. The group also published *Eon/Justice and Truth*, a biennial periodical. Headquarters were in Englewood, Colorado.

★1031★
ORDER OF THELEMA
Current address not obtained for this edition.

The Order of Thelema was a Thelemic magick group which rejected the attempt by various branches of the O.T.O. to establish their authority by reference to a line of succession from Aleister Crowley. It was structured as a Crowleyan study group. There was no system of rituals except those things which members interpreted from Crowley's revelatory bible, *Liber Al vel Legis* (*The Book of the Law*), each according to his own will. The group believed that Aleister Crowley still operated close to this plane of existence as a present and active force, and that it was possible for him to reach the order by psychic means. The written words of Crowley were the only source of Thelemic Law. Strong support was given the perspective of *The Book of the Law*. Headquarters of the Order of Thelema are in San Diego, California. The word "Thelema" means will.

★1032★
ORDO ADEPTORUM INVISIBLUM
% Gerry Ahrens
18 Crampton House
Patmore St.
London, England B

The Ordo Adeptorum Invisiblum (O.A.I.) is a British-based thelemicist order aligned to the Maatian magical "current." It has grown out of the proclamation of the magical Aeon of Ma (or Maat) proclaimed in 1948 by Frater Achad (Charles Stansfeld Jones). Maat is the ancient Egyptian goddess of Truth and Justice. The order looks toward a planetary manifestation of the presence of Maat. The coming of Maat has been heralded by the three twentieth-century trends: the great liberation movements leading to the recognition of human rights, the attempts to balance male-dominated Western magic and the non-elitist androgynous approach to magic practiced by Maatian groups. In recognition of their acceptance of feminist liberation concerns and the non-sexist nature of their magical workin gs, members of the O. A. I. have dropped the use of common designations of male and female members as "frater" and "soror" in favor of the single desination "persona."

The O.A.I. began in England in 1979 in the informal workings of three thelemic magicians (two women and one man). In 1980 they made a formal alignment to the Aeon of Maat and thus the O. A. I. came into existence. At the end of the year, the three original members separated. One went to Fez, Morocco, and the following year, one came to Chicago. The first members of the O.A.I were received in Chicago.

The order has developed as a very loose confederation of otherwise independent magicians pursuing their own magical experiments in alignment to the Maatian Aeon. Periodically, order members will gather for group rituals. New initiates are received after their successful performance of *Liber Samakh He*, a revised version of *Liber Samakh*, a thelemic ritual designed to promote conversation with one's Holy Guardian Angel (higher self). The order is non-hierarchial. Leadership can be exercised by any member and teaching is a matter of sharing the results of individual ritual workings with the larger membership. All members have access to all materials possessed by the order.

Membership: In 1985 members of the order could be found in England, the Chicago metropolitan area, and California. There are less than 100 members.

Sources: Persona Skia, *O.A.I. Manifesto: Origin, History, Organization.* Kenilworth, IL: Ordo Adeptorum Invisiblum, 1982; Persona PVAD MASURUS 1043, *Liber Samakh He.* Chicago: Stellium Press, 1981; *Liber ANDANA.* Chicago: Ordo Adeptorum, 1983.

★1033★
ORDO TEMPLI ASTARTE
Box 3341
Pasadena, CA 91103

The Ordo Templi Astarte (Order of the Temple of Astarte-OTA), which also operates under the name Church of Hermetic Science, is a ritual magick group begun in 1970 to practice Kabbalistic Magick in the Western tradition. Based upon Jungian psychology, the OTA defined magick as a "system of ritual hypnotic induction (conjuration) that calls upon archetypal forms from the unconscious (evocation) and allows them to be visualized (manifestation) whereupon they can be used for numerous purposes ranging from the frankly psychotherapeutic to the more abstract system research and development."

The OTA traces its history to Aleister Crowley through Louis Culling. Culling claims to have a charter from Crowley for an autonomous lodge. This charter was given after Culling left C.F. Russell, who was deviating from Crowley's teachings. Culling turned the charter over to the OTA leadership before his recent death. The group also claims to possess the "secret rituals of the Ordo Templi Orientis in Crowley's original holographs." Though operating with a thelemic charter, the OTA does not consider itself fully thelemic. In describing the order, founder Carroll R. Runyon, Jr. has noted, " We operate a Collegium ad Spiritum Sanctum of the O.T.O. in our Philosophus Grade as a research and study program. In its own context, it is Thelemic; but we do not initiate or operate ceremonially under a Thelemic aegis. We have great respect for the works of Aleister Crowley, but we consider him a Master of the Art in much the same way that Sufis consider Jesus a Great ProphSet--without calling themselves Christians."

The OTA is centered in a single lodge in Pasadena. During the 1970s there was for several years a second lodge in Pittsburgh. The lodge is headed by Carroll Runyon, also known as Frater Aleyin.

Membership: Not reported. There are less than 50 members.

Periodicals: *The Seventh Ray*, Box 3341, Pasadena, CA 91103.

Sources: Robert S. Ellwood, Jr., *Mysticism and Religion.* Englewood Cliffs, NJ: Prentice-Hall, 1980; Cheryl JoAnne Christensen, *Magical Epistemic Communities: The Construction of Specialized Social Realities in Bunyoro, Uganda and Los Angeles, California.* Cambridge, MA: Massachusetts Institute of Technology, Ph.D. dissertation, 1975.

★1034★
ORDO TEMPLI ORIENTIS
% Grand Lodge
JAF Box 7666
New York, NY 10116

The Ordo Templi Orientis, which had become disorganized following the death of Karl Germer (1962) who had succeeded Aleister Crowley as Outer Head of the Order was reborn in 1969 when Grady Louis McMurtry (Hymenaeus Alpha) asserted his authority as head of the O.T.O. McMurty had been given two letters in 1946 from Aleister Crowley giving him authority to reform the order and act as Crowley's representative in the United States, subject to the approval of Karl Johannes Germer (Frater Saturnus). Though these letter were originally intended to apply to the situation of the lodge in Pasadena which McMurtry had been asked to investigate, they did give him broad emergency powers. Crowley died in 1947 and the authorization, though put aside by McMurtry and never used, were never withdrawn. Germer's death in 1962 left McMurtry the only person with power to act.

McMurtry had been initiated into the Agape Lodge of the O.T.O. in Pasadena in the 1930s and during World War II, while stationed in England, was the only American O.T.O. member to be with Crowley. McMurtry took the designation of "Caliph," in 1969 claiming there was no present outer head of the order in a person, only in an international office. He rejected the claims of Kenneth Grant in England and Karl Metzger in Switzerland to be the outer head.

During the thirteen years of McMurtry's leadership, the O.T.O. grew into a substantial body with chapters and lodges across the United States and Canada, and overseas in Germany, Norway, Australia, and New Zealand. There were individual members in other countries, including Poland and Yugoslavia. Membership in the OTO (Dublin, Ca.) requires physical participation in the ceremonies of initiation and the payment of subscription costs and dues.

Several months after McMurtry's death, the IX degree members met and elected one of their number to replace him. He has chosen to remain anonymous except to members of the higher degrees of the order and has assume the name-title of Hymenaeus Beta, X, Caliph, Frater Superior, Outer Head of the Order. The Grand

Lodge and headquarters were moved from Berkeley, California to New York City.

Membership: In 1985 the Order had approximately 500 members in 58 lodges and camps.

Periodicals: *The Magical Link*, Box 2303, Berkeley, CA 94702; *Ecclesia Gnostica*, Camp of the Star and the Raven, 1005 Market St., #207 San Francisco, CA 94103; *In the Continuum*, Box 415, Oroville, CA 95965.

Sources: Aleister Crowley, *Equinox.* New York, Samuel Weiser, n.d. 10 vols.; Aleister Crowley, *I.N.R.I. O.T.O. Introduction.* Berkeley, CA: Ordo Templi Orientis, 1981; Aleister Crowley and Frater 137, *Source Book 93.* San Francisco: Stellar Visions, 1981; *O.T.O. System Outline.* San Francisco: Stellar Visions, 1981; Bill Hiedrick, *Magick and Qabalah.* Berkeley, CA: Ordo Templi Orientis, 1980.

★1035★
ORDO TEMPLI ORIENTIS (GRANT)
Current address not obtained for this edition.

Kenneth Grant emerged in the 1970s as the self-proclaimed leader of the British branch of the Ordo Templi Orientis. He had co-edited *The Confessions of Aleister Crowley* (1969), late head of the order, and had even earlier (in the 1950s) under the direction and charter of Crowley's successor, Karl Germer, established the New Isis Lodge in London. However, Germer's charter had given Grant the charter to work only the first three degrees. Grant began to work all eleven, writing his own materials where they were unavailable. Germer expelled him from the O.T.O. However, when Germer died, and with the O.T.O. almost extinct, they were few who could challenge Grant's leadership. In 1973 he published *Aleister Crowley and the Hidden God*, the first of six substantive books that began to explore the *Qliphoth*, the so-called backside of the Kabbalah, the mystical Tree of Life. His concentration on the magick of this shadowy realm of the consciousness both gave his brand of magick a unique quality and led other magicians, even Thelemites,to accuse him of tampering with black magick.

Except for the concentration on the Qliphoth in the experimental areas of magick, Grant's order follows much traditional O.T.O. tradition and practice, the secret material of the order having become public during the 1970s through the access given to the Crowley papers deposited at the Warburg Institute in London. Like the other thelemic groups, the O.T.O. (Grant) has as its aim the establishment of the law of Thelema. It does not undertake the training of novices and accepts for membership only those who have submitted a record of nine months' magical practice. They must also publish or disseminate *Liber LXXVII*, a brief statement by Aleister Crowley of some major Thelemic principles.

Organizationally, this branch of the O.T. O. has dropped the "quasi-masonic" structures typical of most magical groups, and its ten degrees are no longer conferred in secret, elaborate rituals. There is no set course to study. Advancement beyond the third degree is subject to the invitation of the governing body. Each applicant is aided to discover the great work which is her/his own true will.

The O.T.O. (Grant) came to the United States through individuals who contacted Grant after reading his several books. It grew and spread in the mid-1970s. For several years, a periodical, *Mezla*, appeared. However, in the early 1980s, Soror Tanith (J. R. Ayers), head of the O.T.O. in North America, resigned and no successor has been named.

Membership: Not reported. At present, there are no known lodges and less than 100 members of the O.T.O. branch headed by Kenneth Grant in the United States.

Sources: Kenneth Grant, *Aleister Crowley and the Hidden God.* New York: Samuel Weiser, 1974; Kenneth Grant, *Nightside of Eden.* London: Frederick Muller, 1977; Kenneth Grant, *Outside the Circles of Time.* London: Frederick Muller, 1980.

★1036★
ORDO TEMPLI ORIENTIS (ROANOKE, VIRGINIA)
(Defunct)

The Ordo Templi Orientis headquartered in Roanoke, Virginia, had claimed to be the true O.T.O. It rejected the claims of the other groups which had emerged in the 1970s based on a charter or lineage dating to Aleister Crowley. Its head was Robert E. L. Shell who saw the mission of the OTO as preventing "hard-won knowledge from being lost in the upheavals and birth pangs of the Aeon Horus [the new era announced by Crowley in 1904]...." One must validate claims by proving allegiance to the law of Thelema, or the Will, the primary principle guiding thought and action for Crowley's disciples. The goal is the Great Work, the ultimate lifting of all humanity to the status of gods. Shell claimed contact with the secret chiefs, the entities (much like the theosophical Great White Brotherhood), who guided the order from the inner planes of existence.

★1037★
SHRINE OF SOTHIS
(Defunct)

The Shrine of Sothis made its appearance in 1973 by way of some ads in psychic/occult periodicals. It taught a system of practical theurgy (magick) as the highest and most efficient mode of communication between man and his inner self. A complete set of lessons, which could be obtained on a correspondence basis, took the student step-by-step through the magical disciplines. The student was taught about the pentagram (a disc-shaped talisman), the gods, initiation, reincarnation, black magick, divination, the construction of talismans and invocation. The goal of the lessons was to lift the student into the realization of the "great concealed one," God. Students practiced daily devotions and orations in their own homes. Members joined by paying an initiation fee. Headquarters were in San Francisco. After several years of operation, the order dropped out of sight.

★1038★
SOCIETY ORDO TEMPLI ORIENTIS IN
    AMERICA
Box 90018
Nashville, TN 37209

Among those who made claim to the lineage of the Ordo Templi Orientis following the death of Karl Germer (d. 1962) , who had succeeded Aleister Crowley as Outer Head of the Order, was Marcelo Ramos Motta, a Brazilian member of the O.T.O. He claimed that in the years following Germer's death he had completed his initiatic work and assumed the magical status needed to become the leader of the work. In 1975, through the Society of the Ordo Templi Orientis (S.O.T.O.), as his branch was known, he issued the first of four massive volumes of the *Equinox*, each issue of which contained writings by Crowley, Motta and others. These were seen as a revival of the semi-annual publication issued originally by Crowley (1909-1913). Other publications followed.

The S.O.T.O. immediately ran into a conflict with the Ordo Templi Orientis (see separate entry) over the copyright to the writings of Aleister Crowley that had been left to the O.T.O. in Crowley's will. The S.O.T.O. claimed to be that organization, and writers and organizations not associated with the S.O.T.O. who wrote about or published Crowley's writings were denounced in various issues of the *Equinox*. The tension between O.T.O., S.O.T.O., and Samuel Weiser , (the publisher of the first issue of the new *Equinox*) led to several law suits. In 1985 a libel suit filed by Grady McMurtry (caliph of the O.T.O.) and others, concerning remarks made in the *Equinox*, against Motta and the S.O.T.O. resulted in the awarding of all copyrights and trademarks to the O.T.O. and turned back all claims by Motta to be the Outer Head of the Order of the Ordo Templi Orientis.

Membership: Not reported. There are less than 100 members in the United States.

Periodicals: *Equinox*, Box 90018, Nashville, TN 37209.

Sources: Marcelo Motta, *Letter to a Brazilian Mason*. Nashville, TN: Troll Publishing Company, 1980; Marcelo Motta, *Manifesto*. Nashville, TN: Society Ordo Templi Orientis in America, 1978; Marcelo Motta, *Thelemic Political Morality*. Nashville, TN: Society Ordo Templi Orientis in America, 1978; Marcelo Motta, *The Political Aims of the O. T. O.*. Nashville: TN: Ordo Templi Orientis, 1980.

★1039★
TEMPLE OF TRUTH
Box 3125
Pasadena, CA 91103

One of the prime movers in the founding of the Ordo Templi Astarte was Nelson H. White, who served as its vice-president and, under his magical name Frater Khedemel, its major apologist. In 1973, however, he left the Ordo Templi Astarte and he and his wife, Anne White (Soror Veritas) began the Temple of Truth (TOT). The Temple differs from other occult orders in that it has no grades and no fixed curriculum. It has also dispensed with many of the ceremonial trappings of traditional ritual magick; emphasis is placed on individual independent study and spiritual development. Students adopt an individualized course after an initial series of classes. The teachings are basically Kabbalistic and follow the teachings in the Whites' books.

The T.O.T. is the magica l order sponsored by the Light of Truth Church, a licensed corporation in California. The church is neither evangelistic nor fundamentalistic and recognizes the subjectivity of what most people call "Truth." Membership in both the church and the order is open to all persons.

Headquarters of the church are in Pasadena, where the Whites operate a church-sponsored bookstore, The Magick Circle. *The White Lite*, which began publication in the fall of 1974, has become one of the oldest continuously published magical magazines in the country.

Membership: Not reported. There is one center located in Pasadena, California.

Periodicals: *The White Light*, Box 93124, Pasadena, CA 91109-3124.

Sources: Nelson and Anne White, *Collected Rituals of the T.O.T.* Pasadena, CA: The Technology Group, 1982; Nelson and Anne White, *Working High Magick*. Pasadena, CA: The Technology Group, 1982; Nelson and Anne White, *Secret Magick Revealed*. Pasadena, CA: The Technology Group, 1979; Nelson and Anne White, *The Wizard's Apprentice*. Pasadena, CA: The Technology Group, 1982.

Witchcraft and Neo-Paganism

★1040★
ALEXANDRIAN WICCA
Current address not obtained for this edition.

Most closely related to the older Gardnerian Wicca are the Alexandrians, followers of Alexander Sanders, termed by his biographer "The King of the Witches." According to Sanders, in 1933, as a seven-year old, he surprised his grandmother, who was nude and standing in a circle in the kitchen. She ordered Sanders into the circle and had him strip and bend over with his head between his thighs. She took a knife, nicked his scrotum and declared, "You are one of us now." Sanders realized that he was a witch. He was later initiated by her as third degree witch. In actual fact, all indications are that Sanders was an early member of one of the Gardnerian Wicca covens, and that he took the Gardnerian rituals, modified them slightly and began his own work independently. In any case, in 1967, after the failure of several marriages, Sanders settled in London with his third wife, Maxine Sanders.

In 1969, a sensationalized article on Sanders in a Sunday London newspaper led to a meteoric rise. Other papers and media turned him into a celebrity, and his biography was released during the year. He also made a film, "Legend of the Witches," which further boosted his popularity; he was a frequent guest on television talk shows. His text of the Witchcraft rituals were among the first to be published and become publically available.

The Alexandrians ritually resemble the Gardnerians, upon whom they base their practices. Like the Gardnerians, their rituals are skyclad (i.e., in the nude), and the coven in London became one of the most photographed in all the craft. Alexandrians have become noted for the culmination of the third-degree initiation in the Great Rite, i.e., sexual intercourse, also used at handfasting (marriage) ceremonies. Ideally, the rite is held for two people about to leave and form a new coven. The rite may be symbolic or actual.

The situation of Alexandrian witchcraft as a distinct tradition has been greatly altered by attacks within the Witchcraft community questioning Sanders's credentials and by the defection of a leading member, Stewart Farrar, who, with his wife Janet Farrar, began an independent coven. He has emerged as an important author and ritual innovator. Much of the attention that once came to Sanders now currently flows to the neo-Alexandrian system of Farrar. However, rather than creating a new lineage of covens, Farrar's work has tended to be absorbed into the larger Pagan-Witchcraft community as another source for eclectic covens to draw upon.

Membership: In America a few Alexandrian covens still exist, but their number has steadily decreased.

Sources: June Johns, *King of the Witches*. New York: Coward-McCann, 1970; *The Alex Sanders Lectures*. New York: Magickal Childe, Inc., 1980; Stewart Farrar, *What Witches Do*. New York: Coward, McCann & Geoghegan, 1971; Janet Farrar and Stewart Farrar, *Eight Sabbaths for Witches*. London: Robert Hale, 1981; Janet Farrar and Stewart Farrar, *The Witches' Way*. London: Robert Hale, 1984.

★1041★
ALGARD WICCA
% Mary Nesnick
529 E. 20th St.
New York, NY 10009

Algard (from "Alexandrian" and Gardnerian") Wicca was formed in 1972 by Mary Nesnick, an Alexandrian Wicca high priestess, in New York City. Ms. Nesnick was initiated into the craft in 1964 by a college professor. She was a freshman at the time. The intent of Algard was to lead to a more independent sect of Wicca that would allow more latitude in ritual and action. As the name implies, both Alexandrian and Gardnerian rituals were sources for Algard practices (Alexandrian Wicca and Gardnerian Wicca are discussed in separate entries.) Combining the two was relatively easy, since they were similar and at many points even identical. Algard covens worship both skyclad and robed, at the coven's discretion. All initiation ceremonies are skyclad.

The Algard covens are governed by the grand high priestess (Ms. Nesnick) and a grand high priest, who oversee the covens and settle intercoven problems and who speak for the craft. Each coven is headed by a high priestess and high priest. Twenty elders assist the ten neophyte priestesses and priests in learning craft ways. A one-year waiting period is required before initiation. Homosexuality is grounds for rejection. Members must be eighteen years of age. Screening before initiation was a point at issue with Alexander Sanders, who felt that the first degree was the place for strict screening. Worship is centered on the eight festivals and thirteen full moon esbats. Only initiates attend.

The Algard Wiccans are one of the most highly organized bodies of covens. An *Algard Newsletter*, issued only to members, tied the leaders together. However, in the flux of the Wiccan community during the late 1970s, the tradition seems to have been largely dissipated.

Membership: Not reported. In 1973 there were a reported 48 covens with affiliated groups in England, Canada, and Greece. There was no verification of those claims, and there is good reason to doubt them. In the early 1980s, the tradition has been reduced to one or two covens in the New York area.

★1042★
AMERICAN ORDER OF THE BROTHERHOOD
OF WICCA
% Lady Sheba
Box 3383-G
St. Paul, MN 55415

The American Order of the Brotherhood of Wicca is an eclectic traditional Wiccan group headed by Lady Sheba (Jessie Wicker Bell). American Celtic is the name given the covens which combine Lady Sheba's Celtic heritage and American Indian magical tradition. Lady Sheba was initiated into the craft in the 1930s. She became the focus of controversy in the early 1970s for publishing her *Grimoire* and *Book of Shadows*, thus making public secret rituals and practices. These rituals turned out to be slightly revised versions of the Gardnerian rituals. She also referred to herself as a Witch Queen, a title used in Gardnerian Wicca for a priestess whose has raised coven members to the third degree and sent them out to form a new coven. The title was rejected by many of the more individualistic craft members.

Lady Sheba defines witch as "the wise one" and witchcraft as "magick," denying that it is nature worship or a fertility cult. To her, witchcraft is learning to manipulate and use the natural laws. Nature is the physical manifestation of the creator, who appears as Mother-Father. Astrology is also an important aspect of witchcraft. Lady Sheba's rituals adhere to the traditional Gardnerian Wiccan forms--the circle, the rituals, the three degrees, the eight festivals and covens of thirteen or fewer persons. They differ primarily in espousing a robed tradition (Gardnerian rituals are done in the nude). Couples and family relations are emphasized.

The American Order is organized into dependent covens tied together by their relationship to Lady Sheba, who is recognized as having come from a long line of witches. Covens are located across the country, and there are a few overseas.

During the 1970s, at the time Lady Sheba's books were being published, the American Order was among the most active groups in promoting interaction and cooperation among witches of various traditions. Much of the organizational leadership was assumed by Carl Weschcke, owner-publisher of Llewellyn Publications, who had been initiated by Lady Sheba. In 1973, the Twin Cities Area Council of the American Order of the Brotherhood of Wicca was formed as a council of coven leaders, and all traditions were invited to participate. In 1974, the Order was a strong force behind the formation of the short-lived ecumenical organization, the Council of American Witches. In more recent years the Order has assumed a much lower profile.

Membership: Not reported. There are only a few covens currently associated with the order.

Sources: Lady Sheba (Jessie Wicker Bell), *Witch*. St. Paul, MN: Llewellyn Publications, 1973; Lady Sheba, *The Grimoire of Lady Sheba*. St. Paul, MN: Llewellyn Publications, 1974.

★1043★
ASATRU FREE ASSEMBLY
Box 1754
Breckenridge, TX 76024

The Asatru Free Assembly dates to the formation in 1972 of the Viking Brotherhood by Stephen A. McNallen, then a student at Midwestern University in Wichita Falls, Texas. McNallen had been a follower of the Norse deities for several years as an individual and he decided that the time had come for him to speak publically about them. He began to publish *The Runestone*, a quarterly periodical. Shortly after forming the Brotherhood, McNallen went into the Army and served as an officer with NATO in Europe. During this period *The Runestone* continued to appear, and other groups of Norse Pagans appeared. Upon returning to civilian life in 1976, McNallen began to refine the brotherhood's ritual and doctrine. This refinement led to the adoption of a new name, the Asatru Free Assembly. This change emphasizes the great value placed on individualism, courage, integrity, and independence, and the general opposition to all collective ideologies (including fascism) within the assembly (which is home to a wide variety of belief and practice within its general framework). It also sets itself apart from "Odinism" (the popular name for Norse Paganism) in that the assembly is looking to revive the "cults" of all the Norse deities, not just Odin.

Worship is viewed as a contradiction of the spirit of ego centrality in the Viking religion. However, basic rituals have been devised to celebrate certain events and to recognize the gods, who epitomize certain values. New members are initiated, and name-givings and burials are also occasions for ritual. Adherents celebrate Yule (December 2 5); Ragnar's Day (March 28), in commemoration of Viking Ragnar Lodbrok, who sailed up the Seine River in 845 and sacked Paris; Lindisfarne Day (June 8); and Midsummer Day (summer solstice). *Runestone* regularly carries a calendar of ritual and remembrance days.

Local groups of the Brotherhood are called "Skeppslags" or "ship's crews," and they consist of from two to 15 members. Each Skeppslag operates under the chieftain of the Brotherhood. Also becoming active during the early 1980s were a variety of guilds, groups built around a particualr interest. These vary from sewing guilds to warriors' and brewers' guild. Some guilds publish their own newsletters. The assembly continues to be headed by McNallen, who also edits its journal.

Membership: In 1984 the assembly reported 150 members, 5 centers and 4 priests.

Periodicals: *The Runestone*, Box 1754, Breckenridge, TX 76024; *The Frothing Vat*, Jace Crouch, 7860 W. Jefferson Road, Elwell, MI 48832.

Remarks: Within the larger Pagan community, the Norse groups have, as a whole, been condemned for their overt racism. The Asatru Free Assembly has been largely free of racist expression and has continued to be accepted by non-Norse Pagans.

Sources: Stephen A. McNallen, *Rituals of Asatru*. Breckenridge, TX: Asatru Free Assembly, 1985; Heigi

Hundingsbani, *The Religion of Odin--A Handbook*. Red Wing, MN: Viking House, 1978.

★1044★

ATLANTION WICCA
(Defunct)

Atlantion Wicca, though originating in the 1960s, was based upon the teachings (and dedicated to the memory) of Elizabeth Sawyer, the witch of Edmonton, England. Ms. Sawyer was hung at Tyburn, England, on April 19, 1621, for supposedly killing by witchcraft a neighbor, Agnes Ratcleife. She had been known in the town as a healer and midwife and for helping farmers with their crops. The founding high priest was Don Sawyer, a descendant.

Rituals and teachings of Atlantion Wicca were found in its own *Book of Shadows*, which drew heavily upon Gardnerian Wicca practice. Esbats are held at both the full and new moons, and the sabbats were celebrated. Work was conducted within the circle. Reincarnation was a central belief. The group forbade the use of drugs, orgies, sacrifice, public nudity, and any behavior which might reflect poorly upon the craft.

The Atlantion witches were headquartered in Syracuse, New York and in 1977 they had three covens. For several years they engaged in vigorous activity to establish in the public's mind the image of Witchcraft as a serious religion and to destroy the negative images which connected Wicca to violence, black magic, and the worship of Satan. No sign of the survival of the covens into the mid-1980s has been manifest.

★1045★

CHURCH AND SCHOOL OF WICCA
Box 1502
New Bern, NC 28560

Since the early 1970s advertisements have appeared in various psychic and occult periodicals advertising the School of Wicca, a church which considers itself a representative of Welsh traditional Witchcraft headed by Gavin Frost and his wife, Yvonne Frost, of New Bern, North Carolina. The Church and School of Wicca has been one of the most open and accessible Witchcraft groups, and became a ready means of entry for many people into Witchcraft. It has carried on a campaign to promote what it considers a proper understanding of the craft in the wake of centuries of adverse propaganda and to recruit student witches. To this end, it has produced a course of study in Wicca (the ancient word for "witches," "wise ones") and the Frosts have authored several books.

Emphases of the School of Wicca vary somewhat from other forms. More to the center is magick as the focus of witchcraft; the role of the Mother Goddess is played down, and "spirit guides" as aids to progress are highlighted. Much material is borrowed from British ritual magick. Sexual magick is a major focus of rituals.

Since the early 1970s, the Frosts have been the center of controversy within the Wicca community. They have been accused of not worshipping the Goddess, and of sexual and racial bigotry, particularly bigotry against homosexuals. They were also critized for the title to their first book, *The Witch's Bible*, since is seemed to speak for all the craft while departing in emphassis from some craft distinctives. (That particular controversy seemed to have been resolved at the spring, 1974 , Witch Meet in Minneapolis, primarily by Gavin's winsome personality and forceful intellect.)

Twelve tenets summarize the world view of the Church of Wicca:

1. God is the overseeing intelligence that created the universe and the spirit world or the "other"; 2. The ultimate aim is to reach the sphere of God; 3. As above, so below; 4. Hell is within the mind of man; 5. Good is external; 6. Evil in the soul must be eliminated for progression to higher levels; 7. Reincarnation is for those who have not progressed far enough on earth; 8. All must live in harmony with nature; 9. The development and care of the body is a sacred duty; 10. Power is available from the human mind and from the spirits; 11. Good begets good; and 12. Evil begets evil. The final tenet sets the School of Wicca against the traditional fertility focus. The School of Wicca believes that the fertility plea has been answered and that the overpopulation crisis is the result. As more souls from the spirit side incarnate, the development level of earth is being lowered.

Membership: Covens are found across the United States. Exact locations and figures are not published.

Periodicals: *Survival*, Box 1502, New Bern, NC 28560.

Sources: Gavin Frost and Yvonne Frost, *The Witch's Bible*. New York: Berkley Publishing Company, 1975; Gavin Frost and Yvonne Frost, *A Witch's Guide to Life*. Cottonwood, AZ: Esoteric Publications, 1978; Gavin Frost and Yvonne Frost, *The Magic Power of Witchcraft*. West Nyack, NY: Parker Publishing Company, 1976.

★1046★

CHURCH OF ALL WORLDS
Box 212
Redwood Valley, CA 95470

Among the largest and most influential of all the pagan bodies during the 1970s was the Church of All Worlds, formed in 1967. The church traces its history back to 1961, when a group at Westminster College at Fulton, Missouri, formed around Tim Zell and Louis Christie. During the mid-1960s, it was centered on the University of Oklahoma campus at Norman and operated under the name Atlan Foundation. A periodical, *The Atlan Torch* (later *Atlan Annals*), was published. In 1967 following a move to St. Louis, the Church of All Worlds was incorporated. In 1968, the *Green Egg* appeared. From its inauspicious beginnings as a one-page ditto sheet, it grew into as the most significant periodical in the pagan movement during the 1970s and made Tim Zell, its editor, a major force in Neo-Paganism (a term which Zell coined). It was also the major instrument in the church's expansion.

The Church of All Worlds took much inspiration from the science fiction classic, *Stranger in a Strange Land* by Robert Heinlein. In the novel, the Stranger, Michael Smith, was an earthman born on Mars and raised by Martians. Among his other adventures upon being brought to earth was the formation of the "Church of All Worlds." The "Church" was built around "nests." A basic concepts was "groking," i.e., the ability to be fully intuitive about someone. It also emphasized the experience of co-equal love between the sexes. The nests were places where groking and joful sexual love could find expression. Martian was spoken. The common greeting was, "Thou Art God," a recognition of the divine in each person.

The non-fictional Church of All Worlds is organized around a Central Nest where master records are kept. Autonomous nests are composed of at least nine members located in the same area. There are nine circles of advancement, named after the nine planets; each circle includes study, writings, sensitivity and encounter-group experience, as well as active participation in the life of the church.

Worship in the Church of All Worlds is centered on the Earth- Mother Goddess and the Horned god, who represent the plant and animal kingdoms respectively. The matriarchal aspect is emphasized. The Church of All Worlds is dedicated to the "celebration of life, the maximal actualization of human potential and the realization of ultimate individual freedom and personal responsibility in harmonious exo-psychic relationship with the total Biosphere of Holy Mother Earth." The good is that which is pro-life and nature. The eight seasonal festivals commonly associated with Witchcraft are celebrated.

Though incorporated in 1967, the church had trouble being recognized as a legitimate religious body and was refused recognition by the Missouri Department of Revenue for purposes of state sales tax exemption. The rejection was on the basis of its lack of primary concern about the hereafter, God, the destiny of souls, heaven, hell, sin and its punishment, and other supernatural matters. The ruling was overturned in 1971.

In 1974, the church reported nests located in Missouri, California, Illinois, Kansas, Wisconsin, Iowa, Wyoming, Minnesota, Pennsylvania, Tennessee, New Jersey, New York, and Ohio. It published two periodicals, *The Green Egg* and *The Pagan*. Two years later, Zell, having established the Church, moved from St. Louis to California, for a life more centered upon writing, research in some areas of particular interest and the practice of the religion he had developed. He left the administration and the publication of *The Green Egg* in the hand of leaders. After only a few issues the magazine ceased to appear and much of the church dissolved in the wake of intense internal conflict. By the mid-1980s it survived in California among those attracted to Zell, who renamed himself, Otter G'Zell, and his wife Morning G'Zell.

Membership: Not reported. There are an estimated 50 to 100 people affiliated with the Church as of the mid-1980s.

Remarks: The research initiated by Morning and Otter G'Zell in California in the late 1970s led to the production of a "unicorn," i.e. a goat with but a single horn, produced by an operation on a baby goat. The emergence of the first such goat, named Lancelot, was followed by a national publicity campaign, a shortlived periodical, *The Living Unicorn* (1981-82) and the eventual purchase of it by the Ringling Bros. and Barnum and Bailey Circus. G'Zell then turned his attention to the reports of mermaids being cited in the South Seas.

Sources: *The Living Unicorn.* Los Gatos, CA: The Living Unicorn, [1980]; Tim Zell, *Cataclysm and Consciousness: From the Golden Age to the Age of Iron.* Redwood Valley, CA; The Author, 1977.

★1047★
CHURCH OF PAN
R.R. 3
Box 189
Foster, RI 02825

The Church of Pan was founded in 1970 by Kenneth Walker and members of a nudist colony in rural Rhode Island. The organization of the church was occasioned by the request of two members to be married in the nude and the inability of the group to locate a minister to perform the ceremony. They decided to form a church and Walker became the minister.

The Church of Pan espouses naturalist principles. Reverence and devotion is directed toward the Creator, and actions follow patterns discerned to be in concert with the Creator's designs and purposes. While engaged in altruistic actions which attempt to modify the harshness of nature, in line with the destiny of creation, the church denounces human actions which have destroyed life-supporting systems and polluted nature. Humans have the task of maintaining the balance of life on the planet. The church also opposes the distortions of human society in its treatment of sexuality. Forgetting the naturalness of sex, society tends to view it either as sinful or something to be marketed.

The church is headquartered at a nudist colony managed by Walker. Members are active in the promotion of environmental concerns. As might be expected from the nature of its beginning, the church has experienced difficulties over its status as a tax-exempt religious organization.

Membership: In 1983 the church reported 30 families, all members of the one "congregation" in Rhode Island.

★1048★
CHURCH OF THE ETERNAL SOURCE
Box 7091
Burbank, CA 91510-7091

The Church of the Eternal Source, the most substantial of the Egyptian bodies, was founded in 1970 by Donald D. Harrison and Harold Moss. Harrison, a former Roman Catholic, and Moss were converted to paganism through the study of Greek and Roman religion and the attraction of the fine arts of ancient Egypt. In 1967, Harrison founded the *Julian Review*, which became the organ of the Delphic Fellowship, an early Pagan fellowship based upon Greek motifs. Moss organized a social group professing the Egyptian religion after seeing a movie, "The Egyptian," which focused on Akhenaten. In 1963, the group held an Egyptian costume party. In 1967/68, after an involvement with Fereferia (a group described elsewhere in this chapter) Moss felt called to become a priest of Horus (the god said to be the offspring of Isis and Osiris). The Church of the Eternal Source combines aspects of a number of Egyptian cults. Each priest and priestess acts autonomously in supervising ritual and initiation procedures for his or her cult.

The two basic principles of the Church of the Eternal Source are polytheism, the plurity of gods, and authentic Egyptianism. The church teaches that divinity is a balance of distinct divine vectors. The diversity of the gods, and their transactions, produce reality. Man's task is to achieve balance in his soul in the divine vectors. Authentic Egyptian religion relates to the early period when Egypt was relatively untainted by non-Egyptian ideas. This period becomes a source for all later religious insights. The mastery of Egyptian history is stressed. Many of the church leaders have many pilgrimages to Egypt.

Religious practices center on personal shrines, the study of theology, divination, the fine arts and personal worship with wide variations. Group worship is manifest in the festivals, which are dramatic reenactments of a holy myth. The Egyptian pantheon forms the basic content of faith. A typical myth is the story of the rebirth of Osiris. Osiris was killed by Set, the god of darkness. Isis, the wife of Osiris, sought him, her tears causing the Nile to overflow. She found the body and buried it, but not carefully. Set exhumed it, dismembered it and scattered the pieces through the land. Isis then carefully sought and assembled each piece. Osiris was then resurrected. Osiris and Isis are accompanied in the pantheon by Horus, their son; Bast, the beneficent solar goddess represented as a cat; Thoth,

the god of wisdom; and Ra, the sun god often represented as Khepera, the beetle (believed to be self-generated). The myths are described in ancient literature, such as the *Egyptian Book of the Dead*.

Important festival days are held each full moon; on the birthdays of the deities, the latter occurring in July; and the equinoxes and the solstices. Ritual magick is performed, but no set ritual is prescribed. A typical Egyptian ritual is found in *Magic, An Occult Primer* by David Conway. The newsletter is for members only.

Membership: In 1984 the Church reported four groups (located in the Tucson, Arizona and San Diego and Los Angeles, California areas), eight priests/priestesses, and approximately 100 members. There are also groups in Canada and Great Britain.

Periodicals: *Shen,* Box 7091, Burbank, CA 91510-7091.

Remarks: Don Harrison, one of the Church' founders, is the author of several novels emphasizing both ancient religions and sexual themes.

Sources: David Conway, *Magic, An Occult Primer.* New York: E. P. Dutton, 1972; Henri Frankfort, *Ancient Egyptian Religion, An Interpretation.* New York : Harper & Row, 1961.

★1049★
CHURCH OF THE WYCCAN REDE
(Defunct)

The Church of the Wyccan Rede was a Celtic traditional Witchcraft group headed by Lady Cybele and headquartered in Madison, Wisconsin. The Goddess and Horned God were worshipped, the former taking slight precedence. The Goddess was thought to rule from Yule to Midsummer's Eve, and the God, the other half of the year. The eight sabbats were also celebrated. Midsummer's Eve is the most important. The sabbats were concluded with a shared meal. There are also regular esbats.

Worship was within the circle. Members took turns in being the coven leader and conducting the ceremonies. There were no overt sexual activities involved in the rituals. Oneness with nature was the prime goal. Members were pacifistic and charitable, and refused reward for their services. Black magic and Satanism were strongly condemned.

For several years, Lady Cybele managed The Cauldron, an occult supply store and center. It offered lectures on occult topics, psychic readings, books and health food. Lady Cybele is a herbalist and incorporated her knowledge of herbs into her teachings. Associated with the Church for the Wyccan Rede was a coven in Milwaukee headed by Frederic A. Buchholtz. Buchholtz was the operator of Sanctum Regnum, an occult supply and book shop.

★1050★
CIRCLE
Box 219
Mt. Horeb, WI 53572

As the Witchcraft and Neo-Pagan community developed in the U.S. in the 1970s, it became extremely diverse and eclectic. Typical of the broad eclectism is Circle (incorporated as the Church of Circle Wicca, a wicca group from Madison, Wisconsin, headed by Jim Alan and Selena Fox. From an interest in the occult, the two became attracted to Witchcraft in the early 1970s and in 1974 founded Circle as a coven. They began a newsletter, and because of their music (Jim Alan was a professional musician) and leadership abilities, they were soon taking a prominent role at Pagan gatherings around the United States. Their home outside Madison became a center at which Pagans gathered and from which information flowed. The newsletter grew into a substantial periodical. Further, both Alan and Fox made themselves available to non-Wiccans, including the media (at a time when most Pagans took an extremely low profile and avoided publicity and man even contact outside of the Pagan community. As a result, a Pagan network grew around Circle, a network actively nurtured by *Circle Network News*, by the early 1980s by far the largest circulating periodical in the Pagan community.

In the early 1980s Circle moved to rural Wisconsin, west of Madison and finally settled at Circle Sanctuary, a secluded farm near Mt. Horeb, Wisconsin. Also, around 1980 in response to the disruption of the Midwest Pagan Council, an ecumenical Pagan organization centered in Chicago, in which Circle participated, and the growth of the Covenant of the Goddess (which included only groups which considered themselves "witches"), Circle organized the ecumenical Pagan Spirit Alliance, a national fellowship with included both Neo-Pagan and Witchcraft groups. The first annual Pagan Spirit Gathering was held in 1981.

As it has developed, Circle now sees itself as more than the small family of covens it was in the late 1970s. It is a network for people on the path of the magical ways of nature from a variety of traditions, including the Native American and shamanist. Worship is centered upon the Mother Goddess and all are expected to attune themselves to positive magic and spirituality. Rituals are extremely eclectic and constantly changing, though following the common pattern of meetings for the new and full moons and the eight Pagan festivals. Circle regularly sponsorspublic festivals in Madison and special summer events for Pagans at Circle Sanctuary during the summer. In the early 1980s Circle initiated a formal program for the training of Pagan priests and priestesses leading to formal ordination by the Church of Circle Wicca.

Membership: Not reported. *Circle Network News* circulates over 10,000 copies each issue.

Educational facilities: Circle Seminary, Mt. Horeb, Wisconsin.

Periodicals: *Circle Network News*, Box 219, Mt. Horeb, WI 53572; *Sanctuary Circles Newsletter*, Box 219, Mt. Horeb, WI 53572; *Pagan Spirit Journal*, Box 219, Mt. Horeb, WI 53572.

Sources: Selena Fox, *Circle Guide to Pagan Resources*. Mt. Horeb, WI: Circle, 1984; Jim Alan and Selena Fox, *Circle Magick Songs*. Madison, WI: Circle Publications, 1977; Blacksun, *The Elements of Beginning Ritual Construction*. Madison, WI; Circle, 1982.

★1051★
CONGREGATION OF ATEN
(Defunct)

A growing split within the Pristine Egyptian Orthodox Church (discussed elsewhere in this chapter) led in 1974 to a schism and the withdrawal of Milton J. Neruda, who then formed the Congregation of Aten. At least one issue in the schism was the method of approaching the dominant American Christian faith. Neruda argued that Christianity was heavily reliant on Egyptian religion for such concepts as the Trinity, the virgin birth, Christmas and resurrection. He took a highly polemical stance with respect to the Christian faith. The Egyptian faith of the congregation of Aten offered answers "to one who is not blinded by prejudice and ignorance. Knowledge is the only path to true salvation!" The Pristine Egyptian Orthodox Church had taken a much milder stance. Neruda led the single congregation which existed for several years in Chicago.

★1052★
COVENANT OF THE GODDESS
Box 1226
Berkeley, CA 94704

The Covenant of the Goddess (C.O.G.) was formed in 1975 by members of approximately ten covens in California as a confederation of autonomous covens to facilitate cooperation between covens and to secure legal status and tax exemption for Witchcraft groups. Among the leaders in creating the new organization were Aiden Kelly and Alison Harlow. Largely confined to California in its first years, by the end of the decade it had accepted covens in the East and during the early 1980s became a national organization which had shifted a significant amount of its activity to the Midwest.

Membership is open to witches, both covens and individuals practings as solitaries. New members must be recommended by two active C.O.G. members and follow the worship of Goddess and the Olde Gods. A code of ethics binds members to the Wiccan Rede, "An ye harm none, do as ye will." It also espouses guidelines on finances, the sovereignty of the individual covens, secrecy, and respect for diversity.

Annually member of the Covenant of the Goddess gather for a Grand Council meeting at which business is conducted. The council elects officers and appoints the editor of the newsletter. Where three or more covens exist in close geographic proximity, they may organize a local council for the accomplishment of specific projects and general cooperative endeavor.

Membership: In 1985 there were 63 covens of which 19 were in Northern California.

Periodicals: *The Covenant of the Goddess Newsletter*, Box 194, San Anselmo, CA 94960.

Sources: Starhawk, *The Spiral Dance*. San Francisco: Harper & Row, 1979; Starhawk, *Dreaming the Dark*. Boston: Beacon Press, 1982.

★1053★
CYMRY WICCA
Box 1866
Athens, GA 30602

The Cymry Wicca is a Celtic traditional witchcraft group founded in 1967 in Washington, D.C., by William, or, as he is known in the craft, Rhuddlwm Gawr. The proper name is Cymry ab Prydian or Welsh Sons and Daughters of the Isle of Great Britain. The group was originally the Brotherhood of Wicca but changed the name, so as not to be confused with Lady Sheba's covens. William was initiated in England and afterwards spent four months studying in Wales. The Cymry received its laws and traditions from Great Britain through William. They are contained in eight volumes in manuscript form. The Cymry Wicca moved its headquarters to Georgia in 1973.

The Cymry has three deities: the Goddess, the Horned God, and their son, the Child of Light (corresponding to the Egyptian Isis, Osiris and Horus). Celtic names are employed by the Cymry. Worship is both skyclad (naked) and robed, and both inside and outside the circle, depending on the occasion. Reincarnation is stressed. Major focus of Cymry is on becoming attuned to nature and its forces. Drugs are forbidden.

The Cymry differs from other Wicca groups in that it is organized on seven levels. Each probationer is given a level name and a secret name, both in Welsh. Movement through the levels is occasioned by initiation ceremonies. The first level, the "naming," is coincidental with the members' identification with the coven. The Cymry is organized in autonomous covens. There is no witch king or queen, but there are elders who render binding decisions on questions put to them.

Cymry Wicca covens were most active in the mid-1970s. In 1974, there were approximately fifteen covens located in Georgia, Florida, Tennessee, North Carolina, Alabama and Virginia. Rhuddlwn Gawr compiled two editions of the *Pagan/Occult/New Age Directory*, which included broad segments of the American wicca and neo-pagan community. *The Sword of Dyrnwyn* appeared as a periodical for several years. In September 1978, in upstate Georgia, the Cymry hosted the first of several Gatherings of the Tribes, a conclave of Witches and Neo-Pagans from a wide variety of traditions and perspectives. During the 1980s the covens have been less active.

Membership: Not reported.

Sources: Rhuddlwn Gawr with Marcy Edwards, *The Quest*. Smyrna, GA: Pagan Grove Press, 1979; Rhuddlwn Gawr, *Pagan/Occult/New Age Directory*. Atlanta: Pagan Grove Press, 1980.

★1054★
DANCERS OF THE SACRED CIRCLE
(Defunct)

Closely related to Fereferia, an organization discussed elsewhere in this chapter, were the Dancers of the Sacred Circle, founded in the early 1970s by Richard Stanewick. Stanewick was one of the founders of Fereferia and served as its secretary until he moved to the San Francisco area and formed an autonomous group. Headquarters for the Dancers were near Redway, California, on a forty-acre nature sanctuary.

The Dancers attempted to build a total life based on the central figure of the Maiden divinity. Devotions were daily and seasonal, and had both aesthetic and erotic emphases. Included were wilderness mysteries, henge rites (a henge is an open air ring temple), and work in the maintenance and creation of gardens, orchards and wilderness shrines. The group was small, consisting of Richard, his wife, Phyllis Stanewick, and a few adherents. It disbanded in the early 1980s.

★1055★
DELPHIC COVEN
(Defunct)

Among the early Goddess-worshipping groups in the United States was the Celtic traditional Delphic Coven founded by Bonnie Sherlock, who operated from a small town in Wyoming. According to Sherlock, the tradition had been handed down through the family, which migrated from Scotland in 1570, first to Ireland then to America. Ms. Sherlock was taught the craft by her great-grandmother, who imparted the first two initiations. The third was received from a Sioux medicine man.

The group claimed Celtic origins "in that we take our muse from the Cauldron of the Kerridwen, and will at length become as the radiant browed Taliesin." Egyptian and American Indian elements were added, though a basic dualistic cosmology remained. "The dragon of darkness is the great fetter of ignorance which we must overcome through educational enlightenment, communication, and involvement with others who are likeminded." Included in the group's belief were reincarnation and karma (the consequences of good and bad actions from former incarnations). Creative expression, primarily through arts, was a major theme; ecology and love of nature, especially as expressed in reverence of the mountain environment, were also emphasized. "The earth is a living, breathing thing to be reverenced and looked after, as are all the lesser creatures." Even the Horned God is visualized as a "Big Horned Sheep." Several issues of a periodical, *The Medicine Wheel*, were published. The coven dissolved following Sherlock's death in the late 1970s.

★1056★
DELPHIC FELLOWSHIP
(Defunct)

The Delphic Fellowship originated in 1967 when Michael Kinghorn and Donald Harrison began to publish the *Julian Review* as a forum of discussion of the Pagan religion. The Fellowship was formed the following year with the intent of restoring the heritage of Greece and rightful homage to the gods. A program was begun, to acquaint people of Christian, Jewish and agnostic/atheistic backgrounds with the Pagan option.

The Delphic Fellowship took its inspiration from the ancient oracle at Delphi. The Greek pantheon, headed by Zeus, was worshipped. The Delphian Affirmations asserted belief in the plurality of Gods; in the experience of the wholeness of nature; in the sacred character of the Cosmos (and the denial of its fall); in man as a child of Holy Earth; in moral freedom; in the beauty, purity, and holiness of man's sexuality; that the instinct to survive is natural and pleasing to the gods; that man's posture toward nature should be one of reverence and joyous participation, and in the Sacred Precepts of Elder Delphi, especially his admonition, "Know Thyself; Nothing in Excess."

The Delphic Fellowship was small and largely superceded by the Church of the Eternal Source, an Egyptian Pagan group which Harrison help found. The headquarters of the Delphic Fellowship was in Los Angeles.

★1057★
DIANIC WICCA
% Susan B. Anthony Coven No. 1
Box 11363
Oakland, CA 94611

Dianic Wicca is a name given to those covens which have developed a strong emphasis upon feminism and the role of Witchcraft as the religion of females (wimmin). They have taken the Gardnerian Wicca tradition and wedded it to a worldview which has arisen within modern popular feminism. It is the belief of Dianic witches that the worship of the Goddess in a primeval past co-existed with a period of peace on earth which was destroyed by the rise of men and patriarchial deities. In Dianic covens, the worship of the Mother Goddess alone has replaced that of the worship of God and Goddess together prevalent in most Witchcraft groups. Dianic covens vary from all-female separatist groups, to all-female groups, to mixed male-female groups with a strong feminist emphasis.

Within the coven, the focus is on the high priestess, who represents the Goddess. She is assisted by a maiden and occasionally (where men are allowed) a high priest. They represent the consort and the child. The majority of the all-female covens operate in the nude. Some Dianic covens hold to a belief in the possibility of parthenogenetic birth, that is, birth not requiring male assistance.

Among the first of the Dianic Wiccan groups was a coven in Dallas, Texas, founded by Morgan McFarland and Mark Roberts. High Priestess McFarland was a freelance photographer, writer and feminist who began to explore the Craft in her early teens. She published a short-lived Neo-Pagan periodical, *The Harp*, before going public in 1972. High Priest Roberts was also a freelance writer and photographer. The group had originally been established as an occult group called the Seekers. In 1972, it began to publish *The New Broom*. An article in *The New Broom* described the Dianic aspect as a blending of monotheism and pantheism. The group was monotheistic in that it worships the Goddess as the essential creative force. It was pantheistic in considering every creation in Nature a child of the Goddess.

After the Dallas coven dissolved, the thrust of Dianic Wicca was picked up by several California feminist leaders, the most famous being Zsuzsanna Budapest, leader of the Susan B. Anthony Coven No. 1. Budapest, a lesbian, developed a separatist coven in southern California associated with The Feminist Wicca, a "matriarchial spiritual center" in Venice, California. She moved the coven to Oakland in the early 1980s and was briefly a member of the Covenant of the Goddess. She is the author of several of the most important books in the developing Dianic tradition. Also among the early Dianics is Ann Forfreedom, leader of the Temple of the Goddess Within in Sacramento, and Deborah Bender, editor of *Homebrew*, a feminist Wiccan journal in the early 1980s. Withstanding attacks from those who complain that Dianic Witchcraft has lost the balance implied in the acknowledgement of the God and Goddess, the Dianics persisted and have become recognized as an important part of the Goddess tradition. Besides the separate Dianic covens, Dianic Wicca has found strong advocates within otherwise non-Dianic groups. For example, Starhawk, whose coven is a member of the Covenant of the Goddess (see separate entry), is a popular spokesperson of the Dianic position.

Membership: Statistics not available.

Periodicals: *Thesmophoria*, Susan B. Anthony Coven No. 1, Box 11363, Oakland, CA 94611; *The Wise Woman*, Box 19421, Sacramento, CA 95819.

Remarks: Dianic is a designation which fittingly describes a group of covens and Witchcraft groups. Their inclusion under that label by no means implies any organizational connection or even mutual recognition. While united by an agreement on a feminist approach to Witchcraft, they are frequently at opposition on other issues.

Sources: Morgana, Arduine and Boreas, *Footsteps on a Dianic Path*. [Dallas, TX]: Coven of Morigana, n.d.; Ann Forfreedom, *Book of the Goddess*. Sacramento, CA: Temple of the Goddess Within, 1980; Ann for Freedom, *Feminist Wicca Works*. Sacramento, CA: The Author, 1980; Zsuzsanna Budapest, *The Feminist Book of Lights and Shadows*. Venice, CA: Luna Publications, 1976; Zsuzsanna Budapest, *The Holy Book of Women's Mysteries*. Los Angeles: Susan B. Anthony Coven No. 1, 1979, 1980. 2 vols.; Marion Weinstein, *A Dianic Book of Shadows*. New York: Earth Magic Productions, 1980.

★1058★
DISCORDIAN SOCIETY
Current address not obtained for this edition.

There is one aspect of the Neo-Pagan movement in America which seems to be a complete put-on, the Discordian Society. As described in *Principia Discordia*, the "bible" of the group, Discordians worship Eris, the goddess of chaos. The Society was founded by someone named Malaclypse the Younger who, in 1958, upon evoking the Lady in the Erisian aspect, was told, "We Discordians must stick apart." Among the prominent Neo-Pagans who have identified themselves with the Society is Robert Anton Wilson, also known as Mordecai the Foul. Wilson is a popular writer and and advocate of the Illuminatus conspiracy. He coauthored with Robert Shea a three-volume fantasy novel *Illuminatus!*, describing the Discordian world, including its sister organization, the John Dillinger Died for You Society.

Members in the Discordian Society are initiated as popes. Being infallible, they have the power to excommunicate everyone. As pope, a member is in the Fifth House of Discordia, popularly known as the Out House. The member can then proceed to higher orders-bishop, knight, castle, priest, dupe and finally clown.

In fact the Discordian movement has not functioned as an organization but has been perpetuated as an inside joke and means of relieving tension within Pagan groups. Quite simply it is the Neo-Pagan version of "Murphy's Law." When things go wrong, the Goddess Eris is invoked with the phrase, "Hail, Eris!" Periodically, an individual will take it upon themselves to publish material in the name of the Society. The most well known literature, apart from *Principia Discordia* (which has been kept in print in ever newer editions) was a periodical, *St. John's Bread*, that enjoyed a brief life in the mid-1970s.

Sources: Malacylpse the Younger, *Principia Discordia*. Mason, MI: Loompanics Unlimited, 1978.

★1059★
EARTHSTAR TEMPLE
35 W. 19th St.
New York, NY 10011

The New York Coven of Welsh Traditionalist Witches was headed by Ed Buczynski, better known by his ritual name, Hermes, who had taken the "Celtic" rituals used by Gwen Thompson of the New England Welsh Traditionalist Coven and adapted them for use by a group in Brooklyn, New York. The form of Wicca followed was called "Gwyddoniaid" and is traced to the mixture of Celtic (male deity) and Pictish (female deity) religions in Wales. They worship the Earth Mother in her nine-fold aspects and the Horned God.

Covens are limited to thirteen male and female members, chosen alternately. Each coven is under the guidance of a high priest and high priestess. (Each coven is autonomous, but is tied to others by similar ritual and laws.) The high priestess is ascendent, in keeping with the matriarchal orientation. There are weekly and monthly (on the full moon) rituals as well as the eight sabbats. No magick is worked at the latter. Power usually raised for magick is "given directly to the god in loving sacrifice." Worship is done within a nine-foot circle. Identical red robes are worn, emphasizing the equality of individuals before the gods.

The New York Coven came into prominence in the early 1970s when Buczynski and Harold Slater became public advocates for the craft. They have presented awards to the Inquisitional Bigot of the Year through Friends of the Craft, an affiliated organization. They also operated the Warlock Shop, an occult supplies store in Brooklyn, and, for several years published *Earth Religion News*. In the late 1970s, Slater, who had absorbed some elements of ritual magick in his practice, assumed leadership of the group and store. He moved both to Manhattan. The group was renamed Earthstar and the store is currently known as the Magickal Child. Slater has periodically sponsored large festive gatherings of Neo-Pagans, witches and magicians in New York City.

Membership: Not reported.

Sources: Edmund M. Buczynski, *Witchcraft Fact Book*. New York: Magickal Childe, n.d.; Herman Slater, ed., *The Magickal Formulary*. New York: Magickal Childe, 1981.

★1060★
ESP LABORATORY
Box 216
219 S. Ridge Dr.
Edgewood, TX 75117

The ESP Laboratory was founded in Los Angeles in 1966 by Al G. Manning. Manning was a certified public accountant who, during meditations, was contacted by a Prof. Reinhardt, his spirit teacher and guide. With Reinhardt's help, he wrote his first book and founded the ESP Laboratory, which functions as both psychic interest center and a church. Manning became a minister of Spiritual Science. He has since written several books. The keynote to Manning's approach to the psychic is results. An early program made use of color to aid attunement to the living light in its differing shades so as to attain personal goals of success, power, prosperity, and healing. Instruction in the mystic light was offered in a twenty-lesson correspondence course. Healing is a major emphasis.

Divination and the occult steadily became more important parts of the Laboratory's work. In 1970, a course on the "I Ching" was first offered. In 1971, a course on "White Magic and Witchcraft" was offered, and a new book, *Helping Yourself with White Witchcraft*, appeared the following year. Emphasis was placed not so much on the religion of Wicca but rather upon magick, control and the rituals to use for various purposes. One of the members of the Laboratory who completed the course has formed the Astral Coven.

The ESP Laboratory moved its headquarters from Holloywood to Texas in the early 1980s. Members, via correspondence, are found in all fifty states and some foreign countries. Ordination as a minister is offered after the passing of required courses. A monthly newsletter contains announcements, reports on research, a monthly light exercise and an astrology column.

Membership: Not reported. In 1974 there were ministers with credentials from the laboratory functioning in California, Ohio, Texas, and Virginia.

Periodicals: *E.S.P. Laboratory Newsletter*, Box 216, 219 S. Ridge Drive, Edgewood, TX 75119.

Sources: Al G. Manning, *Helping Yourself with White Witchcraft*. West Nyack, NY: Parker Publishing Company, 1972; Al G. Manning, *Helping Yourself with the Power of Gnostic Magic*. West Nyack, NY: Parker Publishing Company, 1979.

★1061★
FEREFERIA
Box 41363
Eagle Rock, CA 90041

The oldest of the presently existing Neo-Pagan groups is Fereferia, founded in 1957 as the Fellowship of Hesperides by Fred Adams. Adams, as early as 1947 at Stanford University and later the University of Southern California, had become involved in Eleusinian mysteries and ritual magick. In 1956, he had a sudden conversion to the Goddess. He met Robert Graves, author of the *White Goddess*, one of the most influential volumes leading to the contemporary revival of Pagan thought, and by 1958 had become fully paganized. He began to seek a purified paganism of the highly sacramental cultures of Crete and Minoa, and he believed that mankind could develop a utopian, paradisaic life on earth by basing culture on horticulture. In 1959, an open-air temple was established in the Sierra Madre.

Adams has become a significant figure in the movement as a poetic figure and above all a talented artist. His stylized presentation of the Goddess has circulated throughout the Pagan movement. He has also produced some calendars based on Pagan seasons.

Fereferia differs from most Neo-Pagan bodies in that it centers on Kore, the maiden. In the Holy Family of the polytheist pantheon are the Mother, as source and center; the Father, as full outwardness, withdrawal and separation; the Son, as creative separation, and the Daughter, as creative return, configuration, form and mysterious wholeness. Kore is the Daughter, also to be identified with Persephone in the Eleusinian mysteries. Fereferia is the advocate of the Maiden Way. The Maiden Way includes organic gardening, particularly reverence for tree life; a vegetarian diet; reverence for all life; outside living; the realization that health, vitality and rejuvenation are basic to spiritual growth; handicraft technology; dissolution of coercive structures; elimination of artificial conditions; natural safeguards against overpopulation; a maximum of free, creative play and erotic development; veneration of beauty, desire and creative; and affirmation of the divine mystery of sex as the central polarity of cosmic process. Rituals celebrating of nature are carried out in several locations, including Pasadena and the nearby mountains, in specially constructed henges.

Membership: Not reported. There are less than 50 members.

Periodicals: *Korythalia*, Box 41363, Eagle Rock, CA 90041.

★1062★
FIRST WICCAN CHURCH OF MINNESOTA
(Defunct)

The First Wiccan Church of Minnesota grew out of the Camelot of the Star of the North Coven of the American Order of the Brotherhood of Wicca, a Wiccan group founded by Lady Sheba. the church was formed by Carl Weschcke (Gnosticus) and his wife Sandra Weschcke (Kashta in 1973. Carl is head of Llewellyn Publications which during the 1970s published Lady Sheba's books and *Gnostica News*, which was a major voice within the Wicca/Pagan community. Though following much of the material of Lady Sheba, the First Wiccan Church also developed its own practices.

Three foci of coven activity were recognized. Worship occurred at the esbats held during the full moon and at the sabbats on the solstices and equinoxes. It was an effort to tune into the natural rhythms of the sun and moon. Magick is seen as the ceremonial work which brings people-integration. The ritual of the craft focuses on practical mundane success, the use of mind power to gain an object of desire. Like Lady Sheba, this group opposed the secrecy that has traditionally surrounded the craft. The church was dissloved in the late 1970s.

Sources: Lady Sheba (Jessie Wicker Bell); *Witch*. St. Paul, MN: Llewellyn Publications, 1973; Lady Sheba, *The Grimoire of Lady Sheba*. St. Paul, MN: Llewellyn Publications, 1974.

★1063★
GARDNERIAN WICCA
% Theos and Phoenix
Box 56
Commack, NY 11725

Gerald B. Gardner (1884-1964) did more to revive modern Witchcraft than any single individual. He composed rituals with the assistance of a few others , including Doreen Valiente, which became the source of most rituals used by both Witches and Neo-Pagans. Several members of his British covens (for example, Alexander Sanders and Sybil Leek) took copies of his rituals and published their own edited versions of them as the basis for a new form of Wicca. However, the single largest group of Wiccans are those who continue to use the rituals as finally developed by Gardner in the 1960s.

Gardnerian Wicca was brought to America in the 1960s. It came through several individuals who traveled to Great Britain for initiation in one of Gardner's covens. Most of these revised and rewrote the rituals upon their return. Such was not the case with Raymond Buckland and his wife, Rosemary Buckland. Raymond (who claims a Ph.D. in anthropology) and Rosemary Buckland operated the Buckland Museum of Witchcraft and Magick on Long Island. Reared as good members of the Church of England, they began dabbling in occultism and were attracted to Gardner after settling in New York in the early 1960s. They corresponded with him and visited his home on the Isle of Man, where he operated a witchcraft museum. While there, the Bucklands went through a three-week crash program and were initiated in the second degree before they left. (The usual time between any of the three degrees of witchcraft is one year and a day.) Upon their return, they began to organize Gardnerian covens, ens, which spread across the country. This growth was due in part to the widespread media coverage of the museum and the unique religion espoused by the Bucklands.

Each Gardnerian coven is headed by a high priestess and a high priest. Without the former no ceremonies are held. Membership in the covens is by couples, and the size of the coven is limited only by the space available in the nine-foot circle. New covens are usually formed by a witch's leaving a full-size coven and beginning a new one. The high priestess of the original coven becomes the "witch queen" of the new coven. Within Gardnerian covens there is a form of apostolic succession from Rosemary Buckland (who is no longer associated with the Gardnerian covens) through a lineage of witch queens to presently functioning priestesses.

Gardnerian witches worship in the nude, and by so doing have given to the craft a new word, "skyclad." The female witch does wear a necklace, a symbol of reincarnation. The high priest and priestess wear bracelets symbolic of rank, and the witch queen wears a crown and garter.

In 1973, the Bucklands, known in the craft as Robat and Lady Rowen, were divorced. They turned over the leadership of the Gardnerian covens to Judy Kneitel and her husband Tom Kneitel, known as Lady Theos and Phoenix. During 1973/74, they published *Gardnerian Aspects* as a magazine within the Green Egg, but discontinued it with issue No. 63 in favor of an intracoven letter. *The Hidden Path*, begun by Lady Dierdre of the Coven of the Silver Trine in Louisville, Kentucky, continues as a semi-public periodical. Buckland developed an alternative Wicca system called Seax Wicca (see separate entry).

Membership: Membership is not available to the public, but it is estimated that several hundred people are involved in Gardnerian covens recognized by Theos and Phoenix. Many more consider themselves Gardnerian.

Periodicals: *The Hidden Path*, Windwalker, Box 793 F, Wheeling, IL 60090.

Sources: Gerald B. Gardner, *Witchcraft Today*. London: Karrolds, 1968; J. L. Bracelin, *Gerald Gardner: Witch*. London: Octagon Press, 1960; A Witch, *The Devil's Prayerbook*. London: Mayflower, 1975; Doreen Valiente, *Natural Magic*. New York: St. Martin's Press, 1975; Doreen Valiente, *Witchcraft for Tomorrow*. London: Robert Hale Limited, 1978.

★1064★
THE GEORGIAN CHURCH
1908 Verde St.
Bakersfield, CA 93304

The Georgian Church, originally the Church of Wicca at Bakersfield, California, was formed by George E. Patterson (d. 1984). Patterson claimed a 1940 initiation from a Celtic group. After World War II, he settled in California and in the 1970s began to gather a coven. The group was eclectic, combining rituals from Gardnerian Wicca, Alexandrian Wicca and other sources, and was termed Georgian. Eventually a charter came from the Universal Life Church, and Patterson obtained a doctor of divinity degree from the American Bible Institute. As with most witches, there is belief in the gods and goddesses, magick, the unity of life and reincarnation. The group does not accept Satanism, black magicians or groups organized only for sex. There are three degrees in Georgian Wicca. . These degrees acknowledge attainment of knowledge and time devoted to the craft. The church publishes a monthly periodical, noteworthy both for its size and quality as well as its longevity.

Membership: Not reported. By 1973, there were four affiliated covens in Southern California. By 1978 there were associated covens in Missouri, New York, and New Jersey. As of the mid-1980s, there are loosely affiliated covens (many of them led by priests and/or priestesses trained by Patterson) across the United States.

Periodicals: *Georgian Newsletter*, 1908 Verde St., Bakersfield, CA 93304.

★1065★
HOLLYWOOD COVEN
(Defunct)

The Hollywood Coven was formed as a Celtic traditional Wiccan group in 1967 by E. Tanssan of Hollywood, Florida. Tanssan, now in his 70s, had formerly been a member of a coven in Birmingham, Michigan. The Birmingham coven, headed by T. Milligan, had been established in the early part of the century. Tanssan had succeeded his teacher as leader in Birmingham shortly before the coven was disbanded because of police harassment. He and some of the members moved to Florida and established the new coven. Emerging as spokeswoman for the coven was Kitty Lessing, who edited its periodical, *The Black Lite.*

Worship was in the circle. No drugs were allowed. It was a robed tradition. Initiation was allowed only after a year of study of occultism and witchcraft. Initiates were eligible to become a coven lady or grand master. There were no priests or priestesses.

The basic deities were the Great One, the Horned God, and the Lady of Silver, the earth mother. The God was considered the father of all gods and guide to the afterlife.

Nature was seen the creation of the gods, hence sacred. Only four sabbaths--Halloween, Yule, Candlemas (February 2) and Lammas (August 1)--were celebrated. The solstices and equinoxes were not formally celebrated. Esbats were held weekly or biweekly. In 1972 two covens were being operated in Hollywood, the main coven and a student coven. During the mid-1970s, Lessing moved to California, and shortly afterward the Hollywood Coven dropped out of sight. This may have been one of the few genuine pre-Gardnerian covens in the United States.

★1066★
HOLY ORDER OF BRIGET
(Defunct)

The Holy Order of Briget was a Wicca group formed in the late 1960s in Denver by Michael Myers. For several years, a co-op book store, Spell, Book and Candle, was operated in Denver, but it closed in November, 1973. Land was purchased in rural Colorado, and Craftcast Farm was begun as a "monastic" focus within American Wicca.

Craftcast was run during the brief period of its existence on a communal basis and set aside as a place where ritual would be continual. A deep love for the Mother was the motivating force. Witchcraft, viewed as seeking wisdom by changing knowledge into understanding, was practiced. The monastic ideal allows for "one spiritual goal" to become dominant. According to Myers, other covens in various locations throughout the West were affiliated with the Holy Order of Briget; however, since the dissolving of the farm in the late 1970s, considerable doubt has been cast upon Myers's claims.

★1067★
LADY SARA'S COVEN
(Defunct)

Sara Cunningham was an Episcopalian who turned witch. During the late 1960s, she operated the Albion Training Coven and, in 1970, became one of the founders of the Church of the Eternal Source. She separated from that group in 1971 over eclecticism (which she expounded) versus a pure Egyptian religion. She founded the Temple of Tiphereth, which combined elements of Western ritual magick, Egyptian religion and Wicca. The temple was located in Pasadena, where she also ran Stonehenge, an occult supply house. She also met Hans Holzer, who wrote about her psychic abilities in several of his books. In 1973, she moved to Wolf Creek, Oregon, where she formed Lady Sara's Coven, an eclectic Wicca group. She publishes a "Course in Wicca," a year-and-a-day study course which she offers to students around the country. Her coven has dropped out of sight in recent years.

Sources: Lady Sara [Cunningham], *Questions and Answers on Wicca Craft*. Wolf Creek, OR: Stonehenge Farm, 1974; Sara [Cunningham], *Candle Magic*. Hollywood, CA: Phoenix House, 1974; *The Hermetic Art*. Glendale, OR:

First Temple of Tiphareth, 1975; *AUM, The Sacred Word.* Glendale, OR: First Temple of Tipareth, 1975.

★1068★
MENTAL SCIENCE INSTITUTE
Current address not obtained for this edition.

Barney C. (Eli) Taylor, who is the grand master of what is termed druidic witchcraft, is a descendant of Thomas Hartley, who was burned at the stake for practicing witchcraft in England in the early 1550s. Hartley was a healer and herbalist. Because of persecution, others like him fled to America and settled in the mountain country of the Appalachians and the Ozarks. (Taylor grew up in the Ozarks.) The Mental Science Institute was organized in the late 1960s as a focus for Taylor's brand of herbal magick. He traces his particular kind of witchcraft to the druid, and it is thus termed druidic. It is also a robed tradition, in contrast to both the modern "naked ones" (i.e., the practitioners of Gardnerian Wicca, and the clothed ones who emphasize magick. The robed ones emphasize healing.

The membership of the Mental Science Institute is divided into covens of no more than twelve individuals, meeting under a wizard. Wizards in turn meet under a magi; the magis under a master magi; and the master magis under the grand master. Taylor is grand master for the United States. Apprentices are those studying in order to join the group. There are three degrees in the craft: a first degree, a basic member; a second degree, a wise leader; and a third degree, the wise doctor.

Worship is conducted in regular esbats and the four grand sabbats. The institute is the most male oriented of all the Wiccan groups and has a theology closely related to Christianity and to ritual magick. T he universe is seen as a series of levels--celestial, terrestrial and telestial. The celestial is divided into sublevels at the top of which is God the Father, followed by the Lord of Lights, arch-angels and angels. Man, animals and plants are on the terrestrial level. At the lowest level, the telestial, are the mineral, chemical and electrical elements and creative thought. Just as there is a Father, there is a Mother of all people.

In a concept very close to Mormonism, the institute teaches that God the Father was at one time a child. The children will, in like measure, become gods. Reincarnation is part of that process. A complete cycle lasts for approximately 142 years: from birth to death, a year in purgatory, 70 years to integrate the life experience, and a year waiting for rebirth.

Membership: Not reported.

Sources: Eli [Taylor], *The First Book of Wisdom.* n.p.: The Author, 1973; Eli [Taylor], *The Second Book of Wisdom.* n. p.: n. d.

★1069★
NEMETON
(Defunct)

Nemeton was the name of an eclectic Pagan organization formed in 1971 by a group of pagans in the San Francisco Bay area headed by Gwydion Pendderwen. Among the group were witches; some worship the Voudoun and some follow the Sioux medicine wheel, an Indian magical system. Nemeton is an ancient Celtic word for grave or sanctuary. Central to modern Nemeton was Coeden Brith, a secluded tract of 220 acres to which members may go for festivals or just to commune with nature. Dominant in Nemeton were the two Druidic groups, the Brythonic and Goedelic.

The Brythonic group, based on the pantheon of early pagan Teutonic religion, combined the strong influence of western European polytheism with a strong element of matriarchy. The principle deity was the triple Goddess, who is accompanied many lesser deities. The ritual was in Welch. The Goedelic used Irish. Its deities were headed by the Queen of Death (identified with the Queen of Faerie, the Queen of Elphin and Morgan Le Fay of the Arthurian romances). Nemeton published a journal, *Nemeton*, and a for-members-only newsletter *Nemeton Newsletter*. Membership was concentrated in Northern California. Much of the membership became part of the Covenant of the Goddess. Alison Harlow, a Nemeton leader, was one of the Covenant founders.

Sources: Gwydion Pendderwen, *The Rites of Summer.* Redwood Valley, CA: Nemeton, 1980; *Nemeton Directory.* Oakland, CA: Nemeton, 1973.

★1070★
NEO-DIANIC FAITH
(Defunct)

The late W. Holman Keith came to paganism early in the 1940s. He attended the Church of Aphrodite, an early pagan group founded in the 1920s by Gleb Botkin and, in the late 1960s, emerged as head of his own Neo-Dianic Faith. Keith described the revival of paganism as the recovery of the ancient spirituality embodied in the prehistoric nature religion and Mother Goddess worship. Though the Neo-Dianic Faith was confined to a small group in the Los Angeles area, as Paganism grew through the 1970s, Keith emerged as an elder brother for many just discovering Paganism.

Keith thought of the divine, the great mover, as eternal desire, ideally embodied in woman. Man's and woman's oneness with life and nature is expressed in a primal piety which includes an ethic of pleasure, beauty, subordination of the drive for power and its resulting machinations of control, and worship of the feminine. The Greco-Roman pantheon is favored, but not exclusively. The active participation in the experience of being alive, in worshipping the Goddess, brings its own assurance of immortality, the moment in time being identical with the eternal now.

After Keith's death in the late 1970s his small following dissolved.

★1071★
NEW ENGLAND COVEN OF WELSH TRADITIONALIST WITCHES
(Defunct)

The New England Coven of Welsh Traditionalist Witches was founded in the late 1960s by Gwen Thompson of North Haven, Connecticut. It was a Celtic traditionalist coven. Thompson had taken the Gardnerian rituals and rewritten them around a Welsh Celtic theme. Among the early covens, it was considered conservative in its form of worship, which was conducted only in a properly prepared circle or (for outside worship) grove. Members of the coven wore robes with cords and no footwear. Rituals were kept in a *Book of Shadows*. The basic belief in the Earth Mother, the Horned One and a family of pagan deities was set within a basic dualistic cosmology reminiscent of Manichaeism, which taught the release of the spirit from matter.

As Thompson stated, "Our doctrine involves the ancient battle between the hosts of Light and those of Darkness... in which Light lost. Light, in this case, may be referred to as Wisdom, or that force which sought to upgrade mankind from his primitive state into a being able to understand more fully his own nature, that of his planet, and the universe at large. It is our belief that our world is governed by the hosts of Darkness who are responsible for the 'three D's:' Death, Disease, and Disaster. We believe that mankind and his world were originally a perfect creation, but that both have been victimized for many thousands of years. We feel that Light will ultimately prevail."

In 1973 Thompson, the high priestess, moved to Gatlinburg, Tennessee. Lady Kerry and her high priest, Stock, succeeded Thompson as the leaders of the New England coven. Thompson began two covens in the Gatlinburg area. During the 1980s, none of the three covens has been located. They are presumed defunct.

★1072★
NEW REFORMED ORTHODOX ORDER OF THE GOLDEN DAWN
% Robin Goodfellow and Gaia Wildewoode
1625 Woolsey St.
Berkeley, CA 947036

The New Reformed Orthodox Order of the Golden Dawn began in the San Francisco area in 1968 as a group of schoolmates working on an occult project. At Lammas, (August 1), 1968, the study group was transformed into a pagan religious society. Continuing to meet for sabbats into late 1969, the group decided to become a coven and,

in October, held their first skyclad esbat. Out of it, the Coven of the Full Moon emerged. Other covens were formed as leaders worked through the 2 degrees. The Coven of the Horned Moon (later Stone Moon) was formed in 1971; the Coven of the Spiral Dance in 1973.

The Order is governed by a council of elders consisting of all members of the second degree or higher, but their power is strictly advisory and concentrated on planning the major gatherings. Each coven also has a council of elders. There are three degrees of initiation, separated by a year and a day at least. The elders must approve all initiations. The Order differs from most Wiccan groups in that it has no high priest or priestess. It feels that all are equal in the circle before the Goddess.

Gardnerian rituals were adapted and new rituals written for the order's use. On the lesser sabbats the order still meets as a costumed pagan religious society. On the grand sabbats, the covens gather skyclad and only the initiated participate. A periodical, *The Witch's Trine*, was published during most of the 1970s.

Among the founders of the group is Aiden Kelly, who has in recent years left Paganism and returned to the Roman Catholic Church. Glenna Turner, another prominent leader, joined in the formation of the Covenant of the Goddess and many of the covens now hold dual membership.

Membership: Not reported.

Sources: Gini Graham Scott, *Cult and Countercult*. Westport, CT: Greenwood Press, 1980.

★1073★
OPEN GODDESS
(Defunct)

The Open Goddess was an eclectic Wicca group that drew on Alexandrian Wicca revised with insights from a broader perspective on Western occultism. The Kabbalistic symbolism of balance was predominant; both the Goddess (my Lady) and God (my Lord) are worshipped. The Goddess is identified with the sephirot Binah and the god with Chochman. These are the first emanations from Kether, the unseen Godhead. The God is the solar principle, the king to be enthroned. The Goddess is the lunar principle, veiled in the mysteries of nature and the universe. The name is derived from the belief that the various names of the Goddess are all equally valid.

At one point in the mid-1970s, the Open Goddess claimed over fifty affiliated covens scattered from New Hampshire to Florida. Headquarters were in Woodbridge, New Jersey, where High Priestess and Priest, Pennie Robbins and Kevin Robbins, resided.

★1074★
ORDER OF OSIRUS
(Defunct)

The Order of Osirus dates from 1572, with Edward Wharton, a Cambridge graduate and schoolteacher who had early become interested in divination and the occult. During his last year at college, he became interested in witchcraft. He started his first coven in the 1510s, but it was disbanded. The first covens of the new order in 1572 had seven members (to avoid the accusation of being a parody on the twelve apostles). The order considers these the first "white covens," as opposed to popular "black" covens that were involved with Satanism and black magic. It was also Wharton's belief that the smaller, more intimate body could generate unlimited power.

The Osirian Order is said to have spread to Massachusetts in the seventeenth century. In 1676, Mary Austin and Anne Brintone arrived in Boston. They were apprehended by Richard Bellingham, who accused them of witchcraft. They were released, however, upon paying 10 pounds sterling and promising to leave Boston. To Simon Newell, who paid the money, credit is due for preservation of the rituals, spells and incantations. They moved to Salem and began the first Osirian coven. By 1692, there were thirty-seven covens in New England. The order then went underground for two hundred years.

Leading the order in the 1970s was Samuel R. Graves, who was introduced to witchcraft by Chris Newell of North Bristol, Massachusetts, a descendant of Simon Newell. Chris gave Simon's journals to Graves. Graves has led in a contemporary revival of the order and the publication of several books. For the order, witchcraft has to do with the mastering of the power of the mind, the strength of individual will and the power of suggestion. The group is primarily concerned with spells and incantations toward some positive goal. Work is done in a circle. Symbol of the Osirian Order is the goat skull, associated with the Horned God, Pan, and the love of nature.

Headquarters of the order were established in Kearney, Nebraska. Membership was open to all after payment of the five-dollar fee. A bimonthly newsletter was published. No recent evidence of the continuance of the order has been available.

Sources: Samuel R. Graves, *Witchcraft: The Osirian Order.* San Francisco: JBT Marketing, 1971; *Potions and Spells of Witchcraft.* San Francisco: JBT Marketing, 1970.

★1075★
RUNIC SOCIETY
(Defunct)

The Runic Society was formed in 1974 by N. J. Templin. It advocated Wotanism, or Odinism, viewed as the oldest religion in the world and the religion of the Aryans since the late Stone Age. The Society believed that the Nordic Race is the "Chosen Race of Nature" and that only through Odinism can Nordics be true to nature. The Norse gods were worshipped and thought of as manifestations of nature. Since religion was considered a personal matter, there were no religious services. There were, however, religious festivals termed "blots," and priests, whose function it was to perform marriages and funerals. The family unit, self-respect and loyalty to the ancestral heritage were promoted. The Odinist faith is opposed to Christianity. Odinism was seen as this-worldly; immortality is given through the improvement of the future generation. The Society sought to establish a true economic, racial and spiritual community (not as a separate nation but within the nation).

The Runic Society was governed by the supreme council, made up of several Wotanist priests, a secretary, treasurer and advisory personnel. It published *Einherjar*, a quarterly. The associated House of Odin sold Odinist jewelry and articles. Headquarters were in Milwaukee, with a second group in Chicago. Around 1980 the group dissolved after a period of internal dissension.

During its years of existence, the Runic Society kept close association with Da-America (in Pittsburgh), which publishes the journal, *New America*, and with Die Artgemeinschaft (The Old Religion) in Germany. Also closely related to the Runic Society was the Odinist Movement headquartered in Toronto. It was formed in 1971 and published two periodicals, *The Sunwheel* and *The Odinist*.

★1076★
PAGAN WAY, TEMPLE OF THE
(Defunct)

One of the most important groups spreading Neo-Paganism (as opposed to Witchcraft) was the Pagan Way, a loosely associated set of Neo-Pagan groves which emerged in the late 1960s. The group had several sources. Donna Cole, a witch in Chicago, had traveled to England in the 1960s and was initiated into Gardnerian Wicca. Upon her return to the United States, she made contact with Herman Enderle and Virginia Brubaker, who had formed an occult study group. Together they established a Pagan Temple. Cole also composed a set of Pagan rituals which were less magical and more celebratory than the Gardnerian ones. During this period, she met Ed Fitch, a California Pagan. Fitch later composed a second set of rituals similar in perspective to Cole's. During the early 1970s, Cole and Fitch circulated the Pagan Way rituals around the United States with the result that a number of Pagan Way Temples (groves) emerged.

One early grove was in Philadelphia and had among its leaders Penny Novak, Michael Novack, and Thomas (a pseudonym). Thomas became the editor in 1970 of the original Pagan journal *Waxing Moon* (later the *Crystal Well*) when its founder, Joseph Wilson, moved to England.

Wilson began a British *Waxing Moon,* thus precipitating the name change in America. The *Crystal Well* was never the official organ of the Pagan Way, but it had a close informal connection and functioned as a means whereby Pagan Way groups could stay in contact.

The Pagan Way was a celebratory nature religion dedicated to the growth in understanding of the sacred quality of the seasonal rounds and the holy, mystic qualities of everyday life. Unlike most pagan groups, it was not a "magical" group and has no secret rituals. (The rituals were recently published in book form as A Book of Pagan Rituals.) While many individuals practiced magick, the group came together for celebration only. The Goddess was, of course, the central theme of the celebrations.

Pagan Way study centered on three basic steps: first, study of the myths and history of paganism; second, practice of rituals for both individuals and groups; and third, in-depth working in the craft (for those who desired it). In many areas the Pagan Way served as an outer portal to the more secretive craft.

In 1973, Pagan Way groves were functioning in Philadelphia, Pennsylvania; New York City; Wilmington, Delaware; Huron, South Dakota; Loiusville, Kentucky; San Bernadino, California; Passaic, New Jersey; and Chicago, Illinois.. There were also numerous small Pagan Way groups scattered across the country. Ed Fitch headed the California Grove. In 1974, the Chicago Pagan Way became the Uranus Temple (now the Temple of the Pagan Way). There were between 30 and 60 members at Philadelphia. By 1980, the Pagan Way had largely died. Some groups had been destroyed by internal dissension. Most were were simply superceded by numerous Neo-Pagan and Witchcraft groups under the leadership of those trained in the groves, coupled with the retirement of many of the original leaders. The original rituals, which were not copyrighted, have been published in several editions and remain popular among Neo-Pagans in North America and England.

Periodicals: Ed Fitch, *Magical Rites from the Crystal Well.* St. Paul, MN: Llewellyn Publications, 1984; *A Book of Pagan Rituals.* New York: Samuel Weiser, 1978.

★1077★
PRISTINE EGYPTIAN ORTHODOX CHURCH
(Defunct)

The Pristine Egyptian Orthodox Church was founded in 1963 in Chicago by Milton J. Neruda and Charles Renslow. It grew out of a small group in suburban Chicago Heights, Illinois. The original name was the Egyptian Holy Church. Its tradition is traced to 1375 B.C. and Pharoah Amenhotep IV (Ikhnaton the Great). The church saw itself as the heir to the original (Pristine), authentic (Orthodox) Egyptian doctrines.

High priority was placed upon individuality and the right of the individual to reason toward belief. Salvation was equated with knowledge. All religions are man-made as outward expressions of God-given faith. The church believed in one creator (Khepera) but venerated the many gods as physical examples of the attributes of the creator. These found expression in the basic Egyptian pantheon. The church also taught living in harmony with nature, the equality of all humans and the spiritual (magical) powers. It sought not to judge individuals, but to leave questions of adultery, murder, homosexuality, etc., to civil authority. (Neruda was an activist in the Chicago homosexual community.) There were four major Holy Days: Easter (March, spring), the Unity of Hator (June 22), the Seb and Mut Festival (September 22) and the Festival of Lights (December 28). There was but a single congregation of the Egyptian Church, in Chicago. It was headed by the Rev. Charles Renslow, arkon of North and South America. There were three priests. *The Egyptian Bible,* composed of ancient Egyptian materials, formed the scriptures of the church. The church split following a disagreement between Renslow and Neruda over its stance in regard to Christianity. Neruda was more actively against the Christian faith and believed that the church should be vocal in its criticism. He left to found the Congregation of Aten. Neither group survived to the end of the decade.

★1078★
PSYCHEDELIC VENUS CHURCH
(Defunct)

The Psychedelic Venus was formed in 1969 partly as an outgrowth of a former body, the Shiva Fellowship. As its name implies, it combines elements of sexual freedom and psychedelic drugs. The Shiva Fellowship dates from November 1967, when Willie Minzey went to India and was dedicated and marked in the traditional way as a worshipper of Shiva. The practice of the religion includes the smoking of hashish. Minzey returned to the United States and established a temple to Shiva in his home in San Francisco. He also began to hold public services in Golden Gate Park. On April 16, 1969, Minzey was arrested and, in 1971, was sentenced to prison for a term lasting from ten years to life. The Shiva Fellowship disintegrated into other groups.

The Psychedelic Venus Church was founded by Jefferson Poland. As a pagan fellowship dedicated to the worship of the Hindu goddess Kali, who was equated with Venus, the church drew together elements implicit in the Sexual Freedom League, the Gay Liberation Front, emerging paganism, the Shiva Fellowship and various other radical activist groups in the Berkeley/San Francisco area. The Psychedelic Venus Church described itself as a "pantheistic nature religion, humanist hedonism, a religious pursuit of bodily pleasure through sex and marijuana."

Worship in the Psychedelic Venus Church focused upon its celebrations. Until the conviction of Minzey, these were held regularly and openly. Afterwards, they were held irregularly. Typical indoor celebrations would begin with the sacrament- smoking marijuana-during which time a liturgy would be held. After the liturgy, sensitivity sessions and partying in the nude would conclude the evening. Public celebrations would center upon the smoking of marijuana and participation in sexual activity. At one such ceremony, Jefferson Poland was arrested.

The church was governed by a board of directors (four females and three males) elected annually by the membership. The board appointed officers. The president through the late 1970s was Mother Boats. *Intercourse*, a magazine, and *Nelly Heathen*, appeared as occasional periodicals. At its height in 1971, there were 1,000 members, but the church steadily lost support through the 1970s. By 1974 the group reported only 250 members. By the end of the decade the group had disappeared.

★1079★
REFORMED DRUIDS OF NORTH AMERICA
% Live Oak Grove
Box 142
Orinda, CA 94563

The Reformed Druids of North America was formed in 1963 by a group of students at Carleton College, Northfield, Minnesota, as a protest against a compulsory chapel attendance requirement. It began as the result of a conversation between David Fisher, Howard Cherniack and Norman Nelson. The idea emerged of forming a non-bloody, sacrificial Druidic group. If students were denied credit for attending its services, then they would claim religious persecution; if they received credit, the whole project would be revealed as a hoax, thus ridiculing the requirement. The requirement was dropped during the 1963-64 school year, but the group decided that, since it enjoyed the rituals so much, it would continue. At that time, the structure was completed and the major system of beliefs outlined.

Rituals had been constructed by the Reformed Druids from materials in anthropological literature, such as *The Golden Bough*, the classical text by Sir James Fraser. A henge (an open-air ring temple) was constructed on nearby Monument Hill, where the first Protestant service in Minnesota was held. Though frequently destroyed, the henge was constantly replaced. Ritual is directed toward nature and is held outdoors (in an oak grove) where possible. Robes of white are worn. The passing of the waters-of-life is a symbol of oneness with nature. Festival days are Samhain (Nov. 1), Mid-winter, Ormelc (Feb. 1), Beltane (May 1), Mid-summer, and Lugnasadh (Aug. 1). The Celtic/Druidic gods and goddesses are retained to help focus attention on nature. They include Donu, the mother of the gods and humanity, and Taranis, one of her children, the god of thunder and lightning.

The Reformed Druids are organized into autonomous groves. Each grove is headed by an arch-druid, a preceptor (for business matters) and a server (to assist the arch-druid). Three orders of the priesthood are recognized. Higher orders are honorary. *The Druid Chronicles*, consisting of the history, rules and customs of the Reformed Druids of North America, serve as the scriptures. These were composed mainly by Jan Johnson and David Frangquist, who succeeded the first arch-druid.

Over the years, a continuity of organization was effected through a lineage of arch-druids. The original arch-druid entered the priesthood of the Episcopal Church. Others established groves in different parts of the country. In 1978, locally autonomous groves were functioning in Northfield and Minneapolis, Minnesota; Chicago and Evanston, Illinois; Ann Arbor, Michigan; Webster Groves, Missouri; New York City; and Palo Alto and Berkeley, California.

In the mid-1970s, leadership of the Druid movement passed to Isaac Bonewits, who had made national headlines when he graduated from the University of California at Berkeley with a degree in magick. Bonewits headed a Berkeley grove. More importantly, he compiled the Druid writings, adding material he had written on Druidism and in 1977 published the *Druid Chronicles (Evolved)*, which contain the history, rituals, laws, and customs for the Reformed Druids. In 1978 he began *Pentalpha* as a national Druid periodical. After several years of publishing hing the magazine and trying to promote Druidism, Bonewits withdrew from all leadership roles (though he continues to be active in Pagan affairs otherwise). Emmon Bodfish became preceptor of the Berkeley Grove, which was renamed the Live Oak Grove and moved to Orinda, California.

Membership: In 1984 there were three groves: Orinda, California; Garland, Texas; and Keene, New Hampshire.

Periodicals: *Druid Missal-any*, Box 142, Orinda, CA 94563.

Sources: P. E. Isaac Bonewits, *Real Magic*. New York: Coward, McCann & Geoghegan, 1971; P. E. Isaac Bonewits, *Authentic Thaumaturgy*. Albany, CA: The CHAOSium, 1978; *The Druid Chronicles (Evolved)*. Berkeley, CA: Berkeley Drunemetom Press, 1976.

★1080★
SABAEAN RELIGIOUS ORDER OF AMEN
% El Sabarum
3221 N. Sheffield
Chicago, IL 60657

The Sabaean Religious Order of Amen is the continuation of a Mediterranean religion which dates to Ancient Sumer and Babylon. It was brought to America in the 1960s by Frederic de Arechaga, whose mother had been a high priestess of the Sabaeans in Spain. According to de

Arechaga, "Sabaean", which means one who believes in many gods, can probably be traced to Harran, an ancient city in what is now Iraq. Abraham is said to have come from Harran (Genesis 12:4).

The Sabaean Order believes in the Mother Goddess. The religion is described as "henotheistic," an amalgamation of monotheism, polytheism, pantheism, etc. The relation between god and man is within. Divinity is Saba, i.e., all; hence all the gods, the host of heaven, are worshipped. Most important of the gods are the four aspects ts of the Mother Goddess.

The mother appears as four separate identities associated with the races of humankind and the cycle of life. In order, they are: the Red Goddess, birth; the White Goddess, the duality of illusion, life; the Blue Goddess (Astarte), fertility; and the Yellow Goddess, death. The period of the Red Goddess begins with the fall equinox. At that time the feast of Janus, the two- headed god, is celebrated and the year begins.

Astrology is very important to the Sabaean system. The worship cycle is related to the positions of the moon and sun, which are calculated by taking into account the drift of the zodiac over past millennia. Major festivals (greater Sabbaths) are quarterly at the equinoxes and solstices. Lesser Sabbaths are celebrated in accordance with the lunar cycles.

One practice which has met much opposition in the pagan community is the sacrifice of animals. These are made in connection with major festivals and weddings (called eclipses). The sacrificed animal (or vegetable) is then eaten as a communion with the gods. Marriages within the Sabaean system are all for a definite period of time, determined by a divinatory method used during the wedding (eclipse) ceremony. Re-eclipsing is allowed. Homosexual eclipses are also conducted.

The Sabaean Order is headquartered in Chicago, where its Temple of the Moon is located. The group has an occult supply store, El Sabarum, and a mail order house for supplies, Isis Supplies. Osiris Book Service, Ltd. is a mail order bookstore. For several years the group issued a periodical, *Iris* (formerly *Janus*).

Membership: Not reported. There is one group, in Chicago, Illinois.

★1081★
SM CHURCH
% Robin Stewart, Priestess
Box 1407
San Francisco, CA 94101

The SM Church emerged in the mid-1970s in Berkeley, California, among people who defined themselves as being into SM (i.e., sadism and masochism) and who had, in addition, come to believe in the ancient historical practices of Goddess worship (which had appeared in the previous decade throughout the San Francisco Bay area). The church began as discussions of the SM experience led to questions of spiritual meaning associated with intense SM fantasy, beyond simple sexual gratification. Early positive explorations led to the establishment of the "Temple of the Goddess" of the SM Church.

The SM Church opposes the male father image which has dominated Western religion and encourages members to focus upon the feminine aspects of God, which it seeks to uncover in ongoing research in to periods and cultures which emphasized Goddess worship. The church differs from many other Neo-Pagan groups in that it believes in a powerful female deity, equivalent to the male monotheistic God. The church is feminist in orientation and from the beginning excluded male dominant-female submissive patterns from its organization. It allows both homosexual and heterosexual patterns of female dominance within the church's philosophy. Undergirding its approach is a belief in the great transition of Western culture. The church believes that society could collapse and, in that event, females would have to take control. The church is attempting to plan for that possibility.

Ritual life, initially adopted from other Neo-Pagan group patterns, includes a unique emphasis upon the use of controlled pain and mortification experiences as a sacrament of penance. On occassion, such rituals are designed to allow both males and females to experience the extremes of female dominance fantasies, though the church denies that female rule in the envisioned postmodern society would be vindictively harsh. Further, the sacramental atmosphere of the rituals attempts to separate them from any identification with commercialized exploitation of SM practices.

The church has published a set of purposes which includes the following: the purchase and/or erection of church facilities; the continuance of the seminary which trains women for the priesthood; the development of ordered communities as models of a matriarchial society; and assistance in improving the image of the SM community (through various charity projects). The church has initiated plans to build a monastery as a full-scale model of a female-dominated society.

The church is governed by a board of directors. Associated with it is the Essemian Society, a nonreligious social-educational group whose activities derive from SM Church perspectives.

Membership: Not reported. Membership in both the SM Church and Essemian Socity is limited to a single congregation in San Francisco. There are estimated to be less than 100 members.

Educational facilities: The SM Seminary, San Francisco, California.

Sources: Russell Budd, "Interview: The SM Organizations of San Francisco" in *Woman/Slave* no. 14 (October-December 1982) pp. 30-37; Gerald Green and Caroline Green, *SM, the Last Taboo*. New York: Ballantine Books, 1974.

★1082★
SEAX-WICA
Box 7882
Charlottesville, VA 22906

After his divorce in 1973, Raymond Buckland moved to New Hampshire, remarried, and emerged as a spokesperson (along with his new wife Joan Buckland) for a new tradition, Seax-Wica. Seax-Wica differs from other Wicca groups in that it claims no relation to previously existing covens. A Saxon background has been adopted as an alternative to the Gardnerian Wicca tradition (see separate entry). Buckland and his first wife, Rosemary Buckland, brought Gardnerian witchcraft to America in the early 1960s. Woden and Freya are the names chosen for thc male and female deities of Seax-Wicca.

Seax-Wica covens are headed by a high priest and priestess chosen annually by a vote of the coven. Members, including priests, are termed "Gesith" after initiation and "Ceorl" before. Those outside the craft are termed "Theow". There is only one degree of initiation. *The Tree* is the name given the Book of Shadows, the traditional book of rituals.

Besides the matter of tradition, Seax-Wica differs from other groups in several ways. The male deity and the high priest are raised to equality with their female counterparts. Ritual scourging and binding have been dropped. Worship is either skyclad or in a short simple tunic. There is no sexual activity in the rituals.

Headquarters for Seax-Wica are at the Seax-Wica Seminary in Virginia. Autonomous covens had, by 1974, been establsihed in New York, New Jersey, and Massachusetts. A decade later there were covens in most states and several foreign countries. Facilitating the rapid spread of Seax-Wica has been a home study course in witchcraft written by Buckland. *Seax-Wica Voys* was published for several years as the official journal.

Membership: In 1984 Seax-Wica reported approximately 3,000 members in the United States and an additional 1,000 in foreign countries.

Educational facilities: Seax-Wica Seminary, Charlottesville, VA 22906.

Sources: Raymond Buckland, *The Tree*. New York: Samuel Weiser, 1974; Tara Buchland, *Beauty Secrets of the Ancient Egyptians*. Scottsville, VA: Taray Publications, 1982; Raymond Buckland, *Practical Color Magick*. St. Paul, MN: Llewellyn Publications, 1983.

★1083★
TEMPLE OF BACCHUS
RD 2
Box 51
Wells, MA 04090

The Temple of Bacchus was formed in 1978 by Bishop H. Carlisle Estes, the temple's pastor. Bacchus, also known as Dionysus, was the ancient Greek god of food and drink. Estes claimed in 1975 that Bacchus revealed to him the temple's teachings, which have been published in a pamphlet, *The Book of Bacchus*. The Temple believes that there is one God, known by many names, and that Bacchus is His disciple. Bacchus decreed that Estes should form a church to worship God and ordered that it be a place of joy and celebration. Bacchus taught that everything God created is good and humans should enjoy the pleasures of the body-food, wines, music, creative activity, and the arts. However, all should be enjoyed in moderation. Excess in any area leads to illness and pestilence and the disfiguring of bodily form.

According to the revelation, Bacchus has decreed daily worship with feasting and dancing. Six days of bacchanals are followed by a day of fasting and rest. Priests, bishops and cardinals of the church assist in the preparation of the daily feast with a primary responsibility of preventing the rituals from becoming repetitious and stereotyped.

Almost from its founding, the temple has been a subject of controversy. Critics charged Bishop Estes and his assistant, Cardinal Vincent Morino, with operating a restaurant under the guise of a temple in order to circumvent local zoning laws which had previously denied them permission to open a restaurant in the building occupied by the temple. They further charged that the nightly bacchanals (in which those in attendance are asked to contribute a stated donation and in return receive a full meal) are in fact not religious events at all. The controversy has led to several law suits which are, as of the time of this writing, still pending and which will determine the future of the temple.

The temple is one of several religious bodies chartered by the Universal Life Church of Modesto, California.

Membership: In 1979 the church reported 125 members of the single congregation in Maine, with new congregations beginning in Honolulu, Hawaii and in Wiltshire, England.

★1084★
TEMPLE OF THE PAGAN WAY
Box 60151
Chicago, IL 60660

The Temple of the Pagan Way dates from 1966 and the formation of an occult study and worship group led by Herman Enderle and Virginia Brubaker. The group became associated with the British Pagan Front and began to use the rituals written by Donna Cole. However, divergences developed within the Temple over the ascendancy of the Mother Goddess, a prominent theme in the Pagan Way rituals. A system incorporating a balanced view of deity, both male and female, was adopted, with prominent elements from the Kabbalah. Enderle, who was a student of ritual magick, advocated a strong emphasis on magick in addition to "just worshipping the Goddess."

During the 1970s the Temple was the motivating force in the formation of a number of other Neo-Pagan bodies. Most of the currently existing Neo-Pagan and Wicca groups in the Chicago area derive from it. They include the Calumet Pagan Temple, Epiphanes, and the First Temple of the Craft of WICA (all now independent organizations). The Temple of the Sacred Stones, an eclectic witchcraft coven headed by Donna Cole, had a long association with the Temple, and it now meets in the building which formerly housed the Temple.

After several years as the Temple of the Pagan Way, the group adopted a new name in the spring of 1974, Uranus Temple. During this period, its emphasis upon ritual magick was at its height. Uranus was an initiatory temple with its basis in Western occultism and paganism. Members attended regular services associated with the full and new moon as well as the eight festivals. New members begin with a series of ethics classes which introduce them to the basic perspective of the temple. They are then prepared for a Ritual of Dedication where a public declaration of the acceptance of paganism is made. The next step is initiation. There are five degrees, each of which corresponds to the classical elements of the ancients and entails approximately one year of study.

The first degree is Earth, in which the student is taught to gain control over him/herself and is introduced to basic occult material and exercises. The second degree is Water, with emphasis on exploring the psychic and emotional self. The third degree is Fire, and deals directly with self-change through magick. The fourth degree is Air, and expresses the use of what has been learned and the ability to function easily as a magician and pagan. The fifth degree, Spirit, is the completed use of the first four degrees.

The Temple was headed by a high priest and high priestess elected annually from among the priests and priestesses. Members in the second degree can choose studies leading to the priesthood. A General Council consisting of all members is the highest authority, and there is a Council of Elders, composed of senior members of the community, to which the high priest and priestess are responsible.

In 1975 the high priest (Enderle) and high priestess (Brubaker) had sufficient irreconcilable differences that the group split. The majority (and hence the name) followed Brubaker. Enderle then formed the Earthstar Temple. After using the name Uranus for a short while, it was discarded for the original name. The group has since

become a witchcraft coven, though retaining many of the unique ritual and magical emphases from the 1970s. The Temple has taken an active role in the Covenant of the Goddess.

Membership: Not reported. There is one group, located in Chicago, Illinois.

★1085★
TEUTONIC TEMPLE
(Defunct)

In Dallas, Oregon, the Teutonic Temple functioned as a polytheistic religion derived from the folk customs and festivals of the English, German and Scandinavian peoples. Members believed in a supreme God and a pantheon of lesser deities including Tiw, the sky father; Wodan; Thunar; Fria; and Frua, goddess of fertility and magick. The eight pagan festivals were celebrated. Yule, the winter solstice, is the beginning of the Teutonic year. The Teutonic Temple was a conservative religion and is against free love, perversion, pornography, drugs, draft dodging and permissiveness. No evidence of its continuance into the 1980s had been located.

★1086★
VENUSIAN CHURCH
Box 21263
Seattle, WA 98111

The Venusian Church was formed in 1975 by Ron Peterson, a Seattle businessman, and chartered the following year by the Universal Life Church. During the 1960s and early 1970s, Peterson, a former member of the Seventh-Day Adventist Church, followed a spiritual pilgrimage which centered upon the release of sexual feelings repressed by the strict sexual code under which he was raised. He found assistance within the human potential movement and became an advocate of helping others who wished to confront their sexual feelings. Meanwhile, he had also become a professional pornographer.

Peterson gathered around him a group of interested people, including several sex therapists and human potential counselors, and began to explore the potential of sex and sexual experience in releasing human creativity and opening the realm of the spiritual. For a short while, the church operated a Temple of Venus in downtown Seattle which featured both pornographic films and sexually explicit presentations that attempted to communicate the church's attitude about open sexuality to the general public. In 1977 a retreat center, Camp Armac, was opened and became the focus of church activities. A variety of seminars, workshops, social events, and worship services were offered, all in an atmosphere in which clothes were optional and sexual experimentation was condoned and even encouraged.

The leaders of the church resisted any attempts to systematically build a belief system or pattern of worship, and the life of the group slowly emerged out of the spontaneous experiencesof various gatherings of the members. First came the worship of nature in the form of the Goddess and the acknowledgment of Her at communal feasts and in the celebration of the solar equinox and solstice. Then in 1979 church members discovered the preexisting Neo-Pagan movement. Having found in Neo-Paganism a larger movement which already possessed a complete religious system toward which the Venusian Church seemed to be heading, the church began to absorb both thought and practices from their new acquaintances, especially from the Church of All Worlds.

In 1979 Camp Armac closed and for several years the church conducted its programs in the homes of members. In 1981 the church purchased a large tract of land near Redmond, Washington. A former warehouse was converted into a church center named the Longhouse, and a stonehenge was erected for outdoor rituals.

Because of its strong opinions on the centrality of sex and its varied attempts to communicate its beliefs through programs which featured nudity and even overt sexual acts, the church has been in constant tension with legal authorities. On several occasions, people working at the Temple of Aphrodite were arrested for lewd conduct. The church has also been in a long-term battle to reclaim its tax-exempt status which was revoked by the U.S. Internal Revenue Service.

The beliefs of the Venusian Church follow those of Neo-Paganism. The church affirms the centrality of nature and seeks to discover means to reestablish links with those original natural patterns currently distorted by society, especially in its repression of creative sexual expression. Sex is considered divine. The church is self-consciously eclectic in belief and antidogmatic. It encourages the influx of any ideas which prove useful to the overall accomplishments of the church's goals.

The church is formally headed by a board of directors, but management of the church center and program development is placed in a loosely organized council of active members. Ministers are selected from among the members after demonstrating their leadership abilities and competence in dealing with people.

Membership: In 1984 the church had approximately 150 members in the single center outside Seattle, Washington. Most members live in or close to Seattle.

Periodicals: *Longhouse Calendar*, 23301 Redmond-Fall City Road, Redmond, WA 98053.

★1087★
WITCHES INTERNATIONAL CRAFT ASSOCIATES
153 W. 80th St.
New York, NY 10024

Witches International Craft Associates (W.I.C.A.) is the public structure of the Sicilian Strege tradition headed in America by Dr. Leo Louis Martello. It was formed in 1970. Prior to that time Dr. Martello had been an active Spiritualist. In 1955 he was ordained and became the head of the International Guidance Temple of Bible Spiritual Independents, Mother Church & Seminary in New York City. He served the church for five years. He was also a national officer of the American Graphological Society, a hypnotist and popular writer on occult subjects.

According to Martello, witchcraft teaching and practice was passed through his family and was initiated in 1951. During the 1960s he returned to Sicily (from America where his parents had immigrated) and re-established contact with the Strege. In 1969 he published his first book on witchcraft, and the following year he went public. He founded W.I.C.A.

Martello emerged as one of the earliest spokespersons of the new witchcraft. His organization led in the formation of a number of necessary structures serving the emerging community in the early 1970s: Witches Encounter Bureau (to aid witches in contacting each other), the Witches Liberation Movement (which published the "Witch Manifesto"), and the Witches Antidefamation League. He also initiated two periodicals, *Witchcraft Digest* and the *W.I.C.A. Newsletter*.

According to Martello, the actualities of Strege Wicca have never been revealed, though Charles B. Leland's book *Aradia* comes close to revealing them. *Aradia* was meant to be a study of Strege. The basic deity is Diana, the first created before all creation. She divided into darkness and into light (Lucifer). Desiring the light, she tricked Lucifer into lying with her and thus became the mother of Herodias (Aradia). She also became the Queen of the Witches. The basic ritual is the conjuration of Diana and the invocation of Aradia. Cubes of meal, salt and honey in the shape of a crescent moon are consecrated and eaten. The climax of the ritual, performed at the full moon, is dancing and "love in the darkness." The ritual is skyclad (performed in the nude).

One point at which Sicilian Wicca differs from most traditions is its use of spells and incantations that threaten the deity. For example, Diana is addressed:

Or I may truly at another time So conjure thee that thou shalt have no peace Or happiness, for thou shalt ever be In suffering until thou grantest that Which I require in strictest faith from here!

Threats are a recognition of the essential divinity in each person, a sense of personal power which even the gods and goddesses cannot undermine.

Strege functions as an ethnic branch of the craft. Headed in the United States by Martello, who sees it as one with continuing Sicilian practices. In recent years Martello has discontinued the periodicals, but still circulates his many books though the publishing arm Hero Press.

Membership: Not reported.

Sources: Leo Louis Martello, *Witchcraft, The Old Religion.* Secaucus, NJ: University Books, 1973; Leo Louis Martello, *Weird Ways of Witchcraft.* New York: HC Publishers, 1969; Leo Louis Martello, *How to Prevent Psychic Blackmail.* New York: Samuel Weiser, 1975; Leo Louis Martello, *What It Means To Be a Witch.* New York: The Author, [1975]; Leo Louis Martello, *Curses in Verses.* New York: Hero Press, 1971; Charles Godfrey Leland, *The Mystic Will.* New York: Hero Press, 1980.

Voodoo

★1088★
AFRO-AMERICAN VODOUN
Current address not obtained for this edition.

Occassionally, a leader of a voodoo group will allow an outsider (such as a reporter) to gain limited access to their organization. Such a leader was High Priestess Madam Arboo of Afro-American Vodoun. Madam Arboo was active in Harlem in the 1960s as leader of an Afro-American Vodoun group. Born in Georgia, Madam Arboo was reared in voodoo and migrated to New York City. As described in a lengthy article which is the only source of information about her, she described vodoun as an Afro-Christian cult centered on Damballah (the chief voodoo deity), the god of wisdom, personified as a serpent. As high priestess, she is his messenger. Her group differs from Haitian voodoo groups in that it has reduced the remainder of the pantheon to the position of sub-deities or spirits. Damballah is equated with the serpent that Moses elevated in the wilderness (Numbers 21:9).

Healing is a high priority of Vodoun and includes both psychic and psychological counseling and (where permitted) the dispensing of folk remedies such as rattlesnake oil. Worship is held on the evening of the new moon and is centered on ecstatic dance accompanied by flute and drum and led by the papaloi (priest) and mammaloi (priestess). The members, as they dance, enter trancelike states which become occasions for revelations and messages from the spirits. Elements of Christianity survive in the use of spirituals. The threefold way of Vodoun teaches faith, love, and joy as virtues. The pentagram (for females) and the star of David (for males) are major symbols. Animals carry symbolic power: the goat , fertility; rtility; the eagle, majesty; the turtle,

caution; and the vulture is Damballah's sanitation department.

Membership: No direct contact has been established with Madame Arboo and the current status of her group is uncertain. Vodoun groups exist along the East coast and are organized into gatherings of from 15 to 20 persons.

Sources: Madam Arboo as told to Harold Preece, "What Voodoo' Really Is" in *Exploring the Unknown*, vol. 4, no. 6 (April, 1964) pp. 6-19.

★1089★
CHAMBER OF HOLY VOODOO
Box 341
New York, NY 10021

The Chamber of Holy Voodoo emerged in the 1970s as a semi-public voodoo organization which offers to teach voodoo to students via correspondence. While the specific teachings are revealed only to students, the Chamber offers to introduce those who join to the world of Holy Spirits and to teach them how to invoke them for various purposes. After a basic course, students may prepare themselves for the priesthood and learn the secrets of healing, exorcism and the process of spirit possession. The Chamber also has a special section devoted to dealing with the problems of its members, the Room of Blessing, in which voodoo is used to assist individuals in overcoming obstacles and reaching goals. Marriage counseling is a particular concern.

Membership: Not reported.

★1090★
FIRST CHURCH OF VOODOO
Box 2381
Knoxville, TN 37917

Robert W. Pelton, a free-lance journalist, made an extensive study of voodoo in the early 1970s, traveling around the United States visiting magicians, conjure men and women and voodoo practitioners. His research led to a number of books surveying the topic. He also decided to organize a voodoo church which began meeting in the home of Francis Torrance and Candy Torrance, a voodoo priest and priestess in North Knoxville, who taught a course in voodoo magic at the University of Tennessee evening school. The church was incorporated in Tennessee in 1973. The Church teachings combined elements of voodoo, conjureman (hoodoo), and Christianity. Ordination is available by mail.

Membership: Not reported.

Sources: Robert W. Pelton, *The Complete Book of Voodoo.* New York: G. P. Putnam's Sons, 1972; Robert W. Pelton, *Voodoo Secrets from A to Z.* South Brunswick, NJ: A. S. Barnes and Company, 1973; Robert W. Pelton,

Voodoo Charms and Talismans. New York: Drake Publishers, 1973; Robert W. Pelton, *Voodoo Signs and Omens.* South Brunswick, NJ: A. S. Barnes and Company, 1974.

★1091★

OYOTUNJI, YORUBA VILLAGE OF
Box 51
Sheldon, SC 29941

In December, 1973, a group of blacks from Harlem received national news coverage for their establishment of a "voodoo kingdom" in Beauford County, South Carolina. The sacred village of Oyotunji is headed by King Oba Efuntola Oseijeman Adelabu Adefunmi I, born Walter Eugene King in 1928. King abandoned the Baptist Church of his family during his teens and began a search for the ancient gods of Africa. He traveled to Haiti in 1954 and discovered voodoo. Upon his return to the United States in 1955, he founded the Order of Damballah Hwedo Ancestor Priests. Then in 1959 he traveled to Cuba and was initiated in the Orisha-Vodu African priesthood by Afro-Cubans at Matanzas, Cuba. The Order of Damballah was superceded by the Shango Temple and in 1960 he incorporated the African Theological Archministry. The Shango Temple was renamed the Yoruba Temple.

In 1970 King Efuntola, as King became known, moved with most of the temple members to rural South Carolina where the Yoruba Village of Oyotunji was established. He began a complete reform of the Orisha-Vodu priesthood along Nigerian lines. In 1972 he traveled to Nigeria and was initiated into the Ifa priesthood. Upon his return he was proclaimed oba-king (Alashe) of Oyotunji. He opened the first Parliament of Oyotunji chiefs and landowners and founded the priest' council (Igbimolosha) in 1973. These two groups make the rules for the community. They attempt to adhere closely to African models.

Oyotunji has been modeled on a Nigerian village. A palace for the King and his wives (seven by 1982) and children has been constructed. There are also several temples dedicated to the various deities. Only Yoruban is spoken before noon each day.

Yoruba Religion is considered to be the "rain forest version of the Ancient Egyptian Mystery System" It is the source for Afro-Cuban Santeria, but makes no attempt to equate its gods with Christian saints. The system is headed by Chango and the pantheon includes Elegba, god of luck; Ogun, god of metal; Ifa, god of divination; and Eshu the trickster, the messenger of the gods. Practices of the Yoruba system include animal sacrifice, polygamy, ecstatic dancing and the appeasement of the gods by various offerings. Worship centers upon the veneration of the deities. Worship is also directed toward ancestors, the closest level of spiritual forces to individuals.

Membership: In 1982 there were more than 200 residents of Oyotunji.

Remarks: King Efuntola had become a leader in the African Nationalist movement in the 1960s. Since moving to South Carolina, his village has become a pilgrimage site for many blacks, irrespective of their acceptance of his religious stance.

Sources: Oba Efuntola Oseijeman Adelabu Adefunmi I, *Olorisha, A Guidebook into Yoruba Religion.* Sheldon, SC: The Author, 1982; Carl M. Hunt, *Oyotunji Village.* Washington, DC: University Press of America,1979; Carlos Canet, *Oyotunji.* Miami, FL: Editorial AIP, n.d.; Baba Oseijeman Adefunmi, *Ancestors of the Afro-Americans.* Long Island City, NY: Aims of Modzawe, 1973.

★1092★

RELIGIOUS ORDER OF WITCHCRAFT
% Witchcraft Shop
521 St. Philip
New Orleans, LA 70116

The Religious Order of Witchcraft was incorporated in 1972 in New Orleans, Louisana, by Mary Oneida Toups, its high priestess. A housewife and a mother, she began her magical career in 1969 in a Kabbalistic system. In 1970 she opened the Witches' Workshop (now the Witchcraft Shop), a magick/witchcraft/voodoo shop in the city. She continued her study in the ritual magick systems of Aleister Crowley and Israel Regardie and in 1971 reached the point of mystical communion with her holy guardian angel. That communion led to the founding of the order. According to her textbook, *Magick, High and Low*, the order is focused in Kabbalistic magick with a strong emphasis on astrology, Egyptian mythology, and the Tarot. The members venerate the "God of the Witches" popularly known as the Goat of Mendes. They do not worship it, but rather what it symbolizes: the magical light of universal intelligence always available to people when they learn how to use it, the belief that sacrifice must come before complete illumination, the balance between justice and mercy, eternal life, and the dual masculine-feminine nature of the body, among other things.

Membership: Not reported.

Sources: Oneida Troups, *Magick, High and Low.* Jefferson, LA: Hope Publications, 1975.

★1093★

YORUBA THEOLOGICAL ARCHMINISTRY
167 E. 106th St.
New York, NY 10029

Similar in belief to the Yoruban Village of Oyotunji is the Yoruba Theological Archministry, which emerged in the early 1980s in Manhattan. It is headed by John Mason.

The term Yoruba is used to describe any person, regardless of national origin, who while living in the Western Hemisphere has adopted the religious views, philosophy, and traditions of the Yorubas of Southwest Africa.

Membership: Not reported. There is one center in New York City.

Sources: John Mason, *Sin Egun (Ancestor Worship)*. New York: Yoruba Theological Archministry, 1981; John Mason, *Osanyin*. New York: Yoruba Theological Archministry, 1983; John Mason, *Ebo Eje (Blood Sacrifice)*. New York: Yoruba Theological Archministry, 1981; John Mason, *Onje Fun Orisa (Food for the Gods)*. New York: Yoruba Theological Archministry, 1981.

Satanism

★1094★
BROTHERHOOD OF THE RAM
(Defunct)

Operating from the early 1960s into the 1970s, the Brotherhood of the Ram established a bookstore in Los Angeles. Satan was to this group a god of joy and pleasure. Some traditional aspects of Satanism, such as the "pact," were accepted. Members made a pact with Satan renouncing all other devotion and their Christian baptism, and then signed the pact with their own blood. Membership was confined to Southern California. As of the 1980s the store has been closed and the group reportedly disbanded.

★1095★
CHURCH OF SATAN
Box 210082
San Francisco, CA 94121

One story repeated continually in the media is how Anton LaVey shaved his head on Walpurgisnacht (April 30) in 1966, proclaimed the beginning of the Satanic era, and launched the Church of Satan. LaVey became a media event and the object of both features and front page newspaper articles. His early fame came from news coverage of such events as a Satanic funeral service for a Navy man killed in an accident at Treasure Island Navy Base, worship with a nude woman on the altar in his black house in San Francisco, the revelation of actress Jayne Mansfield's association with the church, and a bit part for LaVey in the movie "Rosemary's Baby" (as the Devil). But no little credit must go to LaVey himself.

LaVey is a former animal trainer and carnival organist. (His love for big cats led him to acquire Tagore, a lion cub.) While with the carnival, he became intrigued by the psychic and gained a reputation as a ghosthunter. LaVey is the author of three books--*The Satanic Bible*, *The Satanic Rituals*, and *The Compleat Witch*. Each contains the teachings of the Satanic Church.

The basic themes of LaVey's brand of Satanism are self-assertion, antiestablishmentarianism and the gratification of man's physical or mental nature. Satan is a Promethean figure, representing indulgence, vital existence, undefiled wisdom, kindness to the deserving, vengeance, responsibility to the responsible, the notion that man is just another animal, and so-called sins which lead to physical or mental gratification. It is LaVey's opinion that Satan represents the source of these values. Rituals are conceived both as psychodramas and as magical acts that focus psychokinetic force, as in the ritual magick tradition.

Satanic philosophy is very close to the teachings pf Aleister Crowley in *The Book of the Law*. Each person is seen as living according to his own set of rules. However, the Church of Satan opposes illegal acts at variance with laws established for the common good. Sex is viewed as the strongest instinct (next to self preservation) and natural. Drugs are viewed as escapist and contrary to the realistic view of life as preached by the church.

Ritually, the church celebrates three main holidays. For individuals, the most important day is their birthday. For the group, Walpurgisnacht and Halloween are the major days. Both have sexual implications as the spring rebirth of nature and the harvest festivals. Baptism is a ceremony of glorification of the one baptized. There are various rituals for different magical and celebratory purposes. The Enochian language, which first appeared in print in 1659 in a biography of John Dee(and was later used by the Hermetic Order of the Golden Dawn) is employed in rituals. Missing from the rituals is the black mass.

Operating from the San Francisco headquarters, the Satanic Church spread to urban centers across the United States, surfacing in Miami, Florida; New Orleans, Louisiana; New York City; and throughout the Midwest. By 1977, one spokesperson claimed more than 10,000 members for the church (lifetime membership is available for a $100.00 donation). In the mid-1970s the grottos (local groups) were abandoned and the Church was reorganized as a secret society.

Membership: Not reported. Church membership statistics are confidential. Internationally, however, members are reported in Hong Kong, Israel, Zaire, Iceland, Costa Rica, and Rumania, among other countries.

Periodicals: *The Cloven Hoof* Box 896, Daly City, CA 94017.

Remarks: The number of members of the Church of Satan has been debated. According to ex-members, there were never more than 250 paid members. One participant-observer engaged in research in 1968-69 reported less than 500 members. In 1974 the church was ravaged by the defection of a majority of its members who founded several other groups. The most successful (which inherited over half the Church's membership) was the Temple of Set (see separate entry). There has been a reported upsurge in membership application in the mid-1980s. In 1985, approximately 2,000 copies of the *Cloven Hoof* were being mailed out.

Sources: Burton H. Wolff, *The Devil's Avenger*. New York: Pyramid Books, 1974; Anton Szandor LaVey, *The Satanic Bible*. New York: Avon, 1969; Anton, Szandor LaVey, *The Compleat Witch*. New York: Lancer Books, 1971; Anton Szandor LaVey, *The Satanic Rituals*. Secaucus, NJ: University Books, 1972; Randall H. Alfred, "The Church of Satan" in Charles Y. Glock and Robert N. Bellah, *The New Religious Consciousness*. Berkeley: University of California Press, 1976; Walt Harrington, "The Devil in Anton LaVey" in *The Washington Post Magazine* (February 23, 1986) pp. 6-17.

★1096★
CHURCH OF SATANIC BROTHERHOOD
(Defunct)

In the early 1970s, controversy began to develop among the Midwestern grottoes of the Church of Satan. Among those involved were Wayne West of Detroit and John De Haven of Dayton, Ohio. The dissolution of the Stygian Grotto of the Dayton area of the Church of Satan occurred on February 11, 1973. Anton LaVey had revoked the grotto's charter, accusing it of "having been acting in violation of the law." With members from Ohio, Indiana, and Michigan, the Church of Satanic Brotherhood was formed in March 1973 by John De Haven, Joseph M. Daniels, Ronald E. Lanting, and Harry L. Booth.

The church followed the practices of the Church of Satan with several exceptions that grew out of the controversy. Only those people who "can get along with others" were allowed in the Brotherhood. *The Satanic Rituals* by LaVey was viewed as a collection of butchered rites as used in their original form at the Central Grotto. An intense polemic against LaVey was launched.

After its founding, the Brotherhood spread rapidly. Grottoes were established in St. Petersburg, Florida; Dayton-Centerville, Ohio; Indianapolis, Indiana; Louisville, Kentucky; New York City; and Columbus, Ohio. A Council of the Churches was headed by the bishops (fourth degree). The priesthood made up its third degree. Each grotto was headed by a magister. A periodical, *The True Grimoire*, was published monthly.

The Church of Satanic Brotherhood lasted only a short period. In 1974 John De Haven publically renounced Satanism and proclaimed his conversion to Christianity. He made his announcement in the midst of a gathering of the Church in St. Petersburg during which he smashed many of the altar implements.

★1097★
ORDER OF THE BLACK RAM
Current address not obtained for this edition.

The Order of the Black Ram is a Satanic organization based on the belief in Aryan racial superiority and closely associated with the National Renaissance Party, a neo-Nazi organization. Adherents believe that each race is the embodiment of a racial soul which is expressed in its culture and philosophy. Individuality is stressed. The Order of the Black Ram is eclectic, drawing on the writings of Anton LaVey (founder of the Church of Satan); Robert Heinlein's novel, *Stranger in a Strange Land*; and Neo-Paganism. It was headquartered in suburban Detroit, Michigan, where its grand magister, the Rev. Seth-Klippoth, resided. *Liber Venifica* was an irregular periodical.

★1098★
ORDO TEMPLI SATANAS
(Defunct)

Closely associated with the Church of Satanic Brotherhood was the Ordo Templi Satanas (OTS). Some OTS members were former members of the Brotherhood. Practices, beliefs, and organization are similar. There were two temples of the OTS, one in Indianapolis, Indiana and one in Louisville, Kentucky (headed by Clifford Amos). Leader of the OTS was Joseph Daniels, known as Apollonius, priest of Hermopolis. He was also one of the founders of the Brotherhood. This miniscule group disbanded after a few years.

★1099★
OUR LADY OF ENDOR COVEN
(Defunct)

Existing for many years prior to the establishment of the Church of Satan was Our Lady of Endor Coven, the Ophite Cultus Satanas, founded by Herbert Arthur Sloane of Toledo, Ohio in 1948. Satanas (the Horned God) appeared to him first when Sloane was a child. Later, Sloane saw him as the figure pictured on the dust jacket of Margaret Murray's *The God of the Witches*. (Murray is discussed in the introductory material to this volume.) The Lord Satanas appeared again when Sloane was twenty-five years old.

The system of Our Lady of Endor Coven was based heavily on Gnosticism; *The Gnostic Religion* by Hans Jonas was a highly recommended book. The Christian God, the creator, was identified with the Gnostic Demiurge. The Demiurge is the God beyond the creator God , an emanation of the transcendent God. Satanas is the messenger of the remote God who brought Eve the knowledge that there was a God beyond the God who created the cosmos. The God beyond takes no part of "this world," except as he is concerned with the return of his spirit, now entrapped in matter as the divine within humanity. The return of the divine within humanity to the God beyond is accomplished through Gnosis, occult knowledge which people can attain.

Satanism was believed to be the oldest religion, dating to the worship of the Horned God found in the prehistoric cave paintings in Europe. It differs from witchcraft in not turning the Horned God into a fertility god and thus retaining his spiritual significance. Organization followed a pattern similar to witchcraft, covens being the prime structure. The organization was headed by a priest but has no extra-coven structure.

There was but one coven led by Sloane. It dissolved after his death in the early 1980s.

Remarks: For a brief period of time Sloane was a member of the Church of Satan, but his membership did not visibly alter the coven he led.

★1100★
TEMPLE OF SET
Box 29271
San Francisco, CA 94129

The Temple of Set was founded in 1975 by a group of former members of the Church of Satan. Among the leaders in founding the new temple were Michael A. Aquino, Lilith Sinclair, and Betty Ford. Sinclair had been the priestess of the Lilith Grotto, the largest in the Church of Satan in the early 1970s. The temple describes itself as an initiatory society dedicated to Set, an ancient Egyptian deity, the corrupted legends of which became the basis of the Christian "Satan." Temple members do not believe Set to have been an "evil" figure.

According to the temple teaching, the universe is a nonconscious environment possessed of a mechanical consistency. In contrast to the universe and occasionally violating its laws is Set. Set has, over a period of millenia, altered the genetic makeup of humans in order to create a species possessing unnormal intelligence. Three key phases have been noted, pointing out those people possessing the intellect for the next third level of evolution. These occurred in 1904 (when *The Book of Law* was given to Aleister Crowley); in 1966 (when the Church of Satan was founded); and in 1975 (when the Temple of Set was founded). The techniques and teachings of the Temple of Set are designed to identify and communicate with these individuals.

The Temple is led by a Council of Nine which appoints the High Priest of Set and the Executive Director. There are five degrees reached by successive initiations: setian, adept, priest/ess of Set, master of the temple, and magus. The program is designed for individual progress and few group activities are held. The organization provides a guided reading list containing material on a wide range of occult, scientific, and religious subjects. Topics covered include ancient Egypt, the writings of H. P. Lovecraft, sex, magic, and cybernetics.

Membership: In 1984 the Temple had approximately 500 members.

Periodicals: *Scroll of Set*, Box 29129, San Francisco, CA 94129.

Remarks: The Temple of Set is currently the largest and most substantial of the several Satanic organizations still in existence. At the time of its founding, the Temple inherited the majority of the membership of the Church of Satan.

Sources: Gini Graham Scott, *The Magicians*. New York: Irvington Publishers, 1983; Michael A. Aquino, *Temple of Set Reading List XIX*. San Francisco: Temple of Set, 1984.

★1101★
THEE SATANIC CHURCH
(Defunct)

In 1974 Thee Satanic Church of the Nethilum Rite divided, and a second organization was established by Dr. Evelyn Paglini, one of the original cofounders. Its belief and structure were identical to those of the parent church. The Satanic Church opened a book and occult supply store in a Chicago suburb and Paglini began an occult periodical, *Psychic Standard*, which did not carry any Satanic material. Paglini's group slowly dropped their Satanic trappings. In one of their last public actions, they gathered at Comiskey Park prior to a Chicago White Sox baseball game to do a magical ritual to aid the faltering team.

The *Psychic Standard* ceased publication in 1980. Shortly after that time Paglini moved away from Chicago.

★1102★
**THEE SATANIC ORTHODOX CHURCH OF
    NETHILUM RITE**
(Defunct)

Centered in Chicago was Thee Satanic Orthodox Church of Nethilum Rite headed by High Priest Terry Taylor. Headquarters were at the Occult Book Shop in Chicago. The Church went public in 1971. It was opposed to the Satanism of Anton LaVey and the Church of Satan. Members believed in God as the creator of the universe and in Satan as the creature of God. Satan is the apex of creation who possesses all the power and knowledge of the universe. Members tried to acquire as much of Satan's knowledge and power as possible. This acquisition was to be achieved through magical rituals and psychic development and through the elders, described as an "international group of high ministers in the private end of Thee Satanic Church." The Church disappeared in the mid-1970s.

Only one center, in Chicago, was ever established. It claimed 538 members in 1973. Weekly Saturday night meetings were held including songs, prayers, a ritualistic mass, and introduction of new members. Recruitment was

through evening public discussion sessions, the store, and classes given by Taylor.

Middle Eastern Family
Part 1, Judaism

An historical essay on this family is provided beginning on page 141.

Mainline Judaism

★1103★
CONSERVATIVE JUDAISM
United Synagogue of America
155 Fifth Ave.
New York, NY 10010

As Reform and Orthodox polemics began to polarize the Jewish community, there arose a middle group which advocated an allegiance to traditional Judaism, but without strict attention to all the Orthodox ways. Drawn together by an affront to tradition accompanying the graduation of the first class at Hebrew Union College, Rabbi Sabato Morais, Marcus Jastrow and Henry Pereira Mendes formed a Jewish Theological Seminary Association to counteract the effects of Reform.

Never strong, Conservative Judaism nevertheless found champions in Cyrus Adler and Rabbi Solomon Schechter. The two revived the faltering Jewish Theological Seminary, and Schechter became the mainstay of a Judaism that respected tradition but was saturated with contemporary scholarship. The Conservative synagogue uses English as well as Hebrew, does not separate men and women, and emphasizes modern education. However, many orthodox practices, such as the covered heads during worship, are retained.

The Jewish Theological Seminary in New York and Los Angeles remains the educational center of Conservatism. In 1913, Schechter pulled together the United Synagogue of America. The Rabbinical Assembly was founded six years later.

Membership: In 1980 there were approximately 824 congregations and 1,500,000 affiliated members.

Educational facilities: Jewish Theological Seminary, New York City and Los Angeles, California.

Periodicals: *Conservative Judaism*, 3080 Broadway, New York, NY 10027; *United Synagogue Review*, 155 Fifth Avenue, New York, NY 10010.

Sources: Moshe Davis, *The Emergence of Conservative Judaism*. Philadelphia: The Jewish Publication Society of America, 1963; Abraham J. Karp, *A History of the United Synagogue of America, 1913-1963*. New York: United Synagogue of America, 1964; Marshall Sklare, *Conservative Judaism*. Glencoe, IL: The Free Press, 1955.

★1104★
JEWISH RECONSTRUCTIONIST FOUNDATION
Federation of Reconstructionist Congregations and
 Havurot
2521 Broadway, S.
New York, NY 10025

During the years following World War I, the Jewish community became prosperous and diffuse. In recognition of the not strictly religious nature of much of what was commonly labeled Judaism, conservative scholar Mordecai M. Kaplan proposed in the 1930s a new approach to Judaism, one which would take account of its diverse nature. In his *Judaism as a Civilization* (1934), he argued that Judaism was not so much a religion as a religious civilization. He called for a reconstruction of Judaism not around the synagogue but the community as a whole. Jewish civilization would unite Reform, Conservative and Orthodox religion, Zionism and various other Jewish interests.

The ideas of Kaplan appealed especially to nonreligious Jews who were nonetheless attached to "Jewishness." Thus was founded the Reconstructionist movement, and in 1935 Kaplan began a periodical, *The Reconstructionist*, to propagate his ideas within Conservative Judaism. Kaplan's approach to tradition, his rejection of the divine origin of the Torah and his reevaluation of ritual in light of modern thought, however, proved a constant source of discord, and Kaplan and the Conservatives slowly drifted apart. The Orthodox were so annoyed with him that, in

1945 (after he published a revised prayer book), he was excommunicated. The excommunication was in turn attacked by the Conservative and Reform leadership.

Membership: In 1984 Reconstructionists reported 60,000 members, 50 synangogues and centers, and 120 rabbis. There were an additional 5,000 members outside of the United States in centers in Canada, Israel, and the Netherlands Antilles.

Educational facilities: Reconstructionist Rabbinical College, Wyncote, Pennsylvania.

Periodicals: *The Reconstructionist*, 31 E. 28th Street, New York, NY 10016; *Raayonot*, Reconstructionist Rabbinical Association, 2521 Broadway, S., New York, NY 10025.

Sources: Mordecai M. Kaplan, *Basic Values in Jewish Religion*. New York: Reconstructionist Press, 1948; Mordecai M. Kaplan, *The Meaning of God in Modern Jewish Religion*. New York: Reconstructionist Press, 1962; Mordecai M. Kaplan, *The Future of the American Jew*. New York: Macmillan Company, 1949; Jack J. Cohen, *The Case for Religious Humanism*. New York: Reconstructionist Press, 1958; Eugene Kohn, *Religious Humanism*. New York: Reconstructionist Press, 1953.

★1105★
REFORM JUDAISM
Union of American Hebrew Congregations
838 Fifth Ave.
New York, NY 10021

One of the oldest congregations in America was the Sephardic congregation, Beth Elohim, in Charleston. In the 1820s, some of its younger members began to petition for reform. They wanted some English added for those who spoke no Hebrew. Rejected, they withdrew and in 1824 organized the Reform Society of Israelites, led by Isaac Harby. This effort was but the first of many that were to disturb Israel-in-America through the nineteenth century.

Reform was already a powerful movement in Germany, where educated Jews could reconcile their learning and religious heritage only by removing anachronisms and thoroughly modernizing Jewish thought and life. Ceremonial laws and many practices such as covering the head during worship were discarded as outdated cultural accretions. An openness to the general religious community was advocated.

The leader around whom the various reform efforts coalesced was Rabbi Isaac Wise. The Bohemian-born Wise came to America in 1846 and settled in Albany, New York. Eight years later, he moved to Cincinnati, where his career paralleled the growth in size and status of the German Jewish community. He immediately began to advocate reform. He founded a periodical, *The Israelite*, to oppose the Orthodox periodical *Occident* founded by Isaac

Leeser. In 1857 he published his revised prayer book in both Hebrew and German. He began the *Deborah*, a German-language periodical. He traveled extensively around the country, spreading his ideas and organizing synagogues.

In 1875, Wise founded the Union of American Hebrew Congregations with headquarters in Cincinnati. Two years later its education center, Hebrew Union College, was established. In 1889 the rabbinical structure, the Central Conference of American Rabbis, with Wise as president, was formed.

During the nineteenth century, Cincinnati was a center for German Jews. In the twentieth century, New York has become the Jewish center of the United States. The extension of Judaism in New York beyond its meager German Jewish base was reflected in the founding in 1922 of the Jewish Institute of Religion (now the New York Campus of Hebrew Union College) and the movement in 1951 of the Union to headquarters on Fifth Avenue. Reform activities now largely originate out of the building popularly called the "House of Living Judaism."

Membership: In 1980 there were approximately 715 congregations and 1,200,000 affiliated members.

Educational facilities: Hebrew Union College, Cincinnati, Ohio There are HUC campuses in New York City, Los Angeles, and Jerusalem.

Periodicals: *Journal of Reform Judaism*, 21 E. 40th Street, New York, NY 10016; *Reform Judaism*, 838 5th Avenue, New York, NY 10021.

Sources: W. Gunther Plaut, *The Rise of Reform Judaism*. New York: World Union for Progressive Judaism, 1963; *Reform Judaism*. Cincinnati, OH: Hebrew Union College Press, 1949; Bertram Wallace Korn, *Retrospect and Prospect*. New York: The Central Conference of American Rabbis, 1965; *An Intimate Portrait of the Union of American Hebrew Congregations--A Centennial Documentary*. Cincinnati: The American Jewish Archives, 1973; Frederic A. Doppelt and David Polish, *A Guide for Reform Jews*. The Authors, 1957; Jacob R. Marcus, *Israel Jacobson*. Cincinnati, OH: Hebrew Union College Press, 1972.

★1106★
ORTHODOX JUDAISM
% Rabbinical Council of America
1250 Broadway, Suite 807
New York, NY 10001

The earliest divisions in American Judaism were linguistic. They came about as various national groups settled in America. While all professed a similar Old World form of faith, the groups were differentiated by peculiarities of the various national cultures. Orthodox Judaism remains one of the major facets of the American Jewish experience.

Orthodox Jews are distinctive within the Jewish community in their Old World practices: strict keeping of the Sabbath, kosher food laws and special attention to tradition, the keeping of the exact forms of their elders. The learning and use of Hebrew is emphasized.

In the process of Americanization (and the demand for English in the service), and with the importation of German-based Reform Judaism, champions of Orthodoxy, such as Rabbi Isaac Leeser of the Mikveh Israel Congregation, arose. Orthodoxy is, in a real sense, an American product, arising as a tradition-affirming segment of Judaism in reaction to the Reform movement. Orthodoxy was also the poorest. The Orthodox scattered into urban centers around the country. Thus Orthodoxy, while continuing the much older traditions of European Judaism, only formalized an organization at the end of the nineteenth century.

Preliminary efforts at cooperative endeavor began among Orthodox adherents in the 1880s, in reaction to Reform activities. In 1898 the Union of Orthodox Jewish Congregations of America was formed. Only two years earlier, the first rabbinical school, the Rabbi Elchanan Theological Seminary (now Yeshiva University) had been established. In 1902, the Union of Orthodox Rabbis was formed by the Eastern European rabbis, who had come to control the congregational association. The English-speaking rabbis retained control of the seminary, which grew slowly as the number of English-speaking Orthodox Jews grew. In 1935, the English-speaking rabbis formed the Rabbinical Council of America. Thus Orthodox Jews are served by one congregational and two rabbinical associations.

Publishing has been a major activity in the Orthodox community ever since Leeser began in his teens to write a defense of Judaism and in 1843 to publish his prominent periodical, the Occident and Jewish Advocate. Today, the Rabbinical Council publishes two quarterlies, Tradition, in English, and Hadorom, in Hebrew. Jewish Life is published by the Union of Orthodox Congregations. A second Orthodox school, the Hebrew Theological College in Chicago, was founded in 1922.

Following the common Jewish pattern, Orthodox Jewish congregations are independent and autonomous, and both rabbis and congregations freely associate in the various associations.

Membership: In 1980 there were an estimated 1,000,000 Orthodox Jews in the United States. The Union of Orthodox Jewish Congregations reported 1,000-member congregations.

Educational facilities: Yeshiva University, New York City, New York; Hebrew Theological College, Chicago, Illinois; Isaac Elchanan Theological Seminary, New York City, New York; Ner Israel Rabbinical College, Baltimore, Maryland; Hayin Berlin, New York City, New York.

Periodicals: *Jewish Life*, 45 W. 36th St., New York, NY 10018; *Tradition*, 1250 Broadway, Suite 802, New York, NY 10001.

Sources: Hutchins Hapgood, *The Spirit of the Ghetto*. New York: Schocken Books, 1966; Egon Mayer, *From Suburb to Shtetl*. Philadelphia: Temple University Press, 1979; Elkanah Schwartz, *American Life: Shtetl Style*. New York; Jonathan David, 1967.

Hassidism

★1107★
BLUZHEVER HASIDISM
Belzer Bet Midrash
662 Eastern Pkwy.
Brooklyn, NY 11213

Shapira is an outstanding Polish Hasidic family by which several dynasties were established in the nineteenth century. One was established at Bluzhever. The present Rebbe in Williamsburg is a descendant of Rabbi Elimelekh Shapira of Dinov. He survived the Holocaust; the American Army arrived at the concentration camp just before he was due to be executed.

Membership: Not reported.

★1108★
BOBOV HASIDISM
℅ Rabbi Solomon Halberstamm
Yeshiva Bnai Zion
4909 15th St.
Brooklyn, NY 11219

The Halberstamm family has contributed to the formation of several Hasidic groups. The Bobov dynasty was founded in the nineteenth century by Rabbi Benzion Halberstam. He was a noted composer and his "niggun" (melody), "Yah-Ribbon" ("God of the world"), is still chanted on Sabbath evenings. The Bobov are known for their musical creativity. Under Rabbi Benzion's leadership, Hasidic education spread throughout Galicia in the Carpathian Mountain region of Southern Poland. Rabbi Benzion actively resisted the Nazis and was murdered for his efforts.

He was succeeded by his son, Rabbi Solomon Halbertstamm (b. 1908), who escaped to the United States. Settling in Brooklyn, he built the Yeshiva Kedushat Zion. Kiryat Bobov (Bobov City) is being built in Queens. In 1959 he founded Bobov, a Hasidic town near Bat Yam, Israel and established a Yeshiva Bnei Ziyyon near Jerusalem.

Membership: Not reported.

★1109★
BOSTONER HASIDISM
℅ New England Chasidic Center
1710 Beacon St.
Brookline, MA 02146

The Horowitz family has been a prominent Jewish family for many centuries, producing numerous rabbis. It was frequently divided between those supporting and those opposing Hasidism. Among the first Hasidic rebbes in the United States was Grand Rabbi Pinchas D. Horowitz, who settled in Boston around 1920. He came from that branch of the family which had settled in Jerusalem several generations earlier. The lineage is carried on by descendants, who have centers in Brookline, Massachusetts and Brooklyn, New York. The Brookline center has become well known as a center for young Jews exploring their heritage through Hasidism. The center is led by Rabbis Meier Horowitz and Levi Horowitz.

Membership: Not reported. There are two centers.

Sources: Zmiros Shabbos and Yon Tov, *From the Rebbe's Table.* Brookline, MA: New England Chasidic Center, 1983.

★1110★
BRATSLAV HASIDISM
℅ Rabbi Leo Rosenfeld
864 44th St.
Brooklyn, NY 11219

Nachman of Bratslav (1772-1810) was a Ukrainian great-grandson of Baal Shem Tov. He became known, even as a child, for his asceticism. After he made a trip to the Holy Land, a group formed around him. He died at an early age, thirty-eight, and as he passed away he was heard to say, "My light will glow till the days of the Messiah." His followers interpreted his statement to mean that they would never need another rebbe. Unique in Hasidism without a living rebbe, the Bratslav are referred to by other Hasidic groups as the "dead Hasidim."

The main synagogue of the Bratslav is in Jerusalem and is headed by the Rosh Beth, who, though not a rebbe, is the spiritual leader. Emphasis in the movement is on utter simplicity and warmth of feeling. Prayer is a major activity. Teachings are found in the thirteen stories of Rebbe Nachman which emphasize that the trials of life are to be seen as preludes to new soarings of the spirit.

In Brooklyn, the Bratslav group is headed by Rabbis Leo Rosenfeld and Gedaliah Freer, who have gathered followers of the tradition primarily from young Orthodox Jews attracted to the Hasidic traditions. Through the Breslov Research Institute, attempts have been made to promote studies based on Rabbi Nachman's teachings and to translate his writings into English.

Membership: Not reported.

Sources: Arthur Green, *Tormented Master.* New York: Schrocken Books, 1979; Rabbi Nachman, *Azamra!.* Brooklyn, NY: Breslov Research Institute, 1984; Gedaliah Freer, *Rabbi Nachman's Foundation.* New York: OHR MiBRESLOV, 1976;Gedaliah Freer, *Rabbi Nachman's Fire.* New York: Hermon Press, 1972.

★1111★
CHERNOBYL HASIDISM
℅ Rabbi Israel Jacob Twersky
1520 49th St.
Brooklyn, NY 11232

The Twersky family has given the world of Hasidism several dynasties. The oldest began with Menahem Nahum ben Zevi (1730-1787) of Chernobyl in the Ukraine, a contemporary of the Baal Shem Tov. Never a zaddik himself, he helped the initial spread of Hasidism in the Ukraine and laid stress on purification of moral attributes to make one worthy of the Torah. His son, Mordecai Twersky (1770-1837), was the first zaddik and real founder of the Chernobyl dynasty. Mordecai had eight sons. Aaron Twersky, the eldest, continued the dynasty, and the rest founded their own dynasties, which dominated Russian Ukrainian Jewry in the nineteeth century. Members came to the United States after the Russian Revolution. Three Hasidic groups headed by members of the Twersky family currently function in the United States.

Chernobyl Hasidism is represented in the United States by Rabbi Israel Jacob Twersky.

Membership: Not reported.

★1112★
KLAUSENBURG HASIDISM
Current address not obtained for this edition.

A branch of the Halberstamm family founded the dynasty at Klausenburg-Sandz in the nineteenth century. Rabbi Zevi Halberstamm was killed in the Holocaust. His son, Rabbi Yekutiel Jehudah Halberstamm settled in the United States, but in 1956 migrated to Israel and founded Shikun Kiryat Zanz near Nathania, which attained a population of 2,000. Kiryat Zanz has its own yeshiva, a school for girls, a kindergarten and a diamond factory. Only a remnant of the Klausenburg Hasidim remains in Williamsburg, a section of Brooklyn. In Montreal, there is a Metivta (Yeshiva) under the direction of Rabbi Samuel Undsorfer.

Membership: Not reported.

★1113★
LUBAVITCH HASIDISM
770 Eastern Pkwy.
Brooklyn, NY 11213

By far the largest of the Hasidic bodies is the Lubavitch. The arrival of its rebbe, Rabbi Joseph Isaac Schneersohn, in New York in 1940 signaled the rebirth of Hasidism in the New World. Compared with most Hasidic groups, it is open and evangelistic toward its non-Hasidic Jewish neighbors, and has established Lubavitch Hasidism as a national body. Lubavitch Hasidism began in 1773 in Lithuania under the leadership of Rabbi Schneur Zalman (1745-1813), a child prodigy and student of Rabbi Dov Baer, an outstanding Hasidic scholar. Upon Dov Baer's death in 1772, Rabbi Zalman was sent to Lithuania as a Hasidic missionary. He spent the rest of his life in Lithuania and Russia, teaching and writing. His works include the *Likutic Amarian*, better known as the *Tanya*, the essential text of the *Chabad*, as his teachings became known.

A second Rabbi Dov Baer (1773-1827), the Mittler Rebbe, the son of Rabbi Zalman, succeeded as leader of the Chabad. After his father's death, he settled in Lubavitch in White Russia, the town which gave the dynasty its name. Rabbi Dov Baer was succceeded in turn by Rabbi Menachem Mendel Schneersohn (1789-1866), son of Rabbi Zalman's daughter; Rabbi Samuel Schneersohn (1834-1882), Rabbi Mendel's son; Rabbi Sholom Dov Baer (1860-1920), Rabbi Samuel's son, and Rabbi Joseph Isaac Schneersohn (1880-1950), the son and secretary of Rabbi Dov Baer, who brought the movement to America.

The Lubavitch work actually began in the mid-1920s when Rabbi Schneersohn formed the Agudas Chassidas Chabad of the United States of America and Canada. He visited the United States in 1929, during which time he met with President Herbert Hoover. He had settled in Warsaw after World War 1. When his life was threatened by Hitler's legions, the Rebbe was finally persuaded to migrate to the United States.

Chabad is a combination of the initials of "Chochmah," "Binah," and "Daath," the highest virtues in the Kabbalistic system. Daath (knowledge), Chochmah (wisdom)and Binah (intelligence) are three sephirot on the Kabbalistic tree. Faith and belief in God share an insistence on intellectual study and understanding of religious truth. The emphasis on truth has made education basic to the Lubavitch program. The love of one's fellow Jew (Ahavas Yisroel) is a second emphasis of Lubavitch to an openness to the entire Jewish community,in contrast to most other Hasidim, who generally hold a low opinion of their lax, nonpracticing brethren.

Music and dancing are important to Lubavitcher life. Dancing is the bodily manifestation of inward joy. It is always done by males separately from females, as mixed dancing is prohibited by Jewish law. There are two varieties: circle dancing, in which the hand is placed on the shoulder of the brother in front, and rikkud, jumping and skipping up and down. Dancing is a vital part of the festivals, including Purim and the Hasidic historic anniversaries.

Headquarters of the Lubavitcher Rebbe, Rabbi Menachem Mendel Schneersohn (b. 1902), son-in-law of Rabbi Isaac Schneersohn, are in Brooklyn, where the Tomchoi T'mimim, the Lubavitcher Yeshiva, is located. A year after Rabbi Schneersohn arrived in the United States in 1941, he was placed in charge of the Merkos L'Inyone Chinuch, the educational arm of the Lubavitch movement; more than 67 educational institutions have since been founded. He also guided the development of Merkos Publication Society, the major publisher of Hasidic literature in the United States, and the Ezrat Pleitim Vesidurom, a relief organization in 56 cities across the United States.

Membership: Not reported.

Periodicals: *Talks and Tales*, 770 Eastern Parkway, Brooklyn, NY 11213; *The Uforatzto Journal*, Lubavitch Youth Organization, 770 Eastern Parkway, Brooklyn, NY 11213.

Sources: *Challenge*. London: Lubavitch Foundation of Great Britain, 1970; Naftali Hertz Ehrmann, *The Rav*. New York: Feldheim Publishers, 1977; Mal Warshaw, *Tradition, Orthodox Jewish Life in America*. New York: Schrocken, 1976; Nissan Mindel, *Rabbi Schneur Zalman of Ladi*. Brooklyn, NY: Chabad Research Center, Kehot Publication Society, 1973; M. M. Schneerson, *Letters by the Lubavitcher Rebbe*. Brooklyn, NY: Kehot Publication Society, 1979.

★1114★
MONASTRITSH HASIDISM
Current address not obtained for this edition.

The Rabinowicz family has one of the most outstanding Hasidic lineages and is the source of several dynasties. The founder of the dynasty was Jacob Isaac Rabinowicz (1765-1814). As a wandering preacher, he was guided to Rabbi Jacob Isaac Horwitz, the father of Polish Hasidism, known for his psychic abilities and often referred to as the "sad-eyed Seer of Lubin." The Seer told Jacob Isaac that he was a reincarnation of Patriarch Jacob Mordecai and Rabbi Jacob ben Meir Tam (a twelfth-century scholar). He quickly became known as a Talmudic scholar and a seeker of justice. He gradually separated from the seer and established himself at Przysucha.

The emphasis of Jacob Isaac was introspection, aimed at making an individual a good Jew. He thought it essential that one neither lies to himself nor lives in superficiality. The highest pinnacle of the love of God could be acquired only by painstaking personal striving. He insisted on "Kavanah," concentration and devotion in prayer.

Przysucha services were not always at the proper times; it was better to pray late than to pray without Kavanah. Action and service, charity and loving kindness were seen as the measures of sincerity.

The Biala dynasty was founded by Rabbi Isaac Jacob Rabinowicz (1847-1905), a direct descendant of Jacob Isaac. Rabinowicz became known for his devotion to the Sabbath, a topic that fills most of his writings. The Biala tradition was passed to Rabbi Yechiel Joshua Rabinowicz (b. 1895). He survived the Nazis by fleeing to Siberia, then in 1947 he settled in Israel. He was known as a miracle worker and he established a Yeshiva (a school for Talmudic study) at B'nai Brak. Rabbi Nathan David Rabinowicz heads the Biala in London.

The Monastritsh Hasidic tradition was brought to the United States in the early 1920s in the wave of Russian Jewish migration by Rebbe Joshua Hershal Rabinowicz (1860-1938). Monastyrshchina is a town west of Minsk in present-day Byelorussia.

Membership: Not reported.

★1115★
NOVOMINSK HASIDISM
% Rabbi Nahum M. Perlow
1569 47th St.
Brooklyn, NY 11220

The Novominsk dynasty was founded by Jacob Perlow (1847- 1902) who as a young rabbi was advised to "go to Poland, raise a family and establish a dynasty." He settled at Minsk-Mazowiech, not far from Warsaw. His fame and following grew, and he built a Yeshiva and a large synagogue. Upon his death, his son, Alter Yisrael Shimon Perlow (1874-1933), succeeded him. Known for his intensity of prayer and passion while preaching, the young rabbi moved to Warsaw in 1917 and drew crowds to his Sunday discourses.

In 1925, Rabbi Yehuda Arye Perlow, brother of the Rebbe of Novominsk, arrived in New York and established the Novominsk dynasty. The current rebbe is Rabbi Nahum Perlow, son of A.Y.S. Perlow, who had accompanied his father from Poland.

Membership: Not reported.

★1116★
SATMAR HASIDISM
% Congregation Y L D'Satmar
152 Rodney
Brooklyn, NY 11220

The Satmar Hasidic tradition is one of the newest, having been founded by Rebbe Yoel Teitelbaum (b.1886) in the first decade of the twentieth century. Following the death of his father in 1904, Yoel, the second son, moved from Sighet, his birthplace, and founded his own group at Satmar in Northeast Hungary. Zionism was becoming a growing force in European Jewry in these formative years of Satmar, and from the yeshiva he had established at Orshovah, Yoel began actively to oppose Zionism. After the unexpected death of Rebbe Yoel's brother in 1926, the leadership of the dynasty passed to Yoel instead of to new Rebbe of Sighet. Yoel's prestige grew steadily until 1944, when the Holocaust hit Hungary. The Rebbe was saved, ironically, by his Zionist enemies, and he escaped to Switzerland.

In 1946 Rebbe Yoel settled in Williamsburg in Brooklyn with the few surivors of the Holocaust. The Congregation Yetev Lev D'Satmar, established in 1948, had 860 members by 1961. Many of these were converts. The anti-Zionist stand remains the distinctive feature of Satmar Hasidism. The Natorei Karta (Guardians of the City), an ultra-orthodox anti-Zionist group in Jerusalem, has placed itself under Satmar's care. Members believe that since only the Messiah can re-establish Israel, the attempt to set up a Jewish state is blasphemy. In 1965, Amram Blau, the leader of the Natorei Karta, was relieved of his position for marrying a divorced convert from Catholicism.

Headquarters of the Satmar movement are in Brooklyn, where there are a number of groups. They have purchased land at Monroe, New York, for the establishment of a Satmar Community. Satmar groups are also found in Jerusalem and B'nai Brak, Israel; Antwerp, Belgium; London, england; Montreal, Quebec, Canada; Montevideo, Uruguay; Sao Paulo, Brazil; and Buenos Aires; Argentina. Rebbe Yoel still heads the group though, since his stroke in 1968, he has not been as active as before.

Membership: Not reported. In the early 1970s there were approximately 1,500 members of the group.

Sources: Israel Rubin, *Satmar, An Island in the City*. Chicago: Quadrangle Books, 1972; Harry Gersh and Sam Miller, "Satmar in Brooklyn" in *Commentary* vol. 28 (1959) pp. 31-41.

★1117★
SIGHET HASIDISM
152 Hewes St.
Brooklyn, NY 11211

Rebbe Moses Teitelbaum of Ughely, Hungary, was the founder of the Teitelbaum Hasidic dynasty. The third in the succession, Rebbe Zalmen Leib Teitelbaum, established the center of the work at Sighet (now in northern Rumania). Until 1926, Sighet was a prominent Hasidic center, but the sudden death of Rebbe Hayin Hersch Teitelbaum in that year left his fourteen-year-old son, Zalmen Leib Teitelbaum, as heir to the succession. Since Hasidism is built on the charisma of the rebbe, the Sighet center never regained its former authority. After the Holocaust, the Sighet Hasidic community was disrupted. Finally, it was re-established in Zenta,

Yugoslavia by Rebbe Zalmen Leib's brother, Rebbe Moses Teitelbaum. Rebbe Moses moved to the United States and now leads the survivng members from Brooklyn.

Membership: Not reported.

★1118★
SKVER HASIDISM
Skverer Town
New Square, NY 10977

Isaac Twersky (1812-1895), seventh son of Mordecai Twersky, settled at Skver, southwest of Kiev, and began a new dynasty in the 1830s. Members of the Skver dynasty came to the United States after World War II. In 1963, they purchased more than one hundred and thirty acres in Spring Valley, Rockland County, New York, when they built the village of New Square (supposed to be New Skver, but erroneously recorded at the courthouse). Approximately 700 members live there; others remain in Williamsburg. The Rebbe Jacob Joseph Twersky lives at New Square. The building of the isolated village symbolizes the thrust of the Skver faith: the keeping of the law and no compromise with the modern world. Residents of New Square commute regularly to New York as a place of employment. Nonresident Skver Hasidism is in a thirty-family, self-contained community at nearby Monsey, New York. Rebbe Twersky's son-in-law, Rabbi Mordecai Hagar Twersky, is head of the second group.

Membership: Not reported.

Sources: Joan Gould, "A Village of Slaves to the Torah'" in *The Jewish Digest* (October 1967) pp. 49-52.

★1119★
STOLIN HASIDISM
Stolin Bet Midrash
1818 54th St.
Brooklyn, NY 11211

Possibly the first zaddik to reach the United States was Rabbi Jacob (d. 1946), the son of Rabbi Israel of Stolin. During his life there were four centers for prayer (stieblech) in Brooklyn and one in Detroit. Presently, the headquarters are in Boro Park in Brooklyn.

Membership: Not reported.

★1120★
TALNOYE (TALNER) HASIDISM
Talner Beth David
64 Corey Rd.
Brookline, MA 02146

David Twersky (1808-1882), sixth son of Mordecai Twersky, established his dynasty at Talnoye, south of Kiev in Russia. It is said that he lived luxuriously and sat upon a silver throne with the words, "King David of

Israel lives forever." In the United States, Rabbi Alexander Twersky carries on the tradition.

Membership: Not reported.

Sources: Issac Even, "Chasidism in the New World" in *Communal Register*. New York: Kelillah, 1918. pp. 341-46.

★1121★
WORK OF THE CHARIOT
(Defunct)

The Work of the Chariot was a Jewish mystical group active during the 1970s which made its main objective the translation, publication, and distribution of Jewish, Christian, and Islamic mystical material, particularly Hasidic/Kabbalistic source materials. The work was centered in three groups which met to practice the principles of practical mysticsm. Two were in Los Angeles and one in Hollywood. Affiliate groups were located in England and Israel, and a number of distinguished scholars served as consultants in the translation work.

The Work of the Chariot published its own translation of Kabbalistic texts such as the *Book of Formation*, the *Book of Splendor* and the *Tree of Life* by Rabbi Yitzaq Luria, La'Ari. The Group was heavily Kabbalistic. The Chariot of God of Ezekiel is a major theme in Kabbalistic literature. Its authors attempted to know not the unknowable Ein Soph, but the Throne of God on its Chariot. Such knowledge is one of the "secrets" of God, to be obtained by theurgic (magical) means.

Sources: *Book of Names*. Hollywood, CA: Work of the Chariot, 1971; *Work of the Chariot, Introduction*. Hollywood, CA: Work of the Chariot, 1971; *Book of Formation (Sepher Yetzirah), The Letters of Our Father Abraham*. Hollywood, CA: Work of the Chariot, 1971; *Work of the Chariot, Ezekiel, Isaiah, II Kings*. Hollywood, CA: Work of the Chariot, 1971.

Black Judaism

★1122★
CHURCH OF GOD (BLACK JEWS)
Current address not obtained for this edition.

The Church of God (Black Jews) was founded in the early twentieth century by Prophet F. S. Cherry, who claimed to have had a vision calling him to his office as prophet. He was sent to America and began the church in Philadelphia. A self-educated man, Prophet Cherry became conversant in both Hebrew and Yiddish. He became famous for his homiletic abilities, colloquialisms, and biting slang.

The Church of God is open only to black people, who are identified with the Jews of the Bible. White Jews are viewed as frauds and interlopers. The church does not use the term synagogue, the place of worship of the white Jews (Rev. 3:9). The church teaches that Jesus was a black man. The first men were also black, the first white man being Gehazi, who received his whiteness as a curse (11 Kings 5: 27). The white man continued to mix with the black people, and the yellow race resulted. Esau was the first red man (Gen. 25:25). God is, of course, black. Black people sprang from Jacob.

The New Year begins with Passover in April. Saturday is the true Sabbath. Speaking in tongues is considered nonsense. Eating pork, divorce, taking photographs, and observing Christian holidays are forbidden. The end of the period that started with creation is approaching, and the Black Jews will return in 2000 A.D. to institute the millennium.

Membership: Not reported.

★1123★

CHURCH OF GOD AND SAINTS OF CHRIST
Box 187
Portsmouth, VA 23704

Elder William S. Crowdy, a black cook on the Sante Fe Railroad, claimed to have a vision from God calling him to lead his people to the true religion. He left his job and founded the Church of God and Saints of Christ in 1896 at Lawrence, Kansas. In 1900, he moved to Philadelphia, and the first annual assembly was held. Crowdy died in 1908, and Joseph N. Crowdy and William H. Plummer succeeded him as bishops. Joseph N. Crowdy died in 1917, the same year that the headquarters were moved to Bellville, Virginia, where the church had purchased a large farm. In 1931, Calvin S. Skinner, the last leader appointed by the founder, became bishop, but he lived only three months thereafter. He passed the leadership to Howard Z. Plummer, who held it for many years.

The doctrine of the Church of God is a complicated mixture of Judaism, Christianity and black nationalism. Members are accepted into the church by repentance, baptism by immersion, confession of faith in Christ Jesus, receiving communion of unleavened bread and water, having their feet washed by the elder, and agreeing to keep the Ten Commandments. They must also have been taught how to pray according to Matthew 6:9-13, and they must have been breathed upon with a holy kiss. They believe that black people are the descendants of the ten lost tribes of Israel. They believe in keeping the Ten Commandments and adhering literally to the teachings of both the Old and New testaments as positive guides to salvation., The church observes the Jewish Sabbath and the use of corresponding Hebrew names. The church is a strong advocate of temperance.

The church is headed by its bishop and prophet who is divinely called to his office. He is believed to be in direct communion with God, to utter prophecies, and to perform miracles. When a prophet dies, the office remains vacant until a new call occurs. The prophet presides over the executive board of twelve ordained elders. The church is divided into district, annual, and general assemblies. There are four orders of the ministry: bishops, missionaries, ordained ministers, and nonordained ministers. Deacons care for the temporal affairs of the church. Each local church bears the denominational name and is numbered according to its appearance in the state. The church at Bellville is communalistic, but other churches are not. The Daughters of Jerusalem and Sisters of Mercy is a women's organization whose duty is to look for straying members, to help the sick and needy, and to care for visitors from other local churches.

Membership: Not reported. At last report (1959) there were 217 churches and 38,217 members. There are affiliated congregations in Jamaica.

Educational facilities: Bellville Industrial Institute, Bellville, Virginia.

Sources: Arthur Huff Fauset, *Black Gods of the Metropolis.* Philadelphia: University of Pennsylvania Press, 1944.

★1124★

COMMANDMENT KEEPERS CONGREGATION OF THE LIVING GOD
% Rabbi David M. Dore
1 E. 123rd St.
New York, NY 10035

The Commandment Keepers Congregation of the Living God emerged among West Indian blacks who migrated to Harlem. The group began with the Beth B'nai Abraham congregation founded in 1924 by Arnold Josiah Ford, an early black nationalist and leader in the Universal Negro Improvement Association founded by Marcus Garvey. Ford had repudiated Christianity, adopted Judaism, and learned Hebrew. During the years after the congregation began, Ford met Arthur Wentworth Matthew (1892-1973). Matthew was born in Lagos, West Africa, in 1892. His family moved to St. Kitts in the British West Indies and then, in 1911, to New York. Matthew became a minister in the Church of the Living God, the Pillar and Ground of Truth, a black pentecostal church which had endorsed the U.N.I.A. Then in 1919, with eight other men, he organized his own group, the Commandment Keepers: Holy Church of the Living God, over which he became bishop. In Harlem, he had met white Jews for the first time and in the 1920s came to know A. J. Ford. Possibly from Ford, Matthew began to learn Orthodox Judaism and Hebrew and to acquire ritual materials.

Both also learned of the Falashas, the black Jews of Ethiopia, and began to identify with them. In 1930, Ford's congregation ran into financial trouble. Ford turned over the membership to Matthew's care and left for Ethiopia where he spent the rest of his life. The identification with Ethiopia merely increased through the years. In 1935, when Haile Selassie was crowned emperor, Matthew declared himself the Falashas in America and claimed credentials from Haile Selassie.

The Commandment Keepers believe that the black men are really the Ethiopian Falashas and the Biblical Hebrews who had been stripped of the knowledge of their name and religion during the slavery era. It is impossible for a a black man to conceive of himself as a "Negro" and retain anything but slave mentality. With other black Jews, adherents believe the biblical patriarchs to have been black. Christianity is rejected as the religion of the Gentiles or whites.

An attempt has been made to align the Commandment Keepers with Orthodox Jewish practice. Hebrew is taught and revered as a sacred language. The Jewish holidays are kept, and the Sabbath services are held on Friday evenings and Saturday mornings and afternoons. Kosher food laws are kept. An Ethiopian Hebrew Rabbinical college trains leaders in Jewish history, the Mishnah, Josephus, the Talmud, and legalism. Elements of Christianity are retained--footwashing, healing, and the gospel hymns. Services are free of what Matthew terms "niggeritions," the loud emotionalism of the holiness groups.

Matthew also taught Kabbalistic Science, a practice derived from conjuring, the folk magic of Southern blacks. By conjuring, Matthew believed that he could heal and create changes in situations. The conjuring is worked through four angels. In order to get results, one must call upon the right angel.

Matthew was succeeded by his grandson, David M. Dore, a graduate of Yeshiva University.

Membership: Not reported. In the early 1970s there were a reported 3,000 members in several congregations in the New York metropolitan area and the Northeast; 300 members attended the synagogue on East 123rd Street in New York City.

Sources: Howard M. Brotz, *The Black Jews of Harlem.* New York: Schocken Books, 1970; Albert Ehrman, "The Commandment Keepers: A Negro Jewish Cult in America Today" in *Judaism* vol. 8, no. 3 (Summer 1959) pp. 266-70.

★1125★
HOUSE OF JUDAH
Wetumpka, AL 36092

The House of Judah is a small Black Israelite group founded in 1965 by Prophet William A. Lewis. Alabama-born Lewis was converted to his black Jewish beliefs (which are similar to those of the Church of God and

Saints of Christ) from a street preacher in Chicago in the 1960s. Throughout the decade he gathered a small following out of a storefront on the southside and in 1971 moved the group to a twenty-two-acre tract near Grand Junction, Michigan. The group lived quietly and little noticed until 1983 when a young boy in the group was beaten to death. The incident focused attention on the group for its advocacy of corporal punishment. The mother of the boy was sentenced to prison for manslaughter. By 1985 the group had resettled in Alabama.

The House of Judah teaches that the Old Testament Jews were black, being derived from Jacob and his son Judah, who were black (Jeremiah 14:2). Both Solomon and Jesus were black. Jerusalem, not Africa, is the black man's land. The white Jew is the devil (Rev. 2:9); he occupies the black man's land but will soon be driven out. The House of Judah awaits a deliverer, whom God will send to take the black man from the U.S.A. to Jerusalem. He will be a second Moses to lead his people to the promised land. The group lives communally.

Membership: In 1985 there were approximately 80 members living on the farm in rural Alabama. There is only one center.

Sources: Kate De Smet, "Return to the House of Judah" in *Michigan, the Magazine of the Detroit News*, July 21, 1985.

★1126★
ORIGINAL HEBREW ISRAELITE NATION
% Communicators Press
Box 19504
Chicago, IL 60649

The Black Israelites (members of the Original Hebrew Israelite Nation) emerged in Chicago in the 1960s around Ben Ammi Carter (born G. Parker), a black man who had studied Judaism with a rabbi, and Shaleah Ben-Israel. To the Black Jewish ideas (which were espoused by several groups in Chicago at this time) Carter and Ben-Israel added the concept of Black Zionism and held out the vision of a return to the Holy Land for their members. From headquarters at the A-Beta Cultural Center on Chicago's south side, they began to gather followers. The somewhat anonymous group came into prominence in the late 1960s as a result of their attempts to migrate to Africa and then to Israel. The group mo ved first to Liberia, seen as analogous to the Hebrew children's wandering in the desert for forty years to throw off the effects of slavery. Soon after their arrival, they approached the Israeli ambassador about a further move to Israel. They were unable to negotiate the move to Israel for members in Liberia. In 1968 Carter and 38 members from Chicago flew directly to Israel. Given temporary sanction and work permits, the group from Liberia joined them. By 1971, when strict immigration restrictions were imposed upon members of the group, over 300 had migrated. Other members of the group continued to arrive, however, using tourist visas which were destroyed upon moving into the colony (which had been established at Dimona). By 1980 between 1,500 and 2,000 had settled in Israel.

The Black Israelites feel they are descendants of the ten lost tribes of Israel and thus Jews by birth. They celebrate the Jewish rituals and keep the Sabbath. However, they are distinguished from traditional Jews by their practice of polygamy (a maximum of seven wives is allowed) and their abandonment of the synagogue structure.

The group is currently headed by Carter, the chief rabbi. He is assisted by a divine council of twelve princes (for each of the twelve ancient tribes of Israel). During the early 1980s, the American following was under the direction of Prince Asiel Ben Israel. Under the princes are seven ministers responsible for providing education, distribution of food, clothing and shelter, economics, transportation, sports, recreation and entertainment, life preservation, and sanitation.

In Israel, the group lives communally. According to most reports, the group (due to lack of legal status), lives under harsh conditions and the continual threat of mass deportation. They have been unable to obtain necessary additional housing (for those many members who immigrated illegally) and the children are not allowed to attend public schools. Within Israel, the group has asked for land to settle in order to create their own community.

Membership: Not reported. In 1980 there were an estimated 1,500 members in Israel (900 at Dimona, 400 at Arad, 100 at Mitzpe Ramon, and 100 at Eilat) and 3,000 living in the United States, scattered in black communities in urban centers such as Chicago, Atlanta, Georgia, and Washington, D.C.

Remarks: In the wake of continuous immigration problems with the State of Israel during the 1970s, the group gained new prominence in 1980 when members in the United States were charged with the systematic theft of money, credit cards, and blank airline tickets, all of which were being used to support the group and assist members in their movement to Israel.

Sources: Ben Ammi Carter, *God, the Black Man, and Truth*. Chicago: The Communicators Press, 1982; Shaleak Ben Yehuda, *Black Hebrew Israelites from America to the Promised Land*. New York: Vantage Press, 1975; Israel J. Gerber, *The Heritage Seekers*. Middle Village, NY: Jonathan David Publishers, 1977; Thomas Whitfield, *From Night to Sunlight*. Nashville, TN: Broadman Press, 1980; H. Bashford Fish, "Trouble Among the Children of the Prophets" in *The Washington Post Magazine* (February 7, 1982).

★1127★
PAN AFRICAN ORTHODOX CHRISTIAN CHURCH
13535 Livernois
Detroit, MI 48238

The Pan African Orthodox Christian Church dates to 1953 when 300 members of St. Mark's Presbyterian Church in Detroit walked out and formed Central Congregational Church. In 1957 they moved into facilities at 7625 Linwood in Detroit and over the next decade became intensely involved in community issues, especially those impinging upon the black community. In 1967, the church's pastor, Albert B. Cleage, Jr. preached what has become a famous sermon calling for a new black theology and a black church to articulate it. An eighteen-foot painting of a black Madonna was unveiled and the Black Christian Nationalist Movement was launched. The church building became known as the Shrine of the Black Madonna 1. In 1970 a book store and cultural center were opened. Cleage changed his name to Jaramogi Abebe Agyeman.

The Black Nationalist Creed, printed below, spells out a position which identifies the black man and the Hebrew Nation:

"I Believe that human society stands under the judgment of one God, revealed to all, and known by many names. His creative power is visible in the mysteries of the universe, in the revolutionary Holy Spirit which will not long permit men to endure injustice nor to wear the shackles of bondage, in the rage of the powerless when they struggle to be free, and in the violence and conflict which even now threaten to level the hills and the mountains.

"I Believe that Jesus, the Black Messiah, was a revolutionary leader, sent by God to rebuild the Black Nation Israel and to liberate Black People from powerlessness and from the oppression, brutality, and exploitation of the white gentile world.

"I Believe that the revolutionary spirit of God, embodied in the Black Messiah, is born anew in each generation and that Black Christian Nationalists constitute that living remnant of God's Chosen People in this day, and are charged by him with responsibility for the Liberation of Black People.

"I Believe that both my survival and my salvation depend upon my willingness to reject INDIVIDUALISM, and so I commit my life to the Liberation Struggle of Black people and accept the values, ethics, morals, and program of the Black Nation defined by that struggle and taught by the Black Christian Nationalist Movement."

During the 1970s the organization expanded significantly. Agyeman composed an ordination service and ordained eight ministers, who were given the title "Mwalimu,"

Swahili for "teacher." Agyemnan's own name means "liberator, blessed man, savior of the nation." Other congregations and centers were established in Detroit. In 1974 a shrine was opened in Atlanta, Georgia and in 1977 in Kalamazoo, MIchigan. Also in 1974, a BGN training program to prepare leaders for the liberation struggle of black people was begun.

Educational facilities: Not reported. In 1983 there were six congregations, four in Detroit, one in Kalamazoo, Michigan, and one in Atlanta, Georgia.

Sources: Hiley H. Ward, *Prophet of the Black Nation.* New York: Pilgrim Press, 1969; Albert B. Cleage, Jr., *The Black Messiah.* New York: Sheed and Ward, 1968; Albert E. Cleage, Jr., *Black Christian Nationalism: New Directions for the Black Church.* New York: William Morrow, 1972.

★1128★
RASTAFARIANS
Current address not obtained for this edition.

The Rastafarian Movement, a Jamaican black nationalist movement, grew out of a long history of fascination with Africa in general and Ethiopia in particular among the masses in Jamaica. The movement can be traced directly to the efforts of Marcus Garvey, founder of the Universal Negro Improvement Association, who, among other endeavors, promoted a steamship company that would provide transportation for blacks going back to Africa. In 1927 Garvey predicted the crowning of a black king in Africa as a sign that the redemption of black people from white oppression was near. The 1935 coronation of Haile Selassie as emperor of Ethiopia was seen as a fulfillment of Garvey's words.

Haile Selassie was born Ras Tafari Makonnen out of a lineage claimed to derive from the Queen of Sheba and King Solomon. He proclaimed his title as King of Kings, Lord of Lords, His Imperial Majesty the Conquering Lion of the Tribe of Judah. Elect of God. His name Haile Selassie means "Power of the Holy Trinity." Reading about the coronation, four ministers in Jamaica--Joseph Hibbert, Archibald Dunkley, Robert Hinds, and most prominently, Leonard Howell--saw the new emperor as not only the fulfillment of the Garveyite expectation, but also the completion of Biblical prophecies such as those in Revelation 5:2-5 and 19:16 which refer to the Lion of the Tribe of Judah and the King of Kings. The four, independently of each other, began to proclaim Haile Selassie the Messiah of the black people. Their first successes came in the slums of West Kingston, where they discovered each other and a movement began.

Howell began to proselytize around the island. He raised money by selling pictures of Haile Selassie and telling the buyers that they were passports back to Africa. He was arrested and sentenced to two years in jail for fraud. Upon his release he moved into the hill country jof St.

Catherine's parish and founded a commune, the Pinnacle, which, in spite of government attacks and several moves, became the center of the movement for the next two decades. At the Pinnacle, the smoking of ganga (marijuana) and the wearing of long hair curled to resemble a lion's mane (dread locks) became the marks of identification of the group.

As the Rastafarians matured, they adopted the perspectives of Black Judaism and identified the Hebrews of the Old Testament as black people. Their belief system was distinctly racial and they taught that the whites were inferior to the blacks. More extreme leaders saw whites as the enemies of blacks and believed that, in the near future, blacks will return to Africa and assume their rightful place in world leadership. Haile Selassie is believed to be the embodiment of God and, though no longer visible, he nevertheless still lives. Some Rastafarians believe Selassie is still secretly alive, though most see him as a disembodied spirit.

Relations with white culture have been tense, lived at the point of "dread," a term to describe the confrontation of a people struggling to regain a denied racial selfhood. Most Rastafarians are pacifists, though much support for the movement developed out of intense antiwhite feelings. Violence has been a part of the movement since the destruction of the Pinnacle, though it has been confined to individuals and loosely organized groups. One group, the Nyabingi Rastas, stand apart from most by their espousal of violence.

Rastafarians came to the United States in large numbers as part of the general migration of Jamaicans in the 1960s and 1970s. They have brought with them an image of violence, and frequent news reports have detailed murders committed by individuals identified as Rastafarians. Rastafarian spokespersons have only complained that many young Jamaican-Americans have adopted the outward appearance of Rastafarians (dread locks and ganga-smoking) without adopting Rastafarian beliefs and lifestyle.

A major aspect of Rastafarian life is the unique music developed as its expression. Reaggae, a form of rock music, became popular far beyond Rastafarian circles, and exponents such as Bob Marley and Peter Tosh became international stars. Reggae has immensely helped in the legitimization of Rastafarian life and ideals.

In Jamaica the Rastafarian Movement is divided into a number of organizations and factions, many of which have been brought into the Jamaican community in America. Surveys of American Rastafarians have yet to define the organization in the United States though individual Rastafarians may be found in black communities across America, most noticably Brooklyn, New York, Miami, Florida, and Chicago, Illinois.

Membership: There are an estimated 3,000-5,000 Rastafarians in the United States, though the figures are somewhat distorted by the large number of people who have adopted the outward appearance of Rastafarian life.

Periodicals: *Arise*, Creative Publishers, Ltd., 8 Waterloo Avenue, Kingston, Jamaica, West Indies; *Jahugliman*, c/o Carl Gayle, 19C Annette Cresent, Kingston 10, Jamaica, West Indies.

Sources: Leonard Barrett, *The Rastafarians*. Boston: Beacon Press, 1977; Joseph Owens, *Dread*. Kingston: Sangster, 1976; K. M. Williams, *The Rastafarians*. London: Ward Lock Educational, 1981.

★1129★
UNITED HEBREW CONGREGATION
Current address not obtained for this edition.

The United Hebrew Congregation was the name of about a half dozen congregations of black Jews which during the mid-1970s were centered upon the Ethiopian Hebrew Culture Center in Chicago, which were headed by Rabbi Naphtali Ben Israel. It was this group's belief that Ham's sons were black. Included were the Hebrews of which one reads in the Bible. Abraham came from Chaldea, and the ancient Chaldeans were black. The congregation members believe Solomon was black (Song of Solomon 1:5). Sabbath services were held on Saturday. No sign of their continuance into the 1980s has been found.

Membership: Not reported.

Miscellaneous Jewish Groups

★1130★
COMMUNITY OF MICAH (FABRENGEN)
(Defunct)

The Community of Micah was one of several radical, left-oriented groups which emerged from the wave of social consciousness in the late 1960s. Members attempt to relate all action to the goal of human liberation. A major concern has been the survival of Judaism, and the group has been involved in Jewish consciousness-raising. An urban communal structure, the community in 1972 attempted to establish Kibbutz Micah as an experiment in Jewish rural communal living in central Pennsylvania, but it did not survive.

The Community developed an active study program which included Hasidic literature (especially the books of Martin Buber), mysticism, yoga and radical Jewish politics. The group was disowned by the Washington (D.C.) Jewish Community in 1971. The Community published the *Voice of Micah* and other Jewish and political action material.

Sources: Arthur I. Waskow, *The Bush Is Burning*. New York: The Macmillan Company, 1971.

★1131★
HAVURAH MOVEMENT
National Havurot Coordinating Committee
250 W. 57th St., Suite 216
New York, NY 10019

During the 1960s, as part of the larger wave of communalism which swept America, a variety of primarily young Jews began to combine their exploration of Jewish roots with experiments in communal living. Havurot Shalom was one of the first such experiments. It was established as a traditional Jewish community in Boston in 1968. It was conceived as a core community around which a larger constituency would be oriented. It offered adult education courses in Torah, Hasidism, traditional arts such as challah baking, and more contemporary subjects.

At about the same time and in the years following, other havurot communities emerged within Jewish communities in such widely scattered locations as New York City; Phoenix, Arizona; Madison, Wisconsin; Ithaca, New York; Philadelphia; Washington, DC; Rochester, New York; and Austin, Texas. Some were attached to congregations; many were completely independent enterprises. The movement has tried to draw from each of the three dominant Jewish traditions rather than identifying with any one of them. Full equality of women has been a major commitment of the movement. In 1979, 350 havurot members held a conference at Rutgers University and organized the National Havurot Coordinating Committee which immediately began planning programs to assist havurah communities survive by gaining a greater knowledge of their Jewish heritage.

Membership: Not reported. Recent estimates of the movement suggest that several hundred havurah communities have survived into the mid-1980s.

Sources: Bernard Reisman, "The Havurah: An Approach to Humanizing Jewish Organizational Life" in *Journal of Jewish Communal Service*, vol. 52, no. 2 (Winter 1975) pp. 202-209.

★1132★
LIFE ACTION FOUNDATION
Box 263
Ojai, CA 93023

Among the most famous of the new leaders to rise in the 1960s outside of the normal synagogue structures is Sholomo Carlebach, the "hippie" guitar-strumming rabbi. A exponent of Neo-Hassidism, Carlebach has been involved in a number of structures attempting to revive the Jewish mystical traditions in a contemporary context. He has become the teacher to many Jews scattered around the United States. The Life Action Foundation coordinates his activities.

Among the earliest structures which evolved out of Carlebach's work was the House of Love and Prayer, a Jewish community in San Francisco. It emerged in 1969 among Jews who had rediscovered their Jewishness out of Carlebach's work in the drug culture. The emphasis of the House was on the shared life, Torah and prayer. For several years, Carlebach limited his travels to teach at the house's yeshivah. Similar communities emerged in New York and Jerusalem. The San Francisco group published the *Holy Beggars' Gazette* and *Tree* and operated the Judaic Book Service. There were, in the mid-1970s, between 20 and 40 members at the House. Services are held on Friday evening, Saturday morning, and each day a 6:30 a.m. Open classes are conducted on Hebrew and the Tamud.

Membership: Not reported. Carlebach's following has continued to grow through the 1980s, though the structures have evolved through the years.

Sources: Leo Skir, "Shlomo Carlebach and the House of Love and Prayer" in *Midstream* (February 1970), pp. 31-42.

★1133★
LITTLE SYNAGOGUE
27 E. 20th St.
New York, NY 10003

Hungarian-born Rabbi Joseph H. Gelberman was a leader of a Conservative congregation who left it to found the Little Synagogue (Congregation Tel Aviv), a "modern Hasidic community" located just north of Greenwich Village in Manhattan in New York City. Gelberman's program combines elements of Hasidism, New Thought, and Eastern religious thought. Integral to the program is the Midway Counseling Center, specializing in psychological counseling and based upon the concept that learning to love is the key to growth on all levels of the self.

Rabbi Gelberman has become a popular figure in New Thought metaphysical circles and has often spoken at International New Thought Alliance meetings and at the New York congregation of the Church of the Truth. Science of Mind lessons are a regular part he weekly program. Over the years, Martin Buber's Hasidism has come more and more to the fore in Gelberman's thinking. The Synagogue seeks, through Hasidic thought and techniques, to find personal growth and the joy of worship. Sabbath services include chanting, silent meditation, and spontaneous verbalization leading to mystical and metaphysical encounter. Interpretation of the Zohar is a central feature of the educational program.

Although a single congregation, the Little Synagogue has had immense influence through media coverage and

Gelberman's lecturing and leading workshops around the United States. Gelberman has also developed "Interfaith Seminars" as a means of interfaith dialogue between Jews, Christians, Muslims, and members of Eastern religions. Wisdom Press publishes Rabbi Gelberman's books and tapes, distributing them throughout the country.

Membership: Not reported. There is one center in Manhattan.

Educational facilities: The New Seminary, New York, New York.

Periodicals: *Kabbalah for Today*, 27 E. 20th St., New York, NY 10003.

Sources: Joseph H. Gelberman, *To Be...Fully Alive*. Farmingdale, NY: Coleman Graphics, 1983; Joseph H. Gelberman, *Psychology and Metaphysics*. New York: Little Synagogue Press, n.d.; Joseph H. Gelberman, *Reaching a Mystical Experience: A Kabbalistic Encounter*. (New York: Wisdom Press, 1970); "Kabbala for Moderns" in *Hadassah Magazine*, vol. 54, no. 3 (November 1972).

★1134★
SOCIETY FOR HUMANISTIC JUDAISM
28611 W. Twelve Mile Rd.
Farmington Hills, MI 48018

Within the American Jewish community attempts have been made since the mid-nineteenth century to articulate a secular, humanistic and even atheistic Judaism. Such efforts have resulted in structures such as the Ethical Culture Society (which while predominately Jewish in membership did little to relate to the Jewish community) and a variety of Jewish agricultural communal experiments. Primarily, however, secular Jews were not related to synagogue life. In the 1960s there arose a group of rabbis who wished to combine the religious life and affirmation of their Jewishness within a humanistic perspective. Sherwin T. Wine led the way in the formation of the first humanist congregation, the Birmingham Temple (in suburban Detroit). He was joined by Daniel Friedman who had led Congregation Bnai Or in Deerfield, Illinois to adopt humanistic thought and practice. In 1970 they led in the formation of the Society for Humanistic Judaism and the Association for Humanistic Rabbis.

Humanistic Judaism is a religious community of people who do not believe in God but who exist within the framework of the larger Jewish heritage. Traditional Jewish distinctives such as Torah (a symbol for truth) and the Passover story (a reminder of the human values of freedom, courage, and peace) are retained but reinterpreted. References to God have been eliminated from the liturgies, and prayer is used but rarely. Emphasis is placed upon ethics and the promotion of human values.

Humanistic ethics assert that ethics and morals rest upon a human foundation, and that each person must be responsible for individual ethical decisions and their consequences. Humanistic ethics also assume that people must be treated noncoercively, with respect, and in such a way that their individuality and uniqueness are affirmed. Assisting others to assume responsibility for their lives and to become autonomous adults (not dependent upon others, society, or God) is a prime ethical activity.

Membership: Not reported. In 1979 there were four humanistic congregations in the United States.

Periodicals: *Humanistic Judaism*, 28611 W. Twelve Mile Rd., Farmington Hills, MI 48018.

Sources: Sherwin T. Wine, *Humanistic Judaism*. Buffalo, NY: Prometheus Books, 1978. Saul N. Goodman, *The Faith of Secular Jews*. New York: KTAV Publishing House, 1976; Ruth Feldman, "Beth Or Offers Alternative Form of Judaism, Maintains Low Profile, Earns Activists' Scorn" in *North Shore*, vol. 2,no. 1 (January/February 1979), pp. 56-59; Sidney M. Weisman, "From Orthodox Judaism to Humanism" in *The Humanist*, vol. 39, no. 3 (May/June 1979), pp. 32-35.

★1135★
SOCIETY OF JEWISH SCIENCE
825 Round Swamp Rd.
Old Bethpage, NY 11804

Jewish converts were mentioned in Christian Science literature in the 1890s. In the first decade of the twentieth century, substantial numbers in the still small Jewish community began to look Mary Baker Eddy (who founded the Church of Christ, Scientist) for inspiration. In 1911 the California Grand Lodge of B'nai B'rith adopted a resolution denying membership to Jews adhering to Christian Science and, in 1912, the Central Conference of American Rabbis (Reformed) devoted a session at its annual meeting to a discussion of the issue. Of particular interest were those Jews who insisted that Christian Science only made them better Jews.

Out of this debate came Alfred Geiger Moses, a Reformed rabbi from Mobile, Alabama, who, in 1916, published his *Jewish Science*. Drawing upon Hasidic sources, he translated Chochmah (the Kabbalistic sephirot, generally translated as wisdom). He saw the Baal Shem Tov as the source of Mrs. Eddy's thought and Christian Science as Hasidism with a veneer of Christology. He further emphasized "faith cure" as a genuinely Jewish tradition and recounted incidents of cures he had witnessed. Moses' position was actually nearer New Thought than Christian Science, inasmuch as he refused to deny the existence of matter. He emphasized thinking "right thoughts" and training the mind with affirmations (short statements "affirming" God and creation), following a proper diet, avoiding excesses, and refusing to become angered.

In 1922, Lithuanina-born Rabbi Morris Lichtenstein gave organizational form to Moses' ideas, establishing the Society of Jewish Science in New York City. In 1925, he published *Jewish Science and Health* and, in subsequent years, several other books. From 1923 to 1949, the Society of Jewish Science published the *Jewish Science Interpreter* ten times a year. By 1938, there were 19 practitioners. Rival groups had begun to emerge almost immediately. Rabbi Clifton Harby Levy organized the Center of Christian Science in 1923. Levy published a series of lessons, *The Helpful Manual* and a periodical, the *Jewish Life*. By 1929 he had six active groups in New York City and one each in Baltimore, Maryland; Rochester and Syracuse, New York; and Washington, D.C. The Center continued until the late 1950s. Christian Science Liberals, a group of Jews who had accepted Christian Science, were active proselytizers in the 1920s, but they eventually merged with the Parent Church of Annie C. Bill.

Rabbi Lichtenstein died in 1938 and was succeeded by his wife, Tehilla Lichtenstein, who has since occupied his pulpit. She was the first woman to fill such a role uninterruptedly and for so long (more than three decades). She wrote the basic introductory booklet, "What to Tell Your Friends about Jewish Science." Ms. Lichtenstein draws the distinction between Jewish Science and Christian Science by noting that within Judaism are all the spiritual goals any Jew needs. Jewish science is a way of life which puts into application all the spiritual, ethical, and moral principles of the Jewish faith, and thus enables one to attain health and happiness. That the cure of physical and mental illnesses can be effected by restoring one's mental processes to their natural condition is a central postulate.

Membership: In recent years, statistical data on membership has not been available to the public. Reportedly, several hundred persons are affiliated with the main congregation in New York City, and there are said to be groups in Miami, Florida; Chicago, Illinois; and California. Ms. Lichtenstein has also alluded to thousands of adherents scattered across the country who are affiliated through the Society's literature.

Sources: Morris Lichtenstein, *Jewish Science and Health*. New York: Jewish Science Publishing Company, 1925; Morris Lichtenstein, *Joy of Life*. New York: Jewish Science Publishing Society, 1938; Tehilla Licchtenstein, *What to Tell Your Friends About Jewish Science*. New York: Society of Jewish Science, 1951; John J. Appel, "Christian Science and the Jews" in *Jewish Social Studies*, vol. 31 (April 1969), pp. 100-121; Charles Harby Levy, *The Helpful Maual*. New York: The Centre of Jewish Science, n.d.

★1136★
SOCIETY OF THE BIBLE IN THE HANDS OF ITS CREATORS, INC.
Current address not obtained for this edition.

The Society of the Bible in the Hands of Its Creator, Inc., was formed in 1943. The inspiration for the Society was the work of Moses Guibbory, the Ukrainian-born international president and organizer of the group. He was assisted by British-born radio commentator and Jewish convert Boake Canter and by David Horowitz, founder of the United Israel World Union, who met Guibbory in Jerusalem. The object of the Society was to publish and spread the ideas of *The Bible in the Hands of Its Creators* by Guibbory and both a Hebrew and an English Bible as perfected by Guibbory's research, and to develop and maintain places of devotion and spiritual guidance for members of the Society.

The Bible in the Hands of Its Creators is a massive volume, the chief ideas of which center upon defining the nature of Jehovah, the one God, besides whom there is no other. Jehovah, while one, is also many. He is both male and female, the terrible God, the creator, the merciful and gracious God, the forgiving and long-suffering one. The prophetic day of Jehovah began in 1929 (5689 A.M.) and has since continued.

Guibbory, as the international president, controlled the Society, assisted by an executive board of from five to 13 members. Missionary work was begun in the Society but was stopped by Guibbory. In the late 1970s, the Society closed its New York office and no contact has been re-established. In the 1970s the only known gathering of members was at Guibbory's South Norwalk, Connecticut home for the major Jewish holidays. Gentile converts were included.

Sources: Moses Guibbory, *The Bible in the Hands of Its Creator.* New York: The Society of the Bible in the Hands of Its Creator, 1943.

★1137★
UNITED ISRAEL WORLD UNION
406 E. 42nd St.
New York, NY 10017

The United Israel World Union was formed in 1943 by Swedish-born David Horowitz. The UIWU is based upon "the eternal monotheistic values contained in the Torah and the eternal precepts of Israel as emananting from Sinai under Moses." It accepts the Hebrew Bible as a blueprint not for Israel alone, but for all humanity. As such, a vigorous missionary program to convert people, particularly Christians, to Judaism, was conducted. Among the leaders of the movement are a number of converts from various national, ethnic, religious and racial backgrounds, including black Jewish rabbi Mosha Hailu Paris and former Jehovah's Witness Olin Moyle. Horowitz has developed a special appreciation for Charles Taze Russell, founder of what is today known as the Jehovah's Witnesses, who was one of the earliest voices of Zionism.

Underlying the UIWU is a version of the British-Israel theory which recognized some gentiles as the descendants of the ten lost tribes of Israel. A major goal of UIWU is a reunion of Judah and Israel and it sees itself as a meeting place for this reunion. Some acceptance of the Union has been found among Reform Jews, who also seek to universalize the Jewish message. In America, groups were formed in New York, Michigan, West Virginia, Illinois and other states. In New York, the monthly *United Israel Bulletin* is published by Horowitz. Associated with the New York headquarters is the Brotherhood Synagogue in Manhattan.

Membership: Not reported. By the mid-1970s 24 centers of the UIWU with 13,7000 members had emerged around the globe in England, Spain, Mexico, Germany, Japan, and the United States.

Periodicals: *United Israel Bulletin*, 406 E. 42nd St., New York, NY 10017.

Sources: David Horowitz, *Pastor Charles Taze Russell, An Early American Christian Zionist.* New York: Philosophical Library, 1986.

Middle Eastern Family
Part 2, Islam, Zoroastrianism, Bahaism

An historical essay on this family is provided beginning on page 147.

Islam

★1138★
SHI'A MUSLIMS
% Islamic Center of Detroit
15571 Joy Rd.
Detroit, MI 48228

The Shi'a Muslim Community (one of the two orthodox branches of Islam) is by far the smaller. It includes some Iranian-Americans though Shi'as of other nationalities (Lebanese, Pakistani, Yemeni) are also present in significant numbers. The oldest and among the most prominent Shi'a centers is the Islamic Center of Detroit, a Lebanese center which emerged as the Detroit Islamic community split into the traditional Sunni and Shi'a factions early in the twentieth century. Growth in the Shi'as was marked by its 1949 invitation to Iman Mohamad Jawad Chirri to become the community's spiritual leader and the establishment of the center in the 1960s under his guidance.

More typical of the Shi'a centers established since 1965 is the Islamic Society of Georgia, a Pakistani-American center in Atlanta founded in 1970. It is a major distributor of Shi'a publications from around the world and publishes *Islamic Affairs*. It has made a major priority of its program the circulation of Shi'a literature to "willing readers" at little or no cost. The Midwest Association of Shi'a Organized Muslims is a similar center in Chicago.

A step forward in the organization of the Shi'a community was the 1970 formation of the Shi'a Association of North America by families in New York and New Jersey. Through its newsletter, *Islamic Review*, and other publications, it has led in the establishment of traditional standards of belief and practice in the Shia community nationally. The Iranian Revolution under the Ayatollah Khomeini has had a marked effect of uniting the American Shi'a community, which has responded with strong support. In like measure, the American-Lebanese Shi'as have identified with the Shi'as of Lebanon, though they are somewhat divided in their support of the various factions that emerged in the 1970s.

While the majority of English-language Shia literature still originates from foreign presses, several publishing ventures have emerged in the United States. The Detroit center has published a number of works by Iman Chirri, an eminent Islamic scholar. It is joined by Free Islamic Literature, Inc. of Houston, Texas and Mehfile Shahe Khorasan Charitable Trust of Englewood Cliffs, New Jersey.

Membership: Not reported. There are several dozen Shi'a centers scattered across the United States.

Educational facilities: The Islamic Seminary, 55 W. 42nd St., Suite 1211, New York, NY 10036.

Periodicals: *Islamic Affairs*, Islamic Society of Georgia, 172 Vine St., S.W., Atlanta, GA 30314; *The Islamic Review*, Shia Association of North America, 108 5363 62nd Dr., Forest Hills, New York, NY 11375; *Husaini News*, Husaini Association of Greater Chicago, P.O. Box 6810, Chicago, IL 60645.

Sources: Mohammad Jawad Chirri, *The Brother of the Prophet Mohammad*. Detroit: Islamic Center of Detroit, 1979, 1982. 2 Vols.; Mohammad Jawad Chirri, *Inquiries About Islam*. Detroit: Islamic Center of Detroit, 1965; Ali Shariati, *Islamic View of Man*. Houston, TX: Free Islamic Literature, Inc., 1979; *Iman Khomeini, Pope and Christianity*. Tehran, Iran: Islamic Propaganda Organization, 1983; *The Life of Iman Husain*. Englewood Cliffs, NJ: Mehfile Shahe Khorasan Charitable Trust, n.d. (tract).

★1139★
SUNNI MUSLIMS
% Islamic Center
2551 Massachusetts Ave., N.W.
Washington, DC 20008

The Islamic world, though concentrated in the Arab nations of the Middle East, stretches from Yugoslavia to Indonesia and includes not only a large part of the U.S.S.R. but a growing community in Africa south of the Sahara. Since 1965, the Islamic community which had been concentrated in the Midwest and a few Eastern urban centers, has blossomed into a significant religious element of American life in every part of the United States. Literally millions of immigrants from Islamic Asia, Africa and Europe have settled in North America and begun the generation-long process of building ethnic community centers and facilities for worship (often the same building).

Unlike much of Christendom, Islam is organized into a number of autonomous centers. Each center (which may be called a community center, a mosque, a musajid) will tend to be dominated by one ethnic community, though outside the largest urban centers where a variety of mosques can be found, centers will have welcomed people of various nationalities into affiliation. Many of the major centers will have a periodical, which has both a primary local audience and a national circulation. The mosque, headed by the iman (minister-teacher) is the basic unit of Islam.

Above the level of the local centers, a variety of national and continental organizations have been formed to mobilize the various local Islamic communities, provide the public (largely ignorant of Islam) with information, and coordinate the activities (particlarly the propagation of the faith) of the community at large. These organizations, whose membership will come from a variety of ethnic backgrounds, tend to be divided politically. Each of the different organization will be ideologically aligned to, for example, different factions in the Middle East, and/or atuned to a more-or-less activist role in support of various concerns of the land from which they immigrated. Political activism is particularly noticeable in those groups which serve the large Muslim community on the nation's campuses. Local centers will often affiliate with several of the competing national associations.

Symbolic of Sunni Muslim presence in America is the Islamic Center in Washington, D.C. Begun in 1949, it took seven years to complete. It was officially opened in 1957. While begun as a center for diplomatic personnel, with financial support from seventeen countries, with the growth of Islam in North America it has become a place to which all American Sunnis look as a visible point of unity in the otherwise decentralized Islamic community. The importance of the Center was dramatically underscored in the early 1980s when it was taken over by a group who supported the Iranian Revolution under the Ayatollah Khomeini and opposed the influence of the ambassadors from Saudi Arabia. The takeover disrupted the center for several years and led to the withdrawal of its prominent iman, Dr. Muhammad Abdul Rauf, a leading Islamic apologist in North America.

Among the oldest of the Canadian-United States organizations is the Federation of Islamic Organizations in the United States and Canada. It was founded in 1952, largely as a result of the efforts of Abdullah Ingram of Cedar Rapids, Iowa. He called a meeting attended primarily by Lebanese Muslims, representative of the older American Muslim centers, and formed the International Muslim Society, which two years later became the Federation. The Federation has as its goals the perpetuation of Islam and of Muslim culture and the dissemination of correct information about Muslim society worldwide. It publishes a periodical, *The Muslim Star*, and holds annual conventions, usually in the Midwest. The Federation accomplishments have been related to the fellowship of various Muslim centers across national and ethnic boundaries, and more activist groups, while acknowledging the contribution of the Federation, saw the need for further organizations.

The Islamic Society of North America emerged in the early 1980s out of the Muslim Students Association originally founded in 1952. It represents a broadening focus of concern by former students who moved into roles of leadership in the Muslim, academic and professional communities in America. The Society is headquartered at the Islamic Teaching Center, a large complex in suburban Indianapolis, from which it oversees the network of subsidiary organizations it has fostered and nurtured.

From its original goals, developed to assist graduate students temporarily in the United States study to survive in a non-Muslim environment, the Society has since 1975 refocused its attention on building Islamic structures among a permanent and growing North American Islamic population and actively propagating the faith among the non-Muslim public. To these ends, the society has established the Islamic Medical Association, the Association of Muslim Social Scientists and the Association of Muslim Scientists and Engineers. It has published numerous books (including the proceedings of the many conferences its sponsors) and pamphlets (especially a set designed to introduce Islam to non-Muslims) and several periodicals, most prominently *Al-Ittihad* and *Islamic Horizons*. The Muslim Student Association continues as one department of the Society. The Islamic Teaching Center is the main structure engaged in *dawah*, the propagation of the faith.

Possibly the most inclusive Islamic organization for Sunni Muslims is the Council of Islamic Organizations of America (both the Federation of Islamic Associations and the Islamic Society of North America are affiliates). The idea of the Council emerged in 1973 at a meeting in Saudi Arabia. Then the Muslim World League, an international

Muslim organization with offices in New York City, organized the first Islamic Conference of North America which met April 22-24, 1977 at Newark, New Jersey. The Council was organized at that gathering to meet primary needs for unity and co-ordination of the many Islamic centers in North America. In its lengthy list of goals, it set itself the task of fostering unity, establishing and propagating the faith in its fullness, the perpetuation of modest dress codes, assistance in building mosques and other facilities for Muslims, and the funding of various designated projects of broad Muslim int erest.

Also formed in the 1970s, the Council of Imans in North America formed as a continent-wide professional organization for the leaders of the various mosques and Islamic centers.

The several organizations mentioned above are but a few of the many new structures being established in the Muslim Community. All of the organizations have been assisted by the development of Muslim publishing concerns, such as American Trust Publications, affiliated with the Islamic Society of North America; Kazi Publications in Chicago; and The Crescent Publications, Tacoma Park, Maryland. As of the mid-1980s, however, the majority of English-language literature produced for the American Muslim community is still published overseas.

Membership: Estimates vary on the size of the Sunni Muslim community. As many as 400 mosques and centers have been counted. Approximately 3,000,000 immigrants from predominantly Muslim countries have come to the United States. Together with converts, including large followings in American black communities, the total number of Muslims approaches the size of the Jewish community.

Educational facilities: American Islamic College, Chicago, Illinois.

Periodicals: *Muslim Star*, Federation of Islamic Associations in the U.S.A. and Canada, 25351 Five Mile Rd., Redford Twp., MI 48239; *Islamic Horizons* , Box 38, Plainfield, IN 46168; *Al-Ittihad*, Box 38, Plainfield, IN 46168; *The Minaret*, Islamic Center of Southern California, 434 S. Vermont Ave., Los Angeles, CA 90020; *Path of Righteousness*, Council of Imans in North America, 1214 Cambridge Cresent, Sarnia, ON, Canada N7S 3W4.

Sources: Hammudah Abdalati, *Islam in Focus*. Indianapolis, IN: American Trust Publications, 1975; Kamal Avdich, *Outline of Islam*. Northbrook, IL: The Islamic Cultural Center, n.d.; Suzanne Haneef, *What Everyone Should Know About Islam and Muslims*. Chicago: Kazi Publications, 1979; Muhammad Abdul Rauf, *Islam, Creed and Worship*. Washington, DC: The Islamic Center, 1974; Moulana Mohammad Abdul-Aleem Soddiqui, *Elementary Teachings of Islam*. Tacoma Park,

MD: The Crescent Publications, n.d.; S. Mazhar Hussain, ed., *Proceedings of the First Islamic Conference of North America*. New York: Muslim World League, 1977.

Sufism

★1140★
ARICA INSTITUTE
235 Park Ave., S.
New York, NY 10003

Emerging out of an eclectic background, but drawing heavily upon Sufism and the ideas and methods of Georgei Gurdjieff, is the Arica Institute founded by Oscar Ichazo in 1971. Ichazo was a student at the University of La Paz, Chile, when at the age of nineteen he encountered a small esoteric group from whom he began to learn a variety of teachings from the kabbalah to Zen to Sufism to Gurdjieff. With their encouragement he traveled to Asia for further studies. He eventually settled in the town of Arica to teach a band of dedicated students. In 1970 a group of approximately 50 American stayed at Arica for nine months, following which Ichazo moved his work to New York and founded the Institute named for the town in his home coutry.

Ichazo teaches that early in life humans experience a fall from their perfect essence into personality experienced in part as the contradiction between inner feelings and outer reality. Ego consciousness develops as a mechanism for dealing with the fallen world. In pure essence, there are three centers in the human being: the intellectual (path), the emotional (oth) and the vital (kath). Ideally, the vital center is in control. It allows people to sense their basic unity with life. As humans grow, the intellectual center attempts to rule the person in all aspects. The ego, consisting of learned patterns and idea which fix the individual's manner of dealing with the world. Arica attempts to restore the natural balance through ego reduction and the promotion of the vital function.

To accomplish its goals, Ichazo has combined ined a variety of exercises which commonly begin with the individual's participation in a 40-day session of intensive training, though alternative introductory programs have been developed for those unable to devote a large block of time to the practice. The basic training is followed by a variety classes teaching advanced and specialized meditation and exercise techniques. A nonsectarian form of zhikr, the traditional Sufi practice of the remembrance of God, is taught as are Zen meditation techniques. It is Ichazo's belief that Western culture has reached a point in which a change of consciousness is both necessary and possible. He sees Arica as a method of facilitating that transformation.

Membership: Not reported. There are groups across the United States and Canada.

Periodicals: *Newsletter*, 235 Park Avenue South, New York, NY 10003.

Sources: Oscar Ichazo, *The Human Process for Enlightenment and Freedom*. New York: Arica Institute, 1976; *Interviews with Oscar Ichazo*. New York: Arica Institute Press, 1982; Oscar Ichazo, *The 9 Ways of Zhikr Ritual*. New York: Arica Institute, 1976; Oscar Ichazo, *Arica Psycho-Calisthenics*. New York: Simon & Schuster, 1976.

★1141★
BAWA MUHAIYADDEEN FELLOWSHIP
5820 Overbrook Ave.
Philadelphia, PA 19131

Bawa Muhaiyaddeen Fellowship was founded in 1971. Shaikh Muhaiyaddeen M. R. Guru Bawa is a Ceylonese Sufi teacher said to be over a hundred years old. In the 1930s he was discovered by pilgrims in the Kataragama Forest, and the Serendib Study Group was established in Colombo, the capial of Sri Lanka. He was first brought to Philadelphia in 1971 by a disciple, and as a group began to recognize him as their spiritual teacher, the Guru Bawa Fellowship was organized. During the next years he traveled between Philadelphia and Sri Lanka.

Bawa sees himself not as the teacher of a new religion, but as dealing with the essence of all religion. He teaches the unity of God and human unity in God. A Sufi is one who has lost the self in the Solitary Oneness that is God. It is the individual's sole duty to take the 3,000 qualities of God within him/herself. The soul is the point of divine wisdom at which the consciousness of individuals is known as being one with God. From this point the individual realizes God.

The conditions leading to God realizations are the following: 1) the constant affirmation that nothing but God exists; 2) the continual elimination of evil from one's life; and 3) the conscious effort to become God's qualities--patience, tolerance, peacefulness, compassion, and the assumption that all lives should be treated as one's own. The conditions lead naturally to the practice of *zhikr*, the remembrance of God.

Headquarters of Bawa's followers was established in a large house in a residential section of Philadelphia. Over the years his books have been translated into English (many published by Fellowship Press) and groups established around the United States.

Membership: Not reported. In 1982 there were 16 fellowship groups in the United States and two in Canada.

Periodicals: *God's Light*, 5820 Overbrook Ave., Philadelphia, PA 19131.

Sources: M. R. Bawa Muhaiyaddeen, *God, His Prophets and His Children*. Philadelphia: Fellowship Press, 1978; M. R. Bawa Muhaiyaddeen, *The Guidebook*. Philadelphia: Fellowship Press, 1976. 2 Vols.; M. R. Bawa Muhaiyaddeen, *Mata Veeram, or the Forces of Illusion*. York Beach, ME: Samuel Weiser, 1982; M. R. Guru Bawa Muhaiyaddeen, *Truth and Light*. Guru Bawa Fellowship of Philadelphia, 1974; M. R. Bawa Muhaiyaddeen, *The Truth and Unity of Man*. Philadelphia: Fellowship Press, 1980.

★1142★
CHISHTI ORDER OF AMERICA
℅ Hakim G. M. Chishti
390 Soundview Dr.
Rocky Point, NY 11778

The Chishti Order of America is one of several Sufi groups in the United States which traces its origins to the Chishti Order, one of the four main branches of Sufism. The Chishti Order was founded by Khwaja Abu Ishaq Chishti, who settled at Chishti in Khurasan in what is present-day Iran during the tenth century. The lineage of leaders of the Chishti Order stayed in Persia until the succession of Khwaja Muinuddin Chishti (1142-1236), the most renowned saint in the order's history. He took the order to India and is regarded as the true founder of the modern order.

Khwaja Muinuddin was born in Sistan, Persia, and raised as a Sufi. The constant warfare he witnessed during his early life reinforced the mystic tendencies he inherited through his family. He studied with Hazrat Khwara Usman Harvani, a teaching master of the Chishti Order, for twenty years and was, upon his departure, granted the khalifat, or succession, of his teacher. He traveled to Lahore and Delhi before settling in Ajmer, then the seat of an important Hindu state. He became a major force in establishing Islam in India. His tomb in Ajmer is sacred shrine as well as the location of the international headquarters of the order.

Over the centuries various leaders of the order have founded new branches. The two most important are the Nizami (founded by Nizamu'd-Din Mahbubiilahi) and the Sabiri (founded by Makhdum Ala'u'di-Din Ali Ahmad Sabiri). Both orders were started by students of Baba Farid Shakarganilj in the thirteenth century. The Chishti Order of America derives its lineage from the Sabiri branch of the Chishti Order. The Nizami branch is represented in America by the Sufi Order (see separate entry).

The Chishti Order of America was founded in 1972 by Hakim G. M. Chishti as the Chishti Sufi Mission, an affiliate of the Chishti Sufi Mission Society of India in Ajmer. Hakim was a student of Mirza Wahiduddin Begg who was the senior teacher at Ajmer during the 1970s. When Begg died in 1979, Hakim was granted his succession, a fact confirmed in a ceremony in Ajmer in

1980. At the same time, the Chishti Sufi mission was renamed the Chishti Order of America.

Khwaja Muinuddin stressed the essence of Sufism as the apprehension of Divine reality through spiritual means and the suppression of the lower self. He taught the need of devotion to one's spiritual master (Pir) as a necessity for salvation. He also stressed the obligation of humanitarian action in the face of the caste system

Membership: Not reported. In 1981 sheihks of the order were to be found in New York, Chicago, and Los Angeles.

Sources: W. D. Begg, *The Holy Biography of Hazrat Khwaja Muinuddin Chishti*. Tucson, AZ: Chishti of Mission of America, 1977.

★1143★
CLAYMONT SOCIETY FOR CONTINUOUS EDUCATION
Box 112
Charlestown, WV 25414

John Godolphin Bennett (1897-1974) met Georgei Gurdjieff in 1921 in Constantinople, where Bennett was serving in the British Army. He continued his off-and-on relationship with Gurdjieff until the latter's death in 1949. He subsequently authored a number of books which discussed his work with Gurdjieff and advocated his Fourth Way system (see separate entry on the Gurdjieff Foundation). However, he was not bound by Gurdjieff, and in his mature years he also became enthusiastic about both Subud (discussed elsewhere in this chapter) and the yoga of Shivapuri Baba, an Indian teacher. He wrote an important book introducing each to the English-speaking world.

Bennett claimed that Gurdjieff had left him a commission as a teacher of the Gurdjieff system to the world. Bennett's interest in Sabud, for example, was prompted by his belief that Bapak Subuh, it founder, was identical with Aahiata Shiemash, a coming prophet of conscience, spoken of in Gurdjieff's book, *All and Everything*. Bennett also came to believe that humanity had reached the point in evolution that individuals could assume responsibility for its future course. Through spiritual training, individuals could become transformed and in the process begin to transform the world.

In 1971, to put his ideas into action, Bennett founded the International Academy for Continuous Education at Sherborne, Gloucestershire, near Oxford. The core of the program at Sherborne House consisted of a ten-month resident intensive based directly on Gurdjieff. Bennett died in 1974, and the following year the center was closed.

However, beginning with Bennett's American tour in 1971, and the subsequent circulation of his books in the United States, a cadre of American students arose. In 1975 some of those students picked up the thrust of Sherborne House and created the Claymont Society and School in West Virginia. Under the leadership of Pierre Elliot, who had worked with Gurdjieff's prime student P. D. Ouspensky and then with Bennett for many years, the Claymont Society has established a community and continued the transformative thrust begun by Bennett. Beginning with Gurdjieff's and Bennett's teachings and methods, the group has incorporated a variety of techniques, especially those of the *Khwajagan*, Sufi teachers of Central Asia.

The Society is designed to function as a "Fourth Way" school, i.e., a community whose members are working together towards human transformation within the context of a task to be realized in the world. The particular task is the building of a community capable of surviving under harsh economic and social conditions and to educate others to do likewise. It is seeking to become self-sufficient economically and organizationally and is building an economic base in farming, cottage industry and in managing a school for interested outsiders to learn the life of the community and the transformative teachings which underly its existence.

The Claymont School provides the basic ten-month program developed for Sherborne House, plus a variety of more inclusive programs offered by other teachers from compatible Sufi, Hasidic, and Eastern perspectives. Coombe Springs Press continues from the Sherborne House establishment as publishers of Bennett's books and other literature of a related perspective. In the United States, Claymont Communications distributes Coombe Springs publications as well as Bennett's material published by others.

Membership: Not reported. The Society has a potential for supporting 200 families on its present West Virginia acreage. Less than 100 currently reside there.

Sources: John G. Bennett, *Witness*. Tucson, AZ: Omen Press, 1974; John G. Bennett, *Gurdjieff, Making a New World*. New York: Harper & Row, 1973; John G. Bennett, *Is There "Life" on Earth?* New York: Stonehill Publishing Company, 1973; John G. Bennett, *Creative Thinking*. Sherborne, England: Coombe Springs Press, 1964; John G. Bennett, *Enneagram Studies*. York Beach, ME: Samuel Weiser, 1983.

★1144★
GURDJIEFF FOUNDATION
Box 549
San Francisco, CA 94101

Georgei Gurdjieff (d. 1949) was a modern spiritual teacher greatly influenced by Sufism, but who blended it, with other spiritual teachings, into a unique philosophy which have in the several decades since his death become the springboard for a host of variations. Born in the 1870s in a small town on the Armenian-Turkish border, Gurdjieff studied the mysticism of Greek Orthodoxy and developed an interest in both science and the occult prior to leaving home as a young man. He began a period of wanderings that took him from Tibet to Ethiopia as a member of a legendary band, the Seekers of the Truth, in quest of esoteric wisdom. A significant period was spent among the Turkish Sufi masters.

In 1912 he surfaced in Moscow where he married a countess and met his most important disciple, Pyotr Demianovitch Ouspensky. With his students, he left Russia as the revolution was beginning and settled in Paris, where in 1922 he founded the Institute for the Harmonious Development of Man. Here, the unknown and the famous gathered to study with Gurdjieff. Among his students were Alexander de Salzmann and his wife Jeanne de Salzmann, author Katherine Mansfield, writer/editor A. R. Orage, and Maurice Nicoll.

Gurdjieff taught that humans are asleep, that they are operated like puppets by forces of which they have no awareness. He looked for individuals who had awakened to their contact with the higher force that brought direct awareness (and hence some degree of control) of the other forces of their environment . Gurdjieff developed a variety of techniques to assist the awakening process. Possibly the most famous were the Gurdjieff movements, a series of dancelike exercises. He also generated considerable controversy for placing students in situations of tension and conflict designed to force self-conscious awareness. The system required an individual teacher-student relationship almost of necessity. It came to be known as the "fourth" way, the way of encounter with ordinary life, as opposed to the other ways of the yogi, monk or fakir. The way was symbolized by the enneagram, a nine-pointed design in a circle.

Two years after the opening of the Institute, Gurdjieff toured America with his students presenting demonstrations of the movements. He found a ready audience among people who had read Ouspensky's book, *Tertium Organum* (1920) and/or who had been influenced by Orage. The genesis of his American following dates from this trip. Gurdjieff closed the Institute in 1933, but continued to teach and, possibly more important, to write for the rest of his life. Most of his writings were circulated privately to his students. Only one book, *The Herald of Coming God*, was published before his death.

During his last days, Gurdjieff spent much time with long-time pupil Jeanne de Salzmann, who following Gurdjieff's death founded the Gurdjieff Foundation in Paris. This became the model for similar structures around the world. In 1953, Lord Pentland (1908-1976) established the Gurdjieff Foundation of New York. Born Henry John Sinclair, Lord Pentland was knighted in 1924 at the time of his father's death. The Gurdjieff Foundation of San Francisco was founded a few years later. These oversee a number of Gurdjieff groups in major cities around the United States. Members of the foundation engage in regular meetings, study the writings of Gurdjieff and other teachers, engage in the movements and various forms of work, all designed to awaken the individual. Until recently, the Institutes were under the control of personal students of Gurdjieff, however, leadership has passed to a new generation of students as those original students pass from the scene.

Membership: Not reported. An estimated 500 people are directly related to the Gurdjieff Foundation in New York City. Other groups can currently be found in most major cities.

Sources: J. Walter Driscoll, *Gurdjieff, An Annotated Bibliography*. New York: Garland Publishing, Inc., 1985; Kathleen Riordan Speeth, *The Gurdjieff Work*. Berkeley, CA: And/Or Press, 1976; James Webb, *The Harmonious Circle*. New York: G. P. Putnam's Sons, 1980; P. D. Ouspensky, *The Fourth Way*. New York: Alfred A. Knopf, 1957; Kathleen Riordan Speeth and Ira Freidlander, *Gurdjieff, Seeker of Truth*. New York: Harper & Row, 1980.

★1145★
INSTITUTE FOR RELIGIOUS DEVELOPMENT
Chardavogne Rd.
Warwick, NY 19990

Wilhem A. Nyland, a Dutch chemist and musician and a former member of the Gurdjieff Foundation, left the foundation in 1960 to found his own group. He had studied with Gurdjieff and A. C. Orage in his younger years. The work is headquartered in Warwick, New York, where a community who manage a farm and several cottage industries is located. Study-discussion groups can be found in several cities including New York City and Sebastopol, California. An herb farm in Red Hill, New Jersey is loosely affiliated. Nyland died in 1975.

Membership: Not reported.

Sources: Irmis B. Popoff, *Gurdjieff Group Work with Wilhem Nyland*. York Beach, ME: Samuel Weiser, 1983; Wilhem Nyland, *Firefly*. Warwick, NY: The Author, [1965].

★1146★
HABIBIYYA-SHADHILIYYA SUFIC ORDER
33 Bristol Gardens
London, England

The Habibiyya-Shadhiliyya Sufic Order originated with Shaikh Muhammed Ibn Al-Habib, termed Perfect Shaikh and Gnostic of Allah. The Shadhiliyya Order originated in the thirteenth century with Shaikh Al Shadhili of Fez, Morocco, and subsequently divided into a number of sub-orders of which the Habibiyya is one. Al-Habib is designated the Qutb (head of the spiritual hierarchy of saints) and is venerated as the Light of the Messenger.

Followers are urged to annihilate themselves in him. He is the author of the *Diwan*, a poetic presentation of his teachings.

Al-Habib speaks of God as the beloved; the goal of life is immersion in him. The way of the world is "Jahiliyya," pride and arrogance. Islam's way is submission and the recognition of our place in the harmonious whole. The main practice of the Habibiyya is Dhikr'Allah (or zhikr), the invocation, remembering and calling upon Allah.

The Habibiyya came to the United States in 1973 and opened a center in Berkeley, California. In 1977 the order claimed 5,000 American members. However, no work in the United States has been visible during the 1980s and its present status is unknown.

Membership: Not reported.

Sources: *The Sufic Path*. Berkeley, CA: Privately Printed, n.d.

★1147★
INSTITUTE FOR THE DEVELOPMENT OF THE HARMONIOUS HUMAN BEING
Box 370
Nevada City, CA 95959

In the early 1960s the Institute for the Development of the Harmonious Human Being emerged to present the teachings of E. J. Gold. The teachings and practices, whose theme is voluntary evolution as preparation for service to the Absolute, have been constantly refined and developed over the years through intensive research and work. Among the important, though by no means exclusive, sources which Gold drew upon have been the teachings of Georgei Gurdjieff. The hallmark of Gold's teachings, as presented in his numerous books, is the representation of the being or Essential Self as neither awake nor asleep, but identified, in ordinary life, with the body, emotions and psyche--collectively termed " the machine," which is asleep. In relation to the Essential self, the machine has a transformational function, but only if it is brought into an awakened state.

The awakened state can be brought about by practices and/or special living conditions within a lifestyle based upon the correct use of attention upon, and attitudes towards, the machine's psycho-physical activities. Long-term, gradual erosion--the wind-and-water method--are favored by Gold for achieving the awakening of the machine, activation of its transformational functions, and eventual transformation of the Essential Self in accordance with its true purpose. Gold has emphasized the discernment of the waking state, the use of indirect methods to overcome the fixed habits of the machine, and the individual's study of his/her "chronic," i.e. a defense mechanism against the waking state acquired by each person in early childhood. Over the years Gold's students have made a wide appplication of his teachings in such

diverse field as architecture, psychotherapy, early childhood education, and computer programming.

Membership: In 1984 there were approximately 200 members of the Institute, 25 clergy leaders, and 30 groups. There are additional centers in Canada.

Periodicals: *Talk of the Month*, Box 370, Nevada City, CA 95959; *One-Eyed Journal*, Box 370, Nevada City, CA 95959.

Remarks: There has been much discussion concerning the relation of Gold and Gurdjieff. While there are obvious differences in their teachings, the inspiration of Gurdjieff is quite evident in Gold's choice of a name for his work, his use of the enneagram (a nine-pointed symbol used by Gurdjieff) in his Institute's logo, and his picturing a Gurdjieff look-alike on the cover of several books (such as his *Secret Talks with Mr. G*). Without detracting from the originality of Gold's work and thought, his reliance, especially in his early years, on Gurdjieff is undeniable.

Sources: David Christie et al, eds., *The New American Book of the Dead*. Nevada City, CA: IDHHB Publishing, 1981; E. J. Gold, *Autobiography of a Sufi*. Crestline, CA: IDHHB Publications, 1976; *Secret Talks with Mr. G.* Nevada City, CA: IDHHB Publishing, 1978; E. J. Gold, *Shakti! The Spiritual Science of DNA*. Crestline, CA: Core Group Publications. 1973; *The Avatar's Handbook*. Los Angeles: Institute for the Development of the Harmonious Human Being, n.d.

★1148★
JERRAHI ORDER OF AMERICA
864 S. Main St.
Spring Valley, NY 10977

The Jerrahi Order of America is the North American affiliate of the Halveti-Jerrahi Sufi Order headquartered in Turkey. The Halveti (also spelled Khalwati) is regarded as one of the original source schools of Sufism, and members attribute its founding to several thirteenth-century Muslim ascetics. The Halveti experienced many schisms, one of which was founded in the seventeenth century by Hazreti Pir Nureddin Jerrahi (d. 1733). Born in a prominent Istanbul family , Herrahi studied law and at the age of nineteen was appointed a judge for the Ottoman Empire's province of Egypt. Just as he was due to sail to his new post, he met Halveti Sheikh Ali ₉Ala-ud-din and gave up his legal career to become a dervish. An accomplished student, he soon received *ijazat*, license to teach, from his instructor.

The Halveti orders have been characterized by both a strict program of training and emphasis upon individualism (one cause of the continual splintering). It has also invested great reverence in any of its leaders who could demonstrate power. Jerrahi is considered a qutb, a spiritual pole of the universe, and head of the hierarchy of saints. The order spread throughout the Ottoman Empire and beyond, from Yugoslavia to Indonesia.

The most distinctive practice of the Jerrahi Order is *dhikr* (or zhikr), literally the remembrance of God. Dhikr is the invocation of the unity of God and is performed by the dervishes within a circle headed by their sheikh.

The Jerrahi is currently headed by Sheikh Muzaffer Ozak Al-Jerrahi, who resides in Istanbul. He is the author of a number of books; however, only one, *The Unveiling of Love*, has as yet been translated into English. He established the Jerrahi Order in America within the American-Iranian community in the late 1970s. The Masjid al-Farah, its main center, is located in Manhattan.

Membership: Not reported. Two centers were active in 1982, one in New York City and one in Spring Valley, New York. Periodically, Sheikh Muzaffer visits the United States and invites the general public to participate in dhikr performances, which he has held in cities across the United States and Canada.

Sources: Muzaffer Ozek Al-Jerrahi, *The Unveiling of Love*. New York: Inner Traditions International, 1981.

★1149★
KHANIQAHI-NIMATULLAHI
306 W. 11th St.
New York, NY 10014

The Khaniqahi-Nimatullahi is the Western representative of the Nimatullahi Order of Sufis, an Iranian order founded by Nur ad-din M. Ni'matullah (1330-1431). Ni'matullah was born in Syria, the son of a Sufi master, and studied with several Sufi teachers before meeting his principal teacher, Abdullah al-Yafi-i, in Mecca. After Sheikh Yafi-i's death in 1367, Ni'matullah began a period of traveling, finally settling in Mahan, Persia (Iran), whence the order spread throughout Persia and India.

The present head of the order is Dr. Javad Nurbakhsh, former head of the Department of Psychiatry of the University of Teheran, Iran. Nurbakhsh brought the order to the West in the 1970s and by 1983 had established centers in London, England, and several United States cities. He also created Khaniqahi-Nimatullahi Publications as the publishing arm of the order, and it immediately began to generate English-language Sufi materials.

Nurbakhsh defines a Sufi as one who travels the path of love and devotion towards the Absolutely Real. Knowledge of the Real is accessible only to the Perfected Ones, the prime model being Ali, the son-in-law of Mohammad, to whom Iranian Shi'ite Muslims trace their authority. Ali traveled the path as a disciple of Mohammad and became not just a spiritual master, but the qutb, or spiritual axis, for his time. The head of the Nimatullahi Order continues in the succession of spiritual masters to whom disciples can look for knowledge.

Membership: Not reported. In 1980 in the United States the order had six centers, one each in New York City; Washington, D.C.; Boston; Seattle; San Francisco; and Mission Hills, California. There were an estimated several hundred people involved with the order.

Sources: Javad Nurbakhsh, *Masters of the Path*. New York: Khaniqahi-Nimatullahi Publications,1980; Javad Nurbakhsh, *What the Sufis Say*. New York; Khaniqahi-Nimatullahi Publications, 1980.

★1150★
MEVLANA FOUNDATION
Box 305
Boulder, CO 80306

The Mevlana Foundation was founded in 1976 by Reshad Feild, the first sheikh of the Mevlana school of Sufism to travel to the West. The Mevlana lineage was initiated by Mevlana Jelalu'ddin Rumi (1207-1272), the great thirteenth-century mystic poet. Raised as a Sufi, Rumi was an ecstatic and a visionary. He settled in Qonya, in present-day Turkey, and his tomb became the headquarters of his followers. They formally organized soon after his death.

Sufis share the basic beliefs of Islam but are organized around the leader, the sheikh, of the order who is considered the axis of the conscious universe. Rumi was especially devoted to music, and the Mevlana Order developed a musical emphasis. The order practices the zhikr, the remembrance of God, and became noted for its practice of the Turn, a dance in which individual Sufis attempted to establish a universal axis within themselves. For this practice the Mevlana became famous in popular folklore as the "whirling dervishes."

Reshad Feild was raised in London. He studied with a Gurdjieff/Ouspensky group as well as the Druids, and finally became a professional spiritual healer. In the early 1960s he met Pir Vilayat Khan, leader of the Sufi Order, and was initiated as a Sufi sheikh by him. In the fall of 1969, still on a spiritual pilgrimage, Feild encountered a man referred to simply as Hamid. As a result of this encounter, he traveled to Turkey to study. While there he met Sheikh Suleyman Dede, the head of the Mevlana Order.

In 1976 Feild left Turkey and moved to Los Angeles, where he became a Sufi teacher and healer. Shortly after the move, he assisted Dede's visit to America. During this trip, Dede initiated Feild as the first sheikh in the West. Feild founded the Institute for Conscious Life which later became the Mevlana Foundation.

Membership: Not reported. Groups affiliated with the foundation can be found in the United States, Canada, and England.

Sources: Reshad Feild, *The Last Barrier*. New York: Harper & Row, 1976; Reshad Feild, *The Invisible Way*. San Francisco: Harper & Row, 1979; Reshad Feild, *Cooperation in the Three Worlds*. Los Angeles: The Institute for Conscious Life, 1974; Murat Yagan, *I Come from Behind Kaf Mountain*. Putney, VT: Threshold Books, 1984.

★1151★
PROSPEROS
℅ Inner Space Center
Box 5505
El Monte, CA 91734

Closely paralleling the Gurdjieff movement is the Prosperos, founded in 1956 in Florida by Phez Kahlil and Thane Walker, its present leader. Walker, described by all who have met him as an awe-inspiring, charismatic person, is a former Marine and student of Georgei Gurdjieff. He has modeled himself on Gurdjieff, but has broadened his sources with material from Jung, Freud, modern psychological techniques and the occult. The group was named after the magician in Shakespeare's *The Tempest*. It is described as a "Fourth Way" school.

The overarching reality for the Prosperos is the One Mind. Reality is experienced as one views from the perspectives of that One Mind. Both memory and the senses could be one vision, but via fourth way techniques, the self can be identified with the One. "Translation" is the name given that process. In Translation classes, the pupil is led through five steps: the statement of Being (What are the facts about reality?); Uncovering the Lie, the claims of the senses; Argument, or testing of the claims; Summing up Results; and Establishing the Absolute. Thane relies heavily on Gurdjieff's technique of disorientation of the pupil and the importance of the pupil-teacher relationship. He creates many kinds of experiences in various classes and intensive seminars. Pantomime, improvisation, body exercises and singing are all used as aids.

Headquarters of the Prosperos, termed the Inner Space Center, houses Publishing Programs, which produces the monthly *Newsletter*, instructional materials and Thane's book, *Not So Secret Doctrine*. Leadership is vested in Thane and the Mentors. The Mentors are drawn from the High Watch, an inner circle of advanced students who have completed three classes, submitted two theses and delivered an oral dissertation. There is an annual Prosperos assembly. In the Midwest, Thane operates through the Institute of Advanced Thinking, headquartered in Cleveland, Ohio.

Membership: In 1984, there were an estimated 3,000 members in groups in San Francisco; Hawaii; Oregon; New York; Ohio; New Orleans; and Seattle.

Educational facilities: Prosperos Seminary, El Monte, California.

Periodicals: *Newsletter*, Box 5505, El Monte, CA 91734.

★1152★
SUBUD
℅ Chairman Locksin Thompson
4 Pilot Rd.
Carmel, CA 93924

In Georgei Gurdjieff's book, *All and Everything*, he speaks of Ashiata Shiemash, the Prophet of Conscious. Some of Gurdjieff's students claimed that the passages were prophetic and that the Ashiata Shiemash was yet to come. One of the students with Gurdjieff during the last years of his life claimed students were told that the Ashiata Shiemash was "already preparing himself a long way from here," (i.e., Paris), and that he would be associated with the Malay Archipelago. After Gurdjieff's death, many of his students awaited the coming of a teacher to pick up the master's mantle; many thought they had found him in the person of Bapak Subuh (b. 1901).

Muhammed Subuh was a local government official from Java. Acting on prophecy that he was to die in his twenty-fourth year, be began to search for spiritual guidance and turned to many teachers, including several Sufi shaikhs such as Shaikh Abdurrahman of the Nakshibendi Order of Dervishes. To a man, they told him that he was different, that they had nothing to teach him and that his enlightenment would come directly from God. However, no enlightenment came until 1925, when one evening a ball of light descended upon him, entered through the crown of his head and filled him with radiant light and vibrations. For the next three years, his body experienced spontaneous occurrences of the *latihans*, a cleansing and purifying process. After three years these stopped, and he entered a period of darkness and confusion. Finally in 1933, his true mission was revealed to him, and he was soon contacted by some Sufis whose teacher had requested the contact. Thus Subud became a movement.

Bapak (meaning father) Subud quit his job and devoted his life to the spread of the movement throughout Java. His work continued for twenty-three years. Some Europeans heard of his work and invited him to England in 1956. In England, Bapak soon gained a following, largely built upon former disciples of Gurdjieff. J. G. Bennett was particularly influential the author of the widely read *Concerning Subud*. Bennett, a well-known Gurdjieff disciple, had, in 1946, founded the Institute for the Comparative Study of History, Philosophy and the Sciences at Coome Springs, England, to further Gurdjieff's teachings. The Institute became the center for the spread of Subud in the English-speaking world.

Subud is a contraction of three Sanskrit words: "Sulisa," right living in accordance with the will of God; "Budhi," the inner force residing in the nature of man himself; and "Dharma," surrender and submission to the power of God. The key to Subud is the *latihan*, the process of surrendering to the power of god, and the only group occurrence (usually twice a week) in Subud. Beginners must go through several months of probation before entering the *latihan*. After establishing their sincerity, they are opened. Opening is accomplished through instrumentality of several experienced members (helpers) who are viewed as channels of the higher energies of God. It is believed by Subud that the power originally given directly to Bapak is transmitted by contact with a person in whom it is already established.

The *latihan* proper is a time of moving the consciousness beyond mind and desire and allowing the power to enter and do its work. During this time, males and females are in separate, darkened rooms. Often accompanying the spontaneous period are various body movements and vocal manifestations--cries, moans, laughter and singing. These occur in the voluntary surrender of the self to the power. During this time, people report sensations of love and freedom and, often, healings. All reach a higher level of consciousness.

After coming to England, Subud spread rapidly. The healing of Eva Bartok in 1957 was a major event in its spread. In 1958, Bapak was invited to the United States by a John Cooke, and Subud found a home among Gurdjieff disciples in this country. It spread rapidly. A periodical, *Subud News* (later *Subud North American News*) was founded in 1959, and Dharma Book Company was established to publish the movement's literature. By 1972, Subud had more than seventy centers in North America.

Membership: Not reported.

Remarks: Some difficulty in studying Subud has been experienced because of the sharp distinction drawn between those who have experienced *latihan* and outsiders. Much literature is produced only for members and unavailable for researchers.

Sources: John G. Bennett, *Concerning Sabud*. New York: University Books, 1959; Husein Rofe, *The Path of Subud*. London: Rider & Company, 1959; Muhammad-Subuh Sumohadiwidjojo, *Susila Budhi Dharma*. Subud Publications International, 1975; Anthony Bright-Paul, *Stairway to Subud*. New York: Dharma Book Company, 1965; Eva Bartok, *Worth Living For*. New York: University Books, 1959.

★1153★
SUFI ISLAMIA RUHANIAT SOCIETY
% The Mentorgarten
10 Precita Avenue
San Francisco, CA 94110

In the mid-1970s, the San Francisco Sufi Society, formerly headed by Murshid Samuel L. Lewis (1896-1971), came into increasing conflict with Pir Vilayat Inayat Khan, the head of the Sufi Order. Lewis had been initiated into

Sufism by Rabia Martin the first murshid of the Sufi Order and had known Hazrat Inayat Khan. During the years after World War II, when the Sufi Order was not active in America, Lewis had traveled to Asia and received training and initiation independent of Khan's son and successor, Pir Vilayat. He founded a group in San Francisco in the mid-1960s. In 1968 he aligned his work with Pir Vilayat. Among issues raised by Lewis's followers in the Sufi Order was Pir Vilayat's rejection of homosexuals in the membership. This conflict came to a head in 1977 when Pir Vilayat forbade the use of all conscience-altering drugs, such as marijuana and LSD, and demanded acceptance of himself as the prime spiritual teacher. In rejecting these constraints, leaders of the San Francisco Sufi Society, especially many who considered Samuel Lewis their prime spiritual guide, separated themselves from Pir Vilayat.

The Sufi Islamia Ruhaniat Society continues a program and practice much like the Sufi Order and uses the writings of Hazrat Inayat Khan, the founder of the Sufi Order, and of Samuel L. Lewis as teaching material. Members proceed through a series of studies consisting of twelve grades. Worship services are held on Sunday, and Sufi dancing sessions occur during the week. Heads of the Society are Murshid Moineddin Jablonski and Masheikh Wali Ali Meyer.

Membership: Not reported. In 1980, classes and regular weekly meetings were being held in San Francisco, Palo Alto, San Jose, Berkeley, Marin County, and Sonoma County, California (all locations in the greater San Francisco Bay area).

Periodicals: *Bismullah*, 410 Placita, San Francisco, CA 94110.

Sources: Samuel L. Lewis, *The Jerusalem Trilogy*. Novato, CA: Prophecy Pressworks, 1975; Samuel L. Lewis, *In the Garden*. New York: Harmony Books, 1975; Samuel L. Lewis, *Introduction to Spiritual Brotherhood*. San Francisco: Sufi Islamia, 1981.

★1154★
SUFI ORDER
Sufi Order Secretariat
Box 574
Lebanon Springs, NY 12114

Sufism was brought to the United States in 1910 by Pir Hazrat Inayat Khan (1881-1927). An Indian-born musician, he was initiated into the Nizami branch of the Christi Order, one of the main Sufi schools of India. (The other main branch, the Sabiri, is represented in the United States by the Chishti Order of America.) The Chishti School was brought to India from Persia, and in its new home it absorbed elements of Hindu Vedantic thought which gave it a distinctive position within the Sufi world. The idea in coming to the West was to westernize the Sufi path. By bringing together East and West, it was thought, a basis for unity in the religion of love and wisdom could be laid. Doctrinal bias would be replaced by the power of mysticism.

Khan brought the Sufi Order to America in 1910. His first initiate was Rabia Martin who developed a center in San Francisco prior to World War I, which included among its member Samuel L. Lewis. Pir Inayat died suddenly in 1927 and succession was passed to his then eleven-year old son Vilayat. In the United States, Martin claimed the succession as the first initiate and murshid (minister). The European members and the family refused to recognize her, partly because she was a female, and the American and European work separated. During the last years of her life, Martin (d. 1947) heard of and began to investigate a new Indian teacher, Meher Baba, but died before completing her evaluation. Martin was succeeded by Ivy Oneita Duce, who became a disciple of Meher Baba and led the Sufi following entrusted to her under his care.

The Sufi Order was reintroduced to the United States in the 1960s by Pir Inayat Vilayat Khan (b. 1916). His work on the West Coast was boosted by the encounter with Samuel Lewis. Lewis, a former member of Martin's group, did not accept Meher Baba. After World War II he traveled to Asia and received several independent initiations and recognition as a Sufi murshid. he founded a Sufic group in San Francisco in 1966 which he brought into the Sufi Order in 1968. (Eventually, much of that work was lost when in 1977 some of Lewis's students rejected some of Khan's regulations for the Order and withdrew to form the Sufi Islamia Ruhaniat Society.) Khan succeeded in building a stable national organization during the 1970s, and has become one of the most respected and popular teachers within the loosely organized New Age Movement.

The teachings of Inayat Khan have been summarized in ten "Sufi Thoughts." The Thoughts affirm that there is but one God, Master, Holy Book (i.e., the sacred manuscript of nature), religion, law, brotherhood, moral principle, object of praise, truth and path. Meditation and dervish dancing are the main means to induce the mystic consciousness.

The activity headed by Khan has three aspects. The Sufi Order proper is an esoteric school into which individuals are admitted by initiation (Bayat) and accept Khan as their spiritual counsellor. Initiates follow a study program and follow a set of personal practices, including special breathing techniques and the repetition of a wazifa (or mantrum) usually delineated at the time of initiation. The more esteric religious activity is called the Universal Worship of the Church of All. Universal Worship is built around a liturgy developed by Inayat Khan which attempts to emphasize what is perceived as the essence of religion within all religions. Inayat Khan initiated the building of the Universel, a temple of all religions, in France shortly before his death. The Healing Order is built around the group healing ritual developed by Inayat Khan. Under Vilayat, the healing work has pushed the Sufi Order into the middle of the holistic health movement which became a prominent part of the larger New Age movement during the 1970s.

The American work of the Sufi Order is headed by Pir Khan and the Board of Trustees, which control the property and assets of the Order. An Interstate Council, consisting of the Trustess and representatives of all the branches of the Order, oversees financial transactions and coordinates programs. Center and branch leaders are appointed by Pir Khan. The on-going administration of the order is in the hands of Secretary General. Internationally the Sufi Order is headquartered in France with national branches in England, Holland, France, Germany, Austria, Italy, Switzerland, India, and Canada. Nationally, the order is headquartered at the Abode of the Message, a community near Lebanon Springs, New York on the site of a former Shaker Village.

Membership: Not reported. There are centers across the United States and Canada.

Periodicals: *The Message*, Route 15, Box 270, Tucson, AZ 85715; *Under the Wings*, Sufi Order, Route 15, Box 270, Tucson, AZ 85715; *Ziraat*, 22 Pillow Road, Austin, TX 78745.

Sources: *The Sufi Order*. New Lebanon, NY: The Message, Sufi Order, 1977; Elisabeth de Jong-Keesing, *Inayat Khan*. The Hague: East-West Publications Fonds B. V., 1974; Vilayat Inayat Khan, *The Message in Our Time*. San Francisco: Harper & Row, 1978; *Toward the One*. New York: Harper & Row, 1974; *Initiation*. Lebanon Springs, NY: Sufi Order, 1980.

Black Islam

★1155★
**AHMADIYYA ANJUMAN ISHAAT ISLAM,
   LAHORE, INC**
36911 Walnut St.
Newark, CA 94560

Following the death of Mirza Ghulam Hazrat Ahmad (1835-1908), founder of the Ahmadiyya Movement in Islam, a disagreement arose among his followers concerning the founder's status. Those who followed Ahmad's family proclaimed him a prophet. However, others, led by Maulawi Muhammad Ali, considered Ahmad the Promised Messiah and the greatest *mujaddid*, i.e., renewer of Islam, but denied that Ahmad had ever claimed the special status of "prophet." Ali asserted that Ahmad's use of that term was entirely allegorical. The claim of prophethood for Ahmad has resulted in the assignment of Ahmadiyya Muslims to a status outside of the Muslim community and resulted in their persecution in several Muslim-dominated countries.

Members of the Ahmadiyya branch founded by Ali came to America in the 1970s and incorporated in California.

Membership: Not reported.

Periodicals: *The Islamic Review*, 36911 Walnut St., Newark, CA 94560.

★1156★
AHMADIYYA MOVEMENT OF ISLAM
2141 Leroy Place, N.W.
Washington, DC 20008

The Ahmadiyya movement was not brought to the United States with the intention of its becoming a black man's religion. Ahmadiyya originated in India in 1889 as a Muslim reform movement. It differs from orthodox Islam in that it believes that Mirza Ghulam Hazrat Ahmad (1835-1908) was the promised Messiah, the coming one of all the major Indian faiths. It has, in the years since its founding, developed the most aggressive missionary program in Islam.

Ahmad had concluded, as a result of his studies, that Islam was in a decline and that he had been appointed by Allah to demonstrate its truth, which he began doing by authoring a massive book, *Barahin-i-Ahmaditah*. He assumed the title of *mujaddid*, the renewer of faith for the present age, and declared himself both Madhi, the expected returning savior of Muslims, and the Promised Messiah of Christians. He advocated the view that Jesus had not died on the cross, but had come to Kashmir in his later life and died a normal death there. The second coming is not of a resurrected Jesus, but the appearance of one who bore the power and spirit of Jesus.

Ahmadiyya came to the United States in 1921 and the first center was in Chicago. Its founder, Dr. Mufti Muhammad Sadiq began to publish a periodical, *Muslim Sunrise*. While recruiting some members from among immigrants, the overwhelming majority of converts consisted of blacks. Only since the repeal of the Asian Exclusion Act in 1965 and the resultant emigration of large numbers of Indian and Pakistani nationals has the movement developed a significant Asian constituency in the United States.

A vast missionary literature demonstrating Islam's superiority to Christianity has been produced. Jesus is widely discussed. He is viewed as a great prophet. He only swooned on the cross. He escaped from the tomb to India and continued many years of ministry. He is buried at Srinagar, India, where the legendary Tomb of Issa (Jesus) is a popular pilgrimage site. The denial of the divinity of Jesus is in line with the assertion of Allah as the one true God. Christianity is seen as tritheistic.

At present, the movement is small. Headquarters were moved to Washington, D.C., in 1950 after a quarter century in Chicago.

Membership: Not reported. Active centers in more than twenty cities are in operation, almost all in the Northeast and Midwest.

Periodicals: *The Ahmadiyya Gazette*, 2141 Leroy Place, N.W., Washington, DC 20008; *The Muslim Sunrise*, 2141 Leroy Place, N.W., Washington, DC 20008.

Sources: Muhammad Zafrulla Khan, *Ahmadiyyat, The Renaissance of Islam*. London: Tabshir Publications, 1978; Hazrat Mirza Bashiruddin Mahmud Ahmad, *Ahmadiyyat or the True Islam*. Washington, DC: The American Fazl Mosque, 1951; Hazrat Mirza Bashiruddin Mahmad Ahmad, *Invitation*. Rabwah, Pakistan: Ahmadiyya Muslim Foreign Missions, 1968; A. R. Dard, *Life of Ahmad*. Lahore, Pakistan: Tabshir Publications, 1948; S. Abul Hasan Ali Nadwi, *Qadianism, A Critical Study*. Lucknow, India: Islamic Research and Publications, 1974.

★1157★
AMERICAN MUSLIM MISSION
Masjid Hon. Elijah Muhammad
7351 S. Stony Brook Ave.
Chicago, IL 60649

Though there are a variety of Muslim groups functioning within the black community, when one reads in the media or hears mention of "Black Muslims," the most likely reference is to the Nation of Islam, founded by Master Wallace Fard Muhammad and headed for many years by its prophet, Elijah Muhammad (1897-1975). After Elijah Muhammad's death the organization's name was changed successively to the World Community of Islam in the West and in 1980 the American Muslim Mission. It is the most successful of the Black Muslim bodies, having spread across the nation in the 1960s during the period of the black revolution. Its success and that of one dissident member, Malcolm X, led to numerous books and articles about it.

Following the death of Noble Drew Ali, founder of the Moorish Science Temple of America, there appeared in Detroit one W. D. Fard, a mysterious figure claiming to be Noble Drew Ali reincarnated. He proclaimed that he had been sent from Mecca to secure freedom, justice and equality for his uncle (the Negroes) living in the wilderness of North America, surrounded and robbed by the cave man. (The white man was also referred to as the "Caucasian devil" and "Satan.") He established a temple in 1930 in Detroit. Among his many converts was Elijah Poole.

The 1930s was a time of intense recruiting activity and dispute with the Nation of Islam. Within Fard's ranks discussion focused on his divinity, legitimacy and role. In 1934, a second temple was founded in Chicago, and the following year Fard dropped from sight. By this time, Poole, known as Elijah Muhammad, had risen to leadership.

Under Elijah Muhammad's leadership the Black Muslims emerged as a strong, cohesive unit. Growth was slow, due in part to Muhammad's imprisonment during World War II as a conscientious objector. As the new prophet, he composed the authoritative Message to the Blackman in America, *a summary statement of the Nation of Islam's position.*

The central teaching of the Nation of Islam can be seen as a more sophisticated version of the Moorish Science study of the black man's history. According to Muhammad, Yakub, a mad black scientist, created the white beast, who was then permitted by Allah to reign for six thousand years. That period was over in 1914. Thus the twentieth century is the time for the Nation of Islam to regroup and regain an ascendant position.

Education, economics, and political aspirations were major aspects of the Muslim program. The first University of Islam was opened in 1932, and parochial education (many of the schools being names for Clara Muhammad, Elijah Muhammad's wife) has been a growing and more effective part of the Nation ever since. Besides the common curriculum, Black Muslim history, Islam and Arabic have been stressed. Classes are offered through the twelfth grade. Economically, the Muslims have stressed a work ethic and business development. The weekly newspaper carries numerous ads by businesses owned by Muslims. Politically, Muslims looked to the establishment of a black nation to be owned and operated by blacks.

Muslims excluded whites from the movement and imposed a strict discipline on members to accentuate their new religion and nationality. Foods, dress and behavior patterns are regulated; a ritual life based on, but varying from, Orthodox form, was prescribed.

Black Muslims instituted a far-reaching program in furtherance of their aspirations. An evangelizing effort to make the Muslim program known within the black community was sustained in a weekly newspaper, *Muhammad Speaks.* During the 1960s and into the 1970s, growth was spectacular. By the time of Elijah Muhammad's death there were approximately 70 temples across the nation, including the South and over 100,000 members.

In 1975 Elijah Muhammad died and was succeeded by his son Wallace D. Muhammad. During the decade of Wallace's leadership, a move toward both Orthodox Islam and decentralization of the organization has occurred. These moves have been reflected in the name changes, the schism of conservatives who have left to found movements continuing the peculiar emphases of the Nation of Islam prior to 1975, and the beginning of acceptance of the American Muslim Mission by orthodox Muslims. *Muhammad Speaks* was renamed *Bilalian News.*

In 1985 Wallace Muhammad, with the approval of the Council of Imans (ministers), resigned his post as leader of the American Muslim Mission and disbanded the movement's corporate structure. Property owned by the corporation was to be sold. Wallace remains as the iman of the temple on Chicago's south side. That move represents the establishment of a fully congregational polity by the Muslims whose local centers are now under the guidance of the imans rather than the control of the Chicago headquarters.

Membership: Not reported. There were approximately 200 centers in the mission at the time of its disincorporation. Foreign centers were located in Barbados, Belize, Guyana, Bermuda, Jamaica, the Bahamas, Canada, St. Thomas Island, and Trinidad.

Periodicals: *American Muslim Journal*, 7801 S. Cottage Grove Avenue, Chicago, IL 60619.

Sources: Elijah Muhammad, *Message to the Blackman in America.* Chicago: Muhammad Mosque of Islam, No. 2, 1965; C. Eric Lincoln, *The Black Muslims in America*, Boston: Beacon Press, 1961; Warith Deen Muhammad, *As a Light Shineth from the East.* Chicago: WDM Publishing Co., 1980; Wallace D. Muhammad, *Lectures of Elam Muhammad.* Chicago: Zakat Propagation Fund Publications, 1978; W. D. Muhammad, *Religion on the Line.* Chicago: W. D. Muhammad Publications, 1983.

★1158★
ANSAARU ALLAH COMMUNITY
716 Bushwick Ave.
Brooklyn, NY 11221

Members of the Ansaaru Allah Community , also known as the Nubian Islaamic Hebrew Mission, believe that the nineteenth-century Sudanese leader, Muhammed Ahmed Ibn Al-Sayid Abdullah (1844-1885), was the True Mahdi, the predicted Khaliyfah (successor) to the Prophet Mohammed. After his death, Al Mahdi was buried in the Sudan, and the group he founded (the Ansaars) continued under his successors, mainly: 1) As Sayyid Abdur Rahman Muhammad Al Madhi (the first successor); 2) As Sayyid Al Haadi Abdur Muhammad Rahmaan Al Madhi (the second successor); 3) As Sayyid Isa Al Haadi Muhammad Al Madhi (the third successor). Presently, the third successor, who is also Al Mahdi's great-grandson, leads the mission.

The Community teaches from the Old Testament (Tawrah), the Psalms of David (Dhabuwr), the New Testament (Injiyl), and the *Holy Qur'aan.* The last testament, the *Holy Qur'aan*, was given to the last and seal of the Prophets of the line of Adam, Mustafa Muhammad Al Amin. The group teaches that Allah is Alone in His power, the All (which is Tawhiyd "Oneness"), and does not use the term "God."

Adam and Hawwah (Eve) are believed to have been Nubians. After the flood, during the prophet Nuwh's (Noah) time, his son Ham desired to commit sodomy while looking at his father's nakedness. This act resulted in the curse of leprosy being put upon Ham's fourth son, Canaan, thus turning his skin pale. In such a manner did the pale races come into existence, including the Amorites, Hittites, Jebusites, Sidonites, all the sons of Canaan and their descendants. Mixing the blood with these "subraces" (so-called because they are no longer pure Nubians), is unlawful for Nubians.

From the seed of Ibraahiym (Abraham), two nations were produced, the nation of Isaac, whose descendants later became known as Israelites, through his son Jacob, and the nation of Ishmael, whose descendants are called the Ishmailites. The Israelites were enslaved for four hundred and thirty years in Egypt. The Ishmailites were predicted to be enslaved in a land not of their own for four hundred years. The Nubians of the United States, the West Indies and various other places around the world are the seed of Ishmael (and hence Hebrews). Al Madhi taught that all with straight hair and pale skin were Turks; However, this does not include people of color such as the Latins, Japanese, Koreans, Cubans, Sicilians, etc.

Under As Siddid Al Imaan Isa Al Aaahi Al Madhi's guidance, the Nubian Islaamic Hebrew Mission was begun in the late 1960s in New York. In 1970, the prophesies of the "Opening of the Seventh Seal" (Revelation 8:1) commenced with the opening of the Ansaaru Allah Community and the publishing of literature to help remove the veil of confusion from Nubians. In 1972 communities were established in Philadelphia, Connecticut, Texas, and Albany, New York. The following year centers were opened in Trinidad and Tobaga. In the next decade the movement spread around the world and included centers in England, Ghana, South America and Hawaii.

Symbol of the community is the six-pointed star (made from two triangles) in an inverted cresent. It is considered to be the seal of Allah.

Membership: Not reported.

Periodicals: *Ansar Village Bulletin*, 716 Bushwick Ave., Brooklyn, NY 11221.

Sources: Philip Warner, *Dervish, The Rise of An African Empire*. New York: Taplinger Publishing Company, 1975; Al Hajj Al Iman Isa Ibd'Allah Muhammad Al Madhi, trans., *The Holy Qur'aan*. Brooklyn, NY: Ansaru Allah Community, 1977; *Muslim Prayer Book*. Brooklyn, Ansaru Allah Community, 1984; *What Is a Muslim?*. Brooklyn, NY: Ansaru Allah Community, 1979; *Dietary Laws of a Muslim*. Brooklyn, NY: Ansaru Allah Community, 1979; *Muhammad Ahmad, The Only True Madhi!*. Brooklyn, NY: Ansaru Allah Community, 1979.

★1159★
CALISTRAN
(Defunct)

The Calistran was a short-lived splinter of the original Nation of Islam (now the American Muslim Mission) which came to public attention in the early 1970s, a period of heightened tension and internal violence within the black Muslim community generally. On October 7, 1973, two members of the Calistran who had reportedly "stepped out of line" were shot in Pasadena, California, by a "disciplinarian." No sign of the Calistran has been seen in the 1980s.

★1160★
HANAFI MUSLIM MOVEMENT
7700 16th St., N.W.
Washington, DC 20012

The Hanafi Muslim Movement was founded in 1968 by Hamaas Abdul Khaalis (born Ernest Timothy McGee). He had become a member of the Nation of Islam now the American Muslim Mission in 1950 and by 1956 was the national secretary of the Nation of Islam. His study of Islam convinced him that the orthodox position was correct (i.e., there is no god but Allah, and Mohammed is his prophet-not Elijah Muhammad). In 1968 Khaalis left the Nation of Islam and established the Hanafi Madh-Hab Center. In 1972, he moved the headquarters from New York City to Washington, D.C. into facilities provided by basketball star Kareem Abdul-Jabbar.

In 1973, a series of events began which completely ravaged the Hanafi movement. On January 18, 1973, seven members of the Hanafi Muslims (including two of Khaalis's children) were slain in their Washington, D.C. home and movement headquarters. Khaalis's wife was shot and survived, though she is paralyzed for life. The Nation of Islam was accused of the murders, a charge it vehemently denied. Subsequently, five members of the Philadelphia Nation of Islam group were convicted of the murders, but received relatively light sentences.

Then in 1977, Khaalis and some of his followers, seeking revenge for the murders, took over three buildings in Washington, D.C. and held hostages for 38 hours. In the process, one man was killed. For this action, Khaalis was sentenced to spend from 41 to 120 years in prison, and eleven of his followers were also convicted and sentenced.

The Hanafi Muslis believe in a literal interpretation of the Koran and count themselves among the true followers of Islam. They allow whites to join, but few have taken advantage of the opportunity. In 1977, they numbered fewer than 1,000 members; they had mosques in New York, Chicago, Los Angeles, and Washington, D.C. Authority for the Hanafi Muslims is vested in the chief iman (teacher), and each mosque is headed by an iman appointed by the chief iman.

Membership: Not reported. The movement has declined significantly since the incident in Washington in 1977. It numbers only a few hundred members at most.

Remarks: Basketball star Kareem Abdul-Jabbar has been a member of the Hanafi group since the early 1970s. He was a pallbearer at the funeral for Khaalis's children.

Sources: Kareem Abdul-Jabbar, *Giant Steps.* New York: Bantam Books, 1983; Bill Rhoden, "Kareem" in *Ebony*, vol. 30, no. 6, (April 1975), pp. 54-62.

★1161★
MOORISH SCIENCE TEMPLE OF AMERICA
762 W. Baltimore St.
Baltimore, MD 21201

Timothy Drew (1886-1929), a black man from North Carolina, had concluded from his reading and travels that black people were not Ethiopians (as some early black nationalists were advocating) but Asiatics, specifically Moors. They were descendants of the ancient Moabites and their homeland was Morocco. He claimed that the Continental Congress had stripped American blacks of their nationality and that George Washington had cut down their bright red flag (the cherry tree) and hidden it in a safe in Independence Hall. Blacks were thus assigned to the role of slaves.

As Noble Drew Ali, Drew emerged in 1913 in Newark, New Jersey, to preach the message of Moorish identity. The movement spread slowly with early centers in Pittsburgh, Detroit and several southern cities. In 1925, Ali moved to Chicago and the following year incorporated the Moorish Science Temple of America. In 1927 he published *The Holy Koran* (not to be confused with the *Koran* or *Qur'aan* used by all orthodox Moslem groups). Ali's *Koran* was a pamphlet-size compilation of Moorish beliefs which drew heavily upon *The Aquarian Gospel of Jesus Christ*, a volume received by automatic writing by Spiritualist Levi Dowling in the 1890s. The *Koran* delineates the creation and fall of the race, the origin of black people, the opposition of Christianity to God's people and the modern predicament of the Moors.

It was Noble Drew Ali's belief that only Islam could unite the black man. The black race is Asiatic, Moroccan, hence Moorish. Jesus was a black man who tried to redeem the black Moabites and was executed by the white Romans. Moorish Americans must be united under Allah and his holy prophet. Marcus Garvey is seen as forerunner to Ali. Friday has been accepted as the holy day. Worship forms, particularly music, have been drawn from popular black culture and given Islamic content.

Ali died in 1919 and was succeeded by one of his young colleagues, R. German Ali, who still heads the movement. Shortly after Ali's death, one of the members appeared in Detroit as Wallace Fard Muhammad, the reincarnation of Noble Drew Ali, and began the Nation of Islam (now the American Muslim Mission). In spite of the competition from the Nation of Islam, the temple grew in the years after Ali's death, and during the 1940s temples could be found in Charleston, West Virginia; Hartford, Connecticut; Milwaukee; Richmond, Virginia; Cleveland; Flint, Michigan; Chattanooga, Tennessee; Indianapolis; Toledo and Steubenville, Ohio; Brooklyn; and Indiana Harbor, Indiana. In more recent years, the movement has declined. During the 1970s, the headquarters were moved to Baltimore.

Membership: Not reported.

Sources: Noble Drew Ali *Timothy Drew, The Holy Koran of the Moorish Science Temple of America.* [Baltimore: MD]: Moorish Science Temple of America, 1978; Noble Drew Ali, *Moorish Literature.* The Author, 1928; Arthur Huff Fauset, *Black Gods of the Metropolis.* Philadelphia: University of Pennsylvania Press, 1971.

★1162★
MOORISH SCIENCE TEMPLE, PROPHET ALI REINCARNATED FOUNDER
519 N. Howard St.
Baltimore, MD 21201

In 1975, Richardson Dingle-El, a member of the Moorish Science Temple of America in Baltimore, proclaimed himself Noble Drew Ali 3d, the reincarnation of Noble Drew Ali (1886-1929), the founder of the Moorish Science Temple of America. As such he claimed succession to Noble Drew Ali 2d (d.1945), who had claimed succession in the 1930s. The followers of Noble Drew Ali 3d have established headquarters in Baltimore and have several temples around the United States. A periodical is published by the temple in Chicago. In most ways it follows the beliefs and practices of the Moorish Science Temple of America.

Membership: Not reported.

Periodicals: *Moorish Guide*, 3810 S. Wabash, Chicago, IL 60653.

★1163★
THE NATION OF ISLAM (THE CALIPH)
Muhammad's Temple of Islam No. 1
1233 W. Baltimore St.
Baltimore, MD 21223

As significant changes within the Nation of Islam founded by Elijah Muhammad proceeded under his son and successor Wallace D. Muhammad, the Nation of Islam became a more orthodox Islamic organization. It was renamed the American Muslim Mission and dropped many of the distinctive features of its predecessor. Opposition among those committed to Elijah Muhammad's ideas and programs led to several schisms in the late 1970s. Among the "purist" leaders, Emmanuel Abdullah Muhammad asserted his role as the Caliph of

Islam raised up to guide the people in the absence of Allah (in the person of Wallace Fard Muhammad) and his Messenger (Elijah Muhammad). One Islamic tradition insists that a caliph always follows a messenger.

The Nation of Islam under the caliph continues the beliefs and practices abandoned by the American Muslim Mission. A new school, the University of Islam, was begun and the Fruit of Islam, the disciplined order of Islamic men, reinstituted. A new effort aimed at economic self-sufficiency has been promoted, and businesses have been created to implement the program.

Membership: Not reported. As of 1982, the Nation of Islam under the caliph had only two mosques, one in Baltimore and one in Chicago.

Periodicals: *Muhammad Speaks*, Muhammad's Temple of Islam No. 1, 1233 W. Baltimore St., Baltimore, MD 21223.

★1164★
THE NATION OF ISLAM (FARRAKHAN)
Box 20083
Chicago, IL 60620

Of the several factions which broke away from the American Muslim Mission (formerly known as the Nation of Islam and then as the World Community of Islam in the West) and assumed the group's original name, the most successful has been the Nation of Islam headed by Abdul Haleem Farrakhan. Farrakhan was born Louis Eugene Wolcott. He was a nightclub singer in the mid-1950s when he joined the Nation of Islam headed by Elijah Muhammad. As was common among Muslims at that time, he dropped his last name, which was seen as a name imposed by slavery and white society, and became known as Minister Louis X. His oratorical and musical skills carried him to a leading position as minister in charge of the Boston Mosque and, after the defection and death of Malcolm X, to the leadership of the large Harlem center and designation as the official spokesperson for Elijah Muhammad.

In 1975 Elijah Muhammad died. Though many thought Louis X, by then known by his present name, might become the new leader of the nation, Elijah Muhammad's son, Wallace, was chosen instead. At Wallace Muhammad's request, Farrakhan moved to Chicago to assume a national post. During the next three years, the Nation of Islam moved away from many of its distinctive beliefs and programs and emerged as the American Muslim Mission. It dropped many of its racial policies and began to admit white people into membership. It also began to move away from its black nationalist demands and to accept integration as a proper goal of its programs.

Farrakhan emerged as a leading voice among "purists" who opposed any changes in the major beliefs and programs instituted by Elijah Muhammad. Long-standing disagreements with the new direction of the Black Muslim body led Farrakhan to leave the organization in 1978 and to form a new Nation of Islam. He reinstituted the beliefs and program of the pre-1975 Nation of Islam. He reformed the Fruit of Islam, the internal security force, and demanded a return to strict dress standards.

With several thousand followers, Farrakhan began to rebuild the Nation of Islam. He established mosques and developed an outreach to the black community on radio. He was only slightly noticed until 1984 when he aligned himself with the U.S. presidential campaign of Jesse Jackson, a black minister seeking the nomination of the Democratic Party. Jackson's acceptance of his support and Farrakhan's subsequent controversial statements (some claimed by critics to be anti-Semitic) on radio and at press conferences kept Farrakhan's name in the news during the period of Jackson's candidacy and in subsequent months.

Membership: Not reported. There are an estimated 5,000 to 10,000 members of the Nation of Islam.

Periodicals: *The Final Call*, Box 20083, Chicago, IL 60620.

Sources: Louis E. Lomax, *When the Word Is Given*. Cleveland, OH: World Publishing Company, 1963; Clarence Page, "Deciphering Farrakhan " in *Chicago*, vol. 33, no. 8 (August 1984), pp. 130-35; Tynnetta Muhammad, *The Divine Light*. Phoenix, AZ: H.E.M.E.F, 1982; Elijah Muhammad, *Our Savior Has Arrived*. Chicago: Muhammad's Temple of Islam No. 2, 1974.

★1165★
NATION OF ISLAM (JOHN MUHAMMAD)
Nation of Islam, Temple No. 1
19220 Conat St.
Detroit, MI 48234

John Muhammad, brother of Elijah Muhammad, founder of the Nation of Islam, was among those who rejected the changes in the Nation of Islam and the teachings of ijah Muhammad which led to its change into the American Muslim Mission. In 1978 he left the mission and formed a continuing Nation of Islam designed to perpetuate the programs outlined in Elijah Muhammad's two books, *Message to the Blackman* and *Our Saviour Has Arrived*. According to John Muhammad, who uses the standard title of black Muslim leaders, "Minister" Elijah Muhammad was the last Messenger of Allah and was sent to teach the black man a New Islam.

Membership: Not reported. John Muhammad has support around the United States, but the only temple is in Detroit.

Periodicals: *Minister John Muhammad Speaks*. Nation of Islam, Temple No. 1, 19220 Conant St., Detroit, MI 48234.

Zoroastrianism

MEHER BABA, FRIENDS OF
% Meher Center on the Lakes
Box 487
Myrtle Beach, SC 29577

★1166★
MAZDAZNAN MOVEMENT
1159 S. Norton Ave.
Los Angeles, CA 90019

The first and for many years the only Zoroastrian group in the United States was the Mazdaznan Movement founded by the Rev. Dr. Otoman Zar-Adhusht Hanish (d. 1936). Dr. Hanish claimed to have been sent by the Inner Temple Community of El Khaman to bring Mazdaznan to the world. He began teaching around the turn of the century and formally inaugurated the movement in Chicago in 1902. He also began a periodical, *The Mazdaznan*, published by the Sun Worshippers Press (later the Mazdaznan Press). In 1916, headquarters were moved to Los Angeles.

Mazdaznan emphasizes the monotheistic faith in the Lord God Mazda, the creator. Man is in God and God in him. God is expressed as the Holy Family of Father (male creative principle), Mother (procreative female principle) and Child (destiny/salvation). Man is on earth to reclaim the earth and to turn it into a paradise suitable for God to dwell therein. The means to reclaim the material, the body, and make it as perfect as our spirit, is the power of breath. Mazdaznan teaches a discipline of breathing, rhythmic prayers and chants. These are supplemented by a recommended vegetarian diet and exercises.

Mazdaznan spread across America into Europe in its first decade. By the time Hanish died centers could be found in most urban centers. During the 1970s, centers were active in England (13), as well as Mexico, Belgium, Denmark, France, Germany, Holland, and Switzerland. There is a vegetarian science center in Hawaii.

Membership: Not reported.

Periodicals: *Mazdaznan*, 1159 S. Norton Ave., Los Angeles, CA 90019.

Sources: Otoman Zar-Adhusht Hanish, *Inner Studies*. Mokelumne Hill, CA: Health Research, 1963; O. Z. A. Hanish, *The Power of Breath*. Los Angeles: Mazdaznan Press, 1970; Otoman Zar-Adhusht Hanish, *The Philosophy of Mazdaznan*. Los Angeles: Mazdaznan Press, 1960; Otoman Zar-Adhusht Hanish, *Health and Breath Culture*. [Chicago]: Sun Worshipper Publishing Co., 1902; O. Z. Hanish & O Rauth, *God and Man United*. Santa Fe Springs, CA: Stockton Trade Press, 1975.

Meher Baba (1894-1969), was an Indian teacher born Merwan Sherariarji Irani of Zoroastrian parents living in Poona, India. He was born in the month of Meher, an observation that would later lead a disciple to give him the name by which he is popularly known. As a young man, Meher Baba met Hazrat Babajan, "an ancient Mohammedan woman and one of the five Perfect Masters of the Age." From her, he received what he described as self-realization, and in 1921 another Perfect Master, Upasani Maharaj (a Hindu), pronounced him a satguru, one who had come to full god-realization.

That same year he gathered his first disciples and in 1922 established a center in Bombay. In 1924 he moved to Aranaon, near Ahmednagar, and opened a permanent colony called "Meherabad." He included at the colony a hospital, poorhouse and free school. In 1925, he began his period of silence, unbroken in this life. From that time, he communicated only with a blackboard and, eventually, only with hand gestures.

Meher Baba began recruiting students in England in 1927. Meredith Starr traveled to India a few years later as his first Western disciple. Meher Baba first came to the United States in 1931 and began to contact people for the loosely knit fellowship of Friends of Meher Baba. The number of such friends, tied together by a host of autonomous centers, periodicals, and publishing concerns, grew steadily in the West, spurred by Meher Baba's occasional visits.

Meher Baba, meaning "Compassionate Father," said that he came not to teach but to awaken. He is the Avatar, God incarnate, who has reappeared often in man's history. Since men ignored the words, he remains silent. In the silence followers are able to realize the seven realities: the only real existence is God; the only real love is the love for God; the only real sacrifice is in pursuit of love; the only real renunciation abandons all selfish desires and thoughts; the only real knowledge is that god dwells in all; the only real control is the discipline of the senses; and the only real surrender is that in which the individual is calm in all circumstances.

Within the large body of Baba lovers, there is one special closeknit group called Sufism Reoriented. This group derives from the original Sufi group organized early in the century by Hazrat Inayat Khan, founder of the Sufi Order. Khan appointed Rabia Martin of San Francisco his successor, an appointment not recognized by members in Europe, in large part because Martin was female. Toward the end of her life, Martin heard of Meher Baba and began to correspond with him. She became convinced that he was the Qutb, in Sufi understanding the hub of the spiritual universe. Though Martin never met Meher Baba, her successor, Ivy Oneita Duce, did. Meher Baba confirmed her as the rightful successor, but more importantly, in 1952 during a trip to Myrtle Beach, South Carolina, Baba presented the group with a new plan contained in a document, "Chartered Guidance from Meher Baba for the Reorientation of Sufism as the Highway to the Ultimate Universalized."

Within Sufism Reoriented, the Sufi path begins in submission and obedience to the murshid as the arm of Baba. For the student, there must be a need to know that God exists, to be able to discriminate between the real and unreal, to be indifferent to externals, and to be ready to gain the six mental attitudes (control over thoughts, outward control, tolerance, endurance, faith, and balance).

Membership: Not reported.

Periodicals: *Glow International*,   Meher Baba Work, Box 10, New York, NY 10185; *Meher News Exchange, East/West*, 801 13th Avenue South, North Myrtle Beach, SC 29582.

Sources: Jean Adriel, *Avatar*. Santa Barbara, CA: J. F. Rowny Press, 1947; Naosherwan Anzar, *The Beloved, The Life and Work of Meher Baba*. North Myrtle Beach, SC: Sheriar Press, Inc., 1974; Tom Hopkinson & Dorothy Hopkinson, *Much Silence: Meher Baba, His Life and Work*. New York: Dodd, Mead & Company, 1974; Meher Baba, *God to Man and Man to God*. North Myrtle Beach, SC: Sheriar Press, Inc., 1975. Sufism Reoriented: Ivy Oneita Duce, *How a Master Works*. Walnut Creek, CA: Sufism Reoriented, 1975; *Sufism*. San Francisco: Sufism Reoriented, 1971; Ivy Oneita Duce, *What Am I Doing Here?* San Francisco: Sufism Reoriented, 1966; *Sufism Speaks Out*. Walnut Creek, CA: Sufism Reoriented, 1981.

★1168★
ZOROASTRIAN ASSOCIATIONS IN NORTH AMERICA
% Center for Zoroastrian Research
801 E. Tenth St.
Bloomington, IN 47401

Since 1965 immigration from India, Iran and Pakistan has included a number of Zoroastrians, though in no wise approaching the number of Hindus and Muslims. In the United States, those from India (Parsees) and those from Iran (Zartoshtis) have found a common identity of faith, in spite of the differences of language, nationality, doctrine and practice which separated them in their Asian setting. In those places where a sufficient number reside, associations have been organized and Zoroastrians from all countries belong. Because of the necessary compromise on doctrinal and liturgical issues, the more conservative leadership in Asia has tended to reject the American communities and to leave them in a somewhat isolated condition. American leaders are thus attempting to forge a

new Zoroastrianism which retains the essentials but discards the divisive quarrels of the Old World.

The Center for Zoroastrian Research in Bloomington, Indiana, has been actively gathering information on the American Zoroastrian community as well as actively participating in its ongoing self-examination.

Membership: In 1984 there were ten Zoroastrian Associations in the United States (Los Angeles, San Jose, and Huntington Beach, California; Houston; Hinsdale, Illinois; Silver Spring, Maryland; Pittsburg, Pennsylvania; Randolph, Madison, and Marlton, New Jersey) and four in Canada (Toronto; Vancouver; Edmonton; and Brossard, Quebec).

Bahaism

★1169★
BAHA'I WORLD FAITH
National Spiritual Assembly of the Baha'is of the U.S.
415 Linden Ave.
Wilmette, IL 60091

In Persia (present-day Iran), a predominantly Muslim country, the expectation of the coming of the Mahdi, the successor to Mohammed promised in Islamic writings, was strong. In this environment was born Mirza Ali Muhammed (1819-1850), a Shi'a Muslim who declared himself the Bab or Gate through whom people would know about the advent of another messenger of God. Many people accepted the messianic claims of the Bab after his declaration in 1844, and Babism was founded. The initial enthusiasm of the movement quickly encountered fierce opposition. Persecution followed. In 1850, the Bab was martyred.

Two years later, one of the Babis (followers of the Bab) attempted to kill the Shah, and persecution led to further imprisonments of Babis. Among those thrown in jail was Mirza Husayn Ali (1817-1892), who, while languishing in prison, came to understand himself as the Holy One whom the Bab predicted; however, he kept the revelation to himself for several years. In 1853, he, his family and many of the Bab's followers were exiled. They left Tehran for Bagdad. During the next years, leadership of the Babi movement was in the hands of Mirza Yahya, Husayn Ali's half brother, but gradually it shifted to Husayn Ali because of Mirza Yahya's incompetence. In 1863, Husayn Ali revealed to a few close associates and members of his family of the revelation in prison. From that time an increasing number of individuals began to recognize him as Baha'u'llah (meaning the Glory of God), his religious name, and leader of the exiles.

Bahu'u'llah moved from Bagdad to Adrianople (now Edirne), to the penal colony at Akka (now Acre) in present-day Israel. Arriving in Akka in 1868, he spent the remainder of his life there and while still under house arrest by the ruling Turkish authorities, produced his most important works, considered scripture by his followers.

Bahu'u'llah was succeeded by the third major figure in Baha'i history, Abbas Effendi (1844-1921), known to the world by his religious name, Abdu'l-Baha (meaning Slave of Baha). Abdu'l-Baha, Baha'u'llah's son, is considered the exemplar of the Baha'i Faith. He served Baha'u'llah until his death and later found himself confined by the Turkish authorities until the Revolution of the Young Turks in 1908 brought a gradual easing of restrictions. Abdu'l-Baha then turned his attention to the spread of Baha'ism. Under his guidance, it spread around the world. Upon his death in 1921, Adbu'l-Baha was succeeded by Shoghi Effendi (1897-1957), his grandson, as guardian of the faith.

The Baha'i Faith was brought to America in 1892 by Ibrahim Kheirella, though he later left the movement and founded a rival organization. Kheirella founded a group in Chicago in 1893 and several others sprang up as a result of his efforts. The first convert was Thornton Chase, who joined faith in 1894. The first United States Convention was held in 1907. In 1902, Agnes Baldwin Alexander encountered Baha'ism in Rome and took it to Hawaii. During 1912, Abdu'l-Baha spent eight months in the United States and laid the cornerstone of the Baha'i House of Worship in Wilmette, Illinois. The Temple took forty years to complete and was dedicated in 1953.

The teachings of Baha'ism are contained in the writings of the Bab, Baha'u'llah and Abdu'l-Baha, considered scriptures, and in the writings of Shoghi Effendi and the Universal House of Justice, considered infallible interpretations of the scriptures. They teach the essential oneness of all revealed faiths, which have been given at different stages and ages. Baha'ism is the crown and summation of the eight previous world faiths: Sabeanism, Judaism, Hinduism, Buddhism, Islam, Zoroastrianism, Islam and the Religion of the Bab. "Nine" is a prominent symbol of the faith; all temples are nine-sided and capped with a dome.

Baha'ism teaches that god is, in essence, unknowable, though his word is known through his chosen messenger. This word is summarized in thirteen principles: the independent search for truth, the oneness of the human race, the unity of religion, the condemnation of prejudice, the harmony of science and religion, the equality of the sexes, compulsory education, the adoption of a universal language, the abolition of extremes of wealth and poverty, a world court, work in the spirit of service as worship, justice and universal peace. Baha'ism also teaches the immortality of the soul in continuous progress.

Work is held as a necessity for all and is considered a form of worship. However, regular weekly gatherings featuring prayer and the readings from the sacred writings are held. There are an annual fasting period and eight holidays commemorating various events in the lives of the founders. March 21 is celebrated as New Year's Day. Besides the Temple at Wilmette, others have been built around the world.

After Shoghi Effendi's death, leadership of the faith passed to the Universal House of Justice, an international body headquartered in Haifa, Israel. Members of the Universal House of Justice are elected every five years at an international convention composed of representatives of the numerous national spiritual assemblies which have been formed in most countries of the world. In the United States, the direction of the Baha'i Faith is in the hands of the National Spiritual Assembly, elected annually at the National Baha'i Assembly. There is no clergy. Members are organized into local spiritual assemblies, with a minimum of nine members in each assembly. From its offices in Wilmette, Illinois, it has charge of the national administrative affairs of the faith, including the management of the Baha'i Publishing Trust and a Baha'i Home for the Aged.

The World Center of the Baha'i Faith is in Haifa, Israel, where the Bab shrine is located and Abdu'l-Baha is buried. National assemblies have been organized in over 120 countries and many others have Baha'i assemblies. The national assembly in England is one of the oldest, having been established in the 1930s. The British publishing house of George Ronald is a major publisher of English-language Baha'a books widely circulated in the United States.

Membership: Membership figures not available. The Baha'i Faith has a policy against reporting exact membership figures. In 1980, however, there were over 1,400 local spiritual assemblies (with a minimum of nine members each) in the United States and over 25,000 such assemblies in the world.

Periodicals: *World Order*, 536 Sheridan Road, Wilmette, IL 60091; *U. S. Baha'i Report*, 536 Sheridan Road, Wilmette, IL 60091.

Sources: Mary Perkins and Philip Hainsworth, *The Baha'i Faith*. London: Ward Lock Educational, 1980; H. M. Balyuzi, *Baha'u'llah, The King of Glory*. Oxford: George Ronald,1980; H. M. Balyuzi, *Abdu'l-Baha*. London: George Ronald, 1971; O. Z. Whitehead, *Some Early Baha'is of the West*. Oxford: George Ronald, 1976; William McElwee Miller, *The Baha'i Faith*. South Pasadena, CA: William Carey Library, 1974.

★1170★
FAITH OF GOD
(Defunct)

The Faith of God grew out of the work of Jamshid Maani, a Persian prophet known to the public as simply "The Man," a title used to signify the coming of maturity to humanity and that the real station of man is a spiritual station. The Man announced his mission in 1963 in Israel and then Iran. He began to gather followers in various nations around the world to the Faith of God. The Faith emerged following the death of Shoghi Effendi, the guardian of the Baha'i World Faith, and the failure of another guardian to emerge as his successor. Among the early converts to The Man's cause was John Carre, a lifelong Baha'i, who traveled extensively on his behalf and organized the House of Mankind, the administrative aspect of the Faith, in several countries. He also headed the international umbrella organization, the Universal Palace of Order.

The Man continued the Baha'i belief in progressive revelation to mankind through the various mediators or teachers from Zoroaster to Baha'u'llah, and sees himself as the latest in this series. Evolution is also a key notion. The universe and its various parts are in continuous evolution. The universe is alive. The culmination of material creation is man's moving toward spiritual man. This evolutionary process is part of a divine plan leading creation toward unity.

The overall evolution of humanity is toward perfection on all levels. This goal was the reason for all the prophets. Their teachings are one. All forms of worship are acceptable except those contrary to wisdom or detrimental to others. We must strive to give all persons the attributes of the saintly ones. The individual's progression is aided by thorough meditation and prayer but they must become effective in our thoughts and actions.

The House of Mankind was initially established in each of five areas of the world. Like the Baha'i Faith, there is no clergy. Pictured for the future was the development of the Universal Palace of Order, which will bring to realization the aspirations of mankind for the unity and oneness of government. The House of Mankind functioned for a period of approximately ten years in the United States from its headquarters in the residence of John Carre in Mariposa, California. However, during the 1970s, The Man lived with Carre for a number of months, during which time Carre came to know Maani personally and as a result withdrew his support. The movement, which had only several hundred members, ceased to exist in America soon after that action.

Sources: John Carre, *An Island of Hope*. Mariposa, CA: House of Light, 1975; The Man [Jamshid Maani], *Universal Order*. Mariposa, CA; John Carre, 1971; The Man, *"Heaven"*. Mariposa, CA: John Carre, 1971; The Man, *The Sun of the Word of the Man*. Mariposa, CA: John Carre, 1971.

★1171★
ORTHODOX BAHA'I FAITH, MOTHER BAHA'I COUNCIL OF THE UNITED STATES
3111 Futura
Roswell, NM 88201

The Orthodox Baha'i Faith, Mother Baha'i Council of the United States is one of three organizations of former members of the Baha'i Faith who accept the claims of Charles Mason Remey (see separate entry on Remey Society) to be the successor of Shoghi Effendi, the guardian of the Baha'i Faith who died in 1957. After Remey's death in 1974, Joel B. Marangella was one of two people to assert that Remey had named him the Third Guardian of the Faith. Upon assuming that position, Marangella discovered the organization that Remey had established in America in disarray due to the successful court action initiated by the Baha'i Faith. He moved to reestablish Remey's work through a new organization, the National Bureau of the Orthodox Baha'i Faith in America. In 1972 the headquarters moved from New York City to Albuquerque, New Mexico. Soon after that move a council of nine persons was elected. It assumed the responsibilities of the bureau as the Mother Baha'i Council of the United States. It is composed entirely of individuals residing in the Roswell, New Mexico, area.

The Mother Baha'i Council has continued an aggressive attack upon the organization of the Spiritual Assembly of the Baha'i Faith (the ruling authority for Baha'is), occasionally placing advertisements in Chicago-area newspapers outlining its position. (The United States headquarters of the Baha'i Faith is in Wilmette, Illinois, a Chicago suburb.)

Membership: Not reported. There are an estimated several hundred Orthodox Baha'is connected with the Mother Baha'i Council in the United States. Joel Marangella resides in Germany, and other members can be found throughout Europe.

Periodicals: *Newsletter*, 3111 Futura, Roswell, NM 88201.

★1172★
ORTHODOX BAHA'I FAITH UNDER THE REGENCY
% National House of Justice of the U.S. and Canada
Box 1424
Las Vegas, NV 87701

The Orthodox Baha'i Faith under the Regency is one of three organizations of former members of the Baha'i Faith who accepted the claims of Charles Mason Remey (see separate entry on Remey Society) to be the successor of Shoghi Effendi, the Guardian of the Baha'i Faith who died in 1957. Remey claimed to be the Second Guardian. After Remey's death in 1974, Joel B. Marangella was one of two men who claimed to have been appointed by Remey as the Third Guardian. Marangella organized his followers as the Orthodox Baha'i Faith, represented in the United States by the Mother Baha'i Council of the United States.

Among those appointed to a leadership role by Remey, Reginald B. (Rex) King accepted Marangella as the Third Guardian but later came e to the conclusion that both Remey and Marangella had taken actions which were contrary to Baha'i law. He concluded that Remey, rather than being the Second Guardian, was but the regent who assumed control until such time as the Second Guardian appeared and took his rightful place. Upon reaching that conclusion, King withdrew from Marangella and claimed to be the second regent.

King died in 1977. In his will be appointed four members of his family--Eugene K. King, Ruth L. King, Theodore Q. King, and Thomas King--as a council of regents to succeed him. The Orthodox Baha'is follow the teaching of the Baha'i Faith, differing only in their rejection of the authority of the spiritual assembly in favor of the regency.

Membership: Not reported. There are an estimated several hundred Orthodox Baha'is in the United States.

Periodicals: *The Star of the West*, Orthodox Baha'i Faith, National House of Justice of the United States and Canada, Box 1424, Las Vegas, NV 87701.

★1173★
REMEY SOCIETY
86-11 Commonwealth Blvd.
Bellerose, NY 11426

The Remey Society is one of three organizations of former members of the Baha'i Faith who accept Charles Mason Remey (1874-1974) as the Second Guardian of the Faith. Remey was a prominent Baha'i for many years. He authored a number of books, designed several Baha'i temples, and served as president of the International Baha'i Council. In 1951 he was one of nine people named by Shoghi Effendi as a hand of the cause.

In 1957 Shoghi Effendi died without having fathered a child, left a will, or naming a successor. Remey then joined with the other hands of the cause in proclaiming the formation of a Baha'i World Center made up of nine hands of the cause to assume temporarily the function of the guardian. Remey was one of the nine. However, during the next few years, Remey dissented from the position of the other hands. He argued that the guardianship was a necessary feature of the structure of the faith. He also asserted that, as the president of the International Baha'i Council (a position assigned Remey by Shoghi Effendi), he was the only one in a position to become the Second Guardian. He waited two years for the hands to accept his position. Then, in 1959, he left Haifa, where the Baha'i Faith has its international headquarters, and came to the United States. In 1960 he issued a Proclamation to the Baha'is of the World and circulated it

at the annual gathering of the American Baha'is that year. He also issued a pamphlet, "A Last Appeal to the Hands of the Faith," asking them to abandon plans to elect members of the International Baha'i Council in 1961. The hands continued to reject his claims and expelled him from the faith.

Throughout the 1960s Remey insisted upon his right to be designated the Second Guardian. Finally, in 1968 he appointed the first five Elders of the Baha'i Epoch and announced the organization of his followers under the name The Orthodox Abba World Faith. He retired to Florence, Italy, and lived out the last decade of his life in virtual retirement.

After Remey's death in 1974, two men, Donald Harvey and Joel Marangella, both claimed that he had appointed them as the Third Guardian of the Faith. The Remey Society unites the American followers of Donald Harvey. The society was organized by Francis C. Spataro.

Membership: Not reported. It is estimated that no more than a thousand people recognize Donald Harvey's claims, of whom only a few hundred reside in the United States.

Periodicals: *The Remey Letter*, 86-11 Commonwealth Blvd., Bellerose, New York 11426.

Sources: Charles Mason Remey, *The Baha'i Movement*. Washington, DC: J. D. Milans & Sons, 1912; Charles Mason Remey, *Observations of a Baha'i Traveller*. Washington, DC: J. D. Milans & Sons, 1914; Charles Mason Remey, *Extracts from Daily Observations of the Baha'i Faith Made to the Hands of the Faith in the Holy Land*. Privately published, (1961); Francis Cajetan Spataro, *The Lion of God*. Bellerose, NY: The Remey Society, 1981; Francis Cajetan Spataro, *The Rerum*. Bellerose, NY: The Author, 1980.

★1174★
WORLD UNION OF UNIVERSAL RELIGION AND UNIVERSAL PEACE
Current address not obtained for this edition.

In the years after the death of Abdu'l-Baha and the elevation of his grandson, Shoghi Effendi, to the leadership of the Baha'i Faith as the Guardian of the Faith, an American Baha'i, Ruth White, began to question Shoghi Effendi's authority. In her first book, *Abdul Baha and the Promised Age* (1926), she voiced her opposition to his attempts to develop the Baha'i organization by quoting Abdu'l-Baha to the effect that, "The Baha'i Movement is not an organization. You can never organize the Baha'i Cause." More importantly, she began to voice opposition to Shoghi Effendi's role as guardian, and in her 1929 work, *The Bahai Religion and Its Enemy, the Bahai Organization*, she attacked the authenticity of the Will and Testament of Abdul-Baha, the document upon which Effendi's authority rested.

Though she lectured widely throughout the United States, her only success in recruiting supporters came in Germany where the Baha'i World Union was founded by Wilhelm Herrigel and other Baha'is, who were described as friends of Abdul-Baha. The Baha'i World Union continued until 1937 when the German government outlawed the Baha'i Faith.

Simultaneously with White's attack upon Effendi, though separate from it, Ahmad Sohrab, a close friend of Abdu'l-Baha who had accompanied him on his American tour in 1912, and an American Baha'i, Julie Chandler (Mrs. Lewis Stuyvesant Chandler), formed an independent Baha'i network in New York City. They felt that Effendi's increasing efforts to organize the faith were counterproductive. They established the New History Society which offered lectures by Sohrab and other prominent guests (Albert Einstein addressed it on one occasion) and opened the Baha'i Bookshop. Members of the New History Society considered themselves participants in the Baha'i movement but separate from the organization headed by Effendi. In response, the Baha'i Faith brought suit against Sohrab, Chandler, and the New History Society seeking to prevent their use of the name "Baha'i." The court ruled against them, however, stating that no group of followers of a religion could monopolize the name of that religion or prevent other groups of followers from practicing their faith.

Like the Baha'i World Union, the New History Society found support in Europe and opened offices in Paris in the 1930s, and Sohrab became the major spokesperson for the society. He spoke frequently and authored a number of books, including *Broken Silence*, a response to the 1941 court case.

Ruth White and Ahmad Sohrab both died in 1958 and Julie Chandler in 1961. Since their deaths, their work and thought have been carried on by Hermann Zimmer of Stuttgart, West Germany. Zimmer had returned to Germany in 1948 after being released from a POW camp. He picked up the remnants of Herrigel's organization and formed the World Union for Universal Religion and Universal Peace. In 1950 he published *Die Wiederkunft Christi* in which he equated Baha'u'llah with Christ returned in his Second Advent. Though never a large organization, the World Union remains a rallying point for "Free Baha'is" around the world.

Membership: Not reported. Estimates suggest that only a few hundred "Free Baha'is" reside in the United States.

Sources: *The Baha'i Case against Mrs. Lewis Stuyvesant Chandler and Mirza Ahmad Sohrab.* Wilmette, Il: National Spiritual Assembly of the Baha'is of the United States and Canada, 1941; Mirza Ahmad Sohrab, *Broken Silence*. New York: New History Foundation, 1942; Mirza Ahmad Sohrab, *The Will and Testament of Abdul Baha: An Analysis*. New York: New History Foundation, 1944; Ruth White, *Abdul Baha and the Promised Age*. New York: 1927; Ruth White, *Baha'i Religion and Its Enemy, the Baha'i Organization*. Rutland, VT: Charles Tuttle, 1929; Hermann Zimmer, *A Fraudulent Testament Devalues the Baha'i Religion into Political Shoghism*. Stuttgart, Germany: World Union for Universal Religion and Universal Peace, 1973.

Eastern Family
Part 1, Hinduism, Jainism, Sikhism

An historical essay on this family is provided beginning on page 153.

Hinduism

★1175★
AJAPA YOGA FOUNDATION
% Shri Janardan Ajapa Yogashram
Box 1731
Placerville, CA 95667

Ajapa yoga, *shadba brahman*, the yoga of absolute sound, is one form of yoga based upon the repetition of mantras. Ajapa yoga was rediscovered and given to the modern world by Guru Purnananda Paramahansa. He learned of the practice from Matang Rishi in a hidden monastery in Tibet. He created three ashrams in Bengal to spread the teachings which, while very old, had not been widely available until the last half of the nineteenth century. The work begun by Purnananda was continued by his disciple Guru Bhumanannda Paramahansa who in turn passed the succession to Guru Janardan Paramahansa, (b. 1888). Guru Janardan organized the World Conference on Scientific Yoga in New Delhi, which brought him into contact with many westerners. Following the conference he accepted an invitation to lecture in Czechoslovakia and expanded his Western tour to include Germany, Canada and the United States. After being in the West for over a year, he returned to India.

Some of the Westerners he encountered upon his tour traveled to India in 1973. In 1974, upon their return to New York, they incorporated the Ajapa Yoga Foundation. Guru Janardan made visits in 1974, 1975, and 1976 establishing centers in Hamburg, Germany; Montreal, Quebec; Los Angeles; Baltimore, Atlanta; and Knoxville, Tennessee. A periodical was begun in 1976, and a book summarizing the teachings was published. From that modest beginning the Foundation has steadily grown, spurred by occasional visits by Guru Jarandan.

According to the Foundation's teachings, humans have lost their true identities and are left in a world of pain, want, and illusion. True identity can be gained by the practice of ajapa yoga beginning with the repetition of the mantra given by the guru at the time of initiation, accompanied by specific breathing techniques.

Membership: Not reported.

Periodicals: *The Ajapa Journal*, Shri Janardan Ajapa Yoga Ashram, Box 1731, Placerville, CA 95667.

Sources: *Tattwa Katha: A Tale of Truth.* New York: Ajapa Yoga Foundation, 1976.

★1176★
AMERICAN MEDITATION SOCIETY
Box 244
Bourbonnais, IL 60914

The American Meditation Society is the United States affiliate of the International Foundation for Spiritual Unfoldment founded in 1975 in Capetown, South Africa by Purushottan Narshinhran (b.1932), whom his followers know by his spiritual name, Gururaj Ananda Yogi. As a child in his native Gujurat, he showed a distinct focus upon spiritual realities. Whe he was five years old he ran away from home to visit the temples in the neighborhood. When he was found, he explained to his parents that he had visited many temples, but had found to his frustration that "the Gods were lifeless and would not speak to me." His continued search for the Divine culminated when he discovered that what he sought lay within himself. Having found the inner reality, and having fully and permanently entered the self-realized state, he set himself to the task of becoming a spiritual teacher in the West.

He moved to South Africa and became a successful businessman. In 1975, following a problem with his heart, he retired from business and turned to full-time work as a spiritual teacher. He founded the International Foundation for Spiritual Unfoldment. Within the first year it had spread to nine countries, in the British Commonwealth and throughout Europe. In 1977 it was organized in California as the American Meditation Society.

Gururaj Ananda Yogi teaches not a religion, but the basis which underlies all religions. His task is seen as merely to awaken the individual to the same reality that he discovered and to lead him or her along the path of unfoldment. Meditation is the individual's major tool in turning inward, and it works best if individualized. The society offers basic meditation courses which introduce the variety of ways to meditate. Gururaj assists in the process of individualizing sound which is intoned during meditation. Individuals send their pictures to Gururaj. He meditates upon the picture and hears the sound each person makes with the universe. He presents the distinct sound to each person as a unique personal mantrum.

Membership: In 1984 the Society had approximately 2,000 members in 30 centers. Internationally, the foundation has centers in Canada, Australia, Zimbabwe, Spain, Denmark, Germany, Holland, Ireland, Great Britain, and South Africa.

Periodicals: *American Meditation Society Newsletter*, Box 244, Bourbonnais, IL 60914.

Sources: Ted Partridge, *Jewels of Silence*. Farmborough, Hamps.: St. Michael's Abbey Press, 1981; Savita Taylor, *The Path to Unfoldment*. London: VSM Publications, 1979.

★1177★

AMERICAN VEGAN SOCIETY
501 Old Harding Hwy.
Malaga, NJ 08328

The American Vegan Society was founded in 1960 at Malaga, New Jersey, by H. Jay Dinshah. The basis of the Society is ahimsa, defined as "dynamic harmlessness." The six pillars of ahimsa (one for each letter) are abstinence from all animal products, particularly for food or clothing; harmlessness and reverence for life; integrity of thought, word, and deed; mastery over oneself; service to mankind, nature, and creation; and advancement of understanding and truth. Veganism is conceived as an advanced and comprehensive program for living and draws its inspiration from Mahatma Gandhi, Albert Schweitzer, and the father of the founder. Vegans are vegetarians and ecology-oriented, and most oppose abortion, smoking, and drugs and practice karma yoga. Karma (work) yoga is an action path to perfection-doing good and avoiding harm.

Headquarters for the society are at Suncrest, run as a teaching hotel, at Malaga. A program is conducted during the summer attended by Vegans from across the country. An active lecture program is carried on by the Dinshahs. An annual convention is held in May. The society is affiliated with the North American Vegetarian Society, headquarterd at Dolgeville, New York, and the International Vegetarian Union, headquartered in Leaterhead, Surrey, England.

Membership: The Society reported a membership of less than 1,000 in 1984.

Periodicals: *Ahimsa*, 501 Old Harding Highway, Malaga, NJ 08328.

★1178★
ANANDA
Alleghany Star Route
Nevada City, CA 95959

Ananda is the name of a variety of related activities founded by Swami Kriyananda (also known by his secular name, J. Donald Walters), a direct disciple of Swami Paramahansa Yogananda since 1948. Kriyananda received his monastic name from Yogananda and was a member of the Board of Directors of the Self-Realization Fellowship. He gradually began to feel that administrative functions were not his calling, and he left. In 1967-68 he incorporated the Yoga Fellowship and founded Ananda as a spiritual community on 650 acres of land in rural northern California. Eventually approximately 125 people, moved to Ananda and an increasing number of people who were initiated by Kriyananda has arisen around the United States.

The teachings of Ananda are similar to those of the Self-Realization Fellowship, except that Swami Kriyananda is at the center instead of Yogananda. Kriyananda has also emphasized the ascetic life-style to a much greater extent. The Ananda Cooperative Village is a communal structure. From it a number of businesses have grown and flourished. Jewelry, perfumes, incense, and candies are produced and distributed nationally. Also located at the village is the Ananda High School for the teenage children of the village and the surrounding community.

Yoga is a central feature in the teachings. It is offered as an alternative to the fast-paced American culture, a way to inner happiness and calm. Hatha is taught along with the other forms of yoga, and a seven-month course in yoga is mailed to those who cannot come to the village. Yogic philosophy is stressed, but instructions are included on posture, breathing, food, healing and meditation. Practitioners of the yoga taught to all may be offered initiation into the kriya yoga teachings of Yogananda, the substance of which is revealed only to initiates.

There are four levels of affiliation to Ananda. The Ananda Spiritual Family, formerly called the Circle of Joy is for any interested individual. Provisional members are those who have come to live at Ananda to see if they will be accepted as full-time residents. If accepted they become full members. After five years as full members, individuals may join the Yoga Fellowship.

In the late 1970s a second community was founded on land near Occidental, California, donated to Ananda by Peter Myers. It is called Ocean Song. Ananda House was established in San Francisco in 1979. Other residential centers are located in Stockton, Sacramento, Nevada City, and Atherton, California.

Residents of the Ananda Cooperative Village, the original spiritual community, run a full retreat schedule during the summer, including yoga classes, Sunday devotional services, lectures, and satsangs (sessions with the master). Highlight of the year is the Annual Spiritual Renewal Week in August. It is an intensive week climaxed by the initiation of devotees into kriya yoga. Ananda Publications issues many of Kriyananda's books.

Membership: Not reported. In 1982 there were approximately 100 living at Ananda and over 1,000 in the larger Spiritual Family.

Periodicals: *Ananda*, 14618 Tyler Foote Rd., Nevada City, CA 95959.

Sources: Swami Kriyananda (Donald Walters), *The Path*. Nevada City, CA: Ananda Publications, 1977; Ted A. Nordquist, *Ananda Cooperative Village*. Uppsala, Sweden: Borgstroms Tryckeri Ab, 1978; John Ball, *Ananda, Where Yoga Lives*. Bowling Green, OH: Bowling Green University Popular Press, 1982; Swami Kriyananda, *Cooperative Communities, How to Start Them, and Why*. Nevada City, CA: Ananda Publications, 1968; Swami Kriyananda, *Crises in Modern Thought*. Nevada City, CA: Ananda Publications, 1972; Swami Kriyananda, *Letters to Truth Seekers*. Nevada City, CA: Ananda Publications, 1973.

★1179★
ANANDA ASHRAMA
Box 8555
La Cresenta, CA 91214

The Ananda Ashrama was founded by Swami Paramananda (1885-1940), born Suresh Chandra Gula Thakurta, a former swami with the Vedanta Society. Paramananda came to the United States in 1906 with Swami Abhedananda to be his assistant at the New York Vedanta center. In 1909 he moved to Boston to open a Vedanta center there. In 1915 he traveled to Los Angeles, where a previous attempt to open a center had failed. Paramananda was successful, and he divided his time between the two centers. In 1923 he moved the Los Angeles center to La Cresenta, north of the city in the mountains. Six years later he opened a rural center outside of Boston at Cohasset. During Paramananda's lifetime, these were an integral part of the larger Vedanta Society.

After Paramanada's death, the three centers he had founded severed their connection with the larger Vedanta movement and became independent centers under the leadership of Srimata Gayatri Devi (born Georgina Jones Walton), who met Paramananda in 1919 and who as Sister Devamata edited many of his books as well as authoring his biography. The Boston center was closed,

and it merged with the Cohasset center in 1952. Srimata Gayatri Devi led the center until her death. It is currently headed by her students. The Ananda Ashrama has survived to become the oldest currently existing ashram in the United States.

Membership: Not reported. There are several hundred connected with the two centers.

Sources: Sara Ann Levinsky, *A Bridge of Dreams*. West Stockbridge, MA: Inner Traditions, 1984; Sister Devamata, *Swami Paramananda and His Work*. La Cresenta, CA: Ananda Ashrama, 1926, 1941. 2 Vols.; Swami Paramananda, *The Path of Devotion*. Boston, MA: The Vedanta Center, 1907; Swami Paramananda, *Vedanta in Practice*. Boston, MA: The Vedanta Center, 1917.

★1180★
ANANDA MARGA YOGA SOCIETY
854 Pearl St.
Denver, CO 80203

The Ananda Marga Yoga society was founded in 1955 in Bihar, India by Prabhat Ranjan Sarkar (b.1921), known to his followers as Shrii Shrii Anandamurti, which roughly translated means "one upon seeing Him falls into bliss." He was an accomplished yogi at four and began initiating devotees at age six. He is considered by his followers to be a miracle worker and Maha-Guru (or God incarnate), one of which appears every few thousand years. A former railway clerk, Sankar took the vows of the renounced life at the time he founded Ananda Marga.

Anandamurti teaches a yogic philosophy, the practicing of which places one on the path of bliss. The path begins with initiation, in which the devotee is privately instructed in the method of initiation by a guru (teacher). He is then taught the requirements of yama and niyama (discussed in the introduction to this volume), and meditation (dharmacakra). The initiate is required to learn by heart the "supreme command," which instructs him/her to practice twice-daily meditation, observe yama and niyama, and the obligation to bring all into the path of perfection. Combined with the yogic philosophy was a strong movement toward social service.

Ananda Marga came to the United States in September, 1969, when Acharya Vimalananda was sent by Anandamurti (Dadaji) to establish the work in America. Under his leadership, Ananda Marga made rapid progress and, by 1973, had established more than 100 centers with approximately 3,000 members. A monthly newsletter, *Sadvipra*, was begun in 1973.

Ananda Marga appeared not just as a religious movement, but a political one as well. Sankar's political ideals were articulated as the Progressive Utilization Theory (Prout), based upon which he began to organize the lower classes in opposition to both the Communists and the ruling government. The Proutist Bloc ran candidates for office in the 1967 and 1969 elections. In 1971, however, Sankar was accused by a former follower of having conspired to murder some ex-members. Based upon his testimony Sankar was arrested and jailed awaiting trial. His imprisonment lasted through the national emergency proclaimed by Indira Ghandi in 1975. Ananda Marga was one of the organization she banned nationally. Meanwhile Ananda Margis had been involved in a number of violent incidents, some aimed at protesting Sankar's imprisonment. Sankar was finally brought to trial, under the conditions of the emergency, and convicted. He was unable to call any witnesses in his behalf. He was finally retried in 1978 and found not guilty. Since that date the number of reported incidents has decreased markedly. While still a large movement, Ananda Marga has not recovered its former strength in India.

Ananda Marga brought its social idealism with it. In 1958 Sankar had organized Renaissaince Universal to mobilize intellectuals and others for the improvement of humanity's condition. Renaissance Universal is organized in America and directly sponsored by Ananda Marga through Renaissance Universal Clubs on college campuses, ERAWS (Education, Relief and Welfare Section) working in development of various programs, the *Renaissance Universal* magazine, and RAWA (Renaissance Artists and Writers Association). Proutist Universal, which advocates Sankar's political ideals, is officially independent of Ananda Marga, but informally associated.

Membership: Not reported.

Periodicals: *Sadvipra*, 854 Pearl Street, Denver, CO 80403; *Delaware Valley Prout News*, Proutist Universal, 228 S. 46th Street, Philadelphia, PA 19139.

Remarks: Acharya Vimalananda, who founded Ananda Marag in the United States, left the organization to found the Yoga House Ashram.

Sources: *The Spiritual Philosophy of Shrii Shrii Anandamurti*. Denver, CO: Ananda Marga Publications, 1981; Nandita & Devadatta, *Path of Bliss, Ananda Marga Yoga*. Wichita, KS: Ananda Marga Publishers, 1971; Shrii Shrii Anandamurti, *Baba's Grace*. Denver, CO: Amrit Publications, 1973; Shrii Shrii Anandamurti, *The Great Universe: Discourses on Society*. Los Altos Hills, CA: Ananda Marga Publications, 1973; P. R. Sarkar, *Idea and Ideology*. Calcutta: Acarya Pranavananda Avadhuta, 1978; Acharya Tadbhavananda Avadhuta, *Glimpses of Prout Philosophy*. Copenhagen, Denmark: Central Proutist Publications, 1981.

★1181★
ARUNCHALA ASHRAMA
342 E. 6th St.
New York, NY 10003

Inspired by the life and teachings of Sri Ramana Maharshi (1879-1950), Arunchala Ashrama was founded in New York City on December 7, 1966. At the age of sixteen, Ramana Maharshi was absorbed in a one-pointed quest for truth which resulted in his total abidance in God, or the "self," as he called it. He then left home and resided on the slopes of Arunchala Mountain, a sacred place of pilgrimage in South India. He remained there for the next fifty-four years, until his death in 1950. His most potent teachings are believed by his followers to have been imparted in the silence of his presence, which conferred the peace of God-realization to mature souls. Orally, he taught the path of self-enquiry and self-surrender. He asked seekers to enquire whence the "I-consciousness" springs, to return to its source and abide there. He taught seekers to throw all the burdens of life upon the Divine, and to be at peace and to abide on the Heart of God. He taught all in such a way as not to interfere with outward religious professions or practices. Rather, he taught each to seek his or her own source, as he believed there was only one source and one God.

Arunchala maintains facilities in New York City and in Nova Scotia, Canada. A routine of prayer and meditation is followed at both locations. There are also retreat facilities at the Nova Scotia center.

Membership: The ashrama has not instituted formal membership. There are 2 centers.

Sources: T. M. P. Mahadevan, *Ramana Maharshi, the Sage of Arunchala*. London: George Allen & Unwin, 1977; Paul Brunton, *A Message from Arunchala*. New York: Samuel Weiser, 1971; Arthur Osborne, *Ramana Maharshi and the Path of Self-Knowledge*. New York: Samuel Weiser, 1970; Arthur Osborne, ed., *The Teachings of Ramana Maharshi*. New York: Samuel Weiser, 1962.

★1182★
AUROBINDO, DISCIPLES OF SRI
% Matagiri-Sri Aurobindo Center
High Falls, NY 12440

Of the many Hindu religious leaders who have arisen in the last century, none remains as enigmatic as Sri Aurobindo Ghose (1872-1950). He was given an English education and began to make his mark as a literary figure. When Bengal, his native state, was the center of the independence movement, Aurobindo became a political activist. Thrown in jail on sedition charges, he turned to the Hindu scriptures and began to practice yoga. He had a vision of Krishna which changed the course of his life. Released from jail, he soon fled to French-controlled Pondicherry as a refugee and continued his spiritual practice.

The next years were spent in writing, yoga and the building of an ashram. Most of his famous books appeared in the sixteen years prior to his day of victory, November 24, 1926. On that date, his sadhana (path to enlightenment) ended and he realized the supermind. His chief disciple was Mira Richards (1878-1973), a French divorcee who met Aurobindo prior to World War II. She gradually took over the management of the ashram and after 1926, when Aurobindo ceased to see people, she became the contact between him and his disciples. The "Mother", as she is known, had seen her master in her dreams before she came to Pondicherry in 1914. From 1950 to her death in 1973 she sustained and guarded the work.

Sri Aurobindo's thought has often been compared with Teilhard de Chardin's, as it was an evolutionary philosophy based upon man's growth in consciousness both individually and collectively. God--pure existence, will force--draws man to himself. Creation is a result of his "descent" and the evolution is as much a divine work as man's progress. The divine presence is manifested in the life force or "conscious" force in creation. People are said to be ripe for a new evolutionary consciousness. People will become "gnostic beings," at one with the eternal. The gnostic beings will appear, grow in number, form communities. Eventually all of humanity will enter "the life divine."

The means to achieve the life divine is yoga. Aurobindo taught what is termed "integral yoga," a form of right-hand tantra. It includes the traditional forms of yoga and the psychology of the internal psychic self, including kundalini and the seven chakras. An individual is seen as a complicated self with a higher self, soul, psychic being, mental and vital bodies which enclose the physical, and an ego. Yoga helps people bring forth their psychic selves.

In India, the Sri Aurobindo Society has established an international section to service centers outside of the country. In the United States a number of more-or-less independent centers have arisen. The most prominent is Matagiri, currently located at High Falls, New York. In California, three prominet centers have survived for many years, the East-West Cultural Center founded by Judith Tyberg in 1953; the California Institute of Integral Studies (formerly the California Institute of Asian Studies founded by Haridas Chaudhuri; and the Atmaniketan Ashram, a residence center in Pomoma. There are numerous other smaller centers.

International headquarters remain at the ashram in Pondicherry. In 1972, it published a 30-volume centenary edition of Aurobindo's works. It has also published most of the Mother's writings.

Membership: Not available.

Periodicals: *Collaboration*, Matagiri-Sri Aurobindo Center, High Falls, NY 12440; *Purna Yoga*, Atmaniketan Ashram, 1291 Weber St., Pomona, CA 91768.

Sources: Robert A. McDermott, ed. *Six Pillars*. Chambersburg, PA: Wilson Books, 1974; Robert McDermott, ed., *The Essential Aurobindo*. New York: Schrocken Books, 1973; Robert Neil Minor, *Sri*

Aurobindo: The Perfect and the Good. Columbia, MO: South Asia Books, 1978; Haridas Chaudhuri, *The Evolution of Integral Consciousness*. Wheaton, IL: Theosophical Publishing House, 1977; Morwenna Donnelly, *Founding the Life Divine*. Lower Lake, CA: Dawn Horse Press, 1976; Narayan Prasad, *Life in Sri Aurobindo Ashram*. Pondicherry, India: Sri Aurobindo Ashram, 1968.

★1183★
BLUE MOUNTAIN CENTER OF MEDITATION
Box 477
Petaluma, CA 94953

The Blue Mountain Center of Meditation, established by Eknath Easwaran in 1960, is named for the Nilgiris (Blue) Mountain in South India. It was in the shadow of its peak that Eknath Easwaran made his boyhood home and upon its summit that he later resided. Easwaran became an English professor and in 1959 came to the United States through Fulbright Exchange Program. He settled in Berkeley, and students soon gathered around him to meditate and to learn his spiritual discipline.

He looks upon his mother's mother as his spiritual teacher. She taught him that the supreme goal is to know God through union with God. Family yoga is the name given to the practice of finding fulfillment by putting first the welfare of those around one. Meditation, the discipline adopted to accomplish the goal of union, teaches one to focus the mind and to utilize its full potential. The individual can, by meditation, gain full self-control and cease to be the victim of uncontrolled urges. He is also enabled to live selflessly in family and community. Strong attention is given to problem-solving through meditating.

The Blue Mountain Center opened an ashram, Ramagiri, where full-time students reside. Classes for serious students are offered in Petaluma, California.

Membership: Not reported. Approximately 50 full-time students reside at the ashram.

Periodicals: *The Little Lamp*, Nilgiri Press, Box 477, Petaluma, CA 94953.

Sources: Eknath Easwaran, *The Bhagavad Gita for Daily Living*. Berkeley, CA: Blue Mountain Center of Meditation, 1975; Eknath Easwaran, *Like a Thousand Suns*, Petaluma, CA: Nilgiri Press, 1979; Eknath Easwaran, *The Mantram Handbook*. Petaluma, CA: Nilgiri Press, 1977; Eknath Easwaran, *A Man to Match His Mountains*. Petaluma, CA: Nilgiri Press, 1984; Eknath Easwaran, *The Supreme Ambition*. Petaluma, CA: Nilgiri Press, 1982; Eknath Easwaran, *Dialogue with Death*. Petaluma, CA: Nilgiri Press, 1981.

★1184★
SRI CAITANYA SARASWAT MATH
% Guardian of Devotion
62 S. 13th St.
San Jose, CA 95112

Following the death of A. C. Bhaktivedanta Swami Prabhupada, founder of the International Society for Krishna Consciousness (the Hare Krishna movement in the west), some of his initiated disciples chose not to transfer their loyalty to any of the several initiating gurus who were placed in charge of the movement. Rather, some turned to Bhakti Raksaka Srihara Deva Goswami, one of Swami Prabhupada's God-brothers; i.e., they were initiated by the same guru, Bhaktisiddhanta Saraswati Goswami Maharaja of the Gaudiya Math in India. Srihara Deva was one of several people who founded a separate organization in the wake of the disruption of the Gaudiya Math.

There is one temple of the Sri Caitanya Sarawswat Math in the United States. The Guardian of Devotion Press is its publishing arm.

Membership: Not reported. There are less than one hundred devotees affiliated with the temple in the United States.

Sources: Bhakti Raksaka Srihara Deva Goswami, *Sri Guru and His Grace*. San Jose, CA: Guardian of Devotion Press, 1983; Bhakti Raksaka Srihara Deva Goswami, *The Search for Sri Krsna, Reality the Beautiful*. San Jose, CA: Guardian of Devotion Press, 1983.

★1185★
CHILTERN YOGA FOUNDATION
1029 Hyde St., No. 6
San Francisco, CA 94109

Swami Sivananda Saraswati (1887-1963) (born Kuppuswami Iyer) was one of several renowned Hindu teachers to arise in this century and become revered as a saint and holy man. Reared by devout parents who encouraged his education, he began a medical course of study, cut short by the death of his father. He moved to Malaysia as a hospital administrator, but after ten years, in 1923, he returned to India to pursue a spiritual quest. He was initiated as a *sannyasin*, to follow the renounced life, and settled in Swargashram, near Rishikish, where many sannyasins lived. He began to write, teach and make pilgrimages around India. He advocated a life of devotion (bhakti yoga) and service (karma yoga).

Unwilling to forget the life of service upon which he had embarked as a youth, he moved to Rishikish and established an ashram. As part of the ashram facility, he opened a medical dispensary to serve the local community. By 1936 the work had grown considerably. He formed the Divine Life Trust and the Divine Life Society, an open membership auxiliary. The dispensary grew into a major medical facility. The ashram became a major center for the propagation of yoga, and attracted many of the best teachers from throughout India.

Sivananda's teaching is summarized in the motto, "serve, love, meditate, realize." He led his students upon a sadhana (path to enlightenment) which included bhakti (practicing love) and ahimsa (constant striving to do no harm and cause no pain). He developed a synthesis, integral yoga, which included the four traditional forms of hatha, jnana, karma, and raja, to which he added a fifth, japa (the repetition of mantras).

Sivananda never came to the United States, but he sent his students to the West and received students from Europe and America. As early as 1959 Swami Chidananda, his successor as leader of the ashram in Rishikish, visited the United States. During the 1960s as students scattered around the world, branches of the society were established in many countries. After Sivananda's death, however, these generally separated from the India centers and became a separate corporation under their founder. In the United States several students began teaching Sivananda's yoga and a variety of corporate structures have emerged. The Chiltern Yoga Foundation is one such organization.

Swami Venkatesanda was a leading student of Sivananda, about whom he has written several books. He traveled widely on behalf of the Divine Life Society. During the 1960s he took the lead in establishing the society in South Africa. During the 1970s the work in South Africa separated from the society in India and was renamed the Chiltern Yoga Foundation. In the early 1980s a center of the foundation was established in San Francisco.

Membership: Not reported.

Sources: Swami Sivananda, *Sadhana*. Sivanandanagar, India: Divine Life Society, 1967; N. Ananthanarayanan, *From Man to God-Man*. New Delhi, India: The Author, 1970; Swami Venkatesananda, *Sivananda's Integral Yoga*. Johannesburg, South Africa: Divine Life Society, 1969; K. A. Tawker, *Sivananda, One World Teacher*. Rishikish, India: The Yoga-Vedanta Forest University, 1957; Swami Venkatasananda, *Gurudev Sivananda*. Durban, South Africa: Divine Life Society of South Africa, 1961; Sarat Chandra Behera, *The Holy Stream, The Inspiring Life of Swami Chidananda*. Shivanandanagar, India: Divine Life Society, 1981. Swami Venkatesananda, *Christ, Krishna and You*. San Francisco: Chiltern Yoga Foundation, 1983; Yogeshwari Muni, comp., *Venkatesa*. Elgin, South Africa: Chiltern Yoga Trust, 1977; Swami Venkatesananda, *Living Meditation*. Elgin, South Africa: Chiltern Yoga Foundation, 1980; Swami Venkatesananda, *Yoga, Art of Enlightened Living*. North Fremantle, W. Aust.: Integral Yoga Association, 1974; Swami Venkatesananda, *Sivananda's Integral Yoga*. Johannesburg, South Africa: Divine Life Society, 1969.

★1186★
CHINMAYA MISSION (WEST)
Box 2753
Napa, CA 94558

Swami Chinmayananda is an independent teacher of Vedanta who in 1943 was initiated into sannyas, the renounced life, by Swami Sivananda at Rishikish, India. With Sivananda's blessing, Chinmayananda traveled into the Himalayan Mountains to Uttar Kusi to study with a learned teacher, Swami Tapovanam, known for his knowledge of the Hindu scriptures. He studied with Tapovanam for eight years, leaving in 1951 to share his knowledge with the public. He began teaching and as people responded the Chinmaya Mission evolved.

Chinmaya first came to North America in the 1960s. As he periodically toured the country, groups of disciples came into existence. In 1975 Chinmaya Mission West and its publishing arm, Chinmaya Publications West were incorporated. Once formed, assisted by Chinmayananda's charismatic personality and drive, the Mission spread rapidly, slowed only during the period of Chinmayananda's period of inactivity following a heart operation in 1980, and the resignation of Swami Dayananda, expected successor to the aging leader of the mission. Dayananda had headed Sandeepany West, the university-level school for Vedanta teachers, and had provided energetic leadership for the entire Mission. He wishrd, however, to lead a more unstructured spiritual life.

Chinmaya Mission has been distinguished both by its Vedantic teachings and its emphasis upon knowledge of the Upanishads and the *Bhagavad Gita*, the two main Hindu scriptures. Chinamyananda has authored numerous books, including commentaries on the *Gita* and Upanishads.

Membership: Not reported. Chinmaya missions can be found across North America. There are an estimated several hundred around the world, the largest number being in India.

Periodicals: *Newsletter*, Box 2753, Napa, CA 94558.

Sources: Swami Chinmayananda, *The Way to Self-Perfection*. Napa, CA: Chinmaya Publilcations (West), 1976; Swami Chinmayananda, *A Manual for Self-Unfoldment*. Napa CA; Chinmaya Publication (West), 1975; Swami Chinmayananda, *Kindle Life*. Madras: Chinmaya Publications Trust, n.d.; *The Holy Geeta* with commentary by Swami Chinmayananda. Bombay: Central Chinmaya Mission Trust, n.d.; Swami Chinmayananda, *Meditation (Hasten Slowly)*. Napa, CA: The Family Press, 1974.

★1187★
SRI CHINMOY CENTERS
Box 32433
Jamaica, NY 11431

Sri Chinmoy Kumar Ghose (b.1931) entered the Sri Aurobindo Ashram at the age of twelve and over two decades of practicing intense spiritual disciplines he attained a state of enlightenment. In 1964 he came to the United States from his native Bengal to begin "serving the West." His teachings are centered upon yoga, man's conscious union with God. Yoga is seen as the science that teaches us how the ultimate reality can be discovered in life itself. Students are taught hatha yoga, proper breathing, vegetarianism, and meditation.

Initiation, Siksha (the giving of oneself), is a major step in the life of the disciple. In initiation, the guru gives the disciple a portion of his life-soul, and the disciple gives his soulful promise to serve the master. Sri Chinmoy teaches that while a guru is not absolutely necessary to realize God, a guru does help facilitate inner spiritual progress. He serves as a private tutor for the spiritual life.

As a guru, Sri Chinmoy guides each person's meditative discipline and spiritual growth. He teaches that the path of love, devotion (bhakti) and surrender is the swiftest and easiest way to God. He encourages athletics as a means to illumination of the physical consciousness, and the centers across the country have sponsored many running events. Disciples are urged to be transforming agents in the world. To illustrate this emphasis, headquarters have been established at the United Nations where Sri Chinmoy is the permanent director of the United Nations Meditation Group and delivers the monthly Dag Hammarskjold lecture.

Sri Chinmoy is a prolific author, having written more than 400 books and booklets. An accomplished musician, he has composed over 3,000 devotional songs and frequently gives concerts, often in the cause of world peace.

Membership: Not reported. There are more than 60 Chinmoy centers around the world.

Sources: Madhuri [Nancy Elizabeth Sands], *The Life of Sri Chinmoy*. Jamaica, NY: Sri Chinmoy Lighthouse, 1972; Sri Chinmoy, *A Sri Chinmoy Primer*. Forest Hills, NY: Vishma Press, 1974; Sri Chinmoy, *Astrology, the Supernatural and the Beyond*. Hollis, NY: Vishma Press, 1973; Sri Chinmoy, *Arise! Awake!*. New York: Frederick Fell, 1972; Sri Chinmoy, *My Lord's Secrets Revealed*. New York: Herder and Herder, 1971.

★1188★
CHURCH OF THE CHRISTIAN SPIRITUAL ALLIANCE
Lake Rabun Road
Box 7
Lakemont, GA 30552

The Church of the Christian Spiritual Alliance (CSA) was founded in 1962 by H. Edwin O'Neal, a Baptist; his wife, Lois O'Neal, an adherent of Religious Science; and William Arnold Lapp, a Unitarian. Its stated purpose was to teach the fatherhood of God and brotherhood of man as interpreted in the light of modern-day experience." It emerged as a highly eclectic organization which combined Christian, psychic and Eastern insights. It absorbed *Orion*, a popular independent occult monthly founded by Ural R. Murphy of Charlotte, North Carolina, and continues its publication, now as an annual.

In the late 1960s, the church was joined by Roy Eugene Davis, a former student of Swami Paramahansa Yogananda and leader of the Self-Realization Fellowship center in Phoenix, Arizona. Davis had left SRF and formed New Life Worldwide. He brought his organization and its periodical (which became *Truth Journal*) into CSA. Davis's traveling and speaking gave CSA a national audience.

CSA took a decisive turn in 1977 when O'Neal resigned as chairman of the board and president of the publishing complex and was replaced by Davis. The focus of CSA has in the ensuing years been that of Davis, who has established the church as part of the larger New Age movement with its concerns of astrology, holistic health, and meditation. The yoga teachings of Yogananda as presented through Davis have become the central core of the teachings. Davis keeps a year-round schedule of seminars around the United States. His ecumenical approach to religion is in keeping with the New Age emphases.

The educational arm of the church is the Center for Spiritual Awareness at Lakemont. Each summer a full retreat and workshop progam is held at CSA. Featured is a teacher training seminar designed to prepare CSA ministers. The Shrine of All Faiths and Sacred Initiation Temple are part of the headquarters complex. Initiation into kriya yoga is offered to members.

Membership: Not reported. In 1985 there were 18 groups and study centers inthe United States. Ministers could also be found in Bermuda and Germany.

Periodicals: *Truth Journal*, Lake Rabun Rd., Box 7, Lakemont, GA 30552; *Orion*, Lake Rabun Rd., Box 7, Lakemont, GA 30552.

Sources: Roy Eugene Davis, *An Easy Guide to Meditation*. Lakemont, GA: CSA Press, 1978; Roy Eugene Davis, *The Path of Soul Liberation*. Lakemont, GA: CSA Press, 1975;

Roy Eugene Davis, *The Teachings of the Masters of Perfection*. Lakemont, GA: CSA Press, 1979; Roy Eugene Davis, *The Way of the Initiate*. St. Petersburg, FL: New Life World-Wide, 1968; Roy Eugene Davis, *Yoga-Darshana*. Lakemont, GA: CSA Press, 1976.

★1189★
DEVATMA SHAKTI SOCIETY
Rte. 1, Box 150 C-2
Paige, TX 78659

The Devatma Shakti Society was formed in 1976 by Swami Shivom Tirth (b. 1924) for the practice of the *shaktipat* system of yoga, a system revived by Swami Gangadhar Tirth Maharaj. Little is known of this swami; he lived in solitude and initiated only one disciple, Kali Kishore Gangopadhyay, who became known as Swami Narayan Tirth Dev Maharaj (1870-1935). He founded an meditation center in Madaripur, Faridpur, India and passed his succession to Shri Yoganandaji Maharaj (d.1959). Yoganandaji established an ashram in Rishikish. He initiated Swami Vishnu Tirth Maharaj (d.1969) who established the Narayan Kuti Sanyas Ashram at Dewas.

Swami Shivom Tirth was initiated by Vishnu Tirth in 1959 and took the vows of the sannyasin (the renounced life) in 1963. During the 1970s, Shivom Tirth began to propagate the shaktipat system outside of India, first in Europe and Southeast Asia and then in America. The first ashram in North America was established in central Texas. Shivom Tirth occasionally visits America on lecture tours, visiting his disciples across the United States.

Shaktipat is the descent of the power of the guru upon the disciple, thus activating the disciple's own latent kundalini shakti, often pictured as a serpent sleeping coiled at the base of the spine. The awakening of the energy and its movement up the spinal column to the top of the head produces enlightenment. This way to enlightenment is through the guru's grace and bypasses the years of effort and discipline necessary in other forms of yoga.

Membership: Not reported.

Sources: Shivom Tirth, *A Guide to Shaktipat*. Paige, TX: Devatma Shakti Society, 1985.

★1190★
DHYANYOGA CENTERS
Manu Michael Hannon, Director
2026 Redesdale Ave.
Los Angeles, CA 90039

Indian yoga teacher Dhyanyogi Mahant Madhusudandasji Maharaj left home as a child of 13 to seek enlightenment. He spent the next 40 years as a wandering student, during which time he met and worked with his guru whom he discovered at Mt. Abu in Rajasthan State in northern India. From his guru he received shaktipat, a transmission of power believed to release the latent power of kundalini, pictured as residing at the base of the spine. The emergence of that power and the experience of its traveling up the spine to the crown of the head is considered by many Hindu groups to be the means of enlightenment.

In 1962 Dhyanyogi Madhusudandasji ceased his wanderings and began to teach. He established an ashram at Bandhvadi, Gujurat, the first of several in western India. He authored two books, *Message to Disciples* and *Light on Meditation*. During the 1970s followers moved to England and the United States. He made his first visit to his Western disciples in 1976 and began to build a following among American converts.

Dhyanyogi Madhusudandasji's teachings emphasize meditation (dhyan), or raja yoga, and kundalini yoga. He offers shaktipat to sadhuks (students). As the kundalini awakens the student is open to the guru's continuing influence and is able to shed past encumbrances and to move on the path of enlightennment.

Membership: Not reported. Groups of followers can be found in Illinois, New Jersey, and California.

Sources: Madhusudandasji Maharaj Dhyanyogi Mahant, *Light on Meditation*. Los Angeles: n.p., 1978; Dhyanyogi Madhusudandasji, *Shakti, Hidden Treasure of Power*. Pasadena Dyanyoga Centers, 1979; Dhyanyogi Madhusudandasji, *Message to Disciples*. Bombay: Shri Dhyanyogi Mandal, 1968; Dhyanyogi Madhusudandasji, *Brahmanada: Sound. Mantra and Power*. Pasadena, CA: Dhyanyoga Centers, 1979; Dhyanyogi Madhusudandasji, *Death, Dying and Beyond*. Pasadena, CA: Dhyanyoga Centers, 1979.

★1191★
FIVEFOLD PATH
% Vasant V. Paranjpe
RFD #1, Box 212-C
Madison, VA 22727

The Fivefold Path was founded in Madison, Virginia, in 1973 by Vesant Paranjpe, who had received a divine command to come to the United States and teach kriya yoga, the Fivefold Path. From the Virginia headquarters, Paranjpe began to visit and teach in neighboring cities-- Washington, D.C.; Baltimore; Philadelphia; Riverton, New Jersey--and followers began to form. A semimonthly periodical was begun, and a fire temple consecrated at Param Dham, the name given the headquarters.

The Fivefold Path is a system of kriya yoga which begins in purification of the atmosphere as a step leading to the purification of the mind. Its steps include the following: 1) agnihotra, a fire ceremony done at sunrise and sunset each day (Agni is the Hindu God of fire); 2) daan, sharing one's assets in a spirit of humility; 3) tapa, self-discipline; 4) karma, right action; and 5) swadhyaya, self-study.

Membership: Not reported.

Periodicals: *Satsang*, Box 13, Randallstown, MD 21133.

Sources: Vasant V. Paranjpe, *Grace Alone*. Madison, VA: Fivefold Path, 1971; Vasant V. Paranjpe, *Ten Commandments of Parama Sadguru*. Randallstown, MD: Agnihotra Press, 1976.

★1192★
FOUNDATION OF REVELATION
59 Scott St.
San Francisco, CA 94117

The Foundation of Revelation was formed in 1970 in San Francisco by persons who recognized the existence of perfect knowledge and practical omnipotence in the form of a "beggar" then living in the village of Gorkhara near Calcutta, India. The man had been born of a ruling Brahmin family in 1913 and spent his early years as an avid student of various forms of modern knowledge. On the eve of June 14, 1966, he perceived that the illusions of these limited and disintegrating forms of modern knowledge were burned down by Agni, the fire of knowledge, and on September 9, 1966, the convergence of persisting cosmic existence, the luminous nature of consciousness, was concentrated in the person of this Yogi as Siva, the Destroyer. Thus 1966 is the first year of a new era of Siva Kalpa (meaning the period of time of Lord Siva's omnipotent imagination).

To the Foundation, Siva is the creator of conscious life and the destroyer of ignorance, whose pure love of knowledge moves the forms of ego into intensifying contradictions of their own divisive natures to the point of spontaneous recoil toward the synthesis of body, life and mind. He is considered the most accessible of powers. He never refused the request of a supplicant, perhaps his most dangerous attribute, and he surrounds himself with those from the extremes of the social spectrum whose natural penchant for truth, the power of self-expression, and the ability to manifest same, holds them apart from the world of mediocrity, always gravitating to the heights or depths of existence in the pull toward ultimate perfection.

The first Western contact with the holy man was in 1968 when he made an appearance at the Spiritual Summit Conference sponsored by the Temple of Understanding in Washington, D.C. Several delegates followed him home and one, Charlotte P. Wallace, now president of the foundation, stayed to learn. Word spread of his work, and, in 1969, he was invited to the United States to take up residence in San Francisco, which became the world headquarters of the foundation. Those from countries around the world who witnessed his revelations firsthand returned to their respective countries to organize themselves within the spirit and corporate structure of the foundation to create bases for international communication and activity, with the single purpose of breaking down the barriers of nationality, religion and race and foster the mutually beneficial and harmonious relationships of nations.

The foundation is led by a governing body consisting of the president and seven officers. Each country has a president directly responsible to the world president. Each local leader is responsible to the national president.

Membership: In 1984 the foundation reported 5,000 members in the United States and 25,000 members in the world. There were 21 centers worldwide in 10 countries.

★1193★
HANUMAN FOUNDATION
Box 478
Santa Fe, NM 87501

The Hanuman Foundation is described as the nonorganization focused in the spiritual teaching of Baba Ram Dass. Ram Dass is the name taken by Richard Alpert, the former professor of psychology at Harvard University who was fired along with Timothy Leary because of their LSD experiments. Within a short time he became discouraged with drugs as a means to attain higher states of consciousness and he turned to India. There he met Bhagwan Dass, a young American guru, and his teacher, Maharaji, who lived in the foothills of the Himalayas. From Maharaji he learned raja yoga, the path to God through meditation.

Upon returning to the West, Baba Ram Dass wrote and published *Be Here Now*, which emphasized his ideal of living in the present, other than being tied to the past or contemplating the future. He sees all people on a journey to enlightenment. Each person needs and has a guru to help his progress. Some gurus are on the physical plane, but such is not necessary since the relationship is spiritual. Each person is at a different place on his journey, and, thus, differing exercises are needed by each individual. Some might need yoga, renunciation, mantras, sex or even psychedelic drugs. For Baba Ram Dass, yoga was the path to enlightenment.

For several years, Baba Ram Dass traveled and spoke using his New Hampshire home as headquarters. The Orphalese Foundation controlled a tape library. Another center was the ZBS Foundation in Fort Edwards, New York. The Hanuman Foundation was established in 1974 as a means of focusing the karma yoga and as an alternative to an ashram. It is named for Hanuman, a god who appears in the form of a monkey and who is a main character in Hindu scriptures. He is seen by the Foundation as the perfect embodiment of devoted service. The Foundation is run by a board of directors and has programs in 1) Alternative Metaphors for Dying, a project in helping the individual face death; 2) the Prison Ashram, to aid inmates of penitentiaries on the path to perfection; 3) meditation; 4) Hanuman Temple; and 5) spiritual educational materials. Each of these projects is centered in a different part of the country.

Membership: Not reported.

Sources: Baba Ram Dass, *Remember, Be Here Now*. San Christobal, NM: Lama Foundation, 1971; Baba Ram Dass, *The Only Dance There Is*. New York: Jason Aaronson, 1976; Bab Ram Dass, *Grist for the Mill*. Santa Cruz, CA: Unity Press, 1977; Baba Ram Dass, *Miracle of Love*. New York: E. P. Dutton, 1979; *Inside Out*. Nederland, CO: Prison-Ashram Project, Hanuman Foundation, 1976.

★1194★
HIMALAYAN INTERNATIONAL INSTITUTE OF YOGA SCIENCE & PHILOSOPHY
RD 1
Honesdale, PA 18431

Swami Rama is a learned Hindu philosopher and master yogi who came to the United States to teach. Born in 1925, he was adopted by a Bengalese yogi and became a monk. In 1949, he attained the high position of being a monk in the Shankaracharya Order, an honor he relinquished in 1952 to further his own teaching goals. He founded the Himalayan Institute, which he brought to the United States in 1970.

Yoga and meditation are the main emphases of the Institute. All levels of hatha yoga are taught, and raja yoga is emphasized as a means to balance the body-spirit dichotomy which is man. Yoga leads to a spiritual world-view.

Swami Rama has become a celebrity because of his work with psychologists Elmer Green and Alyce Green in which he has demonstrated amazing physical feats of body-function control. This work highlights what Swami Rama calls superconscious meditation, "a unique system...to awaken the sleeping energy of consciousness, to raise its volume and intensity to that individual awareness becomes one with the Universal Self." It involves relaxation, posture, breathing and mantras.

The Himalayan Institute has published a number of books on yoga, science, psychology, philosphy and meditation. Programs at the centers, especially at the headquarters complex, include a wide range of seminars, special five and ten day health and training programs, residential programs, and training for professionals. It has also developed a program in Eastern Studies and Comparative Psychology leading to a master of science degree from the University of Scranton graduate school.

Membership: In 1984 the Institute reported 12 centers, with foreign work in India, Japan, and Europe.

Periodicals: *Dawn*, R.R. 1, Box 400, Honesdale, PA 18431; *Himalayan News*, RR 1, Box 400, Honesdale, PA: PA 18431.

Sources: Swami Rama, *Living with the Himalayan Masters.* Honesdale, PA: Himalayan International Institute of Yoga Science and Philosophy, 1978; *Inspired Thoughts of Swami Rama.* Honesdale, PA: Himalayan International Institute of Yoga Science and Philosophy, 1983; Swami Rama, *Lectures on Yoga.* Arlington Heights, IL: Himalayan International Institute of Yoga Science and Philosophy, 1972; Swami Rama, *A Practical Guide to Holistic Health.* Honesdale, PA: Himalayan International Institute of Yoga Science and Philosophy, 1978; Swami Rama, Rudolph Ballentine & Swami Ajaya (Allan Weinstock), *Yoga and Psychotherapy.* Glenview, IL: Himalayan Institute, 1976.

★1195★
HOLM
% Anthony Zuccarello, President
Box 25839
Prescott Valley, AZ 86312

Holm, also known as the Church of Divine Influence, was founded during the early 1970s by Lee Lozowick, a former Silva Mind Control instructor. Lozowick gathered a small group of seekers around him and established Holm at Tabor, New Jersey. In 1975 he published his first book, *Beyond Release*, edited from talks he had given, and began to issue a newsletter, *At Holm*. The groups's growth fluctuated for several years, and members began to look for a place where a community could be created. Hence, in 1980 the group moved to Prescott Valley, Arizona, and estalished an ashram.

Lozowick's eclectic spiritual teachings draw heavily upon Hinduism, but also include elements of Georgei Gurdjieff, Meher Baba, and Zen Buddhism. The goal of life, according to Lozowick, is "spiritual slavery," a state in which one has been so blessed and transformed that the indiviual is compelled by inner necessity to fulfill the Will of God. The spiritual life at Holm includes daily *darshan* (sessions with Lozowick), *kirtans* (hymns and chants), and the five life conditions. Members are expected to follow : 1) a daily discipline of exercise (hatha yoga and/or a martial art); 2) a balanced lacto-vegetarian diet free of tobacco, alcohol, and mind-altering drugs; 3) daily study of spiritual literature; 4) celibacy outside of monogamous marriage; and 5) daily meditation. Lozowick also encourages weekly bridge games as a spiritual discipline and to emphasized the spiritual aspect has written a bridge manual entitled, *Zen Gamesmanship*.

Holm recognizes three levels of membership. The core group that manages the affairs of Holm are called the Mandali. The body of full resident members of the community are designated the Order of Ordinary Fools. Other participants, who may attend community activities, participate in Holm study groups in their own community, and offer some minimal financial support, are designated the Order of Divine Fools.

Membership: In 1984 Holm reported 100 members in the United States and an additional 25 members outside the country. Besides the main ashram in Arizona, study groups have been organized in New York City, Los Angeles, and Boulder, Colorado. There are three ministers.

Periodicals: *Divine Slave Gita*, Box 25839, Prescott Valley, AZ 86312.

Sources: Lee Lozowick, *Acting God.* Prescott Valley, AZ: Holm Press, 1980; Lee Lozowick, *Beyond Release.* Tabor, NJ: Holm Press, 1975; Lee Lozowick, *Book of Unenlightenment.* Prescott Valley, AZ: Holm Press, 1980; Lee Lozowick, *The Cheating Buddah.* Tabor, NJ: Holm Press, 1980; Lee Lozowick, *In the Fire.* Tabor, NJ: Holm Press, 1978; Lee Lozowick, *Laughter of the Stones.* Tabor, NJ: Holm Press, n.d.

★1196★
HOLY SHANKARACHARYA ORDER
RD 3, Box 400
Stroudsburg, PA 18360

The Holy Shankaracharya Order had its beginning in 1968 when Swami Lakshmy Devyashram, a disciple of Swami Sivananda Saraswati, established the Sivananda Ashram of Yoga One Science. Through self-study and under Sivananda's spiritual inspiration, she founded samadhi (a mystic state of altered consciousness) in 1963. In 1964, she had a vision of Swami Sivananda and was led by him to the Poconos. The guidance continued in the building of the retreat/camp. In 1969, she was ordained by Swami Swanandashram in the Holy Order of Sannyasa, Saraswati, the order in which Sivananda was ordained. In 1974, Swami Lakshmy was elected Mahamandaleshwari (Great Overlord) of the Holy Shankaracharya Order in the United States.

In 1974 property was purchased in Virginia and a second ashram-temple complex begun. It was dedicated in 1977. In 1978, from her superior in the Shankaracharya Order, Jagadguru Shankaracharya Abhinava Vidyateertha Maharaj, headquartered at Sringeri, the holy seat of the Order, she was requested to establish a shakti peetham (monastery), which was named Sri Rajarajeshwari Peetham. As the Swami gathered students around her, she ordained them, and they have become instructors in the various programs and activities. In the same year a Hindu Heritage Summer Camp was created. The response to this program led to the acceptance of the non-Indian, female swami by the Indian-American community.

In 1981, shortly before Swami Lakshmy died, Hindu priestly services were begun at the peetham. Swami Lakshmy was succeeded by Swami Saraswati Devyashram, one of her female students. Under her leadership the outreach to the Indian community has grown. A center has been opened in Tucson, Arizona and a winter heritage camp initiated in 1982. Today, the Holy Shankacharya

Order is a major traditional Saivite Hindu center. In 1983 Swami Saraswati Devyashram was initiated by the Jagadguru Shankaracharya at Sringeri. In 1984 it joined the ecumenical Council of Hindu Temples. It now provides a full range of temple services at the peetham in the Poconos.

Membership: Not reported.

Periodicals: *Vedic Heritage Newsletter,* Sri Rajarajeshwari Peetham, R.D.3, Box 3430, Stroudsburg, PA 18360.

★1197★
INTEGRAL YOGA INSTITUTE
% Satchidananda Ashram
Rte. 1, Box 172
Buckingham, VA 93921

Swami Satchidananda, one of several disciples of Swami Sivananda Saraswati to carry his teaching around the world, founded the Integral Yoga Institute. Satchidananda, after a life of wandering and dissatisfaction, met Swami Sivananda in 1947. In 1949, he was initiated as a sannyasin, the renounced life, and was given his name which means Existence-Knowledge-Bliss-Absolute. Because of his mastery of yogic science, he was given the title "Yogiraj." After seventeen years of work with Sivanada's Divine Life Society, he came to New York on an intended two-day visit, but stayed to become the founder-director of the Integral Yoga Institute (IYI).

Although the IYI teaches the full scope of Sivananda's work, the emphasis is on hatha yoga, of which Satchidananda is a master. His text, *Integral Yoga Hatha,* is a central study guide and its popularity, in general, is helping spread the movement. Hatha yoga uses various physical positions such as the lotus position (sitting with legs crossed) to discipline the body and allow the mind to concentrate.

In 1975 Satchidananda began a monastic order and initiated the first group of twenty-eight (including fifteen women) in 1975. The sannyasin take the traditional vows of poverty, chastity and obedience but also vow to serve selflessly and to never cause fear to any living being. In 1985 the headquarters of IYI were shifted from the ashram in Connecticut to a new ashram in Virginia.

Membership: Not reported. There are approximately 25 ashrams and teaching centers in the United States. Overseas there is work in India, Sri Lanka, and Australia.

Periodicals: *Integral Yoga,* Sri Satchidananda Ashram, Route 1, Box 172, Buckingham, VA 23921; *IYI News,* 227 West 13th Street, New York, NY 10011.

Remarks: Satchidananda has become known for his involvement in interfaith work. Located at the Virginia ashram is the Light of Truth Universal Shrine, a temple honoring all of the religions of the world. He believes that all religions are in their essence one.

Sources: Sita Weiner, *Swami Satchidananda.* New York: Bantam Books, 1972; Sri Swami Satchidananda, *A Decade of Service.* Pomfret Center, CT: Satchidananda Ashram-Yogaville, 1976; Swami Satchidananda et al, *Living Yoga.* New York: An Interface book, 1977; Swami Satchidananda, *Integral Hatha Yoga.* New York: Holt, Rinehart and Winston, 1970; Swami Satchidananda, *The Glory of Sannyasa.* Pomfret, CT: Satchidananda Ashram-Yogaville, 1975.

★1198★
INTERCOSMIC CENTER OF SPIRITUAL AWARENESS
% Ananda Ashram
Sapphire Rd.
R.D. 2, Box 212-C-1
Monroe, NY 10950

The Intercosmic Center of Spiritual Associations (ICSA), formerly the International Center for Self-Analysis, was founded by Dr. Rammurti S. Mishra, a student of Bhagavan Sri Ramana Maharshi. As a young yogi, Maharshi (discussed elsewhere in this chapter) was able to detach his consciousness from the transient world and experience transcendental reality. Upon returning to his physical body, he posed the question "Who am I?" The question was answered through a technique of self-analysis. ICSA seeks to help its adherents through a similar technique of analysis. Its stated goals are 1) to experience one's self as the cosmic center of vibrations; 2) to establish unity of all beings, especially all nations; 3) to promote global togetherness; 4) to promote a natural way of education, self-discipline and relations; 5) to promote the teaching of sanskrit; 6) to establish modern educational centers; 7) to promote natural, spiritual and psychological methods of healing; 8) to experience automatic and spontaneous psychosynthesis and psychoanalysis; and 9) to assist the individual in realizing the Godhood that always resides within.

The ICSA is the umbrella for a number of ashrams around the world under Mishra's direction. Dr. Mishra is a master of raja and kundalini yoga and a medical doctor with specialities in psychiatry and endocrinology. A significant part of the program centers on intensive self-analysis week-ends held at the Ashram Farm in Pulaski, New York. Srimarti Margaret Coble directs ICSA.

Membership: Not reported. In the United States the main centers are the Ananda Ashram in Monroe, New York; the Rochester Ashram; the I.C.S.A. of Syracuse; and the New York City yoga center (all sponsored by the Yoga Society of New York) and the Brahmananda Ashram, the teaching center of the Yoga Society of San Francisco in California.

Periodicals: *Self-Analysis Bulletin*, Box 805, Monroe, NY 10950.

Sources: Rammurti Mishra, *Fundamentals of Yoga.* New York: Lancer Books, 1969; Ramamurti Mishna, *Self Analysis and Self Knowledge.* Lakemont, GA: CSA Press, 1978; Margaret Coble, *Self-Abidance.* Port Louis, Mauritius: Standard Printing Establishment, 1973; Rammurti Mishra, *Dynamics of Yoga Mudras and Five Suggestions for Meditation.* Pleasant Valley, NY: Kriya Press, 1967; Rammurti S. Mishra, *Isha Upanishad.* Dayton, OH: Yoga Society of Dayton, 1962.

★1199★

INTERNATIONAL BABAJI KRIYA YOGA SANGAM
595 W. Bedford Rd.
Imperial City, CA 92251

The International Babaji Yoga Sangam was founded in 1952 by Yogi S. A. A. Ramaiah. Yogi Ramaiah is the disciple of Kriya Babaji Nagaraj, the satguru of the order. Born and raised in Tamil, Nagaraj was initiated into Kriya Kundalini Pranayam by a sage named Agasthiya who resided at Kuttralam, India. He also traveled to Sri Lanka to study with another Siva Siddhanta teacher under whom he attained enlightenment. He eventually settled in the Himalayas, where he still lives. He has chosen to live quietly and allow his disciples to spread his teachings. The Babaji Yoga Sangam was founded under the guidance of Babaji Nagaraj. It is claimed that Nagaraj was born in 203 A.D. and lives on in defiance of the limitations of death.

Yogi S.A.A. Ramaiah became well-known in the early 1960s as a result of his submitting to a number of scientific tests in which he demonstrated his control over several body functions, including the ability to vary his body temperature over a fifteen-degree range. He brought the movement he had founded in India to America in the 1960s. By the early 1970s, fifteen centers had been opened across the country with headquarters in Norwalk, California. Sadhana centers, for more intense, live-in practice of kriya yoga, were established in several rural California locations. More recently the Yogi Ramaiah established the first shrine to Ayyappa Swami, a figure in the ancient Hindu holy books, the Puranas, in Imperial City, California. Each December, beginning in 1970, members of the sangam make a pilgrimage from the shrine, which also serves as the American headquarters of the group, to Mount Shasta, 800 miles away in the mountains of northern California.

Membership: Not reported.

Sources: Yogi S.A.A. Ramaiah, *Shasta Ayyappa Swami Yoga Pilgrimage.* Imperial City, CA: Pan American Babaji Yoga Sangam, n.d.

★1200★

INTERNATIONAL SOCIETY FOR KRISHNA CONSCIOUSNESS
3764 Watseka Blvd.
Los Angeles, CA 90034

The International Society for Krishna Consciousness (ISKCON) is a major representaive of that form of devotional Vaishnava Hinduism which grew out of the work of Chaitanya Mahaprabhu (1486-1534?), the famed Bengali saint. Caitanya advocated a life of intense devotion centered upon the public chanting of the names of God, primarily through the chanting of the Hare Krishna mantra: Hare Krishna Hare Krishna Hare Hare Krishna Krishna Hare Rama Hare Rama Hare Hare Rama Rama.

ISKCON developed out of the activity of A. C. Bhaktivedanta Swami Prabhupada (1896-1977). Prabhupada was a businessman. He was initiated into the revived Krishna Consciousness movement represented in the Guadiya Mission in 1932. In 1936 his guru told him to take Krishna worship to the West, but he did not take his mission to spread the movement seriously until the 1950s. In 1959, he took his vows for the renounced life as a sannyasin order. In 1965, he traveled to America to build a movement. ISKCON was founded the following year in New York City. A magazine was begun and a San Francisco center opened in 1967. Besides leading the movement and serving as the initiating guru to the several thousands of adherents, Prabhupada was a prolific translator/author. He produced two series of translations and commentaries on the main scriptures of Krishna Consciousness, *The Srimad Bhagavatam* and the *Caitanya-caritamrita.* His primary work, the first one that most new members first encounter, was his translation of and commentary on the Bhagavad-Gita, *The Bhagavad-Gita As It Is.*

The movement grew, though never in the great numbers that its media coverage often suggested. It was a frequent object of media coverage because of its colorful appearance and strange, exotic beliefs and practices. During the 1970s it became one of the major targets for the anti-cult movement.

The central thrust of ISKCON is bhakti yoga, which in this case takes the form of chanting the Hare Krishna mantra. The chanting is the process for receiving the pure consciousness of God (thought of in his prime incarnations of Krishna and Rama) and dispelling the maya or illusion in which the world is immersed. Devotion also includes the following: service to the deity statues found in all Krishna temples; telok, markings of the body with clay in twelve places, each representing a name of God; kirtan, the public chanting and dancing to Krishna; and eating of prasadam, food (all vegetables) offered to Krishna. Devotees also study much traditional Hindu lore (Vedic culture), the history of bhakti yoga and the writings of the founder.

As the society has spread, it has gained fame for its festivals and feasts. Each summer one or more international festivals featuring a mass parade honoring Lord Jagannath are held, and everyone is fed a vegetarian meal. Weekly feasts (open to the public) are part of the normal activity of the local temple.

Prior to Prabhupada's death, he had appointed a 22-member governing body commission (GBC) which had begun to function in the early 1970s and provided a smooth transition of power in 1977. Included in the GBC were the initiating gurus who were assigned hegemony over the temples in various segments (zones) of the global movement. The initiating gurus are in charge of the spiritual work of the religion, while the GBC provides overall coordination and administrative oversight. The various zones are further divided into a number of corporations, each independent and autonomous and directly under the control of the initiating guru in charge. There is no longer any central headquarters or central voice for the entire movement. The decentralization has led to the formation of a variety of publishing concerns and programs in the several zones.

Arising as the most important centers in in the United States during the early 1980s are the complex in Los Angeles and the retreat community, New Vrindaban, near Moundsville, West Virginia. The Los Angeles Center is home to Bhaktivedanta Book Trust, the major publishing arm of the movement. New Vrindaban has become a major tourist attraction with its monumental architecture that features a home built for Prabhupada, the Palace of Gold, and other structures already built as part of a projected park and temple complex. Bhaktipada Books is the publishing concern at New Vrindaban.

Membership: In 1984 the movement reported 3,000 core community members and 250,000 lay constituents. There were 50 center in the United States. There are 8,000 members worldwide. Centers can be found in 60 countries.

Periodicals: *Back to Godhead*, Box 18928, Philadelphia, PA 19119-0428; *Plain Living High Thinking*, Bhaktipada Books, Hare Krishna Ridge, New Vrindaban, WV 26041; *The ISKCON World Review*, 3764 Watseka Avenue, Los Angeles, CA 90034.

Remarks: In Hawaii, ISKCON experienced a temporary schism when a rival group under Sai Young emerged. Young's followers, known as the Haiku Meditation Center and Krishna Yoga Community, followed Bhaktivedanta's teachings but did not don the saffron robes or shave their heads. The group disbanded in 1971 and ISKCON inherited its members.

In 1983 a former member of the movement, Robin George, was awarded $9,700,000 in a lawsuit against the movement. This judgment (now being appealed) could, if sustained, seriously damage the movement in California, New Orleans, New York, and Canada (the temples under direct attack by the suit). Much of the future of the movement is contingent upon the outcome of this litigation.

Sources: A. C. Bhaktivedanta Swami Prabhupada, *Bhagavad-Gita As It Is*. New York: Bhaktivedanta Book Trust, 1972; Satsvarupa dasa Goswami, *Srila Prabhupada-lilamrta*. Los Angeles: Bhaktivedanta Book Trust, 1980-1983. 6 vols.; Steven Gelberg, ed., *Hare Krishna, Hare Krishna*. New York: Grove Press, 1983; Kim Knott, *My Sweet Lord*. Wellingborough, Northamptonshire,: Aquarian Press, 1986; J. Stillson Judah, *Hare Krishna and the Counterculture*. New York: John Wiley & Sons, 1974.

**★1201★
JOHANNINE DAIST COMMUNITY**
℅ Brian O'Mahony
750 Adrian Way
San Rafael, CA 94903

The Johannine Daist Community was founded in 1970 as the Dawn Horse Fellowship by Franklin Jones. In 1960, after a "crisis of despair," he began a period of introspection which led him to study with Swami Rudrananda (discussed elsewhere in this chapter), the American student of Swami Muktananda (also discussed elsewhere in this chapter). At Rudrananda's suggestion, he entered a Lutheran seminary. In 1968 he traveled to India to meet Muktananda. At Muktananda's ashram he had his first adult experience of total absorption in the Transcendental Consciousness.

On September 10, 1970, he entered what he has termed the permanent state of Sahaj Samadhi, which is coessential with the Transcendental Being-Consciousness itself. This is the condition which he is believed to have surrendered at birth, and which he had tried to recover throughout his life. Soon after this experience he began to teach in order to transmit the God-realization he had attained. In 1973 he undertook a pilgrimage to India. During this time he changed his name to Bubba Free John--"Bubba" denoting brother. Upon his return he changed his method of teaching. He involved his students in the many experiences of life, including sexuality, the pursuits of money and material rewards, and spiritual and psychic encounters. Some experiences became quite intense and all were aimed at showing their futility.

After three years of primary interaction with his students, Bubba Free John withdrew into seclusion. In 1979 he entered a new phase of work and adopted the name Da Free John--"Da" signifying "giver." This has been a phase of retirement from active teaching work and institutional involvement to concentrate on the transmission of the "Transcendental Condition." As Da Free John's work has grown and changed, so has the name of the body of believers from Dawn Horse Fellowship to Free Primitive Church of Divine Communion to Johannine Daist Communion.

The teachings of Da Free John have been termed the Way of Radical Understanding. It begins in the denial of the illusion of the separateness of our individual existence. We are the all-comprehensive Reality, Being-Consciousness-Bliss. This condition which is native and natural to us becomes obvious when all egoic motivation toward introversion and extroversion is transcended, i.e., when radical understanding prevails. Enlightenment, thus, already exists; it cannot be attained. It is, however, to be realized. This realization occurs through a process which Da Free John has characterized as the seven stages of life. The seven stages provide a method of evaluating one's individual progress as well as the level of the mass of other spiritual teachings.

Stage one begins at birth and focuses upon adaptation to the world. Stage two, beginning around age seven, focuses upon the integration of the emotional self and the physical. The third stage is a period of development of the mind, will and emotional-sexual functions. The fourth stage marks the beginning of spiritual awakening. The fifth stage relates to the mystical inner search capped with the experience of samahdi. The sixth stage is the profound state of "ego-death", or the transcendence of the separate self-sense, the awakening to Transcendental Consciousness. In the seventh stage, the individual recognizes everything as a modification of the Radiant Transcendental Being.

Membership: In 1984 there were approximately 800 members in the United States and several hundred overseas. Some members now live at the resident retreat center in the Fiji Islands.

Periodicals: *The Laughing Man*, 750 Adrian Way, San Rafael, CA 94903; *Crazy Wisdom*, 750 Adrian Way, San Rafael, CA 94903.

Sources: Franklin Jones, *The Method of the Siddhas.* Los Angeles: Dawn Horse Press, 1973; Bubba Free John [Franklin Jones], *No Remedy.* Lower Lake, CA: Dawn Horse Press, 1976; Da Free John [Franklin Jones], *The Dawn Horse Testament.* San Rafael, CA: Dawn Horse Press, 1985; *The Next Option.* Clearlake, CA: Dawn Horse Press, 1984; Georg Feuerstein, ed., *Humor Suddenly Returns.* Clearlake, CA: Dawn Horse Press, 1984.

★1202★
KIRPALU YOGA FELLOWSHIP
Box 793
Lenox, MA 01240

Yogi Amrit Desai, a disciple of Swami Shri Kkirpalvanandji, a kundalini master of India, came to America in 1960 as a student. While pursuing another career, he began to teach yoga. The response was so great that, in 1966, he founded the Yoga Society of Pennsylvania. In 1970 he returned to India where he was given the shaktipat initiation by his guru. Shaktipat is experienced as a release of kundalini energy believed to be latent at the base of the spine. Upon release it travels upward. When it reaches the crown of the head, it brings enlightenment.

Out of his own experience of kundalini yoga, Desai, while engaged in his daily practice of hatha yoga, began to experience a series of spontaneous postures. At the time his consciousness had left his body and watched the postures as an observer. The experience was repeated and over a period of time the new actions were systematized into a new form of yoga, named for his guru, Kirpalu Yoga. Kirpalu yoga combines a slow performance of postures synchronized with yogic breathing to produce an effortless series of meditative movements having the capacity to produce the higher states of consciousness. He began to teach this to his students.

The first residential community of his disciples emerged in 1971 and the Kirpalu Ashram created at Sumneytown, Pennsylavnia. In 1974, Desai transferred all his ownership interest in his work to a new non-profit corporation, Kirpalu Yoga Fellowship, was created to guide the teachings. A second residential community in Massachusetts has become the headquarters of the fellowship. Meanwhile, kirpalu yoga groups led by teachers trained by Desai have emerged around the United States.

The center in Massachusetts carries on a year-round program focused upon the practice of yoga, holistic health, and a vegetarian diet. Its program offers training in yoga therapy, teacher preparation, and a wide variety of workshops on related concerns. In 1977, the Fellowship sponsored the first visit of Swami Kirpalvanandji to America.

Membership: In 1984 there were two major centers and 40 affiliated centers with approximately 2,500 members. There are also centers in Canada and Germany.

Periodicals: *The Kirpalu Experience*, Kirpalu Yoga Retreat, Box 1061, Summit Station, PA 17979; *The Kirpalu Family Newsletter*.

Sources: Sukanya Warren, *Gurudev, The Life of Yogi Amrit Desai.* Summit Station, PA: Kirpalu Publications, 1982; Amrit Desai, *Guru and Disciple.* Sumneytown, PA: Kirpalu Yoga Ashram, 1975; Swami Kirpalvananda, *Science of Meditation.* Vadodara, Gujarat, India: Sri Dahyabhai Hirabhai Patel, 1977; Swami Kirpalvanandji, *Premyatra.* Summit Station, PA: Kirpalu Yoga Fellowship, 1981.

★1203★
KRISHNAMURTI FOUNDATION OF AMERICA
Ojai, CA 93023

The Krishnamurti Foundation of America is one of several groups in this volume that does not consider itself a religion. It was founded in 1969 to assist in sponsoring

Krishnamurti's lectures, arranging his tours, publishing his books, and producing audio-visuals. Krishnamurti is considered primarily an educator and philosopher. The Foundation is included in this volume because he functions in a role analogous to a spiritual teacher and guide, and his lectures constantly deal with what have traditionally been thought of as "religious" themes.

The work of Jeddu Krishnamurti (1895-1986) really began in 1929 when he dissolved the Order of the Star of the East, which had been created by Annie Besant and the Theosophical Society to promote Krishnamurti as the coming World Savior. This breaking of relations with the society, which became complete 1933, followed an intense period of inner turmoil and questioning of his role and thought. That period had been highlighted by a life-changing three-day spiritual experience much of which took place under a pepper tree adjacent to his home in Oaji, California, August 17-20, 1922. Seven years later he had decided that humans cannot come to truth through any creed, dogma, priest, ritual, philosophic knowledge or psychological technique. They insisted that he was merely a teacher sharing ideas, and not guru in any traditional sense of the word.

Truth lies in observation of the content of mind. Individuals build fences of security consisting of symbols, images and beliefs. These images burden life and relationships. Our individuality is the name given to the form and superficial culture acquired from tradition and the environment. Freedom lies in freedom from the content of our consciousness. It is pure observation without direction, the choiceless awareness of our daily existence and activity.

Krishnamurti began to give talks to those who continued to listen after the break with Theosophy. He regularly lectured in America, Europe and India. Star Publishing Trust, which had previously published his talks, became Krishnamurti Writings, Inc. and had sole charge of reprinting his writings and transcriptions of his lectures. In 1968 he severed his relations with Krishnamurti Writings, Inc. and in 1968 created the Krishnamurti Foundation in England. The American Foundation was established the following year. In India, Krishnamurti's work had been facilitated by the Foundation for New Education which in 1953 had become the Rishi Valley Trust. In 1970 it became the Krishnamurti Foundation of India. There are also foundations in Spain and Canada. Each of the national foundations are independent and autonomous, but operate in close cooperation.

The American foundation sponsors the Oak Grove School, an independent elementary and secondary school whose curriculum is based upon Krishnamurti's philosophy of education. It is located in Ojai, California.

Membership: The Foundation does not have members. It has a mailing list of supporters.

Periodicals: *Bulletin*, Krishnamurti Foundation, Box 216, Ojai, CA 93023-0216.

Remarks: Recently, Krishnamurti died. The Foundation has announced that it will continue to facilitate the distribution of Krishnamurti's tapes and books and to channel suppport to Oak Grove School.

Sources: Mary Lutyens, *Krishnamurti, The Years of Awakening*. New York: Farrar, Straus & Giroux, 1975; Mary Lutyens, *Krishnamurti, The Years of Fulfillment*. London: J. Murray, 1983; Alcyone [Jeddu Krishnamurti], *At the Feet of the Master*. Adyar, India: Theosophical Publishing House, n.d.; Jeddu Krishnamurti, *Commentaries on Living*. Wheaton, IL: Theosophical Publishing House, 3 vols.; Jeddu Krishnamurti and David Bohm, *The Ending of Time*. San Francisco, CA: Harper & Row, 1985.

★1204★
KUNDALINI RESEARCH FOUNDATION
10 E. 39th St.
New York, NY 10016

Gopi Krishna (b. 1903) is a Hindu master of kundalini yoga. After twenty years of meditation, he experienced the kundalini at the age of thirty-seven. He has spent the years since exploring the nature of kundalini and has produced three books on the subject. In 1970, American followers organized the Kundalini Research Foundation to disseminate Gopi Krishna's books and writings and to continue his research.

Kundalini is the name given the divine energy believed to be lodged at the base of the spine. Often pictured as a coiled snake, the awakened energy travels up the spine and remolds the brain. It is identified with prana, the nerve energy which effects altered states of consciousness. The awakened energy is the biological basis of genius. Kundalini, according to Krishna, is concentrated in the sex energy. Awakening the kundalini redirects the prana from the sexual regions to the brain. In the awakening, a fine biological "essence" rises from the reproductive region to the brain through the spinal column. The flow can be felt behind the palate from the middle point of the tongue to the root, and can be objectively measured.

Membership: Not reported.

Periodicals: *Chimo*, Chimo Publications, 79 Victoria St., Toronto, ON, Canada M5C 2B1 (unofficial publication).

Sources: Gopi Krishna, *The Biological Basis of Religion and Genius*. New York: Harper & Row 1972; Gopi Krishna, *The Secret of Yoga*. New York; Harper & Row, 1972; Gopi Krishna, *The Awakening of Kundalini*. New York: E. P. Dutton, 1975; Gopi Krishna, *The Riddle of Consciousness*. New York: Kundalini Research Foundation, 1976; Gopi Krishna, *Yoga, a Vision of Its Future*. New Delhi, India: Kundalini Research and Publication Trust, 1978.

★1205★
LAKSHMI
270 N. Canon Dr., Suite 1280
Beverly Hills, CA 90210

Lakshmi was founded by former English professor Dr. Frederick Lenz. Lenz was a disciple of Sri Chinmoy during the 1960s and studied with him for eleven years. Under the name Atmananda, given to him by his guru, he taught yoga in Los Angeles and Southern California. Spontaneously, his students reported a number of extraordinary experiences during his classes. According to reports, Lenz levitated, disappeared completely, and/or radiated intense beams of light during group meditations. During the 1970s Atmananda left Sri Chinmoy and formed Lakshmi as an independent organization. At a gathering of approximately 100 of his students in the early 1980s, he announced that Eternity had given him a new name, "Rama."

Rama teaches that humanity is at the end of a cycle. The present period, Kali Yuga, is a dark age. At the end of each cycle or age, Vishu (the god of the Hindus) is due to take incarnation. While Rama does not see himself to be the same conscious entity as the historic Rama, a previous incarnation of Vishu, he does claim to be the embodiment of the "particular octave of celestial light which was once incarnated as Rama."

Membership: Not reported. Rama regularly teaches seminars in Malibu and Los Angeles, California. Lakshmi has an estimated several hundred members.

Periodicals: *Self Discovery*, 270 N. Canon Drive, Suite 1280, Beverly Hills, CA 90210.

Sources: Rama, *The Last Incarnation*. Malibu, CA: Lakshmi Publications, 1983; Frederick Lenz, *Life Times*. New York: Fawcett Crest, 1979.

★1206★
MA YOGA SHAKTI INTERNATIONAL MISSION
114-23 Lefferts Blvd.
South Ozone, NY 11420

The Ma Yoga Shakti International Mission was formed in 1979 by Ma Yogashakti Sarawati, an Indian female guru, who migrated to the United States in 1977. She established ashrams in New York and Florida and alternates her time between them. She also has four ashrams in India (Bombay, Calcutta, Delhi, and Gondia). Ma Yogashakti teaches a balanced approach to all yogas-- hatha, raja, bhakti, and karma. Full moon Purnima (devotional services) are held monthly. Her teachings are spelled out in a number of books she has written, including: *Chhandogya Upanishad, Prayers and Poems from Mother's Heart, Shree Satya Narayana Vrata Katha, Adhyatma Sandesh,* and *The Invisible Seven Psychic Lotuses.*

Membership: In 1984 the mission had three centers, one in New York and two in Florida (Deerfield Beach and Palm Bay), with an estimated 200 members.

Periodicals: *Yogashakti Mission Newsletter*, 114-23 Lefferts Blvd., South Ozone, NY 11420.

Sources: Ma Yogashakti Saraswati, *Prayers & Poems from Mother's Heart*. Melbourne, FL: Yogashakti Mission, 1976; Ma Yogashakti Saraswati, trans., *Shree Satya Narayana Vrata Katha*. Melbourne, FL: Yogashakti Mission, n.d.; Ma Yogashakti, *Yoog Vashishtha*. Gondia, India: Yogashakti Mission, [1970 ?]; Guru Chetanaschakti, *Guru Pushpanjali*. Calcutta: Yogashakti Mission Trust, 1977.

★1207★
MOKSHA FOUNDATION
745 31st St.
Boulder, CO 80303

The Moksha Foundation was founded in 1976 as the Self-Enlightenment Meditation Society by Bishwanath Singh, known by his religious name Tantracharya Nityananda. Nityananda began studying yoga at the age of seven. He became a student of Shrii Shrii Anandamurtiji and eventually served as a monk with the Ananda Marga Yoga Society. In 1969 he realized that he was a siddha yogi in his previous incarnation and that he had been reincarnated in this life to teach meditation and yoga. He left the Anada Marga Yoga Society and began independent work, eventually establishing centers in India and England. He also renounced his vows as a monk and married.

In 1973 Nityananda moved to Boulder, Colorado, and established the Self-Enlightenment Meditation Society. The center served as a residence for several of his closest students. He taught meditation , tantric yoga philosophy, and lathi, a martial art, and offered personal instruction and initiation for his followers. From his Colorado headquarters, he regularly journeyed to meet with students in Chicago, Minneapolis, New York, and Los Angeles.

In 1981 Nityananda traveled to Europe on a speaking tour. While on the Continent, he was invited to lecture in Sweden. After leaving the plane in Stockholm, he disappeared. His body was found several months later; he had been murdered. Mira Sussman, a resident student at the Boulder center, succeeded to leadership of the foundation and has continued the program initiated by Nityananda.

Membership: Not reported. At the time of Nityananda's death, he had approximately 50 students in Boulder, with other groups in several U.S. cities. The centers previously founded in London and in Bihar, India, continued, and he regularly visited them.

Periodicals: *The Tantric Way*, 745 31st Street, Boulder, CO 80303.

★1208★

NARAYANANANDA UNIVERSAL YOGA TRUST
N U Yoga Ashram
1418 N. Kedzie
Chicago, IL 60651

The Narayanananda Universal Yoga Trust was created in 1967 by Swami Narayanananda Maharaj (b. April 12, 1902), a native of the hill country of Coorg in Southern India. At the age of twenty-seven, he began his religious quest. He traveled to the Ramakrishna Math in Belur, Bengal (outside of Calcutta). He joined the monks and took his vows as a sannyasin (the renounced life). He studied under Swami Shivananda, the math's president, and in 1932 departed for the Himalayas to complete his spiritual quest. In February, 1933, he experienced nirvikipa samadhi, described as the merger of his individual consciousness with the great Ocean of Consciousness occasioned by the awakening of his kundalini, the latent energy pictured as lying coiled like a serpent at the base of the spine.

After the experience of samadhi, Narayanananda remained a recluse, refusing to take disciples or form an organization. Then in 1947, moved by the suffering of people at the time of the separation of Pakistan from India, he agreed to take disciples. Over the next twenty years the nunmber of disciples grew and included some Europeans. The growth in the number of followers led Narayanananda to create the trust which at its inception included centers in Denmark, Germany, and Switzerland.

Narayanananda teaches what he terms Universal Religion. He emphasizes meditation, strict morality, and mind control (i.e., the detached life) as the path to union with the Divine. He also emphasizes kundalini yoga.

In 1977 Swami Narayanananda authorized Swami Turiyananda to start an ashram in the United States. He settled in Chicago and opened one center. An ashram/ retreat was begun in Winter, Wisconsin. Narayanananda made his first visit to the United States in 1980 and conducted classes at both locations.

Membership: In 1980 the trust had approximately 15 centers in India, Denmark, Sweden, Norway, Germany, and New Zealand. The two centers in the United States serve several hundred members.

Periodicals: *Yoga*, N. U. Yoga Ashrama, Gylling, DK-8300 Odder, Denmark.

Sources: Swami Narayanananda, *The Mysteries of Man, Mind and Mind Functions*. N.p., n.d.; Swami Narayanananda, *A Practical Guide to Samadhi*. Rishikish, India: Narayanananda Universal Yoga Trust, 1966; Swami Narayanananda, *The Secrets of Mind-Control*. Rishikish,

India: Narayanananda Universal Yoga Trust, 1970; Swami Narayanananda, *The Secrets of Prana, Pranayana, and Yoga-Asana*. Gylling, Denmark: N U Yoga Trust & Ashrama, 1979; Swami Narayanananda, *The Primal Power in Man*. Rishikish, India: Narayanananda Universal Yoga Trust, 1970.

★1209★

PRANA YOGA ASHRAM
International Headquarters
% Swami Sivalingam
488 Spruce St.
Berkeley, CA 94708

The Prana Yoga Center was founded by Swami Sivalingam a former in hatha yoga at the Yoga Vedanta Forest Academy established at Rishikish on the Ganges River by Swami Sivananda. Sivalingam began his stay at Sivananda's center in 1959. In 1962 he began his international work by bringing the yoga teachings first to Japan and then in Hong Kong, where he established several Sivananda Yoga Centers. He moved to the United States in 1973 and successsively founded the Prana Yoga Foundation (1974), the Prana Yoga Ashram (1975), the Prana Yoga Center (1976), and the Ayaodhyanagar Retreat (1977). In 1975 he extended his work to Vancouver, British Columbia. As a result of this work and subsequent travels, he has established a string of centers which ring the globe from India to Japan, to North America to Denmark and Spain.

Sivalingam follows the yogic teachings and practices of Sivananda with an emphasis upon hatha yoga asanas (position) and the practice of pranayama (precise breath control). Through this practice, prana, or energy, is manifested and controlled and leads to purification of the nervous system and inner spiritual balance.

Membership: Not reported. In 1980 there were six centers in the United States and nine centers in other countries.

Periodicals: *Prana Yoga Life*, Box 1037, Berkeley, CA 94701.

Sources: Swami Sivalingam, *Wings of Divine Wisdom*. Berkeley, CA: Prana Yoga Ashram, 1977.

★1210★

RAJ-YOGA MATH AND RETREAT
Box 547
Deming, WA 98244

The Raj-Yoga Math and Retreat is a small monastic community formed in 1974 by Father Satchakrananda Bodhisattvaguru. Satchakrananda began the practice when he experienced the raising of the kundalini, an internal energy pictured in Hindu thought as a snake coiled and resting at the base of the spine which, upon awakening, rises to the crown chakra (psychic center at the top of the head). That event produced an awareness of

Satchakrananda's divine heritage. Following that event, he spent a short time in a Trappist monastery, attended Kenyon College, and then became coordinator for the Northwest Free University, where he taught yoga.

In 1973 Satchakrananda was "mystically" initiated as a yogi by the late Swami Sivananda (1887-1963), the founder of the Divine Life Society, through a trilogy of "female Matas" at a retreat he attended on the Olympic (Washington) Peninsula. The following year, with a small group of men and women, he founded the math (monastery). In 1977, he was ordained a priest by Archbishop Herman Adrian Spruit of the Church of Antioch (see separate entry) and has attempted to combine both Hindu and Christian traditions at the math. Spiritual disciplines include the regular celebrations of the mass, though the major practice offered is the Japa Yoga Sadhana, consisting of the sucessive practice of japa (mantra) yoga, meditation, kriyas (cleansings), mudras, asanas (hatha yoga postures), and pranayam (disciplined breathing). Japa yoga allows practitioners to become aware of their divine nature.

The math is located in the foothills of Mt. Baker overlooking the Nooksuck River near Deming, Washington. It accepts resident students for individual instruction, but offers a variety of classes for nonresidents through the Karma Leela Institute. For those unable to travel to the math for instruction, Satchakrananda has put together a japa yoga workshop packet.

Membership: The resident community at the math fluctuates between two and twenty. Several hundred individuals are associated with the math through their attendance at the Karma Leela Institute.

Sources: Yogi Satchakrananda, *Coming and Going, The Mother's Drama*. Deming, WA: Raj-Yoga Math & Retreat, 1975; *Letters to Satchekrananda*. Deming, WA: Raj-Yoag Math & Retreat, 1977.

★1211★
RUDRANANDA ASHRAM
6 Linnaean St.
Cambridge, MA 02138

Swami Rudrananda (1928-1973), born Albert Rudolph, was a spiritual seeker who had participated in groups following the methods of George Gurdjieff and Subud, prior to traveling to India. There, in 1958, he met Swami Nityananda (d. 1961) and his student Swami Muktananda (1908-1982). In these two swamis he found an end to his quest. He also arranged Muktananda's first visit to America in 1970 and helped launch his movement. However, after studying first with Nityananda and later with Muktananda for fifteen years, he broke with Muktananda in 1971 and founded the Shree Gurudev Rudrananda Yoga Ashram. The teachings followed essentially the Saivite Hindu teachings of Nityananda and Muktananda, both of whom emphasized the role of the

guru who gave shaktipat to awaken the kundalini. Kundalini is the cosmic power believed to be resting dormant like a coiled snake at the base of the spine. Its awakening allows the power to travel up the spine to the crown of the head, thus producing enlightenment.

Rudrananda founded a string of ashrams across the United States and wrote one book, *Spiritual Cannibalism*, published within months of his death in an airplane accident. His movement was managed for a short time by a group of eight close disciples but eventually splintered with the various ashrams and their leaders going in independent directions. The largest and most substantial remnant of Rudrananda's following was reorganized under Swami Chetanananda, head of the ashram in Bloomington, Indiana in 1973. Several years later Chetanananda moved his headquarters to Cambridge, Masasachusetts and developed a complex of interrelated organizations.

The ashram is a community of disciples living the practical spiritual life as Savaite Hindus. The Nityananda Institute is a meditation center whose aim is to make the spiritual life of the group accessible to westerners. The Rudi Foundation adopted the broad goal of restating what is termed the "perennial wisdom," i.e, the common affirmation of Indian thought and Western mystical perspectives, in modern terminology and contemporary studies. The Rudra Press is the publishing arm of the organization.

Membership: Not reported. Several hundred people are involved in the ashram in Massachusetts.

Periodicals: *Re-Vision*, Rudi Foundation, Box 316, Cambridge, MA 02238.

Sources: Swami Rudrananda, *Spiritual Cannibalism*. New York: Links, 1973; Swami Chetanananda, *Songs from the Center of the Well*. Cambridge, MA: Rudra Press, 1983; M.U. Hatengdi, *Nityananda, the Divine Presence*. Cambridge, MA: Rudra Press, 1984; . U. Hatengdi and Swami Chrtanananda, *Nitya Sutras*. Cambridge, MA: Rudra Press, 1985; Lucia Nevai, "Rudi, The Spiritual Legacy of an American Original" in *Yoga Journal*, no. 65 (July/August 1985), pp. 36-38, 68-71.

★1212★
S. A. I. FOUNDATION
7911 Willoughby Ave.
Los Angeles, CA 90046

All religions have had their miracle workers, but Satya Sai Baba (b. 1926) is certainly the most outstanding in India today. The first miracle related to Sai Baba concerned a mysterious cobra found under his bed, proclaiming, say his followers, Sai Baba's role as Sheshiasa, Lord of Serpents. As a child he worked miracles for his classmates, producing objects out of nowhere, a favorite practice still continued.

In 1940, he fell into a coma which lasted for two months. Upon awakening suddenly, he announced, "I am Sai Baba of Shirdi." Sai Baba of Shirdi (1856?-1918) was an Indian holy man who had left behind a large following who still venerated him and observed his teachings. Satya Sai Baba, by his statement, claimed to be his reincarnation. Followers assert his ability to recall conversations between individuals who were disciples of the original Sai Baba.

The thrust of the Sai Baba movement is veneration of Sai Baba and recounting the miracle stories about him. Teachings are mainline Hinduism with emphasis on four aspects-Dharma Sthapana (establishing the faith on a firm foundation), Vidwathposhana (fostering scholarship), Vedasamrakshana (preservation of the Vedas) and Bhaktirakshana (protection of the devotees from secularism and materialism).

The Indian headquarters in Prasanthi Nilayam (Home of the Supreme Peace) are the focus of the Sai Baba movement. Here each Thursday devotees gather for a darshan or vision of Sai Baba. Special darshans are held during the Dasara holidays in October and his birthday celebration in November.

Interest in Sai Baba in America began with a set of lectures given in 1967 at the University of California at Santa Barbara. Movies of Prasanthi Nilayam were shown by Indra Devi, who had recently visited Sai Baba. She has since turned her spiritual center at Tecete, California, into an American Nilayam. The movement spread during the 1970s and groups have formed across the United States.

Membership: Not reported.

Periodicals: *Sathya Sai Newsletter*, 1800 East Garvey Avenue, West Covina, CA 91791.

Sources: Samuel H. Sandweiss, *Sai Baba, The Holy Man...and the Psychiatrist*. San Diego, CA: Birth Day Publishing Company, 1975; Howard Murphet, *Sai Baba, Man of Miracles*. New York: Samuel Weiser, 1976; John Hislop, *Conversations with Sathya Sai Baba*. San Diego: Birth Day Publishing Company, 1978; Grace T. McMartin, ed., *A Recapitulation of Sathya Sai Baba's Divine Teachings*. Hyderabad, India: Avon Printing Works, 1982; Tal Brooks, *Avatar of Night*. New Delhi, India: Tarang Paperbacks, 1984; *Lessons for Study Circle*. Prasanti Milayam, India: World Council of Sri Sathya Sai Organizations, n.d.; *Manual of Sri Sathya Sai Seva Dal and Guidelines for Activities*. Bombay: World Council of Sri Sathya Sai Organizations, 1979.

★1213★
SATYANANDA ASHRAMS, U.S.A.
1157 Ramblewood Way
San Mateo, CA 94403

Swami Satyananda Saraswati (b. 1893), a former disciple of Swami Sivananda Saraswati (1887-1963), founder of the Divine Life Society, pioneered the modern opening of the yoga to all, both sannyasins and householders, regardless of sex, nationality, caste, or creed. After working with Sivananda for twelve years, he wandered India for nine more. In 1964, the year after his guru's death, Satyananda founded the Bihar School of Yoga. He built the Sivananda Ashram on the banks of the Ganges and the Ganta Darshan on a hill overlooking the river valley. Satyananda continued Sivananda's broad approach which integrated the various yogic techniques, but gave particular emphasis to tantra. Also, like Sivananda, he actively spread his teachings, first throughout India, and beginning with a world tour in 1968, to the West. During the 1970s he establsihed ten ashrams and many centers in India and outside of India; followers could be found in Australia, Indonesia, Columbia, Greece, France, Sweden, England, and Ireland. As the movement spread, he organized the International Yoga Fellowship.

Satyananda's teachings came to the United States in two separate manners. First, in 1975 Llewellyn Publications, an occult publisher in St. Paul, Minnesota, released a major work by Swami Anandakapila (a.k.a. John Mumford), a leading disciple of Satyananda's in Australia. The publication of *Sexual Occultism* was followed by a United States tour in 1976 and feature articles in *Gnostica*, a major occult periodical. Concurrently with the publication of Anandakapila's book, a New York publisher released *Yoga, Tantra and Meditation* by Swami Janakananda Saraswati, a teacher for Satyananda in Scandinavia. Second, during the 1970s many students of Satyananda immigrated to the United States from India, and as their numbers increased they formed small yoga groups. In 1980 Swami Niranjannan Saraswati (b. 1960), a leading teacher with Satyananda who had traveled extensively and organized ashrams for the International Yoga Fellowship, arrived in the United States. On October 28, 1980, he organized Satyananda Ashrams U.S.A., the American affiliate of the International Yoga Fellowship. Niranjananda remained in the United States teaching and organizing local centers. In the summer of 1982, Swami Amritananda, visited the United States. Her visit was followed immediately by Satyananda's first tour of North America.

While it is not the main emphasis of his teachings, Satyananda has become known as an exponent of the so-called left-hand path of tantric yoga. Tantra is built upon the blending and exchange of male and female sexual enengies and consciousness. In left-hand tantra, sexual intercourse is utilized as a means of reaching ananda (or bliss).

The International Yoga Fellowship is one of the largest yoga groups worldwide. Its extensive membership in the United States is somewhat hidden, being largely confined to the Indian-American community.

Membership: Not reported. Membership is estimated to be in the thousands as ashrams and centers may be found across the United States and Canada.

Periodicals: *Yoga,* Bihar School of Yoga, Lal Darwaja, Monghyr 811201, Bihar, India.

Sources: Swami Satyananda Saraswati, *Taming the Kundalini.* Munger, Bihar, India: Bihar School of Yoga, 1982; Swami Satyananda Saraswati, *Sure Ways to Self-Realization.* Munger, Bihar, India: Bihar School of Yoga, 1983; *Teachings of Swami Satyananda Saraswati.* Mongyar, Bihar, India: Bihar School of Yoga, 1981; John Mumford [Swami Anandakapila], *Sexual Occultism.* St. Paul, MN: Llewellyn Publications, 1975; Swami Janakananda Saraswati, *Yoga, Tantra & Meditation.* New York: Ballantine Books, 1975.

★1214★
SELF-REALIZATION FELLOWSHIP
3880 San Rafael Ave.
Los Angeles, CA 90065

The Self Realization Fellowship traces its beginning to 1861 and the work of Mahavater Babaji, who revived and taught kriya yoga. He chose Swami Paramahansa Yogananda (1893-1952) to bring the teachings to the West. Yogananda was trained by Swami Sri Yukteswar (1855-1936) who left to Yogananda his succession and ashram properties. Yogananda founded the Yogoda Satsang of India in 1917. In 1920 Swami Yogananda came to the United States to attend the Pilgrim Tercentenary Anniversary International Congress of Religious Liberals. Impressed by what he found in America, he decided to stay, and, with those Americans who flocked around him, formed a small center of the Yogoda Satsang in Boston. From that center, he worked throughout the Eastern United States. In 1924 he went to the West Coast. In the later 1920s, he concentrated his activities in the Midwest.

Books, a magazine, *East-West,* and a correspondence course aided the rapid growth of the movement, but nothing was as effective as the personality of Yogananda. Born in India, Yogananda, after his graduation from college, joined the strict Swami Order and became the disciple of Sri Yukteswarji. In 1916 Yogananda discovered the techniques of Yogoda, a system of physical development which, combined with traditional yoga, became the central concern of his teachings.

The spread of the work in America led in 1935 to the formation of the Self-Realization Fellowship with national headquarters in Los Angeles. Other centers were opened in Encinitas, San Diego, Hollywood, Long Beach and Pacific Palisades; smaller groups are located around the country. Yogananda in death was as impressive as in life. His demise was heralded by his disciples as an extraordinary event because of "the absence of any visual signs of decay in the dead body of Paramahansa Yogananda...even twenty days after his death."

The emphasis of the Self-Realization Fellowship is teaching the way to bliss (ananda), or self-realization, or God-realization. The way is through "definite scientific techniques for attaining personal experience of God." The technique is kriya yoga, a system of awakening and energizing the psychic centers or chakras along the spinal column. The basic practice is regular deep meditation which leads to a focusing of spiritual cosmic energies. By the practice of kriya yoga, blood is decomposed and recharged with oxygen, the atoms of which are transmitted into "life current" to rejuvenate the brain and spinal centers.

The essential unity of Eastern and Western religious teachings is stressed in the Fellowship. To highlight this emphasis, an affiliate, Church of All Religions, is connected with the Fellowship. Worship centers on the inner communion (meditation) practices of Yogananda.

Yogananda was succeeded by Swami Rajasi Janakananda (James J. Lynn). Lynn died in 1955 and was succeeded by Sri Daya Mata, the present head of the fellowship.

Membership: Not reported. In 1981 the fellowship listed eight temples and ashram centers; one is in Phoenix and the remainder in California. There were an additonal 78 centers and meditation groups in the United States. There were centers in 37 foreign countries. The Yogoda Satsang of India had 32 centers and a variety of charitable facilities which it operated.

Periodicals: *Self-Realization,* 3880 San Rafael Avenue, Los Angeles, CA 90065.

Sources: Paramahansa Yogananda, *Autobiography of a Yogi.* Los Angeles: Self-Realization Fellowship, 1971; Paramahansa Yogananda, *Descriptive Outlines of Yogoda.* Los Angeles: Yogoda Satsang Society, 1928; *Self-Realization Fellowship Highlights.* Los Angeles: Self-Realization Fellowship, 1980; Sri Daya Mata, *Only Love.* Los Angeles: Self-Realization Fellowship, 1976; *Self-Realization Fellowship Manual of Services.* Los Angeles: Self-Realization Fellowship, 1965; *New Pilgrims of the Spirit.* Boston: Beacon Press, 1921.

★1215★
SELF-REVELATION CHURCH OF ABSOLUTE MONISM
4748 Western Ave., N.W.
Washington, DC 20016

Several movements have grown out of the work of Swami Paramahansa Yogananda's disciples. The Self-Revelation Church of Absolute Monism is an independent church founded by Yogananda in 1927 and turned over to Swami Premananda, called from India in 1928. It now operates independently of the Self-Realization Fellowship. Besides the tradition of Yogananda as taught by Premananda, the life and work of Gandhi are stressed, and the Mahatma

Gandhi Memorial Foundation operates as an affiliate organization.

Membership: Not reported. There is one center in Washington, D.C. and a mission in West Bengal.

Periodicals: *The Mystic Cross*, 4748 Western Avenue N.W., Washington, DC 20016; *The Gandhi Message*, Gandhi Memorial Center, 4748 Western Avenue, Box 9515, Washington, DC 20016.

Sources: Swami Premananda, *Light on Kriya Yoga*. Washington, DC: Swami Premananda Foundation, 1969; Swami Premananda, *The Path of the Eternal Law*. Washington, DC: Self-Realization Fellowship, 1042; Swami Premananda, *Prayers of Self-Realization*. Washington, DC: Self-Realization Fellowship, 1943.

★1216★
SIDDHA YOGA DHAM OF AMERICA
Box 605
South Fallsburg, NY 12779

Swami Muktananda Paramahansa (1908-1982) was the leading disciple of siddha yogi Swami Nityananda (d. 1961), who had established a center at Ganeshpuri, India. After moving from teacher to teacher, he settled at Ganeshpuri in 1947 and decided that Nityananda was his true guru. He was initiated and, in 1955, reached full God-realization. Following Nityananda's death, Muktananda became the leader of the ashram. In 1962 he turned the ashram into a public trust (the Indian equivalent of an non-profit corporation) and renamed it the Shree Gurudev Siddha Yoga Ashram. Muktananda, or Baba, as he is called by his followers, continued Nityananda's ideas and advocated the system of shaktipat as the easiest way to God-realization and gurubhava (devotion to the guru) as the means to obtain the divine grace needed for God-realization.

Muktananda's introduction to the West began with the arrival of western disciples at Ganeshpuri. Among the first was Albert Rudolph (1928-1973) who visited Nityananda in 1958. Rudolph became a disciple. In 1970 he arranged for Muktananda's first American tour. The popular American guru Baba Ram Dass accompanied Muktananda on the tour, which included stops at New York, Dallas, Los Angeles and San Francisco. Afterwards, the S.Y.D.A. Foundation was established in the United States. Original centers were established in New York and Piedmont, California. He returned in 1974 and 1981.

Before his death, Muktananda designated Swami Chidvilasananda and Swami Nityananda, a brother and sister, as his successors. They have led the movement since 1982.

Membership: Not reported. In 1980 there were over 250 centers connected with the foundations, over 100 of which were in the United States.

Periodicals: *Siddha Path*, SYDA Foundation, Box 600, South Fallsburg, NY 12779; *Baba Company*, Box 507, Cupertino, CA 95015; *Shree Gurudev Vani*, Gurudev Siddha Peeth, Geneshpuri, India.

Sources: Swami Muktananda, *Guru*. New York: Harper & Row, 1981; Swami Mukatananda Paramahansa, *Satsang with Baba*. Oakland, CA: S.Y.D.A. Foundation, 1974, 1976. 2 Vols.; *Introduction to Kashmir Shaivism*. Oakland, CA: S.Y.D.A. Foundation, 1977; Swami Prajnananda, *A Search for the Self*. Ganeshpuri, India: Gurudev Siddha Peeth, 1979; Paul Zweig, *Muktananda, Selected Essays*. New York: Harper & Row, 1976.

★1217★
SIVANANDA VEDANTA YOGA CENTERS
5178 St. Lawrence Blvd.
Montreal, PQ, Canada

Swami Vishnu Devananda (born 1927) has been the most succesful of Swami Sivananda Saraswati's chelas (pupils) to arrive in the West. He became a disciple of Sivananda in 1947 after being attracted by his books. Shortly after his arrival at Sivananda's ashram he transcended body-consciousness. In 1957, after rising in the ranks to become a leading disciple, Vishnu Devananda set out on a world tour, arriving in San Francisco in 1958, and settling the following year in Montreal, where he founded the Sivananda Vedanta Yoga Center. From the time of his permanent settlement in North America, continued growth has been the story of his work. Students have been widely attracted by Vishnu Devananda's skill in hatha yoga and his willingness to demonstrate the asanas (postures) for the public. Vishnu Devananda is also called Vishnuswamiji and the shortened form, Swamiji.

True World Order was founded in 1969 to foster world peace and brotherhood. To demonstrate his concern for peace, Swamiji flew around the world in his handpainted Piper Apache, dropping peace leaflets and organizing peace marches in designated trouble spots. The trip was completed in spite of Vishnuswamiji's refusal to carry a passport.

Membership: Not reported. In 1980 there were two ashrams and nine "major" centers in the United States and one ashram and five centers in Canada. Yoga teachers affiliated to Vishnu Devananda are located in numerous places in both the United States and Canada. Other centers were located in Austria, Australia, the Bahamas, France, Germany, Great Britain, India, Israel, Mexico, New Zealand, Spain, Switzerland, and Uruguay.

Periodicals: *Yoga Life*, Sivananda Yoga Vedanta Center, 243 W. 24th Street, New York, NY 10011.

Sources: Swami Vishnudevananda, *The Complete Illustrated Book of Yoga*. New York: Julian Press, 1960; Swami Vishnu Devananda, *Meditations and Mantras*. New York: OM Lotus Publishing Company, 1978.

★1218★
SONORAMA SOCIETY
(Defunct)

The Sonorama Society was formed after the first trip at Maharishi Mahesh Yogi to the United States in 1959 and is devoted to the Maharishi's guru, the late Swami Brahmananda Saraswati Maharaj, the illustrious Jagad-Guru Bhagawan of Jyotir-Math, Bhadrikashraman, India. At the age of nine, Swami Saraswati Maharaj began a forty-year exploration of inner consciousness that allowed him to rediscover the mental technique (transcendental meditation) and become leader of the Shankaracharya Order. He is seen as the perfect master.

The Society was formed as an association of persons who are practicing transcendental meditation. Sonorama Society members were tied together by correspondence lessons and irregular contact with those who have mastered the techniques. Headquarters were established in Los Angeles under the leadership of R. Manley Whitman, the sponsor-director. The society lasted only a few years; its work was superceded by the growth of the TM movement, now organized by the World Plan Executive Council.

★1219★
SRI RAM ASHRAMA
P.O. Box AR
Benson, AR 24259

The Sri Ram Ashrama was founded in 1967 at Millbrook, New York, as the Ananda Ashrama by Swami Abhayananda. Swani Abhayananda's guru was Rammurti Sriram Mishra, and the Ashrama was soon renamed in his honor. During the years in which Timothy Leary and his League for Spiritual Discovery was located at Millbrook, the two groups existed side by side on the Hitchcock Ranch. Later the Ashrama moved to Benson, Arizona. The Ashrama is a center for yoga in its practical, universal and scientific aspects. It is a universal and cosmic religion.

Members of the Ashrama are expected to manifest five resolutions: ahimsa, truthfulness, honesty, direction of all bodily and mental energies toward reality, and the renunciation of worldly goods. They study and follow eight principles: Yama, determination to live in the light of truth; Niyama, the five methods of cleanliness, contentment, critical examination of senses, study and complete self-surrender; Asana, the postures of yoga which leave the mind free for meditation; Pranayama, breath-energy control; Pratyhora, sublimation of psychic energy to high purposes; Dharana, fixation of attention; Dhyana, continuous meditation and focusing attention, and Samadhi, transformation of all attention.

The Ashrama is run by its officers and board of trustees. Kriya Press is the publication arm.

Membership: Not reported. In 1970, the ashrama claimed 2,000 adherents in its greater family.

★1220★
SAIVA SIDDHANTA CHURCH
Box 10
Kapaa, HI 96746

The Saiva Siddhanta Church, originally known as the Subramuniya Yoga Order was founded by Master Subramuniya (b. 1927), a native of California who traveled to Sri Lanka and in 1949 was initiated by a guru Jnaniguru Yaganathan, more popularly known as Siva Yogaswami. He returned to the United States and spent some years in following his sadhana (path). Then in 1957 he founded the Subramuniya Yoga Order and opened the Christian Yoga Church in San Francisco. He founded a periodical, *Christian Yoga World*, developed a radio program, the "Christian Yoga Hour," and wrote a correspondance course. Other Christian yoga centers were founded in Redwood City, California and Reno, Nevada and an ashram was opened in Virginia City, Nevada.

During the 1960s, all remnants of Christianity were dropped as the Saivite Hinduism of Subramuniya's guru became dominant. The Subramuniya Yoga Order became first known as the Wailua University of the Contemplative Arts, in 1973 as the Saiva Siddhanta Yoga Order, and in the late 1970s as the Saiva Siddhanta Church.

Teachings of the church are derived from the ancient Saivite scriptures, the Vedas: the Rig, Sama, Yajur and Atharva. They also use the Saiva Agamas, the authoritative explanation of Saivism, and the Tirumantiram, written by Saint Tirumulkar approximately 2,000 years ago. The later volume is written in Tamil (not Sanskrit) and is a summary of Saivism. The teachings have been passed through a lineage of teachers (the Siva Yogaswami Guru Paramparai) to Yogaswami and Subramuniya.

The church is built around the worship of Siva, known as the only Absolute Reality, both immanent and transcendent. Siva is worshiped under the forms of the Siva Lingam, Ardhanarisava (as Siva/Sakti in whom all apparent opposites are reconciled), and Nataraja, the Divine Dancer. Siva created the other deities and the human soul. Dharma is Siva's divine law which governs creation.

The soul is immortal but veiled by the bonds of ignorance (anava), consequences of thoughts and deeds (karma), and illusions of matter (maya). In order to continue its spiritual evolution the soul periodically reincarnates in a physical body. It is the human task to follow the established dharma (pattern) in his/her personal and social life. Good conduct, as summarized in the yamas and niyamas of classical yoga, is also encouraged.

The communal life of Saivites is centered in the temples of Siva, considered the abode of the deity. Such a temple has been constructed in Hawaii on land adjacent to the church's headquarters. Here puja, the invocation of Siva and the other deities and an expression of love for Siva, is offered daily. Most homes also have a home shrine where the deity is invoked.

The church is headed by Subramuniya and the Saiva Swami Sangam, the ordained priesthood of swamis. Swamis join the order of sannyasin by taking lifetime vows of poverty, obedience and chastity.

In 1970 land was purchased in Hawaii on the island of Kauai for a temple and headquarters complex. It also houses the theological seminary. One education facility, the Himalayan Academy, attached to the church's San Francisco center, distributes the San Marga Master Course, a correspondance course for new and prospective members, as well as the church's periodical, *Hinduism Today*.

Membership: Not reported.

Educational facilities: Wailua University Theological Seminary, Kapaa, Hawaii.

Periodicals: *Hinduism Today*, 2575 Sacramento Street, San Francisco, CA 94118.

Sources: Master Subramuniya, *Raja Yoga*. San Francisco: Comstock House, 1973; *Siva's Cosmic Dance*. San Francisco: Himalayan Academy, [1983]; Sr. Subramuniya, *Gems of Cognition*. San Francisco: Christian Yoga Publications, 1958; Master Subramuniya, *The Self God*. San Francisco: Tad Robert Gilmore and Company, 1971; Master Subramuniya, *Beginning to Meditate*. Kapaa, HI: Wailua University of Contemplative Arts, 1972.

★1221★
SHANTI YOGI INSTITUTE AND YOGA RETREAT
943 Central Ave.
Ocean City, NJ 08226

The Shanti Yogi Institute and Yoga Retreat was founded in 1973 by Shanti Desai, the brother of Amrit Desai, the founder of the Kripalu Yoga Fellowship. Desai had been a student of Swami Kripalvanandji since childhood. He was initiated at the age of fifteen. He came to the United States to pursue graduate studies in chemistry at Drexel University. He earned his master's degree and began a career as a chemist, but in 1972 left his job to devote his life to teaching yoga. He returned to India and received the shaktipat initiation from his guru and established the Shanti Yogi Institute in New Jersey (suburban Philadelphia).

The institute emphasizes hatha and raja yoga, and has aligned itsself with the New Age Movement's concern for holistic health. Each center established by Desai has a vegetarian restaurant and a health food store.

Membership: Not reported. There are two centers, one in Ocean City and one in Glassboro, New Jersey.

Sources: Yogi Shanti Desai, *The Complete Practice Manual of Yoga*. Ocean City, NJ: Shanti Yogi Institute, 1976.

★1222★
SWAMI KUVALAYANANDA YOGA FOUNDATION
527 South St.
Philadelphia, PA 19147

The Swami Kuvalayananda Yoga (SKY) Foundation was founded by Dr. Vijayendra Pratap who earned a Ph.D. in applied psychology at the Bombay University. Dr. Pratap was the student of Swami Kuvalayanandaji, founder of Kaivalyadhama, the famous yoga center in Bombay, and served as its assistant director before coming to the United States. The SKY Foundation offers classes in hatha yoga at all levels, trains teachers, and holds classes on yogic philosophy based on Patanjali (the ancient writer who put into simple, cogent language the theory and techniques of yoga). One of the purposes of the Foundation is to research the older yogic traditions in the light of modern knowledge, and the foundation has sponsored several conferences on science and yoga. Headquarters are in Philadelphia above the Garland of Letters Bookstore, operated by the foundation.

Membership: Not reported. There is one center in Philadelphia.

★1223★
TANTRIK ORDER IN AMERICA
(Defunct)

The Tantrik Order was one of the first Hindu groups founded in the United States, and possibly the first created by a Western student of the Eastern teachings. It was founded in New York City by Pierre Bernard (born 1875 as Peter Coons) (1875-1955), better known by members of the order as Oom the Omnipotent. The order had superceded the Bacchante Academy whose California operation had ceased in the San Francisco earthquake of 1906. Associated with the order was the New York Sanskrit College.

Bernard taught a form of Tantric Hinduism combined with hatha yoga. The sexual aspects of tantra were included as integral aspects of the instruction, and Bernard came under scrutiny during the early days of the order's operation as police began to suspect him of trying to seduce his pupils. He survived several early scandals, however, and in 1924 moved to an estate in Nyack, New York, on Long Island, and continued as leader of the order for the next three decades (closed only briefly during World War II when the estate was used as a center for refugees from Nazi Germany). His clientele included many wealthy people, including several members of the Vanderbilt family. Bernard became a wealthy and influential citizen. He donated a zoo to the community and eventually became president of the bank in nearby Pearl City.

As far as is known, the order died with its founder. There are reports of the existence of an offshoot, the New York Sacred Tantrics, which functioned during the 1096s. However, reports have not been confirmed and if the group existed, it had disbanded by the late 1970s.

Remarks: Pierre Bernard had several famous relatives. He was the cousin-by-marriage of Mary Baker Eddy, founder of the Church of Christ, Scientist. In the early years of his work in New York, he was the guardian of his half-sister, Ora Ray Baker, who became the wife of Hazrat Inayat Khan, founder of the Sufi Order. Bernard's nephew, Pierre Bernard, wrote what is a classic text on yoga as his thesis at Columbia University, *Hatha Yoga: The Report of a Personal Experience*.

Sources: *In Re Fifth Veda*, International Journal of the Tantrik Order. New York: Tantrik Order in America, n.d. [1909]; Charles Boswell, "The Great Fume and Fuss over the Omnipotent Oom" in *True*, (January 1965), pp. 31-33, 86-91; Paul Sann, *Fads, Follies, and Delusions of the American People*. New York: 1967.

★1224★
TEMPLE OF COSMIC RELIGION
4218 16th St., N.W.
Washington, DC 20011

In 1966, while attending the Kumbha Mela (ritual bathing) Festival in the Ganges River, an independent Hindu teacher, later to be known as Satguru Sant Keshavadas, was told by a holy man named Lord Panduranga Vittala, "Go to the West; spread the cosmic religion." When Keshavadas returned to Delhi, the advice was reinforced in a vision. The following year he began a tour of Europe and the Middle East, and arrived in the United States in May. In 1968 he founded a center in Washington D.C., as the American headquarters of the Dasashram International Center in India. In the mid-1970s the American headquarters moved to Southfield, Michigan, near Detroit, and adopted the name of the Temple of Cosmic Religion, a title long used in the movement.

In bringing Hinduism to the West, Keshavadas envisioned the beginning of a world cosmic religion, uniting all religious paths. This cosmic religion will propose that truth is one and that all paths lead to the realization of God. Keshavadas teaches yoga and meditation and devotion to God through chanting and singing (bhakti yoga, as discussed in the introductory material for this volume). He believes karma and reincarnation to be central to the beliefs of the religion.

From the world headquarters of the Temple of Cosmic Religion located in Bangalore, India, at the Panduranga Temple, temples have been established around India in five locations, England, Trinidad and the United States. U.S. temples are located in Washington, D.C.; Southfield, Michigan; and Oakland, California. Books and materials are distributed through the Oakland temple.

Membership: Not reported. In 1980 there were three temples and three study groups (two in Virginia and one in southern California).

Sources: Mukundadas [Michael Allen Makowsky], *Minstrel of Love*. Nevada City, CA: Hansa Publications, 1980; *Life and Teachings of Sadguru Sant Keshavadas, A Commemoration*. Southfield, MI: Temple of Cosmic Religion, 1977; Sant Keshavadasji, *This Is Wisdom*. Privately Printed, 1975; Sant Keshavadas, *The Purpose of Life*, New York: Vantage Press, 1978; Sant Keshavadas, *Sadguru Speaks*. Washington, DC: Temple of Cosmic Religion, 1975.

★1225★
TEMPLE OF KRIYA YOGA
2414 N. Kedzie
Chicago, IL 60647

The Temple of Kriya Yoga was founded by Goswami Kriyananda (born Melvin Higgins), not to be confused with the Swami Kriyananda who founded the Ananda Ashram. The temple is headquartered in a temple building on the northside of Chicago. Kriyananda had studied with a guru, spoken of only as Sri Sri Shelliji in the temple literature, who passed to him the kriya yoga tradition of Swami Paramahansa Yogananda, founder of the Self-Realization Fellowship. Kriyananda began teaching yoga in the 1940s and opened the temple in Chicago in the 1960s. Kriyananda, an accomplished astrologer, also opened the College of Occult Sciences which offered classes in a variety of esoteric subjects.

During the late 1970s, the temple abandoned its rented facilities in downtown Chicago for its new headquarters. Associated with the Chicago center is a retreat facility in South Haven, Michigan. In 1977 the Kriyananda Healing Center was established as a holistic health facility, adjacent to the temple. Traditional western medicine is supplemented by a program emphasizing yoga and meditation, fasting, biofeedback and massage.

Kriyananda follows the yoga system of Yogananda, and over the years he has authored a variety of books delineating kriya yoga, meditation and astrology. He sees religion as providing a deep personal understanding of the nature and purpose of God and the Universe. He teaches the oneness of law, spirit and love and their identity with God. He affirms the meaningfulness of the universe and the possibility of attaining illumination and fulfillment (through the practice of Kriya yoga) in this lifetime.

Membership: Not reported. There are several hundred temple members and many more individuals who receive the services of the temple through its classes, programs and astrology services.

Periodicals: *The Flame of Kriya*, 2414 N. Kedzie, Chicago, IL 60647.

Sources: Goswami Kriyananda, *Yoga, Text for Teachers and Advanced Students*. Chicago: Temple of Kriya Yoga, 1976; Goswami Kriyananda, *Pathway to God-Consciousness*. Chicago: Temple of Kriya Yoga, 1970; Goswami Kriyananda, *The Bhagavad Gita, The Song of God*. Chicago: Temple of Kriya Yoga, n.d.

★1226★
TRUTH CONSCIOUSNESS
% Sacred Mountain Ashram
Gold Hill, Salina Star Route
Boulder, CO 80302

Truth Consciousness, formed in 1973, is the organization of followers of Swami Amar Jyoti. Swamiji, as he is called by his students, was born in 1928 in what is today Pakistan. A few months prior to his graduation from college, he renounced his seemingly destined life of comfort and success to follow an inner dictum, "Know yourself and you shall know everything." He began a ten-year period of solitude and meditation, that he broke in 1960 when he began a pilgrimage around India. He founded Jyoti Ashram in Pune, Maharastra State, and received his first students. In 1961 he took his first trip to the United States, but, even though his first American disciples were drawn to him during that visit, he spent the next decade concentrating on his work in India.

Swamji returned to the United States in 1973 and began his first ashram in the West. Truth Consciousness is the non-profit corporation which ties together the various centers created by a growing following. Swamiji divides his time between the Indian and American ashrams and centers.

The primary focus of life in the ashrams of Truth Consciousness is the regular satsangs, or sessions, in which students sit with Swamiji and discuss various concerns (or listen to tapes in his absence). Swamiji emphasizes the search toward self-knowledge and meditation as means for inner exploration. Individuals already are, in essence, that which they seek. Thus along with meditation, he emphasizes the need of constant reminders that affirm the union of the self with joy, love and peace.

Membership: In the United States, Truth Consciousness consists of three ashrams (Boulder, Colorado; Rockford, Michigan; and Tucson, Arizona). There is no formal membership, but an estimated several hundred individuals are affiliated with the organization. In India, Ananda Niketan Ashrams, the trust headed by Swami Amar Jyoti,

has two ashrams, one in Pune, Maharashstra, and the Rishi Ashram in the Himalayas.

Periodicals: *Truth Consciousness Journal*, Sacred Mountain Ashram, Gold Hill, Salina Route, Boulder, CO 80302.

Sources: Kessler Frey, *Satsang Notes of Swai Amar Jyoti*. Boulder, CO: Truth Consciousness, 1977; Swami Amar Jyoti, *Spirit of Himalaya*. Boulder, CO: Truth Consciousness, 1985.

★1227★
VEDANTA SOCIETY
34 W. 71st St.
New York, NY 10023

Among Hindu groups, none has made as great an impact on America as the Vedanta Society, the only Hindu body established in America before 1900. The Society grew out of the vision of Sri Ramakrishna (1836-1886) and the work of his prime disciple, Swami Vivekananda (1863-1902).

Ramakrishna was a priest in a Calcutta temple of Kali, one of several forms in which God is worshipped as Universal Mother in popular Hinduism. Through long meditation and intense yearning for direct experience of the divine, he attained the state of samadhi or God-consciousness. Continuous samadhi became his goal, and he followed a number of sadhanas or paths to enlightenment, both within and outside the Hindu tradition. He became convinced that: 1) the Divine Mother wished him to remain on the threshold between the Absolute and the relative in order to serve as an instrument for the spiritual uplift of humanity, and 2) all religions (including Hinduism) were different paths to the same goal, and all gods were different aspects of the same Godhead.

A number of disciples, some of them college-trained intellectuals, gathered around Ramakrishna. Before his death some revered him as an avatar, or divine incarnation. Vivekananda, commissioned by Ramakrishna, forged the younger disciples into a monastic brotherhood and gradually convinced them that as Ramakrishna's followers they had a mission not only to seek enlightenment but also to work to alleviate the suffering of humanity through spiritual ministration and social service.

In 1893, Vivekananda came to America to teach the universal religion realized by Ramakrishna. He took the World Parliament of Religions by storm, and for two years he lectured throughout the United States, gathering followers. In November, 1895, the Vedanta Society of New York was formed, and in the next few years centers were added in San Francisco and Boston. Each is autonomous but works under the Ramakrishna Order. In 1897 Vivekananda returned to India and organized the

Ramakrishna Mission, dedicated to serving humanity in a spirit of worship of the divine dwelling within each person.

The central ideas of Vedanta monistic philosophy can be summarized in three propositions:

1. Brahman or God is the underlying unity manifested in all. Each person in essence is divine, and the goal of human life is to realize this divinity within oneself and in all others. This realization is the true basis of unselfishness, as the divine unity is the basis of love.

2. Maya, the illusion of individual separateness, is an interpretation by the mind. We perceive variety rather than the underlying unity because of the condition of our mind, its prejudices, desires and fears. Absolute reality can be known even in this life through the purified mind; this has been verified by the great mystics of all religions.

3. The mind may be purified by a variety of means, and each person's spiritual life evolves according to his or her mental makeup. Four basic yogas or spiritual disciplines have been codified by Vivekanada: devotion, intellectual discrimination, unselfish work and psychic control. These correspond to the four basic aspects of the human mind: the emotional, intellectual, active and reflective. The predominance of one or more of these in an individual determines what path that person should follow.

Vedanta differs from most other Hindu movements in that it stresses principles over personalities. Vivekananda and his successors have emphasized the universal teachings of Vedanta rather than the personality of Ramakrishna. At the same time, freedom is given to the individual follower to worship Ramakrishna or any prophet of any religion as a means to enlightenment. Instruction by a qualified teacher is strongly recommended, although too much emphasis on the personality of the teacher is recognized as a danger.

Vedanta's intellectual approach to Hinduism has found expression in the publication of numerous books, including popular editions of the Upanishads, the Bhagavad-Gita, and the Yoga Aphorisms of Patanjali. Through these, it has stimulated interst in Hinduism among many thinking people. Gerald Heard, Aldous Huxley, and Christopher Isherwood all had a well-known interest in Vedanta.

Membership: In 1984 the Society had over 1,500 members in 13 centers led by 13 swamis. Centers are also found in Argentina, Bangladesh, France, Fiji, Great Britain, India, Mauritius, Singapore, Sri Lanka, and Switzerland.

Periodicals: *Prabuddha Bharata or Awakened India*, 5 Dehi Entally Road, Calcuta, India 700 014. *Vedanta in the West*, published for many years by the Vedanta Press in Hollywood, California, was discontinued in the 1970s.

Sources: Swami Gambhrananda, *History of the Ramakrishna Math and Mission*. Calcutta: Advaita Ashrama, 1957; Christopher Isherwood, *Ramakrishna and His Disciples*. New York: Simon and Schuster, 1965; Christopher Isherwood, ed., *Vedanta for the Western World*. New York: Viking Press, 1945; Clive Johnson, ed., *Vedanta*. New York: Bantam Books, 1974; Romain Rolland, *The Life of Vivekananda and the Universal Gospel*. Calcutta: Advaita Ashrama, 1970.

★1228★
VEDANTIC CULTURAL SOCIETY
2324 Stuart St.
Berkeley, CA 94705

The Vedantic Cultural Society was formed in 1983 by Hansadutta Swami (a.k.a. Hans Kary), a former initiating guru with the International Society for Krishna Consciousness (ISKCON). During the late 1970s, Hansadutta had been the subject of strong criticism by the other gurus in ISKCON because of his unorthodox fund raising, administrative, and recruiting activities. In the spring of 1980, he was arrested for possession of illegal firearms. While the charges were later dropped, his advocacy of survivalism and his possession of a number of weapons led to his being sent to India for a year. After consideration of the sacred nature of the relationship of initiating guru and his disciples (which constituted most of the Berkeley temple), the governing council reinstated him. However, his return to Berkeley did not ease the tension, and in 1983 ISKCON excommunicated Hansadutta. he left and took most of the Berkeley temple with him, forming the Vedantic Cultural Society.

In most ways, the Vedantic Cultural Society follows the beliefs and practices of ISKCON, since the cause of the split was neither doctrinal nor devotional.

Hansadutta's troubles did not end with the break from ISKCON. In September of 1983, he was arrested and accused of shooting out several store windows in Berkeley. Several weapons and empty shells were found in his car. As this volume goes to press, the future of the center and its leader is very much in doubt.

Membership: The Center has several hundred members, all in Berkeley and in one rural center.

Sources: Hansadutta Swami, *The Book, What the Black Sheep Said*. Berkeley, CA: Hansa Books, 1985; Hansadutta Swami, *Kirtan*. Berkeley, CA: Hansa Books, 1984; Hansadutta Swami, *The Hammer for Smashing Illusion*. Berkeley, CA: Hansa Books, 1983.

★1229★
WORLD COMMUNITY
Route 4, Box 265
Bedford, VA 24523

In 1970 Vasudevadas, a Western teacher of mystical and yogic disciplines, and his wife, Devaki-Ma founded Prema Dharmasala as a yoga ashram for dedicated lay-disciples and renunciates anf the World Community as a community of householders and families who looked to Vasudevadas as their spiritual teacher. Throughout the 1970s Prema Dharmasala functioned as the main training center for those who had made a commitment to a life of renunciation and service to God and the human family. However, in the early 1980s, a shift of emphasis to the World Community occurred as a vision of a community to function as a symbol of the oneness of Truth and the transforming power of Prem (Divine Love) emerged. By 1984, Prema Dharmasala had been completely superceded by the Prema World Community.

As developed, the World Community will be located on the acreage previously occupied by the Prema Dharmasala. Centered upon a large Temple of All Religion will be a series of interrelated villages for various types of individuals, an educational center, a holistic health clinic, and a research and training center for the New Age. The outlines of the emerging plan has remained open to allow for new insight as members become more attuned to Truth.

Membership: Not reported. There are several hundred people associated with the community.

Sources: Vasudevadas, *Vasudevadas Speaks to Your Heart.* Bedford, VA: Prema Dharmasala and Fellowship Association, 1976; Vasudevadas, *Running Out of Time and Who Is Watching?* Bedford, VA: Prema Fellowship, 1979; Vasudevadas, *A Time for Eternity.* Bedford, VA: Premadharmasala and Fellowship Association, 1976; *Love Offerings at Thy Lotus Feet.* Bedford, VA: Prema Dharmasala, 1975.

★1230★
WORLD PLAN EXECUTIVE COUNCIL
17310 Sunset Blvd.
Pacific Palisades, CA 90272

There is perhaps at present no more controversial group in the United States than the movement known popularly as Transcendental Meditation (TM) and officially called the World Plan Executive Council. Critics claim that it is a Hindu group masquerading under a non-religious facade. The World Plan Executive Council strongly denies the charge, noting that many people of all religions and no religion are meditators. The U.S. District Court in Newark, New Jersey, decided in 1978 that the pracatice of TM is religious in nature and banned the teaching of TM in New Jersey public high schools. Controversy aside, TM exists in the interface of Eastern religion and the current

human potentials movement and is hence included here. Possibly it is more an answer to what could be called religious needs than it is an actual religious group. It does retain overtones of the Hinduism that gave it birth.

The founder of TM (or rather its modern rediscoverer) was Guru Dev, but its real exponent has become Maharishi Mahesh Yogi, who spent thirteen years in seclusion with Guru Dev and who, upon Guru Dev's death, came forth in 1958 to tell the world about TM. Prior to his life of meditation, he had obtained a B.S. in physics at Allahabad University. In 1959 he made his first world tour, which brought him to the United States. His movement grew slowly until the mid-1960s when the Beatles, Mia Farrow and Jane Fonda joined his following.

In 1972 Maharishi announced the World Plan, the overall strategy which guides the movement and from which the council takes its name. The goal of the World Plan is to share the Science of Creative Intelligence with the whole world. The immediate objective of the plan is to extablish 3,600 World Plan centers (one for each million people on earth) and to staff each center with 1,000 teachers (one for each person on earth). The ultimate goal is to bring in the Age of Enlightenment.

The World Plan Executive Council consists of five task-oriented structures. The International Meditation Society is the main structure for introducing the general public to T.M. The Student International Meditation Society is aimed at the campus population. Maharishi International University is a regular four-year university which offers both bachelor's and master's degrees, but its curriculum is based on the outlook of the TM movement. The University is in Fairfield, Iowa. The American Foundation for the Science of Creative Intelligence is working in the business community. Finally the Spiritual Regeneration Movement works with the "older generation," i.e., those over thirty.

The essence of TM is a form of japa yoga-meditation with a mantra, a sound constantly repeated silently during meditation and upon which the meditator concentrates. Each individual begins his process of meditation with initiation. At this time he is given an individual mantra for his own use which he is not to reveal to others. The mantra is given Maharishi or one of his personal representatives. The initiation ceremony, in which members repeat a number of "prayers" to Hindu deities and offer veneration to a long line of gurus, is a major item cited by critics who claim TM is a religious practice.

The overall philosophy of the World Plan Executive Council is spelled out in Maharishi's book, *The Science of Being and Art of Living*, in which a complete cosmology is presented. According to Maharishi, underneath the universe is the absolute field of pure being-unmanifested and transcendental. Being is the ultimate reality of creation. The science of being teaches how to contact ultimate reality. TM is the tool. Once meditation begins, one begins to "live the being" and Maharishi offers instruction on correct thinking, speaking, action, behavior and health. The goal is God-realization. Maharishi's teaching is "the summation of the practical wisdom of the integrated life as advanced by the Vedic Rishis of ancient India." That is to say, the ultimate goal of TM is "to achieve the spiritual goals of mankind in this generation."

Currently, Maharishi has no legal affiliation to the World Plan Executive Council. He is looked upon the founder of TM and the Science of Creative Intelligence. Through his books, taped lectures and constant presence in picture and thought, he still dominates the organization.

Growth of the movement in the 1970s was spurred by widespread media coverage and by its increased popularity in the business world, schools and the Army. It has even found the approval of the Illinois state legislature. Much of the recent growth is attributable to psychologists who promote the benefits of meditation. Growth began to slow in 1976 and further decrease was noticeable after the 1977 court decision. In 1977 TM announced its siddha program, a course in advanced techniques which allowed the student to gain various supernormal capabilities including levitation, invisibility, mastery over nature, and fulfillment of all desires. The over-all goal was the creation of the "Age of Enlightenment." While many signed up for the course, it caused attacks from many who charged that it could not produce the advertised results.

Membership: Not reported. By 1984 more than 1,000,000 people had taken basic TM courses in the United States; many of those, however, are not continuing to practice TM. In 1978, the organization had more than 7,000 authorized teachers and 400 teaching centers. Researchers have noted that TM peaked in 1976 when it initiated 292,273 people. By the end of that year, however it had begun a radical decline. In 1977 it initiated only 50,000.

Educational facilities: Maharishi International University, Fairfield, Iowa.

Periodicals: *World Government News*, Age of Enlightenment Distribution, Box 186, Livingston Manor, NY 12758.

Sources: William Jefferson, *The Story of the Maharishi*. New York: Pocket Books, 1976; Mahareshi Mahesh Yogi, *The Science of Being and Art of Living*. London: International SRM Publications, 1966; Mahareshi Mahesh Yogi, *Love and God*. N.p.: Age of Enlightenment Press, 1973; Martin Ebon, ed., *Maharishi, the Guru*. New York: New American Library, 1968; Harold H. Bloomfield, Michael Peter Cain and Dennis T. Jaffe, *TM, Discovering Inner Energy and Overcoming Stress*. New York: Delacorte Press, 1975; Nat Goldhaber, *TM: An Alphabetical Guide to the Transcendental Meditation Program*. New York: Ballantine Books, 1976. Controversial and polemical volumes include the following: Gordon R. Lewis, *Transcendental Meditation*. Glendale, CA: G/L Regal Books, 1975; John E. Patton, *The Case Against TM in the Schools*. Grand Rapids, MI: Baker Book House, 1976; Michael A. Persinger; Normand J. Carrey and Lynn A. Suess, *TM and Cult Mania*. North Quincy, MA: Christopher Publishing House, 1980; R. D. Scott, *Transcendental Misconceptions*. San Diego, CA: Beta Books, 1978; John White, *Everything You Want to Know About TM, Including How to Do It*. New York: Pocket Books, 1976; William Sims Bainbridge and Daniel H. Jackson, "The Rise and Decline of Transcendental Meditation." in Rodney Stark and William Sims Bainbridge, *The Future of Religion*. Berkeley: University of California Press, 1985.

★1231★
YASODHARA ASHRAM SOCIETY
Box 9
Kootenay Bay, BC, Canada V0B 1X0

Though physically located in Canada, just north of Idaho near Kootenay Bay, British Columbia, the Yasodhara Ashram Society is very much a part of the Hindu scene in the United States and draws many of its students and instructors from below the border. Its periodical, *Ascent*, is also widely circulated in the United States.

The founder of the Yasodhara Ashram is Sylvia Hellman, a German-born Canadian citizen. As a young adult, she had become influenced by the Self-Realization Fellowship, but while meditating before a picture of Swami Paramahansa Yogananda, she saw the face of Swami Sivananda Saraswati in a vision. She traveled to India, was initiated by Sivananda into the Sanyasa (monastic) Order in 1956 and acquired the name Swami Radha. Under Sivananda's direction, she returned to Canada to establish the Yasodhara Ashram. From 1956 to 1963, the Ashram was in Vancouver, but then was moved to Kootenay Bay.

While teaching the varied yogic disciplines as taught by Sivananda, Swami Radha had also expanded the concerns of the ashram to include other Hindu practices, various psychic and occult systems and an attempt to engage in dialogue with Christian symbols and traditions. Unique to Swami Radha is the Divine Light Invocation learned in India from another guru referred to as Babaji. It is a technique employing a mantra to call down the divine energy, visualized as white light, and to use it for healing. Among the classes offered at the ashram are ones on drama, psychic phenomena, Christian origins and Gestalt psychology. A goal is to build a "Temple of All Religions," a project based upon a belief that all religions are at root the same. Associated with the ashram is the Association for the Development of Human Potential, founded by Sivananda Radha and based in Idaho, and the ashram's publishing arm, Timeless Books.

Membership: Not reported.

Periodicals: *Ascent*, Box 9, Kootenay Bay, BC, Canada V0B 1X0.

Sources: Sivananda Radha, *Mantras, Words of Power.* Porthill, ID: Timeless Books, 1980; Sivananda Radha, *Radha, Diary of a Woman's Search.* Porthill, ID: Timeless Books, 1981; Sivananda Radha, *Kundalini, Yoga for the West.* Spokane, WA: Timeless Books, 1978; Sivannada Radha, *Gods Who Walk the Rainbow.* Porthill, ID: Timeless Books, 1981.

★1232★
YOGA HOUSE ASHRAM
Box 3391
San Rafael, CA 94902

The Yoga House Ashram was formed in the mid-1970s by Dadaji Vimalananda, a former leader of the Ananda Marga Yoga Society. Dadaji was born in 1942 in Badwel, South India, of a Brahmin family. At the age of six he had an intense initiation experience of divine light filling his room and a voice instructing him on the path of enlightenment. He began to pursue the inner life, and at the age of sixteen became an instructor of meditation. In 1962 he met Shrii Anandamurti, founder of the Ananda Marga Yoga Society and was impressed with both his spirituality and his program of service to humanity, especially the sick, the elderly, and the poor. In like measure, Anandamurti was impressed with his young disciple and quickly elevated him to a teacher of yoga. In 1966 Dadaji left India to spread Ananda Marga. He was responsible for starting centers in Thailand, Singapore, Indonesia, Malasia, Hong Kong, and the Philippines. The government and the United Nations honored him for his efforts on behalf of the victims of the 1968 earthquake that struck Manila.

In 1969 Dadaji came to the United States and assisted in the spread of Ananda Marga. However, in the mid-1970s he left Ananda Marga and founded the Yoga House Ashram. Since that time he has spent his time creating his own following in the San Francisco Bay area of California. Dadaji came to the United States with a strong desire to bridge the gap between East and West. He teaches a traditional yoga but has retained the emphasis upon social action he found in Ananda Marga. He teaches his students to keep their role in society as they strive for God.

Membership: Not reported. The work of the Yoga House Ashram is confined to northern California where Dadaji Vimalananda teaches yoga at a variety of locations in the greater San Francisco Bay area.

Sources: Dadaji Vimalananda, *Yogamritam (The Nectar of Yoga).* San Rafael, CA: Yoga House Ashram, 1977.

★1233★
YOGA RESEARCH FOUNDATION
6111 S.W. 74th Ave.
Miami, FL 33143

Swami Jyotir Maya Nanda (b.1931) is a learned teacher who began his religious pilgrimage in the ascetic life, emerged into teaching and editing, and became a leading figure at Swami Sivananda Saraswati's Yoga Vedanta Forest Academy. He came to America in 1962 and founded the Sanantan Dharma Mandir with headquarters in Puerto Rico. The headquarters were moved to Miami under the present name in 1969. Swami Jyotir Maya Nanda teaches integral yoga without using the term, preferring Vedanta. He has developed a vast publishing program centered on his many books and those of his prime disciple, Swami Lalitananda.

Membership: Not reported. There is one center in Miami.

Periodicals: *International Yoga Guide*, Yoga Research Foundation, 6111 S.W. 74th Avenue, Miami, FL 33143; *Integral Light*, 6111 SW 74th Avenue, Miami FL 33143.

Sources: Swami Jyotir Maya Nanda, *Yoga Can Change Your Life.* Miami, FL: International Yoga Society, 1975; Swami Jyotir Maya Nanda, *The Way to Liberation.* Miami, FL: Swami Lalitananda, 1976; Swami Jyotir Maya Nanda, *Yoga of Sex-Sublimation, Truth and Non-violence.* Miami, FL: Swami Lalitananda, 1974; Swami Jyotir Maya Nanda, *Yoga Vasistha.* Miami, FL: Yoga Research Society, 1977; Swami Lalitananda, *Yoga in Life.* Miami, FL: Swami Jyotir Maya Nanada, 1973.

★1234★
YOGANTA MEDITATION CENTER
(Defunct)

The Yoganta Meditation Center was a small eclectic community based upon the concept of spiritual growth through a variety of meditative and yogic techniques. The center provided residential facilities where adherents could practice their own discipline for an extended time. There was no guru; the belief was that the exchange of personal experiences would benefit all.

Seminars were irregularly offered on such topics as mantras, hatha yoga, meditation and miscellaneous psychic topics. A quarterly journal, *The Yoganta Center Newsletter*, was published. During the 1970s there are approximately ten to fifteen residents at the center located at Nederland, Colorado.

★1235★

YOGI GUPTA ASSOCIATION
127 E. 56th St.
New York, NY 10022

Yogi Gupta, born in Kanpur in North India, was a lawyer who left his profession to become a monk in the sannyasa order in Banaras. At that time, he was renamed Swami Kailashananda and became a major teacher of hatha and karma yoga. He also founded the Kailashananda Mission at Rishikesh. Basic to Yogi Gutpa's teaching is hatha yoga with its various postures (asanas). Hatha is the entrance into various other disciplines including psychic development, vegetarianism and yogic philosophy. Through yoga one can learn self-mastery and achieve the many goals of life-happiness, success and freedom. Yogi Gupta first came to the United States in 1954. He founded a center in New York City which is an outpost of the Indian centers.

Membership: Not reported.

Sources: Yogi Gupta, *Shradha and Heavenly Fathers.* New York: Yogi Gupta New York Center, n.d.; Yogi Gupta, *Yoga and Long Life.* New York; Dodd, Mead, 1958; Yogi Gupta, *Yoga and Yogic Powers.* New York: Yogi Gupta New York Center, 1963.

★1236★

YOGIRAJ SECT
(Defunct)

Swami Swanandashram was born in Calcutta in 1921 and in his youth became a yogi. In college he was a student of philosophy, mathematics and sanskrit. In 1950, however, he renounced all possessions and for twenty years lived in a cave at Gangotri. He was initiated in the Shankaracharya Order and is now head of the Yogiraj Sect. In 1970, Swanandashram emerged from his cave and began a public ministry to teach a way of oneness with God through yoga. In his teaching, the essential reality of the unchangeable God is held up as that which is to be seen behind the transitory illusions of commonplace life. The erroneous identification of the body as the real self is the root of all evil, suffering and death. Yoga is the means to overcome the false identification. During the early 1970s there was one American center of Swanadashram's followers in Easton, Pennsylvania. It was absorbed into the Holy Shankaracharya Order.

Jainism

★1237★

INTERNATIONAL NAHAVIR JAIN MISSION
Acharya Sushil Jain Ashram
722 Tomkins Ave.
Staten Island, NY 10305

Since 1965, along with Hindus and Sikhs, Jains began to immigrate to the United States, though due to restrictions on travel over water, not in numbers as great as members of other Indian religious groups. Among the immigrants were individuals associated with the International Mahavir Mission. The Mission had been founded in India in 1970 by Guruji Muni Sushul Kumar (b. 1926). As a teenager, Guruji had entered the Sacred Order of Jain Munis, receiving from his guru two traditional symbols of nonviolence: the mukh-patti, a white mask worn over the face to keep the wearer from accidently swallowing an insect and thus killing a living soul, and a augha, a broom for sweeping surfaces before sitting lest a living entity be harmed. The Mission was brought to Europe and North America by its members. Guruji traveled to the United States in 1975 to visit the Jain communities.

The Mission emphasizes the Jain tenets of vegetarianism, ahimsa (nonviolence) and anekantavada (the many-faceted nature of truth). It teaches hatha yoga, pranayama (breath control), japa yoga (the use of mantric words of power), ayurvadic medicine, and chanting.

In the United States an urban ashram was opened in Staten Island and a rural center, Muni Sushil Yogville, in upstate New York. Centers have also been opened in England, France, Germany and Canada. International headquarters are in New Delhi, India. Guruji has been active in interreligious work (growing out of the Jain belief in anekantavada), and organized the World Fellowship of Religions which periodically sponsors international interreligious conferences. In 1977, Guruji also participated in the first North American Jain Conference held at Berkeley, California in 1981.

Membership: Not reported.

Periodicals: *News from Jain Ashram.* 722 Tomkins Avenue, Staten Island, NY 10305.

★1238★

JAIN MEDITATION INTERNATIONAL CENTER
Box 730, Radio City
New York, NY 10101

Gurudev Shree Chitrabhanu had been a Jain muni (monk) for twenty-nine years. During that time he had become widely known and respected in his native India and had, in 1965, founded the Divine Knowledge Society in Bombay. Then in 1971 he gave up his monastic existence and rejected the millennia-long taboo on traveling over water and by means other than foot, to come to the United States at the invitation the Temple of Understanding to lecture at a conference at Harvard University. Following that conference, he stayed in North America and lectured widely to both other Jains who, like him, had immigrated to America. In 1974, he founded New Life Now, an organization dedicated to the spiritual illumination of the West. New Life Now evolved into the Jain Meditation International Center. Chitrabhanu defines a Jain as one who "speaks of a personal responsibility for his own deeds, regards a person as a master of his own destiny, and refrains from violence."

The Center is headquartered in New York City and teaches meditation, yoga, vegetarianism, and tai chi. While moving among Jains who have immigrated to the United States, Chitrabhanu has had great success among non-Indian-Americans. Groups have been established in Boston, Pittsburgh, Philadelphia, West Orange (New Jersey), and Toronto. He has also worked in Brazil. The associated Jain Peace Fellowship is headquartered in South Norwalk, Connecticut. Chitrabhanu participated in the first North American Jain conference held in Berkeley, California in 1981.

Membership: Not reported.

Periodicals: *JMIC Newsletter*, Box 730, Radio City, New York, NY 10101.

Sources: A. H. A. Baakza, *Half-hours with a Jain Muni.* Bombay: Jaico Publishing House, 1962; Gurudev Chitrabhanu, *The Philosophy of Soul and Matter.* New York: Jain Meditation Center, 1977; Gurudev Shree Chitrabhanu, *The Psychology of Enlightenment.* New York: Dodd, Mead & Company, 1979; Gurudev Shree Chitrabhanu, *Realize What You Are.* New York: Dodd, Mead & Company, 1978; Gurudev Shree Chitrabhanu, *Twelve Facets of Reality.* New York: Dodd, Mead & Company, 1980.

★1239★
RAJNEESH FOUNDATION INTERNATIONAL
Antelope, OR 97741

Bhagwan Shree Rajneesh, born Rajneesh Chandra Mohan in a small town in India in 1931, has become one of the most controversial gurus to travel to the West and establish his teachings. Born of Jain parents, Rajneesh took seriously the Jain belief in anekantavada, the many faceted nature of truth. Rajneesh studied the varied major religious traditions from which he absorbed a variety of teachings. He earned his master's degree in philosophy and began a teaching career. During his college days in 1953, he had what he termed an experience of samadhi. His early adult years were divided between his scholarly career and his work as a spiritual leader. In 1966 he resigned his post at the University of Jabalpur and became a full-time spiritual teacher. In 1974 he purchased land

for an ashram in Poona, which became his headquarters for most of the decade.

During the 1970s he encountered Western humanistic psychology and absorbed several of its emphases, including the high value on self-expression and the release of inner emotions as a means to personal freedom. These emphases and the techniques used to promote them were integrated into the Indian teachings offered by Rajneesh and became embodied in his most distinctive practice, dynamic meditation.

Rajneesh teaches a way to enlightenment and personal freedom. Initiation is into an order of what is termed neo-sannyas. In Hinduism, *sannyas* is the renounced life. Sannyasins renounce home, family attachments, sex, and the material life. Rajneesh redefined sannyas as living consciously. Rather than a denial of the material life, it is a plunge into it. Initiates are asked to do four things: dress in red; wear a mall (a rosary-like necklace of 108 beads) with Rajneesh's picture; use the new name given by the initiator; and meditate regularly. New initiates are introduced to five major meditation formats. Days begin and end with chanting. Periodically, especially at gatherings of Rajneesh disciples, dynamic meditation, which involves widely differing meditation techniques followed in sequence (from regulated breathing to chanting to total silence) is practiced. Consistent with the emphasis upon personal freedom, Rajneesh had encouraged the practice of left-hand tantric yoga and encouraged free sexual expression.

Rajneesh came to the United States in 1981, and after a short stay in New Jersey, he moved to the 64,000 acre Big Muddy Ranch near Antelope, Oregon. The ranch became the site of a proposed new city, Rajneeshpuram. Older residents and eventually many Oregonians began to oppose the proposed plan to bring four to six thousand people to the new city by the end of the century. As the controversy grew, the entire plan came to an abrupt end when, in 1985, Rajneesh was charged with immigration fraud. He was fined and deported from the United States. His former chief assistant, Ma Anand Sheela (Silverman) was also charged on a number of felony counts. Some of his American followers are also under indictment and awaiting trial. The center in Oregon has been offered for sale, and the goals of Rajneeshpuram abandoned. The movement, however, has remained intact. The numerous Rajneesh centers around the United States and the world have been but slightly disturbed by the events in Rajneeshpuram. The movement will remain in flux until Rajneesh is resettled. (In August, 1986, it was reported that Rajneesh had returned to his native India after being denied permanent residence in several other countries.)

Membership: Not reported. In 1984 the Foundation estimated 250,000 followers worldwide. There were an estimated 10,000 to 20,000 initiates in the United States.

Educational facilities: Academy of Rajnesshism (currently being relocated).

Remarks: Rajneesh centers are located in most large cities across the United States. Users are advised to contact local centers for the most current information on this group.

Sources: *Rajneeshism.* Rajneeshpuram, OR, Rajneesh Foundation International, 1983; Bhagwan Shree Rajneesh, *The Great Challenge, A Rajneesh Reader.* New York: Grove Press, 1982; Bhagwan Shree Rajneesh, *I Am the Gate.* New York: Harper & Row, 1977; Bhagwan Shree Rajneesh, *Tantra, Spirituality & Sex.* San Francisco: Rainbow Bridge, 1977; Bhagwan Shree Rajneesh, *The Orange Book.* Rajneeshpuram, OR: Rajneesh Foundation International, 1983. Sally Belfrage, *Flowers of Emptiness.* New York: Dial Press, 1981; Ma Satya Bharti, *Death Comes Dancing.* London: Routledge & Kegan Paul, 1981; Gita Mehta, *Karma Cola.* New York: Simon & Schuster, 1979; Ram Chandra Prasad, *Rajneesh: The Mystic of Feeling.* Delhi: Motilal Banarsidass, 1978.

Sikhism

★1240★
SIKH DHARMA
1620 Pruess Rd.
Los Angeles, CA 90035

A major representative of Sikhism in the United States is Yogi Bhajan, who arrived in 1968 and founded the Healthy, Happy, Holy Organization (better known as 3HO), the educational arm of the Sikh Dharma. Shri Singh Sahib Bhai Sahib Harbhajan Singh Khalsa Yogiji, popularly known as Yogi Bhajan is a priest of the Sikh Dharma, headquartered in Amritsar, India. Teachings are based upon those of Guru Nanak, about whom the organization has published a book, and center on the praise of God and in addition the practice of kundalini yoga (a practice which had earned the Sikh Dharma some criticism from other orthodox Sikhs).

As Sikhs (literally a "student of truth"), members follow Guru Nanak's admonition to rise before sunrise, bathe, and contemplate God's Nam. These individual practices are followed by gathering with the congregation and singing the Guru's hymns. Sikhs bow to the Word of God contained in *Sri Guru Granth Sahib*, the writings compiled by the original ten gurus that now serves as the official Guru (though there will be numerous teachers such as Yogi Bhajan). A copy is enthroned in every Sikh gurdwara (place of worship).

Kundalini yoga, the yoga of awareness, releases the coiled energy at the base of the spine, and according to the teaching, sends it up the spine to the pineal gland, the "seat of the soul." The kundalini (energy) is released through chanting, postures and intense breathing. It is a relatively quick yoga, not requiring years to master. The practice of yoga has as its goal the overcoming of the negative conditions of life-painful thought waves, intellectual discrimination, and obstacles to enlightenment.

Members of the Sikh Dharma are baptized and accept the 5 K's of traditional Sikh practice. A baptized member is called an Amritdhari Sikh. Others affiliated with the group are called Sahajdhari. Members are vegetarian, and every gurdhara has a kitchen attached to it. Several members have opened vegetarian restaurants and grocery stores. Alcohol, tobacco, and intoxicating drugs are forbidden.

Leadership of the Sikh Dharma is invested in the Khalsa Council which functions under Yogi Bhajan. It consists of the Adminstrative and Regional ministers who oversee the local centers and appoint the Singh Sahibs (men) and Sardarni Sahiba (women), the ministers. p. Besides the center in Los Angeles, a second headquarters complex is located in Espanola, New Mexico where Yogi Bhajan resides. It is the sight of the semiannual national gatherings on the summer and winter soltices and several camps (for women and children). The Healthy, Happy, Holy Organization is the educational arm of the Sikh Dharma. It is incorporated separately. There is also a women's auxiliary, the GGM (Grace of God Movement of the Women of America) aimed at dealing with the proper role of women. Women are "Shakti," divine power in manifestation. Women are accorded equal opportunities at all levels of leadership in the organization. Associated is the Kundalini Research Institute which gathered data on the effectiveness of kundalini yoga and publishes much of the movement's literature. Also associated is Spiritual Community Publications, formed by members of the organization in the the San Francisco Bay area, who publish *The New Consciousness Sourcebook*, formerly the *Spiritual Community Guide*, the major directory of Eastern and New Age religious groups.

Membership: In 1984 the Sikh Dharma claimed 250,000 members in the United States, the sum total of Sikhs in the United States. Of these, however, only 5,000 to 10,000 are associated with the Sikh Dharma in any formal relationship. There were approximately 125 teaching centers.

Periodicals: *Beads of Truth*, 3HO Foundation, 1620 Pruess Road, Los Angeles, CA 90035.

Sources: Sahib Harbhajan Singh (Yogi Bhajan), *The Teachings of Yogi Bhajan*. New York: Hawthorn Books, 1977; Sardarni Premka Kaur, *Guru for the Aquarian Age*. San Rafael, CA: Spiritual Community, 1972; Sahib Harbhajan Singh (Yogi Bhajan), *The Experience of*

Consciousness. Pomona, CA: KRI Publications, 1977; *Kundalini Yoga/Sadhana Guidelines.* Pomona, CA: KRI Publications, 1978.

★1241★
DIVINE LIGHT MISSION
Box 390858
Miami Beach, FL 33139

Few new religious movements have grown and spread as quickly as the Divine Light Mission did during its early months in the United States. Beginning in 1971, it had, by 1973, more than 40 centers in North America and was publishing both a monthly publication, *And It is Divine,* and a tabloid, *The Divine Times.* The mission was centered upon the then teenage guru Maharaj Ji (b. 1957) who assumed leadership in 1966 at the time of the death of his father, Shri Hans Ji Maharaj. A former member of the eclectic Brahmo Samaj, Shri Hans Ji Maharaj had met a guru in the Sant Mat tradition, identified only as Dada Guru, who initiated him into surat shabda yoga (the yoga of the sound current) through four techniques or kriyas which were to become the trademark of the Divine Light Mission. In the 1920s, following the death of his guru, Shri Hans began to travel in northern India and around 1930 first arrived in Delhi. His work grew informally for many years, spreading across the northern half of India from Bombay to Calcutta. In 1950 he commissioned the first mahatmas, assistants who had the authority to initiate as his representative, and a short time afterwards he issued the first copies of a monthly magazine,*Hansadesh.* The following was formally organized in 1960 as Divya Sandesh Parishad, i.e., the Divine Light Mission.

Shri Hans was considered a satguru, or perfect master, by his followers. His death was considered a great loss; however, at his funeral, in the midst of the mourning crowd, one of Sri Hans four sons, Prem Pal Singh Rawat, then only eight years old, arose and addressed the crowd, "O You have been illusioned by maya (the delusion that suffering is real). Maharaj Ji [i.e., Shri Hans] is here, very much present amidst you. Recognize him, adore him and obey him." Thus Maharaj Ji proclaimed his lordship and established himself as the new head of his father's mission.

Maharaj Ji had been an unusual child who began meditating age two and giving discourses at age six. He entered his teen years with a curious mixture of "normal" childhood urges and the meditative life of a satguru. Four years later, on November 8, 1970, at the India Gate in Delhi, Maharaj Ji proclaimed the dawn of a new era, and his followers answered his call to mission. Early in 1971, Maharaj Ji made his first tour of the United States, mixing visits to Disneyland and horror movies with sessions with prospective disciples. A second visit was made to a huge meeting of disciples at Montrose, Colorado, in the summer of 1972. Each trip was accompanied by wide advertisement and mass media coverage.

Following Sant Mat tradition, Maharaj Ji is considered a perfect master and, as such, an embodiment of God. He gives initiation (called the giving of knowledge) into the truth of life. Initiation involves instruction in the four yoga techniques taught to Shri Hans by his guru. They are taught to a premie (follower of the guru) by a mahatma (personal representative of the guru). The first involves the placing of the knuckles on the eyes, a process which produces flashes of light in the head (by pinching the optic nerve). The second involves the plugging of the ears and concentrating only on internal sounds. The third involves a concentration on the sound of one's own breathing. Finally, the "nectar" is a technique in which the tongue is curled backward against the roof of the mouth. These techniques are practiced daily by primies (lovers of God). Regular daily practice of these techniques allows the premie to become atuned to the sound and light current emanating from the Divine.

In the early 1970s, the Mission suffered greatly from its "Millennium 73" program which proved unable to attract enough people to fill (and pay for) the Houston Astrodome. This disaster was followed by internal dissent within Maharaj Ji's family. A month after the Houston event, Maharaj Ji turned 16. He took personal adminstrative control of the mission. Then in May 1974, he married his 24-year old secretary. His mother, Mataji, reacted by taking control of the mission in India and declaring an older brother in control. A lawsuit gave Maharaj Ji control of the movement outside of India while the family retained control of the large Indian following. The publicity attendant upon the internal problems, concurrent with attacks by anti-cultists in the United States, led the mission to adopt a low profile. Maharaj Ji ceased to make public appearances and announcements of activities were not made outside of the membership. In the late 1970s both the headquarters of the movement in Denver and Maharaj Ji's residence in Malibu were transferred to Miami, Florida. Recently, Mahara Ji returned to California.

Membership: Not reported. In 1978 the mission reported 50,000 people involved, of which 10,000 to 12,000 were very active. It is estimated that in the intervening years that the number has diminished considerably, though groups can still be found across the United States.

Sources: James V. Downton, Jr., *Sacred Journeys.* New York: Columbia University Press, 1979; Charles Cameron, ed., *Who Is Guru Maharaj Ji?* New York: Bantam Books, 1973; Guru Maharaj Ji, *The Living Master.* Denver, CO: Divine Light Mission, 1978; *Satgurudev Shri Hans Ji Maharaj.* Delhi, India: Divine Light Mission, n.d.; *An Introduction to Divine Light Mission.* London: Shri Hans Production, [1972].

★1242★
ECKANKAR
Box 3100
Menlo Park, CA 94025

ECKANKAR, the Ancient Science of Soul Travel, constitutes the teachings of ECK Master Paul Twitchell (d. 1971). Twitchell, a former journalist, had been an initiate of Sant Mat Master Kirpal Singh, founder of the Ruhani Satsang and teacher of the Divine Science of the Soul. In 1964 he moved to San Francisco and began to teach surat shabda yoga, which emphasized techniques of attuning the soul to the sound and light current emanating from God. It also emphasized bi-location, the ability of the conscious soul to leave the body and travel in the invisible realms. In 1965, Twitchell declared himself the Living ECK Master and formed the first public ECKANKAR group. He is considered by members of ECKANKAR as the 971st MAHANTA and Living ECK Master of the Vairagi Order, taking his place in a line that began before recorded history. To become the ECK Master, Twitchell is believed to have studied with former Masters Sudar Singh in India and Rebazar Tarzs in the Himalayas. The *Shariyat-Ki-Sugmad* is the scripture of ECKANKAR. The original copy is located in the spiritual city of Agam Des, one of the seven golden wisdom temples, which can only be reached in the Soul body. Two volumes copied and translated by Twitchell have been published.

In its basic concepts, ECKANKAR closely follows the Sant Mat teachings of Kirpal Singh and of Western Sant Mat writer Julian Johnson, a disciple (like Kirpal Singh) of Sawan Singh, head of the Radhasoami Satsang, Beas, from whom he developed much of his understanding of the tradition. Twitchell did create a new vocabulary to designate the spiritual realms described in Sant Mat teachings. ECKANKAR teaches that all life flows from God (the SUGMAD) downward to the world. The cosmic current (ECK) is the creative-sustaining reality of all existence and is perceived as sound. To gain the highest spiritual realms, it is necessary to hear the cosmic sound, identified with the Sanskrit Nam and the Christian Logos. Students who are awakened to the divine sound also become aware of the cosmic light. ECKANKAR spiritual exercises teach students, called chelas, to project their inner consciousness through the lower states into the ecstatic states in which they possess total awareness of being.

There are over one hundred exercises in the writings of ECK to aid the student in the various stages of growth. Basic techniques involve the use of chants combined with specific imaginative actions such as the concentration upon the spiritual form of the ECK Master or on leaving the body.

As with all Sant Mat groups, a living master is essential. The Master delivers the chela from the wheel of reincarnation and links him with the ECK current, thus leading him to the realms where total spiritual freedom is attained. The Master guides the chela personally through the lower spiritual or astral realms. Meeting with the ECK Master is termed "darshan" and begins with being with a Living Master in the physical; hence, the necessity of always having a Living ECK Master. Besides the physical meeting, the ECK master is encountered on the spiritual planes and can be contacted through the various exercises. Spiritual travel of the Soul body (Atma Sarup), through dreams, imagination, and direct projection is regularly reported by chelas.

The international headquarters of ECKANKAR is in Menlo Park, California. It relates to its students through correspondence courses (available only to chelas), local ECKANKAR Satsang groups, and conferences which feature the presence of the ECK Master. After Paul Twitchell's death in 1971, he was succeeded by Darwin Gross. Gross married but soon divorced Gail Twitchell, Paul Twitchell's widow. More recently, he has been rejected by the organization which no longer considers him as a true ECK Master. Harold Kemp is the present Living ECK Master.

Twitchell authored over sixty manuscripts on the subject of ECKANKAR, over thirty of which have been published by the Illuminated Way Press. Centers and groups are located across the United States and Canada as well as in Mexico, Europe, Asia, South America, and Africa.

Periodicals: *ECK World News*, Box 3100, Menlo Park, CA 94025; *ECK Meta Journal*, Box 3100, Menlo Park, CA 94025; *The Banyan Tree*, Box 3100, Menlo Park, CA 94025.

Remarks: In the early 1980s, as the nature of ECKANKAR's relationship to the Sant Mat tradition became common knowledge, substantial charges were leveled that Paul Twitchell had not just developed a variant of the tradition but had actually plagierized materials, particularly those of Julian Johnson, to use as basic teaching material. Further, David Cristopher Lane, author of a major book on ECKANKAR, demonstrated that Twitchell had fabricated a spiritual career out of his readings and study with teachers such as Kirpal Singh, L. Ron Hubbard (founder of the Church of Scientology), and Swami Premananda of the Self- R evelation Church of Absolute Monism. Articles written by Twitchell which originally acknowledged his reliance upon these and other teachers were later republished with the names of ECK masters substituted in their stead.

Sources: David Christopher Lane, *The Making of a Spiritual Movement*. Del Mar, CA: Del Mar Press, 1983; Paul Twitchell, *All About ECK*. Las Vegas, NV: The Illuminated Way Press, 1968; Paul Twitchell, *The Tiger's Fang*. New York: Lancer Books, 1969; Paul Twitchell, *ECKANKAR, the Key to Secret Worlds*. New York: Lancer Books, 1969; Darwin Gross, *From Heaven to the*

Prairie. Menlo Park, CA: IWP Publishing, 1980; Harold Kemp, *The Wind of Change*. Menlo Park, CA: IWP Publishing, 1980; ECKANKAR International Office Staff. *A Profile of ECKANKAR*. Menlo Park: ECKANKAR, 1979.

★1243★

KIRPAL LIGHT SATSANG
% Bernadine Chard
442 Beloit
Kensington, CA 94708

Following the death of Kirpal Singh in 1974 (see biographical sketch in separate entry on the Sawan Kirpal Ruhani Mission), Darshan Singh, Kirpal Singh's son, who most thought would succeed his father, was rejected by Madam Hardevi, who had been chosen the temporal chairman of the Sawan Ashran and the Ruhani Satsang in India. She supported Thakar Singh, a leading disciple who had, in the months following Kirpal Singh's death, developed a growing belief in his commission to serve as the movement's guru. Madam Haedevi died in 1979, and Thakar Singh took complete control of the ashram.

In the wake of the refusal of the directors of the American corporation, the Ruhani Satsang-Divine Science of the Soul, some American followers who recognized Thakar Singh reorganized as the Kirpal Light Ashram and established headquarters in the Bay Area of northern California. The small group has grown in the wake of several visits by Thakar Singh to America, but does not yet approach the size of the Sawan Kirpal Ruhani Mission.

Membership: Not reported.

Periodicals: *Sat*, Kirpal Light Satsang, 442 Beloit Avenue, Kensington, CA 94708.

★1244★

MOVEMENT OF SPIRITUAL INNER AWARENESS, CHURCH OF THE
3500 W. Adams Blvd.
Los Angeles, CA 90018

The Church of the Movement of Spiritual Inner Awareness (MSIA--pronounced "messiah") was formed in 1968 by an early ECKANKAR student, Sri John-Roger Hinkins, termed the Mystical Traveler Consciousness. MSIA is an outward reflection of each individual's movement toward a more complete awareness of God. The focal point of the movement is the consciousness of Sri John-Roger. He has total awareness of all levels of consciousness and works with all who ask for his assistance. He is able to assist others in developing awareness. In particular, he helps each person into a consciousness of his soul's perfection. Such soul transcendence frees one from the wheel of incarnations. The work begins on the outer level to direct the student to spiritual consciousness, but then most instruction is on the inner spiritual planes. Here, the student is directed to the light and sound within.

Sri John-Roger is believed to have the ability to "read" the karmic record of each person (good and bad actions of earlier incarnations) and the ability to help students release physical karma (consequences for bad actions) in dream patterns. Acting while they are asleep, he takes students into the higher realms, the soul realm beyond the astral, causal, mental and etheric realms. The soul realm is considered our true home to which we seek return. As one learns soul transcendence (called soul travel in ECK), one's physical environment also changes as one perceives life anew.

Students are aided in their progress by a program of MSIA Light studies, aura balancing, an eight-year series of monthly Awareness Discourses, tapes, publications and seminars. The Light studies are the basic what-to-do and how-to-do it sessions. They are bolstered by the discourses, publications, and tapes. Aura balancing helps release past negative patterns; auras are psychic emanations that people give off and that psychics can interpret. Programming helps one become aware of programmed responses and teaches how to create new responses.

A number of auxiliary organizations have been developed to carry Sri John-Roger's teachings into various areas. Some of these operate as independent corporations though informally tied to the Church. Baraka Books publishes many of Hinkins' books. Insight Transformational Seminars offer short-term intensive growth experiences for individuals. Health concerns have been centered upon the Baraka Holistic Center for Therapy and Research in Santa Monica, California. Baraka Products markets a line of health related products and educational services. The Movement broadly supports holistic health structure and practitioners and encourages individuals affiliated with the Movement to become involved in promoting health-related concerns. There are two schools supported by the Movement. Most of the national offices are located in two buildings in Los Angeles and Santa Monica. Hinkins also has a television show which appears nationally on cable television. Most of these auxiliary organizations and concerns have been brought together as divisions of the John-Roger Foundation.

Membership: Not reported. In the mid-1980s MSIA claimed over 275 centers of activity in the United States and 11 other countries.

Educational facilities: Prana Theological Seminary and College of Philosophy, 3500 W. Adams Blvd., Los Angeles, CA 90018; KOH-E-NOR University, 2101 Wilshire Blvd., Santa Monica, CA 90403.

Periodicals: *The Movement Newspaper*, Box 19458, Los Angeles, CA 90019.

Sources: Sanderson Beck and Mark T. Holmes, eds., *Across the Golden Bridge*. Los Angeles, CA: Golden Age Education Publications, 1974; John-Roger Hinkins, *The Christ Within*. New York: Baraka Press, 1976; John-Roger Hinkins, *Possessions, Projections and Entities*. New York: Baraka Press, 1976; John-Roger Hinkins, *The Sound Current*. New York: Baraka Press, 1976; John-Roger Hinkins, *The Spiritual Family*. New York: Baraka Press, 1976.

★1245★
NIRANKARI UNIVERSAL BROTHERHOOD MISSION
Sant Nirankari Mission (USA)
1015 Thacker St.
Des Plaines, IL 60016

The Nirankari Universal Brotherhood Mission is one of several Sant Mat groups which traces its lineage to Jaimal Singh, founder of the Radhasoami Satsang, Beas. It was founded by Boota Singh (1873-1943) a tatoo artist who in 1929 received a succession from Kahn Singh. Boota Singh became known for his opposition to the rigid conventions and rituals of the Sikhs; he opposed all taboos, castes, creeds and divisions based upon external habits and appearances. He discarded all dictates concerning what one eats, drinks, or wears. Boota Singh was succeeded by Avtar Singh (1899-1969). After the partition of 1947 (which established Pakistan as a separate state), Avtar Singh moved the headquarters of the Nirankari Mission to Delhi and formally established the Sant Nirankari Mandal. He wrote a constitution and gave it its present organizational structure. He authored *Avtar Baani*, which functions as a holy book for the movement. Under Avtar Singh, the mission flourished and a colony was established on the Januma River in Delhi. In 1969 Avtar Singh was succeeded by Gurbachan Singh, who had the year previous traveled to Europe to establish the work there. By 1973 there were 354 branches with work outside of India in England, Hong Kong, Canada, and the United States.

The spread of the Nirankari Mission to the West began in 1955 when Bhag Mal, a member, moved to England. The mission was formally organized in 1962. Soon after becoming head of the mission, Gurbachan Singh, who had helped develop the work in the West, formed a foreign section to focus upon growth outside of India. In 1971 he made his first trip to North America. Beginning in Vancouver, he moved to San Francisco where he appointed Dr. Iqhaljeet Rai as president of the Nirankari Universal Mission in the United States. He continued his journey across the United States and visited Toronto and Montreal before returning home. In 1972 headquarters were moved to Madison, Wisconsin.

Internationally, the mission is headed by the Seven Stars, who are seven men picked by the guru to serve for life. The mission in India, after receiving persecution, organized the Sant Nirankari Seva Dal, a defense force to protect the group against acts of violence directed against it.

Essential to the life of the mission is *gian*, the giving of the knowledge by the guru to each member. This process, the exact nature of which is held confidential within the group, establishes the relationship of guru to disciple. As the mission has grown, specific disciples have been appointed to represent the guru in the giving of knowledge. Members of the mission agree to live by the five principles: 1) Nothing is ours. All possessions--physical, mental, material--are a divine loan which we must utilize only as trustees and not as masters. 2) No discrimination based upon caste, creed, color, religion, or worldly status. 3) No criticism of anyone's diet or dress, as this creates conflict and breeds hatred. 4) No renunciation of the world. One should continue performing one's normal vocations and functions of life and be always righteous. 5) No divulgence of the Divine Secret of the gian except with permission of the True Master.

Membership: In 1982, the Mission reported 2,000 members in 20 centers in the United States. The Mission claims more than 8,000,000 members worldwide in 26 countries.

Periodicals: *Sant Nirankari*, Nirankari Colony, Delhi 1100009, India.

Sources: Balwany Gargi, *Nirankari Baba*. Delhi, India: Thomson Press, 1973.

★1246★
RADHASOAMI SATSANG, BEAS
% Roland DeVries
2922 Los Flores Ave.
Riverside, CA 92503

Several groups presently operating in America derive their existence from the spiritual movement begun in 1861 by Param Guru Shri Shiv Dayal Singh Sahab (1818-1878). This movement is not recognized by orthodox Sikhs because it considers Singh Sahab as a new human guru. By contrast, orthodox Sikhs believe the last human guru died in 1718. Singh Sahab, known as Soamiji Maharaj, passed the leadership of the new movement to a designated disciple, who did the same. Soamiji Maharaj designated Rai Salig Ram (1829-1898) as his successor, and he in turn designated Pandit Brahma Shankar Misra (1861-1907).

In 1907, the death of the third leader was followed by a dispute over the rightful successor. The majority of the Central Committee refused the leadership of Sri Kamta Prasad Sinha (1861-1949) (better known as "Param Guru Sarkar Sahab") while a majority (111-116) of the satsangs accepted his leadership. (A satsang is a gathering of members with their master.) The Central Committee, in charge of the Samadhs, or tombs of the first three leaders, refused the Sahab group access to them. They recognized Maheshwari Devi (d.1913), the sister of the third leader, as the true Sant Satguru. She became known as Buaji Maharaj. The Sahab group became known as the Radhasoami Satsang, Dayalhagh, and the Buaji Maharaj group as the Radhasoami Satsang, Soamibagh.

Another division in the Radhasoami occured in the 1890s over Baba Jaimal Singh (1839-1903), a disciple of Soamiji Maharaj. After an army career of thirty-four years, he settled in Beas and began to hold satsang. His activities led to a break because of innovations which the Radhasoami could not accept. Thus the Radhasoami Satsang, Beas, came into being. Jaimal Singh was succeeded by Sawan Singh (1958-1948). Under his lengthy term as the head of the organization, it expanded radically. Where previous Sant mat leaders had initiated at most several thousand followers, Sawan Singh initiated over 100,000.

A final division of the Radhasoami occurred in 1951, when Kirpal Singh, a long-time disciple, claimed the "spiritual heritage" of Sawan Singh. After Singh's death, Jagat Singh was named his successor, but he lived for only three more years. In his will, Jagat Singh appointed the present leader, Charan Singh (b.1916), the grandson of Sawan Singh, as his successor. Rejecting Charan Singh, Kirpal Singh, who had already left Beas, established his independent ashram in Delhi.

The beliefs of the Radhasoami are very much like the gnostic and Manichean religions of the ancient Mediterranean Basin. (Those religions believed matter to be evil, and only spirit to be good.) The cosmology begins with the Dayalk Radhasoami, the supreme spiritual being, from whom emanated the Mauj or overflow. It is the spirit sound from which came creation. As it descended, it came into contact with "maya" (matter, illusion), which predominates on the lowest level.

The individual soul is also an emanation of the supreme being that descended into the lower regions and became imprisoned beyond any possibility of escape. To teach individuals the way of escape was the purpose of the incarnation of the supreme being in the human form of Soamiji Maharaj.

Surat Shabda Yoga, the only way of return to spirit, consists of 1)Sumiran (the repetition of the holy name "Radhasoami") and Dhyan (contemplation of the holy form), and 2) the "sound practice." The latter, consisting of a set of practices which allows the student to become attuned to the sound and light emanating from God, is revealed to the initiate only by the Sant Satguru. The sound is the "radio wave" that guides the individual home.

The Sant Satguru is given the highest veneration as the incarnation of Nij Dhar or divine emanation. The Nij Dhar is in only one body at a time, which explains the importance placed upon a relationship to the Satguru. His revelation to the faithful occurs after the death of the former Satguru. Disagreement by large segments of the movement over who the new guru was to be has led to the schisms.

The Radhasoami Satsang, Beas, came to the United States in 1907 through Kev Singh Sasmus, a disciple of Sawan Singh, who arrived as an interpreter for a group of Indian immigrants. In Port Angeles, Washington, he encountered Dr. H. M. Brock and his wife to whom he explained Sant Mat (the religion of the saints). They wished to be initiated, and Sawan Singh gave permission to Kev Singh. They were initiated in 1911. The Brocks in turn became teachers and were authorized to give nam (initiation) to believers. Dr. Julian Johnson was initiated in 1931 and became one of the authoritative authors of the movement. The Brocks were succeeded as the master's representatives by Harvey Myers and he by the present representative, Roland de Vries of Riverside, California.

Under the leadership of Charan Singh, the Radhasoami Satsang, Beas, has eclipsed all of the other Sant mat groups in India. He has initiated over 700,000 individuals, more than all the other Sant Mat leaders combined.

Membership: Not reported. In the mid-1970s, there were 41 centers in the United States and three in Canada.

Periodicals: *R. S. Greetings,* Roland Devries, 2922 Las Flores Avenue, Riverside, CA 92503.

Sources: Peter Fripp, *The Mystic Philosophy of Sant Mat.* London: Neville Spearman, 1964; Huzur Maharaj Sawan Singh, *Philosophy of the Masters.* Beas, India: Radhasoami Satsang, Beas, 1963-1967. 5 Vols.; Maharaj Charan Singh, *The Path.* Beas, India: Radhasoami Satsang, Beas, 196; Maharaj Charan Singh, *Light on Sant Mat.* Bras, India: Radha Soami Satsang, Beas, 1958; *Radha Soami Colony Bras and Its Teachings.* Beas, India: Radha Soami Satsang, Beas, n.d.

★1247★
SANT BANI ASHRAM
Franklin, NH 03235

Among the early and more important centers of the followers of Kirpal Singh (see biographical material in item on Sawan Kirpal Ruhani Mission) was the Sant Bani Ashram in Franklin, New Hampshire. Headed by Russell Perkins, the center had handled much of the publishing for the movement over the decades. Among the significant titles are several volumes of Kirpal Singh's collected works. After the death of Kirpal Singh in 1974, Perkins refused to recognize Darshan Singh, the popularly supported candidate as Kirpal Singh's successor. Having heard of Ajaib Singh, he visited his ashram in the Rajasthan desert and eventually recognized him as Kirpal Singh's successor. Joining Perkins was Arran Stephens, Kirpal Singh's Canadian representative, and head of

Kirpal Ashram in Vancouver. Stephens had been the first Westerner to hear of Ajaib Singh and had raised the possibility of his being Kirpal Singh's successor in an issue of the movement's magazine, *Sat Sandesh*.

Ajaib Singh was initiated in 1967 by Kirpal Singh. Ajaib Singh has his major following in North America and has visited his disciples in America on a several occasions. He adopted the name of the New Hamphire center as that of his own work in India.

Membership: Not reported.

Periodicals: *Sant Bani: The Voice of the Saints*, Sant Bani Ashram, Franklin, NH 03235.

Remarks: After promoting Ajaib Singh for several years, Arran Stephens withdrew his support, claiming that Ajaib Singh contradicted many of Kirpal Singh's teachings and had on several occasions misrepresented both events which had occurred to him and his relationship to Kirpal Singh.

Sources: Kirpal Singh, Ajaib Singh, and Sawan Singh, *The Message of Love*. Sanbornton, NH: Sant Bani Ashram, n.d.; Kirpal Singh, *The Way of the Saints*. Sanbornton, NH: Sant Bani Ashram, 1976; Kirpal Singh, *Morning Talks*. Franklin, NH: Sant Bani Ashram, 1974.

★1248★
SAWAN KIRPAL RUHANI MISSION
% T. S. Khanna
8807 Lea Lane
Alexandria, VA 22309

The Sawan Kirpal Ruhani Mission is one of three organizations which claims to continue the work of the Ruhani Satsang founded in 1951 by Kirpal Singh (1896-1974). In 1917 Kirpal Singh had a vision of a "Radiant Form" whom he took to be Guru Nanak (the founder of Sikhism). In 1924, however, he met Sawan Singh (head of the Radhasoami Satsang, Beas) and recognized him as the one in the vision. He stayed with Sawan Singh for the last twenty-four years of his life.

When Jagat Singh received the succession from Sawan Singh, Kirpal Singh left Beas and began the independent Sawan Ashram in Delhi. In 1951, at the time Charan Singh succeeded Jagat Singh, he formed the Ruhani Satsang. In 1949, T. S. Khanna, a disciple of Kirpal Singh, migrated to Canada and established the Ruhani Satsang in Toronto. Several years later he moved to the Washington, D.C. suburb of Alexandria, Virginia.

The growth of the work was accelerated by the two visits of Kirpal Singh in 1955 and 1963, during which time he toured cities in North America and initiated many individuals. As a result, a national association of members and centers was incorporated in California as the "Divine

Science of the Soul." Kirpal Singh, however, had initiated people without regard for their affiliations and religious background. Some preferred to create informal groups and became tied together very loosely under the Ruhani Satsang, incorporated by Khanna in Washington. In 1972 Kirpal Singh ordered the merger of the American work in the California corporation and the Washington corporation was dissolved. Khanna was elected chairman of the board of the merged body, Ruhani Satsang-Divine Science of the Soul.

Kirpal Singh died in 1974. The movement divided anew as various centers became aligned to the several claimants to Kirpal Singh's succession. In both India and the United States, the largest number of initiates and centers followed Darshan Singh (b. 1921), Kirpal Singh's son. Led by T. S. Khanna and other longtime disciples such as Olga Donenberg and Sunnie Cowen, these members reorganized as the Sawan Kirpal Ruhani Mission. (Meanwhile, the broad of the Ruhani Satsang-Divine Science, the continuing corporate structure, has refused to recognize any successor to Kirpal Singh.) Darshan Singh made his first visit to the United States in 1978. Having lost control of Sawan Ashram, due to his rejection by Madam Hardevi, who had been chosen temporal chairman of the Ruhani Satsang in India, he established a new center, Kirpal Ashram, also in Delhi. Following his 1978 tour, he also opened a free kitchen and medical dispensary at the ashram complex. Like his father, Darshan Singh has continued to promote interfaith work and has authored a number of books.

Outside of India, disciples of Darshan Singh could be found in over twenty-five countries of the world. Sawan Kirpal Publications is the publishing arm of the movement, and several structures have emerged to handle various audiovisual material.

Membership: Not reported. In the early 1980s, there were centers in over 100 towns and cities in the United States associated with the Sawan Kirpal Ruhani Mission. There were centers in 10 Canadian cities.

Periodicals: *Sat Sandesh*, Rte .1, Box 24, Bowling Green, VA 22427: *Sawan Kirpal Ruhani Mission Newsletter*, Rte. 1, Box 24, Bowling Green, VA 22427.

Sources: Kirpal Singh, *The Jap Ji*. Bowling Green, KY: Sawan Kirpal Productions, 1981; Darshan Singh, *The Secret of Secrets*. Bowling Green, VA: Sawan Kirpal Productions, 1978; H. C. Chadda, ed., *Seeing Is Above All*. Bowling Green, VA: Sawan Kirpal Productions, 1977; Bhadra Sena, *The Beloved Master*. Delhi, India: Ruhani Satsang, 1963; Kirpal Singh, *Godman*. Delhi, India: Ruhani Satsang Sawan Ashram , 1967; *A Brief Biography of Darshan Singh*. Bowling Green, VA: Sawan Kirpal Publications, [1983].

★1249★
SIKH COUNCIL OF NORTH AMERICA
95-30 118th St.
Richmond Hill, NY 11419

The Sikh Council for North America is the major organization which attempts to provide communication and coordination for those Sikh congregations and temples located across the United States serving predominantly Indian-American Sikhs. Since 1965, the number of Sikhs has risen dramatically, doubling between 1975 and 1985.

The beginning of Sikh organization in America can be traced to the arrival of Jawala Singh and Wisakha Singh, two advocates of Indian independence, who came to California in 1908. They owned a ranch on the Holtville River near Sacramento where they practiced Gurbani Kirtan (singing the songs from *Sri Guru Granth Sahib*). Then in 1912 a lot was purchased at Stockton, California and the *Sri Guru Granth Sahib* installed in a gurdwara (place of worship). The Pacific Coast Khalsa Diwan Society was organized to raise money for a temple, an original wooden temple was constructed in 1916, replaced with a brick structure in 1929. For several decades it was the only Sikh center in the United States and large gathering were held there four times a year.

The temple in Stockton was closely associated with the Ghadar Party, an organization established in 1913 in San Francisco and financed in large part by Jwala Singh, which advocated Indian independence from British rule. Though largely destroyed during World War I, due to its ties with German supporters, it continued into the 1940s and its building has been turned into a memorial to the struggle for Indian independence. In more recent years the Stockton temple has become identified with those Sikhs in the Punjab seeking independence from Indian rule which is largely Hindu.

After World War II and India's gaining of independence in 1948, there was further migration of Punjabis, enought so that a second temple was constructed at El Centro, California. In 1969 the largest Sikh temple in the world was erected in Yuba City, California. By 1974 there were clsoe to 100,000 Sikhs from the Punjab in the United States. Centers can now be found in cities and towns across the United States.

In the 1970s the Sikh Foundation emerged as a public voice for East Indian Sikhs in the United States. From its headquarters in Redwood City, California, it published the quarterly, *Sikh Sandar*, and *Sikhs in the U.S.A. and Canada*, a directory. The Foundation was recently superceded by the Council.

Membership: As of the mid-1980s there are an estimated 250,000 Sikhs in the United States.

Sources: *Sikhs in the U.S.A. & Canada*. Redwood City, CA: The Sikh Foundation, 1972; Wadhawa Singh, *Introduction to the Sikh Temple, Stockton, abd the Ghadar Party*. Stockton, CA: Sikh Temple, 1983; Wadhawa Singh, *Introduction to Sikhism and Its Holy Scripture: Sri Guru Granth Sahib*. Stockton: Sikh Temple, 1981.

Eastern Family
Part 2, Buddhism, Shinto, Japanese New Religions

An historical essay on this family is provided beginning on page 159.

Theravada Buddhism

★1250★

CAMBODIAN BUDDHIST TEMPLE
20622 Pioneer Blvd.
Lakewood, CA 90715

Since 1965, and particularly since the end of the Viet Nam War, Cambodians have migrated to the United States. In the 1970s, they began to establish temples to serve Cambodian communities. These communities have been relatively poor, and most of the temples have been in rented unmarked facilities. Besides the temple in suburban Los Angeles there are centers in Chicago and suburban Washington, D.C.

Membership: Not reported. There are an estimated 160,000 Cambodians in the United States, as of 1985.

★1251★

INSIGHT MEDITATION SOCIETY
Pleasant St.
Barre, MA 01005

The Insight Meditation Society was founded by Jack Kornfield and Joseph Goldstein. On his spiritual pilgrimage in India, Goldstein encountered Anagarika Munindra, a former bkahti Hindu who had turned to Burmese Theravada Buddhism and become an accomplished teacher. During the 1960s Jack Kornfield began his study of Theravada Buddhism, spending six years in Southeast Asia. He studied primarily with two students of Burmese teacher Mahasi Satadaw, Achaan Chaa and U Asabha Thera. Upon their return to the United States in the 1970s, both began to teach insight meditation, that form of meditation which is central to Theravada Buddhism, and both authored books which have become important channels for introducing the practice to American audiences. The Society was created as a means to organize their efforts. It also hosts Theravada teachers visiting from Southeast Asia.

Membership: Not reported.

Sources: Joseph Goldstein, *The Experience of Insight.* Boulder, CO: Shambhala, 1976; Jack Kornfield, *Living Buddhist Masters.* Santa Cruz, CA: Unity Press, 1977.

★1252★

INTERNATIONAL BUDDHIST MEDITATION CENTER
928 S. New Hampshire Ave.
Los Angeles, CA 90006

The International Buddhist Meditation Center was founded in 1970 as a teaching center for Vietnamese Zen Buddhism. In Viet Nam, as in some other Southeast Asian countriues, Zen and Theravada Buddhism has merged to produce some unique and eclectic forms. The center was formed by the Ven. Thich Thien-An (1926-1980), a Vietnamese Buddhist bishop and late professor of Oriental languages at the University of Southern California. Before coming to the United States, he was chairman of the Department of Asian Studies at the University of Saigon.

While emphasizing Zen practice, the Center offers its members "the opportunity to experience the full breadth and depth of Buddhism." The issues surrounding Vietnamese Buddhism are also highlighted, and it is hoped that the Center will emerge as a place for interchange of United States and Vietnamese students. The center is located several blocks from another Vietnamese Buddhist temple which serves primarily first--generation Vietnamese immigrants. After the Ven Thien-An's death, leadership passed to Dr. Leo M. Pruden, the president of the University of Oriental Studies; Ven. Dr. Thich Man-Giac, of the Vietnamese Buddhist Temple of Los Angeles; and Dr. Karuna Dharma.

The center offers a full program of worship, classes and retreats, and draws leadership from several Vietnamese priests now working in this country, but not otherwise connected with the center.

Membership: Not reported. There is one center in Los Angeles, California.

Periodicals: *Monthly Guide*. 928 S. New Hampshire Avenue, Los Angeles, CA 90006.

Sources: Thich Thien-An, *Buddhism and Zen in Vietnam*. Rutland, VT: Charles Tuttle, 1975; Thich Thien-AN, *Zen Philosophy, Zen Practice*. Berkely, CA: Dharma Publishing, 1975.

★1253★
LAO BUDDHIST SANGHA OF THE U.S.A.
938 N. Hobart Blvd.
Los Angeles, CA 90029

Like other southeast Asians, Laotians have come to the United States in significant numbers since 1965, and particularly since the end of the Viet Nam War. The number of new immigrants quadrupled during the period 1980-1985, and the religious scene is in great flux with new work only beginning to be stablized in each Laotian community. Temples have been established in Los Angeles, Chicago, and Washington, D.C.

Membership: Not reported. As of 1985 there are an estimated 220,000 Laotians in the United States.

★1254★
NEO-DHARMA
% Dr. Douglas Burns
2648 Graceland Ave.
San Carlos, CA 94070

Dr. Douglas Murray Burns is a psychiatrist born in Boston and raised in Oregon. As a high school student, he became interested in Buddhism. In 1960, he published his first work, *The Principles of Buddhist Philosophy*. He moved to California in 1961 and gathered around him a group interested, as he was, in a rational Theravada form of Buddhist faith, which he called Neo- Dharma. (Buddha's teachings outline the Dharma, the true way of life. Theravada Buddhism is also called Hinayana, a conservative, monastic Buddhism.) In 1965, Burns went to Thailand with the intent of entering a monastery, but was prevented by his induction into the Army. He has continued to lecture widely and write prolifically.

Burn's ideas can be summarized in a few statements, which obviously represent a neo-Buddhist or modernist approach: 1) The universe is regulated by impartial and unchanging laws. 2) Knowledge of these laws is acquired by insight and by unprejudiced reasoning in the light of one's experiences-not by faith in scriptures or mystical revelations. 3) Moral law, like physical law, is inherent in the workings of nature. Greed, hatred, and egotism result in proportionate amounts of unhappiness for one who is responsible for such motivations. 4) This three dimensional realm of space, time and matter is not the only level of existence. The concrete world of sense perception is a reality, but it is not the only possible dimension of reality. His rational modern approach has found an audience in Thailand and Ceylon, and the American group has continued to function by learning and practicing his ideas. While concentrated in California, they are scattered around the United States.

Membership: Not reported. In 1970 there were approximately 250 people affiliated with the group.

Periodicals: *Neo-Dharma Notes*, 2648 Graceland Avenue, San Carlos, CA 94070.

Sources: Douglas Burns, *Nirvana*. Bankok, Thailand: World Fellowship of Buddhists, 1967; Douglas M. Burns, *Buddhism, Science and Atheism*. Bangkok, Thailand: World Fellowship of Buddhists, 1965.

★1255★
SRI LANKAN (CEYLONESE) BUDDHISM
Buddhist Vihara Society
5017 16th St., N.W.
Washington, DC 20011

In 1964 while visiting the United States, the Most Venerable Madihe Pannaseeha, Maha Nayaka Thera of Ceylon, became aware of both an interest in Buddhism and the lack of a center for Theravada Buddhism. Acting upon his suggestion, the Sasana Sevaka Society of Maharagama, Ceylon, sent the Venerable Thera Bope Vinita to Washington in 1965, where the Buddhist Vihara Society was founded with the help of the Ceylonese Embassy. In 1967, Vinita was succeeded by the Venerable Pandita Mahathera Dickwela Piyananda, who was succeeded in 1968 by his assistant, the Venerable Mahathera Henepola Gunaratana. A permanent home was dedicated in 1968 as the Washington Buddhist Vihara (Temple).

A large percentage of support for the Washington temple has come from the staff of the embassies of Ceylon, Laos, Thailand and Burma who are themselves Theravada Buddhists, though in recent years temples serving the various national groups have been established in the Washington area. An aggressive outreach program has brought some non-Asian following. The temple houses both a bookstore and library which provide Theravada literature.

Worship is centered on Sunday afternoon Vandana (devotion) and the sermon. Special celebrations include Wesak (the spring celebration of Gautama Buddha) and Olcott Day, commemorating the Theosophist Henry Steele Olcott, who is credited with the nineteenth century revival of Ceylonese Buddhism. In 1970, there were 70 members.

Since 1965 a number of Buddhists from Sri Lanka moved to the United States and settled on the West Coast. To the Buddhist Vihara Society, for many years the only Ceylonese temple in the United States, have been added a growing number of temples serving primarily first generation immigrants. The Dharma Vijaya Buddhist Vihara in Los Angeles and the California Buddhist Vihara Society in Berkeley are among the most prominent. Among the scholarly leaders of the Sri Lankan Buddhist community in America is David J. Kalupahana, a professor of philosophy at the University of Hawaii and author of numerous books, both popular and academic. Dr. Dickwela Piyananda Mahathera, president of the Washington Vihara, offers spiritual oversight to the newer temples.

Membership: Not reported.

Periodicals: *The Washington Buddhist*, 5017 16th Street, N.W., Washington, DC 20011.

Sources: Henepola Gunaratana, *Come and See*. Washington, DC: Buddhist Vihara Society, n.d.; David J. Kalupahana, *Buddhist Philosophy, A Historical Analysis*. Honolulu: University of Hawaii Press, 1976; David J. Kalupahana, *The Way of Siddhartha*. Boulder, CO: Shambhala, 1982; Bhikkhu Ananda, *Theravada and Zen*. Colombo, Sri Lanka: M.D. Gunasena & Co., 1962; *Buddha Vandana*. Los Angeles: Dharma Vijava Buddhist Vihara, 1985.

★1256★
STILLPOINT INSTITUTE
2740 Greenwich, #416
San Francisco, CA 94123

The Stillpoint Institute was founded in 1971 as the Susana Yeiktha Meditation Center and Buddhist Society. The founder, an American now known by his Buddhist name, Anagarika Sujata, was a college dropout who went to Ceylon and took training as a monk in Theravada Buddhism. He was ordained in 1967, returned to the United States and, in 1970, founded the Buddhist Society of Clearwater. In 1971, he moved to Denver. From there, Sujata developed his Theravada Buddhist perspective in lectures, in teaching meditation and in leading retreats. Around him a small community developed.

The goal of the Institute is the "integration of body awareness techniques with the Satipatthana Vipassana Insight Meditation," in which the mind is trained to be more observant while refraining from comment on or judgment of what it views. In the mid-1970s the Institute moved to San Jose, California.

The emphasis of Sujata's teaching, as manifested in his book, *Beginning to See*, is on present-mindedness and detachment. Buddhist insight meditation is the key to the laying down of anger, attachment and selfishness, and to the attainment of loving kindness, compassion, sympathetic joy and equanimity.

Membership: Not reported.

Sources: Anagarika Sujata, *Beginning to See*. Denver: Sasana Yeiktha Meditation Center, 1973; Mahasi Sayadaw, *The Satipatthana Vipassana Meditation*. Elgin, AZ: Unity Press, 1957.

★1257★
TAUNGPUPU KABA-AYE DHAMMA CENTER
18335 Big Basin Way
Boulder Creek, CA 95006

The center for Burmese Buddhism in the United States is the Taungpupu Kaba-Aye Dhamma Center and Monastery in Boulder Creek, California and the associated Center in San Francisco. The monastery was founded in 1981 by the Venerable Kaba-Aye Sayadaw, a Burmese monk on a goodwill tour of the United States. He left two monks, Hlaign Tet Sayadaw and U Kaythawa, to head the work. Dr. Rina Sircar, a longtime student of Kaba-Aye Sayadaw, serves as the resident meditation teacher. The monastery offers periodic retreats for those already versed in vipassana meditation, that form of meditation most common to Theravada Buddhists.

In 1979 U Silananda, one of several monks who accompanied Sayadaw on his first trip to America, remained in the United States to provide leadership for Burmese Buddhists. He founded the Dhammananda Vihara in Daly City, California (serving primarily Burmese-Americans) and the Berkeley Vipassana Center, serving non-Asian students. There is also a Burmese center in suburban Washington, D.C.

Membership: Not reported.

★1258★
THAI-AMERICAN BUDDHIST ASSOCIATION
Wat Thai of Los Angeles
12909 Cantara St.
North Hollywood, CA 91506

The general unrest in Southeast Asia and the rescinding of the Oriental Exclusion Act in 1965 combined to increase immigration from Thailand to the United States in the late 1960s. Significant Thai-American communities emerged on the West Coast and in several urban areas further inland. Assisted by leadership from Thailand, the new immigrant communities began to organize their predominantly Buddhist religious life. In 1970, at the invitation of the American Thais, the Ven. Pharkhru Vajirathammasophon of Wat Vajirathamsathit toured the United States. During his visit, the Thai-American Buddhist Association was formally organized in Los Angeles and plans were initiated to build the Wat Thai of Los Angeles, a temple complex which would serve the largest of the Thai communities in the West. Later that year, three priests arrived to take up permanent residence.

The 1971 visit by the Ven. Phra Dhammakosacharn, a leading Thai Buddhist priest, was followed by the incorporation of the Wat Thai as the Theravada Buddhist

Center and the beginning of a fund raising drive. In 1972 the United States government invited the supreme patriarch, Phra Wannarat of Wat Phra Jetuphon, and a group of Thai priests to make an official state visit. During this visit, the presentation of the land-title deed for the future site of the Wat Thai was held in the office of the Consul General in Los Angeles. The cornerstone was laid and construction commenced. It was finished in stages, and in 1980 the statue of Buddha in the main temple was consecrated.

While work on the complex in Los Angeles proceeded, other wats were being organized in other cities from San Francisco and Denver to Houston, Washington, D.C., and New York.

Theravada Buddhism has, as a major practice, insight meditation, described as the practice of mindfulness. Mindfulness is the observation point arrived at by the meditator from which he or she can truly understand mental and physical phenomena as they arise. In general, Theravada Buddhists are among the most conservative in their adherence to the oldest Buddhist traditions and they use the Pali-language texts of early Buddhism, as opposed to the Sanskrit texts used by the Mahayana Buddhists.

Membership: There are over one hundred thousand Thais in the United States, and 40,000 in Los Angeles alone. As of 1985, wats had been established in Los Angeles, San Francisco, and Sunnyvale, California; Denver, Colorado; Ogden, Utah; Chicago, Illinois; Houston, Texas; Washington, D.C.; St. Louis, Missouri; Miami and Tampa, Florida; and Mt. Vernon, New York.

Periodicals: *Duangpratip*, 12909 Cantara Street, North Hollywood, CA 91605-1198.

Sources: M. L. Manich Jumsai, *Understanding Thai Buddhism*. Bangkok, Thailand: Chalermit Press, 1973; Jane Hamilton-Merritt, *A Meditator's Dairy*. New York: Harper & Row, 1976; Phra Maha Singhathon Narasapo, *Buddhism, An Introduction to a Happy Life*. Bangkok: The Preacher's Association, Wat Phrajetubon, 1969.

★1259★
VIET NAM BUDDHISTS
Congregation of Vietnamese Buddhists in the U.S.
863 S. Berendo
Los Angeles, CA 90005

Because of the resettlement of the many Vietnamese Buddhists who entered the United States after the Viet Nam War, the number of Vietnamese temples far exceeds that of other Southeast Asians, and they may be found in all sections of the United States. The temples serve first generation Vietnamese-Americans and services are conducted in Vietnamese. Vietnamese Buddhism is distinctive in the way it has merged Theravada and Zen. Among the leading spokespersons for Vietnamese Buddhism is Thich Nhat Hanh, who became known to

Americans during the Viet Nam War as a peace advocate. He works closely with the Fellowship of Reconciliation.

Membership: Not reported. By 1985, there were an estimated 500,000 Vietnamese in the United States, most Buddhists.

Sources: Thich Nhat Hanh, *The Miracle of Mindfulness*. Boston: Beacon Press, 1976; Thich Nhat Hanh, *Zen Keys*. Garden City, NY: Doubleday, 1974.

★1260★
VIPASSANA FELLOWSHIP OF AMERICA
Chapelbrook
Ashfield Road
Williamsburg, MA 01096

The Vipassana Fellowship of America was formed by Dhirvamsa, a Thai monk, who came to England in 1964 as chief incumbent monk of the Buddhapadipa Temple. He eventually gave up his monk's robe, finding it too confining in his work with Westerners. In 1969 he came to the United States and began to teach vipassana meditation, that form of meditation traditional to Thai Buddhism. An initial center was established in New England. Dhirvamsa now regularly tours the United States speaking, teaching meditation, and holding retreats. Dhirvamsa's students can also be found in Thailand, Canada, Sweden, Switzerland, Australia, and New Zealand.

Membership: Not reported.

Sources: Dhirvamsa, *The Way of Non-Attachment*. New York: Schocken Books, 1977.

Japanese Buddhism

★1261★
BODAIJI MISSION
1251 Elm
Honolulu, HI 96814

The Bodaiji Mission was founded in 1930 by Nisshyo Takao, the Holy Interpreter. It is continued by Roy S. Takakuwa as an independent congregation teaching "True Buddhism." Takakuwa is a baker in Honolulu, but he also serves as the sole teacher and priest. The bakery provides the total support for the mission, because no donations are allowed. The teaching of the mission is described as empirical, moving from fact to the source of facts.

The basic concept of Bodaiji teachings is Dai-O-Kyo, filial piety, the lack of which is a great cause of discord and trouble. Filial piety begins in Yojomanjo, the unconditional salvation of true motherhood. Just as motherhood was the source of our nurture, so cooperation, coexistence, and right living lead us to universal salvation. True Buddhism teaches how to live rightly.

An acceptance of the law of cause and effect underlies the teachings; where there is something wrong, one finds the cause and changes it. Thus, when one adopts a program of right living, salvation will come.

Healing is a concept basic to right living. Each person who comes for healing must stick to a rigid diet and must learn to breathe properly. Holy water is also used. Meditation is advised for all for fifteen minutes each day to replenish energy.

Membership: In 1982 there were approximately 100 members. There is but a single congregation, and no membership roll is kept.

★1262★
BUDDHIST CHURCHES OF AMERICA
1710 Octavia St.
San Francisco, CA 94109

The Honpa Hongwanji goes under different names in its two jurisdictions. In the Hawaiian Islands, it is known as Honpa Hongwanji Mission. In the rest of the country, it is known as the Buddhist Churches of America. As in Japan, the Honpa Hongwanji is the largest of the Buddhist groups. During the twentieth century, it has spread throughout the Japanese/American community and has been a major bridge leading to the accommodation of that community to American mores. The Honpa Hongwangi is one of the three prime groups teaching Pureland or Shin Buddhism.

The Buddhist Churches of America have headquarters in San Francisco. There are sixty independent churches and forty branches, mostly on the Pacific Coast. They are divided into eight administrative districts, six on the Pacific Coast, one for the mountain states and one for the East and Midwest. Since 1977, Bishop Kenryu Tsuji has presided over eighty ministers and more than 60,000 members. A board of directors and a representative national council oversee the administrative functions.

The Honpa Hongwanji Mission of Hawaii, headquartered in Honolulu, has thirty-six missions throughout the islands. A bishop is headquartered in Honolulu and has fifty-three ministers under him. Until World War II, the Honpa Hongwanji in Kyoto appointed the bishop, but since then the Hawaiian members have elected the bishop for a three-year term. In 1967, Kanmo Imamura, son of Bishop Yemyo Imamura, the long-time bishop who did so much for the Buddhist cause in Hawaii prior to World War II, was elected Bishop.

The Jikoen Hongwanji Temple was built in 1938 as a temple for Okinawan Shinshu immigrants who had come to Honolulu during the 1920s and 1930s. It functions as a member of the Honpa Hongwanji.

Membership: In 1984 the Buddhist Churches of America reported 100,000 members, 100 temples (with an additional 40 branches), and 130 priests. Of these, approximately 22,000 members and 36 temples were in Hawaii. The group in America is a mission outpost of the largest of the Japanese Buddhist groups. It claims over 10,000,000 members worldwide.

Educational facilities: Institute of Buddhist Studies, Berkeley, CA 94704; American Buddhist Academy, New York, NY.

Periodicals: Horin (in Japanese), 1710 Octavia Street, San Francisco, CA 94109; Wheel of Dharma (in English), 1710 Octavia Street, San Francisco, CA 94109; Pacific World, 1710 Octavia Street, San Francisco, CA 94109 .

Sources: Traditions of Jososhinshu Hongwanji-Ha. [Los Angeles]: Senshin Buddhist Temple, 1982; Shin Buddhist Handbook. Honolulu: Honpa Hongwanji Mission of Hawaii, 1972; Buddhist Handbook for Shin-shu Followers. Tokyo: The Hokuseido Press, 1969; Buddhist Churches of America, 75 Year History, 1899-1974. Chicago: Norbet, Inc., 1974. 2 Vols.

★1263★
GEDATSU CHURCH OF AMERICA
401 Baker
San Francisco, CA 94115

The Gedatsu Church was formed by Gedatsu Kongpo (posthumous title of Shoken Okano), a priest in the Shugendo sect of Shingon Buddhism. Born in 1881, he rose to the rank of archbishop. In 1929, he founded the Gedatsu movement in his own town. A student of comparative religion, Gedatsu Konpgo borrowed freely from Shinto and Christianity to produce an eclectic Buddhist teaching.

According to Gedatsu, man desires wealth, fame, sex, food and rest. Man runs into trouble whenever the search for these five, so necessary for survival, becomes directed solely to self-satisfaction. He then falls into the tragedies of life and is suffers from ignorance of karmic law, hereditary problems, and selfish thoughts. The object of religion is to move from the problems and suffering of the present to the state of enlightenment--calm resignation and complete peace of mind. (By the law of karma, a person must experience the consequences of his or her actions.)

Gedatsu offers a method of attaining enlightenment through the development of wisdom, the purification of emotion, and the improvement of will power. Wisdom is developed by meditation on the symbol "AJI." The emotions are purified by service to the souls of ancestors and other spiritual entities. Will power is improved by the Way of the Holy Goho, a progressive method of disciplining the mind and spirit that can dissolve the bonds of karma.

Underlying the Gedatsu doctrine is the concept of universal law and universal truth. The universal law is the power of nature, absolutely unchangeable and indestructible. It is seen in the regular cycles of nature. This law also functions to bring to enlightenment those who follow the path.

Center of Gedatsu worship is the Goreichi Spiritual Sanctuary. This shrine is the resting place of all spirits and houses the Tenjinchigi, the spirit of the supreme creator, the source of the universal law. The shrine also contains a statue of Fudo Myo-Oh, who has the power to conquer all evil. Other bodhisattvas are also represented. A semiannual Thanksgiving Festival is observed in the spring and fall, and the Annual Roku Jizo Festival is observed in June. All are noteworthy for their ceremony. Central to all worship is Kuyo, the act of humbly repaying by absolute gratitude all the sources to which one is indebted. Kuyo is ritualized in the Nectar Service during which spirits in a state of unrest are brought to rest.

Gedatsu was brought to the United States in the late 1940s and incorporated in 1951. It has headquarters in San Francisco, and it maintains ten churches, including those in Sacramento, San Jose, Stockton, and Los Angeles, California. The Goreichi Shrine is in Mayhew, a Sacramento suburb. There is one temple in Honolulu.

Membership: Not reported.

Sources: *Manual for Implementation of Gedatsu Practice.* [San Francisco]: Gedatsu Church of America, 1965; Eizan Kishida, *Dynamic Analysis of Illness through Gedatsu.* N.p.: 1962; *Gedatsu Ajikan Kongozen Meditation.* San Francisco: Gedatsu Church of America, 1974.

★1264★
HIGASHI HONGWANJI BUDDHIST CHURCH
505 E. Third St.
Los Angeles, CA 90013

Quickly following the Buddhist Churches of America, the largest of the Shin Buddhist groups, was the Higashi Hongwanji. However, since it has done little to Westernize, it has been slower to spread. In 1899, Shizuka Sazanami began to work on Kauai in Hawaii, where a temple was constructed in Waimea. It was 1916 before a temple appeared in Honolulu. On the mainland, the Higashi Honganji began with Rev. Junjyo Izumida who, in 1904, established the Los Angeles Buddhist Mission as an outpost of the Honpa Hongwanji. Two other churches were also formed in Los Angeles, and soon a rivalry developed between them. In 1917 a merger of the three congregations was ratified. Izumida, however, opposed the merger and, in a court suit, won the property of the congregation he had led. In 1921 he joined the Higashi Honganji and brought the congregation with him. Shortly after the establishment of the Higashi Honganji in Los Angeles, a second temple was opened in Berkeley,

California. A third was added in Chicago after World War II. The Chicago temple, under the leadership of Gyomay Kubose also sponsors a Zen center. Kubose, who serves as both a Shin priest and Zen master, follows in the pattern of the late D. T. Suzuki, the most famous member of the Higashi Honganji (at least to Western audiences). The American branch of the Higashi Honganji is presided over by Gyoko Saito, the priest in Los Angeles.

Membership: In 1982 there were 1,800 members in six churches in Hawaii. There are three temples in the continental United States, though there are several branch churches attached to the Los Angeles temple.

Periodicals: *The Way*, 505 E. Third Street, Los Angeles, CA 90013.

Sources: *Jodo Shinshu.* Tokyo: Otani University, 1961; Haya Akagarasu, *Shout of Buddha.* Trans. by Gyoko Saito & Joan Sweany. Chicago: Orchid Press, 1977; Haya Akegarasu, *The Fundamental Spirit of Buddhism.* Trans. by Gyomay M. Kubose. Chicago: Buddhist Temple of Chicago, 1977; Manshi Kiyozuma, *December Fan.* Trans. by Nobuo Haneda. Kyoto, Japan: Higashi Honganji, 1984; Beatrice Lane Suzuki, *Mahayana Buddhism.* New York: Macmillan, 1969; D. T. Suzuki, *Shin Buddhism.* New York: Harper & Row, 1970; *Higashi Honganji Dedication-1976.* Los Angeles: Higashi Hongwanji Buddhist Church, 1976.

★1265★
JODO MISSION
1429 Kakiki St.
Honolulu, HI 96822

The Buddhist immigrants to Hawaii, tired of several clerical frauds which had been perpetrated upon them soon after their arrival, petitioned the Jodo-shu to send an official representative to lead them in worship. In response, an overseas missionary society was organized. In the 1890s Gakuo Okabe arrived and tramped through the plantations, carrying a statue of Amida Buddha. In 1896, he built the first Jodo-shu temple in Paauhau on the Big Island, Hawaii. In 1903, Shinjun Shimizu was sent to take charge of the work. By the end of the first decade of the twentieth century, a temple in Honolulu had been constructed. Steady growth has proceeded on the islands. The Jodo Mission is headed by Bishop Kyodo Fujuhana, the twelfth to hold the post. An inter-club council coordinates the various mission activities.

Membership: In 1982 there were 2,000 members in 21 churches and 40 priests, all in Hawaii. There is one Jodo center in Los Angeles, California.

Sources: *Light of Asia.* Honolulu, HI: Hawaii Jodo Mission, 1962; Ruth Tabrah, *Buddhism, "A Modern Way of Life and Thought."* Honolulu, HI: Hawaii Jodo Mission, 1969; Kodo Matsunami, *Introducing Buddhism.* Honolulu: Jodo Mission of Hawaii, 1965.

★1266★

KAILAS SHUGENDO
% Dr. Neville Warwick
2362 Pine St.
San Francisco, CA 94115

The Kailas Shugendo was founded by Dr. Neville G. Pemchekov-Warwick, known to his followers as Ajari. Shugendo is an old Buddhist tradition that borrows from pre-Buddhist Japanese shamanism and mountain religion. Ajari has been conducting Shugendo practices since 1940 and is termed Dai Sendatsu, which allows him to start his own movement. His background is Russian Buddhist, and he immigrated to America in the 1960s.

Central to the Shugendo is fire worship. Twice a day, members observe Goma, the fire ceremony. The ritual master conducts while the members chant. Once a week Hiwatari, fire purification, is performed. Members walk the sacred fire but are not burned. At intervals, members go to the mountains for ascetic practices--shugyo (climbing the mountain while chanting mantra), going under ice-cold waterfalls and hanging people off rocks. Music is also a part of daily life. Headquarters of the ashram are in San Francisco, California, where it offers musical and cultural presentations to the Bay Area community and performs emergency community services.

Membership: Not reported.

★1267★

NICHIREN MISSION
3058 Pali Hwy.
Honolulu, HI 96817

Nichiren (1222-1282) was a famous Buddhist reformer. In 1253 he began to preach a new doctrine--that salvation lay in the Lotus Sutra, the most famous Buddhist sanskrit text. The theme of the Lotus Sutra is the nature of Buddha's manifestations. Nichiren believed that the Lotus Sutra taught a combination of the methodologies of the other Buddhist groups--the ways of transformation, bliss and law. Rather than call upon the Amida Buddha, as in Shin Buddhist practice, one should call upon the Lotus Sutra. Daimoku, a repetitive chant of "Namu myoho renge kyo" (reverence to the wonderful law of the Lotus) became and remains the distinctive practice of the Nichiren Buddhists. Nichiren believed that the teachings known as the Lotus Sutra constituted primitive, true Buddhism and could unite the many Buddhist sects.

Nichiren divided history into the following three millennia: shobo, the period of the true law, which was the first millinnium beginning at Buddha's death; zobo, or image law, the second millennium; and mappo, or end of the law, which is to last 10,000 years. During mappo, which began in 1050 C.E., the Lotus was the way of salvation. Since the Lotus was perfect, all Japanese should yield to it and allow it to spread. According to Chinese figuring, Buddha died in 949 B.C.E. (By Western figuring, he died in 486 B.C.E.) Nichiren followed the Chinese date and said each millennium was about 1,000 years. The first was the period of Hinayana Buddhism; the second, of Provisional Mahayana Buddhism; the third, of the True Mahayana Buddhism treated in the Lotus Sutra.

The worship of the Nichiren Buddhist is centered upon the repetition of the Lotus chant. This act is performed in front of the gohonzon, a mandala upon which the chant is inscribed along with the name of Buddhas, bodhisattvas, and other Buddhist deities and personalities.

Nichiren was an ardent advocate of his new cause; so dogmatic were his polemics that he angered other Buddhists. He died seeking the union of his ideas with Japan's national policy. The Nichiren Buddhists never reached their goal, but they have become one of the five largest Japanese groups.

Members of the Nichiren-shu (Nichiren religion) built a temple on the island of Hawaii at Pahala in 1902. This temple served the Japanese immigrants who had come to work on the plantations. In 1912 one more was added on Oahu, now the headquarters of the Nichiren Mission of Hawaii under the leadership of Bishop Senchu Murano.

An independent Nichiren congregation was established on Oahu in 1931 by a priest of the Kempon Hokke Sect (one of the Japanese Nichiren groups) under the name "Honolulu Myohoji." This temple joined the Nichiren Mission in 1979. It enshrines part of the relics of the Buddha. The Pahala Nichiren Temple ceased to exist in 1957 because of the evacuation of the Japanese people from the district, and it has recently been purchased by a Tibetan Buddhist group. Other temples have been added on the various islands. Since World War II Nichiren Buddhism has come to California and headquarters have been established in Sacramento for the several temples. Members are primarily Japanese-Americans.

Membership: In 1984 the Mission in Hawaii reported 600 members in five churches served by eight priests. There are 8,000,000 Nichiren Buddhists worldwide.

Periodicals: *The Newsletter*, Nichiren Mission of Hawaii, 3058 Pali Highway, Honolulu, HI 96817

Sources: Masaharu Anesaki, *Nichiren, the Buddhist Prophet*. Cambridge: Harvard University Press, 1949; Senchu Murano, *An Outline of the Lotus Sutra*. Minobu-San, Japan: Kuonji Temple, 1969; *Hasu No Oshie (The Teachings of the Lotus)*. Honolulu, HI: Nichiren YBA of Honolulu, 1962; *A History of Nichiren Buddhism in Hawaii*. Honolulu: Nichiren Mission of Hawaii, 1982.

★1268★
NICHIREN SHOSHU TEMPLE
7576 Etiwanda Ave.
Etiwanda, CA 91739

In Japan the followers of Nichiren (1222-1282), the Buddhist reformer, divided into several groups. In 1290 one of the six main disciples of Nichiren, Nichiko (1246-1332), separated from the other five in a dispute which in part concerned the question of who had the responsibility for the upkeep of Nichiren's tomb. But the dispute also had a doctrinal element. Nichiko disagreed over the nature of the Lotus Sutra, the document upon which Nichiren had based his reforms and which his followers looked to as containing the teachings of true Buddhism. The Lotus Sutra contains twenty-eight chapters, divided into two sections of fourteen chapters each. Nichiko held that the first section, the Honmon, in which Buddha is revealed in his eternal aspect, was superior to the latter. The other five disciples saw the entire Lotus Sutra to be of equal value. Nichiko founded the Daisekiji temple at the foot of Mt. Fiji. His followers became the Nichiren Shoshu. Nichiren Shoshu was relatively small until after World War II. Then it began to grow rapidly because of the development of an affiliated lay organization whose efforts have made Nichiren Shoshu one of the largest Buddhist organizations in the world.

Soka Gakkai International was founded as Soka Kyoiku Gakkai (Creative Education Society) in 1930 by Makiguchi Tsunesaburo. His beliefs were at odds with Shintoism, the national religion of Japan from 1868 to 1945. During World War II, Makiguchi refused to worship the sun goddess, the head of the Shinto gods. For this refusal he was sent to prison, where he died. However, the Nichiren Shoshu, which numbered only sixty members, was reborn after the war under a vigorous new president, Josei Toda. His impact was clearly manifest when, in 1958, more than 300,000 persons attended his funeral. Toda was succeeded by Daisaku Ikeda, the current international president. Soka Gakkai International was officially created in 1975 in recognition of its transformation from a predominantly Japanese movement to a worldwide organization.

Nichiren Shoshu beliefs follow those of the Nichiren-Shu in most respects. Nichiren is regarded as the Buddha for this age. The Lotus Sutra is revered, and the reverence is reflected in the mantra whose repetition has become the central practice of the Nichiren Shoshu, "namu myoho rengekyo" (adoration to the exquisite law of the Lotus Sutra). Also revered is the Dai-Gohonzin, the supreme object of worship (upon which the mantra is written in Japanese) housed at the head temple in Japan. Members of the Nichiren Shoshu generally have a model of the Dai-Gohozon in their homes and meeting halls. Nichiren Shoshu teaches that those who embrace the same practice of chanting "namu myoho-rengekyo" and reciting parts of the Lotus Sutra, as Nichiren did, can attain enlightenment just as he did. And, when enough people attain this enlightened state, a state of world peace and harmony can be achieved.

Nichiren Shoshu came to the United States through the immigration of its members to Hawaii and the West Coast after World War II. In 1957 Masayasu Sadanaga moved to the United States, and in the following year he began holding Nichiren Shoshu meetings in Washington, D.C. An American chapter of Soka Gakkai was formed in 1960 following the arrival of Ikeda who made his first visit to North America that year. That event has been followed by a period of steady growth and made Nichiren Shoshu possibly the fastest growing Buddhist group in the United States. Sadanaga, who changed his name to George M. Williams, became the director of the work which became known as Nichiren Shoshu of America.

Until 1965, Nichiren Shoshu had been represented in America solely by Soka Gakkai, its lay organization. However, in that year ground was broken in Etiwanda, California for the first Nichiren Shoshu temple. Subsequently, other temples, each headed by one or more priests, have been constructed near Chicago, Washington, D.C., New York City, and in Hawaii. As in Japan, the priesthood and lay organization are incorporated separately, though they work closely together. In the United States, the priesthood is organized as Nichiren Shoshu Temple, and the lay members are organized as Nichiren Shoshu Soka Gakkai of America.

Membership: In 1984 Nichiren Shoshu reported 300,000 members, 40 NSA centers, and 5 temples.

Periodicals: *Soka Gakkai News*, 32 Shinano-machi, Shinjuku-ku, Tokyo 160, Japan.

Remarks: Since World War II, as Soka Gakkai has grown in Japan, it has been strongly opposed by other Buddhist groups. First, Nichiren Shoshu articulated the doctrine of "obutsu myogo," i.e., a government essentially aligned with Buddhism. It called for the unification of imperial authority and Buddhism as well as the designation of Buddhism as the state religion. To this end it entered the field of politics. By 1955, it had manifested a remarkable ability to have its candidates elected. In 1964, a political party, the Komei Kai, was organized and it soon became the third largest party in the Japanese Upper House. In 1965, the party elected 20 members. Secondly, in its evangelical efforts, it taught the practice of shaku-buku, literally "bend and flatten," the name given to the high pressure recruitment tactics used on potential converts. Such tactics were reported by the organization's opponents to include bullying and badgering, applying pressure to the vulnerable, and occasionally, physical assault. (Such practices have not been evident or reported in relation to the movement in the United States.) However, disturbed by Nichiren Shoshu's success, ninety-six Japanese religious bodies united in 1965 to fight it as a political entity. During the 1970s, its political influence waned considerably, though it remains a powerful force.

In 1979 Soka Gakkai International was briefly affected by a scandal which erupted when some members accused Ikeda of personal misconduct. When tried, those who had brought the accusations were found guilty of libel. Meanwhile, the organization lost the support of some members and a few Nichiren Shoshu priests resigned. The organization, however, quickly recovered.

Sources: George M. Williams, *Freedom and Influence.* Santa Monica, CA: World Tribune Press, 1985; Daisaku Ikeda, *Guidance Memo.* Tokyo: Seikyo Press, 1966; Yasuji Kirimura, *Fundamentals of Buddhism.* Tokyo: Nichiren Shoshu Center, 1977; *Soka Gakkai.* Tokyo: Soka Gakkai, 1983; *The Liturgy of Nichiren Shoshu.* N.p.: Nichiren Shoshu Temple, 1979.

★1269★
PALOLO KANNONDO TEMPLE
3326 Paalea St.
Honolulu, HI 96816

The Palolo Kannondo Temple in Honolulu is a small center of worship for Kannon, the Japanese equivalent of Kwan Yin, the goddess of mercy. The temple was founded in 1935 as an outpost of a large Kannon temple in southern Japan. Kannon is thought of in much the same way that Amida is thought of in Shin Buddhism, that is, as a bodhisattva, one who appears spiritually to people to enlighten them. A statue of Kannon, the patron of fishermen, had been placed on the southern shore of Oahu. It was cast into the sea and broken during World War II. After the war, the statue was found and repaired, and it now rests in the dooryard of the temple.

Membership: Not reported.

★1270★
RISSHO KOSEI KAI
℅ Rev. Kazuhiko K. Nagamoto
118 N. Mott
Los Angeles, CA 90033

Rissho Kosei Kai (the Society for the Establishment of Righteous and Friendly Intercourse) is one of the new Nichiren bodies that arose as World War II was beginning. The movement was founded by Nikkyo Niwano, a farmer's son, and Naganuma Myoko. Niwano (b. 1906), a self-taught man, was a member of Reiyukai, a Nichiren sect formed in 1922. Naganuma (1899-1957) was the wife of an iceman in Tokyo, and for she many years suffered from a serious disease. On Niwano's advice, she joined Reiyukai and was healed. Together they seceded and, in 1938, began Rissho Kosei Kai. The motivation seemed to be Niwano's desire for independence as well as a greater leadership role.

Rissho Kosei Kai follows Nichiren's interpretation of Buddhism. Attention is focused on the three Hokke Sutras (the Muryogi Sutra, the Lotus Sutra, and the Kanfugen Sutra). The Daimoku, the repetition of the mantra "Namu Myoho renge kyo," is used. Unlike Nichiren Shoshu, Rissho Kosei Kai does not use the Daimoku for its power. It is an expression of gratitude and faith. Man is bound by the laws of reincarnation and cause and effect. The consequences of these laws can only be broken by repentance and perfect living. The goal of Rissho Kosei Kai is the attainment of perfect Buddhahood through faith and repentance.

Dharma worship takes place in instruction halls. It includes chanting of the Lotus Sutra and the Daimoku and a sermon. After the service, hoza, or group counseling, begins. The congregation divides into small groups for discussions of personal problems and of the deeper aspects of faith. Divinatory practices are often incorporated. There are three annual festivals: the Foundation Festival on March 5; the Flower Festival on Buddha's birthday, April 8; and the Grand Festival on October 13.

While Rissho Kosei Kai has grown strong in Japan, it has penetrated the United States slowly. It began in 1959 when Mrs. Tomoko Ozaki opened her home in Kealakekua, Kona, Hawaii for a gathering of members who had migrated from Japan. The occasion was the visit of Rev. Kazue Yukawe. During the 1960s the movement spread to Honolulu and then to California and Chicago. The group consists mainly of Japanese-Americans. Members are also located in Korea, Hong Kong, Thailand, and Brazil.

Membership: In 1984, the Rissho Kosei-Kai reported 10 centers, serving 1,200 families in the United States. There were four priests. It reported over 5,000,000 members worldwide.

Periodicals: *Dharma World,* Kosei Publishing Co., 2-7-1 Wada, Suginami, Tokyo 166, Japan.

Sources: *Rissho Kosei-Kai.* Tokyo: Kosei Publishing Co., 1966; Nichiko Niwano, *My Father, My Teacher.* Tokyo: Kosei Publishing Co., 1982; Nikkyo Niwano, *Lifetime Beginner.* Yokyo: Kosei Publishing Co., 1978.

★1271★
SHINGON MISSION
915 Sheridan St.
Honolulu, HI 96810

Shingon Buddhism is a Japanese esoteric right-hand tantric sect. It places great emphasis on ritual, imagery, and ceremony, as well as occultism. The central practice is the use of mantras as magical formulas. "Mantra" means "true word, and its use emphasizes the need for the correct formula to accomplish the end. The incorporation of popular magical practices is one secret of Shingon's success. The man who integrated the elements that became Shingon was a monk named Ku Kai or, as he is most popularly known, Kobo Daishi. A student of Chinese religion, he was initiated by the Chinese into esoteric studies. He returned to Japan and began Shingon in 808 A.D. In 816, he received a grant of land to construct a monastery on. The site was Koyasan, a mountain near Osaka, upon which a collection of temples and monasteries were built. It remains the international Shingon headquarters.

Shingon's right-hand tantrism specializes in the worship of masculine gods. The pantheon shows numerous Hindu deities. A central solar divinity is Vairochana, from whom emanates the world. Vairochana is represented by graphic forms--the mandala, a cosmological form which artistically represents the essence of the universe. Art is an important facet of Shingon; Ku Kai believed that only art could convey the inner meaning of the Buddha's teaching. Also to be seen on the mandalas are the Buddhas and bodhisattvas who personify the Godhead. They include Amida, Shakyamuni (Gautama Buddha) and Kannon (Kwan Yin). Practices of the Shingon include meditation (often with the mantra), mudras (symbolic gestures), postures, and handling of ritual instruments.

Shingon was brought to the United States in 1902 by Hogen Yujiri, an immigrant laborer who opened a preaching hall in Hawaii on the island of Maui. He claimed to have been cured of an eye ailment by the "limitless compassion of Kobo Daishi." In 1903, Kodo Yamamoto gathered a Shingon following and built on Kauai the "Eighty-eight Holy Places of Hawaii's Garden Isle," modeled on a Japanese shrine. Before the decade was out, temples had been founded in Honolulu and on the Big Island (Hawaii). The movement spread quickly through the plantations.

In 1914, Eikaku Seki came to Honolulu as an official representative from Koyasan. He considered deplorable the chaotic condition of the popularized manifestation of his faith. He set up headquarters and built a detached temple of the Kongobuji, the main temple on Koyasan. Shingon continued to grow and gradually came under Seki's control.

Shingon reached its peak in the years prior to World War II. Since then, it has declined. It had only thirteen temples in 1972, half of the number reported in 1926. Headquarters are in Honolulu where Bishop Tetsuei Katoda oversees twelve ministers.

Membership: Not reported. Beside the dozen temples in Hawaii, there is also a Shingon temple in Los Angeles, California.

Sources: *Light of Buddha*. Los Angeles: Koyasan Buddhist Temple, 1968.

★1272★
SHINSHU KYOKAI MISSION
Bentenshu Hawaii Kyokai
3871 Old Pali Rd.
Honolulu, HI 86817

The Shinshu Kyokai Mission is a Shinshu congregation in Honolulu which is independent of both the Honpa Hongwanji and the Higashi Hongwanji. As a congregational project, the group maintains a dormitory for students and working men.

Membership: In 1982 there were 800 members in one center.

★1273★
SHINYO-EN
% Bishop Joshin Kuriyama
2348 S. Beretania St.
Honolulu, HI 96814

The Shinyo-En is one of the new Japanese religions founded in 1945 by Lord Shinjo Ito, a former Shingon priest. The first overseas branch was founded in Honolulu in 1972, and the temple was dedicated in May of the following year. Bishop Joshin Kuriyama, a registered pharmacist who abandoned her profession and eventually became a priest and then a bishop, established the work in Hawaii.

Lord Ito had, as a Shingon priest, found his duties irrelevant and wished more directly to help people find enlightenment and happiness. He concentrated on the later teachings of the Buddha and eventually believed himself able to interpret them for the layman.

The teachings center on the rebirth of lost souls. The spirits of the departed who do not rest in peace are the cause of present suffering and illness, and control us daily. Their influence heightens our own greed and selfishness. Services are directed toward Kosanori Sama, the Ground God, and Gezaiten Sama, the Sky God, who work together for the believer and the lost souls. April 8, Buddha's birthday, is a special festival day.

Membership: There is one center in Hawaii.

Periodicals: *Sono Michi*, 2348 S. Beretania, Honolulu, HI 96826.

★1274★
TODAIJI HAWAII BEKKAKU HONZAN
% Bishop Tatsusho Hirai
2426 Luakini St.
Honolulu, HI 96814

The Kegon sect was introduced into Japan from China in the eighth century and was one of the so-called Nara sects. Its basic text was the Avatamsakasutra. The sutra tells of the visit of Sudhana to some Buddhist worthies in order to realize the principle of dharmadhatu, the realization of the domain of Buddha's law. Basic is the idea of mutual interdependence and causation of all that exists. Symbolic of this interdependence is a figure known as Indra's Net, a huge net which bears a jewel at each point of intersection. Each jewel is seen to bear the image of all the others.

Nature is seen to exist in a set of polarities-universality/specialization, integration/differentiation, and similarity/diversity. Kegon is a traditional form of Buddhism. Ancestor worship is of prime importance and is coupled with the offering of food and drink in a gesture of belief in the non-dying of spiritual being. The mutual interaction of this life and the next is a strongly held belief.

There is only one Kegon center in the United States--the Todaiji Hawaii Bekkaku Honzan. The Todaiji was organized in Honolulu by Bishop Tatsusho Hirai, who claims to be the only female Buddhist bishop in the world. After an unsuccessful marriage to a second generation Japanese immigrant to Hawaii, she returned to Japan and entered the Todaiji Temple as a nun. After years of study, she returned to Hawaii as a missionary and, after the war, organized the Branch Temple (officially recognized in 1948). Construction of the present temple began in 1950 and was finished in 1958.

Bishop Hirai has faced opposition from the Buddhist clergy, who claim that she is incapable of expounding Kegon teaching. Nevertheless, she has persisted, aided by her adopted son, Ryowa Hirai, also trained at Nara and ordained by his mother.

Membership: In 1982 the center in Hawaii reported 30,000 adherents (i.e., the number who had received either a healing blessing and/or special amulet from the center).

Sources: Tatsusho Hirai, *Todaiji of Hawaii*. Honolulu: Todaiji Hawaii Bekkaku Honzan, n.d.

Zen Buddhism

★1275★
CALIFORNIA BOSATSUKAI
5632 Green Oak Dr.
Los Angeles, CA 90068

The California Bosatsukai shares the tradition of both Soen Nakagawa Roshi and Nyogen Senzaki (1876-1958), two Japanese Zen Buddhist pioneers in America. A Rinzai Zen monk, Senzaki came to California in 1905 and in 1928 established his own zendo in San Francisco. He started another in 1929 in Los Angeles. He was the Zen master of these two independent zendos until he died in 1958. The California Bosatsukai continues the tradition of Senzaki in Los Angeles.

In the early 1960s, Hakuun Yasutani Roshi, who was a student of Soen Nakagawa Roshi and had been trained on both the Rinzai and Soto Zen traditions, came to the U.S. Hakuun Yasutani accepted the role of Zen master for the California Bosatsukai along with his duties at other centers. He continued working with the California Bosatsukai until his death in 1973. Besides the Los Angeles center, there are branches in Hollywood, Del Mar, Los Gatos, and San Diego, California.

Membership: Not reported. There are approximately 100 members.

Sources: Louis Nordstrom, ed., *Namu Dai Bosa*. New York: Theatre Arts Books, 1976; Nyogen Senzaki and Salidin Reps, trans., *10 Bulls*. Los Angeles: DeVorss & Co, 1935; Nyogen Senzaki and Ruth Stout McCandless, eds., *Buddhism and Zen*. New York: Philosophical Library, 1953.

★1276★
CAMBRIDGE BUDDHIST ASSOCIATION
263 N. Harvard St.
Cambridge, MA 02134

The Cambridge Buddhist Association grew out of interest in Zen that developed on the campus of Harvard University in the 1950s. The Association began during the visit of Dr. Shin-ichi Hisamatsu and Dr. Daisetz Teitaro Suzuki in 1957. A group headed by Dr. Stewart Holmes and Mr. and Mrs. John Mitchell persuaded them to remain in Cambridge to give zazen instruction. A "Western style" zendo was established, and lectures and zazen instruction were given. Zazen means sitting still and is discussed in the introductory material to this volume.

After six months, Suzuki and Hisamatsu departed to other duties and the Association was left to its own resources. Help came from other Buddhists who, though not of Zen persuasion, nevertheless recognized the need for a Buddhist center and the importance of meditation. Suzuki became the group's president in 1959. In 1964, Shunrya Suzuki Roshi, a Zen master who had "learned English and has made every effort to understand...the American ways of Life,'" became the advisor of the Association. Suzuki, head of the Sokoji Temple in San Francisco, had also inspired the Zen Center of San Francisco during its early years.

The Cambridge Buddhist Association has the reputation of being the most intellectual and "scholarly" of all the Zen groups, primarily because of the affiliation of Dr. D.T. Suzuki, its president until his death in 1966. The group publishes an annual recommended reading list as one of the activities of its library. The organization has published three booklets which are excellent for those seeking an introduction to Buddhism in general and Zen in particular.

Because of its campus context and (until recently) isolated condition as the only Zen center in the Boston metropolitan area, the Association has been a central locus of Buddhist and inter-faith dialogues. Results of a particular significant encounter reached the public as *Conversations: Christian and Buddhist.* The Association is led by its president, the Rev. Chimyo Horioka, and a group of officers. Though small, it has made a major impact on American Buddhism and the opinion of Americans about Buddhism.

Membership: Not reported.

Sources: *Cambridge Buddhist Association.* Cambridge, MA: Cambridge Buddhist Association, 1960; Rindo Fujimoto, *The Way of Zazen.* Cambridge, MA: Cambridge Buddhist Association, 1969; Sita Paulickpulle Renfrew, *A Buddhist Guide for Laymen.* Cambridge, MA: Cambridge Buddhist Association, 1963; Daisetz T. Suzuki, *The Chain of Compassion.* Cambridge, MA: Cambridge Buddhist Association, 1966: Aelred Graham, *Conversations: Buddhist and Christian.* New York: Harcourt, Brace and World, 1968.

★1277★
DIAMOND SANGHA
Koko An
2119 Kaloa Way
Honolulu, HI 96822

The Diamond Sangha is the Hawaii Soto Zen organization which also serves as a Zen center for the non-Japanese community in the Islands. It was organized as the Zen Buddhist Association of Hawaii by Robert Aitkin and his wife, Anne Aitken, in 1959, with an initial center in Honolulu. Aitkin first learned about Zen as an internee on Guam during World War II. After the war, he traveled to Japan and became a student of Nyogen Senzaki. He also met Zen masters Soen Nakagawa and Hakuun Yasutani on subsequent visits.

Hakuun Yasutani (1885-1973) was an outstanding Soto master who had been trained in both Rinzai and Soto traditions. In 1954, he separated his following from the main Soto body in Japan and established Sanbokyodan (the Fellowhip of the Three Treasures) as an independent organization. Aitkin, after forming the Diamond Sangha, affiliated with the Sanbokyodan and remains its American representative. When Yasutani Roshi died, he was succeeded by Yamada Koun Roshi, who makes regular visits to Hawaii. There Yamada Koun Roshi leaded sesshin (extended "sitting" meditiation) and confirms the efforts of Aitkin.

Eido Shimano, a monk, was resident director of the Hawaii zendo for the first four years and was succeeded in that capacity by Katsuki Sekida, a lay student. In 1961, *Diamond Sangha*, a newsletter of the zendo, was established, and the present name of the group was adopted. A book of sutras, later adopted by the California

Bosatsukai and other groups, was published in 1963. In 1969, a second center on Maui was developed to help the "dropouts," particularly those involved in drugs. In 1974, Aitken was ordained as Aitken Gyoun Roshi and became the teacher of the Sangha.

Emphasis at the Sangha is away from the ritualism of the predominant Japanese Buddhism of Hawaii and toward the unitive life of meditation and work. The latter is particularly important in the communal life of the Maui zendo. Simplicity is a goal. Koan practice, discussed in the introductory material to thsi volume, is initiated among members before they have progressed very far along the path to self-realization.

Members of the Sangha have been among the leaders in thinking about and reformulating the understanding of the role of women in Zen and in Buddhism in general. The Sangha sponsors *Kahawai*, a feminist journal promoting the full participation of women in Western Buddhist organizations.

Membership: Not reported. There are less than 100 members at the two centers.

Periodicals: *Diamond Sangha*, Koko An, 2119 Kaloa Way, Honolulu, HI 96822; *Blind Donkey*, Maui Zendo, R.R.1, Box 702, Haiku, HI 96708; *Kahawai*, 2119 Kaloa Way, Honolulu, HI 96822.

Sources: Robert Aitken, *Taking the Path of Zen.* San Francisco: North Point Press, 1982

★1278★
FIRST ZEN INSTITUTE
113 E. 30th St.
New York, NY 10016

The First Zen Institute of America was founded in New York in 1930 by Sokei-an Sasaki Roshi, who came to the United States in 1928 with a commission from Ryomo-Zen Institute of Tokyo, a missionary wing of Rinzai Zen in Japan, to establish Rinzai Zen Buddhism in the West. From the beginning, the practice of Zen for lay people was stressed. Until 1945, the name Buddhist Society of America was used. The disruption experienced by Japanese-Americans during World War II also affected the institute. An early attempt to publish Soki- an's writing in a periodical, *Cat's Yawn*, was curtailed by the beginning of the war. In 1941, a zendo, a place set aside for Zen meditation, was set up at the home of Ruth Everett, under the close scrutiny of the FBI. Sokei-an, inturned for a period after the bombing of Pearl Harbor, married Ruth Everett in 1944. Unfortunately, he died a short later, before the war ended.

Sokei-an left no successor, but his students continued to meet and practice what he had taught them. Ruth Fuller moved to Daitaku-ji to continue her study. She became the first woman to become a Zen priest. She also organized the First Zen Institute of America in Japan as a structure to receive American students who wished to study abroad.

In 1954, the institute began a second periodical, *Zen Notes*, which included the writings of Sokai-an an other Zen Masters. In 1969, the Institute moved into its present headquarters in Manhattan. A Regular schedule of zazen meetings is held for members, and a weekly Wednesday evening session is open to newcommers. Still lay led, the institute invites guest roshis to lead sesshins, extened meditation retreats, periodically.

Governance of the Institute is by it members through a council drawn from its senior members. Senior members are "persons who have taken the Three Refuges before a qualified Buddhist priest and who have been accepted as disciples by a Zen Master recognized by the Institute." Senior members bear the title Koji, if a man, and Daishi, if a woman.

Membership: In 1984 the institute had approximately 100 members.

Periodicals: *Zen Notes*, 113 E. 30th St., New York, NY 10016.

Sources: Ruth Fuller Sasaki, *Zen, A Method for Religious Awakening*. Kyoto, Japan: The First Zen Institute of America in Japan, 1959; *Cat's Yawn*. New York: First Zen Institute in America, 1947.

★1279★

MINNESOTA ZEN MEDITATION CENTER
3343 Calhoun Pkwy.
Minneapolis, MN 55408

The Minnesota Zen Meditation Center began in the 1960s with a group of people in Minneapolis who began to practice zazen, Zen meditation. They developed an association with the San Francisco Zen Center and its assistant priest, Dainen Katagiri Roshi, visited them on several occasions. In 1972 the group extended an invitation to Katagiri Roshi to become the leader of a new Zen center they were establishing. He accepted, and the Minnesota Zen Center was formed in January 1973.

Katagiri Roshi was born in Japan in 1928 and became a Zen monk in 1946. He trained at Eiheji Monastery, the original center of the Soto Shu Sect. He came to the United States in 1963 to work with the Japanese-American Soto Buddhists and was assigned to their Los Angeles temple. After five months, however, he was sent to San Francisco to assist Shunryu Suzuki Roshi in both the San Francisco temple (Sokoji) and the independent Zen Center of San Francisco. While there, he assisted in the opening of the Tassajara Zen Mountain Center.

Since coming to Minneapolis, Katagiri Roshi has attracted students throughout the Midwest among whom affiliated centers have emerged. In 1978 the center purchased 280 acres in southeastern Minnesota and has begun construction of a year-round center for intensive Zen practice.

The center is governed by a board of directors which is elected at the annual meeting of members. There are three categories of membership--associate, general and voting-- but only the latter may vote at the annual meetings. Katagiri Roshi is consulted in an advisory capacity on the center's administrative affairs.

Membership: In 1984 the American Zen College reported 2,500 members at its three centers.

Educational facilities: Hokyo-ji (Catching the Moon Zen Monastic Center), Houston, Minnesota.

Periodicals: *Udumbara*, 3343 East Calhoun Parkway, Minneapolis, MN 55408; *MZMC Newsletter*, 3343 East Calhoun Parkway, Minneapolis, MN 55408.

★1280★
RINZAI-JI, INC.
2245 W. 25th St.
Los Angeles, CA 90018

Rinzai-Ji, Inc., is an association of Zen centers in the Rinzai tradition which began in 1968 with the founding of the Cimarron Zen Center in Los Angeles by Joshu Sasaki Roshi. Sasaki Roshi had received his Inka, acknowledgement of his accomplishments as a student, by Joten Miura, later to become leader of the Myoshinji sect of Rinzai Zen in Japan. Sasaki Roshi left the monastery he headed in Japan to come to America in 1962. Rinzai-Ji began as a gathering of students who had responded to his several years of teaching in Southern California. In 1970 a second center began in Redondo Beach, California and that same year the main training center was opened on Mt. Baldy, north of Los Angeles. Sasaki Roshi continued an active schedule visiting centers, training students and lecturing around the United States and other centers developed in the East and in Puerto Rico (1983). A Canadian center in Vancouver can be traced to a group which formed in response to talks given by Sasaki Roshi in 1967. A set of lectures in Austria in 1979 led to the first European affiliated center being formed. Each center of Rinzai-Ji offers an intensive program of zazen ("sitting with the master") and periodic sesshin ("extended sitting meditation"). All are headed by individuals trained by Sasaki Roshi.

Membership: Not reported. In 1985 there were 10 center in the United States and one each in Puerto Rico, Canada and Austria.

Periodicals: *Center of Gravity*, Jemez Bodhi Mandala, Box 8, Jemez Springs, NM 87025

Sources: Joshu Sasaki, *Buddha Is the Center of Gravity*. San Cristobal, NM: Lama Foundation, 1974;

★1281★
SOTO MISSION
Zenshuji Soto Mission
123 S. Hewitt St.
Los Angeles, CA 90012

The Soto Mission is the oldest presently existing Zen group in the United States and is the outgrowth of the work of the Rev. Hosen Isobe, bishop of the North American Mission. Of all the Zen bodies in America, this group has the closest connection with the parent body in Japan. In America, it operates primarily among the Japanese-American community. In comparison with other Zen groups, it is the least Americanized and still does much instruction and prints literature in the mother tongue.

Since its founding in Hawaii in 1915, it has spread throughout the Islands and in 1972 had ten temples. In the continental United States, from the original Zenshuji Mission, centers have spread along the coast and have become the source for other Zen groups, most notably the Zen Center of San Francisco and the Minnesota Zen Meditation Center in Minneapolis.

Zen, like other religions imported from India and the Orient, carries with it a variety of cultural peculiarities, which can pose problems in an occidental environment, as, for instance, language barriers. Other cultural conflicts derive from the extreme authority system of the Japanese monasteries, a cultural form incompatible with individualism of a democratic society. Finally, there is the racial barrier between the Japanese- American community and its Caucasian neighbors, a barrier accentuated by the conflict of World War II. Like other Buddhist groups, Zen bodies tend to be either all Japanese or all Caucasian.

Membership: In 1983 the Soto Mission in Hawaii reported 1,150 members attached to the single center in Honolulu. There are six other Soto temples in Hawaii. California has two Soto Missions, one in Los Angeles and one in San Francisco.

Sources: Ernest Hunt, *Gleanings from Soto-Zen*. Honolulu, HI: The Author, 1953; *A Short Manual of Soto Zen Buddhism*. Tokyo: The Evangelization Department of the Soto Zen Sect, 1962.

★1282★
SOTO ZEN CHURCH
Shasta Abbey
Box 478
Mount Shasta, CA 96067

The Soto Zen Church was established as the Sojiji Foreign Guest Department of the Dai Hon Zen Sojiji, a Soto monastery at Yokohama. It was founded in 1963 to specialize in teaching non-Japanese who wished to enter the Buddhist priesthood. The previous year Jiyu Kennett, an English woman raised as a Buddhist, entered Dai Hon Zen Sojiji. Kennett Roshi rose to the rank of abbess, received the Sei degree (equivalent to a doctor of divinity) and became head of the department. In 1969, the entire organization was moved to San Francisco and became known as the Zen Mission Society. Mt. Shasta (California) Abbey was founded in Novemeber 1970 and the headquarters of the Mission moved there. In 1971, the society declared its temporal independence from its Japanese affiliates, although there is still an unofficial fraternal tie.

Kennett Roshi had a commission to train and ordain others in the priesthood, and the prime thrust of the Soto Zen Church, the name by which the society is currently known, has been to train persons for the Soto Zen Buddhist priesthood. The religious traditions are preserved, but a Western environment is evident. A complete course of study in Theravada and Soto Zen Buddhism is offered, which includes music and temple administration skills. The Church is among those Zen groups which place most emphasis on their Buddhist heritage. Along with zazen, a thorough training in the teachings of Buddha according to Theravada Buddhism is stressed (a strict, monastic Buddhism). A pupil lives full-time at the Shasta monastery.

The publication of Kennett Roshi's several books, her lecture tours, and the development of trained leaders at Shasta has contributed to the growth of a number of affiliated centers. Branch communities are located in Berkeley, Columbia, and Santa Barbara, California; Eugene and Portland, Oregon; and Hexham, England. Meditation groups are located in Eureka, Ukiah, Sacramento, Palo Alto, California; Klamath Falls and Roseburg, Oregon; Seattle, Washington; Kalispell, Montana; and Vancouver and Edmonton, Canada.

Membership: Not reported. In 1985 there were 17 centers in North America.

Periodicals: *The Journal of Shasta Abbey*, Box 478, Mount Shasta, CA 96067; *Berkeley Buddhist Priory Newsletter*, 1358 Marin Avenue, Albany, CA 94706.

Sources: Jiyu Kennett, *Zen Is Eternal Life*. Emeryville, CA: Dharma Publishing, 1976; Jiyu Kennett, *How to Grow a Lotus Blossom*. Mount Shasta, CA: Shasta Abbey, 1977; Jiyu Kennett, *The Wild, White Goose*. Mount Shasta, CA: Shasta Abbey, 1977-78. 2 Vols.; *Zen Meditation*. Mount Shasta, CA: Shasta Abbey Press, 1980; *Zen Training*. Mount Shasta, CA: Shasta Abbey, 1982.

★1283★
ZEN BUDDHIST TEMPLE OF CHICAGO
2230 N. Halsted
Chicago, IL 60614

The largest Zen center in the Midwest is the Zen Buddhist Temple of Chicago, a Soto center established by Rev. Soyu Matsuoka in the late 1950s. The major activity of the group is the meditation service, which includes a lecture by one of the priests. Matsuoka was sent to the United States and served as a priest in California before coming to Chicago. The current head of the Chicago center is the Rev. Kongo Langlois. The Rev. Dale Ver-Kuilen is the instructor at the Long Beach Temple, and Matsuoka Roshi remains as spiritual leader of both. Small groups associated with the Chicago Temple can be found in the states surrounding Lake Michigan. Matsuoka opened a center in Detroit, Michigan in 1973.

Membership: Not reported.

Periodicals: *Diamond Sword*, 2230 N. Halsted Street, Chicago, IL 60614.

★1284★
ZEN CENTER OF LOS ANGELES
923 S. Normandie Ave.
Los Angeles, CA 90006

The Zen Center of Los Angeles was formed in 1967 by a group of students under the leadership of Hakuyu Taizan Maezumi Roshi, a Zen master formerly with the Zenshuji Soto Mission in Los Angeles. The inspiration for the center came from Hakuun Yasutani Roshi's visits in the early 1960s. The Los Angeles center supports a variety of activities including daily zazen, weekly lectures by Maezumi Roshi or one of his associates, and beginning classes. Center members also attend dokusan (master/student interviews) and monthly sesshin (extended "sitting" meditation). A residence program allows a few students to live at the center.

During the 1970s, the Center developed a vigorous publishing program and Maezumi Roshi developed a following across the United States. Groups affiliated with the Zen Center of Los Angeles developed in Arizona, Oregon, Utah and New York. Two rural centers at Mt. Tremper, New York and Mountain Center, California provide accomodations for more intensive Zen practice. The Kuroda Institute develops programs aimed at the academic community. Internationally, affiliated centers have emerged in England, Mexico and the Netherlands.

Membership: Not reported. In 1985 there were 11 centers in the United States and 5 foreign centers.

Periodicals: *Ten Directions*, 923 South Normandie Avenue, Los Angeles, CA 90006.

Sources: Hakuyu Taizan Maezumi and Bernard Tetsugen Glassman, eds., *On Zen Practice*. Los Angeles: Zen Center of Los Angeles, 1976. 2 vols.; Hakuyu Taizan Maezumi and Bernard Tetsugen Glassman, eds., *The Hazy Moon of Enlightenment*. Los Angeles: Zen Center of Los Angeles, 1977; John Daishin Buksbazen, *To Forget the Self*. Los Angeles: Zen Center of California, 1977.

★1285★
ZEN CENTER OF ROCHESTER
Arnold Park
Rochester, NY 14607

The Zen Center of Rochester grew out of and is still largely centered upon the experience of Philip Kapleau. Kapleau had encountered Zen while in Japan as a war crimes trial court reporter. Further spurred by the lectures of lay scholar Daisetz Teitaro Suzuki at Columbia University, he returned to Japan and studied under Soen Nakagawa Roshi, who assigned the "Mu" koan discussed earlier in this chapter. Kapleau later studied at the Soto monastery at Hoshinji. After five years, Kapleau experienced kensho, a deep mystic enlightenment, and followed it with eight more years of training. In 1966, he was sanctioned as a teacher of Zen.

At this same time, Kapleau published one of the most influential Zen books, *The Three Pillars of Zen*. There is strong emphasis on koan work, as well as the zazen meditation of his Rinzai training (with elements of Soto). Zazen means sitting still with a one-pointed stabilized mind.

The Rochester Center was founded in 1966 under Kapleau's leadership. The center grew steadily, and in 1970 a permanent center was dedicated. In 1968, *Zen Bow* began as a quarterly publication. Affiliates of the Rochester Center are located in the Chicago, Denver, and Santa Fe. Foreign affiliates are located in Montreal, Toronto, Mexico City, Stockholm, Warsaw, and Berlin.

Membership: In 1984 there were 520 members in the United States and an additional 180 members worldwide. There are 11 centers and four priests.

Periodicals: *Zen Bow*, Arnold Park, Rochester, NY 14607.

Sources: Philip Kapleau, *Three Pillars of Zen*. Garden City, NY: Doubleday, 1980; Philip Kapleau, *Zen: Dawn in the West*. 1981 ; Philip Kapleau, *To Cherish All Life*. San Francisco: Harper & Row, 1982; Philip Kapleau, ed., *The Wheel of Death*. New York: Harper & Row, 1971; Albert Low, *The Iron Cow of Zen*. Wheaton, IL: Theosophical Publishing House, 1985.

★1286★
ZEN CENTER OF SAN FRANCISCO
300 Page St.
San Francisco, CA 94102

The Zen Center of San Francisco dates from 1959 when students began to gather around the newly arrived Shunryu Suzuki Roshi, head of the Sokoji Temple, the Soto Mission in San Francisco. Apart from the Japanese-Americans who regularly attended, the temple was home to an English-speaking group which had been influenced by the Rinzai-oriented First Zen Institute in New York. After Suzuki Roshi arrived and his English-speaking abilities were recognized, the group began to grow as others, many from the beatnik, hippie and (later) the drug-culture communities, discoved Zen. Emphasis was placed upon zazen and the experience to be derived through it.

From the beginning, the English-speaking practitioners developed a life separate from the Japanese-American group, and gradually emerged as a distinct organization. In 1967 the group purchased the Tassajara Springs in Carmel Valley, California as the site for a rural center, more accomodating to intensive and monastic Zen experiences. In 1969 a large building in San Francisco was purchased as a headquarters for these living in the city. Finally in 1972, Green Gulch Farm in Marin County was purchased and Green Dragon Zen Temple created. Members residing at the farm can both follow an intense Zen practice as well as work on growing organic produce. Products from the farm are marketed in the city at a grocery across the street from the city center. Other affiliated centers have emerged in cities around Northern California including Monterey, Berkeley, Los Altos and Mill Valley.

In 1971, Suzuki Roshi died and was succeeded as chief priest and abbott of the Zen Center by an American disciple, Zentatsu Myoyu Roshi-Richard Baker. Baker left the center in 1983, at which time the control of the center was assumed by the board and the several priests.

Membership: Not reported. In the 1970s over 300 people were associated with the city center in San Francisco and approximately 50 lived at Green Gulch.

Periodicals: *Wind Bell*, 300 Page Street, San Francisco, CA 94102.

Remarks: In 1983 a major crisis was experienced by the Zen Center of San Francisco when Baker Roshi was asked to step down because of sexual improprieties. He first took a year's leave of absence and them severed all connection with the center. The scandal became public at the same time that several other Eastern religious leaders in America were also being accused of similiar conduct. Having ackowledged the seriousness of the affair, the center's leaders assumed control and guided the center through the period of transition.

Sources: Edward Espe Brown, *The Tassajara Bread Book*. Boulder, CO: Shambhala, 1970; Shunryu Suzuki, *Zen Mind, Beginner's Mind*, New York: Westherhill, 1970; Kathy Butler, "Events are the Teacher" in *COEvolution* no. 40 (Winter 1983), pp. 112-123.

★1287★
ZEN STUDIES SOCIETY
223 E. 67th St.
New York, NY 10021

The Zen Studies Society grew out of the work of Daisetz Teitaro Suzuki, a lay scholar credited with helping to bring Zen to America. The Zen Studies Society was founded in 1956 to promote Zen Buddhism as Suzuki had articulated it in his writings and lectures at Columbia University. The founder, Cornelius Cane, died in 1962 (by which time Suzuki had returned to Japan), and the Society became largely inactive. In 1964, members of the zendo made contact with Eido Tai Shimano (b.1932), who had settled in New York. Eido Tai Shimano, a monk who had worked with the Diamond Sangha, became president of the New York zendo in 1965. The zendo had by this time shifted its program from scholarship and study of Zen to the practice of Zen. (A zendo is a place set aside for Zen meditation and study.) Philadelphia and Washington, D.C. groups developed independently in the early 1960s and affiliated with the Zen Studies Society.

In 1960, Shuntetsu Koshi, a monk, came to study at the Philadelphia Quaker center, Pendle Hill. Zen meetings began to be held in a member's home and to grow with the aid of occasional visits by Hakuun Yasutani Roshi. Among the first to join the group was Dr. Albert J. Stunkard, who had served as an army physician in post-World War II Japan and had studied at Engaku-ji Monastery. In 1965, the Philadelphia zendo affiliated with the Zen Studies Society. In 1966, a schism was occasioned by a movement of the zendo to a more central location. The Korean priest, Dr. Kyung Bo Seo, who had led the zendo for a year, remained at the old location and retained his former students. The Philadelphia zendo had approximately 20 members (as of 1970) and no regular leader.

The third arm of Zen Studies Society began with Mervine Rosen who in 1961 attended sessions with Soen Nakagawa Roshi at the home of Dr. Bernard Phillips in Wilmington, Delaware. (Dr. Phillips was an officer of the New York zendo.) Mr. Rosen, after a year in Tokyo studying with Yasutian Roshi, settled in Washington. A number of students began to meet together after a session by Yasutani Roshi in Leesburg, Virginia, in the summer of 1963, and, in the fall, a Washington Zen group, which soon affiliated with the Zen Studies Society, was formed. It had approximately 10 members, as of the mid-1970s.

Zazen and walking meditation are central to the life of Zen Studies Society and members have ample opportunities for regular sessions with supplemental weekend retreats the third weekend of each month and longer sessions each summer. Buddhist holy days are also observed. At the New York zendo, the spiritual center of the society, public meetings are held regularly from which new members are drawn. Their number is limited by consideration of space in the zendo and the number of students a teacher can personally instruct. The New York zendo has approximately 125 students.

Associated with the New York zendo is the Dai Bosatsu Zendo Kongo Ji, a monastery in the Catskill Mountains in New York. At the time of its founding, it was the only monastery in the U.S. that offers full-time traditional Zen monastic life in a Japanese-style temple.

Membership: Not reported. There are several hundred students connected with the society.

Periodicals: *Dharma Season*, 223 East 67th Street, New York, NY 10021.

Sources: *Daily Sutras for Chanting and Recitation*. New York: New York Zendo of the Zen Studies Society, n.d.; Eido Shimano, *Golden Wind*. Tokyo: Japan Publications, 1979; Eido Shimano, ed., *Like a Dream, Like a Fantasy*. Tokyo: Japan Publications, 1978.

Chinese Buddhism

★1288★
BUDDHA'S UNIVERSAL CHURCH
702 Washington St.
San Francisco, CA 94108

The largest of the Buddhist organizations centered upon the San Francisco Chinese community is Buddha's Universal Church, founded in the late 1920s in Chinatown. The church is currently housed in a million-dollar temple begun during the 1950s and dedicated in 1963. It is the largest in the continental United States and contains the first mosaic image of Buddha.

Among the founders of Buddha's Universal Church was the late Dr. Paul F. Fung, a physician, a Doctor of the Dharma, and vice-president of the World Fellowship of Buddhists. Currently the church is led by Dr. George D. Fung and Dr. Frederick Hong. Outstanding scholarly leadership has enabled the church to become an American Buddhist intellectual center which now houses a fine library and research facility. A project of translating Buddhist texts eventuated in the publication of *The Sutra of the Sixth Patriarch of the Pristine Orthodox Dharma* in 1964, the first of several projected volumes.

Public services are held every second and fourth Sunday at 2:30 and 3:00 p.m. and include a lecture and tour. On the roof is a garden with a Bodhi tree, grown from a cutting of the tree under which Buddha sat, and a lotus-shaped pool.

Membership: The are approximately 300 members of the church at the single center in San Francisco.

Sources: Paul F. Fung and George D. Fung, trans., *The Sutra of the Sixth Patriarch on the Pristine Orthodox Dharma*. San Francisco: Buddha's Universal Church, 1964; Frederick Hong and George D. Fung, trans., *Pristine Orthodox Dharma*. San Francisco: Buddha's Universal Church, 1977.

★1289★
BUDDHA'S UNIVERSAL CHURCH AND CH'AN BUDDHIST SANGHA
Current address not obtained for this edition.

Buddha's Universal Church was founded in the 1960s by the Rev. Dr. Calvin C. Vassallo, in Houston, Texas. The church was eclectic and drew upon all of the Buddhist traditions, though the Chinese was preferred. According to Vassallo, the church teaches truth, the common denominator of all religion and philosophy. Truth is universal, and is to non-Buddhists equated with "God." Truth is your father; from truth you were born and from the truth you must go into your savior, the Buddha. Great emphasis was placed on the four basic truths and the noble eightfold path, and a codified presentation of Buddha's teachings.

During the 1970s the Church was located in Houston, but in recent years abandoned its former facilities. During the 1970s it carried on an active program. Worship was centered upon the daily family worship before the family shrine. Sunday services were adopted from the Buddhist Churches of America (Japanese Shin). Adjacent to the Houston headquarters was a nunnery headed by Mother Superior Samma Yasodhara. A Department of Buddhist Education offered courses in T'ai Chi Chuan (Chinese yoga), Buddhism and Kung-Fu; in addition, there was an active social program reaching the needy in Houston through the city's welfare agencies.

Sources: *Truth: An Outline of the Buddhist Churches and Sangha*. Houston, TX: Buddha's Universal Church, 1971.

★1290★
BUDDHIST ASSOCIATION OF THE UNITED STATES
3070 Albany Cresent
New York, NY 10463

The largest of the Buddhist organizations centered in the old Chinese community of New York City is the Buddhist Association of the United States, formed in 1964. An active program presents a varied format attempting a synthesis of several Buddhist trends. The two most important are Ch'an, the Chinese form of Zen, and Pure Land Buddhism, which centers on the worship of Amida Buddha. A library is open to the public, and the Sunday schedule includes meditation, a lecture and discussion. The Association is led by President Log To and Vice

President C. T. Shen. Shen is a popular author and has lectured widely in the East on Buddhism. There are approximately 150 adherents. A number of pamphlets have been produced.

Membership: Not reported. In the 1970s there were approximately 150 adherents.

Sources: C. T. Shen, *A Glimpse of Buddhism*. Taipei, Taiwan: Torch of Wisdom, 1970; C. T. Shin, *What We Can Learn from Buddhism*. Taipei, Taiwan: Torch of Wisdom Publishing House, 1975; Narada Thera, *An Outline of Buddhism*. Bronx, NY: Buddhist Association in the United States, n.d.; T'an Hsu, *On Amidism*. Bronx, NY: Buddhist Association of the United States, 1973; *The Enlightenment Sutra with Annotations*. Bronx, NY: Buddhist Association of the United States, 1955.

★1291★

CHINESE BUDDHIST ASSOCIATION
42 Kawananake Place
Honolulu, HI 96817

The Chinese Buddhist Association, established in 1955 at the suggestion of the Hong Kong Chinese Buddhist Association, received Abbot Sic Tse Ting the following year. The temple in Honolulu has a ten-foot, gold-leaf statue of Buddha as a center of worship; the life of Buddha is depicted on its walls.

Membership: In 1982 there were 1,300 members in one center.

★1292★

CHUNG FU KUAN (TAOIST SANCTUARY)
6020 Craner Ave.
North Hollywood, CA 91606

The Chung Fu Kuan (Inner Truth Looking Place), popularly known as the Taoist Sanctuary, was formed in the 1960s by Dr. Khigh Alx Dhiegh, since 1935 a student of I Ching, the ancient art of Chinese divination. Dhiegh is known to television audiences as a popular character actor. The Sanctuary draws its inspiration from the philosophy of Lao-Tzu, an older contemporary of Confucius.. A lower government official, he became discouraged and abandoned his post. According to tradition, as he was about to leave China, he was asked to write down his teachings. The result was the Tao Te Ching, the chief scripture of Taoism.

Tao (the Way of the universe) is harmony. When events and things are allowed to move naturally, harmony is the result. The chief aim of human existence is to attain fullness of life by attaining harmony with the Tao. The result of Taoist thinking is "Wu-wei," a quietistic, non-interfering style of life. Politically, Wu-wei finds its best expression in laissez-faire and the ideal self- contained village state. The balance of the two forces into yin and yang, encompassing the bsic polarities of the universe, is

also crucial. As Taoism developed, divination emerged as a major practice. The most popular form of divining the future was the I Ching.

The I Ching is built upon a series of trigrams, each a combination of two primary forms-the yang-hsiao, a straight line, the symbol of the male or positive principle, and the yin-hsiao, a broken line, the symbol of the female or negative principle. The two symbols can be arranged into eight different trigrams, and the trigrams can form sixty-four hexagrams. Each hexagram has been ascribed symbolic meanings, correlating with the eight fundamental elements or factors in the universe and sixty-four phenomena in the universe. Together, the hexagrams represent symbolically all the possible situations of creation. They may tell a person to do something or not to do it; to change or not to change, etc.

Associated with the Sanctuary is the International I Ching Studies Institute. Dr. Dhiegh has written a modern commentary on the I Ching, *The Eleventh Wing*. Ceremony-teaching services are regularly held on the first and third Sunday and gatherings on the first and third Friday. Taoist meditation occurs on Wednesday nights. The Institute offers Kung-fu, T'ai Chi Chuan (Chinese yoga) and courses in Chinese herbal practices.

Membership: In 1984 there were approximately 100 members in four centers: North Hollywood, San Diego, and Santa Barbara, California and Tempe, Arizona.

Sources: Khigh Alx Dhiegh, *The Eleventh Wing*. New York: Delta Books, 1973; Robert Meyers, "Khigh Dhiegh Digs I Ching" *in TV Guide*, (February 20, 1971), pp. 45-48.

★1293★

DHARMA REALM BUDDHIST ASSOCIATION
City of Ten Thousand Buddhas
Talmage, CA 95481

The Dharma Realm Buddhist Association was founded as the Sino-American Buddhist Association in 1959 by disciples of Tripitaka Master Hsuan Hua. In 1962 he moved from Hong Kong to San Francisco at their invitation. In 1968 the Buddhist Lecture Hall was established as a center for the study and practice of orthodox Buddhism in the West. Originally founded by Chinese-Americans, the center quickly attracted a large Caucasian membership. The organization expanded rapidly. The Gold Mountain Monastery in San Francisco was opened in 1970; the International Institute for the Translation of Buddhist Texts was founded in 1973; and the City of Ten Thousand Buddhas, a international study center for western Buddhists, opened in 1976. A center, Gold Wheel Monastery, was opened in Los Angeles in 1976.

Master Hsuan Hua had been a longtime student of Master Hsu Yun in China. He moved to Hong Kong after the

Maoist Revolution in 1949. In accepting the invitation to come to the West, he did so with the intention of establishing Buddhism in its entirety. Among the young converts to Buddhism attracted to the lecture hall, he accepted some into monastic vows. In 1969 five disciples went to Taiwan to receive final ordination as bhikshus (monks) and bhikshunis (nuns), and by 1972 there were ten fully-ordained monks and several novices preparing for ordination.

The Dharma Realm Buddhist Association, though based in the Ch'an (Zen) school of Chinese Buddhism, teaches all five main varieties of Chinese Buddhism. New members accept Chinese Buddhist names. Lay members have "Kuo" as part of their name; those destined for the priesthood who received their novice vows from Master Hsuan Hua have "Heng" added to their name; and the fully-ordained monks receive the surname "Shih," the first character of the Chinese word, Sakyamuni (Gautama Buddha). Each new member takes the Three Refuges (a ceremony similar to Christian confirmation, by which the new member promises to take refuge in the Buddha, the Dharma or teachings of Buddha, and the Sangha).

The Association has emphasized the development of a Buddhist monastic community, an element of Buddhist life frequently missing in Western Buddhist organizations, and over 50 persons have entered the orders. Monastics lead a very disciplined life of practice and study. They are strict vegetarians and do not eat before noon. The program emphasizes Sutra study (including language studies and translation, lectures and chanting) and meditation.

The Dharma Realm Buddhist University was the first Buddhist university to be established in the Western World. It offers degreed courses in Buddhist studies, letters and science, and the creative and applied arts. It is located in the City of 10,000 Buddhas near Talmage, California. Through the Sangha Training and Lay Training Programs, the Buddhist equivalent of seminary education is offers for Buddhist leaders. Since its founding in 1973 the International Institute for the Translation of Buddhist Texts has become a major publisher of Buddhist literature. Managed by both Sangha (clergy) and lay scholars under the guidance of Hsuan Hua, it had by 1980 published translations of over 100 volumes of Chinese Buddhist writings in various Western languages.

Membership: In 1984 the Association reported 20,000 members in six centers served by 50 ministers.

Educational facilities: Dharma Realm Buddhist University, Talmage, California.

Periodicals: *Vajra Bodhi Sea*, Gold Mountain Monastery, 1731 15th Street, San Francisco, CA 94103; *The Proper Dharma Seal*, City of Ten Thousand Buddhas, Box 217, Talmage, CA 95481.

Sources: Heng Yin, comp., *Records of the Life of the Venerable Master Hsuan Hua*. San Francisco: Committee for the Publication of the Biography of the Venerable Master Hsuan Hua, 1973, 1975. 2 Vols.; Hsuan Hua, *Buddha Root Farm*. San Francisco: Buddhist Text Translation Society, 1976; *World Peace Gathering*. San Francisco: Sino-American Buddhist Association, 1975; Hsuan Hua, *The Ten Dharma-Realms Are Not Beyond a Single Thought*. San Francisco: Buddhist Text Translation Society, 1976.

★1294★
EAST WEST FOUNDATION
17 Station St.
Brookline, MA 02147

Michio Kushi (b.1926), a student of George Ohsawa (1893-1966), the founder of Macrobiotics, came to the United States in 1949 and became active in the spread of its philosophy. Initially working through the Ohsawa Foundation (now the George Ohsawa Macrobiotic Foundation) headquartered in California, Kushi developed an independent following in New England. After Ohsawa's death, Kushi founded The Order of the Universe Publications and in 1967 began to issue a periodical, *The Order of the Universe*. In 1972 Kushi founded the East West Foundation to oversee the spread of the work of presenting macrobiotics to the public and nurturing the growing number of people who had accepted macrobiotic principles and practice. In 1979 the Kushi Institute was founded to train leaders in the movement.

Kushi's teachings are summarized in a set of theorems and principles which define the nature of yin and yang, the prime differentiation within the universe. All phenomena is composed of a complex of these two polar opposites and macrobiotics defines and assists individuals in relating to the yin-yang composition of the universe. While a major component of macrobiotic philosophy relates to developing a balanced diet, the philosophy encompasses every area of life, as spelled out in numerous publications by the Kushi and the Foundation.

Membership: Not reported. In 1984 there were 13 affiliated East West Foundations in the United States and associated centers in Canada and Germany. A directory of the larger macrobiotic movement listed over 400 individuals, businesses, and centers promoting the teachings.

Educational facilities: Kushi Institute, Brookline, Massachusetts.

Periodicals: *East West Journal*, 17 Station Street, Brookline, MA 02147.

Sources: Michio Kushi with Stephen Blauer, *The Macrobiotic Way*. Wayne, NJ: Avery Publishing Group, 1985; Michio Kushi, *The Book of Macrobiotics*. Tokyo:

Japan Publications, 1977; Michio Kushi, *The Teachings of Michio Kushi*. Boston, MA: East West Foundation, 1971. 2 Vols.; Jean Charles Kohler and Mary Alice Kohler, *Healing Miracles from Macrobiotics*. West Nyack, NY: Parker Publishing Co., 1979.

★1295★
EASTERN STATES BUDDHIST ASSOCIATION OF AMERICA
64 Mott St.
New York, NY 10013

The Eastern States Buddhist Association of America was founded in 1963 as the first New York-area Chinese temple with a priest in attendance. Largely through the help of Mrs. James Ying, the program has grown and developed. In 1971 Dharma Master Bhikshu Hsi Ch'en, who had escaped China when the Communists took over, was brought to the United States to head the Temple Mahayana, an Association retreat center in the Catskill Mountains in New York.

The Eastern States Buddhist Association follows the T'ien-t'ai school founded by Chih-i (558-597), a monk at Mount T'ien- t'ai in China. The members emphasize the Lotus Sutra as inclusive of all Buddha's teachings. Meditation, the study of the Sutras, repeating the name of Amitabha Buddha, and living a disciplined life are emphasized.

Membership: Not reported.

★1296★
GEORGE OHSAWA MACROBIOTIC FOUNDATION
Box 426
Oroville, CA 95965

Closely related to Taoism is macrobiotics, a philosophy developed by George Ohsawa (Yukikazu Sahurazawa) (1893-1966) drawing on Zen, Taoism and Chinese wisdom philosophy. Macrobiotics is based on the concept of yin and yang. All things are differentiated apparatus of one Infinity. Yin and yang are the poles of the Infinity's bifurcation. Everything changes. Yin is centrifugal and yang centripetal. By their attraction and repulsion, energy and all phenomena are produced. All things are made of unequal proportions of yin and yang. All physical forms are yang (male) at the center and yin (female) at the surface.

The object of macrobiotics, for the individual, is to balance the yin and yang as far as possible in one's life. As for diet, one ideally eats foods which are balanced-- cereals and brown rice being good examples. One also learns to live in harmony with the environment.

Macrobiotics was introduced into the West in France by Ohsawa in the 1920s and it gradually spread through Europe. By the time of his death, macrobiotic centers could be found in Belgium, England, Germany, Italy,

Spain, and Sweden. From the center in Japan work had also spread to Brazil and Viet Nam. Macrobiotic teachings spread to America after World War II. During the 1950s, Herman Aihara, a student of Ohsawa's from Japan, migrated to the United States. He founded the Ohsawa Foundation, since renamed the George Ohsawa Macrobiotic Foundation, the first Macrobiotic organization in North America, and in 1961 began a periodical, *Yin Yang*. The Foundation, through its publications and sponsoring of lecturers, became the focus of the early spread of macrobiotic teachings, and continue as one of two national associations of people devoted to macrobiotic principles.

Membership: Not reported. In 1984 there were over 50 centers of activity reported in a foundation directory in the United States and Canada.

Periodicals: *Macrobiotics Today*, Box 426, Oroville, CA 95965.

Sources: George Ohsawa, *Zen Macrobiotics*. Los Angeles: Ohsawa Foundation, 1965; George Ohsawa, *Guidebook for Living*. Los Angeles: Ohsawa Foundation, 1967; George Ohsawa, *The Book of Judgment*. Los Angeles: Ohsawa Foundation, 1966; George Oshawa, *Practical Guide to Far Eastern Macrobiotic Medicine*. Oroville, CA: George Ohsawa Macrobiotic Foundation, 1976; Herman Aihara, *Seven Macrobiotuic Principles*. San Francisco: George Ohsawa Macrobiotic Foundation, 1973.

★1297★
HAWAII CHINESE BUDDHIST SOCIETY
1614 Nuuanu Ave.
Honolulu, HI 96817

In 1953, a number of Chinese-American residents in Hawaii decided to take advantage of the movement of the many Buddhist monks into Hong Kong after the Maoist revolution and to establish work under their leadership. The initial Hawaiian group divided between those who wished to choose the monks from among their acquaintances and those who wished the Hong Kong Chinese Buddhist Association to select the most qualified.

The Hawaii Chinese Buddhist Society chose to make its own selection and brought the Reverend Chuen Wai from Hong Kong to head the temple in Honolulu. He was joined in 1957 by Dharma Master Tsu Yin. They emphasize the Buddhist nature of the society, as opposed to the Taoist influence in some temples. All the statues are of traditional Buddhist bodhisattvas-Omito (Amida), Kwan Yin, Wei Ton (sometimes called General Wei Ton), who was asked by Buddha to protect Buddhist teachings, and Tay Chong Wong, the god of wisdom.

Membership: In 1982 there were 1,000 members in one center in Honolulu.

★1298★
KWAN YIN TEMPLE
170 N. Vineyard St.
Honolulu, HI 96817

The oldest Chinese temple in America is the Kwan Yin Temple begun by Leong Dick Ying, a monk who in 1878 brought to Hawaii two gold-leaf statues--the Taoist Kwan Tai and the Buddhist Kwan Yin, the goddess of mercy. A temple was built in Chinatown in Honolulu and, after several moves, in 1921 found a permanent home on Vineland Street in Honolulu. Along with the statue of Kwan Yin, there are several statues of other deities.

The festival year which regulates the life of the various temples is followed at the Kwan Yin Temple. The Chinese New Year is the biggest festival. In late summer, the Chinese girls pay tribute to the Weaver Maid, who finally married the man she loved. The Chinese Moon Festival (August 15), the winter solstice, and the anniversary of the founding of the Chinese Republic (October 10) are also celebrated.

Membership: In 1982 the temple reported 850 members.

★1299★
SHRINE OF THE ETERNAL BREATH OF TAO
117 Stonehave Way
Los Angeles, CA 90049

The Shrine of the Eternal Breath of Tao was founded by Master Ni, Hua-Ching, who began his study of Taoism as a child in China. After the Chinese Revolution, he moved to Taiwan and continued his studies. Eventually he became a teacher of Taoism and its related martial and healing arts. During the 1970s he moved to the United States and began to teach in Los Angeles.

Master Ni teaches the universal law of subtle energy response. Everything in the universe is a manifestation of energy in either its grosser or its more subtle states. Understanding and developing the proper response to the energies of one's environment will bring harmony to one's life. The practice of Taoist meditation, martial arts (king fu and t'ai chi ch'uan), and medical practices (acupuncture and herbs) assist in attaining a balanced relationship to life. The universal law of response is basic to all spiritual practices.

Membership: Not reported. In 1982 the shrine had two centers, one in Los Angeles and one in Malibu, California. There were an estimated 100 members.

Educational facilities: College of Tao and Traditional Chinese Healing, Los Angeles.

Sources: Hua-Ching Ni, *Tao, the Subtle Universal Law and the Integral Way of Life*. Malibu, CA: Shrine of the Eternal Breath of Tao, 1982.

Korean Buddhism

★1300★
AMERICAN ZEN COLLEGE
16815 Germantown Road (Route 18)
Germantown, MD 20767

The American Zen College began in 1970 as Hui-Neng Zen at Easton, Pennsylvania. The temple was founded by Gosung Shin, the Seventy-seventh Patriarch in the Lin-Che lineage, a line of Zen masters which traces its origin to Buddha Sakyamuni. Gosung Shin had been an abbot in three Korean temples, but came to the United States in 1969 at the request of Zen Master Kyung Bo Seo to permanently establish the World Zen Center which Kyung-Bo-Seo had founded at Spruce Run Mt., Virginia. Shin studied at Harvard University briefly and in 1970 settled in Philadelphia where a Hui-Neng Zen Center Association developed as students gathered around him. In the spring of 1981, at the invitation of Mr. Paul Beidler, the group moved to Easton, Pennsylvania, and changed its name to the Hui-Neng Zen Temple. Soon outgrowing the facilities at Easton, the temple moved to a tract of land in rural New York, near Woodhull. The name was changed to the Kwan-Yin Zen Temple. There being no houses on the property, Shin and his followers lived in tents while the temple was being constructed. Eventually they developed a self-sufficient community supported by the proceeds of a health food store in Corning, New York.

Once the center at Woodhull became a stable and growing concern, Shin began a program of planned expansion. In 1977 an urban center opened in Washington and the following year a second rural center was established near Germantown, Maryland. The new name, American Zen College, was adopted and the focus of activity shifted from New York temple, which remains as a retreat center for advanced students.

The American Zen College center in Washington, D.C., serves primarily the large Korean community in the metropolitan area, while most non-Korean students live at the Seneca Lake Zen Center in Maryland. A daily schedule of chanting, recitation of the sutras, and meditation is followed at the centers, and, on Friday evenings at Seneca Lake, Shin leads a seven-hour period of extended meditation.

Membership: In 1984 the American Zen College reported 2,500 members at its three centers.

Periodicals: *Buddha World*, American Zen College, 16815 Germantown Road (Route 118), Germantown, Maryland 20767.

Sources: Gosung Shin, *Zen Teachings of Emptiness*. Washington, DC: American Zen College Press, 1982.

★1301★
KOREAN BUDDHIST BO MOON ORDER
% Rev. Bup Choon
Bul Sim Sa Temple
5011 N. Damen
Chicago, IL 60625

The Bo Moon Order is one of the eighteen registered Buddhist Orders in Korea. It came to the United States in 1979 when the Bul Sil Sa Temple was organized in Chicago. A second temple was organized in the Los Angeles suburb of Garden Grove in 1980.

Membership: Not reported.

★1302★
KOREAN BUDDHIST CHOGYE ORDER
Kwan Um Sa Temple
451 S. Serrano Ave.
Los Angeles, CA 90020

Not until the 1970s did significant numbers of Korean Buddhists migrate to the United States. Most of these were affiliated with the Chogye Order, the largest in Korea. In February 1973 the Thalmahsa Buddhist Monastery and temple was established in Los Angeles. It was soon followed a second Los Angeles temple and others which folloed in various California locations; Chicago; New York City; Tacoma, Washington; Detroit; and Honolulu. During the 1980s the number continues to grow. These temples are to be distinguished from those of the Kwan Um Zen School (from which they are organizationally separate) as they serve primarily first generation Korean-Americans.

Membership: Not reported. In 1984 there were 23 Chogye Order temples in the United States and three in Canada.

Sources: Baba Moo Har, ed., *Brief Introduction to Korean Buddhism.* Los Angeles: The Korean Buddhist Sangha Association of Western Territories in U.S.A., 1984.

★1303★
KWAN UM ZEN SCHOOL
K. B. C. Hong Poep Won
RFD No. 5
528 Pound Rd.
Cumberland, RI 02864

The Kwan Um Zen School was founded in 1983 to connect the various temples and centers previously founded by Master Seung Sahn Sunim. Soen Sa Nim, as he is generally referred to by his students, is the Seventy-eighth Patriarch in the Chogye Order. As a young man in Korea, he became deeply involved in radica politics but turned to Buddhism during World War II. He became a student of Zen Master Ko Bang and eventually abbot of two temples. After the war, he became a leader in the effort to revive the Chogye sect which had suffered much damage in the final years of Japanese occupation. In 1965

he traveled to Japan and during his stay founded three temples. In 1972 he came to the United States and began a small temple in Providence, Rhode Island. That temple became the headquarters from which he traveled around New England and across the United States. Early branch centers were established in New Haven, Cambridge, and New York City, followed by centers in Los Angeles and Berkeley.

Master Seung Sahn came to the United States with a missionary zeal to plant a new Buddhist tradition in the West. He emphasizes that the purposes of Zen area, first, to understand the True Self, i.e. attain Truth, and, then, to assist other people to attain the "Great Love, Great Compassion, Great Bodhisattva Way." Most people have a significant amount of karma which forms an obstacle to enlightenment, hence the necessity of masters and centers. Like the Japanese Rinzai masters, Seung Sahn uses the koan as a major teaching device. Besides the main practice of daily sitting meditation, each center associated with the school sponsored a silent three or seven day meditation retreat called Yong Maeng Jong Jin (to leap like a tiger while sitting), equivalent to the sesshin or extended meditation sessions at Japanese Zen centers.

The growth of the center in providence led to its purchase of a tract of land in rural Rhode Island upon which it developed a residential community and to which it eventually moved its headquarters. Throughout the early 1980s, Soen Sa Nim extended his travels and developed centers in South America and Europe, with special success in Poland.

Membership: In 1984 the Kwan Um Zen School reported fifteen centers and temples in the United States, seven in Poland and others in England, Spain, Brazil, and Canada.

Periodicals: *Primary Point*, K.B.C. Hong Poep Won, RFD, No. 5, 528 Pound Rd., Cumberland, RI 02864.

Sources: Seung Sahn, *Bone of Space.* San Francisco: Four Season's Foundation, 1982; Seung Sahn, *Dropping Ashes on the Buddha.* Edited by Stephen Mitchell. New York: Grove Press, 1976; Seung Sahn, *Only Don't Know.* San Francisco: Four Season's Foundation, 1982.

★1304★
ZEN LOTUS SOCIETY
Zen Buddhist Temple-Ann Arbor
1214 Packard Rd.
Ann Arbor, MI 48104

The Zen Lotus Society was founded in 1975 in Toronto, Ontario, but dates to the arrival in the United States of an independent Korean Zen monk, Samu Sunim (b. 1941). Samu Sunim was an orphan who became a Zen monk. Forced to choose between his pacifist beliefs and serving out his years in the army (required of all Korean youth), Samu Sunim deserted and fled to Japan. In 1967, with the aid of some friends, he migrated to New York City and began to teach meditation. In 1968 he moved to Montreal where he worked for the next few years improving his English. He also became a Canadian citizen and married. In 1972 he moved to Toronto where a Korean-Canadian community existed, but his initial plans to begin a center were frustrated by a lengthy illness. Only in 1975 did he resume his meditation schedule. By 1979 his support had grown to the point that a building could be purchased, and the Zen Buddhist Temple of Toronto was established and in 1980, incorporated.

In 1981 Alexander Lundquist was sent from Toronto to Ann Arbor, Michigan, to found a temple. The following year Samu Sunim ordained him a monk, with the name Sanbul Sunim. Later that year, the Zen Buddhist Temple-Ann Arbor was incorporated.

Both temples of the Zen Lotus Society conduct daily meditation sessions, instruct beginners in basic meditation, and hold regular weekend meditation retreats. Quarterly, Samu Sunim holds extended five-to seven-day retreats. Temple members are very active in social affairs and devote time to the peace movement. The society is developing a Buddhist Peace Cemetery. Members also participate in the Buddhists Concerned for Animals.

Membership: In 1984 the society reported three centers, one each in Canada, the United States, and Mexico. In the United States, there were 50 members with an additional 150 members in other centers.

Periodicals: *Spring Wind-Buddhist Educational Forum*, 1214 Packard Road, Ann Arbor, Michigan 48104.

Tibetan Buddhism

★1305★
AMERICAN BUDDHIST SOCIETY AND FELLOWSHIP, INC.
% Robert Ernest Dickhoff
600 W. 157th St.
New York, NY 10032

One of the oldest Tibetan Buddhist centers in the United States is the American Buddhist Society and Fellowship founded in 1945 (incorporated in 1947) by Robert Ernest Dickhoff. French-born Dickhoff migrated to the United States in 1927. He became involved in the occult and claims that, "Out of the Invisible Realm of the Spirit of Tibet" he was given recognition by several spiritual entities including Maha Chohan K. H. (i.e., the ascended master Koot Hoomi, first brought to the attention of the West by Theosophist Helena Petrovna Blavatsky). He was given the titles "Red Lama" and "Most Reverend" and instructed to gather the Buddhists in American into a society. In 1950, according to Dickhoff, he was given the title of Grand Lama of the White Lodge of Tibet, See of New York, by the Dalai Lama.

During the 1960s, Dickhoff became known in UFO circles for his advocacy of the theory that UFOs were hostile. He believes that the UFOs are winged garudas (a bird-like demon in Buddhhist thought), capturing humans and killing them for food.

Membership: Not reported. The Society consists of one center in New York City.

Sources: Robert Ernest Dickhoff, *The Eternal Fountain*. Boston, MA: Bruce Humphries, 1947; Robert E. Dickhoff, *Behold...the Venus Garuda*. New York: The Author, 1968; Robert E. Dickhoff, *Aggarta*. Mokelumne Hill, CA: Health Research, 1964.

★1306★
ARYA MAITRYA MANDALA
% Lama Anagarika Govinda
214 Sir Francis Drake Blvd.
San Anselmo, CA 49960

German-born Lama Anagarika Govinda (b.1898) began to think of himself as a Buddhist while still a teenager. Working as an archeologist, he was able to travel freely in southern Asia and also worked for the promotion of an ecumenical Buddhism in Europe. In 1931 he traveled to Tibet and studied under Tomo Geshe Rinpoche. In 1933, in honor of his guru, he founded the Arya Maitreya Mandala as a Buddhist order. (Maitreya, it is noted, was the only bodhisattva (saint) acceptable to all Mahayana Buddhist groups.) Centers of the order were first established in Germany and throughout Europe.

The Home of the Dharma was founded in San Francisco 1967 by the Rev. Iru Price as the American branch of the Arya Maitreya Mandala. The order is held together by a common acceptance of the ideal of the awakening of our innermost spirit, the "Buddha-nature" within us. This ideal is expressed by making Buddhism a way of life, assisting those wishing to understand the Buddha's teaching, and developing methods of religious practice suitable to Western psychology. Lama Govinda made his first visit to the United States in 1969. He lectured and exhibited his paintings at the Zen Center of San Francisco. Since that time, he has made several tours teaching meditation.

The Home of the Dharma holds regular meetings and conducts an annual Wesak celebration in spring to honor Buddha. The Kwan Yin Free School for refugee children is supported in Hong Kong.

Membership: Not reported. There is one American center of the Arya Maitreya Mandala.

Sources: Anagarika Govinda, *Foundations of Tibetan Buddhism*. New York: Humanities Press, 1959; Anagarika Govinda, *Creative Meditation and Multi-Dimensional Consciousness*. Wheaton, IL: Theosophical Publishing House, 1976; "Special Meditation Issue" in *Human*

Dimensions, vol. 1, no. 4, (1972); Anagarika Govinda, *The Psychological Attitude of Early Buddhist Philosophy.* London: Rider & Company, 1961.

★1307★

CHAPORI-LING FOUNDATION SANGHA
% Dr. Norbu Lompas Chen
766 8th Ave.
San Francisco, CA 94118

The Chakpori-Ling Foundation is a Nyingmapa Tibetan Buddhist center founded in the 1970s by Dr. Norbu L. Chen, formerly physician of Dharma Chakra Monastery in Kathmandu, Nepal. He received his basic instruction in Buddhism and Buddhist healing practices from refugees who had fled Tibet to Nepal following the 1959 Chinese invasion. He subsequently came to the United States and established Chakpori-Ling, named for a famous healing center just outside Lhasa, the capital of Tibet.

The Foundation operates a college which offers courses in Buddhism for prospective monks and nuns and training in oriental medicine. There is also a clinic for those who wish to receive treatment from an oriental physician.

Membership: Not reported. There is one center in San Francisco, California.

Educational facilities: College of Oriental Medicine, San Francisco, California.

★1308★

DRIKUNG DHARMA CENTERS
% Drikung Kyabgon
3454 Macomb St., N.W.
Washington, DC 20008

The Drikung Dharma Centers are the American branch of the Drikung Kagyu Order, one school within the Kagyupa Tibetan Buddhist sect (which dates to Milarepa, the famous teacher). The order is unusual in that the lineage is carried by two heads simultaneously. In the early 1960s, one of the heads, His Holiness Drikung Kyabgon Chetsang Rinpoche, left Tibet for India. Unable to leave Tibet, His Holiness Chung Tsang, the other head of the order, was separated from his colleague for over twenty-five years, their first meeting being in India in 1985. The first American Drikung Center was founded under the auspices of the Drikung Kyabgon in 1978.

The Drinkung Order is noted for its teachings on meditation, particularly the Drikung Phowa Meditation, a meditation intimately connected with the experience of death. Traditionally the Phowa Benediction was given every twelve years.

Membership: In 1985, there were two drikung centers, one in Washington, D.C. and one in Los Angeles, California.

★1309★

EWAM CHODEN
254 Cambridge St.
Kensington, CA 94707

Ewam Choden was the first center of the Sakyapa sect of Tibetan Buddhism founded in the United States. Its founder was Lama Kunga Thartse Rinpoche, who came to the United States in the 1960s and settled in Kensington, California. He opened Ewam Choden in 1971. The Sakyapa sect was the last great reform movement in Tibetan Buddhism. It was founded in 1071 C.E.. by K'on-dkon-mch'og rgyal-po, who taught a "reformed" tantra that still retained parts of the older tantra practices (which were highly magical and sexual). Present head of the sect is Sakya Trizin, who paid his first visit to America, and Ewam Choden, in 1977.

Ewan Choden means the integration of method and wisdom, compassion and emptiness, and possessing the Dharma (the true way of life taught by the Buddha). The center was established to practice and study Tibetan religion and culture. Lama Kunga established a program of meditation, classes and ceremonial observation of holy days. The center administers the Tibetan Relief Fund and Tibetan Pen-Pal program. Public meditation services are held on Sunday evenings.

Membership: Not reported. There is one urban center in Kensington, California, overlooking San Francisco Bay, with a second rural center projected for Grass Valley, California.

Sources: "His Holiness Sakya Trizin, An Interview" in *Wings* vol. 1, no. 1 (September/October 1987), pp. 36-38, 51-53.

★1310★

GANDEN TEKCHEN LING
Deer Park
4548 Schneider Dr.
Oregon, WI 53575

The Ganden Mahayana Center was formed in the mid-1970s by a group of students who had gathered around Geshe Lhundup Sopa, a professor in the Buddhist Studies Program at the University of Wisconsin at Madison. Sopa had been a teacher at the monastery at Sera until the Chinese invasion of Tibet. He fled to India but was sent to Labsum Shedrub Ling, the monastery in New Jersey in 1965 as a tutor for young monks. In 1968 he joined the faculty at the University of Wisconsin. Once formed, the center created Deer Park, a grove named after the place near Benares, India, where Buddha first taught, three miles from the university campus. A full program of both academic instruction in Buddhist, Tibetan and related subjects as well as facilities for the practice of traditional Tibetan Buddhism was offered.

The Center follows the branch of Tibetan Buddhism taught by the Dalai Lama and has, on several occasions, hosted the Dalai Lama, including his first American visit in 1979. In 1981, prior to the Dalai Lama's visit, the Center purchased acreage near Oregon, Wisconsin, and transferred its program to the new center. That new center was the site of the first performance in the West of the Kalachakra Initiation Ceremony by the Dalai Lama. The Kalachakra tantric path is one method of practicing Buddhist meditation which is considered for those who wish to progress speedily through intense meditational activity.

Membership: In 1981 the Center had 80 members.

Sources: Geshe Lhundup Sopa and Jeffrey Hopkins, *Practice and Theory of Tibetan Buddhism*. New York: Grove Press, 1976; *Kalachakra Initiation, Madison, 1981*. Madison, WI: Deer Park, 1981; Marcia Keegan, ed., *The Dalai Lama's Historic Visit to North America*. New York: Clear Light Publications, 1981; Tenzin Gyatsho, the 14th Dalai Lama, *The Opening of the Wisdom-Eye*. Wheaton, IL: Theosophical Publishing House, 1972; Tenzin Gyatso, *The Buddhism of Tibet and the Key to the Middle Way*. New York: Harper & Row, 1975.

★1311★
JETSUN SAKYA CENTER
623 W. 129th St.
New York, NY 10027

Jetsun Sakya Center is a small Sakyapa center founded in 1977 by Dezhung Rinpoche. Like Ewam Choden, it is under the Sakya Trizin, the head of the Sakyapa Order who resides in India, but is organizationally separate.

Membership: Not reported.

★1312★
KAGYU DHARMA
127 Sheafe Rd.
Wappinger Falls, NY 12590

Kagyu Dharma is the collective name give the several centers established by and under the direction of Kalu Rinpoche. Rinpoche is a teacher of the Kargyupa sect of Tibetan Buddhism. He studied at the Palpung Monastery in eastern Tibet. He left Tibet in 1957 to establish a monastery in Bhutan, at the request of the queen. He then settled at Sonada, Darjeeling, India, and established his own center, Samdup Tarjeyling Monastery. He has trained a number of monks especially to head centers in the West, and during the 1970s he started centers in Europe and North America. Focus of the European work is in Belgium at the urban center in Antwerp and the rural retreat at Huy. Each center carries on a regular format of worship and meditation which follows a daily, weekly, and lunar month schedule.

Among the American centers, Kagyu Droden Choling in San Francisco is most active. It is headed by Lama Lodo, the author of several books, and administers a publishing arm, KDK Publications, which publishes books in both Tibetan and English. Khawachen Dharma Center in Anchorage, Alaska is an eclectic Buddhist center under the direction of N. Paljor, and it receives guidance from one of Kalu Rinpoche's students, Lama Karma Rinchen of Hawaii.

Membership: Not reported. North American centers can be found in New York, California, Oregon, Washington, Hawaii, and British Columbia, Canada.

Periodicals: *Dundrub Yong* (Song of Fulfillment), Kagyu Droden Kunchab, 3476 21st St., San Francisco, CA 94110.

Sources: Lama Lodo, *Bardo Teachings*. San Francisco: KDK Publications, 1982; Lama Lodru, *Attaining Enlightenment*. San Francisco, CA: Kagyu Droden Kunchab Publications, 1979; Ken McLeod, trans., *The Total Flowering of Activity to Help Others*. Vancouver, BC: Kagyu Kunchab Chuling, 1975; Rikzin Palzang, trans., *Prayers for Generating Guru Devotion*. San Francisco, CA: Kagyu Droden Kunchab Publications, 1979; Kakhyab Dorje, *A Continuous Rain to Benefit Others*. Vancouver, BC: Kagyu Kunhyab Chuling, n.d.

★1313★
LABSUM SHEDRUB LING
Box 306-1, RD. 1
Washington, NJ 07882

The first Tibetan Buddhist group to arrive in America came here in 1951 and settled near Farmington, New Jersey. It included 200 members of the Kalmuck tribe of Mongolia; they had fled the Soviet authorities who wished to "communize" them. In 1955, with the aid of Church World Service (a Christian ecumenical group), Geshe Wangyal, a lama of the Drepung Monastery near Lhasa, Tibet, came from Tibet to America. He helped found Labsum Shedrup Ling (the Lamast Buddhist Monastery of America) and remains the leader of the small Kalmuck community.

The Mahayana Sutra and Tantra Center is a Tibetan Buddhist center located close to Labsum Shedrub Ling. It is under the direction of Geshe Lobsang Tharchin, the resident lama at the monastery, who came to the United States in the 1970s. While the monastery community is composed primarily of Asian immigrants, the center is primarily Caucasian in membership, and Geshe Tharchin has produced a variety of books in English to introduce Americans to Tibetan practice. Members have full access to the library at the monastery. There is a second center in Washington, D.C.

Membership: Not reported. Besides the monastery, there are two centers with Caucasian members.

Sources: Geshe Wangyal, *The Door of Liberation*. New York: Maurice Girodias Associates, 1973; Arturo F. Gonzalez, Jr., "New Jersey's Buddhist Shangri-La" in *Coronet*, (April 1950), pp. 146-55; Geshe Lobsang Tharchin and Barbara D. Taylor, *Methods of Achieving the Paths*. Washington, DC: Mahayana Sutra and Tantric Center, 1981; Geshe Lobsang Tharchin, *A Commentary on Guru Yoga*. Washington, DC: Mahayana Sutra and Tantric Center, 1981.

★1314★
KARMA TRIYANA DHARMACHAKRA
352 Meads Mountain Rd.
Woodstock, NY 12498

The Karma Triyana Dharmachakra was begun in 1976 when Khenpo Karthar Rinpoche came to America to establish a monastery and cultural center at the direction of His Holiness, the Gyalwa Karmapa, head of the Kargyupa branch of Tibetan Buddhism. The Gyalwa Karmapa had developed a vision of the center as a result of his American tour in 1974. Besides establishing the monastery, Rinpoche and his associates have traveled the United States teaching and organizing centers, each of which bear the name, "Karma Thegsum Choling." In 1980, the organization sponsored a visit by the Gyalwa Karmapa in 1980.

Membership: In 1983 there were 17 centers in the United States.

Periodicals: *Monastery Newsletter*, Karma Triyana Dharmachakra, 352 Meads Mountain Road, Woodstock, NY 12498; Gelongma Karma Tsultim Khechog Palmo, *A Garland of Morning Prayers*. Rumtek, Gangtok, Sikkim: The Author, 1976.

★1315★
LONGCHEN NYINGTHIG BUDDHIST SOCIETY
Box 302
Harris, NY 12742

The Longchen Nyingthig Buddhist Society was founded in New York City by the Venerable Tsede Lhamo, Rhenock Chamkusho. The Longchen Nyingthig lineage extends unbroken to Padmasambava, the famous teacher recognized as the founder of the Nyingmapa branch of Tibetan Buddhism. The teachings, which require intensive practice and close contact between student and teacher, offer the possibility of attaining permanent Buddhahood in a single lifetime. Its present leader, a female, Rhenock Chamkusko, was the daughter of Kyungtrul Pema Wangchen, a Nyingmapa rinpoche. Following the death of her father when she was only three years old, she was taken to study with another female guru, Jetsun Lochen Rinpoche. This guru's monastery was on White Brow Mountain where centuries earlier Nyingma lama Gwalwa Longchenpa had founded the Longchen Nyingthig lineage.

In 1948 Chamkusko married Sonam Kazi, and in 1956 went with him to establish a monastery in Sikkim. Discovered by American pilgrims, they were invited to move to the United States, which they did in 1969. They established the Longchen Society. In 1972 the Dzogchen Pema Choling Meditation Center was opened in Philadelphia. The retreat center, which now serves as headquarters, was added in 1975.

Membership: Not reported. There are three centers and less than 200 members.

★1316★
MAHA SIDDHA NYINGMAPA CENTER
Box 257
Conway, MA 63121

The Maha Siddha Nyingmapa Center is a small Nyingmapa center under the direction of Dodrup Chen Rinpoche. Students carry out a daily schedule of meditation and chanting.

Membership: Not reported. There are less than 50 people affiliated with the center.

Sources: Tulku Thondup, *Buddhist Civilization in Tibet*. Cambridge, MA: Maha Siddha Nyingmapa Center, 1982.

★1317★
NECHHUNG DRAYANGLING
Box 281
Pahala, HI 96777

In 1972 the head of the Nyingmapa branch of Tibetan Buddhism visited Hawaii. Inspired by his visit, a group of students initiated efforts to bring a teacher to live on the islands permanently. One of their number consulted with the Dalai Lama concerning that possibility. The students had acquired access to a Nichiran Buddhist temple at Pahala which had been abandoned when Japanese workers moved out of the area. They wished to locate a teacher who could be free of the "sectarian" interests of most teachers. Finally, in 1975, Nechhung Rinpoche moved to Hawaii. He was an accomplished teacher of both the Gelugpa branch of Tibetan Buddhism (that branch directly headed by the Dalai Lama) and the older Nyingmapa (unreformed) branch. Feeling that the Pahala temple, located in rural Wood Valley, was an auspicious place to begin attracting students, Rinpoche moved to Honolulu. Within a few years he had established five centers, one each on Oahu, Maui and Kauai and two on the big island. As the work progressed, and the facilities at Pahala improved, the work was consolidated at Wood Valley, though the Honolulu center remains open. In 1985, Nechhung Drayangling hosted Gangen Tri Rinpoche, one of the leaders of the Gelupga sect.

Membership: Not reported. There are two centers, both in Hawaii.

★1318★
PANSOPHIC INSTITUTE
Box 2422
Reno, NV 89505

The Pansophic Institute was founded in 1973 in Reno, Nevada, by Simon Grimes (Simon Theugos, Choskyi Palden Konchog Chopel). One of its main goals is to bring the concepts of Tibetan Vajrayana (tantric) Buddhism into the mainstream of Western thought. The Pansophic Institute is most closely related to the Gelugpa sect of which the Dalai Lama is the head. In the eleventh century, Atisha Dipankara came from India and began a great reformation of the Tibetan practices. Atisha's work was followed up in the fifteenth century by Tsong Khapa. He introduced strict discipline and the practices of the mendicant monks. Vajradhara is the Buddha, and there is a strong belief in Maitreya, "the coming Buddha." The strong discipline is based on the authority of the Dalai Lama. By the seventeenth century, the Gelugpa sect had become the established religion of Tibet.

One of the leading monasteries of the Gelugpa was Tashilunpo Monastery near Shigatse. The successive reincarnations of its hierarch, beginning with the scholar Kas Grub-Je, were, according to tradition, installed as the Panchen Rinpoche. The sixth Panchen Rinpoche was Choskyi Nuima (1883-1937). It was prophesied that the line of the Panchen Rinpoche would disappear from Asia and reappear in the West with the mission of unifying Eastern and Western thought as the foundation of world culture. Many believe Simon Grimes, the founder of the Pansophic Institute who was born in North China, to be the reincarnation of the sixth Panchen Lama.

According to the Pansophic Institute, the most important concept of Vajrayana Buddhism is "Mahamudra," total awareness of one's consciousness. It contains the seed of enlightenment and is the goal of meditation. A seven-point ethical code is adhered to: abstain from injury to other beings, taking what is not given, sexual obsessions, making false claims and slandering others; work to maintain conscious, clear awareness in oneself and others; cultivate this ethical code in oneself and in mankind.

The Institute has branch centers throughout the United States and in Canada, Australia, India, Nepal, and several countries in West Africa. It functions through its School of Universal Wisdom and Church of Universal Light. Its curriculum includes Tibetan religion and culture, meditation, spiritual healing, parapsychology, comparative religion, esoteric (gnostic) cosmologies, and the four types of theurgy (tantra as adapted to the West). The Institute also promotes planetary understanding, peace, and unity.

Membership: Not reported.

Educational facilities: School of Universal Wisdom, Reno, Nevada.

Periodicals: *Clear Light*, Box 2422, Reno, NV 89505.

Sources: Simon Grimes, *The Flaming Diamond*. Reno, NV: Pansophic Institute, 1974; *The Graduated Path to Liberation*. Reno, NV: Pansophic Institute, 1972.

★1319★
RIGPA
Box 7326
Santa Cruz, CA 95061

Rigpa is an association of Tibetan Buddhist meditation centers under the direction of Sigyal Rinpoche. Rinpoche is an incarnate lama of the Dzogchen lineage who studied first under Jamyang Khyentse Choekyi Lodroe, and then in the mid-1970s he accompanied the Dalai Lama on his first trip to the west, remaining behind in to attend Cambridge University. He founded Orgyen Choe Ling in London and attracted students in France and the United States and most recently in Australia. Rinpoche teaches dzoghen meditation, belived to be the final and ultimate teaching of Buddha, which brings the precise experience of the awakened state. Tapes and booklets by Rinpoche are circulated by Sound of Dharma in Santa Cruz, California. Radio shows consisting of interviews with Rinpoche are distributed to stations by New Dimensions Radio in San Francisco. Rinpoche resides in England but makes regular visits to the United States and conducts an annual weeklong retreat for students. In 1985 Rigpa hosted the first visit to the United States by the Dzogchen Rinpoche, Jugme Losel Wangpo.

Membership: Not reported.

Sources: Sogyal Rinpoche, *View, Meditation and Action*. London: Dzogchen Orgyen Choe Ling, 1979; Sogyal Rinpoche, *Face to Face Meditation Experience*. London: Orgyen Choe Ling, 1978.

★1320★
SAKYA TEGCHEN CHOLING
5042 18th Ave.,N.E.
Seattle, WA 98105

Jigdal Dagchen Sakya Rinpoche is a learned teacher of the Sakya branch of Buddhism who received initiation and the lineage of his father, Trichen Ngawang Thuptok Wangchug. He studied widely under a variety of teachers especially Dzongsar Khyentse Rinpoche and Dingo Khyentse Rinpoche, nonsectarian lamas of the Sakya and Nyingmapa schools respectively. He fled Tibet after the 1959 revolt and the following year came to the University of Washington under a Rockefeller Grant. He founded Sakya Tegchen Choling in 1974. In 1981 a second center, Tsechen Kun Khyab Choling, was opened in Olympia, Washington.

The central practice of the center is meditation upon Chenrezi (also known as Avalokiteshvara), a Buddhist bodhisattva. Such practice is believed to generate love and compassion and is accomplished in two stages in which meditators first visualize themselves as Chenrezi and secondly examines their own mind.

Membership: Not reported. There are two centers, both in Washington.

Periodicals: *Sakya Tegchen Choeling Newsletter*, 5042 18th Avenue N. E., Seattle, WA 98105.

★1321★
THUBTEN DARGYE LING
135 N. St. Andrews Place
Los Angeles, CA 90004

Thupten Dargye Ling was founded by Geshe Tsultrim Gyeltsen, a teacher in the Sakya tradition of Tibetan Buddhism. A graduate of Gyuto Tantric College, he migrated to America and taught first at the University of California-Santa Barbara and presently at the University of Oriental Studies in Los Angeles. Thupten Dargye Ling offers courses in Tibetan studies and a regular schedule of meditation. There is an affiliated center in Minneapolis which began in 1978 by students attracted by the 1978 visit of the Sakya Trizin, the head of the Sakya Buddhist tradition.

Membership: Not reported.

★1322★
TIBETAN NYINGMAPA MEDITATION CENTER
2425 Hillside Ave.
Berkeley, CA 94704

The Tibetan Nyingmapa Meditation Center is the representative of the "unreformed" Tibetan Nyingmapa groups. It was brought to the United States by Tarthang Tulku Rinpoche in 1969. In Tibet, Nyingmapa began with the introduction of Buddhism into the country in 747 A.D. and the merging of Buddhism with pre-Buddhist worship. Of particular importance in unreformed Buddhism is tantrism or Sivaic mysticism, which includes worship of the female energies, the spouses of the Hindu god, Shiva (Siva). The female energies were associated with supernatural powers, as well as sexuality. The Nyingmapa in America claims to possess "the entire range of higher tantric practices."

The Nyingmapa Meditation Center is located in Berkeley, California, in a former fraternity house now named Padma Ling (lotus ground), from which a highly expansionist program has developed. Dharma Publishing is responsible for a number of Tibetan Buddhist books, including some on Tibetan art. The educational wing, the Nyingma Institute was founded in 1973 and conducts a full program of classes and seminars. The Nyingmapa Center has constructed a monastery and retreat center in Sonoma County, California, called Odyian.

Membership: Not reported.

Educational facilities: Nyingma Institute, Berkeley, California.

Periodicals: *Gesar*, 2425 Hillside Avenue, Berkeley, CA 94704.

Sources: *Annals of the Nyingmapa Lineage In America*. Berkeley, CA: Dharma Publishing, 1977-1985. 3 Vols.; Tarthang Tulku, *Knowledge of Freedom*. Berkeley, Dharma Publishing, 1984; Tarthang Tulku, *Kum Nye Relaxation*. Berkeley, CA: Dharma Publishing, 1978. 2 vols.; Tarthang Tulku, *Skillful Means*. Berkeley, CA: Dharma Publishing, 1978; *Calm and Clear*. Berkeley, Tibetan Nyingmapa Meditation Center, 1973.

★1323★
VAJRAHATU
1345 Spruce St.
Boulder, CO 80302

Vajradhatu, the largest of the several Tibetan Buddhist groups in the United States, is a representative of the Kargyupa sect founded by Lama Marpa of Lhagyupa in the eleventh century. It is most known for its famous teacher, Milarepa. The Kargyupa tradition was brought to the United States by Chogyam Trungpa Rinpoche (b.1939). Trungpa is believed to be the incarnation of the Trungpa *tulku* (emanation of a bodhisattva) and abbot of Surmang Monastery, a center of the Kargyupa tradition until the takeover of Tibet by the Chinese.

Trungpa fled Tibet in 1959 and settled in England. While attending Oxford University he discovered a small Buddhist center in Scotland which was in 1967 turned over to him and became Samye-ling Monastery. Two years later he left his monastic orders and became a layperson again. In 1970 he married and migrated to the United States as leader of the Tail of the Tiger Monastery which had been formed by a group of his students in Vermont. He traveled, lectured and established several centers over the next few years. Vajradhatu was created as an umbrella for the several activities in 1973. He had by this time moved to Colorado.

At and near Boulder, a complex of interrelated organizations have been established. Under Vajradhatu proper are all the centers around the United States, called "dharmadatus." Karme-Choling (Tail of the Tiger) and its sister center Karma Dzong in Colorado are used primarily for retreats, study programs and training sessions. Shambhala has become a major publisher of Buddhist books in English.

Trunpa created the Nalanda Foundation to direct several outreach programs. Of these, Naropa Institute, the educational arm, is the most important. It has become a important center for Buddhist scholarship in the west through its varied and creative programs. Maitri

Therapeutic Community is the group's structure for entry into the realm of holistic health. Shambhala Training, reminiscent of Werner Erhard's seminars, EST, provides a Buddhist alternative format of the intensive transformational programs.

Trungpa directs his teaching to awaken the mind of his students through a threefold emphasis upon meditation, work and study. The teachings include secret esoteric teachings which are shared only with advanced students.

Vajradhatu is headed by Trungpa, though in 1975 he named his Dharma successor, Osel Tendzen (Thomas Rich) who as Vakra Regent has assumed much of the responsibility for administering the organization program.

Membership: Not reported. In 1983 there were 37 dharmadatus, including the several major centers in Vermont and Colorado.

Educational facilities: Naropa Institute, Boulder, Colorado.

Periodicals: *The Vajradhatu Sun*, 1345 Spruce Street, Boulder, CO 80302.

Sources: Choegyam Thrungpa, *Born in Tibet*. Boulder, CO: Shambhala, 1976; Choegyam Trungpa, *Cutting Through Spiritual Materialism*. Berkeley, CA: Shambhala, 1973; Herbert V. Guenther and Choegyam Trungapa, *The Dawn of Tantra*. Berkeley, CA: Shambhala, 1975; Tom Clark, *The Great Naropa Poetry Wars*. Santa Barbara, CA; Cadmus Editions, 1980; Karma Thinley, *The History of the Sixteen Karmapas of Tibet*. Boulder, CO: Prajna Press, 1980.

★1324★
VAJRAPANI INSTITUTE FOR WISDOM CULTURE
Box I
Boulder Creek, CA 95006

The Foundation for the Preservation of the Mahayana Tradition is a worldwide association of Tibetan Buddhist centers founded by Lama Thubten Yeshe and Lama Thubten Zopa Rinpoche, both trained in the Gelugpa tradition of Tibetan Buddhism (that tradition directly headed by the Dalai Lama). They met in 1959 when as refugees from Tibet they both settled in Buxaduar, India. The young Zopa Rinpoche was sent to Thubten Yeshe for further instruction. In 1965 the pair met Zina Rachevsky, a Russian who was ordained as a nun in 1967. The three established the Nepal Mahayana Gompa Center near Kathmandu in 1969.

The center in Nepal began to attract Western students and in 1973 the International Mahayana Institute, an organization of Western nuns and monks, was located adjacent to the Center. The first Indian outpost, Tushita

International Retreat Center, was opened in Dharmasala in 1972. That same year the Mount Everest Center for Buddhist Studies opened at Lawudo, Nepal, to educate Nepalese children.

In 1974 the two lamas were invited to tour the West by C. T. Shen of the Institute for the Advanced Study of World Religions in New York. They toured the United States and spoke at most of the Tibetan Buddhist centers then open as well as several universities. In Nashville, Indiana, the Lama's visited Mrs Louis Bob-Wood, a former student at their center in Kathmandu, who had gathered a group of interested students. They founded the Bodhicitta Center for Developing Human Potential, their first American group. The American publication and circulation of the lectures given on this tour brought them more students and the eventual development of other centers. In 1977 students donated 30 acres of land near Boulder Creek, California for the development of a retreat center, currently the American headquarters of the movement.

In the last decade the movement has spread around the world. Western headquarters were established in Italy and a publishing enterprise in England. A new line of English-language books on Tibetan Buddhism, graded to several levels, have appeared as the Wisdom Basic Books (Orange Series), Intermediate Books (White Series), and Advanced Books (Blue Series).

Membership: Not reported. In 1985 there were three centers in the United States and 39 additional centers worldwide.

Periodicals: *Wisdom: Magazine of the FPMT*, Wisdom Publications, 23 Dering Street, London W1, England.

Sources: Geshe Rabten and Geshe Ngawang Dhargyey, *Advice from a Spiritual Friend*. New Delhi, India: Publications for Wisdom Culture, 1977; Jeffrey Hopkins, *The Tantric Distinction*. London: Wisdom Publications, 1984; Thubten Yeshe and Thubten Zopa, *Wisdom Energy*. Honolulu, HI: Conch Press, 1976.

★1325★
YESHE NYINGPO
19 W. 16th St.
New York, NY 10011

Yeshe Nyingpo was founded in 1976 by Dudjom Rinpoche, believed to be a reincarnation of one of Buddha's personal disciples and of Cheuchung Lotsawa, one of Padmasambhava's (who brought Buddhism to Tibet) disciples. Yeshe Nyingpo is envisioned as the instrument for the transmission of the pure Nyingmapa teachings and practice to the west. In 1980 land for an educational-retreat center, Orgyen Cho Dzong, was purchased in the Catskills. Construction on the projected complex is proceeding through the mid-1980s. Affiliated are centers across the United States and in Europe.

Membership: Not reported. In 1983 there were six centers in the United States: two in New York, one in California, and three in Oregon.

Western Buddhism

★1326★
AMERICAN BUDDHIST MOVEMENT
301 W. 45th St.
New York, NY 10036

The American Buddhist Movement was founded in 1980 as an independent Buddhist order to promote Buddhism in America and ordain Buddhist monks. Rather than following any particular school of Buddhism, the movement respects all traditions as equal and encourages the unity of Buddhist thought and practice. Theravada, Mahayana, and Vijrayana Buddhists participated in the movement's founding. In defining its peculiar role, the movement asserts that an American form of Buddhism is possible and that Westerners do not have to adopt Asian cultural forms to be Buddhists.

The movement has established a variety of structures to perpetuate its program. Classes are offered on a variety of Buddhist concerns, including introduction to the several distinctive national traditions. Periodically, an *American Buddhist Directory* is published. Plans have been announced to build a permanent center in the New York City area to house a meditation hall, library, and lecture room.

Membership in the movement is open to all Buddhists and activities have been designed to serve those primarily affiliated with the movement as well as those affiliated with other groups. Leadership is invested in a four-person board of directors. Kevin R. O'Neill has served as its president since its inception.

Membership: In 1984 the movement reported 200 members in three centers.

Educational facilities: Buddhist College, 225 Lafayette St., New York, NY 10012.

Periodicals: *American Buddhist Newsletter*, 301 West 45th Street, New York, NY 10036.

Sources: *The American Buddhist Directory*. New York: The American Buddhist Movement, 1985.

★1327★
BUDDHIST FELLOWSHIP OF NEW YORK
331 Riverside Dr.
New York, NY 10025

The Rev. Boris Erwitt, an American ordained to the Buddhist priesthood in Japan, began the Buddhist Fellowship of New York in 1961. The original group consisted of eight friends of the Rev. Erwitt who banded together to practice, study and propagate Buddhism, and to provide a gathering for Buddhists of non-Buddhist background. The program is centered on bimonthly meetings with a service according to the Pure Land practice and a lengthy discussion in which all participate. A number of pamphlets have been published and distributed.

The membership is small and drawn largely from the intellectual and artistic community. Some were first interested in Buddhism through the "beat" generation's emphasis on Zen. Project Sujata (named after the girl who saved Buddha's life) practices the virtue of "Ooana" (giving) by sponsoring the education of an indigent American Indian child and scholarships for "untouchables" in India.

Membership: Not reported.

Periodicals: *Kantaka*, 331 Riverside Drive, New York, NK 10025.

★1328★
BUDDHIST WORLD PHILOSOPHICAL GROUP
(Defunct)

The Buddhist World Philosophical Group was a small Buddhist fellowship headquartered in Three Rivers, Michigan. Its leader, Marie Harlow (b.1902), took over the longstanding Chicago-based occult periodical, *The Occult Digest*, in the 1940s and began almost immediately to emphasize Eastern religion, particularly Buddhism, over occult topics. In 1944 she renamed the magazine *World Philosophy*, and later moved its editorial office to Three Rivers, Michigan. In 1962 *World Philosophy* became *Buddhist World Philosophy*, and Harlow announced a set of four aims for the magazine: to promote universal brotherhood, to proclaim the sanctity of life, to destroy the "limitations of the negative Semitic religious God-concept," and to turn America toward Buddhism. A small group of people congregated around the ideals articulated by Harlow which continued to meet until her death in recent years.

★1329★
CHOWADO HENJO KYO
% Rev. Reisai Fugita
1757 Algaroba St.
Honolulu, HI 96814

Chowado Henjo Kyo is a Buddhist healing body founded by the Rev. Reisai Fujita, a former priest in the Shingi Shingon Chizan (a Shingon group without representatives in America). The worship and temple arrangement is typical of Shingon practice and Kobo Daishi is worshipped. However, the healing experience and resultant teaching of the Rev. Fujita are the essential aspects of Chowado. Fujita, in spite of his success as a

Shingon priest, was afflicted by chronic stomach and intestinal trouble that led to tuberculosis and paralysis. He tried unsuccessfully the method of Hakuin, the Zen priest, but soon discovered that he needed physical exercises as well as spiritual healing. Beginning with the practice of breathing, he developed a system which led to his cure. In 1906, he decided to devote his life to helping others as he had been helped.

Fujita's physical exercises, which must be mastered by church members, include regulated breathing and harmony exercises of various parts of the body. The stomach, the most important party of the body, is singled out for special consideration; the correctly exercised abdomen, according to Fujita, is "gourd-shaped."

As part of his evangelistic endeavors, Fujita went to Hawaii in 1929 en route to California. In Hawaii he found both a need and an audience ready to listen. He sent his student companion on to California and ministered to the Japanese community in Hawaii, instead of going on to California. The mission flourished during the 1930's but was severely hurt by the war. After the war, Fujita moved to Honolulu and operated from a two-story church in Honolulu. The single congregation has not grown since his death.

Membership: Not reported.

★1330★
CHURCH OF ONE SERMON
Current address not obtained for this edition.

The Church of One Sermon located in Lemon Grove, California, was formed in the 1970s to aid in "the Full Awakening in all people of that special Reality knowledge first testified to by Guatama Siddhartha, the Buddha." Its founder and director was Leonard Enos. An eclectic approach centered on Mahayana Buddhism, but including tantra and Zen and even some Sufism, was taught, with particular interest being given to current research in psychology on the meditative states of consciousness. The program consisted largely of meditation, exercise and discussion sessions. One center was functioning in 1973, but in recent years no evidence of its continued existence had appeared.

★1331★
FRIENDS OF BUDDHISM-WASHINGTON D.C.
% Dr. Kurt Leidecker
306 Caroline St.
Fredericksburg, VA 22401

Alabama-born Robert Stuart Clifton became interested in Buddhism as a student at Columbia University in the 1920s. He moved to San Francisco and lived in the Japanese community. In 1933, he was ordained as a priest in the Honpa Hongwanji Mission, now the Buddhist Churches of America, and began English language work along the West Coast. In 1934, he traveled to Japan and

while there became a Higashi Hongwanji priest. Upon his return to America, he lectured widely and organized a number of "friends of Buddhism" societies, mostly in the East.

The Washington Friends of Buddhism was formed in the home of Mr. and Mrs. Lee Sirat at a gathering of persons Clifton had interested in Buddhism. There were eleven in the original group. The program has always centered on lectures and discussion of Buddhism, but meditation and worship have been included from the beginning. Wesak, the spring fesival honoring Gautama Buddha, is also celebrated.

The only one of the Friends of Buddhism groups, besides the Washington group, to survive through the 1960s was the Friends of Buddhism of New York, founded in the early 1950s. In the late 1960s, following the retirement of its leader, Frank E. Becker, the New York group merged with the Washington group.

Membership: Not reported.

Sources: Kurt F. Leidecker, *History of the Washington Friends of Buddhism.* Washington, DC: United States Information Service, 1960.

★1332★
HARMONY BUDDHIST MISSION
% Rev, Frank Newton
Clarksville, AK 92830

The Harmony Buddhist Mission was founded in 1953 by Frank Newton. It is centered on Buddhist ethical and philosophical teachings. Self-responsibility and attunement to fact are stressed. Leaders in the mission (preceptors) are not allowed to receive any income for religious duties but must work at secular occupations. Frank Newton has gained a reputation as a writer and translator of Buddhist literature. Some 1,500 people have reportedly come into Buddhism through his efforts.

Membership: Not reported.

★1333★
SHIVAPURAM
(Defunct)

Shivapuram was founded in 1963 by Radha Appu (also known as Rakshasi) in the Catskill Mountains of New York. While on a retreat and doing vigorous breathing and concentration exercises to raise the kundalini (creative energy), he became aware of the Master Vijaya Bhattacharya, who appeared to him. Over a period of time, the master gave instructions and told Radha Appu to "Go forward" and found Shivapuram. He remains as the sole contact with the master, though sporadic appearances are made to the shivas, the members of the Shivapuram. In 1967, Rakshasi was given instructions to found a worldwide Crusade of the Spirit to save humanity from self-destruction.

Though borrowing from Hinduism, the Shivapuram is basically Mahayana Buddhist with large portions of tantra. Adherents do not believe in escape into nirvana, but in accepting the world and using it as a means of liberation. They seek Buddhatva, the quality of being enlightened. They use chants and mantras and meditative yoga.

The Shivapuram members were largely drawn from California. There were in 1971 three priests, ten lecturers and approximately 300 members. While committed to spreading the movement, the members are not openly evangelistic and are highly selective about who is invited to join or even attend meetings. There has been no evidence of a continuing movement in recent years.

★1334★
UNIVERSAL BUDDHIST FELLOWSHIP
% Rev. Harold H. Priebe
Box 1079
Ojai, CA 93023

The Universal Buddhist Fellowship was formed in 1951 by the Venerable H. H. (Tissa) Priebe of Ojai, California. It is described as autonomous and non-sectarian. Its purpose is dissemination of the Western Dharma (the true way of life taught by Buddha).

Membership: Not reported.

Periodicals: *Western Bodhi*, Box 1079, Ojai, CA 93023.

Shinto

★1335★
CHURCH OF WORLD MESSIANITY
3068 San Marino St.
Los Angeles, CA 90006

Sekai Kyusei Kyo, generally known by its English name, the Church of World Messianity, was founded by Mokichi Okada (1882-1955), usually referred to by his honorific title, Meishu-sama. Raised in poverty and beset with illness and business failure, in the 1920s Okada turned to religion and joined Omoto, one of the newer religions of Japan. In 1926, however, he began to receive revelations, as a result of which he began to see himself as a channel for the Light of God. He understood his mission as one of the transmission of *johrei*, the Light of God for the purification of the spiritual body. Such purification would lead to healing and a general improvement in life.

In 1934 Okada left Omoto and founded Kannon Kai. As the War approached, innovative religious groups were suppressed and Okada had to give up the practice of

johrei until after the War, though the movement continued to grow. During the War, Okada moved to Hakone Province and constructed a "paradise," a model of a future paradise on earth. A second such model was built at Atari. In 1947 the group was renamed Kippon Kannon Kai and assumed its present name in 1950. He was succeeded by his wife, who died in 1962 and then his daughter, Fujieda Itsuki, the Church's present leader.

In the years after World War II, members of the church migrated to the United States. Okada sent Kiyoko Higuchi and Rev. Henry Ajiki to the United States to organize the church. The first center outside of Japan was incorporated in 1953 in Honolulu. The following year the two missionaries went to California and organized the Los Angeles church. A third was soon added in Valley Center, California. During the next twenty years churches were established along the West Coast from Vancouver to San Diego. Internationally, the church spread to Okinawa, Brazil, and Korea.

Membership: Not reported.

Periodicals: *World Messianity Newsletter*, 369 Junipero Avenue, Long Beach, CA 90814; *MOA Newsletter*, Mokichi Okada Association, 369 Junipero Avenue, Long Beach, CA 90814.

Sources: *The Light from the East: Mokichi Okada*. Atami, Japan: MOA Productions, 1983; *Teachings of Meishu-Sama*. Atami, Japan: Church of World Messianity, 1967-68. 2 Vols.; *M. Okada, A Modern-Day Renaissance Man*. New York: M. Okada Cultural Services Association, 1981; *Members' Handbook'*. [Atami, Japan]: Church of World Messianity, n.d.; *Introductory Course of World Messianity and Joining the Church*. Los Angeles: Church of World Messianity, 1976.

★1336★
HONKYOKU SHINTO
Honkyoku-Daijingu Temple
61 Puiwa Rd.
Honolulu, HI 96817

In 1882 the Japanese designated thirteen shinto sects as approved but withdrew government support from them (as opposed to Buddhism which was not sanctioned by the government). Honkyoku Shinto was among the more traditionalist sects included on the government list. It bases its beliefs on the ancient Shinto text, the *Mojiki*, and sees itself as the Way of Nature, the spontaneous manifestation of the order of being taking form in human life. Worship is centered upon Ame-no-Minaka-Nushi-no-Kami (The Deity Who is Lord of the Center of Heaven), the primary source of all. On the altar of the Honkyoku shrine there is a mirror and a ball which symbolize God. This absolute deity gives rise to two other deities: Taka-Mimusibi-no-Kami and Kami-Musubi-no-Kami. The world arises from the interaction of these two very different deities. From them arise other deities, the

Japanese Imperial family and the Japanese people. Through the ancestors of those now living, the people are tied to the divine as a great spiritual body. Shinto faith is best expressed in practice, reverence to the gods and one's ancestors, devotion to the Imperial family and patriotism. Honkyoku Shinto prospered during the first half of the twentieth century. On the eve of World War II it could report over 3,300 centers and 1,200,000 members in Japan. It was also the earliest Shinto group to establish itself in Hawaii. The Daijingu Temple in Honolulu was founded around 1906 by Rev. Masasato Kawasaki. Because of its intense Japanese nationalism, it was closed, and the property confiscated, during World War II. A new temple was built after the war. In 1949 a statue of one of the Shinto goddesses confiscated and sent to Japan by the United States government was returned and enthroned at the Honolulu temple, then located on Buckle Street.

The Honkyoku temples in Hawaii hold monthly public services, but most worship is individual and private. There are annual festivals on New Year's Day and the second Sunday of September. Bishop Kazoe Kawasaki has succeeded his father as head of the Honkyoku in Hawaii.

Membership: Not reported. There are currently two temples, one in Honolulu and one in Hilo, Hawaii. In 1963 the Honolulu temple claimed to serve over 10,000 families.

★1337★
INARI SHINTO
Hawaii Inari Taisha
2132 S. King St.
Honolulu, HI 96817

In Hawaii the Inari have departed from the Inari deities common to the group in Japan. The Hawaiian Inari worship a main deity, Shoichii Shi Sha. The Wakamiya Shrine in Honolulu was founded in 1912 by the Rev. Yoshio Akizaki. Since his passing in 1951, his son, the Rev. Takeo Akizaki, has been in charge. He has begun to assume the role of pastor and the temple has regular worship services. A second temple is located on Molokai.

Membership: Not reported. There are two Inari shrines in Hawaii, one in Honolulu and one in Molokai.

★1338★
JINGA SHINTO
Hawaii Ichizuchi Jinga
2020 S. King St.
Honolulu, HI 96817

The Rev. Shina Miyake founded the Hawaii Ichizuchi Jinga in Honolulu in 1913. In 1963, on the occasion of their fiftieth anniversary, a rebuilt shrine building was dedicated.

Membership: Not reported. There is one shrine in Honolulu, Hawaii.

★1339★
JINSHA SHINTO
Kotohira Jinsha Temple
1045 Kama Lane
Honolulu, HI 96817

Representative of the Jinsha Shinto are two temples, the Hawaii Kotohira Jinsha Temple in Honolulu and the Maui Jinsha Temple at Wailuku. Jinsha is a form of national Shintoism.

Membership: Not reported.

★1340★
KONKO KYO
% Rev. Alfred Y. Tsyyuki
2924 E. 1st St.
Los Angeles, CA 90033

Konko Kyo was founded in 1859 by Bunjiro Kawate (1814-1883) (later given the title Konko Daijin), a Shinto farmer, who after years of misfortune and illness had a revelation of God as Tenchi Kane-no-Kami, the parent God of the universe. God revealed to him that the prosperity of men is the ultimate purpose of creation and that God without that purpose realized is morally imperfect. In 1882 Konko Kyo was recognized as one of the thirteen approved forms of sectarian Shinto in Japan.

The interrelation of God and man is the key to Konko Kyo teaching. Man cannot exist apart from God, and God's work can only be complete through man. Konko Daijin was the mediator who informed all men of this fellowship. Priests continue to function as mediators, just as Konko Daijin functioned. The process of mediation (*toritsugi*) is quite similar to Roman Catholic confessions.

Rites and ceremonies follow Shinto practice, but are demythologized. Konko Kyo is monotheistic and does not practice divination or magic. Much more emphasis is placed on the sermon, piety and social concern. Belief in God with sincerity and a pious life are cardinal virtues. Social concerns have led to the founding of a hospital, a public library, museum, leper missions and prison work.

Konko Kyo was established in the United States in 1919 by Mr. & Mrs. Bunjiro Hirayama who founded the Konko Kyo Association of Seattle, Washington. A second center was opened in Tacoma in 1925. The following year, the Rev. Kokichi Katashima, a Konko official from Japan, visited the Washington centers and, on his return route to Japan, organized believers who had recently migrated to Los Angeles and Honolulu. The work grew until the disruption of World War II and the internment of most of the leadership. The San Francisco headquarters were reestablished in the fall of 1945. The post-World War II freedom of religion in Japan has allowed Konko

Kyo to grow and spread as a vigorous movement. Setsutane Konko, the present mediator and leader, has supported the work outside of Japan and has spurred the production of English-language materials. In 1965 a radio show was inagurated by Konko minister Masaru Okazaki.

Membership: Not reported. In 1982 there were seven churches in the United States (apart from Hawaii) and two in Canada. The Hawaii Mission had an additional six churches.

Periodicals: *Konko Review,* 2924 East First Street, Los Angeles, CA 90033.

Sources: *Konko Daijin, A Biography.* San Francisco: Konko Churches of America, 1981; *Konko Kyo's 50 Years in America.* San Francisco: Konko Churches of America, 1976; Konkokyo Hombu, ed., *The Sacred Scriptures of Kinkokyo.* Konko-cho, Japan: Konkokyo Hombu, 1933; Yoshiaki Fukuda, *Outline of Sacred Teaching of Konko Religion.* [San Francisco]: Konko Missions of North America, 1955; *Daily Service Book.* [San Francisco]: Ministerial Staff of Konko Churches of America, 1971.

★1341★
MAHIKARI OF AMERICA
Los Angeles Dojo
6470 Foothill Blvd.
Tujunga, CA 91042

Mahikari, one of the newer religions of Japan, was founded by Yoshikasu Okada (1901-1974), a man who had turned to religion after World War II. He joined the Church of World Messianity which taught a form of spiritual healing in which the practitioner directs *johrei,* God's Healing Light, to the patient. In 1959 Okada had a revelation of Su-God (the Lord God) who entrusted a healing mission to him. Though his teachings varied little from the Church of World Messianity, he began to work independently of it. In 1960 he organized the L.H. (Lucky and Happy) Sunshine Children (later the Sekai Mahikari Bunmei Kyodan (Church of World True Light Children)).

Okada taught the practice of *Mahikari-no-Waza,* the use of God's True Light for purification of spiritual, mental and physical pollutions. At the time of initiation, new members receive an *Omitama,* a pendant, used to focus the Light.

Okada claimed to be the physical embodiment of Yonimasu-o-amatsu, a Shinto deity, and received regular revelations during the remaining years of his life. These revelations have been collected into the *Goseigenshu,* the Mahikari scriptures. During the final years of his life he assumed the titles, "Sukuinushisama" (Master of Salvation), and "Oshienushisama" (Spiritual Leader).

Just prior to his death, Okada designated his daughter, Oshienushi Keijusama, as his successor, but she was challenged by a prominent leader, Sekiguchi Sakae. A

lawsuit was settled in Sekiguchi's favor and he took possession of the group's headquarters. Keijusama reorganized her followers into Sukyo Mahikari. The movement is in the process of building a world shrine to Su-no-Omikamasama (Almighty God) at Takayama, Japan.

Membership: Not reported. As of 1985, there were nine centers in the United States and one each in Canada and Puerto Rico under Mahikari of America.

Sources: Winston Davis, *Dojo.*Stanford, CA: Stanford University Press, 1980; A. K. Tebecis, *Mahikari, Thank God for the Answers At Last.* Tokyo, Japan: L. H. Yoko Shuppan, 1982; *Primary Initiation Text.* N.p.: Mahikari, 1978; *Yokoshi Norogoto Shu.* Los Angeles: Sekai Mahikari Bunmei Kyodan of America, 1977.

★1342★
SHINREIKYO
% Mr. Kameo Kiyota
310C Uulani St.
Hilo, HI 96720

Shinreikyo is a post-World War II Japanese healing group based on Kami-no-michi, the Way of God. Shinreikyo was founded by Master Kanichi Otsuka, viewed by his followers as the great sage (who was to appear as Buddhism lost its power) and the messiah that Christians expected at the second coming. The message of Shinreikyo is that Kami-no-michi is the way to happiness and prosperity. It is identified with Nippon Seishin, the Japanese spirit, a way common to all since ancient times, based upon the laws of the universe. The intense nationalism is typical of much Shintoism.

The center of Shinreikyo is its healing miracles. Master Otsuka is said to attack disease in the three existences of past, present, and future. Accounts of healing of serious illnesses fill Shinreikyo literature. Shinreikyo came to the United States in 1963 when Mr. Kameo Kiyoto established a branch in Hilo, Hawaii. Literature in English is distributed by the Metaphysical Scientific Institute in Japan.

Membership: Not reported.

★1343★
SOCIETY OF JOHREI
Box 1321
Brookline, MA 02146

The Society of Johrei was formed in 1971 by former leaders of the Church of World Messianity who felt that it had departed from the teachings of founder Mokichi Okada. They began to work independently of the church and then organized the society. Their following included people in Korea and Brazil. An American office was opened in the 1980s and began to publicize the society through distribution of an edited volume of Okada's writings.

Membership: Not reported.

Sources: Mokichi Okada, *Johrei: Divine Light of Salvation.* Kyoto, Japan: Society of Johrei, 1984.

★1344★
TAISHAKYO SHINTO
215 N. Kukui St.
Honolulu, HI 96817

Taishakyo began as a distinct sect of Shinto in 1873 when Sonfuku Senge organized the devotees of the old shrine at Izumu, Japan. According to legend, the deity Amenohonohi-no-Mikoto, son of the sun goddess Amaterasu-Omi-Kami went to Izumo to negotiate with another deity, Okuninushi-no-Mikoto, the return of the land to the Imperial family. One condition of the transaction was that Amenohonohi-no-Mikoto make adoration to Okuninushi-no-Mikoto. The people of Izumu consider themselves the descendents of the former, preserving a shrine dedicated to the latter. Members of the sect stress the spirit of self-sacrifice of Okuninushi-no-Mikoto, who gave his lands to the Imperial family, and adore Amenohonohi-no-Mikoto, who served the Imperial family.

The Hawaii Izumo Taisha was founded in 1906 as an outpost of the Taishakyo sect (incorporated 1919). The Rev. Katsuyoshi Miyao was the first priest. The movement spread and shrines were developed at Wailuku, Maui, Hilo and Kona. In 1923 a master temple builder was brought from Japan to construct a shrine in Honolulu according to strict Japanese patterns. After World War II began, the members in Honolulu gave that shrine to the city to keep it from being confiscated. After the war the shrine was reestablished in the home of the priest, while members began a lengthy legal battle to have their original building returned. Receiving ownership in 1961, they immediately discovered that it was in the midst of a redevelopment site. It was finally given status as a part of Hawaii's cultural heritage and relocated outside of the development project. A second shrine was built as the negotiations on the old one proceeded and was dedicated in 1969.

Membership: Not reported. There are two temples in Hawaii.

★1345★
TENRIKYO
Tenrikyo Mission Headquarters in America
2727 E. First St.
Los Angeles, CA 90033

Of the various groups termed "new religions," Tenrikyo is the largest, with more than 2,000,000 members. It was founded by a woman, Miki Maegawa Nakayama. In 1837,

she began to go into trances and spoke as if God were speaking through her. Over a period of time, she gave away her possessions to attain ultimate poverty and began to practice spiritual healing. The rise of Tenrikyo coincided with a period of popular revolt, and its leaders were persecuted by the government, but in 1908 it was finally given recognition by the government as an approved Shinto sect.

According to Tenrikyo, God first revealed himself as Kami (the creator) and then as Tsuki-hi (the Moon/Sun God). The pantheon of Shinto is conceived as aspects of the one God. The center of Tenrikyo is Tenri-o-no-mikoto (Lord of divine wisdom), commonly referred to as Oya-gami (God the parent), who spoke through and dwelt in Nakayama. Nakayama is now believed to reside in spirit at her former home in Tenri, Japan.

Humans are essentially good but have during their lives accumulated Nokori (dust). The various kinds of Nokori (greed, stinginess, partiality, hatred, animosity, anger, covetousness and arrogance) stain our minds. As the dust is swept away, individuals will be opened to a happy life (Yokiguraski), or salvation.

In the past there were a number of means to Yokigurashi, but today the main avenues are self-reflection, prayer and "tsutome" or sacred service. A major prayer is "Ashiki o harote tasuke tamae, Tenri-o-no-mikoto" ("Sweep away all evils and save us, parent, Tenri-o-no-mikoto"). The prayer is accompanied by hand motions symbolic of dust being brushed away from the soul. Tsutome is a ceremony performed only at the international headquarters at the city of Tenri in Japan. In the Jiba, the palace, is the Kanodai (sacred stand) around which service and dancing are offered.

In order to manifest the parenthood of God and to realize Yokigurashi, a variety of social service and cultural institutions have been founded. They include orphanages, Tenri University, a library, museum and churches.

Having spread to Korea and China in the first decades after given government recognition, Tenrikyo, as its fortieth anniversary approached in 1926, gave attention to establishing the movement in America. In 1927 two missionaries, Yone Okazaki and Rinzo Torizawa were sent to Seattle and began work among members already living in Portland and Seattle. Within a few years churches were begun in Tacoma, Los Angeles and Honolulu. By the beginning of World War II, the Church had parishes along the West Coast from San Diego to Vancouver. By 1965, there were fifteen congregations in Hawaii and by 1973, congregations had spread as far east as Chicago.

Membership: Not reported. Tenrikyo churches can now be found in Japanese-American communities across the United States and Canada.

Periodicals: *Tenrikyo Newsletter,* 2727 East First Street, Los Angeles, CA 90033.

Sources: *Tenrikyo, Its History and Teachings.* Tenri, Japan: Tenrikyo Overseas Mission Department, 1966; *A Short History of Tenrikyo.* Nara, Japan: Tenrikyo Church, 1956; Teruo Nishiyama, *Introduction to the Teachings of Tenrikyo.* Tenri, Japan: Tenrikyo Overseas Mission Department, 1981; *The Life of Oyasama, Foundress of Tenrikyo.* Tenri, Japan: Tenrikyo Church Headquarters, 1982; Henry van Straelen, *The Religion of Divine Wisdom.* Kyoto: Veritas Shoin, 1957; Tomoji Takano, *The Missionary,* trans by Mitsuru Yuge. Tenri, Japan: Tenrikyo Overseas Missionary Department, 1981.

★1346★

TENSHO KOTAI JINGU KYO

Hawaii Dojo
888 N. King St.
Honolulu, HI 96817

Tensho Kotai Jingu Kyo is a religion built around the remarkable charismatic figure, Kitamura Sayo (1900-1967), usually addressed as "Ogamisama" (The Great God) by her followers. Born in Japan, January 1, 1900, she later married a farmer. Ogamisama had no particular religious convictions until 1943, when a series of divine revelations began. A Shinto god, Tensho- kotai-jin, descended into her body and told her to be the founder of the "Kingdom of God on earth." The new religion spread rapidly and was registered with the government in 1947.

Tensho-Kotai-jin is seen as the absolute God of the universe, the heavenly Father (as in Christianity) and the eternal Buddha. The almighty God is a male-female pair who by possessing Kitamura Sayo formed a trinity. Both she and her followers describe her in deific terms. She is seen to have powers of prophecy and healing. She proclaimed 1946 as the first year of the New Era.

Ogamisama's sermons were sometimes "sung" while in a state of ecstasy and were always delivered without preparation. She has also taught her followers the prayer of the Odoru Shukyo (dancing religion), which functions much as the Lord's Prayer in Christianity. Characteristic of the religion is dance of non-ego performed by the followers as an expression of the inner bliss which follows spiritual purification.

Ogamisama's role is to establish the kingdom here and now by purging the world of the six roots of evil--regret, desire, hatred, fondness, love, and being loved excessively. For the individual, the process begins in the salvation of evil spirits, severing personal karma with the assistance of the prayer of Odoru Shukyo and continuing to polish the soul with sincerity, charity, and brotherhood.

Ogamisama made her first trip to Hawaii in 1959. She advised her listeners to burn the relics of Shintoism and Buddhism, because they belonged to the past. The result of her trip was the establishment of eight branches of her religion. In October 1964 she began a nine-month worldwide tour which brought her to America for the last time. The movement had become worldwide by the time of her death in 1967. She was succeeded by her granddaughter, Kiyokazu Kitamura, revered as "Himegamisama."

An active evangelistic program of the Tensho Kotai Jungu Kyo is supported by a number of publications. The central document is the *Prophet of Tabuse,* a biography of Ogamisama. A periodical appears in both an English and Spanish edition. Branches have been formed throughout the Hawaiian Islands and wherever Japanese-American communities exist on the West Coast.

Membership: Not reported.

Periodicals: *Voice from Heaven,* Tensho-Kotai-Jingu-Kyo, Tabuse, Yamaguchi Pref., Japan.

Sources: *The Prophet of Tabuse.* Tabuse, Japan: Tensho-Kotai-Jingu-Kyo, 1954; *Ogamisama Says....* Tabuse, Japan: Tensho-Kotai-Jingu-Kyo, 1963; Takie Sugiyama Lebra, "Logic of Salvation: The Case of a Japanese Sect in Hawaii" in *The International Journal of Social Psychiatry,* vol. 16, no. 1 (Winter 1969/70) pp. 45-53.

★1347★

THIRD CIVILIZATION

Box 1836
Sante Fe, NM 87501

The Third Civilization is one of the "new religions" of Japan and represents a twentieth-century form of Shintoism based upon the work of Sen-sei Koji Ogasawara. Ogasawara retranslated the *Kojiki* and *Nippon-Syoki* (*Nihongi*), the Shinto scriptures, in such a way as to lift the veil of symbolic mythology and to put the name of God into sound. The Third Civilization is involved in the study of the Kototama principle. "Kototama" is equated with the Biblical "Logos," the Chinese "Tao," and is the underlying life-principle which is the source of all.

According to the Third Civilization, history can be divided into three periods. Ten thousand years ago, our human ancestors perfected the Kototama principle and lived as one family in a peaceful society. This perfect society was the First Civilization and is equated with the Garden of Eden. About 5,000 years ago, the Kototama principle was hidden from society and a new principle guiding society toward the material-scientific or Second Civilization emerged. During this time, man divided into tribes and nations and became competitive. Basic to the Second Civilization is the division between physical and spiritual. The present time, in which the pollution of the planet is monumental, is the hellfire prophesied in prior ages. Our only hope is the "messiah," the capacity of the human soul which has been dormant, the Kototama principle. With this principle, the Third Civilization will emerge.

Membership: Not reported. European centers are located in Paris and Uppsala, Sweden.

Periodicals: *Third Civilization Monthly*, Box 1836, Santa Fe, NM 87501.

Sources: Masahilo Nakazono, *Messiah's Return, The Hidden Kototama Principle*. Santa Fe, NM: Third Civilization, 1972; Masahilo Nakazono, *Kototama*. Sante Fe, NM: Third Civilization, 1976; Masahilo Nakazano, *My Past Way of Budo*. Santa Fe: Kototama Institute, 1979.

Indexes

Religious Organizations and Institutions Index

This index provides an alphabetical listing of religious organizations and groups described or discussed in the *Encyclopedia*. Because of the difference in format between the essay section and the directory section, index citations refer to both page numbers (for items in the essay section) and entry numbers (for items in the directory section). For the convenience of the user, citations referring to entry numbers are signified by a star. The citation referring to an organization's main entry in the directory section is further signified by a boldface italicized number. Index references following a religious organization's name are presented in sequential order, i.e., in the order they appear in the book. Thus, page numbers will precede entry numbers in a string of references.

American Catholic Church 5, ★18, ★32, ★59, ★61, ★68, ★104, ★105, ★*980*, ★981, ★985

American Catholic Church, Archdiocese of New York ★*66*, ★112

American Catholic Church (Malabar Succession) ★29

American Catholic Church (Syro-Antiochean ★980

American Catholic Orthodox Church ★105

American Christian Action Council ★163

American Christian Missionary Society ★553

American Church Union ★56

American Citizens for Honesty in Government ★907

American Conference of Undenominated Churches ★579

American Council of Christian Churches ★163, ★172, ★184, ★186, ★191, ★194, ★195, ★196, ★200, ★523, ★525, ★527, ★571, ★579, ★580

American Council of Christian Churches (ACCC) 73

American Eastern Orthodox Church ★*67*

American Episcopal Church ★17, ★*43*, ★44, ★46, ★51, ★53, ★59

American Esoteric Section 125

American Ethical Union ★*674*, ★675

American Evangelical Christian Churches ★*570*

American Evangelistic Association ★*415*

American Exarchate of the Russian Orthodox Catholic Church ★106, ★110

American Fellowship Church ★*690*

American Foreign Bible Society 61

American Foundation for the Science of Creative Intelligence ★1230

American Friends Service Committee ★490

American Grail Foundation ★*852*

American Graphological Society ★1087

American Holy Orthodox Catholic Apostolic Eastern Church ★105

American Holy Orthodox Catholic Eastern Church ★*68*

American Humanist Association ★*675*

American Independent Orthodox Church (Bridges) ★*69*

American Indian Evangelical Church ★*309*

American Indian Mission ★309

American Leadership College ★927

American Lutheran Church ★*130*

American Meditation Society ★*1176*

American Ministerial Association ★22

American Muslim Mission ★*1157*, ★1159, ★1160, ★1161, ★1163, ★1164, ★1165

American National Baptist Convention 64, ★536

American Nazi Party ★670

American Order of the Brotherhood of Wicca ★*1042*, ★1062

American Orthodox Catholic Church ★2, ★15, ★59, ★72, ★75, ★76, ★84, ★99, ★100, ★107, ★115, ★125

American Orthodox Catholic Church (Healy) ★*71*

American Orthodox Catholic Church (Irene) ★*72*

American Orthodox Catholic Church (Propheta) ★*70*, ★73

American Orthodox Catholic Church in the U.S. and Canada; Archdiocese of the ★2

American Orthodox Catholic Church - Western Rite Mission, Diocese of New York ★*2*

American Orthodox Church 10, ★70, ★*73*, ★101, ★116

American Orthodox Church, Diocese of California ★85

American Orthodox Church, Diocese of Chicago and North America ★115

American Rationalist Federation ★*676*, ★689

American Rescue Workers ★*213*

American Salvation Army ★213

American School of Mentalvivology ★*767*

American Society for Psychical Research (ASPR) 112, ★851

American Theosophical Society 126

American Tract Society ★518

American Unitarian Association 89, ★675, ★687

American Universalist Temple of Divine Wisdom ★*898*

American Vegan Society ★*1177*

American World Patriarchs ★7, ★9, ★12, ★14, ★*75*, ★97

American Zen College ★*1300*

Americans First, Inc. ★*677*

Ames Brethren); Plymouth Brethren (Exclusive: ★*564*

Amica Temple of Radiance ★*1010*

Amish 22, 47, 52, ★740

Amish Mennonite Church; Old Order ★*458*

Amish Mennonite Churches; Beachy ★*455*

Amish; Old Order 53

Anabaptists 16, 21, 22, 48

Ananda ★*1178*

Ananda Ashrama ★*1179*, ★1219

Ananda Cooperative Village ★1178

Ananda House ★1178

Ananda Marga Yoga Society ★*1180*, ★1207, ★1232

Ananda Niketan Ashrams ★1226

Anchor Bay Evangelistic Association ★*310*

Ancient Amethystine Order ★883

Ancient British Church ★52

Ancient Mystic Order of the Rosy Cross ★772

The Ancient Mystical Order of the Fratis Lucis ★996

Ancient and Mystical Order of the Rosae Crucis ★899, ★*947*, ★949

Ancient Order of Oriental Templars ★1028

Anglican Catholic Church ★43, ★*44*, ★46, ★50, ★51, ★53, ★56, ★60

Anglican Catholic Church in Canada ★45

Anglican Church 2, 32

Anglican Church in America ★43

The Anglican Church of America ★46

Anglican Church of the Americas ★76

Anglican Church of Canada ★44, ★45

Anglican Church of Korea ★44

Anglican Church of North America ★44, ★*45*

Anglican Episcopal Church ★43, ★46, ★52

Anglican Episcopal Church of North America ★*46*

Anglican Orthodox Church 3, ★43, ★46, ★*47*

Anglican Rite Jurisdiction of the Americas; Holy Catholic Church, ★*53*

Anglican Universal Church ★48, ★101, ★954

Anglo-Saxon Federation of America ★*664*

Ann Ree Colton Foundation of Niscience ★*1011*

Ansaaru Allah Community ★*1158*

Anthropological Research Foundation ★*853*

Anthroposophical League; Rosicrucian ★*952*

Anthroposophical Society ★953, ★*1012*

Anthroposophical Therapy and Hygiene Association ★1012

Anti-Communist League of America ★575

Antiocean Orthodox Church ★77

Antioch (Archdioceses of the United States and Canada) (Jacobite); Syrian Orthodox Church of ★*128*

Antioch Association of Metaphysical Science ★*768*

Antiochean Orthodox Archdiocese of Toledo, Ohio, and Dependencies ★74

Organizations Index

Northwestern Holiness Association ★247

Norwegian-Danish Evangelical Free Church Association ★179

Nova Hierosolyma; Lord's New Church Which Is ★*802*

Novominsk Hasidism ★*1115*

Nubian Islaamic Hebrew Mission ★1158

Nurbakhshi Order 149

Nyabingi Rastas ★1128

Oasis Fellowship ★*1017*

Oblates of St. Martin of Tours ★29

Occidental Orthodox Parishes; Association of ★77

Occult, Revelatory, Enlightenment Church; Astrological, Metaphysical, ★*900*

Ocean Song ★1178

Odinist Movement ★1075

Odyian ★1322

Ohio Association for Community Churches ★174

Ohio Bible Fellowship ★*583*

Ohio Bible Mission ★583

Ohsawa Foundation ★1294, ★1296

Ohsawa Macrobiotic Foundation; George ★*1296*

Old Brethren ★466

Old Brethren Church ★*472*, ★473

Old Brethren German Baptist Church ★*472*, ★*473*

Old Calendar Greek Orthodox Church ★40

Old Catholic Archdiocese for the Americas and Europe ★33

Old Catholic Church 3, ★15, ★34

Old Catholic Church in America ★5, ★18, ★20, ★33, ★48, ★68, ★104

Old Catholic Church of America; Archdiocese of the ★*3*

Old Catholic Church in America (Brothers) ★*21*

Old Catholic Church in America; Polish ★*33*

Old Catholic Church of British Columbia and Society; St. Raphael's ★*997*

Old Catholic Church of Canada ★19

Old Catholic Church in England ★29

Old Catholic Church; Mariavite ★2

Old Catholic Church in North America (Catholicate of the West) ★*22*

Old Catholic Church in Poland ★15

Old Catholic Church of Poland ★15

Old Catholic Church, Province of North America; Mariavite ★*15*

Old Catholic Church of Texas, Inc. ★21

Old Catholic Church, Ultrajectine Tradition; North American ★*17*

Old Catholic Church of Utrecht ★26

Old Catholic Church-Utrecht Succession ★*23*

Old Catholic Episcopal Church ★985, ★988, ★*992*

Old Catholic Episcopate in the Americas; United Hispanic ★*41*

Old Catholic Orthodox Church of St. Augustine of the Mystical Body of Christ ★16

Old Catholic Patriarchate of America ★118

Old Christian Reformed Church of Canada and America; Free and ★*155*

Old Episcopal Church ★*54*

Old German Baptist Brethren ★464, ★472, ★*474*, ★475

Old Holy Catholic Church, Province of North America ★*993*

Old Laestadians); Apostolic Lutheran Church ★*131*

Old Order Amish 53, ★455

Old Order Amish Mennonite Church ★*458*

Old Order German Baptist Brethren Church ★473

Old Order German Baptist Church ★*475*

Old Order (Horning or Black Bumper) Mennonites; Weaverland Conference ★*450*

Old Order Mennonites ★444

Old Order (Reidenbach) Mennonites ★*444*

Old Order River Brethren ★468

Old Order (Wenger) Mennonites ★444, ★*445*, ★448

Old Order (Wisler) Mennonite Church ★*446*

Old Order (Wisler) Mennonites ★445, ★450

Old Order (or Yorker) River Brethren ★462, ★*476*

Old Orthodox Catholic Patriarchate of America ★75, ★76, ★*104*

Old Regular Baptists ★519

Old Roman Catholic Church ★4, ★16, ★23, ★24, ★26, ★28, ★29, ★30, ★38

Old Roman Catholic Church, Archdiocese of Chicago ★73

Old Roman Catholic Church, Archdiocese of Chicago (Fris) ★*27*

Old Roman Catholic Church (Brown); Thee Orthodox ★*36*

Old Roman Catholic Church; Canonical ★*4*

Old Roman Catholic Church in England ★26

Old Roman Catholic Church in England and America ★4

Old Roman Catholic Church (English Rite) ★24, ★27, ★30, ★35

Old Roman Catholic Church (English Rite) and the Roman Catholic Church of the Ultrajectine Tradition ★*28*

Old Roman Catholic Church (Hamel) ★*25*

Old Roman Catholic Church (Marchenna) ★19, ★*26*

Old Roman Catholic Church in North America ★*24*, ★27

Old Roman Catholic Church; Ontario ★*30*

Old Roman Catholic Church (Orthodox Orders) ★84

Old Roman Catholic Church; Our Lady of Good Hope ★4

Old Roman Catholic Church (Rogers); North American ★*18*

Old Roman Catholic Church (Schweikert); North American ★*19*

Old Roman Catholic Church in the U. S. ★38

Old Roman Catholic Church in the U. S. (Hough) ★*29*

Old Roman Catholic Church-Utrecht Succession; North American ★*20*

Old Roman Catholic Church (Whitehead); United ★*42*

Old Roman Catholic Hungarian Orthodox Church of America; Independent ★*14*

Old Roman Community Catholic Church (Jones); Tridentine ★*40*

Omega Christian Church; Alpha and ★*414*

Omega Pentecostal Church of God of America, Inc.; Alpha and ★*386*

Omniune Church ★*701*

Omoto ★792, ★1335

Shrine of the Black Madonna ★1127

One World Family ★760

One World Family); Universal Industrial Church of the New World Comforter ★*760*

Oneida Community 101

The Only Fair Religion ★*936*

Ontario Old Roman Catholic Church ★25, ★*30*

Ontological Society ★915

Open Bible Church of God ★337

Open Bible Evangelistic Association ★331

Open Bible Standard Churches, Inc. ★*331*

Open Brethren 72

Open Brethren); Plymouth Brethren ★565

Open Goddess ★*1073*

Open Way ★*1018*

Operations Grace World Missions ★572

Order of Antioch ★984

Order of the Black Ram ★*1097*

Order of the Brotherhood of Wicca; American ★*1042*

Order of the Celtic Cross ★35

Order of Christus Rex ★*992*

Order of Damballah Hwedo Ancestor Priests ★1091

Order of the Elect Cohens ★1028

Order of the Golden Dawn (OGD); Hermetic 134
Order of the Golden Grail ★898
Order of the Knights of the Golden Circle ★950
Order of the Lily and the Eagle ★1030
Order of Loving Service ★880
Order of Osirus ★1074
Order of Our Most Blessed Lady, Queen of Peace ★19
Order of the Portal 136
Order of the Red Hand ★883
Order of Saint John Bernadone ★986
Order of Saint Michael ★31
Order of the Sons of Levi; Zion's ★710
Order of St. Germain ★994
Order of St. Germain, Ecclesia Catholica Liberalis ★993, ★994
Order of St. Timothy, Ecclesia Catholica Liberalis ★993
Order of the Star of the East ★979, ★1012, ★1203
Order of Thelema ★1031
Order of the Universe Publications ★1294
Ordo Adeptorum Invisiblum ★1032
Ordo Templi Astarte ★1033, ★1039
Ordo Templi Orientis ★949, ★1028, ★1033, ★1034, ★1035, ★1038
Ordo Templi Orientis in America; Society ★1038
Ordo Templi Orientis (Grant) ★1035
Ordo Templi Orientis (OTO) 135
Ordo Templi Orientis (Roanoke, Virginia) ★1036
Ordo Templi Satanas ★1098
Oregon Conference of the Church of God (Seventh-Day) ★628
Oregon Yearly Meeting ★488
Organization of Awareness ★853, ★857, ★864
Organization of Awareness (Calgary) ★869
Organization of Awareness (Federal Way) ★870
Organization of Awareness; International ★864
Organization of Awareness (Olympia) ★871
Orgyen Cho Dzong ★1325
Oriental Mission Society ★190
Oriental Missionary Society ★235
Oriental Missionary Society Holiness Conference ★255
(Original) Church of God ★297, ★306
Original Church of God (or Sanctified Church) ★261
Original Free Will Baptist Church; General Conference of the ★542
Original Glorious Church of God in Christ Apostolic Faith ★367, ★373
Original Hebrew Israelite Nation ★1126

Original Mountain Assembly; Church of God of the ★290
Original Pentecostal Church of God ★408
Original United Holy Church International ★400
Orphalese Foundation ★1193
Orthodox Abba World Faith ★1173
Orthodox American Catholic Church, Diocese of the Ozarks ★73
Orthodox Baha'i Faith, Mother Baha'i Council of the United States ★1171
Orthodox Baha'i Faith under the Regency ★1172
Orthodox Catholic Church of America ★68, ★96, ★99, ★105
Orthodox Catholic Patriarchate of America ★68, ★104, ★105
Orthodox Catholic Synod of the Syro-Chaldean Rite ★127
Orthodox Christian Reformed Churches ★158
Orthodox Church 10
Orthodox Church; African 11
Orthodox Church in America ★25, ★88, ★106
Orthodox Church of America ★107
Orthodox Church in America ★110
Orthodox Church of France ★77
Orthodox Church of Greece ★114
Orthodox Church in the Philippines ★70
Orthodox Church of the Philippines ★73
Orthodox Judaism ★1106
Orthodox Old Catholic Church ★84
Orthodox Old Roman Catholic Church (Brown); Thee ★36
Orthodox Old Roman Catholic Church II ★84
Orthodox Presbyterian Church ★163, ★165, ★166
Osirus; Order of ★1074
Our Lady of Endor Coven ★1099
Our Lady of Endor Coven, the Ophite Cultus Satanas ★1099
Our Lady of Good Hope Old Roman Catholic Church ★4
Our Lady of the Roses, Mary Help of Mothers Shrine ★31
Overcoming Faith Churches ★343
Overcoming Holy Church of God; Apostolic ★358
Oxford Movement ★57
Oyotunji, Yoruba Village of ★1091
Pacific Apostolic Faith Movement ★283, ★285
Pacific Coast Association of Friends ★489
Pacific Coast Khalsa Diwan Society ★1249
Pacific Yearly Meeting ★483, ★487

Pacific Yearly Meeting of Friends ★489
Pagan Front ★1084
Pagan Spirit Alliance ★1050
Pagan Spirit Gathering ★1050
Pagan Temple ★1076
Pagan Way, Temple of the ★1076
Pagan Way; Temple of the ★1084
Palatine); Pre-Nicene Church (de ★996
Palolo Kannondo Temple ★1269
Palpung Monastery ★1312
Pan African Orthodox Christian Church ★1127
Pan; Church of ★1047
Pansophic Institute ★1318
Paracelsian Order ★986
Paracletian Catholic Church ★995, ★1023
Parent Church ★1135
Particular Baptists 58
Pastoral Bible Institute ★630, ★633, ★637, ★638
Patriarchal Parishes of the Russian Orthodox Church in the United States and Canada ★86
Patriarchial Exarchate of the Russian Orthodox Church in the Americas ★41
Patriarchial Parishes of the; Russian Orthodox Church in the U.S.A., ★110
Peace Mission ★937
Peniel Mission ★224
Peniel Missions ★237
Pentecost Pilgrim Church ★240
Pentecostal Apostolic Church; Bible Way ★363
Pentecostal Assemblies of the World ★365
Pentecostal Assemblies; Association of Seventh-Day ★416
Pentecostal Assemblies of Jesus Christ ★374, ★375, ★381
Pentecostal Assemblies of the U.S.A. ★332
Pentecostal Assemblies of the World ★354, ★362, ★369, ★374, ★375, ★379, ★381
Pentecostal Brethren in Christ ★242
Pentecostal Church; Calvary ★318
Pentecostal Church of Christ ★304
Pentecostal Church of Christ; International ★304
Pentecostal Church of God ★332
Pentecostal Church of God of America ★332, ★334
Pentecostal Church of God of America, Inc.; Alpha and Omega ★386
Pentecostal Church of God of America; True Fellowship ★402
Pentecostal Church of God of New York; Latin-American Council of the ★413

Organizations Index

Educational Institution Index

Lists alphabetically the post-secondary educational institutions sponsored and/or supported by religious organizations described in the *Encyclopedia*. Numbers cited in this index refer to entry numbers, not to page numbers.

Personal Name Index

An alphabetical listing of persons discussed in the essay section and the directory section of the *Encyclopedia*. Numbers cited in this index refer to page numbers (for items in the essay section) and entry numbers (for items in the directory section). Citations referring to entry numbers are signified by a star.

Asbury, Francis ★177, ★182, ★201, ★202
Ashbrook, John ★583
Ashbury, Francis 32
Ashiata Shiemash ★1152
Ashjian, Mesrob ★120
Asoka 160
Assagioli, Robert ★976
Astley, Norman ★958
Astraea ★956
Astrid ★887
Atkinson, W. W. ★796
Atkinson, William Walker 156
Atmananda ★1205
Ato-Hotab, Emmanuel 10
Attakai, Mary ★896
Aubrey, George ★327
Audrey, J. W. ★352
Augustine 78, ★1
Aurobindo Ghose, Sri ★1182
Austin, Mary ★1074
Austin-Sparks, Theodore ★595, ★597
Austin, Tom ★408
Autobindo, Sri ★922
Auxentios of Athens, Metropolitan ★114
Avalokiteshvara ★1320
Awrey, Daniel 40
Ayer, A. J. 90
Ayyappa Swami ★1199
Azrael ★1022
Baal Shem Tov ★1110, ★1111
Baal Shem Tov, Israel 144
Bab ★1169
Baba Premanand Bharati 156
Baba Ram Dass 117
Babbitt, Elwood ★757
Backus, Isaac ★522
Bacon, Francis ★947
Bader, Augustine 79
Bagwell, Elder J. D. 81
Baha'u'llah 150, ★1169, ★1170, ★1174
Bailes, Frederick 108
Bailey, Alice 121, 126, ★973, ★974, ★975, ★976, ★977, ★978, ★979
Bailey, Dorothy ★1010
Bailey, Foster ★975
Bain, Alan 5, ★119
Baker, Charles F. ★589
Baker, Ora Ray ★1223
Baker, Oscar M. ★585, ★592
Baker, Richard ★1286
Baletka, John ★181
Ballard, Edna W. 127, ★1003, ★1005
Ballard, Guy 121, ★811, ★883, ★998, ★999, ★1001, ★1003, ★1004, ★1005
Ballard, Guy W. 127
Ballard, M. P. B. ★13
Ballard, Marlin Paul Bausum ★10
Ballou, Adin 101
Ballou, Hosea 88
Baloran ★888
Baltes, Gloria ★781
Banks, A. A. ★537
Baradeus, Jacob 12

Barbeau, Andre ★39
Barber, Forest ★983
Barber, Forest Gregory ★1028
Barber, Gregory F. E. ★982
Barber, Margaret E. ★595
Barbuiziuk, Rev. ★527
Barcynski, Leonard R. ★995, ★1023
Barcynski, Vivian ★995, ★1023
Barker, Frank ★166
Barlow, John ★711
Barlow, John Y. ★719
Barnabe, Julian ★322
Barnes, Harry Elmer ★675
Barnett, Calvin ★470
Barnett, M. J. 107
Barrett, Francis 132
Barrett, Harrison D. ★831
Barrett, Thomas Ball ★328
Barrington-Evans, W. A. ★24
Barrow, R. G. ★61
Barrows, Charles M 107
Barth, Hattie M. ★304
Barth, Kenneth L. ★580
Barth, Paul T. ★304
Bartholomew, M. L. ★612
Bartkow, Paul ★527
Bartlemen, Frank 41
Bartok, Eva ★1152
Barton, Michael X. 118
Bashir, Anthony ★74
Bashira, Sophonius 10, 11, ★86
Basil ★11
Basilios, Abuna ★125
Basilius, Mar ★10
Basilius Soares, Mar ★126, ★127
Bass, S. C. ★367, ★373
Bateman, Alice La Trobe 126
Bateman, Keith ★712
Bateman, Samuel 96
Bates, Joseph 80, ★606
Bates, Lonnie ★372
Bauer, Roy G. ★23, ★38
Baughman, John L. ★776
Bautista, Margarito ★711, ★719
Baxter, David M. ★107
Baxter, Richard 112, 114
Bayle, Pierre 90
Beachy, Moses ★455
Bean, Scipio ★201
Beane, John S. ★362
Beatty, George ★596
Beckbill, W. W. ★191
Becker, Frank E. ★1331
Becker, Peter 53, ★465
Becket, John Michael ★13
Becket, Thomas a 2
Beckwith, Edwin Burt ★989
Begg, Mirza Wahiduddin ★1142
Beidler, Paul ★460, ★463, ★1300
Beissel, Conrad 65
Beissel, Johann ★549
Beitz, Pastor W. F. ★149
Bekken, Dean ★988
Bell, A. D. ★20
Bell, Jessie Wicker ★1042
Bell, E. N. 43, ★313
Bellingham, Richard ★1074

Ben-Israel, Shaleah ★1126
Benade, William ★800
Bender, Deborah ★1057
Benedict, Samuel Durlin ★18
Benik, Anthony ★845
Benjamine, Elbert ★958
Bennett, J. G. ★1152
Bennett, John Godolphin ★1143
Bennett, Paul ★214
Benning, Frank H. ★46
Benson, Ezra Taft ★708
Bent, Dave W. ★886
Bernard, Pierre 156, ★1223
Bernhardt, Oskar Ernest ★852
Bernowski, Richard A. ★24
Beroth, Ernest ★334
Berry, D. M. ★997
Berry, W. J. ★529
Bertiaux, Michael ★1028
Besant, Annie 125, ★969, ★970, ★971, ★979, ★989, ★1012, ★1203
Besant-Scott, Mabel 138
Beshai, Marcus ★123
Besse, Clair ★459
Besse, G. Henry ★459
Besse, Lynn ★459
Beswarick, John ★820
Bethards, Betty ★926
Bethurum, Truman 117
Bey, Hamid ★912, ★978
Bhagat Singh Thind 158
Bhagwan Dass ★1193
Bhagwan Singh Gyanee 157
Bhajan, Yogi ★1240
Bharati, Premanand ★901
Bhattacharya, Besudeb 156
Bhattacharya, Vijaya ★1333
Bhumanannda Paramahansa, Guru ★1175
Bias, Clifford ★824, ★840, ★850
Bickerton, William ★727
Bilecky, Adam ★75
Bill, Annie C. ★1135
Billet, Grant Timothy ★22
Bingham, Mrs. Frank 107, ★778
Bishop, Beatrice Gaulton ★822
Bishop, Gladden 94
Bishop, Jemima ★257
Bishop, John L. ★656
Bizich, Tracy B. ★659
Blackstone, William E. 69
Blanchard, Charles A. ★582
Blau, Amram ★1116
Blaurock, George 48
Blavatsky, Helena Petrovna 112, 121, 123, ★966, ★967, ★969, ★970, ★971, ★973, ★1004, ★1009, ★1011, ★1012, ★1305
Blessing, John David ★669
Blessing, William Lester ★669
Blighton, Paul W. ★959
Blighton, Ruth ★959
Blob, Charlotte ★880
Boardman, William 36
Bob-Wood, Mrs Louis ★1324
Bodenstein, Andreas 47
Bodfish, Emmon ★1079

Effendi, Abbas 150, ★1169
Egli, Henry ★456
Egly, Henry ★456
Eielsen, Elling ★142
Eikerenkoetter II, Frederick ★771, ★795
Eisen, William ★803
Eklund, John T. ★988, ★989
Eleanore Mary Thedick ★903
Elizabeth I 2
Elliot, Pierre ★1143
Elliott, Ralph H. ★524
Ellis, Henry Milton ★780
Ellison, James D. ★668
Elmer E. Franke ★604
Elsworth Thomas Kaiser ★659
Elton, Eve ★781
Emerson, Ralph Waldo 89, 156, ★759
Emery, George ★915
Emmanuel, Brother ★924
Empson, Stephen ★77
Emry, Sheldon ★666
Enderle, Herman ★1076, ★1084
Engel, C. ★69
Engel, Jacob ★462
Engel, Leopold ★858
Englert, Paul ★682
Enochs, Emmet Neil ★52
Enrico, Rocco ★786
Entfelder, Christian 50
Erdmann, Paul ★750
Erhard, Werner ★1323
Erickson, Elmer ★513
Erickson, Rose Ann ★817
Eris ★1024
Erni, Julian E. ★46
Erwitt, Boris ★1327
Esbjorn, Lars Paul 17
Eschmann, John ★518
Eshai Shimun XXIII, Mar ★122
Eshelman, M. M. 84
Estes, H. Carlisle ★1083
Estrada, Jose Manuel ★1020
Ethel Schroeder ★763
Eusebius ★1
Eutyches, Archimandrite 12
Evans, J. Ellwood ★572
Evans, Jesse E. ★261
Evans, Mark Cardinal ★95
Evans, Warren Felt 106, 107
Everett, Ruth ★1278
Ewart, Frank J. 43
Ewing, Finis ★164
Facione, Francis P. ★24
Faitlovitch, Jacques 144
Falk, Louis W. ★44
Fambough, William ★188
Fanning, Tolbert ★553
Faquaragon, Alezandro B. ★414
Farrakhan, Abdul Haleem ★1164
Farrar, Janet ★1040
Farrar, Stewart ★1040
Farrell, Michael ★4, ★16
Farrow, Mia ★1230
Farrow, Sister Lucy 43
Farwell, William ★770

Fauth, Gordon ★648
Fauth, Naomi Dugger ★648
Fedchenkov, Benjamin ★86, ★110
Fehervary, Thomas ★37, ★39
Feild, Reshad ★1150
Feldman, Mark ★1029
Felicia, Sister ★33
Ferguson, Joseph T. ★798
Ferguson, Mable G. ★412
Ferguson, Manie ★237
Ferguson, Marilyn 119
Ferguson, Robert A. ★804
Ferguson, T. P. ★237
Ferguson, William ★884
Ferrando, Manual ★101
Fesi, John Dominic ★23, ★38
Fetting, Otto ★721, ★722, ★723, ★724
Feuerbach, Ludwig 90
Fields, H. W. ★400
Filer, Clifford ★243
Fillmore, Charles 107, ★774, ★797
Fillmore, Myrtle 107, ★797
Finch, Ralph G. ★227
Finleyson, John 83
Finney, Charles G. 36, ★237
Firmilian, Archimandrite ★113
Firmilian, Bishop ★113
Fisher, David ★1079
Fisher, George ★214
Fisher, J. Henry ★447
Fist, Fletcher ★754
Fitch, Charles 80
Fitch, Ed ★1076
Fitch, Lillian G. ★340
Fitch, William ★340
Fitzgerald, B. J. ★846
Flanders, Lloyd ★729
Flanders, Moroni ★729
Fleischmann, Konrad Anton ★518
Flenner, Millard J. 84
Fletcher, Clyde ★728
Fletcher, Emery ★728
Fletcher, Jack T. ★853
Fletcher, John 40, ★305
Fletcher, Pat ★853
Fletcher, Rupert J. ★728
Flexer, Dorothy ★840, ★850
Flexer, Dorothy Graff ★809
Flexer, Russell J. ★809
Flower, J. Roswell ★313
Flowers, Amanda ★824
Fludd, Robert 122
Fonda, Jane ★1230
Fons, G. F. C. ★334
Forbes, James Alexander ★400
Forbes, William Francis ★99, ★105
Ford, Arnold Josiah 145, ★1124
Ford, Arthur ★821, ★923
Ford, Betty ★1100
Ford, Jack ★243
Ford, Lewis 44, ★407
Ford, Patricia deMont ★35
Forest, Julia ★832
Forfreedom, Ann ★1057
Forgostein, Carolyn ★967
Forgostein, Harold ★967

Forrest, Julia O. ★839
Fosdick, Harry Emerson ★165
Foster, Charles 94
Foster, Harry ★597
Foster, Jane ★1026
Foster, Mrs. Thomas 166
Foster, Randolph S. 36
Foster, Robert 94
Fourier, Charles 100
Foust, James A. ★303
Fox, Arthur H. ★703
Fox, Diane ★703
Fox, Earl G. ★858
Fox, Emmet 108, ★775, ★776
Fox, George 51, 53
Fox, Kate 115
Fox, Margaretta 115
Fox, Selena ★1050
Francesca, Aleuti ★888
Francescon, Louis ★319
Francis of Assisi 99, ★1
Francis, Brother ★879
Francis David 88
Francis, Marianne ★888
Francisco Pagtakhan ★53
Franck, Sebastian 50
Francke, August Hermann 27
Frangquist, David ★1079
Franklin, Ben ★553
Franklin, Benjamin ★947
Franson, Fredrick ★179
Fraser, James ★1079
Frater Aleyin ★1033
Frazee, J. J. ★374
Frazer, Dudley ★327
Frazier, Dudley ★326
Frazier, Henry D. ★906
Frazier, R. O. ★438
Frederick Hong ★1288
Frederick Wilhelm III of Prussia, King ★177
Fredriksen, Norman C. ★838
Freeman, Carole ★859
Freer, Gedaliah ★1110
Freking, F. W. ★17
French, H. Robb 38, ★277
Freytag, F. L. Alexander ★639
Friede, Johannes ★858
Friedman, Daniel ★1134
Fris, Howard ★27, ★28, ★73
Frisby, Neal 44, ★347
Froelich, Samuel Heinrich ★494, ★495
Fromke, DeVern ★597
Frost, Gavin ★1045
Frost, Yvonne ★1045
Frothingham, Octavius Brooks 90
Fry, Daniel ★890
Fry, Russell G. ★46
Fuge, Albert J. ★52
Fujita, Reisai ★1329
Fujuhana, Kyodo ★1265
Fuller, Andrew ★504
Fuller, Richard 61
Fuller, W. E. ★305
Fullerton, Alexander ★970
Fulton, Gilbert A. ★712

Hamid ★1150
Hamiter, I. W. ★373
Hampton, Charles ★981, ★987, ★988, ★989
Han, Han Ja ★923
Hancock, Pauline ★720
Hancock, Samuel N. ★375
Hand, Beth R. ★820
Haney, Milton L. 37
Hanish, Otoman Zar-Adhusht ★1166
Hann, Amos ★273
Hans Ji Maharaj ★1241
Hansadutta Swami ★1228
Hanson, Ernest ★946
Harby, Isaac ★1105
Harden, Tom ★407
Hardevi, Madam ★1243, ★1248
Harding, A. L. Mark ★6
Hardy, Pere Gilles ★77
Hargrove, E. T. ★969
Hariot, Thomas 90
Harlow, Alison ★1052, ★1069
Harlow, Marie ★1328
Harms, Oscar C. ★317
Harper, H. C. ★555
Harris, C. W. ★394
Harris, James Frank ★376
Harris, Martin 94
Harrison, Carl B. ★597
Harrison, Donald ★1056
Harrison, Donald D. ★1048
Harrison, Doyle ★343
Hartley, Thomas 113, ★1068
Hartley, William ★968, ★969
Harvani, Hazrat Khwara Usman ★1142
Harvey, Donald ★1173
Harvey, Robert C. ★43, ★44
Harwood, J. H. ★582
Hash, Ruben K. ★364
Hasketh, Harrison Roy ★810
Haven, Gilbert 36
Hawaweeny, Bishop Raphael 10, ★74, ★106
Hawkins, Israyl Bill ★649
Hawkins, Jacob ★649, ★650
Hayes, Norvel ★343
Hays, Raymond ★407
Haywood, G. T. 43, ★354, ★365
Haywood, Thomas Garfield ★374, ★375
Hazrat Babajan ★1167
Heagy, Henry C. ★210
Healy, Patrick J. ★2, ★71
Heard, Gerald ★1227
Hearn, Charles V. ★22
Heath, Chester H. ★323
Heatwole, Gabriel D. ★446
Hedrick, Granville ★723
Hegg, Verner ★1012
Heideman, A.L. ★136
Heideman, Arthur Leopold 18, ★134
Heideman, Paul A. ★134, ★136
Heidenreich, Alfred ★1012
Heil, W. F. ★209
Heindel, Augusta Foss ★953
Heindel, Max ★953

Heinemann, Barbara ★733
Heinlein, Robert ★1046, ★1097
Heller, Patrick A. ★679
Hellman, Sylvia ★1231
Helwys, Thomas 58
Hembree, Maud ★254
Henninges, H.C. ★631
Henry C. Brooks ★383
Henry VIII 2
Hensley, George Went 44, ★407
Hensley, Kirby J. ★704
Henzsel, Johanna ★858
Hepker, George H. ★904
Herford, Ulric Vernon ★10, ★46, ★79, ★126, ★127
Herman F. Nelson ★53
Herman, Father ★106
Herman, Mordecai 145
Herman A. Spruit ★991
Hermes ★1059
Hermes Mercurious Trismegistus ★942, ★956
Hernandez y Esperon, Angel Maria ★412
Hernandez, J. A. ★411
Herr, Francis ★447
Herr, John ★447
Herrigel, Wilhelm ★1174
Herzl, Theodor 143
Herzog, Bishop 4, ★34
Herzog, Bishop Eduard 4
Hesketh, Harrison Roy ★811
Heughan, Elsie ★240
Hevia, Jose G. Oncins ★91
Heyer, 'Father' J. C. F. ★151
Hibbert, Joseph ★1128
Hickey, L. D. ★729
Hicks, Donald ★273
Hicks, Elias ★481
Hieronimus, Robert ★940
Higbee, C. L. 94
Higbee, Francis 95
Higgins, Jerry ★821
Higgins, Melvin ★1225
Higgins, Minnie ★958
Higginson, Thomas Wentworth 90
Higuchi, Kiyoko ★1335
Hilborn, Harry M. ★824
Hillyer, Nelson D. ★30
Himes, Joshua 80
Hindmarsh, Robert 113
Hinds, Robert ★1128
Hinkins, John-Roger ★1244
Hinkle, George M. 94
Hinkson, G. Duncan ★61, ★62
Hinton, Daniel ★32
Hinton, Daniel C. ★980
Hirai, Ryowa ★1274
Hirai, Tatsusho ★1274
Hirano, Toshio ★255
Hirayama, Bunjiro ★1340
Hirsh, R. H. ★638
Hisamatsu, Shin-ichi ★1276
Hobbs, Donald C. ★325
Hoch, Daniel ★453
Hochweber, Wilhelm ★1012
Hocking, W.E. ★165

Hockley, Fred 134
Hodgson, William B. 148
Hodur, Francis ★34
Hoefle, John J. ★634, ★636
Hoeller, Stephan A. ★982, ★983, ★993
Hoeskema, Herman ★159
Hoffman, George W. ★210
Hoffmann, Christopher ★745
Hofmann, Dr. Albert 116
Hofmann, Melchior 47, 79
Hoiles, C. Douglas ★688
Holdeman, John ★440
Holloway, Gilbert N. ★933
Holloway, June ★933
Holman, Leroy ★318
Holmes, Ernest 107, ★774, ★780, ★789, ★792, ★796
Holmes, Fenwicke ★792, ★796
Holmes, Stewart ★1276
Holmgren, A. A. ★328
Holsinger, Henry R. ★461, ★474
Holstine, Henry ★434
Holz, Richard ★213
Holzer, Hans ★1067
Homer, Alfred ★816
Homer, Gladys A. ★816
Honen 162
Honey, C. A. ★880
Hoo-Kna-Ka ★874
Hooker, Thomas 25
Hooper, Ivy M. ★840
Hoosier, Harry 33
Hoover, Christian ★476
Hopkins, Emma Curtis 107, ★761, ★769, ★778, ★781
Hopkins, Samuel ★165
Hopwood, Freeman ★672
Horioka, Chimyo ★1276
Horner, Ralph G. ★239
Horning, Moses ★445, ★450
Hornshuh, Fred ★331
Horowitz, David ★1136, ★1137
Horowitz, Levi ★1109
Horowitz, Meier ★1109
Horowitz, Pinchas D. ★1109
Horwitz, Jacob Isaac ★1114
Hoskins, I. F. ★638
Hottel, W. B. ★215
Houdini, Harry 115
Hough, Damian ★38
Hough, Joseph Damien ★29
Houser, Alvin E. ★559
Houteff, Victor T. ★601, ★602, ★603
Howard, D. H. ★697
Howard, Luther S. ★333
Howard, W. O. ★373
Howe, Julia Ward 88
Howell, James ★207
Howell, Leonard ★1128
Hoyle, Webster B. ★58
Hoyt, Herman A. ★469
Hua, Hsuan ★1293
Huba, Ihor ★102
Hubbard, L. Ron 135, ★905, ★907, ★1242
Hubbard, Mary Sue ★907

Roberts, James Pickford ★45, ★988
Roberts, Mark ★1057
Roberts, Oral ★339, ★427
Roberts, Robert 66, ★550, ★562
Robertson, W. E. J. ★61
Robinson, Frank B. ★935
Robinson, Herbert ★76
Robinson, Ida ★399
Robinson, John 58
Roby, Jasper C. ★358
Roche, Edmond P. ★646
Rock, John Friedrick ★733
Rockwell, George Lincoln ★670
Rodriguez, Antonio ★21
Rodriguez Y Durand, Alberto Luis
   ★16
Rodriguez y Fairfield, Emelio Federico
   ★16
Rodriguez y Fairfield, Emile ★4
Rodriguez-Fairfield, Emile F. ★16
Rodriguez-Rivera, Juan Francisco
   ★411
Roerich, Helena ★973, ★1009
Roerich, Nicolas ★973, ★1009
Rogers, Clarissa ★657
Rogers, Granville ★273
Rogers, Hubert A. ★14, ★18, ★59
Rogers, James H. ★18
Rollings, Edward B. ★177
Roman, Olga ★815
Ronald Powell ★996
Rosado, Francisco ★410
Rosado, Leoncai ★410
Rosen, Mervine ★1287
Rosenblum, Arthur ★748
Rosencreutz, Christian 121, 122,
   ★1030
Rosenfeld, Leo ★1110
Rosenius, Carl Olof ★178
Rosenkruz, Sergius ★950
Rosete, Lupe ★53
Ross, Martin 62
Rossi, Andrew ★959
Rothmann, Bernard 50, 100
Rouse, James ★731
Rowen, Lady ★1063
Rowinski, Francis C. ★34
Royce, Josiah 112
Rucker, J. L. ★261
Rudenko, Palladij ★102
Rudolph, Albert ★1211, ★1216
Rudometkin, Maksim Gavrilovic
   ★499, ★500
Rudrananda, Swami ★1211
Ruffing, Jennings ★920
Rumi, Mevlana Jelalu'ddin ★1150
Runcorn, Ora ★628
Runyon, Jr., Carroll R. ★1033
Russell, Bertrand 90, ★686
Russell, C.F. ★1033
Russell, Charles Taze 81, ★327,
   ★629, ★630, ★631, ★633, ★634,
   ★635, ★636, ★637, ★638, ★639,
   ★669, ★1137
Russell, H. V. ★997
Russo, M. ★814
Ruth, C. W. ★231

Rutherford, J. F. ★633, ★635, ★637,
   ★638
Rutherford, J. R. 83, ★639
Ryan, Francis J. ★9, ★39
Ryan, James Charles ★43
Ryan, Leo J. ★937
Ryzy, Emigidius J. ★75
Ryzy-Ryski, Uladyslau ★14, ★75,
   ★104
Ryzy-Ryski, Uladyslav ★7, ★9, ★12
Ryzy-Ryski, Ulanyslau ★97
Saarenpaa, Mikko 18
Sabiri, Makhdum Ala'u'di-Din Ali
   Ahmad ★1142
Sadanaga, Masayasu ★1268
Sadiq, Mufti Muhammad ★1156
Sadler, John 83
Sai Baba, Satya ★1212
Sai Baba of Shirdi ★1212
Saint-Charles, Pierre-Antoine ★1028
Saint Germain 127
Saint-Martin, Louis Claude de 132,
   ★1028, ★1030
Saint-Omer, Geoffrey de 132
Saint-Simon, Claude Henri 100
Saito, Gyoko ★1264
Sakae, Sekiguchi ★1341
Sakuma, Henry T. ★255
Sakya Trizin ★1309, ★1311, ★1321
Saliba, Philip ★74
Salisbury, W. L. ★847
Samarin, Paul I. ★500
Samon, Sergius ★87
Sams, Clarence Francis ★530
Sams, James C. ★535
Samuel, Bishop ★123
Samuel, MarAthanasius Y. ★128
Samuel, William ★765
Sananda ★882, ★887, ★1005, ★1006
Sanat Kumara ★1004, ★1005
Sanches, Antonio ★353
Sanches, George ★353
Sandeman, Robert 65
Sander, J. A. ★199
Sanders, Alexander 138, ★1040,
   ★1041, ★1063
Sanders, Maxine ★1040
Sandine, Hilmer B. ★173
Sant Ram Mandal 157
Santamaria, John ★319
Santamaria, Rocco ★319
Saoshyant, Prophet ★910
Sarah, Sister ★412
Saraswati Devyashram, Swami ★1196
Saraswati Goswami Maharaja,
   Bhaktisiddhanta ★1184
Saraydarian, Haroutiun ★973
Saraydarian, Torkom ★973
Sargent, Thomas ★8, ★23, ★40
Sarkar, Prabhat Ranjan ★1180
Sarkissian, Karekin ★120
Sasaki, Joshu ★1280
Sasaki, Ruth Fuller Everett 165
Satchakrananda Bodhisattvaguru,
   Father ★1210
Satchidananda, Swami ★1197
Sattler, Michael 48

Saturnus, Frater ★1034
Satyananda Saraswati, Swami ★1213
Sauer II, Christopher ★465
Saunders, Monroe ★379
Saunders, Willard W. ★374
Savelle, Jerry J. ★343
Sawka, Demetius ★117
Sawyer, Don ★1044
Sawyer, Elizabeth ★1044
Sawyna, Wasyl ★47
Sayadaw, Hlaign Tet ★1257
Sayadaw, Kaba-Aye ★1257
Sayadaw, Mahasi ★1251
Sayo, Kitamura ★1346
Sazanami, Shizuka ★1264
Schaffer, James ★262
Schaffer, Sr., Peter ★496
Schechter, Solomon ★1103
Schellenberg, Abraham ★454
Scheppe, John S. 43
Schiffner, Alexander ★671
Schlatter, Michael ★177
Schlossberg, Bertram S. ★79
Schmitt, Charles P. ★417
Schmitt, Dorothy E. ★417
Schmucker, Samuel S. 17
Schmul, Rev. H. E. 38, ★268
Schneersohn, Joseph Isaac ★1113
Schneersohn, Menachem Mendel
   ★1113
Schneersohn, Samuel ★1113
Schneider, Abe ★233
Schneider, William H. ★59
Scholte, Henrik ★152
Schraub, Philip ★1022
Schroeder, Lynn 112
Schucman, Helen ★785
Schuler, Robert ★594
Schweikert, John E. ★19
Schweitzer, Albert ★1177
Schwenckfeld, Casper 50
Schwenkfeld, Caspar ★501
Scofield, C. I. 69, 71
Scott, F. C. ★390
Scott, George ★178
Scott, Joseph L. ★306
Scott, Orange ★242
Scroggie, William Graham 69
Seabrook, Brian ★807
Seabury, Samuel ★55
Seale, Ervin ★776
Seivertson, Geneva D. ★903
Seivertson, Wayne ★903
Seki, Eikaku ★1271
Selassie, Haile ★124, ★1124, ★1128
Sellers, Ernest William ★412
Sellers, F. E. ★196
Sellers, L. O. ★296
Seltmann, Max ★858
Selzer, Charles L. ★733
Semple, Robert ★329
Sen, Keschub Chunder 156
Seng-ts'an 162
Senge, Sonfuku ★1344
Senntao, Mysikiitta Fa ★914
Sensenig, Aaron ★449
Senzaki, Nyogen ★1275, ★1277

Publication Index

An alphabetical list of periodicals, newsletters, and other publications regularly issued by the religious groups outlined in the directory section. Numbers cited in this index refer to entry numbers, not to page numbers. (This index does not cover source materials listed at the end of each essay chapter nor does it cover publications listed under the heading Sources within each directory entry.)

The Celtic Evangelist ★49
Center of Gravity ★1280
Cerkovny Visnik—Church Messenger ★65
Challenge ★599
Chimes ★832, ★873, ★1022
Chimo ★1204
Christ Is the Answer ★665
Christ for the Nations ★341
Christadelphia ★550
Christadelphia Newsletter ★550
The Christadelphian ★550
The Christadelphian Advocate ★562
Christadelphian Focus on the News ★550
Christadelphian Messenger ★550
Christadelphian Tidings of the Kingdom of God ★550
The Christext ★783
Christian Appeal ★557
The Christian Baptist ★533
The Christian Beacon ★163
Christian Century ★97
Christian Chronicle ★553
The Christian Community ★174
The Christian Community Journal ★1012
Christian Evangel ★313
The Christian Index ★204
The Christian Leader ★454
The Christian Militant ★575
Christian Mission Voice ★440
Christian Missions in Many Lands ★569
Christian Monthly ★131
The Christian Pathway ★533
The Christian Science Journal ★761
The Christian Science Monitor ★761
Christian Science Quarterly ★761
Christian Science Sentinel ★761
The Christian Spiritual Voice ★406
Christian Standard ★239, ★560
Christian Truth for the Household of Faith ★568
Christian Vanguard ★670
The Christian Voice ★244
Christian Yoga World ★1220
Christian Youth ★288
The Christoid Evangel ★910
Chrysostomos ★85
The Church Advocate ★154, ★225
The Church Advocate and Good Way ★226
The Church of Christian Liberty Messenger ★575
Church Directory and Year Book ★32
The Church of God ★293
Church of God Evangel ★285
The Church of God Final Warning ★297
Church of God Herald ★288
The Church Herald ★160
The Church Herald and Holiness Banner ★223
The Church of Light Quarterly ★958
Church Newsletter ★702

Circle Network News ★1050
Circle Seminary ★1050
The Classics Expositor ★587
Clear Light ★1318
The Cloven Hoof ★1095
Collaboration ★1182
The Coming Revolution ★1001
The Communicator ★99
The Concordia Lutheran ★141
Congregational Beacon ★173
Congregational Methodist Messenger ★188
The Congregationalist ★176
Conservative Baptist ★509
Conservative Judaism ★1103
Contact ★544, ★866
The Contender ★339
The Contender for the Faith ★365
Continuum ★993
Contributor's Bulletin ★962
Convention Herald ★268
Conviction ★321
Cosmic Frontiers ★1015
Cosmic Light ★806
Cosmic Voice ★881
Covenant Companion ★178
The Covenant of the Goddess Newsletter ★1052
Covenant Home Altar ★178
Covenant Quarterly ★178
The Covenanter ★273
The Covenanter Witness ★168
Crazy Wisdom ★1201
Creative Thought ★789
Credinta—The Faith ★108
The Crusader ★670
Crystal Well ★1076
The Cumberland Flag ★169
Daily Guide to Richer Living ★796
Daily Meditation ★961
Daily Word ★797
The Dairy ★458
The Dawn ★633
Dawn ★1194
Dawn of a New Day ★344
De Wachter ★152
The Defender ★411
Delaware Valley Prout News ★1180
Der Bote ★453
Deseret News ★708
Destiny Editorial Letter Service ★664
Dharma Season ★1287
Dharma World ★1270
Diamond Sangha ★1277
Diamond Sword ★1283
Diocesean Observer ★114
The Disciple ★551
Divine Slave Gita ★1195
The Divine Times ★1241
Divine Toad Sweat ★897
The Door ★76
The Double Heartline ★941
Druid Missal-any ★1079
Dry Legion ★256
Duangpratip ★1258
Dundrub Yong (Song of Fulfillment) ★1312

Earth Religion News ★1059
East-West ★1214
East West Journal ★1294
Ecclesia ★43
Ecclesia Gnostica ★1034
Echoes of Grace ★568
ECK Meta Journal ★1242
ECK World News ★1242
Einherjar ★1075
El Defensor Hispano ★411
El Mensajero de los Postreros Dias ★412
El Revelator Christiana ★409
The Elijah Messenger ★644
Elim Herald ★320
EMCI Herald ★576
Emmanuel Herald ★227
Emmanuel Holiness Messenger ★296
Emphasis ★234
Ensenznzas de la Mueva Era ★868
The Ensign ★708
Ensign ★714
Eon/Justice and Truth ★1030
Epiphany Studies in the Scriptures ★637
Episcopal Recorder ★57
Episcopal Tidings ★46
The Episcopalian ★55
Equinox ★1038
The Ernest Christian ★274
The Esoterian News ★790
E.S.P. Laboratory Newsletter ★1060
The Etherian Bulletin ★917
The Ethical Outlook ★674
Ethical Platform ★674
The Evangel ★258
Evangelical Baptist ★301
Evangelical Baptist Herald ★521
The Evangelical Beacon ★179
The Evangelical Excerpts ★247
The Evangelical Methodist ★191, ★194
Evangelical Visitor ★462
The Evangelist ★53
The Evening and Morning Star ★723
Ever Increasing Faith Messenger ★343
Exegesis ★680
Expression ★927
The Facing Bench ★480
Facts for Action ★666
Facts of the Faith ★616
The Faith ★646, ★648
Faith and Fellowship ★139
Faith-Life ★149
Faith and Truth ★307
Faith and Victory ★222
The Faithist Journal ★878
Familienfreund ★452
Fate Magazine ★956, ★1028
Fellowship ★341, ★554
Fellowship Echoes ★390
The Fellowship Herald ★623
Fellowship Together ★417
Fifth Year Book ★32
The Final Call ★1164
The Fire ★427

The Living Unicorn ★1046
Longhouse Calendar ★1086
Lorian Journal ★931
The L.O.T.U.S. ★865
Lotus Leaves ★825
The Lund Re-View ★764
The Lutheran ★146
The Lutheran Ambassador ★138
Lutheran Sentinel ★143
The Lutheran Spokesman ★140
Lutheran Standard ★130
The Lutheran Standard ★147
Macrobiotics Today ★1296
The Magical Link ★1034
Magyar Egyhaz ★156
The Mantle ★328
Maranatha Devotions ★598
Maranatha! The Lord Cometh ★84
The Mariavita Monthly ★15
Mark-Age Inform-Nations (MAIN)
  ★887
The Marturion ★742
The Master Key ★655
Master Mind ★781
Master Thoughts ★775
Mater Benevola ★12
Mazdaznan ★1166
The Medicine Wheel ★1055
Megiddo Messenger ★254
Meher News Exchange, East/West
  ★1167
The Mennonite ★453
Mennonite Historical Bulletin ★443
The Mentor ★1000, ★1007
Mercury ★954
Message ★389
The Message ★589, ★1154
Message of the Open Bible ★331
The Messenger ★3, ★306, ★452
Messenger ★465
The Messenger ★522, ★801
Messenger of Truth ★440
The Messenger of Truth ★527
The Metaphysical Messenger ★809
The Minaret ★1139
Minister John Muhammad Speaks
  ★1165
Ministry ★606
Miracle ★348
Miracle Magazine ★348
Miracle News ★785
Miracle Word ★342
Miracles ★785
Missionary Baptist Searchlght ★503
The Missionary Revivalist ★272
The Missionary Signal ★154
The Missionary Tidings ★230
Missionary Tidings ★246
Missions ★221
Missions in Action ★539
MOA Newsletter ★1335
The Monarch Messenger ★695
Monastery Newsletter ★1314
The Monitor of the Reign of Justice
  ★639
Monthly Guide ★1252
Moody Church News ★582

Moody Monthly ★582
The Moon Monk ★856
Moorish Guide ★1162
The Mother Church ★121
The Mount Zion Reporter ★648,
  ★654
The Movement Newspaper ★1244
Mu Eggs Press ★754
Muhammad Speaks ★1163
Muslim Star ★1139
The Muslim Sunrise ★1156
The Mystic Cross ★1215
Mystic, the Magazine of the
  Supernatural ★863
MZMC Newsletter ★1279
N.A.C.C. Update ★560
The NAHC Bulletin ★277
The Narrow Way ★645
Nation ★686
National Baptist Voice ★536
The National Spiritualist Summit
  ★831
The Nationalist Spiritualist Reporter
  ★827
Needed Truth ★563
Nelly Heathen ★1078
Neo-Dharma Notes ★1254
New Age Christian Newsletter ★862
The New Age Forum ★807
New Age Teachings ★868
New America ★1075
The New Angelus for the New Age
  ★1022
The New Aurora ★505
New Birth Christian Newsletter ★862
The New Broom ★1057
New Church Home ★800
New Church Life ★800
The New Creation ★632
New Era ★708
The New Shiloh Messenger ★658
The New Spirit ★811
New Testament Testimonies ★517
The New World Translation of the
  Holy Scriptures ★635
New York Newsletter ★1012
The News ★47
News Bulletin ★170
News from Jain Ashram ★1237
News from Martinus Institute ★866
Newsletter ★494, ★610, ★625, ★690,
  ★854, ★919, ★933, ★1029, ★1140,
  ★1151, ★1171, ★1186
The Newsletter ★1267
Newsletter for Christian Millennial
  Church Members ★632
Newsletter of the New Jersey Chapter
  ★683
Newswatch Magazine ★614
Noohra-Light ★786
The North American Moravian ★180
The North Star Baptist ★515
The Northern Independent ★230
Northwest Vision ★488
The Northwestern Lutheran ★151
Notes from Lollygog ★765
Notes from Out Church Organ ★656

Notes from Woodsong ★765
The Occult Digest ★1328
The Odinist ★1075
The Ohio Fellowship Visitor ★583
The Old Catholic ★985
Old Catholic Church (Utrecht
  Succession) ★27
The Old Catholic Newsletter ★993
Old Faith Contender ★529, ★533
Old Paths Advocate ★555
The Olive Tree ★652
On the March ★216
One Church ★110
One-Eyed Journal ★1147
onflowers ★959
Open Letter ★1005
Oracle of Thoth ★948
The Order of the Universe ★1294
Orion ★1188
Orthodoks Mustakil ★115
The Orthodox Catholic ★73
Orthodox Catholic Herald ★115
The Orthodox Church ★106
Orthodox Life ★111
Orthodox Missionary ★114
Orthodox Observer ★90
The Orthodox Word ★111
Our Anglican Heritage ★45
Our Daily Bread ★801
Our Herald ★360
Our Missionary ★104
Our News and Views ★855
The Outreach ★120
Outside the Camp ★590
Over There ★964
The Overcomer ★331
Pacific World ★1262
The Pagan ★1046
Pagan Spirit Journal ★1050
Paper for All ★639
The Pastor's Journal ★174
The Path of Orthodoxy ★113
Path of Righteousness ★1139
The Path of Truth ★791
Pathways to Health ★899
The PCA Messenger ★166
Pearls of Wisdom ★1001
Peniel Herald ★237
Pentalpha ★1079
Pentecostal Evangel ★313
The Pentecostal Free-Will Baptist
  Messenger ★308
Pentecostal Herald ★332
The Pentecostal Herald ★381
The Pentecostal Leader ★304
The Pentecostal Messenger ★332
Pentecostal Outlook ★374
Pentecostal Power ★314
People of Destiny Magazine ★417
The People's Mouthpieces ★358
The Pilgrim ★472
Pilgrim News ★278
Pillar of Fire ★256
Pisgah Journal ★418
Plain Living High Thinking ★1200
The Plain Truth ★628
Plenty News ★751

The True Light ★64
The True Report ★595
True Witness ★392
The Trumpet ★61
Trumpet ★665
Truth ★589
The Truth ★654, ★719
Truth Consciousness Journal ★1226
Truth on Fire ★216
Truth Journal ★1188
The Truth Seeker ★672
The Truth Teller ★723
Truth for Today ★592
Twentieth Century Watch ★615
U. S. Baha'i Report ★1169
U. S. Orthodox Life ★105
Ubique ★989
U.C.C. Spokesman ★845
UCM Magazine ★846
Udumbara ★1279
The Uforatzto Journal ★1113
Ukrainian Orthodox Herald ★117
Ukrainian Orthodox Word ★116
The Ultimates ★597
Under the Wings ★1154
Understanding ★890
Unification Leader ★608
Unification News ★923
Uniguidance ★861
Union Searchlight ★207
The United Brethren ★208
United Church Herald ★177
The United Evangelical ★209
United Holiness Sentinel ★280
United Israel Bulletin ★1137
United Synagogue Review ★1103
Unity Magazine ★797
Universal Challenger ★281
Universal Life ★704
The Universal Message ★697
The Universal Spiritualist ★850
Unsearchable Riches ★588
Up Lift ★796
Urantia Brotherhood Bulletin ★945
Urantian ★945
UU World ★687
Vajra Bodhi Sea ★1293
The Vajradhatu Sun ★1323
Valor ★964
Valvoju ★132
Vedanta in the West ★1227

Vedic Heritage Newsletter ★1196
Vekrozumu ★676
Venture Inward ★899
The Vindicator ★474
The Vineyard (Vreshta) ★63
The Vision Speaks ★286
Vista ★319
Vital Christianity ★221
Voice ★315, ★541
The Voice ★579, ★597, ★772
Voice of Astara ★956
The Voice of Eternal Life ★732
The Voice of Evangelical Methodism ★190
Voice from the East ★122
Voice from Heaven ★1346
The Voice of Healing ★339, ★341
The Voice of the 'I AM' ★1003
Voice of Micah ★1130
The Voice of Missions ★201, ★387
Voice of the Nazarene ★281
The Voice of Orthodoxy ★94
The Voice of Peace ★725
The Voice of the Synod ★989
The Voice of Unity ★612
The Voice of Universarius ★892
The Voice of Warning ★721
The Voice of the Wilderness ★354
Voice in the Wilderness ★597
Voice of the World ★400
The Voyager ★794
War Cry ★238
The Washington Buddhist ★1255
The Watchman ★667
The Watchtower Announcing
   Jehovah's Kingdom ★635
Waxing Moon ★1076
The Way ★1264
The Way Magazine ★593
Wellspring ★735
The Wesleyan Advocate ★242
Wesleyan World ★242
West Coast Evangel ★557
Western Bodhi ★1334
Western Orthodox Voice ★85
Wheel of Dharma ★1262
The White Light ★1039
White Star Illuminator ★893
White Wing Messenger ★287
The Whole Truth ★366
Whole Truth ★387

W.I.C.A. Newsletter ★1087
Wind Bell ★1286
Window on Bethany ★574
Windows: East and West ★489
Wisconsin Lutheran Quarterly ★151
Wisdom: Magazine of the FPMT ★1324
The Wise Woman ★1057
Witchcraft Digest ★1087
The Witch's Trine ★1072
Witness ★147
The Witness ★818
Women's Chains ★256
The Word ★74, ★642, ★972
The Word of Faith ★343
Word and Witness ★313
Word and Work ★556
World Evangelism ★415
World Goodwill Newsletter ★975
World Government News ★1230
World Insight ★627
World Messianity Newsletter ★1335
World Mission ★224
World Order ★1169
World Philosophy ★1328
The World Today Analyzed ★643
The Worldwide News ★628
Yahweh Nissi ★758
Yearbook of Jehovah's Witnesses ★635
Yin Yang ★1296
Yoga ★1208, ★1213
Yoga Life ★1217
The Yoganta Center Newsletter ★1234
Yogashakti Mission Newsletter ★1206
Young Ideas ★791
Youth ★628
The Youth Messenger ★306
Zen Bow ★1285
Zen Notes ★1278
Zion Trumphet ★205
Zion's Advocate ★723
Zion's Echoes of Truth ★333
Zion's Herald ★477
Zion's Landmark ★531
Zion's Restorer ★667
Zion's Watchman ★667
Ziraat ★1154

Geographic Index

Arranges religious organizations listed in the directory section alphabetically by state and then by city. Numbers cited in this index refer to entry numbers and not to page numbers.

Alabama

Apostolic Overcoming Holy Church of God ★358★
% Bishop Jasper C. Roby
514 W. 10th Ave., N.
Birmingham, AL 35204

House of God Which is the Church of the Living God, the Pillar and Ground of Truth without Controversy (Keith Dominion) ★396★
% Bishop J. W. Jenkins, Chief Overseer
Box 9113
Birmingham, AL 36108

Triumph the Church and Kingdom of God in Christ ★267★
Box 77056
Birmingham, AL 35228

Universal Church of Scientific Truth ★798★
1250 Indiana St.
Birmingham, AL 35224

Bible Methodist Connection of Churches ★270★
Rev. George Vernon
Box 187
Brent, AL 35304

Church of God (World Headquarters) ★293★
% Voy M. Bullen, General Overseer
2504 Arrowwood Dr., S.E.
Huntsville, AL 35803

Second Cumberland Presbyterian Church in U. S. ★169★
226 Church St.
Huntsville, AL 35801

House of Judah ★1125★
Wetumpka, AL 36092

Assembly of Yahvah (Alabama) ★644★
Box 89
Winfield, AL 35594

Alaska

Harmony Buddhist Mission ★1332★
% Rev, Frank Newton
Clarksville, AK 92830

Alaska Yearly Meeting ★478★
Box 268
Kotzebue, AK 99752

Arizona

United Order Effort ★719★
% Leroy Johnson
Colorado City, AZ 86021

Oasis Fellowship ★1017★
Box O
Florence, AZ 85232

Old Episcopal Church ★54★
% Rt. Rev. Jack C. Adam
Box 2424
Mesa, AZ 85204

Berean Bible Fellowship ★585★
52nd & E. Virginia Sts.
Phoenix, AZ 85008

Bethany Bible Church and Related Independent Bible Churches of the (Arizona) Area ★574★
6060 N. Seventh Ave.
Phoenix, AZ 85013

B'nai Shalom ★316★
Gospel of Peace Camp Ground
5607 S. 7th St.
Phoenix, AZ 85040

Church of Basic Truth ★904★
Box 6084
Phoenix, AZ 85005

Church of Essential Science ★807★
% Rev. Brian Seabrook
Box 31022
Phoenix, AZ 85046

Evangelical Orthodox (Catholic) Church in America (Non-
Papal Catholic) ★11★
% Most Rev. Perry R. Sills
3110 W. Voltaire Ave.
Phoenix, AZ 85029

Hall Deliverance Foundation ★342★
Box 9910
Phoenix, AZ 85068

Miracle Life Revival, Inc. ★347★
Box 20707
Phoenix, AZ 85036

Miracle Revival Fellowship ★348★
% Don Stewart Evangelistic Association
Phoenix, AZ

National Colored Spiritualist Association of Churches
★827★
% Rev. Nellie Mae Taylor
1245 West Watkins Rd.
Phoenix, AZ 85007

Theocentric Foundation ★942★
3341 E. Cambridge Ave.
Phoenix, AZ 85008

University of Life Church ★851★
% Rev. Richard Ireland
5600 Sixth St.
Phoenix, AZ 85040

Holm ★1195★
% Anthony Zuccarello, President
Box 25839
Prescott Valley, AZ 86312

Ruby Focus of Magnificent Consummation ★1005★
P.O. Drawer 1188
Sedona, AZ 86336

Foundation for Science of Spiritual Law ★816★
% Rev. Alfred Homer
Tonopah, AZ 85354

Universariun Foundation ★892★
4360 North Bear Claw Way
Tucson, AZ 85749

Ascended Master Fellowship ★998★
Box 603
162 Look-a way
Yarnell, AZ 85362

Infinite Way ★762★
Box 215
Youngtown, AZ 85363

Arkansas

Congregation of Yah ★619★
Box S
Beebe, AR 72012

Sri Ram Ashrama ★1219★
P.O.Box AR
Benson, AR 24259

Baptist Missionary Association of America ★507★
716 Main St.
Little Rock, AR 72201

Orthodox Church of America ★107★
% Most Rev. David Baxter
502 East Childress
Morrilton, AR 72110

Free Christian Zion Church of Christ ★205★
1315 Hutchingson
Nashville, AR 71852

New Life Fellowship ★652★
Box 75
Natural Dam, AR 72948

Sovereign Grace Baptist Churches ★526★
% Rev. E. W. Johnson
Calvary Baptist Church
Pine Bluff, AR

Shiloh Trust ★743★
% Rev. James Janisch
Sulfur Springs, AR 72763

American Baptist Association ★503★
4605 N. State Line Ave.
Texarkana, AR 75501

California

Aquarian Educational Group ★973★
30188 Mulholland Hwy.
Agoura, CA 91301

Home of Truth ★781★
% Rev. Gloria Baltes
1300 Grand St.
Alemeda, CA 94501

The (Local) Church ★595★
% Living Stream Ministry
1853 West Ball Rd.
Anaheim, CA 92804

Esoteric Fraternity ★737★
Box 37
Applegate, CA 95703

Society of Evangelical Agnostics ★686★
Box 515
Auberry, CA 93602

The Synanon Church ★759★
46216 Dry Creek Rd.
Box 112
Badger, CA 93603

The Georgian Church ★1064★
1908 Verde St.
Bakersfield, CA 93304

Lectorium Rosicrucianum ★951★
Box 9246
Bakersfield, CA 93309

Tridentine Old Roman Community Catholic Church
(Jones) ★40★
% Most Rev. Jacques A. Jones
10446 Highdale St.
Bellflower, CA 90706

Covenant of the Goddess ★1052★
Box 1226
Berkeley, CA 94704

New Reformed Orthodox Order of the Golden Dawn
★1072★
% Robin Goodfellow and Gaia Wildewoode
1625 Woolsey St.
Berkeley, CA 947036

Prana Yoga Ashram ★1209★
International Headquarters
% Swami Sivalingam
488 Spruce St.
Berkeley, CA 94708

Tibetan Nyingmapa Meditation Center ★1322★
2425 Hillside Ave.
Berkeley, CA 94704

Vedantic Cultural Society ★1228★
2324 Stuart St.
Berkeley, CA 94705

Lakshmi ★1205★
270 N. Canon Dr., Suite 1280
Beverly Hills, CA 90210

Church of the Gentle Brothers and Sisters ★908★
Box 346
Bolinas, CA 94924

Taungpupu Kaba-Aye Dhamma Center ★1257★
18335 Big Basin Way
Boulder Creek, CA 95006

Vajrapani Institute for Wisdom Culture ★1324★
Box I
Boulder Creek, CA 95006

Missionary Dispensary Bible Research ★651★
Box 5296
Buena Park, CA 90622

Church of the Eternal Source ★1048★
Box 7091
Burbank, CA 91510-7091

The Colony ★736★
Burnt Ranch, CA 95527

Concordant Publishing Concern ★588★
15570 W. Knochaven Drive
Canyon Country, CA 91351

Subud ★1152★
% Chairman Locksin Thompson
4 Pilot Rd.
Carmel, CA 93924

Noohra Foundation ★786★
% Dr. Rocco Enrico
720 Paularino Ave.
Costa Mesa, CA 92626

Theosophical Society (Hartley) ★968★
Covina, CA

Holy Apostolic-Catholic Church of the East (Chaldean-Syrian) ★126★
% Metropolitam Mar Mikhael
190 Palisades Dr.
Daly City, CA 94015

Orthodox Catholic Synod of the Syro-Chaldean Rite
★127★
% Most Rev. Bashir Ahmed
100 Los Banos Ave.
Daly City, CA 94014

Filipino Assemblies of the First Born ★322★
1229 Glenwood
Delano, CA 93215

Fereferia ★1061★
Box 41363
Eagle Rock, CA 90041

Mexican National Catholic Church ★16★
% Rt. Rev. Emile F. Rodriguez-Fairfield
4011 E. Brooklyn Ave.
East Los Angeles, CA 90022

Unarius-Science of Life ★891★
143 S. Magnolia
El Cajon, CA 92022

Prosperos ★1151★
% Inner Space Center
Box 5505
El Monte, CA 91734

American Universalist Temple of Divine Wisdom ★898★
Rte. 4, Box 301
Escondido, CA 92025

Christward Ministry ★1014★
Route 5, Box 206
Escondido, CA 92025

Nichiren Shoshu Temple ★1268★
7576 Etiwanda Ave.
Etiwanda, CA 91739

Sacred Society of the Eth, Inc. ★1006★
Box 3
Forks of Salmon, CA 96031

International Ministerial Federation, Inc. ★581★
723 Clark St.
Fresno, CA 93701

Seicho-No-Ie ★792★
North American Missionary Headquarters
14527 S. Vermont Ave.
Gardena, CA 90247

United Spiritualist Church ★842★
813 W. 165th Place
Gardena, CA 90247

Ann Ree Colton Foundation of Niscience ★1011★
336 W. Colorado
Glendale, CA 91209

Old Catholic Episcopal Church ★992★
% Most Rev. Jay Davis Kirby
923 1/2 E. Briadway
Glendale, CA 91205

Federation of St. Thomas Christian Churches ★984★
% Dr. Joseph L. Vredenburgh
6656 Trigo Road, B
Goleta, CA 93117

Temple of the People ★967★
Box 528-H
Halcyon, CA 93420

Aetherius Society ★881★
6202 Afton Place
Hollywood, CA 90028

Church of Universal Brotherhood ★696★
6311 Yucca Street
Hollywood, CA 90028

International Babaji Kriya Yoga Sangam ★1199★
595 W. Bedford Rd.
Imperial City, CA 92251

Church of Cosmic Science ★806★
Box 61
Jamul, CA 92035

White Star ★893★
Box 307
Joshua Tree, CA 92252

Church of Cosmic Origin and School of Thought ★1015★
Box 257
June Lake, CA 93529

Ewam Choden ★1309★
254 Cambridge St.
Kensington, CA 94707

Kirpal Light Satsang ★1243★
% Bernadine Chard
442 Beloit
Kensington, CA 94708

Ananda Ashrama ★1179★
Box 8555
La Cresenta, CA 91214

American Catholic Church ★980★
% Most Rev. Simon Eugene Talarczyk
430 Park Ave.
Laguna Beach, CA 92651

Cambodian Buddhist Temple ★1250★
20622 Pioneer Blvd.
Lakewood, CA 90715

California Evangelistic Association ★317★
1800 E. Anaheim Rd.
Long Beach, CA 90815

Missionary Christian and Soul Winning Fellowship ★233★
350 E. Market St.
Long Beach, CA 90805

United Libertarian Fellowship ★688★
% Will Buckley, President
1220 Larnel Place
Los Altos, CA 94022

Agasha Temple of Wisdom ★803★
460 Western Ave.
Los Angeles, CA 90004

American Independent Orthodox Church (Bridges) ★69★
2301 Stanford Ave.
Los Angeles, CA 90011

Associated Churches of Christ (Holiness) ★259★
1302 E. Adams Blvd.
Los Angeles, CA 90011

Byzantine Catholic Church ★84★
% Most Rev. Mark I. Miller
Box 3642
Los Angeles, CA 90078

California Bosatsukai ★1275★
5632 Green Oak Dr.
Los Angeles, CA 90068

Chirothesian Church of Faith ★902★
1757 N. Normandie
Los Angeles, CA 90027

Christ Faith Mission ★418★
Los Angeles, CA

Church of Light ★958★
Church of Light
Los Angeles, CA

Church of World Messianity ★1335★
3068 San Marino St.
Los Angeles, CA 90006

Concilio Olazabal de Iglesias Latino Americano ★409★
1925 E. First St.
Los Angeles, CA 90033

Dhyanyoga Centers ★1190★
Manu Michael Hannon, Director
2026 Redesdale Ave.
Los Angeles, CA 90039

Ecclesia Gnostica ★982★
% Most Rev. Stephan Hoeller
4516 Hollywood Blvd.
Los Angeles, CA 90028

Estonian Orthodox Church in Exile ★87★
% Rev. Sergius Samon
5332 Fountain Ave.
Los Angeles, CA 90029

Fellowship of Christian Assemblies ★321★
% Fellowship Press
657 W. 18th St.
Los Angeles, CA 90015

Fellowship of Universal Guidance ★861★
1674 Hillhurst Ave.
Los Angeles, CA 90027

God's Benevolence Orthodox Catholic Church ★12★
% Rt. Rev. Patrick K. McReynolds
801 Levering Ave., 3
Los Angeles, CA 90024

Higashi Hongwanji Buddhist Church ★1264★
505 E. Third St.
Los Angeles, CA 90013

Independent Fundamentalist Bible Churches ★580★
% Dr. M. H. McReynolds, Jr.
205 N. Union Ave.
Los Angeles, CA 90026

Institute of Esoteric Transcendentalism ★783★
% Mr. Robert W. C. Burke
3278 Wilshire Blvd.
Los Angeles, CA 90005

International Buddhist Meditation Center ★1252★
928 S. New Hampshire Ave.
Los Angeles, CA 90006

International Church of the Foursquare Gospel ★329★
% Angelus Temple
1100 Glendale Blvd.
Los Angeles, CA 90026

International Group of Theosophists ★966★
634 S. Gramercy Place, Suite 301
Los Angeles, CA 90005

International Society for Krishna Consciousness ★1200★
3764 Watseka Blvd.
Los Angeles, CA 90034

Konko Kyo ★1340★
% Rev. Alfred Y. Tsyyuki
2924 E. 1st St.
Los Angeles, CA 90033

Korean Buddhist Chogye Order ★1302★
Kwan Um Sa Temple
451 S. Serrano Ave.
Los Angeles, CA 90020

Lao Buddhist Sangha of the U.S.A. ★1253★
938 N. Hobart Blvd.
Los Angeles, CA 90029

Mazdaznan Movement ★1166★
1159 S. Norton Ave.
Los Angeles, CA 90019

Molokan Spiritual Christians (Pryguny) ★500★
% Paul I. Samarin
944 Orme St.
Los Angeles, CA 99923

Movement of Spiritual Inner Awareness, Church of the ★1244★
3500 W. Adams Blvd.
Los Angeles, CA 90018

Old Roman Catholic Church (Marchenna) ★26★
% Most Rev. Derek Lang
2103 S. Portland St.
Los Angeles, CA 90007

Oriental Missionary Society Holiness Conference ★255★
3660 South Gramercy Place
Los Angeles, CA 90018

Peniel Missions ★237★
606 E. 6th St.
Los Angeles, CA 90021

Philosophical Research Society ★962★
3910 Los Feliz Blvd.
Los Angeles, CA 90027

Pre-Nicene Church (de Palatine) ★996★
% Most Rev. Seiji Yamauchi
8136 Ginzaga Ave.
Los Angeles, CA 90045

Rinzai-Ji, Inc. ★1280★
2245 W. 25th St.
Los Angeles, CA 90018

Rissho Kosei Kai ★1270★
% Rev. Kazuhiko K. Nagamoto
118 N. Mott
Los Angeles, CA 90033

S. A. I. Foundation ★1212★
7911 Willoughby Ave.
Los Angeles, CA 90046

Self-Realization Fellowship ★1214★
3880 San Rafael Ave.
Los Angeles, CA 90065

Shrine of the Eternal Breath of Tao ★1299★
117 Stonehave Way
Los Angeles, CA 90049

Sikh Dharma ★1240★
1620 Pruess Rd.
Los Angeles, CA 90035

Society of Christ, Inc. ★837★
% Bishop Dan Boughan
3061 Harrington St.
Los Angeles, CA 90006

Soto Mission ★1281★
Zenshuji Soto Mission
123 S. Hewitt St.
Los Angeles, CA 90012

Superet Light Center ★841★
2512-16 W. Third St.
Los Angeles, CA 90059

Tenrikyo ★1345★
Tenrikyo Mission Headquarters in America
2727 E. First St.
Los Angeles, CA 90033

Thubten Dargye Ling ★1321★
135 N. St. Andrews Place
Los Angeles, CA 90004

United Church of Religious Science ★796★
3251 W. 6th St.
Box 75127
Los Angeles, CA 90075

United Full Gospel Ministers and Churches ★337★
Los Angeles, CA

United Lodge of Theosophists ★971★
% Theosophy Hall
245 W. 33rd St.
Los Angeles, CA 90007

Universal Christ Church, Inc. ★845★
1704 W. Venice Blvd.
Los Angeles, CA 90006

Universal Christian Spiritual Faith and Churches for All Nations ★406★
Los Angeles, CA

Universal White Brotherhood ★1021★
Prosveta U. S. A.
Box 49614
Los Angeles, CA 90049

Universal World Church ★439★
123 N. Lake St.
Los Angeles, CA 90026

Viet Nam Buddhists ★1259★
Congregation of Vietnamese Buddhists in the U.S.
863 S. Berendo
Los Angeles, CA 90005

Zen Center of Los Angeles ★1284★
923 S. Normandie Ave.
Los Angeles, CA 90006

Church of Revelation (Hawaii) ★811★
21475 Summit Rd.
Los Gatos, CA 95030

School of Natural Science ★874★
25355 Spanish Ranch Rd.
Los Gatos, CA 95030

Church Universal and Triumphant ★1001★
Box A
Malibu, CA 90265

Arcana Workshops ★974★
Box 605
Manhattan Beach, CA 90266

ECKANKAR ★1242★
Box 3100
Menlo Park, CA 94025

Universal Life Church ★704★
601 Third St.
Modesto, CA 95351

United Evangelical Churches ★437★
Box 28
Monrovia, CA 91016

American Fellowship Church ★690★
183 Sargent Court
Monterey, CA 93940

Millennial Church of Jesus Christ ★716★
% Leo Peter Evoniuk LeBaron
177 Webster St.
Monterey, CA 93940

Association of Sananda and Sanat Kumara ★882★
Box 35
Mount Shasta, CA 96067

Soto Zen Church ★1282★
Shasta Abbey
Box 478
Mount Shasta, CA 96067

Church of Antioch ★981★
% Most Rev. Herman Adrian Spruit
Box 219
Mountian View, CA 94042

Chinmaya Mission (West) ★1186★
Box 2753
Napa, CA 94558

Ananda ★1178★
Alleghany Star Route
Nevada City, CA 95959

Institute for the Development of the Harmonious Human
    Being ★1147★
Box 370
Nevada City, CA 95959

Ahmadiyya Anjuman Ishaat Islam, Lahore, Inc ★1155★
36911 Walnut St.
Newark, CA 94560

Chung Fu Kuan (Taoist Sanctuary) ★1292★
6020 Craner Ave.
North Hollywood, CA 91606

Tara Center ★979★
Box 6001
North Hollywood, CA 91603

Thai-American Buddhist Association ★1258★
Wat Thai of Los Angeles
12909 Cantara St.
North Hollywood, CA 91506

Inner Light Foundation ★926★
Box 761
Novato, CA 94948

Dianic Wicca ★1057★
% Susan B. Anthony Coven No. 1
Box 11363
Oakland, CA 94611

Diocese of Christ the King ★50★
% Rt. Rev. Robert S. Morse
St. Peter's Pro-Cathedral
6013 Lawton
Oakland, CA 94618

Rosicrucian Fellowship ★953★
2222 Mission Ave.
Box 713
Oceanside, CA 92054

Amica Temple of Radiance ★1010★
Box 304
Ojai, CA 93023

International Liberal Catholic Church ★987★
% Rt. Rev. Edmund W. Sheehan
480 Fairview Rd.
Ojai, CA 93023

Krishnamurti Foundation of America ★1203★
Ojai, CA 93023

Life Action Foundation ★1132★
Box 263
Ojai, CA 93023

Meditation Groups, Inc. ★976★
Box 566
Ojai, CA 93023

Universal Buddhist Fellowship ★1334★
% Rev. Harold H. Priebe
Box 1079
Ojai, CA 93023

Reformed Druids of North America ★1079★
% Live Oak Grove
Box 142
Orinda, CA 94563

George Ohsawa Macrobiotic Foundation ★1296★
Box 426
Oroville, CA 95965

World Plan Executive Council ★1230★
17310 Sunset Blvd.
Pacific Palisades, CA 90272

Anglican Episcopal Church of North America ★46★
% Most Rev. Walter Hollis Adams
789 Allen Ct.
Palo Alto, CA 94303

Ecclesia Gnostica Mysterium ★983★
% Most Rev. Rosa Miller
3437 Alma, 23
Palo Alto, CA 94306

Inner Circle Kethra E'Da Foundation, Inc. ★863★
Box 11672
Palo Alto, CA 94306

Seed Center ★765★
Box 591
Palo Alto, CA 94302

Foundation for Biblical Research ★620★
Box 499
Pasadena, CA 91102

Ordo Templi Astarte ★1033★
Box 3341
Pasadena, CA 91103

Temple of Truth ★1039★
Box 3125
Pasadena, CA 91103

Theosophical Society ★969★
Post Office Bin C
Pasadena, CA 91109

World Insight International ★627★
Box 35
Pasadena, CA 91102

Worldwide Church of God ★628★
300 W. Green St.
Pasadena, CA 91123

Blue Mountain Center of Meditation ★1183★
Box 477
Petaluma, CA 94953

Undenominational Church of the Lord ★240★
% Pastor Robert Wallace
Box 291
Placentia, CA 92677

Ajapa Yoga Foundation ★1175★
% Shri Janardan Ajapa Yogashram
Box 1731
Placerville, CA 95667

Lemurian Fellowship ★960★
Box 397
Ramona, CA 92065

Church of General Psionics ★906★
204 N. Catalina
Redondo Beach, CA 90277

Church of All Worlds ★1046★
Box 212
Redwood Valley, CA 95470

New Order of Glastonbury ★991★
Box 324
Rialto, CA 92376

North American Old Roman Catholic Church-Utrecht
    Succession ★20★
% Rt. Rev. E. R. Verostek
3519 Roosevelt Ave.
Richmond, CA 94805

Radhasoami Satsang, Beas ★1246★
% Roland DeVries
2922 Los Flores Ave.
Riverside, CA 92503

Pyramid Church of Truth and Light ★834★
2426 G St.
Sacramento, CA 95816

Seventh-Day Adventist Church, Reform Movement ★605★
American Union
6380 63rd St.
Sacramento, CA 95824

Arya Maitrya Mandala ★1306★
% Lama Anagarika Govinda
214 Sir Francis Drake Blvd.
San Anselmo, CA 49960

Neo-Dharma ★1254★
% Dr. Douglas Burns
2648 Graceland Ave.
San Carlos, CA 94070

American Association for the Advancement of Atheism
    ★672★
Box 2832
San Diego, CA 92112

Independent Assemblies of God, International ★328★
3840 5th Ave.
San Diego, CA 92103

Johannine Catholic Church ★986★
Archbishop J. Julian Gillmon
Box 8098
San Diego, CA 92102

Liberal Catholic Church International ★988★
% Rt. Rev. Dean Bekken
741 Cerro Gordo Ave.
San Diego, CA 92102

Love Project ★932★
Box 7601
San Diego, CA 92107

New Psychiana ★935★
% Psychiana Study Group
4069 Stephens St.
San Diego, CA 92103

Phoenix Institute ★787★
976 Chalcedony St.
San Diego, CA 92109

Religious Science International ★789★
3130 5th Ave.
San Diego, CA 92103

Teaching of the Inner Christ, Inc. ★941★
% Inner Christ Administrative Center, Inc.
3009 Grape St.
San Diego, CA 92102

Buddha's Universal Church ★1288★
702 Washington St.
San Francisco, CA 94108

Buddhist Churches of America ★1262★
1710 Octavia St.
San Francisco, CA 94109

Catholic Apostolic Church in America ★85★
% Most Rev. Jerome Joachim
540 Jones St., Suite 504
San Francisco, CA 94102

Chapori-Ling Foundation Sangha ★1307★
% Dr. Norbu Lompas Chen
766 8th Ave.
San Francisco, CA 94118

Chiltern Yoga Foundation ★1185★
1029 Hyde St., No. 6
San Francisco, CA 94109

Church of Satan ★1095★
Box 210082
San Francisco, CA 94121

Church of the Tree of Life ★895★
451 Columbus Ave.
San Francisco, CA 94133

Foundation of Revelation ★1192★
59 Scott St.
San Francisco, CA 94117

Gedatsu Church of America ★1263★
401 Baker
San Francisco, CA 94115

Gurdjieff Foundation ★1144★
Box 549
San Francisco, CA 94101

Holy Order of MANS ★959★
20 Steiner St.
San Francisco, CA 94117

Kailas Shugendo ★1266★
% Dr. Neville Warwick
2362 Pine St.
San Francisco, CA 94115

MeBasrim Fellowship ★990★
% Mar Petros
495 Ellis, 137
San Francisco, CA 94102

Molokan Spiritual Christians (Postojannye) ★499★
841 Carolina St.
San Francisco, CA 94107

Pacific Yearly Meeting of Friends ★489★
% The Clerk
2160 Lake St.
San Francisco, CA 94121

SM Church ★1081★
% Robin Stewart, Priestess
Box 1407
San Francisco, CA 94101

Stillpoint Institute ★1256★
2740 Greenwich, 416
San Francisco, CA 94123

Sufi Islamia Ruhaniat Society ★1153★
% The Mentorgarten
10 Precita Avenue
San Francisco, CA 94110

Temple of Set ★1100★
Box 29271
San Francisco, CA 94129

Zen Center of San Francisco ★1286★
300 Page St.
San Francisco, CA 94102

Ancient and Mystical Order of the Rosae Crucis ★947★

San Jose, CA 95191

Christian Assembly ★770★
72 N. 5th St.
San Jose, CA 95112

Church of Inner Wisdom ★772★
% Joan Gibson
Box 4765
San Jose, CA 95126

Sri Caitanya Saraswat Math ★1184★
% Guardian of Devotion
62 S. 13th St.
San Jose, CA 95112

United Christian Scientists ★766★
Box 8048
San Jose, CA 95125

Universal Church of the Master ★846★
% Rev. Birdie Peterson
45 N. First St.
Box 6100
San Jose, CA 95113

Church of the Trinity (Invisible Ministry) ★775★
% A. Stuart Otto
Box 37
San Marcos, CA 92069

Etherian Religious Society of Universal Brotherhood
★917★
Box 446
San Marcos, CA 92069

Satyananda Ashrams, U.S.A. ★1213★
1157 Ramblewood Way
San Mateo, CA 94403

Johannine Daist Community ★1201★
% Brian O'Mahony
750 Adrian Way
San Rafael, CA 94903

Yoga House Ashram ★1232★
Box 3391
San Rafael, CA 94902

Amended Christadelphians ★550★
% Christadelphian Ecclesia
206 Stanley Dr.
Santa Barbara, CA 93105

Hallowed Grounds Fellowship of Spiritual Healing and
Prayer ★818★
% Rev. George Daisley
629 San Ysidro Rd.
Santa Barbara, CA 93108

Cosmic Church of Life and Spiritual Science ★814★
% Rev. M. Russo
2885 Homestead Rd., Suite 1
Santa Clara, CA 95051

Christ Ministry Foundation ★903★
Box 1103
Santa Cruz, CA 95061

Holy Grail Foundation ★819★
% Rev. Leona Richards
1344 Pacific Ave., Suite 100
Santa Cruz, CA 95060

Rigpa ★1319★
Box 7326
Santa Cruz, CA 95061

Church of Eductivism ★905★
3003 Santa Monica Blvd.
Santa Monica, CA 90404

Old Catholic Church in North America (Catholicate of
the West) ★22★
% Rev. Dr. Charles V. Hearn
2210 Wilshire Blvd., Suite 582
Santa Monica, CA 90403

Universal Industrial Church of the New World Comforter
(One World Family) ★760★
Box 3
Stockton, CA 95201

Dharma Realm Buddhist Association ★1293★
City of Ten Thousand Buddhas
Talmage, CA 95481

Mahikari of America ★1341★
Los Angeles Dojo
6470 Foothill Blvd.
Tujunga, CA 91042

Astara Foundation ★956★
800 W. Arrow Hwy.
Box 5003
Upland, CA 91786

Brethren in Christ ★462★
% Bishop R. Donald Shafer
Box 245
Upland, CA 91786

Twentieth Century Church of God ★625★
Box 129
Vacaville, CA 95688

International Evangelism Crusades ★432★
7970 Woodman Ave.
Van Nuys, CA 91402

George Adamski Foundation ★880★
314 Lado de Loma Dr.
Vista, CA 92083

Divine Word Foundation ★858★
26648 San Felipe Rd.
Warner Springs, CA 92086

Inner Powers Society ★782★
Yucca Valley, CA 92284

Institute of Mentalphysics ★929★
59700 - 29 Palms Hwy.
Box 640
Yucca Valley, CA 92284

Colorado

Assembly of YHWHOSANA ★647★
% David K. Johnson
50006 Olson Rd.
Boone, CO 81025

Church of Tzaddi ★813★
2885 Aurora Ave.
Boulder, CO 80303

Mevlana Foundation ★1150★
Box 305
Boulder, CO 80306

Moksha Foundation ★1207★
745 31st St.
Boulder, CO 80303

Truth Consciousness ★1226★
% Sacred Mountain Ashram
Gold Hill, Salina Star Route
Boulder, CO 80302

Vajrahatu ★1323★
1345 Spruce St.
Boulder, CO 80302

Emmanuel Association ★227★
West Cucharas at 27th St.
Colorado Springs, CO 80904

Rocky Mountain Yearly Meeting ★491★
29 N. Garland
Colorado Springs, CO 80909

American Orthodox Catholic Church (Irene) ★72★
% Most Rev. Milton A. Pritts
851 Leyden St.
Denver, CO 80220

Ananda Marga Yoga Society ★1180★
854 Pearl St.
Denver, CO 80203

Bible Missionary Church ★272★
822 S. Simms
Denver, CO 80211

Catholic Life Church ★6★
% Most Rev. A. L. Mark Harding
1955 Arapahoe St., Suite 1603
Denver, CO 80202

Colorado Reform Baptist Church ★540★
% Bishop William Conklin
Box 12514
4344 Bryant St.
Denver, CO 80211

Divine Science Federation International ★778★
1400 Williams St.
Denver, CO 80218

General Conference of the Church of God ★622★
General Conference Offices
Box 33677
Denver, CO 80233

House of Prayer for All People ★669★
Box 837
Denver, CO 80201

Pillar of Fire ★256★
1302 Sherman St.
Denver, CO 80203

Emissaries of Divine Light ★915★
5569 N. Country Rd. 29
Loveland, CO 80537

Apostolic Church of Jesus ★353★
1825 E. River St.
Pueblo, CO 81001

Brotherhood of the White Temple ★957★
Sedalia, CO 80135

Connecticut

Christian Millennial Church ★632★
307 White St.
Hartford, CT 06106

Community of Catholic Churches ★8★
Most Rev. Thomas Sargent
3 Columbia St.
Hartford, CT 06106

Life Study Fellowship Foundation, Inc. ★784★
Noroton, CT 06820

Autocephalous Syro-Chaldean Church of North America
★79★
% Most Rev. Bertram S. Schlossberg (Mar Uzziah)
9 Ellington Ave.
Rockville, CT 06066

Independent Old Roman Catholic Hungarian Orthodox
Church of America ★14★
% Most Rev. Archbishop Edward C. Payne, Catholicos-
Metropolitan
Box 261
Weatherfield, CT 06109

District of Columbia

Ahmadiyya Movement of Islam ★1156★
2141 Leroy Place, N.W.
Washington, DC 20008

Bible Way Church of Our Lord Jesus Christ World Wide,
Inc. ★362★
1130 New Jersey Ave., N.W.
Washington, DC 20001

Church of the Savior ★735★
2025 Massachusetts Avenue, N.W.
Washington, DC 20036

Drikung Dharma Centers ★1308★
% Drikung Kyabgon
3454 Macomb St., N.W.
Washington, DC 20008

Foundation Church of the New Birth ★862★
Box 996, Benjamin Franklin Station
Washington, DC 20044

Gospel Spreading Church ★264★
2030 Georgia Ave., N.W.
Washington, DC 20003

Hanafi Muslim Movement ★1160★
7700 16th St., N.W.
Washington, DC 20012

Highway Christian Church of Christ ★369★
436 W St., N.W.
Washington, DC 20001

Inner Peace Movement ★927★
Box 4897
Washington, DC 20008

International Evangelical Church and Missionary
Association ★431★
Washington, DC

National Spiritual Science Center ★832★
5605 16th St., N.W.
Washington, DC 20011

Progressive National Baptist Convention, Inc. ★538★
39-7 Georgia Ave., N.W.
Washington, DC 20011

Redeemed Assembly of Jesus Christ, Apostolic ★376★
% Bishop Douglas Williams
734 1st St., S.W.
Washington, DC 20024

Roman Catholic Church ★1★
National Conference of Catholic Bishops
1312 Massachusetts Ave., N.W.
Washington, DC 20005

Self-Revelation Church of Absolute Monism ★1215★
4748 Western Ave., N.W.
Washington, DC 20016

Seventh-Day Adventist Church ★606★
6840 Eastern Ave., N.W.
Washington, DC 20012

Seventh Day Pentecostal Church of the Living God
★336★
1443 S. Euclid
Washington, DC 20009

Sri Lankan (Ceylonese) Buddhism ★1255★
Buddhist Vihara Society
5017 16th St., N.W.
Washington, DC 20011

Sunni Muslims ★1139★
% Islamic Center
2551 Massachusetts Ave., N.W.
Washington, DC 20008

Temple of Cosmic Religion ★1224★
4218 16th St., N.W.
Washington, DC 20011

True Grace Memorial House of Prayer ★403★
205 V St., N.W.
Washington, DC 20001

United Church of Jesus Christ (Apostolic) ★379★
% Monroe E. Saunders, Presiding Bishop
2136 32nd Place, S.E.
Washington, DC 20020

United House of Prayer for All People ★405★
1721 1/2 7th St., N.W.
Washington, DC 20001

Way of the Cross Church of Christ ★383★
332 4th St., N.E.
Washington, DC 20003

Witness and Testimony Literature Trust and Related
Centers ★597★
Testimony Book Ministry
Box 34241, Bethesada Dr.
Washington, DC 20034

Florida

American Episcopal Church ★43★
% The Most Rev. Anthony F. M. Clavier
Box 373
Deerfield Beach, FL 33441

Calvary Grace Christian Church of Faith ★693★
% Rev. Herman Keck Jr.
271 N.E. 57th St.
Fort Lauderdale, FL 33308

Mark-Age ★887★
Box 290368
Fort Lauderdale, FL 33329

Laodicean Home Missionary Movement ★636★
Rte. 38
9021 Temple Rd., W.
Fort Myers, FL 33912

Universal Free Life Church ★703★
Hollywood, FL

Confraternity of Deists, Inc. ★682★
Box 179
Homosassa Springs, FL 32647

Church of God by Faith ★419★
3220 Haines St.
Jacksonville, FL 32206

National Baptist Convention of America ★535★
% Dr. James C. Sams, President
954 Kings Rd.
Jacksonville, FL 32204

New Congregational Methodist Church ★197★
% Bishop Joe E. Kelley
354 E. 9th St.
Jacksonville, FL 32206

Southeastern Yearly Meeting ★492★
SEYM Office
1375 Talbot Ave.
Jacksonville, FL 32205

United Baptists ★546★
% Omer E. Baker
8640 Brazil Rd.
Jacksonville, FL 32208

Sologa, Inc. ★1008★
Box 759
Melbourne, FL 32901

Universal Religion of America ★849★
Merritt Island, FL 32953

Endtime Body-Christian Ministries, Inc. ★422★
Miami, FL

Iglesia Bando Evangelico Gedeon/Gilgal Evangelistic
International Church ★412★
636 N.W. 2nd St.
Miami, FL 33128

Roosevelt Spiritual Memorial Benevolent Association
★835★
% Rev. Nellie M. Pickens
Box 68-313
Miami, FL 33138

Yoga Research Foundation ★1233★
6111 S.W. 74th Ave.
Miami, FL 33143

Divine Light Mission ★1241★
Box 390858
Miami Beach, FL 33139

Epiphany Bible Students Association ★634★
Box 97
Mount Dora, FL 32757

African Orthodox Church ★61★
% Most Rev. Stafford J. Sweeting
15801 N.W. 38th Place
Opa-Locka, FL 33054

Church of the Brotherhood ★734★
Box 606
Orange City, FL 32763

American Evangelical Christian Churches ★570★
Waterfront Dr.
Pineland, FL 33945

Canonical Old Roman Catholic Church ★4★
% Most Rev. John J. Humphreys
5501 62nd Ave.
Pinellas Park, FL 33565

Church of the Holy Monarch ★695★
Box 1116
Port Orange, FL 32019

Eastern Orthodox Catholic Church in America ★86★
% Most Rev. Dismas Markle
321 S. Magnolia Ave.
Sanford, FL 32771

Church of Metaphysical Christianity ★809★
2717 Browning St.
Sarasota, FL 33577

Universal Harmony Foundation ★848★
% Rev. Helene Gerling
5903 Seminole Blvd.
Seminole, FL 33542

Church of the Humanitarian God ★681★
% Ron Libert
Box 13236
St. Petersburg, FL 33733

National Spiritual Aid Association ★829★
5239 40th St., N.
St. Petersburg, FL 33714

National Primitive Baptist Convention of the U.S.A.
★530★
Box 2355
Tallahassee, FL 32301

Church of Scientology ★907★
Flag Service Org(anization)
Box 23751
Tampa, FL 33630-3751

Churches of Christ (Non-Instrumental, Conservative)
★558★
% Florida College
119 Glen Arven Ave.
Tampa, FL 33617

Koreshan Unity ★741★
% Claude J. Rahn
2012 28th Avenue
Vero Beach, FL 32960

Georgia

Cymry Wicca ★1053★
Box 1866
Athens, GA 30602

Anglican Church of North America ★45★
% Rt. Rev. Robert T. Shepherd
Chapel of St. Augustine of Canterbury
1906 Forest Green Dr., N.E.
Atlanta, GA 30329

Churches of God, Holiness ★263★
170 Ashby St., N.W.
Atlanta, GA 30314

Fire-Baptized Holiness Church of God of the Americas
★392★
556 Houston St.
Atlanta, GA 30312

First Deliverance Church of Atlanta ★340★
65 Hardwick St., S.E.
Atlanta, GA 30315

First Interdenominational Christian Association ★298★
Calvary Temple Holiness Church
1061 Memorial Dr., S.E.
Atlanta, GA 30315

Gospel Harvesters Evangelistic Association (Atlanta)
★427★
1710 De Foor Ave., N.W.
Atlanta, GA 30318

Sought Out Church of God in Christ ★401★

Brunswick, GA 31520

Sanctified Church of Christ ★257★
2715 18th Ave.
Columbus, GA 31901

Church of God of the Union Assembly ★291★
Box 1323
Dalton, GA 30720

Presbyterian Church in America ★166★
% Stated Clerk
Box 1428
Decatur, GA 30031

Holiness Baptist Association ★302★

Douglas, GA 31533

Asbury Bible Churches ★184★
% Rev. Jack Tondee
Box 1021
Dublin, GA 31021

Congregational Holiness Church ★294★
3888 Fayetteville Hwy.
Griffin, GA 30223

Primitive Baptists-Progressive ★532★
% Banner Bookstore
Box 4
Jessup, GA 31545

Church of the Christian Spiritual Alliance ★1188★
Lake Rabun Road
Box 7
Lakemont, GA 30552

Christ's Sanctified Holy Church (South Carolina) ★220★
CSHC Campground
Perry, GA 31068

Pentecostal Fire-Baptized Holiness Church ★307★

Taccoa, GA 30577

Hawaii

Shinreikyo ★1342★
% Mr. Kameo Kiyota
310C Uulani St.
Hilo, HI 96720

Apostolic Faith (Hawaii) ★355★
1043 Middle St.
Honolulu, HI 96819

Bodaiji Mission ★1261★
1251 Elm
Honolulu, HI 96814

Celtic Evangelical Church ★49★
% Rt. Rev. Wayne W. Gau
1666 St. Louis Dr.
Honolulu, HI 96816

Chinese Buddhist Association ★1291★
42 Kawananake Place
Honolulu, HI 96817

Chowado Henjo Kyo ★1329★
% Rev. Reisai Fugita
1757 Algaroba St.
Honolulu, HI 96814

Diamond Sangha ★1277★
Koko An
2119 Kaloa Way
Honolulu, HI 96822

Filipino Community Churches ★192★
838 Kanoa St.
Honolulu, HI 96827

Hawaii Chinese Buddhist Society ★1297★
1614 Nuuanu Ave.
Honolulu, HI 96817

Honkyoku Shinto ★1336★
Honkyoku-Daijingu Temple
61 Puiwa Rd.
Honolulu, HI 96817

Inari Shinto ★1337★
Hawaii Inari Taisha
2132 S. King St.
Honolulu, HI 96817

International Christian Churches ★430★
2322-22 Kanealii Ave.
Honolulu, HI 96813

Jinga Shinto ★1338★
Hawaii Ichizuchi Jinga
2020 S. King St.
Honolulu, HI 96817

Jinsha Shinto ★1339★
Kotohira Jinsha Temple
1045 Kama Lane
Honolulu, HI 96817

Jodo Mission ★1265★
1429 Kakiki St.
Honolulu, HI 96822

Kwan Yin Temple ★1298★
170 N. Vineyard St.
Honolulu, HI 96817

Lamb of God Church ★330★
612 Isenburg St.
Honolulu, HI 96817

Nichiren Mission ★1267★
3058 Pali Hwy.
Honolulu, HI 96817

Palolo Kannondo Temple ★1269★
3326 Paalea St.
Honolulu, HI 96816

Shingon Mission ★1271★
915 Sheridan St.
Honolulu, HI 96810

Shinshu Kyokai Mission ★1272★
Bentenshu Hawaii Kyokai
3871 Old Pali Rd.
Honolulu, HI 86817

Shinyo-En ★1273★
% Bishop Joshin Kuriyama
2348 S. Beretania St.
Honolulu, HI 96814

Taishakyo Shinto ★1344★
215 N. Kukui St.
Honolulu, HI 96817

Tensho Kotai Jingu Kyo ★1346★
Hawaii Dojo
888 N. King St.
Honolulu, HI 96817

Todaiji Hawaii Bekkaku Honzan ★1274★
% Bishop Tatsusho Hirai
2426 Luakini St.
Honolulu, HI 96814

Saiva Siddhanta Church ★1220★
Box 10
Kapaa, HI 96746

Nechhung Drayangling ★1317★
Box 281
Pahala, HI 96777

Alpha and Omega Christian Church ★414★
96-171 Kamahamaha Hwy.
Pearl City, HI 96782

Idaho

Seventh Day Church of God ★624★
Box 804
Caldwell, ID 83606-0804

Rainbow Family of Living Light ★755★
Route 1, Box 6
McCall, ID 83638

General Council of the Churches of God ★623★
1827 W. 3rd St.
Meridian, ID 83642-1653

Illinois

Plymouth Brethren (Exclusive: The Tunbridge Wells
        Brethren) ★568★
% Bible Truth Publishers
59 Industrial Dr.
Addison, IL 60101

Baptist General Conference ★539★
2002 S. Arlington Heights Rd.
Arlington Heights, IL 60005

American Meditation Society ★1176★
Box 244
Bourbonnais, IL 60914

African Orthodox Church of the West ★62★
% Most Rev. G. Duncan Hinkson
St. Augustine's African Orthodox Church
5831 S. Indiana St.
Chicago, IL 60637

American Muslim Mission ★1157★
Masjid Hon. Elijah Muhammad
7351 S. Stony Brook Ave.
Chicago, IL 60649

Berean Bible Fellowship (Chicago) ★586★
7609 W. Belmont
Chicago, IL 60635

Cosmic Circle of Fellowship ★884★
% Edna Valverde
4857 N. Melvina Ave.
Chicago, IL 60630

Evangelical Covenant Church of America ★178★
5101 N. Francisco Ave.
Chicago, IL 60625

Evangelical Ministers and Churches, International, Inc.
    ★576★
105 Madison
Chicago, IL 60602

Korean Buddhist Bo Moon Order ★1301★
% Rev. Bup Choon
Bul Sim Sa Temple
5011 N. Damen
Chicago, IL 60625

Metropolitan Spiritual Churches of Christ, Inc. ★826★
4315 S. Wabash
Chicago, IL 60653

Monastery of the Seven Rays ★1028★
Box 1554
Chicago, IL 60690-1554

Moody Church ★582★
1630 N. Clark
Chicago, IL 60614

Narayanananda Universal Yoga Trust ★1208★
N U Yoga Ashram
1418 N. Kedzie
Chicago, IL 60651

The Nation of Islam (Farrakhan) ★1164★
Box 20083
Chicago, IL 60620

North American Old Roman Catholic Church (Schweikert)
    ★19★
% Most Rev. John E. Schweikert
4200 N. Kedvale
Chicago, IL 60641

Old Orthodox Catholic Patriarchate of America ★104★
% Most Rev. Peter A. Zurawetzky
5520 W. Dakin St.
Chicago, IL 60641

Old Roman Catholic Church (English Rite) and the
    Roman Catholic Church of the Ultrajectine Tradition
    ★28★
% Most Rev. Robert Lane
4416 N. Malden
Chicago, IL 60640

Original Hebrew Israelite Nation ★1126★
% Communicators Press
Box 19504
Chicago, IL 60649

Sabaean Religious Order of Amen ★1080★
% El Sabarum
3221 N. Sheffield
Chicago, IL 60657

Temple of Kriya Yoga ★1225★
2414 N. Kedzie
Chicago, IL 60647

Temple of the Pagan Way ★1084★
Box 60151
Chicago, IL 60660

Temple of Universal Law ★844★
5030 N. Drake
Chicago, IL 60625

Thee Orthodox Old Roman Catholic Church (Brown)
    ★36★
% Rt. Rev. Peter Charles Brown
Box 49314
Chicago, IL 60649

Traditional Roman Catholic Church in the Americas ★38★
% Most Rev. John D. Fesi
Friary Press
Box 470
Chicago, IL 60690

Urantia Brotherhood ★945★
533 Diversey Pkwy.
Chicago, IL 60614

Zen Buddhist Temple of Chicago ★1283★
2230 N. Halsted
Chicago, IL 60614

Christian Believers Conference ★631★
% Berean Bible Students Church
5930 W. 29th St.
Cicero, IL 60650

Independent Spiritualist Association ★824★
% Rev. Harry M. Hilborn
5130 W. 25th St.
Cicero, IL 60650

Plymouth Brethren (Exclusive: Booth-Continental) ★565★
% Grace and Truth, Inc.
210 Oak St., Hillery
Danville, IL 61832

Nirankari Universal Brotherhood Mission ★1245★
Sant Nirankari Mission (USA)
1015 Thacker St.
Des Plaines, IL 60016

Church of God in Christ, Congregational ★388★
1905 Bond Ave.
East St. Louis, IL 62201

Church of the Brethren ★465★
Church of the Brethren General Offices
1451 Dundee Ave.
Elgin, IL 60120

Ukrainian Evangelical Alliance of North America ★170★
% Rev. Wladimir Borosky
690 Berkeley Ave.
Elmhurst, IL 60126

Ukrainian Evangelical Baptist Convention ★527★
% Rev. Barbuiziuk
690 Berkeley Ave.
Elmhurst, IL 60126

Reba Place Fellowship and Associated Communities ★756★
727 Reba Place
Evanston, IL 60602

Liberal Catholic Church, Province of The United States ★989★
% Rt. Rev. Lawrence J. Smith
9740 S. Avers
Evergreen Park, IL 60642

Christian Apostolic Church (Forest, Illinois) ★496★
Forrest, IL 61741

Serbian Orthodox Church in Diaspora ★114★
% Metropolitan Iriney Kovachevic
Box 371
Grayslake, IL 60030

International Council of Community Churches ★174★
% Rev. J. Ralph Shotwell, Executive Director
900 Ridge Rd., Suite LL 1
Homewood, IL 60430

Serbian Eastern Orthodox Church for the U.S.A. and Canada ★113★
% Rt. Rev. Bishop Firmilian
St. Sava Monastery
Box 519
Libertyville, IL 60048

Mennonite Church ★443★
528 E. Madison St.
Lombard, IL 60148

North American Baptist Conference ★518★
1 S. 210 Summit Ave.
Oakbrook Terrace, IL 60181

Church of God General Conference (Abrahamic Faith) ★599★
313 N. Third St.
Box 100
Oregon, IL 61061

Apostolic Christian Churches of America ★495★
3420 N. Sheridan Rd.
Peoria, IL 61604

Church of Christian Liberty ★575★
203 E. Camp McDonald Rd.
Prospect Heights, IL 60070

New Testament Association of Independent Baptist Churches ★517★
1079 Westview Dr.
Rochelle, IL 61068

Salem Acres ★758★
R.R.1, Box 175A
Rock City, IL 61070

I AM Religious Activity ★1003★
Saint Germain Foundation
1120 Stonehedge Dr.
Schaumberg, IL 60194

General Association of Regular Baptist Churches ★512★
1300 N. Meacham Rd.
Schaumburg, IL 60195

Apostolic Catholic Assyrian Church of the East, North American Diocese ★122★
% His Grace, Mar Aprim Khamis, Bishop of the North American Diocese
744 N. Kildare
Skokie, IL 60076

Protestant Reformed Churches of America ★159★
15615 S. Park Ave.
South Holland, IL 60473

Concordia Lutheran Conference ★141★
Central Ave. at 171st Place
Tingley Park, IL 60477

Apostolic Christian Church (Nazarean) ★494★
Apostolic Christian Church Foundation
Box 151
Tremont, IL 61568

Independent Fundamental Churches of America ★579★
1860 Mannheim Rd.
Westcester, IL 60153

Conservative Baptist Association ★509★
25W560 Geneva Rd., Box 66
Wheaton, IL 60189

Plymouth Brethren (Open Brethren) ★569★
% Stewards Foundation
Box 294
Wheaton, IL 60189

Theosophical Society of America ★970★
Box 270
Wheaton, IL 60187

Baha'i World Faith ★1169★
National Spiritual Assembly of the Baha'is of the U.S.
415 Linden Ave.
Wilmette, IL 60091

Indiana

Church of God (Anderson, Indiana) ★221★
Box 2420
Anderson, IN 46018

Universal Spiritualist Association ★850★
% Rev Clifford Bias
5836 Pendleton Ave.
Anderson, IN 46011

Faith Mission Church ★228★
% Rev. Ray Snow
1318 26th St.
Bedford, IN 47421

Zoroastrian Associations in North America ★1168★
% Center for Zoroastrian Research
801 E. Tenth St.
Bloomington, IN 47401

Old German Baptist Brethren ★474★
% Elder Clement Skiles
Rte. 1, Box 140
Bringhurst, IN 46913

General Assemblies and Church of the First Born ★325★

% Donald C. Hobbs
1008 Center Cross St.
Edinburgh, IN 46124

Bethel Ministerial Association ★361★
Box 5353
Evansville, IN 47715

Conference of the Evangelical Mennonite Church ★456★
1420 Kerrway Court
Fort Wayne, IN 46805

Missionary Church ★234★
3901 S. Wayne Ave.
Fort Wayne, IN 46807

Pentecostal Church of Zion ★333★
% Zion College of Theology
Box 110
French Lick, IN 47432

Macedonian Orthodox Church ★103★
% Rev. Spiro Tanaskaki
51st & Virginia Sts.
Gary, IN 46409

Apostolic Catholic Church of the Americas ★76★
% Most Rev. Gordon I. DaCosta
408 S. 10th St.
Gas City, IN 46933

Church of the Bible Covenant ★273★
Rte. 8, Box 214
450 N. Fortville Pike
Greenfield, IN 46140

Church of the United Brethren in Christ ★208★
% Bishop C. Ray Miller
302 Lake St.
Huntington, IN 46750

Christian Church (Disciples of Christ) ★551★
222 S. Downey Ave.
Box 1986
Indianapolis, IN 46206

Orthodox Catholic Church of America ★105★
% Most Rev. Alfred Lankenau
Box 1222
Indianapolis, IN 45206

Pentecostal Assemblies of the World ★374★
% Willard W. Saunders, Presiding Bishop
3040 N. Illinois St.
Indianapolis, IN 46208

Branham Tabernacle and Related Assemblies ★339★
% Spoken Word Publications
Box 888
Jeffersonville, IN 47131

Christian Israelites ★656★
% Mrs. M. Shafer
4592 Shafer Dr.
LaFayette, IN 47905

Truth for Today Bible Fellowship ★592★
2508 N. 400, E.
Lafayette, IN 47905

Wesleyan Church ★242★
Box 2000
Marion, IN 46952

Soulcraft, Inc. ★964★
Box 192
Noblesville, IN 46060

Friends United Meeting ★482★
101 Quaker Hill Dr.
Richmond, IN 47374

Midwest Congregational Christian Church ★175★
% Rev. Robert Schmitz
Rte. 1, Box 68
Union City, IN 47390

Central Yearly Meeting of Friends ★479★
Box 215
Westfield, IN 46074

Fellowship of Grace Brethren Churches ★469★

Winona Lake, IN 46590

Free Methodist Church of North America ★230★
901 College Ave.
Winona Lake, IN 46590

Iowa

Gospel Assemblies (Sowder) ★327★

% Gospel Assembly Church
7135 Meredith Dr.
Des Moines, IA 50322

Open Bible Standard Churches, Inc. ★331★
2020 Bell Ave.
Des Moines, IA 50315

Amana Community of Inspirationists ★733★
% Charles L. Selzer, President
Homestead, IA 52236

Anglican Catholic Church ★44★
% The Most Rev. Louis W. Falk
4807 Aspen Dr.
West Des Moines, IA 50265

Kansas

Apostolic Faith (Kansas) ★312★
1009 Lincoln Ave.
Baxter Springs, KS 66713

Churches of God (Independent Holiness People) ★226★
1225 E. First St.
Fort Scott, KS 66701

Mennonite Brethren Church of North America
    (Bruedergemeinde) ★454★

Hillsboro, KS 67063

Fire-Baptized Holiness Church (Wesleyan) ★229★
600 College Ave.
Independence, KS 67301

Church of God in Christ, Mennonite ★440★
420 N. Wedel
Moundridge, KS 67107

General Conference Mennonite Church ★453★
722 Main St.
Newton, KS 67114

Church of God (Holiness) ★223★
7415 Metcalf
Overland Park, KS 66204

Dunkard Brethren Church ★467★
% Dale E. Jamison, Chairman
Board of Trustees
Quinter, KS 67752

Christian Apostolic Church (Sabetha, Kansas) ★497★
Sabetha, KS 66534

Fountain of Life Fellowship ★621★
Valley Center, KS 67147

Evangelical Methodist Church ★190★
3000 W. Kellogg Dr.
Wichita, KS 67213

Mid-America Yearly Meeting ★485★
2018 Maple
Wichita, KS 67213

Missouri Valley Friends Conference ★486★
% Corky Stark
719 Brookfield Rd.
Wichita, KS 67206

Kentucky

Kentucky Mountain Holiness Association ★252★
Star Rte. 1, Box 350
Jackson, KY 41339

Separate Baptists in Christ ★522★
% Rev. Roger Popplewell, Moderator
Rte. 5
Russell Springs, KY 42642

Church of God of the Original Mountain Assembly ★290★
Williamsburg, KY 40769

Louisiana

National Baptist Convention of the U.S.A., Inc. ★536★
% Dr. T. G. Jemison, President
915 Spain St.
Baton Rouge, LA 70802

Christ's Sanctified Holy Church (Louisiana) ★219★
S. Cutting Ave. at E. Spencer St.
Jennings, LA 70546

New Christian Crusade Church ★670★
Box 426
Metairie, LA 70004

Volunteers of America ★241★
3813 N. Causeway Blvd.
Metairie, LA 70002

Religious Order of Witchcraft ★1092★
% Witchcraft Shop
521 St. Philip
New Orleans, LA 70116

Congregational Church of Practical Theology ★911★
Star Route, Box 28
Ponchatoula, LA 70454

Maine

United Society of Believers in Christ's Second Appearing
★746★
Sabbathday Lake, ME 04274

Maryland

Alpha and Omega Pentecostal Church of God of America,
Inc. ★386★
3023 Clifton Ave.
Baltimore, MD 21216

American Evangelistic Association ★415★
2200 Mt.Royal Terrace
Baltimore, MD 21217

Evangelical Bible Church ★423★
2499 Washington Blvd.
Baltimore, MD 21230

Evangelical Catholic Communion ★10★
% Most Rev. Marlin Paul Bausum Ballard
8648 Oakleigh Rd.
Baltimore, MD 21234

Grace and Hope Mission ★249★
45 Guy St.
Baltimore, MD 21202

Moorish Science Temple of America ★1161★
762 W. Baltimore St.
Baltimore, MD 21201

Moorish Science Temple, Prophet Ali Reincarnated
Founder ★1162★
519 N. Howard St.
Baltimore, MD 21201

The Nation of Islam (The Caliph) ★1163★
Muhammad's Temple of Islam No. 1
1233 W. Baltimore St.
Baltimore, MD 21223

Savitria ★940★
2405 Ruscombe
Baltimore, MD 21209

True Fellowship Pentecostal Church of God of America
★402★
4238 Pimlico Rd.
Baltimore, MD 21215

Scripture Research Association ★653★
14410 S. Springfield Rd.
Brandywine, MD 20613

American Zen College ★1300★
16815 Germantown Road (Route 18)
Germantown, MD 20767

Conservative Mennonite Conference ★457★
% Ivan J. Miller
Grantsville, MD 21536

Gospel Mission Corps ★248★
Box 175
Hightstown, MD 08520

Regular Baptists ★519★
% Tom Marshall
9023 Contee Rd.
Laurel, MD 20810

Body of Christ Movement ★417★
% Foundational Teachings
Box 6598
Silver Spring, MD 20906

Massachusetts

Insight Meditation Society ★1251★
Pleasant St.
Barre, MA 01005

Albanian Orthodox Archdiocese in America ★63★
% Metropolitan Theodosius
529 E. Broadway
Boston, MA 02127

Church of Christ, Scientist ★761★
Christian Science Service Center
Boston, MA 02115

Old Catholic Church-Utrecht Succession ★23★
% Most Rev. Roy G. Bauer
Box 1981
Boston, MA 02105

Unitarian Universalist Association ★687★
25 Beacon St.
Boston, MA 02108

United Church and Science of Living Institute ★795★
% Rev. Frederick Eikerenkotter II
Box 1000
Boston, MA 02103

New Age Teachings ★868★
37 Maple St.
Brookfield, MA 01506

Bostoner Hasidism ★1109★
% New England Chasidic Center
1710 Beacon St.
Brookline, MA 02146

East West Foundation ★1294★
17 Station St.
Brookline, MA 02147

Society of Johrei ★1343★
Box 1321
Brookline, MA 02146

Talnoye (Talner) Hasidism ★1120★
Talner Beth David
64 Corey Rd.
Brookline, MA 02146

Cambridge Buddhist Association ★1276★
263 N. Harvard St.
Cambridge, MA 02134

Rudrananda Ashram ★1211★
6 Linnaean St.
Cambridge, MA 02138

Maha Siddha Nyingmapa Center ★1316★
Box 257
Conway, MA 63121

Albanian Orthodox Diocese of America ★64★
% The Rev. Ik. Ilia Katra, Vicar General
54 Burroughs St.
Jamaica Plain, MA 02130

National Spiritual Alliance of the U.S.A. ★830★
RFD 1
Lake Pleasant, MA 01347

Kirpalu Yoga Fellowship ★1202★
Box 793
Lenox, MA 01240

Anglo-Saxon Federation of America ★664★
Box 177
Merrimac, MA 01860

General Convention of the New Jerusalem in the United
  States of America ★801★
48 Sargent St.
Newton, MA 02158

New England Evangelical Baptist Fellowship ★516★
% Dr. John Viall
40 Bridge St.
Newton, MA 02158

Renaissance Church of Beauty ★757★
Box 112
Turner's Falls, MA 01376

Temple of Bacchus ★1083★
RD 2
Box 51
Wells, MA 04090

Vipassana Fellowship of America ★1260★
Chapelbrook
Ashfield Road
Williamsburg, MA 01096

Michigan

Hungarian Reformed Church in America ★156★
% Rt. Rev. Dezso Abraham
18700 Midway Ave.
Allen Park, MI 48101

Lower Lights Church ★276★

Ann Arbor, MI

Zen Lotus Society ★1304★
Zen Buddhist Temple-Ann Arbor
1214 Packard Rd.
Ann Arbor, MI 48104

Church of Daniel's Band ★187★
% Rev. Duane Koontz, President
5950 Dale Rd.
Beaverton, MI 48612

Israelite House of David ★657★
Box 1967
Benton Harbor, MI 49022

Israelite House of David as Reorganized by Mary Purnell
★658★
Box 187
Benton Harbor, MI 49022

United Holiness Church of North America ★280★
Cedar Springs, MI 49319

Christian Pilgrim Church ★244★
Coldwater, MI 49036

Church of Universal Triumph/The Dominion of God
★262★
% Rev. James Shaffer
8317 LaSalle Blvd.
Detroit, MI 48206

Nation of Islam (John Muhammad) ★1165★
Nation of Islam, Temple No. 1
19220 Conat St.
Detroit, MI 48234

National Baptist Evangelical Life and Soul Saving
Assembly of the U.S.A. ★537★
441-61 Monroe Ave.
Detroit, MI 48226

Pan African Orthodox Christian Church ★1127★
13535 Livernois
Detroit, MI 48238

Romanian Apostolic Pentecostal Church of God of North
America ★435★
7794 Rosemont
Detroit, MI 48203

Romanian Orthodox Church in America ★108★
% His Eminence The Most Rev. Archbishop Victorin
(Ursache)
19959 Riopelle
Detroit, MI 48203

Shi'a Muslims ★1138★
% Islamic Center of Detroit
15571 Joy Rd.
Detroit, MI 48228

Church of Nature ★680★
Box 407
Dryden, MI 48428

Full Gospel Minister Association ★425★
East Jordan, MI 49727

Society for Humanistic Judaism ★1134★
28611 W. Twelve Mile Rd.
Farmington Hills, MI 48018

Colonial Village Pentecostal Church of the Nazarene
★421★
Flint, MI

Christian Reformed Church in North America ★152★
2850 Kalamazoo Ave.,S.E.
Grand Rapids, MI 49560

Free and Old Christian Reformed Church of Canada and
America ★155★
% Jacob Tamminga
950 Ball Ave., N.E.
Grand Rapids, MI 49503

Grace Gospel Fellowship ★589★
1011 Aldon St., S.W.
Grand Rapids, MI 49509

Spiritual Research Society ★877★
740 Hubbard St., N.E.
Grand Rapids, MI 49505

Orthodox Christian Reformed Churches ★158★
3268 S. Chestnut
Grandville, MI 49418

Assemblies of Yahweh (Michigan) ★646★
Box 102
Holt, MI 48842

Romanian Orthodox Episcopate of America ★109★
% His Eminence Archbishop Valerian (D, Trifa)
2522 Frey Tower Rd.
Jackson, MI 49201

Finnish Orthodox Church ★89★
% Fr. Denis Ericson
Box 174
Lansing, MI 48901

Spiritualist Episcopal Church ★840★
% Rev. Ivy M. Hooper
727 N. Capital Ave.
Lansing, MI 48906

Anchor Bay Evangelistic Association ★310★
Box 188
New Baltimore, MI 48047

Universal Church, the Mystical Body of Christ ★438★
Box 874
Saginaw, MI 48605

Church of Eternal Life and Liberty ★679★
Box 622
Southfield, MI 48037

School of Light and Realization (Solar) ★978★
Route 1, Box 72
Suttons Bay, MI 49682

Old Roman Catholic Church in North America ★24★
% Most Rev. Francis P. Facione
3827 Old Creek Rd.
Troy, MI 48084

Mariavite Old Catholic Church, Province of North
America ★15★
% His Eminence, Most Rev. Robert R. J. M. Zaborowski
2803 Tenth St.
Wyandotte, MI 48192

Coptic Fellowship of America ★912★
1735 Pinnacle, S.W.
Wyoming, MI 48509

Minnesota

Church of the Lutheran Brethren of America ★139★
1007 Westside Dr.
Box 655
Fergus Falls, MN 56537

Evangelical Lutheran Church in America ★142★
% Truman Larson
Rte. 1
Jackson, MN 56143

American Indian Evangelical Church ★309★
1823 Emerson Ave., N.
Minneapolis, MN 55411

American Lutheran Church ★130★
422 S. 5th St.
Minneapolis, MN 55415

Association of Free Lutheran Congregations ★138★
3170 E. Medicine Lake Blvd.
Minneapolis, MN 55427

Church of the Lutheran Confession ★140★
460 75th Ave.
Minneapolis, MN 55432

Evangelical Free Church of America ★179★
1551 E. 66th St.
Minneapolis, MN 55423

Independent Baptist Church of America ★513★
% Elmer Erickson, President
2646 Longfellow
Minneapolis, MN 55407

Minnesota Baptist Association ★515★
% Rev. Richard L. Paige, Jr., Executive Secretary
5000 Golden Valley Rd.
Minneapolis, MN 55422

Minnesota Zen Meditation Center ★1279★
3343 Calhoun Pkwy.
Minneapolis, MN 55408

Plymouth Brethren (Exclusive: Ames Brethren) ★564★
% Christian Literature, Inc.
Box 23082
Minneapolis, MN 55423

Apostolic Lutheran Church (Old Laestadians) ★131★
% Rev. George Wilson, President
New York Mills, MN 56567

American Order of the Brotherhood of Wicca ★1042★
% Lady Sheba
Box 3383-G
St. Paul, MN 55415

Aurum Solis ★1023★
% The Administrator General
Box 43383-OSV
St. Paul, MN 55164

Conservative Congregational Christian Conference ★173★
7582 Currell Blvd., Suite 108
St. Paul, MN 55125

Mississippi

First Congregational Methodist Church of the U.S.A.
★193★

Decatur, MS 39327

Congregational Methodist Church ★188★
Box 155
Florence, MS 39073

Association of Independent Methodists ★185★
Box 4274
Jackson, MS 39216

Church of Christ (Holiness) U.S.A. ★260★
329 E. Monument St.
Jackson, MS 39202

Methodist Protestant Church ★196★
% Rev. F. E. Sellers
Monticello, MS 55362

Missouri

Church of God Evangelistic Association ★614★
11824 Beaverton
Bridgeton, MO 63044

Huna Research Associates ★925★
126 Camillia Drive
Cape Girardeau, MO 63701

Davidian Seventh-Day Adventists Association ★602★
Bashan Hill
Exeter, MO 65647

United Pentecostal Church ★381★
8855 Dunn Rd.
Hazelwood, MO 63042

Christ Catholic Church (Pruter) ★7★
% Most Rev. Karl Pruter
Box 98
Highlandville, MO 65669

Church of Christ (Bible and Book of Mormon Teaching)
★720★
1515 S. Harvard
Independence, MO 64052

Church of Christ (Fetting/Bronson) ★721★
1138 East Gudgell
Independence, MO 64055

Church of Christ (Temple Lot) ★723★
Temple Lot
Independence, MO 65051

Church of Christ with the Elijah Message (Dravesites)
★725★
608 Lacy Rd.
Independence, MO 64050

Church of Jesus Christ (Cutlerite) ★728★
819 S. Cottage St.
Independence, MO 64050

Reorganized Church of Jesus Christ of Latter-Day Saints
★726★
The Auditorium
Box 1059
Independence, MO 64051

Restored Church of Jesus Christ (Walton) ★731★
Box 1651
Independence, MO 64055

True Church of Jesus Christ Restored ★732★
1533 E. Mechanic
Independence, MO 64050

Pentecostal Church of God of America ★332★
Box 850
602 Main St.
Joplin, MO 64802

Church of the Nazarene ★224★
6401 The Paseo
Kansas City, MO 64131

Defenders of the Faith ★411★
928 Linwood Blvd.
Kansas City, MO 64109

Churches of Christ (Non-Instrumental, One Cup) ★555★
% Old Paths Advocate
R.R. 1
Lebanon, MO 65536

Church of Christ (Restored) ★722★
% Mr. Uel Sisk
609 C Lilac Place, John Knox Village
Lee's Summit, MO 64063

Zion's Order of the Sons of Levi ★710★
% Douglas Kilgore
Rte. 2
Mansfield, MO 65704

Covenant, the Sword and the Arm of the Lord ★668★
Rte. 1, Box 128
Pontiac, MO 65729

General Association of General Baptists ★541★
100 Stinson Dr.
Poplar Bluff, MO 63901

Yahweh's Assembly in Messiah ★655★
Rte. 1, Box 364
Rocheport, MO 65279

Church of Christ at Halley's Bluff ★724★

Schell City, MO 64783

Church of Israel ★667★
Box 62-83
Schell City, MO 64783

American Orthodox Church ★73★
% Archbishop Aftimios Harold J. Donovan, Exarch
3332 S. Kings Ave.
Springfield, MO 65807

Association of Fundamental Ministers and Churches
★214★

Springfield, MO

Baptist Bible Fellowship ★506★
Box 191
Springfield, MO 65801

Fundamental Methodist Church ★194★
1034 N. Broadway
Springfield, MO 65802

General Council of the Assemblies of God ★313★
1445 Boonville Ave.
Springfield, MO 65802

American Rationalist Federation ★676★
2001 St. Clair Ave.
St. Louis, MO 63144

Association of Evangelical Lutheran Churches ★137★
St. Louis, MO 63131

Gospel Assemblies (Jolly) ★326★
St. Louis, MO

Lutheran Church-Missouri Synod ★147★
International Center
1333 S. Kirkwood Rd.
St. Louis, MO 63122

Pastoral Bible Institute ★638★
Box 15031, Chouteau Station
St. Louis, MO 63110

Universal Great Brotherhood ★1020★
Administrative Council of the U. S. A.
Box 9154
St. Louis, MO 63117

American School of Mentalvivology ★767★
Cedar Heat of the Ozarks
Thornfield, MO 65762

Unity School of Christianity ★797★
Unity Village, MO 64065

Montana

Hutterian Brethren-Dariusluet ★738★
% Rev. Elias Walter
Surprise Creek Colony
Stanford, MT 59479

Hutterian Brethren-Lehreleut ★739★
% Rev. Joseph Kleinsasser
Milford Colony
Wolf Creek, MT 59648

Nebraska

Evangelical Wesleyan Church ★274★

Grand Island, NE 68801

Reformed Church in the United States ★161★
% Rev. Vernon Polleme, President
3930 Masin Dr.
Lincoln, NE 68521

Berean Fundamental Churches ★573★
Box 549
North Platte, NE 69101

Evangelical Mennonite Brethren Conference ★451★
5800 S. 14th St.
Omaha, NE 68107

Future Foundation ★920★
Box 26
Steinauer, NE 68441

Nevada

Church of Revelation (California) ★810★
517 E. Park Paseo
Las Vegas, NV 89104

Foundation Faith of God ★919★
Faith Center
3055 S. Bronco
Las Vegas, NV 89102

Institute of Cosmic Wisdom ★928★
3528 Franciscan Lane
Las Vegas, NV 89121

Orthodox Baha'i Faith under the Regency ★1172★
% National House of Justice of the U.S. and Canada
Box 1424
Las Vegas, NV 87701

Catholic Christian Church ★5★
% Most Rev. Alan S. Stanford
316 California Ave., Suite 713
Reno, NV 89509

Pansophic Institute ★1318★
Box 2422
Reno, NV 89505

New Hampshire

Sant Bani Ashram ★1247★

Franklin, NH 03235

Homebringing Mission of Jesus Christ ★924★
% Charlotte E. Suprenant
Box 13
Pelham, NH 03076

New Jersey

Bible Presbyterian Church ★163★
756 Haddon Ave.
Collingswood, NJ 12771

African Universal Church ★385★
% Archbishop Clarence C. Addison
14 Webster Place
East Orange, NJ 07018

Dawn Bible Students Association ★633★
199 Railroad Ave.
East Rutherford, NJ 07073

Antiochian Orthodox Christian Archdiocese of North
America ★74★
% Metropolitan Philip, Primate
358 Mountain Rd.
Englewood, NJ 07631

Coptic Orthodox Church ★123★
% Archpriest Fr. Gabriel Abdelsayed
427 West Side Ave.
Jersey City, NJ 07304

Syrian Orthodox Church of Antioch (Archdioceses of the
United States and Canada) (Jacobite) ★128★
% Archbishop MarAthanasius Y. Samuel, Primate
49 Kipp Ave.
Lodi, NJ 07644

American Vegan Society ★1177★
501 Old Harding Hwy.
Malaga, NJ 08328

Philanthropic Assembly ★639★
709 74th St.
North Bergen, NJ 07047

Shanti Yogi Institute and Yoga Retreat ★1221★
943 Central Ave.
Ocean City, NJ 08226

Ukrainian Orthodox Church in the U.S.A. ★116★
% Most Rev. Mstyslav Skrynpyk
Box 495
South Bound Brook, NJ 08880

Byelorussian Orthodox Church ★83★
190 Turnpike Rd.
South River, NJ 08882

Salvation Army ★238★
799 Bloomfield Ave.
Verona, NJ 07044

Labsum Shedrub Ling ★1313★
Box 306-1, RD. 1
Washington, NJ 07882

New Mexico

Understanding, Inc. ★890★
Box 614
Alamagordo, NM 88311

Quimby Center ★939★
Box 453
Alamogordo, NM 88310

Church of Jesus Christ of Latter-Day Saints (Strangite)
★729★
% Vernon Swift
Box 522
Artesia, NM 88210

T.O.M. Religious Foundation ★843★
Box 52
Chimayo, NM 87522

City of the Sun Foundation ★1000★
Box 356
Columbus, NM 88029

New Age Church of Truth ★933★
Star Route 2
Box CLC
Deming, NM 88030

Orthodox Baha'i Faith, Mother Baha'i Council of the
     United States ★1171★
3111 Futura
Roswell, NM 88201

Lama Foundation ★753★
Box 44
San Cristobal, NM 877564

Hanuman Foundation ★1193★
Box 478
Santa Fe, NM 87501

Intermountain Yearly Meeting ★483★
% Sante Fe Friends Meeting
630 Canyon Rd.
Sante Fe, NM 87501

Third Civilization ★1347★
Box 1836
Sante Fe, NM 87501

New York

Pilgrim Holiness Church of New York ★278★
32 Cadillac Ave.
Albany, NY 12205

American Humanist Association ★675★
7 Harwood Dr.
Box 146
Amherst, NY 14226-0146

Our Lady of the Roses, Mary Help of Mothers Shrine
     ★31★
Box 52
Bayside, NY 11361

Remey Society ★1173★
86-11 Commonwealth Blvd.
Bellerose, NY 11426

Tioga River Christian Conference ★561★
% Rev. George Kyrk
Bible School Park, NY 16837

Ausar Auset Society ★948★
% Oracle of Thoth, Inc.
Box 281
Bronx, NY 10462

Damascus Christian Church ★410★
% Rev. Enrique Melendez
179 Mt. Eden Parkway
Bronx, NY 10473

Ethiopian Orthodox Church in the United States of
     America ★124★
% His Eminence Abuna Yeshaq, Archbishop
Holy Trinity Ethiopian Orthodox Church
140-142 W. 176th St.
Bronx, NY 10453

Ansaaru Allah Community ★1158★
716 Bushwick Ave.
Brooklyn, NY 11221

Bluzhever Hasidism ★1107★
Belzer Bet Midrash
662 Eastern Pkwy.
Brooklyn, NY 11213

Bobov Hasidism ★1108★
% Rabbi Solomon Halberstamm
Yeshiva Bnai Zion
4909 15th St.
Brooklyn, NY 11219

Bratslav Hasidism ★1110★
% Rabbi Leo Rosenfeld
864 44th St.
Brooklyn, NY 11219

Chernobyl Hasidism ★1111★
% Rabbi Israel Jacob Twersky
1520 49th St.
Brooklyn, NY 11232

Church of God in Christ, International ★389★
% Rt. Rev. Carl E. Williams, Presiding Bishop
170 Adelphi St.
Brooklyn, NY 11025

Ethiopian Orthodox Coptic Church, Diocese of North and
     South America ★125★
1255 Bedford Ave.
Brooklyn, NY 11216

Jehovah's Witnesses ★635★
25 Columbia Heights
Brooklyn, NY 11201

Lubavitch Hasidism ★1113★
770 Eastern Pkwy.
Brooklyn, NY 11213

Novominsk Hasidism ★1115★
% Rabbi Nahum M. Perlow
1569 47th St.
Brooklyn, NY 11220

Satmar Hasidism ★1116★
% Congregation Y L D'Satmar
152 Rodney
Brooklyn, NY 11220

Sighet Hasidism ★1117★
152 Hewes St.
Brooklyn, NY 11211

Stolin Hasidism ★1119★
Stolin Bet Midrash
1818 54th St.
Brooklyn, NY 11211

Tridentine Catholic Church ★39★
% Archbishop Leonard J. Curreri, Primate
Sacred Heart of Jesus Chapel
1740 W. Seventh St.
Brooklyn, NY 11223

United Hispanic Old Catholic Episcopate in the Americas
    ★41★
% Most Rev. Hector Roa y Gonzalez
10 Stagg St.
Brooklyn, NY 11206

United Old Roman Catholic Church (Whitehead) ★42★
% Most Rev. Armand C. Whitehead
527 82nd St.
Brooklyn, NY 11209

Universal Shrine of Divine Guidance ★118★
% Most Rev. Mark A. G. Karras
30 Malta St.
Brooklyn, NY 11207

True Church of Christ, International ★943★
Box 2, Station G
Buffalo, NY 14213

Servant Catholic Church ★35★
% Most Rev. Robert E. Burns
50 Coventry Lane
Central Islip, NY 11722

Gardnerian Wicca ★1063★
% Theos and Phoenix
Box 56
Commack, NY 11725

Longchen Nyingthig Buddhist Society ★1315★
Box 302
Harris, NY 12742

Aurobindo, Disciples of Sri ★1182★
% Matagiri-Sri Aurobindo Center
High Falls, NY 12440

Church of the Gospel ★245★
% Marion Green
20 1/2 Walnut St.
Hudson Falls, NY 12839

Miracle Experiences, Inc. ★785★
Box 158
Islip Terrace, NY 11752

Sri Chinmoy Centres ★1187★
Box 32433
Jamaica, NY 11431

Ukrainian Orthodox Church in America (Ecumenical
    Patriarchate) ★117★
St. Andrew's Ukrainian Orthodox Diocese
% Most Rev. Metropolitan Andrei Kuschak
90-34 139th St.
Jamaica, NY 11435

New Age Church of Christ ★1004★

Kings Park, NY 11754

National Association of Holiness Churches ★277★
% Rev. Dale L. Hallaway, General Secretary
60 Averyville Rd.
Lake Placid, NY 12946

Sufi Order ★1154★
Sufi Order Secretariat
Box 574
Lebanon Springs, NY 12114

National Spiritualist Association of Churches ★831★
% Rev. Joseph H. Merrill
13 Cleveland St.
Lily Dale, NY 14652

Elim Fellowship ★320★
Lima, NY 14485

United Church of the Apostles ★702★
Lindenhurst, NY 11757

Embassy of the Gheez-Americans ★914★
Mt. Helion Sanctuary
Rock Valley Rd., Box 53
Long Eddy, NY 12760

American Orthodox Catholic Church - Western Rite
    Mission, Diocese of New York ★2★
% Most Rev. Joseph J. Raffaele
318 Expressway Dr., S.
Medford, NY 11763

Intercosmic Center of Spiritual Awareness ★1198★
% Ananda Ashram
Sapphire Rd.
R.D. 2, Box 212-C-1
Monroe, NY 10950

Skver Hasidism ★1118★
Skverer Town
New Square, NY 10977

Agni Yoga Society ★1009★
319 W. 107th St.
New York, NY 10025

Algard Wicca ★1041★
% Mary Nesnick
529 E. 20th St.
New York, NY 10009

American Buddhist Movement ★1326★
301 W. 45th St.
New York, NY 10036

American Buddhist Society and Fellowship, Inc. ★1305★
% Robert Ernest Dickhoff
600 W. 157th St.
New York, NY 10032

American Catholic Church, Archdiocese of New York
    ★66★
% Most Rev. Michael Edward Verra
238 Mott St.
New York, NY 10012

American Ethical Union ★674★
2 W. 64th St.
New York, NY 10023

American Orthodox Catholic Church (Propheta) ★70★
% Archbishop John A. Christian
675 E. 183rd St.
New York, NY 10458

Anthroposophical Society ★1012★
Rudolf Steiner Information Center
211 Madison Ave.
New York, NY 10016

Arcane School ★975★
866 United Nations Plaza
Suite 566-7
New York, NY 10017

Arica Institute ★1140★
235 Park Ave.S.
New York, NY 10003

Armenian Apostolic Church of America ★120★
% Archbishop Mesrob Ashjian
138 E. 39th St.
New York, NY 10016

Armenian Church of America ★121★
% His Eminence Torkom Manoogian, Primate
630 Second Ave.
New York, NY 10016

Arunchala Ashrama ★1181★
342 E. 6th St.
New York, NY 10003

Association of Occidental Orthodox Parishes ★77★
Father Stephen Empson
57 Saint Marks Place
New York, NY 10003

Autocephalous Slavonic Orthodox Catholic Church (In
    Exile) ★78★
2237 Hunter Ave.
New York, NY 10475

Bible Church of Christ ★315★

New York, NY

Buddhist Association of the United States ★1290★
3070 Albany Cresent
New York, NY 10463

Buddhist Fellowship of New York ★1327★
331 Riverside Dr.
New York, NY 10025

Bulgarian Eastern Orthodox Church (Diocese of North
    and South America and Australia) ★80★
Metropolitan Joseph
550 A, W. 50th St.
New York, NY 10019

Chamber of Holy Voodoo ★1089★
Box 341
New York, NY 10021

Church of Our Lord Jesus Christ of the Apostolic Faith
    ★365★
2081 Seventh Ave.
New York, NY 10027

Church of the Truth ★776★
% Dr. John L. Baughman
154 W. 5th St.
New York, NY 10019

Commandment Keepers Congregation of the Living God
    ★1124★
% Rabbi David M. Dore
1 E. 123rd St.
New York, NY 10035

Conservative Judaism ★1103★
United Synagogue of America
155 Fifth Ave.
New York, NY 10010

Earthstar Temple ★1059★
35 W. 19th St.
New York, NY 10011

Eastern States Buddhist Association of America ★1295★
64 Mott St.
New York, NY 10013

Ecumenical Orthodox Catholic Church-Autocephalous ★9★
% Most Rev. Francis J. Ryan, Primate-Apostolos
        WesternRite
Box 637, Grand Central Station
New York, NY 10017

First Church of Divine Immanence ★780★
2109 Broadway
Apt. 8L/144
New York, NY 10023

First Zen Institute ★1278★
113 E. 30th St.
New York, NY 10016

General Assembly of Spiritualists ★817★
% Rev. Rose Ann Erickson
Ansonia Hotel
2107 Broadway
New York, NY 10023

Greek Orthodox Archdiocese of North and South America
    ★90★
% His Eminence Archbishop Iakovos
8-10 E. 79th St.
New York, NY 10021

Havurah Movement ★1131★
National Havurot Coordinating Committee
250 W. 57th St., Suite 216
New York, NY 10019

Holy Orthodox Church in America ★101★
% Most Rev. Mother Serena
321 W. 101st St.
New York, NY 10025

Holy Spirit Association for the Unification of World
    Christianity ★923★
4 W. 43rd St.
New York, NY 10036

Independent Associated Spiritualists ★823★
% Rev. Marion Owens
124 W. 72nd St.
New York, NY 10023

International Metaphysical Association ★763★
20 E. 68th St.
New York, NY 10021

Jain Meditation International Center ★1238★
Box 730, Radio City
New York, NY 10101

Jetsun Sakya Center ★1311★
623 W. 129th St.
New York, NY 10027

Jewish Reconstructionist Foundation ★1104★
Federation of Reconstructionist Congregations and Havurot
2521 Broadway, S.
New York, NY 10025

Khaniqahi-Nimatullahi ★1149★
306 W. 11th St.
New York, NY 10014

Kundalini Research Foundation ★1204★
10 E. 39th St.
New York, NY 10016

Latin-American Council of the Pentecostal Church of God
of New York ★413★
115 E. 125th St.
New York, NY 10035

Little Synagogue ★1133★
27 E. 20th St.
New York, NY 10003

Lutheran Church in America ★146★
231 Madison Ave.
New York, NY 10016

Ordo Templi Orientis ★1034★
% Grand Lodge
JAF Box 7666
New York, NY 10116

Orthodox Judaism ★1106★
% Rabbinical Council of America
1250 Broadway, Suite 807
New York, NY 10001

Presbyterian Church (U.S.A.) ★167★
475 Riverside Dr.
New York, NY 10115

Protestant Episcopal Church in the U.S.A. ★55★
815 Second Ave.
New York, NY 10017

Reform Judaism ★1105★
Union of American Hebrew Congregations
838 Fifth Ave.
New York, NY 10021

Reformed Church in America ★160★
475 Riverside Dr.
New York, NY 10115

Russian Orthodox Church Outside of Russia ★111★
% His Eminence Philaret, Metropolitan
75 E. 93rd St.
New York, NY 10028

Russian Orthodox Church in the U.S.A., Patriarchial
Parishes of the ★110★
St. Nicholas Patriarchal Cathedral
15 E. 97th St.
New York, NY 10029

Sacred Heart Catholic Church (Arrendale) ★112★
1475 Walton Ave.
New York, NY 10452

School of Esoteric Studies ★977★
40 E. 49th St., Suite 1903
New York, NY 10017

Seventh-Day Christian Conference ★607★
246 W. 138th St.
New York, NY 10030

Societas Rosicruciana in America ★954★
321 W. 101st St.
New York, NY 10025

Society of Pragmatic Mysticism ★793★
200 W. 58th St.
New York, NY 10019

Spiritual Science Mother Church ★839★
Carnegie Hall
56th St. & 7th Ave.
New York, NY 10019

Syrian Orthodox Church of Malabar ★129★
% Dr. K. M. Simon
Union Theological Seminary
Broadway and 120th St.
New York, NY 10027

Unification Association of Christian Sabbath Keepers
★608★
255 W. 131st St.
New York, NY 10027

United Church of Christ ★177★
105 Madison Ave.
New York, NY 10016

United Israel World Union ★1137★
406 E. 42nd St.
New York, NY 10017

United Wesleyan Methodist Church of America ★212★
% Rev. David S. Bruno
270 W. 126th St.
New York, NY 10027

Universal Brotherhood ★944★
Box 366, Grand Central Station
New York, NY 10017

Vedanta Society ★1227★
34 W. 71st St.
New York, NY 10023

Witches International Craft Associates ★1087★
153 W. 80th St.
New York, NY 10024

Yeshe Nyingpo ★1325★
19 W. 16th St.
New York, NY 10011

Yogi Gupta Association ★1235★
127 E. 56th St.
New York, NY 10022

Yoruba Theological Archministry ★1093★
167 E. 106th St.
New York, NY 10029

Zen Studies Society ★1287★
223 E. 67th St.
New York, NY 10021

Christian and Missionary Alliance ★217★
350 N. Highland Ave.
Nyack, NY 10960

Society of Jewish Science ★1135★
825 Round Swamp Rd.
Old Bethpage, NY 11804

American World Patriarchs ★75★
% Most Rev. Emigidius J. Ryzy
19 Aqueduct St.
Ossining, NY 10562

Sikh Council of North America ★1249★
95-30 118th St.
Richmond Hill, NY 11419

Society of Brothers ★744★

Rifton, NY 12471

Megiddo Mission ★254★
478 Thurston Rd.
Rochester, NY 14619

Zen Center of Rochester ★1285★
Arnold Park
Rochester, NY 14607

Chishti Order of America ★1142★
% Hakim G. M. Chishti
390 Soundview Dr.
Rocky Point, NY 11778

Sanctuary of the Master's Presence ★1007★
Two Larkin Rd.
Scarsdale, NY 10583

People's Christian Church ★604★
402 Melrose St.
Schenectady, NY 12306

Siddha Yoga Dham of America ★1216★
Box 605
South Fallsburg, NY 12779

Ma Yoga Shakti International Mission ★1206★
114-23 Lefferts Blvd.
South Ozone, NY 11420

Jerrahi Order of America ★1148★
864 S. Main St.
Spring Valley, NY 10977

North American Old Roman Catholic Church (Rogers)
★18★
% Most Rev. Archbishop James H. Rogers
118-09 Farmer Blvd.
St. Albans, NY 11412

International Nahavir Jain Mission ★1237★
Acharya Sushil Jain Ashram
722 Tomkins Ave.
Staten Island, NY 10305

Orthodox Church in America ★106★
% Most Blessed Theodosius, Archbishop of Washington,
    Metropolitan of All America and Canada
Very Rev. Daniel Hubiak, Chancellor
Box 675
Syosset, NY 11791

Kagyu Dharma ★1312★
127 Sheafe Rd.
Wappinger Falls, NY 12590

Institute for Religious Development ★1145★
Chardavogne Rd.
Warwick, NY 19990

Holy Ukrainian Autocephalic Orthodox Church in Exile
    ★102★
103 Evergreen St.
West Babylon, NY 11714

Karma Triyana Dharmachakra ★1314★
352 Meads Mountain Rd.
Woodstock, NY 12498

Mount Hebron Apostolic Temple of Our Lord Jesus of
    the Apostolic Faith ★371★
Mount Hebron Apostolic Temple
27 Vineyard Ave.
Yonkers, NY 10703

North Carolina

General Conference of the Original Free Will Baptist
    Church ★542★

Ayden, NC 28513

Emmanuel Holiness Church ★296★
Box 818
Bladenboro, NC 28320

Advent Christian Church ★598★
Box 23152
Charlotte, NC 28212

African Methodist Episcopal Zion Church ★202★
Box 23843
Charlotte, NC 28232

Carolina Evangelistic Association ★284★
200 Tuckaseegee Rd.
Charlotte, NC 28208

Essene Teachings Inc. ★1002★
% Mary Myers
3427 Denison Place
Charlotte, NC 28215

Shiloh True Light Church of Christ ★660★
% Elder James Ronnie Purser
4001 Sheridan Rd.
Charlotte, NC 28205

Pentecostal Free Will Baptist Church ★308★
Box 1081
Dunn, NC 28334

Mount Calvary Holy Church of America ★266★
% Bishop Harold Williams
1214 Chowan St.
Durham, NC 27713

Original United Holy Church International ★400★
% Bishop H. W. Fields
Box 263
Durham, NC 27702

Black Primitive Baptists ★529★
% Primitive Baptist Library
Rte. 2
Elon College, NC 27244

Christian Spirit Center ★805★
Box 114
Elon College, NC 27244

Primitive Baptists-Absolute Predestinarians ★531★
% Primitive Baptist Library
Rte. 2
Elon College, NC 27244

Primitive Baptists-Regulars ★533★
% Primitive Baptist Library
Rte. 2
Elon College, NC 27244

General Conference of the Evangelical Baptist Church
★301★
Kavetter Bldg.
3400 E. Ash St.
Goldsboro, NC 27530

Holiness Church of God ★303★
% Bishop B. McKinney
602 E. Elm St.
Graham, NC 27253

Holiness Church of God, Inc. ★250★
% Bishop B. McKinney
602 Elm St.
Graham, NC 27253

United Free-Will Baptist Church ★547★
% Kingston College
Kingston, NC 28501

Church of God, Body of Christ ★611★
Rte. 1
Mocksville, NC 27028

Shiloh True Light Church of Christ (Braswell) ★661★

Monroe, NC 28110

Missionary Methodist Church of America ★235★
Rte. 7
Morganton, NC 28655

Church and School of Wicca ★1045★
Box 1502
New Bern, NC 28560

Lumber River Annual Conference of the Holiness
Methodist Church ★253★
% Bishop C. N. Lowry
Rowland, NC 28383

Anglican Orthodox Church ★47★
% Most Rev. James Parker Dees
323 E. Walnut St.
Box 128
Statesville, NC 28677

Southern Appalachian Yearly Meeting and Association
★493★
% Mrs. Ruth O. Szittya
Box 545
Swannanoa, NC 28778

Christian Unity Baptist Association ★508★
% Elder Thomas T. Reynolds
Thomasville, NC 27360

Apostolic Church of Christ ★351★
2044 Stadium Dr.
Winston-Salem, NC 27107

Apostolic Church of Christ in God ★352★
% Bethlehem Apostolic Church
1217 E. 15th St.
Winston-Salem, NC 27105

Ohio

Rex Humbard Ministry ★584★

Akron, OH 44331

Brethren Church (Ashland, Ohio) ★461★
524 College Ave.
Ashland, OH 44805

Religious Society of Friends (Conservative) ★490★
% Olney Friends School
Barnesville, OH 43713

Association of Fundamental Gospel Churches ★459★
9189 Grubb Court
Canton, OH 44721

Evangelical Friends Church, Eastern Division ★480★
1201 30th St., N.W.
Canton, OH 44709

North American Christian Convention ★560★
3533 Epley Rd.
Cincinnati, OH 45239

Wesleyan Tabernacle Association ★258★
626 Elliott Ave.
Cincinnati, OH 45215

Churches of Christ in Christian Union ★246★
1427 Lancaster Pike
Circleville, OH 43113

Church of God (Cleveland, Ohio) ★612★
% Pastor M. L. Bartholomew
Box 02026
Cleveland, OH 44102

Church of God (O'Beirn) ★613★
Box 81224
Cleveland, OH 44181

Old Order (Reidenbach) Mennonites ★444★
% Henry W. Riehl
Rte. 1
Columbiana, OH 44408

Old Order (Wenger) Mennonites ★445★
% Henry W. Riehl
Rte. 1
Columbiana, OH 44408

Old Order (Wisler) Mennonite Church ★446★
% Bishop Henry W. Riehl
Rte. 1
Columbiana, OH 44408

Holy Catholic Church, Anglican Rite Jurisdiction of the
    Americas ★53★
% Most. Rev. G. Wayne Craig, Archbishop
2535 Sunbury Dr.
Columbus, OH 43219

United Methodist Church ★182★
% Council on Ministries
601 W. Riverside Ave.
Dayton, OH 45406

Wesleyan Holiness Association of Churches ★282★
108 Carter
Dayton, OH 45405

Leroy Jenkins Evangelistic Association ★346★
Box F
Delaware, OH 43015

Churches of God, General Conference ★154★
700 E. Melrose Ave.
Box 926
Findlay, OH 45839

Churches of God, General Conference ★225★
700 E. Melrose Ave.
Box 926
Findlay, OH 45839

Conservative Mennonite Fellowship (Non-Conference)
    ★442★
Box 36
Hartville, OH 44632

International Pentecostal Church of Christ ★304★
Box 439
2245 U.S. 42, S.W.
London, OH 43140

Ohio Bible Fellowship ★583★
% Rev. John Ashbrook
5733 Hopkins Rd.
Mentor, OH 44060

The Way International ★593★
Box 328
New Knoxville, OH 45871

Bulgarian Eastern Orthodox Church, Diocese of North
    and South America ★81★
519 Brynhaven Dr.
Oregon, OH

Beachy Amish Mennonite Churches ★455★
9675 Iams Rd.
Plain City, OH 43064

Allegheny Wesleyan Methodist Connection ★268★
2161 Woodsdale Rd.
Salem, OH 44460

Christian Nation Church, U.S.A. ★218★
% Rev. Harvey Monjar, General Overseer
Box 142
South Lebanon, OH 45065

Light of the Universe ★865★
161 N. Sandusky Rd.
Tiffin, OH 44883

Oklahoma

International Pentecostal Holiness Church ★305★
7300 N.W. 39th Expressway
Bethany, OK 73008

United Seventh-Day Brethren ★626★
% Myrtle Ortiz
Box 225
Enid, OK 73701

Church of God (Guthrie, Oklahoma) ★222★
% Faith Publishing House
7415 W. Monsur Ave.
Guthrie, OK 73044

Bible Churches (Classics Expositor) ★587★
% Dr. C. E. McLain
1429 N.W. 100th St.
Oklahoma City, OK 73114

Church of the Living God (Christian Workers for
    Fellowship) ★390★
% Bishop F. C. Scott
801 N.E. 17th St.
Oklahoma City, OK 73105

Gnostic Orthodox Church ★985★
% Abbot-Bishop George Burke
3500 Coltrane Rd.
Oklahoma City, OK 73121

Law of Life Ascended Master Groups ★999★
% A. D. K. Luk
1124 N. Meta Ave.
Oklahoma City, OK 73107

Old Holy Catholic Church, Province of North America
    ★993★
% Most Rev. George Brister
Box 69235
Oklahoma City, OK 73146

Universal Life Mission Church ★705★
610 N. Second St.
Sapulpa, OK 74066

Assembly of Yahvah (Oregon) ★643★
% Elder L. D. Snow
Box 1010
Stilwell, OK 74960

Church of God of the Apostolic Faith ★288★
2530 W. Cameron
Tulsa, OK 74127

International Convention of Faith Churches and Ministers
    ★343★
4500 S. Garnett
Exchange Tower, Suite 910
Tulsa, OK 74146

Lighthouse Gospel Fellowship ★433★
% Lighthouse Gospel Center
636 E. 3rd St.
Tulsa, OK 74120

Oregon

Crown of Life Fellowship ★697★
Route 2, Box 190
Albany, OR 97321

Rajneesh Foundation International ★1239★

Antelope, OR 97741

Solar Light Center ★888★
7700 Avenue of the Sun
Central Point, OR 97501

Church of God, the Eternal ★618★
Box 755
Eugene, OR 97440

Evangelical Church of North America ★247★
7525 S.E. Lake Rd., Suite 7
Milwaukie, OR 97222

Northwest Yearly Meeting of Friends Church ★488★
Box 190
Newberg, OR 97132

The Apostolic Faith ★283★
6615 S.E. 52nd Ave.
Portland, OR 97206

Grace Gospel Evangelistic Association International Inc.
★429★
% Rev. John D. Kennington
909 N.E. 30th St.
Portland, OR 97232

Last Day Messenger Assemblies ★590★
Box 17056
Portland, OR 97217

Pentecostal Evangelical Church of God, National and
International ★335★

Riddle, OR 97469

Mu Farm ★754★
Box 143
Yoncalla, OR 97499

Pennsylvania

Western Orthodox Church in America ★119★
% Most Rev. C. David Luther
1529 Pleasant Valley Blvd.
Altoona, PA 16602

Assemblies of Yahweh ★645★

Bethel, PA 19507

Moravian Church in America ★180★
Northern Province
69 W. Church St.
Box 1245
Bethlehem, PA 18018

General Church of the New Jerusalem ★800★
% Rt. Rev. L. B. King, Executive Bishop
Bryn Athyn, PA 19009

Lord's New Church Which Is Nova Hierosolyma ★802★
Rev. Philip Odhner
Box 4
Bryn Athyn, PA 19009

Layman's Home Missionary Movement ★637★

Chester Springs, PA 19425

United Zion Church ★477★
% Bishop Alvin H. Eberly
Rte. 2
Denver, PA 17517

Old Order (or Yorker) River Brethren ★476★
% Bishop Daniel M. Sipling
356 E. High St.
Elizabethtown, PA 17022

Stauffer Mennonite Church ★448★
% Bishop Jacob S. Stauffer
Rte. 3
Ephrata, PA 17522

Holiness Gospel Church ★251★
Rte. 2, Box 13
Etters, PA 17319

Free Gospel Church, Inc. ★323★
% Rev. Chester H. Heath
Box 477
Export, PA 15632

Voice of the Nazarene Association of Churches ★281★
Box 1
Finleyville, PA 15332

Holiness Christian Church of the United States of
America ★231★

Gibraltar, PA 19524

Emmanuel's Fellowship ★468★
% Rev. Paul Goodling
Rte. 2
Greencastle, PA 17275

Himalayan International Institute of Yoga Science &
Philosophy ★1194★
RD 1
Honesdale, PA 18431

American Carpatho-Russian Orthodox Greek Catholic
Church ★65★
% Most Rev. John R. Martin
312 Garfield St.
Johnstown, PA 15906

United Christian Church ★210★
% Elder Henry C. Heagy, Moderator
Lebanon R.D. 4
Lebanon County, PA 17042

Congregational Bible Church ★441★
% Congregational Bible Church
Marietta, PA 17547

Church of God, the House of Prayer ★292★
% Rev. Charles Mackenin
Marklesburg, PA 15459

Reformed Mennonite Church ★447★
% J. Henry Fisher
448 N. Prince St.
Millersville, PA 17551

Church of Jesus Christ (Bickertonite) ★727★
Sixth & Lincoln Sts.
Monogahela, PA 15603

African Union First Colored Methodist Protestant Church ★203★
515 Jefferson, Plymouth Township
Morristown, PA 19401

Evangelical Congregational Church ★209★
100 W. Park Ave.
Box 186
Myerstown, PA 17067

Weaver Mennonites ★449★
% Pike Meeting House
New Holland, PA 17557

Weaverland Conference Old Order (Horning or Black Bumper) Mennonites ★450★
% Bishop H. O. Weaver
Weaverland Meeting House
New Holland, PA 17557

Schwenkfelder Church in America ★501★

Pennsburg, PA 18073

American Rescue Workers ★213★
% General Paul E. Martin, Commander-In-Chief
2827 Frankford Ave.
Philadelphia, PA 19134

Apostolic Church ★311★
142 N. 17th St.
Philadelphia, PA 19103

Aquarian Research Foundation ★748★
5620 Morton St.
Philadelphia, PA 19144

Bawa Muhaiyaddeen Fellowship ★1141★
5820 Overbrook Ave.
Philadelphia, PA 19131

Calvary Holiness Church ★243★
3415-19 N. Second St.
Philadelphia, PA 19140

Church of the Lord Jesus Christ of the Apostolic Faith (Philadelphia) ★366★
22nd & Bainbridge Sts.
Philadelphia, PA 19146

Friends General Conference ★481★
1520-B Race St.
Philadelphia, PA 19102

Full Gospel Defenders Conference of America ★424★
% Grover S. Smith
3311 Hartel Ave.
Philadelphia, PA 19152

Holy Eastern Orthodox Church of the United States ★97★
% Most Rev. Trevor W. Moore
1611 Wallace St.
Philadelphia, PA 19130

House of God, Which Is the Church of the Living God, the Pillar and Ground of Truth, Inc. ★395★
6107 Cobbs Creek Pkwy.
Philadelphia, PA 19143

Kodesh Church of Emmanuel ★265★
% Rev. Fred Almond
5104 Haverford Ave.
Philadelphia, PA 19131

Mount Sinai Holy Church ★399★
% Bishop Mary E. Jackson
1601 Broad St.
Philadelphia, PA 19148

Orthodox Presbyterian Church ★165★
7401 Old York Rd.
Philadelphia, PA 19126

Reformed Episcopal Church ★57★
% Board of National Church Extension
4225 Chestnut St.
Philadelphia, PA 19140

Russian/Ukrainian Evangelical Baptist Union of the U.S.A., Inc. ★521★
Roosevelt Blvd. & 7th St.
Philadelphia, PA 19120

Shiloh Apostolic Temple ★377★
1516 W. Master
Philadelphia, PA 19121

Swami Kuvalayananda Yoga Foundation ★1222★
527 South St.
Philadelphia, PA 19147

United Holy Church of America ★404★
Box 19846
Philadelphia, PA 19144

Universal Church of Psychic Science ★847★
4740 Taconey St.
Philadelphia, PA 19124

Associated Gospel Churches ★571★
1919 Beach St.
Pittsburgh, PA 15221

The Church of Holy Light ★694★
Box 4478
Pittsburgh, PA 15205

Lake Erie Yearly Meeting ★484★
% Clerk, Samuel B. Pellwitz
572 Briar Cliff Rd.
Pittsburgh, PA 15221

Reformed Presbyterian Church of North America ★168★
% Louis D. Hutmire, Stated Clerk
7418 Penn Ave.
Pittsburgh, PA 15208

Seventh-Day Baptists (German) ★549★
% Crist M. King
238 S. Aiken St.
Pittsburgh, PA 15206

Bible Protestant Church ★186★
Rte. 1, Box 12
Port Jarvis, PA 12771

Fraternitas Rosae Crucis ★949★
Beverly Hall
Quakertown, PA 18951

Calvary Grace Churches of Faith ★692★
Box 333
Rillton, PA 19140

Polish National Catholic Church ★34★
% Most Rev. Francis C. Rowinski
529 E. Locust St.
Scranton
Scranton, PA 18505

Holy Shankaracharya Order ★1196★
RD 3, Box 400
Stroudsburg, PA 18360

God's Missionary Church ★275★
% Rev. Paul Miller
Swengal, PA 17880

Bible Fellowship Church ★215★
% Pastor W. B. Hottel
404 W. Main St.
Terre Hill, PA 17581

Christian Church of North America, General Council
★319★
Rte. 18 & Rutledge Rd.
Box 141-A, R.D. 1
Transfer, PA 16154

Association of Evangelicals for Italian Missions ★505★
314 Richfield Rd.
Upper Darby, PA 19082

United Episcopal Church of North America ★60★
% Most Rev. C. Dale D. Doren
2293 Country Club Dr.
Upper St. Clair, PA 15241

American Baptist Churches in the U.S.A. ★504★

Valley Forge, PA 19481

Primitive Methodist Church ★211★
40 E. Northampton St.
Wilkes-Barre, PA 18702

International Church of Ageless Wisdom ★820★
Box 502
Wyalusing, PA 18853

Puerto Rico

Mita Movement ★349★
Calle Duarte 235
Hata Rey, PR 60919

Rhode Island

Kwan Um Zen School ★1303★
K. B. C. Hong Poep Won
RFD No. 5
528 Pound Rd.
Cumberland, RI 02864

Church of Pan ★1047★
R.R. 3
Box 189
Foster, RI 02825

General Six-Principle Baptists ★543★
Rhode Island Conference
% Edgar S. Kirk, President
38 Church St.
West Warwick, RI 02893

South Carolina

Reformed Methodist Union Episcopal Church ★206★
% Rt. Rev. Leroy Gethers
1136 Brody Ave.
Charleston, SC 20407

United Episcopal Church of America ★59★
% Rt. Rev. Richard C. Acker
6317 N. Trenholm Rd.
Columbia, SC 29206

Free Will Baptist Church of the Pentecostal Faith ★299★
Box 278
Elgin, SC 29045

Associate Reformed Presbyterian Church (General Synod)
★162★
Associate Reformed Presbyterian Center
One Cleveland St.
Greenville, SC 29601

South Carolina Baptist Fellowship ★523★
% Rev. John Waters
Faith Baptist Church
1600 Greenwood Rd.
Laurens, SC 29360

Southwide Baptist Fellowship ★525★
% Rev. John Waters
Faith Baptist Church
1607 Greenwood Rd.
Laurens, SC 39360

Meher Baba, Friends of ★1167★
% Meher Center on the Lakes
Box 487
Myrtle Beach, SC 29577

Southern Methodist Church ★200★
% Rev. W. Lynn Corbett
Box 132
Orangeburg, SC 29116-0132

General Association of Davidian Seventh-Day Adventists
★603★
Rte. 1, Box 174
Salem, SC 29676

Oyotunji, Yoruba Village of ★1091★
Box 51
Sheldon, SC 29941

South Dakota

Hutterian Brethren-Schmiedeleut ★740★
% Rev. David D. Decker
Tachetter Colony
Olivet, SD 57052

Tennessee

Holy Orthodox Church, American Jurisdiction ★99★
% Most Rev. W. Francis Forbes
Box 400
Antioch, TN 37013

Fellowship of Independent Evangelical Churches ★577★
% Howard Boyll
2311 Anderson St.
Bristol, TN 73620

Westminster Biblical Fellowship ★172★
% Rev. Earl Pinckney
Bristol, TN 37620

Open Way ★1018★
Box 217
Celina, TN 38551

(Original) Church of God ★306★
Box 3086
Chattanooga, TN 37404

Church of God (Cleveland, Tennessee) ★285★
Keith St. at 25th St., N.W.
Cleveland, TN 37311

Church of God (Jerusalem Acres) ★286★
% John A. Looper, Chief Bishop
Box 1207
1826 Dalton Pike (Jerusalem Acres)
Cleveland, TN 37311

Church of God of Prophecy ★287★
Bible Place
Cleveland, TN 37311

United Christian Ministerial Association ★436★
Box 754
Cleveland, TN 37311

Yahweh's Temple ★384★
Box 652
Cleveland, TN 37311

Upper Cumberland Presbyterian Church ★171★
% Roaring River Upper Cumberland Presbyterian Church
Gainesboro, TN 38562

Assemblies of the Called Out Ones of Yah ★641★
231 Cedar St.
Jackson, TN 38301

Church of God of the Mountain Assembly ★289★

Jellico, TN 37762

Evangelical Methodist Church of America ★191★
Box 751
Kingsport, TN 37662

Bible Methodist Connection of Tennessee ★271★
Box 10408
Knoxville, TN 37919

First Church of Voodoo ★1090★
Box 2381
Knoxville, TN 37917

Christian Congregation ★552★
% Rev. Ora Wilbert Eads, General Supt.
804 W. Hemlock St.
La Follette, TN 37766

People of the Living God ★742★
Rt. 2 Box 423
McMinnville, TN 37110

Christian Methodist Episcopal Church ★204★
564 Frank Ave.
Memphis, TN 38101

Church of God in Christ ★387★
% Mason Temple
939 Mason St.
Memphis, TN 38103

Cumberland Presbyterian Church ★164★
Cumberland Presbyterian Center
1978 Union Ave.
Memphis, TN 38104

African Methodist Episcopal Church ★201★
500 8th Ave., S.
Nashville, TN 37203

Church of God (Sanctified Church) ★261★
1037 Jefferson St.
Nashville, TN 37208

Church of the Living God, the Pillar and Ground of
    Truth (Lewis Dominion) ★391★
4520 Hydes Ferry Pike
Box 5735
Nashville, TN 37208

Disciples of Faith ★777★
Box 50322
Nashville, TN 37205

National Association of Free Will Baptists ★544★
Box 1088
Nashville, TN 37202

Society Ordo Templi Orientis in America ★1038★
Box 90018
Nashville, TN 37209

Southern Baptist Convention ★524★
% Executive Committee
460 James Robertson Pkwy.
Nashville, TN 37219

Southern Episcopal Church ★58★
% Most Rev. B. H. Webster
2315 Valley Brook Rd.
Nashville, TN 37215

The Farm ★751★
156-C Drakes Lane
Summertown, TN 38483

Duck River (and Kindred) Association of Baptists ★510★
Duck River Association
% Elder A. B. Ray, Moderator
500 Regan St.
Tullahoma, TN 37388

Texas

House of Yahweh (Abilene, Texas) ★649★
Box 242
Abilene, TX 79604

Full Gospel Church Association ★300★
Box 265
Amarillo, TX 79105

World Baptist Fellowship ★528★
3001 W. Division
Arlington, TX 76012

American Atheists, Inc. ★673★
% Madalyn Murray O'Hair
Box 2117
Austin, TX 78767

Churches of Christ (Non-Instrumental) ★553★
% Firm Foundation
Box 610
Austin, TX 78767

Old Catholic Church in America (Brothers) ★21★
% Metropolitan Hilarion
1905 S. Third St.
Austin, TX 78704

Asatru Free Assembly ★1043★
Box 1754
Breckenridge, TX 76024

Full Gospel Fellowship of Churches and Ministers
   International ★341★
1545 W. Mockingbird Ln., Suite 1012
Dallas, TX 75235

Holy Orthodox Catholic Church ★98★
% Most Rev. Paul G. Russell
5831 Tremont
Dallas, TX 75214

International Deliverance Churches ★344★
Box 353
Dallas, TX 75221

New Testament Church of God ★236★
% Rev. G. W. Pendleton
307 Cockrell Hill Rd.
Dallas, TX 75211

Wisdom Institute of Spiritual Education ★799★
1236 S. Marlborough
Dallas, TX 75208

Word Foundation ★972★
Box 18235
Dallas, TX 75218

Churches of Christ (Non-Instrumental, Liberal) ★554★
% Restoration Review
1201 Windsor Dr.
Denton, TX 76201

ESP Laboratory ★1060★
Box 216
219 S. Ridge Dr.
Edgewood, TX 75117

Church of the First Born of the Fullness of Times ★714★
5854 Mira Serana
El Paso, TX 79912

Lotus Ashram ★825★
% Rev. Noel Street
Box 39
Fabens, TX 79838

Christ Truth League ★769★
2400 Canton Dr.
Fort Worth, TX 76112

Stelle Group ★965★
405 Mayfield Ave.
Garland, TX 75041

Churches of Christ (Non-Instrumental, Non-Sunday
   School) ★557★
% Gospel Tidings
500 E. Henry
Hamilton, TX 76531

Berachah Church ★572★
5139 W. Alabama
Houston, TX 77056

Full Gospel Evangelistic Association ★324★
5828 Chippewa Blvd.
Houston, TX 70086

Independent Bible Church Movement ★578★
% Church Multiplication, Inc.
Box 79203
Houston, TX 77279

International Ministerial Association ★370★
4003 Bellaire Blvd.
Houston, TX 77025

Timely Messenger Fellowship ★591★
% R. B. Shiflet
Box 473
Mineral Wells, TX 76067

House of Yahweh (Odessa, Texas) ★650★
% Jacob Hawkins
Box 4938
Odessa, TX 79760

Devatma Shakti Society ★1189★
Rte. 1, Box 150 C-2
Paige, TX 78659

Today Church ★794★
Box 832366
Richardson, TX 75083-2366

Unity of the Brethren ★181★
% Rev. John Baletka, President
3829 Sandstone
San Angelo, TX 76904

Mayan Order ★961★
Box 2710
San Antonio, TX 78299

Omniune Church ★701★
309 Breckenridge
Texarkana, TX 75501

Church of God, International ★615★
Box 2525
Tyler, TX 75710

Branch SDA's ★601★
Box 4666
Waco, TX 76705

St. Paul's Church of Aquarian Science ★836★
312 S. Texas Blvd.
Weslaco, TX 78596

Utah

Church of Jesus Christ in Solemn Assembly ★712★
% Alexander Joseph, Presiding King
Long Haul, Box 151
Big Water, UT 84741

Apostolic United Order ★711★
1194 W. 16600, S.
Bluffsdale, UT 84065

Aaronic Order ★706★
% Dr. Robert J. Conrad
Box 7095
Salt Lake City, UT 84107

The Builders ★749★
Box 2278
Salt Lake City, UT 84110

Church of Jesus Christ (Bulla) ★707★
% Art Bulla
2928 S. State St.
Salt Lake City, UT 84115

Church of Jesus Christ of Latter-Day Saints ★708★
50 E. North Temple
Salt Lake City, UT 84150

Universal Brotherhood of Faithists ★878★
% Universal Faithists of Kosmon
Box 664
Salt Lake City, UT 84110

Sons Ahman Israel ★718★
Box 186
Washington, UT 84780

Virginia

Sawan Kirpal Ruhani Mission ★1248★
% T. S. Khanna
8807 Lea Lane
Alexandria, VA 22309

World Community ★1229★
Route 4, Box 265
Bedford, VA 24523

Integral Yoga Institute ★1197★
% Satchidananda Ashram
Rte. 1, Box 172
Buckingham, VA 93921

Seax-Wica ★1082★
Box 7882
Charlottesville, VA 22906

Friends of Buddhism-Washington D.C. ★1331★
% Dr. Kurt Leidecker
306 Caroline St.
Fredericksburg, VA 22401

Fivefold Path ★1191★
% Vasant V. Paranjpe
RFD 1, Box 212-C
Madison, VA 22727

True Vine Pentecostal Churches of Jesus ★378★
% Dr. Robert L. Hairston
New Bethel Apostolic Church
Martinsville, VA 24112

Fellowship of the Inner Light ★860★
Rte. 1, Box 390
New Market, VA 22844

International General Assembly of Spiritualists ★821★
1809 E. Bayview Blvd.
Norfolk, VA 23503

Church of God and Saints of Christ ★1123★
Box 187
Portsmouth, VA 23704

Unamended Christadelphians ★562★
% Lawrence Dodl
5104 Cavedo Lane
Richmond, VA 23231

Reformed Zion Union Apostolic Church ★207★
% Deacon James C. Feggins
416 South Hill Ave.
South Hill, VA 23970

Association for Research and Enlightenment ★899★
Box 595
Virginia Beach, VA 23451

Washington

Raj-Yoga Math and Retreat ★1210★
Box 547
Deming, WA 98244

Calvary Pentecostal Church ★318★
% Rev. Leroy Holman
1775 Yew, N.E.
Olympia, WA 98506

Calvary Fellowships, Inc. ★665★
Box 128
Rainer, WA 98576

Bethel Temple ★314★
2033 Second Ave.
Seattle, WA 98121

Church of Armageddon ★750★
617 W. McGraw St.
Seattle, WA 98119

Cosmic Awareness Communications ★857★
Box 115
Seattle, WA 98507

Evangelical Orthodox Church ★88★
% Rt. Rev. Peter Gillquist, Presiding Bishop
Box 17074
Seattle, WA 98107

North Pacific Yearly Meeting ★487★
% University Friends Center
4001 9th Ave., N.E.
Seattle, WA 98105

Sakya Tegchen Choling ★1320★
5042 18th Ave.,N.E.
Seattle, WA 98105

Venusian Church ★1086★
Box 21263
Seattle, WA 98111

Western Bible Students Association ★640★
12739 14th St.
Seattle, WA 98125

Pentecostal Evangelical Church ★334★
% Rev. Ernest Beroth
Box 4218
Spokane, WA 99202

Sabian Assembly ★963★
2324 Norman Rd.
Stanwood, WA 98292

Association of Seventh-Day Pentecostal Assemblies ★416★
% Elder Garver C. Gray, Chairman
4700 N.E. 119th St.
Vancouver, WA 98665

Associated Churches of God ★610★
% Association for Christian Development
The Pine Building
Winslow, WA 98110

West Virginia

Church of God (Apostolic) ★364★
Saint Peter's Church of God (Apostolic)
125 Meadows St.
Beckley, WV 25801

Claymont Society for Continuous Education ★1143★
Box 112
Charlestown, WV 25414

Church of God (Seventh-Day, Salem, West Virginia)
★617★
79 Water St.
Salem, WV 26426

Primitive Advent Christian Church ★600★
% Eliza Moss, President
Sissonville, WV 25185

Wisconsin

Seventh-Day Baptist General Conference USA and Canada
Ltd. ★548★
Seventh Day Baptist Center
3120 Kennedy Rd., P.O. Box 1678
Janesville, WI 53547

Metropolitan Church Association ★232★
323 Broad St.
Lake Geneva, WI 53147

Evangelical Lutheran Synod ★143★
% Rev. George Orvick, President
2670 Milwaukee St.
Madison, WI 53704

Freedom from Religion Foundation ★683★
Box 750
Madison, WI 53701

The Protestant Conference ★149★
728 N. 9th St.
Manitowoc, WI 54220

Lorian Association ★931★
Box 147
Middleton, WI 53562

Archdiocese of the Old Catholic Church of America ★3★
% Most Rev. Walter X. Brown
2450 N. 50th St.
Milwaukee, WI 53210

Wisconsin Evangelical Lutheran Synod ★151★
2929 N. Mayfair Rd.
Milwaukee, WI 53222

Circle ★1050★
Box 219
Mt. Horeb, WI 53572

North American Old Catholic Church, Ultrajectine
Tradition ★17★
% For My God and My Country
Necedah, WI 54646

National Association of Congregational Christian Churches
★176★
8473 S. Howell Ave.
Box 1620
Oak Creek, WI 53154

Ganden Tekchen Ling ★1310★
Deer Park
4548 Schneider Dr.
Oregon, WI 53575

CANADA

British Columbia

Yasodhara Ashram Society ★1231★
Box 9
Kootenay Bay, BC, Canada V0B 1X0

Bible Holiness Movement ★216★
Box 223
Postal Station A
Vancouver, BC, Canada V6C 2M3

Glad Tidings Missionary Society ★426★
3456 Fraser St.
Vancouver, BC, Canada

International Spiritualist Alliance ★822★
% Rev. Beatrice G. Bishop
3381 Findlay St.
Vancouver, BC, Canada

St. Raphael's Old Catholic Church of British Columbia
and Society ★997★
715 E. 51st Ave.
Vancouver, BC, Canada V5X 1E2

Manitoba

Evangelical Mennonite Conference (Kleine Gemeinde)
★452★
Box 1268
400 Main St.
Steinbach, MB, Canada R0A 2A0

New Brunswick

Primitive Baptist Conference of New Brunswick, Maine
and Nova Scotia ★545★
% St. John Valley Bible Camp
Box 355
Harland, NB, Canada

Ontario

Old Order Amish Mennonite Church ★458★
Pathway Publishers
Rte. 4
Aylmer, ON, Canada N5H 2R3

Standard Church of America ★239★

Brockville, ON, Canada

Churches of God in the British Isles and Overseas
(Needed Truth) ★563★
% Mr. J. Ramage
44 Tweedsmuir Ave.
Dundas, ON, Canada

Netherlands Reformed Congregations ★157★
% Rev. A.M. Doer
Main St., Box 42
Norwich, ON, Canada N0J 1P0

Old Roman Catholic Church (Hamel) ★25★
% H. H. Claudius I
Box 2608, Station D
Ottawa, ON, Canada K1P 5W7

Byelorussian Autocephalic Orthodox Church in the U.S.A.
★82★
% Archbishop Mikalay, Primate
Church of St. Cyril of Turau
524 St. Clarens Ave.
Toronto, ON, Canada

Ontario Old Roman Catholic Church ★30★
% Most Rev. Nelson D. Hillyer
5 Manor Rd., W. Suite 5
Toronto, ON, Canada M5P 1E6

Quebec

Latvian Evangelical Lutheran Church in America ★145★
% Rev. Arturs Voitkus, President
3438 Rosedale Ave.
Montreal, PQ, Canada H4B 2G6

Sivananda Vedanta Yoga Centers ★1217★
5178 St. Lawrence Blvd.
Montreal, PQ, Canada

FOREIGN

Australia

Temple Society ★745★
% Dr. Richard Hoffman
152 Tucker
Bentleigh, Australia

American Grail Foundation ★852★
% Verlag Alexander Bernhardt
Vomperberg, A-6134 Vomp
Tirol, Australia

Denmark

Martinus Institute of Spiritual Science ★866★
94-96 Mariendalsvej
Copenhagen, Denmark

England

Plymouth Brethren (Exclusive: Raven-Taylor Brethren)
★567★
% Stow Hill Bible and Tract Depot
5 Fife Rd.
Kingston-on-Thames, England

Habibiyya-Shadhiliyya Sufic Order ★1146★
33 Bristol Gardens
London, England

Ordo Adeptorum Invisiblum ★1032★
% Gerry Ahrens
18 Crampton House
Patmore St.
London, England

Universal Link ★879★
1, St. Georges Square
St. Annes, Lancashire, England

Israel

Church of God (Jerusalem) ★648★
Box 10184
Jerusalem, Israel

Workers Together with Elohim ★654★
Box 14411
Jerusalem, Israel

South Africa

School of Truth ★791★
% Dr. Nicol Campbell
Box 5582
Johannesburg, South Africa

Subject Index

Provides access to the material in both the essay section and the directory section through a selected list of subject terms. Numbers cited in this index refer to both page numbers (for items in the essay section) and entry numbers (for items in the directory section). Citations referring to entry numbers are signified by a star.

Bible—Literal interpretation 50

Bible—Verbal inspiration 72, 73, ★186, ★506, ★524, ★590

Bible—Versions—American Revised ★588

Bible—Versions—Concordant ★588

Bible—Versions—Douay-Rheims ★31

Bible—Versions—Inspired (Joseph Smith's) ★731

Bible—Versions—King James Version (KJV) 63, ★46, ★171, ★188, ★289, ★300, ★514, ★588, ★651

Bible—Versions—Kravitz 28

Bible—Versions—New World Translation ★470, ★635

Bible—Versions—Peshitta 11, ★126, ★593, ★786

Bible—Versions—Revised Standard Version (RSV) ★72, ★163, ★171, ★525, ★588, ★705

Bible—Versions—Rotherham ★651

Bible—Versions—Sacred Name versions ★651, ★653

Bible—Versions—Schofield Reference Bible

Bible—Versions—True Complete Bible ★943

Black Magic(k) 131, 132, 139, ★1028, ★1035, ★1037, ★1049, ★1064, ★1076

Black Mass ★1044, ★1095

Blood transfusions ★635

Bodhisattvas 160

Body-fely salvation ★342

Boy Scouts ★144

Breaking of Bread

Breathing exercises 155, 162, ★1166, ★1175, ★1187, ★1194, ★1209, ★1219, ★1237, ★1239, ★1240

British-Israelism 83, 84, ★628, ★1137

Bruja 137

Calendar, Julian ★90, ★94

Camp meetings 36, ★211, ★222, ★231, ★232, ★236, ★251, ★252, ★283, ★299, ★302, ★307, ★324, ★325, ★327

Canon law ★1

Canons of Dort 22, 23, ★152, ★160

Cardinals ★1

Catechisms—Baltimore ★23

Catechisms—Heidelberg 22, 23, ★156

Catechisms—Luther's ★177

Catechism preaching ★152

Celibacy 9, 11, 15, 101, 148, ★1, ★2, ★11, ★22, ★41, ★737, ★746, ★923

Cellular cosmology ★741

Chakras ★854

Chanting ★801, ★1108, ★1133, ★1166, ★1200, ★1224, ★1237, ★1239, ★1240, ★1242, ★1267, ★1268, ★1270, ★1293, ★1300, ★1333

Chastity 99, 101, 136

Christmas 61, ★132

Church-State, Separation of 10, 16, 22, 47, 51, ★185, ★672, ★675, ★676, ★683, ★684, ★689

Circumcision ★656

Circumcision of the heart ★133

Civil disobedience ★163

Civil Rights Movement 88, ★185, ★538, ★540, ★673

Clairvoyance 111, 112, 113, 114, 121

Class meetings ★194, ★206

Classis ★152, ★159, ★160

College of Cardinals ★1

Colonizations, attempts at 64, ★601

Come Out Movement 37, 80, ★223

Common grace controversy ★159

Communalism 50, 51, 65, 89, 99, 100, 101, 102, ★232, ★418, ★657, ★658, ★659, ★668, ★706, ★710, ★714, ★717, ★728, ★731, ★733, ★734, ★735, ★736, ★737, ★738, ★739, ★740, ★741, ★742, ★743, ★744, ★745, ★746, ★747, ★748, ★749, ★750, ★751, ★752, ★753, ★754, ★756, ★757, ★758, ★759, ★760, ★878, ★916, ★937, ★940, ★960, ★967, ★978, ★1017, ★1066, ★1123, ★1125, ★1126, ★1128, ★1130, ★1131, ★1132, ★1134, ★1143, ★1178, ★1179, ★1195, ★1277

Communion, sacrament or ordinance of 28, 36, ★1, ★180, ★201, ★454, ★503, ★540, ★821, ★1123

Communion, sacrament or ordinance of—by intincture

Communion, sacrament or ordinance of—closed communion 49, 63, 66, ★518, ★519, ★541, ★546

Communion, sacrament or ordinance of—consubstantiation 16

Communion, sacrament or ordinance of—in the hand ★31

Communion, sacrament or ordinance of—Lord's supper 29, 31, 50, 65, 66, 72, 74, ★160, ★208, ★213, ★283, ★286, ★306, ★311, ★325, ★360, ★364, ★374, ★385, ★387, ★390, ★397, ★398, ★454, ★494, ★539, ★569, ★574, ★579, ★604, ★607, ★611, ★612, ★614, ★656, ★660, ★727, ★742, ★758, ★801, ★844

Communion, sacrament or ordinance of—of the saints ★88

Communion, sacrament or ordinance of—not practiced ★327, ★333, ★591, ★594, ★770

Communion, sacrament or ordinance of—open communion ★2, ★13, ★55, ★152, ★181, ★182, ★501, ★508

Communion, sacrament or ordinance of—transubstantiation 16, 31, ★1

Conclusions of Utrecht ★152

Confession ★1

Confession—auricular ★11, ★659

Confession—public 18, ★134

Confessions of faith 16, ★504, ★512, ★517, ★518, ★524

Confessions of faith—Augsburg 16, ★177

Confessions of faith—Belgic 22, ★152, ★157, ★160

Confessions of faith—Heidelberg ★152, ★157, ★160, ★161, ★177

Confessions of faith—of 1913 (Congregational) ★177

Confessions of faith—Schleitheim ★442, ★740

Confessions of faith—Second Helvetic 22, ★156

Confessions of faith—Utrecht ★7

Confessions of faith—Westminster 22, 24, 25, 59, ★162, ★163, ★164, ★166, ★168

Confirmation 3, ★1, ★461

Conscientious objection to war 29, 66, ★227, ★229, ★257, ★355, ★359, ★360, ★381, ★388, ★397, ★398, ★420, ★423, ★425, ★444, ★445, ★513, ★549, ★563, ★594, ★601, ★603, ★605, ★607, ★641, ★645, ★656, ★1157

Consistory 22, ★159

Continuing revelation ★482

Conventicles ★745

Council of Seven Lights

Court (legal) cases 117, 128, 156, 158, ★200, ★673, ★677, ★683, ★704, ★723, ★759, ★761, ★894, ★896, ★897, ★907, ★918, ★988, ★989, ★1003, ★1038, ★1174, ★1180, ★1200, ★1341, ★1344

Creeds ★981

Creeds—Apostles ★442

Creeds—Chalcedonian 2, 11, 12

Creeds—Nicene ★959

Cryogenics ★679

Curia ★1

Dancing ★138, ★740, ★746, ★1087, ★1088, ★1113, ★1345, ★1346

Deacons/Deaconesses ★2, ★12

Dead Sea Scrolls ★916

Decrees 79, 88, 112, 114, 128, ★675, ★1001, ★1003, ★1004, ★1005

Deism ★682

Dhikr, see Zhikr

Dianetics ★905, ★907

Diet 81, ★752, ★758, ★860, ★909, ★1135, ★1240, ★1261

Diet—Dietary restrictions 147, ★412, ★500, ★611, ★622, ★626, ★643, ★646, ★647, ★654, ★954, ★1122, ★1245

Missions—Germany ★15, ★57, ★147,
★176, ★179, ★209, ★221, ★342,
★365, ★416, ★453, ★469, ★527,
★557, ★633, ★639, ★725, ★726,
★744, ★796, ★858, ★866, ★947,
★951, ★959, ★976, ★1034, ★1154,
★1166, ★1171, ★1174, ★1176,
★1202, ★1208, ★1217, ★1285,
★1296, ★1306

Missions—Ghana ★147, ★216, ★293,
★319, ★342, ★374, ★437, ★525,
★599, ★1158

Missions—Gold Coast ★385

Missions—Great Britain 41, 65, 124,
★82, ★147, ★151, ★176, ★221,
★223, ★229, ★239, ★243, ★256,
★293, ★342, ★365, ★366, ★374,
★377, ★550, ★563, ★565, ★566,
★568, ★569, ★572, ★599, ★605,
★633, ★643, ★645, ★726, ★744,
★764, ★789, ★791, ★796, ★802,
★841, ★855, ★858, ★859, ★866,
★878, ★879, ★881, ★907, ★925,
★947, ★959, ★969, ★970, ★971,
★976, ★979, ★988, ★989, ★996,
★1032, ★1035, ★1083, ★1084,
★1121, ★1149, ★1154, ★1158,
★1166, ★1176, ★1177, ★1190, ★1

Missions—Greece ★176, ★221, ★255,
★293, ★556, ★605, ★633, ★1213

Missions—Guam ★152, ★541

Missions—Guatamala ★211, ★214,
★227, ★323, ★324, ★437, ★440,
★751

Missions—Guyana 28, ★334, ★399,
★801, ★937

Missions—Haiti 64, ★234, ★255,
★258, ★293, ★307, ★366, ★373,
★375, ★415, ★652, ★726, ★1028

Missions—Holland, see Netherlands

Missions—Honduras ★185, ★208,
★437

Missions—Hong Kong ★147, ★151,
★160, ★164, ★178, ★179, ★201,
★208, ★214, ★255, ★304, ★316,
★415, ★437, ★453, ★556, ★1245,
★1270, ★1291, ★1293, ★1297,
★1306

Missions—India 41, 62, 124, 125,
126, 153, 154, 155, 156, 157, 158,
★47, ★57, ★147, ★151, ★176,
★209, ★210, ★216, ★221, ★222,
★224, ★232, ★234, ★240, ★255,
★304, ★308, ★310, ★316, ★318,
★319, ★321, ★323, ★334, ★342,
★358, ★373, ★415, ★418, ★428,
★429, ★437, ★440, ★451, ★453,
★461, ★465, ★480, ★544, ★557,
★561, ★575, ★598, ★599, ★605,
★616, ★624, ★633, ★643, ★725,
★726, ★764, ★796, ★970, ★971,
★1142, ★1154, ★1156, ★1168,
★1175, ★1180, ★1182, ★1184,
★1186, ★1190, ★

Missions—Indonesia 28, ★151, ★152,
★178, ★209, ★255, ★295, ★310,
★314, ★418, ★539, ★1152, ★1324

Missions—Iran 150, ★437, ★1168,
★1169

Missions—Ireland ★1176, ★1213

Missions—Israel ★316, ★338, ★453,
★648, ★654, ★841, ★1108, ★1110,
★1112, ★1116, ★1121, ★1132,
★1169, ★1217

Missions—Italy ★176, ★200, ★317,
★319, ★571, ★632, ★639, ★725,
★971, ★976, ★1154, ★1324

Missions—Ivory Coast ★319, ★342,
★544

Missions—Jamaica ★124, ★191, ★208,
★210, ★223, ★231, ★234, ★261,
★316, ★365, ★366, ★373, ★374,
★379, ★418, ★427, ★429, ★437,
★482, ★535, ★608, ★615, ★623,
★624, ★643, ★789, ★1123, ★1128,
★1157

Missions—Japan 161, 162, ★139,
★147, ★151, ★152, ★160, ★164,
★168, ★178, ★179, ★209, ★210,
★221, ★226, ★304, ★314, ★321,
★429, ★437, ★451, ★462, ★518,
★525, ★539, ★541, ★544, ★556,
★575, ★598, ★726, ★792, ★801,
★802, ★923, ★959, ★1209, ★1262,
★1263, ★1264, ★1265, ★1267,
★1268, ★1269, ★1270, ★1271,
★1272, ★1273, ★1274, ★1277,
★1278, ★1279, ★1280, ★1281,
★1282, ★1283, ★1284, ★1335,
★1336, ★1337, ★1338, ★1339,
★1340, ★1341, ★1342, ★1343,
★1344, ★1345, ★1346

Missions—Jordan 28, ★366, ★482

Missions—Kenya ★209, ★215, ★216,
★221, ★342, ★571, ★575, ★725

Missions—Korea 161, ★147, ★152,
★178, ★221, ★240, ★415, ★418,
★437, ★453, ★484, ★575, ★576,
★726, ★923, ★1270, ★1300,
★1301, ★1302, ★1303, ★1304,
★1335, ★1343, ★1345

Missions—Kuwait ★160

Missions—Lebanon ★147, ★221

Missions—Lesotho ★453, ★751

Missions—Liberia 64, ★147, ★209,
★216, ★256, ★366, ★374, ★375,
★400, ★608

Missions—Madagascar ★47

Missions—Malawi ★557, ★564, ★567,
★860

Missions—Malaysia ★179, ★209,
★461, ★598

Missions—Maldive Islands ★366

Missions—Mexico ★125, ★147, ★151,
★152, ★160, ★162, ★190, ★200,
★209, ★222, ★226, ★232, ★234,
★247, ★260, ★288, ★300, ★304,
★307, ★308, ★310, ★317, ★324,
★342, ★379, ★412, ★418, ★437,
★453, ★461, ★469, ★482, ★489,
★509, ★539, ★557, ★575, ★599,
★633, ★711, ★714, ★719, ★726,
★796, ★1166, ★1217, ★1242,
★1284, ★1285

Missions—Nepal ★1318, ★1324

Missions—Netherlands ★800, ★802,
★860, ★866, ★951, ★959, ★969,
★971, ★976, ★987, ★988, ★1095,
★1154, ★1166, ★1176, ★1284

Missions—Netherland Antilles ★413

Missions—New Guinea ★147, ★209

Missions—New Zealand ★147, ★342,
★572, ★633, ★726, ★859, ★951,
★998, ★1034, ★1208, ★1217,
★1260

Missions—Nicaraugua ★208, ★308,
★462, ★525

Missions—Nigeria ★47, ★147, ★151,
★152, ★222, ★234, ★240, ★293,
★294, ★304, ★316, ★342, ★374,
★416, ★427, ★440, ★465, ★518,
★525, ★571, ★598, ★599, ★608,
★616, ★725, ★726, ★775, ★796,
★807, ★841

Missions—Norway ★800, ★1208

Missions—Okinawa ★295, ★726,
★1335

Missions—Oman ★160

Missions—Pakistan ★47, ★162, ★1156

Missions—Panama ★293, ★412, ★535,
★544, ★841

Missions—Paraguay ★147, ★191,
★453, ★527, ★744

Missions—Peru ★143, ★179, ★324,
★561, ★883

Missions—Philippines ★147, ★152,
★160, ★176, ★179, ★209, ★216,
★222, ★295, ★300, ★308, ★310,
★319, ★323, ★334, ★342, ★414,
★423, ★428, ★430, ★440, ★539,
★541, ★556, ★571, ★586, ★598,
★599, ★605, ★616, ★623, ★624,
★643, ★645, ★655, ★726, ★796

Missions—Poland ★15, ★34, ★1034,
★1285, ★1303

Missions—Polynesia ★726

Missions—Portugal ★366, ★576

Missions—Puerto Rico ★41, ★151,
★304, ★349, ★411, ★413, ★469,
★525, ★544, ★589, ★1280, ★1341

Missions—Russia ★1120

Missions—St. Lucia ★624

Mission—Saudia Arabia ★998, ★1139

Missions—Serbia

Missions—Sierra Leone ★147, ★201,
★208, ★234, ★323, ★954

Missions—Singapore ★179, ★437,
★1227